Rand McNally
Universal World Atlas

Rand McNally

Universal

WORLD ATLAS

NEW REVISED EDITION

RAND McNALLY & COMPANY   Chicago / New York / San Francisco

Title page photo by David Muench

UNIVERSAL WORLD ATLAS

Copyright © 1991 by Rand McNally & Company

PRINTED IN THE UNITED STATES OF AMERICA

Library of Congress Catalog Card Number: 87-42862

ISBN 0-528-83198-4

Contents

World Reference Maps ———— vi

Maps and Map Projections ——— vii

Map Scale ———————— viii

Reference Maps 1–128

Map Symbols ———————— 1

The World and Special Regions 2–7

The World ———————— 2
Polar Map of the World ———— 4
Atlantic Ocean ——————— 5
Pacific Ocean ——————— 6
Antarctica ————————— 7

Europe 8–29

Europe and Western Asia ——— 8
British Isles ———————— 10
Ireland —————————— 11
England and Wales ————— 12
Scotland and Northern England — 13
Norway, Sweden and Finland — 14
Denmark and Northern Germany — 15
France and the Low Countries — 16
Belgium, Netherlands, Luxembourg
  and Western Germany ——— 17
Germany, Austria and Switzerland — 18
Central Germany ——————— 19
Alpine Regions ——————— 20
Switzerland ————————— 21
Spain and Portugal ————— 22
Italy ——————————— 23
Yugoslavia, Hungary, Romania
  and Bulgaria ——————— 24
Greece, Albania and Western Turkey — 25
Poland and Czechoslovakia —— 26
Western Soviet Union ———— 27
South Central Soviet Union —— 28
Soviet Union ———————— 29

Asia 30–41

Asia ——————————— 30
China, Mongolia, Korea,
  Japan and Taiwan ———— 31
Northeastern China ————— 32
Japan and Korea —————— 33
Indonesia and the Philippines — 34
Kampuchea (Cambodia), Laos, Vietnam,
  Thailand and Malaysia ——— 35
India, Pakistan, Bangladesh, Burma
  and Sri Lanka —————— 36
Central India and Nepal ——— 37
Middle East ———————— 38
Iran and Afghanistan ———— 39
Turkey, Cyprus, Syria, Jordan,
  Israel and Lebanon ———— 40
Israel and Northern Egypt —— 41

Africa 42–49

Africa —————————— 42
Northeast Africa —————— 43
Northwest Africa —————— 44
West Africa ———————— 45
Equatorial Africa —————— 46
East Africa ———————— 47
Central Africa ——————— 48
Southern Africa —————— 49

Australia and Oceania 50–52

Australia ————————— 50
Southeastern Australia
  and New Zealand ———— 51
Pacific Islands ——————— 52

South America 53–60

South America ——————— 53
Central and Southern Argentina
  and Chile ———————— 54
Bolivia, Paraguay, Northern Argentina
  and Chile ———————— 55
Uruguay and Southern Brazil — 56
Eastern Brazil ——————— 57
Peru and Ecuador —————— 58
Guyana, Suriname, French Guiana
  and Northern Brazil ———— 59
Colombia and Venezuela —— 60

North America 61–127

North America ——————— 61
Central America —————— 62
Mexico —————————— 63
West Indies ———————— 64
Caribbean Islands ————— 65

Canada 66

Alberta ————— 68
British
  Columbia —— 69
Manitoba ——— 70
Maritime
  Provinces — 71
Newfoundland — 72
Ontario ———— 73
Quebec ——— 74
Saskatchewan — 75

United States of America 76

Alabama ——— 78
Alaska ———— 79
Arizona ——— 80
Arkansas ——— 81
California ——— 82
Colorado ——— 83
Connecticut — 84
Delaware ——— 85
Florida ———— 86
Georgia ——— 87
Hawaii ———— 88
Idaho ———— 89
Illinois ——— 90
Indiana ——— 91
Iowa ———— 92
Kansas ——— 93
Kentucky ——— 94
Louisiana ——— 95
Maine ———— 96
Maryland ——— 97
Massachusetts — 98
Michigan ——— 99
Minnesota —— 100
Mississippi —— 101
Missouri ——— 102
Montana ——— 103
Nebraska ——— 104
Nevada ——— 105
New Hampshire 106
New Jersey — 107
New Mexico — 108
New York — 109
North Carolina 110
North Dakota — 111
Ohio ———— 112
Oklahoma —— 113
Oregon ——— 114
Pennsylvania — 115
Rhode Island — 116
South Carolina 117
South Dakota — 118
Tennessee —— 119
Texas ———— 120
Utah ———— 121
Vermont ——— 122
Virginia ——— 123
Washington — 124
West Virginia — 125
Wisconsin —— 126
Wyoming —— 127

North Polar Regions ———— 128

Index to World Reference Maps 129–224

Introduction to the Index
  and List of Abbreviations ——— 129
Index to World Reference Maps — 130

World Geographical Information 225–256

World Political Information ——— 225

General; The Continents;
  Historical Populations;
  Largest Countries: Population;
  Largest Countries: Area ——— 229

Principal Mountains —————— 230

Oceans, Seas, and Gulfs;
  Principal Lakes; Principal
  Rivers; Principal Islands ——— 231

World Metropolitan Areas —— 232

World Populations —————— 233

World Reference Maps

The world is made up of seven major land-masses: the continents of Europe, Asia, Africa, Australia, South America, North America, and Antarctica. To allow for the inclusion of detail, each continent is broken down into a series of maps, and this grouping is arranged so that as consecutive pages are turned, a continuous and successive part of the continent is shown. Larger-scale maps are used for regions of greater detail (having many cities, for example) or for areas of global significance.

The continental sequence of the maps is as follows: Europe (traditionally first in atlases), Asia (connected to Europe and forming the Eurasian landmass), Africa, Australia and Oceania, South America, and North America.

All the *regional* maps within each continent are drawn on the same scale. Thus it is possible to make direct visual comparisons of the sizes of countries and the distances between places by turning from one map to another. For instance, North America is mapped in three regions—Mexico, United States, Canada — all

at the scale of 1:12,000,000. South America's regions are shown at the scale of 1:8,000,000, Europe's, Asia's, and Australia's regions at the scale of 1:16,000,000, and Africa's at the scale of 1:11,400,000. Smaller areas are shown in detail on larger scale sectional maps, which use even multiples of the regional scales. The United States and Canada have individual maps of each state and province.

The maps carry as many political subdivisions as space will permit. Counties are shown on all U.S. state maps and on the maps of appropriate Canadian provinces. Other countries may not be mapped on a large enough scale to show administrative subdivisions. For some of these countries, the names of larger administrative subdivisions appear without the boundaries. In others, regions with historical significance are shown.

The following three pages discuss funda-mental concepts about maps which will aid in the use of the atlas: projections, scale, and map symbols.

Maps and Map Projections

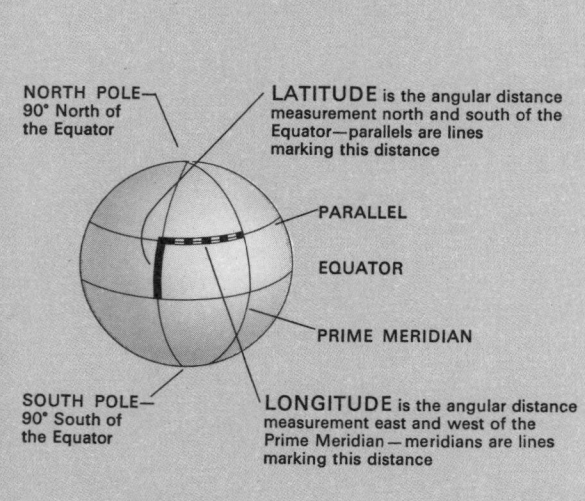

NORTH POLE—
90° North of
the Equator

LATITUDE is the angular distance
measurement north and south of the
Equator—parallels are lines
marking this distance

PARALLEL

EQUATOR

PRIME MERIDIAN

SOUTH POLE—
90° South of
the Equator

LONGITUDE is the angular distance
measurement east and west of the
Prime Meridian—meridians are lines
marking this distance

CONIC PROJECTIONS

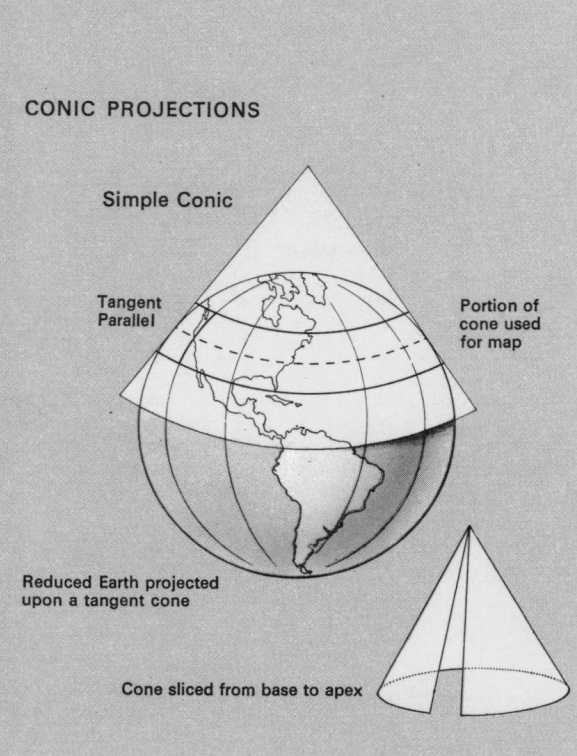

Simple Conic

Tangent
Parallel

Portion of
cone used
for map

Reduced Earth projected
upon a tangent cone

Cone sliced from base to apex

Cone developed
onto a flat surface

radius = side of cone

limit of projection band

projection band

From the earliest crude drawing to the latest highly
accurate, skillful execution, maps have played a
very important part in man's understanding of the
planet upon which he lives. Maps expand our
conceptions about areas. The following pages are de-
signed to point up some significant elements of maps
which are useful in intelligently interpreting them
and the variety of information they contain. These
sections are *Map Projections*, *Map Scale*, *Map Symbols*,
and the *Index Reference System*.

MAP PROJECTIONS
The systematic arrangement of parallels and meridians
on a plane or flat surface is the framework upon which a
map is constructed, and this orderly network is called a
map projection. Projections are actually developed
through the use of mathematical formulae. The process
can best be comprehended by visualizing the following
four steps.
1. The earth reduced to a small sphere.
2. Geometric forms—cone, cylinder, plane surface—
   placed upon or around this sphere.
3. Transferral of the Earth's imaginary grid of parallels and meridians to one of these forms.
4. The form flattened, producing the projection.

Conic Projections
The Simple Conic or Conic as it is often called, the
Lambert Conformal Conic, and the Polyconic, as their
names imply, are all conically derived. Most of the maps
in the atlas utilize these three conic projections. Parallels
and meridians are projected onto a cone that is tangent
to the reduced earth. Slicing the cone from its base to
apex and flattening it onto a flat surface results in the
Simple Conic Projection. Along the line that is tangent to
the surface, the scale of the map is true. This line, usually a parallel, is called a *standard parallel*. As regions
away from this line are mapped, the alterations of scale,
shape, areal size, and direction increase.

Cylindrical Projections
By projecting the Earth's grid onto a tangent cylinder, we can achieve a series of parallels and meridians
at right angles to one another, as they are on the Earth.
The three cylindrical projections illustrated here show
how the same outlined regions look on all three. Notice
that on all the maps there is a difference between the
regions' areal extent; however, the difference is mini-
mized by the Miller Projection. Comparison of the shapes
of the regions with those on a globe shows the Mercator
indicating this property most accurately. Other cylindrical projections enable the areas to be correctly shown
while distorting the shapes of the landmasses.

Plane Projections
Here transformation of the sphere directly to a tangent flat surface is the method of projection. The *Lambert
Azimuthal Equal Area Projection* is one upon which the
correct relationships between areas have been main-
tained. For instance, Greenland and the lower portion
of the Arabian Peninsula, which are approximately the
same in areal extent, appear to be so on the Lambert
Azimuthal Equal Area Projection. Notice, however, that
although Africa's area is shown correctly, it has been
stretched in one direction and compressed in another,
thus altering its shape and the scale of the projection.

Equal Area Projections of the World
To show the world in its entirety on a flat surface
so that areas may be compared intelligently, is extremely
difficult without altering the shapes of areas beyond rec-
ognition. Cylindrical projections do not accomplish this,
and plane and conic projections also do not represent
the whole world this way. Two projections are frequently
used today to accomplish this—the *Homolographic* and
the *Sinusoidal*. Each retains the equal area property of
the sphere, although each sacrifices uniform scale and
invites some extreme shape compression and shearing
in the polar areas of the projections.

In summary, where maps cover approximately a hem-
isphere of the Earth's surface, extreme distortion of some
type is evidenced. On most of the maps in the atlas,
however, individual choices of projections have been
made to present a realistic picture of the Earth. With
these maps the user may compare sizes of areas, shapes
of landmasses, and measure distances and directions
as accurately as necessary.

CYLINDRICAL PROJECTIONS

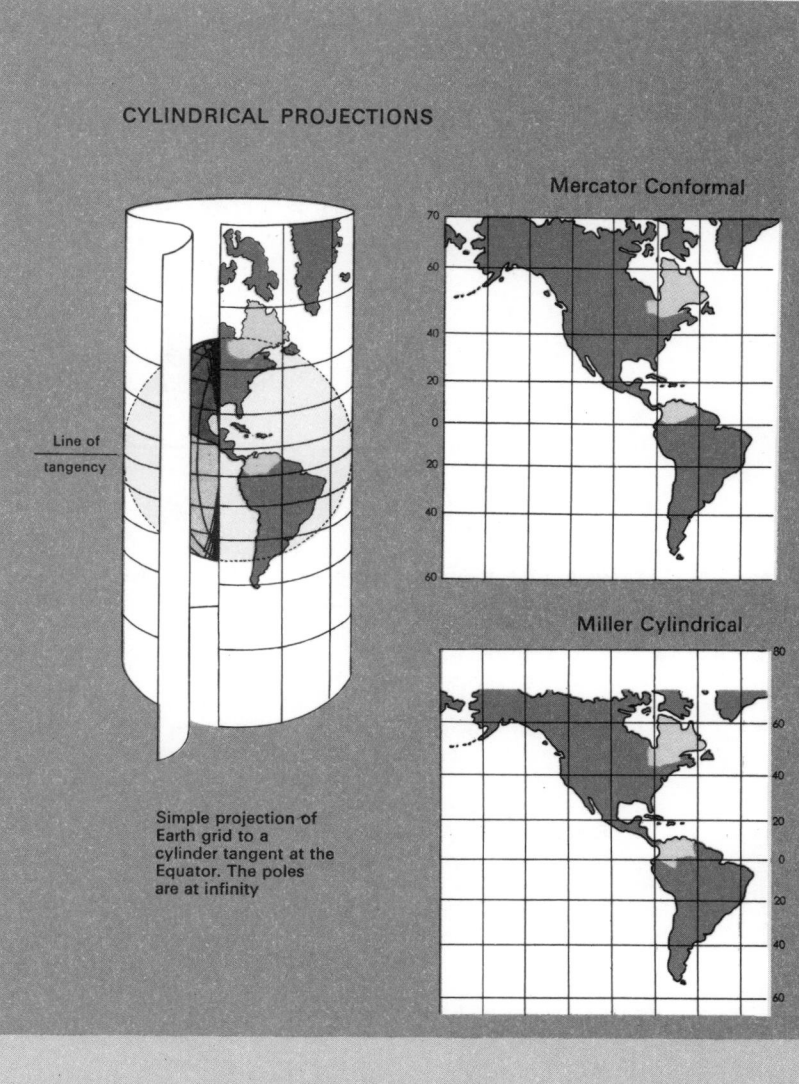

Line of
tangency

Simple projection of
Earth grid to a
cylinder tangent at the
Equator. The poles
are at infinity

Mercator Conformal

Miller Cylindrical

PLANE PROJECTIONS

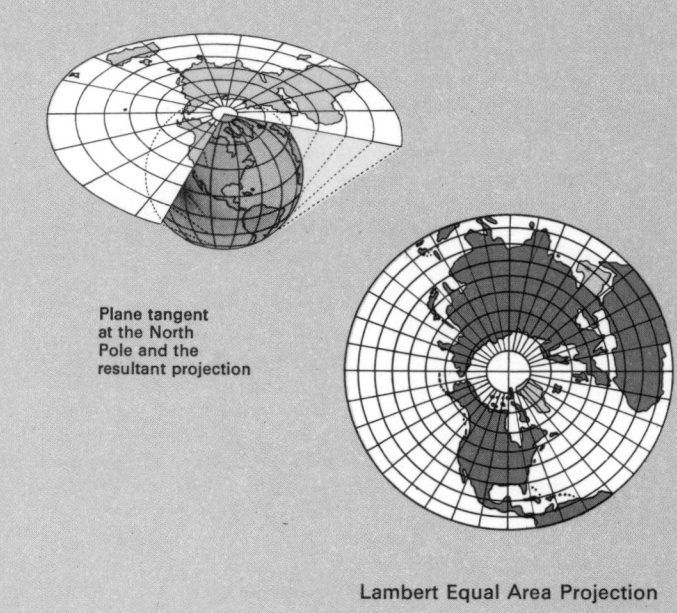

Plane tangent
at the North
Pole and the
resultant projection

Lambert Equal Area Projection

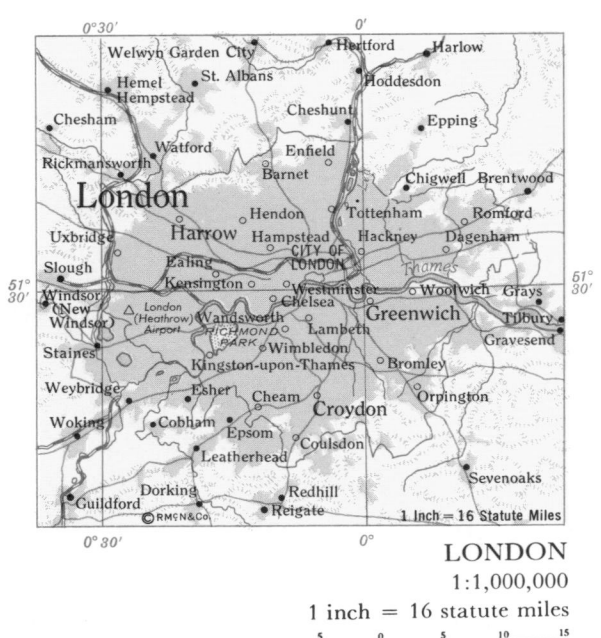

LONDON
1:1,000,000
1 inch = 16 statute miles

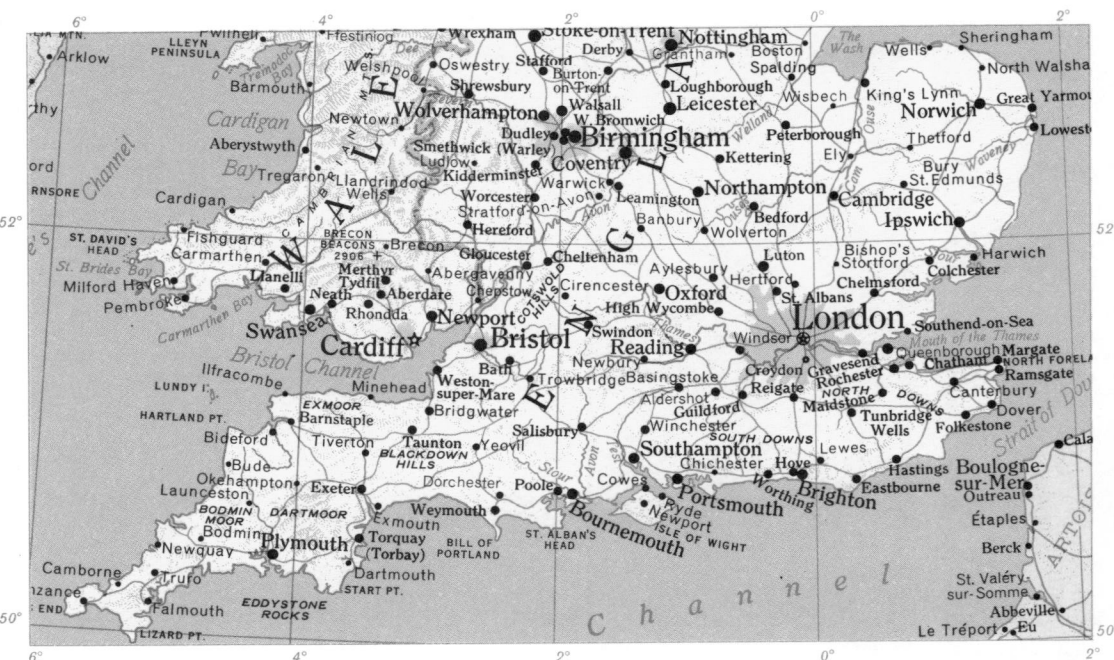

LONDON AND VICINITY
1:2,000,000
1 inch = 32 statute miles

MAP SCALE

The scale of a map is the relationship it has with the area it represents. It usually is determined by measuring the distance between two places on the map and relating this to the distance between the same two places on the Earth's surface. This relationship may be stated in a number of different ways. Three commonly used methods are the representative fraction, a written statement, and a graphic portrayal. Each of the four maps on this page has its scale stated by these three methods.

The *representative fraction* is written either $\frac{1}{1,000,000}$ or 1:1,000,000. The map unit is always given as one, and the number of similar units this map unit represents on the Earth's surface is written as the denominator of the fraction, or after the colon. Thus, 1 inch or 1 centimeter on the London map in the upper left of the page represents 1,000,000 inches or 1,000,000 centimeters on the Earth's surface. In order to determine how many miles on the Earth 1 inch on the map represents, divide 63,360 (the number of inches in one mile) into 1,000,000. This results in the *written scale* being stated 1 inch represents approximately 16 miles. To further simplify the written scale by a *graphic portrayal*, a distance measured on the map may be converted to the Earth miles it represents by reading directly off the scale. The measured distance from London to Glasgow on the 1:16,000,000 scale map is 1.35 inches, which represents approximately 340 miles, the actual distance on the Earth's surface.

Because the Earth is spherical in shape and the map representing this sphere is flat, a degree of stretching and compressing has taken place in the projection of the sphere to the flat surface. (See the preceding section on projections). Inconsistency of scale from place to place on all maps is one of the results of this flattening process. The size relationship of map measurement to Earth measurement (scale) may not be exactly as stated on all parts of the map. Generally, as one moves away from the standard parallels, or the midsection of the map, toward the periphery, the stated scale changes. Because most of the Cosmo Series Maps encompass relatively small portions of the Earth's surface, the change in scale is of little consequence for general map use.

On world maps, however, where the scale varies greatly from one latitude to another, a varying graphic scale is employed. See the Graphic Linear Scale employed on the world map on pages 2 and 3. This permits accurate measurements at various parallels of latitude. At parallel 45°, 1 inch represents approximately 1,000 miles; at parallel 60° 1 inch represents approximately 700 miles.

As the scale of a map increases, the amount of information and detail shown increases, that is, the representative fraction and scale become larger. Notice in the four examples on this page how the increase in scale makes possible an increase in the number of cities shown, in the detail of the coastline, and in the intricacy and number of rivers.

SOUTHERN ENGLAND
1:4,000,000
1 inch = 64 statute miles

NORTHWEST EUROPE
1:16,000,000
1 inch = 252 statute miles

Reference Maps

MAP SYMBOLS

CULTURAL FEATURES

Political Boundaries

International
Secondary (State, province, etc.)
County

Populated Places

Cities, towns, and villages

•••••• Symbol size represents population of the place

Chicago
Gary
Racine
Glenview
Edgewood

Type size represents relative importance of the place.

Corporate area of large U.S. and Canadian cities and urban area of other foreign cities

Major Urban Area
Area of continuous commercial, industrial, and residential development in and around a major city

○ Community within a city
⊛ Capital of major political unit
☆ Capital of secondary political unit
◉ Capital of U.S. state or Canadian province
◦ County Seat
▲ Military Installation
⊙ Scientific Station

Miscellaneous

National Park
National Monument
Provincial Park
Indian Reservation
△ Point of Interest
∴ Ruins
■ ⚒ Buildings
▭ Race Track
Railroad – International Maps
Tunnel
Underground or Subway
Dam
Bridge
Dike

Highway – U.S. and Canadian Maps
Railroad – U.S. and Canadian Maps

LAND FEATURES

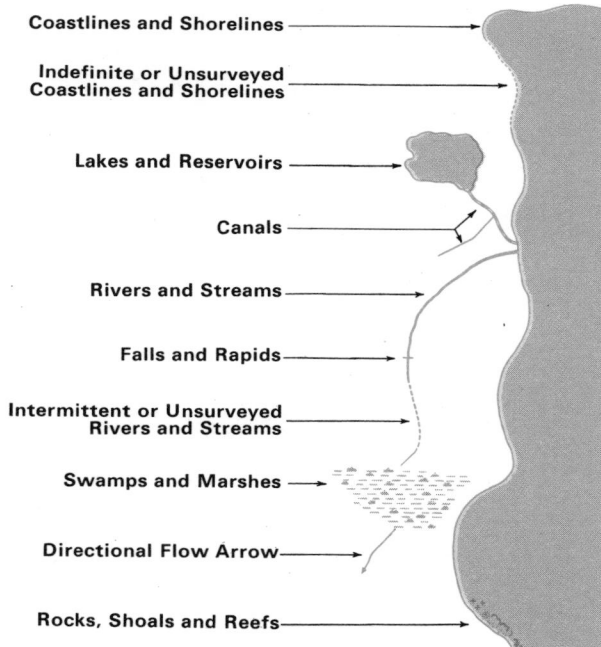

Ranges →
Peaks →
Passes → LITTLE PASS
Point of Elevation above sea level — 8,520 FT.
Escarpments, Bluffs, Cliffs, and Plateaus — PLATEAU
Glaciers →
Volcanoes →
Lava Flows →
Sand Dunes →
Deserts →

WATER FEATURES

Coastlines and Shorelines ——→
Indefinite or Unsurveyed Coastlines and Shorelines ——→
Lakes and Reservoirs ——→
Canals ——→
Rivers and Streams ——→
Falls and Rapids ——→
Intermittent or Unsurveyed Rivers and Streams ——→
Swamps and Marshes ——→
Directional Flow Arrow ——→
Rocks, Shoals and Reefs ——→

TYPE STYLES USED TO NAME FEATURES

A S I A	Continent	PANTELLERIA (ITALY) Country of which unit is a dependency in parentheses	U I N T A DESERT Major Terrain Features
DENMARK CANADA	Country, State, or Province	SRI LANKA (CEYLON) Former or alternate name	MT. MORIAH Individual Mountain
BÉARN	Region, Province, or Historical Region	Rome (Roma) Local or alternate city name	STROMBOLI NUNIVAK Island or Coastal Feature
		Naval Air Station Military Installation	Ocean Lake River Canal Hydrographic Features
CROCKETT	County	MESA VERDE SAN XAVIER National Park or Monument, Provincial Park, Indian Res.,	

Note: Size of type varies according to importance and available space. Letters for names of major features are spread across the extent of the feature.

THE INDEX REFERENCE SYSTEM

Place	Location	Index Key	Page
Cadillac, Que., Can	*h11	73
Cadillac, Sask., Can	H2	70
Cadillac, Fr	E3	14
Cadillac, Wexford, Mich	B4	90
Cadiz, San Bernardino, Calif.	E6	82
Cadiz, Trigg, Ky	D2	94
Cadron, creek, Ark	B3	81
Caen, Fr	C3	14
Caetité, Braz	D2	57
Calcutta, India	D8	39
Cambridge, Eng	B8	12
Catania, It	F5	21
Ceará, state, Braz	C3	57
Chamblee, DeKalb, Ga	h8	87
Chambly, Que., Can	D4	73
Chambord, Que., Can	A5	73
Champagne, former prov., Fr.	C5	14
Champaign, Champaign, Ill.	B4	90
Champdoré, lake, Que., Can	g8	75
Champerico, Guat	C2	62
Champéry, Switz	D2	19
Champex, Switz	D3	19
Champigneulles, Fr	F6	15
Champion, Chase, Nebr	D4	103
Champlain, co., Que., Can	B4	73
Champlain, lake, N.Y., Vt.	B2	120
Champotón, Mex	D6	63
Changchou, China	E8	33
Chanthaburi, Thai	F5	38
Chaparral, Col	C2	60
Charleville-Mézières, Fr	C6	14
Chatham, Eng	C8	12
Chiapa de Corzo, Mex	D6	63
Chiapas, state, Mex	D6	63
Chiba, Jap	I10, n19	37
Chiba, pref., Jap	*I10	37
Chibemba, Ang	E1	48
Chibougamau, Que., Can	k12	73
Chicago, Cook, Ill	B4	90
Chichaoua, Mor	C3	44
Chichen Itzá, ruins, Mex	C7	63
Chichester, Eng	D7	12
Chickasaw, co., Iowa	A5	92
Chiclana, Sp	D2	20
Chiclayo, Peru	C2	58
Columbus, Franklin, Ohio	C3	111

The indexing system used in this atlas is based upon the conventional pattern of parallels and meridians used to indicate latitude and longitude. The index samples beside the map indicate that the cities of *Chicago, Cadillac,* and *Champaign* are all located in *B4.* Each index key letter, *in this case "B,"* is placed between corresponding degree numbers of latitude in the vertical borders of the map. Each index key number, *in this case "4,"* is placed between corresponding degree numbers of longitude in the horizontal borders of the map. Crossing of the parallels above and below the index letter with the meridians on each side of the index number forms a confining "box" in which the given place is certain to be located. It is important to note that location of the place may be anywhere in this confining "box."

Insets on many foreign maps are indexed independently of the main maps by separate index key letters and figures. All places indexed to these insets are identified by the lower case reference letter in the index key. A diamond-shaped symbol in the margin of the map is used to separate the insets from the main map and also to separate key letters and numbers where the spacing of the parallels and meridians is great.

Place-names are indexed to the location of the city symbol. Political divisions and physical features are indexed to the location of their names on the map.

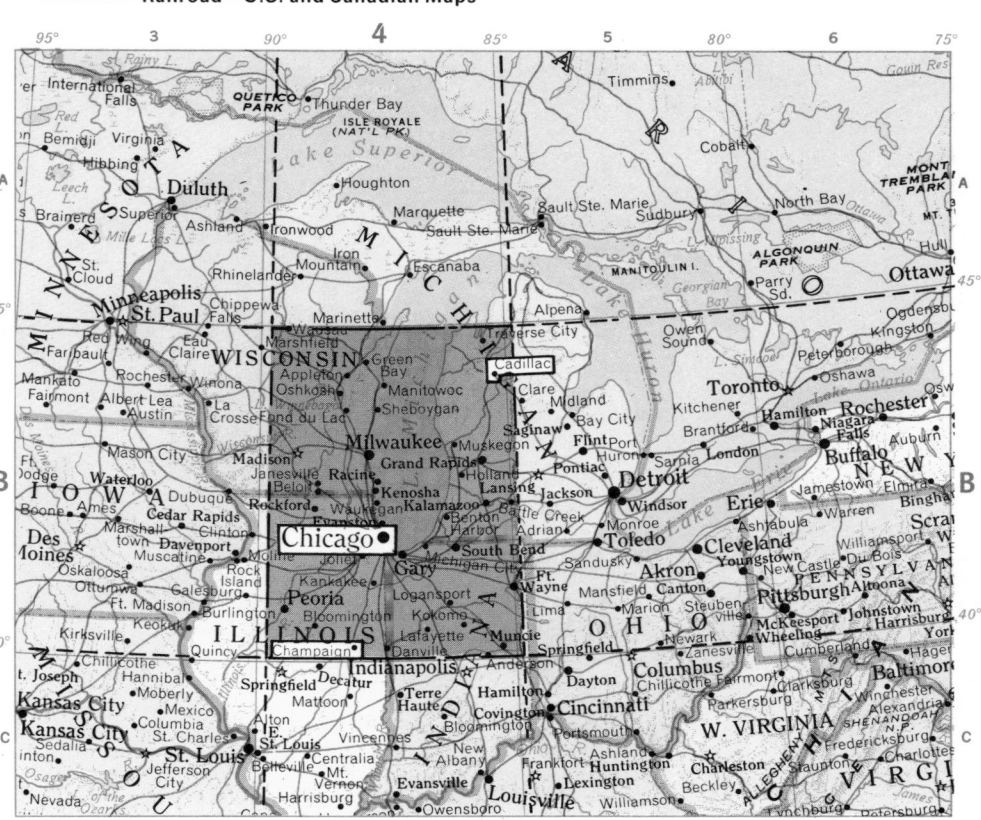

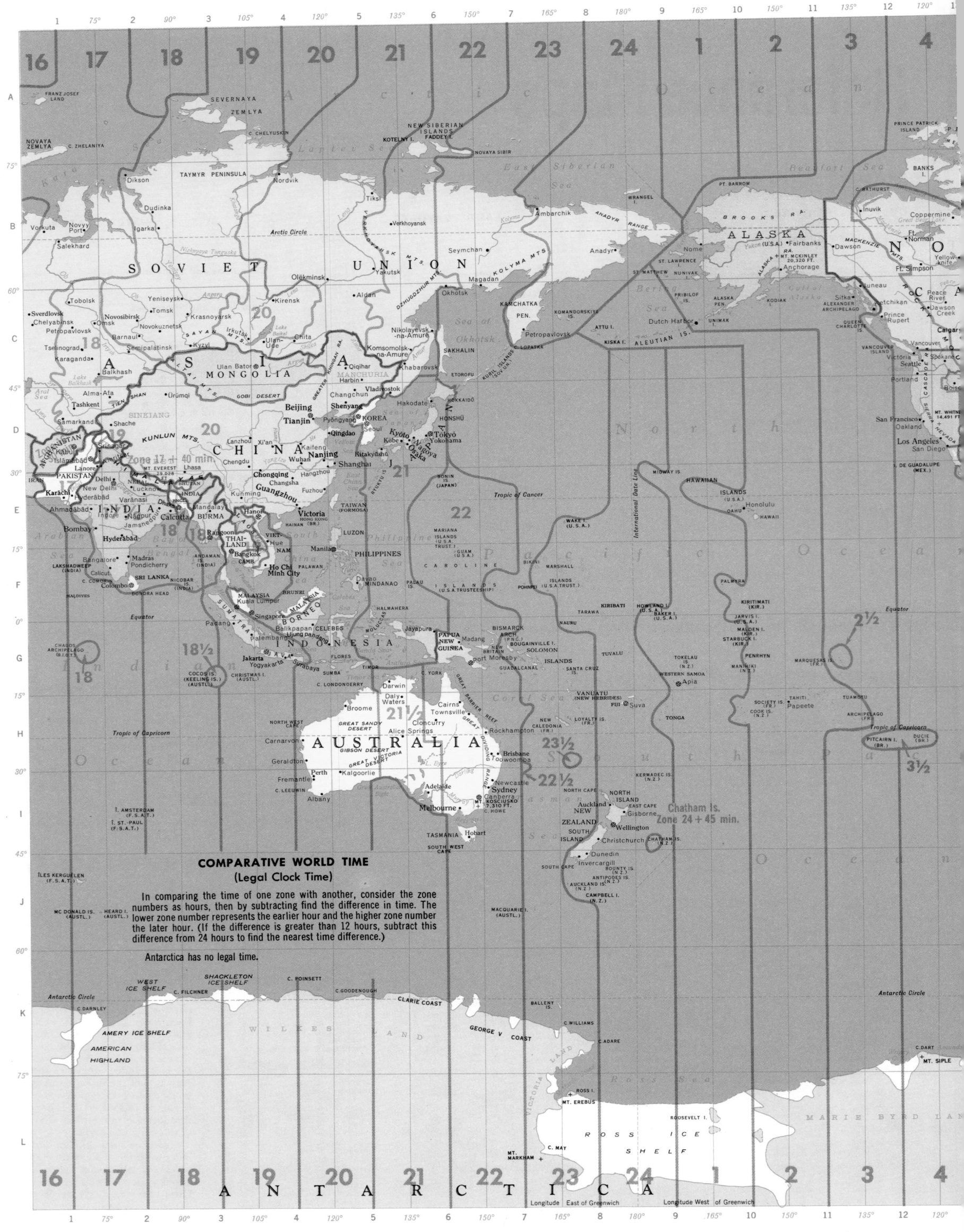

COMPARATIVE WORLD TIME
(Legal Clock Time)

In comparing the time of one zone with another, consider the zone numbers as hours, then by subtracting find the difference in time. The lower zone number represents the earlier hour and the higher zone number the later hour. (If the difference is greater than 12 hours, subtract this difference from 24 hours to find the nearest time difference.)

Antarctica has no legal time.

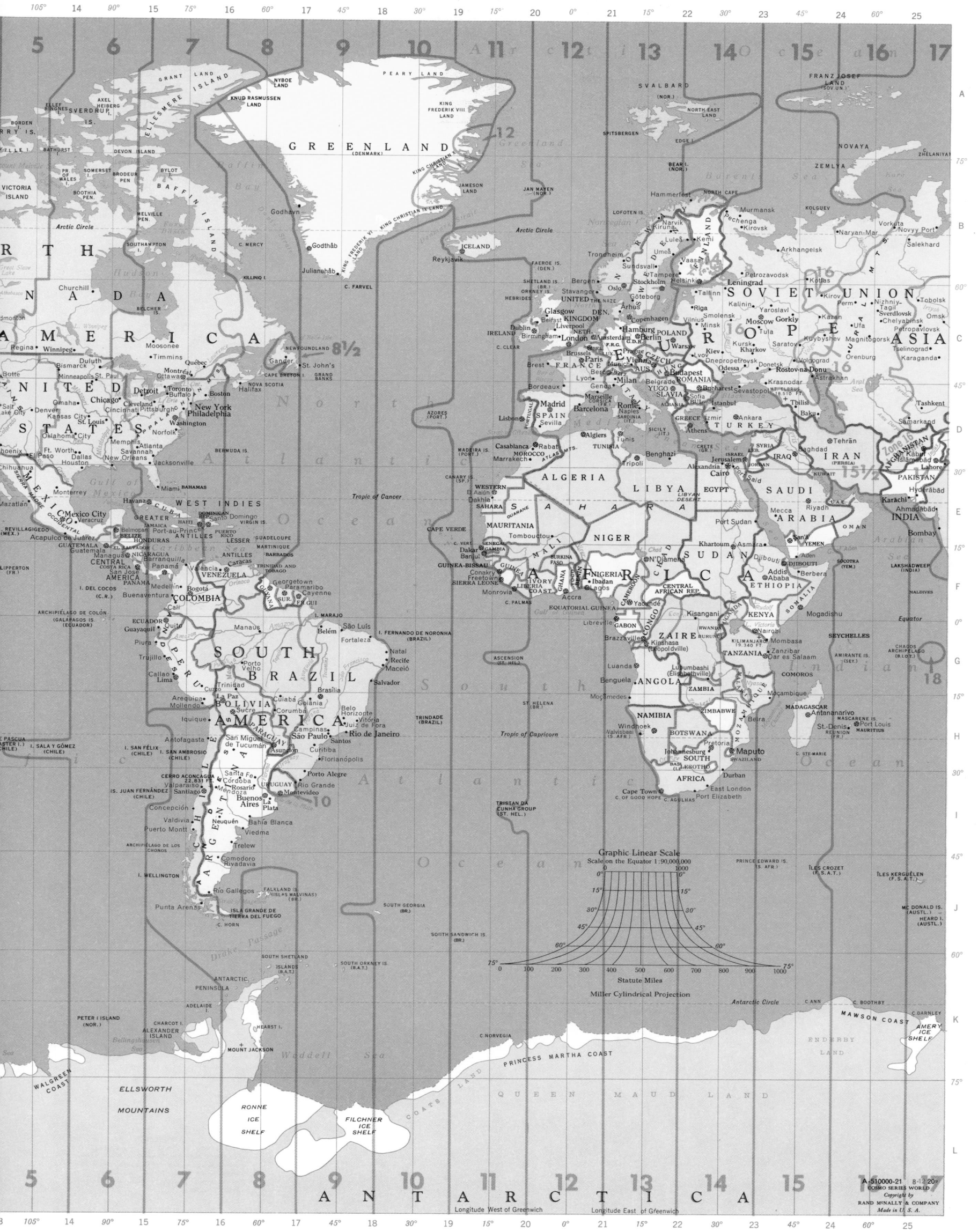

Graphic Linear Scale
Scale on the Equator 1:90,000,000

Statute Miles

Miller Cylindrical Projection

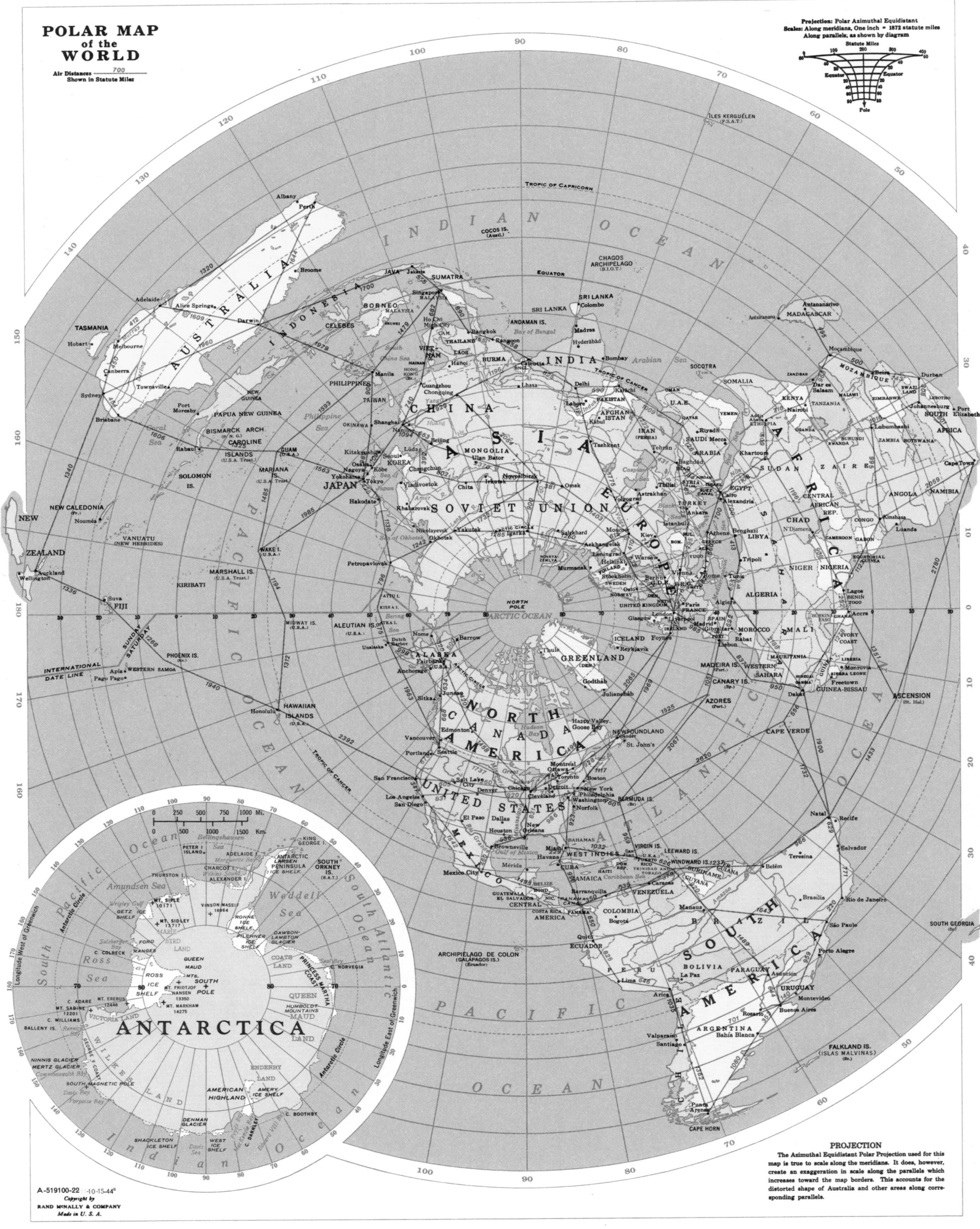

POLAR MAP
of the
WORLD

Air Distances 700 / Shown in Statute Miles

Projection: Polar Azimuthal Equidistant
Scales: Along meridians, One inch = 1872 statute miles
Along parallels, as shown by diagram

PROJECTION

The Azimuthal Equidistant Polar Projection used for this map is true to scale along the meridians. It does, however, create an exaggeration in scale along the parallels which increases toward the map borders. This accounts for the distorted shape of Australia and other areas along corresponding parallels.

A-519100-22 · -40-15-44⁶
Copyright by
RAND McNALLY & COMPANY
Made in U. S. A.

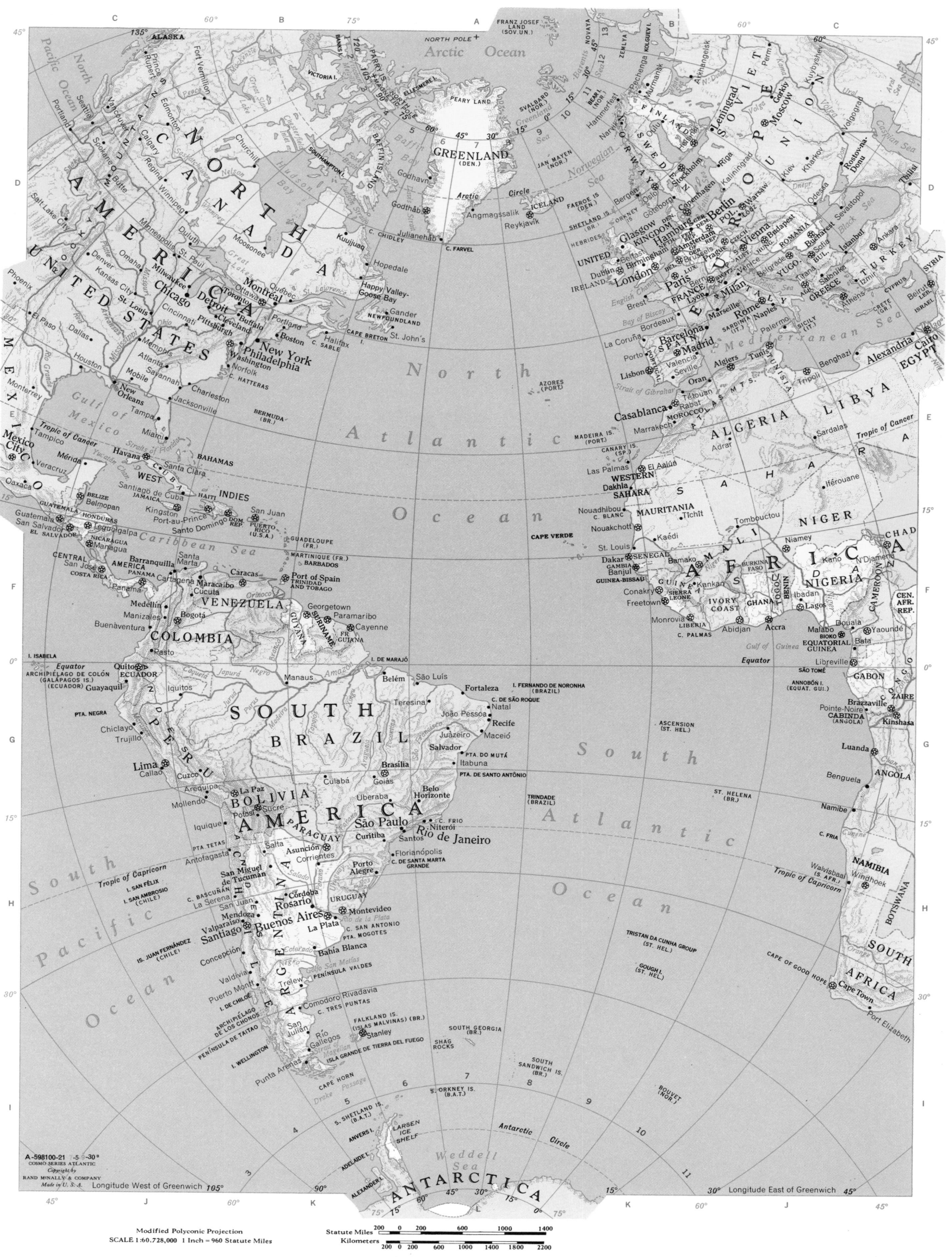

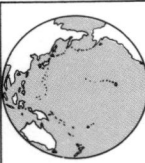

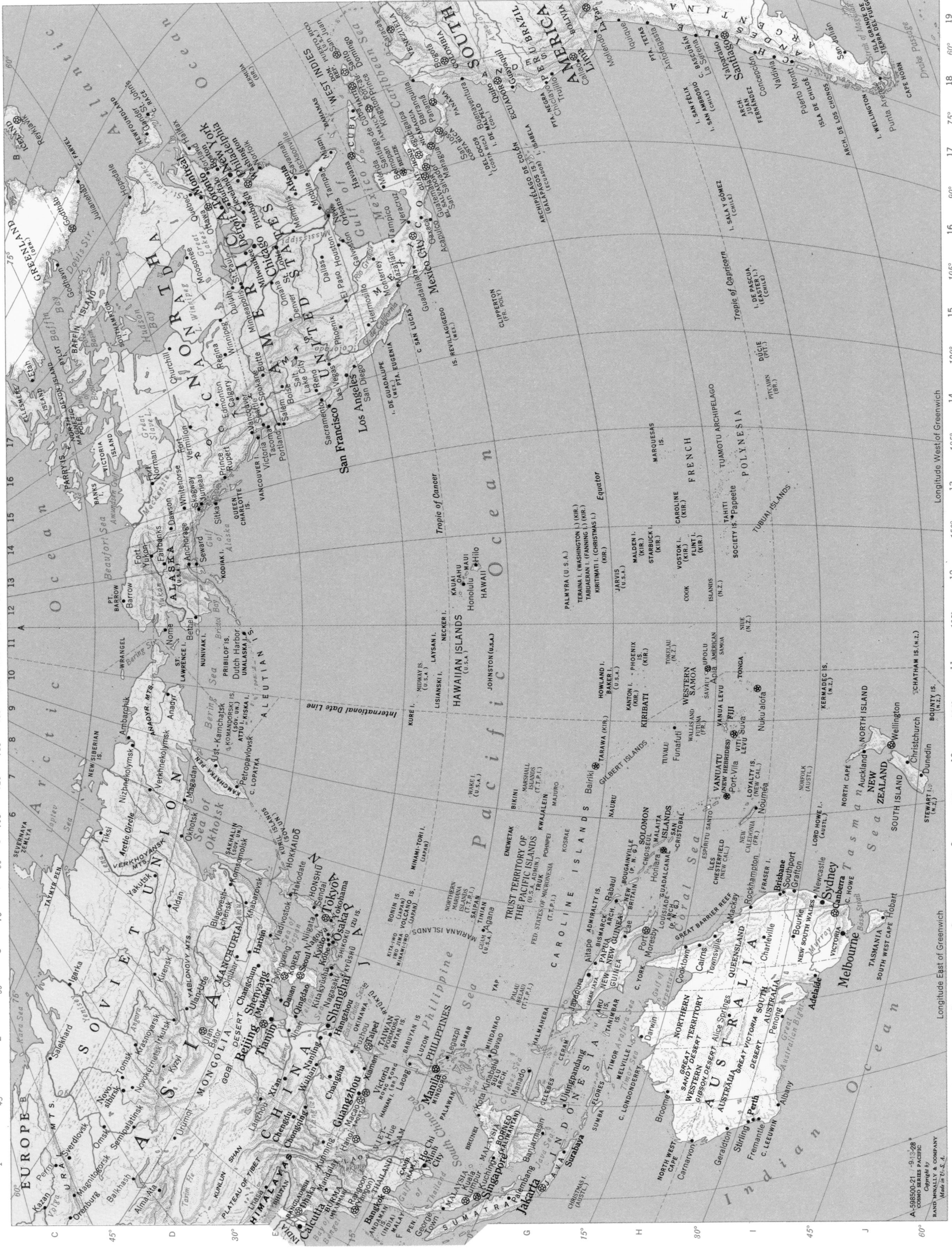

Modified Secant Conic Projection
SCALE 1:66,800,000   1 Inch = 1,040 Statute Miles

Statute Miles 200 0 200 600 1000 1400
Kilometers 200 0 200 600 1000 1400 1800 2200

Modified Secant Conic Projection
SCALE 1:66,800,000   1 Inch = 1,040 Statute Miles

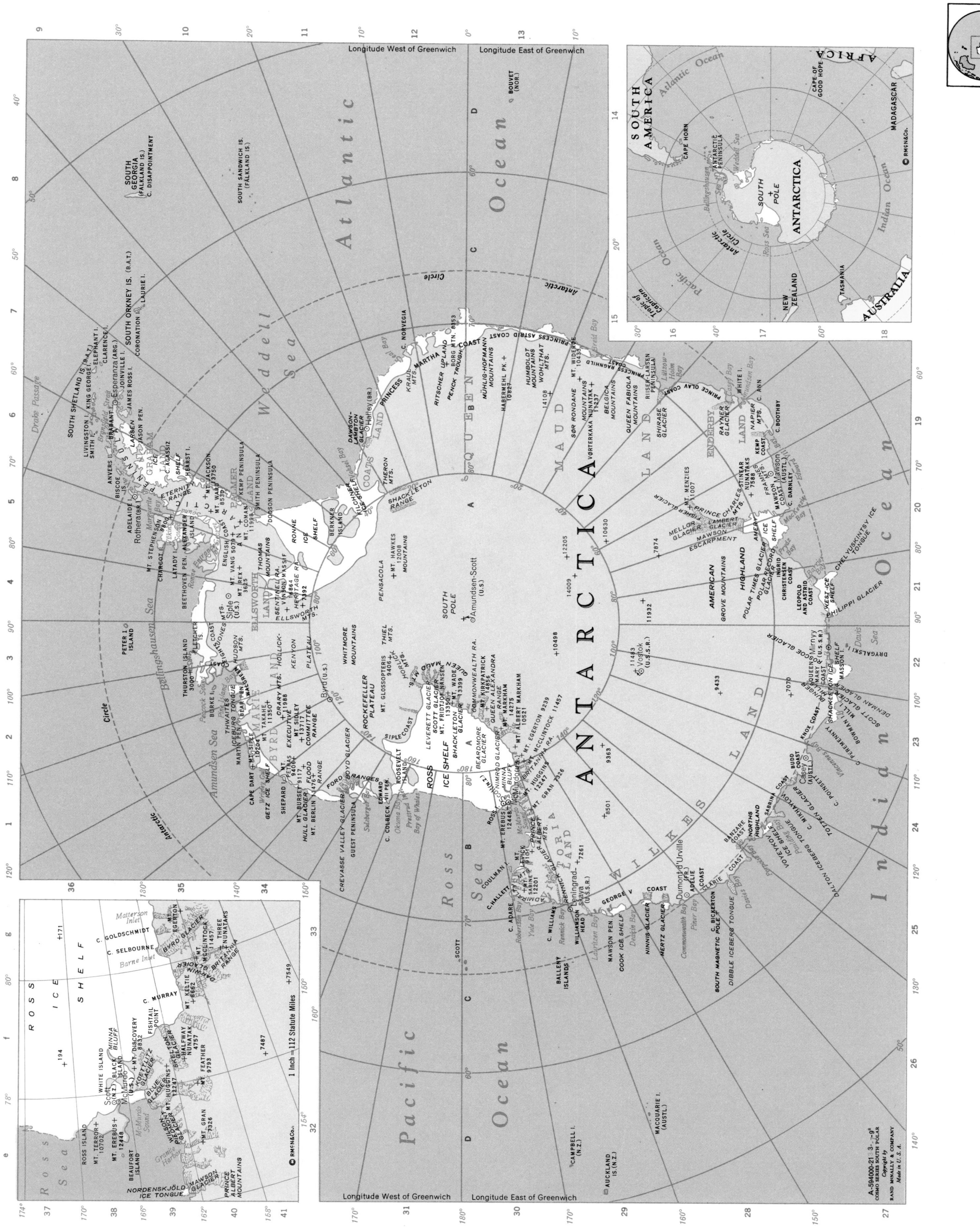

Lambert Azimuthal Equal Area Projection
SCALE 1:28,000,000   1 Inch = 442 Statute Miles

Statute Miles
100 0 100 200 300 400 500

Kilometers
100 0 100 300 500 700

1 Inch = 112 Statute Miles

A-59000-21-3·-9⁵
COSMO SERIES SOUTH POLAR
Copyright by
RAND McNALLY & COMPANY
Made in U.S.A.

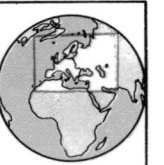

SOVIET UNION

RUSSIAN SOVIET FEDERATIVE SOCIALIST REPUBLIC

WEST SIBERIAN LOWLAND

CENTRAL SIBERIAN UPLANDS

KAZAKH S. S. R.

UZBEK S.S.R.

TURKMEN S.S.R.

KARA-KUM DESERT

KYZYL KUM DESERT

MOINKUM DESERT

UST-URT PLATEAU

MONGOLIA

CHINA

AFGHANISTAN

PAKISTAN

INDIA

IRAN (PERSIA)

PLATEAU OF IRAN

DASHT-E KAVIR

DASHT-E LUT

DASHT-E SISTAN

RIGESTAN

IRAQ

SYRIA

SYRIAN DESERT

SAUDI ARABIA

JORDAN

LEBANON

ISRAEL

ASIA MINOR

KEY

HINDU KUSH

TIEN SHAN

Ocean

Kara Sea

White Sea

Caspian Sea

Aral Sea

Black Sea

Persian Gulf

Arabian Sea

NOVAYA ZEMLYA

VAYGACH I.

KOLGUYEV ISLAND

KOLA PENINSULA

YAMAL PEN.

Arctic Circle

Moscow (Moskva)
Gorkiy
Kharkov
Kiev
Volgograd
Dnepropetrovsk
Donetsk
Rostov-na-Donu
Baku
Tbilisi
Yerevan
Tashkent
Tehrān
Baghdad
Damascus (Dimashq)
Beirut (Bayrūt)
Aleppo (Halab)
Mosul (Al Mawṣil)
Basra (Al Baṣrah)
Kuwait
Karachi
Rawalpindi
Peshawar
Kābul
Qandahār
Mashhad
Eṣfahān
Shiraz
Arkhangelsk
Leningrad

MT. NARODNAYA 6,217 FT.
MT. ELBRUS 18,510 FT.
MT. ARARAT 16,804 FT.
MT. AKSORAN 5,135 FT.

Conic Projection
SCALE 1:16,000,000   1 Inch = 252 Statute Miles

Longitude East of Greenwich

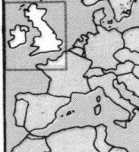

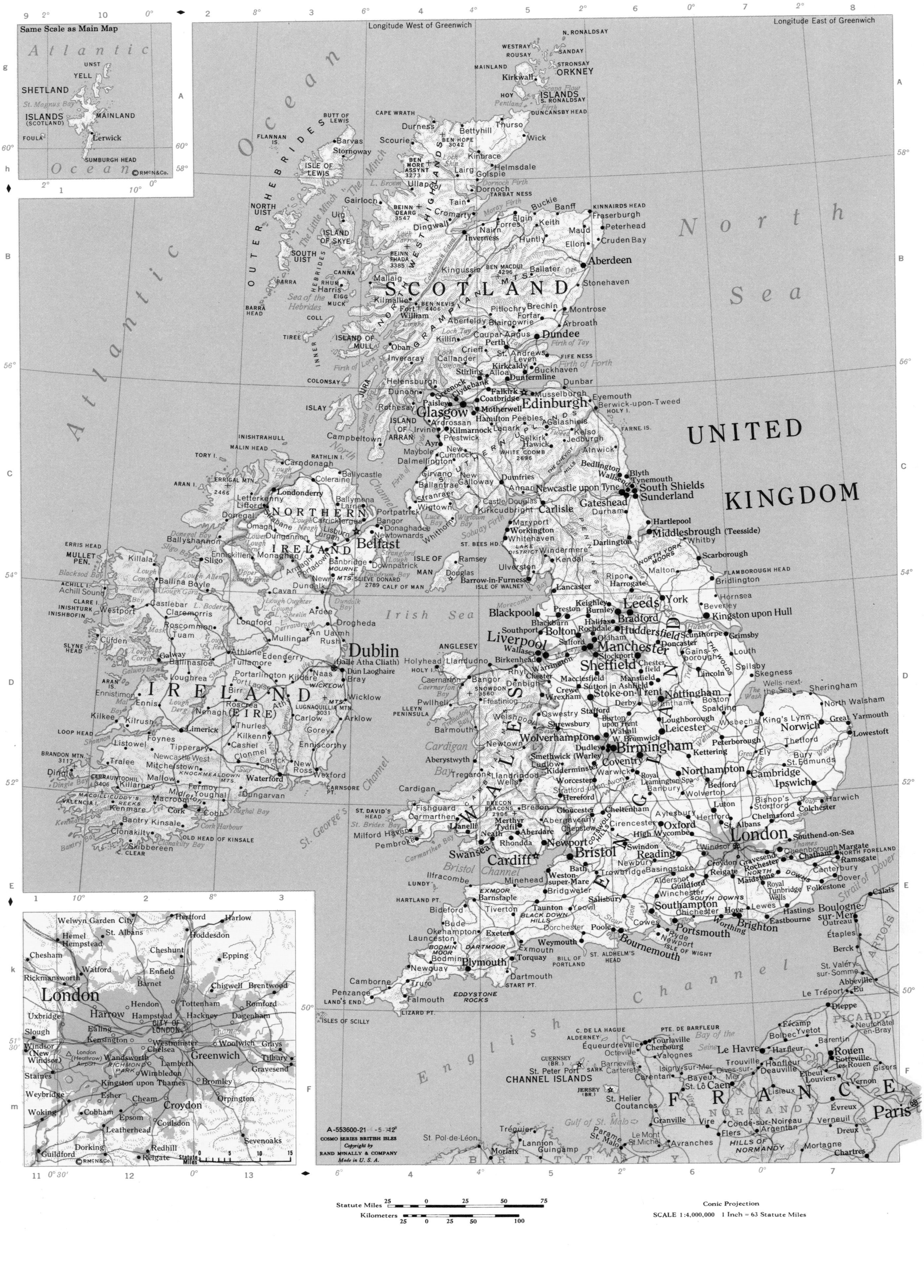

Lambert Conformal Conic Projection
SCALE 1 : 2,000,000 1 Inch = 32 Statute Miles

Statute Miles 5 0 5 10 20 30 40 50
Kilometers 5 0 5 10 20 30 40 50 60

A-551700-21-4 -6-7°
COSMO SERIES IRELAND
Copyright by
RAND McNALLY & COMPANY
Made in U.S.A.

Longitude West of Greenwich

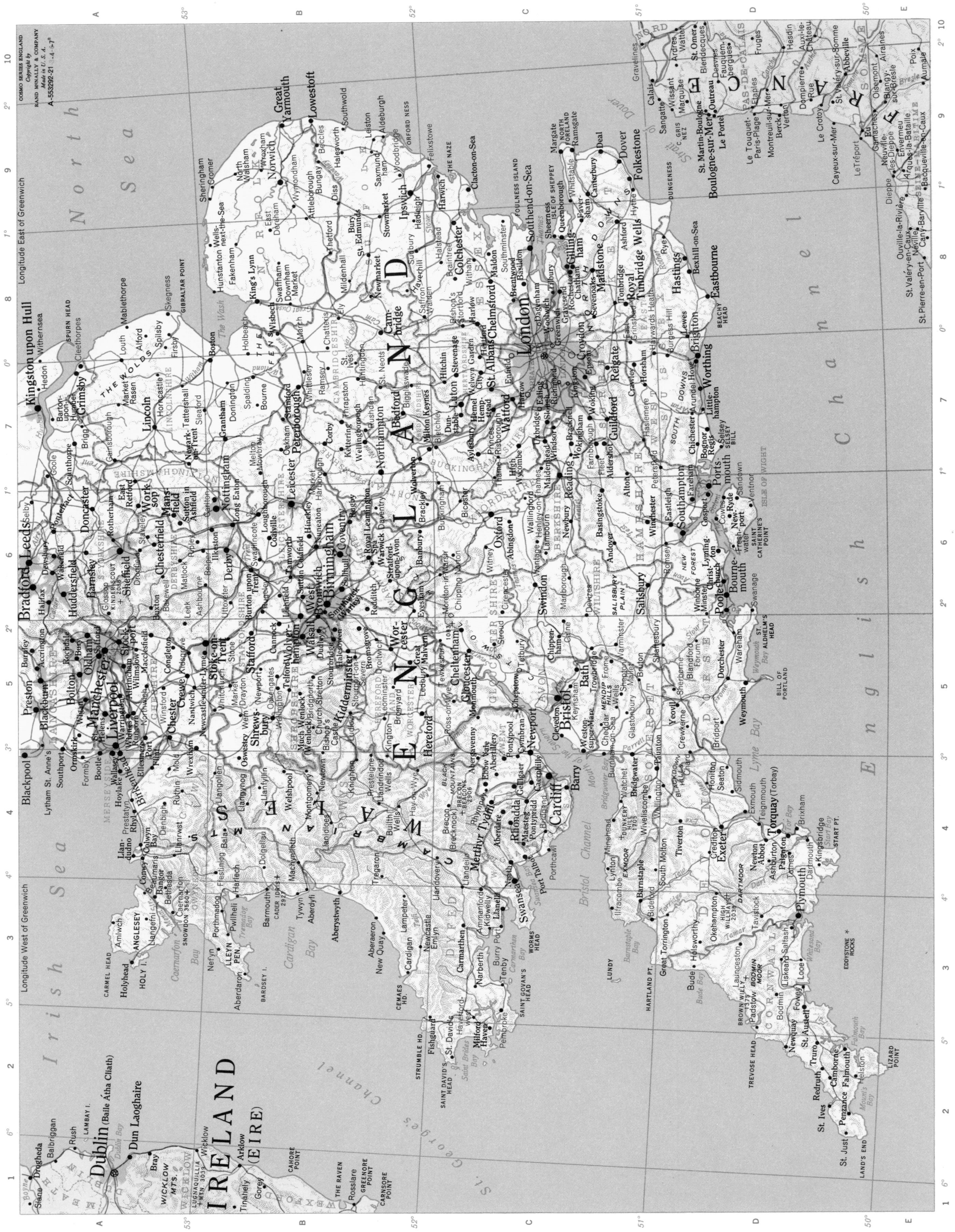

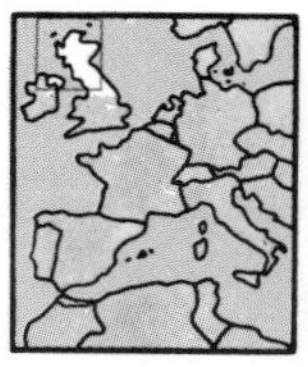

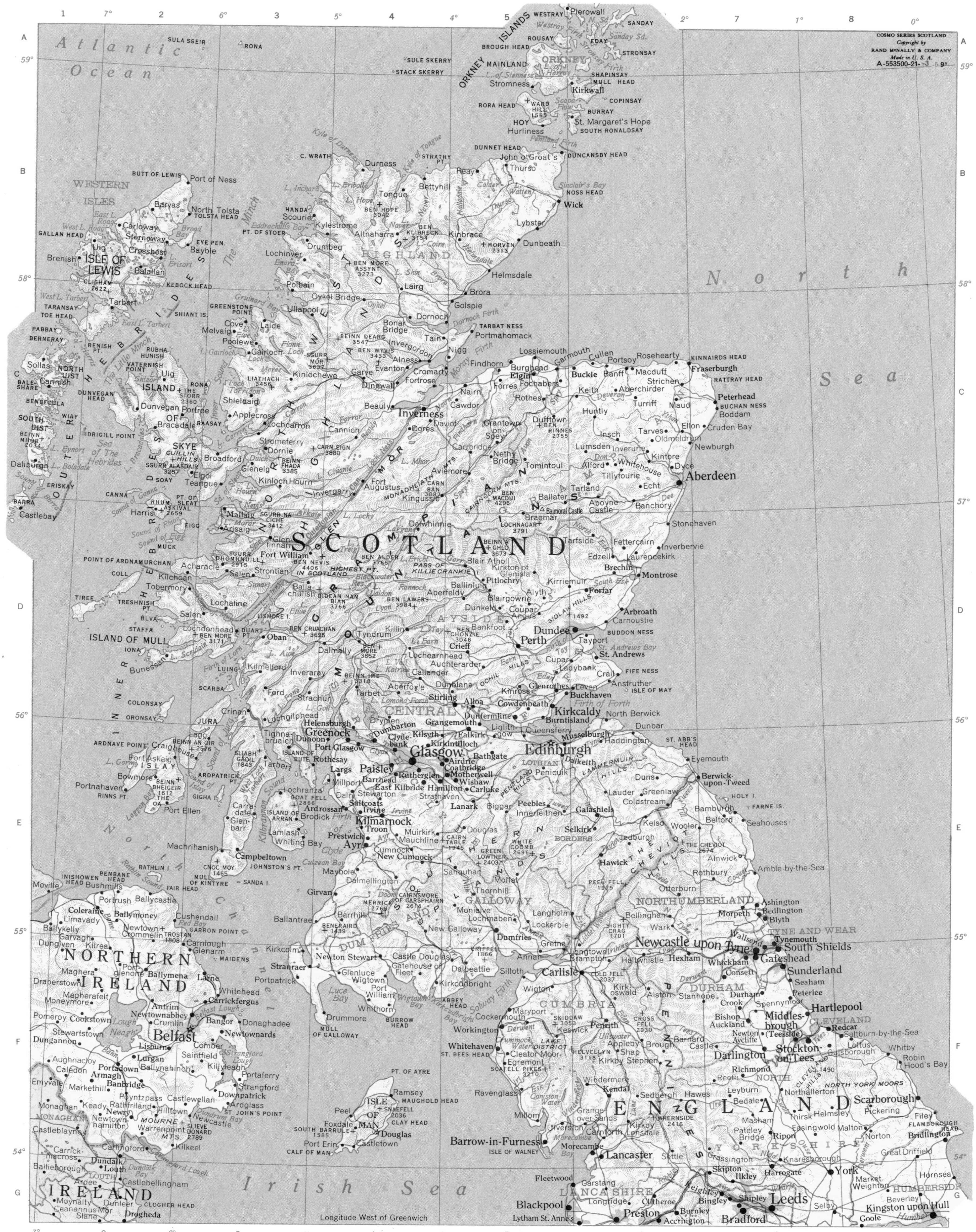

COSMO SERIES SCOTLAND
Copyright by
RAND M⁹NALLY & COMPANY
Made in U. S. A.
A-553500-21-

Lambert Conformal Conic Projection
SCALE 1 : 2,000,000 1 Inch = 32 Statute Miles

Statute Miles
Kilometers

Longitude West of Greenwich

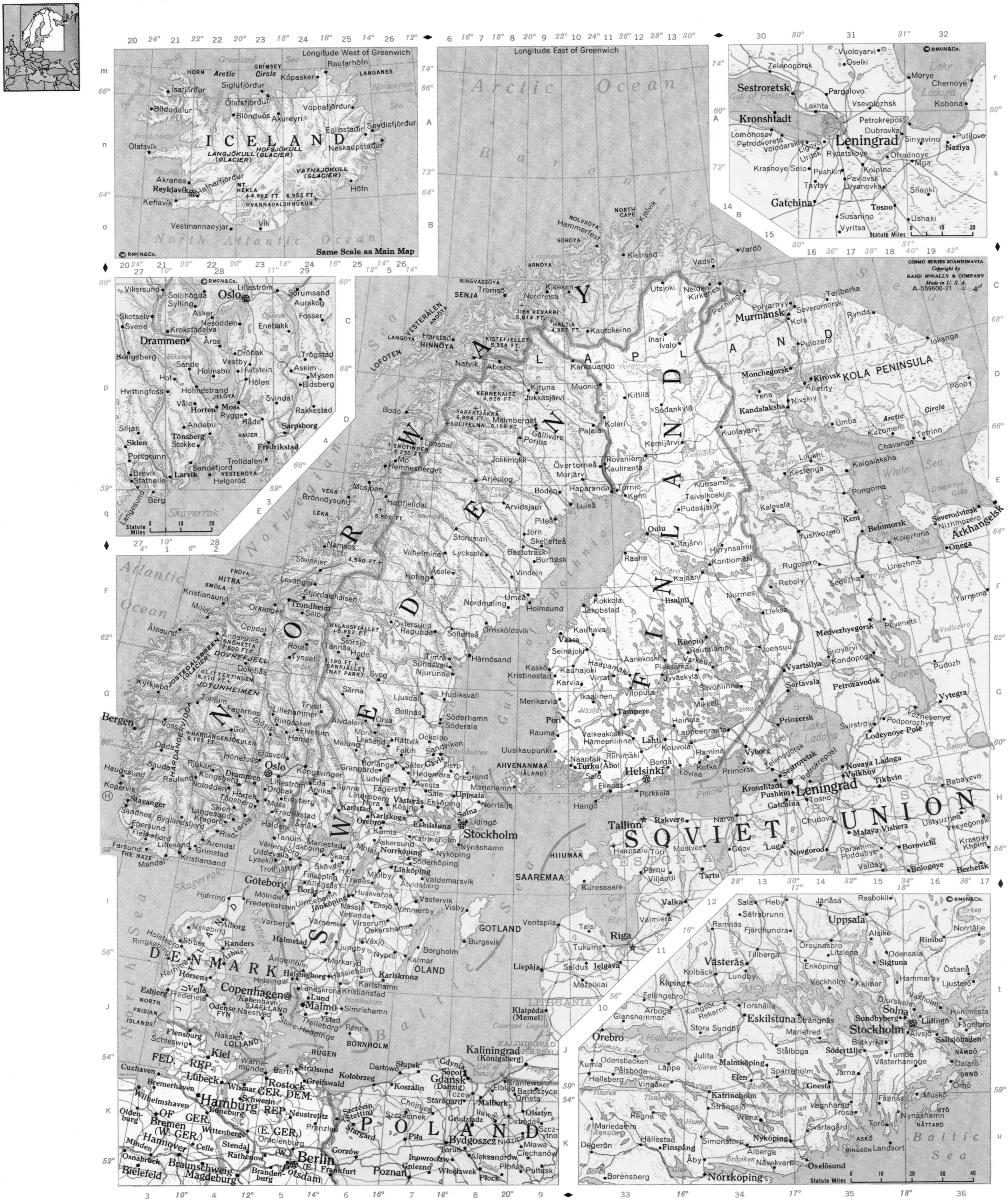

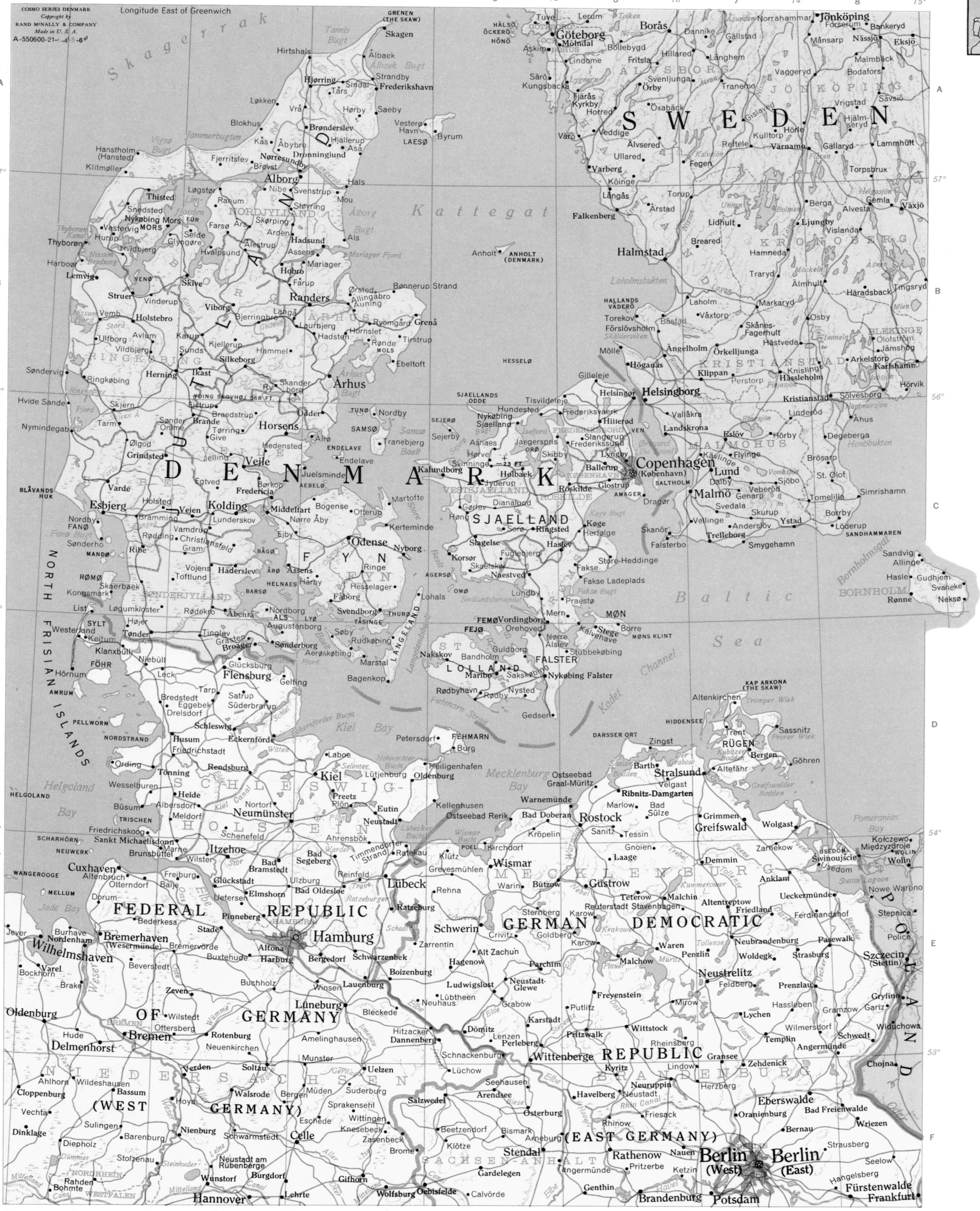

SCALE 1:2,000,000   1 Inch = 32 Statute Miles

Lambert Conformal Conic Projection

Statute Miles

Kilometers

Longitude East of Greenwich

COSMO SERIES DENMARK

Copyright by
RAND M9NALLY & COMPANY
Made in U.S.A.
A-550600-21-... 4...-6²

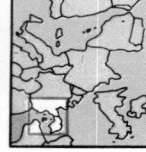

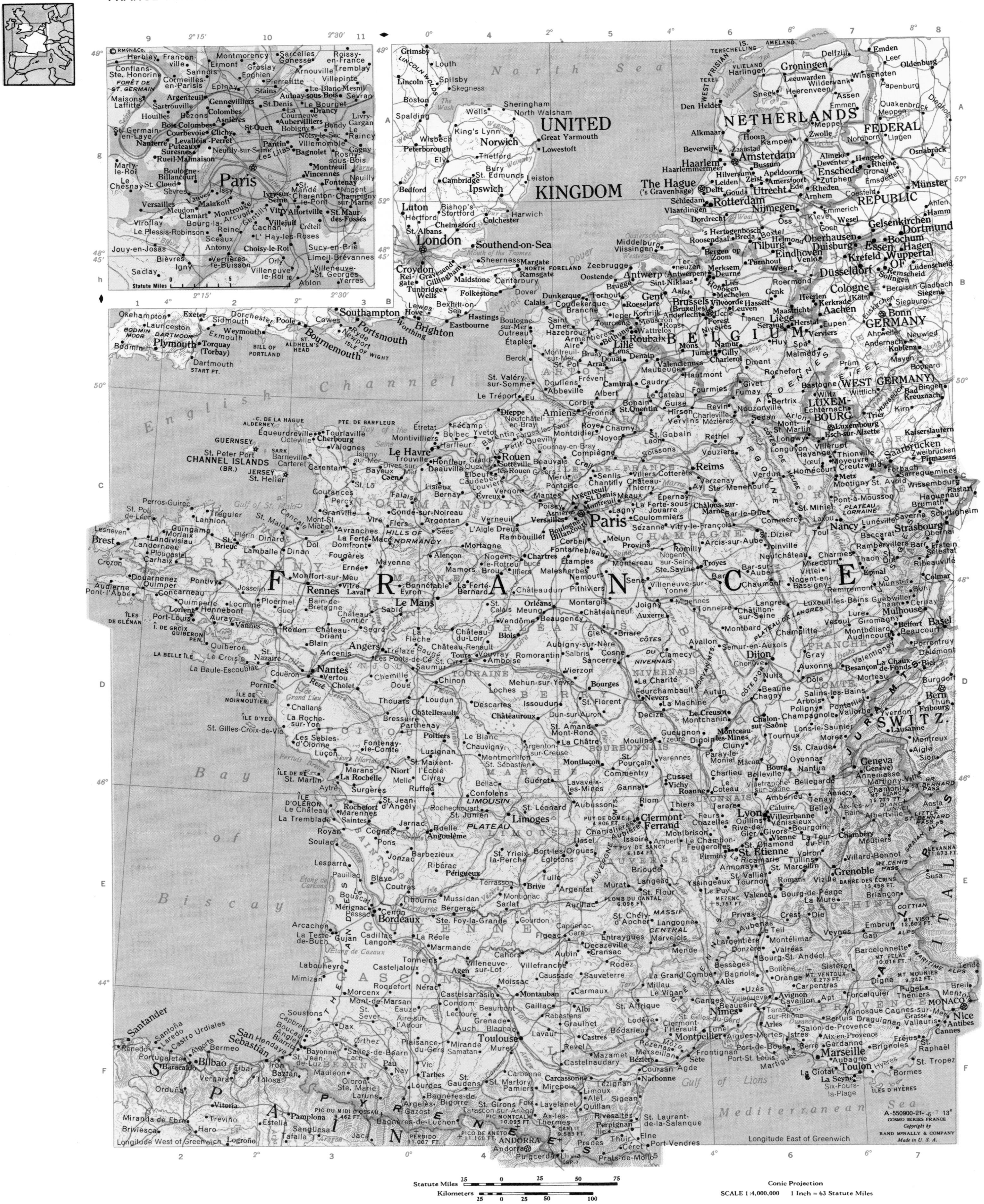

FRANCE AND THE LOW COUNTRIES

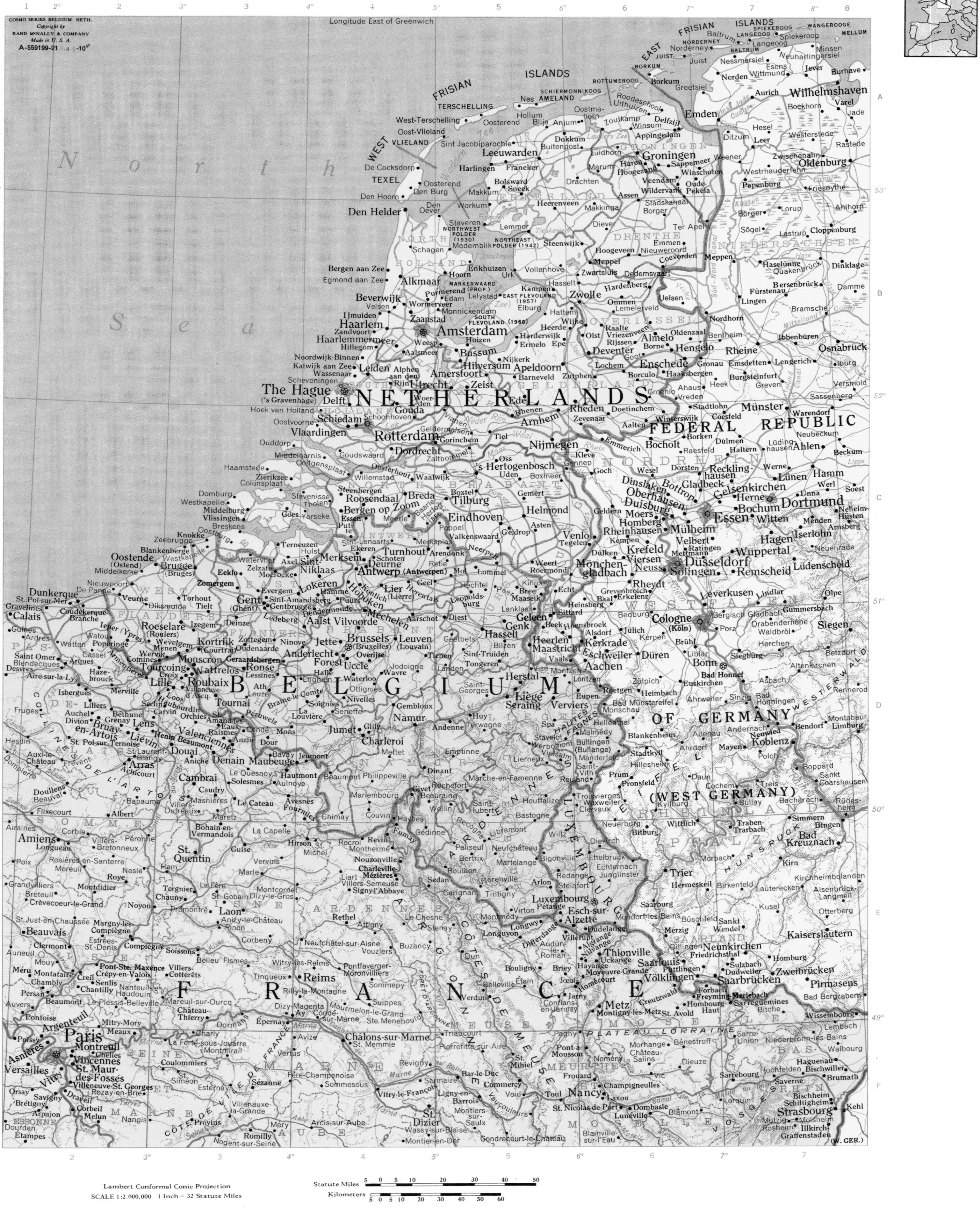

SCALE 1:2,000,000 1 Inch = 32 Statute Miles
Lambert Conformal Conic Projection

Kilometers
Statute Miles

Longitude East of Greenwich

COSMO SERIES BELGIUM NETH.
Copyright by
RAND M^{c}NALLY & COMPANY
Made in U.S.A.
A-559199-21

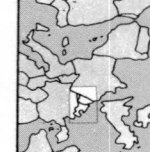

BELGIUM, NETHERLANDS, LUXEMBOURG AND WESTERN GERMANY

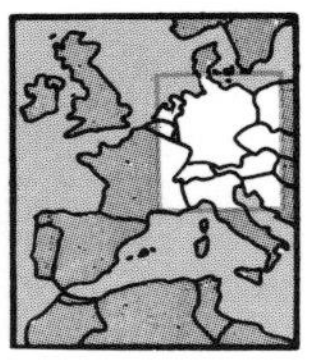

GERMANY, AUSTRIA AND SWITZERLAND

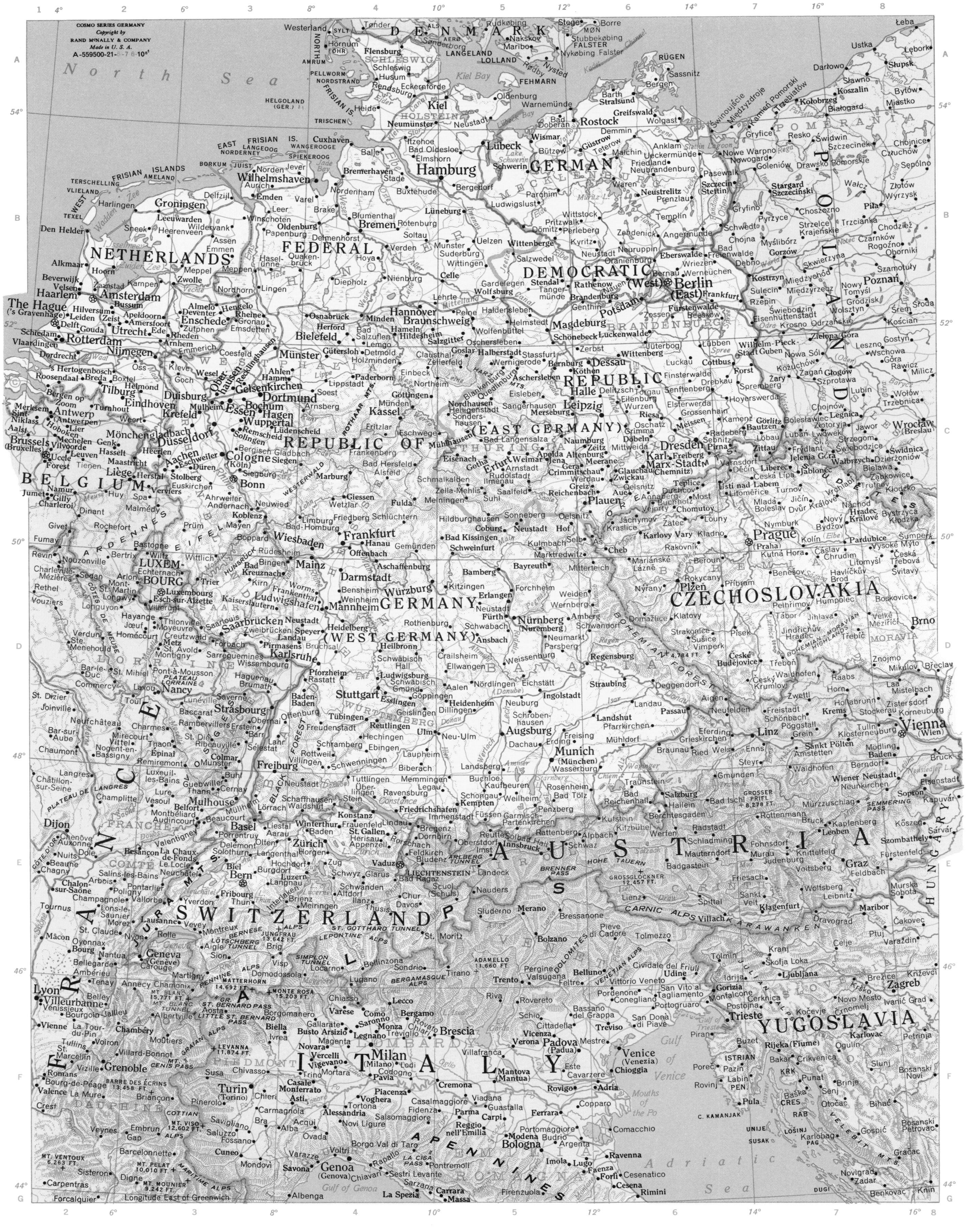

COSMO SERIES GERMANY

Copyright by
RAND McNALLY & COMPANY
Made in U.S.A.
A-559500-21-7 6-10"

Conic Projection

SCALE 1:4,000,000 1 Inch = 63 Statute Miles

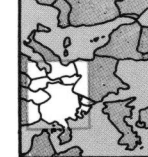

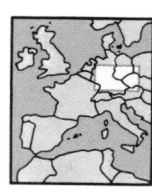

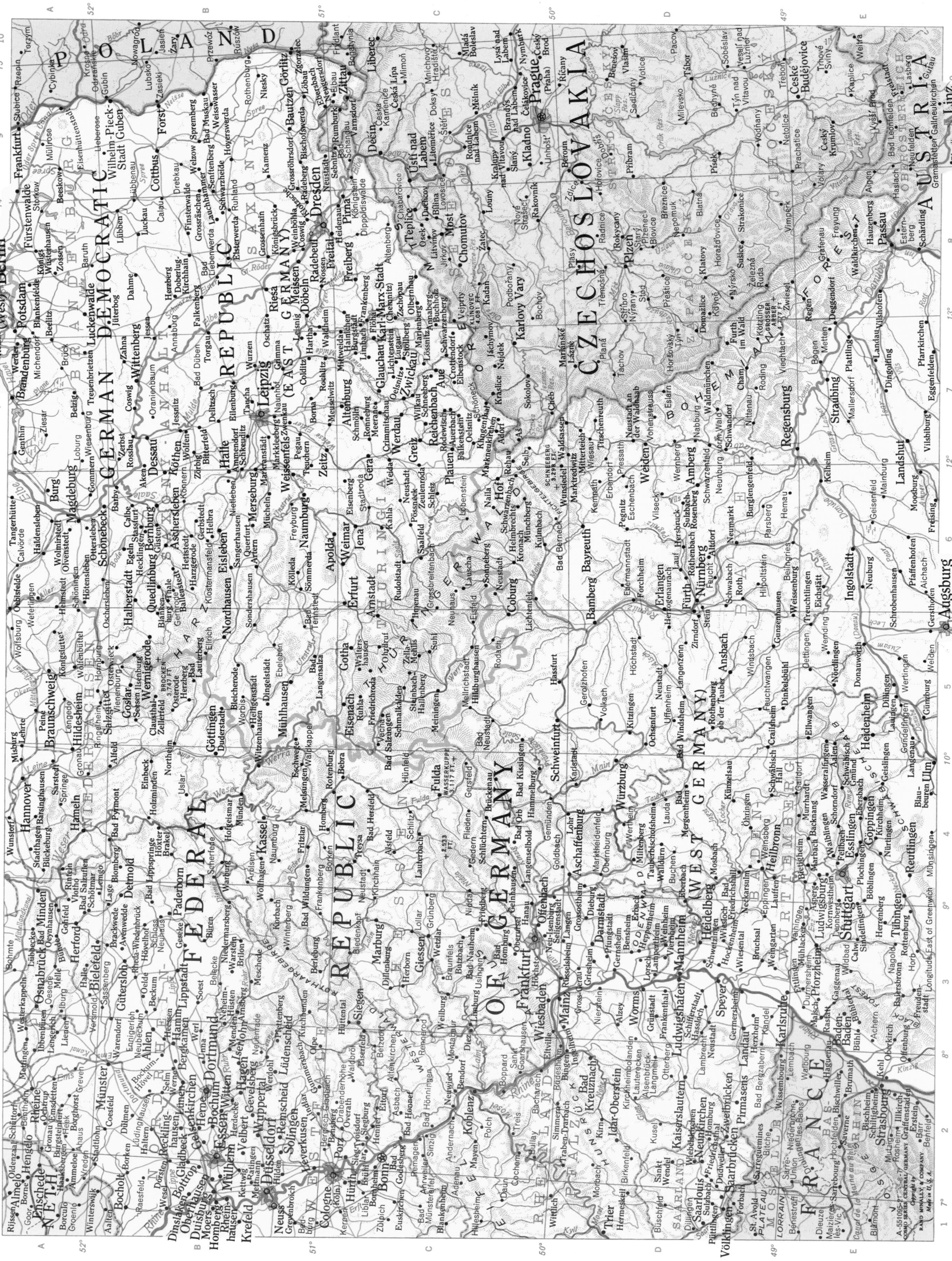

Lambert Conformal Conic Projection
SCALE 1:2,000,000 1 Inch = 32 Statute Miles

Statute Miles 5 0 5 10 20 30 40 50
Kilometers 5 0 5 10 20 30 40 50 60

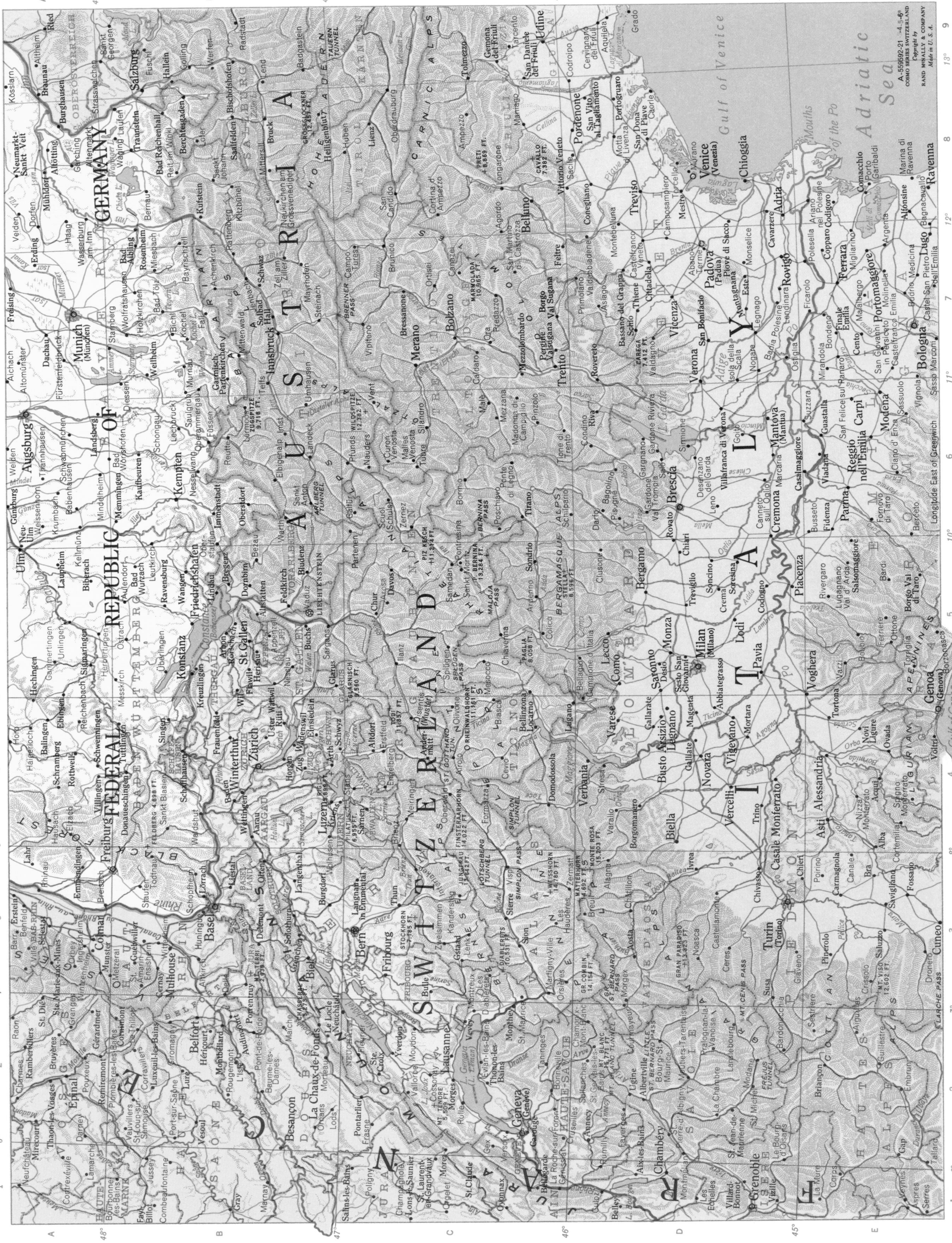

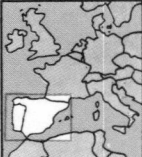

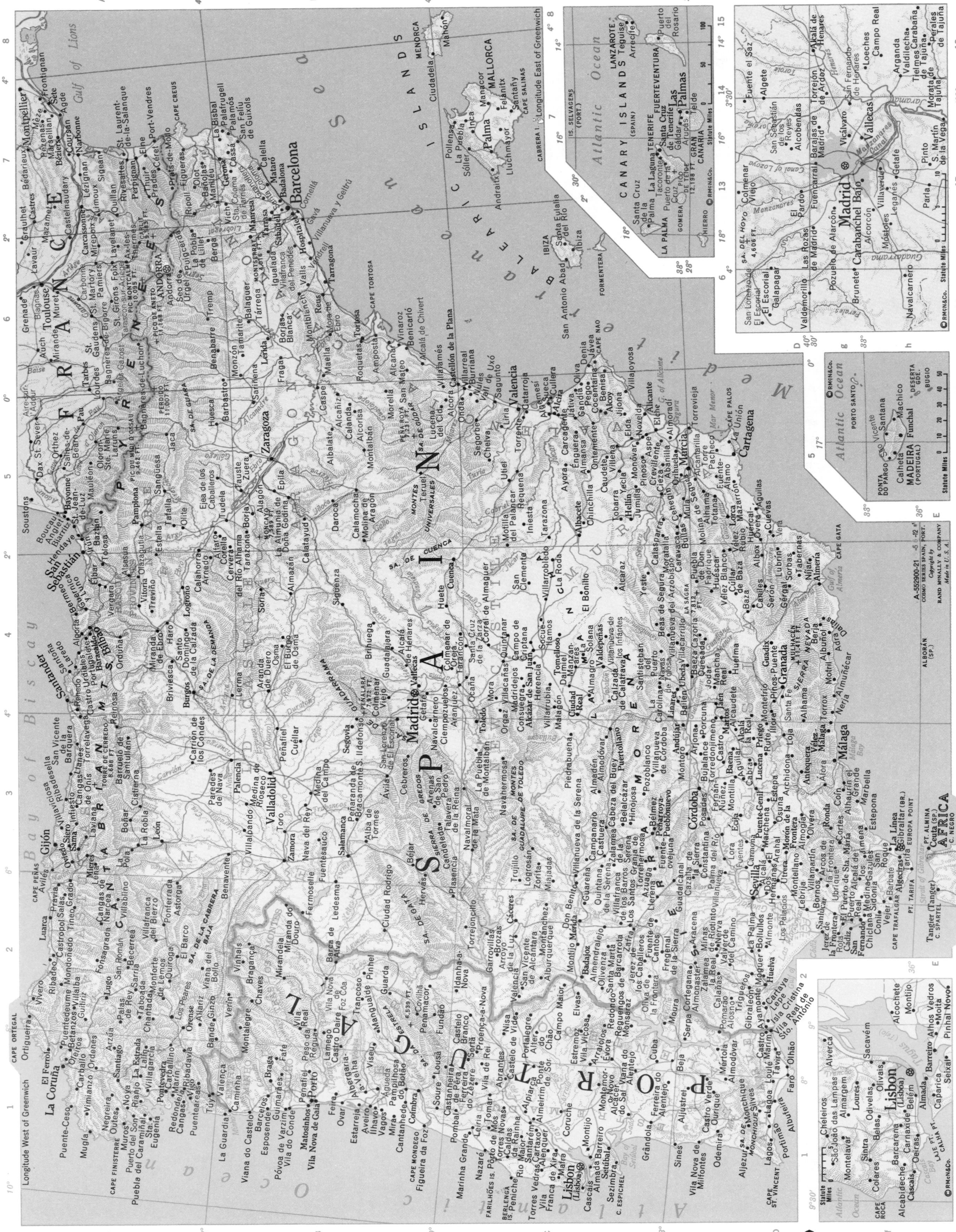

Statute Miles 25 0 25 50 75
Kilometers 25 0 25 50 100

Conic Projection
SCALE 1:4,000,000 1 inch = 63 Statute Miles

Conic Projection
SCALE 1:4,000,000 1 Inch = 63 Statute Miles

Statute Miles
Kilometers

Longitude East of Greenwich

A-551800-21 -5-4-10
COSMO SERIES ITALY
Copyright by
RAND McNALLY & COMPANY
Made in U.S.A.

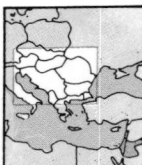

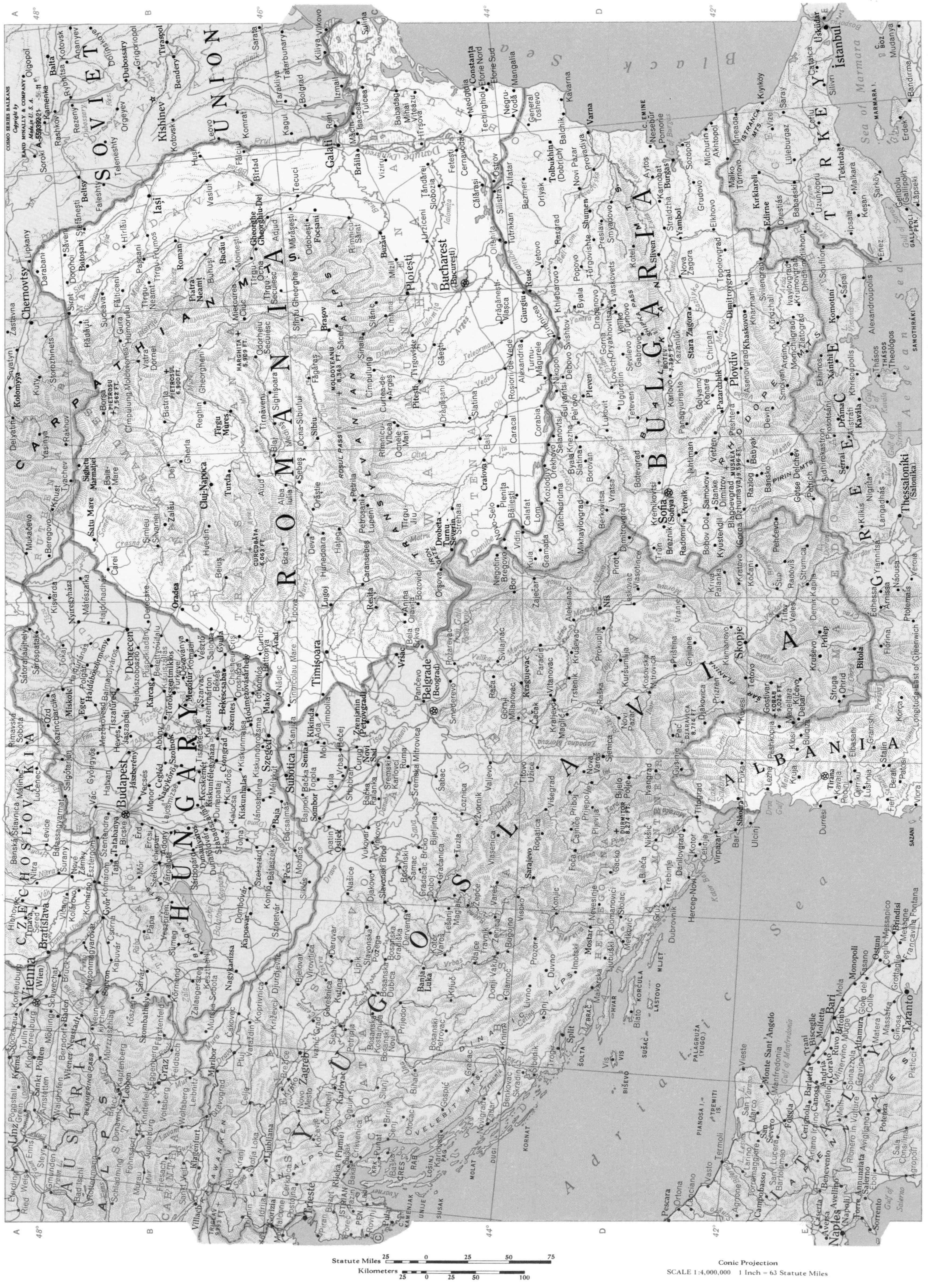

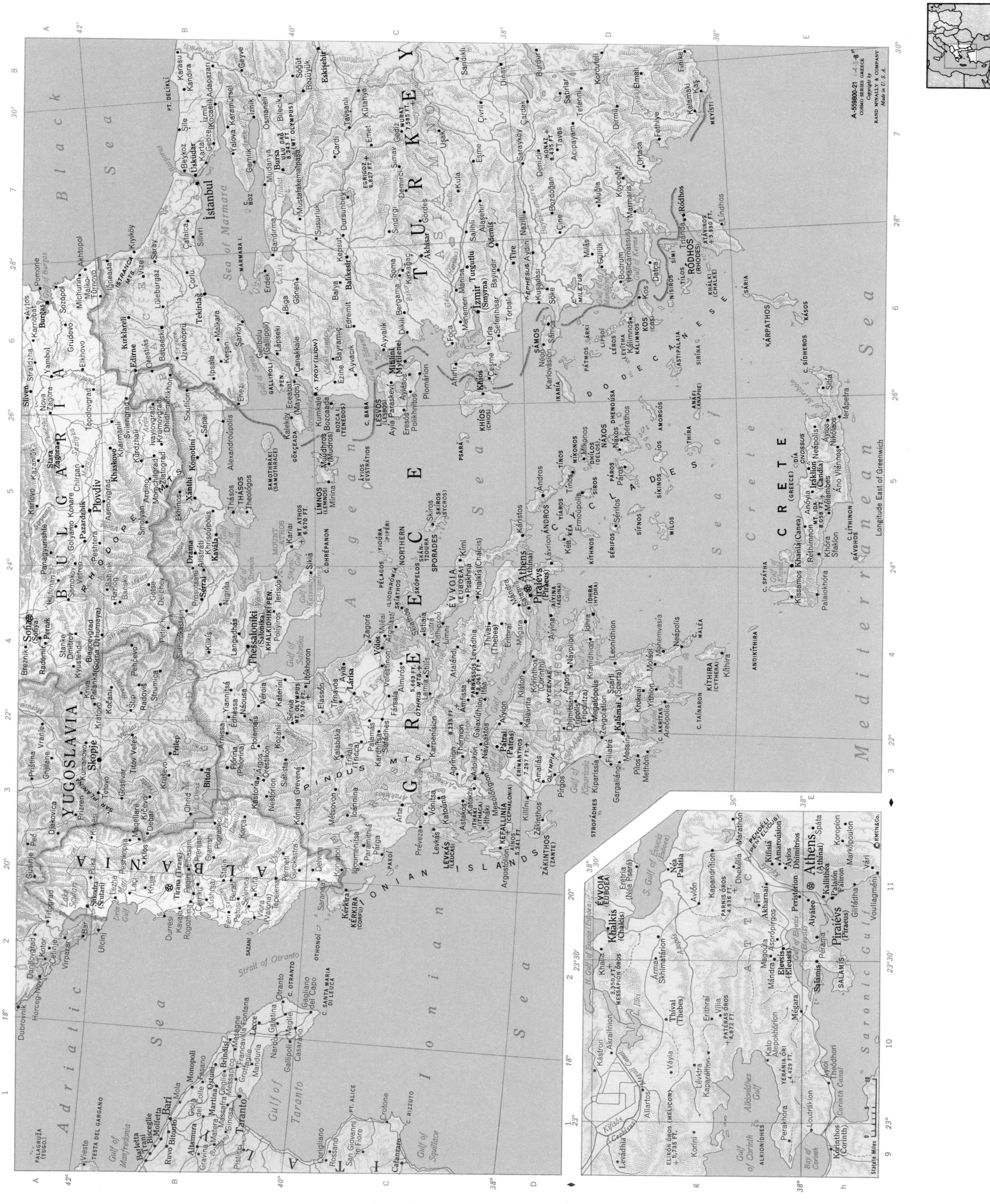

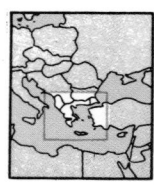

Conic Projection
SCALE 1:4,000,000 1 Inch = 63 Statute Miles

Statute Miles

Kilometers

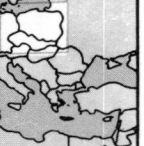

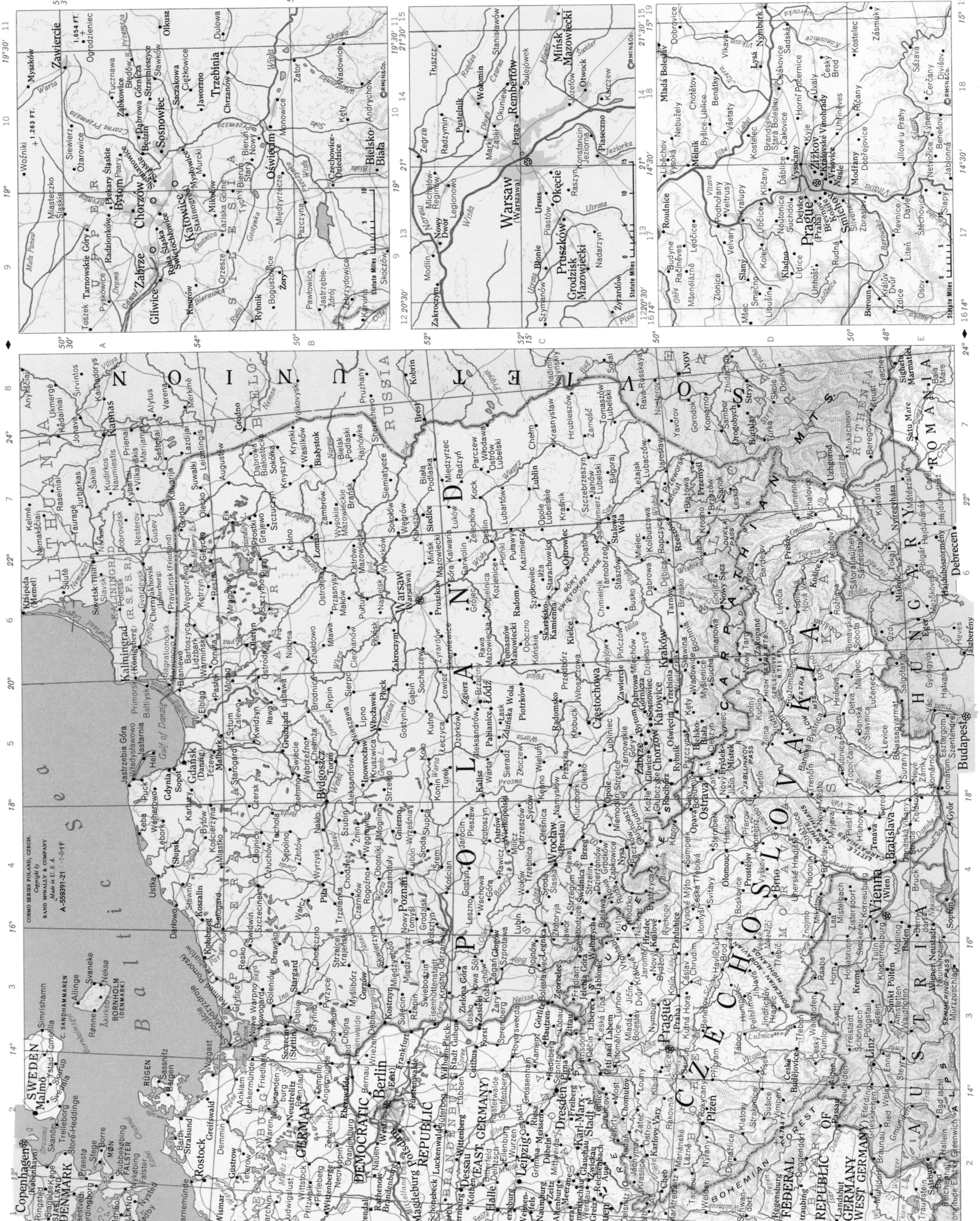

Conic Projection

SCALE 1:4,000,000   1 Inch = 63 Statute Miles

Statute Miles 25 0 25 50 75

Kilometers 25 0 25 50 100

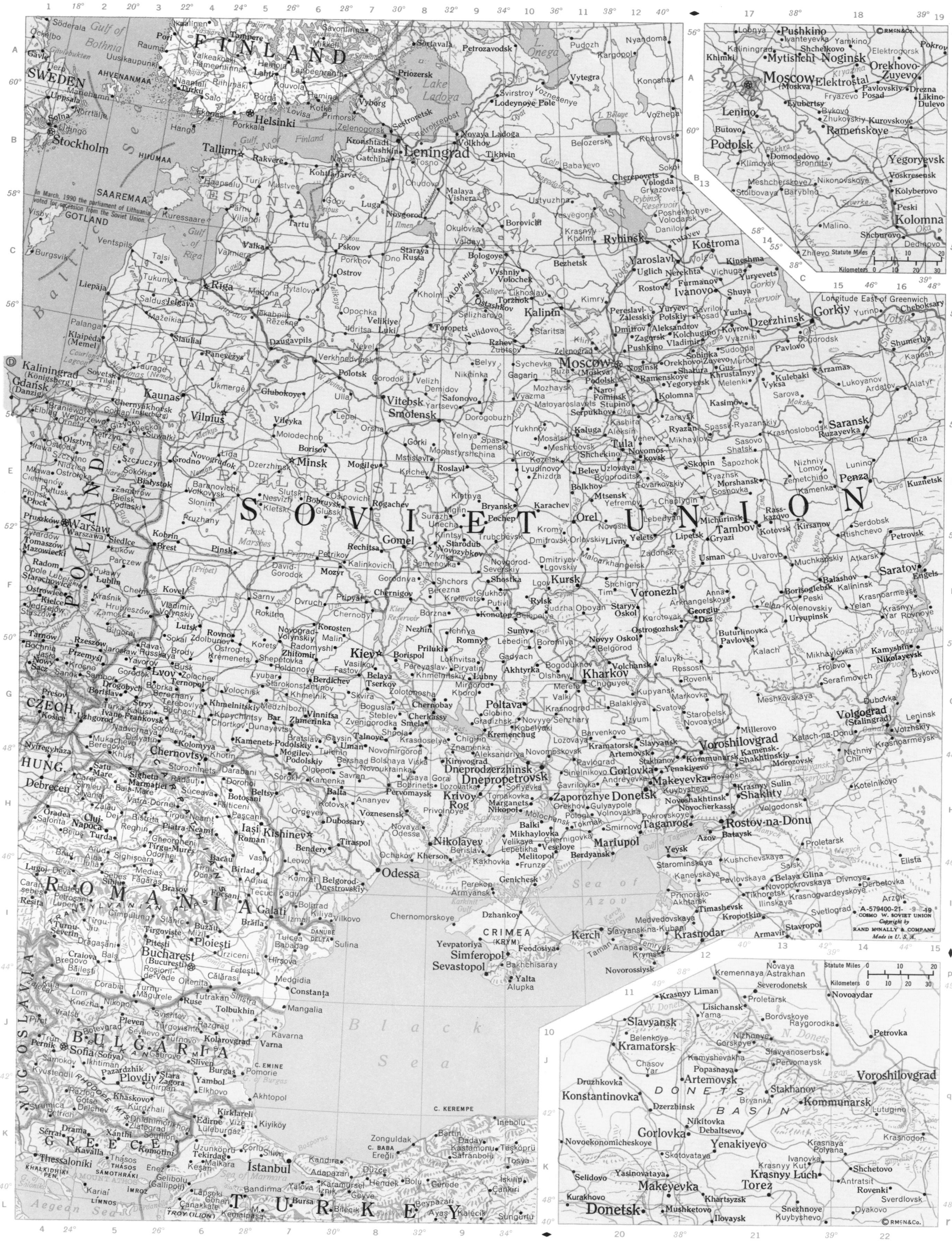

Statute Miles 50 0 50 100 150 200 250

Kilometers 50 0 50 100 150 200 250 300

Sinusoidal Projection

SCALE 1 : 11,400,000   1 Inch = 180 Statute Miles

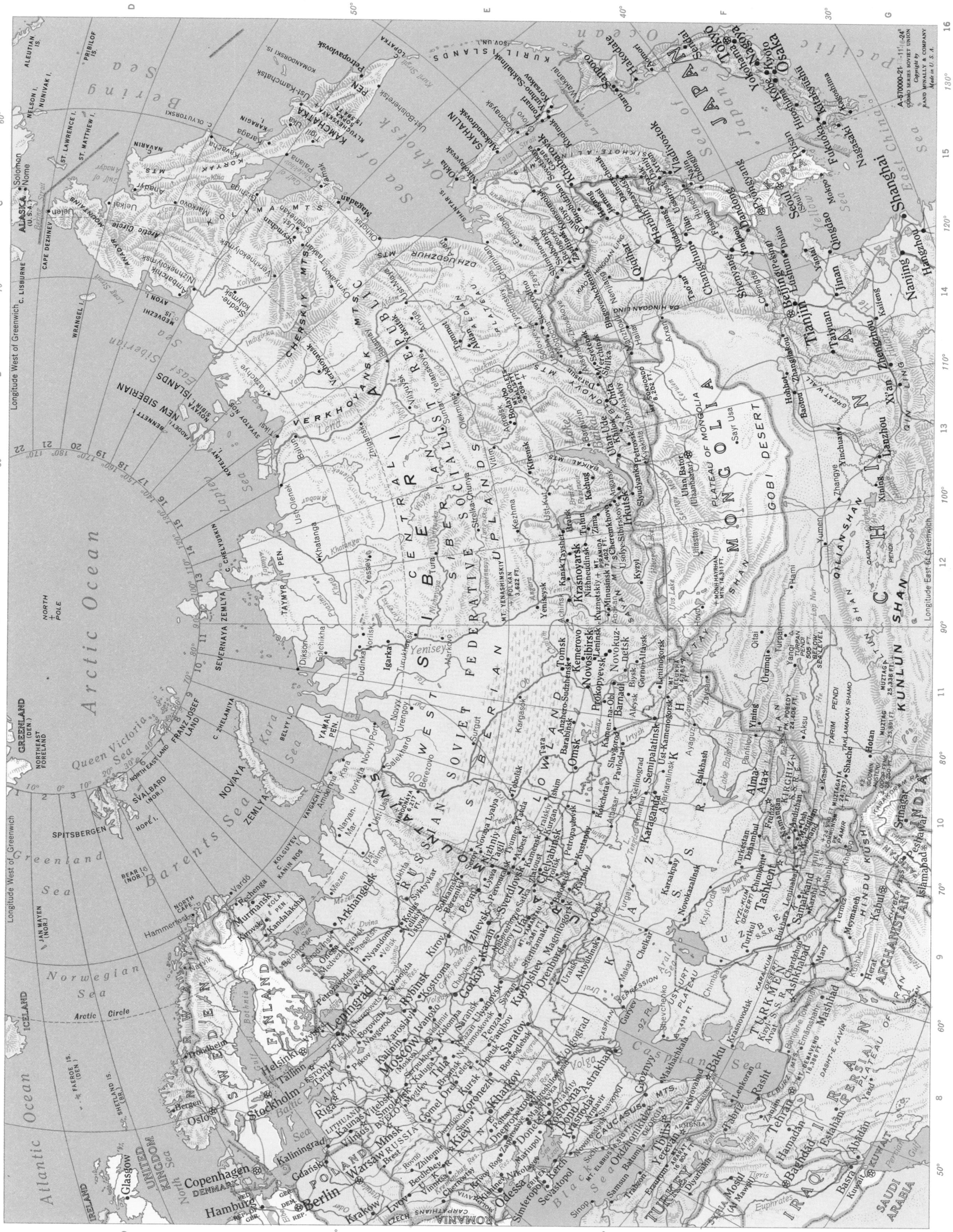

Lambert Azimuthal Equal Area Projection
SCALE 1:28,000,000   1 Inch = 442 Statute Miles

Statute Miles
100 0 100 200 300 400 500

Kilometers
100 0 100 300 500 700

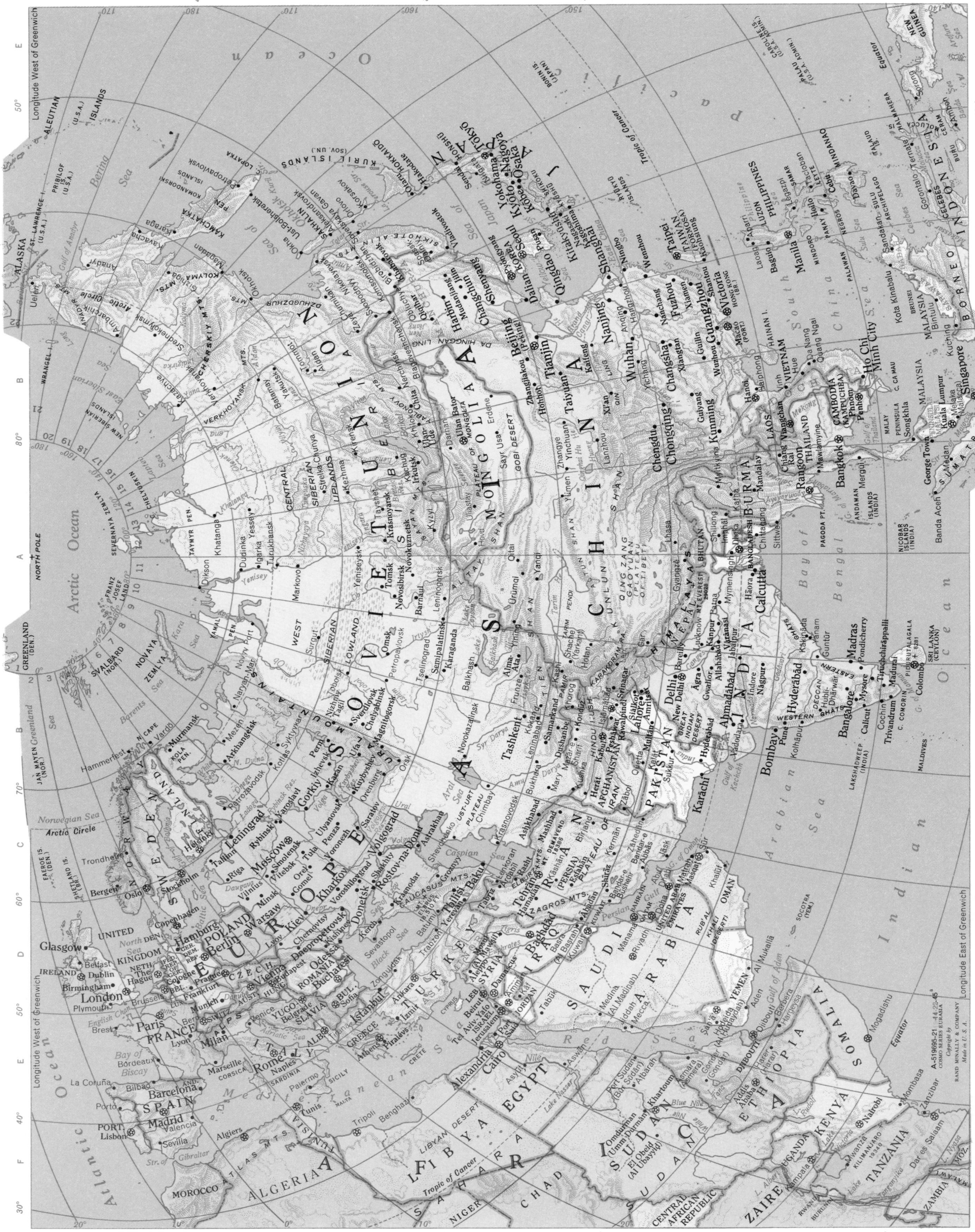

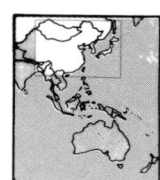

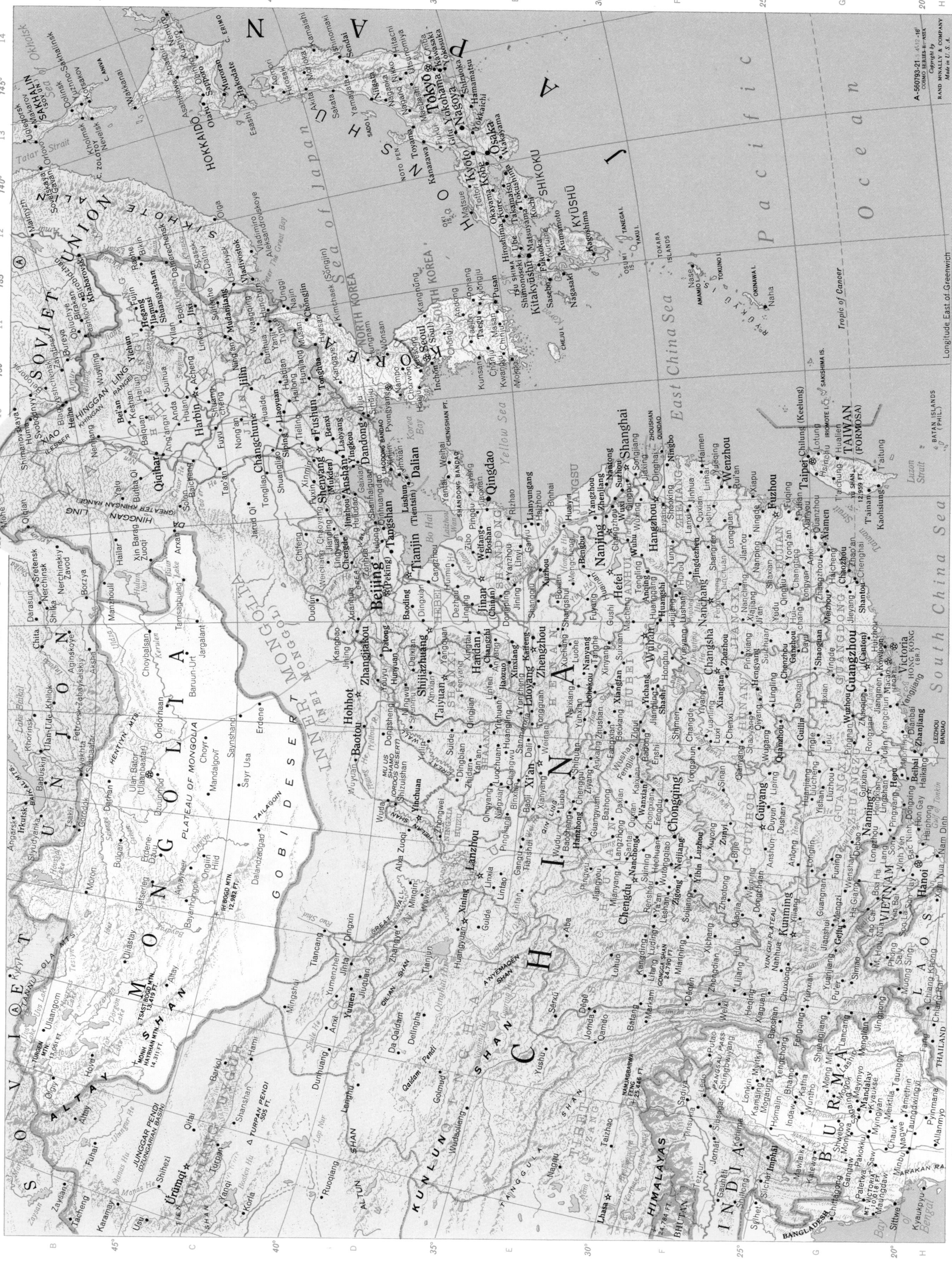

Polyconic Projection
SCALE 1:16,000,000 1 Inch = 252 Statute Miles

Statute Miles 100 0 100 200 300
Kilometers 100 0 100 200 300 400

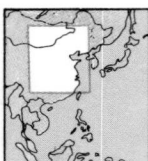

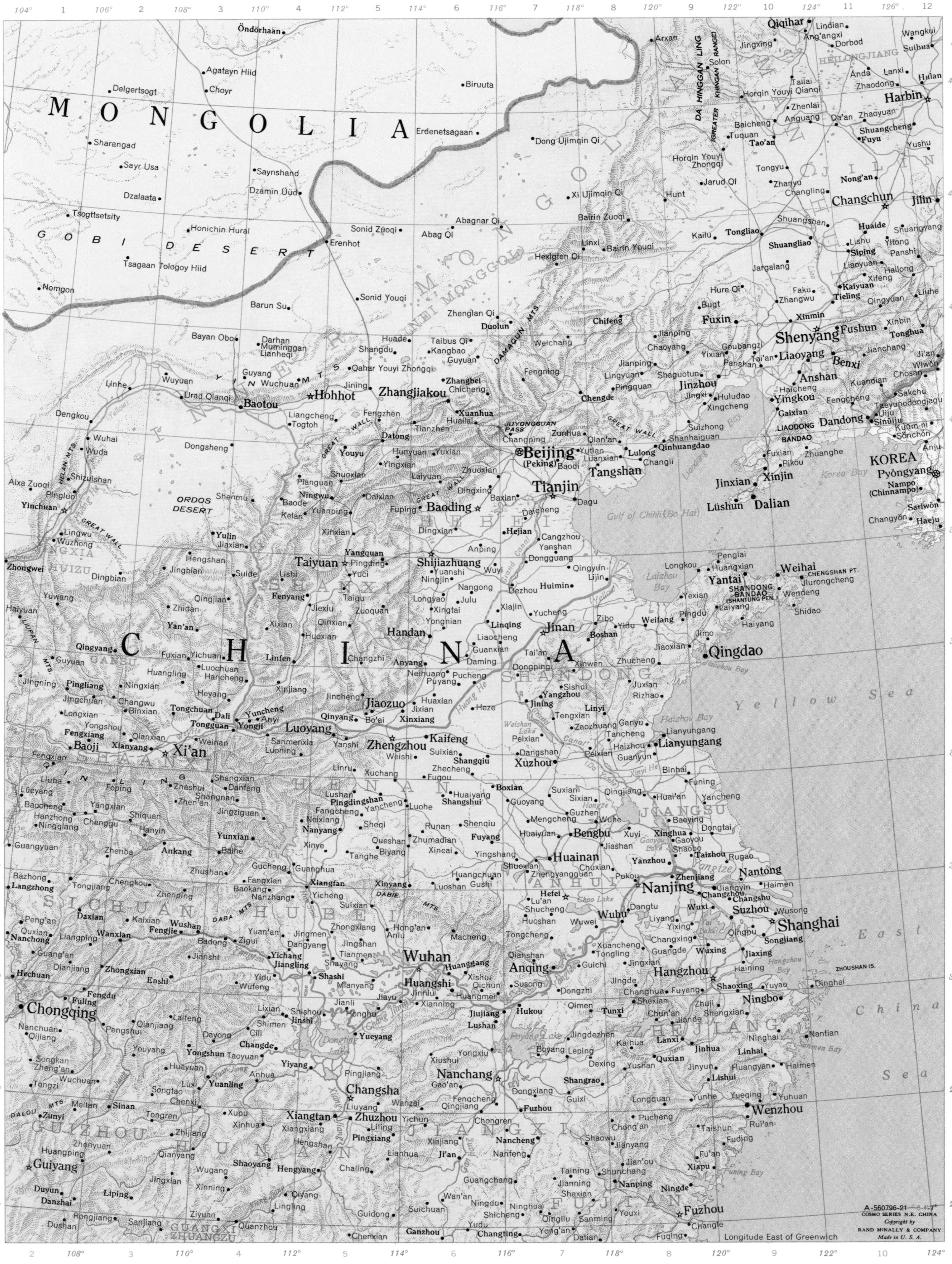

Statute Miles 50 0 50 100 150
Kilometers 50 0 50 100 200

Lambert Conformal Conic Projection
SCALE 1 : 8,000,000   1 Inch = 126 Statute Miles

Longitude East of Greenwich

A-560796-21—5-4-7
COSMO SERIES N.E. CHINA
Copyright by
RAND M9NALLY & COMPANY
Made in U.S.A.

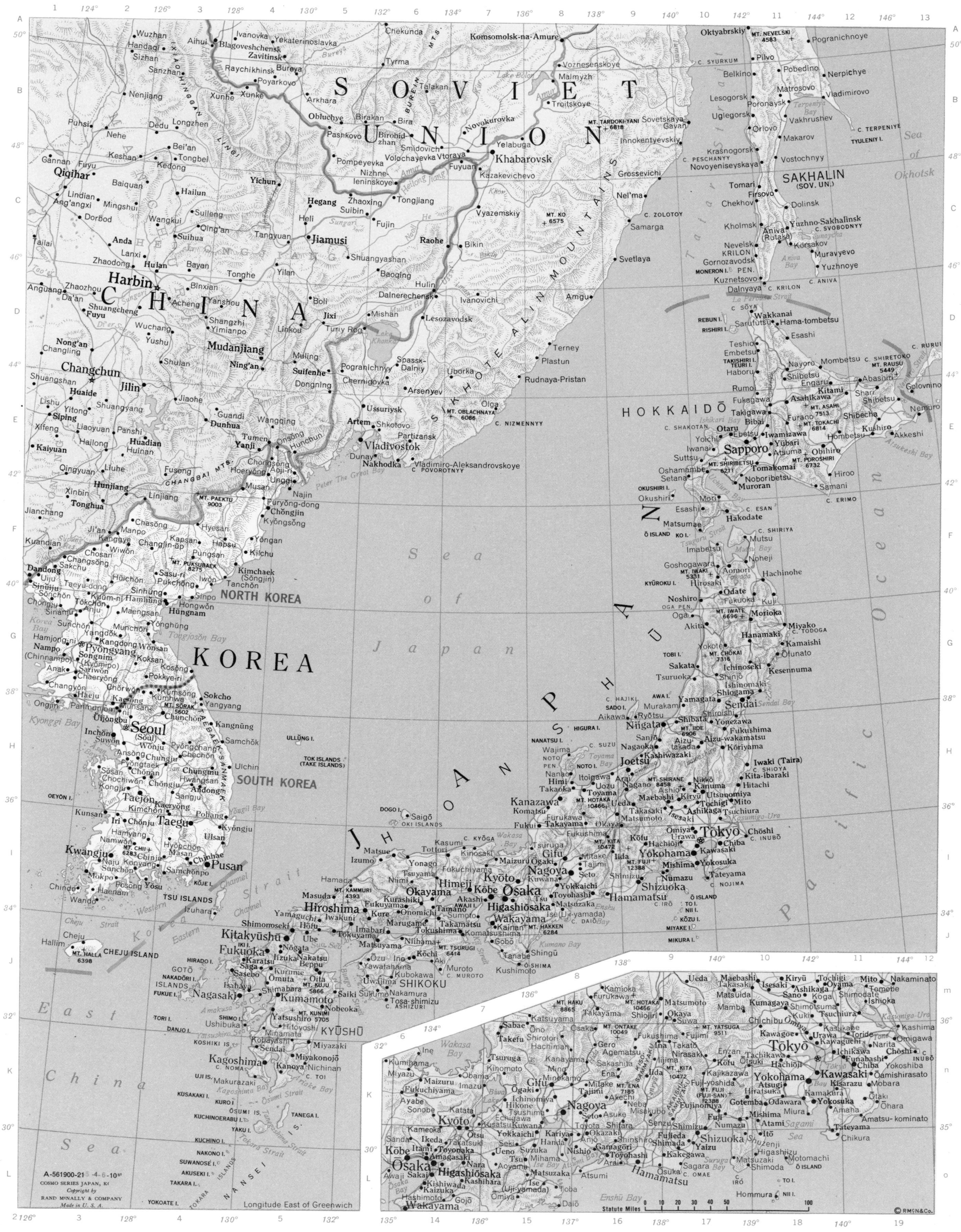

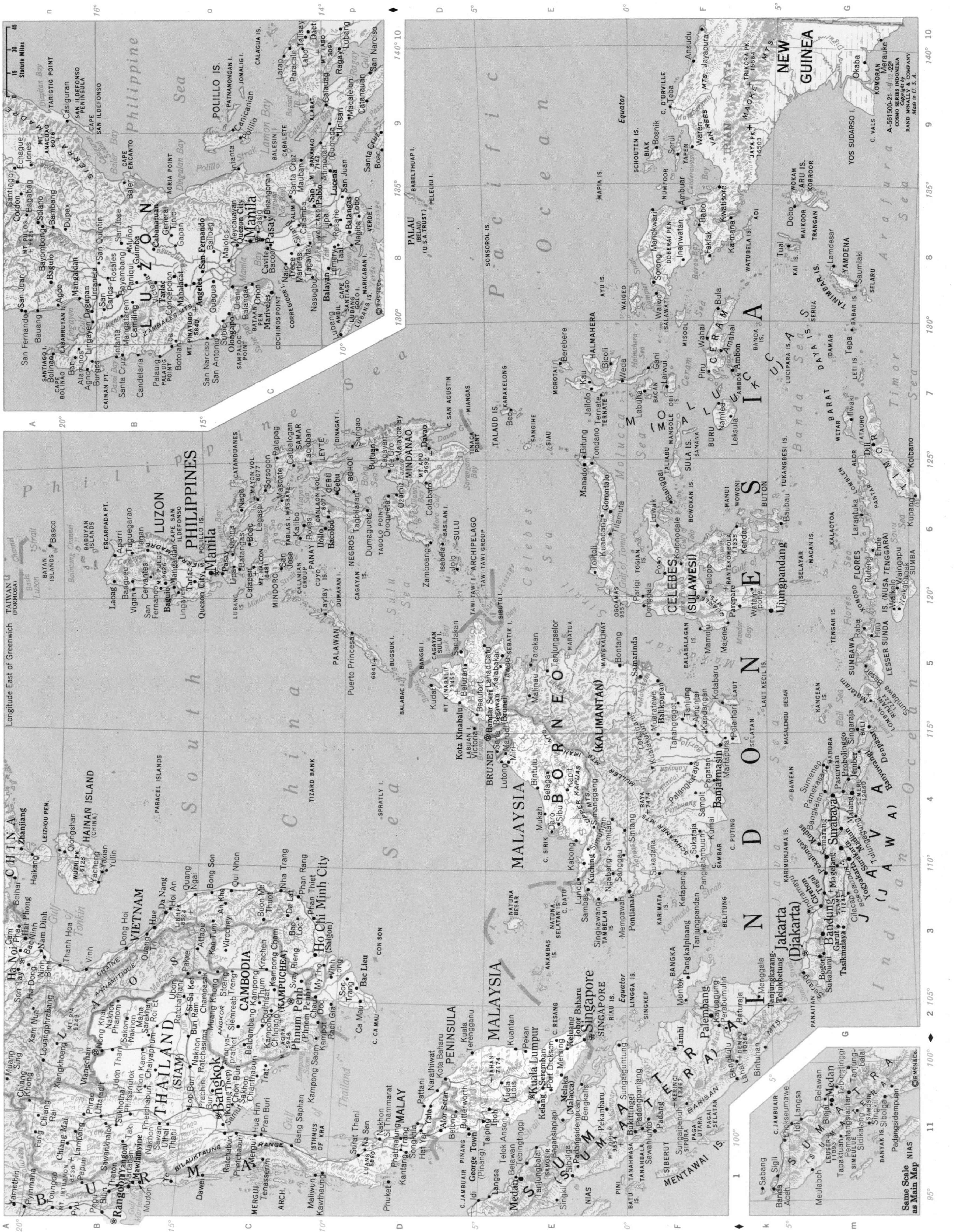

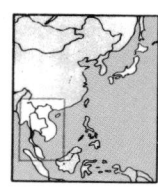

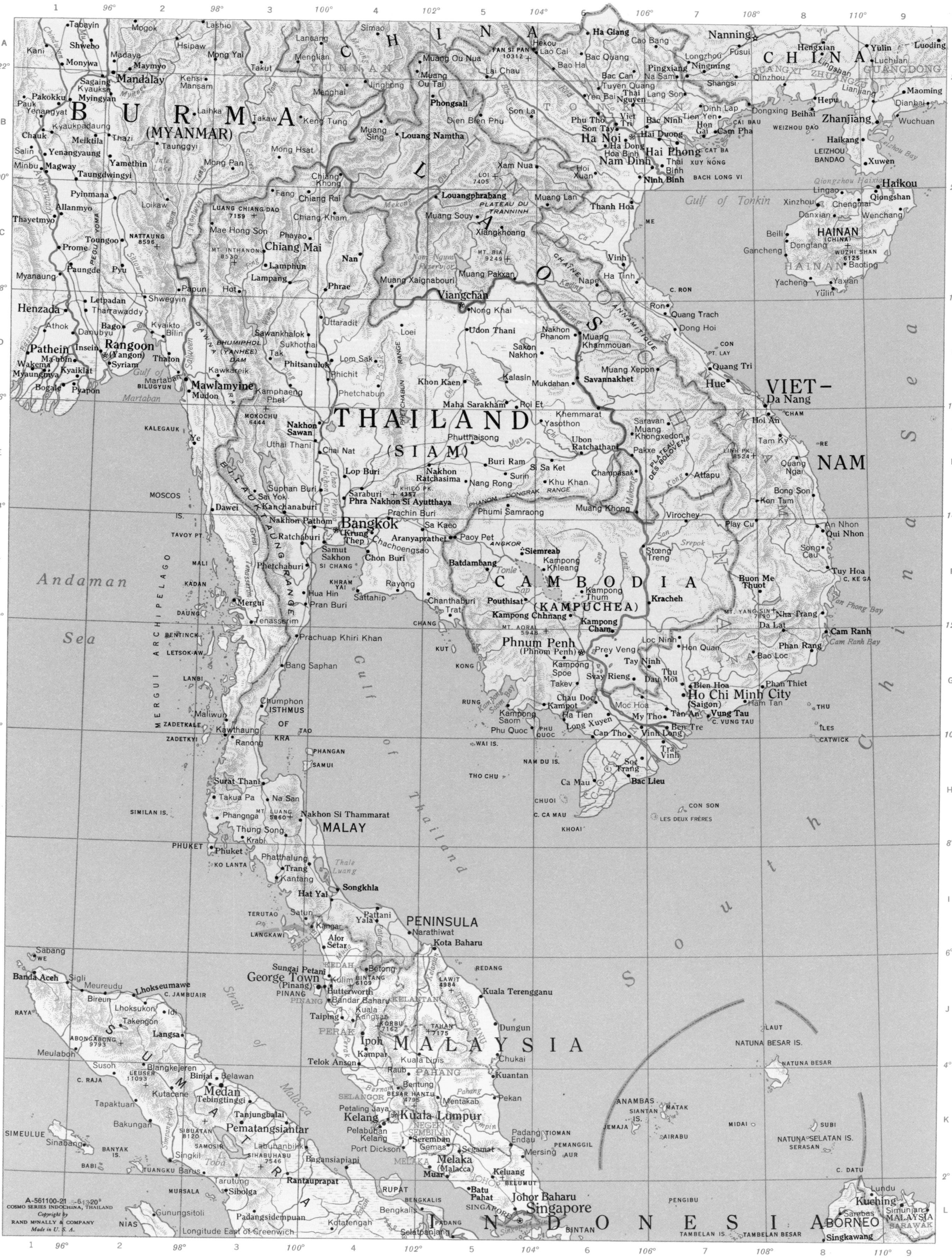

Lambert Conformal Conic Projection
SCALE 1:8,000,000 1 Inch = 126 Statute Miles

Statute Miles 50 0 50 100 150
Kilometers 50 0 50 100 200

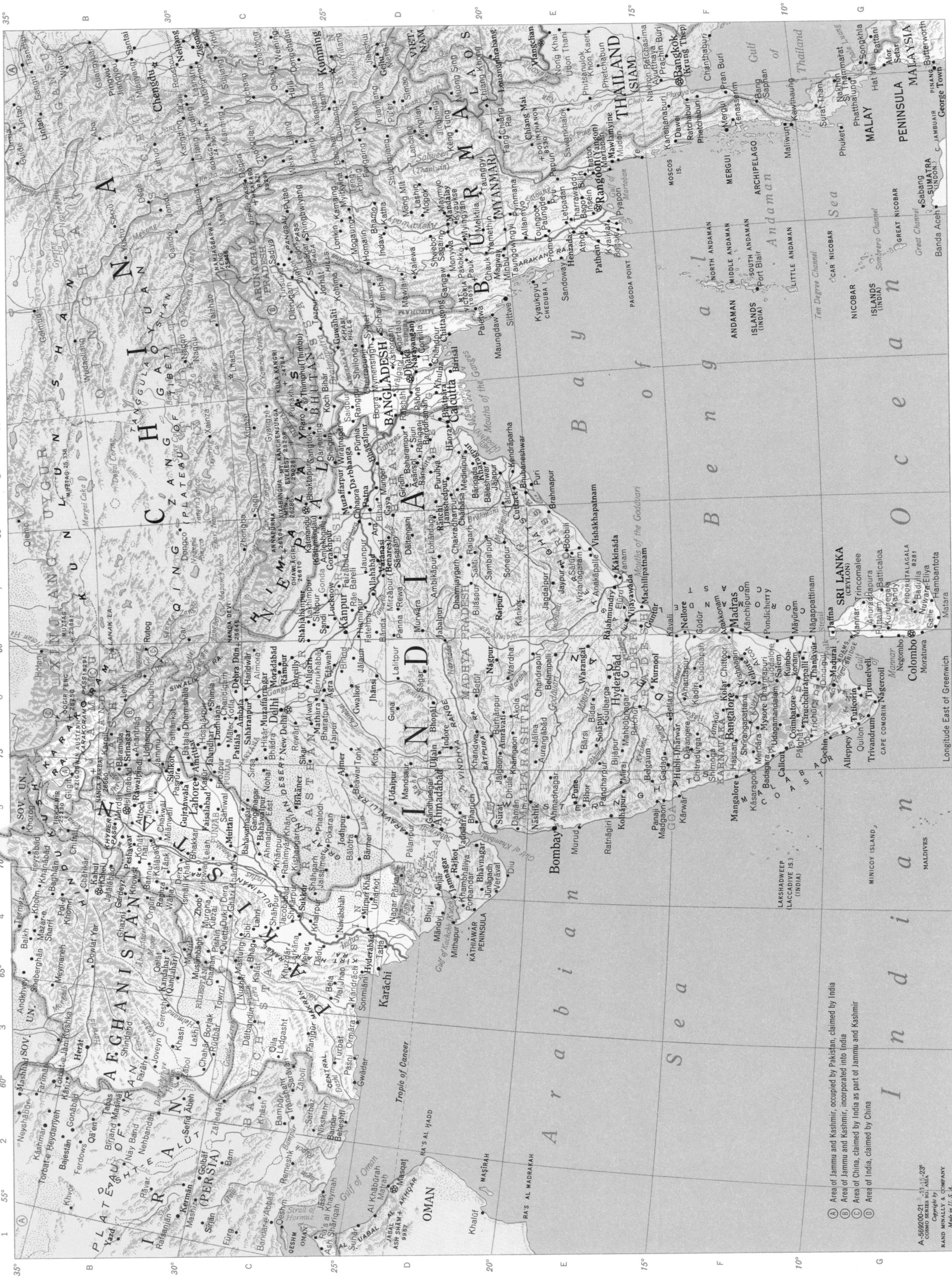

Lambert Conformal Conic Projection

SCALE 1 : 8,000,000   1 Inch = 126 Statute Miles

Statute Miles

Kilometers

A-561095-21
COSMO SERIES CENTRAL INDIA
Copyright by
RAND McNALLY & COMPANY
Made in U.S.A.

SOVIET UNION

PAKISTAN
Same Scale as Main Map

U N I O N

S O V I E T

TURKMEN S.S.R.

UZBEK S.S.R.

Samarkand

Ashkhabad

Baku

Caspian Sea

Tehrān

I R A N

PLATEAU OF IRAN (PERSIA)

A F G H A N I S T A N

Kābul (Kābol)

Kandahār (Qandahār)

Herāt

Mashhad

Eṣfahān

Shīrāz

Kermān

Zāhedān

P A K I S T A N

B A L U C H I S T A N

KIRTHAR RANGE

SULAIMAN RANGE

Quetta

Karāchi

Hyderābād

Arabian Sea

Gulf of Oman

Persian Gulf

QATAR

Doha (Ad Dawḥah)

BAHRAIN

UNITED ARAB EMIRATES

OMAN

S A U D I   A R A B I A

KUWAIT

Kuwait

Basra (Al Baṣrah)

Baghdad

I R A Q

T U R K E Y

DASHT-E LŪT

DASHT-E KAVĪR

ELBURZ MTS

KOPET MTS

INDIA

Lambert Conformal Conic Projection
SCALE 1 : 8,000,000 1 Inch = 126 Statute Miles

Statute Miles

Kilometers

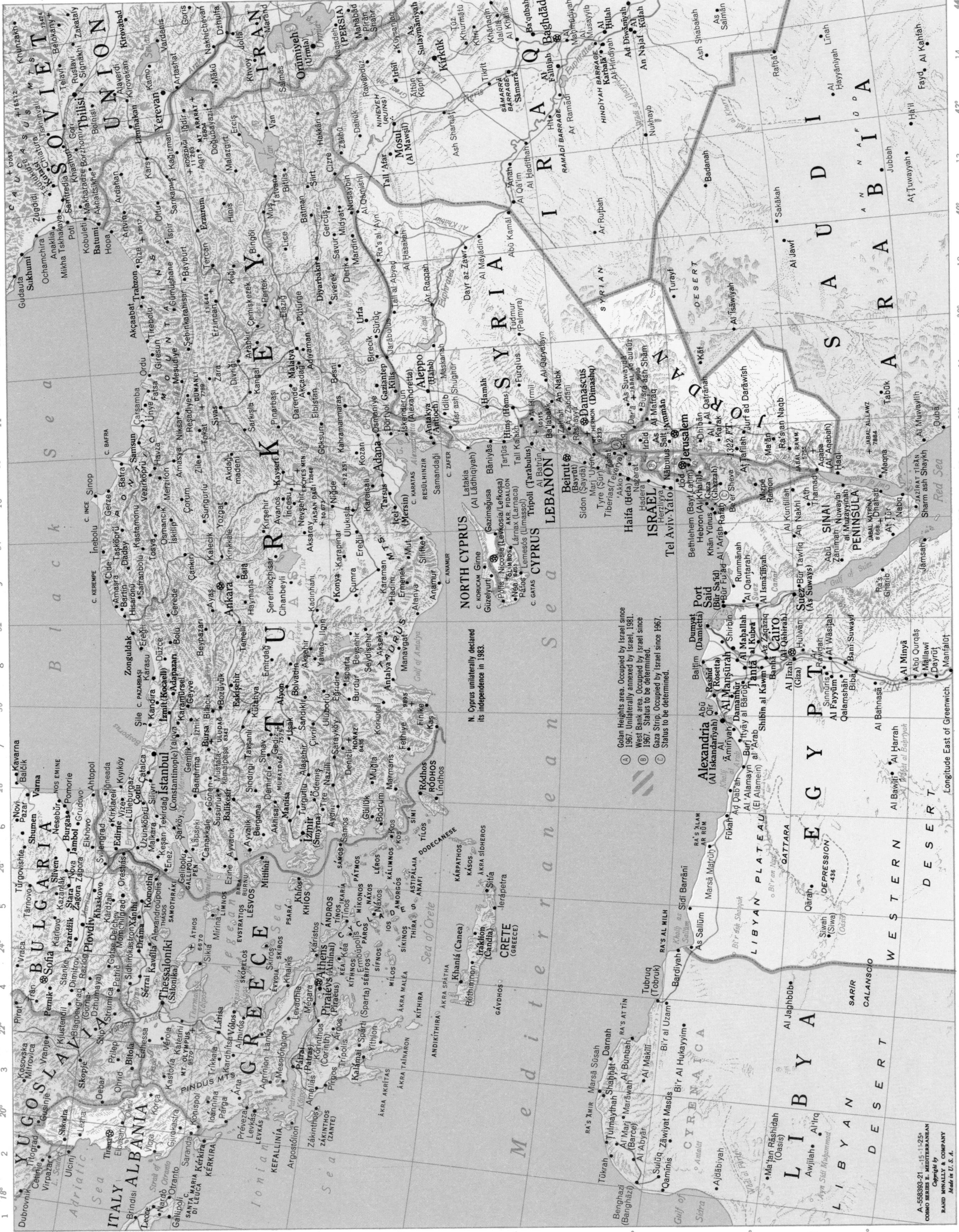

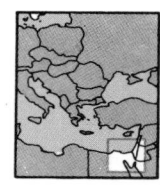

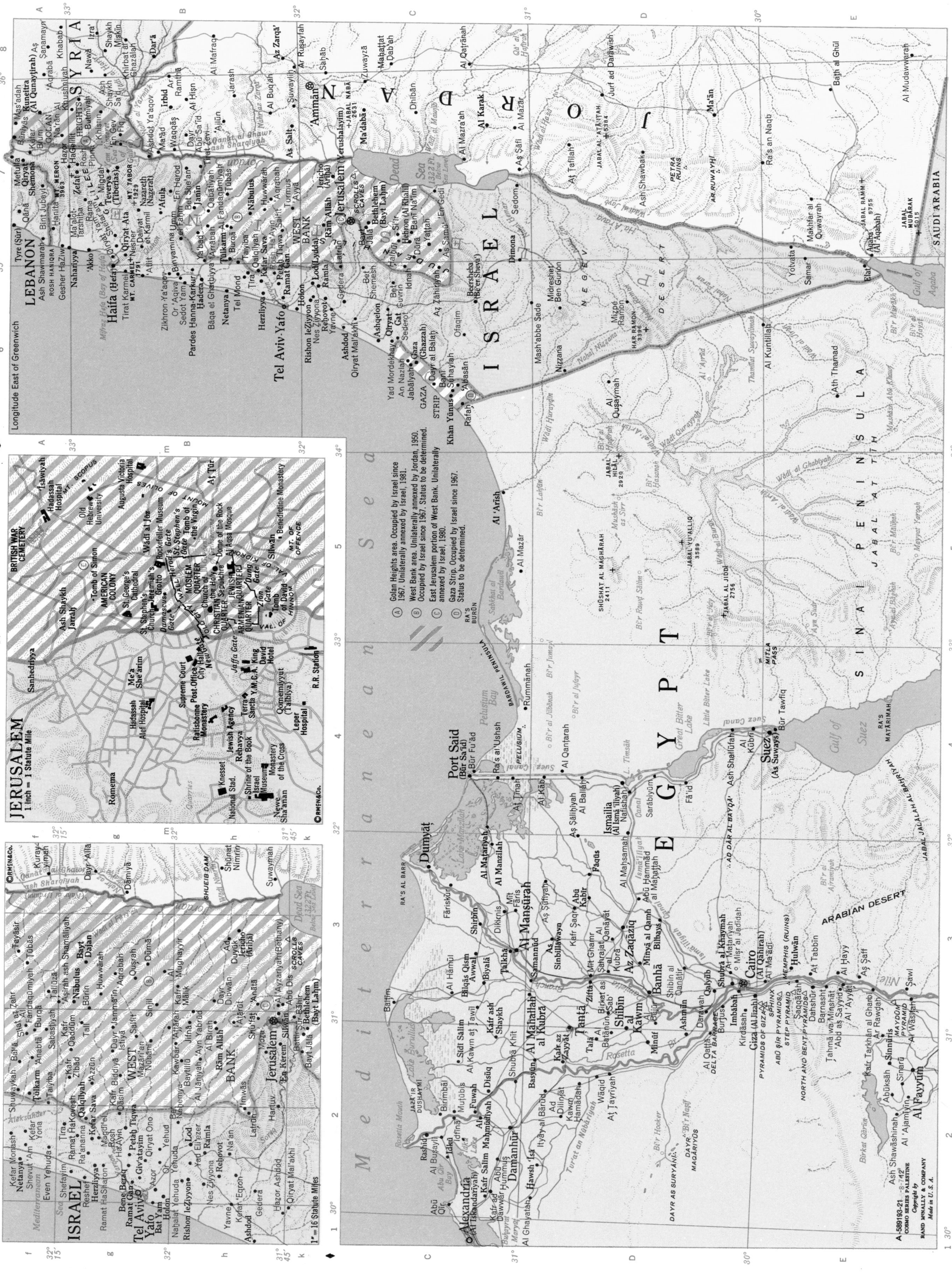

ISRAEL AND NORTHERN EGYPT

SYRIA · LEBANON · ISRAEL · JORDAN · WEST BANK · GAZA STRIP · SAUDI ARABIA · EGYPT · SINAI PENINSULA · ARABIAN DESERT

Mediterranean Sea

Dead Sea

Gulf of Aqaba · Gulf of Suez · Suez Canal

A Golan Heights area. Occupied by Israel since 1967. Unilaterally annexed by Israel 1981.
B West Bank area. Unilaterally occupied by Israel since 1967. Status to be determined. East Jerusalem portion of West Bank, unilaterally annexed by Israel, 1980.
C Gaza Strip. Occupied by Israel since 1967. Status to be determined.

JERUSALEM
1 Inch = 1 Statute Mile

BRITISH WAR CEMETERY · MOSLEM QUARTER · CHRISTIAN QUARTER · ARMENIAN QUARTER · JEWISH QUARTER · Dome of the Rock · Church of the Holy Sepulchre · MT. OF OFFENCE · VALLEY OF HINNOM

1 = 16 Statute Miles

Lambert Conformal Conic Projection
SCALE 1:2,000,000   1 Inch = 32 Statute Miles

Statute Miles 5 0 5 10 20 30 40 50
Kilometers 5 0 5 10 20 30 40 50 60

A-589193-21
COSMO SERIES PALESTINE
Copyright by
RAND M^cNALLY & COMPANY
Made in U.S.A.

41

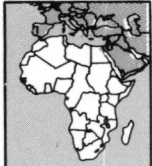

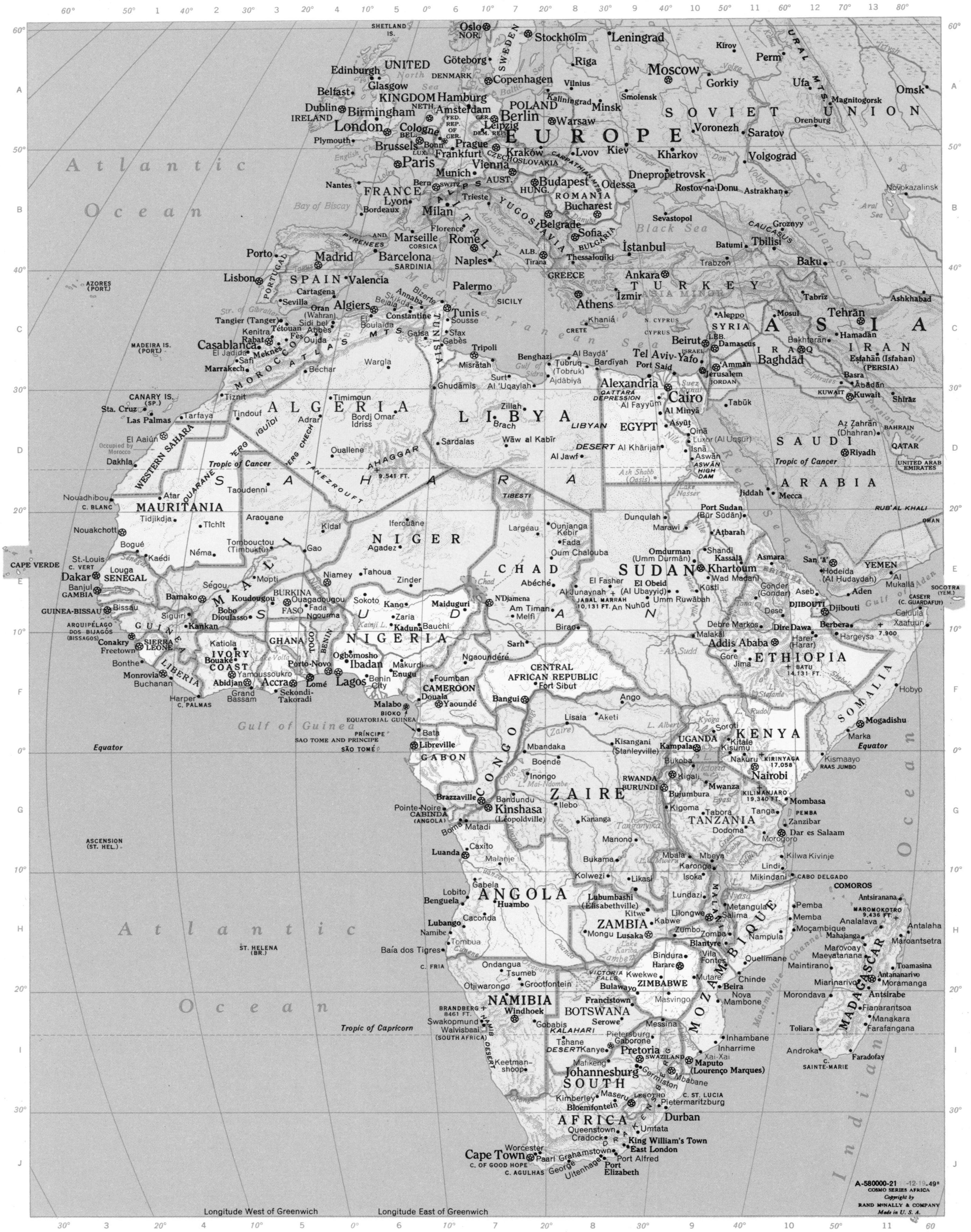

AFRICA

Atlantic Ocean

EUROPE

Shetland Is.
Oslo NOR.
Stockholm
Leningrad
Kirov
Perm
Omsk
Edinburgh UNITED
Göteborg
Riga
Moscow
Gorkiy
Ufa
Magnitogorsk
Glasgow DENMARK
Copenhagen
Vilnius
Smolensk
Belfast KINGDOM Hamburg
Amsterdam
Berlin
Minsk
SOVIET UNION
Dublin Birmingham NETH.
GER.
Warsaw
Voronezh
Saratov
Orenburg
IRELAND London Cologne BEL.
Bonn GER.
Prague
Kraków
Lvov
Kiev
Kharkov
Volgograd
Plymouth Brussels LUX.
Frankfurt
Vienna
Odessa
Rostov-na-Donu
Astrakhan
Novokazalinsk
Paris
Munich
Budapest
Bucharest
Dnepropetrovsk
Nantes FRANCE
Bern SWITZ.
Trieste
ROMANIA
Sevastopol
Aral Sea
Lyon
Milan
Belgrade
Black Sea
Caucasus
Groznyy
Bordeaux
Florence
Rome
Sofia
İstanbul
Batumi
Tbilisi
Baku
Porto
Marseille
Naples
Thessaloniki
Ankara
Trabzon
TURKEY
Lisbon SPAIN
Madrid
Barcelona
Palermo
GREECE
İzmir
ASIA
Tehrān
Ashkhabad
Valencia
Athens
Aleppo
Mosul
Tabrīz
IRAN
Cartagena
SICILY
SYRIA
Hamadān
Esfahān
Sevilla
Tunis
Beirut LEB.
Damascus
Baghdād
Basra
Tangier
Constantine
ISRAEL
Jerusalem
Amman
KUWAIT
Kuwait
Abādān
Shīrāz
Casablanca
Tripoli
Benghazi
Port Said
JORDAN
Az Zahrān
BAHRAIN

CAPE VERDE

Atlantic Ocean

Indian Ocean

Longitude West of Greenwich | Longitude East of Greenwich

Statute Miles
Kilometers

Sinusoidal Projection
SCALE 1:36,313,000 1 Inch = 565 Statute Miles

A-580000-21 12-19-49*
COSMO SERIES AFRICA
Copyright by
RAND McNALLY & COMPANY
Made in U.S.A.

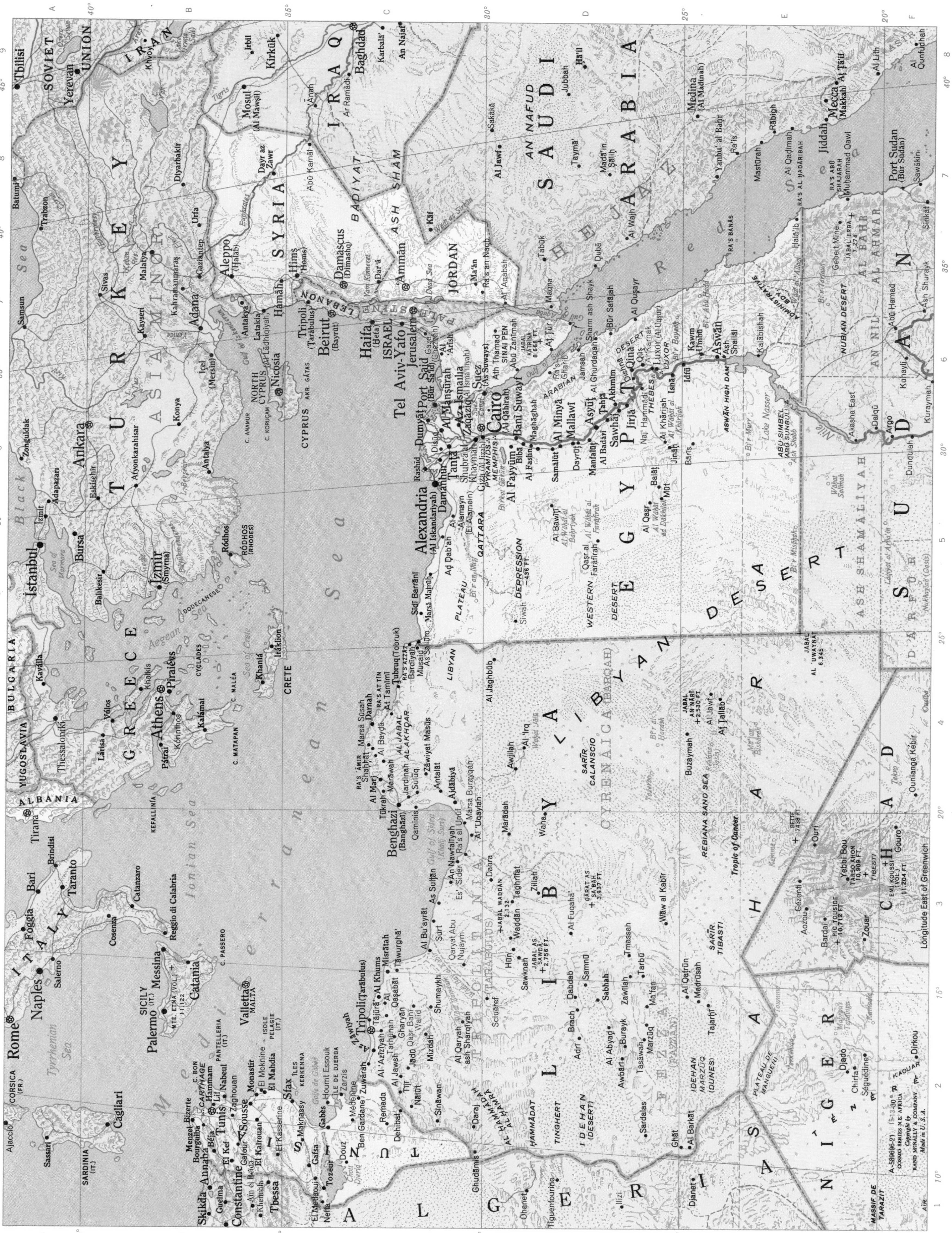

Sinusoidal Projection
SCALE 1:11,400,000   1 Inch = 180 Statute Miles

Statute Miles

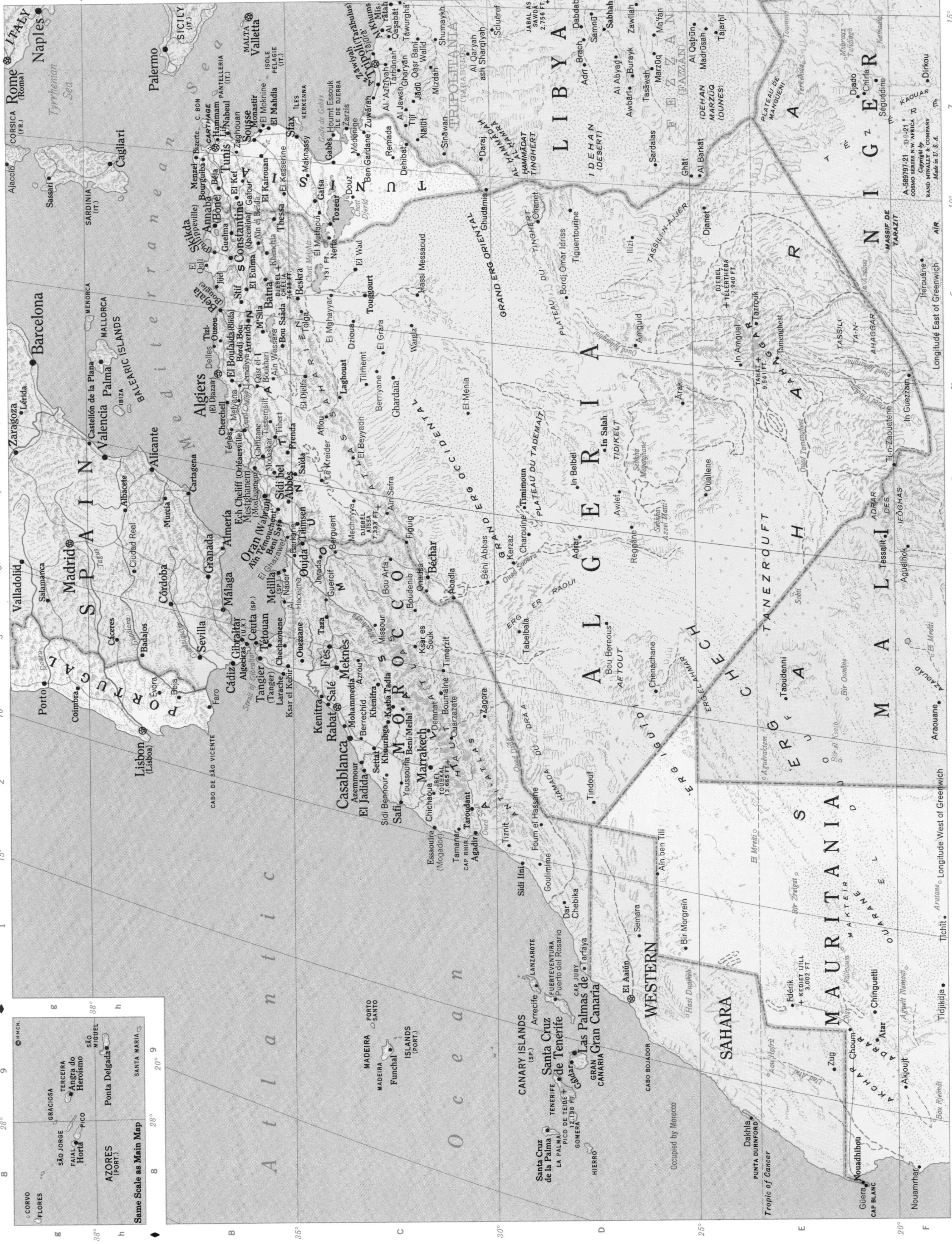

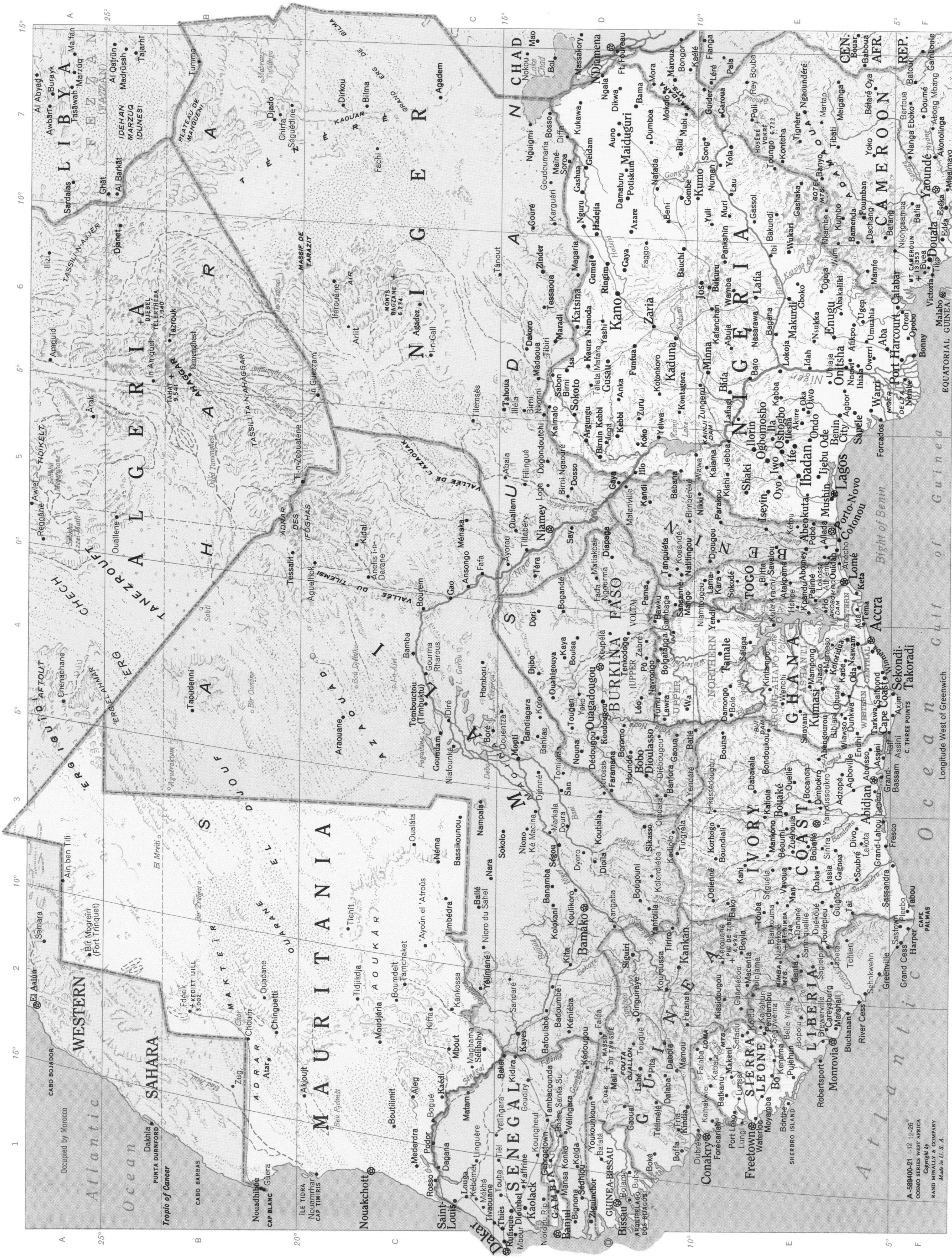

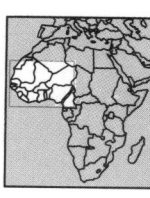

Sinusoidal Projection
SCALE 1:11,400,000   1 Inch = 180 Statute Miles

Statute Miles

Kilometers

A-59400-21

COSMO SERIES WEST AFRICA
Copyright by
RAND M^cNALLY & COMPANY
Made in U.S.A.

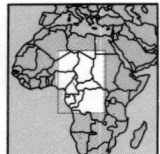

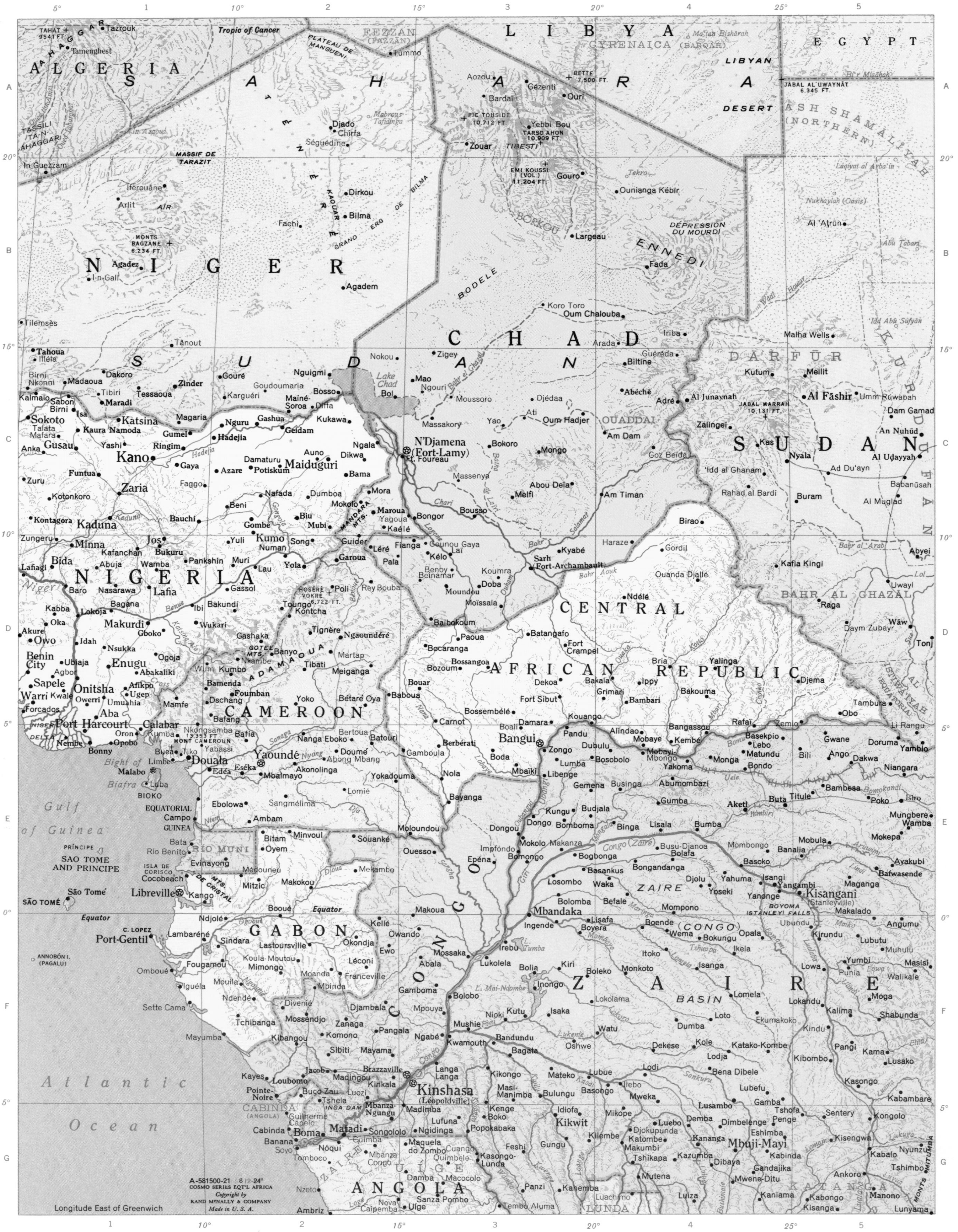

ALGERIA

TAHAT 9541 FT.
AHAGGAR
Tazrouk
Tamanghest

MASSIF DE TARAZIT

NIGER

Tibiri
In Guezzam
Iferouâne
Arlit
MONTS BAGZANE 6,234 FT.
Agadez
I-n-Gall

Tilemsès
Tahoua
Illéla
Birni Nkonni
Mádaoua
Dakoro
Tânout
Agadem
Kalmalo
Sabon Birni
Isa
Tibira
Tessaoua
Zinder
Gouré
Goudoumaria
Maïné-Soroa
Diffa

Sokoto
Talata Mafara
Katsina
Magaria
Nguru
Gashua
Geidam
Kukawa
Anka
Gusau
Kaura Namoda
Gumel
Hadejia
Damaturu
Auno
Dikwa
Ngala

Kano
Ringim
Potiskum
Maiduguri
Bama
Zuru
Funtua
Gaya
Azare
Faggo
Mora
Mokolo
Kontagora
Zaria
Faggo
Nafada
Dumboa
Maroua
Kaduna
Bauchi
Beni
Gombe
Biu
Mubi
Yagoua
Kaélé

NIGERIA

Zungeru
Minna
Jos
Bukuru
Yuli
Kumo
Numan
Song
Guider
Léré
Fianga
Abuja
Wamba
Pankshin
Muri
Lau
Yola
Garoua
Pala
Lafiagi
Bida
Kafanchan
Nasarawa
Lafia
Ibi
Wukari
Rey Bouba

Baro
Bagana
Gboko
Gashaka
Tignère
Ngaoundéré
Kabba
Lokoja
Makurdi
BOTEL GOTEL MTS.
Banyo
Tibati
Meiganga

Oka
Idah
Nsukka
Ogoja
Nkambe
Martap
Akure
Owo
Enugu
Abakaliki
Bamenda
Foumban
Yoko
Bétaré Oya
Babaua
Bouar

Benin City
Agbo
Afikpo
Ugep
Kumbo
Dschang
Bafoussam
Bangui

CAMEROON

Sapele
Warri
Onitsha
Owerri
Umuahia
Mamfe
Bafia
Nanga Eboko
Batouri
Berbérati
Nola
Forcados
Port Harcourt
Calabar
Nkongsamba
Yabassi
Doumé
Abong Mbang
Gamboula
Boda
Mbaiki

Bonny
Opobo
Buea
Tiko
Limbe
Douala
Eséka
Yaoundé
Akonolinga
Yokadouma

Malabo
Luba
Edéa
Mbalmayo
Lomié
Bayanga

BIOKO
EQUATORIAL GUINEA
Campo
Ebolowa
Sangmélima
Moloundou

Gulf of Guinea

PRÍNCIPE
SAO TOME AND PRINCIPE

Bata
Río Benito
RIO MUNI
Bitam
Oyem
Souanké
Ouesso

ISLA DE CORISCO
Evinayong
Minvoul
Médouneu
Mekambo

SÃO TOMÉ
Cocobeach
Kango
Mitzic
Makokou

Equator

Libreville
Ndjolé
Booué
Makoua

GABON

C. LOPEZ
Port-Gentil
Lambaréné
Sindara
Lastoursville
Okondja
Ewo
Owando
Kellé

ANNOBÓN I. (PAGALU)
Omboué
Fougamou
Koula-Moutou
Mimongo
Moanda
Léconi
Abala

Iguéla
Moulla
Franceville
Mbinda
Gamboma

Ndendé
Divénie
Mpouya
Sette Cama
Tchibanga
Mossendjo
Zanaga
Pangala
Ngabé

Mayumba
Kibangou
Komono
Mayama

CONGO

Divénie
Sibiti
Brazzaville
Kinkala

Kayes
Loubomo
Madingou
Pointe-Noire
Buco Zau
Luozi
Tshela
Kinshasa (Léopoldville)

CABINDA (ANGOLA)
Cabinda
Mbanza-Ngungu
Madimba
Boma
Matadi
Songololo

Atlantic Ocean

Banana
Soyo
Nóqui
Mbanza Congo
Tomboco

ANGOLA

Nzeto
Ambriz
Nova Caipemba
Uíge

LIBYA

FEZZAN (PAZZAN)
Fummo
CYRENAICA (BARQAH)

SAHARA

PLATEAU DE MANGUENI
Djado
Chirfa
Séguédine

Aozou
Gézenti
Ouri
BETTE 7,500 FT.
Bardai
PIC TOUSIDE 10,712 FT.
Zouar
Yebbi Bou
TARSO AHON 10,909 FT.
TIBESTI

EMI KOUSSI (VOL.) 11,204 FT.
Gouro

BORKOU
ENNEDI
Fada

BODELE

Koro Toro
Oum Chalouba
Iriba
Arada
Guéréda
Biltine

CHAD

Nokou
Zigey
Mao
Ngouri
Moussoro
Djédaa
Ati
Oum Hadjer
Abéché
Adré

Bol
Massakory
Yao
Bokoro
Mongo
Am Dam
Goz Beïda

N'Djamena (Fort-Lamy)
Ft. Foureau
Massenya
Bongor
Bousso
Melfi
Am Timan
Birao

Kyabé
Sarh (Fort-Archambault)
Gordil

CENTRAL AFRICAN REPUBLIC

Laï
Kélo
Benoy
Beïnamar
Koumra
Ouanda Djallé
Kaga

Baïbokoum
Moundou
Doba
Moissala
Ndélé

Batangafo
Fort Crampel
Bria
Yalinga
Djema

Bocaranga
Bossangoa
Bozoum
Dekoa
Bakala
Grimari
Ippy
Bakouma
Obo

Paoua
Damara
Bambari
Rafaï
Zemio
Li Rangu

Bouar
Bossembélé
Fort Sibut
Kouango
Yambio

Carnot
Bangui
Kembé
Bangassou
Basekpio
Lebo
Gwane
Ango
Dakwa
Niangara

Zongo
Dubulu
Mobaye
Mobayi
Monga
Bondo
Doruma

Pandu
Alindao
Mbongo
Yakoma

ZAIRE

Lumba
Bosobolo
Yakoma
Bili
Buta
Titule
Bambesa
Poko
Isiro

Libenge
Gemena
Businga
Abumombazi
Mungbere
Wamba
Mokepa

Dongou
Impfondo
Mokolo Makanza
Kungu
Budjala
Gumba
Aketi
Banalia
Ayakubi
Bafwasende

Epéna
Bomongo
Dongo
Bomboma
Binga
Lisala
Bumba
Mobula

CONGO

Bozene
Busu-Djanoa
Bolafa
Basoko
Mombongo
Banalia

Mossaka
Bogbonga
Basankusu
Bongandanga
Djolu
Yahuma
Kisangani (Stanleyville)
BOYOMA (STANLEY) FALLS

Lukolela
Bolobo
Bolomba
Befale
Mompono
Yangambi
Yanonge
Makalado

Mbandaka
Lisafa
Boyera
Bokungu
Yoseki
Maganga

Equator

Ingende
Boende
Wema
Opala
Ubundu
Angumu

Irebu
Tumba
Bokungu
Itoko
Ikela
Punia
Lowa
Yumbi
Masisi

Abala
Lukolela
Bolia
Kiri
Boleko
Monkoto
Isanga
Kirundu
Lubutu
Muhulu

Gamboma
L. Mai-Ndombe
Inongo
Kutu
Lokolama
Lomela
Lokandu
Kalima
Moga
Walikale

Ngabé
Kwamouth
Bandundu
Mushie
Isaka
Dekese
Kole
Katako-Kombe
Kindu
Pangi
Kama
Lusaka

ZAIRE

Bagata
Oshwe
Lodja
Kibombo
Kasongo

Kikongo
Mateko
Lubue
Lebo
Lusambo
Luebo
Demba
Lubefu
Gamba
Kabambare

Kinshasa (Léopoldville)
Masi-Manimba
Bulungu
Basongo
Mweka
Lusambo
Sentery
Kongolo

KASAI
Kenge
Boko
Idiofa
Mikope
Kananga
Eshimba
Kisengwa

Kikwit
Feshi
Gungu
Kilembe
Makumbi
Mbuji-Mayi
Kabinda
Nyunzu

Popokabaka
Kasongo-Lunda
Kazumba
Tshikapa
Mutena
Dibaya
Kabalo
Tshibombo

Panzi
Kahemba
Luiza
Luebo
Gandajika
Mwene-Ditu
Kongolo
Kisanga

Tembo Aluma
LUNDA
Kaniama
Manono
Lunyama

Statute Miles 50 25 0 50 100 150 200 250

Sinusoidal Projection
SCALE 1:11,400,000   1 Inch = 180 Statute Miles

A-581500-21 8·12·24
COSMO SERIES EQT'L AFRICA
Copyright by
RAND M?NALLY & COMPANY
Made in U.S.A.

Longitude East of Greenwich

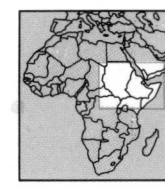

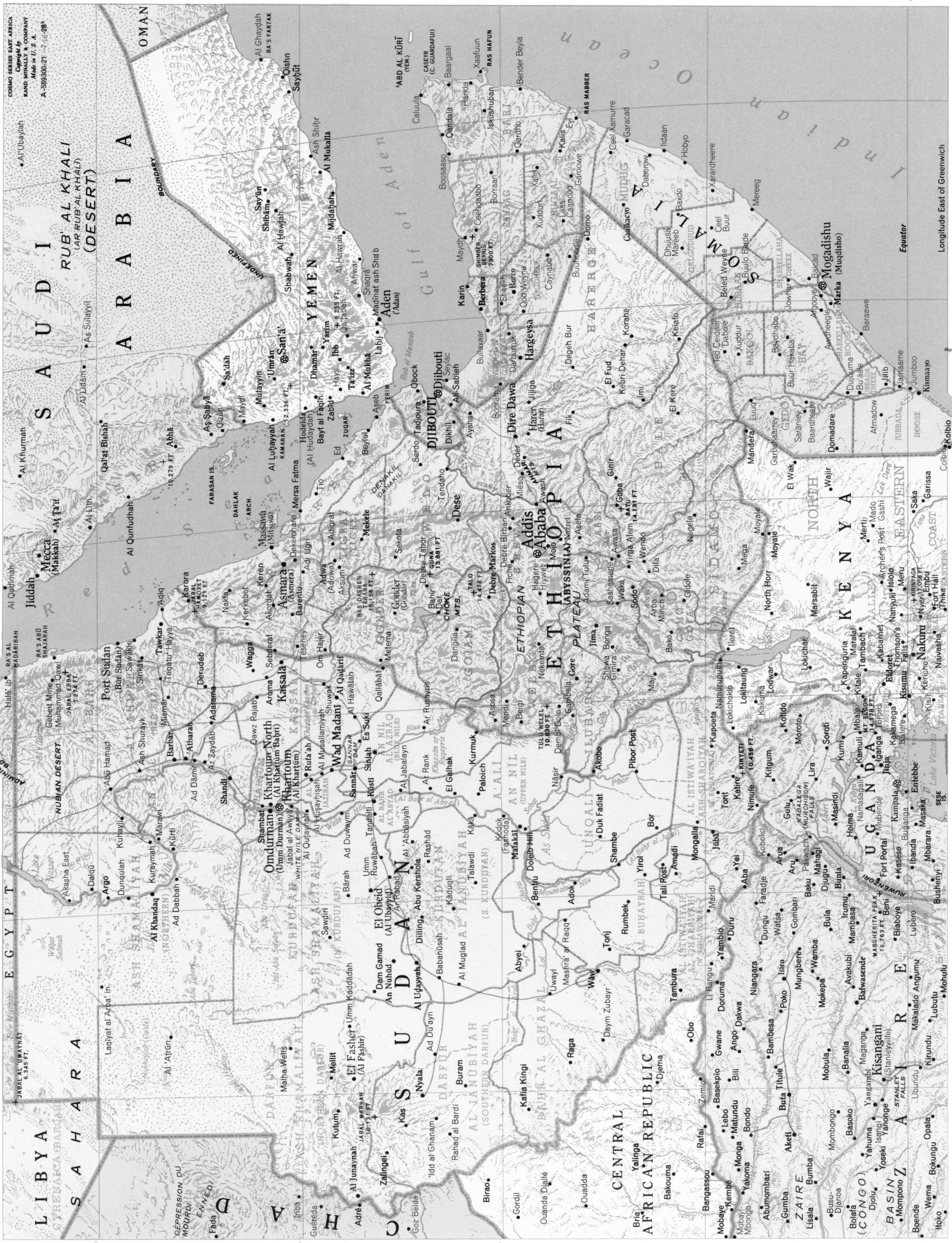

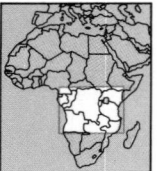

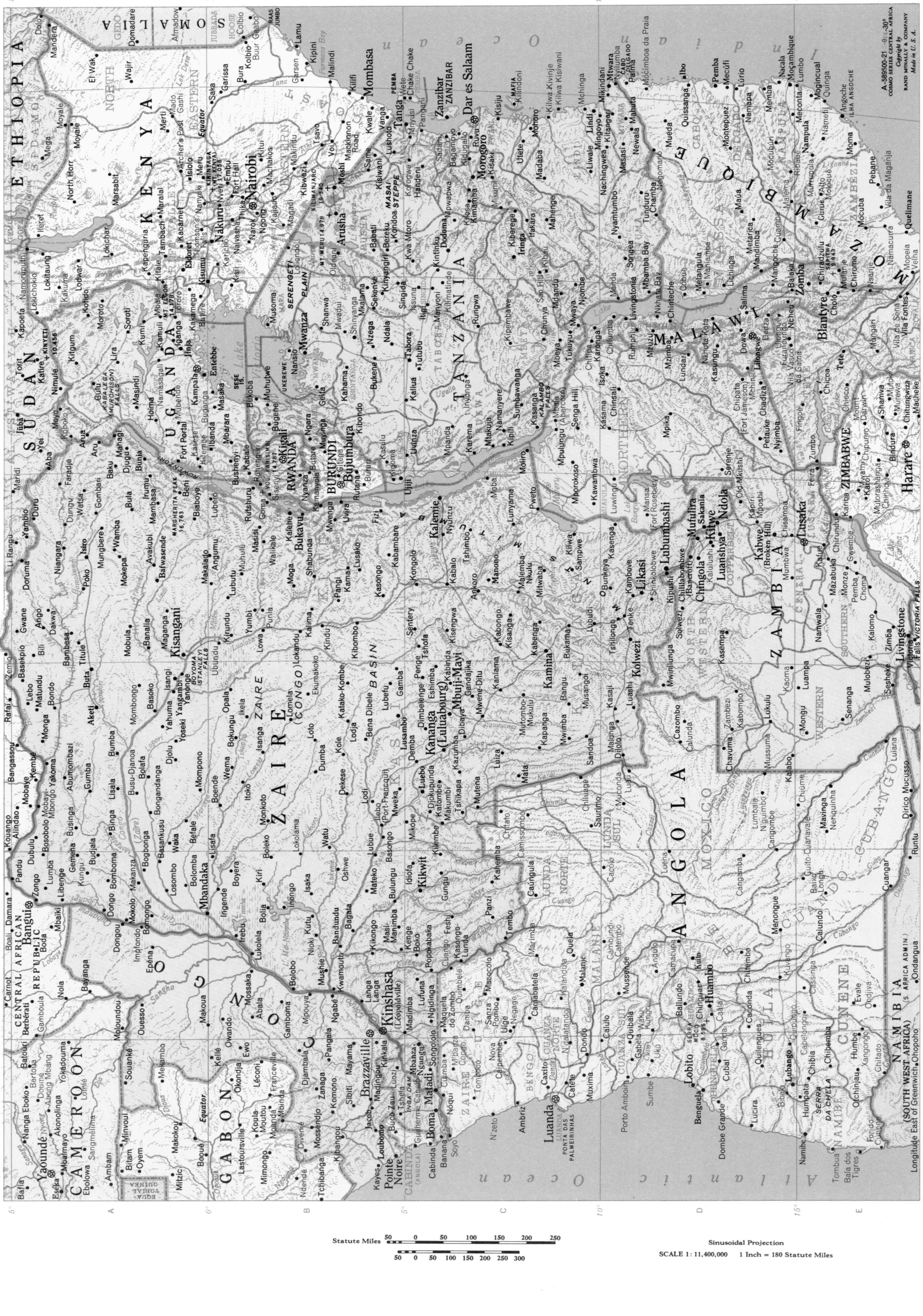

ETHIOPIA
SUDAN
KENYA
UGANDA
SOMALIA
TANZANIA
RWANDA
BURUNDI
ZAIRE
CONGO
GABON
CAMEROON
CENTRAL AFRICAN REPUBLIC
ANGOLA
ZAMBIA
MALAWI
MOZAMBIQUE
ZIMBABWE
NAMIBIA (SOUTH WEST AFRICA)
Nairobi
Kampala
Kigali
Bujumbura
Dar es Salaam
Kinshasa
Brazzaville
Luanda
Lusaka
Harare
Bangui
Yaoundé
Mombasa
Atlantic Ocean
Longitude East of Greenwich
A-589500-21
COSMO SERIES CENTRAL AFRICA
Copyright by RAND McNALLY & COMPANY
Made in U. S. A.
Statute Miles 50 0 50 100 150 200 250
50 0 50 100 150 200 250 300
Sinusoidal Projection
SCALE 1: 11,400,000 1 Inch = 180 Statute Miles

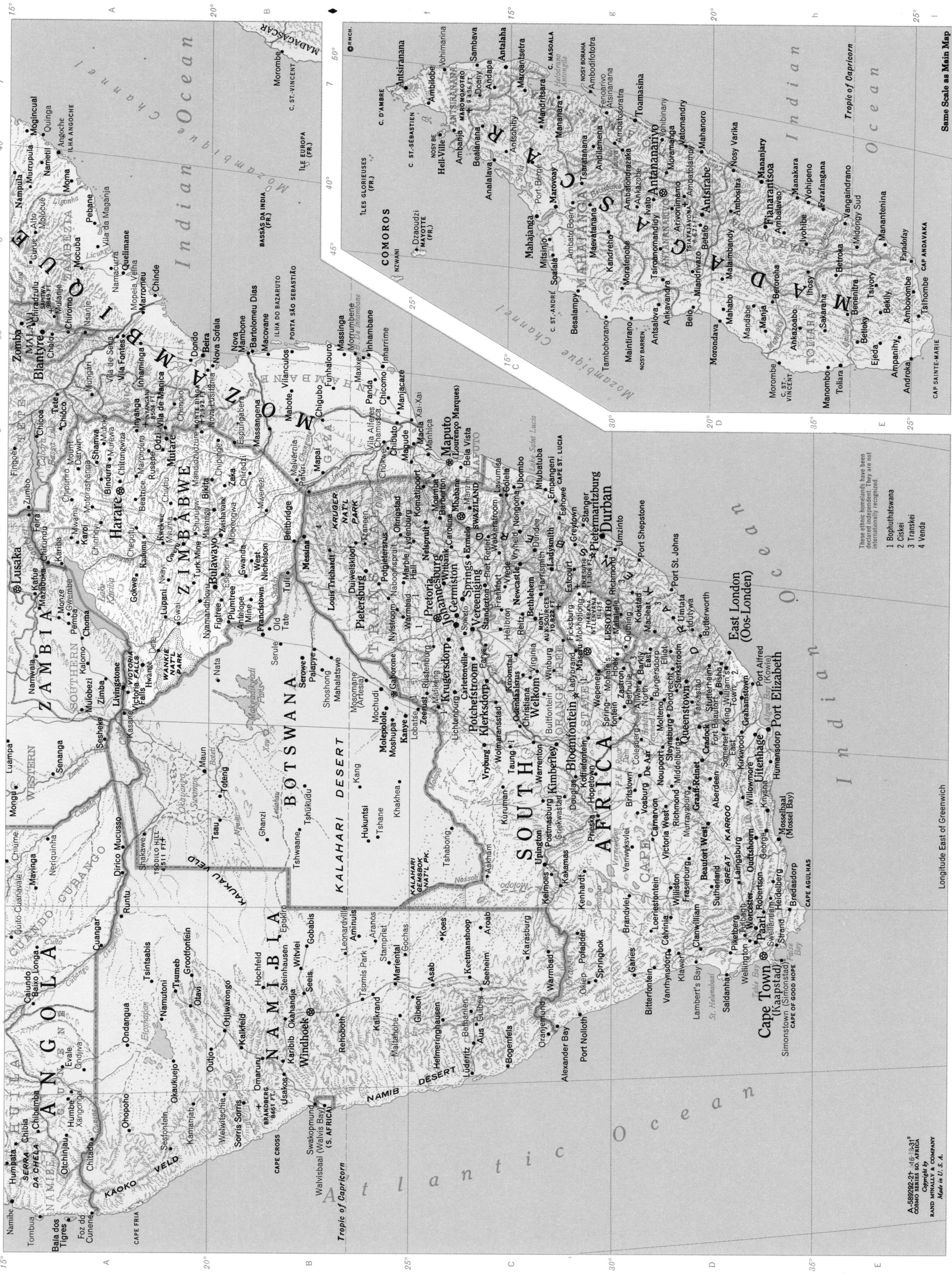

Same Scale as Main Map

These ethnic homelands have been declared independent. They are not internationally recognized.

1 Bophuthatswana
2 Ciskei
3 Transkei
4 Venda

A-589292-21 -46-i-31ª
COSMO SERIES SO. AFRICA
Copyright by
RAND M9NALLY & COMPANY
Made in U.S.A.

Sinusoidal Projection
SCALE 1 : 11,400,000   1 Inch = 180 Statute Miles

Statute Miles   50 25 0   50   100   150   200   250
Kilometers   50 0 50 100 150 200 250 300

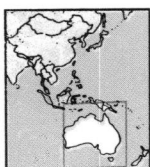

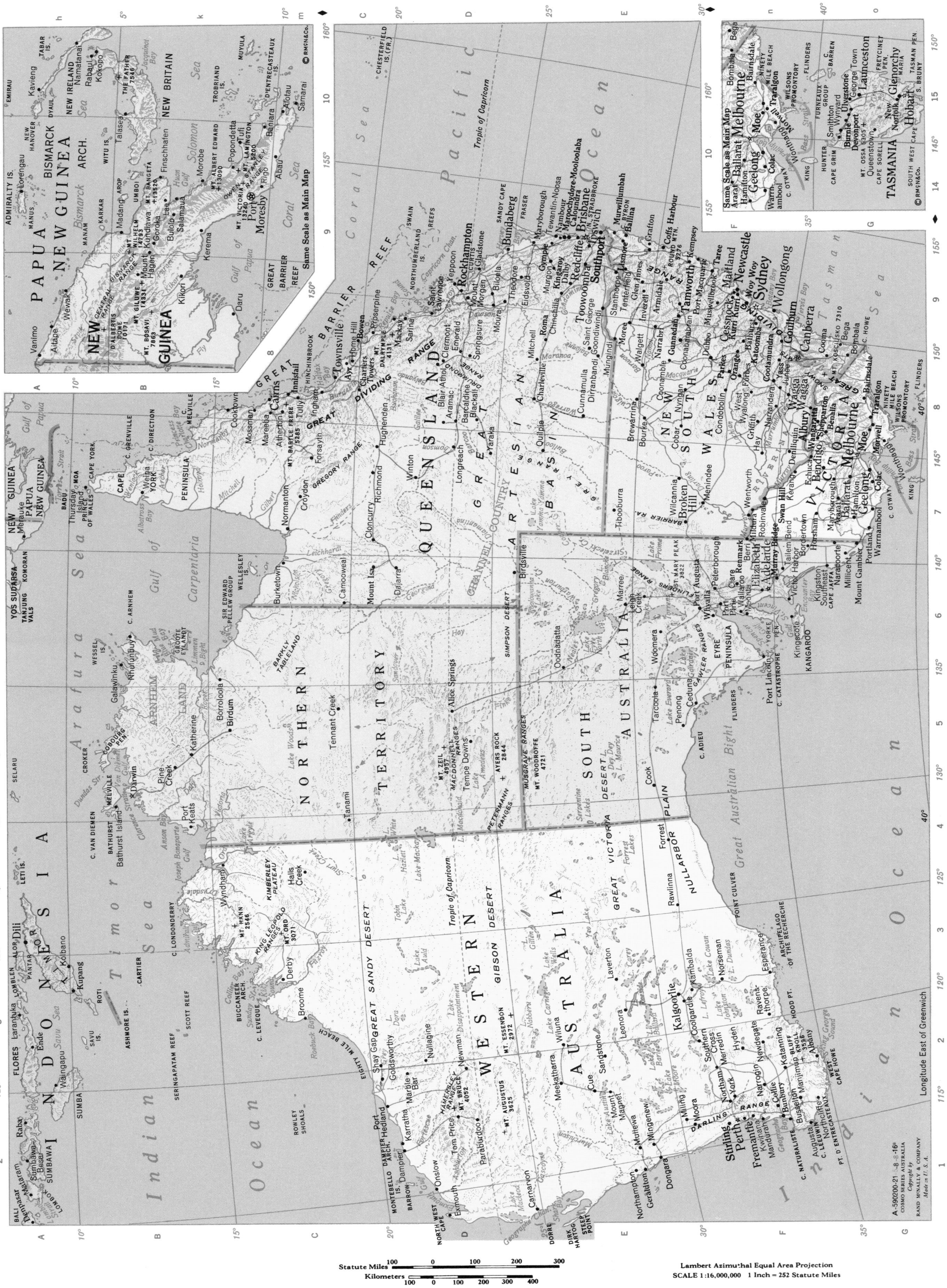

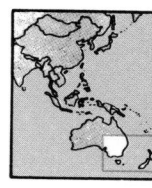

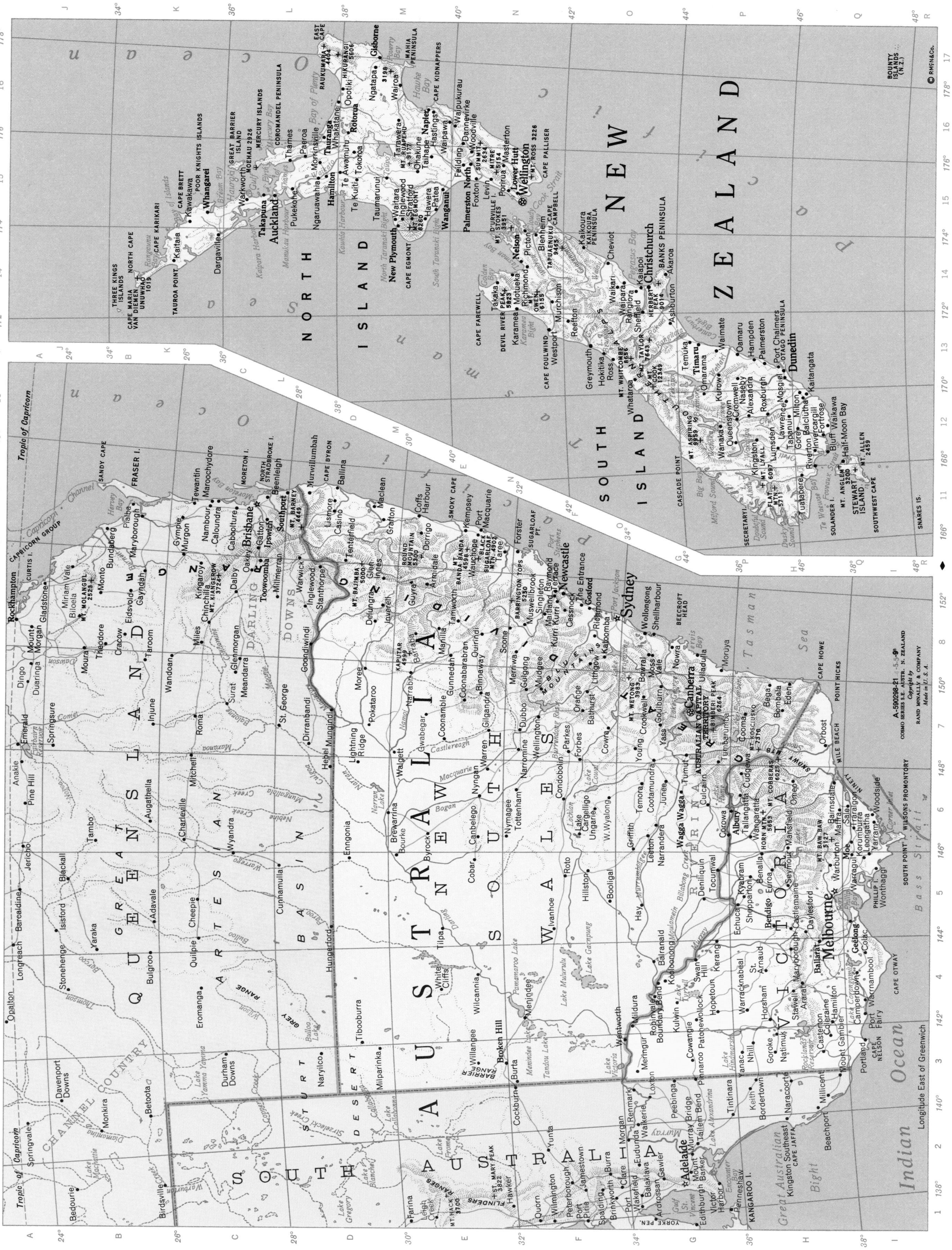

Lambert Conformal Conic Projection

SCALE 1 : 8,000,000 1 Inch = 126 Statute Miles

Statute Miles 50 0 50 100 150

Kilometers 50 0 50 100 200

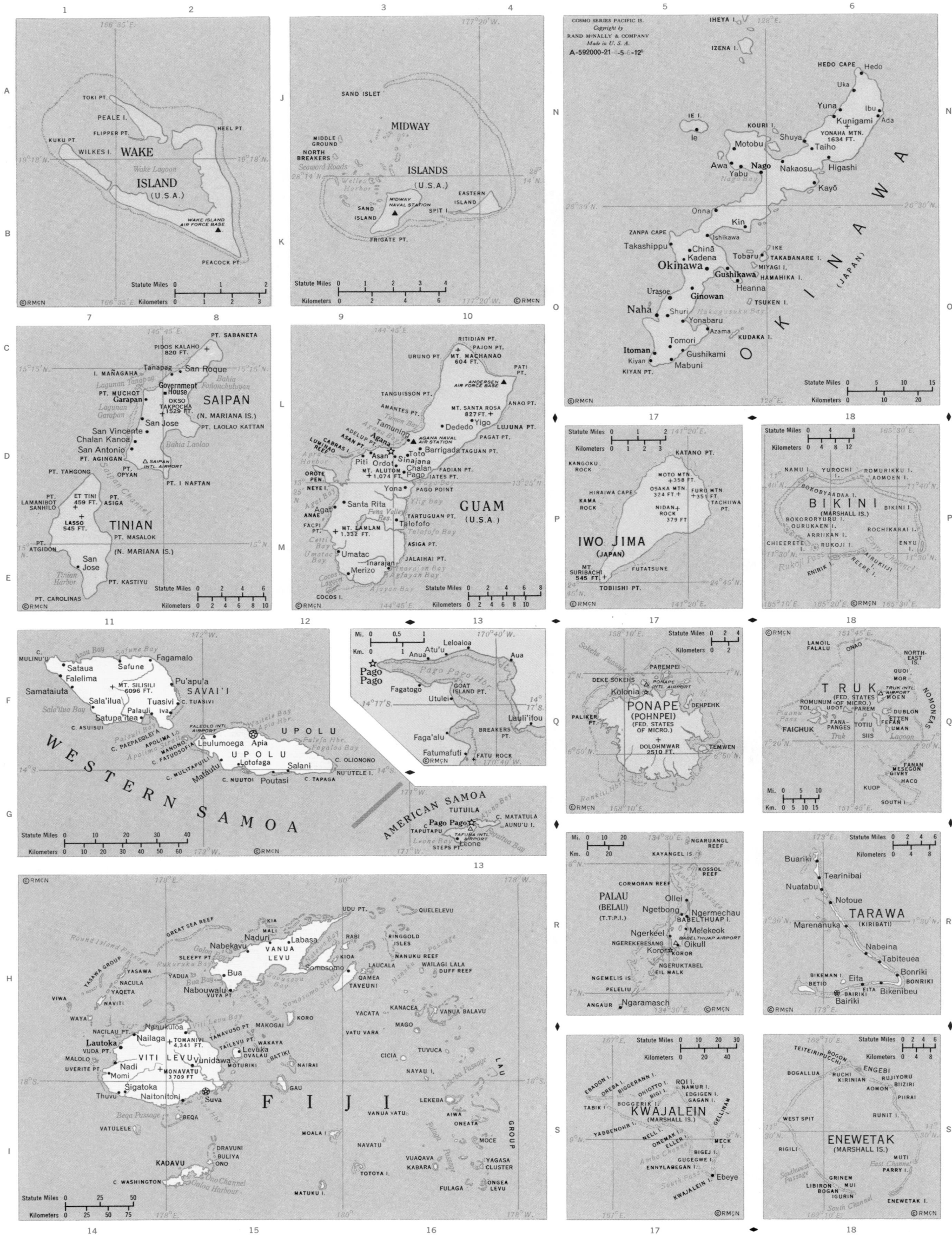

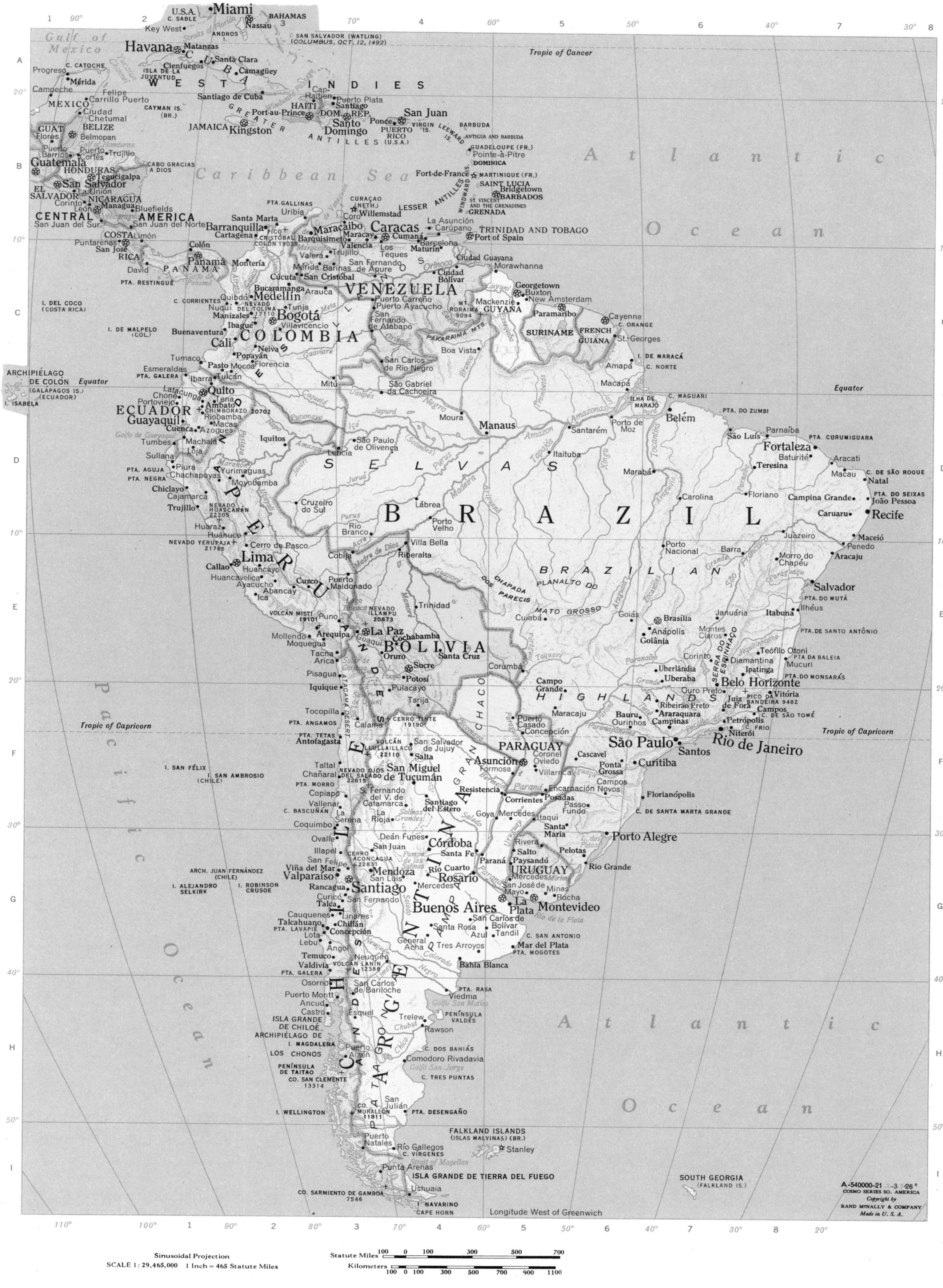

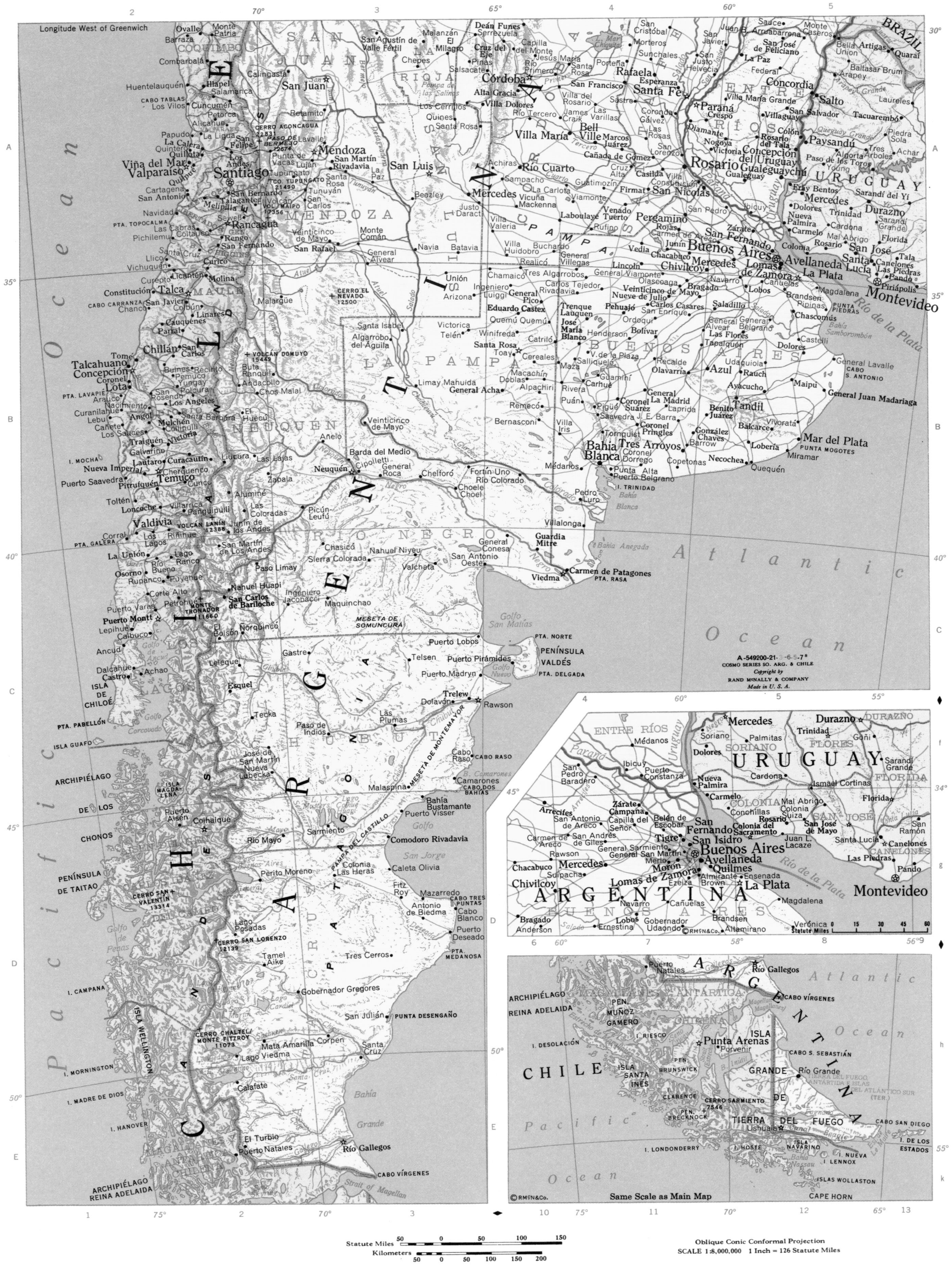

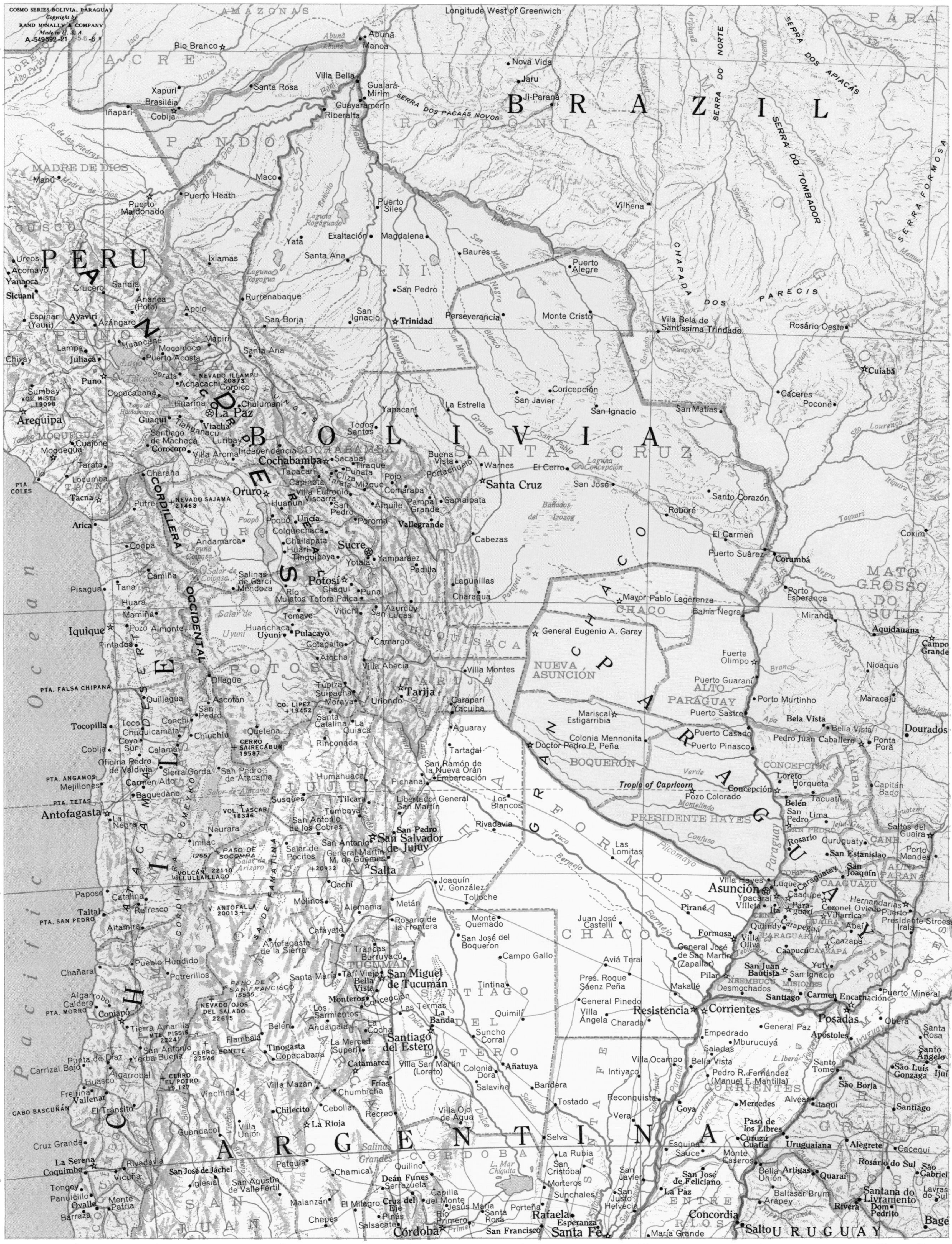

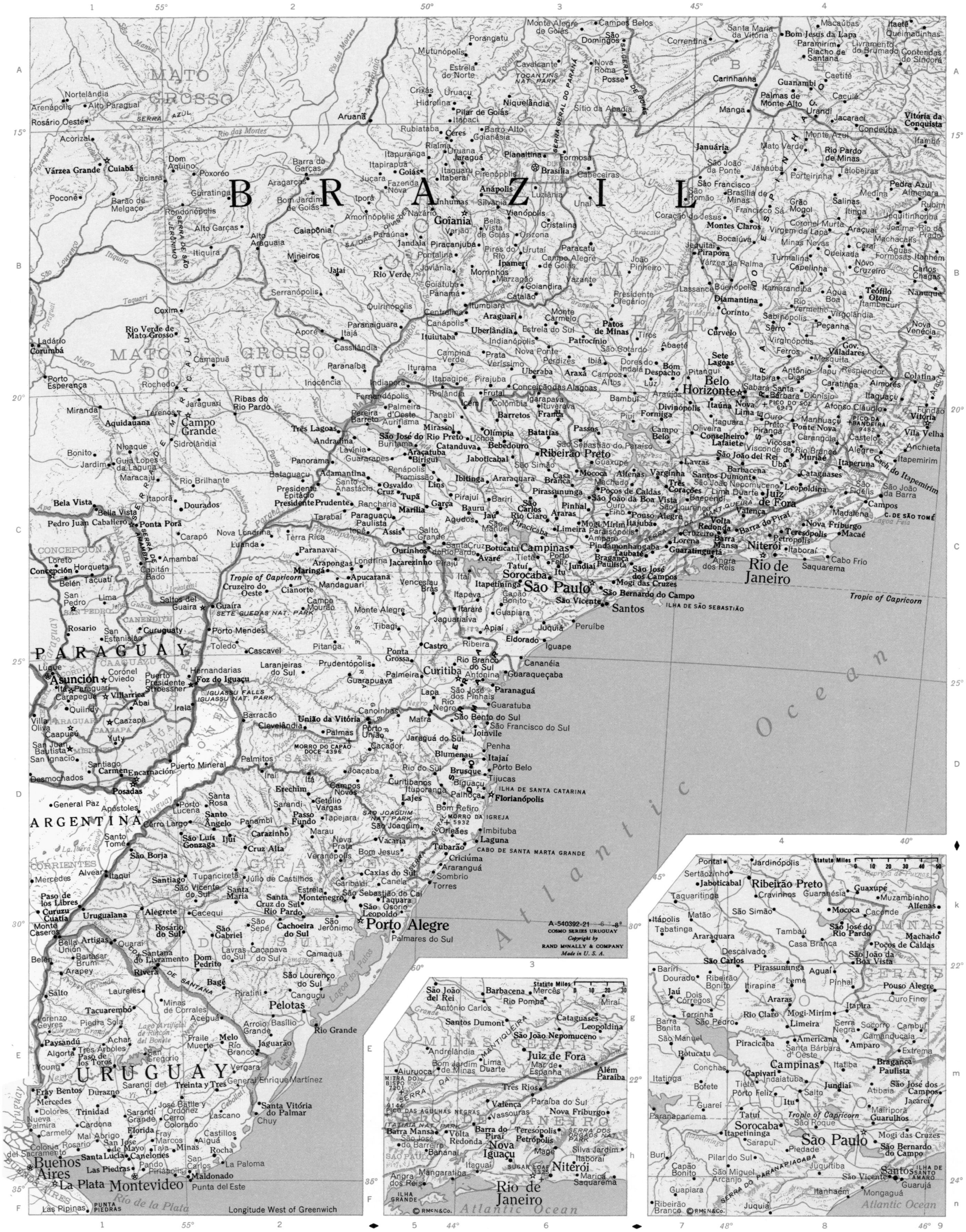

BRAZIL

MATO GROSSO

MATO GROSSO DO SUL

MINAS GERAIS

PARAGUAY

ARGENTINA

URUGUAY

Atlantic Ocean

Tropic of Capricorn

Major cities and towns include:

Cuiabá, Várzea Grande, Goiânia, Anápolis, Brasília, Belo Horizonte, Ribeirão Preto, São Paulo, Campinas, Sorocaba, Santos, São Vicente, Curitiba, Paranaguá, Florianópolis, Blumenau, Joinvile, Porto Alegre, Pelotas, Rio Grande, Campo Grande, Três Lagoas, Presidente Prudente, Marília, Bauru, Londrina, Maringá, Foz do Iguaçu, Asunción, Encarnación, Posadas, Uruguaiana, Santa Maria, Caxias do Sul, Rivera, Tacuarembó, Melo, Paysandú, Salto, Durazno, Trinidad, Minas, Maldonado, Montevideo, Buenos Aires, La Plata, Rio de Janeiro, Niterói, Juiz de Fora, Volta Redonda, Nova Friburgo, Petrópolis, Teresópolis, Campos, Macaé, Cabo Frio

Rio de Janeiro (inset)

São Paulo (inset)

Ribeirão Preto (inset)

COSMO SERIES URUGUAY
Copyright by
Rand McNally & Company
Made in U.S.A.
A-540392-21

Longitude West of Greenwich

Statute Miles
50   0   50   100   150

Kilometers
50   0   50   100   150   200

Oblique Conic Conformal Projection
SCALE 1:8,000,000   1 inch = 126 Statute Miles

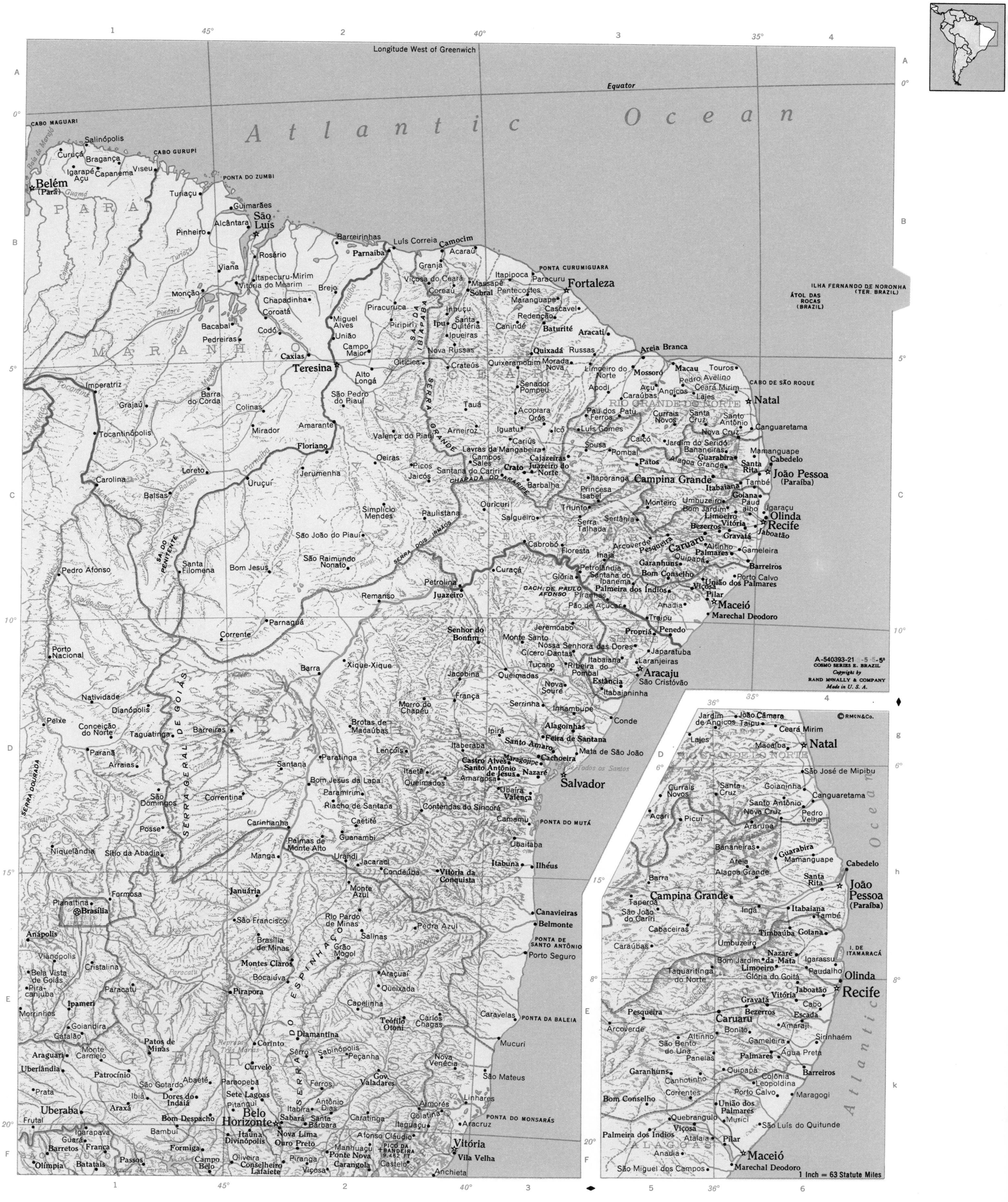

A t l a n t i c   O c e a n

Longitude West of Greenwich

Equator

PARÁ
MARANHÃO

Belém
(Pará)
CABO MAGUARI
Salinópolis
Curuçá
Bragança
Igarapé Açu
Capanema
Viseu
CABO GURUPI
Turiaçu
PONTA DO ZUMBI
Guimarães
Alcântara
São Luís
Pinheiro
Viana
Rosário
Barreirinhas
Luís Correia
Camocim
Acaraú
Parnaíba
Granja
Viçosa do Ceará
Massapê
Paracuru
Itapipoca
PONTA CURUMIGUARA
Fortaleza
Itapecuru-Mirim
Vitória do Mearim
Brejo
Coreaú
Sobral
Pentecostes
Cascavel
Monção
Chapadinha
Coroatá
Miguel Alves
Piripiri
Ipu
Santa Quitéria
Inhuçu
Ipueiras
Redenção
Maranguape
Bacabal
Codó
União
Campo Maior
Nova Russas
Caxias
Teresina
Oiticica
Crateús
Quixeramobim
Morada Nova
Baturité
Aracati
Areia Branca
Alto Longá
São Pedro do Piauí
Tauá
Senador Pompeu
Quixadá
Russas
Macau
Touros
Imperatriz
Grajaú
Barra do Corda
Colinas
Acopiara
Orós
Iguatu
Icó
Limoeiro do Norte
Mossoró
Açu
Pedro Avelino
Ceará Mirim
CABO DE SÃO ROQUE
RIO GRANDE DO NORTE
Natal
Mirador
Amarante
Arneiroz
Cariús
Sousa
Luís Gomes
Pau dos Ferros
Apodi
Caraúbas
Angicos
Lajes
Santa Cruz
Santo Antônio
Nova Cruz
Canguaretama
Tocantinópolis
Floriano
Valença do Piauí
Oeiras
Picos
Lavras da Mangabeira
Campos Sales
Cajazeiras
Juazeiro do Norte
Pombal
Caicó
Jardim do Seridó
Bananeiras
Mamanguape
Cabedelo
Loreto
Jaicós
Santana do Cariri
Crato
Barbalha
Iporanga
Patos
Alagoa Grande
Guarabira
Santa Rita
João Pessoa
(Paraíba)
Carolina
Balsas
Simplício Mendes
CHAPADA DO ARARIPE
Princesa Isabel
Triunfo
Monteiro
Campina Grande
Itabaiana
També
Goiana
Olinda
Recife
Pedro Afonso
Santa Filomena
Bom Jesus
São Raimundo Nonato
São João do Piauí
Paulistana
Ouricuri
Salgueiro
Serra Talhada
Sertânia
Bom Jardim
Limoeiro
Paudalho
Vitória
Igaraçu
Jaboatão
Porto Nacional
Remanso
Curaçá
Cabrobó
Floresta
Arcoverde
Bezerros
Gravatá
Gameleira
Natividade
Dianópolis
Parnaguá
Parnaíba
Petrolina
Juazeiro
CACH. DE PAULO AFONSO
Inajá
Petrolândia
Caruaru
Altinho
Palmares
Peixe
Conceição do Norte
Paranã
Arraias
Corrente
Barra
Xique-Xique
Glória
Santana do Ipanema
Palmeira dos Índios
Garanhuns
Bom Conselho
Quipapá
União dos Palmares
Barreiras
Porto Calvo
Taguatinga
Barreiras
Senhor do Bonfim
Jeremoabo
Monte Santo
Nossa Senhora das Dores
Propriá
Penedo
Viçosa
Pilar
Maceió
Marechal Deodoro
Morro do Chapéu
Jacobina
Queimadas
Cícero Dantas
Tucano
Ribeira do Pombal
Itabaiana
Laranjeiras
Japaratuba
Formosa
Brasília
Niquelândia
Sítio da Abadia
Brotas de Macaúbas
França
Serrinha
Inhambupe
Conde
Aracaju
São Cristóvão
Estância
Itabaianinha
Ipirá
Alagoinhas
Feira de Santana
Anápolis
Vianópolis
Bela Vista de Goiás
Paracatu
Ipameri
Morrinhos
Goiandira
Catalão
Monte Carmelo
Araguari
Uberlândia
Patrocínio
Prata
Uberaba
Frutal
Igarapava
Guará
Barretos
Franca
Batatais
Olímpia
Passos
Cristalina
Planaltina
Formosa
Januária
Monte Azul
São Francisco
Rio Pardo de Minas
Salinas
Grão Mogol
Pedra Azul
Montes Claros
Bocaiúva
Araçuaí
Capelinha
Teófilo Otoni
Carlos Chagas
Caravelas
PONTA DA BALEIA
Mucuri
São Mateus
Linhares
Aracruz
PONTA DO MONSARÁS
Vitória
Vila Velha
Anchieta
Belo Horizonte
Diamantina
Pirapora
Piranga
Ouro Preto
Formiga
SERRA DO ESPINHAÇO
SERRA GERAL DE GOIÁS

Lençóis
Itaberaba
Santo Amaro
Cachoeira
Mata de São João
Castro Alves
Santo Antônio de Jesus
Nazaré
Salvador
Maragojipe
Amargosa
Ubaíra
Valença
Camamu
PONTA DO MUTÁ
Ubaitaba
Itabuna
Ilhéus
Canavieiras
Belmonte
Porto Seguro
PONTA DE SANTO ANTÔNIO
Vitória da Conquista
Condeúba
Itambé
Santana
Paratinga
Itaeté
Queimados
Paramirim
Riacho de Santana
Caetité
Contendas do Sincorá
Bom Jesus da Lapa
Correntina
São Domingos
Posse
Palmas de Monte Alto
Manga
Urandi
Jacaraci
Guanambi

ILHA FERNANDO DE NORONHA
(TER. BRAZIL)
ÁTOL DAS ROCAS
(BRAZIL)

A-540393-21 -5-5-5°
COSMO SERIES E. BRAZIL
Copyright by
RAND McNALLY & COMPANY
Made in U.S.A.

[Inset map — Rio Grande do Norte / Paraíba / Pernambuco / Alagoas]

Jardim de Ângicos
João Câmara
Taipu
Ceará Mirim
Lajes
Macaíba
Natal
RIO GRANDE DO NORTE
Currais Novos
Santa Cruz
Goianinha
São José de Mipibu
Acari
Picuí
Santo Antônio
Canguaretama
Araruna
Nova Cruz
Pedro Velho
Bananeiras
Guarabira
Mamanguape
Cabedelo
Barra
Alagoa Grande
Santa Rita
João Pessoa
(Paraíba)
Campina Grande
Taperoá
Inga
Itabaiana
També
São João do Cariri
Timbaúba
Goiana
Cabaceiras
Umbuzeiro
I. DE ITAMARACÁ
Caraúbas
Nazaré da Mata
Igarassu
Taquaritinga do Norte
Bom Jardim
Limoeiro
Paudalho
Glória do Goitá
Vitória
Olinda
Recife
Pesqueira
Arcoverde
Caruaru
Bezerros
Gravatá
Taboão
Cabo
Escada
Amaraji
Sirinhaém
Altinho
Bonito
São Bento do Una
Panelas
Gameleira
Palmares
Água Preta
Garanhuns
Canhotinho
Quipapá
Colônia Leopoldina
Barreiros
Bom Conselho
Correntes
Porto Calvo
Maragogi
União dos Palmares
Viçosa
Murici
São Luís de Quitunde
Quebrangulo
Anadia
Palmeira dos Índios
Pilar
Maceió
ALAGOAS
São Miguel dos Campos
Marechal Deodoro

O c e a n
A t l a n t i c

1 Inch = 63 Statute Miles

Oblique Conic Conformal Projection
SCALE 1:8,000,000   1 Inch = 126 Statute Miles

Statute Miles 50 0 50 100 150
Kilometers 50 0 50 100 150 200

©RMcN&Co.

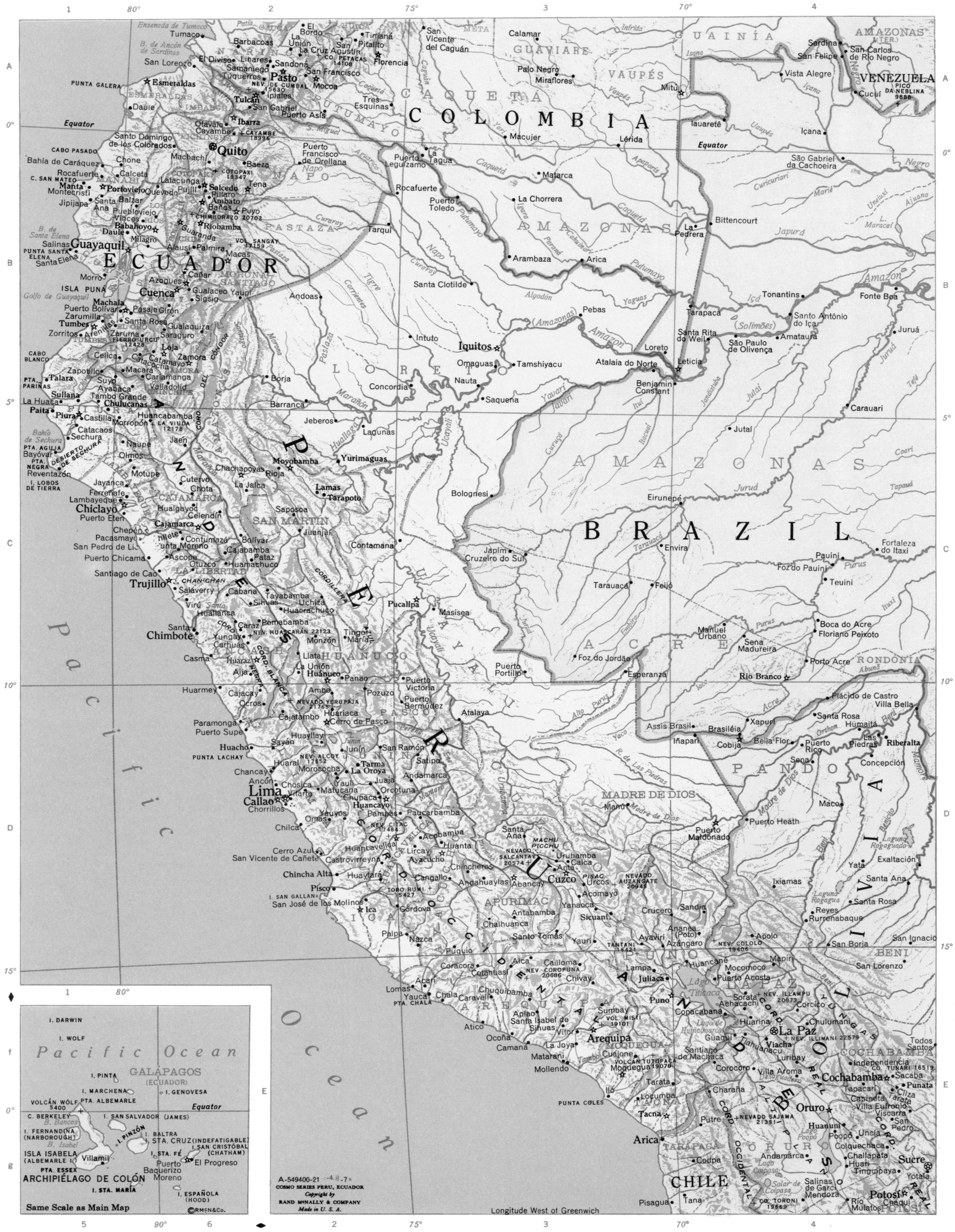

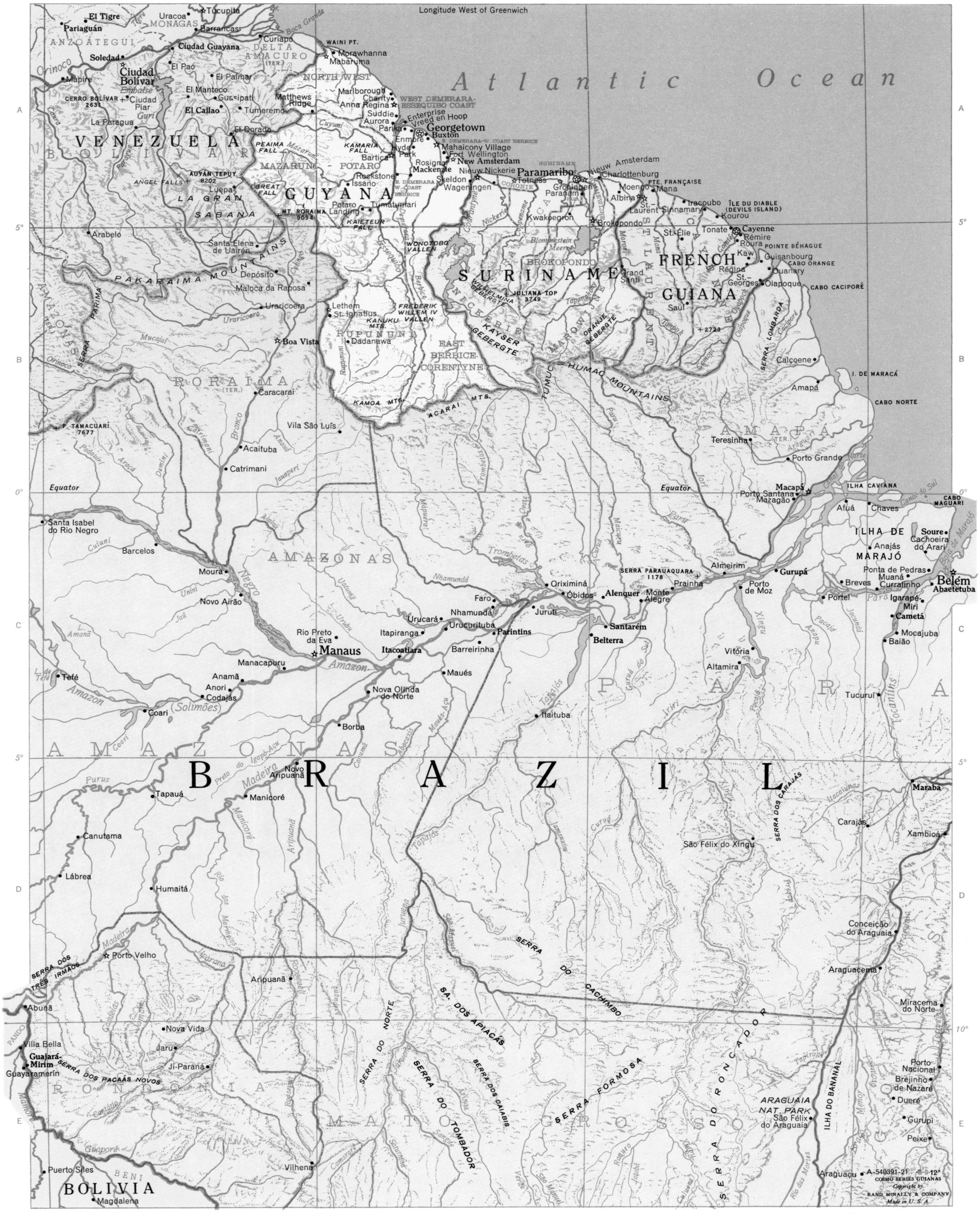

Longitude West of Greenwich

Atlantic Ocean

VENEZUELA

GUYANA

SURINAME

FRENCH GUIANA

BRAZIL

BOLIVIA

Georgetown
Paramaribo
Cayenne
ÎLE DU DIABLE (DEVILS ISLAND)

Manaus
Boa Vista
Macapá
Belém
ILHA DE MARAJÓ
Maraba

Equator

PAKARAIMA MOUNTAINS
TUMUC-HUMAC MOUNTAINS
SERRA DO CACHIMBO
SERRA FORMOSA
SERRA DO RONCADOR

ARAGUAIA NAT. PARK

AMAZONAS
PARÁ
RONDONIA
MATO GROSSO
RORAIMA (TER.)
AMAPÁ (TER.)

Oblique Conic Conformal Projection
SCALE 1:8,000,000   1 Inch = 126 Statute Miles

Statute Miles
Kilometers

A-540391-21
RAND McNALLY & COMPANY
Made in U.S.A.

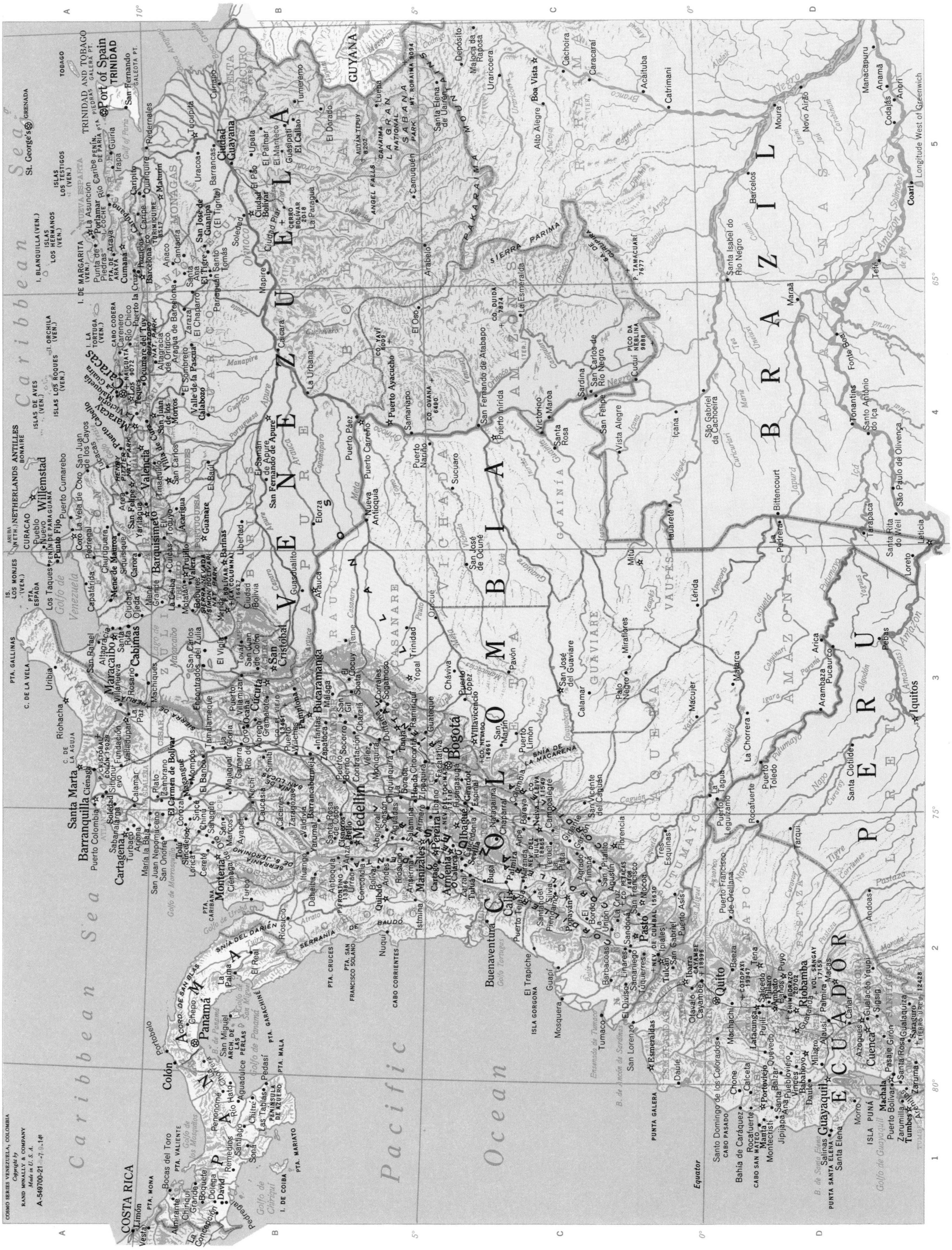

Statute Miles 50 0 50 100 150

Kilometers 50 0 50 100 150 200

Oblique Conic Conformal Projection
SCALE 1:8,000,000 1 Inch = 126 Statute Miles

COSMO SERIES VENEZUELA, COLOMBIA
Copyright by
RAND MCNALLY & COMPANY
Made in U.S.A.
A-549700-21-27-51.1p

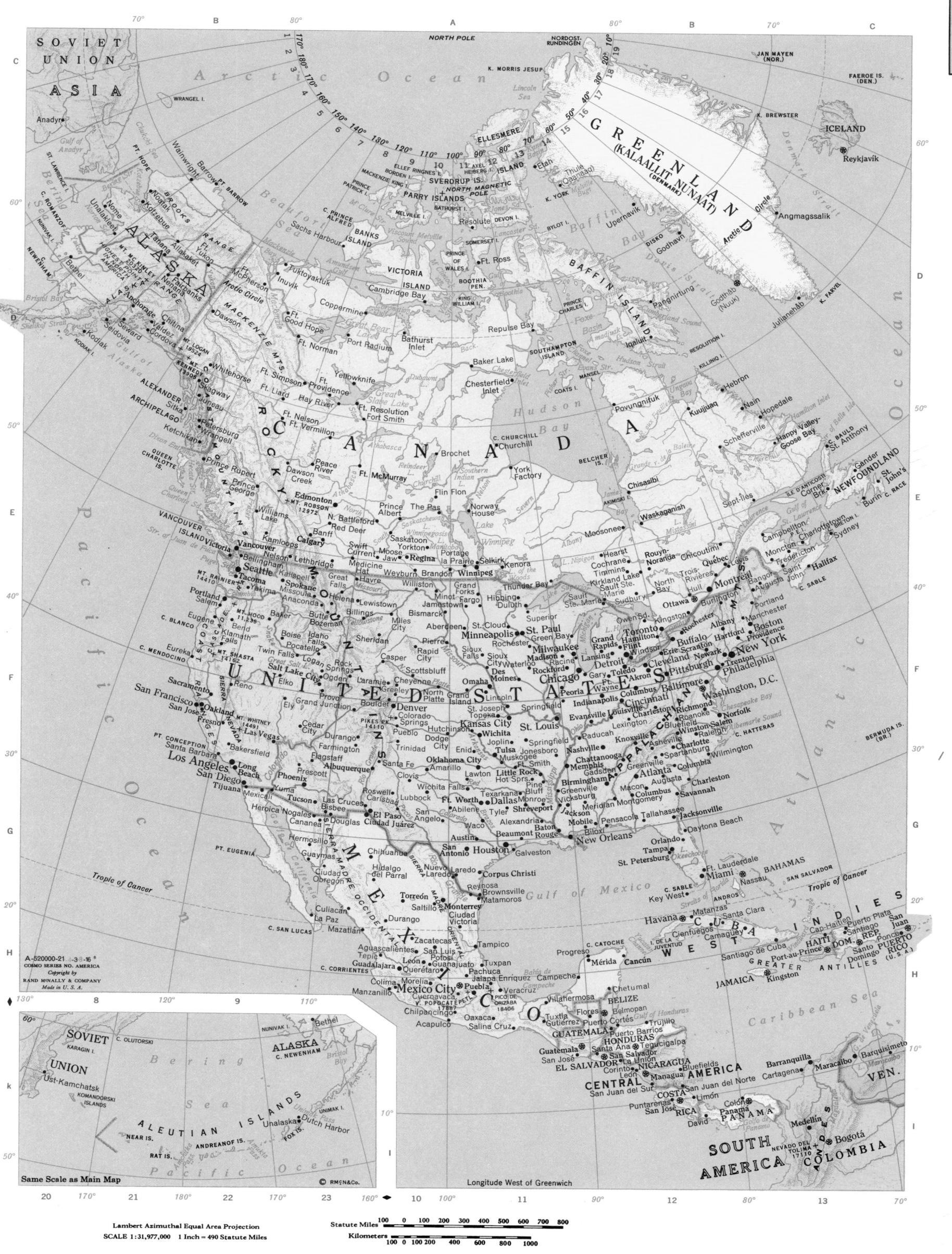

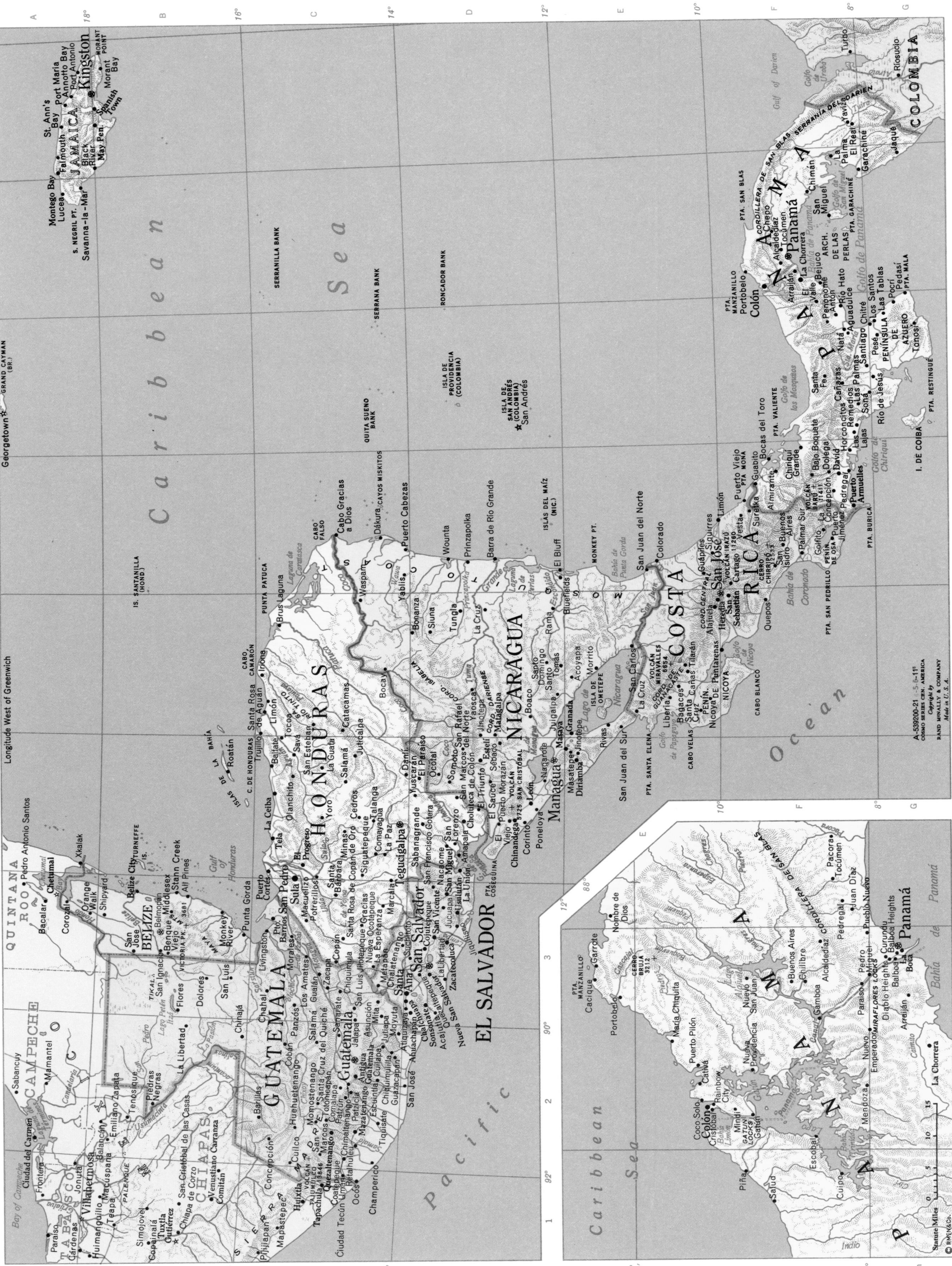

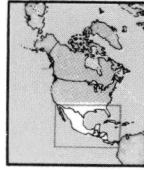

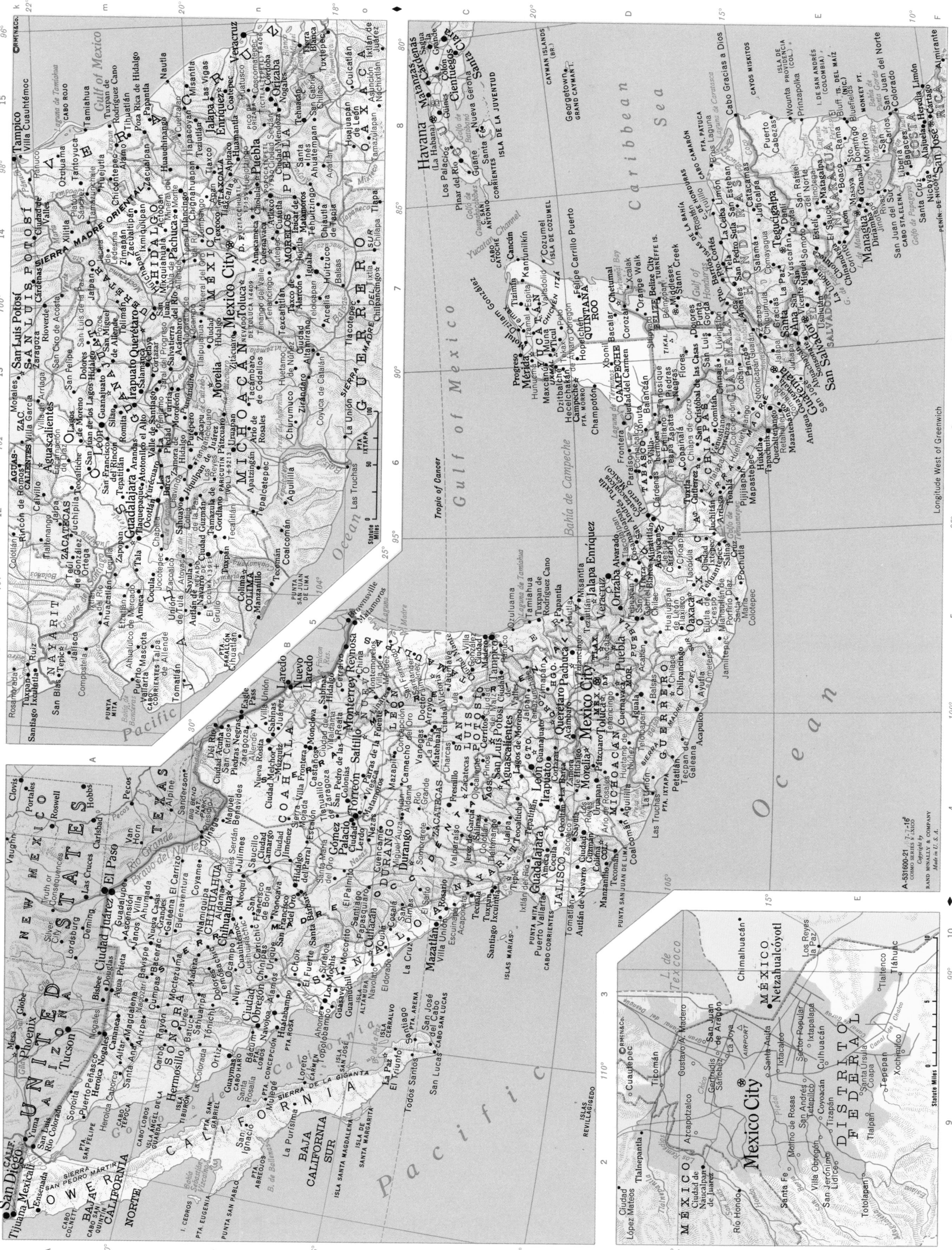

Oblique Conic Conformal Projection
SCALE 1:12,000 000 1 Inch = 189 Statute Miles

Statute Miles 50 25 0 50 100 150 200 250

Kilometers 50 0 100 200 300

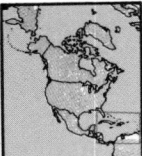

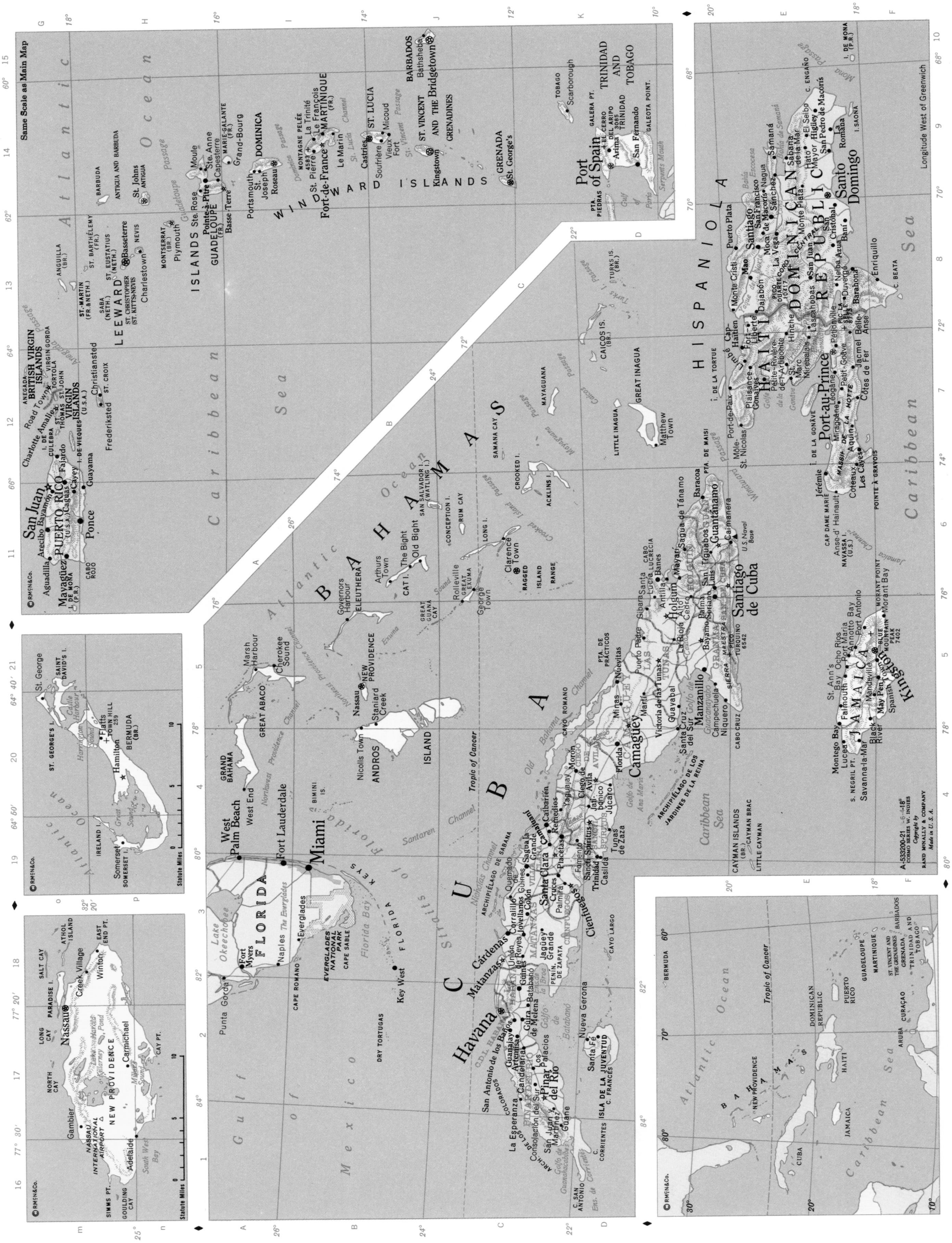

Same Scale as Main Map

Atlantic Ocean

Caribbean Sea

BAHAMAS

CUBA

HISPANIOLA

DOMINICAN REPUBLIC

HAITI

JAMAICA

PUERTO RICO

LEEWARD ISLANDS

WINDWARD ISLANDS

TRINIDAD AND TOBAGO

San Juan
Havana
Santiago de Cuba
Camagüey
Port-au-Prince
Santo Domingo
Kingston
Port of Spain
Bridgetown
BARBADOS
GRENADA
ST. VINCENT AND THE GRENADINES
ST. LUCIA
MARTINIQUE (FR.)
DOMINICA
GUADELOUPE (FR.)
ANTIGUA AND BARBUDA
MONTSERRAT (BR.)
ST. CHRISTOPHER (ST. KITTS)-NEVIS
BRITISH VIRGIN ISLANDS
VIRGIN ISLANDS (U.S.A.)

Gulf of Mexico

FLORIDA
Miami
Fort Lauderdale
West Palm Beach
Key West
Fort Myers

Tropic of Cancer

BERMUDA (BR.)
Hamilton

CAYMAN ISLANDS

NEW PROVIDENCE
Nassau

Oblique Conic Conformal Projection
SCALE 1:6,000,000 1 Inch = 95 Statute Miles

Statute Miles 25 0 25 75 125
Kilometers 25 0 25 75 125 175

A-533200-21
Copyright by
RAND McNALLY & COMPANY
Made in U.S.A.

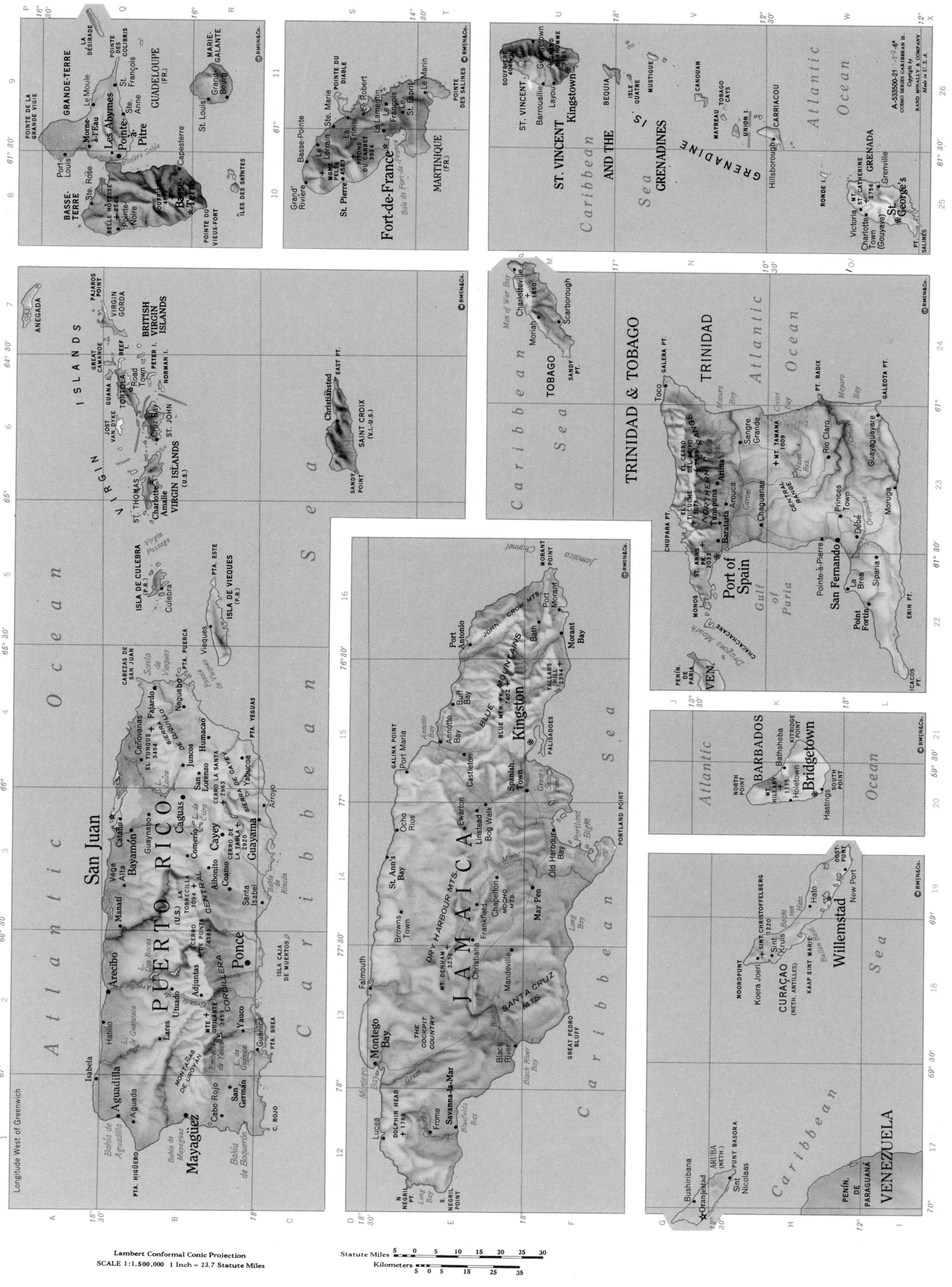

Lambert Conformal Conic Projection
SCALE 1:1,500,000   1 Inch = 23.7 Statute Miles

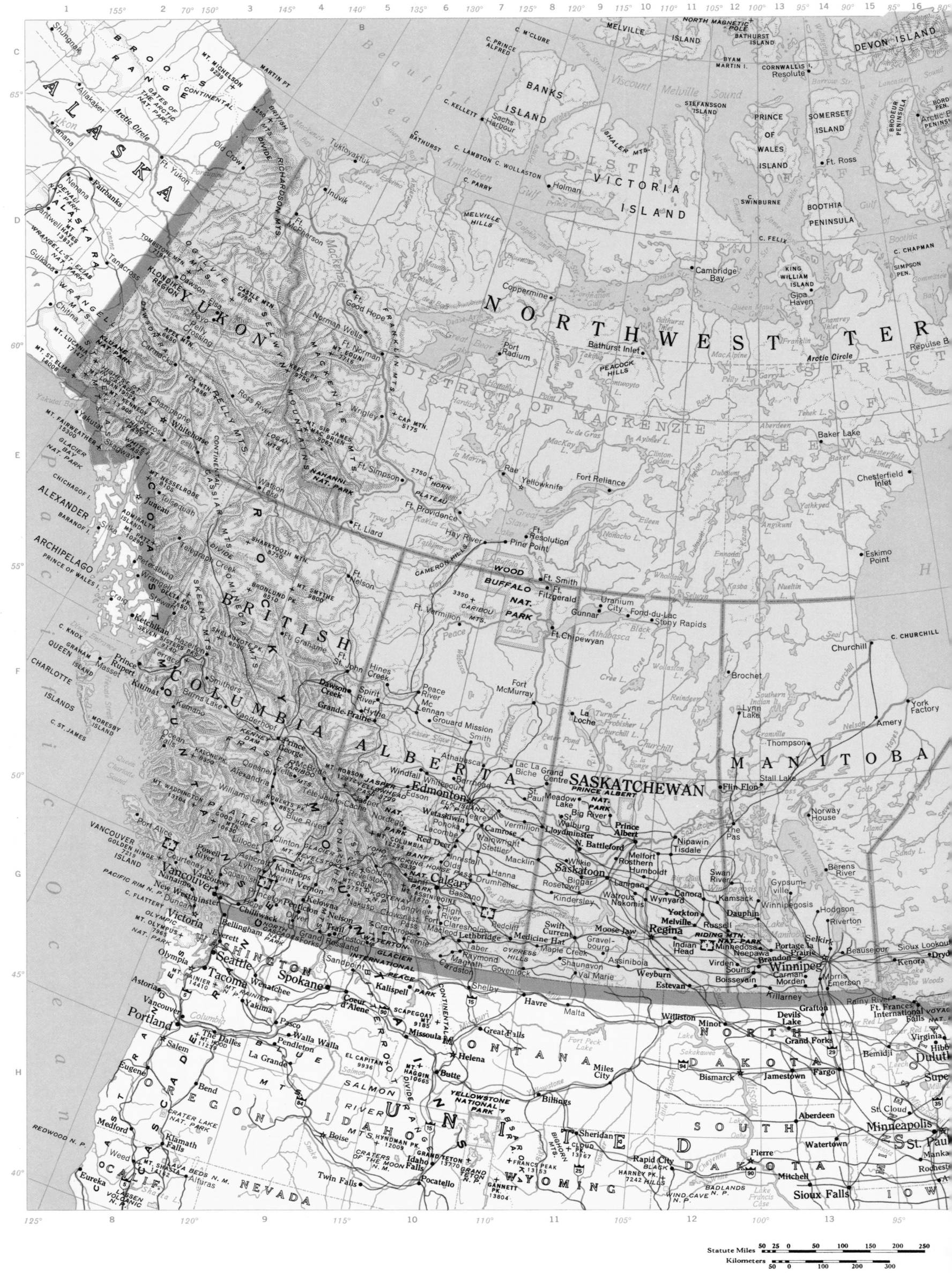

Inset map (top right):

QUEEN
CAPE
STALLWORTHY
ELIZABETH MEIGHEN I.
AXEL
HEIBERG
Eureka
ISLANDS BORDEN ISLAND Isachsen ELLEF RINGNES ISLAND SVERDRUP IS. Grise Fiord
BROCK MACKENZIE AMUND RINGNES ISLAND
PRINCE PATRICK ISLAND KING ISLAND LOUGHEED CORNWALL I. GRAHAM I. Grise Fiord COBURG ISLAND
Mould Bay CAMERON NORTH MAGNETIC POLE GRINNELL PEN.
EGLINTON PARRY ISLANDS BATHURST ISLAND DEVON ISLAND
MELVILLE ISLAND BYAM MARTIN CORNWALLIS ISLAND
BANKS ISLAND Resolute
Viscount
STEFANSSON ISLAND PRINCE OF WALES ISLAND SOMERSET ISLAND BORDEN PEN. BYLOT ISLAND
VICTORIA ISLAND BAFFIN ISLAND

Same Scale as Main Map ©R.M & N & Co.

C. COLUMBIA
BARBEAU PK. 8544
Alert
GREENLAND (DENMARK)

Main map labels (selection):

BAFFIN BAY

GREENLAND (DENMARK)

ITORIES

NEWFOUNDLAND

QUEBEC

ONTARIO

NEW BRUNSWICK

NOVA SCOTIA

PRINCE EDWARD ISLAND

St. John's
Montreal
Ottawa
Toronto
Quebec
Halifax
Boston
New York
Philadelphia
Chicago

Hudson Bay

James Bay

Lake Superior

Lake Michigan

Lake Huron

Lake Erie

Lake Ontario

Atlantic Ocean

All islands within Hudson Bay, James Bay and Ungava Bay lie within Northwest Territories

Longitude West of Greenwich

A-520200·72 ·8·8·12°
COSMO SERIES CANADA
Copyright by
RAND McNALLY & COMPANY
Made in U.S.A.

Lambert Conformal Conic Projection
SCALE 1:12,000,000   1 Inch = 189 Statute Miles

67

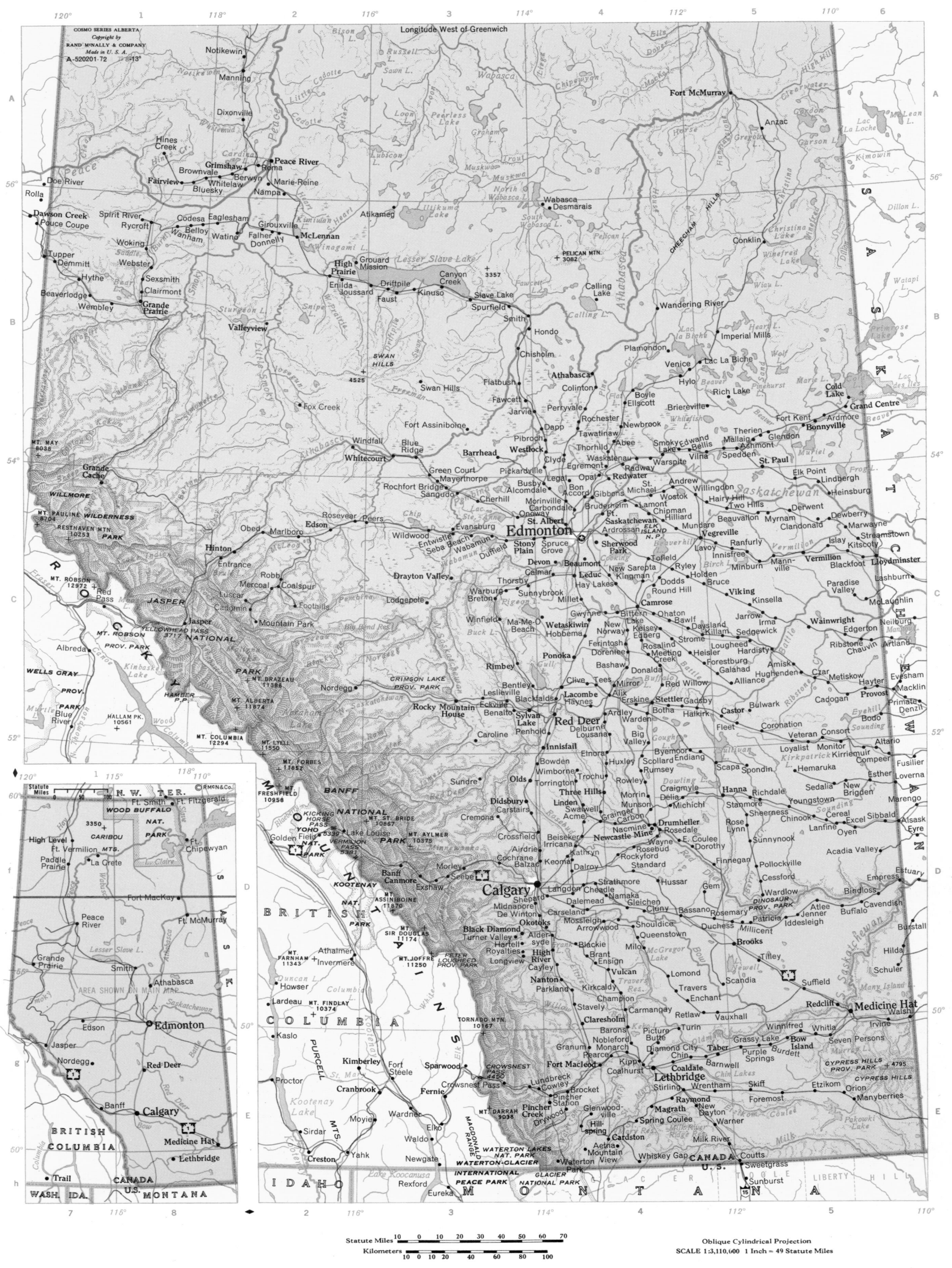

Oblique Cylindrical Projection
SCALE 1:4,255,000 1 Inch = 67 Statute Miles

Statute Miles

Kilometers

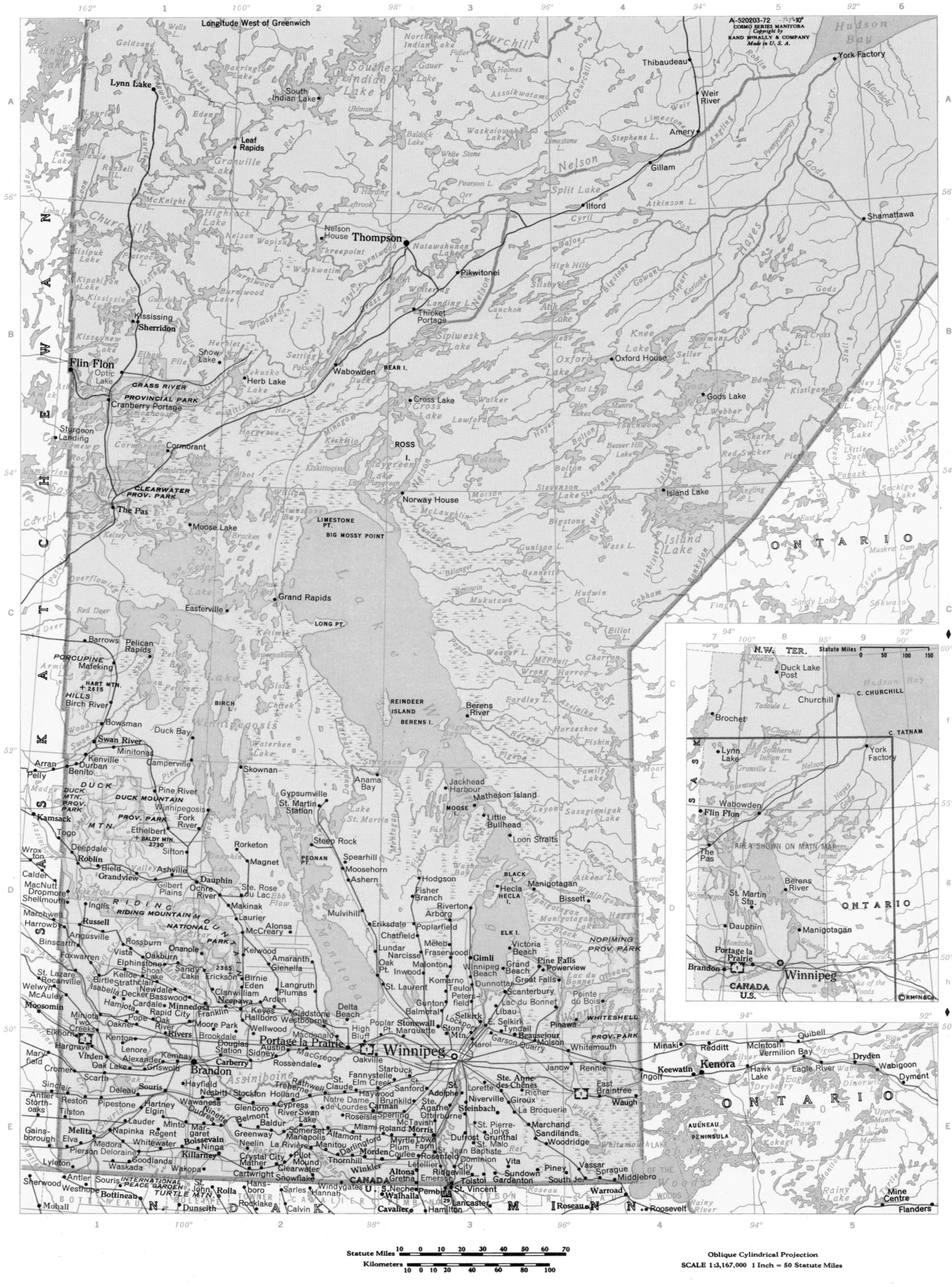

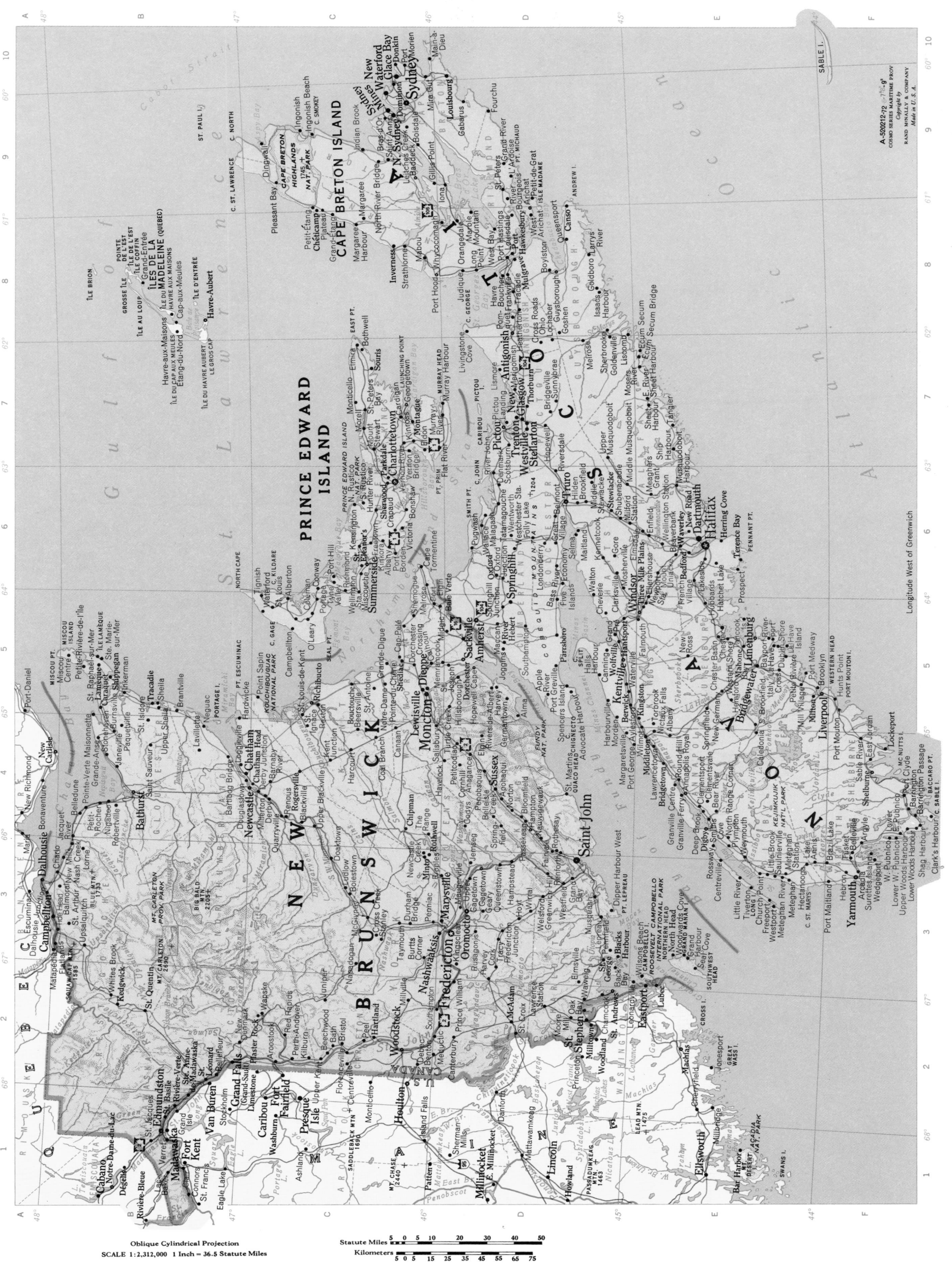

PRINCE EDWARD ISLAND

CAPE BRETON ISLAND

NEW BRUNSWICK

NOVA SCOTIA

Gulf of St. Lawrence

Atlantic Ocean

Bay of Fundy

Halifax

Sydney

Saint John

Fredericton

Moncton

Charlottetown

Oblique Cylindrical Projection
SCALE 1:2,312,000   1 Inch = 36.5 Statute Miles

Statute Miles
5 0 5   10   20   30   40   50

Kilometers
5 0 5   15   25   35   45   55   65   75

Longitude West of Greenwich

A-520212-72
COSMO SERIES MARITIME PROV.
Copyright by
RAND McNALLY & COMPANY
Made in U. S. A.

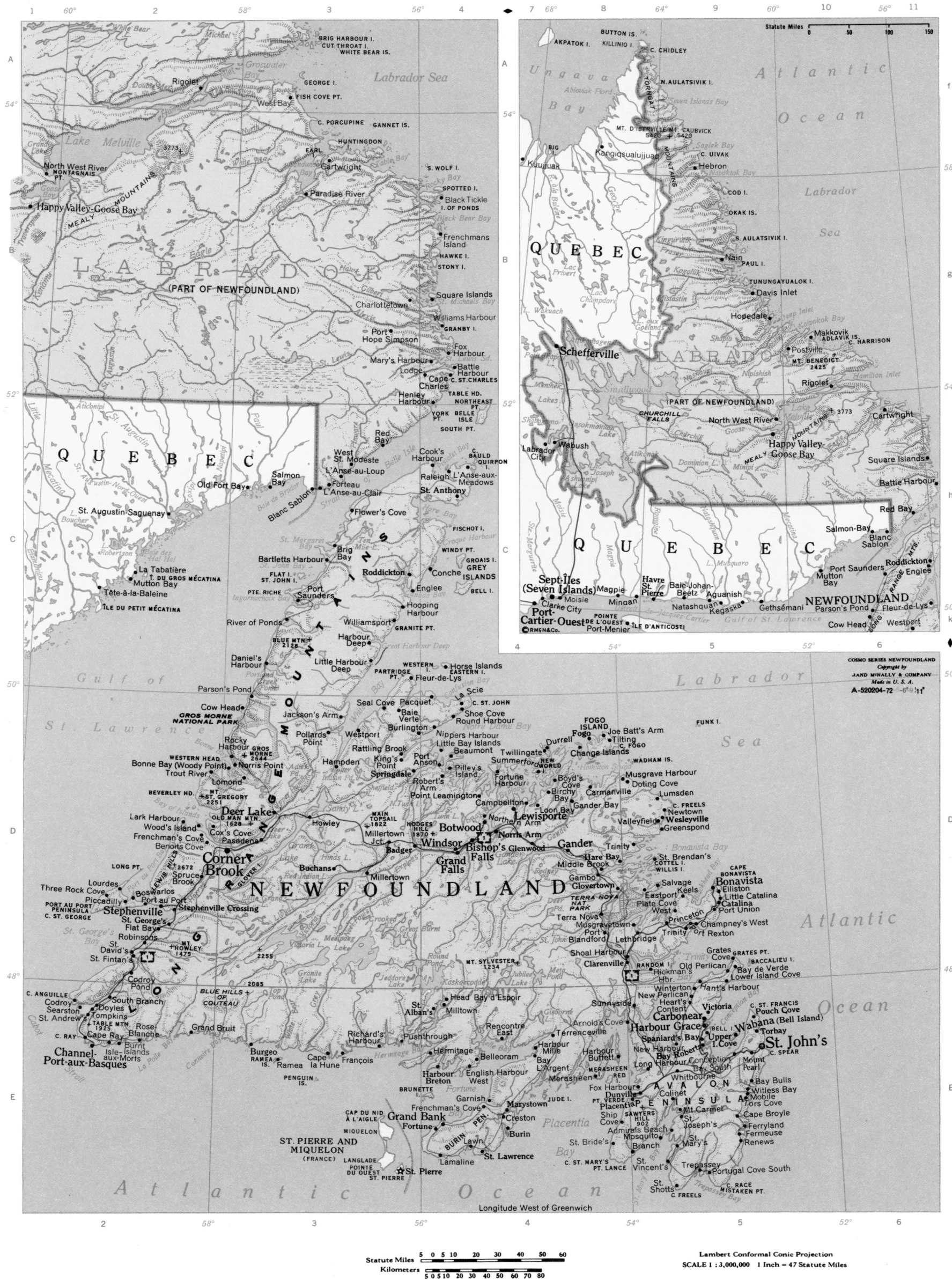

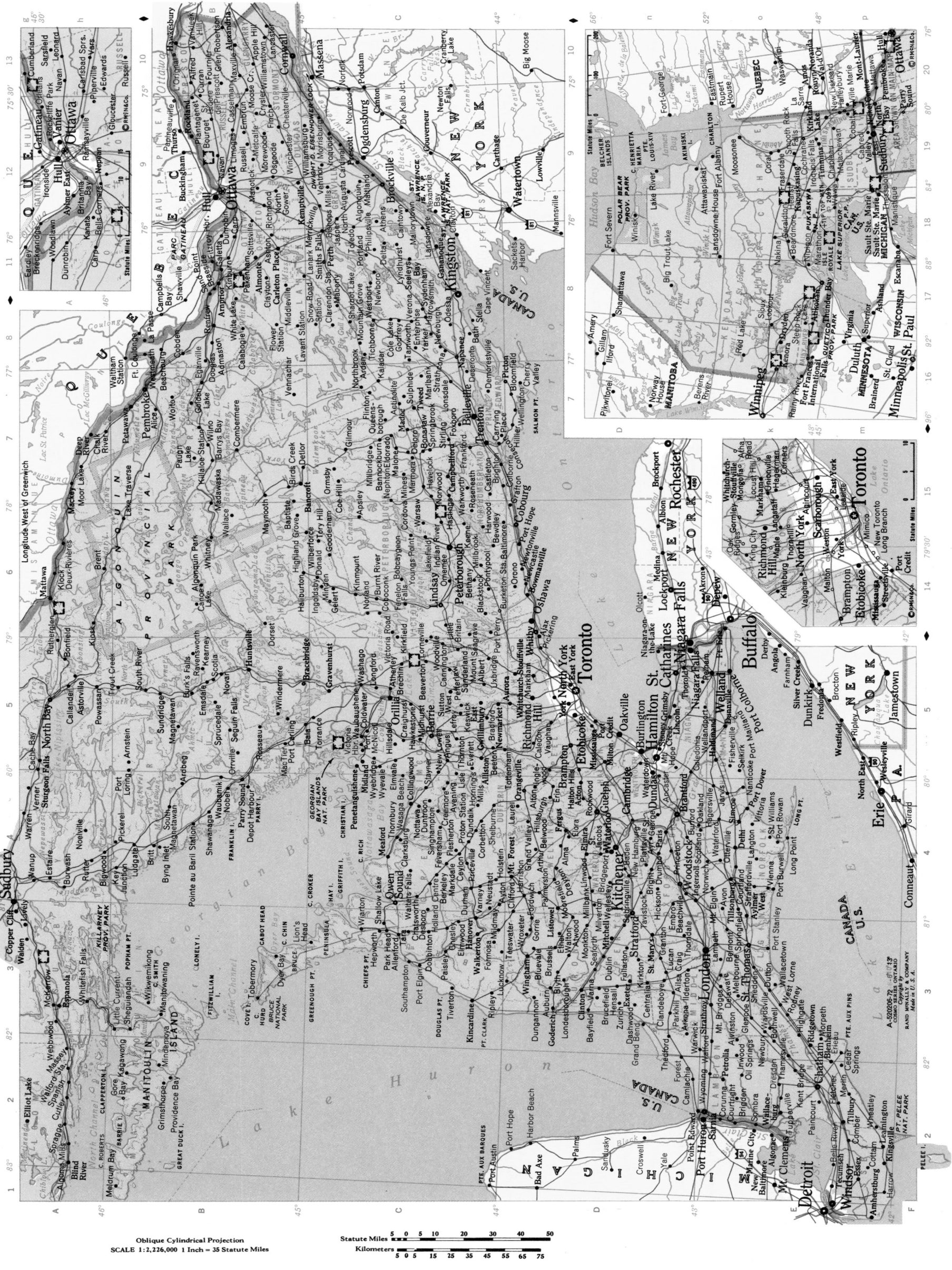

Oblique Cylindrical Projection
SCALE 1:2,226,000 1 Inch = 35 Statute Miles

Statute Miles 5 0 5 10 20 30 40 50

Kilometers 5 0 5 15 25 35 45 55 65 75

A-520206-72   Copyright
RAND M?NALLY & COMPANY
Made in U.S.A.

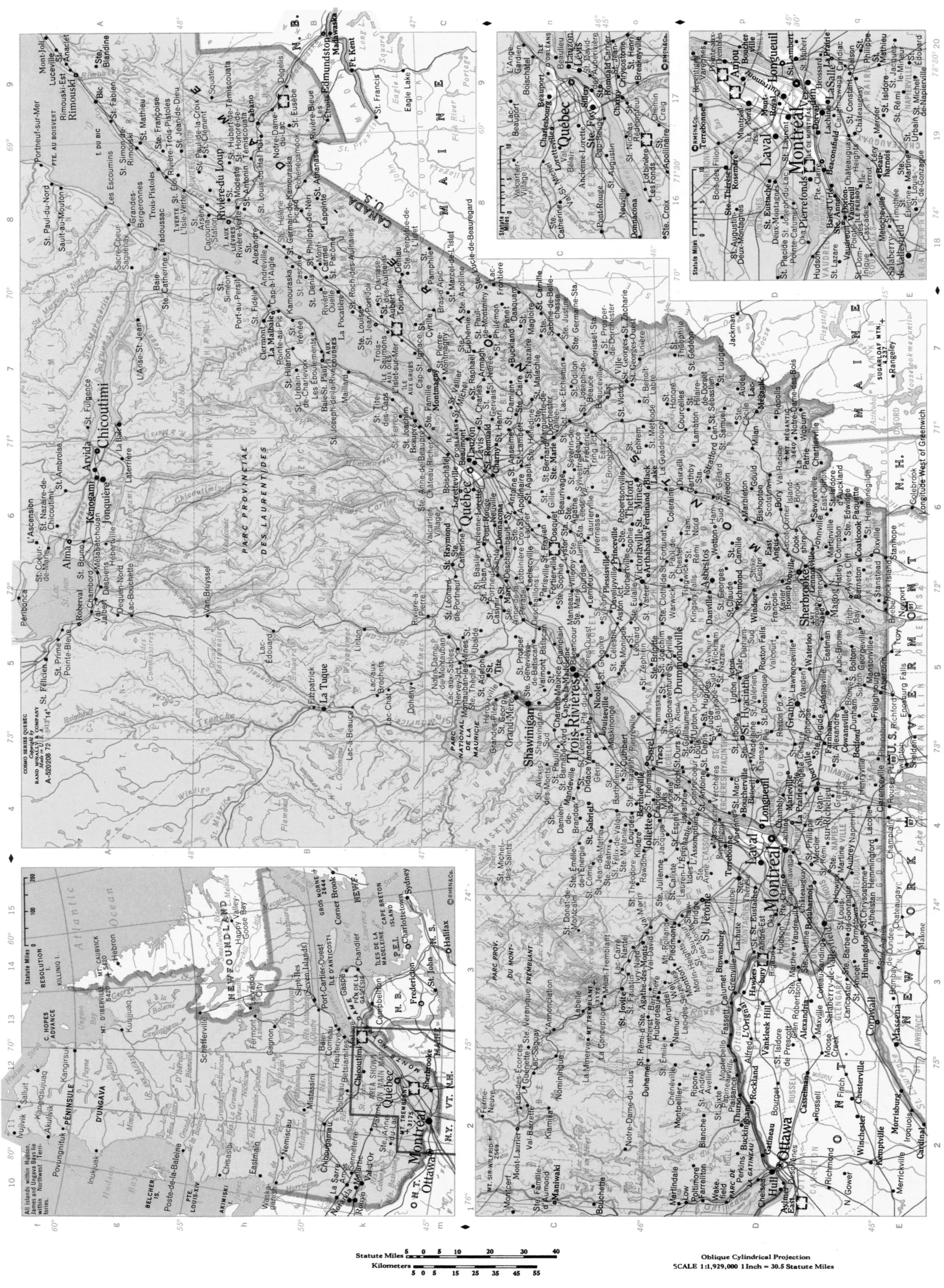

Statute Miles 5 0 5 10   20   30   40

Kilometers 5 0 5 15   25   35   45   55

Oblique Cylindrical Projection
SCALE 1:1,929,000 1 Inch = 30.5 Statute Miles

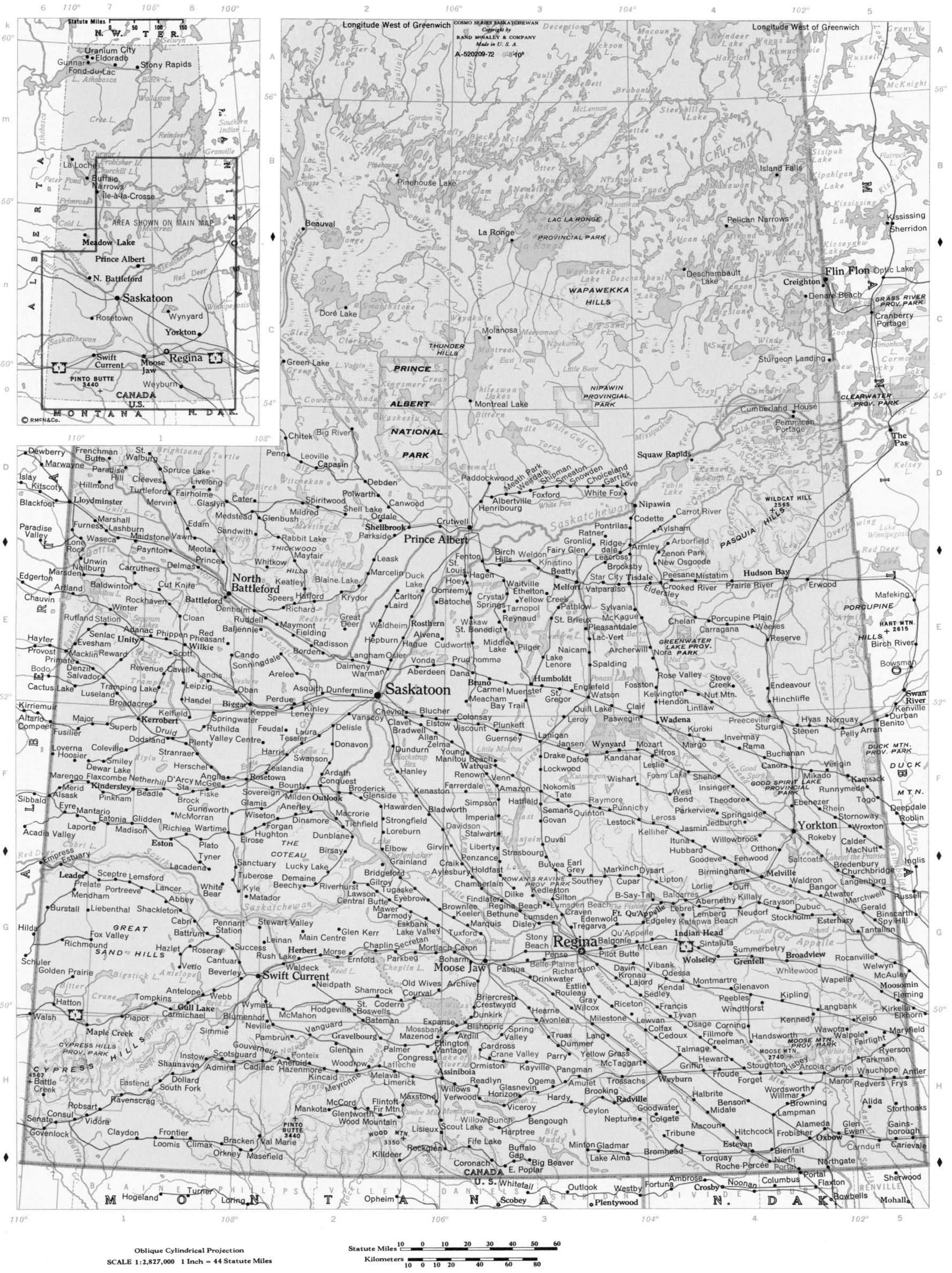

Longitude West of Greenwich

Lambert Conformal Conic Projection
SCALE 1:12,000,000   1 Inch = 189 Statute Miles

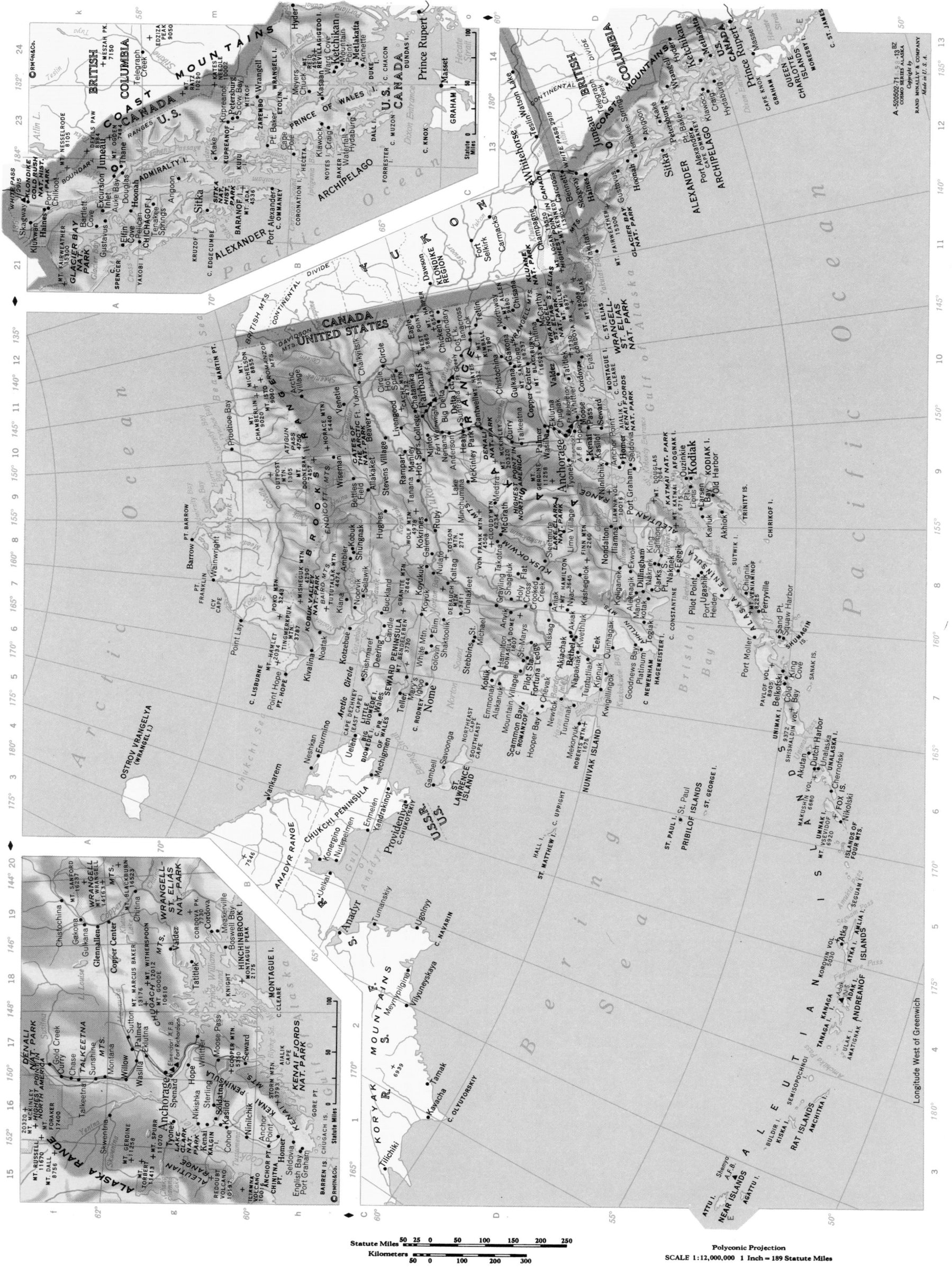

Statute Miles 50 25 0 50 100 150 200 250
Kilometers 50 0 100 200 300

Polyconic Projection
SCALE 1:12,000,000 1 Inch = 189 Statute Miles

A-500502/71.51-13 BZ
Copyright by
COSMO SERIES ALASKA
RAND McNALLY & COMPANY
Made in U.S.A.

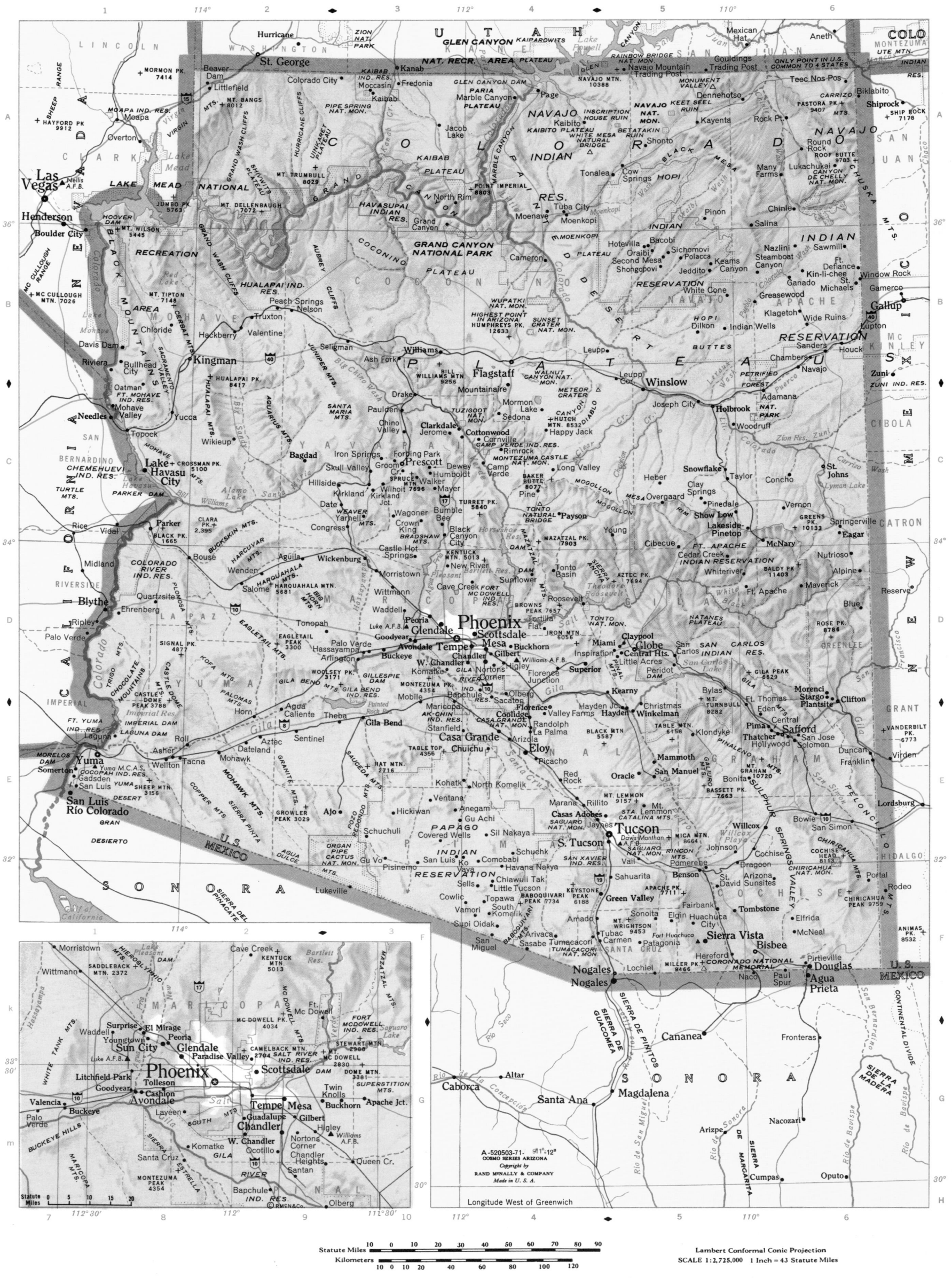

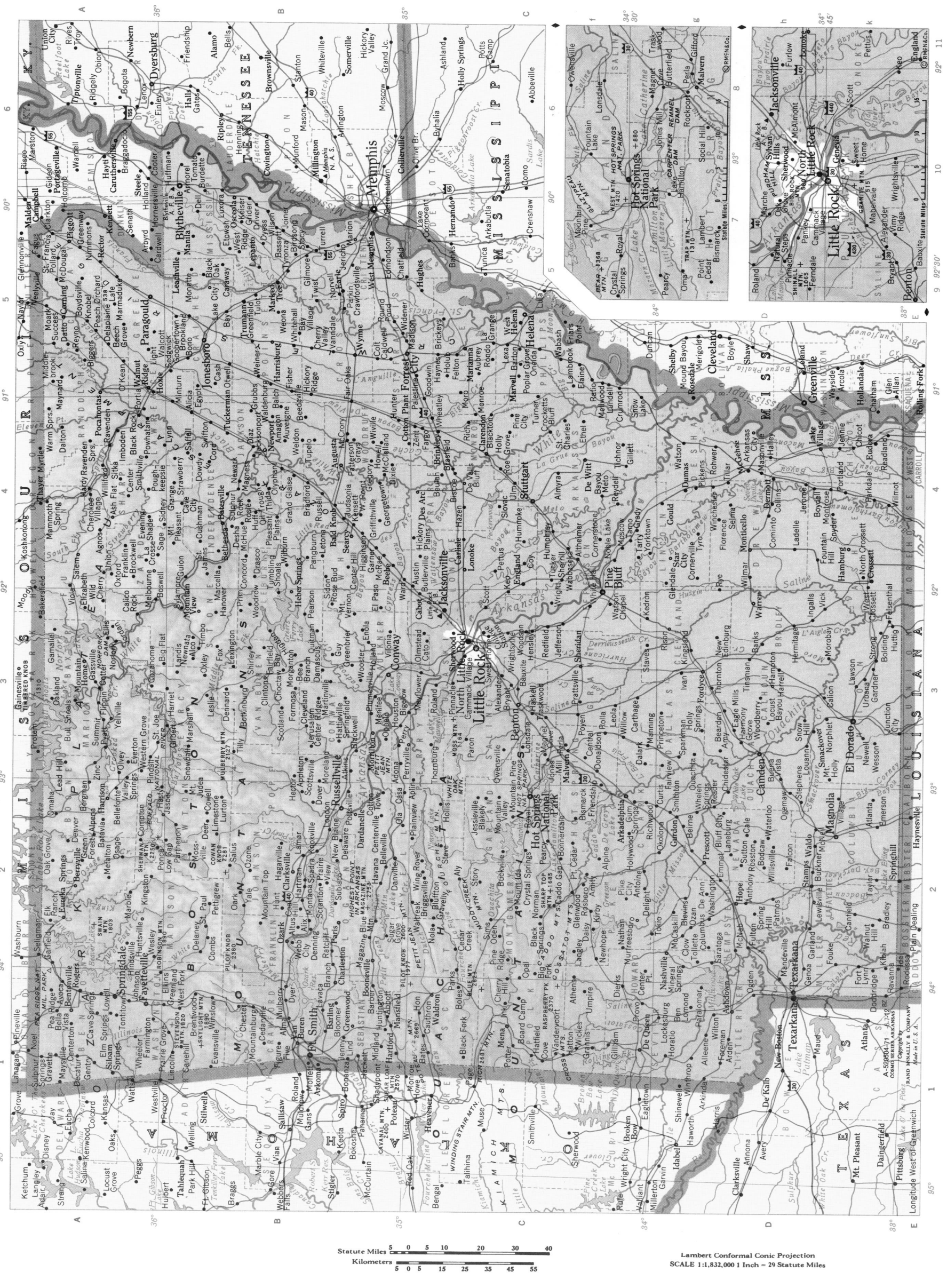

Statute Miles 5 0 5 10 20 30 40
Kilometers 5 0 5 15 25 35 45 55

Lambert Conformal Conic Projection
SCALE 1:1,832,000 1 Inch = 29 Statute Miles

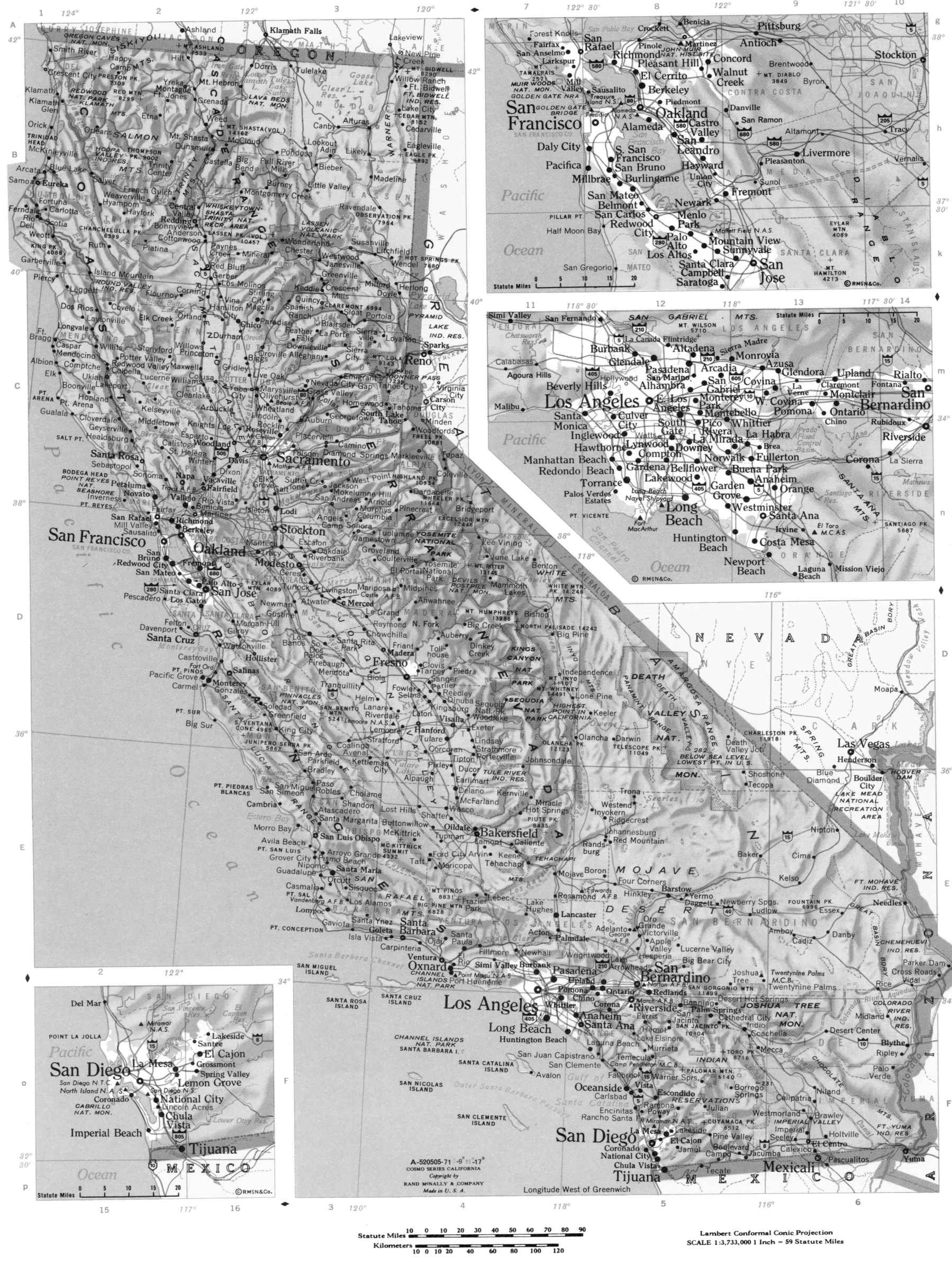

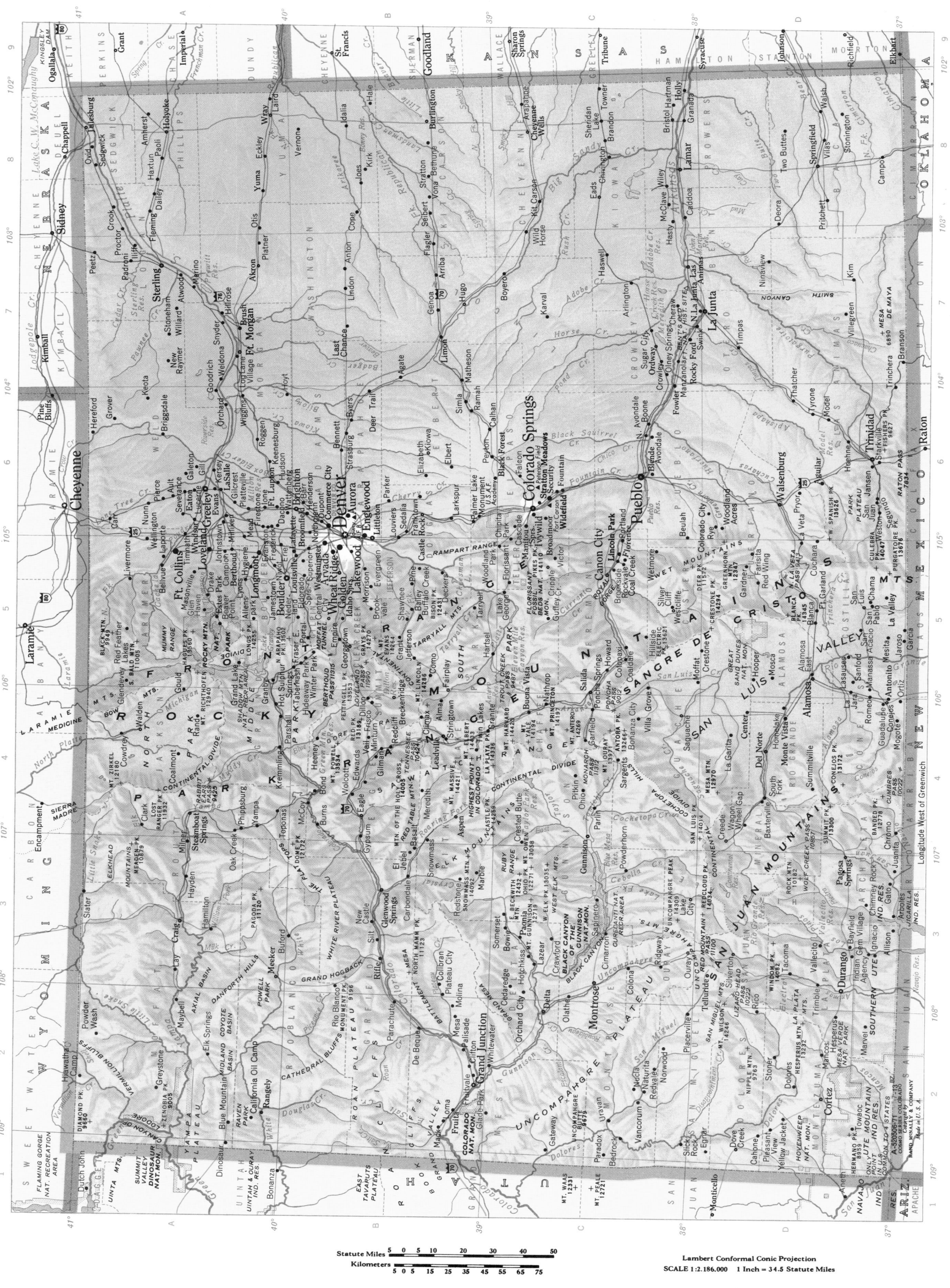

Statute Miles 5 0 5 10 20 30 40 50
Kilometers 5 0 5 15 25 35 45 55 65 75

Lambert Conformal Conic Projection
SCALE 1:2,186,000   1 Inch = 34.5 Statute Miles

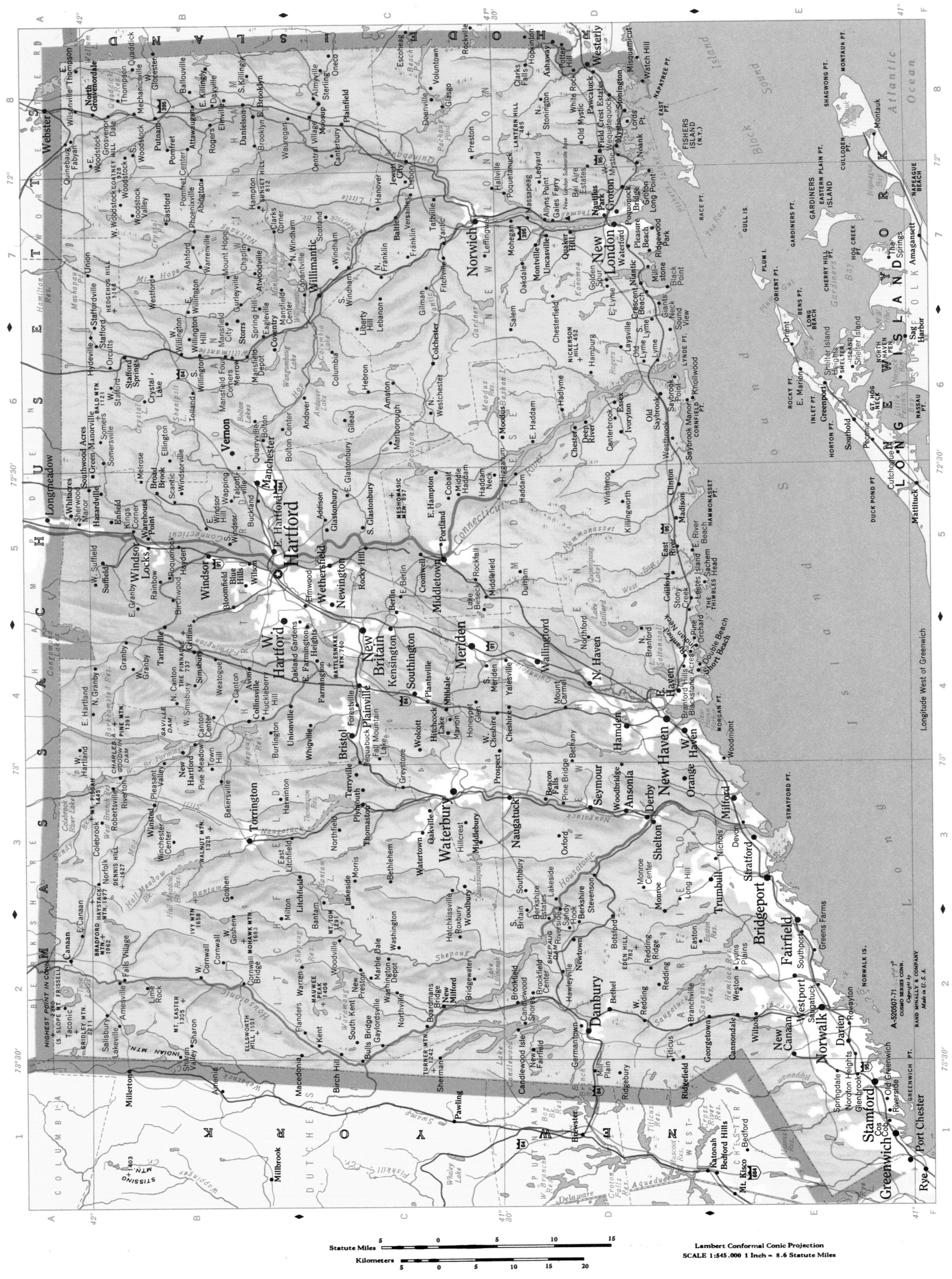

Statute Miles

Kilometers

Lambert Conformal Conic Projection
SCALE 1:545,000 1 Inch = 8.6 Statute Miles

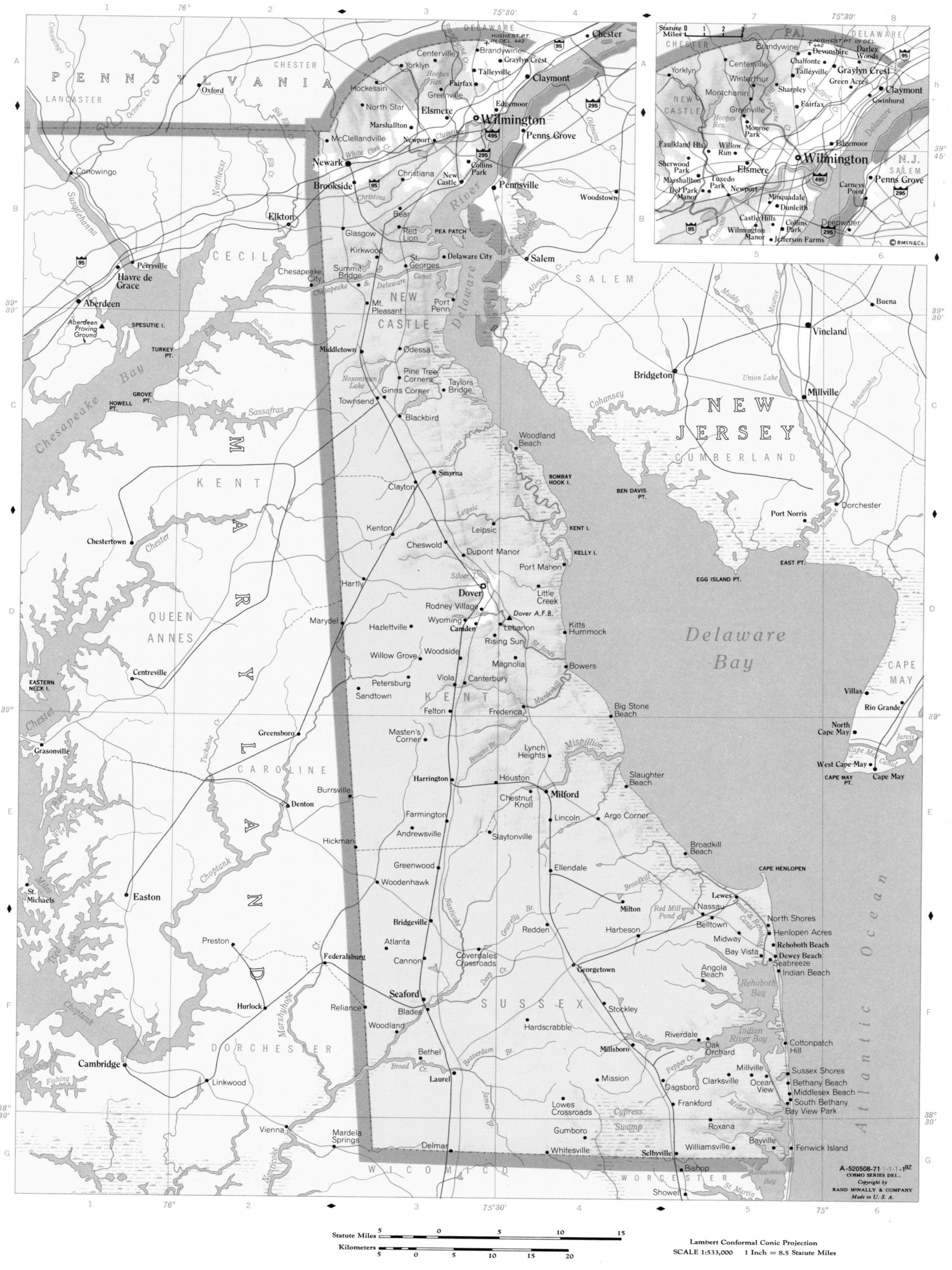

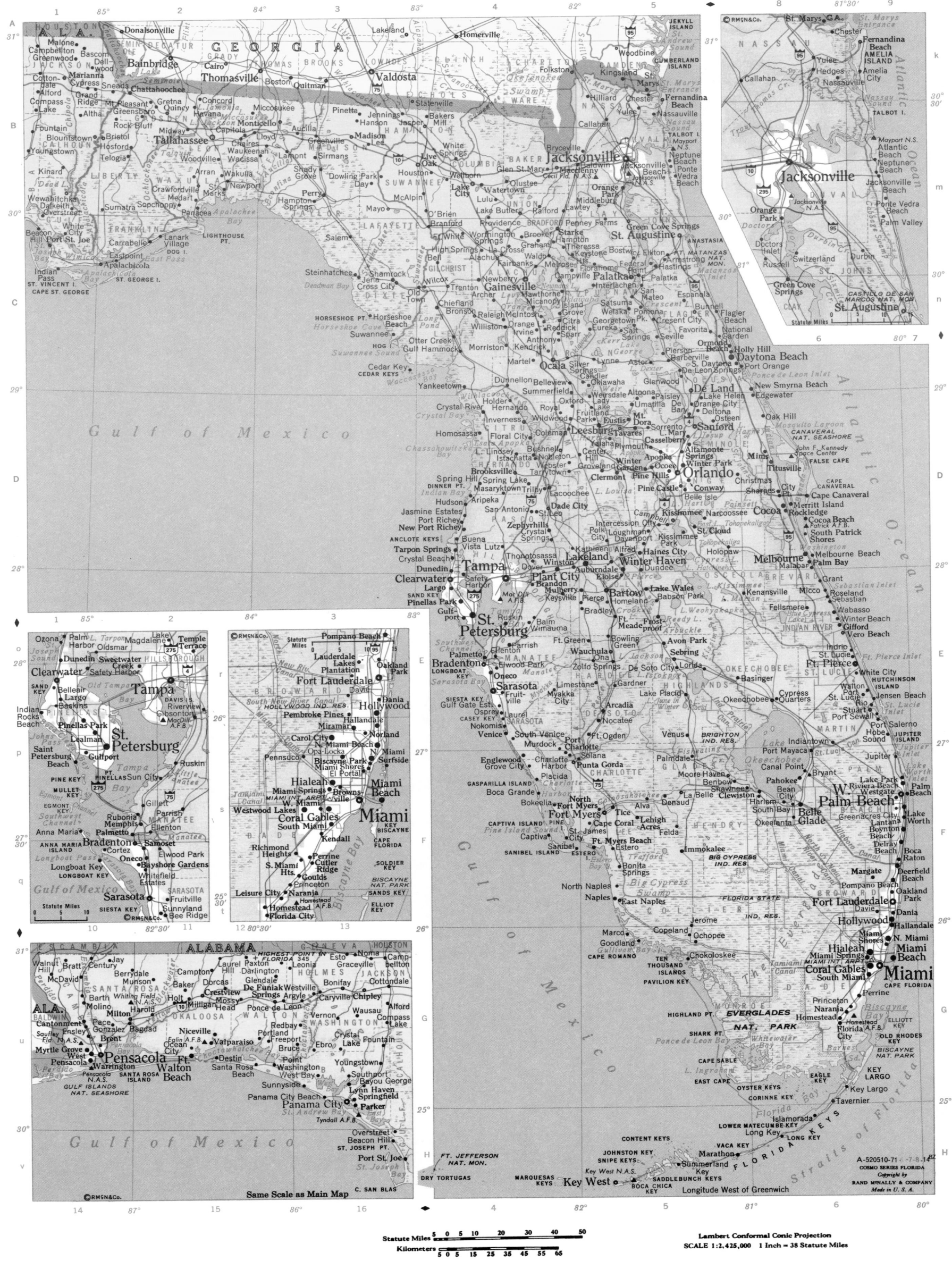

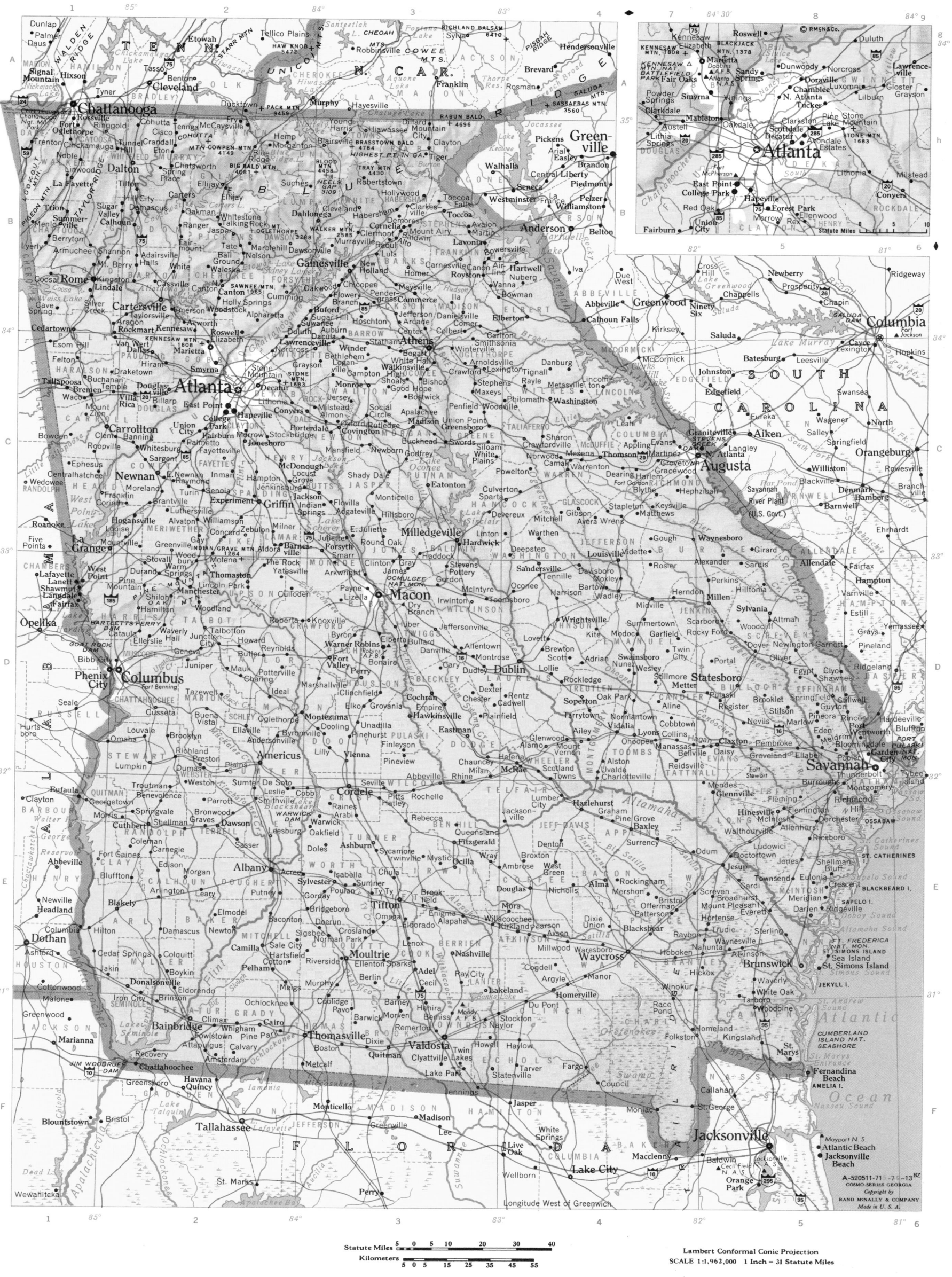

Statute Miles

Kilometers

Lambert Conformal Conic Projection
SCALE 1:1,962,000   1 Inch = 31 Statute Miles

A-520511-71-7-13

COSMO SERIES GEORGIA

Copyright by
RAND McNALLY & COMPANY
Made in U.S.A.

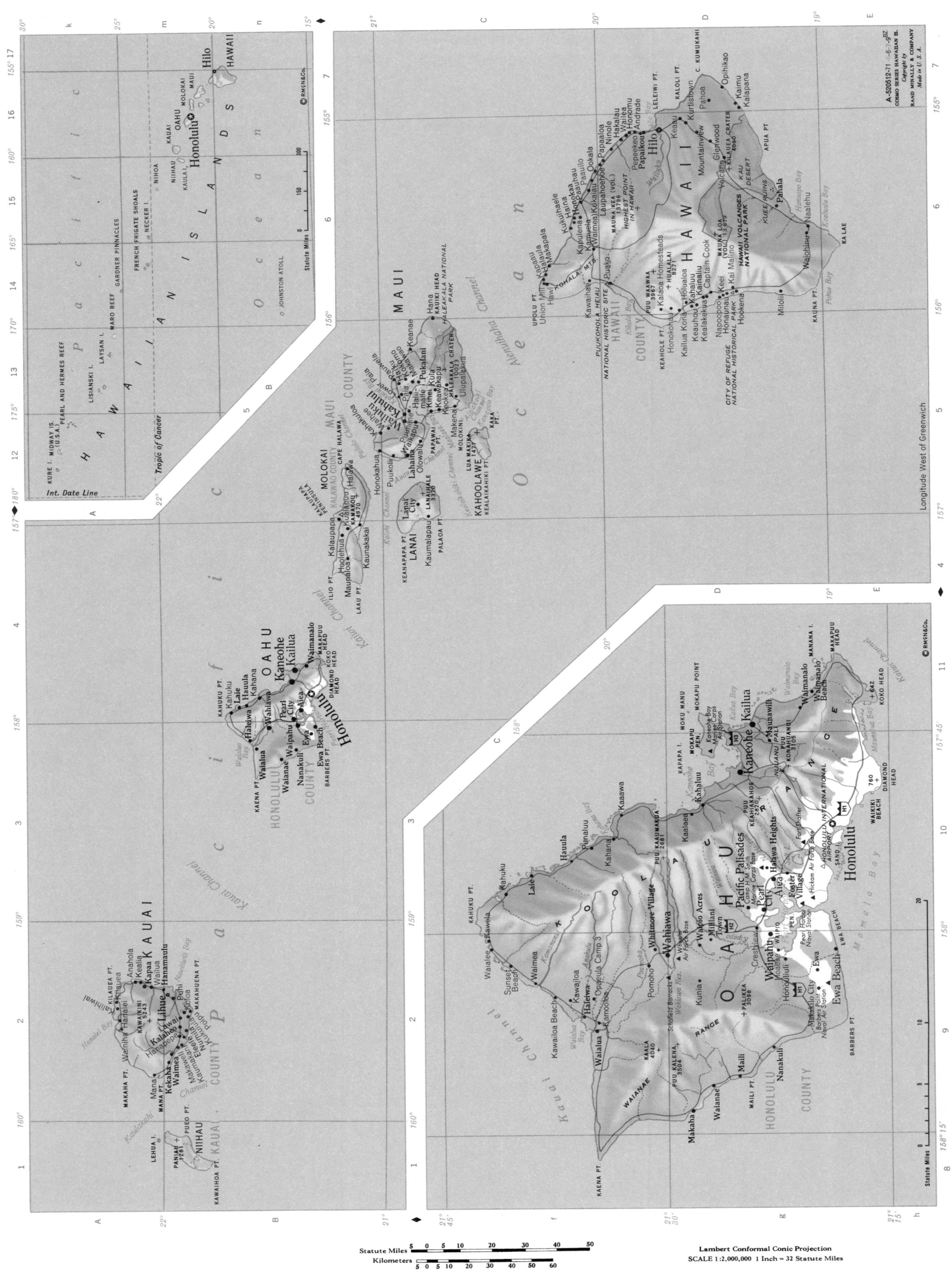

Lambert Conformal Conic Projection
SCALE 1:2,000,000 1 Inch = 32 Statute Miles

Statute Miles 5 0 5 10 20 30 40 50

Kilometers 5 0 5 10 20 30 40 50 60

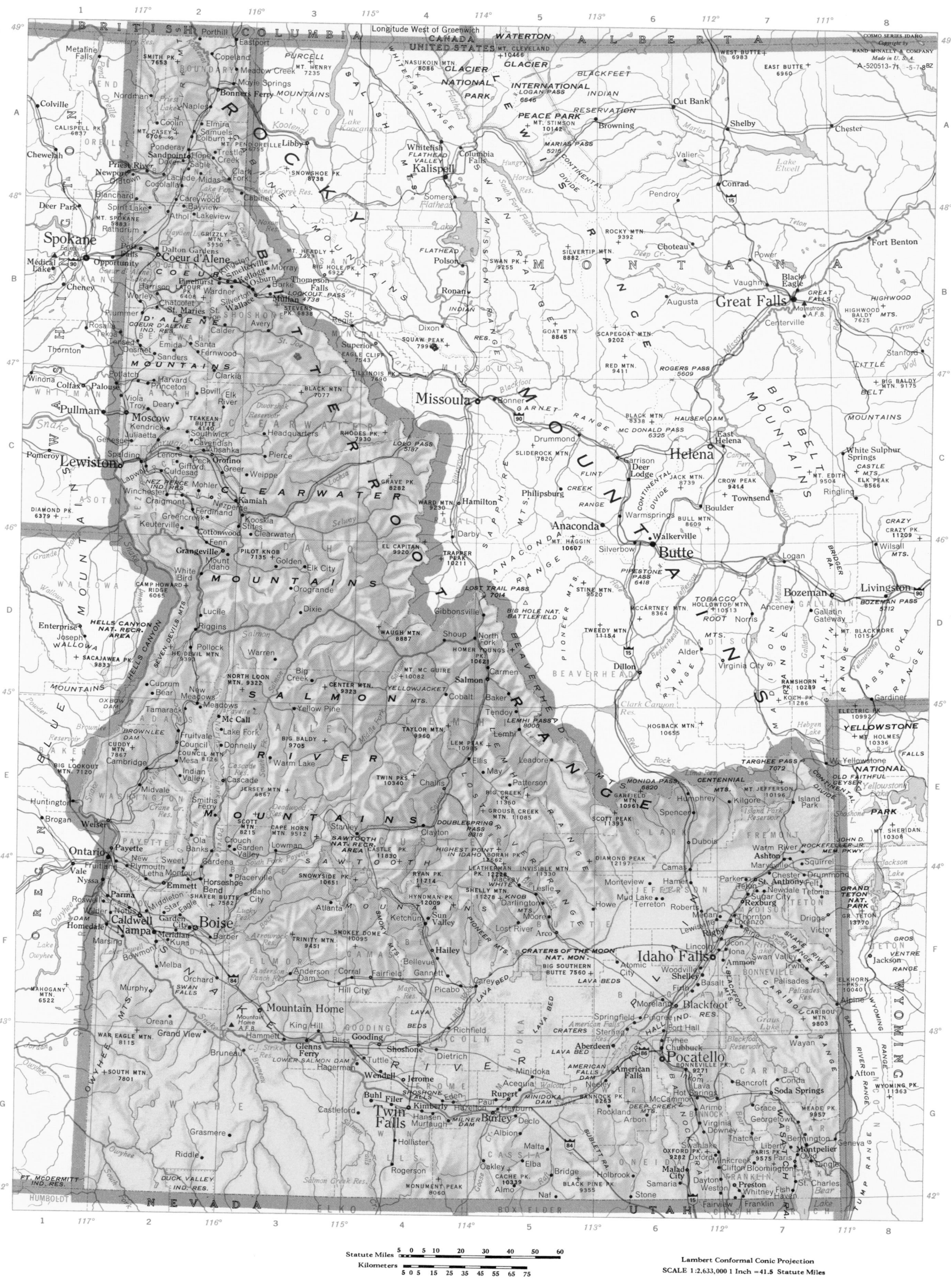

Statute Miles

Kilometers

Lambert Conformal Conic Projection
SCALE 1:2,633,000 1 Inch = 41.5 Statute Miles

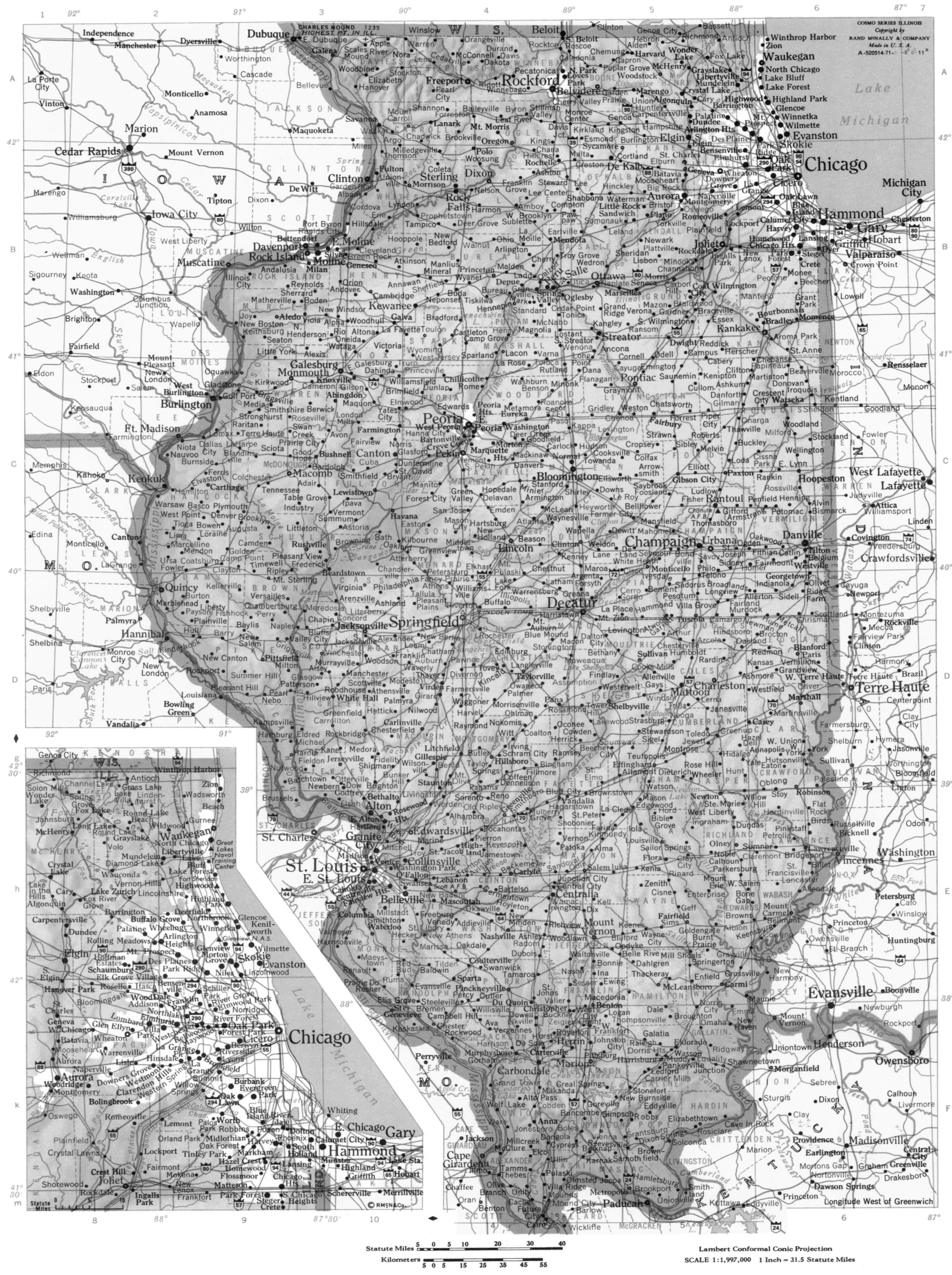

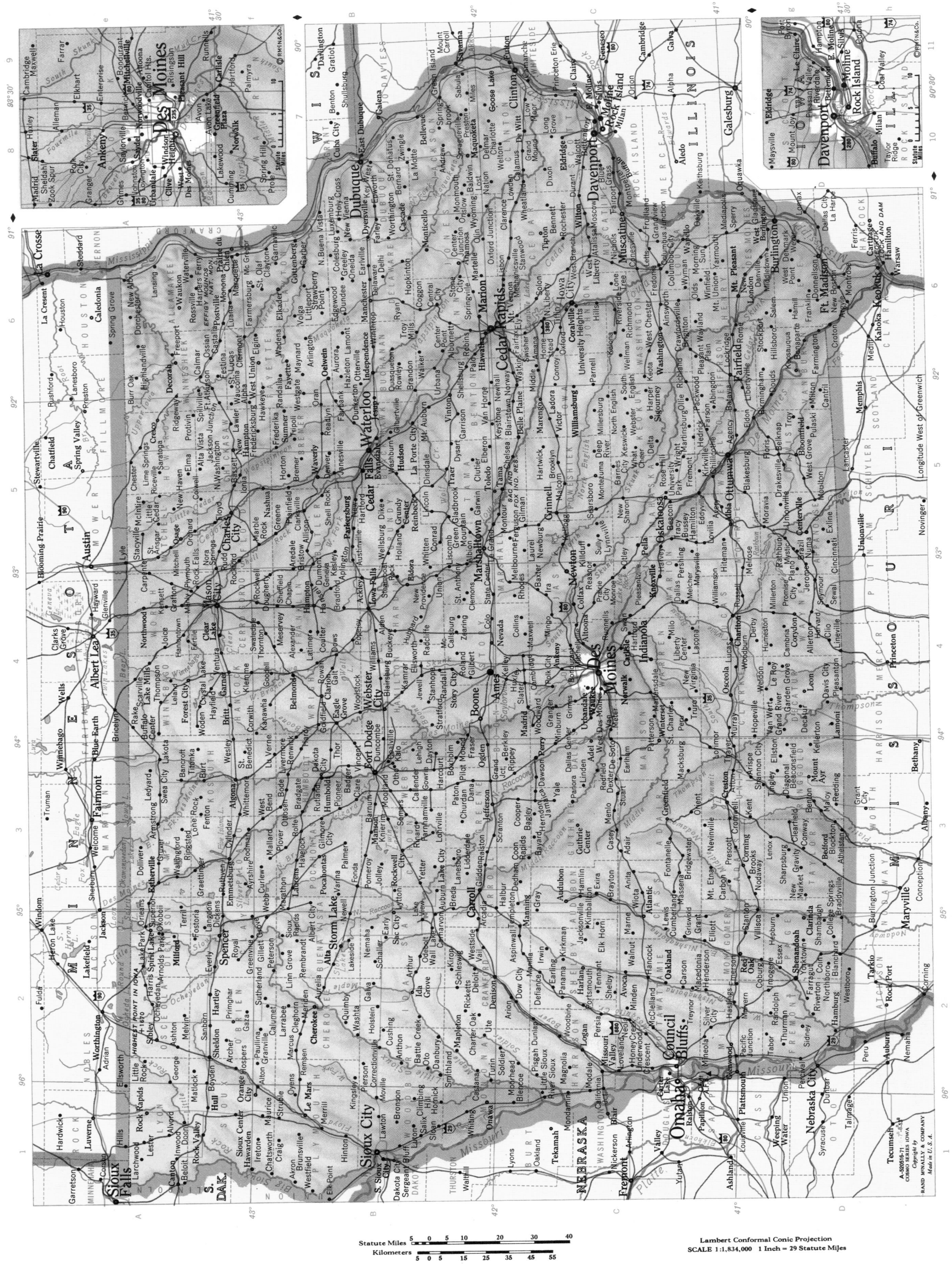

Lambert Conformal Conic Projection
SCALE 1:1,834,000   1 Inch = 29 Statute Miles

Statute Miles
Kilometers

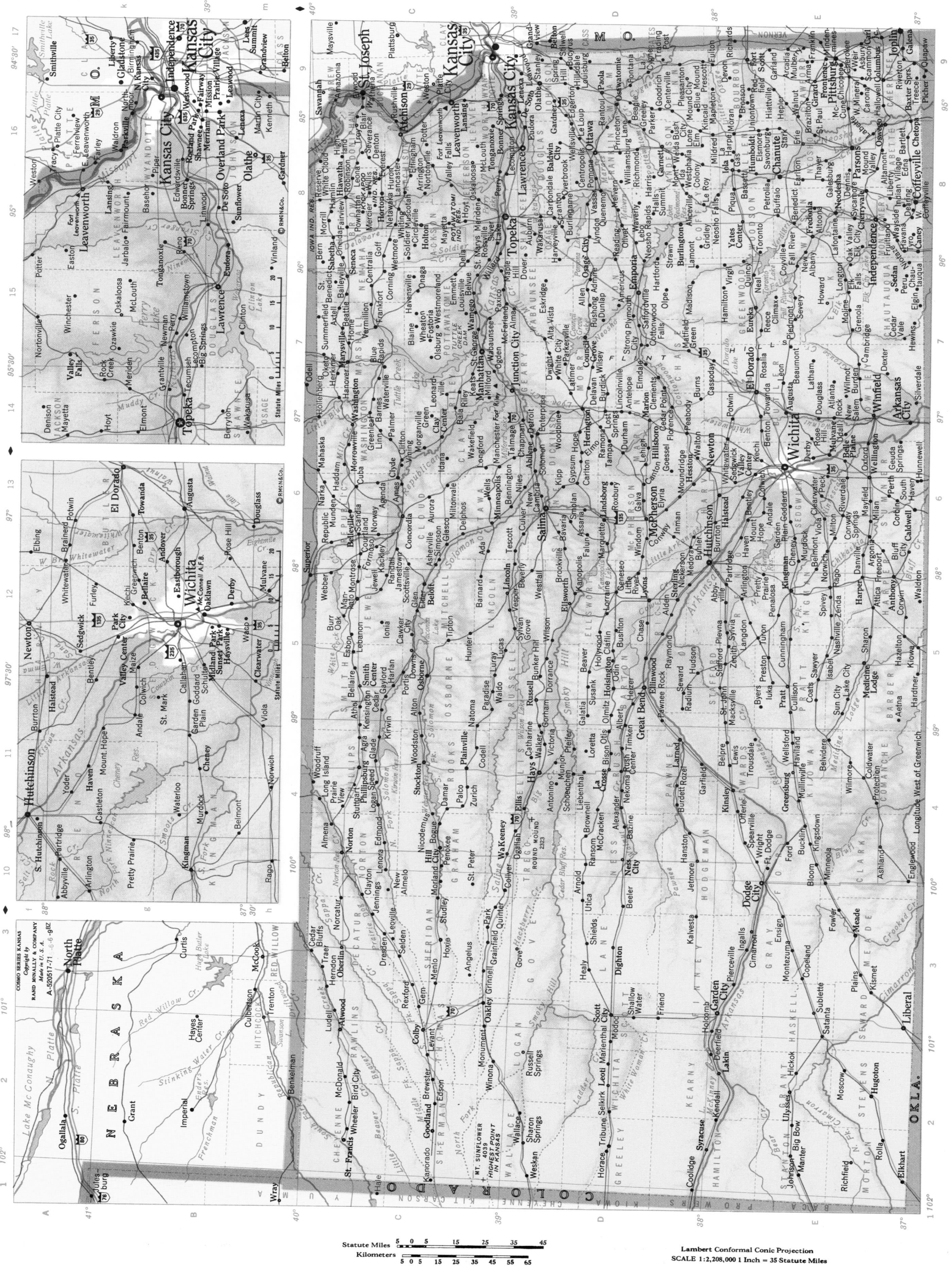

Statute Miles 5 0 5 15 25 35 45
Kilometers 5 0 5 15 25 35 45 55 65

Lambert Conformal Conic Projection
SCALE 1:2,208,000 1 Inch = 35 Statute Miles

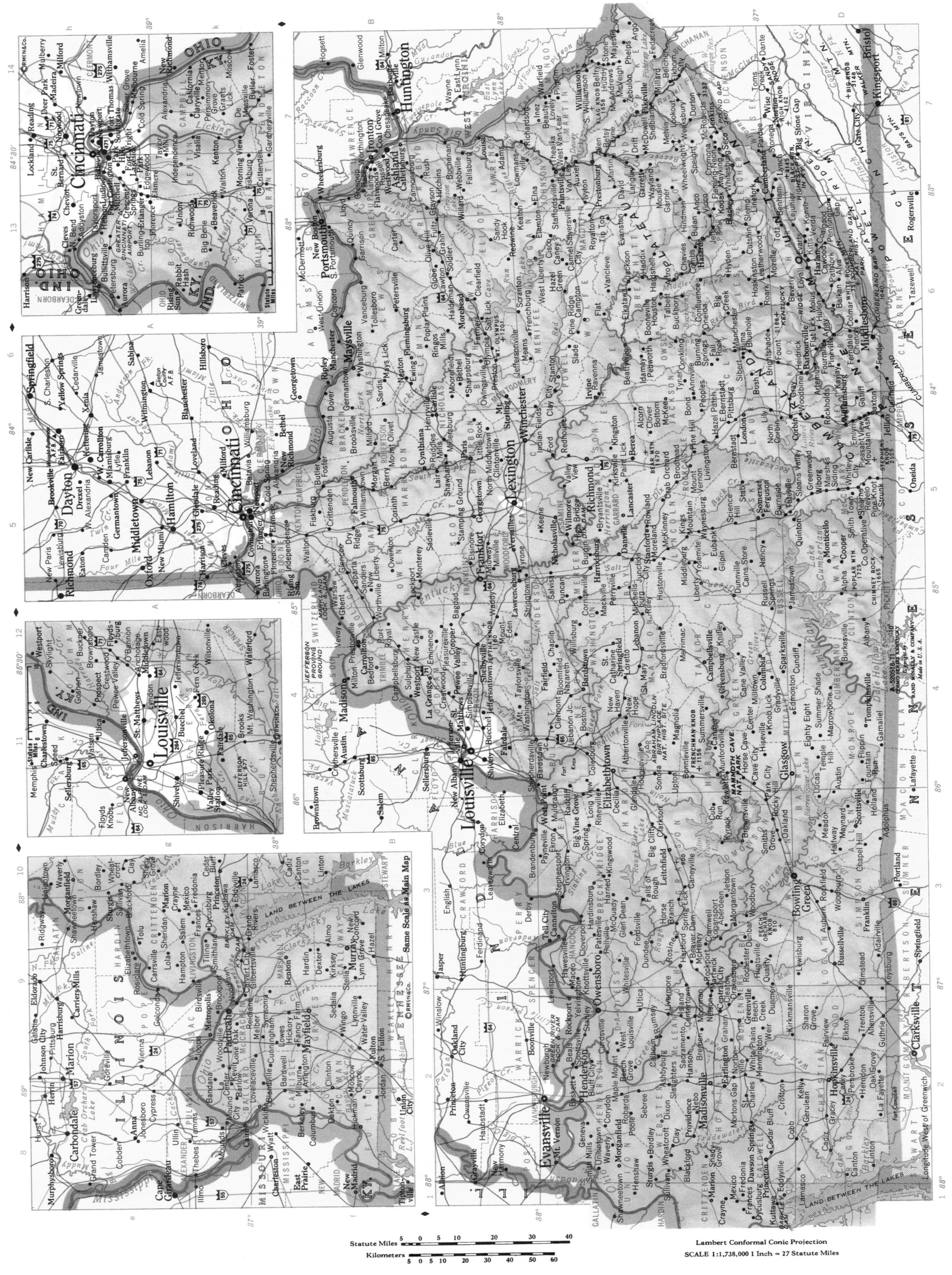

Lambert Conformal Conic Projection
SCALE 1:1,738,000 1 Inch = 27 Statute Miles

Statute Miles
Kilometers

Statute Miles
Kilometers

Lambert Conformal Conic Projection
SCALE 1:2,083,000   1 Inch = 33 Statute Miles

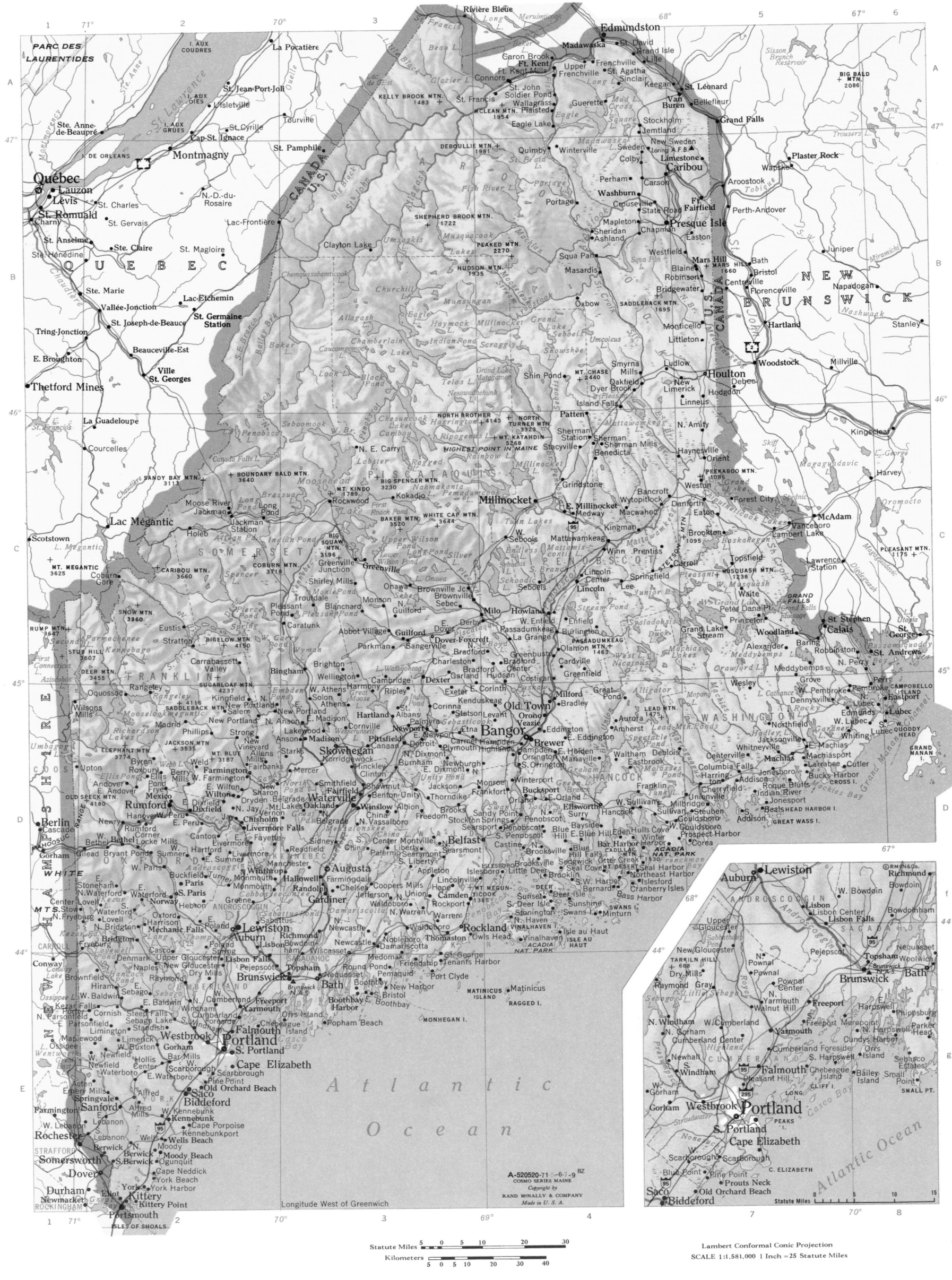

Statute Miles 5 0 5 10 20 30
Kilometers 5 0 5 10 20 30 40

A-520520-71 6-7-9 BZ
COSMO SERIES MAINE
Copyright by
RAND McNALLY & COMPANY
Made in U.S.A.

Longitude West of Greenwich

Lambert Conformal Conic Projection
SCALE 1:1,581,000 1 Inch = 25 Statute Miles

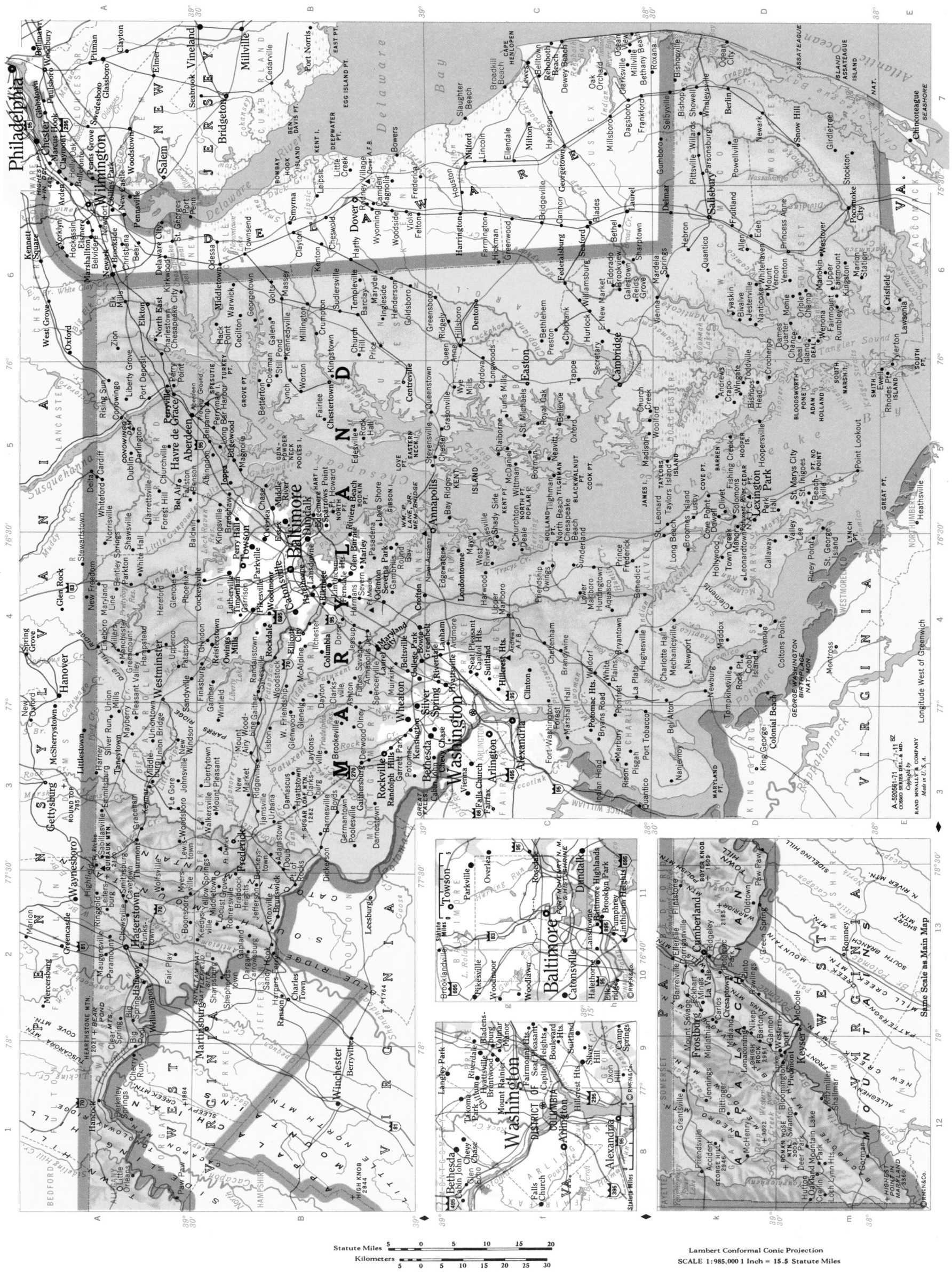

Statute Miles
Kilometers

Lambert Conformal Conic Projection
SCALE 1:985,000 1 Inch = 15.5 Statute Miles

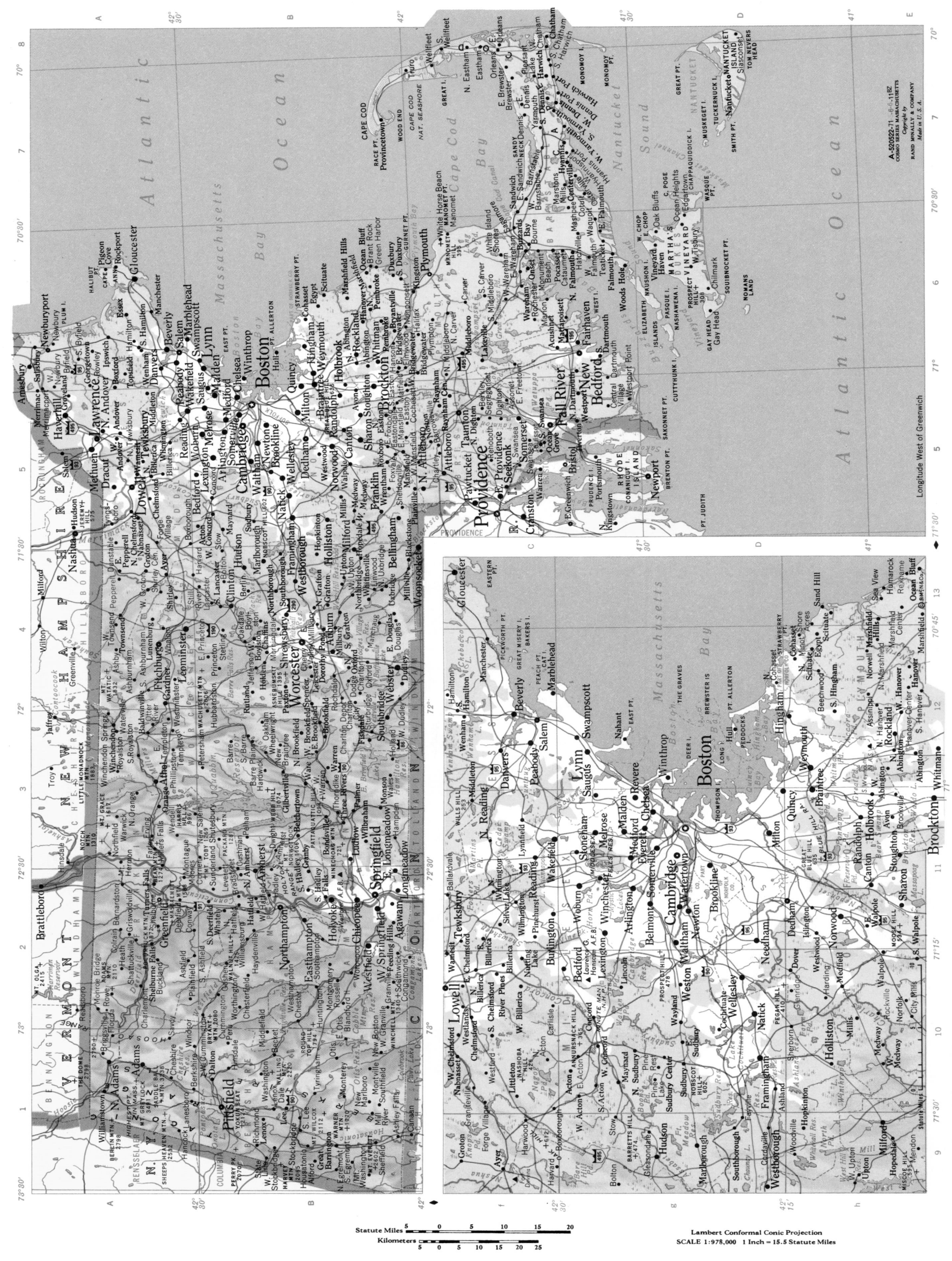

Statute Miles
Kilometers

Lambert Conformal Conic Projection
SCALE 1:978,000   1 Inch = 15.5 Statute Miles

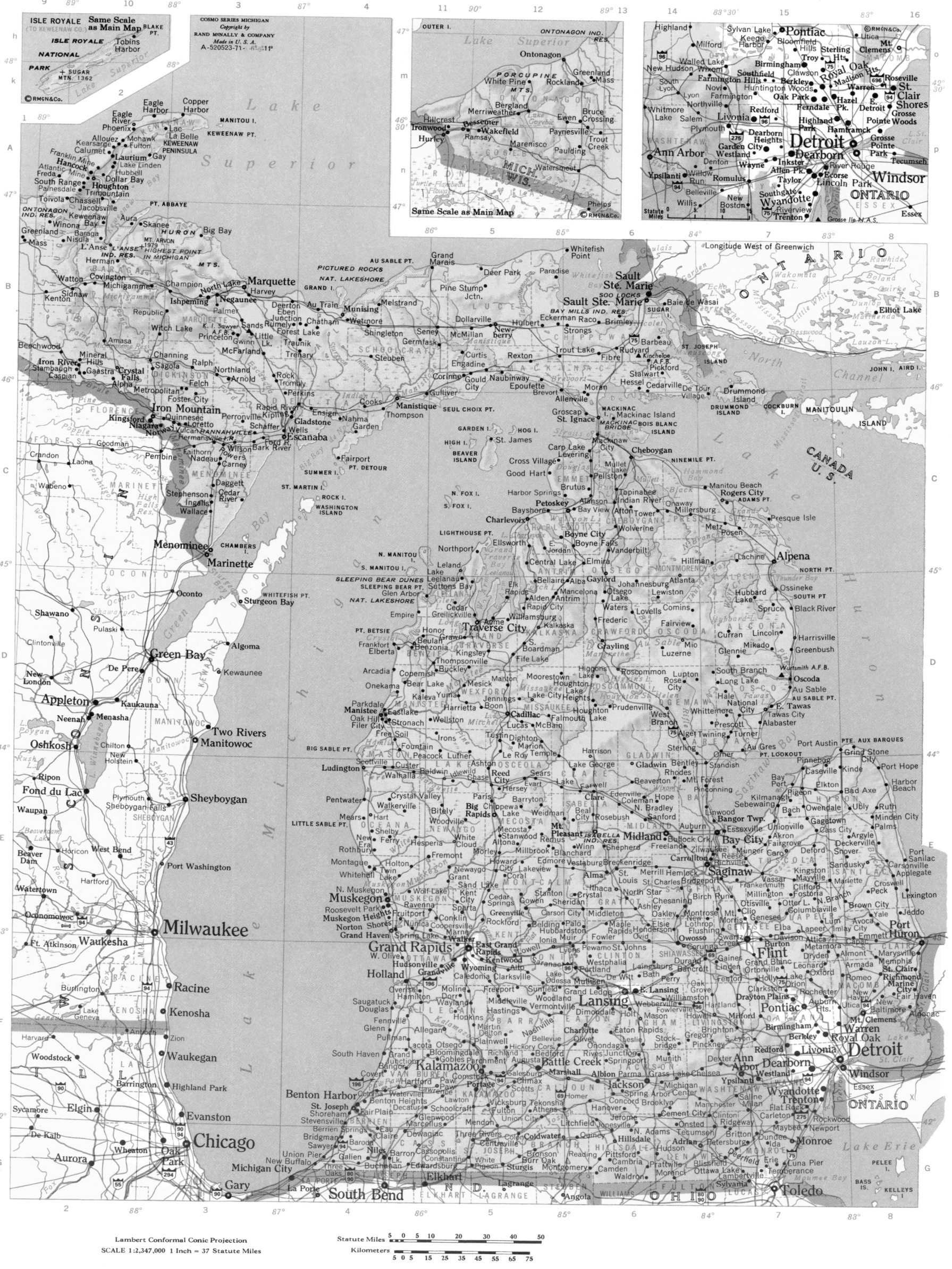

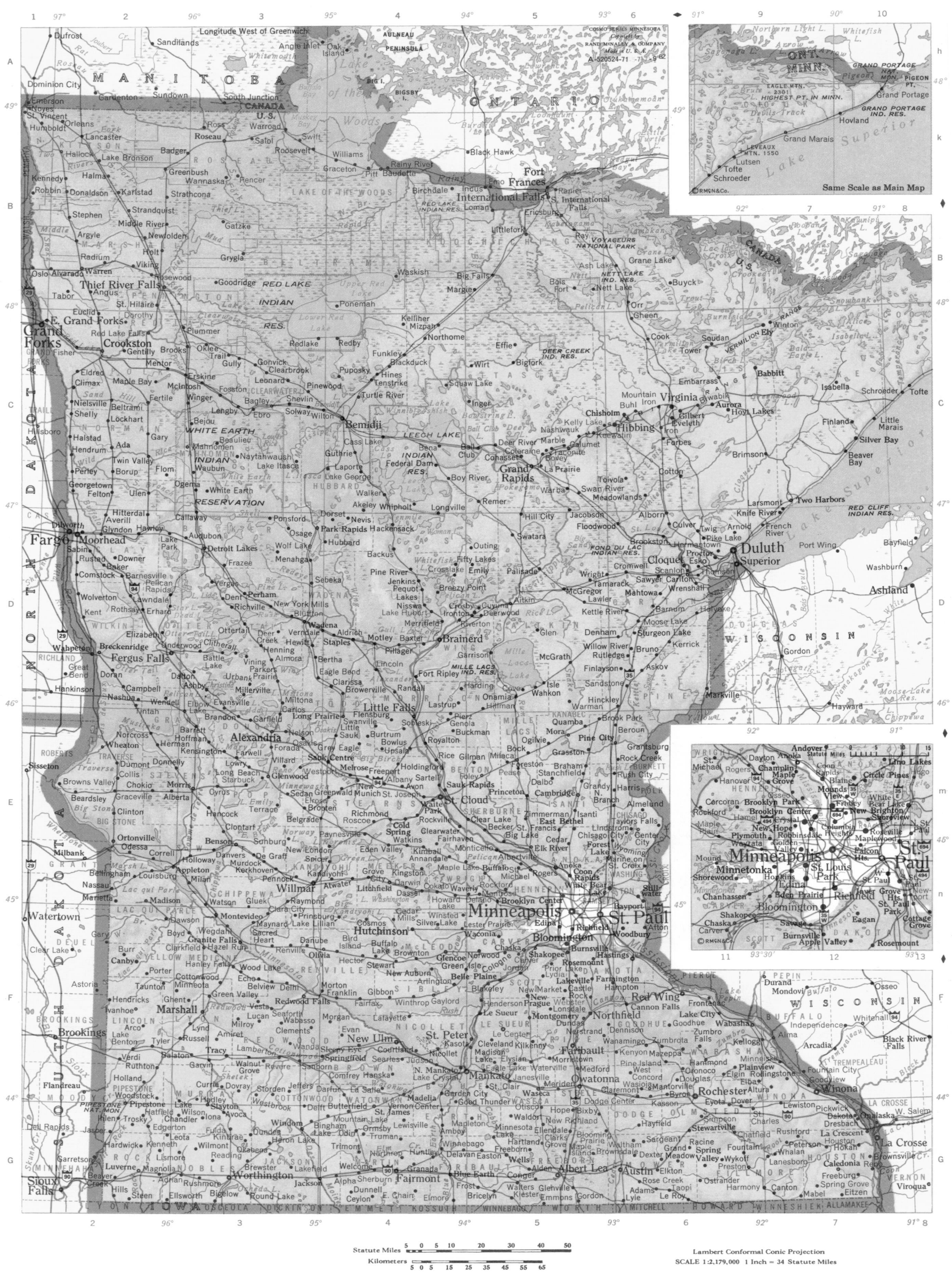

Lambert Conformal Conic Projection
SCALE 1:2,179,000 1 Inch = 34 Statute Miles

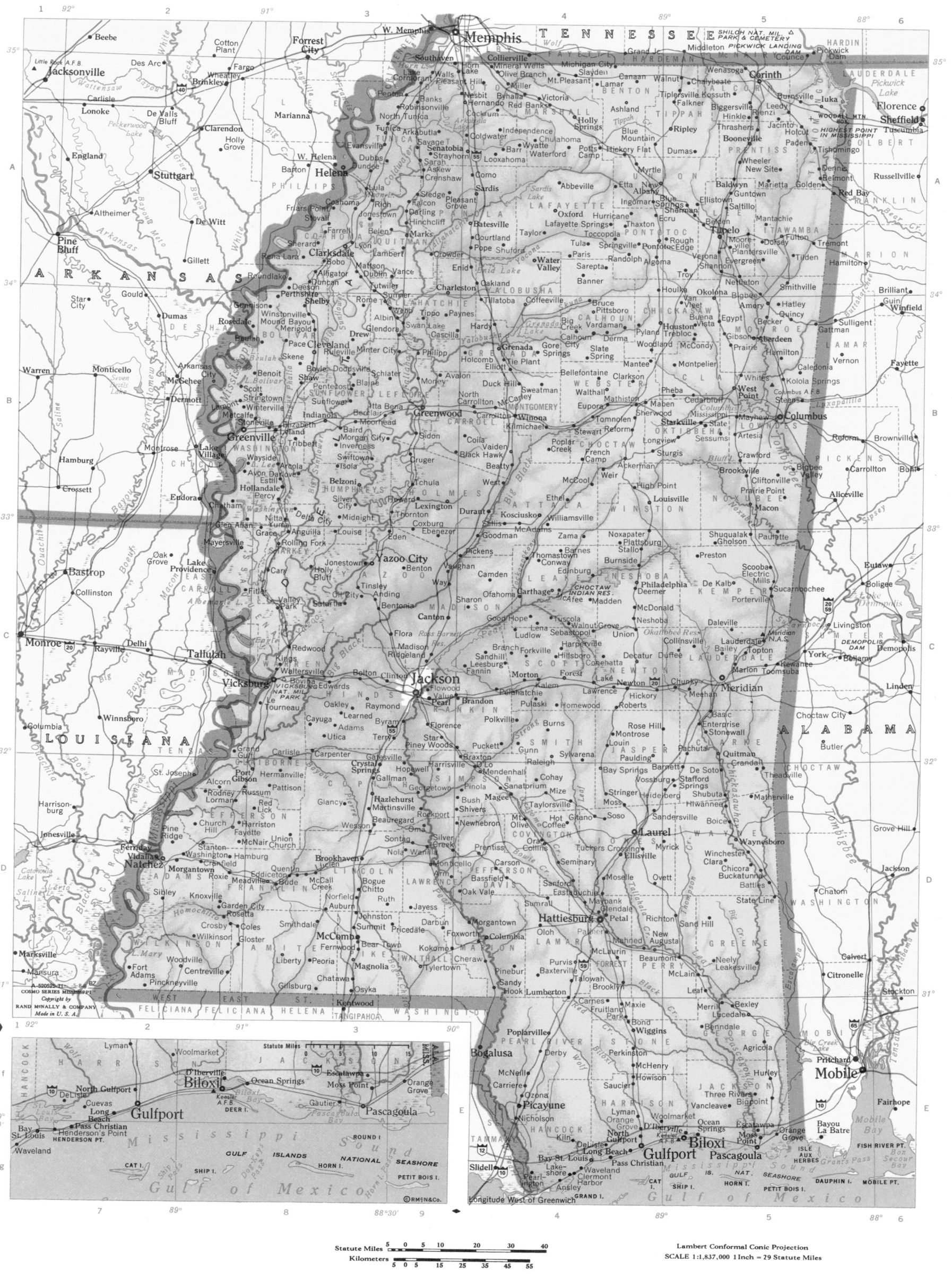

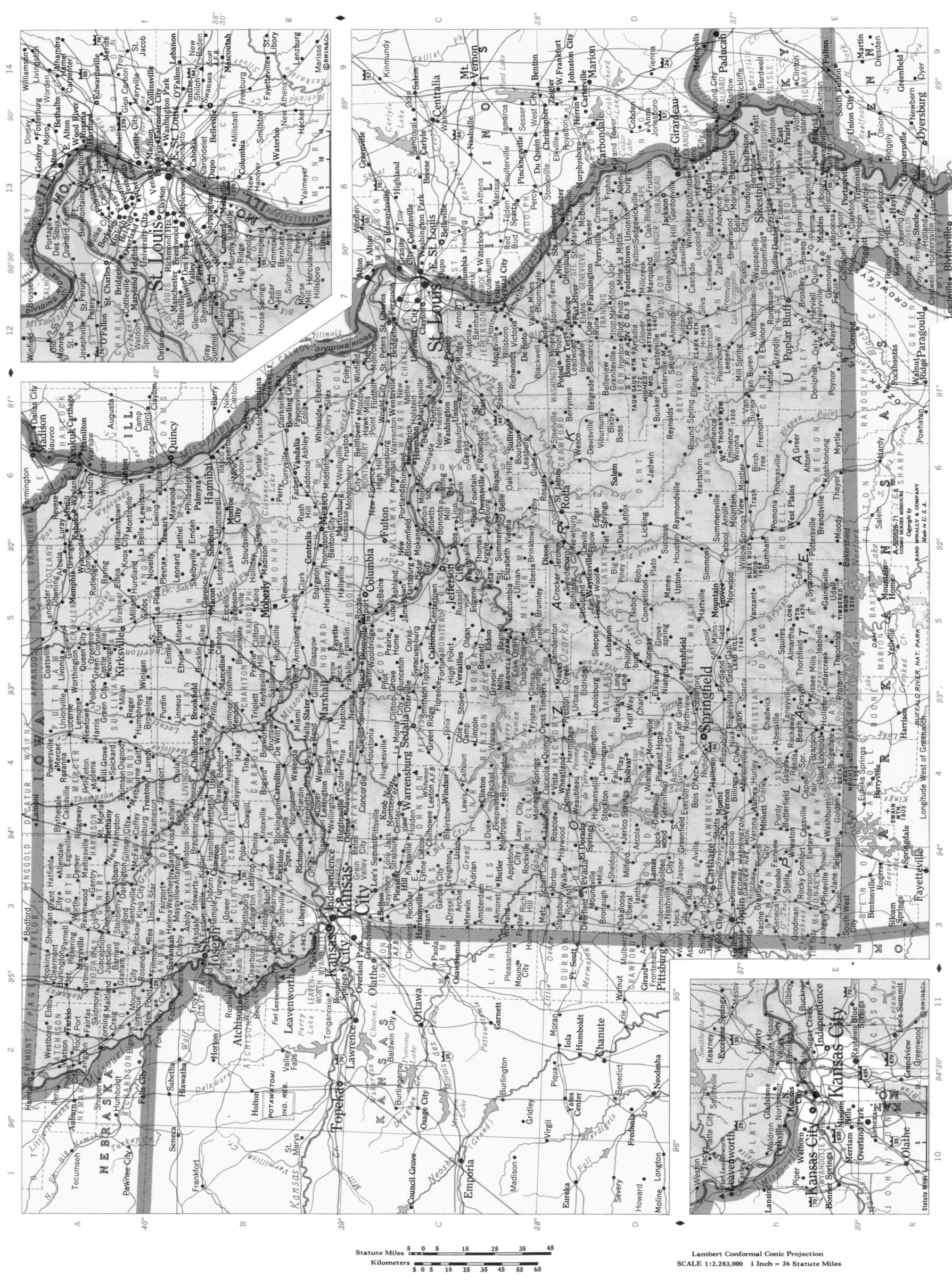

Statute Miles 5 0 5 15 25 35 45

Kilometers 5 0 5 15 25 35 45 55 65

Lambert Conformal Conic Projection
SCALE 1:2,283,000   1 Inch = 36 Statute Miles

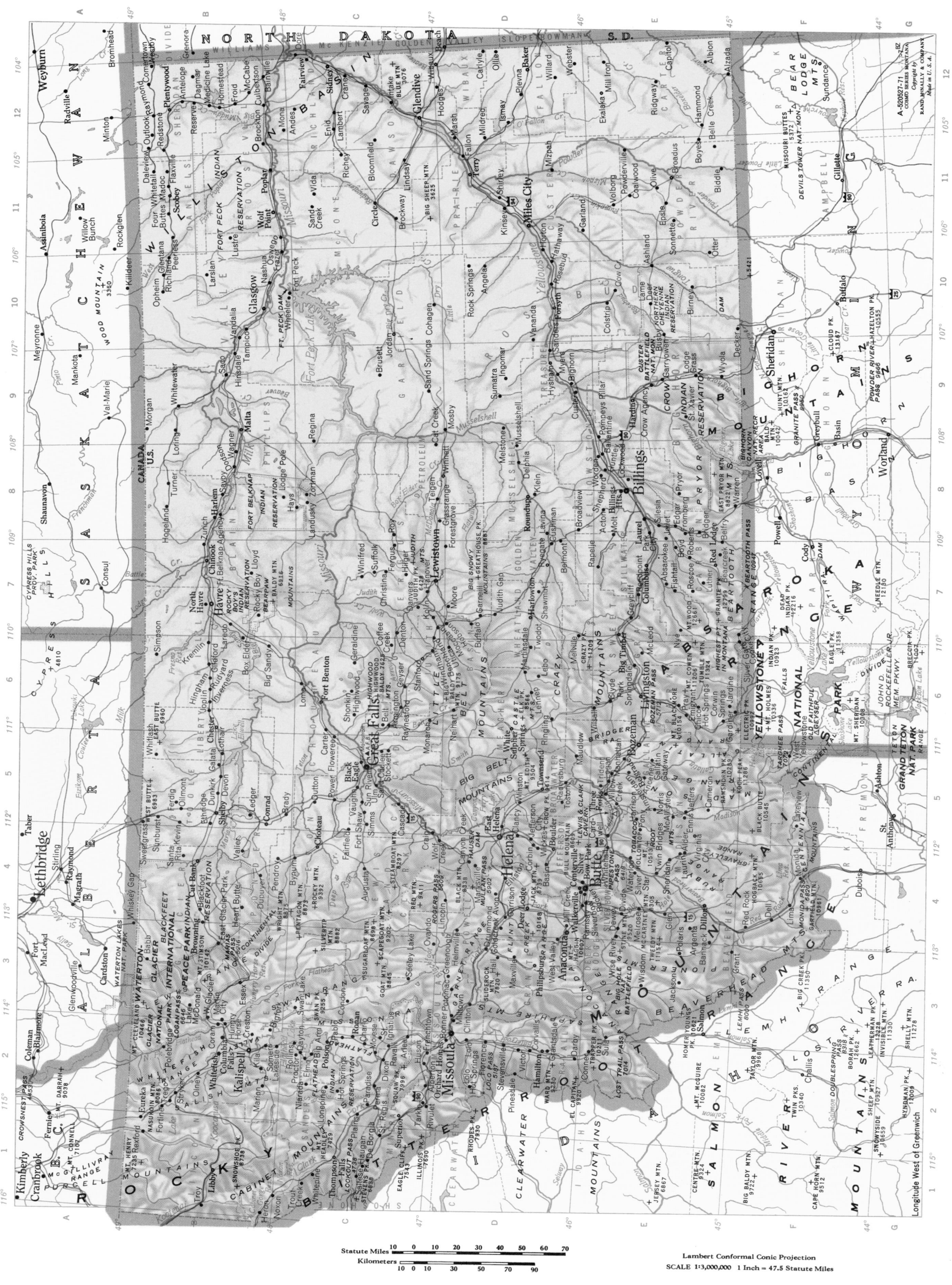

Statute Miles
Kilometers

Lambert Conformal Conic Projection
SCALE 1:3,000,000   1 Inch = 47.5 Statute Miles

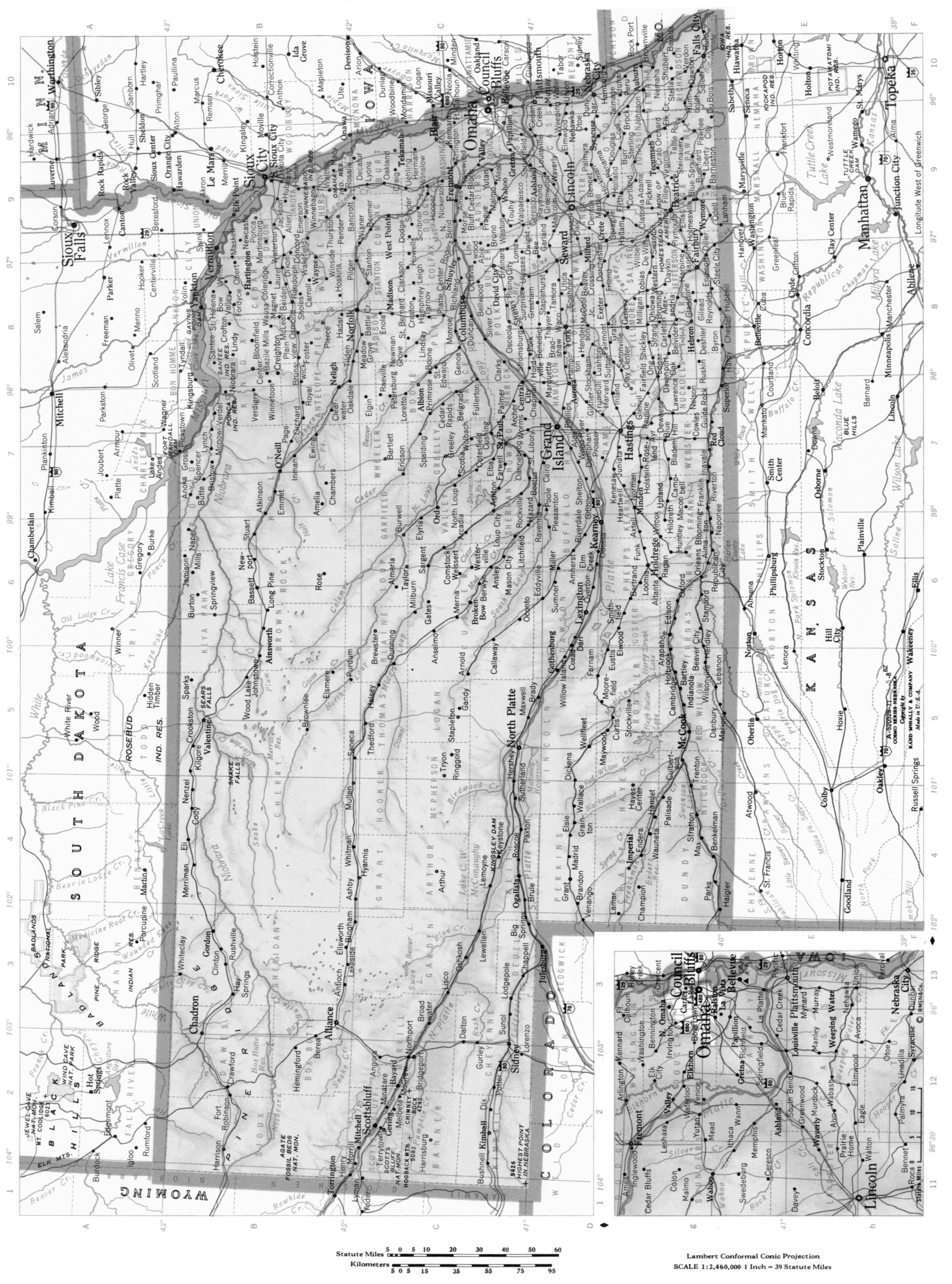

Statute Miles 5 0 5 10 20 30 40 50 60
Kilometers 5 0 5 15 35 55 75 95

Lambert Conformal Conic Projection
SCALE 1:2,460,000 1 Inch = 39 Statute Miles

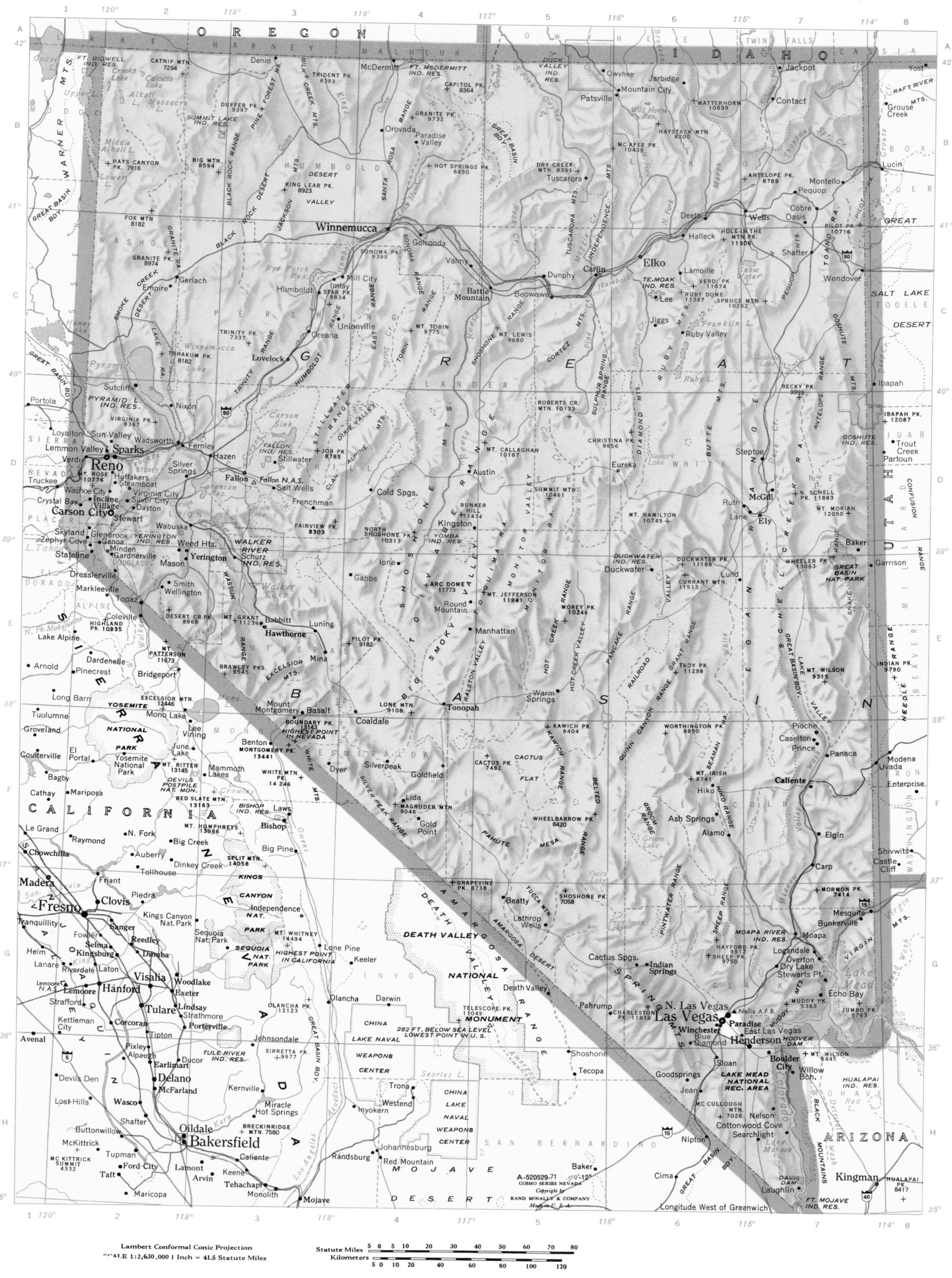

Lambert Conformal Conic Projection
SCALE 1:2,630,000 1 Inch = 41.5 Statute Miles

Statute Miles 5 0 5 10 20 30 40 50 60 70 80
Kilometers 5 0 10 20 40 60 80 100 120

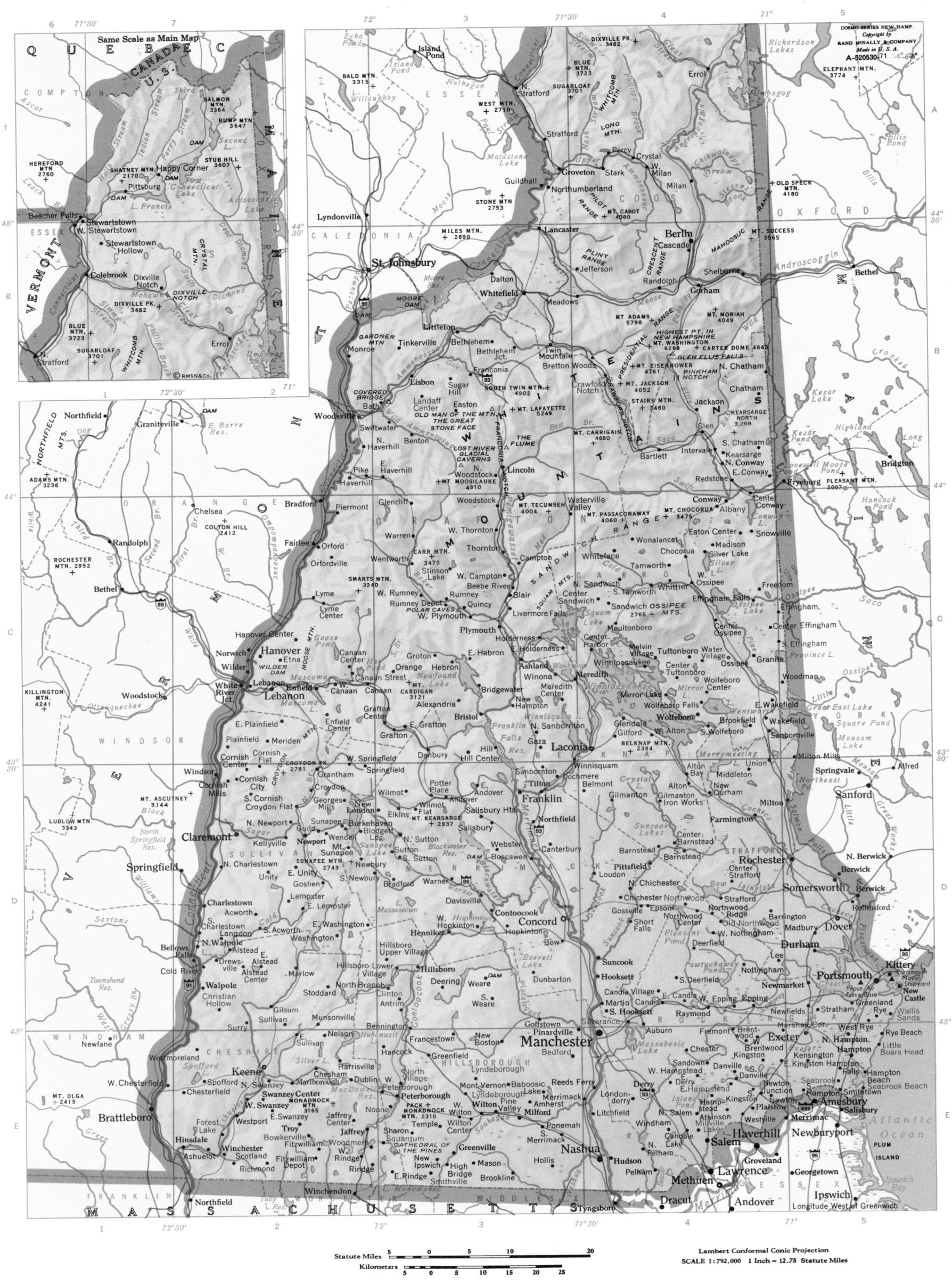

Same Scale as Main Map

Statute Miles

Kilometers

Lambert Conformal Conic Projection
SCALE 1:792,000   1 Inch = 12.75 Statute Miles

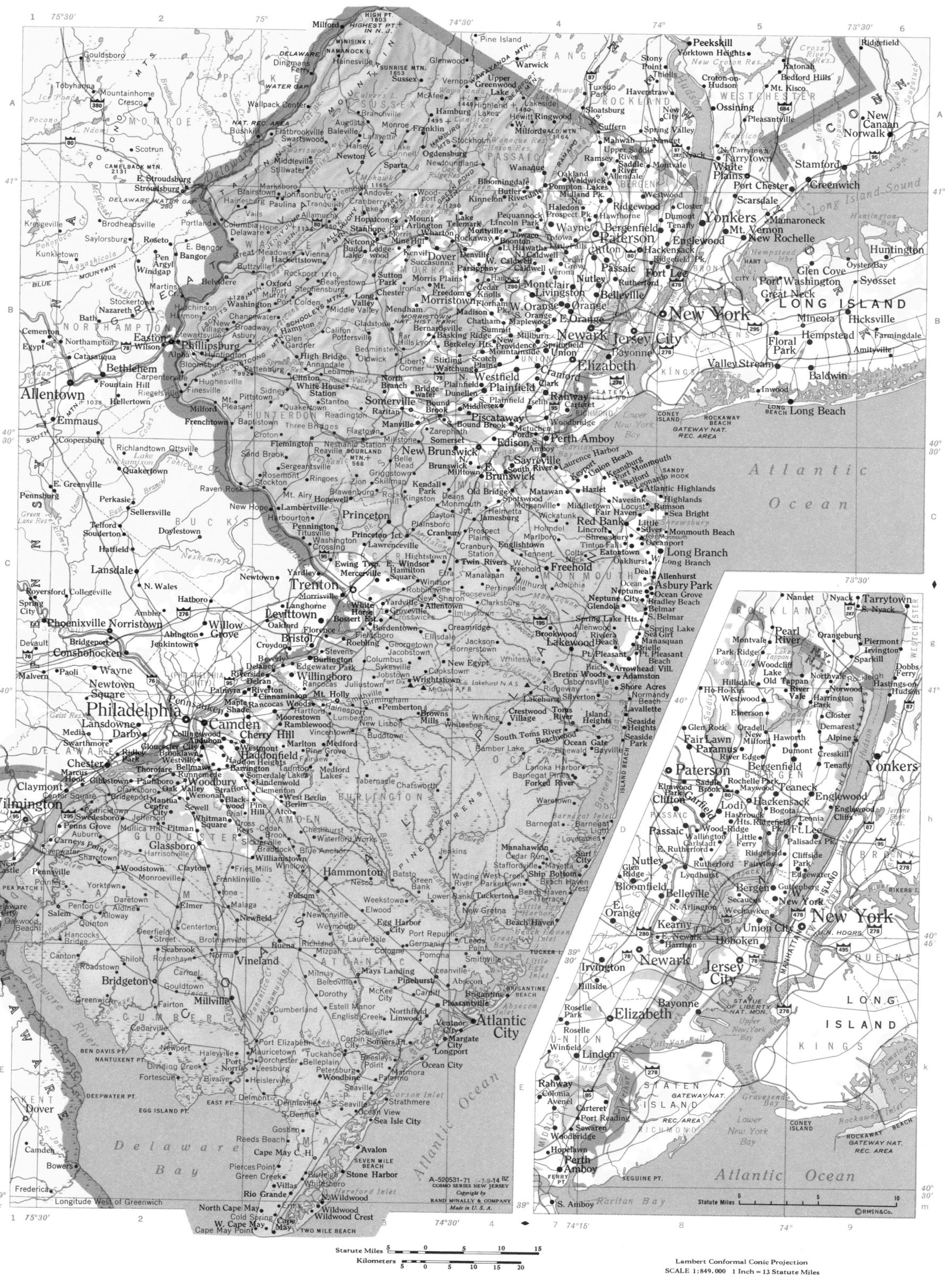

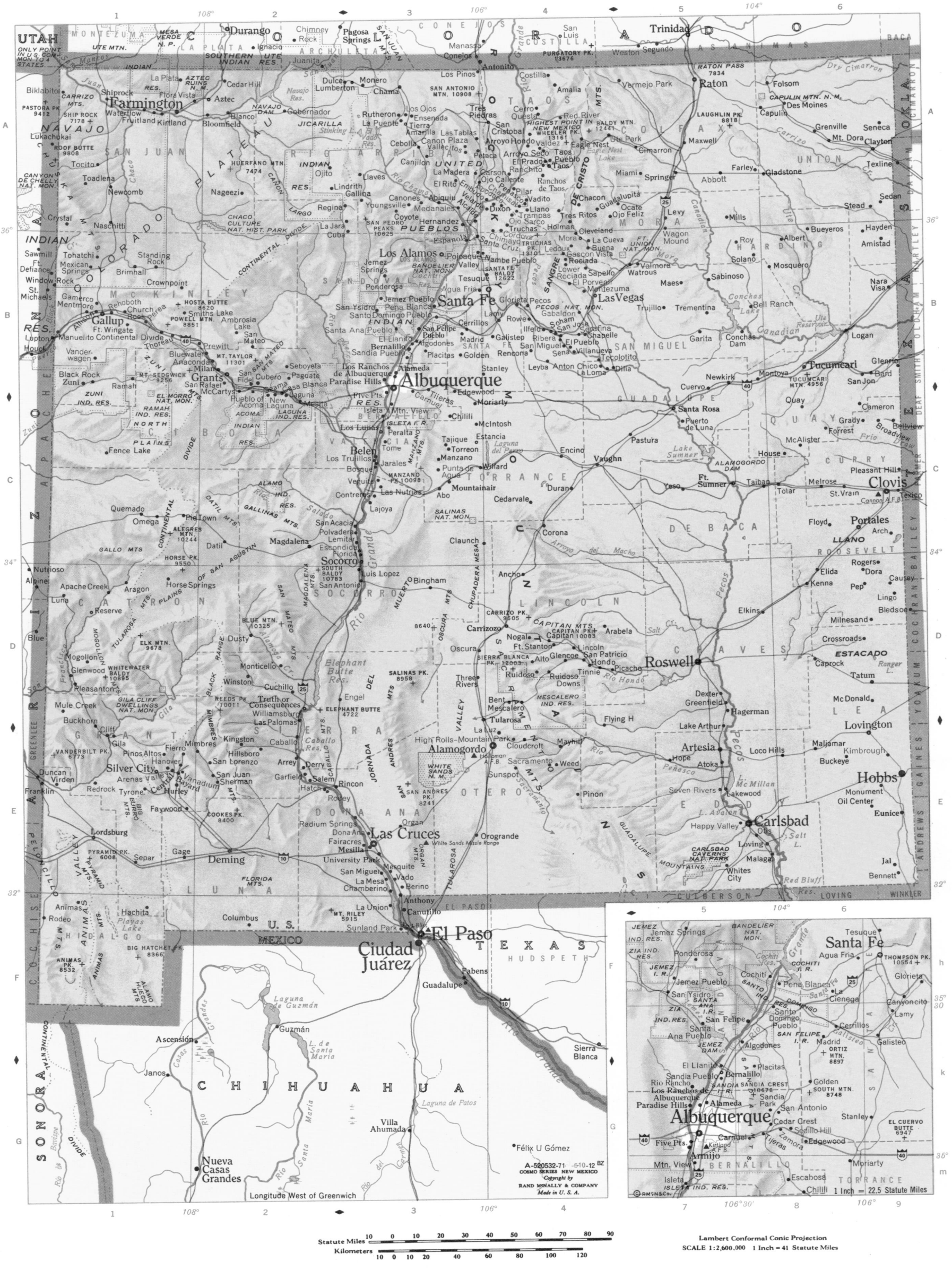

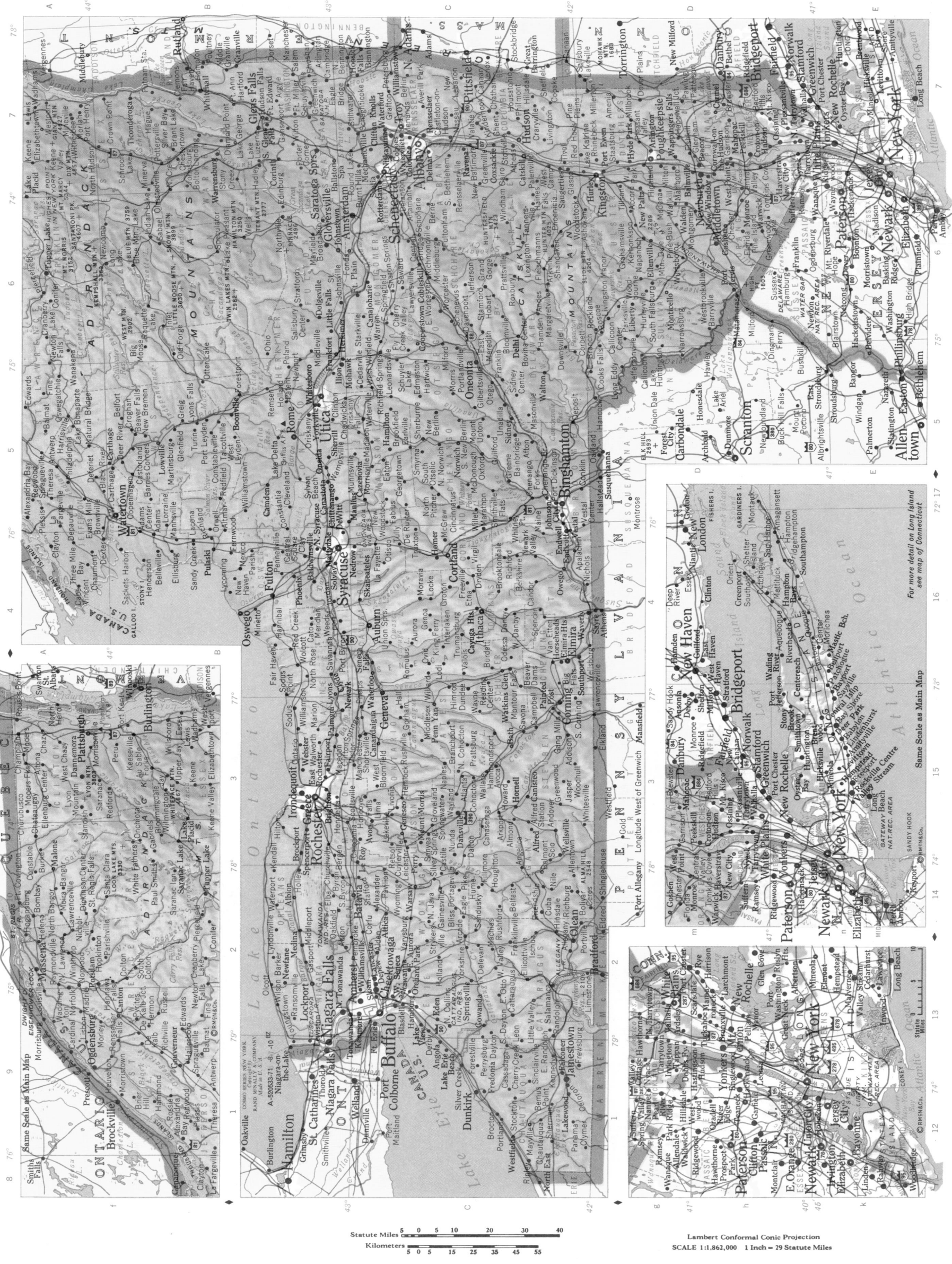

Statute Miles 5 0 5 10 20 30 40

Kilometers 5 0 5 15 25 35 45 55

Lambert Conformal Conic Projection
SCALE 1:1,862,000 1 Inch = 29 Statute Miles

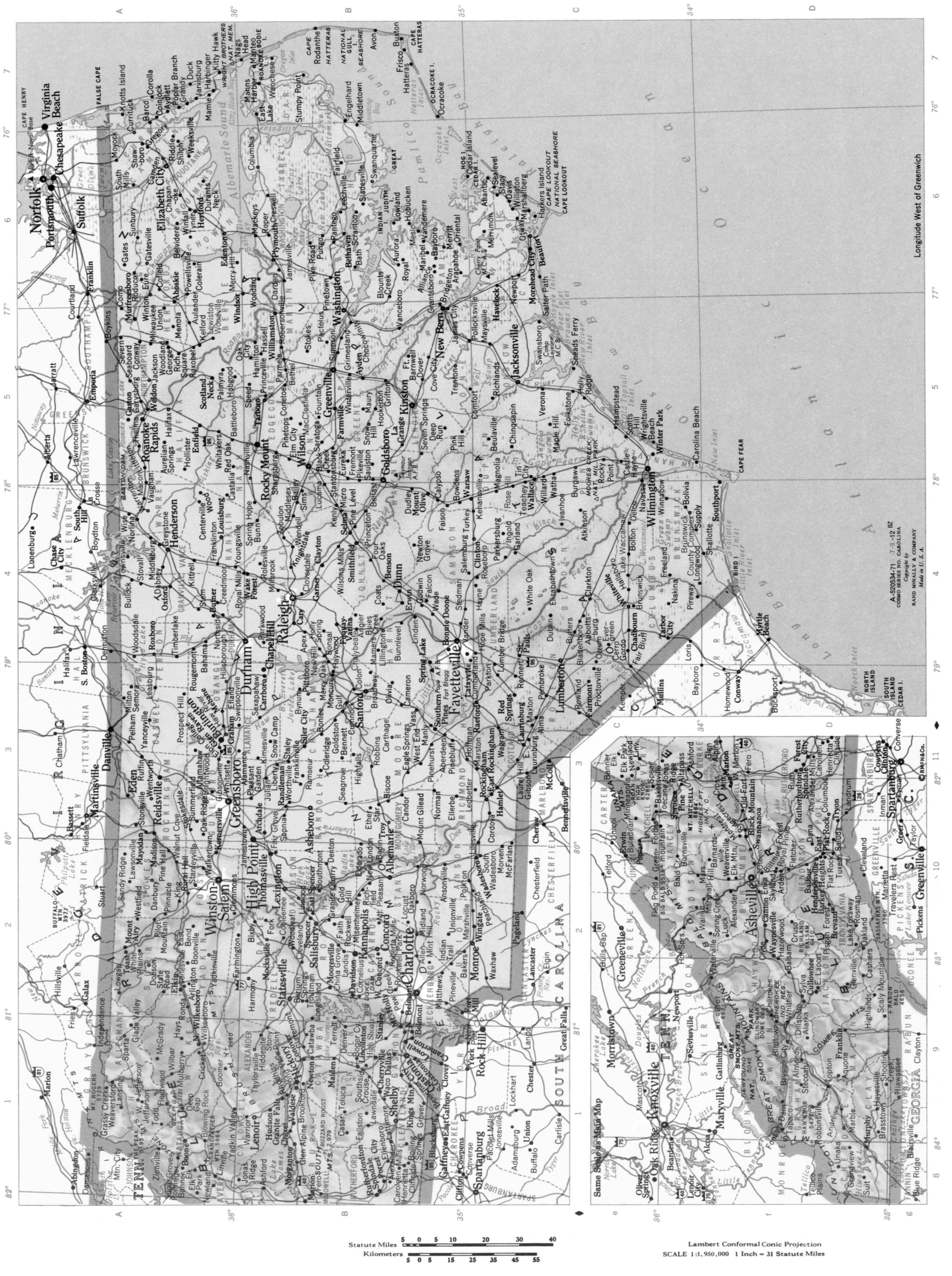

Statute Miles
Kilometers

Lambert Conformal Conic Projection
SCALE 1:1,950,000 1 Inch = 31 Statute Miles

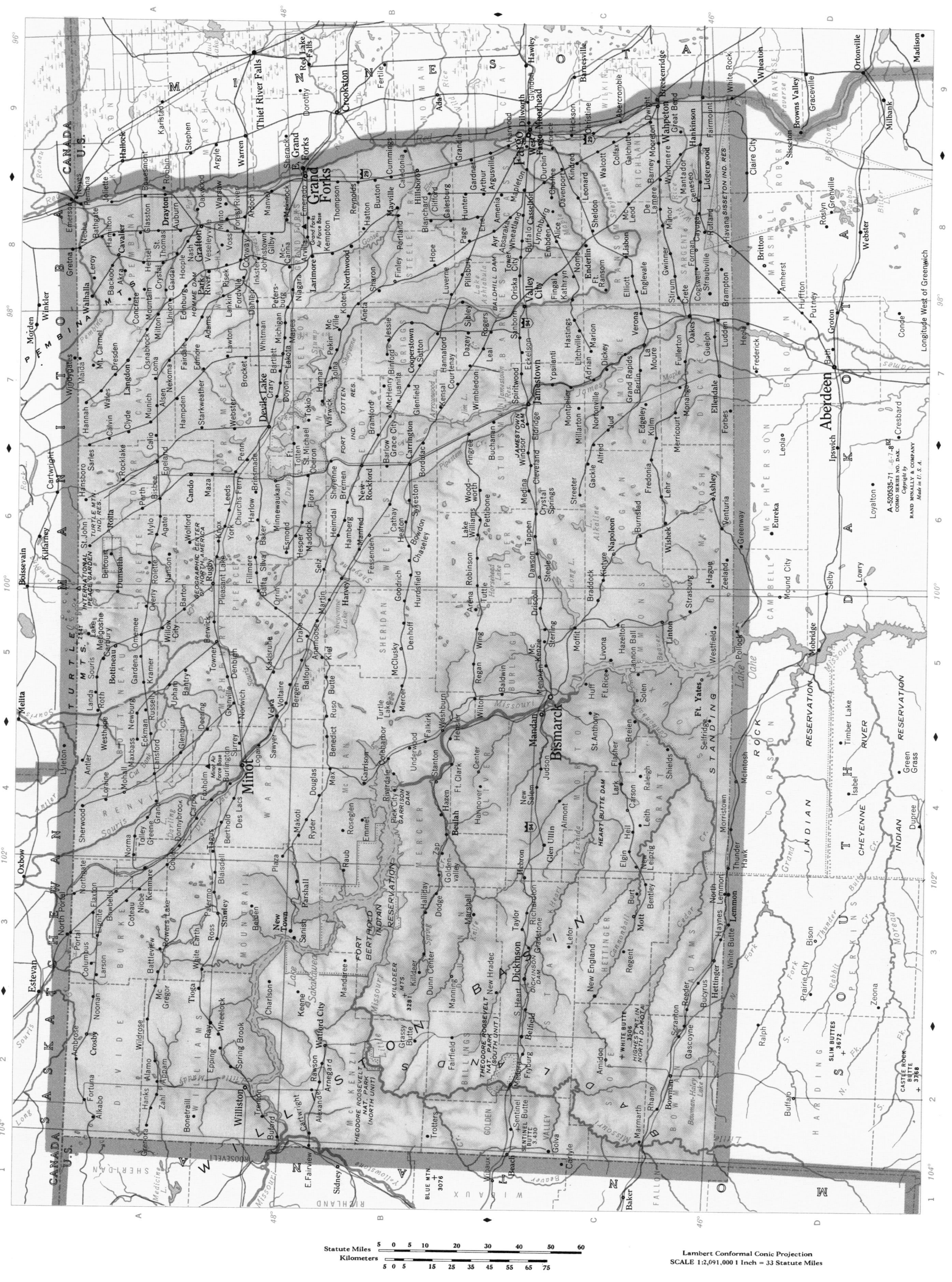

Statute Miles 5 0 5 10 20 30 40 50 60
Kilometers 5 0 5 15 25 35 45 55 65 75

Lambert Conformal Conic Projection
SCALE 1:2,091,000 1 Inch = 33 Statute Miles

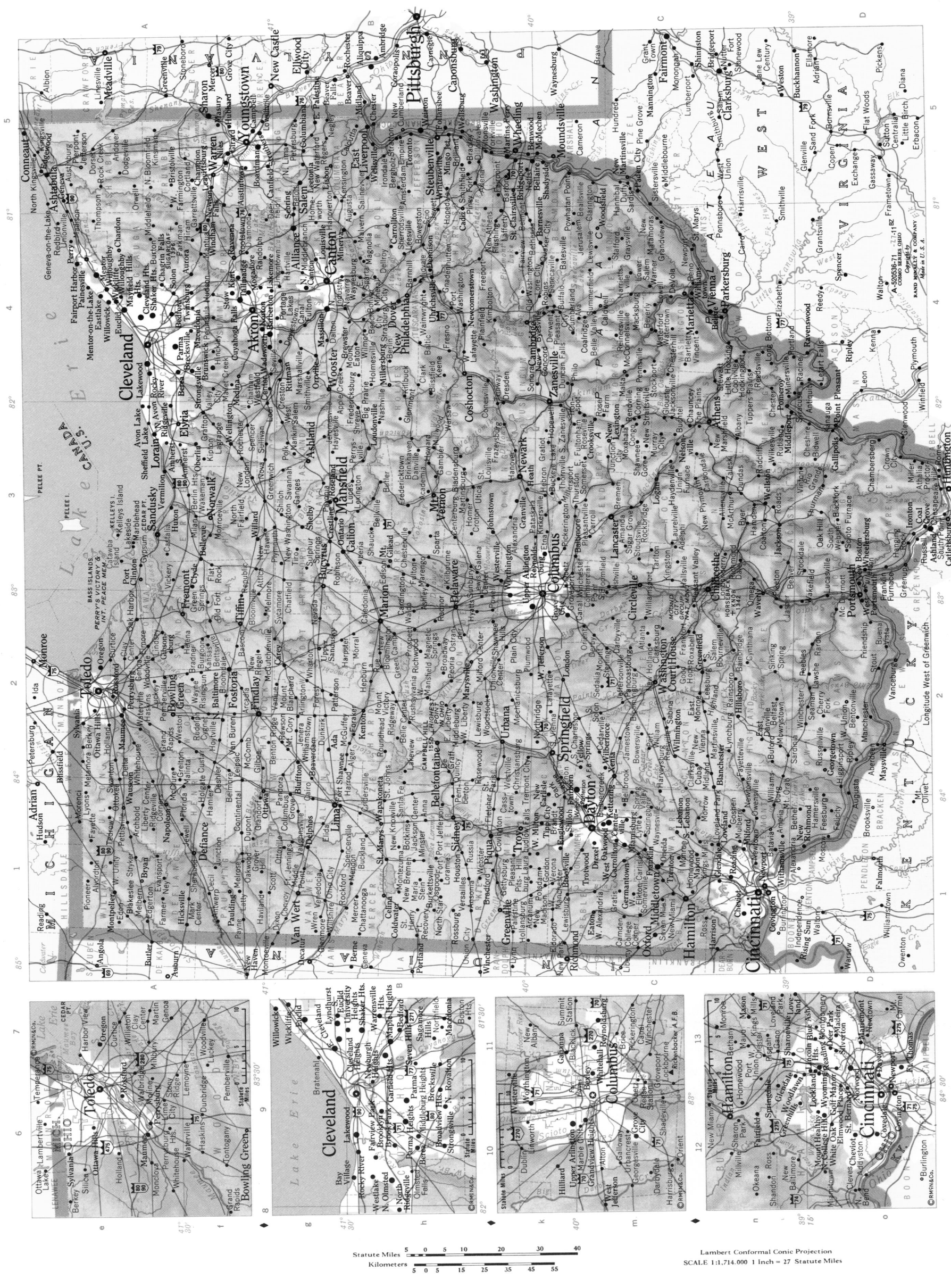

Statute Miles 5 0 5 10 20 30 40
Kilometers 5 0 5 15 25 35 45 55

Lambert Conformal Conic Projection
SCALE 1:1,714,000 1 Inch = 27 Statute Miles

Statute Miles 5 0 5 10 20 30 40
Kilometers 5 0 5 15 25 35 45 55

Lambert Conformal Conic Projection
SCALE 1:1,957,000 1 Inch = 31 Statute Miles

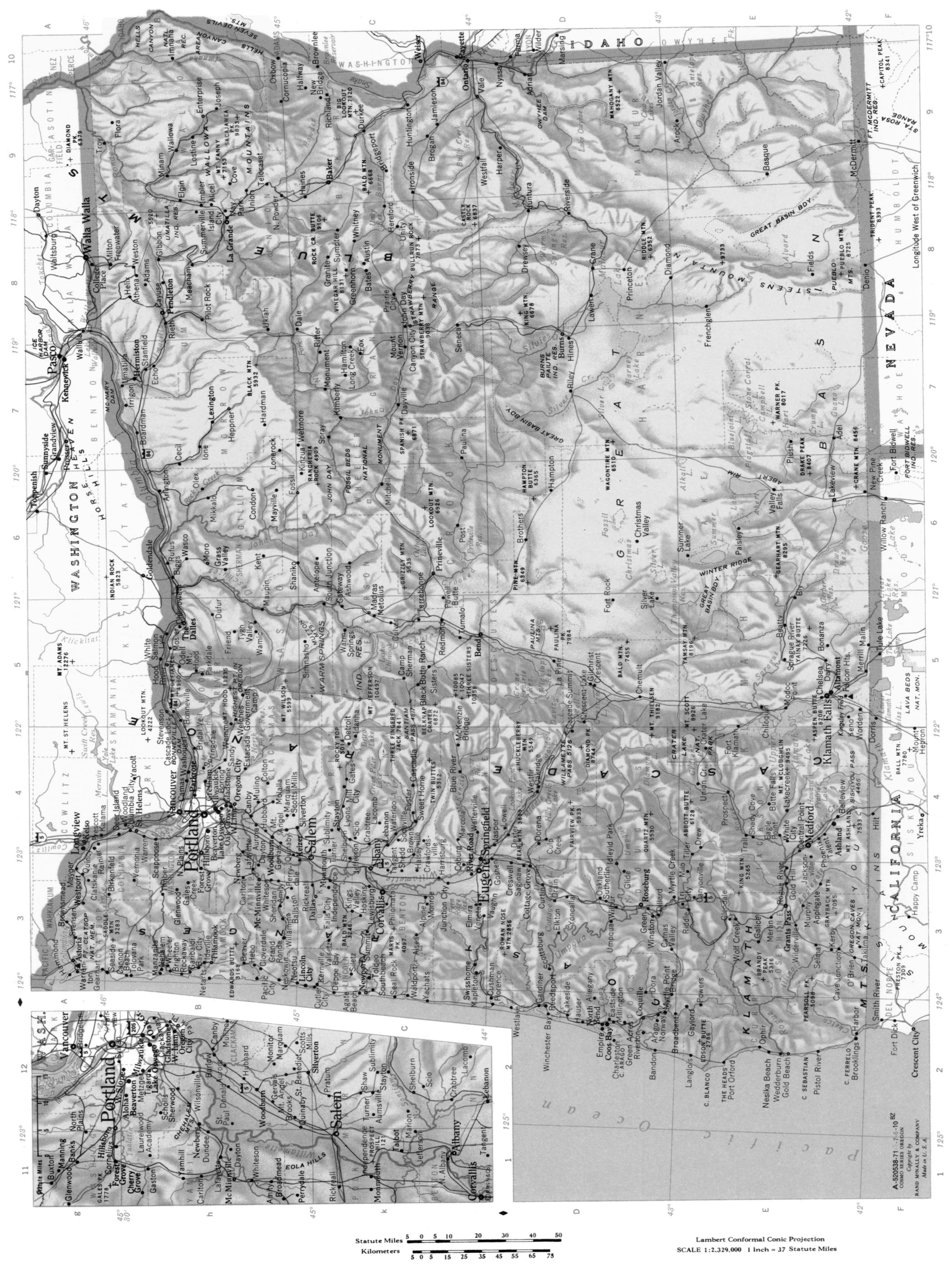

Lambert Conformal Conic Projection
SCALE 1:2,329,000   1 Inch = 37 Statute Miles

Statute Miles
Kilometers

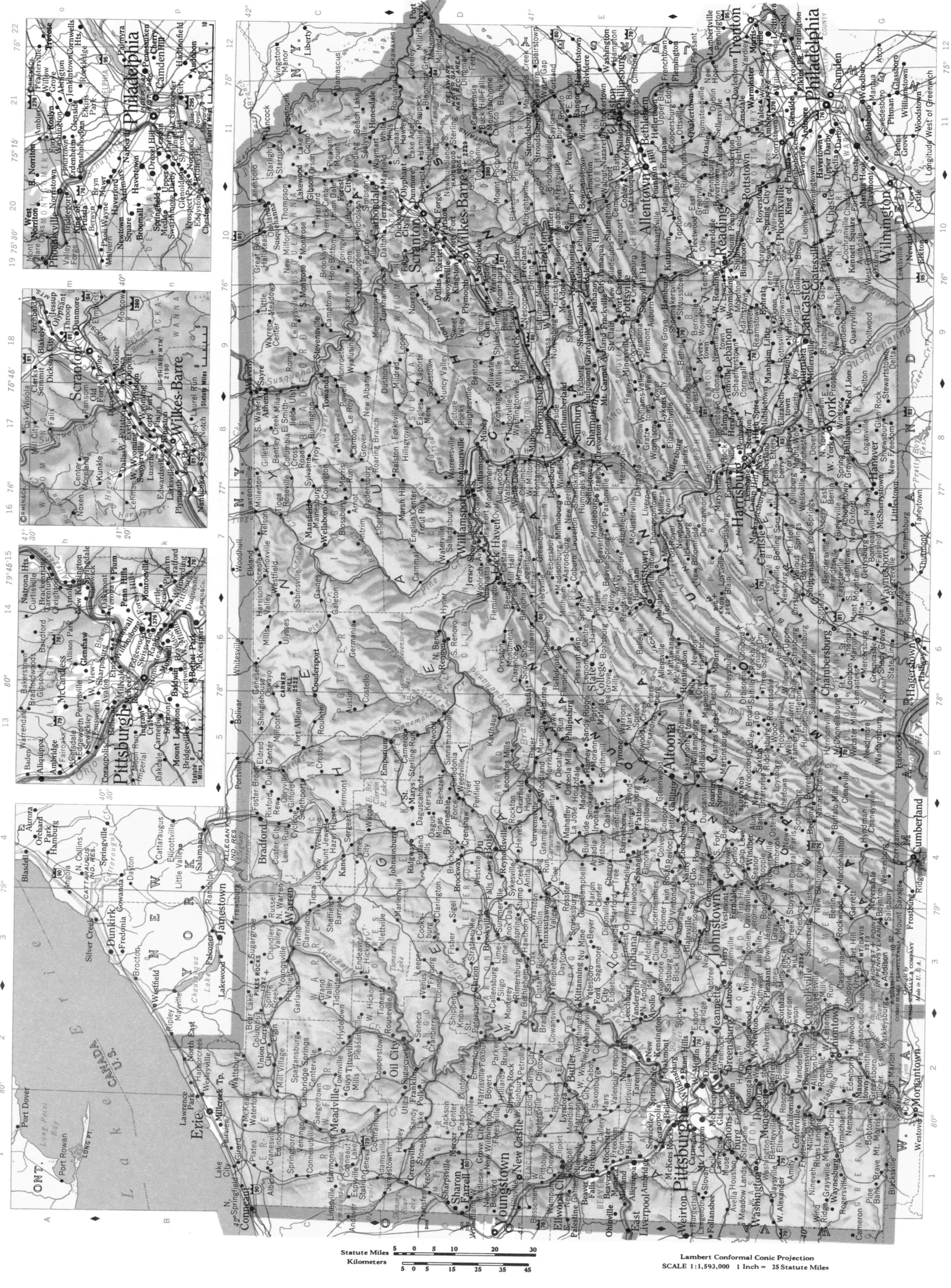

Statute Miles
Kilometers

Lambert Conformal Conic Projection
SCALE 1:1,593,000   1 Inch = 25 Statute Miles

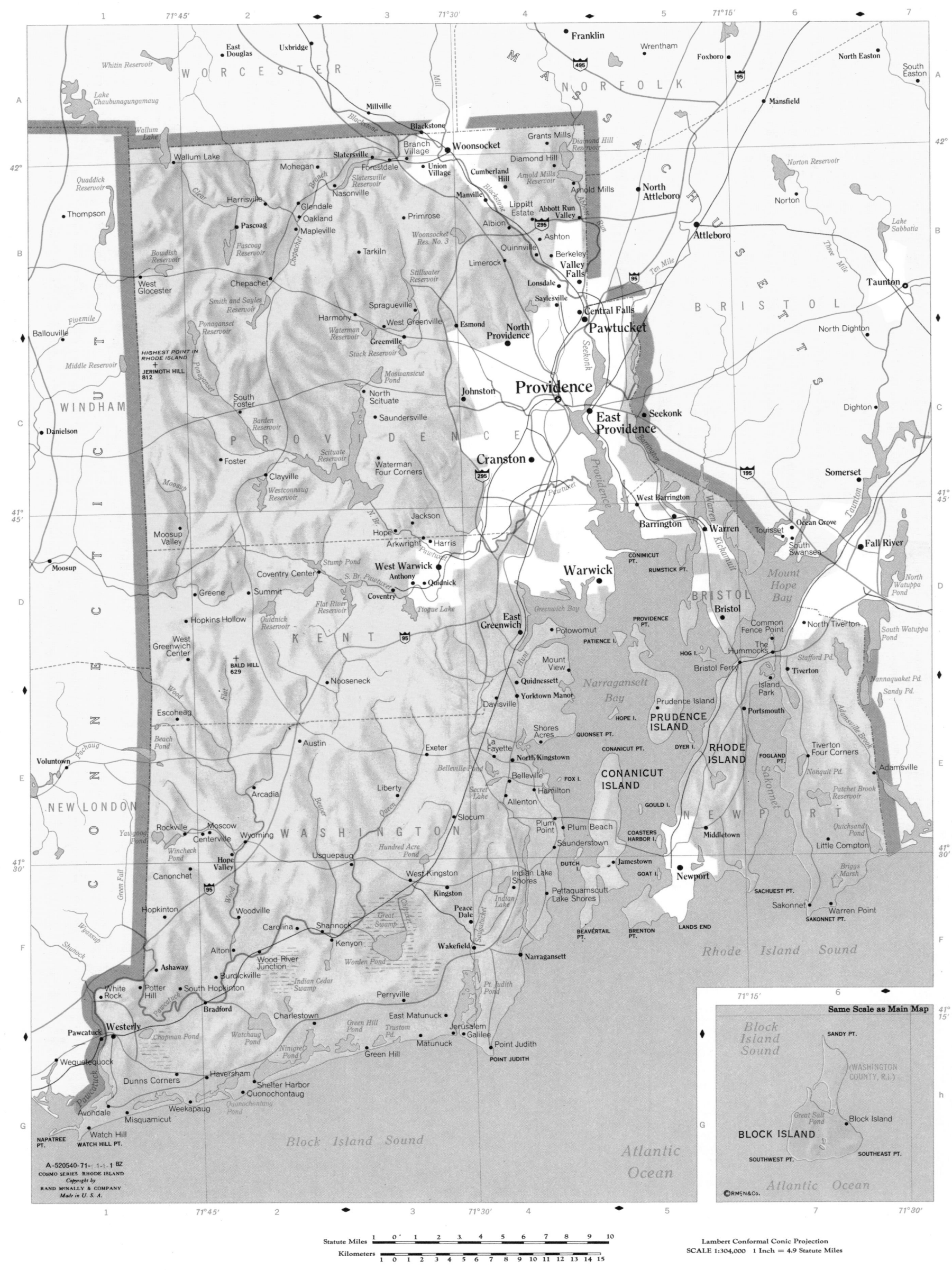

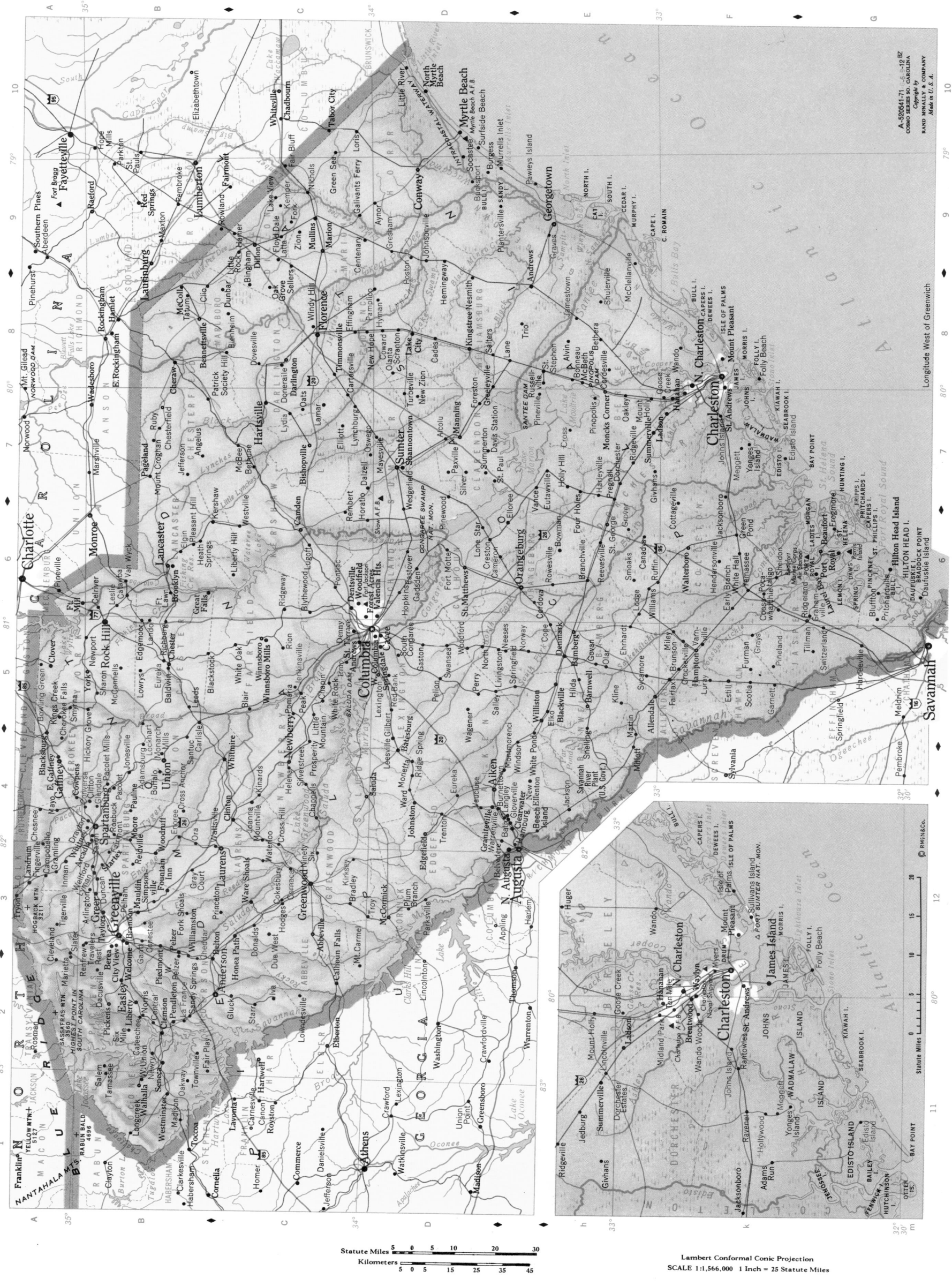

Lambert Conformal Conic Projection
SCALE 1:1,566,000 1 Inch = 25 Statute Miles

Statute Miles
Kilometers

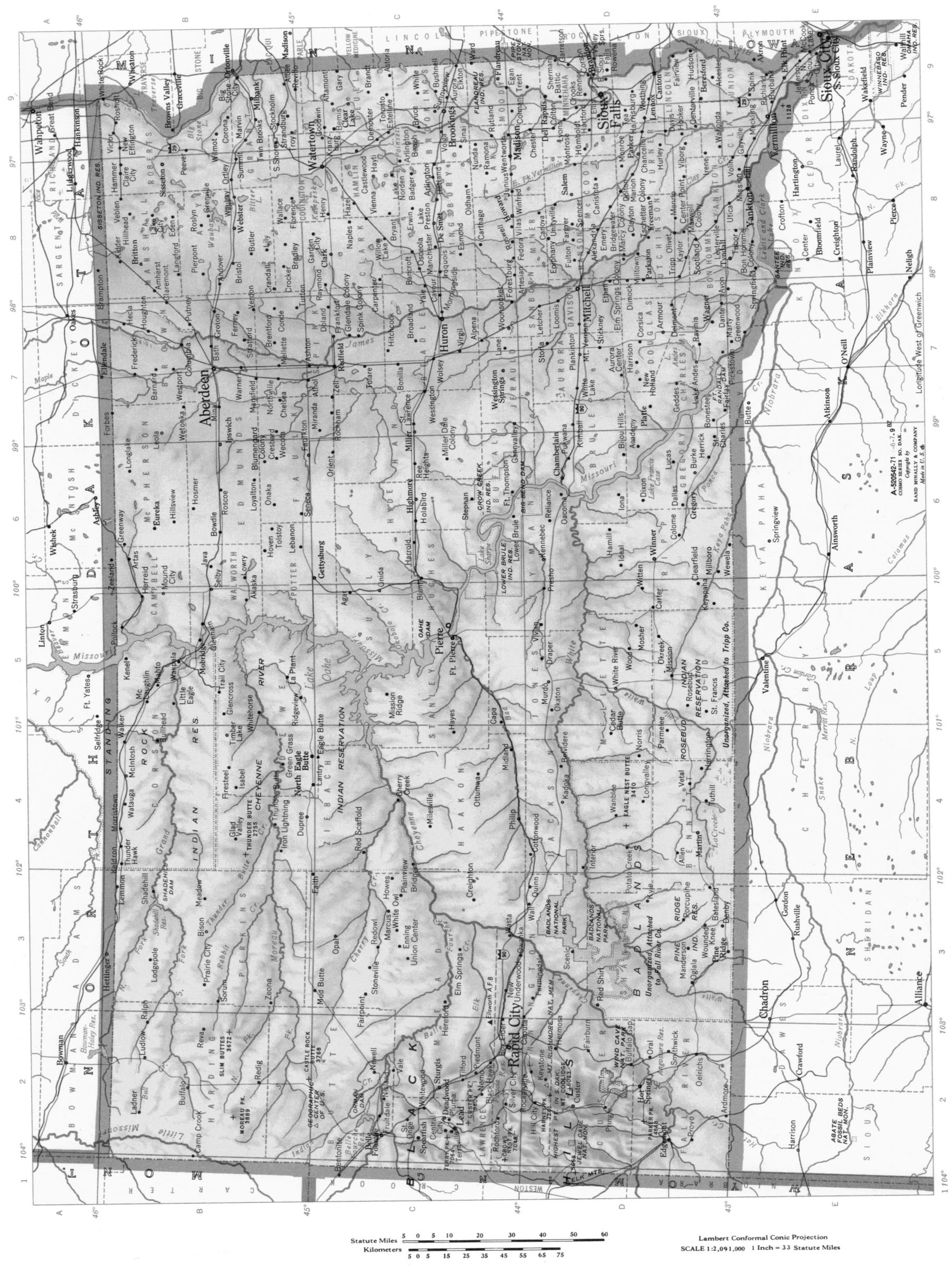

Statute Miles
Kilometers

Lambert Conformal Conic Projection
SCALE 1:2,091,000   1 Inch = 33 Statute Miles

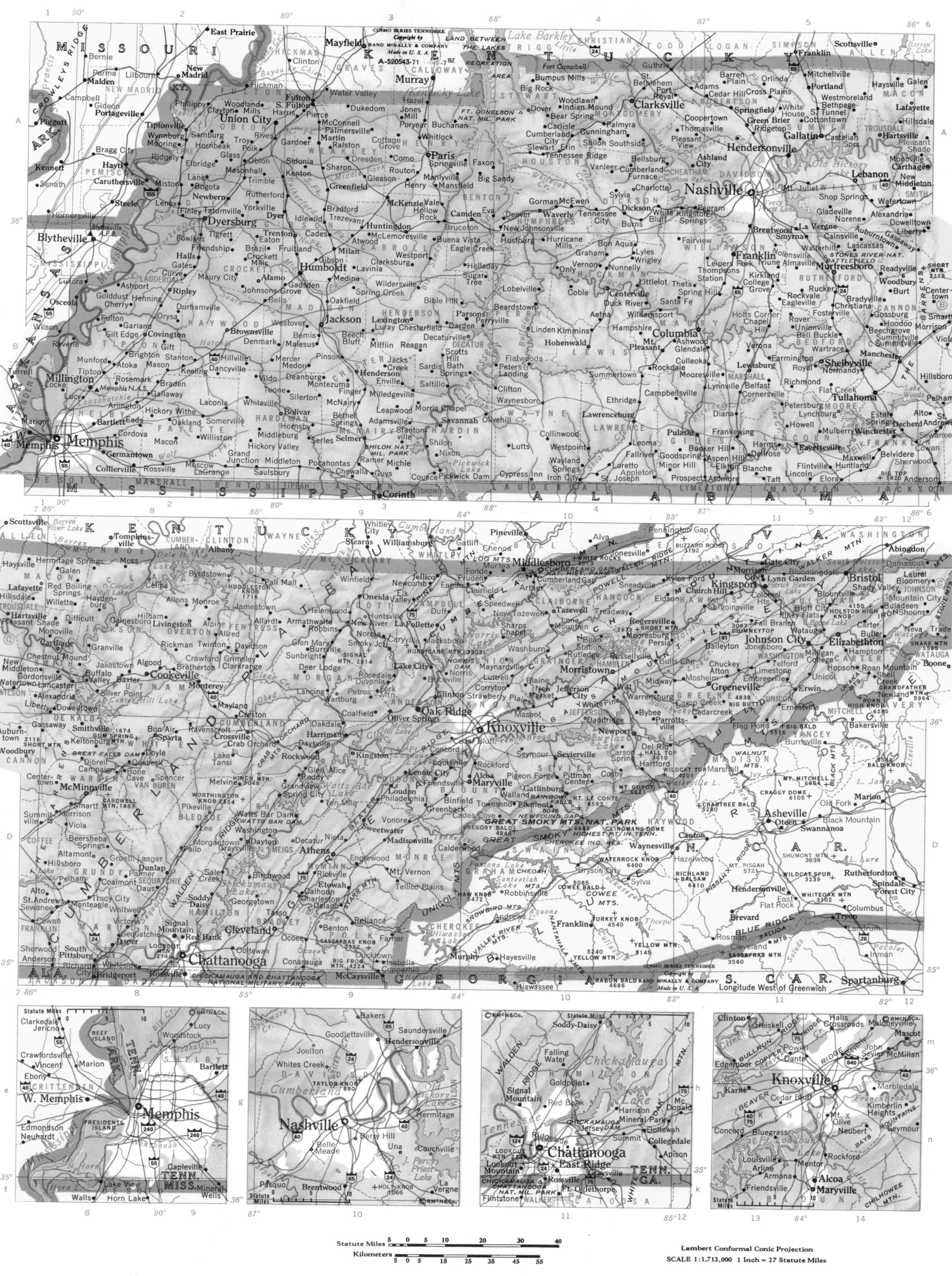

Statute Miles 5 0 5 10 20 30 40
Kilometers 5 0 5 15 25 35 45 55

Lambert Conformal Conic Projection
SCALE 1:1,713,000 1 Inch = 27 Statute Miles

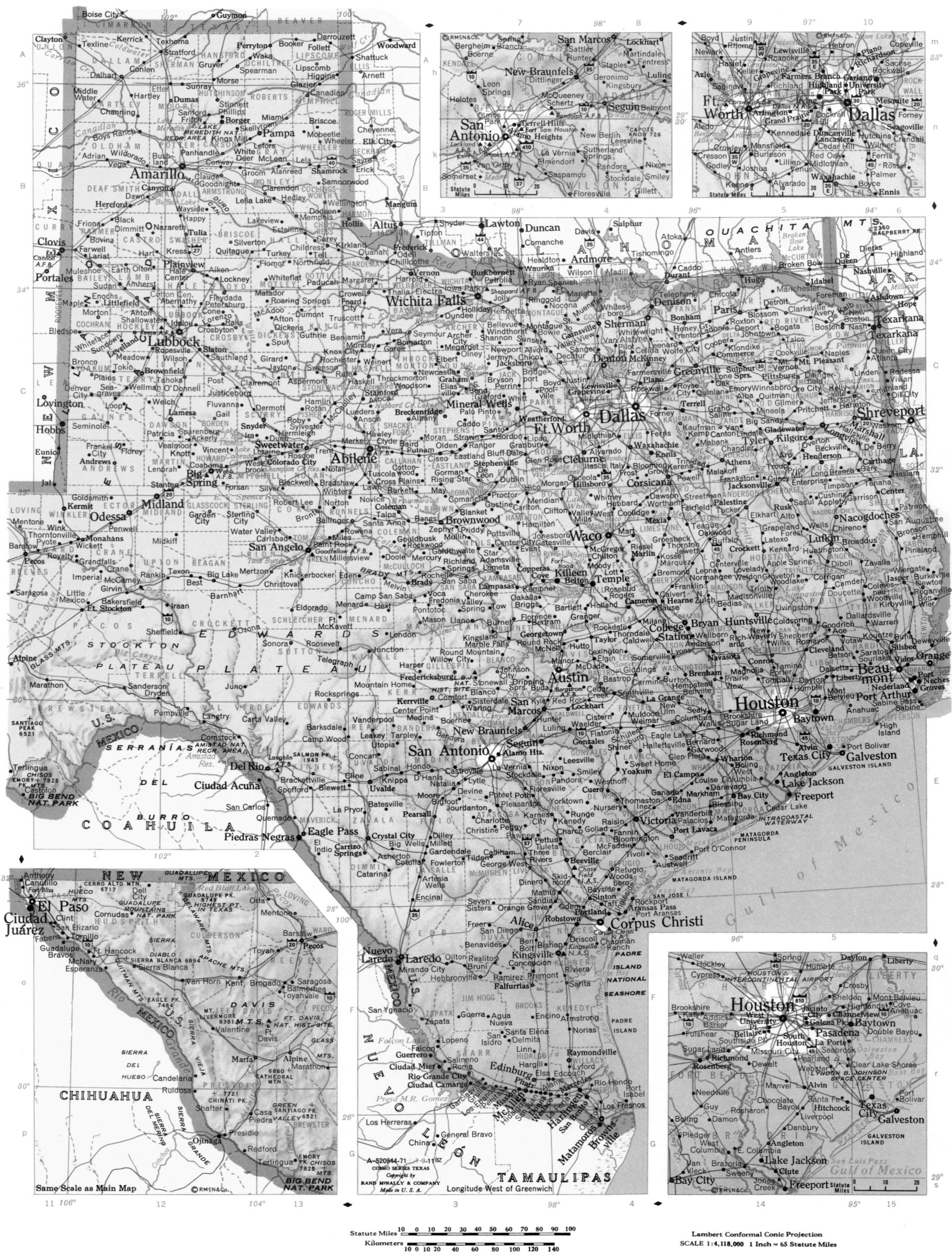

Statute Miles 10 0 10 20 30 40 50 60 70 80 90 100

Kilometers 10 0 10 20 40 60 80 100 120 140

Lambert Conformal Conic Projection
SCALE 1:4,118,000 1 Inch = 65 Statute Miles

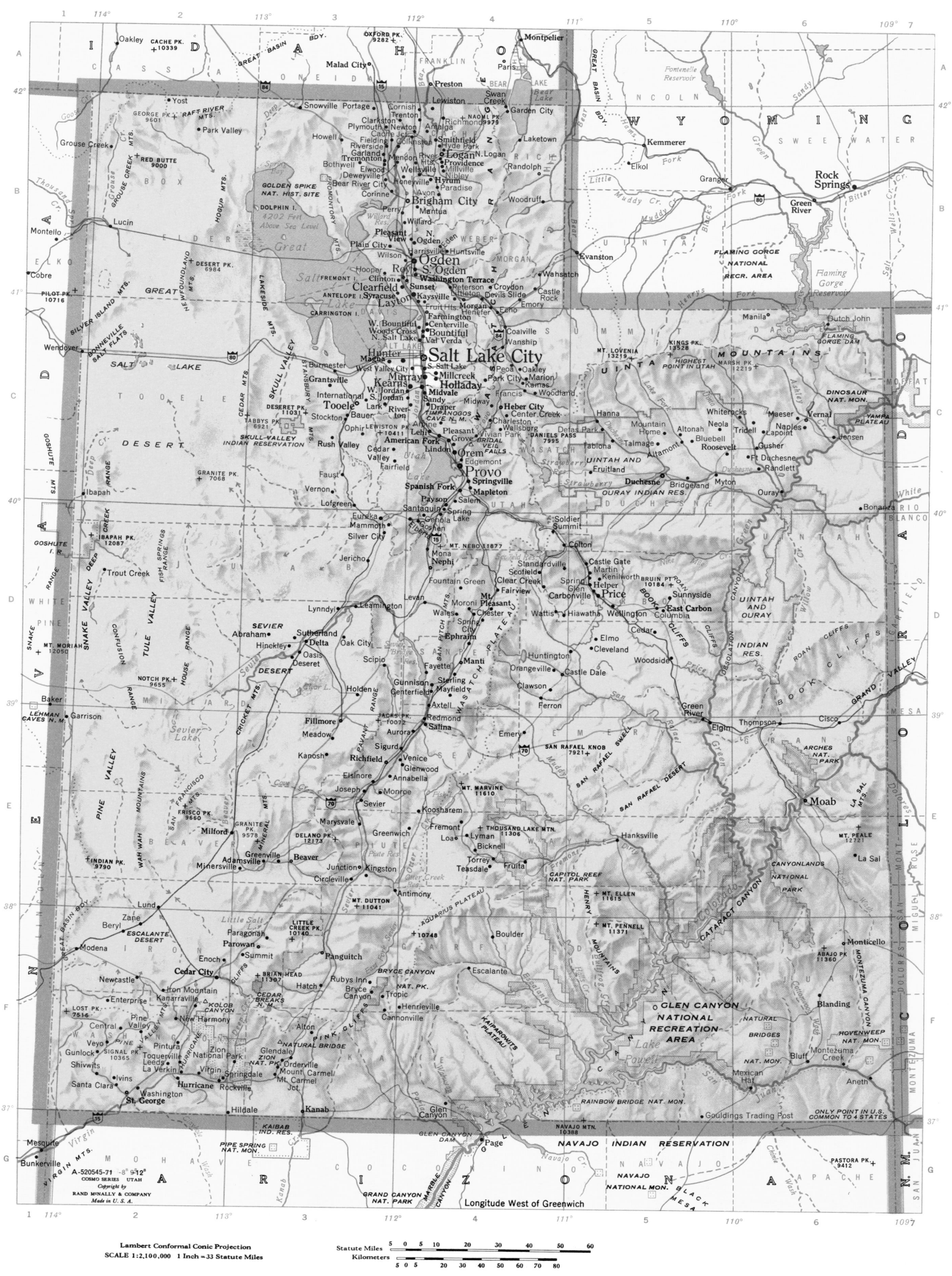

Lambert Conformal Conic Projection
SCALE 1:2,100,000   1 Inch = 33 Statute Miles

Statute Miles

Kilometers

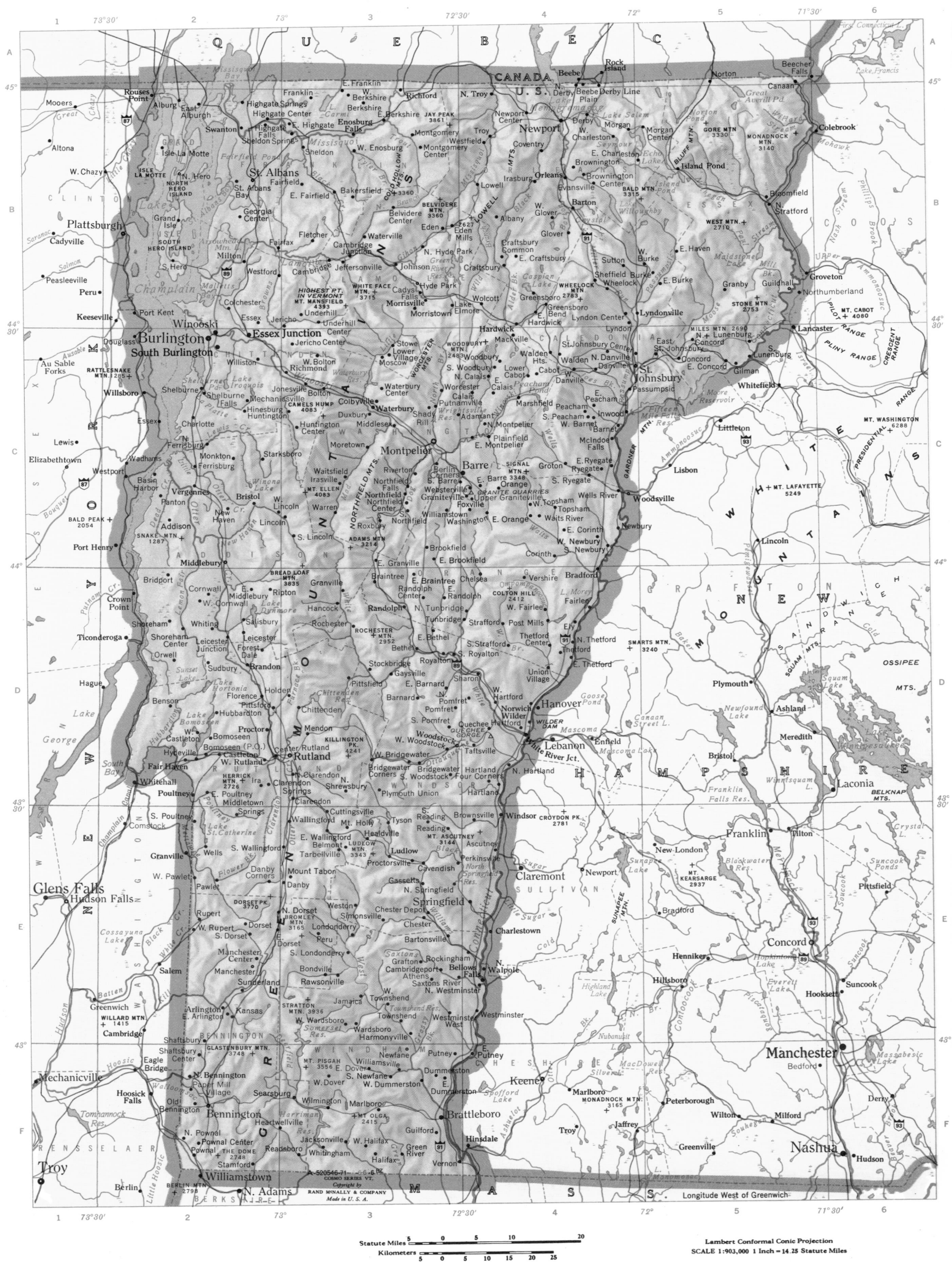

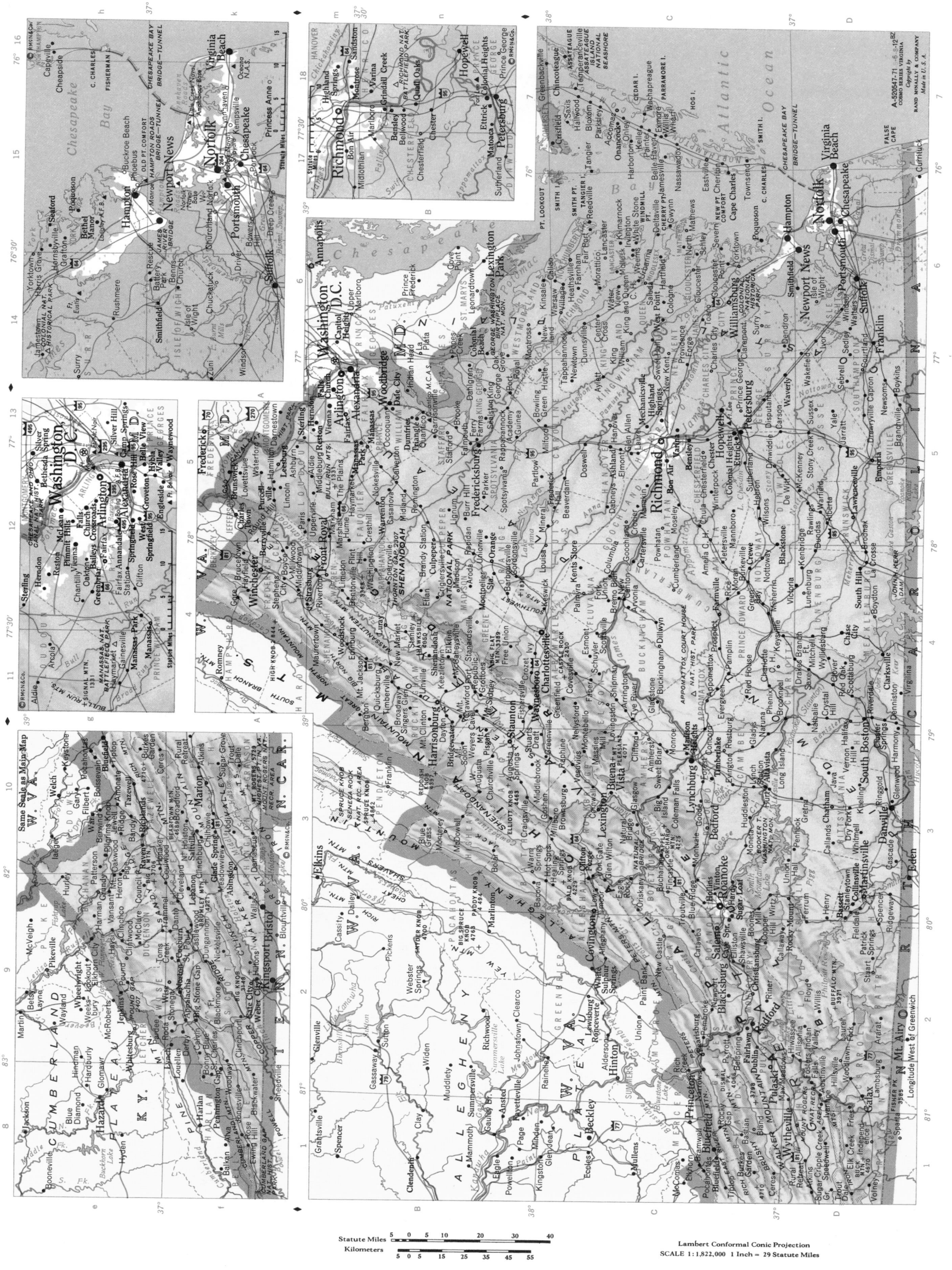

Statute Miles
Kilometers

Lambert Conformal Conic Projection
SCALE 1:1,822,000 1 Inch = 29 Statute Miles

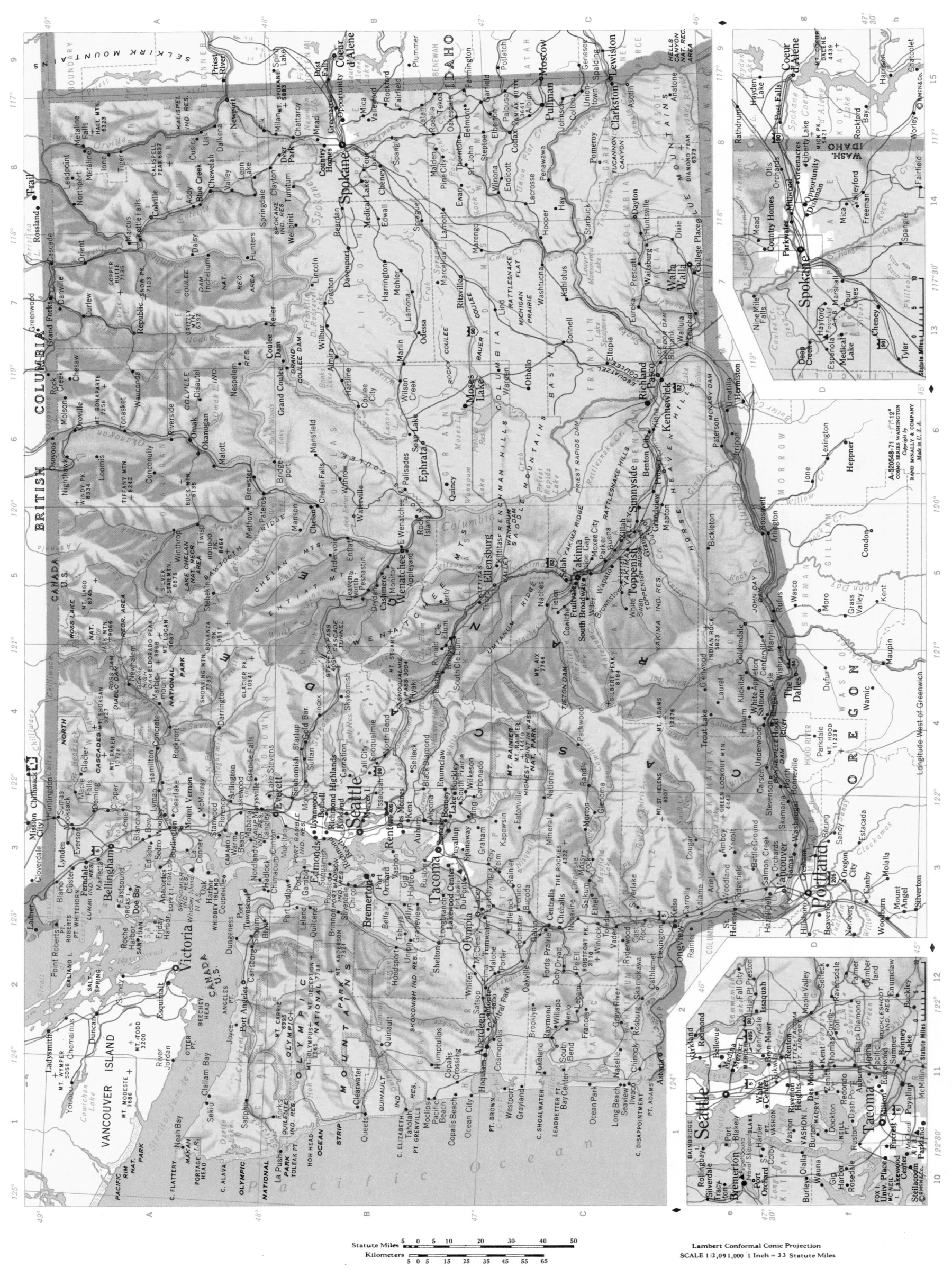

Statute Miles
Kilometers

Lambert Conformal Conic Projection
SCALE 1:2,091,000 1 Inch = 33 Statute Miles

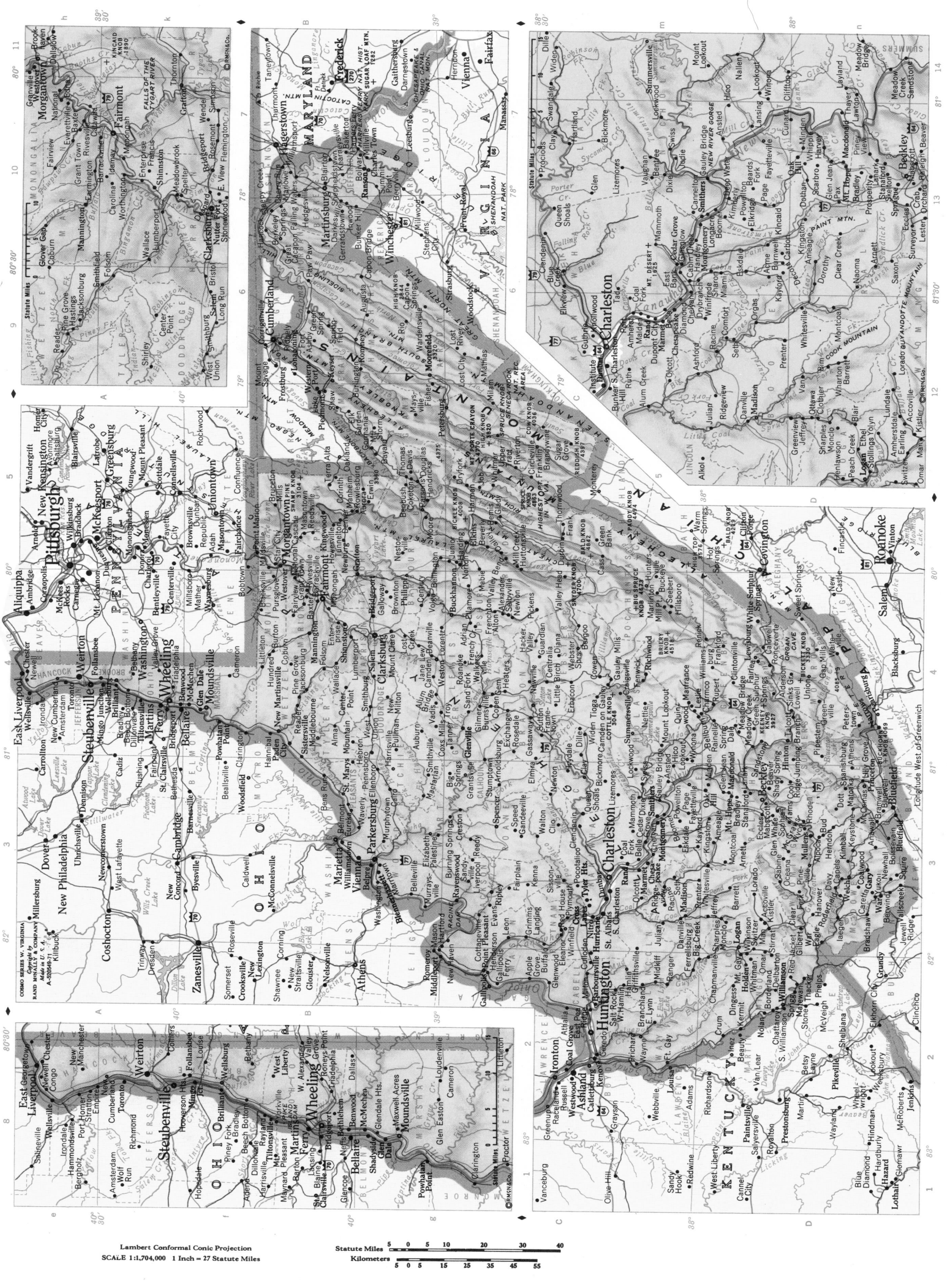

Lambert Conformal Conic Projection
SCALE 1:1,704,000   1 Inch = 27 Statute Miles

Statute Miles 5 0 5 10   20   30   40
Kilometers 5 0 5 15 25 35 45 55

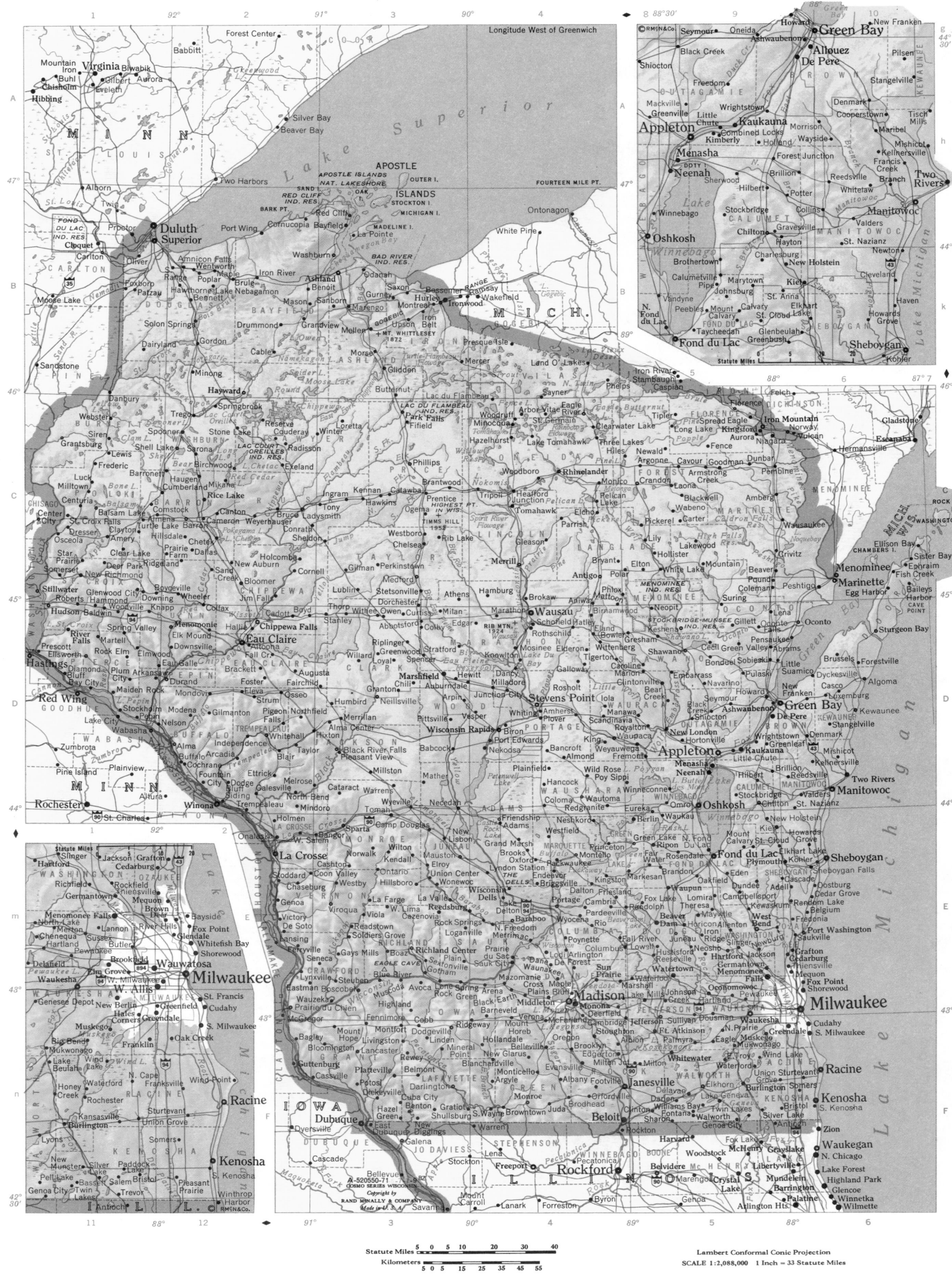

Longitude West of Greenwich

Lake Superior

APOSTLE
ISLANDS

Lake Michigan

Lambert Conformal Conic Projection
SCALE 1:2,088,000   1 Inch = 33 Statute Miles

Statute Miles

Kilometers

A-520550-71
COSMO SERIES WISCONSIN
Copyright by
RAND McNALLY & COMPANY
Made in U.S.A.

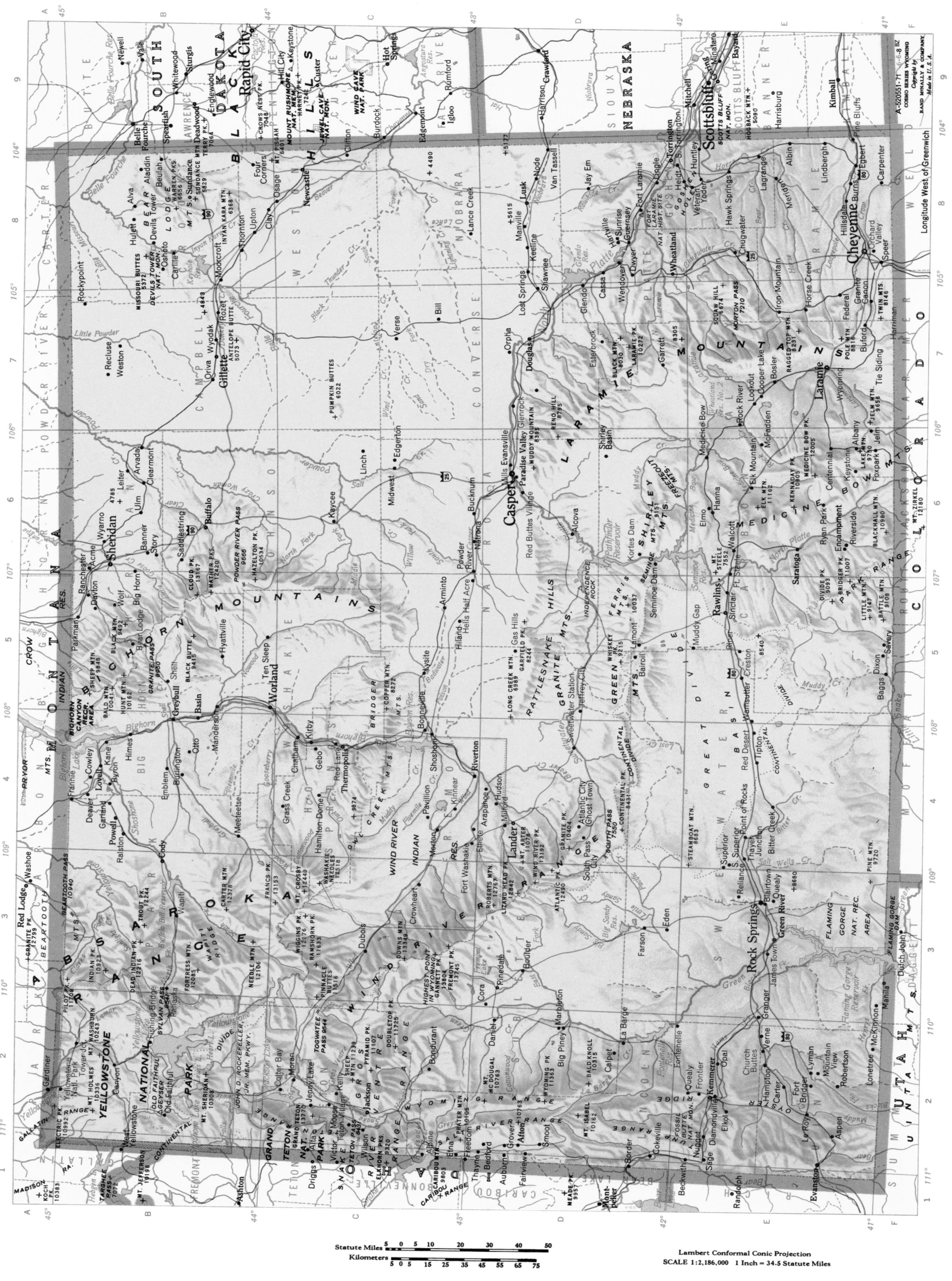

Statute Miles

Kilometers

Lambert Conformal Conic Projection
SCALE 1:2,186,000 1 Inch = 34.5 Statute Miles

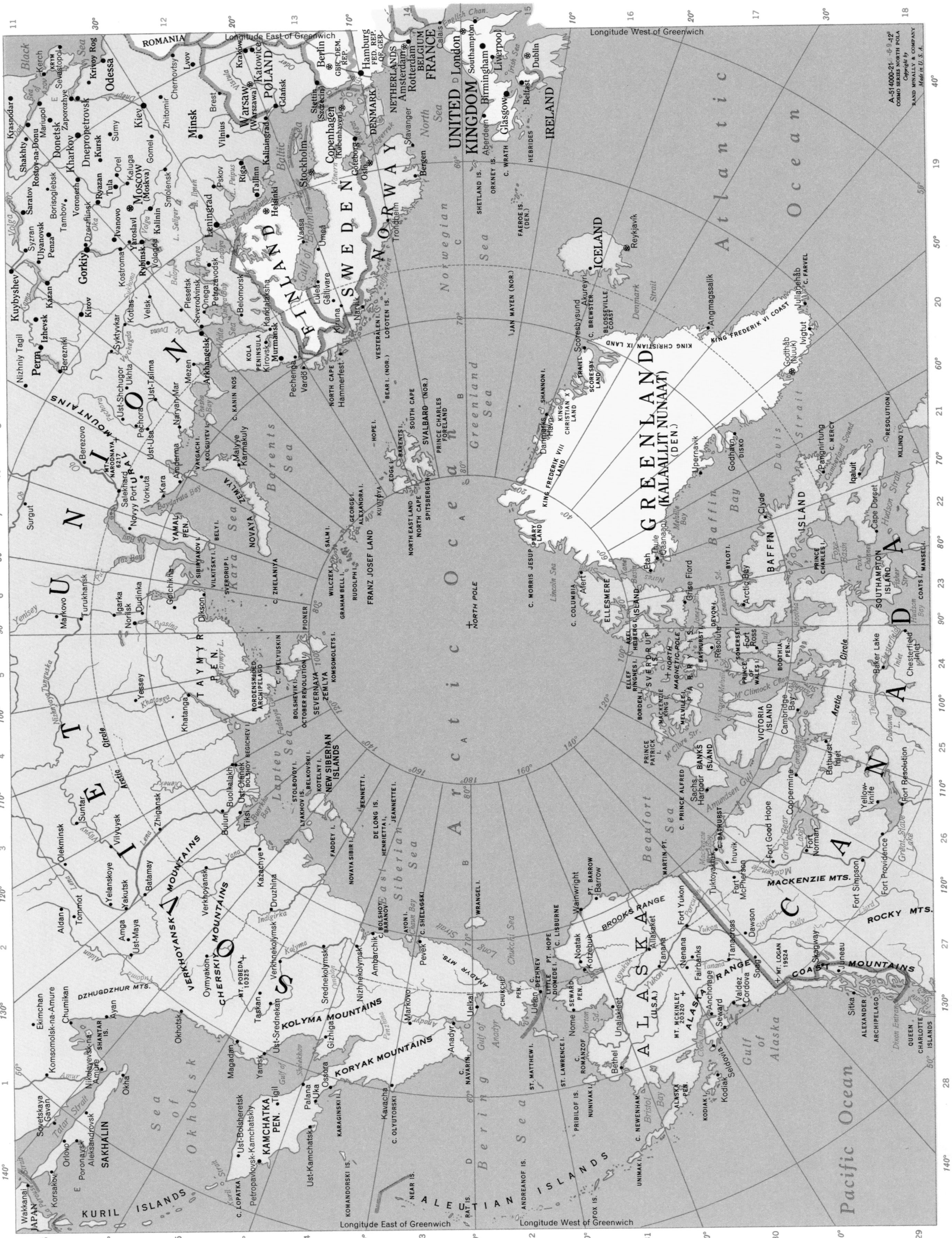

INDEX TO WORLD REFERENCE MAPS

INTRODUCTION TO THE INDEX

This universal index includes in a single alphabetical list approximately 78,000 names of features that appear on the reference maps. Each name is followed by the name of the country or continent in which it is located, a map-reference key and a page reference.

Names The names of cities appear in the index in regular type. The names of all other features appear in *italics*, followed by descriptive terms (hill, mtn., state) to indicate their nature.

Names that appear in shortened versions on the maps due to space limitations are spelled out in full in the index. The portions of these names omitted from the maps are enclosed in brackets — for example, Acapulco [de Juárez].

Abbreviations of names on the maps have been standardized as much as possible. Names that are abbreviated on the maps are generally spelled out in full in the index.

Country names and names of features that extend beyond the boundaries of one country are followed by the name of the continent in which each is located. Country designations follow the names of all other places in the index. The locations of places in the United States, Canada, and the United Kingdom are further defined by abbreviations that indicate the state, province, or political division in which each is located.

All abbreviations used in the index are defined in the List of Abbreviations below.

Alphabetization Names are alphabetized in the order of the letters of the English alphabet. Spanish *ll* and *ch*, for example, are not treated as distinct letters. Furthermore, diacritical marks are disregarded in alphabetization — German or Scandinavian *ä* or *ö* are treated as *a* or *o*.

The names of physical features may appear inverted, since they are always alphabetized under the proper, not the generic, part of the name, thus: 'Gibraltar, Strait of'. Otherwise every entry, whether consisting of one word or more, is alphabetized as a single continuous entity. 'Lakeland', for example, appears after 'La Crosse' and before 'La Salle'. Names beginning with articles (Le Havre, Den Helder, Al Manşūrah) are not inverted. Names beginning 'St.', 'Ste.' and 'Sainte' are alphabetized as though spelled 'Saint'.

In the case of identical names, towns are listed first, then political divisions, then physical features. Entries that are completely identical are listed alphabetically by country name.

Map-Reference Keys and Page References The map-reference keys and page references are found in the last two columns of each entry.

Each map-reference key consists of a letter and number. The letters appear along the sides of the maps. Lowercase letters indicate reference to inset maps. Numbers appear across the tops and bottoms of the maps.

Map reference keys for point features, such as cities and mountain peaks, indicate the locations of the symbols. For extensive areal features, such as countries or mountain ranges, locations are given for the approximate centers of the features. Those for linear features, such as canals and rivers, are given for the locations of the names.

Names of some important places or features that are omitted from the maps due to space limitations are included in the index. Each of these places is identified by an asterisk (*) preceding the map-reference key.

The page number generally refers to the main map for the country in which the feature is located. Page references to two-page maps always refer to the left-hand page.

LIST OF ABBREVIATIONS

Afg.	Afghanistan	De., U.S.	Delaware, U.S.	Ks., U.S.	Kansas, U.S.	Nmb.	Namibia	St. Luc.	St. Lucia

Afg. — Afghanistan
Afr. — Africa
Ak., U.S. — Alaska, U.S.
Al., U.S. — Alabama, U.S.
Alb. — Albania
Alg. — Algeria
Alta. — Alberta, Can.
Am. Sam. — American Samoa
anch. — anchorage
And. — Andorra
Ang. — Angola
Ant. — Antarctica
Antig. — Antigua and Barbuda
Ar., U.S. — Arkansas, U.S.
Arg. — Argentina
Aus. — Austria
Austl. — Australia
Az., U.S. — Arizona, U.S.
b. — bay, gulf, inlet, lagoon
Bah. — Bahamas
Bahr. — Bahrain
Barb. — Barbados
B.A.T. — British Antarctic Territory
B.C. — British Columbia, Can.
Bdi. — Burundi
Bel. — Belgium
Ber. — Bermuda
Bhu. — Bhutan
B.I.O.T. — British Indian Ocean Territory
Bngl. — Bangladesh
Bol. — Bolivia
Boph. — Bophuthatswana
Bots. — Botswana
Braz. — Brazil
Bru. — Brunei
Bul. — Bulgaria
Burkina — Burkina Faso
c. — cape, point
Ca., U.S. — California, U.S.
Cam. — Cameroon
Camb. — Cambodia
Can. — Canada
Cay. Is. — Cayman Islands
Cen. Afr. Rep. — Central African Republic
Christ. I. — Christmas Island
clf. — cliff, escarpment
co. — county, parish
Co., U.S. — Colorado, U.S.
Col. — Colombia
Com. — Comoros
cont. — continent
C.R. — Costa Rica
crat. — crater
Ct., U.S. — Connecticut, U.S.
ctry. — country
C.V. — Cape Verde
Cyp. — Cyprus
Czech. — Czechoslovakia
D.C., U.S. — District of Columbia, U.S.

De., U.S. — Delaware, U.S.
Den. — Denmark
dep. — dependency, colony
depr. — depression
dept. — department, district
des. — desert
Dji. — Djibouti
Dom. — Dominica
Dom. Rep. — Dominican Republic
Ec. — Ecuador
Eg. — Egypt
E. Ger. — German Democratic Republic
El Sal. — El Salvador
Eng., U.K. — England, U.K.
Eq. Gui. — Equatorial Guinea
est. — estuary
Eth. — Ethiopia
Eur. — Europe
Faer. Is. — Faeroe Islands
Falk. Is. — Falkland Islands
Fin. — Finland
Fl., U.S. — Florida, U.S.
for. — forest, moor
Fr. — France
Fr. Gu. — French Guiana
Fr. Poly. — French Polynesia
F.S.A.T. — French Southern and Antarctic Territory
Ga., U.S. — Georgia, U.S.
Gam. — Gambia
Gib. — Gibraltar
Grc. — Greece
Gren. — Grenada
Grnld. — Greenland
Guad. — Guadeloupe
Guat. — Guatemala
Gui. — Guinea
Gui.-B. — Guinea-Bissau
Guy. — Guyana
Hi., U.S. — Hawaii, U.S.
hist. — historic site, ruins
hist. reg. — historic region
H.K. — Hong Kong
Hond. — Honduras
Hung. — Hungary
i. — island
Ia., U.S. — Iowa, U.S.
I.C. — Ivory Coast
Ice. — Iceland
ice — ice feature, glacier
Id., U.S. — Idaho, U.S.
Il., U.S. — Illinois, U.S.
In., U.S. — Indiana, U.S.
Indon. — Indonesia
I. of Man — Isle of Man
Ire. — Ireland
is. — islands
Isr. — Israel
Isr. Occ. — Israeli Occupied Territories
Jam. — Jamaica
Jord. — Jordan
Kir. — Kiribati

Ks., U.S. — Kansas, U.S.
Kuw. — Kuwait
Ky., U.S. — Kentucky, U.S.
l. — lake, pond
La., U.S. — Louisiana, U.S.
Leb. — Lebanon
Leso. — Lesotho
Lib. — Liberia
Liech. — Liechtenstein
Lux. — Luxembourg
Ma., U.S. — Massachusetts, U.S.
Madag. — Madagascar
Malay. — Malaysia
Mald. — Maldives
Man. — Manitoba, Can.
Marsh. Is. — Marshall Islands
Mart. — Martinique
Maur. — Mauritania
May. — Mayotte
Md., U.S. — Maryland, U.S.
Me., U.S. — Maine, U.S.
Mex. — Mexico
Mi., U.S. — Michigan, U.S.
Micron. — Federated States of Micronesia
Mid. Is. — Midway Islands
mil. — military installation
Mn., U.S. — Minnesota, U.S.
Mo., U.S. — Missouri, U.S.
Mon. — Monaco
Mong. — Mongolia
Monts. — Montserrat
Mor. — Morocco
Moz. — Mozambique
Mrts. — Mauritius
Ms., U.S. — Mississippi, U.S.
Mt., U.S. — Montana, U.S.
mth. — river mouth or channel
mtn. — mountain
mts. — mountains
Mwi. — Malawi
N.A. — North America
N.B. — New Brunswick, Can.
N.C., U.S. — North Carolina, U.S.
N. Cal. — New Caledonia
N. Cyp. — North Cyprus
N.D., U.S. — North Dakota, U.S.
Ne., U.S. — Nebraska, U.S.
Neth. — Netherlands
Neth. Ant. — Netherlands Antilles
Newf. — Newfoundland, Can.
N.H., U.S. — New Hampshire, U.S.
Nic. — Nicaragua
Nig. — Nigeria
N. Ire., U.K. — Northern Ireland, U.K.
N.J., U.S. — New Jersey, U.S.
N. Kor. — North Korea
N.M., U.S. — New Mexico, U.S.
N. Mar. Is. — Northern Mariana Islands

Nmb. — Namibia
Nor. — Norway
Norf. I. — Norfolk Island
N.S. — Nova Scotia, Can.
Nv., U.S. — Nevada, U.S.
N.W. Ter. — Northwest Territories, Can.
N.Y., U.S. — New York, U.S.
N.Z. — New Zealand
Oc. — Oceania
Oh., U.S. — Ohio, U.S.
Ok., U.S. — Oklahoma, U.S.
Ont. — Ontario, Can.
Or., U.S. — Oregon, U.S.
Pa., U.S. — Pennsylvania, U.S.
Pak. — Pakistan
Pan. — Panama
Pap. N. Gui. — Papua New Guinea
Para. — Paraguay
P.E.I. — Prince Edward Island, Can.
pen. — peninsula
Phil. — Philippines
Pit. — Pitcairn
pl. — plain, flat
plat. — plateau, highland
Pol. — Poland
Port. — Portugal
P.R. — Puerto Rico
prov. — province, region
Que. — Quebec, Can.
reg. — physical region
res. — reservoir
Reu. — Reunion
rf. — reef, shoal
R.I., U.S. — Rhode Island, U.S.
Rom. — Romania
Rw. — Rwanda
S.A. — South America
S. Afr. — South Africa
Sask. — Saskatchewan, Can.
Sau. Ar. — Saudi Arabia
S.C., U.S. — South Carolina, U.S.
sci. — scientific station
Scot., U.K. — Scotland, U.K.
S.D., U.S. — South Dakota, U.S.
Sen. — Senegal
Sey. — Seychelles
Sing. — Singapore
S. Kor. — South Korea
S.L. — Sierra Leone
S. Mar. — San Marino
Sol. Is. — Solomon Islands
Som. — Somalia
Sov. Un. — Soviet Union
Sp. N. Afr. — Spanish North Africa
Sri L. — Sri Lanka
state — state, republic, canton
St. C.-N. — St. Christopher-Nevis
St. Hel. — St. Helena

St. Luc. — St. Lucia
stm. — stream (river, creek)
S. Tom./P. — Sao Tome and Principe
St. P./M. — St. Pierre and Miquelon
strt. — strait, channel, sound
St. Vin. — St. Vincent and the Grenadines
Sud. — Sudan
Sur. — Suriname
sw. — swamp, marsh
Swaz. — Swaziland
Swe. — Sweden
Switz. — Switzerland
Tai. — Taiwan
Tan. — Tanzania
T./C. Is. — Turks and Caicos Islands
ter. — territory
Thai. — Thailand
Tn., U.S. — Tennessee, U.S.
Tok. — Tokelau
Trin. — Trinidad and Tobago
T.T.P.I. — Trust Territory of the Pacific Islands
Tun. — Tunisia
Tur. — Turkey
Tx., U.S. — Texas, U.S.
U.A.E. — United Arab Emirates
Ug. — Uganda
U.K. — United Kingdom
Ur. — Uruguay
U.S. — United States
Ut., U.S. — Utah, U.S.
Va., U.S. — Virginia, U.S.
val. — valley, watercourse
Vat. — Vatican City
Ven. — Venezuela
V.I., Br. — Virgin Islands, British
Viet. — Vietnam
V.I.U.S. — Virgin Islands (U.S.)
vol. — volcano
Vt., U.S. — Vermont, U.S.
Wa., U.S. — Washington, U.S.
Wal./F. — Wallis and Futuna
W. Ger. — Federal Republic of Germany
Wi., U.S. — Wisconsin, U.S.
W. Sah. — Western Sahara
W. Sam. — Western Samoa
wtfl. — waterfall
W.V., U.S. — West Virginia, U.S.
Wy., U.S. — Wyoming, U.S.
Yugo. — Yugoslavia
Yukon — Yukon Territory, Can.
Zam. — Zambia
Zimb. — Zimbabwe

INDEX

A

Name	Map Ref.	Page

Name	Ref.	Page
Aachen, W. Ger.	C3	18
Aalen, W. Ger.	D5	18
A'alī an Nīl (Upper Nile), prov., Sud.	D3	47
Aalsmeer, Neth.	B4	17
Aalst (Alost), Bel.	B6	17
Aalten, Neth.	C6	17
Äänekoski, Fin.	F11	14
Aarau, Switz.	E4	18
Aare, stm., Switz.	E3	18
Aargau, state, Switz.	E4	18
Aaronsburg, Pa., U.S.	E7	115
Aarschot, Bel.	D4	17
Aba, China	E5	31
Aba, Nig.	E6	45
Aba, Zaire	A5	48
Abacaxis, stm., Braz.	C3	59
Abādān, Iran	B4	38
Ābādeh, Iran	F6	39
Abadla, Alg.	C4	44
Abaeté, Braz.	C5	59
Abaetetuba, Braz.	C7	32
Abagnar Qi, China	C6	32
Abag Qi, China	E4	55
Abaí, Para.	F6	121
Abajo Peak, mtn., Ut., U.S.	E6	45
Abakaliki, Nig.	D12	29
Abakan, Sov. Un.	B2	48
Abala, Congo	D5	45
Abala, Niger	D3	58
Abancay, Peru	B4	78
Abanda, Al., U.S.	C5	22
Abanilla, Spain	B3	23
Abano Terme, Italy	D6	43
Abar Kūh, Iran	F6	39
'Abasān, Isr. Occ.	E4	41
Abashiri, Japan	C13	31
Abau, Pap. N. Gui.	m12	50
Abaya, Lake, l., Eth.	D4	47
Abbaye, Point, c., Mi., U.S.	B2	99
Abbeville, Fr.	B4	16
Abbeville, Al., U.S.	D4	78
Abbeville, Ga., U.S.	E3	87
Abbeville, La., U.S.	E3	95
Abbeville, Ms., U.S.	A4	101
Abbeville, S.C., U.S.	C3	117
Abbeville, co., S.C., U.S.	C2	117
Abbey, Sask.	G1	75
Abbeydorney, Ire.	E2	11
Abbeyfeale, Ire.	E2	11
Abbeyleix, Ire.	E4	11
Abbiategrasso, Italy	B2	23
Abbotsford, B.C.	f13	69
Abbotsford, Wi., U.S.	D3	126
Abbott, Ar., U.S.	B1	81
Abbott Butte, mtn., Or., U.S.	E4	114
Abbott Run, stm., U.S.	B4	116
Abbott Run Valley, R.I., U.S.	B4	116
Abbottsburg, N.C., U.S.	C4	110
Abbottstown, Pa., U.S.	G7	115
Abbot Village, Me., U.S.	C3	96
Abbyville, Ks., U.S.	E5	93
'Abd al Kūrī, i., Yemen	D5	38
Abdulino, Sov. Un.	E19	8
Abe, Lake, l., Afr.	C5	47
Abéché, Chad	C4	46
Abee, Alta.	B4	68
Abejorral, Col.	B2	60
Abengourou, I.C.	E4	45
Åbenrå, Den.	C3	15
Abeokuta, Nig.	E5	45
Aberaeron, Wales, U.K.	B3	12
Aberchirder, Scot., U.K.	C6	13
Abercorn, Que.	D5	74
Abercrombie, N.D., U.S.	C9	111
Aberdare, Wales, U.K.	E5	10
Aberdaron, Wales, U.K.	B3	12
Aberdeen, Sask.	E2	75
Aberdeen, S. Afr.	D3	49
Aberdeen, Scot., U.K.	B5	10
Aberdeen, Id., U.S.	G6	89
Aberdeen, In., U.S.	G8	91
Aberdeen, Ky., U.S.	C3	94
Aberdeen, Md., U.S.	A5	97
Aberdeen, Ms., U.S.	B5	101
Aberdeen, N.C., U.S.	B3	110
Aberdeen, Oh., U.S.	D2	112
Aberdeen, S.D., U.S.	B7	118
Aberdeen, Wa., U.S.	C2	124
Aberdeen Lake, l., N.W. Ter.	D13	66
Aberdeen Proving Ground, mil., Md., U.S.	A5	97
Aberdeen Township, N.J., U.S.	*C4	107
Aberdyfi, Wales, U.K.	B3	12
Aberfeldy, Scot., U.K.	B5	10
Aberfoyle, Scot., U.K.	D4	13
Abergavenny, Wales, U.K.	E5	10
Abernant, Al., U.S.	B2	78
Abernathy, Tx., U.S.	C2	120
Abernethy, Sask.	G4	75
Abert, Lake, l., Or., U.S.	E6	114
Abert Rim, clf., Or., U.S.	E6	114
Aberystwyth, Wales, U.K.	D4	10
Abhā, Sau. Ar.	D4	38
Abhar, Iran	E4	38
Abidjan, I.C.	E4	45
Abie, Ne., U.S.	C9	104
Abilene, Ks., U.S.	D6	93
Abilene, Tx., U.S.	C3	120
Abingdon, Eng., U.K.	C6	12
Abingdon, Il., U.S.	C3	90
Abingdon, Md., U.S.	B5	97
Abingdon, Va., U.S.	f10	123
Abington, Ct., U.S.	B7	84
Abington, Ma., U.S.	B6	98
Abington [Township], Pa., U.S.	o21	115
Abiquiu, N.M., U.S.	A3	108
Abisko, Swe.	C8	14
Abita Springs, La., U.S.	D5	95
Abitibi, stm., Ont.	o19	73
Abitibi, Lake, l., Ont.	G16	66
Ablon, Fr.	h10	16
Abloviak Fiord, Que.	f8	72
Aboisso, I.C.	E4	45
Abomey, Benin	E5	45
Abong Mbang, Cam.	E2	46
Abony, Hung.	B5	24
Abou Deïa, Chad	C3	46
Aboyne, Scot., U.K.	C6	13
Abraham Lake, res., Alta.	C2	68
Abraham Lincoln Birthplace National Historic Site, hist., Ky., U.S.	C4	94
Abrams, Wi., U.S.	D5	126
Abrantes, Port.	C1	22
Ábrego, Col.	B3	60
Abreojos, Punta, c., Mex.	B2	63
Abruzzi, prov., Italy	C4	23
Absaraka, N.D., U.S.	C8	111
Absarokee, Mt., U.S.	E7	103
Absaroka Range, mts., U.S.	F7	127
Absecon, N.J., U.S.	E4	107
Absecon Inlet, b., N.J., U.S.	E4	107
Abū 'Alī, i., Sau. Ar.	H4	39
Abu Dhabi (Abū Ẓaby), U.A.E.	C5	38
Abū Dīs, Isr. Occ.	h12	41
Abū Ḥadd, Bi'r, well, Eg.	E6	43
Abū Ḥamad, Sud.	B3	47
Abū Ḥammād al Maḥaṭṭah, Eg.	D3	41
Abū Ḥummuṣ, Eg.	C2	41
Abuja, Nig.	E6	45
Abū Kabīr, Eg.	D3	41
Abū Kamāl, Syria	B4	38
Abu Kershola, Sud.	C3	47
Abū Khawf, Mushāsh, well, Eg.	E6	41
Abūkshāh, Eg.	E2	41
Abumombazi, Zaire	A3	48
Abū Mūsā, i., U.A.E.	I7	39
Abunã, Braz.	A2	55
Abuná (Abunã), stm., S.A.	A2	55
Abuná (Abunã), stm., S.A.	A2	55
Abū Qīr, Eg.	C2	41
Abū Qīr Bay, b., Eg.	C2	41
Abū Qurqāṣ, Eg.	I8	40
Abū Road, India	E4	37
Abū Shajarah, Ra's, c., Sud.	A4	47
Abu Simbel (Abū Sunbul), hist., Eg.	E6	43
Abū Sufyān, 'Idd, well, Sud.	B2	47
Abū Ṭabarī, well, Sud.	B2	47
Abū 'Urūq, well, Sud.	B3	47
Abū Zanīmah, Eg.	D6	43
Åby (part of Norrköping), Swe.	u34	14
Åbybro, Den.	A3	15
Abyei, Sud.	D2	47
Abyssinia see Ethiopia, ctry., Afr.	D4	47
Academia, Oh., U.S.	B3	112
Academy, S.D., U.S.	D6	118
Acadia, co., La., U.S.	D3	95
Acadia National Park, Me., U.S.	D4	96
Acadia Valley, Alta.	D5	68
Acaituba, Braz.	B2	59
Acajutla, El Sal.	D3	62
Acámbaro, Mex.	C4	63
Acaponeta, Mex.	C3	63
Acapulco [de Juárez], Mex.	B3	59
Acarai Mountains, mts., S.A.	B3	59
Acaraú, Braz.	B2	57
Acaray, stm., Para.	E5	55
Acari, Braz.	h5	57
Acarí, Peru	E3	58
Acarigua, Ven.	B4	60
Acatlán [de Osorio], Mex.	D5	63
Acayucan, Mex.	D6	63
Accident, Md., U.S.	k12	97
Accomac, Va., U.S.	C7	123
Accomack, co., Va., U.S.	C7	123
Accord, N.Y., U.S.	D6	109
Accoville, W.V., U.S.	D3	125
Accra, Ghana	E4	45
Accrington, Eng., U.K.	A5	12
Ace, Tx., U.S.	D5	120
Aceguá, Braz.	B2	56
Acequia, Id., U.S.	G5	89
Achacachi, Bol.	C2	55
Achalpur, India	C6	54
Achao, Chile	E1	56
Achar, Ur.	D3	13
Acharacle, Scot., U.K.	B10	31
Achenkirch, Aus.	B7	20
Achen Lake, l., Aus.	B7	20
Achern, W. Ger.	E3	19
Achicourt, Fr.	C3	16
Achille, Ok., U.S.	D5	113
Achill Head, c., Ire.	D1	11
Achill Island, i., Ire.	D1	11
Achill Sound, b., Ire.	D1	11
Achinsk, Sov. Un.	D12	29
Achiras, Arg.	A4	54
Achisay, Sov. Un.	E7	28
Achtubinsk, Sov. Un.	D3	28
Acipayam, Tur.	D7	25
Acireale, Italy	F5	23
Ackerly, Tx., U.S.	C2	120
Ackerman, Ms., U.S.	B4	101
Ackley, Ia., U.S.	B4	92
Acklins Island, i., Bah.	C5	108
Acmar, Al., U.S.	B3	78
Acme, Alta.	D4	68
Acme, La., U.S.	C4	95
Acme, Mi., U.S.	D5	99
Acme, Wa., U.S.	A3	124
Acme, W.V., U.S.	m13	125
Acme, Wy., U.S.	B6	127
Acobamba, Peru	D3	58
Acoma Indian Reservation, N.M., U.S.	C2	108
Acomayo, Peru	D3	58
Aconcagua, Cerro, mtn., Arg.	A3	54
Acopiara, Braz.	B1	56
Acorizal, Braz.	B1	56
Acosta, Pa., U.S.	F3	115
Acoyapa, Nic.	E4	62
Acquarossa, Switz.	D6	21
Acqui [Terme], Italy	B2	23
Acre, state, Braz.	C4	58
Acre, stm., S.A.	C4	58
Acree, Ga., U.S.	E2	87
Actinolite, Ont.	C7	73
Acton, Ont.	D4	73
Acton, Ca., U.S.	E4	82
Acton, Me., U.S.	E2	96
Acton, Ma., U.S.	B5	98
Acton Vale, Que.	D5	74
Actopan, Mex.	C4	63
Açu, Braz.	B1	57
Acushnet, Ma., U.S.	C6	98
Acworth, Ga., U.S.	B2	87
Acworth, N.H., U.S.	D2	106
Ada, Ghana	E5	45
Ada, Yugo.	C5	24
Ada, co., Id., U.S.	F2	89
Ada, Mount, mtn., Ak., U.S.	m22	79
Adair, Il., U.S.	C3	90
Adair, Ia., U.S.	C3	92
Adair, Ok., U.S.	A6	113
Adair, co., Ia., U.S.	C3	92
Adair, co., Ky., U.S.	C4	94
Adair, co., Mo., U.S.	A5	102
Adair, co., Ok., U.S.	B7	113
Adairsville, Ga., U.S.	B2	87
Adairville, Ky., U.S.	D3	94
Adak Island, i., Ak., U.S.	E4	79
Adak Naval Station, mil., Ak., U.S.	E4	79
Adamant, Vt., U.S.	C3	122
Adamantina, Braz.	C2	56
Adamaoua, mts., Afr.	D2	46
Adam Island, i., Md., U.S.	D5	97
Adami Tulu, Eth.	D4	47
Adams, Ky., U.S.	F6	91
Adams, Ma., U.S.	A1	98
Adams, Mn., U.S.	G6	100
Adams, Ne., U.S.	D9	104
Adams, N.Y., U.S.	B4	109
Adams, N.D., U.S.	A7	111
Adams, Ok., U.S.	e9	113
Adams, Or., U.S.	B8	114
Adams, Tn., U.S.	A4	119
Adams, Wi., U.S.	E4	126
Adams, co., Co., U.S.	B6	83
Adams, co., Id., U.S.	E2	89
Adams, co., Il., U.S.	D2	90
Adams, co., In., U.S.	C8	91
Adams, co., Ia., U.S.	C3	92
Adams, co., Ms., U.S.	D2	101
Adams, co., Ne., U.S.	D7	104
Adams, co., N.D., U.S.	C3	111
Adams, co., Oh., U.S.	D2	112
Adams, co., Pa., U.S.	G7	115
Adams, co., Wa., U.S.	B7	124
Adams, co., Wi., U.S.	D4	126
Adams, Mount, mtn., N.H., U.S.	B4	106
Adams, Mount, mtn., Wa., U.S.	C4	124
Adams, Mount, mtn., Vt., U.S.	C3	122
Adams Bridge, rf., Asia	G6	36
Adams Center, N.Y., U.S.	B5	109
Adams City, Co., U.S.	*B6	83
Adams Lake, l., B.C.	D8	69
Adams Mountain, mtn., Ma., U.S.	A2	98
Adams Point, c., Mi., U.S.	C7	99
Adams Run, S.C., U.S.	k11	117
Adamstown, N.J., U.S.	C4	107
Adamstown, Md., U.S.	B3	97
Adamstown, Pa., U.S.	F9	115
Adamsville, Que.	D5	74
Adamsville, Al., U.S.	f7	78
Adamsville, Pa., U.S.	D1	115
Adamsville, R.I., U.S.	E6	116
Adamsville, Tn., U.S.	B3	119
Adamsville, Tx., U.S.	D3	120
Adamsville Brook, stm., R.I., U.S.	E6	116
Adana, Tur.	D10	25
Adanac, Sask.	E1	75
Adapazarı, Tur.	B4	47
Adarama, Sud.	E3	11
Adare, Ire.	B30	7
Adare, Cape, c., Ant.	A5	12
Adavale, Austl.	B5	51
Adda, stm., Italy	B2	23
Ad Dab'ah, Eg.	C5	43
Ad Dabbah, Sud.	C8	40
Ad Dahnā', des., Sau. Ar.	C4	38
Ad Dāmir, Sud.	C2	54
Ad Dammām, Sau. Ar.	E1	56
Ad Dibdibah, pl., Sau. Ar.	D3	13
Addicks Barker, Tx., U.S.	r14	120
Addieville, Il., U.S.	E4	90
Ad Dilinjāt, Eg.	D2	41
Addington, Ok., U.S.	C4	113
Addis, La., U.S.	D4	95
Addis Ababa (Addis Abeba), Eth.	D4	47
Addison, Al., U.S.	A2	78
Addison, Ct., U.S.	C5	84
Addison, Il., U.S.	k8	90
Addison, Me., U.S.	D5	96
Addison, N.Y., U.S.	C3	109
Addison, Pa., U.S.	G3	115
Addison, Tx., U.S.	*n10	120
Addison, Vt., U.S.	C2	122
Addison, co., Vt., U.S.	C2	122
Ad Dīwānīyah, Iraq	B4	38
Ad Du'ayn, Sud.	C2	47
Ad Duwaym, Sud.	C3	47
Ad Duyūk, Isr. Occ.	h12	41
Addy, Wa., U.S.	A8	124
Addyston, Oh., U.S.	o12	112
Adel, Ga., U.S.	E3	87
Adel, Ia., U.S.	C3	92
Adel, Or., U.S.	E7	114
Adelaide, Austl.	F6	50
Adelaide, Bah.	m17	64
Adelaide Island, i., Ant.	C6	7
Adelanto, Ca., U.S.	E5	82
Adelboden, Switz.	C26	7
Adell, Wi., U.S.	*B4	97
Adelphi, Md., U.S.	C3	112
Adelphi, Oh., U.S.	C3	112
Aden (Adan), Yemen	D3	38
Aden, Gulf of, b.	B5	112
Adena, Oh., U.S.	C1	19
Adenau, W. Ger.	E6	87
Adgateville, Ga., U.S.	B2	78
Adi, i., Indon.	F8	34
Adieu, Cape, c., Austl.	F5	50
Adige, stm., Italy	A4	81
Adigrat, Eth.	H7	37
Adilābād, India	B3	82
Adin, Ca., U.S.	C8	20
Adirondack Mountains, mts., N.Y., U.S.	A6	109
Adıyaman, Tur.	C12	40
Adjud, Rom.	B8	24
Adjuntas, P.R.	g10	112
Adlavik Islands, is., Newf.	B6	21
Adliswil, Switz.	E5	101
Admaston, Ont.	H1	75
Admiral, Sask.	H1	75
Admirals Beach, Newf.	E5	72
Admiralty Bay, b., Ak., U.S.	A9	79
Admiralty Gulf, b., Austl.	B4	50
Admiralty Inlet, b., N.W. Ter.	B15	66
Admiralty Inlet, b., Wa., U.S.	m22	79
Admiralty Islands, is., Pap. N. Gui.	h12	50
Admiralty Mountains, mts., Ant.	B29	7
Admire, Ks., U.S.	D7	93
Adobe Acres, N.M., U.S.	B3	108
Adobe Creek, stm., Co., U.S.	C7	83
Adobe Creek Reservoir, res., Co., U.S.	C7	83
Ado-Ekiti, Nig.	*E6	45
Adok, Sud.	D3	47
Adolphus, Ky., U.S.	D3	94
Adona, Ar., U.S.	B3	81
Ādoni, India	*E6	36
Adony, Hung.	B4	24
Adour, stm., Fr.	F3	16
Adowa see Adwa, Eth.	C4	47
Adra, Spain	D4	22
Adrano, Italy	F5	23
Adrar, Alg.	D4	44
Adrar, reg., Maur.	B2	45
Adré, Chad	C4	46
Adri, Libya	D2	43
Adria, Italy	B4	23
Adrian, Ga., U.S.	D4	87
Adrian, Mi., U.S.	G6	99
Adrian, Mn., U.S.	G3	100
Adrian, Mo., U.S.	C3	102
Adrian, N.D., U.S.	C7	111
Adrian, Or., U.S.	D9	114
Adrian, Tx., U.S.	B1	120
Adrian, W.V., U.S.	C4	125
Adriatic Sea, Eur.	G12	8
Adrigole, Ire.	F2	11
Advance, In., U.S.	D5	91
Advance, Mo., U.S.	D8	102
Advocate Harbour, N.S.	D5	71
Adwa (Adowa), Eth.	C4	47
Adzopé, I.C.	E4	45
Æbelø, i., Den.	C4	15
Aegean Sea	C5	40
Aegeri, Lake, l., Switz.	B4	25
Aegina see Aíyina, i., Grc.	D4	25
Ærø, i., Den.	D4	15
Ærøskøbing, Den.	D4	15
Aesch, Switz.	B4	21
Aetna, Ks., U.S.	E4	68
Aetna, Tn., U.S.	B4	119
Afars and Issas see Djibouti, ctry., Afr.	C5	47
Affoltern am Albis, Switz.	B5	21
Afft on, Mo., U.S.	*f13	102
Afghanistan, ctry., Asia	B3	36
Afgooye, Som.	E6	47
Afif, Sau. Ar.	C3	38
Afikpo, Nig.	E6	45
Aflou, Alg.	C5	44
Afmadow, Som.	E5	47
Afognak Island, i., Ak., U.S.	D9	79
Afono Bay, b., Am. Sam.	G13	52
Afonso Cláudio, Braz.	C4	56
Africa, cont.	*A4	85
Afton, De., U.S.	C3	92
Afton, Ia., U.S.	C6	99
Afton, Mi., U.S.	F6	100
Afton, Mn., U.S.	C5	109
Afton, N.Y., U.S.	A7	113
Afton, Ok., U.S.	C11	119
Afton, Tn., U.S.	C2	120
Afton, Tx., U.S.	D2	127
Afton, Wy., U.S.	D4	44
Afula, Isr.	B7	41
Afyon, Tur.	C8	40
Agadem, Niger	C7	45
Agadez, Niger	C6	45
Agadir, Mor.	C3	44
Agana, Guam	L9	52
Agana Bay, b., Guam	L9	52
Agana Heights, Guam	*L9	52
Agana Naval Air Station, mil., Guam	L10	52
Agar, India	F5	37
Agar, S.D., U.S.	C5	118
Agartala, India	D9	36
Agassiz, B.C.	E7	69
Agassiz, Cape, c., Ant.	C6	7
Agat, Guam	M9	52
Agat Bay, b., Guam	M9	52
Agate, N.D., U.S.	B7	83
Agate, N.D., U.S.	A6	111
Agate Beach, Or., U.S.	C2	114
Agate Fossil Beds National Monument, Ne., U.S.	B2	104
Agattu Island, i., Ak., U.S.	E2	79
Agawam, Ok., U.S.	C3	98
Agawam, Mt., U.S.	C4	113
Agboville, I.C.	E4	45
Agde, Fr.	F5	16
Agematsu, Japan	*E5	45
Agen, Fr.	n16	33
Agency, Ia., U.S.	E4	16
Agency, Mo., U.S.	D5	92
Agenda, Ks., U.S.	B3	102
Ageo, Japan	C6	93
Agerola, Italy	*I9	33
Agersø, i., Den.	B4	20
Agfayan Bay, b., Guam	C5	15
Aghleam, Ire.	M10	52
Aghā Jārī, Iran	C1	11
Agincourt (part of Scarborough), Ont.	k15	73
Agingan, Puntan, c., N. Mar. Is.	D7	52
Aginskoye, Sov. Un.	A7	31
Agira, Italy	F5	23
Agno, Phil.	n12	34
Agno, stm., Phil.	o13	34
Agnone, Italy	D5	23
Agogna, stm., Italy	A4	81
Agogo, Ghana	n13	34
Agordo, Italy	C6	20
Agoura Hills, Ca., U.S.	m11	82
Agra, India	A6	109
Agra, Ks., U.S.	C6	36
Agra, Ok., U.S.	B5	113
Agri, stm., Italy	F8	34
Agrigento, Italy	F4	23
Agrínion, Grc.	C3	40
Agripoli, Italy	D19	8
Agryz, Sov. Un.	B4	56
Água Boa, Braz.	B1	65
Aguada, P.R.	B2	62
Aguadas, Col.	G11	64
Aguadilla, P.R.	B1	65
Aguadilla, Bahía de, b., P.R.	B1	65
Aguadulce, Pan.	F7	62
Agua Dulce Mountains, mts., Az., U.S.	E2	80
Agua Fria, N.M., U.S.	B3	108
Agua Fria, stm., Az., U.S.	D3	80
Aguaí, Braz.	m8	57
Aguán, stm., Hond.	h9	72
Aguanish, Que.	F3	120
Aguapey, stm., Arg.	k6	57
Agua Preta, Braz.	A3	63
Agua Prieta, Mex.	D3	55
Aguaray, Arg.	B2	58
Aguarico, stm., S.A.	C4	63
Aguascalientes, Mex.	C3	56
Aguascalientes, state, Mex.	B4	56
Agudos, Braz.	B1	22
Águeda, Port.	B2	22
Águeda, stm., Eur.	C5	45
Aguelhok, Mali	B3	45
Aguéraktem, well, Mali	D2	80
Aguilar, Spain	D6	83
Aguilar, Co., U.S.	D5	22
Aguilas, Spain	D4	63
Aguililla, Mex.	A3	60
Aguja, Cabo de la, c., Col.	C1	58
Aguja, Punta, c., Peru	D3	49
Agulhas, Cape, c., S. Afr.	h5	56
Agulhas Negras, Pico das, mtn., Braz.	D7	34
Ahaggar, mts., Alg.	E6	44
Ahaggar, Tassili ta-n-, plat., Alg.	E6	44
Ahar, Iran	B3	39
Ahascragh, Ire.	D3	11
Ahaus, W. Ger.	A2	19
Ahlen, W. Ger.	C6	25
Ahlhorn, W. Ger.	F2	15
Ahmadābād (Ahmedabad), India	D5	36
Ahmadnagar, India	C5	36
Ahmadpur East, Pak.	E4	44
Ahmic Lake, l., Ont.	B5	73
Ahoada, Nig.	B3	63
Ahome, Mex.	C5	44
Ahon, Tarso, mtn., Chad	A3	46
Ahoskie, N.C., U.S.	A6	110
Ahousat, B.C.	E4	69
Ahrensbök, W. Ger.	D4	15
Ahrweiler, W. Ger.	C3	18
Ahtanum Creek, stm., Wa., U.S.	C5	124
Ahuacatlán, Mex.	m11	63
Ahuachapán, El Sal.	E7	63
Ahualulco de Mercado, Mex.	m11	63
Ahwahnee, Ca., U.S.	D4	82
Ahvāz (Nāsiri), Iran	B4	38
Ahvenanmaa (Åland), is., Fin.	G9	14
Ahwar, Yemen	D4	38
Aialik, Cape, c., Ak., U.S.	D10	79
Aibonito, P.R.	B3	65
Aichach, W. Ger.	E6	19
Aiea, Hi., U.S.	B4	88
Aiken, S.C., U.S.	D4	117
Aiken, co., S.C., U.S.	D4	117
Aikens Lake, l., Man.	D4	70
Ailey, Ga., U.S.	D4	87
Ailsa Craig, Ont.	D3	73
Aimorés, Braz.	C2	59
Ain, dept., Fr.	C1	20
Aïn ben Tili, Maur.	A3	45
Aïn Beïda, Alg.	B6	44
Ainslie Lake, l., N.S.	C6	71
Ainsworth, Ne., U.S.	B6	104
Aïn Témouchent, Alg.	B4	44
Aïn Wessara, Alg.	B5	44
Aipe, Col.	C2	60
Aiquile, Bol.	C6	45
Aïr, mts., Niger	K7	35
Airabu, i., Indon.	B2	22
Airaines, Fr.	D3	68
Airdrie, Alta.	E5	13
Airdrie, Scot., U.K.	D5	92
Aire, stm., Eng., U.K.	A6	12
Aire-sur-l'Adour, Fr.	F3	16
Aire [-sur-la-Lys], Fr.	B5	16
Air Force Island, i., N.W. Ter.	C18	66
Airline, Ga., U.S.	B3	87
Air Park West, Ne., U.S.	D9	104
Aisch, stm., W. Ger.	F4	39
Aisén del General Carlos Ibáñez del Campo, prov., Chile	D7	52
Aishihik Lake, l., Yukon	D5	66
Aisne, dept., Fr.	C6	16
Aisne, stm., Fr.	C4	16
Aïssa, Djebel, mtn., Alg.	h11	50
Aitape, Pap. N. Gui.	D5	100
Aitkin, Mn., U.S.	D5	100
Aitkin, co., Mn., U.S.	G7	101
Aitolikón, Grc.	B6	24
Aiud, Rom.	m15	63
Aix, Mount, mtn., Wa., U.S.	C4	124
Aix-en-Provence, Fr.	F6	16
Aix-les-Bains, Fr.	E6	16
Aíyina (Aegina), i., Grc.	C4	25
Aíyion, Grc.	F4	23
Aizu-takada, Japan	H9	33
Aizu-wakamatsu, Japan	H9	33
Ajaccio, Fr.	D2	23
Ajaccio, Gulf of, b., Fr.	D2	23
Ajax, Ont.	D6	73
Ajayan Bay, b., Guam	M9	52
Ajdābiyā, Libya	C4	43
Ajjer, Tassili-n-, plat., Alg.	D6	44
'Ajlūn, Jord.	B7	41
Ajmer, India	C5	36
Ajo, Az., U.S.	E3	80
Ajo, Az., U.S.	E3	41
'Ajramīyah, Bi'r al, well, Eg.	E3	41
Akaishi-sammyaku, mts., Japan	n17	33
Akaki Beseka, Eth.	*D4	47
Akalkot, India	I6	37
Akaroa, N.Z.	O14	51
'Akasha East, Sud.	A3	47
Akashi, Japan	I7	33
Akaska, S.D., U.S.	B5	118
Akbulak, Sov. Un.	E20	8
Akçaabat, Tur.	B12	40
Akçadağ, Tur.	C11	40
Ak-Chin Indian Reservation, Az., U.S.	E3	80
Akdağmadeni, Tur.	C10	40
Akechi, Japan	n16	33
Akeld, Mn., U.S.	C4	100
Aken, E. Ger.	B7	19
Akers, La., U.S.	D5	95
Aketi, Zaire	A3	48
Akhaltsikhe, Sov. Un.	B14	40
Akharnaí, Grc.	g11	25
Akhdar, Al Jabal al, mts., Libya	C4	43
Akhdar, Al Jabal al, mts., Oman	C5	38
Akhelóös, stm., Grc.	C3	25
Akhiok, Ak., U.S.	D9	79
Akhisar, Tur.	C6	40
Akhmīm, Eg.	C3	38
Akhtopol, Bul.	E6	44
Akhtyrka, Sov. Un.	F10	27
Aki, Japan	J6	33
Akiachak, Ak., U.S.	C7	79
Akimiski Island, i., N.W. Ter.	F16	66
Akita, Japan	D13	31
Akjoujt, Maur.	C2	45
Akkeshi, Japan	E12	33
'Akko, Isr.	F10	40
Akobo, Sud.	D3	47
Akobo, stm., Afr.	D3	47
Akola, India	D6	36
Akonolinga, Cam.	E2	46
Akordat, Eth.	B4	47
Akosombo Dam, Ghana	E5	45
Akpatok Island, i., N.W. Ter.	D19	66
Akra, N.D., U.S.	A8	111
Akrahamn, Grc.	g10	25
Akranes, Ice.	n21	14
Akrítas, Akra, c., Grc.	D3	40
Akron, Al., U.S.	C2	78
Akron, Co., U.S.	A7	83
Akron, In., U.S.	B5	91
Akron, Mi., U.S.	E7	99
Akron, N.Y., U.S.	B2	109
Akron, Oh., U.S.	A4	112
Akron, Pa., U.S.	F9	115
Aksaray, Tur.	C10	40
Akşehir, Tur.	C8	40
Akşehir, Lake, l., Tur.	C8	40
Akseki, Tur.	D8	40
Aksenovo-Zilovskoye, Sov. Un.	D14	29
Aksha, Sov. Un.	A7	31
Akshimrau, Sov. Un.	E4	28
Aksoran, Mount, mtn., Sov. Un.	F24	8
Aksu, China	E11	29
Aksum, Eth.	C4	47
Aktogay, Sov. Un.	D9	28
Aktumsyk, Sov. Un.	D8	29
Aktyubinsk, Sov. Un.	D8	29
Akulivik, Que.	f11	74
Akure, Nig.	E6	45
Akureyri, Ice.	n23	14
Akuseki Island, i., Japan	L4	33
Akutan, Ak., U.S.	D6	79
Akyab see Sittwe, Burma	D9	36
Alabama, state, U.S.	C3	78
Alabama, stm., Al., U.S.	D2	78
Alabama Port, Al., U.S.	E1	78
Alabaster, Al., U.S.	B3	78
Alabaster, Mi., U.S.	D7	99
Alabat, i., Phil.	o14	34
Al 'Abbāsīyah, Sud.	C3	47
Al Abyad, Libya	D2	43
Al Abyār, Libya	F3	40
Alachua, Fl., U.S.	C4	86
Alachua, co., Fl., U.S.	C4	86
Aladdin, Wy., U.S.	B8	127
Alagna [Valsesia], Italy	C3	23
Alagoa Grande, Braz.	C3	57
Alagoas, state, Braz.	C3	57
Alagoinhas, Braz.	C3	57
Alagón, Spain	B2	22
Alagón, stm., Spain	C2	22
Al 'Ajamīyīn, Eg.	D3	41
Al 'Ajrūd, well, Eg.	D6	41
Alajuela, C.R.	E5	63
Alajuela, Lago, res., Pan.	k11	62
Alakanuk, Ak., U.S.	C7	79
Alakol, Lake, l., Sov. Un.	D10	28
Alalakeiki Channel, strt., Hi., U.S.	C5	88
Al Alamayn, Eg.	B2	38
Alalaú, stm., Braz.	C2	59
Alamance, co., N.C., U.S.	A3	110
Alamance, N.C., U.S.	B3	110
'Alam ar Rūm, Ra's, c., Egypt	G6	40
Alameda, Sask.	H4	75
Alameda, Ca., U.S.	h8	82
Alameda, N.M., U.S.	B3	108
Alameda, co., Ca., U.S.	D3	82
Alameda Naval Air Station, mil., Ca., U.S.	h8	82
Alaminos, Phil.	n12	34
Al 'Āmirīyah, Eg.	G7	40
Alamito Creek, stm., Tx., U.S.	m15	120
Alamo, Mex.	*D2	82
Alamo, Ca., U.S.	D4	87
Alamo, Ga., U.S.	D4	87
Alamo, Nv., U.S.	F6	105
Alamo, N.D., U.S.	A2	111
Alamo, Tn., U.S.	B2	119
Alamo, Tx., U.S.	F3	120
Alamogordo, N.M., U.S.	E4	108
Alamogordo Dam, N.M., U.S.	C5	108
Alamo Heights, Tx., U.S.	E3	120

Name	Map Ref.	Page
Alamo Hueco Mountains, mts., N.M., U.S.	F1	108
Alamo Indian Reservation, N.M., U.S.	C2	108
Alamo Lake, res., Az., U.S.	C2	80
Alamos, Mex.	B3	63
Alamosa, Co., U.S.	D5	83
Alamosa, co., Co., U.S.	D5	83
Alamosa, stm., Co., U.S.	D4	83
Alamosa Creek, stm., N.M., U.S.	D2	108
Alamosa East, Co., U.S.	D5	83
Åland see Ahvenanmaa, is., Fin.	G9	14
Alanreed, Tx., U.S.	B2	120
Alanson, Mi., U.S.	C6	99
Alanya, Tur.	D9	40
Alaotra, Lac, l., Madag.	g9	49
Alapaha, Ga., U.S.	E3	87
Alapaha, stm., U.S.	E3	87
Alapayevsk, Sov. Un.	B6	28
Al 'Aqabah, Jord.	C3	38
Al 'Aqsa Mosque, Isr. Occ.	m14	41
Al 'Arīsh, Egypt	C6	43
Alasdair, Sgurr, mtn., Scot., U.K.	C2	13
Alaşehir, Tur.	C7	40
Alaska, state, U.S.	C9	79
Alaska, Gulf of, b., Ak., U.S.	D10	79
Alaska Peninsula, pen., Ak., U.S.	D8	79
Alaska Range, mts., Ak., U.S.	C9	79
Alassio, Italy	C2	23
Alatna, stm., Ak., U.S.	B9	79
Al 'Atrūn, Sud.	B2	47
Alatyr, Sov. Un.	D16	27
Alausí, Ec.	B2	58
Alava, Cape, c., Wa., U.S.	A1	124
Alaverdi, Sov. Un.	B15	40
Al 'Ayyāt, Egypt	E3	41
Al 'Ayzarīyah (Bethany), Isr.	h12	41
Al 'Azīzīyah, Libya	C2	43
Alb, stm., W. Ger.	A5	21
Alba, Italy	B2	23
Alba, Mi., U.S.	D6	99
Alba, Mo., U.S.	D3	102
Alba, Pa., U.S.	C8	115
Alba, Tx., U.S.	E5	120
Albacete, Spain	C5	22
Al Badārī, Egypt	D6	43
Alba de Tormes, Spain	B3	22
Ålbæk, Den.	A4	15
Ålbæk Bugt, b., Den.	A4	15
Al Bahnasā, Egypt	H8	40
Al Bahr al Abyad, prov., Sud.	C3	47
Al Bahr al Ahmar (Red Sea), prov., Sud.	B4	47
Alba Iulia, Rom.	B6	24
Al Bājūr, Egypt	D3	41
Albalate [del Arzobispo], Spain	B5	22
Al Ballah, Egypt	D4	41
Albanel, Lac, l., Que.	F18	66
Albani, Colli, hills, Italy	h9	23
Albania, ctry., Eur.	B2	40
Albano, Lake, l., Italy	h9	23
Albano Laziale, Italy	h9	23
Albany, Austl.	F2	50
Albany, N.S.	E4	71
Albany, P.E.I.	C6	71
Albany, Ca., U.S.	*h8	82
Albany, Ga., U.S.	E2	87
Albany, Il., U.S.	B3	90
Albany, In., U.S.	D7	91
Albany, Ky., U.S.	D4	94
Albany, La., U.S.	g10	95
Albany, Mn., U.S.	E4	100
Albany, Mo., U.S.	A3	102
Albany, N.H., U.S.	C4	106
Albany, N.Y., U.S.	C7	109
Albany, Oh., U.S.	C3	112
Albany, Ok., U.S.	D5	113
Albany, Or., U.S.	C3	114
Albany, Tx., U.S.	C3	120
Albany, Vt., U.S.	B4	122
Albany, Wi., U.S.	F4	126
Albany, co., N.Y., U.S.	C6	109
Albany, co., Wy., U.S.	E7	127
Albany, stm., Ont.	o18	73
Al Ba'kāt, Egypt	E2	43
Al Batānūn, Egypt	D2	41
Albatross Bay, b., Austl.	B7	50
Al Batrūn, Leb.	E10	40
Al Bawītī, Egypt	D5	43
Al Bayda, Libya	C4	43
Albee, S.D., U.S.	B9	118
Albemarle, N.C., U.S.	B2	110
Albemarle, co., Va., U.S.	C4	123
Albemarle, Punta, c., Ec.	f5	58
Albemarle Lake, l., Ms., U.S.	C2	101
Albemarle Sound, strt., N.C., U.S.	A6	110
Albenga, Italy	B2	23
Alberche, stm., Spain	B3	22
Ålberga (part of Eskilstuna), Swe.	u34	14
Albergaria-a-Velha, Port.	B1	22
Albersdorf, W. Ger.	D3	15
Albert, Fr.	B5	16
Albert, Ks., U.S.	D4	93
Albert, N.M., U.S.	B6	108
Albert, Ok., U.S.	B3	113
Albert, co., N.B.	D5	71
Albert, Lake, l., Afr.	A5	48
Albert, Al., U.S.	C4	78
Alberta, Mn., U.S.	E2	100
Alberta, prov., Can.	C4	69
Alberta, Mount, mtn., Alta.	C2	68
Albert Canyon, B.C.	D9	69
Albert City, Ia., U.S.	B3	92
Albert Edward, Mount, mtn., Pap. N. Gui.	k12	50
Albert Lea, Mn., U.S.	G5	100
Albert Markham, Mount, mtn., Ant.	A28	7
Albert Nile, stm., Ug.	A5	48
Alberton, P.E.I.	C5	71
Alberton, Mt., U.S.	C2	103
Albertson, N.Y., U.S.	k13	109
Albertville, Sask.	D3	75
Albertville, Al., U.S.	A3	78
Albertville, Fr.	E7	16
Albertville, Mn., U.S.	E5	100
Albeuve, Switz.	C3	21
Albi, Fr.	F5	16
Albia, Ia., U.S.	C5	92
Albin, Wy., U.S.	E8	127
Albina, Sur.	A4	59
Albino, Italy	E8	21
Albion, Id., U.S.	G5	89
Albion, Il., U.S.	E5	90
Albion, In., U.S.	B7	91
Albion, Ia., U.S.	B5	92
Albion, Me., U.S.	D3	96
Albion, Mi., U.S.	F6	99
Albion, Ne., U.S.	C7	104
Albion, N.Y., U.S.	B2	109
Albion, Pa., U.S.	C1	115
Albion, R.I., U.S.	B4	116
Albion, Wa., U.S.	C8	124
Albion, Wi., U.S.	F4	126
Alborán, i., Spain	E4	22
Ålborg, Den.	I3	14
Ålborg Bugt, b., Den.	B4	15
Alborn, Mn., U.S.	D6	100
Albox, Spain	D4	22
Albreda, B.C.	C8	69
Albrightsville, Pa., U.S.	D10	115
Albufeira, Port.	D1	22
Al Buhayrah, prov., Sud.	D2	47
Al Bu'ayrāt, Libya	C3	43
Albuñol, Spain	D4	22
Albuq'ah, Jord.	B7	41
Albuquerque, N.M., U.S.	B3	108
Al Buraymi, Oman	C5	38
Alburg, Vt., U.S.	B2	122
Alburnett, Ia., U.S.	B6	92
Alburquerque, Spain	C2	22
Alburtis, Pa., U.S.	F10	115
Albury, Austl.	G8	50
Al Buşayli, Egypt	C2	41
Alca, Peru	E3	58
Alcabideche, Port.	f9	22
Alcácer do Sal, Port.	C1	22
Alcalá de Chivert, Spain	B6	22
Alcalá [de Guadaira], Spain	D3	22
Alcalá de Henares, Spain	B4	22
Alcalá de los Gazules, Spain	D3	22
Alcalá la Real, Spain	D4	22
Alcalde, N.M., U.S.	A3	108
Alcaledíaz, Pan.	F8	62
Alcamo, Italy	F4	23
Alcanar, Spain	B6	22
Alcañiz, Spain	B5	22
Alcántara, Braz.	B2	57
Alcantarilla, Spain	D5	22
Alcaraz, Spain	C4	22
Alcaudete, Spain	D3	22
Alcázar de San Juan, Spain	C4	22
Alcester, S.D., U.S.	D9	118
Alcira, Spain	C5	22
Alco, Ar., U.S.	B3	81
Alco, La., U.S.	C2	95
Alcoa, Tn., U.S.	D10	119
Alcobendas, Spain	o17	22
Alcochete, Port.	f10	22
Alcolu, S.C., U.S.	D7	117
Alcomdale, Alta.	C4	68
Alcona, co., Mi., U.S.	D7	99
Alcora, Spain	B5	22
Alcorcón, Spain	p17	22
Alcorisa, Spain	B5	22
Alcorn, co., Ms., U.S.	A5	101
Alcovy, stm., Ga., U.S.	C3	87
Alcoy, Spain	C5	22
Alcoy, Nevado, mtn., Peru	D2	58
Aldama, Mex.	B3	63
Aldan, Sov. Un.	D15	29
Aldan, stm., Sov. Un.	C16	29
Aldan Plateau, plat., Sov. Un.	D15	29
Al Dār al Baydā', hist., Eg.	D3	41
Aldeburgh, Eng., U.K.	B12	12
Alden, Ia., U.S.	B4	92
Alden, Ks., U.S.	D5	93
Alden, Mi., U.S.	D5	99
Alden, Mn., U.S.	G5	100
Alden, N.Y., U.S.	C2	109
Alden, Pa., U.S.	D9	115
Alder, Mt., U.S.	E4	103
Alder, Ben, mtn., Scot., U.K.	D4	13
Alder Brook, stm., Vt., U.S.	B2	122
Alderney, i., Guernsey	F5	10
Aldershot, Eng., U.K.	E6	10
Alderson, W.V., U.S.	D4	125
Alderwood Manor, Wa., U.S.	*B3	124
Aldie, Va., U.S.	B5	123
Aldora, Ga., U.S.	C2	87
Aldrich, Al., U.S.	B3	78
Aldrich, Mn., U.S.	D4	100
Aledo, Il., U.S.	B3	90
Aledo, Tx., U.S.	C4	120
Aleg, Maur.	C2	45
Alegre, Braz.	C4	56
Alegrete, Braz.	D1	56
Alegros Mountain, mtn., N.M., U.S.	C2	108
Alejandro Selkirk, Isla, i., Chile	G2	53
Aleknagik, Ak., U.S.	D8	79
Aleksandriya, Sov. Un.	G9	27
Aleksandrov, Sov. Un.	C12	27
Aleksandrovskoye, Sov. Un.	A9	28
Aleksandrovsk [Sakhalinskiy], Sov. Un.	D17	29
Aleksandrów [Kujawski], Pol.	B5	26
Aleksandrów [Łódzki], Pol.	C5	26
Aleksin, Sov. Un.	D11	27
Aleksinac, Yugo.	D5	24
Alemania, Arg.	E2	55
Além Paraíba, Braz.	g6	56
Alençon, Fr.	C4	16
Alenquer, Braz.	C4	59
Alentejo, hist. reg., Port.	C2	22
Alenuihaha Channel, strt., Hi., U.S.	C5	88
Aleppo (Halab), Syria	B3	38
Aléria, Fr.	C2	23
Alert, N.W. Ter.	k39	66
Alert Bay, B.C.	D4	69
Alès, Fr.	E6	16
Alessandria, Italy	B3	23
Ålestrup, Den.	B3	15
Ålesund, Nor.	F5	14
Alet, Fr.	F5	16
Aleutian Islands, is., Ak., U.S.	E3	79
Aleutian Range, mts., Ak., U.S.	D8	79
Alex, Ok., U.S.	C4	113
Alexander, Man.	E1	70
Alexander, Ar., U.S.	C3	81
Alexander, Ga., U.S.	C5	87
Alexander, Ks., U.S.	D4	93
Alexander, Me., U.S.	C5	96
Alexander, N.Y., U.S.	C2	109
Alexander, N.C., U.S.	f10	110
Alexander, N.D., U.S.	B2	111
Alexander, W.V., U.S.	C4	125
Alexander, co., Il., U.S.	F4	90
Alexander, co., N.C., U.S.	B1	110
Alexander, stm., Isr.	f10	41
Alexander Archipelago, is., Ak., U.S.	D12	79
Alexander Bay, S. Afr.	C2	49
Alexander City, Al., U.S.	C4	78
Alexander Island, i., Ant.	B5	7
Alexander Mills, N.C., U.S.	B1	110
Alexandra, N.Z.	P12	51
Alexandretta, Gulf of, b., Tur.	D10	40
Alexandretta see İskenderun, Tur.	D11	40
Alexandria, B.C.	C6	69
Alexandria, Ont.	B10	73
Alexandria (Al Iskandarīyah), Eg.	B2	38
Alexandria, Rom.	B8	24
Alexandria, Al., U.S.	B4	78
Alexandria, In., U.S.	D6	91
Alexandria, Ky., U.S.	B5	94
Alexandria, La., U.S.	C3	95
Alexandria, Mn., U.S.	E3	100
Alexandria, Mo., U.S.	A6	102
Alexandria, Ne., U.S.	D8	104
Alexandria, N.H., U.S.	C3	106
Alexandria, Oh., U.S.	B3	112
Alexandria, S.D., U.S.	D8	118
Alexandria, Tn., U.S.	A5	119
Alexandria, Va., U.S.	B5	123
Alexandria Bay, N.Y., U.S.	A5	109
Alexandrina, Lake, l., Austl.	G2	51
Alexandroúpolis, Grc.	B5	40
Alexis, stm., Newf.	B3	72
Alexis Creek, B.C.	C6	69
Aley, stm., Sov. Un.	E25	8
Aleysk, Sov. Un.	D11	29
Alfalfa, co., Ok., U.S.	A3	113
Al Fallūjah, Iraq	F14	40
Al Fandaqūmīyah, Isr. Occ.	B7	41
Alfaro, Spain	A5	22
Al Fashn, Egypt	D6	43
Alfatar, Bul.	D8	24
Al Fāw, Iraq	G4	39
Al Fayyūm, Egypt	C3	38
Alfeld, W. Ger.	B4	19
Alfenas, Braz.	C6	56
Alfiós (Alpheus), stm., Grc.	D3	25
Alfonsine, Italy	E8	20
Alford, Eng., U.K.	A8	12
Alford, Scot., U.K.	C6	13
Alford, Fl., U.S.	B1	86
Alford, In., U.S.	H3	91
Alford, Ma., U.S.	B1	98
Alfordsville, In., U.S.	G4	91
Alfortville, Fr.	g10	16
Alfred, Ont.	B10	73
Alfred, Me., U.S.	E2	96
Alfred, N.Y., U.S.	C3	109
Alfred, N.D., U.S.	C6	111
Alfred Lake, l., Me., U.S.	B3	96
Alfred Mills, Me., U.S.	E2	96
Alfred Station, N.Y., U.S.	C3	109
Al Fujayrah, U.A.E.	C5	38
Al Fuqahā', Libya	D3	43
Al Ghayatah, Egypt	D2	41
Al Ghaydah, Yemen	B7	47
Alghero, Italy	D2	23
Al Ghurdaqah, Egypt	D6	43
Algiers (El Djazaïr), Alg.	B5	44
Algoa Bay, b., S. Afr.	D4	49
Algodón, stm., Peru	B3	58
Algodones, N.M., U.S.	B3	108
Algoma, Ms., U.S.	A4	101
Algoma, Wi., U.S.	D6	126
Algoma, dept., Ont.	A2	73
Algoma Mills, Ont.	A2	73
Algona, Ia., U.S.	A3	92
Algona, Wa., U.S.	B3	124
Algonac, Mi., U.S.	F8	99
Algonquin, Il., U.S.	A5	90
Algonquin Park, Ont.	B6	73
Algonquin Provincial Park, Ont.	B6	73
Algood, Tn., U.S.	C8	119
Algorta (Guecho), Spain	A4	22
Algorta, Ur.	E1	56
Algrange, Fr.	C5	16
Alhama [de Granada], Spain	D4	22
Alhama [de Murcia], Spain	D5	22
Alhambra, Ca., U.S.	m12	82
Alhambra, Il., U.S.	E4	90
Al Hāmūl, Egypt	C3	41
Al Harrah, Egypt	H7	40
Al Hasakah, Syria	D13	40
Alhaurín el Grande, Spain	D3	22
Al Hawātah, Sud.	C3	47
Al Hawrah, Yemen	C6	47
Al Hayy, Egypt	C1	22
Al Hayy, Iraq	E3	41
Al Hayyānīyah, Sau. Ar.	H14	40
Al Hillah (Hilla), Iraq	B4	38
Al Hindīyah, Iraq	F15	40
Al Hirmil, Leb.	E11	40
Al Hisn, Jord.	B7	41
Al Hoceïma, Mor.	A4	44
Alhos Vedros, Port.	f9	22
Al Hufūf (Hofuf), Sau. Ar.	C4	38
Al Husayhisah, Sud.	C3	47
Al Husn, Jord.	B3	41
'Alī al Gharbī, Iraq	E3	39
Alíartos, Grc.	g10	25
Alībāg, India	H4	37
Alicante, Spain	C5	22
Alicante, Gulf of, b., Spain	C5	22
Alice, Ont.	B7	73
Alice, N.D., U.S.	C8	111
Alice, Tx., U.S.	F3	120
Alice, Point, c., Italy	E6	23
Alice Lake, l., Mn., U.S.	C7	100
Alice Springs, Austl.	D5	50
Aliceville, Al., U.S.	B1	78
Aliceville, Ks., U.S.	D8	93
Alicia, Ar., U.S.	B4	81
Alicudi, i., Italy		
Alida, Sask.	H5	75
Aligarh, India	G6	36
Aligūdarz, Iran	E4	39
Alindao, Cen. Afr. Rep.	C5	47
Aline, Ga., U.S.	D4	87
Aline, Ok., U.S.	A3	113
Alingsås, Swe.	I5	14
Alīpur Duār, India	D12	37
Aliquippa, Pa., U.S.	E1	115
Al 'Irq, Libya	D4	43
Ali-Sabieh, Dji.	C5	47
Al Istiwa'iyah al Gharbīyah (Western Equatoria), prov., Sud.	D2	47
Al Istiwa'iyah ash Sharqīyah (Eastern Equatoria), prov., Sud.	E3	47
Alistráti, Grc.	B4	25
Aliwal North, S. Afr.	D4	49
Alix, Alta.	C4	68
Alix, Ar., U.S.	B2	81
Al Jabalayn, Sud.	C3	47
Al Jafūrah, des., Sau. Ar.	I5	39
Al Jaghbūb, Libya	B10	43
Al Jahrah, Kuw.	G3	39
Al Jānīyah, Isr. Occ.	h11	41
Al Jawf, Libya	E4	43
Al Jawf, Sau. Ar.	C3	38
Al Jazīrah, prov., Sud.	C3	47
Aljezur, Port.	D1	22
Al Jubayl, Sau. Ar.	H4	39
Al Jazīrah, prov., Sud.	C3	47
Al Junaynah, Sud.	C1	47
Al Kāb, Eg.	D2	41
Alkabo, N.D., U.S.	A2	111
Al Kahfah, Sau. Ar.	I14	40
Alkali Lake, l., Nv., U.S.	B2	105
Alkali Lake, l., Or., U.S.	E6	114
Alkaline Lake, l., N.D., U.S.	C6	111
Al Karak, Jord.	G10	40
Al Karnak, Egypt	D6	43
Al Kawm al Tawīl, Eg.	C3	41
Al Khābūr, stm., Syria	B4	38
Al Khābūrah, Oman	C5	38
Al Khāliş, Iraq	E15	40
Al Khandaq, Sud.	B3	47
Al Khārijah, Egypt	C3	38
Al Khartūm, prov., Sud.	C3	47
Al Khasab, Oman	C5	38
Al Khums, Libya	C3	43
Al Khurmah, Sau. Ar.	C4	38
Al Khushnīyah, Isr. Occ.	A7	41
Alkionídhes, is., Grc.	g9	25
Alkionídhes Gulf, b., Grc.	g10	25
Alkmaar, Neth.	A6	16
Alkol, W.V., U.S.	m12	125
Al Kūbrī, Eg.	D4	41
Al Kūfah, Iraq	F14	40
Al Kuntillah, Egypt	E6	41
Al Kūt, Iraq	B4	38
Allada, Benin	E5	45
Allagash, Me., U.S.	B3	96
Allagash, stm., Me., U.S.	B3	96
Allagash Lake, l., Me., U.S.	B3	96
Allahābād, India	C7	36
Allakaket, Ak., U.S.	B9	79
Allamakee, co., Ia., U.S.	A6	92
Allamuchy Mountain, mtn., N.J., U.S.	B3	107
Allanridge, S. Afr.	F2	75
Allardt, Tn., U.S.	C9	119
Allariz, Spain	A2	22
Allatoona Lake, res., Ga., U.S.	B2	87
Alleene, Ar., U.S.	D1	81
Allegan, Mi., U.S.	F5	99
Allegan, co., Mi., U.S.	F5	99
Allegany, N.Y., U.S.	C2	109
Allegany, Or., U.S.	D2	114
Allegany, co., Md., U.S.	k13	97
Allegany, co., N.Y., U.S.	C2	109
Allegany Indian Reservation, N.Y., U.S.	C2	109
Alleghany, Ca., U.S.	C3	82
Alleghany, co., N.C., U.S.	A1	110
Alleghany, co., Va., U.S.	C2	123
Allegheny, co., Pa., U.S.	E1	115
Allegheny, stm., U.S.	E2	115
Allegheny Front, mtn., W.V., U.S.	B5	125
Allegheny Mountain, mts., U.S.	B3	123
Allegheny Plateau, plat., U.S.	C1	126
Allegheny Reservoir, res., U.S.	B4	115
Allemands, Bayou Des, stm., La., U.S.	k11	95
Allemands, Lac Des, l., La., U.S.	E5	95
Allen, Al., U.S.	D2	78
Allen, Ks., U.S.	D7	93
Allen, Ky., U.S.	C7	94
Allen, Md., U.S.	D6	97
Allen, Ne., U.S.	B9	104
Allen, Ok., U.S.	C5	113
Allen, Tx., U.S.	C4	120
Allen, S.D., U.S.	D4	118
Allen, co., In., U.S.	B7	91
Allen, co., Ks., U.S.	E8	93
Allen, co., Ky., U.S.	D3	94
Allen, co., La., U.S.	D3	95
Allen, co., Oh., U.S.	B1	112
Allen, Lough, l., Ire.	G4	13
Allen, Mount, mtn., N.Z.	Q11	51
Allen, Mount, mtn., Ak., U.S.	C11	79
Allendale, Il., U.S.	E6	90
Allendale, Mo., U.S.	A3	102
Allendale, N.J., U.S.	A4	107
Allendale, S.C., U.S.	E5	117
Allendale, co., S.C., U.S.	E5	117
Allende, Mex.	B4	63
Allenford, Ont.	C3	73
Allenhurst, N.J., U.S.	C5	107
Allens Mills, Me., U.S.	D2	96
Allensville, Ky., U.S.	D3	94
Allensville, Oh., U.S.	C3	112
Allentown, Ga., U.S.	D3	87
Allenton, Al., U.S.	D2	78
Allenton, Mo., U.S.	f12	102
Allenton, R.I., U.S.	E4	116
Allenton, Wi., U.S.	E5	126
Allentown, N.J., U.S.	C3	107
Allentown, N.Y., U.S.	C2	109
Allentown, Pa., U.S.	E11	115
Allenville, Il., U.S.	D5	90
Allenwood, N.J., U.S.	C4	107
Allenwood, Pa., U.S.	D8	115
Alleppey, India	G6	36
Aller, stm., Eur.	B4	18
Allerton, Il., U.S.	D6	90
Allerton, Ia., U.S.	D4	92
Allerton, Point, c., Ma., U.S.	B6	98
Allgood, Al., U.S.	B3	78
Allgäuer Alps, mts., Eur.	B9	21
Alliance, Alta.	C5	68
Alliance, Ne., U.S.	B3	104
Alliance, co., Mi., U.S.	D7	99
Alliance, Oh., U.S.	B4	112
Allihies, Ire.	F11	13
Allingåbro, Den.	B4	15
Allinge [-Sandvig], Den.	C8	15
Allison, Co., U.S.	D3	83
Allison, Ia., U.S.	B5	92
Allison, N.M., U.S.	B1	108
Allison, Pa., U.S.	G2	115
Allison Park, Pa., U.S.	h14	115
Alliston, Ont.	C4	73
Al Lith, Sau. Ar.	C4	38
Alloa, Scot., U.K.	B5	10
Allons, Tn., U.S.	C8	119
Allouez, Mi., U.S.	A2	99
Allouez, Wi., U.S.	h9	126
Alloway, N.J., U.S.	D2	107
Alloway Creek, stm., N.J., U.S.	D2	107
Al Luhayyah, Yemen	B5	47
Allumette Lake, l., Can.	B7	73
Alluwe, Ok., U.S.	A6	113
Ally, Wa., U.S.	B3	124
Alma, N.B.	D5	71
Alma, Ont.	D4	73
Alma, Que.	A6	74
Alma, Ar., U.S.	B1	81
Alma, Co., U.S.	B4	83
Alma, Ga., U.S.	E4	87
Alma, Il., U.S.	E5	90
Alma, Ks., U.S.	C7	93
Alma, Mi., U.S.	E6	99
Alma, Mo., U.S.	B4	102
Alma, Ne., U.S.	D6	104
Alma, N.C., U.S.	C3	110
Alma, Ok., U.S.	C4	113
Alma, W.V., U.S.	B4	125
Alma, Wi., U.S.	D1	126
Alma Center, Wi., U.S.	D3	126
Almada, Port.	C1	22
Almadén, Spain	C3	22
Al Mafraq, Jord.	C2	41
Almagro, Spain	C4	22
Al Mahallah al Kubrá, Eg.	D3	41
Alma Hill, hill, N.Y., U.S.	C2	109
Al Mahmūdīyah, Iraq	F15	40
Al Mahmūdīyah, Eg.	C2	41
Al Mahsamah, Eg.	D4	41
Al Makīlī, Libya	F4	40
Almanor, Lake, l., Ca., U.S.	B3	82
Almansa, Spain	C5	22
Al Mansūrah, Eg.	B3	38
Al Manzilah, Eg.	C3	41
Almanzora, stm., Spain	D4	22
Al Marj, Libya	C4	43
Almargem, Port.	f9	22
Almartha, Mo., U.S.	E5	102
Al Matarīyah, Eg.	D3	41
Al Matarīyah, Eg.	D3	41
Al Mayādīn, Syria	B4	38
Almazán, Spain	B4	22
Al Mazār, Eg.	C5	41
Al Mazār, Jord.	C7	41
Al Mazra'ah, Jord.	C7	41
Almeirim, Braz.	A4	59
Almeirim, Port.	C1	22
Almelo, Neth.	A7	16
Almelund, Mn., U.S.	E6	100
Almena, Ks., U.S.	C4	93
Almena, Wi., U.S.	C1	126
Almenara, Braz.	B4	56
Almendralejo, Spain	C2	22
Almería, Spain	D4	22
Almería, Ne., U.S.	C6	104
Almería, Gulf of, b., Spain	D4	22
Almetyevsk, Sov. Un.	*D8	29
Älmhult, Swe.	B8	15
Al Minyā, Eg.	C3	38
Al Miqdādīyah, Iraq	E2	39
Almira, Wa., U.S.	B7	124
Almirante, Pan.	F6	62
Almirante Brown, Arg.	g7	54
Almirós, Grc.	C4	40
Almo, Id., U.S.	G5	89
Almo, Ky., U.S.	f9	94
Almodóvar [del Campo], Spain	C3	22
Almogía, Spain	D3	22
Almonaster [la Real], Spain	D2	22
Almond, N.Y., U.S.	C3	109
Almond, N.C., U.S.	f9	110
Almond, Wi., U.S.	D4	126
Almont, Mi., U.S.	F8	99
Almont, N.D., U.S.	C4	111
Almonte, Ont.	B8	73
Almonte, Spain	D2	22
Almora, India	C6	36
Almoradí, Spain	C5	22
Al Mubarraz, Sau. Ar.	C4	38
Al Mughayyir, Isr. Occ.	g12	41
Al Mukallā, Yemen	D4	38
Al Mukhā, Yemen	D4	38
Almuñécar, Spain	D4	22
Al Musallamīyah, Sud.	C3	47
Al Musayyib, Iraq	F15	40
Al Muwaylih, Sau. Ar.	I10	40
Almyra, Ar., U.S.	C4	81
Alness, Scot., U.K.	C4	13
Alnwick, Eng., U.K.	F6	10
Alondra, Ca., U.S.	*n12	82
Alonsa, Man.	D2	70
Alor, i., Indon.	G6	34
Álora, Spain	D3	22
Alor Setar, Malay.	D2	34
Alosno, Spain	D2	22
Alotau, Pap. N. Gui.	m13	50
Alpachiri, Arg.	B4	54
Alpaugh, Ca., U.S.	E4	82
Alpbach, Aus.	E5	18
Alpena, Ar., U.S.	A2	81
Alpena, Mi., U.S.	C7	99
Alpena, co., Mi., U.S.	D7	99
Alpena, S.D., U.S.	C7	118
Alpha, Il., U.S.	B3	90
Alpha, Ky., U.S.	C6	94
Alpha, Mi., U.S.	B2	99
Alpha, Mn., U.S.	G4	100
Alpha, N.J., U.S.	B2	107
Alpharetta, Ga., U.S.	B2	87
Alpine, Al., U.S.	B3	78
Alpine, Az., U.S.	D6	80
Alpine, Ar., U.S.	C2	81
Alpine, Ca., U.S.	*F5	82
Alpine, N.J., U.S.	h9	107
Alpine, Or., U.S.	C3	114
Alpine, Tn., U.S.	C8	119
Alpine, Tx., U.S.	D1	120
Alpine, Ut., U.S.	C4	121
Alpine, Wy., U.S.	C1	127
Alpine, co., Ca., U.S.	C4	82
Alpine Junction, Wy., U.S.	*C1	127
Alpoca, W.V., U.S.	D3	125
Alps, mts., Eur.	E4	18
Al Qadārif, Sud.	C4	47
Al Qadīmah, Sau. Ar.	C3	38
Al Qāmishlī, Syria	A4	38
Al Qantarah, Eg.	D4	41
Al Qaryah ash Sharqīyah, Libya	C2	43
Al Qaryatayn, Syria	E11	40
Al Qaşabāt, Libya	D4	43
Al Qaşr, Eg.	C2	38
Al Qatīf, Sau. Ar.	C4	38
Al Qatrānah, Jord.	G11	40
Al Qatrūn, Libya	D2	43
Al Qattah, Eg.	D2	41
Al Qunfudhah, Sau. Ar.	D4	38
Al Qurnah, Iraq	F3	39
Al Quşaymah, Eg.	D6	41
Al Quşayr, Eg.	C3	38
Al Qutaynah, Sud.	C3	47
Alrø, Den.	C4	15
Als, i., Den.	D3	15
Alsace, hist. reg., Fr.	C7	16
Alsask, Sask.	F1	75
Alsasua, Spain	A4	22
Alsdorf, W. Ger.	D6	17
Alsea, Or., U.S.	C3	114
Alsek, stm., N.A.	D5	66
Alsen, N.D., U.S.	A7	111
Alsenbrück-Langmeil, W. Ger.	D2	19
Alsfeld, W. Ger.	C4	18
Alsike (part of Uppsala), Swe.	t35	14
Alsip, Il., U.S.	*k9	90
Alstead, N.H., U.S.	D2	106
Alstead, stm., Sask.	B2	75
Alstead Center, N.H., U.S.	D2	106
Alston, Eng., U.K.	F6	10
Alston, Ga., U.S.	D4	87
Alta, Ia., U.S.	B2	92
Alta, Ut., U.S.	*C4	121
Alta, Wy., U.S.	C1	127
Alta, Or., U.S.	C3	114
Alta Gracia, Arg.	A4	54
Altagracia de Orituco, Ven.	A3	60
Altamaha, stm., Ga., U.S.	E4	87
Altamaha Sound, strt., Ga., U.S.	E5	87
Altamahaw, N.C., U.S.	A3	110
Altamira, Braz.	C4	59
Altamira, Chile	E2	55
Altamirano, Arg.	g7	54
Altamont, Il., U.S.	D5	90
Altamont, Ks., U.S.	E8	93
Altamont, Mo., U.S.	B3	102
Altamont, N.Y., U.S.	C6	109
Altamont, Or., U.S.	E5	114
Altamont, Tn., U.S.	D8	119
Altamont, Ut., U.S.	C5	121
Altamonte Springs, Fl., U.S.	D5	86
Altamura, Italy	D6	23
Altamura, Isla, i., Mex.	C3	63
Altar, Mex.	A2	63
Altario, Alta.	C5	68
Alta Vista, Ia., U.S.	A5	92
Alta Vista, Ks., U.S.	C7	93
Altavista, Va., U.S.	C3	123
Altay, China	B2	31
Altay, Mong.	B4	31
Altay Shan, mts., Asia	B3	31
Altdorf, Switz.	E4	21
Altdorf [bei Nürnberg], W. Ger.	D6	19
Altefähr, E. Ger.	D7	15
Altenberg, E. Ger.	C8	19
Altenbruch, W. Ger.	B4	18
Altenburg, E. Ger.	C7	19
Altenburg, Mo., U.S.	D8	102
Altenkirchen, W. Ger.	C2	19
Altenmarkt [an der Alz], W. Ger.	A8	20
Altentreptow, E. Ger.	C7	15
Alter do Chão, Port.	C2	22
Altha, Fl., U.S.	B1	86
Altheim, Aus.	A9	20
Altheimer, Ar., U.S.	C4	81
Altinho, Braz.	E5	57
Altkirch, Fr.	E7	16
Altmar, N.Y., U.S.	B5	109
Altmühl, stm., W. Ger.	D5	19
Altnaharra, Scot., U.K.	B4	13
Alto, Ga., U.S.	B3	87
Alto, La., U.S.	B4	95
Alto, Mi., U.S.	F5	99
Alto, N.M., U.S.	D4	108
Alto, Tn., U.S.	D8	119
Alto, Tx., U.S.	D5	120
Alto Araguaia, Braz.	D5	56
Alto Cedro, Cuba	D5	64

Index

Name	Map Ref.	Page
Alto Garças, Braz.	B2	56
Alto Longá, Braz.	C2	57
Alto Molócuè, Moz.	A6	49
Altomünster, W. Ger.	A7	20
Alton, Ont.	D4	73
Alton, Eng., U.K.	C7	12
Alton, Al., U.S.	B3	78
Alton, Il., U.S.	E3	90
Alton, Ia., U.S.	B2	92
Alton, Ks., U.S.	C5	93
Alton, La., U.S.	h12	95
Alton, Mo., U.S.	E6	102
Alton, N.H., U.S.	D4	106
Alton, Oh., U.S.	m10	112
Alton, R.I., U.S.	F2	116
Alton, Ut., U.S.	F3	121
Alton, W.V., U.S.	C4	125
Altona, Man.	E3	70
Altona (part of Hamburg), W. Ger.	E3	15
Altona, Il., U.S.	B3	90
Altona, In., U.S.	B7	91
Altona, N.Y., U.S.	f11	109
Altona, Ut., U.S.	C5	121
Alton Bay, N.H., U.S.	D4	106
Altoona, Al., U.S.	A3	78
Altoona, Fl., U.S.	D5	86
Altoona, Ia., U.S.	C4	92
Altoona, Ks., U.S.	E8	93
Altoona, Pa., U.S.	E5	115
Altoona, Wi., U.S.	D2	126
Alto Paraguai, Braz.	A1	56
Alto Paraguay, dept., Para.	D4	55
Alto Paraná, dept., Para.	D5	55
Alto Pass, Il., U.S.	F4	90
Alto Purus, stm., Peru	D3	58
Altötting, W. Ger.	A8	20
Altrincham, Eng., U.K.	A5	12
Altro, Ky., U.S.	C6	94
Altstätten, Switz.	B5	20
Ältün Küprï, Iraq	E15	40
Altun Shan, mts., China	D2	31
Altura, Mn., U.S.	F7	100
Alturas, Ca., U.S.	B3	82
Altus, Ar., U.S.	B2	81
Altus, Ok., U.S.	C2	113
Altus Air Force Base, mil., Ok., U.S.	C2	113
Altus Reservoir, res., Ok., U.S.	C2	113
Altusried, W. Ger.	A9	20
Al 'Ubaylah, Sau. Ar.	C5	38
Al Uqayah, Sud.	C2	47
Alum Bank, Pa., U.S.	F4	115
Alum Bridge, W.V., U.S.	B4	125
Alum Creek, W.V., U.S.	m12	125
Alum Creek, stm., Oh., U.S.	k11	112
Aluminé, Arg.	B2	54
Alum Rock, Ca., U.S.	*k9	82
Alupka, Sov. Un.	I10	27
Al 'Uqaylah, Libya	C3	43
Al 'Uqayr, Sau. Ar.	I5	39
Alutom, Mount, hill, Guam	L9	52
Alva, Fl., U.S.	F5	86
Alva, Ky., U.S.	D6	94
Alva, Ok., U.S.	A3	113
Alva, Wy., U.S.	B8	127
Alvarado, Mex.	D5	63
Alvarado, Mn., U.S.	B2	100
Alvarado, Tx., U.S.	C4	120
Alvaton, Ga., U.S.	C2	87
Älvdalen, Swe.	G6	14
Alvear, Arg.	E4	55
Alvena, Sask.	E2	75
Alverca, Port.	f9	22
Alverton, Pa., U.S.	F2	115
Alvesta, Swe.	B8	15
Alvin, Il., U.S.	C6	90
Alvin, S.C., U.S.	E8	117
Alvin, Tx., U.S.	E5	120
Alvinston, Ont.	E3	73
Alvo, Ne., U.S.	h12	104
Alvord, Ia., U.S.	A1	92
Alvord, Tx., U.S.	C4	120
Alvord Lake, l., Or., U.S.	E8	114
Alvordton, Oh., U.S.	A1	112
Älvsborg, co., Swe.	A6	15
Älvsered, Swe.	A6	15
Älvsjö (part of Stockholm), Swe.	t36	14
Al Wajh, Sau. Ar.	C3	38
Alwar, India	C6	36
Al Wāsiṭah, Eg.	E3	41
Alxa Zuoqi, China	D6	31
Alyat, Sov. Un.	F3	28
Alyth, Scot., U.K.	D5	13
Alytus, Sov. Un.	A8	26
Alz, stm., W. Ger.	D6	18
Alzada, Mt., U.S.	E12	103
Alzey, W. Ger.	D3	19
Ama, La., U.S.	k11	95
Amacuzac, stm., Mex.	n14	63
Amadeus, Lake, l., Austl.	D5	50
Amadi, Sud.	D3	47
Amadjuak Lake, l., N.W. Ter.	C18	66
Amado, Az., U.S.	F4	80
Amador, co., Ca., U.S.	C3	82
Amagansett, N.Y., U.S.	n16	109
Amagasaki, Japan	o14	33
Amager, i., Den.	C6	15
Amagon, Ar., U.S.	B4	81
Amaha, Japan	n18	33
Amahai, Indon.	F7	34
Amakusa Sea, Japan	J4	33
Åmål, Swe.	H5	14
Amalfi, Italy	D5	23
Amalga, Ut., U.S.	B4	121
Amalia, N.M., U.S.	A4	108
Amaliás, Grc.	G5	25
Amalner, India	G5	37
Amambaí, Braz.	C1	56
Amambaí, Serra de, mts., S.A.	C1	56
Amambay, dept., Para.	D4	55
Amamio Island, i., Japan	F10	31
Amana, Ia., U.S.	C6	92
Amancey, Fr.	C6	16
Amanda, Oh., U.S.	C3	112
Amangeldy, Sov. Un.	E6	28
Amantea, Italy	E6	23
Amantes Point, c., Guam	L10	52
Amapá, Braz.	B4	59
Amapá, ter., Braz.	B4	59
Amapala, Hond.	D4	62
Amaraji, Braz.	k6	57
Amarante, Braz.	D2	57
Amaranth, Man.	D2	70
Amargosa, Braz.	C5	57
Amargosa, stm., U.S.	D5	105
Amargosa Desert, des., U.S.	G5	105
Amargosa Range, mts., U.S.	G5	105
Amarillo, Tx., U.S.	B2	120
Amaro, Mount, mtn., Italy	C5	23
Amaroúsion, Grc.	g11	25
Amasa, Mi., U.S.	B2	99
Amasra, Tur.	B9	40
Amasya, Tur.	B10	40
Amataurá, Braz.	B4	58
Amatignak Island, i., Ak., U.S.	E4	79
Amatsu-kominato, Japan	n19	33
Amazon (Solimões) (Amazonas), stm., S.A.	D5	53
Amazonas, state, Braz.	C2	59
Amazonas, dept., Col.	D3	60
Amazonas, dept., Peru	C2	58
Amazonas, ter., Ven.	C4	60
Amazonia, Mo., U.S.	B3	102
Ambājōgāi, India	H6	37
Ambāla, India	B6	36
Ambalavao, Madag.	h9	49
Ambam, Cam.	E2	49
Ambanja, Madag.	f9	49
Ambarchik, Sov. Un.	C19	29
Ambato, Ec.	B2	58
Ambato Boeny, Madag.	g9	49
Ambatolampy, Madag.	g9	49
Ambatondrazaka, Madag.	g9	49
Ambatosoratra, Madag.	g9	49
Amber, Ok., U.S.	B4	113
Amberg, W. Ger.	D5	18
Amberg, Wi., U.S.	C6	126
Ambérieu [-en-Bugey], Fr.	E6	16
Amberson, Pa., U.S.	F6	115
Ambert, Fr.	E5	16
Ambia, In., U.S.	D2	91
Ambikāpur, India	D7	36
Ambil Island, i., Phil.	p13	34
Ambilobe, Madag.	f9	49
Amble-by-the-Sea, Eng., U.K.	B7	13
Ambler, Ak., U.S.	B8	79
Ambler, Pa., U.S.	F11	115
Ambo, Peru	D2	58
Ambo Channel, strt., Marsh Is.	S17	52
Ambodifototra, Madag.	g9	49
Amboina see Ambon, Indon.		
Amboise, Fr.	D4	16
Ambon, Indon.	F7	34
Ambon, i., Indon.	F7	34
Ambositra, Madag.	h9	49
Ambovombe, Madag.	h9	49
Amboy, Ca., U.S.	E6	82
Amboy, Il., U.S.	B4	90
Amboy, In., U.S.	C6	91
Amboy, Mn., U.S.	G4	100
Amboy, Wa., U.S.	D3	124
Ambridge, Pa., U.S.	E1	115
Ambriz, Ang.	C1	48
Ambrose, N.D., U.S.	A2	111
Ambrosia Lake, N.M., U.S.	B2	108
Ambur, Indon.	F8	34
Amchitka Island, i., Ak., U.S.	E3	79
Amchitka Pass, strt., Ak., U.S.	E4	79
Am Dam, Chad	C4	46
Amderma, Sov. Un.	C9	29
Ameagle, W.V., U.S.	D3	125
Ameca, Mex.	C4	63
Amecameca [de Juárez], Mex.	n14	63
Ameland, i., Neth.	A6	16
Amelia, La., U.S.	E4	95
Amelia, Ne., U.S.	B7	104
Amelia, Oh., U.S.	C1	112
Amelia, co., Va., U.S.	C4	123
Amelia City, Fl., U.S.	k9	86
Amelia Court House, Va., U.S.	C5	123
Amelia Island, i., Fl., U.S.	k9	86
Amelinghausen, W. Ger.	E4	15
Amendolara, Italy	E6	23
Amenia, N.Y., U.S.	D7	109
Amenia, N.D., U.S.	B8	111
American, stm., Ca., U.S.	C3	82
American, South Fork, stm., Ca., U.S.	C3	82
Americana, Braz.	m8	57
American Canyon, Ca., U.S.	*C2	82
American Falls, Id., U.S.	G6	89
American Falls Dam, Id., U.S.	G6	89
American Falls Reservoir, res., Id., U.S.	F5	89
American Fork, Ut., U.S.	C4	121
American Highland, plat., Ant.	B20	7
American Samoa, dep., Oc.	G11	6
Americus, Ga., U.S.	D2	87
Americus, Ks., U.S.	D7	93
Americus, Mo., U.S.	C6	102
Amersfoort, Neth.	A6	16
Amery, Man.	A4	70
Amery, Wi., U.S.	C1	126
Amery Ice Shelf, ice, Ant.	C20	7
Ames, Ia., U.S.	B4	92
Ames, Ks., U.S.	C6	93
Ames, Ne., U.S.	C9	104
Ames, Ok., U.S.	A3	113
Amesbury, Ma., U.S.	A6	98
Ameson, Ont.	B2	84
Amfissa, Grc.	C4	25
Amga, Sov. Un.	C16	29
Amguid, Alg.	D6	44
Amgun, stm., Sov. Un.	D16	29
Amherst, N.S.	D5	71
Amherst, Me., U.S.	D4	96
Amherst, Ma., U.S.	B2	98
Amherst, Ne., U.S.	D6	104
Amherst, N.H., U.S.	E3	106
Amherst, N.Y., U.S.	C2	109
Amherst, Oh., U.S.	A3	112
Amherst, S.D., U.S.	B8	118
Amherst, Tx., U.S.	B1	120
Amherst, Va., U.S.	C3	123
Amherst, Wi., U.S.	D4	126
Amherst, co., Va., U.S.	C3	123
Amherstdale, W.V., U.S.	n12	125
Amherstburg, Ont.	E1	73
Amidon, N.D., U.S.	C2	111
Amiens, Fr.	C5	16
Aminuis, Nmb.	D3	48
'Āmir, Ra's, c., Libya	C4	43
Amirante Islands, is., Sey.	G24	2
Amiret, Mn., U.S.	F3	100
Amir Kabir Dam, Iran	C5	39
Amisk, Alta.	C5	68
Amisk Lake, l., Sask.	C4	75
Amistad, N.M., U.S.	B6	108
Amistad National Recreation Area, Tx., U.S.	E2	120
Amistad Reservoir, res., N.A.	E2	120
Amite, La., U.S.	D5	95
Amite, co., Ms., U.S.	D3	101
Amite, stm., La., U.S.	D5	95
Amity, Ar., U.S.	C2	81
Amity, Mo., U.S.	B3	102
Amity, Or., U.S.	B3	114
Amity, Pa., U.S.	F1	115
Amityville, N.Y., U.S.	E7	109
Amlekhgañj, Nepal	C7	36
Amlia Island, i., Ak., U.S.	E3	79
Amlwch, Wales, U.K.	A3	12
'Ammān, Jord.	B3	38
Ammanford, Wales, U.K.	C3	12
Ammeloe, W. Ger.	B6	19
Ammon, Id., U.S.	F7	89
Ammonoosuc, stm., N.H., U.S.	B3	106
Amne Machin Shan see A'nyêmaqên Shan, mts., China	E4	31
Amnicon Falls, Wi., U.S.	B2	126
Amo, In., U.S.	E4	91
Āmol, Iran	C6	39
Amonate, Va., U.S.	e10	123
Amoret, Mo., U.S.	C3	102
Amorgós, i., Grc.	D5	40
Amorinópolis, Braz.	B2	56
Amorita, Ok., U.S.	A3	113
Amory, Ms., U.S.	B5	101
Amos, Que.	k11	74
Amoy see Xiamen, China	G8	31
Ampanihy, Madag.	h8	49
Amparo, Braz.	C5	56
Amper, stm., W. Ger.	C8	20
Ampezzo, Italy	B6	22
Amposta, Spain	D6	22
Amrāvati (Amraoti), India	D6	36
Amreli, India	A7	21
Amriswil, Switz.	A7	21
Amritsar, India	B5	36
Amroha, India	C7	37
Amrum, i., W. Ger.	A4	18
Amsteg, Switz.	C6	21
Amstelveen, Neth.	*B4	17
Amsterdam, Neth.	A6	16
Amsterdam, Ga., U.S.	F2	87
Amsterdam, Mo., U.S.	C3	102
Amsterdam, Mt., U.S.	E5	103
Amsterdam, N.Y., U.S.	C6	109
Amsterdam, Oh., U.S.	B5	112
Amsterdam, Île, i., F.S.A.T.	I2	2
Amstetten, Aus.	C6	84
Am Timan, Chad	C4	46
Amu Darya, stm., Asia	F9	29
Amukta Pass, strt., Ak., U.S.	E3	79
Amulet, Sask.	H3	75
Amund Ringnes Island, i., N.W. Ter.	m32	66
Amundsen Bay, b., Ant.	C17	7
Amundsen Gulf, b., N.W. Ter.	B8	66
Amundsen-Scott, sci., Ant.	A17	7
Amundsen Sea, Ant.	B36	7
Amuntai, Indon.	F5	34
Amur (Heilong Jiang), stm., Asia	E16	29
Amvrakia, Gulf of, b., Grc.	C3	25
Amy, Ar., U.S.	D3	81
Amzi, Oued ti-n-, val., Afr.	E5	44
'Anabtā, Isr. Occ.	B14	41
Anaco, Ven.	B5	60
Anacoco, La., U.S.	C2	95
Anacoco, Bayou, stm., La., U.S.	D2	95
Anaconda, Mt., U.S.	D4	103
Anaconda Range, mts., Mt., U.S.	E3	103
Anacortes, Wa., U.S.	A3	124
Anacostia, stm., U.S.	C3	97
Anacostia, Northwest Branch, stm., U.S.	B3	97
Anacuao, Mount, mtn., Phil.	n13	34
Anadarko, Ok., U.S.	B3	113
Anadia, Braz.	C3	57
Anadyr, Sov. Un.	C20	29
Anadyr, stm., Sov. Un.	C20	29
Anadyr, Gulf of, b., Sov. Un.	C21	29
Anadyr Mountains, mts., Sov. Un.	C20	14
Anae, i., Guam	M9	52
Anáfi (Anaphe), i., Grc.	D5	40
Anagance, N.B.	D4	71
'Ānah, Iraq	E13	40
Anaheim, Ca., U.S.	F5	82
Anahim Lake, B.C.	C5	69
Anahola, Hi., U.S.	A2	88
Anahuac, Tx., U.S.	E5	120
Anahulu, stm., Hi., U.S.	f9	88
Anajás, Braz.	C5	59
Anak, N. Kor.	G2	33
Anakāpalle, India	E7	36
Anakie, Austl.	A6	51
Anaklia, Sov. Un.	A13	40
Analalava, Madag.	f9	49
Anamã, Braz.	C2	59
Anama Bay, Man.	D2	70
Ana Maria, Golfo de, b., Cuba	D4	64
Anambas Islands, is., Indon.	E3	34
Anamoose, N.D., U.S.	B5	111
Anamosa, Ia., U.S.	B6	92
Anamur, Tur.	D9	40
Anamur, Cape, c., Tur.	D9	40
Anándale, La., U.S.	*C3	95
Ananea (Poto), Peru	F4	58
Anantapur, India	E6	36
Anantnāg, India	B6	36
Anao Point, c., Guam	L10	52
Anapa, Sov. Un.	I11	27
Anaphe see Anáfi, i., Grc.		
Anápolis, Braz.	B5	56
Anapu, stm., Braz.	C4	59
Anār, Iran	F7	39
Anārak, Iran	E10	39
Añatuya, Arg.	E3	55
Anauá, stm., Braz.	B1	21
Anawalt, W.V., U.S.	D3	125
Ancash, dept., Peru	C2	58
Ancaster, Ont.	D4	73
Ancenis, Fr.	E4	16
Ancha, Sierra, mts., Az., U.S.	D4	80
Anchieta, Braz.	E8	57
Anching see Anqing, China	E8	31
Anchorage, Ak., U.S.	C10	79
Anchorage, Ky., U.S.	g11	94
Anchor Point, Ak., U.S.	D9	79
Anchor Point, c., Ak., U.S.	h15	79
Ancienne-Lorette, Que.	C6	74
Anclote Keys, is., Fl., U.S.	D4	86
Anco, Ky., U.S.	C6	94
Ancón, Peru	D2	58
Ancona, Italy	C4	23
Ancona, Il., U.S.	B5	90
Ancón de Sardinas, Bahía de, b., S.A.	C2	60
Ancud, Chile	C2	54
Ancud, Golfo de, b., Chile	C2	54
Anda, China	B10	31
Andacollo, Arg.	B2	54
Andahuaylas, Peru	D3	58
Andale, Ks., U.S.	E6	93
Andalgalá, Arg.	E2	55
Andalsnes, Nor.	F2	14
Andalusia, Al., U.S.	D3	78
Andalusia, Il., U.S.	B3	90
Andalusia, hist. reg., Spain	D3	22
Andaman and Nicobar Islands, ter., India	*F9	36
Andaman Islands, is., India	F9	36
Andaman Sea, Asia	F10	36
Andamarca, Bol.	C2	55
Andapa, Madag.	f9	49
Andavaka, Cap, c., Madag.	i9	49
Andebu, Nor.	p28	14
Andenne, Bel.	C7	21
Andermatt, Switz.	D5	17
Andernach, W. Ger.	C4	20
Andersen Air Force Base, mil., Guam	L10	52
Anderslöv, Swe.	C7	15
Angostura Reservoir, res., S.D., U.S.	g6	54
Anderson, Arg.	A2	78
Anderson, Al., U.S.	A2	78
Anderson, Ak., U.S.	C10	79
Anderson, Ca., U.S.	B2	82
Anderson, In., U.S.	D6	91
Anderson, Mo., U.S.	E3	102
Anderson, S.C., U.S.	B2	117
Anderson, Tn., U.S.	D8	119
Anderson, Tx., U.S.	D4	120
Anderson, co., Ks., U.S.	D8	93
Anderson, co., Ky., U.S.	C4	94
Anderson, co., S.C., U.S.	B2	117
Anderson, co., Tn., U.S.	C9	119
Anderson, co., Tx., U.S.	D5	120
Anderson, stm., N.W. Ter.	C7	66
Anderson, Mount, mtn., Wa., U.S.	B2	124
Anderson Ranch Reservoir, res., Id., U.S.	F3	89
Andersonville, Ga., U.S.	D2	87
Andersonville, In., U.S.	F7	91
Andes, Col.	B2	60
Andes, N.Y., U.S.	C6	109
Andes, mts., S.A.	E4	53
Andes, Lake, l., S.D., U.S.	D7	118
Andfjorden, strt., Nor.	C7	14
Andhra Pradesh, state, India	E6	36
Andikíthira, i., Grc.	E4	40
Andilamena, Madag.	g9	49
Andímeshk, Iran	E4	39
Andizhan, Sov. Un.	E10	29
Andkhvoy, Afg.	A4	36
Andoas, Peru	B2	58
Andong, S. Kor.	D10	31
Andorra, And.	A6	22
Andorra, ctry., Eur.	C6	12
Andover, Eng., U.K.	C6	6
Andover, Ct., U.S.	B6	84
Andover, Ks., U.S.	E6	93
Andover, Me., U.S.	D2	96
Andover, Ma., U.S.	A5	98
Andover, Mn., U.S.	m12	100
Andover, N.J., U.S.	B3	107
Andover, N.Y., U.S.	C3	109
Andover, Oh., U.S.	A5	112
Andover, S.D., U.S.	B8	118
Andover Lake, res., Ct., U.S.	C6	84
Andøya, i., Nor.	C6	14
Andradina, Braz.	D6	45
Andraitx, Spain	C7	22
Andreanof Islands, is., Ak., U.S.	E4	79
Andrelândia, Braz.	g5	56
Andréville, Que.	B8	74
Andrew, Alta.	C4	68
Andrew, Ia., U.S.	B7	92
Andrew, co., Mo., U.S.	B3	102
Andrew Island, i., N.S.	D9	71
Andrews, In., U.S.	C6	91
Andrews, Md., U.S.	D5	97
Andrews, N.C., U.S.	f9	110
Andrews, S.C., U.S.	E8	117
Andrews, Tx., U.S.	C1	120
Andrews, co., Tx., U.S.	C1	120
Andrews Air Force Base, mil., Md., U.S.	C4	97
Andrewsville, De., U.S.	E3	85
Andreyevka, Sov. Un.	G11	27
Andria, Italy	D6	23
Androka, Madag.	h8	49
Andros, Grc.	D5	25
Ándros, i., Grc.	D5	40
Androscoggin, co., Me., U.S.	D2	96
Androscoggin, stm., Me., U.S.	D2	96
Androscoggin Lake, l., Me., U.S.	D2	96
Andros Island, i., Bah.	B5	64
Andrychów, Pol.	h10	26
Andújar, Spain	C3	22
Andulo, Ang.	D2	48
Anécho, Togo	E5	45
Anefis i-n-Darane, Mali	C5	45
Anegada, i., V.I. Br.	G12	64
Anegada, Bahía, b., Arg.	C4	54
Anegada Passage, strt., N.A.	G13	64
Anegam, Az., U.S.	E3	80
Añelo, Arg.	B3	54
Anerley, Sask.	F2	75
Aneroid, Sask.	H2	75
Aneta, N.D., U.S.	B8	111
Aneth, Ut., U.S.	F6	121
Aneto, Pico de, mtn., Spain	A6	22
Angamos, Punta, c., Chile	D1	55
Ang'angxi, China	B9	31
Angara, stm., Sov. Un.	D12	29
Angarsk, Sov. Un.	D13	29
Angaur, i., Palau	R17	52
Ángel de la Guarda, Isla, i., Mex.	B2	63
Angeles, Phil.	o13	34
Angeles, Point, c., Wa., U.S.	A2	124
Angel Falls, wtfl., Ven.	B5	60
Ängelholm, Swe.	I5	14
Angelica, N.Y., U.S.	C2	109
Angelina, co., Tx., U.S.	D5	120
Angelina, stm., Tx., U.S.	D5	120
Angels Camp, Ca., U.S.	C3	82
Angelus, Ks., U.S.	C3	93
Angelus, S.C., U.S.	B7	117
Angermanälven, stm., Swe.	F7	14
Angermünde, E. Ger.	B6	18
Angers, Fr.	D3	16
Angicos, Braz.	C3	57
Angie, La., U.S.	D6	95
Angier, N.C., U.S.	B4	110
Angikuni Lake, l., N.W. Ter.	D13	66
Angkor, hist., Camb.	C2	34
Angle Inlet, Mn., U.S.	*B3	124
Angle Lake, Wa., U.S.	Q11	51
Anglem, Mount, mtn., N.Z.	Q11	51
Anglesey, i., Wales, U.K.	D4	10
Anglet, Fr.	F3	16
Angleton, Tx., U.S.	E5	120
Anglia, Sask.	F1	75
Angliers, Que.	G17	66
Anglin, stm., Man.	A5	70
Angling Lake, l., N.W. Ter.	C5	70
Ango, Zaire	A4	48
Angoche, Moz.	A6	49
Angoche, Ilha, i., Moz.	A6	49
Angol, Chile	B2	54
Angola, In., U.S.	A8	91
Angola, N.Y., U.S.	C1	109
Angola, ctry., Afr.	D2	48
Angola Beach, De., U.S.	F5	85
Angola Swamp, sw., N.C., U.S.	C5	110
Angoon, Ak., U.S.	D13	79
Angora, Ne., U.S.	C2	104
Angora see Ankara, Tur.	C9	40
Angostura Reservoir, res., S.D., U.S.	D2	118
Angoulême, Fr.	E4	16
Angra do Heroísmo, Port.	g10	44
Angra dos Reis, Braz.	C4	56
Angren, Sov. Un.	E7	28
Anguang, China	B10	32
Anguilla, Ms., U.S.	C3	101
Anguilla, ctry., N.A.	G13	64
Anguillara [Sabazia], Italy	g8	23
Anguille, Cape, c., Newf.	E2	72
Angumu, Zaire	B4	48
Angus, Ont.	C5	73
Angus, Mn., U.S.	B2	100
Angusville, Man.	D1	70
Anholt, Den.	B5	15
Anholt, i., Den.	B5	15
Anhua, China	J4	32
Anhui, prov., China	E8	31
Anhwei see Anhui, prov., China	E8	31
Aniak, Ak., U.S.	C8	79
Aniche, Fr.	D3	17
Aniene (Teverone), stm., Italy	h9	23
Anina, Rom.	F1	108
Anita, Ia., U.S.	C3	92
Anita, Pa., U.S.	D4	115
Aniva, Sov. Un.	C11	33
Aniva, Cape, c., Sov. Un.	B13	31
Aniva, Bay, b., Sov. Un.	C11	33
Aniwa, Wi., U.S.	C4	126
Anizy-le-Château, Fr.	E3	17
Anjār, India	D5	36
Anjō, Japan	o16	33
Anjou, Que.	p19	74
Anjou, hist. reg., Fr.	D3	16
Anju, N. Kor.	G2	33
Anjum, Neth.	A6	17
Anka, Nig.	E6	45
Ankang, China	E6	31
Ankara, Tur.	C9	40
Ankavandra, Madag.	g9	49
Ankazoabo, Madag.	h8	49
Ankazobe, Madag.	g9	49
Ankeny, Ia., U.S.	C4	92
An Khe, Viet.	C3	34
Anklam, E. Ger.	B6	18
Ankober, Eth.	D6	47
Ankoro, Zaire	C5	48
Anlong, China	F6	31
Anlu, China	I5	32
Ann, Cape, c., Ant.	C18	7
Ann, Cape, c., Ma., U.S.	A6	98
Anna, Sov. Un.	F13	27
Anna, Il., U.S.	F4	90
Anna, Oh., U.S.	B1	112
Anna, Lake, res., Va., U.S.	B5	123
Annaba (Bône), Alg.	B6	44
Annabella, Ut., U.S.	E4	121
Annaberg-Buchholz, E. Ger.	C6	18
An Nabk, Syria	B8	19
Annaburg, E. Ger.	B7	102
An Nafūd, des., Sau. Ar.	C4	38
An Najaf, Iraq	E3	39
An Nakhl, Eg.	H9	40
Annalee Heights, Va., U.S.	*B5	123
Annam, hist. reg., Viet.	E7	35
An Nāṣirīyah, Iraq	A2	39
Annapolis, Il., U.S.	D6	90
Annapolis, Mo., U.S.	D7	102
Annapolis, Md., U.S.	C4	97
Annapolis, stm., N.S.	E4	71
Annapolis, co., N.S.	E4	71
Annapolis Junction, Md., U.S.	B4	97
Annapolis Royal, N.S.	E4	71
Annapurna, mtn., Nepal	F7	75
Ann Arbor, Mi., U.S.	F7	99
Anne Arundel, co., Md., U.S.	B4	97
Annecy, Fr.	E7	16
Annecy, Lake, l., Fr.	E7	16
Annecy-le-Vieux, Fr.	E1	21
Annemasse, Fr.	D7	16
Annette, Ak., U.S.	n24	79
An Nhon, Viet.	F8	35
An Nīl, prov., Sud.	B3	47
An Nīl al Azraq (Blue Nile), prov., Sud.	C3	47
Annobón Island (Pagalu), i., Eq. Gui.	F1	46
Annona, Tx., U.S.	C5	120
Annone, Lago di, l., Italy	E7	21
Annotto Bay, Jam.	E5	64
Annotto Bay, b., Jam.	E15	65
Annsjön, l., Swe.	u33	14
An Nuhūd, Sud.	C2	47
An Nu'mānīyah, Iraq	E2	39
Annursnack Hill, hill, Ma., U.S.	g10	98
Annville, Ky., U.S.	C6	94
Annville, Pa., U.S.	F8	115
Anoka, Mn., U.S.	E5	100
Anoka, Ne., U.S.	B7	104
Anoka, co., Mn., U.S.	E5	100
Anori, Braz.	C2	59
Anóyia, Grc.	E5	25
Anping, China	E6	32
Anqing, China	E8	31
Ansbach, W. Ger.	D5	18
Anse d'Hainault, Haiti	C6	64
Anselmo, Ne., U.S.	C6	104
Anserma, Col.	B2	60
Anshan, China	C9	31
Anshun, China	F6	31
Ansley, Al., U.S.	D3	78
Ansley, Ms., U.S.	E4	101
Ansley, Ne., U.S.	C6	104
Anson, Me., U.S.	D3	96
Anson, Tx., U.S.	C3	120
Anson, co., N.C., U.S.	B2	110
Anson Bay, b., Austl.	B5	50
Ansong, S. Kor.	H3	33
Ansonia, Ct., U.S.	D3	84
Ansonia, Oh., U.S.	B1	112
Ansonville, Ont.	G16	66
Ansonville, N.C., U.S.	B2	110
Ansted, W.V., U.S.	C3	125
Anstruther, Scot., U.K.	D6	13
Ansudu, Indon.	F9	34
Anta, Peru	D3	58
Antabamba, Peru	D3	58
Antakya (Antioch), Tur.	D11	40
Antalaha, Madag.	f10	49
Antalāt, Libya	C4	43
Antalāt, well, Libya	G3	40
Antalya, Tur.	D8	40
Antalya, Gulf of, b., Tur.	D8	40
Antananarivo, Madag.	g9	49
Antananarivo, prov., Madag.	g9	49
Antarctica, cont.	A19	7
Antarctic Peninsula, pen., Ant.	C6	7
Antelope, Sask.	G1	75
Antelope, Ks., U.S.	D7	93
Antelope, Mt., U.S.	B12	103
Antelope, Or., U.S.	C6	114
Antelope, S.D., U.S.	*D5	118
Antelope, co., Ne., U.S.	B7	104
Antelope Butte, mtn., Wy., U.S.	B7	127
Antelope Creek, stm., Wy., U.S.	C7	127
Antelope Island, i., Ut., U.S.	C4	121
Antelope Lake, l., Sask.	G1	75
Antelope Mine, Zimb.	B4	49
Antelope Peak, mtn., Nv., U.S.	B7	105
Antelope Range, mts., Nv., U.S.	D7	105
Antelope Reservoir, res., Or., U.S.	E9	114
Antelope Valley, val., Nv., U.S.	D5	105
Antequera, Spain	D3	22
Antero, Mount, mtn., Co., U.S.	C4	83
Antero Reservoir, res., Co., U.S.	C5	83
Antes Fort, Pa., U.S.	D7	115
Anthony, Fl., U.S.	C4	86
Anthony, Ks., U.S.	E5	93
Anthony, N.M., U.S.	F3	108
Anthony, R.I., U.S.	D3	116
Anthony Creek, stm., W.V., U.S.	C4	125
Anti-Atlas, mts., Mor.	C3	44
Antibes, Fr.	F7	16
Anticosti, Île d', i., Que.	k14	74
Antietam Creek, stm., Md.	B2	97
Antietam National Battlefield Site, hist., Md., U.S.	B2	97
Antigo, Wi., U.S.	C4	126
Antigonish, N.S.	D8	71
Antigonish, co., N.S.	D7	71
Antigua, i., Antig.	H14	64
Antigua and Barbuda, ctry., N.A.	H14	64
Antigua Guatemala, Guat.	D6	64
Antilla, Cuba	D6	64
Antioch, Ca., U.S.	h9	82
Antioch, Il., U.S.	A5	90
Antioch, In., U.S.	D5	91
Antioch, Ne., U.S.	B3	104
Antioch see Antakya, Tur.	D11	40
Antioquia, Col.	B2	60
Antioquia, dept., Col.	B2	60
Antipodes Islands, is., N.Z.	J8	2
Antiquity, Oh., U.S.	D4	112
Antler, N.D., U.S.	A4	111
Antler, stm., N.A.	E1	75
Antlers, Ok., U.S.	C6	113
Antofagasta, Chile	D1	55
Antofagasta, prov., Chile	D2	55
Antofagasta de la Sierra, Arg.	D2	55
Antofalla, Volcán, vol., Arg.	E2	55
Antoine, Pan.	F7	62
Antón, Pan.	B7	83
Anton, Co., U.S.	B7	83
Anton, Tx., U.S.	C1	120
Anton Chico, N.M., U.S.	B4	108
Antongila, Helodrano, b., Madag.	g9	49
Antonina, Braz.	B7	56
Antônio Carlos, Braz.	g6	57
Antônio de Biedma, Arg.	B4	54
Antônio Dias, Braz.	g6	57
Antonito, Co., U.S.	D4	83
Antony, Fr.	g10	16
Antratsit, Sov. Un.	q22	17
Antrim, N.Ire., U.K.	D5	13
Antrim, N.H., U.S.	E3	106
Antrim, Pa., U.S.	C7	115
Antrim, co., Mi., U.S.	D5	99
Antrim, co., N.Ire., U.K.	D5	13
Antsalova, Madag.	g8	49
Antsirabe, Madag.	g9	49
Antsiranana, Madag.	f9	49
Antsiranana, prov., Madag.	f9	49
Antsohihy, Madag.	f9	49
Antwerp (Antwerpen), Bel.	A5	109
Antwerp, N.Y., U.S.	A5	109
Antwerp, Oh., U.S.	A1	112
Antwerp, prov., Bel.	C4	17

Name | **Map Ref.** | **Page**

Antwerpen see Antwerp, Bel. ... B5 16
Anua, Am. Sam. ... F13 52
An Uaimh (Navan), Ire. ... D3 10
Anuradhapura, Sri L. ... G7 36
Anvers Island, i., Ant. ... C6 7
Anvik, Ak., U.S. ... C7 79
Anxi, China ... F8 31
Anxi, China ... C4 31
Anyang, China ... D7 31
Anyang, S. Kor. ... *H3 31
Anyi, China ... G4 32
Anykščiai, Sov. Un. ... A8 26
Anzá, Col. ... B2 60
Anza, stm., Italy ... E5 21
Anzac, Alta. ... A5 68
Anzhero-Sudzhensk, Sov. Un. ... D11 29
Anzin, Fr. ... D3 17
Anzio, Italy ... D4 23
Anzoátegui, state, Ven. ... B5 60
Aoji-ri, N. Kor. ... E5 33
Aomen see L'Aquila, Italy ...
Aomoen Strait, Marsh Is. ... P18 52
Aomon, i., Marsh Is. ... S18 52
Aomori, Japan ... C13 31
Aoral, Mount, mtn., Camb. ... C2 34
Aosta, Italy ... B1 23
Aou Hofrit, well, W. Sah. ... E2 44
Aouk, Bahr, stm., Afr. ... D3 46
Aoukâr, reg., Maur. ... C2 45
Aoyama, Japan ... o15 33
Aozou, Chad ... A3 46
Apa, stm., S.A. ... D4 55
Apache, Ok., U.S. ... C3 113
Apache, co., Az., U.S. ... B6 80
Apache Creek, N.M., U.S. ... D1 108
Apache Junction, Az., U.S. ... m9 80
Apache Peak, mtn., Az., U.S. ... F5 80
Apalachee, Ga., U.S. ... C3 87
Apalachee Bay, b., Fl., U.S. ... B2 86
Apalachicola, Fl., U.S. ... C2 86
Apalachicola, stm., Fl., U.S. ... B1 86
Apalachicola Bay, b., Fl., U.S. ... C2 86
Apalachin, N.Y., U.S. ... C4 109
Apan, Mex. ... n14 63
Apaporis, stm., S.A. ... D3 60
Aparri, Phil. ... B6 34
Apatin, Yugo. ... C4 24
Apatity, Sov. Un. ... D15 14
Apatzingán [de la Constitución], Mex. ... n12 63
Apeldoorn, Neth. ... A6 16
Apennines, mts., Italy ... C4 23
Apennine Tunnel, Italy ... B3 23
Apérathos, Grc. ... D5 25
Apex, N.C., U.S. ... B4 110
Apex Mountain, mtn., Yukon ... D5 66
Api, mtn., Nepal ... C8 37
Apia, W. Sam. ... F12 52
Apiacás, Serra dos, plat., Braz. ... E3 59
Apia Harbour, b., W. Sam. ... F12 52
Apiaí, Braz. ... C3 56
Apishapa, stm., Co., U.S. ... D6 83
Apison, Tn., U.S. ... h11 119
Apizaco, Mex. ... n14 63
Aplao, Peru ... E3 58
Aplin, Ar., U.S. ... C3 81
Aplington, Ia., U.S. ... B5 92
Apo, Mount, mtn., Phil. ... D7 34
Apodi, Braz. ... C3 57
Apohaqui, N.B. ... D4 71
Apolda, E. Ger. ... C5 18
Apolima Island, i., W. Sam. ... F11 52
Apolima Strait, strt., W. Sam. ... F11 52
Apollo, Pa., U.S. ... E2 115
Apolo, Bol. ... B2 55
Apopka, Fl., U.S. ... D5 86
Apopka, Lake, l., Fl., U.S. ... D5 86
Aporé, Braz. ... B2 56
Aporé, stm., Braz. ... B2 56
Apostle Islands, is., Wi., U.S. ... A3 126
Apostle Islands National Lakeshore, Wi., U.S. ... A3 126
Apóstoles, Arg. ... E4 55
Appalachia, Va., U.S. ... f9 123
Appalachian Mountains, mts., N.A. ... C11 76
Appam, N.D., U.S. ... A2 111
Appanoose, co., Ia., U.S. ... D5 92
Appenzell, Switz. ... E4 18
Appenzell-Ausser Rhoden, state, Switz. ... B5 20
Appenzell-Inner Rhoden, state, Switz. ... B5 20
Apperson, Ok., U.S. ... A5 113
Appingedam, Neth. ... A6 17
Apple, stm., Wi., U.S. ... C1 126
Appleby, Eng., U.K. ... F6 13
Appleby, Tx., U.S. ... D5 120
Applecreek, Oh., U.S. ... B4 112
Applecross, Scot., U.K. ... C3 13
Applegate, Mi., U.S. ... E8 99
Applegate, Or., U.S. ... E3 114
Applegate, stm., Or., U.S. ... E3 114
Apple Grove, W.V., U.S. ... C2 125
Apple Hill, Ont. ... B10 73
Apple Orchard Mountain, mtn., Va., U.S. ... C3 123
Apple River, N.S. ... D5 71
Apple River, Il., U.S. ... A3 90
Apple Springs, Tx., U.S. ... D5 120
Appleton, Ar., U.S. ... B3 81
Appleton, Me., U.S. ... D3 96
Appleton, Mn., U.S. ... E2 100
Appleton, Wa., U.S. ... D4 124
Appleton, Wi., U.S. ... D5 126
Appleton City, Mo., U.S. ... C3 102
Apple Valley, Ca., U.S. ... E5 82
Apple Valley, Mn., U.S. ... n12 100
Apple Valley, N.D., U.S. ... *C5 111
Applewood, Co., U.S. ... B5 83
Appleyard, Wa., U.S. ... B5 124
Appling, Ga., U.S. ... C4 87
Appling, co., Ga., U.S. ... E4 87
Appomattox, Va., U.S. ... C4 123
Appomattox, co., Va., U.S. ... C4 123
Appomattox, stm., Va., U.S. ... C4 123
Appomattox Court House National Historical Park, Va., U.S. ... C4 123
Apra Harbor, b., Guam ... L9 52
Aprelsk, Sov. Un. ... D14 29
Aprilia, Italy ... D4 23
Apsheron Peninsula, pen., Sov. Un. ... G19 8
Apsley, Ont. ... C6 73
Apt, Fr. ... F6 16
Aptos, Ca., U.S. ... *D3 82
Apua Point, c., Hi., U.S. ... D6 88
Apucarana, Braz. ... C2 56
Apulia (Puglia), prov., Italy ... D6 23
Apure, state, Ven. ... B4 60
Apure, stm., Ven. ... B4 60
Apurímac, dept., Peru ... D3 58

Apurímac, stm., Peru ... D3 58
'Aqaba, Gulf of, b. ... C3 38
'Aqiq, Sud. ... B4 47
'Aqrabā, Syria ... A8 41
'Aqrabah, Isr. Occ. ... B7 41
Aquarius Mountains, mts., Az., U.S. ... C2 80
Aquarius Plateau, plat., Ut., U.S. ... E4 121
Aquasco, Md., U.S. ... C4 97
Aquebogue, N.Y., U.S. ... n16 109
Aquidauana, Braz. ... C1 56
Aquila see L'Aquila, Italy ... C4 23
Aquileia, Italy ... D9 20
Aquiles Serdán, Mex. ... B3 63
Aquin, Haiti ... E7 64
Aquone, N.C., U.S. ... f9 110
Arab, Al., U.S. ... A3 78
'Arab, Baḥr al, stm., Sud. ... D2 47
'Arab, Khalīj al, b., Egypt ... G7 40
'Arab, Shatt al, stm., Iraq ... B4 38
Arabelo, Ven. ... C5 60
Arabi, Ga., U.S. ... E3 87
Arabi, La., U.S. ... k11 95
Arabian Desert, des., Eg. ... C3 38
Arabian Sea ... H9 30
'Arabian, stm., Braz. ... B2 59
Araçá, Braz. ... D3 57
Aracati, Braz. ... B3 57
Araçatuba, Braz. ... C2 56
Aracena, Spain ... D2 22
Aracruz, Braz. ... B4 56
Araçuaí, Braz. ... B4 56
Arad, Rom. ... B5 24
Arada, Chad ... A3 46
Arafura Sea ... G7 6
Aragarças, Braz. ... B2 56
Arago, Or., U.S. ... D2 114
Arago, Cape, c., Or., U.S. ... D2 114
Aragon, Ga., U.S. ... B1 87
Aragon, N.M., U.S. ... D1 108
Aragon, hist. reg., Spain ... B5 22
Aragón, stm., Spain ... A5 22
Aragua, state, Ven. ... A4 60
Araguacema, Braz. ... D5 59
Araguaçu, Braz. ... E5 59
Aragua de Barcelona, Ven. ... B5 60
Araguaia, Braço Menor, stm., Braz. ... E5 59
Araguaia National Park, Braz. ... E4 59
Araguao, Boca, mth., Ven. ... B5 60
Araguari, Braz. ... B4 56
Araguari, stm., Braz. ... B4 59
Arai, Japan ... H9 33
Arai, Japan ... o16 33
Arai, Alg. ... D5 44
Arāk, Iran ... B4 38
Arakan Range, mts., Burma ... E9 36
Arakhthos, stm., Grc. ... C3 25
Arakonam, India ... F6 36
Araks, stm., Asia ... B3 39
Aral Sea, Sov. Un. ... D6 28
Aralsk, Sov. Un. ... D6 28
Aramac, Austl. ... D8 50
Aramac, Col. ... D8 60
Ārān, Iran ... D5 39
Aranda de Duero, Spain ... B4 22
Arandas, Mex. ... m12 63
Aran Island, i., Ire. ... C2 10
Aran Islands, is., Ire. ... D2 10
Aranjuez, Spain ... B4 22
Aranos, Nmb. ... B2 49
Aransas, co., Tx., U.S. ... E4 120
Aransas Bay, b., Tx., U.S. ... E4 120
Aransas Pass, Tx., U.S. ... F4 120
Aranyaprathet, Thai. ... C2 34
Araouane, Mali ... C4 45
Arapahoe, Co., U.S. ... C8 83
Arapahoe, Ne., U.S. ... D6 104
Arapahoe, N.C., U.S. ... B6 110
Arapahoe, Wy., U.S. ... D4 127
Arapahoe, co., Co., U.S. ... B6 83
Arapey, Ur. ... E1 56
Arapey Grande, stm., Ur. ... E1 56
Arapkir, Tur. ... C12 40
Arapongas, Braz. ... C2 56
Araranguá, Braz. ... D3 56
Araraquara, Braz. ... C3 56
Araras, Braz. ... C3 56
Ararat, Austl. ... G7 50
Ararat, Austl. ... D2 123
Ararat, Mount, mtn., Tur. ... C15 40
Araripe, Chapada do, plat., Braz. ... D3 57
Araruna, Braz. ... h6 57
Arauca, Col. ... B3 60
Arauca, dept., Col. ... B3 60
Arauca, stm., S.A. ... B3 60
Arauco, Chile ... B2 54
Araújos, Braz. ... B3 56
Arāvalli Range, mts., India ... D5 36
Araxá, Braz. ... B4 56
Araya, Ven. ... A5 60
Araya, Punta de, c., Ven. ... A5 60
Arba Minch, Eth. ... A5 47
Arbela, Braz. ... A5 102
Arboga, Swe. ... t33 14
Arbois, Fr. ... D6 16
Arboles, Co., U.S. ... D3 83
Arbon, Switz. ... B5 20
Arbon, Id., U.S. ... G6 89
Arborea (Mussolinia), Italy ... E2 23
Arborfield, Sask. ... D4 75
Arborg, Man. ... D3 70
Arbor Vitae, Wi., U.S. ... C4 126
Arbroath, Scot., U.K. ... B5 10
Arbuckle, Ca., U.S. ... C2 82
Arbuckle, Lake, l., Fl., U.S. ... E5 86
Arbuckle Mountains, mts., Ok., U.S. ... C4 113
Arbuckles, Lake of the, res., Ok., U.S. ... C5 113
Arbyrd, Mo., U.S. ... E7 102
Arc, Bayou des, stm., Ar., U.S. ... B4 81
Arcachon, Fr. ... E3 16
Arcade, Ca., U.S. ... c3 82
Arcade, N.Y., U.S. ... C2 109
Arcadia, N.S. ... F3 71
Arcadia, Fl., U.S. ... E5 86
Arcadia, In., U.S. ... D5 91
Arcadia, Ia., U.S. ... B2 92
Arcadia, Ks., U.S. ... E9 93
Arcadia, La., U.S. ... B3 95
Arcadia, Mi., U.S. ... D4 99
Arcadia, Mo., U.S. ... D7 102
Arcadia, Ne., U.S. ... C6 104
Arcadia, Oh., U.S. ... A2 112
Arcadia, Ok., U.S. ... B4 113
Arcadia, Pa., U.S. ... E4 115

Arcadia, R.I., U.S. ... E2 116
Arcadia, S.C., U.S. ... B4 117
Arcadia, Wi., U.S. ... D2 126
Arcanum, Oh., U.S. ... C1 112
Arcata, Ca., U.S. ... B1 82
Arc Dome, mtn., Nv., U.S. ... E4 105
Arcelia, Mex. ... n13 63
Arcey, Fr. ... A2 21
Archambault, Lac, l., Que. ... C3 74
Archbald, Pa., U.S. ... m18 115
Archbold, Oh., U.S. ... A1 112
Archdale, N.C., U.S. ... B3 110
Archer, Ia., U.S. ... A2 92
Archer, Ne., U.S. ... C7 104
Archer, co., Tx., U.S. ... C3 120
Archer, Lake, l., Austl. ... B7 50
Archer City, Tx., U.S. ... C3 120
Archer's Post, Kenya ... A6 48
Archerwill, Sask. ... E4 75
Arches National Park, Ut., U.S. ... E6 121
Archidona, Spain ... D3 22
Archie, Mo., U.S. ... C3 102
Archive, Sask. ... G3 75
Archuleta, co., Co., U.S. ... D3 83
Arco, Id., U.S. ... F5 89
Arco, Mn., U.S. ... F2 100
Arcola, Ont. ... D8 71
Arcola, Il., U.S. ... D5 90
Arcola, In., U.S. ... B7 91
Arcola, Ms., U.S. ... B3 101
Arcola, Va., U.S. ... g11 123
Arcos de la Frontera, Spain ... D3 22
Arcot, India ... F6 36
Arcoverde, Braz. ... C3 57
Arctic Bay, N.W. Ter. ... B16 66
Arctic Ocean ... A1 128
Arctic Village, Ak., U.S. ... B10 79
Arcueil, Fr. ... g10 16
Arcverde, Braz. ... E7 24
'Arīsh, Wādī al, val., Eg. ... D6 41
Arda, stm., Eur. ... H7 25
Ardabīl (Ardebil), Iran ... B4 38
Ardahan, Tur. ... E2 11
Ardakān, Iran ... B5 38
Ardakān, Iran ... E6 39
Ardara, Ire. ... C3 11
Ardath, Sask. ... F2 75
Ardatov, Sov. Un. ... D16 27
Ardbeg, Ont. ... B4 73
Ardea, Italy ... h9 23
Ardebil see Ardabīl, Iran ... B4 38
Arden, Ire. ... E2 10
Arden, Man. ... D2 70
Arden, Ont. ... C8 73
Arden, Den. ... B3 15
Arden, Ar., U.S. ... D1 81
Arden, Ca., U.S. ... *C2 82
Arden, N.C., U.S. ... f10 110
Arden Hills, Mn., U.S. ... *m12 100
Ardennes, dept., Fr. ... E4 17
Ardennes, reg., Eur. ... B6 16
Ardenno, Italy ... C5 20
Ardenvoir, Wa., U.S. ... B5 124
Ārdestān, Iran ... D4 11
Ardglass, N. Ire., U.K. ... C6 11
Ardgroom, Ire. ... F2 11
Ardila, stm., Eur. ... C2 22
Ardill, Sask. ... H3 75
Ardino, Bul. ... H7 24
Ardley, Alta. ... C4 68
Ardmore, Ire. ... F4 11
Ardmore, Al., U.S. ... A3 78
Ardmore, In., U.S. ... A5 91
Ardmore, Md., U.S. ... C4 97
Ardmore, Ok., U.S. ... C4 113
Ardmore, Pa., U.S. ... F11 115
Ardmore, S.D., U.S. ... D2 118
Ardmore, Tn., U.S. ... B5 119
Ardnamurchan, Point of, c., Scot., U.K. ... D2 13
Ardnave Point, c., Scot., U.K. ... C2 11
Ardoch, N.D., U.S. ... A8 111
Ardpatrick Point, c., Scot., U.K. ... E3 13
Ardres, Fr. ... D1 17
Ardrossan, Austl. ... G1 51
Ardrossan, Alta. ... C4 68
Ardrossan, Scot., U.K. ... C4 13
Ardsley, N.Y., U.S. ... g13 109
Arecibo, P.R. ... G11 64
Aredale, Ia., U.S. ... B5 92
Areia, Braz. ... h6 57
Areia Branca, Braz. ... B3 57
Arelee, Sask. ... E2 75
Arena, Wi., U.S. ... E4 126
Arena, Point, c., Ca., U.S. ... C2 82
Arena, Punta, c., Mex. ... C3 63
Arenac, co., Mi., U.S. ... D7 99
Arenápolis, Braz. ... A1 56
Arenas de San Pedro, Spain ... B3 22
Arenas Valley, N.M., U.S. ... E1 108
Arendal, Nor. ... H3 14
Arendonk, Bel. ... C5 17
Arendsee, E. Ger. ... F5 15
Arendtsville, Pa., U.S. ... G7 115
Arenillas, Ec. ... B1 58
Arenzville, Il., U.S. ... D3 90
Arequipa, Grc. ... D4 25
Arequipa, Peru ... E3 58
Arequipa, dept., Peru ... E3 58
Arezzo, Italy ... C3 23
Argalastí, Grc. ... C4 25
Arganda, Spain ... p18 22
Argelès-Gazost, Fr. ... F3 16
Argen, stm., W. Ger. ... A8 21
Argenta, Italy ... B3 23
Argenta, Il., U.S. ... D5 90
Argentan, Fr. ... C6 16
Argenteuil, Fr. ... C5 16
Argenteuil, co., Que. ... C3 74
Argentina, ctry., S.A. ... G4 53
Argentina, stm., Braz. ... E2 56
Argenton-sur-Creuse, Fr. ... D4 16
Argeș, stm., Rom. ... E7 24
Arghandāb, stm., Afg. ... E13 39
Arghandāb, Band-e, res., Afg. ... F13 39
Argo, Sud. ... B3 47
Argo, Al., U.S. ... B3 78
Argo, Il., U.S. ... A3 90
Argo, Ky., U.S. ... C7 94
Argo Corner, De., U.S. ... E4 85
Argolis, Gulf of, b., Grc. ... D4 25
Argonia, Ks., U.S. ... E6 93
Argonne, Wi., U.S. ... C5 126
Argonne, reg., Fr. ... C6 16

Argonne, Forêt d', for., Fr. ... E4 17
Árgos, Grc. ... D4 40
Argos, In., U.S. ... B5 91
Árgos Orestikón, Grc. ... B3 25
Argostólion, Grc. ... C3 40
Argun, stm., Asia ... D14 29
Argungu, Nig. ... D5 45
Argusville, N.D., U.S. ... B9 111
Argyle, N.S. ... F4 71
Argyle, Fl., U.S. ... u15 86
Argyle, Ga., U.S. ... E4 87
Argyle, Ia., U.S. ... D6 92
Argyle, Mi., U.S. ... E8 99
Argyle, Mn., U.S. ... B2 100
Argyle, Mo., U.S. ... C5 102
Argyle, N.Y., U.S. ... B7 109
Argyle, Tx., U.S. ... F4 120
Argyle, Wi., U.S. ... F4 126
Argyle, Lake, res., Austl. ... C4 50
Århus, co., Den. ... I4 14
Århus, Den. ... B4 15
Arhus Bugt, b., Den. ... B4 15
Ari, In., U.S. ... B7 91
Ariake Bay, b., Japan ... K5 33
Ariano Irpino, Italy ... D5 23
Ariano nel Polesine, Italy ... E8 20
Ariari, stm., Col. ... C3 60
Arica, Chile ... C1 55
Arica, Col. ... D3 60
Arichat, N.S. ... D8 71
Ariège, stm., Fr. ... F4 16
Ariel, Wa., U.S. ... C3 124
Ariès, stm., Rom. ... B6 24
Arikaree, stm., U.S. ... B8 83
Arima, Trin. ... K14 64
Arimo, Id., U.S. ... G6 89
Arinos, stm., Braz. ... B4 55
Ario de Rosales, Mex. ... D4 63
Arion, Ia., U.S. ... C2 92
Aripeka, Fl., U.S. ... D4 86
Aripo, El Cerro del, mtn., Trin. ... K14 64
Aripuanã, Braz. ... D2 59
Aripuanã, stm., Braz. ... D2 59
Arisaig, Scot., U.K. ... D3 13
Arispe, Ia., U.S. ... D3 92
Aristazabal Island, i., B.C. ... C3 69
Ariton, Al., U.S. ... D4 78
Arivaca, Az., U.S. ... F4 80
Arivonimamo, Madag. ... g9 49
Arizaro, Salar de, pl., Arg. ... D2 55
Arizona, Arg. ... B3 54
Arizona, state, U.S. ... C4 80
Arizona Sunsets, Az., U.S. ... F6 80
Arizpe, Mex. ... A2 63
Arjay, Ky., U.S. ... D6 94
Arjeplog, Swe. ... D8 14
Arjona, Col. ... A2 60
Arjona, Spain ... D3 22
Arkabutla, Ms., U.S. ... A3 101
Arkabutla Lake, res., Ms., U.S. ... A3 101
Arkadelphia, Al., U.S. ... B3 78
Arkadelphia, Ar., U.S. ... C2 81
Arkadhía, reg., Grc. ... D3 13
Arkaig, Loch, l., Scot., U.K. ... D3 13
Arkalyk, Sov. Un. ... D7 28
Arkansas, co., Ar., U.S. ... C4 81
Arkansas, state, U.S. ... C3 81
Arkansas, stm., U.S. ... C9 76
Arkansas, Salt Fork, stm., U.S. ... A3 113
Arkansas City, Ar., U.S. ... D4 81
Arkansas City, Ks., U.S. ... E6 93
Arkansaw, Wi., U.S. ... D1 126
Arkelstorp, Swe. ... B8 15
Arkhangelsk, Sov. Un. ... C7 29
Arkhangelskoye, Sov. Un. ... F13 27
Arkhara, Sov. Un. ... B5 33
Arki, i., Grc. ... D6 25
Arkika, Ar., U.S. ... D1 81
Arklow, Ire. ... D3 10
Arkoma, Ok., U.S. ... B7 113
Arkona, Ont. ... D3 73
Arkona, Kap (The Skaw), c., E. Ger. ... A6 21
Arkport, N.Y., U.S. ... C3 109
Arkville, N.Y., U.S. ... C6 109
Arkwright, Ga., U.S. ... D3 87
Arkwright, R.I., U.S. ... D3 116
Arlanza, stm., Spain ... A4 22
Arlanzón, stm., Spain ... A4 22
Arlberg Tunnel, Aus. ... A5 18
Arlee, Mt., U.S. ... C2 103
Arles, Fr. ... F6 16
Arley, Al., U.S. ... A2 78
Arlington, Az., U.S. ... D3 80
Arlington, Co., U.S. ... C7 83
Arlington, Ga., U.S. ... E2 87
Arlington, In., U.S. ... E6 91
Arlington, Ia., U.S. ... B6 92
Arlington, Ks., U.S. ... E5 93
Arlington, Ky., U.S. ... f9 94
Arlington, Mn., U.S. ... F4 100
Arlington, Ne., U.S. ... C9 104
Arlington, N.Y., U.S. ... D7 109
Arlington, N.C., U.S. ... A2 110
Arlington, Oh., U.S. ... B2 112
Arlington, S.C., U.S. ... B6 114
Arlington, S.D., U.S. ... C8 118
Arlington, Tn., U.S. ... B2 119
Arlington, Vt., U.S. ... E2 122
Arlington, Va., U.S. ... A5 123
Arlington, Wa., U.S. ... A3 124
Arlington, co., Va., U.S. ... g12 123
Arlington, Lake, res., Tx., U.S. ... n9 120
Arlington Beach, S.D., U.S. ... C8 118
Arlington Heights, Il., U.S. ... A5 90
Arlon, Bel. ... C6 16
Arly, stm., Fr. ... D2 20
Arma, Ks., U.S. ... D3 101
Arm, stm., Sask. ... F3 75
Arma, Grc. ... g10 25
Armada, Mi., U.S. ... F8 99
Armagh, Que. ... C7 74
Armagh, N. Ire., U.K. ... C3 10
Armagh, co., N. Ire., U.K. ... E2 11
Armagh, Fr. ... F3 16
Armathwaite, Tn., U.S. ... C9 119
Armavir, Sov. Un. ... E7 29
Armenia, Col. ... C2 60
Armenia, state, Sov. Un. ... E16 29
Armentières, Fr. ... B5 16
Armería, stm., Mex. ... n12 63
Armero, Col. ... C2 60
Armidale, Austl. ... F9 50
Armijo, N.M., U.S. ... k7 108
Armington, Il., U.S. ... C4 90
Armington, Mt., U.S. ... C6 103
Arminto, Wy., U.S. ... C5 127
Armit Lake, l., Can. ... C1 70

Armley, Sask. ... D3 75
Armonk, N.Y., U.S. ... *g13 109
Armorel, Ar., U.S. ... B6 81
Armour, S.D., U.S. ... D7 118
Armstead, Al., U.S. ... B3 78
Armstrong, B.C. ... D8 69
Armstrong, Fl., U.S. ... C5 86
Armstrong, Il., U.S. ... C6 90
Armstrong, Ia., U.S. ... A3 92
Armstrong, Mo., U.S. ... B5 102
Armstrong, Ok., U.S. ... C5 113
Armstrong, Tx., U.S. ... F4 120
Armstrong, co., Pa., U.S. ... E2 115
Armstrong, co., Tx., U.S. ... B2 120
Armstrong, Wi., U.S. ... C5 126
Armstrong Creek, stm., W.V., U.S. ... m13 125
Armstrong Station, Ont. ... F15 66
Armuchee, Ga., U.S. ... B1 87
Armyansk, Sov. Un. ... H9 27
Arnaud, stm., Que. ... E18 66
Arnaudville, La., U.S. ... D4 95
Arneburg, E. Ger. ... F5 15
Arnedo, Spain ... A4 22
Arnegard, N.D., U.S. ... B2 111
Arneiroz, Braz. ... C2 57
Arnett, Ok., U.S. ... A2 113
Arnett, W.V., U.S. ... D3 125
Arney, stm., N. Ire., U.K. ... C4 11
Arnhem, Neth. ... B6 16
Arnhem, Cape, c., Austl. ... B6 50
Arnhem Land, reg., Austl. ... B5 50
Arnissa, Grc. ... B3 25
Arno, stm., Italy ... C3 23
Arnold, Ca., U.S. ... C3 82
Arnold, Ks., U.S. ... D3 93
Arnold, Md., U.S. ... *B4 97
Arnold, Mi., U.S. ... B3 99
Arnold, Mn., U.S. ... C6 100
Arnold, Mo., U.S. ... C7 102
Arnold, Ne., U.S. ... C5 104
Arnold, Pa., U.S. ... h14 115
Arnold Mills, R.I., U.S. ... B4 116
Arnold Mills Reservoir, res., R.I., U.S. ... B4 116
Arnoldsburg, W.V., U.S. ... C3 125
Arnold's Cove, Newf. ... E4 72
Arnolds Park, Ia., U.S. ... A2 92
Arnoldsville, Ga., U.S. ... C3 87
Arnot, Pa., U.S. ... C7 115
Arnouville, Fr. ... g10 16
Arnøya, i., Nor. ... B9 14
Arnprior, Ont. ... B8 73
Arnstadt, E. Ger. ... C5 18
Arnstein, Ont. ... B5 73
Arø, i., Den. ... C3 15
Aroa, Ven. ... A4 60
Aroab, Nmb. ... C2 49
Arock, Or., U.S. ... E9 114
Aroda, Va., U.S. ... B4 123
Arolla, Switz. ... B3 21
Arolsen, W. Ger. ... B4 18
Aroma, Sud. ... B4 47
Aroma Park, Il., U.S. ... B6 90
Arona, Italy ... E6 21
Aroostook, N.B. ... C2 71
Aroostook, co., Me., U.S. ... B4 96
Aroostook, stm., N.A. ... B4 96
Arop, i., Pap. N. Gui. ... k12 50
Aros, Nor. ... p28 14
Arosa, Switz. ... C5 20
Arouca, Trin. ... N23 64
Arp, Tx., U.S. ... C5 120
Arpajon, Fr. ... F2 17
Arpin, Wi., U.S. ... D3 126
Arques, Fr. ... D2 17
Arques-la-Bataille, Fr. ... E9 12
'Arrābah, Isr. Occ. ... B7 41
Ar Rahad, Sud. ... B3 47
Arraias, Braz. ... D1 57
Arraijola, Pan. ... F8 62
Arraiolos, Port. ... C2 22
Ar Ramādī, Iraq ... B4 38
Ar Ramthā, Jord. ... B7 41
Arran, Fl., U.S. ... B5 86
Arran, Island of, i., Scot., U.K. ... C4 10
Ar Rank, Sud. ... C3 47
Ar Raqqah, Syria ... B3 38
Arras, Fr. ... B5 16
Ar Rawdah, Eg. ... E3 41
Arrecifes, Arg. ... m15 22
Arrecifes, stm., Arg. ... g7 54
Arrey, N.M., U.S. ... E2 108
Arriaga, Mex. ... D6 63
Arriba, Co., U.S. ... B7 83
Arriikan Island, i., Marsh Is. ... P18 52
Arrington, Va., U.S. ... C8 93
Arrington, Va., U.S. ... C4 123
Arroio Grande, Braz. ... E2 56
Arroll, Mo., U.S. ... C9 104
Arrone, stm., Italy ... h8 23
Arrow, Lough, l., Ire. ... C3 11
Arrow Creek, stm., Mt., U.S. ... C6 103
Arrow Head Lodge, Wy., U.S. ... *B5 127
Arrowhead Mountain Lake, res., Vt., U.S. ... B2 122
Arrowhead Village, N.J., U.S. ... C4 107
Arrow Rock, Mo., U.S. ... B5 102
Arrowrock Reservoir, res., Id., U.S. ... F3 89
Arrowsmith, Il., U.S. ... C5 90
Arrowwood, Alta. ... D4 68
Arrowwood Lake, res., N.D., U.S. ... B7 111
Arroyo, P.R. ... C3 65
Arroyo de la Luz, Spain ... C2 22
Arroyo Grande, Ca., U.S. ... E3 82
Arroyo Hondo, N.M., U.S. ... A4 108
Arroyo Seco, N.M., U.S. ... A4 108
Ar Rumaythah, Iraq ... F2 39
Ar Ruṣayfah, Jord. ... B8 41
Ar Ruṣayris, Sud. ... F3 75
Ar Ruṭbah, Iraq ... B4 38
Ar Ruwaytt̄, hist., Jord. ... D7 41
Ar Fork, Az., U.S. ... B3 80
Arsenyev, Sov. Un. ... D6 33
Arṣṭa, Sov. Un. ... D6 33
Arsinöe prov., Eth. ... H9 33
Årstad, Swe. ... H9 33
Árta, Grc. ... B3 25
Árta, dept., Grc. ... *C3 25
Ártabro, Cabo, c., Japan ... H9 33
Artashat, Sov. Un. ... B2 39
Ar Ṭayyān, well, Sau. Ar. ... H13 40
Artem, Sov. Un. ... E16 29
Artemisa, Cuba ... C2 64
Artemovsk, Sov. Un. ... E27 29
Artemovsk, Sov. Un. ... G11 29
Artemovskiy, Sov. Un. ... D6 28
Artena, Italy ... h9 23
Arter, Mount, mtn., Wy., U.S. ... D4 127
Artern, E. Ger. ... B6 19

Artesia, Ca., U.S. ... *n12 82
Artesia, Ms., U.S. ... B5 101
Artesia, N.M., U.S. ... E5 108
Artesian, S.D., U.S. ... C8 118
Artesia Wells, Tx., U.S. ... E3 120
Arth, Switz. ... B4 20
Arthabaska, Que. ... C6 74
Arthabaska, co., Que. ... C5 74
Arthur, Ont. ... D4 73
Arthur, Il., U.S. ... D5 90
Arthur, Ia., U.S. ... B2 92
Arthur, Ne., U.S. ... C4 104
Arthur, N.D., U.S. ... B8 111
Arthur, Tn., U.S. ... C10 119
Arthur, co., Ne., U.S. ... C4 104
Arthur, Lake, l., La., U.S. ... D3 95
Arthur, Lake, l., Pa., U.S. ... E1 115
Arthur Kill, stm., N.J., U.S. ... k8 107
Arthurs Town, Bah. ... B6 64
Artibonite, stm., Haiti ... E7 64
Artigas, Ur. ... E1 56
Artois, hist. reg., Fr. ... B5 16
Artois, Collines de l', hills, Fr. ... D2 17
Artvin, Tur. ... B13 40
Aru, Zaire ... A5 48
Arua, Ug. ... A5 48
Aruanã, Braz. ... C2 57
Aruba, ctry., N.A. ... H17 65
Arucas, Spain ... m14 22
Aru Islands, is., Indon. ... G8 34
Arun, stm., Eur. ... D7 12
Arunachal Pradesh, state, India ... C10 37
Arundel, Que. ... D3 74
Arundel, Eng., U.K. ... D7 12
Arundel Village, Md., U.S. ... *h11 97
Arusha, Tan. ... B6 48
Arusha, prov., Tan. ... B6 48
Aruwimi, stm., Zaire ... A4 48
Arvada, Co., U.S. ... B5 83
Arvada, Wy., U.S. ... B6 127
Arvagh, Ire. ... D4 11
Arvayheer, Mong. ... B5 31
Arve, stm., Eur. ... D2 20
Arvida, Que. ... A6 74
Arvidsjaur, Swe. ... E8 14
Arvika, Swe. ... H5 14
Arvilla, N.D., U.S. ... B8 111
Arvin, Ca., U.S. ... E4 82
Arvon, Mount, mtn., Mi., U.S. ... B2 99
Arvonia, Va., U.S. ... C4 123
Arxan, China ... B8 31
Arys, Sov. Un. ... E7 28
Arzamas, Sov. Un. ... D14 27
Arzgir, Sov. Un. ... I15 27
Arzúa, Spain ... A1 22
Aš, Czech. ... C2 26
Aså, Den. ... A4 15
Asab, Nmb. ... C2 49
Asad, Lake, res., Syria ... B12 40
Asahi, Mount, mtn., Japan ... E11 33
Asahi, Japan ... C13 31
Asahikawa, Japan ... C13 31
Asan Bay, b., S. Kor. ... H3 33
Asan Point, c., Guam ... L9 52
Āsānsol, India ... D8 36
Asbach, W. Ger. ... C2 19
Asbest, Sov. Un. ... D9 29
Asbestos, Que. ... D6 74
Asbury, Mo., U.S. ... D3 102
Ascención, Mex. ... A3 63
Ascension, co., La., U.S. ... D5 95
Ascension, i., St. Hel. ... G4 42
Aschaffenburg, W. Ger. ... C4 18
Aschersleben, E. Ger. ... C5 18
Ascoli Piceno, Italy ... C4 23
Ascona, Switz. ... D6 21
Ascope, Peru ... C2 58
Ascotán, Chile ... D3 55
Ascot-Corner, Que. ... D6 74
Ascutney, Vt., U.S. ... E4 122
Ascutney, Mount, mtn., Vt., U.S. ... E4 122
Aseb, Eth. ... C5 47
Asela, Eth. ... D4 47
Åsele, Swe. ... E7 14
Asenovgrad, Bul. ... E7 24
Asha, Sov. Un. ... B5 28
Ashanti, prov., Ghana ... E4 45
Ashaway, R.I., U.S. ... F1 116
Ashbourne, Eng., U.K. ... A6 12
Ashburn, Ga., U.S. ... E3 87
Ashburn, Mo., U.S. ... B6 102
Ashburnham, Ma., U.S. ... A4 98
Ashburton, Eng., U.K. ... O13 51
Ashburton, stm., Austl. ... D2 50
Ashby, Al., U.S. ... B3 78
Ashby, Ma., U.S. ... A4 98
Ashby, Mn., U.S. ... D3 100
Ashbyburg, Ky., U.S. ... C2 94
Ashcroft, B.C. ... D7 69
Ashdod, Isr. ... C6 41
Ashdot Ya'aqov, Isr. ... B5 102
Ashdown, Ar., U.S. ... D1 81
Ashe, co., N.C., U.S. ... A1 110
Asheboro, N.C., U.S. ... B3 110
Ashepoo, stm., S.C., U.S. ... C5 113
Asher, Ok., U.S. ... B7 111
Ashern, Man. ... C3 65
Asherton, Tx., U.S. ... E3 120
Asherville, Ks., U.S. ... C5 93
Asheville, N.C., U.S. ... f10 110
Ashfield, Ma., U.S. ... A4 81
Ash Flat, Ar., U.S. ... A4 81
Ashford, Al., U.S. ... D4 78
Ashford, Eng., U.K. ... D8 12
Ashford, Ct., U.S. ... B7 84
Ashford, W.V., U.S. ... m12 125
Ash Fork, Az., U.S. ... B3 80
Ash Grove, Mo., U.S. ... D4 102
Ashikaga, Japan ... H9 33
Ashio, Japan ... H9 33
Ashizuri, Cape, c., Japan ... J6 33
Ashkhabad, Sov. Un. ... G6 29
Ashkum, Il., U.S. ... C6 90
Ash Lake, Mn., U.S. ... B6 100
Ashland, Al., U.S. ... B4 78
Ashland, Ca., U.S. ... *h8 82
Ashland, Il., U.S. ... D3 90
Ashland, Ks., U.S. ... E4 93
Ashland, Ky., U.S. ... B7 94
Ashland, Me., U.S. ... B4 96
Ashland, Ma., U.S. ... g10 98
Ashland, Ms., U.S. ... A4 101

Name	Map Ref.	Page
Ashland, Mo., U.S.	C5	102
Ashland, Mt., U.S.	E10	103
Ashland, Ne., U.S.	C9	104
Ashland, N.H., U.S.	C3	106
Ashland, Oh., U.S.	B3	112
Ashland, Ok., U.S.	C5	113
Ashland, Or., U.S.	E4	114
Ashland, Pa., U.S.	E9	115
Ashland, Va., U.S.	C5	123
Ashland, Wi., U.S.	B3	126
Ashland, co., Oh., U.S.	B3	112
Ashland, co., Wi., U.S.	B3	126
Ashland, Mount, mtn., Or., U.S.	E4	114
Ashland City, Tn., U.S.	A4	119
Ashland Reservoir, res., Ma., U.S.	h10	98
Ashley, Il., U.S.	E4	90
Ashley, In., U.S.	A7	91
Ashley, Mi., U.S.	E6	99
Ashley, Mo., U.S.	B6	102
Ashley, N.D., U.S.	C6	111
Ashley, Oh., U.S.	B3	112
Ashley, Pa., U.S.	n17	115
Ashley, co., Ar., U.S.	D4	81
Ashley, stm., S.C., U.S.	F7	117
Ashley Creek, stm., Ut., U.S.	C7	121
Ashley Falls, Ma., U.S.	B1	98
Ashmont, Alta.	B5	68
Ashmore, Il., U.S.	D5	90
Ashmore Islands, is., Austl.	B3	50
Ashmūn, Eg.	D2	41
Ashnola, stm., N.A.	A5	124
Ashokan, N.Y., U.S.	D6	109
Ashokan Reservoir, res., N.Y., U.S.	D6	109
Ashport, Tn., U.S.	B2	119
Ashqelon, Isr.	B3	38
Ash Shabakah, Iraq	B4	38
Ash Shallāl, Eg.	E5	43
Ash Shallāl, Eg.	E6	43
Ash Shallūfah, Eg.	D4	41
Ash Shāmīyah (Northern), prov., Sud.	B2	47
Ash Shāriqah, U.A.E.	C5	38
Ash Sharqāt, Iraq	B4	38
Ash Shaṭrah, Iraq	F3	39
Ash Shawāshinah, Eg.	E2	41
Ash Shawbak, Jord.	D7	41
Ash Shawmarah, Leb.	A7	41
Ash Shaykh Jarrāh (part of Jerusalem), Isr. Occ.	m14	41
Ash Shaykh Sa'd, Syria	B7	41
Ash Shiḥr, Yemen	D4	38
Ash Shumlul, Sau. Ar.	H3	39
Ash Shurayk, Sud.	A3	47
Ash Springs, Nv., U.S.	F6	105
Ashtabula, Oh., U.S.	A5	112
Ashtabula, co., Oh., U.S.	A5	112
Ashtabula, Lake, res., N.D., U.S.	B8	111
Ashton, Ont.	B8	73
Ashton, Id., U.S.	E7	89
Ashton, Il., U.S.	A2	92
Ashton, Md., U.S.	B3	97
Ashton, Mi., U.S.	E5	99
Ashton, Ne., U.S.	C7	104
Ashton, R.I., U.S.	B4	116
Ashton, S.D., U.S.	C7	118
Ashuanipi Lake, l., Newf.	h8	72
Ashuelot, N.H., U.S.	E2	106
Ashuelot, stm., N.H., U.S.	E2	106
Ashville, Man.	D1	70
Ashville, Al., U.S.	B3	78
Ashville, Oh., U.S.	C3	112
Ashwaubenon, Wi., U.S.	D5	126
Ashwood, Or., U.S.	C6	114
Ashwood, Tn., U.S.	B4	119
Asia, cont.	E11	30
Asia Minor, reg., Tur.	C10	40
Asifābād, India	H7	37
Asiga, Puntan, c., N. Mar. Is.	D7	52
Asiga Point, c., Guam	M10	52
Asinara, Gulf of, b., Italy	D2	23
Asinara Island, i., Italy	D2	23
Asino, Sov. Un.	B11	28
'Asīr, reg., Sau. Ar.	D4	38
'Asīrah ash Shamālīyah, Isr. Occ.	g12	41
Asker, Nor.	p28	14
Askersund, Swe.	H6	14
Askew, Ms., U.S.	A3	101
Askham, S. Afr.	C3	49
Askim, Nor.	p29	14
Askim, Swe.	A5	15
Askival, mtn., Scot., U.K.	D2	13
Askö, l., Swe.	u35	14
Askov, Mn., U.S.	D6	100
Āsmār, Afg.	D15	39
Asmara (Asmera), Eth.	B4	47
Asnæs, Den.	C5	15
Asnebumskit Hill, hill, Ma., U.S.	B4	98
Åsnen, l., Swe.	B8	15
Asnières [-sur-Seine], Fr.	g10	16
Asopós, stm., Grc.	g11	25
Asosa, Eth.	C3	47
Asotin, Wa., U.S.	C8	124
Asotin, co., Wa., U.S.	C8	124
Asotin Creek, stm., Wa., U.S.	C8	124
Aspe, Spain	C5	22
Aspen, Co., U.S.	B4	83
Aspen Butte, mtn., Or., U.S.	E4	114
Aspen Hill, Md., U.S.	*B3	97
Aspen Hill, Tn., U.S.	B5	119
Asperg, W. Ger.	E4	19
Aspermont, Tx., U.S.	C2	120
Aspers, Pa., U.S.	G7	115
Aspinall, Pa., U.S.	C2	92
Aspinwall, Pa., U.S.	k14	115
Aspiring, Mount, mtn., N.Z.	P12	51
Aspres [-sur-Buëch], Fr.	E2	17
Aspsropirgos, Grc.	g11	25
Aspy Bay, b., N.S.	E2	75
Asquith, Sask.	g9	98
Assabet, stm., Ma., U.S.	D4	38
As Saffānīyah, Sau. Ar.	C4	38
Aş Şāfī, Jord.	C7	41
Assaikwatamo, stm., Man.	A3	70
Aş Şāliḥīyah, Eg.	D4	41
As Sallūm, Eg.	B2	38
As Salmān, Iraq	B4	38
Aş Şalt, Jord.	F10	40
Assam, state, India	C9	36
Aş Şamū', Isr. Occ.	C7	41
Aş Şanamayn, Syria	A8	41
Assaria, Ks., U.S.	D6	93
Assateague Island, i., U.S.	D7	97
Assateague Island National Seashore, U.S.	D7	97
Assawoman Bay, b., Md., U.S.	D7	97
Assawompset Pond, l., Ma., U.S.	C6	98
Assen, Neth.	A7	16
Assens, Den.	C3	15
Assens, Den.	B4	15
As Sinbillāwayn, Eg.	D3	41
Assini, I.C.	E4	45
Assiniboia, Sask.	H2	75
Assiniboine, stm., Can.	E2	70
Assiniboine, Mount, mtn., Can.	D3	68
Assinika, stm., Man.	C4	70
Assinippi, Ma., U.S.	h12	98
Assis, Braz.	C2	56
Assis Brasil, Braz.	D4	58
Assisi, Italy	C4	23
Asso, Italy	E7	21
Assonet, Ma., U.S.	C5	98
As Sudd, reg., Sud.	D3	47
Aş Şūfīyah, Eg.	D3	41
Aş Sulaymānīyah, Iraq	B4	38
Aş Sulaymānīyah, Sau. Ar.	C4	38
As Sulayyil, Sau. Ar.	A6	47
As Sulṭān, Libya	D4	43
Aş Şummān, plat., Sau. Ar.	H3	39
As Suwaydā', Syria	F11	40
Astakós, Grc.	C3	25
Āstānā, Iran	B4	39
Astara, Iran	B5	39
Asten, Neth.	C5	17
Asterābād see Gorgān, Iran	B5	38
Asti, Italy	B2	23
Astipálaia, i., Grc.	G8	25
Astola, i., Pak.	I11	39
Aston, Pa., U.S.	*p20	115
Aston Jonction, Que.	C5	74
Astor, Fl., U.S.	C5	86
Astorga, Spain	A2	22
Astoria, Il., U.S.	C3	90
Astoria, Or., U.S.	A3	114
Astoria, S.D., U.S.	C9	118
Astrakhan, Sov. Un.	h9	23
Astura, stm., Italy	h9	23
Asturias, hist. reg., Spain	A2	22
Asuisui, Cape, c., W. Sam.	F11	52
Asuke, Japan	n16	33
Asunción, Para.	E4	55
Asunción Mita, Guat.	C3	62
Asunción Nochixtlán, Mex.	o15	63
Āsunden, l., Swe.	A7	15
Aswān, Eg.	C3	38
Aswān High Dam, Eg.	C3	38
Asyūṭ, Eg.	C3	38
Atacama, prov., Chile	E2	55
Atacama, Salar de, pl., Chile	B3	58
Atacama Desert, des., Chile	D2	55
'Aṭāʾiṭah, Jabal al, mtn., Jord.	D7	41
Atakpamé, Togo	E5	45
Atalaia, Braz.	k5	57
Atalaia do Norte, Braz.	B3	58
Atalándi, Grc.	C4	25
Atalaya, Peru	D3	58
Atalissa, Ia., U.S.	C6	92
Atami, Japan	n18	33
Atascadero, Ca., U.S.	E3	82
Atascosa, co., Tx., U.S.	E3	120
Atasu, Sov. Un.	D8	28
Atauro, i., Indon.	G7	34
Atáviros, mtn., Grc.	D6	25
'Aṭbarah, Sud.	B3	47
'Aṭbarah, stm., Afr.	B4	47
Atbasar, Sov. Un.	D9	29
Atchafalaya, stm., La., U.S.	D4	95
Atchafalaya Bay, b., La., U.S.	E4	95
Atchison, Ks., U.S.	C8	93
Atchison, co., Ks., U.S.	C8	93
Atchison, co., Mo., U.S.	A2	102
Atco, N.J., U.S.	D3	107
Atgidon, Puntan, c., N. Mar. Is.	E7	52
Ath, Bel.	D3	17
Athabasca, Alta.	B4	68
Athabasca, stm., Alta.	f8	68
Athabasca, Lake, l., Can.	m7	75
Athalia, Oh., U.S.	D3	112
Athboy, Ire.	D10	69
Athapapuskow Lake, l., Man.	B1	70
Atha Road (part of Pickering), Ont.	k15	73
Athboy, Ire.	D5	11
Athelstan, Que.	D3	74
Athenry, Ire.	D3	11
Athens, Ont.	C9	73
Athens (Athínai), Grc.	D4	40
Athens, Al., U.S.	A3	78
Athens, Ar., U.S.	C2	81
Athens, Ga., U.S.	C3	87
Athens, Il., U.S.	D4	90
Athens, In., U.S.	B5	91
Athens, La., U.S.	B2	95
Athens, Me., U.S.	D3	96
Athens, Mi., U.S.	F5	99
Athens, N.Y., U.S.	C7	109
Athens, Oh., U.S.	C3	112
Athens, Pa., U.S.	C8	115
Athens, Tn., U.S.	D9	119
Athens, Tx., U.S.	C5	120
Athens, Vt., U.S.	E3	122
Athens, W.V., U.S.	D3	125
Athens, Wi., U.S.	C3	126
Athens, co., Oh., U.S.	C3	112
Athensville, Il., U.S.	D3	90
Atherley, Ont.	C5	73
Atherton, Austl.	C8	50
Atherton, Ca., U.S.	*k8	82
Athertonville, Ky., U.S.	C4	94
Athiémé, Benin	E5	45
Athínai see Athens, Grc.	D3	11
Athlone, Ire.	D3	11
Athok, Burma	E10	36
Athol, Id., U.S.	B2	89
Athol, Ks., U.S.	C5	93
Athol, Ma., U.S.	A3	98
Athol, S.D., U.S.	C7	118
Atholl Island, i., Bah.	m18	64
Áthos, mtn., Grc.	B5	40
Ath Thamad, Eg.	D6	43
Athy, Ire.	D3	10
Ati, Chad	C3	46
Atibaia, Braz.	E3	56
Atico, Peru	D3	58
Aticonipi, Lac, l., Que.	C2	72
Atikameg, Alta.	B3	68
Atik Lake, l., Man.	B4	70
Atikokan, Ont.	o17	73
Atikonak Lake, l., Newf.	h8	72
Atiquizaya, El Sal.	D3	62
Atka, Ak., U.S.	E5	79
Atka Island, i., Ak., U.S.	E5	79
Atkarsk, Sov. Un.	F15	27
Atkins, Ar., U.S.	B3	81
Atkins, Va., U.S.	D1	123
Atkinson, Ga., U.S.	E5	87
Atkinson, Il., U.S.	B3	90
Atkinson, Ne., U.S.	B7	104
Atkinson, N.H., U.S.	E4	106
Atkinson, N.C., U.S.	C4	110
Atkinson, co., Ga., U.S.	E4	87
Atkinson Lake, l., Man.	A4	70
Atlanta, Ar., U.S.	D2	81
Atlanta, Ga., U.S.	C2	87
Atlanta, Id., U.S.	F3	89
Atlanta, Il., U.S.	C4	90
Atlanta, In., U.S.	D5	91
Atlanta, Ks., U.S.	E7	93
Atlanta, La., U.S.	C3	95
Atlanta, Mi., U.S.	C6	99
Atlanta, Mo., U.S.	B5	102
Atlanta, Ne., U.S.	D6	104
Atlanta, N.Y., U.S.	C3	109
Atlanta, Oh., U.S.	C2	112
Atlanta, Tx., U.S.	C5	120
Atlantic, Ia., U.S.	C2	92
Atlantic, N.C., U.S.	C6	110
Atlantic, co., N.J., U.S.	E3	107
Atlantic Beach, Fl., U.S.	m9	86
Atlantic City, N.J., U.S.	E4	107
Atlantic City, Wy., U.S.	D4	127
Atlantic Highlands, N.J., U.S.	C4	107
Atlantic Mine, Mi., U.S.	A2	99
Atlantic Ocean		
Atlántico, dept., Col.	A2	60
Atlantic Peak, mtn., Wy., U.S.	D3	127
Atlas Mountains, mts., Afr.	C4	44
Atlas Saharien, mts., Alg.	C5	44
Atlee, Alta.	D5	68
Atlin, B.C.	m16	69
Atlin Lake, l., Can.	E6	66
'Atlit, Isr.	B6	41
Atlixco, Mex.	n14	63
Atmore, Al., U.S.	D2	78
Atna Peak, mtn., B.C.	C3	69
Atocha, Bol.	D2	55
Atoka, N.M., U.S.	E5	108
Atoka, Ok., U.S.	C5	113
Atoka, Tn., U.S.	B2	119
Atoka, co., Ok., U.S.	C5	113
Atoka Reservoir, res., Ok., U.S.	C5	113
Atomic City, Id., U.S.	F6	89
Atotonilco el Alto, Mex.	m12	63
Atoyac, Mex.	m12	63
Atoyac, stm., Mex.	n14	63
Atrak, stm., Asia	B5	38
Ätran, stm., Swe.	B6	15
Atrato, stm., Col.	B2	60
Atrek (Atrak), stm., Asia	C7	39
Atsugi, Japan	n18	33
Atsukeshi Bay, b., Japan	E12	33
Atsuma, Japan	E10	33
Atsumi, Japan	o16	33
Atsumi Bay, b., Japan	o16	33
At Tabbīn, Eg.	E3	41
Aṭ Ṭafīlah, Jord.	G10	40
At Ṭā'if, Sau. Ar.	C4	38
Attala, co., Ms., U.S.	B4	101
Attalla, Al., U.S.	A3	78
Aṭ Ṭallāb, Libya	E4	43
At Tamīmī, Libya	C4	43
Attapu, Laos	C3	34
Attapulgus, Ga., U.S.	F2	87
'Aṭṭārah, Isr. Occ.	h11	41
Attawapiskat, Ont.	n19	73
Attawapiskat, stm., Ont.	n18	73
Aṭ Ṭayrīyah, Eg.	D2	41
Attean Pond, l., Me., U.S.	C2	96
Atterberry, Il., U.S.	D3	91
Attica, In., U.S.	E5	93
Attica, Ks., U.S.	E7	99
Attica, Mi., U.S.	C2	109
Attica, N.Y., U.S.	A3	112
Attica, Oh., U.S.	A3	112
Attica, hist. reg., Grc.	g11	25
Attica, Ind., U.S.	C5	73
Attleboro, Ma., U.S.	C5	98
Attleborough, Eng., U.K.	B9	12
Attock, Pak.		
Attu Island, i., Ak., U.S.	E2	79
Attoy, Ire.	D5	11
Aṭ Ṭūr, Eg.	D6	43
Aṭ Ṭūr, Isr. Occ.	m14	41
Aṭ Ṭuwayyah, Sau. Ar.	I13	40
Attymon, Ire.	D3	11
Atuel, stm., Arg.	B3	54
Atui, Uad, val., Afr.	B2	45
Atu'u, Am. Sam.	F13	52
Atvidaberg, Swe.	H6	14
Atwater, Ca., U.S.	D3	82
Atwater, Mn., U.S.	E4	100
Atwater, Oh., U.S.	D3	73
Atwood, Ont.	A7	83
Atwood, Co., U.S.	D5	90
Atwood, Il., U.S.	B6	91
Atwood, Ks., U.S.	C2	93
Atwood, Ok., U.S.	C5	113
Atwood, Tn., U.S.	B3	119
Atwood Lake, res., Oh., U.S.	B4	112
Atwoodville, Ct., U.S.	B7	84
Aua, Am. Sam.	F13	52
Auau Channel, strt., Hi., U.S.	F6	16
Aubagne, Fr.	E4	17
Aubange, Bel.	F4	17
Aube, dept., Fr.	C8	50
Aubenas, Fr.	D4	82
Auberry, Ca., U.S.	g10	11
Aubervilliers, Fr.	E5	16
Aubière, Fr.	E5	16
Aubin, Fr.	E3	16
Aubrey, Que.	C5	81
Aubrey, Ar., U.S.	C5	81
Aubrey Cliffs, clf., Az., U.S.	B2	80
Auburn, Ont.	D3	73
Auburn, Al., U.S.	C4	78
Auburn, Ca., U.S.	C3	82
Auburn, Ga., U.S.	B3	87
Auburn, Il., U.S.	D4	90
Auburn, In., U.S.	B7	91
Auburn, Ky., U.S.	D3	94
Auburn, Me., U.S.	D2	96
Auburn, Ma., U.S.	B4	98
Auburn, Mi., U.S.	E6	99
Auburn, Ne., U.S.	D10	104
Auburn, N.H., U.S.	D4	106
Auburn, N.J., U.S.	D2	107
Auburn, N.Y., U.S.	C4	109
Auburn, N.D., U.S.	A8	111
Auburn, Pa., U.S.	E9	115
Auburn, Wa., U.S.	B3	124
Auburn, W.V., U.S.	B4	125
Auburn, Wy., U.S.	D1	127
Auburndale, Fl., U.S.	D5	86
Auburndale, Wi., U.S.	D3	126
Auburn Heights, Mi., U.S.	F7	99
Auburntown, Tn., U.S.	B5	119
Aubusson, Fr.	E5	16
Auch, Fr.	F4	16
Auchel, Fr.	D2	17
Auchterarder, Scot., U.K.	D5	13
Aucilla, Fl., U.S.	B3	86
Aucilla, stm., Fl., U.S.	B3	86
Auckland, N.Z.	L15	51
Auckland Islands, is., N.Z.	J8	2
Aude, stm., Fr.	F5	16
Audet, Que.	D7	74
Audierne, Fr.	C1	16
Audincourt, Fr.	D7	16
Audrain, co., Mo., U.S.	B6	102
Audubon, Ia., U.S.	C3	92
Audubon, Mn., U.S.	D3	100
Audubon, N.J., U.S.	D2	107
Audubon, Pa., U.S.	C2	92
Audubon, co., Ia., U.S.	C2	92
Audubon, Lake, res., N.M., U.S.	C2	92
Audun-le-Roman, Fr.	C6	18
Aue, E. Ger.	C7	19
Auerbach, E. Ger.	C6	18
Augathella, Austl.	B6	51
Auggen, W. Ger.	A4	21
Aughnacloy, N. Ire., U.K.	C5	11
Aughrim, Ire.	E5	11
Auglaize, co., Oh., U.S.	B1	112
Auglaize, stm., Oh., U.S.	A1	112
Au Gres, Mi., U.S.	D7	99
Augsburg, W. Ger.	*D5	18
August, Ca., U.S.	*D3	82
Augusta, Austl.	F2	50
Augusta, Italy	F5	23
Augusta, Ar., U.S.	B4	81
Augusta, Ga., U.S.	C5	87
Augusta, Il., U.S.	C3	90
Augusta, Ks., U.S.	E7	93
Augusta, Ky., U.S.	B6	94
Augusta, Me., U.S.	D3	96
Augusta, Mi., U.S.	F5	99
Augusta, Mo., U.S.	C7	102
Augusta, Mt., U.S.	C4	103
Augusta, Oh., U.S.	B4	112
Augusta, W.V., U.S.	B6	125
Augusta, Wi., U.S.	D2	126
Augusta, co., Va., U.S.	B3	123
Augusta Springs, Va., U.S.	B3	123
Augusta Victoria Hospital, Isr. Occ.	m14	41
Augustenborg, Den.	D3	15
Augustów, Pol.	B7	26
Augustus, Mount, mtn., Austl.	A5	110
Aulander, N.C., U.S.	A5	110
Auld, Lake, l., Austl.	D3	50
Aulendorf, W. Ger.	B5	20
Aulnay-sous-Bois, Fr.	g11	16
Aulne, stm., Fr.	C2	16
Aulneau Peninsula, pen., Ont.	E3	41
Aulnoye [-Aymeries], Fr.	D3	17
Ault, Co., U.S.	A6	83
Ault, Piz, mtn., Switz.	C7	21
Aumale, Fr.	E9	12
Aumsville, Or., U.S.	k12	114
Auning, Den.	B2	17
Auno, Nig.	G13	52
Aunu'u Island, i., Am. Sam.	K6	35
Aur, i., Malay.	B2	60
Aura, Hi., U.S.	D7	37
Auraiya, India	B2	56
Aurangābād, India	D2	16
Auray, Fr.	C2	16
Aurelia, Ia., U.S.	A5	110
Aurelian Springs, N.C., U.S.	B3	18
Aurich, W. Ger.	C2	56
Auriflama, Braz.	C5	73
Aurillac, Fr.	A3	59
Aurora, Ont.	B6	83
Aurora, Guy.	B3	90
Aurora, Il., U.S.	F8	91
Aurora, In., U.S.	C6	93
Aurora, Ks., U.S.	C6	100
Aurora, Mn., U.S.	E4	102
Aurora, Mo., U.S.	D7	104
Aurora, Ne., U.S.	C4	109
Aurora, N.Y., U.S.	B6	110
Aurora, N.C., U.S.	A4	112
Aurora, Oh., U.S.	B4	114
Aurora, Or., U.S.	C9	118
Aurora, S.D., U.S.	E4	121
Aurora, Ut., U.S.	D6	125
Aurora, W.V., U.S.	C5	126
Aurora, Wi., U.S.	C2	49
Aurora, co., S.D., U.S.	D7	118
Aurora Center, S.D., U.S.	p29	14
Aurskog, Nor.	C2	49
Aus, Nmb.	D7	99
Au Sable, Mi., U.S.	C7	99
Au Sable, stm., Mi., U.S.	f11	109
Au Sable, North Branch, stm., Mi., U.S.	D6	99
Au Sable Forks, N.Y., U.S.	f11	109
Au Sable Point, c., Mi., U.S.	B4	99
Au Sable Point, c., Mi., U.S.	D7	99
Auschwitz see Oświęcim, Pol.	C5	26
Aussa, stm., Italy	h7	87
Austell, Ga., U.S.	C2	87
Austerlitz see Slavkov, Czech.	C4	81
Austin, In., U.S.	G6	91
Austin, Ky., U.S.	D3	94
Austin, Mn., U.S.	G6	100
Austin, Nv., U.S.	D4	105
Austin, Pa., U.S.	C5	115
Austin, Tx., U.S.	D4	120
Austin, co., Tx., U.S.	E4	120
Austin, Lake, l., Austl.	E3	50
Austintown, Oh., U.S.	A5	112
Austinville, Va., U.S.	D2	123
Australia, ctry., Oc.	E6	50
Australian Capital Territory, ter., Austl.	E7	51
Austria, ctry., Eur.	F4	45
Austwell, Tx., U.S.	E4	120
Axim, Ghana	G3	101
Autauga, co., Al., U.S.	C3	78
Autaugaville, Al., U.S.	C3	78
Authie, stm., Fr.	D1	16
Autlán de Navarro, Mex.	H7	62
Au Train, Mi., U.S.	B4	99
Autun, Fr.	B4	16
Auvergne, Ar., U.S.	B4	81
Auvergne, hist. reg., Fr.	E5	16
Auvergne Mountains, mts., Fr.	E5	16
Auvers [-sur-Oise], Fr.	E2	17
Auxerre, Fr.	E5	16
Auxi-le-Château, Fr.	D6	16
Auxonne, Fr.	B6	102
Auxvasse, Mo., U.S.	E5	16
Auzangate, Nevado, mtn., Peru	D3	58
Ava, Il., U.S.	E5	102
Ava, Mo., U.S.	C4	112
Ava, Oh., U.S.	A4	48
Avakubi, Zaire	A4	98
Ayer, Ma., U.S.	D5	74
Avallon, Fr.	B3	87
Avalon, Ca., U.S.	B3	101
Avalon, Ms., U.S.	B4	112
Avalon, N.J., U.S.	E3	107
Avalon, Pa., U.S.	h13	115
Avalon, Lake, res., N.M., U.S.	E5	108
Avalon Peninsula, pen., Newf.	E5	72
Avanos, Tur.	C10	40
Avant, Ok., U.S.	A5	113
Avard, Ok., U.S.	A3	113
Avaré, Braz.	A4	60
Avdira, Grc.	C5	11
Avella, Pa., U.S.	F1	115
Avellaneda, Arg.	A5	54
Avellino, Italy	D5	23
Avenal, Ca., U.S.	E3	82
Avenches, Switz.	C3	21
Avenel, Md., U.S.	*B4	97
Avenel, N.J., U.S.	k7	107
Avening, Ont.	C4	73
Aventura, Fl., U.S.	*G6	86
Avenue, Md., U.S.	D4	97
Avenwedde, W. Ger.	E5	20
Avera, Ga., U.S.	C4	87
Averill, Mn., U.S.	D2	100
Averill Park, N.Y., U.S.	C7	109
Aversa, Italy	D5	23
Avery, Id., U.S.	B3	89
Avery, Ia., U.S.	C5	92
Avery, Mt., U.S.	C4	103
Avery, Ok., U.S.	B4	112
Avery, Tx., U.S.	C5	120
Avery, co., N.C., U.S.	e11	110
Avery Island, La., U.S.	E4	95
Aves, Islas de, is., Ven.	A4	60
Avesnes, Fr.	D3	17
Avesta, Swe.	G7	14
Avezzano, Italy	C4	23
Aviemore, Scot., U.K.	C5	13
Avigliano, Italy	D5	23
Avignon, Fr.	F6	16
Ávila, Spain	B3	22
Avila Beach, Ca., U.S.	E3	82
Avilés, Spain	A3	22
Avilla, In., U.S.	B7	91
Avilla, Mo., U.S.	D3	102
Avis, Pa., U.S.	D7	115
Avisio, stm., Italy	E4	90
Avlón, Grc.	g11	25
Avlum, Den.	A2	78
Avoca, Al., U.S.	A1	81
Avoca, Ar., U.S.	G4	91
Avoca, Ia., U.S.	C2	92
Avoca, In., U.S.	E8	99
Avoca, Mi., U.S.	G3	100
Avoca, Mn., U.S.	B2	92
Avoca, Ne., U.S.	h12	104
Avoca, N.Y., U.S.	C3	109
Avoca, Tx., U.S.	C3	120
Avoca, Wi., U.S.	E3	126
Avocado Heights, Ca., U.S.	*m13	82
Avola, B.C.	D8	69
Avola, Italy	F5	23
Avon, Ont.	E3	73
Avon, Ct., U.S.	B4	84
Avon, Il., U.S.	C3	90
Avon, In., U.S.	e8	92
Avon, Ma., U.S.	B5	98
Avon, Mn., U.S.	E4	100
Avon, N.Y., U.S.	C3	109
Avon, N.C., U.S.	B7	110
Avon, Oh., U.S.	A4	112
Avon, S.D., U.S.	D8	118
Avon, stm., Eng., U.K.	E5	12
Avon, stm., Eng., U.K.	D6	10
Avon, stm., Eng., U.K.	E6	12
Avon, stm., Scot., U.K.	D5	13
Avon by the Sea, N.J., U.S.	C4	107
Avondale, Az., U.S.	D3	80
Avondale, Co., U.S.	C6	83
Avondale, La., U.S.	*E5	95
Avondale, Mo., U.S.	h10	102
Avondale, Oh., U.S.	*C1	112
Avondale, Pa., U.S.	G10	115
Avondale, R.I., U.S.	G1	116
Avondale Estates, Ga., U.S.	h8	87
Avon Lake, Oh., U.S.	A3	112
Avonmore, Pa., U.S.	E3	115
Avonmore, Pa., U.S.	E5	86
Avon Park, Fl., U.S.	E5	86
Avoyelles, co., La., U.S.	C3	95
Awa, Japan	C4	81
Awa Island, i., Japan	G9	33
Awaji Island, i., Japan	I7	33
Awasa, Eth.	D4	47
Awash, Eth.	C5	47
Awash, stm., Eth.	C5	47
Awbārī, Libya	D3	43
Awdheegle, Som.	D4	43
Awe, Loch, l., Scot., U.K.	D4	13
Awjilah, Libya	B5	92
Awka, Nig.	D4	43
Awlef, Alg.	C6	44
Axel, Neth.	E5	108
Axel Heiberg Island, i., N.W. Ter.	A2	83
Axial Basin, Co., U.S.	A2	83
Axim, Ghana	F4	45
Axminster, Eng., U.K.	E4	120
Axis, Al., U.S.	C3	78
Axmansen, W. Ger.	D10	104
Axtell, Ks., U.S.	C7	93
Axtell, Ne., U.S.	D6	104
Axtell, Ut., U.S.	D4	121
Auvergne, hist. reg., Fr.	E5	16
Aÿ, Fr.	C5	16
Ay, stm., Sov. Un.	B5	28
Ayabaca, Peru	n14	33
Ayabe, Japan	B5	54
Ayacucho, Arg.	D3	58
Ayacucho, Peru	D2	17
Ayacucho, dept., Peru	E11	29
Ayaguz, Sov. Un.	D2	22
Ayamonte, Spain	D16	29
Ayan, Sov. Un.	B2	60
Ayapel, Col.	B9	40
Ayaş, Tur.	D3	58
Aydar, stm., Sov. Un.	G12	27
Ayden, N.C., U.S.	B5	110
Aydin, Tur.	A7	110
Aydlett, N.C., U.S.	A4	98
Ayer, Ma., U.S.	D5	74
Ayers Cliff, Que.	B3	87
Ayers Rock, mtn., Austl.	D10	36
Ayeyarwady, stm., Burma	C4	25
Ayia, Grc.	C6	25
Ayia Paraskeví, Grc.	h10	25
Ayiásos, Grc.	g11	25
Áyioi Theódhoroi, Grc.	C5	25
Áyios Dhimítrios, Grc.	C5	25
Áyios Evstrátios, i., Grc.	B7	73
Áyios Nikólaos, Grc.	G3	75
Aylen Lake, l., Ont.	E6	10
Aylesbury, Eng., U.K.	D5	71
Aylesford, N.S.	C5	123
Aylett, Va., U.S.	D3	102
Aylmer, Mount, mtn., Alta.	D2	74
Aylmer East, Que.	E4	73
Aylmer Lake, l., N.W. Ter.	D11	66
Aylmer West, Ont.	D4	75
Aylsham, Sask.	D9	117
Aynor, S.C., U.S.	h11	41
'Ayn Yabrūd, Isr. Occ.	B9	29
Ayon Island, i., Sov. Un.	C5	22
Ayora, Spain	D5	45
Ayorou, Niger	C3	45
'Ayoûn el 'Atroûs, Maur.	C8	50
Ayr, Austl.	D4	73
Ayr, Ont.	C4	10
Ayr, Scot., U.K.	D7	104
Ayr, N.D., U.S.	B8	111
Ayr, stm., Scot., U.K.	E4	13
Ayre, Point of, c., I. of Man.	F4	13
Ayrshire, In., U.S.	H3	91
Ayrshire, Ia., U.S.	A3	92
Aysary, Sov. Un.	C8	28
Aysha, Eth.	C4	73
Ayton, Ont.	D8	24
Aytos, Bul.	D3	16
Aytré, Fr.	E8	34
Ayu Islands, is., Indon.	D5	63
Ayutla [de los Libres], Mex.	C6	40
Ayvacık, Tur.	C6	40
Azalea, Park, Fl., U.S.	*D5	86
Azalia, In., U.S.	F6	91
Azama, Japan	O5	52
Āzamgarh, India	D9	36
Azángaro, Peru	D3	58
Azaouad, reg., Mali	C4	45
Azaouak, Vallée de l', val., Afr.	C5	45
Azare, Nig.	D7	45
Āžar Shahr, Iran	B4	38
Azcapotzalco (part of Mexico City), Mex.	h9	63
Azemmour, Mor.	C3	44
Azerbaijan, hist. reg., Iran	B4	38
Azerbaijan S.S.R., state, Sov. Un.	E7	29
Aziscohos Lake, l., Me., U.S.	C1	96
Azle, Tx., U.S.	n9	120
Azogues, Ec.	B2	58
Azores, is., Port.	g9	44
Azov, Sov. Un.	H12	27
Azov, Sea of, Sov. Un.	E6	29
Azoyú, Mor.	C3	44
Aztec, N.M., U.S.	A2	108
Aztec Peak, mtn., Az., U.S.	D5	80
Aztec Ruins National Monument, N.M., U.S.	A1	108
Azua, Dom. Rep.	E8	64
Azuaga, Spain	C3	22
Azuay, prov., Ec.	B2	58
Azuero, Peninsula de, pen., Pan.	G7	62
Azul, Arg.	B5	54
Azul, Cordillera, mts., Peru	C2	58
Azul, Serra, plat., Braz.	A2	56
Azusa, Ca., U.S.	m13	82
Az Zabdānī, Syria	F11	40
Az Zāhirīyah, Isr. Occ.	C4	41
Az Zahrān (Dhahran), Sau. Ar.	C4	38
Az Zaqāzīq, Eg.	C6	43
Az Zarqā', Jord.	B3	38
Az Zāwiyah, Libya	C2	43
Az Zaydāb, Sud.	B3	47
'Azzāz, Ra's, c., Libya	D3	43
Azzel Matti, Sebkha, pl., Alg.	D5	44
Az Zubayr, Iraq	F3	39
'Azzūn, Isr. Occ.	g11	41

B

Baal, W. Ger.	C6	17
Baalbek, Leb.	B3	38
Baar, Switz.	B6	21
Baardheere, Som.	E5	47
Baargaal, Som.	C7	47
Baarle-Hertog, Bel.	C4	17
Baarn, Neth.	C6	40
Baba Burnu, c., Tur.	C9	24
Babaeski, Tur.	B6	25
Babahoyo, Ec.	B2	58
Babana, Nig.	D5	45
Babanūsah, Sud.	C2	47
Babar Islands, is., Indon.	G7	34
Babati, Tan.	B6	48
Babayevo, Sov. Un.	B11	27
Babb, Mt., U.S.	B3	103
Babb Creek, stm., Pa., U.S.	C7	115
Babbie, Al., U.S.	D3	78
Babbitt, Nv., U.S.	E3	105
Babbitt, Mn., U.S.	C7	100
Babcock, Wi., U.S.	D3	126
Babelthuap International Airport, Palau	R17	52
Babelthuap Island, i., Palau	R17	52
Babenhausen, W. Ger.	A6	20
Babi, i., Indon.	K2	35
Babine, stm., B.C.	B4	69
Babine Lake, l., B.C.	B5	69
Babine Range, mts., B.C.	B4	69
Babo, Indon.	F8	34

134

Name	Map Ref.	Page

Bābol, Iran — B5 38
Bābol Sar, Iran — C6 39
Baboosic Lake, N.H., U.S. — E3 106
Baboquivari Mountains, mts., Az., U.S. — F4 80
Baboquivari Peak, mtn., Az., U.S. — F4 80
Baboua, Cen. Afr. Rep. — D2 46
Babson Park, Fl., U.S. — E5 86
Babushkin, Sov. Un. — A6 31
Babuyan Islands, is., Phil. — B6 34
Babyak, Bul. — E6 24
Babylon, N.Y., U.S. — n15 109
Baca, co., Co., U.S. — D8 83
Bacabal, Braz. — B2 56
Bacajá, stm., Braz. — C4 59
Bacalar, Mex. — D7 63
Bacan, i., Indon. — F7 34
Bacău, Rom. — B8 24
Baccalieu Island, i., Newf. — D5 72
Baccarat, Fr. — C7 16
Baccaro Point, c., N.S. — F4 71
Bacerac, Mex. — A3 63
Bach, Mi., U.S. — E7 99
Bacharach, W. Ger. — C2 19
Bach Long Vi, i., Viet. — B7 35
Back, stm., N.W. Ter. — C12 66
Back, stm., S.C., U.S. — h12 117
Bačka Palanka, Yugo. — C4 24
Bačka Topola, Yugo. — C4 24
Back Bay, N.B. — D3 71
Backbone Mountain, mtn., U.S. — m12 97
Backnang, W. Ger. — E4 19
Backoo, N.D., U.S. — A8 111
Backus, Mn., U.S. — D4 100
Bac Lieu, Viet. — D3 34
Bac Ninh, Viet. — A3 34
Bacobi, Az., U.S. — B5 80
Bacolod, Phil. — C6 34
Bacon, co., Ga., U.S. — E4 87
Baconton, Ga., U.S. — E2 87
Bacoor, Phil. — o13 34
Bacova, Va., U.S. — B3 123
Bac Quang, Viet. — A6 35
Bacqueville-en-Caux, Fr. — E9 12
Bácsalmás, Hung. — B5 24
Bácum, Mex. — B2 63
Bad, stm., S.D., U.S. — C5 118
Bad, stm., Wi., U.S. — B3 126
Badagara, India — F6 36
Bad Aibling, W. Ger. — B7 20
Badajoz, Spain — C2 22
Badalona, Spain — B7 22
Badanah, Sau. Ar. — B3 38
Bad Axe, Mi., U.S. — E8 99
Bad Bergzabern, W. Ger. — D2 19
Bad Berneck, W. Ger. — C6 19
Bad Bramstedt, W. Ger. — E3 15
Bad Doberan, E. Ger. — A5 18
Bad Düben, E. Ger. — B7 19
Baden, Ont. — D4 73
Baden, Switz. — E4 18
Baden, Pa., U.S. — E1 115
Baden, hist. reg., W. Ger. — D4 19
Baden-Baden, W. Ger. — D4 19
Baden [bei Wien], Aus. — D8 19
Baden-Württemberg, state, W. Ger. — D4 19
Bad Freienwalde, E. Ger. — B7 18
Bad Friedrichshall, W. Ger. — D4 19
Badgastein, Aus. — E6 18
Badger, Newf. — D3 72
Badger, Ia., U.S. — B3 92
Badger, Mn., U.S. — B2 100
Badger, S.D., U.S. — C8 118
Badger Creek, stm., Co., U.S. — B7 83
Bad Godesberg, W. Ger. — C2 19
Bad Hersfeld, E. Ger. — C4 18
Bad Homburg [vor der Höhe], W. Ger. — C4 18
Bad Honnef, W. Ger. — C2 19
Bad Hönningen, W. Ger. — C2 19
Badia Polesine, Italy — D7 20
Badin, Pak. — E2 37
Badin, N.C., U.S. — B2 110
Badin Lake, res., N.C., U.S. — B2 110
Bad Ischl, Aus. — E6 18
Bad Kissingen, W. Ger. — C5 18
Bad Kreuznach, W. Ger. — D3 18
Badlands, hills, S.D., U.S. — D2 90
Badlands, reg., — C2 111
Badlands National Park, S.D., U.S. — D3 118
Bad Langensalza, E. Ger. — B5 18
Bad Lauterberg, E. Ger. — B5 18
Bad Leonfelden, Aus. — E9 19
Bad Liebenwerda, E. Ger. — B8 19
Bad Lippspringe, W. Ger. — B3 19
Bad Mergentheim, W. Ger. — D4 19
Bad Münstereifel, W. Ger. — C1 19
Bad Muskau, W. Ger. — B9 19
Bad Nauheim, W. Ger. — C3 19
Bad Neustadt [an der Saale], W. Ger. — C5 19
Bad Oeynhausen, W. Ger. — A3 19
Bad Oldesloe, W. Ger. — B5 18
Badong, China — E7 31
Bad Orb, W. Ger. — C4 19
Badoumbé, Mali — D2 45
Bad Pyrmont, W. Ger. — B4 19
Bad Ragaz, Switz. — E4 18
Bad Reichenhall, W. Ger. — E8 19
Bad River Indian Reservation, Wi., U.S. — B3 126
Bad Salzungen, E. Ger. — B4 18
Bad Salzungen, E. Ger. — C5 19
Bad Schandau, E. Ger. — C8 19
Bad Segeberg, W. Ger. — E4 15
Bad Sülze, E. Ger. — D6 15
Bad Tennstedt, E. Ger. — B5 18
Bad Tölz, W. Ger. — B7 20
Badu, i., Austl. — A7 50
Badulla, Sri L. — G7 36
Badwater Creek, stm., Wy., U.S. — C5 127
Bad Wildungen, W. Ger. — B4 19
Bad Windsheim, W. Ger. — D5 19
Bad Wörishofen, W. Ger. — B6 20
Bad Wurzach, W. Ger. — B5 20
Baena, Spain — D3 22
Baependi, Braz. — C4 56
Baeza, Ec. — B2 58
Baeza, Spain — D4 22
Bafang, Cam. — D2 46
Bafatá, Gui.-B. — C2 45
Baffin Bay, b., N.A. — B14 61
Baffin Bay, b., Tx., U.S. — E4 120
Baffin Island, i., N.W. Ter. — C18 66
Bafia, Cam. — E2 46
Bafoulabé, Mali — D2 45
Bafoussam, Cam. — *D2 46
Bāfq, Iran — B5 38

Bafra, Tur. — B10 40
Bâft, Iran — G8 39
Bafwasende, Zaire — A4 48
Bagabag, Phil. — n13 34
Bagaces, C.R. — E7 63
Bagamoyo, Tan. — C6 48
Bagana, Nig. — E6 45
Baganga, Phil. — E6 34
Bagansiapiapi, Indon. — E2 34
Bagata, Zaire — B2 48
Bagdad, Az., U.S. — C2 80
Bagdad, Fl., U.S. — u14 86
Bagdad, Ky., U.S. — B4 94
Bagé, Braz. — E2 56
Bāgerhāt, Bngl. — F12 37
Baggs, Wy., U.S. — E5 127
Baghdād, Iraq — B4 38
Bagheria, Italy — E4 23
Baghlān, Afg. — A4 36
Bagley, Ia., U.S. — C3 92
Bagley, Mn., U.S. — C3 100
Bagley, Wi., U.S. — F2 126
Bakhchisaray, Sov. Un. — I9 27
Bagnacavallo, Italy — E7 20
Bagnara [Calabra], Italy — E5 23
Bagnell Dam, Mo., U.S. — C5 102
Bagnell, Mo., U.S. — C5 102
Bagnères-de-Bigorre, Fr. — F4 16
Bagnères-de-Luchon, Fr. — F4 16
Bagnolet, Fr. — g10 16
Bagnols, Fr. — E6 16
Bago, Burma — E10 36
Bâgø, i., Den. — D3 15
Bagolino, Italy — D6 20
Bagot, co., Que. — D5 74
Bagrationovsk, Sov. Un. — A6 26
Baguio, Phil. — B6 34
Bagzane, Monts, mts., Niger — C6 45
Bahama, N.C., U.S. — A4 110
Bahamas, ctry., N.A. — B5 64
Bahār, Iran — D4 39
Baharampur, India — D8 36
Bahāwalnagar, Pak. — C5 36
Bahāwalpur, Pak. — C5 36
Bahia, state, Braz. — D2 57
Bahía, Islas de la, is., Hond. — D7 63
Bahía Blanca, Arg. — B4 54
Bahía Bustamante, Arg. — D3 54
Bahía de Caráquez, Ec. — B1 58
Bahía Negra, Para. — D4 55
Bahir Dar, Eth. — C4 47
Bahraich, India — D8 37
Bahrain, ctry., Asia — C5 38
Bahr al Ghazāl, prov., Sud. — D2 47
Bahr aş Şāfī, des., Asia — D4 38
Bahrīyah, Al Wāhāt al, well, Eg. — D5 43
Bāhū Kalāt, Iran — I10 39
Baía dos Tigres, Ang. — E1 48
Baia-Mare, Rom. — B6 24
Baião, Braz. — C5 59
Baibokoum, Chad — D3 46
Baicheng, China — B9 31
Baie-Comeau, Que. — k13 74
Baie de Wasai, Mi., U.S. — B6 99
Baie-d'Urfé, Que. — q19 74
Baie-Johan-Beetz, Que. — h9 72
Baiersbronn, W. Ger. — E3 19
Baie-Sainte-Catherine, Que. — A8 74
Baie-Saint-Paul, Que. — B7 74
Baie Verte, N.B. — C5 71
Baie Verte, Newf. — D3 72
Baihe, China — H4 32
Baikal, Lake, l., Sov. Un. — D13 29
Baikal Mountains, mts., Sov. Un. — D13 29
Baikunthpur, India — F9 37
Bailén, Spain — C4 22
Băilești, Rom. — C6 24
Bailey, Ms., U.S. — C5 101
Bailey, N.C., U.S. — B4 110
Bailey, co., Tx., U.S. — B1 120
Bailey Island, Me., U.S. — g8 96
Bailey Island, i., S.C., U.S. — k11 117
Baileys Crossroads, Va., U.S. — g12 123
Baileys Harbor, Wi., U.S. — C6 126
Baileyton, Al., U.S. — A3 78
Baileyton, Tn., U.S. — C11 119
Baileyville, Il., U.S. — A4 90
Baileyville, Ks., U.S. — C7 93
Baileyville, Me., U.S. — D5 11
Bailieborough, Ire. — D5 11
Bailundo, Ang. — D2 48
Bainbridge, Ga., U.S. — F2 87
Bainbridge, In., U.S. — E4 91
Bainbridge, N.Y., U.S. — C5 109
Bainbridge, Oh., U.S. — C2 112
Bainbridge Island, i., Wa., U.S. — e10 124
Bain-de-Bretagne, Fr. — D3 16
Bains, La., U.S. — D4 95
Bainville, Mt., U.S. — B12 103
Baiquan, China — B10 31
Baird, Ms., U.S. — B3 101
Baird, Tx., U.S. — C3 120
Bairdford, Pa., U.S. — h14 115
Baird Inlet, b., Ak., U.S. — C7 79
Baird Mountains, mts., Ak., U.S. — B7 79
Bairiki, Kir. — R18 52
Bairiki, i., Kir. — R18 52
Bairin Youqi, China — C8 32
Bairin Zuoqi, China — B8 32
Bairnsdale, Austl. — G8 50
Bairoil, Wy., U.S. — D5 127
Baïse, stm., Fr. — F4 16
Baixo Longa, Ang. — E2 48
Baja, Hung. — B4 24
Baja California Norte, state, Mex. — A1 63
Baja California Sur, state, Mex. — B2 63
Bajestān, Iran — D9 39
Bajmok, Yugo. — C4 24
Bajo Boquete, Pan. — F6 63
Bajram-Ali, Sov. Un. — C11 29
Bakala, Cen. Afr. Rep. — D4 46
Bakar, Yugo. — C2 24
Bakel, Sen. — C2 45
Baker, Ca., U.S. — E5 82
Baker, Fl., U.S. — u15 86
Baker, La., U.S. — D4 95
Baker, Mn., U.S. — D6 100
Baker, Mt., U.S. — D12 103
Baker, Nv., U.S. — D7 105
Baker, N.D., U.S. — A6 111
Baker, Or., U.S. — C9 114
Baker, co., Fl., U.S. — B4 86
Baker, co., Ga., U.S. — E2 87
Baker, co., Or., U.S. — C9 114
Baker, stm., N.H., U.S. — C3 106

Baker, Mount, mtn., Wa., U.S. — A4 124
Baker Butte, mtn., Az., U.S. — C4 80
Baker Hill, Al., U.S. — D4 78
Baker Island, i., Oc. — F11 6
Baker Island, i., Ak., U.S. — n22 79
Baker Lake, N.W. Ter. — D13 66
Baker Lake, l., N.W. Ter. — D13 66
Baker Lake, l., Me., U.S. — B3 96
Baker Lake, res., Wa., U.S. — A4 124
Baker Mountain, mtn., Me., U.S. — C3 96
Bakers, N.C., U.S. — B2 110
Bakers Bayou, stm., Ar., U.S. — k11 81
Bakersfield, Ca., U.S. — E4 82
Bakersfield, Mo., U.S. — E5 102
Bakersfield, Vt., U.S. — B3 122
Bakers Island, i., Ma., U.S. — f12 98
Bakers Mill, Fl., U.S. — B4 86
Bakerstown, Pa., U.S. — h14 115
Bakersville, Ct., U.S. — B3 84
Bakersville, N.C., U.S. — e10 110
Bakerton, W.V., U.S. — B7 125
Bakewell, Eng., U.K. — A6 12
Bakhmut, stm., Sov. Un. — q21 27
Bākhtarān (Kermānshāh), Iran — B4 38
Bakır, stm., Tur. — C6 25
Bako, Eth. — D4 47
Bako, Ks., U.S. — C7 93
Bakony Mountains, mts., Hung. — B3 24
Bakool, prov., Som. — E5 47
Bakouma, Cen. Afr. Rep. — D4 46
Bakoye, stm., Afr. — D3 45
Baku, Sov. Un. — E7 29
Baku, Zaire — A5 48
Bakundi, Nig. — E7 45
Bakungan, Indon. — K2 35
Bal, Ont. — B5 73
Bal'ā, Isr. Occ. — f11 41
Bala, Wales, U.K. — A4 12
Bala, Ks., U.S. — C7 93
Balabac Island, i., Phil. — D5 34
Balabac Strait, strt., Asia — D5 34
Balabalagan Islands, is., Indon. — F5 34
Balad, Iraq — D2 39
Bālāghāt, India — G8 37
Balaguer, Spain — B6 22
Balakhna, Sov. Un. — D17 8
Balakhta, Sov. Un. — D27 8
Balaklava, Austl. — G2 51
Balaklava, Sov. Un. — G11 27
Balakleya, Sov. Un. — F1 11
Balakovo, Sov. Un. — *D7 29
Bālā Morghāb, Afg. — D11 39
Balancán [de Domínguez], Mex. — D6 63
Balanga, Phil. — o13 34
Balāngīr, India — G9 37
Balashov, Sov. Un. — F14 27
Balassagyarmat, Hung. — A4 24
Balaton, Mn., U.S. — F3 100
Balaton, Lake, l., Hung. — B3 24
Balayan, Phil. — p13 34
Balayan Bay, b., Phil. — p13 34
Balbi, mtn., Pap. N. Gui. — *G9 6
Balboa, Pan. — m11 62
Balboa Heights, Pan. — m11 62
Balbriggan, Ire. — D5 11
Balcad, Som. — E6 47
Balcarce, Arg. — B5 54
Balcarres, Sask. — G4 75
Balch Springs, Tx., U.S. — *n10 120
Balclutha, N.Z. — Q12 51
Balcones, N.C., U.S. — f10 110
Bald Eagle Lake, l., Mn., U.S. — m12 100
Bald Eagle Lake, l., Mn., U.S. — C7 100
Baldegger Lake, l., Switz. — B5 21
Baldhill Dam, N.D., U.S. — B7 111
Bald Knob, Ar., U.S. — B4 81
Bald Knob, mtn., Va., U.S. — c3 123
Bald Knob, mtn., W.V., U.S. — C5 125
Bald Knoll, mtn., Wy., U.S. — D2 127
Bald Mountain, mtn., Ct., U.S. — B6 84
Bald Mountain, mtn., N.J. — A4 107
Bald Mountain, mtn., Or., U.S. — D5 114
Bald Mountain, mtn., Or., U.S. — C9 114
Bald Mountain, mtn., Vt., U.S. — B5 122
Bald Mountain, mtn., Wy. — B5 127
Bald Mountains, mts., N.C. — f10 110
Baldock Lake, l., Man. — A3 70
Baldur, Man. — E2 70
Baldwin, Fl., U.S. — B5 86
Baldwin, Il., U.S. — E4 90
Baldwin, La., U.S. — E4 95
Baldwin, Md., U.S. — B5 97
Baldwin, Mi., U.S. — E5 99
Baldwin, N.D., U.S. — B5 111
Baldwin, Pa., U.S. — k13 115
Baldwin, S.C., U.S. — B5 117
Baldwin, Wi., U.S. — D1 126
Baldwin, co., Al., U.S. — E2 78
Baldwin, co., Ga., U.S. — C3 87
Baldwin City, Ks., U.S. — D8 93
Baldwin Heights, U.S. — H2 91
Baldwin Park, Ca., U.S. — *E4 82
Baldwinsville, N.Y., U.S. — B4 109
Baldwinton, Sask. — E1 75
Baldwinville, Ma., U.S. — A3 98
Baldwyn, Ms., U.S. — A5 101
Baldy Mountain, mtn., B.C. — D7 69
Baldy Mountain, mtn., Man. — D1 70
Baldy Mountain, mtn., Mt. — B7 103
Baldy Mountain, mtn., N.M. — A4 108
Baldy Peak, mtn., Az., U.S. — D6 80
Bale, prov., Eth. — D5 47
Balearic Islands, is., Spain — C7 22
Baleia, Ponta da, c., Braz. — E3 57
Baleine, Rivière à la, stm. — g13 74
Baler, Phil. — o13 34
Baler Bay, b., Phil. — o13 34
Baleshare, i., Scot., U.K. — C1 13
Baleshwar, India — J12 37
Balesin, i., Phil. — o14 34
Baleville, N.J., U.S. — A3 107
Balfate, Hond. — A4 62
Balfour, N.C., U.S. — f10 110
Balfour, N.D., U.S. — B5 111
Balgonie, Sask. — G3 75
Bāli, India — E4 37

Bali, i., Indon. — G5 34
Balıkesir, Tur. — C6 40
Balikpapan, Indon. — F5 34
Balingen, W. Ger. — A4 20
Balintang Channel, strt., Phil. — B6 34
Bali Sea, Indon. — G5 34
Baliuag, Phil. — o13 34
Balje, W. Ger. — B4 18
Baljenie, Sask. — E2 75
Balkan, Ky., U.S. — D6 94
Balkan Mountains, mts., Eur. — C3 96
Balkh, Afg. — A4 36
Balkhash, Sov. Un. — H9 29
Balkhash, Lake, l., Sov. Un. — E10 29
Balki, Sov. Un. — H10 27
Balko, Ok., U.S. — e10 113
Ball, La., U.S. — C3 95
Balla, Ire. — D3 11
Ballachulish, Scot., U.K. — D3 13
Ballagh, Ire. — E4 11
Ballaghaderreen, Ire. — D3 11
Ballantine, Mt., U.S. — E8 103
Ballantrae, Scot., U.K. — C4 10
Ballarat (Ballaarat), Austl. — G7 50
Ballard, Ok., U.S. — A7 113
Ballard, co., Ky., U.S. — e8 94
Ballard, Lake, l., Austl. — E3 50
Ballardvale, Ma., U.S. — f11 98
Ball Club, Mn., U.S. — C5 100
Ballé, Mali — C3 45
Ballenas, Bahía de, b., Mex. — B2 63
Ballenstedt, E. Ger. — B6 19
Balleny Islands, is., Ant. — C29 7
Ballerup [-Målov], Den. — C6 15
Ball Ground, Ga., U.S. — B2 87
Ballia, India — E10 37
Ballina, Austl. — E9 50
Ballina, Ire. — C2 10
Ballina, Ire. — E3 11
Ballinakill, Ire. — D4 11
Ballinalack, Ire. — D4 11
Ballinasloe, Ire. — D3 11
Ballinen, Ire. — D3 11
Ballingarry, Ire. — F3 11
Ballingeary, Ire. — E3 11
Ballinger, Tx., U.S. — D3 120
Ballinluig, Scot., U.K. — D5 13
Ballinrobe, Ire. — D2 11
Ballinskelligs Bay, b., Ire. — F1 11
Ballintra, Ire. — C3 11
Ballitore, Ire. — D5 11
Ball Mountain Lake, res., Vt. — E3 122
Ballouville, Ct., U.S. — B8 84
Ballston, Or., U.S. — B3 114
Ballston Spa, N.Y., U.S. — B7 109
Ballwin, Mo., U.S. — f12 102
Bally, Pa., U.S. — F10 115
Ballybofey, Ire. — C4 11
Ballybunnion, Ire. — E2 11
Ballycanew, Ire. — E5 11
Ballycastle, Ire. — C2 11
Ballycastle, N. Ire., U.K. — C3 10
Ballyconneely, Ire. — D1 11
Ballyconnell, Ire. — C4 11
Ballycroy, Ire. — C2 11
Ballyduff, Ire. — E3 11
Ballyduff, Ire. — E1 11
Ballyferriter, Ire. — D1 11
Ballygar, Ire. — D3 11
Ballygorman, Ire. — B4 11
Ballyhaunis, Ire. — D3 11
Ballyheige, Ire. — E2 11
Ballyhoura Mountains, mts., Ire. — E3 11
Ballyjamesduff, Ire. — D4 11
Ballykelly, N. Ire., U.K. — B4 11
Ballylongford, Ire. — E2 11
Ballymahon, Ire. — D4 11
Ballymena, N. Ire., U.K. — C3 10
Ballymoe, Ire. — D3 11
Ballymoney, N. Ire., U.K. — B5 11
Ballymote, Ire. — C3 11
Ballymurray, Ire. — D4 11
Ballynahinch, N. Ire., U.K. — C6 11
Ballyneety, Ire. — E3 11
Ballynoe, Ire. — E3 11
Ballysadare, Ire. — C3 11
Ballyshannon, Ire. — C3 11
Ballyteige Bay, b., Ire. — E5 11
Ballyvaghan, Ire. — D2 11
Ballyvourney, Ire. — F2 11
Balm, Fl., U.S. — E4 86
Balmat, N.Y., U.S. — A5 109
Balmazújváros, Hung. — B5 24
Balmhorn, mtn., Switz. — D4 21
Balmoral, Man. — D3 70
Balmoral, N.B. — B3 71
Balmoral Castle, hist., Scot., U.K. — C5 13
Balmorhea, Tx., U.S. — o13 120
Balmville, N.Y., U.S. — D6 109
Baloda Bāzār, India — G9 37
Balonne, stm., Austl. — E8 50
Bālotra, India — C5 36
Balrāmpur, India — D9 37
Balranald, Austl. — G4 51
Balș, Rom. — C7 24
Balsam, N.C., U.S. — f9 110
Balsam Lake, Wi., U.S. — C1 126
Balsam Lake, l., Ont. — C6 73
Balsam Lake, l., Wi., U.S. — C1 126
Balsas, Mex. — D5 63
Balsas, stm., Braz. — C1 57
Balsas, stm., Mex. — D4 63
Balsthal, Switz. — B4 21
Baltanás, Spain — D7 22
Balta, Sov. Un. — H7 27
Balta, N.D., U.S. — A5 111
Baltasar Brum, Ur. — E1 56
Baltic, Ct., U.S. — C7 84
Baltic, Oh., U.S. — B4 112
Baltic, S.D., U.S. — D9 118
Baltic Sea, Eur. — I8 14
Baltim, Eg. — C3 41
Baltimore, Ont. — C7 73
Baltimore, Ire. — F2 11
Baltimore, Md., U.S. — B4 97
Baltimore, Oh., U.S. — C3 112
Baltimore Highlands, Md., U.S. — h11 97
Baltinglass, Ire. — E5 11
Baltiysk, Sov. Un. — A5 26
Baltra, Isla, i., Ec. — g5 58
Baltrum, i., W. Ger. — A7 17
Baluchistan, hist. reg., Asia — C6 36
Balya, Tur. — C6 25
Balzac, Alta. — D3 68
Balzar, Ec. — B2 58

Balzers, Liech. — B8 21
Bam, Iran — C5 38
Bama, Nig. — D7 45
Bamako, Mali — D3 45
Bamba, Mali — C4 45
Bambang, Phil. — n13 34
Bambari, Cen. Afr. Rep. — D4 46
Bamberg, W. Ger. — D5 18
Bamberg, S.C., U.S. — E5 117
Bamberg, co., S.C., U.S. — E5 117
Bambesa, Zaire — A4 48
Bambili, Braz. — C3 56
Bamburgh, Eng., U.K. — E7 13
Bam Co, l., China — B9 36
Bamenda, Cam. — D2 46
Bampūr, Iran — H10 39
Bampūr, stm., Iran — H9 39
Ban, Carn, mtn., Scot., U.K. — C4 13
Banagher, Ire. — D4 11
Banahao, Mount, mtn., Phil. — o13 34
Banalia, Zaire — A4 48
Banamba, Mali — D3 45
Banana, Zaire — C1 48
Bananal, Braz. — h5 56
Bananal, Ilha do, i., Braz. — E4 59
Banana River, b., Fl., U.S. — D6 86
Bananeiras, Braz. — C3 57
Banās, stm., India — C3 38
Banās, Ra's, c., Eg. — C3 38
Banat, hist. reg., Eur. — C5 24
Banbridge, N. Ire., U.K. — C6 11
Banbury, Eng., U.K. — D6 10
Banchory, Scot., U.K. — C6 13
Bancos, Ec. — g5 58
Bancroft, Ont. — B7 73
Bancroft, Id., U.S. — G7 89
Bancroft, Ia., U.S. — A3 92
Bancroft, Me., U.S. — C4 96
Bancroft, Ne., U.S. — B9 104
Bancroft, S.D., U.S. — C8 118
Bancroft, Wi., U.S. — D4 126
Bānda, India — C7 36
Banda Aceh, Indon. — k11 34
Banda Banda, Mount, mtn., Austl. — E9 51
Banda Islands, is., Indon. — F7 34
Bandama, stm., I.C. — E3 45
Bandana, Ky., U.S. — e9 94
Bandar see Machilipatnam, India — E7 36
Bandar Baharu, Malay. — J4 35
Bandar Beheshtī, Iran — I10 39
Bandar-e 'Abbās, Iran — G5 39
Bandar-e Anzalī (Bandar-e Pahlavī), Iran — B4 38
Bandar-e Būshehr, Iran — G5 39
Bandar-e Deylam, Iran — F5 39
Bandar-e Khomeynī (Bandar-e Shāhpūr), Iran — F4 39
Bandar-e Lengeh, Iran — H7 39
Bandar-e Māhshahr, Iran — *F4 39
Bandar-e Pahlavī see Bandar-e Anzalī, Iran — B4 38
Bandar-e Rīg, Iran — G5 39
Bandar-e Shāh see Bandar-e Torkeman, Iran — B5 38
Bandar-e Shāhpūr see Bandar-e Khomeynī, Iran — F4 39
Bandar-e Torkeman (Bandar-e Shāh), Iran — B5 38
Bandar Maharani see Muar, Malay. — K5 35
Bandar Seri Begawan (Brunei), Bru. — E5 34
Banda Sea, Indon. — G7 34
Bande, Spain — A2 22
Banded Peak, mtn., Co., U.S. — D4 83
Bandeira, Pico da, mtn., Braz. — C4 56
Bandelier National Monument, N.M., U.S. — B3 108
Bandera, Arg. — B4 54
Bandera, Tx., U.S. — E3 120
Bandera, co., Tx., U.S. — E3 120
Banderas, Bahía de, b., Mex. — m11 63
Bandholm, Den. — D5 15
Bandiagara, Mali — D4 45
Bāndīkūi, India — D6 37
Bandırma, Tur. — B7 40
Bandon, Ire. — F3 11
Bandon, Or., U.S. — D2 114
Bandon, stm., Ire. — F3 11
Bandundu, Zaire — B2 48
Bandung, Indon. — G3 34
Bandy, Va., U.S. — e10 123
Bāneh, Iran — D2 39
Banes, Cuba — D6 64
Banff, Alta. — D3 68
Banff, Scot., U.K. — D5 13
Banff National Park, Alta. — D2 68
Banfora, Burkina — D4 45
Bangalore, India — F5 36
Bangassou, Cen. Afr. Rep. — E4 46
Bangeta, Mount, mtn., Pap. N. Gui. — k12 50
Banggai, Indon. — F6 34
Banggi Island, i., Malay. — D5 34
Banggong Co, l., China — D6 36
Bangka, i., Indon. — F3 34
Bangkalan, Indon. — G4 51
Bangkok (Krung Thep), Thai. — C2 34
Bangladesh, ctry., Asia — f9 110
Bangor, Sask. — G4 75
Bangor, N. Ire., U.K. — C4 10
Bangor, Wales, U.K. — A3 12
Bangor, Me., U.S. — D4 96
Bangor, Mi., U.S. — F4 99
Bangor, N.Y., U.S. — f10 109
Bangor, Pa., U.S. — E11 115
Bangor Township, Mi., U.S. — E7 99
Bangs, Mount, mtn., Az., U.S. — A2 80
Bang Saphan, Thai. — C2 34
Bangued, Phil. — n13 34
Bangui, Cen. Afr. Rep. — E3 46
Bangweulu, Lake, l., Zam. — C5 48
Banhã, Eg. — B3 38
Ban Hat Yai see Hat Yai, Thai. — D2 34
Baní, Dom. Rep. — E8 64
Bani, stm., Mali — D3 45
Baní, stm., Mali — n12 34
Bania, Pap. N. Gui. — k12 50
Banister, stm., Va., U.S. — D4 123
Banī Na'īm, Isr. Occ. — C7 41
Banī Suhaylah, Isr. Occ. — C6 41
Banī Suwayf, Eg. — C3 38
Bāniyās, Isr. Occ. — B3 38
Banja Luka, Yugo. — C3 24
Banjarmasin, Indon. — F4 34
Banjul, Gam. — D1 45

Bankas, Mali — D4 45
Bankeryd, Swe. — A8 15
Bankfoot, Scot., U.K. — D5 13
Bankhead, Al., U.S. — A2 78
Bankhead Lake, res., Al., U.S. — B2 78
Banks, Al., U.S. — D4 78
Banks, Ar., U.S. — D3 81
Banks, Id., U.S. — E2 89
Banks, Ms., U.S. — A3 101
Banks, Or., U.S. — g11 114
Banks, co., Ga., U.S. — B3 87
Banksian, stm., Can. — C4 70
Banks Island, i., B.C. — C2 69
Banks Island, i., N.W. Ter. — B8 66
Banks Lake, res., Ga., U.S. — E3 87
Banks Lake, res., Wa., U.S. — B6 124
Banks Peninsula, pen., N.Z. — O14 51
Bankston, Al., U.S. — B2 78
Bankstown, Austl. — *F9 50
Bānkura, India — I12 37
Bann, stm., N. Ire., U.K. — B5 11
Bannack, Mt., U.S. — E4 103
Banner, Ms., U.S. — A4 101
Banner, Wy., U.S. — B6 127
Banner, co., Ne., U.S. — C2 104
Banner Elk, N.C., U.S. — A1 110
Banning, Ca., U.S. — F5 82
Bannister, Mi., U.S. — E6 99
Bannockburn, Ont. — C7 73
Bannock, co., Id., U.S. — G6 89
Bannock Range, mts., Id., U.S. — G6 89
Bannu, Pak. — B5 36
Bañolas, Spain — A7 22
Baños, Ec. — B2 58
Banská Bystrica, Czech. — D5 26
Banská Štiavnica, Czech. — D5 26
Bansko, Bul. — E6 24
Bānswāra, India — F5 37
Bantam, Ct., U.S. — C3 84
Bantam, stm., Ct., U.S. — B3 84
Bantam Lake, l., Ct., U.S. — C3 84
Banteer, Ire. — E3 11
Bantry, Ire. — E2 10
Bantry, N.D., U.S. — A5 111
Bantry Bay, b., Ire. — F2 11
Banyak Islands, is., Indon. — m11 34
Banyo, Cam. — D2 46
Banyuwangi, Indon. — G4 34
Banzare Coast, Ant. — C25 7
Baocheng, China — E6 31
Baode, China — E4 32
Baodi, China — E7 32
Baoding, China — D8 32
Bao Ha, Viet. — A6 35
Baoji, China — E6 31
Baokang, China — E7 31
Bao Loc, Viet. — C3 34
Baoqing, China — C3 34
Baoshan, China — F4 31
Baotou, China — C8 31
Baoulé, stm., Afr. — D3 45
Baoulé, stm., Mali — D3 45
Baoying, China — H8 32
Bapaume, Fr. — D2 17
Bapchule, Az., U.S. — D4 80
Baptiste, Ont. — B6 73
Baptistown, N.J., U.S. — B2 107
Bāqa el Gharbiyya, Isr. — B7 41
Ba'qūbah, Iraq — B4 38
Baquedano, Chile — D2 55
Bar, Fr. — C6 16
Bar, Sov. Un. — G6 27
Bar, Yugo. — D4 24
Barabinsk, Sov. Un. — D10 29
Baraboo, Wi., U.S. — E3 126
Baraboo, stm., Wi., U.S. — E3 126
Baracaldo, Spain — A4 22
Baracoa, Cuba — D6 64
Barada, stm., Asia — D10 104
Baradero, Arg. — f7 54
Baraga, Mi., U.S. — B2 99
Baraga, co., Mi., U.S. — B2 99
Bārah, Sud. — E8 64
Barahona, Dom. Rep. — E8 64
Barajas de Madrid, Spain — p17 22
Bārākpur, India — F12 37
Bārāmūla, India — D2 114
Bārān, India — E6 37
Baranagar, India — *D8 36
Baranof Island, i., Ak., U.S. — m22 79
Baranovichi, Sov. Un. — E7 27
Barataria, Trin. — N23 64
Barataria, La., U.S. — E5 95
Barataria Bayou, stm., La., U.S. — k11 95
Barataria Bay, b., La., U.S. — E6 95
Barat Daya Islands, is., Indon. — G7 34
Baraya, Col. — C2 60
Barbacena, Braz. — C4 56
Barbacoas, Col. — C2 60
Barbado, stm., Braz. — D3 55
Barbados, ctry., N.A. — J15 64
Barbalha, Braz. — C3 57
Barbar, Sud. — B3 47
Barbastro, Spain — A6 22
Barbate [de Franco], Spain — D2 22
Barbeau, Sask. — B6 99
Barbeau Peak, mtn., N.W. Ter. — k37 66
Barber, co., Ks., U.S. — E5 93
Barbers Point, c., Hi., U.S. — B3 88
Barbers Point Naval Air Station, mil., Hi., U.S. — g9 88
Barberton, Ont. — C5 49
Barberton, Oh., U.S. — A4 112
Barberville, Fl., U.S. — C5 86
Barbezieux, Fr. — E5 16
Barbil, India — F10 37
Barbour, co., Al., U.S. — D4 78
Barbour, co., W.V., U.S. — B4 125
Barboursville, Va., U.S. — B4 125
Barboursville, W.V., U.S. — C2 125
Barbourville, Ky., U.S. — D6 94
Barbuda, i., Antig. — H14 64
Barby, E. Ger. — B6 19
Barca de Alva, Port. — B2 22
Barcaldine, Austl. — D8 50
Barcarena, Port. — f9 22
Barcarrota, Spain — C2 22
Barcellona [Pozzo di Gotto], Italy — E5 23
Barcelona, Spain — B7 22
Barcelona, Ven. — A7 60
Barcelonnette, Fr. — E7 16
Barcelos, Braz. — B3 59
Barcelos, Port. — B1 22
Barclay, Md., U.S. — B6 97

Name	Map Ref.	Page
Barco, N.C., U.S.	A7	110
Barcoo, stm., Austl.	D7	50
Barcroft, Lake, res., Va., U.S.	g12	123
Bard, N.M., U.S.	B6	108
Barda del Medio, Arg.	A3	46
Bardaï, Chad	C5	41
Bardawîl, Sabkhat al, sw., Eg.	C4	41
Bardawil Peninsula, spit, Eg.	C4	41
Barddhamān, India	D6	36
Bardejov, Czech.	D6	26
Barden Reservoir, res., R.I., U.S.	C2	116
Bardi, Italy	E5	20
Bardīyah, Libya	C5	43
Bardolph, Il., U.S.	C3	90
Bardonecchia, Italy	D2	20
Bardsey Island, i., Wales, U.K.	B3	12
Bardstown, Ky., U.S.	C4	94
Bardstown Junction, Ky., U.S.	C4	94
Bardswell Group, is., B.C.	C3	69
Bardwell, Ky., U.S.	f9	94
Bardwell Lake, res., Tx., U.S.	C4	120
Bare Hill Pond, l., Ma., U.S.	g9	98
Bareilly, India	C6	36
Barenburg, W. Ger.	F2	15
Barentin, Fr.	C4	16
Barre des Écrins, mtn., Fr.	E7	16
Barents, i., Nor.	B12	128
Barents Sea, Eur.	B6	29
Barentu, Eth.	B4	47
Barfleur, Pointe de, c., Fr.	C3	16
Bargarh, India	G9	37
Bargersville, In., U.S.	E5	91
Barguzin, Sov. Un.	D13	29
Bar Harbor, Me., U.S.	D4	96
Bari, Italy	D6	23
Bari, prov., Som.	D6	47
Barillas, Guat.	C2	62
Barinas, Ven.	B3	60
Barinas, state, Ven.	B4	60
Baring, Me., U.S.	C5	96
Baring, Mo., U.S.	A5	102
Bāripada, India	D8	36
Bariri, Braz.	C3	56
Bārīs, Eg.	E6	43
Barisāl, Bngl.	D9	36
Barisan Mountains, mts., Indon.	F2	34
Barito, stm., Indon.	F4	34
Barium Springs, N.C., U.S.	B2	110
Barker, N.Y., U.S.	B2	109
Barker Heights, N.C., U.S.	f10	110
Barkerville, B.C.	C7	69
Barkeyville, Pa., U.S.	D2	115
Barkhamsted Reservoir, res., Ct., U.S.	B3	84
Bark Lake, l., Ont.	E4	73
Barkley, La., U.S.	f10	94
Barkley Dam, Ky., U.S.	e9	94
Barkley Sound, strt., B.C.	E5	69
Barkly East, S. Afr.	H5	49
Barkly Tableland, plat., Austl.	C6	50
Barkmere, Que.	C3	74
Barkol, China	C3	31
Bark Point, c., Wi., U.S.	B2	126
Bark River, Mi., U.S.	C3	99
Barksdale, Tx., U.S.	E2	120
Barksdale Air Force Base, mil., La., U.S.	B2	95
Bar Lake, l., Sask.	B2	75
Bar-le-Duc, Fr.	C6	16
Barlee, Lake, l., Austl.	E2	50
Barletta, Italy	D6	23
Barling, Ar., U.S.	B1	81
Barlow, Ky., U.S.	e8	94
Barlow, N.D., U.S.	B6	111
Barlow, Or., U.S.	h12	114
Bärmer, India	C5	36
Bar Mills, Me., U.S.	E2	96
Barmouth, Wales, U.K.	D4	10
Barna, Ire.	D2	11
Barnaby River, N.B.	C4	71
Barnard, Ks., U.S.	C5	93
Barnard, Mo., U.S.	A3	102
Barnard, S.D., U.S.	B7	118
Barnard, Vt., U.S.	D3	122
Barnard Castle, Eng., U.K.	g17	13
Barnardsville, N.C., U.S.	f10	110
Barnasht, Sov. Un.	E3	41
Barnaul, Sov. Un.	D11	29
Barnegat, N.J., U.S.	D4	107
Barnegat Bay, b., N.J., U.S.	D4	107
Barnegat Inlet, b., N.J., U.S.	D4	107
Barnegat Light, N.J., U.S.	D4	107
Barnegat Pines, N.J., U.S.	D4	107
Barne Inlet, b., Ant.	q10	7
Barnes, Ks., U.S.	C7	93
Barnes, Pa., U.S.	C3	115
Barnes, co., N.D., U.S.	B7	111
Barnesboro, Pa., U.S.	E4	115
Barnes City, U.S.	C5	92
Barnes Corners, N.Y., U.S.	B5	109
Barnes Creek, stm., La., U.S.	D2	95
Barnes Sound, strt., Fl., U.S.	G6	86
Barneston, Ne., U.S.	D9	104
Barnesville, Ga., U.S.	C2	87
Barnesville, Md., U.S.	B3	97
Barnesville, Mn., U.S.	D2	100
Barnesville, Oh., U.S.	C4	112
Barnet (part of London), Eng., U.K.	k12	10
Barnet, Vt., U.S.	C4	122
Barnett, Mo., U.S.	C5	102
Barneveld, Neth.	B5	17
Barneveld, Wi., U.S.	E4	126
Barneville-Carteret, Fr.	F6	10
Barney, Ga., U.S.	F3	87
Barney, N.D., U.S.	C8	111
Barney, Mount, mtn., Austl.	D9	51
Barnhart, Mo., U.S.	C7	102
Barnhart, Tx., U.S.	D2	120
Barnhill, Oh., U.S.	B4	112
Barnsdall, Ok., U.S.	A5	113
Barnsley, Eng., U.K.	A6	12
Barnstable, Ma., U.S.	C7	98
Barnstable, co., Ma., U.S.	C7	98
Barnstaple, Eng., U.K.	E4	10
Barnstaple Bay, b., Eng., U.K.	C3	12
Barnstead, N.H., U.S.	D6	74
Barnston, Que.	D6	74
Barnum, Ia., U.S.	B3	92
Barnum, Mn., U.S.	D6	100
Barnwell, Alta.	E4	68
Barnwell, S.C., U.S.	E5	117
Barnwell, co., S.C., U.S.	E5	117
Baro, Nig.	E6	45
Baro, stm., Afr.	D3	47
Baroda, Mi., U.S.	G4	99
Baroda see Vadodara, India		
Baron, Ok., U.S.	B7	113
Barons, Alta.	E4	68
Barques, Pointe aux, c., Mi., U.S.	D8	99
Barquisimeto, Ven.	A4	60
Barr, Fr.	C7	16
Barr, Co., U.S.	B6	83
Barr, Ra's al, c., Eg.	C3	41
Barra, Braz.	h5	57
Barra, Braz.	D2	57
Barra, i., Scot., U.K.	B3	10
Barra, Sound of, strt., Scot., U.K.	C1	13
Barraba, Austl.	E8	51
Barra Bonita, Braz.	m7	56
Barracão, Braz.	D2	56
Barrackville, W.V., U.S.	B4	125
Barra de Río Grande, Nic.	D6	62
Barra do Corda, Braz.	C1	57
Barra do Garças, Braz.	B2	56
Barra do Piraí, Braz.	C4	56
Barra Head, c., Scot., U.K.	B3	10
Barra Mansa, Braz.	C4	56
Barranca, Peru	A6	34
Barranca, N.M., U.S.	*A3	108
Barrancabermeja, Col.	B3	60
Barrancas, Ven.	B5	60
Barrancos, Port.	C2	112
Barranco, Peru	*D2	58
Barranquilla, Col.	A3	60
Barras, Chile	A2	54
Barre, Ma., U.S.	B3	98
Barre, Vt., U.S.	C4	122
Barre, Lake, l., La., U.S.	E5	95
Barre Falls Reservoir, res., Ma., U.S.	B4	98
Barreiras, Braz.	D2	57
Barreirinha, Braz.	C3	59
Barreirinhas, Braz.	B2	57
Barreiro, Port.	C1	22
Barreiros, Braz.	C3	57
Barrhead, Alta.	B3	68
Barrhead, Scot., U.K.	E4	13
Barrhill, Scot., U.K.	E4	13
Barrie, Ont.	C5	73
Barrie Island, i., Ont.	B2	73
Barrière, B.C.	D7	69
Barrier Lake, l., Sask.	E4	75
Barrier Range, mts., Austl.	F7	50
Barrigada, Guam	L10	52
Barrington, N.S.	F4	71
Barrington, Il., U.S.	A5	90
Barrington, N.H., U.S.	D4	106
Barrington, N.J., U.S.	D2	107
Barrington, R.I., U.S.	D5	116
Barrington, co., R.I., U.S.	C5	116
Barrington Lake, l., Man.	A1	70
Barrington Passage, N.S.	F4	71
Barrington Tops, mtn., Austl.	F8	51
Barrio Obrero Industrial, Peru	*D2	58
Barro Alto, Braz.	B3	56
Barron, Wi., U.S.	C2	126
Barron, co., Wi., U.S.	C2	126
Barronett, Wi., U.S.	C2	126
Barron Lake, Mi., U.S.	G4	99
Barroualie, St. Vin.	U26	65
Barrow, Arg.	B4	54
Barrow, Ak., U.S.	A8	79
Barrow, co., Ga., U.S.	B3	87
Barrow, i., Austl.	D2	50
Barrow, stm., Ire.	D3	10
Barrow, Point, c., Ak., U.S.	A8	79
Barrow-in-Furness, Eng., U.K.	C5	10
Barrow Strait, strt., N.W. Ter.	B14	66
Barrows, Man.	C5	98
Barrowsville, Ma., U.S.	C5	98
Barruelo de Santullán, Spain	A3	22
Barry (Vale of Glamorgan), Wales, U.K.	C4	12
Barry, Il., U.S.	D2	90
Barry, co., Mi., U.S.	F5	99
Barry, co., Mo., U.S.	E4	102
Barrys Bay, Ont.	B7	73
Barryton, Mi., U.S.	E5	99
Barryville, N.Y., U.S.	D6	109
Barsinghausen, W. Ger.	A4	19
Bārsi, India	D2	41
Barstow, Ca., U.S.	E5	82
Barstow, Tx., U.S.	D1	120
Bar-sur-Aube, Fr.	C6	16
Bartel, E. Ger.	E4	90
Barth, Fl., U.S.	u14	86
Bartholomew, co., In., U.S.	F6	91
Bartholomew, Bayou, stm., U.S.	D4	81
Bartibog Bridge, N.B.	B4	71
Bartica, Guy.	A3	59
Bartin, Tur.	B9	40
Bartle Frere, Mount, mtn., Austl.	C8	50
Bartlesville, Ok., U.S.	A6	113
Bartlett, Il., U.S.	*k8	90
Bartlett, Ks., U.S.	E8	93
Bartlett, Ne., U.S.	C7	104
Bartlett, N.H., U.S.	B4	106
Bartlett, Oh., U.S.	C4	112
Bartlett, Tn., U.S.	B2	119
Bartlett, Tx., U.S.	D4	120
Bartlett Cove, Ak., U.S.	k22	79
Bartlett Reservoir, res., Az., U.S.	D4	80
Bartletts Ferry Dam, U.S.	C4	87
Bartlett Harbour, Newf.	C3	72
Barton, Al., U.S.	A2	78
Barton, Md., U.S.	k12	97
Barton, N.D., U.S.	A5	111
Barton, Oh., U.S.	B5	112
Barton, Vt., U.S.	B4	122
Barton, co., Ks., U.S.	D5	93
Barton, co., Mo., U.S.	D3	102
Barton, stm., Vt., U.S.	B4	122
Bartonsville, Il., U.S.	C3	90
Barton-upon-Humber, Eng., U.K.	A7	12
Bartonville, Il., U.S.	C4	90
Bartoszyce, Pol.	A6	26
Bartow, Fl., U.S.	E5	86
Bartow, Ga., U.S.	D4	87
Bartow, co., Ga., U.S.	B2	87
Barú, Volcán, vol., Pan.	F6	62
Barun Su, China	C4	32
Barus, Indon.	K3	35
Baruth, E. Ger.	A8	19
Barun-Urt, Mong.	B7	31
Barvas, Scot., U.K.	A3	10
Barvenkovo, Sov. Un.	G11	27
Barview, Or., U.S.	*D2	114
Barwāni, India	F5	37
Barwick, Ga., U.S.	F3	87
Barwon, stm., Austl.	B3	10
Barybino, Sov. Un.	n17	27
Barycz, stm., Pol.	C4	26
Barysh, Sov. Un.	B4	71
Bashi, Al., U.S.	D2	78
Bashi Channel, strt., Asia	A6	34
Basiad Bay, b., Phil.	o14	34
Basilan Island, i., Phil.	D6	34
Basildon, Eng., U.K.	C8	12
Basile, La., U.S.	D3	95
Basile (Lucania), prov., Italy	E2	56
Basílio, Braz.	C6	56
Basin, Mt., U.S.	D4	103
Basin, Wy., U.S.	B4	127
Basinger, Fl., U.S.	E5	86
Basingstoke, Eng., U.K.	C6	12
Basin Harbor, Vt., U.S.	C2	122
Basin Lake, l., Sask.	E3	75
Baška, Yugo.	C2	24
Baskahegan Lake, l., Me., U.S.	C5	96
Baskatong, Réservoir, res., Que.	k11	74
Baskett, Ky., U.S.	C2	94
Baskin, Fl., U.S.	p10	86
Baskin, La., U.S.	B4	95
Basking Ridge, N.J., U.S.	B3	107
Basoko, Zaire	A3	48
Basongo, Zaire	B3	48
Basora, Punt, c., Neth. Ant.	H17	65
Basque Provinces, hist. reg., Sp.	A4	22
Basra (Al Başrah), Iraq	B4	38
Bas-Rhin, dept., Fr.	F7	17
Bassano, Alta.	D4	68
Bassano del Grappa, Italy	B3	23
Bassas da India, rf., Reu.	B6	49
Basse-Pointe, Mart.	S10	65
Basse Santa Su, Gam.	D2	45
Basse-Terre, Guad.	I14	64
Basseterre, St. C.-N.	H13	64
Basse-Terre, i., Guad.	Q8	65
Bassett, Ar., U.S.	B5	81
Bassett, Ia., U.S.	A5	92
Bassett, Ks., U.S.	E8	93
Bassett, Ne., U.S.	B6	104
Bassett, Va., U.S.	D3	123
Bassett, Wi., U.S.	n11	126
Bassett Creek, stm., Al., U.S.	D2	78
Bassett Peak, mtn., Az., U.S.	E5	80
Bassfield, Ms., U.S.	D4	101
Bassikounou, Maur.	C3	45
Bassum, W. Ger.	F2	15
Basswood, Man.	D1	70
Basswood Lake, l., Mn., U.S.	B7	100
Bástad, Swe.	H5	14
Bastak, Iran	D2	23
Bastelica, Fr.	D9	37
Basti, India	B1	123
Bastia, Fr.	C1	123
Bastogne, Bel.	E5	17
Bastrop, La., U.S.	B4	95
Bastrop, Tx., U.S.	D4	120
Bastrop, co., Tx., U.S.	D4	120
Bastuträsk, Swe.	E9	14
Basyūn, Eg.	D2	41
Bata, Eq. Gui.	B1	48
Bataan Peninsula, pen., Phil.	o13	34
Batabanó, Cuba	C6	64
Batabanó, Golfo de, b., Cuba	C2	64
Bataguaçu, Braz.	C2	56
Batala, India	B6	36
Batamay, Sov. Un.	C15	29
Batang, China	E4	31
Batangafo, Cen. Afr. Rep.	D3	46
Batangas, Phil.	C6	34
Batan Islands, is., Phil.	A6	34
Batászék, Hung.	B4	24
Batatais, Braz.	C3	56
Batavia, Arg.	A3	54
Batavia, Ar., U.S.	A2	81
Batavia, Il., U.S.	B5	90
Batavia, Ia., U.S.	D5	92
Batavia, N.Y., U.S.	C2	109
Batavia, Oh., U.S.	C1	112
Bataysk, Sov. Un.	H12	27
Batchelor, La., U.S.	D4	95
Batchelor Bay, b., N.C., U.S.	B6	110
Batchtown, Il., U.S.	D3	90
Batdambang, Camb.	C2	34
Bateman, Sask.	G2	75
Bates, Ar., U.S.	C1	81
Bates, co., Mo., U.S.	C3	102
Bates City, Mo., U.S.	D4	117
Batesburg, S.C., U.S.	D4	117
Bates City, Mo., U.S.	D3	118
Batesland, S.D., U.S.	D3	118
Batesville, Ar., U.S.	B4	81
Batesville, In., U.S.	F7	91
Batesville, Ms., U.S.	A4	101
Batesville, Tx., U.S.	E3	120
Bath, N.B.	C2	71
Bath, Ont.	C8	73
Bath, Jam.	F16	64
Bath, Eng., U.K.	C5	10
Bath, Il., U.S.	C3	90
Bath, In., U.S.	E8	91
Bath, Me., U.S.	E3	96
Bath, N.H., U.S.	B3	106
Bath, N.Y., U.S.	C3	109
Bath, N.C., U.S.	B6	110
Bath, Pa., U.S.	E11	115
Bath, S.C., U.S.	D4	117
Bath, S.D., U.S.	B7	118
Bath, co., Ky., U.S.	B6	94
Bath, co., Va., U.S.	B3	123
Bathgate, Scot., U.K.	E5	13
Bathgate, N.D., U.S.	A8	111
Bathinda, India	B5	37
Bathsheba, Barb.	J15	64
Bath Springs, Tn., U.S.	B3	119
Bathurst, Austl.	F8	50
Bathurst, N.B.	B4	71
Bathurst see Banjul, Gam.	D1	45
Bathurst, i., Austl.	B5	50
Bathurst, Cape, c., N.W. Ter.	B7	66
Bathurst Inlet, N.W. Ter.	C11	66
Bathurst Inlet, b., N.W. Ter.	C11	66
Bathurst Island, i., Austl.	B5	50
Bathurst Island, i., N.W. Ter.	m31	66
Batié, Burkina	E4	45
Batiki, i., Fiji	H15	52
Batiscan, Que.	C5	74
Batiscan, stm., Que.	B5	74
Batkanu, S.L.	E2	45
Batman, Tur.	D13	40
Batna, Alg.	B6	44
Batoche, Sask.	E2	75
Baton Rouge, La., U.S.	D4	95
Batouri, Cam.	E2	46
Batson, Tx., U.S.	D5	120
Batsto, N.J., U.S.	D3	107
Batsto, stm., N.J., U.S.	D3	107
Batten Kill, stm., U.S.	E2	122
Battery Park, Va., U.S.	k14	123
Batticaloa, Sri L.	G7	36
Battiest, Ok., U.S.	C7	113
Battle, stm., Can.	F11	66
Battleboro, N.C., U.S.	A5	110
Battle Creek, Sask.	H1	75
Battle Creek, Ia., U.S.	B2	92
Battle Creek, Mi., U.S.	C5	99
Battle Creek, Ne., U.S.	C8	104
Battle Creek, stm., N.A.	B7	103
Battleford, Sask.	E1	75
Battle Ground, In., U.S.	C4	91
Battle Ground, Wa., U.S.	D3	124
Battle Lake, Mn., U.S.	D3	100
Battlement Mesa, mtn., Co., U.S.	B2	83
Battle Mountain, mtn., Wy., U.S.	C5	105
Battle Mountain, mtn., Wy., U.S.	E5	127
Battles, Ms., U.S.	D5	101
Battles Wharf, Al., U.S.	E2	78
Battletview, N.D., U.S.	A3	111
Battonya, Hung.	B5	24
Battrum, Sask.	G1	75
Batu, Indon.	A4	22
Batu, mtn., Eth.	D4	47
Batu, i., Indon.	B2	63
Batu Gajah, Malay.	F1	34
Batu Islands, is., Indon.	E7	29
Batumi, Sov. Un.	E7	29
Batu Pahat, Malay.	L5	35
Baturaja, Indon.	F2	34
Baturino, Sov. Un.	B11	28
Baturité, Braz.	B3	57
Bat Yam, Isr.	g9	41
Baubau, Indon.	G6	34
Bauchi, Nig.	A5	22
Baudette, Mn., U.S.	B4	100
Baudó, Serranía de, mts., Col.	B2	60
Bauer, Ut., U.S.	C3	121
Bauer Coulee, val., Wa., U.S.	B6	124
Baugé, Fr.	D3	16
Bauld, Cape, c., Newf.	C4	72
Bauma, Switz.	B6	21
Baume-les-Dames, Fr.	D2	23
Baunei, Italy	B3	57
Baures, Bol.	B3	59
Baures, stm., Bol.	D6	71
Baurtregaum, mtn., Ire.	E2	11
Bauru, Braz.	C3	56
Bauska, Sov. Un.	C7	18
Bautzen, E. Ger.	C3	19
Bauxite, Ar., U.S.	C3	81
Bavaria, Ks., U.S.	D6	93
Bavaria, hist. reg., W. Ger.	B5	18
Bavarian Alps, mts., Eur.	B7	20
Bavay, Fr.	E3	16
Båven, l., Swe.	t34	14
Bavispe, Mex.	B5	63
Bawcomville, La., U.S.	*B3	95
Bawean, i., Indon.	G4	34
Bawku, Ghana	A4	45
Bawlf, Alta.	C4	68
Baxdo, Som.	D6	47
Baxian, China	E7	32
Baxley, Ga., U.S.	E4	87
Baxter, Ia., U.S.	C4	92
Baxter, Mn., U.S.	D4	100
Baxter, Tn., U.S.	C8	119
Baxter, co., Ar., U.S.	A3	81
Baxter Springs, Ks., U.S.	E9	93
Baxterville, Co., U.S.	D4	83
Baxterville, Ms., U.S.	D4	101
Bay, Ar., U.S.	B5	81
Bay, prov., Som.	E5	47
Bay, co., Fl., U.S.	u16	86
Bay, co., Mi., U.S.	E7	99
Bay, Laguna de, l., Phil.	o13	34
Bay al Kabīr, Wādī, val., Libya	C2	43
Bayamang, Phil.	o13	34
Bayamo, Cuba	D5	64
Bayamón, P.R.	G11	64
Bayan, China	C9	28
Bayanaul, Sov. Un.	D3	32
Bayanga, Cen. Afr. Rep.	B5	31
Bayan Obo, China	D3	32
Bayard, Ia., U.S.	C3	92
Bayard, Ne., U.S.	C2	104
Bayard, N.M., U.S.	E1	108
Bayard, W.V., U.S.	B5	125
Bayberry, N.Y., U.S.	B4	109
Bayboro, N.C., U.S.	B6	110
Bayble, Scot., U.K.	o18	13
Baybunt, Tur.	B13	40
Bay Center, Wa., U.S.	C2	124
Bay City, Mi., U.S.	E7	99
Bay City, Or., U.S.	B3	114
Bay City, Tx., U.S.	E5	120
Bay City, Wi., U.S.	D1	126
Baydarata Bay, b., Sov. Un.	B22	27
Baydhabo, Som.	E5	47
Baydrag, stm., Mong.	B5	31
Bayern, state, W. Ger.	D6	19
Bayeux, Fr.	C5	16
Bayfield, Ont.	D3	73
Bayfield, Co., U.S.	D3	83
Bayfield, Wi., U.S.	B3	126
Bayfield, co., Wi., U.S.	B2	126
Bay Head, N.J., U.S.	*C4	107
Bayındır, Tur.	C6	25
Baykonyr, Sov. Un.	D7	28
Bay L'Argent, Newf.	E4	72
Baylis, Il., U.S.	D3	90
Baylor, co., Tx., U.S.	C3	120
Baymak, Sov. Un.	C5	28
Bay Mills Indian Reservation, Mi., U.S.	B6	99
Bay Minette, Al., U.S.	E2	78
Bayombong, Phil.	n13	34
Bayonet Point, Fl., U.S.	*D4	86
Bayonne, Fr.	F3	16
Bayonne, N.J., U.S.	B4	107
Bayou Bodcau Reservoir, res., La., U.S.	B2	95
Bayou Cane, La., U.S.	*E5	95
Bayou D'Arbonne Lake, res., La., U.S.	B3	95
Bayou George, Fl., U.S.	u16	86
Bayou Goula, La., U.S.	E1	78
Bayou La Batre, Al., U.S.	C1	58
Bayóvar, Peru	*E4	86
Bay Pines, Fl., U.S.	G7	117
Bay Point, c., S.C., U.S.	E5	71
Bayport, N.S.	E7	99
Bayport, Mi., U.S.	E6	100
Bayport, Mn., U.S.	n15	109
Bayport, N.Y., U.S.	C6	25
Bayramiç, Tur.	D5	18
Bayreuth, W. Ger.	C5	97
Bay Ridge, Md., U.S.	B7	20
Bayrischzell, W. Ger.	E2	122
Bay Roberts, Newf.	k14	123
Bays, Lake of, l., Ont.	B5	73
Bay Saint Louis, Ms., U.S.	E4	101
Bay Shore, N.Y., U.S.	E7	109
Bayshore-Est, Que.	C7	74
Bayshore Gardens, Fl., U.S.	q10	86
Bayside, Tx., U.S.	E4	120
Bayside, Wi., U.S.	m12	126
Baysun, Sov. Un.	B13	39
Bayt al Faqīh, Yemen	C5	47
Bayt Dajan, Isr. Occ.	g12	41
Baytown, Tx., U.S.	E5	120
Bay Trail, Sask.	E3	75
Bayt Jālā, Isr. Occ.	g12	41
Baytullū, Isr. Occ.	h11	41
Bayt Jālā, Isr. Occ.	C7	41
Bay Village, Oh., U.S.	g9	112
Baza, Spain	D4	22
Bazaruto, Ilha do, i., Moz.	B6	49
Bazemore, Al., U.S.	E6	31
Bazhong, China	B8	104
Bazile Mills, Ne., U.S.	D4	93
Bazine, Ks., U.S.	G10	39
Bazmān, Kūh-e, mtn., Iran	A5	22
Baztán, Spain	h9	49
Be, Nosy, i., Madag.	h9	90
Beach, II., U.S.	C1	111
Beach, N.D., U.S.	B8	73
Beachburg, Ont.	B4	112
Beach City, Oh., U.S.	D9	115
Beach Haven, N.J., U.S.	D4	107
Beach Haven, Pa., U.S.	D4	107
Beach Haven Crest, N.J., U.S.	D4	107
Beach Haven Inlet, b., N.J., U.S.	D4	107
Beach Haven Terrace, N.J., U.S.	C7	94
Beach Lake, Pa., U.S.	C11	115
Beach Pond, res., U.S.	C8	84
Beachport, Austl.	H3	51
Beachville, Ont.	D4	73
Beachville, Md., U.S.	D5	97
Beachwood, N.J., U.S.	D4	107
Beachwood, Oh., U.S.	*h10	112
Beachy Head, c., Eng., U.K.	D8	12
Beacon, N.Y., U.S.	D7	109
Beacon, N.Y., U.S.	C5	92
Beacon Falls, Ct., U.S.	D3	84
Beaconsfield, Que.	q19	74
Beaconsfield, Que.	D6	47
Beacon Square, Fl., U.S.	*D4	86
Beadle, Sask.	F1	75
Beadle, co., S.D., U.S.	C7	118
Beagh, Slieve, hill, N. Ire., U.K.	C4	11
Beagle, Ont.	D9	93
Beagle, Canal, strt., S.A.	h12	54
Bealanana, Madag.	f9	49
Beale, Cape, c., B.C.	E5	69
Beale Air Force Base, mil., Ca., U.S.	C3	82
Beall, Oh., U.S.	C4	112
Beals, Ky., U.S.	C2	94
Beal City, Mi., U.S.	E6	99
Bean Lake, Mo., U.S.	C10	119
Bean Station, Tn., U.S.	C10	119
Bear, De., U.S.	D5	64
Bear, stm., U.S.	G11	64
Bearcreek, Mt., U.S.	C3	33
Bear Creek, Al., U.S.	A2	78
Bear Creek, Wi., U.S.	D5	126
Bear Creek, stm., U.S.	A7	103
Bear Creek, stm., Al., U.S.	A1	78
Bear Creek, stm., Or., U.S.	E4	114
Bear Creek, stm., Wy., U.S.	E8	127
Bearden, Ar., U.S.	D3	81
Bearden, Ok., U.S.	o18	73
Beardmore Glacier, ice, Ant.	A30	7
Beardmore, Ont.	m13	125
Beards Fork, W.V., U.S.	B4	109
Beardsley, Mn., U.S.	E5	72
Beardstown, Il., U.S.	B4	119
Bearfort Mountain, mtn., N.J., U.S.	A4	107
Bear Island, i., Man.	B3	70
Bear Island, i., Ire.	F2	11
Bear Lake, Mi., U.S.	D4	99
Bear Lake, Pa., U.S.	C3	115
Bear Lake, co., Id., U.S.	G7	89
Bear Lake, l., Alta.	B4	31
Bear Lake, l., Man.	B1	70
Bear Lake, l., Man.	A4	121
Bear Lodge Mountains, Wy., U.S.	B8	127
Bear Mountain, mtn., Ar., U.S.	f7	81
Bear Mountain, mtn., Ky., U.S.	C5	94
Bear Mountain, mtn., Ma.	A3	98
Bear Mountain, mtn., Or., U.S.	D4	114
Béarn, hist. reg., Fr.	F3	16
Bearpaw Mountains, mts., Mt., U.S.	B7	103
Bear Peninsula, pen., Ant.	B1	7
Bear Pond Mountains, mts., Md., U.S.	A2	97
Bear River, N.S.	E4	71
Bear River City, Ut., U.S.	B3	121
Bear Spring, Tn., U.S.	A4	119
Bear Swamp, sw., Ma., U.S.	h11	98
Bear Tooth Pass, Wy., U.S.	B3	127
Beartooth Range, mts., U.S.	E7	103
Bear Town, Ms., U.S.	D3	101
Beartown Mountain, mtn., Va., U.S.	f10	123
Beas de Segura, Spain	C4	22
Beason, Il., U.S.	C4	90
Beata, Cabo, c., Dom. Rep.	F8	64
Beaton, B.C.	D9	69
Beatrice, Al., U.S.	D2	78
Beatrice, Ne., U.S.	D9	104
Beatrice, Zimb.	A5	49
Beattie, Ks., U.S.	C7	93
Beatton, stm., B.C.	E3	75
Beatty, Sask.	E3	75
Beatty, Nv., U.S.	G5	105
Beatty, Or., U.S.	E5	114
Beattyville, Ky., U.S.	C6	94
Beatyestown, N.J., U.S.	B3	107
Beaucaire, Fr.	F6	16
Beauce, co., Que.	C7	74
Beauceville, Que.	C7	74
Beaucourt, Fr.	D7	16
Beaufort, Fr.	E2	21
Beaufort, Malay.	D5	34
Beaufort, Mo., U.S.	C6	102
Beaufort, N.C., U.S.	C6	110
Beaufort, S.C., U.S.	G6	117
Beaufort, co., N.C., U.S.	B5	110
Beaufort, co., S.C., U.S.	G6	117
Beaufort Island, i., Ant.	e38	7
Beaufort Marine Corps Air Station, mil., S.C., U.S.	F6	117
Beaufort Sea, N.A.	B7	61
Beaufort West, S. Afr.	D3	49
Beaugency, Fr.	D4	16
Beauharnois, Que.	D4	74
Beauharnois, co., Que.	D3	74
Beau Lake, l., Me., U.S.	A3	96
Beaulieu, Que.	n17	74
Beaulieu, Mn., U.S.	C3	100
Beauly, Scot., U.K.	C4	13
Beauly, stm., Scot., U.K.	C4	13
Beaumaris, Wales, U.K.	A3	12
Beaumont, Bel.	D4	17
Beaumont, Alta.	C4	68
Beaumont, Newf.	C4	72
Beaumont, Que.	C6	74
Beaumont, Fr.	F4	16
Beaumont, Ca., U.S.	*F5	82
Beaumont, Ks., U.S.	E7	93
Beaumont, Ms., U.S.	D5	101
Beaumont, Tx., U.S.	D5	120
Beaumont [-sur-Oise], Fr.	E2	17
Beaune, Fr.	D6	16
Beauport, Que.	n17	74
Beaupré, Que.	B7	74
Beauraing, Bel.	D4	17
Beauregard, Ms., U.S.	D3	101
Beauregard, co., La., U.S.	D2	95
Beaurivage, Que.	C6	74
Beausejour, Man.	D3	70
Beauty, Ky., U.S.	C7	94
Beauvais, Fr.	C5	16
Beauval, Sask.	B2	75
Beauvallon, Alta.	C5	68
Beaver, Ak., U.S.	B10	79
Beaver, Ar., U.S.	*A2	81
Beaver, Ks., U.S.	D5	93
Beaver, Oh., U.S.	C3	112
Beaver, Ok., U.S.	A1	113
Beaver, Pa., U.S.	E1	115
Beaver, Ut., U.S.	E3	121
Beaver, Wi., U.S.	C6	126
Beaver, co., Ok., U.S.	e10	113
Beaver, co., Pa., U.S.	E1	115
Beaver, co., Ut., U.S.	E2	121
Beaver, stm., Can.	B2	75
Beaver, stm., N.Y., U.S.	B6	109
Beaver, stm., R.I., U.S.	E2	116
Beaver, stm., Ut., U.S.	E6	71
Beaver, stm., U.S.	A2	113
Beaverbank, N.S.	C7	100
Beaver Bay, Mn., U.S.	C7	100
Beaver Brook, stm., U.S.	E4	106
Beaver City, Ne., U.S.	D6	104
Beaver Creek, B.C.	E5	69
Beaver Creek, Mn., U.S.	G2	100
Beaver Creek, Oh., U.S.	C1	112
Beaver Creek, stm., Sask.	F2	75
Beaver Creek, stm., U.S.	E4	104
Beaver Creek, stm., U.S.	C8	127
Beaver Creek, stm., Co., U.S.	B7	83
Beaver Creek, stm., Ks., U.S.	e8	93
Beaver Creek, stm., Ky., U.S.	C7	94
Beaver Creek, stm., Mo., U.S.	E5	102
Beaver Creek, stm., Mt., U.S.	B9	103
Beaver Creek, stm., N.D., U.S.	C5	111
Beaver Creek, stm., Or., U.S.	C5	111
Beaver Creek, stm., Tn., U.S.	m13	119
Beaver Creek, stm., Wy., U.S.	D4	127
Beaver Creek Mountains, mts., U.S.	B3	78
Beaver Crossing, Ne., U.S.	D8	104
Beaverdale, Pa., U.S.	F4	115
Beaver Dam, Az., U.S.	A2	80
Beaver Dam, Ky., U.S.	C3	94
Beaver Dam, Wi., U.S.	E5	126
Beaverdam Branch, stm., De., U.S.	F3	85
Beaverdam Lake, res., Wi., U.S.	E5	126
Beaver Dams, N.Y., U.S.	C4	109
Beaverdell, B.C.	E8	69
Beaver Falls, N.Y., U.S.	B5	109
Beaver Falls, Pa., U.S.	E1	115
Beaverhead, co., Mt., U.S.	A2	103
Beaverhead, stm., Mt., U.S.	E4	103

Name	Map Ref.	Page

Beaverhead Mountains, mts., U.S. — D5 89
Beaverhill Lake, l., Alta. — C4 68
Beaver Hill Lake, l., Man. — B4 70
Beaver Island, i., Mi., U.S. — C5 99
Beaver Island, i., Alta. — B5 68
Beaver Lake, res., Ar., U.S. — A2 81
Beaverlick, Ky., U.S. — k13 94
Beaverlodge, Alta. — B1 68
Beaver Meadows, Pa., U.S. — E10 115
Beaver Point, Co., U.S. — A5 83
Beaver Ridge, mtn., Tn., U.S. — D9 119
Beaver Run Reservoir, res., Pa., U.S. — F2 115
Beaver Springs, Pa., U.S. — E7 115
Beavertail Point, c., R.I., U.S. — F4 116
Beaverton, Ont. — C5 73
Beaverton, Al., U.S. — B1 78
Beaverton, Mi., U.S. — E6 99
Beaverton, Or., U.S. — B4 114
Beavertown, Pa., U.S. — E7 115
Beaver Town, India — C5 36
Beāwar, India — C5 36
Beazley, Arg. — A3 54
Bebedouro, Braz. — C3 56
Bebra, W. Ger. — C4 19
Bécancour, Que. — C5 74
Bécancour, stm., Que. — C6 74
Beccles, Eng., U.K. — B9 12
Bečej, Yugo. — C5 24
Becerreá, Spain — A2 22
Béchar, Alg. — C4 44
Becharof Lake, l., Ak., U.S. — D8 79
Bechyně, Czech. — D9 19
Beckemeyer, Il., U.S. — E4 90
Becker, Mn., U.S. — E5 100
Becker, Ms., U.S. — B5 101
Becker, co., Mn., U.S. — D3 100
Becket, Ma., U.S. — B1 98
Beckham, co., Ok., U.S. — B2 113
Beckley, W.V., U.S. — D3 125
Beckum, W. Ger. — B3 18
Beckville, Tx., U.S. — C5 120
Beckwith Creek, stm., La., U.S. — D2 95
Becky Peak, mtn., Nv., U.S. — D7 105
Bedale, Eng., U.K. — F7 13
Bédarieux, Fr. — F5 16
Bedburg, W. Ger. — C1 19
Bederkesa, W. Ger. — E2 15
Bedford, N.S. — E6 71
Bedford, Que. — D5 74
Bedford, Eng., U.K. — D6 10
Bedford, In., U.S. — G5 91
Bedford, Ia., U.S. — D3 92
Bedford, Ky., U.S. — B4 94
Bedford, Ma., U.S. — B5 98
Bedford, Mi., U.S. — F5 99
Bedford, Mo., U.S. — B4 102
Bedford, N.H., U.S. — E3 106
Bedford, Oh., U.S. — A4 112
Bedford, Pa., U.S. — F4 115
Bedford, Tx., U.S. — *n9 120
Bedford, Va., U.S. — C3 123
Bedford, Wy., U.S. — D2 127
Bedford, co., Pa., U.S. — G4 115
Bedford, co., Tn., U.S. — B5 119
Bedford, co., Va., U.S. — C3 123
Bedford Heights, Oh., U.S. — *h9 112
Bedford Hills, N.Y., U.S. — D7 109
Bedfordshire, co., Eng., U.K. — B7 12
Bedias, Tx., U.S. — D5 120
Bedlington, Eng., U.K. — C6 10
Bedminster, N.J., U.S. — B3 107
Bedourie, Austl. — B2 51
Bedrock, Co., U.S. — C2 83
Bedzin, Pol. — g10 26
Bee, Ne., U.S. — C8 104
Bee, Ok., U.S. — C5 113
Bee, co., Tx., U.S. — E4 120
Beebe, Que. — D5 74
Beebe, Ar., U.S. — B4 81
Beebe Plain, Vt., U.S. — A4 122
Beebe River, N.H., U.S. — C3 106
Bee Branch, Ar., U.S. — B3 81
Beech Bluff, Tn., U.S. — B3 119
Beech Bottom, W.V., U.S. — f8 125
Beech Creek, Ky., U.S. — C2 94
Beech Creek, Pa., U.S. — D6 115
Beecher, Il., U.S. — B6 90
Beecher, Mi., U.S. — E7 99
Beecher City, Il., U.S. — D5 90
Beechey Head, c., B.C. — h12 69
Beech Fork, stm., Ky., U.S. — C4 94
Beech Grove, Ar., U.S. — A5 81
Beech Grove, In., U.S. — E5 91
Beech Grove, Tn., U.S. — B5 119
Beech Island, S.C., U.S. — E4 117
Beechwood, N.B. — C2 71
Beechwood, Ma., U.S. — h12 98
Beechwood, Mi., U.S. — B2 99
Beechy, Sask. — G2 75
Beecroft Head, c., Austl. — G8 51
Beedeville, Ar., U.S. — B4 81
Beef Island, i., Tn., U.S. — e8 119
Beef Island, i., V.I., Br. — B6 65
Beek, Neth. — D5 17
Beeler, Ks., U.S. — D3 93
Beemer, Ne., U.S. — C9 104
Beenleigh, Austl. — C9 51
Bee Ridge, Fl., U.S. — q11 86
Beersheba Springs, Tn., U.S. — D8 119
Beersheba (Be'er Sheva'), Isr. — B3 38
Beersville, N.B. — C4 71
Beeskow, E. Ger. — B7 18
Beesleys Point, N.J., U.S. — E3 107
Beethoven Peninsula, pen., Ant. — B5 7
Beeton, Ont. — C5 73
Beetzendorf, E. Ger. — F5 15
Beeville, Tx., U.S. — E4 120
Befale, Zaire — B4 48
Beg, Lough, l., N. Ire., U.K. — C5 11
Bega, Austl. — G8 51
Beggs, Ok., U.S. — B5 113
Begicheva, i., Sov. Un. — B13 29
Béhague, Pointe, c., Fr. Gu. — B4 59
Behāla (South Suburban), India — *D8 36
Behbahān, Iran — F5 39
Behm Canal, strt., Ak., U.S. — n24 79
Behshahr, Iran — C6 39
Bei'an, China — B10 31
Beigi, China — D3 47
Beihai, China — G6 31
Beijing (Peking), China — D8 31
Beili, China — C8 35
Beilngries, W. Ger. — D6 19
Beinamar, Chad — D3 46
Beipiao, China — *C9 31
Beira, Moz. — A5 49
Beira, hist. reg., Port. — E2 22
Beirne, Ar., U.S. — D2 81

Beirut (Bayrūt), Leb. — B3 38
Beiseker, Alta. — D4 68
Beitbridge, Zimb. — B5 49
Beiuș, Rom. — B6 24
Beja, Port. — C2 22
Béja, Tun. — B6 44
Bejaïa (Bougie), Alg. — B4 44
Béjar, Spain — B3 22
Bejou, Mn., U.S. — C3 100
Bejuco, Pan. — F8 62
Bekabad, Sov. Un. — G22 8
Bekdash, Sov. Un. — E4 28
Békés, Hung. — B5 24
Békéscsaba, Hung. — B5 24
Bekily, Madag. — h9 49
Bela, India — E8 37
Bela, Pak. — C4 36
Bela Crkva, Yugo. — C5 24
Belaga, Malay. — E4 34
Bel Air, Md., U.S. — A5 97
Bel Aire, Ks., U.S. — g12 93
Bel Aire Estates, Ct., U.S. — D7 84
Belalcázar, Spain — C3 22
Bel Alton, Md., U.S. — D4 97
Belampalli, India — E6 36
Bélanger, stm., Man. — C3 70
Bélanger, stm., Sask. — B2 75
Belas, Port. — f9 22
Bela Vista, Braz. — C1 56
Bela Vista, Moz. — C5 49
Bela Vista de Goiás, Braz. — D5 57
Belawan, Indon. — E1 34
Belaya, stm., Sov. Un. — B4 28
Belaya Glina, Sov. Un. — H13 27
Belaya Tserkov, Sov. Un. — G8 27
Belcamp, Md., U.S. — B5 97
Belcher, Ky., U.S. — C7 94
Belcher, La., U.S. — B2 95
Belcherāgh, Afg. — D12 39
Belcher Islands, is., N.W. Ter. — E17 66
Belchertown, Ma., U.S. — B3 98
Belcourt, N.D., U.S. — A6 111
Belcoville, N.J., U.S. — E3 107
Belden, Ms., U.S. — A5 101
Belden, Ne., U.S. — B8 104
Belden, N.D., U.S. — A3 111
Belding, Mi., U.S. — E5 99
Belecke, W. Ger. — B3 19
Beled Weyne, Som. — E6 47
Belém (Pará), Braz. — B1 57
Belém, Arg. — E2 55
Belén, Para. — D4 55
Belen, Ms., U.S. — A3 101
Belen, N.M., U.S. — C3 108
Belén, Ur. — E1 56
Belén de Escobar, Arg. — g7 54
Belenkoye, Sov. Un. — q20 27
Belev, Sov. Un. — E11 27
Belfair, Wa., U.S. — B3 124
Belfast, N. Ire., U.K. — C4 10
Belfast, Me., U.S. — D3 96
Belfast, N.Y., U.S. — C2 109
Belfast, N.C., U.S. — B5 110
Belfast, Oh., U.S. — C2 112
Belfast, Pa., U.S. — B5 115
Belfast Lough, b., N. Ire., U.K. — C6 11
Belfield, N.D., U.S. — C2 111
Belford, Eng., U.K. — E7 13
Belford, N.J., U.S. — C4 107
Belfort, Fr. — D7 16
Belfort, N.Y., U.S. — B5 109
Belfort, ter., Fr. — B2 20
Belfry, Ky., U.S. — C7 94
Belfry, Mt., U.S. — E8 103
Belgaum, India — B2 36
Belgica Mountains, mts., Ant. — B16 7
Belgium, Il., U.S. — C6 90
Belgium, Wi., U.S. — E6 126
Belgium, ctry., Eur. — B6 16
Belgorod, Sov. Un. — F11 27
Belgorod-Dnestrovskiy, Sov. Un. — H8 27
Belgrade, Me., U.S. — D3 96
Belgrade, Mo., U.S. — D7 102
Belgrade, Mt., U.S. — E5 103
Belgrade, Ne., U.S. — C7 104
Belgrade (Beograd), Yugo. — C5 24
Belgrade Lakes, Me., U.S. — D3 96
Belgreen, Al., U.S. — A2 78
Belhaven, N.C., U.S. — B6 110
Belice, stm., Italy — F4 23
Beli Lom, stm., Bul. — D8 24
Belington, W.V., U.S. — B5 125
Belitung, i., Indon. — F3 34
Belize, ctry., N.A. — D7 63
Belize, stm., Belize — B3 62
Belize City, Belize — D7 63
Belkino, Sov. Un. — B11 33
Belknap, Il., U.S. — F5 90
Belknap, Ia., U.S. — D5 92
Belknap, co., N.H., U.S. — C3 106
Belknap Crater, crat., Or., U.S. — C5 114
Belknap Mountain, mtn., N.H., U.S. — C4 106
Belkovski, stm., Sov. Un. — B1 28
Bell, Ca., U.S. — *E4 82
Bell, Fl., U.S. — C4 86
Bell, co., Ky., U.S. — D6 94
Bell, co., Tx., U.S. — D4 120
Bella Bella, B.C. — C3 69
Bellac, Fr. — A4 16
Bella Coola, B.C. — C4 69
Bella Coola, stm., B.C. — C4 69
Bellagio, Italy — D5 20
Bellahy, Ire. — D3 11
Bellaire, Mi., U.S. — D5 99
Bellaire, Oh., U.S. — B5 112
Bellaire, Tx., U.S. — r14 120
Bellamy, Al., U.S. — C1 78
Bellano, Italy — D7 21
Bellary, India — E6 36
Bella Unión, Ur. — E1 56
Bella Vista, Arg. — B5 54
Bella Vista, Arg. — A3 54
Bella Vista, Para. — D4 55
Bellavista, Peru — B2 60
Bella Vista, Tx., U.S. — A1 81
Bellbrook, Oh., U.S. — C1 112
Bell Buckle, Tn., U.S. — B5 119
Bell Burn, W.V., U.S. — C4 125
Bell City, La., U.S. — D3 95
Bell City, Mo., U.S. — D8 102
Belle, W.V., U.S. — C3 125
Belle, stm., La., U.S. — k9 95
Bellair, Fl., U.S. — p10 86
Belle-Anse, Haiti — E7 64
Belle Bay, b., Newf. — E4 72
Belle Center, Oh., U.S. — B2 112
Belle Chasse, La., U.S. — E5 95
Bellechasse, co., Que. — C7 74
Belle Creek, Mt., U.S. — E11 103

Belledune, N.B. — B4 71
Belleek, N. Ire., U.K. — C3 11
Bellefleur, N.B. — B2 71
Bellefontaine, Ms., U.S. — B4 101
Bellefontaine, Oh., U.S. — B2 112
Bellefontaine Neighbors, Mo., U.S. — *f13 102
Bellefonte, Ar., U.S. — A2 81
Bellefonte, De., U.S. — *A3 85
Bellefonte, Pa., U.S. — E6 115
Belle Fourche, S.D., U.S. — C2 118
Belle Fourche, stm., U.S. — C3 118
Belle Fourche Reservoir, res., S.D., U.S. — C2 118
Belle Glade, Fl., U.S. — F6 86
Belle Haven, Va., U.S. — C7 123
Belleherbe, Fr. — B2 21
Belle Hôtesse, mtn., Guad. — Q8 65
Belle Isle, Fl., U.S. — D5 86
Belle Isle, i., Newf. — C4 72
Belle Isle, Strait of, strt., Newf. — C3 72
Belleisle Creek, N.B. — D4 71
Belle Mead, N.J., U.S. — C3 107
Belle Meade, Tn., U.S. — g10 119
Belle Mina, Al., U.S. — A3 78
Belleoram, Newf. — E4 72
Belleplain, N.J., U.S. — E3 107
Belle-Plaine, Sask. — G3 75
Belle Plaine, Ia., U.S. — C5 92
Belle Plaine, Ks., U.S. — E6 93
Belle Plaine, Mn., U.S. — F5 100
Belle Rive, Il., U.S. — E5 90
Belle River, Ont. — E2 73
Belle Rose, La., U.S. — D4 95
Belleu, Fr. — E3 17
Belle Union, In., U.S. — E4 91
Belle Valley, Oh., U.S. — C4 112
Belle Vernon, Pa., U.S. — F2 115
Belleview, Fl., U.S. — C4 86
Belleview, Mo., U.S. — D7 102
Belle View, Va., U.S. — g12 123
Belleville, N.S. — F4 71
Belleville, Ont. — C7 73
Belleville, Fr. — D6 16
Belleville, Ar., U.S. — B2 81
Belleville, Il., U.S. — E4 90
Belleville, Ks., U.S. — C6 93
Belleville, Mi., U.S. — p15 99
Belleville, N.J., U.S. — B4 107
Belleville, N.Y., U.S. — B4 109
Belleville, Pa., U.S. — E6 115
Belleville, R.I., U.S. — E4 116
Belleville, W.V., U.S. — B3 125
Belleville, Wa., U.S. — e11 124
Belley, Fr. — E6 16
Bellflower, Ca., U.S. — n12 82
Bellflower, Il., U.S. — C5 90
Bellflower, Mo., U.S. — B6 102
Bell Gardens, Ca., U.S. — *n12 82
Bellingham, Eng., U.K. — E6 13
Bellingham, Ma., U.S. — B5 98
Bellingham, Mn., U.S. — E2 100
Bellingham, Wa., U.S. — A3 124
Bellingshausen Sea, Ant. — B3 7
Bellinzona, Switz. — E4 18
Bell Island, i., Newf. — E5 72
Bellmawr, N.J., U.S. — D2 107
Bellmead, Tx., U.S. — D4 120
Bellmont, Il., U.S. — E6 90
Bellmore, In., U.S. — E3 91
Bellmore, N.Y., U.S. — *m15 109
Bello, Col. — B2 60
Bellona Falls, Vt., U.S. — E4 122
Belloy, Alta. — B1 68
Bellport, N.Y., U.S. — n16 109
Bell Ranch, N.M., U.S. — B5 108
Bellsburg, Tn., U.S. — A4 119
Bells Corners, Ont. — h12 73
Bells Creek, stm., W.V., U.S. — m13 125
Bellshill, Scot., U.K. — *E4 13
Belltown, Vt., U.S. — F5 85
Belluno, Italy — A4 23
Bellview, N.M., U.S. — C6 108
Bell Ville, Arg. — A4 54
Bellville, Ga., U.S. — D5 87
Bellville, Oh., U.S. — B3 112
Bellville, Tx., U.S. — E4 120
Bellwood, Al., U.S. — D4 78
Bellwood, Il., U.S. — k9 90
Bellwood, Ne., U.S. — C8 104
Bellwood, Pa., U.S. — E5 115
Bellwood, Va., U.S. — n18 123
Belly, stm., N.A. — E4 68
Belmar, N.J., U.S. — C4 107
Bélmez, Spain — C3 22
Belmond, Ia., U.S. — B4 92
Belmont, Man. — E2 70
Belmont, Fl., U.S. — D6 71
Belmont, Ca., U.S. — h8 82
Belmont, Ks., U.S. — C5 93
Belmont, La., U.S. — C2 95
Belmont, Ma., U.S. — g11 98
Belmont, Ms., U.S. — A5 101
Belmont, N.H., U.S. — D4 106
Belmont, N.Y., U.S. — C2 109
Belmont, N.C., U.S. — B1 110
Belmont, Oh., U.S. — B4 112
Belmont, Tx., U.S. — k8 120
Belmont, Vt., U.S. — E3 122
Belmont, Wa., U.S. — B8 124
Belmont, Wi., U.S. — F3 126
Belmont, co., Oh., U.S. — B5 112
Belmonte, Braz. — E3 57
Belmont Heights, Ut., U.S. — *C4 121
Belmopan, Belize — D7 63
Belmullet, Ire. — C1 11
Belo, Madag. — g8 49
Beloeil, Que. — D4 74
Belogorsk, Sov. Un. — D15 29
Belo Horizonte, Braz. — B4 56
Beloit, Man. — D1 70
Beloit, Ia., U.S. — A1 92

Beloit, Ks., U.S. — C5 93
Beloit, Oh., U.S. — B5 112
Beloit, Wi., U.S. — F4 126
Beloit North, Wi., U.S. — F4 126
Belokany, Sov. Un. — B16 40
Belomorsk, Sov. Un. — C6 29
Belopolye, Sov. Un. — F10 27
Beloretsk, Sov. Un. — D8 29
Beloye, Lake, l., Sov. Un. — A11 27
Belozersk, Sov. Un. — B11 27
Belp, Switz. — C4 21
Belper, Eng., U.K. — A6 12
Belpre, Ks., U.S. — E4 93
Belpre, Oh., U.S. — C4 112
Belshaw, In., U.S. — B3 91
Belsprings, Va., U.S. — C2 123
Belt, Mt., U.S. — C6 103
Belt Creek, stm., Mt., U.S. — C6 103
Belted Range, mts., Nv., U.S. — F5 105
Belterra, Braz. — C4 59
Belton, Mo., U.S. — C3 102
Belton, S.C., U.S. — B3 117
Belton, Tx., U.S. — D4 120
Belton Lake, res., Tx., U.S. — D4 120
Beltra, Ire. — C3 11
Beltrami, Mn., U.S. — C2 100
Beltrami, co., Mn., U.S. — B3 100
Beltsville, Md., U.S. — B4 97
Beltsy, Sov. Un. — H6 27
Belturbet, Ire. — C4 11
Belukha, Mount, mtn., Sov. Un. — E11 29
Beluran, Malay. — D5 34
Belvedere, Ga., U.S. — *C2 87
Belvedere, S.C., U.S. — D4 117
Belvedere Marittimo, Italy — E5 23
Belvedere Park, Ga., U.S. — *h8 87
Belvidere, De., U.S. — *B3 85
Belvidere, Il., U.S. — A5 90
Belvidere, Ks., U.S. — E4 93
Belvidere, Ne., U.S. — D8 104
Belvidere, N.J., U.S. — B2 107
Belvidere, N.C., U.S. — A6 110
Belvidere, S.D., U.S. — D4 118
Belvidere, Tn., U.S. — B5 119
Belvidere Center, Vt., U.S. — B3 122
Belvidere Mountain, mtn., Vt., U.S. — B3 122
Belview, Mn., U.S. — F3 100
Belvue, Ks., U.S. — C7 93
Belwood, Ont. — D4 73
Belyando, stm., Austl. — D8 50
Belyy, Sov. Un. — D9 27
Belyy Island, i., Sov. Un. — B9 29
Belyy Yar, Sov. Un. — B11 28
Belzig, E. Ger. — A7 19
Belzoni, Ms., U.S. — B3 101
Bembézar, stm., Spain — C3 22
Bemidji, Mn., U.S. — C4 100
Bemidji, Lake, l., Mn., U.S. — C4 100
Bemis, S.D., U.S. — C9 118
Bemis, Tn., U.S. — B3 119
Bemis, W.V., U.S. — C5 125
Bemiss, Ga., U.S. — F3 87
Bena, stm., N.A. — E4 68
Benāb, Iran — C3 39
Benabarre, Spain — A6 22
Bena Dibele, Zaire — B3 48
Benalla, Austl. — G8 50
Benalto, Alta. — C3 68
Benares see Vārānasi, India — C7 36
Benátky [nad Jizerou], Czech. — n18 26
Benavente, Spain — A3 22
Benavides, Tx., U.S. — F3 120
Benbane Head, c., N. Ire., U.K. — B5 11
Benbecula, i., Scot., U.K. — C1 13
Ben Bolt, Tx., U.S. — F3 120
Benbow, Fl., U.S. — F5 86
Benbrook, Tx., U.S. — *n9 120
Benbrook Lake, res., Tx., U.S. — n9 120
Benbush, W.V., U.S. — B5 125
Benchland, Mt., U.S. — C7 103
Bend, Or., U.S. — C5 114
Ben Davis Point, c., N.J., U.S. — E2 107
Bendeleben, Mount, mtn., Ak., U.S. — n16 109
Bender Beyla, Som. — D7 47
Bendersville, Pa., U.S. — G7 115
Bendigo, Austl. — G7 50
Bendorf, W. Ger. — C2 19
Bene Beraq, Isr. — g10 41
Benedict, Ks., U.S. — E8 93
Benedict, Md., U.S. — C4 97
Benedict, Ne., U.S. — C8 104
Benedict, N.D., U.S. — B4 111
Benedict, Mount, mtn., Newf. — g10 72
Benedicta, Me., U.S. — C4 96
Benenitra, Madag. — h9 49
Beneraird, mtn., Scot., U.K. — E4 13
Benešov, Czech. — D3 26
Bénestroff, Fr. — F6 17
Benevento, Italy — D5 23
Benevolence, Ga., U.S. — E2 87
Benewah, co., Id., U.S. — B2 89
Benfeld, Fr. — A3 20
Benfleet, Eng., U.K. — A7 12
Bengal, hist. reg., Asia — D8 36
Bengal, Bay of, b., Asia — F8 36
Ben Gardane, Tun. — C7 44
Benghazi (Banghāzī), Libya — C4 43
Bengkalis, i., Indon. — L5 35
Bengkulu, Indon. — g11 34
Bengo, dept., Ang. — B2 48
Benguela, Ang. — H3 75
Benguela, dept., Ang. — D1 48
Beni, Zaire — A4 48
Beni, dept., Bol. — B2 55
Beni, stm., Bol. — B2 55
Beni Abbas, Alg. — C4 44
Benicarló, Spain — B6 22
Benicia, Ca., U.S. — C2 82
Benin, ctry., Afr. — E5 45
Benin, Bight of, Afr. — E5 45
Benin City, Nig. — E6 45
Beni Saf, Alg. — B4 44
Benito, Man. — D1 70
Benito Juárez, Arg. — B5 54

Benjamin, Tx., U.S. — C3 120
Benjamin Constant, Braz. — B3 58
Benkelman, Ne., U.S. — D4 104
Benkovac, Yugo. — C2 24
Benld, Il., U.S. — D4 90
Ben Lomond, Ar., U.S. — D1 81
Ben Lomond, Ca., U.S. — *D2 82
Benmore, Lake, res., N.Z. — P12 51
Bennet, Ne., U.S. — D9 104
Bennett, Co., U.S. — B6 83
Bennett, La., U.S. — C7 92
Bennett, N.C., U.S. — B3 110
Bennett, Wi., U.S. — B2 126
Bennett, co., S.D., U.S. — D4 118
Bennett Creek, stm., Md., U.S. — B3 97
Bennett Lake, l., Man. — C3 70
Bennettsbridge, Ire. — E4 11
Bennettsville, S.C., U.S. — B8 117
Bennington, Id., U.S. — G7 89
Bennington, Ks., U.S. — C6 93
Bennington, Ne., U.S. — g12 104
Bennington, N.H., U.S. — E3 106
Bennington, Ok., U.S. — C5 113
Bennington, Vt., U.S. — F2 122
Bennington, co., Vt., U.S. — E2 122
Bennion, Ut., U.S. — *C4 121
Benns Church, Va., U.S. — k14 123
Benoit, Ms., U.S. — B2 101
Benoit, Wi., U.S. — B2 126
Benoits Cove, Newf. — D2 72
Benoy, Chad — D3 46
Benque Viejo, Belize — B3 62
Bensalem, Pa., U.S. — *F12 115
Bensenville, Il., U.S. — B6 90
Bensheim, W. Ger. — D4 18
Bensley, Va., U.S. — C5 123
Benson, Sask. — H4 75
Benson, Az., U.S. — F5 80
Benson, Il., U.S. — C4 90
Benson, Mn., U.S. — E3 100
Benson, N.C., U.S. — B4 110
Benson, co., N.D., U.S. — A6 111
Bens Run, W.V., U.S. — B3 125
Bent, N.M., U.S. — D3 108
Bentheim, W. Ger. — A2 19
Bentinck, i., Burma — G2 35
Bentiu, Sud. — D2 47
Bentley, Alta. — C3 68
Bentley, Ks., U.S. — E6 93
Bentley, La., U.S. — C3 95
Bentley, N.D., U.S. — C3 111
Bentley, Ok., U.S. — C5 113
Bentley Creek, Pa., U.S. — C8 115
Bentley Springs, Md., U.S. — A4 97
Bentleyville, Pa., U.S. — F1 115
Benton, N.B. — D2 71
Benton, Ar., U.S. — C3 81
Benton, Ca., U.S. — D4 82
Benton, Il., U.S. — E5 90
Benton, In., U.S. — B6 91
Benton, Ia., U.S. — C4 92
Benton, Ks., U.S. — E6 93
Benton, Ky., U.S. — f9 94
Benton, La., U.S. — B2 95
Benton, Me., U.S. — D3 96
Benton, Ms., U.S. — C3 101
Benton, Mo., U.S. — D8 102
Benton, Pa., U.S. — D9 115
Benton, Tn., U.S. — D9 119
Benton, Wi., U.S. — F3 126
Benton, co., Ar., U.S. — A1 81
Benton, co., In., U.S. — C3 91
Benton, co., Ia., U.S. — B5 92
Benton, co., Mn., U.S. — E4 100
Benton, co., Ms., U.S. — A4 101
Benton, co., Mo., U.S. — C4 102
Benton, co., Or., U.S. — C3 114
Benton, co., Tn., U.S. — A3 119
Benton, co., Wa., U.S. — C6 124

Benton Harbor, Mi., U.S. — F4 99
Benton Heights, Mi., U.S. — F4 99
Benton Ridge, Oh., U.S. — A2 112
Bentonia, Ms., U.S. — C3 101
Bentonville, Ar., U.S. — A1 81
Bentonville, In., U.S. — E7 91
Bentonville, Oh., U.S. — D2 112
Bentonville, Va., U.S. — B4 123
Bentree, W.V., U.S. — m13 125
Bent's Old Fort National Historic Site, hist., Co., U.S. — C7 83
Bentung, Malay. — K4 35
Benue (Bénoué), stm., Afr. — E6 45
Benwee Head, c., Ire. — C2 11
Benwood, W.V., U.S. — f8 125
Benxi, China — C9 31
Benzie, co., Mi., U.S. — D4 99
Benzonia, Mi., U.S. — D4 99
Beo, Indon. — E7 34
Béoumi, I.C. — E3 45
Beowawe, Nv., U.S. — C5 105
Beppu, Japan — J5 33
Beqa, i., Fiji — I15 52
Beqa Passage, strt., Fiji — I14 52
Berach, stm., India — E5 36
Berat, Alb. — B2 25
Berau Bay, b., Indon. — F8 34
Berbera, Som. — E5 47
Berbérati, Cen. Afr. Rep. — E3 46
Berbice, stm., Guy. — E3 59
Berceto, Italy — E5 20
Berchtesgaden, W. Ger. — E6 18
Berck, Fr. — A3 16
Berclair, Tx., U.S. — E4 120
Berdichev, Sov. Un. — G7 27
Berdyansk, Sov. Un. — H11 27
Berea, Ky., U.S. — C5 94
Berea, Ne., U.S. — B3 104
Berea, Oh., U.S. — A4 112
Berea, S.C., U.S. — B3 117
Berebere, Indon. — E7 34
Beregovo, Sov. Un. — G4 27
Bereku, Tan. — B6 48
Berens, stm., Can. — C3 70
Berens Island, i., Man. — C3 70
Berens River, Man. — C3 70
Beresford, S.D., U.S. — D9 118

Berettyóújfalu, Hung. — B5 24
Berezhany, Sov. Un. — G5 27
Berezina, stm., Sov. Un. — E7 27
Berezna, Sov. Un. — F8 27
Berezniki, Sov. Un. — C9 29
Berezovo, Sov. Un. — C9 29
Berg, Nor. — q27 17
Berga, Spain — A6 22
Berga, Swe. — B8 15
Bergama, Tur. — C6 25
Bergamasque Alps, mts., Italy — A2 23
Bergamo, Italy — B2 23
Bergedorf, W. Ger. — B5 18
Bergen, W. Ger. — F3 15
Bergen, Nor. — G1 14
Bergen, N.Y., U.S. — B3 109
Bergen, co., N.J., U.S. — A4 107
Bergen aan Zee, Neth. — B4 17
Bergen [auf Rügen], E. Ger. — A6 18
Bergenfield, N.J., U.S. — B4 107
Bergen see Mons, Bel. — B5 16
Bergen op Zoom, Neth. — C6 16
Berger, Mo., U.S. — C6 102
Bergerac, Fr. — B4 16
Bergheim, Tx., U.S. — h7 120
Bergholz, Oh., U.S. — B5 112
Bergisch Gladbach, W. Ger. — C3 18
Bergkamen, W. Ger. — B2 19
Bergland, Mi., U.S. — m12 99
Bergman, Ar., U.S. — A2 81
Bergoo, W.V., U.S. — C4 125
Bergstrom Air Force Base, mil., Tx., U.S. — D4 120
Bergton, Va., U.S. — B4 123
Berguent, Mor. — C4 44
Bergün, Switz. — C8 21
Bering Sea — D32 128
Bering Strait, strt. — C6 79
Berino, N.M., U.S. — E3 108
Berislav, Sov. Un. — H9 27
Berja, Spain — D4 22
Berkane, Mor. — C4 44
Berkeley, Ont. — C4 73
Berkeley, Ca., U.S. — D2 82
Berkeley, Il., U.S. — *k9 90
Berkeley, Ky., U.S. — f8 94
Berkeley, Mo., U.S. — f13 102
Berkeley, R.I., U.S. — B4 116
Berkeley, co., S.C., U.S. — E8 117
Berkeley, co., W.V., U.S. — B6 125
Berkeley, Cabo de, c., Ec. — f5 58
Berkeley Heights, N.J., U.S. — B4 107
Berkeley Springs, W.V., U.S. — B6 125
Berkey, Oh., U.S. — A2 112
Berkley, Ma., U.S. — C5 98
Berkley, Mi., U.S. — F7 99
Berkner Island, i., Ant. — B7 7
Berks, co., Pa., U.S. — F9 115
Berkshire, Ma., U.S. — A1 98
Berkshire, N.Y., U.S. — C4 109
Berkshire, Vt., U.S. — B3 122
Berkshire, co., Eng., U.K. — C6 12
Berkshire, co., Ma., U.S. — B1 98
Berkshire Estates, Ct., U.S. — D2 84
Berkshire Hills, hills, Ma., U.S. — B1 98
Berland, stm., Alta. — C1 68
Berleburg, W. Ger. — B3 19
Berlenga Islands, is., Port. — C1 22
Berlin, E. Ger. — B6 18
Berlin (West), W. Ger. — B6 18
Berlin, Ct., U.S. — C5 84
Berlin, Ga., U.S. — E3 87
Berlin, Md., U.S. — D7 97
Berlin, Ma., U.S. — B4 98
Berlin, N.H., U.S. — B4 106
Berlin, N.J., U.S. — D3 107
Berlin, N.Y., U.S. — C7 109
Berlin, Pa., U.S. — G3 115
Berlin, Wi., U.S. — E5 126
Berlin, mtn., mtn., Ant. — B35 7
Berlin Corners, Vt., U.S. — C3 122
Berlin Heights, Oh., U.S. — A3 112
Berlin Lake, res., Oh., U.S. — A4 112
Berlin Mountain, mtn., Ma., U.S. — A1 98
Berlin [West], state, W. Ger. — F7 15
Bermejo, stm., Arg. — A3 54
Bermejo, stm., S.A. — A4 55
Bermeo, Spain — A4 22
Bermuda, dep., N.A. — F14 61
Bermuda, i., N.A. — p20 64
Bern, Switz. — E3 18
Bern, Ks., U.S. — C8 93
Bern, state, Switz. — E3 21
Bernalillo, N.M., U.S. — B3 108
Bernalillo, co., N.M., U.S. — C3 108
Bernam, stm., Malay. — K4 35
Bernard, Ia., U.S. — B7 92
Bernard, Me., U.S. — D4 96
Bernard Lake, l., Ont. — B3 73
Bernardston, Ma., U.S. — A2 98
Bernardsville, N.J., U.S. — B3 107
Bernasconi, Arg. — B4 54
Bernau [bei Berlin], E. Ger. — B6 18
Bernay, Fr. — C4 16
Bernburg, E. Ger. — C5 18
Berndorf, Aus. — E8 18
Berne, N.Y., U.S. — C6 109
Berneray, i., Scot., U.K. — C1 13
Bernese Alps, mts., Switz. — E3 18
Bernice, La., U.S. — B3 95
Bernice, Ok., U.S. — A7 113
Berne, W. Ger. — E8 102
Bernina, Piz, mtn., Eur. — C5 20
Bernina Pass, Switz. — C8 21
Bernville, Pa., U.S. — F9 115
Beroroha, Madag. — h9 49
Beroun, Czech. — D3 26
Berounka, stm., Czech. — C2 26
Berrechid, Mor. — C3 44
Berre [-l'Étang], Fr. — F7 16
Berri, Austl. — F7 50
Berrien, co., Ga., U.S. — E3 87
Berrien, co., Mi., U.S. — F4 99
Berrien Springs, Mi., U.S. — G4 99
Berriyane, Alg. — C5 44
Berry, Al., U.S. — B2 78
Berry, Ky., U.S. — B5 94
Berry, hist. reg., Fr. — A5 16
Berry Creek, stm., Alta. — D5 68
Berryessa, Lake, res., Ca., U.S. — C2 82
Berry Hill, Tn., U.S. — g10 119
Berryman, Mo., U.S. — D6 102
Berryton, Ga., U.S. — B1 87

Name	Map Ref.	Page
Berryton, Ks., U.S.	m14	93
Berryville, Ar., U.S.	A2	81
Berryville, Va., U.S.	A5	123
Bersenbrück, W. Ger.	B7	17
Bershad, Sov. Un.	G7	27
Bertha, Mn., U.S.	D3	100
Berthier, co., Que.	C4	74
Berthierville, Que.	C4	74
Berthold, N.D., U.S.	A4	111
Berthoud, Co., U.S.	A5	83
Berthoud Pass, Co., U.S.	B5	83
Bertie, co., N.C., U.S.	A5	110
Bertoua, Cam.	E2	46
Bertraghboy Bay, b., Ire.	D2	11
Bertram, Tx., U.S.	D4	120
Bertrand, co., Tx., U.S.	E3	120
Bertrand, Mo., U.S.	*G5	99
Bertrand, Mo., U.S.	E8	102
Bertrand, Ne., U.S.	D6	104
Bertrandville, La., U.S.	E5	95
Bertrix, Bel.	C6	16
Berwick, N.S.	D5	71
Berwick, Il., U.S.	C3	90
Berwick, Ia., U.S.	e8	92
Berwick, La., U.S.	E4	95
Berwick, Me., U.S.	E2	96
Berwick, N.D., U.S.	A5	111
Berwick, Pa., U.S.	D9	115
Berwick-upon-Tweed, Eng., U.K.	C6	10
Berwind, W.V., U.S.	D3	125
Berwyn, Alta.	A2	68
Berwyn, Il., U.S.	k9	90
Berwyn, Ne., U.S.	C6	104
Berwyn, Pa., U.S.	o20	115
Beryl, Ut., U.S.	F2	121
Besalampy, Madag.	g8	49
Besançon, Fr.	D7	16
Besar Hantu, mtn., Malay.	K4	35
Beskid Mountains, mts., Eur.	D5	26
Besnard Lake, l., Sask.	B2	75
Besni, Tur.	D11	40
Bessèges, Fr.	E6	16
Bessemer, Al., U.S.	B3	78
Bessemer, Mi., U.S.	n11	99
Bessemer, Pa., U.S.	E1	115
Bessemer City, N.C., U.S.	B1	110
Bessie, Ok., U.S.	B3	113
Best, Tx., U.S.	D2	120
Bestfield, De., U.S.	*B3	85
Bestobe, Sov. Un.	C8	28
Betafo, Madag.	g9	49
Betanzos, Spain	A1	22
Bétaré Oya, Cam.	D2	46
Betatakin Ruin, hist., Az., U.S.	A5	80
Bet Guvrin, Isr.	C6	41
Bethalto, Il., U.S.	E3	90
Bethanien, Nmb.	C2	49
Bethany, Ont.	C6	73
Bethany, Ct., U.S.	D4	84
Bethany, Il., U.S.	D5	90
Bethany, In., U.S.	F5	91
Bethany, La., U.S.	B1	95
Bethany, Mo., U.S.	A3	102
Bethany, Oh., U.S.	n13	112
Bethany, Ok., U.S.	B4	113
Bethany, W.V., U.S.	A5	125
Bethany see Al 'Ayzarīyah, Isr. Occ.	h12	41
Bethany Beach, De., U.S.	F5	85
Bethel, Ak., U.S.	C7	79
Bethel, Ct., U.S.	D2	84
Bethel, Ky., U.S.	B6	94
Bethel, Me., U.S.	D2	96
Bethel, Mo., U.S.	B5	102
Bethel, N.C., U.S.	B5	110
Bethel, Oh., U.S.	D1	112
Bethel, Ok., U.S.	C7	113
Bethel, Pa., U.S.	F9	115
Bethel, Vt., U.S.	D3	122
Bethel Acres, Ok., U.S.	#C2	113
Bethel Park, Pa., U.S.	k14	115
Bethel Springs, Tn., U.S.	B3	119
Bethera, S.C., U.S.	E8	117
Bethesda, Wales, U.K.	A3	12
Bethesda, Ar., U.S.	B4	81
Bethesda, Md., U.S.	C3	97
Bethesda, Oh., U.S.	B4	112
Bethlehem (Bayt Laḥm), Isr. Occ.	G10	40
Bethlehem, S. Afr.	C4	49
Bethlehem, Ct., U.S.	C3	84
Bethlehem, Ga., U.S.	C3	87
Bethlehem, In., U.S.	G7	91
Bethlehem, Md., U.S.	C6	97
Bethlehem, N.H., U.S.	B3	106
Bethlehem, Pa., U.S.	E11	115
Bethlehem, W.V., U.S.	f8	125
Bethlehem Junction, N.H., U.S.	B3	106
Bethpage, N.Y., U.S.	*E7	109
Bethulie, S. Afr.	A5	49
Bethune, Sask.	G3	75
Béthune, Fr.	B5	16
Bethune, Co., U.S.	B8	83
Bethune, S.C., U.S.	C7	117
Betio, i., Kir.	R18	52
Betioky, Madag.	h8	49
Bet Nehemya, Isr.	h10	41
Betong, Thai.	D2	34
Betoota, Austl.	B3	51
Betroka, Madag.	h9	49
Bet Sh'ean, Isr.	B7	41
Bet Shemesh, Isr.	C4	41
Betsiamites, Que.	k13	74
Betsiboka, stm., Madag.	g9	49
Betsie, Point, c., Mi., U.S.	D4	99
Betsy Layne, Ky., U.S.	C7	94
Bette, mtn., Libya	E3	43
Bettendorf, Ia., U.S.	C7	92
Betterton, Md., U.S.	B5	97
Bettiah, India	D10	37
Bettles Field, Ak., U.S.	B9	79
Bettsville, Oh., U.S.	A2	112
Bettyhill, Scot., U.K.	A4	10
Betül, India	D6	36
Betwa, stm., India	D6	36
Betzdorf, W. Ger.	C2	15
Beulah, Co., U.S.	C6	83
Beulah, Mi., U.S.	D4	99
Beulah, Ms., U.S.	B3	101
Beulah, N.D., U.S.	B4	111
Beulah, Wy., U.S.	B8	127
Beulah, Lake, l., Ms., U.S.	B3	101
Beulaville, N.C., U.S.	C5	110
Beuthen see Bytom, Pol.	C5	26
B. Everett Jordan Lake, res., N.C., U.S.	B3	110
Beverley, Sask.	G1	75
Beverley, Eng., U.K.	D6	10
Beverley Head, c., Newf.	D2	72
Beverly, Ks., U.S.	C6	93
Beverly, Ma., U.S.	A6	98
Beverly, N.J., U.S.	C3	107
Beverly, Oh., U.S.	C4	112
Beverly, Tn., U.S.	m14	119
Beverly, W.V., U.S.	C5	125
Beverly Hills, Ca., U.S.	m12	82
Beverly Hills, Mi., U.S.	*o15	99
Beverly Shores, In., U.S.	A4	91
Bewdley, Ont.	C6	73
Bex, Switz.	D3	21
Bexar, co., Tx., U.S.	E3	120
Bexhill-on-Sea, Eng., U.K.	D8	12
Bexley, Ms., U.S.	E5	101
Beyer, Pa., U.S.	E3	115
Beyla, Gui.	G4	45
Beykoz, Tur.	B7	25
Beylul, Eth.	G3	45
Beypazar, Tur.	D8	40
Beyşehir, Tur.	D8	40
Bezau, Aus.	B5	20
Bezerros, Braz.	C3	57
Bezhetsk, Sov. Un.	C11	27
Béziers, Fr.	F5	16
Bezmer, Bul.	D8	24
Bezons, Fr.	g9	16
Bhadra, India	C6	36
Bhadrachalam, India	I8	37
Bhadrak, India	G11	37
Bhag, Pak.	C4	36
Bhagalpur, India	C8	36
Bhakkar, Pak.	B5	36
Bhaktapur, Nepal	C8	36
Bhamo, Burma	D10	36
Bhandara, India	G7	37
Bharatpur, India	C6	36
Bharatpur, Nepal	D10	37
Bharuch, India	D5	36
Bhatpara, India	D8	36
Bhavnagar, India	D5	36
Bhawanipatna, India	H9	37
Bheigeir, Beinn, hill, Scot., U.K.	E2	13
Bhilai (Bhilainagar), India	*D7	37
Bhilai, India	G8	37
Bhilwara, India	E5	37
Bhima, stm., India	E6	36
Bhind, India	C6	36
Bhiwani, India	C6	37
Bhola, Bngl.	F13	37
Bhopal, India	D6	36
Bhor, India	E5	36
Bhubaneshwar, India	D8	36
Bhuj, India	D4	36
Bhumiphol (Yanhee) Dam, Thai.	D3	35
Bhusawal, India	G5	37
Bhutan, ctry., Asia	C9	36
Bia, Mount, mtn., Laos	B2	34
Biaboye, Zaire	A4	48
Biak, i., Indon.	F9	34
Biala, stm., Pol.	h10	26
Biala Podlaska, Pol.	B7	26
Biala Przemsza, stm., Pol.	g11	26
Bialogard (Belgard), Pol.	A4	26
Bialystok, Pol.	B7	26
Bian, Bidean nam, mtn., Scot., U.K.	D4	13
Bianco, Italy	E6	23
Biankouma, I.C.	E3	45
Biarritz, Fr.	F2	16
Biasca, Switz.	C4	20
Bibai, Japan	E10	33
Bibala, Ang.	D1	48
Bibb, co., Al., U.S.	C2	78
Bibb, co., Ga., U.S.	D3	87
Bibb City, Ga., U.S.	D2	87
Biberach, W. Ger.	D4	18
Biberist, Switz.	B4	21
Bibiani, Ghana	E4	45
Bible Grove, Il., U.S.	E5	90
Bible Hill, Tn., U.S.	B3	119
Bic, Que.	A9	74
Bic, Île du, i., Que.	A9	74
Bicaz, Lake, res., Rom.	B8	24
Bicester, Eng., U.K.	C6	12
Biche, Lac la, l., Alta.	B4	68
Bichl, W. Ger.	B7	20
Bickerton, Cape, c., Ant.	C26	7
Bickett Knob, mtn., W.V., U.S.	E11	115
Bickle Knob, mtn., W.V., U.S.	C5	125
Bickleton, Wa., U.S.	D5	124
Bickmore, W.V., U.S.	C3	125
Bicknell, In., U.S.	G3	91
Bicknell, Ut., U.S.	E4	121
Bicoli, Indon.	E8	34
Bicske, Hung.	H5	37
Bida, Nig.	E6	45
Bidar, India	E6	36
Biddeford, Me., U.S.	E2	96
Biddiya, Isr. Occ.	g11	41
Biddle, Mt., U.S.	E11	103
Bideford, Eng., U.K.	E4	11
Bidwell, Oh., U.S.	D3	112
Bidwell, Mount, mtn., Ca., U.S.	B3	82
Bié, dept., Ang.	D2	48
Biebrza, stm., Pol.	B7	26
Biedenkopf, W. Ger.	C3	18
Biel, Switz.	E3	18
Biel (Bienne), Lake, l., Switz.	B3	20
Bielawa, Pol.	C2	26
Bield, Man.	D1	70
Bielefeld, W. Ger.	B4	18
Biella, Italy	B2	23
Bielsk Podlaski, Pol.	B7	26
Bielsko-Biała, Pol.	B7	26
Bienfait, Sask.	H4	75
Bien Hoa, Viet.	G7	35
Bienville, co., La., U.S.	B2	95
Bienville, Lac, l., Que.	g12	74
Bierawka, stm., Pol.	g9	26
Biese, stm., E. Ger.	F5	15
Biesenthal, W. Ger.	E4	19
Bièvre, stm., Fr.	g9	16
Bièvres, Fr.	h9	16
Biferno, stm., Italy	D5	23
Big, stm., Mo., U.S.	m22	102
Big, stm., Mo., U.S.	c7	102
Biga, Tur.	B6	25
Big A Mountain, mtn., Va., U.S.	e9	123
Big Bald, mtn., Ga., U.S.	B2	87
Big Bald Mountain, mtn., N.B.	E5	71
Big Baldy, mtn., Id., U.S.	E3	89
Big Baldy Mountain, mtn., Mt., U.S.	D6	103
Big Bay, b., N.Z.	P11	51
Big Bay De Noc, b., Mi., U.S.	C4	99
Big Bayou, stm., Ar., U.S.	D4	81
Big Bear, Ca., U.S.	*E5	82
Big Bear City, Ca., U.S.	E5	82
Big Beaver, Sask.	H3	75
Bigbee Valley, Ms., U.S.	B5	101
Big Belt Mountains, mts., Mt., U.S.	D5	103
Big Bend, Ca., U.S.	B3	82
Big Bend, La., U.S.	C4	95
Big Bend, Wi., U.S.	n11	126
Big Bend Dam, S.D., U.S.	C6	118
Big Bend National Park, Tx., U.S.	E1	120
Big Bend Reservoir, res., Alta.	C3	68
Big Birch Lake, l., Mn., U.S.	E4	100
Big Black, stm., Me., U.S.	B3	96
Big Black, stm., Ms., U.S.	C3	101
Big Blue, stm., In., U.S.	E6	91
Big Bone, Ky., U.S.	k13	94
Big Bow, Ks., U.S.	E2	93
Big Burro Mountains, mts., N.M., U.S.	E1	108
Big Butt, mtn., Tn., U.S.	C11	119
Big Cabin, Ok., U.S.	A6	113
Big Cabin Creek, stm., Ok., U.S.	A6	113
Big Canyon, val., Tx., U.S.	D1	120
Big Chino Wash, val., Az., U.S.	B3	80
Big Clifty, Ky., U.S.	C3	94
Big Coal, stm., W.V., U.S.	C3	125
Big Corney Bayou, stm., U.S.	D3	81
Big Costilla Peak, mtn., N.M., U.S.	A4	108
Big Creek, B.C.	D6	69
Big Creek, Ca., U.S.	D4	82
Big Creek, Id., U.S.	D3	89
Big Creek, Ky., U.S.	C6	94
Big Creek, Ms., U.S.	B4	101
Big Creek, W.V., U.S.	C2	125
Big Creek, stm., B.C.	D6	69
Big Creek, stm., Ar., U.S.	C5	81
Big Creek, stm., In., U.S.	H2	91
Big Creek, stm., Ks., U.S.	D4	93
Big Creek, stm., La., U.S.	B4	95
Big Creek, stm., Mo., U.S.	C3	102
Big Creek, stm., U.S.	C4	119
Big Creek Lake, res., Al., U.S.	E1	78
Big Creek Peak, mtn., Id., U.S.	E5	89
Big Cypress Indian Reservation, Fl., U.S.	F5	86
Big Cypress Swamp, sw., Fl., U.S.	F5	86
Big Darby Creek, stm., Oh., U.S.	C2	112
Big Delta, Ak., U.S.	C10	79
Big Dry Creek, stm., Mt., U.S.	C10	103
Big Duke Dam, N.C., U.S.	B2	110
Big Eau Pleine, stm., Wi., U.S.	D3	126
Big Eau Pleine Reservoir, res., Wi., U.S.	D4	126
Bigei Island, i., Marsh Is.	S17	52
Big Elk Creek, stm., Md., U.S.	A6	97
Bigelow, Ar., U.S.	B3	81
Bigelow, Mn., U.S.	G3	100
Bigelow, Mount, mtn., Me., U.S.	C2	96
Big Escambia Creek, stm., U.S.	D2	78
Big Falls, Mn., U.S.	B5	100
Big Flat, Ar., U.S.	A3	81
Big Flat Mountain, mtn., Va., U.S.	B4	123
Big Flats, N.Y., U.S.	C4	109
Bigfoot, Tx., U.S.	E3	120
Bigfork, Mn., U.S.	B5	100
Bigfork, Mt., U.S.	B2	103
Big Fork, stm., Mn., U.S.	B5	100
Big Frog Mountain, mtn., Tn., U.S.	D9	119
Biggar, Sask.	E1	75
Biggar, Scot., U.K.	E5	13
Biggarsville, Ms., U.S.	A5	101
Biggers, Ar., U.S.	A5	81
Biggersville, Ms., U.S.	A5	101
Biggleswade, Eng., U.K.	B7	12
Biggs, Ca., U.S.	C3	82
Biggs, Or., U.S.	B6	114
Biggsville, Il., U.S.	C3	90
Big Gull Lake, l., Ont.	C8	73
Big Gully Creek, stm., Sask.	D1	75
Big Hatchet Peak, mtn., N.M., U.S.	F1	108
Big Hole, stm., Mt., U.S.	E4	103
Big Hole National Battlefield, hist., Mt., U.S.	E3	103
Bighorn, Wy., U.S.	B6	127
Big Horn, co., Mt., U.S.	E9	103
Big Horn, co., Wy., U.S.	B4	127
Bighorn, stm., U.S.	B4	76
Bighorn Canyon National Recreation Area, U.S.	E8	103
Bighorn Lake, res., U.S.	E8	103
Bighorn Mountains, mts., U.S.	B5	127
Big Horn Mountains, mts., Az., U.S.	D2	80
Bigi Island, i., Marsh Is.	S17	52
Big Island, i., Va., U.S.	C3	123
Big Island, i., N.W. Ter.	D18	66
Big Kandiyohi Lake, l., Mn., U.S.	F4	100
Big Knob, mtn., Pa., U.S.	F6	115
Big Knob, mtn., Pa., U.S.	f9	123
Big Lake, Mn., U.S.	E5	100
Big Lake, Tx., U.S.	D2	120
Big Lake, l., Me., U.S.	C5	96
Bigler, Pa., U.S.	E5	115
Biglerville, Pa., U.S.	G7	115
Big Lookout Mountain, mtn., Or., U.S.	C9	114
Big Lost, stm., Id., U.S.	F5	89
Big Moose, N.Y., U.S.	B6	109
Big Mossy Point, c., Man.	D3	70
Big Mountain, mtn., Nv., U.S.	B2	105
Big Muddy, stm., Il., U.S.	F4	90
Big Muddy Creek, stm., Mt., U.S.	B12	103
Big Muddy Lake, l., Sask.	H3	75
Big Nemaha, stm., Ne., U.S.	D10	104
Bignona, Sen.	D1	45
Big North Mountain, mts., Va., U.S.	B4	123
Bigonville, Lux.	E5	17
Big Otter, stm., Va., U.S.	C3	123
Big Pine, Ca., U.S.	D4	82
Big Pine Creek, stm., In., U.S.	D3	91
Big Pine Mountain, mtn., Ca., U.S.	E4	82
Big Piney, Mo., U.S.	D5	102
Big Piney, Wy., U.S.	D2	127
Big Piney, stm., Mo., U.S.	D5	102
Big Piney Creek, stm., Ar., U.S.	B2	81
Big Pipe Creek, stm., Md., U.S.	A3	97
Bigpoint, Ms., U.S.	E5	101
Big Pool, Md., U.S.	A1	97
Big Prairie, Oh., U.S.	B3	112
Big Quill Lake, l., Sask.	F3	75
Big Raccoon Creek, stm., In., U.S.	E4	91
Big Rapids, Mi., U.S.	E5	99
Big Rib, stm., Wi., U.S.	C3	126
Big River, Sask.	D2	75
Big Rock, Il., U.S.	B5	90
Big Rock, Tn., U.S.	A4	119
Big Rock Mountain, mtn., Ar., U.S.	B1	81
Big Run, Pa., U.S.	E4	115
Big Sable Point, c., Mi., U.S.	D4	99
Big Sandy, Mt., U.S.	B6	103
Big Sandy, Tn., U.S.	A3	119
Big Sandy, Tx., U.S.	C5	120
Big Sandy, stm., Az., U.S.	C2	80
Big Sandy, stm., Tn., U.S.	A3	119
Big Sandy, stm., Wy., U.S.	D3	127
Big Sandy Creek, stm., Co., U.S.	C8	83
Big Sandy Creek, stm., Mt., U.S.	B6	103
Big Sandy Creek, stm., W.V., U.S.	B5	125
Big Sandy Lake, l., Ont.	E5	70
Big Sandy Lake, l., Sask.	C3	75
Big Sandy Lake, l., Mn., U.S.	D5	100
Big Sandy Reservoir, res., Wy., U.S.	D3	127
Big Satilla Creek, stm., Ga., U.S.	E4	87
Big Savage Mountain, mtn.,	k12	97
Big Sheep Mountain, mtn., Mt., U.S.	C11	103
Big Shiney Mountain, mtn., Pa., U.S.	n18	115
Big Sioux, stm., U.S.	E9	118
Big Slough, stm., Ga., U.S.	F2	87
Big Smoky Valley, val., Nv., U.S.	E4	105
Big Snowy Mountains, mts., Mt., U.S.	D7	103
Big Southern Butte, mtn., Id., U.S.	F5	89
Big South Fork, stm., Ky., U.S.	k13	94
Big Spencer Mountain, mtn., Me., U.S.	C3	96
Big Spring, Ky., U.S.	C3	94
Big Spring, Md., U.S.	A2	97
Big Spring, Tx., U.S.	C2	120
Big Springs, Ks., U.S.	k15	93
Big Springs, Ne., U.S.	C3	104
Big Springs, W.V., U.S.	C3	125
Big Spruce Knob, mtn., W.V., U.S.	C4	125
Big Squaw Mountain, mtn., Me., U.S.	C2	96
Bigstick Lake, l., Sask.	G1	75
Big Stone, co., Mn., U.S.	E2	100
Bigstone, stm., Man.	B4	70
Big Stone City, S.D., U.S.	B9	118
Big Stone Gap, Va., U.S.	f9	123
Bigstone Lake, l., Man.	B4	70
Bigstone Lake, l., Sask.	C4	75
Big Stone Lake, l., U.S.	E2	100
Big Sunflower, stm., Ms., U.S.	B3	101
Big Sur, Ca., U.S.	D3	82
Big Thompson, stm., Co., U.S.	A5	83
Big Timber, Mt., U.S.	E7	103
Big Top, mtn., Tn., U.S.	D9	119
Big Trout Lake, l., Ont.	n17	73
Big Trout Lake, l., Ont.	n17	73
Biguaçu, Braz.	D3	56
Big Valley, Alta.	C4	68
Big Walnut Creek, stm., Oh., U.S.	m11	112
Big Wells, Tx., U.S.	E3	120
Big Wills Creek, stm., Al., U.S.	A3	78
Big Wills Valley, val., Al., U.S.	A4	78
Bigwood, Ont.	A4	73
Big Wood, stm., Id., U.S.	F4	89
Bihać, Yugo.	C2	24
Bihar, India	C8	36
Bihār, state, India	D8	36
Biiziri, i., Marsh Is.	S18	52
Bijagós, Arquipélago dos, is., Gui.-B.	D1	45
Bijapur, India	E6	36
Bijar, Iran	D3	39
Bijeljina, Yugo.	C4	24
Bijelo Polje, Yugo.	D4	24
Bijie, China	F6	31
Bijnor, India	C7	37
Bijou Creek, stm., Co., U.S.	B6	83
Bijou Hills, S.D., U.S.	D6	118
Bikaner, India	C5	36
Bikeman Island, i., Kir.	R18	52
Bikenibeu, Kir.	R18	52
Bikin, Sov. Un.	B11	31
Bikin, stm., Sov. Un.	C7	30
Bikini, atoll, Marsh Is.	F10	6
Bikini Island, i., Marsh Is.	P18	52
Bikita, Zimb.	B5	49
Bilāspur, India	D9	36
Bilauktaung Range, mts., Asia	C1	34
Bilbao, Spain	A4	22
Bilbays, Eg.	C2	41
Bildudalur, Ice.	n21	14
Bileća, Yugo.	C1	21
Bilecik, Tur.	B7	40
Bilgoraj, Pol.	g10	26
Bili, Zaire	A4	48
Bilin, Burma	E10	36
Bilina, Czech.	C8	19
Bilk Creek Mountains, mts., Nv., U.S.	B3	105
Bill, Wy., U.S.	D7	127
Billarp, Ga., U.S.	C2	87
Billerica, Ma., U.S.	A5	98
Billet, Il., U.S.	E6	90
Billings, Mo., U.S.	D4	102
Billings, Mt., U.S.	E8	103
Billings, co., N.D., U.S.	B2	111
Billings Heights, Mt., U.S.	E8	103
Billingsley, Al., U.S.	C3	78
Bill Williams, stm., Az., U.S.	C1	80
Bill Williams Mountain, mtn., Az., U.S.	B3	80
Bilma, Niger	D9	50
Biloela, Austl.	D9	51
Biloxi, Ms., U.S.	E5	101
Biloxi, stm., Ms., U.S.	E4	101
Biloxi Bay, b., Ms., U.S.	f8	101
Bilqas Qism Awwal, Eg.	C3	41
Biltine, Chad	C4	46
Biltmore Forest, N.C., U.S.	f10	110
Bilugyun, i., Burma	D2	35
Bilzen, Bel.	D5	17
Bimbéréké, Benin	D5	45
Bimberi Peak, mtn., Austl.	G7	51
Bimini Islands, is., Bah.	B4	64
Bina-Etāwa, India	E7	37
Binangonan, Phil.	o13	34
Bindloss, Alta.	D5	68
Bindura, Zimb.	A5	49
Binfield, Tn., U.S.	D9	119
Binford, N.D., U.S.	B7	111
Binga, Zaire	A3	48
Binga, Monte, mtn., Afr.	A5	49
Bingamon Creek, stm., W.V., U.S.	k10	125
Bingen, W. Ger.	D3	18
Bingen, Wa., U.S.	D4	124
Bingham, Il., U.S.	D4	90
Bingham, Me., U.S.	C3	96
Bingham, Ne., U.S.	B3	104
Bingham, N.M., U.S.	D3	108
Bingham, co., Id., U.S.	F6	89
Bingham Lake, Mn., U.S.	G3	100
Binghamton, N.Y., U.S.	C5	109
Bingley, Eng., U.K.	G7	13
Bingöl, Tur.	C13	40
Binhai, China	E8	31
Binjai, Indon.	m11	34
Binnaway, Austl.	E7	51
Binningen, Switz.	A4	21
Binscarth, Man.	D1	70
Bintan, i., Indon.	L6	35
Bintang, mtn., Malay.	J4	35
Bintuhan, Indon.	F2	34
Bintulu, Malay.	E4	34
Bint Jubayl, Leb.	A7	41
Binyamina, Isr.	B6	41
Biobío, prov., Chile	B2	54
Biobío, stm., Chile	D2	54
Bioko, i., Eq. Gui.	E1	46
Biola, Ca., U.S.	D3	82
Bippus, In., U.S.	C6	91
Bira, Sov. Un.	B11	31
Birak, Libya	G4	40
Bi'r al Uzaym, Libya	C4	46
Birao, Cen. Afr. Rep.	C4	46
Birch, stm., W.V., U.S.	C4	125
Birchdale, Mn., U.S.	B4	100
Birch Hill, Ct., U.S.	C2	84
Birch Hills, Sask.	E3	75
Birch Island, B.C.	D8	69
Birch Island, i., Man.	C5	70
Birch Lake, l., Alta.	C5	68
Birch Lake, l., Sask.	D1	75
Birch Lake, l., Sask.	C7	75
Birch River, Man.	C1	70
Birch Rock Hill, mtn., Pa., U.S.	F3	115
Birch Run, Mi., U.S.	E7	99
Birch Tree, Mo., U.S.	E6	102
Birchwood, Ct., U.S.	B5	84
Birchwood, Tn., U.S.	D9	119
Birchwood, Wi., U.S.	C2	126
Birchwood Park, De., U.S.	*B3	85
Birchy Bay, Newf.	D4	72
Bird City, Ks., U.S.	C2	93
Bird Creek, stm., Ok., U.S.	A6	113
Bird Island, Mn., U.S.	F4	100
Bird Island, i., N.C., U.S.	D4	110
Birdsboro, Pa., U.S.	F10	115
Bird's Hill, Man.	*D3	70
Birds, Il., U.S.	E6	90
Birdseye, In., U.S.	H4	91
Birds Creek, Ont.	B7	73
Birdsong, Ar., U.S.	B5	81
Birdsville, Austl.	E6	50
Birdsville, Ky., U.S.	e9	94
Birdtail Creek, stm., Man.	D1	70
Birdtown, N.C., U.S.	f9	110
Birdum, Austl.	C5	50
Birdwood, stm., Ne., U.S.	C4	104
Birecik, Tur.	D11	40
Bireun, Indon.	J2	35
Birganj, Nepal	D10	37
Birigui, Braz.	C2	56
Birimbau, Eg.	C2	41
Birjand, Iran	B5	38
Birk, Wādī, val., Sau. Ar.	C4	38
Birkat as Sab', Isr.	D3	41
Birkenfeld, W. Ger.	D2	19
Birkenfeld, Or., U.S.	B3	114
Birkenhead, Eng., U.K.	D5	12
Bîrlad, Rom.	B8	24
Bîrlad, stm., Rom.	B8	24
Birmingham, Sask.	G4	75
Birmingham, Al., U.S.	B3	78
Birmingham, Eng., U.K.	D6	10
Birmingham, Ia., U.S.	D6	92
Birmingham, Mi., U.S.	F7	99
Birmingham, Mo., U.S.	h11	102
Birmingham, N.J., U.S.	D3	107
Birnamwood, Wi., U.S.	D4	126
Birney, Mt., U.S.	E10	103
Birni Ngaouré, Niger	D5	45
Birni Kebbi, Niger	D5	45
Birni Nkonni, Niger	D6	45
Biron, Wi., U.S.	D4	126
Birobidzhan, Sov. Un.	E16	29
Birr, Ire.	D5	11
Birs, stm., Switz.	A4	21
Birsay, Sask.	F2	75
Birsk, Sov. Un.	D20	27
Birtle, Man.	D1	70
Biruaca, Ven.	A6	58
Bisbee, N.D., U.S.	A6	111
Biscay, Bay of, b., Eur.	G8	8
Biscayne, Key, i., Fl., U.S.	s13	86
Biscayne Bay, b., Fl., U.S.	G6	86
Biscayne Gardens, Fl., U.S.	*s13	86
Biscayne National Monument, Fl., U.S.	G6	86
Biscayne Park, Fl., U.S.	s13	86
Bischheim, Fr.	F7	17
Bischofshofen, Aus.	B9	20
Bischofswerda, E. Ger.	B9	19
Bischwiller, Fr.	F7	17
Biscoe, Ar., U.S.	C4	81
Biscoe, N.C., U.S.	B3	110
Biscoe Islands, is., Ant.	C6	7
Bisceglie, Italy	D6	23
Biševo, i., Yugo.	D3	24
Bishārah, Ma'tan, well, Libya	E4	43
Bishnupur, India	F11	37
Bisho, Ciskei	D4	49
Bishop, Ca., U.S.	D4	82
Bishop, Ga., U.S.	C3	87
Bishop, Md., U.S.	D7	97
Bishop, Tx., U.S.	F4	120
Bishop Auckland, Eng., U.K.	F7	13
Bishopric, Sask.	H3	75
Bishop's Castle, Eng., U.K.	B5	12
Bishop's Falls, Newf.	D4	72
Bishops Head, Md., U.S.	D5	97
Bishops Mills, Ont.	C9	73
Bishopton, Que.	D6	74
Bishopville, Md., U.S.	D7	97
Bishopville, S.C., U.S.	C7	117
Bishop's Stortford, Eng., U.K.	E7	10
Bismarck, Ar., U.S.	C2	81
Bismarck, Il., U.S.	C6	90
Bismarck, Mo., U.S.	D7	102
Bismarck, N.D., U.S.	C5	111
Bismarck, Cape, c., Grnld.	A16	128
Bismarck Archipelago, is., Pap. N. Gui.	h12	50
Bismarck Range, mts., Pap. N. Gui.	k11	50
Bismarck Sea, Pap. N. Gui.	h12	50
Bismark, E. Ger.	F5	15
Bison, Ks., U.S.	D4	93
Bison, Ok., U.S.	A4	113
Bison, S.D., U.S.	B3	118
Bison Lake, l., Alta.	A2	68
Bison Peak, mtn., Co., U.S.	B5	83
Bissau, Gui.-B.	D1	45
Bissett, Man.	D4	70
Bistineau, Lake, res., La., U.S.	B2	95
Bistrița, Rom.	B7	24
Bistrița, stm., Rom.	B7	24
Bitam, Gabon	E2	46
Bitburg, W. Ger.	E6	17
Bitche, Fr.	E7	17
Bitely, Mi., U.S.	E5	99
Bitlis, Tur.	C14	40
Bitola, Yugo.	E5	24
Bitonto, Italy	D6	23
Bittencourt, Braz.	B4	58
Bitter Creek, stm., Wy., U.S.	E4	127
Bitterfeld, E. Ger.	B7	19
Bitterfontein, S. Afr.	D2	49
Bitter Lake, l., Sask.	G1	75
Bitter Lake, l., S.D., U.S.	B8	118
Bitterroot Range, mts., U.S.	B3	89
Bitterroot, stm., Mt., U.S.	D2	103
Bittern Lake, l., Alta.	C4	68
Bittern Lake, l., Sask.	D3	75
Bittinger, Md., U.S.	k12	97
Bitung, Indon.	E7	34
Bityug, stm., Sov. Un.	F13	27
Biu, Nig.	D7	45
Bivalve, Md., U.S.	D5	97
Bivalve, N.J., U.S.	E2	107
Biwabik, Mn., U.S.	C6	100
Biwa Lake, l., Japan	n15	33
Bixby, Mn., U.S.	G5	100
Bixby, Mo., U.S.	D6	102
Bixby, N.C., U.S.	B2	110
Bixby, Ok., U.S.	B6	113
Biyala, Eg.	C3	41
Biyang, China	H5	32
Biysk, Sov. Un.	D11	29
Bizerte, Tun.	B6	44
Bjelovar, Yugo.	C3	24
Bjerringbro, Den.	B3	15
Bjork Lake, l., Sask.	E4	75
Bjorkdale, Sask.	E4	75
Black, Al., U.S.	D4	78
Black, stm., Sask.	B5	75
Black, stm., Man.	D4	70
Black, stm., Jam.	E13	65
Black, stm., N.A.	B3	96
Black, stm., Az., U.S.	D5	80
Black, stm., Ar., U.S.	B4	81
Black, stm., Mi., U.S.	E8	99
Black, stm., N.Y., U.S.	B5	109
Black, stm., N.C., U.S.	C4	110
Black, stm., S.C., U.S.	D8	117
Black, stm., Vt., U.S.	E3	122
Black, stm., Vt., U.S.	B4	122
Black, stm., Wi., U.S.	D3	126
Black, Bayou, stm., La., U.S.	E5	95
Blackall, Austl.	D8	50
Black Bear Bay, b., Newf.	B4	72
Black Bear Creek, stm., Ok., U.S.	A4	113
Black Bear Island Lake, l., Sask.	B3	75
Blackbird, De., U.S.	C3	85
Blackburn, Eng., U.K.	D5	10
Blackburn, Mo., U.S.	B4	102
Blackburn, Ok., U.S.	A5	113
Blackburn, Mount, mtn., Ak., U.S.	C11	79
Black Butte, mtn., U.S.	F5	103
Black Butte, mtn., Wy., U.S.	B5	127
Black Butte Lake, res., Ca., U.S.	C2	82
Black Butte Ranch, Or., U.S.	C5	114
Black Canyon, val., Co., U.S.	C3	83
Black Canyon City, Az., U.S.	C3	80
Black Canyon of the Gunnison National Monument, Co., U.S.	C3	83
Black Creek, B.C.	E5	69
Black Creek, Wi., U.S.	D5	126
Black Creek, stm., Ms., U.S.	D4	101
Black Creek, stm., S.C., U.S.	B7	117
Black Diamond, Alta.	D3	68
Black Diamond, Al., U.S.	B2	78
Black Diamond, Wa., U.S.	B4	124
Black Down Hills, hills, Eng., U.K.	E5	10
Blackduck, Mn., U.S.	C4	100
Black Eagle, Mt., U.S.	C5	103
Black Earth, Wi., U.S.	E4	126
Blackey, Ky., U.S.	C7	94
Blackfalds, Alta.	C4	68

Name	Map Ref.	Page
Blackfeet Indian Reservation, Mt., U.S.	B4	103
Blackfoot, Alta.	C5	68
Blackfoot, Id., U.S.	F6	89
Blackfoot, Mt., U.S.	B4	103
Blackfoot, stm., Mt., U.S.	C3	103
Blackfoot Mountains, mts., Id., U.S.	F7	89
Blackfoot Reservoir, res., Id., U.S.	G7	89
Blackford, Ky., U.S.	C2	94
Blackford, co., In., U.S.	D7	91
Black Forest, Co., U.S.	C6	83
Black Forest, mts., W. Ger.	D4	18
Blackfork, Oh., U.S.	D3	112
Blackhall Mountain, mtn., Wy., U.S.	E6	127
Black Hawk, Ms., U.S.	B3	101
Black Hawk, S.D., U.S.	C2	118
Black Hawk, co., Ia., U.S.	B5	92
Blackhead Bay, b., Newf.	D5	72
Black Hills, mts., U.S.	C2	118
Blackie, Alta.	D4	68
Black Island, i., Ant.	f38	7
Black Island, i., Man.	D3	70
Black Jack, Mo., U.S.	*f13	102
Blackjack Mountain, mtn., Ga., U.S.	h7	87
Black Lake, Que.	C6	74
Black Lake, l., Sask.	m7	75
Black Lake, l., Mi., U.S.	C6	99
Black Lake, l., N.Y., U.S.	f9	109
Black Lake Bayou, stm., La., U.S.	B2	95
Blacklick, Oh., U.S.	m11	112
Black Lick, Pa., U.S.	F3	115
Blacklick Estates, Oh., U.S.	m11	112
Black Mesa, mtn., Az., U.S.	A5	80
Black Mesa, mtn., Ok., U.S.	e8	113
Black Mingo Creek, stm., S.C., U.S.	D9	117
Blackmore, Mount, mtn., Mt., U.S.	E6	103
Black Mountain, N.C., U.S.	f10	110
Black Mountain, mtn., U.S.	D7	94
Black Mountain, mtn., Az., U.S.	E4	80
Black Mountain, mtn., Co., U.S.	A5	83
Black Mountain, mtn., Id., U.S.	C3	89
Black Mountain, mtn., Mt., U.S.	D4	103
Black Mountain, mtn., Or., U.S.	B7	114
Black Mountain, mtn., Wy., U.S.	D7	127
Black Mountain, mtn., Wy., U.S.	B5	127
Black Mountains, mts., Wales, U.K.	C4	12
Black Mountains, mts., Az., U.S.	B1	80
Black Oak, Ia., U.S.	C3	92
Black Oak, In., U.S.	A3	91
Black Peak, mtn., Az., U.S.	C1	80
Black Pine Peak, mtn., Id., U.S.	G5	89
Black Point, Ct., U.S.	D7	84
Black Point Beach Club, Ct., U.S.	*D7	84
Black Pond, l., Me., U.S.	B3	96
Blackpool, Eng., U.K.	D5	10
Black Range, mts., N.M., U.S.	D2	108
Black River, Jam.	E5	64
Black River, Mi., U.S.	D7	99
Black River, N.Y., U.S.	A5	109
Black River Bay, b., Jam.	F13	65
Black River Falls, Wi., U.S.	D3	126
Black Rock, Ar., U.S.	A4	81
Black Rock, N.M., U.S.	B1	108
Black Rock Desert, des., Nv., U.S.	B3	105
Black Rock Range, mts., Nv., U.S.	B3	105
Blacksburg, S.C., U.S.	A4	117
Blacksburg, Va., U.S.	C2	123
Black Sea	G15	8
Blacks Fork, stm., U.S.	E3	127
Blacks Harbour, N.B.	D3	71
Blackshear, Ga., U.S.	E4	87
Blackshear, Lake, res., Ga., U.S.	E2	87
Blacksod Bay, b., Ire.	C1	10
Black Springs, Ar., U.S.	C2	81
Black Springs, Nv., U.S.	*D2	105
Black Squirrel Creek, stm., Co., U.S.	C6	83
Blackstock, Ont.	C6	73
Blackstock, S.C., U.S.	B5	117
Blackstone, Ma., U.S.	B4	98
Blackstone, Va., U.S.	C5	123
Blackstone, Alta.	C2	68
Blackstone, stm., R.I., U.S.	B4	116
Blackstrap Reservoir, res., Sask.	F2	75
Black Sugarloaf Mountain, mtn., Austl.	E9	51
Blacksville, W.V., U.S.	B4	125
Black Thunder Creek, stm., Wy., U.S.	C8	127
Black Tickle, Newf.	B4	72
Blacktown, Austl.	*F9	50
Blackville, N.B.	C4	71
Blackville, S.C., U.S.	E5	117
Black Volta (Volta Noire), stm., Afr.	E4	45
Blackwalnut Point, c., Md., U.S.	C5	97
Black Warrior, stm., Al., U.S.	C2	78
Blackwater, Ire.	C5	10
Blackwater, Mo., U.S.	C5	102
Blackwater, Va., U.S.	C1	123
Blackwater, stm., Ire.	E3	11
Blackwater, stm., Fl., U.S.	u15	86
Blackwater, stm., Md., U.S.	D5	97
Blackwater, stm., N.H., U.S.	D3	106
Blackwater, stm., Va., U.S.	D6	123
Blackwater Reservoir, res., Scot., U.K.	D4	13
Blackwater Reservoir, res., N.H., U.S.	D3	106
Blackwell, Ar., U.S.	B3	81
Blackwell, Mo., U.S.	C7	102
Blackwell, Tx., U.S.	A4	113
Blackwell, Tx., U.S.	C2	120
Blackwell, Wi., U.S.	C5	126
Blackwood, N.J., U.S.	D2	107
Blackwood Creek, stm., Ne., U.S.	D4	104
Bladen, Ne., U.S.	D7	104
Bladen, co., N.C., U.S.	C4	110
Bladenboro, N.C., U.S.	C4	110
Bladensburg, Md., U.S.	f9	97
Bladensburg, Oh., U.S.	B3	112
Blades, De., U.S.	F3	85
Bladon Springs, Al., U.S.	D1	78
Bladworth, Sask.	F2	75
Blaeberry, stm., B.C.	D2	68
Blagnac, Fr.	F4	16
Blagodarnoye, Sov. Un.	D2	28
Blagoevgrad (Gorna Dzhumaya), Bul.	D6	24
Blagoveshchensk, Sov. Un.	D20	8
Blagoveshchensk, Sov. Un.	D15	29
Blain, Fr.	D3	16
Blain, Pa., U.S.	F7	115
Blaine, Ks., U.S.	C7	93
Blaine, Me., U.S.	B5	96
Blaine, Mn., U.S.	m12	100
Blaine, Tn., U.S.	C10	119
Blaine, Wa., U.S.	A3	124
Blaine, co., Id., U.S.	F4	89
Blaine, co., Mt., U.S.	B7	103
Blaine, co., Ne., U.S.	C6	104
Blaine, co., Ok., U.S.	B3	113
Blaine Creek, stm., Ky., U.S.	B7	94
Blair, Ne., U.S.	C9	104
Blair, Ok., U.S.	C2	113
Blair, S.C., U.S.	C5	117
Blair, W.V., U.S.	n12	125
Blair, co., Pa., U.S.	E5	115
Blair Athol, Austl.	D8	50
Blair Athol, Scot., U.K.	D5	13
Blairgowrie, Scot., U.K.	B5	10
Blairsburg, Ia., U.S.	B4	92
Blairsden, Ca., U.S.	C3	82
Blairstown, Ia., U.S.	C5	92
Blairstown, Mo., U.S.	C4	102
Blairsville, Ga., U.S.	B3	87
Blairsville, Pa., U.S.	F3	115
Blairton, W.V., U.S.	B7	125
Blaisdell, N.D., U.S.	A3	111
Blaj, Rom.	B6	24
Blake Island, i., Wa., U.S.	e11	124
Blakeley, Mn., U.S.	F5	100
Blakely, Ar., U.S.	C2	81
Blakely, Ga., U.S.	E2	87
Blakely, Pa., U.S.	m18	115
Blake Point, c., Mi., U.S.	h10	99
Blakesburg, Ia., U.S.	D5	92
Blakeslee, Oh., U.S.	A1	112
Blakeslee, Pa., U.S.	D10	115
Blâmont, Fr.	F6	17
Blanc, Cap, c., Afr.	B1	45
Blanc, Cap, c., Tun.	F2	23
Blanc, Mont, mtn., Eur.	E7	16
Blanca, Co., U.S.	D5	83
Blanca, Bahía, b., Arg.	B4	54
Blanca, Cordillera, mts., Peru	C2	58
Blanca, Sierra, mtn., Tx., U.S.	o12	120
Blanca Peak, mtn., Co., U.S.	D5	83
Blanchard, Id., U.S.	A2	89
Blanchard, Ia., U.S.	D2	92
Blanchard, Me., U.S.	C3	96
Blanchard, Mi., U.S.	E5	99
Blanchard, N.D., U.S.	B8	111
Blanchard, Ok., U.S.	B4	113
Blanchard, Pa., U.S.	D6	115
Blanchard, Wa., U.S.	A3	124
Blanchard, stm., Oh., U.S.	A1	112
Blanchardville, Wi., U.S.	F4	126
Blanche, Que.	D2	74
Blanche, Tn., U.S.	B5	119
Blanche, Lake, l., Austl.	E6	50
Blanchester, Oh., U.S.	C2	112
Blanco, N.M., U.S.	A2	108
Blanco, Ok., U.S.	C6	113
Blanco, Tx., U.S.	D3	120
Blanco, co., Tx., U.S.	D3	120
Blanco, stm., Arg.	E2	114
Blanco, stm., Mex.	n15	63
Blanco, Cabo, c., C.R.	F5	62
Blanco, Cabo, c., Peru	B1	58
Blanco, Cape, c., Or., U.S.	E2	114
Blanc Sablon, Que.	C3	72
Bland, Mo., U.S.	C6	102
Bland, Va., U.S.	C1	123
Bland, co., Va., U.S.	C1	123
Blandburg, Pa., U.S.	E5	115
Blandford, Ma., U.S.	B2	98
Blandford Forum, Eng., U.K.	D5	12
Blanding, Ut., U.S.	F6	121
Blandinsville, Il., U.S.	C3	90
Blanford, In., U.S.	E2	91
Blangkejeren, Indon.	K2	35
Blangy-sur-Bresle, Fr.	E9	12
Blankenberge, Bel.	C3	17
Blankenburg, E. Ger.	C5	18
Blankenfelde, E. Ger.	A8	19
Blankenheim, W. Ger.	C11	19
Blanket, Tx., U.S.	A3	101
Blanquilla, Isla, i., Ven.	A5	60
Blantyre, Mwi.	E6	48
Blarney, Ire.	F3	11
Blasdell, N.Y., U.S.	C2	109
Blatná, Czech.	D8	19
Blato, Yugo.	D3	24
Blaubeuren, W. Ger.	D4	18
Blauvelt, N.Y., U.S.	*g13	109
Blåvands Huk, c., Den.	C2	15
Blawenburg, N.J., U.S.	C3	107
Blawnox, Pa., U.S.	k14	109
Blaye, Fr.	E3	16
Błażowa, Pol.	D7	26
Bleckede, W. Ger.	E4	15
Bleckley, co., Ga., U.S.	D3	87
Bled, Yugo.	B2	24
Błędów, Pol.	g10	26
Bledsoe, co., Tn., U.S.	D8	119
Bleeker, Al., U.S.	C4	78
Bleicherode, E. Ger.	B5	19
Blekinge, co., Swe.	B8	15
Blencoe, Ia., U.S.	C1	92
Blende, Co., U.S.	C6	83
Blendecques, Fr.	E3	16
Blenheim, Ont.	E3	73
Blenheim, N.Z.	N14	51
Blenheim, S.C., U.S.	B8	117
Blennerhassett, W.V., U.S.	B4	125
Blessing, Tx., U.S.	E4	120
Blessington, Ire.	D5	11
Bletchley, Eng., U.K.	C7	12
Blevins, Ar., U.S.	D2	81
Blida, Alg.	E9	45
Blija, Neth.	A5	17
Blind, stm., La., U.S.	h10	95
Blind River, Ont.	A2	73
Bliss, Id., U.S.	G4	89
Bliss, N.Y., U.S.	C2	109
Blissfield, Mi., U.S.	G7	99
Blissfield, Oh., U.S.	B4	112
Blitar, Indon.	*G4	34
Blitta, Togo	E5	45
Blocher, In., U.S.	G6	91
Blocker, Ok., U.S.	B6	113
Block Island, R.I., U.S.	h7	116
Block Island, i., R.I., U.S.	h7	116
Block Island Sound, strt., U.S.	D2	116
Blockton, Ia., U.S.	D3	92
Blodgett, Mo., U.S.	D8	102
Blodgett Landing, N.H., U.S.	D2	106
Bloedel, B.C.	D5	69
Bloemfontein, S. Afr.	C4	49
Blois, Fr.	D4	16
Blokhus, Den.	A3	15
Blomberg, W. Ger.	B4	19
Blommesteinmeer, res., Sur.	B3	59
Błonie, Pol.	m13	26
Blood Mountain, mtn., Ga., U.S.	B3	87
Bloodsworth Island, i., Md., U.S.	D5	97
Bloodvein, stm., Can.	D3	70
Bloody Foreland, c., Ire.	B3	11
Bloom, Ks., U.S.	E4	93
Bloom, Slieve, mts., Ire.	D4	11
Bloomdale, Oh., U.S.	A2	112
Bloomer, Ar., U.S.	B1	81
Bloomer, Wi., U.S.	C2	126
Bloomfield, N.B.	D4	71
Bloomfield, Ont.	D7	73
Bloomfield, Ct., U.S.	B5	84
Bloomfield, In., U.S.	F4	91
Bloomfield, Ia., U.S.	D5	92
Bloomfield, Ky., U.S.	C4	94
Bloomfield, Mo., U.S.	E8	102
Bloomfield, Mt., U.S.	C12	103
Bloomfield, Ne., U.S.	B8	104
Bloomfield, N.J., U.S.	h8	107
Bloomfield, N.M., U.S.	A2	108
Bloomfield, Vt., U.S.	B5	122
Bloomfield Hills, Mi., U.S.	o15	99
Bloomfield Township, Mi., U.S.	*F7	99
Bloomingburg, Oh., U.S.	C2	112
Bloomingdale, Ga., U.S.	D5	87
Bloomingdale, Il., U.S.	k8	90
Bloomingdale, In., U.S.	E3	91
Bloomingdale, Mi., U.S.	F5	99
Bloomingdale, N.J., U.S.	A4	107
Bloomingdale, N.Y., U.S.	f10	109
Bloomingdale, Tn., U.S.	C11	119
Blooming Grove, Pa., U.S.	D11	115
Blooming Grove, Tx., U.S.	C4	120
Blooming Prairie, Mn., U.S.	G5	100
Bloomington, Ca., U.S.	*m14	82
Bloomington, Id., U.S.	G7	89
Bloomington, Il., U.S.	C4	90
Bloomington, In., U.S.	F4	91
Bloomington, Md., U.S.	m12	97
Bloomington, Mn., U.S.	F5	100
Bloomington, Ne., U.S.	D6	104
Bloomington, Tx., U.S.	E4	120
Bloomington, Ut., U.S.	*F2	121
Bloomington, Wi., U.S.	F3	126
Bloomington, Lake, res., Il., U.S.	C5	90
Bloomsburg, Pa., U.S.	E9	115
Bloomsdale, Mo., U.S.	C7	102
Bloomville, N.Y., U.S.	C6	109
Bloomville, Oh., U.S.	A2	112
Blossburg, Pa., U.S.	C7	115
Blosseville Coast, Grnld.	C17	128
Blossom, Tx., U.S.	C5	120
Blount, co., Al., U.S.	B3	78
Blount, co., Tn., U.S.	D10	119
Blounts Creek, N.C., U.S.	B6	110
Blount Springs, Al., U.S.	B3	78
Blountstown, Fl., U.S.	B1	86
Blountsville, Al., U.S.	A3	78
Blountville, Tn., U.S.	C11	119
Blovice, Czech.	D8	19
Blowing Rock, N.C., U.S.	A1	110
Blown, Va., U.S.	C7	123
Blucher, Sask.	E2	75
Bludenz, Aus.	E4	18
Blue, Az., U.S.	D6	80
Blue, Ok., U.S.	C5	113
Blue, stm., Co., U.S.	B4	83
Blue, stm., In., U.S.	H5	91
Blue, stm., Mo., U.S.	k10	102
Blue, Bayou, stm., La., U.S.	E5	95
Blue, Mount, mtn., Me., U.S.	D2	96
Blue Anchor, N.J., U.S.	D3	107
Blue Ash, Oh., U.S.	o13	112
Bluebell, Ut., U.S.	C5	121
Blue Buck Knob, hill, Mo., U.S.	E5	102
Blue Buck Point, c., La., U.S.	E2	95
Blue Creek, Wa., U.S.	A8	124
Blue Creek, W.V., U.S.	m13	125
Blue Creek, stm., Ne., U.S.	C3	104
Blue Creek, stm., W.V., U.S.	m13	125
Blue Cypress Lake, l., Fl., U.S.	E6	86
Blue Diamond, Nv., U.S.	G6	105
Blue Earth, Mn., U.S.	G4	100
Blue Earth, co., Mn., U.S.	G4	100
Blue Earth, stm., Mn., U.S.	G4	100
Bluefield, Va., U.S.	C1	123
Bluefield, W.V., U.S.	D3	125
Bluefields, Nic.	C4	58
Bluefields Bay, b., Jam.	E12	65
Blue Glacier, ice, Ant.	e39	7
Blue Grass, Ia., U.S.	C7	92
Blue Grass, Va., U.S.	B3	123
Blue Hill, Me., U.S.	D4	96
Blue Hill, Ne., U.S.	D7	104
Blue Hill Falls, Me., U.S.	D4	96
Blue Hill Range, hills, Ma., U.S.	h11	98
Blue Hills, Ct., U.S.	B5	84
Blue Hills of Couteau, hills, Newf.	E3	72
Bluehole, Id., U.S.	C6	90
Blue Island, Il., U.S.	B6	90
Bluejacket, Ok., U.S.	A6	113
Bluejoint Lake, l., Or., U.S.	E7	114
Blue Knob, mtn., Pa., U.S.	F4	115
Blue Lake, Ca., U.S.	B2	82
Blue Mesa Reservoir, res., Co., U.S.	C3	83
Blue Mound, Il., U.S.	D4	90
Blue Mound, Ks., U.S.	D8	93
Blue Mountain, Ar., U.S.	B2	81
Blue Mountain, Ms., U.S.	A4	101
Blue Mountain, mtn., Ar., U.S.	B2	81
Blue Mountain, mtn., Mt., U.S.	C12	103
Blue Mountain, mtn., Newf.	D3	72
Blue Mountain, mtn., N.B.	B7	110
Blue Mountain, mtn., N.H., U.S.	A4	106
Blue Mountain, mtn., N.M., U.S.	D2	108
Blue Mountain, mtn., N.Y., U.S.	B6	109
Blue Mountain, mtn., Pa., U.S.	F6	115
Blue Mountain Lake, N.Y., U.S.	B6	109
Blue Mountain Lake, res., Ar., U.S.	B2	81
Blue Mountain Peak, mtn., Jam.	E5	64
Blue Mountains, mts., Austl.	F8	51
Blue Mountains, mts., Jam.	E5	64
Blue Mountains, mts., U.S.	A4	76
Blue Mud Bay, b., Austl.	B6	50
Blue Nile, stm., Afr.	C3	47
Bluenose Lake, l., N.W. Ter.	C9	66
Blue Point, Me., U.S.	g7	96
Blue Rapids, Ks., U.S.	C7	93
Blue Ridge, Alta.	B3	68
Blue Ridge, Ga., U.S.	B2	87
Blue Ridge, In., U.S.	E6	91
Blue Ridge, Va., U.S.	C3	123
Blue Ridge, mtn., U.S.	C11	76
Blue Ridge Lake, res., Ga., U.S.	B2	87
Blue Ridge Summit, Pa., U.S.	G7	115
Blue River, B.C.	C8	69
Blue River, Or., U.S.	C4	114
Blue River, Wi., U.S.	E3	126
Blue Springs, Al., U.S.	D4	78
Blue Springs, Ms., U.S.	A5	101
Blue Springs, Mo., U.S.	h11	102
Blue Springs, Ne., U.S.	D9	104
Blue Stack Mountains, mts., Ire.	C3	11
Bluestone, stm., W.V., U.S.	D3	125
Bluestone, Lake, res., U.S.	D4	125
Bluevale, Ont.	D3	73
Bluewater, N.M., U.S.	B2	108
Bluewell, W.V., U.S.	D3	125
Bluff, N.Z.	Q12	51
Bluff, Ut., U.S.	F6	121
Bluff City, Ar., U.S.	D2	81
Bluff City, Il., U.S.	D4	90
Bluff City, Ks., U.S.	E6	93
Bluff City, Ky., U.S.	C2	94
Bluff City, Tn., U.S.	C11	119
Bluff Creek, stm., Ks., U.S.	E5	93
Bluff Creek, stm., Ok., U.S.	A4	113
Bluff Dale, Tx., U.S.	C3	120
Bluffdale, Ut., U.S.	*C4	121
Bluff Knoll, mtn., Austl.	F2	50
Bluff Lake, res., Ms., U.S.	B5	101
Bluff Mountain, mtn., Vt., U.S.	B5	122
Bluff Park, Al., U.S.	g7	78
Bluffs, Il., U.S.	D3	90
Bluffton, Ar., U.S.	C2	81
Bluffton, Ga., U.S.	E2	87
Bluffton, In., U.S.	C7	91
Bluffton, Mn., U.S.	D3	100
Bluffton, Oh., U.S.	B2	112
Bluffton, S.C., U.S.	G6	117
Bluford, Il., U.S.	E5	90
Blumenau, Braz.	D3	56
Blumenfeld, W. Ger.	A6	21
Blumenfeld Colony, S.D., U.S.	B6	118
Blumenhof, Sask.	G2	75
Blumenthal (part of Bremen), W. Ger.	B4	18
Blunt, S.D., U.S.	C6	118
Bly, Or., U.S.	E5	114
Blying Sound, strt., Ak., U.S.	h17	79
Blyth, Ont.	D3	73
Blyth, Eng., U.K.	C6	10
Blythe, Ca., U.S.	F6	82
Blythe, Ga., U.S.	C4	87
Blythedale, Mo., U.S.	A4	102
Blytheville, Ar., U.S.	B6	81
Blytheville Air Force Base, mil., Ar., U.S.	B6	81
Blythewood, S.C., U.S.	C6	117
Boom, Va., U.S.	C7	123
Bo, S.L.	E2	45
Boac, Phil.	C6	34
Boaco, Nic.	E7	63
Bo'ai (Qinghua), China	G5	32
Boali, Cen. Afr. Rep.	E3	46
Boalsburg, Pa., U.S.	E6	115
Board Camp, Ar., U.S.	C1	81
Boardman, Oh., U.S.	A5	112
Boardman, Or., U.S.	B7	114
Boa Vista, Braz.	B2	59
Boaz, Al., U.S.	A3	78
Boaz, Ky., U.S.	f9	94
Bobbili, India	E7	36
Bobbio, Italy	E5	20
Bobcaygeon, Ont.	C6	73
Böblingen, W. Ger.	E4	19
Bobo Dioulasso, Burkina	D4	45
Bobov Dol, Bul.	D6	24
Bôbr, stm., Pol.	C3	26
Bobrinets, Sov. Un.	G9	27
Bobruysk, Sov. Un.	E7	27
Bobtown, Pa., U.S.	G2	115
Boca Chica Key, i., Fl., U.S.	H5	86
Boca Ciega Bay, b., Fl., U.S.	p10	86
Bôca do Acre, Braz.	C4	58
Boca Grande, Fl., U.S.	F4	86
Bocaiúva, Braz.	B4	56
Bocanda, I.C.	E4	45
Bocaranga, Cen. Afr. Rep.	D3	46
Boca Raton, Fl., U.S.	F6	86
Boca del Toro, Pan.	F6	62
Bocay, Nic.	E7	63
Bocay (Buxus), Italy	h8	23
Bochnia, Pol.	D6	26
Bochov, Czech.	C3	18
Bochum, W. Ger.	C3	18
Bock, Mn., U.S.	E5	100
Bockhorn, W. Ger.	E2	15
Bockum-Hövel, W. Ger.	B2	19
Bocognano, Fr.	n12	34
Bodafors, Swe.	A8	15
Bodaybo, Sov. Un.	D14	29
Bodcau Creek, stm., Ar., U.S.	D2	81
Boddam, Scot., U.K.	C7	13
Bode, stm., E. Ger.	B6	19
Bodega Harbor, b., Ca., U.S.	C2	82
Bode, stm., E. Ger.	B4	78
Bodele, reg., Chad	B3	46
Boden, Swe.	E9	14
Boden, Il., U.S.	B3	90
Bodenham, Lough, l., Ire.	D2	11
Bodie Island, i., N.C., U.S.	B7	110
Bodine, stm., B.C.	B5	69
Bodkin Point, c., Md., U.S.	B5	97
Bodmin, Eng., U.K.	E4	10
Bodmin Moor, for., Eng., U.K.	E4	10
Bodo, Alta.	C5	68
Bodö, Nor.	D6	14
Bodrog, stm., Eur.	A5	24
Bodrum, Tur.	D6	40
Bódva, stm., Eur.	A5	24
Boelus, Ne., U.S.	C7	104
Boende, Zaire	B3	48
Boerne, Tx., U.S.	E3	120
Boeuf, stm., La., U.S.	C4	95
Boeuf, Bayou, stm., La., U.S.	D3	95
Boeuf, Lake, l., La., U.S.	k10	95
Bofete, Braz.	m7	56
Boffa, Gui.	F2	45
Bofin, Lough, l., Ire.	C3	11
Bogale, Burma	E10	36
Bogalusa, La., U.S.	D6	95
Bogan, stm., Austl.	E6	51
Bogandé, Burkina	D4	45
Bogard, Mo., U.S.	B4	102
Bogart, Ga., U.S.	C3	87
Bogata, Tx., U.S.	C5	120
Bogatynia, Pol.	*C4	26
Bogatynia, Pol.	C9	19
Bogen, W. Ger.	E7	19
Bogenfels, Nmb.	C2	49
Bogense, Den.	C4	15
Boger City, N.C., U.S.	B1	110
Boggeragh Mountains, mts., Ire.	I4	11
Boggstown, In., U.S.	E6	91
Bogno, Switz.	D7	21
Bognor Regis, Eng., U.K.	D7	12
Bogodukhov, Sov. Un.	F10	27
Bogong, i., Marsh Is.	S18	52
Bogor (Buitenzorg), Indon.	G3	34
Bogoroditsk, Sov. Un.	E12	27
Bogorodsk, Sov. Un.	C14	27
Bogotá, Col.	C3	60
Bogota, N.J., U.S.	h8	107
Bogota, Tn., U.S.	A2	119
Bogotol, Sov. Un.	D26	8
Bogra, Bngl.	D8	36
Boguchany, Sov. Un.	D28	8
Bogué, Maur.	C2	45
Bogue, Ks., U.S.	C4	93
Bogue Chitto, Ms., U.S.	D3	101
Bogue Chitto, stm., U.S.	D5	95
Bogue Inlet, b., N.C., U.S.	C5	110
Bogue Phalia, stm., Ms., U.S.	B3	101
Boguslav, Sov. Un.	G8	27
Bo Hai, b., China	D8	31
Bohain-[en-Vermandois], Fr.	C5	16
Boharm, Sask.	G3	75
Bohemia, La., U.S.	E6	95
Bohemia, N.Y., U.S.	*n15	109
Bohemia, hist. reg., Czech.	D3	26
Bohemian Forest, mts., Eur.	D6	18
Bohemian-Moravian Highlands, plat., Czech.	D3	26
Böhme, stm., W. Ger.	F3	15
Bohmte, W. Ger.	A3	19
Bohol, i., Phil.	D6	34
Bohol Sea, Phil.	E4	46
Boiestown, N.B.	C3	71
Boiling Springs, N.C., U.S.	B1	110
Boiling Springs, Pa., U.S.	F7	115
Bois, Lac des, l., N.W. Ter.	C6	66
Bois, Rio dos, stm., Braz.	B5	56
Bois Blanc Island, i., Mi., U.S.	C6	99
Boischâtel, Que.	C6	74
Bois-Colombes, Fr.	g10	16
Boisdale, N.S.	C9	71
Boisdale, Loch, b., Scot., U.K.	C1	13
Bois D'Arc, Mo., U.S.	D4	102
Bois-des-Filion, Que.	p19	74
Bois de Sioux, stm., Mn., U.S.	E2	100
Boise, Id., U.S.	F2	89
Boise, co., Id., U.S.	F3	89
Boise City, Ok., U.S.	e8	113
Boissevain, Man.	E1	70
Boissevain, Va., U.S.	e10	123
Boistfort Peak, mtn., Wa., U.S.	C2	124
Boisvert, Pointe au, c., Que.	A8	74
Boizenburg, E. Ger.	A4	15
Bojador, Cabo, c., W. Sah.	B2	45
Bojnürd, Iran	B5	38
Bokchito, Ok., U.S.	C5	113
Boké, Gui.	D2	45
Bokeelia, Fl., U.S.	F4	86
Bokhoma, Ok., U.S.	D7	113
Boko, Zaire	C2	48
Bokobyaadaa Island, i., Marsh Is.	P18	52
Bokoro, Chad	C3	46
Bokororyuru Island, i., Marsh Is.	P18	52
Bokoshe, Ok., U.S.	B7	113
Bokungu, Zaire	B3	48
Bol, Chad	C3	46
Bolafa, Zaire	A3	48
Bolama, Gui.-B.	D2	45
Bolar, Va., U.S.	B3	123
Bolbec, Fr.	C4	16
Bolckow, Mo., U.S.	B3	102
Bole, Ghana	E4	45
Boleko, Zaire	C1	48
Boles, Ar., U.S.	C1	81
Boles, Il., U.S.	E5	90
Boles, N.M., U.S.	*E4	108
Bolesławiec, Pol.	C3	26
Boley, Ok., U.S.	B5	113
Bolgatanga, Ghana	D4	45
Bolgrad, Sov. Un.	I7	27
Boli, China	B12	31
Bolia, Zaire	B2	48
Bolinao, Phil.	n12	34
Bolinao, Cape, c., Phil.	n12	34
Boling, Tx., U.S.	E5	120
Bolingbrook, Il., U.S.	k8	90
Bolivar, Arg.	B4	54
Bolívar, Col.	B2	60
Bolivar, Mo., U.S.	D4	102
Bolivar, N.Y., U.S.	C2	109
Bolivar, Oh., U.S.	B4	112
Bolivar, Peru	B2	58
Bolivar, Tn., U.S.	B3	119
Bolivar, co., Ms., U.S.	B3	101
Bolívar, dept., Col.	B2	60
Bolívar, prov., Ec.	H4	60
Bolivar, Cerro, mtn., Ven.	B5	60
Bolivar, Lake, l., Ms., U.S.	B3	101
Bolívar, Pico, mtn., Ven.	B3	60
Bolivia, N.C., U.S.	C4	110
Bolivia, ctry., S.A.	C2	55
Bolkhov, Sov. Un.	E11	27
Bollebygd, Swe.	A6	15
Bollène, Fr.	E6	16
Bolligen, Switz.	C4	21
Bolling, Al., U.S.	D3	78
Bollinger, co., Mo., U.S.	D7	102
Bollnäs, Swe.	F6	14
Bollullos [par del Condado], Spain	D2	22
Bolmen, l., Swe.	B7	15
Bolnisi, Sov. Un.	B15	40
Bolobo, Zaire	C2	48
Bologna, Italy	E6	20
Bolognesi, Peru	C3	58
Bologoye, Sov. Un.	C10	27
Bolomba, Zaire	A2	48
Bolon, Lake, l., Sov. Un.	B8	33
Bolotnoye, Sov. Un.	B10	28
Bolovens, Plateau des, plat., Laos	E7	35
Bolsena, Lake, l., Italy	C3	23
Bolshaya Kamenka, stm., Sov. Un.	q22	27
Bolshaya Viska, Sov. Un.	G8	27
Bolshevik, i., Sov. Un.	B4	128
Bolshoy Irgiz, stm., Sov. Un.	C3	28
Bolshoy Uzen, stm., Sov. Un.	D3	28
Bolshoy Yugan, stm., Sov. Un.	B8	28
Bolsward, Neth.	A5	17
Bolton, Eng., U.K.	D5	10
Bolton, Ms., U.S.	C3	101
Bolton, N.C., U.S.	C4	110
Bolton, Vt., U.S.	C3	122
Bolton, stm., Man.	B4	70
Bolton Center, Ct., U.S.	B6	84
Bolton Lake, l., Man.	B4	70
Bolton Lakes, l., Ct., U.S.	B6	84
Bolton Landing, N.Y., U.S.	B7	109
Bolu, Tur.	B8	40
Bolus Head, c., Ire.	F1	11
Bolvadin, Tur.	C8	40
Bolzano, Italy	A3	23
Boma, Zaire	C1	48
Bomarton, Tx., U.S.	C3	120
Bombala, Austl.	G8	50
Bombay, India	E5	36
Bombay Hook Island, i., De., U.S.	C4	85
Bomboma, Zaire	A2	48
Bom Conselho, Braz.	A2	56
Bom Despacho, Braz.	C3	57
Bom Jardim, Braz.	C3	57
Bom Jardim de Goiás, Braz.	B2	56
Bom Jardim de Minas, Braz.	g5	56
Bom Jesus, Braz.	C2	57
Bom Jesus da Lapa, Braz.	A4	56
Bomokandi, stm., Zaire	A4	48
Bomongo, Zaire	A2	48
Bomoseen, Vt., U.S.	D2	122
Bomoseen, Lake, l., Vt., U.S.	D2	122
Bom Retiro, Braz.	D3	56
Bon, Cap, c., Tun.	B7	44
Bon Accord, Alta.	C4	68
Bonaigarh, India	G10	37
Bon Air, Al., U.S.	B3	78
Bon Air, Tn., U.S.	D8	119
Bon Air, Va., U.S.	C5	123
Bonaire, Ga., U.S.	D3	87
Bonaire, i., Neth. Ant.	A4	60
Bonanza, Nic.	D5	62
Bonanza, Ar., U.S.	B1	81
Bonanza, Or., U.S.	E5	114
Bonanza, Ut., U.S.	C6	121
Bonanza City, Co., U.S.	C4	83
Bonanza Peak, mtn., Wa., U.S.	A5	124
Bonaparte, Ia., U.S.	D6	92
Bonaparte, stm., B.C.	D7	69
Bonaparte, Mount, mtn., Wa., U.S.	A6	124
Bonaparte Lake, l., B.C.	D7	69
Bon Aqua, Tn., U.S.	B4	119
Boñar, Spain	A3	22
Bonar Bridge, Scot., U.K.	C4	13
Bonarlaw, Ont.	C7	73
Bonasila Dome, mtn., Ak., U.S.	C7	79
Bonaventure, Que.	A4	71
Bonaventure, Fl., U.S.	*F6	86
Bonavista, Newf.	D5	72
Bonavista, Cape, c., Newf.	D5	72
Bonavista Bay, b., Newf.	D5	72
Bond, Co., U.S.	B4	83
Bond, Ky., U.S.	C5	94
Bond, Ms., U.S.	E4	101
Bond, co., Il., U.S.	E4	90
Bondeno, Italy	E6	20
Bondo, Zaire	A4	48
Bondo, Zaire	A3	48
Bondoukou, I.C.	E4	45
Bondsville, Ma., U.S.	B3	98
Bonduel, Wi., U.S.	D5	126
Bondurant, Ia., U.S.	C4	92
Bondurant, Wy., U.S.	C2	127
Bondville, Il., U.S.	C5	90
Bondville, Vt., U.S.	E3	122
Bondy, Fr.	g10	16
Bone, Gulf of, b., Indon.	F6	34
Bone Cave, Tn., U.S.	D8	119
Bone Lake, l., Wi., U.S.	C1	126
Bonete, Cerro, mtn., Arg.	E2	54
Bonetraill, N.D., U.S.	A2	111
Bonfield, Ont.	A5	73
Bonfouca, La., U.S.	h12	95
Bonga, Eth.	D4	47
Bongandanga, Zaire	A3	48
Bongor, Chad	C3	46
Bong Son, Viet.	C4	35
Bonham, Tx., U.S.	C4	120
Bon Homme, co., S.D., U.S.	E8	118
Bon Homme Colony, S.D., U.S.	E8	118
Bonifacio, Fr.	n12	34
Bonifacio, Strait of, strt., Eur.	D2	23
Bonifay, Fl., U.S.	u16	86
Bonilla, S.D., U.S.	C7	118
Bonin Islands, is., Japan	*E8	9
Bonita, La., U.S.	B4	95
Bonita, La., U.S.	B4	95
Bonita Springs, Fl., U.S.	F5	86
Bonito, Braz.	C1	56
Bonlee, N.C., U.S.	B3	110
Bonn, W. Ger.	C3	18
Bonneau, S.C., U.S.	E8	117
Bonneauville, Pa., U.S.	G7	115

Name	Map Ref.	Page
Bonne Bay (Woody Point), Newf.	D3	72
Bonne Bay, b., Newf.	D3	72
Bonne Idee, Bayou, stm., La., U.S.	B4	95
Bonner, Mt., U.S.	D3	103
Bonner, co., Id., U.S.	A2	89
Bonnerdale, Ar., U.S.	C2	81
Bonners Ferry, Id., U.S.	A2	89
Bonner Springs, Ks., U.S.	C9	93
Bennerup Strand, Den.	D1	21
Bonnet, Lac du, l., Man.	C4	70
Bonnétable, Fr.	C4	16
Bonnet Clare Floodway, La., U.S.	h11	95
Bonne Terre, Mo., U.S.	D7	102
Bonneville, Fr.	C2	20
Bonneville, Or., U.S.	B5	114
Bonneville, co., Id., U.S.	F7	89
Bonneville Dam, U.S.	B4	114
Bonneville Peak, mtn., Id., U.S.	F6	89
Bonneville Salt Flats, pl., Ut., U.S.	C2	121
Bonnevoie-Sud, Lux.	*E6	17
Bonney Lake, Wa., U.S.	B3	124
Bonnie, Il., U.S.	E5	90
Bonnie Doone, N.C., U.S.	B4	110
Bonnieville, Ky., U.S.	C4	94
Bonnots Mill, Mo., U.S.	C6	102
Bonny, Nig.	F6	45
Bonny Blue, Va., U.S.	f8	123
Bonny Reservoir, res., Co., U.S.	B8	83
Bonnyville, Alta.	B5	68
Bono, Ar., U.S.	B5	81
Bono, Oh., U.S.	*A2	112
Bonorva, Italy	D2	23
Bonriki, Kir.	R18	52
Bonriki, i., Kir.	R18	52
Bons, Fr.	D1	21
Bonsal, N.C., U.S.	B4	110
Bon Secour, Al., U.S.	E2	78
Bonshaw, P.E.I.	C6	71
Bontang, Indon.	E5	34
Bonthe, S.L.	E2	45
Bon Wier, Tx., U.S.	D6	121
Book Cliffs, clf., U.S.	D6	121
Booker, Tx., U.S.	A2	120
Booker T. Washington National Monument, Va., U.S.	C3	123
Booligal, Austl.	F5	51
Boolyglass, Ire.	E4	11
Boomer, N.C., U.S.	A1	110
Boomer, W.V., U.S.	C3	125
Boon, Mi., U.S.	D5	99
Boone, Co., U.S.	C6	83
Boone, Ia., U.S.	B4	92
Boone, N.C., U.S.	A1	110
Boone, co., Ar., U.S.	A2	81
Boone, co., Il., U.S.	A5	90
Boone, co., In., U.S.	D4	91
Boone, co., Ia., U.S.	B3	92
Boone, co., Ky., U.S.	B5	94
Boone, co., Mo., U.S.	B5	102
Boone, co., Ne., U.S.	C7	104
Boone, co., W.V., U.S.	C3	125
Boone, stm., Ia., U.S.	B4	92
Boone Grove, In., U.S.	B3	91
Boone Lake, res., Tn., U.S.	C11	119
Boones Mill, Va., U.S.	C3	123
Booneville, Ar., U.S.	B2	81
Booneville, Ky., U.S.	C6	94
Booneville, Ms., U.S.	A5	101
Boonsboro, Md., U.S.	A2	97
Boons Pond, l., Ma., U.S.	g10	98
Boonton, N.J., U.S.	B4	107
Boonville, Ca., U.S.	C2	82
Boonville, In., U.S.	H3	91
Boonville, Mo., U.S.	C5	102
Boonville, N.Y., U.S.	B5	109
Boonville, N.C., U.S.	A2	110
Boorama, Som.	C4	47
Boosaaso, Som.	C6	47
Booth, Al., U.S.	C3	78
Boothbay, Me., U.S.	E3	96
Boothbay Harbor, Me., U.S.	E3	96
Boothby, Cape, c., Ant.	C18	7
Boothia, Gulf of, b., N.W. Ter.	B14	66
Boothia Peninsula, pen., N.W. Ter.	B14	66
Booths Creek, stm., W.V., U.S.	h11	125
Boothville, La., U.S.	E6	95
Bootle, Eng., U.K.	A4	12
Booué, Gabon	F2	46
Bophuthatswana, ctry., Afr.	C4	49
Bopolu, Lib.	E2	45
Boppard, W. Ger.	C3	18
Boquerón, dept., Para.	D3	55
Boquerón, Pan.	k11	62
Boquerón, Bahía de b., P.R.	B1	65
Bor, Sud.	D3	47
Bor, Yugo.	C6	24
Boraha, Nosy, i., Madag.	g10	49
Borah Peak, mtn., Id., U.S.	E5	89
Borås, Swe.	I5	14
Borāzjān, Iran	G5	39
Borba, Braz.	C3	59
Borculo, Neth.	B6	17
Bordeaux, Fr.	C4	16
Bordelonville, La., U.S.	C4	95
Borden, Sask.	E2	75
Borden, In., U.S.	H6	91
Borden, co., Tx., U.S.	C2	120
Borden Island, i., N.W. Ter.	m29	66
Borden Peninsula, pen., N.W. Ter.	B16	66
Borden Springs, Al., U.S.	B4	78
Bordentown, N.J., U.S.	C3	107
Borderland, W.V., U.S.	D2	125
Borders, prov., Scot., U.K.	E5	13
Bordertown, Austl.	G7	50
Bordighera, Italy	C1	23
Bordj Bou Arreridj, Alg.	B5	44
Bordley, Ky., U.S.	C2	94
Bordulac, N.D., U.S.	B7	111
Boré, Mali	C4	45
Boren, i., Swe.	u33	14
Borensberg, Swe.	u33	14
Borgå, Fin.	G11	14
Börger, W. Ger.	B7	17
Borger, Neth.	B6	17
Borger, Tx., U.S.	B2	120
Borgholm, Swe.	I7	14
Borghorst, W. Ger.	A2	18
Borg Mountain, mtn., Ant.	B12	7
Borgne, Switz.	D3	21
Borgne, Lake, b., La., U.S.	D6	95
Borgomanero, Italy	C2	23
Borgo Piave, Italy	k9	23
Borgosesia, Italy	E5	21
Borgo Val di Taro, Italy	B2	23
Borgo Val Sugana, Italy	C7	20
Boring, Or., U.S.	B4	114
Borislav, Sov. Un.	G4	27
Borisoglebsk, Sov. Un.	D7	29
Borisov, Sov. Un.	D7	27
Borispol, Sov. Un.	F8	27
Borja, Peru	B2	58
Borja, Spain	B5	22
Borjas Blancas, Spain	B6	22
Borken, W. Ger.	B1	19
Borken, W. Ger.	B4	19
Børkop, Den.	C3	15
Borkou, hist. reg., Chad	B3	46
Borkum, i., W. Ger.	A6	17
Borkum, W. Ger.	B3	18
Borlänge, Swe.	G6	14
Bormes, Fr.	F7	16
Bormida, stm., Italy	E4	20
Bormio, Italy	C6	20
Borna, E. Ger.	B7	19
Borne, Neth.	B6	17
Borneo (Kalimantan), i., Asia	E4	34
Bornheim, W. Ger.	C1	19
Bornholm, co., Den.	C8	15
Bornholm, i., Den.	J6	14
Bornholmsgat, strt., Eur.	C8	15
Bornos, Spain	D3	22
Borobudur, hist., Indon.	G4	34
Boromlya, Sov. Un.	F10	27
Boromo, Burkina	D4	45
Boron, Ca., U.S.	E5	82
Borovan, Bul.	D6	24
Borovichi, Sov. Un.	D6	29
Borovskoye, Sov. Un.	q21	27
Borrby, Swe.	C8	15
Borre, Den.	D6	15
Borrego Springs, Ca., U.S.	F5	82
Borriskane, Ire.	E3	11
Borrisoleigh, Ire.	E4	11
Borroloola, Austl.	C6	50
Borşa, Rom.	B7	24
Bort-les-Orgues, Fr.	E5	16
Borūjen, Iran	F5	39
Borūjerd, Iran	B4	38
Borup, Mn., U.S.	C2	100
Borzomi, Sov. Un.	B14	40
Borzna, Sov. Un.	F9	27
Borzonasca, Italy	E5	20
Borzya, Sov. Un.	A8	31
Bosa, Italy	D2	23
Bosanska Dubica, Yugo.	C3	24
Bosanska Gradiška, Yugo.	C3	24
Bosanska Kostajnica, Yugo.	C3	24
Bosanski Novi, Yugo.	C3	24
Bosanski Petrovac, Yugo.	C3	24
Bosanski Šamac, Yugo.	C4	24
Bosavi, Mount, mtn., Pap. N. Gui.	k11	51
Boscawen, N.H., U.S.	D3	106
Boscobel, Wi., U.S.	E3	126
Boshan, China	D8	31
Boshrūyeh, Iran	E8	39
Boskovice, Czech.	D4	26
Bosler, Wy., U.S.	E7	127
Bosna, stm., Yugo.	C3	24
Bosnia, hist. reg., Yugo.	C3	24
Bosnik, Indon.	F9	34
Bosobolo, Zaire	A2	48
Bosporus, strt.	B7	40
Bosque, N.M., U.S.	C3	108
Bosque, co., Tx., U.S.	D4	120
Bosque Farms, N.M., U.S.	B3	108
Boss, Mo., U.S.	D6	102
Bossangoa, Cen. Afr. Rep.	D3	46
Bossembélé, Cen. Afr. Rep.	D3	46
Bossert Estates, N.J., U.S.	C3	107
Bossier, co., La., U.S.	B2	95
Bossier City, La., U.S.	B2	95
Bosso, Niger	D7	45
Bosso, Dallol, val., Niger	C2	31
Bosten Lake, l., China	C2	31
Boston, Eng., U.K.	D7	13
Boston, Ga., U.S.	F3	87
Boston, In., U.S.	E8	91
Boston, Ky., U.S.	C4	94
Boston, Ma., U.S.	B5	98
Boston Bar, B.C.	E7	69
Boston Heights, Oh., U.S.	h9	112
Boston Mountains, mts., Ar., U.S.	B2	81
Bostonnais, stm., Que.	B5	74
Bostwick, Fl., U.S.	C5	86
Bostwick, Ga., U.S.	C3	87
Boswarlos, Newf.	D2	72
Boswell, B.C.	E9	69
Boswell, Al., U.S.	D4	78
Boswell, In., U.S.	C3	91
Boswell, Ok., U.S.	C6	113
Boswell, Pa., U.S.	F3	115
Bosworth, Mo., U.S.	B4	102
Botany Bay, b., Austl.	F9	50
Boteti, stm., Bots.	B3	49
Botetourt, co., Va., U.S.	C3	123
Botev, mtn., Bul.	D7	24
Botevgrad, Bul.	D6	24
Botha, Alta.	C4	68
Bothell, Wa., U.S.	B3	124
Bothnia, Gulf of, b., Eur.	F9	14
Bothwell, Ont.	E3	73
Bothwell, P.E.I.	C7	71
Botkins, Oh., U.S.	B1	112
Botkyrka, Swe.	t35	14
Botolan, Phil.	o13	34
Botoşani, Rom.	B8	24
Botsford, Ct., U.S.	D2	84
Botswana, ctry., Afr.	B3	49
Bottineau, N.D., U.S.	A5	111
Bottineau, co., N.D., U.S.	A4	111
Bottrop, W. Ger.	B1	19
Botucatu, Braz.	D3	56
Botwood, Newf.	D4	72
Bouaflé, I.C.	E3	45
Bouaké, I.C.	E3	45
Bouar, Cen. Afr. Rep.	D3	46
Bou Arfa, Mor.	C4	44
Boucau, Fr.	F3	16
Boucher, Lac, l., Que.	C2	72
Bouchette, Que.	C2	74
Bouctouche, N.B.	C5	71
Boudenib, Mor.	C4	44
Boudreaux, Lake, l., La., U.S.	E5	95
Boudry, Switz.	C2	21
Bougainville, i., Pap. N. Gui.	G9	6
Bougouni, Mali	D3	45
Bouillon, Bel.	E5	17
Boulder, Co., U.S.	A5	83
Boulder, Mt., U.S.	D4	103
Boulder, Ut., U.S.	F4	121
Boulder, Wy., U.S.	D3	127
Boulder, co., Co., U.S.	A5	83
Boulder City, Nv., U.S.	H7	105
Boulder Creek, Ca., U.S.	*D2	82
Boulder Hill, Il., U.S.	*B5	90
Boulevard Heights, Md., U.S.	f9	97
Boulevard Park, Wa., U.S.	*B3	124
Bouligny, Fr.	E5	17
Boulogne-Billancourt, Fr.	C5	16
Boulogne-sur-Mer, Fr.	B4	16
Boulsa, Burkina	D4	45
Boumalne, Mor.	C3	44
Boumdeït, Maur.	C2	45
Bouna, I.C.	E4	45
Boundary, Ak., U.S.	C11	79
Boundary, co., Id., U.S.	A2	89
Boundary Bald Mountain, mtn., Me., U.S.	C2	96
Boundary Bay, b., Wa., U.S.	A3	124
Boundary Bend, Austl.	G4	51
Boundary Peak, mtn., Nv., U.S.	F3	105
Boundary Ranges, mts., N.A.	k22	79
Bound Brook, N.J., U.S.	B3	107
Boundiali, I.C.	E3	45
Bountiful, Ut., U.S.	C4	121
Bounty, Sask.	F2	75
Bounty Islands, is., N.Z.	Q17	51
Bourbeuse, stm., Mo., U.S.	C6	102
Bourbon, In., U.S.	B5	91
Bourbon, Mo., U.S.	C6	102
Bourbon, co., Ks., U.S.	E9	93
Bourbon, co., Ky., U.S.	B5	94
Bourbonnais, Il., U.S.	B6	90
Bourbonnais, hist. reg., Fr.	D5	16
Bourbonne-les-Bains, Fr.	B12	20
Bourem, Mali	C4	45
Bourg, La., U.S.	E5	95
Bourg-de-Péage, Fr.	E6	16
Bourg [-en-Bresse], Fr.	D6	16
Bourges, Fr.	D5	16
Bourget, Ont.	B9	73
Bourget, Lake, l., Fr.	D1	20
Bourg-la-Reine, Fr.	g10	16
Bourgoin [-Jallieu], Fr.	E6	16
Bourg-Saint-Andéol, Fr.	E6	16
Bourg-Saint-Maurice, Fr.	D2	20
Bou Rjeïmat, well, Maur.	C2	45
Bourke, Austl.	F8	50
Bourne, Eng., U.K.	B7	12
Bourne, Ma., U.S.	C6	98
Bournemouth, Eng., U.K.	C2	112
Bou Saâda, Alg.	D2	80
Bouse, Az., U.S.	C3	46
Bousso, Chad	C2	45
Boutilimit, Maur.	k11	95
Boutte, La., U.S.	D13	7
Bouvet, i., Ant.	C5	100
Bovey, Mn., U.S.	C2	89
Bovill, Id., U.S.	C3	101
Bovina, Ms., U.S.	B1	120
Bovina, Tx., U.S.	C6	109
Bovina Center, N.Y., U.S.	D3	106
Bow, N.H., U.S.	A3	124
Bow, Wa., U.S.	D4	68
Bow, stm., Alta.	A3	111
Bowbells, N.D., U.S.	D4	68
Bowden, Alta.	A5	113
Bowden, Ok., U.S.	B4	110
Bowdens, N.C., U.S.	B1	116
Bowdish Reservoir, res., R.I., U.S.	B6	118
Bowdle, S.D., U.S.	f8	96
Bowdoin, Me., U.S.	C1	87
Bowdoinham, Me., U.S.	B7	111
Bowdon, Ga., U.S.	C8	50
Bowdon, N.D., U.S.	C2	90
Bowen, Austl.	D4	85
Bowen, Il., U.S.	B4	112
Bowers, De., U.S.	B3	87
Bowerston, Oh., U.S.	C2	112
Bowersville, Ga., U.S.	A8	111
Bowersville, Oh., U.S.	E6	80
Bowesmont, N.D., U.S.	C3	83
Bowie, Az., U.S.	C4	97
Bowie, Co., U.S.	C4	120
Bowie, Md., U.S.	C5	120
Bowie, Tx., U.S.	D4	101
Bowie, co., Tx., U.S.	E5	68
Bowie Creek, stm., Ms., U.S.	E2	106
Bow Island, Alta.	D4	106
Bowkerville, N.H., U.S.	B5	113
Bow Lake, l., N.H., U.S.	D5	126
Bowlegs, Ok., U.S.	E5	86
Bowler, Wi., U.S.	F4	91
Bowling Green, Fl., U.S.	D3	94
Bowling Green, In., U.S.	B6	102
Bowling Green, Ky., U.S.	A2	112
Bowling Green, Mo., U.S.	A5	117
Bowling Green, Oh., U.S.	B5	123
Bowling Green, Va., U.S.	E4	100
Bowman, Ga., U.S.	B3	87
Bowman, N.D., U.S.	C2	111
Bowman, S.C., U.S.	E6	117
Bowman, co., N.D., U.S.	C2	111
Bowman Creek, stm., Pa., U.S.	m16	115
Bowman-Haley Lake, res., N.D., U.S.	C2	111
Bowman Island, i., Ant.	C23	7
Bowmanstown, Pa., U.S.	E10	115
Bowmanville (part of Newcastle), Ont.	D6	73
Bow Mar, Co., U.S.	*B5	83
Bowmont, Id., U.S.	F2	89
Bowmore, I.C.	F6	34
Bowokan Islands, is., Indon.	G8	51
Bowral, Austl.	A5	113
Bowring, Ok., U.S.	C7	69
Bowron, stm., B.C.	C7	69
Bowron Lake Provincial Park, B.C.	A3	69
Bowser Lake, l., B.C.	C1	70
Bowsman, Man.	C5	100
Bowstring Lake, l., Mn., U.S.	B8	104
Bow Valley, Ne., U.S.	A5	98
Boxborough, Ma., U.S.	B2	104
Box Butte, co., Ne., U.S.	B3	104
Box Butte Creek, stm., Ne., U.S.	B3	104
Box Butte Reservoir, res., Ne., U.S.	C2	118
Box Elder, S.D., U.S.	B2	121
Box Elder, co., Ut., U.S.	A6	83
Box Elder Creek, stm., Co., U.S.	E12	103
Boxelder Creek, stm., Mt., U.S.	C8	103
Box Elder Creek, stm., Mt., U.S.	A6	98
Boxford, Ma., U.S.	B3	92
Boxholm, Ia., U.S.	E8	31
Boxian, China	C5	17
Boxmeer, Neth.	B6	16
Boxtel, Neth.	B3	60
Boyacá, dept., Col.	J7	32
Boyang, China	C3	95
Boyce, La., U.S.	A4	123
Boyce, Va., U.S.	C1	126
Boyceville, Wi., U.S.	F3	100
Boyd, Mn., U.S.	E7	103
Boyd, Mt., U.S.	C4	120
Boyd, Tx., U.S.	D2	126
Boyd, Wi., U.S.	B7	94
Boyd, co., Ky., U.S.	B7	104
Boyd, co., Ne., U.S.	D4	81
Boydell, Ar., U.S.	A2	92
Boyden, Ia., U.S.	B34	7
Boyd Glacier, ice, Ant.	C4	96
Boyd Lake, l., Me., U.S.	B3	97
Boyds, Md., U.S.	D4	72
Boyd's Cove, Newf.	C7	83
Boydton, Va., U.S.	D4	123
Boyer, stm., Ia., U.S.	C2	92
Boyer Knob, mtn., Md., U.S.	k13	97
Boyers, Pa., U.S.	E2	115
Boyertown, Pa., U.S.	F10	115
Boyes, Mt., U.S.	E11	103
Boykin, Al., U.S.	C2	78
Boykin, Ga., U.S.	D5	123
Boykins, Va., U.S.	B4	68
Boyle, Alta.	C2	10
Boyle, Ire.	B3	101
Boyle, Ms., U.S.	C5	94
Boyle, co., Ky., U.S.	D8	71
Boylston, N.S.	B4	98
Boylston, Ma., U.S.	C6	99
Boyne City, Mi., U.S.	C6	99
Boyne Falls, Mi., U.S.	B6	113
Boynton, Ok., U.S.	G3	115
Boynton, Pa., U.S.	F6	86
Boynton Beach, Fl., U.S.	A4	48
Boyoma Falls (Stanley Falls), wtfl., Zaire	C4	100
Boy River, Mn., U.S.	C4	127
Boysen Reservoir, res., Wy., U.S.	B1	120
Boys Ranch, Tx., U.S.	g12	104
Boys Town, Ne., U.S.	B7	25
Boz, Cape, c., Tur.	C6	25
Bozcaada, Tur.	C6	25
Bozca Island (Tenedos), i., Tur.	D7	25
Bozdoğan, Tur.	E5	103
Bozeman, Mt., U.S.	E6	103
Bozeman Pass, Mt., U.S.	C5	97
Bozman, Md., U.S.	D3	46
Bozoum, Cen. Afr. Rep.	C5	24
Bozovici, Rom.	C3	39
Bozqūsh, Kūh-e, mts., Iran	C8	40
Bozüyük, Tur.	D1	23
Bra, Italy	D4	17
Brabant, prov., Bel.	C6	7
Brabant, i., Ant.	A4	75
Brabant Lake, l., Sask.	D3	24
Brač, i., Yugo.	C2	13
Bracadale, Scot., U.K.	C2	13
Bracadale, Loch, b., Scot., U.K.	g8	23
Bracciano, Italy	C4	23
Bracciano, Lake, l., Italy	B5	73
Bracebridge, Ont.	B5	90
Braceville, Il., U.S.	D2	43
Brach, Libya	H1	75
Bracken, Sask.	B5	94
Bracken, co., Ky., U.S.	C2	70
Bracken Lake, l., Man.	h15	115
Brackenridge, Pa., U.S.	D2	126
Brackett, Wi., U.S.	E2	120
Brackettville, Tx., U.S.	B6	12
Brackley, Eng., U.K.	C6	12
Bracknell, Eng., U.K.	B3	19
Brackwede, W. Ger.	D6	23
Brad, Rom.	D6	23
Bradano, stm., Italy	C5	111
Braddock, N.D., U.S.	k14	115
Braddock, Pa., U.S.	B2	97
Braddock Heights, Md., U.S.	G6	117
Braddock Point, c., S.C., U.S.	D2	92
Braddyville, Ia., U.S.	E4	86
Bradenton, Fl., U.S.	F3	115
Bradenton Beach, Fl., U.S.	C5	73
Bradford, Ont.	B4	81
Bradford, Eng., U.K.	B4	81
Bradford, Ar., U.S.	A4	90
Bradford, Ia., U.S.	C4	96
Bradford, Me., U.S.	D3	106
Bradford, N.H., U.S.	B1	112
Bradford, Oh., U.S.	C4	115
Bradford, Pa., U.S.	F1	116
Bradford, R.I., U.S.	A3	119
Bradford, Tn., U.S.	D4	122
Bradford, Vt., U.S.	C4	86
Bradford, co., Fl., U.S.	C8	115
Bradford, co., Pa., U.S.	B2	84
Bradford Mountain, mtn., Ct., U.S.	h13	115
Bradfordwoods, Pa., U.S.	B3	92
Bradgate, Ia., U.S.	D2	81
Bradley, Ar., U.S.	E3	82
Bradley, Ca., U.S.	E5	86
Bradley, Fl., U.S.	B6	90
Bradley, Il., U.S.	D4	96
Bradley, Me., U.S.	B5	112
Bradley, Oh., U.S.	C4	113
Bradley, Ok., U.S.	C3	117
Bradley, S.C., U.S.	B8	118
Bradley, S.D., U.S.	D3	125
Bradley, W.V., U.S.	D3	81
Bradley, co., Ar., U.S.	D9	119
Bradley, co., Tn., U.S.	A2	112
Bradner, Oh., U.S.	D2	72
Brador, Baie de b., Que.	B5	97
Bradshaw, Md., U.S.	D8	104
Bradshaw, Ne., U.S.	D3	125
Bradshaw, W.V., U.S.	C3	80
Bradshaw Mountains, mts., Az., U.S.	C3	80
Bradstreet, Ma., U.S.	F2	75
Bradwell, Sask.	F2	75
Brady, Mt., U.S.	B5	103
Brady, Ne., U.S.	C5	104
Brady, Tx., U.S.	D3	120
Bradyville, Tn., U.S.	B5	119
Brædstrup, Den.	C3	15
Braemar, Scot., U.K.	D5	13
Braeside, Ont.	B8	73
Braga, Port.	B1	22
Bragado, Arg.	B4	54
Bragança, Braz.	A4	57
Bragança, Port.	B2	22
Bragança Paulista, Braz.	A6	57
Braggadocio, Mo., U.S.	E8	102
Braggs, Ok., U.S.	B6	113
Braham, Mn., U.S.	E5	100
Brāhmani, stm., India	D7	36
Brahmapur, India	E7	36
Brahmaputra (Yarlung Zangbo Jiang), stm., Asia	C9	36
Braidwood, Il., U.S.	B5	90
Braila, Rom.	C9	24
Brainard, Ne., U.S.	C8	104
Braine-le-Comte, Bel.	D4	17
Brainerd, Ks., U.S.	g12	93
Brainerd, Mn., U.S.	D4	100
Braintree, Eng., U.K.	C8	12
Braintree, Ma., U.S.	B5	98
Braintree, Vt., U.S.	D3	122
Braithwaite, La., U.S.	k12	95
Brake, W. Ger.	B4	18
Brakel, W. Ger.	B4	19
Brakpan, S. Afr.	*C4	49
Bralorne, B.C.	D6	69
Braman, Ok., U.S.	A4	113
Bramming, Den.	C2	15
Brampton, Ont.	D5	73
Brampton, Eng., U.K.	F6	13
Brampton, N.D., U.S.	C8	111
Bramsche, W. Ger.	B7	17
Bramwell, W.V., U.S.	D3	125
Branch, Newf.	E5	72
Branch, Ar., U.S.	B2	81
Branch, La., U.S.	D3	95
Branch, Wi., U.S.	h10	126
Branch, co., Mi., U.S.	G5	99
Branch, co., R.I., U.S.	B3	116
Branch, stm., Wi., U.S.	h10	126
Branchland, W.V., U.S.	C2	125
Branchport, N.Y., U.S.	C3	109
Branch Village, R.I., U.S.	B3	116
Branchville, Al., U.S.	B3	78
Branchville, Ct., U.S.	D2	84
Branchville, S.C., U.S.	E6	117
Branco, stm., Braz.	D5	55
Branco, stm., Braz.	D4	55
Brandberg, mtn., Nmb.	B1	49
Brande, Den.	C3	15
Brandenburg, E. Ger.	B6	18
Brandenburg, Ky., U.S.	C3	94
Brandenburg, hist. reg., E. Ger.	B6	18
Brandon, Man.	E2	70
Brandon, Co., U.S.	C8	83
Brandon, Fl., U.S.	E4	86
Brandon, Mn., U.S.	E3	100
Brandon, Ms., U.S.	C4	101
Brandon, S.C., U.S.	B3	117
Brandon, Vt., U.S.	D2	122
Brandon, Wi., U.S.	E5	126
Brandon Head, c., Ire.	D1	10
Brandon Mountain, mtn., Ire.	D1	10
Brandsen, Arg.	B5	54
Brandsville, Mo., U.S.	E6	102
Brandt, Oh., U.S.	C1	112
Brandt, S.D., U.S.	C9	118
Brandvlei, S. Afr.	D3	49
Brandý nad Labem, Czech.	C9	19
Brandýs-Stará Boleslav, Czech.	n18	26
Brandy Station, Va., U.S.	B5	123
Brandywine, Md., U.S.	C4	97
Brandywine, W.V., U.S.	C5	125
Brandywine Creek, stm., Pa., U.S.	A5	85
Braniewo, Pol.	C7	7
Brańsk, Pol.	B7	26
Bransfield Strait, strt., Ant.	C6	7
Branson, Co., U.S.	D7	83
Branson, Mo., U.S.	E4	102
Brant, Alta.	D4	68
Brant, co., Ont.	D4	73
Brantford, Ont.	D4	73
Brantford, N.D., U.S.	B7	111
Brant Lake, N.Y., U.S.	B7	109
Brantley, Al., U.S.	D3	78
Brantley, co., Ga., U.S.	E4	87
Brant Rock, Ma., U.S.	B6	98
Brantville, N.B.	B5	71
Brescia, Italy	B3	23
Breskens, Neth.	C3	17
Breslau see Wrocław, Pol.	C4	26
Bresle, stm., Fr.	E9	12
Bressanone, Italy	A3	23
Bressuire, Fr.	D3	16
Brest, Fr.	E1	16
Brest (Brest-Litovsk), Sov. Un.	D5	29
Brétigny [-Notre-Dame], Fr.	F2	17
Breton, Alta.	C3	68
Breton, Pertuis, strt., Fr.	D3	16
Breton Islands, is., La., U.S.	E6	95
Breton Sound, strt., La., U.S.	E6	95
Brett, Cape, c., N.Z.	K15	51
Bretton Woods, N.H., U.S.	B4	106
Breuil, Italy	D3	20
Brevard, N.C., U.S.	f10	110
Brevard, co., Fl., U.S.	E6	86
Breves, Braz.	C4	59
Brevik (part of Porsgrunn), Nor.	p27	14
Břevnov (part of Prague), Czech.	n17	26
Brevoort Lake, l., Mi., U.S.	B5	99
Brevort, Mi., U.S.	B5	99
Brewarrina, Austl.	F8	50
Brewer, Me., U.S.	D4	96
Brewerville, Lib.	E2	45
Brewster, Ks., U.S.	C2	93
Brewster, Mn., U.S.	G3	100
Brewster, Ne., U.S.	C6	104
Brewster, N.Y., U.S.	D7	109
Brewster, Oh., U.S.	B4	112
Brewster, Wa., U.S.	A6	124
Brewster, co., Tx., U.S.	E1	120
Brewster, Kap, c., Grnld.	B18	61
Brazil, In., U.S.	E3	91
Brazil, Ne., U.S.	D5	92
Brazil, Tn., U.S.	B2	119
Brazil, ctry., S.A.	D5	53
Brazilian Highlands, plat.	D5	53
Brazil Lake, N.S.	E4	71
Brazilton, Ks., U.S.	E9	93
Brazoria, Tx., U.S.	r14	120
Brazoria, co., Tx., U.S.	E5	120
Brazos, co., Tx., U.S.	D4	120
Brazos, stm., Tx., U.S.	D4	120
Brazzaville, Congo	B2	48
Brčko, Yugo.	C4	24
Brda, stm., Pol.	B4	26
Brea, Ca., U.S.	n13	82
Brea, Punta, c., P.R.	C2	65
Bread Loaf Mountain, mtn., Vt., U.S.	D3	122
Breakenridge, Mount, mtn., B.C.	E7	69
Breakers Point, c., Am. Sam.	F13	52
Breakeyville, Que.	o17	74
Bream Bay, b., N.Z.	K15	51
Breared, Swe.	B7	15
Breathitt, co., Ky., U.S.	C6	94
Breaux Bridge, La., U.S.	D4	95
Brechin, Ont.	C5	73
Brechin, Scot., U.K.	B5	10
Breckenridge, Co., U.S.	B4	83
Breckenridge, Mi., U.S.	E6	99
Breckenridge, Mn., U.S.	D2	100
Breckenridge, Mo., U.S.	B4	102
Breckenridge, Ok., U.S.	A4	113
Breckenridge, Tx., U.S.	C3	120
Breckenridge Hills, Mo., U.S.	*f13	102
Breckinridge, co., Ky., U.S.	C3	94
Brecknock, Península, pen., Chile	h11	54
Brecksville, Oh., U.S.	A4	112
Břeclav, Czech.	D4	26
Brecon (Brecknock), Wales, U.K.	E5	10
Brecon Beacons, mtn., Wales, U.K.	E5	10
Breda, Neth.	B6	16
Bredasdorp, S. Afr.	D3	49
Bredenbury, Sask.	G4	75
Bredstedt, W. Ger.	D2	15
Bredy, Sov. Un.	E21	8
Bree, Bel.	C5	17
Breese, Il., U.S.	E4	90
Breezy Point, Mn., U.S.	D4	100
Bregalnica, stm., Yugo.	E6	24
Bregenz, Aus.	E4	18
Bregenzerach, stm., Aus.	B8	22
Bregovo, Bul.	C6	24
Bréhal, Fr.	C5	16
Breidafjördur, b., Ice.	n21	14
Breid Bay, b., Ant.	B15	7
Breien, N.D., U.S.	C5	111
Breil, Fr.	F7	16
Breisach, Fr.	A3	20
Brejinho de Nazaré, Braz.	E5	59
Brejo, Braz.	B2	57
Bremen, W. Ger.	B4	18
Bremen, Al., U.S.	A2	78
Bremen, Ga., U.S.	C1	87
Bremen, In., U.S.	B5	91
Bremen, Ky., U.S.	C2	94
Bremen, N.D., U.S.	B6	111
Bremen, Oh., U.S.	C3	112
Bremen, state, W. Ger.	E2	15
Bremer, Ia., U.S.	B5	92
Bremer, co., Ia., U.S.	B5	92
Bremerhaven (Wesermünde), W. Ger.	B4	18
Bremervörde, W. Ger.	B3	124
Bremond, Tx., U.S.	C4	123
Breña, Peru	D4	120
Brenham, Tx., U.S.	*D2	58
Brenner Pass, Eur.	D4	120
Brent, Ont.	B1	13
Brent, Al., U.S.	A3	23
Brenta, stm., Italy	A6	73
Brentford, Fl., U.S.	C2	78
Brenton, W.V., U.S.	u14	86
Brenton Point, c., R.I., U.S.	D7	20
Brentwood, Eng., U.K.	B7	118
Brentwood, Ca., U.S.	*D3	125
Brentwood, Md., U.S.	F5	116
Brentwood, Mo., U.S.	k13	10
Brentwood, N.H., U.S.	h9	82
Brentwood, N.Y., U.S.	f9	97
Brentwood, Oh., U.S.	f13	102
Brentwood, Pa., U.S.	E4	106
Brentwood, S.C., U.S.	E7	109
Brentwood, Tn., U.S.	*o12	112

Name	Map Ref.	Page

Brewster Islands, is., Ma., U.S. — g12 98
Brewton, Al., U.S. — D2 78
Brewton, Ga., U.S. — D4 87
Brezhnev see Naberezhnyye Chelny, Sov. Un. — D8 29
Brežice, Yugo. — C2 24
Březnice, Czech. — D8 19
Breznik, Bul. — D6 24
Brezno, Czech. — D5 26
Bria, Cen. Afr. Rep. — D4 46
Brian Boru Peak, mtn., B.C. — B4 69
Briançon, Fr. — E7 16
Brian Head, mtn., Ut., U.S. — F3 121
Briarcliff, Pa., U.S. — p20 115
Briarcliff Manor, N.Y., U.S. — *D7 109
Briare, Fr. — D5 16
Briartown, Ok., U.S. — B6 113
Brice, Oh., U.S. — m11 112
Bricelyn, Mn., U.S. — G5 100
Briceville, Tn., U.S. — C9 119
Brickeys, Ar., U.S. — C5 81
Brick [Township], N.J., U.S. — C4 107
Bridal Veil, Or., U.S. — B4 114
Bridal Veil Falls, wtfl., Ut., U.S. — C4 121
Bride, stm., Ire. — E3 11
Bridesville, B.C. — E8 69
Bridge, stm., B.C. — D6 69
Bridgeboro, Ga., U.S. — E3 87
Bridge City, La., U.S. — *E5 95
Bridge City, Tx., U.S. — *D6 120
Bridge Creek, stm., Sask. — H1 75
Bridgeford, Sask. — G2 75
Bridgehampton, N.Y., U.S. — n16 109
Bridgeland, Ut., U.S. — C5 121
Bridge Lake, B.C. — D7 69
Bridgend, Wales, U.K. — C4 12
Bridgeport (part of Kitchener), Ont. — D4 73
Bridgeport, Al., U.S. — A4 78
Bridgeport, Ca., U.S. — C4 82
Bridgeport, Ct., U.S. — E3 84
Bridgeport, Il., U.S. — E6 90
Bridgeport, Mi., U.S. — E7 99
Bridgeport, Ne., U.S. — C2 104
Bridgeport, N.J., U.S. — D2 107
Bridgeport, Oh., U.S. — B5 112
Bridgeport, Ok., U.S. — B3 113
Bridgeport, Or., U.S. — o39 114
Bridgeport, Pa., U.S. — o20 115
Bridgeport, Tx., U.S. — C4 120
Bridgeport, Wa., U.S. — B6 124
Bridgeport, W.V., U.S. — B4 125
Bridger, Mt., U.S. — E8 103
Bridger, S.D., U.S. — C4 118
Bridger Mountains, mts., Wy., U.S. — C5 127
Bridger Peak, mtn., Wy., U.S. — E5 127
Bridger Range, mts., Mt., U.S. — E6 103
Bridgeton, In., U.S. — E3 91
Bridgeton, Mo., U.S. — C7 102
Bridgeton, N.J., U.S. — E2 107
Bridgeton, N.C., U.S. — B5 110
Bridgetown, Barb. — J15 64
Bridgetown, N.S. — E4 71
Bridgetown, Oh., U.S. — *o12 112
Bridgeview, Il., U.S. — *k9 90
Bridgeville, N.S. — D7 71
Bridgeville, De., U.S. — F3 85
Bridgeville, Pa., U.S. — k13 115
Bridgewater, N.S. — E5 71
Bridgewater, Ct., U.S. — C2 84
Bridgewater, Ia., U.S. — C3 92
Bridgewater, Me., U.S. — B5 96
Bridgewater, Ma., U.S. — C6 98
Bridgewater, N.H., U.S. — C3 106
Bridgewater, N.J., U.S. — B3 107
Bridgewater, S.D., U.S. — D8 118
Bridgewater, Vt., U.S. — D3 122
Bridgewater, Va., U.S. — B4 123
Bridgewater Corners, Vt., U.S. — D3 122
Bridgman, Mi., U.S. — G4 99
Bridgnorth, Eng., U.K. — B5 12
Bridgton, Me., U.S. — D2 96
Bridgwater, Eng., U.K. — E5 10
Bridgwater Bay, b., Eng., U.K. — C4 12
Bridlington, Eng., U.K. — C6 10
Bridport, Eng., U.K. — E5 12
Brielle, N.J., U.S. — C4 107
Brienz, Switz. — E4 18
Brienz, Lake, l., Switz. — C3 20
Brier Creek, stm., Ga., U.S. — C5 87
Briercrest, Sask. — G3 75
Briereville, Alta. — B5 68
Brierfield, Al., U.S. — B3 78
Brier Hill, N.Y., U.S. — f9 109
Briery Knob, mtn., W.V., U.S. — C4 125
Briey, Fr. — E5 17
Brig, Switz. — E3 18
Brigantine, N.J., U.S. — E4 107
Brigantine Beach, N.J., U.S. — E4 107
Brig Bay, Newf. — C3 72
Brigden, Ont. — E2 73
Brigg, Eng., U.K. — A7 12
Briggs, Ne., U.S. — *C10 104
Briggs, Tx., U.S. — D4 120
Briggsdale, Co., U.S. — A6 83
Briggs Marsh, sw., R.I., U.S. — F6 116
Briggsville, Ar., U.S. — C2 81
Briggsville, Ma., U.S. — A1 98
Briggsville, Wi., U.S. — E4 126
Brigham City, Ut., U.S. — B3 121
Brig Harbour Island, i., Newf. — A3 72
Bright, Ont. — D4 73
Brighton, Ont. — C7 73
Brighton, Eng., U.K. — E6 10
Brighton, Al., U.S. — B3 78
Brighton, Co., U.S. — B6 83
Brighton, Il., U.S. — D3 90
Brighton, Ia., U.S. — C6 92
Brighton, Me., U.S. — C3 96
Brighton, Mi., U.S. — F7 99
Brighton, N.Y., U.S. — B3 109
Brighton, Or., U.S. — B3 114
Brighton, Tn., U.S. — B2 119
Brighton, Ut., U.S. — *C4 121
Brighton Indian Reservation, Fl., U.S. — E5 86
Brightsand Lake, l., Sask. — D1 75
Brightshade, Ky., U.S. — C6 94
Brignoles, Fr. — F7 16
Brihuega, Spain — B4 22
Brilhante, stm., Braz. — C1 56
Brilliant, B.C. — E9 69
Brilliant, Al., U.S. — A2 78
Brilliant, Oh., U.S. — B5 112
Brillion, Wi., U.S. — D5 126
Brilon, W. Ger. — C3 18
Brimfield, Il., U.S. — C4 90
Brimfield, Ma., U.S. — *B3 98
Brimhall, N.M., U.S. — B1 108
Brimley, Mi., U.S. — B6 99
Brimson, Mn., U.S. — C7 100
Brimson, Mo., U.S. — A4 102

Brindisi, Italy — D6 23
Bringhurst, In., U.S. — C5 91
Brinje, Yugo. — C2 24
Brinkhaven, Oh., U.S. — B3 112
Brinkley, Ar., U.S. — C4 81
Brinkman, Ok., U.S. — B2 113
Brinktown, Mo., U.S. — C5 102
Brinkworth, Austl. — F2 51
Brinnon, Wa., U.S. — B3 124
Brinsmade, N.D., U.S. — A6 111
Brinson, Ga., U.S. — F2 87
Brion, Île, i., Que. — B8 71
Brione (Verzasca), Switz. — D6 21
Brioude, Fr. — E5 16
Brisbane, Austl. — E9 50
Briscoe, Tx., U.S. — B2 120
Briscoe, co., Tx., U.S. — B2 120
Brissago, Switz. — D6 21
Bristol, N.B. — C2 71
Bristol, Eng., U.K. — E5 12
Bristol, Co., U.S. — C8 83
Bristol, Ct., U.S. — C4 84
Bristol, Fl., U.S. — B2 86
Bristol, Ga., U.S. — E4 87
Bristol, Il., U.S. — B5 90
Bristol, In., U.S. — A6 91
Bristol, Me., U.S. — *E3 96
Bristol, N.H., U.S. — C3 106
Bristol, R.I., U.S. — D5 116
Bristol, S.D., U.S. — B8 118
Bristol, Tn., U.S. — C11 119
Bristol, Vt., U.S. — C2 122
Bristol, Va., U.S. — f9 123
Bristol, W.V., U.S. — k9 125
Bristol, Wi., U.S. — F5 126
Bristol, co., Ma., U.S. — C5 98
Bristol, co., R.I., U.S. — D5 116
Bristol Bay, b., Ak., U.S. — D7 79
Bristol Channel, strt., U.K. — E4 10
Bristol Ferry, R.I., U.S. — *D5 116
Bristolville, Oh., U.S. — A5 112
Bristow, In., U.S. — H4 91
Bristow, Ia., U.S. — B5 92
Bristow, Ne., U.S. — B7 104
Bristow, Ok., U.S. — B5 113
Britannia Bay (part of Ottawa), Ont. — h12 73
Britannia Beach, B.C. — E6 69
Britannia Range, mts., Ant. — B28 7
British Antarctic Territory, dep., S.A. — *C7 7
British Columbia, prov., Can. — C6 69
British Indian Ocean Territory, dep., Afr. — *G25 2
British Mountains, mts., N.A. — B12 79
British Virgin Islands, dep., N.A. — G12 64
Britstown, S. Afr. — D3 49
Britt, Ont. — B4 73
Britt, Ia., U.S. — A4 92
Brittany, hist. reg., Fr. — C2 16
Britton, Mi., U.S. — G7 99
Britton, S.D., U.S. — B8 118
Brive [-la-Gaillarde], Fr. — E4 11
Briviesca, Spain — A4 22
Brixham, Eng., U.K. — D4 12
Brno, Czech. — D4 26
Broa, Ensenada de la, b., Cuba — C3 64
Broad, stm., Ga., U.S. — B4 87
Broad, stm., S.C., U.S. — C5 117
Broadacres, Sask. — E1 75
Broadalbin, N.Y., U.S. — B6 109
Broadback, stm., Que. — F17 66
Broadbent, Or., U.S. — E2 114
Broad Brook, Ct., U.S. — B5 84
Broad Creek, stm., De., U.S. — F5 85
Broaddus, Tx., U.S. — D5 120
Broadford, Scot., U.K. — C3 13
Broadford, Va., U.S. — f10 123
Broad Haven, b., Ire. — C2 11
Broadhurst, Ga., U.S. — E5 87
Broadkill, stm., De., U.S. — E4 85
Broadkill Beach, De., U.S. — E5 85
Broadland, S.D., U.S. — C7 118
Broadlands, Il., U.S. — D6 90
Broadmeadows, Austl. — *G7 50
Broadmoor, Co., U.S. — C6 83
Broadmoor, Ca., U.S. — *D3 95
Broad Run, stm., Va., U.S. — g11 123
Broad Sound, strt., Austl. — D8 50
Broad Top, Pa., U.S. — F5 115
Broadus, Mt., U.S. — E11 103
Broadview, Sask. — G4 75
Broadview, Il., U.S. — *k9 90
Broadview, Mt., U.S. — D8 103
Broadview, N.M., U.S. — C6 108
Broadview Heights, Oh., U.S. — *h9 112
Broadview Park, Fl., U.S. — F6 86
Broadwater, co., Mt., U.S. — D5 103
Broadway, N.J., U.S. — B2 107
Broadway, N.C., U.S. — B3 110
Broadway, Oh., U.S. — B2 112
Broadway, Va., U.S. — B4 123
Broager, Den. — I3 15
Brochet, Man. — f7 70
Brock, Sask. — F1 75
Brock, Ne., U.S. — D10 104
Brocken, mtn., E. Ger. — B5 19
Brocket, Alta. — E4 68
Brocket, N.D., U.S. — A7 111
Brock Island, i., N.W. Ter. — m29 66
Brockport, N.Y., U.S. — B3 109
Brockport, Pa., U.S. — D4 115
Brockton, Ma., U.S. — B5 98
Brockton, Mt., U.S. — B12 103
Brockton Reservoir, res., Ma., U.S. — h11 98
Brockville, Ont. — C9 73
Brockway, Mt., U.S. — C11 103
Brockway, Pa., U.S. — D4 115
Brockwell, Ar., U.S. — A4 81
Brocton, Il., U.S. — D6 90
Brocton, N.Y., U.S. — C1 109
Brodeur Peninsula, pen., N.W. Ter. — B15 66
Brodhead, Ky., U.S. — C5 94
Brodhead, Wi., U.S. — F4 126
Brodheadsville, Pa., U.S. — E11 115
Brodick, Scot., U.K. — E3 13
Brodnax, Va., U.S. — D4 123
Brodnica, Pol. — B5 26
Brody, Sov. Un. — F5 27
Brogan, Or., U.S. — C9 114
Brokaw, Wi., U.S. — C4 126
Broken Arrow, Ok., U.S. — A6 113
Broken Bow, Ne., U.S. — C6 104
Broken Bow, Ok., U.S. — C7 113
Broken Bow Lake, res., Ok., U.S. — C7 113
Broken Hill, Austl. — F7 50

Brokopondo, Sur. — A3 59
Brokopondo, dept., Sur. — B3 59
Brome, Que. — D5 74
Brome, W. Ger. — F4 15
Brome, co., Que. — D5 74
Brome, Lac, l., Que. — D5 74
Bromhead, Sask. — H4 75
Bromide, Ok., U.S. — C5 113
Bromley (part of London), Eng., U.K. — m13 10
Bromley Mountain, mtn., Vt., U.S. — E3 122
Bromptonville, Que. — D6 74
Bromsgrove, Eng., U.K. — B5 12
Bromyard, Eng., U.K. — B5 12
Bronaugh, Mo., U.S. — D3 102
Bronco, Tx., U.S. — C1 120
Brong-Ahafo, prov., Ghana — E4 45
Bronlund Peak, mtn., B.C. — E7 66
Brönnöysund, Nor. — E5 14
Bronnitsy, Sov. Un. — n18 27
Bronson, Fl., U.S. — C4 86
Bronson, Ia., U.S. — B1 92
Bronson, Ks., U.S. — E8 93
Bronson, Mi., U.S. — G5 99
Bronson, Tx., U.S. — D6 120
Bronwood, Ga., U.S. — E2 87
Bronx, co., N.Y., U.S. — E7 109
Bronxville, N.Y., U.S. — h13 109
Brook, In., U.S. — C3 91
Brookdale, Man. — D2 70
Brooke, co., W.V., U.S. — A4 125
Brooke, Va., U.S. — B5 123
Brooker, Fl., U.S. — C4 86
Brookeville, Md., U.S. — B3 97
Brookfield, N.S. — D6 71
Brookfield, Ct., U.S. — D2 84
Brookfield, Ga., U.S. — E3 87
Brookfield, Il., U.S. — k9 90
Brookfield, Ma., U.S. — B3 98
Brookfield, Mo., U.S. — B4 102
Brookfield, N.H., U.S. — C4 106
Brookfield, N.Y., U.S. — C5 109
Brookfield, Vt., U.S. — C3 122
Brookfield, Va., U.S. — B5 123
Brookfield, Wi., U.S. — m11 126
Brookfield Center, Ct., U.S. — D2 84
Brookford, N.C., U.S. — B1 110
Brookhaven, Ms., U.S. — D3 101
Brookhaven, Pa., U.S. — *p20 115
Brookhaven, W.V., U.S. — h11 125
Brooking, Sask. — H3 75
Brookings, Or., U.S. — E2 114
Brookings, S.D., U.S. — C9 118
Brookings, co., S.D., U.S. — C9 118
Brookland, Ar., U.S. — B5 81
Brooklandville, Md., U.S. — g10 97
Brooklawn, N.J., U.S. — D2 107
Brooklet, Ga., U.S. — D5 87
Brooklin, Me., U.S. — D4 96
Brookline, Ma., U.S. — B5 98
Brookline, N.H., U.S. — E3 106
Brooklyn, N.S. — E5 71
Brooklyn, Al., U.S. — D3 78
Brooklyn, Ct., U.S. — B8 84
Brooklyn, Ga., U.S. — D2 87
Brooklyn, Il., U.S. — C3 90
Brooklyn, Ia., U.S. — C5 92
Brooklyn, Mi., U.S. — F6 99
Brooklyn, Ms., U.S. — D4 101
Brooklyn, Oh., U.S. — h9 112
Brooklyn, Pa., U.S. — C10 115
Brooklyn, S.C., U.S. — B6 117
Brooklyn, Wi., U.S. — F4 126
Brooklyn Center, Mn., U.S. — m12 100
Brooklyn Park, Md., U.S. — h11 97
Brooklyn Park, Mn., U.S. — m12 100
Brookmere, B.C. — E7 69
Brookneal, Va., U.S. — C4 123
Brook Park, Mn., U.S. — E5 100
Brook Park, Oh., U.S. — h9 112
Brookport, Il., U.S. — F5 90
Brookridge, Co., U.S. — *B6 83
Brooks, Alta. — D5 68
Brooks, Ia., U.S. — D3 92
Brooks, Ky., U.S. — g11 94
Brooks, Me., U.S. — D3 96
Brooks, Mn., U.S. — C2 100
Brooks, Or., U.S. — h12 114
Brooks, Wi., U.S. — E4 126
Brooks, co., Ga., U.S. — F3 87
Brooks, co., Tx., U.S. — F3 120
Brooks Air Force Base, mil., Tx., U.S. — k7 120
Brooksby, Sask. — E3 75
Brookshire, Tx., U.S. — E5 120
Brookside, Al., U.S. — f7 78
Brookside, Co., U.S. — C5 83
Brookside, De., U.S. — B3 85
Brooks Peninsula, pen., B.C. — D4 69
Brooks Place, Ma., U.S. — *B5 98
Brooks Range, mts., Ak., U.S. — B9 79
Brookston, In., U.S. — C4 91
Brookston, Mn., U.S. — D6 100
Brooksville, Fl., U.S. — D4 86
Brooksville, Ky., U.S. — B5 94
Brooksville, Me., U.S. — D4 96
Brooksville, Ms., U.S. — B5 101
Brooksville, Ok., U.S. — B5 113
Brookton, Me., U.S. — C5 96
Brooktondale, N.Y., U.S. — C4 109
Brookvale, Co., U.S. — B5 83
Brookview, Md., U.S. — C6 97
Brookville, Il., U.S. — A4 90
Brookville, In., U.S. — F8 91
Brookville, Ks., U.S. — D6 93
Brookville, Ma., U.S. — *h11 98
Brookville, N.Y., U.S. — *E7 109
Brookville, Oh., U.S. — C1 112
Brookville, Pa., U.S. — D3 115
Brookville Lake, res., In., U.S. — F8 91
Brookwood, Al., U.S. — B2 78
Broom, Loch, b., Scot., U.K. — B4 10
Broomall, Pa., U.S. — p20 115
Broome, Austl. — C3 50
Broome, co., N.Y., U.S. — C5 109
Broomes Island, Md., U.S. — D4 97
Broomfield, Co., U.S. — B5 83
Brooten, Mn., U.S. — E3 100
Brora, Scot., U.K. — B5 13
Brora, stm., Scot., U.K. — B4 13
Broseley, Mo., U.S. — E7 102
Brosna, stm., Ire. — D4 11
Brossard, Que. — q20 74
Brotas de Macaúbas, Braz. — D2 56
Brothers, Or., U.S. — D6 114
Brotherton, Tn., U.S. — C8 119
Brothertown, Wi., U.S. — k9 126

Brotmanville, N.J., U.S. — D2 107
Brough, Eng., U.K. — F6 13
Brough Head, c., Scot., U.K. — A5 13
Broughton, Il., U.S. — F5 90
Broussard, La., U.S. — D4 95
Brovary, Sov. Un. — F9 27
Brovst, Den. — A3 15
Broward, co., Fl., U.S. — F6 86
Browardale, Fl., U.S. — r13 86
Browerville, Mn., U.S. — D4 100
Brown, co., Il., U.S. — D3 90
Brown, co., In., U.S. — F5 91
Brown, co., Ks., U.S. — C8 93
Brown, co., Mn., U.S. — F4 100
Brown, co., Ne., U.S. — B6 104
Brown, co., Oh., U.S. — D2 112
Brown, co., S.D., U.S. — B7 118
Brown, co., Tx., U.S. — D3 120
Brown, co., Wi., U.S. — D6 126
Brown, Point, c., Wa., U.S. — C1 124
Brown City, Mi., U.S. — E8 99
Brown Deer, Wi., U.S. — m12 126
Brownell, Ks., U.S. — D4 93
Brownfield, Il., U.S. — F5 90
Brownfield, Me., U.S. — E2 96
Brownfield, Tx., U.S. — C1 120
Brownfields, La., U.S. — *D4 95
Browning, Sask. — H4 75
Browning, Il., U.S. — C3 90
Browning, Mo., U.S. — A4 102
Browning, Mt., U.S. — B3 103
Browning Entrance, strt., B.C. — C2 69
Brownington Center, Vt., U.S. — B4 122
Brownlee, Sask. — G2 75
Brownlee, Ne., U.S. — B5 104
Brownlee Dam, U.S. — E2 89
Brownlee Reservoir, res., U.S. — C10 114
Browns, Il., U.S. — E6 90
Browns, stm., Vt., U.S. — B2 122
Brownsboro, Ky., U.S. — g11 94
Browns Branch, stm., De., U.S. — E3 85
Brownsburg, In., U.S. — E5 91
Brownsburg, Que. — D3 74
Brownsdale, Mn., U.S. — G6 100
Browns Inlet, b., N.C., U.S. — C5 110
Browns Mills, N.J., U.S. — D3 107
Browns Peak, mtn., Az., U.S. — D4 80
Browns Town, Jam. — E14 65
Brownstown, Il., U.S. — E5 90
Brownstown, In., U.S. — G5 91
Brownstown, Pa., U.S. — F9 115
Brownstown, Wa., U.S. — C5 124
Brownstown Head, c., Ire. — E4 11
Browns Valley, In., U.S. — E4 91
Browns Valley, Mn., U.S. — E2 100
Brownsville, Fl., U.S. — s13 86
Brownsville, In., U.S. — E8 91
Brownsville, Ky., U.S. — C3 94
Brownsville, Mn., U.S. — G7 100
Brownsville, Or., U.S. — C4 114
Brownsville, Pa., U.S. — F2 115
Brownsville, Tn., U.S. — B2 119
Brownsville, Tx., U.S. — G4 120
Brownsville, Vt., U.S. — E3 122
Brownton, Mn., U.S. — F4 100
Brownton, W.V., U.S. — B4 125
Brownvale, Alta. — B2 68
Brownville, Me., U.S. — C3 96
Brownville, Ne., U.S. — D10 104
Brownville, N.Y., U.S. — A5 109
Brownville Junction, Me., U.S. — C3 96
Brownwood, Mo., U.S. — D8 102
Brownwood, Tx., U.S. — D3 120
Brownwood, Lake, res., Tx., U.S. — D3 120
Broxton, Ga., U.S. — E4 87
Broye, stm., Switz. — C2 20
Broyhill Park, Va., U.S. — *B5 123
Brozas, Spain — C5 22
Bruay [-en-Artois], Fr. — B5 16
Bruce, Alta. — C4 68
Bruce, Fl., U.S. — u16 86
Bruce, Ms., U.S. — B4 101
Bruce, S.D., U.S. — C9 118
Bruce, Wi., U.S. — C2 126
Bruce, co., Ont. — C3 73
Bruce, Mount, mtn., Austl. — D3 50
Bruce Crossing, Mi., U.S. — m12 99
Bruce National Park, Ont. — B3 73
Bruce Peninsula, pen., Ont. — B3 73
Bruceton, Tn., U.S. — A3 119
Bruceton Mills, W.V., U.S. — B5 125
Brucetown, Va., U.S. — A4 123
Bruchsal, W. Ger. — D5 19
Bruck, Aus. — B8 20
Brück, E. Ger. — A7 19
Bruck [an der Leitha], Aus. — D8 18
Bruck [an der Mur], Aus. — E7 18
Brückenau, W. Ger. — C4 19
Bückeburg, W. Ger. — A4 19
Bruderheim, Alta. — C4 68
Bruff, Ire. — E3 11
Bruges see Brugge, Bel. — B5 16
Brugg, Switz. — B5 21
Brugge (Bruges), Bel. — B5 16
Brühl, W. Ger. — C1 19
Bruin Point, mtn., Ut., U.S. — D5 121
Bruja, Cerro, mtn., Pan. — k11 62
Brule, Ne., U.S. — C4 104
Brule, Wi., U.S. — B2 126
Brule, co., S.D., U.S. — D6 118
Brule, stm., U.S. — C6 126
Brûlé Lake, l., Ont. — B1 73
Brûlé Lake, l., Mn., U.S. — k9 100
Brumado, Braz. — D7 56
Brumath, Fr. — C7 16
Brumley, Mo., U.S. — C5 102
Brumley Mountain, mtn., Va., U.S. — f9 123
Brundidge, Al., U.S. — D4 78
Bruneau, Id., U.S. — G3 89
Bruneau, stm., U.S. — G3 89
Brunei, ctry., Asia — E4 34
Brunei Bay, b., Asia — E5 34
Brunete, Spain — p16 22
Brunette Island, i., Newf. — E4 72
Bruni, Tx., U.S. — F3 120
Brunico, Italy — C6 21
Brüning, Ne., U.S. — D8 104
Brunkild, Man. — E3 70
Brunnen, Switz. — C5 21
Brunner, Lake, l., N.Z. — O13 51
Bruno, Sask. — E3 75
Bruno, Mn., U.S. — D6 100

Bruno, Ne., U.S. — C9 104
Brunsbüttel, W. Ger. — E3 15
Brunson, S.C., U.S. — F5 117
Brunsville, Ia., U.S. — B1 92
Brunswick, Ga., U.S. — E5 87
Brunswick, Me., U.S. — E3 96
Brunswick, Md., U.S. — B2 97
Brunswick, Mo., U.S. — B4 102
Brunswick, Ne., U.S. — B8 104
Brunswick, Oh., U.S. — A4 112
Brunswick, co., N.C., U.S. — C4 110
Brunswick, co., Va., U.S. — D5 123
Brunswick, Península, pen., Chile — h11 54
Brunswick see Braunschweig, W. Ger. — B5 18
Brunswick Naval Air Station, mil., Me., U.S. — E3 96
Bruree, Ire. — E3 11
Brusett, Mt., U.S. — C9 103
Brush, Co., U.S. — A7 83
Brushy Mountain, mtn., Va., U.S. — C1 123
Brushy Mountains, mts., N.C., U.S. — B1 110
Brus Laguna, Hond. — D8 63
Brusly, La., U.S. — D4 95
Brusque, Braz. — D3 56
Brussels (Bruxelles), Bel. — B6 16
Brussels, Ont. — D3 73
Brussels, Il., U.S. — E3 90
Brussels, Wi., U.S. — D6 126
Bruton, Eng., U.K. — C5 12
Brutus, Mi., U.S. — B6 99
Bruyères, Fr. — A2 20
Bruzual, Zaire — A2 48
Bryan, Oh., U.S. — A1 112
Bryan, Tx., U.S. — D4 120
Bryan, co., Ga., U.S. — D5 87
Bryan, co., Ok., U.S. — D5 113
Bryanka, Sov. Un. — g21 27
Bryansk, Sov. Un. — D6 29
Bryans Road, Md., U.S. — C3 97
Bryant, Ar., U.S. — C3 81
Bryant, Fl., U.S. — F6 86
Bryant, Il., U.S. — C3 90
Bryant, In., U.S. — C8 91
Bryant, S.D., U.S. — C8 118
Bryant, Wi., U.S. — C4 126
Bryant Creek, stm., Mo., U.S. — E5 102
Bryant Mountain, mtn., Ma., U.S. — B2 98
Bryant Pond, Me., U.S. — D2 96
Bryantsville, Ky., U.S. — C5 94
Bryantville, Ma., U.S. — B6 98
Bryce Canyon, Ut., U.S. — F3 121
Bryce Canyon National Park, Ut., U.S. — F3 121
Bryceland, La., U.S. — B3 95
Bryceville, Fl., U.S. — B5 86
Bryn Mawr, Pa., U.S. — o20 115
Bryn Mawr, Wa., U.S. — e11 124
Bryson, Tx., U.S. — C3 120
Bryson City, N.C., U.S. — f9 110
Bryte, Ca., U.S. — C3 82
B-Say-Tah, Sask. — G4 75
Bua, Fiji — H15 52
Bu'aale, Som. — E5 47
Bua Bay, b., Fiji — H15 52
Buariki, Kir. — R18 52
Buba, Gui.-B. — D2 45
Bübiyān, i., Kuw. — C4 38
Buccaneer Archipelago, is., Austl. — C3 50
Buchach, Sov. Un. — G5 27
Buchanan, Sask. — F4 75
Buchanan, Lib. — E2 45
Buchanan, Ga., U.S. — C1 87
Buchanan, Mi., U.S. — G4 99
Buchanan, N.D., U.S. — B7 111
Buchanan, Tn., U.S. — A3 119
Buchanan, Va., U.S. — C3 123
Buchanan, co., Ia., U.S. — B6 92
Buchanan, co., Mo., U.S. — B3 102
Buchanan, co., Va., U.S. — e9 123
Buchanan, Lake, l., Austl. — D8 50
Buchanan, Lake, l., Tx., U.S. — D3 120
Buchans, Newf. — D3 72
Bucharest (București), Rom. — C8 24
Buchholz, W. Ger. — B8 21
Buchen, W. Ger. — D4 19
Buchenberg, W. Ger. — A9 21
Buchholz, W. Ger. — E3 15
Buchloe, W. Ger. — B5 20
Buchon, Point, c., Ca., U.S. — E3 82
Buchs, Switz. — B6 20
Buckatunna, Ms., U.S. — D5 101
Buck Creek, In., U.S. — D4 91
Buck Creek, stm., Ga., U.S. — D2 87
Buck Creek, stm., In., U.S. — m11 91
Buck Creek, stm., Ky., U.S. — C4 94
Buckeye, Az., U.S. — D3 80
Buckeye, W.V., U.S. — C4 125
Buckeyestown, Md., U.S. — B3 97
Buckeye Lake, Oh., U.S. — C3 112
Buckeye Lake, l., Oh., U.S. — C3 112
Buckfield, Me., U.S. — D2 96
Buckhannon, W.V., U.S. — C4 125
Buckhannon, stm., W.V., U.S. — C4 125
Buckhaven, Scot., U.K. — B5 10
Buckhead, Ga., U.S. — C3 87
Buckhorn, Ont. — C6 73
Buckhorn, N.M., U.S. — D1 108
Buckhorn Knob, mtn., W.V., U.S. — D4 125
Buckhorn Lake, res., Ky., U.S. — C6 94
Buckie, Scot., U.K. — B5 10
Buckingham, Que. — D2 74
Buckingham, Eng., U.K. — C6 12
Buckingham, co., Va., U.S. — C4 123
Buckinghamshire, co., Eng., U.K. — C7 12
Buck Lake, l., Alta. — C3 68

Buck Mountain, mtn., Va., U.S. — D1 123
Buck Mountain, mtn., Wa., U.S. — A6 124
Bucknell Manor, Va., U.S. — *B5 123
Buckner, Ar., U.S. — D2 81
Buckner, Il., U.S. — F4 90
Buckner, Ky., U.S. — g12 94
Buckner, Mo., U.S. — h11 102
Bucks, Al., U.S. — D1 78
Bucks, co., Pa., U.S. — F11 115
Bucks Harbor, Me., U.S. — D5 96
Buckskin, In., U.S. — H3 91
Buckskin Mountains, mts., Az., U.S. — C2 80
Bucksport, Me., U.S. — D4 96
Bucksport, S.C., U.S. — D9 117
Buckville, Ar., U.S. — C2 81
Bucoda, Wa., U.S. — C3 124
Buco Zau, Ang. — B1 48
Bucyrus, Ks., U.S. — D9 93
Bucyrus, N.D., U.S. — C3 111
Bucyrus, Oh., U.S. — B3 112
Bud, W.V., U.S. — D3 125
Buda, Tx., U.S. — D4 120
Buda, Il., U.S. — B4 90
Budapest, Hung. — B4 24
Budaun, India — C7 37
Budd Coast, Ant. — C24 7
Budd Lake, l., N.J., U.S. — B3 107
Buddon Ness, c., Scot., U.K. — B6 13
Budennovsk, Sov. Un. — G17 8
Buddtown, N.J., U.S. — D3 107
Bude, Eng., U.K. — E4 10
Bude, Ms., U.S. — D3 101
Bude Bay, b., Eng., U.K. — D3 12
Budjala, Zaire — A2 48
Budrio, Italy — B3 23
Budyně [nad Ohří], Czech. — n17 26
Buea, Cam. — E1 46
Buechel, Ky., U.S. — B4 94
Buena, N.J., U.S. — D3 107
Buena Park, Ca., U.S. — n12 82
Buenaventura, Col. — C2 60
Buenaventura, Mex. — B3 63
Buena Vista, Bol. — C3 56
Buena Vista, Al., U.S. — D2 78
Buena Vista, Ar., U.S. — D3 81
Buena Vista, Co., U.S. — C4 83
Buena Vista, Fl., U.S. — D4 86
Buena Vista, Ms., U.S. — B5 101
Buena Vista, N.M., U.S. — A4 108
Buena Vista, Oh., U.S. — D2 112
Buena Vista, Tn., U.S. — B3 119
Buena Vista, Va., U.S. — C3 123
Bueno, stm., Chile — C2 54
Buenópolis, Braz. — A4 56
Buenos Aires, Arg. — A5 54
Buenos Aires, C.R. — F6 62
Buenos Aires, Pan. — k11 62
Buenos Aires, prov., Arg. — B4 54
Buenos Aires, Lago (Lago General Carrera), l., S.A. — F2 54
Bueyeros, N.M., U.S. — B6 108
Buffalo, Alta. — C4 68
Buffalo, Al., U.S. — C4 78
Buffalo, In., U.S. — C4 91
Buffalo, Ia., U.S. — C7 92
Buffalo, Ks., U.S. — E8 93
Buffalo, Mn., U.S. — E5 100
Buffalo, Mo., U.S. — D4 102
Buffalo, N.Y., U.S. — C2 109
Buffalo, Oh., U.S. — C4 112
Buffalo, Ok., U.S. — A2 113
Buffalo, S.C., U.S. — B4 117
Buffalo, S.D., U.S. — B2 118
Buffalo, Tx., U.S. — D5 120
Buffalo, W.V., U.S. — C3 125
Buffalo, Wy., U.S. — B6 127
Buffalo, co., Ne., U.S. — D6 104
Buffalo, co., S.D., U.S. — C6 118
Buffalo, co., Wi., U.S. — D2 126
Buffalo, stm., Ar., U.S. — B3 81
Buffalo, stm., Mn., U.S. — D2 100
Buffalo, stm., Tn., U.S. — B4 119
Buffalo, stm., Wi., U.S. — D2 126
Buffalo Bill Reservoir, res., Wy., U.S. — B3 127
Buffalo Center, Ia., U.S. — A4 92
Buffalo Creek, Co., U.S. — B5 83
Buffalo Creek, stm., W.V., U.S. — f8 125
Buffalo Creek, stm., W.V., U.S. — h10 125
Buffalo Creek, stm., W.V., U.S. — n12 125
Buffalo Gap, Sask. — H3 75
Buffalo Gap, S.D., U.S. — D2 118
Buffalo Grove, Il., U.S. — h9 90
Buffalo Lake, Mn., U.S. — F4 100
Buffalo Lake, l., Alta. — C4 68
Buffalo Lake, l., N.W. Ter. — D9 66
Buffalo Lake, res., Tx., U.S. — B1 120
Buffalo Lake, res., Wi., U.S. — E4 126
Buffalo Mills, Pa., U.S. — G4 115
Buffalo Mountain, mtn., Va., U.S. — D2 123
Buffalo Narrows, Sask. — m7 75
Buffalo Pound Lake, l., Sask. — G3 75
Buffalo Valley, Tn., U.S. — C8 119
Buff Bay, Jam. — E15 65
Buffumville Lake, res., Ma., U.S. — B4 98
Buford, Ga., U.S. — B3 87
Buford, N.D., U.S. — B2 111
Buford, Oh., U.S. — C2 112
Buford, Wy., U.S. — E7 127
Bug, stm., Eur. — E4 27
Buga, Col. — C2 60
Buganga, Ug. — B5 48
Bugene, Tan. — B5 48
Bugio, i., Port. — h12 22
Bugojno, Yugo. — C3 24
Bugsuk Island, i., Phil. — D5 34
Bugt, China — C9 32
Buguruslan, Sov. Un. — C4 28
Buhl, Id., U.S. — G4 89
Buhl, Mn., U.S. — C6 100
Buhler, Ks., U.S. — D6 93
Bühl, W. Ger. — E3 19
Buhuşi, Rom. — B8 24
Bui Dam, Ghana — E4 45
Buies Creek, N.C., U.S. — B4 110

Name	Map Ref.	Page
Builth Wells, Wales, U.K.	B4	12
Buitenpost, Neth.	A6	17
Bujalance, Spain	D3	22
Bujumbura, Bdi.	B4	48
Bukama, Zaire	C4	48
Bukene, Tan.	B5	48
Bukhara, Sov. Un.	F9	29
Bukittinggi, Indon.	F2	34
Bukoba, Tan.	B5	48
Bukovina, hist. reg., Eur.	B7	24
Bula, Indon.	F8	34
Bula, Zaire	A4	48
Bülach, Switz.	A6	21
Buladean, N.C., U.S.	e10	110
Buladeen, Tn., U.S.	C11	119
Bulan, Ky., U.S.	C6	94
Bulawayo, Zimb.	B4	49
Buldir Island, i., Ak., U.S.	E3	79
Bulgan, Mong.	B5	31
Bulgaria, ctry., Eur.	D7	24
Bulgroo, Austl.	B4	51
Buliya, Fiji	I15	52
Bulkley, stm., B.C.	B4	69
Bulkley Ranges, mts., B.C.	B4	69
Bull, stm., B.C.	E10	69
Bullange see Büllingen, Bel.	D6	17
Bullaque, stm., Spain	C3	22
Bullard, Ga., U.S.	D3	87
Bullas, Spain	C5	22
Bullaxaar, Som.	C5	47
Bullay, W. Ger.	C2	19
Bull Creek, stm., Nv., U.S.	E6	105
Bull Creek, stm., S.D., U.S.	C2	118
Bulle, Switz.	C3	20
Bullen Baai, b., Neth. Ant.	H18	65
Bullfrog Creek, stm., Ut., U.S.	F5	121
Bullhead, S.D., U.S.	B4	118
Bullhead City, Az., U.S.	B1	80
Büllingen (Bullange), Bel.	D6	17
Bull Island, i., S.C., U.S.	G6	117
Bull Island, i., S.C., U.S.	F8	117
Bull Island, i., S.C., U.S.	D9	117
Bullitt, co., Ky., U.S.	C4	94
Bullittsville, Ky., U.S.	h13	94
Bull Mountain, mtn., Mt., U.S.	D4	103
Bullock, co., Ga., U.S.	D5	87
Bullock, N.C., U.S.	A4	110
Bullock, co., Al., U.S.	C4	78
Bullock Creek, Mi., U.S.	E6	99
Bulloo, stm., Austl.	E7	50
Bulloo Lake, l., Austl.	E4	51
Bull Run, stm., Va., U.S.	g11	123
Bull Run Mountains, mts., Va., U.S.	B5	123
Bullrun Ridge, mtn., Tn., U.S.	m13	119
Bullrun Rock, mtn., Or., U.S.	C8	114
Bulls Bay, b., S.C., U.S.	F8	117
Bulls Bridge, Ct., U.S.	C1	84
Bulls Gap, Tn., U.S.	C10	119
Bull Shoals, Ar., U.S.	A3	81
Bull Shoals Lake, res., U.S.	A3	81
Bull Sluice Lake, res., Ga., U.S.	h8	87
Bully Creek Reservoir, res., Or., U.S.	C9	114
Bulnes, Chile	B2	54
Bulolo, Pap. N. Gui.	k12	50
Bulsār, India	G4	37
Bultfontein, S. Afr.	C4	49
Bulun, Sov. Un.	B15	29
Bulungu, Zaire	B2	48
Bulwark, Alta.	C5	68
Bulyea, Sask.	G3	75
Bumba, Zaire	A3	48
Bumping, stm., Wa., U.S.	C4	124
Bumpus Mills, Tn., U.S.	A4	119
Buna, Tx., U.S.	D6	120
Bunbury, Austl.	F2	50
Bunceton, Mo., U.S.	C5	102
Bunch, Ok., U.S.	B7	113
Bunche Park, Fl., U.S.	*s13	86
Buncombe, Il., U.S.	F5	90
Buncombe, co., N.C., U.S.	f10	110
Buncrana, Ire.	B4	11
Bundaberg, Austl.	D9	50
Bünde, W. Ger.	A3	19
Bündi, India	E5	37
Bundick Creek, stm., La., U.S.	D2	95
Bundoran, Ire.	C3	11
Bunessan, Scot., U.K.	D2	13
Bungay, Eng., U.K.	D7	12
Bunger Hills, hills, Ant.	C23	7
Bungo Strait, strt., Japan	J6	33
Bunia, Zaire	A5	48
Bunker, Mo., U.S.	D6	102
Bunker Hill, Il., U.S.	D4	90
Bunker Hill, In., U.S.	C5	91
Bunker Hill, Ks., U.S.	D5	93
Bunker Hill, Or., U.S.	*D2	114
Bunker Hill, W.V., U.S.	B6	125
Bunker Hill, W.V., U.S.	m12	125
Bunker Hill, mtn., Nv., U.S.	D4	105
Bunkerville, Nv., U.S.	G7	105
Bunkeya, Zaire	D4	48
Bunkie, La., U.S.	D3	95
Bunn, N.C., U.S.	B4	110
Bunnahowen, Ire.	C2	11
Bunnell, Fl., U.S.	C5	86
Bunnlevel, N.C., U.S.	B4	110
Buolkalakh, Sov. Un.	B12	28
Buon Me Thuot, Viet.	C3	34
Buor-Khaya Bay, b., Sov. Un.	B11	28
Bura, Kenya	B7	48
Buram, Sud.	C2	47
Buras, La., U.S.	E6	95
Buraydah, Sau. Ar.	C4	38
Burayk, Lib.	D2	43
Burbank, Ca., U.S.	E4	82
Burbank, Il., U.S.	k9	90
Burbank, Ok., U.S.	A5	113
Burbank, S.D., U.S.	E9	118
Burbank, Wa., U.S.	C7	124
Burchard, Ne., U.S.	D9	104
Burco, Som.	D6	47
Burdekin, stm., Austl.	C9	50
Burden, Ks., U.S.	E7	93
Burdett, Alta.	E5	68
Burdett, Ks., U.S.	D4	93
Burdett, N.Y., U.S.	C4	109
Burdette, Ar., U.S.	B6	81
Burdick, Ks., U.S.	D7	93
Burdickville, R.I., U.S.	F2	116
Burdur, Tur.	B4	40
Bureau, Il., U.S.	B4	90
Bureau, co., Il., U.S.	B4	90
Burein Mountains, mts., Sov. Un.	B6	29
Büren, W. Ger.	B3	19
Büren [an der Aare], Switz.	B3	21
Bureya, Sov. Un.	B10	31
Bureya, stm., Sov. Un.	D4	33
Burford, Ont.	D4	73
Bür Fu'ād, Eg.	C4	41
Burg, E. Ger.	A6	19
Burg, W. Ger.	D5	15
Burgas, Bul.	D8	24
Burgas, Gulf of, b., Bul.	D8	24
Burgaw, N.C., U.S.	C5	110
Burgdorf, W. Ger.	F3	15
Burgdorf, Switz.	E3	21
Burgeo, Newf.	E3	72
Burgersdorp, S. Afr.	D4	49
Burgess, S.C., U.S.	D9	117
Burgess Hill, Eng., U.K.	D7	12
Burgettstown, Pa., U.S.	F1	115
Burghausen, W. Ger.	A8	20
Burghead, Scot., U.K.	C5	13
Burgin, Ky., U.S.	C5	94
Burglengenfeld, W. Ger.	D7	19
Burgoon, Oh., U.S.	A2	112
Burgos, Phil.	n12	34
Burgos, Spain	A4	22
Burgstädt, E. Ger.	C7	19
Burgsteinfurt, W. Ger.	A2	19
Burgsvik, Swe.	I8	14
Burgundy, hist. reg., Fr.	D6	16
Burhānpur, India	D6	36
Burhave, W. Ger.	E2	15
Burhi Gandak, stm., India	E10	37
Buri, Braz.	m7	56
Burica, Punta, c., N.A.	F6	62
Burien, Wa., U.S.	*f11	124
Burin, Newf.	E4	72
Bürin, Isr. Occ.	g12	41
Burin Peninsula, pen., Newf.	E4	72
Buri Ram, Thai.	C2	34
Buritama, Braz.	C2	56
Burj al 'Arab, Eg.	G7	40
Burkburnett, Tx., U.S.	B3	120
Burke, Id., U.S.	B3	89
Burke, N.Y., U.S.	f10	109
Burke, S.D., U.S.	D6	118
Burke, Vt., U.S.	B5	122
Burke, Va., U.S.	*B5	123
Burke, co., Ga., U.S.	C4	87
Burke, co., N.C., U.S.	B1	110
Burke, co., N.D., U.S.	A3	111
Burke Channel, strt., B.C.	C4	69
Burkesville, Ky., U.S.	D4	94
Burket, In., U.S.	B6	91
Burketon Station (part of Newcastle), Ont.	C6	73
Burketown, Austl.	C6	50
Burkett, Tx., U.S.	C3	120
Burkettsville, Oh., U.S.	B1	112
Burkeville, Tx., U.S.	D6	120
Burkeville, Va., U.S.	C4	123
Burkina Faso, ctry., Afr.	F5	45
Burk's Falls, Ont.	B5	73
Burkville, Al., U.S.	C3	78
Burleigh, N.J., U.S.	E3	107
Burleigh, co., N.D., U.S.	C5	111
Burleson, Tx., U.S.	n9	120
Burleson, co., Tx., U.S.	D4	120
Burley, Id., U.S.	G5	89
Burley, Wa., U.S.	f10	124
Burlingame, Ca., U.S.	h8	82
Burlingame, Ks., U.S.	D8	93
Burlington, Newf.	D3	72
Burlington, Ont.	D5	73
Burlington, Co., U.S.	B8	83
Burlington, Ct., U.S.	B4	84
Burlington, Il., U.S.	A5	90
Burlington, In., U.S.	C5	91
Burlington, Ia., U.S.	D6	92
Burlington, Ks., U.S.	D8	93
Burlington, Ky., U.S.	A5	94
Burlington, Ma., U.S.	f11	98
Burlington, N.J., U.S.	C3	107
Burlington, N.C., U.S.	A3	110
Burlington, N.D., U.S.	A4	111
Burlington, Ok., U.S.	A3	113
Burlington, Pa., U.S.	C8	115
Burlington, Vt., U.S.	C2	122
Burlington, Wa., U.S.	A3	124
Burlington, W.V., U.S.	B6	125
Burlington, Wi., U.S.	F5	126
Burlington, Wy., U.S.	B4	127
Burlington, co., N.J., U.S.	D3	107
Burlington Beach, In., U.S.	A3	91
Burlington Junction, Mo., U.S.	A2	102
Burlyu-Tobe, Sov. Un.	D10	29
Burma (Myanmar), ctry., Asia	D10	36
Burnaby, B.C.	E6	69
Burnaby Island, i., B.C.	C2	69
Burnet, Tx., U.S.	D3	120
Burnet, co., Tx., U.S.	D3	120
Burnett, In., U.S.	E3	91
Burnett, co., Wi., U.S.	C1	126
Burnett, stm., Austl.	E9	50
Burnettown, S.C., U.S.	D4	117
Burnettsville, In., U.S.	C4	91
Burney, Ca., U.S.	B3	82
Burney, In., U.S.	F6	91
Burneyville, Ok., U.S.	D4	113
Burnham, Me., U.S.	D3	96
Burnham, Mo., U.S.	E6	102
Burnham, Pa., U.S.	E6	115
Burnham-on-Sea / Highbridge, Eng., U.K.	J6	12
Burnie, Austl.	o15	50
Burning Springs, Ky., U.S.	C6	94
Burning Springs, W.V., U.S.	C3	125
Burnley, Eng., U.K.	D5	10
Burns, Co., U.S.	B4	83
Burns, Ks., U.S.	D7	93
Burns, Or., U.S.	D7	114
Burns, Tn., U.S.	A4	119
Burns, Wy., U.S.	E8	127
Burns City, In., U.S.	G4	91
Burns Flat, Ok., U.S.	B2	113
Burnside, Il., U.S.	C2	90
Burnside, Ky., U.S.	D5	94
Burnside, Pa., U.S.	E4	115
Burns Lake, B.C.	B5	69
Burns Paiute Indian Reservation, Or., U.S.	D7	114
Burnstad, N.D., U.S.	C6	111
Burnsville, Al., U.S.	C3	78
Burnsville, Ms., U.S.	A5	101
Burnsville, N.C., U.S.	f10	110
Burnsville, W.V., U.S.	C4	125
Burnsville Lake, res., W.V., U.S.	C4	125
Burnt Cabins, Pa., U.S.	F6	115
Burnt Corn, Al., U.S.	D2	78
Burnt Hills, N.Y., U.S.	C7	109
Burntisland, Scot., U.K.	B5	13
Burnt Islands, Newf.	E2	72
Burnt Mills, Lake, l., Va., U.S.	k14	123
Burnt Prairie, Il., U.S.	E5	90
Burnt River, Ont.	C6	73
Burntside Lake, l., Mn., U.S.	C6	100
Burntwood, stm., Man.	B2	70
Burntwood Lake, l., Man.	B1	70
Burnwell, Al., U.S.	f6	78
Burnwell, W.V., U.S.	m13	125
Burqā, Isr. Occ.	b7	41
Burr, Mn., U.S.	F2	100
Burr, Ne., U.S.	D9	104
Burra, Austl.	F2	51
Burragorang, Lake, l., Austl.	G8	51
Burray, i., Scot., U.K.	B6	13
Burrendong Reservoir, res., Austl.	F7	51
Burr Ferry, La., U.S.	C2	95
Burr Hill, Va., U.S.	B5	123
Burriana, Spain	C5	22
Burr Oak, Ks., U.S.	A6	92
Burr Oak, Mi., U.S.	G5	99
Burr Oak Reservoir, res., Oh., U.S.	C3	112
Burroughs, Ga., U.S.	E5	87
Burrow Head, c., Scot., U.K.	F4	13
Burrows, In., U.S.	C5	91
Burruyacú, Arg.	E3	55
Burr Ridge, Il., U.S.	*B6	90
Burrton, Ks., U.S.	D6	93
Burrville, Tn., U.S.	C9	119
Burrwood, La., U.S.	F6	95
Burry Port, Wales, U.K.	C3	12
Bursa, Tur.	B7	40
Burstall, Sask.	G1	75
Bursey, Mount, mtn., Ant.	B35	7
Burt, Ia., U.S.	A3	92
Burt, N.D., U.S.	C3	111
Burt, co., Ne., U.S.	C9	104
Burta, Austl.	F3	51
Burt Lake, l., Mi., U.S.	C6	99
Burton, B.C.	D9	69
Burton, Il., U.S.	D2	90
Burton, Mi., U.S.	E7	99
Burton, Ne., U.S.	B6	104
Burton, Oh., U.S.	A4	112
Burton, Tx., U.S.	D4	120
Burton, Wa., U.S.	f11	124
Burton, W.V., U.S.	B4	125
Burton, Lake, res., Ga., U.S.	B3	87
Burtonport, Ire.	C3	11
Burton upon Trent, Eng., U.K.	D6	10
Burträsk, Swe.	E9	14
Burtrum, Mn., U.S.	E4	100
Burtts Corner, N.B.	C3	71
Burtus, Eg.	D3	41
Buru, i., Indon.	F7	34
Buru, Wādī al, val., Eg.	D5	41
Burullus, Lake, l., Eg.	C2	41
Burūn, Ra's, c., Eg.	C4	41
Burundi, ctry., Afr.	B5	48
Burwash, Ont.	A4	73
Burwell, Ne., U.S.	C6	104
Bury, Que.	D6	74
Bury, Eng., U.K.	A5	12
Burynshik, Sov. Un.	D4	28
Bury Saint Edmunds, Eng., U.K.	D7	10
Busby, Alta.	C4	68
Busby, Mt., U.S.	E10	103
Buschfeld, W. Ger.	D1	19
Busch, Ky., U.S.	C6	94
Bush, La., U.S.	D6	95
Bush City, Ks., U.S.	D8	93
Bushenyi, Ug.	B5	48
Bushimaie, stm., Zaire	B3	48
Bushiribana, Aruba	G17	65
Bushkill, Pa., U.S.	D11	115
Bushland, Tx., U.S.	B1	120
Bushmills, N. Ire., U.K.	B6	11
Bushnell, Fl., U.S.	D4	86
Bushnell, Il., U.S.	C3	90
Bushnell, Ne., U.S.	C2	104
Bushnell, S.D., U.S.	C9	118
Bushong, Ks., U.S.	D7	93
Bush River, b., Md., U.S.	B5	97
Bushton, Ks., U.S.	D5	93
Bushugu, Zaire	A3	48
Busk, Sov. Un.	G5	27
Busko [Zdrój], Pol.	C5	26
Buşra ash Shām, Syria	F11	40
Bussa, Nig.	G6	45
Busselton, Austl.	F2	50
Bussey, Ia., U.S.	C5	92
Bussum, Neth.	A6	16
Busto Arsizio, Italy	B2	23
Buso-Djanoa, Zaire	A3	48
Büsum, W. Ger.	D2	15
Buta, Zaire	A3	48
Buta Ranquil, Arg.	B3	54
Butare, Rw.	B5	48
Bute, Island of, i., Scot., U.K.	E3	13
Butedale, B.C.	C3	69
Bute Inlet, b., B.C.	D5	69
Butha Qi, China	B9	31
Buthier, stm., Italy	D3	20
Butler, Al., U.S.	C1	78
Butler, Ga., U.S.	D2	87
Butler, Il., U.S.	D4	90
Butler, In., U.S.	B8	91
Butler, Ky., U.S.	B5	94
Butler, Mo., U.S.	C3	102
Butler, N.J., U.S.	B4	107
Butler, Oh., U.S.	B3	112
Butler, Ok., U.S.	B2	113
Butler, Pa., U.S.	E2	115
Butler, S.D., U.S.	C8	118
Butler, Tn., U.S.	C11	119
Butler, Wi., U.S.	m11	126
Butler, co., Al., U.S.	D3	78
Butler, co., Ia., U.S.	B5	92
Butler, co., Ks., U.S.	E7	93
Butler, co., Ky., U.S.	C3	94
Butler, co., Mo., U.S.	E7	102
Butler, co., Ne., U.S.	C8	104
Butler, co., Oh., U.S.	C1	112
Butler, co., Pa., U.S.	E2	115
Butlers Bridge, Ire.	C4	11
Butmīyah, Isr. Occ.	B7	41
Butner, N.C., U.S.	A4	110
Butovo, Sov. Un.	n17	27
Buttahatchee, stm., U.S.	B5	101
Butte, Mt., U.S.	E4	103
Butte, Ne., U.S.	B7	104
Butte, N.D., U.S.	B5	111
Butte, co., Ca., U.S.	C3	82
Butte, co., Id., U.S.	F5	89
Butte, co., S.D., U.S.	C2	118
Butte des Morts, Lake, l., Wi., U.S.	D5	126
Butte Falls, Or., U.S.	E4	114
Butte Mountains, mts., Nv., U.S.	D6	105
Butterfield, Ar., U.S.	g8	81
Butterfield, Mn., U.S.	G4	100
Butterfield, Mo., U.S.	E4	102
Butternut, Wi., U.S.	B3	126
Butternut Lake, l., Wi., U.S.	C5	126
Butterworth, Malay.	D2	34
Butterworth, Transkei	D4	49
Buttevant, Ire.	E3	11
Button Islands, is., N.W. Ter.	f8	72
Button Islands, is., N.W. Ter.	f8	72
Buttonwillow, Ca., U.S.	E4	82
Butts, co., Ga., U.S.	C3	87
Butuan, Phil.	D7	34
Buturlinovka, Sov. Un.	F13	27
Butzbach, W. Ger.	C3	19
Bützow, E. Ger.	B5	18
Buuhoodle, Som.	D6	47
Buulo Berde, Som.	E6	47
Buur Gaabo, Som.	F5	47
Buur Hakaba, Som.	E5	47
Buxtehude, W. Ger.	B4	18
Buxton, Guy.	A3	59
Buxton, Eng., U.K.	A6	12
Buxton, N.C., U.S.	B7	110
Buxton, N.D., U.S.	B8	111
Buxton, Or., U.S.	g11	114
Buxton Center, Me., U.S.	*E2	96
Buy, Sov. Un.	B2	28
Buyck, Mn., U.S.	B6	100
Buynaksk, Sov. Un.	E3	28
Buy Lake, l., Asia	B8	31
Büyükliman see Vakfıkebir, Tur.	B12	40
Büyükmenderes, stm., Tur.	D7	40
Buzachi Peninsula, pen., Sov. Un.	E4	28
Buzancy, Fr.	E4	17
Buzău, Rom.	C8	24
Buzău, stm., Rom.	C8	24
Buzaymah, Libya	E4	43
Buzet, Yugo.	C1	24
Buzuluk, Sov. Un.	C4	28
Buzzard Roost, mtn., N.C., U.S.	B1	110
Buzzards Bay, Ma., U.S.	C6	98
Buzzards Bay, b., Ma., U.S.	C6	98
Byala, Bul.	D7	24
Byala Slatina, Bul.	D6	24
Byam Martin Island, i., N.W. Ter.	m31	66
Byars, Ok., U.S.	C4	113
Bybee, Tn., U.S.	C10	119
Bydgoszcz, Pol.	B5	26
Byelorussia (White Russia), state, Sov. Un.	D5	29
Byemoor, Alta.	D4	68
Byer, Oh., U.S.	C3	112
Byers, Co., U.S.	B6	83
Byers, Ks., U.S.	E5	93
Byers, Tx., U.S.	B3	120
Byersville, Oh., U.S.	C4	112
Byesville, Oh., U.S.	C4	112
Byfield, Ma., U.S.	A6	98
Byglandsfjord, Nor.	H2	14
Byhalia, Ms., U.S.	A4	101
Bykovo, Sov. Un.	n18	27
Bykovo, Sov. Un.	G15	27
Bylas, Az., U.S.	D5	80
Bylot Island, i., N.W. Ter.	B17	66
Byng, Ok., U.S.	C5	113
Byng Inlet, Ont.	B4	73
Bynum, Mt., U.S.	C4	103
Bynum, N.C., U.S.	B3	110
Bynumville, Mo., U.S.	B5	102
Byram, Ms., U.S.	C3	101
Byrd, sci., Ant.	A36	7
Byrd Glacier, ice, Ant.	g40	7
Byrdstown, Tn., U.S.	C8	119
Byrnedale, Pa., U.S.	D5	115
Byrock, Austl.	E6	51
Byromville, Ga., U.S.	D3	87
Byron, Ca., U.S.	h9	82
Byron, Il., U.S.	A4	90
Byron, Me., U.S.	D2	96
Byron, Mn., U.S.	F6	100
Byron, Ne., U.S.	D8	104
Byron, N.Y., U.S.	B2	109
Byron, Wy., U.S.	B4	127
Byron, Cape, c., Austl.	E9	50
Byrum, Den.	A5	15
Byšice-Liblice, Czech.	n18	26
Bystrzyca [Kłodzka], Pol.	C4	26
Bytom (Beuthen), Pol.	C5	26
Bytów, Pol.	A4	26
Byzantium see İstanbul, Tur.	B7	40

C

Name	Map Ref.	Page
Ca, stm., Asia	C6	35
Caacupé, Para.	E4	55
Caaguazú, dept., Para.	E4	55
Čaǎk, Yugo.	D5	24
Caála, Ang.	D2	48
Caamaño Sound, strt., B.C.	C3	69
Caapucú, Para.	E4	55
Caazapá, Para.	E4	55
Caazapá, dept., Para.	E4	55
Cabaceiras, Braz.	h5	57
Caballo, N.M., U.S.	E2	108
Caballo Mountains, mts., N.M., U.S.	E2	108
Caballo Reservoir, res., N.M., U.S.	E2	108
Cabana, Peru	C2	58
Cabanatuan, Phil.	o13	34
Cabano, Que.	B9	74
Cabarita, stm., Jam.	E12	65
Cabarrus, co., N.C., U.S.	B2	110
Cabarruyan Island, i., Phil.	n12	34
Cabbage Swamp, sw., Fl., U.S.	m9	86
Cabeceiras, Braz.	B3	56
Cabedelo, Braz.	E12	57
Cabell, co., W.V., U.S.	C2	125
Cabeza del Buey, Spain	C3	22
Cabezas, Bol.	C3	60
Cabimas, Ven.	A3	60
Cabin Creek, W.V., U.S.	m13	125
Cabin Creek, stm., W.V., U.S.	m13	125
Cabinda, Ang.	C1	48
Cabinda, dept., Ang.	C1	48
Cabinet Gorge Reservoir, res., U.S.	B1	103
Cabinet Mountains, mts., Mt., U.S.	B1	103
Cabin John, Md., U.S.	C3	97
Cable, Wi., U.S.	B2	126
Cabo, Braz.	k6	57
Cabo Blanco, Arg.	D3	54
Cabo Delgado, dept., Moz.	D6	48
Cabo Frio, Braz.	C4	56
Cabo Gracias a Dios, Nic.	D8	63
Cabonga, Réservoir, res., Que.	k11	74
Cabool, Mo., U.S.	D5	102
Caboolture, Austl.	C9	51
Cabora Bassa Lake, res., Moz.	A5	49
Cabot, Ar., U.S.	C3	81
Cabot, Pa., U.S.	E2	115
Cabot, Vt., U.S.	C4	122
Cabot, Mount, mtn., N.H., U.S.	A4	106
Cabot Head, c., Ont.	B3	73
Cabot Strait, strt., Can.	G20	66
Cabras Island, i., Guam	L9	52
Cabrera Baja, Sierra de la, mts., Spain	A2	22
Cabrera Island, i., Spain	C7	22
Cabri, Sask.	G1	75
Cabriel, stm., Spain	C5	22
Cabri Lake, l., Sask.	F1	75
Cabrillo National Monument, Ca., U.S.	o15	82
Cabrobó, Braz.	D3	57
Caçador, Braz.	D2	56
Caçapava do Sul, Braz.	E2	56
Cacapon, stm., W.V., U.S.	B6	125
Cacequi, Braz.	D2	56
Cáceres, Braz.	C4	55
Cáceres, Col.	B2	60
Cáceres, Spain	C2	22
Cachan, Fr.	g10	16
Cache, Ok., U.S.	C3	113
Cache, co., Ut., U.S.	B4	121
Cache, stm., Il., U.S.	F4	90
Cache Bay, Ont.	A5	73
Cache Creek, B.C.	D7	69
Cache Creek, stm., Ca., U.S.	C2	82
Cache Junction, Ut., U.S.	B3	121
Cache la Poudre, stm., Co., U.S.	A5	83
Cache la Poudre, North Fork, stm., Co., U.S.	A5	83
Cache Mountain, mtn., Ak., U.S.	B10	79
Cache Peak, mtn., Id., U.S.	G5	89
Cachi, Arg.	E2	55
Cachimbo, Serra do, mts., Braz.	D4	59
Cachoeira, Braz.	D3	57
Cachoeira de Arari, Braz.	C5	59
Cachoeira do Sul, Braz.	E2	56
Cachoeiro do Itapemirim, Braz.	C4	56
Caçiporé, Braz.	B4	59
Caçiporé, Cabo, c., Braz.	B4	59
Cacique, Pan.	h11	62
Cacolo, Ang.	D2	48
Caconda, Ang.	D2	48
Caçonde, Braz.	k8	56
Cacouna-Station, Que.	B8	74
Cactus Flat, pl., Nv., U.S.	F5	105
Cactus Lake, Sask.	E1	75
Cactus Peak, mtn., Nv., U.S.	F5	105
Cactus Springs, Nv., U.S.	G6	105
Caculé, Braz.	A4	56
Caddo, Ok., U.S.	C5	113
Caddo, Tx., U.S.	C3	120
Caddo, co., La., U.S.	B2	95
Caddo, co., Ok., U.S.	B3	113
Caddo, stm., Ar., U.S.	C2	81
Caddo Creek, stm., Ok., U.S.	C4	113
Caddo Gap, Ar., U.S.	C2	81
Caddo Lake, res., U.S.	B2	95
Caddo Mountains, mtn., Ar., U.S.	C2	81
Cade, La., U.S.	D4	95
Cader Idris, mtn., Wales, U.K.	I9	12
Cades, S.C., U.S.	D8	117
Cades, Tn., U.S.	D10	119
Cades Cove, Tn., U.S.	D10	119
Cadet, Mo., U.S.	C7	102
Cadillac, Sask.	H2	75
Cadillac, Fr.	E3	16
Cadillac, Mi., U.S.	D5	99
Cadillac Mountain, mtn., Me., U.S.	D4	96
Cádiz, Spain	D2	22
Cadiz, Ky., U.S.	D2	94
Cadiz, Oh., U.S.	B4	112
Cadiz, Phil.	C6	34
Cadiz, Gulf of, b., Eur.	D2	22
Cadogan, Alta.	C5	68
Cadogan, Pa., U.S.	E2	115
Cadomin, Alta.	C2	68
Cadott, Wi., U.S.	D2	126
Cadotte, stm., Alta.	A2	68
Cadron Creek, stm., Ar., U.S.	B3	81
Cadwell, Ga., U.S.	D4	87
Cadys Falls, Vt., U.S.	B3	122
Caen, Fr.	C6	16
Caernarfon, Wales, U.K.	D4	10
Caernarfon Bay, b., Wales, U.K.	D4	10
Caerphilly, Wales, U.K.	J5	12
Caesar Creek Lake, res., Oh., U.S.	C2	112
Caetité, Braz.	A4	56
Cafayate, Arg.	E2	55
Cagayan, stm., Phil.	B6	34
Cagayan de Oro, Phil.	D6	34
Cagayan Islands, is., Phil.	D5	34
Cagayan Sulu Island, i., Phil.	D5	34
Cagliari, Italy	E2	23
Cagliari, Gulf of, b., Italy	E2	23
Cagnes-sur-Mer, Fr.	C7	20
Caguán, stm., Col.	C3	60
Caguas, P.R.	G11	64
Cahaba, stm., Al., U.S.	C2	78
Cahaba Heights, Al., U.S.	*B3	78
Cahaba Valley, val., Al., U.S.	B3	78
Caher, Ire.	E4	11
Cahersiveen, Ire.	F1	11
Cahokia, Il., U.S.	E3	90
Cahone, Co., U.S.	D2	83
Cahore Point, c., Ire.	E6	11
Cahors, Fr.	E4	16
Cahuinari, stm., Col.	C3	60
Cahuita, Serra dos, plat., Braz.	E3	59
Caiapônia, Braz.	B2	56
Caibarién, Cuba	C4	64
Cai Bau, i., Viet.	B7	35
Caicara, Ven.	B4	60
Caicedonia, Col.	C2	60
Caicó, Braz.	C3	57
Caicos Islands, is., T./C. Is.	D8	63
Caicos Passage, strt., N.A.	C7	64
Cailloma, Peru	E3	58
Caillou Bay, b., La., U.S.	E5	95
Caillou Lake, l., La., U.S.	E6	95
Caimanera, Cuba	E6	64
Caiman Point, c., Phil.	o12	34
Caimito, stm., Pan.	m11	62
Cains, stm., N.B.	C4	71
Cains Store, Ky., U.S.	C5	94
Cainsville, Mo., U.S.	A4	102
Cainsville, Tn., U.S.	B5	119
Caintown, Ont.	C9	73
Cairnbrook, Pa., U.S.	F4	115
Cairngorm Mountains, mts., Scot., U.K.	C5	13
Cairns, Austl.	C8	50
Cairnsmore of Carsphairn, mtn., Scot., U.K.	E4	13
Cairn Table, mtn., Scot., U.K.	E5	13
Cairo (Al Qāhirah), Eg.	B3	38
Cairo, Ga., U.S.	F2	87
Cairo, Il., U.S.	F4	90
Cairo, Mo., U.S.	B5	102
Cairo, Ne., U.S.	D7	104
Cairo, N.Y., U.S.	C7	109
Cairo, Oh., U.S.	B1	112
Cairo, W.V., U.S.	B3	125
Caiundo, Ang.	E2	48
Cajabamba, Peru	C2	58
Cajamarca, Peru	C2	58
Cajamarca, dept., Peru	C2	58
Cajacay, Peru	C2	58
Caja de Muertos, Isla, i., P.R.	C2	65
Cajatambo, Peru	C2	58
Cajazeiras, Braz.	C3	57
Čajniče, Yugo.	D4	24
Čakovec, Yugo.	B3	24
Čakovice, Czech.	n18	26
Calabar, Nig.	F6	45
Calabasas, Ca., U.S.	m11	82
Calabogie, Ont.	B8	73
Calabogie Lake, l., Ont.	B8	73
Calabozo, Ven.	B4	60
Calabria, prov., Italy	E6	23
Calafat, Rom.	D6	24
Calafate, Arg.	E2	54
Calagua Islands, is., Phil.	o14	34
Calahorra, Spain	A5	22
Calais, Fr.	B4	16
Calais, Me., U.S.	C5	96
Calais, Vt., U.S.	C4	122
Calama, Chile	D2	55
Calamar, Col.	A3	60
Calamar, Col.	C3	60
Calamba, Phil.	o13	34
Calamian Group, is., Phil.	C6	34
Calamocha, Spain	B5	22
Calamus, Ia., U.S.	C7	92
Calamus, stm., Ne., U.S.	B6	104
Calañas, Spain	D2	22
Calanda, Spain	B5	22
Calanscio, Sarīr, des., Afr.	H5	40
Calanscio, Sarīr, des., Libya	D4	43
Calapan, Phil.	C6	34
Călărași, Rom.	C8	24
Calarcá, Col.	C2	60
Calasparra, Spain	C5	22
Calatayud, Spain	B5	22
Calau, E. Ger.	B8	19
Calauag, Phil.	p14	34
Calauag Bay, stm., Phil.	o14	34
Calaveras, co., Ca., U.S.	*C3	82
Calavo Gardens, Ca., U.S.	*o16	82
Calbe, E. Ger.	B6	19
Calbuco, Chile	C2	54
Calca, Peru	D3	58
Calcasieu, co., La., U.S.	D2	95
Calcasieu, stm., La., U.S.	D2	95
Calcasieu Lake, l., La., U.S.	E2	95
Calcasieu Pass, strt., La., U.S.	E2	95
Calceta, Ec.	B1	60
Calchaquí, Arg.	E3	55
Calçoene, Braz.	B4	59
Calcutta, India	D8	36
Calcutta, Oh., U.S.	B5	112
Calcutta Lake, l., Nv., U.S.	B2	105
Caldaro, Italy	C3	20
Caldas, dept., Col.	B2	60
Caldas da Rainha, Port.	C1	22
Calder, Sask.	F5	75
Calder, stm., Eng., U.K.	A6	12
Calder, Loch, l., Scot., U.K.	B5	13
Caldera, Chile	E1	55
Calderwood, Tn., U.S.	D10	119
Caldron Falls Reservoir, res., Wi., U.S.	C5	126
Caldwell, Ar., U.S.	B5	81
Caldwell, Id., U.S.	F2	89
Caldwell, Ks., U.S.	E6	93
Caldwell, N.J., U.S.	B4	107
Caldwell, Oh., U.S.	C4	112
Caldwell, Tx., U.S.	D4	120
Caldwell, W.V., U.S.	D4	125
Caldwell, co., Ky., U.S.	C2	94
Caldwell, co., Mo., U.S.	B3	102
Caldwell, co., N.C., U.S.	B1	110
Caldwell, co., Tx., U.S.	E4	120
Cale, Ar., U.S.	D2	81
Caledon, Ont.	D5	73
Caledon, stm., Afr.	C4	49
Caledonia, Ont.	D5	73
Caledonia, Mi., U.S.	F5	99
Caledonia, Mn., U.S.	G7	100
Caledonia, Ms., U.S.	B5	101
Caledonia, N.Y., U.S.	C3	109
Caledonia, Oh., U.S.	B3	112
Caledonia, co., Vt., U.S.	B4	122
Caledonian Canal, Scot., U.K.	C4	13
Calella, Spain	B7	22
Calera, Al., U.S.	B3	78
Calera, Ok., U.S.	D5	113
Caleta Olivia, Arg.	D3	54
Calexico, Ca., U.S.	F6	82
Calf of Man, i., I. of Man	D4	10
Calgary, Alta.	D3	68
Calhan, Co., U.S.	B6	83
Calheta, Port.	h11	22
Calhoun, Al., U.S.	C3	78
Calhoun, Ga., U.S.	B2	87
Calhoun, Il., U.S.	E5	90

Name	Map Ref.	Page
Calhoun, Ky., U.S.	C2	94
Calhoun, La., U.S.	B3	95
Calhoun, Mo., U.S.	C4	102
Calhoun, Tn., U.S.	D9	119
Calhoun, co., Al., U.S.	B4	78
Calhoun, co., Ar., U.S.	D3	81
Calhoun, co., Fl., U.S.	B1	86
Calhoun, co., Ga., U.S.	E2	87
Calhoun, co., Il., U.S.	D3	90
Calhoun, co., Ia., U.S.	B3	92
Calhoun, co., Mi., U.S.	F5	99
Calhoun, co., Ms., U.S.	B4	101
Calhoun, co., S.C., U.S.	D6	117
Calhoun, co., Tx., U.S.	E4	120
Calhoun, co., W.V., U.S.	C3	125
Calhoun City, Ms., U.S.	B4	101
Calhoun Falls, S.C., U.S.	C2	117
Cali, Col.	C2	60
Calico Rock, Ar., U.S.	A3	81
Calicut (Kozhikode), India	F6	36
Caliente, Ca., U.S.	E4	82
Caliente, Nv., U.S.	F7	105
Califon, N.J., U.S.	B3	107
California, Ky., U.S.	k14	94
California, Md., U.S.	*D4	97
California, Mo., U.S.	C5	102
California, Pa., U.S.	F2	115
California, state, U.S.	D4	82
California, Golfo de, b., Mex.	B2	63
California Aqueduct, Ca., U.S.	E4	82
California Junction, Ia., U.S.	A3	54
California Oil Camp, Co., U.S.	A2	83
Calingasta, Arg.	A3	54
Calio, N.D., U.S.	A7	111
Calion, Ar., U.S.	D3	81
Calipatria, Ca., U.S.	F6	82
Calispell Peak, mtn., Wa., U.S.	A8	124
Calistoga, Ca., U.S.	C2	82
Callabonna, stm., Austl.	D1	51
Callabonna, Lake, l., Austl.	D3	51
Callaghan, Mount, mtn., Nv., U.S.	D5	105
Callahan, Fl., U.S.	B5	86
Callahan, Ks., U.S.	g12	93
Callahan, co., Tx., U.S.	C3	120
Callan, Ire.	E4	11
Callander, Ont.	A5	73
Callander, Scot., U.K.	B4	10
Callands, Va., U.S.	D3	123
Callao, Peru	F3	58
Callao, Mo., U.S.	B5	102
Callao, Ut., U.S.	C6	123
Callao, dept., Peru	*D2	58
Callaway, Fl., U.S.	*u16	86
Callaway, Md., U.S.	D4	97
Callaway, Mn., U.S.	D3	100
Callaway, Ne., U.S.	C6	104
Callaway, Va., U.S.	C2	123
Callaway, co., Mo., U.S.	C6	102
Callender, Ia., U.S.	B3	92
Callensburg, Pa., U.S.	D2	115
Callery, Pa., U.S.	E1	115
Callicoon, N.Y., U.S.	D5	109
Callicoon Center, N.Y., U.S.	D6	109
Calliham, Tx., U.S.	E3	120
Calling Lake, Alta.	B4	68
Calling Lake, l., Alta.	B4	68
Calloway, co., Ky., U.S.	f9	94
Calmar, Alta.	C4	68
Calmar, Ia., U.S.	A6	92
Calne, Eng., U.K.	C5	12
Caloosahatchee, stm., Fl., U.S.	F5	86
Caloundra, Austl.	E9	50
Calpella, Ca., U.S.	C2	82
Calpet, Wy., U.S.	D2	127
Caltagirone, Italy	F5	23
Caltanissetta, Italy	F5	23
Caltra, Ire.	D3	11
Caluire [-et-Cuire], Fr.	E6	16
Calulo, Ang.	D1	48
Calumet, Que.	D3	74
Calumet, Ia., U.S.	A2	92
Calumet, Mi., U.S.	B2	99
Calumet, Mn., U.S.	C5	100
Calumet, co., Wi., U.S.	D5	126
Calumet, Lake, l., Il., U.S.	k9	90
Calumet City, Il., U.S.	B6	90
Calumet Park, Il., U.S.	*k9	90
Calumet Sag Channel, Il., U.S.	k9	90
Calumetville, Wi., U.S.	k9	126
Calunda, Ang.	D3	48
Caluula, Som.	C7	47
Calvary, Ga., U.S.	F2	87
Calvary, Wi., U.S.	k9	126
Calvert, Al., U.S.	D1	78
Calvert, Tx., U.S.	D4	120
Calvert, co., Md., U.S.	C4	97
Calvert City, Ky., U.S.	e9	94
Calvert Island, i., B.C.	D3	69
Calverton, Md., U.S.	B4	97
Calverton, Va., U.S.	B5	123
Calverton Park, Mo., U.S.	f13	102
Calvi, Fr.	C2	23
Calvillo, Mex.	m12	63
Calvin, La., U.S.	C3	95
Calvin, N.D., U.S.	A7	111
Calvin, Ok., U.S.	C5	113
Calvinia, S. Afr.	D2	49
Calvörde, E. Ger.	A6	19
Calw, W. Ger.	E3	19
Calwa, Ca., U.S.	*D4	82
Calypso, N.C., U.S.	B4	110
Calzada de Calatrava, Spain	C4	22
Cam, stm., Eng., U.K.	D7	10
Camabatela, Ang.	C2	48
Camacho, Mex.	C4	63
Camacupa, Ang.	D2	48
Camagüey, Cuba	D5	64
Camagüey, prov., Cuba	C4	64
Camajuani, Cuba	C4	64
Camak, Ga., U.S.	C4	87
Camamu, Braz.	D3	57
Camaná, Peru	E3	58
Camanche, Ia., U.S.	C7	92
Camanducaia, Braz.	m8	56
Camano Island, i., Wa., U.S.	A3	124
Camapuã, Braz.	B2	56
Camaquã, Braz.	E2	56
Camaquã, stm., Braz.	E2	56
Camararé, stm., Braz.	E3	59
Camargo, Bol.	D2	55
Camargo, Il., U.S.	D5	90
Camarillo, Ca., U.S.	*E4	82
Camarón, Cabo, c., Hond.	D7	63
Camarones, Bahía, b., Arg.	C3	54
Camas, Wa., U.S.	D3	124
Camas, co., Id., U.S.	F4	89
Camas Valley, Or., U.S.	D3	114
Ca Mau, Viet.	D3	34
Ca Mau, Cape, c., Viet.	D2	34

Camberwell, Austl.	*G8	50
Cambodia, ctry., Asia	C3	34
Camborne [-Redruth], Eng., U.K.	E4	10
Cambrai, Fr.	B5	16
Cambria, Pa., U.S.	D9	115
Cambria, Ca., U.S.	E3	82
Cambria, Ia., U.S.	D4	92
Cambria, Mi., U.S.	G6	99
Cambria, Wi., U.S.	E4	126
Cambria, co., Pa., U.S.	E4	115
Cambrian Mountains, mts., Wales, U.K.	D5	10
Cambrian Park, Ca., U.S.	*D3	82
Cambridge, Ont.	D4	73
Cambridge, Eng., U.K.	D7	10
Cambridge, Il., U.S.	B3	90
Cambridge, Ks., U.S.	E7	93
Cambridge, Me., U.S.	C3	96
Cambridge, Md., U.S.	C5	97
Cambridge, Ma., U.S.	B5	98
Cambridge, Mn., U.S.	E5	100
Cambridge, Ne., U.S.	D5	104
Cambridge, N.Y., U.S.	B7	109
Cambridge, Oh., U.S.	B4	112
Cambridge, Vt., U.S.	B3	122
Cambridge Bay, N.W. Ter.	C12	66
Cambridge City, In., U.S.	E7	91
Cambridge Junction, Vt., U.S.	B3	122
Cambridgeport, Vt., U.S.	E3	122
Cambridge Reservoir, res., Ma., U.S.	g10	98
Cambridge Springs, Pa., U.S.	C1	115
Cambuí, Braz.	m8	56
Cambundi-Catembo (Nova Gaia), Ang.	D2	48
Camden, Al., U.S.	D2	78
Camden, Ar., U.S.	D3	81
Camden, De., U.S.	D3	85
Camden, Il., U.S.	C3	90
Camden, In., U.S.	C4	91
Camden, Me., U.S.	D3	96
Camden, Mi., U.S.	G6	99
Camden, Mo., U.S.	B3	102
Camden, N.J., U.S.	D2	107
Camden, N.Y., U.S.	B5	109
Camden, N.C., U.S.	A6	110
Camden, Oh., U.S.	C1	112
Camden, S.C., U.S.	C6	117
Camden, Tn., U.S.	A3	119
Camden, Tx., U.S.	D5	120
Camden, W.V., U.S.	B4	125
Camden, co., Ga., U.S.	F5	87
Camden, co., Mo., U.S.	C5	102
Camden, co., N.J., U.S.	D3	107
Camden, co., N.C., U.S.	A6	110
Camden on Gauley, W.V., U.S.	C4	125
Camdenton, Mo., U.S.	D5	102
Camelback Mountain, mtn., Az., U.S.	k9	80
Camelot, Wa., U.S.	*B3	124
Camels Hump, mtn., Vt., U.S.	C3	122
Camerino, Italy	C4	23
Cameron, Az., U.S.	B4	80
Cameron, Il., U.S.	C3	90
Cameron, La., U.S.	E2	95
Cameron, Mo., U.S.	B3	102
Cameron, Mt., U.S.	E5	103
Cameron, N.C., U.S.	B3	110
Cameron, Ok., U.S.	B7	113
Cameron, Pa., U.S.	D5	115
Cameron, S.C., U.S.	D6	117
Cameron, Tx., U.S.	D4	120
Cameron, W.V., U.S.	B4	125
Cameron, Wi., U.S.	C2	126
Cameron, co., La., U.S.	E2	95
Cameron, co., Pa., U.S.	D5	115
Cameron, co., Tx., U.S.	F4	120
Cameron Hills, hills, Can.	f7	66
Cameron Island, i., N.W. Ter.	m31	66
Cameron Park, Ca., U.S.	*C3	82
Cameroon, ctry., Afr.	D2	46
Cameroon, Mont, mtn., Cam.	E1	46
Cametá, Braz.	D4	59
Camiling, Phil.	o13	34
Camilla, Ga., U.S.	E2	87
Camiña, Chile	C2	55
Camino, Ca., U.S.	C3	82
Camissombo (Veríssimo Sarmento), Ang.	C3	48
Camlachie, Ont.	D2	73
Cammack Village, Ar., U.S.	C3	81
Cammal, Pa., U.S.	D7	115
Camocim, Braz.	B2	57
Camooweal, Austl.	C1	50
Camopi, stm., Fr. Gu.	B4	59
Camp, co., Tx., U.S.	C5	120
Campagna di Roma, reg., Italy	h9	23
Campaign, Tn., U.S.	D8	119
Campana, Arg.	g7	54
Campana, i., Chile	D1	54
Campanario, Spain	C3	22
Campania, prov., Italy	D5	23
Campania Island, i., B.C.	C3	69
Campbell, Al., U.S.	D2	78
Campbell, Ca., U.S.	k8	82
Campbell, Fl., U.S.	D5	86
Campbell, Mn., U.S.	D2	100
Campbell, Mo., U.S.	E7	102
Campbell, Ne., U.S.	D7	104
Campbell, N.Y., U.S.	C3	109
Campbell, Oh., U.S.	A5	112
Campbell, co., Ky., U.S.	B5	94
Campbell, co., S.D., U.S.	B5	118
Campbell, co., Tn., U.S.	C9	119
Campbell, co., Va., U.S.	C3	123
Campbell, co., Wy., U.S.	B7	127
Campbell, Cape, c., N.Z.	N15	51
Campbellford, Ont.	C7	73
Campbell Hill, Il., U.S.	F4	90
Campbell Hill, hill, Oh., U.S.	B2	112
Campbell Island, B.C.	C3	69
Campbell Island, i., N.Z.	J8	2
Campbell Lake, l., Or., U.S.	E7	114
Campbell River, B.C.	D5	69
Campbells Bay, Que.	B8	73
Campbellsburg, In., U.S.	G5	91
Campbellsburg, Ky., U.S.	B4	94
Campbells Creek, stm., W.V., U.S.	m13	125
Campbellsport, Wi., U.S.	E5	126
Campbellsville, Ky., U.S.	C4	94
Campbellsville, Tn., U.S.	B4	119
Campbellton, N.B.	A3	71
Campbellton, Newf.	D4	72
Campbellton, P.E.I.	C5	71

Campbellton, Fl., U.S.	B1	86
Campbelltown, Austl.	*F9	50
Campbeltown, Scot., U.K.	C4	10
Camp Creek, Tn., U.S.	C11	119
Camp Crook, S.D., U.S.	B2	118
Camp Douglas, Wi., U.S.	E3	126
Campeche, Mex.	D6	63
Campeche, state, Mex.	D6	63
Campeche, Bahía de, b., Mex.	C6	63
Campechuela, Cuba	D5	64
Camperdown, Austl.	I4	51
Camperville, Man.	D1	70
Camp Grove, Il., U.S.	B4	90
Camp Hill, Al., U.S.	C4	78
Camp Hill, Pa., U.S.	F8	115
Camp H. M. Smith Marine Corps Base, mil., Hi., U.S.	g10	88
Camp Howard Ridge, mtn., Id., U.S.	D2	89
Campiglia Marittima, Italy	C3	23
Campina Grande, Braz.	C3	57
Campinas, Braz.	C3	56
Campina Verde, Braz.	B3	56
Campion, Co., U.S.	A5	83
Campione d'Italia, Italy	D4	20
Camp Lejeune Marine Corps Base, mil., N.C., U.S.	C5	110
Campo, Cam.	E1	46
Campo, Ca., U.S.	F5	82
Campo, Co., U.S.	D8	83
Campoalegre, Col.	C2	60
Campo Alegre de Goiás, Braz.	B3	56
Campobasso, Italy	D5	23
Campobello, S.C., U.S.	A3	117
Campobello Island, i., N.B.	E3	71
Campo Belo, Braz.	C3	56
Campo de Criptana, Spain	C4	22
Campodolcino, Italy	D7	21
Campo Gallo, Arg.	E3	55
Campo Grande, Braz.	C2	56
Campo Maior, Braz.	B2	57
Campo Maior, Port.	C2	22
Campo Mourão, Braz.	C2	56
Campo Real, Spain	p18	22
Campos, Braz.	C4	56
Campos Altos, Braz.	B3	56
Camposampiero, Italy	D7	20
Campos Belos, Braz.	A3	56
Campos Novos, Braz.	D2	56
Campos Sales, Braz.	C2	57
Campo Tencia, mtn., Switz.	D6	21
Campo Tures, Italy	C7	20
Camp Pendleton Marine Corps Base, mil., Ca., U.S.	F5	82
Camp Point, Il., U.S.	C2	90
Camp San Saba, Tx., U.S.	D3	120
Camp Sherman, Or., U.S.	C5	114
Camp Springs, Md., U.S.	f9	97
Campti, La., U.S.	C2	95
Campton, Fl., U.S.	v15	86
Campton, Ga., U.S.	C3	87
Campton, Ky., U.S.	C6	94
Campton, N.H., U.S.	C3	106
Campton, Pa., U.S.	C9	115
Camptonville, In., U.S.	I4	91
Campton, W.V., U.S.	m13	125
Cannes, Fr.	F7	16

Candle Lake, l., Sask.	D3	75
Candler, Fl., U.S.	C5	86
Candler, co., Ga., U.S.	D4	87
Candlewood, Lake, l., Ct., U.S.	D1	84
Candlewood Isle, Ct., U.S.	D2	84
Candlewood Knolls, Ct., U.S.	*D2	84
Candlewood Shores, Ct., U.S.	D2	84
Candlewood Trails, Ct., U.S.	*C2	84
Cando, Sask.	E1	75
Cando, N.D., U.S.	A6	111
Candor, N.Y., U.S.	C4	109
Candor, N.C., U.S.	B3	110
Cane, stm., U.S.	C2	95
Canea see Khaniá, Grc.	E5	40
Canehill, Ar., U.S.	B1	81
Canela, Braz.	D2	56
Canelones, Ur.	E1	56
Canelones, dept., Ur.	g8	54
Canendiyu, dept., Para.	A5	55
Cañete, Chile	B2	54
Caney, Ks., U.S.	E8	93
Caney, Ok., U.S.	C6	94
Caney, stm., Ok., U.S.	A5	113
Caney Creek, stm., Tx., U.S.	r14	120
Caney Fork, stm., Tn., U.S.	C8	119
Caneyville, Ky., U.S.	C3	94
Canfield, Ar., U.S.	D2	81
Canfield, Oh., U.S.	A5	112
Cangallo, Peru	D3	58
Cangamba, Ang.	D2	48
Cangas, Spain	A1	22
Cangas de Narcea, Spain	A2	22
Cangas de Onís, Spain	A3	22
Cangombe, Ang.	D3	48
Canguaretama, Braz.	C3	57
Canguçu, Braz.	E2	56
Cangzhou, China	D8	31
Canhotinho, Braz.	k5	57
Caniapiscau, stm., Que.	g13	74
Caniapiscau, Lac, l., Que.	h12	74
Canicanian, Phil.	o14	34
Canicattì, Italy	F4	23
Caniles, Spain	D4	22
Canim Lake, B.C.	D7	69
Canim Lake, l., B.C.	D7	69
Canindé, Braz.	B3	57
Canindé, stm., Braz.	C2	57
Canistear Reservoir, res., N.J., U.S.	A4	107
Canisteo, N.Y., U.S.	C3	109
Canisteo, stm., N.Y., U.S.	C3	109
Canistota, S.D., U.S.	D8	118
Canjilon, N.M., U.S.	A3	108
Canjinlon, Tur.	B9	40
Canlaon Volcano, vol., Phil.	C6	34
Canmore, Alta.	D3	68
Canna, i., Scot., U.K.	C4	94
Canna, Sound of, strt., Scot., U.K.	C2	13
Cannelburg, In., U.S.	G5	91
Cannel City, Ky., U.S.	C6	94
Cannelton, In., U.S.	I4	91
Cannelton, Pa., U.S.	B5	90
Cannes, Fr.	F7	16
Canneto sull'Oglio, Italy	D6	20
Cannich, Scot., U.K.	C4	8
Canning, Austl.	*F2	50
Canning, N.S.	D5	71
Cannington, Ont.	C5	73
Cannock, Eng., U.K.	B5	12
Cannon, De., U.S.	F3	85
Cannon, co., Tn., U.S.	B5	119
Cannon, stm., Mn., U.S.	F5	100
Cannon Air Force Base, mil., N.M., U.S.	C6	108
Cannonball, N.D., U.S.	C5	111
Cannonball, stm., N.D., U.S.	C5	111
Cannon Beach, Or., U.S.	B3	114
Cannondale, Ct., U.S.	E2	84
Cannon Falls, Mn., U.S.	F6	100
Cannonsburg, Ky., U.S.	B7	94
Cannonsville Reservoir, res., N.Y., U.S.	C5	109
Cannonville, Ut., U.S.	F3	121
Canoas, stm., Braz.	D2	56
Canoe, B.C.	D8	69
Canoe, Al., U.S.	D2	78
Canoe, stm., B.C.	C8	69
Canoe Lake, Ont.	B6	73
Canoinhas, Braz.	D2	56
Canon, Al., U.S.	B3	87
Canon City, Co., U.S.	C5	83
Canones, N.M., U.S.	A3	108
Canon Plaza, N.M., U.S.	A3	108
Canoochee, stm., Ga., U.S.	D5	87
Canora, Sask.	F4	75
Canosa di Puglia, Italy	D6	23
Canouan, i., St. Vin.	V26	65
Canova, S.D., U.S.	D8	118
Canso, N.S.	D8	71
Cantabrian Mountains, mts., U.S.	A3	22
Cantanhede, Port.	B1	22
Cantário, stm., Braz.	E2	59
Cantaura, Ven.	B5	60
Canterbury, Austl.	*F9	50
Canterbury, N.B.	D2	71
Canterbury, Eng., U.K.	E7	10
Canterbury, Ct., U.S.	C8	84
Canterbury, De., U.S.	D3	85
Canterbury, N.H., U.S.	D3	106
Canterbury Bight, N.Z.	P13	51
Can Tho, Viet.	G6	35
Canton, Ct., U.S.	B4	84
Canton, Ga., U.S.	B2	87
Canton, Il., U.S.	C3	90
Canton, Ks., U.S.	D6	93
Canton, Ky., U.S.	D2	94
Canton, Me., U.S.	D2	96
Canton, Ma., U.S.	B5	98
Canton, Mi., U.S.	*p15	99
Canton, Ms., U.S.	C3	101
Canton, Mo., U.S.	A6	102
Canton, N.Y., U.S.	f9	109
Canton, N.C., U.S.	f10	110
Canton, Oh., U.S.	B4	112
Canton, Ok., U.S.	A3	113
Canton, Pa., U.S.	C8	115
Canton, S.D., U.S.	D9	118
Canton, Tx., U.S.	C5	120
Canton Center, Ct., U.S.	B4	84
Canton see Guangzhou, China	G7	31

Canton Lake, res., Ok., U.S.	A3	113
Cantril, Ia., U.S.	D5	92
Cantù, Italy	B2	23
Cantuar, Sask.	G1	75
Cantwell, Ak., U.S.	C10	79
Cañuelas, Arg.	B5	54
Canumã, stm., Braz.	C3	59
Canutama, Braz.	D2	59
Canute, Ok., U.S.	B2	113
Canutillo, Tx., U.S.	o11	120
Canwood, Sask.	D2	75
Cany-Barville, Fr.	E8	12
Canyon, Tx., U.S.	B2	120
Canyon, co., Id., U.S.	F2	89
Canyoncito, N.M., U.S.	h9	108
Canyon City, Or., U.S.	C8	114
Canyon Country, Ca., U.S.	*E4	82
Canyon Creek, Alta.	B3	68
Canyon de Chelly National Monument, Az., U.S.	A6	80
Canyon Ferry Lake, res., Mt., U.S.	D5	103
Canyon Lake, Tx., U.S.	E3	120
Canyon Lake, res., Tx., U.S.	E3	120
Canyonlands National Park, Ut., U.S.	E6	121
Canyonville, Or., U.S.	E3	114
Cao Bang, Viet.	A7	35
Caonao, stm., Cuba	D4	64
Caorle, Italy	D8	20
Capac, Mi., U.S.	F8	99
Capakçur see Bingöl, Tur.	C13	40
Capanaparo, stm., Ven.	B7	74
Capanema, Braz.	B1	57
Capão Bonito, Braz.	C3	56
Capão Doce, Morro do, mtn., Braz.	D2	56
Caparica, Port.	f9	22
Caparo, stm., Ven.	B3	60
Capasin, Sask.	E4	75
Capatárida, Ven.	A3	60
Cap-aux-Meules, Que.	B8	71
Cap aux Meules, Île du, i., Que.	B8	71
Capbreton, Fr.	F3	16
Cap-Chat, Que.	G19	66
Cap-de-la-Madeleine, Que.	C5	74
Capdenac-Gare, Fr.	E5	16
Cape, prov., S. Afr.	D3	49
Cape Barren, i., Austl.	o15	51
Cape Breton, co., N.S.	C9	71
Cape Breton Highlands National Park, N.S.	C9	71
Cape Breton Island, i., N.S.	C9	71
Cape Broyle, Newf.	E5	72
Cape Canaveral, Fl., U.S.	D6	86
Cape Charles, Newf.	B4	72
Cape Charles, Va., U.S.	C6	123
Cape Coast, Ghana	E4	45
Cape Cod Bay, b., Ma., U.S.	C6	98
Cape Cod Canal, Ma., U.S.	C6	98
Cape Cod National Seashore, Ma., U.S.	C7	98
Cape Coral, Fl., U.S.	F5	86
Cape Dorset, N.W. Ter.	D17	66
Cape Elizabeth, Me., U.S.	E2	96
Cape Fair, Mo., U.S.	E4	102
Cape Fear, stm., N.C., U.S.	C4	110
Cape Girardeau, Mo., U.S.	D8	102
Cape Girardeau, co., Mo., U.S.	D8	102
Cape Hatteras National Seashore, N.C., U.S.	B7	110
Cape Horn Mountain, mtn., Id., U.S.	E3	89
Cape Island, i., S.C., U.S.	E9	117
Cape la Hune, Newf.	E3	72
Cape Lookout National Seashore, N.C., U.S.	C6	110
Capelinha, Braz.	B4	56
Capelongo, Ang.	E2	48
Cape May, N.J., U.S.	F3	107
Cape May, co., N.J., U.S.	E3	107
Cape May Court House, N.J., U.S.	E3	107
Cape May Point, N.J., U.S.	F3	107
Cape Neddick, Me., U.S.	E2	96
Cape Pole, Ak., U.S.	n23	79
Cape Porpoise, Me., U.S.	E2	96
Cape Ray, Newf.	E2	72
Capers Inlet, b., S.C., U.S.	k12	117
Capers Island, i., S.C., U.S.	G6	117
Capers Island, i., S.C., U.S.	F8	117
Cape Sable Island, i., N.S.	F4	71
Cape Saint Claire, Md., U.S.	*B5	97
Capesterre, Guad.	H14	64
Cape Tormentine, N.B.	C6	71
Cape Town (Kaapstad), S. Afr.	D3	49
Cape Verde, ctry., Afr.	E3	42
Cape Vincent, N.Y., U.S.	A4	109
Cape York Peninsula, pen., Austl.	B7	50
Cap-Haïtien, Haiti	E11	64
Capim, stm., Braz.	D4	59
Capinota, Bol.	C2	55
Capitan, N.M., U.S.	D4	108
Capitan Bado, Para.	A4	55
Capitan Mountains, mts., N.M., U.S.	D4	108
Capitan Peak, mtn., N.M., U.S.	D4	108
Capitol, Mt., U.S.	E12	103
Capitol Heights, Ia., U.S.	e8	92
Capitol Heights, Md., U.S.	C4	97
Capitol Peak, mtn., Nv., U.S.	B4	105
Capitol Reef National Park, Ut., U.S.	E4	121
Capitol View, S.C., U.S.	*D6	117
Capitola, Fl., U.S.	B2	86
Capitola, Ca., U.S.	*D3	82
Capleville, Tn., U.S.	e9	119
Cap Mountain, mtn., N.W. Ter.	B6	125
Capon Bridge, W.V., U.S.	B6	125
Capon Springs, W.V., U.S.	B6	125
Capote Knob, mtn., Tx., U.S.	k8	120
Cappoquin, Ire.	E4	11
Capreol, Ont.	p19	73
Capri, Italy	D5	23
Capricorn Channel, strt., Austl.	D9	50
Capricorn Group, is., Austl.	A8	51
Caprock, N.M., U.S.	D6	108
Capron, Il., U.S.	A5	90

Capron, Ok., U.S.	A3	113
Capron, Va., U.S.	D5	123
Cap-Rouge, Que.	n17	74
Cap-Saint-Ignace, Que.	B7	74
Cap-Santé, Que.	C6	74
Capshaw, Al., U.S.	A3	78
Captain Cook, Hi., U.S.	D6	88
Captiva, Fl., U.S.	F4	86
Captiva Island, i., Fl., U.S.	F4	86
Capua, Italy	D5	23
Capulin, N.M., U.S.	A6	108
Capulin Mountain National Monument, N.M., U.S.	A6	108
Caputa, S.D., U.S.	D3	118
Caquetá, dept., Col.	C3	60
Caquetá (Japurá), stm., S.A.	C3	60
Carabaña, Spain	p18	22
Carabanchel Bajo, Spain	p17	22
Carabinani, stm., Braz.	D5	60
Carabobo, state, Ven.	A4	60
Caracal, Rom.	C7	24
Caracaraí, Braz.	B2	59
Caracas, Ven.	A4	60
Caraguatay, Para.	B4	55
Caraí, Braz.	B4	56
Carajás, Braz.	D5	59
Carajás, Serra dos, mts., Braz.	D4	59
Carangola, Braz.	C4	56
Caransebeș, Rom.	C6	24
Carapari, Bol.	D3	55
Carapeguá, Para.	E4	55
Carapó, Braz.	C1	56
Caratasca, Laguna de, b., Hond.	D8	63
Caratinga, Braz.	B4	56
Caratunk, Me., U.S.	C3	96
Carauari, Braz.	B4	58
Caraúbas, Braz.	h5	57
Caraúbas, Braz.	C3	57
Caravaca, Spain	C5	22
Caravelas, Braz.	E3	57
Caraveli, Peru	E3	58
Caraway, Ar., U.S.	B5	81
Caraz, Peru	C2	58
Carazinho, Braz.	D1	56
Carballino, Spain	A1	22
Carballo, Spain	A1	22
Carberry, Man.	E2	70
Carbet, Pitons du, mts., Mart.	S10	65
Carbó, Mex.	B2	63
Carbon, In., U.S.	E3	91
Carbon, Tx., U.S.	C3	120
Carbon, W.V., U.S.	m13	125
Carbon, co., Mt., U.S.	E7	103
Carbon, co., Pa., U.S.	E10	115
Carbon, co., Ut., U.S.	D5	121
Carbon, co., Wy., U.S.	E5	127
Carbonado, Wa., U.S.	B3	124
Carbonara, Cape, c., Italy	E2	23
Carbondale, Alta.	C4	68
Carbondale, Co., U.S.	B3	83
Carbondale, Il., U.S.	F4	90
Carbondale, Ks., U.S.	D8	93
Carbondale, Pa., U.S.	C10	115
Carbonear, Newf.	E5	72
Carbon Hill, Al., U.S.	B2	78
Carbon Hill, Il., U.S.	B5	90
Carbonia, Italy	E2	23
Carbonne, Fr.	F4	16
Carbonville, Ut., U.S.	D5	121
Carbury, N.D., U.S.	A5	111
Carcagente, Spain	C5	22
Carcans, Étang de, b., Fr.	F5	16
Carcassonne, Fr.	F5	16
Carcross, Yukon	D6	66
Cardale, Man.	D1	70
Cardardale, Tur.	D7	25
Cárdenas, Cuba	m14	63
Cárdenas, Mex.	D6	63
Cárdenas, Mex.	C4	63
Çardi, Tur.	D2	54
Cardiel, Lago, l., Arg.	D2	54
Cardiff, Wales, U.K.	E5	10
Cardiff, Al., U.S.	f7	78
Cardiff, Md., U.S.	A5	97
Cardiff, N.J., U.S.	E3	107
Cardigan, P.E.I.	C7	71
Cardigan, Wales, U.K.	D4	10
Cardigan, Mount, mtn., N.H., U.S.	C3	106
Cardigan Bay, b., P.E.I.	C7	71
Cardigan Bay, b., Wales, U.K.	D4	10
Cardinal, Ont.	C9	73
Cardinal Lake, l., Alta.	A2	68
Cardington, Oh., U.S.	B3	112
Cardona, Ur.	E1	56
Cardona, Spain	B1	22
Cardross, Sask.	H3	75
Cardston, Alta.	E4	68
Cardville, Me., U.S.	C4	96
Cardwell, Mo., U.S.	E7	102
Cardwell Mountain, mtn., Tn., U.S.	D8	119
Carega, mtn., Italy	D7	20
Carei, Rom.	B6	24
Carencro, La., U.S.	D3	95
Carenero, Ven.	A4	60
Carentan, Fr.	C3	16
Caretta, W.V., U.S.	D3	125
Carey, Id., U.S.	F5	89
Carey, Oh., U.S.	B2	112
Carey, Tx., U.S.	B2	120
Carey, Lake, l., Austl.	E3	50
Careysburg, Lib.	G3	45
Careywood, Id., U.S.	A2	89
Carhaix, Fr.	C2	16
Carhuás, Peru	C2	58
Carhué, Arg.	B4	54
Cariamanga, Ec.	B2	58
Cariati, Italy	E6	23
Caribana, Punta, c., Col.	B2	60
Caribbean Sea	—	—
Cariboo Mountains, mts., B.C.	C7	69
Caribou, Me., U.S.	B5	96
Caribou, co., Id., U.S.	G7	89
Caribou Lake, l., Me., U.S.	C3	96
Caribou Mountain, mtn., Id., U.S.	F7	89
Caribou Mountain, mtn., Me., U.S.	C2	96
Caribou Mountains, mts., Alta.	B4	68
Caribou Range, mts., Id., U.S.	F7	89
Carichic, Mex.	B3	63
Carievale, Sask.	H5	75
Carignan, Fr.	C6	16
Carinhanha, Braz.	A4	56
Carini, Italy	E4	23
Carinish, Scot., U.K.	C1	13
Carinthia, hist. reg., Aus.	E6	18

Cari-Ceda

Index

Name	Map Ref.	Page
Caripe, Ven.	A5	60
Caripito, Ven.	A5	60
Cariús, Braz.	C3	57
Carl Blackwell, Lake, res., Ok., U.S.	A4	113
Carle Place, N.Y., U.S.	*n15	109
Carleton, Mi., U.S.	F7	99
Carleton, Ne., U.S.	D8	104
Carleton, co., N.B.	C2	71
Carleton, Mount, mtn., N.B.	B3	71
Carleton Place, Ont.	B8	73
Carletonville, S. Afr.	C4	49
Carlile, Wy., U.S.	B8	127
Carlin, Nv., U.S.	C5	105
Carlingford, Ire.	C5	11
Carlingford Lough, b., Eur.	C5	11
Carlinville, Il., U.S.	D4	90
Carlisle, Eng., U.K.	C5	10
Carlisle, Ar., U.S.	C4	81
Carlisle, In., U.S.	G3	91
Carlisle, Ia., U.S.	C4	92
Carlisle, Ky., U.S.	B5	94
Carlisle, Ma., U.S.	f10	98
Carlisle, Ms., U.S.	C3	101
Carlisle, Oh., U.S.	C1	112
Carlisle, Pa., U.S.	F7	115
Carlisle, S.C., U.S.	B5	117
Carlisle, Tn., U.S.	A4	119
Carlisle, co., Ky., U.S.	f8	94
Carlit, Pic, mtn., Fr.	F4	16
Carl Junction, Mo., U.S.	D3	102
Carlock, Il., U.S.	C4	90
Carloforte, Italy	E2	23
Carlos, Md., U.S.	k13	97
Carlos, Mn., U.S.	E3	100
Carlos Casares, Arg.	B4	54
Carlos Chagas, Braz.	B4	56
Carlos City, In., U.S.	D7	91
Carlos Tejedor, Arg.	B4	54
Carlota, Ca., U.S.	B1	82
Carlow, Ire.	D3	10
Carlow, co., Ire.	E5	11
Carloway, Scot., U.K.	B2	13
Carlowville, Al., U.S.	C2	78
Carlsbad, Ca., U.S.	F5	82
Carlsbad, N.M., U.S.	E5	108
Carlsbad, Tx., U.S.	D2	120
Carlsbad Caverns National Park, N.M., U.S.	E5	108
Carlsbad Springs, Ont.	h13	73
Carlsborg, Wa., U.S.	A2	124
Carlstadt, N.J., U.S.	h8	107
Carlton, Sask.	E2	75
Carlton, Eng., U.K.	B6	12
Carlton, Al., U.S.	D2	78
Carlton, Ga., U.S.	B3	87
Carlton, Ks., U.S.	D6	93
Carlton, Mn., U.S.	D6	100
Carlton, Or., U.S.	B3	114
Carlton, Tx., U.S.	D3	120
Carlton, co., Mn., U.S.	D6	100
Carluke, Scot., U.K.	E5	13
Carlyle, Sask.	H4	75
Carlyle, Il., U.S.	E4	90
Carlyle, Mt., U.S.	D12	103
Carlyle Lake, res., Il., U.S.	E4	90
Carmacks, Yukon	D5	66
Carmagnola, Italy	B1	23
Carman, Man.	E2	70
Carmangay, Alta.	D4	68
Carmanville, Newf.	D4	72
Carmarthen, Wales, U.K.	E4	10
Carmarthen Bay, b., Wales, U.K.	E4	10
Carmaux, Fr.	E5	16
Carmel, Ca., U.S.	D3	82
Carmel, In., U.S.	E5	91
Carmel, La., U.S.	B2	95
Carmel, Me., U.S.	D3	96
Carmel, N.J., U.S.	E2	107
Carmel, N.Y., U.S.	D7	109
Carmel, Mount, mtn., Isr.	B7	41
Carmel Head, c., Wales, U.K.	A3	12
Carmelo, Ur.	E1	56
Carmen, Az., U.S.	F4	80
Carmen, Id., U.S.	D5	89
Carmen, Ok., U.S.	A3	113
Carmen, Isla, i., Mex.	B2	63
Carmen, Río del, stm., Chile	D2	55
Carmen Alto, Chile	D2	55
Carmen de Areco, Arg.	A5	54
Carmen [del Paraná], Para.	E4	55
Carmen de Patagones, Arg.	E4	54
Carmer Hill, hill, Pa., U.S.	C6	115
Carmi, Il., U.S.	E5	90
Carmi, Lake, l., Vt., U.S.	B3	122
Carmichael, Bah.	m17	64
Carmichael, Sask.	G1	75
Carmichael, Ca., U.S.	*C3	82
Carmichaels, Pa., U.S.	G2	115
Carmine, Tx., U.S.	D3	120
Carmona, Spain	D3	22
Carnarvon, Austl.	D1	50
Carnarvon, S. Afr.	D3	49
Carnation, Wa., U.S.	B4	124
Carnaxide, Port.	f9	22
Carndonagh, Ire.	B4	11
Carnduff, Sask.	H5	75
Carnegie, Ga., U.S.	E2	87
Carnegie, Ok., U.S.	B3	113
Carnegie, Pa., U.S.	F1	115
Carnegie, Lake, l., Austl.	E3	50
Carnes, Ms., U.S.	E4	101
Carnesville, Ga., U.S.	B3	87
Carnew, Ire.	E5	11
Carney, Md., U.S.	*B4	97
Carney, Mi., U.S.	C3	99
Carney, Ok., U.S.	B4	113
Carneys Point, N.J., U.S.	D2	107
Carnforth, Eng., U.K.	F6	13
Carnic Alps, mts., Eur.	A4	23
Car Nicobar, i., India	G9	36
Carnlough, N. Ire., U.K.	C6	11
Carnot, Cen. Afr. Rep.	D3	46
Carnoustie, Scot., U.K.	*F1	115
Carnsore Point, c., Ire.	D6	13
Carnuel, N.M., U.S.	D3	10
Caro, Mi., U.S.	B3	108
Carol City, Fl., U.S.	E7	99
Caroleen, N.C., U.S.	s13	86
Carolina, Braz.	B1	110
Carolina, P.R.	E10	54
Carolina, S. Afr.	*B4	65
Carolina, W.V., U.S.	C5	49
Carolina Beach, N.C., U.S.	k10	125
Carolinas, Puntan, c., N. Mar. Is.	C5	110
Caroline, Alta.	E7	52
Caroline, Wi., U.S.	C3	68
Caroline, co., Md., U.S.	D5	126
Caroline, co., Va., U.S.	C6	97
	C5	123
Caroline, atoll, Kir.	G13	6
Caroline Islands, is., T.T.P.I.	F8	6
Carol Stream, Il., U.S.	*k8	90
Caron, Sask.	G3	75
Carona, Ks., U.S.	E9	93
Caroni, stm., Trin.	N23	65
Caroní, stm., Ven.	B5	60
Carora, Ven.	A3	60
Carouge, Switz.	E3	18
Carp, Ont.	B8	73
Carpathian Mountains, mts., Eur.	F13	8
Carpentaria, Gulf of, b., Austl.	B6	50
Carpenter, Ia., U.S.	A4	92
Carpenter, S.D., U.S.	C8	118
Carpenter, Wy., U.S.	E8	127
Carpenter Dam, Ar., U.S.	g7	81
Carpentersville, Il., U.S.	A5	90
Carpentersville, N.J., U.S.	B2	107
Carpentras, Fr.	E6	16
Carpi, Italy	B3	23
Carpinteria, Ca., U.S.	E4	82
Carpio, N.D., U.S.	A4	111
Carp Lake, l., B.C.	C6	99
Carpolac see Morea, Austl.	B6	69
Carr, Co., U.S.	D3	10
Carrabassett Valley, Me., U.S.	C2	96
Carrabelle, Fl., U.S.	C2	86
Carradale, Scot., U.K.	E3	13
Carragana, Sask.	E4	75
Carraraza, Cabo, c., Chile	B2	54
Carrara, Italy	B3	23
Carrauntoohil, mtn., Ire.	E2	23
Carrboro, N.C., U.S.	B3	110
Carrbridge, Scot., U.K.	C5	13
Carrcroft Crest, De., U.S.	*A3	85
Carriacou, i., Gren.	W26	65
Carrickfergus, N. Ire., U.K.	C4	10
Carrickmacross, Ire.	D5	11
Carrick on Shannon, Ire.	D3	11
Carrick on Suir, Ire.	D3	10
Carrie, Mount, mtn., Wa., U.S.	B2	124
Carrier, Que.	o17	74
Carrier, Ms., U.S.	A3	113
Carriere, Ms., U.S.	E4	101
Carrier Mills, Il., U.S.	F5	90
Carrigaholt, Ire.	D3	11
Carrigaline, Ire.	F3	11
Carrigan, Mount, mtn., N.H., U.S.	B4	106
Carrigan Head, c., Ire.	C3	11
Carrington, N.D., U.S.	B6	111
Carrington Island, i., Ut., U.S.	C3	121
Carrión, stm., Spain	A3	22
Carrión de los Condes, Spain	A3	22
Carrizal Bajo, Chile	E1	55
Carrizo Creek, stm., U.S.	A1	120
Carrizo Mountain, mtn., N.M., U.S.	D4	108
Carrizo Mountains, mts., U.S.	A6	80
Carrizo Springs, Tx., U.S.	E3	120
Carrizo Wash, val., U.S.	C6	80
Carrizozo, N.M., U.S.	D4	108
Carr Mountain, mtn., N.H., U.S.	C3	106
Carroll, Ia., U.S.	B3	92
Carroll, Me., U.S.	C4	96
Carroll, Ne., U.S.	B8	104
Carroll, Oh., U.S.	C3	112
Carroll, co., Ar., U.S.	A2	81
Carroll, co., Ga., U.S.	C1	87
Carroll, co., Il., U.S.	A4	90
Carroll, co., In., U.S.	C4	91
Carroll, co., Ia., U.S.	B3	92
Carroll, co., Ky., U.S.	B4	94
Carroll, co., Md., U.S.	A3	97
Carroll, co., Ms., U.S.	B4	101
Carroll, co., Mo., U.S.	B4	102
Carroll, co., N.H., U.S.	C4	106
Carroll, co., Oh., U.S.	B4	112
Carroll, co., Tn., U.S.	B3	119
Carroll, co., Va., U.S.	D2	123
Carroll Lake, l., Can.	D4	70
Carrolls, Wa., U.S.	C3	124
Carrollton, Al., U.S.	B1	78
Carrollton, Ga., U.S.	C1	87
Carrollton, Il., U.S.	D3	90
Carrollton, Ky., U.S.	B4	94
Carrollton, Mi., U.S.	E7	99
Carrollton, Ms., U.S.	B4	101
Carrollton, Mo., U.S.	B4	102
Carrollton, Oh., U.S.	B4	112
Carrollton, Tx., U.S.	*n10	120
Carrolltown, Pa., U.S.	E4	115
Carrollwood, Fl., U.S.	*E4	86
Carron, stm., Scot., U.K.	C3	13
Carron, Loch, b., Scot., U.K.	B4	10
Carrot, stm., Can.	D4	75
Carrot River, Sask.	D4	75
Carrowmore, Lake, l., Ire.	C2	11
Carrsville, Ky., U.S.	e9	94
Caruthers, Sask.	E1	75
Carville, Al., U.S.	C4	78
Carry Falls Reservoir, res., N.Y., U.S.	f10	109
Carrying Place, Ont.	C7	73
Çarşamba, Tur.	B11	40
Carseland, Alta.	D4	68
Carson, Ca., U.S.	*E4	82
Carson, Ia., U.S.	C2	92
Carson, Ms., U.S.	D4	101
Carson, N.M., U.S.	A4	108
Carson, N.D., U.S.	C4	111
Carson, Wa., U.S.	C5	124
Carson, co., Tx., U.S.	B2	120
Carson, stm., Nv., U.S.	D2	105
Carson City, Mi., U.S.	E6	99
Carson City, Nv., U.S.	D2	105
Carson Lake, l., Nv., U.S.	D3	105
Carson Sink, l., Nv., U.S.	D3	105
Carson Spring, Tn., U.S.	D10	119
Carsonville, Mi., U.S.	E8	99
Carstairs, Alta.	D3	68
Carswell Air Force Base, mil., Tx., U.S.	n9	120
Cartagena, Chile	A2	54
Cartagena, Col.	A2	60
Cartagena, Spain	D5	22
Cartago, Col.	E2	60
Cartago, C.R.	F8	63
Carta Valley, Tx., U.S.	E2	120
Cartaxo, Port.	C1	22
Cartaya, Spain	D2	22
Carter, Ky., U.S.	B6	94
Carter, Mt., U.S.	F8	103
Carter, Ok., U.S.	B2	113
Carter, S.D., U.S.	D5	118
Carter, Tn., U.S.	C11	119
Carter, Wy., U.S.	E2	127
Carter, co., Ky., U.S.	B6	94
Carter, co., Mo., U.S.	E7	102
Carter, co., Mt., U.S.	E12	103
Carter, co., Ok., U.S.	C4	113
Carter, co., Tn., U.S.	C11	119
Carter Dome, mtn., N.H., U.S.	B4	106
Carteret, N.J., U.S.	B4	107
Carteret, co., N.C., U.S.	C6	110
Carter Lake, Ia., U.S.	C2	92
Carter Mountain, mtn., Wy., U.S.	B3	127
Carters, Ga., U.S.	B2	87
Cartersburg, In., U.S.	E5	91
Carters Lake, res., Ga., U.S.	B2	87
Cartersville, Ga., U.S.	B2	87
Cartersville, S.C., U.S.	C7	117
Cartersville, Va., U.S.	C4	123
Carterville, Il., U.S.	F4	90
Carterville, Mo., U.S.	D3	102
Carthage, Ar., U.S.	C3	81
Carthage, Il., U.S.	C2	90
Carthage, In., U.S.	E6	91
Carthage, Ms., U.S.	C4	101
Carthage, Mo., U.S.	D3	102
Carthage, N.Y., U.S.	B5	109
Carthage, N.C., U.S.	B3	110
Carthage, S.D., U.S.	C8	118
Carthage, Tn., U.S.	C8	119
Carthage, Tx., U.S.	C5	120
Carthage, hist., Tun.	B7	44
Cartier, i., Austl.	B3	50
Cartwright, Man.	E2	70
Cartwright, Newf.	B3	72
Cartwright, N.D., U.S.	B2	111
Cartwright, Ok., U.S.	D5	113
Caruaru, Braz.	C3	57
Carúpano, Ven.	A5	60
Caruthersville, Mo., U.S.	E8	102
Carver, Ma., U.S.	C6	98
Carver, Mn., U.S.	F5	100
Carver, co., Mn., U.S.	F5	100
Carver Ranch Estates, Fl., U.S.	*r13	86
Carville, La., U.S.	h9	95
Carvin, Fr.	D2	17
Cary, Ga., U.S.	D3	87
Cary, Il., U.S.	A5	90
Cary, Ms., U.S.	C3	101
Cary, N.C., U.S.	B4	110
Caryville, Fl., U.S.	u16	86
Caryville, Tn., U.S.	C9	119
Casa, Ar., U.S.	B2	81
Casablanca, Mor.	C3	44
Casa Blanca, N.M., U.S.	B2	108
Casa Branca, Braz.	C3	56
Casa de Oro, Ca., U.S.	*F5	82
Casa Grande, Az., U.S.	E4	80
Casa Grande National Monument, Az., U.S.	E4	80
Casale Monferrato, Italy	B2	23
Casalmaggiore, Italy	B3	23
Casanare, dept., Col.	B3	60
Casanare, stm., Col.	B3	60
Casanova, Va., U.S.	B5	123
Casape, Italy	h9	23
Casa Piedra, Tx., U.S.	p12	120
Casar, N.C., U.S.	B1	110
Casarano, Italy	D7	23
Casas Adobes, Az., U.S.	E5	80
Cascade, B.C.	E8	69
Cascade, Co., U.S.	C6	83
Cascade, Id., U.S.	E3	89
Cascade, Ia., U.S.	B6	92
Cascade, Mo., U.S.	D7	102
Cascade, Mt., U.S.	C5	103
Cascade, N.H., U.S.	B4	106
Cascade, Va., U.S.	D3	123
Cascade, W.V., U.S.	E5	125
Cascade, Wi., U.S.	E5	126
Cascade, co., Mt., U.S.	C5	103
Cascade Locks, Or., U.S.	B5	114
Cascade Point, c., N.Z.	O12	51
Cascade Range, mts., U.S.	B3	76
Cascade Reservoir, res., Id., U.S.	E3	89
Cascade Summit, Or., U.S.	D4	114
Cascade Tunnel, Wa., U.S.	B5	124
Cascade Vista, Wa., U.S.	*B3	124
Cascadia, Or., U.S.	C4	114
Cascais, Port.	C1	22
Cascais Bay, b., Port.	f9	22
Cascajal, stm., Pan.	h11	62
Cascavel, Braz.	C2	56
Cascavel, Braz.	B3	57
Cascilla, Ms., U.S.	B3	101
Casco, Me., U.S.	D2	96
Casco, Wi., U.S.	D6	126
Casco Bay, b., Me., U.S.	E3	96
Caseyr (Cape Guardafui), c., Som.	C7	47
Cash, Ar., U.S.	B5	81
Cashel, Ire.	C3	10
Cashiers, N.C., U.S.	f9	110
Cashion, Az., U.S.	m8	80
Cashion, Ok., U.S.	B4	113
Cashmere, Wa., U.S.	B5	124
Cashton, Wi., U.S.	E3	126
Cashtown, Pa., U.S.	G7	115
Casiguran, Phil.	n14	34
Casiguran Sound, strt., Phil.	n13	34
Casilda, Arg.	A4	54
Casilda, Cuba	D3	64
Casino, Austl.	D9	51
Casiquiare, stm., Ven.	C4	60
Casjaks, Ky., U.S.	C5	94
Čáslav, Czech.	D26	26
Casma, Peru	E3	58
Casmalia, Ca., U.S.	E3	82
Caspar, Ca., U.S.	C1	82
Caspe, Spain	B5	22
Casper, Wy., U.S.	D6	127
Caspian, Mi., U.S.	B2	99
Caspian Depression, pl., Sov. Un.		
Caspian Lake, l., Vt., U.S.	B4	122
Caspian Sea		
Cass, In., U.S.	F3	91
Cass, W.V., U.S.	C4	125
Cass, co., Il., U.S.	D3	90
Cass, co., In., U.S.	C5	91
Cass, co., Ia., U.S.	C3	92
Cass, co., Mi., U.S.	G4	99
Cass, co., Mn., U.S.	D4	100
Cass, co., Ne., U.S.	D9	104
Cass, co., N.D., U.S.	C8	111
Cass, co., Tx., U.S.	C5	120
Cassadaga, N.Y., U.S.	C1	109
Cassano [de la Selva], Spain	B7	22
Cassai (Kasai), stm., Afr.	D3	48
Cassano, Italy	E5	99
Casselberry, Fl., U.S.	D5	86
Cassel see Kassel, W. Ger.	C4	18
Casselman, Ont.	B9	73
Casselman, Pa., U.S.	G3	115
Casselton, N.D., U.S.	C8	111
Cassia, co., Id., U.S.	G5	89
Cassiar, B.C.	m17	69
Cassiar Mountains, mts., Can.	E6	66
Cassidy, B.C.	f12	69
Cassilândia, Braz.	B2	56
Cassinga, Ang.	E2	48
Cassino, Italy	D4	23
Cass Lake, Mn., U.S.	C4	100
Cass Lake, l., Mn., U.S.	C4	100
Cassoday, Ks., U.S.	D7	93
Cassopolis, Mi., U.S.	G4	99
Cassville, Ga., U.S.	B1	112
Cassville, Mo., U.S.	E4	102
Cassville, Wi., U.S.	F3	126
Castalia, Ia., U.S.	A6	92
Castalia, N.C., U.S.	A4	110
Castalia, Oh., U.S.	A3	112
Castalian Springs, Tn., U.S.	A5	119
Castana, Ia., U.S.	B2	92
Castanea, Pa., U.S.	D7	115
Castanheira de Pêra, Port.	E2	22
Castaños, Mex.	C4	63
Castel di Guido, Italy	h8	23
Castelfranco Emilia, Italy	E7	20
Castelfranco Veneto, Italy	D7	20
Castel Gandolfo, Italy	h9	23
Castel Giuliano, Italy	g8	23
Casteljaloux, Fr.	E4	16
Castella, Ca., U.S.	B2	82
Castellammare, Italy	D3	20
Castelli, Arg.	B5	54
Castellón de la Plana, Spain	C5	22
Castel Madama, Italy	h9	23
Castelnaudary, Fr.	F4	16
Castelo, Braz.	C4	56
Castelo Branco, Port.	C2	22
Castelo de Vide, Port.	C2	22
Castel San Pietro dell'Emilia, Italy	E7	20
Castelsarrasin, Fr.	E4	16
Castelvetrano, Italy	F4	23
Castilla, Pampa del, pl., Arg.	D3	54
Castile, N.Y., U.S.	C2	109
Castine, Me., U.S.	D4	96
Castione [della Presolana], Italy	E9	21
Castle, Ok., U.S.	B5	113
Castle Air Force Base, mil., Ca., U.S.	D3	82
Castlebar, Ire.	D2	10
Castlebay, Scot., U.K.	D1	13
Castlebellingham, Ire.	D5	11
Castleberry, Al., U.S.	D2	78
Castleblayney, Ire.	C5	11
Castlecomer, Ire.	E4	11
Castle Dale, Ut., U.S.	D4	121
Castlederg, N. Ire., U.K.	C4	11
Castle Dome Mountains, mts., Az., U.S.	D1	80
Castle Dome Peak, mtn., Az., U.S.	D1	80
Castle Douglas, Scot., U.K.	C5	10
Castlefinn, Ire.	C4	11
Castleford, Id., U.S.	G4	89
Castlegar, B.C.	E9	69
Castlegregory, Ire.	E1	11
Castle Harbour, b., Ber.	o20	64
Castle Hayne, N.C., U.S.	C5	110
Castle Hills, De., U.S.	i7	85
Castle Hot Springs, Az., U.S.	D3	80
Castleisland, Ire.	E2	11
Castlemaine, Austl.	H5	51
Castlemaine, Ire.	E2	11
Castlemartyr, Ire.	F3	11
Castle Mountain, mtn., Yukon	D5	66
Castle Mountains, mts., Mt., U.S.	D6	103
Castle Park, Ca., U.S.	*o15	82
Castle Peak, mtn., Co., U.S.	B4	83
Castle Peak, mtn., Id., U.S.	E4	89
Castle Point, Mo., U.S.	f13	102
Castlepollard, Ire.	D4	11
Castlerea, Ire.	D3	11
Castlereagh, N. Ire., U.K.	*C6	11
Castlereagh, stm., Austl.	E7	51
Castle Rock, Co., U.S.	B6	83
Castle Rock, Wa., U.S.	F5	100
Castle Rock, Wa., U.S.	C3	124
Castle Rock, mtn., Or., U.S.	C8	114
Castle Rock, mtn., Va., U.S.	C4	123
Castle Rock Butte, mtn., S.D., U.S.	B2	118
Castle Rock Lake, res., Wi., U.S.	E4	126
Castle Shannon, Pa., U.S.	*k13	115
Castleton, Ont.	C7	73
Castleton, Jam.	E15	65
Castleton, Il., U.S.	B4	90
Castleton, Ks., U.S.	g11	93
Castleton, Vt., U.S.	D2	122
Castleton on Hudson, N.Y., U.S.	C7	109
Castletown, I. of Man	F4	13
Castletown Geoghegan, Ire.	D4	11
Castletownroche, Ire.	E3	11
Castlewellan, N. Ire., U.K.	C6	11
Castlewood, S.D., U.S.	C8	118
Castlewood, Va., U.S.	f9	123
Castor, Alta.	C5	68
Castor, La., U.S.	B2	95
Castor, stm., Mo., U.S.	D7	102
Castor Creek, stm., La., U.S.	B3	95
Castorland, N.Y., U.S.	B5	109
Castres, Fr.	F5	16
Castries, St. Luc.	J14	64
Castro, Braz.	C2	56
Castro, Chile	E2	55
Castro, co., Tx., U.S.	B1	120
Castro Alves, Braz.	B3	57
Castro Daire, Port.	B2	22
Castro [del Río], Spain	D3	22
Castro Marim, Port.	D2	22
Castropol, Spain	A2	22
Castrop-Rauxel, W. Ger.	*C3	18
Castro Urdiales, Spain	A4	22
Castro Valley, Ca., U.S.	h8	82
Castro Verde, Port.	D1	22
Castrovillari, Italy	E6	23
Castroville, Ca., U.S.	D3	82
Castroville, Tx., U.S.	E3	120
Castrovirreyna, Peru	D2	58
Castuera, Spain	C3	22
Caswell, co., N.C., U.S.	A3	110
Catacamas, Hond.	E7	63
Catacaos, Peru	C1	58
Catacocha, Ec.	B2	58
Catacombs, hist., Italy	h9	23
Cataguases, Braz.	C4	56
Cataguuamo, stm., U.S.	k12	97
Catahoula, co., La., U.S.	C4	95
Catahoula Lake, l., La., U.S.	C3	95
Catalão, Braz.	B3	56
Çatalca, Tur.	D5	72
Catalina, Newf.	E5	55
Catalina, Chile	E2	55
Catalina Foothills, Az., U.S.	*E5	80
Catalina Island, i., Ca., U.S.	F4	82
Catalonia, hist. reg., Spain	B6	22
Catamarca, Arg.	B2	54
Catamarca, prov., Arg.	B2	54
Catamayo, Ec.	p14	34
Catanauan, Phil.	C6	34
Catanduva, Braz.	C3	56
Catanduanes, i., Phil.	C5	91
Catania, Italy	F5	23
Catania, Gulf of, b., Italy	F5	23
Cataño, P.R.	B3	65
Catanzaro, Italy	E6	23
Cataract, In., U.S.	F4	91
Cataract, Wi., U.S.	D3	126
Cataract Canyon, val., Ut., U.S.	E5	121
Catarina, Tx., U.S.	E3	120
Catarroja, Spain	C5	22
Catasauqua, Pa., U.S.	E11	115
Catastrophe, Cape, c., Austl.	F6	50
Cataula, Ga., U.S.	D2	87
Cataumet, Ma., U.S.	C6	98
Catawba, N.C., U.S.	B1	110
Catawba, S.C., U.S.	B6	117
Catawba, Va., U.S.	C2	123
Catawba, W.V., U.S.	h10	125
Catawba, Wi., U.S.	C3	126
Catawba, co., N.C., U.S.	B1	110
Catawba, stm., S.C., U.S.	B6	117
Catawba, South Fork, stm., N.C., U.S.	B1	110
Catawba Island, Oh., U.S.	A3	112
Catawissa, Pa., U.S.	E9	115
Cat Ba, i., Viet.	B7	35
Catbalogan, Phil.	C6	34
Cat Creek, Mt., U.S.	C8	103
Cateechee, S.C., U.S.	B2	117
Cates, In., U.S.	E3	91
Cathance, Lake, l., Me., U.S.	D5	96
Cathay, N.D., U.S.	B6	111
Cathedral Bluffs, clf., Co., U.S.	B2	83
Cathedral Caverns, Al., U.S.	A3	78
Cathedral City, Ca., U.S.	F5	82
Cathedral Mountain, mtn., Tx., U.S.	o13	120
Cathedral of the Pines, N.H., U.S.	E3	106
Catherine, Al., U.S.	C2	78
Catherine, Lake, res., Ar., U.S.	C3	81
Cathlamet, Wa., U.S.	C2	124
Cat Island, i., Bah.	B6	64
Cat Island, i., Ma., U.S.	f12	98
Cat Island, i., S.C., U.S.	E9	117
Cativá, Pan.	k11	62
Catlettsburg, Ky., U.S.	B7	94
Catlin, Il., U.S.	C6	90
Catlin, In., U.S.	E3	91
Catnip Mountain, mtn., Nv., U.S.	B2	105
Cato, N.Y., U.S.	B4	109
Catoche, Cabo, c., Mex.	C7	63
Catoctin Mountain, mtn., U.S.	B2	97
Catonsville, Md., U.S.	B4	97
Catoosa, Ok., U.S.	A6	113
Catoosa, co., Ga., U.S.	B1	87
Catriló, Arg.	B4	54
Catrimani, Braz.	B2	59
Catrimani, stm., Braz.	B2	59
Catron, co., N.M., U.S.	D1	108
Catron, Mo., U.S.	E8	102
Catskill, N.Y., U.S.	C7	109
Catskill Mountains, mts., N.Y., U.S.	C6	109
Catt, Mount, mtn., B.C.	B3	69
Cattaraugus, N.Y., U.S.	C2	109
Cattaraugus, co., N.Y., U.S.	C2	109
Cattaraugus Creek, stm., N.Y., U.S.	C2	109
Cattaraugus Indian Reservation, N.Y., U.S.	C2	109
Cattolica, Italy	C4	23
Catumbela, stm., Ang.	D1	48
Catwick, Îles is., Viet.	G8	35
Caubvick, Mount (Mont d'Iberville), mtn., Can.	f9	72
Cauca, dept., Col.	C2	60
Cauca, stm., Col.	B2	60
Caucasia, Col.	B2	60
Caucasus Mountains, mts., Sov. Un.	E7	29
Cauchon Lake, l., Man.	B3	70
Caucomgomoc Lake, l., Me., U.S.	B3	96
Caudete, Spain	C5	22
Caudry, Fr.	B5	16
Caughnawaga, Que.	q19	74
Caulfield, Austl.	*G8	50
Caúngula, Ang.	C3	48
Cauquenes, Chile	B2	54
Caura, stm., Ven.	B5	60
Causey, N.M., U.S.	C6	108
Caussade, Fr.	E4	16
Cauthron, Ar., U.S.	C1	81
Caution, Cape, c., B.C.	D3	69
Cauto, stm., Cuba	D5	64
Cauvery, stm., India	F6	36
Cavaillon, Fr.	F6	16
Cavalcante, Braz.	A3	56
Cavalier, N.D., U.S.	A8	111
Cavalier, co., N.D., U.S.	A7	111
Cavallo, mtn., Italy	C8	20
Cavan, Ire.	D4	11
Cavan, co., Ire.	D4	11
Cavarzere, Italy	B4	23
Cave, Italy	h9	23
Cave City, Ar., U.S.	B4	81
Cave City, Ky., U.S.	C4	94
Cave Creek, Az., U.S.	D4	80
Cave In Rock, Il., U.S.	F5	90
Cave Junction, Or., U.S.	E3	114
Cavell, Sask.	D5	68
Cavendish, Id., U.S.	C2	89
Cavendish, Vt., U.S.	E3	122
Cavendish, i., Wi., U.S.	D6	126
Cave Point, c., Wi., U.S.	B6	94
Cave Run Lake, res., Ky., U.S.	B1	87
Cave Spring, Ga., U.S.	C2	123
Cave Spring, Va., U.S.	h9	23
Cave Springs, Ar., U.S.	A1	81
Cavetown, Md., U.S.	A2	97
Cavetown, Md., U.S.	B4	59
Caviana, Ilha, i., Braz.	o13	34
Cavite, Phil.	C7	118
Cavour, S.D., U.S.	C5	126
Cavour, Wi., U.S.	C5	13
Cawdor, Scot., U.K.	D6	94
Cawker City, Ks., U.S.	C5	93
Cawood, Ky., U.S.	E8	69
Cawston, B.C.	B2	58
Caxambu, Braz.	D2	56
Caxias, Braz.	B2	58
Caxias do Sul, Braz.	C1	48
Caxito, Ang.	A2	58
Cayambe, Ec.	A2	58
Cayambe, vol., Ec.	f8	94
Cayce, Ky., U.S.	D5	117
Cayce, S.C., U.S.	B4	59
Cayenne, Fr. Gu.	B4	59
Cayenne, ter., Fr. Gu.	D9	12
Cayeux-sur-Mer, Fr.	G11	64
Cayey, P.R.	B3	65
Cayey, Sierra de, mts., P.R.	D2	56
Cayley, Alta.	B4	59
Caynabo, Som.	D6	47
Cay Point, c., Bah.	n17	64
Cayuga, Ont.	E5	73
Cayuga, In., U.S.	E3	91
Cayuga, Ms., U.S.	C3	101
Cayuga, N.D., U.S.	C8	111
Cayuga, co., N.Y., U.S.	C4	109
Cayuga Heights, N.Y., U.S.	C4	109
Cayuga Lake, l., N.Y., U.S.	C4	109
Cayuse, Or., U.S.	B8	114
Cazalla de la Sierra, Spain	D3	22
Cazaux, Étang de, b., Fr.	E3	16
Cazenovia, N.Y., U.S.	C5	109
Cazenovia, Wi., U.S.	E3	126
Cazombo, Ang.	D3	48
Cazorla, Spain	D4	22
Cea, stm., Spain	A3	22
Ceanannus Mór (Kells), Ire.	D5	11
Ceará, state, Braz.	C3	57
Ceará Mirim, Braz.	C3	57
Ceará-Mirim, stm., Braz.	g6	57
Cebolla, N.M., U.S.	A3	108
Cebolla Creek, stm., Co., U.S.	C3	83
Cebollar, Arg.	B2	55
Cebollati, stm., Ur.	E2	56
Cebreros, Spain	B3	22
Cebu, Phil.	C6	34
Cebu, i., Phil.	C6	34
Cecil, Al., U.S.	C3	78
Cecil, Ga., U.S.	E3	87
Cecil, Oh., U.S.	A1	112
Cecil, Pa., U.S.	F1	115
Cecil, Wi., U.S.	D5	126
Cecil, co., Md., U.S.	A6	97
Cecil Field Naval Air Station, mil., Fl., U.S.	B5	86
Cecilia, Ky., U.S.	C4	94
Cecilton, Md., U.S.	B6	97
Cecina, Italy	C3	23
Cedar, Ks., U.S.	C5	93
Cedar, Mn., U.S.	E5	100
Cedar, co., Ia., U.S.	C6	92
Cedar, co., Mo., U.S.	D4	102
Cedar, co., Ne., U.S.	B8	104
Cedar, stm., Ia., U.S.	B7	104
Cedar, stm., Ne., U.S.	C7	104
Cedar, stm., Wa., U.S.	B4	124
Cedar Bluff, Al., U.S.	A4	78
Cedar Bluff, Va., U.S.	C2	94
Cedarbluff, Ms., U.S.	B5	101
Cedar Bluff, Tn., U.S.	D9	119
Cedar Bluff Reservoir, res., Ks., U.S.	D4	93
Cedar Bluffs, Ks., U.S.	C3	93
Cedar Bluffs, Ne., U.S.	C9	104
Cedar Breaks National Monument, Ut., U.S.	F3	121
Cedar City, Mo., U.S.	C5	102
Cedar City, Ut., U.S.	F2	121
Cedar Creek, Az., U.S.	D5	80
Cedarcreek, Mo., U.S.	E5	102
Cedar Creek, stm., U.S.	C2	109
Cedar Creek, stm., In., U.S.	A7	91
Cedar Creek, stm., Ia., U.S.	D6	92
Cedar Creek, stm., Mo., U.S.	C5	102
Cedar Creek, stm., N.J., U.S.	D4	107
Cedar Creek, stm., N.D., U.S.	C3	111
Cedar Creek, stm., Oh., U.S.	e7	112
Cedar Creek Lake, res., Tx., U.S.	C4	120
Cedaredge, Co., U.S.	C3	83
Cedar Falls, Ia., U.S.	B5	92
Cedar Gap, Mo., U.S.	D5	102
Cedar Grove, In., U.S.	F8	91
Cedar Grove, N.J., U.S.	B4	107
Cedar Grove, W.V., U.S.	C3	125
Cedar Grove, Wi., U.S.	E6	126
Cedar Hill, Mo., U.S.	g12	102
Cedar Hill, N.M., U.S.	A2	108
Cedar Hill, Tn., U.S.	A5	119
Cedar Hill, Tx., U.S.	n10	120
Cedar Hills, Or., U.S.	*h12	114
Cedarhurst, N.Y., U.S.	k13	109
Cedar Island, i., N.C., U.S.	C6	110
Cedar Island, i., S.C., U.S.	E9	117
Cedar Island, i., Va., U.S.	C7	123
Cedar Key, Fl., U.S.	C3	86
Cedar Keys, is., Fl., U.S.	C3	86
Cedar Knolls, N.J., U.S.	B3	107
Cedar Lake, In., U.S.	B3	91
Cedar Lake, l., Ont.	C1	70
Cedar Lake, rès., Il., U.S.	F4	90
Cedar Mills, Mn., U.S.	F4	100
Cedar Mountain, mtn., Ca., U.S.	B3	82
Cedar Mountains, mts., Ut., U.S.	C2	121
Cedar Point, Il., U.S.	B4	90

Cedar Point, Ks., U.S. — D7 93
Cedar Point, c., Md., U.S. — D5 97
Cedar Point, c., Oh., U.S. — A3 112
Cedar Point, c., Oh., U.S. — e7 112
Cedar Rapids, Ia., U.S. — C6 92
Cedar Rapids, Ne., U.S. — C7 104
Cedar River, Mi., U.S. — C3 99
Cedar Run, Pa., U.S. — D4 107
Cedar Springs, Ont. — E2 73
Cedar Springs, Ga., U.S. — E1 87
Cedar Springs, Mi., U.S. — E5 99
Cedar Swamp, sw., Ma., U.S. — f11 98
Cedartown, Ga., U.S. — B1 87
Cedarvale, B.C. — B3 69
Cedar Vale, Ks., U.S. — E7 93
Cedarvale, N.M., U.S. — C4 108
Cedar Valley, Ut., U.S. — C3 121
Cedarville, Al., U.S. — B1 81
Cedarville, Ca., U.S. — B3 82
Cedarville, Il., U.S. — A4 90
Cedarville, In., U.S. — B7 91
Cedarville, Ma., U.S. — *C6 98
Cedarville, Mi., U.S. — A6 99
Cedarville, N.J., U.S. — E2 107
Cedarville, N.Y., U.S. — C5 109
Cedarville, Oh., U.S. — C2 112
Cedoux, Sask. — H4 75
Cedros, Hond. — C4 62
Cedros, Isla, i., Mex. — B1 63
Ceduna, Austl. — F5 50
Ceel Buur, Som. — E6 47
Ceel Xamurre, Som. — D6 47
Ceepeecee, B.C. — E4 69
Ceerigaabo, Som. — C6 47
Cefalù, Italy — E6 23
Cega, stm., Spain — B3 22
Cegléd, Hung. — B4 24
Ceglie Messapico, Italy — D6 23
Çehegín, Spain — C5 22
Čelákovice, Czech. — n18 26
Celaya, Mex. — m13 63
Celebes (Sulawesi), i., Indon. — F6 34
Celebes Sea, Asia — E6 34
Celendín, Peru — C2 58
Celestine, In., U.S. — H4 91
Celica, Ec. — B2 58
Celina, Oh., U.S. — B1 112
Celina, Tn., U.S. — C8 119
Celina, Tx., U.S. — C4 120
Celje, Yugo. — B2 24
Celle, W. Ger. — B5 18
Cellina, stm., Italy — C8 20
Celoron, N.Y., U.S. — C1 109
Celriver, S.C., U.S. — B6 117
Celtic Sea, Eur. — F5 11
Cemaes Head, c., Wales, U.K. — F5 11
Cement, Ok., U.S. — C3 113
Cement City, Mi., U.S. — F6 99
Cementon, Pa., U.S. — E10 115
Çemişgezek, Tur. — C12 40
Cenderawasih Bay, b., Indon. — F9 34
Cenon, Fr. — E3 16
Centenary, S.C., U.S. — C9 117
Centennial, Wy., U.S. — E6 127
Centennial Lake, res., Ont. — B7 73
Centennial Mountains, mts., Id., U.S. — E7 89
Center, Co., U.S. — D4 83
Center, Ga., U.S. — B3 87
Center, In., U.S. — D5 91
Center, Ky., U.S. — C4 94
Center, Mo., U.S. — B6 102
Center, N.D., U.S. — B4 111
Center, Ok., U.S. — C5 113
Center, Tx., U.S. — D5 120
Center Barnstead, N.H., U.S. — D4 106
Centerbrook, Ct., U.S. — D6 84
Centerburg, Oh., U.S. — B3 112
Center City, Mn., U.S. — E6 100
Center City, Tx., U.S. — D3 120
Center Conway, N.H., U.S. — C4 106
Center Cross, Va., U.S. — C6 123
Centereach, N.Y., U.S. — n15 109
Center Effingham, N.H., U.S. — C4 106
Centerfield, Ut., U.S. — D4 121
Center Harbor, N.H., U.S. — C4 106
Center Hill, Ar., U.S. — B4 81
Center Hill, Fl., U.S. — D5 86
Center Hill Lake, res., Tn., U.S. — C8 119
Center Junction, Ia., U.S. — B6 92
Center Line, Mi., U.S. — *p15 99
Center Lovell, Me., U.S. — D2 96
Center Montville, Me., U.S. — D3 96
Center Moreland, Pa., U.S. — m17 115
Center Moriches, N.Y., U.S. — n16 109
Center Mountain, mtn., Id., U.S. — D3 89
Center Ossipee, N.H., U.S. — C4 106
Center Point, Al., U.S. — f7 78
Centerpoint, In., U.S. — F3 91
Center Point, Ia., U.S. — B6 92
Center Point, La., U.S. — C3 95
Center Point, S.D., U.S. — D8 118
Center Point, Tx., U.S. — E3 120
Center Point, W.V., U.S. — B4 125
Center Ridge, Ar., U.S. — B3 81
Center Rutland, Vt., U.S. — D2 122
Center Sandwich, N.H., U.S. — C4 106
Center Square, N.J., U.S. — A2 78
Center Star, Al., U.S. — A2 78
Center Strafford, N.H., U.S. — D5 106
Centerton, Ar., U.S. — A1 81
Centerton, In., U.S. — E5 91
Centerton, N.J., U.S. — D2 107
Centertown, Ky., U.S. — C3 94
Centertown, Mo., U.S. — C5 102
Centerview, Mo., U.S. — C4 102
Center Tuftonboro, N.H., U.S. — C4 106
Centerview, Mo., U.S. — C4 102
Centerville, N.B. — C2 71
Centerville, Al., U.S. — B2 81
Centerville, De., U.S. — A3 85
Centerville, In., U.S. — E8 91
Centerville, Ia., U.S. — D5 92
Centerville, Ks., U.S. — D8 93
Centerville, La., U.S. — E4 95
Centerville, Me., U.S. — D5 96
Centerville, Ma., U.S. — *C7 98
Centerville, Mo., U.S. — *D7 102
Centerville, Nv., U.S. — *E2 105
Centerville, N.C., U.S. — A4 110
Centerville, Oh., U.S. — C1 112
Centerville, Pa., U.S. — F2 115
Centerville, Pa., U.S. — C2 115
Centerville, R.I., U.S. — E2 116
Centerville, S.D., U.S. — D9 118
Centerville, Tn., U.S. — B4 119
Centerville, Tx., U.S. — D5 120
Centerville, Ut., U.S. — C4 121
Centerville, Wa., U.S. — D5 124
Cento, Italy — E7 20
Centrahoma, Ok., U.S. — C5 113
Central, Al., U.S. — C3 78

Central, Az., U.S. — E6 80
Central, In., U.S. — H5 91
Central, N.M., U.S. — E1 108
Central, S.C., U.S. — B2 117
Central, Ut., U.S. — F2 121
Central, prov., Ghana — E4 45
Central, prov., Kenya — B6 48
Central, prov., Mwi. — D5 48
Central, prov., Scot., U.K. — D4 13
Central, prov., Zam. — E4 48
Central, dept., Para. — E4 55
Central, Cordillera, mts., Col. — C2 60
Central, Cordillera, mts., C.R. — E5 62
Central, Cordillera, mts., Dom. Rep. — E8 64
Central, Cordillera, mts., P.R. — B2 65
Central African Republic, ctry., Afr. — D4 46
Central Barren, In., U.S. — H5 91
Central Bridge, N.Y., U.S. — C6 109
Central Butte, Sask. — G2 75
Central City, Co., U.S. — B5 83
Central City, Il., U.S. — E4 90
Central City, Ia., U.S. — B6 92
Central City, Ky., U.S. — C2 94
Central City, Ne., U.S. — C7 104
Central City, Pa., U.S. — F4 115
Central City, S.D., U.S. — C2 118
Central Falls, R.I., U.S. — B4 116
Centralhatchee, Ga., U.S. — C1 87
Central Heights, Az., U.S. — D5 80
Centralia, Ont. — D3 73
Centralia, Il., U.S. — E4 90
Centralia, Ks., U.S. — C7 93
Centralia, Mo., U.S. — B5 102
Centralia, Wa., U.S. — A6 113
Centralia, Wa., U.S. — C3 124
Centralia, W.V., U.S. — C4 125
Central Islip, N.Y., U.S. — n15 109
Central Lake, Mi., U.S. — C5 99
Central Makrān Range, mts., Pak. — C3 36
Central Park, Wa., U.S. — C2 124
Central Point, Or., U.S. — E4 114
Central Range, mts., Pap. N. Gui. — h11 50
Central Range, hills, Trin. — O23 65
Central Siberian Uplands, plat., Sov. Un. — C13 29
Central Square, N.Y., U.S. — B4 109
Central Valley, Ca., U.S. — B2 82
Central Valley, N.Y., U.S. — D6 109
Central Village, Ct., U.S. — C8 84
Central Village, Ma., U.S. — C5 98
Centre, Al., U.S. — A4 78
Centre, co., Pa., U.S. — E6 115
Centre Hall, Pa., U.S. — E6 115
Centre Peak, mtn., B.C. — B4 69
Chalan Kanoa, N. Mar. Is. — D7 52
Chalan Pago, Guam — L10 52
Chalatenango, El Sal. — C3 62
Chalchuapa, El Sal. — D3 62
Chalchuhuites, Mex. — C7 62
Chalco, Canal de, Mex. — h9 63
Chaleur Bay, b., Can. — B4 71
Chalfant, Pa., U.S. — h7 85
Chalfonte, De., U.S. — D5 120
Chalhuanca, Peru — D3 58
Chaling, China — K5 32
Chalk, co., Grc. — D6 25
Chalke see Khálki, i., Grc. — C3 40
Chalk River, Ont. — A7 73
Chalkyitsik, Ak., U.S. — B11 79
Challapata, Bol. — C5 55
Challis, Id., U.S. — E4 89
Chalmers, In., U.S. — C4 91
Chalmette, La., U.S. — E6 95
Châlons-sur-Marne, Fr. — C6 16
Châlon-sur-Saône, Fr. — D6 16
Chaltel, Cerro see Fitzroy, Monte, mtn., S.A. — D2 54
Chālūs, Iran — C5 39
Chalybeate, Ms., U.S. — A5 101
Chalybeate, N.C., U.S. — B4 110
Cham, W. Ger. — D7 19
Cham, Switz. — B5 21
Cham, i., Viet. — E8 35
Chama, stm., Ven. — D5 83
Chama, N.M., U.S. — A3 108
Chama, Rio, stm., N.M., U.S. — A3 108
Chamaicó, Arg. — B4 54
Chamaizí, Arg. — E5 16
Chaman, Pak. — B4 36
Chamba, Tan. — D6 48
Chamba, stm., India — C6 36
Chamberino, N.M., U.S. — E3 108
Chamberlain, Sask. — G3 75
Chamberlain, S.D., U.S. — D6 118
Chamberlain Lake, l., Me. — B3 96
Chamberlin, Mount, mtn., Ak., U.S. — B10 79
Chambers, Az., U.S. — B6 80
Chambers, Ne., U.S. — B7 104
Chambers, co., Al., U.S. — C4 78
Chambers, co., Tx., U.S. — E5 120
Chambersburg, Il., U.S. — D3 90
Chambersburg, Oh., U.S. — D3 112
Chambersburg, Pa., U.S. — G6 115
Chambers Island, i., Wi., U.S. — C6 126
Chambeshi, stm., Zam. — D5 48
Chamblee, Ga., U.S. — h8 87
Chambly, Que. — D4 74
Chambly, Fr. — E2 17
Chambly, co., Que. — D4 74
Chamblyn, Sov. Un. — G2 75
Chamela, stm., India — C6 36
Chamical, Arg. — F2 55
Chamisal, N.M., U.S. — A4 108
Chamois, Mo., U.S. — C6 102
Chamonix [-Mont-Blanc], Fr. — E7 16
Champ, Md., U.S. — D6 97
Champagne, Yukon — D5 66
Champagne, hist. reg., Fr. — C6 16
Champagney, Fr. — A2 21
Champagnole, Fr. — D6 16
Champaign, Il., U.S. — C5 90
Champaign, co., Il., U.S. — C5 90
Champaign, co., Oh., U.S. — B2 112
Champasak, Laos — D4 35
Champdoré, Lac, l., Que. — g8 72
Champerico, Guat. — G1 62
Champéry, Switz. — D2 21
Champigneulles, Fr. — F6 17
Champigny-sur-Marne, Fr. — g11 17
Champion, Alta. — D4 68
Champion, Mi., U.S. — B3 99
Champion, Ne., U.S. — D4 104
Champlain, Que. — A5 112
Champion Creek Reservoir, res., Tx., U.S. — C2 120
Champions, Tx., U.S. — *E5 120

Ceylon, Sask. — H3 75
Ceylon, In., U.S. — C8 91
Ceylon, Mn., U.S. — G4 100
Ceylon see Sri Lanka, ctry., Asia — G7 36
Chabařovice, Czech. — C8 19
Chacabuco, Arg. — A4 54
Chacachacare, i., Trin. — N22 65
Chacahoula, La., U.S. — E5 95
Chachapoyas, Peru — C2 58
Chachoengsao, Thai. — F4 35
Chāchro, Pak. — E3 37
Chaco, prov., Arg. — E3 55
Chaco, dept., Para. — D3 55
Chaco, stm., N.M., U.S. — A1 108
Chaco Culture National Historic Park, N.M., U.S. — A2 108
Chacon, N.M., U.S. — A4 108
Chacon, Cape, c., Ak., U.S. — n24 79
Chacuaco Creek, stm., Co., U.S. — D7 83
Chadan, stm., Ak., U.S. — B10 79
Chandausi, India — C7 37
Chandeleur Islands, is., La., U.S. — E7 95
Chandeleur Sound, strt., La., U.S. — E6 95
Chandigarh, India — B6 36
Chandigarh, ter., India — *B6 36
Chandler, Que. — k14 74
Chandler, Az., U.S. — D4 80
Chandler, In., U.S. — H3 91
Chandler, Mn., U.S. — G3 100
Chandler, Ok., U.S. — B5 113
Chandler, Tx., U.S. — C5 120
Chandler Heights, Az., U.S. — m9 80
Chandlers Valley, Pa., U.S. — C3 115
Chandlerville, Il., U.S. — C3 90
Chandos Lake, l., Ont. — C6 73
Chāndpur, Bngl. — D9 36
Chandrapur, India — E6 36
Chaneysville, Pa., U.S. — G5 115
Chang, i., Thai. — F5 35
Changane, stm., Moz. — F5 35
Changbai Mountains, mts., Asia — E3 33
Changchou see Zhangzhou, China — G8 31
Changchun, China — C10 31
Changde, China — F7 31
Change Islands, Newf. — D4 72
Changewater, N.J., U.S. — B3 107
Changhua, China — I8 32
Chang Jiang see Yangtze, stm., China — E8 31
Changjin-ŭp, N. Kor. — F3 33
Changle, China — L8 32
Changli, China — E8 32
Changling, China — B10 32
Changping, China — D7 32
Changsha, China — F7 31
Changshu, China — I9 32
Changsŏng, N. Kor. — F2 33
Changting, China — F8 31
Changwu, China — D6 31
Changxing, China — I8 32
Changyŏn, N. Kor. — G2 33
Changzhi, China — D7 31
Changzhou, China — E8 31
Chanhassen, Mn., U.S. — n11 100
Channahon, Il., U.S. — B6 90
Channel Country, reg., Austl. — D6 50
Channel Islands, is., Eur. — F5 10
Channel Islands National Park, Ca., U.S. — F4 82
Channel Lake, Il., U.S. — H8 90
Channelview, Tx., U.S. — r14 120
Channing, Mi., U.S. — B2 99
Channing, Tx., U.S. — B1 120
Chantada, Spain — A2 22
Chanthaburi, Thai. — C2 34
Chantilly, Fr. — C5 16
Chantilly, Va., U.S. — g12 123
Chantrey Inlet, b., N.W. Ter. — C13 66
Chanute, Ks., U.S. — E8 93
Chanute Air Force Base, mil., Il., U.S. — C5 90
Chany, Lake, l., Sov. Un. — D10 29
Chao'an, China — G8 31
Chao Lake, l., China — I7 32
Chao Phraya, stm., Thai. — C2 34
Chaor He, stm., China — B9 31
Chaoyang, China — C9 31
Chaoyang, China — *G8 31
Chapadinha, Braz. — B2 57
Chapala, Mex. — m12 63
Chapala, Lago de, l., Mex. — m12 63
Chaparral, Col. — C2 60
Chapayevsk, Sov. Un. — C3 28
Chapel Hill, Ky., U.S. — D3 94
Chapel Hill, N.C., U.S. — B3 110
Chapel Hill, Tn., U.S. — B5 119
Chapelle, N.B. — C2 71
Chapel Square, Va., U.S. — *B5 123
Chapin, Jam. — E14 65
Chapin, Il., U.S. — D3 90
Chapin, Ia., U.S. — B4 92
Chapin, S.C., U.S. — C5 117
Chapleau, Ont. — p19 73
Chapleau, Sask. — G2 75
Chaplin, Ct., U.S. — B7 84
Chaplin, Ky., U.S. — C4 94
Chaplin Lake, l., Sask. — G2 75
Chaplygin, Sov. Un. — E12 27
Chapman, Al., U.S. — D3 78
Chapman, Ks., U.S. — D6 93
Chapman, Ne., U.S. — C7 104
Chapman, co., N.W. Ter. — C15 66
Chapman Pond, l., R.I., U.S. — F1 116
Chapman Ranch, Tx., U.S. — F4 120
Chapmanville, W.V., U.S. — C2 125
Chappaquiddick, N.Y., U.S. — *D7 109
Chappell, Ne., U.S. — C3 104
Chappells, S.C., U.S. — C4 117
Chaptico Creek, stm., Md., U.S. — D4 97
Chaqui, Bol. — D2 55
Char, well, Maur. — A2 44
Charadai, Arg. — E4 55
Charagua, Bol. — C3 55
Charaña, Bol. — D2 55
Charcas, Mex. — C4 63
Charco, Id., U.S. — G6 89
Charcot Island, i., Ant. — C5 7
Chard, Eng., U.K. — F5 10
Chardarinsk Reservoir, res., Sov. Un. — E7 28
Chardon, Oh., U.S. — A4 112

Champlain, Que. — C5 74
Champlain, N.Y., U.S. — f11 109
Champlain, co., Que. — A5 74
Champlain, Lake, l., N.A. — B2 122
Champlin, Mn., U.S. — m12 100
Champney's West, Newf. — D5 72
Champotón, Mex. — D6 63
Chana, Il., U.S. — B4 90
Chañaral, Chile — E1 55
Chança, stm., Eur. — D2 22
Chancay, Peru — D2 58
Chance, Al., U.S. — D2 78
Chance, Md., U.S. — D6 97
Chancellor, Al., U.S. — D4 78
Chancellor, S.D., U.S. — D8 118
Chan Chan, hist., Peru — B2 58
Chanchelulla Peak, mtn., Ca., U.S. — B2 82
Chanco, Chile — B2 54
Chandalar, stm., Ak., U.S. — B10 79
Channel-Port-aux-Basques, Newf. — E2 72
Channelview, Tx., U.S. — r14 120
Channing, Mi., U.S. — B2 99
Chard, well, Maur. — A2 44
Charadai, Arg. — E4 55
Charente, stm., Fr. — E3 16
Charenton, La., U.S. — E4 95
Charenton-le-Pont, Fr. — g10 16
Charette, Que. — C5 74
Chari, stm., Afr. — C3 46
Chārīkār, Afg. — A4 36
Charing, Ga., U.S. — D2 87
Chariton, co., Mo., U.S. — B4 102
Chariton, Ia., U.S. — C4 92
Chariton, stm., U.S. — A5 102
Charity, Guy. — A3 59
Charity, Mo., U.S. — D4 102
Charlemont, Ma., U.S. — A2 98
Charleroi, Bel. — B6 16
Charleroi, Pa., U.S. — F2 115
Charles, co., Md., U.S. — C3 97
Charles, stm., Ma., U.S. — B5 98
Charles A. Goodwin Dam, Ct., U.S. — B3 84
Charlesbourg, Que. — n17 74
Charlesburg, Wi., U.S. — k9 126
Charles City, Ia., U.S. — A5 92
Charles City, co., Va., U.S. — C5 123
Charles Mix, co., S.D., U.S. — D7 118
Charles Mound, hill, Il., U.S. — A3 90
Charleston, Ar., U.S. — B1 81
Charleston, Il., U.S. — D5 90
Charleston, Me., U.S. — C4 96
Charleston, Ms., U.S. — A3 101
Charleston, Mo., U.S. — E8 102
Charleston, Or., U.S. — D2 114
Charleston, S.C., U.S. — F8 117
Charleston, Tn., U.S. — D9 119
Charleston, Ut., U.S. — C4 121
Charleston, W.V., U.S. — C3 125
Charleston, co., S.C., U.S. — F7 117
Charleston Air Force Base, mil., S.C., U.S. — k11 117
Charleston Naval Shipyard, mil., S.C., U.S. — k12 117
Charleston Park, Nv., U.S. — *G6 105
Charleston Peak, mtn., Nv., U.S. — G6 105
Charlestown, Ire. — D3 11
Charlestown, St. C.-N. — H13 64
Charlestown, In., U.S. — H6 91
Charlestown, Md., U.S. — A6 97
Charlestown, N.H., U.S. — D2 106
Charlestown, R.I., U.S. — F2 116
Charlestown, Tn., U.S. — D8 119
Charleville, Austl. — E8 50
Charleville-Mézières, Fr. — C6 16
Charlevoix, Mi., U.S. — C5 99
Charlevoix, co., Mi., U.S. — C5 99
Charlevoix, Lake, l., Mi., U.S. — C5 99
Charlevoix-Est, co., Que. — B7 74
Charlevoix-Ouest, co., Que. — B7 74
Charlie Lake, B.C. — A7 69
Charlieu, Fr. — D6 16
Charlo, N.B. — B3 71
Charlo, Mt., U.S. — C2 103
Charlotte, Ia., U.S. — C7 92
Charlotte, Mi., U.S. — F6 99
Charlotte, N.C., U.S. — B2 110
Charlotte, Tn., U.S. — A4 119
Charlotte, Tx., U.S. — E3 120
Charlotte, Vt., U.S. — C2 122
Charlotte, co., N.B. — D2 71
Charlotte, co., Fl., U.S. — F5 86
Charlotte, co., Va., U.S. — C4 123
Charlotte Amalie, V.I.U.S. — G12 64
Charlotte Court House, Va., U.S. — C4 123
Charlotte Hall, Md., U.S. — D4 97
Charlotte Harbor, Fl., U.S. — F4 86
Charlotte Harbor, b., Fl., U.S. — F4 86
Charlottenburg, Sur. — A4 59
Charlottesville, In., U.S. — E6 91
Charlottesville, Va., U.S. — B4 123
Charlottetown, Newf. — C6 72
Charlottetown, P.E.I. — C6 71
Charlotte Town (Gouyave), Gren. — W25 65
Charlotteville, Trin. — M24 65
Charlotteville, Ga., U.S. — B4 87
Charlson, N.D., U.S. — A3 111
Charlton, Ma., U.S. — B4 98
Charlton, co., Ga., U.S. — F4 87
Charlton City, Ma., U.S. — B4 98
Charlton Depot, Ma., U.S. — B4 98
Charlton Island, i., N.W. Ter. — n20 73
Charly [-sur-Marne], Fr. — C5 16
Charmco, W.V., U.S. — C4 125
Charmes, Fr. — C7 16
Charmey, Switz. — C3 21
Charny, Que. — C6 74
Charouine, Alg. — D4 44
Charquemont, Fr. — B2 21
Charron Lake, l., Man. — C4 70
Charsk, Sov. Un. — D10 28
Charter Oak, Ca., U.S. — *E5 82
Charter Oak, Ia., U.S. — B2 92
Charters Towers, Austl. — D9 50
Chartierville, Que. — D6 74
Chartley, Ma., U.S. — C5 98
Chartres, Fr. — C4 16
Charysh, stm., Sov. Un. — C10 28
Chascomús, Arg. — B5 54
Chase, Ks., U.S. — D5 93
Chase, Mi., U.S. — E5 99
Chase, co., Ks., U.S. — D7 93
Chase, co., Ne., U.S. — D4 104
Chase, Mount, mtn., Me., U.S. — B4 96
Chaseburg, Wi., U.S. — E2 126
Chase City, Va., U.S. — D4 123
Chase Field Naval Air Station, mil., Tx., U.S. — E4 120
Chaseley, N.D., U.S. — B6 111
Chase River, B.C. — f12 69
Chasicó, Arg. — C3 54
Chasov Yar, Sov. Un. — H5 27
Chassahowitzka Bay, b., Fl., U.S. — D4 86
Chassell, Mi., U.S. — A2 99
Chasseral, mtn., Switz. — B3 20
Chasseron, Mont, mtn., Switz. — C2 21
Chataignier, La., U.S. — D3 95
Chataniaka, Al., U.S. — B10 79
Chatawa, Ms., U.S. — D3 101
Château-du-Loir, Fr. — D4 16
Châteaudun, Fr. — C4 16
Château-Gontier, Fr. — D3 16

Chardzhou, Sov. Un. — F9 29
Charente, stm., Fr. — E3 16
Charenton, La., U.S. — E4 95
Charenton-le-Pont, Fr. — g10 16
Charette, Que. — C5 74
Chari, stm., Afr. — C3 46
Chārīkār, Afg. — A4 36
Charing, Ga., U.S. — D2 87
Chariton, co., Mo., U.S. — B4 102
Chariton, Ia., U.S. — C4 92
Chariton, stm., U.S. — A5 102
Charity, Guy. — A3 59
Charity, Mo., U.S. — D4 102
Charlemont, Ma., U.S. — A2 98
Charleroi, Bel. — B6 16
Charleroi, Pa., U.S. — F2 115
Charles, co., Md., U.S. — C3 97
Charles, stm., Ma., U.S. — B5 98
Charles A. Goodwin Dam, Ct., U.S. — B3 84
Charlesbourg, Que. — n17 74
Charlesburg, Wi., U.S. — k9 126
Charles City, Ia., U.S. — A5 92
Charles City, co., Va., U.S. — C5 123
Charles Mill Lake, res., Oh., U.S. — B3 112
Charles Mix, co., S.D., U.S. — D7 118
Charles Mound, hill, Il., U.S. — A3 90
Charleston, Ar., U.S. — B1 81
Charleston, Il., U.S. — D5 90
Charleston, Me., U.S. — C4 96
Charleston, Ms., U.S. — A3 101
Charleston, Mo., U.S. — E8 102
Charleston, Or., U.S. — D2 114
Charleston, S.C., U.S. — F8 117
Charleston, Tn., U.S. — D9 119
Charleston, Ut., U.S. — C4 121
Charleston, W.V., U.S. — C3 125
Charleston, co., S.C., U.S. — F7 117
Charleston Air Force Base, mil., S.C., U.S. — k11 117
Charleston Naval Shipyard, mil., S.C., U.S. — k12 117
Charleston Park, Nv., U.S. — *G6 105
Charleston Peak, mtn., Nv., U.S. — G6 105
Charlestown, Ire. — D3 11
Charlestown, St. C.-N. — H13 64
Charlestown, In., U.S. — H6 91
Charlestown, Md., U.S. — A6 97
Charlestown, N.H., U.S. — D2 106
Charlestown, R.I., U.S. — F2 116
Charlestown, Tn., U.S. — D8 119
Charleville, Austl. — E8 50
Charleville-Mézières, Fr. — C6 16
Charlevoix, Mi., U.S. — C5 99
Charlevoix, co., Mi., U.S. — C5 99
Charlevoix, Lake, l., Mi., U.S. — C5 99
Charlevoix-Est, co., Que. — B7 74
Charlevoix-Ouest, co., Que. — B7 74
Charlie Lake, B.C. — A7 69
Charlieu, Fr. — D6 16
Charlo, N.B. — B3 71
Charlo, Mt., U.S. — C2 103
Charlotte, Ia., U.S. — C7 92
Charlotte, Mi., U.S. — F6 99
Charlotte, N.C., U.S. — B2 110
Charlotte, Tn., U.S. — A4 119
Charlotte, Tx., U.S. — E3 120
Charlotte, Vt., U.S. — C2 122
Charlotte, co., N.B. — D2 71
Charlotte, co., Fl., U.S. — F5 86
Charlotte, co., Va., U.S. — C4 123
Charlotte Amalie, V.I.U.S. — G12 64
Charlotte Court House, Va., U.S. — C4 123
Charlotte Hall, Md., U.S. — D4 97
Charlotte Harbor, Fl., U.S. — F4 86
Charlotte Harbor, b., Fl., U.S. — F4 86
Charlottenburg, Sur. — A4 59
Charlottesville, In., U.S. — E6 91
Charlottesville, Va., U.S. — B4 123
Charlottetown, Newf. — C6 72
Charlottetown, P.E.I. — C6 71
Charlotte Town (Gouyave), Gren. — W25 65
Charlotteville, Trin. — M24 65
Charlotteville, Ga., U.S. — B4 87
Charlson, N.D., U.S. — A3 111
Charlton, Ma., U.S. — B4 98
Charlton, co., Ga., U.S. — F4 87
Charlton City, Ma., U.S. — B4 98
Charlton Depot, Ma., U.S. — B4 98
Charlton Island, i., N.W. Ter. — n20 73
Charly [-sur-Marne], Fr. — C5 16
Charmco, W.V., U.S. — C4 125
Charmes, Fr. — C7 16
Charmey, Switz. — C3 21
Charny, Que. — C6 74
Charouine, Alg. — D4 44
Charquemont, Fr. — B2 21
Charron Lake, l., Man. — C4 70
Charsk, Sov. Un. — D10 28
Charter Oak, Ca., U.S. — *E5 82
Charter Oak, Ia., U.S. — B2 92
Charters Towers, Austl. — D9 50
Chartierville, Que. — D6 74
Chartley, Ma., U.S. — C5 98
Chartres, Fr. — C4 16
Charysh, stm., Sov. Un. — C10 28
Chascomús, Arg. — B5 54
Chase, Ks., U.S. — D5 93
Chase, Mi., U.S. — E5 99
Chase, co., Ks., U.S. — D7 93
Chase, co., Ne., U.S. — D4 104
Chase, Mount, mtn., Me., U.S. — B4 96
Chaseburg, Wi., U.S. — E2 126
Chase City, Va., U.S. — D4 123
Chase Field Naval Air Station, mil., Tx., U.S. — E4 120
Chaseley, N.D., U.S. — B6 111
Chase River, B.C. — f12 69
Chasicó, Arg. — C3 54
Chasov Yar, Sov. Un. — H5 27
Chassahowitzka Bay, b., Fl., U.S. — D4 86
Chassell, Mi., U.S. — A2 99
Chasseral, mtn., Switz. — B3 20
Chasseron, Mont, mtn., Switz. — C2 21
Chataignier, La., U.S. — D3 95
Chatanika, Al., U.S. — B10 79
Chatawa, Ms., U.S. — D3 101
Château-du-Loir, Fr. — D4 16
Châteaudun, Fr. — C4 16

Château-Gontier, Fr. — D3 16
Châteauguay, Que. — D4 74
Châteauguay, co., Que. — D4 74
Châteauguay Heights, Que. — q19 74
Châteauneuf, Fr. — D5 16
Château-Renault, Fr. — D4 16
Château-Richer, Que. — C6 74
Châteauroux, Fr. — D4 16
Château-Salins, Fr. — F6 17
Château-Thierry, Fr. — C5 16
Châtellerault, Fr. — D4 16
Châtel-Saint-Denis, Switz. — C2 21
Chatfield, Man. — D3 70
Chatfield, Mn., U.S. — G6 100
Chatfield, Oh., U.S. — B3 112
Chatham, N.B. — B4 71
Chatham, Ont. — E2 73
Chatham, Eng., U.K. — E7 10
Chatham, Il., U.S. — D4 90
Chatham, La., U.S. — B3 95
Chatham, Ma., U.S. — C8 98
Chatham, Mi., U.S. — B4 99
Chatham, Ms., U.S. — B2 101
Chatham, N.H., U.S. — B4 106
Chatham, N.J., U.S. — B4 107
Chatham, N.Y., U.S. — C7 109
Chatham, Oh., U.S. — A3 112
Chatham, Va., U.S. — D3 123
Chatham, Wy., U.S. — C4 127
Chatham, co., Ga., U.S. — E5 87
Chatham, co., N.C., U.S. — B3 110
Chatham Head, N.B. — C4 71
Chatham Islands, is., N.Z. — I11 6
Chatham Sound, strt., B.C. — B2 69
Chatham Strait, strt., Ak., U.S. — m22 79
Châtillon, Italy — D3 20
Châtillon-sur-Seine, Fr. — D6 16
Chatkal Range, mts., Sov. Un. — E8 28
Chatsworth, Ont. — C4 73
Chatsworth, Ga., U.S. — B2 87
Chatsworth, Il., U.S. — C5 90
Chatsworth, Ia., U.S. — B1 92
Chatsworth, N.J., U.S. — D3 107
Chatsworth Reservoir, res., Ca., U.S. — m11 82
Chattahoochee, Fl., U.S. — B2 86
Chattahoochee, co., Ga., U.S. — D2 87
Chattahoochee, stm., U.S. — E1 87
Chattanooga, Oh., U.S. — B1 112
Chattanooga, Ok., U.S. — C3 113
Chattanooga, Tn., U.S. — D8 119
Chattaroy, Wa., U.S. — B8 124
Chattaroy, W.V., U.S. — D2 125
Chatteris, Eng., U.K. — I13 8
Chattooga, co., Ga., U.S. — B1 87
Chattooga, stm., U.S. — B1 117
Chatuge Lake, res., U.S. — g9 110
Chaudière, stm., Que. — C7 74
Chau Doc, Viet. — C3 34
Chauk, Burma — D9 36
Chaumont, Fr. — C6 16
Chaumont, N.Y., U.S. — A4 109
Chaun Bay, b., Sov. Un. — B34 128
Chauncey, Ga., U.S. — D3 87
Chauncey, Oh., U.S. — C3 112
Chauncy Lake, l., Ma., U.S. — g9 98
Chauny, Fr. — C5 16
Chautauqua, Ks., U.S. — E7 93
Chautauqua, N.Y., U.S. — C1 109
Chautauqua, S.D., U.S. — *D8 118
Chautauqua, co., Ks., U.S. — E7 93
Chautauqua, co., N.Y., U.S. — C1 109
Chautauqua Lake, l., N.Y., U.S. — C1 109
Chauvigny, Fr. — C5 16
Chauvin, Alta. — C5 68
Chauvin, La., U.S. — E5 95
Chavanga, Sov. Un. — D17 14
Chaves, Braz. — C5 59
Chaves, Port. — B2 22
Chaves, co., N.M., U.S. — D5 108
Chavies, Ky., U.S. — C6 94
Chavinda, Mex. — m12 63
Cháviva, Col. — C3 60
Chavuma, Zam. — D3 48
Chazelles, Fr. — E6 16
Chazy, N.Y., U.S. — f11 109
Cheadle, Alta. — D4 68
Cheaha Mountain, mtn., Al., U.S. — B4 78
Cheam (part of London), Eng., U.K. — m12 10
Cheapside, Va., U.S. — h16 123
Cheat, Shavers Fork, stm., W.V., U.S. — B5 125
Cheatham, co., Tn., U.S. — A4 119
Cheatham Reservoir, res., Tn., U.S. — A4 119
Cheat Mountain, mtn., W.V., U.S. — C5 125
Cheb, Czech. — C2 26
Chebacco Lake, l., Ma., U.S. — f12 98
Chebanse, Il., U.S. — C6 90
Chebeague Island, Me., U.S. — E2 96
Cheboksary, Sov. Un. — D7 28
Cheboygan, Mi., U.S. — C6 99
Cheboygan, co., Mi., U.S. — C6 99
Chech, 'Erg. des., Afr. — E4 44
Chechaouene, Mor. — B3 44
Chechŏn, S. Kor. — H4 33
Checotah, Ok., U.S. — B6 113
Chedabucto Bay, b., N.S. — D8 71
Cheddar, Eng., U.K. — C5 12
Cheduba Island, i., Burma — E9 36
Cheektowaga, N.Y., U.S. — C2 109
Cheepie, Austl. — C5 51
Cheesman Lake, res., Co., U.S. — B5 83
Chegutu, Zimb. — A5 49
Chehalem Mountains, mts., Or., U.S. — h12 114
Chehalis, stm., Wa., U.S. — C2 124
Chehalis, Wa., U.S. — C2 124
Cheju, S. Kor. — J3 33
Cheju Island, i., S. Kor. — D10 31
Cheju Strait, strt., S. Kor. — J3 33
Chekhov, Sov. Un. — C10 33
Chekiang see Zhejiang, prov., China — F9 31
Chekunda, Sov. Un. — A6 33
Chela, Serra da, mtn., Ang. — E1 48
Chela, Sask. — E4 75
Chelan, Wa., U.S. — B5 124
Chelan, co., Wa., U.S. — B4 124
Chelan, Lake, l., Wa., U.S. — A5 124
Chelan Falls, Wa., U.S. — B5 124
Chelan Mountains, mts., Wa., U.S. — A5 124
Cheleiros, Port. — f9 22
Cheleken, Sov. Un. — B6 39

Name	Map Ref.	Page
Cheleken Peninsula, pen., Sov. Un.	B6	39
Chelforó, Arg.	B3	54
Chélia, Djebel, mtn., Alg.	B6	44
Chéliff, Oued, stm., Alg.	B5	44
Chelkar, Sov. Un.	E8	29
Chelles, Fr.	F2	17
Chelm, Pol.	C7	26
Chelmno, Pol.	B5	26
Chelmsford, Eng., U.K.	E7	10
Chelmsford, Ma., U.S.	A5	98
Chelmza, Pol.	B5	26
Chelsea, Que.	D2	74
Chelsea (part of London), Eng., U.K.	m12	10
Chelsea, Al., U.S.	g7	78
Chelsea, Ia., U.S.	C5	92
Chelsea, Me., U.S.	D3	96
Chelsea, Ma., U.S.	B5	98
Chelsea, Mi., U.S.	F6	99
Chelsea, Ok., U.S.	A6	113
Chelsea, S.D., U.S.	B7	118
Chelsea, Vt., U.S.	D4	122
Chelsea, Wi., U.S.	C3	126
Chelsea Estates, De., U.S.	*B3	85
Cheltenham, Eng., U.K.	E5	10
Cheltenham, Md., U.S.	C4	97
Cheltenham Township, Pa., U.S.	*o21	115
Chelva, Spain	C5	22
Chelyabinsk, Sov. Un.	D9	29
Chelyan, W.V., U.S.	C3	125
Chelyuskin, Cape, c., Sov. Un.	B13	29
Chelyuskintsy Ice Tongue, ice, Ant.	C21	7
Chemainus, B.C.	E6	69
Chemal, Sov. Un.	E26	8
Chemehuevi Indian Reservation, Ca., U.S.	E6	82
Chemillé, Fr.	D3	16
Chemin Craig, Que.	o17	74
Chemnitz see Karl-Marx-Stadt, E. Ger.	C6	18
Chemquasabamticook Lake (Ross Lake), l., Me., U.S.	B3	96
Chemult, Or., U.S.	D5	114
Chemung, Il., U.S.	A5	90
Chemung, co., N.Y., U.S.	C4	109
Chemung, stm., Pa., U.S.	C5	115
Chemung Lake, l., Ont.	C6	73
Chenāb, stm., Asia	D4	44
Chenachane, Alg.	C5	44
Chenango, co., N.Y., U.S.	C5	109
Chenango, stm., N.Y., U.S.	C5	109
Chenango Bridge, N.Y., U.S.	C5	109
Chenango Forks, N.Y., U.S.	C5	109
Chenārān, Iran	C9	39
Chene, Bayou, stm., La., U.S.	k9	95
Chenequa, Wi., U.S.	m11	126
Chenes, River Aux, b., La., U.S.	k12	95
Chénéville, Que.	D2	74
Cheney, Ks., U.S.	E6	93
Cheney, Wa., U.S.	B8	124
Cheney Reservoir, res., Ks., U.S.	E6	93
Cheneyville, La., U.S.	C3	95
Chengchou see Zhengzhou, China	E7	31
Chengde, China	C8	31
Chengdu (Chengtu), China	E5	31
Chenggu, China	E8	31
Chenghai, China	G8	31
Chengkou, China	I3	32
Chengmai, China	C8	35
Chengshan Shan, c., China	D9	31
Chengtu see Chengdu, China	E5	31
Chenoa, Il., U.S.	C5	90
Chenoa, Ky., U.S.	D6	94
Chenôve, Fr.	D6	16
Chenoweth, Or., U.S.	B5	114
Chenxi, China	F7	31
Chenzhou, China	F7	31
Chepachet, R.I., U.S.	B2	116
Chepachet, stm., R.I., U.S.	B2	116
Chepén, Peru	C2	58
Chepes, Arg.	A3	54
Chepo, Pan.	F8	62
Chepstow, Wales, U.K.	E5	10
Cheptsa, stm., Sov. Un.	D19	8
Chequamegon Bay, b., Wi., U.S.	B3	126
Cher, stm., Fr.	D4	16
Cheraw, Co., U.S.	C7	83
Cheraw, S.C., U.S.	B8	117
Cherbourg, Fr.	C3	16
Cherchell, Alg.	B5	44
Cherdyn, Sov. Un.	A5	28
Cheremkhovo, Sov. Un.	D13	29
Cherepanovo, Sov. Un.	C10	29
Cherepovets, Sov. Un.	D6	29
Cherhill, Alta.	C3	68
Cheriton, Va., U.S.	C7	123
Cherkassy, Sov. Un.	G9	27
Cherkessk, Sov. Un.	G17	8
Cherlakskiy, Sov. Un.	C8	29
Chernigov, Sov. Un.	D6	33
Chernigovka, Sov. Un.	H11	27
Chernobay, Sov. Un.	G9	27
Chernobyl, Sov. Un.	F8	27
Chernogorsk, Sov. Un.	E27	8
Chernomorskoye, Sov. Un.	I9	27
Chernovtsy, Sov. Un.	E5	29
Chernoye, Sov. Un.	r32	14
Chernyakhovsk (Insterburg), Sov. Un.	D3	27
Cherokee, Al., U.S.	A2	78
Cherokee, Ia., U.S.	B2	92
Cherokee, Ks., U.S.	E9	93
Cherokee, N.C., U.S.	f9	110
Cherokee, Ok., U.S.	A3	113
Cherokee, Tx., U.S.	D3	120
Cherokee, co., Al., U.S.	A4	78
Cherokee, co., Ga., U.S.	B2	87
Cherokee, co., Ia., U.S.	B2	92
Cherokee, co., Ks., U.S.	E9	93
Cherokee, co., N.C., U.S.	f8	110
Cherokee, co., Ok., U.S.	B6	113
Cherokee, co., S.C., U.S.	A4	117
Cherokee, co., Tx., U.S.	D5	120
Cherokee Falls, S.C., U.S.	A4	117
Cherokee Indian Reservation, N.C., U.S.	f9	110
Cherokee Lake, res., Tn., U.S.	C10	119
Cherokees, Lake O' The, res., Ok., U.S.	A7	113
Cherokee Sound, Bah.	*A4	81
Cherokee Village, Ar., U.S.	*A4	81
Cherquenco, Chile	B2	54
Cherrapunji, India	C9	36
Cherry, Il., U.S.	B4	90
Cherry, Tn., U.S.	B2	119
Cherry, co., Ne., U.S.	B4	104
Cherry Creek, N.Y., U.S.	C1	109
Cherry Creek, S.D., U.S.	C4	118
Cherry Creek, stm., Co., U.S.	B6	83
Cherry Creek, stm., S.D., U.S.	C3	118
Cherryfield, Me., U.S.	D5	96
Cherry Fork, Oh., U.S.	D2	112
Cherry Grove, Or., U.S.	g11	114
Cherry Hill, N.J., U.S.	D2	107
Cherry Hills Village, Co., U.S.	*B6	83
Cherryland, Ca., U.S.	*D2	82
Cherry Point, c., Va., U.S.	C6	123
Cherry Point Marine Corps Air Station, mil., N.C., U.S.	C6	110
Cherry Run, W.V., U.S.	B6	125
Cherry Tree, Pa., U.S.	E4	115
Cherryvale, Ks., U.S.	E8	93
Cherry Valley, Ont.	D7	73
Cherry Valley, Ar., U.S.	B5	81
Cherry Valley, Ca., U.S.	*F5	82
Cherry Valley, Il., U.S.	A5	90
Cherry Valley, Ma., U.S.	B4	98
Cherry Valley, N.Y., U.S.	C6	109
Cherryville, N.C., U.S.	B1	110
Cherskiy Mountains, mts., Sov. Un.	C17	29
Chesaning, Mi., U.S.	E6	99
Chesapeake, Oh., U.S.	D3	112
Chesapeake, Va., U.S.	D6	123
Chesapeake, W.V., U.S.	C3	125
Chesapeake and Delaware Canal, U.S.	B3	85
Chesapeake Bay, b., U.S.	C12	76
Chesapeake Bay Bridge-Tunnel, tr., U.S.	D7	123
Chesapeake Beach, Md., U.S.	C4	97
Chesapeake City, Md., U.S.	A6	97
Chesaw, Wa., U.S.	A6	124
Chesdin, Lake, res., Va., U.S.	C5	123
Chesha Bay, b., Sov. Un.	B18	8
Chesham, Eng., U.K.	k11	10
Cheshire, Ct., U.S.	D4	84
Cheshire, Ma., U.S.	A1	98
Cheshire, Oh., U.S.	D3	112
Cheshire, co., Eng., U.K.	A5	12
Cheshire, co., N.H., U.S.	E2	106
Cheshire Reservoir, res., Ma., U.S.	A1	98
Cheshunt, Eng., U.K.	k12	10
Cheslatta, N.J., U.S.	D3	107
Chesley, Ont.	C3	73
Chesnee, S.C., U.S.	A4	117
Chester, N.S.	E5	71
Chester, Eng., U.K.	D5	10
Chester, Ca., U.S.	B3	82
Chester, Ct., U.S.	D6	84
Chester, Fl., U.S.	B5	86
Chester, Ga., U.S.	D3	87
Chester, Id., U.S.	F7	89
Chester, Il., U.S.	F4	90
Chester, Ia., U.S.	A5	92
Chester, Md., U.S.	C5	97
Chester, Ma., U.S.	B2	98
Chester, Mt., U.S.	B6	103
Chester, Ne., U.S.	D8	104
Chester, N.H., U.S.	E4	106
Chester, N.J., U.S.	B3	107
Chester, N.Y., U.S.	D6	109
Chester, Oh., U.S.	C4	112
Chester, Ok., U.S.	A3	113
Chester, Pa., U.S.	G11	115
Chester, S.C., U.S.	B5	117
Chester, S.D., U.S.	D9	118
Chester, Ut., U.S.	D4	121
Chester, Vt., U.S.	E3	122
Chester, Va., U.S.	C5	123
Chester, W.V., U.S.	A4	125
Chester, co., Pa., U.S.	G10	115
Chester, co., S.C., U.S.	B5	117
Chester, co., Tn., U.S.	B3	119
Chester, stm., Md., U.S.	B5	97
Chester Basin, N.S.	E5	71
Chester Depot, Vt., U.S.	E3	122
Chesterfield, Eng., U.K.	D6	10
Chesterfield, Il., U.S.	D3	90
Chesterfield, In., U.S.	D6	91
Chesterfield, Ma., U.S.	B2	98
Chesterfield, N.H., U.S.	E2	106
Chesterfield, S.C., U.S.	B7	117
Chesterfield, Tn., U.S.	B3	119
Chesterfield, Va., U.S.	C5	123
Chesterfield, co., S.C., U.S.	B7	117
Chesterfield, co., Va., U.S.	C5	123
Chesterfield, Îles, is., N. Cal.	H9	6
Chesterfield Inlet, N.W. Ter.	D14	66
Chesterfield Inlet, b., N.W. Ter.	D14	66
Chesterhill, Oh., U.S.	C4	112
Chesterton, In., U.S.	A3	91
Chestertown, Md., U.S.	B5	97
Chestertown, N.Y., U.S.	B7	109
Chester Township, Pa., U.S.	*p20	115
Chesterville, Ont.	B9	73
Chesterville, Il., U.S.	D5	90
Chesterville, Oh., U.S.	B3	112
Chestnut, Il., U.S.	C4	90
Chestnut, La., U.S.	B2	95
Chestnut Hill Estates, De., U.S.	*B3	85
Chestnut Knoll, De., U.S.	*B3	85
Chestnut Mound, Tn., U.S.	C8	119
Chestnut Ridge, N.Y., U.S.	*D6	109
Chesuncook Lake, l., Me., U.S.	C3	96
Cheswick, Pa., U.S.	h14	115
Cheswold, De., U.S.	D3	85
Chetac, Lake, l., Wi., U.S.	C2	126
Chetco, stm., Or., U.S.	E2	114
Chetek, Wi., U.S.	C2	126
Chetek, Lake, l., Wi., U.S.	C2	126
Chetopa, Ks., U.S.	E8	93
Chetumal, Mex.	D7	63
Chetumal Bay, b., N.A.	D7	63
Chetwynd, B.C.	B7	69
Chevak, Ak., U.S.	C6	79
Chevelon Creek, stm., Az., U.S.	C5	80
Cheverie, N.S.	D5	71
Cheverly, Md., U.S.	*C4	97
Cheviot, Sask.	E2	75
Cheviot, N.Z.	O14	51
Cheviot, Oh., U.S.	C1	112
Chevreuil, Bayou, stm., La., U.S.	k10	95
Chevreuil, Point, c., La., U.S.	E4	95
Chevy Chase, Md., U.S.	C3	97
Chewack, stm., Wa., U.S.	A5	124
Chewalla, Tn., U.S.	B3	119
Chewelah, Wa., U.S.	A8	124
Chewsville, Md., U.S.	A2	97
Chewton, Pa., U.S.	E1	115
Cheyenne, Ok., U.S.	B2	113
Cheyenne, Wy., U.S.	E8	127
Cheyenne, co., Co., U.S.	C8	83
Cheyenne, co., Ks., U.S.	C2	93
Cheyenne, co., Ne., U.S.	C2	104
Cheyenne, stm., S.D., U.S.	C4	118
Cheyenne, Dry Fork, stm., Wy., U.S.	C7	127
Cheyenne River Indian Reservation, S.D., U.S.	B4	118
Cheyenne Wells, Co., U.S.	C8	83
Chhapra, India	C7	36
Chhatarpur, India	E7	37
Chhatrapur, India	H10	37
Chhindwāra, India	F7	37
Chhukha Dzong, Bhu.	D12	37
Chi, stm., Thai.	E6	35
Chiang Kham, Thai.	C4	35
Chiang Khong, Thai.	A2	34
Chiang Mai, Thai.	B1	34
Chiang Rai, Thai.	B1	34
Chiapa de Corzo, Mex.	D6	63
Chiapas, state, Mex.	D6	63
Chiari, Italy	B2	23
Chiasso, Switz.	E7	21
Chiatura, Sov. Un.	A14	40
Chiautla de Tapia, Mex.	n14	63
Chiavari, Italy	B2	23
Chiavenna, Italy	C5	20
Chiawuli Tak, Az., U.S.	F4	80
Chiba, Japan	D13	36
Chibemba, Ang.	E1	48
Chibia, Ang.	E1	48
Chiblow Lake, l., Ont.	A1	73
Chibougamau, Que.	k12	74
Chibuto, Moz.	B5	49
Chicago, Il., U.S.	B6	90
Chicago Heights, Il., U.S.	B6	90
Chicago Ridge, Il., U.S.	*k9	90
Chicago Sanitary and Ship Canal, Il., U.S.	k8	90
Chicamacomico, stm., Md., U.S.	D6	97
Chicapa, stm., Afr.	C3	48
Chichagof Island, i., Ak., U.S.	m22	79
Chichaoua, Mor.	C3	44
Chicheng, China	D6	32
Chichén Itzá, hist., Mex.	C7	63
Chichester, Eng., U.K.	E6	10
Chichester, N.H., U.S.	D4	106
Chichibu, Japan	n18	33
Chickahominy, stm., Va., U.S.	C5	123
Chickamauga, Ga., U.S.	B1	87
Chickamauga and Chattanooga National Military Park, U.S.	k11	119
Chickamauga Dam, Tn., U.S.	h11	119
Chickamauga Lake, l., Tn., U.S.	D8	119
Chickasaw, Al., U.S.	E1	78
Chickasaw, co., Ia., U.S.	A5	92
Chickasaw, co., Ms., U.S.	B5	101
Chickasawhay, stm., Ms., U.S.	D5	101
Chickasaw National Recreation Area, Ok., U.S.	C5	113
Chickasha, Ok., U.S.	B4	113
Chickasha, Lake, res., Ok., U.S.	B3	113
Chicken, Ak., U.S.	C11	79
Chickwolnepy Stream, stm., N.H., U.S.	A4	106
Chiclana [de la Frontera], Spain	D2	22
Chiclayo, Peru	C2	58
Chico, Ca., U.S.	C3	82
Chico, Tx., U.S.	C4	120
Chico, Wa., U.S.	B3	124
Chico, stm., Arg.	D3	54
Chico, stm., Arg.	h9	54
Chicoa, Moz.	A5	49
Chico Creek, stm., Co., U.S.	C6	83
Chico Hot Springs, Mt., U.S.	E6	103
Chicomo, Moz.	B5	49
Chicontepec, Mex.	m14	63
Chicopee, Ga., U.S.	B3	87
Chicopee, Ks., U.S.	E9	93
Chicopee, Ma., U.S.	B2	98
Chicora, Ms., U.S.	D5	101
Chicora, Pa., U.S.	E2	115
Chicot, co., Ar., U.S.	D4	81
Chicot, Lake, l., Ar., U.S.	D4	81
Chicota, Tx., U.S.	C5	120
Chicot Island, i., La., U.S.	E6	95
Chicoutimi, Que.	A6	74
Chicoutimi, co., Que.	A6	74
Chicoutimi, stm., Que.	A6	74
Chico West, Ca., U.S.	*C3	82
Chidester, Ar., U.S.	D2	81
Chidley, Cape, c., Can.	f8	72
Chiefland, Fl., U.S.	C4	86
Chiefs Point, c., Ont.	C3	73
Chiem Lake, l., W. Ger.	E6	18
Chien, Bayou de, stm., Ky., U.S.	f8	94
Chieri, Italy	B1	23
Chiers, stm., Eur.	E5	17
Chiese, stm., Italy	D6	20
Chieti, Italy	C5	20
Chifeng, China	C8	31
Chigasaki, Japan	*I9	33
Chigirin, Sov. Un.	G9	27
Chignahuapan, Mex.	n14	63
Chignecto, Cape, c., N.S.	D5	71
Chignecto Bay, b., Can.	D7	71
Chignik, Ak., U.S.	D8	79
Chigubo, Moz.	B5	49
Chigwell, Eng., U.K.	k13	10
Chihli, Gulf of see Bo Hai, b., China	D8	31
Chihuahua, Mex.	B3	63
Chihuahua, state, Mex.	B3	63
Chii, Mount, mtn., S. Kor.	I3	33
Chikaskia, stm., U.S.	A4	113
Chikura, Japan	o18	33
Chilapa [de Alvarez], Mex.	D5	63
Chilca, Peru	C2	58
Chilcotin, stm., B.C.	C6	69
Childersburg, Al., U.S.	B3	78
Childress, Tx., U.S.	B2	120
Childress, co., Tx., U.S.	B2	120
Chile, ctry., S.A.	G3	53
Chilecito, Arg.	A3	54
Chililabombwe (Bancroft), Zam.	D4	48
Chilkat Pass, B.C.	E5	66
Chilko Lake, l., B.C.	D5	69
Chillán, Chile	B2	54
Chilli, Sov. Un.	E7	28
Chillicothe, Il., U.S.	C4	90
Chillicothe, Ia., U.S.	C5	92
Chillicothe, Mo., U.S.	B4	102
Chillicothe, Oh., U.S.	C3	112
Chillicothe, Tx., U.S.	B3	120
Chilliwack, B.C.	E7	69
Chilliwack, stm., N.A.	A4	124
Chillum, Md., U.S.	f9	97
Chilmark, Ma., U.S.	D6	98
Chilocco, Ok., U.S.	A4	113
Chiloé, Isla de, i., Chile	C2	54
Chiloquin, Or., U.S.	E5	114
Chilpancingo [de los Bravos], Mex.	D5	63
Chilton, Tx., U.S.	D4	120
Chilton, Wi., U.S.	D5	126
Chilton, co., Al., U.S.	C3	78
Chiluage, Ang.	C3	48
Chilumba, Mwi.	D5	48
Chilung (Keelung), Tai.	F9	31
Chilwa, Lake, l., Afr.	E6	48
Chimacum, Wa., U.S.	A3	124
Chimalhuacán, Mex.	h10	63
Chimaltenango, Guat.	F8	62
Chimán, Pan.	F8	62
Chimayo, N.M., U.S.	A4	108
Chimbay, Sov. Un.	E7	28
Chimborazo, prov., Ec.	B2	58
Chimborazo, vol., Ec.	B2	58
Chimbote, Peru	C2	58
Chimkent, Sov. Un.	E9	29
Chimney Rock, Co., U.S.	D3	83
Chimney Rock, mtn., Ky., U.S.	C5	94
Chimney Rock, mtn., Ne., U.S.	C2	104
Chimneytop, mtn., Tn., U.S.	C11	119
Chimoio, Moz.	A5	49
Chin, Cape, c., Ont.	B3	73
Chinā, Japan	O5	33
China, Mex.	B5	63
China, ctry., Asia	E6	31
China Grove, N.C., U.S.	B2	110
Chinajá, Guat.	D6	63
China Lake, l., Me., U.S.	D3	96
Chinan see Jinan, China	D8	31
Chinandega, Nic.	E7	63
Chinati Peak, mtn., Tx., U.S.	p12	120
Chincha Alta, Peru	D2	58
Chincheros, Peru	D3	58
Chinchilla, Austl.	E9	50
Chinchilla [de Monte Aragón], Spain	C5	22
Chincoteague, Va., U.S.	C7	123
Chincoteague Bay, b., U.S.	D7	97
Chinde, Moz.	A6	49
Chindo, S. Kor.	I3	33
Chindwinn, stm., Burma	C10	36
Chingola, Zam.	D4	48
Chinguar, Ang.	D2	48
Chinguetti, Maur.	B2	45
Chinhae, S. Kor.	I4	33
Chinhoyi, Zimb.	A5	49
Chiniot, Pak.	B3	63
Chinipas, Mex.	B3	63
Chinit, stm., Camb.	F6	35
Chinju, S. Kor.	I4	33
Chinko, stm., Cen. Afr. Rep.	D4	46
Chinle, Az., U.S.	A6	80
Chinle Wash, stm., Az., U.S.	A6	80
Chinnampo see Nampo, N. Kor.	D10	31
Chino, Ca., U.S.	F5	82
Chinon, Fr.	D5	16
Chinook, Alta.	D5	68
Chinook, Mt., U.S.	B7	103
Chinook, Wa., U.S.	C2	124
Chinook, Lake, res., Or., U.S.	C5	114
Chinook Cove, B.C.	D7	69
Chino Valley, Az., U.S.	C3	80
Chinquapin, N.C., U.S.	C5	110
Chinsali, Zam.	D5	48
Chinteche, Mwi.	D5	48
Chinú, Col.	B2	60
Chioco, Moz.	A5	49
Chioggia, Italy	B4	23
Chios see Khios, i., Grc.	C5	40
Chipata (Fort Jameson), Zam.	A4	49
Chipewyan, stm., Alta.	A4	68
Chipinge, Zimb.	B5	49
Chipita Park, Co., U.S.	C6	83
Chip Lake, l., Alta.	C3	68
Chipley, Fl., U.S.	u16	86
Chipman, Alta.	C4	68
Chipman, N.B.	C4	71
Chipola, stm., Fl., U.S.	B1	86
Chippenham, Eng., U.K.	C5	12
Chippewa, co., Mi., U.S.	B6	99
Chippewa, co., Mn., U.S.	E3	100
Chippewa, co., Wi., U.S.	C2	126
Chippewa, stm., Mn., U.S.	E3	100
Chippewa, stm., Wi., U.S.	D2	126
Chippewa, East Branch, stm., Wi., U.S.	C3	126
Chippewa, East Fork, stm., Wi., U.S.	C2	126
Chippewa Falls, Wi., U.S.	D2	126
Chippewa Lake, l., Mi., U.S.	E5	99
Chipping Norton, Eng., U.K.	C6	12
Chipurupalle, India	G5	37
Chiputneticook Lakes, l., N.A.	C5	96
Chipuxet, stm., R.I., U.S.	E3	116
Chiquimula, Guat.	F7	62
Chiquimulilla, Guat.	G3	62
Chiquinquirá, Col.	B3	60
Chira, stm., S.A.	B1	58
Chiradzulu, Mwi.	E6	48
Chirchik, Sov. Un.	E9	29
Chiredzi, Zimb.	B5	49
Chireno, Tx., U.S.	n18	120
Chirfa, Niger	B7	45
Chiricahua Mountains, mts., Az., U.S.	F6	80
Chiricahua National Monument, Az., U.S.	F6	80
Chiricahua Peak, mtn., Az., U.S.	F6	80
Chirikof Island, i., Ak., U.S.	D8	79
Chiriquí, Golfo de, b., Pan.	G6	62
Chiriquí Grande, Pan.	E6	62
Chiromo, Mwi.	E6	48
Chirpan, Bul.	D7	24
Chirripó, Cerro, mtn., C.R.	F6	62
Chirundu, Zimb.	A4	49
Chisago, co., Mn., U.S.	E6	100
Chisago City, Mn., U.S.	E6	100
Chisamba, Zam.	D4	48
Chisana, Ak., U.S.	C11	79
Chisasibi, Que.	h11	74
Chisholm, Alta.	B3	68
Chisholm, Me., U.S.	D2	96
Chisholm, Mn., U.S.	C6	100
Chisholm, Tx., U.S.	B5	85
Chisos Mountains, mts., Tx., U.S.	E1	120
Chistochina, Ak., U.S.	C11	79
Chistopol, Sov. Un.	B4	28
Chita, Sov. Un.	D14	29
Chitado, Ang.	E1	48
Chitato, Ang.	C3	48
Chitek, Sask.	D2	75
Chitek Lake, l., Man.	C2	70
Chitembo, Ang.	D2	48
Chitina, Ak., U.S.	C11	79
Chitina, stm., Ak., U.S.	g19	79
Chitipa, Mwi.	C5	48
Chitose, Japan	*E10	33
Chitradurga, India	F4	37
Chitrāl, Pak.	A5	36
Chitré, Pan.	E6	62
Chittagong, Bngl.	D9	36
Chittaurgarh, India	H5	37
Chittenango, N.Y., U.S.	B5	109
Chittenden, Vt., U.S.	D3	122
Chittenden, co., Vt., U.S.	C2	122
Chittenden Reservoir, res., Vt., U.S.	D3	122
Chittoor, India	F5	37
Chitungwiza, Zimb.	A5	49
Chiuchiu, Chile	D2	55
Chiume, stm., Afr.	C3	48
Chiúme, Ang.	C3	48
Chiusi, Italy	C3	23
Chivasso, Italy	B1	23
Chivay, Peru	E3	58
Chivhu, Zimb.	A5	49
Chivilcoy, Arg.	A4	54
Chivington, Co., U.S.	C8	83
Chixoy, stm., Guat.	C2	62
Chizhapka, stm., Sov. Un.	B9	28
Chloride, Az., U.S.	B1	80
Chmielnik, Pol.	C6	26
Choapa, stm., Chile	A2	54
Choapan, Mex.	D5	63
Chobe, stm., Afr.	A3	49
Choccolocco, Al., U.S.	B4	78
Choccolocco Creek, stm., Al., U.S.	B3	78
Chochiwŏn, S. Kor.	H3	33
Chocó, dept., Col.	B2	60
Chocolate Mountains, mts., U.S.	E2	82
Chocontá, Col.	B3	60
Chocowinity, N.C., U.S.	B5	110
Choctaw, Ar., U.S.	B3	81
Choctaw, Ok., U.S.	B4	113
Choctaw, co., Al., U.S.	C1	78
Choctaw, co., Ms., U.S.	B4	101
Choctaw, co., Ok., U.S.	C6	113
Choctawhatchee, East Fork, stm., Al., U.S.	D4	78
Choctawhatchee, West Fork, stm., Al., U.S.	D4	78
Choctawhatchee Bay, b., Fl., U.S.	u15	86
Choctaw Indian Reservation, Ms., U.S.	C4	101
Chodzież, Pol.	B4	26
Choele Choel, Arg.	B3	54
Chōfu, Japan	*I9	33
Choiceland, Sask.	D3	75
Choiseul, i., Sol. Is.	A5	51
Choisy-le-Roi, Fr.	g10	16
Choix, Mex.	B3	63
Chojna, Pol.	B2	26
Chojnice, Pol.	B4	26
Chojnów, Pol.	B3	26
Chōkai, Mount, mtn., Japan	G10	33
Choke, mts., Eth.	C4	47
Chokio, Mn., U.S.	E2	100
Chokoloskee, Fl., U.S.	G5	86
Chokwé, Moz.	B5	49
Cholame, Ca., U.S.	E3	82
Cholet, Fr.	E6	16
Cholo, Mwi.	E6	48
Cholula [de Rivadabia], Mex.	n14	63
Choluteca, Hond.	E7	63
Choluteca, stm., Hond.	E7	63
Choma, Zam.	D4	48
Chomo Lhāri, mtn., Asia	D12	37
Chomutov, Czech.	C2	26
Chonan, S. Kor.	H3	33
Chon Buri, Thai.	C2	34
Chone, Ec.	B1	58
Chong'an, China	K8	32
Chŏngju, N. Kor.	C10	31
Chŏngju, S. Kor.	G3	33
Chongqing (Chungking), China	F6	31
Chongren, China	K6	32
Chongsŏng, N. Kor.	D10	31
Chŏnju, S. Kor.	I3	33
Chonos, Archipiélago de los, is., Chile	C2	54
Chopim, stm., Braz.	D2	56
Choptank, Md., U.S.	C6	97
Choptank, stm., Md., U.S.	C6	97
Chōru, India	C5	37
Chortkov, Sov. Un.	G5	27
Chŏrwŏn, N. Kor.	D10	31
Chosan, N. Kor.	C5	31
Chōshi, Japan	I10	33
Chosica, Peru	D2	58
Chos Malal, Arg.	B2	54
Choszczno, Pol.	B3	26
Choteau, Mt., U.S.	C4	103
Chotěboř, Czech.	n18	63
Choudrant, La., U.S.	B3	95
Choudrant, Bayou, stm., La., U.S.	B3	95
Choum, Maur.	B2	45
Choushan Islands see Zhoushan Islands, is., China	E9	31
Chouteau, Ok., U.S.	A6	113
Chouteau, co., Mt., U.S.	C6	103
Chowan, co., N.C., U.S.	A6	110
Chowan, stm., N.C., U.S.	A6	110
Chowchilla, Ca., U.S.	D3	82
Chowchilla, stm., Ca., U.S.	D3	82
Choybalsan, Mong.	B7	31
Choyr, Mong.	B6	31
Chrisman, Il., U.S.	D6	90
Chrisney, In., U.S.	H3	91
Christchurch, Eng., U.K.	D6	12
Christchurch, N.Z.	O14	51
Christian, co., Il., U.S.	D4	90
Christian, co., Ky., U.S.	D2	94
Christian, co., Mo., U.S.	E4	102
Christiana, Jam.	E9	64
Christiana, S. Afr.	G5	49
Christiana, De., U.S.	B3	85
Christiana, Pa., U.S.	G9	115
Christiana, Tn., U.S.	B5	119
Christian Island, dep., Oc.	D2	106
Christian Hollow, N.H., U.S.	C4	73
Christian Island, i., Ont.	B1	112
Christiansburg, Va., U.S.	C2	123
Christiansfeld, Den.	C3	15
Christian Sound, strt., Ak., U.S.	n22	79
Christiansted, V.I.U.S.	H12	64
Christina, stm., Alta.	A5	68
Christina, stm., De., U.S.	B3	85
Christina, Lake, l., Alta.	B5	68
Christina, Lake, l., Mn., U.S.	D3	100
Christina Peak, mtn., Nv., U.S.	D6	105
Christine, N.D., U.S.	C9	111
Christine, Tx., U.S.	E3	120
Christmas, Fl., U.S.	D5	86
Christmas Island see Kiritimati, Island, i., Kir.	F12	6
Christmas Lake, l., Or., U.S.	D6	114
Christmas Valley, Or., U.S.	D6	114
Christopher, Il., U.S.	F4	90
Christoval, Tx., U.S.	D2	120
Chromo, Co., U.S.	D4	83
Chrudim, Czech.	B11	26
Chrysler, Al., U.S.	D2	78
Chrzanów, Pol.	g10	26
Chu, Sov. Un.	E8	28
Chu, stm., Sov. Un.	G23	8
Chubbuck, Id., U.S.	G6	89
Chubut, prov., Arg.	C3	54
Chubut, stm., Arg.	C3	54
Chuckey, Tn., U.S.	C11	119
Chudovo, Sov. Un.	B8	27
Chugach Islands, is., Ak., U.S.	h16	79
Chugach Mountains, mts., Ak., U.S.	g18	79
Chuguyev, Sov. Un.	G11	27
Chugwater, Wy., U.S.	E8	127
Chugwater Creek, stm., Wy., U.S.	E8	127
Chuiuis Mountain, mtn., B.C.	B5	69
Chukai (Kemaman), Malay.	J5	35
Chukchi Sea	C32	128
Chukotsk Peninsula, pen., Sov. Un.	C32	128
Chula, Ga., U.S.	E3	87
Chula, Mo., U.S.	B4	102
Chula, Va., U.S.	C5	123
Chula Vista, Ca., U.S.	F5	82
Chulucanas, Peru	B1	58
Chulumani, Bol.	C5	55
Chulym, Sov. Un.	B10	28
Chulym, stm., Sov. Un.	D11	29
Chumbicha, Arg.	E2	55
Chumikan, Sov. Un.	D16	29
Chumphon, Thai.	G3	35
Chumysh, stm., Sov. Un.	C10	28
Chun'an, China	J8	32
Chunchŏn, S. Kor.	H3	33
Chunchula, Al., U.S.	E1	78
Chungju, S. Kor.	H3	33
Chungking see Chongqing, China	F6	31
Chungmu, S. Kor.	H4	33
Chunya, Tan.	C5	48
Chupaca, Peru	D2	58
Chupadera Mesa, mtn., N.M., U.S.	D3	108
Chupadero, N.M., U.S.	*B4	108
Chupara Point, c., Trin.	N23	65
Chuquibamba, Peru	E3	58
Chuquicamata, Chile	D2	55
Chuquisaca, dept., Bol.	D5	55
Chur, Switz.	E4	18
Churchbridge, Sask.	G5	75
Church Creek, Md., U.S.	C5	97
Church Hill, Md., U.S.	B6	97
Church Hill, Ms., U.S.	D2	101
Church Hill, Tn., U.S.	C11	119
Churchill, Man.	*I9	70
Churchill, co., Nv., U.S.	D3	105
Churchill, stm., Can.	E13	66
Churchill, stm., Newf.	h9	72
Churchill, Cape, c., Man.	f9	70
Churchill Falls, wtfl., Newf.	h8	72
Churchill Lake, l., Me., U.S.	B3	96
Churchill Lake, l., Sask.	m7	75
Church Mountain, mtn., B.C.	f14	69
Church Point, N.S.	E3	71
Church Point, La., U.S.	D3	95
Church Rock, N.M., U.S.	B1	108
Churchs Ferry, N.D., U.S.	A6	111
Church Stretton, Eng., U.K.	B5	12
Churchton, Md., U.S.	C4	97
Churchville, N.Y., U.S.	B3	109
Churchville, Va., U.S.	B3	123
Churdan, Ia., U.S.	B3	92
Chūru, India	C5	37
Churubusco, In., U.S.	B7	91
Churuguara, Ven.	A4	60
Churumuco, Mex.	n13	63
Chushul, India	B6	36
Chuska Mountains, mts., Az., U.S.	A6	80
Chusovaya, stm., Sov. Un.	D20	8
Chusovoy, Sov. Un.	B5	28
Chust, Sov. Un.	G23	8
Chuxian, China	H8	32
Chuxiong, China	F5	31
Chuy, Ur.	E2	56
Cianjur, Indon.	*G3	34
Cianorte, Braz.	C2	56
Cibecue, Az., U.S.	C5	80
Cibola, co., N.M., U.S.	C1	108
Cibolo Creek, stm., Tx., U.S.	h7	120
Cicero, Il., U.S.	B6	90
Cicero, In., U.S.	D5	91
Cicero, N.Y., U.S.	B4	109
Cicero Dantas, Braz.	B3	57
Ciche, Sgurr na, mtn., Scot., U.K.	D3	13
Cicia, i., Fiji	H16	52
Cide, Tur.	B9	40

Name	Map Ref.	Page
Cidra, Lago de, res., P.R.	B3	65
Ciechanów, Pol.	B6	26
Ciego de Avila, Cuba	D4	64
Ciego de Avila, prov., Cuba	C4	64
Ciempozuelos, Spain	B4	22
Ciénaga, Col.	A3	60
Ciénaga de Oro, Col.	B2	60
Cienfuegos, Cuba	C3	64
Cienfuegos, prov., Cuba	C3	64
Cieszyn, Pol.	D5	26
Cieza, Spain	C5	22
Ciężkowice, Pol.	g10	26
Cigüela, stm., Spain	C4	22
Cihanbeyli, Tur.	C9	40
Cihuatlán, Mex.	n11	63
Cilacap, Indon.	G3	34
Cili, China	J4	32
Cima, Ca., U.S.	E6	82
Cimarron, Co., U.S.	C3	83
Cimarron, Ks., U.S.	E3	93
Cimarron, N.M., U.S.	A5	108
Cimarron, co., Ok., U.S.	e8	113
Cimarron, stm., U.S.	C8	76
Cimarron, North Fork, stm., U.S.	E2	93
Cimarron Hills, Co., U.S.	*C6	83
Cîmpina, Rom.	C7	24
Cîmpulung, Rom.	C7	24
Cîmpulung Moldovenesc, Rom.	B7	24
Cincinnati, Ia., U.S.	D5	92
Cincinnati, Oh., U.S.	C1	112
Cincinnatus, N.Y., U.S.	C5	109
Cinconsine, Lac, l., Que.	B4	74
Çine, Tur.	D7	25
Cinnaminson, N.J., U.S.	D3	107
Cintalapa [de Figueroa], Mex.	D6	63
Cinto, Monte, mtn., Fr.	C2	23
Cipolletti, Arg.	B3	54
Circle, Ak., U.S.	B11	79
Circle, Mt., U.S.	C11	103
Circle Hot Springs, Ak., U.S.	B11	79
Circle Pines, Mn., U.S.	m12	100
Circleville, Ks., U.S.	C8	93
Circleville, Oh., U.S.	C3	112
Circleville, Ut., U.S.	E3	121
Circleville, W.V., U.S.	C5	125
Cirebon, Indon.	G3	34
Cirencester, Eng., U.K.	E6	10
Ciri, stm., Pan.	m10	62
Cisco, Ga., U.S.	B2	87
Cisco, S.D., U.S.	C5	90
Cisco, Ky., U.S.	C6	94
Cisco, Tx., U.S.	C3	120
Cisco, Ut., U.S.	E6	121
Ciskei, ctry., Afr.	D4	49
Cisne, Il., U.S.	E5	90
Cisneros, Col.	B2	60
Cisnes, stm., Chile	C2	54
Cispus, stm., Wa., U.S.	C4	124
Cissna Park, Il., U.S.	C6	90
Cistern, Tx., U.S.	E4	120
Cisterna di Latina, Italy	h9	23
Cistierna, Spain	A3	22
Citac, Nevado, mtn., Peru	D2	58
Citra, Fl., U.S.	C5	86
Citronelle, Al., U.S.	D1	78
Citrus, Ca., U.S.	*E5	82
Citrus, co., Fl., U.S.	D4	86
Citrus Heights, Ca., U.S.	*C3	82
Cittadella, Italy	B3	23
Città di Castello, Italy	C4	23
City Mills, Ma., U.S.	h10	98
City of Commerce, Ca., U.S.	n12	82
City of Refuge National Historical Park, Hi., U.S.	D5	88
City Point, Hi., U.S.	D6	86
City View, S.C., U.S.	B3	117
Ciudad Acuña, Mex.	B4	63
Ciudad Altamirano, Mex.	n13	63
Ciudad Bolívar, Ven.	B3	60
Ciudad Bolivia, Ven.	B3	60
Ciudad Camargo, Mex.	B3	63
Ciudad de la Habana, prov., Cuba	C2	64
Ciudad del Carmen, Mex.	D6	63
Ciudad del Maíz, Mex.	C5	63
Ciudad de Naucalpan de Juárez, Mex.	h9	63
Ciudad de Valles, Mex.	C5	63
Ciudad Villaldama, Mex.	B4	63
Ciudadela, Spain	B7	22
Ciudad Guayana, Ven.	B6	60
Ciudad Guzmán, Mex.	D4	63
Ciudad Hidalgo, Mex.	n13	63
Ciudad Ixtepec, Mex.	D5	63
Ciudad Jiménez, Mex.	B4	63
Ciudad Juárez, Mex.	A3	63
Ciudad Lerdo, Mex.	B4	63
Ciudad López Mateos, Mex.	g9	63
Ciudad Madero, Mex.	C5	63
Ciudad Mante, Mex.	C5	63
Ciudad Melchor Múzquiz, Mex.	B4	63
Ciudad Mendoza, Mex.	n15	63
Ciudad Obregón, Mex.	B3	63
Ciudad Ojeda, Ven.	A3	60
Ciudad Piar, Ven.	B5	60
Ciudad Real, Spain	C4	22
Ciudad Rodrigo, Spain	B3	22
Ciudad Serdán, Mex.	n15	63
Ciudad Tecún Umán, Guat.	C1	62
Ciudad Victoria, Mex.	C5	63
Cividale del Friuli, Italy	A4	23
Civitanova Marche, Italy	C4	23
Civitavecchia, Italy	C3	23
Civray, Fr.	D4	16
Çivril, Tur.	C7	40
Cizre, Tur.	D14	40
C.J. Strike Reservoir, res., Id., U.S.	G3	89
Clackamas, Or., U.S.	h12	114
Clackamas, co., Or., U.S.	B4	114
Clacton-on-Sea, Eng., U.K.	D5	93
Claflin, Ks., U.S.	D5	93
Claiborne, Al., U.S.	D2	78
Claiborne, La., U.S.	B3	95
Claiborne, Md., U.S.	*B3	97
Claiborne, co., La., U.S.	B2	95
Claiborne, co., Ms., U.S.	D3	101
Claiborne, co., Tn., U.S.	C10	119
Claiborne, Lake, res., La., U.S.	B3	95
Clair, N.B.	B1	71
Clair, Sask.	E3	75
Claire, Lake, l., Alta.	f8	68
Claire City, S.D., U.S.	B8	118
Clair Engle Lake, res., Ca., U.S.	B2	82
Clairfield, Tn., U.S.	*C10	119
Clair-Mel City, Fl., U.S.	*E4	86
Clairmont, Alta.	B1	68
Clairton, Pa., U.S.	F2	115
Clallam, co., Wa., U.S.	B1	124
Clallam Bay, Wa., U.S.	A1	124
Clamart, Fr.	g10	16
Clamecy, Fr.	D5	16
Clam Lake, l., Sask.	B3	75
Clam Lake, l., Wi., U.S.	C1	126
Clan Alpine Mountains, mts., Nv., U.S.	D4	105
Clancy, Mt., U.S.	D5	103
Clandeboye, Ont.	D3	73
Clandonald, Alta.	C5	68
Clanton, Al., U.S.	C3	78
Clanwilliam, Man.	D2	70
Clara, Ms., U.S.	D5	101
Clara, Ire.	F3	100
Clara City, Mn., U.S.	F3	100
Clara Peak, mtn., Az., U.S.	C2	80
Clare, Austl.	F6	50
Clare, In., U.S.	D6	91
Clare, Ia., U.S.	B3	92
Clare, Mi., U.S.	E6	99
Clare, co., Ire.	E3	11
Clare, co., Mi., U.S.	E6	99
Clare, stm., Ire.	D3	11
Clarecastle (Clare), Ire.	E3	11
Claregalway, Ire.	D3	11
Clare Island, i., Ire.	D1	10
Claremont, Ca., U.S.	m13	82
Claremont, Mn., U.S.	F6	100
Claremont, N.H., U.S.	D2	106
Claremont, N.C., U.S.	B1	110
Claremont, S.D., U.S.	B7	118
Claremont, Va., U.S.	C6	123
Claremont, mtn., Ca., U.S.	C3	82
Claremore, Ok., U.S.	A6	113
Claremorris, Ire.	D2	10
Clarence, Al., U.S.	A3	78
Clarence, Ia., U.S.	C6	92
Clarence, La., U.S.	C2	95
Clarence, Mo., U.S.	B5	102
Clarence, Pa., U.S.	D6	115
Clarence, stm., N.Z.	O14	51
Clarence, Isla, i., Chile	h11	54
Clarence Cannon Lake, res., Mo., U.S.	B6	102
Clarence Island, i., B.A.T.	C7	7
Clarence Strait, strt., Austl.	B5	50
Clarence Strait, strt., Ak., U.S.	n23	79
Clarence Town, Bah.	C6	64
Clarenceville, Que.	D4	74
Clarendon, Ar., U.S.	C4	81
Clarendon, Pa., U.S.	C3	115
Clarendon, Tx., U.S.	B2	120
Clarendon, Vt., U.S.	D2	122
Clarendon, co., S.C., U.S.	D7	117
Clarendon Hills, Il., U.S.	k9	90
Clarendon Springs, Vt., U.S.	D2	122
Clarendon Station, Ont.	C8	73
Clarenville, Newf.	D4	72
Claresholm, Alta.	D4	68
Clarie Coast, Ant.	C26	7
Clarinda, Ia., U.S.	D2	92
Clarington, Oh., U.S.	C5	112
Clarion, Pa., U.S.	D3	115
Clarion, Ia., U.S.	B4	92
Clarion, co., Pa., U.S.	D3	115
Clarion, stm., Pa., U.S.	D3	115
Clarissa, Mn., U.S.	D4	100
Clarita, Ok., U.S.	C5	113
Clark, Mo., U.S.	B5	102
Clark, N.J., U.S.	B4	107
Clark, S.D., U.S.	C8	118
Clark, co., Ar., U.S.	C2	81
Clark, co., Id., U.S.	E6	89
Clark, co., Il., U.S.	D6	90
Clark, co., In., U.S.	H6	91
Clark, co., Ks., U.S.	E4	93
Clark, co., Ky., U.S.	C5	94
Clark, co., Mo., U.S.	A6	102
Clark, co., Nv., U.S.	G6	105
Clark, co., Oh., U.S.	C2	112
Clark, co., S.D., U.S.	C8	118
Clark, co., Wa., U.S.	D3	124
Clark, co., Wi., U.S.	D3	126
Clark, Lake, l., Ak., U.S.	C9	79
Clark, Point, c., Ont.	C3	73
Clark Colony, S.D., U.S.	*C8	118
Clarkdale, Az., U.S.	C3	80
Clarkdale, Ga., U.S.	h7	87
Clarke, co., Al., U.S.	D2	78
Clarke, co., Ga., U.S.	C3	87
Clarke, co., Ia., U.S.	C4	92
Clarke, co., Ms., U.S.	C5	101
Clarke, co., Va., U.S.	A4	123
Clarke City, Que.	h8	72
Clarke Lake, l., Sask.	C2	75
Clarkesville, Ga., U.S.	B3	87
Clarkfield, Mn., U.S.	F3	100
Clark Fork, Id., U.S.	A2	89
Clark Fork, stm., U.S.	C1	103
Clarkia, Id., U.S.	B2	89
Clark Mountain, mtn., Mo., U.S.	D7	102
Clarkrange, Tn., U.S.	C8	119
Clarks, Ne., U.S.	C8	104
Clarks, stm., Ky., U.S.	f9	94
Clarks, West Fork, stm., Ky., U.S.	f9	94
Clarksboro, N.J., U.S.	D2	107
Clarksburg, Ont.	C4	73
Clarksburg, Md., U.S.	B3	97
Clarksburg, Mo., U.S.	C5	102
Clarksburg, Oh., U.S.	C2	112
Clarksburg, W.V., U.S.	B4	125
Clarksdale, Ms., U.S.	A3	101
Clarksdale, Mo., U.S.	B3	102
Clarks Falls, Ct., U.S.	D8	84
Clarks Grove, Mn., U.S.	G5	100
Clark's Harbour, N.S.	F4	71
Clarks Hill, In., U.S.	D4	91
Clarkson, Ky., U.S.	C3	94
Clarkson, Ne., U.S.	C8	104
Clarks Point, Ak., U.S.	D8	79
Clarks Summit, Pa., U.S.	m18	115
Clarkston, Ga., U.S.	h8	87
Clarkston, Mi., U.S.	F7	99
Clarkston, Ut., U.S.	B3	121
Clarkston, Wa., U.S.	C8	124
Clarksville, Ar., U.S.	B2	81
Clarksville, De., U.S.	F5	85
Clarksville, Fl., U.S.	B1	86
Clarksville, Ia., U.S.	B5	92
Clarksville, In., U.S.	H6	91
Clarksville, Md., U.S.	B4	97
Clarksville, Mi., U.S.	F5	99
Clarksville, Mo., U.S.	B7	102
Clarksville, Oh., U.S.	C2	112
Clarksville, Tn., U.S.	A4	119
Clarksville, Tx., U.S.	C5	120
Clarksville, Va., U.S.	D4	123
Clarkton, Mo., U.S.	E8	102
Clarkton, N.C., U.S.	C4	110
Claryville, Ky., U.S.	k14	94
Claryville, Mo., U.S.	D8	102
Clashmore, Ire.	E4	11
Clatonia, Ne., U.S.	D9	104
Clatskanie, Or., U.S.	A3	114
Clatsop, co., Or., U.S.	A3	114
Claude, Tx., U.S.	B2	120
Claudy, N. Ire., U.K.	C4	11
Claunch, N.M., U.S.	C3	108
Clausthal-Zellerfeld, W. Ger.	C5	18
Clavet, Sask.	F2	75
Clawson, Mi., U.S.	o15	99
Clawson, Ut., U.S.	D4	121
Claxton, Ga., U.S.	D5	87
Clay, Al., U.S.	f7	78
Clay, Ky., U.S.	C2	94
Clay, La., U.S.	B3	95
Clay, N.Y., U.S.	B4	109
Clay, W.V., U.S.	C3	125
Clay, Wy., U.S.	B8	127
Clay, co., Al., U.S.	B4	78
Clay, co., Ar., U.S.	A5	81
Clay, co., Fl., U.S.	B5	86
Clay, co., Ga., U.S.	E2	87
Clay, co., Il., U.S.	E5	90
Clay, co., In., U.S.	F3	91
Clay, co., Ia., U.S.	A2	92
Clay, co., Ks., U.S.	C6	93
Clay, co., Ky., U.S.	C6	94
Clay, co., Mn., U.S.	D2	100
Clay, co., Ms., U.S.	B5	101
Clay, co., Mo., U.S.	B3	102
Clay, co., Ne., U.S.	D7	104
Clay, co., N.C., U.S.	f9	110
Clay, co., S.D., U.S.	E8	118
Clay, co., Tn., U.S.	C8	119
Clay, co., Tx., U.S.	C3	120
Clay, co., W.V., U.S.	C3	125
Clay Center, Ks., U.S.	C6	93
Clay Center, Ne., U.S.	D7	104
Clay Center, Oh., U.S.	A2	112
Clay City, Il., U.S.	E5	90
Clay City, In., U.S.	F3	91
Clay City, Ky., U.S.	C6	94
Clay Creek, stm., Co., U.S.	D8	83
Claydon, Sask.	H1	75
Clayhatchee, Al., U.S.	D4	78
Claymont, De., U.S.	A4	85
Claypool, Az., U.S.	D5	80
Claypool, In., U.S.	B6	91
Claysburg, Pa., U.S.	F5	115
Claysville, Pa., U.S.	F1	115
Clayton, Ont.	B8	73
Clayton, Al., U.S.	D4	78
Clayton, De., U.S.	C3	85
Clayton, Ga., U.S.	B3	87
Clayton, Id., U.S.	E4	89
Clayton, Il., U.S.	C3	90
Clayton, In., U.S.	E4	91
Clayton, Ia., U.S.	B6	92
Clayton, Ks., U.S.	C3	93
Clayton, La., U.S.	C4	95
Clayton, Mo., U.S.	C7	102
Clayton, N.J., U.S.	D2	107
Clayton, N.M., U.S.	A6	108
Clayton, N.Y., U.S.	A4	109
Clayton, N.C., U.S.	B4	110
Clayton, Ok., U.S.	C6	113
Clayton, S.D., U.S.	D8	118
Clayton, Tn., U.S.	A2	119
Clayton, Wa., U.S.	B8	124
Clayton, Wi., U.S.	C1	126
Clayton, co., Ga., U.S.	C2	87
Clayton, co., Ia., U.S.	B6	92
Clayton Lake, Me., U.S.	B3	96
Claytor Lake, res., Va., U.S.	C2	123
Clayville, R.I., U.S.	C2	116
Clear, stm., Alta.	A1	68
Clear, stm., R.I., U.S.	B2	116
Clear, Cape, c., Ire.	E2	10
Clear Boggy Creek, stm., Ok., U.S.	C5	113
Clearbrook, Mn., U.S.	C3	100
Clear Creek, In., U.S.	F4	91
Clear Creek, Ut., U.S.	D4	121
Clear Creek, W.V., U.S.	n13	125
Clear Creek, co., Co., U.S.	B5	83
Clear Creek, stm., Az., U.S.	C4	80
Clear Creek, stm., Ne., U.S.	C6	104
Clear Creek, stm., Tn., U.S.	C9	119
Clear Creek, stm., Wy., U.S.	B6	127
Cleary, Cape, c., Ak., U.S.	D10	79
Clearfield, Ia., U.S.	D3	92
Clearfield, Ky., U.S.	B6	94
Clearfield, Pa., U.S.	D5	115
Clearfield, S.D., U.S.	D5	118
Clearfield, Ut., U.S.	B3	121
Clearfield, co., Pa., U.S.	D5	115
Clear Fork, W.V., U.S.	D3	125
Clear Fork, stm., W.V., U.S.	n13	125
Clear Fork, stm., W.V., U.S.	D3	125
Clear Island, i., Ire.	F2	11
Clearlake, Ca., U.S.	C2	82
Clear Lake, Ia., U.S.	A4	92
Clear Lake, Mn., U.S.	E5	100
Clear Lake, S.D., U.S.	C9	118
Clearlake, Wa., U.S.	A3	124
Clear Lake, Wi., U.S.	C1	126
Clear Lake, l., Man.	D1	70
Clear Lake, l., Ia., U.S.	A4	92
Clear Lake, l., Ut., U.S.	D3	121
Clear Lake City, Tx., U.S.	r14	120
Clear Lake Reservoir, res., Ca., U.S.	B3	82
Clear Lake Shores, Tx., U.S.	r15	120
Clearmont, Mo., U.S.	A2	102
Clearmont, Wy., U.S.	B6	127
Clear Spring, Md., U.S.	A2	97
Clear Springs, Mo., U.S.	C4	102
Clear Stream, stm., N.H., U.S.	g7	106
Clearview, Ok., U.S.	B5	113
Clearview City, Ks., U.S.	g12	93
Clearwater, B.C.	D7	69
Clearwater, Man.	E2	70
Clearwater, Fl., U.S.	D4	86
Clearwater, Ks., U.S.	E6	93
Clearwater, Mn., U.S.	E5	100
Clearwater, S.C., U.S.	E4	117
Clearwater, co., Id., U.S.	C3	89
Clearwater, co., Mn., U.S.	C3	100
Clearwater, stm., Alta.	D3	68
Clearwater, stm., Can.	A5	68
Clearwater, stm., B.C.	C7	69
Clearwater, stm., Id., U.S.	C2	89
Clearwater, stm., Mn., U.S.	C3	100
Clearwater Lake, Wi., U.S.	C4	126
Clearwater Lake, l., B.C.	C7	69
Clearwater Lake, l., Man.	B1	70
Clearwater Lake, res., Mo., U.S.	D7	102
Clearwater Mountains, mts., Id., U.S.	C2	89
Clearwater Provincial Park, Man.	C1	70
Cleator Moor, Eng., U.K.	F5	13
Cleburne, Tx., U.S.	C4	120
Cleburne, co., Al., U.S.	B4	78
Cleburne, co., Ar., U.S.	B3	81
Cle Elum, Wa., U.S.	B5	124
Cle Elum, stm., Wa., U.S.	f7	78
Cle Elum Lake, res., Wa., U.S.	B4	124
Cleethorpes, Eng., U.K.	A7	12
Cleeves, Sask.	D1	75
Cleggan, Ire.	D1	11
Cleghorn, Ia., U.S.	B2	92
Cleland Heights, De., U.S.	*B3	85
Clem, Ga., U.S.	C1	87
Clementon, N.J., U.S.	D3	107
Clements, Ks., U.S.	D7	93
Clements, Md., U.S.	D4	97
Clements, Mn., U.S.	F3	100
Clementsport, N.S.	E4	71
Clementsvale, N.S.	E4	71
Clemmons, N.C., U.S.	A2	110
Clemons, Ia., U.S.	B4	92
Clemons, N.Y., U.S.	B7	109
Clemscot, Ok., U.S.	C4	113
Clendenin, W.V., U.S.	C3	125
Clendening Lake, res., Oh., U.S.	B4	112
Cleona, Pa., U.S.	F9	115
Cleo Springs, Ok., U.S.	A3	113
Clermont, Austl.	D8	50
Clermont, Que.	B7	74
Clermont, Fr.	E2	17
Clermont, Fl., U.S.	D5	86
Clermont, Ga., U.S.	B3	87
Clermont, Ia., U.S.	A6	92
Clermont, Ky., U.S.	C4	94
Clermont, co., Oh., U.S.	C1	112
Clermont-Ferrand, Fr.	E5	16
Clermont Harbor, Ms., U.S.	E4	101
Clermont-l'Hérault, Fr.	F5	16
Clerval, Fr.	B1	21
Clervaux, Lux.	E6	12
Clevedon, Eng., U.K.	C5	12
Cleveland, Al., U.S.	A3	78
Cleveland, Ar., U.S.	B3	81
Cleveland, Il., U.S.	B3	90
Cleveland, Mn., U.S.	F5	100
Cleveland, Mo., U.S.	B3	101
Cleveland, N.M., U.S.	A4	108
Cleveland, N.Y., U.S.	B5	109
Cleveland, N.C., U.S.	B2	110
Cleveland, N.D., U.S.	C6	111
Cleveland, Oh., U.S.	A4	112
Cleveland, Ok., U.S.	A5	113
Cleveland, S.C., U.S.	A2	117
Cleveland, Tn., U.S.	D9	119
Cleveland, Tx., U.S.	D5	120
Cleveland, Ut., U.S.	D5	121
Cleveland, Va., U.S.	f9	123
Cleveland, co., Ar., U.S.	D3	81
Cleveland, co., N.C., U.S.	B1	110
Cleveland, co., Ok., U.S.	B4	113
Cleveland, Mount, mtn., Mt., U.S.	B2	103
Cleveland, co., Eng., U.K.	F7	13
Cleveland Heights, Oh., U.S.	A4	112
Cleveland Heights, hills, Eng., U.K.	F7	13
Clevelândia, Braz.	D2	56
Clever, Mo., U.S.	D4	102
Cleves, Oh., U.S.	o12	112
Cleves see Kleve, W. Ger.	C3	18
Clew Bay, b., Ire.	D2	10
Clewiston, Fl., U.S.	F6	86
Clichy, Fr.	g10	16
Clifden, Ire.	D1	10
Cliff, N.M., U.S.	E1	108
Cliff Island, i., Me., U.S.	g7	96
Clifford, Ont.	D4	73
Clifford, In., U.S.	F6	91
Clifford, Mi., U.S.	E7	99
Clifford, N.D., U.S.	B8	111
Clifford, Pa., U.S.	C10	115
Clifford, Va., U.S.	C3	123
Cliffside, N.C., U.S.	B1	110
Cliffside Park, N.J., U.S.	h9	107
Clifftop, W.V., U.S.	m14	125
Clifton, Az., U.S.	D6	80
Clifton, Co., U.S.	B2	83
Clifton, co., Pa., U.S.	G7	89
Clifton, Il., U.S.	C6	90
Clifton, Ks., U.S.	C6	93
Clifton, N.J., U.S.	B4	107
Clifton, S.C., U.S.	B4	117
Clifton, Tn., U.S.	B4	119
Clifton, Tx., U.S.	C4	120
Clifton, Va., U.S.	g12	123
Clifton City, Mo., U.S.	*C4	123
Clifton Forge, Va., U.S.	C3	123
Clifton Heights, Pa., U.S.	*p20	115
Clifton Hill, Mo., U.S.	B5	102
Clifton Knolls, N.Y., U.S.	*C7	109
Clifton Springs, N.Y., U.S.	C3	109
Climax, Ms., U.S.	B5	101
Climax, Sask.	H1	75
Climax, Co., U.S.	B4	83
Climax, Ga., U.S.	F2	87
Climax, Ks., U.S.	E7	93
Climax, Mi., U.S.	F5	99
Climax Springs, Mo., U.S.	C4	102
Climbing Hill, Ia., U.S.	B1	92
Clinch, co., Ga., U.S.	F4	87
Clinch, stm., U.S.	D9	119
Clinchco, Va., U.S.	e9	123
Clinchfield, Ga., U.S.	D3	87
Clinch Mountain, mtn., U.S.	C10	119
Clinchport, Va., U.S.	f9	123
Clingmans Dome, mtn., U.S.	D10	119
Clint, Tx., U.S.	o11	120
Clinton, B.C.	D7	69
Clinton, Ont.	D3	73
Clinton, Ar., U.S.	B3	81
Clinton, Ct., U.S.	D5	84
Clinton, Ga., U.S.	D3	87
Clinton, Il., U.S.	C5	90
Clinton, In., U.S.	E3	91
Clinton, Ky., U.S.	f9	94
Clinton, La., U.S.	D4	95
Clinton, Me., U.S.	D3	96
Clinton, Md., U.S.	C4	97
Clinton, Ma., U.S.	B4	98
Clinton, Mi., U.S.	F7	99
Clinton, Mn., U.S.	E2	100
Clinton, Mo., U.S.	C4	102
Clinton, Mt., U.S.	D3	103
Clinton, Ne., U.S.	B3	104
Clinton, N.J., U.S.	B3	107
Clinton, N.Y., U.S.	B5	109
Clinton, N.C., U.S.	C4	110
Clinton, Ok., U.S.	B3	113
Clinton, S.C., U.S.	C4	117
Clinton, Tn., U.S.	C9	119
Clinton, Ut., U.S.	B3	121
Clinton, Wa., U.S.	B3	124
Clinton, Wi., U.S.	F5	126
Clinton, co., Il., U.S.	E4	90
Clinton, co., In., U.S.	D4	91
Clinton, co., Ia., U.S.	C7	92
Clinton, co., Ky., U.S.	D4	94
Clinton, co., Mi., U.S.	F6	99
Clinton, co., Mo., U.S.	B3	102
Clinton, co., N.Y., U.S.	f11	109
Clinton, co., Oh., U.S.	C2	112
Clinton, co., Pa., U.S.	D6	115
Clinton, Lake, res., Il., U.S.	C5	90
Clinton-Colden Lake, l., N.W. Ter.	D11	66
Clinton Lake, res., Ks., U.S.	m15	93
Clinton Reservoir, res., N.J., U.S.	A4	107
Clinton Township, Mi., U.S.	*F8	99
Clintonville, Ky., U.S.	B5	94
Clintonville, Pa., U.S.	D2	115
Clintonville, W.V., U.S.	D4	125
Clintonville, Wi., U.S.	D5	126
Clintwood, Va., U.S.	e9	123
Clio, Al., U.S.	D4	78
Clio, Ca., U.S.	C3	82
Clio, Mi., U.S.	E7	99
Clio, S.C., U.S.	B8	117
Clio, W.V., U.S.	C3	125
Clipperton, atoll, Fr. Poly.	F15	6
Clisham, mtn., Scot., U.K.	C2	6
Clitheroe, Eng., U.K.	G6	13
Clive, Alta.	C4	68
Clive, Ia., U.S.	e8	92
Cliza, Bol.	C2	55
Cloan, Sask.	E1	75
Cloe, Pa., U.S.	E4	115
Cloghan, Ire.	C4	11
Cloghan, Ire.	D4	11
Cloghane, Ire.	E1	11
Clogheen, Ire.	E3	11
Clogher, Ire.	D4	11
Clogher Head, c., Ire.	D5	11
Clonakilty, Ire.	E2	11
Clonakilty Bay, b., Ire.	E2	11
Cloncurry, Austl.	D7	50
Clones, Ire.	C4	11
Clonmany, Ire.	B4	11
Clonmel, Ire.	E3	11
Clonmellon, Ire.	D4	11
Clontarf, Mn., U.S.	E3	100
Cloone, Ire.	D4	11
Clo-oose, B.C.	g12	69
Cloppenburg, W. Ger.	F2	15
Clopton, Al., U.S.	D4	78
Cloquet, Mn., U.S.	D6	100
Cloquet, stm., Mn., U.S.	C6	100
Closter, N.J., U.S.	B5	107
Clothier, W.V., U.S.	n12	125
Cloud, co., Ks., U.S.	C6	93
Cloud Chief, Ok., U.S.	B3	103
Cloudcroft, N.M., U.S.	E4	108
Cloud Peak, mtn., Wy., U.S.	C6	113
Cloudy Bay, b., Ar.	N15	51
Cloudy Mountain, mtn., Ar.,	C8	79
Clovelândia, Braz.	D2	56
Clover, S.C., U.S.	A5	117
Clover, Va., U.S.	D4	123
Clover Bottom, Ky., U.S.	C6	94
Cloverdale, Al., U.S.	A2	78
Cloverdale, Ca., U.S.	C2	82
Cloverdale, In., U.S.	E4	91
Cloverdale, Or., U.S.	B3	114
Cloverleaf, Tx., U.S.	*r14	120
Cloverport, Ky., U.S.	C3	94
Clovis, Ca., U.S.	D4	82
Clovis, N.M., U.S.	C6	108
Clow, Ar., U.S.	h11	125
Cloyne, Ire.	F3	11
Clute, Tx., U.S.	r14	120
Clutha, stm., N.Z.	P12	51
Clwyd, co., Wales, U.K.	A4	12
Clyattville, Ga., U.S.	F3	87
Clyde, Alta.	B4	68
Clyde, N.W. Ter.	B19	66
Clyde, Ks., U.S.	C6	93
Clyde, Mo., U.S.	A3	102
Clyde, N.Y., U.S.	B4	109
Clyde, N.C., U.S.	f10	110
Clyde, N.D., U.S.	A7	111
Clyde, Oh., U.S.	A3	112
Clyde, Tx., U.S.	C3	120
Clyde, stm., Scot., U.K.	E4	13
Clyde, Firth of, est., Scot., U.K.	C4	10
Clydebank, Scot., U.K.	C4	10
Clyde Park, Mt., U.S.	E6	103
Clymer, N.Y., U.S.	C1	109
Clymer, Pa., U.S.	E3	115
Clyo, Ga., U.S.	D5	87
Cnossus, hist., Grc.	E5	25
Côa, stm., Port.	E2	22
Coachella, Ca., U.S.	F5	82
Coachella Canal, Ca., U.S.	F6	82
Coachford, Ire.	E3	11
Coahoma, Tx., U.S.	C2	120
Coahoma, co., Ms., U.S.	A3	101
Coahuayana, stm., Mex.	n12	63
Coahuila, state, Mex.	B4	63
Coal, co., Ok., U.S.	C5	113
Coal, stm., W.V., U.S.	C3	125
Coal Bluff, In., U.S.	E3	91
Coal Branch, N.B.	C4	71
Coal City, Il., U.S.	B5	90
Coal City, In., U.S.	F3	91
Coalcomán [de Matamoros], Mex.	D4	63
Coal Creek, Co., U.S.	C5	83
Coal Creek, stm., U.S.	E3	91
Coal Creek, stm., Ok., U.S.	B6	113
Coaldale, Alta.	E4	68
Coaldale, Co., U.S.	C5	83
Coaldale, Nv., U.S.	E4	105
Coaldale, Pa., U.S.	E10	115
Coalfield, Tn., U.S.	C9	119
Coal Fork, W.V., U.S.	C3	125
Coal Fork, stm., W.V., U.S.	m13	125
Coalgate, Ok., U.S.	C5	113
Coal Grove, Oh., U.S.	D3	112
Coal Harbour, B.C.	D4	69
Coal Hill, Ar., U.S.	B2	81
Coalhurst, Alta.	E4	68
Coaling, Al., U.S.	B2	78
Coalinga, Ca., U.S.	D3	82
Coalmont, Co., U.S.	A4	83
Coalmont, In., U.S.	F3	91
Coalmont, Tn., U.S.	D8	119
Coalridge, Oh., U.S.	C4	112
Coalspur, Alta.	C2	68
Coalton, Il., U.S.	D4	90
Coalton, Oh., U.S.	C3	112
Coalville, Eng., U.K.	B6	12
Coalville, Ut., U.S.	C4	121
Coalwood, W.V., U.S.	D3	125
Coamo, P.R.	B3	65
Coari, Braz.	C2	59
Coari, stm., Braz.	C2	59
Coast, prov., Kenya	B7	47
Coasters Harbor Island, i., R.I., U.S.	E5	116
Coast Mountains, mts., N.A.	E6	66
Coast Ranges, mts., U.S.	B3	76
Coatbridge, Scot., U.K.	C5	10
Coatepec, Mex.	n15	63
Coatepeque, Guat.	C2	62
Coatesville, Pa., U.S.	G10	115
Coaticook, Que.	D6	74
Coatney Hill, mtn., Ct., U.S.	B7	84
Coatopa, Al., U.S.	C1	78
Coats, Ks., U.S.	E5	93
Coats, N.C., U.S.	B4	110
Coatsburg, Il., U.S.	C2	90
Coats Island, i., N.W. Ter.	D16	66
Coats Land, reg., Ant.	B9	7
Coatsville, Mo., U.S.	A5	102
Coatzacoalcos (Puerto México), Mex.	D6	63
Cobalt, Ont.	p19	73
Cobalt, Ct., U.S.	C5	84
Cobán, Guat.	D6	63
Cobar, Austl.	F8	50
Cobb, Ky., U.S.	D2	94
Cobb, Ok., U.S.	C5	113
Cobb, Wi., U.S.	F3	126
Cobb, co., Ga., U.S.	C2	87
Cobb, stm., Mn., U.S.	G5	100
Cobberas, Mount, mtn., Austl.	H7	51
Cobble Hill, B.C.	g12	69
Cobble Mountain Reservoir, res., Ma., U.S.	B2	98
Cobbosseecontee Lake, l., Me., U.S.	D3	96
Cobbtown, Ga., U.S.	D5	87
Cobden, Ont.	B8	73
Cobden, Il., U.S.	F4	90
Cobequid Mountains, mts., N.S.	D5	71
Cobh, Ire.	E2	10
Cobham, Eng., U.K.	m12	10
Cobham, stm., Can.	C4	70
Cobija, Bol.	B2	55
Cobija, Chile	D2	55
Coble, Tn., U.S.	B4	119
Coblence see Koblenz, W. Ger.	C3	18
Cobleskill, N.Y., U.S.	C6	109
Coboconk, Ont.	C6	73
Cobourg, Ont.	D6	73
Cobourg Peninsula, pen., Austl.	B5	50
Cobre, Nv., U.S.	B7	105
Côbuè, Moz.	D6	48
Cobun Creek, stm., W.V., U.S.	h11	125
Coburg, Austl.	*G7	51
Coburg, W. Ger.	C5	18
Coburg, Ia., U.S.	D2	92
Coburg, Or., U.S.	C3	114
Coburg Island, i., N.W. Ter.	m36	66
Coburn Gore, Me., U.S.	C2	96
Coburn Mountain, mtn., Me., U.S.	C2	96
Cocentaina, Spain	C5	22
Cochabamba, Bol.	C2	55
Cochabamba, dept., Bol.	C2	55
Coche, Isla, i., Ven.	A5	60
Cocheco, stm., N.H., U.S.	D5	106
Cochem, W. Ger.	C2	18
Cochesett, Ma., U.S.	B5	98
Cochetopa Creek, stm., Co., U.S.	C4	83
Cochetopa Hills, mts., Co., U.S.	C4	83
Cochin, India	H6	37
Cochin China, hist. reg., Viet.	H6	35
Cochinos Point, c., Phil.	o13	34
Cochise, Az., U.S.	E6	80
Cochise, co., Az., U.S.	E6	80
Cochise Head, mtn., Az., U.S.	h8	108
Cochiti Indian Reservation, N.M., U.S.	h8	108
Cochiti Reservoir, res., N.M., U.S.	B3	108
Cochituate, Ma., U.S.	g10	98
Cochituate, Lake, l., Ma., U.S.	g10	98
Cochran, Ga., U.S.	D3	87
Cochran, co., Tx., U.S.	C1	120
Cochrane, Alta.	D3	68
Cochrane, Ont.	o19	73
Cochrane, Wi., U.S.	D2	126
Cochrane, dept., Ont.	o19	73
Cochranville, Pa., U.S.	G10	115

Name	Map Ref.	Page
Cockburn, Austl.	F3	51
Cocke, co., Tn., U.S.	D10	119
Cockermouth, Eng., U.K.	F5	13
Cockeysville, Md., U.S.	B4	97
Cockpit Country, reg., Jam.	E13	65
Cockrell Hill, Tx., U.S.	n10	120
Cockrum, Ms., U.S.	A4	101
Coco, stm., N.A.	E8	63
Coco, Isla del, i., C.R.	C2	53
Cocoa, Fl., U.S.	D6	86
Cocoa Beach, Fl., U.S.	D6	86
Cocoa West, Fl., U.S.	*D6	86
Cocobeach, Gabon	E1	46
Cocolalla, Id., U.S.	A2	89
Coconino, co., Az., U.S.	B3	80
Coconino Plateau, plat., Az., U.S.	B3	80
Coconut Creek, Fl., U.S.	*F6	86
Cocopah Indian Reservation, Az., U.S.	E1	80
Cocos Bay, b., Trin.	O23	65
Cocos Island, i., Guam	M9	52
Cocos Islands (Keeling Islands), is., Oc.	G3	2
Cocos Lagoon, b., Guam	M9	52
Coco Solo, Pan.	k11	62
Cocula, Mex.	C4	63
Codajás, Braz.	C2	59
Codell, Ks., U.S.	C4	93
Coden, Al., U.S.	E1	78
Codera, Cabo, c., Ven.	A4	60
Coderre, Sask.	G2	75
Codesa, Alta.	B1	68
Codette, Sask.	D3	75
Codigoro, Italy	E8	20
Codington, co., S.D., U.S.	C8	118
Cod Island, i., Newf.	g9	72
Codó, Braz.	B2	57
Codogno, Italy	B2	23
Codpa, Chile	C2	55
Codroipo, Italy	D8	20
Codroy, Newf.	E2	72
Codroy Pond, Newf.	D2	72
Cody, Ne., U.S.	B4	104
Cody, Wy., U.S.	B3	127
Codys, N.B.	D4	71
Coeburn, Va., U.S.	f9	123
Coe Hill, Ont.	C7	73
Coesfeld, W. Ger.	C3	18
Coesse, In., U.S.	B7	91
Coeur d'Alene, Id., U.S.	B2	89
Coeur d'Alene, stm., Id., U.S.	B2	89
Coeur d'Alene Indian Reservation, Id., U.S.	B2	89
Coeur d'Alene Lake, res., Id., U.S.	B2	89
Coeur d'Alene Mountains, mts., Id., U.S.	B2	89
Coevorden, Neth.	B6	17
Coffee, co., Al., U.S.	D3	78
Coffee, co., Ga., U.S.	E4	87
Coffee, co., Tn., U.S.	B5	119
Coffee Creek, Mt., U.S.	C6	103
Coffeen, Il., U.S.	D4	90
Coffee Springs, Al., U.S.	D4	78
Coffeeville, Al., U.S.	D1	78
Coffeeville, Ms., U.S.	B4	101
Coffey, Mo., U.S.	A3	102
Coffey, co., Ks., U.S.	D8	93
Coffeyville, Ks., U.S.	E8	93
Coffin, Île, i., Que.	B8	71
Coffs Harbour, Austl.	F9	50
Cofield, N.C., U.S.	A6	110
Cogdell, Ga., U.S.	E4	87
Coggon, Ia., U.S.	B6	92
Coghinas, stm., Italy	D2	23
Cognac, Fr.	E3	16
Cogswell, N.D., U.S.	C8	111
Cohagen, Mt., U.S.	C10	103
Cohansey, stm., N.J., U.S.	E2	107
Cohasset, Ma., U.S.	B6	98
Cohasset, Mn., U.S.	C5	100
Cohocton, N.Y., U.S.	C3	109
Cohocton, stm., N.Y., U.S.	C3	109
Cohoe, Ak., U.S.	g16	79
Cohoes, N.Y., U.S.	C7	109
Cohoon, Lake, res., Va., U.S.	k14	123
Cohutta, Ga., U.S.	B2	87
Cohutta Mountain, mtn., Ga., U.S.	B2	87
Coiba, Isla de, i., Pan.	G7	62
Coig, stm., Arg.	E2	54
Coihaique, Chile	E2	54
Coila, Ms., U.S.	B4	101
Coils Creek, stm., Nv., U.S.	D5	105
Coimbatore, India	F6	36
Coimbra, Port.	B1	22
Coimbra, Port.	D3	22
Coín, Spain	D3	22
Coin, Ia., U.S.	D2	92
Coinjock, N.C., U.S.	A7	110
Coipasa, Laguna, l., Bol.	C2	55
Coipasa, Salar de, pl., Bol.	C2	55
Coire, Loch, l., Scot., U.K.	B4	13
Cojedes, state, Ven.	B4	60
Cojutepeque, El Sal.	D3	62
Cokato, Mn., U.S.	E4	100
Coke, co., Tx., U.S.	D2	120
Coker, Al., U.S.	B2	78
Coketon, W.V., U.S.	B5	125
Cokeville, Wy., U.S.	D2	127
Colàba Point, c., India	H4	37
Colac, Austl.	G7	50
Colares, Port.	f9	22
Colatina, Braz.	B4	56
Colbeck, Cape, c., Ant.	B33	7
Colbert, Ok., U.S.	D5	113
Colbert, co., Al., U.S.	A2	78
Colbert Heights, Al., U.S.	A2	78
Colbio, Som.	F5	47
Colborne, Ont.	C7	73
Colbún, Chile	B2	54
Colburn, Id., U.S.	A2	89
Colburn, In., U.S.	C4	91
Colby, Ks., U.S.	C2	93
Colby, Me., U.S.	B4	96
Colby, Wi., U.S.	D3	126
Colbyville, Vt., U.S.	C3	122
Colchester, Eng., U.K.	E7	10
Colchester, Ct., U.S.	C6	84
Colchester, Il., U.S.	C3	90
Colchester, Vt., U.S.	B2	122
Colchester, co., N.S.	D6	71
Colcord, Ok., U.S.	A7	113
Cold, stm., N.H., U.S.	C4	106
Cold, stm., N.H., U.S.	D2	106
Cold Bay, Ak., U.S.	E7	79
Cold Fell, mtn., Eng., U.K.	F6	13
Cold Hollow Mountains, mts., Vt., U.S.	B3	122
Colditz, E. Ger.	B7	19
Cold Lake, Alta.	B5	68
Cold Lake, l., Can.	B5	68
Cold River, N.H., U.S.	D2	106
Cold Spring, Ky., U.S.	A5	94
Cold Spring, Mn., U.S.	E4	100
Cold Spring, N.J., U.S.	F3	107
Cold Spring, Tx., U.S.	D5	120
Cold Spring Harbor, N.Y., U.S.	*n15	109
Coldspring, Tx., U.S.	D5	120
Cold Stream Pond, l., Me., U.S.	C4	96
Coldstream, Ont.	C5	73
Coldstream, Scot., U.K.	E6	13
Coldwater, Ks., U.S.	E4	93
Coldwater, Mi., U.S.	G5	99
Coldwater, Ms., U.S.	A4	101
Coldwater, Oh., U.S.	B1	112
Coldwater, stm., Ms., U.S.	A3	101
Coldwater Creek, stm., U.S.	e9	113
Cole, Ok., U.S.	B4	113
Cole, co., Mo., U.S.	C5	102
Cole Camp, Mo., U.S.	C4	102
Coleen, stm., Ak., U.S.	B11	79
Colebrook, Ct., U.S.	B3	84
Colebrook, N.H., U.S.	g7	106
Colebrook River Lake, res., Ct., U.S.	A3	84
Coleharbor, N.D., U.S.	B4	111
Cole Lake, Ont.	C8	73
Coleman, P.E.I.	C5	71
Coleman, Fl., U.S.	D4	86
Coleman, Ga., U.S.	E2	87
Coleman, Mi., U.S.	B5	97
Coleman, Mi., U.S.	E6	99
Coleman, Ok., U.S.	C5	113
Coleman, Tx., U.S.	D3	120
Coleman, co., Tx., U.S.	D3	120
Coleman Falls, Va., U.S.	C3	123
Colen Lakes, l., Man.	B4	70
Colerain, N.C., U.S.	A6	110
Coleraine, Austl.	H3	51
Coleraine, Que.	D6	74
Coleraine, N. Ire., U.K.	C3	10
Coleraine, Mn., U.S.	C5	100
Coleridge, Ne., U.S.	B8	104
Coleridge, N.C., U.S.	B3	110
Coles, Ms., U.S.	D2	101
Coles, co., Il., U.S.	D5	90
Coles, Punta, c., Peru	E3	58
Colesberg, S. Afr.	D4	49
Colesburg, Ia., U.S.	B6	92
Colesburg, Ky., U.S.	C4	94
Coleta, Il., U.S.	B4	90
Coleville, Sask.	F1	75
Coleville, Ca., U.S.	H4	75
Colfax, Sask.	F1	75
Colfax, Ca., U.S.	C3	82
Colfax, Il., U.S.	C5	90
Colfax, In., U.S.	D4	91
Colfax, Ia., U.S.	C4	92
Colfax, La., U.S.	C3	95
Colfax, N.D., U.S.	C9	111
Colfax, Wi., U.S.	D2	126
Colfax, co., Ne., U.S.	C8	104
Colfax, co., N.M., U.S.	A5	108
Colgate, Sask.	H4	75
Colhué Huapi, Lago, l., Arg.	D3	54
Colibris, Pointe des, c., Guad.	Q9	65
Colico, Italy	C5	20
Colijnsplaat, Neth.	C3	17
Colima, Mex.	D4	63
Colima, state, Mex.	D4	63
Colima, Nevado de, mtn., Mex.	n12	63
Colinas, Braz.	C2	57
Colinet, Newf.	E5	72
Colinton, Alta.	B4	68
Coll, i., Scot., U.K.	B3	10
Collbran, Co., U.S.	B3	83
College, Ak., U.S.	B10	79
College City, Ar., U.S.	*A5	81
College Corner, Oh., U.S.	C1	112
Collegedale, Tn., U.S.	h11	119
College Grove, Tn., U.S.	B5	119
College Park, Ga., U.S.	C2	87
College Park, Md., U.S.	C4	97
College Place, Wa., U.S.	C7	124
College Springs, Ia., U.S.	D2	92
College Station, Ar., U.S.	C3	81
College Station, Tx., U.S.	D4	120
Collegeville, Ar., U.S.	*C3	81
Collegeville, In., U.S.	C3	91
Collegeville, Pa., U.S.	F11	115
College Ward, Ut., U.S.	*B4	121
Colleton, co., S.C., U.S.	F6	117
Colleyville, Tx., U.S.	*n9	120
Collie, stm., U.S.	F2	50
Collier, co., Fl., U.S.	F5	86
Collier Bay, b., Austl.	C3	50
Collier City, Fl., U.S.	*F6	86
Colliers, W.V., U.S.	f8	125
Collierville, Tn., U.S.	B2	119
Collin, co., Tx., U.S.	C4	120
Collingdale, Pa., U.S.	p20	115
Collingwood, N.J., U.S.	D2	107
Collingsworth, co., Tx., U.S.	B2	120
Collingwood, Ont.	C4	73
Collins, Ar., U.S.	D4	81
Collins, Ga., U.S.	D4	87
Collins, Ia., U.S.	C4	92
Collins, Ms., U.S.	D4	101
Collins, Mo., U.S.	C4	102
Collins, Wi., U.S.	h10	126
Collins Park, De., U.S.	B3	85
Collinston, La., U.S.	B4	95
Collinston, Ut., U.S.	B3	121
Collinsville, Al., U.S.	A4	78
Collinsville, Ct., U.S.	B4	84
Collinsville, Il., U.S.	E4	90
Collinsville, Ms., U.S.	C5	101
Collinsville, Ok., U.S.	A6	113
Collinsville, Tn., U.S.	B4	119
Collinwood, Tn., U.S.	B4	119
Collipulli, Chile	B2	54
Collins, Mn., U.S.	E2	100
Collooney, Ire.	C3	11
Collyer, Ks., U.S.	C3	93
Colmar, Fr.	D6	16
Colmar Manor, Md., U.S.	f9	97
Colmenar de Oreja, Spain	B4	22
Colmenar Viejo, Spain	B4	22
Colmesneil, Tx., U.S.	D5	120
Colnett, Cabo, c., Mex.	A1	63
Cologne (Köln), W. Ger.	C3	18
Cologne, Mn., U.S.	F5	100
Cologne, N.J., U.S.	E3	107
Cologne, Va., U.S.	*C6	123
Coloma, Mi., U.S.	F4	99
Coloma, Wi., U.S.	D4	126
Colombes, Fr.	g10	16
Colômbia, Braz.	C3	56
Colombia, Col.	C3	60
Colombia, ctry., S.A.	C3	60
Colombo, Sri L.	G6	36
Colome, S.D., U.S.	D6	118
Colón, Arg.	A5	54
Colón, Cuba	C3	64
Colón, Pan.	F8	62
Colon, Mi., U.S.	G5	99
Colon, Ne., U.S.	g11	104
Colon, N.C., U.S.	B3	110
Colón, Archipiélago de (Galapagos Islands), is., Ec.	g5	58
Colona, Co., U.S.	C3	83
Colonia, N.J., U.S.	k7	107
Colonia, dept., Ur.	g8	54
Colonia del Sacramento, Ur.	E1	56
Colonia Dora, Arg.	D3	54
Colonia Las Heras, Arg.	D3	54
Colonial Beach, Va., U.S.	B6	123
Colônia Leopoldina, Braz.	k6	57
Colonial Heights, Tn., U.S.	C11	119
Colonial Heights, Va., U.S.	C5	123
Colonial National Historical Park, Va., U.S.	C6	123
Colonial Park, Pa., U.S.	*F8	115
Colonia Mennonita, Para.	D5	55
Colonia Suiza, Ur.	g8	54
Colonie, N.Y., U.S.	C7	109
Colony, Ks., U.S.	D8	93
Colony, Ok., U.S.	B3	113
Colorado, C.R.	E8	63
Colorado, state, U.S.	B5	83
Colorado, stm., Arg.	B4	54
Colorado, stm., N.A.	D5	76
Colorado, stm., Tx., U.S.	D3	120
Colorado City, Az., U.S.	A3	80
Colorado City, Co., U.S.	D6	83
Colorado City, Tx., U.S.	C2	120
Colorado City, Lake, res., Tx., U.S.	C2	120
Colorado National Monument, Co., U.S.	B2	83
Colorado Plateau, plat., U.S.	B4	80
Colorado River Aqueduct, Ca., U.S.	F6	82
Colorado River Indian Reservation, U.S.	D1	80
Colorados, stm., La., U.S.	C4	95
Colorados, Archipiélago de los, is., Cuba	C1	64
Colorado Springs, Co., U.S.	C6	83
Colotlán, Mex.	C4	63
Colquechaca, Bol.	C2	55
Colquitt, Ga., U.S.	E2	87
Colquitt, co., Ga., U.S.	E3	87
Colrain, Ma., U.S.	A2	98
Colstrip, Mt., U.S.	E10	103
Colt, Ar., U.S.	B5	81
Coltauco, Chile	A2	54
Colton, Ca., U.S.	*E5	82
Colton, N.Y., U.S.	f10	109
Colton, Or., U.S.	B4	114
Colton, S.D., U.S.	D9	118
Colton, Wa., U.S.	C8	124
Colton Hill, mtn., Vt., U.S.	B3	122
Coltons Point, Md., U.S.	D4	97
Colts Neck, N.J., U.S.	C4	107
Columbia, Al., U.S.	D4	78
Columbia, Ca., U.S.	C3	82
Columbia, Ct., U.S.	C6	84
Columbia, Il., U.S.	E3	90
Columbia, Ky., U.S.	C4	94
Columbia, Md., U.S.	B4	97
Columbia, Ms., U.S.	D4	101
Columbia, Mo., U.S.	C5	102
Columbia, N.C., U.S.	B6	110
Columbia, Pa., U.S.	F9	115
Columbia, S.C., U.S.	C5	117
Columbia, S.D., U.S.	B7	118
Columbia, Tn., U.S.	B4	119
Columbia, Va., U.S.	C4	123
Columbia, co., Ar., U.S.	D2	81
Columbia, co., Fl., U.S.	B4	86
Columbia, co., Ga., U.S.	C4	87
Columbia, co., N.Y., U.S.	C7	109
Columbia, co., Or., U.S.	B3	114
Columbia, co., Pa., U.S.	D9	115
Columbia, co., Wa., U.S.	C7	124
Columbia, co., Wi., U.S.	E4	126
Columbia, stm., N.A.	A7	76
Columbia, Cape, c., N.W. Ter.	k37	66
Columbia, Mount, mtn., Can.	C2	68
Columbia Basin, Wa., U.S.	C6	124
Columbia City, In., U.S.	B7	91
Columbia City, Or., U.S.	B4	114
Columbia Cross Roads, Pa., U.S.	C8	115
Columbia Falls, Me., U.S.	D5	96
Columbia Falls, Mt., U.S.	B2	103
Columbia Heights, Mn., U.S.	m12	100
Columbia Lake, l., B.C.	D10	69
Columbia Lake, res., Ct., U.S.	C6	84
Columbia Mountains, mts., B.C.	C7	69
Columbiana, Al., U.S.	B3	78
Columbiana, Oh., U.S.	B5	112
Columbiana, co., Oh., U.S.	B5	112
Columbiaville, Mi., U.S.	E7	99
Columbine, Co., U.S.	A5	83
Columbus, Ga., U.S.	D1	87
Columbus, In., U.S.	F6	91
Columbus, Ks., U.S.	E9	93
Columbus, Ky., U.S.	f8	94
Columbus, Ms., U.S.	B5	101
Columbus, Mt., U.S.	E7	103
Columbus, Ne., U.S.	C8	104
Columbus, N.J., U.S.	C3	107
Columbus, N.M., U.S.	F2	108
Columbus, N.C., U.S.	f10	110
Columbus, N.D., U.S.	A3	111
Columbus, Oh., U.S.	C2	112
Columbus, Tx., U.S.	E4	120
Columbus, Wi., U.S.	E4	126
Columbus, co., N.C., U.S.	C4	110
Columbus Air Force Base, mil., Ms., U.S.	B5	101
Columbus City, Ia., U.S.	C6	92
Columbus Grove, Oh., U.S.	B1	112
Columbus Junction, Ia., U.S.	C6	92
Columbus Lake, res., Ms., U.S.	B5	101
Colville Indian Reservation, Wa., U.S.	A6	124
Colville Lake, l., N.W. Ter.	C7	66
Colvin Mountain, mtn., Al., U.S.	B4	78
Colvos Passage, strt., Wa., U.S.	f10	124
Colwell, Ia., U.S.	A5	92
Colwich, Ks., U.S.	E6	93
Colwood, B.C.	h12	69
Colwyn Bay, Wales, U.K.	A5	12
Colyell Creek, stm., La., U.S.	h10	95
Coman, Mount, mtn., Ant.	B6	7
Comanche, Ok., U.S.	C4	113
Comanche, Tx., U.S.	D3	120
Comanche, co., Ks., U.S.	E4	93
Comanche, co., Ok., U.S.	C3	113
Comanche, co., Tx., U.S.	D3	120
Comarapa, Bol.	C5	55
Comandine, stm., Austl.	E9	50
Comayagua, Hond.	E7	63
Combahee, stm., S.C., U.S.	F6	117
Combarbalá, Chile	A2	54
Combeaufontaine, Fr.	B1	20
Combee Settlement, Fl., U.S.	*D5	86
Comber, Ont.	E2	73
Comber, N. Ire., U.K.	C6	11
Combermere, Ont.	B7	73
Combined Locks, Wi., U.S.	h9	126
Combs, Ar., U.S.	B2	81
Combs, Ky., U.S.	C6	94
Comer, Al., U.S.	C4	78
Comer, Ga., U.S.	B3	87
Comerío, P.R.	B3	65
Comet, stm., Austl.	B7	51
Comfort, N.C., U.S.	B5	110
Comfort, Tx., U.S.	E3	120
Comfort, W.V., U.S.	m12	125
Comfrey, Mn., U.S.	F4	100
Comilla, Bngl.	D9	36
Comines, Bel.	D2	17
Comino, Cape, c., Italy	D2	23
Comins, Mi., U.S.	D6	99
Cominto, Ar., U.S.	D4	81
Comiso, Italy	F5	23
Comitán [de Domínguez], Mex.	D6	63
Commack, N.Y., U.S.	*n15	109
Commentry, Fr.	D5	16
Commerce, Ga., U.S.	B3	87
Commerce, Mo., U.S.	D8	102
Commerce, Ok., U.S.	A7	113
Commerce City, Co., U.S.	B6	83
Commerce, Tx., U.S.	C5	120
Commercial Point, Oh., U.S.	C2	112
Commercy, Fr.	C6	16
Commewijne, dept., Sur.	A4	59
Commiskey, In., U.S.	G6	91
Commissaires, Lac des, l., Que.	A5	74
Committee Bay, b., N.W. Ter.	C15	66
Common Fence Point, R.I., U.S.	D6	116
Commonwealth Bay, b., Ant.	C27	7
Commonwealth Range, mts., Ant.	A30	7
Communism Peak, mtn., Sov. Un.	F10	29
Como, Italy	B2	23
Como, Co., U.S.	B5	83
Como, Ms., U.S.	A4	101
Como, N.C., U.S.	A5	110
Como, Tn., U.S.	A3	119
Como, Lake, l., Italy	B2	23
Comobabi, Az., U.S.	E4	80
Comodoro Rivadavia, Arg.	D3	54
Comorin, Cape, c., India	G6	36
Comoros, ctry., Afr.	H10	42
Comox, B.C.	E5	69
Compass Lake, Fl., U.S.	B1	86
Compeer, Alta.	D5	68
Competition, Mo., U.S.	D5	102
Compiègne, Fr.	C5	16
Compostela, Mex.	m11	63
Comptche, Ca., U.S.	C2	82
Compton, Que.	D6	74
Compton, Ca., U.S.	*n12	82
Compton, Il., U.S.	B4	90
Compton, co., Que.	D6	74
Comstock, Mi., U.S.	F5	99
Comstock, Mn., U.S.	D2	100
Comstock, Ne., U.S.	C6	104
Comstock, Tx., U.S.	E2	120
Comstock, Wi., U.S.	C1	126
Comté, stm., Fr. Gu.	B4	59
Con, i., Viet.	D7	35
Conakry, Gui.	G3	44
Conanicut Island, i., R.I., U.S.	E5	116
Conanicut Point, c., R.I., U.S.	E5	116
Conasauga, Tn., U.S.	D9	119
Conasauga, stm., U.S.	B2	87
Concan, Tx., U.S.	E3	120
Conceição das Alagoas, Braz.	B5	56
Conceição do Araguaia, Braz.	D5	59
Conceição do Norte, Braz.	D1	57
Concepción, Arg.	B3	54
Concepción, Bol.	C5	55
Concepción, Chile	B2	54
Concepción, Para.	D4	55
Concepción, Phil.	o13	34
Concepción, Tx., U.S.	F3	120
Concepción, dept., Para.	A4	55
Concepción, Laguna, l., Bol.	C5	55
Concepción del Oro, Mex.	C4	63
Concepción del Uruguay, Arg.	A5	54
Conception, Mo., U.S.	A3	102
Conception, Point, c., Ca., U.S.	E3	82
Conception Bay, b., Newf.	E5	72
Conception Bay South, Newf.	E5	72
Conception Island, i., Bah.	C6	64
Conception Junction, Mo., U.S.	A3	102
Conchas, Braz.	m7	56
Conchas Dam, N.M., U.S.	B5	108
Conchas Lake, l., N.M., U.S.	B5	108
Conche, Newf.	C4	72
Conchi, Chile	D2	55
Conchillas, Ur.	g7	54
Concho, Az., U.S.	C6	80
Concho, co., Tx., U.S.	D3	120
Concho, stm., Tx., U.S.	D2	120
Conchos, stm., Mex.	C4	63
Conconully, Wa., U.S.	A6	124
Concord, Ar., U.S.	B4	81
Concord, Ca., U.S.	h8	82
Concord, Fl., U.S.	B2	86
Concord, Ga., U.S.	C2	87
Concord, Il., U.S.	D3	90
Concord, Ky., U.S.	B6	94
Concord, Ma., U.S.	B5	98
Concord, Mi., U.S.	F6	99
Concord, Mo., U.S.	g13	102
Concord, Ne., U.S.	B9	104
Concord, N.H., U.S.	D3	106
Concord, N.C., U.S.	B2	110
Concord, Pa., U.S.	F6	115
Concord, Tn., U.S.	D9	119
Concord, Vt., U.S.	C5	122
Concord, Va., U.S.	C4	123
Concord, stm., Ma., U.S.	A5	98
Concordia, Arg.	A5	54
Concordia, Col.	B2	60
Concordia, Peru	B3	58
Concordia, Ks., U.S.	C6	93
Concordia, Mo., U.S.	C4	102
Concordia, co., La., U.S.	C4	95
Concrete, N.D., U.S.	A8	111
Concrete, Wa., U.S.	A4	124
Conda, Id., U.S.	G7	89
Condamine, stm., Austl.	E9	50
Conde, Braz.	D3	57
Condé [-sur-l'Escaut], Fr.	D13	17
Condé-sur-Marne, Fr.	E4	17
Condé-sur-Noireau, Fr.	C3	16
Condeúba, Braz.	A4	56
Condino, Italy	D6	20
Condobolin, Austl.	F8	50
Condom, Fr.	F4	16
Condon, Mt., U.S.	C3	103
Condon, Or., U.S.	B6	114
Cóndor, Cordillera del, mts., S.A.	B2	58
Cone, Tx., U.S.	C2	120
Conecuh, co., Al., U.S.	D2	78
Conecuh, stm., U.S.	D3	78
Conegliano [Veneto], Italy	B4	23
Conehatta, Ms., U.S.	C4	101
Conejos, Co., U.S.	D4	83
Conejos, co., Co., U.S.	D4	83
Conejos, stm., Co., U.S.	D4	83
Conejos Peak, mtn., Co., U.S.	D4	83
Conemaugh, Pa., U.S.	F4	115
Conemaugh River Lake, res., Pa., U.S.	F3	115
Conestee, S.C., U.S.	B3	117
Conesville, Ia., U.S.	C6	92
Conesville, Oh., U.S.	B4	112
Conetoe, N.C., U.S.	B5	110
Coney Island (part of New York), N.Y., U.S.	k13	109
Conflans-en-Jarnisy, Fr.	E5	17
Conflans-Sainte-Honorine, Fr.	g9	16
Confluence, Ky., U.S.	C6	94
Confluence, Pa., U.S.	G3	115
Confolens, Fr.	D6	16
Confuso, stm., Para.	A4	55
Congamond, Ma., U.S.	B2	98
Congamond Lakes, l., U.S.	A4	84
Congaree, stm., S.C., U.S.	D6	117
Congaree Swamp National Monument, S.C., U.S.	D6	117
Conger, Mn., U.S.	G5	100
Congers, N.Y., U.S.	*D7	109
Congleton, Eng., U.K.	A5	12
Congo, Oh., U.S.	C3	112
Congo, W.V., U.S.	e8	125
Congo (Zaïre), stm., Afr.	B2	48
Congo, ctry., Afr.	B2	48
Congress, Sask.	H2	75
Congress, Az., U.S.	C3	80
Conifer, N.Y., U.S.	A6	109
Coniston, Ont.	A4	73
Conklin, Alta.	B5	68
Conklin, Mi., U.S.	E5	99
Conklin, N.Y., U.S.	C5	109
Conley, Ga., U.S.	*C2	87
Conn, Lough, l., Ire.	C2	10
Connacht (Connaught), hist. reg., Ire.	D2	11
Connaught see Connacht, hist. reg., Ire.	D2	11
Conneaut, Oh., U.S.	A5	112
Conneaut Creek, stm., Oh., U.S.	A5	112
Conneaut Lake, Pa., U.S.	C1	115
Conneaut Lake, l., Pa., U.S.	C1	115
Conneautville, Pa., U.S.	C1	115
Connecticut, state, U.S.	C5	84
Connecticut, stm., U.S.	C5	84
Connell, Wa., U.S.	C7	124
Connellsville, Pa., U.S.	F2	115
Connells Mills, Mo., U.S.	A5	102
Conner, Mt., U.S.	E2	103
Connerville, Ok., U.S.	C5	113
Connersville, In., U.S.	E7	91
Connoire Bay, b., Newf.	E2	72
Connors, N.B.	B1	71
Conococheague Creek, stm., Md., U.S.	A2	97
Conover, N.C., U.S.	B1	110
Conowingo, Md., U.S.	A5	97
Conowingo Dam, Md., U.S.	A5	97
Conquest, Sask.	F2	75
Conrad, Ia., U.S.	B5	92
Conrad, Mt., U.S.	B5	103
Conrath, Wi., U.S.	C2	126
Conroe, Tx., U.S.	D5	120
Conroy, Ia., U.S.	C6	92
Conselheiro Lafaiete, Braz.	C4	56
Consett, Eng., U.K.	F7	13
Consolación del Sur, Cuba	C6	64
Con Son, i., Viet.	D7	35
Consort, Alta.	C5	68
Constableville, N.Y., U.S.	B5	109
Constance, Lake, l., Eur.	C9	24
Constance see Konstanz, W. Ger.	E4	18
Constanța, Rom.	C9	24
Constantia, N.Y., U.S.	B5	109
Constantina, Spain	D3	22
Constantine, Mi., U.S.	G5	99
Constantine (Qacentina), Alg.	B6	44
Constantine, Cape, c., Ak., U.S.	D8	79
Constantinople see İstanbul, Tur.	B7	40
Constitución, Chile	B2	54
Consuegra, Spain	C4	22
Consul, Sask.	H1	75
Contact, Nv., U.S.	B7	105
Contai, India	G11	37
Contamana, Peru	C3	58
Contas, Rio de, stm., Braz.	D3	57
Contendas do Sincorá, Braz.	A4	56
Content Keys, is., Fl., U.S.	H5	86
Continental, Oh., U.S.	A1	112
Continental Divide, N.M., U.S.	B1	108
Continental Peak, mtn., Wy., U.S.	D4	127
Continental Reservoir, res., Co., U.S.	D3	83
Contoocook, N.H., U.S.	D3	106
Contoocook, stm., N.H., U.S.	D3	106
Contra Costa, co., Ca., U.S.	D3	82
Contratación, Col.	B3	60
Contrecoeur, Que.	D4	74
Contreras, N.M., U.S.	C3	108
Contrexéville, Fr.	A1	20
Contumazá, Peru	C2	58
Contwoyto Lake, l., N.W. Ter.	C10	66
Convent, La., U.S.	D5	95
Converse, In., U.S.	C6	91
Converse, La., U.S.	C2	95
Converse, S.C., U.S.	B4	117
Converse, Tx., U.S.	*E3	120
Converse, co., Wy., U.S.	C7	127
Convoy, Oh., U.S.	B1	112
Conway, P.E.I.	C6	71
Conway, Ar., U.S.	B3	81
Conway, Fl., U.S.	D5	86
Conway, Ia., U.S.	D3	92
Conway, Ks., U.S.	D6	93
Conway, Ma., U.S.	A2	98
Conway, Mo., U.S.	D5	102
Conway, N.H., U.S.	C4	106
Conway, N.C., U.S.	A5	110
Conway, N.D., U.S.	A8	111
Conway, S.C., U.S.	D9	117
Conway, co., Ar., U.S.	B3	81
Conway, Lake, res., Ar., U.S.	B3	81
Conway Lake, l., N.H., U.S.	C4	106
Conway Springs, Ks., U.S.	E6	93
Conwy, Wales, U.K.	A4	12
Conyers, Ga., U.S.	C2	87
Cook, Austl.	F5	50
Cook, Ne., U.S.	D9	104
Cook, co., Ga., U.S.	E3	87
Cook, co., Il., U.S.	B6	90
Cook, co., Mn., U.S.	k9	100
Cook, Cape, c., B.C.	D4	69
Cook, Mount, mtn., N.Z.	O13	51
Cooke, co., Tx., U.S.	C4	120
Cooke City, Mt., U.S.	E7	103
Cookes Peak, mtn., N.M., U.S.	E2	108
Cookeville, Tn., U.S.	C8	119
Cook Ice Shelf, ice, Ant.	C28	7
Cooking Lake, l., Alta.	C4	68
Cook Inlet, b., Ak., U.S.	D9	79
Cook Islands, ctry., Oc.	G12	6
Cook Mountain, mtn., W.V., U.S.	n12	125
Cook Point, c., Md., U.S.	C5	97
Cooks, Mi., U.S.	C4	99
Cooksburg, Pa., U.S.	D3	115
Cooks Falls, N.Y., U.S.	D6	109
Cookshire, Que.	D6	74
Cooks Mills, Il., U.S.	D5	90
Cookson, Ok., U.S.	B7	113
Cookstown, N. Ire., U.K.	C5	11
Cookstown, Ont.	C5	73
Cook Strait, strt., N.Z.	N15	51
Cooksville, Il., U.S.	C5	90
Cookville, Tx., U.S.	C5	120
Cooktown, Austl.	C8	50
Coolah, Austl.	F8	50
Coolaney, Ire.	C3	11
Cooleemee, N.C., U.S.	B2	110
Coolgardie, Austl.	F3	50
Coolidge, Az., U.S.	E4	80
Coolidge, Ga., U.S.	E3	87
Coolidge, Ks., U.S.	D2	93
Coolidge, Tx., U.S.	D4	120
Coolidge, Mount, mtn., S.D., U.S.	D2	118
Coolin, Id., U.S.	A2	89
Cool Ridge, W.V., U.S.	D3	125
Coolspring, Pa., U.S.	D2	115
Coolville, Oh., U.S.	C4	112
Cooma, Austl.	G8	50
Coonabarabran, Austl.	F8	50
Coonamble, Austl.	F8	50
Coon Rapids, Ia., U.S.	C3	92
Coon Rapids, Mn., U.S.	E5	100
Coon Valley, Wi., U.S.	E2	126
Cooper, Ia., U.S.	C3	92
Cooper, Tx., U.S.	C5	120
Cooper, co., Mo., U.S.	C5	102
Cooper, East Branch, stm., S.C., U.S.	E8	117
Cooper, West Branch, stm., S.C., U.S.	E8	117
Cooper Creek, stm., Austl.	E7	50
Cooper Mountain, mtn., Ak., U.S.	g17	79
Cooper Road, La., U.S.	*B2	95
Coopersburg, Pa., U.S.	F11	115
Coopers Mills, Me., U.S.	D3	96
Cooperstown, N.Y., U.S.	C6	109
Cooperstown, N.D., U.S.	B7	111
Cooperstown, Wi., U.S.	h10	126
Coopersville, Mi., U.S.	E5	99
Coopertown, Tn., U.S.	A5	119
Coos, co., N.H., U.S.	A4	106
Coos, co., Or., U.S.	D2	114
Coos, stm., Or., U.S.	D2	114
Coosa, Ga., U.S.	B1	87
Coosa, co., Al., U.S.	C3	78
Coosa, stm., U.S.	C3	78
Coosada, Al., U.S.	C3	78
Coosawattee, stm., Ga., U.S.	B2	87
Coosawhatchie, S.C., U.S.	F6	117
Coosawhatchie, stm., S.C., U.S.	F5	117
Coos Bay, Or., U.S.	D2	114
Cootamundra, Austl.	F8	50
Cootehill, Ire.	C4	11
Copacabana, Arg.	E2	55
Copacabana, Bol.	C2	55
Copainalá, Mex.	D6	63
Copalis Beach, Wa., U.S.	B1	124
Copalis Crossing, Wa., U.S.	B1	124
Copán, Hond.	C3	62

Name	Map Ref.	Page
Copan, Ok., U.S.	A6	113
Copan Reservoir, res., Ok., U.S.	A6	113
Cope, Co., U.S.	B8	83
Cope, S.C., U.S.	E5	117
Copeland, Fl., U.S.	G5	86
Copeland, Ks., U.S.	E3	93
Copemish, Mi., U.S.	D5	99
Copen, W.V., U.S.	C4	125
Copenhagen (København), Den.	J5	14
Copenhagen, N.Y., U.S.	B5	109
Copetonas, Arg.	B4	54
Copeville, Tx., U.S.	m10	120
Copiah, co., Ms., U.S.	D3	101
Copiapó, Chile	E1	55
Copiapó, stm., Chile	E1	55
Copinsay, i., Scot., U.K.	B6	13
Coplay, Pa., U.S.	E10	115
Copparo, Italy	B3	23
Coppename, stm., Sur.	A3	59
Copper, stm., Ak., U.S.	C11	79
Copperas Cove, Tx., U.S.	D4	120
Copperbelt, prov., Zam.	D4	48
Copper Butte, mtn., Wa., U.S.	A7	124
Copper Center, Ak., U.S.	C10	79
Copper Cliff (part of Sudbury), Ont.	A3	73
Copper Harbor, Mi., U.S.	A3	99
Copperhill, Tn., U.S.	D9	119
Copper Hill, Va., U.S.	C2	123
Coppermine, N.W. Ter.	C9	66
Coppermine, stm., N.W. Ter.	C10	66
Copper Mountain, B.C.	E7	69
Copper Mountain, mtn., Wy., U.S.	C5	127
Copper Mountains, mts., Az., U.S.	E2	80
Copper Ridge, mtn., U.S.	m13	119
Copper Ridge, mtn., Va., U.S.	f9	123
Copperton, Ut., U.S.	*C3	121
Coppet, Switz.	D1	21
Copton Creek, stm., Alta.	B1	68
Coqên, China	B10	37
Coquet, stm., Eng., U.K.	E7	13
Coquille, Or., U.S.	D2	114
Coquimbo, Chile	E1	55
Coquimbo, prov., Chile	F1	55
Cora, Wy., U.S.	D3	127
Corabia, Rom.	D7	24
Coração de Jesus, Braz.	B4	56
Coracora, Peru	F3	58
Coral, Ont.	o19	73
Coral, Mi., U.S.	E5	99
Coral, Pa., U.S.	F3	115
Coral Gables, Fl., U.S.	G6	86
Coral Hills, Md., U.S.	*C4	97
Coral Sea, Oc.	G9	6
Coral Springs, Fl., U.S.	*F6	86
Coral Terrace, Fl., U.S.	*G6	86
Coralville, Ia., U.S.	C6	92
Coralville Lake, res., Ia., U.S.	C5	92
Coral Way Village, Fl., U.S.	*G6	86
Coram, Mt., U.S.	B2	103
Coram, N.Y., U.S.	*n15	109
Corangamite, Lake, l., Austl.	I4	51
Coraopolis, Pa., U.S.	E1	115
Corato, Italy	D6	23
Corbeil [-Essonnes], Fr.	C5	16
Corbeny, Fr.	E3	17
Corbett, N.Y., U.S.	C5	109
Corbetton, Ont.	C4	73
Corbie, Fr.	C5	16
Corbin, Ks., U.S.	E6	93
Corbin, Ky., U.S.	D5	94
Corbin, Mt., U.S.	D4	103
Corbin City, N.J., U.S.	E3	107
Corby, Eng., U.K.	B7	12
Corcoran, Ca., U.S.	D4	82
Corcoran, Mn., U.S.	m11	100
Corcovado, Golfo, b., Chile	C2	54
Cord, Ar., U.S.	B4	81
Cordaville, Ma., U.S.	g9	98
Cordele, Ga., U.S.	E3	87
Cordell, Ok., U.S.	B3	113
Cordell Hull Lake, res., Tn., U.S.	C8	119
Corder, Mo., U.S.	B4	102
Cordesville, S.C., U.S.	E8	117
Cordillera, dept., Para.	A4	55
Córdoba, Arg.	A4	54
Córdoba, Mex.	n15	63
Córdoba, Spain	D7	22
Córdoba, prov., Arg.	A4	54
Córdoba, dept., Col.	B2	60
Cordon, Phil.	n13	34
Córdova, Peru	D2	58
Cordova, Al., U.S.	B2	78
Cordova, Ak., U.S.	C10	79
Cordova, Il., U.S.	B3	90
Cordova, Md., U.S.	C6	97
Cordova, Ne., U.S.	*D8	104
Cordova, N.M., U.S.	A4	108
Cordova, N.C., U.S.	C3	110
Cordova, S.C., U.S.	E6	117
Cordova, Tn., U.S.	B2	119
Cordova Mines, Ont.	C7	73
Cordova Peak, mtn., Ak., U.S.	C10	79
Corea, Me., U.S.	D5	96
Corella, Spain	A5	22
Corfu, N.Y., U.S.	C2	109
Corfu see Kérkira, i., Grc.	C2	40
Cori, Italy	h9	23
Corigliano, Italy	E6	23
Corinna, Me., U.S.	D3	96
Corinne, Mi., U.S.	B5	99
Corinne, Ut., U.S.	B3	121
Corinne, W.V., U.S.	*D3	125
Corinne Key, i., Fl., U.S.	G6	86
Corinth see Kórinthos, Grc.		
Corinth, Ky., U.S.	B5	94
Corinth, Me., U.S.	D4	96
Corinth, Ms., U.S.	A5	101
Corinth, N.Y., U.S.	B7	109
Corinth, Vt., U.S.	C4	122
Corinth, W.V., U.S.	B5	125
Corinth, Bay of, b., Grc.	h9	25
Corinth, Gulf of, b., Grc.	C4	25
Corinth Canal, Grc.	h10	25
Corinto, Braz.	B4	56
Corinto, Nic.	E7	64
Corisco, Isla de, i., Eq. Gui.	E1	46
Cork, N.B.	D3	71
Cork, Ire.	E2	10
Cork, co., Ire.	F3	11
Cork Harbour, b., Ire.	F4	23
Corleone, Italy	L2	23
Çorlu, Tur.	B6	40
Cormeilles-en-Parisis, Fr.	g9	16
Cormoran Reef, rf., Palau	R17	52
Cormorant, Man.	B1	70
Cormorant Lake, l., Man.	B1	70
Corn, Ok., U.S.	B3	113
Cornaca, S.C., U.S.	C3	117
Cornelia, Ga., U.S.	B3	87
Cornelius, N.C., U.S.	B2	110
Cornelius, Or., U.S.	g11	114
Cornell, Il., U.S.	C5	90
Cornell, Wi., U.S.	C2	126
Cornellà, Spain	B7	22
Corner Brook, Newf.	D3	72
Corner Inlet, b., Austl.	I6	51
Cornersville, Tn., U.S.	B5	119
Cornerville, Ar., U.S.	C4	81
Cornfield Point, c., Ct., U.S.	D6	84
Cornhill, N.B.	D4	71
Corning, Sask.	H4	75
Corning, Ar., U.S.	A5	81
Corning, Ca., U.S.	C2	82
Corning, Ia., U.S.	D3	92
Corning, Ks., U.S.	C7	93
Corning, Mo., U.S.	A2	102
Corning, N.Y., U.S.	C3	109
Corning, Oh., U.S.	C3	112
Cornish, Me., U.S.	E2	96
Cornish, Ok., U.S.	C4	113
Cornish, Ut., U.S.	B4	121
Cornish Center, N.H., U.S.	D2	106
Cornish Flat, N.H., U.S.	D2	106
Cornish Mills, N.H., U.S.	D2	106
Cornishville, Ky., U.S.	C5	94
Cornville, Az., U.S.	C4	80
Cornville, Me., U.S.	D3	96
Corno Grande, mtn., Italy	C4	23
Cornucopia, Wi., U.S.	B2	126
Cornwall, Ont.	B10	73
Cornwall, Ct., U.S.	B2	84
Cornwall, Pa., U.S.	F9	115
Cornwall, Vt., U.S.	D2	122
Cornwall, co., Eng., U.K.	D3	12
Cornwall Bridge, Ct., U.S.	B2	84
Cornwallis Island, i., N.W. Ter.	m33	66
Cornwallis Island, i., N.W. Ter.	m32	66
Cornwall-on-Hudson, N.Y., U.S.	D6	109
Cornwells Heights, Pa., U.S.	o22	115
Coro, Ven.	A4	60
Corocoro, Bol.	C2	55
Coroico, Bol.	C2	55
Corolla, N.C., U.S.	A7	110
Coromandel Coast, India	F7	36
Coromandel Peninsula, pen., N.Z.	L15	51
Corona, Al., U.S.	B2	78
Corona, Ca., U.S.	F5	82
Corona, N.M., U.S.	C5	83
Corona, S.D., U.S.	B9	118
Coronach, Sask.	H3	75
Coronado, Ca., U.S.	F5	82
Coronado, Bahía de, b., C.R.	*B6	62
Coronado National Memorial, Az., U.S.	F5	80
Coronation, Alta.	C5	68
Coronation Gulf, b., N.W. Ter.	C10	66
Coronation Island, i., B.A.T.	C8	7
Coronation Island, i., Ak., U.S.	n22	79
Coronel, Chile	B2	54
Coronel Dorrego, Arg.	B4	54
Coronel Murta, Braz.	B4	56
Coronel Oviedo, Para.	E4	55
Coronel Pringles, Arg.	B4	54
Coronel Suárez, Arg.	B4	54
Coronie, dept., Sur.	A3	59
Coropuna, Nevado, mtn., Peru	E3	58
Corowa, Austl.	G6	51
Corozal, Belize	D7	63
Corozal, Col.	B2	60
Corpataux, Switz.	C3	21
Corpen, Arg.	D3	54
Corps, Fr.	E1	20
Corpus Christi, Tx., U.S.	F4	120
Corpus Christi Naval Air Station, mil., Tx., U.S.	F4	120
Corral, Chile	D4	54
Corral, Id., U.S.	F4	89
Corral de Almaguer, Spain	C4	22
Corrales, Col.	B3	60
Corralillo, Cuba	C3	64
Corraun, Ire.	D2	11
Correctionville, Ia., U.S.	B2	92
Corregidor Island, i., Phil.	o10	34
Correll, Mn., U.S.	E2	100
Corrente, Braz.	D1	57
Corrente, stm., Braz.	k5	57
Correntina, Braz.	A4	56
Corrib, Lough, l., Ire.	D2	10
Corrientes, Arg.	E4	55
Corrientes, prov., Arg.	E4	55
Corrientes, stm., Arg.	E4	55
Corrientes, stm., S.A.	A3	59
Corrientes, Cabo, c., Col.	B2	60
Corrientes, Cabo, c., Cuba	D1	64
Corrientes, Cabo, c., Mex.	C3	63
Corrientes, Ensenada de, b., Cuba	D1	64
Corrigan, Tx., U.S.	D5	120
Corriganville, Md., U.S.	k13	97
Corrofin, Ire.	E2	11
Corry, Pa., U.S.	C2	115
Corryton, Tn., U.S.	C10	119
Corse, Cap, c., Fr.	C2	23
Corsica, Pa., U.S.	D3	115
Corsica, S.D., U.S.	D7	118
Corsica, i., Fr.	C2	23
Corsicana, Tx., U.S.	C4	120
Corson, co., S.D., U.S.	B4	118
Corson Inlet, b., N.J., U.S.	E3	107
Cortazar, Mex.	C2	62
Corte, Fr.	C2	23
Corte Alto, Chile	C2	54
Cortegana, Spain	D2	22
Corte Madera, Ca., U.S.	*h7	82
Cortemilia, Italy	E2	23
Cortes [de la Frontera], Spain	E2	22
Cortez, Co., U.S.	D2	83
Cortez, Fl., U.S.	q10	86
Cortez Mountains, mts., Nv., U.S.	C5	105
Cortina d'Ampezzo, Italy	A4	23
Cortland, Il., U.S.	B5	90
Cortland, In., U.S.	G6	91
Cortland, Ne., U.S.	D9	104
Cortland, N.Y., U.S.	C4	109
Cortland, Oh., U.S.	A5	112
Cortland, co., N.Y., U.S.	C4	109
Cortona, Italy	C3	23
Coruche, Port.	C1	22
Çoruh, stm., Asia	B13	40
Çorum, Tur.	B10	40
Corumbá, Braz.	B1	56
Corumbá, stm., Braz.	B3	56
Corunna, Ont.	E2	73
Corunna, In., U.S.	B7	91
Corunna, Mi., U.S.	F6	99
Corvallis, Mt., U.S.	D2	103
Corvallis, Or., U.S.	C3	114
Corvo, i., Port.	g8	44
Corwin, Ks., U.S.	E5	93
Corwin Springs, Mt., U.S.	E6	103
Corwith, Ia., U.S.	B4	92
Cory, In., U.S.	F3	91
Corydon, In., U.S.	H5	91
Corydon, Ia., U.S.	D4	92
Corydon, Ky., U.S.	C2	94
Coryell, co., Tx., U.S.	D4	120
Cos see Kos, i., Grc.	D6	40
Cosalá, Mex.	E6	62
Cosamaloapan [de Carpio], Mex.	D5	63
Cosby, Mo., U.S.	A3	102
Cosby, Tn., U.S.	D10	119
Coscomatepec [de Bravo], Mex.	n15	63
Cosegüina, Punta, c., Nic.	D4	62
Cosenza, Italy	E6	23
Coshocton, Oh., U.S.	B4	112
Coshocton, co., Oh., U.S.	B4	112
Cosmopolis, Wa., U.S.	C2	124
Cosmos, Mn., U.S.	F4	100
Cosne, Fr.	D5	16
Cossatot, stm., Ar., U.S.	C1	81
Cossatot Mountains, mtn., Ar., U.S.	C2	81
Cossonay, Switz.	C2	20
Costa Mesa, Ca., U.S.	n13	82
Costa Rica, ctry., N.A.	F6	62
Costello, Pa., U.S.	C5	115
Costelloe, Ire.	D2	11
Costigan, Me., U.S.	C4	96
Costilla, N.M., U.S.	A4	108
Costilla, co., Co., U.S.	D5	83
Coswig, E. Ger.	B8	19
Coswig, E. Ger.	B7	19
Cotabato, Phil.	D6	34
Cotagaita, Bol.	D2	55
Cotahuasi, Peru	E3	58
Coteau, N.D., U.S.	A3	111
Coteau-Landing, Que.	D3	74
Coteaux, Haiti	E6	64
Côte d'Or, reg., Fr.	D6	16
Côtes de Fer, Haiti	E7	64
Cotesfield, Ne., U.S.	C7	104
Cotija de la Paz, Mex.	n12	63
Cotingo, stm., Braz.	B2	59
Cotonou, Benin	E5	45
Cotopaxi, Co., U.S.	C5	83
Cotopaxi, prov., Ec.	B2	58
Cotopaxi, vol., Ec.	B2	58
Cotswold Hills, hills, Eng., U.K.	E5	10
Cottage Grove, Mn., U.S.	n13	100
Cottage Grove, Or., U.S.	D3	114
Cottage Grove, Tn., U.S.	A3	119
Cottage Grove Reservoir, res., Or., U.S.	D3	114
Cottageville, S.C., U.S.	F7	117
Cottageville, W.V., U.S.	C3	125
Cottbus, E. Ger.	C7	18
Cottel Island, i., Newf.	D5	72
Cotter, Ar., U.S.	A3	81
Cottian Alps, mts., Eur.	E7	16
Cottle, co., Tx., U.S.	B2	120
Cottleville, Mo., U.S.	f12	102
Cotton, Ga., U.S.	E2	87
Cotton, Mn., U.S.	C6	100
Cotton, co., Ok., U.S.	C3	113
Cotton Center, Tx., U.S.	B1	120
Cottondale, Al., U.S.	B2	78
Cottondale, Fl., U.S.	B1	86
Cottonpatch Hill, De., U.S.	F5	85
Cotton Plant, Ar., U.S.	B4	81
Cottonton, Al., U.S.	C4	78
Cottontown, Tn., U.S.	A5	119
Cotton Valley, La., U.S.	B2	95
Cottonwood, Al., U.S.	D4	78
Cottonwood, Az., U.S.	C3	80
Cottonwood, Ca., U.S.	B2	82
Cottonwood, Id., U.S.	C2	89
Cottonwood, Mn., U.S.	F3	100
Cottonwood, Ok., U.S.	C5	113
Cottonwood, S.D., U.S.	D4	118
Cottonwood, Tx., U.S.	C3	120
Cottonwood, Ut., U.S.	*C4	121
Cottonwood, co., Mn., U.S.	F3	100
Cottonwood, stm., Ks., U.S.	D7	93
Cottonwood, stm., Mn., U.S.	F3	100
Cottonwood Cove, Nv., U.S.	H7	105
Cottonwood Creek, stm., Wy., U.S.	D2	127
Cottonwood Creek, stm., Wy., U.S.	C4	127
Cottonwood Falls, Ks., U.S.	D7	93
Cottonwood Heights, Ut., U.S.	*C4	121
Cottonwood Wash, val., Ut., U.S.	F6	121
Cotuit, Ma., U.S.	C7	98
Cotulla, Tx., U.S.	E3	120
Couchiching, Lake, l., Ont.	C5	73
Couchwood, La., U.S.	B2	95
Coudekerque-Branche, Fr.	B5	16
Couderay, Wi., U.S.	C2	126
Coudersport, Pa., U.S.	C5	115
Coudres, Île aux, i., Que.	B7	74
Couëron, Fr.	D3	16
Cougar, Wa., U.S.	C3	124
Cougar Reservoir, res., Or., U.S.	C4	114
Coulee, N.D., U.S.	A3	111
Coulee City, Wa., U.S.	B6	124
Coulee Dam, Wa., U.S.	B7	124
Coulee Dam National Recreation Area, Wa., U.S.	A7	124
Coulman Island, i., Ant.	B29	7
Coulommiers, Fr.	C5	16
Coulsdon (part of London), Eng., U.K.	m12	10
Coulterville, Ca., U.S.	D3	82
Coulwood, Va., U.S.	f9	123
Council, Ga., U.S.	F4	87
Council, Id., U.S.	E2	89
Council, Va., U.S.	e9	123
Council Bluffs, Ia., U.S.	C2	92
Council Grove, Ks., U.S.	D7	93
Council Grove Lake, res., Ks., U.S.	D7	93
Council Mountain, mtn., Id., U.S.	E2	89
Country Club Hills, Il., U.S.	*k9	90
Country Homes, Wa., U.S.	B8	124
Countryside, Il., U.S.	*k9	90
Countyline, Ok., U.S.	C4	113
Coupar Angus, Scot., U.K.	B5	10
Coupeville, Wa., U.S.	A3	124
Coupon, Pa., U.S.	E4	115
Courantyne, stm., S.A.	A3	59
Courbevoie, Fr.	g10	16
Courcelles, Que.	D7	74
Courland Lagoon, b., Sov. Un.	D3	27
Courmayeur, Italy	D2	20
Coursan, Fr.	F5	16
Courtenay, N.D., U.S.	B7	111
Courtenay, B.C.	E5	69
Courtmacsherry, Ire.	F3	11
Courtrai see Kortrijk, Bel.	B5	16
Courtright, Ont.	E2	73
Courval, Sask.	G2	75
Coushatta, La., U.S.	B2	95
Coutances, Fr.	C3	16
Coutras, Fr.	E3	16
Coutts, Alta.	E5	68
Couvin, Bel.	D4	17
Cove, Ar., U.S.	C1	81
Cove, Or., U.S.	B9	114
Cove City, N.C., U.S.	B5	110
Cove Creek, stm., Ut., U.S.	E3	121
Covedale, Oh., U.S.	o12	112
Covelo, Ca., U.S.	C2	82
Coventry, Eng., U.K.	D6	10
Coventry, Ct., U.S.	B6	84
Coventry, De., U.S.	*B3	85
Coventry, R.I., U.S.	D3	116
Coventry, Vt., U.S.	B4	122
Cove Point, Md., U.S.	D5	97
Cove Point, c., Md., U.S.	D5	97
Coverdales Crossroads, De., U.S.	F3	85
Covered Wells, Az., U.S.	E3	80
Covert, Mi., U.S.	F4	99
Covesville, Va., U.S.	C4	123
Covilhã, Port.	B2	22
Covina, Ca., U.S.	m13	82
Covington, Ga., U.S.	C3	87
Covington, In., U.S.	D3	91
Covington, Ky., U.S.	A5	94
Covington, La., U.S.	D5	95
Covington, Mi., U.S.	B2	99
Covington, Oh., U.S.	B1	112
Covington, Ok., U.S.	A4	113
Covington, Tn., U.S.	B2	119
Covington, Va., U.S.	C2	123
Covington, Wa., U.S.	f11	124
Covington, co., Al., U.S.	D3	78
Covington, co., Ms., U.S.	D4	101
Cowal, Lake, l., Austl.	F6	51
Cowan, Tn., U.S.	B5	119
Cowan, Lake, l., Sask.	C7	75
Cowan, Lake, l., Austl.	F3	50
Cowangie, Austl.	G3	51
Cowan Knob, mtn., Ar., U.S.	B2	81
Cowansville, Que.	D5	74
Cowansville, Pa., U.S.	E2	115
Coward, S.C., U.S.	D8	117
Cowarts, Al., U.S.	D4	78
Cow Creek, stm., Ks., U.S.	D5	93
Cow Creek, stm., Wa., U.S.	C7	124
Cowden, Il., U.S.	D5	90
Cowdenbeath, Scot., U.K.	B3	13
Cowdrey, Co., U.S.	A4	83
Cowee Mountains, mts., N.C., U.S.	f9	110
Cowen, W.V., U.S.	C4	125
Cowen, Mount, mtn., Mt., U.S.	E6	103
Cowes, Eng., U.K.	E6	10
Coweta, Ok., U.S.	B6	113
Coweta, co., Ga., U.S.	C2	87
Cowiche, Wa., U.S.	C5	124
Cowichan Bay, B.C.	g12	69
Cowichan Lake, l., B.C.	E5	69
Cow Knob, mtn., W.V., U.S.	C5	125
Cow Lakes, l., Or., U.S.	D9	114
Cowles, Ne., U.S.	D7	104
Cowley, Alta.	E3	68
Cowley, Wy., U.S.	B4	127
Cowley, co., Ks., U.S.	E7	93
Cowlic, Az., U.S.	F4	80
Cowling, Il., U.S.	E6	90
Cowlington, Ok., U.S.	B7	113
Cowlitz, co., Wa., U.S.	C3	124
Cowlitz, stm., Wa., U.S.	C3	124
Cowpasture, stm., Va., U.S.	B3	123
Cowpen Mountain, mtn., Ga., U.S.	B2	87
Cowpens, S.C., U.S.	A4	117
Cowra, Austl.	F7	51
Coxburg, Ms., U.S.	B3	101
Coxsackie, N.Y., U.S.	C7	109
Cox's Cove, Newf.	D2	72
Coxs Mills, W.V., U.S.	B4	125
Coy, Al., U.S.	D2	78
Coy, Ar., U.S.	C4	81
Coyame, Mex.	B3	62
Coyanosa Draw, Tx., U.S.	D1	120
Coyle, Ok., U.S.	B4	113
Coyoacán (part of Mexico City), Mex.	h9	63
Coyote Basin, Co., U.S.	A2	83
Coyuca de Catalán, Mex.	n13	63
Coyville, Ks., U.S.	E8	93
Cozad, Ne., U.S.	D6	104
Cozahome, Ar., U.S.	A3	81
Cozumel, Mex.	C7	63
Cozumel, Isla de, i., Mex.	C7	63
Crab Creek, stm., Wa., U.S.	C6	124
Crab Orchard, Ky., U.S.	C5	94
Crab Orchard, Ne., U.S.	D9	104
Crab Orchard, Tn., U.S.	D9	119
Crab Orchard, W.V., U.S.	n13	125
Crab Orchard Lake, res., Il., U.S.	F4	90
Crab Orchard Mountains, mts., Tn., U.S.	D9	119
Crabtree, Or., U.S.	C4	114
Crabtree, Pa., U.S.	F3	115
Crabtree Mills, Que.	D4	74
Cracking, stm., Sask.	D4	75
Cracow, Austl.	D7	51
Cradock, S. Afr.	D4	49
Craftsbury, Vt., U.S.	B4	122
Craftsbury Common, Vt., U.S.	B4	122
Cragford, Al., U.S.	B4	78
Craig, Ak., U.S.	D13	79
Craig, Co., U.S.	A3	83
Craig, Mo., U.S.	A2	102
Craig, Mt., U.S.	C5	103
Craig, Ne., U.S.	C9	104
Craig, co., Ok., U.S.	A6	113
Craig, co., Va., U.S.	C2	123
Craig Air Force Base, mil., Al., U.S.	C3	78
Craig Creek, stm., Va., U.S.	C2	123
Craigellachie, B.C.	D8	69
Craighead, co., Ar., U.S.	B5	81
Craighouse, Scot., U.K.	E3	13
Craighurst, Ont.	C5	73
Craigmont, Id., U.S.	C2	89
Craigmyle, Alta.	D4	68
Craigsville, Va., U.S.	B3	123
Craigsville, W.V., U.S.	C4	125
Craik, Sask.	F3	75
Crail, Scot., U.K.	D6	13
Crailsheim, W. Ger.	D5	18
Craiova, Rom.	C6	24
Cramerton, N.C., U.S.	B1	110
Cranberry, Pa., U.S.	D2	115
Cranberry Isles, Me., U.S.	D4	96
Cranberry Lake, N.Y., U.S.	A6	109
Cranberry Lake, l., N.Y., U.S.	A6	109
Cranberry Portage, Man.	B1	70
Cranbrook, B.C.	E10	69
Cranbury, N.J., U.S.	C3	107
Crandall, Ga., U.S.	B2	87
Crandall, S.D., U.S.	B8	118
Crandall, Tx., U.S.	n10	120
Crandon, Wi., U.S.	C5	126
Crane, Az., U.S.	E1	80
Crane, In., U.S.	G4	91
Crane, Mo., U.S.	E4	102
Crane, Or., U.S.	D8	114
Crane, Tx., U.S.	D1	120
Crane, co., Tx., U.S.	D1	120
Crane Creek, stm., Oh., U.S.	e7	112
Crane Creek Reservoir, res., Id., U.S.	E2	89
Crane Hill, Al., U.S.	A2	78
Crane Lake, Mn., U.S.	B6	100
Crane Lake, l., Sask.	G1	75
Crane Lake, l., Mn., U.S.	B6	100
Crane Mountain, mtn., Or., U.S.	E6	114
Crane Prairie Reservoir, res., Or., U.S.	D5	114
Cranesville, Pa., U.S.	C1	115
Cranfield, Ms., U.S.	D2	101
Cranford, N.J., U.S.	B4	107
Cransac, Fr.	E5	16
Cranston, R.I., U.S.	C4	116
Cranstown, Cape, c., Grnld.	B20	128
Crapaud, P.E.I.	C6	71
Crary, N.D., U.S.	A7	111
Crary Mountains, mts., Ant.	B1	7
Craryville, N.Y., U.S.	C7	109
Crasna, stm., Eur.	B7	24
Crater Lake, Or., U.S.	E4	114
Crater Lake, l., St. Vin.	U26	65
Crater Lake, l., Or., U.S.	E4	114
Crater Lake National Park, Or., U.S.	E4	114
Craters of the Moon National Monument, Id., U.S.	F5	89
Crateús, Braz.	C2	57
Crato, Braz.	E11	57
Craughwell, Ire.	D3	11
Craven, Sask.	G3	75
Craven, co., N.C., U.S.	B5	110
Cravinhos, Braz.	k8	56
Crawford, Ga., U.S.	C3	87
Crawford, Ms., U.S.	B5	101
Crawford, Ne., U.S.	B2	104
Crawford, Tn., U.S.	C8	119
Crawford, co., Ar., U.S.	B1	81
Crawford, co., Ga., U.S.	D2	87
Crawford, co., Il., U.S.	D6	90
Crawford, co., In., U.S.	H4	91
Crawford, co., Ia., U.S.	B2	92
Crawford, co., Ks., U.S.	E9	93
Crawford, co., Mi., U.S.	D6	99
Crawford, co., Mo., U.S.	D6	102
Crawford, co., Oh., U.S.	B3	112
Crawford, co., Pa., U.S.	C1	115
Crawford, co., Wi., U.S.	E3	126
Crawford Lake, l., Me., U.S.	C5	96
Crawford Notch, N.H., U.S.	B4	106
Crawford Notch State Park, N.H., U.S.	B4	106
Crawfordsville, Ar., U.S.	B5	81
Crawfordsville, In., U.S.	D4	91
Crawfordsville, Or., U.S.	C4	114
Crawfordville, Fl., U.S.	B2	86
Crawfordville, Ga., U.S.	C4	87
Crawley, Eng., U.K.	J13	12
Crayne, Ky., U.S.	C2	94
Crazy Mountains, mts., Mt., U.S.	D6	103
Crazy Peak, mtn., Mt., U.S.	D6	103
Crazy Woman Creek, stm., Wy., U.S.	B6	127
Creal Springs, Il., U.S.	F5	90
Creamridge, N.J., U.S.	C3	107
Crean Lake, l., Sask.	C2	75
Cree, stm., Sask.	E11	66
Cree Lake, l., Sask.	m7	75
Creede, Co., U.S.	D4	83
Creedmoor, N.C., U.S.	A4	110
Creek, co., Ok., U.S.	B5	113
Creekside, Pa., U.S.	E3	115
Creel, Fr.	C4	16
Creighton, Mo., U.S.	C3	102
Creighton, Ne., U.S.	B8	104
Creighton, Pa., U.S.	h14	115
Creighton, S.D., U.S.	C3	118
Creil, Fr.	C4	16
Crellin, Md., U.S.	m12	97
Crema, Italy	B2	23
Cremona, Alta.	D3	68
Cremona, Italy	B3	23
Crenshaw, Ms., U.S.	A3	101
Crenshaw, co., Al., U.S.	D3	78
Creola, Al., U.S.	E1	78
Creole, La., U.S.	E2	95
Crépy-en-Valois, Fr.	E2	17
Cres, i., Yugo.	C2	24
Cresaptown, Md., U.S.	k13	97
Cresbard, S.D., U.S.	B7	118
Crescent, Ga., U.S.	E5	87
Crescent, Ia., U.S.	C2	92
Crescent, Mo., U.S.	f12	102
Crescent, Ok., U.S.	B4	113
Crescent, Or., U.S.	D5	114
Crescent, Lake, l., Wa., U.S.	A2	124
Crescent City, Ca., U.S.	B1	82
Crescent City, Fl., U.S.	C5	86
Crescent City, Il., U.S.	C6	90
Crescent Lake, Or., U.S.	D5	114
Crescent Lake, l., Or., U.S.	D5	114
Crescent Mills, Ca., U.S.	B3	82
Crescent Range, mtn., N.H., U.S.	B4	106
Crescent Springs, Ky., U.S.	h13	94
Crescent Spur, B.C.	C7	69
Cresco, Ia., U.S.	A5	92
Cresco, Pa., U.S.	D11	115
Crespo, Arg.	A4	54
Cresskill, N.J., U.S.	h9	107
Cresson, Pa., U.S.	F4	115
Cresson, Tx., U.S.	n9	120
Cressona, Pa., U.S.	E9	115
Crest, Fr.	E6	16
Cresta, Switz.	C4	21
Crested Butte, Co., U.S.	C4	83
Cresthaven, Fl., U.S.	*F6	86
Crest Hill, Il., U.S.	k8	90
Crestline, Ca., U.S.	*E5	82
Crestline, Oh., U.S.	B3	112
Creston, B.C.	E9	69
Creston, Newf.	E4	72
Creston, Il., U.S.	B5	90
Creston, Ia., U.S.	C3	92
Creston, Mt., U.S.	B2	103
Creston, Ne., U.S.	C8	104
Creston, Oh., U.S.	B4	112
Creston, Wa., U.S.	B7	124
Creston, W.V., U.S.	C3	125
Creston, Wy., U.S.	E5	127
Crestone, Co., U.S.	D5	83
Crestone Peak, mtn., Co., U.S.	D5	83
Crestview, Fl., U.S.	u15	86
Crestview, Hi., U.S.	g10	88
Crestwood, Il., U.S.	*k9	90
Crestwood, Ky., U.S.	B4	94
Crestwood, Mo., U.S.	*f13	102
Crestwood Village, N.J., U.S.	D4	107
Crestwynd, Sask.	G3	75
Creswell, N.C., U.S.	B6	110
Creswell, Or., U.S.	D3	114
Crete, Il., U.S.	B6	90
Crete, Ne., U.S.	D9	104
Crete, N.D., U.S.	C8	111
Crete, i., Grc.	D5	40
Crete, Sea of, Grc.	D5	40
Créteil, Fr.	g10	16
Cretone, Italy	g9	23
Creus, Cape, c., Spain	A7	22
Creuse, stm., Fr.	D4	16
Creutzwald, Fr.	C7	16
Crevasse Valley Glacier, ice, Ant.	B34	7
Creve Coeur, Il., U.S.	C4	90
Creve Coeur, Mo., U.S.	*f13	102
Crèvecœur-le-Grand, Fr.	E2	17
Crevillente, Spain	G5	22
Crewe, Eng., U.K.	D5	10
Crewe, Va., U.S.	C4	123
Crewkerne, Eng., U.K.	D5	12
Criciúma, Braz.	B7	56
Cricket, N.C., U.S.	A1	110
Cricket Mountains, mts., Ut., U.S.	D3	121
Cridersville, Oh., U.S.	B1	112
Crieff, Scot., U.K.	B4	13
Criffel, mtn., Scot., U.K.	F5	13
Criglersville, Va., U.S.	B4	123
Crikvenica, Yugo.	C2	24
Crimea, pen., Sov. Un.	E6	29
Crimmitschau, E. Ger.	C7	18
Crimson Lake Provincial Park, Alta.	C3	68
Crinan, Scot., U.K.	C4	13
Cripple Creek, Co., U.S.	C5	83
Cripple Creek, Va., U.S.	D1	123
Crișana-Maramureș, hist. reg., Rom.	B6	24
Crisfield, Md., U.S.	E6	97
Crisp, co., Ga., U.S.	E3	87
Criss Creek, B.C.	D7	69
Crissolo, Italy	E2	23
Cristal, Monts de, mts., Gabon	E2	46
Cristalina, Braz.	C5	57
Cristina, Braz.	B6	56
Cristóbal, Pan.	k11	62
Cristóbal Colón, Pico, mtn., Col.	A3	60
Crișul Alb, stm., Rom.	C5	24
Crittenden, Ky., U.S.	B5	94
Crittenden, co., Ar., U.S.	B5	81
Crittenden, co., Ky., U.S.	e9	94
Crivitz, E. Ger.	E5	15
Crivitz, Wi., U.S.	C6	126
Crixás, Braz.	A3	56
Crna, stm., Yugo.	C2	24
Crnomelj, Yugo.	C2	24
Croatia, hist. reg., Yugo.	C2	24
Croche, stm., Que.	A5	74
Crocheron, Md., U.S.	D5	97
Crocker, Mo., U.S.	D5	102
Crockett, Ca., U.S.	g8	82
Crockett, Tx., U.S.	D5	120
Crockett, co., Tn., U.S.	B2	119
Crockett, co., Tx., U.S.	D2	120
Crockett Mills, Tn., U.S.	B2	119
Crocketts Bluff, Ar., U.S.	C4	81
Crocketville, S.C., U.S.	F5	117
Crofton, Ky., U.S.	C2	94
Crofton, Md., U.S.	B4	97
Crofton, Ne., U.S.	B8	104
Croghan, N.Y., U.S.	B5	109

Name	Map Ref.	Page
Croghan Mountain, mtn., Ire.	E5	11
Crohy Head, c., Ire.	C3	11
Croix, Fr.	D3	17
Croix, Lac la, l., Mn., U.S.	B6	100
Croker, i., Austl.	B5	50
Croker, Cape, c., Ont.	C4	73
Cromarty, Scot., U.K.	B4	10
Cromer, Man.	E1	70
Cromer, Eng., U.K.	B9	12
Cromona, Ky., U.S.	C7	94
Cromwell, N.Z.	P12	51
Cromwell, Al., U.S.	C1	78
Cromwell, Ct., U.S.	C5	84
Cromwell, In., U.S.	B6	91
Cromwell, Ia., U.S.	C3	92
Cromwell, Ky., U.S.	C3	94
Cromwell, Mn., U.S.	D6	100
Cromwell, Ok., U.S.	B5	113
Crook, Eng., U.K.	F7	13
Crook, co., Or., U.S.	C6	114
Crook, co., Wy., U.S.	B8	127
Crooked, stm., B.C.	B6	69
Crooked, stm., Or., U.S.	C6	114
Crooked Creek, Ak., U.S.	C8	79
Crooked Creek, stm., U.S.	E3	93
Crooked Creek, stm., Ar., U.S.	A3	81
Crooked Creek, stm., In., U.S.	k10	91
Crooked Creek, stm., Pa., U.S.	C7	115
Crooked Creek Lake, res., Pa., U.S.	E3	115
Crooked Island, i., Bah.	C6	64
Crooked Island Passage, strt., Bah.	C6	64
Crooked Lake, l., Newf.	D3	72
Crooked Lake, l., Sask.	G4	75
Crooked Lake, l., Fl., U.S.	E5	86
Crooked Lake, l., Mn., U.S.	B7	100
Crooked River, Sask.	E4	75
Crooks, S.D., U.S.	D9	118
Crooks Lake, l., Nv., U.S.	B2	105
Crookston, Mn., U.S.	C2	100
Crookston, Ne., U.S.	B5	104
Crookstown, Ire.	F3	11
Crooksville, Oh., U.S.	C3	112
Crookwell, Austl.	G7	51
Croom, Ire.	E3	11
Cropper, Ky., U.S.	B4	94
Cropsey, Il., U.S.	C5	90
Croque Harbour, b., Newf.	C4	72
Crosby, Mn., U.S.	D5	100
Crosby, Ms., U.S.	D2	101
Crosby, N.D., U.S.	A2	111
Crosby, Pa., U.S.	C5	115
Crosby, Tx., U.S.	r14	120
Crosby, co., Tx., U.S.	C2	120
Crosby, Mount, mtn., Wy., U.S.	C3	127
Crosbyton, Tx., U.S.	C2	120
Crosland, Ga., U.S.	E3	87
Cross, S.C., U.S.	E7	117
Cross, co., Ar., U.S.	B5	81
Cross, stm., Afr.	E6	45
Cross, Cape, c., Nmb.	B1	49
Cross Anchor, S.C., U.S.	B4	117
Cross Bay, b., Man.	C2	70
Crossbost, Scot., U.K.	B2	13
Cross City, Fl., U.S.	C3	86
Cross Creek, N.B.	C3	71
Cross Creek, stm., W.V., U.S.	f8	125
Crossett, Ar., U.S.	D4	81
Cross Fell, mtn., Eng., U.K.	F6	13
Crossfield, Alta.	D3	68
Crosshaven, Ire.	F3	11
Cross Hill, S.C., U.S.	C4	117
Cross Island, i., Me., U.S.	D5	96
Cross Keys, N.J., U.S.	D2	107
Cross Lake, Man.	B3	70
Crosslake, Mn., U.S.	D4	100
Cross Lake, l., Man.	B3	70
Cross Lake, l., Me., U.S.	A4	96
Cross Lake, res., La., U.S.	B2	95
Cross Lanes, W.V., U.S.	C3	125
Crossman Peak, mtn., Az., U.S.	C1	80
Cross Mill, N.C., U.S.	f10	110
Crossmolina, Ire.	C2	11
Cross Mountains, mts., Ar., U.S.	C1	81
Cross Plains, In., U.S.	G7	91
Cross Plains, Tn., U.S.	A5	119
Cross Plains, Tx., U.S.	C3	120
Cross Plains, Wi., U.S.	E4	126
Crossroads, N.M., U.S.	D6	108
Cross Roads Ohio, N.S.	D7	71
Cross Sound, strt., Ak., U.S.	k21	79
Cross Timbers, Mo., U.S.	C4	102
Crosstown, Mo., U.S.	D8	102
Cross Village, Mi., U.S.	C5	99
Crossville, Al., U.S.	A4	78
Crossville, Il., U.S.	E5	90
Crossville, Tn., U.S.	D8	119
Crosswicks, N.J., U.S.	C3	107
Croswell, Mi., U.S.	E8	99
Crothersville, In., U.S.	G6	91
Croton, Ia., U.S.	D6	92
Croton, N.J., U.S.	B3	107
Croton, Oh., U.S.	B3	112
Crotone (Croton), Italy	E6	23
Croton-on-Hudson, N.Y., U.S.	D7	109
Crottendorf, E. Ger.	C7	19
Crouch, Id., U.S.	E3	89
Crouse, N.C., U.S.	B1	110
Crouseville, Me., U.S.	B4	96
Crow, stm., Mn., U.S.	F4	100
Crow, North Fork, stm., Mn., U.S.	E4	100
Crow Agency, Mt., U.S.	E9	103
Crow Creek, stm., U.S.	A6	83
Crow Creek Indian Reservation, S.D., U.S.	C6	118
Crowder, Ms., U.S.	A3	101
Crowder, Ok., U.S.	B6	113
Crowduck Lake, l., Man.	D4	70
Crowell, Tx., U.S.	C3	120
Crowheart, Wy., U.S.	C3	127
Crow Indian Reservation, Mt., U.S.	E9	103
Crowley, La., U.S.	D3	95
Crowley, Tx., U.S.	n9	120
Crowley, co., Co., U.S.	C7	83
Crowley, Lake, res., Ca., U.S.	D4	82
Crowleys Ridge, mtn., U.S.	B5	81
Crown City, Oh., U.S.	D3	112
Crown King, Az., U.S.	C3	80
Crown Point, In., U.S.	B3	91
Crown Point, La., U.S.	k11	95
Crownpoint, N.M., U.S.	B1	108
Crown Point, N.Y., U.S.	B7	109
Crow Peak, mtn., Mt., U.S.	D5	103
Crowsnest, B.C.	E10	69
Crowsnest Pass, Alta.	E3	68
Crowsnest Pass, Can.	E3	68
Crows Nest Peak, mtn., S.D., U.S.	C2	118
Crowville, La., U.S.	B4	95
Crow Wing, co., Mn., U.S.	D4	100
Crow Wing, stm., Mn., U.S.	D4	100
Croydon, Austl.	C7	50
Croydon (part of London), Eng., U.K.	E6	10
Croydon, N.H., U.S.	D2	106
Croydon, Pa., U.S.	F12	115
Croydon, Ut., U.S.	B4	121
Croydon Flat, N.H., U.S.	D2	106
Croydon Peak, mtn., N.H., U.S.	D2	106
Crozet, Va., U.S.	B4	123
Crozet, Îles, is., F.S.A.T.	J24	2
Crozier, Va., U.S.	C5	123
Crozon, Fr.	C1	16
Cruachan, Ben, mtn., Scot., U.K.	D3	13
Cruagh Island, i., Ire.	D1	11
Crucero, Peru	D3	58
Cruces, Cuba	C3	64
Cruces, Punta, c., Col.	B2	60
Crucible, Pa., U.S.	G1	115
Cruden Bay, Scot., U.K.	B6	10
Cruger, Ms., U.S.	B3	101
Crum, W.V., U.S.	D2	125
Crumlin, N. Ire., U.K.	C5	11
Crummock Water, l., Eng., U.K.	F5	13
Crump Lake, l., Or., U.S.	E7	114
Crumpton, Md., U.S.	B6	97
Crumrod, Ar., U.S.	C5	81
Crumstown, In., U.S.	A5	91
Cruseilles, Fr.	C2	20
Crusheen, Ire.	E3	11
Cruso, N.C., U.S.	f10	110
Crutwell, Sask.	D2	75
Cruz, Cabo, c., Cuba	E5	64
Cruz Alta, Arg.	A4	54
Cruz Alta, Braz.	D2	56
Cruz Bay, V.I.U.S.	B6	65
Cruz del Eje, Arg.	A4	56
Cruzeiro, Braz.	C4	56
Cruzeiro do Oeste, Braz.	C2	56
Cruzeiro do Sul, Braz.	C3	58
Cruz Grande, Chile	C1	56
Crysler, Ont.	B9	73
Crystal, Mn., U.S.	m12	100
Crystal, N.D., U.S.	A8	111
Crystal, stm., Co., U.S.	B3	83
Crystal Bay, Nv., U.S.	D1	105
Crystal Bay, b., Fl., U.S.	D4	86
Crystal Beach, Fl., U.S.	D4	86
Crystal City, Man.	E2	70
Crystal City, Mo., U.S.	C7	102
Crystal City, Tx., U.S.	E3	120
Crystal Falls, Mi., U.S.	B2	99
Crystal Hill, Va., U.S.	D4	123
Crystal Lake, Ct., U.S.	B6	84
Crystal Lake, Fl., U.S.	u16	86
Crystal Lake, Il., U.S.	A5	90
Crystal Lake, l., U.S.	A4	92
Crystal Lake, l., Ct., U.S.	B6	84
Crystal Lake, l., Mi., U.S.	D4	99
Crystal Lake, l., N.H., U.S.	D4	106
Crystal Lake, l., Vt., U.S.	B4	122
Crystal Lawns, Il., U.S.	k8	90
Crystal Manor, Il., U.S.	k8	90
Crystal Mountain, mtn., N.H., U.S.	g7	106
Crystal Pond, res., Ct., U.S.	B7	84
Crystal River, Fl., U.S.	D4	86
Crystal Springs, Sask.	E3	75
Crystal Springs, Ar., U.S.	C2	81
Crystal Springs, Fl., U.S.	D4	86
Crystal Springs, Ms., U.S.	D3	101
Crystal Springs, N.D., U.S.	C6	111
Crystal Valley, Mi., U.S.	E4	99
Csongrád, Hung.	B5	26
Csorna, Hung.	B3	24
Cuajone, Peru	E3	58
Cuamba, Moz.	D6	48
Cuando, stm., Afr.	H8	42
Cuando Cubango, dept., Ang.	E2	48
Cuangar, Ang.	E2	48
Cuango, Ang.	C2	48
Cuango (Kwango), stm., Afr.	C2	48
Cuanza, stm., Ang.	C2	48
Cuanza-Norte, dept., Ang.	C1	48
Cuanza-Sul, dept., Ang.	D1	48
Cuarto, stm., Arg.	A4	54
Cuauhtémoc, Mex.	B3	63
Cuautepec (part of Mexico City), Mex.	g9	63
Cuautla [Morelos], Mex.	n14	63
Cuba, Port.	C2	22
Cuba, Al., U.S.	C1	78
Cuba, Il., U.S.	C3	90
Cuba, Ks., U.S.	C6	93
Cuba, Mo., U.S.	C6	102
Cuba, N.M., U.S.	A3	108
Cuba, N.Y., U.S.	C2	109
Cuba, Oh., U.S.	C2	112
Cuba, ctry., N.A.	C4	64
Cuba City, Wi., U.S.	F3	126
Cubal, Ang.	D1	48
Cubero, N.M., U.S.	B2	108
Cub Run, Ky., U.S.	C3	94
Cucamonga, Ca., U.S.	*m13	82
Cuchara, Co., U.S.	D5	83
Cucharas, stm., Co., U.S.	D6	83
Cuchillo, N.M., U.S.	D2	108
Cuchivero, stm., Ven.	B4	60
Cúcuta, Col.	C4	60
Cudahy, Ca., U.S.	*E4	82
Cudahy, Wi., U.S.	F6	126
Cuddalore, India	F6	36
Cuddapah, India	F6	36
Cuddy Mountain, mtn., Id., U.S.	E2	89
Cudgewa, Austl.	H6	51
Cudworth, Sask.	E3	75
Cue, Austl.	E2	50
Cuéllar, Spain	B3	22
Cuenca, Ec.	B2	58
Cuenca, Spain	B4	22
Cuenca, Sierra de, mts., Spain	B4	22
Cuencamé [de Ceniceros], Mex.	C4	63
Cuernavaca, Mex.	D5	63
Cuero, Tx., U.S.	E4	120
Cuervo, N.M., U.S.	B5	108
Cuetzalan, Mex.	m15	63
Cuevas, Ms., U.S.	E4	101
Cuevas [del Almanzora], Spain	D5	22
Cuglieri, Italy	D2	23
Cuiabá, Braz.	B1	56
Cuiabá, stm., Braz.	B1	56
Cuicas, Ven.	B3	60
Cuicatlán, Mex.	o15	63
Cuilapa, Guat.	C2	62
Cuilcagh, mtn., Eur.	C4	11
Cuilco, Guat.	C2	62
Cuillin Hills, hills, Scot., U.K.	C2	13
Cuimba, Ang.	C1	48
Cuipo, Pan.	k10	62
Cuíto, stm., Ang.	E2	48
Cuíto-Cuanavale, Ang.	E2	48
Cuitzeo, Lago de, l., Mex.	n13	63
Cuiuni, stm., Braz.	C2	59
Cuivre, West Fork, stm., Mo., U.S.	B6	102
Culberson, co., Tx., U.S.	o12	120
Culbertson, Mt., U.S.	B12	103
Culbertson, Ne., U.S.	D5	104
Culcairn, Austl.	G6	51
Culdaff Bay, b., Ire.	B4	11
Culdesac, Id., U.S.	C2	89
Culebra, P.R.	B5	65
Culebra, Isla de, i., P.R.	G12	64
Culebra Peak, mtn., Co., U.S.	D5	83
Culgoa, stm., Austl.	E8	50
Culhuacán (part of Mexico City), Mex.	h9	63
Culiacán, Mex.	C3	63
Cúllar de Baza, Spain	D4	22
Cullen, Scot., U.K.	C6	13
Cullen, La., U.S.	B2	95
Culleoka, Tn., U.S.	B5	119
Cullera, Spain	C5	22
Cullison, Ks., U.S.	E5	93
Cullman, Al., U.S.	A3	78
Cullman, co., Al., U.S.	A3	78
Culloden, Ga., U.S.	D2	87
Culloden, W.V., U.S.	C2	125
Cullom, Il., U.S.	C5	90
Cullomburg, Al., U.S.	D1	78
Cullowhee, N.C., U.S.	f9	110
Culoz, Fr.	D1	20
Culp Creek, Or., U.S.	D4	114
Culpeper, Va., U.S.	B5	123
Culpeper, co., Va., U.S.	B5	123
Cultus Lake, B.C.	f14	69
Culuene, stm., Braz.	A2	56
Culver, In., U.S.	B5	91
Culver, Ks., U.S.	D5	93
Culver, Mn., U.S.	D6	100
Culver, Or., U.S.	C5	114
Culver, Point, c., Austl.	F3	50
Culver City, Ca., U.S.	m12	82
Culvers Lake, l., N.J., U.S.	A3	107
Culverton, Ga., U.S.	C4	87
Culzean Bay, b., Scot., U.K.	E4	13
Cumaná, Ven.	A5	60
Cumbal, Nevado de, mtn., Col.	C2	60
Cumberland, B.C.	E5	69
Cumberland, Ont.	g13	73
Cumberland, Ky., U.S.	C3	92
Cumberland, Ky., U.S.	D7	94
Cumberland, Md., U.S.	k13	97
Cumberland, N.J., U.S.	E3	107
Cumberland, N.C., U.S.	B4	110
Cumberland, Oh., U.S.	C4	112
Cumberland, Va., U.S.	C5	123
Cumberland, Wi., U.S.	C1	126
Cumberland, co., N.S.	D5	71
Cumberland, co., Il., U.S.	D5	90
Cumberland, co., Ky., U.S.	D4	94
Cumberland, co., Me., U.S.	E2	96
Cumberland, co., N.J., U.S.	E2	107
Cumberland, co., N.C., U.S.	B4	110
Cumberland, co., Pa., U.S.	F7	115
Cumberland, co., Tn., U.S.	D8	119
Cumberland, co., Va., U.S.	C4	123
Cumberland, stm., U.S.	C11	76
Cumberland, Lake, res., Ky., U.S.	D5	94
Cumberland, South Fork, stm., U.S.	D5	94
Cumberland Center, Me., U.S.	g7	96
Cumberland City, Tn., U.S.	A4	119
Cumberland Foreside, Me., U.S.	g7	96
Cumberland Furnace, Tn., U.S.	A4	119
Cumberland Gap, Tn., U.S.	C10	119
Cumberland Gap, U.S.	D6	94
Cumberland Gap National Historical Park, U.S.	D6	94
Cumberland Hill, R.I., U.S.	B4	116
Cumberland House, Sask.	D4	75
Cumberland Island National Seashore, Ga., U.S.	F5	87
Cumberland Lake, l., Sask.	C4	75
Cumberland Mountain, mtn., Tn., U.S.	C9	119
Cumberland Peninsula, pen., N.W. Ter.	C20	66
Cumberland Plateau, plat., U.S.	D8	119
Cumberland Sound, strt., N.W. Ter.	C19	66
Cumbernauld, Scot., U.K.	*E5	13
Cumbres Pass, Co., U.S.	D4	83
Cumbria, co., Eng., U.K.	F6	13
Cuming, co., Ne., U.S.	C9	104
Cumming, Ga., U.S.	B2	87
Cumming, Ia., U.S.	f8	92
Cummings, N.D., U.S.	B8	111
Cummington, Ma., U.S.	B2	98
Cumnock, N.C., U.S.	B3	110
Cumnock [and Holmhead], Scot., U.K.	E4	13
Cumpas, Mex.	A3	63
Cumra, Tur.	D9	40
Cunard, W.V., U.S.	n13	125
Cunco, Chile	D2	54
Cuncumén, Chile	A2	54
Cundiff, Ky., U.S.	*C3	94
Cundinamarca, dept., Col.	C3	60
Cundiyo, N.M., U.S.	*B4	108
Cundys Harbor, Me., U.S.	g8	96
Cunene, dept., Ang.	E1	48
Cunene, stm., Afr.	E1	48
Cuneo, Italy	E1	23
Cuney, Tx., U.S.	C5	120
Cunnamulla, Austl.	E8	50
Cunningham, Ky., U.S.	f9	94
Cunningham, Tn., U.S.	A4	119
Cupar, Sask.	G3	75
Cupar, Scot., U.K.	D5	13
Cupertino, Ca., U.S.	*k8	82
Curaçá, Braz.	E5	57
Curaçao, i., Neth. Ant.	H18	65
Curacautín, Chile	D2	54
Curacó, stm., Arg.	B3	54
Curanilahue, Chile	D1	54
Curaray, stm., Braz.	B3	58
Curcubâta, mtn., Rom.	B6	24
Curdsville, Ky., U.S.	C2	94
Curecanti National Recreation Area, Co., U.S.	C3	83
Curepto, Chile	B2	54
Curiapo, Ven.	B5	60
Curicó, Chile	A2	54
Curicuriari, stm., Braz.	D4	60
Curimataú, stm., Braz.	h6	57
Curitiba, Braz.	D3	56
Curitibanos, Braz.	D2	56
Curlew, Ia., U.S.	B3	92
Curlew, Wa., U.S.	A7	124
Curlew Creek, stm., Wa., U.S.	A7	124
Curlew Lake, l., Wa., U.S.	A7	124
Curon Venosta, Italy	C6	20
Currais Novos, Braz.	C3	57
Curralinho, Braz.	B5	57
Curran, Ont.	B10	73
Curran, Mi., U.S.	D7	99
Currans, Ire.	E2	11
Currant, Nv., U.S.	*D7	105
Currant Creek, stm., Co., U.S.	C5	83
Currant Mountain, mtn., Nv., U.S.	E6	105
Current, stm., U.S.	A5	81
Currie, Mn., U.S.	F3	100
Currituck, N.C., U.S.	A6	110
Currituck, co., N.C., U.S.	A6	110
Curry, co., N.M., U.S.	C6	108
Curry, co., Or., U.S.	E2	114
Curryville, Mo., U.S.	B6	102
Curtea-de-Argeş, Rom.	C7	24
Curtice, Oh., U.S.	A2	112
Curtin, Or., U.S.	D3	114
Curtis, Ar., U.S.	D2	81
Curtis, Mi., U.S.	B5	99
Curtis, Ne., U.S.	D5	104
Curtis, i., Austl.	D9	50
Curtiss, Wi., U.S.	D3	126
Curtisville, Pa., U.S.	E2	115
Curuá, stm., Braz.	C4	59
Curuá, stm., Braz.	D4	59
Curuá do Sul, stm., Braz.	C4	59
Curuçá, Braz.	B1	57
Curug, Yugo.	C4	24
Curuguaty, Para.	D5	55
Curum: Sierra de, mts., S.A.	C5	60
Curundu, Pan.	m11	62
Curuzú Cuatiá, Arg.	B5	54
Curvelo, Braz.	E7	57
Curver, stm., Switz.	C8	21
Curwensville, Pa., U.S.	E4	115
Curwensville Lake, res., Pa., U.S.	E4	115
Curwood, Mount, mtn., Mi., U.S.	B2	99
Cushendall, N. Ire., U.K.	B5	11
Cushing, Ia., U.S.	B2	92
Cushing, Ne., U.S.	C7	104
Cushing, Ok., U.S.	B5	113
Cushing, Tx., U.S.	D5	120
Cushman, Ar., U.S.	B4	81
Cushman, Ma., U.S.	B2	98
Cushman, Lake, res., Wa., U.S.	B2	124
Cusick, Wa., U.S.	A8	124
Cusihuiriáchic, Mex.	B3	63
Cusset, Fr.	D5	16
Cusseta, Al., U.S.	C4	78
Cusseta, Ga., U.S.	D2	87
Custar, Oh., U.S.	A2	112
Custer, Mi., U.S.	E4	99
Custer, Mt., U.S.	D9	103
Custer, S.D., U.S.	D2	118
Custer, Wa., U.S.	A3	124
Custer, co., Co., U.S.	C5	83
Custer, co., Id., U.S.	E4	89
Custer, co., Mt., U.S.	D11	103
Custer, co., Ne., U.S.	C6	104
Custer, co., Ok., U.S.	B2	113
Custer, co., S.D., U.S.	D2	118
Custer Battlefield National Monument, Mt., U.S.	E9	103
Custer City, Ok., U.S.	B3	113
Custer City, Pa., U.S.	C2	118
Custer Peak, mtn., S.D., U.S.	C2	118
Cut Bank, Mt., U.S.	B4	103
Cutbank, stm., Alta.	B1	68
Cut Bank Creek, stm., N.D., U.S.	A4	111
Cut Beaver Lake, l., Sask.	D4	75
Cutchogue, N.Y., U.S.	m16	109
Cutervo, Peru	C2	58
Cuthbert, Ga., U.S.	E2	87
Cut Knife, Sask.	E1	75
Cutler, Ont.	A2	73
Cutler, Fl., U.S.	*G6	86
Cutler, In., U.S.	C5	91
Cutler, Me., U.S.	D5	96
Cutler Ridge, Fl., U.S.	s13	86
Cutlerville, Mi., U.S.	*F5	99
Cut Off, La., U.S.	E5	95
Cutshin, Ky., U.S.	C6	94
Cuttack, India	D8	36
Cut Throat Island, i., Newf.	A3	72
Cuttingsville, Vt., U.S.	E3	122
Cuttyhunk Island, i., Ma., U.S.	D6	98
Cutzamalá, stm., Mex.	n13	63
Cuvo, stm., Ang.	D1	48
Cuxhaven, W. Ger.	B4	18
Cuyahoga, co., Oh., U.S.	A4	112
Cuyahoga, stm., Oh., U.S.	A4	112
Cuyahoga Falls, Oh., U.S.	A4	112
Cuyama, stm., Ca., U.S.	E4	82
Cuyama, Ca., U.S.	E4	82
Cuyamaca Peak, mtn., Ca., U.S.	F5	82
Cuyamungue, N.M., U.S.	*B4	108
Cuylerville, N.Y., U.S.	*C3	109
Cuyo Islands, is., Phil.	C6	34
Cuyo, N.M., U.S.	D5	108
Cuyuni, stm., S.A.	A3	59
Cuzco, Peru	D3	58
Cuzco, In., U.S.	H4	91
Cuzco, dept., Peru	D3	58
Cwmbran, Wales, U.K.	C5	12
C.W. McConaughy, Lake, res., Ne., U.S.	C4	104
Cybinka, Pol.	A9	19
Cyclades, is., Grc.	D7	40
Cyclone, Pa., U.S.	C4	115
Cygnet, Oh., U.S.	A2	112
Cylinder, Ia., U.S.	A3	92
Cynthiana, In., U.S.	H2	91
Cynthiana, Ky., U.S.	B5	94
Cynthiana, Oh., U.S.	C2	112
Cypress, Al., U.S.	*B4	108
Cypress, Ca., U.S.	*n12	82
Cypress, Fl., U.S.	B4	86
Cypress, Il., U.S.	F4	90
Cypress, Tx., U.S.	r14	120
Cypress Bayou, stm., Ar., U.S.	B3	81
Cypress Creek, stm., Tx., U.S.	r14	120
Cypress Hills, hills, Can.	G10	66
Cypress Hills Provincial Park, Alta.	E5	68
Cypress Hills Provincial Park, Sask.	H1	75
Cypress Inn, Tn., U.S.	B3	119
Cypress Lake, Fl., U.S.	*F6	86
Cypress Lake, l., Sask.	H1	75
Cypress Lake, l., Fl., U.S.	D5	86
Cypress Quarters, Fl., U.S.	E6	86
Cypress River, Man.	E2	70
Cypress Swamp, sw., U.S.	F4	85
Cyprus, ctry., Asia	E9	40
Cyprus, North, ctry., Asia	E9	40
Cyrenaica (Barqah), hist. reg., Libya	D4	43
Cyril, Ok., U.S.	C3	113
Cyril, stm., Man.	B4	70
Cyrus, Mn., U.S.	E3	100
Cythera see Kíthira, i., Grc.	D4	40
Czar, Alta.	C5	68
Czarna, stm., Pol.	k14	26
Czarna Przemsza, stm., Pol.	g10	26
Czarnków, Pol.	B4	26
Czechoslovakia, ctry., Eur.	D4	26
Czechowice-Dziedzice, Pol.	h10	26
Czersk, Pol.	B4	26
Częstochowa, Pol.	C5	26
Człuchów, Pol.	B4	26

D

Da'an, China	B11	32
Daaquam, Que.	C7	74
Dabakala, I.C.	E4	45
Daba Mountains, mts., China	I4	32
Dabdab, Libya	D2	43
Dabeiba, Col.	B3	26
Dabie (part of Szczecin), Pol.	*B3	60
Dabie Mountains, mts., China	I5	32
Dáblice, Czech.	n18	26
Dabneys, Va., U.S.	C5	123
Dabola, Gui.	D2	45
Daborow, Som.	D4	47
Dabou, I.C.	E4	45
Dąbrowa Białostocka, Pol.	B7	26
Dąbrowa Górnicza, Pol.	C5	26
Dąbrowa [Tarnowska], Pol.	C6	26
Dacca see Dhaka, Bngl.	D9	36
Dachau, W. Ger.	D5	18
Dacoma, Ok., U.S.	A3	113
Dacono, Co., U.S.	A6	83
Dacula, Ga., U.S.	C3	87
Dadanawa, Guy.	B3	59
Daday, Tur.	B9	40
Dade, co., Fl., U.S.	B1	87
Dade, co., Ga., U.S.	B1	87
Dade, co., Mo., U.S.	D4	102
Dade City, Fl., U.S.	D4	86
Dadeville, Al., U.S.	C4	78
Dadeville, Mo., U.S.	D4	102
Dādra and Nagar Haveli, ter., India	*D5	36
Dadu, Pak.	H2	36
Daet, Phil.	o14	34
Dafoe, Sask.	F3	75
Dafoe, stm., Man.	B4	70
Dagana, Sen.	C1	45
Dagenham (part of London), Eng., U.K.	k13	10
Daggett, Ca., U.S.	E5	82
Daggett, Mi., U.S.	C3	99
Daggett, co., Ut., U.S.	C6	121
Dagmar, Mt., U.S.	B12	103
Dagsboro, De., U.S.	F5	85
Dagua, China	E2	32
Daguscahonda, Pa., U.S.	D4	115
Dagus Mines, Pa., U.S.	D4	115
Dahinda, Il., U.S.	C3	90
Da Hinggan Ling (Greater Khingan Range), mts., China	B9	31
Dahlak Archipelago, is., Eth.	B5	47
Dahlen, N.D., U.S.	A8	111
Dahlgren, Il., U.S.	E5	90
Dahlgren, Va., U.S.	B5	123
Dahlonega, Ga., U.S.	B3	87
Dahme, E. Ger.	B8	19
Dāhod, India	F5	37
Dahomey see Benin, ctry., Afr.	E5	45
Dahra, Libya	E5	43
Dahük, Iraq	D14	41
Daicheng, China	E7	32
Dailey, W.V., U.S.	C5	125
Daimiel, Spain	C4	22
Daingean, Ire.	D4	11
Daingerfield, Tx., U.S.	C5	120
Daiō, Japan	o15	33
Daiō, Cape, c., Japan	I8	33
Dairen see Dalian, China	D9	31
Dairy, Or., U.S.	E5	114
Dairyland, Wi., U.S.	B1	126
Daisetta, Tx., U.S.	D5	120
Daisy, Ar., U.S.	C2	81
Daisy, Ok., U.S.	C6	113
Daixian, China	D7	31
Dajabón, Dom. Rep.	E8	64
Dajarra, Austl.	D6	50
Dakar, Sen.	D1	45
Dākhilah, Al Wāḥat ad, well, Eg.	D5	43
Dakhla, W. Sah.	E1	44
Dakoro, Niger	D6	45
Dakota, Mn., U.S.	F5	100
Dakota, co., Mn., U.S.	F5	100
Dakota, co., Ne., U.S.	B9	104
Dakota City, Ia., U.S.	B3	92
Dakota City, Ne., U.S.	B9	104
Dākura, Nic.	C6	62
Dakwa, Zaire	A4	48
Daláas, Aus.	B9	21
Dalaba, Gui.	D2	45
Dalälven, stm., Swe.	C4	9
Dalandzadgad, Mong.	C5	31
Dalarö, Swe.	t36	14
Dālbandin, Pak.	C3	36
D'Albertis Dome, mtn., Pap. N. Gui.	k11	50
Dalbo, Mn., U.S.	E5	100
Dalby, Austl.	E9	50
Dalby, Swe.	C7	15
Dalcahue, Chile	E2	54
Dale, Il., U.S.	F5	90
Dale, In., U.S.	H4	91
Dale, Ok., U.S.	B4	113
Dale, Or., U.S.	C8	114
Dale, co., Al., U.S.	D4	78
Dale City, Va., U.S.	B5	123
Dale Hollow Lake, res., U.S.	C8	119
Dalemead, Alta.	D4	68
Daleville, Al., U.S.	D4	78
Daleville, In., U.S.	D6	91
Daleville, Ms., U.S.	C5	101
Dalhart, Tx., U.S.	A1	120
Dalhousie, N.B.	A3	71
Dalhousie, India	A5	37
Dalhousie Junction, N.B.	A3	71
Dali, China	E6	31
Dalian (Lüda), China	D9	31
Dalías, Spain	D4	22
Daliburgh, Scot., U.K.	C1	13
Daliyat et Karmil, Isr.	B7	41
Dalkeith, Scot., U.K.	E5	13
Dalkeith, Il., U.S.	B1	86
Dalkena, Wa., U.S.	A8	124
Dalkey, Ire.	D5	11
Dall, Mount, mtn., Ak., U.S.	f15	79
Dallardsville, Tx., U.S.	D5	120
Dallas, Al., U.S.	B3	78
Dallas, Ga., U.S.	C2	87
Dallas, Ia., U.S.	C4	92
Dallas, N.C., U.S.	B1	110
Dallas, Or., U.S.	C3	114
Dallas, Pa., U.S.	D10	115
Dallas, S.D., U.S.	D6	118
Dallas, Tx., U.S.	C4	120
Dallas, W.V., U.S.	f8	125
Dallas, Wi., U.S.	C2	126
Dallas, co., Al., U.S.	C2	78
Dallas, co., Ar., U.S.	D3	81
Dallas, co., Ia., U.S.	C3	92
Dallas, co., Mo., U.S.	D4	102
Dallas, co., Tx., U.S.	C4	120
Dallas Center, Ia., U.S.	C4	92
Dallas City, Il., U.S.	C2	90
Dallas Naval Air Station, mil., Tx., U.S.	n9	120
Dallastown, Pa., U.S.	G8	115
Dall Island, i., Ak., U.S.	n23	79
Dalmally, Scot., U.K.	D4	13
Dalmatia, Pa., U.S.	E8	115
Dalmatia, hist. reg., Yugo.	D3	24
Dalmellington, Scot., U.K.	C4	10
Dalmeny, Sask.	E2	75
Dalnerechensk, Sov. Un.	E16	29
Dalnyaya, Sov. Un.	D11	33
Daloa, I.C.	E3	45
Dalou Mountains, mts., China	K2	32
Dalqū, Sud.	A3	47
Dalroy, Alta.	D4	68
Dalry, Scot., U.K.	E4	13
Dalrymple, Mount, mtn., Austl.	D7	36
Dāltenganj, India	D7	36
Dalton, Ar., U.S.	A4	81
Dalton, Ga., U.S.	B1	98
Dalton, Ma., U.S.	B1	98
Dalton, Mn., U.S.	D3	100
Dalton, Mo., U.S.	B5	102
Dalton, Ne., U.S.	C3	104
Dalton, N.H., U.S.	B3	106
Dalton, N.Y., U.S.	C3	109
Dalton, Oh., U.S.	B4	112
Dalton, Pa., U.S.	C10	115
Dalton, Wi., U.S.	E4	126
Dalton City, Il., U.S.	D5	90
Dalton Gardens, Id., U.S.	B2	89
Dalton Iceberg Tongue, ice, Ant.	C25	7
Dalwhinnie, Scot., U.K.	D4	13
Daly, stm., Austl.	B5	50
Daly City, Ca., U.S.	h8	82
Dalzell, Il., U.S.	B4	90
Dalzell, S.C., U.S.	C7	117
Damán, India	D5	36
Damān and Diu, ter., India	*D5	36
Damanhūr, Eg.	C6	43
Damaqun Mountains, mts., China	D7	32
Damar, Ks., U.S.	C4	93
Damar, i., Indon.	G7	34
Damara, Cen. Afr. Rep.	D3	46
Damariscotta, Me., U.S.	D3	96
Damariscotta Lake, l., Me., U.S.	D3	96
Damascus, Ar., U.S.	B3	81
Damascus (Dimashq), Syria	B3	38
Damascus, Ga., U.S.	E2	87
Damascus, Md., U.S.	B3	97
Damascus, Pa., U.S.	C11	115
Damascus, Va., U.S.	f10	123
Damascus Gate, hist., Isr. Occ.	m14	41
Damaturu, Nig.	D7	45
Damba, Ang.	C2	48
Dame Marie, Cap, c., Haiti	E6	64
Dames Quarter, Md., U.S.	D6	97
Dam Gamad, Sud.	C2	47
Dāmghān, Iran	B5	38
Damietta Branch, stm., Eg.	D3	41
Damietta see Dumyāṭ, Eg.	F6	32
Daming, China	G13	41
Dāmiyā, Jord.		
Damme, W. Ger.	B8	17
Dāmodar, stm., India	F10	37
Damoh, India	F7	37
Damon, Tx., U.S.	r14	120
Damongo, Ghana	E4	45
Dampier Archipelago, is., Austl.	D2	50
Dampier Strait, strt., Indon.	F8	34
Damvant, Switz.	B2	21
Dan, stm., U.S.	D3	123
Dana, Sask.	E3	75
Dana, In., U.S.	E3	91
Dana, Ky., U.S.	B6	94
Dana, N.C., U.S.	f10	110
Danané, I.C.	E3	45
Da Nang, Viet.	B3	34
Dana Point, Ca., U.S.	*F5	82
Dānāpur, India	E10	37
Danbury, Ct., U.S.	D2	84
Danbury, Ia., U.S.	B2	92
Danbury, N.H., U.S.	C3	106
Danbury, N.C., U.S.	A2	110
Danbury, Tx., U.S.	r14	120
Danbury, Wi., U.S.	B1	126
Danby, Vt., U.S.	E2	122
Danby Corners, Vt., U.S.	E2	122
Dancy, Wi., U.S.	D3	126
Dancyville, Tn., U.S.	B2	119
Dande, stm., Ang.		
Dandenong, Austl.	*G8	50
Dandong, China	C9	31
Dandridge, Tn., U.S.	C10	119

Name	Map Ref.	Page
Dane, Wi., U.S.	E4	126
Dane, co., Wi., U.S.	E4	126
Danevang, Tx., U.S.	E4	120
Danfeng, China	H4	32
Danforth, Il., U.S.	C6	90
Danforth, Me., U.S.	C5	96
Danforth Hills, mts., Co., U.S.	A2	83
Dangila, Eth.	C4	47
Dangshan, China	G7	32
Dangtu, China	I8	32
Dangyang, China	I4	32
Dania, Fl., U.S.	F6	86
Daniel, Ut., U.S.	*C4	121
Daniel, Wy., U.S.	D2	127
Daniels, co., Mt., U.S.	B11	103
Daniel's Harbour, Newf.	C3	72
Danielson, Ct., U.S.	B8	84
Daniels Pass, Ut., U.S.	C4	121
Danielsville, Ga., U.S.	B3	87
Danilov, Sov. Un.	B13	27
Danilovgrad, Yugo.	C4	24
Danjo Island, i., Japan	J4	33
Danlí, Hond.	E7	63
Dannebrog, Ne., U.S.	C7	104
Dannemara, N.Y., U.S.	f11	109
Dannemarie, Fr.	A3	21
Dannenberg, W. Ger.	E5	15
Dannevirke, N.Z.	N16	51
Dannike, Swe.	A7	15
Dans Mountain, mtn., Md., U.S.	k13	97
Dansville, N.Y., U.S.	C3	109
Dante, S.D., U.S.	D7	118
Dante, Tn., U.S.	m14	119
Dante, Va., U.S.	f9	123
Dantewāra, India	H8	37
Danube, Mn., U.S.	F3	100
Danube, stm., Eur.	G14	8
Danube Delta, Eur.	I7	27
Danubyu, Burma	D1	35
Danvers, Il., U.S.	C4	90
Danvers, Ma., U.S.	A6	98
Danvers, Mn., U.S.	E3	100
Danvers, Mt., U.S.	C7	103
Danville, Que.	D5	74
Danville, Al., U.S.	A2	78
Danville, Ar., U.S.	B2	81
Danville, Ca., U.S.	h9	82
Danville, Ga., U.S.	D3	87
Danville, Il., U.S.	C6	90
Danville, In., U.S.	E4	91
Danville, Ia., U.S.	D6	92
Danville, Ks., U.S.	E6	93
Danville, Ky., U.S.	C5	94
Danville, La., U.S.	B3	95
Danville, N.H., U.S.	E4	106
Danville, Oh., U.S.	B3	112
Danville, Pa., U.S.	F8	115
Danville, Vt., U.S.	C4	122
Danville, Va., U.S.	D3	123
Danville, Wa., U.S.	A7	124
Danville, W.V., U.S.	C3	125
Danxian, China	C8	35
Danzhai, China	C8	35
Danzig, Gulf of, b., Eur.	A5	26
Danzig see Gdańsk, Pol.	A5	26
Daosa, India	D6	37
Daoxian, China	F7	31
Daphne, Al., U.S.	E2	78
Dapp, Alta.	B4	68
Da Qaidam, China	D4	31
Daqing (Anda), China	*B10	31
Dar'ā, Syria	F11	40
Dārāb, Iran	G7	39
Darabani, Rom.	A8	24
Daraj, Libya	C2	43
Darasun, Sov. Un.	D14	29
Darawah, Eg.	D3	41
Darbandi Khan Dam, Iraq	D2	39
Darbhanga, India	C8	36
D'Arbonne, Bayou, stm., La., U.S.	B3	95
Darburruk, Som.	D5	47
Darby, Mt., U.S.	D2	103
Darby, Pa., U.S.	G11	115
Darbydale, Oh., U.S.	m10	112
Darby Township, Pa., U.S.	*G11	115
Darbyville, Oh., U.S.	C2	112
Dar Chebika, Mor.	D2	44
D'Arcy Station, Sask.	F1	75
Dardanelle, Ar., U.S.	B2	81
Dardanelle, Ca., U.S.	C4	82
Dardanelle Lake, res., Ar., U.S.	B2	81
Dardanelles, strt.	B5	40
Darden, N.C., U.S.	B6	110
Darden, Tn., U.S.	B3	119
Dardenne Creek, stm., Mo., U.S.	f12	102
Dare, co., N.C., U.S.	B7	110
Darende, Tur.	C11	40
Dar es Salaam, Tan.	C6	48
Daretown, N.J., U.S.	D2	107
Darfo, Italy	D6	20
Darfur, Mn., U.S.	F4	100
Dārfūr al Janūblyah (Southern Darfur), prov., Sud.	C1	47
Dārfūr ash Shamālīyah (Northern Darfur), prov., Sud.		
Dargan, Md., U.S.	B2	97
Dargan-Ata, Sov. Un.	A11	39
Dargaville, N.Z.	K14	51
Darhan, Mong.	B6	31
Darhan Muminggan Lianheqi, China	D4	32
Darien, Ct., U.S.	E2	84
Darien, Ga., U.S.	E5	87
Darien, Il., U.S.	*k9	90
Darien, Wi., U.S.	F5	126
Darien, Gulf of, b.	F9	62
Darién, Serranía del, mts.	D5	62
Dariense, Cordillera, mts., Nic.	D5	62
Darjeeling, India	C8	36
Darke, co., Oh., U.S.	B1	112
Darkesville, W.V., U.S.	B6	125
Darley Woods, De., U.S.	h8	85
Darling, stm., Austl.	A3	101
Darling, stm., Austl.	F7	50
Darling, Lake, res., N.D., U.S.	A4	111
Darling Downs, reg., Austl.	C8	51
Darlingford, Man.		
Darling Range, mts., Austl.	F2	50
Darlington, Eng., U.K.	C6	10
Darlington, Al., U.S.	v15	86
Darlington, Id., U.S.	F5	89
Darlington, In., U.S.	D4	91
Darlington, Md., U.S.	A5	97
Darlington, Mo., U.S.	A3	102
Darlington, S.C., U.S.	C8	117
Darlington, Wi., U.S.	F3	126
Darlington, co., S.C., U.S.	C8	117
Darlowo, Pol.	A4	26
Darmody, Sask.	G2	75
Darmstadt, W. Ger.	D4	18
Darnah, Libya	C4	43
Darnell, La., U.S.	B4	95
Darnestown, Md., U.S.	B3	97
Darney, Fr.	A2	20
Darnley, Cape, c., Ant.	C19	7
Daro, Malay.	E4	34
Daroca, Spain	B5	22
Darr, Ne., U.S.	D6	104
Darreh Gaz, Iran	C9	39
Darrington, Wa., U.S.	A4	124
Darrouzett, Tx., U.S.	A2	120
Darrow, La., U.S.	h10	95
Dart, stm., Eng., U.K.	D4	12
Dart, Cape, c., Ant.	B36	7
Dartmoor, for., Eng., U.K.	E5	10
Dartmouth, N.S.	E6	71
Dartmouth, Eng., U.K.	E5	10
Dartmouth, Ma., U.S.	C5	98
Dartmouth Woods, De., U.S.	*A3	85
Daru, Pap. N. Gui.	k11	50
Daruvar, Yugo.	C3	24
Darvel Bay, b., Malay.	E5	34
Darwin, Austl.	B5	50
Darwin, Ca., U.S.	D5	82
Darwin, Mn., U.S.	E4	100
Darwin, Isla i., Ec.	f5	58
Darwin Glacier, ice, Ant.	f41	7
Dasht, stm., Pak.	C3	36
Dashwood, Ont.	D3	73
Dasol Bay, b., Phil.	o12	34
Dassel, Mn., U.S.	E4	100
Datça, Tur.	D6	25
Dateland, Az., U.S.	E2	80
Datia, India	E7	37
Datian, China	L7	32
Datil, N.M., U.S.	C2	108
Datil Mountains, mts., N.M., U.S.	C2	108
Datong, China	C7	31
Datto, Ar., U.S.	A5	81
Datu, Cape, c., Asia	E3	34
Datze, stm., E. Ger.	E7	15
Daudnagar, India	E10	37
Daufuskie Island, S.C., U.S.	G6	117
Daufuskie Island, i., S.C., U.S.	G6	117
Daugava (Western Dvina), stm., Sov. Un.	C2	108
Daugavpils (Dvinsk), Sov. Un.	D6	27
Daule, Ec.	A2	58
Daule, Ec.	B2	58
Daun, W. Ger.	C1	19
Daund, India	H5	37
Daung, i., Burma	F3	35
Dauphin, Man.	D1	70
Dauphin, co., Pa., U.S.	F8	115
Dauphin, co., Pa., U.S.	F8	115
Dauphin, Man.	D2	70
Dauphiné, hist. reg., Fr.	E6	16
Dauphin Island, Al., U.S.	E1	78
Dauphin Island, i., Al., U.S.	E1	78
Dauphin Lake, l., Man.	D2	70
Daus, Tn., U.S.	D8	119
Dāvangere, India	F6	36
Davant, La., U.S.	E6	95
Davao, Phil.	D7	34
Davao Gulf, b., Phil.	D7	34
Dävar Panāh, Iran	H11	39
Daveluyville, Que.	C5	74
Davenport, Ca., U.S.	D2	82
Davenport, Fl., U.S.	D5	86
Davenport, Ia., U.S.	C7	92
Davenport, Ne., U.S.	D8	104
Davenport, N.Y., U.S.	C6	109
Davenport, N.D., U.S.	C8	111
Davenport, Ok., U.S.	B5	113
Davenport, Wa., U.S.	B7	124
Davenport Downs, Austl.	B3	51
Daventry, Eng., U.K.	B6	12
Davey, Ne., U.S.	h11	104
David, Pan.	F6	62
David, Ky., U.S.	C7	94
David City, Ne., U.S.	C8	104
David-Gorodok, Sov. Un.	E6	27
Davidson, Sask.	F3	75
Davidson, N.C., U.S.	B2	110
Davidson, Ok., U.S.	C2	113
Davidson, co., N.C., U.S.	B2	110
Davidson, co., Tn., U.S.	A5	119
Davidson Mountains, mts., Ak., U.S.	B11	79
Davidsville, Pa., U.S.	F4	115
Davie, Fl., U.S.	F6	86
Davie, co., N.C., U.S.	B2	110
Davin, Sask.	G3	75
Davis, Il., U.S.	A4	90
Davis, N.C., U.S.	C6	110
Davis, Ok., U.S.	C4	113
Davis, S.D., U.S.	D9	118
Davis, W.V., U.S.	B5	125
Davis, co., Ia., U.S.	D5	92
Davis, co., Ut., U.S.	C3	121
Davis, Mount, mtn., Pa., U.S.	G3	115
Davisboro, Ga., U.S.	D4	87
Davis City, Ia., U.S.	D4	92
Davis Creek, stm., W.V., U.S.	m12	125
Davis Dam, Az., U.S.	B1	80
Davis Inlet, Newf.	g9	72
Davis Islands, i., Fl., U.S.	p11	86
Davis Junction, Il., U.S.	A4	90
Davis-Monthan Air Force Base, mil., Az., U.S.	E5	80
Davis Mountains, mts., Tx., U.S.	o12	120
Davison, Mi., U.S.	E7	99
Davison, co., S.D., U.S.	D7	118
Davisville, N.H., U.S.	D3	106
Davle, Czech.	o17	26
Dāvar Panāh, Iran		
Davy, W.V., U.S.	D3	125
Dawa, China	*C9	31
Dawa, stm., Afr.	E5	47
Dawei, Burma	F10	36
Dawes, co., Ne., U.S.	B2	104
Dawn, Mo., U.S.	B4	102
Dawn, Tx., U.S.	B1	120
Dawna Range, mts., Burma	D3	35
Dawros Head, c., Ire.	C3	11
Daws Island, i., S.C., U.S.	G6	117
Dawson, Yukon	D5	66
Dawson, Ga., U.S.	E2	87
Dawson, Ia., U.S.	C3	92
Dawson, Mn., U.S.	F2	100
Dawson, Ne., U.S.	D10	104
Dawson, N.D., U.S.	C6	111
Dawson, Pa., U.S.	F2	115
Dawson, Tx., U.S.	D4	120
Dawson, co., Ga., U.S.	B2	87
Dawson, co., Mt., U.S.	C11	103
Dawson, co., Ne., U.S.	D6	104
Dawson, co., Tx., U.S.	C1	120
Dawson, stm., Austl.	D8	50
Dawson, Mount, mtn., B.C.	D9	69
Dawson Creek, B.C.	B7	69
Dawson-Lambton Glacier, ice, Ant.	B10	7
Dawson Range, mts., Yukon	D5	66
Dawson Springs, Ky., U.S.	C2	94
Dawsonville, Ga., U.S.	B2	87
Dax, Fr.	F3	16
Daxian, China	E6	31
Day, Fl., U.S.	B3	86
Day, co., S.D., U.S.	B8	118
Daykin, Ne., U.S.	D8	104
Daylesford, Austl.	H5	51
Daym Zubayr, Sud.	D2	47
Dayong, China	J4	32
Dayr Abū Sa'īd, Jord.	B7	41
Dayr al Balaḥ, Isr. Occ.	C6	41
Dayr 'Allā, Jord.	g13	41
Dayr az Zawr, Syria	B4	38
Dayr Dibwān, Isr. Occ.	h12	41
Dayr Istiyā, Isr. Occ.	g11	41
Dayrūṭ, Eg.	D6	43
Daysland, Alta.	C4	68
Daysville, Tn., U.S.	D9	119
Dayton, Al., U.S.	C2	78
Dayton, Id., U.S.	G7	89
Dayton, In., U.S.	D4	91
Dayton, Ia., U.S.	B3	92
Dayton, Ky., U.S.	h14	94
Dayton, Md., U.S.	m12	100
Dayton, Mn., U.S.	D2	105
Dayton, Nv., U.S.	C3	107
Dayton, N.J., U.S.	C2	109
Dayton, N.Y., U.S.	C1	112
Dayton, Oh., U.S.	B3	114
Dayton, Or., U.S.	E3	115
Dayton, Pa., U.S.	D8	119
Dayton, Tn., U.S.	D5	120
Dayton, Tx., U.S.	B4	123
Dayton, Va., U.S.	C8	124
Dayton, Wa., U.S.	B5	127
Dayton, Wy., U.S.	C5	86
Daytona Beach, Fl., U.S.	F7	31
Dayu, China	B8	84
Dayville, Ct., U.S.	C7	114
Dayville, Or., U.S.	B7	111
Dazey, N.D., U.S.	D3	49
De Aar, S. Afr.	D1	70
Dead, North Branch, stm., Me., U.S.	C2	96
Dead, South Branch, stm., Me., U.S.	C2	96
Dead Creek, stm., Vt., U.S.	C2	122
Dead Diamond, stm., N.H., U.S.	g7	106
Dead Indian Peak, mtn., Wy., U.S.	B3	127
Dead Lake, l., Mn., U.S.	D3	100
Dead Lake, res., Fl., U.S.	B1	86
Deadman Bay, b., Fl., U.S.	C3	86
Deadman Creek, stm., Wa., U.S.	g14	124
Dead Sea, l., Asia	B3	38
Deadwood, S.D., U.S.	C2	118
Deadwood Reservoir, res., Id., U.S.	E3	89
Deaf Smith, co., Tx., U.S.	B1	120
Deakin Bay, b., Ant.	C28	7
Deal, Eng., U.K.	C9	12
Deal, N.J., U.S.	C4	107
Deale, Md., U.S.	C4	97
Deal Island, Md., U.S.	D6	97
Deal Island, i., Md., U.S.	D6	97
Deam, stm., B.C.	C4	69
Deanburg, Tn., U.S.	B3	119
Dean Channel, strt., B.C.	C4	69
Deán Funes, Arg.	A4	54
Deanville, W.V., U.S.	B4	125
Dearborn, Mi., U.S.	F7	99
Dearborn, Mo., U.S.	B3	102
Dearborn, co., In., U.S.	F7	91
Dearborn Heights, Mi., U.S.	p15	99
Dearg, Beinn, mtn., Scot., U.K.	B4	10
Dearing, Ga., U.S.	C4	87
Dearing, Ks., U.S.	E8	93
Dearing, Mo., U.S.	E8	102
De Armanville, Al., U.S.	B4	78
Deary, Id., U.S.	C2	89
Dease Arm, b., N.W. Ter.	C8	66
Dease Lake, B.C.	m16	69
Dease Strait, strt., N.W. Ter.	C11	66
Death Valley, val., Ca., U.S.	D5	82
Death Valley Junction, Ca., U.S.	D5	82
Death Valley National Monument, Ca., U.S.	D5	82
Deatsville, Al., U.S.	C3	78
Deauville, Fr.	C7	16
Deaver, Wy., U.S.	B4	127
Deba, Nig.	*D6	45
De Baca, co., N.M., U.S.	C5	108
Debaltsevo, Sov. Un.	q21	27
Debao, China	C6	31
Debar, Yugo.	E5	24
De Bary, Fl., U.S.	D5	86
Debauch Mountain, mtn., Ak., U.S.	C8	79
Debden, Sask.	D2	75
Débé, Trin.	O23	65
Debec, N.B.	C2	71
De Beque, Co., U.S.	B2	83
De Berry, Tx., U.S.	C5	83
Debica, Pol.	C6	26
Deblin, Pol.	C6	26
Deblois, Me., U.S.	D5	96
Debno, Pol.	B3	26
Debo, Lac, l., Mali	C4	45
Debolt, Alta.	B1	68
De Borgia, Mt., U.S.	C1	103
Debovo, Bul.	D7	24
Debre Birhan, Eth.	D4	47
Debrecen, Hung.	B5	24
Debre Markos, Eth.	C4	47
Debre Tabor, Eth.	C4	47
Debre Zeyit, Eth.	*D4	47
De Cade, Lake, l., La., U.S.	E5	95
Decatur, Ar., U.S.	A1	81
Decatur, Ga., U.S.	C2	87
Decatur, Il., U.S.	D5	90
Decatur, In., U.S.	C8	91
Decatur, Ia., U.S.	D4	92
Decatur, Mi., U.S.	F5	99
Decatur, Ms., U.S.	C4	101
Decatur, Ne., U.S.	B9	104
Decatur, Tn., U.S.	D9	119
Decatur, Tx., U.S.	C4	120
Decatur, co., Ga., U.S.	F2	87
Decatur, co., In., U.S.	F6	91
Decatur, co., Ia., U.S.	D4	92
Decatur, co., Ks., U.S.	C3	93
Decatur, co., Tn., U.S.	B3	119
Decatur, Lake, res., Il., U.S.	D5	90
Decaturville, Tn., U.S.	B3	119
Decazeville, Fr.	E5	16
Deccan, plat., India	E6	36
Deception, Mount, mtn., Wa., U.S.	B2	124
Deception Lake, l., Sask.	A3	75
Decherd, Tn., U.S.	B5	119
Dččín, Czech.	C3	26
Decize, Fr.	D5	16
Decker, Man.	D1	70
Decker, In., U.S.	G2	91
Decker, Mt., U.S.	E10	103
Decker Lake, B.C.	B5	69
Deckers, Co., U.S.	B5	83
Deckerville, Mi., U.S.	E8	99
Declo, Id., U.S.	G5	89
De Cocksdorp, Neth.	A4	17
Decorah, Ia., U.S.	A6	92
Decota, W.V., U.S.	m13	125
Dededo, Guam	L10	52
Dedemsvaart, Neth.	B6	17
Deder, Eth.	C4	68
Dedham, Ia., U.S.	C3	92
Dedham, Ma., U.S.	B5	98
Dedinovo, Sov. Un.	n19	27
Dédougou, Burkina	D4	45
Dedu, China	B3	33
Dedza, Mwi.	D5	48
Dee, stm., U.K.	B5	10
Deedsville, In., U.S.	C5	91
Deel, stm., Ire.	E3	11
Deemer, Ms., U.S.	C4	101
Deep, stm., N.C., U.S.	B3	110
Deep Brook, N.S.	E4	71
Deep Creek, stm., De., U.S.	F3	85
Deep Creek, stm., Mt., U.S.	C4	103
Deep Creek, stm., Ut., U.S.	B3	121
Deep Creek, stm., Ut., U.S.	C3	121
Deep Creek, stm., Ut., U.S.	F3	121
Deep Creek, stm., Wa., U.S.	g13	124
Deep Creek Lake, res., Md., U.S.	K12	97
Deep Creek Mountains, mts., Id., U.S.	G6	89
Deep Creek Range, mts., Ut., U.S.	D2	121
Deepdale, Man.	D1	70
Deep Fork, stm., Ok., U.S.	B5	113
Deep Gap, N.C., U.S.	A1	110
Deep Gap, N.C., U.S.	A1	110
Deep Inlet, b., Newf.	g10	72
Deep Red Creek, stm., Ok., U.S.	C3	113
Deep River, Ont.	A7	73
Deep River, Ct., U.S.	D6	84
Deep River, N.C., U.S.	C5	92
Deep Run, N.C., U.S.	B5	110
Deepstep, Ga., U.S.	C4	87
Deepwater, Mo., U.S.	C4	102
Deepwater, N.J., U.S.	D2	107
Deep Water, W.V., U.S.	m13	125
Deer, Ar., U.S.	B2	81
Deer Creek, Il., U.S.	C4	90
Deer Creek, In., U.S.	C5	91
Deer Creek, Mn., U.S.	D3	100
Deer Creek, stm., In., U.S.	C5	91
Deer Creek, stm., Md., U.S.	A5	97
Deer Creek, stm., Ms., U.S.	B3	101
Deer Creek, stm., Oh., U.S.	C2	112
Deer Creek Indian Reservation, Mn., U.S.	C5	100
Deerfield, Il., U.S.	h9	90
Deerfield, Ks., U.S.	D8	91
Deerfield, Ma., U.S.	A2	98
Deerfield, Mi., U.S.	G7	99
Deerfield, Mo., U.S.	D3	102
Deerfield, N.H., U.S.	D4	106
Deerfield, Oh., U.S.	A4	112
Deerfield, Wi., U.S.	E4	126
Deerfield, stm., U.S.	A2	98
Deerfield Beach, Fl., U.S.	F6	86
Deerfield Street, N.J., U.S.	D2	107
Deer Grove, Il., U.S.	B4	90
Deering, Ak., U.S.	B7	79
Deering, Mo., U.S.	E8	102
Deering, N.H., U.S.	D3	106
Deering, N.D., U.S.	A4	111
Deer Island, Or., U.S.	B4	114
Deer Island, pen., U.S.	g12	98
Deer Island, l., Ms., U.S.	f8	101
Deer Isle, Me., U.S.	D4	96
Deer Isle, i., Me., U.S.	D4	96
Deer Lake, Newf.	D3	72
Deer Lake, l., Newf.	D3	72
Deer Lake, l., Mn., U.S.	C5	100
Deer Lodge, Mt., U.S.	D4	103
Deer Lodge, Tn., U.S.	C9	119
Deer Lodge, co., Mt., U.S.	E3	103
Deer Mountain, mtn., Me., U.S.	C2	96
Deer Park, Fl., U.S.	D5	86
Deer Park, Md., U.S.	m12	97
Deer Park, Mi., U.S.	B5	99
Deer Park, N.Y., U.S.	n15	109
Deer Park, Oh., U.S.	o13	112
Deer Park, Tx., U.S.	*r14	120
Deer Park, Wa., U.S.	B8	124
Deer Park, Wi., U.S.	C1	126
Deer Peak, mtn., Co., U.S.	C5	83
Deer Pond, l., Newf.	D4	72
Deer River, Mn., U.S.	C5	100
Deer River, N.Y., U.S.	B5	109
Deerton, Mi., U.S.	B3	99
Deer Trail, Co., U.S.	B6	83
Deerwood, Mn., U.S.	D5	100
Deeth, Nv., U.S.	B6	105
Deex Nugaaleed, stm., Som.	C5	47
Defeet Park, Ut., U.S.	B5	121
Deferiet, N.Y., U.S.	A5	109
Defiance, Ia., U.S.	C2	92
Defiance, Mo., U.S.	f12	102
Defiance, Oh., U.S.	A1	112
Defiance, co., Oh., U.S.	A1	112
Defiance, Mount, mtn., Or., U.S.	B5	114
Deford, Mi., U.S.	E7	99
De Forest, Wi., U.S.	E4	126
De Funiak Springs, Fl., U.S.	u15	86
Dêgê, China	E4	31
Degeberga, Swe.	C8	15
Degeh Bur, Eth.	D5	47
Dégelis, Que.	B9	74
Degerön, Swe.	B2	92
Degersheim, Switz.	u33	14
Deggendorf, W. Ger.	D6	18
De Graff, Mn., U.S.	E3	100
De Graff, Oh., U.S.	B2	112
De Gray Lake, res., Ar., U.S.	C2	81
De Grey, stm., Austl.	D2	50
Deh Bīd, Iran	B5	38
Dehibat, Tun.	C7	44
Dehiwala-Mount Lavinia, Sri L.	*G6	36
Deh Kord, Iran	E4	39
Dehlorān, Iran	E3	39
Dehpehk i, Micron.	Q17	52
Dehra Dūn, India	B6	36
Deh Shū, Afg.	F11	39
Deinze, Bel.	D3	17
Dej, Rom.	B6	24
Dejvice (part of Prague), Czech.	n17	26
De Kalb, Il., U.S.	B5	90
De Kalb, In., U.S.	C5	101
De Kalb, Mo., U.S.	B3	102
De Kalb, N.Y., U.S.	f9	109
De Kalb, Tx., U.S.	C5	120
De Kalb, co., Al., U.S.	A4	78
De Kalb, co., Ga., U.S.	C2	87
De Kalb, co., Il., U.S.	B5	90
De Kalb, co., In., U.S.	B7	91
De Kalb, co., Mo., U.S.	B3	102
De Kalb, co., Tn., U.S.	D8	119
De Kalb Junction, N.Y., U.S.	f9	109
Dekemhare, Eth.	B4	47
Dekese, Zaire	B3	48
Deke Sokehs, i., Micron.	Q17	52
Dekoa, Cen. Afr. Rep.	D3	46
Delacroix, La., U.S.	k12	95
Delafield, Wi., U.S.	m11	126
De Lamere, N.D., U.S.	C8	111
Delanco, N.J., U.S.	C3	107
De Land, Fl., U.S.	C5	86
De Land, Il., U.S.	C5	90
Delaney, Ar., U.S.	B2	81
Delano, Ca., U.S.	E4	82
Delano, Mn., U.S.	E5	100
Delano Peak, mtn., Ut., U.S.	E3	121
Delanson, N.Y., U.S.	C6	109
Delaplaine, Ar., U.S.	A5	81
Delarām, Afg.	E11	39
Delaronde Lake, l., Sask.	C2	75
Delavan, Il., U.S.	C4	90
Delavan, Ks., U.S.	D7	93
Delavan, Mn., U.S.	G4	100
Delavan, Wi., U.S.	F5	126
Delavan Lake, Wi., U.S.	*F5	126
Delaware, Ont.	E3	73
Delaware, Ar., U.S.	B2	81
Delaware, Ia., U.S.	B6	92
Delaware, Oh., U.S.	B2	112
Delaware, Ok., U.S.	A6	113
Delaware, co., In., U.S.	D7	91
Delaware, co., Ia., U.S.	B6	92
Delaware, co., N.Y., U.S.	C5	109
Delaware, co., Oh., U.S.	B2	112
Delaware, co., Ok., U.S.	A7	113
Delaware, co., Pa., U.S.	G11	115
Delaware, state, U.S.	D3	85
Delaware, stm., U.S.	C8	93
Delaware, East Branch, stm., N.Y., U.S.	C5	109
Delaware, West Branch, stm., U.S.	C5	109
Delaware Bay, b., U.S.	C12	76
Delaware City, De., U.S.	B3	85
Delaware Lake, res., Oh., U.S.	B3	112
Delaware Mountains, mts., Tx., U.S.	o12	120
Delaware Water Gap, Pa., U.S.	E11	115
Delaware Water Gap National Recreation Area, U.S.	B2	107
Delbarton, W.V., U.S.	D2	125
Delburne, Alta.	C4	68
Delcambre, La., U.S.	E4	95
Del City, Ok., U.S.	B4	113
Delco, N.C., U.S.	C4	110
Deleau, Man.	E1	70
Delémont, Switz.	E3	18
De Leon, Tx., U.S.	C3	120
De Leon Springs, Fl., U.S.	C5	86
Delevan, N.Y., U.S.	C2	109
Delft, Neth.	A6	16
Delfzijl, Neth.	A7	16
Delgada, Punta, c., Arg.	C4	54
Delgado, Cabo, c., Moz.	D7	48
Delgertsogt, Mong.	A2	32
Delhi, India	B6	36
Delhi, Ia., U.S.	B6	92
Delhi, La., U.S.	B4	95
Delhi, N.Y., U.S.	C6	109
Delhi, Ok., U.S.	B2	113
Delhi, ter., India	*C6	36
Delhi Hills, Oh., U.S.	*o12	112
Delia, Alta.	D4	68
Delia, Ks., U.S.	C8	93
Delicias, Mex.	C7	60
Delight, Ar., U.S.	C2	81
Delingha, China	B5	31
Delisle, Sask.	F2	75
De Lisle, Ms., U.S.	E4	101
Delitzsch, E. Ger.	B6	18
Dell, Mt., U.S.	E4	103
Dell, co., Ar., U.S.	B5	81
Dell City, Tx., U.S.	F4	103
Delle, Fr.	B3	20
Dellenbaugh, Mount, mtn., Az., U.S.	A2	80
Delles, Alg.	B5	44
Dell Rapids, S.D., U.S.	D9	118
Dellrose, Tn., U.S.	B4	119
Dellroy, Oh., U.S.	B4	112
Dellslow, W.V., U.S.	h11	125
Dellwood, Fl., U.S.	B1	86
Dellwood, Mo., U.S.	*f13	102
Delmar, Al., U.S.	A2	78
Delmar, De., U.S.	G3	85
Delmar, Ia., U.S.	B7	92
Delmar, Md., U.S.	D6	97
Delmar, N.Y., U.S.	C7	109
Delmas, Sask.	E1	75
Delmenhorst, W. Ger.	B4	18
Delmita, Tx., U.S.	F3	120
Delmont, N.J., U.S.	E3	107
Delmont, S.D., U.S.	D7	118
Del Norte, Co., U.S.	D4	83
Del Norte, co., Ca., U.S.	B2	82
Deloit, Ia., U.S.	B2	92
Delong, In., U.S.	B5	91
De Long Islands, is., Sov. Un.	B35	128
Deloraine, Man.	E1	70
Delorme, Lac, l., Que.	F18	66
Deloro, Ont.	C7	73
Delos see Dhílos, i., Grc.	D5	25
Del Park Manor, De., U.S.	i7	85
Delphi, In., U.S.	C4	91
Delphi, Mt., U.S.	D8	103
Delphos, Ks., U.S.	C6	93
Delphos, Oh., U.S.	B1	112
Delran, N.J., U.S.	C3	107
Delray Beach, Fl., U.S.	F6	86
Del Rio, Tn., U.S.	D10	119
Del Rio, Tx., U.S.	E2	120
Delson, Que.	q19	74
Delta, Ont.	C8	73
Delta, Al., U.S.	B4	78
Delta, Co., U.S.	C2	83
Delta, Ia., U.S.	C5	92
Delta, La., U.S.	B5	95
Delta, Mo., U.S.	D8	102
Delta, Oh., U.S.	A1	112
Delta, Pa., U.S.	G9	115
Delta, co., Co., U.S.	C3	83
Delta, co., Mi., U.S.	C3	99
Delta, co., Tx., U.S.	C5	120
Delta, reg., Ms., U.S.	B3	101
Delta Amacuro, ter., Ven.	B5	60
Delta Barrage, Eg.	D3	41
Delta Beach, Man.	D2	70
Delta City, Ms., U.S.	B3	101
Delta Junction, Ak., U.S.	C10	79
Delta Peak, mtn., B.C.	A3	69
Delta Reservoir, res., N.Y., U.S.	B5	109
Deltaville, Va., U.S.	C6	123
Delton, Mi., U.S.	F5	99
Delungra, Austl.	D8	51
Delvin, Ire.	D4	11
Delvina, Alb.	C3	25
Delyatin, Sov. Un.	G5	27
Demaine, Sask.	G2	75
Demanda, Sierra de la, mtn., Spain	A4	22
Demarest, N.J., U.S.	h9	107
Demba, Zaire	C3	48
Dembi Dolo, Eth.	D3	47
Demerara, stm., Guy.	A3	59
Demidov, Sov. Un.	D8	27
Deming, N.M., U.S.	E2	108
Deming, Wa., U.S.	A3	124
Demini, stm., Braz.	B2	59
Demirci, Tur.	C7	40
Demir Kapija, Yugo.	E6	24
Demmitt, Alta.	B1	68
Demmin, E. Ger.	B6	18
Demopolis, Al., U.S.	C2	78
Demopolis Dam, Al., U.S.	C2	78
Demorest, Ga., U.S.	B3	87
Demorestville, Ont.	C7	73
De Mossville, Ky., U.S.	k14	94
Demotte, In., U.S.	B3	91
Dempo, mtn., Indon.	F2	34
Dempster, S.D., U.S.	C9	118
Dêmqog, China	A7	37
Demyanka, stm., Sov. Un.	B8	28
Denain, Fr.	B5	16
Denakil (Danakil), pl., Eth.	C5	47
Denali National Park, Ak., U.S.	C9	79
Denare Beach, Sask.	C4	75
Denau, Sov. Un.	H22	8
Denaud, Fl., U.S.	F5	86
Denbigh, Wales, U.K.	D5	10
Denbigh, N.D., U.S.	A5	111
Den Burg, Neth.	A4	17
Denby, S.D., U.S.	D3	118
Dendermonde, Bel.	C4	17
Dendron, Va., U.S.	C6	123
Denezhkin Kamen, Mount, mtn., Sov. Un.	A5	28
Dengkou, China	D2	32
Denham, In., U.S.	B4	91
Denham, Mn., U.S.	D6	100
Denham, Mount, mtn., Jam.	E13	65
Denham Springs, La., U.S.	D5	95
Den Helder, Neth.	A6	16
Denhoff, N.D., U.S.	B5	111
Denholm, Sask.	E1	75
Den Hoorn, Neth.	C6	22
Denia, Spain	C6	22
Deniau, Que.	B8	74
Deniliquin, Austl.	G7	50
Denio, Nv., U.S.	B3	105
Denison, Ia., U.S.	B2	92
Denison, Ks., U.S.	C5	93
Denison, Tx., U.S.	C4	120
Denison Dam, U.S.	D5	113
Denizli, Tur.	D7	40
Denman Glacier, ice, Ant.	C22	7
Denmark, Ia., U.S.	D6	71
Denmark, Me., U.S.	E2	96
Denmark, S.C., U.S.	E5	117
Denmark, Tn., U.S.	B2	119
Denmark, Wi., U.S.	D6	126
Denmark, ctry., Eur.	I3	14
Denmark Strait, strt.	C17	128
Dennard, Ar., U.S.	B3	81
Dennehotso, Az., U.S.	A6	80
Denning, Ar., U.S.	B2	81
Dennis, Ks., U.S.	E8	93
Dennis, Ma., U.S.	C7	98
Dennis, Mt., U.S.	A5	101
Dennis Hill, Ct., U.S.	B3	84
Dennison, Mn., U.S.	F5	100
Dennison, Oh., U.S.	B4	112
Dennis Port, Ma., U.S.	C7	98
Dennison, Scot., U.K.	*D5	13
Denny Terrace, S.C., U.S.	C5	96
Denover, Neth.	B7	16
Denpasar, Indon.	G5	34
Dent, Mn., U.S.	D3	100
Dent, co., Mo., U.S.	D6	102
Dentan, Al., U.S.	A2	78
Denton, Ks., U.S.	C8	93
Denton, Md., U.S.	C6	97
Denton, Mi., U.S.	p14	99
Denton, Mt., U.S.	C7	103
Denton, N.C., U.S.	B2	110
Denton, Tx., U.S.	C4	120

Name	Map Ref.	Page

Denton, co., Tx., U.S. — C4 120
D'Entrecasteaux, Point, c., Austl. — F2 50
D'Entrecasteaux Islands, is., Pap. N. Gui. — k13 50
Dents Du Midi, mts., Switz. — D2 21
Dentsville, S.C., U.S. — C6 117
Denver, Ar., U.S. — A2 81
Denver, Co., U.S. — B6 83
Denver, Il., U.S. — C2 90
Denver, In., U.S. — C5 91
Denver, Ia., U.S. — B5 92
Denver, Mo., U.S. — A3 102
Denver, N.C., U.S. — B1 110
Denver, Pa., U.S. — F9 115
Denver, Tn., U.S. — A4 119
Denver, W.V., U.S. — B5 125
Denver, co., Co., U.S. — B6 83
Denver City, Tx., U.S. — C1 120
Denville, N.J., U.S. — B4 107
Denzil, Sask. — E1 75
Deoghar, India — E11 37
De Panne, Bel. — C2 17
Departure Bay, B.C. — f12 69
Depauville, N.Y., U.S. — A4 109
Depauw, In., U.S. — H5 91
De Pere, Wi., U.S. — D5 126
Depew, N.Y., U.S. — C2 109
Depew, Ok., U.S. — B5 113
Depoe Bay, Or., U.S. — C2 114
Depok, Indon. — *G3 34
Deport, Tx., U.S. — C5 120
Deposit, N.Y., U.S. — C5 109
Depósito, Braz. — B2 59
Depot Harbour, Ont. — B4 73
Depue, Il., U.S. — B4 90
Deputy, In., U.S. — G6 91
Dêqên, China — F4 31
De Queen, Ar., U.S. — C1 81
De Queen Lake, res., Ar., U.S. — C1 81
Dequen-Nord, Que. — A5 74
De Quincy, La., U.S. — D2 95
Dera, stm., Ar., U.S. — E5 47
Dera Ghāzi Khān, Pak. — B5 36
Dera Ismāīl Khān, Pak. — B5 36
Derbent, Sov. Un. — E3 28
Derbetovka, Sov. Un. — I14 27
Derby, Austl. — C3 50
Derby, N.B. — D6 71
Derby, Eng., U.K. — D6 10
Derby, Ct., U.S. — D3 84
Derby, In., U.S. — H4 91
Derby, Ks., U.S. — E6 93
Derby, Me., U.S. — C4 96
Derby, Ms., U.S. — E4 101
Derby, N.Y., U.S. — C2 109
Derby, Oh., U.S. — B4 112
Derby, Va., U.S. — f9 123
Derby Junction, N.B. — C4 71
Derby Line, Vt., U.S. — A4 122
Derbyshire, co., Eng., U.K. — A6 12
Derecske, Hung. — B5 24
Derg, Lough, l., Ire. — D2 10
Der Grabow, b., E. Ger. — D6 15
De Ridder, La., U.S. — D2 95
Derik, Tur. — D13 40
Derma, Ms., U.S. — B4 101
Dermott, Ar., U.S. — D4 81
Dernieres, Isles, is., La., U.S. — E5 95
Derravaragh, Lough, l., Ire. — D3 10
Derrieusseaux Creek, stm., Ar., U.S. — C3 81
Derry, La., U.S. — C3 95
Derry, N.H., U.S. — E4 106
Derry, Pa., U.S. — F3 115
Derrybrien, Ire. — D3 11
Derry see Londonderry, N. Ire., U.K.
De Ruyter, N.Y., U.S. — C5 109
Derventa, Yugo. — C3 24
Derwent, Alta. — C4 68
Derwent, Oh., U.S. — C4 112
Derwent, stm., Eng., U.K. — F8 13
Derwent, stm., Eng., U.K. — F6 13
Derwent, stm., Eng., U.K. — F5 13
Derwood, Md., U.S. — B3 97
Derzhavinsk, Sov. Un. — C7 28
Desaguadero, stm., Arg. — A3 54
Desaguadero, stm., Bol. — C2 55
Des Allemands, La., U.S. — E5 95
Desamparados, C.R. — *F5 62
Des Arc, Ar., U.S. — C4 81
Des Arc, Mo., U.S. — D7 102
Desbiens, Que. — A6 74
Desboro, Ont. — C3 73
Descalvado, Braz. — k8 56
Descartes, Fr. — D4 16
Deschaillons [-sur-Saint-Laurent], Que. — C5 74
Deschambault, Que. — C6 74
Deschambault Lake, Sask. — C4 75
Deschambault Lake, l., Sask. — C4 75
Deschênes, Que. — D2 74
Deschutes, co., Or., U.S. — D5 114
Deschutes, stm., Or., U.S. — B6 114
Dese, Eth. — C4 47
Deseado, stm., Arg. — D3 54
Desengaño, Punta, c., Arg. — D3 54
Desenzano del Garda, Italy — D6 20
Deseret, Ut., U.S. — D3 121
Deseret Peak, mtn., Ut., U.S. — C3 121
Deseronto, Ont. — C7 73
Desert, Mount, mtn., W.V., U.S. — m13 125
Deserta Grande, i., Port. — h12 22
Desert Center, Ca., U.S. — F6 82
Desert Creek Peak, mtn., Nv., U.S. — E2 105
Desert Hot Springs, Ca., U.S. — F5 82
Desert Peak, mtn., Ut., U.S. — B2 121
Desert Valley, val., Nv., U.S. — B3 105
Desha, Ar., U.S. — B4 81
Desha, co., Ar., U.S. — D4 81
Deshler, Ne., U.S. — D8 104
Deshler, Oh., U.S. — A2 112
Desio, Italy — D5 20
Des Lacs, N.D., U.S. — A4 111
Des Lacs, stm., N.D., U.S. — A4 111
Desloge, Mo., U.S. — D7 102
Desmarais, Alta. — B4 68
Desmet, Id., U.S. — B2 89
De Smet, S.D., U.S. — C8 118
Desmochados, Para. — E4 55
Des Moines, Ia., U.S. — C4 92
Des Moines, N.M., U.S. — A6 108
Des Moines, Wa., U.S. — B3 124
Des Moines, co., Ia., U.S. — D5 92
Des Moines, stm., U.S. — D5 92
Des Moines, East Fork, stm., U.S. — A3 92
Desna, stm., Sov. Un. — F8 27
Desolación, Isla, i., Chile — h11 54

Desolation Canyon, val., Ut., U.S. — D5 121
De Soto, Ga., U.S. — E2 87
De Soto, Il., U.S. — F4 90
De Soto, Ia., U.S. — C3 92
De Soto, Ks., U.S. — D9 93
De Soto, Mo., U.S. — C7 102
De Soto, Wi., U.S. — E2 126
De Soto, co., Fl., U.S. — E5 86
De Soto, co., La., U.S. — B2 95
De Soto, co., Ms., U.S. — A3 101
De Soto City, Fl., U.S. — E5 86
Despard, W.V., U.S. — k10 125
Des Peres, Mo., U.S. — f13 102
Des Plaines, Il., U.S. — A6 90
Des Plaines, stm., U.S. — k8 90
Dessau, E. Ger. — C6 18
Destin, Fl., U.S. — u15 86
Destrehan, La., U.S. — E5 95
Desvres, Fr. — D1 17
Dete, Zimb. — A4 49
Detlor, Ont. — B7 73
Detmold, W. Ger. — C4 18
Detour, Point, c., Mi., U.S. — C4 99
De Tour Village, Mi., U.S. — C7 99
Detroit, Al., U.S. — A1 78
Detroit, Ks., U.S. — D6 93
Detroit, Me., U.S. — D3 96
Detroit, Mi., U.S. — F7 99
Detroit, Or., U.S. — C4 114
Detroit, Tx., U.S. — C5 120
Detroit, stm., N.A. — F7 99
Detroit Lake, res., Or., U.S. — C4 114
Detroit Lakes, Mn., U.S. — D3 100
Detva, Czech. — D5 26
Deuel, co., Ne., U.S. — C3 104
Deuel, co., S.D., U.S. — C9 118
Deurne (part of Antwerp), Bel. — B6 16
Deux Frères, Les, is., Viet. — H7 35
Deux-Montagnes, Que. — p19 74
Deux Montagnes, Lac des, l., Que. — q19 74
Deux-Rivières, Ont. — A6 73
Deva, Rom. — C6 24
De Valls Bluff, Ar., U.S. — C4 81
Dévaványa, Hung. — B5 24
Deventer, Neth. — A7 16
Devereux, Ga., U.S. — C3 87
Deveron, stm., Scot., U.K. — C6 13
DeView, Bayou, stm., Ar., U.S. — B4 81
Devil River Peak, mtn., N.Z. — N14 51
Devils Elbow, Mo., U.S. — D5 102
Devils Island see Diable, Île du, i., Fr. Gu. — A4 59
Devils Lake, N.D., U.S. — A7 111
Devils Lake, l., N.D., U.S. — A6 111
Devils Paw, mtn., Ak., U.S. — k23 79
Devils Postpile National Monument, Ca., U.S. — D4 82
Devils Slide, Ut., U.S. — B4 121
Devils Tower, Wy., U.S. — B8 127
Devils Tower National Monument, Wy., U.S. — B8 127
Devil Track Lake, l., Mn., U.S. — k9 100
Devine, Tx., U.S. — E3 120
Devizes, Eng., U.K. — C6 12
Devol, Ok., U.S. — C3 113
Devola, Oh., U.S. — C4 112
Devon, Alta. — C4 68
Devoll, stm., Alb. — B3 25
Devon, Ks., U.S. — E9 93
Devon, Mt., U.S. — B5 103
Devon, co., Eng., U.K. — D4 12
Devon Island, i., N.W. Ter. — m34 66
Devonport, Austl. — o15 51
Devonshire, De., U.S. — r14 120
Dewar, Ok., U.S. — B6 113
Dewart Lake, l., In., U.S. — B6 91
Dewberry, Alta. — C5 68
Dewdney, B.C. — E6 69
Deweese, Ne., U.S. — D7 104
Dewees Inlet, b., S.C., U.S. — k12 117
Dewees Island, i., S.C., U.S. — F8 117
Dewey, Az., U.S. — C3 80
Dewey, Ok., U.S. — A6 113
Dewey, co., Ok., U.S. — B2 113
Dewey, co., S.D., U.S. — B4 118
Dewey Beach, De., U.S. — F5 85
Dewey Lake, res., Ky., U.S. — C7 94
Deweyville, Tx., U.S. — D6 120
Deweyville, Ut., U.S. — B3 121
De Witt, Alta. — D3 68
De Witt, Ar., U.S. — C4 81
Dewitt, Ia., U.S. — C7 92
Dewitt, Mi., U.S. — F6 99
De Witt, Mo., U.S. — B4 102
De Witt, Ne., U.S. — D9 104
De Witt, N.Y., U.S. — B4 109
Dewitt, Va., U.S. — C5 123
De Witt, co., Il., U.S. — C4 90
De Witt, co., Tx., U.S. — E4 120
Dewsbury, Eng., U.K. — A6 12
Dexing, China — J7 32
Dexter, Ga., U.S. — D3 87
Dexter, Ks., U.S. — E7 93
Dexter, Ky., U.S. — f9 94
Dexter, Me., U.S. — C3 96
Dexter, Mi., U.S. — F7 99
Dexter, Mn., U.S. — G6 100
Dexter, Mo., U.S. — E8 102
Dexter, N.M., U.S. — D5 108
Dexter, N.Y., U.S. — A4 109
Dexter, Or., U.S. — D4 114
Dexter, Lake, l., Fl., U.S. — C5 86
Dey-Dey, Lake, l., Austl. — E5 50
Deyhūk, Iran — E8 39
Deyyer, Iran — H6 39
Dez, stm., Iran — E4 39
Dezfūl, Iran — D5 39
Dezhnev, Cape, c., Sov. Un. — C21 29
Dezhou, China — D8 31
Dhahab, Eg. — H10 40
Dhahran see Az Zahrān, Sau. Ar. — C4 38
Dhaka (Dacca), Bngl. — D9 36
Dhamār, Yemen — D4 38
Dhamtari, India — G8 37
Dhangadhi, Nepal — C8 37
D'Hanis, Tx., U.S. — E3 120
Dhankuta, Nepal — D11 37
Dhār, India — F5 37
Dharmapuri, India — F6 36
Dharmjaygarh, India — D7 36
Dharmshāla, India — B6 37

Dhaulpur, India — D6 37
Dhawlāgiri, mtn., Nepal — C7 36
Dhekélia, Grc. — g11 25
Dhenoûsa, i., Grc. — D5 25
Dhiban, Jord. — G10 40
Dhidhimótikhon, Grc. — B6 25
Dhíkti (Delos), i., Grc. — D5 25
Dhímitsána, Grc. — D4 25
Dhomhnuill, Sgurr, mtn., Scot., U.K. — D3 13
Dhorāji, India — G3 37
Dhrépanon, Cape, c., Grc. — C4 25
Dhuburi, India — D12 37
Dhule, India — D5 36
Dhuusa Mareeb, Som. — D4 47
Día, i., Grc. — E5 25
Diable, Île du (Devils Island), i., Fr. Gu. — A4 59
Diable, Pointe du, c., Mart. — S11 65
Diablerets, mtn., Switz. — C3 20
Diablo, Canyon, val., Az., U.S. — C4 80
Diablo, Mount, mtn., Ca., U.S. — h9 82
Diablo Dam, Wa., U.S. — A4 124
Diablo Heights, Pan. — m11 62
Diablo Lake, res., Wa., U.S. — A4 124
Diablo Range, mts., Ca., U.S. — D3 82
Diamante, Arg. — A4 54
Diamantina, Braz. — B4 56
Diamantina, stm., Austl. — D7 50
Diamond, Oh., U.S. — A4 112
Diamond, W.V., U.S. — m12 125
Diamond Bar, Ca., U.S. — *n13 82
Diamond Bluff, Wi., U.S. — D1 126
Diamond City, Alta. — E4 68
Diamond Harbour, India — F12 37
Diamond Head, crat., Hi., U.S. — B4 88
Diamond Hill, R.I., U.S. — B4 116
Diamond Hill Reservoir, res., R.I., U.S. — A4 116
Diamond Lake, Il., U.S. — h9 90
Diamond Lake, l., Or., U.S. — D4 114
Diamond Mountains, mts., Nv., U.S. — D6 105
Diamond Peak, mtn., Co., U.S. — A2 83
Diamond Peak, mtn., Id., U.S. — E5 89
Diamond Peak, mtn., Or., U.S. — D4 114
Diamond Peak, mtn., Wa., U.S. — C8 124
Diamond Point, N.Y., U.S. — B7 109
Diamond Springs, Ca., U.S. — C3 82
Diamondville, Wy., U.S. — E2 127
Diana, Tn., U.S. — B5 119
Diana, W.V., U.S. — C4 125
Dianalund, Den. — C5 15
Dianbai, China — G7 31
Dianjiang, China — I2 32
Dianópolis, Braz. — D1 57
Diapaga, Burkina — D5 45
Diapitan Bay, b., Phil. — n14 34
Diaz, Ar., U.S. — B4 81
Dibaya, Zaire — C3 48
Dibble, Ok., U.S. — B4 113
Dibble Iceberg Tongue, ice, Ant. — C26 7
Dibbrell, Tn., U.S. — D8 119
Dibrugarh, India — C9 36
Dickens, Ia., U.S. — A2 92
Dickens, Ne., U.S. — D5 104
Dickens, Tx., U.S. — C2 120
Dickens, co., Tx., U.S. — C2 120
Dickenson, co., Va., U.S. — e9 123
Dickerson, Md., U.S. — B3 97
Dickey, N.D., U.S. — C7 111
Dickey, co., N.D., U.S. — C7 111
Dickeyville, Wi., U.S. — F3 126
Dickinson, Al., U.S. — D2 78
Dickinson, N.D., U.S. — C3 111
Dickinson, Tx., U.S. — *r14 120
Dickinson, co., Ia., U.S. — A2 92
Dickinson, co., Ks., U.S. — D6 93
Dickinson, co., Mi., U.S. — B3 99
Dickinson Center, N.Y., U.S. — f10 109
Dickinson Dam, N.D., U.S. — C3 111
Dickson, Ok., U.S. — C5 113
Dickson, Tn., U.S. — A4 119
Dickson, co., Tn., U.S. — A4 119
Dickson City, Pa., U.S. — D10 115
Dicle (Tigris), stm., Asia — D13 40
Didcot, Eng., U.K. — C6 12
Didsbury, Alta. — D3 68
Didwāna, India — F5 37
Diébougou, Burkina — D4 45
Diefenbaker, Lake, res., Sask. — F2 75
Diégo-Suarez see Antsiranana, Madag. — f9 49
Diekirch, Lux. — E6 17
Diemel, stm., W. Ger. — B9 18
Dien Bien Phu, Viet. — B5 35
Diepholz, W. Ger. — B8 18
Dieppe, N.B. — C5 71
Dieppe, Fr. — C8 16
Dierks, Ar., U.S. — C1 81
Di er Songhua, stm., China — B12 31
Diessen, W. Ger. — D7 20
Diest, Bel. — D5 17
Dieterich, Il., U.S. — D5 90
Dietikon, Switz. — B5 21
Dietrich, Id., U.S. — G4 89
Dieuze, Fr. — C7 16
Diever, Neth. — B6 17
Diez, W. Ger. — E7 18
Diffa, Niger — D7 45
Differdange, Lux. — F5 17
Difficult, Tn., U.S. — C8 119
Digboi, India — C10 36
Digby, N.S. — E4 71
Digby, co., N.S. — E4 71
Dighton, Ks., U.S. — D3 93
Dighton, Ma., U.S. — C5 98
Digne, Fr. — E13 16
Digoin, Fr. — F5 16
Digul, stm., Indon. — G10 34
Dijon, Fr. — D6 16
Dikhil, Dji. — C5 47
Dikirnis, Eg. — g11 40
Dikili, Tur. — C3 25
Dikson, Sov. Un. — B11 29
Dikwa, Nig. — D7 45
Dila, Eth. — D4 47
Dili, Indon. — G7 34
Dilia, stm., Niger — B4 108
Dilkon, Az., U.S. — B5 80
Dilke, Sask. — G3 75
Dillard, Or., U.S. — D3 114
Dillard, Ga., U.S. — B3 87
Dill City, Ok., U.S. — B2 113
Dille, W.V., U.S. — C4 125

Dillenburg, W. Ger. — C3 19
Diller, Ne., U.S. — D9 104
Dilley, Tx., U.S. — E3 120
Dilliner, Pa., U.S. — G2 115
Dilling, Sud. — C2 47
Dillingen, W. Ger. — D1 19
Dillingen [an der Donau], W. Ger. — D5 18
Dillingham, Ak., U.S. — D8 79
Dillon, Co., U.S. — B4 83
Dillon, Mt., U.S. — E4 103
Dillon, S.C., U.S. — C9 117
Dillon, co., S.C., U.S. — C9 117
Dillon, stm., Can. — B5 68
Dillon Lake, res., Oh., U.S. — B3 112
Dillon Reservoir, res., Co., U.S. — B4 83
Dillonvale, Oh., U.S. — B5 112
Dillsboro, In., U.S. — F7 91
Dillsboro, N.C., U.S. — f9 110
Dillsburg, Pa., U.S. — F7 115
Dillwyn, Va., U.S. — C4 123
Dilolo, Zaire — D3 48
Dimbelenge, Zaire — C3 48
Dimbokro, I.C. — E4 45
Dîmbovița, stm., Rom. — C7 24
Dimitrovgrad, Bul. — D6 24
Dimitrovgrad, Yugo. — C7 24
Dimitrovgrad, Sov. Un. — E3 28
Dimmit, Tx., U.S. — B1 120
Dimmit, co., Tx., U.S. — E3 120
Dimmitt, Tx., U.S. — B1 120
Dimock, S.D., U.S. — D8 118
Dimona, Isr. — D4 40
Dimondale, Mi., U.S. — F6 99
Dinagat Island, i., Phil. — C7 34
Dinājpur, Bngl. — E12 37
Dinan, Fr. — D4 16
Dinant, Bel. — D4 17
Dinar, Tur. — C5 40
Dinard, Fr. — C2 16
Dinaric Alps, mts., Yugo. — C3 24
Dindigul, India — F6 36
Dinero, Tx., U.S. — E4 120
Dingalan Bay, b., Phil. — o13 34
Dingbian, China — D6 31
Dingelständt, E. Ger. — B5 19
Dingess, W.V., U.S. — D2 125
Dinghai, China — E9 31
Dingle, Ire. — D1 10
Dingle, Id., U.S. — G7 89
Dingle Bay, b., Ire. — D1 10
Dingmans Ferry, Pa., U.S. — D12 115
Dingo, Austl. — A7 51
Dingolfing, W. Ger. — E7 19
Dinguiraye, Gui. — D2 45
Dingwall, N.S. — C9 71
Dingwall, Scot., U.K. — B4 10
Dingxian, China — D8 31
Dingxin, China — C4 31
Dingxing, China — E6 32
Dinh Lap, Viet. — B7 35
Dinkelsbühl, W. Ger. — D5 19
Dinkey Creek, Ca., U.S. — D4 82
Dinklage, W. Ger. — F2 15
Dinner Point, c., Fl., U.S. — D4 86
Dinorwic Lake, l., Ont. — E5 70
Dinosaur, Co., U.S. — A1 83
Dinosaur National Monument, U.S. — C6 121
Dinosaur Provincial Park, Alta. — D5 68
Dinsdale, Ia., U.S. — B5 92
Dinslaken, W. Ger. — B1 19
Dinsmore, Sask. — F2 75
Dinuba, Ca., U.S. — D4 82
Dinwiddie, Va., U.S. — C5 123
Dinwiddie, co., Va., U.S. — C5 123
Dioïla, Mali — C7 45
Dionisio, Braz. — B4 56
Diourbel, Sen. — D1 45
Diphu Pass, Asia — C10 36
Diplo, Pak. — D3 36
Dipper Harbour West, N.B. — D3 71
Dippoldiswalde, E. Ger. — C8 19
Diré, Mali — C4 45
Direction, Cape, c., Austl. — B7 50
Dire Dawa, Eth. — D5 47
Diriamba, Nic. — E7 63
Dirico, Ang. — E3 48
Dirk Hartog, i., Austl. — E1 50
Dirkou, Niger — C7 45
Dirmil, Tur. — D7 40
Dirranbandi, Austl. — E8 50
Dirty Devil, stm., Ut., U.S. — E5 121
Disappointment, Cape, c., Falk. Is. — D9 54
Disappointment, Cape, c., Wa., U.S. — C1 124
Disappointment, Lake, l., Austl. — D3 50
Disappointment Creek, stm., Co., U.S. — D2 83
Discovery, Mount, mtn., Ant. — f39 7
Disentis (Mustér), Switz. — g14 19
Dishman, Wa., U.S. — g14 124
Dishnā, Eg. — D6 43
Disko, i., Grnld. — C15 61
Disley, Sask. — G3 75
Dismal, stm., Ne., U.S. — C5 104
Dismal, stm., N.C., U.S. — C5 104
Disney, Ok., U.S. — A6 113
Disputanta, Va., U.S. — C5 123
Disraëli, Que. — D6 74
Diss, Eng., U.K. — B9 12
Distant, Pa., U.S. — E3 115
District Heights-Forestville, Md., U.S. — *C4 97
District of Columbia, dept., U.S. — f8 97
Distrito Especial (Bogotá), dept., Col. — C3 60
Distrito Federal (Federal District), state, Mex. — D5 63
Distrito Federal, dept., Arg. — g7 54
Distrito Federal, dept., Braz. — B3 56
Distrito Federal, dept., Ven. — A6 60
Disūq, Eg. — C6 43
Ditzum, W. Ger. — A7 17
Diu, India — D5 36
Divenié, Congo — B1 48
Divernon, Il., U.S. — D4 90
Dives-sur-Mer, Fr. — C3 16
Divide, co., N.D., U.S. — A2 111
Divide Peak, mtn., Wy., U.S. — E5 127
Dividing Creek, N.J., U.S. — E2 107
Dividing Creek, stm., Md., U.S. — D6 97
Divinópolis, Braz. — B2 56
Divion, Fr. — D2 17
Divisões, Serra das, hills, Braz. — B2 56
Divišov, Czech. — o18 26
Divnoye, Sov. Un. — I14 27

Divo, I.C. — E3 45
Divriği, Tur. — C12 40
Dix, Ne., U.S. — C2 104
Dix, Il., U.S. — E5 90
Dix, stm., Ky., U.S. — C5 94
Dix Dam, Ky., U.S. — C5 94
Dixence, stm., Switz. — D3 21
Dixfield, Me., U.S. — D2 96
Dix Hills, N.Y., U.S. — *n15 109
Dixiana, Al., U.S. — B3 78
Dixie, Ar., U.S. — B4 81
Dixie, Ga., U.S. — F3 87
Dixie, Id., U.S. — D3 89
Dixie, Wa., U.S. — B2 124? — C7 124
Dixie, W.V., U.S. — C3 125
Dixie, co., Fl., U.S. — C3 86
Dixie Union, Ga., U.S. — E4 87
Dixie Valley, val., Nv., U.S. — A7 105
Dixmont, Me., U.S. — D3 96
Dixon, Ca., U.S. — C3 82
Dixon, Il., U.S. — B4 90
Dixon, In., U.S. — C6 91
Dixon, Ia., U.S. — C7 92
Dixon, Ky., U.S. — C2 94
Dixon, Mo., U.S. — C5 102
Dixon, Mt., U.S. — B9 104
Dixon, Ne., U.S. — A4 104
Dixon, N.M., U.S. — B1 112
Dixon, S.D., U.S. — E5 127
Dixon, Wy., U.S. — E5 127
Dixon, co., Ne., U.S. — B9 104
Dixon Entrance, strt., N.A. — B1 69
Dixons Mills, Al., U.S. — C2 78
Dixon Springs, Il., U.S. — F5 90
Dixonville, Alta. — A2 68
Dixonville, Pa., U.S. — E3 115
Dixville, Que. — D6 74
Dixville Notch, N.H., U.S. — g7 106
Dixville Notch, N.H., U.S. — g7 106
Dixville Peak, mtn., N.H., U.S. — g7 106
Diyarbakir, Tur. — D13 40
Dizy-le-Gros, Fr. — E3 17
Dizy-Magenta, Fr. — E2 17
Dja, stm., Afr. — E2 46
Djado, Niger — B7 45
Djakarta see Jakarta, Indon. — G3 34
Djakovica, Yugo. — C4 24
Djakovo, Yugo. — C4 24
Djambala, Congo — E6 44
Djanet, Alg. — E6 44
Djaravica, mtn., Yugo. — C3 24
Djédaa, Chad — D5 46? — E2 46
Djedeida, Tun. — F2 46
Djema, Cen. Afr. Rep. — D5 46
Djénné, Mali — C9 45
Djerba, Île de, i., Tun. — C7 44
Djerid, Chott, sw., Tun. — C6 44
Djibo, Burkina — D4 45
Djibouti, Dji. — C5 47
Djibouti, ctry., Afr. — C5 47
Djokupunda, Zaire — C3 48
Djolu, Zaire — A4 48
Djougou, Benin — A5 48
Djuju, Zaire — B2 48
Djurdjevac, Yugo. — t36 14
Djursholm, Swe. — D4 101
D'Lo, Ms., U.S. — D4 101
Dluga, stm., Pol. — k14 26
Dmitriyev-Lgovskiy, Sov. Un. — E10 27
Dmitrov, Sov. Un. — C11 27
Dmitrovsk-Orlovskiy, Sov. Un. — E10 27
Dnepr, stm., Sov. Un. — D5 29
Dneprodzerzhinsk, Sov. Un. — D5 29
Dnepropetrovsk, Sov. Un. — G10 27
Dnestr, stm., Sov. Un. — H7 27
Dnieper see Dnepr, stm., Sov. Un. — D5 29
Dno, Sov. Un. — D5 27
Doaktown, N.B. — C3 71
Doany, Madag. — f9 49
Doba, Chad — D3 46
Dobbins Air Force Base, mil., Ga., U.S. — h7 87
Dobbinton, Ont. — C3 73
Dobbs Ferry, N.Y., U.S. — g13 109
Döbeln, E. Ger. — C6 18
Doberai Peninsula, pen., Indon. — F8 34
Doberlug-Kirchhain, E. Ger. — B8 19
Doblas, Arg. — B4 54
Dobo, Indon. — G8 34
Doboj, Yugo. — C4 24
Doboy Sound, b., Ga., U.S. — o18 87
Dobříš, Czech. — D9 19
Dobšiná, Czech. — D6 26
Dobšiná, Czech. — n18 26
Dobrovice, Czech. — A7 26
Dobruja, reg., Eur. — C9 24
Dobruš, Sov. Un. — D6 27
Doce, stm., Braz. — E8 57
Docena, Al., U.S. — f7 78
Dock Junction, Ga., U.S. — E5 87
Doctor Arroyo, Mex. — f11 124
Doctor Pedro P. Peña, Para. — D3 55
Doctors Inlet, Fl., U.S. — m8 86
Doctors Lake, l., Fl., U.S. — m8 86
Doctortown, Ga., U.S. — E5 87
Doddridge, Ar., U.S. — D2 81
Doddridge, co., W.V., U.S. — B4 125
Dodds, Alta. — C4 68
Doddsville, Ms., U.S. — B3 101
Dodecanese, is., Grc. — D6 40
Dodge, Ne., U.S. — C9 104
Dodge, N.D., U.S. — B3 111
Dodge, Wi., U.S. — D1 126
Dodge, co., Ga., U.S. — D3 87
Dodge, co., Mn., U.S. — G6 100
Dodge, co., Ne., U.S. — C9 104
Dodge, co., Wi., U.S. — E5 126
Dodge Center, Mn., U.S. — F6 100
Dodge City, Ks., U.S. — E3 93
Dodge Park, Md., U.S. — *C4 97
Dodgeville, Mi., U.S. — A5 99
Dodgeville, Wi., U.S. — F3 126
Dodoma, Tan. — C6 48
Dodoma, prov., Tan. — C6 48
Dodsland, Sask. — F1 75
Dodson, La., U.S. — B3 95
Dodson, Mt., U.S. — B8 103
Dodson, Tx., U.S. — B2 120
Dodson Peninsula, pen., Ant. — A17 7
Doe River, B.C. — A7 69
Doerun, Ga., U.S. — E2 87
Doe Run, Mo., U.S. — D7 102
Doetinchem, Neth. — C6 16
Dog, stm., Vt., U.S. — C3 122
Dogai Coring, l., China — D6 69

Dog Island, i., Fl., U.S. — C2 86
Dog Keys Pass, strt., Ms., U.S. — g8 101
Dog Lake, l., Man. — D2 70
Dog Lake, l., Man. — H6 33
Dōgo Island, i., Japan — *F5 39
Do Gonbadān, Iran — D5 45
Dogondoutchi, Niger — C15 40
Doğubayazit, Tur. — C15 40
Doha (Ad Dawhah), Qatar — B5 38
Doheny, Que. — B5 74
Doiran, Lake, l., Eur. — m7 24
Dois Córregos, Braz. — A6 17
Dokkum, Neth. — A5 16
Doksy, Czech. — C3 16
Dol, Fr. — C3 16
Doland, S.D., U.S. — C7 118
Dolavón, Arg. — k12 74
Dolbeau, Que. — D6 16
Dôle, Fr. — F6 62
Dolega, Pan. — F6 62
Doleib Hill, Sud. — D3 47
Doles, Ga., U.S. — E2 87
Dolgellau, Wales, U.K. — B4 12
Dolgeville, N.Y., U.S. — B6 109
Dolina, Sov. Un. — D8 26
Dolinsk, Sov. Un. — B13 31
Dolinskoye, Sov. Un. — B9 24
Dollar Bay, Mi., U.S. — A2 99
Dollard, Sask. — H1 75
Dollart, b., Eur. — A7 17
Dollarville, Mi., U.S. — B5 99
Dolliver, Ia., U.S. — A3 92
Dolný Kubín, Czech. — D5 26
Dolohmwar, mtn., Micron. — Q17 52
Dolomite, Al., U.S. — B3 78
Dolomites, mts., Italy — A3 23
Dolores, Arg. — B5 54
Dolores, Guat. — D7 63
Dolores, Mex. — B3 63
Dolores, Co., U.S. — D2 83
Dolores, Ur. — E1 56
Dolores, co., Co., U.S. — D2 83
Dolores, stm., U.S. — E7 121
Dolores Hidalgo, Mex. — m13 63
Dolphin and Union Strait, strt., N.W. Ter. — C9 66
Dolphin Head, mtn., Jam. — E12 65
Dolphin Island, i., Ut., U.S. — B3 121
Dolton, Il., U.S. — k9 90
Dolton, S.D., U.S. — D8 118
Dom, mtn., Switz. — D4 21
Domadare, Som. — B2 56
Dom Aquino, Braz. — B2 56
Domat-Ems, Switz. — C7 21
Domažlice, Czech. — D2 26
Dombarovskiy, Sov. Un. — F3 14
Dombås, Nor. — F6 17
Dombasle[-sur-Meurthe], Fr. — D1 48
Dombe Grande, Ang. — B4 24
Dombóvár, Hung. — C3 17
Domburg, Neth. — C3 16
Dôme, Puy de, mtn., Fr. — E5 16
Dome Mountain, mtn., Az., U.S. — k9 80
Dome of the Rock, Isr. Occ. — m14 41
Dome Peak, mtn., Co., U.S. — B3 83
Domeyko, Cordillera, mts., Chile — D2 55
Domfront, Fr. — D4 16
Dominica, ctry., N.A. — i14 64
Dominica Passage, strt., N.A. — I14 64
Dominican Republic, ctry., N.A. — E8 64
Dominion, Cape, c., N.W. Ter. — C18 66
Dominion City, Man. — E3 70
Dominion Lake, l., Newf. — h9 72
Dömitz, E. Ger. — B5 18
Dommel, stm., Eur. — C5 17
Domo, Eth. — D6 47
Domodedovo, Sov. Un. — n17 27
Domodossola, Italy — A2 23
Dom Pedrito, Braz. — E2 56
Dompierre [-sur-Authie], Fr. — D1 17
Domremy, Sask. — E3 75
Domuyo, Volcán, vol., Arg. — B2 54
Don, stm., Scot., U.K. — H13 27
Don, stm., Sov. Un. — H13 27
Dona Ana, co., N.M., U.S. — E2 108
Donaghadee, N. Ire., U.K. — C4 10
Donald, Ont. — h12 114
Donalda, Alta. — C4 68
Donaldson, S.C., U.S. — C3 117
Donaldson, Ar., U.S. — C3 81
Donaldson, Mn., U.S. — B2 100
Donaldson, Pa., U.S. — E9 115
Donaldsonville, La., U.S. — D4 95
Donalsonville, Ga., U.S. — E2 87
Donard, Ire. — D5 11
Donaueschingen, W. Ger. — E4 18
Donauwörth, W. Ger. — E5 19
Don Benito, Spain — C3 22
Doncaster, Eng., U.K. — D6 10
Doncaster and Templestowe, Austl. — *G8 50
Dondo, Ang. — C1 48
Dondo, Moz. — A5 49
Donegal, co., Ire. — C4 11
Donegal, Ire. — C4 11
Donegal Bay, b., Ire. — E2 11
Donegal Point, c., Ire. — E2 11
Donets Basin, Sov. Un. — q21 27
Dongara, Austl. — E1 50
Dongchuan, China — F5 31
Dongco, China — D7 36
Donggang, China — B7 36
Donggala, Indon. — F5 34
Dong Hoi, Viet. — B3 34
Dongning, China — D5 32
Dongo, Zaire — A2 48
Dongou, Congo — A2 48
Dongsheng, China — D6 31
Dongtai, China — H9 32
Dongting Hu, l., China — B7 32
Dong Ujimqin Qi, China — J7 32
Dongxiang, China — G6 31
Dongzhi, China — B7 32
Doniphan, Mo., U.S. — E7 102
Doniphan, Ne., U.S. — D7 104
Doniphan, co., Ks., U.S. — C8 93
Donji Vakuf, Yugo. — C3 24
Dogai Coring, l., China — D6 69
Donkey Creek, stm., Wy., U.S. — B7 127

Name	Map Ref.	Page
Donkin, N.S.	C10	71
Donley, co., Tx., U.S.	B2	120
Donna, Tx., U.S.	F3	120
Donnaconna, Que.	C6	74
Donnellson, Il., U.S.	D4	90
Donnellson, Ia., U.S.	D6	92
Donnelly, Alta.	B2	68
Donnelly, Id., U.S.	E2	89
Donnelly, Mn., U.S.	E2	100
Donner, La., U.S.	E5	95
Donner Pass, Ca., U.S.	C3	82
Donnybrook, N.D., U.S.	A4	111
Donora, Pa., U.S.	F2	115
Donovan, Il., U.S.	C6	90
Don Peninsula, pen., B.C.	C3	69
Donzère, Fr.	E6	16
Dooagh, Ire.	D1	11
Doogort, Ire.	C1	11
Doole, Tx., U.S.	D3	120
Dooling, Ga., U.S.	D3	87
Doolittle, Mo., U.S.	D6	102
Dooly, co., Ga., U.S.	D3	87
Doon, Ia., U.S.	A1	92
Doon, Loch, l., Scot., U.K.	E4	13
Doonbeg, Ire.	E2	11
Doonerak, Mount, mtn., Ak., U.S.	B9	79
Door, co., Wi., U.S.	D6	126
Doornik see Tournai, Bel.	D3	17
Dora, Al., U.S.	B2	78
Dora, Mo., U.S.	E5	102
Dora, N.M., U.S.	D6	108
Dora, Lake, l., Austl.	D3	50
Dora Baltea, stm., Italy	B1	20
Doran, Mn., U.S.	D2	100
Doraville, Ga., U.S.	h8	87
Dorbod, China	A11	32
Dorcas, Fl., U.S.	u15	86
Dorcheat, Bayou, stm., U.S.	B2	95
Dorchester, N.B.	D5	71
Dorchester, Eng., U.K.	E5	10
Dorchester, Ia., U.S.	A6	92
Dorchester, Ne., U.S.	D8	104
Dorchester, N.J., U.S.	E3	107
Dorchester, S.C., U.S.	E7	117
Dorchester, Wi., U.S.	C3	126
Dorchester, co., Que.	C7	74
Dorchester, co., Md., U.S.	D5	97
Dorchester, co., S.C., U.S.	E7	117
Dorchester, Cape, c., N.W. Ter.	C17	66
Dorchester Crossing, N.B.	C5	71
Dorchester Estates, S.C., U.S.	k11	117
Dorcyville, La., U.S.	*D4	95
Dordogne, stm., Fr.	h9	95
Dordrecht, Neth.	E4	16
Dordrecht, S. Afr.	B6	16
Doré, stm., Sask.	C2	75
Doré Lake, Sask.	C2	75
Doré Lake, l., Ont.	B7	73
Doré Lake, l., Sask.	C2	75
Dorena, Or., U.S.	D3	114
Dorena Lake, res., Or., U.S.	D3	114
Dorenlee, Alta.	C4	68
Dores, Scot., U.K.	C4	13
Dores do Indaiá, Braz.	B3	56
Dorfen, W. Ger.	A8	20
Dorgali, Italy	D2	23
Dörgön Lake, l., Mong.	B3	31
Dori, Burkina	D4	45
Dorion-Vaudreuil, Que.	q18	74
Dorking, Eng., U.K.	m12	10
Dormans, Fr.	E3	17
Dormont, Pa., U.S.	k13	115
Dornbirn, Aus.	E4	18
Dornie, Scot., U.K.	C3	13
Dornoch, Scot., U.K.	C4	13
Dornoch Firth, est., Scot., U.K.	B5	10
Dorogobuzh, Sov. Un.	D9	27
Dorohoi, Rom.	B8	24
Dorothy, Alta.	D4	68
Dorothy, Mn., U.S.	C2	100
Dorothy, N.J., U.S.	E3	107
Dorothy, W.V., U.S.	n13	125
Dorothy Pond, Ma., U.S.	B4	98
Dorr, Mi., U.S.	F5	99
Dorrance, Ks., U.S.	D5	93
Dorre, i., Austl.	E1	50
Dorrigo, Austl.	E9	51
Dorris, Ca., U.S.	B3	82
Dorris Heights, Il., U.S.	F5	90
Dorset, Ont.	B6	73
Dorset, Mn., U.S.	D4	100
Dorset, Oh., U.S.	A5	112
Dorset, Vt., U.S.	E2	122
Dorset, co., Eng., U.K.	E5	10
Dorset Peak, mtn., Vt., U.S.	E2	122
Dorsey, Md., U.S.	B4	97
Dorsey, Ms., U.S.	A5	101
Dorsten, W. Ger.	B1	19
Dortmund, W. Ger.	C3	18
Dortmund Ems Canal, W. Ger.	B7	18
Dorton, Ky., U.S.	C7	94
Dörtyol, Tur.	D11	40
Do Rūd, Iran	E4	39
Dorum, W. Ger.	E2	15
Doruma, Zaire	A4	48
Dorval, Que.	q19	74
Dos Bahías, Cabo, c., Arg.	C3	54
Dos Bocas, Lago, res., P.R.	E3	65
Dos Hermanas, Spain	D3	22
Dos Quebradas, Col.	*C2	22
Dosquet, Que.	C6	74
Dos Rios, Ca., U.S.	C2	82
Dosso, Niger	D5	45
Dossor, Sov. Un.	D4	28
Doswell, Va., U.S.	C5	123
Dothan, Al., U.S.	D4	78
Dothan, W.V., U.S.	n13	125
Doting Cove, Newf.	D5	72
Dot Lake, Ak., U.S.	C11	79
Dott, W.V., U.S.	D3	125
Doty, Wa., U.S.	C2	124
Douai, Fr.	B5	16
Douala, Cam.	E1	46
Douarnenez, Fr.	C1	16
Double Bayou, Tx., U.S.	r15	120
Double Beach, Ct., U.S.	D4	84
Double Mer, b., Newf.	A2	72
Double Mountain, mtn., Al., U.S.	g7	78
Double Oak Mountain, mtn., Al., U.S.	g7	78
Doublespring Pass, Id., U.S.	E5	89
Doubletop Peak, mtn., Wy., U.S.	C2	127
Doubs, Md., U.S.	B3	97
Doubs, dept., Fr.	B2	20
Doubs, stm., Eur.	D7	16
Doubtful Sound, strt., N.Z.	P11	51
Doucette, Tx., U.S.	D5	120
Douds, Ia., U.S.	D5	92
Doué, Fr.	D3	16
Douentza, Mali	D4	45
Dougherty, Ia., U.S.	B4	92
Dougherty, Ok., U.S.	C4	113
Dougherty, co., Ga., U.S.	E2	87
Douglas, I. of Man	C4	10
Douglas, S. Afr.	C3	49
Douglas, Az., U.S.	F6	80
Douglas, Ga., U.S.	E4	87
Douglas, Ma., U.S.	B4	98
Douglas, Mi., U.S.	F4	99
Douglas, Ne., U.S.	F6	100
Douglas, N.D., U.S.	B4	111
Douglas, Ok., U.S.	A4	113
Douglas, W.V., U.S.	B5	125
Douglas, Wy., U.S.	D7	127
Douglas, co., Co., U.S.	B6	83
Douglas, co., Ga., U.S.	C2	87
Douglas, co., Il., U.S.	D5	90
Douglas, co., Ks., U.S.	D8	93
Douglas, co., Mn., U.S.	E3	100
Douglas, co., Mo., U.S.	E5	102
Douglas, co., Ne., U.S.	C9	104
Douglas, co., Nv., U.S.	E2	105
Douglas, co., Or., U.S.	D3	114
Douglas, co., S.D., U.S.	D7	118
Douglas, co., Wa., U.S.	B6	124
Douglas, co., Wi., U.S.	B2	126
Douglas, Mount, mtn., Ak., U.S.	D9	79
Douglas Channel, strt., B.C.	C3	69
Douglas Creek, stm., Co., U.S.	B2	83
Douglas Lake, B.C.	D7	69
Douglas Lake, l., Mi., U.S.	C6	99
Douglas Lake, res., Tn., U.S.	D10	119
Douglas Point, c., Ont.	C3	73
Douglass, Ks., U.S.	E7	93
Douglas Station, Man.	E2	70
Douglasville, Ga., U.S.	C2	87
Doullens, Fr.	B5	16
Doumé, Cam.	E2	46
Dour, Bel.	D3	17
Doura, Mali	D3	45
Dourados, Braz.	m7	56
Dourados, Braz.	C2	56
Dourdan, Fr.	F2	17
Douro (Duero), stm., Eur.	B12	22
Dousman, Wi., U.S.	E5	126
Douz, Tun.	C6	44
Dove Creek, Co., U.S.	D2	83
Dover, Eng., U.K.	E7	10
Dover, Ar., U.S.	B2	81
Dover, De., U.S.	D3	85
Dover, Fl., U.S.	D4	86
Dover, Id., U.S.	A2	89
Dover, Ks., U.S.	D8	93
Dover, Ky., U.S.	B6	94
Dover, Ma., U.S.	h10	98
Dover, Mo., U.S.	B4	102
Dover, N.H., U.S.	D5	106
Dover, N.J., U.S.	B3	107
Dover, N.C., U.S.	B5	110
Dover, Oh., U.S.	B4	112
Dover, Pa., U.S.	F8	115
Dover, Tn., U.S.	A4	119
Dover, stm., Alta.	A4	68
Dover, Strait of, strt., Eur.	B5	16
Dover Air Force Base, mil., De., U.S.	D4	85
Dover-Foxcroft, Me., U.S.	C3	96
Dover Hill, In., U.S.	G4	91
Dover Plains, N.Y., U.S.	D7	109
Dovesville, S.C., U.S.	C8	117
Dovray, Mn., U.S.	F3	100
Dow, Il., U.S.	D3	90
Dow, Ok., U.S.	C6	113
Dowa, Mwi.	D5	48
Dowagiac, Mi., U.S.	G4	99
Dow City, Ia., U.S.	C2	92
Dowell, Il., U.S.	F4	90
Dowell, Md., U.S.	D5	97
Dowelltown, Tn., U.S.	C8	119
Dowlatābād, Afg.	C13	39
Dowlat Yar, Afg.	B4	36
Dowling Lake, l., Alta.	D4	68
Dowling Park, Fl., U.S.	B3	86
Downer, Mn., U.S.	D2	100
Downers Grove, Il., U.S.	B5	90
Downey, Ca., U.S.	n12	82
Downey, Id., U.S.	G6	89
Downham Market, Eng., U.K.	B8	12
Downieville, Ca., U.S.	C3	82
Downing, Mo., U.S.	A5	102
Downing, Wi., U.S.	C1	126
Downingtown, Pa., U.S.	F10	115
Downpatrick, N. Ire., U.K.	C4	11
Downpatrick Head, c., Ire.	C2	11
Downs, Il., U.S.	C5	90
Downs, Ks., U.S.	C5	93
Downs Mountain, mtn., Wy., U.S.	C3	127
Downsville, La., U.S.	B3	95
Downsville, N.Y., U.S.	C6	109
Downsville, Wi., U.S.	D2	126
Downton, Mount, mtn., B.C.	C5	69
Dows, Ia., U.S.	B4	92
Dowshī, Afg.	D14	39
Doyle, Ca., U.S.	B3	82
Doyle, Tn., U.S.	D8	119
Doyles, Newf.	E2	72
Doylestown, Oh., U.S.	B4	112
Doylestown, Pa., U.S.	F11	115
Doyline, La., U.S.	B2	95
Doyon, N.D., U.S.	A7	111
Dozier, Al., U.S.	D3	78
Dra'a, Hamada du, des., Alg.	D3	44
Drâa, Oued, val., Mor.	D3	44
Drabenderhöhe, W. Ger.	C2	19
Drachten, Neth.	A6	17
Dracut, Ma., U.S.	A5	98
Drăgănești-Vlașca, Rom.	D7	24
Drăganovo, Bul.	D7	24
Drăgășani, Rom.	D7	24
Draguignan, Fr.	F7	16
Dragvograd, Yugo.	B2	24
Drain, Or., U.S.	D3	114
Drake, Sask.	F3	75
Drake, Az., U.S.	C3	80
Drake, Co., U.S.	A5	83
Drake, N.D., U.S.	B5	111
Drakensberg, mts., Afr.	D4	49
Drake Passage, strt.	J16	2
Drake Peak, mtn., Or., U.S.	E6	114
Drakesboro, Ky., U.S.	C2	94
Drakes Branch, Va., U.S.	D4	123
Drakes Creek, stm., Ky., U.S.	D3	94
Drakes Creek, West Fork, stm., Ky., U.S.	D3	94
Drakesville, Ia., U.S.	D5	92
Draketown, Ga., U.S.	C1	87
Dráma, Grc.	B5	40
Drama, stm., Pol.	g9	26
Drammen, Nor.	H4	14
Dramselva, stm., Nor.	p27	14
Drancy, Fr.	g10	16
Dranse, stm., Fr.	C2	20
Draper, S.D., U.S.	D5	118
Draper, Ut., U.S.	C4	121
Draperstown, N. Ire., U.K.	C5	11
Drasco, Ar., U.S.	B4	81
Draveil, Fr.	F2	17
Drava (Drau), stm., Eur.	C4	24
Dravuni, i., Fiji	I15	52
Drawsko [Pomorskie], Pol.	B3	26
Drayton, Ont.	D4	73
Drayton, N.D., U.S.	A8	111
Drayton, S.C., U.S.	B4	117
Drayton Plains, Mi., U.S.	F7	99
Drayton Valley, Alta.	C3	68
Dreamland Villa, Az., U.S.	*D4	80
Drebkau, E. Ger.	C7	18
Drelsdorf, W. Ger.	D5	15
Drenthe, prov., Neth.	B6	17
Dresbach, Mn., U.S.	G7	100
Dresden, Ont.	E2	73
Dresden, E. Ger.	C6	18
Dresden, Ks., U.S.	C3	93
Dresden, Oh., U.S.	B3	112
Dresden, Tn., U.S.	A3	119
Dresser, In., U.S.	F3	91
Dresser, Wi., U.S.	C1	126
Dresslerville, Nv., U.S.	*E2	105
Dreux, Fr.	C4	16
Drew, Ms., U.S.	B3	101
Drew, co., Ar., U.S.	D4	81
Drewryville, Va., U.S.	D5	123
Drews Reservoir, res., Or., U.S.	E6	114
Drewsville, N.H., U.S.	D2	106
Drexel, Mo., U.S.	C3	102
Drexel, N.C., U.S.	B1	110
Drexel Hill, Pa., U.S.	p20	115
Drifton, Pa., U.S.	D10	115
Driftwood, Ok., U.S.	A3	113
Driftwood, stm., In., U.S.	F5	91
Driftwood Creek, stm., Ne., U.S.	D4	104
Driggs, Id., U.S.	F7	89
Drimoleague, Ire.	F2	11
Drina, stm., Yugo.	C4	24
Drin Gulf, b., Alb.	B2	25
Drini, stm., Alb.	A3	25
Drinkwater, Sask.	G3	75
Dripping Springs, Tx., U.S.	D3	120
Driscoll, N.D., U.S.	C5	111
Driscoll, Tx., U.S.	F4	120
Driskill Mountain, hill, La., U.S.	B3	95
Driver, Ar., U.S.	B5	81
Drøbak, Nor.	H4	14
Drobeta-Turnu-Severin, Rom.	C6	24
Drogheda, Ire.	D5	11
Drogobych, Sov. Un.	G4	27
Droitwich, Eng., U.K.	B5	12
Dromahair, Ire.	C3	11
Dromod, Ire.	D4	11
Dromore, N. Ire., U.K.	C4	11
Dromore West, Ire.	C3	11
Dronero, Italy	E3	20
Dronfield, Eng., U.K.	A6	12
Dronninglund, Den.	A4	15
Dropmore, Man.	D1	70
Druid, Sask.	F1	75
Druid Hills, Ga., U.S.	*C2	87
Drulingen, Fr.	E2	19
Drumbeg, Scot., U.K.	B3	13
Drumbo, Ont.	D4	73
Drumcliff, Ire.	C3	11
Drumheller, Alta.	D4	68
Drum Island, i., S.C., U.S.	k12	117
Drumlish, Ire.	D4	11
Drummond, Id., U.S.	F7	89
Drummond, Mt., U.S.	D3	103
Drummond, Ok., U.S.	A3	113
Drummond, Wi., U.S.	B2	126
Drummond, co., Que.	D5	74
Drummond, Lake, l., Va., U.S.	D6	123
Drummond Island, i., Mi., U.S.	B7	99
Drummond Island, i., Mi., U.S.	C7	99
Drummond Range, mts., Austl.	D8	50
Drummondville, Que.	D5	74
Drummondville-Sud, Que.	D5	74
Drummore, Scot., U.K.	F4	13
Drumquin, N. Ire., U.K.	C4	11
Drumright, Ok., U.S.	B5	113
Drumshanbo, Ire.	C3	11
Druzhba, Sov. Un.	C36	128
Druzhkovka, Sov. Un.	q20	27
Drwęca, stm., Pol.	B5	26
Dryad, Wa., U.S.	C2	124
Drybranch, W.V., U.S.	m13	125
Dry Branch, Ga., U.S.	D3	87
Dry Cimarron, stm., U.S.	A6	108
Dry Creek, La., U.S.	D2	95
Dry Creek, stm., Ks., U.S.	g12	93
Dry Creek Mountain, mtn., Nv., U.S.	B5	105
Dryden, Ont.	o16	73
Dryden, Ar., U.S.	*B5	81
Dryden, Me., U.S.	D2	96
Dryden, Mi., U.S.	F7	99
Dryden, N.Y., U.S.	C4	109
Dryden, Tx., U.S.	D1	120
Dryden, Va., U.S.	f9	123
Dryfork, W.V., U.S.	C5	125
Dry Fork, Va., U.S.	D3	123
Dry Fork, stm., Mo., U.S.	D6	102
Dry Fork, stm., W.V., U.S.	B5	125
Dry Fork, stm., W.V., U.S.	B5	125
Dry Harbour Mountains, mts., Jam.	E14	65
Dry Mills, Me., U.S.	E2	96
Dry Prong, La., U.S.	C3	95
Dry Ridge, Ky., U.S.	B5	94
Dry Run, Pa., U.S.	F6	115
Drysdale, stm., Austl.	B4	50
Dry Tortugas, is., Fl., U.S.	H5	86
Drywood, Alta.	E4	68
Dschang, Cam.	D2	46
Duaiheb, Hasi, well, W. Sah.	C2	44
Duaringa, Austl.	A7	51
Duarte, Ca., U.S.	*E5	82
Duarte, Pico, mtn., Dom. Rep.	E8	64
Duart Point, c., Scot., U.K.	D3	13
Dubā, Sau. Ar.	C3	38
Dubach, La., U.S.	B3	95
Dubai (Dubayy), U.A.E.	C5	38
Dubawnt, stm., N.W. Ter.	D12	66
Dubawnt Lake, l., N.W. Ter.	D12	66
Du Bay, Lake, res., Wi., U.S.	D4	126
Dubberly, La., U.S.	B2	95
Dubbo, Austl.	F8	51
Dübendorf, Switz.	B6	21
Dublin (Baile Átha Cliath), Ire.	D5	11
Dublin, Al., U.S.	C3	78
Dublin, Ca., U.S.	*D3	82
Dublin, Ga., U.S.	D4	87
Dublin, In., U.S.	E7	91
Dublin, Md., U.S.	A5	97
Dublin, N.H., U.S.	E2	106
Dublin, N.C., U.S.	C4	110
Dublin, Oh., U.S.	k10	112
Dublin, Pa., U.S.	F11	115
Dublin, Tx., U.S.	C3	120
Dublin, co., Ire.	D5	11
Dublin Bay, b., Ire.	D5	11
Dublin Shore, N.S.	E5	71
Dublon, i., Micron.	Q18	52
Dubnica [nad Váhom], Czech.	D5	26
Dubois, Id., U.S.	E6	89
Dubois, Il., U.S.	E4	90
Dubois, Pa., U.S.	D4	115
Du Bois, Ne., U.S.	D9	104
Du Bois, Pa., U.S.	D4	115
Dubois, Wy., U.S.	C3	127
Dubois, co., In., U.S.	H4	91
Duboistown, Pa., U.S.	D7	115
Dubossary, Sov. Un.	H7	27
Dubossary Reservoir, res., Sov. Un.	B9	24
Dubovka, Sov. Un.	D22	28
Dubréka, Gui.	E2	45
Dubrovka, Sov. Un.	s31	14
Dubrovnik, Yugo.	D4	24
Dubuc, Sask.	G4	75
Dubulu, Zaire	A3	48
Dubuque, Ia., U.S.	B7	92
Dubuque, co., Ia., U.S.	B7	92
Duchcov, Czech.	C2	26
Duchesne, Ut., U.S.	C5	121
Duchesne, co., Ut., U.S.	C5	121
Duchesne, stm., Ut., U.S.	C5	121
Duchess, Alta.	D5	68
Ducie, atoll, Pit.	H14	6
Duck, N.C., U.S.	A7	110
Duck, stm., Tn., U.S.	B4	119
Duck Bay, Man.	C1	70
Duck Creek, stm., De., U.S.	C4	85
Duck Creek, stm., Nv., U.S.	D7	105
Duck Creek, stm., Oh., U.S.	C4	112
Duck Creek, stm., Wi., U.S.	h9	126
Duck Hill, Ms., U.S.	B4	101
Duck Lake, Sask.	E2	75
Duck Lake, l., Man.	B2	70
Duck Lake, l., Me., U.S.	C4	96
Duck Lake Post, Man.	f8	70
Duck Mountain, hills, Man.	D1	70
Duck Mountain Provincial Park, Man.	D1	70
Duck Mountain Provincial Park, Sask.	F5	75
Duck River, Tn., U.S.	B4	119
Ducktown, Tn., U.S.	D9	119
Duck Valley Indian Reservation, U.S.	B5	105
Duckwater, Nv., U.S.	E6	105
Duckwater Indian Reservation, Nv., U.S.	E6	105
Duckwater Peak, mtn., Nv., U.S.	E6	105
Ducor, Ca., U.S.	E4	82
Dudelange, Lux.	E6	17
Duderstadt, W. Ger.	B5	19
Dudinka, Sov. Un.	C11	29
Dudley, Eng., U.K.	D5	10
Dudley, Ga., U.S.	D3	87
Dudley, Ma., U.S.	B4	98
Dudley, Mo., U.S.	E7	102
Dudley, N.C., U.S.	B4	110
Dudley, Pa., U.S.	F5	115
Dudweiler, W. Ger.	D2	19
Duékoué, I.C.	E3	45
Dueré, Braz.	E5	59
Due West, S.C., U.S.	C3	117
Duero (Douro), stm., Eur.	B3	22
Duff, In., U.S.	H3	91
Duff, Sask.	G4	75
Duff, Tn., U.S.	C9	119
Duffee, Ms., U.S.	C5	101
Dufferin, co., Ont.	C4	73
Duffer Peak, mtn., Nv., U.S.	B3	105
Duffield, Va., U.S.	f9	123
Duff Reef, rf., Fiji	H16	52
Dufftown, Scot., U.K.	C5	13
Dufur, Or., U.S.	B5	114
Dugdemona, stm., La., U.S.	B3	95
Dugger, In., U.S.	F3	91
Dug Hill Ridge, mtn., Md., U.S.	A3	119
Dugi, i., Yugo.	C2	24
Duhamel, Que.	C2	74
Duich, Loch, b., Scot., U.K.	C3	13
Duida, Cerro, mtn., Ven.	C4	60
Duisburg, W. Ger.	B6	19
Duiwelskloof, S. Afr.	B5	49
Dujuma, Som.	B3	47
Dukan Dam, Iraq	E5	37
Duke, Al., U.S.	B4	78
Duke, Ok., U.S.	C2	113
Dukedom, Tn., U.S.	A3	119
Dukes, co., Ma., U.S.	D6	98
Duki, Pak.	B3	36
Dukou, China	*F5	31
Dulac, La., U.S.	E5	95
Dulce, N.M., U.S.	A2	108
Dulce, stm., Arg.	E3	55
Dülken, W. Ger.	B6	17
Dülmen, W. Ger.	B2	19
Dulowa, Pol.	g11	26
Duluth, Ga., U.S.	B2	87
Duluth, Mn., U.S.	D6	100
Dūmā, Isr. Occ.	g12	41
Dūmā, Syria	*F11	41
Dumaguete, Phil.	D6	34
Dumanli, mtn., Tur.	B11	40
Dumaran Island, i., Phil.	C5	34
Dumas, Ar., U.S.	D4	81
Dumas, Ga., U.S.	D2	87
Dumas, Ms., U.S.	A5	101
Dumas, Tx., U.S.	B2	120
Dumbarton, Scot., U.K.	E4	13
Dumbéa, Zaire	B3	48
Dumboa, Nig.	B4	91
Dumfries, Scot., U.K.	C5	10
Dumfries, Va., U.S.	B5	123
Dumfries and Galloway, prov., Scot., U.K.	E4	13
Dumka, India	E11	37
Dummer, l., W. Ger.	F2	15
Dummerston, Vt., U.S.	F3	122
Dumont, Ia., U.S.	B5	92
Dumont, Mn., U.S.	E2	100
Dumont, N.J., U.S.	B5	107
Dumont, Tx., U.S.	C2	120
Dumont d'Urville, sci., Ant.	C27	7
Dumont Loring Woods, Va., U.S.	*B5	123
Dumyāṭ (Damietta), Eg.	B3	38
Dunaff Head, c., Ire.	B4	11
Dunaföldvár, Hung.	B4	24
Dunaire, Ga., U.S.	*h8	87
Dunajec, stm., Eur.	B6	26
Dunajská Streda, Czech.	D5	26
Dunany Point, c., Ire.	D5	11
Dunapataj, Hung.	B4	24
Dunaújváros, Hung.	B4	24
Dunay, Sov. Un.	E6	33
Dunayevtsy, Sov. Un.	G6	27
Dunbar, Scot., U.K.	C5	13
Dunbar, Ky., U.S.	C3	94
Dunbar, Ne., U.S.	D9	104
Dunbar, Pa., U.S.	G2	115
Dunbar, S.C., U.S.	B8	117
Dunbar, W.V., U.S.	C3	125
Dunbarton, N.H., U.S.	D3	106
Dunbeath, Scot., U.K.	B5	13
Dunblane, Sask.	F2	75
Dunblane, Scot., U.K.	E4	13
Dunboyne, Ire.	D5	11
Dunbridge, Oh., U.S.	f6	112
Duncan, B.C.	E6	69
Duncan, Az., U.S.	E6	80
Duncan, Ms., U.S.	A3	101
Duncan, Ok., U.S.	C4	113
Duncan, S.C., U.S.	B3	117
Duncan, stm., B.C.	D9	69
Duncan Falls, Oh., U.S.	C4	112
Duncan Lake, res., B.C.	D9	69
Duncannon, Pa., U.S.	F7	115
Duncansby Head, c., Scot., U.K.	A5	10
Duncansville, Pa., U.S.	F5	115
Duncanville, Al., U.S.	B2	78
Duncanville, Tx., U.S.	n10	120
Duncombe, Ia., U.S.	B4	92
Duncormick, Ire.	E5	11
Dundalk, Ont.	C4	73
Dundalk, Ire.	C3	11
Dundalk, Md., U.S.	B4	97
Dundalk Bay, b., Ire.	D3	11
Dundas, Ont.	D5	73
Dundas, Il., U.S.	E5	90
Dundas, Mn., U.S.	F5	100
Dundas, Oh., U.S.	C3	112
Dundas, co., Ont.	B9	73
Dundas, co., Austl.	F3	50
Dundas Island, i., B.C.	B2	69
Dundas Strait, strt., Austl.	B5	50
Dundee, S. Afr.	C5	49
Dundee, Scot., U.K.	C5	10
Dundee, Fl., U.S.	D5	86
Dundee, Ia., U.S.	B6	92
Dundee, Ky., U.S.	C3	94
Dundee, Mi., U.S.	G7	99
Dundee, Mn., U.S.	G3	100
Dundee, N.Y., U.S.	C4	109
Dundee, Oh., U.S.	B4	112
Dundee, Or., U.S.	h11	114
Dundee, Tx., U.S.	C3	120
Dundee, Wi., U.S.	E5	126
Dundrum, Ire.	D4	104
Dundrum, N. Ire., U.K.	D5	11
Dundrum Bay, b., N. Ire., U.K.	C4	10
Dundy, co., Ne., U.S.	D4	104
Dunean, N.C., U.S.	*D3	117
Dunedin, N.Z.	P13	51
Dunedin, Fl., U.S.	D4	86
Duneland Beach, In., U.S.	A4	91
Dunellen, N.J., U.S.	B4	107
Dunfanaghy, Ire.	B4	11
Dunfermline, Scot., U.K.	B5	10
Dungannon, Ont.	C3	73
Dungannon, N. Ire., U.K.	C4	11
Dungannon, Va., U.S.	f9	123
Dungarpur, India	I4	37
Dungarvan, Ire.	E4	11
Dungarvan Harbour, b., Ire.	E4	11
Dungarvon, stm., N.B.	C3	71
Dungeness, c., Eng., U.K.	D8	12
Dung Gate, hist., Isr. Occ.	m14	41
Dungiven, N. Ire., U.K.	C5	11
Dunglow, Ire.	B3	11
Dungu, Zaire	A5	48
Dungun, Malay.	J5	35
Dunham, Que.	D5	74
Dunhua, China	C10	31
Dunhuang, China	C3	31
Dunkard Creek, stm., U.S.	B4	125
Dunkeld, Scot., U.K.	C5	13
Dunkerque, Fr.	B5	16
Dunkerton, Ia., U.S.	B5	92
Dunkineely, Ire.	B3	11
Dunkirk, In., U.S.	D7	91
Dunkirk, N.Y., U.S.	C1	109
Dunkirk, Oh., U.S.	B2	112
Dunklin, co., Mo., U.S.	E7	102
Dunkwa, Ghana	E4	45
Dún Laoghaire, Ire.	D5	11
Dunlap, Il., U.S.	C4	90
Dunlap, In., U.S.	A6	91
Dunlap, Ia., U.S.	C2	92
Dunlap, Ks., U.S.	D7	93
Dunlap, Tn., U.S.	D8	119
Dunlavin, Ire.	D5	11
Dunleer, Ire.	D5	11
Dunleith, De., U.S.	i7	85
Dunlo, Pa., U.S.	F4	115
Dunloup Creek, stm., W.V., U.S.	n13	125
Dunmanway, Ire.	F2	11
Dunmore, Ky., U.S.	C2	94
Dunmore, Pa., U.S.	D10	115
Dunmore, Lake, l., Vt., U.S.	D2	122
Dunmore East, Ire.	E5	11
Dunn, N.C., U.S.	B4	110
Dunn, Tx., U.S.	C2	120
Dunn, co., N.D., U.S.	B3	111
Dunn, co., Wi., U.S.	D2	126
Dunnamanagh, N. Ire., U.K.	C4	11
Dunn Center, N.D., U.S.	B3	111
Dunnegan, Mo., U.S.	D4	102
Dunnell, Mn., U.S.	G4	100
Dunnellon, Fl., U.S.	C4	86
Dünnern, stm., Switz.	B4	21
Dunnet Head, c., Scot., U.K.	B5	13
Dunning, Ne., U.S.	C5	104
Dun Loring Woods, Va., U.S.	*B5	123
Dunnottar, Man.	D3	70
Dunns Bridge, In., U.S.	C4	91
Dunns Corners, R.I., U.S.	G1	116
Dunnsville, Va., U.S.	C6	123
Dunnville, Ont.	E5	73
Dunoon, Scot., U.K.	C4	10
Dunphy, Nv., U.S.	C5	105
Dunqulah, Sud.	B3	47
Dunrea, Man.	E2	70
Dunrobin, Ont.	B8	73
Duns, Scot., U.K.	E6	13
Dunseith, N.D., U.S.	A5	111
Dunsmuir, Ca., U.S.	B2	82
Dunstable, Eng., U.K.	C7	12
Dunstable, Ma., U.S.	A5	98
Dun-sur-Auron, Fr.	D5	16
Dun [-sur-Meuse], Fr.	E5	17
Dunvegan, Ont.	C4	73
Dunvegan, Scot., U.K.	C2	13
Dunvegan, Loch, b., Scot., U.K.	C2	13
Dunvegan Head, c., Scot., U.K.	C2	13
Dunville, Newf.	E5	72
Dunwoody, Ga., U.S.	h8	87
Duolun, China	C8	31
Du Page, co., Il., U.S.	B5	90
Du Page, stm., Il., U.S.	k8	90
Dupax, Phil.	n13	34
Duplessis, La., U.S.	h10	95
Duplin, co., N.C., U.S.	C5	110
Du Pont, Ga., U.S.	F4	87
Dupont, In., U.S.	G6	91
Dupont, Oh., U.S.	A1	112
Dupont, Wa., U.S.	B3	124
Dupont, Bayou, stm., La., U.S.	k11	95
Dupont City, W.V., U.S.	m13	125
Dupont Manor, De., U.S.	D3	85
Dupree, S.D., U.S.	B4	118
Dupuyer, Mt., U.S.	B4	103
Duquesne, Pa., U.S.	F2	115
Du Quoin, Il., U.S.	E4	90
Dūrā, Isr. Occ.	C7	41
Duran, N.M., U.S.	C4	108
Durance, stm., Fr.	F6	16
Durand, Il., U.S.	A4	90
Durand, Ga., U.S.	C2	87
Durand, Mi., U.S.	F7	99
Durand, Wi., U.S.	D2	126
Durango (Victoria de Durango), Mex.	C4	63
Durango, Co., U.S.	D3	83
Durango, state, Mex.	C4	63
Durant, Ia., U.S.	C7	92
Durant, Ms., U.S.	B4	101
Durant, Ok., U.S.	D5	113
Durants Neck, N.C., U.S.	A6	110
Duraton, stm., Spain	E1	22
Durazno, Ur.	E1	55
Durazno, dept., Ur.	f8	54
Durban, Man.	D1	70
Durban, S. Afr.	C5	49
Durbin, N.D., U.S.	C8	111
Durbin, W.V., U.S.	C5	125
Durbin Creek, stm., Fl., U.S.	m8	86
Düren, W. Ger.	C3	18
Durg, India	*D7	37
Durgāpur, India	F11	37
Durham, Ont.	C4	73
Durham, Eng., U.K.	C6	10
Durham, Ca., U.S.	C3	82
Durham, Ct., U.S.	C5	84
Durham, Ks., U.S.	D6	93
Durham, Mo., U.S.	B6	102
Durham, N.H., U.S.	D5	106
Durham, N.C., U.S.	B4	110
Durham, co., Eng., U.K.	C6	10
Durham, co., N.C., U.S.	A4	110
Durham (Regional Municipality), co., Ont.	C6	73
Durham Downs, Austl.	E7	51
Durham Bridge, N.B.	C3	71
Durham-Sud, Que.	D5	74
Durhamville, Tn., U.S.	B2	119
Durkee, Or., U.S.	C9	114
Durmersheim, W. Ger.	D3	19
Durmitor, mtn., Yugo.	D4	24
Durness, Scot., U.K.	A4	10
Durness, Kyle of, b., Scot., U.K.	B4	10
Durnford, Punta, c., W. Sah.	E1	44
Dürrboden, Switz.	C8	21
Durrell, Newf.	D4	72
Durrës, Alb.	B1	25
Durrow, Ire.	E4	11
Durrus, Ire.	F2	11
Dursey Island, i., Ire.	F1	11
Dursunbey, Tur.	A4	40
Duru, Zaire	A4	48
Durūz, Jabal ad, mtn., Syria	F9	34
D'Urville, Cape, c., Indon.	F9	34
D'Urville Island, i., N.Z.	D10	51
Duryea, Pa., U.S.	D10	115
Dushan, China	F9	31
Dushanbe, Sov. Un.	J11	29
Dushaymāt, Jazā'ir, is., Eg.	C2	41
Dushore, Pa., U.S.	C9	115
Dusky Sound, strt., N.Z.	P11	51
Duson, La., U.S.	D3	95
Düsseldorf, W. Ger.	C3	18
Dusty, N.M., U.S.	D1	108
Dutch Creek, stm., Ar., U.S.	C2	81
Dutchess, co., N.Y., U.S.	D7	109
Dutch Harbor, Ak., U.S.	E6	79
Dutch Island, i., R.I., U.S.	F4	116

Name	Map Ref.	Page
Dutch John, Ut., U.S.	C6	121
Dutchtown, Mo., U.S.	D8	102
Dutton, Ont.	E3	73
Dutton, Al., U.S.	A4	78
Dutton, Mt., U.S.	C5	103
Dutton, Mount, mtn., Ut., U.S.	E3	121
Dutzow, Mo., U.S.	C7	102
Duval, co., Fl., U.S.	B5	86
Duval, co., Tx., U.S.	F3	120
Duvergé, Dom. Rep.	E8	64
Duvno, Yugo.	D3	24
Duxbury, Ma., U.S.	B6	98
Duxbury, Vt., U.S.	C3	122
Duyun, China	F6	31
Düzce, Tur.	B8	40
Dvina Bay, b., Sov. Un.	C16	8
Dvůr Králové [nad Labem], Czech.	C3	26
Dwārka, India	F2	37
Dwight, Il., U.S.	B5	90
Dwight, Ks., U.S.	D7	93
Dwight, Ma., U.S.	B3	98
Dwight, Ne., U.S.	C8	104
Dwight, N.D., U.S.	C9	111
Dwight D. Eisenhower Lock, N.Y., U.S.	f9	109
Dworshak Reservoir, res., Id., U.S.	C3	89
Dwyer, Wy., U.S.	D8	127
Dyakovo, Sov. Un.	r22	27
Dyatkovo, Sov. Un.	E10	27
Dyaul, i., Pap. N. Gui.	h13	51
Dyce, Scot., U.K.	C6	13
Dyckesville, Wi., U.S.	D6	126
Dycusburg, Ky., U.S.	e9	94
Dyer, In., U.S.	A2	91
Dyer, Nv., U.S.	F3	105
Dyer, Tn., U.S.	A3	119
Dyer, co., Tn., U.S.	A2	119
Dyer Bay, Ont.	B3	73
Dyer Bay, b., Ont.	B3	73
Dyer Brook, Me., U.S.	B4	96
Dyer Island, i., R.I., U.S.	E5	116
Dyero, Mali	D3	45
Dyersburg, Tn., U.S.	A2	119
Dyersville, Ia., U.S.	B6	92
Dyess, Ar., U.S.	B5	81
Dyess Air Force Base, mil., Tx., U.S.	C3	120
Dyfed, co., Wales, U.K.	C3	12
Dyje, stm., Eur.	D3	26
Dykh-Tau, Mount, mtn., Sov. Un.	*E7	29
Dyment, Ont.	E5	70
Dysart, Sask.	G3	75
Dysart, Ia., U.S.	B5	92
Dzalaata, Mong.	B2	32
Dzamïn Üüd, Mong.	B4	32
Dzaoudzi, May.	f9	49
Dzaudzhikau see Ordzhonikidze, Sov. Un.	E7	29
Dzavhan, stm., Mong.	B3	31
Dzerzhinsk, Sov. Un.	C14	27
Dzerzhinsk, Sov. Un.	E6	27
Dzhalal-Abad, Sov. Un.	E8	28
Dzhambul, Sov. Un.	E10	29
Dzhankoy, Sov. Un.	I10	27
Dzhebel, Sov. Un.	B7	39
Dzhetygara, Sov. Un.	C6	28
Dzhezkazgan, Sov. Un.	D7	28
Dzhizak, Sov. Un.	G22	8
Dzhugdzhur Mountains, mts., Sov. Un.	D16	29
Dzhungarian Alatau Mountains, mts., Asia	D9	28
Dzhusaly, Sov. Un.	D6	28
Działdowo, Pol.	B6	26
Działoszyce, Pol.	C6	26
Dzierżoniów, Pol.	C4	26
Dzilam González, Mex.	C7	63
Dzioua, Alg.	C6	44
Dzitbalché, Mex.	C6	63
Dzulfa, Sov. Un.	C15	40
Dzungarian Basin see Junggar Pendi, China	B2	31
Dzuunmod, Mong.	B6	31
E		
Eads, Co., U.S.	C8	83
Eads, Tn., U.S.	B2	119
Eagan, Mn., U.S.	n12	100
Eagan, Tn., U.S.	C10	119
Eagar, Az., U.S.	C6	80
Eagle, Ak., U.S.	C11	79
Eagle, Id., U.S.	F2	89
Eagle, Ne., U.S.	h12	104
Eagle, N.Y., U.S.	C2	109
Eagle, Wi., U.S.	F5	126
Eagle, co., Co., U.S.	B4	83
Eagle, stm., Newf.	B2	72
Eagle Bend, Mn., U.S.	D3	100
Eagle Bridge, N.Y., U.S.	C7	109
Eagle Butte, S.D., U.S.	C4	118
Eagle Cave, Wi., U.S.	E3	126
Eagle City, Ok., U.S.	B3	113
Eagle Cliff, mtn., U.S.	B3	89
Eagle Creek, Tn., U.S.	B4	119
Eagle Creek, stm., Sask.	F2	75
Eagle Creek, stm., In., U.S.	D5	91
Eagle Creek, stm., Ky., U.S.	B5	94
Eagle Creek Reservoir, res., In., U.S.	E5	91
Eagle Dam, Ia., U.S.	E4	91
Eagle Grove, Ia., U.S.	B4	92
Eagle Harbor, Mi., U.S.	A2	99
Eagle Key, i., Fl., U.S.	G6	86
Eagle Lake, Mn., U.S.	A4	96
Eagle Lake, Me., U.S.	F5	100
Eagle Lake, Tx., U.S.	E4	120
Eagle Lake, Wi., U.S.	*F5	126
Eagle Lake, l., Ont.	E5	70
Eagle Lake, l., Ca., U.S.	B3	82
Eagle Lake, l., Me., U.S.	A4	96
Eagle Lake, l., Me., U.S.	B3	96
Eagle Lake, l., Wi., U.S.	C4	126
Eagle Mills, Ar., U.S.	D3	81
Eagle Mountain, mtn., Mn., U.S.	k9	100
Eagle Mountain Lake, res., Tx., U.S.	m9	120
Eagle Nest, N.M., U.S.	A4	108
Eagle Nest Butte, mtn., S.D., U.S.	D4	118
Eaglenest Lake, l., Can.	A4	70
Eagle Nest Lake, l., N.M., U.S.	A4	108
Eagle Pass, Tx., U.S.	E2	120
Eagle Peak, mtn., Ca., U.S.	B3	82
Eagle Peak, mtn., Tx., U.S.	o12	120
Eagle Point, Or., U.S.	E4	114
Eagle River, Ont.	E5	70
Eagle River, Mi., U.S.	A2	99
Eagle River, Wi., U.S.	C4	126
Eagle Rock, Va., U.S.	C3	123
Eaglesham, Alta.	B2	68
Eagles Mere, Pa., U.S.	D8	115
Eagle Springs, N.C., U.S.	B3	110
Eagletail Mountains, mts., Az., U.S.	D2	80
Eagletail Peak, mtn., Az., U.S.	D2	80
Eagleton Village, Tn., U.S.	*D10	119
Eagletown, Ok., U.S.	C7	113
Eagleville, Ca., U.S.	B3	82
Eagleville, Ct., U.S.	B6	84
Eagleville, Mo., U.S.	A4	102
Eagleville, Tn., U.S.	B5	119
Eakly, Ok., U.S.	B3	113
Ealing (part of London), Eng., U.K.	k12	10
Eardley, Que.	g11	73
Eardley Lake, l., Man.	C3	70
Earle, Ar., U.S.	B5	81
Earl Grey, Sask.	G3	75
Earlham, Ia., U.S.	C3	92
Earlimart, Ca., U.S.	E4	82
Earling, Ia., U.S.	C2	92
Earling, W.V., U.S.	n12	125
Earlington, Ky., U.S.	C2	94
Earl Island, i., Newf.	B3	72
Earl Park, In., U.S.	C3	91
Earlsboro, Ok., U.S.	B5	113
Earlton, Ks., U.S.	E8	93
Earlville, Il., U.S.	B5	90
Earlville, Ia., U.S.	B6	92
Earlville, N.Y., U.S.	C5	109
Early, co., Ga., U.S.	E2	87
Early Branch, S.C., U.S.	F6	117
Earn, stm., Scot., U.K.	D5	13
Earn, Loch, l., Scot., U.K.	D4	13
Earth, Tx., U.S.	B1	120
Easingwold, Eng., U.K.	F7	13
Easky, Ire.	C3	11
Easley, S.C., U.S.	B2	117
East, stm., Ont.	B5	73
East, stm., Ct., U.S.	D5	84
East, stm., N.Y., U.S.	k13	109
East, stm., Wi., U.S.	h9	126
East Acton, U.S.	g10	98
East Alburgh, Vt., U.S.	B2	122
East Alstead, N.H., U.S.	D2	106
East Alton, Il., U.S.	E3	90
East Andover, Me., U.S.	D2	96
East Andover, N.H., U.S.	D3	106
East Angus, Que.	D6	74
East Arlington, Vt., U.S.	E2	122
East Aurora, N.Y., U.S.	C2	109
East Baldwin, Me., U.S.	E2	96
East Bangor, Pa., U.S.	E11	115
East Bank, W.V., U.S.	m13	125
East Barnard, Vt., U.S.	D3	122
East Barre, Vt., U.S.	C4	122
East Baton Rouge, co., La., U.S.	D4	95
East Bay, b., Fl., U.S.	u16	86
East Bay, b., Tx., U.S.	R15	120
East Beckwith Mountain, mtn., Co., U.S.	C3	83
East Bend, N.C., U.S.	A2	110
East Berbice-Corentyne, dept., Guy.	B3	59
East Berlin, Ct., U.S.	C5	84
East Berlin, Pa., U.S.	G8	115
East Bernard, Tx., U.S.	E4	120
East Bernstadt, Ky., U.S.	C5	94
East Bethel, Mn., U.S.	E5	100
East Bethel, Vt., U.S.	D3	122
East Billerica, Ma., U.S.	f11	98
East Blue Hill, Me., U.S.	D4	96
East Bonne Terre, Mo., U.S.	D7	102
East Boothbay, Me., U.S.	E3	96
Eastborough, Ks., U.S.	g12	93
Eastbourne, Eng., U.K.	E7	10
East Brady, Pa., U.S.	E2	115
East Braintree, Man.	E4	70
East Braintree, Vt., U.S.	D3	122
East Branch Clarion River Lake, res., Pa., U.S.	C4	115
East Brewster, Ma., U.S.	C7	98
East Brewton, Al., U.S.	D2	78
East Bridgewater, Ma., U.S.	B6	98
East Brimfield Lake, res., Ma., U.S.	B3	98
Eastbrook, Me., U.S.	D4	96
East Brookfield, Ma., U.S.	B3	98
East Brooklyn, Ct., U.S.	C8	84
East Broughton, Que.	C6	74
East Brunswick, N.J., U.S.	C4	107
East Burke, Vt., U.S.	B5	122
East Butler, Pa., U.S.	E2	115
East Butte, mtn., Mt., U.S.	B5	103
East Cache Creek, stm., Ok., U.S.	C3	113
East Calais, Vt., U.S.	C4	122
East Canaan, Ct., U.S.	A2	84
East Candia, N.H., U.S.	D4	106
East Cape, c., N.Z.	L17	51
East Cape, c., Fl., U.S.	G5	86
East Carbon, Ut., U.S.	D5	121
East Carroll, co., La., U.S.	B4	95
East Chain, Mn., U.S.	G3	100
East Channel, strt., Marsh Is.	S18	52
East Charleston, Vt., U.S.	B5	122
East Chelmsford, Ma., U.S.	f10	98
Eastchester, N.Y., U.S.	*n15	109
East Chicago, In., U.S.	A3	91
East Chicago Heights, Il., U.S.	*k9	90
East China Sea, Asia	F10	31
East Chop, Ma., U.S.	D6	98
East Cleveland, Oh., U.S.	g9	112
East-Clifton, Que.	D6	74
East Columbia, Tx., U.S.	r14	120
East Compton, Ca., U.S.	*F4	82
East Concord, Vt., U.S.	C5	122
East Conway, N.H., U.S.	B4	106
East Corinth, Me., U.S.	D3	96
East Corinth, Vt., U.S.	C4	122
East Cote Blanche Bay, b., La., U.S.	E4	95
East Coulee, Alta.	D4	68
East Danville, Oh., U.S.	C2	112
East Demerara-West Coast Berbice, dept., Guy.	A3	59
East Dennis, Ma., U.S.	C7	98
East Dereham, Eng., U.K.	B8	12
East Derry, N.H., U.S.	E4	106
East Detroit, Mi., U.S.	p16	99
East Dixfield, Me., U.S.	D3	96
East Dixmont, Me., U.S.	D3	96
East Dorset, Vt., U.S.	E2	122
East Douglas, Ma., U.S.	B4	98
East Dover, Ma., U.S.	C3	96
East Dover, Vt., U.S.	F3	122
East Dubuque, Il., U.S.	A3	90
East Dummerston, Vt., U.S.	F3	122
East Eddington, Me., U.S.	D4	96
East Ellijay, Ga., U.S.	B2	87
Eastend, Sask.	H1	75
East End Point, c., Bah.	m18	64
East Enterprise, In., U.S.	G8	91
Easter, Mount, mtn., Ct., U.S.	B2	84
Easter Island see Pascua, Isla de, i., Chile	H15	6
Eastern, prov., Ghana	E5	45
Eastern, prov., Kenya	B6	48
Eastern Bay, b., Md., U.S.	C5	97
Eastern Channel, strt., Japan	J4	33
Eastern Ghâts, mts., India	E7	36
Eastern Island, i., Newf.	C4	72
Eastern Island, i., Mid. Is.	K4	52
Eastern Neck Island, i., Md., U.S.	C5	97
Eastern Point, c., Ma., U.S.	f13	98
Easterville, Man.	C2	70
East Fairfield, Vt., U.S.	B3	122
East Fairview, N.D., U.S.	B1	111
East Falmouth, Ma., U.S.	C6	98
East Farmingdale, N.Y., U.S.	*E7	109
East Farmington Heights, Ct., U.S.	C4	84
East Feliciana, co., La., U.S.	D4	95
East Flanders, prov., Bel.	C3	17
East Flat Rock, N.C., U.S.	f10	110
East Flevoland, reg., Neth.	B5	17
Eastford, Ct., U.S.	B7	84
East Fork, stm., Wy., U.S.	D3	127
East Fork Lake, res., Oh., U.S.	C1	112
East Foxboro, Ma., U.S.	B5	98
East Franklin, Vt., U.S.	B3	122
East Freetown, Ma., U.S.	C6	98
East Fultonham, Oh., U.S.	C3	112
East Gaffney, S.C., U.S.	A4	117
East Galesburg, Il., U.S.	C3	90
Eastgate, Wa., U.S.	*e11	124
East German Democratic Republic see German Democratic Republic, ctry., Eur.	B6	18
East Glacier Park, Mt., U.S.	B3	103
East Glastonbury, Ct., U.S.	C5	84
East Glenville, N.Y., U.S.	*C7	109
East Grafton, N.H., U.S.	C3	106
East Granby, Ct., U.S.	B5	84
East Grand Forks, Mn., U.S.	C2	100
East Grand Rapids, Mi., U.S.	F5	99
East Granville, Vt., U.S.	C3	122
East Greenville, Pa., U.S.	F10	115
East Greenwich, R.I., U.S.	D4	116
East Grinstead, Eng., U.K.	C8	12
East Gwillimbury, Ont.	C5	73
East Haddam, Ct., U.S.	D6	84
East Half Hollow Hills, N.Y., U.S.	*n15	109
East Hampden, Me., U.S.	*D4	96
East Hampstead, N.H., U.S.	E4	106
East Hampton, Ct., U.S.	C5	84
Easthampton, Ma., U.S.	B2	98
East Hampton, N.Y., U.S.	n16	109
East Hanover, N.J., U.S.	*B4	107
East Hardwick, Vt., U.S.	B4	122
East Harpswell, Me., U.S.	g8	96
East Hartford, Ct., U.S.	B5	84
East Hartland, Ct., U.S.	A4	84
East Haven, Ct., U.S.	D4	84
East Haven, Vt., U.S.	B5	122
East Haverhill, N.H., U.S.	B3	106
East Hebron, N.H., U.S.	C3	106
East Helena, Mt., U.S.	D5	103
East Hemet, Ca., U.S.	*F5	82
East Hickory, Pa., U.S.	C3	115
East Highgate, Vt., U.S.	B3	122
East Hills, N.Y., U.S.	*E7	109
East Holden, Me., U.S.	D4	96
East Holderness, N.H., U.S.	C3	106
East Islip, N.Y., U.S.	*n15	109
East Jordan, N.S.	F4	71
East Jordan, Mi., U.S.	C5	99
East Juliette, Ga., U.S.	C3	87
East Kelowna, B.C.	E8	69
East Kilbride, Scot., U.K.	E4	13
East Killingly, Ct., U.S.	B8	84
East Kingston, N.H., U.S.	E4	106
Eastlake, Mi., U.S.	D4	99
East Lake, N.C., U.S.	B7	110
Eastlake, Oh., U.S.	A4	112
East Lake, l., Ont.	C5	70
East Lake Tohopekaliga, l., Fl., U.S.	D5	86
Eas La Mirada, Ca., U.S.	*F5	82
Eastland, Tx., U.S.	C3	120
Eastland, co., Tx., U.S.	C3	120
Eastland Township, Ut., U.S.	*F6	121
East Lansing, Mi., U.S.	F6	99
East Laport, Pa., U.S.	f9	110
East Las Vegas, Nv., U.S.	G6	105
East Laurinburg, N.C., U.S.	C3	110
East Lebanon, Me., U.S.	E2	96
East Lempster, N.H., U.S.	D2	106
East Liberty, Oh., U.S.	B2	112
East Litchfield, Ct., U.S.	B3	84
East Livermore, Me., U.S.	D2	96
East Liverpool, Oh., U.S.	B5	112
East Longmeadow, Ma., U.S.	B2	98
East Los Angeles, Ca., U.S.	m12	82
East Lyme, Ct., U.S.	D7	84
East Lynn, Il., U.S.	C6	90
East Lynn, W.V., U.S.	C2	125
East Lynne, Mo., U.S.	C3	102
East Lynn Lake, res., W.V., U.S.	C2	125
East Machias, Me., U.S.	D5	96
East Madison, Me., U.S.	D3	96
Eastmain, Que.	h11	74
Eastmain, stm., Que.	F18	66
Eastman, Que.	D5	74
Eastman, Ga., U.S.	D3	87
Eastman, Wi., U.S.	E2	126
East Mansfield, Ma., U.S.	B5	98
East Marietta, Ga., U.S.	*C2	87
East Marion, Ma., U.S.	*C6	98
East Marion, N.Y., U.S.	*m16	109
East Matunuck, R.I., U.S.	F3	116
East Meadow, N.Y., U.S.	*n15	109
East Meredith, N.Y., U.S.	C6	109
East Middlebury, Vt., U.S.	D2	122
East Midvale, Ut., U.S.	*C4	121
East Millbury, Ma., U.S.	B4	98
East Millinocket, Me., U.S.	C4	96
East Moline, Il., U.S.	B3	90
East Monroe, Oh., U.S.	C2	112
East Montpelier, Vt., U.S.	C4	122
East Naples, Fl., U.S.	F5	86
East Newark, N.J., U.S.	k8	107
East New Market, Md., U.S.	C6	97
East Newnan, Ga., U.S.	C2	87
East Newport, Me., U.S.	D3	96
East Nishnabotna, stm., Ia., U.S.	C2	92
East Norriton, Pa., U.S.	o20	115
East Northport, N.Y., U.S.	*n15	109
East Olympia, Wa., U.S.	C3	124
East Orange, N.J., U.S.	B4	107
East Orange, Vt., U.S.	C4	122
East Orland, Me., U.S.	D4	96
East Orleans, Ma., U.S.	C8	98
East Otis, Ma., U.S.	B1	98
East Otto, N.Y., U.S.	C2	109
East Palatka, Fl., U.S.	C5	86
East Palestine, Oh., U.S.	B5	112
East Palo Alto, Ca., U.S.	*D2	82
East Parsonfield, Me., U.S.	E2	96
East Pass, strt., Fl., U.S.	u15	86
East Patchogue, N.Y., U.S.	*n16	109
East Peacham, Vt., U.S.	C4	122
East Pea Ridge, W.V., U.S.	C2	125
East Peoria, Il., U.S.	C4	90
East Pepperell, Ma., U.S.	A4	98
East Peru, Me., U.S.	D2	96
East Petersburg, Pa., U.S.	F9	115
East Pine, B.C.	B7	69
East Pittsburgh, Pa., U.S.	k14	115
Eastpoint, Fl., U.S.	C2	86
East Point, Ga., U.S.	C2	87
East Point, La., U.S.	C3	95
East Point, c., P.E.I.	C8	71
East Point, c., Ma., U.S.	B6	98
East Point, c., N.J., U.S.	E2	107
East Point, c., V.I.U.S.	C6	65
East Poland, Me., U.S.	D2	96
East Poplar, Sask.	H3	75
East Portal, Co., U.S.	B5	83
East Porterville, Ca., U.S.	*D5	82
East Poultney, Vt., U.S.	D2	122
East Prairie, Mo., U.S.	E8	102
East Princeton, Ma., U.S.	B4	98
East Prospect, Pa., U.S.	G8	115
East Providence, R.I., U.S.	C4	116
East Pryor Mountain, mtn., Mt., U.S.	E8	103
East Quogue, N.Y., U.S.	n16	109
East Randolph, N.Y., U.S.	C2	109
East Randolph, Vt., U.S.	D3	122
East Range, mts., Nv., U.S.	C4	105
East Retford, Eng., U.K.	A7	12
East Ridge, Tn., U.S.	h11	119
East Rindge, N.H., U.S.	E3	106
Eastriver, Ct., U.S.	D5	84
East River Mountain, mts., U.S.	C1	123
East River Sheet Harbour, N.S.	E7	71
East Rochester, N.Y., U.S.	B3	109
East Rockaway, N.Y., U.S.	*k13	109
East Rockingham, N.C., U.S.	C3	110
East Rutherford, N.J., U.S.	h8	107
East Ryegate, Vt., U.S.	C4	122
East Saint Johnsbury, Vt., U.S.	C5	122
East Saint Louis, Il., U.S.	E3	90
East Salt Creek, stm., Co., U.S.	B2	83
East Sandwich, Ma., U.S.	C7	98
East Sebago, Me., U.S.	E2	96
East Selkirk, Man.	D3	70
East Siberian Sea, Sov. Un.	B18	29
Eastside, Or., U.S.	D2	114
East Sioux Falls, S.D., U.S.	D9	118
East Smithfield, Pa., U.S.	C8	115
East Sparta, Oh., U.S.	B4	112
East Spencer, N.C., U.S.	B2	110
East Springfield, N.Y., U.S.	C6	109
East Stoneham, Me., U.S.	D2	96
East Stroudsburg, Pa., U.S.	D11	115
East Sudbury, Ma., U.S.	g10	98
East Sullivan, Me., U.S.	D4	96
East Sullivan, N.H., U.S.	E2	106
East Sumner, Me., U.S.	D2	96
East Swanzey, N.H., U.S.	E2	106
East Tawas, Mi., U.S.	D7	99
East Templeton, Ma., U.S.	A3	98
East Thermopolis, Wy., U.S.	*C4	127
East Thetford, Vt., U.S.	D4	122
East Thompson, Ct., U.S.	A8	84
East Troy, Wi., U.S.	F5	126
East Tustin, Ca., U.S.	*n13	82
East Unity, Me., U.S.	D3	96
East Vandergrift, Pa., U.S.	E2	115
East Vestal, N.Y., U.S.	C5	109
East View, W.V., U.S.	k10	125
Eastville, Va., U.S.	C7	123
East Wakefield, N.H., U.S.	C4	106
East Walker, stm., U.S.	E2	105
East Wallingford, Vt., U.S.	E3	122
East Walpole, Ma., U.S.	h11	98
East Wareham, Ma., U.S.	C6	98
East Waterboro, Me., U.S.	E2	96
East Waterford, Me., U.S.	D2	96
East Wenatchee, Wa., U.S.	*B5	124
East Wilton, Me., U.S.	D2	96
East Windsor, N.J., U.S.	C3	107
East Windsor Hill, Ct., U.S.	B5	84
Eastwood, Ky., U.S.	g12	94
Eastwood Hills, Ut., U.S.	*C4	121
East Worcester, N.Y., U.S.	C6	109
East York, Ont.	D5	73
Eaton, Co., U.S.	A6	83
Eaton, In., U.S.	D7	91
Eaton, Me., U.S.	C5	96
Eaton, N.Y., U.S.	C5	109
Eaton, Oh., U.S.	C1	112
Eaton, Tn., U.S.	B2	119
Eaton, co., Mi., U.S.	F6	99
Eaton Center, N.H., U.S.	C4	106
Eatonia, Sask.	F1	75
Eatonton, Ga., U.S.	C3	87
Eatontown, N.J., U.S.	C4	107
Eatonville, Wa., U.S.	C3	124
Eau Claire, Mi., U.S.	G4	99
Eau Claire, Wi., U.S.	D2	126
Eau Claire, co., Wi., U.S.	D2	126
Eau Claire, stm., Wi., U.S.	D2	126
Eau Galle, Wi., U.S.	D1	126
Eauze, Fr.	F4	16
Ebadon Island, i., Marsh Is.	S17	52
Ebb and Flow Lake, l., Man.	D2	70
Ebbw Vale (Blaenau Gwent), Wales, U.K.	C4	12
Ebeleben, E. Ger.	B5	19
Ebeltoft, Den.	B4	15
Ebenezer, Sask.	F4	75
Ebenezer, Ms., U.S.	C3	101
Ebenezer, Oh., U.S.	A1	112
Eben Junction, Mi., U.S.	B4	99
Ebensburg, Pa., U.S.	F4	115
Eberbach, W. Ger.	D3	19
Ebermannstadt, W. Ger.	D6	19
Ebersbach, E. Ger.	B9	19
Ebersbach, W. Ger.	E4	19
Eberswalde [-Finow], E. Ger.	B6	18
Ebetsu, Japan	E10	33
Ebeye, Marsh Is.	S17	52
Ebingen, W. Ger.	D5	23
Eboli, Italy	D5	23
Ebolowa, Cam.	E2	46
Ebro, Fl., U.S.	u16	86
Ebro, Mn., U.S.	C3	100
Ebro, stm., Spain	B6	22
Eccles, W.V., U.S.	n13	125
Eceabat, Tur.	B6	25
Echague, Phil.	n13	34
Echallens, Switz.	C2	21
Ech Cheliff (Orléansville), Alg.	B5	44
Echeconnee Creek, stm., Ga., U.S.	D3	87
Echigawa, Japan	n15	33
Echo, Al., U.S.	D4	78
Echo, La., U.S.	C3	95
Echo, Mn., U.S.	F3	100
Echo, Or., U.S.	B7	114
Echo, Ut., U.S.	C4	121
Echo Bay, Nv., U.S.	G7	105
Echoing, stm., Can.	B6	70
Echoing Lake, l., Ont.	B5	70
Echola, Al., U.S.	B2	78
Echo Lake, l., Me., U.S.	D3	96
Echo Lake, l., Vt., U.S.	B5	122
Echt, Neth.	C5	17
Echt, Scot., U.K.	C6	13
Echternach, Lux.	C7	16
Echuca, Austl.	G7	50
Écija, Spain	D3	22
Eckelson, N.D., U.S.	C7	111
Eckerman, Mi., U.S.	B5	99
Eckernförde, W. Ger.	A5	18
Eckernförder Bucht, b., W. Ger.	D4	15
Eckerty, In., U.S.	H4	91
Eckhart Mines, Md., U.S.	k13	97
Eckley, Co., U.S.	A8	83
Eckman, N.D., U.S.	A4	111
Eckman, W.V., U.S.	*D3	125
Eckville, Alta.	C3	68
Eclectic, Al., U.S.	C3	78
Eclipse Sound, strt., N.W. Ter.	B17	66
Econfina, stm., Fl., U.S.	B3	86
Economy, N.S.	D6	71
Economy, Pa., U.S.	h13	115
Écorces, Rivière aux, stm., Que.	A6	74
Ecorse, Mi., U.S.	p15	99
Ecru, Ms., U.S.	A4	101
Ector, co., Tx., U.S.	D1	120
Ecuador, ctry., S.A.	D3	58
Ed, Swe.	H5	14
Edam, Sask.	D1	75
Edam, Neth.	B5	17
Édouard, Lac, l., Que.	B5	74
Eday, i., Scot., U.K.	A6	13
Edberg, Alta.	C4	68
Edcouch, Tx., U.S.	F4	120
Eddiceton, Ms., U.S.	D3	101
Eddington, Me., U.S.	D4	96
Eddrachillis Bay, b., Scot., U.K.	B3	13
Eddy, co., N.M., U.S.	E5	108
Eddy, co., N.D., U.S.	B7	111
Eddystone, Pa., U.S.	p20	115
Eddystone Rocks, Eng., U.K.	K8	8
Eddyville, Il., U.S.	F5	90
Eddyville, Ia., U.S.	C5	92
Eddyville, Ky., U.S.	e9	94
Eddyville, Ne., U.S.	C6	104
Ede, Neth.	B5	17
Ede, Nig.	*E5	45
Edéa, Cam.	E2	46
Eden, Austl.	H7	51
Eden, Man.	D2	70
Eden, Az., U.S.	E6	80
Eden, Ga., U.S.	D5	87
Eden, Id., U.S.	G4	89
Eden, Md., U.S.	D6	97
Eden, Ms., U.S.	C3	101
Eden, N.Y., U.S.	C2	109
Eden, N.C., U.S.	A3	110
Eden, S.D., U.S.	B8	118
Eden, Tx., U.S.	D3	120
Eden, Ut., U.S.	B4	121
Eden, Vt., U.S.	B3	122
Eden, Wi., U.S.	E5	126
Eden, Wy., U.S.	D3	127
Eden, stm., Eng., U.K.	G10	8
Edenborn, Pa., U.S.	G2	115
Edenderry, Ire.	C4	11
Eden Lake, l., Man.	A1	70
Eden Mills, Vt., U.S.	B3	122
Eden Prairie, Mn., U.S.	n12	100
Eden Valley, Mn., U.S.	E4	100
Edenville, Mi., U.S.	E6	99
Edenwold, Sask.	G3	75
Eder, stm., W. Ger.	C4	18
Edesville, Md., U.S.	B5	97
Edgar, Ne., U.S.	D8	104
Edgar, Wi., U.S.	D4	126
Edgar, co., Il., U.S.	D6	90
Edgard, La., U.S.	D5	95
Edgar Springs, Mo., U.S.	D6	102
Edgartown, Ma., U.S.	D6	98
Edge, i., Nor.	B12	128
Edgecombe, co., N.C., U.S.	B5	110
Edgecumbe, Cape, c., Ak., U.S.	m21	79
Edgefield, S.C., U.S.	D4	117
Edgefield, co., S.C., U.S.	D4	117
Edgeley, Sask.	G4	75
Edgeley, N.D., U.S.	C7	111
Edgemere, Md., U.S.	B5	97
Edgemont, Ar., U.S.	*B3	81
Edgemont, Ca., U.S.	*F5	82
Edgemont, S.D., U.S.	D2	118
Edgemoor, De., U.S.	A3	85
Edgemoor, S.C., U.S.	B5	117
Edgemoor, Tn., U.S.	m13	119
Edgerly, La., U.S.	D2	95
Edgerton, Alta.	C5	68
Edgerton, Ks., U.S.	D8	93
Edgerton, Mn., U.S.	G2	100
Edgerton, Mo., U.S.	B3	102
Edgerton, Oh., U.S.	A1	112
Edgerton, Wi., U.S.	F4	126
Edgerton, Wy., U.S.	C6	127
Edgewater, Al., U.S.	f7	78
Edgewater, Co., U.S.	*B5	83
Edgewater, Fl., U.S.	D6	86
Edgewater, Md., U.S.	C4	97
Edgewater, N.J., U.S.	h9	107
Edgewater Park, N.J., U.S.	C3	107
Edgewood, B.C.	E8	69
Edgewood, Il., U.S.	E5	90
Edgewood, In., U.S.	D6	91
Edgewood, Ky., U.S.	h13	94
Edgewood, Md., U.S.	B5	97
Edgewood, N.M., U.S.	B3	108
Edgewood, Oh., U.S.	A5	112
Edgewood, Pa., U.S.	k14	115
Edgewood, Wa., U.S.	f11	124
Edgeworth, Pa., U.S.	h13	115
Edgeworthstown see Mostrim, Ire.		
Ediggen Island, i., Marsh Is.	S17	52
Édhessa, Gr.	B4	40
Edina, Mn., U.S.	F5	100
Edina, Mo., U.S.	A5	102
Edinboro, Pa., U.S.	C1	115
Edinburg, Il., U.S.	D4	90
Edinburg, Ms., U.S.	C4	101
Edinburg, N.Y., U.S.	B6	109
Edinburg, N.D., U.S.	A8	111
Edinburg, Tx., U.S.	F3	120
Edinburg, Va., U.S.	B4	123
Edinburgh, Scot., U.K.	C5	10
Edinburgh, In., U.S.	F6	91
Edirne, Tur.	B6	40
Edison, Ga., U.S.	E2	87
Edison, Ne., U.S.	D6	104
Edison, N.J., U.S.	B4	107
Edison, Oh., U.S.	B3	112
Edison, Wa., U.S.	A3	124
Edisto, stm., S.C., U.S.	E6	117
Edisto, North Fork, stm., S.C., U.S.	D5	117
Edisto, South Fork, stm., S.C., U.S.	E5	117
Edisto Island, S.C., U.S.	F7	117
Edisto Island, i., S.C., U.S.	F7	117
Edith, Mount, mtn., Mt., U.S.	D5	103
Edithburgh, Austl.	G1	51
Edmeston, N.Y., U.S.	C5	109
Edmond, Ks., U.S.	C4	93
Edmond, Ok., U.S.	B4	113
Edmonds, Wa., U.S.	B3	124
Edmondson, Ar., U.S.	B5	81
Edmondson Heights, Md., U.S.	g10	97
Edmonson, co., Ky., U.S.	C3	94
Edmonton, Alta.	C4	68
Edmonton, Ky., U.S.	D4	94
Edmore, Mi., U.S.	E5	99
Edmore, N.D., U.S.	A7	111
Edmund Lake, l., Man.	B5	70
Edmunds, co., S.D., U.S.	B6	118
Edmundston, N.B.	B1	71
Edna, Ks., U.S.	E8	93
Edna, Tx., U.S.	E4	120
Edna, W.V., U.S.	h10	125
Edna Bay, Ak., U.S.	n23	79
Edolo, Italy	D9	21
Edon, Oh., U.S.	A1	112
Edremit, Tur.	C6	25
Edremit, Gulf of, b., Tur.	C6	25
Edson, Alta.	C2	68
Edson, Ks., U.S.	C2	93
Edson Butte, mtn., Or., U.S.	E2	114
Eduni, Mount, mtn., N.W. Ter.	D7	66
Edwall, Wa., U.S.	B8	124
Edwand, Alta.	B4	68
Edward, Lake, l., Afr.	B5	48
Edwards, Ont.	h13	73
Edwards, Co., U.S.	C4	83
Edwards, Il., U.S.	C4	90
Edwards, Ms., U.S.	C3	101
Edwards, N.Y., U.S.	A5	109
Edwards, co., Il., U.S.	E4	90
Edwards, co., Ks., U.S.	E4	93
Edwards, co., Tx., U.S.	E2	120
Edwards Air Force Base, mil., Ca., U.S.	E5	82
Edwardsburg, Mi., U.S.	G4	99
Edwards Butte, mtn., Or., U.S.	B3	114
Edwards Plateau, plat., Tx., U.S.	D2	120
Edwardsport, In., U.S.	G3	91
Edwardsville, Il., U.S.	E4	90
Edwardsville, Ks., U.S.	k16	93
Edwardsville, Pa., U.S.	n17	115
Edward VIII Bay, b., Ant.	C18	7
Edward VII Peninsula, pen., Ant.	B33	7
Edwin, Al., U.S.	D4	78
Edzell, Scot., U.K.	D6	13
Eek, Ak., U.S.	C7	79
Eek, stm., Ak., U.S.	C7	79
Eeklo, Bel.	C3	17
Eel, stm., Ca., U.S.	B2	82
Eel, stm., In., U.S.	C5	91
Eel, stm., In., U.S.	F3	91
Eferding, Aus.	D7	18
Effie, La., U.S.	C3	95
Effie, Mn., U.S.	C5	100
Effigy Mounds National Monument, Ia., U.S.	A6	92

Name	Map Ref.	Page
Effingham, Il., U.S.	D5	90
Effingham, Ks., U.S.	C8	93
Effingham, N.H., U.S.	C5	106
Effingham, S.C., U.S.	C8	117
Effingham, co., Ga., U.S.	D5	87
Effingham, co., Il., U.S.	D5	90
Effingham Falls, N.H., U.S.	C4	106
Effon-Alaiye, Nig.	*E5	45
Efland, N.C., U.S.	A3	110
Eforie Nord, Rom.	C9	24
Eforie Sud (Vasile Roaită), Rom.	C9	24
Ega, stm., Spain	A4	22
Egadi Islands, is., Italy	E4	23
Egan, S.D., U.S.	D9	118
Egan Range, mts., Nv., U.S.	E7	105
Eganville, Ont.	B7	73
Egbert, Wy., U.S.	E8	127
Egedesminde, Grnld.	*C15	61
Egegik, Ak., U.S.	D8	79
Egeland, N.D., U.S.	A6	111
Egeln, E. Ger.	B6	19
Eger, Hung.	B5	24
Egersund, Nor.	H2	14
Egerton, Mount, mtn., Ant.	A28	7
Eggebek, W. Ger.	D3	15
Eggenfelden, W. Ger.	E7	19
Egg Harbor, Wi., U.S.	C6	126
Egg Harbor City, N.J., U.S.	D3	107
Egg Harbor Point, c., N.J., U.S.	E2	107
Egg Lake, l., Sask.	C3	75
Egilsstadir, Ice.	n25	14
Égletons, Fr.	E5	16
Eglin Air Force Base, mil., Fl., U.S.	u15	86
Eglinton Island, i., N.W. Ter.	m28	66
Eglisau, Switz.	A6	21
Egmond aan Zee, Neth.	B4	17
Egmont, Cape, c., N.Z.	M14	51
Egmont, Mount, mtn., N.Z.	M15	51
Egmont Bay, b., P.E.I.	C5	71
Egmont Channel, strt., Fl., U.S.	p10	86
Egmont Key, i., Fl., U.S.	p10	86
Egnar, Co., U.S.	D2	83
Egremont, Alta.	B4	68
Egremont, Eng., U.K.	F5	13
Eğridir, Tur.	D8	40
Eğridir, Lake, l., Tur.	C8	40
Egrigoz, mtn., Tur.	C7	25
Egtved, Den.	C3	15
Egypt, Ar., U.S.	B5	81
Egypt, Ga., U.S.	D5	87
Egypt, Ma., U.S.	B6	98
Egypt, Ms., U.S.	B5	101
Egypt, ctry., Afr.	C2	38
Egypt, Lake of, res., Il., U.S.	F5	90
Egypt Lake, Fl., U.S.	*D4	86
Ehrenberg, Az., U.S.	D1	80
Ehrenfeld, Pa., U.S.	F4	115
Ehrhardt, S.C., U.S.	E5	117
Éibar, Spain	A4	22
Eibau, E. Ger.	C9	19
Eibenstock, E. Ger.	C7	19
Eichstätt, W. Ger.	D5	19
Eider, stm., W. Ger.	A4	18
Eidsberg, Nor.	H4	14
Eidson, Tn., U.S.	C10	119
Eidsvold, Austl.	E9	50
Eidsvoll, Nor.	G4	14
Eielson Air Force Base, mil., Ak., U.S.	C10	79
Eifel, mts., W. Ger.	C3	18
Eige, Carn, mtn., Scot., U.K.	C3	13
Eiger, mtn., Switz.	C5	21
Eigg, i., Scot., U.K.	B3	10
Eigg, Sound of, strt., Scot., U.K.	D2	13
Eightmile Creek, stm., Ks., U.S.	h12	93
Eights Coast, Ant.	B3	7
Eighty Eight, Ky., U.S.	D4	94
Eikeren, l., Nor.	p28	14
Eildon, Lake, res., Austl.	H6	51
Eileen Lake, l., N.W. Ter.	D11	66
Eilenburg, E. Ger.	C6	18
Eiler Rasmussen, Cape, c., Grnld.	A16	128
Eil Malk, i., Palau	R17	52
Einbeck, W. Ger.	C4	18
Eindhoven, Neth.	B6	16
Einsiedeln, Switz.	B4	20
Eirunepé, Braz.	C4	58
Eisenach, E. Ger.	C6	19
Eisenberg, E. Ger.	C6	19
Eisenhower, Mount, mtn., N.H., U.S.	B4	106
Eisenhüttenstadt, E. Ger.	B6	18
Eisenstadt, Aus.	E8	18
Eiserfeld, W. Ger.	C2	19
Eisfeld, E. Ger.	C5	19
Eisleben, E. Ger.	C6	18
Eita, Kir.	R18	52
Eita, i., Kir.	R18	52
Eitzen, Mn., U.S.	G7	100
Ejby, Den.	C3	15
Ejea de los Caballeros, Spain	A5	22
Ejeda, Madag.	h8	49
Ejigbo, Nig.	*E5	45
Ejstrup, Den.	C3	15
Ejutla de Crespo, Mex.	D5	63
Ekalaka, Mt., U.S.	E12	103
Ekenäs, Fin.	G10	14
Ekeren (part of Antwerp), Bel.	C4	17
Ekhínos, Grc.	B5	25
Ekimchan, Sov. Un.	D16	29
Ekoln, l., Swe.	t35	14
Ekron, Ky., U.S.	C3	94
Eksjö, Swe.	I6	14
Ekukmakoko, Zaire	B3	48
Ekwan, stm., Ont.	F15	66
Ekwok, Ak., U.S.	D8	79
El Aaiún, W. Sah.	D2	44
Elaine, Ar., U.S.	C5	81
Elamanchili, India	I9	37
Elamton, Ky., U.S.	C6	94
Elamville, Al., U.S.	D4	78
Eland, Wi., U.S.	D4	126
El Aranal, Spain	D3	22
Elassón, Grc.	C4	25
Elat, Isr.	E6	41
Elazığ, Tur.	C12	40
Elba, Al., U.S.	D3	78
Elba, Mi., U.S.	E7	99
Elba, Ne., U.S.	C7	104
Elba, N.Y., U.S.	B2	109
Elba, i., Italy	C3	23
El Banco, Col.	B5	60
Elbasani, Alb.	B3	40
El Baúl, Ven.	B4	60
Elbe (Labe), stm., Eur.	B4	18
Elberfeld, In., U.S.	H3	91
Elberon, Ia., U.S.	B5	92
Elbert, Co., U.S.	B6	83
Elbert, Tx., U.S.	C3	120
Elbert, co., Co., U.S.	B6	83
Elbert, co., Ga., U.S.	B4	87
Elbert, Mount, mtn., Co., U.S.	B4	83
Elberta, Al., U.S.	E2	78
Elberta, Ga., U.S.	D3	87
Elberta, Mi., U.S.	D4	99
Elberta, Ut., U.S.	D4	121
Elberton, Ga., U.S.	B4	87
Elbeuf, Fr.	C4	16
Elbigenalp, Aus.	B6	20
Elbing, Ks., U.S.	f12	93
Elblag, Pol.	A5	26
El Bluff, Nic.	E8	63
El Bolsón, Arg.	C2	54
El Bonillo, Spain	C4	22
El Bordo, Col.	C2	60
El Boulaïda (Blida), Alg.	B5	44
El Burgo de Osma, Spain	B4	22
Elburn, Il., U.S.	B5	90
Elburz Mountains, mts., Iran	B5	38
El Cajon, Ca., U.S.	F5	82
El Callao, Ven.	B5	60
El Campo, Tx., U.S.	E4	120
El Capitan, mtn., Mt., U.S.	D2	103
El Capitan Reservoir, res., Ca., U.S.	o16	82
El Carmen, Bol.	C4	55
El Carmen de Bolívar, Col.	B2	60
El Carrizo, Mex.	B3	63
El Centro, Ca., U.S.	F6	82
El Cerrito, Ca., U.S.	h8	82
El Cerro, Bol.	C3	55
El Chaparro, Ven.	B4	60
Elche, Spain	C5	22
Elcho, Wi., U.S.	C4	126
Elco, Il., U.S.	F4	90
El Cocuy, Col.	B3	60
El Cuervo Butte, mtn., N.M., U.S.	k9	108
Elda, Spain	C5	22
Elde, stm., E. Ger.	B5	18
Elderon, Wi., U.S.	D4	126
Eldersley, Sask.	E4	75
Elderton, Pa., U.S.	E3	115
El Diviso, Col.	C2	60
El Djelfa, Alg.	C5	44
El Djouf, des., Afr.	B3	45
El Dorado, Ar., U.S.	D3	81
Eldorado, Braz.	C3	56
Eldorado, Ont.	C7	73
Eldorado, Sask.	m7	75
Eldorado, Mex.	C3	63
Eldorado, Ga., U.S.	E3	87
Eldorado, Il., U.S.	F5	90
El Dorado, Ks., U.S.	E7	93
Eldorado, Md., U.S.	C6	97
Eldorado, N.C., U.S.	B2	110
Eldorado, Oh., U.S.	C1	112
El Dorado, Ok., U.S.	C2	113
Eldorado, Tx., U.S.	D2	120
El Dorado, co., Ca., U.S.	C3	82
El Dorado Peak, mtn., Ca., U.S.	A4	124
Eldorado Springs, Co., U.S.	B5	83
El Dorado Springs, Mo., U.S.	D3	102
Eldorendo, Ga., U.S.	E2	87
Eldoret, Kenya	A6	48
Eldred, Il., U.S.	D3	90
Eldred, Mn., U.S.	C2	100
Eldred, Pa., U.S.	C5	115
Eldridge, Al., U.S.	B2	78
Eldridge, Ia., U.S.	C7	92
Eldridge, Mo., U.S.	D5	102
Eldridge, N.D., U.S.	C7	111
Eleanor, W.V., U.S.	C3	125
Electra, Tx., U.S.	B3	120
Electra Lake, res., Co., U.S.	D3	83
Electric Mills, Ms., U.S.	C5	101
Electric Peak, mtn., Co., U.S.	C5	83
Electric Peak, mtn., Mt., U.S.	E6	103
Elektrogorsk, Sov. Un.	n18	27
Elektrostal, Sov. Un.	n18	27
Elephant Butte, mtn., N.M., U.S.	*E4	82
Elephant Butte Reservoir, res., N.M., U.S.	D2	108
Elephant Island, i., B.A.T.	C7	7
Elephant Mountain, mtn., Me., U.S.	D2	96
Eleuthera, i., Bah.	B5	64
Eleva, Wi., U.S.	D2	126
Eleven Mile Canyon Reservoir, res., Co., U.S.	C5	83
Eleven Point, stm., U.S.	A4	81
Elevsís (Eleusis), Grc.	g11	25
Elevsís, Gulf of, b., Grc.	g11	25
Elfers, Fl., U.S.	D4	86
Elfin Cove, Ak., U.S.	k21	79
Elfrida, Az., U.S.	F6	80
Elfros, Sask.	F4	75
El Fud, Eth.	D5	47
El Fuerte, Mex.	B3	63
El Galhak, Sud.	C3	47
El Ghazawet, Alg.	B4	44
Elgin, Man.	E1	70
Elgin, N.B.	D4	71
Elgin, Scot., U.K.	B5	10
Elgin, Az., U.S.	F5	80
Elgin, Il., U.S.	B5	90
Elgin, Ia., U.S.	B6	92
Elgin, Mn., U.S.	F6	100
Elgin, Ne., U.S.	C7	104
Elgin, N.D., U.S.	C4	111
Elgin, Ok., U.S.	C3	113
Elgin, Or., U.S.	B9	114
Elgin, S.C., U.S.	B6	117
Elgin, Tx., U.S.	D4	120
Elgin, co., Ont.	E3	73
Elgol, Scot., U.K.	D2	13
Elgon, Mount, mtn., Afr.	A5	48
El Grara, Alg.	C5	44
El Grullo, Mex.	n11	63
El Huecú, Arg.	B2	54
Eli, Ne., U.S.	B4	104
Eliasville, Tx., U.S.	C3	120
Elida, N.M., U.S.	D6	108
Elida, Oh., U.S.	B1	112
Elikón Óros (Helicon), mtn., Grc.	g9	25
Elila, stm., Zaire	B4	48
Elim, Ak., U.S.	C7	79
El Indio, Tx., U.S.	E2	120
Eliot, Me., U.S.	E2	96
Elisabethville see Lubumbashi, Zaire		
Elista, Sov. Un.	H15	27
Elizabeth, Austl.	F6	50
Elizabeth, Ar., U.S.	A3	81
Elizabeth, Co., U.S.	B6	83
Elizabeth, Il., U.S.	A3	90
Elizabeth, In., U.S.	H6	91
Elizabeth, La., U.S.	D3	95
Elizabeth, Mn., U.S.	D2	100
Elizabeth, N.J., U.S.	B4	107
Elizabeth, W.V., U.S.	B3	125
Elizabeth, Cape, c., Wa., U.S.	B1	124
Elizabeth City, N.C., U.S.	A6	110
Elizabeth Islands, is., Ma., U.S.	D6	98
Elizabethton, Tn., U.S.	C11	119
Elizabethtown, Il., U.S.	F5	90
Elizabethtown, In., U.S.	F6	91
Elizabethtown, Ky., U.S.	C4	94
Elizabethtown, N.Y., U.S.	A7	109
Elizabethtown, N.C., U.S.	C4	110
Elizabethtown, Pa., U.S.	F8	115
Elizabethville, Pa., U.S.	E8	115
El Jadida, Mor.	C3	44
El Jebel, Co., U.S.	B3	83
Efk, Pol.	B7	26
Elk, Ca., U.S.	C2	82
Elk, Wa., U.S.	A8	124
Elk, co., Ks., U.S.	E7	93
Elk, co., Pa., U.S.	D4	115
Elk, stm., B.C.	D10	69
Elk, stm., U.S.	A2	78
Elk, stm., Co., U.S.	A4	83
Elk, stm., Ks., U.S.	E7	93
Elk, stm., W.V., U.S.	C3	125
Elk, stm., Wi., U.S.	C3	126
Elkader, Ia., U.S.	B6	92
El Kairouan, Tun.	B7	44
El Kala, Alg.	F2	23
El Kasserine, Tun.	B6	44
Elkatawa, Ky., U.S.	C6	94
Elk City, Id., U.S.	D3	89
Elk City, Ks., U.S.	E7	93
Elk City, Ne., U.S.	g12	104
Elk City, Ok., U.S.	B2	113
Elk City, Lake, res., Ks., U.S.	E7	93
Elk Creek, Ca., U.S.	C2	82
Elk Creek, Ne., U.S.	D9	104
Elk Creek, Va., U.S.	D1	123
Elk Creek, stm., Ok., U.S.	B2	113
Elk Creek, stm., S.D., U.S.	C3	118
El Kef, Tun.	B6	44
El Kere, Eth.	D5	47
Elk Falls, Ks., U.S.	E7	93
Elkford, B.C.	D10	69
Elk Garden, W.V., U.S.	B5	125
Elk Grove, Ca., U.S.	C3	82
Elk Grove Village, Il., U.S.	h9	90
Elkhart, Il., U.S.	C4	90
Elkhart, In., U.S.	A6	91
Elkhart, Ia., U.S.	e8	92
Elkhart, Ks., U.S.	E2	93
Elkhart, Tx., U.S.	D5	120
Elkhart, co., In., U.S.	A6	91
Elkhart, stm., In., U.S.	B6	91
Elkhart Lake, Wi., U.S.	E5	126
Elkhead Mountains, mts., Co., U.S.	A3	83
Elkhorn, Man.	E1	70
Elk Horn, Ia., U.S.	C2	92
Elkhorn, Ne., U.S.	g12	104
Elkhorn, W.V., U.S.	*D3	125
Elkhorn, Wi., U.S.	F5	126
Elkhorn, stm., Ne., U.S.	B7	104
Elkhorn, North Fork, stm., Ne., U.S.	B8	104
Elkhorn, South Fork, stm., Ne., U.S.	B7	104
Elkhorn City, Ky., U.S.	C7	94
Elkhorn Peaks, mts., Id., U.S.	F7	89
Elkhovo, Bul.	D8	24
Elkin, N.C., U.S.	A2	110
Elkins, Ar., U.S.	A1	81
Elkins, N.H., U.S.	D3	106
Elkins, W.V., U.S.	C5	125
Elkins Park, Pa., U.S.	o21	115
Elk Island National Park, Alta.	C4	68
Elkland, Ks., U.S.	D7	93
Elkland, Mo., U.S.	D4	102
Elkland, Pa., U.S.	C7	115
Elk Mills, Md., U.S.	A6	97
Elkmont, Al., U.S.	A3	78
Elkmont, Tn., U.S.	D10	119
Elk Mound, Wi., U.S.	D2	126
Elk Mountain, mtn., N.M., U.S.	D1	108
Elk Mountain, mtn., Wy., U.S.	E6	127
Elk Mountains, mts., U.S.	D1	118
Elk Mountains, mts., Co., U.S.	B3	83
Elko, B.C.	E10	69
Elko, Ga., U.S.	D3	87
Elko, Nv., U.S.	C6	105
Elko, S.C., U.S.	E5	117
Elko, co., Nv., U.S.	B6	105
Elk Peak, mtn., Mt., U.S.	D6	103
Elk Point, Alta.	C5	68
Elk Point, S.D., U.S.	E9	118
Elk Rapids, Mi., U.S.	D5	99
Elk Ranch, Ar., U.S.	A2	81
Elk River, Id., U.S.	C2	89
Elk River, Mn., U.S.	E5	100
Elk Springs, Co., U.S.	D1	108
Elkton, Ga., U.S.	E2	87
Elkton, Ky., U.S.	D2	94
Elkton, Md., U.S.	A6	97
Elkton, Mi., U.S.	E7	99
Elkton, Mn., U.S.	G6	100
Elkton, Or., U.S.	D3	114
Elkton, S.D., U.S.	C9	118
Elkton, Tn., U.S.	B5	119
Elkton, Va., U.S.	B4	123
Elk Valley, Tn., U.S.	C9	119
Elkview, W.V., U.S.	m13	125
Elkville, Il., U.S.	F4	90
Ellabell, Ga., U.S.	D5	87
Ellamore, W.V., U.S.	C4	125
Ellaville, Ga., U.S.	D2	87
Ellef Ringnes Island, i., N.W. Ter.	m31	66
Ellen, Mount, mtn., Ut., U.S.	E5	121
Ellen, Mount, mtn., Vt., U.S.	C3	122
Ellenboro, N.C., U.S.	B1	110
Ellenboro, W.V., U.S.	B3	125
Ellenburg Center, N.Y., U.S.	f11	109
Ellendale, De., U.S.	E4	85
Ellendale, Mn., U.S.	G5	100
Ellendale, N.D., U.S.	C7	111
Ellensburg, Wa., U.S.	C5	124
Ellenton, Fl., U.S.	E4	86
Ellenton, Ga., U.S.	E3	87
Ellenville, N.Y., U.S.	D6	109
Ellenwood, Ga., U.S.	h8	87
Ellerbe, N.C., U.S.	B3	110
Eller Island, i., Marsh Is.	S17	52
Ellershouse, N.S.	E6	71
Ellerslie, Ga., U.S.	D2	87
Ellerslie, Md., U.S.	k13	97
Ellesmere Island, i., N.W. Ter.	m35	66
Ellesmere Port, Eng., U.K.	A5	12
Ellettsville, In., U.S.	F4	91
Ellice Islands see Tuvalu, ctry., Oc.	G10	6
Ellichpur see Achalpur, India	G6	37
Ellicott City, Md., U.S.	B4	97
Ellicottville, N.Y., U.S.	C2	109
Ellijay, Ga., U.S.	B2	87
Ellington, Ct., U.S.	B6	84
Ellington, Mo., U.S.	D7	102
Ellinwood, Ks., U.S.	D5	93
Elliot, S. Afr.	H5	49
Elliot Lake, Ont.	A2	73
Elliott, Ia., U.S.	C2	92
Elliott, Ms., U.S.	B4	101
Elliott, N.D., U.S.	C8	111
Elliott, co., Ky., U.S.	B6	94
Elliott Bay, b., Wa., U.S.	e11	124
Elliott Key, i., Fl., U.S.	G6	86
Elliott Knob, mtn., Va., U.S.	B3	123
Ellis, Id., U.S.	E4	89
Ellis, Ks., U.S.	D4	93
Ellis, Ne., U.S.	D9	104
Ellis, S.D., U.S.	D9	118
Ellis, co., Ks., U.S.	D4	93
Ellis, co., Ok., U.S.	A2	113
Ellis, co., Tx., U.S.	C4	120
Ellisburg, N.Y., U.S.	B4	109
Ellisdale, N.J., U.S.	C3	107
Ellis Grove, Il., U.S.	E4	90
Ellis Pond, l., Me., U.S.	D2	96
Elliston, Newf.	D5	72
Elliston, Mt., U.S.	D4	103
Elliston, Va., U.S.	C2	123
Ellisville, Ms., U.S.	D4	101
Ellisville, Mo., U.S.	f12	102
Ellon, Scot., U.K.	B5	10
Ellore see Elūru, India	E7	36
Elloree, S.C., U.S.	D6	117
Ellport, Pa., U.S.	E1	115
Ellrich, E. Ger.	B5	19
Ells, stm., Alta.	A4	68
Ellscott, Alta.	B4	68
Ellsinore, Mo., U.S.	E7	102
Ellston, Ia., U.S.	D3	92
Ellsworth, Il., U.S.	C5	90
Ellsworth, Ia., U.S.	B4	92
Ellsworth, Ks., U.S.	D5	93
Ellsworth, Me., U.S.	D4	96
Ellsworth, Mi., U.S.	C5	99
Ellsworth, Mn., U.S.	G2	100
Ellsworth, Ne., U.S.	B3	104
Ellsworth, Pa., U.S.	F1	115
Ellsworth, Wi., U.S.	D1	126
Ellsworth, co., Ks., U.S.	D5	93
Ellsworth Air Force Base, mil., S.D., U.S.	C2	118
Ellsworth Hill, mtn., Ct., U.S.	B2	84
Ellsworth Land, reg., Ant.	B4	7
Ellsworth Mountains, mts., Ant.	B4	7
Ellwangen, W. Ger.	D5	18
Ellwood City, Pa., U.S.	E1	115
Elm, stm., N.D., U.S.	B8	111
Elm, stm., N.D., U.S.	B7	111
Elma, Ia., U.S.	A5	92
Elma, Wa., U.S.	C2	124
El Mahdia, Tun.	B7	44
Elmali, Tur.	D7	25
El Manteco, Ven.	B5	60
Elm City, N.C., U.S.	B5	110
Elm Creek, Man.	E2	70
Elm Creek, Ne., U.S.	D6	104
Elm Creek, stm., Mn., U.S.	G4	100
Elm Grove, La., U.S.	B2	95
Elm Grove, Wi., U.S.	m11	126
Elmhurst, Il., U.S.	B6	90
Elmhurst, Pa., U.S.	D10	115
Elmira, Ont.	D4	73
Elmira, P.E.I.	C7	71
Elmira, Mi., U.S.	C6	99
Elmira, Mo., U.S.	B3	102
Elmira, N.Y., U.S.	C4	109
Elmira, Or., U.S.	C3	114
Elmira Heights, N.Y., U.S.	C4	109
Elmo, Ks., U.S.	D6	93
Elmo, Mt., U.S.	C2	103
Elmo, Ut., U.S.	D5	121
Elmodel, Ga., U.S.	E2	87
El Moknine, Tun.	B7	44
Elmont, Ks., U.S.	k14	93
Elmont, N.Y., U.S.	k13	109
Elmont, Va., U.S.	C5	123
El Monte, Ca., U.S.	*E4	82
Elmore, Al., U.S.	C3	78
Elmore, Mn., U.S.	G4	100
Elmore, Oh., U.S.	A2	112
Elmore, co., Al., U.S.	C3	78
Elmore, co., Id., U.S.	F3	89
Elmore City, Ok., U.S.	C4	113
El Morro National Monument, N.M., U.S.	B1	108
Elmsdale, N.S.	E6	71
Elmshorn, W. Ger.	B4	18
Elm Springs, Ar., U.S.	A1	81
Elm Springs, S.D., U.S.	C3	118
Elm Springs Colony, S.D., U.S.	C8	111
Elmsville, N.B.	D3	71
Elmvale, Ont.	C5	73
Elmville, Ct., U.S.	B8	84
Elmwood, Ont.	C3	73
Elmwood, Il., U.S.	C3	90
Elmwood, Ma., U.S.	B6	98
Elmwood, Ne., U.S.	D9	104
Elmwood, Ok., U.S.	A1	113
Elmwood, Wi., U.S.	D1	126
Elmwood Park, Il., U.S.	k9	90
Elmwood Park, N.J., U.S.	h8	107
Elmwood Place, Oh., U.S.	o13	112
Elna, Ky., U.S.	C7	94
Elnora, Alta.	D4	68
Elnora, In., U.S.	G3	91
El Nevado, Cerro, mtn., Arg.	B3	54
Elon College, N.C., U.S.	A3	110
Elora, Ont.	D4	73
Elora, Tn., U.S.	B5	119
El Oro, prov., Ec.	B2	58
Eloise, Fl., U.S.	E5	86
Elorza, Ven.	B4	60
El Oso, Ven.	B4	60
Eloy, Az., U.S.	E4	80
El Palmar, Ven.	B5	60
El Palmito, Mex.	B3	63
El Pao, Ven.	B5	60
El Paraíso, Hond.	D4	62
El Pardo, Spain	o17	22
El Paso, Ar., U.S.	B3	81
El Paso, Il., U.S.	C4	90
El Paso, Tx., U.S.	o11	120
El Paso, co., Co., U.S.	C6	83
El Paso, co., Tx., U.S.	o11	120
Elphin, Ire.	D3	11
Elphinstone, Man.	D1	70
El Porvenir, N.M., U.S.	B4	108
El Portal, Ca., U.S.	D4	82
El Portal, Fl., U.S.	s13	86
El Porvenir, N.M., U.S.	B4	108
El Prado, N.M., U.S.	A4	108
El Progreso, Ec.	g6	58
El Progreso, Hond.	C4	62
El Puerto de Santa María, Spain	D2	22
El Qoll, Alg.	B6	44
El Real, Pan.	F9	62
El Reno, Ok., U.S.	B4	113
El Rio, Ca., U.S.	E4	82
El Rito, N.M., U.S.	C3	108
Elrod, Al., U.S.	B2	78
Elrosa, Mn., U.S.	E4	100
Elrose, Sask.	F1	75
Elroy, Wi., U.S.	E3	126
Elsa, Yukon	D5	66
Elsa, Tx., U.S.	F4	120
Elsah, Il., U.S.	E3	90
El Salto, Mex.	E3	63
El Salvador, ctry., N.A.	E7	63
El Samán de Apure, Ven.	B4	60
El Sauce, Nic.	E7	63
Elsberry, Mo., U.S.	B7	102
El Segundo, Ca., U.S.	*n12	82
El Seibo, Dom. Rep.	E9	64
Elsie, Mi., U.S.	E6	99
Elsie, Ne., U.S.	D4	104
Elsinore see Helsingør, Den.	I5	9
Elsinore, Ky., U.S.	C5	94
Elsinore, De., U.S.	E3	121
Elsmere, De., U.S.	B3	85
Elsmere, Ne., U.S.	B5	104
Elsmere, N.Y., U.S.	*n15	109
El Sobrante, Ca., U.S.	*h8	82
El Sombrero, Ven.	B4	60
Elsterwerda, E. Ger.	B7	18
Elstow, Sask.	F2	75
El Tarf, Alg.	F2	23
El Tigre, Ven.	B5	60
El Tocuyo, Ven.	B4	60
Elton, La., U.S.	D3	95
Elton, Wi., U.S.	C5	126
Eltopia, Wa., U.S.	C7	124
El Toro Marine Corps Air Station, mil., Ca., U.S.	n13	82
El Tránsito, Chile	E1	55
El Trapiche, Col.	C2	60
El Triunfo, Hond.	D4	62
El Triunfo, Mex.	G4	100
El Tucuche, mtn., Trin.	N23	65
El Turbio, Arg.	G2	54
Eltville, W. Ger.	C3	19
Elūru (Ellore), India	E7	36
Elva, Port.	E1	70
Elvaston, Il., U.S.	C2	90
Elverson, Pa., U.S.	F10	115
Elverum, Nor.	G4	14
El Viejo, Nic.	E7	63
El Vigía, Ven.	B3	60
Elvins, Mo., U.S.	D7	102
El Volcán, Chile	A2	54
El Wad, Alg.	C6	44
El Wak, Kenya	A7	48
Elwell, Lake, res., Mt., U.S.	B5	103
Elwha, stm., Wa., U.S.	A2	124
Elwood, Ont.	D6	73
Elwood, Il., U.S.	k8	90
Elwood, In., U.S.	D6	91
Elwood, Ks., U.S.	C9	93
Elwood, Ne., U.S.	D6	104
Elwood, N.J., U.S.	D3	107
Elwood, N.Y., U.S.	*n15	109
Elwood Park, Fl., U.S.	E4	86
Ely, Eng., U.K.	I13	13
Ely, Ia., U.S.	C6	92
Ely, Mn., U.S.	C7	100
Ely, Nv., U.S.	D7	105
Ely, Vt., U.S.	C4	122
Elyria, Ks., U.S.	D6	93
Elyria, Ne., U.S.	C7	104
Elyria, Oh., U.S.	A3	112
Elysburg, Pa., U.S.	E8	115
Elysian, Mn., U.S.	F5	100
El Yunque, mtn., P.R.	n15	64
Elzach, W. Ger.	A4	20
Emāmshahr (Shāhrūd), Iran	B5	38
Emanuel, co., Ga., U.S.	D4	87
Emba, Sov. Un.	D5	28
Emba, stm., Sov. Un.	D5	28
Embarcación, Arg.	D3	55
Embarrass, stm., Il., U.S.	E6	90
Embarrass, Mn., U.S.	C6	100
Embarrass, Wi., U.S.	D5	126
Embarrass, stm., Wi., U.S.	D5	126
Embden, N.D., U.S.	C8	111
Embden, W. Ger.	B3	18
Embden Pond, l., Me., U.S.	D3	96
Embetsu, Japan	D10	33
Embira, stm., Braz.	C3	58
Emblem, Wy., U.S.	B4	127
Embreeville, Tn., U.S.	C11	119
Embro, Ont.	D4	73
Embrun, Ont.	B9	73
Embrun, Fr.	E7	16
Embudo, N.M., U.S.	A4	108
Emden, W. Ger.	B3	18
Emden, Il., U.S.	C4	90
Emden, Mo., U.S.	B6	102
Emelle, Al., U.S.	C1	78
Emerald, Austl.	D8	50
Emerald, *D9	114	
Emerson, Man.	E3	70
Emerson, Ar., U.S.	D2	81
Emerson, Ga., U.S.	B2	87
Emerson, Ia., U.S.	C2	92
Emerson, Ne., U.S.	B9	104
Emerson, N.J., U.S.	h8	107
Emery, S.D., U.S.	D8	118
Emery, Ut., U.S.	E5	121
Emery, co., Ut., U.S.	E5	121
Emery Mills, Me., U.S.	E2	96
Emet, Tur.	C7	25
Emida, Id., U.S.	B2	89
Emigrant, Mt., U.S.	E6	103
Emigrant Gap, Ca., U.S.	C3	82
Emiliano Zapata, Mex.	D6	63
Emilia-Romagna, prov., Italy	B3	23
Emily, Mn., U.S.	D5	100
Emily, Lake, l., Mn., U.S.	E3	100
Emine, Cape, c., Bul.	D8	24
Eminence, In., U.S.	F4	91
Eminence, Ky., U.S.	B4	94
Eminence, Mo., U.S.	D6	102
Emington, Il., U.S.	C5	90
Emirau, i., Pap. N. Gui.	h13	57
Emirdağ, Tur.	C8	40
Emison, In., U.S.	G3	91
Emlenton, Pa., U.S.	D2	115
Emlyn, Ky., U.S.	D5	94
Emma, Mo., U.S.	C4	102
Emma Lake, l., Sask.	D2	75
Emmaus, Pa., U.S.	E11	115
Emmaus, Wi.	B4	21
Emmeline Lake, l., Sask.	C2	75
Emmen, Neth.	A7	16
Emmen, Switz.	B5	21
Emmendingen, W. Ger.	A3	20
Emmerich, W. Ger.	C3	18
Emmet, Ar., U.S.	D2	81
Emmet, Ne., U.S.	B7	104
Emmet, co., Ia., U.S.	A3	92
Emmet, co., Mi., U.S.	C6	99
Emmetsburg, Ia., U.S.	A3	92
Emmett, Id., U.S.	F2	89
Emmett, Ks., U.S.	C7	93
Emmett, Mi., U.S.	F8	99
Emmitsburg, Md., U.S.	A3	97
Emmonak, Ak., U.S.	C7	79
Emmons, Mn., U.S.	G5	100
Emmons, co., N.D., U.S.	C5	111
Emory, Tx., U.S.	C5	120
Emory Peak, mtn., Tx., U.S.	E1	120
Empangeni, S. Afr.	C5	49
Empedrado, Arg.	B5	54
Empire, Co., U.S.	B5	83
Empire, Ga., U.S.	D3	87
Empire, La., U.S.	E6	95
Empire, Mi., U.S.	D4	99
Empire, Nv., U.S.	C2	105
Empoli, Italy	C5	23
Emporia, Ks., U.S.	D7	93
Emporia, Va., U.S.	D5	123
Emporium, Pa., U.S.	D5	115
Empress, Alta.	D5	68
Emptinne, Bel.	D5	17
Ems, stm., Eur.	B3	18
Emsdale, Ont.	B5	73
Emsdetten, W. Ger.	C3	18
Ems Jade Canal, W. Ger.	B3	18
Emsworth, Pa., U.S.	h13	115
Emyvale, Ire.	C5	11
Ena, Japan	n16	33
Ena, Mount, mtn., Japan	n16	33
Enard Bay, b., Scot., U.K.	B3	13
Encampment, Wy., U.S.	E6	127
Encampment, stm., U.S.	E6	127
Encantadas, Cape, c., Phil.	o13	34
Encarnación, Para.	C5	54
Encarnación de Díaz, Mex.	m12	63
Enchant, Alta.	D4	68
Enchi, Ghana	E4	45
Encinal, N.M., U.S.	*B2	108
Encinal, Tx., U.S.	E3	120
Encinitas, Ca., U.S.	F5	82
Encino, N.M., U.S.	C4	108
Encino, Tx., U.S.	F3	120
Encontrados, Ven.	B3	60
Encounter Bay, b., Austl.	G6	50
Endako, B.C.	B5	69
Endako, stm., B.C.	B5	69
Ende, Indon.	G6	35
Endeavor, Wi., U.S.	E4	126
Endeavour, Sask.	C4	75
Endelave, Den.	C4	15
Endelave, i., Den.	C4	15
Enderby, B.C.	D8	69
Enderby Land, reg., Ant.	C18	7
Enderlin, N.D., U.S.	C8	111
Enders Reservoir, res., Ne., U.S.	D4	68
Endiang, Alta.	D4	68
Endicott, Ne., U.S.	D8	104
Endicott, N.Y., U.S.	C4	109
Endicott, Wa., U.S.	C8	124
Endicott Mountains, mts., Ak., U.S.	B9	79
Endless Lake, l., Me., U.S.	C4	96
Endwell, N.Y., U.S.	C4	109
Ene, stm., Peru	F4	58
Enebakk, Nor.	p29	14
Energetik, Sov. Un.	F9	28
Enewetak, atoll, Marsh Is.	F9	6
Enewetak Island, i., Marsh Is.	S18	52
Enez, Tur.	B6	40
Enfield, Austl.	*F6	50
Enfield, N.S.	E6	71

Enfield (part of London), Eng., U.K. — k12 10
Enfield, Ct., U.S. — B5 84
Enfield, Il., U.S. — E5 90
Enfield, Me., U.S. — C4 96
Enfield, N.H., U.S. — C2 106
Enfield, N.C., U.S. — A5 110
Enfield Center, N.H., U.S. — C2 106
Engadine, Mi., U.S. — B5 99
Engaño, Cabo, c., Dom. Rep. — D11 33
Engebi, i., Marsh Is. — S18 52
'En Gedi, Isr. — C7 41
Engelberg, Switz. — C4 20
Engelhard, N.C., U.S. — B7 110
Engels, Sov. Un. — F16 27
Engels, W. Ger. — A6 21
'En Gev, Isr. — B7 41
Enghien, Bel. — D4 17
Enghien, Fr. — g10 16
England, Ar., U.S. — C4 81
England, ter., U.K. — D6 10
England Air Force Base, mil., La., U.S. — C3 95
Englee, Newf. — C3 72
Engleféld, Sask. — E3 75
Engleside, Va., U.S. — g12 123
Englevale, N.D., U.S. — C8 111
Englewood, Co., U.S. — B6 83
Englewood, Fl., U.S. — F4 86
Englewood, Ks., U.S. — E4 93
Englewood, N.J., U.S. — B5 107
Englewood, Oh., U.S. — C1 112
Englewood, Tn., U.S. — D9 119
Englewood Cliffs, N.J., U.S. — h9 107
English, In., U.S. — H5 91
English Bay, Ak., U.S. — h16 79
English Center, Pa., U.S. — D7 115
English Channel, strt., Eur. — F5 10
English Coast, Ant. — B5 7
English Creek, N.J., U.S. — E3 107
English Lake, In., U.S. — B4 91
Englishtown, N.J., U.S. — C4 107
Enguera, Spain — C5 22
'En Harod, Isr. — B7 41
Enid, Ms., U.S. — A4 101
Enid, Mt., U.S. — C12 103
Enid, Ok., U.S. — A4 113
Enid Lake, res., Ms., U.S. — A4 101
Enigma, Ga., U.S. — E3 87
Enilda, Alta. — B2 68
Enirik Island, i., Marsh Is. — P18 52
eNjesuthi, mtn., S. Afr. — C4 49
Enka, N.C., U.S. — f10 110
'En Kerem, Isr. — h11 41
Enkhuizen, Neth. — B5 17
Enköping, Swe. — H7 14
Enmore, Guy. — A3 59
Enna, Italy — F5 23
Ennadai Lake, l., N.W. Ter. — D12 66
Ennedi, plat., Chad — B4 46
Ennell, Lough, l., Ire. — D4 11
Enngonia, Austl. — D5 51
Ennigerloh, W. Ger. — B3 19
Enning, S.D., U.S. — C3 118
Ennis, Ire. — D2 10
Ennis, Mt., U.S. — E5 103
Ennis, Tx., U.S. — C4 120
Enniscorthy, Ire. — D3 10
Enniskillen, N. Ire., U.K. — C3 10
Ennistimon, Ire. — D2 10
Enns, Aus. — D7 18
Enns, stm., Aus. — D7 18
Ennylabegan Island, i., Marsh Is. — S17 52
Enoch, Ut., U.S. — F3 121
Enochs, Tx., U.S. — C1 120
Enola, Ar., U.S. — B3 81
Enola, Ne., U.S. — C8 104
Enon, Al., U.S. — C4 78
Enon, Oh., U.S. — C2 112
Enoree, S.C., U.S. — B4 117
Enoree, stm., S.C., U.S. — B3 117
Enos, In., U.S. — B3 91
Enosburg Falls, Vt., U.S. — B3 122
Enriquillo, Dom. Rep. — F8 64
Enriquillo, Lago, l., Dom. Rep. — E8 64
Enschede, Neth. — A7 16
Ensenada, Arg. — g8 54
Ensenada, Mex. — A1 63
Ensenada, N.M., U.S. — A3 108
Enshi, China — E6 31
Enshu Bay, b., Japan — I8 33
Ensign, Alta. — D4 68
Ensign, Ks., U.S. — E3 93
Ensign, Mi., U.S. — C4 99
Ensisheim, Fr. — g10 16
Ensley, Fl., U.S. — u14 86
Entebbe, Ug. — A5 48
Enterprise, Ont. — C8 73
Enterprise, Guy. — A3 59
Enterprise, Al., U.S. — D4 78
Enterprise, Il., U.S. — E5 90
Enterprise, Ia., U.S. — e8 92
Enterprise, Ks., U.S. — D6 93
Enterprise, La., U.S. — C4 95
Enterprise, Ms., U.S. — C5 101
Enterprise, Ok., U.S. — B6 113
Enterprise, Or., U.S. — B9 114
Enterprise, Ut., U.S. — F2 121
Enterprise, W.V., U.S. — B4 125
Entiat, Wa., U.S. — B5 124
Entiat, stm., Wa., U.S. — B5 124
Entiat, Lake, l., Wa., U.S. — B5 124
Entiat Mountains, mts., Wa., U.S. — B5 124
Entrance, Alta. — C2 68
Entraygues, Fr. — E5 16
Entrée, Île d', i., Que. — B8 71
Entre Minho e Douro, hist. reg., Port. — B1 22
Entre Ríos, prov., Arg. — A5 54
Entwistle, Alta. — C3 68
Enugu, Nig. — E6 45
Enumclaw, Wa., U.S. — B4 124
Envermeu, Fr. — E9 12
Envigado, Col. — *B2 60
Enville, Tn., U.S. — B3 119
Envira, Braz. — C3 58
Enyu Channel, strt., Marsh Is. — P18 52
Enyu Island, i., Marsh Is. — P18 52
Enz, stm., W. Ger. — D4 18
Enza, stm., Italy — E6 20
Enzan, Japan — n17 33
Eola, La., U.S. — D3 95
Eola Hills, hills, Or., U.S. — h11 114
Eolia, Mo., U.S. — B6 102
Eolie Islands, is., Italy — E5 23
Eoline, Al., U.S. — C2 78
Epe, Neth. — B5 17
Epéna, Congo — A2 48
Épernay, Fr. — C5 16
Epes, Al., U.S. — C1 78

Ephesus, Ga., U.S. — C1 87
Ephesus, hist., Tur. — D6 25
Ephraim, Ut., U.S. — D4 121
Ephraim, Wi., U.S. — C6 126
Ephrata, Pa., U.S. — F9 115
Ephrata, Wa., U.S. — B6 124
Épila, Spain — B5 22
Épinal [-sur-Seine], Fr. — g10 16
Épinay, Fr. — C7 16
Epiphany, S.D., U.S. — D8 118
Epirus, hist. reg., Grc. — C3 25
Epping, Eng., U.K. — k13 10
Epping, N.H., U.S. — D4 106
Epping, N.D., U.S. — A2 111
Eppingen, W. Ger. — D3 19
Epps, La., U.S. — B4 95
Epsom, In., U.S. — G3 91
Epsom [and Ewell], Eng., U.K. — m12 10
Epukiro, Nmb. — B2 49
Epworth, Ia., U.S. — B7 92
Eqlid, Iran — F6 39
Equality, Al., U.S. — C3 78
Equality, Il., U.S. — F5 90
Equatorial Guinea, ctry., Afr. — E1 46
Équeurdreville, Fr. — C3 16
Equinunk, Pa., U.S. — C11 115
Erath, La., U.S. — E3 95
Erath, co., Tx., U.S. — C3 120
Erba, Italy — E7 21
Erba, Jabal, mtn., Sud. — A4 47
Erbach, W. Ger. — D3 19
Erbacon, W.V., U.S. — C4 125
Erciş, Tur. — C14 40
Erciyes Mountain, mtn., Tur. — C10 40
Ercsi, Hung. — B4 24
Érd, Hung. — B4 24
Erdek, Tur. — B6 25
Erdene, Mong. — C7 31
Erdene-Dzuu, Mong. — B5 31
Erdenetsagaan, Mong. — B6 32
Erdenheim, Pa., U.S. — o21 115
Erding, W. Ger. — D5 18
Erebus, Mount, mtn., Ant. — B29 7
Erechim, Braz. — D2 56
Ereğli, Tur. — D10 40
Ereğli, Tur. — B8 40
Erenhot, China — C4 32
Eresós, Grc. — C5 25
Erétria (Néa Psará), Grc. — g11 25
Erfurt, E. Ger. — C5 18
Ergene, stm., Tur. — B6 40
Erhard, Mn., U.S. — D2 100
Eria, stm., Spain — A2 22
Erial, N.J., U.S. — D2 107
Eriboll, Loch, b., Scot., U.K. — B4 13
Erice, Italy — E4 23
Ericht, Loch, l., Scot., U.K. — D4 13
Erick, Ok., U.S. — B2 113
Erickson, B.C. — E9 69
Erickson, Man. — D2 70
Ericsburg, Mn., U.S. — B5 100
Ericson, Ne., U.S. — C7 104
Erie, Co., U.S. — A5 83
Erie, Il., U.S. — B3 90
Erie, Ks., U.S. — E8 93
Erie, Mi., U.S. — G7 99
Erie, N.D., U.S. — B8 111
Erie, Pa., U.S. — B1 115
Erie, co., N.Y., U.S. — C2 109
Erie, co., Oh., U.S. — A3 112
Erie, co., Pa., U.S. — C1 115
Erie, Lake, l., N.A. — B11 76
Erieau, Ont. — E3 73
Erie Canal, N.Y., U.S. — B5 109
Eriksdale, Man. — D2 70
Erímanthos, mtn., Grc. — D3 25
Erimo, Cape, c., Japan — C13 31
Erin, Ont. — D4 73
Erin, Tn., U.S. — A4 119
Erin Point, c., Trin. — O22 65
Erin Springs, Ok., U.S. — C4 113
Eriskay, i., Scot., U.K. — C1 13
Erisort, Loch, b., Scot., U.K. — B2 13
Erithraí, Grc. — C4 25
Eritrea, prov., Eth. — B4 47
Erkelenz, W. Ger. — C6 17
Erken, l., Swe. — t36 14
Erlangen, W. Ger. — D5 18
Erlanger, Ky., U.S. — A5 94
Erling, Lake, res., Ar., U.S. — D2 81
Erma, N.J., U.S. — F3 107
Ermelo, Neth. — B5 17
Ermelo, S. Afr. — C5 49
Ermenek, Tur. — D9 40
Ermont, Fr. — g10 16
Ermoúpolis (Syros), Grc. — D5 40
Erne, Upper Lough, l., Eur. — C3 10
Ernée, Fr. — C3 16
Ernest, Pa., U.S. — E3 115
Ernestina, Arg. — g7 54
Ernestville, Tn., U.S. — C11 119
Ernfold, Sask. — G2 75
Erode, India — *F6 36
Eromanga, Austl. — C4 51
Eros, La., U.S. — B3 95
Errigal Mountain, mtn., Ire. — C2 10
Erris Head, c., Ire. — C1 10
Errol, N.H., U.S. — A4 106
Errol Heights, Or., U.S. — *h12 114
Erskine, Alta. — C4 68
Erskine, Mn., U.S. — C3 100
Erstein, Fr. — C7 16
Erstfeld, Switz. — C4 20
Erving, Ma., U.S. — A3 98
Erwin, N.C., U.S. — B4 110
Erwin, S.D., U.S. — C8 118
Erwin, Tn., U.S. — C11 119
Erwin, W.V., U.S. — B5 125
Erwinville, La., U.S. — D4 95
Erwood, Sask. — E4 75
Erzincan, Tur. — C12 40
Erzurum, Tur. — C13 40
Esan, Cape, c., Japan — F10 33
Esashi, Japan — C13 31
Esbjerg, Den. — J3 14
Esbon, Ks., U.S. — C5 93
Escada, Braz. — k6 57
Escalante, Ut., U.S. — F4 121
Escalante, stm., Ut., U.S. — F4 121
Escalante Creek, stm., Co., U.S. — C2 83
Escalante Desert, des., Ut., U.S. — F2 121
Escalón, Mex. — B4 63
Escalon, Ca., U.S. — D3 82
Escambia, co., Al., U.S. — D2 78
Escambia, stm., Fl., U.S. — u14 86
Escanaba, Mi., U.S. — C3 99

Escanaba, stm., Mi., U.S. — B3 99
Escarpada Point, c., Phil. — B6 34
Escatawpa, Ms., U.S. — E5 101
Escatawpa, stm., U.S. — D5 101
Eschede, W. Ger. — F4 15
Eschenbach, W. Ger. — D6 19
Escholzmatt, Switz. — C4 21
Esch-sur-Alzette, Lux. — C7 16
Eschwege, W. Ger. — C5 18
Eschweiler, W. Ger. — C3 18
Escobal, Pan. — k11 62
Escocesa, Bahía, b., Dom. Rep. — E9 64
Escoheag, R.I., U.S. — E1 116
Escondido, N.M., U.S. — C3 108
Escondido, Ca., U.S. — F5 82
Escondido, stm., Nic. — D6 62
Escoumins, Rivière des, stm., Que. — A8 74
Escuinapa [de Hidalgo], Mex. — C3 63
Escuintla, Guat. — C2 62
Escuminac, Que. — A3 71
Escuminac, Point, c., N.B. — B5 71
Eséka, Cam. — E2 46
Esens, W. Ger. — A7 17
Eşfahān (Isfahan), Iran — B5 38
Esguevas, stm., Spain — B3 22
Esher (part of London), Eng., U.K. — m12 10
Eshimba, Zaire — C3 48
Eshkāshem, Afg. — C15 39
Eshowe, S. Afr. — C5 49
Esigodini, Zimb. — B4 49
Esk, stm., U.K. — E6 13
Esk, stm., Eng., U.K. — F5 13
Eskbank, Sask. — G2 75
Eskdale, W.V., U.S. — C3 125
Eske, Lough, l., Ire. — C3 11
Eskilstuna, Swe. — H7 14
Eskimo Lakes, l., N.W. Ter. — C6 66
Eskimo Point, N.W. Ter. — D14 66
Eskişehir, Tur. — C8 40
Esko, Mn., U.S. — D6 100
Eskridge, Ks., U.S. — D7 93
Esla, stm., Spain — B3 22
Eslāmābād, Iran — *D3 39
Eslarn, W. Ger. — D7 19
Eslava, stm., Mex. — h9 63
Eslöv, Swe. — C7 15
Eşme, Tur. — C7 25
Esmeralda, co., Nv., U.S. — F4 105
Esmeraldas, Ec. — A2 58
Esmeraldas, prov., Ec. — A2 58
Esmond, Il., U.S. — A5 90
Esmond, N.D., U.S. — A6 111
Esmond, R.I., U.S. — B4 116
Esmont, Va., U.S. — C4 123
Esom Hill, Ga., U.S. — C1 87
Espada, Punta, c., Col. — A3 60
Espanola, Ont. — A4 73
Espanola, Fl., U.S. — C5 86
Espanola, N.M., U.S. — B3 108
Española, Wa., U.S. — g13 124
Española, Isla (Hood), i., Ec. — g6 58
Esparto, Ca., U.S. — C2 82
Esperance, Austl. — F3 50
Esperance, Wa., U.S. — *B3 124
Esperanza, Peru — C3 58
Esperanza, Tx., U.S. — o12 120
Esperanza, stm., Pan. — k12 62
Esperanza, sci., Ant. — C7 7
Espichel, Cape, c., Port. — C1 22
Espinal, Col. — C5 60
Espinhaço, Serra do, mts., Braz. — E6 53
Espírito Santo, state, Braz. — B4 56
Espírito Santo, i., Vanuatu — H10 6
Espita, Mex. — C7 63
Espoo, Fin. — *G11 14
Esposende, Port. — B1 22
Espungabera, Moz. — B5 49
Espy, Pa., U.S. — D9 115
Espyville Station, Pa., U.S. — C1 115
Esquatzel Coulee, val., Wa., U.S. — C6 124
Esquel, Arg. — C2 54
Esquimalt, B.C. — E6 69
Esquina, Arg. — F4 55
Essaouira (Mogador), Mor. — C4 17
Essen, Bel. — B7 17
Essen, W. Ger. — C3 18
Essendon, Austl. — *G7 50
Essendon, Mount, mtn., Austl. — D3 50
Essequibo, stm., Guy. — B3 59
Essex, Ont. — E2 73
Essex, Ca., U.S. — E6 82
Essex, Ct., U.S. — D6 84
Essex, Ia., U.S. — D2 92
Essex, Md., U.S. — B4 97
Essex, Ma., U.S. — A6 98
Essex, Mo., U.S. — E8 102
Essex, Mt., U.S. — B3 103
Essex, N.Y., U.S. — f11 109
Essex, Vt., U.S. — B2 122
Essex, co., Ont. — E2 73
Essex, co., Eng., U.K. — C8 12
Essex, co., Ma., U.S. — A5 98
Essex, co., N.J., U.S. — B4 107
Essex, co., N.Y., U.S. — A7 109
Essex, co., Vt., U.S. — B5 122
Essex, co., Va., U.S. — C6 123
Essex, Punta, c., Ec. — g5 58
Essex Fells, N.J., U.S. — *B4 107
Essex Junction, Vt., U.S. — C2 122
Essexville, Mi., U.S. — E7 99
Es' Sider, Libya — C3 43
Esslingen, W. Ger. — D4 18
Essonne, dept., Fr. — F2 17
Est, Île de l', i., Que. — B8 71
Est, Pointe de l', c., Que. — B8 71
Estacada, Or., U.S. — B4 114
Estacado, Llano, pl., U.S. — C1 120
Estados, Isla de los, i., Arg. — h13 54
Eşţahbān, Iran — F9 39
Estaire, Ont. — A4 73
Estância, Braz. — B3 57
Estancia, N.M., U.S. — C3 108
Estarreja, Port. — B1 22
Estcourt, S. Afr. — C5 49
Este, Italy — B3 23
Este, Punta, c., P.R. — B3 64
Estelí, Nic. — E7 63
Estella, Spain — A4 22
Estelle, La., U.S. — *E5 95
Estelline, S.D., U.S. — C9 118
Estelline, Tx., U.S. — B2 120
Estell Manor, N.J., U.S. — D3 107
Estepa, Spain — D3 22
Estepona, Spain — D3 22
Esterbrook, Wy., U.S. — D7 127
Esterhazy, Sask. — G4 75
Esternay, Fr. — F3 17

Esternberg, Aus. — E8 19
Estero, Fl., U.S. — F5 86
Estero Bay, b., Ca., U.S. — E3 82
Estero Bay, b., Fl., U.S. — F5 86
Estero Island, i., Fl., U.S. — F5 86
Estes Park, Co., U.S. — A5 83
Estevan, Sask. — H4 75
Estevan Group, is., B.C. — C3 69
Estevan Point, B.C. — E4 69
Esther, Alta. — D5 68
Estherville, Ia., U.S. — A3 92
Estherwood, La., U.S. — D3 95
Estill, Ms., U.S. — B3 101
Estill, S.C., U.S. — F5 117
Estill, co., Ky., U.S. — C6 94
Estillfork, Al., U.S. — A3 78
Estill Springs, Tn., U.S. — B5 119
Estlin, Sask. — G3 75
Eston, Sask. — F1 75
Estonia, state, Sov. Un. — D5 29
Estrées-Saint-Denis, Fr. — E2 17
Estrela, Braz. — *B2 22
Estrela, mtn., Port. — *B2 22
Estrela, Serra da, mts., Port. — B2 22
Estrela do Norte, Braz. — A3 56
Estrela do Sul, Braz. — B3 56
Estremadura, hist. reg., Port. — C1 22
Estremadura, hist. reg., Spain — C2 22
Estremoz, Port. — C2 22
Esztergom, Hung. — B4 24
Etah, Grnld. — B13 61
Étain, Fr. — E5 17
Étalans, Fr. — B1 21
Étampes, Fr. — C5 16
Étang-du-Nord, Que. — B8 71
Étaples, Fr. — B4 16
Etāwah, India — G8 37
Eternity Range, mts., Ant. — C6 7
Ethan, S.D., U.S. — D8 118
Ethel, Ont. — D3 73
Ethel, Mo., U.S. — B5 102
Ethel, Ms., U.S. — C4 101
Ethel, W.V., U.S. — n12 125
Ethelbert, Man. — D1 70
Ethelsville, Al., U.S. — B1 78
Ethete, Wy., U.S. — C4 127
Ether, N.C., U.S. — B3 110
Ethiopia, ctry., Afr. — D4 47
Ethiopian Plateau, plat., Eth. — D4 47
Ethridge, Mt., U.S. — B5 103
Ethridge, Tn., U.S. — B4 119
Etive, Loch, l., Scot., U.K. — D3 13
Etlan, Va., U.S. — B4 123
Etna, Ca., U.S. — B2 82
Etna, Me., U.S. — D3 96
Etna, N.H., U.S. — C2 106
Etna, N.Y., U.S. — C4 109
Etna, Oh., U.S. — C3 112
Etna, Pa., U.S. — k14 115
Etna, Wy., U.S. — C1 127
Etna, Mount, mtn., Italy — F5 23
Etna Green, In., U.S. — B5 91
Etobicoke, Ont. — D5 73
Etolin Island, i., Ak., U.S. — m23 79
Etolin Strait, strt., Ak., U.S. — C6 79
Eton, Ga., U.S. — B2 87
Etoshapan, pl., Nmb. — A2 49
Etowah, Ar., U.S. — B5 81
Etowah, Tn., U.S. — D9 119
Etowah, co., Al., U.S. — A3 78
Etowah, stm., Ga., U.S. — B2 87
Etra, N.J., U.S. — C3 107
Étreat, Fr. — C4 16
Étroubles, Italy — E3 21
Etta, Ms., U.S. — A4 101
Ettelbruck, Lux. — E6 17
Etten, i., Micron. — Q18 52
Etter, Tx., U.S. — B2 120
Ettersbeek, Bel. — *D4 17
Etters, Pa., U.S. — F8 115
Ettlingen, W. Ger. — E5 19
Ettrick, Va., U.S. — C5 123
Ettrick, Wi., U.S. — D2 126
Etzatlán, Mex. — m11 63
Etzikom, Alta. — E5 68
Etzikom Coulee, stm., Alta. — E5 68
Eu, Fr. — B4 16
Euboea see Évvoia, i., Grc. — C4 40
Eucha, Ok., U.S. — A7 113
Euclid, Mn., U.S. — C2 100
Euclid, Oh., U.S. — A4 112
Eucumbene, Lake, l., Austl. — H7 51
Eudora, Ar., U.S. — D4 81
Eudora, Ks., U.S. — D8 93
Eudunda, Austl. — G2 51
Eufaula, Al., U.S. — D4 78
Eufaula, Ok., U.S. — B6 113
Eufaula Lake, res., Ok., U.S. — B6 113
Eugene, Mo., U.S. — C5 102
Eugene, Or., U.S. — C3 114
Eugenia, Punta, c., Mex. — B1 63
Eulaton, Al., U.S. — B3 78
Euless, Tx., U.S. — *n9 120
Eulonia, Ga., U.S. — E5 87
Eunice, La., U.S. — D3 95
Eunice, N.M., U.S. — E6 108
Eupen, Bel. — B7 16
Euphrates, stm., Asia — B3 38
Eupora, Ms., U.S. — B4 101
Eure, stm., Fr. — C4 16
Eure, dept., Fr. — C4 16
Eure-et-Loir, dept., Fr. — C4 16
Eureka, N.W. Ter. — m34 66
Eureka, Ca., U.S. — B1 82
Eureka, Il., U.S. — C4 90
Eureka, Ks., U.S. — E7 93
Eureka, Mt., U.S. — B1 103
Eureka, Nv., U.S. — D6 105
Eureka, N.C., U.S. — B5 110
Eureka, S.C., U.S. — D5 117
Eureka, S.D., U.S. — B6 118
Eureka, Ut., U.S. — D3 121
Eureka, W.V., U.S. — B3 124
Eureka, co., Nv., U.S. — D5 105
Eureka Sound, strt., N.W. Ter. — m34 66
Eureka Springs, Ar., U.S. — A2 81
Euroa, Austl. — H5 51
Europa, Île, i., Reu. — B7 49
Europa Point, c., Gib. — D3 22
Europe, cont. — E13 8
Euskirchen, W. Ger. — C3 18
Eustis, Fl., U.S. — D5 86
Eustis, Me., U.S. — C2 96
Eustis, Ne., U.S. — D5 104

Eutaw, Al., U.S. — C2 78
Eutawville, S.C., U.S. — E7 117
Eutin, W. Ger. — D4 15
Eutsuk Lake, l., B.C. — C4 69
Eva, Tn., U.S. — A3 119
Evale, Ang. — E2 48
Evangeline, stm., Italy — E4 21
Evangeline, co., La., U.S. — D3 95
Evangeline, La., U.S. — D3 95
Evans, Co., U.S. — A6 83
Evans, Ga., U.S. — C4 87
Evans, La., U.S. — C2 95
Evans, W.V., U.S. — C3 125
Evans, co., Ga., U.S. — D5 87
Evans, Lac, l., Que. — o20 73
Evans, Mount, mtn., Co., U.S. — B5 83
Evansburg, Alta. — C3 68
Evans City, Pa., U.S. — E1 115
Evansdale, Ia., U.S. — B5 92
Evans Mills, N.Y., U.S. — A5 109
Evansport, Oh., U.S. — A1 112
Evanston, Il., U.S. — A6 90
Evanston, Ky., U.S. — C6 94
Evanston, Wy., U.S. — E2 127
Evansville, Ar., U.S. — B1 81
Evansville, Il., U.S. — E4 90
Evansville, In., U.S. — I2 91
Evansville, Mn., U.S. — D3 100
Evansville, Ms., U.S. — A3 101
Evansville, Vt., U.S. — B4 122
Evansville, Wi., U.S. — F4 126
Evansville, Wy., U.S. — D6 127
Evant, Tx., U.S. — D3 120
Evanton, Scot., U.K. — C4 13
Evart, Mi., U.S. — E5 99
Evarts, Ky., U.S. — D6 94
Eveleth, Mn., U.S. — C6 100
Evelyn, La., U.S. — C2 95
Evening Shade, Ar., U.S. — A4 81
Even Yehuda, Isr. — f10 41
Everard, Lake, l., Austl. — F5 50
Everest, Ks., U.S. — C8 93
Everest, Mount, mtn., Asia — C5 36
Everett, Ont. — E5 73
Everett, Ga., U.S. — E5 87
Everett, Ma., U.S. — g11 98
Everett, Pa., U.S. — F5 115
Everett, Wa., U.S. — B3 124
Everett, Mount, mtn., Ma., U.S. — B1 98
Everett Lake, res., N.H., U.S. — D3 106
Everettville, W.V., U.S. — h10 125
Evergem, Bel. — C3 17
Everglades National Park, Fl., U.S. — G5 86
Evergreen, Al., U.S. — D3 78
Evergreen, Co., U.S. — B5 83
Evergreen, La., U.S. — D3 95
Evergreen, Ms., U.S. — A5 101
Evergreen, N.C., U.S. — C4 110
Evergreen, Va., U.S. — C4 123
Evergreen Park, Il., U.S. — k9 90
Everly, Ia., U.S. — A2 92
Everman, Tx., U.S. — *n9 120
Everson, Pa., U.S. — F2 115
Everson, Wa., U.S. — A3 124
Everton, Ar., U.S. — A3 81
Everton, Mo., U.S. — D4 102
Evesham, Eng., U.K. — B6 12
Évian-les-Bains, Fr. — C2 20
Evington, Va., U.S. — C3 123
Evolène, Switz. — D3 21
Évora, Port. — C2 22
Évreux, Fr. — C4 16
Évron, Fr. — C3 16
Évros (Maritsa) (Meriç), stm., Eur. — B6 25
Évvoia (Euboea), i., Grc. — C4 40
Évvoia, Gulf of, b., Grc. — C4 40
Ewa, Hi., U.S. — B3 88
Ewa Beach, Hi., U.S. — g9 88
Ewan, Wa., U.S. — B8 124
Ewarton, Jam. — E14 65
Ewell, Md., U.S. — D5 97
Ewen, Mi., U.S. — m12 99
Ewing, Il., U.S. — E5 90
Ewing, Mo., U.S. — A6 102
Ewing, Ne., U.S. — B7 104
Ewing Township, N.J., U.S. — C3 107
Ewo, Congo — B1 48
Exaltación, Bol. — B2 55
Excel, Alta. — D5 68
Excel, Al., U.S. — D2 78
Excello, Mo., U.S. — B5 102
Excelsior Mountain, mtn., Ca., U.S. — C4 82
Excelsior Mountains, mts., Nv., U.S. — E3 105
Excelsior Springs, Mo., U.S. — B3 102
Exchange, Pa., U.S. — D8 115
Exchange, W.V., U.S. — C4 125
Exe, stm., Eng., U.K. — D4 12
Executive Committee Range, mts., Ant. — B36 7
Exeland, Wi., U.S. — C2 126
Exeter, Ont. — D3 73
Exeter, Eng., U.K. — E5 10
Exeter, Ca., U.S. — D4 82
Exeter, Me., U.S. — D3 96
Exeter, Mo., U.S. — E4 102
Exeter, N.H., U.S. — E5 106
Exeter, Pa., U.S. — D10 115
Exeter, R.I., U.S. — D3 116
Exeter, stm., N.H., U.S. — E5 106
Exira, Ia., U.S. — C3 92
Exmoor, for., Eng., U.K. — E5 10
Exmore, Va., U.S. — C7 123
Exmouth, Austl. — D1 50
Exmouth, Eng., U.K. — E5 10
Exmouth Gulf, b., Austl. — D1 50
Expanse, Sask. — H3 75
Experiment, Ga., U.S. — C2 87
Exploits, stm., Newf. — D3 72
Exploits, Bay of, b., Newf. — D4 72
Exploits Point, c., Newf. — D4 72
Extension, B.C. — f12 69
Extrema, Braz. — m8 56
Exuma Sound, strt., Bah. — B5 64
Eyak, Ak., U.S. — C10 79

Eyasi, Lake, l., Tan. — B6 48
Eyebrow, Sask. — G2 75
Eyehill Creek, stm., Can. — C5 68
Eyemouth, Scot., U.K. — C5 10
Eye Peninsula, pen., Scot., U.K. — B2 13
Eyl, Som. — D6 47
Eylar Mountain, mtn., Ca., U.S. — D3 82
Eynort, Loch, b., Scot., U.K. — C1 13
Eyota, Mn., U.S. — G6 100
Eyre, Sask. — F1 75
Eyre North, Lake, l., Austl. — E6 50
Eyre Peninsula, pen., Austl. — F6 50
Ezeiza, Arg. — g7 54
Ezine, Tur. — C6 25

F

Fabens, Tx., U.S. — o11 120
Faber, Va., U.S. — C4 123
Faber Lake, l., N.W. Ter. — D9 66
Fabius, N.Y., U.S. — C5 109
Fabius, stm., Mo., U.S. — A6 102
Fåborg, Den. — C4 15
Fabriano, Italy — C4 23
Fabyan, Ct., U.S. — A8 84
Facatativá, Col. — C3 60
Fachi, Niger — C7 45
Fackler, Al., U.S. — A4 78
Facpi Point, c., Guam — M9 52
Factoryville, Pa., U.S. — C10 115
Fada, Chad — B4 46
Fada Ngourma, Burkina — D5 45
Faddeya Gulf, b., Sov. Un. — B3 128
Faddey Island, i., Sov. Un. — B17 29
Fadian Point, c., Guam — L10 52
Faenza, Italy — B3 23
Faeroe Islands, ctry., Eur. — C7 8
Fafa, Mali — C5 45
Fafe, Port. — B1 22
Fafen, stm., Eth. — D5 47
Faga'alu, Am. Sam. — F13 52
Fagaitua Bay, b., Am. Sam. — G13 52
Fagaloa Bay, b., Am. Sam. — F12 52
Fagamalo, W. Sam. — F11 52
Fågăraş, Rom. — C7 24
Fagatogo, Am. Sam. — F13 52
Fågelbro, Swe. — t36 14
Fagernes, Nor. — G3 14
Fagersta, Swe. — G6 14
Fago, Nig. — D6 45
Faguibine, Lac, l., Mali — C4 45
Fagus, Mo., U.S. — E7 102
Faial, i., Port. — g8 44
Faichuk, is., Micron. — Q18 52
Faiacres, N.M., U.S. — E3 108
Fairbairn Reservoir, res., Austl. — A7 51
Fairbank, Az., U.S. — F5 80
Fairbank, Ia., U.S. — B5 92
Fairbanks, Ak., U.S. — C10 79
Fairbanks, Fl., U.S. — C4 86
Fairbanks, In., U.S. — F2 91
Fairbanks, La., U.S. — B3 95
Fairborn, Oh., U.S. — C1 112
Fairburn, Ga., U.S. — C2 87
Fairburn, S.D., U.S. — D2 118
Fairbury, Il., U.S. — C5 90
Fairbury, Ne., U.S. — D8 104
Fairchance, Pa., U.S. — G2 115
Fairchild, Wi., U.S. — D3 126
Fairchild Air Force Base, mil., Wa., U.S. — g13 124
Fairdale, Ky., U.S. — B4 94
Fairdale, N.D., U.S. — A7 111
Fairfax, Ca., U.S. — C2 82
Fairfax, De., U.S. — A3 85
Fairfax, Ia., U.S. — C6 92
Fairfax, Mn., U.S. — F4 100
Fairfax, Mo., U.S. — A2 102
Fairfax, Ok., U.S. — A5 113
Fairfax, S.C., U.S. — F5 117
Fairfax, S.D., U.S. — D7 118
Fairfax, Vt., U.S. — B2 122
Fairfax, Va., U.S. — B5 123
Fairfax, co., Va., U.S. — g12 123
Fairfax Station, Va., U.S. — *F9 50
Fairfield, Austl. — *F9 50
Fairfield, Al., U.S. — B3 78
Fairfield, Ca., U.S. — C2 82
Fairfield, Ct., U.S. — E2 84
Fairfield, Id., U.S. — F4 89
Fairfield, Il., U.S. — E5 90
Fairfield, Ia., U.S. — C6 92
Fairfield, Ky., U.S. — C4 94
Fairfield, Me., U.S. — D3 96
Fairfield, Mt., U.S. — C5 103
Fairfield, Ne., U.S. — D7 104
Fairfield, N.J., U.S. — *B4 107
Fairfield, N.C., U.S. — B6 110
Fairfield, Oh., U.S. — n12 112
Fairfield, Tx., U.S. — D4 120
Fairfield, Vt., U.S. — B2 122
Fairfield, co., Ct., U.S. — D2 84
Fairfield, co., Oh., U.S. — C3 112
Fairfield, co., S.C., U.S. — C5 117
Fairfield Bay, Ar., U.S. — B3 81
Fairfield Pond, l., Vt., U.S. — B3 122
Fairgrove, Mi., U.S. — E7 99
Fair Grove, Mo., U.S. — D4 102
Fair Grove, N.C., U.S. — B2 110
Fairhaven, Ma., U.S. — C6 98
Fair Haven, Mi., U.S. — F8 99
Fair Haven, Mn., U.S. — E4 100
Fair Haven, N.J., U.S. — C4 107
Fair Haven, N.Y., U.S. — B4 109
Fair Haven, Vt., U.S. — D2 122
Fair Head, c., N. Ire., U.K. — D1 75
Fairholme, Sask. — D1 75
Fairland, Il., U.S. — D5 90
Fairland, Ok., U.S. — A7 113
Fair Lawn, N.J., U.S. — h8 107
Fairlawn, Oh., U.S. — *A4 112
Fairlea, W.V., U.S. — D4 125
Fairlee, Md., U.S. — B5 97
Fairlee, Vt., U.S. — D4 122
Fairlight, Sask. — H5 75
Fairmont, Il., U.S. — C6 90
Fairmont, Mn., U.S. — G4 100
Fairmont, Ne., U.S. — D8 104

Name	Map Ref.	Page
Fairmont, N.C., U.S.	C3	110
Fairmont, Ok., U.S.	A4	113
Fairmont, S.C., U.S.	B3	117
Fairmont, W.V., U.S.	g12	123
Fairmount, Ga., U.S.	B2	87
Fairmount, Il., U.S.	C6	90
Fairmount, In., U.S.	D6	91
Fairmount, Ks., U.S.	k16	93
Fairmount, Md., U.S.	D6	97
Fairmount, N.Y., U.S.	*B4	109
Fairmount, N.D., U.S.	C9	111
Fairmount Heights, Md., U.S.	f9	97
Fair Oaks, Ar., U.S.	B4	81
Fair Oaks, Ca., U.S.	*C3	82
Fair Oaks, Ga., U.S.	h7	87
Fair Oaks, In., U.S.	B3	91
Fairoaks, Pa., U.S.	h13	115
Fair Plain, Mi., U.S.	F4	99
Fairplay, Co., U.S.	B5	83
Fair Play, Md., U.S.	A2	97
Fair Play, Mo., U.S.	D4	102
Fair Play, S.C., U.S.	B2	117
Fairpoint, Oh., U.S.	B5	112
Fairpoint, S.D., U.S.	C3	118
Fairport, Ia., U.S.	C7	92
Fairport, Mi., U.S.	C4	99
Fairport, Mo., U.S.	B3	102
Fairport, N.Y., U.S.	B3	109
Fair Port, Va., U.S.	C6	123
Fairton, N.J., U.S.	E2	107
Fairvale, N.B.	D4	71
Fairview, Alta.	A1	68
Fairview, Ar., U.S.	*D4	81
Fairview, Il., U.S.	C3	90
Fairview, In., U.S.	D7	91
Fairview, Ks., U.S.	C8	93
Fairview, Ky., U.S.	D2	94
Fairview, Mi., U.S.	D6	99
Fairview, Mt., U.S.	E3	102
Fairview, Mt., U.S.	C12	103
Fairview, N.J., U.S.	D3	107
Fairview, N.J., U.S.	h8	107
Fairview, N.Y., U.S.	*D7	109
Fairview, Oh., U.S.	B4	112
Fairview, Ok., U.S.	A3	113
Fairview, Or., U.S.	*B4	114
Fairview, Pa., U.S.	B1	115
Fairview, S.D., U.S.	D9	118
Fairview, Tn., U.S.	B4	119
Fairview, Ut., U.S.	D4	121
Fairview, W.V., U.S.	B3	125
Fairview, Wy., U.S.	D2	127
Fairview Heights, Il., U.S.	E3	90
Fairview Park, In., U.S.	E3	91
Fairview Park, Oh., U.S.	h9	112
Fairview Peak, mtn., Nv., U.S.	D3	105
Fairview Peak, mtn., Or., U.S.	D4	114
Fairview Shores, Fl., U.S.	*D5	86
Fair Water, Wi., U.S.	E5	126
Fairway, Ks., U.S.	k16	93
Fairweather, Mount, mtn., N.A.	D12	79
Fairwood, Wa., U.S.	*B8	124
Fairwood, Wa., U.S.	*B3	124
Fairy Glen, Sask.	D3	75
Faisalabad (Lyallpur), Pak.	B5	36
Faison, N.C., U.S.	B4	110
Faith, N.C., U.S.	B2	110
Faith, S.D., U.S.	B3	118
Faithorn, Mi., U.S.	C3	99
Faizābād (Fyzabad), India	C7	36
Fajardo, P.R.	G12	64
Fakenham, Eng., U.K.	B8	12
Fakfak, Indon.	F8	34
Fakse, Den.	C6	15
Fakse Bugt, b., Den.	C6	15
Fakse Ladeplads, Den.	C6	15
Faku, China	C10	32
Fal, stm., Eng., U.K.	D3	12
Falaba, S.L.	E2	45
Falaise, Fr.	C3	16
Falalu, i., Micron.	Q18	52
Fălciu, Rom.	B9	24
Falcon, Ar., U.S.	D2	81
Falcon, Co., U.S.	C6	83
Falcon, Ms., U.S.	A3	101
Falcon, N.C., U.S.	B4	110
Falcón, state, Ven.	A4	60
Falconer, N.Y., U.S.	C1	109
Falcon Heights, Mn., U.S.	n12	100
Falcon Heights, Or., U.S.	E5	114
Falcon Lake, res., N.A.	F3	120
Faléa, Mali	D2	45
Falefa Harbour, b., W. Sam.	F12	52
Falelima, W. Sam.	F11	52
Falémé, stm., Afr.	D2	45
Faleolo International Airport, W. Sam.	F12	52
Faleshty, Sov. Un.	B8	24
Falfurrias, Tx., U.S.	F3	120
Falher, Alta.	B2	68
Falkenberg, E. Ger.	B8	19
Falkenberg, Swe.	B6	15
Falkenstein, E. Ger.	C7	19
Falkirk, Scot., U.K.	C5	10
Falkland, N.D., U.S.	B4	111
Falkland, B.C.	D8	69
Falkland Islands (Islas Malvinas), dep., S.A.	I5	53
Falkner, Ms., U.S.	A5	101
Falköping, Swe.	H5	14
Falkville, Al., U.S.	A3	78
Fall, W. Ger.	B7	20
Fall, stm., Ks., U.S.	E7	93
Fall Branch, Tn., U.S.	C11	119
Fallbrook, Ca., U.S.	F5	82
Fall City, Wa., U.S.	B4	124
Fall Creek, Wi., U.S.	D2	126
Fall Creek, stm., In., U.S.	k10	91
Fallentimber, Pa., U.S.	E4	115
Falling Creek, stm., Va., U.S.	n17	123
Falling Rock Creek, stm., W.V., U.S.	m13	125
Falling Water, Tn., U.S.	h11	119
Falling Waters, W.V., U.S.	B6	125
Fallis, Ok., U.S.	B4	113
Fall Mountain Lake, Ct., U.S.	C4	84
Fällnäs, Swe.	u35	14
Fallon, Mt., U.S.	D11	103
Fallon, Nv., U.S.	D3	105
Fallon, co., Mt., U.S.	D12	103
Fallon Indian Reservation, Nv., U.S.	D3	105
Fallon Naval Air Station, mil., Nv., U.S.	D3	105
Fall River, Ks., U.S.	E7	93
Fall River, Ma., U.S.	C5	98
Fall River, Wi., U.S.	E4	126
Fall River, co., S.D., U.S.	D2	118
Fall River Lake, res., Ks., U.S.	E7	93
Fall River Mills, Ca., U.S.	B3	82
Fall Rock, Ky., U.S.	C6	94
Falls, Pa., U.S.	D10	115
Falls, co., Tx., U.S.	D4	120
Fallsburg, N.Y., U.S.		
Falls Church, Va., U.S.	g12	123
Falls City, Ne., U.S.	D10	104
Falls City, Tx., U.S.		
Falls Creek, Pa., U.S.	D4	115
Fallston, Md., U.S.	A5	97
Fallston, N.C., U.S.	B1	110
Falls Township, Pa., U.S.	*F12	115
Falmouth, Jam.	E5	71
Falmouth, Eng., U.K.	E4	10
Falmouth, Il., U.S.	E7	91
Falmouth, Ky., U.S.	B5	94
Falmouth, Me., U.S.	E2	96
Falmouth, Ma., U.S.	C6	98
Falmouth, Mi., U.S.	D5	99
Falmouth, Va., U.S.	B5	123
Falmouth Bay, b., Eng., U.K.	D2	12
Falsa Chipana, Punta, c., Chile	D1	55
False Bay, b., S. Afr.	D2	49
False Cape, c., Fl., U.S.	D6	86
False Cape, c., Va., U.S.	D7	123
Falso, Cabo, c., Hond.	C6	62
Falster, i., Den.	D5	15
Falsterbo, Swe.	J6	14
Fălticeni, Rom.	B8	24
Falun, Swe.	G6	14
Falun, Ks., U.S.	D6	93
Famagusta see Gazimağusa, N. Cyp.	E9	40
Famatina, Sierra de, mts., Arg.	E2	55
Family Lake, l., Man.	D4	70
Fanan, i., Micron.	Q18	52
Fanapanges, i., Micron.	Q18	52
Fancy Farm, Ky., U.S.	f9	94
Fancy Prairie, Il., U.S.	D4	90
Fang, Thai.	B1	34
Fangcheng, China	H5	32
Fangxian, China	E7	31
Fannettsburg, Pa., U.S.	F6	115
Fannin, Tx., U.S.	E4	120
Fannin, co., Ga., U.S.	B2	87
Fannin, co., Tx., U.S.	C4	120
Fanning Island see Tabuaeran Island, atoll, Kir.	F12	6
Fanny, Mount, mtn., Or., U.S.	B9	114
Fanny Bay, B.C.	E5	69
Fannystelle, Man.	E3	70
Fano, Italy	C4	23
Fanø, i., Den.	C2	15
Fanø Bugt, b., Den.	C2	15
Fan Si Pan, mtn., Viet.	A5	35
Fanwood, N.J., U.S.	*B4	107
Fāqūs, Eg.	D3	41
Faradje, Zaire	A4	48
Faradofay, Madag.	h9	49
Farafangana, Madag.	h9	49
Farafirah, Al Wāḥat al, well, Eg.	C2	38
Farāh, Afg.	B3	36
Farah, stm., Afg.	B3	36
Farallón, Punta, c., Mex.	n11	63
Faramana, Burkina	D4	45
Faranah, Gui.	D4	45
Farasan Islands, is., Sau. Ar.	D4	38
Farber, Mo., U.S.	B6	102
Fareham, Eng., U.K.	D6	12
Farewell, Cape, c., N.Z.	N14	51
Fargo, Ga., U.S.	F4	87
Fargo, N.D., U.S.	C9	111
Fargo, Ok., U.S.	A2	113
Faribault, Mn., U.S.	F5	100
Faribault, co., Mn., U.S.	G4	100
Farīdpur, Bngl.	F12	37
Fārigh, Wādī al, val., Libya	G3	40
Farīmān, Iran	D9	39
Farina, Austl.	E2	51
Farina, Il., U.S.	E5	90
Fāriskūr, Eg.	C3	41
Farley, Ia., U.S.	B6	92
Farley, Mo., U.S.	B3	102
Farley, N.M., U.S.	A5	108
Farmer, Oh., U.S.	A1	112
Farmer, S.D., U.S.	D8	118
Farmer City, Il., U.S.	C5	90
Farmers, Ky., U.S.	B6	94
Farmers Branch, Tx., U.S.	n10	120
Farmersburg, In., U.S.	F3	91
Farmersburg, Ia., U.S.	B6	92
Farmersville, Ca., U.S.	*D4	82
Farmersville, Il., U.S.	D4	90
Farmersville, Tx., U.S.	C4	120
Farmerville, La., U.S.	B3	95
Farmingdale, Me., U.S.	D3	96
Farmingdale, N.J., U.S.	*C4	107
Farmingdale, N.Y., U.S.	*n15	109
Farmington, Ar., U.S.	A1	81
Farmington, Ct., U.S.	C4	84
Farmington, De., U.S.	E3	85
Farmington, Il., U.S.	C3	90
Farmington, Ia., U.S.	D6	92
Farmington, Me., U.S.	D2	96
Farmington, Mi., U.S.	p15	99
Farmington, Mn., U.S.	F5	100
Farmington, Mo., U.S.	D7	102
Farmington, N.H., U.S.	D4	106
Farmington, N.M., U.S.	A1	108
Farmington, N.C., U.S.	A2	110
Farmington, Pa., U.S.	G2	115
Farmington, Ut., U.S.	B4	121
Farmington, Wa., U.S.	B8	124
Farmington, stm., Ct., U.S.	B4	84
Farmington, West Branch, stm., U.S.	B4	84
Farmington Hills, Mi., U.S.	o15	99
Farmingville, N.Y., U.S.	*n15	109
Farmland, In., U.S.	D7	91
Farm Pond, l., Ma., U.S.	h10	98
Farmville, N.C., U.S.	B5	110
Farmville, Va., U.S.	C4	123
Farnam, Ne., U.S.	D5	104
Farne Islands, is., Eng., U.K.	C6	12
Farner, Tn., U.S.	D9	119
Farnham, Que.	D5	74
Farnham, Va., U.S.	C6	123
Farnham, Mount, mtn., B.C.	D9	69
Farnhamville, Ia., U.S.	B3	92
Färnigen, Switz.	C6	21
Faro, Braz.	C3	59
Faro, Port.	D2	22
Farragut, Ia., U.S.	D2	92
Farragut, Tn., U.S.	*D9	119
Farrar, Ia., U.S.	e9	92
Farrar, stm., Scot., U.K.	C4	13
Farrāshband, Iran	G6	39
Farrell, Ms., U.S.	A3	101
Farrell, Pa., U.S.	D1	115
Farrellton, Que.	D2	74
Farrerdale, Sask.	F3	75
Farris, Ok., U.S.	C6	113
Farris, l., Nor.	p27	14
Farrukhābād, India	C6	36
Fars, hist. reg., Iran	C5	38
Fars, prov., Iran	C5	38
Farsala (Pharsalus), Grc.	E4	25
Farsø, Den.	B3	15
Farson, Ia., U.S.	C5	92
Farson, Wy., U.S.	D3	127
Farsund, Nor.	H2	14
Fartak, Ra's, c., Yemen	D5	38
Farvel, Kap, c., Grnld.	D16	61
Farwell, Mi., U.S.	E6	99
Farwell, Mn., U.S.	E3	100
Farwell, Ne., U.S.	C7	104
Farwell, Tx., U.S.	B1	120
Fasā, Iran	G6	39
Fasano, Italy	D6	23
Fashoda see Kodok, Sudan	D3	47
Fassett, Que.	D3	74
Fastov, Sov. Un.	F7	27
Fatehpur, India	C7	36
Fatsa, Tur.	B11	40
Fatuatulfu, Am. Sam.	F13	52
Fatuosofia, Cape, c., W. Sam.	F11	52
Fatu Rock, rock, Am. Sam.	F13	52
Faucett, Mo., U.S.	B3	102
Faucilles, Monts, mts., Fr.		
Faulk, co., S.D., U.S.	B6	118
Faulkland Heights, De., U.S.	i7	85
Faulkner, co., Ar., U.S.	B3	81
Faulkton, S.D., U.S.	B6	118
Faunsdale, Al., U.S.	C2	78
Fauquembergues, Fr.	D10	12
Fauquier, B.C.	E8	69
Fauquier, co., Va., U.S.	B5	123
Faust, Alta.	B3	68
Favara, Italy	F4	23
Faverges, Fr.	D2	20
Faversham, Eng., U.K.	C8	12
Favorita, Fl., U.S.	C5	86
Fawcett, Lake, l., Alta.	B4	68
Fawcett, Alta.	B3	68
Fawnie Nose, mtn., B.C.	C5	69
Fawnie Range, mts., B.C.	C5	69
Faxaflói, b., Ice.	n21	14
Faxälven, stm., Swe.	F6	14
Faxon, Ok., U.S.	C3	113
Faxon, Pa., U.S.	D8	115
Fayd, Sau. Ar.	I14	40
Fayette, Al., U.S.	B2	78
Fayette, In., U.S.	E5	91
Fayette, Ia., U.S.	B6	92
Fayette, Me., U.S.	D2	96
Fayette, Ms., U.S.	D2	101
Fayette, Mo., U.S.	B5	102
Fayette, Oh., U.S.	A1	112
Fayette, Ut., U.S.	D4	121
Fayette, co., Al., U.S.	B7	78
Fayette, co., Ga., U.S.	C2	87
Fayette, co., Il., U.S.	D5	90
Fayette, co., In., U.S.	E7	91
Fayette, co., Ia., U.S.	B6	92
Fayette, co., Ky., U.S.	B5	94
Fayette, co., Oh., U.S.	C2	112
Fayette, co., Pa., U.S.	G2	115
Fayette, co., Tn., U.S.	B2	119
Fayette, co., Tx., U.S.	E4	120
Fayette, co., W.V., U.S.	C3	125
Fayetteville, Ar., U.S.	A1	81
Fayetteville, Ga., U.S.	C2	87
Fayetteville, N.C., U.S.	B4	110
Fayetteville, Oh., U.S.	C2	112
Fayetteville, Pa., U.S.	G6	115
Fayetteville, Tn., U.S.	B5	119
Fayetteville, W.V., U.S.	C3	125
Faylakah, i., Kuw.	G4	39
Fays-Billot, Fr.		
Fayville, Ma., U.S.	g9	98
Faywood, N.M., U.S.	E1	108
Fazenda Nova, Braz.	B2	56
Fderik, Maur.	B2	45
Fear, Cape, c., N.C., U.S.	D5	110
Feasterville, Pa., U.S.	o21	115
Feather, stm., Ca., U.S.	C3	82
Feather, Middle Fork, stm., Ca., U.S.	C3	82
Feather, Mount, mtn., Ant.	e40	7
Feather Falls, Ca., U.S.	C3	82
Featherston, N.Z.	N15	51
Featherstone, Ok., U.S.	B6	113
Fécamp, Fr.	C4	16
Federal, Arg.	A5	54
Federal Dam, Mn., U.S.	C4	100
Federal Heights, Co., U.S.	*B6	83
Federal Point, Fl., U.S.	C5	86
Federalsburg, Md., U.S.	C6	97
Federal Way, Wa., U.S.	*f11	124
Fedora, S.D., U.S.	C8	118
Fedscreek, Ky., U.S.	C7	94
Feeding Hills, Ma., U.S.	B2	98
Feesburg, Oh., U.S.	D1	112
Fefan, i., Micron.	Q18	52
Fegen, Swe.	A7	15
Fehmarn, i., W. Ger.	A5	18
Fehmarn Strait, strt., Eur.	D5	15
Feia, Lagoa, b., Braz.	C4	56
Feijó, Braz.	E3	54
Feilding, N.Z.	N15	51
Feira, Port.	E2	22
Feira (Luangwa), Zam.	E5	48
Feira de Santana, Braz.	D5	54
Fejø, i., Den.	D5	15
Felanitx, Spain	C7	22
Felch, Mi., U.S.	C3	99
Felda, Fl., U.S.	A6	92
Feldberg, mtn., W. Ger.	E3	18
Feldbach, Aus.	E7	21
Feldberg, E. Ger.	B8	19
Feldkirch, Aus.	B2	21
Felicity, Oh., U.S.	D1	112
Felipe Carrillo Puerto, Mex.	D7	63
Felix, Cape, c., N.W. Ter.	C13	66
Felixstowe, Eng., U.K.	C9	12
Felixville, La., U.S.	D5	95
Fellbach, W. Ger.	C5	18
Fellingsbro, Swe.	t33	14
Fellowship, N.J., U.S.	*D3	107
Fellsmere, Fl., U.S.	E6	86
Felsenthal, Ar., U.S.	D3	81
Felt, Id., U.S.	F7	89
Felt, Ok., U.S.	e8	113
Felton, Ca., U.S.	D2	82
Felton, De., U.S.	D3	85
Felton, Ga., U.S.	C1	87
Felton, Mn., U.S.	C2	100
Felton, Pa., U.S.	G8	115
Feltre, Italy	A3	23
Femunden, l., Nor.	D5	15
Femund, i., Den.	F4	14
Fena Valley Reservoir, res., Guam	M9	52
Fence, Wi., U.S.	C5	126
Fence, stm., Mi., U.S.	B2	99
Fence Lake, N.M., U.S.	C1	108
Fence Lake, l., Wi., U.S.	C4	126
Fenelon Falls, Ont.	C6	73
Fengcheng, China	D11	32
Fengcheng, China	E6	31
Fengdu, China	E8	31
Fengjie, China	E8	31
Fengning, China	D7	32
Fengqing, China	G4	31
Fengxiang, China	G2	32
Fengyang, China	H2	32
Fengyang, China	D5	32
Fenimore Pass, strt., Ak., U.S.	E4	79
Fenn, Id., U.S.	D2	89
Fennimore, Wi., U.S.	F3	126
Fenton, Sask.	D3	75
Fenton, La., U.S.	D3	95
Fenton, Mi., U.S.	F7	99
Fenton, Mo., U.S.	f13	102
Fentress, Tx., U.S.	E4	120
Fentress, co., Tn., U.S.	C9	119
Fenwick, W.V., U.S.	C4	125
Fenwick Island, i., S.C., U.S.	G5	85
Fenwood, Sask.	G4	75
Fenyang, China	D7	31
Feodosiya, Sov. Un.	I10	27
Fer, Point au, c., La., U.S.	E4	95
Ferbane, Ire.	D4	11
Ferdig, Mt., U.S.	B5	103
Ferdinand, Id., U.S.	C2	89
Ferdinand, In., U.S.	H4	91
Ferdinandshof, E. Ger.	E7	15
Ferdows, Iran	B5	38
Fère-Champenoise, Fr.	F3	17
Ferentino, Italy	D4	23
Fergana, Sov. Un.	E8	28
Fergana Mountains, mts., Sov. Un.	E8	28
Fergus, Ont.	D4	73
Fergus, Mt., U.S.	C7	103
Fergus, co., Mt., U.S.	C7	103
Fergus Falls, Mn., U.S.	D2	100
Ferguson, B.C.	D9	69
Ferguson, Ia., U.S.	C5	92
Ferguson, Ky., U.S.	C5	94
Ferguson, Mo., U.S.	C7	102
Ferintosh, Alta.	C4	68
Ferkéssédougou, I.C.	E3	45
Ferme-Neuve, Que.	C2	74
Fermeuse, Newf.	E5	72
Fermo, Italy	C4	23
Fermont, Que.	h13	74
Fermoselle, Spain	B2	22
Fermoy, Ire.	D2	10
Fernandina, Isla (Narborough), i., Ec.	g5	58
Fernandina Beach, Fl., U.S.	B5	86
Fernando de Noronha, Ilha, i., Braz.	B4	57
Fernandópolis, Braz.	C2	56
Fernando Póo see Bioko, i., Eq. Gui.	E1	46
Fernán-Núñez, Spain	D3	22
Fernbank, Al., U.S.	B1	78
Fern Creek, Ky., U.S.	g11	94
Fern Creek, stm., Ky., U.S.	g11	94
Ferndale, Ar., U.S.	h9	81
Ferndale, Ca., U.S.	B1	82
Ferndale, Ky., U.S.	D6	94
Ferndale, Md., U.S.	B4	97
Ferndale, Mi., U.S.	p15	99
Ferndale, Pa., U.S.	F4	115
Ferndale, Wa., U.S.	A3	124
Ferney, S.D., U.S.	C7	118
Fernie, B.C.	E10	69
Fernley, Nv., U.S.	D2	105
Fern Park, Fl., U.S.	*D5	86
Fern Ridge Lake, res., Or., U.S.	C3	114
Ferns, Ire.	E5	11
Fernwood, Id., U.S.	B2	89
Fernwood, Ms., U.S.	D3	101
Fernwood, N.Y., U.S.	B4	109
Ferrara, Italy	B3	23
Ferreira do Alentejo, Port.	C1	22
Ferreira do Zêzere, Port.	C2	22
Ferrellsburg, W.V., U.S.	C2	125
Ferreñafe, Peru	C2	58
Ferret, Cape, c., Or., U.S.	C2	114
Ferriday, La., U.S.	C4	95
Ferrier, Il., U.S.	C5	90
Ferriere, Italy	E5	20
Ferron, Ut., U.S.	D4	121
Ferros, Braz.	B4	56
Ferrum, Va., U.S.	D2	123
Ferry, co., Wa., U.S.	A7	124
Ferry Farms, Va., U.S.	B5	123
Ferry Point, c., N.J., U.S.	k7	107
Ferryville, Wi., U.S.	E2	126
Ferrysburg, Mi., U.S.	E4	99
Fertile, Ia., U.S.	A4	92
Fertile, Mn., U.S.	C2	100
Fertilia, Italy	D2	23
Fès, Mor.	C3	44
Fessenden, N.D., U.S.	B6	111
Festina, Ia., U.S.	A6	92
Festus, Mo., U.S.	C7	102
Feteşti, Rom.	E4	11
Fethard, Ire.	D4	11
Fethiye, Tur.	D7	40
Fetisovo, Sov. Un.	I7	28
Fetsund, Nor.	E4	14
Feucht, W. Ger.	D6	19
Feuchtwangen, W. Ger.	D5	18
Feudal, Sask.	F2	75
Feuilles, Rivière aux, stm., Que.	g12	74
Fevik, Nor.	H3	14
Feversham, Ont.	C4	73
Feyzabad, Afg.	D1	36
Fez see Fès, Mor.	C3	44
Fezzan (Fazzan), hist. reg., Libya	C2	43
Ffestiniog, Wales, U.K.	D5	10
Fhada, Beinn, mtn., Scot., U.K.	B4	10
Fiambalá, Arg.	E2	55
Fianarantsoa, Madag.	h9	49
Fianarantsoa, prov., Madag.	h9	49
Fianga, Chad	D3	46
Fibre, Mi., U.S.	B6	99
Ficarolo, Italy	E7	20
Fiche, Eth.	A4	47
Fichtelgebirge, mts., W. Ger.	C6	19
Ficksburg, S. Afr.	C4	49
Fidalgo Island, i., Wa., U.S.	A3	124
Fidelity, Il., U.S.	D3	90
Fidenza, Italy	B3	23
Fidler Lake, l., Man.	A3	70
Field, B.C.	D9	69
Fieldale, Va., U.S.	D3	123
Field Crest Estates, Ct., U.S.	D8	84
Fielding, Sask.	E2	75
Fielding, Ut., U.S.	B3	121
Fieldon, Il., U.S.	D3	90
Fields, La., U.S.	D2	95
Fields, Or., U.S.	E8	114
Fields Lake, l., La., U.S.	k10	95
Fieldsboro, N.J., U.S.	C3	107
Fier, Alb.	B2	25
Fierro Urco, mtn., Ec.	B2	58
Fiesch, Switz.	D5	21
Fiesole, Italy	C3	23
Fife, prov., Scot., U.K.	C5	13
Fife, co., Scot., U.K.	C5	13
Fife Lake, Mi., U.S.	D5	99
Fife Lake, l., Sask.	H3	75
Fife Lake, l., Mi., U.S.	D5	99
Fife Lake, l., Sask.	H3	75
Fife Ness, c., Scot., U.K.	B5	10
Fifield, Wi., U.S.	C3	126
Fifteenmile Creek, stm., Wy., U.S.	B4	127
Fifteen Mile Falls Reservoir, res., U.S.	C5	122
Fifty Lakes, Mn., U.S.	D4	100
Figeac, Fr.	D8	16
Fig Garden, Ca., U.S.	*D4	82
Figtree, Zimb.	B4	49
Figueira da Foz, Port.	B1	22
Figueras, Spain	A7	22
Figuig, Mor.	C4	44
Fiji, ctry., Oc.	H10	6
Fik, Eth.	D5	47
Filchner Ice Shelf, ice, Ant.	B1	7
File, stm., Man.	B1	70
File Lake, l., Man.	B1	70
Filer, Id., U.S.	G4	89
Filer City, Mi., U.S.	D4	99
Filey, Eng., U.K.	F8	13
Fili, Grc.	g11	25
Filiatrá, Grc.	D3	25
Filicudi, i., Italy	E5	23
Filingué, Niger	D5	45
Filisur, Switz.	C8	21
Filley, Ne., U.S.	D9	104
Fillmore, Sask.	H4	75
Fillmore, Ca., U.S.	E4	82
Fillmore, In., U.S.	E4	91
Fillmore, Mo., U.S.	A3	102
Fillmore, N.Y., U.S.	C2	109
Fillmore, N.D., U.S.	A6	111
Fillmore, Ok., U.S.	C5	113
Fillmore, Ut., U.S.	D4	121
Fillmore, co., Mn., U.S.	G6	100
Fillmore, co., Ne., U.S.	D8	104
Fimi, stm., Zaire	B2	48
Finale Emilia, Italy	E7	20
Fincastle, Va., U.S.	C3	123
Finch, Ont.	B9	73
Findhorn, Scot., U.K.	C5	13
Findhorn, stm., Scot., U.K.	C5	13
Findlater, Sask.	F3	75
Findlay, Il., U.S.	D5	90
Findlay, Oh., U.S.	A2	112
Findlay, Mount, mtn., B.C.	D9	69
Fine, N.Y., U.S.	A5	109
Finesville, N.J., U.S.	B2	107
Fingal, N.D., U.S.	C8	111
Finger, Tn., U.S.	B3	119
Finger Lake, l., Ont.	C5	70
Fingerville, S.C., U.S.	A3	117
Fingoè, Moz.	A5	49
Finike, Tur.	D8	40
Finland, Mn., U.S.	C7	100
Finland, ctry., Eur.	E12	14
Finland, Gulf of, b., Eur.	H12	14
Finlay, stm., B.C.	m17	69
Finlayson, Mn., U.S.	D6	100
Finley, N.D., U.S.	B8	111
Finley, Ok., U.S.	C6	113
Finley, Tn., U.S.	A2	119
Finleyson, Ga., U.S.	D3	87
Finly, In., U.S.	E6	91
Finmoore, B.C.	C6	69
Finnegan, Alta.	D4	68
Finney, co., Ks., U.S.	D3	93
Finn Mountain, mtn., Ak., U.S.	C8	79
Finnsnes, Nor.	k12	50
Finspång, Swe.	u33	14
Finsteraarhorn, mtn., Switz.	C4	20
Finsterwalde, E. Ger.	C6	19
Fintona, N. Ire., U.K.	C3	11
Fintown, Ire.	C3	11
Fionn Loch, l., Scot., U.K.	C3	13
Fiora, stm., Italy	D5	21
Fiorenzuola d'Arda, Italy	E5	20
Firat (Euphrates), stm., Asia	C3	38
Fir, stm., Sask.	F10	124
Fircrest, Wa., U.S.	f10	124
Firebaugh, Ca., U.S.	D3	82
Firenze (Florence), Italy	C3	23
Firesteel, S.D., U.S.	B4	118
Firestone, Co., U.S.	A6	83
Firmat, Arg.	A4	54
Firminy, Fr.	E6	16
Firozabad, India	D8	36
Firozpur, India	B5	36
Firozābād, Iran	G6	39
Firsovo, Sov. Un.	C11	33
First Connecticut Lake, l., N.H., U.S.	f7	106
First Roach Pond, l., Me., U.S.	C3	96
Firth, Id., U.S.	F6	89
Firth, Ne., U.S.	D9	104
Firth, stm., N.A.	C4	66
Firūzābād, Iran	G6	39
Firūzkūh, Iran	B5	38
Fischamend Markt, Aus.		
Fischot Island, i., Newf.	C4	72
Fish, stm., Nmb.	C2	49
Fish, stm., Al., U.S.	E2	78
Fish, stm., Me., U.S.	A4	96
Fish Creek, stm., W.V., U.S.	g8	125
Fisheating Creek, stm., Fl., U.S.	F5	86
Fisher, Ar., U.S.	B5	81
Fisher, Il., U.S.	C5	90
Fisher, La., U.S.	C2	95
Fisher, Mn., U.S.	C2	100
Fisher, W.V., U.S.	B5	125
Fisher, co., Tx., U.S.	C2	120
Fisher, stm., Man.	D3	70
Fisher Bay, b., Man.	D3	70
Fisher Branch, Man.	D3	70
Fisher Glacier, ice, Ant.	B19	7
Fishermans Island, i., Va., U.S.	h15	123
Fishers, I., N.S.	E4	71
Fishers Island, i., N.Y., U.S.	m16	109
Fishers Peak, mtn., Co., U.S.	D6	83
Fisher Strait, strt., N.W. Ter.	D16	66
Fishersville, Va., U.S.	B4	123
Fishertown, Pa., U.S.	F4	115
Fisherville, Ont.	E5	73
Fishguard [and Goodwick], Wales, U.K.	E4	10
Fish Haven, Id., U.S.	G7	89
Fishhook, Il., U.S.	D3	90
Fishing Bay, b., Md., U.S.	D5	97
Fishing Creek, Md., U.S.	D5	97
Fishing Creek, stm., N.C., U.S.	A5	110
Fishing Creek, stm., S.C., U.S.	B5	117
Fishing Creek, stm., W.V., U.S.	B4	125
Fishing Creek, North Fork, stm., W.V., U.S.	h9	125
Fishing Creek, South Fork, stm., W.V., U.S.	h9	125
Fishing Creek Reservoir, res., S.C., U.S.	B6	117
Fishing Lake, l., Sask.	F4	75
Fishkill, N.Y., U.S.	D7	109
Fish Lake, l., Ut., U.S.	E4	121
Fish River Lake, l., Me., U.S.	A4	96
Fish Springs Range, mts., Ut., U.S.	D2	121
Fishtail, Mt., U.S.	E7	103
Fishtail Point, c., Ant.	f39	7
Fishtrap Lake, res., Ky., U.S.	C7	94
Fishville, La., U.S.	C3	95
Fisk, Mo., U.S.	E7	102
Fiskdale, Ma., U.S.	B3	98
Fiske, Sask.	F1	75
Fismes, Fr.	C5	16
Fitch-Bay, Que.	D5	74
Fitchburg, Ma., U.S.	A4	98
Fitchburg, Wi., U.S.	*F4	126
Fitchville, Ct., U.S.	C7	84
Fithian, Il., U.S.	C6	90
Fitler, Ms., U.S.	C2	101
Fittstown, Ok., U.S.	C5	113
Fitzgerald, Ga., U.S.	E3	87
Fitzhugh, Ok., U.S.	C5	113
Fitz Hugh Sound, strt., B.C.	D4	69
Fitzpatrick, Que.	B5	74
Fitz Roy, Arg.	D3	53
Fitzroy, stm., Austl.	C3	50
Fitzroy, stm., Austl.	D9	50
Fitzroy, Monte (Cerro Chaltel), mtn., S.A.	D2	54
Fitzroy Harbour, Ont.	B8	73
Fitzwilliam, N.H., U.S.	E2	106
Fitzwilliam Depot, N.H., U.S.	E2	106
Fitzwilliam Island, i., Ont.	B3	73
Fiume see Rijeka, Yugo.	C2	24
Fiumicino, Italy	h8	23
Five Island Lake, l., Ia., U.S.	A3	92
Five Islands, N.S.	D5	71
Fivemile Creek, stm., Wy., U.S.	C4	127
Fivemiletown, N. Ire., U.K.	C4	11
Five Points, Al., U.S.	B4	78
Five Points, N.M., U.S.	B3	108
Fizi, Zaire	B5	48
Fjårås Kyrkby, Swe.	A6	15
Fjärdhundra, Swe.	t34	14
Fjerritslev, Den.	A3	15
Flagg Mountain, hill, Al., U.S.	B3	78
Flag Knob, mtn., Ky., U.S.	C7	94
Flagler, Co., U.S.	B7	83
Flagler, co., Fl., U.S.	C5	86
Flagler Beach, Fl., U.S.	C5	86
Flag Pond, Tn., U.S.	C11	119
Flagstaff, Az., U.S.	B4	80
Flagstaff Lake, l., Or., U.S.	E7	114
Flagtown, N.J., U.S.	B3	107
Flamand, Lac, l., Que.	B4	74
Flambeau, stm., Wi., U.S.	C3	126
Flambeau, South Fork, stm., Wi., U.S.	C3	126
Flamborough Head, c., Eng., U.K.	C6	10
Flaming Gorge Dam, Ut., U.S.	C6	121
Flaming Gorge National Recreation Area, U.S.	E3	127
Flaming Gorge Reservoir, res., U.S.	E3	127
Flanagan, Il., U.S.	C5	90
Flanders, Ont.	*E5	72
Flanders, Ct., U.S.	C2	84
Flanders, N.J., U.S.	*B3	107
Flanders, hist. reg., Eur.	B5	16
Flandreau, S.D., U.S.	C9	118
Flandreau Indian Reservation, S.D., U.S.	C9	118
Flannan Islands, is., Scot., U.K.	A3	10
Flåren, i., Swe.	A8	15
Flasher, N.D., U.S.	C4	111
Flat, Ak., U.S.	C8	79
Flat, Ky., U.S.	C6	94
Flat, Mo., U.S.	D6	102
Flat, stm., Mi., U.S.	E5	99
Flat, stm., N.C., U.S.	A4	110
Flat, stm., R.I., U.S.	E2	116
Flat Bay, Newf.	D2	72
Flat Brook, stm., N.J., U.S.	A3	107
Flatbrookville, N.J., U.S.	A3	107
Flatbush, Alta.	B3	68
Flat Creek, Tn., U.S.	B5	119
Flathead, co., Mt., U.S.	B2	103
Flathead, stm., N.A.	E10	69
Flathead, North Fork, stm., N.A.	B2	103
Flathead, South Fork, stm., Mt., U.S.	C3	103
Flathead Indian Reservation, Mt., U.S.	C2	103
Flathead Lake, l., Newf.	C2	103
Flathead Valley, val., Mt., U.S.	C2	103
Flat Lake, l., Alta.	B4	68
Flat Lake, l., La., U.S.	k9	95
Flatlands, N.B.	B3	71
Flat Lick, Ky., U.S.	D6	94
Flat Mountain, mtn., N.Z.	P11	51

Name	Map Ref.	Page
Flatonia, Tx., U.S.	E4	120
Flat River, P.E.I.	C7	71
Flat River, Mo., U.S.	D7	102
Flat River Reservoir, res., R.I., U.S.	D3	116
Flat Rock, Al., U.S.	A4	78
Flat Rock, Il., U.S.	E6	90
Flat Rock, Mi., U.S.	F6	91
Flat Rock, Mi., U.S.	F7	99
Flat Rock, N.C., U.S.	f10	110
Flat Rock, Oh., U.S.	A3	112
Flatrock, Il., U.S.	F6	91
Flatrock Lake, l., Man.	B1	70
Flattery, Cape, c., Wa., U.S.	A1	124
Flatts, Ber.	p20	64
Flatwood, Al., U.S.	C2	78
Flatwoods, Ky., U.S.	B7	94
Flatwoods, La., U.S.	C3	95
Flatwoods, Tn., U.S.	B4	119
Flatwoods, W.V., U.S.	*C4	125
Flawil, Switz.	B5	20
Flaxcombe, Sask.	F1	75
Flaxton, N.D., U.S.	A3	111
Flaxville, Mt., U.S.	B11	103
Fleet, Eng., U.K.	C5	68
Fleet, Eng., U.K.	C7	12
Fleetwood, Eng., U.K.	G5	13
Fleetwood, N.C., U.S.	A1	110
Fleetwood, Pa., U.S.	F10	115
Fleischmanns, N.Y., U.S.	C6	109
Flekkefjord, Nor.	H2	14
Fleming, Sask.	G5	75
Fleming, Co., U.S.	A8	83
Fleming, Ga., U.S.	E5	87
Fleming, Pa., U.S.	E6	115
Fleming, co., Ky., U.S.	B6	94
Fleming-Neon, Ky., U.S.	C7	94
Flemingsburg, Ky., U.S.	B6	94
Flemington, Ga., U.S.	E5	87
Flemington, Mo., U.S.	D4	102
Flemington, N.J., U.S.	B3	107
Flemington, Pa., U.S.	D7	115
Flemington, W.V., U.S.	k10	125
Flen, Swe.	t34	14
Flensburg, W. Ger.	A4	18
Flensburg, Mn., U.S.	E4	100
Flensburg Fjord, b., Eur.	D3	15
Flers, Fr.	C3	16
Flesherton, Ont.	C4	73
Fletcher, Ont.	E2	73
Fletcher, N.C., U.S.	f10	110
Fletcher, Oh., U.S.	B1	112
Fletcher, Ok., U.S.	C3	113
Fletcher, Vt., U.S.	B3	122
Fletcher Islands, is., Ant.	B3	7
Fleur-de-Lys, Newf.	C3	72
Fleurier, Switz.	C2	20
Flieden, W. Ger.	C4	19
Flims, Switz.	C7	21
Flinders, stm., Austl.	C8	50
Flinders Island, i., Austl.	F5	50
Flinders Range, mts., Austl.	F6	50
Flin Flon, Man.	B1	70
Flint, Wales, U.K.	A4	12
Flint, In., U.S.	A7	91
Flint, Mi., U.S.	E7	99
Flint, stm., Ga., U.S.	E2	87
Flint City, Al., U.S.	A3	78
Flint Creek, stm., Al., U.S.	A3	78
Flint Creek Range, mts., Mt., U.S.	D3	103
Flinthill, Mo., U.S.	C7	102
Flint Hill, Va., U.S.	B4	123
Flint Hills, hills, Ks., U.S.	D7	93
Flint Island, i., Kir.	G12	6
Flintoft, Sask.	H2	75
Flinton, Ont.	C7	73
Flint Run, stm., W.V., U.S.	k9	125
Flintstone, Md., U.S.	k13	97
Flintville, Tn., U.S.	B5	119
Flipper Point, c., Wake I.	A2	52
Flippin, Ar., U.S.	A3	81
Flippin, Ky., U.S.	D4	94
Flixecourt, Fr.	D2	17
Flöha, E. Ger.	C8	19
Flom, Mn., U.S.	C2	100
Flomaton, Al., U.S.	D2	78
Flomot, Tx., U.S.	B2	120
Floodwood, Mn., U.S.	D6	100
Flood Range, mts., Ant.	B35	7
Flora, Il., U.S.	E5	90
Flora, In., U.S.	C4	91
Flora, Ms., U.S.	C3	101
Florahome, Fl., U.S.	C5	86
Floral, Al., U.S.	D3	78
Floral City, Fl., U.S.	D4	86
Floral Park, N.Y., U.S.	*k13	109
Flora Vista, N.M., U.S.	A1	108
Florence (Firenze), Italy	C3	23
Florence, Al., U.S.	A2	78
Florence, Az., U.S.	D4	80
Florence, Ca., U.S.	*n12	82
Florence, Co., U.S.	C5	83
Florence, In., U.S.	G8	91
Florence, Ks., U.S.	D7	93
Florence, Ky., U.S.	A5	94
Florence, Ms., U.S.	C3	101
Florence, Mo., U.S.	C5	102
Florence, Mt., U.S.	D2	103
Florence, N.J., U.S.	C3	107
Florence, Or., U.S.	D2	114
Florence, S.C., U.S.	C8	117
Florence, S.D., U.S.	B8	118
Florence, Tx., U.S.	D4	120
Florence, Vt., U.S.	D2	122
Florence, Wi., U.S.	C5	126
Florence, co., S.C., U.S.	C8	117
Florence, co., Wi., U.S.	C5	126
Florence Junction, Az., U.S.	D4	80
Florenceville, N.B.	C2	71
Florencia, Col.	C2	60
Florenville, Bel.	E5	17
Flores, Guat.	D7	63
Flores, dept., Ur.	f8	54
Flores, i., Indon.	G6	34
Flores, i., Port.	g8	44
Flores Island, i., B.C.	E4	69
Flores Sea, Indon.	G5	34
Floresta, Braz.	C3	57
Floresville, Tx., U.S.	E3	120
Florham Park, N.J., U.S.	B4	107
Floriano, Braz.	C2	57
Floriano Peixoto, Braz.	C4	58
Florianópolis, Braz.	D3	56
Florida, Cuba	D4	64
Florida, Ma., U.S.	A1	98
Florida, N.M., U.S.	D3	108
Florida, N.Y., U.S.	D6	109
Florida, Oh., U.S.	A1	112
Florida, Ur.	E1	56
Florida, dept., Ur.	f8	54
Florida, state, U.S.	E5	86
Florida, Cape, c., Fl., U.S.	G6	86
Florida, Straits of, strt., N.A.	F11	76
Florida Bay, b., Fl., U.S.	H6	86
Floridablanca, Col.	*B3	60
Florida City, Fl., U.S.	G6	86
Florida Keys, is., Fl., U.S.	H6	86
Florida Mountains, mts., N.M., U.S.	E2	108
Florida State Indian Reservation, Fl., U.S.	F5	86
Florien, La., U.S.	C2	95
Flórina (Phlorina), Grc.	B3	25
Floris, Ia., U.S.	D5	92
Florissant, Co., U.S.	C5	83
Florissant, Mo., U.S.	f13	102
Florissant Fossil Beds National Monument, Co., U.S.	C5	83
Flossmoor, Il., U.S.	k9	90
Flournoy, Ca., U.S.	C2	82
Flovilla, Ga., U.S.	C3	87
Flower Brook, stm., Vt., U.S.	E2	122
Floweree, Mt., U.S.	C5	103
Flower Hill, N.Y., U.S.	*E7	109
Flower's Cove, Newf.	C3	72
Flowery Branch, Ga., U.S.	B3	87
Flowood, Ms., U.S.	C3	101
Floyd, Ia., U.S.	A5	92
Floyd, N.M., U.S.	C6	108
Floyd, Va., U.S.	D2	123
Floyd, co., Ga., U.S.	B1	87
Floyd, co., In., U.S.	H6	91
Floyd, co., Ia., U.S.	A5	92
Floyd, co., Ky., U.S.	C7	94
Floyd, co., Tx., U.S.	B2	120
Floyd, co., Va., U.S.	D2	123
Floyd, stm., Ia., U.S.	B1	92
Floydada, Tx., U.S.	C2	120
Floyd Dale, S.C., U.S.	C9	117
Floydsburg, Ky., U.S.	g12	94
Floyds Fork, stm., Ky., U.S.	B4	94
Floyds Knobs, In., U.S.	H6	91
Fluchthorn, mtn., Eur.	C9	21
Fluessen, l., Neth.	B5	17
Flumendosa, stm., Italy	E2	23
Flums, Switz.	B7	21
Flushing, Mi., U.S.	E7	99
Flushing, Oh., U.S.	B4	112
Fluvanna, Tx., U.S.	C2	120
Fluvanna, co., Va., U.S.	C4	123
Fly, stm.	k11	50
Fly Creek, N.Y., U.S.	C6	109
Flyinge, Swe.	C7	15
Flying H, N.M., U.S.	D4	108
Foam Lake, Sask.	F4	75
Foam Lake, l., Sask.	F4	75
Foard, co., Tx., U.S.	B3	120
Foça, Tur.	C6	25
Foča, Yugo.	D4	24
Fochabers, Scot., U.K.	C5	13
Focşani, Rom.	C8	24
Foggia, Italy	D5	23
Fogland Point, c., R.I., U.S.	E6	116
Fogliano, Italy	k9	23
Fogo, Newf.	D4	72
Fogo, Cape, c., Newf.	D5	72
Fogo Island, i., Newf.	D4	72
Fohnsdorf, Aus.	E7	18
Föhr, i., W. Ger.	A4	18
Foix, Fr.	F4	16
Folcroft, Pa., U.S.	*p20	115
Foley, Al., U.S.	E2	78
Foley, Mn., U.S.	E5	100
Foley, Mo., U.S.	B7	102
Foley Island, i., N.W. Ter.	C17	66
Foligno, Italy	C4	23
Folkestone, Eng., U.K.	E7	10
Folkston, Ga., U.S.	F4	87
Folkstone, N.C., U.S.	C5	110
Follansbee, W.V., U.S.	A4	125
Follett, Tx., U.S.	A2	120
Follonica, Italy	C3	23
Folly Beach, S.C., U.S.	F8	117
Folly Island, i., S.C., U.S.	F8	117
Folly Lake, N.S.	D6	71
Folsom, Ca., U.S.	C3	82
Folsom, La., U.S.	D5	95
Folsom, N.J., U.S.	D3	107
Folsom, N.M., U.S.	A6	108
Folsom, W.V., U.S.	B4	125
Folsomville, In., U.S.	H3	91
Fomento, Cuba	C4	64
Fonda, Ia., U.S.	B3	92
Fonda, N.Y., U.S.	C6	109
Fond-du-Lac, Sask.	m7	75
Fond du Lac, Wi., U.S.	E5	126
Fond du Lac Indian Reservation, Mn., U.S.	D6	100
Fonde, Ky., U.S.	D6	94
Fondi, Italy	D4	23
Fonsagrada, Spain	A2	22
Fonseca, Golfo de, b., N.A.	E7	63
Fontainebleau, Fr.	C5	16
Fontana, Ca., U.S.	m14	82
Fontana, Ks., U.S.	D9	93
Fontana, Wi., U.S.	F5	126
Fontana Dam, N.C., U.S.	f9	110
Fontana Lake, res., N.C., U.S.	f9	110
Fontanelle, Ia., U.S.	C3	92
Fontanet, In., U.S.	E3	91
Fontenay-le-Comte, Fr.	D3	16
Fontenay [-sous-Bois], Fr.	g10	16
Fontenelle, In., U.S.	E2	127
Fontenelle Reservoir, res., Wy., U.S.	D2	127
Foosland, Il., U.S.	C5	90
Foothill Farms, Ca., U.S.	*C3	82
Foothills, Alta.	C2	68
Footville, Wi., U.S.	F4	126
Foping, China	H2	32
Forada, Mn., U.S.	E3	100
Foraker, Ok., U.S.	A5	113
Foraker, Mount, mtn., Ak., U.S.	f16	79
Forbach, Fr.	C7	16
Forbes, Austl.	F8	50
Forbes, Il., U.S.	D5	90
Forbes, Mn., U.S.	C6	100
Forbes, Mo., U.S.	B2	102
Forbes, N.D., U.S.	D7	111
Forbes, Lac, l., Que.	C3	74
Forbes, Mount, mtn., Alta.	D2	68
Forcados, Nig.	E6	45
Force, Pa., U.S.	D4	115
Forcalquier, Fr.	E6	16
Forchheim, W. Ger.	D5	18
Ford, Scot., U.K.	D3	13
Ford, Ks., U.S.	E4	93
Ford, Ky., U.S.	C6	94
Ford, co., Il., U.S.	C5	90
Ford, co., Ks., U.S.	E4	93
Ford, stm., Mi., U.S.	C3	99
Ford City, Ca., U.S.	E4	82
Ford City, Pa., U.S.	E2	115
Fordland, Mo., U.S.	D5	102
Fordoche, La., U.S.	D4	95
Ford Ranges, mts., Ant.	B34	7
Ford River, Mi., U.S.	C3	99
Fords, N.J., U.S.	B4	107
Fords Prairie, Wa., U.S.	C2	124
Fordsville, Ky., U.S.	C3	94
Fordville, N.D., U.S.	A8	111
Fordwich, Ont.	D3	73
Fordyce, Ar., U.S.	D3	81
Fordyce, Ne., U.S.	B8	104
Forécariah, Gui.	E2	45
Foreman, Ar., U.S.	D1	81
Foremost, Alta.	E5	68
Foresman, In., U.S.	C3	91
Forest, Bel.	B6	16
Forest, Ont.	D2	73
Forest, Ms., U.S.	C4	101
Forest, Oh., U.S.	B2	112
Forest, Tx., U.S.	D5	120
Forest, Va., U.S.	C3	123
Forest, co., Pa., U.S.	C3	115
Forest, co., Wi., U.S.	C5	126
Forest, stm., N.D., U.S.	A8	111
Forest Acres, S.C., U.S.	C6	117
Forestburg, Alta.	C4	68
Forestburg, S.D., U.S.	C7	118
Forest City, Il., U.S.	C4	90
Forest City, Ia., U.S.	A4	92
Forest City, Me., U.S.	C5	96
Forest City, Mo., U.S.	B2	102
Forest City, N.C., U.S.	B1	110
Forest City, Pa., U.S.	C11	115
Forestdale, R.I., U.S.	B3	116
Forest Dale, Vt., U.S.	D2	122
Forest Glen, La., U.S.	h12	95
Forest Green, Mo., U.S.	B5	102
Forestgrove, Mt., U.S.	D7	103
Forest Grove, Or., U.S.	B3	114
Forest Hill, La., U.S.	C3	95
Forest Hill, Md., U.S.	A5	97
Forest Hill, Tx., U.S.	*n9	120
Forest Hills, Pa., U.S.	k14	115
Forest Home, Al., U.S.	D3	78
Forest Junction, Wi., U.S.	h9	126
Forest Knolls, Ca., U.S.	g7	82
Forest Lake, Mn., U.S.	E6	100
Forest Lake, N.H., U.S.	E5	106
Foreston, Mn., U.S.	E5	100
Foreston, S.C., U.S.	D7	117
Forest Park, Ga., U.S.	h8	87
Forest Park, Il., U.S.	k9	90
Forest Park, La., U.S.	B3	95
Forest Park, Oh., U.S.	n12	112
Forestport, N.Y., U.S.	B5	109
Forest River, N.D., U.S.	A8	111
Forestville, Md., U.S.	*C4	97
Forestville, N.Y., U.S.	C1	109
Forestville, Pa., U.S.	D1	115
Forestville, Wi., U.S.	D6	126
Forfar, Scot., U.K.	B5	10
Forgan, Sask.	F2	75
Forgan, Ok., U.S.	A1	113
Forges-les-Eaux, Fr.	C4	16
Forget, Sask.	H4	75
Forge Village, Ma., U.S.	A5	98
Forillon, Parc National de, Que.	k14	74
Fork, N.C., U.S.	B2	110
Fork, S.C., U.S.	C9	117
Fork Creek, stm., W.V., U.S.	m12	125
Forked Deer, stm., Tn., U.S.	B2	119
Forked Deer, Middle Fork, stm., Tn., U.S.	D3	119
Forked Deer, North Fork, stm., Tn., U.S.	B3	119
Forked Deer, South Fork, stm., Tn., U.S.	B2	119
Forked Island, La., U.S.	E3	95
Forked River, N.J., U.S.	D4	107
Forkland, Al., U.S.	C2	78
Fork Mountain, Tn., U.S.	C9	119
Fork River, Man.	D1	70
Forks, Wa., U.S.	B1	124
Fork Shoals, S.C., U.S.	B3	117
Forksville, Pa., U.S.	D8	115
Fork Union, Va., U.S.	C4	123
Forkville, Ms., U.S.	C4	101
Forlì, Italy	B4	23
Forman, N.D., U.S.	C8	111
Formazza, Italy	A4	12
Formby, Eng., U.K.	g8	12
Formello, Italy	g8	23
Formentera, i., Spain	C6	22
Formiga, Braz.	F6	56
Formosa, Arg.	B5	56
Formosa, Braz.	C3	56
Formosa, Ont.	D3	73
Formosa, Arg.	B3	81
Formosa, prov., Arg.	D3	55
Formosa, Serra, plat., Braz.	E4	57
Formosa Bay, b., Kenya	B7	48
Formosa see Taiwan, ctry., Asia	G9	31
Formoso, Ks., U.S.	C6	93
Formoso, stm., Braz.	A6	56
Formoso, stm., Braz.	E5	59
Forney, Tx., U.S.	n10	120
Fornovo di Taro, Italy	E6	20
Forres, Scot., U.K.	B5	10
Forrest, Austl.	F4	50
Forrest, Il., U.S.	C5	90
Forrest, co., Ms., U.S.	D4	101
Forrest City, Ar., U.S.	B5	81
Forrester Island, i., Ak., U.S.	n23	79
Forrest Lakes, l., Austl.	A4	50
Forreston, Il., U.S.	A4	90
Forsan, Tx., U.S.	C2	120
Forsayth, Austl.	C7	50
Forserum, Swe.	A8	15
Förslövsholm, Swe.	B6	15
Forster, Austl.	F9	51
Forst [Lausitz], E. Ger.	C7	18
Forsyth, Ga., U.S.	C3	87
Forsyth, Il., U.S.	D5	90
Forsyth, Mo., U.S.	E4	102
Forsyth, Mt., U.S.	D10	103
Forsyth, co., Ga., U.S.	B2	87
Forsyth, co., N.C., U.S.	A2	110
Fort Adams, Ms., U.S.	D2	101
Fort Albany, Ont.	n19	73
Fortaleza, Braz.	B5	57
Fortaleza de Ituxi, Braz.	C4	58
Fort Ann, N.Y., U.S.	B7	109
Fort Apache, Az., U.S.	D6	80
Fort Apache Indian Reservation, Az., U.S.	D5	80
Fort-Archambault see Sarh, Chad	D3	46
Fort Ashby, W.V., U.S.	B6	125
Fort Assiniboine, Alta.	B3	68
Fort Atkinson, Ia., U.S.	A6	92
Fort Atkinson, Wi., U.S.	F5	126
Fort Augustus, Scot., U.K.	C4	13
Fort Barnwell, N.C., U.S.	B5	110
Fort Beaufort, S. Afr.	D4	49
Fort Belknap Agency, Mt., U.S.	B8	103
Fort Belknap Indian Reservation, Mt., U.S.	B8	103
Fort Belvoir, mil., Va., U.S.	g12	123
Fort Benjamin Harrison, mil., In., U.S.	k10	91
Fort Benning, Ga., U.S.	D2	87
Fort Benton, Mt., U.S.	C6	103
Fort Berthold Indian Reservation, N.D., U.S.	B3	111
Fort Bidwell, Ca., U.S.	B3	82
Fort Bidwell Indian Reservation, Ca., U.S.	B3	82
Fort Blackmore, Va., U.S.	f9	123
Fort Bliss, mil., Tx., U.S.	o11	120
Fort Bragg, Ca., U.S.	C2	82
Fort Bragg, mil., N.C., U.S.	B3	110
Fort Branch, In., U.S.	H2	91
Fort Bridger, Wy., U.S.	E2	127
Fort Calhoun, Ne., U.S.	C9	104
Fort Campbell, mil., U.S.	A4	119
Fort Carson, mil., Co., U.S.	C6	83
Fort Chipewyan, Alta.	f8	68
Fort Clark, N.D., U.S.	B4	111
Fort Clatsop National Memorial, hist., Or., U.S.	A3	114
Fort Cobb, Ok., U.S.	B3	113
Fort Cobb Reservoir, res., Ok., U.S.	B3	113
Fort Collins, Co., U.S.	A5	83
Fort Coulonge, Que.	B8	73
Fort Covington, N.Y., U.S.	f10	109
Fort Crampel, Cen. Afr. Rep.	D3	46
Fort Davis, Al., U.S.	C4	78
Fort Davis, Tx., U.S.	o13	120
Fort Davis National Historic Site, hist., Tx., U.S.	o13	120
Fort Defiance, Az., U.S.	B6	80
Fort-de-France, Mart.	I14	64
Fort-de-France, Baie de, b., Mart.	S10	65
Fort Deposit, Al., U.S.	D3	78
Fort Detrick, mil., Md., U.S.	B3	97
Fort Devens, mil., Ma., U.S.	f9	98
Fort Dix, mil., N.J., U.S.	C3	107
Fort Dodge, Ia., U.S.	B3	92
Fort Dodge, Ks., U.S.	E4	93
Fort Donelson National Military Park, Tn., U.S.	A4	119
Fort Duchesne, Ut., U.S.	C6	121
Forteau, Newf.	C3	72
Fort Edward, N.Y., U.S.	B7	109
Fort Erie, Ont.	E6	73
Fortescue, Mo., U.S.	A2	102
Fortescue, stm., Austl.	D2	50
Fort Eustis, mil., Va., U.S.	h14	123
Fort Fairfield, Me., U.S.	B5	96
Fort Fitzgerald, Alta.	f8	68
Fort Foureau, Cam.	C3	46
Fort Foureau, Chad	C3	46
Fort Frances, Ont.	o16	73
Fort Fraser, B.C.	B5	69
Fort Frederica National Monument, Ga., U.S.	E5	87
Fort Gaines, Ga., U.S.	E1	87
Fort Garland, Co., U.S.	D5	83
Fort Gay, W.V., U.S.	C2	125
Fort Gibson, Ok., U.S.	B6	113
Fort Gibson Lake, res., Ok., U.S.	A6	113
Fort Good Hope, N.W. Ter.	C7	66
Fort Gordon, mil., Ga., U.S.	C4	87
Fort Grahame, B.C.	E8	66
Fort Greely, mil., Ak., U.S.	C10	79
Fort Green, Fl., U.S.	E5	86
Fort Hall, Kenya	B6	48
Fort Hall, Id., U.S.	F6	89
Fort Hall Indian Reservation, Id., U.S.	F6	89
Fort Hancock, Tx., U.S.	o12	120
Fort Hill, Pa., U.S.	G3	115
Fort Hood, mil., Tx., U.S.	D4	120
Fort Howard, Md., U.S.	B5	97
Fort Huachuca, mil., Az., U.S.	F5	80
Fortierville, Que.	C5	74
Fortin, Mt., U.S.	B2	103
Fortín Uno, Arg.	B3	54
Fort Jackson, mil., S.C., U.S.	C6	117
Fort Jefferson National Monument, Fl., U.S.	H4	86
Fort Jennings, Oh., U.S.	B1	112
Fort Jones, Ca., U.S.	B2	82
Fort Kent, Alta.	B5	68
Fort Kent, Me., U.S.	A4	96
Fort Kent Mills, Me., U.S.	A4	96
Fort Klamath, Or., U.S.	E5	114
Fort Knox, mil., Ky., U.S.	B4	94
Fort-Lamy see N'Djamena, Chad	C3	46
Fort Langley, B.C.	f13	69
Fort Laramie, Wy., U.S.	D8	127
Fort Laramie National Historic Site, hist., Wy., U.S.	D8	127
Fort Lauderdale, Fl., U.S.	F6	86
Fort Lawn, S.C., U.S.	B6	117
Fort Leavenworth, mil., Ks., U.S.	C9	93
Fort Lee, N.J., U.S.	B5	107
Fort Lee, mil., Va., U.S.	C5	123
Fort Leonard Wood, mil., Mo., U.S.	D5	102
Fort Lewis, mil., Wa., U.S.	B3	124
Fort Liard, N.W. Ter.	D8	66
Fort-Liberté, Haiti	E8	64
Fort Littleton, Pa., U.S.	F5	115
Fort Loramie, Oh., U.S.	B1	112
Fort Loudon, Pa., U.S.	G6	115
Fort Loudoun Lake, res., Tn., U.S.	D9	119
Fort Lupton, Co., U.S.	A6	83
Fort MacArthur, mil., Ca., U.S.	n12	82
Fort MacKay, Alta.	f8	68
Fort Macleod, Alta.	E4	68
Fort Madison, Ia., U.S.	D6	92
Fort Matanzas National Monument, Fl., U.S.	C5	86
Fort McClellan, mil., Al., U.S.	B4	78
Fort McDermitt Indian Reservation, U.S.	B4	105
Fort McDowell, Az., U.S.	k9	80
Fort McDowell Indian Reservation, Az., U.S.	D4	80
Fort McHenry National Monument And Historic Shrine, Md., U.S.	g11	97
Fort McKavett, Tx., U.S.	D2	120
Fort McKinley, Oh., U.S.	*C1	112
Fort McMurray, Alta.	A5	68
Fort McPherson, N.W. Ter.	C6	66
Fort Meade, Fl., U.S.	E5	86
Fort Meade, mil., Md., U.S.	B4	97
Fort Meadow Reservoir, res., Ma., U.S.	g9	98
Fort Mill, S.C., U.S.	A6	117
Fort Miller, N.Y., U.S.	B7	109
Fort Mitchell, Al., U.S.	C4	78
Fort Mitchell, Ky., U.S.	h13	94
Fort Mitchell, Va., U.S.	D4	123
Fort Mojave Indian Reservation, U.S.	C1	80
Fort Monmouth, mil., N.J., U.S.	C4	107
Fort Monroe, mil., Va., U.S.	h15	123
Fort Morgan, Al., U.S.	E1	78
Fort Morgan, Co., U.S.	A7	83
Fort Motte, S.C., U.S.	D6	117
Fort Myer, mil., Va., U.S.	g12	123
Fort Myers, Fl., U.S.	F5	86
Fort Myers Beach, Fl., U.S.	F5	86
Fort Necessity, La., U.S.	B4	95
Fort Nelson, B.C.	m18	69
Fort Norman, N.W. Ter.	D7	66
Fort Ogden, Fl., U.S.	E5	86
Fort Oglethorpe, Ga., U.S.	B1	87
Fort Ord, mil., Ca., U.S.	D3	82
Fort Payne, Al., U.S.	A4	78
Fort Peck, Mt., U.S.	B10	103
Fort Peck Dam, Mt., U.S.	B10	103
Fort Peck Indian Reservation, Mt., U.S.	B11	103
Fort Peck Lake, res., Mt., U.S.	C9	103
Fort Pierce, Fl., U.S.	E6	86
Fort Pierce Inlet, b., Fl., U.S.	E6	86
Fort Pierre, S.D., U.S.	C5	118
Fort Plain, N.Y., U.S.	C6	109
Fort Portal, Ug.	A5	48
Fort Providence, N.W. Ter.	D9	66
Fort Qu'Appelle, Sask.	G4	75
Fort Randall Dam, S.D., U.S.	D7	118
Fort Ransom, N.D., U.S.	C8	111
Fort Recovery, Oh., U.S.	B1	112
Fort Reliance, N.W. Ter.	D11	66
Fort Resolution, N.W. Ter.	D10	66
Fort Rice, N.D., U.S.	C5	111
Fort Richardson, mil., Ak., U.S.	C10	79
Fort Riley, mil., Ks., U.S.	C7	93
Fort Ripley, Mn., U.S.	D4	100
Fort Ritchie, mil., Md., U.S.	A3	97
Fort Ritner, In., U.S.	G5	91
Fort Robinson, Ne., U.S.	B2	104
Fort Rock, Or., U.S.	D5	114
Fortrose, N.Z.	Q12	51
Fortrose, Scot., U.K.	C4	13
Fort Ross, N.W. Ter.	B14	66
Fort Rucker, mil., Al., U.S.	D4	78
Fort Saint James, B.C.	B5	69
Fort Saint John, B.C.	A7	69
Fort Sam Houston, mil., Tx., U.S.	k7	120
Fort Saskatchewan, Alta.	C4	68
Fort Scott, Ks., U.S.	E9	93
Fort Severn, Ont.	n18	73
Fort Shafter, mil., Hi., U.S.	g10	88
Fort Shaw, Mt., U.S.	C5	103
Fort Shawnee, Oh., U.S.	B1	112
Fort Sheridan, mil., Il., U.S.	h9	90
Fort-Shevchenko, Sov. Un.	E4	28
Fort Sibut, Cen. Afr. Rep.	D3	46
Fort Sill, mil., Ok., U.S.	C3	113
Fort Simpson, N.W. Ter.	D8	66
Fort Smith, Alta.	f8	68
Fort Smith, N.W. Ter.	D10	66
Fort Smith, Ar., U.S.	B1	81
Fort Stanton, N.M., U.S.	D4	108
Fort Steele, B.C.	E10	69
Fort Steele, Wy., U.S.	E6	127
Fort Stewart, mil., Ga., U.S.	D5	87
Fort Stockton, Tx., U.S.	D1	120
Fort Sumner, N.M., U.S.	C5	108
Fort Sumter National Monument, S.C., U.S.	k12	117
Fort Supply, Ok., U.S.	A2	113
Fort Supply Lake, res., Ok., U.S.	A2	113
Fort Thomas, Az., U.S.	D6	80
Fort Thomas, Ky., U.S.	h14	94
Fort Thompson, S.D., U.S.	C6	118
Fort Totten, N.D., U.S.	B7	111
Fort Totten Indian Reservation, N.D., U.S.	B7	111
Fort Towson, Ok., U.S.	C6	113
Fort Union National Monument, N.M., U.S.	B5	108
Fort Valley, Ga., U.S.	D3	87
Fort Vermilion, Alta.	f7	68
Fortville, In., U.S.	E6	91
Fort Wainwright, mil., Ak., U.S.	C10	79
Fort Walton Beach, Fl., U.S.	u15	86
Fort Washakie, Wy., U.S.	C4	127
Fort Washington, Pa., U.S.	o21	115
Fort Washington Forest, Md., U.S.	C4	97
Fort Wayne, In., U.S.	B7	91
Fort Wellington, Guy.	A3	59
Fort White, Fl., U.S.	C4	86
Fort William, Scot., U.K.	B4	10
Fort Wingate, N.M., U.S.	B1	108
Fort Worth, Tx., U.S.	C4	120
Fort Wright, Ky., U.S.	h13	94
Fort Yates, N.D., U.S.	C5	111
Forty Fort, Pa., U.S.	D10	115
Fort Yukon, Ak., U.S.	B10	79
Fort Yuma Indian Reservation, Ca., U.S.	F6	82
Forūr, i., Iran	H7	39
Foss Reservoir, res., Ok., U.S.	B2	113
Fosston, Sask.	E4	75
Fosston, Mn., U.S.	C3	100
Foster, In., U.S.	D3	91
Foster, Ky., U.S.	B5	94
Foster, Mo., U.S.	C3	102
Foster, Ne., U.S.	B8	104
Foster, Ok., U.S.	C4	113
Foster, Or., U.S.	C4	114
Foster, R.I., U.S.	C2	116
Foster, co., N.D., U.S.	B6	111
Foster, stm., Sask.	A3	75
Foster Brook, Pa., U.S.	C4	115
Foster City, Ca., U.S.	*h8	82
Foster City, Mi., U.S.	C4	99
Fosters, Al., U.S.	B2	78
Fosters Falls, Va., U.S.	D2	123
Fosters Pond, l., Ma., U.S.	f11	98
Fosterville, Tn., U.S.	B5	119
Fostoria, Al., U.S.	C3	78
Fostoria, Ia., U.S.	A2	92
Fostoria, Ks., U.S.	C7	93
Fostoria, Mi., U.S.	E7	99
Fostoria, Oh., U.S.	A2	112
Fougamou, Gabon	F2	46
Fougères, Fr.	C3	16
Fouke, Ar., U.S.	D2	81
Foula, i., Scot., U.K.	g9	10
Foulness Island, i., Eng., U.K.	C8	12
Foulwind, Cape, c., N.Z.	N13	51
Foumban, Cam.	D2	46
Foum el Hassane, Mor.	D3	44
Fount, Ky., U.S.	D6	94
Fountain, Al., U.S.	D2	78
Fountain, Co., U.S.	C6	83
Fountain, Fl., U.S.	B1	86
Fountain, Mn., U.S.	G6	100
Fountain, N.C., U.S.	B5	110
Fountain, co., In., U.S.	D3	91
Fountain City, In., U.S.	E8	91
Fountain City, Wi., U.S.	D2	126
Fountain Creek, stm., Co., U.S.	C6	83
Fountain Green, Ut., U.S.	D4	121
Fountain Hill, Ar., U.S.	D4	81
Fountain Hill, Pa., U.S.	E11	115
Fountain Inn, S.C., U.S.	B3	117
Fountain Lake, Ar., U.S.	f8	81
Fountain Peak, mtn., Ca., U.S.	E6	82
Fountain Place, La., U.S.	D4	95
Fountain Run, Ky., U.S.	D4	94
Fountaintown, In., U.S.	E6	91
Fountain Valley, Ca., U.S.	*n13	82
Four Buttes, Mt., U.S.	B11	103
Fourchambault, Fr.	D5	16
Fourche, Ar., U.S.	*C3	81
Fourche Creek, stm., Ar., U.S.	k10	81
Fourche LaFave, stm., Ar., U.S.	C2	81
Fourche Maline, stm., Ok., U.S.	C6	113
Fourche Mountain, mtn., Ar., U.S.	C2	81
Fourchu, N.S.	D9	71
Four Corners, Ca., U.S.	E5	82
Four Corners, Or., U.S.	*C4	114
Four Corners, Wy., U.S.	B8	127
Four Lakes, Wa., U.S.	B8	124
Fourmies, Fr.	B6	16
Fourmile, Ky., U.S.	D6	94
Fourmile Creek, stm., Ia., U.S.	e8	92
Four Mountains, Islands of, is., Ak., U.S.	E6	79
Fournier, Ont.	B10	73
Four Oaks, N.C., U.S.	B4	110
Fouta Djallon, reg., Gui.	D2	45
Foveaux Strait, strt., N.Z.	Q11	51
Fowey, Eng., U.K.	D3	12
Fowler, Ca., U.S.	D4	82
Fowler, Co., U.S.	C6	83
Fowler, Il., U.S.	C2	90
Fowler, In., U.S.	C3	91
Fowler, Ks., U.S.	E3	93
Fowler, Mi., U.S.	E6	99
Fowlerton, In., U.S.	D6	91
Fowlerton, Tx., U.S.	E3	120
Fowlerville, Mi., U.S.	F6	99
Fowlkes, Tn., U.S.	B2	119
Fownhope, Eng., U.K.	F2	87
Fox, Ar., U.S.	B3	81
Fox, Ok., U.S.	C4	113
Fox, Or., U.S.	C8	114
Fox, stm., Man.	B4	70
Fox, stm., Mi., U.S.	B4	99
Fox, stm., Mi., U.S.	A6	102
Fox, stm., Wi., U.S.	D5	126
Foxboro, Ont.	C7	73
Foxboro, Ma., U.S.	B5	98
Foxborough, Ma., U.S.	B5	98
Fox Chapel, Pa., U.S.	*h14	115
Fox Creek, Alta.	B2	68
Foxdale, I. of Man	F4	13
Foxe Basin, b., N.W. Ter.	C17	66
Foxe Channel, strt., N.W. Ter.	D16	66
Foxe Peninsula, pen., N.W. Ter.	C17	66
Foxford, Ire.	D2	11
Fox Harbour, Newf.	E5	72
Fox Harbour, Newf.	B4	72
Fox Island, i., R.I., U.S.	E4	116
Fox Island, i., Wa., U.S.	f10	124
Fox Islands, is., Ak., U.S.	E6	79
Fox Lake, Il., U.S.	h8	90
Fox Lake, Wi., U.S.	E5	126
Fox Mountain, mtn., Yukon	D6	66
Fox Mountain, mtn., Nv., U.S.	B2	105
Foxpark, Wy., U.S.	E6	127
Fox River Grove, Il., U.S.	h8	90
Foxton, N.Z.	N15	51
Foxvale, Ma., U.S.	B5	98
Fox Valley, Sask.	G1	75
Foxville, Vt., U.S.	C4	122
Foxwarren, Man.	D1	70
Foxworth, Ms., U.S.	D4	101
Foyil, Ok., U.S.	A6	113
Foyle, stm., Eur.	C4	11
Foyle, Lough, b., Eur.	C4	11
Foynes, Ire.	I3	39
Foz do Cunene, Ang.	E1	48
Foz do Iguaçu, Braz.	C3	58
Foz do Jordão, Braz.	C3	58
Foz do Pauíni, Braz.	C3	58
Frackville, Pa., U.S.	E9	115
Fraga, Spain	B6	22
Fraile Muerto, Ur.	E2	56
Frametown, W.V., U.S.	C4	125
Framingham, Ma., U.S.	B5	98

Name	Map Ref.	Page
Framnes Mountains, mts., Ant.	C19	7
Franca, Braz.	C3	56
França, Braz.	D2	57
Française, Pointe, c., Fr. Gu.	A4	59
Francavilla Fontana, Italy	D6	23
France, ctry., Eur.	D5	16
Frances, Ky., U.S.	e9	94
Francés, Cabo, c., Cuba	D2	64
Francestown, N.H., U.S.	E3	106
Francesville, In., U.S.	C4	91
Franceville, Gabon	F2	46
Franche-Comté, hist. reg., Fr.	D6	16
Francis, Sask.	G4	75
Francis, Ok., U.S.	C5	113
Francis, Ut., U.S.	C4	121
Francis, W.V., U.S.	k10	125
Francis, Lake, l., N.H., U.S.	f7	106
Francis Case, Lake, res., S.D., U.S.	D6	118
Francisco, In., U.S.	H3	91
Francisco Sá, Braz.	B4	56
Francis Creek, Wi., U.S.	h10	126
Francistown, Bots.	B4	49
François, Newf.	E3	72
François Lake, l., B.C.	C5	69
Franconia, N.H., U.S.	B3	106
Franconia, Va., U.S.	*B5	123
Franconia Notch, N.H., U.S.	B3	106
Franconville, Fr.	g9	16
Francs Peak, mtn., Wy., U.S.	C3	127
Franeker, Neth.	A5	17
Frank, W.V., U.S.	C5	125
Frankel City, Tx., U.S.	C1	120
Frankenberg, E. Ger.	C8	19
Frankenberg [-Eder], W. Ger.	C4	18
Frankenmuth, Mi., U.S.	E7	99
Frankenthal, W. Ger.	D4	18
Frankewing, Tn., U.S.	B5	119
Frankfield, Jam.	E14	65
Frankford, Ont.	C7	73
Frankford, De., U.S.	F5	85
Frankford, Mo., U.S.	B6	102
Frankford, W.V., U.S.	D4	125
Frankford see Kilcormac, Ire.	D4	11
Frankfort, S. Afr.	C4	49
Frankfort, Il., U.S.	m9	90
Frankfort, In., U.S.	D4	91
Frankfort, Ks., U.S.	C7	93
Frankfort, Ky., U.S.	B5	94
Frankfort, Me., U.S.	D4	96
Frankfort, Mi., U.S.	D4	99
Frankfort, N.Y., U.S.	B5	109
Frankfort, Oh., U.S.	C2	112
Frankfort, S.D., U.S.	C7	118
Frankfurt [am Main], W. Ger.	C4	18
Frankfurt [an der Oder], E. Ger.	B7	18
Fränkische Saale, stm., W. Ger.	C5	19
Frank Lake, l., Alta.	D4	68
Franklin, Man.	D2	70
Franklin, Al., U.S.	D2	78
Franklin, Az., U.S.	E6	80
Franklin, Ar., U.S.	A4	81
Franklin, Ct., U.S.	C7	84
Franklin, Ga., U.S.	C1	87
Franklin, Id., U.S.	G7	89
Franklin, Il., U.S.	D3	90
Franklin, In., U.S.	F5	91
Franklin, Ia., U.S.	D6	92
Franklin, Ks., U.S.	E9	93
Franklin, Ky., U.S.	D3	94
Franklin, La., U.S.	E4	95
Franklin, Me., U.S.	D4	96
Franklin, Ma., U.S.	B5	98
Franklin, Mn., U.S.	F4	100
Franklin, Mo., U.S.	B5	102
Franklin, Ne., U.S.	D7	104
Franklin, N.H., U.S.	D3	106
Franklin, N.J., U.S.	A3	107
Franklin, N.Y., U.S.	C5	109
Franklin, N.C., U.S.	f9	110
Franklin, Oh., U.S.	C1	112
Franklin, Pa., U.S.	D2	115
Franklin, Tn., U.S.	B5	119
Franklin, Tx., U.S.	D4	120
Franklin, Va., U.S.	D6	123
Franklin, W.V., U.S.	C5	125
Franklin, Wi., U.S.	n11	126
Franklin, dept., N.W. Ter.	B15	66
Franklin, co., Al., U.S.	A2	78
Franklin, co., Ar., U.S.	B2	81
Franklin, co., Fl., U.S.	C2	86
Franklin, co., Ga., U.S.	B3	87
Franklin, co., Id., U.S.	G7	89
Franklin, co., Il., U.S.	E4	90
Franklin, co., In., U.S.	F7	91
Franklin, co., Ia., U.S.	B4	92
Franklin, co., Ks., U.S.	D8	93
Franklin, co., Ky., U.S.	B5	94
Franklin, co., La., U.S.	B4	95
Franklin, co., Ma., U.S.	A2	98
Franklin, co., Ms., U.S.	D3	101
Franklin, co., Mo., U.S.	C6	102
Franklin, co., Ne., U.S.	D7	104
Franklin, co., N.Y., U.S.	f10	109
Franklin, co., N.C., U.S.	A4	110
Franklin, co., Oh., U.S.	B2	112
Franklin, co., Pa., U.S.	G6	115
Franklin, co., Tn., U.S.	B5	119
Franklin, co., Tx., U.S.	C5	120
Franklin, co., Vt., U.S.	B2	122
Franklin, co., Va., U.S.	D3	123
Franklin, co., Wa., U.S.	C6	124
Franklin, Point, c., Ak., U.S.	A8	79
Franklin D. Roosevelt Lake, res., Wa., U.S.	B7	124
Franklin Falls Reservoir, res., N.H., U.S.	C3	106
Franklin Grove, Il., U.S.	B4	90
Franklin Island, i., Ont.	B4	73
Franklin Lake, l., N.W. Ter.	C13	66
Franklin Lake, l., Nv., U.S.	C6	105
Franklin Lakes, N.J., U.S.	*B4	107
Franklin Mine, Mi., U.S.	A2	99
Franklin Mountains, mts., N.W. Ter.	C8	66
Franklin Park, Il., U.S.	k9	90
Franklin Park, Pa., U.S.	h13	115
Franklin Square, N.Y., U.S.	*E7	109
Franklin Strait, strt., N.W. Ter.	B13	66
Franklinton, La., U.S.	D5	95
Franklinton, N.C., U.S.	A4	110
Franklinville, N.J., U.S.	D2	107
Franklinville, N.Y., U.S.	C2	109
Franklinville, N.C., U.S.	B3	110
Frankston, Austl.	*G8	50
Frankston, Tx., U.S.	C5	120
Frankville, Wi., U.S.	n12	126
Franktown, In., U.S.	D6	91
Franktown, Co., U.S.	B6	83
Frankville, Que.	D5	74
Frankville, Al., U.S.	D1	78
Frannie, Wy., U.S.	B4	127
Franz Josef Land, is., Sov. Un.	B8	29
Frascati, Italy	D4	23
Fraser, Co., U.S.	B5	83
Fraser, Ia., U.S.	B4	92
Fraser, Mi., U.S.	*o16	99
Fraser, i., Austl.	E9	50
Fraser, stm., B.C.	E7	69
Fraser, stm., Newf.	g9	72
Fraserburg, S. Afr.	D3	49
Fraserburgh, Scot., U.K.	B6	10
Fraserdale, Ont.	o19	73
Fraser Lake, B.C.	B5	69
Fraser Lake, l., B.C.	B5	69
Fraser Plateau, plat., B.C.	D6	69
Fraserwood, Man.	D3	70
Frasne, Fr.	C2	20
Frauenfeld, Switz.	E4	18
Fray Bentos, Ur.	E1	56
Fray Marcos, Ur.	E1	56
Frazee, Mn., U.S.	D3	100
Frazer, Mt., U.S.	B10	103
Frazeysburg, Oh., U.S.	B3	112
Frazier Park, Ca., U.S.	E4	82
Freda, Mi., U.S.	A2	99
Frederic, Mi., U.S.	D6	99
Frederica, De., U.S.	D4	85
Fredericia, Den.	J3	14
Frederick, Co., U.S.	A6	83
Frederick, Il., U.S.	C3	90
Frederick, Md., U.S.	B3	97
Frederick, Ok., U.S.	C2	113
Frederick, S.D., U.S.	B7	118
Frederick, co., Md., U.S.	B3	97
Frederick, co., Va., U.S.	A4	123
Frederick Hall, Va., U.S.	C5	123
Fredericksburg, In., U.S.	H5	91
Fredericksburg, Ia., U.S.	B5	92
Fredericksburg, Oh., U.S.	B4	112
Fredericksburg, Pa., U.S.	F9	115
Fredericksburg, Tx., U.S.	D3	120
Fredericksburg, Va., U.S.	B5	123
Frederick Sound, strt., Ak., U.S.	m23	79
Fredericktown, Mo., U.S.	D7	102
Fredericktown, Oh., U.S.	B3	112
Fredericktown, Pa., U.S.	F1	115
Fredericton, N.B.	D3	71
Fredericton Junction, N.B.	D3	71
Frederika, Ia., U.S.	B5	92
Frederiksberg, Den.	*J5	14
Frederiksberg, co., Den.	C6	15
Frederikshavn, Den.	I4	14
Frederikssund, Den.	C6	15
Frederiksted, V.I.U.S.	H12	64
Frederiksværk, Den.	C6	15
Fredonia, Al., U.S.	C4	78
Fredonia, Az., U.S.	A3	80
Fredonia, In., U.S.	H5	91
Fredonia, Ia., U.S.	C6	92
Fredonia, Ks., U.S.	E8	93
Fredonia, Ky., U.S.	C1	94
Fredonia, N.Y., U.S.	C1	109
Fredonia, Pa., U.S.	D1	115
Fredonia, Tx., U.S.	D3	120
Fredonia, Wi., U.S.	E6	126
Fredrikstad, Nor.	H4	14
Freeborn, Mn., U.S.	G5	100
Freeborn, co., Mn., U.S.	G5	100
Freeburg, Il., U.S.	E4	90
Freeburg, Mo., U.S.	C6	102
Freeburg, Pa., U.S.	E8	115
Freedom, Ca., U.S.	*D3	82
Freedom, Me., U.S.	D3	96
Freedom, N.H., U.S.	C4	106
Freedom, Ok., U.S.	A2	113
Freedom, Pa., U.S.	E1	115
Freedom, Wi., U.S.	h9	126
Freedom, Wy., U.S.	D2	127
Freehold, N.J., U.S.	C4	107
Freeland, Mi., U.S.	E6	99
Freeland, N.C., U.S.	C4	110
Freeland, Pa., U.S.	D10	115
Freeland Park, In., U.S.	C3	91
Freelandville, In., U.S.	G3	91
Freel Peak, mtn., Ca., U.S.	C4	82
Freels, Cape, c., Newf.	E5	72
Freels, Cape, c., Newf.	D5	72
Freeman, Mo., U.S.	C3	102
Freeman, S.D., U.S.	D8	118
Freeman, Wa., U.S.	g14	124
Freeman, stm., Alta.	B3	68
Freeman Lake, l., In., U.S.	C4	91
Freemansburg, Pa., U.S.	E11	115
Freemanville, Al., U.S.	D2	78
Freemason Island, is., La., U.S.	E7	95
Freemount, Ire.	E3	11
Freeport, Bah.	*A4	64
Freeport, N.S.	E3	71
Freeport, Fl., U.S.	u15	86
Freeport, Il., U.S.	A4	90
Freeport, Ks., U.S.	E6	93
Freeport, Me., U.S.	E2	96
Freeport, Mi., U.S.	F5	99
Freeport, N.Y., U.S.	n15	109
Freeport, Oh., U.S.	B4	112
Freeport, Pa., U.S.	E2	115
Freeport, Tx., U.S.	E5	120
Freer, Tx., U.S.	F3	120
Free Soil, Mi., U.S.	D4	99
Freestone, co., Tx., U.S.	D4	120
Freetown, P.E.I.	C6	71
Freetown, S.L.	G2	45
Freetown, In., U.S.	G5	91
Free Union, Va., U.S.	B4	123
Freeville, N.Y., U.S.	C4	109
Freezeout Mountains, mts., Wy., U.S.	D6	127
Fregenal de la Sierra, Spain	C2	22
Fregene, Italy	h8	23
Freiberg, E. Ger.	C6	18
Freiberger Mulde, stm., Eur.	B8	19
Freiburg [im Breisgau], W. Ger.	D3	18
Freienbach, Switz.	B6	21
Freirina, Chile	E1	55
Freising, W. Ger.	D5	18
Freistadt, Aus.	D7	18
Freital, E. Ger.	B8	19
Fréjus, Fr.	F7	16
Fréjus Tunnel, Eur.	D2	20
Frelighsburg, Que.	D5	74
Fremantle, Austl.	F2	50
Fremont, Ca., U.S.	D2	82
Fremont, In., U.S.	A8	91
Fremont, Ia., U.S.	C5	92
Fremont, Mo., U.S.	E6	102
Fremont, Ne., U.S.	C9	104
Fremont, N.H., U.S.	E4	106
Fremont, N.C., U.S.	B5	110
Fremont, Oh., U.S.	A2	112
Fremont, Ut., U.S.	E4	121
Fremont, Wi., U.S.	D5	126
Fremont, co., Co., U.S.	C5	83
Fremont, co., Id., U.S.	E7	89
Fremont, co., Ia., U.S.	D2	92
Fremont, co., Wy., U.S.	C4	127
Fremont, stm., Ut., U.S.	E5	121
Fremont Island, i., Ut., U.S.	B3	121
Fremont Peak, mtn., Wy., U.S.	C3	127
French, stm., Ont.	A4	73
French Broad, stm., U.S.	D10	119
Frenchburg, Ky., U.S.	C6	94
French Camp, Ms., U.S.	B4	101
French Creek, W.V., U.S.	C4	125
French Creek, stm., Man.	A5	70
French Creek, stm., Pa., U.S.	C2	115
French Frigate Shoals, rf., Hi., U.S.	m14	88
Frenchglen, Or., U.S.	E8	114
French Guiana, dep., S.A.	B4	59
French Gulch, Ca., U.S.	B2	82
French Island, Wi., U.S.	*E2	126
French Lick, In., U.S.	G4	91
Frenchman, Nv., U.S.	D3	105
Frenchman Bay, b., Me., U.S.	D4	96
Frenchman Butte, Sask.	D1	75
Frenchman Creek, stm., U.S.	A4	123
Frenchman Hills, hills, Wa., U.S.	C6	124
Frenchman Knob, mtn., Ky., U.S.	C4	94
Frenchman Lake, l., Nv., U.S.	G6	105
Frenchman Park, Fl., U.S.	D5	86
Frenchman's Cove, Newf.	D2	72
Frenchman's Cove, Newf.	E4	72
Frenchmans Island, Newf.	B4	72
Frenchpark, Ire.	D3	11
French Polynesia, dep., Oc.	H13	6
French River, Mn., U.S.	D7	100
French Settlement, La., U.S.	D5	95
French Southern and Antarctic Territories, dep., Afr.	*J1	2
Frenchton, W.V., U.S.	C4	125
Frenchtown, Mt., U.S.	C2	103
Frenchtown, N.J., U.S.	B2	107
French Village, N.S.	E6	71
Frenchville, Me., U.S.	A4	96
Frenda, Alg.	B5	44
Fresco, I.C.	E3	45
Fresco, stm., Braz.	D4	59
Freshfield, Mount, mtn., Can.	D2	69
Freshford, Ire.	E4	11
Freshwater, Eng., U.K.	D6	12
Fresnillo [de González Echeverría], Mex.	C4	63
Fresno, Ca., U.S.	D4	82
Fresno, Oh., U.S.	B4	112
Fresno, co., Ca., U.S.	D4	82
Fresno Reservoir, res., Mt., U.S.	B6	103
Freudenstadt, W. Ger.	D4	18
Frévent, Fr.	B5	16
Frewsburg, N.Y., U.S.	C1	109
Freyburg, E. Ger.	B6	19
Freycinet Peninsula, pen., Austl.	o15	50
Freyenstein, E. Ger.	E6	15
Freyming-Merlebach, Fr.	E6	17
Freyung, W. Ger.	E8	19
Fria, Gui.	D2	45
Fria, Cape, c., Nmb.	A1	49
Friant, Ca., U.S.	D4	82
Friars Point, Ms., U.S.	A3	101
Frias, Arg.	E2	55
Fribourg, Switz.	E3	18
Fribourg, state, Switz.	C3	20
Friday Harbor, Wa., U.S.	A2	124
Fridtjof Nansen, Mount, mtn., Ant.	A32	7
Friedberg, W. Ger.	C4	18
Friedens, Pa., U.S.	F3	115
Friedland, E. Ger.	B6	18
Friedrichroda, E. Ger.	C5	19
Friedrichshafen, W. Ger.	E4	18
Friedrichskoog, W. Ger.	D2	15
Friedrichstadt, W. Ger.	D3	15
Friedrichsthal, W. Ger.	D2	19
Friend, Ne., U.S.	D8	104
Friendship, Ar., U.S.	C3	81
Friendship, In., U.S.	G7	91
Friendship, Me., U.S.	E3	96
Friendship, N.Y., U.S.	C2	109
Friendship, Oh., U.S.	D2	112
Friendship, Tn., U.S.	B2	119
Friendship, Wi., U.S.	E4	126
Friendsville, Md., U.S.	k12	97
Friendsville, Tn., U.S.	D9	119
Friendswood, In., U.S.	E5	91
Friendswood, Tx., U.S.	*r14	120
Frierson, La., U.S.	B2	95
Fries, Va., U.S.	D2	123
Friesach, Aus.	E7	18
Friesack, E. Ger.	C7	18
Friesland, Wi., U.S.	E4	126
Friesland, prov., Neth.	A5	17
Fries Mills, N.J., U.S.	D2	107
Friesoythe, W. Ger.	B4	18
Frigate Point, c., Mid. Is.	K3	52
Frio, co., Tx., U.S.	E3	120
Frio, stm., Tx., U.S.	E3	120
Frio Draw, val., U.S.	C6	108
Friona, Tx., U.S.	B1	120
Fripps Island, i., S.C., U.S.	G7	117
Frisco, Co., U.S.	B4	83
Frisco City, Al., U.S.	D2	78
Frisco Peak, mtn., Ut., U.S.	E2	121
Frissell, Mount, mtn., U.S.	A2	84
Fristoe, Mo., U.S.	C4	102
Fritch, Tx., U.S.	B2	120
Fritzlar, W. Ger.	C4	18
Friuli-Venezia Giulia, prov., Italy	C8	20
Frobisher, Sask.	H4	75
Frobisher Bay, b., N.W. Ter.	D19	66
Frobisher Lake, l., Sask.	m7	75
Frog Lake, l., Alta.	C5	68
Frogmore, La., U.S.	C4	95
Frogmore, S.C., U.S.	G6	117
Frohna, Mo., U.S.	D8	102
Froid, Mt., U.S.	B12	103
Frolovo, Sov. Un.	G14	27
Fromberg, Mt., U.S.	E8	103
Frome, Jam.	E12	65
Frome, Eng., U.K.	C5	12
Frome, stm., Eng., U.K.	D5	12
Frome, Lake, l., Austl.	F6	50
Frontenac, Ks., U.S.	E9	93
Frontenac, Mn., U.S.	F6	100
Frontenac, co., Ont.	C8	73
Frontenac, co., Que.	D7	74
Frontera, Mex.	D6	63
Frontier, Sask.	H1	75
Frontier, Wy., U.S.	E2	127
Frontier, co., Ne., U.S.	D5	104
Frontignan, Fr.	F5	16
Frontino, Páramo, mtn., Col.	B2	60
Front Range, mts., Co., U.S.	A5	83
Front Royal, Va., U.S.	B4	123
Frosinone, Italy	D2	23
Frost, Mn., U.S.	G5	100
Frost, Tx., U.S.	C4	120
Frostburg, Md., U.S.	k13	97
Frostproof, Fl., U.S.	E5	86
Frouard, Fr.	F6	17
Froude, Sask.	H4	75
Frøya, i., Nor.	F3	14
Fruges, Fr.	D2	17
Fruita, Co., U.S.	B2	83
Fruitdale, Al., U.S.	D1	78
Fruitdale, S.D., U.S.	C2	118
Fruithurst, Al., U.S.	B4	78
Fruitland, Id., U.S.	F2	89
Fruitland, Ia., U.S.	C6	92
Fruitland, Ks., U.S.	E8	93
Fruitland, Md., U.S.	D6	97
Fruitland, Mo., U.S.	D8	102
Fruitland, N.M., U.S.	A1	108
Fruitland, Tn., U.S.	B3	119
Fruitland, Ut., U.S.	C5	121
Fruitland Park, Fl., U.S.	D5	86
Fruitland Park, Ms., U.S.	E4	101
Fruitport, Mi., U.S.	E4	99
Fruitvale, B.C.	E9	69
Fruitvale, Co., U.S.	B2	83
Fruitvale, Id., U.S.	E2	89
Fruitvale, Wa., U.S.	C5	124
Fruitville, Fl., U.S.	E4	86
Frunze, Sov. Un.	H10	28
Frunze, Sov. Un.	E10	29
Frutal, Braz.	C3	56
Frutigen, Switz.	C4	21
Fry, Ga., U.S.	B2	87
Fryazevo, Sov. Un.	n18	27
Fryburg, Pa., U.S.	D2	115
Fryeburg, La., U.S.	B2	95
Fryeburg, Me., U.S.	D2	96
Frys, Sask.	H5	75
Fu'an, China	K8	32
Fuchou see Fuzhou, China	F8	31
Fuchū, Japan	*I9	33
Fuding, China	K9	32
Fuencarral, Spain	p17	22
Fuente-Álamo [de Murcia], Spain	D5	22
Fuente de Cantos, Spain	C2	22
Fuente el Saz, Spain	o17	22
Fuente Obejuna, Spain	C3	22
Fuentesaúco, Spain	B3	22
Fuentes [de Andalucía], Spain	B3	22
Fuerte, stm., Mex.	B3	63
Fuerte Olimpo, Para.	D4	55
Fuerteventura, i., Spain	m14	22
Fuglebjerg, Den.	C5	15
Fugou, China	G6	32
Fuhai, China	B2	31
Fuji, Mount, vol., Japan	I9	33
Fujian, prov., China	F9	32
Fujieda, Japan	o17	33
Fujimi, Japan	n17	33
Fujin, China	B11	31
Fujinomiya, Japan	n17	33
Fujisawa, Japan	*I9	33
Fuji-yoshida, Japan	n17	33
Fukagawa, Japan	E10	33
Fūkah, Egypt	G6	40
Fukien see Fujian, prov., China	F8	31
Fukuchiyama, Japan	I7	33
Fukue Island, i., Japan	J4	33
Fukui, Japan	D12	31
Fukuoka, Japan	E11	31
Fukuoka, Japan	F10	33
Fukushima, Japan	I8	33
Fukushima, Japan	H10	33
Fukuyama, Japan	I6	33
Fulaga, i., Fiji	I16	52
Fulaga Passage, strt., Fiji	I16	52
Fulda, W. Ger.	C4	18
Fulda, In., U.S.	H4	91
Fulda, Mn., U.S.	G3	100
Fulda, stm., W. Ger.	B4	19
Fuling, China	J2	32
Fullerton, Ont.	D3	73
Fullerton, Ca., U.S.	n13	82
Fullerton, La., U.S.	D3	95
Fullerton, Ne., U.S.	C8	104
Fulton, Al., U.S.	D2	78
Fulton, Ar., U.S.	D2	81
Fulton, Il., U.S.	B3	90
Fulton, In., U.S.	C5	91
Fulton, Ks., U.S.	D9	93
Fulton, Ky., U.S.	f9	94
Fulton, Md., U.S.	B4	97
Fulton, Mo., U.S.	C6	102
Fulton, Ms., U.S.	A5	101
Fulton, N.Y., U.S.	B4	109
Fulton, Oh., U.S.	B3	112
Fulton, S.D., U.S.	D8	118
Fulton, Tx., U.S.	E4	120
Fulton, co., Ar., U.S.	A4	81
Fulton, co., Ga., U.S.	C2	87
Fulton, co., Il., U.S.	C3	90
Fulton, co., In., U.S.	B5	91
Fulton, co., Ky., U.S.	f8	94
Fulton, co., N.Y., U.S.	B6	109
Fulton, co., Oh., U.S.	A1	112
Fulton, co., Pa., U.S.	G6	115
Fultondale, Al., U.S.	f7	78
Fultonham, N.Y., U.S.	C6	109
Fultz, Ky., U.S.	B6	94
Fumay, Fr.	C6	16
Funabashi, Japan	n19	33
Funafuti, Tuvalu	G10	6
Funchal, Port.	h12	22
Fundación, Col.	A3	60
Fundão, Braz.	B4	56
Fundão, Port.	B2	22
Fundy, Bay of, b., Can.	D4	71
Fundy National Park, N.B.	D4	71
Funhalouro, Moz.	B5	49
Funing, China	G6	32
Funing, China	H8	32
Funing Bay, b., China	K9	32
Funk, Ne., U.S.	D6	104
Funkley, Mn., U.S.	C4	100
Funkstown, Md., U.S.	A2	97
Funtua, Nig.	D6	45
Fuping, China	E9	32
Fuping, China	E8	32
Fuqing, China	F8	31
Fuquay-Varina, N.C., U.S.	B4	110
Fur, i., Den.	B3	15
Furancungo, Moz.	D6	47
Furano, Japan	E11	33
Fürg, Iran	C5	38
Furka Pass, Switz.	C5	21
Furley, Ks., U.S.	g12	93
Furmanov, Sov. Un.	C13	27
Furmanovka, Sov. Un.	E8	28
Furnace Brook, stm., Vt., U.S.	D3	122
Furnas, co., Ne., U.S.	D6	104
Furnas, Represa de, res., Braz.	C3	56
Furneaux Group, is., Austl.	o15	50
Furness, Sask.	D1	75
Furqlus, Syria	E11	40
Fürstenau, W. Ger.	B7	17
Fürstenfeld, Aus.	E8	18
Fürstenfeldbruck, W. Ger.	A7	20
Fürstenwalde [Spree], E. Ger.	B7	18
Fürth, W. Ger.	D5	18
Furth im Wald, W. Ger.	D7	19
Furukawa, Japan	H9	33
Furu Mountain, hill, Japan	P17	52
Fusagasugá, Col.	C3	60
Fuschl [am See], Aus.	B9	20
Fushan, China	D5	31
Fushan, China	C9	31
Fushun, China	C11	32
Fusilier, Sask.	F1	75
Fusong, China	E3	33
Füssen, W. Ger.	E5	18
Fusui, China	A7	35
Futatsune, rock, Japan	P17	52
Futrono, Sov. Un.	H10	28
Futrono, Chile	E10	29
Future City, Il., U.S.	F4	90
Fuwah, Eg.	C2	41
Fuxian, China	E9	32
Fuxian Hu, l., China	G5	31
Fuxin, China	C9	31
Fuyang, China	E8	31
Fuyang, China	E8	31
Fuyang, stm., China	B9	31
Fuyu, China	C2	33
Fuyu, China	B7	33
Fuyuan, China	B7	33
Fuzhou, China	J7	32
Fuzhou (Fuchou), China	F8	31
Fuzhou, China	J7	32
Fyn, co., Den.	C4	15
Fyn, i., Den.	J4	14
Fyne, Loch, b., Scot., U.K.	B4	10

G

Gaalkacyo, Som.	D6	47
Gaastra, Mi., U.S.	B2	99
Gabaldon, N.M., U.S.	B4	108
Gabarus, N.S.	D9	71
Gabbs, Nv., U.S.	E4	105
Gabela, Ang.	D1	48
Gabès, Tun.	C7	44
Gabès, Golfe de, b., Tun.	C7	44
Gabin, Pol.	B5	26
Gabon, ctry., Afr.	A2	46
Gaborone, Bots.	B4	49
Gabriel, Mount, hill, Ire.	F2	11
Gabriels, N.Y., U.S.	f10	109
Gabriola, B.C.	f12	69
Gabrovo, Bul.	D7	24
Gachsārān, Iran	F5	39
Gackle, N.D., U.S.	C6	111
Gacko, Yugo.	D4	24
Gadag, India	E6	36
Gadmen, Switz.	C5	21
Gadsby, Alta.	C4	68
Gadsden, Az., U.S.	E1	80
Gadsden, Al., U.S.	A3	78
Gadsden, S.C., U.S.	D6	117
Gadsden, Tn., U.S.	B3	119
Gadsden, co., Fl., U.S.	B2	86
Gadyach, Sov. Un.	F10	27
Găeşti, Rom.	C7	24
Gaeta, Italy	D4	23
Gaeta, Gulf of, b., Italy	D4	23
Gaffney, S.C., U.S.	A4	117
Gafsa, Tun.	B6	44
Gafour, Tun.	B6	44
Gage, Ok., U.S.	A2	113
Gage, co., Ne., U.S.	D9	104
Gage, Cape, c., P.E.I.	C7	71
Gagetown, N.B.	D3	71
Gagetown, Mi., U.S.	E7	99
Gagnoa, I.C.	G4	45
Gagliano del Capo, Italy	I13	23
Gagnon, Que.	h13	74
Gahanna, Oh., U.S.	k11	112
Gaibandha, Bngl.	E12	37
Gail, Tx., U.S.	C2	120
Gaildorf, W. Ger.	E4	19
Gaillac, Fr.	F4	16
Gaillard, Lake, l., Ct., U.S.	D5	84
Gaines, Mi., U.S.	F7	99
Gaines, Pa., U.S.	C6	115
Gaines, co., Tx., U.S.	C1	120
Gainesboro, Tn., U.S.	C8	119
Gaines Creek, stm., Ok., U.S.	C6	113
Gainesville, Fl., U.S.	C4	86
Gainesville, Ga., U.S.	B3	87
Gainesville, Mo., U.S.	E5	102
Gainesville, Tx., U.S.	C4	120
Gainesville, Va., U.S.	g11	123
Gainsborough, Eng., U.K.	D6	12
Gairloch, Scot., U.K.	C3	10
Gairloch, Loch, b., Scot., U.K.	C3	10
Gaither, Md., U.S.	B4	97
Gaithersburg, Md., U.S.	B3	97
Gaixian, China	C9	31
Gakona, Ak., U.S.	C10	79
Galahad, Alta.	C5	68
Galapagar, Spain	o16	22
Galápagos, ter., Ec.	g5	58
Galapagos Islands see Colón, Archipiélago de, is., Ec.	g5	58
Galashiels, Scot., U.K.	C5	10
Galata, Mt., U.S.	B5	103
Galaţi (Galacz), Rom.	C9	24
Galatia, Il., U.S.	F5	90
Galatia, Ks., U.S.	D5	93
Galátsion, Grc.	*C4	25
Galax, Va., U.S.	D2	123
Galaxídhion, Grc.	C4	25
Gáldar, Spain	m14	22
Galeana, Mex.	A3	63
Galen, Tn., U.S.	C8	119
Galena, Ak., U.S.	C7	79
Galena, Il., U.S.	A3	90
Galena, Ks., U.S.	E9	93
Galena, Md., U.S.	B6	97
Galena, Mo., U.S.	E4	102
Galena, Oh., U.S.	B3	112
Galena Park, Tx., U.S.	r14	120
Galeota Point, c., Trin.	K14	64
Galera, Punta, c., Chile	B2	54
Galera, Punta, c., Ec.	A1	58
Galera, Punta, c., Trin.	K14	64
Galesburg, Il., U.S.	C3	90
Galesburg, Ks., U.S.	E8	93
Galesburg, Mi., U.S.	F5	99
Galesburg, N.D., U.S.	B8	111
Gales Creek, Or., U.S.	B3	114
Gales Ferry, Ct., U.S.	D7	84
Galestown, Md., U.S.	C6	97
Galesville, Md., U.S.	C4	97
Galesville, Wi., U.S.	D2	126
Galeton, Co., U.S.	A6	83
Galeton, Pa., U.S.	C6	115
Galette, Ont.	*B8	73
Galeville, N.Y., U.S.	*B4	109
Galguduud, prov., Som.	D6	47
Galiano Island, i., B.C.	E6	69
Galich, Sov. Un.	D6	26
Galicia, hist. reg., Eur.	A1	22
Galicia, hist. reg., Spain	A1	22
Galien, Mi., U.S.	G4	99
Galilee, R.I., U.S.	F3	116
Galilee, hist. reg., Isr.	B7	41
Galilee, Lake, l., Austl.	D8	50
Galilee, Sea of see Kinneret, Yam, l., Isr.	B7	41
Galion, Oh., U.S.	B3	112
Galisteo Creek, stm., N.M., U.S.	k8	108
Galite Channel, strt., Tun.	F2	23
Galiuro Mountains, mts., Az., U.S.	E5	80
Galivants Ferry, S.C., U.S.	C9	117
Gallan Head, c., Scot., U.K.	B1	13
Gallant, Al., U.S.	B3	78
Gallarate, Italy	B2	23
Gällaryd, Swe.	A8	15
Gallatin, Tn., U.S.	A5	119
Gallatin, co., Il., U.S.	F5	90
Gallatin, co., Ky., U.S.	B5	94
Gallatin, co., Mt., U.S.	E5	103
Gallatin, stm., Mt., U.S.	E5	103
Gallatin Gateway, Mt., U.S.	E5	103
Gallatin Range, mts., Mt., U.S.	E5	103
Gallaway, Tn., U.S.	B2	119
Galle, Sri L.	G7	36
Gallegos, stm., Arg.	G2	54
Gallery Head, c., Ire.	F3	11
Galli, co., Oh., U.S.	D3	112
Galliano, La., U.S.	E5	95
Galliate, Italy	D4	20
Gallicano nel Lazio, Italy	h9	23
Gallina, N.M., U.S.	A3	108
Gallinas, Punta, c., Col.	A3	60
Gallinas Mountains, mts., N.M., U.S.	C2	108
Gallipoli, Italy	I12	23
Gallipoli see Gelibolu, Tur.	B6	40
Gallipoli Peninsula, pen., Tur.	B6	40
Gallipolis, Oh., U.S.	D3	112
Gallipolis Ferry, W.V., U.S.	C2	125
Gällivare, Swe.	D9	14
Gallneukirchen, Aus.	E9	19
Gallo, stm., Spain	B5	22
Gallo Mountains, mts., N.M., U.S.	C1	108
Galloo Island, i., N.Y., U.S.	A4	109
Galloway, Oh., U.S.	m10	112
Galloway, W.V., U.S.	B4	125
Galloway, Wi., U.S.	D4	126
Galloway, Mull of, c., Scot., U.K.	F4	13
Gällstad, Swe.	A7	15
Gallup, N.M., U.S.	B1	108
Galoa Bay, b., Fiji	H15	52
Galoa Harbour, b., Fiji	H15	52
Galt, Ca., U.S.	C3	82
Galt, Mo., U.S.	A4	102
Galten, Swe.	t34	14
Galtür, Aus.	C6	20
Galtymore Mountain, mtn., Ire.	E3	11
Galva, Il., U.S.	B3	90
Galva, Ks., U.S.	D6	93
Galveston, In., U.S.	C5	91
Galveston, Tx., U.S.	E5	120
Galveston, co., Tx., U.S.	E5	120
Galveston Bay, b., Tx., U.S.	E5	120
Galveston Island, i., Tx., U.S.	E5	120
Galvez, Arg.	A4	54
Galway, Ire.	D2	11
Galway, co., Ire.	D2	11
Galway Bay, b., Ire.	D2	11
Gamagōri, Japan	o16	33
Gamaliel, Ar., U.S.	A3	81
Gamaliel, Ky., U.S.	D4	94
Gamarra, Col.	B3	60
Gamba, China	C12	37
Gamba, Zaire	B3	48
Gambaga, Ghana	D4	45
Gambela, Eth.	D3	47
Gambell, Ak., U.S.	C5	79
Gambia, ctry., Afr.	D1	45
Gambia, stm., Afr.	F2	42
Gambier, Bah.	m17	64
Gambier, Oh., U.S.	B3	112
Gamboa, Pan.	k11	62
Gambo, Newf.	D4	72
Gamboma, Congo	B2	48

Name	Map Ref.	Page
Gamboula, Cen. Afr. Rep.	E3	46
Gambrills, Md., U.S.	B4	97
Gameleira, Braz.	C3	57
Gamerco, N.M., U.S.	B1	108
Gammertingen, W. Ger.	A5	20
Gammon, stm., Can.	D4	70
Gamo Gofa, prov., Eth.	D4	47
Gamph, Slieve, mts., Ire.	C3	11
Ganado, Az., U.S.	B6	80
Ganado, Tx., U.S.	E4	120
Gananoque, Ont.	C8	73
Gancheng, China	C8	35
Ganda, Ang.	D1	48
Gandajika, Zaire	C3	48
Gandak, stm., Asia	D10	37
Gandeeville, W.V., U.S.	C3	125
Gander, Newf.	D4	72
Gander, stm., Newf.	D4	72
Gander Bay, Newf.	D4	72
Gander Lake, l., Newf.	D4	72
Gāndhīnagar, India	D5	36
Gandhi Reservoir, res., India	E5	37
Gandía, Spain	C5	22
Gandy, Ne., U.S.	C5	104
Gangānagar, India	C5	36
Gangāpur, India	D6	37
Gangaw, Burma	D9	36
Gangdise Mountains, mts., China	B9	37
Ganges, B.C.	g12	69
Ganges, Fr.	F5	16
Ganges, Oh., U.S.	B3	112
Ganges, stm., Asia	D8	36
Ganges, Mouths of the, mth., Asia	D8	36
Gang Mills, N.Y., U.S.	C3	109
Gangtok, India	C8	36
Gangu, China	E6	31
Gani, Indon.	F7	34
Gan Jiang, stm., China	K6	32
Gannan, China	C1	33
Gannat, Fr.	D5	16
Gannet Islands, is., Newf.	F7	72
Gannett Peak, mtn., Wy., U.S.	C3	127
Gannon, Md., U.S.	k12	97
Gannvalley, S.D., U.S.	C7	118
Gano, Oh., U.S.	n13	112
Gans, Ok., U.S.	B7	113
Gansevoort, N.Y., U.S.	B7	109
Gansu, prov., China	D5	31
Ganta, Lib.	E3	45
Gantt, Al., U.S.	D3	78
Gantt, S.C., U.S.	B3	117
Gantt Lake, res., Al., U.S.	D3	78
Gantts Quarry, Al., U.S.	B3	78
Ganyu, China	E8	31
Ganzhou, China	F7	31
Gao, Mali	C5	45
Gao'an, China	J6	32
Gaoil, Sliabh, mtn., Scot., U.K.	E3	13
Gaoua, Burkina	D4	45
Gaoual, Gui.	D2	45
Gaoyou, China	H8	32
Gaoyou Lake, l., China	H8	32
Gap, Fr.	E7	16
Gap, Pa., U.S.	G9	115
Gapan, Phil.	o13	34
Gapland, Md., U.S.	B2	97
Gap Mills, W.V., U.S.	D4	125
Gar, China	B7	36
Gara, Lough, l., Ire.	D2	10
Garacad, Som.	D6	47
Garachiné, Pan.	F8	62
Garachiné, Punta, c., Pan.	F8	62
Garanhuns, Braz.	C3	57
Garapan, N. Mar. Is.	D7	52
Garapan, Lagunan, b., N. Mar. Is.	D7	52
Garau, Canal de, Mex.	h9	63
Garbahaarrey, Som.	E5	47
Garber, Ia., U.S.	B6	92
Garber, Ok., U.S.	A4	113
Garberville, Ca., U.S.	B2	82
Garbsen, W. Ger.	*B4	18
Garça, Braz.	G3	57
Garching [an der Alz], W. Ger.	A8	20
Garcia, Co., U.S.	D5	83
Garciasville, Tx., U.S.	F3	120
Gard, stm., Fr.	E6	16
Gardane, Fr.	F6	16
Gardar, N.D., U.S.	A8	111
Gardelegen, E. Ger.	B5	18
Garden, Mi., U.S.	C3	99
Garden, co., Ne., U.S.	C3	104
Gardena, Ca., U.S.	n12	82
Gardena, N.D., U.S.	A5	111
Garden City, Al., U.S.	A3	78
Garden City, Co., U.S.	*A6	83
Garden City, Ga., U.S.	D5	87
Garden City, Id., U.S.	F2	89
Garden City, In., U.S.	F6	91
Garden City, Ks., U.S.	E3	93
Garden City, La., U.S.	E4	95
Garden City, Mi., U.S.	p15	99
Garden City, Mn., U.S.	F4	100
Garden City, Mo., U.S.	C3	102
Garden City, N.Y., U.S.	*E7	109
Garden City, S.D., U.S.	C8	118
Garden City, Tx., U.S.	D2	120
Garden City, Ut., U.S.	B4	121
Garden City Park, N.Y., U.S.	*n15	109
Gardendale, Al., U.S.	B3	78
Gardendale, Tx., U.S.	E3	120
Garden Grove, Ca., U.S.	n13	82
Garden Grove, Ia., U.S.	D4	92
Garden Home, Or., U.S.	*B4	114
Garden Island, i., Mi., U.S.	C5	99
Garden of Gethsemane, Isr. Occ.	m14	41
Garden Plain, Il., U.S.	B3	90
Garden Plain, Ks., U.S.	E6	93
Garden Prairie, Il., U.S.	A5	90
Garden Reach, India	*D8	36
Gardenton, Man.	E3	70
Garden Valley, Id., U.S.	E3	89
Gardey, Arg.	D5	54
Gardi, Ga., U.S.	E5	87
Gardiner, Me., U.S.	D3	96
Gardiner, Mt., U.S.	E6	103
Gardiner, Or., U.S.	D2	114
Gardiners Island, i., N.Y., U.S.	m16	109
Gardner, Ar., U.S.	D3	81
Gardner, Co., U.S.	D5	83
Gardner, Fl., U.S.	E5	86
Gardner, Il., U.S.	B5	90
Gardner, Ks., U.S.	D9	93
Gardner, Ma., U.S.	A4	98
Gardner, N.D., U.S.	B9	111
Gardner, Tn., U.S.	A3	119
Gardner Canal, strt., B.C.	C3	69
Gardner Lake, l., Ct., U.S.	C6	84
Gardner Lake, l., Me., U.S.	D5	96
Gardner Mountain, mtn., N.H., U.S.	B3	106
Gardner Pinnacles, Hi., U.S.	k14	88
Gardnersville, Ky., U.S.	k14	94
Gardnerville, Nv., U.S.	E2	105
Gardone Riviera, Italy	D6	20
Gardone Val Trompia, Italy	D6	20
Garešnica, Yugo.	C3	24
Garfield, Ar., U.S.	A2	81
Garfield, Co., U.S.	C4	83
Garfield, Ga., U.S.	D4	87
Garfield, Ks., U.S.	D4	93
Garfield, Mn., U.S.	E3	100
Garfield, N.J., U.S.	h8	107
Garfield, Wa., U.S.	B8	124
Garfield, co., Co., U.S.	B2	83
Garfield, co., Mt., U.S.	C9	103
Garfield, co., Ne., U.S.	C6	104
Garfield, co., Ok., U.S.	A4	113
Garfield, co., Ut., U.S.	F4	121
Garfield, co., Wa., U.S.	C8	124
Garfield Heights, Oh., U.S.	h9	112
Garfield Mountain, mtn., Mt., U.S.	F4	103
Garfield Park, U.S.	*B3	85
Garfield Peak, mtn., Wy., U.S.	D5	127
Gargaliános, Grc.	D3	25
Gargano Peninsula, pen., Italy	D5	23
Gargnano, Italy	D6	20
Garibaldi, Braz.	D2	56
Garibaldi, Or., U.S.	B3	114
Garibaldi, Mount, mtn., B.C.	E6	69
Garibaldi Provincial Park, B.C.	D6	69
Garies, S. Afr.	D2	49
Garissa, Kenya	B6	48
Garita, N.M., U.S.	B5	108
Garland, Al., U.S.	D3	78
Garland, Ar., U.S.	D2	81
Garland, Ks., U.S.	E9	93
Garland, Me., U.S.	C3	96
Garland, Ne., U.S.	D9	104
Garland, N.C., U.S.	C4	110
Garland, Pa., U.S.	C3	115
Garland, Tn., U.S.	B2	119
Garland, Tx., U.S.	n10	120
Garland, Ut., U.S.	B3	121
Garland, Wy., U.S.	B4	127
Garland, co., Ar., U.S.	C2	81
Garm, Sov. Un.	H23	8
Garmisch-Partenkirchen, W. Ger.	E5	18
Garmouth, Scot., U.K.	C5	13
Garnavillo, Ia., U.S.	B6	92
Garneill, Mt., U.S.	D7	103
Garner, Ar., U.S.	B4	81
Garner, Ia., U.S.	A4	92
Garner, Ky., U.S.	C7	94
Garner, N.C., U.S.	B4	110
Garner Range, mts., Mt., U.S.	D3	103
Garnett, Ks., U.S.	D8	93
Garnett, S.C., U.S.	F5	117
Garnish, Newf.	E4	72
Garnpung, Lake, l., Austl.	F4	51
Garonne, stm., Eur.	E3	16
Garoowe, Som.	C4	47
Garou, Lac, l., Mali	C4	45
Garoua, Cam.	D2	46
Garrard, co., Ky., U.S.	C5	94
Garretson, S.D., U.S.	D9	118
Garrett, Il., U.S.	D5	90
Garrett, In., U.S.	B7	91
Garrett, Ky., U.S.	C7	94
Garrett, Pa., U.S.	G3	115
Garrett, Wy., U.S.	D7	127
Garrett, co., Md., U.S.	k12	97
Garrett Park, Md., U.S.	B3	97
Garrettsville, Oh., U.S.	A4	112
Garrick, Sask.	D3	75
Garrison, Ia., U.S.	B5	92
Garrison, Ky., U.S.	B6	94
Garrison, Md., U.S.	B4	97
Garrison, Mn., U.S.	D5	100
Garrison, Mt., U.S.	D4	103
Garrison, N.Y., U.S.	D7	109
Garrison, N.D., U.S.	B4	111
Garrison, Tx., U.S.	D5	120
Garrison, Ut., U.S.	E1	121
Garrison Dam, N.D., U.S.	B4	111
Garrisonville, Va., U.S.	B5	123
Garristown, Ire.	D5	11
Garron Point, c., N. Ire., U.K.	A6	11
Garrote, Pan.	h11	62
Garrovillas, Spain	C2	22
Garry, stm., Scot., U.K.	D5	13
Garry Lake, l., N.W. Ter.	C13	66
Garryowen, Mt., U.S.	E9	103
Garsen, Kenya	B7	48
Garson Lake, l., Can.	A5	68
Garson Quarry, Man.	D3	70
Garstang, Eng., U.K.	G6	13
Garth, Al., U.S.	A3	78
Garthby Station (Beaulac), Que.	D6	74
Gartz, E. Ger.	E8	15
Garut, Indon.	G3	34
Garvagh, N. Ire., U.K.	C5	11
Garvin, Mn., U.S.	F3	100
Garvin, Ok., U.S.	D7	113
Garvin, co., Ok., U.S.	C4	113
Garwin, Ia., U.S.	B5	92
Garwolin, Pol.	C6	26
Garwood, N.J., U.S.	*B4	107
Garwood, Tx., U.S.	E4	120
Gary, In., U.S.	A3	91
Gary, Mn., U.S.	C7	100
Gary, S.D., U.S.	C9	118
Gary, Tx., U.S.	C5	120
Gary, W.V., U.S.	D3	125
Garyarsa, China	B8	37
Garysburg, N.C., U.S.	A5	110
Garyville, La., U.S.	D5	95
Garza, co., Tx., U.S.	C2	120
Garza García, Mex.	*B4	63
Garza-Little Elm Reservoir, res., Tx., U.S.	C4	120
Garzón, Col.	C2	60
Gas, Ks., U.S.	E8	93
Gas City, In., U.S.	D6	91
Gasconade, Mo., U.S.	C6	102
Gasconade, co., Mo., U.S.	C6	102
Gasconade, stm., Mo., U.S.	C6	102
Gasconade, Osage Fork, stm., Mo., U.S.	D5	102
Gascony, hist. reg., Fr.	E3	16
Gascoyne, N.D., U.S.	C2	111
Gascoyne, stm., Austl.	E2	50
Gashaka, Nig.	E7	45
Gasherbrum, mtn., Asia	*A6	36
Gashua, Nig.	D7	45
Gasparilla Island, i., Fl., U.S.	F4	86
Gaspé, Que.	k14	74
Gaspé, Cap, c., Que.	G20	66
Gaspésie, Péninsule de la, pen., Que.	k13	74
Gasport, N.Y., U.S.	B2	109
Gasque, Al., U.S.	E2	78
Gassaway, Tn., U.S.	D8	119
Gassaway, W.V., U.S.	C4	125
Gassetts, Vt., U.S.	E3	122
Gassol, Nig.	E7	45
Gassville, Ar., U.S.	A3	81
Gaston, In., U.S.	D7	91
Gaston, N.C., U.S.	A5	110
Gaston, Or., U.S.	h11	114
Gaston, S.C., U.S.	D5	117
Gaston, co., N.C., U.S.	B1	110
Gaston Dam, N.C., U.S.	A5	110
Gastonia, N.C., U.S.	B1	110
Gastre, Arg.	C3	54
Gata, Cape, c., Spain	D4	22
Gata, Sierra de, mts., Spain	B2	22
Gatas, Cape, c., Cyp.	E9	40
Gatchina, Sov. Un.	B8	27
Gate, Ok., U.S.	A1	113
Gate City, Va., U.S.	f9	123
Gatehouse of Fleet, Scot., U.K.	F4	13
Gates, N.C., U.S.	A6	110
Gates, N.Y., U.S.	B3	109
Gates, Or., U.S.	C4	114
Gates, Tn., U.S.	B2	119
Gates, co., N.C., U.S.	A6	110
Gateshead, Eng., U.K.	C6	10
Gates of the Arctic National Park, Ak., U.S.	B9	79
Gatesville, Ms., U.S.	B3	101
Gatesville, N.C., U.S.	A6	110
Gatesville, Tx., U.S.	D4	120
Gateway, Ar., U.S.	*A2	81
Gateway, Co., U.S.	C2	83
Gateway, Or., U.S.	C5	114
Gatineau, Que.	D2	74
Gatineau, co., Que.	C2	74
Gatineau, stm., Que.	D2	74
Gatineau, Parc de la, Que.	D2	74
Gatliff, Ky., U.S.	D5	94
Gatlinburg, Tn., U.S.	D10	119
Gato, Co., U.S.	D3	83
Gattman, Ms., U.S.	B5	101
Gatton, Austl.	C9	51
Gatún, Pan.	k11	62
Gatún, Lago, res., Pan.	k11	62
Gatun Locks, Pan.	k11	62
Gatzke, Mn., U.S.	B3	100
Gau, i., Fiji	I15	52
Gauer Lake, l., Man.	A3	70
Gauja, stm., Sov. Un.	C5	27
Gaula, stm., Nor.	F4	14
Gauley Bridge, W.V., U.S.	C3	125
Gauley Mills, W.V., U.S.	C4	125
Gause, Tx., U.S.	D4	120
Gautier, Ms., U.S.	f8	101
Gávdhos, i., Grc.	E5	40
Gavins Point Dam, U.S.	B8	104
Gäv Khūnī, Bātlāq-e, sw., Iran	E6	39
Gävlebukten, b., Swe.	G7	14
Gavrilovka, Sov. Un.	G11	27
Gavrilov Posad, Sov. Un.	C13	27
Gawler, Austl.	G2	51
Gawler Ranges, mts., Austl.	F6	50
Gay, Ga., U.S.	C2	87
Gay, Mi., U.S.	A2	99
Gaya, India	D7	36
Gaya, Niger	D5	45
Gaya, Nig.	D6	45
Gay Head, Ma., U.S.	D6	98
Gay Head, c., Ma., U.S.	D6	98
Gaylesville, Al., U.S.	A4	78
Gaylord, Ks., U.S.	C5	93
Gaylord, Mi., U.S.	C6	99
Gaylord, Mn., U.S.	F4	100
Gaylord, Or., U.S.	E2	114
Gaylordsville, Ct., U.S.	C2	84
Gayndah, Austl.	B8	51
Gays, Il., U.S.	D5	90
Gaysin, Sov. Un.	G7	27
Gays Mills, Wi., U.S.	E3	126
Gaysville, Vt., U.S.	D3	122
Gaza (Ghazzah), Isr. Occ.	B3	38
Gaza, prov., Moz.	B5	49
Gaza Strip, ter., Isr. Occ.	C6	41
Gaziantep, Tur.	D11	40
Gazimağusa, N. Cyp.	E9	40
Gboko, Nig.	E6	45
Gdańsk (Danzig), Pol.	A5	26
Gdov, Sov. Un.	B6	27
Gdynia, Pol.	A5	26
Gearhart Mountain, mtn., Or., U.S.	E6	114
Geary, N.B.	D3	71
Geary, Ok., U.S.	B3	113
Geary, co., Ks., U.S.	D7	93
Geauga, co., Oh., U.S.	A4	112
Gebeit Mine, Sud.	A4	47
Gebze, Tur.	B7	25
Ged, La., U.S.	D2	95
Geddes, S.D., U.S.	D7	118
Gedera, Isr.	D3	41
Gedinne, Bel.	E4	17
Gediz, Tur.	C7	40
Gediz, stm., Tur.	C6	40
Gedo, prov., Som.	B10	128
Gedser, Den.	D5	15
Geel, Bel.	B5	16
Geelong, Austl.	G7	50
Geetbets, Bel.	D5	17
Geff, Il., U.S.	E5	90
Geiger, Al., U.S.	C1	78
Geiselhöring, W. Ger.	E6	19
Geisenfeld, W. Ger.	E6	19
Geislingen, W. Ger.	E5	19
Geismar, La., U.S.	h9	95
Geistown, Pa., U.S.	F4	115
Geist Reservoir, res., In., U.S.	E6	91
Geita, Tan.	B5	48
Gejiu, China	G5	31
Gela, Italy	F5	23
Gelderland, prov., Neth.	B5	17
Geldermalsen, Neth.	C5	17
Geldern, W. Ger.	C5	17
Geldrop, Neth.	C5	17
Geleen, Neth.	D5	17
Gelfingen, Switz.	B5	16
Gelibolu (Gallipoli), Tur.	B6	25
Gelinam Island, i., Marsh Is.	S17	52
Gelnhausen, W. Ger.	C4	19
Gelsenkirchen, W. Ger.	C3	18
Gelting, W. Ger.	D3	15
Gem, Alta.	D4	68
Gem, Id., U.S.	*B3	89
Gem, Ks., U.S.	C3	93
Gem, W.V., U.S.	C4	125
Gem, co., Id., U.S.	E2	89
Gemas, Malay.	K5	35
Gemena, Zaire	A2	48
Gemert, Neth.	C5	17
Gemla, Swe.	B7	40
Gemlik, Tur.	B7	40
Gemona del Friuli, Italy	C9	20
Gemünden, W. Ger.	C4	18
Gem Village, Co., U.S.	D3	83
Genale (Jubba), stm., Afr.	C7	47
Genarp, Swe.	C4	15
Gene Autry, Ok., U.S.	C5	113
General Acha, Arg.	B4	54
General Alvear, Arg.	B5	54
General Alvear, Arg.	A3	54
General Belgrano, Arg.	B5	54
General Carrera, Lago (Lago Buenos Aires), l., S.A.	D2	54
General Conesa, Arg.	C4	54
General Enrique Martínez, Ur.	E2	56
General Eugenio A. Garay, Para.	D3	55
General José de San Martín Zapallar, Arg.	E4	55
General Juan Madariaga, Arg.	B5	54
General La Madrid, Arg.	B4	54
General Lavalle, Arg.	B5	54
General Martín Miguel de Güemes, Arg.	D2	55
General Paz, Arg.	E4	55
General Pico, Arg.	B4	54
General Pinedo, Arg.	E3	55
General Roca, Arg.	B3	54
General San Martin, Arg.	g7	54
General Sarmiento, Arg.	g7	54
General Tinio, Phil.	o13	34
General Toshevo, Bul.	D9	24
General Viamonte, Arg.	B4	54
General Villegas, Arg.	B4	54
Genesee, Id., U.S.	C2	89
Genesee, Mi., U.S.	E7	99
Genesee, Pa., U.S.	C6	115
Genesee, co., Mi., U.S.	E7	99
Genesee, co., N.Y., U.S.	B2	109
Genesee, stm., N.Y., U.S.	C2	109
Genesee Depot, Wi., U.S.	n11	126
Geneseo, Il., U.S.	B3	90
Geneseo, Ks., U.S.	D5	93
Geneseo, N.Y., U.S.	C3	109
Geneseo, N.D., U.S.	C8	111
Geneva (Genève), Switz.	E3	18
Geneva, Al., U.S.	D4	78
Geneva, Ga., U.S.	D2	87
Geneva, Id., U.S.	G7	89
Geneva, Il., U.S.	B5	90
Geneva, In., U.S.	C8	91
Geneva, Ky., U.S.	C2	94
Geneva, Ne., U.S.	D8	104
Geneva, N.Y., U.S.	C4	109
Geneva, Oh., U.S.	A5	112
Geneva, Pa., U.S.	C1	115
Geneva, co., Al., U.S.	D4	78
Geneva, Lake, l., Eur.	E3	18
Geneva, Lake, l., Wi., U.S.	F5	126
Geneva-on-the-Lake, Oh., U.S.	A5	112
Genève, state, Switz.	C2	20
Genichesk, Sov. Un.	H10	27
Genil, stm., Spain	D3	22
Genk, Bel.	B6	16
Gennep, Neth.	C5	17
Gennevilliers, Fr.	g10	16
Genoa (Genova), Italy	B2	23
Genoa, Ar., U.S.	D2	81
Genoa, Co., U.S.	B7	83
Genoa, Il., U.S.	A5	90
Genoa, Ne., U.S.	C8	104
Genoa, Nv., U.S.	D2	105
Genoa, N.Y., U.S.	C4	109
Genoa, Oh., U.S.	A2	112
Genoa, Wi., U.S.	E2	126
Genoa, Gulf of, b., Italy	B2	23
Genoa City, Wi., U.S.	F5	126
Genola, Mn., U.S.	D5	100
Genola, Ut., U.S.	D4	121
Genoni, Switz.	D1	21
Genova see Genoa, Italy	B3	23
Genovesa, Isla, i., Ec.	f6	58
Gent (Ghent), Bel.	B5	16
Gentbrugge (part of Gent), Bel.	C3	17
Genthin, E. Ger.	B6	18
Gentilly, Fr.	g10	16
Gentilly, Mn., U.S.	C2	100
Gentofte, Den.	*C6	15
Gentry, Ar., U.S.	A1	81
Gentry, Mo., U.S.	A3	102
Gentry, co., Mo., U.S.	A3	102
Gentryville, In., U.S.	H3	91
Genzano di Roma, Italy	h9	23
Geographe Bay, b., Austl.	F2	50
Geographe Channel, strt., Austl.	D1	50
Geographical Society Island, i., Grnld.	B16	128
Geokchay, Sov. Un.	G18	8
George, S. Afr.	D3	49
George, Ia., U.S.	A2	92
George, N.C., U.S.	A5	110
George, co., Ms., U.S.	E5	101
George, i., Sov. Un.	B10	128
George, stm., Que.	g13	74
George, Cape, c., N.S.	D8	71
George, Lake, l., Austl.	G7	51
George, Lake, l., N.S.	E3	71
George, Lake, l., Fl., U.S.	C5	86
George, Lake, l., N.Y., U.S.	B7	109
George Air Force Base, mil., Ca., U.S.	E5	82
George B. Stevenson Reservoir, res., Pa., U.S.	D6	115
George Hill, mtn., Md., U.S.	k12	97
George Island, i., Newf.	A3	72
George Peak, mtn., Ut., U.S.	B2	121
Georgesville, Oh., U.S.	m10	112
Georgetown, Austl.	o15	50
Georgetown, Bah.	C6	64
Georgetown, Guy.	B7	59
Georgetown, P.E.I.	C7	71
Georgetown, Cay. U.S.	D8	63
George Town, Gam.	D2	45
Georgetown, Guy.	B7	59
Georgetown, St. Vin.	U26	65
Georgetown, Ar., U.S.	B4	81
Georgetown, Ca., U.S.	C3	82
Georgetown, Co., U.S.	B5	83
Georgetown, Ct., U.S.	D2	84
Georgetown, De., U.S.	F4	85
Georgetown, Fl., U.S.	C5	86
Georgetown, Ga., U.S.	E1	87
Georgetown, Id., U.S.	G7	89
Georgetown, Il., U.S.	D6	90
Georgetown, In., U.S.	H6	91
Georgetown, Ky., U.S.	B5	94
Georgetown, La., U.S.	C3	95
Georgetown, Ma., U.S.	A6	98
Georgetown, Mn., U.S.	C2	100
Georgetown, Ms., U.S.	D3	101
Georgetown, N.J., U.S.	C3	107
Georgetown, N.Y., U.S.	C5	109
Georgetown, Oh., U.S.	D2	112
Georgetown, S.C., U.S.	E9	117
Georgetown, Tn., U.S.	D9	119
Georgetown, Tx., U.S.	D4	120
Georgetown, co., S.C., U.S.	E9	117
George V Coast, Ant.	C28	7
Georgeville, Que.	D5	74
George VI Sound, strt., Ant.	B6	7
George Washington Birthplace National Monument, Va., U.S.	B6	123
George Washington Carver National Monument, Mo., U.S.	E3	102
George West, Tx., U.S.	E3	120
Georgia, state, Sov. Un.	E7	29
Georgia, state, U.S.	D3	87
Georgia, Strait of, strt., N.A.	E5	69
Georgia Center, Vt., U.S.	B2	122
Georgian Bay, b., Ont.	B3	73
Georgiana, Al., U.S.	D3	78
Georgina, stm., Austl.	C3	51
Georgiu-Dez, Sov. Un.	F12	27
Georgiyevsk, Sov. Un.	G17	8
Gera, E. Ger.	C6	18
Geraardsbergen, Bel.	D3	17
Geral, Serra, clf., Braz.	D2	56
Geral do Paraná, Serra, mts., Braz.	A3	56
Geraldine, Al., U.S.	A4	78
Geraldine, Mt., U.S.	C6	103
Geraldton, Austl.	E1	50
Geraldton, Ont.	o18	73
Gérardmer, Fr.	A2	20
Gerber, Ca., U.S.	B2	82
Gerber Reservoir, res., Or., U.S.	E5	114
Gerbstedt, E. Ger.	C6	18
Gercüş, Tur.	D13	40
Gerdau, stm., W. Ger.	F4	15
Gerdine, Mount, mtn., Ak., U.S.	C9	79
Gerede, Tur.	B9	40
Gereshk, Afg.	B3	36
Gérgal, Spain	D4	22
Gering, Ne., U.S.	C2	104
Gerlach, Nv., U.S.	C2	105
Gerlachovka, mtn., Czech.	D6	26
German Democratic Republic (East Germany), ctry., Eur.	B6	18
Germania, N.J., U.S.	D3	107
Germania, Pa., U.S.	C6	115
Germansen Lake, l., B.C.	B5	69
Germantown, N.B.	D5	71
Germantown, Il., U.S.	E4	90
Germantown, Ky., U.S.	B6	94
Germantown, Md., U.S.	B3	97
Germantown, Oh., U.S.	C1	112
Germantown, Tn., U.S.	B2	119
Germantown, Wi., U.S.	E5	126
Germany, Federal Republic of (West Germany), ctry., Eur.	C4	18
Germersheim, W. Ger.	D5	19
Germfask, Mi., U.S.	B5	99
Germiston, S. Afr.	C4	49
Gernrode, E. Ger.	B6	19
Gernsheim, W. Ger.	D4	19
Gero, Japan	n16	33
Gerolzhofen, W. Ger.	D5	19
Gerona, Spain	B7	22
Geronimo, Ok., U.S.	C3	113
Geronimo, Tx., U.S.	h8	120
Gerrardstown, W.V., U.S.	B6	125
Gersfeld, W. Ger.	C5	19
Gersthofen, W. Ger.	E5	19
Gertrudis Sánchez (part of Mexico City), Mex.	h9	63
Gerty, Ok., U.S.	C5	113
Gervais, Or., U.S.	B4	114
Gerze, Tur.	B10	40
Geseke, W. Ger.	B3	19
Gesher HaZiw, Isr.	A7	41
Gessie, In., U.S.	D3	91
Getafe, Spain	B4	22
Gethsémani, Que.	h9	72
Gettysburg, Pa., U.S.	G7	115
Gettysburg, S.D., U.S.	C6	118
Getúlio Vargas, Braz.	D2	56
Getz Ice Shelf, ice, Ant.	B36	7
Geuda Springs, Ks., U.S.	E6	93
Gevelsberg, W. Ger.	B2	19
Gex, Fr.	C2	20
Geyser, Mt., U.S.	C6	103
Geyserville, Ca., U.S.	C2	82
Geyve, Tur.	B8	40
Gézenti, Chad	A3	46
Ghabīyah, Wādī al, val., Eg.	E5	41
Ghaggar, stm., India	C5	37
Ghāghara, stm., India	E9	37
Ghaghar Reservoir, res., India	E9	37
Ghana, ctry., Afr.	E4	45
Ghanzi, Bots.	B3	49
Ghardaïa, Alg.	C5	45
Gharyān, Libya	C2	43
Ghawr ash Sharqīyah, Qanāt al, Jord.	B7	41
Ghazāl, Bahr al, stm., Sud.	D3	47
Ghazāl, Bahr al, stm., Chad	D3	46
Ghāziābād, India	*C6	36
Ghazīpur, India	E9	37
Ghaznī, Afg.	B4	36
Ghazzah see Gaza, Isr. Occ.	C6	41
Gheens, La., U.S.	E5	95
Ghent, Ky., U.S.	B4	94
Ghent, Mn., U.S.	F3	100
Ghent, N.Y., U.S.	C7	109
Ghent see Gent, Bel.	B5	16
Gheorghe Gheorghiu-Dej, Rom.	B8	24
Gheorgheni, Rom.	B7	24
Gherla, Rom.	B6	24
Ghilizane, Alg.	B5	44
Ghlò, Beinn a', mtn., Scot., U.K.	D5	13
Ghudāmis, Libya	C1	43
Ghūrīān, Afg.	D10	39
Giannutri, i., Italy	C3	23
Giant Mountain, mtn., N.Y., U.S.	A7	109
Giants Neck, Ct., U.S.	D7	84
Giaveno, Italy	D3	20
Gibara, Cuba	D5	64
Gibbon, Ne., U.S.	D7	104
Gibbons, Alta.	C4	68
Gibbonsville, Id., U.S.	D5	89
Gibbs, Mo., U.S.	A5	102
Gibbstown, N.J., U.S.	D2	107
Gibeon, Nmb.	C2	49
Gibraleón, Spain	D2	22
Gibraltar, dep., Eur.	D3	22
Gibraltar, Strait of, strt.	E3	22
Gibraltar Point, c., Eng., U.K.	B2	13
Gibsland, La., U.S.	B2	95
Gibson, Ga., U.S.	C4	87
Gibson, La., U.S.	E5	95
Gibson, Ms., U.S.	B5	101
Gibson, Mo., U.S.	E7	102
Gibson, N.C., U.S.	C3	110
Gibson, Pa., U.S.	C10	115
Gibson, Tn., U.S.	B3	119
Gibson, co., In., U.S.	H2	91
Gibson, co., Tn., U.S.	A3	119
Gibsonburg, Oh., U.S.	A2	112
Gibson City, Il., U.S.	C5	90
Gibson Desert, des., Austl.	D3	50
Gibsonia, Fl., U.S.	*D5	86
Gibsonia, Pa., U.S.	h14	115
Gibson Island, i., Md., U.S.	B5	97
Gibsons, B.C.	E6	69
Gibsonton, Fl., U.S.	p11	86
Gibsonville, N.C., U.S.	A3	110
Giddings, Tx., U.S.	D4	120
Gideon, Mo., U.S.	E8	102
Gidole, Eth.	D4	47
Gien, Fr.	D5	16
Giessen, W. Ger.	C4	18
Gifford, Ar., U.S.	g8	81
Gifford, Fl., U.S.	E6	86
Gifford, Id., U.S.	C2	89
Gifford, Il., U.S.	C5	90
Gifford, Pa., U.S.	C4	115
Giffre, stm., Fr.	C2	21
Gifhorn, W. Ger.	F4	15
Gift, Tn., U.S.	B2	119
Gifu, Japan	D12	31
Giganta, Sierra de la, mts., Mex.	B2	63
Gigante, Col.	C2	60
Gigha Island, i., Scot., U.K.	E3	13
Gig Harbor, Wa., U.S.	B3	124
Giglio, i., Italy	C3	23
Gihon, stm., Vt., U.S.	B3	122
Gijón, Spain	A3	22
Gila, co., Az., U.S.	D5	80
Gila, stm., Az., U.S.	D5	76
Gila Bend, Az., U.S.	E3	80
Gila Bend Indian Reservation, Az., U.S.	D3	80
Gila Bend Mountains, mts., Az., U.S.	D2	80
Gila Cliff Dwellings National Monument, N.M., U.S.	D1	108
Gila Mountains, mts., Az., U.S.	D6	80
Gila Peak, mtn., Az., U.S.	D6	80
Gila River Indian Reservation, Az., U.S.	D4	80
Gilbert, Ar., U.S.	B3	81
Gilbert, Ia., U.S.	B4	92
Gilbert, La., U.S.	B4	95
Gilbert, Mn., U.S.	C6	100
Gilbert, Or., U.S.	*B4	114
Gilbert, S.C., U.S.	D5	117
Gilbert, W.V., U.S.	D3	125
Gilbert, stm., Newf.	B3	72
Gilbert Islands see Kiribati, ctry., Oc.	G11	6
Gilbert Islands, is., Kir.	G10	6
Gilbertown, Al., U.S.	D1	78
Gilbert Peak, mtn., Wa., U.S.	C4	124
Gilbert Plains, Man.	D1	70
Gilbertsville, Ky., U.S.	f9	94
Gilbertsville, N.Y., U.S.	C5	109
Gilbertsville, Pa., U.S.	F10	115
Gilbertville, Ia., U.S.	B5	92
Gilbertville, Ma., U.S.	B3	98
Gilboa, Oh., U.S.	B1	112
Gilby, N.D., U.S.	A8	111
Gilchrist, Or., U.S.	D5	114
Gilchrist, co., Fl., U.S.	C4	86
Gilcrest, Co., U.S.	A6	83
Gildford, Mt., U.S.	B6	103
Gilead, Ct., U.S.	C6	84
Gilead, Me., U.S.	D2	96
Gilead, Ne., U.S.	D8	104
Giles, co., Tn., U.S.	B4	119
Giles, co., Va., U.S.	C2	123
Gilford, N. Ire., U.K.	C5	11
Gilford Island, i., B.C.	D4	69
Gilford Park, N.J., U.S.	*D4	107
Gilgandra, Austl.	E7	51
Gil Island, i., B.C.	C3	69
Gill, Co., U.S.	A6	83
Gill, Lough, l., Ire.	C3	11
Gillam, Man.	A4	70
Gilleleje, Den.	B6	15
Gillen, Lake, l., Austl.	E3	50
Gillespie, Il., U.S.	D4	90
Gillespie, co., Tx., U.S.	D3	120
Gillespie Dam, Az., U.S.	D3	80
Gillett, Ar., U.S.	C4	81
Gillett, Fl., U.S.	p10	86
Gillett, Tx., U.S.	E3	120
Gillett, Wi., U.S.	D5	126
Gillett Grove, Ia., U.S.	B2	92
Gillette, Wy., U.S.	B7	127
Gillham, Ar., U.S.	C1	81
Gilliam, Mo., U.S.	B4	102
Gilliam, co., Or., U.S.	B6	114
Gillingham, Eng., U.K.	C8	12
Gillis, La., U.S.	D2	95
Gilman, Ct., U.S.	C7	84
Gilman, Il., U.S.	C5	90
Gilman, Ia., U.S.	C5	92
Gilman, Mn., U.S.	E5	100

Name	Map Ref.	Page

Gilman, Vt., U.S. — C5 122
Gilman, Wi., U.S. — C3 126
Gilman City, Mo., U.S. — A4 102
Gilmanton, N.H., U.S. — D4 106
Gilmanton, Wi., U.S. — D2 126
Gilmanton Iron Works, N.H., U.S. — D4 106
Gilmer, Tx., U.S. — C5 120
Gilmer, W.V., U.S. — C4 125
Gilmer, co., Ga., U.S. — B2 87
Gilmer, co., W.V., U.S. — C4 125
Gilmore, Ar., U.S. — B5 81
Gilmore City, Ia., U.S. — B3 92
Gilmour, Ont. — C7 73
Gilo, stm., Eth. — D3 47
Gilpin, Ky., U.S. — C5 94
Gilpin, co., Co., U.S. — B5 83
Gilroy, Sask. — G2 75
Gilroy, Ca., U.S. — D3 82
Gilson, Il., U.S. — C3 90
Gilsum, N.H., U.S. — D2 106
Gilt Edge, Tn., U.S. — B2 119
Giltner, Ne., U.S. — D7 104
Giluwe, Mount, mtn., Pap. N. Gui. — k11 50
Gimli, Man. — D3 70
Ginir, Eth. — D5 47
Ginns Corner, De., U.S. — C3 85
Ginosa, Italy — D6 23
Ginowan, Japan — O5 52
Ginzo [de Limia], Spain — A2 22
Gioia del Colle, Italy — D6 23
Gioiosa Ionica, Italy — E6 23
Girard, Ga., U.S. — C5 87
Girard, Il., U.S. — D4 90
Girard, Ks., U.S. — E9 93
Girard, La., U.S. — B4 95
Girard, Oh., U.S. — A5 112
Girard, Pa., U.S. — B1 115
Girard, Tx., U.S. — C2 120
Girardot, Col. — C3 60
Girardville, Pa., U.S. — E9 115
Girdletree, Md., U.S. — D7 97
Giresun, Tur. — B12 40
Giri, stm., Zaire — A2 48
Girīdih, India — D8 36
Girna, stm., India — G5 37
Girne, N. Cyp. — E9 40
Giromagny, Fr. — D7 16
Girón, Ec. — B2 58
Gironde, est., Fr. — D5 16
Giroux, Man. — E3 70
Girouxville, Alta. — B2 68
Girvan, Scot., U.K. — C4 10
Girvin, Sask. — F3 75
Girvin, Tx., U.S. — D1 120
Gisborne, N.Z. — M17 51
Gisborne Lake, l., Newf. — E4 72
Giscome, B.C. — B6 69
Gisenyi, Rw. — B4 48
Gislaved, Swe. — A7 15
Gisors, Fr. — C4 16
Gitega, Bdi. — B4 48
Giulianova, Italy — C4 23
Giurgiu, Rom. — D7 24
Giv'atayim, Isr. — g10 41
Give, Den. — C3 15
Givet, Fr. — B6 16
Givhans, S.C., U.S. — E7 117
Givors, Fr. — E6 16
Givry, i., Micron. — Q18 52
Giza (Al Jīzah), Eg. — B3 38
Giza, Pyramids of, hist., Egypt — E3 41
Gīzāb, Afg. — E13 39
Gizhiga, Sov. Un. — C19 29
Giżycko, Pol. — A6 26
Gjirokastra, Alb. — B3 40
Gjoa Haven, N.W. Ter. — C13 66
Gjøvik, Nor. — G4 14
Glace Bay, N.S. — C10 71
Glacier, B.C. — D9 69
Glacier, Wa., U.S. — A4 124
Glacier, co., Mt., U.S. — B3 103
Glacier Bay, b., Ak., U.S. — k21 79
Glacier Bay National Park, Ak., U.S. — D12 79
Glacier National Park, B.C. — D9 69
Glacier National Park, Mt., U.S. — B2 103
Glacier Peak, mtn., Wa., U.S. — A4 124
Gladbeck, W. Ger. — B1 19
Gladbrook, Ia., U.S. — B5 92
Glade, Ks., U.S. — C4 93
Glade Creek, stm., Wa., U.S. — C6 124
Glade Creek, stm., W.V., U.S. — n14 125
Glade Creek, stm., W.V., U.S. — n13 125
Glade Park, Co., U.S. — B2 83
Glades, co., Fl., U.S. — F5 86
Glade Spring, Va., U.S. — f10 123
Glade Valley, N.C., U.S. — A1 110
Gladeview, Fl., U.S. — *G6 86
Gladeville, Tn., U.S. — A5 119
Gladewater, Tx., U.S. — C5 120
Gladmar, Sask. — H3 75
Gladstone, Austl. — D9 50
Gladstone, Man. — D2 70
Gladstone, Il., U.S. — C3 90
Gladstone, Mi., U.S. — C4 99
Gladstone, Mo., U.S. — h10 102
Gladstone, Ne., U.S. — D8 104
Gladstone, N.J., U.S. — B3 107
Gladstone, N.M., U.S. — A6 108
Gladstone, N.D., U.S. — C3 111
Gladstone, Or., U.S. — B4 114
Gladstone, Va., U.S. — C4 123
Glad Valley, S.D., U.S. — B4 118
Gladwin, Mi., U.S. — E6 99
Gladwin, co., Mi., U.S. — D6 99
Glady, W.V., U.S. — C5 125
Gladys, Va., U.S. — C3 123
Glåma, stm., Nor. — G5 14
Glamis, Sask. — F2 75
Glamoč, Yugo. — E11 23
Glan, l., Swe. — u33 14
Glan, stm., W. Ger. — F3 18
Gland, Switz. — D1 21
Glandorf, Oh., U.S. — A1 112
Glanshammar (part of Örebro), Swe. — t33 14
Glärnisch, mts., Switz. — C4 20
Glarus, Switz. — E4 18
Glarus, state, Switz. — B5 20
Glarus Alps, mts., Switz. — C6 21
Glasco, Ks., U.S. — C6 93
Glasco, N.Y., U.S. — C7 109
Glascock, co., Ga., U.S. — C4 87
Glasford, Il., U.S. — C4 90
Glasgo, Ct., U.S. — C8 84
Glasgow, Scot., U.K. — C4 10
Glasgow, N.Z. — D3 90
Glasgow, Ky., U.S. — C4 94
Glasgow, Mo., U.S. — B5 102
Glasgow, Mt., U.S. — B10 103
Glasgow, Va., U.S. — C3 123
Glasgow, W.V., U.S. — m13 125

Glasgow Village, Mo., U.S. — *f13 102
Glaslyn, Sask. — D1 75
Glasnevin, Sask. — H3 75
Glass, Tn., U.S. — A2 119
Glassboro, N.J., U.S. — D2 107
Glasscock, co., Tx., U.S. — D2 120
Glassmanor, Md., U.S. — *C4 97
Glass Mountains, mts., Tx., U.S. — D1 120
Glassport, Pa., U.S. — F2 115
Glasston, N.D., U.S. — A8 111
Glastenbury Mountain, mtn., Vt., U.S. — F2 122
Glastonbury, Eng., U.K. — C5 12
Glastonbury, Ct., U.S. — C5 84
Glauchau, E. Ger. — C6 18
Glazier, Tx., U.S. — A2 120
Glazier Lake, l., Me., U.S. — A3 96
Glazov, Sov. Un. — B4 28
Glazypeau Mountain, mtn., Ar., U.S. — f7 81
Gleason, Tn., U.S. — A3 119
Gleason, Wi., U.S. — C4 126
Gleasondale, Ma., U.S. — g9 98
Gleichen, Alta. — D4 68
Gleiwitz see Gliwice, Pol. — C5 26
Glen, Mn., U.S. — D5 100
Glen, Ms., U.S. — E4 103
Glen, N.H., U.S. — B4 106
Glen, W.V., U.S. — m13 125
Glenade, Ire. — C3 11
Glen Alice, Tn., U.S. — D9 119
Glen Allan, Ms., U.S. — B2 101
Glen Allen, Al., U.S. — B2 78
Glenallen, Mo., U.S. — D7 102
Glen Allen, Va., U.S. — C5 123
Glen Alpine, N.C., U.S. — B1 110
Glenamaddy, Ire. — D3 11
Glenamoy, Ire. — C2 11
Glénan, Îles de, is., Fr. — D1 16
Glen Arbor, Mi., U.S. — D4 99
Glenarm, N. Ire., U.K. — G4 11
Glenavon, Sask. — G4 75
Glen Avon, Ca., U.S. — m14 82
Glenbain, Sask. — H2 75
Glenbarr, Scot., U.K. — E3 13
Glenbeigh, Ire. — E2 11
Glenbeulah, Wi., U.S. — k9 126
Glenboro, Man. — E2 70
Glenbrook, Nv., U.S. — D2 105
Glenburn, N.D., U.S. — A4 111
Glen Burnie, Md., U.S. — B4 97
Glen Burnie Park, Md., U.S. — *B4 97
Glenbush, Sask. — D1 75
Glen Campbell, Pa., U.S. — E4 115
Glen Canyon, Ut., U.S. — F4 121
Glen Canyon, val., U.S. — G4 121
Glen Canyon Dam, Az., U.S. — A4 80
Glen Canyon National Recreation Area, U.S. — F5 121
Glencar, Ire. — *E2 11
Glen Carbon, Il., U.S. — *E4 90
Glencliff, N.H., U.S. — C3 106
Glencoe, Ont. — E3 73
Glencoe, Al., U.S. — B4 78
Glencoe, Il., U.S. — A6 90
Glencoe, Ky., U.S. — B5 94
Glencoe, La., U.S. — E4 95
Glencoe, Md., U.S. — A4 97
Glencoe, Mn., U.S. — F4 100
Glencoe, Mo., U.S. — f12 102
Glencoe, N.M., U.S. — D4 108
Glencoe, Ok., U.S. — A5 113
Glencolumbkille, Ire. — C3 11
Glen Cove, N.Y., U.S. — h13 109
Glencross, S.D., U.S. — B5 118
Glendale, Az., U.S. — D3 80
Glendale, Ar., U.S. — D4 81
Glendale, Ca., U.S. — m12 82
Glendale, Co., U.S. — *B6 83
Glendale, Fl., U.S. — v15 86
Glendale, Ky., U.S. — C4 94
Glendale, Ma., U.S. — *B1 98
Glendale, Ms., U.S. — D4 101
Glendale, N.H., U.S. — *f13 102
Glendale, N.H., U.S. — C4 106
Glendale, Oh., U.S. — C1 112
Glendale, Or., U.S. — E3 114
Glendale, R.I., U.S. — B2 116
Glendale, S.C., U.S. — B4 117
Glendale, Tn., U.S. — B5 119
Glendale, Ut., U.S. — F3 121
Glendale, Wi., U.S. — m12 126
Glendale Colony, S.D., U.S. — C7 118
Glendale Heights, Il., U.S. — *k8 90
Glendale Heights, W.V., U.S. — g8 125
Glen Dean, Ky., U.S. — C3 94
Glendive, Mt., U.S. — C12 103
Glendo, Wy., U.S. — D7 127
Glendon, N.J., U.S. — *C4 107
Glendon, Alta. — B5 68
Glendora, Ca., U.S. — m13 82
Glendora, Ms., U.S. — B3 101
Glendora, N.J., U.S. — *D2 107
Glendo Reservoir, res., Wy., U.S. — D8 127
Glendowan, Ire. — C4 11
Glen Easton, W.V., U.S. — g8 125
Glen Echo, Md., U.S. — f8 97
Glen Elder, Ks., U.S. — C5 93
Glenelg, Scot., U.K. — C3 13
Glenelg, Md., U.S. — B4 97
Glenella, Man. — D2 70
Glen Ellis Falls, wtfl., N.H., U.S. — B4 106
Glen Ellyn, Il., U.S. — k8 90
Glen Ewen, Sask. — H4 75
Glenfarne, Ire. — C4 11
Glen Ferris, W.V., U.S. — *C3 125
Glenfield, N.Y., U.S. — B5 109
Glenfield, N.D., U.S. — B7 111
Glenfinnan, Scot., U.K. — D3 13
Glen Flora, Tx., U.S. — E4 120
Glengad Head, c., Ire. — B4 11
Glen Gardner, N.J., U.S. — B3 107
Glengarriff, Ire. — F2 11
Glengarry, co., Ont. — B10 73
Glenham, N.Y., U.S. — D7 109
Glenham, S.D., U.S. — B5 118
Glen Haven, Co., U.S. — A5 83
Glen Head, N.Y., U.S. — *h13 109
Glen Innes, Austl. — E9 50
Glen Jean, W.V., U.S. — D3 125
Glen Kerr, Sask. — G2 75
Glen Lake, l., Mi., U.S. — D5 99
Glen Lyon, Pa., U.S. — D9 115
Glenmont, Oh., U.S. — B3 112
Glenmora, La., U.S. — D3 95
Glenmore, Ok., U.S. — B1 112
Glenmorgan, Austl. — C7 51
Glenn, Mi., U.S. — F4 99
Glenn, co., Ca., U.S. — C2 82

Glennallen, Ak., U.S. — f19 79
Glenn Dale, Md., U.S. — *C4 97
Glennie, Mi., U.S. — D7 99
Glennonville, Mo., U.S. — E7 102
Glenns Ferry, Id., U.S. — G3 89
Glennville, Ga., U.S. — E5 87
Glenolden, Pa., U.S. — p20 115
Glenoma, Wa., U.S. — C3 124
Glenorchy, Austl. — o15 50
Glenpool, Ok., U.S. — B5 113
Glenridge, N.J., U.S. — h10 98
Glen Raven, N.C., U.S. — A3 110
Glenrio, N.M., U.S. — B6 108
Glen Robertson, Ont. — B10 73
Glen Rock, N.J., U.S. — h8 107
Glen Rock, Pa., U.S. — G8 115
Glenrock, Wy., U.S. — D7 127
Glen Rose, Tx., U.S. — C4 120
Glenrothes, Scot., U.K. — C5 13
Glen Saint Mary, Fl., U.S. — B4 86
Glens Falls, N.Y., U.S. — B7 109
Glenshaw, Pa., U.S. — h14 115
Glenside, Sask. — F2 75
Glenside, Pa., U.S. — F11 115
Glentana, Mt., U.S. — B10 103
Glenties, Ire. — C3 11
Glentworth, Sask. — H2 75
Glen Ullin, N.D., U.S. — C4 111
Glenview, Il., U.S. — h9 90
Glenview Naval Air Station, mil., Il., U.S. — h9 90
Glenvil, Ne., U.S. — D7 104
Glenville, Ire. — E3 11
Glenville, Mn., U.S. — G5 100
Glenville, N.C., U.S. — f9 110
Glenville, W.V., U.S. — C4 125
Glen White, W.V., U.S. — D3 125
Glen Wilton, Va., U.S. — C3 123
Glenwood, Newf. — D4 72
Glenwood, Al., U.S. — D3 78
Glenwood, Ar., U.S. — C2 81
Glenwood, Fl., U.S. — C5 86
Glenwood, Ga., U.S. — D4 87
Glenwood, Il., U.S. — *k9 90
Glenwood, In., U.S. — E7 91
Glenwood, Ia., U.S. — C2 92
Glenwood, Md., U.S. — B3 97
Glenwood, Mn., U.S. — E3 100
Glenwood, Mo., U.S. — A5 102
Glenwood, N.M., U.S. — D1 108
Glenwood, Or., U.S. — B3 114
Glenwood, Ut., U.S. — E4 121
Glenwood, Va., U.S. — D3 123
Glenwood, Wa., U.S. — C4 124
Glenwood, Wi., U.S. — C2 125
Glenwood City, Wi., U.S. — C1 126
Glenwood Farms, Va., U.S. — *C5 123
Glenwood Hills, Ga., U.S. — *C2 87
Glenwood Springs, Co., U.S. — B3 83
Glenwoodville, Alta. — E4 68
Gletsch, Switz. — C5 21
Glezen, In., U.S. — H3 91
Glidden, Sask. — F1 75
Glidden, Ia., U.S. — B3 92
Glidden, Wi., U.S. — B3 126
Glide, Or., U.S. — D3 114
Glifádha, Grc. — h11 25
Glin, Ire. — E2 11
Glittertinden, mtn., Nor. — G3 14
Globe, Az., U.S. — D5 80
Globe, Ky., U.S. — B6 94
Globino, Sov. Un. — G9 27
Glogów, Pol. — C4 26
Glória, Braz. — C3 57
Glória de Goitá, Braz. — k6 57
Glorieta, N.M., U.S. — B4 108
Glorieuses, Îles, is., Reu. — f9 49
Glossop, Eng., U.K. — A6 12
Glossopteris, Mount, mtn., Ant. — A1 7
Gloster, Ga., U.S. — h8 87
Gloster, La., U.S. — B2 95
Gloster, Ms., U.S. — D2 101
Gloucester, Ont. — h12 73
Gloucester, Eng., U.K. — E5 10
Gloucester, Ma., U.S. — A6 98
Gloucester, co., N.B. — B4 71
Gloucester, co., N.J., U.S. — D2 107
Gloucester, co., Va., U.S. — C6 123
Gloucester City, N.J., U.S. — D2 107
Gloucester Point, Va., U.S. — C6 123
Gloucestershire, co., Eng., U.K. — C7 12
Glouster, Oh., U.S. — C3 112
Glover, Mo., U.S. — D7 102
Glover, Vt., U.S. — B4 122
Glover Gap, W.V., U.S. — h10 125
Glover Island, i., Newf. — D3 72
Gloversville, N.Y., U.S. — B6 109
Gloverville, S.C., U.S. — D4 117
Glovertown, Newf. — D4 72
Głubczyce, Pol. — C4 26
Glubokoye, Sov. Un. — D6 27
Głuchołazy, Pol. — C4 26
Gluck, S.C., U.S. — C2 117
Glücksburg, W. Ger. — D3 15
Glückstadt, W. Ger. — B4 18
Glukhov, Sov. Un. — F9 27
Glussk, Sov. Un. — E7 27
Glyndon, Md., U.S. — B4 97
Glyndon, Mn., U.S. — D2 100
Glyngøre, Den. — B2 15
Gmünd, Aus. — E7 18
Gmunden, Aus. — E6 18
Gnadenhutten, Oh., U.S. — B4 112
Gnesta, Swe. — t35 14
Gniezno, Pol. — B4 26
Gnjilane, Yugo. — D5 24
Gniezno, Pol. — B4 26
Gnojno, Pol. — B9 20
Goa, state, India — E5 36
Goalpāra, India — D13 37
Goat Fell, mtn., Scot., U.K. — E3 13
Goat Island, i., R.I., U.S. — E5 116
Goat Island Point, c., Am. Sam. — F13 52
Goat Mountain, mtn., Mt., U.S. — C3 103
Goat Rock Dam, U.S. — C4 78
Gobabis, Nmb. — B2 49
Gobernador Gregores, Arg. — D2 54
Gobernador Udaondo, Arg. — g7 54
Gobi Desert, des., Asia — C5 31
Gobles, Mi., U.S. — F5 99
Gobō, Japan — J7 33
Gochas, Nmb. — B2 49
Godāvari, stm., India — E6 36

Godāvari, Mouths of the, mth., India — E7 36
Goddard, Ks., U.S. — E6 93
Goderich, Ont. — D3 73
Godfrey, Ont. — C8 73
Godfrey, Ga., U.S. — C3 87
Godfrey, Il., U.S. — E3 90
Godhavn, Grnld. — C15 61
Godhra, India — F4 37
Godley, Tx., U.S. — n9 120
Gods, stm., Man. — A5 70
Gods Lake, Man. — B4 70
Gods Lake, l., Man. — B4 70
Godthåb (Nuuk), Grnld. — C15 61
Godwin, N.C., U.S. — B4 110
Godwin Austen, see K2, mtn., Asia — A6 36
Goehner, Ne., U.S. — D8 104
Goélands, Lac aux, l., Que. — g8 72
Goes, Neth. — C3 17
Goessel, Ks., U.S. — D6 93
Goff, Ks., U.S. — C8 93
Goff Creek, stm., Ok., U.S. — e9 113
Goffstown, N.H., U.S. — D3 106
Gogebic, co., Mi., U.S. — n12 99
Gogebic, Lake, l., Mi., U.S. — m12 99
Gogebic Range, hills, U.S. — B3 126
Goglio, Italy — D5 21
Gohfeld, W. Ger. — A3 19
Göhren, E. Ger. — D7 15
Goiana, Braz. — C4 57
Goiandira, Braz. — B5 56
Goianésia, Braz. — B5 56
Goiânia, Braz. — C5 56
Goianinha, Braz. — h6 57
Goiás, Braz. — B5 56
Goiás, state, Braz. — B5 56
Goiatuba, Braz. — B5 56
Goil, Loch, b., Scot., U.K. — D4 13
Goito, Italy — D6 20
Gojam, prov., Eth. — C4 47
Gojō, Japan — o14 33
Gökçeada, i., Tur. — B5 25
Göksun, Tur. — C11 40
Gokwe, Zimb. — A4 49
Gol, Nor. — G3 14
Gola Island, i., Ire. — B3 11
Golam Head, c., Ire. — D2 11
Golan Heights, ter., Syria — A7 41
Golbāf, Iran — C5 38
Golchikha, Sov. Un. — B11 29
Golconda, Il., U.S. — F5 90
Golconda, Nv., U.S. — C4 105
Goldach, Switz. — B7 21
Goldap, Pol. — A7 26
Goldbach, W. Ger. — C4 19
Gold Bar, Wa., U.S. — B4 124
Gold Beach, Or., U.S. — E2 114
Goldberg, E. Ger. — E6 15
Goldboro, N.S. — D8 71
Gold Bridge, B.C. — D6 69
Gold Coast see Southport, Austl. — E9 50
Goldcreek, Ak., U.S. — f17 79
Goldcreek, Mt., U.S. — D4 103
Goldcrest, Tn., U.S. — B2 119
Golden, B.C. — D9 69
Golden, Ire. — E4 11
Golden, Co., U.S. — B5 83
Golden, Il., U.S. — C2 90
Golden, Ms., U.S. — A5 101
Golden, Mo., U.S. — E4 102
Golden, N.M., U.S. — B3 108
Golden, Ok., U.S. — C7 113
Golden Bay, b., N.Z. — N14 51
Golden Beach, Fl., U.S. — *G6 86
Golden City, Mo., U.S. — D3 102
Goldendale, Wa., U.S. — D5 124
Golden Ears Provincial Park, B.C. — E6 69
Golden Gate Bridge, Ca., U.S. — h7 82
Golden Gate National Recreation Area, Ca., U.S. — h7 82
Golden Glades, Fl., U.S. — *G6 86
Golden Hinde, mtn., B.C. — E5 69
Golden Lake, l., Ont. — B7 73
Golden Meadow, La., U.S. — E5 95
Golden Prairie, Sask. — G1 75
Golden Spike National Historic Site, hist., Ut., U.S. — B3 121
Golden Spur, Ut., U.S. — D7 84
Golden Valley, Mn., U.S. — n12 100
Golden Valley, N.D., U.S. — B3 111
Golden Valley, co., Mt., U.S. — D7 103
Golden Valley, co., N.D., U.S. — B3 111
Goldenville, N.S. — D7 71
Goldfield, Ia., U.S. — B4 92
Goldfield, Nv., U.S. — F4 105
Gold Hill, N.C., U.S. — B2 110
Gold Hill, Or., U.S. — E3 114
Goldonna, La., U.S. — B3 95
Goldsand Lake, l., Man. — A1 70
Goldsboro, Md., U.S. — B6 97
Goldsboro, N.C., U.S. — B5 110
Goldsby, Ok., U.S. — B4 113
Goldschmidt, Cape, c., Ant. — g40 7
Goldsmith, In., U.S. — D5 91
Goldsmith, Tx., U.S. — D1 120
Goldston, N.C., U.S. — B3 110
Goldsworthy, Austl. — D2 50
Goldthwaite, Tx., U.S. — D3 120
Goleen, Ire. — F2 11
Golela, S. Afr. — C5 49
Goleniów, Pol. — B3 26
Goleta, Ca., U.S. — E4 82
Golets-Skalistyy, Mount, mtn., Sov. Un. — D14 29
Golfito, C.R. — F6 62
Golf Manor, Oh., U.S. — o13 112
Golfo, Tx., U.S. — E4 120
Goliad, Tx., U.S. — E4 120
Goliad, co., Tx., U.S. — E4 120
Golmud, China — D3 31
Golo Island, i., Phil. — p13 34
Golovin, Sov. Un. — C7 79
Golpāyegān, Iran — B5 38
Goltry, Ok., U.S. — A3 113
Golts, Md., U.S. — B6 97
Golva, N.D., U.S. — C2 111
Golyamo Konare, Bul. — D7 24
Goma, Zaire — B5 48
Gomati, stm., India — C7 36
Gombari, Zaire — A4 48
Gombe, Nig. — D7 45
Gomel, Sov. Un. — E8 27
Gomera, i., Spain — m13 22
Gómez Palacio, Mex. — B4 60
Gonābād, Iran — C8 39
Gonaïves, Haiti — E7 64
Gonâve, Golfe de la, b., Haiti — E7 64

Gonâve, Île de la, i., Haiti — E7 64
Gonbad-e Qābūs, Iran — C7 39
Gonda, India — C7 36
Gonder (Gondar), Eth. — C4 47
Gonder, prov., Eth. — C4 47
Gondia, India — G8 37
Gondrecourt-le-Château, Fr. — F5 17
Gönen, Tur. — B6 40
Gonesse, Fr. — g10 16
Gongga Shan, mtn., China — F5 31
Gongola, stm., Nig. — D7 45
Goñi, Ur. — f8 54
Gonvick, Mn., U.S. — C3 100
Gonzales, Ca., U.S. — D3 82
Gonzales, La., U.S. — D5 95
Gonzales, Tx., U.S. — E4 120
Gonzales, co., Tx., U.S. — E4 120
Gonzalez, Fl., U.S. — u14 86
González Chaves, Arg. — B4 54
Goochland, Va., U.S. — C5 123
Goochland, co., Va., U.S. — C5 123
Goode, Va., U.S. — C3 123
Goode, Mount, mtn., Ak., U.S. — g18 79
Goodell, Ia., U.S. — B4 92
Gooderham, Ont. — C6 73
Goodeve, Sask. — F4 75
Goodfellow Air Force Base, mil., Tx., U.S. — D2 120
Goodfield, Il., U.S. — C4 90
Good Hart, Mi., U.S. — C5 99
Good Hope, Ga., U.S. — C3 87
Good Hope, Il., U.S. — C3 90
Good Hope, Ms., U.S. — C4 101
Good Hope, Oh., U.S. — C2 112
Good Hope, Cape of, c., S. Afr. — D2 49
Good Hope Mountain, mtn., B.C. — D5 69
Goodhue, Mn., U.S. — F6 100
Goodhue, co., Mn., U.S. — F6 100
Gooding, Id., U.S. — G4 89
Gooding, co., Id., U.S. — G4 89
Goodland, Fl., U.S. — G5 86
Goodland, In., U.S. — C3 91
Goodland, Ks., U.S. — C2 93
Goodland, Mi., U.S. — D6 113
Goodlands, Man. — E1 70
Goodlettsville, Tn., U.S. — g10 119
Goodman, Ms., U.S. — C4 101
Goodman, Mo., U.S. — E3 102
Goodman, Wi., U.S. — C5 126
Goodnews Bay, Ak., U.S. — D7 79
Goodnight, Tx., U.S. — B2 120
Good Pine, La., U.S. — C3 95
Goodrich, Co., U.S. — A6 83
Goodrich, Ks., U.S. — D8 93
Goodrich, N.D., U.S. — B5 111
Goodrich, Tx., U.S. — D5 120
Goodridge, Mn., U.S. — B3 100
Good Spirit Lake, l., Sask. — F4 75
Good Spirit Lake Provincial Park, Sask. — F4 75
Goodspring, Tn., U.S. — B4 119
Goodsprings, Al., U.S. — B2 78
Goodsprings, Nv., U.S. — H6 105
Good Thunder, Mn., U.S. — F4 100
Goodview, Mn., U.S. — F7 100
Goodwater, Sask. — H4 75
Goodwater, Al., U.S. — B3 78
Goodway, Al., U.S. — D2 78
Goodwell, Ok., U.S. — e9 113
Goodwin, Ar., U.S. — C4 81
Goodwin, S.D., U.S. — C9 118
Goodyear, Az., U.S. — D3 80
Goole, Eng., U.K. — A7 12
Goolwa, Austl. — F7 50
Goondiwindi, Austl. — E9 50
Goor, Neth. — C7 17
Goose, stm., Newf. — h9 72
Goose, stm., N.D., U.S. — B8 111
Goose Bay, b., Newf. — B1 72
Goose Bay see Happy Valley-Goose Bay, Newf. — B1 72
Gooseberry Creek, stm., Wy., U.S. — B4 127
Goose Creek, S.C., U.S. — F7 117
Goose Creek, stm., Ne., U.S. — B5 104
Goose Creek, stm., Va., U.S. — C3 123
Goose Creek Reservoir, res., S.C., U.S. — k11 117
Goose Island, i., B.C. — C7 92
Goose Lake, l., Ia., U.S. — B7 92
Goose Lake, l., Sask. — F2 75
Goose Lake, l., Sask. — F2 75
Goose Lake, l., B.C. — B3 82
Goose Pond, l., N.H., U.S. — C2 106
Gopālganj, India — D10 37
Gopto Lake, l., Pol. — B5 26
Göppingen, W. Ger. — D4 18
Gorakhpur, India — C7 36
Gorday, Ga., U.S. — E3 87
Gordes, Tur. — C7 40
Gordil, Cen. Afr. Rep. — A2 78
Gordo, Al., U.S. — B2 78
Gordon, Al., U.S. — D4 78
Gordon, Ga., U.S. — D3 87
Gordon, Mn., U.S. — G5 100
Gordon, Ne., U.S. — B3 104
Gordon, Tx., U.S. — C3 120
Gordon, Wi., U.S. — B2 126
Gordon, co., Ga., U.S. — B2 87
Gordon Creek, stm., Ne., U.S. — B5 104
Gordon Horne Peak, mtn., B.C. — D8 69
Gordon Lake, l., Alta. — A5 68
Gordon's Corner, N.J., U.S. — *C4 107
Gordonsville, Tn., U.S. — C8 119
Gordonsville, Va., U.S. — B4 123
Gordonville, Mo., U.S. — D8 102
Gore, N.S. — D6 71
Gore, Eth. — C4 47
Gore, N.Z. — Q12 51
Gore, Ok., U.S. — B6 113
Gore Bay, Ont. — B2 73
Gore Mountain, mtn., Vt., U.S. — B5 122
Gore Point, c., Ak., U.S. — h16 79
Gore Range, mts., Co., U.S. — B4 83
Gore Springs, Ms., U.S. — B4 101
Goreville, Il., U.S. — F5 90
Gorey, Ire. — E5 11
Gorgān (Asterābād), Iran — B5 38
Gorgān, stm., Iran — B5 38
Gorgān Bay, b., Iran — B5 39
Gorge High Dam, Wa., U.S. — A4 124
Gorgona, Isla, i., Col. — C2 60
Gorgona, Isola, i., Italy — C3 23
Gorham, Il., U.S. — F4 90

Gorham, Ks., U.S. — D4 93
Gorham, Me., U.S. — E2 96
Gorham, N.H., U.S. — B4 106
Gorham, N.Y., U.S. — C3 109
Gori, Sov. Un. — E2 28
Gorin, Mo., U.S. — A5 102
Gorinchem, Neth. — C5 17
Goris, Sov. Un. — B3 39
Gorizia, Italy — B4 23
Gorkha, Nepal — C10 37
Gorkiy, Sov. Un. — D7 29
Goñi...
Gorkiy Reservoir, res., Sov. Un. — D7 29
Gørlev, Den. — C5 15
Gorlice, Pol. — D6 26
Görlitz, E. Ger. — C7 18
Gorlovka, Sov. Un. — G12 27
Gorman, Md., U.S. — m12 97
Gorman, Tn., U.S. — A4 119
Gorman, Tx., U.S. — C3 120
Gormania, W.V., U.S. — B5 125
Gormley (part of Whitchurch-Stouffville), Ont. — k15 73
Gorna Oryakhovitsa, Bul. — D7 24
Gornji Milanovac, Yugo. — C5 24
Gorno-Altaysk, Sov. Un. — D11 29
Gornozavodsk, Sov. Un. — C10 33
Gorodenka, Sov. Un. — G5 27
Gorodets, Sov. Un. — D17 8
Gorodnya, Sov. Un. — F8 27
Gorodok, Sov. Un. — A5 24
Gorodok, Mong. — A3 31
Gorodok, Sov. Un. — G4 27
Gorodok, Sov. Un. — D8 27
Goroka, Pap. N. Gui. — k12 50
Gorontalo, Indon. — E6 34
Gorrie, Ont. — D3 73
Gorskoye, Sov. Un. — q21 27
Gort, Ire. — D3 11
Gortahork, Ire. — B3 11
Goruma, i., Ire. — D2 11
Goryn, stm., Sov. Un. — F6 27
Gorzów [Wielkopolski], Pol. — B3 26
Gosford, Austl. — F8 51
Goshen, Newf. — D8 71
Goshen, Al., U.S. — D3 78
Goshen, Ca., U.S. — D4 82
Goshen, In., U.S. — A6 91
Goshen, Ky., U.S. — g11 94
Goshen, Ma., U.S. — B2 98
Goshen, N.H., U.S. — D2 106
Goshen, N.J., U.S. — E3 107
Goshen, N.Y., U.S. — D6 109
Goshen, Oh., U.S. — C1 112
Goshen, Or., U.S. — D3 114
Goshen, Ut., U.S. — D4 121
Goshen, Va., U.S. — C3 123
Goshen, co., Wy., U.S. — D8 127
Goshen Hole, Wy., U.S. — D8 127
Goshogawara, Japan — F10 33
Goshute Indian Reservation, U.S. — D7 105
Goshute Lake, l., Nv., U.S. — C7 105
Goshute Mountains, mts., Nv., U.S. — C7 105
Goslar, W. Ger. — B3 18
Gosnell, Ar., U.S. — *B6 81
Gosnells, Austl. — *F2 50
Gosper, co., Ne., U.S. — D6 104
Gospić, Yugo. — C2 24
Gosport, Eng., U.K. — D6 12
Gosport, Al., U.S. — D2 78
Gosport, In., U.S. — F4 91
Gossau, Switz. — B7 21
Gossville, N.H., U.S. — D4 106
Gostivar, Yugo. — E5 24
Gostyń, Pol. — C4 26
Gostynin, Pol. — B5 26
Gostynka, stm., Pol. — g9 26
Göteborg (Gothenburg), Swe. — I4 14
Göteborg och Bohus, co., Swe. — A5 15
Gotel Mountains, mts., Afr. — G7 45
Gotemba, Japan — n18 33
Gotha, E. Ger. — C5 18
Gothenburg, Ne., U.S. — D5 104
Gotland, i., Swe. — I8 14
Gotō Islands, is., Japan — J4 33
Gotse Delchev (Nevrokop), Bul. —
Göttingen, W. Ger. — C4 18
Gottwaldov (Zlín), Czech. — D4 26
Götzis, Aus. — B8 21
Goubangzi, China — D9 32
Gouda, Neth. — A6 16
Goudeau, La., U.S. — D3 95
Goudiry, Sen. — D2 45
Goudoumaria, Niger — D7 45
Goudsward, Neth. — C4 17
Gough, Ga., U.S. — C4 87
Gough Island, i., St. Hel. — I9 5
Gough Lake, l., Alta. — C4 68
Gouin, Réservoir, res., Que. — k12 74
Goulburn, Austl. — F8 50
Gould, Que. — D6 74
Gould, Ar., U.S. — D4 81
Gould, Co., U.S. — A4 83
Gould, Ok., U.S. — C2 113
Gouldbusk, Tx., U.S. — D3 120
Gould City, Mi., U.S. — B5 99
Goulding Cay, i., Bah. — m16 64
Gouldings Trading Post, Ut., U.S. — F5 121
Gould Island, i., R.I., U.S. — E5 116
Goulds, Fl., U.S. — s13 86
Gouldsboro, Me., U.S. — D4 96
Gouldsboro, Pa., U.S. — D11 115
Gouldtown, N.J., U.S. — E2 107
Goulimine, Mor. — D2 44
Goumamitz, stm., N.B. — C4 71
Goundam, Mali — C4 45
Gounou Gaya, Chad — G8 45
Gourdon, Fr. — E4 16
Gouré, Niger — D7 45
Gourma Rharous, Mali — C4 45
Gournay-en-Bray, Fr. — C4 16
Gouro, Chad — E8 46
Gouverneur, Sask. — H2 75
Gouverneur, N.Y., U.S. — f9 109
Govan, Sask. — F3 75
Govan, Scot., U.K. — E5 13
Gove, Ks., U.S. — C3 93
Gove, co., Ks., U.S. — D3 93
Govenlock, Sask. — H1 75
Government Camp, Or., U.S. — B5 114
Governador Valadares, Braz. — E4 56
Governors Harbour, Bah. — B5 64

Name	Map Ref.	Page

Govind Ballabh Pant Reservoir, res., India — F9 37
Govind Reservoir, res., India — B6 37
Gowan, stm., Man. — B4 70
Gowanda, N.Y., U.S. — C2 109
Gowen, Mi., U.S. — E5 99
Gowen, Ok., U.S. — C6 113
Gower, Mo., U.S. — B3 102
Gowna, Lough, l., Ire. — D3 10
Gowrie, Ia., U.S. — B3 92
Goya, Arg. — E4 55
Goz Beïda, Chad — C4 46
Graaff-Reinet, S. Afr. — D3 49
Grabill, In., U.S. — B8 91
Grabow, E. Ger. — E5 15
Gračac, Yugo. — C2 24
Gračanica, Yugo. — C4 24
Grace, Id., U.S. — G7 89
Grace, Ms., U.S. — C3 101
Grace, Mount, mtn., Ma., U.S. — A3 98
Grace City, N.D., U.S. — B7 111
Graceham, Md., U.S. — A3 97
Gracemont, Ok., U.S. — B3 113
Graceton, Mn., U.S. — B4 100
Graceville, Fl., U.S. — u16 86
Graceville, Mn., U.S. — E2 100
Gracewood, Ga., U.S. — C4 87
Gracey, Ky., U.S. — D2 94
Gracias, Hond. — E7 63
Graciosa, i., Port. — g9 44
Gradačac, Yugo. — C4 24
Gradizhsk, Sov. Un. — G9 27
Grado, Italy — D9 20
Grado, Spain — A2 22
Grady, Ar., U.S. — C4 81
Grady, N.M., U.S. — C6 108
Grady, Ok., U.S. — C4 113
Grady, co., Ga., U.S. — F2 87
Grady, co., Ok., U.S. — C4 113
Gradyville, Ky., U.S. — A3 92
Graettinger, Ia., U.S. — A3 92
Grafenau, W. Ger. — C3 120
Grafton, Austl. — E9 50
Grafton, Ont. — D6 73
Grafton, Il., U.S. — E3 90
Grafton, Ia., U.S. — A4 92
Grafton, Ma., U.S. — B4 98
Grafton, Ne., U.S. — D8 104
Grafton, N.H., U.S. — C3 106
Grafton, N.Y., U.S. — C7 109
Grafton, N.D., U.S. — A8 111
Grafton, Oh., U.S. — A3 112
Grafton, Vt., U.S. — E3 122
Grafton, Va., U.S. — h15 123
Grafton, W.V., U.S. — B4 125
Grafton, Wi., U.S. — E6 126
Grafton, co., N.H., U.S. — C3 106
Grafton Center, N.H., U.S. — C3 106
Graham, Al., U.S. — B4 78
Graham, Ca., U.S. — *n12 82
Graham, Fl., U.S. — C4 86
Graham, Ga., U.S. — E4 87
Graham, Ky., U.S. — C2 94
Graham, Mo., U.S. — A2 102
Graham, N.C., U.S. — A3 110
Graham, Ok., U.S. — C4 113
Graham, Tn., U.S. — B4 119
Graham, Tx., U.S. — C3 120
Graham, Wa., U.S. — B3 124
Graham, co., Az., U.S. — E5 80
Graham, co., Ks., U.S. — C4 93
Graham, co., N.C., U.S. — f9 110
Graham, stm., B.C. — A6 69
Graham, Lake, res., Tx., U.S. — C3 120
Graham, Mount, mtn., Az., U.S. — E6 80
Graham Bell, i., Sov. Un. — A7 128
Graham Creek, stm., In., U.S. — G6 91
Graham Island, i., B.C. — C1 69
Graham Island, i., N.W. Ter. — m33 66
Graham Lake, l., Alta. — A3 68
Graham Lake, l., Me., U.S. — D4 96
Graham Land, reg., Ant. — C6 7
Grahamstown, S. Afr. — D4 49
Grahamsville, N.Y., U.S. — D6 109
Grahamsville, S.C., U.S. — G6 117
Grahn, Ky., U.S. — B6 94
Graian Alps, mts., Eur. — E7 16
Grainfield, Ks., U.S. — C3 93
Grainger, Alta. — D4 68
Grainger, co., Tn., U.S. — C10 119
Grainland, Sask. — F2 75
Grainola, Ok., U.S. — A5 113
Grainton, Ne., U.S. — D4 104
Grain Valley, Mo., U.S. — B3 102
Grajaú, Braz. — C1 57
Grajaú, stm., Braz. — B1 57
Grajewo, Pol. — B7 26
Gram, Den. — C3 15
Gramada, Bul. — D6 24
Gramalote, Col. — B3 60
Gramastetten, Aus. — E9 19
Grambling, La., U.S. — B3 95
Gramercy, La., U.S. — h10 95
Gramling, S.C., U.S. — A3 117
Grammer, In., U.S. — F6 91
Grammichele, Italy — F5 23
Grampian, Pa., U.S. — E4 115
Grampian, prov., Scot., U.K. — C6 13
Grampian Mountains, mts., Scot., U.K. — B4 13
Gramshi, Alb. — B3 25
Gramzow, E. Ger. — E8 15
Gran, Mount, mtn., Ant. — B29 7
Granada, Nic. — E7 63
Granada, Spain — D4 22
Granada, Co., U.S. — C8 83
Granada, Mn., U.S. — G4 100
Granard, Ire. — D4 11
Granbury, Tx., U.S. — C4 120
Granby, Que. — D5 74
Granby, Ct., U.S. — A5 83
Granby, Ma., U.S. — B4 84
Granby, Mo., U.S. — E3 102
Granby, Vt., U.S. — B5 122
Granby, Lake, res., Co., U.S. — A5 83
Granby Island, i., Newf. — B4 72
Gran Canal del Desagüe, Mex. — g9 63
Gran Canaria, i., Spain — n14 22
Gran Chaco, pl., S.A. — D3 55
Grand, Co., U.S. — A4 83
Grand, co., Co., U.S. — A4 83
Grand, co., Ut., U.S. — E6 121
Grand, stm., Ont. — D4 73
Grand, stm., Mi., U.S. — E5 99
Grand, stm., Mo., U.S. — A3 102
Grand, stm., Oh., U.S. — A4 112
Grand, stm., S.D., U.S. — B4 118
Grand, North Fork, stm., S.D., U.S. — B3 118
Grand, South Fork, stm., S.D., U.S. — B3 118
Grand Bahama, i., Bah. — A4 64
Grand-Bank, Newf. — E4 72
Grand-Bassam, I.C. — E4 45

Grand Bay, N.B. — D3 71
Grand Bay, Al., U.S. — E1 78
Grand Bayou, stm., La., U.S. — k10 95
Grand Bayou, stm., La., U.S. — h9 95
Grand Bend, Ont. — D3 73
Grand Blanc, Mi., U.S. — F7 99
Grand Bonhomme, mtn., St. Vin. — U26 65
Grand-Bourg, Guad. — I14 64
Grand Bruit, Newf. — E2 72
Grand Caillou, La., U.S. — E5 95
Grand Canal (Da Yunhe), China — E8 31
Grand Canal, Ire. — D4 11
Grand Cane, La., U.S. — B2 95
Grand Canyon, Az., U.S. — A3 80
Grand Canyon, co., Az., U.S. — A3 80
Grand Canyon National Park, Az., U.S. — B3 80
Grand Cayman, i., Cay. Is. — D8 63
Grand Centre, Alta. — B5 68
Grand Cess, Lib. — F3 45
Grand Chenier, La., U.S. — E3 95
Grand Codroy, stm., Newf. — E2 72
Grand Combin, mtn., Switz. — D3 20
Grand Coteau, La., U.S. — D3 95
Grand Coulee, Wa., U.S. — B6 124
Grand Coulee Dam, Wa., U.S. — B6 124
Grande, stm., Arg. — B3 54
Grande, stm., Arg. — D2 55
Grande, stm., Bol. — C3 55
Grande, stm., Braz. — B2 56
Grande, stm., Braz. — D2 57
Grande, stm., Braz. — E3 54
Grande, Bahía, b., Arg. — E3 54
Grande, Boca, mth., Ven. — B5 60
Grande, Ilha, i., Braz. — h5 56
Grande, Rio, stm., Braz. — E7 76
Grande, Serra, mts., Braz. — C2 57
Grande-Anse, N.B. — B4 71
Grande Cache, Alta. — C1 68
Grande de Arecibo, stm., P.R. — B2 65
Grande [de Matagalpa], stm., Nic. — E8 63
Grande de Santiago, stm., Mex. — C3 63
Grande de Tarija, stm., S.A. — D3 55
Grande-Digue, N.B. — C5 71
Grande-Ligne, Que. — D4 74
Grande-Entrée, Que. — B8 71
Grande Prairie, Alta. — B1 68
Grand Erg de Bilma, des., Niger — C7 45
Grand Erg Occidental, des., Alg. — C5 44
Grand Erg Oriental, des., Alg. — C6 44
Grande rivière de la Baleine, stm., Que. — g11 74
Grande Ronde, stm., U.S. — C8 124
Grandes, Salinas, pl., Arg. — F2 55
Grandes-Bergeronnes, Que. — A8 74
Grandes-Piles, Que. — C5 74
Grande-Terre, i., Guad. — Q9 65
Grande Vigie, Pointe de la, c., Guad. — P9 65
Grand Falls (Grand-Sault), N.B. — B2 71
Grand Falls, Newf. — D4 72
Grandfalls, Tx., U.S. — D1 120
Grand Falls Lake, l., N.A. — C5 96
Grandfather Mountain, mtn., N.C., U.S. — A1 110
Grandfield, Ok., U.S. — C3 113
Grand Forks, B.C. — E8 69
Grand Forks, N.D., U.S. — B8 111
Grand Forks, co., N.D., U.S. — B8 111
Grand Forks Air Force Base, mil., N.D., U.S. — B8 111
Grand Glaise, Ar., U.S. — B4 81
Grand Gorge, N.Y., U.S. — C6 109
Grand Gulf, Ms., U.S. — C2 101
Grand Harbour, N.B. — E3 71
Grand Haven, Mi., U.S. — E4 99
Grand Hogback, mtn., Co., U.S. — B3 83
Grandin, N.D., U.S. — B9 111
Grand Island, Ne., U.S. — D7 104
Grand Island, i., La., U.S. — D6 95
Grand Island, i., Mi., U.S. — B4 99
Grand Isle, La., U.S. — E6 95
Grand Isle, Me., U.S. — A4 96
Grand Isle, Vt., U.S. — B2 122
Grand Isle, co., Vt., U.S. — B2 122
Grand Junction, Co., U.S. — B2 83
Grand Junction, Ia., U.S. — B3 92
Grand Junction, Mi., U.S. — F4 99
Grand Junction, Tn., U.S. — B2 119
Grand lac Bostonnais, l., Que. — B5 74
Grand-Lahou, I.C. — E3 45
Grand Lake, Co., U.S. — A5 83
Grand Lake, l., N.B. — D3 71
Grand Lake, l., Newf. — B1 72
Grand Lake, l., Newf. — D3 72
Grand Lake, l., N.A. — C5 96
Grand Lake, l., La., U.S. — E6 95
Grand Lake, l., La., U.S. — E3 95
Grand Lake, l., Mi., U.S. — C7 99
Grand Lake, l., Oh., U.S. — B1 112
Grand Lake Matagamon, l., Me., U.S. — B4 96
Grand Lake Seboeis, l., Me., U.S. — B4 96
Grand Lake Stream, Me., U.S. — C5 96
Grand Ledge, Mi., U.S. — F6 99
Grand Lieu, Lac de l., l., Fr. — D3 16
Grand Manan Channel, strt., N.A. — D6 96
Grand Manan Island, i., N.B. — E3 71
Grand Marais, Mi., U.S. — B5 99
Grand Marais, Mn., U.S. — k9 100
Grand Marsh, Wi., U.S. — E4 126
Grand Meadow, Mn., U.S. — G6 100
Grand-Mère, Que. — C5 74
Grand Mesa, mtn., Co., U.S. — C3 83
Grand Mound, Ia., U.S. — C7 92
Grândola, Port. — G3 22
Grand Pass, Mo., U.S. — B4 102
Grand Portage Indian Reservation, Mn., U.S. — k10 100
Grand Portage National Monument, Mn., U.S. — h10 100
Grand Prairie, Tx., U.S. — n10 120
Grand Pré, N.S. — D5 71
Grand Rapids, Man. — C2 70
Grand Rapids, Mi., U.S. — F5 99
Grand Rapids, Mn., U.S. — C5 100
Grand Rapids, N.D., U.S. — C7 111
Grand Rapids, Oh., U.S. — f6 112
Grand Ridge, Fl., U.S. — B1 86
Grand Ridge, Il., U.S. — B5 90

Grand River, N.S. — D9 71
Grand River, Ia., U.S. — D4 92
Grand Ronde, Or., U.S. — B3 114
Grand Rivers, Ky., U.S. — f9 94
Grand' Rivière, Mart. — S10 65
Grand Saline, Tx., U.S. — C5 120
Grand Santi, Fr. Gu. — B4 59
Grandson, Switz. — C2 21
Grand Terrace, Ca., U.S. — *E5 82
Grand Terre Islands, is., La., U.S. — E6 95
Grand Teton, mtn., Wy., U.S. — C2 127
Grand Teton National Park, Wy., U.S. — C2 127
Grand Tower, Il., U.S. — F4 90
Grand Traverse, co., Mi., U.S. — D5 99
Grand Traverse Bay, b., Mi., U.S. — C5 99
Grand Traverse Bay, East Arm, b., Mi., U.S. — D5 99
Grand Traverse Bay, West Arm, b., Mi., U.S. — D5 99
Grand Valley, Pa., U.S. — C2 115
Grand Valley, val., U.S. — B2 83
Grandview, Man. — D1 70
Grand View, Id., U.S. — G2 89
Grandview, Il., U.S. — D6 90
Grandview, In., U.S. — I4 91
Grandview, Ia., U.S. — C6 92
Grandview, Mo., U.S. — C3 102
Grandview, Oh., U.S. — C4 112
Grandview, Tn., U.S. — D9 119
Grandview, Wa., U.S. — C6 124
Grand View, Wi., U.S. — B2 126
Grandview Heights, Oh., U.S. — m10 112
Grandville, Mi., U.S. — F5 99
Grandvilliers, Fr. — E1 17
Grand Wash Cliffs, clf., Az., U.S. — B2 80
Grandy, Mn., U.S. — E5 100
Grandy, N.C., U.S. — A7 110
Grängärde (part of Ludvika), Swe. — G6 14
Grangeburg, Al., U.S. — D4 78
Grange-over-Sands, Eng., U.K. — F6 13
Granger, In., U.S. — A5 91
Granger, Ia., U.S. — C4 92
Granger, Mo., U.S. — A6 102
Granger, Tx., U.S. — D4 120
Granger, Wa., U.S. — C5 124
Granger, Wy., U.S. — E3 127
Granges [-sur-Vologne], Fr. — A2 20
Grangeville, Id., U.S. — D2 89
Grangeville, La., U.S. — D5 95
Granisle, B.C. — B4 69
Granite, Co., U.S. — B4 83
Granite, Ok., U.S. — C2 113
Granite, Or., U.S. — C8 114
Granite, Ut., U.S. — *C4 121
Granite, co., Mt., U.S. — D3 103
Granite Canon, Wy., U.S. — E7 127
Granite City, Il., U.S. — E3 90
Granite Falls, Mn., U.S. — F3 100
Granite Falls, N.C., U.S. — B1 110
Granite Falls, Wa., U.S. — A4 124
Granite Harbor, b., Ant. — e39 7
Granite Lake, res., Newf. — D3 72
Granite Mountain, mtn., Ak., U.S. — B7 79
Granite Mountain, mtn., Co., U.S. — B3 83
Granite Mountains, mts., Az., U.S. — E2 80
Granite Park, Ut., U.S. — *C4 121
Granite Pass, U.S. — B5 127
Granite Peak, mtn., Mt., U.S. — E7 103
Granite Peak, mtn., Nv., U.S. — C2 105
Granite Peak, mtn., Nv., U.S. — B4 105
Granite Peak, mtn., Ut., U.S. — E3 121
Granite Peak, mtn., Ut., U.S. — C2 121
Granite Peak, mtn., Wy., U.S. — D4 127
Granite Point, c., Newf. — C3 72
Granite Quarry, N.C., U.S. — B2 110
Granite Range, mts., Nv., U.S. — C2 105
Graniteville, Ma., U.S. — f10 98
Graniteville, Mo., U.S. — D7 102
Graniteville, S.C., U.S. — D4 117
Graniteville, Vt., U.S. — C4 122
Granja, Braz. — B2 57
Granja de Torrehermosa, Spain — C3 22
Granma, prov., Cuba — D5 64
Grannis, Ar., U.S. — C1 81
Grano, N.D., U.S. — A4 111
Granollers, Spain — B7 22
Gran Paradiso, mtn., Italy — D3 20
Gransee, E. Ger. — E7 15
Grant, Al., U.S. — A3 78
Grant, Co., U.S. — B5 83
Grant, Fl., U.S. — E6 86
Grant, Ia., U.S. — C2 92
Grant, La., U.S. — E5 95
Grant, Mt., U.S. — E3 103
Grant, Ne., U.S. — D4 104
Grant, Ok., U.S. — C5 113
Grant, co., Ar., U.S. — C3 81
Grant, co., In., U.S. — C6 91
Grant, co., Ks., U.S. — E2 93
Grant, co., Ky., U.S. — B5 94
Grant, co., La., U.S. — C3 95
Grant, co., Mn., U.S. — E2 100
Grant, co., Ne., U.S. — C4 104
Grant, co., N.M., U.S. — E1 108
Grant, co., N.D., U.S. — C4 111
Grant, co., Ok., U.S. — A4 113
Grant, co., Or., U.S. — C7 114
Grant, co., S.D., U.S. — B8 118
Grant, co., Wa., U.S. — B6 124
Grant, co., W.V., U.S. — B5 125
Grant, co., Wi., U.S. — F3 126
Grant, mtn., Nv., U.S. — F6 105
Grant City, Mo., U.S. — A3 102
Grantham, Eng., U.K. — I5 13
Grantham, N.H., U.S. — D2 106
Granton, Wi., U.S. — D3 126
Grantown-on-Spey, Scot., U.K. — D5 13
Grant Park, Il., U.S. — B6 90
Grant Range, mts., Nv., U.S. — E6 105
Grants, N.M., U.S. — B2 108
Grantsboro, N.C., U.S. — B6 110
Grantsburg, In., U.S. — H5 91
Grantsburg, Wi., U.S. — C1 126
Grantsdale, Mt., U.S. — D2 103
Grants Lick, Ky., U.S. — k14 94
Grants Pass, Or., U.S. — E3 114
Grantsville, Md., U.S. — k12 97
Grantsville, Ut., U.S. — C3 121
Grantsville, W.V., U.S. — C3 125

Grant Town, W.V., U.S. — B4 125
Grantville, Ga., U.S. — C2 87
Grantville, Ks., U.S. — k14 93
Grantville, Pa., U.S. — F8 115
Granum, Alta. — E4 68
Granville, Fr. — C3 16
Granville, Il., U.S. — B4 90
Granville, Ia., U.S. — B2 92
Granville, Ma., U.S. — B2 98
Granville, N.Y., U.S. — B7 109
Granville, N.D., U.S. — A5 111
Granville, Oh., U.S. — B3 112
Granville, Vt., U.S. — D3 122
Granville, co., N.C., U.S. — A4 110
Granville Centre, N.S. — E4 71
Granville Ferry, N.S. — E4 71
Granville Lake, l., Man. — A1 70
Grão Mogol, Braz. — D5 57
Grapeland, Tx., U.S. — D5 120
Grapeview, Wa., U.S. — B3 124
Grapevine, Tx., U.S. — C4 120
Grapevine Lake, res., Tx., U.S. — n9 120
Grapevine Peak, mtn., Nv., U.S. — G4 105
Gras, Lac de, l., N.W. Ter. — D10 66
Grasonville, Md., U.S. — C5 97
Grass, stm., Man. — B2 70
Grass, stm., N.Y., U.S. — f9 109
Grass Creek, In., U.S. — C5 91
Grass Creek, Wy., U.S. — C4 127
Grasse, Fr. — F7 16
Grasselli, Al., U.S. — B3 78
Grassflat, Pa., U.S. — D5 115
Grassington, Eng., U.K. — F7 13
Grass Lake, Il., U.S. — h8 90
Grass Lake, Mi., U.S. — F6 99
Grass Lake, l., Il., U.S. — h8 90
Grassrange, Mt., U.S. — C8 103
Grass River Provincial Park, Man. — B1 70
Grasston, Mn., U.S. — E5 100
Grass Valley, Ca., U.S. — C3 82
Grass Valley, Or., U.S. — B6 114
Grassy Brook, stm., Vt., U.S. — E3 122
Grassy Butte, N.D., U.S. — B2 111
Grassy Creek, N.C., U.S. — A1 110
Grassy Lake, Alta. — E5 68
Grassy Lake, l., La., U.S. — k9 95
Grates Cove, Newf. — D5 72
Grates Point, c., Newf. — D5 72
Gratiot, Oh., U.S. — C3 112
Gratiot, Wi., U.S. — F3 126
Gratiot, co., Mi., U.S. — E6 99
Gratis, Oh., U.S. — C1 112
Gratz, Pa., U.S. — E8 115
Graubünden, state, Switz. — C5 20
Graulhet, Fr. — I8 16
Gravatá, Braz. — E11 57
Grave Creek, stm., W.V., U.S. — g8 125
Gravedona, Italy — D7 21
Gravelbourg, Sask. — H2 75
Gravelines, Fr. — D2 17
Gravelly, Ar., U.S. — C2 81
Gravelly Branch, stm., De., U.S. — F4 85
Gravelly Range, mts., Mt., U.S. — E4 103
Gravenhurst, Ont. — C5 73
Grave Peak, mtn., Id., U.S. — C4 89
Graves, Ga., U.S. — E2 87
Graves, co., Ky., U.S. — f9 94
Gravesend, Eng., U.K. — E7 10
Gravette, Ar., U.S. — A1 81
Gravina [in Puglia], Italy — D6 23
Gravity, Ia., U.S. — D3 92
Gravois, Pointe à, c., Haiti — E7 64
Gravois Mills, Mo., U.S. — C5 102
Grawn, Mi., U.S. — D5 99
Gray, Sask. — G3 75
Gray, Fr. — D6 16
Gray, Ga., U.S. — C3 87
Gray, Ia., U.S. — C3 92
Gray, Ky., U.S. — D5 94
Gray, La., U.S. — k10 95
Gray, Me., U.S. — g7 96
Gray, Pa., U.S. — F3 115
Gray, co., Ks., U.S. — E3 93
Gray, co., Tx., U.S. — B2 120
Grayback Mountain, mtn., Or., U.S. — E3 114
Gray Court, S.C., U.S. — B3 117
Gray Gables, Ma., U.S. — *C6 98
Gray Horse, Ok., U.S. — A5 113
Grayland, Wa., U.S. — C1 124
Grayling, Ak., U.S. — C7 79
Grayling, Mi., U.S. — D6 99
Graylyn Crest, De., U.S. — A3 85
Graymont, Il., U.S. — B5 90
Grays, Eng., U.K. — m13 10
Grays Harbor, co., Wa., U.S. — B2 124
Grays Harbor, b., Wa., U.S. — C1 124
Grayslake, Il., U.S. — A5 90
Grays Lake, sw., Id., U.S. — F7 89
Grayson, Sask. — G4 75
Grayson, Al., U.S. — A2 78
Grayson, Ga., U.S. — C3 87
Grayson, Ky., U.S. — B7 94
Grayson, co., Ky., U.S. — C3 94
Grayson, co., Tx., U.S. — C4 120
Grayson, co., Va., U.S. — D1 123
Grayson Lake, res., Ky., U.S. — B7 94
Grays Peak, mtn., Co., U.S. — B5 83
Grays River, Wa., U.S. — C2 124
Gray Summit, Mo., U.S. — g12 102
Graysville, Al., U.S. — f7 78
Graysville, In., U.S. — F2 91
Graysville, Oh., U.S. — C4 112
Graysville, Tn., U.S. — D8 119
Grayville, Il., U.S. — E5 90
Greasewood, Az., U.S. — B6 80
Great Abaco, i., Bah. — A5 64
Great Alföld, pl., Hung. — B5 24
Great Artesian Basin, Austl. — D7 50
Great Australian Bight, Austl. — F4 50
Great Averill Pond, l., Vt., U.S. — B5 122
Great Barrier Island, i., N.Z. — L15 51
Great Barrier Reef, rf., Austl. — C8 50
Great Barrington, Ma., U.S. — B1 98
Great Basin National Park, Nv., U.S. — E7 105
Great Bay, b., N.H., U.S. — D5 106
Great Bay, b., N.J., U.S. — D4 107

Great Bear Lake, l., N.W. Ter. — C8 66
Great Bend, Ks., U.S. — D5 93
Great Bend, N.D., U.S. — C9 111
Great Bend, Pa., U.S. — C10 115
Great Bitter Lake, l., Eg. — D4 41
Great Blasket Island, i., Ire. — I2 11
Great Blue Hill, hill, Ma., U.S. — B5 98
Great Burnt Lake, l., Newf. — D3 72
Great Cacapon, W.V., U.S. — B6 125
Great Camanoe, i., V.I., Br. — B6 65
Great Captain Island, i., Ct., U.S. — F1 84
Great Channel, strt., Asia — G9 36
Great Deer, Sask. — E2 75
Great Dismal Swamp, sw., U.S. — D6 123
Great Divide Basin, Wy., U.S. — E4 127
Great Dividing Range, mts., Austl. — F9 50
Great Driffield, Eng., U.K. — F8 13
Great Duck Island, i., Ont. — B2 73
Great East Lake, l., U.S. — C5 106
Great Egg Harbor, stm., N.J., U.S. — D3 107
Greater Antilles, is., N.A. — H13 61
Greater Cincinnati Airport, Ky., U.S. — h13 94
Greater Khingan Range see Da Hinggan Ling, mts., China — B9 31
Greater London, co., Eng., U.K. — *A5 12
Greater Manchester, co., Eng., U.K. — *A5 12
Great Exuma, i., Bah. — C6 64
Great Falls, Man. — D3 70
Great Falls, Mt., U.S. — C5 103
Great Falls, S.C., U.S. — B6 117
Great Falls, wtfl., U.S. — B3 97
Great Falls Dam, Tn., U.S. — D6 119
Great Guana Cay, i., Bah. — B5 64
Great Harbour Deep, b., Newf. — C3 72
Greathouse Peak, mtn., Mt., U.S. — D7 103
Great Inagua, i., Bah. — D7 64
Great Indian Desert (Thar Desert), des., Asia — C5 36
Great Island, spit, Ma., U.S. — C7 98
Great Island, i., N.C., U.S. — B6 110
Great Karroo, plat., S. Afr. — D3 49
Great Lake, l., Austl. — o15 50
Great Lakes Naval Training Center, mil., Il., U.S. — h9 90
Great Malvern, Eng., U.K. — B5 12
Great Miami, stm., U.S. — C1 112
Great Misery Island, i., Ma., U.S. — f12 98
Great Moose Lake, l., Me., U.S. — D3 96
Great Neck, N.Y., U.S. — h13 109
Great Neck Estates, N.Y., U.S. — *E7 109
Great Nicobar, i., India — G9 36
Great North Mountain, mtn., U.S. — C6 125
Great Ouse, stm., Eng., U.K. — D7 10
Great Pedro Bluff, c., Jam. — F13 65
Great Pee Dee, stm., U.S. — D9 117
Great Point, c., Ma., U.S. — D7 98
Great Pond, l., Me., U.S. — D3 96
Great Pond, l., Me., U.S. — C4 96
Great Pond, l., Ma., U.S. — h12 98
Great Pond, l., Ma., U.S. — h11 98
Great Quittacas Pond, l., Ma., U.S. — C6 98
Great Ruaha, stm., Tan. — C6 48
Great Sacandaga Lake, l., N.Y., U.S. — C6 109
Great Saint Bernard Pass, Eur. — B1 23
Great Salt Lake, l., Ut., U.S. — B3 121
Great Salt Lake Desert, des., Ut., U.S. — C2 121
Great Salt Plains Lake, res., Ok., U.S. — A3 113
Great Salt Pond, l., R.I., U.S. — h7 116
Great Salt Pond, l., Jam. — F15 65
Great Sand Dunes National Monument, Co., U.S. — D5 83
Great Sand Hills, Sask. — G1 75
Great Sandy Desert, des., Austl. — D3 50
Great Sea Reef, rf., Fiji — H15 52
Great Seneca Creek, stm., Md., U.S. — B3 97
Great Skellig Island, i., Ire. — F1 11
Great Slave Lake, l., N.W. Ter. — D10 66
Great Smoky Mountains, mtn., U.S. — D1 110
Great Smoky Mountains National Park, U.S. — D1 110
Great Sound, strt., Ber. — p19 64
Great Swamp, sw., R.I., U.S. — F3 116
Great Tenasserim, stm., Burma — F3 35
Great Torrington, Eng., U.K. — J9 12
Great Victoria Desert, des., Austl. — E4 50
Great Village, N.S. — D6 71
Great Wall, hist., China — C8 31
Great Wass Island, i., Me., U.S. — D5 96
Great Yarmouth, Eng., U.K. — D7 10
Great Zab, stm., Asia — D14 40
Gredos, Sierra de, mts., Spain — B3 22
Greece, N.Y., U.S. — B3 109
Greece, ctry., Eur. — A6 83
Greeley, Co., U.S. — A6 83
Greeley, Ia., U.S. — B6 92
Greeley, Ne., U.S. — C7 104
Greeley, Pa., U.S. — D12 115
Greeley, co., Ks., U.S. — D2 93
Greeley, co., Ne., U.S. — C7 104
Greeleyville, S.C., U.S. — D7 117
Greely Fiord, N.W. Ter. — k35 66
Green, Ks., U.S. — C6 93
Green, Or., U.S. — D3 114
Green, co., Ky., U.S. — C4 94
Green, co., Wi., U.S. — F4 126
Green, stm., N.B. — B1 71
Green, stm., U.S. — C6 76
Green, stm., Ky., U.S. — C2 94
Green, stm., Wa., U.S. — B4 124

Greenbackville, Va., U.S. — C7 123
Green Bank, N.J., U.S. — D3 107
Green Bank, W.V., U.S. — C5 125
Green Bay, Va., U.S. — C4 123
Green Bay, Wi., U.S. — D6 126
Green Bay, b., U.S. — D3 99
Greenbelt, Md., U.S. — C4 97
Greenbriar, Va., U.S. — g12 123
Greenbrier, Al., U.S. — A3 78
Greenbrier, Ar., U.S. — B3 81
Green Brier, Tn., U.S. — A5 119
Greenbrier, co., W.V., U.S. — D4 125
Greenbrier, stm., W.V., U.S. — D4 125
Green Brook, N.J., U.S. — *B4 107
Greenburr, Pa., U.S. — D7 115
Greenbush, Me., U.S. — D4 96
Greenbush, Mi., U.S. — D7 99
Greenbush, Mn., U.S. — B2 100
Greenbush, Wi., U.S. — k9 126
Green Camp, Oh., U.S. — B2 112
Greencastle, In., U.S. — E4 91
Greencastle, Mo., U.S. — A5 102
Greencastle, Pa., U.S. — G6 115
Green City, Mo., U.S. — A5 102
Green Court, Alta. — B3 68
Green Cove Springs, Fl., U.S. — C5 86
Greencreek, Id., U.S. — C2 89
Greendale, In., U.S. — F8 91
Greendale, Ut., U.S. — *C6 121
Greendale, Wi., U.S. — m11 126
Greendell, N.J., U.S. — B3 107
Greene, Ia., U.S. — B5 92
Greene, Me., U.S. — D2 96
Greene, N.Y., U.S. — C5 109
Greene, N.D., U.S. — A4 111
Greene, co., Al., U.S. — C1 78
Greene, co., Ar., U.S. — A5 81
Greene, co., Ga., U.S. — C3 87
Greene, co., Il., U.S. — D3 90
Greene, co., In., U.S. — F4 91
Greene, co., Ia., U.S. — B3 92
Greene, co., Ms., U.S. — D5 101
Greene, co., Mo., U.S. — D4 102
Greene, co., N.Y., U.S. — C6 109
Greene, co., N.C., U.S. — B5 110
Greene, co., Oh., U.S. — C2 112
Greene, co., Pa., U.S. — G1 115
Greene, co., Tn., U.S. — C11 119
Greene, co., Va., U.S. — B4 123
Greeneville, Tn., U.S. — C11 119
Green Fall, stm., U.S. — F1 116
Greenfield, Ar., U.S. — B5 81
Greenfield, Ca., U.S. — D3 82
Greenfield, Il., U.S. — D3 90
Greenfield, In., U.S. — E6 91
Greenfield, Ia., U.S. — C3 92
Greenfield, Me., U.S. — D4 96
Greenfield, Ma., U.S. — A2 98
Greenfield, Mo., U.S. — D4 102
Greenfield, N.H., U.S. — E3 106
Greenfield, Oh., U.S. — C2 112
Greenfield, Ok., U.S. — B3 113
Greenfield, Tn., U.S. — A3 119
Greenfield, Wi., U.S. — n11 126
Greenfield Plaza, Ia., U.S. — e8 92
Green Forest, Ar., U.S. — A2 81
Green Grass, S.D., U.S. — B4 118
Green Harbor, Ma., U.S. — B6 98
Greenhill, Al., U.S. — A2 78
Green Hill, R.I., U.S. — G3 116
Green Hill Pond, l., R.I., U.S. — G3 116
Greenhills, Oh., U.S. — n12 112
Greenhorn Creek, stm., Co., U.S. — D6 83
Green Island, Ia., U.S. — B7 92
Green Island, N.Y., U.S. — *C7 109
Green Isle, Mn., U.S. — F4 100
Green Lake, Sask. — C2 75
Green Lake, Ut., U.S. — *C6 121
Green Lake, Wi., U.S. — E5 126
Green Lake, co., Wi., U.S. — E4 126
Green Lake, l., B.C. — D7 69
Green Lake, l., Me., U.S. — D4 96
Green Lake, l., Wi., U.S. — E5 126
Greenland, Ar., U.S. — B1 81

Greenland, Mi., U.S. — B1 99
Greenland, N.H., U.S. — D5 106
Greenland (Kalaallit Nunaat), ctry., N.A. — B16 61
Greenland Sea — B15 128
Greenlaw, Scot., U.K. — E6 13
Greenlawn, N.Y., U.S. — *h13 109
Greenleaf, Ks., U.S. — C7 93
Greenleaf, Wi., U.S. — D5 126
Greenlee, co., Az., U.S. — D6 80
Green Lookout Mountain, mtn., Wa., U.S. — D3 124
Green Lowther, mtn., Scot., U.K. — E5 13
Greenmanville, Ct., U.S. — B5 84
Greenmount, Md., U.S. — A4 97
Greenmountain, N.C., U.S. — f10 110
Green Mountain Falls, Co., U.S. — *C6 83
Green Mountain Reservoir, res., Co., U.S. — B4 83
Green Mountains, mts., Vt., U.S. — F2 122
Greenock, Scot., U.K. — C4 10
Greenore Point, c., Ire. — E5 11
Greenough, Mt., U.S. — D3 103
Greenough Point, c., Ont. — C3 73
Green Peter Lake, res., Or., U.S. — C4 114
Green Pond, Al., U.S. — B2 78
Green Pond, S.C., U.S. — F6 117
Green Pond, l., N.J., U.S. — A4 107
Green Pond Mountain, mtn., N.J., U.S. — B3 107
Greenport, N.Y., U.S. — m16 109
Green Ridge, Mo., U.S. — C4 102
Green River, Ut., U.S. — E5 121
Green River, Wy., U.S. — E3 127
Green River Lake, res., Ky., U.S. — C4 94
Green River Lock and Dam, U.S. — I2 91
Green River Reservoir, res., Vt., U.S. — B3 122
Green Rock, Il., U.S. — B3 90
Greensboro, Al., U.S. — C2 78
Greensboro, Fl., U.S. — B2 86
Greensboro, Ga., U.S. — C3 87
Greensboro, Md., U.S. — C6 97

Name	Map Ref.	Page

Greensboro, N.C., U.S. — A3 110
Greensboro, Pa., U.S. — G2 115
Greensboro, Vt., U.S. — B4 122
Greensboro Bend, Vt., U.S. — B4 122
Greensburg, In., U.S. — F7 91
Greensburg, Ks., U.S. — E4 93
Greensburg, Ky., U.S. — C4 94
Greensburg, La., U.S. — D5 95
Greensburg, Pa., U.S. — F2 115
Green Sea, S.C., U.S. — C10 117
Greens Fork, In., U.S. — E7 91
Greens Peak, mtn., Az., U.S. — C6 80
Greenspond, Newf. — D5 72
Green Spring, W.V., U.S. — B6 125
Green Springs, Oh., U.S. — A2 112
Greenstone Point, c., Scot., U.K. — C3 13
Green Sulphur Springs, W.V., U.S. — D4 125
Greensville, co., Va., U.S. — D5 123
Green Swamp, sw., N.C., U.S. — C4 110
Greentop, Mo., U.S. — A5 102
Greentown, In., U.S. — D6 91
Green Tree, Pa., U.S. — *k13 115
Greenup, Il., U.S. — D5 90
Greenup, Ky., U.S. — B7 94
Greenup, co., Ky., U.S. — B7 94
Green Valley, Az., U.S. — F5 80
Green Valley, Il., U.S. — C4 90
Green Valley, Mn., U.S. — F3 100
Green Valley, Wi., U.S. — D5 126
Green Valley, val., Tx., U.S. — p13 120
Greenview, Il., U.S. — C4 90
Greenview, W.V., U.S. — n12 125
Greenville, Lib. — E3 45
Greenville, Al., U.S. — D3 78
Greenville, Ca., U.S. — B3 82
Greenville, De., U.S. — A3 85
Greenville, Fl., U.S. — B3 86
Greenville, Ga., U.S. — C2 87
Greenville, Il., U.S. — E4 90
Greenville, In., U.S. — H6 91
Greenville, Ia., U.S. — A2 92
Greenville, Ky., U.S. — C2 94
Greenville, Me., U.S. — C3 96
Greenville, Mi., U.S. — E5 99
Greenville, Ms., U.S. — B2 101
Greenville, Mo., U.S. — D7 102
Greenville, N.H., U.S. — E3 106
Greenville, N.Y., U.S. — *n15 109
Greenville, N.C., U.S. — B5 110
Greenville, Oh., U.S. — B1 112
Greenville, Pa., U.S. — D1 115
Greenville, R.I., U.S. — C3 116
Greenville, S.C., U.S. — B3 117
Greenville, Tx., U.S. — C4 120
Greenville, Ut., U.S. — E3 121
Greenville, W.V., U.S. — D4 125
Greenville, Wi., U.S. — h8 126
Greenville, co., S.C., U.S. — B3 117
Greenville Creek, stm., Oh., U.S. — B1 112
Greenville Junction, Me., U.S. — C3 96
Greenwald, Mn., U.S. — E4 100
Greenwater Lake Provincial Park, Sask. — E4 75
Greenway, Man. — E2 70
Greenway, Ar., U.S. — A5 81
Greenwell Springs, La., U.S. — D5 95
Greenwich (part of London), Eng., U.K. — m13 10
Greenwich, Ct., U.S. — E1 84
Greenwich, Ks., U.S. — g12 93
Greenwich, N.J., U.S. — C2 107
Greenwich, N.Y., U.S. — B7 109
Greenwich, Oh., U.S. — A3 112
Greenwich, Ut., U.S. — E4 121
Greenwich, Va., U.S. — *B5 123
Greenwich Bay, b., R.I., U.S. — D4 116
Greenwich Hill, N.B. — D3 71
Greenwich Point, c., Ct., U.S. — E1 84
Greenwood, B.C. — E8 69
Greenwood, Ar., U.S. — B1 81
Greenwood, De., U.S. — A3 85
Greenwood, In., U.S. — B1 86
Greenwood, In., U.S. — E5 91
Greenwood, Ky., U.S. — D5 94
Greenwood, La., U.S. — B2 95
Greenwood, Ms., U.S. — B3 101
Greenwood, Mo., U.S. — k11 102
Greenwood, Ne., U.S. — D9 104
Greenwood, N.Y., U.S. — C4 96
Greenwood, Pa., U.S. — E5 115
Greenwood, S.C., U.S. — C3 117
Greenwood, S.D., U.S. — C4 118
Greenwood, Wi., U.S. — D3 126
Greenwood, co., Ks., U.S. — E7 93
Greenwood, co., S.C., U.S. — C3 117
Greenwood, Lake, res., In., U.S. — G4 91
Greenwood, Lake, res., S.C., U.S. — C4 117
Greenwood Lake, N.Y., U.S. — D6 109
Greenwood Lake, l., N.J., U.S. — A4 107
Greenwood Lake, l., N.J., U.S. — C7 100
Greenwood Village, Co., U.S. — *B6 83
Greer, Id., U.S. — C2 89
Greer, Mo., U.S. — E6 102
Greer, S.C., U.S. — B3 117
Greer, co., Ok., U.S. — C2 113
Greers Ferry Lake, res., Ar., U.S. — B3 81
Greeson, Lake, res., Ar., U.S. — C2 81
Gregg, co., Tx., U.S. — C5 120
Gregoire Lake, l., Alta. — A5 68
Gregory, Ar., U.S. — B4 81
Gregory, Mi., U.S. — F6 99
Gregory, N.C., U.S. — A6 110
Gregory, S.D., U.S. — D6 118
Gregory, co., S.D., U.S. — D6 118
Gregory, stm., Austl. — C6 50
Gregory, Lake, l., Austl. — E6 50
Gregory Bald, mtn., Tn., U.S. — D10 119
Gregory Range, mts., Austl. — C7 50
Greifswald, E. Ger. — A6 18
Greifswalder Bodden, b., E. Ger. — D7 15
Greig, N.Y., U.S. — B5 109
Greilickville, Mi., U.S. — D5 99
Grein, Aus. — D7 18
Greiz, E. Ger. — C6 18
Gretton, Oh., U.S. — A11 112
Gremyachinsk, Sov. Un. — D20 8
Grená, Den. — B4 15
Grenada, Ca., U.S. — B2 82
Grenada, Ms., U.S. — B4 101
Grenada, co., Ms., U.S. — B4 101
Grenada, ctry., N.A. — J14 64
Grenada Lake, res., Ms., U.S. — B4 101
Grenade, Fr. — F4 16
Grenadine Islands, is., N.A. — V26 61
Grenagh, Ire. — E3 11
Grenay, Fr. — D2 17

Grenchen, Switz. — B3 20
Grenen (The Skaw), spit, Den. — A4 15
Grenfell, Sask. — G4 75
Grenoble, Fr. — E6 16
Grenola, Ks., U.S. — E7 93
Grenora, N.D., U.S. — A2 111
Grenville, Que. — D3 74
Grenville, Gren. — W25 65
Grenville, N.M., U.S. — A6 108
Grenville, S.D., U.S. — B8 118
Grenville, co., Ont. — C9 73
Grenville, Cape, c., Austl. — B7 50
Grenville, Point, c., Wa., U.S. — B1 124
Grenville Channel, strt., B.C. — C3 69
Gresham, Or., U.S. — C8 104
Gresham, Or., U.S. — B4 114
Gresham, S.C., U.S. — D9 117
Gresham, Wi., U.S. — D5 126
Gresham Park, Ga., U.S. — *h8 87
Gretna, Man. — E3 70
Gretna, Scot., U.K. — F5 13
Gretna, Fl., U.S. — B2 86
Gretna, La., U.S. — E5 95
Gretna, Ne., U.S. — C9 104
Greven, W. Ger. — D3 123
Greven, W. Ger. — A2 19
Grevená, Grc. — B3 25
Grevenbroich, W. Ger. — B1 19
Grevesmühlen, E. Ger. — E5 15
Grey, co., Ont. — C4 73
Grey, stm., Newf. — E3 72
Grey, stm., N.Z. — O13 51
Greybull, Wy., U.S. — B4 127
Greybull, stm., Wy., U.S. — B4 127
Greycliff, Mt., U.S. — E7 103
Grey Eagle, Mn., U.S. — E4 100
Grey Islands, is., Newf. — C4 72
Greylock, Mount, mtn., Ma., U.S. — A1 98
Greymouth, N.Z. — O13 51
Grey Range, mts., Austl. — E7 50
Greys, stm., Wy., U.S. — C2 127
Greystone, Ct., U.S. — C3 84
Greystone, N.C., U.S. — A4 110
Gribbell Island, i., B.C. — C3 69
Gridley, Ca., U.S. — C3 82
Gridley, Il., U.S. — C5 90
Gridley, Ks., U.S. — D8 93
Gridley Mountain, mtn., Ct., U.S. — A2 84
Griekwastad, S. Afr. — C3 49
Griesheim, W. Ger. — D3 19
Grieskirchen, Aus. — D6 18
Griffin, Sask. — H4 75
Griffin, Ga., U.S. — C2 87
Griffin, In., U.S. — H2 91
Griffiss Air Force Base, mil., N.Y., U.S. — B5 109
Griffith, Austl. — F8 50
Griffith, In., U.S. — A3 91
Griffith Island, i., Ont. — C4 73
Griffithsville, W.V., U.S. — C3 125
Griffithville, Ar., U.S. — B4 81
Grifton, N.C., U.S. — B5 110
Griggs, Ok., U.S. — e8 113
Griggs, co., N.D., U.S. — B7 111
Griggstown, N.J., U.S. — C3 107
Griggsville, Il., U.S. — D3 90
Grigoriopol, Sov. Un. — B9 24
Grijalva, stm., Mex. — D6 63
Grim, Cape, c., Austl. — o14 50
Grimari, Cen. Afr. Rep. — D4 46
Grimes, Al., U.S. — D4 78
Grimes, Ia., U.S. — C4 92
Grimes, co., Tx., U.S. — D4 120
Grimesland, N.C., U.S. — B5 110
Grimma, E. Ger. — C6 18
Grimma, E. Ger. — D7 15
Grimmialp, Switz. — C4 21
Grimms Landing, W.V., U.S. — C3 125
Grimsby, Ont. — D5 73
Grimsby, Eng., U.K. — D7 13
Grimsey, i., Ice. — m23 11
Grimshaw, Alta. — A2 68
Grimsley, Tn., U.S. — C9 119
Grimstad, Nor. — H3 14
Grimsthorpe, Ont. — B2 73
Grindall Creek, Wa., U.S. — n18 123
Grindelwald, Switz. — C5 21
Grindstone, Den. — C2 15
Grindstone, Me., U.S. — C4 96
Grind Stone City, Mi., U.S. — D8 99
Grindstone, i., Marsh Is. — S18 52
Grinnell, Ia., U.S. — C5 92
Grinnell, Ks., U.S. — C3 93
Grinnell Peninsula, pen., N.W. Ter. — m32 66
Grise Fiord, N.W. Ter. — m35 66
Gris-Nez, Cap, c., Fr. — D9 12
Grissom Air Force Base, mil., In., U.S. — C5 91
Griswold, Man. — E1 70
Griswold, Ia., U.S. — C2 92
Griswoldville, Ma., U.S. — A2 98
Grizzly Mountain, mtn., Id., U.S. — B2 89
Grizzly Mountain, mtn., Or., U.S. — C6 114
Grizzly Mountain, mtn., Wa., U.S. — A7 124
Groais Island, i., Newf. — C4 72
Grodków, Pol. — C4 26
Grodno, Sov. Un. — E4 28
Grodzisk Mazowiecki, Pol. — m13 26
Grodzisk [Wielkopolski], Pol. — B4 26
Groenlo, Neth. — B6 17
Groesbeck, Oh., U.S. — *o12 112
Groesbeck, Tx., U.S. — D4 120
Groix, Île de, i., Fr. — D2 16
Grójec, Pol. — C6 26
Grombalia, Tun. — F3 23
Gronau, W. Ger. — B3 18
Gronau, W. Ger. — A2 19
Groningen, Neth. — A7 16
Groningen, Sur. — A7 59
Groningen, prov., Neth. — A6 17
Grónlid, Sask. — D3 75
Groom, Tx., U.S. — B2 120
Groom Lake, l., Nv., U.S. — F6 105
Groom Range, mts., Nv., U.S. — F6 105
Groote Eylandt, i., Austl. — B6 50
Grootfontein, Nmb. — A2 49
Grootvloer, pl., S. Afr. — C3 49
Groscap, Mi., U.S. — C6 99
Grosio, Italy — D9 21
Groslay, Fr. — g10 16
Gros-Mécatina, Île du, i., Que. — C2 72
Gros Morne, mtn., Newf. — D3 72
Gros Morne National Park, Newf. — D3 72
Gross, Ne., U.S. — B7 104
Grossbreitenbach, E. Ger. — C6 19
Grosse Île, i., Que. — *F7 99
Grosse Île, i., Que. — B8 71

Grosse Isle Naval Air Station, mil., Mi., U.S. — p15 99
Grosse Laaber, stm., W. Ger. — E7 19
Grossenhain, E. Ger. — C6 18
Grosse Pointe, Mi., U.S. — p16 99
Grosse Pointe Farms, Mi., U.S. — *F8 99
Grosse Pointe Park, Mi., U.S. — p16 99
Grosse Pointe Woods, Mi., U.S. — p16 99
Grosser Arber, mtn., W. Ger. — D8 19
Grosse Röder, stm., E. Ger. — B8 19
Grösser Plön, l., W. Ger. — D4 15
Grosser Priel, mtn., Aus. — E7 18
Grosse Tete, La., U.S. — D4 95
Grosseto, Italy — C3 23
Grossglockner, mtn., Aus. — E6 18
Grossmont, Ca., U.S. — o16 82
Grossostheim, W. Ger. — D4 19
Grossräschen, E. Ger. — B9 19
Grossröhrsdorf, E. Ger. — B9 19
Grosvenor Dale, Ct., U.S. — B8 84
Gros Ventre, stm., Wy., U.S. — C2 127
Gros Ventre Range, mts., Wy., U.S. — C2 127
Groswater Bay, b., Newf. — A3 72
Groton, Ct., U.S. — D7 84
Groton, Ma., U.S. — A4 98
Groton, N.H., U.S. — C3 106
Groton, N.Y., U.S. — C4 109
Groton, S.D., U.S. — B7 118
Groton, Vt., U.S. — C4 122
Groton Long Point, Ct., U.S. — D7 84
Grottaferrata, Italy — h9 23
Grottaglie, Italy — D6 23
Grottoes, Va., U.S. — B4 123
Grouard Mission, Alta. — B2 68
Grouse Creek, Ut., U.S. — B2 121
Grouse Creek, stm., Ks., U.S. — E7 93
Grouse Creek, stm., Ut., U.S. — B2 121
Grouse Creek Mountain, mtn., Id., U.S. — E5 89
Grouse Creek Mountains, mts., Ut., U.S. — B2 121
Grovania, Ga., U.S. — D3 87
Grove, Me., U.S. — C5 96
Grove, Ok., U.S. — A7 113
Grove City, Fl., U.S. — F4 86
Grove City, Mn., U.S. — E4 100
Grove City, Oh., U.S. — C2 112
Grove City, Pa., U.S. — D1 115
Grove Hill, Al., U.S. — D2 78
Groveland, Ca., U.S. — D3 82
Groveland, Fl., U.S. — D5 86
Groveland, Ga., U.S. — D5 87
Groveland, Ma., U.S. — A5 98
Groveland, N.Y., U.S. — C3 109
Grove Mountains, mts., Ant. — B21 7
Grove Point, c., Md., U.S. — B5 97
Groveport, Oh., U.S. — C3 112
Grover, Co., U.S. — A6 83
Grover, N.C., U.S. — B1 110
Grover, Pa., U.S. — C8 115
Grover, S.C., U.S. — E6 117
Grover, Wy., U.S. — D2 127
Grover City, Ca., U.S. — E3 82
Grover Hill, Oh., U.S. — A1 112
Grovertown, In., U.S. — B4 91
Groves, Tx., U.S. — E6 120
Grovespring, Mo., U.S. — D5 102
Groveton, N.H., U.S. — A3 106
Groveton, Tx., U.S. — D5 120
Groveton Gardens, Va., U.S. — *B5 123
Groveton, Va., U.S. — C4 87
Groveville, N.J., U.S. — C3 107
Groznyy, Sov. Un. — E7 29
Grudovo, Bul. — D8 24
Grudziądz, Pol. — B5 26
Grues, Île aux, i., Que. — B7 74
Gruetli-Laager, Tn., U.S. — D8 119
Gruinard Bay, b., Scot., U.K. — C3 13
Grulla, Tx., U.S. — F3 120
Grünberg, W. Ger. — C3 19
Grundy, Va., U.S. — e9 123
Grundy, co., Il., U.S. — B5 90
Grundy, co., Ia., U.S. — B5 92
Grundy, co., Mo., U.S. — A4 102
Grundy, co., Tn., U.S. — D8 119
Grundy Center, Ia., U.S. — B5 92
Grünstadt, W. Ger. — D3 19
Grunthal, Man. — E3 70
Grüsch, Switz. — C8 21
Gruver, Ia., U.S. — A3 92
Gruver, Tx., U.S. — A2 120
Gruyères, Switz. — C3 21
Gruž (part of Dubrovnik), Yugo. — D4 24
Gryazi, Sov. Un. — E13 27
Gryazovets, Sov. Un. — B13 27
Gryfice, Pol. — B3 26
Gryfino, Pol. — B2 26
Grygla, Mn., U.S. — B3 100
Gstaad, Switz. — C3 20
Guabito, Pan. — F6 62
Guacanayabo, Golfo de, b., Cuba — D5 64
Guachi, Arg. — B4 54
Guadalajara, Mex. — C4 63
Guadalajara, Spain — B4 22
Guadalcanal, Spain — C3 22
Guadalcanal, i., Sol.Is. — G9 6
Guadalentín, stm., Spain — D5 22
Guadalhorce, stm., Spain — D3 22
Guadalmena, stm., Spain — C4 22
Guadalope, stm., Spain — B5 22
Guadalquivir, stm., Spain — D2 22
Guadalupe, Mex. — *B4 63
Guadalupe, Az., U.S. — m9 80
Guadalupe, Ca., U.S. — E3 82
Guadalupe, co., N.M., U.S. — C5 108
Guadalupe, co., Tx., U.S. — E4 120
Guadalupe, Isla de, i., Mex. — E15 6
Guadalupe, Sierra de, mts., Spain — C3 22
Guadalupe [Bravos], Mex. — A3 63
Guadalupe Mountains, mts., U.S. — E5 108
Guadalupe Mountains National Park, Tx., U.S. — o12 120
Guadalupe Peak, mtn., Tx., U.S. — o12 120
Guadalupita, N.M., U.S. — A4 108
Guadalupe, i., Lee.Is. — C7 64
Guadarrama, stm., Spain — p17 22
Guadarrama, Sierra de, mts., Spain — B4 22
Guadeloupe, dep., N.A. — H14 64
Guadeloupe Passage, strt., N.A. — H14 64
Guadiana, stm., Eur. — D2 22

Guadiana Menor, stm., Spain — D4 22
Guadiela, stm., Spain — B4 22
Guadilla, Bahía de b., P.R. — B1 65
Guadix, Spain — D4 22
Guafo, Isla, i., Chile — C2 54
Guagua, Phil. — o13 34
Guainía, dept., Col. — C4 60
Guainía, stm., S.A. — C4 60
Guaíra, Braz. — B1 57
Guairá, dept., Para. — E4 55
Guajará Mirim, Braz. — E5 59
Guajataca, Lago de, res., P.R. — B2 65
Guajira, dept., Col. — A3 60
Gualaceo, Ec. — B2 58
Gualala, Ca., U.S. — C1 82
Gualán, Guat. — D7 63
Gualaquiza, Ec. — B2 58
Gualeguay, Arg. — A5 54
Gualeguaychú, Arg. — A5 54
Guam, dep., Oc. — F8 6
Guamá, stm., Braz. — B1 57
Guaminí, Arg. — B4 54
Guamúchil, Mex. — B3 63
Guanacaste, Cordillera de, mts., C.R. — E5 62
Guanahacabibes, Golfo de, b., Cuba — C1 64
Guana Island, i., V.I., Br. — B6 65
Guanajay, Cuba — C2 64
Guanajuato, Mex. — C4 63
Guanajuato, state, Mex. — C4 63
Guanambi, Braz. — A4 56
Guanare, Ven. — B4 60
Guandacol, Arg. — E2 55
Guane, Cuba — C1 64
Guang'an, China — I2 32
Guangchang, China — K7 32
Guangde, China — K7 32
Guangdong, prov., China — G7 31
Guangnan, China — B2 32
Guangxi Zhuangzu, prov., China — G6 31
Guangyuan, China — H4 32
Guangzhou (Canton), China — G7 31
Guánica, P.R. — C2 65
Guánica, Laguna de, l., P.R. — C2 65
Guano Lake, l., Or., U.S. — E7 114
Guantánamo, Cuba — D6 64
Guantánamo, prov., Cuba — D6 64
Guanxian, China — F6 32
Guanyun, China — G8 32
Guapí, Col. — C2 60
Guapiara, Braz. — D2 56
Guápiles, C.R. — E6 62
Guaporé (Iténez), stm., S.A. — B3 55
Guaqui, Bol. — C2 55
Guará, Braz. — F1 57
Guarabira, Braz. — C3 57
Guaranda, Ec. — B2 58
Guaranésia, Braz. — k8 56
Guarapuava, Braz. — D2 56
Guaraqueçaba, Braz. — D3 56
Guararapes, Braz. — C2 56
Guaratinguetá, Braz. — C3 56
Guaratuba, Braz. — D3 56
Guarda, Port. — B2 22
Guardafui, Cape see Caseyr, c., Som. — C7 47
Guardia Mitre, Arg. — C4 54
Guardian, W.V., U.S. — C4 125
Guareí, Braz. — m7 56
Guareña, stm., Ven. — C2 22
Guárico, state, Ven. — B4 60
Guárico, stm., Ven. — B4 60
Guaruja, Braz. — n8 56
Guarulhos, Braz. — m8 56
Guasave, Mex. — B3 63
Guasdualito, Ven. — B3 60
Guasipati, Ven. — B6 60
Guastalla, Italy — B3 23
Guatemala, Guat. — E6 63
Guatemala, ctry., N.A. — D6 63
Guateque, Col. — A4 54
Guatimozín, Arg. — B4 54
Guatopo National Park, Ven. — C3 60
Guaviare, dept., Col. — C3 60
Guaviare, stm., Col. — C4 60
Guaxupé, Braz. — C3 56
Guayabal, Cuba — D5 64
Guayaguayare, Trin. — O23 65
Guayama, P.R. — H11 64
Guayaquil, Ec. — B2 58
Guayaquil, Golfo de, b., S.A. — B1 58
Guayaramerín, Bol. — B1 55
Guayas, prov., Ec. — B1 58
Guaymas, Mex. — B2 63
Guaynabo, P.R. — B3 65
Guazacapán, Guat. — C2 62
Gubakha, Sov. Un. — B5 28
Gubbio, Italy — C4 23
Gubin, Pol. — B9 19
Gucheng, China — H4 32
Gúdar, Sierra de, mts., Spain — B5 22
Gudauta, Sov. Un. — A13 40
Gudená, stm., Den. — B3 15
Gudermes, Sov. Un. — E3 28
Gudhjem, Den. — C8 15
Gudivada, India — F6 36
Gudiv4r, India — D7 36
Güeckédou, Gui. — E2 45
Guelma, Alg. — B6 44
Guelph, Ont. — D4 73
Guelph, N.D., U.S. — C7 111
Guénette, Que. — C2 74
Güera, W. Sah. — E1 44
Guercif, Mor. — C4 44
Guéréda, Chad — C4 46
Guéret, Fr. — D4 16
Guerette, Me., U.S. — A4 96
Guernica y Luno, Spain — A4 22
Guernsey, Sask. — F3 75
Guernsey, Wy., U.S. — D8 127
Guernsey, co., Oh., U.S. — B4 112
Guernsey, dep., Eur. — F5 10
Guernsey, i., Guernsey — F5 10
Guerrero, state, Mex. — D4 63
Guerrero Peak, pen., Ant. — B34 7
Guethary, Fr. — D6 16
Gueugnon, Fr. — D6 16
Guérnie, Ar., U.S. — B3 81
Gueydan, La., U.S. — D3 95
Guffey, Co., U.S. — C5 83
Gúgú, Mt., Marsh Is. — S17 52
Guia Lopes da Laguna, Braz. — C1 56
Guidan, Nmb. — C2 49
Guichi, China — I7 32
Guide, Fr. — D5 31
Guide Rock, Ne., U.S. — D7 104
Guidong, China — K5 32
Guidonia (Montecelio), Italy — D4 23
Guiglio, I.C. — E3 45
Guilarte, Monte, mtn., P.R. — D2 65
Guild, N.H., U.S. — D2 106

Guildford, Eng., U.K. — E6 10
Guildhall, Vt., U.S. — B5 122
Guilford, Ct., U.S. — D5 84
Guilford, In., U.S. — F8 91
Guilford, Me., U.S. — C3 96
Guilford, Mo., U.S. — A3 102
Guilford, N.Y., U.S. — C5 109
Guilford, Vt., U.S. — F3 122
Guilford, co., N.C., U.S. — A3 110
Guilherme Capelo, Ang. — C1 48
Guillaume-Delisle, Lac, l., Que. — E17 66
Guillestre, Fr. — E2 20
Guimarães, Braz. — B2 57
Guimarães, Port. — B2 22
Guimba, Phil. — o13 34
Guin, Al., U.S. — B2 78
Guinea, Va., U.S. — B5 123
Guinea, ctry., Afr. — D2 45
Guinea, Gulf of, b., Afr. — F6 42
Guinea-Bissau, ctry., Afr. — D1 45
Guiné-Bissau, Braz. — B1 57
Güines, Cuba — C2 64
Güines, Fr. — D11 12
Guingamp, Fr. — C2 16
Guion, Ar., U.S. — B4 81
Güira de Melena, Cuba — C2 64
Güiratinga, Braz. — B2 56
Güiria, Ven. — A5 60
Guisanbourg, Fr. Gu. — B4 59
Guisborough, Eng., U.K. — F7 13
Guise, Fr. — C5 16
Guist Creek, stm., Ky., U.S. — B4 94
Guitiriz, Spain — A2 22
Guixi, China — J7 32
Guiyang, China — G6 31
Guiyang, China — F6 31
Guizhou, prov., China — F6 31
Gujan, Fr. — E3 16
Gujarat, state, India — D5 36
Gujrānwāla, Pak. — B5 36
Gujrāt, Pak. — B5 36
Gulbarga, India — E6 36
Guldborg, Den. — D5 15
Gulf, N.C., U.S. — B3 110
Gulf Breeze, Fl., U.S. — C1 86
Gulf Gate Estates, Fl., U.S. — *u14 86
Gulf Hammock, Fl., U.S. — C4 86
Gulf Islands National Seashore, U.S. — E5 101
Gulfport, Fl., U.S. — E4 86
Gulf Port, Il., U.S. — C2 90
Gulfport, Ms., U.S. — E4 101
Gulf Shores, Al., U.S. — E2 78
Gulgong, Austl. — F7 51
Gulkana, Ak., U.S. — C10 79
Gullion, Slieve, mtn., N. Ire., U.K. — C5 11
Gull Island, i., N.C., U.S. — B7 110
Gullivan Bay, b., Fl., U.S. — G5 86
Gulliver, Mi., U.S. — B5 99
Gull Lake, Sask. — G1 75
Gull Lake, l., Alta. — C4 68
Gull Lake, l., Mn., U.S. — D4 100
Güllük, Tur. — D6 40
Gully, Mn., U.S. — C3 100
Gulu, Ug. — A5 48
Gumaca, Phil. — p14 34
Gumba, Zaire — A3 48
Gumboro, De., U.S. — G4 85
Gumefens, Switz. — C3 21
Gumel, Nig. — D6 45
Gummersbach, W. Ger. — B2 19
Gum Spring Mountain, mtn., Tn., U.S. — D8 119
Gum Springs, Ar., U.S. — C2 81
Gum Swamp Creek, stm., Ga., U.S. — D3 87
Gümüşhane, Tur. — B12 40
Guna, India — D6 36
Guna, mtn., Eth. — A4 47
Gundelfingen, W. Ger. — C5 19
Gungu, Zaire — C3 48
Gunisao, stm., Man. — C3 70
Gunisao Lake, l., Man. — C3 70
Gunlock, Ut., U.S. — F2 121
Gunn, Ms., U.S. — C4 101
Gunnar, Sask. — m7 75
Gunnbjørn Fjeld, mtn., Grnld. — *C17 128
Gunnedah, Austl. — F9 50
Gunnison, Co., U.S. — C4 83
Gunnison, Ms., U.S. — B3 101
Gunnison, Ut., U.S. — D4 121
Gunnison, co., Co., U.S. — C3 83
Gunnison, stm., Co., U.S. — C2 83
Gunnison, Mount, mtn., Co., U.S. — C3 83
Gunnworth, Sask. — F1 75
Gunpowder Creek, stm., Ky., U.S. — k13 94
Gunpowder Neck, c., Md., U.S. — B5 97
Gunpowder River, b., Md., U.S. — B5 97
Gunter Air Force Base, mil., Al., U.S. — C3 78
Guntersville, Al., U.S. — A3 78
Guntersville Dam, Al., U.S. — A3 78
Guntersville Lake, res., Al., U.S. — A3 78
Guntown, Ms., U.S. — A5 101
Guntūr, India — E7 36
Günzburg, W. Ger. — D5 19
Günz, stm., W. Ger. — D5 19
Gunzenhausen, W. Ger. — D5 19
Guoyang, China — H7 32
Gura Humorului, Rom. — A7 24
Gurdāspur, India — B6 36
Gurdon, Ar., U.S. — D2 81
Gurgei, stm., Braz. — D2 57
Gurguéia, stm., Braz. — E8 57
Guri, Embalse, res., Ven. — B5 60
Gurk, stm., Aus. — E14 18
Gurley, Al., U.S. — A3 78
Gurley, Ne., U.S. — C2 104
Gurleyville, Ct., U.S. — B7 84
Gurnee, Il., U.S. — h9 90
Gurnet Point, c., Ma., U.S. — B6 98
Gurney, Wi., U.S. — B3 126
Gurué, Moz. — A6 49
Gurupá, Braz. — B1 57
Gurupi, Braz. — E5 59
Gurupi, stm., Braz. — B1 57
Gurupi, Cabo, c., Braz. — B1 57
Gusau, Nig. — D6 45
Gusev, Sov. Un. — A7 26
Gusher, Ut., U.S. — C6 121
Gushi, China — E8 31

Gushikawa, Japan — O5 52
Gusinje, Yugo. — D4 24
Gus-Khrustalnyy, Sov. Un. — D13 27
Gustavo A. Madero (part of Mexico City), Mex. — h9 63
Gustavus, Ak., U.S. — D12 79
Güsten, E. Ger. — B6 19
Gustine, Ca., U.S. — D3 82
Gustine, Tx., U.S. — D3 120
Gutau, Aus. — E9 19
Gütersloh, W. Ger. — C4 18
Guthrie, Ky., U.S. — D2 94
Guthrie, Mn., U.S. — C4 100
Guthrie, Ok., U.S. — B4 113
Guthrie, Tx., U.S. — C2 120
Guthrie, co., Ia., U.S. — C3 92
Guthrie Center, Ia., U.S. — C3 92
Guthrie Lake, l., Man. — B1 70
Guttenberg, Ia., U.S. — B6 92
Guttenberg, N.J., U.S. — h8 107
Guwāhāti, India — C9 36
Guy, Ar., U.S. — B3 81
Guyana, ctry., S.A. — A3 59
Güira, Ven. — A5 60
Guyandotte, stm., W.V., U.S. — C2 125
Guyandotte Mountain, mtn., W.V., U.S. — n12 125
Guyenne, hist. reg., Fr. — E4 16
Guymon, Ok., U.S. — e9 113
Guyot, Mount, mtn., U.S. — D10 119
Guyra, Austl. — E8 51
Guys, Tn., U.S. — B3 119
Guysborough, N.S. — D7 71
Guysborough, co., N.S. — D7 71
Guys Mills, Pa., U.S. — C2 115
Guyton, Ga., U.S. — D5 87
Guyuan, China — G2 32
Guyuan, China — D6 32
Güzelyurt, N. Cyp. — E9 40
Guzhen, China — H7 32
Gvardeysk, Sov. Un. — A6 26
Gwabegar, Austl. — E7 51
Gwadar, Pak. — C3 36
Gwai, Zimb. — A4 49
Gwalior, India — C6 36
Gwanda, Zimb. — B4 49
Gwane, Zaire — A4 48
Gweebarra Bay, b., Ire. — C3 11
Gwda, stm., Pol. — B4 26
Gweedore, Ire. — C2 11
Gwembe, Zam. — E4 48
Gwent, co., Wales, U.K. — C5 12
Gweru, Zimb. — A4 49
Gwinhurst, De., U.S. — h8 85
Gwinn, Mi., U.S. — B3 99
Gwinner, N.D., U.S. — C8 111
Gwinnett, co., Ga., U.S. — C2 87
Gwydyr Bay, b., Ak., U.S. — A10 79
Gwynedd, co., Wales, U.K. — A3 12
Gwynn, Va., U.S. — C6 123
Gwynne, Alta. — C4 68
Gwynneville, In., U.S. — E6 91
Gwynns Falls, stm., Md., U.S. — g10 97
Gyangzê, China — C8 36
Gyaring Co, l., China — B8 36
Gyaring Hu, l., China — E4 31
Gyirong, China — C10 37
Gympie, Austl. — E9 50
Gyöngyös, Hung. — B4 24
Györ (Raab), Hung. — B3 24
Gypsera, Switz. — C3 21
Gypsum, Co., U.S. — B4 83
Gypsum, Ks., U.S. — C6 93
Gypsum, Oh., U.S. — A3 112
Gypsumville, Man. — D2 70
Gyula, Hung. — B5 24

H

Haag [in Oberbayern], W. Ger. — A8 20
Haakon, co., S.D., U.S. — C4 118
Haaksbergen, Neth. — B6 17
Haamstede, Neth. — C3 17
Haapamäki, Fin. — F11 14
Haapsalu, Sov. Un. — B4 27
Ha Arava (Wādī al Jayb), val., Asia — D7 41
Haarlem, Neth. — A6 16
Haarlemmermeer, Neth. — A6 16
Hab, stm., Pak. — I13 39
Habermehl Peak, mtn., Ant. — B13 7
Habersham, Ga., U.S. — B3 87
Habersham, co., Ga., U.S. — B3 87
Haboru, Japan — D10 52
Hachiman, Japan — n15 35
Hachinohe, Japan — F10 35
Hachiōji, Japan — I9 35
Hachita, N.M., U.S. — F1 108
Hacienda Heights, Ca., U.S. — *n13 82
Hack, Mount, mtn., Austl. — E2 51
Hackberry, Az., U.S. — B1 80
Hackberry, La., U.S. — E2 95
Hackberry Creek, stm., Ks., U.S. — D3 93
Hackensack, Mn., U.S. — D4 100
Hackensack, N.J., U.S. — B4 107
Hackensack, stm., N.J., U.S. — h8 107
Hacker Valley, W.V., U.S. — C4 125
Hackettstown, Ire. — C4 11
Hackett, Ar., U.S. — B1 81
Hackettstown, N.J., U.S. — B3 107
Hackleburg, Al., U.S. — A2 78
Hackney (part of London), Eng., U.K. — k12 10
Hack Point, Md., U.S. — B6 97
Hacoda, Japan — D3 78
Hacq, i., Micron. — Q18 52
Hadar, Ne., U.S. — B8 104
Haddam, Ct., U.S. — D5 84
Haddam, Ks., U.S. — C6 93
Haddington, Scot., U.K. — E6 13
Haddix, Ky., U.S. — C6 94
Haddock, Ga., U.S. — C3 87
Haddon Heights, N.J., U.S. — D2 107
Haddonfield, N.J., U.S. — D2 107
Haddon Heights, N.J., U.S. — D2 107
Hadejia, Nig. — D7 45
Hadejia, stm., Nig. — D7 45
Hadera, Isr. — F10 41
Haderslev, Den. — C3 15
Hadim, Tur. — D9 40
Ḩaḑḑam, Bi'r al, well, Eg. — B6 41
Hadleigh, Eng., U.K. — B8 12
Hadley, Ma., U.S. — B2 98
Hadley, Mi., U.S. — F7 99
Hadley, N.Y., U.S. — B7 109
Hadley, Pa., U.S. — D1 115

Hadley Bay, b., N.W. Ter. — B11 66
Hadley Lake, l., Me., U.S. — D5 96
Hadlock, Wa., U.S. — A3 124
Hadlyme, Ct., U.S. — D6 84
Ha Dong, Viet. — A3 34
Hadramawt, reg., Yemen — D4 38
Hadsten, Den. — B4 15
Hadsund, Den. — B4 15
Haeju, N. Kor. — C10 31
Haenam, S. Kor. — I3 33
Haerhpin see Harbin, China — B10 31
Hafford, Sask. — E2 75
Hafira, Qâ'al, pl., Jord. — C8 41
Hafnarfjördur, Ice. — n22 14
Haft Gel, Iran — F4 39
Hafun, Ras, c., Som. — C7 47
Hagan, Ga., U.S. — D5 87
Hagari, stm., India — F6 36
Hagen, W. Ger. — C3 18
Hagenow, E. Ger. — E5 15
Hagensborg, B.C. — C4 69
Hagere Hiywet, Eth. — G4 47
Hagerman, Id., U.S. — G4 89
Hagerman, N.M., U.S. — D5 108
Hagerman Corners, Ont. — k15 73
Hagerstown, In., U.S. — E7 91
Hagerstown, Md., U.S. — A2 97
Hagersville, Ont. — E4 73
Haggart Lake, l., Ont. — D4 70
Haggin, mtn., Mt., U.S. — D3 103
Ha Giang, Viet. — A6 35
Hags Head, c., Ire. — E2 11
Hague, Sask. — E2 75
Hague, N.Y., U.S. — B7 109
Hague, N.D., U.S. — C6 111
Hague, Cap de la, c., Fr. — C3 16
Haguenau, Fr. — C7 16
Hagues Peak, mtn., Co., U.S. — A5 83
Ha! Ha!, Baie des, b., Que. — C2 72
Ha! Ha!, Lac, l., Que. — A7 74
Hahira, Ga., U.S. — F3 87
Hahnville, La., U.S. — E5 95
Haicheng, China — G8 31
Haicheng, China — D10 32
Haichow Bay see Haizhou Bay, b., China — G8 32
Haifa (Hefa), Isr. — B3 38
Haifa, Bay of see Hefa, Mifraz, b., Isr. — B6 41
Haigerloch, W. Ger. — A4 20
Haigler, Ne., U.S. — D4 104
Haikang, China — G6 31
Haikou, China — B4 34
Haiku, Hi., U.S. — C5 88
Hā'il, Sau. Ar. — C4 38
Hailar, China — B8 31
Haile, La., U.S. — B3 95
Hailesboro, N.Y., U.S. — f9 109
Hailey, Id., U.S. — F4 89
Haileybury, Ont. — p20 73
Haileyville, Ok., U.S. — C6 113
Hailong, China — C10 31
Hailun, China — B10 31
Haimen, China — F9 31
Haimen, China — I9 32
Hainan Island, i., China — B3 34
Hainaut, prov., Bel. — D3 17
Haines, Ak., U.S. — D12 79
Haines, Or., U.S. — C9 114
Hainesburg, N.J., U.S. — B2 107
Haines City, Fl., U.S. — D5 86
Haines Falls, N.Y., U.S. — C6 109
Hainesport, N.J., U.S. — D3 107
Hainesville, N.J., U.S. — A3 107
Hainichen, E. Ger. — C8 19
Haining, China — I9 32
Hai Phong, Viet. — A3 34
Hairy Hill, Alta. — C5 68
Haiti, ctry., N.A. — E7 64
Haiyang, China — F9 32
Haiyuan, China — F1 32
Haizhou, China — E8 31
Haizhou Bay, b., China — G8 32
Hajdúböszörmény, Hung. — B5 24
Hajdúhadház, Hung. — B5 24
Hajdúnánás, Hung. — B5 24
Hajdúszoboszló, Hung. — B5 24
Hajiki, Cape, c., Japan — G9 33
Hajnówka, Pol. — B7 26
Hakalau, Hi., U.S. — D6 88
Hakkâri, Tur. — D14 40
Hakken, Mount, mtn., Japan — I7 33
Hakodate, Japan — C13 31
Hākra Branch, stm., Pak. — C4 37
Haku, Mount, mtn., Japan — m15 33
Halabjah, Iraq — D2 39
Halâ'ib, Eg. — E7 43
Halaula, Hi., U.S. — C6 88
Halawa, Cape, c., Hi., U.S. — B5 88
Halawa Heights, Hi., U.S. — g10 88
Halberstadt, E. Ger. — C5 18
Halbrite, Sask. — H4 75
Halbur, Ia., U.S. — C3 92
Halcon, Mount, mtn., Phil. — C6 34
Haldeman, Ky., U.S. — B6 94
Halden, Nor. — H4 14
Haldensleben, E. Ger. — B5 18
Haldimand, Ont. — E5 73
Haldimand, co., Ont. — E5 73
Hale, Co., U.S. — B8 83
Hale, Mi., U.S. — D7 99
Hale, Mo., U.S. — B4 102
Hale, co., Al., U.S. — C2 78
Hale, co., Tx., U.S. — B2 120
Haleakala Crater, crat., Hi., U.S. — C5 88
Haleakala National Park, Hi., U.S. — C6 88
Haleburg, Al., U.S. — D4 78
Hale Center, Tx., U.S. — B2 120
Haledon, N.J., U.S. — *B4 107
Haleiwa, Hi., U.S. — B3 88
Hales Corners, Wi., U.S. — n11 126
Halesowen, Eng., U.K. — B5 12
Halesworth, Eng., U.K. — B9 12
Halethorpe, Md., U.S. — B4 97
Haleyville, Al., U.S. — A2 78
Haleyville, N.J., U.S. — E2 107
Half Assini, Ghana — E4 45
Half Hollow Hills, N.Y., U.S. — *h13 109
Half-Moon Bay, N.Z. — Q12 51
Half Moon Bay, Ca., U.S. — k8 82
Halfway, Ky., U.S. — D3 94
Halfway, Md., U.S. — A2 97
Half Way, Mo., U.S. — D4 102
Halfway, Or., U.S. — C9 114
Halfway, stm., B.C. — A6 69
Halfway Nunatak, mtn., Ant. — f40 7
Ḥalḥūl, Isr. Occ. — C7 41

Haliburton, Ont. — B6 73
Haliburton, co., Ont. — B6 73
Halibut Point, c., Ma., U.S. — A6 98
Halifax, N.S. — E6 71
Halifax, Eng., U.K. — D6 10
Halifax, Ma., U.S. — C6 98
Halifax, N.C., U.S. — A5 110
Halifax, Pa., U.S. — F8 115
Halifax, Va., U.S. — D4 123
Halifax, Vt., U.S. — F3 122
Halifax, co., N.C., U.S. — A5 110
Halifax, co., Va., U.S. — D4 123
Halifax, co., N.S. — E6 71
Halifax Bay, b., Austl. — C8 50
Haliimaile, Hi., U.S. — C5 88
Halkirk, Scot., U.K. — C5 10
Halkirk, Alta. — C4 68
Hall, In., U.S. — E4 91
Hall, Mt., U.S. — D3 103
Hall, N.Y., U.S. — C3 109
Hall, co., Ga., U.S. — B3 87
Hall, co., Ne., U.S. — D7 104
Hall, co., Tx., U.S. — B2 120
Halla, Mount, mtn., S. Kor. — J3 33
Halladale, stm., Scot., U.K. — B5 13
Hallam, Ne., U.S. — D9 104
Hallam Peak, mtn., B.C. — C8 69
Halland, co., Swe. — B6 15
Hallandale, Fl., U.S. — G6 86
Hallands Väderö, i., Swe. — B6 15
Halle, Bel. — D4 17
Halle, E. Ger. — C5 18
Halle, W. Ger. — A3 19
Halleck, Nv., U.S. — C6 105
Hallein, Aus. — E6 18
Halle-Neustadt, E. Ger. — *C6 18
Hällestad, Swe. — u33 14
Hallett, Ok., U.S. — A5 113
Hallett, Cape, c., Ant. — B30 7
Hallettsville, Tx., U.S. — E4 120
Halley, Ar., U.S. — D4 81
Halley Bay, sci., Ant. — B10 7
Halliday, N.D., U.S. — B3 111
Hallie, Wi., U.S. — D2 126
Hall Island, i., Ak., U.S. — C5 79
Hall Meadow Brook, stm., Ct., U.S. — B3 84
Hall Meadow Brook Reservoir, res., Ct., U.S. — B3 84
Hall Mountain, mtn., Wa., U.S. — A8 124
Hallock, Mn., U.S. — B2 100
Hallowell, Ks., U.S. — E9 93
Hallowell, Me., U.S. — D3 96
Hall Peninsula, pen., N.W. Ter. — D19 66
Halls, Ga., U.S. — B3 87
Halls, Tn., U.S. — B2 119
Halls, Hi., U.S. — *C10 119
Hallsberg, Swe. — t33 14
Halls Creek, Austl. — C4 50
Halls Creek, stm., Ut., U.S. — F5 121
Halls Crossroads, Tn., U.S. — m14 119
Halls Harbour, N.S. — D5 71
Halls Stream, stm., N.H., U.S. — f7 106
Halls Summit, Ks., U.S. — D8 93
Hallstead, Pa., U.S. — C10 115
Hall Summit, La., U.S. — B2 95
Hallsville, Mo., U.S. — B5 102
Hallsville, Oh., U.S. — C3 112
Hallsville, Tx., U.S. — C5 120
Halltown, Mo., U.S. — D4 102
Hallville, Ct., U.S. — C7 84
Hallwood, Va., U.S. — C7 123
Hallwil Lake, l., Switz. — B4 20
Halma, Mn., U.S. — B2 100
Halmahera, i., Indon. — E7 34
Halmahera Sea, Indon. — F7 34
Halmstad, Swe. — I5 14
Hals, Den. — B4 15
Halsell, Al., U.S. — C1 78
Halsey, Ne., U.S. — C5 104
Halsey, N.J., U.S. — A3 107
Halsey, Or., U.S. — C3 114
Halstad, Mn., U.S. — C2 100
Halstead, Eng., U.K. — C8 12
Halstead, Ks., U.S. — E6 93
Haltern, W. Ger. — B2 19
Haltia, mtn., Eur. — C9 14
Haltom City, Tx., U.S. — *n9 120
Halton, co., Ont. — D5 73
Halton Hills, Ont. — D5 73
Haltwhistle, Eng., U.K. — F6 13
Ham, Fr. — E3 17
Hamada, Japan — I6 33
Hamadān, Iran — B4 38
Hamāhika Island, i., Japan — O5 52
Hamamatsu, Japan — E12 31
Hamar, Nor. — G4 14
Hama-tombetsu, Japan — D11 33
Hambantota, Sri L. — G7 36
Hamberg, N.D., U.S. — B6 111
Hamber Provincial Park, B.C. — C8 69
Hamblen, co., Tn., U.S. — C10 119
Hamburg, W. Ger. — B5 18
Hamburg, Ar., U.S. — D4 81
Hamburg, Ct., U.S. — D6 84
Hamburg, Il., U.S. — D3 90
Hamburg, Ia., U.S. — D2 92
Hamburg, Ms., U.S. — D2 101
Hamburg, N.J., U.S. — A3 107
Hamburg, N.Y., U.S. — C2 109
Hamburg, Pa., U.S. — E10 115
Hamburg, Wi., U.S. — C4 126
Hamburg, state, W. Ger. — B5 18
Hamburg Mountains, mts., N.J., U.S. — A3 107
Ḥamḍ, Wādī al, val., Sau. Ar. — C3 38
Hamden, Ct., U.S. — D4 84
Hamden, N.Y., U.S. — C6 109
Hamden, Oh., U.S. — C3 112
Hämeenlinna, Fin. — G11 14
Hamel, Mn., U.S. — m11 100
Hamel, W. Ger. — B5 18
Hamer, Id., U.S. — F6 89
Hamer, S.C., U.S. — C9 117
Hamersley Range, mts., Austl. — D2 50
Hamhŭng, N. Kor. — C3 33
Hami, China — C3 31
Hamill, Ia., U.S. — D6 92
Hamill, S.D., U.S. — D6 118
Hamilton, Austl. — G7 50
Hamilton, Ber. — p20 64
Hamilton, Ont. — D5 73
Hamilton, Scot., U.K. — C4 10
Hamilton, N.Z. — L15 51
Hamilton, Al., U.S. — A2 78
Hamilton, Ak., U.S. — C7 79

Hamilton, Co., U.S. — A3 83
Hamilton, Ga., U.S. — D2 87
Hamilton, Il., U.S. — C2 90
Hamilton, In., U.S. — A8 91
Hamilton, Ia., U.S. — C5 92
Hamilton, Ks., U.S. — E7 93
Hamilton, Ma., U.S. — A6 98
Hamilton, Mi., U.S. — F4 99
Hamilton, Ms., U.S. — B5 101
Hamilton, Mo., U.S. — B3 102
Hamilton, Mt., U.S. — D2 103
Hamilton, N.Y., U.S. — C5 109
Hamilton, N.C., U.S. — B5 110
Hamilton, N.D., U.S. — A8 111
Hamilton, Oh., U.S. — C1 112
Hamilton, Or., U.S. — C7 114
Hamilton, R.I., U.S. — E4 116
Hamilton, Tx., U.S. — D3 120
Hamilton, Wa., U.S. — A4 124
Hamilton, co., Fl., U.S. — B3 86
Hamilton, co., Il., U.S. — E5 90
Hamilton, co., In., U.S. — D5 91
Hamilton, co., Ia., U.S. — B4 92
Hamilton, co., Ks., U.S. — E2 93
Hamilton, co., Ne., U.S. — D7 104
Hamilton, co., N.Y., U.S. — B6 109
Hamilton, co., Oh., U.S. — C1 112
Hamilton, co., Tn., U.S. — D8 119
Hamilton, co., Tx., U.S. — D3 120
Hamilton, Lake, res., Ar., U.S. — C2 81
Hamilton, Mount, mtn., Ak., U.S. — C8 79
Hamilton, Mount, mtn., Ca., U.S. — k9 82
Hamilton, Mount, mtn., Nv., U.S. — D6 105
Hamilton City, Ca., U.S. — C2 82
Hamilton Dome, Wy., U.S. — C4 127
Hamilton Inlet, b., Newf. — A2 72
Hamilton Mountain, mtn., N.Y., U.S. — B6 109
Hamilton Reservoir, res., Ma., U.S. — B3 98
Hamilton Sound, strt., Newf. — D4 72
Hamilton Square, N.J., U.S. — C3 107
Hamina, Fin. — G12 14
Hamiota, Man. — D1 70
Hamlet, Oh., U.S. — A1 112
Hamlet, In., U.S. — B4 91
Hamlet, Ne., U.S. — D4 104
Hamlet, N.C., U.S. — C3 110
Hamlet, Mount, mtn., Ak., U.S. — C5 79
Hamletsburg, Il., U.S. — F5 90
Hamlin, N.Y., U.S. — B3 109
Hamlin, Pa., U.S. — D11 115
Hamlin, Tx., U.S. — C2 120
Hamlin, W.V., U.S. — C2 125
Hamlin, co., S.D., U.S. — C8 118
Hamlin Lake, l., Mi., U.S. — D4 99
Hammam Lif, Tun. — B7 44
Hammār, Hawr al, l., Iraq — F3 39
Hammarby, Swe. — t35 14
Hamme, Bel. — C4 17
Hammel, Den. — B3 15
Hammelburg, W. Ger. — C4 19
Hammer, S.D., U.S. — B8 118
Hammerfest, Nor. — B10 14
Hammett, Id., U.S. — G3 89
Hamm [in Westfalen], W. Ger. — B2 19
Hammon, Ok., U.S. — B2 113
Hammonasset, stm., Ct., U.S. — D5 84
Hammonasset Point, c., Ct., U.S. — E5 84
Hammond, Il., U.S. — D5 90
Hammond, In., U.S. — A2 91
Hammond, La., U.S. — D5 95
Hammond, Mn., U.S. — F6 100
Hammond, Mt., U.S. — E12 103
Hammond, N.Y., U.S. — f9 109
Hammond, Or., U.S. — A3 114
Hammond, Wi., U.S. — C1 126
Hammond Bay, b., Mi., U.S. — C6 99
Hammondsport, N.Y., U.S. — C3 109
Hammonton, N.J., U.S. — D3 107
Hamnavoe, Scot. — B7 13
Hamoyet, Jabal, mtn., Afr. — B4 47
Hampden, Newf. — D3 72
Hampden, N.Z. — P13 51
Hampden, Me., U.S. — D4 96
Hampden, N.D., U.S. — A7 111
Hampden, co., Ma., U.S. — B2 98
Hampden Highlands, Me., U.S. — D4 96
Hampshire, Il., U.S. — A5 90
Hampshire, Tn., U.S. — B4 119
Hampshire, co., Eng., U.K. — C6 12
Hampshire, co., Ma., U.S. — B2 98
Hampshire, co., W.V., U.S. — B6 125
Hampstead, Md., U.S. — A4 97
Hampstead, N.H., U.S. — E4 106
Hampstead, N.C., U.S. — C5 110
Hampstead, N.B. — D4 71
Hampton, Ar., U.S. — D3 81
Hampton, Ct., U.S. — B7 84
Hampton, Fl., U.S. — C4 86
Hampton, Ga., U.S. — C2 87
Hampton, Ia., U.S. — B4 92
Hampton, Ky., U.S. — e9 94
Hampton, Md., U.S. — *B4 97
Hampton, Mn., U.S. — F5 100
Hampton, N.J., U.S. — B3 107
Hampton, N.H., U.S. — E5 106
Hampton, S.C., U.S. — F5 117
Hampton, Tn., U.S. — C11 119
Hampton, Va., U.S. — C6 123
Hampton, co., S.C., U.S. — F5 117
Hampton Bays, N.Y., U.S. — n16 109
Hampton Beach, N.H., U.S. — E5 106
Hampton Butte, mtn., Or. — D6 114
Hampton Falls, N.H., U.S. — E5 106
Hampton Roads, anch., Va. — k15 123
Hampton Roads Bridge-Tunnel, Va., U.S. — k15 123
Hams Fork, stm., Wy., U.S. — D6 127
Hams-Sud, Que. — D6 74
Ham Tan, Viet. — I9 35
Hamtramck, Mi., U.S. — p15 99
Hamyang, S. Kor. — I3 33
Han, stm., Asia — H4 33

Hana, Hi., U.S. — C6 88
Hanahan, S.C., U.S. — F7 117
Hanalei, Hi., U.S. — A2 88
Hanalei Bay, b., Hi., U.S. — A2 88
Hanamaki, Japan — G10 33
Hanamaulu, Hi., U.S. — B2 88
Hanapepe, Hi., U.S. — B2 88
Hanau, W. Ger. — C4 18
Hanceville, B.C. — D6 69
Hanceville, Al., U.S. — A3 78
Hancheng, China — G4 32
Hancock, Ia., U.S. — C2 92
Hancock, Me., U.S. — D4 96
Hancock, Md., U.S. — A1 97
Hancock, Ma., U.S. — A1 98
Hancock, Mi., U.S. — A2 99
Hancock, Mn., U.S. — E3 100
Hancock, N.H., U.S. — E3 106
Hancock, N.Y., U.S. — C5 109
Hancock, Vt., U.S. — D3 122
Hancock, Wi., U.S. — D4 126
Hancock, W.V., U.S. — B6 125
Hancock, co., Ga., U.S. — C3 87
Hancock, co., Il., U.S. — C2 90
Hancock, co., In., U.S. — E6 91
Hancock, co., Ia., U.S. — A4 92
Hancock, co., Ky., U.S. — C3 94
Hancock, co., Me., U.S. — D4 96
Hancock, co., Ms., U.S. — E4 101
Hancock, co., Oh., U.S. — A2 112
Hancock, co., Tn., U.S. — C10 119
Hancock, co., W.V., U.S. — A4 125
Hancock Pond, l., Me., U.S. — D2 96
Hancocks Bridge, N.J., U.S. — D2 107
Hand, co., S.D., U.S. — C6 118
Handa, Japan — o15 33
Handa, Som. — C7 47
Handa, i., Scot., U.K. — B3 13
Handan, China — D7 31
Handaqi, China — A3 33
Handel, Sask. — E1 75
Handeni, Tan. — C6 48
Handley, W.V., U.S. — m13 125
Handsworth, Sask. — H4 75
Hardin, Il., U.S. — D3 90
Hardin, Ky., U.S. — f9 94
Hardin, Mo., U.S. — B4 102
Hardin, Mt., U.S. — E9 103
Hardin, co., Il., U.S. — F5 90
Hardin, co., Ia., U.S. — B4 92
Hardin, co., Ky., U.S. — C4 94
Hardin, co., Oh., U.S. — B2 112
Hardin, co., Tn., U.S. — B3 119
Hardin, co., Tx., U.S. — D5 120
Harding, Ma., U.S. — h10 98
Harding, co., N.M., U.S. — B6 108
Harding, co., S.D., U.S. — B2 118
Harding, Lake, res., U.S. — C4 78
Harding Lake, l., Man. — A2 70
Hardinsburg, In., U.S. — H5 91
Hardinsburg, Ky., U.S. — C3 94
Hardinville, Il., U.S. — E6 90
Hardisty, Alta. — C5 68
Hardisty Lake, l., N.W. Ter. — D9 66
Hardman, Or., U.S. — B7 114
Hardoi, India — D8 37
Hardshell, Ky., U.S. — C6 94
Hardtner, Ks., U.S. — E5 93
Hardwick, Ga., U.S. — C3 87
Hardwick, Ma., U.S. — B3 98
Hardwick, Mn., U.S. — G2 100
Hardwick, Ne., U.S. — C2 104
Hardwick, Vt., U.S. — B4 122
Hardwicke, N.B. — B5 71
Hardwood Ridge, mtn., Pa., U.S. — D11 115
Hardy, Sask. — H3 75
Hardy, Ar., U.S. — A4 81
Hardy, Ia., U.S. — B3 92
Hardy, Ms., U.S. — B4 101
Hardy, Ne., U.S. — D8 104
Hardy, Ok., U.S. — A5 113
Hardy, co., W.V., U.S. — B6 125
Hardy, Lake, l., Fl., U.S. — E5 86
Hare Bay, Newf. — D4 72
Hare Bay, b., Newf. — C4 72
Haren, Neth. — A6 17
Haren (Harar), W. Ger. — B7 17
Harergge, prov., Eth. — D4 47
Harfleur, Fr. — C7 16
Harford, Pa., U.S. — C10 115
Harford, co., Md., U.S. — A5 97
Hargeysa, Som. — D5 47
Harghita, mtn., Rom. — B7 24
Hargill, Tx., U.S. — F3 120
Hargrave, Man. — E1 70
Hargrave, stm., Man. — B2 70
Hargrave Lake, l., Man. — B2 70
Hari, stm., Indon. — F2 34
Haridwār, India — C6 36
Ḥarīr, Wādī al, val., Syria — B8 41
Harīrūd, stm., Asia — B3 36
Harker Heights, Tx., U.S. — *D4 120
Harkers Island, N.C., U.S. — C6 110
Harlan, In., U.S. — B8 91
Harlan, Ia., U.S. — C2 92
Harlan, Ky., U.S. — D6 94
Harlan, co., Ky., U.S. — D6 94
Harlan, co., Ne., U.S. — D6 104
Harlan County Lake, res., Ne., U.S. — E6 104
Harlech, Wales, U.K. — B3 12
Harlem, Fl., U.S. — F5 86
Harlem, Mt., U.S. — B8 103
Harleyville, S.C., U.S. — E7 117
Harlingen, Neth. — A6 16
Harlingen, Tx., U.S. — F4 120
Harlow, Eng., U.K. — C8 12
Harlow, N.D., U.S. — B6 111
Harlowton, Mt., U.S. — D7 103
Harman, W.V., U.S. — C5 125
Harmans, Md., U.S. — B4 97
Harmarville, Pa., U.S. — k14 115
Harmon, Il., U.S. — B4 90
Harmon, Ok., U.S. — A2 113
Harmon, co., Ok., U.S. — C2 113
Harmony, In., U.S. — E3 91
Harmony, Me., U.S. — D3 96
Harmony, Mn., U.S. — G6 100
Harmony, N.C., U.S. — A2 110
Harmony, Pa., U.S. — E1 115
Harmony, R.I., U.S. — B3 116
Harmonsburg, Pa., U.S. — C1 115
Harmony Grove, Ar., U.S. — D3 81
Harmony Hills, Oh., U.S. — *B3 112
Harms, Tn., U.S. — B5 119
Harned, Ky., U.S. — C3 94

Harnett, co., N.C., U.S. — B4 110
Harney, Md., U.S. — A3 97
Harney, co., Or., U.S. — D7 114
Harney, Lake, l., Fl., U.S. — D5 86
Harney Lake, l., Or., U.S. — D7 114
Harney Peak, mtn., S.D., U.S. — D2 118
Härnösand, Swe. — F8 14
Haro, Spain — A4 22
Haro, Cabo, c., Mex. — B2 63
Harold, Fl., U.S. — u15 86
Harold Pond, l., Bah. — m17 64
Haro Strait, strt., Wa., U.S. — A2 124
Harper, Lib. — F3 45
Harper, Ks., U.S. — E5 93
Harper, Or., U.S. — D9 114
Harper, Tx., U.S. — D3 120
Harper, Wa., U.S. — e10 124
Harper, co., Ks., U.S. — E5 93
Harper, co., Ok., U.S. — A2 113
Harper, Mount, mtn., Ak., U.S. — C11 79
Harpers Ferry, Ia., U.S. — A6 92
Harpers Ferry, W.V., U.S. — B7 125
Harpers Ferry National Historical Park, W.V., U.S. — B7 125
Harpersville, Al., U.S. — B3 78
Harpersville, Ms., U.S. — C4 101
Harper Woods, Mi., U.S. — *p16 99
Harpster, Oh., U.S. — B2 112
Harpswell Center, Me., U.S. — *E3 96
Harptree, Sask. — H3 75
Harquahala Mountain, mtn., Az., U.S. — D2 80
Harquahala Mountains, mts., Az., U.S. — D2 80
Harrah, Ok., U.S. — B4 113
Harrah, Wa., U.S. — C5 124
Harray, Loch of, l., Scot., U.K. — A5 13
Harrell, Ar., U.S. — D3 81
Harricana, stm., Can. — F17 66
Harrietta, Mi., U.S. — D5 99
Harriettsville, Oh., U.S. — C4 112
Harriman, Tn., U.S. — D9 119
Harriman Reservoir, res., Vt., U.S. — F3 122
Harrington, De., U.S. — E8 85
Harrington, Me., U.S. — D5 96
Harrington, Wa., U.S. — B7 124
Harrington Park, N.J., U.S. — h9 107
Harrington Pond, l., Me., U.S. — o20 64
Harrington Sound, strt., Ber. — o20 64
Harriott Lake, l., Sask. — A4 75
Harris, Sask. — F2 75
Harris, Scot., U.K. — B3 10
Harris, Ia., U.S. — A2 92
Harris, Mn., U.S. — E6 100
Harris, Mo., U.S. — A4 102
Harris, Ok., U.S. — D7 113
Harris, R.I., U.S. — D3 116
Harris, Tn., U.S. — A3 119
Harris, co., Ga., U.S. — D2 87
Harris, co., Tx., U.S. — E5 120
Harris, Lake, l., Fl., U.S. — D5 86
Harris, Sound of, strt., Scot., U.K. — C1 13
Harrisburg, Ar., U.S. — B5 81
Harrisburg, Il., U.S. — F5 90
Harrisburg, Mo., U.S. — B5 102
Harrisburg, Ne., U.S. — C2 104
Harrisburg, Oh., U.S. — C3 112
Harrisburg, Or., U.S. — C3 114
Harrisburg, Pa., U.S. — F8 115
Harris Grove, Va., U.S. — h15 123
Harris Hill, hill, Ma., U.S. — A3 98
Harrismith, S. Afr. — C4 49
Harrison, Ar., U.S. — A2 81
Harrison, Id., U.S. — B2 89
Harrison, Me., U.S. — D2 96
Harrison, Mi., U.S. — D6 99
Harrison, Mt., U.S. — E5 103
Harrison, Ne., U.S. — B2 104
Harrison, N.J., U.S. — k8 107
Harrison, N.Y., U.S. — h13 109
Harrison, Oh., U.S. — C1 112
Harrison, S.D., U.S. — D7 118
Harrison, Tn., U.S. — h11 119
Harrison, co., In., U.S. — H5 91
Harrison, co., Ia., U.S. — C2 92
Harrison, co., Ky., U.S. — B5 94
Harrison, co., Ms., U.S. — E5 101
Harrison, co., Mo., U.S. — A3 102
Harrison, co., Oh., U.S. — B4 112
Harrison, co., Tx., U.S. — C5 120
Harrison, co., W.V., U.S. — B4 125
Harrison, Cape, c., Newf. — g10 72
Harrison Bay, b., Ak., U.S. — A9 79
Harrisonburg, La., U.S. — C4 95
Harrisonburg, Va., U.S. — B4 123
Harrison Hot Springs, B.C. — f14 69
Harrison Lake, l., B.C. — D7 69
Harrison Township, Mi., U.S. — *F8 99
Harrison Valley, Pa., U.S. — C6 115
Harrisonville, Il., U.S. — E3 90
Harrisonville, Mo., U.S. — C3 102
Harrisonville, N.J., U.S. — D2 107
Harrisonville, Pa., U.S. — G5 115
Harriston, Ont. — D4 73
Harriston, Ms., U.S. — D2 101
Harrisville, Mi., U.S. — D7 99
Harrisville, Ms., U.S. — D3 101
Harrisville, N.H., U.S. — E2 106
Harrisville, N.Y., U.S. — A5 109
Harrisville, Pa., U.S. — D1 115
Harrisville, R.I., U.S. — B2 116
Harrisville, W.V., U.S. — B3 125
Harrodsburg, In., U.S. — F4 91
Harrodsburg, Ky., U.S. — B5 94
Harrods Creek, stm., Ky., U.S. — g11 94
Harrogate, Eng., U.K. — C6 10
Harrold, S.D., U.S. — C6 118
Harrop Lake, l., Man. — C4 70
Harrow, Ont. — E2 73
Harrowby, Man. — D1 70
Harrowsmith, Ont. — C8 73
Harrys, stm., Newf. — D2 72
Harry S. Truman Reservoir, res., Mo., U.S. — C4 102
Harry Strunk Lake, res., Ne., U.S. — D5 104
Harsin, Iran — D3 39
Harstad, Nor. — C7 14
Hart, Mi., U.S. — E4 99
Hart, Tx., U.S. — B1 120
Hart, co., Ga., U.S. — B4 87

Name	Map Ref.	Page
Hart, co., Ky., U.S.	C4	94
Hart, Lake, l., Fl., U.S.	D5	86
Hartell, Alta.		
Hartfield, Va., U.S.	C6	123
Hartford, Ar., U.S.	D4	78
Hartford, Ct., U.S.	B5	84
Hartford, Il., U.S.	E3	90
Hartford, In., U.S.	*G8	91
Hartford, Ia., U.S.	C4	92
Hartford, Ks., U.S.	D8	93
Hartford, Ky., U.S.	C3	94
Hartford, Me., U.S.	D2	96
Hartford, Mi., U.S.	F4	99
Hartford, N.J., U.S.	D3	107
Hartford, N.Y., U.S.	B7	109
Hartford, S.D., U.S.	D9	118
Hartford, Tn., U.S.	D10	119
Hartford, Vt., U.S.	D4	122
Hartford, W.V., U.S.	C3	125
Hartford, Wi., U.S.	E5	126
Hartford, co., Ct., U.S.	B4	84
Hartford City, In., U.S.	D7	91
Hartha, E. Ger.	B7	19
Hartington, Ne., U.S.	B8	104
Hart Island, i., U.S.	B5	97
Hart Lake, l., Or., U.S.	E7	114
Hartland, N.B.	C2	71
Hartland, Me., U.S.	D3	96
Hartland, Mi., U.S.	F7	99
Hartland, Mn., U.S.	G5	100
Hartland, Vt., U.S.	D4	122
Hartland, W.V., U.S.	m13	125
Hartland, Wi., U.S.	E5	126
Hartland Four Corners, Vt., U.S.	D4	122
Hartland Point, c., Eng., U.K.	E4	10
Hartlepool, Eng., U.K.		
Hartley, Ia., U.S.	A2	92
Hartley, Tx., U.S.	B1	120
Hartley, co., Tx., U.S.	B1	120
Hartline, Wa., U.S.	B6	124
Hartly, De., U.S.	D3	85
Hartman, Ar., U.S.	B2	81
Hartman, Co., U.S.	C8	83
Hart Mountain, mtn., Man.	C1	70
Hartney, Man.	E1	70
Hartsburg, Il., U.S.	C4	90
Hartsburg, Mo., U.S.	C5	102
Hartsdale, N.Y., U.S.	*n15	109
Hartsel, Co., U.S.	B5	83
Hartselle, Al., U.S.	A3	78
Hartsfield, Ga., U.S.	E3	87
Hartshorn, Mo., U.S.	D6	102
Hartshorne, Ok., U.S.	C6	113
Hartsville, In., U.S.	F6	91
Hartsville, S.C., U.S.	C7	117
Hartsville, Tn., U.S.	A5	119
Hartuv, Isr.	h11	41
Hartville, Mo., U.S.	D5	102
Hartville, Oh., U.S.	B4	112
Hartville, Wy., U.S.	D8	127
Hartwell, Ga., U.S.	B4	87
Hartwell Lake, res., U.S.	B1	117
Hartwick, Ia., U.S.	C5	92
Hartwick, N.Y., U.S.	C5	109
Har Us Lake, l., Mong.	B3	31
Harvard, Id., U.S.	C2	89
Harvard, Il., U.S.	A5	90
Harvard, Ma., U.S.	A4	98
Harvard, Ne., U.S.	D7	104
Harvard, Mount, mtn., Co., U.S.	C4	83
Harvel, Il., U.S.	D4	90
Harvest, Al., U.S.	A3	78
Harvey, N.B.	D3	71
Harvey, N.B.	D5	71
Harvey, Il., U.S.	B6	90
Harvey, La., U.S.	E5	95
Harvey, Mi., U.S.	B3	99
Harvey, N.D., U.S.	B6	111
Harvey, W.V., U.S.	n13	125
Harvey, co., Ks., U.S.	D6	93
Harvey Lake, res., Pa., U.S.	m16	115
Harvey Mountain, mtn., U.S.	B1	98
Harveysburg, Oh., U.S.	C1	112
Harveys Creek, stm., Pa., U.S.	n16	115
Harveyville, Ks., U.S.	D8	93
Harwich, Eng., U.K.	E7	10
Harwich, Ma., U.S.	C7	98
Harwich Port, Ma., U.S.	C7	98
Harwinton, Ct., U.S.	B3	84
Harwood, Md., U.S.	C4	97
Harwood, Ma., U.S.	f9	98
Harwood, Mo., U.S.	D3	102
Harwood, N.D., U.S.	*C9	111
Harwood Heights, Il., U.S.	*k9	90
Haryāna, state, India	C6	36
Harzgerode, E. Ger.		
Harz Mountains, mts., Eur.	C5	18
Ḥasā, Wādī al, Jord.	D5	41
Ḥasanah, Bi'r, well, Eg.	F9	37
Hase, stm., W. Ger.	B3	18
Haselünne, W. Ger.	B3	18
Hashimoto, Japan	o14	35
Haskell, Ar., U.S.	C3	81
Haskell, Ok., U.S.	B6	113
Haskell, Tx., U.S.	C3	120
Haskell, co., Ks., U.S.	E3	93
Haskell, co., Ok., U.S.	B6	113
Haskell, co., Tx., U.S.	C3	120
Haskins, Oh., U.S.	A2	112
Haslach, Aus.	E9	19
Hasle, Den.		
Haslemere, Eng., U.K.	C7	12
Haslet, Tx., U.S.	n9	120
Haslett, Mi., U.S.	*F6	99
Haslev, Den.		
Hassan, India		
Hassayampa, stm., Az., U.S.	D3	80
Hassell, N.C., U.S.	B5	110
Hasselt, Bel.	B6	16
Hasselt, Neth.	B6	16
Hassfurt, W. Ger.	C5	19
Hassi Messaoud, Alg.	C6	44
Hässleholm, Swe.	I5	14
Hässloch, W. Ger.	D3	19
Hastings, Barb.	K20	65
Hastings, Ont.	C7	73
Hastings, N.Z.	M16	51
Hastings, Eng., U.K.	E7	10
Hastings, Fl., U.S.	C5	86
Hastings, Ia., U.S.	C2	92
Hastings, Mi., U.S.	F5	99
Hastings, Mn., U.S.	F6	100
Hastings, Ne., U.S.	D7	104
Hastings, N.D., U.S.	C7	111
Hastings, Ok., U.S.	C3	113
Hastings, Pa., U.S.	E4	115
Hastings, W.V., U.S.	h9	125
Hastings, co., Ont.	C7	73
Hastings-on-Hudson, N.Y., U.S.	h13	109
Hästveda, Swe.	B7	15
Hasty, Ar., U.S.	A2	81
Hasty, Co., U.S.	C8	83
Hatch, N.M., U.S.	E2	108
Hatch, Ut., U.S.	F3	121
Hatchechubbee, Al., U.S.	C4	78
Hatchet Creek, stm., Al., U.S.	B3	78
Hatchet Lake, N.S.	E6	71
Hatchie, stm., Tn., U.S.	B2	119
Hatchineha, Lake, l., Fl., U.S.	D5	86
Hatchville, Ma., U.S.	C6	98
Hatch Wash, val., Ut., U.S.	E6	121
Hatfield, Sask.	F3	75
Hatfield, Ar., U.S.	C1	81
Hatfield, In., U.S.	I3	91
Hatfield, Ma., U.S.	B2	98
Hatfield, Mn., U.S.	G2	100
Hatfield, Pa., U.S.	F11	115
Hathaway, Mt., U.S.	D10	103
Hāthras, India	D7	37
Ha Tien, Viet.	G6	35
Hatillo, P.R.	B2	65
Ha Tinh, Viet.	C6	35
Hatley, Ga., U.S.	E3	87
Hatley, Ms., U.S.	B5	101
Hatley, Wi., U.S.	D4	126
Hat Mountain, mtn., Az., U.S.	E3	80
Hato, Neth. Ant.	H19	65
Hato, Bocht van, b., Neth. Ant.	H19	65
Hato Mayor [del Rey], Dom. Rep.	E9	64
Hatta, India	E7	37
Hatteras, N.C., U.S.	B7	110
Hatteras, Cape, c., N.C., U.S.	B7	110
Hatteras Inlet, b., N.C., U.S.	B7	110
Hattfjelldal, Nor.	E6	14
Hattiesburg, Ms., U.S.	D4	101
Hattieville, Ar., U.S.	B3	81
Hattingen, W. Ger.	*C3	18
Hatton, Sask.	G1	75
Hatton, Al., U.S.	A2	78
Hatton, Ar., U.S.	C1	81
Hatton, N.D., U.S.	B8	111
Hatvan, Hung.	B4	24
Hatzic, B.C.	f13	69
Haubourdin, Fr.	D3	17
Haubstadt, In., U.S.	H2	91
Haugan, Mt., U.S.	C1	103
Haugen, Wi., U.S.	C2	126
Haugesund, Nor.	H1	14
Haughton, La., U.S.	B2	95
Haultain, stm., Sask.	A2	75
Hauppauge, N.Y., U.S.	*n15	109
Hauraki Gulf, b., N.Z.	L15	51
Hausach, W. Ger.	A4	20
Hauser, Or., U.S.	D2	114
Hauser Dam, Mt., U.S.	D5	103
Haus Stock, mtn., Switz.	C7	21
Haut, Isle au, i., Me., U.S.	D4	96
Haut Atlas, mts., Mor.	C3	44
Haute-Marne, dept., Fr.	A1	20
Hauterive (part of Baie-Comeau), Que.	k13	74
Hautes-Alpes, dept., Fr.	E2	20
Haute-Saône, dept., Fr.	B2	20
Haute-Savoie, dept., Fr.	C2	20
Hautes Fagnes, mts., Eur.	D6	17
Hautmont, Fr.	B5	16
Haut-Rhin, dept., Fr.	B3	20
Hauula, Hi., U.S.	B4	88
Hauzenberg, W. Ger.	E8	19
Havana (La Habana), Cuba	C2	64
Havana, Al., U.S.	C2	78
Havana, Ar., U.S.	B2	81
Havana, Fl., U.S.	B2	86
Havana, Il., U.S.	C3	90
Havana, Ks., U.S.	E8	93
Havana, N.D., U.S.	D8	111
Havana Nakya, Az., U.S.	A4	80
Havasu, Lake, res., U.S.	C1	80
Havasupai Indian Reservation, Az., U.S.	A3	80
Havel, stm., Eur.	F6	15
Havelberg, E. Ger.	F6	15
Havelock, N.B.	D4	71
Havelock, Ont.	C7	73
Havelock, Ia., U.S.	B3	92
Havelock, N.C., U.S.	C6	110
Haven, Ks., U.S.	E6	93
Havensville, Ks., U.S.	C7	93
Haverford [Township], Pa., U.S.	o20	115
Haverfordwest, Wales, U.K.	C3	12
Haverhill, Ma., U.S.	A5	98
Haverhill, N.H., U.S.	B2	106
Haversham, R.I., U.S.	G2	116
Havertown, Pa., U.S.	G11	115
Haviland, Ks., U.S.	E4	93
Haviland, Oh., U.S.	A1	112
Havířov, Czech.	*D5	26
Havlíčkův Brod, Czech.	D3	26
Havre, Mt., U.S.	B7	103
Havre-Aubert, Que.	B8	71
Havre Aubert, Île du, i., Que.	B7	71
Havre-aux-Maisons, Que.	B8	71
Havre aux Maisons, Île du, i., Que.	B7	71
Havre Boucher, N.S.	D8	71
Havre de Grace, Md., U.S.	A5	97
Havre North, Mt., U.S.	B7	103
Havre Saint Pierre, Que.	h9	72
Havza, Tur.	B10	40
Haw, stm., N.C., U.S.	B3	110
Hawaii, co., Hi., U.S.	D6	88
Hawaii, i., Hi., U.S.	D6	88
Hawaii, state, U.S.	D6	88
Hawaiian Gardens, Ca., U.S.	*n12	82
Hawaiian Islands, is., Hi., U.S.	m14	88
Hawaii Volcanoes National Park, Hi., U.S.	D6	88
Hawarden, Sask.	F2	75
Hawarden, Ia., U.S.	A1	92
Hawea, Lake, l., N.Z.	P12	51
Hawera, N.Z.	M15	51
Hawes, Eng., U.K.	F6	13
Hawesville, Ky., U.S.	C3	94
Hawi, Hi., U.S.	C6	88
Hawick, Scot., U.K.	C5	10
Hawke, stm., Newf.	B3	72
Hawke Bay, b., N.Z.	M16	51
Hawke Island, i., Newf.	B4	72
Hawker, Austl.	E2	51
Hawkes, Mount, mtn., Ant.	A7	7
Hawkesbury, Ont.	B10	73
Hawkesbury Island, i., B.C.	C3	69
Hawkestone, Ont.	C5	73
Hawkeye, Ia., U.S.	B6	92
Hawkins, Wi., U.S.	C3	126
Hawkins, co., Tn., U.S.	C11	119
Hawkinsville, Ga., U.S.	D3	87
Hawk Lake, Ont.	E5	70
Hawk Point, Mo., U.S.	C6	102
Hawk Run, Pa., U.S.	E5	115
Hawksbill, mtn., Va., U.S.	B4	123
Hawk Springs, Wy., U.S.	E8	127
Hawley, Mn., U.S.	D2	100
Hawley, Pa., U.S.	D11	115
Hawley, Tx., U.S.	C3	120
Hawleyville, Ct., U.S.	D2	84
Haworth, N.J., U.S.	h9	107
Haworth, Ok., U.S.	D7	113
Haw River, N.C., U.S.	A3	110
Ḥawsh ʿĪsā, Eg.	D2	41
Hawthorn, Pa., U.S.	n12	82
Hawthorne, Ca., U.S.	C4	86
Hawthorne, Fl., U.S.	C4	86
Hawthorne, Nv., U.S.	E3	105
Hawthorne, N.J., U.S.	B4	107
Hawthorne, N.Y., U.S.	g13	109
Haxtun, Co., U.S.	A8	83
Hay, Austl.	F7	50
Hay, stm., Austl.	D6	50
Hay, stm., Can.	E9	66
Hayange, Fr.	C7	16
Haybes, Fr.	D4	17
Hayden, Al., U.S.	B3	78
Hayden, Az., U.S.	E5	80
Hayden, Co., U.S.	A3	83
Hayden, Id., U.S.	*B2	89
Hayden, In., U.S.	G6	91
Haydenburg, Tn., U.S.	C8	119
Hayden Lake, l., Id., U.S.	B2	89
Haydenville, Ma., U.S.	B2	98
Haydenville, Oh., U.S.	C3	112
Hayes, La., U.S.	D3	95
Hayes, S.D., U.S.	C4	118
Hayes, co., Ne., U.S.	D4	104
Hayes, stm., Man.	B5	70
Hayes, Mount, mtn., Ak., U.S.	C10	79
Hayes Center, Ne., U.S.	D4	104
Hayesville, N.C., U.S.	f9	110
Hayesville, Oh., U.S.	B3	112
Hayesville, Or., U.S.	*C4	114
Hayfield, Man.	E1	70
Hayfield, Ia., U.S.	A4	92
Hayfield, Va., U.S.	*B5	123
Hayford, Wa., U.S.	g13	124
Hayford Peak, mtn., Nv., U.S.	G6	105
Hayfork, Ca., U.S.	B2	82
Hay Lake, l., Ont.	C4	73
Hay Lakes, Alta.	C4	68
Hayman, Tur.	C9	40
Haymarket, Va., U.S.	B5	123
Haymock Lake, l., Me., U.S.	B3	96
Haymond, Va., U.S.	F7	91
Haynes, Alta.	C4	68
Haynes, Ar., U.S.	C5	81
Haynes, N.D., U.S.	D3	111
Haynesville, La., U.S.	B2	95
Haynesville, Me., U.S.	C5	96
Hayneville, Al., U.S.	C3	78
Hay-on-Wye, Wales, U.K.	B4	12
Hay River, N.W. Ter.	D9	66
Hays, Ks., U.S.	D4	93
Hays, Mt., U.S.	C8	103
Hays, N.C., U.S.	A1	110
Hays, Yemen	C5	47
Hays, co., Tx., U.S.	D3	120
Hays Canyon Peak, mtn., Nv., U.S.	B2	105
Haysi, Va., U.S.	e9	123
Haysville, Ks., U.S.	g12	93
Haysville, Tn., U.S.	A5	119
Hay Springs, Ne., U.S.	B3	104
Haystack Mountain, mtn., Ct., U.S.	B3	84
Haystack Mountain, mtn., Nv., U.S.	B6	105
Hayter, Alta.	C5	68
Hayti, Mo., U.S.	E8	102
Hayti, S.D., U.S.	C8	118
Hayti Heights, Mo., U.S.	E8	102
Hayton, Wi., U.S.	h9	126
Hayward, Ca., U.S.	h8	82
Hayward, Ok., U.S.	A4	113
Hayward Addition, S.D., U.S.	*D8	118
Hayward, Wi., U.S.	C2	126
Haywards Heath, Eng., U.K.	C7	12
Haywood, Man.	E2	70
Haywood, N.C., U.S.	B3	110
Haywood, co., N.C., U.S.	f10	110
Haywood, co., Tn., U.S.	B2	119
Hazard, Ky., U.S.	C6	94
Hazard, Ne., U.S.	C6	104
Hazardville, Ct., U.S.	B5	84
Hazārībāgh, India	E10	37
Hazel, Ky., U.S.	f9	94
Hazel Crest, Il., U.S.	k9	90
Hazel Dell, Il., U.S.	D5	90
Hazel Dell, Wa., U.S.	D3	124
Hazel Green, Al., U.S.	A3	78
Hazel Green, Ky., U.S.	C6	94
Hazel Green, Wi., U.S.	F3	126
Hazel Hurst, Pa., U.S.	C4	115
Hazel Park, Mi., U.S.	p15	99
Hazel Patch, Ky., U.S.	C5	94
Hazel Run, Mn., U.S.	F3	100
Hazelton, B.C.	B4	69
Hazelton, Id., U.S.	G4	89
Hazelton, Ks., U.S.	E5	93
Hazelton, N.D., U.S.	C5	111
Hazelton Peak, mtn., Wy., U.S.	B5	127
Hazelwood, Mo., U.S.	*f13	102
Hazelwood, N.C., U.S.	f9	110
Hazen, Ar., U.S.	C4	81
Hazen, Nv., U.S.	D2	105
Hazen, N.D., U.S.	B4	111
Hazen Bay, b., Ak., U.S.	C6	79
Hazenmore, Sask.	H2	75
Hazen Strait, strt., N.W. Ter.	m29	66
Hazlehurst, Ga., U.S.	E4	87
Hazlehurst, Ms., U.S.	D3	101
Hazlet, Sask.	G1	75
Hazlet, N.J., U.S.	C4	107
Hazleton, In., U.S.	H2	91
Hazleton, Ia., U.S.	B6	92
Hazleton, Pa., U.S.	E10	115
Hazlett, Lake, l., Austl.	D4	50
Hazlettville, De., U.S.	D3	85
Ḥaẓōr Ashdod, Isr.	h9	41
Ḥaẓor HaGelilit, Isr.	B7	41
Head Bay d'Espoir (part of Milltown-Head Bay d'Espoir), Newf.	E4	72
Headford, Ire.	D2	11
Head Harbor Island, i., Me., U.S.	D4	96
Headland, Al., U.S.	D4	78
Headley, Mount, mtn., Mt., U.S.	C1	103
Head of Island, La., U.S.	h10	95
Headquarters, Id., U.S.	C3	89
Headrick, Ok., U.S.	C2	113
Heafford Junction, Wi., U.S.	C4	126
Healdsburg, Ca., U.S.	C2	82
Healdton, Ok., U.S.	C4	113
Healdville, Vt., U.S.	E3	122
Healing Springs, Va., U.S.	C3	123
Healy, Ak., U.S.	C10	79
Healy, Ks., U.S.	D3	93
Heanna, Japan	O5	52
Heard, co., Ga., U.S.	C1	87
Heard Island, i., Austl.	J1	2
Hearne, Sask.	G3	75
Hearne, Tx., U.S.	D4	120
Hearst, Ont.	o19	73
Heart, stm., Alta.	B2	68
Heart, stm., N.D., U.S.	C3	111
Heart Butte, Mt., U.S.	B4	103
Heart Butte Dam, N.D., U.S.	C3	111
Hearthstone Mountain, mtn., Md., U.S.	A2	97
Heart Lake, l., Alta.	B5	68
Heart Lake, l., Wy., U.S.	B2	127
Heart's Content, Newf.	E5	72
Heartwell, Ne., U.S.	D7	104
Heath, Al., U.S.	D3	78
Heath, Ma., U.S.	A2	98
Heath, Oh., U.S.	B3	112
Heatherton, N.S.	D8	71
Heath Springs, S.C., U.S.	B6	117
Heathsville, Va., U.S.	C6	123
Heaton, N.D., U.S.	B6	111
Heaundā, Nepal	D10	37
Heavener, Ok., U.S.	C7	113
Hebbronville, Tx., U.S.	F3	120
Hebei, prov., China	D8	31
Hebel, Austl.	E8	50
Heber, Az., U.S.	C5	80
Heber, Ut., U.S.	C4	121
Heber Springs, Ar., U.S.	B3	81
Hébertville, Que.	A6	74
Hebgen Lake, res., Mt., U.S.	*F5	103
Hebi, China	*D7	31
Hebrides, Sea of the, Scot., U.K.	B3	10
Hebron, Newf.	f9	72
Hebron, N.S.	F3	71
Hebron (Al Khalīl), Isr. Occ.	G10	40
Hebron, Ct., U.S.	C6	84
Hebron, Il., U.S.	A5	90
Hebron, In., U.S.	B3	91
Hebron, Ky., U.S.	h13	94
Hebron, Me., U.S.	D2	96
Hebron, Ne., U.S.	D8	104
Hebron, N.D., U.S.	C3	111
Hebron, N.H., U.S.	C3	106
Hebron, Oh., U.S.	C3	112
Hebron, Tx., U.S.	m10	120
Hebron, W.V., U.S.	B3	125
Heby, Swe.	t34	14
Hecate Strait, strt., B.C.	C2	69
Hecelchakán, Mex.	C6	63
Heceta Island, i., Ak., U.S.	n23	79
Hechingen, W. Ger.	D4	18
Hechtel, Bel.	C5	17
Hechuan, China	E6	31
Hecker, Il., U.S.	E4	90
Hecla, Man.	D3	70
Hecla, S.D., U.S.	B7	118
Hecla, Isl., i., Man.	D3	70
Hectanooga, N.S.	E3	71
Hector, Mn., U.S.	F4	100
Hede, Swe.	F5	14
Hedemora, Swe.	G6	14
Hedgehog Hill, hill, Ct., U.S.	B7	84
Hedges, Fl., U.S.	k8	86
Hedgesville, W.V., U.S.	B7	125
Hedley, B.C.	E7	69
Hedley, Tx., U.S.	B2	120
Hedo, Japan	N6	52
Hedo Cape, c., Japan	N6	52
Hedon, Eng., U.K.	A7	12
Hedrick, Ia., U.S.	C5	92
Heeia, Hi., U.S.	*B4	88
Heel Point, c., Wake I.		
Heeney, Co., U.S.	B4	83
Heerde, Neth.	B6	16
Heerenveen, Neth.	A6	16
Heerlen, Neth.	B6	16
Heessen, W. Ger.	C8	18
Hefa, Mitraz (Bay of Haifa), b., Isr.	B6	41
Hefei, China	E8	31
Heflin, Al., U.S.	B4	78
Heflin, La., U.S.	B2	95
Hegang, China	B11	31
Hegins, Pa., U.S.	E9	115
Heide, W. Ger.	A4	18
Heidelberg, Austl.	*G8	50
Heidelberg, W. Ger.	F4	19
Heidelberg, S. Afr.	D3	49
Heidelberg, Ms., U.S.	D5	101
Heidenau, E. Ger.	C8	19
Heidenheim, W. Ger.	D5	18
Heidrick, Ky., U.S.	D6	94
Heihe (Aihui), China	A10	31
Heil, N.D., U.S.	C4	111
Heilbron, S. Afr.	C4	49
Heilbronn, W. Ger.	D4	18
Heiligenblut, Aus.	B8	20
Heiligenhafen, W. Ger.	D4	15
Heiligenstadt, E. Ger.	C5	18
Heilongjiang, prov., China	B10	31
Heilong Jiang (Amur), stm., Asia	B10	31
Heilungkiang see Heilongjiang, prov., China	B10	31
Heilwood, Pa., U.S.	E4	115
Heimbach, W. Ger.	D6	17
Heimdal, N.D., U.S.	B6	111
Heimenkirch, W. Ger.	A8	21
Heinola, Fin.	G12	14
Heinsberg, W. Ger.	C6	17
Heiskell, Tn., U.S.	m13	119
Heisler, Alta.	C4	68
Heislerville, N.J., U.S.	E3	107
Heizer, Ks., U.S.	D5	93
Hejaz, reg., Sau. Ar.	C2	38
Hejian, China	E7	32
Hekla, Mount, vol., Ice.	n23	14
Hekou, China	A5	35
Hel, Pol.	A5	26
Helagsfjället, mtn., Swe.	F5	14
Helan Shan, mts., China	D6	31
Helbra, E. Ger.	D6	17
Helena, Ar., U.S.	C5	81
Helena, Ga., U.S.	D4	87
Helena, Mo., U.S.	B3	102
Helena, Mt., U.S.	D4	103
Helena, N.Y., U.S.	f10	109
Helena, Oh., U.S.	A2	112
Helena, Ok., U.S.	A3	113
Helena, S.C., U.S.	C4	117
Helendale, Ca., U.S.	E5	82
Helensburgh, Scot., U.K.	B4	10
Helenwood, Tn., U.S.	C9	119
Helga å, stm., Swe.	B8	15
Helgasjön, l., Swe.	B8	15
Helgeröd, Nor.	p28	14
Helgoland, i., W. Ger.	A3	18
Helgoland Bay, b., W. Ger.	D2	15
Heli, China	C5	33
Helicon see Elikón Óros, mtn., Grc.	g9	25
Helix, Or., U.S.	B8	114
Hellam, Pa., U.S.	G8	115
Hellenthal, W. Ger.	D6	17
Hellertown, Pa., U.S.	E11	115
Hellín, Spain	C5	22
Hells Canyon, val., U.S.	B10	114
Hells Canyon National Recreation Area, U.S.	B10	114
Hell-Ville, Madag.	f9	49
Helm, Ca., U.S.	D3	82
Helmand, stm., Asia	B3	36
Helmbrechts, W. Ger.	C6	19
Helmer, Id., U.S.	*C2	89
Helmer, In., U.S.	A7	91
Helmeringhausen, Nmb.	C2	49
Helmetta, N.J., U.S.	C4	107
Helmond, Neth.	B6	16
Helmsburg, In., U.S.	F5	91
Helmsdale, stm., Scot., U.K.	A5	10
Helmsley, Eng., U.K.	B5	13
Helmstedt, W. Ger.	B5	18
Helotes, Tx., U.S.	h7	120
Helper, Ut., U.S.	D5	121
Helsingborg, Swe.	I5	14
Helsingør, Den.	I5	14
Helsinki, Fin.	G11	14
Helston, Eng., U.K.	D2	12
Heltonville, In., U.S.	G5	91
Helvecia, Arg.	A4	54
Helvellyn, mtn., Eng., U.K.	F6	13
Helvetia, Pa., U.S.	D4	115
Helvick Head, c., Ire.	E4	11
Hemaruka, Alta.	D5	68
Hematite, Mo., U.S.	C7	102
Hemau, W. Ger.	D6	19
Hemel Hempstead, Eng., U.K.	k12	10
Hemet, Ca., U.S.	F5	82
Hemford, N.S.	E5	71
Hemingford, Ne., U.S.	B2	104
Hemingway, S.C., U.S.	D9	117
Hemlock, Mi., U.S.	E6	99
Hemlock, N.Y., U.S.	C3	109
Hemlock Reservoir, res., Ct., U.S.	E2	84
Hemmesta, Swe.	t36	14
Hemmingford, Que.	D4	74
Hemnesberget, Nor.	D5	14
Hemphill, Tx., U.S.	D6	120
Hemphill, co., Tx., U.S.	B2	120
Hemple, Mo., U.S.	B3	102
Hempstead, N.Y., U.S.	n15	109
Hempstead, Tx., U.S.	D4	120
Hempstead, co., Ar., U.S.	D2	81
Henagar, Al., U.S.	A4	78
Henan, prov., China	E9	31
Henares, stm., Spain	B4	22
Hendaye, Fr.		
Henderson, Arg.	B4	54
Henderson, Co., U.S.	B6	83
Henderson, Ia., U.S.	C2	92
Henderson, Ky., U.S.	C2	94
Henderson, La., U.S.	D4	95
Henderson, Md., U.S.	B6	97
Henderson, Mn., U.S.	F5	100
Henderson, Ne., U.S.	D8	104
Henderson, Nv., U.S.	G7	105
Henderson, N.C., U.S.	A4	110
Henderson, Tn., U.S.	B3	119
Henderson, Tx., U.S.	C5	120
Henderson, W.V., U.S.	C2	125
Henderson, co., Il., U.S.	C3	90
Henderson, co., Ky., U.S.	C2	94
Henderson, co., N.C., U.S.	f10	110
Henderson, co., Tn., U.S.	B3	119
Henderson, co., Tx., U.S.	C5	120
Henderson's Point, Ms., U.S.	g7	101
Hendersonville, N.C., U.S.	f10	110
Hendersonville, Tn., U.S.	A5	119
Hendijān, Iran	F4	39
Hendley, Ne., U.S.	D6	104
Hendon, Sask.	E4	75
Hendon (part of London), Eng., U.K.	k12	10
Hendricks, Mn., U.S.	F2	100
Hendricks, W.V., U.S.	B5	125
Hendricks, co., In., U.S.	E4	91
Hendrik Verwoerd Dam, res., S. Afr.	D4	49
Hendrum, Mn., U.S.	C2	100
Hendry, co., Fl., U.S.	F5	86
Henefer, Ut., U.S.	C4	121
Hengelo, Neth.	A7	16
Hengshan, China	F3	32
Hengshan, China	K5	32
Hengyang, China	F7	31
Hengxian, China	G6	31
Hénin-Beaumont, Fr.	D2	17
Henlawson, W.V., U.S.	n12	125
Henley Harbour, Newf.	B4	72
Henley-on-Thames, Eng., U.K.	C7	12
Henlopen, Cape, c., De., U.S.	E5	85
Henlopen Acres, De., U.S.	F5	85
Hennebont, Fr.	D2	16
Hennef, W. Ger.	C2	19
Hennepin, Il., U.S.	B4	90
Hennepin, Ok., U.S.	C4	113
Hennepin, co., Mn., U.S.	E5	100
Henniker, N.H., U.S.	D3	106
Henning, Il., U.S.	C6	90
Henning, Mn., U.S.	D3	100
Henning, Tn., U.S.	B2	119
Henribourg, Sask.	D3	75
Henrico, co., Va., U.S.	C5	123
Henrietta, Mo., U.S.	B4	102
Henrietta, N.Y., U.S.	B3	109
Henrietta, N.C., U.S.	B1	110
Henrietta, Tx., U.S.	C3	120
Henrietta Island, i., Sov. Un.	B35	128
Henrietta Maria, Cape, c., Ont.	n19	73
Henrieville, Ut., U.S.	F4	121
Henry, Il., U.S.	B4	90
Henry, Ne., U.S.	C1	104
Henry, S.D., U.S.	C8	118
Henry, Va., U.S.	D3	123
Henry, co., Al., U.S.	D4	78
Henry, co., Ga., U.S.	C2	87
Henry, co., Il., U.S.	B3	90
Henry, co., In., U.S.	E7	91
Henry, co., Ia., U.S.	C6	92
Henry, co., Ky., U.S.	B4	94
Henry, co., Mo., U.S.	C4	102
Henry, co., Oh., U.S.	A1	112
Henry, co., Tn., U.S.	A3	119
Henry, co., Va., U.S.	D3	123
Henry, Mount, mtn., Mt., U.S.	B1	103
Henry Kater, Cape, c., N.W. Ter.	C19	66
Henry Mountains, mts., Ut., U.S.	E5	121
Henry Pittier National Park, Ven.	A4	60
Henrys Fork, stm., U.S.	E2	127
Henryetta, Ok., U.S.	B6	113
Henryville, Que.	D4	74
Henryville, In., U.S.	G6	91
Hensall, Ont.	D3	73
Hensel, N.D., U.S.	A8	111
Henshaw, Ky., U.S.	e9	94
Hensler, N.D., U.S.	B4	111
Hensley, Ar., U.S.	C3	81
Henson Creek, stm., Md., U.S.	f9	97
Hentiyn Mountains, mts., Mong.	B6	31
Henzada, Burma	E10	36
Hepburn, Sask.	E2	75
Hepburn, Oh., U.S.	B2	112
Hephzibah, Ga., U.S.	C4	87
Hepler, Ks., U.S.	E9	93
Heppenheim, W. Ger.	D3	19
Heppner, Or., U.S.	B7	114
Hepu, China	G6	31
Hepworth, Ont.	C3	73
Heqing, China	F5	31
Herāt, Afg.	B3	36
Herbert, Sask.	G2	75
Herbertingen, W. Ger.	A5	20
Herbert Peak, mtn., N.Z.	O14	51
Herbes, Isle aux, i., Al., U.S.	E1	78
Herblay, Fr.	g9	16
Herbon, W. Ger.	B2	19
Herceg-Novi, Yugo.	D4	24
Hercegovina, hist. reg., Yugo.	C7	102
Herculaneum, Mo., U.S.	C7	102
Hercules, Ca., U.S.	*g8	82
Herdecke, W. Ger.	B2	19
Heredia, C.R.		
Hereford, Eng., U.K.	D5	10
Hereford, Az., U.S.	F5	80
Hereford, Co., U.S.	A6	83
Hereford, Md., U.S.	A5	97
Hereford, Or., U.S.	C8	114
Hereford, S.D., U.S.	C2	118
Hereford, Tx., U.S.	B1	120
Hereford and Worcester, co., Eng., U.K.	B5	12
Hereford Inlet, b., N.J., U.S.	E3	107
Hérémence, Switz.	D3	21
Herencia, Spain	C4	22
Herentals, Bel.	C4	17
Herfølge, Den.	B4	15
Herford, W. Ger.	B4	18
Héricourt, Fr.	B2	21
Herington, Ks., U.S.	D7	93
Herisau, Switz.	E4	18
Heritage Range, mts., Ant.	B4	7
Heritage Village, Ct., U.S.	*D3	84
Herkimer, Ks., U.S.	C7	93
Herkimer, N.Y., U.S.	B6	109
Herkimer, co., N.Y., U.S.	B5	109
Herman, Mi., U.S.	B2	99
Herman, Mn., U.S.	E2	100
Herman, Ne., U.S.	C9	104
Herman, Pa., U.S.	E2	102
Hermano Peak, mtn., Co., U.S.	D2	83
Hermansville, Mi., U.S.	C3	99
Hermanville, Ms., U.S.	D3	101
Hermeskeil, W. Ger.	F2	115
Hermiston, Or., U.S.	B7	114
Hermitage, Newf.	E4	72
Hermitage, Ar., U.S.	D3	81
Hermitage, Mo., U.S.	D4	102
Hermitage, Pa., U.S.	*D1	115
Hermitage Bay, b., Newf.	E3	72
Hermitage Springs, Tn., U.S.	C5	119
Hermleigh, Tx., U.S.	C2	120
Hermon, Me., U.S.	*D4	96
Hermon, N.Y., U.S.	f9	109
Hermon, Mount, mtn., Asia	F11	40
Hermosa, S.D., U.S.	D2	118

Hermosa Beach, Ca., U.S. — *n12 82
Hermosillo, Mex. — B2 63
Hernád, stm., Eur. — A5 24
Hernandarias, Para. — E5 55
Hernandez, N.M., U.S. — A3 108
Hernando, Fl., U.S. — D4 86
Hernando, Ms., U.S. — A4 101
Hernando, co., Fl., U.S. — D4 86
Herndon, Ga., U.S. — D4 87
Herndon, Ia., U.S. — C3 92
Herndon, Ks., U.S. — C3 93
Herndon, Ky., U.S. — D2 94
Herndon, Pa., U.S. — E8 115
Herndon, Va., U.S. — B5 123
Herndon, W.V., U.S. — D3 125
Herne, W. Ger. — B2 19
Herning, Den. — I3 14
Herod's Gate, hist., Isr. Occ. — m14 41
Heroica Caborca, Mex. — A2 63
Heroica Nogales, Mex. — A2 63
Heron, Mt., U.S. — B1 103
Heron Bay, Al., U.S. — E1 78
Heron Lake, Mn., U.S. — G3 100
Hérouxville, Que. — C5 74
Herreid, S.D., U.S. — B5 118
Herrenberg, W. Ger. — E3 19
Herrick, Il., U.S. — D5 90
Herrick, S.D., U.S. — D6 118
Herrick Center, Pa., U.S. — C11 115
Herrick Creek, stm., B.C. — B7 69
Herrick Mountain, mtn., Vt., U.S. — D2 122
Herriman, Ut., U.S. — *C3 121
Herrin, Il., U.S. — F4 90
Herring Bay, b., Md., U.S. — C4 97
Herring Cove, N.S. — E6 71
Herring Run, stm., Md., U.S. — g11 97
Herrington Lake, res., Ky., U.S. — C5 94
Hersbruck, W. Ger. — D6 19
Herschel, Sask. — F1 75
Herscher, Il., U.S. — B5 90
Hersey, Mi., U.S. — E5 99
Hershey, Ne., U.S. — C5 104
Hershey, Pa., U.S. — F8 115
Herstal, Bel. — B6 16
Herten, W. Ger. — *C3 19
Hertford, Eng., U.K. — E6 10
Hertford, N.C., U.S. — A6 110
Hertford, co., N.C., U.S. — A5 110
Hertfordshire, co., Eng., U.K. — C7 12
Hervás, Spain — B3 22
Hervey Bay, Austl. — D9 50
Hervey-Jonction, Que. — C5 74
Herxheim, W. Ger. — D3 19
Herzberg, E. Ger. — F7 15
Herzberg, E. Ger. — B8 19
Herzberg [am Harz], W. Ger. — B5 19
Herzliyya, Isr. — F10 40
Herzogenaurach, W. Ger. — D5 19
Herzogenbuchsee, Switz. — B4 21
Hesdin, Fr. — D2 17
Hesel, W. Ger. — A7 17
Hesper, Ia., U.S. — B6 111
Hesperia, Ca., U.S. — E5 82
Hesperia, Mi., U.S. — E4 99
Hesperus, Co., U.S. — D2 83
Hesperus Mountain, mtn., Co., U.S. — D2 83
Hess, Ok., U.S. — C2 113
Hesse, hist. reg., W. Ger. — C4 18
Hessel, Mi., U.S. — B6 99
Hesselager, Den. — C4 15
Hesselø, i., Den. — B5 15
Hessen, state, W. Ger. — C3 19
Hessmer, La., U.S. — C3 95
Hesston, Ks., U.S. — D6 93
Hetland, S.D., U.S. — C8 118
Hettick, Il., U.S. — D3 90
Hettinger, N.D., U.S. — D3 111
Hettinger, co., N.D., U.S. — C3 111
Hettstedt, E. Ger. — B6 19
Heusler, In., U.S. — I2 91
Heuvelton, N.Y., U.S. — f9 109
Heves, Hung. — B5 24
Heward, Sask. — H4 75
Hewins, Ks., U.S. — E7 93
Hewitt, Mn., U.S. — D3 100
Hewitt, N.J., U.S. — A4 107
Hewitt, Tx., U.S. — *D4 120
Hewitt, Wi., U.S. — D3 126
Hewlett, N.Y., U.S. — *n14 109
Hexham, Eng., U.K. — F6 13
Hexian, China — G7 31
Hexigten Qi, China — C7 32
Hext, Tx., U.S. — D3 120
Heyang, China — G4 32
Heyburn, Id., U.S. — G5 89
Heyworth, Il., U.S. — C5 90
Heze (Caozhou), China — *D8 31
Heze, China — G6 32
Hialeah, Fl., U.S. — G6 86
Hiattville, Ks., U.S. — E9 93
Hiawassee, Ga., U.S. — B3 87
Hiawatha, Ia., U.S. — B6 92
Hiawatha, Ks., U.S. — C8 93
Hiawatha, Ut., U.S. — D5 121
Hiawatha Camp, Co., U.S. — A2 83
Hibbard, In., U.S. — B5 91
Hibbing, Mn., U.S. — C6 100
Hickam Air Force Base, mil., Hi., U.S. — g10 88
Hickiwan, Az., U.S. — E3 80
Hickman, De., U.S. — E3 85
Hickman, Ky., U.S. — f8 94
Hickman, Ne., U.S. — D9 104
Hickman, co., Ky., U.S. — f8 94
Hickman, co., Tn., U.S. — B4 119
Hickman's Harbour, Newf. — D5 72
Hickok, Ks., U.S. — E2 93
Hickory, Ms., U.S. — f9 94
Hickory, N.C., U.S. — B1 110
Hickory, co., Mo., U.S. — D4 102
Hickory Corners, Mi., U.S. — F5 99
Hickory Flat, Ms., U.S. — A4 101
Hickory Grove, S.C., U.S. — B5 117
Hickory Hills, Il., U.S. — *k9 90
Hickory Plains, Ar., U.S. — C4 81
Hickory Ridge, Ar., U.S. — B5 81
Hickory Valley, Tn., U.S. — B2 119
Hickory Withe, Tn., U.S. — B2 119
Hickox, Ga., U.S. — E5 87
Hicks, La., U.S. — C2 95
Hicks, Point, c., Austl. — H7 51
Hickson, Ont. — D4 73
Hickson Lake, l., Sask. — A3 75
Hicksville, N.Y., U.S. — E7 109
Hicksville, Oh., U.S. — A1 112
Hico, Tx., U.S. — D3 120
Hico, W.V., U.S. — n11 99
Hida, stm., Japan — n16 33
Hidalgo, Il., U.S. — D5 90
Hidalgo, Tx., U.S. — F3 120

Hidalgo, state, Mex. — C5 63
Hidalgo, co., N.M., U.S. — F1 108
Hidalgo, co., Tx., U.S. — F3 120
Hidalgo del Parral, Mex. — B3 63
Hiddenite, N.C., U.S. — B1 110
Hiddensee, i., E. Ger. — D7 15
Hideaway Park, Co., U.S. — B5 83
Hidrolina, Braz. — A3 56
Hieroglyphic Mountains, mts., Az., U.S. — k8 80
Hierro, i., Spain — n13 22
Higashi, Japan — N6 52
Higashiizu, Japan — o18 33
Higashiōsaka, Japan — I7 33
Higbee, Mo., U.S. — B5 102
Higden, Ar., U.S. — B3 81
Higdon, Al., U.S. — A4 78
Higganum, Ct., U.S. — D5 84
Higgins, Tx., U.S. — A2 120
Higgins Lake, l., Mi., U.S. — D6 99
Higgins Lake, l., Mi., U.S. — D6 99
Higgins Millpond, res., Md., U.S. — C6 97
Higginson, Ar., U.S. — B4 81
Higginsport, Oh., U.S. — D2 112
Higginsville, Mo., U.S. — B4 102
High Bluff, Man. — D2 70
High Bridge, Ky., U.S. — C5 94
High Bridge, N.H., U.S. — E3 106
High Bridge, N.J., U.S. — B3 107
Highfalls, N.C., U.S. — B3 110
High Falls Reservoir, res., Wi., U.S. — C5 126
Highfield, Md., U.S. — A3 97
Highgate, Ont. — E3 73
Highgate Falls, Vt., U.S. — B2 122
High Hill, Mo., U.S. — C6 102
High Hill, stm., Can. — A5 68
High Hill Lake, l., Man. — B4 70
High Island, Tx., U.S. — E5 120
High Island, i., Mi., U.S. — C5 99
High Knob, mtn., Va., U.S. — A4 123
High Knob, mtn., W.V., U.S. — C5 125
Highland, Ca., U.S. — *E5 82
Highland, Il., U.S. — E4 90
Highland, In., U.S. — A3 91
Highland, Ks., U.S. — C8 93
Highland, Mi., U.S. — o14 99
Highland, N.Y., U.S. — D7 109
Highland, Wi., U.S. — E3 126
Highland, co., Oh., U.S. — C2 112
Highland, co., Va., U.S. — B3 123
Highland Falls, N.Y., U.S. — *D6 109
Highland Grove, Ont. — B7 73
Highland Heights, Oh., U.S. — *g10 112
Highland Home, Al., U.S. — D3 78
Highland Lake, l., Me., U.S. — g7 96
Highland Lakes, N.J., U.S. — A4 107
Highland Park, Il., U.S. — A6 90
Highland Park, Mi., U.S. — p15 99
Highland Park, N.J., U.S. — *C4 107
Highland Park, Tx., U.S. — n10 120
Highland Peak, mtn., Ca., U.S. — C4 82
Highland Point, c., Fl., U.S. — G5 86
Highlands, N.J., U.S. — C5 107
Highlands, N.C., U.S. — f9 110
Highlands, Tx., U.S. — r14 120
Highlands, co., Fl., U.S. — E5 86
Highland Springs, Va., U.S. — C5 123
Highlandville, Ia., U.S. — A6 92
High Level, Alta. — F7 68
Highmore, S.D., U.S. — C6 118
High Point, Ms., U.S. — B4 101
High Point, Mo., U.S. — C5 102
High Point, N.C., U.S. — B2 110
High Point, N.J., U.S. — e12 124
High Prairie, Alta. — B2 68
High Ridge, Mo., U.S. — g12 102
High River, Alta. — D4 68
High Rock, mtn., Md., U.S. — k12 97
High Rock Lake, l., Man. — B1 70
High Rock Lake, res., N.C., U.S. — B2 110
High Rolls Mountain Park, N.M., U.S. — E4 108
High Shoals, Ga., U.S. — C3 87
High Shoals, N.C., U.S. — B1 110
High Spire, Pa., U.S. — F8 115
High Springs, Fl., U.S. — C4 86
High Tatra Mountains, mts., Eur. — D5 26
High Top, mtn., W.V., U.S. — C5 125
Hightstown, N.J., U.S. — C3 107
Highview, Ky., U.S. — *g11 94
High Willhays, mtn., Eng., U.K. — K9 10
Highwood, Il., U.S. — A6 90
Highwood, Mt., U.S. — C6 103
Highwood Baldy, mtn., Mt., U.S. — C6 103
Highwood Mountains, mts., Mt., U.S. — C6 103
High Wycombe, Eng., U.K. — E6 10
Higley, Az., U.S. — D4 80
Higüero, Punta, c., P.R. — B1 65
Higüey, Dom. Rep. — E9 64
Higura Iri, prov., Som. — E6 47
Hiiraan, prov., Som. — E6 47
Hiiumaa, i., Sov. Un. — B4 27
Hiko, Nv., U.S. — F6 105
Hikone, Japan — n15 33
Hiko Range, mts., Nv., U.S. — F6 105
Hikurangi, mtn., N.Z. — L17 51
Hilāl, Jabal, mts., Eg. — D5 41
Hilbert, Wi., U.S. — D5 126
Hilda, Alta. — D5 68
Hilda, S.C., U.S. — E5 117
Hildale, Ut., U.S. — F3 121
Hildburghausen, E. Ger. — C5 18
Hilden, N.S. — D6 71
Hildesheim, W. Ger. — B4 18
Hildreth, Ne., U.S. — D6 104
Hiles, Wi., U.S. — C4 126
Hilger, Mt., U.S. — C7 103
Hilham, Tn., U.S. — C8 119
Hill, N.H., U.S. — C3 106
Hill, co., Mt., U.S. — B6 103
Hill, co., Tx., U.S. — D4 120
Hillaby, Mount, mtn., Barb. — K20 65
Hillared, Swe. — A7 15
Hill City, Id., U.S. — F4 89
Hill City, Ks., U.S. — C4 93
Hill City, Mn., U.S. — D5 100
Hill City, S.D., U.S. — D2 118
Hillcrest, Il., U.S. — B4 90
Hillcrest, Mi., U.S. — n11 99
Hillcrest, N.Y., U.S. — *n15 109
Hillcrest Center, Ca., U.S. — *E4 82
Hillcrest Heights, Md., U.S. — *C4 97
Hillegom, Neth. — B4 17

Hillerage, Ne., U.S. — *C2 104
Hillerød, Den. — C6 15
Hillesheim, W. Ger. — C1 19
Hillhead, S.D., U.S. — B8 118
Hilliard, Alta. — C4 68
Hilliard, Fl., U.S. — B5 86
Hilliard, Oh., U.S. — k10 112
Hilliards, Pa., U.S. — D2 115
Hillier, Ont. — D7 73
Hillisburg, In., U.S. — D5 91
Hill Lake, l., Ar., U.S. — h10 81
Hillman, Mi., U.S. — C7 99
Hillman, Mn., U.S. — D5 100
Hillmond, Sask. — D1 75
Hillrose, Co., U.S. — A7 83
Hills, Ia., U.S. — C6 92
Hills, Mn., U.S. — G2 100
Hillsboro, N.B. — D5 71
Hillsboro, Al., U.S. — A2 78
Hillsboro, Ga., U.S. — C3 87
Hillsboro, Il., U.S. — D4 90
Hillsboro, Ia., U.S. — D6 92
Hillsboro, Ks., U.S. — D6 93
Hillsboro, Md., U.S. — C6 97
Hillsboro, Ms., U.S. — C4 101
Hillsboro, Mo., U.S. — C7 102
Hillsboro, N.H., U.S. — D3 106
Hillsboro, N.D., U.S. — B8 111
Hillsboro, Oh., U.S. — C2 112
Hillsboro, Or., U.S. — B4 114
Hillsboro, Tn., U.S. — D8 119
Hillsboro, Tx., U.S. — C4 120
Hillsboro, W.V., U.S. — C4 125
Hillsboro, Wi., U.S. — E3 126
Hillsboro, co., Fl., U.S. — E4 86
Hillsboro, co., N.H., U.S. — E3 106
Hillsboro Bay, b., Fl., U.S. — F6 86
Hillsboro Canal, Fl., U.S. — F6 86
Hillsborough, N.B. — D5 71
Hillsborough, Gren. — W25 65
Hillsborough, St. Vin. — W26 65
Hillsborough, co., Fl., U.S. — E4 86
Hillsborough, co., N.H., U.S. — E3 106
Hillsborough Bay, b., P.E.I. — C6 71
Hillsborough Lower Village, N.H., U.S. — D3 106
Hillsborough Upper Village, N.H., U.S. — D3 106
Hills Creek Lake, res., Or., U.S. — D4 114
Hillsdale, Ont. — C5 73
Hillsdale, Il., U.S. — B3 90
Hillsdale, In., U.S. — E3 91
Hillsdale, Ks., U.S. — D9 93
Hillsdale, Mi., U.S. — G6 99
Hillsdale, N.J., U.S. — g8 107
Hillsdale, N.Y., U.S. — C7 109
Hillsdale, Ok., U.S. — A4 113
Hillsdale, Wi., U.S. — C2 126
Hillsdale, Wy., U.S. — E8 127
Hillsdale, co., Mi., U.S. — G6 99
Hillside, Az., U.S. — C3 80
Hillside, Co., U.S. — C5 83
Hillside, Il., U.S. — *k9 90
Hillside, N.J., U.S. — k8 107
Hillside Heights, De., U.S. — *B3 85
Hillspring, Alta. — E4 68
Hillston, Austl. — F5 51
Hillsview, S.D., U.S. — B6 118
Hillsville, Pa., U.S. — D1 115
Hillsville, Va., U.S. — D2 123
Hilltonia, Ga., U.S. — D5 87
Hilltown, N. Ire., U.K. — C5 11
Hillview, Il., U.S. — D3 90
Hillview, Ky., U.S. — *g11 94
Hillville, Tn., U.S. — B2 119
Hilo, Hi., U.S. — D6 88
Hilo Bay, b., Hi., U.S. — D6 88
Hilpoltstein, W. Ger. — D6 19
Hilton, Ga., U.S. — E1 87
Hilton, N.Y., U.S. — B3 109
Hilton Head Island, S.C., U.S. — G6 117
Hilton Head Island, i., S.C., U.S. — G6 117
Hiltons, Va., U.S. — f9 123
Hilversum, Neth. — A6 16
Hima, Ky., U.S. — C6 94
Himachal Pradesh, state, India — B6 37
Himalayas, mts., Asia — C8 36
Himeji, Japan — I7 33
Himi, Japan — H8 33
Himrod, N.Y., U.S. — C4 109
Hinche, Haiti — E7 64
Hinchinbrook, i., Austl. — C8 50
Hinchinbrook Island, i., Ak., U.S. — g18 79
Hinchliffe, Sask. — E4 75
Hinch Mountain, mtn., Tn., U.S. — D9 119
Hinckley, Eng., U.K. — B6 12
Hinckley, Il., U.S. — B5 90
Hinckley, Me., U.S. — D3 96
Hinckley, Mn., U.S. — D6 100
Hinckley, Oh., U.S. — A4 112
Hinckley, Ut., U.S. — D3 121
Hinckley Reservoir, res., N.Y., U.S. — B5 109
Hindīyah Barrage, Iraq — F15 40
Hindman, Ky., U.S. — C7 94
Hindmarsh, Lake, l., Austl. — G3 51
Hinds, co., Ms., U.S. — C3 101
Hindsboro, Il., U.S. — D5 90
Hinds Lake, l., Newf. — D3 72
Hindsville, Ar., U.S. — A2 81
Hindu Kush, mts., Asia — A5 36
Hines, Mn., U.S. — C4 100
Hines, Or., U.S. — D7 114
Hinesburg, Vt., U.S. — C2 122
Hines Creek, Alta. — A1 68
Hineston, La., U.S. — C3 95
Hinesville, Ga., U.S. — E5 87
Hingham, Ma., U.S. — B6 98
Hingham, Mt., U.S. — B6 103
Hingham Bay, b., Ma., U.S. — g12 98
Hingoli, India — H6 37
Hınıs, Tur. — C6 40
Hinkle, Ms., U.S. — A5 101
Hinkley, Ca., U.S. — E5 82
Hinnom, Valley of, val., Isr. Occ. — m14 41
Hinnøya, i., Nor. — C6 14
Hinojosa [del Duque], Spain — C6 22
Hinsdale, Il., U.S. — k9 90
Hinsdale, Ma., U.S. — B1 98
Hinsdale, Mt., U.S. — B9 103
Hinsdale, N.H., U.S. — E2 106
Hinsdale, N.Y., U.S. — C2 109
Hinsdale, co., Co., U.S. — D4 83
Hinterrhein, Switz. — C7 21
Hinterrhein, stm., Switz. — C7 21
Hinton, Alta. — C2 68

Hinton, Ia., U.S. — B1 92
Hinton, Ok., U.S. — B3 113
Hinton, W.V., U.S. — D4 125
Hirado Island, i., Japan — J4 33
Hiraiwa Cape, c., Japan — P17 52
Hirakata, Japan — *I7 33
Hirākūd Reservoir, res., India — G9 37
Hiram, Ga., U.S. — C2 87
Hiram, Me., U.S. — E2 96
Hiram, Oh., U.S. — A4 112
Hiratsuka, Japan — n17 33
Hîrlău, Rom. — B8 24
Hiroo, Japan — E11 33
Hirosaki, Japan — C13 31
Hiroshima, Japan — E11 31
Hirschberg see Jelenia Góra, Pol. — C3 26
Hirson, Fr. — C6 16
Hîrşova, Rom. — C8 24
Hirtshals, Den. — A3 15
Hisār, India — C6 36
Hisarönü, Tur. — B9 40
Hitachi, Japan — D13 31
Hitchcock, Ok., U.S. — B3 113
Hitchcock, S.D., U.S. — C7 118
Hitchcock, Tx., U.S. — r14 120
Hitchcock, co., Ne., U.S. — D4 104
Hitchcock Lake, Ct., U.S. — C4 84
Hitchin, Eng., U.K. — C7 12
Hitchins, Ky., U.S. — B7 94
Hitchita, Ok., U.S. — B6 113
Hiteman, Ia., U.S. — C5 92
Hitoyoshi, Japan — J5 33
Hitra, i., Nor. — F3 14
Hitterdal, Mn., U.S. — D2 100
Hittisau, Aus. — B8 21
Hitzacker, W. Ger. — E5 15
Hiwannee, Ms., U.S. — D5 101
Hiwassee, stm., Tn., U.S. — D9 119
Hiwassee Lake, res., N.C., U.S. — f8 110
Hixon, B.C. — C6 69
Hixton, Wi., U.S. — D2 126
Hjalleru, Den. — A4 15
Hjälmaren, l., Swe. — H7 14
Hjälmseröd, Swe. — A8 15
Hjo, Swe. — H6 14
Hjørring, Den. — I3 14
Hkakabo Razi, mtn., Burma — C10 36
Hlohovec, Czech. — D4 26
Ho, Ghana — E5 45
Hoa Binh, Viet. — B6 35
Hoaeae, Hi., U.S. — g9 88
Hoagland, In., U.S. — C8 91
Hoback, stm., Wy., U.S. — C2 127
Hobart, Austl. — o15 50
Hobart, In., U.S. — A3 91
Hobart, N.Y., U.S. — C6 109
Hobart, Ok., U.S. — B2 113
Hobbema, Alta. — C4 68
Hobbieville, In., U.S. — G4 91
Hobbs, In., U.S. — D6 91
Hobbs, N.M., U.S. — E6 108
Hobe Sound, Fl., U.S. — E6 86
Hobgood, N.C., U.S. — A5 110
Hoboken (part of Antwerp), Bel. — B6 16
Hoboken, Ga., U.S. — E4 87
Hoboken, N.J., U.S. — k8 107
Hobro, Den. — B3 15
Hobson, Mt., U.S. — D7 103
Hobson Lake, l., B.C. — C7 69
Hobucken, N.C., U.S. — B6 110
Hochdorf, Switz. — B4 18
Hochfeld, Nmb. — B2 49
Hochfelden, Fr. — F7 17
Ho Chi Minh City (Saigon), Viet. — C3 34
Höchst (part of Frankfurt am Main), W. Ger. — C3 19
Höchstadt [an der Aisch], W. Ger. — D5 19
Hockenheim, W. Ger. — D3 19
Hockerville, Ok., U.S. — A7 113
Hockessin, De., U.S. — A3 85
Hocking, co., Oh., U.S. — C3 112
Hocking, stm., Oh., U.S. — C3 112
Hockingport, Oh., U.S. — C4 112
Hockley, Tx., U.S. — q14 120
Hockley, co., Tx., U.S. — C1 120
Hoddesdon, Eng., U.K. — k13 10
Hodeida (Al Ḩudaydah), Yemen — D4 38
Hodge, La., U.S. — B3 95
Hodgeman, co., Ks., U.S. — D4 93
Hodgenville, Ky., U.S. — C4 94
Hodges, Al., U.S. — A2 78
Hodges, S.C., U.S. — C3 117
Hodges Hill, hill, Newf. — D4 72
Hodges Village Reservoir, res., Ma., U.S. — B4 98
Hodgeville, Sask. — G2 75
Hodgson, Man. — D3 70
Hódmezővásárhely, Hung. — B5 24
Hodonín, Czech. — D4 26
Hoehne, Co., U.S. — D6 83
Hoek van Holland (part of Rotterdam), Neth. — C4 17
Hoensbroek, Neth. — D5 17
Hoeryŏng, N. Kor. — E4 33
Hoey, Sask. — E3 75
Hof, W. Ger. — C5 18
Hof, Nor. — p28 14
Hoffman, Mn., U.S. — E3 100
Hoffman, N.C., U.S. — B3 110
Hoffman Estates, Il., U.S. — h8 90
Hofgeismar, W. Ger. — B4 19
Höfn, Ice. — n25 14
Höfu, Japan — I5 33
Höganäs, Swe. — B6 15
Hoganville, Ga., U.S. — C2 87
Hogback Mountain, mtn., Mt., U.S. — F4 103
Hogback Mountain, mtn., Ne., U.S. — C2 104
Hogback Mountain, mtn., S.C., U.S. — A3 117
Hogeland, Mt., U.S. — B8 103
Hog Island, i., Fl., U.S. — D3 86
Hog Island, i., Mi., U.S. — C5 99
Hog Island, i., N.C., U.S. — B6 110
Hog Island, i., R.I., U.S. — D5 116
Hog Island, i., Va., U.S. — C7 123
Hogup Mountains, mts., Ut., U.S. — B2 121

Holman, N.W. Ter. — B9 66
Holmdel, N.J., U.S. — C4 107
Holmen, Wi., U.S. — E2 126
Holmes, co., Fl., U.S. — u16 86
Holmes, co., Ms., U.S. — B3 101
Holmes, co., Oh., U.S. — B4 112
Holmes, Mount, mtn., Wy., U.S. — B2 127
Holmes Lake, l., Man. — A3 70
Holmestrand, Nor. — p28 14
Holmesville, Ne., U.S. — D9 104
Holmesville, Oh., U.S. — B4 112
Holmsbu, Nor. — p28 14
Holmsund, Swe. — F9 14
Holon, Isr. — B6 41
Holopaw, Fl., U.S. — D5 86
Holroyd, Austl. — *F9 50
Holroyd, stm., Austl. — B7 50
Holstebro, Den. — C2 15
Holstein, Ont. — C4 73
Holstein, Ia., U.S. — B2 92
Holstein, Ne., U.S. — D7 104
Holsteinsborg, Grnld. — *C15 61
Holston, stm., Tn., U.S. — C11 119
Holston, Middle Fork, stm., Va., U.S. — f10 123
Holston High Knob, mtn., Tn., U.S. — C11 119
Holsworthy, Eng., U.K. — D3 12
Holt, Al., U.S. — B2 78
Holt, Fl., U.S. — u15 86
Holt, Mi., U.S. — F6 99
Holt, Mn., U.S. — B2 100
Holt, Mo., U.S. — B3 102
Holt, co., Mo., U.S. — A2 102
Holt, co., Ne., U.S. — B7 104
Holt Creek, stm., Ne., U.S. — B6 104
Holt Knob, mtn., Tn., U.S. — g10 119
Holton, In., U.S. — F7 91
Holton, Ks., U.S. — C8 93
Holton, Mi., U.S. — E4 99
Holts Corner, Tn., U.S. — B5 119
Holtsville, N.Y., U.S. — *n15 109
Holtville, Al., U.S. — C3 78
Holtville, Ca., U.S. — F6 82
Holtwood, Pa., U.S. — G9 115
Holualoa, Hi., U.S. — D6 88
Holy Cross, Ire. — E4 11
Holy Cross, Ak., U.S. — C8 79
Holy Cross, Ia., U.S. — B7 92
Holy Cross, Mountain of the, mtn., Co., U.S. — B4 83
Holyhead, Wales, U.K. — D4 10
Holy Island, i., Eng., U.K. — C6 10
Holy Island, i., Wales, U.K. — D4 10
Holyoke, Co., U.S. — A8 83
Holyoke, Ma., U.S. — B2 98
Holyoke, Mn., U.S. — D6 100
Holyoke Range, hills, Ma., U.S. — B2 98
Holyrood, Ks., U.S. — D5 93
Holy Sepulchre, The Church of the, Isr. Occ. — m14 41
Holy Trinity, Al., U.S. — C4 78
Holzgau, Aus. — B9 21
Holzkirchen, W. Ger. — B7 20
Holzminden, W. Ger. — C4 18
Homalin, Burma — D9 36
Homathko, stm., B.C. — D5 69
Homberg, W. Ger. — B4 19
Homberg, W. Ger. — B1 19
Hombetsu, Japan — E11 33
Homborn, Mali — C4 45
Hombourg-Haut, Fr. — E6 17
Homburg, W. Ger. — D2 19
Homburg see Bad Homburg, W. Ger. — C4 18
Home, Ks., U.S. — C7 93
Home Bay, b., N.W. Ter. — C19 66
Home Corner, In., U.S. — C6 91
Homécourt, Fr. — C6 16
Homecroft, In., U.S. — m10 91
Homedale, Id., U.S. — F2 89
Home Gardens, Ca., U.S. — *n13 82
Home Hill, Austl. — C8 50
Homelake, Co., U.S. — D4 83
Homeland, Fl., U.S. — E5 86
Homeland, Ga., U.S. — F4 87
Homeland Park, S.C., U.S. — *B2 117
Home Place, In., U.S. — E5 91
Homer, Ak., U.S. — D9 79
Homer, Ga., U.S. — B3 87
Homer, Il., U.S. — C6 90
Homer, In., U.S. — E6 91
Homer, La., U.S. — B2 95
Homer, Mi., U.S. — F6 99
Homer, Ne., U.S. — B9 104
Homer, N.Y., U.S. — C4 109
Homer City, Pa., U.S. — E3 115
Homer Youngs Peak, mtn., Mt., U.S. — E3 103
Homestead, Fl., U.S. — G6 86
Homestead, Ia., U.S. — C6 92
Homestead, Mt., U.S. — B12 103
Homestead, Ok., U.S. — A3 113
Homestead, Pa., U.S. — k14 115
Homestead Air Force Base, mil., Fl., U.S. — G6 86
Homestead National Monument of America, Ne., U.S. — D9 104
Hometown, Il., U.S. — *k9 90
Homewood, Al., U.S. — g7 78
Homewood, Ca., U.S. — C3 82
Homewood, Il., U.S. — B6 90
Homewood, Ms., U.S. — C4 101
Homeworth, Oh., U.S. — B4 112
Hominy, Ok., U.S. — A5 113
Hominy Creek, stm., Ok., U.S. — A5 113
Homma Dam, N.D., U.S. — A8 111
Hommura, Japan — o18 33
Homochitto, stm., Ms., U.S. — D2 101
Homosassa, Fl., U.S. — D4 86
Homs (Ḩimṣ), Syria — B3 38
Hon, Ar., U.S. — C1 81
Honaker, Va., U.S. — e10 123
Honan see Henan, prov., China — E7 31
Honaunau, Hi., U.S. — D6 88
Honda, Col. — B3 60
Hondo, Alta. — B3 68
Hondo, N.M., U.S. — D4 108
Hondo, Tx., U.S. — E3 120
Hondo, stm., Mex. — h9 63
Hondo, stm., N.A. — A3 62
Hondo, Rio, stm., N.M., U.S. — D7 108
Honduras, ctry., N.A. — D7 63
Honduras, Cabo de, c., Hond. — D7 63
Honduras, Gulf of, b., N.A. — D7 63
Honea Path, S.C., U.S. — C3 117
Honefoss, Nor. — G4 14
Honeoye Falls, N.Y., U.S. — C3 109
Honesdale, Pa., U.S. — C11 115

Name	Map Ref.	Page
Honey Brook, Pa., U.S.	F10	115
Honey Creek, Ia., U.S.	C2	92
Honey Creek, Wi., U.S.	n11	126
Honey Grove, Tx., U.S.	C5	120
Honey Lake, l., Ca., U.S.	B3	82
Honeymoon Bay, B.C.	E5	69
Honeypot Glen, Ct., U.S.	C4	84
Honeyville, Ut., U.S.	B3	121
Honfleur, Fr.	C4	16
Høng, Den.	C5	15
Hon Gai, Viet.	B7	35
Hong'an, China	I6	32
Honga River, b., Md., U.S.	D5	97
Honghu, China	F7	31
Hong Kong, dep., Asia	G7	31
Hongshui He, stm., China	G6	31
Hongwŏn, N. Kor.	C12	31
Hongze Hu, l., China	E8	31
Honiara, Sol.Is.	G9	6
Honichin Hural, Mong.	C3	32
Honiton, Eng., U.K.	D4	12
Hönö, i., Swe.	A5	15
Honobia, Ok., U.S.	C7	113
Honokaa, Hi., U.S.	C6	88
Honokahua, Hi., U.S.	B5	88
Honokohau, Hi., U.S.	D6	88
Honolulu, Hi., U.S.	B4	88
Honolulu, co., Hi., U.S.	B3	88
Honolulu International Airport, Hi., U.S.	g10	88
Honomu, Hi., U.S.	D6	88
Honor, Mi., U.S.	D4	99
Honoraville, Al., U.S.	D3	78
Honouliuli, Hi., U.S.	g9	88
Hon Quan, Viet.	G7	35
Honshū, i., Japan	D12	31
Honuapo Bay, b., Hi., U.S.	D6	88
Hood, co., Tx., U.S.	C4	120
Hood, Mount, mtn., Or., U.S.	B5	114
Hood Canal, b., Wa., U.S.	B2	124
Hoodoo, Tn., U.S.	B5	119
Hoodoo Peak, mtn., Wa., U.S.	A5	124
Hood Point, c., Austl.	F2	50
Hood River, Or., U.S.	B5	114
Hood River, co., Or., U.S.	B5	114
Hoodsport, Wa., U.S.	B2	124
Hoogeveen, Neth.	B6	17
Hoogezand, Neth.	A6	17
Hookena, Hi., U.S.	D6	88
Hooker, Ok., U.S.	e9	113
Hooker, S.D., U.S.	D8	118
Hooker, co., Ne., U.S.	C4	104
Hooker, Bi'r, well, Eg.	D2	41
Hooker, Mount, mtn., Can.	C8	69
Hookerton, N.C., U.S.	B5	110
Hook Head, c., Ire.	E5	11
Hooksett, N.H., U.S.	D4	106
Hoolehua, Hi., U.S.	B4	88
Hoonah, Ak., U.S.	D12	79
Hoopa Valley Indian Reservation, Ca., U.S.	B2	82
Hooper, Ne., U.S.	C9	104
Hooper, Co., U.S.	D5	83
Hooper, Ut., U.S.	B3	121
Hooper, Wa., U.S.	C7	124
Hooper Bay, Ak., U.S.	C6	79
Hooper Creek, stm., Ne., U.S.	h12	104
Hooper Islands, is., Md., U.S.	D5	97
Hooper Strait, strt., Md., U.S.	D5	97
Hoopersville, Md., U.S.	D5	97
Hoopes Reservoir, res., De., U.S.	A3	85
Hoopeston, Il., U.S.	C6	90
Hooping Harbour, Newf.	C3	72
Hoople, N.D., U.S.	A8	111
Hooppole, Il., U.S.	B4	90
Hoorn, Neth.	A6	16
Hoosac Range, mts., U.S.	A1	98
Hoosic, stm., U.S.	C7	109
Hoosick Falls, N.Y., U.S.	C7	109
Hoosier, Sask.	F1	75
Hoosuc Range, mts., U.S.	D1	96
Hoover, Al., U.S.	*g7	78
Hoover Dam, U.S.	G7	105
Hoover Reservoir, res., Oh., U.S.	B3	112
Hooverson Heights, W.V., U.S.	f8	125
Hooversville, Pa., U.S.	F4	115
Hopa, Tur.	B13	40
Hopatcong, N.J., U.S.	B3	107
Hopatcong, Lake, l., N.J., U.S.	A4	107
Hop Bottom, Pa., U.S.	C10	115
Hope, B.C.	E7	69
Hope, Ak., U.S.	C10	79
Hope, Ar., U.S.	D2	81
Hope, Id., U.S.	A2	89
Hope, In., U.S.	F6	91
Hope, Ks., U.S.	D6	93
Hope, Me., U.S.	D3	96
Hope, Mi., U.S.	E6	99
Hope, Mn., U.S.	G5	100
Hope, N.M., U.S.	E5	108
Hope, N.D., U.S.	B8	111
Hope, i., Nor.	B12	128
Hope, Ben, mtn., Scot., U.K.	B4	13
Hope, Loch, l., Scot., U.K.	B4	13
Hope, Point, c., Ak., U.S.	B6	79
Hopedale, Newf.	g9	72
Hopedale, Il., U.S.	C4	90
Hopedale, La., U.S.	E6	95
Hopedale, Ma., U.S.	B4	98
Hopedale, Oh., U.S.	B5	112
Hopeh see Hebei, prov., China	D8	31
Hope Hull, Al., U.S.	C3	78
Hope Island, i., B.C.	D4	69
Hope Island, i., R.I., U.S.	E5	116
Hopelawn, N.J., U.S.	k7	107
Hopelchén, Mex.	D7	63
Hope Mills, N.C., U.S.	B4	110
Hopes Advance, Cap, c., Que.	f13	74
Hopeton, Ok., U.S.	A3	113
Hopetoun, Austl.	G4	51
Hopetown, S. Afr.	G4	48
Hope Valley, R.I., U.S.	E2	116
Hopeville, Ia., U.S.	D4	92
Hopewell, N.S.	D7	71
Hopewell, Ms., U.S.	D3	101
Hopewell, N.J., U.S.	C3	107
Hopewell, Oh., U.S.	C3	112
Hopewell, Pa., U.S.	F5	115
Hopewell, Va., U.S.	C5	123
Hopewell Cape, N.B.	D5	71
Hopewell Junction, N.Y., U.S.	D7	109
Hopi Buttes, mtn., Az., U.S.	B5	80
Hopi Indian Reservation, Az., U.S.	A5	80
Hopkins, Mi., U.S.	F5	99
Hopkins, Mn., U.S.	n12	100
Hopkins, Mo., U.S.	A3	102
Hopkins, S.C., U.S.	D6	117
Hopkins, co., Ky., U.S.	C2	94
Hopkins, co., Tx., U.S.	C5	120
Hopkinsville, Ky., U.S.	D2	94
Hopkinton, Ia., U.S.	B6	92
Hopkinton, Ma., U.S.	B4	98
Hopkinton, N.H., U.S.	D3	106
Hopkinton, N.Y., U.S.	f10	109
Hopkinton, R.I., U.S.	F1	116
Hopkinton Lake, res., N.H., U.S.	D3	106
Hopland, Ca., U.S.	C2	82
Hopson, Tn., U.S.	C11	119
Hopwood, Pa., U.S.	G2	115
Hoquiam, Wa., U.S.	C2	124
Horace, Ks., U.S.	D2	93
Horace, N.D., U.S.	C9	111
Horace Mountain, mtn., Ak., U.S.	B10	79
Horatio, Ar., U.S.	D1	81
Horatio, S.C., U.S.	C6	117
Horažďovice, Czech.	D8	19
Horb, W. Ger.	E3	19
Hørby, Den.	A4	15
Hörby, Swe.	C7	15
Hordville, Ne., U.S.	C8	104
Hord, Il., U.S.	E5	90
Horgen, Switz.	E4	18
Horicon, Wi., U.S.	E5	126
Horine, Mo., U.S.	C7	102
Horizon, Sask.	H3	75
Hörle, Swe.	A7	15
Horlick Mountains, mts., Ant.	A36	7
Hormoz, i., Iran	H8	39
Hormuz, Strait of, strt., Asia	C5	38
Horn, Aus.	D7	18
Horn, c., Ice.	m21	14
Horn, Cape, c., Chile	k12	54
Hornavan, l., Swe.	D7	14
Hornbeak, Tn., U.S.	A2	119
Hornbeck, La., U.S.	C2	95
Hornburg, W. Ger.	A5	19
Horncastle, Eng., U.K.	A7	12
Hornell, N.Y., U.S.	C3	109
Hornerstown, N.J., U.S.	C3	107
Hornersville, Mo., U.S.	E7	102
Horning's Mills, Ont.	C4	73
Hornick, Ia., U.S.	B1	92
Horní Počernice, Czech.	n18	26
Horn Island, i., Ms., U.S.	E5	101
Horn Island Pass, strt., Ms., U.S.	g8	101
Horn Lake, Ms., U.S.	A3	101
Horn Mountain, mtn., Al., U.S.	B3	78
Horn Plateau, plat., N.W. Ter.	D9	66
Horn Pond, l., Ma., U.S.	g11	98
Hornsby, Tn., U.S.	B3	119
Hornsbyville, Va., U.S.	h15	123
Hornsea, Eng., U.K.	D6	10
Hornslet, Den.	B4	15
Hörnum, W. Ger.	A4	18
Hořovice, Czech.	D8	19
Horqin Youyi Qianqi, China	A10	32
Horqin Youyi Zhongqi, China	B9	32
Horqueta, Para.	D4	55
Horred, Swe.	A6	15
Horry, co., S.C., U.S.	D10	117
Horse, stm., Alta.	A5	68
Horse, stm., Ct., U.S.	C6	84
Horseback Knob, hill, Oh., U.S.	C2	112
Horse Branch, Ky., U.S.	C3	94
Horse Cave, Ky., U.S.	C4	94
Horse Creek, Wy., U.S.	E7	127
Horse Creek, stm., U.S.	E8	127
Horse Creek, stm., Co., U.S.	C7	83
Horse Creek, stm., Mo., U.S.	D4	102
Horse Creek Reservoir, res., Co., U.S.	C7	83
Horsefly, B.C.	C7	69
Horsefly Lake, l., B.C.	C7	69
Horsehead Lake, l., N.D., U.S.	B6	111
Horseheads, N.Y., U.S.	C4	109
Horse Heaven Hills, hills, Wa., U.S.	C6	124
Horse Islands, Newf.	C4	72
Horse Mountain, mtn., N.M., U.S.	D1	108
Horsens, Den.	J3	14
Horseshoe Bend, Fl., U.S.	C3	86
Horseshoe Bend, Id., U.S.	F2	89
Horseshoe Bend National Military Park, Al., U.S.	C4	78
Horseshoe Cove, b., Fl., U.S.	C3	86
Horseshoe Lake, l., Man.	C4	70
Horseshoe Point, c., Fl., U.S.	C3	86
Horseshoe Reservoir, res., Az., U.S.	D4	80
Horse Springs, N.M., U.S.	D1	108
Horsham, Austl.	G7	50
Horsham, Eng., U.K.	C7	12
Horsham, Pa., U.S.	*F11	115
Horšovský Týn, Czech.	D7	19
Horta, Port.	g8	44
Horten, Nor.	H4	14
Hortense, Ga., U.S.	E5	87
Horton, Ga., U.S.	A3	78
Horton, In., U.S.	D5	91
Horton, Ks., U.S.	C8	93
Horton, Mi., U.S.	F6	99
Horton, Ne., U.S.	B5	104
Horton, stm., N.W. Ter.	C8	66
Hortonia, Lake, l., Vt., U.S.	D2	122
Hortonville, Wi., U.S.	D5	126
Hørve, Den.	C5	15
Hörvik, Swe.	B8	15
Horw, Switz.	E4	18
Hoschton, Ga., U.S.	B3	87
Hoséré Vokré, mtn., Cam.	D2	46
Hosford, Fl., U.S.	B2	86
Hoshāb, Pak.	H11	39
Hoshiārpur, India	B6	36
Hoskins, Ne., U.S.	B8	104
Hoskins, Or., U.S.	C3	114
Hoskinston, Ky., U.S.	C6	94
Hosmer, B.C.	E10	69
Hosmer, S.D., U.S.	B6	118
Hospers, Ia., U.S.	A2	92
Hospital, Ire.	I4	11
Hospitalet, Spain	B7	22
Hosston, La., U.S.	B2	95
Hosta Butte, mtn., N.M., U.S.	B1	108
Hoste, Isla, i., Chile	k12	54
Hot, Thai.	C3	35
Hotaka, Mount, mtn., Japan	H8	36
Hotan, China	A7	36
Hotan, stm., China	A7	36
Hotchkiss, Co., U.S.	C3	83
Hotchkissville, Ct., U.S.	C3	84
Hot Coffee, Ms., U.S.	D4	101
Hot Creek Range, mts., Nv., U.S.	E5	105
Hot Creek Valley, val., Nv., U.S.	E5	105
Hotevilla, Az., U.S.	B5	80
Hoting, Swe.	C7	14
Hot Springs, Mt., U.S.	C2	103
Hot Springs see Truth or Consequences, N.M., U.S.		
Hot Springs, N.C., U.S.	f10	110
Hot Springs, S.D., U.S.	D2	118
Hot Springs, Va., U.S.	C3	123
Hot Springs, co., Wy., U.S.	C4	127
Hot Springs National Park, Ar., U.S.	C2	81
Hot Springs National Park, Ar., U.S.	C2	81
Hot Springs Peak, mtn., Ca., U.S.	B3	82
Hot Springs Peak, mtn., Nv., U.S.	B4	105
Hot Sulphur Springs, Co., U.S.	A4	83
Hottah Lake, l., N.W. Ter.	C9	66
Hotte, Massif de la, mts., Haiti	E7	64
Houck, Az., U.S.	B6	80
Houffalize, Bel.	D5	17
Houghton, Mi., U.S.	A2	99
Houghton, N.Y., U.S.	C2	109
Houghton, S.D., U.S.	B7	118
Houghton, co., Mi., U.S.	B2	99
Houghton Lake, Mi., U.S.	D6	99
Houghton Lake, l., Mi., U.S.	D6	99
Houghton Lake Heights, Mi., U.S.	D6	99
Houilles, Fr.	g9	16
Houlka, Ms., U.S.	A4	101
Houlton, Me., U.S.	B5	96
Houltonville, La., U.S.	h11	95
Houma, La., U.S.	E5	95
Houma Essouk, Tun.	C7	44
Houndé, Burkina	D4	45
Hourn, Loch, b., Scot., U.K.	C3	13
Housatonic, Ma., U.S.	B1	98
Housatonic, stm., U.S.	D3	84
House, B.C.	B4	68
House, stm., Alta.	B4	68
House Range, mts., Ut., U.S.	D2	121
House Springs, Mo., U.S.	g12	102
Houston, B.C.	B4	69
Houston, Ar., U.S.	B3	81
Houston, De., U.S.	E3	85
Houston, Mn., U.S.	G7	100
Houston, Ms., U.S.	B4	101
Houston, Mo., U.S.	D6	102
Houston, Oh., U.S.	B1	112
Houston, Pa., U.S.	F1	115
Houston, Tx., U.S.	E5	120
Houston, co., Al., U.S.	D4	78
Houston, co., Ga., U.S.	D3	87
Houston, co., Mn., U.S.	G7	100
Houston, co., Tn., U.S.	A4	119
Houston, co., Tx., U.S.	D5	120
Houston, stm., La., U.S.	D2	95
Houston, Lake, res., Tx., U.S.	r14	120
Houston Intercontinental Airport, Tx., U.S.	r14	120
Houstonia, Mo., U.S.	C4	102
Houtzdale, Pa., U.S.	E5	115
Hove, Eng., U.K.	E6	10
Hovelhof, W. Ger.	B3	19
Hoven, S.D., U.S.	B6	118
Hovenweep National Monument, Ut., U.S.	F6	121
Hövsgöl Lake, l., Mong.	A5	31
Howar, Wādī, val., Afr.	B2	47
Howard, Ga., U.S.	D2	87
Howard, Ks., U.S.	E7	93
Howard, Pa., U.S.	E7	115
Howard, S.D., U.S.	C8	118
Howard, Wi., U.S.	D5	126
Howard, co., Ar., U.S.	C2	81
Howard, co., In., U.S.	C5	91
Howard, co., Ia., U.S.	A5	92
Howard, co., Md., U.S.	B4	97
Howard, co., Mo., U.S.	B5	102
Howard, co., Ne., U.S.	C7	104
Howard, co., Tx., U.S.	C2	120
Howard City, Mi., U.S.	E5	99
Howard Hanson Reservoir, res., Wa., U.S.	B4	124
Howard Lake, Mn., U.S.	E4	100
Howard Prairie Lake, res., Or., U.S.	E4	114
Howards Grove-Millersville, Wi., U.S.	E6	126
Howardville, Mo., U.S.	E8	102
Howe, Id., U.S.	F6	89
Howe, In., U.S.	A7	91
Howe, Ok., U.S.	C7	113
Howe, Cape, c., Austl.	G9	50
Howe, Mount, mtn., Newf.	D2	72
Howell, Mi., U.S.	F7	99
Howell, Ut., U.S.	B3	121
Howell, co., Mo., U.S.	E6	102
Howells, Ne., U.S.	C8	104
Howes, S.D., U.S.	C3	118
Howesville, W.V., U.S.	B5	125
Howick, Que.	D4	74
Howison, Ms., U.S.	E4	101
Howland, Me., U.S.	C4	96
Howland, Oh., U.S.	*A5	112
Howland Island, i., Oc.	F11	6
Howley, Newf.	D3	72
Howley, Mount, mtn., Newf.	D2	72
Howser, B.C.	D9	69
Hoxie, Ar., U.S.	A5	81
Hoxie, Ks., U.S.	C3	93
Höxter, W. Ger.	B4	19
Hoy, i., Scot., U.K.	A5	10
Hoya, W. Ger.	B4	19
Hoyerswerda, E. Ger.	C7	18
Hoylake, Eng., U.K.	H9	10
Hoyleton, Il., U.S.	E4	90
Hoyo, Sierra del, mts., Spain	o17	22
Hoyt, N.B.	D3	71
Hoyt, Co., U.S.	B6	83
Hoyt, Ks., U.S.	C8	93
Hoyt Lakes, Mn., U.S.	C6	100
Hoytville, Oh., U.S.	A2	112
Hradec Králové, Czech.	E11	26
Hranice, Czech.	D6	26
Hřiňová, Czech.	D5	26
Hron, stm., Czech.	H4	26
Hrubieszów, Pol.	C7	26
Hsinchu, Tai.	G9	31
Hsipaw, Burma	A2	35
Huacho, Peru	D2	58
Huachuca City, Az., U.S.	F5	80
Huacrachuco, Peru	C2	58
Huade, China	D5	32
Huadian, China	C10	31
Hua Hin, Thai.	C1	34
Huai'an (Huaicheng), China	H8	32
Huaibei, China	*E8	31
Huaide, China	C9	31
Huailai, China	D6	32
Huainan, China	C6	31
Huaiyang, China	H6	32
Huaiyin, China	H7	32
Huaiyuan, China	D5	31
Huajuapan de León, Mex.	I10	62
Hualalai, vol., Hi., U.S.	D6	88
Hualapai Indian Reservation, Az., U.S.	B2	80
Hualapai Mountains, mts., Az., U.S.	B2	80
Hualapai Peak, mtn., Az., U.S.	B2	80
Hualgayoc, Peru	C2	58
Hualien, Tai.	G9	31
Huallaga, stm., Peru	D7	50
Huallanca, Peru	C2	58
Huamachuco, Peru	C2	58
Huamantla, Mex.	n15	63
Huambo, Ang.	D2	48
Huambo, dept., Ang.	D2	48
Huancabamba, Peru	C2	58
Huancané, Peru	E4	58
Huancavelica, Peru	D2	58
Huancavelica, dept., Peru	D2	58
Huancayo, Peru	D2	58
Huanchaca, Bol.	D2	55
Huangchuan, China	H6	32
Huanggang, China	E8	31
Huang He (Yellow), stm., China	D8	31
Huangling, China	D6	31
Huangmei, China	I6	32
Huangping, China	K2	32
Huangshi, China	E8	31
Huangxian, China	F9	32
Huangyan, China	J9	32
Huangyuan, China	D5	31
Huanta, Peru	D3	58
Huánuco, Peru	C2	58
Huánuco, dept., Peru	C2	58
Huanuni, Bol.	C2	55
Huara, Chile	C2	55
Huaral, Peru	D2	58
Huaráz, Peru	C2	58
Huari, Bol.	C2	55
Huariaca, Peru	C2	58
Huarina, Bol.	C2	55
Huarmey, Peru	D2	58
Huascarán, Nevado, mtn., Peru	C2	58
Huasco, Chile	E1	55
Huasco, stm., Chile	E1	55
Huatabampo, Mex.	B3	63
Huatusco [de Chicuellar], Mex.	n15	63
Huauchinango, Mex.	m14	63
Huautla [de los Figueroa], Mex.	n14	63
Huaylas, Peru	C2	58
Huaytará, Peru	D2	58
Huayuan, China	J3	32
Hubbard, Ia., U.S.	B4	92
Hubbard, Mn., U.S.	D4	100
Hubbard, Ne., U.S.	B9	104
Hubbard, Oh., U.S.	A5	112
Hubbard, Or., U.S.	B4	114
Hubbard, Tx., U.S.	D4	120
Hubbard, co., Mn., U.S.	C4	100
Hubbard Creek Lake, res., Tx., U.S.	C3	120
Hubbard Lake, Mi., U.S.	D7	99
Hubbard Lake, l., Mi., U.S.	D7	99
Hubbards, N.S.	E5	71
Hubbardston, Ma., U.S.	B3	98
Hubbardston, Mi., U.S.	E6	99
Hubbardton, stm., Vt., U.S.	D2	122
Hubbell, Mi., U.S.	A2	99
Hubbell, Ne., U.S.	D8	104
Hubei, prov., China	E7	31
Huben, Aus.	C8	20
Huber, Ga., U.S.	D3	87
Huberdeau, Que.	D3	74
Huber Heights, Oh., U.S.	*C1	112
Huber Ridge, Oh., U.S.	*B3	112
Hubli-Dhārwār, India	E6	36
Huckleberry Hill, Ct., U.S.	B4	84
Huckleberry Mountain, mtn., Or., U.S.	D4	114
Huddersfield, Eng., U.K.	D6	10
Huddinge, Swe.	*H7	14
Huddleston, Va., U.S.	C3	123
Huddleston Knob, mtn., Tn., U.S.	C8	119
Hude, W. Ger.	E2	19
Hudiksvall, Swe.	G7	14
Hudson, Co., U.S.	A6	83
Hudson, Fl., U.S.	D4	86
Hudson, Il., U.S.	C5	90
Hudson, In., U.S.	A7	91
Hudson, Ia., U.S.	B5	92
Hudson, Ks., U.S.	D5	93
Hudson, Me., U.S.	C4	96
Hudson, Ma., U.S.	B4	98
Hudson, Mi., U.S.	G6	99
Hudson, N.H., U.S.	E4	106
Hudson, N.Y., U.S.	C7	109
Hudson, N.C., U.S.	B1	110
Hudson, Oh., U.S.	A4	112
Hudson, S.D., U.S.	D9	118
Hudson, Wi., U.S.	D1	126
Hudson, Wy., U.S.	D4	127
Hudson, co., N.J., U.S.	B4	107
Hudson, stm., U.S.	E7	109
Hudson, Lake, res., Ok., U.S.	A6	113
Hudson Bay, Can.	D15	66
Hudson Bay, Sask.	F4	75
Hudson Falls, N.Y., U.S.	B7	109
Hudson Hope, B.C.	A6	69
Hudson Lake, In., U.S.	A4	91
Hudson Mountains, mts., Ant.	B3	7
Hudsonville, Mi., U.S.	F5	99
Hudspeth, co., Tx., U.S.	o12	120
Hudwin Lake, l., Man.	C4	70
Hue, Viet.	B3	34
Huedin, Rom.	B6	24
Huehuetenango, Guat.	D6	63
Huejotzingo, Mex.	n14	63
Huejutla [de Reyes], Mex.	m14	63
Huelma, Spain	D4	22
Huelva, Spain	D2	22
Huentelauquén, Chile	C2	58
Huércal-Overa, Spain	D5	22
Huerfano, co., Co., U.S.	D5	83
Huerfano, stm., Co., U.S.	D6	83
Huerfano Mountain, mtn., N.M., U.S.	A2	108
Huesca, Spain	B5	22
Huéscar, Spain	D4	22
Huetamo de Núñez, Mex.	D4	63
Huete, Spain	B4	22
Huetter, Id., U.S.	*B2	89
Hueytown, Al., U.S.	g6	78
Huff, N.D., U.S.	C5	111
Huffakers, Nv., U.S.	D2	105
Huggins, Mount, mtn., Ant.	B29	7
Hugh Butler Lake, res., Ne., U.S.	D5	104
Hughenden, Austl.	D7	50
Hughenden, Alta.	C5	68
Hughes, Ak., U.S.	B9	79
Hughes, Ar., U.S.	C5	81
Hughes, co., Ok., U.S.	B5	113
Hughes, co., S.D., U.S.	C5	118
Hughes, stm., Man.	A1	70
Hughes, North Fork, stm., W.V., U.S.	B3	125
Hughes, South Fork, stm., W.V., U.S.	B3	125
Hughesville, Md., U.S.	C4	97
Hughesville, Mo., U.S.	C4	102
Hughesville, N.J., U.S.	B2	107
Hughesville, Pa., U.S.	D8	115
Hughton, Sask.	F2	75
Hugli, stm., India	D6	36
Hugo, Co., U.S.	B7	83
Hugo, Mn., U.S.	m13	100
Hugo, Ok., U.S.	C6	113
Hugo, Lake, res., Ok., U.S.	C6	113
Hugoton, Ks., U.S.	E2	93
Huguley, Al., U.S.	*C4	78
Huichang, China	F8	31
Huichapan, Mex.	m14	63
Hüichŏn, N. Kor.	F3	33
Huila, dept., Ang.	D2	48
Huila, dept., Col.	C2	60
Huila, Nevado del, mtn., Col.	C2	60
Huili, China	F5	31
Huimanguillo, Mex.	B1	62
Huimin, China	D8	31
Huinan, China	E4	33
Huitzuco [de los Figueroa], Mex.	n14	63
Huixtla, Mex.	D6	63
Huizen, Neth.	C5	17
Huizhou, China	G7	31
Hukou, China	F8	31
Hukuntsi, Bots.	B3	49
Hulah Lake, res., Ok., U.S.	A5	113
Hulan, China	B10	31
Hulbert, Mi., U.S.	B5	99
Hulbert, Ok., U.S.	B6	113
Hulen, Ky., U.S.	D6	94
Hulett, Wy., U.S.	B8	127
Hulin, China	C13	31
Hull, Que.	D2	74
Hull, Il., U.S.	D2	90
Hull, Ia., U.S.	A1	92
Hull, Ma., U.S.	B6	98
Hull, co., Que.	D2	74
Hull see Kingston upon Hull, Eng., U.K.	D6	10
Hulls Cove, Me., U.S.	D4	96
Hulst, Neth.	C4	17
Huludao, China	C9	31
Hulun Hu, l., China	B8	31
Hulwān, Eg.	E3	41
Huma, China	A10	31
Humacao, P.R.		
Humahuaca, Arg.	A3	56
Humaitá, Braz.	D2	59
Humansdorp, S. Afr.	H4	48
Humansville, Mo., U.S.	D4	102
Humber, stm., Eng., U.K.	G8	10
Humberside, co., Eng., U.K.	G8	10
Humble, Tx., U.S.	r14	120
Humboldt, Sask.	E3	75
Humboldt, Az., U.S.	C3	80
Humboldt, Il., U.S.	D5	90
Humboldt, Ia., U.S.	B3	92
Humboldt, Ks., U.S.	E8	93
Humboldt, Ne., U.S.	D10	104
Humboldt, Nv., U.S.	C3	105
Humboldt, S.D., U.S.	D8	118
Humboldt, Tn., U.S.	B3	119
Humboldt, co., Ca., U.S.	B2	82
Humboldt, co., Ia., U.S.	B3	92
Humboldt, co., Nv., U.S.	B3	105
Humboldt, stm., Nv., U.S.	C3	105
Humboldt, North Fork, stm., Nv., U.S.	B6	105
Humboldt Mountains, mts., Ant.	B14	7
Humboldt Range, mts., Nv., U.S.	C3	105
Hume, Il., U.S.	D6	90
Hume, Mo., U.S.	C3	102
Hume, N.Y., U.S.	C2	109
Hume, Va., U.S.	B5	123
Hume, Lake, res., Austl.	G6	51
Humeston, Ia., U.S.	D4	92
Hummels Wharf, Pa., U.S.	E8	115
Humnoke, Ar., U.S.	C4	81
Humpata, Ang.	E1	48
Humphrey, Ar., U.S.	C4	81
Humphrey, Ne., U.S.	C8	104
Humphreys, Mo., U.S.	A4	102
Humphreys, co., Ms., U.S.	B3	101
Humphreys, co., Tn., U.S.	A4	119
Humphreys, Mount, mtn., Ca., U.S.	D4	82
Humphreys Peak, mtn., Az., U.S.	B4	80
Humpolec, Czech.		
Humptulips, Wa., U.S.	B2	124
Hūn, Libya	D3	43
Hunan, prov., China	F7	31
Hunchun, China	C13	31
Hundested, Den.	C5	15
Hundred, W.V., U.S.	B4	125
Hundred Acre Pond, l., R.I., U.S.	E3	116
Hunedoara, Rom.	C6	24
Hünfeld, W. Ger.	C4	19
Hungary, ctry., Eur.	B4	24
Hungerford, Austl.	D5	51
Hüngnam, N. Kor.	D10	31
Hungry Hill, mtn., Ire.	F2	11
Hungry Horse, Mt., U.S.	B2	103
Hungry Horse Reservoir, res., Mt., U.S.	B3	103
Huningue, Fr.	B3	20
Hunish, Rubha, c., Scot., U.K.	C2	13
Hunjiang, China	C10	31
Hunn, l., Swe.	u33	14
Hunnewell, Ks., U.S.	E6	93
Hunnewell, Mo., U.S.	B6	102
Hunstanton, Eng., U.K.	B8	12
Hunt, China	B9	32
Hunt, Ar., U.S.	B2	81
Hunt, Il., U.S.	D5	90
Hunt, co., Tx., U.S.	C4	120
Hunt, stm., R.I., U.S.	D4	116
Hunter, Ar., U.S.	B4	81
Hunter, Ks., U.S.	C5	93
Hunter, N.D., U.S.	B8	111
Hunter, Ok., U.S.	A4	113
Hunter, i., Austl.	o14	50
Hunter, Cape, c., N.W. Ter.	B18	66
Hunterdon, co., N.J., U.S.	B3	107
Hunter Island, i., B.C.	D3	69
Hunter Mountain, mtn., N.Y., U.S.	C6	109
Hunter River, P.E.I.	C6	71
Hunters, Wa., U.S.	A7	124
Huntersfield Mountain, mtn., N.Y., U.S.	C6	109
Huntersville, W.V., U.S.	C4	125
Huntertown, In., U.S.	B7	91
Huntingburg, In., U.S.	H4	91
Hunting Creek, stm., Md., U.S.	C4	97
Huntingdon, B.C.	f13	69
Huntingdon, Que.	D3	74
Huntingdon, Eng., U.K.	B7	12
Huntingdon, Pa., U.S.	F6	115
Huntingdon, Tn., U.S.	A3	119
Huntingdon, co., Que.	D3	74
Huntingdon, co., Pa., U.S.	F5	115
Huntingdon Island, i., Newf.	B3	72
Huntington, Ar., U.S.	B1	81
Huntington, In., U.S.	C7	91
Huntington, Ma., U.S.	B2	98
Huntington, N.J., U.S.	B2	107
Huntington, N.Y., U.S.	E7	109
Huntington, Or., U.S.	C9	114
Huntington, Tx., U.S.	D5	120
Huntington, Ut., U.S.	D5	121
Huntington, Vt., U.S.	C3	122
Huntington, Va., U.S.	*B5	123
Huntington, W.V., U.S.	C2	125
Huntington, co., In., U.S.	C6	91
Huntington Bay, N.Y., U.S.	*E7	109
Huntington Beach, Ca., U.S.	F4	82
Huntington Center, Vt., U.S.	C3	122
Huntington Creek, stm., Nv., U.S.	C6	105
Huntington Lake, res., In., U.S.	C7	91
Huntington Park, Ca., U.S.	*E4	82
Huntington Station, N.Y., U.S.	*E7	109
Huntington Woods, Mi., U.S.	p15	99
Huntingtown, Md., U.S.	C4	97
Huntland, Tn., U.S.	B5	119
Huntley, Il., U.S.	A5	90
Huntley, Mn., U.S.	G4	100
Huntley, Mt., U.S.	E8	103
Huntley, Ne., U.S.	D6	104
Huntley, Wy., U.S.	E8	127
Huntly, Scot., U.K.	B5	10
Hunt Mountain, mtn., Wy., U.S.	B5	127
Hunts Point, N.S.	F5	71
Huntsville, Ont.	B5	73
Huntsville, Al., U.S.	A3	78
Huntsville, Ar., U.S.	A2	81
Huntsville, In., U.S.	E6	91
Huntsville, Ky., U.S.	C3	94
Huntsville, Mo., U.S.	B5	102
Huntsville, Oh., U.S.	B2	112
Huntsville, Tn., U.S.	C9	119
Huntsville, Tx., U.S.	D5	120
Huntsville, Ut., U.S.	B4	121
Hunucmá, Mex.	C7	63
Hunyuan, China	D6	31
Huon Gulf, b., Pap. N. Gui.	k12	50
Huoshan, China	I7	32
Huoxian, China	F4	32
Hupeh see Hubei, prov., China	E7	31
Huraydin, Wādī, val., Eg.	D6	41
Hurd, Cape, c., Ont.	B3	73
Hurdland, Mo., U.S.	A5	102
Hurdsfield, N.D., U.S.	B6	111
Hure Qi, China	C9	32
Hurley, Ms., U.S.	E5	101
Hurley, Mo., U.S.	D4	102
Hurley, N.M., U.S.	E1	108
Hurley, N.Y., U.S.	D6	109
Hurley, S.D., U.S.	D8	118
Hurley, Va., U.S.	e9	123
Hurley, Wi., U.S.	B3	126
Hurleyville, N.Y., U.S.	D6	109
Hurliness, Scot., U.K.	B5	13
Hurlock, Md., U.S.	C6	97
Hurmagai, Pak.	G12	39
Huron, In., U.S.	G4	91
Huron, Ks., U.S.	C8	93
Huron, Oh., U.S.	A3	112
Huron, S.D., U.S.	C7	118
Huron, co., Mi., U.S.	E7	99
Huron, co., Oh., U.S.	A3	112
Huron, stm., Mi., U.S.	p14	99
Huron, Lake, l., N.A.	C11	76
Huron Mountains, hills, Mi., U.S.	B3	99
Hurricane, Al., U.S.	E2	78
Hurricane, Ut., U.S.	F2	121
Hurricane, W.V., U.S.	C2	125
Hurricane Cliffs, clf., U.S.	A2	80
Hurricane Creek, stm., Ar., U.S.	C3	81
Hurricane Creek, stm., Ga., U.S.	E4	87
Hurricane Mills, Tn., U.S.	B4	119
Hurricane Mountain, mtn., Tn., U.S.	C9	119
Hurst, Il., U.S.	F4	90
Hurst, Tx., U.S.	*n9	120
Hurstville, Austl.	*F9	50
Hurt, Va., U.S.	C3	123
Hurtsboro, Al., U.S.	C4	78
Hurup, Den.	B2	15
Huşi, Rom.	B9	24

Name	Map Ref.	Page
Huskvarna (part of Jönköping), Swe.	I6	14
Huson, Mt., U.S.	C2	103
Hussar, Alta.	D4	68
Husser, La., U.S.	D5	95
Hustburg, Tn., U.S.	B4	119
Hustisford, Wi., U.S.	E5	126
Hustle, Va., U.S.	B5	123
Hustontown, Pa., U.S.	F5	115
Hustonville, Ky., U.S.	C5	94
Husum, W. Ger.	A4	18
Husum, Wa., U.S.	D4	124
Hutchins, Tx., U.S.	n10	120
Hutchinson, Ks., U.S.	D6	93
Hutchinson, Mn., U.S.	F4	100
Hutchinson, N.J., U.S.	B2	107
Hutchinson, co., S.D., U.S.	D8	118
Hutchinson, co., Tx., U.S.	B2	120
Hutchinson Island, i., Fl., U.S.	E6	86
Hutchinson Island, i., S.C., U.S.	k11	117
Hutch Mountain, mtn., Az., U.S.	C4	80
Hutsonville, Il., U.S.	D6	90
Huttig, Ar., U.S.	C3	81
Hutto, Tx., U.S.	D4	120
Hutton, Md., U.S.	m12	97
Huttonsville, W.V., U.S.	C5	125
Huttwil, Switz.	B4	21
Hutuo He, stm., China	E5	32
Huu, Indon.	G5	34
Ḥuwwārah, Isr. Occ.	g12	41
Ḥuwwārah, Isr. Occ.	B7	41
Huxford, Al., U.S.	D2	78
Huxley, Alta.	D4	68
Huxley, Ia., U.S.	C4	92
Huy, Bel.	B6	16
Hūzgān, Iran	F4	39
Huzhou, China	*E9	31
Hvalpsund, Den.	B3	15
Hvannadalshnúkur, mtn., Ice.	n24	14
Hvar, i., Yugo.	D3	24
Hvidbjerg, Den.	B2	15
Hvide Sande, Den.	C2	15
Hvidovre, Den.	*C6	15
Hvitsten, Nor.	p28	14
Hvittingfoss (part of Kongsberg), Nor.	p28	14
Hwange, Zimb.	A4	49
Hwang Ho see Huang He, stm., China	D8	31
Hyak, Wa., U.S.	B4	124
Hyampom, Ca., U.S.	B2	82
Hyannis, Ma., U.S.	C7	98
Hyannis, Ne., U.S.	C4	104
Hyannis Port, Ma., U.S.	C7	98
Hyargas Lake, l., Mong.	B3	31
Hyas, Sask.	F4	75
Hyatts, Oh., U.S.	B3	112
Hyattstown, Md., U.S.	B3	97
Hyattsville, Md., U.S.	C4	97
Hyattville, Wy., U.S.	B5	127
Hybart, Al., U.S.	D2	78
Hybla Valley, Va., U.S.	g12	123
Hyco, stm., U.S.	D3	123
Hyco Lake, res., N.C., U.S.	A3	110
Hydaburg, Ak., U.S.	D13	79
Hyde, Pa., U.S.	D5	115
Hyde, co., N.C., U.S.	B6	110
Hyde, co., S.D., U.S.	C6	118
Hyden, Austl.	F2	50
Hyden, Ky., U.S.	C6	94
Hyde Park, Guy.	A3	59
Hyde Park, N.Y., U.S.	D7	109
Hyde Park, Ut., U.S.	B4	121
Hyde Park, Vt., U.S.	B3	122
Hyder, Ak., U.S.	D13	79
Hyderābād, India	E6	36
Hyderābād, Pak.	C4	36
Hydetown, Pa., U.S.	C2	115
Hydeville, Ct., U.S.	B6	84
Hydeville, Vt., U.S.	D2	122
Hydra see Ídhra, i., Grc.	D4	25
Hydraulic, B.C.	C7	69
Hydro, Ok., U.S.	B3	113
Hyères, Fr.	F7	16
Hyères, Îles d', is., Fr.	F7	16
Hyesan, N. Kor.	C10	31
Hygiene, Co., U.S.	A5	83
Hylo, Alta.	B4	68
Hyman, S.C., U.S.	D8	117
Hymera, In., U.S.	F3	91
Hyndman, Pa., U.S.	G4	115
Hyndman Peak, mtn., Id., U.S.	F5	89
Hyner, Pa., U.S.	D6	115
Hyŏpchon, S. Kor.	I4	33
Hyrum, Ut., U.S.	B4	121
Hyrynsalmi, Fin.	E13	14
Hysham, Mt., U.S.	D9	103
Hythe, Alta.	B1	68
Hythe, Eng., U.K.	C9	12
Hyvinkää, Fin.	*G11	14

I

Name	Map Ref.	Page
Iaco (Yaco), stm., S.A.	D4	58
Iaeger, W.V., U.S.	D3	125
Ialomiţa, stm., Rom.	C8	24
Iamonia, Lake, l., Fl., U.S.	B2	86
Iantha, Mo., U.S.	D3	102
Iapu, Braz.	B4	56
Iaşi, Rom.	B8	24
Iatan, Mo., U.S.	B3	102
Iates Point, c., Guam	L10	52
Iatt, Lake, res., La., U.S.	C3	95
Iauaretê, Braz.	C4	60
Iba, Phil.	o12	34
Ibadan, Nig.	E5	45
Ibagué, Col.	C2	60
Ibanda, Ug.	B5	48
Ibapah, Ut., U.S.	C2	121
Ibapah Peak, mtn., Ut., U.S.	D2	121
Ibar, stm., Yugo.	D5	24
Ibaraki, Japan	*I7	33
Ibarra, Ec.	A2	58
Ibb, Yemen	C5	47
Ibbenbüren, W. Ger.	A2	19
Iberá, Laguna, l., Arg.	E4	55
Iberia, Oh., U.S.	B3	112
Iberia, co., La., U.S.	E4	95
Iberville, Que.	D4	74
Iberville, La., U.S.	D4	95
Iberville, co., La., U.S.	D4	95
Iberville, co., Que.	D4	74
Iberville, Mont d' (Mount Caubvick), mtn., Can.	g14	74
Ibi, Nig.	E6	45
Ibi, stm., Japan	n15	33
Ibiá, Braz.	E5	57
Ibiapaba, Serra da, mts., Braz.	B2	57
Ibicuí, stm., Braz.	D1	56
Ibicuy, Arg.	A5	54
Ibirapuitã, stm., Braz.	E1	56
Ibitinga, Braz.	C3	56
Ibiza (Iviza), Spain	C6	22
Ibiza, i., Spain	C6	22
Ibo, Moz.	D7	48
Ibri, Oman	C5	38
Ibu, Japan	N6	52
Iburg, W. Ger.	A3	19
Ica, Peru	D2	58
Ica, dept., Peru	D2	58
Içá (Putumayo), stm., S.A.	D4	60
Icaraí, Braz.	C3	56
Icacos Point, c., Trin.	O22	63
Içana, Braz.	A4	58
Içana (Isana), stm., S.A.	C4	60
Ice Harbor Dam, Wa., U.S.	D10	40
İçel (Mersin), Tur.	n23	14
Iceland, ctry., Eur.	C3	56
Icém, Braz.	B7	69
Ice Mountain, mtn., B.C.	n18	33
Ichikawa, Japan	n15	33
Ichinomiya, Japan	G10	33
Ichinoseki, Japan	F9	27
Ichnya, Sov. Un.	B5	124
Icicle Creek, stm., Wa., U.S.	F7	115
Ickesburg, Pa., U.S.	C3	57
Ico, Braz.	A7	79
Icy Cape, c., Ak., U.S.	k22	79
Icy Strait, strt., Ak., U.S.	A2	95
Ida, La., U.S.	G7	99
Ida, Mi., U.S.	D3	100
Ida, Lake, l., Mn., U.S.	E5	25
Ida, Mount, mtn., Grc.	B2	92
Ida Grove, Ia., U.S.	D7	113
Idabel, Ok., U.S.	E6	45
Idah, Nig.	D3	89
Idaho, co., Id., U.S.	E3	89
Idaho, state, U.S.	F3	89
Idaho City, Id., U.S.	F6	89
Idaho Falls, Id., U.S.	B5	83
Idaho Springs, Co., U.S.	B8	83
Idalia, Co., U.S.	C2	120
Idalou, Tx., U.S.	k10	125
Idamay, W.V., U.S.	C6	93
Idanha, Ks., U.S.	C4	114
Idanha, Or., U.S.	C2	22
Idanha-a-Nova, Port.	D2	19
Idar-Oberstein, W. Ger.	C4	91
Idaville, In., U.S.	B3	114
Idaville, Or., U.S.	D5	68
Iddesleigh, Alta.	D2	87
Ideal, Ga., U.S.	D6	118
Ideal, S.D., U.S.	C2	43
Idehan, des., Libya	A4	78
Idélès, Niger	B4	31
Ider, Al., U.S.	C2	41
Ider, stm., Mong.	C3	38
Idfu, Eg.	D4	25
Ídhra, Grc.	D4	25
Ídhra (Hydra), i., Grc.	D1	34
Idi, Indon.	C2	48
Idiofa, Zaire	C2	41
Idkū, Eg.	C2	41
Idkū Lake, l., Eg.	E5	99
Idlewild, Mi., U.S.	A3	119
Idlewild, Tn., U.S.	D3	114
Idleyld Park, Or., U.S.	E11	40
Idlib, Syria	D4	22
Illora, Spain	D4	22
Ilmen, Lake, l., Sov. Un.	B8	27
Ilmenau, E. Ger.	C5	18
Ilmenau, stm., W. Ger.	B5	18
Ilo, Peru	E3	58
Ilobu, Nig.	*E5	45
Iloilo, Phil.	C6	34
Ilorin, Nig.	E5	45
Ilovaysk, Sov. Un.	r21	27
Ilovlya, Sov. Un.	D2	28
Ilsenburg, E. Ger.	B5	19
Ilwaco, Wa., U.S.	C1	124
Ilwaki, Indon.	G7	34
Iłża, Pol.	C6	26
Imabari, Japan	I6	33
Imabetsu, Japan	F10	33
Imambaba, Japan	C11	31
Iman, stm., Sov. Un.	B11	31
Imandra, Lake, l., Sov. Un.	B15	8
Imatra, Fin.	*G13	14
Imazu, Japan	n14	33
Imbābah (part of Giza), Eg.	a2	58
Imbabura, prov., Ec.	A2	58
Imbituba, Braz.	C5	59
Imbler, Or., U.S.	B9	114
Imboden, Ar., U.S.	A4	81
Ime, Beinn, mtn., Scot., U.K.	D4	13
Imgyt Marsh, sw., Sov. Un.	E5	80
Imeni, Eth.	D5	47
Imilac, Chile	F2	55
Imlay, Nv., U.S.	C3	105
Imlay City, Mi., U.S.	E7	99
Imlaystown, N.J., U.S.	C3	107
Immeln, l., Swe.	B8	15
Immenstadt, W. Ger.	E5	18
Immokalee, Fl., U.S.	F5	86
Imnaha, Or., U.S.	B10	114
Imnaha, stm., Or., U.S.	B10	114
Imogene, Ia., U.S.	D2	92
Imola, Italy	B3	23
Imotski, Yugo.	D3	24
Imperatriz, Braz.	C1	57
Imperia, Italy	C2	23
Imperial, Sask.	F3	75
Imperial, Ca., U.S.	F6	82
Imperial, Mo., U.S.	C7	102
Imperial, Ne., U.S.	D4	104
Imperial, Pa., U.S.	k13	115
Imperial, Tx., U.S.	D1	120
Imperial, co., Ca., U.S.	F6	82
Imperial Beach, Ca., U.S.	o15	82
Imperial Dam, U.S.	E1	80
Imperial Mills, Alta.	B5	68
Imperial Reservoir, res., U.S.	E1	80
Imperial Valley, val., Ca., U.S.	F6	82
Impfondo, Congo	A2	48
Imphal, India	H9	36
Imst, Aus.	E5	18
'Imwās, Isr. Occ.	h11	41
Ina, Japan	n16	33
Ina, Il., U.S.	E5	90
Ina, stm., Pol.	B5	26
Ina, stm., Asia	B3	26
Ine, Japan	J6	33
Inebolu, Tur.	B9	40
İnegöl, Tur.	B7	40
Inez, Ky., U.S.	C7	94
Inez, Tx., U.S.	E4	120
Infanta, Phil.	o13	34
Infanta, Phil.	B3	34
Infantas, Col.	B3	60
Infiernillo, Presa del, res., Mex.	h6	51
Inga Dam, Zaire	C1	48
I-n-Gall, Niger	D6	45
In Azaoua, well, Niger	B6	45
Ikela, Zaire	B3	48
Ikerre, Nig.	*E6	45
Ikhtiman, Bul.	D6	24
Iki Island, i., Japan	J4	33
Ikire, Nig.	*E5	45
Ikirun, Nig.	*E5	45
Ikole, Nig.	*E6	45
Ikorodu, Nig.	*E5	45
Ikot Ekpene, Nig.	E5	45
Ila, Ga., U.S.	B3	87
Ila, Nig.	B6	34
Ilagan, Phil.	E3	39
Īlām, Iran	E4	18
Ilanz, Switz.	B6	102
Ilasco, Mo., U.S.	B5	26
Ilawa, Pol.	*E6	45
Ilawe-Ekiti, Nig.	B4	97
Ilchester, Md., U.S.	D3	73
Ilderton, Ont.	m7	75
Île-à-la-Crosse, Sask.	B2	75
Île-à-la-Crosse, Lac, l., Sask.	B3	48
Ilebo (Port-Francqui), Zaire	C5	16
Île-de-France, hist. reg., Fr.	E20	
Ilek, stm., Sov. Un.	q19	74
Île-Perrot, Que.	A6	48
Ileret, Kenya	B6	68
Îles, Lac des, l., Sask.	E5	45
Ilesha, Nig.	B4	108
Ilfeld, N.M., U.S.	A4	70
Ilford, Man.	E4	10
Ilfracombe, Eng., U.K.	C8	40
Ilgin, Tur.	B1	22
Ilhavo, Port.	D3	57
Ilhéus, Braz.	E10	29
Ili, stm., Asia	D8	79
Iliamna, Ak., U.S.	D8	79
Iliamna Lake, l., Ak., U.S.	C9	79
Iliamna Volcano, vol., Ak., U.S.	A7	83
Iliff, Co., U.S.	g10	
Iliki, Lake, l., Grc.	I13	27
Ilinskaya, Sov. Un.	C4	25
Iliodhrómia, i., Grc.	B5	109
Ilion, N.Y., U.S.	B4	88
Ilio Point, c., Hi., U.S.	*D4	25
Ilioúpolis, Grc.	B6	12
Ilkeston, Eng., U.K.	G7	13
Ilkley, Eng., U.K.	E4	18
Ill, stm., Aus.	C2	55
Illampu, Nevado, mtn., Bol.	D6	34
Illana Bay, b., Phil.	A2	54
Illapel, Chile	F5	16
Ille, Fr.	D6	45
Illéla, Niger	D5	18
Iller, stm., W. Ger.	A3	21
Illertissen, W. Ger.	C4	16
Illiers, Fr.	C4	90
Illinois, state, U.S.	A7	113
Illinois, stm., Il., U.S.	B5	90
Illinois, stm., Or., U.S.	B3	90
Illinois City, Il., U.S.	B3	89
Illinois Peak, mtn., Id., U.S.	D4	90
Illiopolis, Il., U.S.	F7	17
Illkirch-Graffenstaden, Fr.	In Belbel, Alg.	D5	44
Ince, Spain	C7	22
Incastro, stm., Italy	h9	23
Ince, Cape, c., Tur.	A10	40
Incesu, Tur.	C10	40
Inchard, Loch, b., Scot., U.K.	B3	13
Inchelium, Wa., U.S.	A7	124
Inch'ŏn, S. Kor.	D10	31
Incline Village, Nv., U.S.	D2	105
Indaiatuba, Braz.	m8	56
Indalsälven, stm., Swe.	F7	14
Indaw, Burma	D10	36
Independence, Ca., U.S.	D4	82
Independence, In., U.S.	D3	91
Independence, Ia., U.S.	B6	92
Independence, Ks., U.S.	E8	93
Independence, Ky., U.S.	B5	94
Independence, La., U.S.	D5	95
Independence, Mo., U.S.	B3	102
Independence, Oh., U.S.	*h9	112
Independence, Or., U.S.	C3	114
Independence, Va., U.S.	D1	123
Independence, Wi., U.S.	D2	126
Independence, co., Ar., U.S.	B4	81
Independence, stm., N.Y., U.S.	B5	109
Independence Mountains, mts., Nv., U.S.	C5	105
Independence National Historical Park, Pa., U.S.	p21	115
Independence Rock, mtn., Wy., U.S.	D5	127
Independencia, Bol.	C2	55
Inderborskiy, Sov. Un.	D4	28
Index, Wa., U.S.	B4	124
India, ctry., Asia	D6	36
Indiahoma, Ok., U.S.	C3	113
Indian, stm., Ont.	B7	73
Indian, stm., De., U.S.	F4	85
Indian, stm., Mi., U.S.	B4	99
Indian, stm., N.Y., U.S.	A5	109
Indiana, Pa., U.S.	E3	115
Indiana, co., Pa., U.S.	E3	115
Indiana, state, U.S.	E5	91
Indiana Dunes National Lakeshore, In., U.S.	A3	91
Indian Agency, Co., U.S.	E5	83
Indian Bay, b., Fl., U.S.	E5	91
Indian Beach, De., U.S.	D4	86
Indian Brook, N.S.	C9	71
Indian Cedar Swamp, sw., R.I., U.S.	F2	116
Indian Cove, Ct., U.S.	*D4	84
Indian Creek, stm., In., U.S.	H5	91
Indian Creek, stm., Md., U.S.	C3	97
Indian Creek, stm., Oh., U.S.	C1	112
Indian Creek, stm., S.D., U.S.	B3	118
Indian Creek, stm., Tn., U.S.	B3	119
Indian Creek, stm., W.V., U.S.	k9	125
Indian Creek, stm., W.V., U.S.	D4	125
Indian Grave Mountain, hill, Ga., U.S.	C2	87
Indian Harbour Beach, Fl., U.S.	*D6	86
Indian Head, Sask.	G4	75
Indian Head, Md., U.S.	C3	97
Indian Heights, In., U.S.	*D5	91
Indian Hills, Co., U.S.	*B5	83
Indian Lake, N.Y., U.S.	B6	109
Indian Lake, l., Mi., U.S.	C4	99
Indian Lake, l., N.Y., U.S.	B6	109
Indian Lake, l., Oh., U.S.	*E5	112
Indian Lake, l., R.I., U.S.	F4	116
Indian Lake Shores, R.I., U.S.	F4	116
Indian Mound, Tn., U.S.	A4	119
Indian Mound Beach, Ma., U.S.	C6	98
Indian Mountain, mtn., Ct., U.S.	B2	84
Indian Neck, Ct., U.S.	D4	84
Indian Ocean	G2	2
Indianola, Il., U.S.	D6	90
Indianola, Ia., U.S.	C4	92
Indianola, Ms., U.S.	B3	101
Indianola, Ne., U.S.	D5	104
Indianola, Pa., U.S.	B15	8
Indianópolis, Braz.	*G13	14
Indian Peak, mtn., Ut., U.S.	E2	121
Indian Peak, mtn., Wy., U.S.	B3	127
Indian Pond, l., Me., U.S.	C3	96
Indian Pond, l., Me., U.S.	D3	96
Indian Prairie Canal, Fl., U.S.	E5	86
Indian River, Ont.	C6	73
Indian River, Me., U.S.	D5	96
Indian River, Mi., U.S.	C6	99
Indian River, co., Fl., U.S.	E6	86
Indian River, b., Fl., U.S.	D6	86
Indian River Bay, b., De., U.S.	F5	85
Indian Rock, mtn., Wa., U.S.	D5	124
Indian Rocks Beach, Fl., U.S.	p10	86
Indian Springs, Ga., U.S.	C3	87
Indian Springs, In., U.S.	G4	91
Indian Springs, Nv., U.S.	G6	105
Indian Stream, stm., N.H., U.S.	f7	106
Indiantown, Fl., U.S.	E6	86
Indian Trail, N.C., U.S.	B2	110
Indian Valley, Id., U.S.	E2	89
Indian Valley, Va., U.S.	D2	123
Indian Village, Ks., U.S.	E8	93
Indian Village, In., U.S.	D3	91
Indian Wells, Az., U.S.	B5	80
Indiaporã, Braz.	B3	56
Indigirka, stm., Sov. Un.	C17	29
Indio, Ca., U.S.	F5	82
Indio, stm., Pan.	k10	62
Indochina, reg., Asia	B3	34
Indonesia, ctry., Asia	F5	34
Indore, India	B6	36
Indragiri, stm., Indon.	F2	34
Indramayu, Indon.	G3	34
Indrāvati, stm., India	E7	36
Indus, Mn., U.S.	B5	100
Indus, stm., Asia	C3	36
Industry, Il., U.S.	C3	90
Ine, Japan	n14	33
Inebolu, Tur.	B9	40
İnegöl, Tur.	*B7	40
Inez, Ky., U.S.	C7	94
Inez, Tx., U.S.	E4	120
Infanta, Phil.	o13	34
Infanta, Phil.	B3	34
Infantas, Col.	B3	60
Infiernillo, Presa del, res., Mex.	h6	51
Inga Dam, Zaire	C1	48
I-n-Gall, Niger	D6	45
In Azaoua, well, Niger	B6	45
Ingalls, Ar., U.S.	D3	81
Ingalls, In., U.S.	E6	91
Ingalls, Ks., U.S.	E3	93
Ingalls, Mi., U.S.	C3	99
Ingalls, Ok., U.S.	A5	113
Ingalls Park, Il., U.S.	B5	90
Ingelheim, W. Ger.	D3	19
Ingende, Zaire	B2	48
Ingeniero Jacobacci, Arg.	C3	54
Ingeniero Luiggi, Arg.	B4	54
Ingenika, stm., B.C.	A5	69
Inger, Mn., U.S.	C5	100
Ingersheim, Fr.	A3	20
Ingersoll, Ont.	A3	113
Ingham, Austl.	C4	50
Ingham, co., Mi., U.S.	F6	99
Ingleside, Md., U.S.	B6	97
Ingleside, Ont.	D5	73
Ingleside, Ca., U.S.	F4	120
Ingleside, Tx., U.S.	B6	125
Inglewood, Ont.	D5	73
Inglewood, N.Z.	M15	51
Inglewood, Ca., U.S.	n12	82
Inglewood, Ne., U.S.	C9	104
Inglewood, Tx., U.S.	*B3	124
Inglis, Man.	D1	70
Ingoda, stm., Sov. Un.	B7	31
Ingold, N.C., U.S.	C4	110
Ingoldsby, Ont.	C6	73
Ingolf, Ont.	A4	70
Ingolstadt, W. Ger.	D5	18
Ingomar, Ms., U.S.	A4	101
Ingomar, Mt., U.S.	D9	103
Ingonish, N.S.	C9	71
Ingonish Beach, N.S.	C9	71
Ingornachoix Bay, b., Newf.	C3	72
Ingraham, Il., U.S.	E5	90
Ingram, Pa., U.S.	k13	115
Ingram, Wi., U.S.	C3	126
Ingram, Tx., U.S.	A5	109
Ingrid Christensen Coast, Ant.	C20	7
In Guezzam, Alg.	F6	44
Ingul, stm., Sov. Un.	H9	27
Ingulets, stm., Sov. Un.	H9	27
Inhambane, Moz.	B6	49
Inhambane, dept., Moz.	B5	49
Inhambane, Baía de, b., Moz.	B6	49
Inhambupe, Braz.	D3	57
Inhaminga, Moz.	A5	49
Inharrime, Moz.	B6	49
Inhuçu, Braz.	B2	57
Inhumas, Braz.	B3	56
Inírida, stm., Col.	C4	60
Inisa, Nig.	*E5	45
Inishark, i., Ire.	D1	11
Inishbofin, i., Ire.	D1	10
Inishcrone, Ire.	D2	11
Inishkea Islands, is., Ire.	C1	11
Inishmaan, i., Ire.	D2	11
Inishmore, i., Ire.	D1	11
Inishmurray, i., Ire.	C2	11
Inishowen Head, c., Ire.	B5	11
Inishtooskert, i., Ire.	E1	11
Inishtrahull, rock, Ire.	C3	10
Inishturk, i., Ire.	D1	11
Inishvickillane, i., Ire.	E1	11
Inistioge, Ire.	E4	11
Injune, Austl.	B7	51
Inkerman, N.B.	A5	51
Inkom, Id., U.S.	G6	89
Inkster, Mi., U.S.	p15	99
Inkster, N.D., U.S.	A8	111
Inland, Ne., U.S.	D7	104
Inle Lake, l., Burma	B2	35
Inlet, N.Y., U.S.	B6	109
Inman, Ga., U.S.	C2	87
Inman, Ks., U.S.	D6	93
Inman, Ne., U.S.	B7	104
Inman, S.C., U.S.	A3	117
Inn, stm., Eur.	D6	18
Inner Hebrides, is., Scot., U.K.	E5	13
Inner Mongolia (Nei Mongol), prov., China	C7	31
Inner Sound, strt., Scot., U.K.	B4	10
Innisfail, Austl.	C8	50
Innisfail, Alta.	C4	68
Innisfree, Alta.	C5	68
Inniswold, La., U.S.	*D4	95
Innokentyevskiy, Sov. Un.	B10	33
Innsbruck, Aus.	E5	18
Inny, stm., Ire.	C4	11
Ino, Japan	J6	33
Inola, Ok., U.S.	A6	113
Inongo, Zaire	B2	48
Inowrocław, Pol.	B5	26
Ins, Switz.	B3	21
In Salah, Alg.	D5	44
Inscription House Ruin, hist., Az., U.S.	A5	80
Insein, Burma	E10	36
Insinger, Sask.	F4	75
Inspiration, Az., U.S.	D5	80
Institute, W.V., U.S.	m12	125
Instow, Sask.	H1	75
Inta, Sov. Un.	D8	28
Intercession City, Fl., U.S.	D5	86
Interior, S.D., U.S.	D4	118
Interlachen, Fl., U.S.	C5	86
Interlaken, Switz.	E3	18
Interlaken, Ma., U.S.	*B1	98
Interlaken, N.Y., U.S.	C4	109
International Falls, Mn., U.S.	B5	100
International Peace Garden, N.A.	A5	111
Intersection Mountain, mtn., Can.	C8	69
Intervale, N.H., U.S.	B4	106
Intiyaco, Arg.	B4	54
Intracoastal City, La., U.S.	E3	95
Intracoastal Waterway, U.S.	E4	95
Intuto, Peru	B3	58
Inukjuak, Que.	g11	74
Inútil, Bahía, b., Chile	h12	55
Inuvik, N.W. Ter.	h12	66
Inver Bay, b., Ire.	C3	11
Inverbervie, Scot., U.K.	E6	13
Invercargill, N.Z.	Q12	51
Inverell, Austl.	E9	50
Invergarry, Scot., U.K.	C4	13
Invergordon, Scot., U.K.	C5	13
Inver Grove Heights, Mn., U.S.	n12	100
Invermay, Sask.	F4	75
Invermere, B.C.	D9	69
Inverness, N.S.	C8	71
Inverness, Scot., U.K.	B4	10
Inverness, Al., U.S.	C4	78
Inverness, Ca., U.S.	C2	82
Inverness, Fl., U.S.	D4	86
Inverness, Il., U.S.	*A5	90
Inverness, Ms., U.S.	B3	101
Inverness, Mt., U.S.	B6	103
Inverness, co., N.S.	C8	71
Inverurie, Scot., U.K.	C6	13
Invisible Mountain, mtn., Id., U.S.	F5	89
Inwood, Man.	D3	70
Inwood, Ont.	E3	73
Inwood, Fl., U.S.	*D5	86
Inwood, Ia., U.S.	A1	92
Inwood, N.Y., U.S.	k13	109
Inwood, W.V., U.S.	B6	125
Inwood, Vt., U.S.	C4	122
Inyanga, Zimb.	A5	49
Inyangani, mtn., Zimb.	A5	49
Inyan Kara Creek, stm., Wy., U.S.	B8	127
Inyan Kara Mountain, mtn., Wy., U.S.	B8	127
Inyo, co., Ca., U.S.	D5	82
Inyo, Mount, mtn., Ca., U.S.	D5	82
Inyokern, Ca., U.S.	E5	82
Inyo Mountains, mts., Ca., U.S.	D4	82
Inyonga, Tan.	E16	27
Inza, Sov. Un.	B5	69
Inzana Lake, l., B.C.	C3	69
Ioánnina, Grc.	D18	14
Iokanga, Sov. Un.	E5	90
Iola, Il., U.S.	E8	93
Iola, Ks., U.S.	D4	126
Iola, Wi., U.S.	D9	71
Iona, N.S.	F7	89
Iona, Id., U.S.	G3	100
Iona, Mn., U.S.	D2	107
Iona, N.J., U.S.	D6	118
Iona, S.D., U.S.	D2	13
Iona, i., Scot., U.K.	C3	82
Ione, Ca., U.S.	A6	83
Ione, Co., U.S.	E4	105
Ione, Nv., U.S.	B7	114
Ione, Or., U.S.	A8	124
Ione, Wa., U.S.	A5	92
Ionia, Ia., U.S.	F5	99
Ionia, Mi., U.S.	C4	102
Ionia, Mo., U.S.	F5	99
Ionia, co., Mi., U.S.	C3	25
Ionian Islands, is., Grc.	H12	14
Ionian Sea, Eur.	D5	40
Íos, i., Grc.	D7	99
Iosco, co., Mi., U.S.	B2	68
Iosegun, stm., Alta.	D3	95
Iota, La., U.S.	D2	95
Iowa, La., U.S.	C5	92
Iowa, co., Ia., U.S.	E3	126
Iowa, co., Wi., U.S.	C4	92
Iowa, state, U.S.	B4	92
Iowa, West Branch, stm., Ia., U.S.	C6	92
Iowa City, Ia., U.S.	B4	92
Iowa Falls, Ia., U.S.	A3	92
Iowa Indian Reservation, U.S.	A3	92
Iowa Lake, l., U.S.	C3	120
Iowa Park, Tx., U.S.	B3	56
Ipameri, Braz.	C3	90
Ipava, Il., U.S.	D5	26
Ipel' (Ipoly), stm., Eur.	C2	60
Ipiales, Col.	D3	57
Ipiaú, Braz.	D3	57
Ipirá, Braz.	E2	34
Ipoh, Malay.	D5	26
Ipoly (Ipel'), stm., Eur.	D4	46
Ippy, Cen. Afr. Rep.	D6	18
ipsala, Tur.	E9	50
Ipswich, Austl.	D7	10
Ipswich, Eng., U.K.	A6	98
Ipswich, Ma., U.S.	B6	118
Ipswich, S.D., U.S.	A5	98
Ipswich, stm., Ma., U.S.	B2	57
Ipu, Braz.	B2	57
Ipueiras, Braz.	D19	66
Iqaluit, N.W. Ter.	D1	55
Iquique, Chile	B3	58
Iquitos, Peru	C4	92
Ira, Tx., U.S.	C2	120
Ira, Vt., U.S.	D2	122
Iraan, Tx., U.S.	D2	120
Iracoubo, Fr. Gu.	A4	59
Iraí, Braz.	D2	56
Íráklion (Candia), Grc.	E5	40
Irala, Para.	B5	55
Iran, ctry., Asia	B5	38
Iran, Plateau of, plat., Asia	C6	38
Iran Mountains, mts., Asia	E4	34
Īrānshahr, Iran	H10	39
Irapa, Ven.	A5	60
Irapuato, Mex.	C4	63
Iraq, ctry., Asia	B4	38
Irasburg, Vt., U.S.	B4	122
Irasville, Vt., U.S.	C3	122
Irazú, Volcán, vol., C.R.	F6	62
Irbid, Jord.	B3	38
Irbil, Iraq	B4	38
Irebu, Zaire	B2	48
Iredell, co., N.C., U.S.	B2	110
Ireland, In., U.S.	H3	91
Ireland, ctry., Eur.	D3	10
Ireland Island, i., Ber.	p19	64
Irene, S.D., U.S.	D8	118
Ireton, Ia., U.S.	B1	92
Irgiz, stm., Sov. Un.	D6	28
Irgiz, Sov. Un.	D6	28
Iri, S. Kor.	I3	33
Irian Jaya, prov., Indon.	F9	34
Iriba, Chad	B4	46
Iriklinskoye Reservoir, res., Sov. Un.	C5	28
Iringa, Tan.	C6	48
Iriomote Island, i., Japan	G9	31
Iriona, Hond.	C5	62
Irion, co., Tx., U.S.	D2	120
Iriri, stm., Braz.	C4	59
Irish, Mount, mtn., Nv., U.S.	F6	105
Irish Sea, Eur.	D4	10
Irkutsk, Sov. Un.	D13	29
Irma, Alta.	C5	68
Irmo, S.C., U.S.	C5	117
Irō, Cape, c., Japan	I9	33
Iron, co., Mi., U.S.	C6	100
Iron, co., Mo., U.S.	D7	102
Iron, co., Ut., U.S.	F2	121
Iron, co., Wi., U.S.	B3	126

Name — Map Ref. — Page

Iron Belt, Wi., U.S. B3 126
Iron City, Ga., U.S. E2 87
Iron City, Tn., U.S. B4 119
Irondale, Al., U.S. f7 78
Irondale, Mo., U.S. D7 102
Irondale, Oh., U.S. B5 112
Irondequoit, N.Y., U.S. B3 109
Iron Gate, Va., U.S. C3 123
Iron Gate, val., Eur. C6 24
Iron Gate Reservoir, res., Eur. C5 24
Iron Gate Reservoir, res., Ca., U.S. B2 82
Ironia, N.J., U.S. B3 107
Iron Lightning, S.D., U.S. B4 118
Iron Mountain, Mi., U.S. C2 99
Iron Mountain, Mo., U.S. D7 102
Iron Mountain, Wy., U.S. E7 127
Iron Mountain, mtn., Az., U.S. D4 80
Iron Mountains, mts., U.S. D1 123
Iron Ridge, Wi., U.S. E5 126
Iron River, Mi., U.S. B2 99
Iron River, Wi., U.S. B2 126
Irons, Mi., U.S. D5 99
Ironside, Que. h12 73
Ironside, Or., U.S. C9 114
Ironspot, Oh., U.S. C3 112
Iron Springs, Az., U.S. C3 80
Ironton, Mn., U.S. D5 100
Ironton, Mo., U.S. D7 102
Ironton, Oh., U.S. D3 112
Ironwood, Mi., U.S. n11 99
Iroquois, Ont. C9 73
Iroquois, Il., U.S. C6 90
Iroquois, S.D., U.S. C8 118
Iroquois, co., Il., U.S. C6 90
Iroquois, stm., U.S. C6 90
Iroquois, Lake, l., Vt., U.S. B2 122
Iroquois Falls, Ont. o19 73
Irrawaddy see Ayeyarwady, stm., Burma D10 36
Irricana, Alta. D4 68
Irrigon, Or., U.S. B7 114
Irt, stm., Eng., U.K. F5 13
Irthing, stm., Eng., U.K. F6 13
Irtysh, Sov. Un. C8 28
Irtysh, stm., Sov. Un. D9 29
Irumu, Zaire A4 48
Irún, Spain A5 22
Irvine, Alta. E5 68
Irvine, Scot., U.K. C4 10
Irvine, Ca., U.S. n13 82
Irvine, Fl., U.S. C4 86
Irvine, Ky., U.S. C6 94
Irvine, Pa., U.S. C3 115
Irvine, stm., Scot., U.K. E4 13
Irvines Landing, B.C. E5 69
Irving, Il., U.S. D4 90
Irving, Tx., U.S. n10 120
Irvington, Al., U.S. E1 78
Irvington, Il., U.S. E4 90
Irvington, Ky., U.S. C3 94
Irvington, Ne., U.S. g12 104
Irvington, N.J., U.S. k8 107
Irvington, N.Y., U.S. g13 109
Irvington, Va., U.S. C6 123
Irvona, Pa., U.S. E4 115
Irwin, Id., U.S. F7 89
Irwin, Ia., U.S. C2 92
Irwin, Pa., U.S. F2 115
Irwin, co., Ga., U.S. E3 87
Irwinton, Ga., U.S. D3 87
Irwinville, Ga., U.S. E3 87
Isa, Nig. D6 45
Isaac Lake, l., B.C. C7 69
Isaacs Harbour, N.S. D8 71
Isabel, Ks., U.S. E5 93
Isabel, S.D., U.S. B4 118
Isabel, Bahía, b., Ec. g5 58
Isabel, Mount, mtn., Wy., U.S. D2 127
Isabela, Phil. D6 34
Isabela, P.R. A1 65
Isabela, Isla (Albemarle Island), i., Ec. g5 58
Isabelia, Cordillera, mts., Nic. D5 62
Isabella, Man. D1 70
Isabella, Ga., U.S. E3 87
Isabella, Mn., U.S. C7 100
Isabella, Mo., U.S. E5 102
Isabella, Ok., U.S. A3 113
Isabella, Pa., U.S. G2 115
Isabella, Tn., U.S. D9 119
Isabella, co., Mi., U.S. E6 99
Isabella Indian Reservation, Mi., U.S. E6 99
Isabella Lake, l., Mn., U.S. C7 100
Isaccea, Rom. C9 24
Isachsen, N.W. Ter. m31 66
Ísafjarðardjúp, Ice. m21 14
Ísafjörður, Ice. m21 14
Isahaya, Japan J5 33
Isaka, Zaire B2 48
Isana (Içana), stm., S.A. C4 60
Isanga, Zaire B3 48
Isangi, Zaire A3 48
Isanti, Mn., U.S. E5 100
Isanti, co., Mn., U.S. E5 100
Isar, stm., Eur. D6 18
Isarco, stm., Italy A3 23
ʿĪsāwīyah, Isr. Occ. m14 41
ʿĪsāwīyah, Sau. Ar. G12 40
Isbergues, Fr. D2 17
Isbister, stm., Man. C4 70
Ischgl, Aus. B9 21
Ischia, i., Italy D4 23
Ischua, N.Y., U.S. C2 109
Ise (Uji-yamada), Japan I8 33
Ise, stm., W. Ger. F4 15
Ise Bay, b., Japan o15 33
Isefjord, b., Den. C5 15
Isel, stm., Aus. E6 18
Iselin, N.J., U.S. B4 107
Iselin, Pa., U.S. E3 115
Isen, stm., W. Ger. A8 20
Isenthal, Switz. C6 21
Iseo, Lake, l., Italy B3 23
Isère, dept., Fr. D1 20
Isère, stm., Fr. E6 16
Iserlohn, W. Ger. B2 19
Isernia, Italy D5 23
Isesaki, Japan H9 33
Iseyin, Nig. E5 45
Isfahan see Eşfahān, Iran B5 38
Ishikari Bay, b., Japan E10 33
Ishikawa, Japan O5 52
Ishim, Sov. Un. D9 29
Ishim, stm., Sov. Un. D9 29
Ishimbay, Sov. Un. C5 28
Ishinomaki, Japan D13 31
Ishioka, Japan m19 33
Ishpeming, Mi., U.S. B3 99
Isigny-sur-Mer, Fr. C3 16
Isil-Kul, Sov. Un. C8 28
Isinglass, stm., N.H., U.S. D4 106
Isiolo, Kenya A6 48
Isiro, Zaire A4 48
Isisford, Austl. B5 51
İskenderun (Alexandretta), Tur. D11 40
İskilip, Tur. B10 40
Iskitim, Sov. Un. E25 8
Iskŭr, stm., Bul. D6 24
Iskushuban, Som. C7 47
Iskwatikan Lake, l., Sask. B3 75
Isla Cristina, Spain D2 22
Islāmābād, Pak. B5 36
Islamorada, Fl., U.S. H6 86
Island, Ky., U.S. C2 94
Island, co., Wa., U.S. A3 124
Island Beach, N.J., U.S. D4 107
Island-Brook, Que. D6 74
Island City, Or., U.S. B8 114
Island Creek, Ma., U.S. *B6 98
Island Falls, Sask. B4 75
Island Falls, Me., U.S. B4 96
Island Grove, Fl., U.S. C4 86
Island Heights, N.J., U.S. D4 107
Island Lake, Man. C4 70
Island Lake, l., Man. C4 70
Island Lake, stm., Man. B4 70
Island Park, Id., U.S. E7 89
Island Park, N.Y., U.S. *E7 109
Island Park, R.I., U.S. E6 116
Island Park Reservoir, res., Id., U.S. E7 89
Island Pond, Vt., U.S. B5 122
Island Pond, l., N.H., U.S. E4 106
Islands, Bay of, b., Newf. D2 72
Islands, Bay of, b., N.Z. K15 51
Isla Vista, Ca., U.S. E4 82
Islay, Alta. C5 68
Islay, i., Scot., U.K. C3 10
Islay, Sound of, strt., Scot., U.K. E3 13
Isle, Mn., U.S. D5 100
Isle, stm., Fr. E4 16
Isle au Haut, Me., U.S. D4 96
Isle-aux-Morts, Newf. E2 72
Isle La Motte, Vt., U.S. B2 122
Isle of Man, ctry., Eur. C4 10
Isle of Palms, S.C., U.S. k12 117
Isle of Wight, Va., U.S. D6 123
Isle of Wight, co., Eng., U.K. D6 12
Isle of Wight, co., Va., U.S. D6 123
Isle of Wight Bay, b., Md., U.S. D7 97
Isle Pierre, B.C. C6 69
Isle Royale National Park, Mi., U.S. h9 99
Islesboro, Me., U.S. D4 96
Islesboro Island, i., Me., U.S. D4 96
Islesford, Me., U.S. D4 96
Isleta, N.M., U.S. C3 108
Isleta Indian Reservation, N.M., U.S. C3 108
Isleton, Ca., U.S. C3 82
Islington, Ma., U.S. h11 98
Islip, N.Y., U.S. *n15 109
Islip Terrace, N.Y., U.S. *n15 109
Ismael Cortinas, Ur. f5 54
Ismailia, Eg. B3 38
Ismāʿīlīyah Canal, Eg. D3 41
Ismay, Mt., U.S. D12 103
Isnā, Eg. C3 38
Isny, W. Ger. A9 21
Isoka, Zam. D5 48
Isola, Ms., U.S. B3 101
Isola della Scala, Italy D7 20
Isola di Capo Rizzuto, Italy E6 23
Isonzo, stm., Eur. A4 23
Isparta, Tur. D8 40
İspir, Tur. B13 40
Israel, ctry., Asia B3 38
Israel, stm., N.H., U.S. B3 106
Israeli Occupied Areas, dep., Asia B7 41
Issano, Guy. A3 59
Issaquah, Wa., U.S. B3 124
Issaquena, co., Ms., U.S. C2 101
Issia, I.C. E3 45
Issoire, Fr. E5 16
Issoudun, Fr. D4 16
Issuna, Tan. C5 48
Issy, Fr. g10 16
Issyk-Kul, Lake, l., Sov. Un. E10 29
Istachatta, Fl., U.S. D4 86
Īstādeh-ye Moqor, Āb-e, l., Afg. B4 36
İstanbul (Constantinople) (Byzantium), Tur. B7 40
Istiaía, Grc. C4 25
Istmina, Col. B2 60
Isto, Mount, mtn., Ak., U.S. B11 79
Istokpoga, Lake, l., Fl., U.S. E5 86
Istranca Mountains, mts., Tur. B6 25
Istres, Fr. F6 16
Istrian Peninsula, pen., Yugo. C1 24
Itá, Braz. D2 56
Itá, Para. E4 55
Itabaiana, Braz. C3 57
Itabaiana, Braz. D3 57
Itabaianinha, Braz. D3 57
Itabapoana, stm., Braz. C4 56
Itaberaba, Braz. D2 57
Itaberaí, Braz. B3 56
Itabira, Braz. B4 56
Itaboraí, Braz. C4 56
Itabuna, Braz. D3 57
Itacaiunas, stm., Braz. D4 59
Itacoatiara, Braz. C3 59
Itacuaí, stm., Braz. C3 58
Itaetê, Braz. D2 57
Itaguaçu, Braz. B4 56
Itaguaí, Braz. h6 56
Itaguara, Braz. C4 56
Itaguaru, Braz. B3 56
Itagüí, Col. *B2 60
Itaí, Braz. C3 56
Itaituba, Braz. C3 59
Itajá, Braz. B2 56
Itajaí, Braz. D3 56
Itajubá, Braz. C3 56
Italy, Tx., U.S. C4 120
Italy, ctry., Eur. C4 23
Italy Cross, N.S. E5 71
Itamaracá, Ilha de, i., Braz. h6 57
Itamarandiba, Braz. B4 56
Itambacuri, Braz. B4 56
Itambé, Braz. B4 56
Itami, Japan o14 33
Itanhaém, Braz. n8 56
Itapaci, Braz. A3 56
Itapagipe, Braz. B3 56
Itapecuru, stm., Braz. B2 57
Itapecuru-Mirim, Braz. B2 57
Itapemirim, Braz. C4 56
Itaperuna, Braz. C4 56
Itapetininga, Braz. C3 56
Itapetininga, stm., Braz. m7 56
Itapeva, Braz. C3 56
Itapicuru, stm., Braz. D3 57
Itapipoca, Braz. B3 57
Itapira, Braz. m8 56
Itapiranga, Braz. C3 59
Itapirapuã, Braz. B2 56
Itápolis, Braz. k7 56
Itaporã, Braz. C2 56
Itaporanga, Braz. C3 57
Itapúa, dept., Para. E4 55
Itapuranga, Braz. B2 56
Itaqui, Braz. D1 56
Itararé, Braz. C3 56
Itararé, stm., Braz. C3 56
Itārsi, India F6 37
Itasca, Il., U.S. k8 90
Itasca, Tx., U.S. C4 120
Itasca, co., Mn., U.S. C5 100
Itasca, Lake, l., Mn., U.S. C3 100
Itatiaia National Park, Braz. h5 56
Itatiba, Braz. m8 56
Itatinga, Braz. m7 56
Itaúna, Braz. C4 56
Itawamba, co., Ms., U.S. A5 101
Itéa, Grc. C4 25
Iténez (Guaporé), stm., S.A. B3 55
Itenhém, Braz. B4 56
Ithaca, Mi., U.S. E6 99
Ithaca, Ne., U.S. g11 104
Ithaca, N.Y., U.S. C4 109
Ithaca see Itháki, i., Grc. C3 25
Itháki, Grc. C3 25
Itháki (Ithaca), i., Grc. C3 25
Itigi, Tan. C5 48
Itimbiri, stm., Zaire A3 48
Itinga, Braz. B4 56
Itiquira, Braz. B2 56
Itiquira, stm., Braz. *B1 56
Itiquira, stm., Braz. B1 56
Itirapina, Braz. m8 56
Itō, Japan o18 33
Itoigawa, Japan H8 33
Itoko, Zaire B3 48
Itoman, Japan O5 52
Itta Bena, Ms., U.S. B3 101
Itu, Braz. C3 56
Ituango, Col. B2 60
Ituí, stm., Braz. B3 58
Ituiutaba, Braz. B3 56
Itumbiara, Braz. B3 56
Ituna, Sask. F4 75
Ituporanga, Braz. D3 56
Iturama, Braz. B2 56
Ituverava, Braz. C3 56
Ituxi, stm., Braz. C4 58
Ityāy al Bārūd, Eg. D2 41
Itzehoe, W. Ger. B4 18
Iuka, Il., U.S. E5 90
Iuka, Ks., U.S. E5 93
Iuka, Ms., U.S. A5 101
Iva, S.C., U.S. C2 117
Iva, W. Sam. F11 52
Ivaí, stm., Braz. C2 56
Ivalo, Fin. C12 14
Ivan, Ar., U.S. D3 81
Ivangrad, Yugo. D4 24
Ivanhoe, Austl. F5 51
Ivanhoe, Mn., U.S. F2 100
Ivanhoe, N.C., U.S. C4 110
Ivanhoe, Va., U.S. D2 123
Ivanić Grad, Yugo. C3 24
Ivano-Frankovsk, Sov. Un. G5 27
Ivanovichi, Sov. Un. D7 33
Ivanovka, Sov. Un. q21 27
Ivanovka, Sov. Un. A4 33
Ivanovo, Sov. Un. D7 29
Ivanteyevka, Sov. Un. n17 27
Ivato, Madag. g9 49
Ivaylovgrad, Bul. E8 24
Ivdel, Sov. Un. A6 28
Ivesdale, Il., U.S. D5 90
Ives Estates, Fl., U.S. *G6 86
Ivigtut, Grnld. C19 128
Ivinheima, stm., Braz. C2 56
Ivins, Ut., U.S. F2 121
Ivohibe, Madag. h9 49
Ivor, Va., U.S. D6 123
Ivory Coast, ctry., Afr. E3 45
Ivoryton, Ct., U.S. D6 84
Ivösjön, l., Swe. B8 15
Ivrea, Italy B1 23
Ivry-Nord, Que. C3 74
Ivry-sur-Seine, Fr. g10 16
Ivujivik, Que. f11 74
Ivy, Va., U.S. B4 123
Ivydale, W.V., U.S. C3 125
Ivy Mountain, mtn., Ct., U.S. B3 84
Ivyton, Ky., U.S. C7 94
Ivywild, Co., U.S. C6 83
Iwaki (Taira), Japan H10 33
Iwaki, Mount, mtn., Japan F10 33
Iwakuni, Japan I6 33
Iwamizawa, Japan E10 33
Iwanai, Japan E10 33
Iwate, Mount, mtn., Japan G10 33
Iwo, Nig. E5 45
Iwo Jima, i., Japan E8 6
Iwŏn, N. Kor. F4 33
Ixelles (Elsene), Bel. *D4 17
Ixiamas, Bol. B2 55
Ixmiquilpan, Mex. m14 63
Ixtacalco (part of Mexico City), Mex. h9 63
Ixtapa, Punta, c., Mex. D4 63
Ixtapalapa (part of Mexico City), Mex. h9 63
Ixtlán de Juárez, Mex. o15 63
Ixtlán del Río, Mex. C4 63
Izabal, Lago de, l., Guat. D7 63
Īzad Khvāst, Iran F6 39
Izamal, Mex. C7 63
Izard, co., Ar., U.S. A4 81
Izberbash, Sov. Un. E3 28
Izegem, Bel. D3 17
Izena Island, i., Japan N5 52
Izhevsk (Ustinov), Sov. Un. D8 29
Izhma, stm., Sov. Un. C19 8
Izmail, Sov. Un. I7 27
İzmir (Smyrna), Tur. C6 40
İzmir, Gulf of, b., Tur. C6 25
İzmit (Kocaeli) (Nicomedia), Tur. B7 40
İznik (Nicaea), Tur. B7 40
İznik Lake, l., Tur. B7 25
Izozog, Bañados de, sw., Bol. C3 55
Izraʿ, Syria B8 41
Iztaccíhuatl, vol., Mex. n14 63
Izúcar de Matamoros, Mex. n14 63
Izuhara, Japan I4 33
Izu Islands, is., Japan D8 6
Izumo, Japan I6 33
Izyum, Sov. Un. G11 27

J

Jabal al Awliyā', Sud. B3 47
Jabalón, stm., Spain C4 22
Jabalpur, India D6 36
Jabālyah, Isr. Occ. C6 41
Jablonec [nad Nisou], Czech. C3 26
Jablonná, Czech. o17 26
Jablunkov Pass, Czech. D5 26
Jaboatão, Braz. C4 57
Jaboticabal, Braz. C3 56
Jabrīn, i., Iran C5 38
Jaca, Spain A5 22
Jacala de Ledesma, Mex. m14 63
Jacaraci, Braz. A4 56
Jacaré, stm., Braz. D2 57
Jacareí, Braz. m9 56
Jacarezinho, Braz. C2 56
Jachin, Al., U.S. C1 78
Jáchymov, Czech. C2 26
Jaciara, Braz. B1 56
Jacinto, Ms., U.S. A5 101
Jacinto City, Tx., U.S. r14 120
Jack, Al., U.S. D4 78
Jack, co., Tx., U.S. C3 120
Jackfish Lake, l., Sask. D1 75
Jackhead Harbour, Man. D3 70
Jackman, Me., U.S. C2 96
Jackman Station, Me., U.S. C2 96
Jack Mountain, mtn., Mt., U.S. D4 103
Jack Mountain, mtn., Va., U.S. B3 123
Jack Mountain, mtn., Wa., U.S. A5 124
Jackpot, Nv., U.S. B7 105
Jacksboro, Tn., U.S. C9 119
Jacksboro, Tx., U.S. C3 120
Jacks Creek, Tn., U.S. B3 119
Jacks Mountain, mtn., Pa., U.S. E6 115
Jackson, Al., U.S. D2 78
Jackson, Ca., U.S. C3 82
Jackson, Ga., U.S. C3 87
Jackson, Ky., U.S. C6 94
Jackson, La., U.S. D4 95
Jackson, Me., U.S. D3 96
Jackson, Mi., U.S. F6 99
Jackson, Mn., U.S. G4 100
Jackson, Ms., U.S. C3 101
Jackson, Mo., U.S. D8 102
Jackson, Mt., U.S. E3 103
Jackson, Ne., U.S. B9 104
Jackson, N.H., U.S. B4 106
Jackson, N.J., U.S. C4 107
Jackson, N.C., U.S. A5 110
Jackson, Oh., U.S. C3 112
Jackson, R.I., U.S. D3 116
Jackson, S.C., U.S. E4 117
Jackson, Tn., U.S. B3 119
Jackson, Wi., U.S. E5 126
Jackson, Wy., U.S. C2 127
Jackson, co., Al., U.S. A3 78
Jackson, co., Ar., U.S. B4 81
Jackson, co., Co., U.S. A4 83
Jackson, co., Fl., U.S. B1 86
Jackson, co., Ga., U.S. B3 87
Jackson, co., Il., U.S. F4 90
Jackson, co., In., U.S. G5 91
Jackson, co., Ia., U.S. B7 92
Jackson, co., Ks., U.S. C8 93
Jackson, co., Ky., U.S. C5 94
Jackson, co., La., U.S. B3 95
Jackson, co., Mi., U.S. F6 99
Jackson, co., Mn., U.S. G3 100
Jackson, co., Ms., U.S. E5 101
Jackson, co., Mo., U.S. B3 102
Jackson, co., N.C., U.S. f9 110
Jackson, co., Oh., U.S. C3 112
Jackson, co., Ok., U.S. C2 113
Jackson, co., Or., U.S. E4 114
Jackson, co., S.D., U.S. D4 118
Jackson, co., Tn., U.S. C8 119
Jackson, co., Tx., U.S. E4 120
Jackson, co., W.V., U.S. C3 125
Jackson, co., Wi., U.S. D3 126
Jackson, stm., Va., U.S. C3 123
Jackson, Lake, l., Fl., U.S. E5 86
Jackson, Lake, l., Fl., U.S. B2 86
Jackson, Mount, mtn., Ant. B6 7
Jackson, Mount, mtn., N.H., U.S. B4 106
Jackson, Port, b., Austl. F8 51
Jacksonboro, S.C., U.S. F7 117
Jacksonburg, W.V., U.S. B4 125
Jackson Center, Oh., U.S. B1 112
Jackson Center, Pa., U.S. D1 115
Jackson Dam, Al., U.S. D2 78
Jackson Hill, In., U.S. F3 91
Jackson Junction, Ia., U.S. A5 92
Jackson Lake, res., Ga., U.S. C3 87
Jackson Lake, res., Wy., U.S. C2 127
Jackson Mountain, mtn., Me., U.S. D2 96
Jackson Mountains, mts., Nv., U.S. B3 105
Jacksonport, Ar., U.S. B4 81
Jackson's Arm, Newf. D3 72
Jacksons Gap, Al., U.S. C4 78
Jacksonville, Al., U.S. B4 78
Jacksonville, Ar., U.S. C3 81
Jacksonville, Fl., U.S. B5 86
Jacksonville, Ga., U.S. E4 87
Jacksonville, Il., U.S. D3 90
Jacksonville, Me., U.S. D5 96
Jacksonville, Mo., U.S. B5 102
Jacksonville, N.C., U.S. C5 110
Jacksonville, Oh., U.S. C3 112
Jacksonville, Or., U.S. E4 114
Jacksonville, Tx., U.S. D5 120
Jacksonville, Vt., U.S. F3 122
Jacksonville Beach, Fl., U.S. B5 86
Jacksonville Naval Air Station, mil., Fl., U.S. B5 86
Jacks Peak, mtn., Ut., U.S. E3 121
Jacktown, Ok., U.S. B4 113
Jacmel, Haiti E7 64
Jacob, Congo B1 48
Jacobābād, Pak. C4 36
Jacobina, Braz. D2 57
Jacob Lake, Az., U.S. A3 80
Jacobson, Mn., U.S. D5 100
Jacobstown, N.J., U.S. C3 107
Jacobsville, Mi., U.S. B2 99
Jacques-Cartier, stm., Que. B6 74
Jacques-Cartier, Détroit de, strt., Que. h8 72
Jacques-Cartier, Mont, mtn., Que. G19 66
Jacquet, stm., N.B. B3 71
Jacquet River, N.B. B4 71
Jacquinot Bay, b., Pap. N. Gui. k13 50
Jacuí, stm., Braz. D2 56
Jacuípe, stm., Braz. D3 57
Jacumba, Ca., U.S. F5 82
Jacundá, stm., Braz. C4 59
Jadabpur, India *D8 36
Jaddi, Rās, c., Pak. I11 39
Jade, W. Ger. A8 17
Jade Bay, b., W. Ger. B4 18
Jādū, Libya C2 43
Jadwin, Mo., U.S. D6 102
Jægerspris, Den. C5 15
Jaén, Peru C2 58
Jaén, Spain D4 22
Jaffa, Cape, c., Austl. G6 50
Jaffa Gate, hist., Isr. Occ. m14 41
Jaffna, Sri L. G7 36
Jaffrey, N.H., U.S. E2 106
Jaffrey Center, N.H., U.S. E2 106
Jagādhri, India B6 37
Jagdalpur, India E7 36
Jaggayyapeta, India I8 37
Jagīn, stm., Iran H9 39
Jagst, stm., W. Ger. D4 19
Jaguarão, Braz. E2 56
Jaguariaíva, Braz. C3 56
Jagüey Grande, Cuba C3 64
Jahrom, Iran C5 38
Jaicós, Braz. C2 57
Jailolo, Indon. E7 34
Jaipur, India C6 36
Jaisalmer, India C5 36
Jājapur, India D8 36
Jajce, Yugo. C3 24
Jakarta (Djakarta), Indon. G3 34
Jakestown, Tn., U.S. C8 119
Jakin, Ga., U.S. E2 87
Jakobstad, Fin. F10 14
Jal, N.M., U.S. E6 108
Jalaihai Point, c., Guam M10 52
Jalālābād, Afg. B5 36
Jalālah al Baḥrīyah, Jabal, plat., Eg. E4 41
Jalandhar, India B6 36
Jalapa, Guat. E6 63
Jalapa Enríquez, Mex. D5 63
Jālaun, India C6 36
Jālgaon, India D6 36
Jalisco, Mex. m11 63
Jalisco, state, Mex. C3 63
Jālna, India E6 36
Jalón, stm., Spain B5 22
Jālor, India E4 37
Jalpa, Mex. C4 63
Jalpan, Mex. C5 63
Jālū, Wāḥat, well, Libya D4 43
Jalūlā, Iraq D2 39
Jamaame, Som. E5 47
Jamaica, Ia., U.S. C3 92
Jamaica, Vt., U.S. E3 122
Jamaica, ctry., N.A. E5 64
Jamaica Bay, b., N.Y., U.S. k13 109
Jamaica Channel, strt., N.A. E6 64
Jamālpur, Bngl. E12 37
Jamanxim, stm., Braz. D3 59
Jamari, stm., Braz. D2 59
Jambi, Indon. F2 34
Jambuair, Cape, c., Indon. D1 34
James, Ga., U.S. D3 87
James, stm., Alta. D3 68
James, stm., U.S. A8 76
James, stm., Mo., U.S. E4 102
James, stm., Va., U.S. C5 123
James, Lake, l., In., U.S. A7 91
James, Lake, res., N.C., U.S. B1 110
James Bay, b., Can. F16 66
James Branch, stm., De., U.S. F3 85
Jamesburg, N.J., U.S. C4 107
James City, N.C., U.S. B5 110
James City, Pa., U.S. C4 115
James City, co., Va., U.S. C6 123
James Craik, Arg. A4 54
James Creek, Pa., U.S. F5 115
James Island, B.C. g12 69
James Island, S.C., U.S. k12 117
James Island, i., Md., U.S. C5 97
James Island, i., S.C., U.S. F8 117
Jameson, Mo., U.S. A4 102
Jamesport, Mo., U.S. B4 102
James River Bridge, Va., U.S. k15 123
James Ross Island, i., Ant. C7 7
James Ross Strait, strt., N.W. Ter. C13 66
Jamestown, Austl. F2 51
Jamestown, Ire. D3 11
Jamestown, Al., U.S. A4 78
Jamestown, Ca., U.S. D3 82
Jamestown, Co., U.S. A5 83
Jamestown, Il., U.S. E4 90
Jamestown, In., U.S. E4 91
Jamestown, Ks., U.S. C6 93
Jamestown, Ky., U.S. D4 94
Jamestown, La., U.S. B2 95
Jamestown, Mo., U.S. C5 102
Jamestown, N.Y., U.S. C1 109
Jamestown, N.C., U.S. B3 110
Jamestown, N.D., U.S. C7 111
Jamestown, Oh., U.S. C2 112
Jamestown, Pa., U.S. D1 115
Jamestown, R.I., U.S. F5 116
Jamestown, S.C., U.S. E8 117
Jamestown, Tn., U.S. C9 119
James Town, Wy., U.S. E3 127
Jamestown Dam, N.D., U.S. C7 111
Jamestown Reservoir, res., N.D., U.S. C7 111
Jamesville, N.C., U.S. B6 110
Jamesville, Va., U.S. C7 123
Jamieson, Or., U.S. C9 114
Jamiltepec, Mex. D5 63
Jamison, Ne., U.S. B6 104
Jammāʿīn, Isr. Occ. g11 41
Jammerbugten, b., Den. A3 15
Jammu, India B5 36
Jammu and Kashmir, dep., Asia A6 36
Jamnagar (Navanagar), India D5 36
Jāmpur, Pak. C3 37
Jamsah, Eg. D6 43
Jamshedpur, India D8 36
Jämshög, Swe. B8 15
Jamul, Ca., U.S. F5 82
Jamuna, stm., Bngl. E12 37
Janaúba, Braz. B4 56
Jandaia, Braz. B2 56
Jandaq, Iran D7 39
Jandiatuba, stm., Braz. B4 58
Jándula, stm., Spain C4 22
Jane, Mo., U.S. E3 102
Jane Lew, W.V., U.S. B4 125
Janesville, Ca., U.S. B3 82
Janesville, Il., U.S. D5 90
Janesville, Ia., U.S. B5 92
Janesville, Mn., U.S. F5 100
Janesville, Wi., U.S. F4 126
Janeville, N.B. B4 71
Jangīpur, India E12 37
Janīn, Isr. Occ. B7 41
Jan Lake, l., Sask. C4 75
Jan Mayen, i., Nor. B15 128
Janos, Mex. A3 63
Jánoshalma, Hung. B4 24
Janow, Man. E4 70
Janów Lubelski, Pol. C7 26
Jansen, Sask. F3 75
Jansen, Co., U.S. D6 83
Jansen, Ne., U.S. D8 104
Januária, Braz. B4 56
Japan, ctry., Asia D12 31
Japan, Sea of, Asia C12 31
Japaratuba, Braz. D3 57
Japim, Braz. C3 58
Japurá (Caquetá), stm., S.A. D4 60
Jaqué, Pan. G8 62
Jarābulus, Syria D12 40
Jaraguá, Braz. B3 56
Jaraguá do Sul, Braz. D3 56
Jaraguari, Braz. C2 56
Jaral del Progreso, Mex. m13 63
Jarales, N.M., U.S. C3 108
Jarama, stm., Spain B4 22
Jaramānah, Syria *F11 40
Jarash, Jord. B7 41
Jarbalo, Ks., U.S. k15 93
Jarbidge, Nv., U.S. B6 105
Jardim, Braz. C1 56
Jardim de Angicos, Braz. g6 57
Jardim do Seridó, Braz. C3 57
Jardīnah, Libya C4 43
Jardine, Mt., U.S. E6 103
Jardines de la Reina, Archipiélago de los, is., Cuba D4 64
Jardinópolis, Braz. k8 56
Järfälla, Swe. *H7 14
Jargalang, China C10 32
Jargalant, Mong. B7 31
Jari, stm., Braz. B4 59
Järlåsa (part of Uppsala), Swe. t35 14
Järna (part of Södertälje), Swe. t35 14
Jarnac, Fr. E3 16
Jarny, Fr. E5 17
Jarocin, Pol. C4 26
Jaroměř, Czech. C3 26
Jarosław, Pol. C7 26
Jaroso, Co., U.S. D5 83
Jarratt, Va., U.S. D5 123
Jarrettsville, Md., U.S. A5 97
Jarrow, Alta. C5 68
Jaru, Braz. B3 55
Jarud Qi, China C9 31
Jarvie, Alta. B4 68
Jarvis, Ont. E4 73
Jarvis, i., Oc. G12 6
Jarvisburg, N.C., U.S. A7 110
Jasień, Pol. B10 19
Jāsk, Iran I8 39
Jasło, Pol. D6 26
Jasmin, Sask. F4 75
Jasmine Estates, Fl., U.S. D4 86
Jason Peninsula, pen., Ant. C6 7
Jasonville, In., U.S. F3 91
Jasper, Alta. C1 68
Jasper, Ont. C9 73
Jasper, Al., U.S. B2 78
Jasper, Ar., U.S. B2 81
Jasper, Fl., U.S. B4 86
Jasper, Ga., U.S. B2 87
Jasper, In., U.S. H4 91
Jasper, Mn., U.S. G2 100
Jasper, Mo., U.S. D3 102
Jasper, N.Y., U.S. C3 109
Jasper, Oh., U.S. C2 112
Jasper, Or., U.S. D4 114
Jasper, Tn., U.S. D8 119
Jasper, Tx., U.S. D6 120
Jasper, co., Ga., U.S. C3 87
Jasper, co., Il., U.S. D5 90
Jasper, co., In., U.S. B3 91
Jasper, co., Ia., U.S. C4 92
Jasper, co., Ms., U.S. C4 101
Jasper, co., Mo., U.S. D3 102
Jasper, co., S.C., U.S. G5 117
Jasper, co., Tx., U.S. D5 120
Jasper Lake, l., Alta. C1 68
Jasper National Park, Alta. C1 68
Jastarnia, Pol. A5 26
Jastrzebia Góra, Pol. A5 26
Jastrzębie-Zdrój, Pol. h9 26
Jászapáti, Hung. B5 24
Jászberény, Hung. B4 24
Jataí, Braz. B2 56
Jāti, Pak. E2 37
Jatibonico, Cuba D4 64
Játiva, Spain C5 22
Jatni, India G10 37
Jatobá, stm., Braz. E4 59
Jaú, Braz. C3 56
Jaú, stm., Braz. C2 59
Jauaperi, stm., Braz. B2 59
Jaumave, Mex. C5 63
Jaunpur, India C7 36
Java, S.D., U.S. B6 118
Java, Va., U.S. D3 123
Java (Jawa), i., Indon. G3 34
Javari see Yavarí, stm., S.A. B3 58
Java Sea, Indon. G4 34
Jávea, Spain C6 22
Jawhār, India H4 37
Jawor, Pol. C4 26
Jaworzno, Pol. g10 26
Jay, Fl., U.S. u14 86
Jay, La., U.S. E5 95
Jay, Me., U.S. D2 96
Jay, N.Y., U.S. f11 109
Jay, Ok., U.S. A7 113
Jay, co., In., U.S. D7 91
Jayanca, Peru C2 58
Jaya Peak, mtn., Indon. F9 34
Jayapura, Indon. F10 34
Jay Em, Wy., U.S. D8 127
Jayess, Ms., U.S. D3 101
Jay Peak, mtn., Vt., U.S. B3 122
Jaypur, India E7 36
Jayton, Tx., U.S. C2 120
Jaz Mūrīān, Hāmūn-e, l., Iran H9 39
J. B. Thomas, Lake, res., Tx., U.S. C2 120
Jean, Nv., U.S. H6 105
Jeanerette, La., U.S. E4 95
Jean Lafitte National Historical Park, La., U.S. k12 95
Jeannette, Pa., U.S. F2 115
Jeannette Island, i., Sov. Un. B35 128
Jebba, Nig. E5 45
Jeberos, Peru C2 58
Jedburg, S.C., U.S. h11 117
Jedburgh, Sask. F4 75
Jedburgh, Scot., U.K. C5 10
Jeddito, Az., U.S. B5 80
Jeddo, Mi., U.S. E8 99
Jeddore Lake, res., Newf. D3 72
Jędrzejów, Pol. C6 26
Jeetze, stm., Eur. B5 18
Jeff, Ky., U.S. C6 94
Jeff Davis, co., Ga., U.S. E4 87
Jeff Davis, co., Tx., U.S. o12 120
Jeffers, Mn., U.S. F3 100

Name	Map Ref.	Page
Jeffers, Mt., U.S.	E5	103
Jefferson, Al., U.S.	C2	78
Jefferson, Ar., U.S.	C3	81
Jefferson, Co., U.S.	B5	83
Jefferson, Ga., U.S.	B3	87
Jefferson, In., U.S.	D4	91
Jefferson, Ia., U.S.	B3	92
Jefferson, La., U.S.	k11	95
Jefferson, Me., U.S.	D3	96
Jefferson, Md., U.S.	B2	97
Jefferson, Md., U.S.	B4	98
Jefferson, N.H., U.S.	B4	106
Jefferson, N.J., U.S.	D2	107
Jefferson, N.Y., U.S.	C6	109
Jefferson, N.C., U.S.	A1	110
Jefferson, Oh., U.S.	A5	112
Jefferson, Ok., U.S.	A4	113
Jefferson, Or., U.S.	C3	114
Jefferson, Pa., U.S.	*F2	115
Jefferson, S.C., U.S.	B7	117
Jefferson, S.D., U.S.	E9	118
Jefferson, Tx., U.S.	C5	120
Jefferson, Wi., U.S.	E5	126
Jefferson, co., Al., U.S.	B3	78
Jefferson, co., Ar., U.S.	C3	81
Jefferson, co., Co., U.S.	B5	83
Jefferson, co., Fl., U.S.	B3	86
Jefferson, co., Ga., U.S.	C4	87
Jefferson, co., Id., U.S.	F6	89
Jefferson, co., Il., U.S.	E5	90
Jefferson, co., In., U.S.	C5	92
Jefferson, co., Ia., U.S.	C5	92
Jefferson, co., Ks., U.S.	B4	94
Jefferson, co., Ky., U.S.	B4	94
Jefferson, co., La., U.S.	E5	95
Jefferson, co., Ms., U.S.	D2	101
Jefferson, co., Mo., U.S.	C5	102
Jefferson, co., Mt., U.S.	D4	103
Jefferson, co., Ne., U.S.	D8	104
Jefferson, co., N.Y., U.S.	A5	109
Jefferson, co., Oh., U.S.	B5	112
Jefferson, co., Ok., U.S.	C4	113
Jefferson, co., Or., U.S.	C5	114
Jefferson, co., Pa., U.S.	D3	115
Jefferson, co., Tn., U.S.	C10	119
Jefferson, co., Tx., U.S.	E5	120
Jefferson, co., Wa., U.S.	B1	124
Jefferson, co., W.V., U.S.	B7	125
Jefferson, co., Wi., U.S.	E5	126
Jefferson, stm., Mt., U.S.	E5	103
Jefferson, Mount, mtn., Id., U.S.	E7	89
Jefferson, Mount, mtn., Nv., U.S.	E5	105
Jefferson, Mount, mtn., Or., U.S.	C5	114
Jefferson City, Mo., U.S.	C5	102
Jefferson City, Mt., U.S.	D5	103
Jefferson City, Tn., U.S.	C10	119
Jefferson Davis, co., La., U.S.	D3	95
Jefferson Davis, co., Ms., U.S.	D4	101
Jefferson Farms, De., U.S.	i7	85
Jefferson Hill, hill, R.I., U.S.	g11	94
Jefferson Manor, Va., U.S.	*B5	123
Jefferson Proving Ground, mil., In., U.S.	G7	91
Jeffersontown, Ky., U.S.	B4	94
Jefferson Valley, N.Y., U.S.	*D7	109
Jefferson Village, Va., U.S.	*B5	123
Jeffersonville, Ga., U.S.	D3	87
Jeffersonville, In., U.S.	H6	91
Jeffersonville, Ky., U.S.	C6	94
Jeffersonville, Oh., U.S.	C2	112
Jeffersonville, Vt., U.S.	B3	122
Jeffrey, W.V., U.S.	D3	125
Jeffrey City, Wy., U.S.	D5	127
Jeffries Creek, stm., S.C., U.S.	C8	117
Jega, Nig.	F5	45
Jehossee Island, i., S.C., U.S.	k11	117
Jeju-Guazú, stm., Para.	D4	55
Jékabpils, Sov. Un.	C5	27
Jekyll Island, i., Ga., U.S.	E5	87
Jelenia Góra (Hirschberg), Pol.	C3	26
Jelgava (Yelgava), Sov. Un.	C4	27
Jellico, Tn., U.S.	C9	119
Jelling, Den.	C3	15
Jelm, Wy., U.S.	E6	127
Jelm Mountain, mtn., Wy., U.S.	E7	127
Jelöya, i., Nor.	p28	14
Jemaja, i., Indon.	K6	35
Jember, Indon.	G4	34
Jemez, stm., N.M., U.S.	k7	108
Jemez Dam, N.M., U.S.	k7	108
Jemez Indian Reservation, N.M., U.S.	h7	108
Jemez Pueblo, N.M., U.S.	B3	108
Jemez Springs, N.M., U.S.	B3	108
Jemison, Al., U.S.	C3	78
Jemseg, N.B.	D3	71
Jena, E. Ger.	C5	18
Jena, Fl., U.S.	C3	86
Jena, La., U.S.	C3	95
Jenaz, Switz.	C8	21
Jenbach, Aus.	B7	20
Jendouba, Tun.	F2	23
Jenera, Oh., U.S.	B2	112
Jenison, Mi., U.S.	*F5	99
Jenkins, Ky., U.S.	C7	94
Jenkins, Mn., U.S.	D4	100
Jenkins, N.J., U.S.	D3	107
Jenkins, co., Ga., U.S.	D5	87
Jenkinsburg, Ga., U.S.	C2	87
Jenkinsville, S.C., U.S.	C5	117
Jenkintown, Pa., U.S.	o21	115
Jenks, Ok., U.S.	A6	113
Jenner, Alta.	D5	68
Jenners, Pa., U.S.	F3	115
Jennie, Ar., U.S.	D4	81
Jennings, Fl., U.S.	B3	86
Jennings, Ks., U.S.	C3	93
Jennings, La., U.S.	D3	95
Jennings, Md., U.S.	k12	97
Jennings, Mi., U.S.	D5	99
Jennings, Mo., U.S.	f13	102
Jennings, Ok., U.S.	A5	113
Jennings, co., In., U.S.	G6	91
Jennings Lodge, Or., U.S.	*B4	114
Jenny Jump Mountain, mtn., N.J., U.S.	B3	107
Jenny Lind, Ar., U.S.	B1	81
Jensen, Ut., U.S.	C6	121
Jensen Beach, Fl., U.S.	E6	86
Jeptha Knob, hill, Ky., U.S.	B4	94
Jequié, Braz.	C4	57
Jequitaí, Braz.	C4	44
Jequitinhonha, Braz.	E2	57
Jequitinhonha, stm., Braz.	E2	57
Jerada, Mor.	C4	44
Jerauld, co., S.D., U.S.	C7	118
Jérémie, Haiti	E6	64
Jeremoabo, Braz.	D3	57
Jerez de García Salinas, Mex.	C4	63
Jerez de la Frontera, Spain	D2	22
Jerez de los Caballeros, Spain	C2	22
Jericho, Austl.	A6	51
Jericho (Arīḥā), Isr. Occ.	C7	41
Jericho, Ar., U.S.	B5	81
Jericho, N.Y., U.S.	*E7	109
Jericho Center, Vt., U.S.	C3	122
Jerico Springs, Mo., U.S.	D4	102
Jerimoth Hill, hill, R.I., U.S.	C1	116
Jermyn, Pa., U.S.	C10	115
Jermyn, Tx., U.S.	C3	120
Jerome, Az., U.S.	C3	80
Jerome, Fl., U.S.	F5	86
Jerome, Id., U.S.	G4	89
Jerome, Ia., U.S.	D4	92
Jerome, Mi., U.S.	F6	99
Jerome, Mo., U.S.	D5	102
Jerome, Pa., U.S.	F4	115
Jerome, co., Id., U.S.	G4	89
Jeromesville, Oh., U.S.	B3	112
Jersey, Ga., U.S.	C3	87
Jersey, co., Il., U.S.	D3	90
Jersey, dep., Eur.	F5	10
Jersey City, N.J., U.S.	B4	107
Jersey Mountain, mtn., Id., U.S.	E3	89
Jersey Shore, Pa., U.S.	D7	115
Jerseyville, Il., U.S.	D3	90
Jerumenha, Braz.	C2	57
Jerusalem (Yerushalayim), Isr.	B3	38
Jerusalem, Ar., U.S.	B3	81
Jerusalem, Oh., U.S.	C4	112
Jervis Bay, b., Austl.	G9	50
Jervis Inlet, b., B.C.	D6	69
Jesenice Reservoir, res., Czech.	C7	19
Jesenik, Czech.	C4	26
Jessamine, co., Ky., U.S.	C5	94
Jessen, E. Ger.	B7	18
Jessie, N.D., U.S.	B7	111
Jessieville, Ar., U.S.	C2	81
Jessnitz, E. Ger.	B7	19
Jessore, Bngl.	F12	37
Jessup, Md., U.S.	B4	97
Jessup, Pa., U.S.	m18	115
Jesup, Ga., U.S.	E5	87
Jesup, Ia., U.S.	B5	92
Jesup, Lake, l., Fl., U.S.	D5	86
Jésus, Île, i., Que.	p19	74
Jesús Carranza, Mex.	D5	63
Jesús Maria, Arg.	A4	54
Jesús María, Peru	*D2	58
Jet, Ok., U.S.	A3	113
Jetersville, Va., U.S.	C4	123
Jetmore, Ks., U.S.	D4	93
Jetson, Ky., U.S.	C3	94
Jette, Bel.	D4	17
Jeumont, Fr.	D4	17
Jever, W. Ger.	B3	18
Jewell Cave National Monument, S.D., U.S.	D2	118
Jewell, Ia., U.S.	B4	92
Jewell, Ks., U.S.	C5	93
Jewell, Oh., U.S.	A1	112
Jewell, co., Ks., U.S.	C5	93
Jewell Ridge, Va., U.S.	e10	123
Jewett, Il., U.S.	D5	90
Jewett, Oh., U.S.	B4	112
Jewett, Tx., U.S.	D4	120
Jewett City, Ct., U.S.	C8	84
Jewett Lake, l., Sask.		
Jeziorka, stm., Pol.	m14	26
Jhal, Pak.	C1	37
Jhālāwār, India	E6	37
Jhal Jhao, Pak.	C4	37
Jhang Sadar, Pak.	B4	37
Jhānsi, India	H8	37
Jharia, India		
Jhelum, Pak.	B5	36
Jhelum, stm., Asia	B5	36
Jhunjhunūn, India	C5	37
Ji'an, China	E6	31
Jiamusi, China	B11	31
Ji'an, China	F7	31
Jianchang, China	D12	32
Jiande, China	J8	32
Jiande, China	E7	31
Jiangling, China	E7	31
Jiangsu, prov., China	E9	31
Jiangxi, prov., China	F8	31
Jiangyin (Chengjiang), China	I9	32
Jiangyou, China	E5	31
Jianli, China	J5	32
Jianning, China	K7	32
Jian'ou, China	C8	31
Jianping, China	C8	31
Jianshi, China	I3	32
Jianshui, China	G5	31
Jianyang, China	E3	33
Jiaohe, China	D9	31
Jiaoxian, China	F9	32
Jiaozhou Bay, b., China	F9	32
Jiaozuo, China	D7	31
Jiashan, China	H8	32
Jiaxian, China	E4	32
Jiaxing, China	E9	31
Jiayu, China	I5	32
Jicarilla Indian Reservation, N.M., U.S.	A2	108
Jičín, Czech.	C3	26
Jiddah, Sau. Ar.	C3	38
Jiddi, Jabal al, mtn., Eg.	D5	41
Jidy, Bi'r al, well, Eg.	D5	41
Jiek'kevarri, mtn., Nor.	C8	14
Jiexiu, China	F4	32
Jieyang, China	G8	31
Jifnā, Isr. Occ.	h11	41
Jigger, La., U.S.	B4	95
Jiggs, Nv., U.S.	C6	105
Jihlava, Czech.	D3	26
Jihočeský, prov., Czech.	D9	19
Jijel, Alg.	B6	44
Jijia, stm., Rom.	B8	24
Jijiga, Eth.	D5	47
Jijona, Spain	C5	22
Jilib, Som.	E5	47
Jilin, China	C10	31
Jilin, prov., China	C10	31
Jiloca, stm., Spain	B5	22
Jílové u Prahy, Czech.	o18	19
Jima, Eth.	D4	47
Jimbolia, Rom.	C5	24
Jimena [de los Frontera], Spain	D3	22
Jim Falls, Wi., U.S.	C2	126
Jima, Eth.		
Jim Hogg, co., Tx., U.S.	F3	120
Jim Lake, res., N.D., U.S.	B7	111
Jim Thorpe, Pa., U.S.	E10	115
Jim Wells, co., Tx., U.S.	F3	120
Jinān, Eg.	D6	43
Jincheng, China	G5	32
Jindřichův Hradec, Czech.	D3	26
Jingbian, China	F3	32
Jingchuan, China	G2	32
Jingde, China	I8	32
Jingdezhen, China	F8	31
Jing He, stm., China	G3	32
Jinghong, China	G5	31
Jingmen, China	I5	32
Jingning, China	G1	32
Jingshan, China	I5	32
Jingxi, China	D9	32
Jingxian, China	K3	32
Jingxian, China	I8	32
Jingxian, China	A10	32
Jingziguan, China	H4	32
Jinhua, China	F8	31
Jining, China	D8	31
Jining, China	C7	31
Jinja, Ug.	A5	48
Jinniu, China	I6	32
Jinotega, Nic.	E7	63
Jinotepe, Nic.	E7	63
Jinsha Jiang, stm., China	F4	31
Jinshi, China	J4	32
Jinxi, China	*C9	31
Jinxian, China	D9	31
Jinyun, China	J9	32
Jinzhou, China	C9	31
Ji-Paraná, Braz.	B3	55
Jiparaná, stm., Braz.	D2	59
Jipijapa, Ec.	B1	58
Jiquilisco, El Sal.	D3	62
Jiquilpan de Juárez, Mex.	n12	63
Jirāfī, Wādī al (Naḥal Paran), val.	E6	41
Jirkov, Czech.	C8	19
Jisr ash Shughūr, Syria	E11	40
Jiu, stm., Rom.	C6	24
Jiujiang, China	F8	31
Jiuquan, China	D4	31
Jiurongcheng, China	F10	31
Jixi, China	B11	31
Jixian, China	G6	32
Jizera, stm., Czech.	C9	19
Joaçaba, Braz.	D2	56
Joaíma, Braz.	B4	56
João Belo see Xai-Xai, Moz.	C5	49
João Câmara, Braz.	g6	57
João Pessoa (Paraíba), Braz.	B5	56
João Pinheiro, Braz.	B5	56
Joaquín V. González, Arg.	E3	55
Jódar, Spain	D3	22
Jodhpur, India	A3	90
Jodie, W.V., U.S.	m13	125
Jodoigne, Bel.	D4	17
Joe Batt's Arm [-Barr'd Islands-Shoal Bay], Newf.	D4	72
Joensuu, Fin.	F13	14
Joes, Co., U.S.	B8	83
Joes Brook, stm., Vt., U.S.	C4	122
Joes Creek, stm., W.V., U.S.	m12	125
Joetsu, Japan	H9	33
Jœuf, Fr.	C6	16
Joffre, Mount, mtn., Can.	D3	68
Joggins, N.S.	D5	71
Jogjakarta see Yogyakarta, Indon.	G4	34
Johannesburg, S. Afr.	C4	49
Johannesburg, Mi., U.S.	D6	99
Johannesburg, Ca., U.S.	E5	82
Johansfors, Swe.		
John Crow Mountains, mts., Jam.	E16	65
John Day, Or., U.S.	C8	114
John Day, stm., Or., U.S.	B6	114
John Day, North Fork, stm., Or., U.S.	C7	114
John Day Dam, Or., U.S.	D5	124
John Day Fossil Beds National Monument, Or., U.S.	C6	114
John F. Kennedy Space Center, sci., Fl., U.S.	D6	86
John H. Kerr Dam, Va., U.S.	D4	123
John H. Kerr Reservoir, res., U.S.	D4	123
John Martin Reservoir, res., Co., U.S.	C7	83
John Muir National Historical Site, hist., Ca., U.S.	h8	82
John o'Groats, Scot., U.K.	B5	13
John Redmond Reservoir, res., Ks., U.S.	D8	93
Johnsburg, Il., U.S.	h8	90
Johnsburg, N.Y., U.S.	B7	109
Johnsburg, Wi., U.S.	k9	126
John Sevier, Tn., U.S.	m14	119
Johns Island, S.C., U.S.	F7	117
Johns Island, i., S.C., U.S.	F7	117
Johnson, Ar., U.S.	A1	81
Johnson, Ks., U.S.	H2	91
Johnson, Ne., U.S.	D10	104
Johnson, Vt., U.S.	B3	122
Johnson, Wa., U.S.	C8	124
Johnson, co., Ar., U.S.	B2	81
Johnson, co., Ga., U.S.	D4	87
Johnson, co., Il., U.S.	F5	90
Johnson, co., In., U.S.	F5	91
Johnson, co., Ia., U.S.	C6	92
Johnson, co., Ks., U.S.	D9	93
Johnson, co., Ky., U.S.	C7	94
Johnson, co., Mo., U.S.	C4	102
Johnson, co., Ne., U.S.	D9	104
Johnson, co., Tn., U.S.	C12	119
Johnson, co., Tx., U.S.	C4	120
Johnson, co., Wy., U.S.	B6	127
Johnsonburg, Pa., U.S.	D4	115
Johnson City, N.Y., U.S.	C5	109
Johnson City, Tn., U.S.	C11	119
Johnson City, Tx., U.S.	D3	120
Johnson Creek, Wi., U.S.	E5	126
Johnsondale, Ca., U.S.	E4	82
Johnson's Bayou, La., U.S.	E2	95
Johnsons Grove, Tn., U.S.	B2	119
Johnsonville, S.C., U.S.	D9	117
Johns Pass, strt., Fl., U.S.	p10	86
Johnston, Ia., U.S.	e8	92
Johnston, R.I., U.S.	C4	116
Johnston, S.C., U.S.	D4	117
Johnston, co., N.C., U.S.	B4	110
Johnston, co., Ok., U.S.	C5	113
Johnston, i., C.S., U.S.	E11	6
Johnston, Lake, l., Austl.	F3	50
Johnston City, Il., U.S.	F5	90
Johnstone, Scot., U.K.	*E4	13
Johnstone Strait, strt., B.C.	D4	69
Johnstone Key, i., Fl., U.S.	H5	86
Johnston's Point, c., Scot., U.K.	E3	13
Johnstown, Co., U.S.	A6	83
Johnstown, Ne., U.S.	B5	104
Johnstown, N.Y., U.S.	B6	109
Johnstown, N.D., U.S.	A8	111
Johnstown, Oh., U.S.	B3	112
Johnstown, Pa., U.S.	F4	115
Johnstown, Tx., U.S.	C5	120
Johnville, Que.	D6	74
John W. Flannagan Reservoir, res., Va., U.S.	e9	123
Johor, state, Malay.	K5	35
Johor Baharu, Malay.	E2	34
Joice, Ia., U.S.	A4	92
Joigny, Fr.	D5	16
Joiner, Ar., U.S.	B5	81
Joinville, Braz.	D3	56
Joinville Island, i., Ant.	C7	7
Jojutla, Mex.	n14	63
Jokkmokk, Swe.	D8	14
Jolfā, Iran	B2	39
Joliet, Il., U.S.	B5	90
Joliet, Mt., U.S.	E8	103
Joliette, Que.	C4	74
Joliette, co., Que.	C3	74
Jolley, Ia., U.S.	B3	92
Jolo, Phil.	D6	34
Jomalig Island, i., Phil.	o14	34
Jomda, China	E4	31
Jonava, Sov. Un.	A8	26
Jonas Ridge, N.C., U.S.	B1	110
Jones, Phil.	n13	34
Jones, Al., U.S.	C3	78
Jones, Ga., U.S.	E5	87
Jones, La., U.S.	B4	95
Jones, Ok., U.S.	B4	113
Jones, co., Ga., U.S.	C3	87
Jones, co., Ia., U.S.	B6	92
Jones, co., Ms., U.S.	D4	101
Jones, co., N.C., U.S.	B5	110
Jones, co., S.D., U.S.	D5	118
Jones, co., Tx., U.S.	C3	120
Jonesboro, Ar., U.S.	B5	81
Jonesboro, Ga., U.S.	C2	87
Jonesboro, Il., U.S.	F4	90
Jonesboro, In., U.S.	D6	91
Jonesboro, La., U.S.	B3	95
Jonesboro, Me., U.S.	D5	96
Jonesboro, Tn., U.S.	C11	119
Jonesboro, Tx., U.S.	D4	120
Jonesburg, Mo., U.S.	C6	102
Jones Creek, Tx., U.S.	s14	120
Jones Mill, Ar., U.S.	C3	81
Jones Mill, Tn., U.S.	A3	119
Jones Mills, Pa., U.S.	F3	115
Jones Mountains, mts., Ant.	B7	7
Jonesport, Me., U.S.	D5	96
Jones Sound, strt., N.W. Ter.	m34	66
Jonestown, Ms., U.S.	A3	101
Jonestown, Ms., U.S.	C3	101
Jonestown, Pa., U.S.	F9	115
Jonesville, In., U.S.	F6	91
Jonesville, La., U.S.	C4	95
Jonesville, Mi., U.S.	G6	99
Jonesville, N.C., U.S.	A2	110
Jonesville, S.C., U.S.	B4	117
Jonesville, Vt., U.S.	C3	122
Jonesville, Va., U.S.	f8	123
Jonquière, Que.	A6	74
Jonuta, Mex.	D6	63
Jonzac, Fr.	E3	16
Joplin, Mo., U.S.	D3	102
Joplin, Mt., U.S.	B6	103
Joppa, Al., U.S.	A3	78
Joppa, Il., U.S.	F5	90
Joppa, Md., U.S.	B5	97
Jordan, Mn., U.S.	F5	100
Jordan, Mt., U.S.	C10	103
Jordan, N.Y., U.S.	B4	109
Jordan, cty., Asia	B7	41
Jordan, stm., Asia	B3	41
Jordan, stm., Ut., U.S.	C4	121
Jordan Creek, stm., U.S.	E4	71
Jordan Lake, l., N.S.	E4	71
Jordan Lake, res., Al., U.S.	C3	78
Jordan Valley, Or., U.S.	E9	114
Jordânia, Braz.	D8	56
Jorhāt, India	H16	37
Jörn, Swe.	D8	14
Jornado del Muerto, des., N.M., U.S.	D3	108
Jos, Nig.	E6	45
José Battle y Ordóñez, Ur.	C5	54
José de San Martín, Arg.	C2	54
Joseph, Or., U.S.	B9	114
Joseph, Lake, l., Ont.	B5	73
Joseph, Lake, l., Newf.	h8	72
Joseph Bonaparte Gulf, b., Austl.	B4	50
Joseph City, Az., U.S.	C5	80
Josephine, co., Or., U.S.	E3	114
Josephville, Mo., U.S.	f12	102
Joshua, Tx., U.S.	n9	120
Joshua Tree, Ca., U.S.	E5	82
Joshua Tree National Monument, Ca., U.S.	F6	82
Josselin, Fr.	C2	16
Jostedalsbreen, ice, Nor.	G2	14
Jost Van Dyke, i., V.I., Br.	B6	65
Jotunheimen, mts., Nor.	G2	14
Jourdanton, Tx., U.S.	E3	120
Joussard, Alta.	B3	68
Joux, Lake, l., Switz.		
Jouy-en-Josas, Fr.	g9	16
Jovellanos, Cuba	C3	64
Joveyn, Afg.	B3	36
Joviânia, Braz.	E4	47
Jowhar, Som.	E6	47
Joy, Il., U.S.	B3	90
Joy, Ok., U.S.	C4	113
Joyce, La., U.S.	C3	95
Joyce, Wa., U.S.	A2	124
Juab, co., Ut., U.S.	D2	121
Juaja, Peru	D2	58
Juan Aldama, Mex.	C4	63
Juan B. Arruabarrena, Arg.	A5	54
Juan de Fuca, Strait of, strt., N.A.	A1	124
Juan Díaz (part of Panamá), Pan.	k12	62
Juan E. Barra, Arg.	B4	54
Juan Fernández, Archipiélago, is., Chile	G2	53
Juanita, N.D., U.S.	B7	111
Juanita, U.S.	*B3	124
Juan José Castelli, Arg.	E3	55
Juanjui, Peru	C2	58
Juan L. Lacaze, Ur.	g8	54
Juárez, Mex.	B4	63
Juaso, Ghana	E4	45
Juazeiro, Braz.	C3	57
Juazeiro do Norte, Braz.	C3	57
Jubba (Genale), stm., Afr.	E5	47
Jubbada Dhexe, prov., Som.	E5	47
Jubbada Hoose, prov., Som.	E5	47
Jubbah, Sau. Ar.	I13	40
Jubilee Lake, l., Newf.	D4	72
Juby, Cap, c., Mor.	D2	44
Júcar, stm., Spain	C5	22
Juçara, Braz.	B2	56
Júcaro, Cuba	D4	64
Juchipila, Mex.	m12	63
Juchipila, stm., Mex.	m12	63
Juchitán [de Zaragoza], Mex.	D5	63
Jucuapa, El Sal.	D3	62
Jud, N.D., U.S.	C7	111
Juda, Wi., U.S.	F4	126
Judean Hills, hills, Asia	C7	41
Jude Island, i., Newf.	E4	72
Judenburg, Aus.	E7	18
Judique, N.S.	D8	71
Judith, Arg.	C7	103
Judith, Point, c., R.I., U.S.	G4	85
Judith Basin, co., Mt., U.S.	C6	103
Judith Gap, Mt., U.S.	D7	103
Judith Island, i., N.C., U.S.	B6	110
Judith Mountains, mts., Mt., U.S.	C7	103
Judith Peak, mtn., Mt., U.S.	C7	103
Judson, Mn., U.S.	F4	100
Judson, In., U.S.	C4	111
Judsonia, Ar., U.S.	B4	81
Judyville, In., U.S.	D3	91
Juelsminde, Den.	C4	15
Jufayr, Bi'r al, well, Eg.	D4	41
Juigalpa, Nic.	E5	63
Juist, W. Ger.	A6	17
Juist, i., W. Ger.	B3	18
Juiz de Fora, Braz.	C4	56
Jujuy, prov., Arg.	D2	55
Jukkasjärvi (part of Kiruna), Swe.	D9	14
Julesburg, Co., U.S.	A8	83
Juliaca, Peru	E3	58
Juliaetta, Id., U.S.	C2	89
Julian, Ca., U.S.	F5	82
Julian, Ne., U.S.	D10	104
Julian, N.C., U.S.	B3	110
Julian, W.V., U.S.	C3	125
Julian Alps, mts., Eur.	C1	24
Juliana Top, mtn., Sur.	B3	59
Julianehåb, Grnld.	C16	61
Jülich, W. Ger.	D6	17
Juliette, Ga., U.S.	C3	87
Julimes, Mex.	B3	63
Júlio de Castilhos, Braz.	D2	56
Julita, Swe.	t34	14
Juliustown, N.J., U.S.	C3	107
Julu, China	F6	32
Jumayl, Bi'r, well, Eg.	D5	41
Jumboo, Som.	F5	47
Jumbo Peak, mtn., Nv., U.S.	G7	105
Jumet (part of Charleroi), Bel.	B6	16
Jumilla, Spain	C5	22
Jump, Wi., U.S.	C3	126
Jump, North Fork, stm., Wi., U.S.	C3	126
Jump, South Fork, stm., Wi., U.S.	C3	126
Jumping Branch, W.V., U.S.	D3	125
Jumping Lake, l., Sask.	E3	75
Jūnāgadh, India	J4	37
Juncos, P.R.	n15	65
Junction, Il., U.S.	F5	90
Junction, Oh., U.S.	A1	112
Junction, Tx., U.S.	D3	120
Junction, Ut., U.S.	E3	121
Junction City, Ar., U.S.	D3	81
Junction City, Ga., U.S.	D2	87
Junction City, Il., U.S.	E5	90
Junction City, Ks., U.S.	C7	93
Junction City, Ky., U.S.	C5	94
Junction City, La., U.S.	A3	95
Junction City, Oh., U.S.	C3	112
Junction City, Or., U.S.	C3	114
Junction City, Wi., U.S.	D4	126
Jundiaí, Braz.	G5	57
Juneau, Ak., U.S.	D13	79
Juneau, Wi., U.S.	E5	126
Juneau, co., Wi., U.S.	E3	126
Junee, Austl.	F8	50
June in Winter, Lake, l., Fl., U.S.	E5	86
June Lake, Ca., U.S.	D4	82
Jungfrau, mtn., Switz.	E3	21
Junggar Pendi (Dzungarian Basin), China	B4	31
Junglinster, Lux.	E6	17
Juniata, Ne., U.S.	D7	104
Juniata, co., Pa., U.S.	F7	115
Juniata, Pa., U.S.	F7	115
Juniata, Raystown Branch, stm., Pa., U.S.	F6	115
Juniata Terrace, Pa., U.S.	E6	115
Junín, Peru	D2	58
Junín, Arg.	C4	54
Junín, Lago, l., Peru	D2	58
Junin de los Andes, Arg.	C2	54
Junior, W.V., U.S.	C4	125
Junior Lake, l., Me., U.S.	C4	96
Juniper, N.B.	C2	71
Juniper Mountains, mts., Az., U.S.	B2	80
Junipero Serra Peak, mtn., Ca., U.S.	D3	82
Junius, S.D., U.S.	C8	118
Juno, Tx., U.S.	D2	120
Juntura, Or., U.S.	D8	114
Jupiter, Fl., U.S.	F6	86
Jupiter Inlet, b., Fl., U.S.	F6	86
Jupiter Island, i., Fl., U.S.	E6	86
J. Percy Priest Lake, res., Tn., U.S.	A5	119
Juquiá, Braz.	D2	56
Juquitiba, Braz.	m8	56
Jura, state, Switz.	C1	20
Jura, dept., Fr.	D2	58
Júra, i., Scot., U.K.	*C3	10
Jura, dept., Fr.	C1	20
Jura, Sound of, strt., Scot., U.K.	A5	54
Jura Mountains, mts., Eur.	E3	18
Jurbarkas, Sov. Un.	A7	26
Jurf ad Darāwīsh, Jord.	G10	40
Juruá, Braz.	B4	58
Juruá, stm., S.A.	B4	58
Juruena, stm., Braz.	C3	59
Juruti, Braz.	C3	59
Juskatla, B.C.	C1	69
Jussey, Fr.	B1	20
Justice, Il., U.S.	*k9	90
Justiceburg, Tx., U.S.	C2	120
Justin, Tx., U.S.	C4	120
Justo Daract, Arg.	A3	54
Jutaí, Braz.	C4	58
Jutaí, stm., Braz.	B4	58
Jüterbog, E. Ger.	C6	18
Jutiapa, Guat.	E7	63
Juticalpa, Hond.	E7	63
Jutland, pen., Den.	I3	14
Juventud, Isla de la (Isle of Pines), i., Cuba	D2	64
Juxian, China	D7	32
Juyongguan Pass, China	D7	32
Južna Morava, stm., Yugo.	C5	15
Jyderup, Den.		
Jyväskylä, Fin.	F11	14

K

Name	Map Ref.	Page
K2 (Godwin Austen), mtn., Asia	A6	36
Kaaawa, Hi., U.S.	f10	88
Kaala, mtn., Hi., U.S.	f9	88
Kaalualu Bay, b., Hi., U.S.	E6	88
Kaaumakua, Puu, mtn., Hi., U.S.	f10	88
Kabala, S.L.	E2	45
Kabale, Ug.	B4	48
Kabalega Falls (Murchison Falls), wtfl., Ug.	A5	48
Kabalo, Zaire	C4	48
Kabambare, Zaire	C4	48
Kabara, i., Fiji	I16	52
Kabarnet, Kenya	A6	48
Kabba, Nig.	E6	45
Kabenga, Zaire	C4	48
Kabetogama Lake, l., Mn., U.S.	B5	100
Kabinda, Zaire	C4	48
Kabīr Kūh, mts., Iran	E3	39
Kabompo, Zam.	D3	48
Kabompo, stm., Zam.	D3	48
Kabong, Malay.	E4	34
Kabongo, Zaire	C4	48
Kabul (Kābol), Afg.	B4	36
Kabul, stm., Asia	D13	39
Kabwe (Broken Hill), Zam.	D4	49
Kachchh, Gulf of (Kutch), b., India	D4	36
Kachess Lake, l., Wa., U.S.	B4	124
Kachug, Sov. Un.	D13	29
Kackley, Ks., U.S.	C6	93
Kadaň, Czech.	C2	26
Kadan, i., Burma	F3	35
Kadavu, i., Fiji	I15	52
Kade, Ghana	E4	45
Kadena, Japan	O5	33
Kadett Channel, strt., Eur.	A6	18
Kading, stm., Laos	C6	35
Kadinhanı, Tur.	C9	40
Kadiolo, Mali	D3	45
Kadiri, India	F6	36
Kadirli, Tur.	*D11	40
Kadoka, S.D., U.S.	D4	118
Kadoma, Zimb.	A4	49
Kadom, Nig.	D6	45
Kaduna, Nig.	D6	45
Kaduna, stm., Nig.	D6	45
Kāduqlī, Sud.	C2	47
Kaédi, Maur.	C2	46
Kaélé, Cam.	C2	46
Kaena Point, c., Hi., U.S.	B3	88
Kaeryŏng, S. Kor.	H4	33
Kaesŏng, N. Kor.	D10	31
Kāf, Sau. Ar.	E6	45
Kafanchan, Nig.	E6	45
Kaffrine, Sen.	D5	36
Kafia Kingi, Sud.	D1	47
Kafr ad Dawwār, Eg.	C2	41
Kafr ash Shaykh, Eg.	A1	112
Kafr az Zayyāt, Eg.	D2	120
Kafr Mālik, Isr. Occ.	h12	41
Kafr Qaddūm, Isr. Occ.	g11	41
Kafr Qāsim, Isr.	g10	41
Kafr Salīm, Eg.	C2	41
Kafr Saqr, Eg.	D3	41
Kafr Ṭarkhān al Gharbī, Eg.	E3	41
Kafr Zībād, Isr. Occ.	g11	41
Kafue, Zam.	E4	48
Kafue, stm., Zam.	E4	48
Kagan, Sov. Un.	B12	39
Kagawong, Ont.	B2	73
Kagera, stm., Afr.	B5	48
Kagoshima, Japan	E11	31
Kagoshima Bay, b., Japan	K5	33
Kagul, Sov. Un.	I7	27
Kahakuloa, Hi., U.S.	B5	88
Kahaluu, Hi., U.S.	g10	88
Kahaluu, Hi., U.S.	D6	88
Kahana, Tan.	B5	48
Kahana Bay, b., Hi., U.S.	f10	88
Kahayan, stm., Indon.	F4	34
Kahemba, Zaire	C6	119
Kahla, E. Ger.	C6	119
Kahlotus, Wa., U.S.	C5	38
Kahnūj, Iran	A6	102
Kahoka, Mo., U.S.	C5	88
Kahoolawe, i., Hi., U.S.	C5	88
Kahramanmaraş, Tur.	D11	40
Kahuku, Hi., U.S.	B4	88
Kahuku Point, c., Hi., U.S.	B4	88
Kahului, Hi., U.S.	C5	88
Kahului Bay, b., Hi., U.S.	C5	88
Kaiama, Nig.	E5	45
Kaiapoi, N.Z.	O14	51
Kaibab, Az., U.S.	A3	80
Kaibab Indian Reservation, Az., U.S.	A3	80
Kaibab Plateau, plat., Az., U.S.	A3	80
Kaibito, Az., U.S.	A4	80
Kaibito Plateau, plat., Az., U.S.	A4	80
Kaieteur Fall, wtfl., Guy.	A3	59
Kaifeng, China	E7	31
Kaijiang, China	J8	32
Kai Islands, is., Indon.	G8	34
Kaikoura, N.Z.	O14	51
Kaikoura Peninsula, pen., N.Z.	O14	51
Kailas Range see Gangdise Mountains, mts., China	B9	37
Kailu, China	C9	32
Kailua, Hi., U.S.	B4	88
Kailua Bay, b., Hi., U.S.	g11	88

Name — Map Ref. — Page

Kailua Kona, Hi., U.S. — D6 — 88
Kai Malino, Hi., U.S. — D6 — 88
Kaimana, Indon. — F8 — 34
Kaimu, Hi., U.S. — D7 — 88
Kainaliu, Hi., U.S. — D6 — 88
Kainan, Japan — I7 — 33
Kainji Dam, Nig. — E5 — 45
Kainji Lake, res., Nig. — E5 — 45
Kaipara Harbour, b., N.Z. — L15 — 51
Kaiparowits Plateau, plat., Ut., U.S. — F4 — 121
Kaipokok Bay, b., Newf. — g10 — 72
Kaiserslautern, W. Ger. — D3 — 18
Kaiserstuhl, Switz. — A5 — 21
Kaišiadorys, Sov. Un. — A8 — 26
Kaitaia, N.Z. — K14 — 51
Kaitangata, N.Z. — Q12 — 51
Kaithal, India — C6 — 37
Kaiwi Channel, strt., Hi., U.S. — B4 — 88
Kaixian, China — E6 — 31
Kaiyuan, China — C11 — 32
Kaizuka, Japan — o14 — 33
Kajaani, Fin. — E12 — 14
Kajakī, Band-e, res., Afg. — E12 — 36
Kajiado, Kenya — B6 — 48
Kajikazawa, Japan — n17 — 33
Kākā, Sud. — C3 — 47
Kakagi Lake, l., Ont. — E5 — 70
Kakamas, S. Afr. — C3 — 49
Kakamega, Kenya — A5 — 48
Kaka Point, c., Hi., U.S. — C5 — 88
Kake, Ak., U.S. — D13 — 79
Kakegawa, Japan — o17 — 33
Kakhovka, Sov. Un. — H9 — 27
Kakhovka Reservoir, res., Sov. Un. — E6 — 29
Kākināda (Cocanada), India — E7 — 36
Kakisa Lake, l., N.W. Ter. — D9 — 66
Kakogawa, Japan — *I7 — 33
Kakuma, Kenya — A5 — 48
Kakwa, stm., Can. — B1 — 68
Kālābagh, Pak. — B5 — 36
Kalabáka, Grc. — C3 — 25
Kalabakan, Malay. — E5 — 34
Kalābishah, Eg. — E6 — 43
Kalabo, Zam. — D3 — 48
Kalach, Sov. Un. — F13 — 27
Ka Lae, c., Hi., U.S. — E6 — 88
Kalahari Desert, des., Afr. — B3 — 49
Kalahari Gemsbok National Park, S. Afr. — C3 — 49
Kalaheo, Hi., U.S. — B2 — 88
Kalaho, Pidos, hill, N. Mar. Is. — C8 — 52
Kalai-Mor, Sov. Un. — D11 — 39
Kalama, Wa., U.S. — C3 — 124
Kalámai, Grc. — D4 — 40
Kalamaki, Tur. — D7 — 25
Kalamariá, Grc. — *B4 — 25
Kalamazoo, Mi., U.S. — F5 — 99
Kalamazoo, co., Mi., U.S. — F5 — 99
Kalamazoo, stm., Mi., U.S. — F5 — 99
Kalambo Falls, wtfl., Afr. — C5 — 48
Kalandula, Ang. — C2 — 48
Kalaoa Homesteads, Hi., U.S. — D6 — 88
Kalaotoa, i., Indon. — G6 — 34
Kalapana, Hi., U.S. — D7 — 88
Kalasin, Thai. — D5 — 35
Kalāt, Pak. — C4 — 36
Kalaupapa, Hi., U.S. — B5 — 88
Kalaupapa Peninsula, pen., Hi., U.S. — B5 — 88
Kalávrita, Grc. — C4 — 25
Kalawao, co., Hi., U.S. — B5 — 88
Kalb, Ra's al, c., Yemen — D4 — 47
Kalba', U.A.E. — C5 — 38
Kalecik, Tur. — B9 — 40
Kaleden, B.C. — E8 — 69
Kalegauk, i., Burma — E2 — 35
Kalehe, Zaire — B4 — 48
Kaleköy, Tur. — B5 — 40
Kalemie (Albertville), Zaire — C4 — 48
Kalema, Puu, mtn., Hi., U.S. — g9 — 88
Kaleva, Mi., U.S. — D4 — 99
Kalevala, Sov. Un. — E14 — 14
Kalewa, Burma — D9 — 36
Kalgalaksha, Sov. Un. — E16 — 14
Kalgin Island, i., Ak., U.S. — g16 — 79
Kalgoorlie, Austl. — F3 — 50
Kalibo, Phil. — C6 — 34
Kalihiwai, Hi., U.S. — A2 — 88
Kalima, Zaire — B4 — 48
Kálimnos, Grc. — D6 — 40
Kálimnos, i., Grc. — D6 — 40
Kaliningrad, Sov. Un. — n17 — 29
Kaliningrad (Königsberg), Sov. Un. — D5 — 29
Kalinkovichi, Sov. Un. — F15 — 27
Kalis, Som. — D6 — 47
Kāli Sindh, stm., India — E6 — 37
Kalispel Indian Reservation, Wa., U.S. — A8 — 124
Kalispell, Mt., U.S. — B2 — 103
Kalisz, Pol. — C5 — 26
Kaliua, Tan. — C5 — 48
Kalix älven, stm., Swe. — D10 — 14
Kalkaska, Mi., U.S. — D5 — 99
Kalkaska, co., Mi., U.S. — D5 — 99
Kalkfeld, Nmb. — B2 — 49
Kalkrand, Nmb. — B2 — 49
Kallithéa, Grc. — h11 — 25
Kalllsjön, l., Swe. — F5 — 14
Kalmalo, Nig. — D6 — 45
Kalmar, Swe. — t35 — 14
Kalmarsund, strt., Swe. — I7 — 14
Kalmykovo, Sov. Un. — D4 — 28
Kalo, Ia., U.S. — B3 — 92
Kalocsa, Hung. — B4 — 24
Kalohi Channel, strt., Hi., U.S. — C4 — 88
Kaloli Point, c., Hi., U.S. — D7 — 88
Kalomo, Zam. — E4 — 48
Kalona, Ia., U.S. — C6 — 92
Kalone Peak, mtn., B.C. — C4 — 69
Kālpi, India — D7 — 37
Kalskag, Ak., U.S. — C7 — 79
Kaltag, Ak., U.S. — C8 — 79
Kaluga, Sov. Un. — E11 — 27
Kalulushi, Zam. — D4 — 48
Kalundborg, Den. — C5 — 15
Kalush, Sov. Un. — G5 — 27
Kaluszyn, Pol. — B6 — 26
Kalvarija, Sov. Un. — A7 — 26
Kalvehave, Den. — C5 — 15
Kalvesta, Ks., U.S. — D3 — 93
Kalvsjön, l., Swe. — A7 — 26
Kalyān, India — H4 — 37
Kama, Japan — B4 — 49
Kama, stm., Sov. Un. — D8 — 29
Kamaing, Burma — C10 — 36
Kamaishi, Japan — D13 — 31
Kamakou, mtn., Hi., U.S. — B5 — 88

Kamakura, Japan — n18 — 33
Kamakwie, S.L. — E2 — 45
Kamananui Stream, stm., Hi., U.S. — f9 — 88
Kamaniskeg Lake, l., Ont. — B7 — 73
Kamanjab, Nmb. — A1 — 49
Kamanyola, Zaire — B4 — 48
Kamarān, i., Yemen — D4 — 38
Kama Reservoir, res., Sov. Un. — D8 — 29
Kāmārhāti, India — *D8 — 36
Kamaria Fall, wtfl., Guy. — A3 — 59
Kama Rock, i., Japan — P17 — 52
Kamas, Ut., U.S. — C4 — 121
Kamatsi Lake, l., Sask. — A4 — 75
Kambalda, Austl. — F3 — 50
Kambove, Zaire — D4 — 48
Kamchatka Peninsula, pen., Sov. Un. — D18 — 29
Kamenets-Podolskiy, Sov. Un. — G6 — 27
Kamenjak, Cape, c., Yugo. — C1 — 24
Kamenka, Sov. Un. — G7 — 27
Kamenka, Sov. Un. — C2 — 28
Kamen-na-Obi, Sov. Un. — D11 — 29
Kamensk-Shakhtinskiy, Sov. Un. — G13 — 27
Kamensk-Uralskiy, Sov. Un. — D9 — 29
Kamenz, E. Ger. — C7 — 18
Kameoka, Japan — o14 — 33
Kamet, mtn., Asia — B7 — 37
Kamiah, Id., U.S. — C2 — 89
Kamiak Butte, mtn., Wa., U.S. — C8 — 124
Kamień Pomorski, Pol. — B3 — 26
Kamina, Zaire — C4 — 48
Kamioka, Japan — m16 — 33
Kamloops, B.C. — D7 — 69
Kammuri, Mount, mtn., Japan — I6 — 33
Kamo, Sov. Un. — B15 — 40
Kamoa Mountains, mts., Guy. — B3 — 59
Kamooloa, Hi., U.S. — f9 — 88
Kamouraska, Que. — B8 — 74
Kamouraska, co., Que. — B8 — 74
Kampala, Ug. — A5 — 48
Kampar, Malay. — J4 — 35
Kampar, stm., Indon. — E2 — 34
Kampen, Neth. — A6 — 16
Kampeska Lake, l., S.D., U.S. — C8 — 118
Kamphaeng Phet, Thai. — D3 — 35
Kampong Cham, Camb. — C3 — 34
Kampong Chhnang, Camb. — C2 — 34
Kampong Khleang, Camb. — F6 — 35
Kampong Saom, Camb. — C2 — 34
Kampong Saom Bay, b., Camb. — C2 — 34
Kampong Spoe, Camb. — G6 — 35
Kampong Thum, Camb. — C2 — 34
Kampot, Camb. — C2 — 34
Kampsville, Il., U.S. — D3 — 90
Kampuchea see Cambodia, ctry., Asia — F6 — 34
Kamsack, Sask. — B4 — 92
Kamuchawie Lake, l., Can. — A4 — 75
Kamuela (Waimea), Hi., U.S. — C6 — 88
Kamuli, Ug. — A5 — 48
Kamyshevakha, Sov. Un. — q21 — 27
Kamyshin, Sov. Un. — F15 — 27
Kamyshlov, Sov. Un. — B6 — 28
Kanab, Ut., U.S. — F3 — 121
Kanab Creek, stm., U.S. — A3 — 80
Kanabec, co., Mn., U.S. — E5 — 100
Kanaceа, i., Fiji — H16 — 52
Kanaga Island, i., Ak., U.S. — E4 — 79
Kanairiktok, stm., Newf. — g9 — 72
Kananaskis, stm., Alta. — D3 — 68
Kananga (Luluabourg), Zaire — C3 — 48
Kanapou Bay, b., Hi., U.S. — C5 — 88
Kanarraville, Ut., U.S. — F2 — 121
Kanash, Sov. Un. — D16 — 27
Kanata, Ont. — B9 — 73
Kanauga, Oh., U.S. — D3 — 112
Kanawha, Ia., U.S. — B4 — 92
Kanawha, co., W.V., U.S. — C3 — 125
Kanawha, stm., W.V., U.S. — C3 — 125
Kanayama, Japan — n16 — 33
Kanazawa, Japan — D12 — 31
Kanbe, Burma — *E10 — 36
Kanchanaburi, Thai. — E3 — 35
Känchenjunga, mtn., Asia — C8 — 36
Kānchipuram (Conjeeveram), India — F7 — 36
Känchrāpāra, India — *D8 — 36
Kandahar (Qandahār), Afg. — B4 — 36
Kandahar, Sask. — F3 — 75
Kandalaksha, Sov. Un. — C6 — 29
Kandalaksha Bay, b., Sov. Un. — B15 — 8
Kandangan, Indon. — F5 — 34
Kandel, W. Ger. — D3 — 19
Kandern, W. Ger. — A4 — 21
Kandersteg, Switz. — C3 — 20
Kandi, Benin — D5 — 45
Kandira, Tur. — B8 — 40
Kandiyohi, Mn., U.S. — E4 — 100
Kandiyohi, co., Mn., U.S. — E3 — 100
Kandla, India — F3 — 37
Kandrāch, India — C4 — 36
Kandreho, Madag. — g9 — 49
Kandy, Sri L. — G7 — 36
Kane, Il., U.S. — D3 — 90
Kane, Pa., U.S. — C4 — 115
Kane, co., Il., U.S. — B5 — 90
Kane, co., Ut., U.S. — F3 — 121
Kane Basin, strt., N.A. — m38 — 66
Kaneohe, Hi., U.S. — B4 — 88
Kaneohe Bay, b., Hi., U.S. — g10 — 88
Kaneohe Bay Marine Corps Air Station, Hi., U.S. — g10 — 88
Kanevskaya, Sov. Un. — H12 — 27
Kang, Bots. — B3 — 49
Kangaba, Mali — D3 — 45
Kangal, Tur. — C11 — 40
Kangar, Malay. — I4 — 35
Kangaroo, i., Austl. — G6 — 50
Kangbao, China — C7 — 31
Kangding, China — E5 — 31
Kangdong, N. Kor. — G3 — 33
Kangean Islands, is., Indon. — G5 — 34
Kanggye, N. Kor. — C10 — 31
Kangiqsualujjuaq, Que. — f8 — 72
Kangiqsujuaq, Que. — f12 — 74
Kangirsuk, Que. — f12 — 74
Kangley, Il., U.S. — B5 — 90
Kangnung, S. Kor. — D10 — 31
Kango, Gabon — E2 — 46
Kangoku Rock, i., Japan — P17 — 52
Kangrinboqê Mountain, mtn., China — B8 — 37
Kani, Burma — A1 — 35
Kani, I.C. — E3 — 45
Kaniama, Zaire — C3 — 48
Kanimekh, Sov. Un. — A12 — 39
Kanin Nos, Cape, c., Sov. Un. — C7 — 29
Kanjiža, Yugo. — B5 — 24
Kankakee, Il., U.S. — B6 — 90
Kankakee, co., Il., U.S. — B6 — 90

Kankakee, stm., U.S. — B5 — 90
Kankan, Gui. — D3 — 45
Kankossa, Maur. — C2 — 45
Kannapolis, N.C., U.S. — B2 — 110
Kannauj, India — D7 — 37
Kano, Nig. — D6 — 45
Kanopolis, Ks., U.S. — D5 — 93
Kanopolis Lake, res., Ks., U.S. — D5 — 93
Kanorado, Ks., U.S. — C1 — 93
Kanosh, Ut., U.S. — E3 — 121
Kanoya, Japan — K5 — 33
Kānpur, India — C7 — 36
Kansas, Al., U.S. — B2 — 78
Kansas, Il., U.S. — D6 — 90
Kansas, Ok., U.S. — A7 — 113
Kansas, state, U.S. — D5 — 93
Kansas, stm., Ks., U.S. — C7 — 93
Kansas City, Ks., U.S. — C9 — 93
Kansas City, Mo., U.S. — B3 — 102
Kansasville, Wi., U.S. — n11 — 126
Kansk, Sov. Un. — D12 — 29
Kansu see Gansu, prov., China — D5 — 31
Kantang, Thai. — D1 — 34
Kanton Island, i., Kir. — G11 — 6
Kantunilkín, Mex. — C7 — 63
Kanturk, Ire. — E3 — 11
Kanuku Mountains, mts., Guy. — B3 — 59
Kanuma, Japan — H9 — 33
Kanye, Bots. — B4 — 49
Kaohsiung, Tai. — G9 — 31
Kaoko Veld, plat., Nmb. — A1 — 49
Kaolack, Sen. — D1 — 45
Kaoma, Zam. — D3 — 48
Kaouar, reg., Niger — C7 — 45
Kapaa, Hi., U.S. — A2 — 88
Kapaau, Hi., U.S. — C6 — 88
Kapandrition, Grc. — g11 — 25
Kapanga, Zaire — C3 — 48
Kapapa Island, i., Hi., U.S. — g10 — 88
Kaparéllion, Grc. — g10 — 25
Kapchagay, Sov. Un. — E9 — 28
Kapchagay Reservoir, res., Sov. Un. — E9 — 28
Kapenguria, Kenya — A6 — 48
Kapfenberg, Aus. — E7 — 18
Kapiri Mposhi, Zam. — D4 — 48
Kapit, Malay. — E4 — 34
Kaplan, La., U.S. — D3 — 95
Kaplice, Czech. — E9 — 19
Kapoeta, Sud. — E3 — 47
Kaposvár, Hung. — B3 — 24
Kaposvar Creek, stm., Sask. — G4 — 75
Kapowsin, Wa., U.S. — C3 — 124
Kappa, Il., U.S. — C4 — 90
Kapsan, N. Kor. — F4 — 33
Kapuas, stm., Indon. — F4 — 34
Kapulena, Hi., U.S. — C6 — 88
Kapuskasing, Ont. — o19 — 73
Kapustin Yar, Sov. Un. — D3 — 28
Kaputar, mtn., Austl. — E8 — 51
Kapuvár, Hung. — B3 — 24
Kara, stm., Sov. Un. — C9 — 29
Karabash, Sov. Un. — D21 — 8
Kara-Bogaz-Gol, Sov. Un. — E4 — 28
Kara-Bogaz-Gol Gulf, b., Sov. Un. — E4 — 28
Karabük, Tur. — *B9 — 40
Karachev, Sov. Un. — E10 — 27
Karāchi, Pak. — *D4 — 36
Karāchi Cantonment, Pak. — *D4 — 36
Karaganda, Sov. Un. — E10 — 29
Karagiz Island, i., Sov. Un. — D19 — 29
Karaisalı, Tur. — D10 — 40
Karaj, Iran — D5 — 39
Karakas, Sov. Un. — D10 — 29
Karakelong, i., Indon. — E7 — 34
Karakoram Pass, Asia — A6 — 36
Karakoram Range, mts., Asia — A6 — 36
Karaköse see Ağrı, Tur. — C14 — 40
Karakul, India — n16 — 33
Kara-Kum Canal, Sov. Un. — H21 — 8
Karamay, China — B1 — 31
Karamea, N.Z. — N14 — 51
Karamea Bight, N.Z. — N13 — 51
Karamürsel, Tur. — B7 — 40
Karapinar, Tur. — D9 — 40
Karasburg, Nmb. — C2 — 49
Kara Sea, Sov. Un. — B9 — 29
Karasu, Tur. — C6 — 28
Karasu, stm., Tur. — B8 — 40
Karasuk, Sov. Un. — C9 — 29
Karatal, stm., Sov. Un. — D9 — 29
Karatas, Cape, c., Tur. — D10 — 40
Karatau Range, mts., Sov. Un. — E7 — 28
Karatobe, Sov. Un. — D4 — 28
Karatsu, Japan — J4 — 33
Karauli, India — D6 — 37
Karaulkeldy, Sov. Un. — D5 — 28
Karawanken, mts., Eur. — E7 — 18
Karbalā', Iraq — F15 — 40
Karcag, Hung. — B5 — 24
Karczew, Pol. — m14 — 27
Kardhítsa, Grc. — C3 — 40
Kárdla, Tan. — C5 — 48
Karema, Tan. — C5 — 48
Karesuando (part of Kiruna), Swe. — C10 — 14
Kargasok, Sov. Un. — D11 — 29
Kargat, Sov. Un. — D25 — 8
Kargil, India — B6 — 36
Kargopol, Sov. Un. — A12 — 27
Kariba, Zimb. — A4 — 49
Kariba, Lake, res., Afr. — A4 — 49
Karibib, Nmb. — B2 — 49
Karikari, Cape, c., N.Z. — K14 — 51
Karimata Islands, is., Indon. — F3 — 34
Karimata Strait, strt., Indon. — F3 — 34
Karīmnagar, India — H7 — 37
Karimunjawa Islands, is., Indon. — G4 — 34
Karisimbi, Volcán, vol., Afr. — B4 — 48
Káristos, Grc. — C6 — 40
Kariya, Japan — o15 — 33
Kārīz, Iran — *D10 — 39
Karkar, i., Pap. N. Gui. — h12 — 50
Karkheh, stm., Iran — E3 — 39
Karkinit Gulf, b., Sov. Un. — I9 — 27
Karl-Marx-Stadt (Chemnitz), E. Ger. — C6 — 18
Karlobag, Yugo. — C2 — 24
Karlovac, Yugo. — C2 — 24
Karlovo, Bul. — D7 — 24
Karlovy Vary, Czech. — C2 — 26
Karlsham, Swe. — I6 — 14
Karlskoga, Swe. — H6 — 14

Karlskrona, Swe. — I6 — 14
Karlsruhe, W. Ger. — D4 — 18
Karlsruhe, N.D., U.S. — A5 — 111
Karlstad, Swe. — H5 — 14
Karlstad, Mn., U.S. — B2 — 100
Karlstadt, W. Ger. — D4 — 19
Karluk, Ak., U.S. — D9 — 79
Karnak, Il., U.S. — F5 — 90
Karnāl, India — *C6 — 30
Karnāli, stm., Nepal — C8 — 37
Karnataka, state, India — F6 — 36
Karnes, co., Tx., U.S. — E4 — 120
Karnes City, Tx., U.S. — E4 — 120
Karnobat, Bul. — D8 — 24
Karns, Tn., U.S. — n13 — 119
Karns City, Pa., U.S. — E2 — 115
Kärnten, state, Aus. — E6 — 18
Karoi, Zimb. — A4 — 49
Karonga, Mwi. — C5 — 48
Karora, Sud. — B4 — 47
Karow, E. Ger. — E6 — 15
Kárpathos, i., Grc. — E6 — 40
Karpenísion, Grc. — C3 — 25
Karratha, Austl. — D2 — 50
Karsakpay, Sov. Un. — E9 — 29
Karsha, Sov. Un. — D4 — 28
Karshi, Sov. Un. — F9 — 29
Karstädt, E. Ger. — E5 — 15
Kartal, Tur. — B6 — 25
Kartaly, Sov. Un. — D9 — 29
Karthaus, Pa., U.S. — D5 — 115
Kartuzy, Pol. — A4 — 26
Kārūn, stm., Iran — F4 — 39
Karup, Den. — B3 — 15
Karup Å, stm., Den. — B3 — 15
Karval, Col. — C7 — 83
Karvia, Fin. — F10 — 14
Karviná, Czech. — D5 — 26
Kawsi, India — F8 — 37
Kārwār, India — D12 — 31
Kås, Den. — A3 — 15
Kas, Sur. — C1 — 47
Kaş, Tur. — D7 — 40
Kasaan, Ak., U.S. — n23 — 79
Kasai (Cassai), stm., Afr. — B3 — 48
Kasai, hist. reg., Zaire — B3 — 48
Kasaji, Zaire — D3 — 48
Kasama, Zam. — D5 — 48
Kasane, Bots. — A4 — 49
Kasanga, Tan. — C5 — 48
Kasaragod, India — F5 — 36
Kasba, India — E11 — 37
Kasba Lake, l., N.W. Ter. — D12 — 66
Kasba Tadla, Mor. — C3 — 44
Kasempa, Zam. — D4 — 48
Kasenga, Zaire — D5 — 48
Kasese, Ug. — A5 — 48
Kashan, Iran — B5 — 38
Kashi, China — F10 — 29
Kashihara, Japan — o14 — 33
Kashima, Japan — n19 — 33
Kashira, stm., Sov. Un. — D12 — 27
Kashirka, stm., Sov. Un. — n18 — 27
Kashmor, Pak. — H9 — 33
Kasilof, Ak., U.S. — C2 — 37
Kasimov, Sov. Un. — C9 — 79
Kaskaskia, Il., U.S. — D13 — 27
Kaskaskia, stm., Il., U.S. — F4 — 90
Kaskö, Fin. — E9 — 14
Kaslo, B.C. — E9 — 69
Kasongo, Zaire — B4 — 48
Kasongo-Lunda, Zaire — C2 — 48
Kásos, i., Grc. — E6 — 40
Kasota, Mn., U.S. — F5 — 100
Kassalā, Sud. — B4 — 47
Kassalā, prov., Sud. — B4 — 47
Kassandra, Gulf of, b., Grc. — B4 — 25
Kassel (Cassel), W. Ger. — C4 — 18
Kastamonu, Tur. — B9 — 40
Kastiyu, Puntan, c., N. Mar. Is. — E7 — 52
Kastoría, Grc. — B3 — 40
Kástron, Grc. — g10 — 25
Kasukabe, Japan — n18 — 33
Kasulu, Tan. — B5 — 48
Kasumi, Japan — I7 — 33
Kasumiga-Ura, l., Japan — H10 — 33
Kasungu, Mwi. — D5 — 48
Kasūr, Pak. — B5 — 36
Katako-Kombe, Zaire — B3 — 48
Katanga, hist. reg., Zaire — C4 — 48
Katanning, Austl. — F2 — 50
Katano, Point, c., Japan — P17 — 52
Katata, Japan — n14 — 33
Katepwa Beach, Sask. — G4 — 75
Katerini, Grc. — B4 — 40
Kates Needle, mtn., Ak., U.S. — m24 — 79
Katha, Burma — D10 — 36
Katherine, Austl. — B5 — 50
Kāthiāwār Peninsula, pen., India — D4 — 36
Kathleen, Fl., U.S. — D4 — 86
Kathmandu (Kāthmāndāū), Nepal — C8 — 36
Kathryn, Alta. — D4 — 68
Kathryn, N.D., U.S. — C8 — 111
Kathua, India — A5 — 37
Katihār, India — C4 — 113
Katimik Lake, l., Man. — C2 — 70
Katiola, I.C. — E3 — 45
Katlatie, Sud. — E3 — 47
Katlehong, S. Afr. — *C4 — 49
Katmai, Mount, mtn., Ak., U.S. — D9 — 79
Katmai National Park, Ak., U.S. — D9 — 79
Kato Alepokhórion, Grc. — g10 — 25
Katoomba, Austl. — F9 — 50
Katomba, Zaire — C3 — 48
Katoúna, Grc. — C3 — 25
Katowice (Stalinogród), Pol. — C5 — 26
Kātrīnā, Jabal, mtn., Eg. — D6 — 43
Katrineholm, Swe. — H7 — 14
Katsina, Nig. — D6 — 45
Katsina Ala, stm., Afr. — *E6 — 45
Katsura, Japan — *H10 — 33
Katsuyama, Japan — m15 — 33
Kattegat, strt., Eur. — I4 — 14
Katwijk aan Zee, Neth. — B4 — 17
Katy, Tx., U.S. — r14 — 120
Kau, Indon. — E7 — 34
Kauai, co., Hi., U.S. — B1 — 88
Kauai, i., Hi., U.S. — A2 — 88
Kauai Channel, strt., Hi., U.S. — B2 — 88
Kau Desert, des., Hi., U.S. — D6 — 88
Kaufbeuren, W. Ger. — E5 — 18
Kaufman, Tx., U.S. — C4 — 120
Kaufman, co., Tx., U.S. — C4 — 120

Kauhajoki, Fin. — F10 — 14
Kauhava, Fin. — F10 — 14
Kauiki Head, c., Hi., U.S. — C6 — 88
Kaukauna, Wi., U.S. — D5 — 126
Kaukau Veld, plat., Afr. — B3 — 49
Kaula, i., Hi., U.S. — m15 — 88
Kaulakahi Channel, strt., Hi., U.S. — A2 — 88
Kauliranta, Fin. — D10 — 14
Kaumakani, Hi., U.S. — B2 — 88
Kaumalapau, Hi., U.S. — C5 — 88
Kaunakakai, Hi., U.S. — B4 — 88
Kauna Point, c., Hi., U.S. — D6 — 88
Kaunas, Sov. Un. — D5 — 29
Kaura Namoda, Nig. — D6 — 45
Kautokeino, Nor. — C10 — 14
Kavacha, Sov. Un. — C19 — 29
Kavaja, Alb. — B3 — 25
Kavála, Grc. — B5 — 40
Kavála, Gulf of, b., Grc. — B5 — 40
Kāvali, India — F6 — 36
Kavarna, Bul. — F9 — 24
Kavieng, Pap. N. Gui. — h13 — 50
Kavīr, Dasht-e, des., Iran — E9 — 29
Kävlinge, Swe. — C7 — 15
Kaw, Fr. Gu. — B4 — 59
Kawagama Lake, l., Ont. — B6 — 73
Kawagoe, Japan — n18 — 33
Kawaguchi, Japan — n18 — 33
Kawaihae, Hi., U.S. — C6 — 88
Kawaihoa Point, c., Hi., U.S. — B1 — 88
Kawaikini, mtn., Hi., U.S. — A2 — 88
Kawailoa, Hi., U.S. — f9 — 88
Kawailoa Beach, Hi., U.S. — f9 — 88
Kawakawa, N.Z. — K15 — 51
Kawambwa, Zam. — C4 — 48
Kawardha, India — F8 — 37
Kawasaki, Japan — D12 — 31
Kawawachikamach, Que. — g13 — 74
Kawbar, Isr. Occ. — h11 — 41
Kaweenakumik Lake, l., Man. — C2 — 70
Kawela, Hi., U.S. — f9 — 88
Kawela Bay, Hi., U.S. — M15 — 51
Kawhia Harbour, b., N.Z. — M15 — 51
Kawich Peak, mtn., Nv., U.S. — F5 — 105
Kawich Range, mts., Nv., U.S. — F5 — 105
Kawkareik, Burma — D3 — 35
Kaw Lake, res., Ok., U.S. — A5 — 113
Kawm Hamādah, Eg. — D3 — 41
Kawm Umbū, Eg. — C3 — 38
Kawthaung, Burma — F10 — 35
Kay, co., Ok., U.S. — A4 — 113
Kaya, Burkina — D4 — 45
Kayan, stm., Indon. — E5 — 34
Kayangel Islands, is., Palau — R17 — 52
Kaycee, Wy., U.S. — C6 — 127
Kayenta, Az., U.S. — A5 — 80
Kayes, Congo — B1 — 48
Kayes, Mali — D2 — 45
Kayford, W.V., U.S. — C3 — 125
Kayjay, Ky., U.S. — D6 — 94
Kaylor, S.D., U.S. — D8 — 118
Kayō, Japan — N6 — 52
Kayser Gebergte, mts., Sur. — B3 — 59
Kayseri, Tur. — C10 — 40
Kaysville, Ut., U.S. — B4 — 121
Kayuagung, Indon. — F2 — 34
Kayville, Sask. — H3 — 75
Kazachye, Sov. Un. — B16 — 29
Kazakevichevo, Sov. Un. — D7 — 33
Kazakh Hills, hills, Sov. Un. — D7 — 28
Kazakh S.S.R., state, Sov. Un. — E9 — 29
Kazalinsk, Sov. Un. — D6 — 28
Kazan, Sov. Un. — D7 — 29
Kazan, stm., N.W. Ter. — D12 — 66
Kazanlŭk, Bul. — D7 — 24
Kazbek, mtn., Sov. Un. — I7 — 8
Kāzerūn, Iran — G5 — 39
Kazhim, Sov. Un. — C24 — 8
Kazi-Magomed, Sov. Un. — E3 — 28
Kazimierz [Dolny], Pol. — B6 — 26
Kazincbarcika, Hung. — A5 — 24
Kazumba, Zaire — C3 — 48
Kazym, stm., Sov. Un. — C22 — 8
Kdyně, Czech. — D5 — 19
Kéa, Grc. — g10 — 25
Kéa, i., Grc. — D5 — 40
Keaau, Hi., U.S. — D6 — 88
Keady, N. Ire., U.K. — C5 — 11
Keahiakahoe, Puu, mtn., Hi., U.S. — g10 — 88
Keahole Point, c., Hi., U.S. — D5 — 88
Kealaikahiki Channel, strt., Hi., U.S. — C5 — 88
Kealaikahiki Point, c., Hi., U.S. — C5 — 88
Kealakekua, Hi., U.S. — D6 — 88
Kealia, Hi., U.S. — A2 — 88
Keams Canyon, Az., U.S. — B5 — 80
Keanae, Hi., U.S. — C5 — 88
Keanapapa Point, c., Hi., U.S. — C4 — 88
Kearney, Mo., U.S. — B3 — 102
Kearney, Ne., U.S. — D7 — 104
Kearney, co., Ne., U.S. — D7 — 104
Kearneysville, W.V., U.S. — B7 — 125
Kearns, Ut., U.S. — C4 — 121
Kearny, Az., U.S. — D5 — 80
Kearny, N.J., U.S. — h8 — 107
Kearny, co., Ks., U.S. — D2 — 93
Kearsarge, Mi., U.S. — A2 — 99
Kearsarge, N.H., U.S. — B4 — 106
Kearsarge, Mount, mtn., N.H., U.S. — D3 — 106
Kearsarge North, mtn., N.H., U.S. — — —
Keatchie, La., U.S. — B2 — 95
Keating, Or., U.S. — C9 — 114
Keaton, Ky., U.S. — C7 — 94
Keauhou, Hi., U.S. — D6 — 88
Keban Reservoir, res., Tur. — C12 — 40
Kebbi, Nig. — D5 — 45
Kebnekaise, mtn., Swe. — D8 — 14
Kebock Head, c., Scot., U.K. — D5 — 10
Kebri Dehar, Eth. — D5 — 47
Kecskemét, Hung. — B4 — 24
Kedah, state, Malay. — J4 — 35
Keddie, Ca., U.S. — B3 — 82
Kedges Straits, strt., Md., U.S. — D5 — 97
Kediri, Indon. — G5 — 34
Kedon, China — B3 — 33
Kédougou, Sen. — D2 — 45
Kedzierzyn-Koźle, Pol. — *C5 — 26
Keedysville, Md., U.S. — B2 — 97
Keefers, B.C. — D7 — 69
Keego Harbor, Mi., U.S. — o15 — 99
Keele Peak, mtn., Yukon — D6 — 66

Keeler, Sask. — G3 — 75
Keeler, Ca., U.S. — D5 — 82
Keeline, Wy., U.S. — D8 — 127
Keeling, Tn., U.S. — B2 — 119
Keeling, Va., U.S. — D3 — 123
Keels, Newf. — D5 — 72
Keelung see Chilung, Tai. — F9 — 31
Keene, Ont. — C6 — 73
Keene, Ca., U.S. — E4 — 82
Keene, Ky., U.S. — C5 — 94
Keene, N.H., U.S. — E2 — 106
Keene, N.Y., U.S. — A7 — 109
Keene, N.D., U.S. — B3 — 111
Keene, Oh., U.S. — B4 — 112
Keene, Tx., U.S. — n9 — 120
Keenes, Il., U.S. — E5 — 90
Keenesburg, Co., U.S. — A6 — 83
Keene Valley, N.Y., U.S. — f11 — 109
Keeney Knob, mtn., W.V., U.S. — D4 — 125
Keensburg, Il., U.S. — E6 — 90
Keeseville, N.Y., U.S. — f11 — 109
Keesler Air Force Base, mil., Ms., U.S. — E5 — 101
Keetmanshoop, Nmb. — C2 — 49
Keet Seel Ruin, hist., Az., U.S. — A5 — 80
Keewatin, Mn., U.S. — C5 — 100
Keewatin, dept., N.W. Ter. — D13 — 66
Keewatin, stm., Man. — A1 — 70
Keezletown, Va., U.S. — B4 — 123
Kefa, prov., Eth. — D4 — 47
Kefallinía (Cephalonia), i., Grc. — C3 — 40
Kefar Blum, Isr. — A7 — 41
Kefar 'Eqron, Isr. — f10 — 41
Kefar Monash, Isr. — f10 — 41
Kefar Sava, Isr. — B6 — 41
Kefar Yona, Isr. — f10 — 41
Keffi, Nig. — *E6 — 45
Keflavik, Ice. — o21 — 14
Ke Ga, Cape, c., Viet. — F8 — 35
Kegaska, Que. — h9 — 72
Kegonsa, Lake, l., Wi., U.S. — F4 — 126
Kehl, W. Ger. — E2 — 19
Keho Lake, l., Alta. — E4 — 68
Kehsi Mansam, Burma — B2 — 35
Keighley, Eng., U.K. — D6 — 10
Keilor, Austl. — *G7 — 50
Keimoes, S. Afr. — C3 — 49
Keiser, Ar., U.S. — B5 — 81
Keitele, l., Fin. — F11 — 14
Keith, Austl. — H3 — 51
Keith, Scot., U.K. — B5 — 10
Keithley Creek, B.C. — C7 — 69
Keithsburg, Il., U.S. — B3 — 90
Keithville, La., U.S. — B2 — 95
Keitum, W. Ger. — D2 — 15
Keizer, Or., U.S. — C3 — 114
Kejimkujik Lake, l., N.S. — E4 — 71
Kejimkujik National Park, N.S. — E4 — 71
Kekaha, Hi., U.S. — B1 — 88
Kékes, mtn., Hung. — *B5 — 24
Kelafo, Eth. — D5 — 47
Kelan, China — E4 — 32
Kelang, Malay. — *J4 — 35
Kelantan, state, Malay. — J4 — 35
Kelantan, stm., Malay. — J5 — 35
Keldron, S.D., U.S. — B4 — 118
Kelfield, Sask. — F1 — 75
Kelford, N.C., U.S. — A5 — 110
Kelheim, W. Ger. — D6 — 18
Kelibia, Tun. — F3 — 23
Kelkit, stm., Tur. — B11 — 40
Kell, Il., U.S. — E5 — 90
Kellé, Congo — B1 — 48
Kellenhusen, W. Ger. — D5 — 15
Keller, Tx., U.S. — n9 — 120
Keller, Va., U.S. — C7 — 123
Keller Lake, l., Sask. — A2 — 75
Kellerman, Al., U.S. — B2 — 78
Kellerton, Ia., U.S. — D3 — 92
Kellerville, Il., U.S. — D3 — 90
Kellett, Cape, c., N.W. Ter. — B7 — 66
Kellettville, Pa., U.S. — D3 — 115
Kelley, Ia., U.S. — C4 — 92
Kelleys Island, Oh., U.S. — A3 — 112
Kelleys Island, i., Oh., U.S. — A3 — 112
Kelliher, Sask. — G3 — 75
Kelliher, Mn., U.S. — C4 — 100
Kellmünz, W. Ger. — A6 — 20
Kellnersville, Wi., U.S. — D6 — 126
Kelloe, Man. — D1 — 70
Kellogg, Id., U.S. — B2 — 89
Kellogg, Ia., U.S. — C5 — 92
Kellogg, Mn., U.S. — F6 — 100
Kells see Ceanannus Mór, Ire. — C5 — 11
Kelly, Ky., U.S. — D2 — 94
Kelly, La., U.S. — C3 — 95
Kelly, Wy., U.S. — C2 — 127
Kelly Air Force Base, mil., Tx., U.S. — k7 — 120
Kelly Brook Mountain, mtn., Me., U.S. — A3 — 96
Kelly Island, i., De., U.S. — D4 — 85
Kelly Lake, B.C. — C7 — 69
Kelly Lake, Mn., U.S. — C5 — 100
Kellyton, Al., U.S. — B3 — 78
Kellyville, N.H., U.S. — D2 — 106
Kellyville, Ok., U.S. — B5 — 113
Kellyville, Tx., U.S. — C5 — 120
Kélo, Chad — E8 — 46
Kelowna, B.C. — E8 — 69
Kelsey, Alta. — — —
Kelsey Lake, l., Man. — C1 — 70
Kelseyville, Ca., U.S. — C2 — 82
Kelso, Scot., U.K. — C5 — 10
Kelso, Sask. — H5 — 75
Kelso, Mo., U.S. — E8 — 102
Kelso, Wa., U.S. — C3 — 124
Keltie, Mount, mtn., Ant. — f40 — 7
Keltonburg, Tn., U.S. — D8 — 119
Keluang (Kluang), Malay. — E2 — 34
Kelvedon, Sask. — E4 — 75
Kelvin, Sov. Un. — E16 — 14
Kelvington, Sask. — F4 — 75
Kelwood, Man. — D2 — 70
Ké Macina, Mali — D3 — 45
Kemano, B.C. — C3 — 69
Kembé, Cen. Afr. Rep. — E4 — 46
Kemerovo, Sov. Un. — D11 — 29
Kemi, Fin. — E11 — 14
Kemijärvi, Fin. — D12 — 14
Kemijoki, stm., Fin. — D12 — 14
Kemme, well, Libya — E3 — 43
Kemmerer, Wy., U.S. — E2 — 127
Kemnath, W. Ger. — D6 — 19
Kemnay, Man. — E1 — 70
Kemp, Ok., U.S. — D5 — 113
Kemp, Tx., U.S. — C4 — 120
Kemp, Lake, res., Tx., U.S. — C3 — 120

Name	Map Ref.	Page

Kemp Coast, Ant. ... C18 7
Kempen, W. Ger. ... C6 17
Kemper, S.C., U.S. ... C9 117
Kemper, co., Ms., U.S. ... C5 101
Kempner, Tx., U.S. ... D4 120
Kemp Peninsula, pen., Ant. ... B6 7
Kempsey, Austl. ... F9 50
Kempshall Mountain, mtn., N.Y., U.S. ... A6 109
Kempten [in Allgäu], W. Ger. ... E5 18
Kempton, Il., U.S. ... C5 90
Kempton, In., U.S. ... D5 91
Kempton, N.D., U.S. ... B8 111
Kemptville, Ont. ... B9 73
Kenai, Ak., U.S. ... C9 79
Kenai Fjords National Park, Ak., U.S. ... D10 79
Kenai Mountains, mts., Ak., U.S. ... h16 79
Kenai Peninsula, pen., Ak., U.S. ... h16 79
Kenamu, stm., Newf. ... B1 72
Kenansville, Fl., U.S. ... E6 86
Kenansville, N.C., U.S. ... C5 110
Kenaston, Sask. ... F2 75
Kenbridge, Va., U.S. ... D4 123
Ken Caryl, Co., U.S. ... *B5 83
Kendal, Sask. ... G4 75
Kendal, Eng., U.K. ... C5 10
Kendall, Fl., U.S. ... s13 86
Kendall, Ks., U.S. ... E2 93
Kendall, N.Y., U.S. ... B2 109
Kendall, Wi., U.S. ... E3 126
Kendall, co., Il., U.S. ... B5 90
Kendall, co., Tx., U.S. ... *E3 120
Kendall Green, Fl., U.S. ... *F6 86
Kendall Park, N.J., U.S. ... C3 107
Kendallville, In., U.S. ... B7 91
Kendari, Indon. ... F6 34
Kendrāparha, India ... D8 36
Kendrick, Id., U.S. ... C2 89
Kendrick, Ok., U.S. ... B5 113
Kendujhargarh, India ... G10 37
Kenduskeag, Me., U.S. ... D4 96
Kenedy, Tx., U.S. ... E4 120
Kenedy, co., Tx., U.S. ... F4 120
Kenefic, S.D., U.S. ... C5 113
Kenel, S.D., U.S. ... B5 118
Kenema, S.L. ... E2 45
Kenge, Zaire ... B2 48
Kēng Tung, Burma ... D10 36
Kenhardt, S. Afr. ... C3 49
Kéniéba, Mali ... D2 45
Kenilworth, Il., U.S. ... h9 90
Kenilworth, N.J., U.S. ... *B4 107
Kenilworth, Ut., U.S. ... D5 121
Kenitra, Mor. ... C3 44
Kenly, N.C., U.S. ... B4 110
Kenmare, Ire. ... E2 10
Kenmare, N.D., U.S. ... A3 111
Kenmare, stm., Ire. ... E1 10
Kenmore, N.Y., U.S. ... C2 109
Kenmore, Wa., U.S. ... *B3 124
Kenna, N.M., U.S. ... D6 108
Kenna, W.V., U.S. ... C3 125
Kennaday Peak, mtn., Wy., U.S. ... E6 127
Kennan, Wi., U.S. ... C3 126
Kennard, In., U.S. ... E6 91
Kennard, Ne., U.S. ... C9 104
Kennard, Tx., U.S. ... D5 120
Kennebago Lake, l., Me., U.S. ... C2 96
Kennebec, S.D., U.S. ... D5 118
Kennebec, co., Me., U.S. ... D3 96
Kennebec, stm., Me., U.S. ... D3 96
Kennebunk, Me., U.S. ... E2 96
Kennebunkport, Me., U.S. ... E2 96
Kennedale, Tx., U.S. ... n9 120
Kennedy, Sask. ... G4 75
Kennedy, Al., U.S. ... B2 78
Kennedy, Mn., U.S. ... B2 100
Kennedy, N.Y., U.S. ... C1 109
Kennedy, Mount, mtn., Yukon ... D5 66
Kennedy Channel, strt., N.A. ... k38 66
Kennedy Entrance, strt., Ak., U.S. ... D9 79
Kennedy Heights, La., U.S. ... *E5 95
Kennedy Lake, l., Sask. ... D4 75
Kennedy Township, Pa., U.S. ... *F1 115
Kennedyville, Md., U.S. ... B5 97
Kenner, La., U.S. ... E5 95
Kennesaw, Ga., U.S. ... B2 87
Kennesaw Mountain, mtn., Ga., U.S. ... *C2 87
Kennesaw Mountain National Battlefield Park, Ga., U.S. ... h7 87
Kennet, stm., Eng., U.K. ... C6 12
Kennetcook, N.S. ... D6 71
Kenneth, Ks., U.S. ... m16 93
Kenneth, Mn., U.S. ... G2 100
Kennett, Mo., U.S. ... E7 102
Kennett Square, Pa., U.S. ... G10 115
Kennewick, Wa., U.S. ... C6 124
Kenney, Il., U.S. ... C4 90
Kenney Dam, B.C. ... C5 69
Kennisis Lake, l., Ont. ... B6 73
Kennydale, Wa., U.S. ... e11 124
Keno, Or., U.S. ... E5 114
Kénogami, Que. ... A6 74
Kénogami, Lac, l., Que. ... A6 74
Kenora, Ont. ... o16 73
Kenora, dept., Ont. ... o17 73
Kenosha, Wi., U.S. ... F6 126
Kenosha, co., Wi., U.S. ... F5 126
Kenova, W.V., U.S. ... C2 125
Ken Rock, Il., U.S. ... *A4 90
Kensal, N.D., U.S. ... B7 111
Kensett, Ar., U.S. ... B4 81
Kensett, Ia., U.S. ... A4 92
Kensico Reservoir, res., N.Y., U.S. ... g13 109
Kensington, P.E.I. ... C6 71
Kensington (part of London), Eng., U.K. ... k12 10
Kensington, Ca., U.S. ... *h8 82
Kensington, Ct., U.S. ... C4 84
Kensington, Ks., U.S. ... C4 93
Kensington, Md., U.S. ... B3 97
Kensington, Mn., U.S. ... E3 100
Kensington, N.H., U.S. ... E5 106
Kensington, Oh., U.S. ... B5 112
Kent, Al., U.S. ... C4 78
Kent, Ct., U.S. ... C2 84
Kent, In., U.S. ... G6 91
Kent, Mn., U.S. ... D2 100
Kent, Oh., U.S. ... A4 112
Kent, Or., U.S. ... B6 114
Kent, Tx., U.S. ... o12 120
Kent, Wa., U.S. ... B3 124
Kent, co., N.B. ... C4 71
Kent, co., Ont. ... E2 73
Kent, co., Eng., U.K. ... C8 12
Kent, co., De., U.S. ... D3 85

Kent, co., Md., U.S. ... B5 97
Kent, co., Mi., U.S. ... E5 99
Kent, co., R.I., U.S. ... D2 116
Kent, co., Tx., U.S. ... C2 120
Kent Bridge, Ont. ... E2 73
Kent City, Mi., U.S. ... E5 99
Kent Island, i., De., U.S. ... D4 85
Kent Island, i., Md., U.S. ... C5 97
Kent Junction, N.B. ... C4 71
Kentland, In., U.S. ... C3 91
Kenton, Man. ... E1 70
Kenton, De., U.S. ... D3 85
Kenton, Ky., U.S. ... k14 94
Kenton, Mi., U.S. ... B2 99
Kenton, Oh., U.S. ... B2 112
Kenton, Ok., U.S. ... e8 113
Kenton, Tn., U.S. ... A2 119
Kenton, co., Ky., U.S. ... B5 94
Kent Point, c., Md., U.S. ... C5 97
Kentucky, state, U.S. ... C4 94
Kentucky, stm., Ky., U.S. ... B5 94
Kentucky, Middle Fork, stm., Ky., U.S. ... C6 94
Kentucky, North Fork, stm., Ky., U.S. ... C6 94
Kentucky, South Fork, stm., Ky., U.S. ... C6 94
Kentucky Lake, res., U.S. ... C10 76
Kentucky Ridge, mtn., Ky., U.S. ... D6 94
Kentville, N.S. ... D5 71
Kentwood, La., U.S. ... D5 95
Kentwood, Mi., U.S. ... F5 99
Kenvil, N.J., U.S. ... B3 107
Kenville, Man. ... D1 70
Kenvir, Ky., U.S. ... D6 94
Kenwood, Oh., U.S. ... *A4 112
Kenwood, Ok., U.S. ... A7 113
Kenya, ctry., Afr. ... A6 48
Kenya, Mount see Kirinyaga, mtn., Kenya ... B6 48
Kenyon, Mn., U.S. ... F6 100
Kenyon, R.I., U.S. ... F2 116
Keo, Ar., U.S. ... C3 81
Keokea, Hi., U.S. ... C5 88
Keokuk, Ia., U.S. ... D6 92
Keokuk, co., Ia., U.S. ... C5 92
Keokuk Lock and Dam, U.S. ... D6 92
Keoma, Alta. ... D4 68
Keosauqua, Ia., U.S. ... D6 92
Keota, Co., U.S. ... A6 83
Keota, Ia., U.S. ... C6 92
Keota, Ok., U.S. ... B7 113
Keowee, Lake, res., S.C., U.S. ... B2 117
Kepno, Pol. ... C5 26
Keppel, Sask. ... E2 75
Kepsut, Tur. ... B5 25
Kerala, state, India ... F6 36
Kerang, Austl. ... G7 50
Keratsinion, Grc. ... *D4 25
Kerby, Or., U.S. ... E3 114
Kerch, Sov. Un. ... E6 29
Kerchemya, Sov. Un. ... C19 8
Kerch Strait, strt., Sov. Un. ... I11 27
Kerema, Pap. N. Gui. ... k12 50
Keremeos, B.C. ... E8 69
Kerempe, Cape, c., Tur. ... A9 40
Keren, Eth. ... B4 47
Kerend, Iran ... D3 39
Kerens, Tx., U.S. ... C4 120
Kerguélen, Îles, is., F.S.A.T. ... J1 2
Kerhonkson, N.Y., U.S. ... D6 109
Kericho, Kenya ... B6 48
Kerinci, mtn., Indon. ... F2 34
Kerkebet, Eth. ... B4 47
Kerkenna, Îles, is., Tun. ... C7 44
Kerkhoven, Mn., U.S. ... E3 100
Kerki, Sov. Un. ... H22 8
Kérkira, Grc. ... C2 40
Kérkira (Corfu), i., Grc. ... C2 40
Kerkrade, Neth. ... B7 16
Kermadec Islands, is., N.Z. ... I11 6
Kermān, Iran ... B5 38
Kermānshāh see Bakhtarān, Iran ... B4 38
Kerme, Gulf of, b., Tur. ... D6 25
Kermit, Tx., U.S. ... D1 120
Kermit, W.V., U.S. ... D2 125
Kermode, Mount, mtn., B.C. ... C2 69
Kern, co., Ca., U.S. ... E4 82
Kern, stm., Ca., U.S. ... E4 82
Kernersville, N.C., U.S. ... A2 110
Kernville, Ca., U.S. ... E4 82
Kernville, Or., U.S. ... C3 114
Kérouané, Gui. ... E3 45
Kerpen, W. Ger. ... C1 19
Kerr, Lake, l., Fl., U.S. ... C5 86
Kerrick, Mn., U.S. ... D6 100
Kerrick, Tx., U.S. ... A1 120
Kerrobert, Sask. ... F1 75
Kerrville, Tx., U.S. ... D3 120
Kerry, co., Ire. ... E2 11
Kerry Head, c., Ire. ... E2 11
Kersey, Pa., U.S. ... D4 115
Kershaw, S.C., U.S. ... B6 117
Kershaw, co., S.C., U.S. ... C6 117
Kersley, B.C. ... C6 69
Kerteminde, Den. ... C4 15
Kerulen, stm., Asia ... B7 31
Kerzaz, Alg. ... D4 44
Kerzers, Switz. ... C3 21
Keşan, Tur. ... B6 40
Kesch, Piz, mtn., Switz. ... C5 20
Kesennuma, Japan ... G10 33
Kesh, N. Ire., U.K. ... C4 11
Keshan, China ... B10 31
Keshena, Wi., U.S. ... D5 126
Kesley, Ia., U.S. ... B5 92
Kestenga, Sov. Un. ... E14 14
Keswick, Ont. ... C5 73
Keswick, Eng., U.K. ... C5 10
Keswick, Ia., U.S. ... C5 92
Keswick, Va., U.S. ... C4 123
Keszthely, Hung. ... B3 24
Keta, Ghana ... E5 45
Ketapang, Indon. ... F3 34
Ketchikan, Ak., U.S. ... D13 79
Ketchum, Ok., U.S. ... A6 113
Ketmen Range, mts., Asia ... E10 28
Ketona, Al., U.S. ... f7 78
Kétou, Benin ... E5 45
Kętrzyn, Pol. ... A6 26
Kettering, Eng., U.K. ... D6 10
Kettering, Md., U.S. ... *C4 97
Kettering, Oh., U.S. ... C1 112
Kettle, stm., N.A. ... A7 69
Kettle, stm., Mn., U.S. ... D6 100

Kettle Creek, stm., Pa., U.S. ... D6 115
Kettle Creek Lake, res., Pa., U.S. ... D6 115
Kettle Falls, Wa., U.S. ... A7 124
Kettleman City, Ca., U.S. ... E4 82
Kettle River, Mn., U.S. ... D6 100
Kettwig, W. Ger. ... B1 19
Kety, Pol. ... D5 26
Ketzin, E. Ger. ... A7 19
Keuka Lake, l., N.Y., U.S. ... C3 109
Keuterville, Id., U.S. ... C2 89
Kevil, Ky., U.S. ... e9 94
Kevin, Mt., U.S. ... B5 103
Kewanee, Il., U.S. ... B4 90
Kewanee, Ms., U.S. ... C5 101
Kewanee, Mo., U.S. ... E8 102
Kewanna, In., U.S. ... B5 91
Kewaskum, Wi., U.S. ... E5 126
Kewaunee, Wi., U.S. ... D6 126
Kewaunee, co., Wi., U.S. ... D6 126
Keweenaw, co., Mi., U.S. ... A2 99
Keweenaw Bay, Mi., U.S. ... B2 99
Keweenaw Bay, b., Mi., U.S. ... B2 99
Keweenaw Peninsula, pen., Mi., U.S. ... A3 99
Keweenaw Point, c., Mi., U.S. ... A3 99
Keyapaha, S.D., U.S. ... D5 118
Keya Paha, co., Ne., U.S. ... B6 104
Keya Paha, stm., U.S. ... A5 104
Key Biscayne, Fl., U.S. ... *G6 86
Keyes, Man. ... D2 70
Keyes, Ok., U.S. ... e8 113
Keyesport, Il., U.S. ... E4 90
Keyhole Reservoir, res., Wy., U.S. ... B8 127
Key Junction, Ont. ... B4 73
Key Largo, Fl., U.S. ... G6 86
Keymar, Md., U.S. ... A3 97
Keynsham, Eng., U.K. ... C5 12
Keyport, N.J., U.S. ... C4 107
Keysburg, Ky., U.S. ... D2 94
Keyser, W.V., U.S. ... B6 125
Keystone, In., U.S. ... C7 91
Keystone, Ia., U.S. ... C5 92
Keystone, Ne., U.S. ... C4 104
Keystone, S.D., U.S. ... D2 118
Keystone, W.V., U.S. ... D3 125
Keystone, Wy., U.S. ... E6 127
Keystone Heights, Fl., U.S. ... C4 86
Keystone Lake, res., Ok., U.S. ... A5 113
Keystone Peak, mtn., Az., U.S. ... F4 80
Keysville, Ga., U.S. ... C4 87
Keysville, Va., U.S. ... C4 123
Keytesville, Mo., U.S. ... B5 102
Key West, Fl., U.S. ... H5 86
Key West, Ia., U.S. ... B7 92
Key West Naval Air Station, mil., Fl., U.S. ... H5 86
Kezar Falls, Me., U.S. ... E2 96
Kezar Lake, l., Me., U.S. ... *D4 96
Kezar Pond, l., Me., U.S. ... D2 96
Kezhma, Sov. Un. ... D13 29
Kežmarok, Czech. ... D6 26
Khabab, Syria ... A8 41
Khabarovsk, Sov. Un. ... E16 29
Khabis see Shahdād, Iran ... F8 39
Khachmas, Sov. Un. ... E3 28
Khaïdhárion, Grc. ... *C4 25
Khairpur, Pak. ... C4 36
Khakhea, Bots. ... B3 49
Khalándrion, Grc. ... *C4 25
Khalia, Grc. ... g11 25
Khálki (Chalke), i., Grc. ... D6 25
Khalkidhikí Penninsula, pen., Grc. ... B4 25
Khalkís, Grc. ... C4 40
Khalūf, Oman ... C5 38
Khambhāliya, India ... D4 36
Khambhāt, India ... F4 37
Khambhāt, Gulf of, b., India ... D5 36
Khāmgaon, India ... B3 36
Khammam, India ... I8 37
Khanabad, Afg. ... A4 36
Khānaqīn, Iraq ... A4 38
Khānderi, i., India ... H4 37
Khandwa, India ... B4 36
Khaniá (Canea), Grc. ... E5 40
Khaniá, Gulf of, b., Grc. ... E4 25
Khānka, Lake see Xingkai Hu, l., Asia ... B11 31
Khānpur, Pak. ... C5 36
Khanty-Mansiysk, Sov. Un. ... A7 28
Kharagpur, India ... D8 36
Khārān, Pak. ... G12 39
Kharānaq, Iran ... E7 39
Kharg Island, i., Iran ... D4 38
Khargon, India ... G5 37
Khārijah, Al Wāḥāt al, well, Eg. ... C12 43
Kharkov, Sov. Un. ... D6 29
Kharmān, Kūh-e, mtn., Iran ... C6 38
Kharmanli, Bul. ... E7 24
Kharovsk, Sov. Un. ... B13 27
Khartoum (Al Kharṭūm), Sud. ... B3 47
Khartoum North (Al Kharṭūm Baḥrī), Sud. ... B3 47
Khartsyzsk, Sov. Un. ... q21 27
Khasavyurt, Sov. Un. ... G18 8
Khāsh, Afg. ... B3 36
Khāsh, Iran ... G10 39
Khāsh, stm., Afg. ... B3 36
Khashm al Qirbah, Khazzān, res., Sud. ... B7 47
Khashuri, Sov. Un. ... B14 40
Khasi Hills, mts., India ... C9 36
Khaskovo, Bul. ... E7 24
Khatanga, Sov. Un. ... B13 29
Khatanga, stm., Sov. Un. ... B13 29
Khavast, Sov. Un. ... E7 28
Khemmarat, Thai. ... D6 35
Khenchla, Alg. ... C3 44
Khenifra, Mor. ... C3 44
Kherson, Sov. Un. ... H9 27
Kheta, stm., Sov. Un. ... B12 29
Khieo Peak, mtn., Thai. ... E5 35
Khilok, Sov. Un. ... D14 29
Khimki, Sov. Un. ... n17 27
Khíos, Grc. ... C6 40
Khíos (Chios), i., Grc. ... E2 40
Khirbat al Ghazālah, Syria ... B8 41
Khisfin, Isr. Occ. ... B8 41
Khiva, Sov. Un. ... E6 28
Khlebarovo (Tsar Kaloyan), Bul. ... D8 24
Khmelnik, Sov. Un. ... E7 24
Khmelnitskiy, Sov. Un. ... G6 27
Khoai, i., Viet. ... H6 35
Khodzheyli, Sov. Un. ... D6 28
Kholm, Afg. ... A3 36
Kholm, Sov. Un. ... C8 27
Kholmsk, Sov. Un. ... E17 29
Khomeyn, Iran ... E5 39

Khomeynīshahr, Iran ... E5 39
Khon Kaen, Thai. ... B2 34
Khoper, stm., Sov. Un. ... F14 27
Khor, stm., Sov. Un. ... B12 31
Khóra Sfakíon, Grc. ... E5 25
Khordha, India ... G10 37
Khorinsk, Sov. Un. ... A6 31
Khorog, Sov. Un. ... F10 29
Khorol, Sov. Un. ... G9 27
Khorramābād, Iran ... E4 39
Khorramshahr, Iran ... B4 38
Khotin, Sov. Un. ... G6 27
Khouribga, Mor. ... C3 44
Khowst, Afg. ... B4 36
Khram Yai, i., Thai. ... F4 35
Khrisoúpolis, Grc. ... B5 25
Khromtau, Sov. Un. ... C5 28
Khu Khan, Thai. ... E6 35
Khulna, Bngl. ... D8 36
Khunzakh, Sov. Un. ... A16 40
Khurja, India ... C6 37
Khurr, Wādī al, val., Asia ... G14 40
Khushāb, Pak. ... A4 37
Khust, Sov. Un. ... G4 27
Khuzdār, Pak. ... C4 36
Khvāf, Iran ... B6 38
Khvor, Iran ... E7 39
Khvormūj, Iran ... G5 39
Khvoy, Iran ... B4 38
Khwae Noi, stm., Thai. ... E3 35
Khyber Pass, Asia ... B5 36
Kia, i., Fiji ... H15 52
Kiamichi, stm., Ok., U.S. ... C6 113
Kiamika, Que. ... C2 74
Kiamika, stm., Que. ... C2 74
Kiana, Ak., U.S. ... B7 79
Kiangarow, Mount, mtn., Austl. ... C8 51
Kiangsi see Jiangxi, prov., China ... F8 31
Kiangsu see Jiangsu, prov., China ... E9 31
Kiantajärvi, l., Fin. ... E13 14
Kiáton, Grc. ... C4 25
Kiawah Island, i., S.C., U.S. ... F7 117
Kibangou, Congo ... C8 48
Kibau, Tan. ... C6 48
Kiberege, Tan. ... C6 48
Kibombo, Zaire ... B4 48
Kibondo, Tan. ... B5 48
Kibwezi, Kenya ... B6 48
Kičevo, Yugo. ... D5 24
Kickamuit, stm., R.I., U.S. ... D5 116
Kickapoo, stm., Wi., U.S. ... E3 126
Kickapoo, Lake, res., Tx., U.S. ... C3 120
Kickapoo Indian Reservation, Ks., U.S. ... C8 93
Kicking Horse Pass, Can. ... D2 68
Kidal, Mali ... C5 45
Kidder, Mo., U.S. ... B3 102
Kidder, S.D., U.S. ... B8 118
Kidder, co., N.D., U.S. ... C6 111
Kidderminster, Eng., U.K. ... D2 12
Kidira, Sen. ... D2 45
Kidnappers, Cape, c., N.Z. ... M16 51
Kidron, Valley of, val., Isr. Occ. ... m14 41
Kidsgrove, Eng., U.K. ... A5 12
Kidugallo, Tan. ... C6 48
Kidwelly, Wales, U.K. ... C3 12
Kief, N.D., U.S. ... B5 111
Kiefer, Ok., U.S. ... B5 113
Kiel, W. Ger. ... A5 18
Kiel, Wi., U.S. ... E5 126
Kiel Bay, b., W. Ger. ... A5 18
Kiel Canal, W. Ger. ... A4 18
Kielce, Pol. ... C6 26
Kiental, Switz. ... C4 21
Kiester, Mn., U.S. ... G5 100
Kiev, Sov. Un. ... D6 29
Kiev Reservoir, res., Sov. Un. ... F8 27
Kiffa, Maur. ... C2 45
Kifisiá, Grc. ... g11 25
Kifisós (Cephisus), stm., Grc. ... g9 25
Kifisós, stm., Grc. ... g11 25
Kifrī, Iraq ... E15 40
Kigali, Rw. ... B5 48
Kiği, Tur. ... C13 40
Kigoma, Tan. ... B4 48
Kigoma, prov., Tan. ... B5 48
Kihei, Hi., U.S. ... C5 88
Kiholo Bay, b., Hi., U.S. ... D5 88
Kii Strait, strt., Japan ... J7 33
Kikinda, Yugo. ... C5 25
Kikongo, Zaire ... B2 48
Kikori, Pap. N. Gui. ... k11 50
Kikori, stm., Pap. N. Gui. ... k11 50
Kikwit, Zaire ... C4 48
Kila, Mt., U.S. ... B2 103
Kilauea, Hi., U.S. ... A2 88
Kilauea Crater, crat., Hi., U.S. ... D6 88
Kilauea Point, c., Hi., U.S. ... A2 88
Kilbaha, Ire. ... E2 11
Kilbeggan, Ire. ... D4 11
Kilbourne, Il., U.S. ... C4 90
Kilbourne, Oh., U.S. ... B3 112
Kilbrannan Sound, strt., Scot., U.K. ... E3 13
Kilburn, N.B. ... C3 71
Kilcar, Ire. ... C3 11
Kilchoan, Scot., U.K. ... D3 13
Kilchreest, Ire. ... D3 11
Kilchu, N. Kor. ... D5 11

Kilcock, Ire. ... D5 11
Kilcolgan, Ire. ... D3 11
Kilconnell, Ire. ... D3 11
Kilcoole, Ire. ... D4 11
Kilcormac (Frankford), Ire. ... D4 11
Kilcullen, Ire. ... D5 11
Kildare (Saint-Ambroise-de-Kildare), Que. ... C4 74
Kildare, Ok., U.S. ... A4 113
Kildare, co., Ire. ... D5 11
Kildorrery, Ire. ... E3 11
Kilembe, Ug. ... A5 48
Kilfenora, Ire. ... D2 11
Kilfinnane, Ire. ... E3 11
Kilgarvan, Ire. ... F2 11
Kilgore, Ne., U.S. ... B5 104
Kilgore, Tx., U.S. ... C5 120
Kilifi, Kenya ... B6 48
Kilifi, prov., Kenya ... B6 48
Kilimanjaro, mtn., Tan. ... B6 48
Kilimatinde, Tan. ... C6 48
Kilindoni, Tan. ... C6 48
Kilis, Tur. ... D11 40
Kiliya, Sov. Un. ... I7 27
Kilkee, Ire. ... D2 11
Kilkeel, N. Ire., U.K. ... C6 11
Kilkenny, Ire. ... D5 11
Kilkenny, Mn., U.S. ... F5 100
Kilkenny, co., Ire. ... E4 11
Kilkerrin, Ire. ... D3 11
Kilkieran, Ire. ... D2 11
Kilkieran Bay, b., Ire. ... D2 11
Kilkis, Grc. ... B4 25
Killadoon, Ire. ... D2 11
Killadysert, Ire. ... E2 11
Killala, Ire. ... C2 10
Killala Bay, b., Ire. ... C2 11
Killaloe, Ire. ... E3 11
Killaloe Station, Ont. ... B7 73
Killam, Alta. ... C5 68
Killarney, Man. ... D2 70
Killarney, Ire. ... E2 11
Killarney, Lake, l., Bah. ... m17 64
Killarney Provincial Park, Ont. ... A3 73
Killavally, Ire. ... D2 11
Killbuck, Oh., U.S. ... B4 112
Killdeer, Sask. ... H2 75
Killdeer, N.D., U.S. ... B3 111
Killdeer Mountains, mts., N.D., U.S. ... B3 111
Killduff, Ia., U.S. ... C5 92
Killearn, Fl., U.S. ... *B2 86
Killeen, Tx., U.S. ... D4 120
Killen, Al., U.S. ... A2 78
Killenaule, Ire. ... E4 11
Killeter, N. Ire., U.K. ... C4 11
Killian, La., U.S. ... h10 95
Killiecrankie, Pass of, Scot., U.K. ... D5 13
Killik, stm., Ak., U.S. ... B9 79
Killilan, Scot., U.K. ... B4 10
Killin, Scot., U.K. ... A4 90 — (see note)
Killingly Center, Ct., U.S. ... *B8 84
Killington Peak, mtn., Vt., U.S. ... D3 122
Killingworth, Ct., U.S. ... D5 84
Killini, Grc. ... D3 25
Killini Island, l., Can. ... f8 72
Killona, La., U.S. ... h11 95
Killorglin, Ire. ... E2 11
Killucan, Ire. ... D4 11
Killybegs, Ire. ... C3 11
Killyleagh, N. Ire., U.K. ... C6 11
Kilmacthomas, Ire. ... E4 11
Kilmaine, Ire. ... D2 11
Kilmallock, Ire. ... E3 11
Kilmanagh, Mi., U.S. ... E7 99
Kilmarnock, Scot., U.K. ... C4 10
Kilmarnock, Va., U.S. ... C6 123
Kilmelford, Scot., U.K. ... D3 13
Kilmez, Sov. Un. ... B4 28
Kilmichael, Ms., U.S. ... B4 101
Kiln, Ms., U.S. ... E4 101
Kilosa, Tan. ... C6 48
Kilrush, Ire. ... D2 11
Kilsyth, Scot., U.K. ... E4 13
Kilteen, Ire. ... D5 11
Kiltimagh, Ire. ... D3 11
Kiltoom, Ire. ... D3 11
Kilwa, Zaire ... C4 48
Kilwa Kisiwani, Tan. ... C6 48
Kilwa Kivinje, Tan. ... C6 48
Kim, Co., U.S. ... D7 83
Kimamba, Tan. ... C6 48
Kimball, Mn., U.S. ... E4 100
Kimball, Ne., U.S. ... C2 104
Kimball, S.D., U.S. ... D7 118
Kimball, W.V., U.S. ... D3 125
Kimball, co., Ne., U.S. ... C2 104
Kimball, Mount, mtn., Ak., U.S. ... C11 79
Kimballton, Ia., U.S. ... C2 92
Kimberley, B.C. ... E9 69
Kimberley, S. Afr. ... C4 49
Kimberley Plateau, plat., Austl. ... C4 50
Kimberlin Heights, Tn., U.S. ... n14 119
Kimberly, Al., U.S. ... B3 78
Kimberly, Id., U.S. ... G4 89
Kimberly, Or., U.S. ... C7 114
Kimberly, W.V., U.S. ... m13 125
Kimberly, Wi., U.S. ... h9 126
Kimble, co., Tx., U.S. ... D3 120
Kimbolton, Oh., U.S. ... B4 112
Kimbrough, Al., U.S. ... D2 78
Kimch'aek (Sŏngjin), N. Kor. ... C10 31
Kimch'ŏn, S. Kor. ... H4 33
Kimesville, N.C., U.S. ... B3 110
Kími, Grc. ... C5 25
Kimiwan Lake, l., Alta. ... B2 68
Kimmell, In., U.S. ... B6 91
Kimmins, Tn., U.S. ... B4 119
Kimmswick, Mo., U.S. ... g13 102
Kimowin, stm., Sask. ... A6 68
Kimry, Sov. Un. ... C11 27
Kimvula, Zaire ... C3 48
Kin, Japan ... O5 52
Kinabalu, Mount, mtn., Malay. ... D5 34
Kinard, Fl., U.S. ... B1 86
Kinbasket Lake, res., B.C. ... D8 69
Kinbrace, Scot., U.K. ... B5 13
Kinbrae, Mn., U.S. ... G3 100
Kinburn, Ont. ... B8 73
Kincaid, Sask. ... H2 75
Kincaid, Il., U.S. ... D4 90
Kincaid, Ks., U.S. ... D8 93
Kincaid, W.V., U.S. ... m13 125
Kincaid, Lake, res., Il., U.S. ... D4 90
Kincardine, Ont. ... C3 73

King City, Ca., U.S. ... D3 82
King City, Mo., U.S. ... A3 102
King Cove, Ak., U.S. ... E7 79
King David Hotel, Isr. ... m14 41
King Ferry, N.Y., U.S. ... C4 109
Kingfield, Me., U.S. ... D2 96
Kingfisher, Ok., U.S. ... B4 113
Kingfisher, co., Ok., U.S. ... B3 113
King Frederik VI Coast, Grnld. ... C19 128
King Frederik VIII Land, reg., Grnld. ... B17 128
King George, Va., U.S. ... B5 123
King George, co., Va., U.S. ... B5 123
King George, Mount, mtn., B.C. ... D10 69
King George Island, i., B.A.T. ... C7 7
King George Sound, strt., Austl. ... G2 50
King Hill, Id., U.S. ... F3 89
King Island, i., B.C. ... C4 69
King Lake, Ne., U.S. ... *C9 104
King Lear Peak, mtn., Nv., U.S. ... B3 105
King Leopold Ranges, mts., Austl. ... C4 50
Kingman, Alta. ... C4 68
Kingman, Az., U.S. ... B1 80
Kingman, In., U.S. ... E3 91
Kingman, Ks., U.S. ... E5 93
Kingman, Me., U.S. ... C4 96
Kingman, co., Ks., U.S. ... E5 93
King Mountain, mtn., Ok., U.S. ... C2 113
King Mountain, mtn., Or., U.S. ... E3 114
King Mountain, mtn., Or., U.S. ... D8 114
King of Prussia, Pa., U.S. ... F11 115
King Peak, mtn., Ca., U.S. ... B1 82
Kings, Il., U.S. ... A4 90
Kings, Ms., U.S. ... C3 101
Kings, co., N.B. ... D4 71
Kings, co., N.S. ... E5 71
Kings, co., P.E.I. ... C7 71
Kings, co., Ca., U.S. ... D4 82
Kings, co., N.Y., U.S. ... E7 109
Kings, stm., Ar., U.S. ... A2 81
Kings, stm., Ca., U.S. ... D4 82
Kings, stm., Nv., U.S. ... B3 105
Kings Salmon, Ak., U.S. ... D8 79
Kingsbridge, Eng., U.K. ... D4 12
Kingsburg, Ca., U.S. ... D4 82
Kingsbury, In., U.S. ... A4 91
Kingsbury, Tx., U.S. ... h8 120
Kingsbury, co., S.D., U.S. ... C8 118
Kings Canyon National Park, Ca., U.S. ... D4 82
Kingsclear, N.B. ... D3 71
Kings Corner, Ct., U.S. ... B5 84
Kingscote, Austl. ... G6 50
Kings Creek, S.C., U.S. ... A5 117
Kingsdown, Ks., U.S. ... E4 93
Kingsey-Falls, Que. ... D5 74
Kingsford, Mi., U.S. ... C2 99
Kingsgate, B.C. ... E9 69
Kingsgate, Wa., U.S. ... *B3 124
Kingsland, Ar., U.S. ... D3 81
Kingsland, Ga., U.S. ... F5 87
Kingsland, Tx., U.S. ... D3 120
Kingsley, Ia., U.S. ... B2 92
Kingsley, Mi., U.S. ... D5 99
Kingsley Dam, Ne., U.S. ... C4 104
King's Lynn, Eng., U.K. ... D7 10
Kingsmere Lake, l., Sask. ... C2 75
Kings Mill, Tx., U.S. ... B2 120
Kings Mills, Oh., U.S. ... C1 112
Kings Mountain, Ky., U.S. ... C5 94
Kings Mountain, N.C., U.S. ... B1 110
King Sound, strt., Austl. ... C2 92
Kings Park, N.Y., U.S. ... *E7 109
Kings Park, Va., U.S. ... *B5 123
Kings Park West, Va., U.S. ... B5 123
Kings Peak, mtn., Ut., U.S. ... C5 121
Kingsport, Tn., U.S. ... C11 119
Kingston, Ont. ... C8 73
Kingston, Jam. ... F5 64
Kingston, N.Z. ... P12 51
Kingston, Ar., U.S. ... A2 81
Kingston, Ga., U.S. ... B2 87
Kingston, Id., U.S. ... B2 89
Kingston, Il., U.S. ... A5 90
Kingston, Ma., U.S. ... C6 98
Kingston, Mi., U.S. ... E7 99
Kingston, Mo., U.S. ... B3 102
Kingston, N.H., U.S. ... E4 106
Kingston, N.J., U.S. ... C4 107
Kingston, N.Y., U.S. ... D6 109
Kingston, Oh., U.S. ... C3 112
Kingston, Ok., U.S. ... D5 113
Kingston, Pa., U.S. ... D10 115
Kingston, R.I., U.S. ... F3 116
Kingston, Tn., U.S. ... D9 119
Kingston, Ut., U.S. ... E3 121
Kingston, Wa., U.S. ... B3 124
Kingston, Wi., U.S. ... E4 126
Kingston Southeast, Austl. ... G6 50
Kingston Springs, Tn., U.S. ... A4 119
Kingston upon Hull, Eng., U.K. ... D7 10
Kingston upon Thames (part of London), Eng., U.K. ... m12 10
Kingstown, St. Vin. ... J14 64
Kingstown, Md., U.S. ... B5 97
Kingstree, S.C., U.S. ... D8 117
Kingsville, Ont. ... E2 73
Kingsville, Md., U.S. ... B5 97
Kingsville, Mo., U.S. ... C3 102
Kingsville, Tx., U.S. ... F4 120
Kingsville Naval Air Station, mil., Tx., U.S. ... F4 120
Kingswood, Ky., U.S. ... C6 94
Kington, Eng., U.K. ... D4 12
Kingurutik Lake, l., Newf. ... g9 72
Kingussie, Scot., U.K. ... B4 10
King William, Va., U.S. ... C5 123
King William Island, i., N.W. Ter. ... C13 66
King William's Town, S. Afr. ... D4 49
Kingwood, Tx., U.S. ... *E5 120
Kingwood, W.V., U.S. ... B5 125
Kinistino, Sask. ... E3 75
Kinkaid Lake, res., Il., U.S. ... F4 90
Kinkala, Congo ... C3 48
Kinkora, P.E.I. ... C6 71
Kinley, Sask. ... E2 75
Kin-Li-Chee, Az., U.S. ... B6 80

Name	Map Ref.	Page
Kinloch, Mo., U.S.	f13	102
Kinlochewe, Scot., U.K.	C3	13
Kinloch Hourn, Scot., U.K.	C3	13
Kinmount, Ont.	C6	73
Kinmundy, Il., U.S.	E5	90
Kinnairds Head, c., Scot., U.K.	B6	90
Kinnear, Wa., U.S.	C4	127
Kinnelon, N.J., U.S.	B4	107
Kinneret, Yam (Sea of Galilee), l., Isr.	B7	41
Kinney, co., Tx., U.S.	E2	120
Kinomoto, Japan	n15	33
Kinosaki, Japan	I7	33
Kinrooi, Bel.	C5	17
Kinross, P.E.I.	C7	71
Kinross, Scot., U.K.	D5	13
Kinsale, Ire.	E2	10
Kinsale, Va., U.S.	B6	123
Kinsella, Alta.	C5	68
Kinsey, Al., U.S.	D4	78
Kinsey, Mt., U.S.	D11	103
Kinshasa (Léopoldville), Zaire	B2	48
Kinsley, Ks., U.S.	E4	93
Kinsman, Oh., U.S.	A5	112
Kinsman, India	D11	37
Kinston, Al., U.S.	D3	78
Kinston, N.C., U.S.	B5	110
Kinta, Ok., U.S.	B6	113
Kintampo, Ghana	E4	45
Kintinku, Tan.	C6	48
Kintore, Scot., U.K.	C6	13
Kintyre, N.D., U.S.	C6	111
Kintyre, Mull of, c., Scot., U.K.	C6	13
Kinuso, Alta.	B3	68
Kinvarra, Ire.	D3	11
Kinyangiri, Tan.	B5	48
Kinyeti, mtn., Sudan	E3	47
Kinzig, stm., W. Ger.	C4	19
Kinzig, stm., W. Ger.	B4	19
Kinzua, Or., U.S.	C6	114
Kioa, i., Fiji	H15	52
Kiona, Wa., U.S.	C6	124
Kioshkokwi Lake, l., Ont.	A6	73
Kiosk, Ont.	A6	73
Kiowa, Co., U.S.	B6	83
Kiowa, Ks., U.S.	E5	93
Kiowa, Ok., U.S.	C6	113
Kiowa, co., Co., U.S.	C8	83
Kiowa, co., Ks., U.S.	E3	93
Kiowa, co., Ok., U.S.	C2	113
Kiowa Creek, stm., Co., U.S.	B6	83
Kiowa Creek, stm., Ok., U.S.	A1	113
Kipahigan Lake, l., Can.	B5	75
Kipahulu, Hi., U.S.	*C5	88
Kipapa Stream, stm., Hi., U.S.	g9	88
Kiparissía, Grc.	D3	25
Kiparissía, Gulf of, b., Grc.	D3	25
Kipembawe, Tan.	C5	48
Kipili, Tan.	C5	48
Kipini, Kenya	B7	48
Kipling, Sask.	G4	75
Kipling, Mi., U.S.	C3	99
Kipnuk, Ak., U.S.	C7	79
Kipp, Alta.	E4	68
Kipp, Ks., U.S.	D6	93
Kipton, Oh., U.S.	A3	112
Kipushi, Zaire	D4	48
Kirby, Ar., U.S.	C2	81
Kirby, Tx., U.S.	*E3	120
Kirby, Wy., U.S.	C4	127
Kirbyville, Tx., U.S.	D6	120
Kirchberg, Switz.	*B7	21
Kirchdorf, E. Ger.	E5	15
Kirchhain, W. Ger.	C3	19
Kirchheimbolanden, W. Ger.	D2	19
Kirchheim [unter Teck], W. Ger.	E4	19
Kirchhundem, W. Ger.	B3	19
Kirensk, Sov. Un.	D13	29
Kirghiz S.S.R., state, Sov. Un.	E10	29
Kirgiz Range, mts., Sov. Un.	E8	28
Kiri, Zaire	B2	48
Kiribati, ctry., Oc.	G11	6
Kırıkhan, Tur.	*D11	40
Kırıkkale, Tur.	C9	40
Kirin see Jilin, prov., China	C10	31
Kirinian, i., Marsh Is.	S18	52
Kirinyaga (Mount Kenya), mtn., Kenya	B6	48
Kiritimati Island (Christmas Island), i., Kir.	F12	6
Kirk, Co., U.S.	B8	83
Kirkby Lonsdale, Eng., U.K.	F6	13
Kirkby Stephen, Eng., U.K.	F6	13
Kirkcaldy, Scot., U.K.	D4	68
Kirkcolm, Scot., U.K.	F3	13
Kirkcudbright, Scot., U.K.	C5	10
Kirkcudbright Bay, b., Scot., U.K.	F4	13
Kirkenes, Nor.	C13	14
Kirkersville, Oh., U.S.	C3	112
Kirkfield, Ont.	C5	73
Kirkintilloch, Scot., U.K.	E4	13
Kirkland, Al., U.S.	D2	78
Kirkland, Az., U.S.	C3	80
Kirkland, Ga., U.S.	E4	87
Kirkland, Il., U.S.	A5	90
Kirkland, Tn., U.S.	B5	119
Kirkland, Wa., U.S.	B3	124
Kirkland Lake, Ont.	o19	73
Kırklareli, Tur.	B6	40
Kırklin, In., U.S.	D5	91
Kirkman, Ia., U.S.	C2	92
Kirkmansville, Ky., U.S.	D2	94
Kirkoswald, Eng., U.K.	F6	13
Kirkpatrick, Mount, mtn., Ant.	A29	7
Kirkpatrick Lake, l., Alta.	D5	68
Kirksey, Ky., U.S.	f9	94
Kirksey, S.C., U.S.	C3	117
Kirksville, Ky., U.S.	C5	94
Kirksville, Mo., U.S.	A5	102
Kirkton, Ont.	D3	73
Kirkton of Glenisla, Scot., U.K.	D5	13
Kirkūk, Iraq	B4	38
Kirkville, Ia., U.S.	C5	92
Kirkwall, Scot., U.K.	A5	10
Kirkwood, S. Afr.	D4	49
Kirkwood, De., U.S.	B3	85
Kirkwood, Il., U.S.	C3	90
Kirkwood, Mo., U.S.	f13	102
Kirn, W. Ger.	D3	18
Kiron, Ia., U.S.	B2	92
Kirov, Sov. Un.	D7	29
Kirovabad, Sov. Un.	E7	29
Kirovakan, Sov. Un.	B15	40
Kirov Bay, b., Sov. Un.	B4	39
Kirovgrad, Sov. Un.	B6	28
Kirovograd, Sov. Un.	G9	27
Kirovsk, Sov. Un.	C6	29
Kirriemuir, Alta.	D5	68
Kirriemuir, Scot., U.K.	D5	13
Kirsanov, Sov. Un.	E14	27
Kırşehir, Tur.	C10	40
Kırthar Range, mts., Pak.	C4	36
Kirtland, N.M., U.S.	A1	108
Kirtland, Oh., U.S.	*C1	112
Kirtland Air Force Base, mil., N.M., U.S.	k7	108
Kiruna, Swe.	D9	14
Kirundu, Zaire	B4	48
Kirwin, Ks., U.S.	C4	93
Kirwin Reservoir, res., Ks., U.S.	C4	93
Kiryū, Japan	H9	33
Kisaki, Tan.	C6	48
Kisanga, Zaire	C4	48
Kisangani (Stanleyville), Zaire	A4	48
Kisarazu, Japan	n18	33
Kisatchie, La., U.S.	C2	95
K.I. Sawyer Air Force Base, mil., Mi., U.S.	B3	99
Kisbey, Sask.	H4	75
Kiselevsk, Sov. Un.	C11	28
Kisengwa, Zaire	C4	48
Kīsh, i., Iran	H6	39
Kishanganj, India	D11	37
Kishangarh, India	C5	36
Kishi, Nig.	E5	45
Kishinev, Sov. Un.	E6	29
Kishiwada, Japan	o14	33
Kishorganj, Bngl.	D9	36
Kishwaukee, stm., Il., U.S.	A5	90
Kisii, Kenya	B5	48
Kisiju, Tan.	C6	48
Kisiwa Creek, stm., Ks., U.S.	g11	93
Kisiwani, Tan.	B6	48
Kiska Island, i., Ak., U.S.	E3	79
Kiskatinaw, stm., B.C.	B7	69
Kiskittogisu Lake, l., Man.	B2	70
Kiskitto Lake, l., Man.	B2	70
Kiskőrös, Hung.	B4	24
Kiskundorozsma (part of Szeged), Hung.	B5	24
Kiskunfélegyháza, Hung.	B4	24
Kiskunhalas, Hung.	B4	24
Kiskunmajsa, Hung.	B4	24
Kislovodsk, Sov. Un.	E2	28
Kismaayo, Som.	F5	47
Kismet, Ks., U.S.	E3	93
Kiso-sammyaku, mts., Japan	n16	33
Kissamos, Grc.	E4	25
Kissee Mills, Mo., U.S.	E4	102
Kisseynew Lake, l., Can.	B1	70
Kissidougou, Gui.	E2	45
Kissimmee, Fl., U.S.	D5	86
Kissimmee, stm., Fl., U.S.	E5	86
Kissimmee, Lake, l., Fl., U.S.	E5	86
Kissimmee Park, Fl., U.S.	E5	86
Kississing, Man.	B1	70
Kississing Lake, l., Man.	B1	70
Kississing Lake, l., Man.	B1	70
Kisslegg, W. Ger.	A8	21
Kistefjellet, mtn., Nor.	C8	14
Kistigan Lake, l., Man.	B5	70
Kistler, W.V., U.S.	D3	125
Kistrand, Nor.	B11	14
Kisújszállás, Hung.	B5	24
Kisumu, Kenya	A5	48
Kisvárda, Hung.	A6	24
Kita, Mali	D3	45
Kita, Mount, mtn., Japan	I9	33
Kita-ibaraki, Japan	H10	33
Kita-iwo-, Japan	E8	6
Kitakyūshū, Japan	E11	31
Kitale, Kenya	A5	48
Kitami, Japan	E11	33
Kitangari, Tan.	D6	48
Kit Carson, Co., U.S.	C8	83
Kit Carson, co., Co., U.S.	C8	83
Kitchell, In., U.S.	E8	91
Kitchener, Ont.	D4	73
Kite, Ga., U.S.	D4	87
Kitgum, Ug.	A5	48
Kíthira (Cythera), i., Grc.	D4	40
Kíthnos, i., Grc.	D4	25
Kitimat, B.C.	B3	69
Kitridge Point, c., Barb.	K21	61
Kitsap, co., Wa., U.S.	B3	124
Kitscoty, Alta.	C5	68
Kittanning, Pa., U.S.	E2	115
Kittatinny Mountain, mtn., U.S.	E2	115
Kittery, Me., U.S.	E2	96
Kittery Point, Me., U.S.	E2	96
Kittilä, Fin.	D11	14
Kittitas, Wa., U.S.	C5	124
Kittitas, co., Wa., U.S.	B4	124
Kittitas Valley, val., Wa., U.S.	B4	124
Kittrell, N.C., U.S.	A4	110
Kitts, Ky., U.S.	D6	94
Kitts Hummock, De., U.S.	D4	85
Kittson, co., Mn., U.S.	B2	100
Kitty Hawk, N.C., U.S.	A7	110
Kitty Hawk Bay, b., N.C., U.S.	A7	110
Kitui, Kenya	B6	48
Kitwanga, B.C.	B3	69
Kitwe, Zam.	D4	48
Kitzbühel, Aus.	E6	18
Kitzingen, W. Ger.	D5	18
Kitzmiller, Md., U.S.	m12	97
Kivalina, Ak., U.S.	B7	79
Kivu, hist. reg., Zaire	B5	48
Kivu, Lac, l., Afr.	A5	48
Kiya, stm., Sov. Un.	D26	8
Kiyan, Japan	o19	33
Kiyan Point, c., Japan	O5	52
Kıyıköy, Tur.	B7	40
Kiyiu Lake, l., Sask.	F1	75
Kizil, stm., Tur.	B10	40
Kizlyar, Sov. Un.	E2	28
Kizyl-Arvat, Sov. Un.	F8	29
Kjaekan, Nor.	C10	14
Kjellerup, Den.	B3	15
Kjøllefjord, Nor.	B12	14
Kladno, Czech.	C3	26
Klagenfurt, Aus.	E6	18
Klageton, Az., U.S.	B6	80
Klaipėda (Memel), Sov. Un.	D7	29
Klamath, Ca., U.S.	B1	82
Klamath, co., Or., U.S.	E5	114
Klamath, stm., U.S.	B2	82
Klamath Falls, Or., U.S.	E5	114
Klamath Glen, Ca., U.S.	B2	82
Klamath Mountains, mts., U.S.	E2	114
Klanxbüll, W. Ger.	D2	15
Klarälven, stm., Eur.	C6	14
Klatovy, Czech.	D2	26
Klawock, Ak., U.S.	D13	79
Kleberg, co., Tx., U.S.	F4	120
Kleena Kleene, B.C.	D5	69
Klein, Tx., U.S.	*D5	120
Kleinburg, Ont.	k14	73
Klemme, Ia., U.S.	A4	92
Klerksdorp, S. Afr.	C4	49
Kletnya, Sov. Un.	E9	27
Kletsk, Sov. Un.	E6	27
Kleve (Cleves), W. Ger.	C3	18
Klibreck, Ben, mtn., Scot., U.K.	B4	13
Kličany, Czech.	n17	26
Klickitat, Wa., U.S.	D4	124
Klickitat, co., Wa., U.S.	D4	124
Klickitat, stm., Wa., U.S.	C4	124
Klimovsk, Sov. Un.	n17	27
Klin, Sov. Un.	C11	27
Klinaklini, stm., B.C.	D5	69
Kline, S.C., U.S.	E5	117
Klingenthal, E. Ger.	C7	19
Klínovec, mtn., Czech.	C7	19
Klintsy, Sov. Un.	E9	27
Klippan, Swe.	B7	15
Klitmøller, Den.	A2	15
Ključ, Yugo.	C3	24
Kłobuck, Pol.	C5	26
Kloch Lake, l., B.C.	B5	69
Klock, Ont.	A6	73
Kłodnica, stm., Pol.	g9	26
Kłodzko, Pol.	C4	26
Klondike, In., U.S.	D4	91
Klondike, Tx., U.S.	C5	120
Klondike Gold Rush National Historical Park, Ak., U.S.	k22	79
Klondike Region, hist. reg., Yukon	D5	66
Klondyke, Az., U.S.	E5	80
Klos, Alb.	B3	25
Klostermansfeld, E. Ger.	B6	19
Klosterneuburg, Aus.	D8	18
Klosters [-Serneus], Switz.	C8	21
Kloten, Switz.	B6	21
Kloten, N.D., U.S.	B7	111
Klötze, E. Ger.	F5	15
Klotzsche, E. Ger.	B9	15
Klotzville, La., U.S.	h9	95
Kluane Lake, l., Yukon	D5	66
Kluane National Park, Yukon	D5	66
Kluczbork, Pol.	C5	26
Klukwan, Ak., U.S.	k22	79
Klutina Lake, l., Ak., U.S.	g19	79
Klütz, E. Ger.	E5	15
Klyazma, stm., Sov. Un.	C13	27
Klyuchevskaya Sopka, vol., Sov. Un.	D18	29
Knapp, Wi., U.S.	D1	126
Knapp Creek, stm., W.V., U.S.	C5	125
Knaresborough, Eng., U.K.	F7	13
Knee Lake, l., Man.	B4	70
Knee Lake, l., Sask.	B2	75
Knesebeck, W. Ger.	F4	15
Knesset, Isr.	m14	41
Knezha, Bul.	D7	24
Knickerbocker, Tx., U.S.	D2	120
Knierim, Ia., U.S.	B3	92
Knife, stm., N.D., U.S.	B3	111
Knife River, Mn., U.S.	D7	100
Knifley, Ky., U.S.	C4	94
Knight Inlet, b., B.C.	D5	69
Knight Island, i., Ak., U.S.	g18	79
Knighton, Wales, U.K.	B4	12
Knights Landing, Ca., U.S.	C3	82
Knights Town, Ire.	F1	11
Knightstown, In., U.S.	E6	91
Knightsville, In., U.S.	E3	91
Knightville Reservoir, res., Ma., U.S.	B2	98
Knin, Yugo.	C3	24
Knippa, Tx., U.S.	E3	120
Knislinge, Swe.	B8	15
Knittelfeld, Aus.	E6	18
Knob Creek, stm., Ky., U.S.	g11	94
Knobel, Ar., U.S.	A5	81
Knob Lick, Ky., U.S.	C4	94
Knob Lick, Mo., U.S.	D7	102
Knobly Mountain, mtn., W.V., U.S.	B5	125
Knob Noster, Mo., U.S.	C4	102
Knobsville, Pa., U.S.	F6	115
Knock, Ire.	E2	11
Knockadoon Head, c., Ire.	F4	11
Knockalongy, mtn., Ire.	C3	11
Knockanefune, hill, Ire.	E2	11
Knockboy, mtn., Ire.	F2	11
Knocklong, Ire.	E3	11
Knockmealdown Mountains, mts., Ire.	D2	10
Knokke [-Heist], Bel.	B2	17
Knollwood, Ct., U.S.	D6	84
Knollwood, W.V., U.S.	m12	125
Knops Pond, l., Ma., U.S.	f9	98
Knott, Tx., U.S.	C2	120
Knott, co., Ky., U.S.	C6	94
Knotts Island, N.C., U.S.	A7	110
Knottsville, Ky., U.S.	C3	94
Knowles, Ok., U.S.	A1	113
Knowlton, Wi., U.S.	D4	126
Knox, Austl.	*G8	50
Knox, In., U.S.	B4	91
Knox, N.D., U.S.	A6	111
Knox, Pa., U.S.	D2	115
Knox, co., Il., U.S.	B3	90
Knox, co., In., U.S.	G3	91
Knox, co., Ky., U.S.	D6	94
Knox, co., Me., U.S.	D4	96
Knox, co., Mo., U.S.	A5	102
Knox, co., Ne., U.S.	B8	104
Knox, co., Oh., U.S.	B3	112
Knox, co., Tn., U.S.	C10	119
Knox, co., Tx., U.S.	C3	120
Knox, Cape, c., B.C.	B1	69
Knox City, Mo., U.S.	A5	102
Knox City, Tx., U.S.	C3	120
Knox Coast, Ant.	C7	7
Knox Dale, Pa., U.S.	D3	115
Knoxville, Al., U.S.	C2	78
Knoxville, Ar., U.S.	B2	81
Knoxville, Ga., U.S.	D3	87
Knoxville, Il., U.S.	C3	90
Knoxville, Ia., U.S.	C4	92
Knoxville, Md., U.S.	B2	97
Knoxville, Ms., U.S.	D2	101
Knoxville, Pa., U.S.	C7	115
Knoxville, Tn., U.S.	D10	119
Knurów, Pol.	g9	26
Knysna, S. Afr.	D3	49
Knyszyn, Pol.	B6	26
Ko, Mount, mtn., Hi., U.S.	C5	33
Kobayashi, Japan	K5	33
Kōbe, Japan	E11	31
Kobelyaki, Sov. Un.	G10	27
København, co., Den.	C6	15
Koblenz (Coblence), W. Ger.	C2	18
Koboko, Ug.	A5	48
Kobona, Sov. Un.	r32	14
Kobroor, i., Indon.	G8	34
Kobuk, Ak., U.S.	B8	79
Kobuk, stm., Ak., U.S.	B8	79
Kobuk Valley National Park, Ak., U.S.	B8	79
Kobuleti, Sov. Un.	B13	40
Köca, stm., Tur.	D7	25
Kocába, stm., Czech.	o17	26
Kocaeli see İzmit, Tur.	B7	40
Kočani, Yugo.	E6	24
Koch Bihār, India	C8	36
Kochel, W. Ger.	B7	20
Kochel Lake, l., W. Ger.	B7	20
Kocher, stm., W. Ger.	D4	19
Kōchi, Japan	E11	31
Koch Peak, mtn., Mt., U.S.	E5	103
Kock, Pol.	C7	26
Kodari, Ky., U.S.	C6	94
Kodari, Nepal	D10	37
Kodiak, Ak., U.S.	D9	79
Kodiak Island, i., Ak., U.S.	D9	79
Kodok (Fashoda), Sud.	D3	47
Koeda Joeri, Neth. Ant.	H18	65
Koes, Nmb.	C2	49
Kofa Mountains, mts., Az., U.S.	D2	80
Koffiefontein, S. Afr.	C3	49
Koforidua, Ghana	E4	45
Kōfu, Japan	I9	33
Kōfu, Japan	m18	33
Koga, Japan		
Kogaluk, stm., Newf.	g9	72
Køge, Den.	C6	15
Køge Bugt, b., Den.	C6	15
Kohala Mountains, mts., Hi., U.S.	C6	88
Kohat, Pak.	B5	36
Kohatk, Az., U.S.	E3	80
Kohima, India	C9	36
Kohler, Wi., U.S.	E6	126
Kohtla-Järve, Sov. Un.	B7	27
Koidu, S.L.	E2	45
Köinge, Swe.	A6	15
Ko Island, i., Japan	F9	33
Köje Island, i., S. Kor.	I4	33
Kokand, Sov. Un.	E10	29
Kokanee Glacier Provincial Park, B.C.	E9	69
Kokchetav, Sov. Un.	D9	29
Kokkola, Fin.	F10	14
Koko, Nig.	D5	45
Koko Head, c., Hi., U.S.	B4	88
Kokolik, stm., Ak., U.S.	B7	79
Kokomo, Hi., U.S.	C5	88
Kokomo, In., U.S.	D5	91
Kokomo, Ms., U.S.	D3	101
Koko Nor see Qinghai Hu, l., China	D4	31
Kokopo, Pap. N. Gui.	h13	50
Kokosing, stm., Oh., U.S.	B3	112
Kokrines, Ak., U.S.	C9	79
Koksoak, stm., Que.	E19	66
Koksilah, B.C.	g12	69
Kokstad, S. Afr.	D4	49
Ko Lanta, i., Thai.	I3	35
Kola Peninsula, pen., Sov. Un.	C6	29
Kolār, India	F6	36
Kolar Gold Fields, India	*F6	36
Kolari, Fin.	D10	14
Kolárovo, Czech.	E4	26
Kolāyat, India	D4	37
Kolbäck, Swe.	t34	14
Kolbano, Indon.	G6	34
Kolbio, Kenya	B7	48
Kolbuszowa, Pol.	C6	26
Kolchugino, Sov. Un.	C12	27
Kolczewo, Pol.	E8	15
Koldewey, i., Grnld.	B16	128
Kole, Zaire	B3	48
Koleč, Czech.	n17	26
Koleen, In., U.S.	G4	91
Kolezhma, Sov. Un.	E16	14
Kolguyev Island, i., Sov. Un.	C7	29
Kolhāpur, India	D8	79
Koliganek, Ak., U.S.	D8	79
Kolimbine, stm., Afr.	C2	45
Kolín, Czech.	C3	26
Kolin, La., U.S.	C3	95
Kölleda, E. Ger.	B6	19
Kolno, Pol.	B6	26
Koło, Pol.	B5	26
Koloa, Hi., U.S.	B2	88
Kolob Canyon, val., Ut., U.S.	F2	121
Kołobrzeg, Pol.	A3	26
Kolola Springs, Ms., U.S.	B5	101
Kolomna, Sov. Un.	C12	27
Kolomyya, Sov. Un.	G5	27
Kolonia, Micron.	Q17	52
Kolonodale, Indon.	F6	34
Kolp, stm., Sov. Un.	B10	27
Kolpashevo, Sov. Un.	B10	28
Kolpino, Sov. Un.	s31	14
Kolwezi, Zaire	D4	48
Kolyberovo, Sov. Un.	n18	27
Kolyma, stm., Sov. Un.	C18	29
Kolyma Mountains, mts., Sov. Un.	C18	29
Komádi, Hung.	B5	24
Komandorski Islands, is., Sov. Un.	D19	29
Komárno, Czech.	E5	26
Komárno Marsh, sw., Sov. Un.	D7	26
Komárom, Hung.	B4	24
Komatipoort, S. Afr.	C5	49
Komatke, Az., U.S.	D3	80
Komatsu, Japan	H8	33
Komatsushima, Japan	I7	33
Komló, Hung.	B4	24
Kommunarsk, Sov. Un.	G12	27
Komodo, i., Indon.	G5	34
Komoé, stm., Afr.	E4	45
Komono, Congo	B1	48
Komoran, i., Indon.	G9	34
Komotiní, Grc.	B8	25
Komrat, Sov. Un.	H7	27
Komsomolets, i., Sov. Un.	A4	128
Komsomolsk [-na-Amure], Sov. Un.	D16	29
Konahuanui, Puu, mtn., Hi., U.S.	g10	88
Konar, stm., Asia	A5	36
Konar-e Khās, Afg.	D15	39
Konawa, Ok., U.S.	C5	113
Kondinskoye, Sov. Un.	B7	28
Kondoa, Tan.	B6	48
Kondopoga, Sov. Un.	F5	29
Kondūz, Afg.	C14	39
Konechnaya, Sov. Un.	B6	28
Kong, i., Camb.	G5	35
Kong, i., Asia	C3	34
Kongeå, stm., Den.	C2	15
Kongju, S. Kor.	H3	33
Kongolo, Zaire	C4	48
Kongsberg, Nor.	H3	14
Kongsmark, Den.	C2	15
Kongsvinger, Nor.	G5	14
Königsberg see Kaliningrad, Sov. Un.	D5	29
Königsbrück, E. Ger.	B8	19
Königslutter, W. Ger.	A5	19
Königstein, E. Ger.	C9	19
Königs Wusterhausen, E. Ger.	A8	19
Konin, Pol.	B5	26
Konispol, Alb.	C3	40
Kónitsa, Grc.	B3	25
Köniz, Switz.	C3	21
Konjic, Yugo.	D4	24
Konkouré, stm., Gui.	D2	45
Könnern, E. Ger.	B6	19
Konolfingen, Switz.	C2	21
Konomoc, Lake, res., Ct., U.S.	D7	84
Konosha, Sov. Un.	A13	27
Konotop, Sov. Un.	F9	27
Końskie, Pol.	C6	26
Konstancin-Jeziorna, Pol.	m14	26
Konstantinovka, Sov. Un.	q20	27
Konstanz (Constance), W. Ger.	E4	18
Kontagora, Nig.	D6	45
Kontcha, Cam.	D2	46
Kontich, Bel.	C4	17
Kontiomäki, Fin.	E13	14
Kon Tum, Viet.	C3	34
Konya, Tur.	D9	40
Konyang, S. Kor.	I3	33
Konzhakovskiy Kamen, mtn., Sov. Un.	B5	28
Koocanusa, Lake, res., N.A.	B1	103
Koochiching, co., Mn., U.S.	B4	100
Koolan, Austl.	G4	51
Kooloonong, Austl.	G4	51
Koolau Range, mts., Hi., U.S.	f10	88
Koontz Lake, In., U.S.	B5	91
Koosharem, Ut., U.S.	E4	121
Kooskia, Id., U.S.	C3	89
Kootenai, Id., U.S.	*A2	89
Kootenai, co., Id., U.S.	B2	89
Kootenay National Park, B.C.	D9	69
Kootenay Lake, l., B.C.	E9	69
Kootenay, stm., N.A.	E9	69
Kópasker, Ice.	m24	14
Kopervik, Nor.	H1	14
Kopet Mountains, mts., Asia	B8	39
Kopeysk, Sov. Un.	B8	28
Köping, Swe.	H6	14
Köppany, stm., Hung.	B4	24
Koppel, Pa., U.S.	E1	115
Koprivnica, Yugo.	B3	24
Kopychintsy, Sov. Un.	G6	27
Korab, mtn., Eur.	E5	24
Korahe, Eth.	D5	47
Korarou, Lac, l., Mali	C4	45
Korba, India	B9	36
Korba, Tun.	F3	23
Korbach, W. Ger.	B3	19
Korbu, mtn., Malay.	J4	35
Korçë, Alb.	B3	40
Korčula, i., Yugo.	D3	24
Kord Kūy, Iran	C7	39
Korea, North, ctry., Asia	D10	31
Korea, South, ctry., Asia	D10	31
Korea Bay, b., Asia	D9	31
Korea Strait, strt., Asia	E10	31
Korets, Sov. Un.	F6	27
Korhogo, I.C.	E3	45
Kori Creek, stm., India	F2	37
Korinthiakós, Grc.	*D4	25
Kórinthos (Corinth), Grc.	D4	40
Kōriyama, Japan	H10	33
Korkino, Sov. Un.	E21	8
Korkuteli, Tur.	D8	40
Körmend, Hung.	B3	24
Kornat, i., Yugo.	D2	24
Korneuburg, Aus.	D8	18
Kornwestheim, W. Ger.	E4	19
Koro, Mali	D4	45
Koro, i., Fiji	H15	52
Korogwe, Tan.	C6	48
Koronis, Lake, l., Mn., U.S.	E4	100
Koropion, Grc.	h11	25
Koror, Palau	R17	52
Koror, i., Palau	R17	52
Korosten, Sov. Un.	F7	27
Koro Toro, Chad	B3	46
Korotoyak, Sov. Un.	F12	27
Korovin Volcano, vol., Ak., U.S.	E5	79
Korsakov, Sov. Un.	E17	29
Korsør, Den.	C5	15
Kortrijk (Courtrai), Bel.	C2	17
Korucam, Cape, c., N. Cyp.	E9	40
Korumburra, Austl.	I5	51
Koryak Mountains, mts., Sov. Un.	C19	29
Kos, Grc.	D6	40
Kos (Cos), i., Grc.	D6	40
Koschagyl, Sov. Un.	D4	28
Kościan, Pol.	B4	26
Kościerzyna, Pol.	A4	26
Kosciusko, Ms., U.S.	B4	101
Kosciusko, co., In., U.S.	B6	91
Kosciusko, Mount, mtn., Austl.	I8	51
Kösdağı, mtn., Tur.	C14	40
Koshigaya, Japan	*I9	33
Koshiki Islands, is., Japan	K3	33
Koshkonong, Lake, l., Wi., U.S.	F5	126
Koshkonong, Mo., U.S.	E6	102
Koskaecodde Lake, l., Newf.	D4	72
Košice, Czech.	D6	26
Košíře (part of Prague), Czech.	n17	26
Koslan, Sov. Un.	A4	28
Koszalin (Köslin), Pol.	A4	26
Köszeg, Hung.	B3	24
Kota, India	D5	36
Kota Baharu, Malay.	C6	34
Kotabumi, Indon.	F2	34
Kota Kinabalu, Malay.	D6	34
Kotatengah, Indon.	L4	35
Kotcha, stm., Sov. Un.	A5	28
Kotelnich, Sov. Un.	A7	28
Kotelnikovo, Sov. Un.	H14	27
Kotelny Island, i., Sov. Un.	B16	29
Köthen, E. Ger.	C5	18
Kotido, Ug.	A5	48
Kotka, Fin.	C7	29
Kotlas, Sov. Un.	C7	29
Kotlik, Ak., U.S.	C7	79
Kotonkoro, Nig.	D6	45
Kotor, Yugo.	D4	24
Kotor Bay, b., Yugo.	D4	24
Kotor Varoš, Yugo.	C3	24
Kotovsk, Sov. Un.	E13	27
Kotovsk, Sov. Un.	H7	27
Kotri, Pak.	E2	37
Kottagüdem, India	I8	37
Kotte, Sri L.	*G6	36
Kotto, stm., Cen. Afr. Rep.	D4	46
Kotzebue, Ak., U.S.	B6	79
Kotzebue Sound, strt., Ak., U.S.	B7	79
Kötzting, W. Ger.	D7	19
Kouandé, Benin	D5	45
Kouango, Cen. Afr. Rep.	D3	46
Kouchibouguacis, stm., N.B.	C4	71
Kouchibouguac National Park, N.B.	C5	71
Koudougou, Burkina	D4	45
Koula-Moutou, Gabon	F2	46
Koulikoro, Mali	D3	45
Koumra, Chad	D3	46
Koungheul, Sen.	D2	45
Kounradskiy, Sov. Un.	D9	28
Kountze, Tx., U.S.	D5	120
Koupéla, Burkina	D4	45
Kouri Channel, strt., Japan	N6	52
Kourou, Fr. Gu.	A4	59
Kouroussa, Gui.	D3	45
Koussi, Emi, mtn., Chad	B3	46
Koutiala, Mali	D3	45
Kouts, In., U.S.	B3	91
Kouvola, Fin.	G12	14
Ko Vaya, Az., U.S.	E4	80
Kovel, Sov. Un.	F5	27
Kovrov, Sov. Un.	C13	27
Kowloon, H.K.	D7	25
Köyceğiz, Tur.	D7	25
Koyuk, Ak., U.S.	C8	79
Koyukuk, Ak., U.S.	C8	79
Koyukuk, stm., Ak., U.S.	B8	79
Kozan, Tur.	D10	40
Kozáni, Grc.	B3	25
Kozelsk, Sov. Un.	D10	27
Kožle, Pol.	C5	26
Kozienice, Pol.	C6	26
Kozłowa Bul.	D6	24
Kozuchów, Pol.	C3	26
Kōzu Island, i., Japan	I9	33
Kpandu, Ghana	E5	45
Kra, Isthmus of, Asia	C1	34
Krabi, Thai.	I3	35
Kracheh, Camb.	C3	34
Kraemer, La., U.S.	k10	95
Kragerö, Nor.	H3	14
Kragujevac, Yugo.	C5	24
Kraków, Pol.	C5	26
Krakower, l., E. Ger.	E6	15
Kraljevo, Yugo.	D5	24
Královské Vinohrady (part of Prague), Czech.	n17	26
Kralupy [nad Vltavou], Czech.	n17	26
Králův Dvůr, Czech.	o17	26
Kramatorsk, Sov. Un.	G11	27
Kramer, In., U.S.	D3	91
Kramer, N.D., U.S.	A5	111
Kranidhion, Grc.	D4	25
Kranj, Yugo.	B2	24
Kranzburg, S.D., U.S.	C9	118
Kraslice, Czech.	C2	26
Krasnaya Polyana, Sov. Un.	q22	27
Krašnik, Pol.	C6	26
Krasnoarmeysk, Sov. Un.	F15	27
Krasnoarmeysk, Sov. Un.	G15	27
Krasnodar, Sov. Un.	D6	29
Krasnodon, Sov. Un.	G12	27
Krasnogorsk, Sov. Un.	q22	27
Krasnograd, Sov. Un.	G10	27
Krasnogvardeyskoye, Sov. Un.	I13	27
Krasnokamsk, Sov. Un.	B5	28
Krasnoperekopsk, Sov. Un.	B25	8
Krasnoselsk, Sov. Un.	s31	14
Krasnoslobodsk, Sov. Un.	D14	27
Krasnoslobodsk, Sov. Un.	G14	27
Krasnoturinsk, Sov. Un.	B6	28
Krasnoufimsk, Sov. Un.	B5	28
Krasnoural'sk, Sov. Un.	D21	8
Krasnovishersk, Sov. Un.	A5	28
Krasnovodsk, Sov. Un.	E8	29
Krasnoye Selo, Sov. Un.	s31	14
Krasnoyarsk, Sov. Un.	D12	29
Krasnoznamenskiy, Sov. Un.	C7	26
Krasnystaw, Pol.	C7	26
Krasnyy Kholm, Sov. Un.	B11	27
Krasnyy Kut, Sov. Un.	q21	27
Krasnyy Liman, Sov. Un.	q20	27
Krasnyy Luch, Sov. Un.	q21	27
Krasnyy Sulin, Sov. Un.	H13	27
Krasnyy Yar, Sov. Un.	D6	24
Kratovo, Yugo.	E6	24
Kraul Mountains, mts., Ant.	B11	7
Kraut, Indon.	*G3	34
Krebs, Ok., U.S.	C6	113
Krefeld, W. Ger.	C3	18
Kremenchug Reservoir, res., Sov. Un.	G9	27
Kremenets, Sov. Un.	F5	27
Kremennaya, Sov. Un.	p21	27
Kremlin, Ok., U.S.	A4	113
Kremlin, Mt., U.S.	B6	103
Kremmling, Co., U.S.	A4	83
Krems [am der Donau], Aus.	D7	18
Kress, Tx., U.S.	B2	120
Kretinga, Sov. Un.	E10	115
Kreuzlingen, Switz.	D6	29
Krichev, Sov. Un.	E8	27
Kriel, S. Afr.	C4	49
Krishna, stm., India	E6	36
Krishnanagar, India	F12	37
Kristiansand, Swe.	H2	14
Kristiansand, Nor.	I6	14
Kristianstad, Swe.	F2	14
Kristianstad, co., Swe.	D6	14
Kristiansund, Nor.	F2	14
Kristinestad, Fin.	B3	24
Kriva Palanka, Yugo.	D6	24
Krivoy Rog, Sov. Un.	H9	27
Križevci, Yugo.	B3	24
Krk, i., Yugo.	C2	24
Krka, stm., Yugo.	D3	24

Name	Map Ref.	Page
Krnov, Czech.	C4	26
Krokeaí, Grc.	D4	25
Krokstadelva, Nor.	p28	14
Krolevets, Sov. Un.	D4	26
Kroměříž, Czech.	E10	27
Kromy, Sov. Un.	C6	19
Kronach, W. Ger.	G3	18
Kronau, Sask.	B8	75
Kronoberg, co., Swe.	B7	15
Kronshtadt, Sov. Un.	C4	6
Kroonstad, S. Afr.	D5	49
Kröpelin, E. Ger.	I13	27
Kropotkin, Sov. Un.	D6	26
Krosno, Pol.	B3	26
Krosno Odrzańskie, Pol.	C4	26
Krotoszyn, Pol.	C4	26
Krotz Springs, La., U.S.	D4	95
Krško, Yugo.	B5	24
Kruger National Park, S. Afr.	C4	49
Krugersdorp, S. Afr.	B2	49
Kruja, Alb.	A6	25
Krumbach, W. Ger.	E7	18
Krumovgrad, Bul.	D5	25
Kruševac, Yugo.	E5	24
Kruševo, Yugo.	E5	24
Kruszwica, Pol.	B5	26
Kruzof Island, i., Ak., U.S.	m21	79
Kryzor, Sask.	E2	75
Krymsk, Sov. Un.	I11	27
Krynica, Pol.	D6	26
Krynki, Pol.	B7	26
Ksar el Kebir, Mor.	B3	44
Ksar es Souk, Mor.	C4	44
Kuala Kangsar, Malay.	J4	35
Kualakurun, Indon.	F4	34
Kuala Lipis, Malay.	E2	34
Kuala Lumpur, Malay.	E2	34
Kuala Terengganu, Malay.	D2	34
Kualapu'u, Hi., U.S.	B4	88
Kuandang, Indon.	E6	34
Kuandian, China	D11	31
Kuantan, Malay.	E2	34
Kuba, Sov. Un.	I7	26
Kuban, stm., Sov. Un.	I13	27
Kubitzer Bodden, b., E. Ger.	D7	15
Kubokawa, Japan	J6	33
Kuching, Malay.	E4	34
Kuchinoerabu Island, i., Japan	K5	33
Kuchino Island, i., Japan	L4	33
Kuçovë see Stalin, Alb.	B2	25
Kudaka Island, i., Japan	O5	33
Kudat, Malay.	D5	34
Kudirkos Naumiestis, Sov. Un.	A7	26
Kudus, Indon.	G4	34
Kudymkar, Sov. Un.	B4	28
Kuee Ruins, hist., Hi., U.S.	D6	88
Kufstein, Aus.	E6	18
Kuhayyl, Sov. Un.	B3	47
Kühēsi, Alb.	A3	25
Kūh Lab, Ra's-e, c., Iran	I10	39
Kūhpāyeh, Iran	E6	39
Kuito, Ang.	D2	48
Kuiu Island, i., Ak., U.S.	m23	79
Kuji, Japan	F10	33
Kujū, Mount, mtn., Japan	J5	33
Kukaiau, Hi., U.S.	C6	88
Kukawa, Nig.	D7	45
Kuki, Japan	m18	33
Kukuihaele, Hi., U.S.	C6	88
Kukuiula, Hi., U.S.	B2	88
Kuku Point, c., Wake I.	A1	52
Kula, Bul.	D6	24
Kula, Tur.	C7	25
Kula, Hi., U.S.	C5	88
Kula, Yugo.	C4	24
Kula Kangri, mtn., Bhu.	C9	36
Kulebaki, Sov. Un.	D14	27
Kulim, Malay.	J4	35
Kulltorp, Swe.	A7	15
Kulm, N.D., U.S.	C7	111
Kulmbach, W. Ger.	C5	18
Kulpmont, Pa., U.S.	E9	115
Kulunda, Sov. Un.	C9	28
Kulunda Lake, l., Sov. Un.	C9	28
Kulwin, Austl.	G4	51
Kulyab, Sov. Un.	H22	8
Kūm, stm., S. Kor.	H3	33
Kuma, stm., Sov. Un.	F18	8
Kumagaya, Japan	m18	33
Kumai, Indon.	F4	34
Kumamoto, Japan	E11	31
Kumano Bay, b., Japan	J8	33
Kumanovo, Yugo.	D5	24
Kumasi, Ghana	E4	44
Kumba, Cam.	E1	46
Kumba-konam, India	F6	36
Kumbo, Cam.	D2	46
Kūmhwa, S. Kor.	G3	33
Kumi, Ug.	A5	48
Kumihama, Japan	n14	33
Kumla, Swe.	H6	14
Kummerower Lake, l., E. Ger.	E6	15
Kumo, Nig.	D7	45
Kumukahi, Cape, c., Hi., U.S.	F2	89
Kuna, Id., U.S.	B2	37
Kundar, stm., Asia	B2	36
Kundiawa, Pap. N. Gui.	k11	50
Kuneitra (Al Qunayṭirah), Isr. Occ.	A7	41
Kunggyü Lake, l., China	B9	37
Kunghit Island, i., B.C.	C2	69
Kungrad, Sov. Un.	E5	28
Kungsbacka, Swe.	A6	15
Kungsör, Swe.	t34	14
Kungu, Zaire	A2	48
Kungur, Sov. Un.	B5	28
Kunia, Hi., U.S.	g9	88
Kunigami, Japan	N6	52
Kunimi, Mount, mtn., Japan	J5	33
Kunkle, Oh., U.S.	m17	115
Kunlun Shan, mts., China	F11	30
Kunming, China	F5	31
Kunsan, S. Kor.	D10	31
Kunszentmárton, Hung.	B5	24
Künzelsau, W. Ger.	D4	19
Kuolayarvi, Sov. Un.	D13	14
Kuop, atoll, Micron.	Q18	52
Kuopio, Fin.	F12	14
Kupa, stm., Yugo.	C2	24
Kupang, Indon.	G6	34
Kupino, Sov. Un.	C2	28
Kupreanof, Ak., U.S.	m23	79
Kupreanof Island, i., Ak., U.S.	m23	79
Kupyansk, Sov. Un.	G11	27
Kur, stm., Sov. Un.	B7	33
Kura, stm., Asia	E3	26
Kurakhovo, Sov. Un.	r20	27
Kurashiki, Japan	I6	33
Kuray, Sov. Un.	E26	8
Kuraymah, Sud.	B3	47
Kurayyimah, Jord.	f13	41
Kurdistan, hist. reg., Asia	B4	38
Kurdufān al Janūbīyah (Southern Kurdufan), prov., Sud.	C2	47
Kurdufān ash Shamālīyah (Northern Kurdufan), prov., Sud.	C2	47
Kürdzhali, Bul.	E7	24
Kure, Japan	E11	31
Kure Island, i., Hi., U.S.	k12	88
Kuressaare, Sov. Un.	B4	27
Kureyka, stm., Sov. Un.	C12	29
Kurgaldzhinskiy, Sov. Un.	C8	28
Kurgan, Sov. Un.	D9	29
Kurganinsk, Sov. Un.	G17	8
Kurgan-Tyube, Sov. Un.	H22	8
Kuria Muria Islands (Khūryān Mūryān), is., Oman	D5	38
Kurigram, Bngl.	E12	37
Kuril Islands, is., Sov. Un.	E17	29
Kuril Strait, strt., Sov. Un.	D18	29
Kurinskaya, Cape, c., Sov. Un.	H18	8
Kurmuk, Sud.	C3	47
Kurnool, India	E6	36
Kuro Island, i., Japan	K4	33
Kuroki, Sask.	F4	75
Kurovskoye, Sov. Un.	n18	27
Kurow, N.Z.	P13	51
Kurri Kurri, Austl.	F9	50
Kursk, Sov. Un.	D6	29
Kuršumlija, Yugo.	D5	24
Kurthwood, La., U.S.	C2	95
Kurtistown, Hi., U.S.	D6	88
Kurtz, In., U.S.	G5	91
Kuruman, S. Afr.	C3	49
Kurume, Japan	E11	31
Kurunegala, Sri L.	G7	36
Kuşadası, Tur.	D6	25
Kusakaki Islands, i., Japan	K4	33
Kusatsu, Japan	n14	33
Kusel, W. Ger.	D2	19
Kushchevskaya, Sov. Un.	H12	27
Kushimoto, Japan	J7	33
Kushiro, Japan	C13	31
Kushka, Sov. Un.	F9	29
Kushmurun, Sov. Un.	C6	28
Kushmurun, Lake, l., Sov. Un.	C6	28
Kuskokwim, stm., Ak., U.S.	C7	79
Kuskokwim Bay, b., Ak., U.S.	D7	79
Kuskokwim Mountains, mts., Ak., U.S.	C8	79
Kuş Lake, l., Tur.	B6	25
Küsnacht, Switz.	B6	21
Küssnacht [am Rigi], Switz.	B5	21
Kustanay, Sov. Un.	D9	29
Küsten Canal, W. Ger.	B7	17
Küstī, Sud.	C3	47
Kut, i., Thai.	G5	35
Kuta, Alb.	B2	25
Kutacane, Indon.	K2	35
Kütahya, Tur.	C7	40
Kutaisi, Sov. Un.	G17	8
Kutawagan Lake, l., Sask.	F3	75
Kutch, Gulf of see Kachchh, Gulf of, b., India	D4	36
Kutch, Rann of, pl., Asia	D4	36
Kutina, Yugo.	C3	24
Kutno, Pol.	B5	26
Kuttawa, Ky., U.S.	e9	94
Kutu, Zaire	B2	48
Kutum, Sud.	C1	47
Kuturaja see Banda Aceh, Indon.	k11	34
Kuty, Sov. Un.	A7	24
Kutztown, Pa., U.S.	E10	115
Kuujjuaq, Que.	g13	74
Kuúm-ni, N. Kor.	G2	33
Kuusamo, Fin.	E13	14
Kuvango (Capelongo), Ang.	D2	48
Kuwait (Al Kuwayt), Kuw.	C4	38
Kuwait, ctry., Asia	C4	38
Kuwait Bay, b., Kuw.	G4	39
Kuybyshev, Sov. Un.	B9	28
Kuybyshev, Sov. Un.	D8	29
Kuybyshevo, Sov. Un.	H12	27
Kuybyshev Reservoir, res., Sov. Un.	D7	29
Kūysanjaq, Iraq	D15	40
Kuyto, l., Sov. Un.	E14	14
Kuznetsk, Sov. Un.	E16	27
Kuznetsk Basin, Sov. Un.	D25	8
Kuznetsovo, Sov. Un.	C10	33
Kuzomen, Sov. Un.	D17	14
Kvarner, b., Yugo.	C2	24
Kvismare Kanal, Swe.	t33	14
Kvitøya, i., Nor.	A11	128
Kwajalein, atoll, Marsh Is.	F10	6
Kwajalein Island, i., Marsh Is.	S17	52
Kwakoegron, Sur.	A3	59
Kwale, Kenya	B6	48
Kwa Mashu, S. Afr.	*C5	49
Kwamouth, Zaire	B2	48
Kwa Mtoro, Tan.	C6	48
Kwangju, S. Kor.	D10	31
Kwangju (Cuango), stm., Afr.	C2	48
Kwangsi Chuang see Guangxi Zhuangzu, prov., China	G6	31
Kwangtung see Guangdong, prov., China	G7	31
Kwatisore, Indon.	F8	34
Kweichow see Guizhou, prov., China	F6	31
Kwekwe, Zimb.	A4	49
Kwenge, stm., Afr.	C2	48
Kwethluk, Ak., U.S.	C7	79
Kwidzyn, Pol.	B5	26
Kwigillingok, Ak., U.S.	D7	79
Kwilu, stm., Afr.	B2	48
Kwinana, Austl.	F3	50
Kyabé, Chad	D3	46
Kyabram, Austl.	H5	51
Kyaiklat, Burma	E10	36
Kyaikto, Burma	D3	35
Kyakhta, Sov. Un.	D13	29
Kyaukpadaung, Burma	B1	35
Kyaukpyu, Burma	D10	36
Kyaukse, Burma	B3	35
Kybartai, Sov. Un.	n18	26
Kyle, Sask.	G1	75
Kyle, S.D., U.S.	D3	118
Kyle, Tx., U.S.	E4	120
Kyles Ford, Tn., U.S.	C10	119
Kylestrome, Scot., U.K.	C6	13
Kyll, stm., W. Ger.	E6	17
Kyllburg, W. Ger.	r20	17
Kyōga, Cape, c., Japan	I7	33
Kyōga, Lake, l., Ug.	A5	48
Kyōmipo see Songnim, N. Kor.	G2	33
Kyonggi Bay, b., Asia	H2	33
Kyŏngju, S. Kor.	D10	31
Kyŏngsŏng, N. Kor.	F4	33
Kyōto, Japan	D12	31
Kyritz, E. Ger.	B6	18
Kyrkjebö, Nor.	G1	14
Kyshtovka, Sov. Un.	D24	8
Kyshtym, Sov. Un.	B6	28
Kyuquot, B.C.	D4	69
Kyuquot Sound, strt., B.C.	E4	69
Kyūroku Island, i., Japan	F9	33
Kyūshū, i., Japan	E11	31
Kyustendil, Bul.	D6	24
Kyzyl, Sov. Un.	D12	29
Kyzyl-Kiya, Sov. Un.	E8	28
Kyzyl-Kum, des., Sov. Un.	E9	28
Kyzyltas Mountains, mts., Sov. Un.	D9	28
Kzyl-Orda, Sov. Un.	E9	29

L

Laa [an der Thaya], Aus.	D8	18
Laage, E. Ger.	E6	15
La Almunia de Doña Godina, Spain	B5	22
La Araucanía, prov., Chile	B2	54
Laas Caanood, Som.	D6	47
La Asunción, Ven.	A5	60
Laau Point, c., Hi., U.S.	B4	88
Labadie, Mo., U.S.	C7	102
Labadieville, La., U.S.	E5	95
La Banda, Arg.	B4	54
La Barca, Mex.	C4	63
La Barge, Wy., U.S.	D2	127
La Barge Creek, stm., Wy., U.S.	D2	127
Labasa, Fiji	H15	52
Labe, Gui.	D2	45
Labé, Gui.	D2	45
Labe (Elbe), stm., Eur.	C7	14
Labelle, co., Que.	A6	74
La Belle, Fl., U.S.	F5	86
La Belle, Mo., U.S.	A6	102
Labelle, co., Que.	D5	66
La Belle-Île, i., Fr.	D2	16
Labette, Ks., U.S.	E8	93
Labette, co., Ks., U.S.	E8	93
Labette Creek, stm., Ks., U.S.	E8	93
Labin, Yugo.	C2	24
La Bisbal, Spain	B7	22
Labo, Phil.	o14	34
Labo, Mount, mtn., Phil.	p14	34
La Boca, Pan.	m11	62
Laboe, W. Ger.	D4	15
La Bolt, S.D., U.S.	*B9	118
Labouheyre, Fr.	E3	16
Laboulaye, Arg.	A4	54
Labrador, reg., Newf.	g9	72
Labrador City, Newf.	h8	72
Labrador Sea, N.A.	g10	72
Lábrea, Braz.	D2	59
La Broquerie, Man.	E3	70
Labuan Island, i., Malay.	D5	34
Labuha, Indon.	F7	34
Labuhanbilik, Indon.	K4	35
Labuk Bay, b., Malay.	D5	34
Lac-à-Beauce, Que.	B5	74
Lacadena, Sask.	G1	75
La Calera, Chile	A2	54
Lacamp, La., U.S.	C3	95
La Canada Flintridge, Ca., U.S.	m12	82
La Capelle [-en-Thiérache], Fr.	B3	17
La Carlota, Arg.	A4	54
La Carolina, Spain	C4	22
Lac-aux-Brochets, Que.	B5	74
Lac-aux-Sables, Que.	C5	74
Lac-Baker, N.B.	B1	71
Lac-Beauport, Que.	n17	74
Lac-Bouchette, Que.	A5	74
Lac-Brome, Que.	D5	74
Laccadive, Minicoy and Amīndīvi Islands see Lakshadweep, ter., India	*F5	36
Laccadive Islands see Lakshadweep, is., India	F5	36
Lac-Carré, Que.	C3	74
Lac-Chat, Que.	B5	74
La Courte Oreilles Indian Reservation, Wi., U.S.	C2	126
Lac-des-Écorces, Que.	C2	74
Lac-des-Seize-Îles, Que.	D3	74
Lac du Bonnet, Man.	D3	70
Lac du Flambeau, Wi., U.S.	C4	126
Lac du Flambeau Indian Reservation, Wi., U.S.	C3	126
Lac-Édouard, Que.	B5	74
La Ceiba, Hond.	D7	63
La Ceiba, Ven.	B3	60
La Center, Ky., U.S.	e9	94
Lac-Etchemin, Que.	C7	74
Lacey, Wa., U.S.	B3	124
Laceys Spring, Al., U.S.	A3	78
Laceyville, Pa., U.S.	C9	115
Lac-Frontière, Que.	C7	74
La Chambre, Fr.	D2	20
Lachapelle [-sous-Rougemont], Fr.	A3	21
La Charité, Fr.	D5	16
La Chartre, Fr.	D5	16
La Chaux-de-Fonds, Switz.	E3	18
Lachay, Punta, c., Peru	B6	58
Lachen, Switz.	B6	21
Lachine, Que.	D5	74
Lachine, Mi., U.S.	C7	99
Lachlan, stm., Austl.	F8	50
La Chorrera, Col.	D3	60
La Chorrera, Pan.	F8	62
Lachute, Que.	D3	74
Laçi, Alb.	B2	25
La Cienega, N.M., U.S.	h8	108
La Ciotat, Fr.	F6	16
La Cisa Pass, Italy	B2	23
Lackawanna, N.Y., U.S.	D1	109
Lackawanna, co., Pa., U.S.	D12	115
Lackawaxen, Pa., U.S.	D12	115
Lackland Air Force Base, mil., Tx., U.S.	k7	120
Lac La Belle, Wi., U.S.	*E5	126
Lac La Biche, Alta.	B5	68
Lac La Hache, B.C.	D7	69
Lac la Ronge Provincial Park, Sask.	B3	75
Laclede, Id., U.S.	A2	89
Laclede, Mo., U.S.	B5	102
Laclede, co., Mo., U.S.	D5	102
Lac-Mégantic, Que.	D7	74
La Cocha, Arg.	B3	54
Lacolle, Que.	D4	74
La Colorada, Mex.	B2	63
Lago Posadas, Arg.	D2	54
Lago Ranco, Chile	D2	54
Lagos, Nig.	E5	45
Lacombe, Alta.	C4	68
Lacombe, La., U.S.	D6	95
Lacombe Bayou, stm., La., U.S.	h12	95
Lacon, Il., U.S.	B4	90
Lacona, Ia., U.S.	C4	92
Lacona, N.Y., U.S.	B4	109
La Concepción, Pan.	F6	62
La Conception, Que.	C3	74
Laconia, In., U.S.	H5	91
Laconia, N.H., U.S.	C4	106
Laconia, Tn., U.S.	B2	119
Laconia, Gulf of, b., Grc.	D4	25
La Conner, Wa., U.S.	A3	124
Lacoochee, Fl., U.S.	D4	86
La Coruña, Spain	A1	22
La Courneuve, Fr.	g10	16
Lacq, Fr.	F3	16
Lac qui Parle, co., Mn., U.S.	F2	100
Lac qui Parle, l., Mn., U.S.	F2	100
Lac qui Parle, West Branch, stm., Mn., U.S.	F2	100
La Creek Lake, l., S.D., U.S.	D4	118
La Crescent, Mn., U.S.	G7	100
La Crescenta, Ca., U.S.	*m12	82
La Creste, Alta.	f7	68
La Crosse, Ar., U.S.	A4	81
La Crosse, Fl., U.S.	C4	86
La Crosse, In., U.S.	B4	91
La Crosse, Ks., U.S.	D4	93
La Crosse, Va., U.S.	D4	123
La Crosse, Wi., U.S.	E2	126
La Crosse, co., Wi., U.S.	E2	126
La Crosse, stm., Wi., U.S.	E3	126
La Cruz, Col.	G4	60
La Cruz, C.R.	E5	62
La Cruz, Mex.	C3	63
La Cruz [de Río Grande], Nic.	D5	62
Lac-Saguay, Que.	C2	74
Lac-Saint-Jean-Est, co., Que.	A6	74
Lac-Saint-Jean-Ouest, co., Que.	A5	74
Lac-Vert, Sask.	E3	75
La Cygne, Ks., U.S.	D9	93
Ladainha, Braz.	B1	56
Ladário, Braz.	B1	56
Ladd, Il., U.S.	B4	90
Ladder Creek, stm., Ks., U.S.	D2	93
Laddonia, Mo., U.S.	B6	102
Ladelle, Ar., U.S.	D4	81
Ladera Heights, Ca., U.S.	*m12	82
La Désirade, i., Guad.	Q9	65
Ladies Island, i., S.C., U.S.	G6	117
Ladispoli, Italy	h8	23
Ladner, S.D., U.S.	B2	118
Lādnūn, India	D5	36
Ladoga, In., U.S.	E4	91
Ladoga, Tx., U.S.	C5	120
Ladora, Ia., U.S.	C5	92
Ladoga, Lake, l., Sov. Un.	C6	29
La Dorada, Col.	B3	60
Ladson, S.C., U.S.	F7	117
Ladue, Mo., U.S.	*C7	102
Ladue, Mo., U.S.	C7	102
Ladybank, Scot., U.K.	E5	13
Ladybrand, S. Afr.	C4	49
Ladysmith, B.C.	E6	69
Ladysmith, S. Afr.	C4	49
Ladysmith, Wi., U.S.	C2	126
Lae, Pap. N. Gui.	k12	50
La Esmeralda, Ven.	C4	60
Læsø, i., Den.	A4	15
La Esperanza, Cuba	C2	63
La Esperanza, Hond.	C3	62
La Estrada, Spain	A1	22
La Estrella, Bol.	E3	55
La Farge, Wi., U.S.	A5	109
LaFargeville, N.Y., U.S.	A4	109
Lafayette, Al., U.S.	*h8	82
Lafayette, Co., U.S.	B5	83
Lafayette, Co., U.S.	B1	87
Lafayette, Ga., U.S.	B1	87
Lafayette, Il., U.S.	B4	90
Lafayette, In., U.S.	D4	91
Lafayette, La., U.S.	D3	95
Lafayette, N.J., U.S.	A3	107
Lafayette, N.Y., U.S.	C4	109
Lafayette, N.C., U.S.	A4	110
Lafayette, Oh., U.S.	C2	112
Lafayette, Or., U.S.	B3	114
Lafayette, R.I., U.S.	E4	116
Lafayette, Tn., U.S.	A5	119
Lafayette, co., U.S.	D2	81
Lafayette, co., Fl., U.S.	C3	86
Lafayette, co., Ms., U.S.	A4	101
Lafayette, co., Mo., U.S.	B4	102
Lafayette, co., Wi., U.S.	F3	126
Lafayette, Mount, mtn., N.H., U.S.	B3	106
Lafayette Southwest, La., U.S.	*D3	81
Lafe, Ar., U.S.	A5	81
La Fère, Fr.	B5	16
La Feria, Tx., U.S.	F4	120
La Ferté-Bernard, Fr.	C4	16
La Ferté-Macé, Fr.	C3	16
La Ferté-sous-Jouarre, Fr.	C5	16
Lafferty, Oh., U.S.	B4	112
Lafia, Nig.	E6	45
Lafiagi, Nig.	E6	45
Lafitte, La., U.S.	k11	95
Laflèche, Sask.	H2	75
La Flèche, Fr.	D3	16
La Follette, Tn., U.S.	C9	119
La Fontaine, In., U.S.	C6	91
Lafontaine, Ks., U.S.	E8	93
Lafourche, co., La., U.S.	E5	95
Lafourche, Bayou, stm., La., U.S.	E5	95
La France, S.C., U.S.	B2	117
La Galera, stm., Italy	h8	23
La Galite, i., Tun.	F2	23
Lagan, stm., Swe.	I5	14
Lage, W. Ger.	B3	17
Lågen, stm., Nor.	G3	14
Lagg, Scot., U.K.	B3	13
Laggan, Loch, res., Scot., U.K.	D4	13
Lagny, Fr.	D5	16
Lago, Mount, mtn., Wa., U.S.	A5	124
Lagoa, Port.	D1	22
Lagoa Vermelha, Braz.	C6	57
Lagos, Port.	D1	22
Lagos de Moreno, Mex.	C4	63
La Goulette, Tun.	*B7	44
Lago Viedma, Arg.	D2	54
La Grand'Combe, Fr.	E6	16
La Grande, Or., U.S.	B8	114
La Grande, stm., Que.	h11	74
La Grande Deux, Réservoir, res., Que.	h11	74
La Grande Quatre, Réservoir, res., Que.	F18	66
La Grange, Ar., U.S.	C5	81
Lagrange, In., U.S.	A7	91
La Grange, Ga., U.S.	C1	87
Lagrange, In., U.S.	A7	91
La Grange, Il., U.S.	B6	90
Lagrange, In., U.S.	A7	91
La Grange, Ky., U.S.	B4	94
La Grange, Me., U.S.	C4	96
La Grange, Mo., U.S.	A6	102
La Grange, N.C., U.S.	B5	110
La Grange, Oh., U.S.	A3	112
La Grange, Tx., U.S.	E4	120
Lagrange, Wy., U.S.	E8	127
Lagrange, co., In., U.S.	A7	91
La Grange Highlands, Il., U.S.	*k9	90
La Grange Park, Il., U.S.	k9	90
La Gran Sabana, pl., Ven.	C6	60
Lagro, In., U.S.	C6	91
La Grue Bayou, stm., Ar., U.S.	C4	81
La Guadeloupe (Saint-Evariste), Que.	D7	74
La Guaira, Ven.	A4	60
La Guardia, Spain	B1	22
La Guata, Hond.	C4	62
Laguna, Braz.	D3	56
Laguna, N.M., U.S.	B2	108
Laguna Beach, Ca., U.S.	F5	82
Laguna Dam, U.S.	E1	80
Laguna Hills, Ca., U.S.	*n13	82
Laguna Indian Reservation, N.M., U.S.	C2	108
Laguna Niguel, Ca., U.S.	*F5	82
Lagunas, Peru	C2	58
Lagunillas, Bol.	C5	55
La Habana, prov., Cuba	C2	64
La Habra, Ca., U.S.	n13	82
Lahad Datu, Malay.	E5	34
Lahaina, Hi., U.S.	C5	88
La Harpe, Il., U.S.	C3	90
La Harpe, Ks., U.S.	E8	93
Lahat, Indon.	F2	34
La Harpe, stm., ...		
La Have, stm., N.S.	E5	71
La Have, N.S.	E5	71
La Have Island, N.S.	E5	71
Lahījān, Iran	C5	39
Lahn, stm., W. Ger.	C4	18
Lahnstein, W. Ger.	E7	17
Laholm, Swe.	H9	14
Laholmsbukten, b., Swe.	B6	15
Lahontan Reservoir, res., Nv., U.S.	D2	105
Lahore, Pak.	B5	36
Lahore Cantonment, Pak.	*B5	36
Lahr, W. Ger.	D3	18
Lahti, Fin.	G11	14
La Huaca, Peru	B1	58
Laï, Chad	D3	46
Lai Chau, Viet.	A5	35
Laichow Bay see Laizhou Wan, b., China	C3	31
Laide, Scot., U.K.	D4	13
Laifeng, China	B4	88
Laie, Hi., U.S.	B4	88
Laifeng, China	F2	31
L'Aigle, Fr.	C4	16
L'Aigle Creek, stm., Ar., U.S.	C4	81
Laihka, Burma	B3	35
Laingsburg, S. Afr.	E6	127
Laingsburg, Mi., U.S.	F6	99
Lair, Ky., U.S.	B5	94
Laird, Sask.	E2	75
Laird, Co., U.S.	A8	83
Laird, Co., U.S.	A4	91
Lairg, Scot., U.K.	C4	13
Laïri, Batha de, stm., Chad	C3	46
Laiwui, Indon.	F7	34
Laiyang, China	D9	31
Laiyuan, China	D8	31
Laizhou Wan, b., China	D8	31
La Jalca, Peru	C2	58
La Jara, Co., U.S.	D5	83
La Jara, N.M., U.S.	A3	108
Laje Point, c., Port.	f9	22
Lajeado, Braz.	D2	56
Lajes, Braz.	C3	57
La Jolla, Point, c., Ca., U.S.	o15	82
La Joya, Mex.	G3	75
La Joya (part of Mexico City), Mex.	h9	63
La Joya, Peru	D3	58
Lajord, Sask.	G3	75
Lajosmizse, Hung.	B4	24
La Junta, Co., U.S.	D7	83
Lake, Mi., U.S.	E5	99
Lake, Ms., U.S.	C4	101
Lake, co., Ca., U.S.	C2	82
Lake, co., Co., U.S.	B4	83
Lake, co., Fl., U.S.	D5	86
Lake, co., Il., U.S.	A6	90
Lake, co., In., U.S.	B3	91
Lake, co., Mi., U.S.	E5	99
Lake, co., Mn., U.S.	C7	100
Lake, co., Mt., U.S.	C2	103
Lake, co., Oh., U.S.	A4	112
Lake, co., Or., U.S.	E6	114
Lake, co., S.D., U.S.	C8	118
Lake, co., Tn., U.S.	A2	119
Lake Alfred, Fl., U.S.	D5	86
Lake Almanor, Ca., U.S.	H3	75
Lake Andes, S.D., U.S.	D7	118
Lake Annis, N.S.	E4	71
Lake Ariel, Pa., U.S.	D11	115
Lake Arrowhead, Ca., U.S.	E5	82
Lake Arthur, La., U.S.	D3	95
Lake Arthur, N.M., U.S.	D5	108
Lake Barcroft, Va., U.S.	*B5	123
Lake Benton, Mn., U.S.	F2	100
Lake Beulah, Wi., U.S.	n11	126
Lake Bluff, Il., U.S.	A6	90
Lake Bonaparte, N.Y., U.S.	A5	109
Lake Bronson, Mn., U.S.	B2	100
Lake Bruce, In., U.S.	C5	91
Lake Butler, Fl., U.S.	B4	86
Lake Cargelligo, Austl.	F8	50
Lake Carmel, N.Y., U.S.	*D7	109
Lake Carroll, Il., U.S.	*D4	90
Lake Charles, La., U.S.	D2	95
Lake Chelan National Recreation Area, Wa., U.S.	A5	124
Lake City, Ar., U.S.	B5	81
Lake City, Ca., U.S.	B3	82
Lake City, Co., U.S.	C3	83
Lake City, Fl., U.S.	B4	86
Lake City, Ia., U.S.	B3	92
Lake City, Ks., U.S.	E5	93
Lake City, Mi., U.S.	D5	99
Lake City, Mn., U.S.	F6	100
Lake City, Pa., U.S.	B1	115
Lake City, S.C., U.S.	D8	117
Lake City, S.D., U.S.	B8	118
Lake City, Tn., U.S.	C9	119
Lake Clark National Park, Ak., U.S.	C11	115
Lake Como, Ms., U.S.	A3	101
Lake Cormorant, Ms., U.S.	A3	101
Lake Cowichan, B.C.	g11	69
Lake Creek, stm., Wa., U.S.	B7	124
Lake Crystal, Mn., U.S.	F4	100
Lake Delta, N.Y., U.S.	B5	109
Lake Delton, Wi., U.S.	E4	126
Lake District, reg., Eng., U.K.	C5	10
Lake Elmo, Mn., U.S.	*n13	127
Lake Elmore, Vt., U.S.	B3	122
Lake Elsinore, Ca., U.S.	F5	82
Lake Erie Beach, N.Y., U.S.	C1	109
Lakefield, Ont.	C6	73
Lake Forest, Il., U.S.	A6	90
Lake Forest, Il., U.S.	*s13	86
Lake Fork, Id., U.S.	E2	89
Lake Fork, Il., U.S.	D4	90
Lake Fork, stm., Co., U.S.	C3	83
Lake Fork, stm., Ut., U.S.	C5	121
Lake Geneva, Wi., U.S.	F5	126
Lake George, Co., U.S.	C5	83
Lake George, Mi., U.S.	E6	99
Lake George, Mn., U.S.	C4	100
Lake George, N.Y., U.S.	B7	109
Lake Grinnell, N.J., U.S.	A3	107
Lake Grove, N.Y., U.S.	*E7	109
Lake Hamilton, Ar., U.S.	g7	81
Lake Harbour, N.W. Ter.	D19	66
Lake Havasu City, Az., U.S.	C1	80
Lake Helen, Fl., U.S.	D5	86
Lake Hiawatha, N.J., U.S.	B4	107
Lake Hubert, Mn., U.S.	D4	100
Lake Hughes, Ca., U.S.	E4	82
Lake Huntington, N.Y., U.S.	D5	109
Lakehurst, N.J., U.S.	C4	107
Lakehurst Naval Air Station, mil., N.J., U.S.	C4	107
Lake in the Hills, Il., U.S.	h8	90
Lake Itasca, Mn., U.S.	C3	100
Lake Jackson, Tx., U.S.	E5	120
Lake Katrine, N.Y., U.S.	D7	109
Lakeland, Fl., U.S.	D5	86
Lakeland, Ga., U.S.	E3	87
Lakeland Highlands, Fl., U.S.	*E5	86
Lake Leelanau, Mi., U.S.	D5	99
Lake Lenore, Sask.	E3	75
Lake Lillian, Mn., U.S.	F4	100
Lake Linden, Mi., U.S.	A2	99
Lake Lindsey, Fl., U.S.	D4	86
Lake Lorraine, Fl., U.S.	*u15	86
Lake Louise, Alta.	B7	109
Lake Luzerne, N.Y., U.S.	B7	109
Lake Mary, Fl., U.S.	o11	86
Lake Magdalene, Fl., U.S.	*D5	86
Lake McDonald, Mt., U.S.	B3	103
Lake Mead National Recreation Area, U.S.	H7	105
Lake Meredith National Recreation Area, Tx., U.S.	B2	120
Lake Metigoshe, N.D., U.S.	A5	111
Lake Mills, Ia., U.S.	A4	92
Lake Mills, Wi., U.S.	E5	126
Lake Minchumina, Ak., U.S.	C9	79
Lakemont, Oh., U.S.	F5	115
Lakemore, Oh., U.S.	A4	112
Lake Mountain, mtn., Wy., U.S.	E6	127
Lakenan, Mo., U.S.	B5	102
Lake Nebagamon, Wi., U.S.	B2	126
Lake Norden, S.D., U.S.	C8	118
Lake Odessa, Mi., U.S.	F5	99
Lake Of The Woods, co., Mn., U.S.	B4	100
Lake Orion, Mi., U.S.	F7	99
Lake Oswego, Or., U.S.	B4	114
Lake Ozark, Mo., U.S.	C5	102
Lake Park, Fl., U.S.	F6	86
Lake Park, Ga., U.S.	F3	87
Lake Park, Ia., U.S.	A2	92
Lake Park, Mn., U.S.	D2	100
Lake Placid, Fl., U.S.	E5	86
Lake Placid, N.Y., U.S.	A7	109
Lake Pleasant, N.Y., U.S.	B6	109
Lake Pontchartrain Causeway, La., U.S.	h11	95
Lakeport, Ca., U.S.	C2	82
Lake Preston, S.D., U.S.	C8	118
Lake Providence, La., U.S.	B4	95
Lake Range, mts., Nv., U.S.	*E2	105
Lake Ridge, Va., U.S.	n19	73
Lake River, Ont.	n19	73
Lake Ronkonkoma, N.Y., U.S.	*n15	109
Lake Shore, Md., U.S.	*B4	101
Lakeshore, Ms., U.S.	E4	101
Lake Shore, Ut., U.S.	*C4	121
Lakeshore, N.S.	E6	71
Lakeside, Az., U.S.	B3	91
Lakeside, Ca., U.S.	*B5	82
Lakeside, Ct., U.S.	C3	84
Lakeside, Fl., U.S.	B5	86
Lakeside, Ia., U.S.	B2	92
Lakeside, Mt., U.S.	B2	103
Lakeside, Ne., U.S.	B3	104
Lakeside, Oh., U.S.	A3	112
Lakeside, Or., U.S.	D2	114
Lakeside, Va., U.S.	*C5	123
Lakeside Mountains, mts., Ut., U.S.	B3	121
Lakeside-Pinetop, Az., U.S.	C6	80
Lake Station, In., U.S.	A3	91
Lake Station, Ok., U.S.	A5	113
Lake Stevens, Wa., U.S.	A3	124
Lake Superior Provincial Park, Ont.	p18	73
Lake Swamp, stm., S.C., U.S.	B3	117
Lake Tansi, Tn., U.S.	D8	119
Lake Telemark, N.J., U.S.	B4	107
Lake Tomahawk, Wi., U.S.	C4	126
Laketon, Tx., U.S.	B2	120
Laketown, Ut., U.S.	B4	121
Lake Toxaway, N.C., U.S.	f10	110
Lake Traverse, Ont.	B6	73
Lake Valley, Sask.	G2	75
Lake Valley, val., Nv., U.S.	*E7	105
Lakeview, Ga., U.S.	*B1	87

Name	Map Ref.	Page
Lakeview, Id., U.S.	B2	89
Lake View, Ia., U.S.	B2	92
Lakeview, Mi., U.S.	E5	99
Lakeview, Mt., U.S.	F5	103
Lakeview, N.Y., U.S.	*E7	109
Lake View, N.Y., U.S.	C2	109
Lakeview, Or., U.S.	E6	114
Lake View, S.C., U.S.	C9	117
Lakeview, Tx., U.S.	B2	120
Lake Villa, Il., U.S.	h8	90
Lake Village, Ar., U.S.	D4	81
Lake Village, In., U.S.	B3	91
Lakeville, Ct., U.S.	B2	84
Lakeville, In., U.S.	A5	91
Lakeville, Ma., U.S.	C6	98
Lakeville, Mn., U.S.	F5	100
Lakeville, N.Y., U.S.	C3	109
Lake Waccamaw, N.C., U.S.	C4	110
Lake Wales, Fl., U.S.	E5	86
Lake Williams, N.D., U.S.	B6	111
Lake Wilson, Mn., U.S.	G3	100
Lake Winola, Pa., U.S.	m17	115
Lake Wissota, Wi., U.S.	*D2	126
Lakewood, Ca., U.S.	n12	82
Lakewood, Co., U.S.	B5	83
Lakewood, Il., U.S.	D5	90
Lakewood, Ia., U.S.	f8	92
Lakewood, Me., U.S.	D3	96
Lakewood, N.J., U.S.	C4	107
Lakewood, N.M., U.S.	E5	108
Lakewood, N.Y., U.S.	C1	109
Lakewood, Oh., U.S.	A4	112
Lakewood, Pa., U.S.	C10	115
Lakewood, Wa., U.S.	A3	124
Lakewood, Wi., U.S.	C5	126
Lakewood Center, Wa., U.S.	B3	124
Lake Worth, Fl., U.S.	F6	86
Lake Worth Inlet, b., Fl., U.S.	F7	86
Lake Zurich, Il., U.S.	h8	90
Lakhī, Afg.	B3	36
Lakhīmpur, India	C7	36
Lakhta (part of Leningrad), Sov. Un.	r31	14
Lakin, Ks., U.S.	E2	93
Lakota, I.C.	E3	45
Lakota, Ia., U.S.	A3	92
Lakota, N.D., U.S.	A7	111
Laksefjorden, Nor.	B12	14
Lakshadweep (Laccadive, Minicoy and Amīndīvi Islands), ter., India	*F5	36
Lakshadweep (Laccadive Islands), is., India	F5	36
La Laguna, Spain	m13	22
La Libertad, El Sal.	D3	62
La Libertad, Guat.	B2	62
La Libertad, dept., Peru	C2	58
La Ligua, Chile	A2	54
Lalín, Spain	A1	22
La Línea, Spain	D3	22
La Loche, Sask.	m7	75
La Loche, Lac, l., Sask.	A6	68
La Loma, N.M., U.S.	B4	108
La Louvière, Bel.	D4	17
La Luz, N.M., U.S.	D4	108
La Macarena, Serranía de, mts., Col.	C3	60
La Machine, Fr.	D5	16
La Maddalena, Italy	D2	23
La Madera, N.M., U.S.	A3	108
Lama-Kara, Togo	E5	45
La Malbaie, Que.	B7	74
Lamaline, Newf.	E4	72
La Mancha, reg., Spain	C4	22
Lamanibot Sanhilo, Puntan, c., N. Mar. Is.	D7	52
Lamar, Ar., U.S.	B2	81
Lamar, Co., U.S.	C8	83
Lamar, In., U.S.	H4	91
Lamar, Ms., U.S.	A4	101
Lamar, Mo., U.S.	D3	102
Lamar, Ne., U.S.	D4	104
Lamar, Ok., U.S.	B5	113
Lamar, Pa., U.S.	D7	115
Lamar, S.C., U.S.	C7	117
Lamar, co., Al., U.S.	B1	78
Lamar, co., Ga., U.S.	C2	87
Lamar, co., Ms., U.S.	D4	101
Lamar, co., Tx., U.S.	C5	120
Lamar, stm., Wy., U.S.	B2	127
Lamarche, Fr.	A1	20
La Marmora, Punta, mtn., Italy	D2	23
La Marque, Tx., U.S.	*r15	120
Lamas, Peru	C2	58
Lamasco, Ky., U.S.	f10	94
La Mauricie, Parc National de, Que.	C5	74
Lamb, co., Tx., U.S.	B1	120
Lamballe, Fr.	D3	16
Lambaréné, Gabon	F2	46
Lambayeque, Peru	C2	58
Lambayeque, dept., Peru	C2	58
Lambay Island, i., Ire.	D5	11
Lambert, Ms., U.S.	A3	101
Lambert, Mt., U.S.	C12	103
Lambert, Ok., U.S.	A3	113
Lambert Glacier, ice, Ant.	B19	7
Lambert Lake, Me., U.S.	C5	96
Lamberton, Mn., U.S.	F3	100
Lambert's Bay, S. Afr.	D2	49
Lambertville, Mi., U.S.	G7	99
Lambertville, N.J., U.S.	C3	107
Lambeth, Ont.	E3	73
Lambeth (part of London), Eng., U.K.	m12	10
Lambourn, Eng., U.K.	C6	12
Lambrecht (Pfalz), W. Ger.	D3	19
Lambro, stm., Italy	D5	20
Lambrook, Ar., U.S.	C5	81
Lambsburg, Va., U.S.	D2	123
Lamb's Head, c., Ire.	F1	11
Lambton, Que.	D6	74
Lambton, co., Ont.	E2	73
Lambton, Cape, c., N.W. Ter.	B8	66
Lamdesar, Indon.	G8	34
Lame Deer, Mt., U.S.	E10	103
Lamego, Port.	B2	22
Lamèque, N.B.	B5	71
Lamèque, Île, i., N.B.	B5	71
La Merced (Superí), Arg.	E2	55
La Mesa, Ca., U.S.	F5	82
La Mesa, N.M., U.S.	E3	108
Lamesa, Tx., U.S.	C2	120
Lamía, Grc.	C4	40
La Minerve, Que.	C3	74
Lamington, Mount, mtn., Pap. N. Gui.	k12	50
La Mirada, Ca., U.S.	*E4	82
Lamlam, Mount, mtn., Guam	M9	50
Lamlash, Scot., U.K.	E3	13
Lammermuir Hills, hills, Scot., U.K.	E6	13
Lammhult, Swe.	A8	15
Lamoil, i., Micron.	Q18	52
La Moille, Il., U.S.	B4	90
Lamoille, Nv., U.S.	C6	105
Lamoille, co., Vt., U.S.	B3	122
Lamoille, stm., Vt., U.S.	B3	122
Lamoille, North Branch, stm., Vt., U.S.	B3	122
La Moine, stm., Il., U.S.	C3	90
Lamona, Wa., U.S.	B7	124
Lamon Bay, b., Phil.	C6	34
Lamoni, Ia., U.S.	D4	92
Lamont, Alta.	C4	68
Lamont, Ca., U.S.	E4	82
Lamont, Fl., U.S.	B3	86
Lamont, Ia., U.S.	B6	92
Lamont, Ks., U.S.	D7	93
Lamont, Ms., U.S.	B2	101
Lamont, Ok., U.S.	A4	113
Lamont, Wa., U.S.	B8	124
La Monte, Mo., U.S.	C4	102
La Motte, Isle, i., Vt., U.S.	B2	122
La Moure, N.D., U.S.	C7	111
La Moure, co., N.D., U.S.	C7	111
Lampa, Peru	E3	58
Lampang, Thai.	B1	34
Lampasas, Tx., U.S.	D3	120
Lampasas, co., Tx., U.S.	D3	120
Lampeter, Wales, U.K.	B3	12
Lampertheim, W. Ger.	D3	19
Lamphun, Thai.	C3	35
Lampman, Sask.	H4	75
Lamprey, stm., N.H., U.S.	D4	106
Lamu, Kenya	B7	48
La Mure, Fr.	E6	16
Lamy, N.M., U.S.	B4	108
Lanagan, Mo., U.S.	E3	102
Lanai, i., Hi., U.S.	C5	88
Lanai City, Hi., U.S.	C5	88
Lanaihale, mtn., Hi., U.S.	C5	88
Lanao, Lake, l., Phil.	D6	34
Lanare, Ca., U.S.	D4	82
Lanark, Ont.	C8	73
Lanark, Scot., U.K.	C5	10
Lanark, Il., U.S.	A4	90
Lanark, W.V., U.S.	D3	125
Lanark, co., Ont.	B8	73
Lanark Village, Fl., U.S.	C2	86
Lance, Point, c., Newf.	E4	72
Lance Creek, Wy., U.S.	C8	127
Lance Creek, stm., Wy., U.S.	C8	127
Lancer, Sask.	G1	75
Lanchou see Lanzhou, China		
Lanciano, Italy	C5	23
Lancing, Tn., U.S.	C8	119
Lancy, Switz.	D1	21
Landa, N.D., U.S.	A5	111
Landaff Center, N.H., U.S.	B3	106
Landau [an der Isar], W. Ger.	D6	18
Landau [in der Pfalz], W. Ger.	D3	19
Land Between the Lakes, U.S.	f9	94
Landeck, Aus.	E5	18
Landen, Bel.	D5	17
Lander, Wy., U.S.	D4	127
Lander, co., Nv., U.S.	C4	105
Landerneau, Fr.	C1	16
Landess, In., U.S.	C6	91
Landing Lake, l., Man.	B3	70
Landis, Sask.	E1	75
Landis, N.C., U.S.	B2	110
Landisburg, Pa., U.S.	F7	115
Landivisiau, Fr.	C1	16
Lando, S.C., U.S.	B6	117
Land O' Lakes, Wi., U.S.	B4	126
Landover, Md., U.S.	*C4	97
Landquart, Switz.	E9	21
Landquart, stm., Switz.	E9	21
Landrum, S.C., U.S.	A3	117
Landsberg, W. Ger.	D5	18
Land's End, c., Eng., U.K.	E4	10
Lands End, c., R.I., U.S.	F5	116
Landshut, W. Ger.	D6	18
Landskrona, Swe.	J5	14
Landsman Creek, stm., Co., U.S.	B8	83
Landsort, Swe.	u35	14
Landusky, Mt., U.S.	C8	103
Lane, Il., U.S.	C5	90
Lane, Ks., U.S.	D8	93
Lane, Nv., U.S.	D7	105
Lane, Ok., U.S.	C6	113
Lane, S.C., U.S.	D8	117
Lane, S.D., U.S.	C7	118
Lane, Tn., U.S.	A2	119
Lane, co., Ks., U.S.	D3	93
Lane, co., Or., U.S.	C4	114
Laneburg, Ar., U.S.	D2	81
La Negra, Chile	D1	55
Lanesboro, Ma., U.S.	A1	98
Lanesboro, Mn., U.S.	G7	100
Lanesboro, Pa., U.S.	C10	115
Lanesville, In., U.S.	H6	91
Lanett, Al., U.S.	C4	78
Lanfine, Alta.	D5	68
Lang, Sask.	H3	75
Langå, Den.	C3	15
Langadhás, Grc.	B4	25
Langa Langa, Zaire		
Langanes, c., Ice.	m25	14
Langarüd, Iran	C5	39
Langås, Swe.	B6	15
Langbank, Sask.	G4	75
Lang Bay, B.C.	E5	69
Langdale, Al., U.S.	C4	78
Langdon, Alta.	D4	68
Langdon, Ia., U.S.	A2	92
Langdon, Ks., U.S.	E5	93
Langdon, Mo., U.S.	A2	102
Langdon, N.H., U.S.	D2	106
Langdon, N.D., U.S.	A7	111
L'Ange-Gardien, Que.	n17	74
Langeac, Fr.	E5	16
Langeland, i., Den.	D4	15
Langelandsbælt, strt., Den.	D4	15
Langeloth, Pa., U.S.	F1	115
Langen, W. Ger.	D3	19
Langenau, W. Ger.	E5	19
Langenburg, Sask.	G5	75
Langenselbold, W. Ger.	C4	19
Langenthal, Switz.	E3	18
Langenzenn, W. Ger.	D5	19
Langeoog, W. Ger.	A7	17
Langeoog, i., W. Ger.	B3	18
Langerak, strt., Den.	A4	15
Langesund, Nor.	H3	14
Langeten, stm., Switz.	B4	21
Langford, B.C.	h12	69
Langford, S.D., U.S.	B8	118
Långhalsen, l., Swe.	u34	14
Langham, Sask.	E2	75
Länghem, Swe.	A7	15
Langholm, Scot., U.K.	E5	13
Langhorne, Pa., U.S.	F12	115
Langjökull, ice, Ice.	n22	14
Langkawi, i., Malay.	I3	35
Langlade, i., St. P./M.	E2	72
Langley, B.C.	f13	69
Langley, Ar., U.S.	C2	81
Langley, Ky., U.S.	C7	94
Langley, Ok., U.S.	A6	113
Langley, S.C., U.S.	E4	117
Langley, Wa., U.S.	A3	124
Langley Air Force Base, mil., Va., U.S.	h15	123
Langley Park, Md., U.S.	f9	97
Langleyville, Il., U.S.	D4	90
Langlois, Or., U.S.	E2	114
Langnau [in Emmental], Switz.	E3	18
Langogne, Fr.	E5	16
Langon, Fr.	E3	16
Langoya, i., Nor.	C6	14
Langres, Fr.	D6	16
Langres, Plateau de, plat., Fr.	D6	16
Langruth, Man.	D2	70
Langsa, Indon.	E1	34
Lang Son, Viet.	B7	36
Langstaff, Ont.	k15	73
Langston, Al., U.S.	A3	78
Langston, Ok., U.S.	B4	113
Langton, Ont.	E4	73
Langtry, Tx., U.S.	E2	120
Languedoc, hist. reg., Fr.	F5	16
L'Anguille, stm., Ar., U.S.	B5	81
Langzhong, China	E6	31
Lanham, Md., U.S.	C4	97
Lanier, co., Ga., U.S.	E3	87
Lanigan, Sask.	F3	75
Lanigan Creek, stm., Sask.	F3	75
Lanin, Volcán, vol., S.A.	B2	54
Lankin, N.D., U.S.	A8	111
Lanklaar, Bel.	C5	17
Lannon, Wi., U.S.	m11	126
Lannion, Fr.	C2	16
L'Annonciation, Que.	C3	74
Lanoka Harbor, N.J., U.S.	D4	107
Lanoraie, Que.	D4	74
Lansdale, Pa., U.S.	F11	115
Lansdowne, Ont.	C8	73
Lansdowne, Md., U.S.	*B4	97
Lansdowne, Pa., U.S.	*p20	115
Lansdowne House, Ont.	n18	73
Lansford, N.D., U.S.	A4	111
Lansford, Pa., U.S.	E10	115
Lansing, Il., U.S.	B6	90
Lansing, Ia., U.S.	A6	92
Lansing, Ks., U.S.	C9	93
Lansing, Mi., U.S.	F6	99
Lansing, N.C., U.S.	A1	110
Lansing, W.V., U.S.	m13	125
Lanslebourg, Fr.	D2	20
Lantana, Fl., U.S.	F6	86
Lantern Hill, hill, Ct., U.S.	D8	84
Lantry, S.D., U.S.	B4	118
Lanusei, Italy	E2	23
Lanuvio, Italy	h9	23
Lanxi, China	F8	31
Lanxi, China	A12	32
Lanzada, Italy	D6	21
Lanzarote, i., Spain	m15	22
Lanzhou (Lanchow), China	D7	31
Laoag, Phil.	A6	35
Lao Cai, Viet.	A6	35
Laohekou, China	E7	31
Laoighis see Laois, co., Ire.	D4	11
Laois, co., Ire.	D4	11
Laolao, Bahia, b., N. Mar. Is.	D8	52
Laolao Kattan, Puntan, c., N. Mar. Is.	D8	52
Laon, Fr.	C5	16
Laona, Wi., U.S.	C5	126
La Oroya, Peru	D2	58
Laos, ctry., Asia	B3	34
Laotto, In., U.S.	B7	91
Lapa, Braz.	D3	56
La Palma, Pan.	F8	62
La Palma, Az., U.S.	E4	80
La Palma, Ca., U.S.	*n12	82
La Palma, i., Spain	m13	22
La Palma [del Condado], Spain	D2	22
La Paloma, Ur.	E2	56
La Pampa, prov., Arg.	B3	54
La Paragua, Ven.	B3	62
La Passe, Ont.	B7	73
La Patrie, Que.	D6	74
La Paz, Arg.	A3	54
La Paz, Bol.	C1	55
La Paz, Col.	A3	60
La Paz, Hond.	C3	62
La Paz, Mex.	E4	63
La Paz, Mex.	D6	63
Lapaz, In., U.S.	B5	91
La Paz, dept., Bol.	C2	55
La Paz, Bahía de, b., Mex.	D2	63
La Pedrera, Col.	D4	60
Lapeer, Mi., U.S.	E7	99
Lapeer, co., Mi., U.S.	E7	99
Lapel, In., U.S.	D6	91
La Perouse Strait, strt., Asia	D10	33
La Piedad [Cavadas], Mex.	m12	63
Lapine, Al., U.S.	D3	78
La Pine, Or., U.S.	D5	114
La Place, Il., U.S.	D5	90
La Place, La., U.S.	h11	95
La Plant, S.D., U.S.	B5	118
La Plata, Arg.	A5	54
La Plata, Col.	C2	60
La Plata, Md., U.S.	C4	97
La Plata, Mo., U.S.	A5	102
La Plata, N.M., U.S.	A1	108
La Plata, co., Co., U.S.	D3	83
La Plata Mountains, mts., Co., U.S.	D3	83
La Plata Peak, mtn., Co., U.S.	B4	83
La Platte, Ne., U.S.	g13	104
La Platte, stm., Vt., U.S.	C2	122
La Pobla de Lillet, Spain	A6	22
La Pocatière, Que.	B7	74
La Poile Bay, b., Newf.	E2	72
Lapoint, Ut., U.S.	C6	121
La Pointe, Wi., U.S.	B3	126
La Pola [de Gordón], Spain	A3	22
La Porte, Ca., U.S.	C3	82
Laporte, Co., U.S.	A5	83
La Porte, In., U.S.	A4	91
Laporte, Pa., U.S.	D9	115
La Porte, Tx., U.S.	r14	120
La Porte, co., In., U.S.	A4	91
La Porte City, Ia., U.S.	B5	92
Läppe, Swe.	t33	14
Lappeenranta, Fin.	G13	14
La Prairie, Que.	D4	74
La Prairie, Mn., U.S.	C5	100
Laprairie, co., Que.	D4	74
Laprida, Arg.	B4	54
La Pryor, Tx., U.S.	E3	120
Läpşeki, Tur.	B6	40
La Puebla de Montalbán, Spain	C3	22
La Puente, Ca., U.S.	*m13	82
La Puente, N.M., U.S.	A3	108
La Push, Wa., U.S.	B1	124
Lapwai, Id., U.S.	C2	89
La Quiaca, Arg.	A2	54
L'Aquila (Aquila), Italy	C4	23
Lār, Iran	C5	38
Lara, state, Ven.	A3	60
Larache, Mor.	B3	44
Larak, i., Iran	H8	39
Laramie, Wy., U.S.	E7	127
Laramie, co., Wy., U.S.	E8	127
Laramie, stm., Wy., U.S.	E7	127
Laramie Mountains, mts., Wy., U.S.	D7	127
Laramie Peak, mtn., Wy., U.S.	D7	127
Larantuka, Indon.	G6	34
Larap, Phil.	o14	34
Larche Pass, Eur.	E3	16
Larchmont, N.Y., U.S.	h13	109
Larchmont North, N.Y., U.S.	*h13	109
Larchwood, Ia., U.S.	A1	92
Lardeau, B.C.	D9	69
Laredo, Spain	A4	22
Laredo, Mo., U.S.	A4	102
Laredo, Tx., U.S.	F3	120
Laredo Sound, strt., B.C.	C3	69
La Réole, Fr.	E4	16
Lares, P.R.	E14	64
Largeau, Chad	B4	46
Largentière, Fr.	E6	16
Largo, Fl., U.S.	E4	86
Largo, Cañon, val., N.M., U.S.	A2	108
Largo, Cayo, i., Cuba	D3	64
Largo, Key, i., Fl., U.S.	G6	86
Largs, Scot., U.K.	E4	13
Lariat, Tx., U.S.	B1	120
La Ricamarie, Fr.	E6	16
Larimer, co., Co., U.S.	A5	83
Larimore, N.D., U.S.	B8	111
Larino, Italy	C5	23
La Rioja, Arg.	E2	55
La Rioja, Cuba	D5	64
La Rioja, prov., Arg.	E2	55
Lárisa, Grc.	C4	40
Laristan, hist. reg., Iran	H6	37
La Riviera, Ca., U.S.	*C3	82
La Rivière, Man.	E2	70
Lark, N.D., U.S.	C4	111
Lark, Ut., U.S.	C3	121
Lārkāna, Pak.	D2	36
Lark Harbour, Newf.	D2	72
Larkinsville, Al., U.S.	A3	78
Larkspur, Ca., U.S.	h7	82
Larksville, Pa., U.S.	n17	115
Larnaca see Lárnax, Cyp.	E9	41
Lárnax (Larnaca), Cyp.	B3	38
Larne, N. Ire., U.K.	C4	10
Larned, Ks., U.S.	D4	93
La Robla, Spain	A3	22
La Rochelle, Fr.	D3	16
La-Roche-sur-Foron, Fr.	C2	20
La-Roche-sur-Yon, Fr.	D3	16
La Roda, Spain	C4	22
La Romana, Dom. Rep.	E9	64
La Ronge, Sask.	B3	75
La Rose, Il., U.S.	C4	90
Larose, La., U.S.	E5	95
Larrabee, Ia., U.S.	B2	92
Larrys River, N.S.	D8	71
Larsen Bay, Ak., U.S.	D9	79
Larsen Ice Shelf, ice, Ant.	C6	7
Larslan, N.D., U.S.	B10	103
Larsmont, Mn., U.S.	D7	100
Larson, N.D., U.S.	A3	111
La Rubia, Arg.	C4	55
La Rue, Oh., U.S.	B2	112
Larue, co., Ky., U.S.	C4	94
Laruns, Fr.	F3	16
Larvik, Nor.	G4	14
Larwill, In., U.S.	B7	91
Laryak, Sov. Un.	C25	8
La Sagra, mtn., Spain	D4	22
La Sal, Ut., U.S.	E6	121
LaSalle, Que.	q19	74
La Salle, Co., U.S.	A6	83
La Salle, Il., U.S.	B4	90
La Salle, Mn., U.S.	F4	100
La Salle, S.D., U.S.	C9	118
La Salle, co., Il., U.S.	B4	90
La Salle, co., La., U.S.	C3	95
La Salle, co., Tx., U.S.	E3	120
La Sal Mountains, mts., Ut., U.S.	E6	121
Las Animas, Co., U.S.	C7	83
Las Animas, co., Co., U.S.	D6	83
La Santa, Cerro, mtn., P.R.	B3	65
La Sarre, Que.	k11	74
Lasberg, Aus.	E9	19
Las Cabras, Chile	A2	54
Lascahobas, Haiti	E8	64
Lascano, Ur.	E2	56
Lascar, Volcán, vol., Chile	D2	55
Las Coloradas, Arg.	B2	54
Las Cruces, N.M., U.S.	E3	108
La Serena, Chile	E1	55
La Seyne [-sur-Mer], Fr.	F6	16
Las Flores, Arg.	B5	54
Lashburn, Sask.	D1	75
Lashio, Burma	D10	36
Las Lajas, Arg.	B2	54
Las Lajas, Pan.	F7	62
Las Lomitas, Arg.	D3	55
Las Marismas, sw., Spain	D2	22
La Solana, Spain	C4	22
Las Palmas, Pan.	F7	62
Las Palmas [de Gran Canaria], Spain	m14	22
La Spezia, Italy	B2	23
Las Piedras, Ur.	E1	56
Las Piedras, Río de, stm., Peru	D3	58
Las Plumas, Arg.	C3	54
Las Rosas, Arg.	A4	54
Las Rozas de Madrid, Spain	p17	22
Lassance, Braz.	B4	56
Lassen, co., Ca., U.S.	B3	82
Lassen Peak, vol., Ca., U.S.	B3	82
Lassen Volcanic National Park, Ca., U.S.	B3	82
Lasso, l., N. Mar. Is.	D7	52
L'Assomption, Que.	D4	74
L'Assomption, co., Que.	D4	74
Las Tablas, Pan.	G7	62
Las Tablas, Pan.	A3	108
Last Chance, Co., U.S.	B7	83
Last Mountain Lake, l., Sask.	F3	75
Las Termas, Arg.	E3	55
Lastoursville, Gabon	F2	46
Lastovo, i., Yugo.	D3	24
Las Truchas, Mex.	D4	63
Lastrup, W. Ger.	B7	17
Las Tunas, prov., Cuba	D5	64
Las Varillas, Arg.	A4	54
Las Vegas, Nv., U.S.	G6	105
Las Vegas, N.M., U.S.	B4	108
Las Vigas, Mex.	n15	63
La Tabatière, Que.	C2	72
Latacunga, Ec.	B2	58
Latady Island, i., Ant.	B5	7
La Tagua, Col.	D3	60
Latah, co., Id., U.S.	C2	89
Latah, Wa., U.S.	B8	124
Latakia (Al Lādhiqīyah), Syria	B3	38
Laterrière, Que.	A6	74
La Teste-de-Buch, Fr.	E3	16
Latexo, Tx., U.S.	D5	120
Latham, Il., U.S.	D4	90
Latham, Ks., U.S.	E7	93
Latham, N.Y., U.S.	*m15	109
Lathrop, Mo., U.S.	B3	102
Lathrop Wells, Nv., U.S.	G5	105
Latimer, Ia., U.S.	B4	92
Latimer, Ks., U.S.	D7	93
Latimer, co., Ok., U.S.	C6	113
Latina, Italy	D4	23
Latium (Lazio), prov., Italy	C4	23
Laton, Ca., U.S.	D4	82
Latoritsa (Latorica), stm., Sov. Un.	D7	26
La Torrecilla, mtn., P.R.	B3	65
La Tortuga, Isla, i., Ven.	A4	60
Latour, Mo., U.S.	C3	102
La Tour-du-Pin, Fr.	E6	16
Latour Peak, mtn., Id., U.S.	B2	89
La Tremblade, Fr.	E3	16
La Trinité, Mart.	I14	64
Latrobe, Pa., U.S.	F3	115
Latrūn, Isr. Occ.	C6	41
Latta, S.C., U.S.	C9	117
Lattimer Mines, Pa., U.S.	E10	115
Lattimore, N.C., U.S.	B1	110
Latty, Oh., U.S.	A1	112
La Tuque, Que.	B5	74
La Unión, Chile	D2	54
La Unión, Col.	C3	60
La Unión, El Sal.	D4	62
La Unión, Mex.	D4	63
La Unión, Peru	C2	58
La Unión, Spain	D5	22
La Unión, Ven.	D4	60
La Urbana, Ven.	B4	60
Laurbjerg, Den.	B3	15
Laurel, Ont.	D4	73
Laurel, De., U.S.	F3	85
Laurel, Fl., U.S.	E4	86
Laurel, In., U.S.	F7	91
Laurel, Ia., U.S.	C5	92
Laurel, Md., U.S.	B4	97
Laurel, Ms., U.S.	D4	101
Laurel, Ne., U.S.	B8	104
Laurel, Va., U.S.	C5	123
Laurel, co., Ky., U.S.	C5	94
Laurel, stm., Ky., U.S.	D5	94
Laurel Bay, S.C., U.S.	G6	117
Laurel Bloomery, Tn., U.S.	C12	119
Laurel Creek, stm., W.V., U.S.	n14	125
Laurel Creek, stm., W.V., U.S.	m12	125
Laureldale, N.J., U.S.	D3	107
Laureldale, Pa., U.S.	F10	115
Laureles, Ur.	E1	56
Laurel Fork, Va., U.S.	D2	123
Laurel Fork, stm., W.V., U.S.	C5	125
Laurel Hill, Fl., U.S.	u15	86
Laurel Hill, N.C., U.S.	C3	110
Laurel Mountain, mtn., W.V., U.S.	B5	125
Laurel River Lake, res., Ky., U.S.	D5	94
Laurel Run, Pa., U.S.	n17	115
Laurelton, Pa., U.S.	E7	115
Laurelville, Oh., U.S.	C3	112
Laurelwood Academy, Or., U.S.	h11	114
Laurence G. Hanscom Air Force Base, mil., Ma., U.S.	g10	98
Laurence Harbor, N.J., U.S.	C4	107
Laurencekirk, Scot., U.K.	E10	13
Laurens, Ia., U.S.	B3	92
Laurens, S.C., U.S.	C3	117
Laurens, co., Ga., U.S.	D4	87
Laurens, co., S.C., U.S.	C4	117
Laurentides, Que.	D4	74
Laurentides, Parc Provincial des, Que.	B6	74
Laurentum, hist., Italy	h8	23
Lauria Inferiore, Italy	D5	23
Laurie, stm., Man.	A1	70
Laurie Island, i., B.A.T.	C8	7
Laurie Lake, l., Can.	A1	70
Laurier, Man.	D2	70
Laurier, Que.	C6	74
Laurierville, Que.	C6	74
Laurin, Mt., U.S.	E4	103
Laurinburg, N.C., U.S.	C3	110
Lauritzen Bay, b., Ant.	C28	7
Laurium, Mi., U.S.	A2	99
Laurium see Lávrion, Grc.	D5	25
Lausanne, Switz.	E3	18
Lauscha, E. Ger.	C6	19
Laut, i., Indon.	F5	34
Laut, i., Indon.	J8	35
Lautaro, Chile	B2	54
Lauterbach, W. Ger.	C4	19
Lauterbrunnen, Switz.	C4	21
Lauterecken, W. Ger.	D2	19
Laut Kecil Islands, is., Indon.	F5	34
Lautoka, Fiji	H14	51
Lauzon, Que.	C6	74
Lava Beds National Monument, Ca., U.S.	B3	82
Lavaca, Al., U.S.	C1	78
Lavaca, Ar., U.S.	B1	81
Lavaca, co., Tx., U.S.	E4	120
Lava Hot Springs, Id., U.S.	G6	89
Laval, Que.	D4	74
Laval, Fr.	C3	16
La Vale, Md., U.S.	k13	97
Lavalle, Arg.	A3	54
La Valle, Wi., U.S.	E3	126
Lavallette, N.J., U.S.	D4	107
Lavaltrie, Que.	D4	74
Lāvān, i., Iran	H6	39
Lavant Station, Ont.	B8	73
Lavapié, Punta, c., Chile	B2	54
Lavaur, Fr.	F4	16
Lavaveix-les-Mines, Fr.	D5	16
Laveen, Az., U.S.	m8	80
La Vega, Dom. Rep.	E8	64
La Vela de Coro, Ven.	F4	64
Lavelanet, Fr.	F4	16
Lavello, Italy	C5	23
L'Avenir, Que.	D5	74
La Vergne, Tn., U.S.	A5	119
La Verkin, Ut., U.S.	F2	121
La Verne, Ca., U.S.	*m13	82
Laverne, Ok., U.S.	A2	113
La Vernia, Tx., U.S.	E3	120
La Veta, Co., U.S.	D5	83
Laviana, Spain	A3	22
La Victoria, Peru	*D2	58
La Victoria, Ven.	A4	60
Laville, Mi., U.S.	D8	103
Lavina, Mt., U.S.	D8	103
Lavinia, Braz.	C2	56
Lavinia, Tn., U.S.	B3	119
La Vista, Ga., U.S.	h8	87
La Vista, Ne., U.S.	g12	104
La Viuda, mtn., Peru	C2	58
Lavonia, Ga., U.S.	B3	87
Lavon Lake, res., Tx., U.S.	m10	120
Lavoy, Alta.	C5	68
Lavras, Braz.	F6	57
Lavras da Mangabeira, Braz.	C3	57
Lavras do Sul, Braz.	C3	56
Lávrion (Laurium), Grc.	D5	25
Lavumisa, Swaz.	C5	49
Lawai, Hi., U.S.	B2	88
Lawers, Ben, mtn., Scot., U.K.	E8	13
Lawford Lake, l., Man.	B3	70
Lawit, mtn., Malay.	J5	35
Lawler, Ia., U.S.	A5	92
Lawley, Mn., U.S.	D5	100
Lawn, Newf.	E4	72
Lawn, Tx., U.S.	F8	115
Lawndale, Ca., U.S.	*E4	82
Lawndale, N.C., U.S.	B1	110
Lawnside, N.J., U.S.	*D2	107
Lawra, Ghana	D4	45
Lawrence, N.Z.	P12	51
Lawrence, In., U.S.	E5	91
Lawrence, Ks., U.S.	D8	93
Lawrence, Ma., U.S.	A5	98
Lawrence, Mi., U.S.	F4	99
Lawrence, N.Y., U.S.	k13	109
Lawrence, Pa., U.S.	F1	115
Lawrence, co., Al., U.S.	A2	78
Lawrence, co., Ar., U.S.	A4	81

Name	Map Ref.	Page
Lawrence, co., Il., U.S.	E6	90
Lawrence, co., In., U.S.	G4	91
Lawrence, co., Ky., U.S.	B7	94
Lawrence, co., Ms., U.S.	D3	101
Lawrence, co., Mo., U.S.	D4	102
Lawrence, co., Oh., U.S.	D3	112
Lawrence, co., Pa., U.S.	E1	115
Lawrence, co., S.D., U.S.	E2	32
Lawrence, co., Tn., U.S.	B4	119
Lawrenceburg, In., U.S.	F8	91
Lawrenceburg, Ky., U.S.	B5	94
Lawrenceburg, Tn., U.S.	B4	119
Lawrence Park, Pa., U.S.	B1	115
Lawrenceport, In., U.S.	G5	91
Lawrence Station, N.B.	D2	71
Lawrencetown, N.S.	E4	71
Lawrenceville, Que.	D5	74
Lawrenceville, Ga., U.S.	C3	87
Lawrenceville, Il., U.S.	E6	90
Lawrenceville, N.J., U.S.	C3	107
Lawrenceville, N.Y., U.S.	f10	109
Lawrenceville, Pa., U.S.	C7	115
Lawrenceville, Va., U.S.	D5	123
Lawshe, Oh., U.S.	D2	112
Lawson, Sask.	G2	75
Lawson, Ar., U.S.	D3	81
Lawson, Mo., U.S.	B3	102
Lawsonia, Md., U.S.	E6	97
Lawsonville, N.C., U.S.	A2	110
Lawtell, La., U.S.	D3	95
Lawtey, Fl., U.S.	B4	86
Lawton, Ia., U.S.	B1	92
Lawton, Ky., U.S.	B6	94
Lawton, Mi., U.S.	F5	99
Lawton, N.D., U.S.	A7	111
Lawton, Ok., U.S.	C3	113
Lawyersville, N.Y., U.S.	C6	109
Lawz, Jabal al, mtn., Sau. Ar.	H10	40
Lax Kw'alaams, B.C.	B2	69
Laxou, Fr.	C7	16
Lay, Point, c., Viet.	D7	35
Lay Dam, Al., U.S.	C3	78
Lay Lake, res., Al., U.S.	C3	78
Layland, W.V., U.S.	n14	125
Layou, St. Vin.	U26	65
Laysan Island, i., Hi., U.S.	k13	88
Laysville, Ct., U.S.	D6	84
Layton, Ut., U.S.	B4	121
Laytonsville, Md., U.S.	B3	97
Laytonville, Ca., U.S.	C2	82
Lazdijai, Sov. Un.	A7	26
Lazear, Co., U.S.	C3	83
Łaziska Górne, Pol.	g9	26
Lea, co., N.M., U.S.	D6	108
Lea, stm., Eng., U.K.	k12	10
Leach, Ok., U.S.	A7	113
Leachville, Ar., U.S.	B5	81
Leacross, Sask.	D3	75
Lead, S.D., U.S.	C2	118
Leadbetter Point, c., Wa., U.S.	C1	124
Leader, Sask.	G1	75
Lead Hill, Ar., U.S.	A3	81
Lead Hill, hill, Mo., U.S.	D5	102
Lead Mountain, mtn., Me., U.S.	D4	96
Lead Mountain Ponds, l., Me., U.S.	D4	96
Leadore, Id., U.S.	E5	89
Leadville, Co., U.S.	B4	83
Leadwood, Mo., U.S.	D7	102
Leaf, Ms., U.S.	D5	101
Leaf, stm., Ms., U.S.	D5	101
Leaf Lake, l., Sask.	E4	75
Leaf Rapids, Man.	A1	70
Leaf River, Il., U.S.	A4	90
League City, Tx., U.S.	*r14	120
Leah, Ga., U.S.	C4	87
Leake, co., Ms., U.S.	C4	101
Leakesville, Ms., U.S.	D5	101
Leakey, Tx., U.S.	E3	120
Leal, N.D., U.S.	B7	111
Lealman, Fl., U.S.	p10	86
Leamington, Ont.	E2	73
Leamington, Ut., U.S.	D3	121
Leamington see Royal Leamington Spa Eng., U.K.	D6	10
Leane, Lough, l., Ire.	E2	11
Leapwood, Tn., U.S.	B3	119
Learned, Ms., U.S.	C3	101
Leary, Ga., U.S.	E2	87
Leasburg, Mo., U.S.	C6	102
Leasburg, N.C., U.S.	A3	110
Leaside (part of East York), Ont.	m15	73
Leask, Sask.	E2	75
Leatherhead, Eng., U.K.	m12	10
Leatherman Peak, mtn., Id., U.S.	E5	89
Leatherwood, Ky., U.S.	C6	94
L'Eau Frais Creek, stm., Ar., U.S.	C3	81
Leavenworth, In., U.S.	H5	91
Leavenworth, Ks., U.S.	C9	93
Leavenworth, Wa., U.S.	B5	124
Leavenworth, co., Ks., U.S.	C8	93
Leavittsburg, Oh., U.S.	A5	112
Leawood, Ks., U.S.	D9	93
Łeba, Pol.	A4	26
Lebam, Wa., U.S.	C2	124
Lebanon, Ct., U.S.	C7	84
Lebanon, De., U.S.	D4	85
Lebanon, Il., U.S.	E4	90
Lebanon, In., U.S.	D5	91
Lebanon, Ks., U.S.	C5	93
Lebanon, Ky., U.S.	C4	94
Lebanon, Mo., U.S.	D5	104
Lebanon, Ne., U.S.	C2	106
Lebanon, N.H., U.S.	D3	107
Lebanon, N.J., U.S.	B3	107
Lebanon, Oh., U.S.	C1	112
Lebanon, Ok., U.S.	D5	113
Lebanon, Or., U.S.	C4	114
Lebanon, Pa., U.S.	F9	115
Lebanon, S.D., U.S.	B6	118
Lebanon, Tn., U.S.	A5	119
Lebanon, Va., U.S.	f9	123
Lebanon, co., Pa., U.S.	F8	115
Lebanon, ctry., Asia	B3	38
Lebanon Junction, Ky., U.S.	C4	94
Le Beau, Tun.	*B7	44
Lebec, Ca., U.S.	E4	82
Lebedin, Sov. Un.	F10	27
Lebedyan, Sov. Un.	E12	27
Le Biot, Fr.	D2	21
Le Blanc, Fr.	D4	16
Le Blanc-Mesnil, Fr.	g10	16
Lebo, Ks., U.S.	D8	93
Lebo, Zaire	A3	48
Lebork, Pol.	A4	26
Le Bourg-d'Oisans, Fr.	D2	21
Le Bourget, Fr.	g10	16
Le Bouscat, Fr.	E3	16
Le Brassus, Switz.	C1	21
Lebret, Sask.	G4	75
Lebrija, Spain	D2	22
Lebu, Chile	B2	54
Lebyazhye, Sov. Un.	B7	28
Le Cateau, Fr.	B5	16
Lecce, Italy	D7	23
Lecco, Italy	B2	23
Lecco, Lake, l., Italy	E7	21
Le Center, Mn., U.S.	F5	100
Lech, stm., Eur.	D5	20
Le Chambon-Feugerolles, Fr.	E6	16
Le-Château, Fr.	E3	16
Lechbruck, W. Ger.	B6	20
Le Chesnay, Fr.	g9	16
Le Chesne, Fr.	E4	17
Leck, W. Ger.	D2	15
Le Claire, Ia., U.S.	C7	92
Leclercville, Que.	C6	74
Lecompte, La., U.S.	C3	95
Lecompton, Ks., U.S.	C8	93
Léconi, Gabon	F2	46
Leconte, Mount, mtn., Tn., U.S.	D10	119
Lecontes Mills, Pa., U.S.	D5	115
Le Coteau, Fr.	D6	16
Le Creusot, Fr.	D6	16
Le Croisic, Fr.	D2	16
Le Crotoy, Fr.	D9	12
Lectoure, Fr.	F4	16
Łęczyca, Pol.	B5	26
Ledbetter, N.C., U.S.	C3	110
Ledbury, Eng., U.K.	B5	12
Ledčice, Czech.	n17	26
Ledeberg (part of Gent), Bel.	C3	17
Ledesma, Spain	B2	22
Ledford, Il., U.S.	F5	90
Ledger, Mt., U.S.	B5	103
Ledgewood, N.J., U.S.	B3	107
Ledo, India	C10	36
Ledoux, N.M., U.S.	B4	108
Leduc, Alta.	C4	68
Ledyard, Ct., U.S.	D7	84
Ledyard, Ia., U.S.	A3	92
Lee, Fl., U.S.	B3	86
Lee, Il., U.S.	B5	90
Lee, Ma., U.S.	C4	96
Lee, Me., U.S.	B1	98
Lee, Nv., U.S.	C6	105
Lee, N.H., U.S.	D4	106
Lee, Tn., U.S.	D8	119
Lee, co., Al., U.S.	C4	78
Lee, co., Ar., U.S.	C5	81
Lee, co., Fl., U.S.	F5	86
Lee, co., Ga., U.S.	E2	87
Lee, co., Il., U.S.	B4	90
Lee, co., Ia., U.S.	D6	92
Lee, co., Ky., U.S.	C6	94
Lee, co., Ms., U.S.	A5	101
Lee, co., N.C., U.S.	B3	110
Lee, co., S.C., U.S.	C7	117
Lee, co., Tx., U.S.	D4	120
Lee, co., Va., U.S.	f8	123
Lee, stm., Ire.	E2	10
Lee, Lake, l., Ms., U.S.	B3	101
Lee Center, Il., U.S.	B4	90
Leechburg, Pa., U.S.	E2	115
Leech Lake, l., Sask.	F4	75
Leech Lake, l., Mn., U.S.	C4	100
Leech Lake Indian Reservation, Mn., U.S.	C4	100
Leechville, N.C., U.S.	B6	110
Leedey, Ok., U.S.	B2	113
Leedom Estates, De., U.S.	*B3	85
Leeds, Eng., U.K.	D6	10
Leeds, Al., U.S.	B3	78
Leeds, N.D., U.S.	A6	111
Leeds, S.C., U.S.	B5	117
Leeds, Ut., U.S.	F2	121
Leeds [and Grenville], co., Ont.	C8	73
Leeds Point, N.J., U.S.	E4	107
Leeds-Village, Que.	C6	74
Leek, Eng., U.K.	A5	12
Leelanau, co., Mi., U.S.	C5	99
Leelanau, Lake, l., Mi., U.S.	C5	99
Leenaun, Ire.	D2	11
Lee Park, Pa., U.S.	n17	115
Leeper, Mo., U.S.	D7	102
Leeper, Pa., U.S.	D2	115
Leer, W. Ger.	B3	18
Leesburg, Al., U.S.	A4	78
Leesburg, Fl., U.S.	D5	86
Leesburg, Ga., U.S.	E2	87
Leesburg, In., U.S.	B6	91
Leesburg, N.J., U.S.	E3	107
Leesburg, Oh., U.S.	C2	112
Leesburg, Va., U.S.	A5	123
Lees Landing, La., U.S.	h11	95
Lees Summit, Mo., U.S.	C3	102
Leesville, La., U.S.	C3	95
Leesville, Oh., U.S.	B4	112
Leesville, S.C., U.S.	D4	117
Leesville, Tx., U.S.	E4	120
Leesville Lake, res., Va., U.S.	C3	123
Leetes Island, Ct., U.S.	D5	84
Leeton, Austl.	G6	51
Leeton, Mo., U.S.	C4	102
Leetonia, Oh., U.S.	B5	112
Leetsdale, Pa., U.S.	h13	115
Leeuwarden, Neth.	A6	16
Leeuwin, Cape, c., Austl.	F2	50
Leeville, La., U.S.	E5	95
Lee Vining, Ca., U.S.	D4	82
Leeward Islands, is., N.A.	H13	64
Le Ferriere, Italy	h9	23
Leffingwell, Ct., U.S.	C7	84
Leflore, Ok., U.S.	C7	113
Leflore, co., Ms., U.S.	B3	101
Le Flore, co., Ok., U.S.	C7	113
Lefor, N.D., U.S.	C3	111
Lefors, Tx., U.S.	B2	120
Le François, Mart.	I14	64
Lefroy, Ont.	C5	73
Lefroy, Lake, l., Austl.	F3	50
Leftrook Lake, l., Man.	A2	70
Legal, Alta.	C4	68
Leganés, Spain	p17	22
Legaspi, Phil.	B7	34
Legau, W. Ger.	E5	18
Leggett, Ca., U.S.	C2	82
Leghorn see Livorno, Italy	C3	23
Legionowo, Pol.	k13	26
Legnago, Italy	D7	23
Legnano, Italy	C4	16
Legnica (Liegnitz), Pol.	C4	26
Lehigh, Ia., U.S.	B3	92
Lehigh, Ks., U.S.	D6	93
Lehigh, Ok., U.S.	C5	113
Lehigh, co., Pa., U.S.	E10	115
Lehigh, stm., Pa., U.S.	E10	115
Lehigh Acres, Fl., U.S.	F5	86
Lehighton, Pa., U.S.	E10	115
Lehinch, Ire.	E2	11
Lehman, Pa., U.S.	n16	115
Lehr, N.D., U.S.	C6	111
Lehrte, W. Ger.	B4	18
Lehua Island, i., Hi., U.S.	A1	88
Leiah, Pak.	B5	36
Leibnitz, Aus.	E7	18
Leicester, Eng., U.K.	D6	10
Leicester, Ma., U.S.	B4	98
Leicester, N.Y., U.S.	C3	109
Leicester, Vt., U.S.	D2	122
Leicester Junction, Vt., U.S.	D2	122
Leicestershire, co., Eng., U.K.	B6	12
Leichhardt, Austl.	*F9	50
Leichhardt, stm., Austl.	C7	50
Leiden, Neth.	A6	16
Leigh, Ne., U.S.	C8	104
Leigh Creek, Austl.	F6	50
Leighlinbridge, Ire.	E5	11
Leighton, Al., U.S.	A2	78
Leinan, Sask.	G2	75
Leine, stm., Eur.	B4	18
Leinster, hist. reg., Ire.	D4	11
Leinster, Mount, mtn., Ire.	E5	11
Leipalingis, Sov. Un.	A7	26
Leipers Fork, Tn., U.S.	B5	119
Leipsic, De., U.S.	D3	85
Leipsic, In., U.S.	G5	91
Leipsic, Oh., U.S.	A2	112
Leipsic, stm., De., U.S.	C3	85
Leipzig, Sask.	E1	75
Leipzig, E. Ger.	C6	18
Leiria, Port.	C1	22
Leisnig, E. Ger.	B7	19
Leiston, Eng., U.K.	B9	12
Leisure City, Fl., U.S.	s13	86
Leitches Creek, N.S.	C9	71
Leitchfield, Ky., U.S.	C3	94
Leiter, Wy., U.S.	B6	127
Leitersburg, Md., U.S.	A2	97
Leiters Ford, In., U.S.	B5	91
Leith, N.D., U.S.	C4	111
Leitha, stm., Eur.	B3	24
Leitrim, co., Ire.	C3	11
Leiva, Cerro, mtn., Col.	C3	60
Leixlip, Ire.	D5	11
Leizhou Bandao, pen., China	G7	31
Leizhou Bay, b., China	B9	35
Lejunior, Ky., U.S.	D6	94
Lek, stm., Neth.	C4	17
Leka, i., Nor.	E4	14
Lekeba, i., Fiji	I16	52
Lekoa, S. Afr.	*C4	49
Le Kreïder, Alg.	C3	44
Leksand, Swe.	G6	14
Leksula, Indon.	F7	34
Lela, Tn., U.S.	B2	120
Leland, Il., U.S.	B5	90
Leland, Ia., U.S.	A4	92
Leland, Mi., U.S.	C5	99
Leland, Ms., U.S.	B3	101
Leland, N.C., U.S.	C4	110
Leleiwi Point, c., Hi., U.S.	D7	88
Leleque, Arg.	C2	54
Lelia Lake, Tx., U.S.	B2	120
Leloaloa, Am. Sam.	F13	52
Le Locle, Switz.	E3	18
Le Lorrain, Mart.	S10	65
Leloup, Ks., U.S.	D8	93
Lelystad, Neth.	A6	16
Le Maire, Estrecho de, strt., Arg.	h12	54
Le Mans, Fr.	C4	16
Le Marin, Mart.	I14	64
Le Mars, Ia., U.S.	B1	92
Lemasters, Pa., U.S.	G6	115
Lemay, Mo., U.S.	*g13	102
Lembach, Fr.	F7	17
Lemberg, Sask.	G4	75
Lemdiyya, Alg.	B5	44
Leme, Braz.	m8	56
Lemelerveld, Neth.	B6	17
Lemery, Phil.	p13	34
Lemesós (Limassol), Cyp.	E9	40
Lemgo, W. Ger.	B4	18
Lemhi, Id., U.S.	E5	89
Lemhi, co., Id., U.S.	E5	89
Lemhi, stm., Id., U.S.	E5	89
Lemhi Pass, Id., U.S.	E5	89
Lemhi Range, mts., Id., U.S.	E5	89
Lemieux, Que.	C5	74
Lemitar, N.M., U.S.	C3	108
Lemmer, Neth.	B5	17
Lemmon, S.D., U.S.	B3	118
Lemmon, Mount, mtn., Az., U.S.	E5	80
Lemmon Valley, Nv., U.S.	D2	105
Lemon Grove, Ca., U.S.	o15	82
Lemon Island, i., S.C., U.S.	G6	117
Lemons, Mo., U.S.	A4	102
Lemont, Il., U.S.	B5	90
Lemont, Pa., U.S.	E6	115
Lemoore, Ca., U.S.	D4	82
Lemoore Naval Air Station, mil., Ca., U.S.	*D4	82
Lemoore Station, Ca., U.S.	*D4	82
Le Moyen, La., U.S.	D3	95
Lemoyne, Ne., U.S.	C4	104
Lempa, stm., N.A.	D2	63
Lem Peak, mtn., Id., U.S.	E5	89
Lempster, N.H., U.S.	D2	106
Lemsford, Sask.	G1	75
Lemvig, Den.	B2	15
Lena, Il., U.S.	A4	90
Lena, In., U.S.	G5	91
Lena, La., U.S.	C3	95
Lena, Ms., U.S.	C4	101
Lena, Spain	A3	22
Lena, Wi., U.S.	C5	126
Lena, stm., Sov. Un.	C15	29
Lenapah, Ok., U.S.	A6	113
Lenawee, co., Mi., U.S.	G6	99
Lençóis, Braz.	B4	57
Lend, Aus.	B9	20
Lendinara, Italy	D7	23
Lenexa, Ks., U.S.	D9	93
Leney, Sask.	E2	75
Lengby, Mn., U.S.	C3	100
Lengede, W. Ger.	B5	18
Lenger, Sov. Un.	E7	28
Lengerich, W. Ger.	A3	19
Lenghu, China	D3	31
Lengshuijiang, China	*F7	31
Lenhartsville, Pa., U.S.	E10	115
Leninabad, Sov. Un.	E9	29
Leninakan, Sov. Un.	E2	28
Leningrad, Sov. Un.	n17	27
Lenino, Sov. Un.	n17	27
Leninogorsk, Sov. Un.	D11	29
Lenin Peak, mtn., Sov. Un.	*F10	29
Leninsk, Sov. Un.	G15	27
Leninsk-Kuznetskiy, Sov. Un.	D11	29
Leninskoye, Sov. Un.	C7	28
Lenkoran, Sov. Un.	F7	29
Lenne, stm., W. Ger.	B2	19
Lennox, Ca., U.S.	*n12	82
Lennox, S.D., U.S.	D9	118
Lennox, Isla, i., Chile	k12	54
Lennox and Addington, co., Ont.	C7	73
Lennoxville, Que.	D6	74
Lenoir, N.C., U.S.	B1	110
Lenoir, co., N.C., U.S.	B5	110
Lenoir City, Tn., U.S.	D9	119
Lenora, Ks., U.S.	C4	93
Lenorah, Tx., U.S.	C2	120
Lenore, Man.	E1	70
Lenore, Id., U.S.	C2	89
Lenore Lake, l., Sask.	E3	75
Lenore Lake, l., Wa., U.S.	B6	124
Lenox, Al., U.S.	D2	78
Lenox, Ga., U.S.	E3	87
Lenox, Ia., U.S.	D3	92
Lenox, Ma., U.S.	B1	98
Lenox, Mo., U.S.	D6	102
Lenox, Tn., U.S.	A2	119
Lenox Dale, Ma., U.S.	B1	98
Lens, Fr.	B5	16
Lentner, Mo., U.S.	B5	102
Lenzburg, Switz.	E5	21
Lenzen, W. Ger.	E5	15
Lenzerheide, Switz.	C8	21
Léo, Burkina	D4	45
Leoben, Aus.	E7	18
Léogâne, Haiti	E7	64
Leola, Ar., U.S.	C3	81
Leola, S.D., U.S.	B7	118
Leoma, Tn., U.S.	B4	119
Leominster, Eng., U.K.	B5	12
Leominster, Ma., U.S.	A4	98
Leon, Nic.	E7	63
León, Spain	A3	22
Leon, Ia., U.S.	A1	92
Leon, Ks., U.S.	E7	93
Leon, N.Y., U.S.	C1	109
Leon, Ok., U.S.	D4	113
Leon, co., Fl., U.S.	B2	86
Leon, co., Tx., U.S.	D4	120
León, hist. reg., Spain	B3	22
Leonard, Mi., U.S.	F7	99
Leonard, Mn., U.S.	C3	100
Leonard, Mo., U.S.	B5	102
Leonard, N.D., U.S.	C8	111
Leonard, Ok., U.S.	B6	113
Leonard, Tx., U.S.	C4	120
Leonardo, N.J., U.S.	C4	107
Leonardsville, N.Y., U.S.	C5	109
Leonardtown, Md., U.S.	D4	97
Leonardville, N.B.	E3	71
Leonardville, Nmb.	B2	49
Leonardville, Ks., U.S.	C7	93
Leonberg, W. Ger.	E3	19
Leone, Am. Sam.	G13	52
Leone, Bay, b., Am. Sam.	G13	52
Leonforte, Italy	F5	23
Leonia, N.J., U.S.	h8	107
Leonia, Id., U.S.	A2	89
Leonidi, Grc.	D5	25
Leonídion, Grc.	D4	25
Leonora, Austl.	E3	50
Leon Valley, Tx., U.S.	*E3	120
Leonville, La., U.S.	D4	95
Leopold, Mo., U.S.	D8	102
Leopold and Astrid Coast, Ant.	C21	7
Leopoldina, Braz.	C4	56
Leopoldsburg, Bel.	C5	17
Léopoldville see Kinshasa, Zaire	B2	48
Leoti, Ks., U.S.	D2	93
Leoville, Sask.	D2	75
Leoville, Ks., U.S.	C3	93
Leovo, Sov. Un.	H7	27
Lepanto, Ar., U.S.	B5	81
Lepe, Spain	D2	22
Lepel, Sov. Un.	D7	27
Lepihué, Chile	C2	54
Lepontine Alps, mts., Eur.	A3	23
Le Portel, Fr.	D9	12
Lepreau, N.B.	D3	71
Lepreau, Point, c., N.B.	D3	71
Lepsinsk, Sov. Un.	F25	8
Lepsy, Sov. Un.	D9	28
Le Puy [-en-Velay], Fr.	E5	16
Le Quesnoy, Fr.	B5	16
Le Raysville, Pa., U.S.	C9	115
Lercara Friddi, Italy	F4	23
Léré, Chad	F2	46
Lerici, Italy	D2	23
Lérida, Col.	m13	63
Lérida, Spain	B6	22
Lerma, stm., Mex.	m13	63
Lerna, Il., U.S.	D5	90
Le Robert, Mart.	S11	65
Léros, i., Grc.	E7	40
Leross, Sask.	F4	75
Leroux Wash, val., Az., U.S.	B5	80
Leroy, Sask.	F3	75
Leroy, Al., U.S.	D1	78
Leroy, Ks., U.S.	D8	93
Le Roy, Il., U.S.	C5	90
Leroy, Mi., U.S.	E5	99
Leroy, Mn., U.S.	G6	100
Le Roy, N.Y., U.S.	C3	109
Leroy, N.D., U.S.	A8	111
Le Roy, Pa., U.S.	C8	115
Lerum, Swe.	A6	15
Le Russey, Fr.	B2	21
Lerwick, Scot., U.K.	g10	10
Léry, Que.	q19	74
Léry, Lake, l., La., U.S.	k12	95
Les Abymes, Guad.	Q8	65
Les Cayes, Haiti	E7	64
Les Diablerets, Switz.	C3	20
Les Éboulements, Que.	B7	74
Les Echelles, Fr.	D1	20
Les Escoumins, Que.	A8	74
Les Étroits, Que.	B9	74
Les Fonds, Que.	o16	74
Les Haudères, Switz.	C3	20
Leshan, China	F5	31
Leshara, Ne., U.S.	g12	104
Lesina, Lake, b., Italy	D5	23
Lesko, Pol.	D7	26
Leskovac, Yugo.	D5	24
Leslie, Sask.	F4	75
Leslie, Ar., U.S.	B3	81
Leslie, Ga., U.S.	E2	87
Leslie, Id., U.S.	F5	89
Leslie, Mi., U.S.	F6	99
Leslie, S.C., U.S.	B6	117
Leslie, W.V., U.S.	C4	125
Leslie, co., Ky., U.S.	C6	94
Leslieville, Alta.	C3	68
Lesneven, Fr.	C1	16
Lesnoy, Sov. Un.	B4	28
Lesogorsk, Sov. Un.	B11	33
Lesosibirsk, Sov. Un.	B9	29
Lesotho, ctry., Afr.	C4	49
Lesozavodsk, Sov. Un.	E16	29
Lesparre, Fr.	E3	16
Les Ponts-de-Cé, Fr.	D3	16
Les Rousses, Fr.	D1	21
Les Sables-d'Olonne, Fr.	D3	16
Lesser Antilles, is.	B4	53
Lesser Khing Range see Xiao Hinggan Ling), mts., China		
Lesser Slave Lake, l., Alta.	B3	68
Lesser Sunda Islands (Nusa Tenggara), is., Indon.	G5	34
Lessines, Bel.	D3	17
Lester, Al., U.S.	A2	78
Lester, Ia., U.S.	A1	92
Lester, W.V., U.S.	n13	125
Lester Prairie, Mn., U.S.	F4	100
Lesterville, Mo., U.S.	D7	102
Lesterville, S.D., U.S.	D8	118
Lestock, Sask.	F3	75
Le Sueur, Mn., U.S.	F5	100
Le Sueur, co., Mn., U.S.	F5	100
Les Verrières, Switz.	C1	21
Leszno, Pol.	C4	26
Letart Falls, Oh., U.S.	C3	112
Letcher, S.D., U.S.	D7	118
Letcher, co., Ky., U.S.	C7	94
Le Teil, Fr.	E6	16
Letellier, Man.	E3	70
Letha, Id., U.S.	F2	89
Lethbridge, Alta.	E4	68
Lethbridge, Newf.	D5	72
Lethem, Guy.	B3	59
Le Thillot, Fr.	B2	20
Letiahau, stm., Bots.	B3	49
Leticia, Col.	D4	60
Leti Islands, is., Indon.	G7	34
Letlhakane, Bots.	A4	49
Letona, Ar., U.S.	B4	81
Le Touquet-Paris-Plage, Fr.	D9	17
Le Tourneau, Ms., U.S.	C5	101
Letpadan, Burma	E10	36
Le Tréport, Fr.	B4	16
Letsok-Aw, i., Burma	G3	35
Letterfrack, Ire.	D2	11
Letterkenny, Ire.	C3	10
Lettermullan, Ire.	D2	11
Letts, In., U.S.	F6	91
Letts, Ia., U.S.	C6	92
Lettsworth, La., U.S.	D4	95
Leucas see Levkás, i., Grc.	C3	40
Leuchars, Scot., U.K.	C5	13
Leuctra see Lévktra, Grc.	g10	25
Leuk, Switz.	D4	21
Leukerbad, Switz.	D4	21
Leulumoega, W. Sam.	F12	52
Leupp, Az., U.S.	B5	80
Leupp Corner, Az., U.S.	B5	80
Leuser, mtn., Indon.	m11	34
Leutkirch, W. Ger.	B6	20
Leuven (Louvain), Bel.	B6	16
Leuze, Bel.	D3	17
Levádhia, Grc.	C4	40
Levallois-Perret, Fr.	g10	16
Levan, Ut., U.S.	D4	121
Levanger, Nor.	F4	14
Levanna, Eur.	E7	16
Levant, Me., U.S.	D4	96
Levant, Ks., U.S.	C2	93
Levelland, Tx., U.S.	C1	120
Leven, Scot., U.K.	B5	10
Leveque, Cape, c., Austl.	C3	50
Leverett Glacier, ice, Ant.	A32	7
Leverkusen, W. Ger.	B1	19
Levice, Czech.	C5	26
Levick, Mount, mtn., Ant.	B29	7
Levie, Fr.	k9	16
Le Vigan, Fr.	E5	16
Levin, N.Z.	N15	51
Lévis, Que.	C6	74
Lévis, co., Que.	C6	74
Levisa Fork, stm., U.S.	C7	94
Levittown, N.Y., U.S.	E7	109
Levittown, Pa., U.S.	F12	115
Levkás (Leucas), i., Grc.	C3	40
Levkás, Grc.	C3	40
Lévktra (Leuctra), Grc.	g10	25
Levy, co., Fl., U.S.	C4	86
Levy Lake, l., Fl., U.S.	C4	86
Lewellen, Ne., U.S.	C3	104
Lewes, Eng., U.K.	E7	10
Lewes, De., U.S.	F5	85
Lewes and Rehoboth Canal, De., U.S.	F5	85
Lewis, In., U.S.	F3	91
Lewis, Ia., U.S.	C2	92
Lewis, Ks., U.S.	E4	93
Lewis, Mo., U.S.	C4	102
Lewis, N.Y., U.S.	A7	109
Lewis, Wi., U.S.	C1	126
Lewis, co., Id., U.S.	C2	89
Lewis, co., Ky., U.S.	B6	94
Lewis, co., Mo., U.S.	A6	102
Lewis, co., N.Y., U.S.	B5	109
Lewis, co., Tn., U.S.	B4	119
Lewis, co., Wa., U.S.	C3	124
Lewis, co., W.V., U.S.	C4	125
Lewis, stm., Wy., U.S.	B2	127
Lewis, Butt of, c., Scot., U.K.	A3	10
Lewis, Isle of, i., Scot., U.K.	A3	10
Lewis, Mount, mtn., Nv., U.S.	C5	105
Lewis and Clark, co., Mt., U.S.	C4	103
Lewis and Clark Cavern, Mt., U.S.	D5	103
Lewis and Clark Lake, res., U.S.	E8	118
Lewisberry, Pa., U.S.	F8	115
Lewisburg, Ky., U.S.	D3	94
Lewisburg, La., U.S.	D3	95
Lewisburg, Oh., U.S.	C1	112
Lewisburg, Pa., U.S.	E8	115
Lewisburg, Tn., U.S.	B5	119
Lewisburg, W.V., U.S.	D4	125
Lewis Center, Oh., U.S.	B2	112
Lewis Creek, stm., Sask.	F3	75
Lewis Creek, stm., Vt., U.S.	C2	122
Lewis Hills, hills, Newf.	D2	72
Lewis Lake, l., Wy., U.S.	B2	127
Lewisporte, Newf.	D4	72
Lewis Range, mts., N.A.	A5	76
Lewis Run, Pa., U.S.	C4	115
Lewis Smith Lake, res., Al., U.S.	B2	78
Lewiston, Ca., U.S.	B2	82
Lewiston, Id., U.S.	C1	89
Lewiston, Me., U.S.	D2	96
Lewiston, Mi., U.S.	D6	99
Lewiston, Mn., U.S.	G7	100
Lewiston, N.Y., U.S.	B1	109
Lewiston, Ut., U.S.	B4	121
Lewiston Peak, mtn., Ut., U.S.	C3	121
Lewiston Woodville, N.C., U.S.	A5	110
Lewistown, Il., U.S.	C3	90
Lewistown, Md., U.S.	B3	97
Lewistown, Mo., U.S.	A6	102
Lewistown, Mt., U.S.	C7	103
Lewistown, Pa., U.S.	E6	115
Lewisville, N.B.	C5	71
Lewisville, Ar., U.S.	D2	81
Lewisville, Id., U.S.	F6	89
Lewisville, In., U.S.	E7	91
Lewisville, Mn., U.S.	G4	100
Lewisville, Oh., U.S.	C4	112
Lewisville, Tx., U.S.	C4	120
Lewisville Lake, res., Tx., U.S.	C4	120
Lexa, Ar., U.S.	C5	81
Lexington, Al., U.S.	A2	78
Lexington, Ga., U.S.	C3	87
Lexington, Il., U.S.	C5	90
Lexington, In., U.S.	G6	91
Lexington, Ky., U.S.	B5	94
Lexington, Ma., U.S.	B5	98
Lexington, Mi., U.S.	E8	99
Lexington, Mn., U.S.	m12	100
Lexington, Mo., U.S.	B4	102
Lexington, Ne., U.S.	D6	104
Lexington, N.C., U.S.	B2	110
Lexington, Oh., U.S.	B3	112
Lexington, Or., U.S.	B7	114
Lexington, S.C., U.S.	D5	117
Lexington, Tn., U.S.	B3	119
Lexington, Tx., U.S.	D4	120
Lexington, Va., U.S.	C3	123
Lexington, co., S.C., U.S.	D5	117
Lexington Park, Md., U.S.	D5	97
Leyba, N.M., U.S.	*D4	108
Leyburn, Eng., U.K.	F7	13
Leyond, stm., Man.	A4	108
Leysin, Switz.	C4	21
Leyte, i., Phil.	C6	34
Lezajsk, Pol.	C7	26
Lezha, Alb.	B2	40
Lézignan, Fr.	F5	16
Lgov, Sov. Un.	F10	27
Lhasa, China	F3	31
Lhaže, China	C11	37
Lhokseumawe, Indon.	k11	34
Lhoksukon, Indon.	J2	35
Liangcheng, China	D5	32
Liangping, China	I2	32
Lianhua, China	K5	32
Lianjiang, China	B9	35
Lianyungang, China	E8	31
Lianyuan, China	G8	32
Liaocheng, China	F6	32
Liaodong Bay, b., China	E9	32
Liao He, stm., China	C9	31
Liaoning, China	C9	31
Liaotung Bay see Liaodong Bay, b., China	E9	32
Liaotung Peninsula, pen., China	D9	31
Liaoyang, China	C9	31
Liaoyuan, China	C10	31
Liard, stm., Can.	E7	66
Liart, Fr.	E4	17
Liathach, mtn., Scot., U.K.	C3	13
Libano, Col.	C2	60
Libau, Man.	D3	70
Libby, Mt., U.S.	B1	103
Libčice [nad Vltavou], Czech.	n17	26
Libčchov, Czech.	n17	26
Libenge, Zaire	A2	48
Liberal, Ks., U.S.	E3	93
Liberec, Czech.	C6	26
Liberia, ctry., Afr.	E3	45
Libertad General Bernardo O'Higgins, prov., Chile	A2	54
Libertad General San Martín, Arg.	B3	55
Liberty, Sask.	F3	75
Liberty, Il., U.S.	D2	90
Liberty, In., U.S.	E8	91
Liberty, Ks., U.S.	E8	93
Liberty, Ky., U.S.	C4	94
Liberty, Me., U.S.	D3	96
Liberty, Ms., U.S.	D3	101
Liberty, Mo., U.S.	B3	102
Liberty, N.Y., U.S.	D6	109

Name	Map Ref.	Page
Liberty, N.C., U.S.	B3	110
Liberty, Pa., U.S.	C7	115
Liberty, S.C., U.S.	B2	117
Liberty, Tn., U.S.	C8	119
Liberty, Wa., U.S.	D5	120
Liberty, Wa., U.S.	B5	124
Liberty, co., Fl., U.S.	B2	86
Liberty, co., Ga., U.S.	E5	87
Liberty, co., Mt., U.S.	B5	103
Liberty, co., Tx., U.S.	D5	120
Liberty Acres, Ca., U.S.	*n12	82
Liberty Center, In., U.S.	C7	91
Liberty Center, Ia., U.S.	C4	92
Liberty Center, Oh., U.S.	A1	112
Liberty Corner, N.J., U.S.	B3	107
Liberty Grove, Md., U.S.	A5	97
Liberty Hill, Ct., U.S.	C6	84
Liberty Hill, S.C., U.S.	C6	117
Liberty Lake, Wa., U.S.	g14	124
Liberty Lake, res., Md., U.S.	B4	97
Liberty Mills, In., U.S.	B6	91
Libertytown, Md., U.S.	B3	97
Libertyville, Il., U.S.	A6	90
Libertyville, Ia., U.S.	D5	92
Libiron, i., Marsh Is.	S18	52
Liblar, W. Ger.	C1	19
Libourne, Fr.	E5	16
Libramont, Bel.	E5	17
Libreville, Gabon	E1	46
Libuse, La., U.S.	C3	95
Libušín, Czech.	n17	26
Libya, ctry., Afr.	D3	43
Libyan Desert, des., Afr.	D4	43
Libyan Plateau, plat., Afr.	C4	43
Licantén, Chile	B2	54
Licata, Italy	F4	23
Lice, Tur.	C13	40
Licenza, Italy	g9	23
Lichfield, Eng., U.K.	B6	12
Lichinga, Moz.	D6	48
Lichtenburg, S. Afr.	C4	49
Lichtenfels, W. Ger.	C6	18
Lichtenstein, E. Ger.	C7	19
Lick Creek, stm., Tn., U.S.	C11	119
Licking, Mo., U.S.	D6	102
Licking, co., Oh., U.S.	B3	112
Licking, stm., Ky., U.S.	B6	94
Licking, North Fork, stm., Ky., U.S.	B5	94
Licking, South Fork, stm., Ky., U.S.	B5	94
Licosa, Point, c., Italy	D5	23
Licungo, stm., Moz.	A6	49
Lida, Sov. Un.	E5	27
Lida, Lake, l., Mn., U.S.	D3	100
Liddel Water, stm., U.K.	E6	13
Lidderdale, Ia., U.S.	B3	92
Lidgerwood, N.D., U.S.	C8	111
Lidhult, Swe.	B7	15
Lidice, Czech.	C3	26
Lidingö, Swe.	H8	14
Lidköping, Swe.	H5	14
Lido di Roma, Italy	h8	23
Lidzbark Warmiński, Pol.	A6	26
Liebenthal, Sask.	G1	75
Liebenthal, Ks., U.S.	D4	93
Lieberose, E. Ger.	B9	19
Liechtenstein, ctry., Eur.	E4	18
Liège (Luik), Bel.	B6	16
Liège, prov., Bel.	D5	17
Liège, stm., Alta.	A4	68
Liegnitz see Legnica, Pol.	C4	26
Lieksa, Fin.	F14	14
Lienen, W. Ger.	A2	19
Lienz, Aus.	C3	18
Liepāja, Sov. Un.	C3	27
Lier (Lierre), Bel.	D5	17
Lierneux, Bel.	D5	17
Lierre see Lier, Bel.	B6	16
Liestal, Switz.	E3	18
Liévin, Fr.	C7	16
Lièvre, Rivière du, stm., Que.	D2	74
Lièvres, Île aux, i., Que.	B8	74
Liffey, stm., Ire.	C3	10
Lifford, Ire.	C3	10
Liftwood, De., U.S.	*A3	85
Light, Ar., U.S.	A5	81
Lighthouse Inlet, b., S.C., U.S.	k12	117
Lighthouse Point, Fl., U.S.	*F6	86
Lighthouse Point, c., Fl., U.S.	C2	86
Lighthouse Point, c., La., U.S.	E3	95
Lighthouse Point, c., Mi., U.S.	C5	99
Lightning Creek, stm., Wy., U.S.	C8	127
Lightning Ridge, Austl.	D6	51
Lignite, N.D., U.S.	A3	111
Lignum, Va., U.S.	B5	123
Ligny-en-Barrois, Fr.	F5	17
Ligonha, stm., Moz.	E6	48
Ligonier, In., U.S.	B6	91
Ligonier, Pa., U.S.	F3	115
Ligovo (part of Leningrad), Sov. Un.	s31	14
Liguria, prov., Italy	E4	20
Liguria, prov., Italy	B2	22
Ligurian Apennines, mts., Italy	E4	20
Ligurian Sea, Eur.	C2	23
Lihue, Hi., U.S.	B2	88
Lijiang, China	F5	31
Lijin, China	F8	32
Likasi, Zaire	D4	48
Likely, B.C.	C7	69
Likely, Ca., U.S.	B3	82
Likhoslavl, Sov. Un.	C10	27
Likino-Dulevo, Sov. Un.	n18	27
Lilbourn, Mo., U.S.	E8	102
Lilburn, Ga., U.S.	h8	87
L'Île-Rousse, Fr.	C2	23
Lilesville, N.C., U.S.	C3	110
Liling, China	K5	32
Lille, Fr.	B5	16
Lille, Ma., U.S.	A4	96
Lille Bælt, strt., Den.	C3	15
Lillehammer, Nor.	G4	14
Lillers, Fr.	D2	17
Lillesand, Nor.	H3	14
Lillestrøm, Nor.	H4	14
Lillian, Al., U.S.	E2	78
Lillian, Tx., U.S.	n9	120
Lillie, La., U.S.	B3	95
Lillington, N.C., U.S.	B4	110
Lillinonah, Lake, l., Ct., U.S.	C2	84
Lilly, Ga., U.S.	D3	87
Lilly, Pa., U.S.	F4	115
Lilly Fork, stm., W.V., U.S.	m13	125
Lilly Grove, W.V., U.S.	D3	125
Lilongwe, Mwi.	D5	48
Lily, Ky., U.S.	C5	94
Lily, S.D., U.S.	B8	118
Lily, Wi., U.S.	C5	126
Lim, stm., Yugo.	D4	24
Lima, Para.	D4	55
Lima, Peru	D2	58
Lima, Il., U.S.	C2	90
Lima, Mt., U.S.	F4	103
Lima, N.Y., U.S.	C3	109
Lima, Oh., U.S.	B1	112
Lima, dept., Peru	D2	58
Lima, stm., Eur.	B1	22
Lima Duarte, Braz.	C4	56
Lima Reservoir, res., Mt., U.S.	F4	103
Limanowa, Pol.	D6	26
Limassol see Lemesós, Cyp.	E9	40
Limavady, N. Ire., U.K.	B5	11
Limay, stm., Arg.	B3	54
Limay Mahuida, Arg.	B3	54
Limbach [-Oberfrohna], E. Ger.	C7	19
Limbe, Cam.	E1	46
Limbé, Haiti	E7	64
Limburg, W. Ger.	C4	18
Limburg, prov., Bel.	D5	17
Limburg, prov., Neth.	D5	17
Lime City, Oh., U.S.	e6	112
Limeil-Brévannes, Fr.	h10	16
Limeira, Braz.	C3	56
Limerick, Sask.	H2	75
Limerick, Ire.	D2	10
Limerick, Me., U.S.	E2	96
Limerick, co., Ire.	E3	11
Lime Rock, Ct., U.S.	B2	84
Limerock, R.I., U.S.	B4	116
Lime Springs, Ia., U.S.	A5	92
Limestone, Ar., U.S.	B2	81
Limestone, Fl., U.S.	E5	86
Limestone, Me., U.S.	B5	96
Limestone, N.Y., U.S.	C2	109
Limestone, Pa., U.S.	D3	115
Limestone, co., Al., U.S.	A2	78
Limestone, co., Tx., U.S.	D4	120
Limestone, stm., Man.	A4	70
Limestone Bay, b., Man.	C2	70
Limestone Lake, l., Man.	A4	70
Limestone Point, pen., Man.	C2	70
Limestone, Va., U.S.	B4	123
Lime Village, Ak., U.S.	C8	79
Limfjorden, strt., Den.	B3	15
Limington, Me., U.S.	E2	96
Limmen Bight, Austl.	B6	50
Limní, Grc.	C4	25
Límnos (Lemnos), i., Grc.	C5	40
Limoeiro, Braz.	C3	57
Limoeiro do Norte, Braz.	C3	57
Limoges, Ont.	B9	73
Limoges, Fr.	E4	16
Limón, C.R.	E8	63
Limón, Hond.	D7	63
Limon, Co., U.S.	B7	83
Limón, Bahía de, b., Pan.	k12	62
Limousin, hist. reg., Fr.	E4	16
Limousin Plateau, plat., Fr.	E4	16
Limoux, Fr.	F5	16
Limpopo, stm., Afr.	E5	48
Līnah, Sau. Ar.	H14	40
Linard, mtn., Switz.	C9	21
Linares, Chile	B2	54
Linares, Col.	C2	60
Linares, Mex.	C5	63
Linares, Spain	C4	22
Linaro, Cape, c., Italy	C3	23
Lince, Peru	*D2	58
Lin, Wy., U.S.	C6	127
Linchuan, China	F8	31
Lincoln, Arg.	A4	54
Lincoln, Ont.	D5	73
Lincoln, Eng., U.K.	D6	10
Lincoln, Al., U.S.	B3	78
Lincoln, Ar., U.S.	B1	81
Lincoln, Ca., U.S.	C3	82
Lincoln, De., U.S.	E4	85
Lincoln, Id., U.S.	F7	89
Lincoln, Il., U.S.	C4	90
Lincoln, Ia., U.S.	B5	92
Lincoln, Ks., U.S.	C5	93
Lincoln, Me., U.S.	C4	96
Lincoln, Ma., U.S.	g10	98
Lincoln, Mi., U.S.	D7	99
Lincoln, Mo., U.S.	C4	102
Lincoln, Mt., U.S.	D4	103
Lincoln, Ne., U.S.	D9	104
Lincoln, N.H., U.S.	B3	106
Lincoln, N.M., U.S.	D4	108
Lincoln, Tn., U.S.	B5	119
Lincoln, Vt., U.S.	C2	122
Lincoln, Va., U.S.	A5	123
Lincoln, co., Ar., U.S.	D4	81
Lincoln, co., Co., U.S.	C7	83
Lincoln, co., Ga., U.S.	C4	87
Lincoln, co., Id., U.S.	G4	89
Lincoln, co., Ks., U.S.	C5	93
Lincoln, co., Ky., U.S.	C5	94
Lincoln, co., La., U.S.	B3	95
Lincoln, co., Me., U.S.	D3	96
Lincoln, co., Mn., U.S.	F2	100
Lincoln, co., Mo., U.S.	C6	102
Lincoln, co., Mt., U.S.	B1	103
Lincoln, co., Ne., U.S.	D5	104
Lincoln, co., Nv., U.S.	F6	105
Lincoln, co., N.M., U.S.	D4	108
Lincoln, co., N.C., U.S.	B1	110
Lincoln, co., Ok., U.S.	B5	113
Lincoln, co., Or., U.S.	C3	114
Lincoln, co., S.D., U.S.	D9	118
Lincoln, co., Tn., U.S.	B5	119
Lincoln, co., Wa., U.S.	B7	124
Lincoln, co., W.V., U.S.	C2	125
Lincoln, co., Wi., U.S.	C4	126
Lincoln, Mount, mtn., Co., U.S.	B4	83
Lincoln Acres, Ca., U.S.	o15	82
Lincoln Center, Me., U.S.	C4	96
Lincoln City, In., U.S.	H4	91
Lincoln City, Or., U.S.	C3	114
Lincoln Heights, Oh., U.S.	o13	112
Lincoln Park, Ca., U.S.	*g10	82
Lincoln Park, Ga., U.S.	D2	87
Lincoln Park, Mi., U.S.	p15	99
Lincoln Park, Nv., U.S.	*D2	105
Lincoln Park, N.J., U.S.	B4	107
Lincoln Sea, N.A.	A15	61
Lincolnshire, Il., U.S.	h9	90
Lincolnshire, co., Eng., U.K.	A7	12
Lincoln Tomb State Memorial, hist., Il., U.S.	D4	90
Lincolnton, Ga., U.S.	C4	87
Lincolnton, N.C., U.S.	B1	110
Lincoln Village, Ca., U.S.	*g10	82
Lincoln Village, Oh., U.S.	*m10	112
Lincolnville, Me., U.S.	D3	96
Lincolnville, S.C., U.S.	h11	117
Lincolnwood, Il., U.S.	h9	90
Lincroft, N.J., U.S.	C4	107
Li Rangu, Sud.	E2	47
Lind, Wa., U.S.	C7	124
Linda, Ca., U.S.	*C3	82
Lindale, Ga., U.S.	B1	87
Lindale, Tx., U.S.	C5	120
Lindau, W. Ger.	E4	18
Lindbergh, Alta.	C5	68
Linden, Alta.	D4	68
Linden, Al., U.S.	C2	78
Linden, In., U.S.	D4	91
Linden, Ia., U.S.	C3	92
Linden, Mi., U.S.	F7	99
Linden, N.J., U.S.	k8	107
Linden, N.C., U.S.	B4	110
Linden, Pa., U.S.	D7	115
Linden, Tn., U.S.	B4	119
Linden, Tx., U.S.	C5	120
Linden, Wi., U.S.	F3	126
Lindenhurst, Il., U.S.	h8	90
Lindenhurst, N.Y., U.S.	n15	109
Lindenwold, N.J., U.S.	D3	107
Linderöd, Swe.	C7	15
Lindesberg, Swe.	H6	14
Lindi, Tan.	C6	48
Lindi, prov., Tan.	C6	48
Lindi, stm., Zaire	A5	48
Lindian, China	A11	32
Lindlar, W. Ger.	B2	19
Lindome, Swe.	A6	15
Lindon, Co., U.S.	B7	83
Lindon, Ut., U.S.	C4	121
Lindrith, N.M., U.S.	A2	108
Lindsay, Ont.	C6	73
Lindsay, Ca., U.S.	D4	82
Lindsay, Mt., U.S.	C11	103
Lindsay, Ne., U.S.	C8	104
Lindsay, Ok., U.S.	C4	113
Lindsborg, Ks., U.S.	D6	93
Lindsey, Oh., U.S.	A2	112
Lindstrom, Mn., U.S.	E6	100
Lindy, Ne., U.S.	B8	104
Lineboro, Md., U.S.	A4	97
Linefork, Ky., U.S.	C7	94
Lineville, Al., U.S.	B4	78
Lineville, Ia., U.S.	D4	92
Linfen, China	D7	31
Linganore Creek, stm., Md., U.S.	B3	97
Lingayen, Phil.	B6	34
Lingayen Gulf, b., Phil.	n13	34
Lingen, W. Ger.	B3	18
Lingga Islands, is., Indon.	F2	34
Lingle, Wy., U.S.	D8	127
Linglestown, Pa., U.S.	F8	115
Lingling, China	F7	31
Lingo, N.M., U.S.	D6	108
Lingshan, China	G6	31
Linguère, Sen.	C1	45
Lingwu, China	E2	32
Lingyuan, China	C8	31
Linhai, China	F9	31
Linhares, Braz.	E2	57
Linhe, China	D2	32
Liniers, Arg.	A4	54
Linière, Que.	C7	74
Linkou, China	B11	31
Linköping, Swe.	H6	14
Linlithgow, Scot., U.K.	E5	13
Linn, Ks., U.S.	C6	93
Linn, Mo., U.S.	C6	102
Linn, Tx., U.S.	F3	120
Linn, co., Ia., U.S.	B6	92
Linn, co., Ks., U.S.	D9	93
Linn, co., Mo., U.S.	B4	102
Linn, co., Or., U.S.	C4	114
Linn Creek, Mo., U.S.	C5	102
Linn Grove, Ia., U.S.	B2	92
Linn Grove, In., U.S.	C7	91
Linneus, Me., U.S.	B5	96
Linneus, Mo., U.S.	B4	102
Linnhe, Loch, b., Scot., U.K.	B4	10
Lino Lakes, Mn., U.S.	m12	100
Linqing, China	D8	31
Linru, China	C3	32
Lins, Braz.	C3	56
Linstead, Jam.	E14	65
Lintan, China	E5	31
Lintao, China	D5	31
Linth, stm., Switz.	C7	21
Linthal, Switz.	C7	21
Linthicum Heights, Md., U.S.	B4	97
Lintlaw, Sask.	E4	75
Linton, Que.	B5	74
Linton, Ga., U.S.	C3	87
Linton, In., U.S.	F3	91
Linton, Ky., U.S.	D2	94
Linton, N.D., U.S.	C5	111
Linville, Va., U.S.	B4	123
Linwood, Ont.	D4	73
Linwood, In., U.S.	D6	91
Linwood, Ks., U.S.	m15	93
Linwood, Ma., U.S.	B4	98
Linwood, Mi., U.S.	E7	99
Linwood, N.J., U.S.	E3	107
Linwood, N.C., U.S.	B2	110
Linworth, Oh., U.S.	k10	112
Linxi, China	D3	32
Linxia, China	D5	31
Linyi, China	D8	31
Linz, Aus.	D7	18
Lions, La., U.S.	h10	95
Lions, Gulf of, b., Fr.	F6	16
Lion's Head, Ont.	C3	73
Lionville, Pa., U.S.	F10	115
Lipa, Phil.	C6	34
Lipan, Tx., U.S.	C4	120
Lipari, Italy	E5	23
Lipari, i., Italy	E5	23
Lipetsk, Sov. Un.	G5	27
Lipez, Cerro, mtn., Bol.	D2	55
Lipik, Yugo.	C3	24
Liping, China	F6	31
Lipkany, Sov. Un.	B5	26
Lipno, Pol.	B5	26
Lipno Reservoir, res., Czech.	E9	19
Lipova, Rom.	B5	24
Lippe, stm., W. Ger.	C4	18
Lippstadt, W. Ger.	B4	18
Lipscomb, Al., U.S.	B3	78
Lipscomb, Tx., U.S.	A2	120
Lipscomb, co., Tx., U.S.	A2	120
Lipsoí, i., Grc.	D6	25
Lipton, Sask.	G4	75
Lipu, China	G7	31
Lira, Ug.	A5	48
Lircay, Peru	D3	58
Liri, stm., Italy	D4	23
Liria, Spain	C5	22
Lisafa, Zaire	B2	48
Lisala, Zaire	A3	48
Lisbon (Lisboa), Port.	C1	22
Lisbon, Ct., U.S.	C7	84
Lisbon, Il., U.S.	B5	90
Lisbon, Ia., U.S.	C6	92
Lisbon, La., U.S.	B3	95
Lisbon, Md., U.S.	B3	97
Lisbon, N.H., U.S.	B3	106
Lisbon, N.Y., U.S.	f9	109
Lisbon, N.D., U.S.	C8	111
Lisbon, Oh., U.S.	B5	112
Lisbon Center, Me., U.S.	f7	96
Lisbon Falls, Me., U.S.	E2	96
Lisburne, Cape, c., Ak., U.S.	B6	79
Liscannor Bay, b., Ire.	E2	11
Liscarney, Ire.	D2	11
Lisco, Ne., U.S.	C3	104
Liscomb, N.S.	D7	71
Liscomb, Ia., U.S.	B5	92
Lisdoonvarna, Ire.	D2	11
Lishi, China	F4	32
Lishu, China	C11	31
Lishui, China	F8	31
Lisianski Island, i., Hi., U.S.	k13	88
Lisichansk, Sov. Un.	q21	27
Lisieux, Sask.	H2	75
Lisieux, Fr.	C4	16
Liskeard, Eng., U.K.	D3	12
L'Isle, Switz.	C1	21
L'Isle [-sur-le-Doubs], Fr.	B2	20
L'Islet, Que.	B7	74
L'Islet, co., Que.	B7	74
L'Islet-sur-Mer, Que.	B7	74
L'Isle-Verte, Que.	A8	74
Lisman, Al., U.S.	C1	78
Lismore, Austl.	E9	51
Lismore, N.S.	D7	71
Lismore, Ire.	E4	11
Lismore, Mn., U.S.	G3	100
Lismore Island, i., Scot., U.K.	D3	13
Lisnaskea, N. Ire., U.K.	C4	11
Listafjorden, b., Nor.	H2	14
Lister, B.C.	E9	69
Listie, Pa., U.S.	F3	115
Listowel, Ont.	D4	73
Listowel, Ire.	D2	10
Litang, China	F5	31
Litava, stm., Czech.	o16	26
Litchfield, Ca., U.S.	B3	82
Litchfield, Ct., U.S.	C3	84
Litchfield, Il., U.S.	D4	90
Litchfield, Mi., U.S.	F6	99
Litchfield, Mn., U.S.	E4	100
Litchfield, Ne., U.S.	C6	104
Litchfield, Oh., U.S.	A3	112
Litchfield, co., Ct., U.S.	B2	84
Litchfield Park, Az., U.S.	m8	80
Litchville, N.D., U.S.	C7	111
Liteň, Czech.	o17	26
Literberry, Il., U.S.	D3	90
Lithgow, Austl.	F8	51
Lithia Springs, Ga., U.S.	h7	87
Lithinon, Cape, c., Grc.	E5	25
Lithonia, Ga., U.S.	C2	87
Lithuania, state, Sov. Un.	D5	29
Lititz, Pa., U.S.	F9	115
Litókhoron, Grc.	B4	25
Litoměřice, Czech.	C3	26
Litomyšl, Czech.	D4	26
Litslena, Swe.	t35	14
Littau, Switz.	B5	21
Little, stm., U.S.	B5	81
Little, stm., Ct., U.S.	C7	84
Little, stm., Ga., U.S.	C3	87
Little, stm., Ga., U.S.	E3	87
Little, stm., Ga., U.S.	C4	87
Little, stm., Ky., U.S.	D2	94
Little, stm., La., U.S.	C3	95
Little, stm., N.C., U.S.	B3	110
Little, stm., Ok., U.S.	C5	113
Little, stm., S.C., U.S.	C2	117
Little, stm., Tn., U.S.	n14	119
Little, stm., Vt., U.S.	C3	122
Little, stm., Va., U.S.	D2	123
Little Alföld, pl., Hung.	B3	24
Little America, Wy., U.S.	*E3	127
Little Andaman, i., India	F9	36
Little Arkansas, stm., Ks., U.S.	D4	93
Little Bay Islands, Newf.	D4	72
Little Bear Lake, l., Sask.	C3	75
Little Beaver Creek, stm., Ks., U.S.	C2	93
Little Belt Mountains, mts., Mt., U.S.	D6	103
Little Bighorn, stm., U.S.	E9	103
Little Birch, W.V., U.S.	C4	125
Little Bitter Lake, l., Eg.	D4	41
Little Black, stm., Me., U.S.	A3	96
Little Blue, stm., U.S.	C6	93
Little Blue, stm., In., U.S.	H5	91
Little Boars Head, N.H., U.S.	E5	106
Little Bow, stm., Alta.	D4	68
Little Britain, Ont.	C6	73
Little Brook, N.S.	E3	71
Little Bullhead, Man.	D3	70
Little Cacapon, stm., W.V., U.S.	B6	125
Little Cadotte, stm., Alta.	A2	68
Little Canada, Mn., U.S.	*m12	100
Little Carpathians, mts., Czech.	D4	26
Little Catalina, Newf.	D5	72
Little Cayman, i., Cay. Is.	E7	64
Little Cedar, stm., Ia., U.S.	A5	92
Little Chief, Ok., U.S.	A5	113
Little Choptank River, b., Md., U.S.	C5	97
Little Churchill, stm., Man.	A4	70
Little Chute, Wi., U.S.	D5	126
Little Colorado, stm., Az., U.S.	B4	80
Little Compton, R.I., U.S.	E6	116
Little Creek, De., U.S.	C4	85
Little Creek Naval Amphibious Base, mil., Va., U.S.	k15	123
Little Creek Peak, mtn., Ut., U.S.	F3	121
Little Current, Ont.	B3	73
Little Deer Isle, Me., U.S.	D4	96
Little Diomede Island, i., Ak., U.S.	B6	79
Little Dry Creek, stm., Mt., U.S.	C10	103
Little Eagle, S.D., U.S.	B5	118
Little Egg Harbor, b., N.J., U.S.	D4	107
Little Egg Inlet, b., N.J., U.S.	E4	107
Little Falls, Mn., U.S.	E4	100
Little Falls, N.Y., U.S.	B6	109
Little Ferry, N.J., U.S.	h8	107
Littlefield, Az., U.S.	A2	80
Littlefield, Tx., U.S.	C1	120
Little Fishing Creek, stm., W.V., U.S.	h9	125
Littlefork, Mn., U.S.	B5	100
Little Fork, stm., Mn., U.S.	B5	100
Little Frog Mountain, mtn., Tn., U.S.	D9	119
Little Goose Creek, stm., Wy., U.S.	B6	127
Little Grand Lake, l., Newf.	D3	72
Little Gunpowder Falls, stm., Md., U.S.	A4	97
Little Harbour Deep, Newf.	C3	72
Little Hocking, Oh., U.S.	C4	112
Little Humboldt, stm., Nv., U.S.	B4	105
Little Humboldt, North Fork, stm., Nv., U.S.	B4	105
Little Humboldt, South Fork, stm., Nv., U.S.	B5	105
Little Kanawha, stm., W.V., U.S.	C4	125
Little Kanawha, West Fork, stm., W.V., U.S.	C4	125
Little Lake, Mi., U.S.	B3	99
Little Lake, l., La., U.S.	E5	95
Littlelot, Tn., U.S.	B4	119
Little Lynches, stm., S.C., U.S.	C7	117
Little Manatee, stm., Fl., U.S.	p11	86
Little Manitou Lake, l., Sask.	F3	75
Little Marais, Mn., U.S.	C7	100
Little Mazarn Creek, stm., Ar., U.S.	g7	81
Little Meadows, Pa., U.S.	C9	115
Little Mecatina, stm., Can.	h9	72
Little Mexico, Tx., U.S.	D1	120
Little Miami, stm., Oh., U.S.	C1	112
Little Miami, East Fork, stm., Oh., U.S.	C1	112
Little Missouri, stm., U.S.	A7	76
Little Missouri, stm., Ar., U.S.	D2	81
Little Moose Mountain, mtn., N.Y., U.S.	B6	109
Little Mountain, S.C., U.S.	C5	117
Little Mountain, mtn., Wy., U.S.	E3	127
Little Muddy, stm., Il., U.S.	E4	90
Little Muddy, stm., N.D., U.S.	A2	111
Little Orleans, Md., U.S.	A1	97
Little Osage, stm., U.S.	E9	93
Little Otter Creek, stm., Vt., U.S.	C2	122
Little Owyhee, stm., U.S.	B5	105
Little Pee Dee, stm., S.C., U.S.	C9	117
Little Pigeon Creek, stm., In., U.S.	I3	91
Little Pipe Creek, stm., Md., U.S.	A3	97
Little Playgreen Lake, l., Man.	B3	70
Littleport, Ia., U.S.	B6	92
Little Powder, stm., U.S.	F11	103
Little Quill Lake, l., Sask.	F3	75
Little Rann of Kachchh, pl., India	F3	37
Little Red, stm., Ar., U.S.	B4	81
Little Red, Middle Fork, stm., Ar., U.S.	B3	81
Little River, Al., U.S.	D2	78
Little River, Ga., U.S.	D3	87
Little River, Ks., U.S.	D5	93
Little River, S.C., U.S.	D10	117
Little River, co., Ar., U.S.	D1	81
Little River Inlet, b., S.C., U.S.	D10	117
Little Rock, Ar., U.S.	C3	81
Little Rock, Il., U.S.	B5	90
Little Rock, Ia., U.S.	A2	92
Little Rock, S.C., U.S.	C9	117
Little Rock, Wa., U.S.	C2	124
Little Rock Air Force Base, mil., Ar., U.S.	C3	81
Little Sable Point, c., Mi., U.S.	E4	99
Little Sachigo Lake, l., Ont.	B5	70
Little Saint Bernard Pass, Eur.	E7	16
Little Salt Lake, l., Ut., U.S.	F3	121
Little Sand Creek, stm., Mn., U.S.	D6	100
Little Sandy, stm., Ky., U.S.	B6	94
Little Sandy Creek, stm., Wy., U.S.	D3	127
Little Sauk, Mn., U.S.	E4	100
Little Sebago Lake, l., Me., U.S.	g7	96
Little Silver, N.J., U.S.	C4	107
Little Sioux, Ia., U.S.	C1	92
Little Sioux, stm., Ia., U.S.	B2	92
Little Sioux, West Fork, stm., Ia., U.S.	B2	92
Little Smoky, stm., Alta.	B2	68
Little Southwest Miramichi, stm., N.B.	C3	71
Little Spokane, stm., Wa., U.S.	B8	124
Little Suamico, Wi., U.S.	D6	126
Little Tallapoosa, stm., U.S.	B4	78
Little Tenmile Creek, stm., W.V., U.S.	k10	125
Little Tennessee, stm., U.S.	D9	119
Littleton, Co., U.S.	B6	83
Littleton, Il., U.S.	C3	90
Littleton, Ma., U.S.	B5	98
Littleton, N.H., U.S.	B3	106
Littleton, N.C., U.S.	A5	110
Littleton, W.V., U.S.	B4	125
Littleville, Al., U.S.	A2	78
Little Valley, Ca., U.S.	B3	82
Little Valley, N.Y., U.S.	C2	109
Little Wabash, stm., Il., U.S.	E5	90
Little Walnut, stm., Ks., U.S.	g13	93
Little West Fork, stm., Tn., U.S.	A4	119
Little White, stm., S.D., U.S.	D5	118
Little Wolf, stm., Wi., U.S.	D4	126
Little Wood, stm., Id., U.S.	F4	89
Little York, Il., U.S.	B3	90
Little York, In., U.S.	G6	91
Little Zab, stm., Asia	E15	40
Littoria see Latina, Italy	D4	23
Litvínov, Czech.	C8	19
Liuba, China	E6	31
Liucheng, China	G6	31
Liucura, Chile	B2	54
Liuhe, China	C11	31
Liupan Mountains, mts., China	F1	32
Liuyang, China	J5	32
Liuzhou, China	G6	31
Livelong, Sask.	D1	75
Lively, Ont.	A3	73
Livengood, Ak., U.S.	B10	79
Livenza, stm., Italy	D8	20
Live Oak, Ca., U.S.	*D3	82
Live Oak, Fl., U.S.	B4	86
Live Oak, Tx., U.S.	*E3	120
Live Oak, co., Tx., U.S.	E3	120
Live Oak Manor, La., U.S.	*E5	95
Livermore, Ca., U.S.	h9	82
Livermore, Co., U.S.	A5	83
Livermore, Ia., U.S.	B3	92
Livermore, Ky., U.S.	C2	94
Livermore, Me., U.S.	D2	96
Livermore, Mount, mtn., Tx., U.S.	o12	120
Livermore Falls, Me., U.S.	D2	96
Livermore Falls, N.H., U.S.	C3	106
Liverpool, N.S.	E5	71
Liverpool, Eng., U.K.	D5	10
Liverpool, Pa., U.S.	E7	115
Liverpool, Tx., U.S.	r14	120
Liverpool, W.V., U.S.	C3	125
Liverpool Bay, b., N.W. Ter.	B7	66
Livigno, Italy	C9	21
Livingston, Guat.	D7	63
Livingston, Al., U.S.	C1	78
Livingston, Ca., U.S.	D3	82
Livingston, Il., U.S.	E4	90
Livingston, Ky., U.S.	C5	94
Livingston, La., U.S.	D5	95
Livingston, Mt., U.S.	E6	103
Livingston, N.J., U.S.	B4	107
Livingston, N.Y., U.S.	C7	109
Livingston, S.C., U.S.	D5	117
Livingston, Tn., U.S.	C8	119
Livingston, Tx., U.S.	D5	120
Livingston, Wi., U.S.	F3	126
Livingston, co., Il., U.S.	C5	90
Livingston, co., Ky., U.S.	e9	94
Livingston, co., La., U.S.	D5	95
Livingston, co., Mi., U.S.	F6	99
Livingston, co., Mo., U.S.	B4	102
Livingston, co., N.Y., U.S.	C3	109
Livingston, Lake, res., Tx., U.S.	D5	120
Livingstone, Zam.	E4	48
Livingstone Cove, N.S.	D8	71
Livingstone Falls, wtfl., Afr.	*C1	48
Livingstonia, Mwi.	D5	48
Livingston Island, i., B.A.T.	C6	7
Livingston Manor, N.Y., U.S.	D6	109
Livno, Yugo.	D3	24
Livny, Sov. Un.	E11	27
Livona, N.D., U.S.	C5	111
Livonia, In., U.S.	G5	91
Livonia, La., U.S.	D4	95
Livonia, Mi., U.S.	F7	99
Livonia, Mo., U.S.	A5	102
Livonia, N.Y., U.S.	C3	109
Livorno (Leghorn), Italy	E5	23
Livramento do Brumado, Braz.	A4	56
Livry-Gargan, Fr.	g11	16
Liwale, Tan.	C6	48
Lixian, China	J4	32
Liyang, China	I8	32
Lizard Creek, stm., Ia., U.S.	B3	92
Lizard Head Pass, Co., U.S.	D3	83
Lizard Head Peak, mtn., Wy., U.S.	D3	127
Lizard Point, c., Eng., U.K.	F4	10
Lizella, Ga., U.S.	D3	87
Lizemores, W.V., U.S.	C3	125
Lizton, In., U.S.	E4	91
Ljubljana, Yugo.	B2	24
Ljubuški, Yugo.	D3	24
Ljungby, Swe.	I5	14
Ljusdal, Swe.	G7	14
Ljusterö, Swe.	I36	14
Llandeilo, Wales, U.K.	C4	12
Llandovery, Wales, U.K.	C4	12
Llandrindod Wells, Wales, U.K.	D5	10
Llandudno, Wales, U.K.	B4	12
Llanelli, Wales, U.K.	E4	10
Llanes, Spain	A3	22
Llanfyllin, Wales, U.K.	B4	12
Llangefni, Wales, U.K.	A3	12
Llangollen Estates, De., U.S.	*B3	85
Llanidloes, Wales, U.K.	B4	12
Llano, N.M., U.S.	A4	108
Llano, Tx., U.S.	D3	120
Llano, co., Tx., U.S.	D3	120
Llano, stm., Tx., U.S.	D3	120
Llanos, pl., S.A.	B3	60
Llanquihue, Lago, l., Chile	C2	54
Llata, Peru	C2	58
Llaves, N.M., U.S.	A3	108
Llera, Spain	C2	22
Lleyn Peninsula, pen., Wales, U.K.	D4	10
Llico, Chile	A2	55
Llobregat, stm., Spain	B6	22
Lloyd, Fl., U.S.	B2	86
Lloyd, Ky., U.S.	B7	94
Lloyd, Mt., U.S.	B7	103
Lloyd Harbor, N.Y., U.S.	*E7	109
Lloydminster (Alta. and Sask.), Sask.	D1	75
Lloyds, stm., Newf.	D3	72
Lluchmayor, Spain	C7	22
Llullaillaco, Volcán, vol., S.A.	D2	55
Loa, Ut., U.S.	E4	121
Loa, stm., Chile	A2	55
Loachapoka, Al., U.S.	C4	78
Loami, Il., U.S.	D4	90
Loange, stm., Afr.	C2	48
Lobatse, Bots.	C4	49
Löbau, E. Ger.	C7	19
Lobaye, stm., Cen. Afr. Rep.	E3	46
Lobelville, Tn., U.S.	B4	119
Lobenstein, E. Ger.	C6	19
Lobería, Arg.	B5	54
Lobito, Ang.	D1	48

Name	Map Ref.	Page
Lobnya, Sov. Un.	m17	27
Lobo, Phil.	p13	34
Lobos, Arg.	B5	54
Lobos, Cabo, c., Mex.	B2	63
Lobos, Punta, c., Mex.	B2	63
Lobos de Tierra, Isla, i., Peru	C1	58
Lobster Lake, l., Me., U.S.	C3	96
Loburg, E. Ger.	A7	19
Locarno, Switz.	E4	18
Lochaber, N.S.	D7	71
Lochaline, Scot., U.K.	D3	13
Lochcarron, Scot., U.K.	C3	13
Lochdonhead, Scot., U.K.	D3	13
Lochearnhead, Scot., U.K.	D4	13
Lochem, Neth.	B6	17
Loches, Fr.	D4	16
Lochgilphead, Scot., U.K.	D3	13
Lochinver, Scot., U.K.	B3	13
Loch Lomond, Va., U.S.	B5	123
Loch Lynn Heights, Md., U.S.	m12	97
Lochmere, N.H., U.S.	C5	13
Lochnagar, mtn., Scot., U.K.	D5	13
Lochranza, Scot., U.K.	E3	13
Loch Raven Reservoir, res., Md., U.S.	B4	97
Lochsa, stm., Id., U.S.	C3	89
Lochy, Loch, l., Scot., U.K.	D4	13
Lockbourne, Oh., U.S.	m11	112
Locke, In., U.S.	B5	91
Locke, N.Y., U.S.	C4	109
Locke, Tn., U.S.	B1	119
Locke Mills, Me., U.S.	D2	96
Lockeport, N.S.	F4	71
Lockerbie, Scot., U.K.	E5	13
Lockesburg, Ar., U.S.	D1	81
Lockhart, Al., U.S.	D3	78
Lockhart, Fl., U.S.	*D5	86
Lockhart, Mn., U.S.	C2	100
Lockhart, S.C., U.S.	B5	117
Lockhart, Tx., U.S.	E4	120
Lock Haven, Pa., U.S.	D7	115
Lockland, Oh., U.S.	o13	112
Lockney, Tx., U.S.	B2	120
Lockport, Man.	D3	70
Lockport, Il., U.S.	B5	90
Lockport, Ky., U.S.	B5	94
Lockport, La., U.S.	E5	95
Lockport, N.Y., U.S.	B2	109
Lockridge, Ia., U.S.	C6	92
Lock Springs, Mo., U.S.	B4	102
Lockwood, Sask.	F3	75
Lockwood, Mo., U.S.	D4	102
Lockwood, Mt., U.S.	E8	103
Lockwood, W.V., U.S.	C3	125
Loc Ninh, Viet.	G7	35
Loco, Ok., U.S.	C4	113
Loco Hills, N.M., U.S.	E6	108
Locumba, Peru	E3	58
Locust, N.J., U.S.	C4	107
Locust, N.C., U.S.	B2	110
Locust Bayou, Ar., U.S.	D3	81
Locust Creek, stm., Mo., U.S.	B4	102
Locust Fork, stm., Al., U.S.	B3	78
Locust Grove, Ga., U.S.	C2	87
Locust Grove, Md., U.S.	B5	97
Locust Grove, N.Y., U.S.	*C7	109
Locust Grove, Ok., U.S.	A6	113
Locust Hill (part of Markham), Ont.	k15	73
Lod, Isr.	G10	40
Loda, Il., U.S.	C5	90
Loděnice, stm., Czech.	n17	26
Löderup, Swe.	C8	15
Lodève, Fr.	F5	16
Lodeynoye Pole, Sov. Un.	A9	27
Lodge, Newf.	B4	72
Lodge, S.C., U.S.	E6	117
Lodge Creek, stm., N.A.	B7	103
Lodge Grass, Mt., U.S.	E9	103
Lodgepole, Alta.	C3	68
Lodge Pole, Mt., U.S.	B8	103
Lodgepole, Ne., U.S.	C3	104
Lodgepole, S.D., U.S.	B3	118
Lodgepole Creek, stm., U.S.	C3	104
Lodi, Italy	B2	23
Lodi, Ca., U.S.	C3	82
Lodi, N.J., U.S.	h8	107
Lodi, N.Y., U.S.	C4	109
Lodi, Oh., U.S.	A3	112
Lodi, Wi., U.S.	E4	126
Lodi, Zaire	B3	48
Lodja, Zaire	B3	48
Lodore, Canyon of, val., Co., U.S.	A2	83
Lodosa, Spain	B2	20
Lodwar, Kenya	A6	48
Łódź, Pol.	C5	26
Loeches, Spain	p18	22
Loei, Thai.	D4	35
Loelli, l., Sud.	D3	47
Loeriesfontein, S. Afr.	D2	49
Lofer, Aus.	B8	20
Lofoten, is., Nor.	C5	14
Loftus, Eng., U.K.	F8	13
Loga, Niger	D5	45
Logan, Il., U.S.	F5	90
Logan, Ia., U.S.	C2	92
Logan, Ks., U.S.	C4	93
Logan, Mt., U.S.	E5	103
Logan, N.M., U.S.	B6	108
Logan, N.D., U.S.	A4	111
Logan, Oh., U.S.	C3	112
Logan, Ok., U.S.	A1	113
Logan, Ut., U.S.	B4	121
Logan, W.V., U.S.	D3	125
Logan, co., Ar., U.S.	B2	81
Logan, co., Co., U.S.	A7	83
Logan, co., Il., U.S.	C4	90
Logan, co., Ks., U.S.	D2	93
Logan, co., Ky., U.S.	D3	94
Logan, co., Ne., U.S.	C5	104
Logan, co., N.D., U.S.	C6	111
Logan, co., Oh., U.S.	B2	112
Logan, co., Ok., U.S.	B4	113
Logan, co., W.V., U.S.	D3	125
Logan, Mount, mtn., Yukon	D4	66
Logan, Mount, mtn., Wa., U.S.	A5	124
Logan, Creek, stm., Ne., U.S.	B9	104
Logandale, Nv., U.S.	G7	105
Logan Lake, B.C.	D7	69
Logan Martin Lake, res., Al., U.S.	B3	78
Logan Mountains, mts., Yukon	B3	66
Logan Pass, Mt., U.S.	B2	103
Logansport, In., U.S.	C5	91
Logansport, Ky., U.S.	C3	94
Logansport, La., U.S.	C2	95
Loganton, Pa., U.S.	D7	115
Loganville, Ga., U.S.	C3	87
Loganville, Pa., U.S.	G8	115
Loge, stm., Ang.	C1	48
Loggieville, N.B.	B4	71
Log Lane Village, Co., U.S.	A7	83
Logone, stm., Afr.	C3	46
Logroño, Spain	C3	22
Logrosán, Spain	B3	15
Løgstør, Den.	C2	15
Logumkloster, Den.	C4	15
Lohals, Den.	D7	36
Lohārdaga, India	D4	19
Lohr, W. Ger.	C3	19
Lohrville, Ia., U.S.	B3	92
Loi, mtn., Laos	C2	35
Loikaw, Burma	D4	16
Loir, stm., Fr.	D3	16
Loire, stm., Fr.	B3	65
Loíza, Lago, res., P.R.	B2	58
Loja, Ec.	D2	22
Loja, prov., Ec.	D3	22
Loja, Spain	D3	22
Lokan Reservoir, res., Fin.	C13	14
Lokandu, Zaire	C3	17
Løkeren, Bel.	C3	17
Lokhvitsa, Sov. Un.	F9	27
Lokichar, Kenya	A6	48
Lokichokio, Kenya	A5	48
Lokitaung, Kenya	A6	48
Løkken, Den.	A3	15
Lokoja, Nig.	E6	45
Lokolama, Zaire	B2	48
Lokoro, stm., Zaire	B3	48
Lokossa, Benin	E5	45
Lol, stm., Sud.	D2	47
Lola, Ky., U.S.	e9	94
Lola, Mount, mtn., Ca., U.S.	C3	82
Loliondo, Tan.	B6	48
Lolland, i., Den.	J4	14
Lollar, W. Ger.	C3	19
Lollie, Ga., U.S.	D4	87
Lolo, Mt., U.S.	D3	103
Lolo Hot Springs, Mt., U.S.	D2	103
Lolo Pass, U.S.	C4	89
Lom, Bul.	D6	24
Loma, Co., U.S.	B2	83
Loma, Mt., U.S.	C6	103
Loma, Ne., U.S.	C9	104
Loma, N.D., U.S.	A7	111
Loma Linda, Ca., U.S.	*E5	82
Lomami, stm., Zaire	B3	48
Loma Mountains, mts., S.L.	E2	45
Loman, Mn., U.S.	B5	100
Lomas, Peru	E3	58
Lomas de Zamora, Arg.	A5	54
Lomax, Il., U.S.	C2	90
Lombarda, Serra, plat., Braz.	B4	59
Lombardia (Lombardy), prov., Italy	B2	23
Lomblen, i., Indon.	G6	34
Lombok, i., Indon.	G5	34
Lombok Strait, strt., Indon.	G5	34
Lomela, Zaire	B3	48
Lomela, stm., Zaire	B3	48
Lometa, Tx., U.S.	D3	120
Lomié, Cam.	E2	46
Lomira, Wi., U.S.	E5	126
Lomita, Ca., U.S.	*E4	82
Lommel, Bel.	C5	17
Lomond, Alta.	D4	68
Lomond, Newf.	D3	72
Lomond, Loch, l., Scot., U.K.	B4	10
Lomonosov, Sov. Un.	s30	14
Lomonosovka, Sov. Un.	C7	28
Lompoc, Ca., U.S.	E3	82
Lom Sak, Thai.	D4	35
Łomża, Pol.	B7	26
Lonaconing, Md., U.S.	k13	97
Loncoche, Chile	B2	54
Londesborough, Ont.	D3	73
London, Ont.	E3	73
London, Eng., U.K.	E6	10
London, Ar., U.S.	B2	81
London, In., U.S.	E6	91
London, Ky., U.S.	C5	94
London, Oh., U.S.	C2	112
London, Tx., U.S.	D3	120
London (Heathrow) Airport, Eng., U.K.	m12	10
Londonderry, N.S.	D6	71
Londonderry (Derry), N. Ire., U.K.	C3	10
Londonderry, N.H., U.S.	E4	106
Londonderry, Vt., U.S.	E3	122
Londonderry, Cape, c., Austl.	B5	50
Londonderry, Isla, i., Chile	k11	54
London Mills, Il., U.S.	C3	90
Londontowne, Md., U.S.	C4	97
Londrina, Braz.	A6	54
Lone Elm, Ks., U.S.	D8	93
Lone Grove, Ok., U.S.	C4	113
Lone Jack, Mo., U.S.	C3	102
Lonely Island, i., Ont.	B3	73
Lone Mountain, Tn., U.S.	C10	119
Lone Mountain, mtn., Nv., U.S.	E4	105
Lone Oak, Ky., U.S.	e9	94
Lone Oak, Tx., U.S.	C5	120
Lone Pine, Ca., U.S.	D4	82
Lonepine, Mt., U.S.	C2	103
Lone Rock, Sask.	D1	75
Lone Rock, Ia., U.S.	A3	92
Lone Rock, Wi., U.S.	E3	126
Lonerock, Or., U.S.	B7	114
Lone Star, S.C., U.S.	D6	117
Lone Tree, Ia., U.S.	C6	92
Lonetree, Wy., U.S.	E2	127
Lone Tree Creek, stm., Co., U.S.	A6	83
Lone Wolf, Ok., U.S.	C2	113
Long, co., Ga., U.S.	E5	87
Longa, stm., Ang.	D1	48
Longá, stm., Braz.	B2	57
Longarone, Italy	B6	20
Long Bar Harbor, Md., U.S.	B5	97
Longboat Key, Fl., U.S.	E4	86
Longboat Key, i., Fl., U.S.	q10	86
Longboat Pass, strt., Fl., U.S.	q10	86
Long Bottom, Oh., U.S.	C4	112
Long Branch (part of Etobicoke), Ont.	m14	73
Long Branch, N.B.	B4	71
Long Branch, N.J., U.S.	C5	107
Long Branch, Tx., U.S.	C5	120
Longbranch, Wa., U.S.	B3	124
Long Cay, i., Bah.	m17	64
Long Creek, Or., U.S.	C7	114
Longcreek, S.C., U.S.	B1	117
Long Creek, stm., N.A.	H3	75
Long Creek Mountain, mtn., Wy., U.S.	D5	127
Longdale, Ok., U.S.	A3	113
Long Eaton, Eng., U.K.	B6	12
Long Eddy, N.Y., U.S.	D5	109
Longford, Ont.	C5	73
Longford, Ire.	D3	10
Longford, Ks., U.S.	C6	93
Longford, co., Ire.	D4	11
Long Grove, Ia., U.S.	C7	92
Long Harbour [-Mount Arlington Heights], Newf.	E5	72
Long Hill, Ct., U.S.	*D7	84
Longiram, Indon.	F5	34
Long Island, Ks., U.S.	C4	93
Long Island, N.C., U.S.	B2	110
Longisland, Va., U.S.	C3	123
Long Island, i., Bah.	C6	64
Long Island, i., Me., U.S.	E3	71
Long Island, i., Me., U.S.	g7	96
Long Island, i., Ma., U.S.	g12	98
Long Island, i., N.Y., U.S.	E7	109
Long Island Sound, strt., U.S.	E7	109
Long Key, Fl., U.S.	H6	86
Long Key, i., Fl., U.S.	H6	86
Longkou, China	F9	32
Longlac, Ont.	G15	66
Long Lake, Il., U.S.	h8	90
Long Lake, Mi., U.S.	D7	99
Long Lake, N.Y., U.S.	B6	109
Longlake, S.D., U.S.	B6	118
Long Lake, Wi., U.S.	C5	126
Long Lake, l., N.B.	B3	71
Long Lake, l., Me., U.S.	A4	96
Long Lake, l., Me., U.S.	D2	96
Long Lake, l., Mi., U.S.	C6	99
Long Lake, l., Mi., U.S.	C7	99
Long Lake, l., Mn., U.S.	D4	100
Long Lake, l., N.Y., U.S.	B6	109
Long Lake, l., N.D., U.S.	C6	111
Long Lake, l., Wa., U.S.	f10	124
Long Lake, l., Wi., U.S.	*C2	126
Long Lake Colony, S.D., U.S.	*B7	118
Long Lane, Mo., U.S.	D5	102
Longleaf, La., U.S.	C3	95
Longlin, China	G6	31
Longmeadow, Ma., U.S.	B2	98
Longmont, Co., U.S.	A5	83
Long Mountain, mtn., Mo., U.S.	E5	102
Long Mountain, mtn., N.H., U.S.	A4	106
Long Pine, Ne., U.S.	B6	104
Long Point, N.S.	D8	71
Long Point, Ont.	E4	73
Long Point, Il., U.S.	B5	90
Long Point, c., Man.	C2	70
Long Point, c., Newf.	D2	72
Long Point, pen., Ont.	E4	73
Long Pond, l., Me., U.S.	C3	96
Long Pond, l., Me., U.S.	C6	96
Long Pond, l., Ma., U.S.	C6	98
Long Pond, res., Fl., U.S.	C4	86
Long Prairie, Mn., U.S.	E4	100
Longquan, China	F8	31
Long Range Mountains, mts., Newf.	D3	72
Longreach, Austl.	D7	50
Longridge, Eng., U.K.	G6	13
Long Run, W.V., U.S.	k9	125
Longs Peak, mtn., Co., U.S.	A5	83
Long Strait, strt., Sov. Un.	B20	29
Longstreet, La., U.S.	B2	95
Longton, Ks., U.S.	E7	93
Longtown, Eng., U.K.	E6	13
Longtown, Mo., U.S.	D8	102
Longueau, Fr.	E2	17
Longueuil, Que.	D4	74
Longuyon, Fr.	C6	16
Longvale, Ca., U.S.	C2	82
Long Valley, Az., U.S.	C4	80
Long Valley, N.J., U.S.	B3	107
Longvalley, S.D., U.S.	D4	118
Longview, Alta.	D3	68
Longview, Il., U.S.	D5	90
Long View, N.C., U.S.	B1	110
Longview, Ms., U.S.	B5	101
Long View, N.C., U.S.	B1	110
Longview, Tx., U.S.	C5	120
Longview, Wa., U.S.	C3	124
Longville, La., U.S.	D2	95
Longville, Mn., U.S.	C5	100
Longwood, Fl., U.S.	*D5	86
Longwood, N.C., U.S.	C4	110
Longwoods, Md., U.S.	C5	97
Longwy, Fr.	C6	16
Longxian, China	G2	32
Long Xuyen, Viet.	G6	35
Longyan, China	F8	31
Longyao, China	F6	32
Longzhen, China	B3	33
Longzhou, China	G6	31
Lonkin, Burma	C10	36
Lonoke, Ar., U.S.	C4	81
Lonoke, co., Ar., U.S.	C4	81
Lönsdal, Nor.	D6	14
Lonsdale, Ont.	C7	73
Lonsdale, Ar., U.S.	C3	81
Lonsdale, Mn., U.S.	F5	100
Lons-le-Saunier, Fr.	E6	16
Lontzen, Bel.	D5	17
Looc, Phil.	C7	34
Looe, Eng., U.K.	D4	12
Loogootee, In., U.S.	G4	91
Lookeba, Ok., U.S.	B3	113
Lookout, Ca., U.S.	B3	82
Lookout, Ky., U.S.	C7	94
Lookout, W.V., U.S.	C4	125
Lookout, Cape, c., N.C., U.S.	C7	110
Lookout, Point, c., Mi., U.S.	d7	99
Lookout Mountain, Tn., U.S.	h11	119
Lookout Mountain, mtn., U.S.	D8	119
Lookout Mountain, mtn., U.S.	C6	114
Lookout Pass, U.S.	B3	89
Lookout Point Lake, res., Or., U.S.	C4	114
Loon, stm., Alta.	A3	68
Loon, stm., Man.	A1	70
Loon Bay, Newf.	D4	72
Loon Lake, Wa., U.S.	A8	124
Loon Lake, l., Alta.	A3	68
Loon Lake, l., Can.	B1	70
Loon Lake, l., Me., U.S.	B3	96
Loon Lake Mountains, mtn., N.Y., U.S.	f10	109
Loon Straits, Man.	D3	70
Loop, Tx., U.S.	C1	120
Loop Creek, stm., W.V., U.S.	m13	125
Loop Head, c., Ire.	D3	11
Loos, Fr.	D3	17
Loosahatchie, stm., Tn., U.S.	B2	119
Loose Creek, Mo., U.S.	C6	102
Looxahoma, Ms., U.S.	A4	101
Lopatka, Cape, c., Sov. Un.	D18	29
Lop Buri, Thai.	C2	34
Lopeno, Tx., U.S.	F3	120
Lopez, Pa., U.S.	D9	115
Lopez, Cap, c., Gabon	F1	46
Lopez Bay, b., Phil.	p14	34
Lopez Island, i., Wa., U.S.	A3	124
Lop Nur, l., China	D3	31
Lopori, stm., Zaire	A3	48
Lopphavet, b., Nor.	B9	14
Lora, Hāmūn-i, l., Asia	G12	39
Lora [del Río], Spain	D3	22
Lorado, W.V., U.S.	D3	125
Lorain, Oh., U.S.	A3	112
Lorain, co., Oh., U.S.	A3	112
Loraine, Il., U.S.	C2	90
Loraine, N.D., U.S.	A4	111
Loraine, Tx., U.S.	C2	120
Loralai, Pak.	B2	37
Loramie, Lake, res., Oh., U.S.	B1	112
Loranger, La., U.S.	D5	95
Lorca, Spain	D5	22
Lord Howe Island, i., Austl.	I9	6
Lordsburg, N.M., U.S.	E1	108
Lords Point, Ct., U.S.	D8	84
Loreauville, La., U.S.	D4	95
Loreburn, Sask.	F2	75
Lore City, Oh., U.S.	C4	112
Lorena, Braz.	C3	56
Lorengau, Pap. N. Gui.	h12	50
Lorentz, W.V., U.S.	B4	125
Lorenzo, Id., U.S.	F7	89
Lorenzo, Ne., U.S.	C2	104
Lorenzo, Tx., U.S.	C2	120
Lorenzo Geyres, Ur.	C1	57
Loreto, Braz.	D3	60
Loreto, Col.	D3	60
Loreto, Italy	C4	23
Loreto, Mex.	B2	63
Loreto, Para.	B3	55
Loreto, dept., Peru	B3	58
Loretta, Ks., U.S.	C4	93
Loretta, Wi., U.S.	C3	126
Lorette, Man.	C6	70
Loretteville, Que.	C6	74
Loretto, Ky., U.S.	C4	94
Loretto, Mi., U.S.	C3	99
Loretto, Ne., U.S.	C3	104
Loretto, Pa., U.S.	F4	115
Loretto, Tn., U.S.	B4	119
Lorica, Col.	B2	60
Lorida, Fl., U.S.	E5	86
Lorient, Fr.	D2	16
L'Orignal, Ont.	B10	73
Lorimor, Ia., U.S.	C3	92
Loring, Mt., U.S.	B9	103
Loring Air Force Base, mil., Me., U.S.	B5	96
Loris, S.C., U.S.	C10	117
Lorlie, Sask.	G4	75
Lorman, Ms., U.S.	D2	101
Lorn, Firth of, est., Scot., U.K.	B3	10
Lorne, N.B.	B3	71
Lorneville, Ont.	C5	73
Lorquin, Fr.	F6	16
Lörrach, W. Ger.	E3	18
Lorraine, Il., U.S.	D5	93
Lorraine, N.Y., U.S.	B5	109
Lorraine, hist. reg., Fr.	C6	16
Lorraine Plateau, plat., Fr.	D3	19
Lorsch, W. Ger.	D3	19
Lorton, Va., U.S.	*B5	123
Lorup, W. Ger.	B7	17
Los Alamitos, Ca., U.S.	*F5	82
Los Alamos, Ca., U.S.	*E3	82
Los Alamos, N.M., U.S.	B3	108
Los Alamos, co., N.M., U.S.	B3	108
Los Altos, Ca., U.S.	k8	82
Los Altos Hills, Ca., U.S.	*k8	82
Los Amates, Guat.	D7	63
Los Andes, Chile	A2	54
Los Ángeles, Chile	B2	54
Los Ángeles, Ca., U.S.	E4	82
Los Angeles, co., Ca., U.S.	E4	82
Los Angeles Aqueduct, Ca., U.S.	E4	82
Losantville, In., U.S.	D7	91
Los Banos, Ca., U.S.	D3	82
Los Blancos, Arg.	A3	54
Loup City, Ne., U.S.	C6	104
Los Cerrillos, Arg.	A3	54
Los Ebanos, Tx., U.S.	F3	120
Los Fresnos, Tx., U.S.	F4	120
Los Gatos, Ca., U.S.	k8	82
Los Hermanos, Islas, is., Ven.	A5	60
Lošinj, i., Yugo.	C2	23
Los Lagos, Chile	B2	54
Los Lagos, prov., Chile	C2	54
Los Lunas, N.M., U.S.	C3	108
Los Mochis, Mex.	B3	63
Los Molinos, Ca., U.S.	B2	82
Los Monjes, Islas, is., Ven.	A3	60
Los Nietos, Ca., U.S.	*n12	82
Los Ojos, N.M., U.S.	A3	108
Losombo, Zaire	A3	48
Los Osos, Ca., U.S.	*E3	82
Los Padillas, N.M., U.S.	*B3	108
Los Palacios, Cuba	C6	64
Los Palacios [y Villafranca], Spain	D3	22
Los Peares, Spain	A2	22
Los Pinos, N.M., U.S.	A3	108
Los Pinos, stm., Co., U.S.	D3	83
Los Ranchos de Albuquerque, N.M., U.S.	B3	108
Los Remedios, stm., Mex.	g9	63
Los Reyes [de Salgado], Mex.	D4	63
Los Reyes de La Paz, Mex.	h10	63
Los Ríos, prov., Ec.	B2	58
Los Roques, Islas, is., Ven.	A4	60
Los Santos, Pan.	G7	62
Los Santos [de Maimona], Spain	C2	22
Los Sarmientos, Arg.	E2	55
Los Sauces, Chile	B2	54
Lossiemouth, Scot., U.K.	C5	13
Lössnitz, E. Ger.	C12	19
Lost, stm., In., U.S.	G4	91
Lost, stm., Wa., U.S.	A5	124
Lost, stm., W.V., U.S.	B6	125
Lostant, Il., U.S.	B5	90
Los Taques, Ven.	A3	60
Lost City, W.V., U.S.	B6	125
Lost Creek, W.V., U.S.	B4	125
Lost Creek, stm., Ar., U.S.	C5	81
Lost Creek, stm., Wy., U.S.	D4	127
Los Teques, Ven.	A4	60
Los Testigos, Islas, is., Ven.	A5	60
Lost Hills, Ca., U.S.	E4	82
Lostine, Or., U.S.	B9	114
Lost Nation, Ia., U.S.	C7	92
Lost Peak, mtn., Ut., U.S.	F2	121
Lost Ranger Peak, mtn., Co., U.S.	A4	83
Lost River, Id., U.S.	F5	89
Lost River, W.V., U.S.	C6	125
Lost River Glacial Caverns, N.H., U.S.	B3	106
Lost River Range, mts., Id., U.S.	E5	89
Lost Springs, Ks., U.S.	D7	93
Lost Springs, Wy., U.S.	D8	127
Lost Trail Pass, U.S.	D5	89
Lost Vigiles, N.M., U.S.	*B4	108
Lotawana, Lake, res., Mo., U.S.	k11	102
Lotbinière, Que.	C6	74
Lotbinière, co., Que.	C6	74
Lothair, Mt., U.S.	B5	103
Lothian, prov., Scot., U.K.	E5	13
Loto, Zaire	B2	48
Lotofaga, W. Sam.	F12	52
Lötschberg Tunnel, Switz.	E3	18
Lott, Tx., U.S.	D4	120
Lotung, Tai.	G9	31
Louang Namtha, Laos	B4	35
Louangphrabang, Laos	B2	34
Louann, Ar., U.S.	D3	81
Loubomo, Congo	g8	125
Loudéac, Fr.	D3	16
Loudon, N.H., U.S.	D4	106
Loudon, Tn., U.S.	D9	119
Loudon, co., Tn., U.S.	D9	119
Loudonville, N.Y., U.S.	*C7	109
Loudonville, Oh., U.S.	B3	112
Loudoun, co., Va., U.S.	A5	123
Loudun, Fr.	D4	16
Louga, Sen.	C1	45
Loughborough, Eng., U.K.	D6	10
Lougheed, Alta.	C4	23
Lougheed Island, i., N.W. Ter.	m31	66
Loughman, Fl., U.S.	D5	86
Loughrea, Ire.	D2	10
Loughros More Bay, b., Ire.	C3	11
Louin, Ms., U.S.	C4	101
Louisa, Ky., U.S.	B7	94
Louisa, Va., U.S.	C5	123
Louisa, co., Ia., U.S.	C6	92
Louisa, co., Va., U.S.	C5	123
Louisa, Lake, l., Fl., U.S.	D5	86
Louisbourg, N.S.	D10	71
Louisburg, Ks., U.S.	D9	93
Louisburg, Mn., U.S.	E2	100
Louisburg, Mo., U.S.	D4	102
Louisburg, N.C., U.S.	A4	110
Louisburgh, Ire.	D2	11
Louisdale, N.S.	D8	71
Louise, Ms., U.S.	C3	101
Louise, Tx., U.S.	E4	120
Louise, W.V., U.S.	f8	125
Louise, Lake, l., Ak., U.S.	f18	79
Louise Island, i., B.C.	C2	69
Louisiade Archipelago, is., Pap. N. Gui.	G9	6
Louisiana, Mo., U.S.	B6	102
Louisiana, state, U.S.	C3	95
Louisiana Point, c., La., U.S.	E2	95
Louis Trichardt, S. Afr.	D4	49
Louisville, Al., U.S.	D4	78
Louisville, Ga., U.S.	C4	87
Louisville, Il., U.S.	E5	90
Louisville, Ky., U.S.	B4	94
Louisville, Ms., U.S.	B4	101
Louisville, Ne., U.S.	D9	104
Louisville, N.Y., U.S.	f9	109
Louisville, Oh., U.S.	B4	112
Louisville, Tn., U.S.	D10	119
Louis-XIV, Pointe, c., Que.	h11	74
Loukhi, Sov. Un.	D15	14
Loulé, Port.	D1	22
Louny, Czech.	C2	26
Loup, co., Ne., U.S.	C6	104
Loup, stm., Ne., U.S.	C8	104
Loup, Île au, i., Que.	B8	71
Loup, Rivière du, stm., Que.	C4	74
Loup, Rivière du, stm., Que.	B8	74
Lourdes, Newf.	D2	72
Lourdes, Fr.	F3	16
Lourdes, Que.	C6	74
Lourenço Marques see Maputo, Moz.	C5	49
Loures, Port.	B1	22
Louros, stm., Grc.	B2	24
Lousã, Port.	E3	22
Louth, Ire.	C4	11
Louth, Eng., U.K.	D7	10
Louth, co., Ire.	D5	11
Loutrá Aidhipsoú, Grc.	*n12	24
Loutrákion, Grc.	h9	25
Loutre, Bayou de, stm., La., U.S.	B3	95
Louvain see Leuven, Bel.	D4	17
Louvale, Ga., U.S.	D2	87
Louviers, Co., U.S.	B6	83
Louviers, Fr.	C4	16
Lovászi, Hung.	I7	32
Love, Sask.	D3	75
Love, co., Ok., U.S.	D4	113
Lovech, Bul.	D7	24
Lovelaceville, Ky., U.S.	f9	94
Loveladies, N.J., U.S.	D4	107
Lovelady, Tx., U.S.	D5	120
Loveland, Co., U.S.	A5	83
Loveland, Ia., U.S.	C2	92
Loveland, Oh., U.S.	C1	112
Loveland Park, Oh., U.S.	C1	112
Loveland Pass, Co., U.S.	B5	83
Lovell, Me., U.S.	D2	96
Lovell, Wy., U.S.	B4	127
Lovells, Mi., U.S.	D6	99
Lovelock, Nv., U.S.	C3	105
Lovely, Ky., U.S.	C7	94
Lovenia, Mount, mtn., Ut., U.S.	C5	121
Love Point, c., Md., U.S.	B5	97
Loverna, Sask.	F1	75
Loves Park, Il., U.S.	A4	90
Lovett, Ga., U.S.	D4	87
Lovett, In., U.S.	G6	91
Lovettsville, Va., U.S.	A5	123
Lovewell Pond, l., Me., U.S.	D2	96
Lovick, Al., U.S.	f7	78
Lovilia, Ia., U.S.	C5	92
Loving, N.M., U.S.	E5	108
Loving, co., Tx., U.S.	D1	120
Lovingston, Va., U.S.	C4	123
Lovington, Il., U.S.	D5	90
Lovington, N.M., U.S.	E6	108
Lovosice, Czech.	C9	19
Low, Que.	D2	74
Lowa, Zaire	B4	48
Lowa, stm., Zaire	B5	48
Lowden, Ia., U.S.	C7	92
Low Farm, Man.	E3	70
Lowell, Ar., U.S.	A1	81
Lowell, In., U.S.	B3	91
Lowell, Ma., U.S.	A5	98
Lowell, Mi., U.S.	F5	99
Lowell, N.C., U.S.	B1	110
Lowell, Oh., U.S.	C4	112
Lowell, Or., U.S.	D4	114
Lowell, Vt., U.S.	B4	122
Lowell, W.V., U.S.	C4	125
Lowell, Wi., U.S.	E5	126
Lowell, Lake, res., Id., U.S.	F2	89
Lowell Mountains, mts., Vt., U.S.	B4	122
Lowellville, Oh., U.S.	A5	112
Lower Arrow Lake, res., B.C.	E8	69
Lower Bank, N.J., U.S.	D3	107
Lower Brule, S.D., U.S.	C6	118
Lower Brule Indian Reservation, S.D., U.S.	C6	118
Lower Burrell, Pa., U.S.	*h15	115
Lower Cabot, Vt., U.S.	C4	122
Lower California, pen., Mex.	B2	63
Lower East Pubnico, N.S.	F4	71
Lower Hutt, N.Z.	N15	51
Lower Island Cove, Newf.	D5	72
Lower Klamath Lake, l., Ca., U.S.	B3	82
Lower Loch Erne, l., N. Ire., U.K.	C3	10
Lower Manitou Lake, l., Ont.	E5	70
Lower Marlboro, Md., U.S.	C4	97
Lower Matecumbe Key, i., Fl., U.S.	H6	86
Lower Merion Township, Pa., U.S.	*F11	115
Lower Monumental Lake, res., Wa., U.S.	C7	124
Lower Moreland Township, Pa., U.S.	*F11	115
Lower New York Bay, b., N.J., U.S.	B4	107
Lower Otay Reservoir, res., Ca., U.S.	o16	82
Lower Paia, Hi., U.S.	C5	88
Lower Peach Tree, Al., U.S.	D2	78
Lower Red Lake, l., Mn., U.S.	C3	100
Lower Rice Lake, l., Mn., U.S.	C3	100
Lower Salem, Oh., U.S.	C4	112
Lower Salmon Dam, Id., U.S.	G4	89
Lower Southampton Township, Pa., U.S.	*G11	115
Lower Village, Vt., U.S.	*C3	122
Lower West Pubnico, N.S.	F4	71
Lower Wilson Pond, l., Me., U.S.	C3	96
Lower Woods Harbour, N.S.	f9	94
Lowes, Ky., U.S.	f9	94
Lowestoft, Eng., U.K.	D7	10
Łowicz, Pol.	B5	26
Lowland, N.C., U.S.	B6	110
Lowman, Id., U.S.	E3	89
Lowmansville, Ky., U.S.	C7	94
Low Moor, Ia., U.S.	C7	92
Lowmoor, Va., U.S.	C3	123
Lowndes, co., Al., U.S.	C3	78
Lowndes, co., Ga., U.S.	F3	87
Lowndes, co., Ms., U.S.	B5	101
Lowndesboro, Al., U.S.	C3	78
Lowndesville, S.C., U.S.	C2	117
Lowry, Mn., U.S.	E3	100
Lowry, S.D., U.S.	B6	118
Lowry Air Force Base, mil., Co., U.S.	B6	83
Lowry City, Mo., U.S.	C4	102
Lowrys, S.C., U.S.	B5	117
Low Tatra Mountains, mts., Czech.	D5	26
Loxley, Al., U.S.	E2	78
Loxton, Austl.	G3	51
Loyal, Ok., U.S.	B3	113
Loyal, Wi., U.S.	D3	126
Loyalist, Alta.	D5	68
Loyall, Ky., U.S.	D6	94
Loyalsock Creek, stm., Pa., U.S.	D8	115
Loyalton, Ca., U.S.	C3	82
Loyalty Islands, is., N. Cal.	H10	6
Loysburg, Pa., U.S.	F5	115
Loysville, Pa., U.S.	F7	115
Loznica, Yugo.	C4	24
Lozova, Sov. Un.	G9	27
Lozovaya, Sov. Un.	G11	27
Lozoya, Canal of, Spain	o17	22
Lu'an, China	I7	32
Luana, stm., Sov. Un.	A6	92
Luanda, Ang.	C1	48
Luanda, Braz.	C2	56
Luanda, dept., Ang.	C1	48
Luang Chiang Dao, mtn., Thai.	C3	35
Luanguinga, stm., Afr.	D5	48
Luangwa, stm., Afr.	D5	48
Luan He, stm., China	C8	31
Luanshya, Zam.	D5	48
Luanxian, China	E8	32
Luapula, prov., Zam.	D4	48
Luarca, Spain	A2	22
Luashi, Zaire	D3	48
Luau, Ang.	D4	48
Luba, Eq. Gui.	E1	46
Lubang, Phil.	p13	34
Lubang, i., Phil.	p13	34
Lubang Islands, is., Phil.	C6	34
Lubango, Ang.	D1	48
Lubartów, Pol.	C7	26
Lubawa, Pol.	B5	26
Lübbecke, W. Ger.	A3	19
Lübben, E. Ger.	C6	19

Name	Map Ref.	Page
Lübbenau, E. Ger.	B8	19
Lubbock, Tx., U.S.	C2	120
Lubbock, co., Tx., U.S.	C2	120
Lubec, Me., U.S.	D6	96
Lübeck, W. Ger.	B5	18
Lübeck Bay, b., Eur.	A5	18
Lubefu, Zaire	B3	48
Lubero, Zaire	B4	48
Lubicon Lake, l., Alta.	A3	68
Lubilash, stm., Zaire	C3	48
Lublin, Pol.	C4	26
Lubliniec, Pol.	C5	26
Lubny, Sov. Un.	F9	27
Luboń, Pol.	B4	26
Lubsko, Pol.	C3	26
Lübtheen, E. Ger.	E5	15
Lubudi, Zaire	C4	48
Lubudi, stm., Zaire	C3	48
Lubue, Zaire	B2	48
Lubumbashi (Élisabethville), Zaire	D4	48
Lubutu, Zaire	B4	48
Lucama, N.C., U.S.	B4	110
Lucan, Ont.	D3	73
Lucan, Ire.	D5	11
Lucan, Mn., U.S.	F3	100
Lucania, Mount, mtn., Yukon	D4	66
Lucas, Ia., U.S.	C4	92
Lucas, Ks., U.S.	C5	93
Lucas, Ky., U.S.	D3	94
Lucas, Mi., U.S.	D5	99
Lucas, Oh., U.S.	B3	112
Lucas, S.D., U.S.	D6	118
Lucas, co., Ia., U.S.	C4	92
Lucas, co., Oh., U.S.	A2	112
Lucasville, Oh., U.S.	D3	112
Lucca, Italy	C3	23
Lucé, Fr.	C4	16
Luce, co., Mi., U.S.	B5	99
Lucea, Jam.	E4	64
Luce Bay, b., Scot., U.K.	C4	10
Lucedale, Ms., U.S.	E5	101
Lucena, Phil.	C6	34
Lucena, Spain	D3	22
Lucena del Cid, Spain	B5	22
Lučenec, Czech.	D5	26
Lucera, Italy	D5	23
Lucerne, Ca., U.S.	C2	82
Lucerne, Co., U.S.	A6	83
Lucerne, In., U.S.	C5	91
Lucerne, Mo., U.S.	A4	102
Lucerne, Lake of, l., Switz.	E4	18
Lucernemines, Pa., U.S.	E3	115
Lucerne Valley, Ca., U.S.	E5	82
Luceville, Que.	A9	74
Luchou see Luzhou, China	F6	31
Lüchow, W. Ger.	F5	15
Luchuan, China		
Lucien, La., U.S.	D3	101
Lucien, Ok., U.S.	A4	113
Lucile, Id., U.S.	D2	89
Lucille, Al., U.S.	B2	78
Lucinda, Pa., U.S.	D2	115
Lucipara Islands, is., Indon.	G7	34
Lucira, Ang.	D1	48
Luck, Wi., U.S.	C1	126
Luckau, E. Ger.	B6	18
Luckenwalde, E. Ger.	A2	112
Luckey, Oh., U.S.	A2	112
Luck Lake, l., Sask.	G2	75
Lucknow, Ont.	D3	73
Lucknow, India	C7	36
Lucky Lake, Sask.	G2	75
Lucky MacCamp, Wy., U.S.	*D5	127
Lucky Peak Lake, res., Id., U.S.	F3	89
Luçon, Fr.	D3	16
Lucrecia, Cabo, c., Cuba	D6	64
Lucy, La., U.S.	h10	95
Lucy, Tn., U.S.	B2	119
Lüda see Dalian, China	D9	31
Luda Kamchiya, stm., Bul.	D8	24
Ludden, N.D., U.S.	C7	111
Ludell, Ks., U.S.	C3	93
Lüdenscheid, W. Ger.	C3	18
Ludgate, Ont.	B4	73
Ludhiāna, India	B6	36
Luding, China	F5	31
Lüdinghausen, W. Ger.	B2	19
Ludington, Mi., U.S.	E4	99
Ludlow, N.B.	C3	71
Ludlow, Eng., U.K.	D5	10
Ludlow, Il., U.S.	C5	90
Ludlow, Ky., U.S.	h13	94
Ludlow, Me., U.S.	B4	96
Ludlow, Ma., U.S.	B3	98
Ludlow, Mo., U.S.	B4	102
Ludlow, Pa., U.S.	C4	115
Ludlow, S.D., U.S.	B2	118
Ludlow, Vt., U.S.	E3	122
Ludlow Falls, Oh., U.S.	B1	112
Ludlow Mountain, mtn., Vt., U.S.	E3	122
Ludowici, Ga., U.S.	E5	87
Ludvika, Swe.	G6	14
Ludwigsburg, W. Ger.	D4	18
Ludwigshafen [am Rhein], W. Ger.	D4	18
Ludwigslust, E. Ger.	B5	18
Luebo, Zaire	C4	48
Lueders, Tx., U.S.	C3	120
Luena, Ang.	D2	48
Luepa, Ven.	B5	60
Lüeyang, China	H2	32
Lufkin, Tx., U.S.	D5	120
Luga, Sov. Un.	B7	27
Luga, stm., Sov. Un.	B7	27
Lugagnano Val d'Arda, Italy	E5	20
Lugan, stm., Sov. Un.	q22	27
Luganchik, stm., Sov. Un.	q22	27
Lugano, Switz.	E4	18
Lugano, Lake, l., Eur.	E7	21
Lugau, E. Ger.	C7	18
Lugenda, stm., Moz.	D6	48
Lugnaquillia Mountain, mtn., Ire.	D3	10
Lugo, Italy	B3	23
Lugo, Spain	A2	22
Lugoff, S.C., U.S.	C6	117
Lugoj, Rom.	C5	24
Lugovoy, Sov. Un.	E8	28
Luhuo, China	E5	31
Luiana, Ang.	E3	48
Luidhorn, Neth.	A6	17
Luik see Liège, Bel.	B6	16
Luing, i., Scot., U.K.	D3	13
Luís Correia, Braz.	D10	54
Luís Gomes, Braz.	E3	57
Luís Lopez, N.M., U.S.	D3	108
Luiza, Zaire	C3	48
Lujuna Point, c., Guam	L10	52
Lukachukai, Az., U.S.	A6	80
Luke, Md., U.S.	m12	97
Luke Air Force Base, mil., Az., U.S.	D3	80
Lukenie, stm., Zaire	B2	48
Lukeville, Az., U.S.	F3	80
Lukolela, Zaire	B2	48
Lukovit, Bul.	D7	24
Łuków, Pol.	C7	26
Lukoyanov, Sov. Un.	D15	27
Lukuga, stm., Zaire	C4	48
Lukulu, Zam.	D3	48
Lula, Ga., U.S.	B3	87
Lula, Ms., U.S.	A3	101
Lula, Wi., U.S.	C5	113
Luleå, Swe.	D9	14
Luleälven, stm., Swe.	D9	14
Lüleburgaz, Tur.	B6	40
Luling, La., U.S.	k11	95
Luling, Tx., U.S.	E4	120
Lulong, China	D8	31
Lulu, Fl., U.S.	B4	86
Lulua, stm., Zaire	C3	48
Luluabourg see Kananga, Zaire	C3	48
Lum, Mi., U.S.	E7	99
Lumba, Zaire	A2	48
Lumbala N'guimbo, Ang.	D3	48
Lumber, stm., U.S.	C9	117
Lumber Bridge, N.C., U.S.	C3	110
Lumber City, Ga., U.S.	E4	87
Lumberport, W.V., U.S.	B4	125
Lumberton, Ms., U.S.	D4	101
Lumberton, N.J., U.S.	D3	107
Lumberton, N.M., U.S.	A3	108
Lumberton, N.C., U.S.	C3	110
Lumberton, Moz.	E7	48
Lumby, B.C.	D8	69
Lumby, Swe.	t34	14
Lumsden, Newf.	D5	72
Lumsden, Sask.	G3	75
Lumsden, N.Z.	P12	51
Lumsden, Sask.	C6	13
Lumsden Beach, Sask.	G3	75
Luna, N.M., U.S.	D1	108
Luna, co., N.M., U.S.	E2	108
Luna Pier, Mi., U.S.	G7	99
Lund, Swe.	J5	14
Lund, Nv., U.S.	E6	105
Lund, i., Eng., U.K.	n12	125
Lunda Norte, dept., Ang.	C2	48
Lunda Sul, dept., Ang.	D3	48
Lundazi, Zam.	D5	48
Lundbreck, Alta.	E3	68
Lundby, Den.	C5	15
Lundby, Swe.	t34	14
Lunderskov, Den.	C3	15
Lundu, Malay.	E3	34
Lundy, i., Eng., U.K.	E4	10
Lune, stm., Eng., U.K.	F6	13
Lünen, W. Ger.	B5	18
Lüneburg, W. Ger.	F6	16
Lunenburg, N.S.	E5	71
Lunenburg, Ma., U.S.	A4	98
Lunenburg, Vt., U.S.	C5	122
Lunenburg, Va., U.S.	D4	123
Lunenburg, co., N.S.	E5	71
Lunenburg, co., Va., U.S.	D4	123
Lunéville, Fr.	C7	16
Lungi, S.L.	E2	45
Lungué-Bungo, stm., Afr.	D3	48
Lūni, stm., India	C5	36
Lunino, Sov. Un.	E15	27
Lunsar, S.L.	E2	45
Luochuan, China	D6	31
Luoding, China	A9	35
Luohe, China	E7	31
Luoning, China	G4	32
Luoshan, China	H6	32
Luoyang, China	E7	31
Luozi, Zaire	B1	48
Lupani, Zimb.	A4	49
Lupeni, Rom.	C6	24
Lupton, Az., U.S.	B6	80
Lupton, Mi., U.S.	D6	99
Lupus, Mo., U.S.	C5	102
Luque, Para.	B5	56
Luquillo, Sierra de, mts., P.R.	E4	65
Lūrah, stm., Afg.	C5	36
Luray, Ks., U.S.	C5	93
Luray, Mo., U.S.	A6	102
Luray, S.C., U.S.	F5	117
Luray, Tn., U.S.	B3	119
Luray, Va., U.S.	B4	123
Lure, Fr.	D7	16
Lure, Lake, l., N.C., U.S.	f10	110
Lurgan, N. Ire., U.K.	C3	10
Luribay, Bol.	C2	55
Lúrio, Moz.	D7	48
Lúrio, stm., Moz.	D6	48
Lurton, Ar., U.S.	B2	81
Lusaka, Zam.	E4	48
Lusaka, prov., Zam.	E4	48
Lusako, Zaire	B4	48
Lusambo, Zaire	B3	48
Lusby, Md., U.S.	D5	97
Luscar, Alta.	C2	68
Luseland, Sask.	E1	75
Lushan, China	H5	32
Lushan, China	F8	32
Lushnja, Alb.	D3	24
Lushoto, Tan.	B6	48
Lushton, Ne., U.S.	D8	104
Lüshun, China	D9	31
Lusignan, Fr.	D4	16
Lusk, Wy., U.S.	D8	127
Lustre, Mt., U.S.	B11	103
Lüt, Dasht-e, des., Iran	B5	38
Lutcher, La., U.S.	D5	95
Lutesville, Mo., U.S.	D8	102
Luther, Mi., U.S.	D5	99
Luther, Ia., U.S.	E7	13
Luther, Ok., U.S.	B4	113
Luthersville, Ga., U.S.	C2	87
Lutherville-Timonium, Md., U.S.	B5	97
Lutie, Ok., U.S.	C6	113
Lütjenburg, W. Ger.	A2	18
Luton, Eng., U.K.	E6	10
Luton, Ia., U.S.	B1	92
Lutong, Malay.	E4	34
Lutsen, Mn., U.S.	k9	100
Lutsk, Sov. Un.	F5	27
Luttrell, Tn., U.S.	C10	119
Lutts, Tn., U.S.	B4	119
Lutugino, Sov. Un.	q22	27
Lutz, Fl., U.S.	D4	86
Lützow-Holm Bay, b., Ant.	C16	7
Luuq, Som.	E5	47
Luverne, Al., U.S.	D3	78
Luverne, Ia., U.S.	B3	92
Luverne, Mn., U.S.	G2	100
Luverne, N.D., U.S.	B8	111
Luvua, stm., Zaire	C4	48
Luwingu, Zam.	D4	48
Luwuk, Indon.	F6	34
Luxapallila Creek, stm., U.S.	B5	101
Luxembourg, Lux.	C7	16
Luxembourg, prov., Bel.	E5	17
Luxembourg, ctry., Eur.	C7	16
Luxemburg, Ia., U.S.	B6	92
Luxemburg, Wi., U.S.	D6	126
Luxeuil-les-Bains, Fr.	D7	16
Luxi, China	F7	31
Luxomni, Ga., U.S.	h8	87
Luxor (Al Uqşur), Eg.	C3	38
Luxor, hist., Egypt	D6	43
Luxora, Ar., U.S.	B6	81
Luz, Braz.	B3	56
Luza, Sov. Un.	A3	28
Luza, stm., Sov. Un.	A3	28
Lvov, Sov. Un.	E5	29
Lyakhov Islands, is., Sov. Un.	B18	128
Lyall, Mount, mtn., N.Z.	P11	51
Lyallpur see Faisalabad, Pak.	B5	36
Lyaskovets, Bul.	D7	24
Lybster, Scot., U.K.	B5	13
Lychen, E. Ger.	E7	15
Lycksele, Swe.	E8	14
Lycoming, N.Y., U.S.	B4	109
Lycoming, co., Pa., U.S.	D7	115
Lycoming Creek, stm., Pa., U.S.	D7	115
Lydenburg, S. Afr.	C5	49
Lydia, Mn., U.S.	F5	100
Lydia, S.C., U.S.	C7	117
Lyell, Mount, mtn., Can.	D2	68
Lyell Island, i., B.C.	C2	69
Lyerly, Ga., U.S.	B1	87
Lyford, Tx., U.S.	F4	120
Lygnern, l., Swe.	A6	15
Lykens, Pa., U.S.	E8	115
Lyle, Mn., U.S.	G6	100
Lyle, Wa., U.S.	D4	124
Lyles, Tn., U.S.	B4	119
Lyleton, Man.	E1	70
Lyman, Ms., U.S.	E4	101
Lyman, Ne., U.S.	C1	104
Lyman, S.C., U.S.	B3	117
Lyman, Ut., U.S.	E4	121
Lyman, Wy., U.S.	E2	127
Lyman, co., S.D., U.S.	D6	118
Lyman Lake, res., Az., U.S.	C6	80
Lyme, Ct., U.S.	D6	84
Lyme, N.H., U.S.	C2	106
Lyme Bay, b., Eng., U.K.	D5	12
Lyme Center, N.H., U.S.	C2	106
Lymington, Eng., U.K.	D6	12
Lynbrook, N.Y., U.S.	*E7	109
Lynch, Ky., U.S.	D7	94
Lynch, Md., U.S.	B5	97
Lynch, Ne., U.S.	B7	104
Lynchburg, N.D., U.S.	C8	111
Lynchburg, Oh., U.S.	C2	112
Lynchburg, S.C., U.S.	C7	117
Lynchburg, Tn., U.S.	B5	119
Lynchburg, Va., U.S.	C3	123
Lynches, stm., S.C., U.S.	D8	117
Lynch Heights, De., U.S.	E4	85
Lynch Station, Va., U.S.	C3	123
Lynd, Mn., U.S.	F3	100
Lyndeborough, N.H., U.S.	E3	106
Lynden, Wa., U.S.	A3	124
Lynde Point, c., Ct., U.S.	D6	84
Lyndhurst, Ont.	C8	73
Lyndhurst, N.J., U.S.	h8	107
Lyndhurst, Oh., U.S.	g10	112
Lyndon, Il., U.S.	B4	90
Lyndon, Ks., U.S.	D8	93
Lyndon, Ky., U.S.	g11	94
Lyndon, Vt., U.S.	B4	122
Lyndon B. Johnson National Historical Site, hist., Tx., U.S.	D3	120
Lyndon B. Johnson Space Center, sci., Tx., U.S.	r14	120
Lyndon Center, Vt., U.S.	B4	122
Lyndon Station, Wi., U.S.	E4	126
Lyndonville, N.Y., U.S.	B2	109
Lyndonville, Vt., U.S.	B4	122
Lyndora, Pa., U.S.	E2	115
Lyngby [-Tårbæk], Den.	C6	15
Lynn, Al., U.S.	A2	78
Lynn, Ar., U.S.	A4	81
Lynn, In., U.S.	D8	91
Lynn, Ma., U.S.	B6	98
Lynn, Pa., U.S.	C10	115
Lynn, co., Tx., U.S.	C2	120
Lynn, Lake, res., W.V., U.S.	B5	125
Lynn Canal, b., Ak., U.S.	k22	79
Lynndyl, Ut., U.S.	D3	121
Lynne Acres, Md., U.S.	*B4	97
Lynnfield, Ma., U.S.	f11	98
Lynn Garden, Tn., U.S.	C11	119
Lynn Grove, Ky., U.S.	f9	94
Lynnhaven Roads, b., Va., U.S.	k15	123
Lynn Lake, Man.	A1	70
Lynnport, Pa., U.S.	E10	115
Lynnville, In., U.S.	H3	91
Lynnville, Ia., U.S.	C5	92
Lynnville, Ky., U.S.	f9	94
Lynnville, Tn., U.S.	B4	119
Lynnwood, Wa., U.S.	B3	124
Lynton, Eng., U.K.	E4	10
Lynwood, Ca., U.S.	n12	82
Lynxville, Wi., U.S.	E2	126
Lyon, co., Ia., U.S.	A1	92
Lyon, co., Ks., U.S.	D7	93
Lyon, co., Ky., U.S.	C1	94
Lyon, co., Mn., U.S.	F3	100
Lyon, co., Nv., U.S.	D2	105
Lyon, stm., Scot., U.K.	C5	8
Lyon Creek, stm., Ks., U.S.	D7	93
Lyon Mountain, N.Y., U.S.	f11	109
Lyon Mountain, mtn., N.Y., U.S.	f11	109
Lyonnais, hist. reg., Fr.	E6	16
Lyons, Co., U.S.	A5	83
Lyons, Ga., U.S.	D4	87
Lyons, Il., U.S.	k9	90
Lyons, In., U.S.	G3	91
Lyons, Ks., U.S.	D5	93
Lyons, Mi., U.S.	F6	99
Lyons, Ne., U.S.	C9	104
Lyons, N.Y., U.S.	B3	109
Lyons, Oh., U.S.	A1	112
Lyons, Or., U.S.	C4	114
Lyons, S.D., U.S.	D9	118
Lyons, Tx., U.S.	D4	120
Lyons Falls, N.Y., U.S.	B5	109
Lyons Plains, Ct., U.S.	E2	84
Lyracrumpane, Ire.	E2	11
Lys, stm., Eur.	D3	17
Lysá [nad Labem], Czech.	n18	26
Lysaya Gora, Sov. Un.	G8	27
Lysekil, Swe.	H4	14
Lysite, Wy., U.S.	C5	127
Lyss, Switz.	B3	21
Lysva, Sov. Un.	D8	29
Lytham Saint Anne's, Eng., U.K.	A5	12
Lytle, Oh., U.S.	C1	112
Lytle, Tx., U.S.	E3	120
Lytton, B.C.	D7	69
Lytton, Ia., U.S.	B3	92
Lyubar, Sov. Un.	G6	27
Lyubertsy, Sov. Un.	n17	27
Lyudinovo, Sov. Un.	E10	27

M

Name	Map Ref.	Page
Ma, stm., Asia	A2	34
Ma'ād, Jord.	B7	41
Maalaea, Hi., U.S.	*C5	88
Maalaea Bay, b., Hi., U.S.	C5	88
Ma'alot-Tarshiha, Isr.	B7	41
Maam Cross, Ire.	D2	11
Maamoura, Cap, c., Tun.	F3	23
Ma'ān, Jord.	G10	40
Ma'anshan, China	*E8	31
Ma'arrat an Nu'mān, Syria	*E11	40
Maas, Ire.	C3	11
Maas (Meuse), stm., Eur.	B6	16
Maaseik, Bel.	C5	17
Maastricht, Neth.	B6	16
Mabalacat, Phil.	o13	34
Mabana, Wa., U.S.	A3	124
Mabank, Tx., U.S.	C4	120
Mabaruma, Guy.	A3	59
Mabber, Ras, c., Som.	D7	47
Mabel, Mn., U.S.	G7	100
Mabel Lake, l., B.C.	D8	69
Mabelvale, Ar., U.S.	k10	81
Maben, Ms., U.S.	B4	101
Mabie, W.V., U.S.	C5	125
Mableton, Ga., U.S.	h7	87
Mablethorpe, Eng., U.K.	A8	12
Mabote, Moz.	B5	49
Mabou, N.S.	C8	71
Mabrous Tafidinga, well, Niger	B7	45
Mabscott, W.V., U.S.	D3	125
Mabton, Wa., U.S.	C5	124
Mabuni, Japan	O5	52
Macachin, Arg.	B4	54
Macaé, Braz.	C4	56
Macaíba, Braz.	g6	57
Macajuba, Braz.	B4	56
Macaloge, Phil.	p14	34
Macalester, B.C.	C6	69
MacAlpine Lake, l., N.W. Ter.	C12	66
Macan Islands, is., Indon.	G6	34
Macao, dep., Asia	C9	31
Macapá, Braz.	B4	59
Macará, Ec.	B2	58
Macas, Ec.	B2	58
Macau, Braz.	C3	57
Macaúbas, Braz.	A4	56
Maccagno [Superiore], Italy	D6	21
Maccan, N.S.	D5	71
Maccarese, Italy	h8	23
MacClenny, Fl., U.S.	B4	86
Macclesfield, Eng., U.K.	D5	10
Macclesfield, N.C., U.S.	B5	110
Macculloch, Cape, c., N.W. Ter.	B18	66
MacDill Air Force Base, mil., Fl., U.S.	E4	86
Macdonald, Man.	D2	70
Macdonald, W.V., U.S.	D3	125
Macdonald, Lake, l., Austl.	D4	50
Macdonald Range, mts., B.C.	E10	69
Macdonaldton, Pa., U.S.	G4	115
Macdonnell Ranges, mts., Austl.	D5	50
McDowell Reservoir, res., N.H., U.S.	E2	106
Macduff, Scot., U.K.	C6	13
Macdui, Ben, mtn., Scot., U.K.	B4	10
Mace, In., U.S.	D4	91
Macedon, N.Y., U.S.	B3	109
Macedonia, Il., U.S.	E5	90
Macedonia, Oh., U.S.	A4	112
Macedonia, hist. reg., Eur.	B4	25
Maceió, Braz.	D3	57
Macenta, Gui.	E3	45
Maceo, Ky., U.S.	C3	94
Macerata, Italy	C4	23
Maces Bay, b., N.B.	D3	71
Macfarlan, W.V., U.S.	B3	125
Macgillycuddy's Reeks, mts., Ire.	E2	10
MacGregor, Man.	B4	56
Machacalis, Braz.	B4	56
Machachi, Ec.	*C3	56
Machakos, Kenya	B6	48
Machala, Ec.	B2	58
Machattie, Lake, l., Austl.	L10	52
Macheng, China	*A4	90
Machesney Park, Il., U.S.	*A4	90
Machias, Me., U.S.	D5	96
Machias, N.Y., U.S.	C2	109
Machias, stm., Me., U.S.	D5	96
Machias Bay, b., Me., U.S.	D5	96
Machias Lakes, l., Me., U.S.	C5	96
Machiasport, Me., U.S.	D5	96
Machichi, stm., Man.	A6	70
Machico, Port.	h12	22
Machida, Japan	*I9	33
Machilipatnam, India	E7	36
Machiques, Ven.	A3	60
Macho, Arroyo del, val., N.M., U.S.	C4	108
Machrihanish, Scot., U.K.	E3	13
Machu Picchu, hist., Peru	D3	58
Machynlleth, Wales, U.K.	B4	12
Macia, Moz.	C5	49
Măcin, Rom.	C9	24
Macina, reg., Mali	A4	45
Macintyre, stm., Austl.	D7	51
Mack, Co., U.S.	B2	83
Mackay, Austl.	D8	50
Mackay, Id., U.S.	F5	89
MacKay, stm., Alta.	A4	68
Mackay, Lake, l., Austl.	D4	50
MacKay Lake, l., N.W. Ter.	D10	66
Mackenzie, B.C.	B6	69
Mackenzie, Guy.	A3	59
Mackenzie, dept., N.W. Ter.	D11	66
Mackenzie, stm., N.W. Ter.	C6	66
MacKenzie Bay, b., Ant.	C20	7
Mackenzie Bay, b., Can.	C5	66
Mackenzie King Island, i., N.W. Ter.	m29	66
Mackenzie Mountains, mts., Can.	D7	66
Mackey, Ont.	A7	73
Mackey, In., U.S.	H3	91
Mackeys, N.C., U.S.	B6	110
Mackeyville, Pa., U.S.	D7	115
Mackinac, co., Mi., U.S.	B5	99
Mackinac, Straits of, strt., Mi., U.S.	C6	99
Mackinac Bridge, Mi., U.S.	C6	99
Mackinac Island, Mi., U.S.	C6	99
Mackinac Island, i., Mi., U.S.	C6	99
Mackinaw, Il., U.S.	C4	90
Mackinaw, stm., Il., U.S.	C4	90
Mackinaw City, Mi., U.S.	C6	99
Mackinnon Road, Kenya	B6	48
Macksburg, Oh., U.S.	C4	112
Macks Creek, Mo., U.S.	D5	102
Macksville, Ks., U.S.	E5	93
Mackville, Ky., U.S.	C4	94
Mackville, Wi., U.S.	h9	126
Maclean, Austl.	D9	51
Maclean Strait, strt., N.W. Ter.	m31	66
Maclear, S. Afr.	D4	49
Macleod, Lake, l., Austl.	D1	50
MacNutt, Sask.	F5	75
Maco, Bol.	C2	
Macocolo, Ang.	C2	48
Macomb, Il., U.S.	C3	90
Macomb, Ok., U.S.	B5	113
Macomb, co., Mi., U.S.	F8	99
Mâcon, Fr.	D6	16
Macon, Ga., U.S.	D3	87
Macon, Il., U.S.	D5	90
Macon, Ms., U.S.	B5	101
Macon, Mo., U.S.	B5	102
Macon, Ne., U.S.	D7	104
Macon, N.C., U.S.	A4	110
Macon, Tn., U.S.	B2	119
Macon, co., Al., U.S.	C4	78
Macon, co., Ga., U.S.	D2	87
Macon, co., Il., U.S.	D5	90
Macon, co., Mo., U.S.	B5	102
Macon, co., N.C., U.S.	f9	110
Macon, co., Tn., U.S.	A5	119
Macon, Bayou, stm., U.S.	B4	95
Macoun, Sask.	H4	75
Macoun Lake, l., Sask.	A4	75
Macoupin, co., Il., U.S.	D4	90
Macoupin Creek, stm., Il., U.S.	D3	90
Macovane, Moz.	B6	49
Macquarie, stm., Austl.	F8	50
Macquarie Island, i., Austl.	J7	2
Macroom, Ire.	E2	10
Macrorie, Sask.	F2	75
MacTier, Ont.	B5	73
Macuelizo, Hond.	C3	62
Macungie, Pa., U.S.	E10	115
Macwahoc, Me., U.S.	C4	96
Macy, In., U.S.	C5	91
Macy, Ne., U.S.	B9	104
Mad, stm., Ct., U.S.	B3	84
Mad, stm., N.H., U.S.	C3	106
Mad, stm., Oh., U.S.	C2	112
Mad, stm., Vt., U.S.	C3	122
Ma'dabā, Jord.	C7	41
Madadi, Tan.	C6	48
Madagascar, ctry., Afr.	g9	49
Madā'in Şāliḥ, Sau. Ar.	D7	38
Madalena, Braz.	C4	56
Madame, Isle, i., N.S.	D9	71
Madang, Pap. N. Gui.	k12	50
Madaoua, Niger	D6	45
Madawaska, Ont.	B7	73
Madawaska, Me., U.S.	A4	96
Madawaska, stm., N.B.	B9	74
Madawaska, stm., Ont.	B9	74
Madawaska Lake, l., Me., U.S.	A4	96
Madaya, Burma	A2	35
Madbury, N.H., U.S.	D5	106
Madden, Ms., U.S.	C4	101
Maddock, N.D., U.S.	B6	111
Maddox, Md., U.S.	D5	97
Madeira, Oh., U.S.	o13	112
Madeira, stm., S.A.	D2	59
Madeira Islands, is., Port.	m11	20a
Madeleine, Îles de la, is., Que.	B8	71
Madeline, Ca., U.S.	B3	82
Madeline Island, i., Wi., U.S.	B3	126
Madera, Mex.	B3	63
Madera, Ca., U.S.	D4	82
Madera, co., Ca., U.S.	D4	82
Madera, Pa., U.S.	E5	115
Madge Lake, l., Sask.	D1	70
Madhupur, India	E11	37
Madhya Pradesh, state, India	D6	36
Madill, Ok., U.S.	C5	113
Madimba, Zaire	C2	48
Madīnat ash Sha'b, Yemen	B1	48
Madingou, Congo	B1	48
Madison, Sask.	F1	75
Madison, Al., U.S.	A3	78
Madison, Ar., U.S.	B5	81
Madison, Ca., U.S.	C3	82
Madison, Fl., U.S.	B3	86
Madison, Ga., U.S.	C3	87
Madison, Il., U.S.	E3	90
Madison, In., U.S.	G7	91
Madison, Ks., U.S.	D7	93
Madison, Me., U.S.	D3	96
Madison, Md., U.S.	C5	97
Madison, Mn., U.S.	E2	100
Madison, Ms., U.S.	C3	101
Madison, Mo., U.S.	B5	102
Madison, Ne., U.S.	C8	104
Madison, N.H., U.S.	C4	106
Madison, N.J., U.S.	B4	107
Madison, N.Y., U.S.	C5	109
Madison, N.C., U.S.	A3	110
Madison, Oh., U.S.	A4	112
Madison, S.D., U.S.	C8	118
Madison, Va., U.S.	B4	123
Madison, W.V., U.S.	C3	125
Madison, Wi., U.S.	E4	126
Madison, co., Al., U.S.	A3	78
Madison, co., Ar., U.S.	B2	81
Madison, co., Fl., U.S.	B3	86
Madison, co., Ga., U.S.	B3	87
Madison, co., Id., U.S.	F7	89
Madison, co., Il., U.S.	E4	90
Madison, co., In., U.S.	D6	91
Madison, co., Ia., U.S.	C3	92
Madison, co., Ky., U.S.	C5	94
Madison, co., La., U.S.	B4	95
Madison, co., Ms., U.S.	C4	101
Madison, co., Mo., U.S.	D7	102
Madison, co., Mt., U.S.	E5	103
Madison, co., Ne., U.S.	C8	104
Madison, co., N.Y., U.S.	C5	109
Madison, co., N.C., U.S.	f10	110
Madison, co., Oh., U.S.	C2	112
Madison, co., Tn., U.S.	B3	119
Madison, co., Tx., U.S.	D5	120
Madison, co., Va., U.S.	B4	123
Madison, stm., Mt., U.S.	E5	103
Madison Heights, Mi., U.S.	o15	99
Madison Heights, Va., U.S.	C3	123
Madison Range, mts., Mt., U.S.	E5	103
Madisonville, Ky., U.S.	C2	94
Madisonville, La., U.S.	D5	95
Madisonville, Tn., U.S.	D9	119
Madisonville, Tx., U.S.	D5	120
Madiun, Indon.	G4	34
Madoc, Ont.	C7	73
Madoc, Mt., U.S.	B11	103
Mado Gashi, Kenya	A6	48
Madon, stm., Fr.	A2	20
Madras, Or., U.S.	C5	114
Madras see Tamil Nadu, state, India	G6	36
Madras, India	F7	36
Madre, Laguna, b., Mex.	C5	63
Madre, Laguna, b., Tx., U.S.	F4	120
Madre, Sierra, mts., N.A.	D6	63
Madre, Sierra, mts., Phil.	B6	34
Madre de Dios, dept., Peru	D3	58
Madre de Dios, stm., S.A.	D4	58
Madre de Dios, Isla, i., Chile	E1	54
Madre del Sur, Sierra, mts., Mex.	D4	63
Madre Occidental, Sierra, mts., Mex.	B3	63
Madre Oriental, Sierra, mts., Mex.	C5	63
Madrid, Spain	B4	22
Madrid, Al., U.S.	D4	78
Madrid, Ia., U.S.	C4	92
Madrid, Me., U.S.	D2	96
Madrid, Ne., U.S.	D4	104
Madrid, N.Y., U.S.	f9	109
Madridejos, Spain	C4	22
Madrūsah, Libya		
Madura, i., Indon.	G4	34
Madurai, India	G6	36
Maebashi, Japan	D12	31
Mae Hong Son, Thai.	B6	
Maella, Spain		
Maengsan, N. Kor.	G3	33
Maeser, Ut., U.S.	C6	121
Maesteg, Wales, U.K.		
Maestra, Sierra, mts., Cuba	D5	64
Maevatanana, Madag.	g9	49
Maeystown, Il., U.S.	E3	90
Ma'fan, Libya	D2	43
Mafeking, Man.	C1	70
Mafeking see Mafikeng, S. Afr.		
Maffra, Austl.	H6	51
Mafia, i., Tan.	C6	48
Mafikeng, S. Afr.	C4	49
Mafra, Braz.	B3	56
Mafra, Port.	C1	22
Magadan, Sov. Un.	D18	29
Magadi, Kenya	B6	48
Magadi, Lake, l., Kenya	B6	48
Magaguadavic Lake, l., N.B.	D2	71
Magalia, Ca., U.S.	C3	82
Magallanes y Antártica Chilena, prov., Chile	h11	54
Maganey, Ire.	E5	11
Maganga, Zaire	A4	48
Magangué, Col.	B3	60
Magaria, Niger	D6	45
Magat, stm., Phil.	n13	34
Magazine, Ar., U.S.	B2	81
Magazine Mountain, mtn., Ar., U.S.	B5	81
Magdalena, Arg.	B5	54
Magdalena, Bol.	B3	60
Magdalena, N.M., U.S.	C2	108
Magdalena, dept., Col.	A3	60
Magdalena, stm., Col.	B3	60
Magdalena, Mex.	h9	63
Magdalena, Isla, i., Chile	C2	54
Magdalena [de Kino], Mex.		
Magdalena del Mar, Peru	*D2	58
Magdalena Mountains, mts., N.M., U.S.	D2	108
Magdeburg, E. Ger.	B5	18
Magdī'el, Isr.	g10	41
Magee, Ms., U.S.	D4	101
Magelang, Indon.	G4	34
Magellan, Strait of (Estrecho de Magallanes), strt., S.A.	h11	54
Magenta, Italy	C4	23
Maggia, stm., Switz.	C4	20
Maggie Creek, stm., Nv., U.S.	C5	105
Maggiore, Lake, l., Eur.	A2	23
Maghāghah, Eg.		
Maghama, Maur.	C2	45
Maghera, N. Ire., U.K.	C5	11
Magherafelt, N. Ire., U.K.	C5	11
Magic Reservoir, res., Id., U.S.	F4	89
Magilligan Point, c., N. Ire., U.K.	B5	11
Maglaj, Yugo.	C4	24

Name	Map Ref.	Page

Maglić, Yugo. — D5 24
Maglie, Italy — D7 23
Magna, Ut., U.S. — C3 121
Magness, Ar., U.S. — B4 81
Magnet, In., U.S. — H5 91
Magnet, Ne., U.S. — B8 104
Magnetawan, Ont. — B5 73
Magnetawan, stm., Ont. — B4 73
Magnet Cove, Ar., U.S. — C3 81
Magnetic Springs, Oh., U.S. — B2 112
Magnitogorsk, Sov. Un. — D8 29
Magnolia, Ar., U.S. — D2 81
Magnolia, De., U.S. — D4 85
Magnolia, Il., U.S. — B4 90
Magnolia, Ia., U.S. — C2 92
Magnolia, Ky., U.S. — C4 94
Magnolia, Md., U.S. — B5 97
Magnolia, Mn., U.S. — G2 100
Magnolia, Ms., U.S. — D3 101
Magnolia, N.J., U.S. — *D2 107
Magnolia, N.C., U.S. — C4 110
Magnolia, Oh., U.S. — B4 112
Magnolia, Tx., U.S. — D5 120
Magnolia Springs, Al., U.S. — E2 78
Mago, i., Fiji — H16 52
Magoffin, co., Ky., U.S. — C6 94
Magog, Que. — D5 74
Magothy River, b., Md., U.S. — B5 97
Magoúla, Grc. — g11 25
Magpie, Que. — h8 72
Magpie, stm., Que. — h8 72
Magrath, Alta. — E4 68
Magruder Mountain, mtn., Nv., U.S. — F4 105
Maguari, Cabo, c., Braz. — B1 57
Magude, Moz. — B5 49
Magway, Burma — D9 36
Mahābād, Iran — B4 38
Mahabo, Madag. — h8 49
Mahaffey, Pa., U.S. — E4 115
Mahagi, Zaire — A5 48
Mahaicony Village, Guy. — A3 59
Mahajanga, Madag. — g9 49
Mahajanga, prov., Madag. — g9 49
Mahakam, stm., Indon. — F5 34
Mahalatswe, Bots. — B4 49
Mahallāt, Iran — E5 39
Mahānadi, stm., India — D7 36
Mahanoro, Madag. — g9 49
Mahanoy City, Pa., U.S. — E9 115
Mahārāshtra, state, India — D6 36
Maha Sarakham, Thai. — B2 34
Mahaska, Ks., U.S. — C6 93
Mahaska, co., Ia., U.S. — C5 92
Mahattat Dab'ah, Jord. — C8 41
Mahbūbnagar, India — E6 36
Mahenge, Tan. — C6 48
Mahesāna, India — F4 37
Mahi, stm., India — D5 36
Mahia Peninsula, pen., N.Z. — M16 51
Mahned, Iran — D4 101
Mahnomen, Mn., U.S. — C3 100
Mahnomen, co., Mn., U.S. — C3 100
Mahoba, India — E7 37
Mahogany Mountain, mtn., Or., U.S. — D9 114
Mahomet, Il., U.S. — C5 90
Mahón, Spain — C8 22
Mahone Bay, N.S. — E5 71
Mahoning, co., Oh., U.S. — B5 112
Mahoning, stm., U.S. — A5 112
Mahoosuc Range, mts., N.H., U.S. — B4 106
Mahopac, N.Y., U.S. — D7 109
Mahto, S.D., U.S. — B5 118
Mahtowa, Mn., U.S. — D6 100
Mahuta, Tan. — D7 48
Mahuva, India — G3 37
Mahwah, N.J., U.S. — A4 107
Maîche, Fr. — B2 20
Maicurú, stm., Braz. — C4 59
Maida, N.D., U.S. — A7 111
Maiden, N.C., U.S. — B1 110
Maidenhead, Eng., U.K. — C7 12
Maiden Rock, Wi., U.S. — D1 126
Maidens, rock, N. Ire., U.K. — C6 11
Maidstone, Sask. — D1 75
Maidstone, Eng., U.K. — E7 12
Maidstone Lake, l., Vt., U.S. — B5 122
Maidsville, W.V., U.S. — B5 125
Maiduguri, Nig. — F8 45
Maihar, India — E8 37
Maikala Range, mts., India — F8 37
Maiko, stm., Zaire — B4 48
Maikoor, i., Indon. — G8 34
Maili, Hi., U.S. — g9 88
Maili Point, c., Hi., U.S. — B7 88
Maillard, Que. — A1 21
Mailley-et-Chazelot, Fr. — D4 18
Main, stm., W. Ger. — E6 19
Main, stm., N. Ire., U.K. — C5 11
Main-à-Dieu, N.S. — C10 71
Mainburg, W. Ger. — E6 19
Main Centre, Sask. — G2 75
Main Channel, strt., Ont. — B3 73
Mai-Ndombe, Lac, l., Zaire — B2 48
Maine, N.Y., U.S. — C4 109
Maine, hist. reg., Fr. — C4 16
Maine, state, U.S. — C3 96
Mainesburg, Pa., U.S. — C7 115
Mainé-Soroa, Niger — D7 45
Mainland, i., Scot., U.K. — g10 11
Mainland, i., Scot., U.K. — A5 11
Mainland, stm., Man. — C4 70
Main Pass, strt., La., U.S. — E6 95
Maintirano, Madag. — g8 49
Main Topsail, mtn., Newf. — D3 72
Mainz (Mayence), W. Ger. — D4 18
Maipo, Volcán, vol., S.A. — A3 54
Maipú, Arg. — C5 54
Maiquetía, Ven. — A4 60
Maira, stm., Italy — E3 23
Mairiporã, Braz. — m8 56
Maisí, Punta de, c., Cuba — D6 64
Maisonnette, N.B. — B4 71
Maisons-Laffitte, Fr. — g9 16
Maitland, Austl. — F9 50
Maitland, N.S. — D6 71
Maitland, Ont. — C9 73
Maitland, Fl., U.S. — *D5 86
Maitland, Mo., U.S. — A2 102
Maíz, Islas del, is., Nic. — E6 63
Maize, Ks., U.S. — g12 93
Maiziéres-lès-Vic, Fr. — E1 19
Maizuru, Japan — I7 33
Majagual, Col. — F5 34
Majene, Indon. — F5 34
Majenica, In., U.S. — C7 91
Majestic, Ky., U.S. — C7 94
Maji, Eth. — D4 47
Major, Sask. — F1 75
Major, co., Ok., U.S. — A3 113
Majuro, atoll, Marsh Is. — F10 6
Makaha, Hi., U.S. — g9 88

Makaha Point, c., Hi., U.S. — A2 88
Makah Indian Reservation, Wa., U.S. — A1 124
Makahuena Point, c., Hi., U.S. — g9 88
Makakilo City, Hi., U.S. — A4 48
Makalado, Zaire — E4 55
Makallé, Arg. — *C8 36
Makāku, mtn., Asia — *F4 90
Makanda, Il., U.S. — F4 90
Makanza, Zaire — A2 48
Makapala, Hi., U.S. — C6 88
Makapuu Head, c., Hi., U.S. — B4 88
Makarov, Sov. Un. — B13 31
Makarska, Yugo. — D3 24
Makasar see Ujungpandang, Indon. — G5 34
Makassar Strait, strt., Indon. — F5 34
Makat, Sov. Un. — E8 29
Makawao, Hi., U.S. — C5 88
Makaweli, Hi., U.S. — B2 88
Makeni, S.L. — E2 45
Makeyevka, Sov. Un. — E6 29
Makgadikgadi Pans, pl., Bots. — B4 49
Makhachkala, Sov. Un. — E7 29
Makharadze, Sov. Un. — B14 40
Makhfar al Quwayrah, Jord. — E7 41
Makinak, Man. — D2 70
Makindu, Kenya — B6 48
Makinsk, Sov. Un. — C8 28
Makkinga, Neth. — B6 17
Makkovik, Newf. — g10 72
Makkum, Neth. — A5 17
Maknassy, Tun. — C6 44
Makó, Hung. — B5 24
Makogai, i., Fiji — H15 52
Makokou, Gabon — E2 46
Makoti, N.D., U.S. — B4 111
Maków [Mazowiecki], Pol. — B6 26
Makteïr, reg., Maur. — B2 45
Mākū, Iran — B3 39
Makumbi, Zaire — C3 48
Makurazaki, Japan — K5 33
Makurdi, Nig. — E6 45
Makushin Volcano, vol., Ak., U.S. — E6 79
Mala, Punta, c., Pan. — Q8 62
Malabar, Fl., U.S. — D6 86
Malabar Coast, India — F6 36
Malabo, Eq. Gui. — E1 46
Mal Abrigo, Ur. — E1 56
Malacca, Strait of, strt., Asia — E2 34
Malacca see Melaka, Malay. — E2 34
Malad City, Id., U.S. — G6 89
Malafede, stm., Italy — h8 23
Málaga, Col. — D6 58
Málaga, Spain — D7 22
Malaga, N.J., U.S. — D2 107
Malaga, N.M., U.S. — E5 108
Málaga Bay, b., Spain — D7 22
Malagash, N.S. — C4 71
Malagón, Spain — C4 22
Malaimbandy, Madag. — h9 49
Malaita, i., Sol.Is. — D3 47
Malakal, Sud. — g10 16
Malakoff, Fr. — g10 16
Malakoff, Tx., U.S. — C4 120
Malalbergo, Italy — E6 23
Malambo, Col. — *A3 60
Malang, Indon. — G4 34
Malange see Malanje, Ang. — C2 48
Malanje, Ang. — C2 48
Malanje, dept., Ang. — C2 48
Malanzán, Arg. — A3 54
Malapane, stm., Pol. — f9 26
Mälaren, l., Swe. — t34 14
Malartic, Que. — k11 74
Malaspina, Arg. — C3 54
Malaspina Glacier, ice, Ak., U.S. — D11 79
Malatya, Tur. — C12 40
Malawi, ctry., Afr. — D5 48
Malaya Vishera, Sov. Un. — B9 27
Malaybalay, Phil. — D7 34
Malāyer, Iran — D4 39
Malay Peninsula, pen., Asia — D2 34
Malaysia, ctry., Asia — E4 34
Malazgirt, Tur. — C14 40
Malbaie, stm., Que. — B7 74
Malbork, Pol. — A5 26
Malchin, E. Ger. — B6 15
Malchow, E. Ger. — B5 15
Malcolm, Ne., U.S. — C5 104
Malcolm, Il., U.S. — B4 90
Malden, Ma., U.S. — B5 98
Malden, Mo., U.S. — E8 102
Malden, Wa., U.S. — B8 124
Malden, W.V., U.S. — m12 125
Malden Island, i., Kir. — G12 6
Maldives, ctry., Asia — G5 36
Maldon, Eng., U.K. — C8 12
Maldonado, Ur. — E2 56
Malè, Italy — C6 20
Maléa, Ákra, c., Grc. — D4 40
Malegaon, India — G5 37
Malema, Moz. — D6 48
Malheur, co., Or., U.S. — D9 114
Malheur, stm., Or., U.S. — D9 114
Malheur Lake, l., Or., U.S. — D8 114
Mali, Gui. — D2 45
Mali, ctry., Afr. — C4 45
Mali, i., Fiji — H15 52
Malibu, Ca., U.S. — m11 82
Maligne Lake, l., Alta. — C2 68
Mālīhah, Bi'r, well, Sud. — E5 41
Malik, Wādī al, val., Sud. — B3 47
Malin, Ire. — B4 11
Malin, Sov. Un. — F7 27
Malin, Or., U.S. — E5 114
Malinau, Indon. — E6 34
Malindi, Kenya — B7 48
Malin Beg, Ire. — B5 26
Malin Head, c., Ire. — A4 11
Malino, Sov. Un. — n18 27
Malinta, Oh., U.S. — A2 112
Maliwun, Burma — F10 36
Malkara, Tur. — I11 40
Mallacoota, Austl. — G9 50
Mallaig, Scot., U.K. — B4 11
Mallaig, Alta. — B5 68

Mallawī, Eg. — C3 38
Mallersdorf, W. Ger. — E7 19
Mallés Venosta, Italy — C6 20
Mallet Creek, Oh., U.S. — A4 112
Malletts Bay, b., Vt., U.S. — B2 122
Mallorca, i., Spain — C7 22
Mallorytown, Ont. — C9 73
Mallow, Ire. — D2 10
Malmbäck, Swe. — A8 15
Malmberget, Swe. — D9 14
Malmédy, Bel. — B7 16
Malmö, Swe. — J5 14
Malmo, Ne., U.S. — C9 104
Malmöhus, co., Swe. — C7 15
Malmyzh, Sov. Un. — B12 31
Maloarkhangelsk, Sov. Un. — E11 27
Maloggia (Maloja), Switz. — D8 21
Maloja Pass, Switz. — C5 20
Malolo, i., Fiji — H14 52
Malolos, Phil. — o13 34
Malone, Ont. — C7 73
Malone, Fl., U.S. — B1 86
Malone, N.Y., U.S. — f10 109
Maloney Reservoir, res., Ne., U.S. — C5 104
Malonga, Zaire — D3 48
Malonno, Italy — D9 21
Malonton, Man. — D3 70
Malott, Wa., U.S. — A6 124
Maloy, Ia., U.S. — D3 92
Maloyaroslavets, Sov. Un. — D11 27
Malpelo, Isla de, i., Col. — C2 53
Malpeque Bay, b., P.E.I. — C6 71
Mālpura, India — D5 37
Malsch, W. Ger. — E3 19
Malta, Id., U.S. — G5 89
Malta, Il., U.S. — B5 90
Malta, Mt., U.S. — B9 103
Malta, Oh., U.S. — C4 112
Malta, ctry., Eur. — H11 8
Malta Bend, Mo., U.S. — B4 102
Maltahöhe, Nmb. — B2 49
Malton (part of Mississauga), Ont. — m14 73
Malton, Eng., U.K. — C6 10
Malung, Swe. — G4 14
Malvern, Ar., U.S. — C3 81
Malvern, Ia., U.S. — D2 92
Malvern, Oh., U.S. — B4 112
Malvern, Pa., U.S. — o19 115
Malverne, N.Y., U.S. — k13 109
Malvérnia, Moz. — B5 49
Malyye Karmakuly, Sov. Un. — B9 128
Malyy Uzen, stm., Sov. Un. — D3 28
Mamala Bay, b., Hi., U.S. — g10 88
Mamanguape, Braz. — C3 57
Mamantel, Mex. — A2 62
Mamaroneck, N.Y., U.S. — h13 109
Mamba, Japan — m17 33
Mambasa, Zaire — A4 48
Mamberamo, stm., Indon. — G10 34
Mamelodi, S. Afr. — *C4 49
Ma-Me-O Beach, Alta. — C4 68
Mamers, Fr. — C4 16
Mamers, N.C., U.S. — B4 110
Mamfe, Cam. — D1 46
Mamiña, Chile — D2 55
Mammern, Switz. — A6 21
Mammoth, Az., U.S. — E5 80
Mammoth, Ut., U.S. — D3 121
Mammoth, W.V., U.S. — C3 125
Mammoth Cave National Park, Ky., U.S. — C4 94
Mammoth Lakes, Ca., U.S. — D4 82
Mammoth Spring, Ar., U.S. — A4 81
Mamonovo, Sov. Un. — A5 26
Mamoré, stm., S.A. — B2 55
Mamou, Gui. — D2 45
Mamou, La., U.S. — D3 95
Mampong, Ghana — E4 45
Mamry, Lake, l., Pol. — A6 26
Mamuju, Indon. — F5 34
Man, I.C. — E3 45
Man, W.V., U.S. — D3 125
Man, stm., Sask. — D4 75
Man, Isle of, i., I. of Man — A4 10
Mana, Fr. Gu. — A4 59
Mana, Hi., U.S. — A2 88
Mana, stm., Fr. Gu. — B4 59
Manabí, prov., Ec. — B1 58
Manacacías, stm., Col. — C5 58
Manacapuru, Braz. — C2 59
Manacor, Spain — B8 22
Manado, Indon. — E6 34
Managua, Nic. — D4 62
Managua, Lago de, l., Nic. — D4 62
Manahawkin, N.J., U.S. — D4 107
Manakara, Madag. — h9 49
Manakin, Va., U.S. — C5 123
Manalapan, N.J., U.S. — C4 107
Manam, i., Pap. N. Gui. — h12 50
Manama, Bahr. — C5 38
Manana Island, i., Hi., U.S. — g11 88
Mananara, Madag. — g9 49
Mananara, stm., Madag. — h9 49
Mananjary, Madag. — h9 49
Manantenina, Madag. — h9 49
Manantico Creek, stm., N.J., U.S. — E3 107
Manapire, stm., Ven. — B4 60
Mana Point, c., Hi., U.S. — A2 88
Manas He, stm., China — B2 31
Manas Hu, l., China — B2 31
Manasquan, N.J., U.S. — C4 107
Manasquan, stm., N.J., U.S. — C4 107
Manassa, Co., U.S. — D5 83
Manassas, Ga., U.S. — E4 87
Manassas, Va., U.S. — B5 123
Manassas National Battlefield Park, Va., U.S. — g11 123
Manassas Park, Va., U.S. — g11 123
Manatee, co., Fl., U.S. — E4 86
Manatee, stm., Fl., U.S. — E4 86
Manatí, P.R. — B7 65
Manaus, Braz. — C2 59
Manavgat, Tur. — h10 126
Manawa, Wi., U.S. — D5 126
Manawan Lake, l., Sask. — B4 75
Mancelona, Mi., U.S. — D5 99
Manchac, Bayou, stm., La., U.S. — h10 95
Mancha Real, Spain — D8 22
Manchatang, Ma., U.S. — B4 98
Manchester, Eng., U.K. — D5 10
Manchester, Ct., U.S. — B5 84
Manchester, Ga., U.S. — D2 87
Manchester, Il., U.S. — D3 90

Manchester, Ia., U.S. — B6 92
Manchester, Ks., U.S. — C6 93
Manchester, Ky., U.S. — C6 94
Manchester, Me., U.S. — D3 96
Manchester, Md., U.S. — A4 97
Manchester, Ma., U.S. — A6 98
Manchester, Mi., U.S. — F6 99
Manchester, Mo., U.S. — f12 102
Manchester, N.H., U.S. — E4 106
Manchester, N.Y., U.S. — C3 109
Manchester, Oh., U.S. — D2 112
Manchester, Ok., U.S. — A3 113
Manchester, Pa., U.S. — F8 115
Manchester, S.D., U.S. — C8 118
Manchester, Tn., U.S. — B5 119
Manchester, Tx., U.S. — C5 120
Manchester, Vt., U.S. — E2 122
Manchester Center, Vt., U.S. — E2 122
Manchuria, hist. reg., China — B10 31
Mancos, Co., U.S. — D2 83
Mancos, stm., U.S. — D2 83
Manda, Tan. — D5 48
Mandabe, Madag. — h8 49
Mandaguari, Braz. — C2 56
Mandal, Nor. — H2 14
Mandalay, Burma — D10 36
Mandalgovi, Mong. — B6 31
Mandali, Iraq — E2 39
Mandalya, Gulf of, b., Tur. — D6 25
Mandan, N.D., U.S. — C5 111
Mandara Mountains, mts., Afr. — C2 46
Mandar Bay, b., Indon. — F5 34
Mandaree, N.D., U.S. — B3 111
Mandeb, Bab el, strt. — D4 38
Mandel, Afg. — E10 39
Mandera, Kenya — A7 48
Manderfield, Bel. — D6 17
Manderson, S.D., U.S. — D3 118
Manderson, Wy., U.S. — B5 127
Mandeure, Fr. — B2 21
Mandeville, Que. — C4 74
Mandeville, Jar. — E5 64
Mandeville, Ar., U.S. — D2 81
Mandeville, La., U.S. — D5 95
Mandiana, Gui. — A5 49
Mandidzudzura, Zimb. — A5 49
Mandimba, Moz. — D6 48
Mandla, India — I8 37
Mandra, Grc. — C4 25
Mandritsara, Madag. — g9 49
Mandsaur, India — D6 36
Mandurah, Austl. — F2 50
Mandvi, Italy — D2 23
Māndvi (Cutch Māndvi), India — D4 36
Manes, Mo., U.S. — D5 102
Manfalūt, Eg. — C3 38
Manfred, N.D., U.S. — B6 111
Manfredonia, Italy — D5 23
Manfredonia, Gulf of, b., Italy — D6 23
Manga, Braz. — A4 56
Mangaldan, Phil. — A2 62
Mangalia, Rom. — B9 24
Mangalore, India — F5 36
Mangaratiba, Braz. — h5 56
Mangatarem, Phil. — o13 34
Mangerton Mountain, mtn., Ire. — D2 10
Mangham, La., U.S. — B4 95
Mangkalihat, Cape, c., Indon. — E6 34
Mangoche, Mwi. — D6 48
Mangoky, stm., Madag. — h8 49
Mangole, i., Indon. — F7 34
Mangualde, Port. — B2 22
Mangueni, Plateau de, plat., Niger — B7 45
Mangum, Ok., U.S. — C2 113
Manhasset, N.Y., U.S. — *h13 109
Manhattan, Ks., U.S. — C7 93
Manhattan, Mt., U.S. — E5 103
Manhattan, Nv., U.S. — E4 105
Manhattan Beach, Ca., U.S. — n12 82
Manhattan Island, i., N.Y., U.S. — h13 109
Manheim, Pa., U.S. — F9 115
Manhein, W.V., U.S. — B5 125
Manhiça, Moz. — C5 49
Manhuaçu, Braz. — C8 56
Maniago, Italy — D6 20
Maniamba, Moz. — D6 48
Manica, dept., Moz. — A5 49
Manicoré, stm., Braz. — D2 59
Manicouagan, stm., Que. — G19 66
Manicouagan, Réservoir, res., Que. — h13 74
Manifest, La., U.S. — C4 95
Manigotagan, Man. — D3 70
Manigotagan, stm., Man. — D3 70
Manigotagan Lake, l., Man. — D4 70
Manila, Phil. — o13 34
Manila, Ar., U.S. — B5 81
Manila, Ut., U.S. — C6 121
Manila Bay, b., Phil. — o13 34
Manilla, Austl. — E8 51
Manilla, Ia., U.S. — C2 92
Manilla, In., U.S. — E6 91
Manipur, state, India — D9 36
Manisa, Tur. — C2 40
Manistee, Mi., U.S. — D4 99
Manistee, co., Mi., U.S. — D4 99
Manistee, stm., Mi., U.S. — D5 99
Manistique, Mi., U.S. — B4 99
Manistique, stm., Mi., U.S. — B4 99
Manistique Lake, l., Mi., U.S. — B5 99
Manito, Il., U.S. — C4 90
Manitoba, prov., Can. — D2 70
Manitoba, Lake, l., Man. — D2 70
Manitou, Man. — E2 70
Manitou, Ok., U.S. — C3 113
Manitou, Lake, l., Ont. — B3 73
Manitou, stm., Ont. — o18 73
Manitou Beach, Sask. — F3 75
Manitou Beach, Mi., U.S. — G7 99
Manitou Lake, l., Ont. — A3 99
Manitou Lake, l., Ont. — o18 73
Manitoulin, dept., Ont. — g11 73
Manitoulin Island, i., Ont. — B2 73
Manitou Springs, Co., U.S. — C6 83
Manitowaning, Ont. — B3 73
Manitowoc, Wi., U.S. — D6 126
Manitowoc, co., Wi., U.S. — D6 126
Manitowoc, North Branch, stm., Wi., U.S. — h9 126
Manitowoc, South Branch, stm., Wi., U.S. — k9 126
Maniwaki, Que. — C2 74
Manizales, Col. — B2 60
Manja, Madag. — h8 49
Manjacaze, Moz. — B5 49
Manjimup, Austl. — F2 50
Manjra, stm., India — E6 36
Mankato, Ks., U.S. — C5 93

Mankato, Mn., U.S. — F5 100
Mankono, I.C. — E3 45
Mankota, Sask. — H2 75
Manley, Ne., U.S. — h12 104
Manley Hot Springs, Ak., U.S. — B9 79
Manlius, Il., U.S. — B4 90
Manlius, N.Y., U.S. — C5 109
Manlléu, Spain — A7 22
Manly, Ia., U.S. — A4 92
Manlyville, Tn., U.S. — A3 119
Manmad, India — G5 37
Mannar, Sri L. — G6 36
Mannar, Gulf of, b., Asia — G6 36
Mannboro, Va., U.S. — C5 123
Mannford, Ok., U.S. — A5 113
Mannheim, W. Ger. — D4 18
Manning, Alta. — A2 68
Manning, Ar., U.S. — C3 81
Manning, Ia., U.S. — C2 92
Manning, N.D., U.S. — B3 111
Manning, Or., U.S. — g11 114
Manning, S.C., U.S. — D7 117
Manning Provincial Park, B.C. — E7 69
Mannington, Ky., U.S. — C2 94
Mannington, W.V., U.S. — B4 125
Manns Choice, Pa., U.S. — G4 115
Manns Creek, stm., W.V., U.S. — n14 125
Mannsville, N.Y., U.S. — B4 109
Mannsville, Ok., U.S. — C5 113
Mannu, stm., Italy — E2 23
Mannville, Alta. — C5 68
Manoa, Bol. — A2 55
Man of War Bay, b., Trin. — M24 65
Manokin, Md., U.S. — D6 97
Manokin, stm., Md., U.S. — D6 97
Manokotak, Ak., U.S. — D8 79
Manokwari, Indon. — F8 34
Manombo, Madag. — h8 49
Manomet, Ma., U.S. — C6 98
Manomet Hill, hill, Ma., U.S. — C6 98
Manomet Point, c., Ma., U.S. — C6 98
Manono, Zaire — C4 48
Manono, i., W. Sam. — F11 52
Manor, Sask. — H4 75
Manor, Ga., U.S. — E4 87
Manor, Tx., U.S. — D4 120
Manorhamilton, Ire. — C4 11
Manorhaven, N.Y., U.S. — *h13 109
Manorville, Pa., U.S. — E2 115
Manosque, Fr. — F6 16
Manotick, Ont. — B9 73
Manouane, Lac, l., Que. — h12 74
Manpo, N. Kor. — F3 33
Manresa, Spain — B6 22
Mansa (Fort Rosebery), Zam. — D1 45
Mansa Konko, Gam. — F2 45
Mansel Island, i., N.W. Ter. — D17 66
Manseau, Que. — C5 74
Mansfield, Austl. — H6 51
Mansfield, Eng., U.K. — D6 10
Mansfield, Ar., U.S. — B1 81
Mansfield, Ga., U.S. — C3 87
Mansfield, Il., U.S. — C5 90
Mansfield, La., U.S. — B2 95
Mansfield, Ma., U.S. — B5 98
Mansfield, Mo., U.S. — D5 102
Mansfield, Oh., U.S. — B3 112
Mansfield, Pa., U.S. — C7 115
Mansfield, S.D., U.S. — B7 118
Mansfield, Tn., U.S. — A3 119
Mansfield, Tx., U.S. — n9 120
Mansfield, Wa., U.S. — B6 124
Mansfield, Mount, mtn., Vt., U.S. — B3 122
Mansfield Center, Ct., U.S. — B7 84
Mansfield Depot, Ct., U.S. — B6 84
Mansfield Four Corners, Ct., U.S. — B6 84
Mansfield Hollow Lake, res., Ct., U.S. — B7 84
Manson, Ia., U.S. — B3 92
Manson, Wa., U.S. — B5 124
Manson Creek, B.C. — B5 69
Mansonville, Que. — D5 74
Mansura, La., U.S. — C3 95
Manta, Ec. — B1 58
Mantachie, Ms., U.S. — A5 101
Mantador, N.D., U.S. — C9 111
Mantagao, stm., Man. — D3 70
Mantario, Sask. — F1 75
Mantaro, stm., Peru — D3 58
Manteca, Ca., U.S. — D3 82
Mantee, Ms., U.S. — B4 101
Manteno, Il., U.S. — B6 90
Manteo, N.C., U.S. — B7 110
Manter, Ks., U.S. — E2 93
Mantes [-la-Jolie], Fr. — C4 16
Manti, Ut., U.S. — D4 121
Mantiqueira, Serra da, mts., Braz. — C4 56
Manton, Mi., U.S. — D5 99
Mantorville, Mn., U.S. — F6 100
Mantova (Mantua), Italy — D2 23
Mantua, Oh., U.S. — A4 112
Mantua, Ut., U.S. — B4 121
Mantua Hills, Va., U.S. — B4 121
Manú, Peru — D3 58
Manuel Benavides, Mex. — B4 63
Manuel Urbano, Braz. — C2 59
Manui, i., Indon. — F7 34
Manukau Harbour, b., N.Z. — L15 51
Manukuru, Indon. — f9 34
Manulla, stm., Ire. — C2 11
Manus, i., Pap. N. Gui. — k16 50
Manvel, N.D., U.S. — A8 111
Manvel, Tx., U.S. — r14 120
Manville, N.J., U.S. — B3 107
Manville, R.I., U.S. — B4 116
Manville, Wy., U.S. — D8 127
Many, La., U.S. — C2 95
Many, Lake, l., Tn., U.S. — B6 119
Manyberries, Alta. — H8 68
Manych, stm., Sov. Un. — H13 27
Manych Lake, l., Sov. Un. — H14 27
Many Farms, Az., U.S. — A6 80
Many Island Lake, l., Can. — D5 68
Manyoni, Tan. — h10 126
Manzanares, Spain — C4 22
Manzanares Canal, Spain — p17 22
Manzanillo, Cuba — D5 64
Manzanillo, Mex. — H6 63
Manzanillo, Punta, c., Pan. — B3 114
Manzanita, Or., U.S. — B3 114
Manzano, N.M., U.S. — C3 108
Manzanola, Co., U.S. — C7 83
Manzano Mountains, mts., N.M., U.S. — C3 108

Manzano Peak, mtn., N.M., U.S. — C3 108
Manzhouli, China — C8 31
Manziana, Italy — g8 23
Manzilah, Lake, l., Eg. — C3 41
Manzini, Swaz. — C5 49
Mao, Chad — C3 46
Mao, Dom. Rep. — E8 64
Maoke Mountains, mts., Indon. — F9 34
Maoming, China — G7 31
Mapai, Moz. — B5 49
Mapam Yumco, l., China — B7 36
Mapastepec, Mex. — D6 63
Mapaville, Mo., U.S. — C7 102
Mapes, N.D., U.S. — A7 111
Mapia, Kepulauan, is., Indon. — B5 34
Mapire, Ven. — B5 60
Mapiri, Bol. — C2 55
Maple (part of Vaughan), Ont. — k14 73
Maple, Tx., U.S. — C1 120
Maple, Wi., U.S. — B2 126
Maple, stm., Ia., U.S. — A7 118
Maple, stm., Mi., U.S. — B2 92
Maple, stm., N.D., U.S. — C2 100
Maple Bay, Mn., U.S. — E4 126
Maple Bluff, Wi., U.S. — H1 75
Maple Creek, Sask. — C9 104
Maple Creek, stm., Ne., U.S. — C9 104
Maple Falls, Wa., U.S. — A3 124
Maple Grove, Mn., U.S. — m12 100
Maple Heights, Oh., U.S. — h9 112
Maple Hill, Ks., U.S. — C7 93
Maple Hill, N.C., U.S. — C5 110
Maple Island, Mn., U.S. — G5 100
Maple Lake, Mn., U.S. — E5 100
Maple Mount, Ky., U.S. — C2 94
Maple Plain, Mn., U.S. — m11 100
Maple Rapids, Mi., U.S. — E6 99
Maple Ridge, B.C. — E6 69
Maples, In., U.S. — B8 91
Maple Shade, N.J., U.S. — D2 107
Maplesville, Al., U.S. — C3 78
Mapleton, Ia., U.S. — B2 92
Mapleton, Ks., U.S. — D9 93
Mapleton, Me., U.S. — B4 96
Mapleton, Mn., U.S. — G5 100
Mapleton, N.D., U.S. — C8 111
Mapleton, Or., U.S. — C3 114
Mapleton, Ut., U.S. — C4 121
Mapleton Depot, Pa., U.S. — F6 115
Maple Valley, Wa., U.S. — f11 124
Mapleview, R.I., U.S. — B2 116
Maplewood, Me., U.S. — n12 100
Maplewood, Mn., U.S. — n12 100
Maplewood, Mo., U.S. — f13 102
Maplewood, N.J., U.S. — B4 107
Mapuera, stm., Braz. — C5 59
Maputo (Lourenço Marques), Moz. — C5 49
Maputo, dept., Moz. — C5 49
Maqāriyūs, Dayr, hist., Eg. — D2 41
Maquela do Zombo, Ang. — C2 48
Maquinchao, Arg. — B2 54
Maquoketa, Ia., U.S. — B7 92
Maquoketa, Mo., U.S. — B6 92
Maquoketa, North Fork, stm., Ia., U.S. — B6 92
Maquon, Il., U.S. — C3 90
Mar, Serra do, clf., Braz. — D5 56
Mara, prov., Tan. — B5 48
Maraã, Braz. — D4 60
Marabá, Braz. — D5 59
Maracá, Ilha de, i., Braz. — B4 59
Maracaibo, Ven. — A3 60
Maracaibo, Lago de, l., Ven. — C1 56
Maracaju, Braz. — C2 56
Maracaju, Serra de, hills, S.A. — A4 60
Maracay, Ven. — A4 60
Marādah, Libya — D3 43
Maradi, Niger — D6 45
Marāgheh, Iran — B4 38
Maragogi, Braz. — k6 57
Maragojipe, Braz. — B3 57
Marais des Cygnes, stm., U.S. — D8 93
Marajó, Baía de, b., Braz. — C5 59
Marajó, Ilha de, i., Braz. — C5 59
Maralal, Kenya — A6 48
Maramec, Ok., U.S. — A5 113
Marana, Az., U.S. — E4 80
Marand, Iran — B4 38
Maranguape, Braz. — B3 57
Maranhão, state, Braz. — B1 57
Marano, Laguna di, b., Italy — D7 23
Marans, Fr. — D3 16
Marañón, stm., Peru — B2 58
Marathón, Grc. — g11 25
Marathon, Ont. — o18 73
Marathon, Fl., U.S. — H5 86
Marathon, Ia., U.S. — B3 92
Marathon, N.Y., U.S. — C4 109
Marathon, Tx., U.S. — D1 120
Marathon, Wi., U.S. — D4 126
Marathon, co., Wi., U.S. — D4 126
Maratua, i., Indon. — E5 34
Marau, Braz. — D2 56
Maravatío de Ocampo, Mex. — n13 63
Marāwah, Libya — B3 47
Marawī, Sud. — *B5 123
Marbach [am Neckar], W. Ger. — E4 19
Marbella, Spain — A2 22
Marble, Ar., U.S. — A2 81
Marble, Co., U.S. — B3 83
Marble, Mn., U.S. — C5 100
Marble, N.C., U.S. — f9 110
Marble Bar, Austl. — D2 50
Marble Canyon, Az., U.S. — A4 80
Marble Canyon, val., Az., U.S. — A4 80
Marble City, Ok., U.S. — B7 113
Marble Cliff, Oh., U.S. — m10 112
Marble Dale, Ct., U.S. — C2 84
Marbledale, Pa., U.S. — n14 119
Marble Falls, Tx., U.S. — D3 120
Marble Hall, S. Afr. — B4 49
Marblehead, Il., U.S. — D2 90
Marblehead, Ma., U.S. — B6 98
Marblehead, Oh., U.S. — A3 112
Marble Hill, Mo., U.S. — D8 102
Marblemount, Wa., U.S. — A4 124
Marble Mountain, N.S. — D8 71
Marble Rock, Ia., U.S. — B5 92
Marbleton, Que. — D6 74
Marbleton, Wy., U.S. — D2 127
Marburg, W. Ger. — C4 18
Marbury, Al., U.S. — C3 78
Marbury, Md., U.S. — C3 97
Marcaria, Italy — D6 20
Marcelin, Sask. — E2 75
Marceline, Mo., U.S. — B5 102

Name	Map Ref.	Page
Marcella, Ar., U.S.	B4	81
Marcelline, Il., U.S.	C2	90
Marcellus, Mi., U.S.	F5	99
March, Eng., U.K.	B8	12
March Air Force Base, mil., Ca., U.S.	F5	82
Marchand, Man.	E3	70
Marche, hist. reg., Fr.	D4	16
Marche-en-Famenne, Bel.	D5	17
Marchena, Spain	D3	22
Marchena, Isla, i., Ec.	f5	58
Marches (Marche), prov., Italy	C4	23
Mar Chiquita, Laguna, l., Arg.	A4	54
Marchwell, Sask.	G5	75
Marco, Fl., U.S.	G5	86
Marco, In., U.S.	G3	91
Marcola, Or., U.S.	C4	114
Marcos Juárez, Arg.	A4	54
Marcus, Ia., U.S.	B2	92
Marcus, S.D., U.S.	C3	118
Marcus, Wa., U.S.	A7	124
Marcus Baker, Mount, mtn., Ak., U.S.	g18	79
Marcus Hook, Pa., U.S.	G11	115
Marcy, Mount, mtn., N.Y., U.S.	A7	109
Marcy Colony, S.D., U.S.	D8	118
Mardān, Pak.	B5	36
Mar de Espanha, Braz.	g6	56
Mardela Springs, Md., U.S.	D6	97
Mar del Plata, Arg.	B5	54
Mardin, Tur.	D13	40
Marechal Deodoro, Braz.	C3	57
Maree, Loch, l., Scot., U.K.	C3	13
Mareeba, Austl.	C8	50
Marenanuka, Kir.	R18	52
Marengo, Sask.	F1	75
Marengo, Il., U.S.	A5	90
Marengo, In., U.S.	H5	91
Marengo, Ia., U.S.	C5	92
Marengo, Oh., U.S.	B3	112
Marengo, Wa., U.S.	B7	124
Marengo, Wi., U.S.	B3	126
Marengo, co., Al., U.S.	C2	78
Marenisco, Mi., U.S.	n12	99
Marennes, Fr.	E3	16
Maretz, Fr.	D3	17
Mareuil-sur-Ourcq, Fr.	E3	17
Marfa, Tx., U.S.	o12	120
Marfrance, W.V., U.S.	C4	125
Margai Co, l., China	A8	36
Marganets, Sov. Un.	H10	27
Margaree, N.S.	C8	71
Margaree Harbour, N.S.	C8	71
Margaret, Man.	E2	70
Margaret, Al., U.S.	B3	78
Margaret, Tx., U.S.	B3	120
Margaretsville, N.S.	D4	71
Margaretville, N.Y., U.S.	C6	109
Margarita, Isla de, i., Ven.	A5	60
Margate, Eng., U.K.	E7	10
Margate, Fl., U.S.	F6	86
Margate, Md., U.S.	*B4	97
Margate City, N.J., U.S.	E3	107
Margerum, Al., U.S.	A1	78
Margherita Peak, mtn., Afr.	A4	44
Marghāb, Afg.	D13	39
Marghīb, Kūh-e, mtn., Iran	E8	39
Margie, Mn., U.S.	B5	100
Margilan, Sov. Un.	E10	29
Margny-lès-Compiègne, Fr.	E2	17
Margo, Sask.	F4	75
Mārgow, Dasht-e, des., Afg.	F11	39
Margrethe, Lake, l., Mi., U.S.	D6	99
Marguerite, Bay, b., Ant.	C6	7
Maria, Que.	A3	71
Maria, i., Austl.	o15	50
María Chiquita, Pan.	k11	62
Mariager, Den.	B3	15
Mariager Fjord, Den.	B3	15
Mariah Hill, In., U.S.	H4	91
María la Baja, Col.	A2	60
Marian, Lake, l., Fl., U.S.	E5	86
Mariana Islands, is., Oc.	E8	6
Marianna, Ar., U.S.	C5	81
Marianna, Fl., U.S.	B1	86
Mariánské Lázně, Czech.	D2	26
Mariapolis, Man.	E2	70
Marias, stm., Mt., U.S.	B4	103
Marías, Islas, is., Mex.	C3	62
Marias Pass, Mt., U.S.	B3	103
Maria Stein, Oh., U.S.	B1	112
Maria van Diemen, Cape, c., N.Z.	K14	51
Mariaville, Me., U.S.	D4	96
Maribel, N.C., U.S.	B6	110
Maribel, Wi., U.S.	h10	126
Maribo, Den.	D5	15
Maribor, Yugo.	B2	24
Maricá, Braz.	h6	56
Maricaban Island, i., Phil.	p13	34
Maricopa, Az., U.S.	E3	80
Maricopa, Ca., U.S.	E4	82
Maricopa, co., Az., U.S.	D3	80
Maricopa Mountains, mts., Az., U.S.	m7	80
Maridī, Sud.	E2	47
Marié, stm., Braz.	D4	60
Marie Byrd Land, reg., Ant.	B1	7
Mariedamm, Swe.	u33	14
Mariefred, Swe.	u33	14
Marie-Galante, i., Guad.	I14	64
Mariehamn, Fin.	t35	14
Marie Lake, l., Alta.	B5	68
Mariembourg, Bel.	D4	17
Mariemont, Oh., U.S.	o13	112
Marienberg, E. Ger.	C7	19
Mariental, Nmb.	B2	49
Marienthal, Ks., U.S.	D2	93
Marienville, Pa., U.S.	D3	115
Marie-Reine, Alta.	B2	68
Maries, co., Mo., U.S.	C6	102
Mariestad, Swe.	H5	14
Marietta, Ga., U.S.	C2	87
Marietta, Mn., U.S.	F6	91
Marietta, Mn., U.S.	E2	100
Marietta, Ms., U.S.	A5	101
Marietta, Oh., U.S.	C4	112
Marietta, Ok., U.S.	D4	113
Marietta, S.C., U.S.	A2	117
Marietta, Wa., U.S.	A3	124
Marieville, Que.	D4	74
Mariinsk, Sov. Un.	B11	29
Marijampolé, Sov. Un.	A7	26
Mari Lake, l., Sask.	B4	75
Marilia, Braz.	C2	56
Marimba, Ang.	C2	48
Marín, Spain	A1	22
Marin, co., Ca., U.S.	C2	82
Marina, Ca., U.S.	*D3	82
Marina del Rey, Ca., U.S.	*n12	82
Marine, Il., U.S.	E4	90
Marine City, Mi., U.S.	F8	99
Marine On St. Croix, Mn., U.S.	E6	100
Marinette, Wi., U.S.	C6	126
Marinette, co., Wi., U.S.	C5	126
Maringá, Braz.	C2	56
Maringa, stm., Zaire	A3	48
Maringouin, La., U.S.	D4	95
Marinha Grande, Port.	C1	22
Marino, Italy	h9	23
Marion, Austl.	*G6	50
Marion, Al., U.S.	C2	78
Marion, Ar., U.S.	B5	81
Marion, Ct., U.S.	C4	84
Marion, Il., U.S.	F5	90
Marion, In., U.S.	C6	91
Marion, Ia., U.S.	B6	92
Marion, Ks., U.S.	D6	93
Marion, Ky., U.S.	e9	94
Marion, La., U.S.	B3	95
Marion, Ma., U.S.	C6	98
Marion, Mi., U.S.	D5	99
Marion, Ms., U.S.	C5	101
Marion, Mt., U.S.	B2	103
Marion, Ne., U.S.	D5	104
Marion, N.Y., U.S.	B3	109
Marion, N.C., U.S.	B1	110
Marion, N.D., U.S.	C7	111
Marion, Oh., U.S.	B2	112
Marion, Or., U.S.	C4	114
Marion, Pa., U.S.	G6	115
Marion, S.C., U.S.	C9	117
Marion, S.D., U.S.	D8	118
Marion, Ut., U.S.	C4	121
Marion, Va., U.S.	f10	123
Marion, Wi., U.S.	D5	126
Marion, co., Al., U.S.	A2	78
Marion, co., Ar., U.S.	A3	81
Marion, co., Fl., U.S.	C4	86
Marion, co., Ga., U.S.	D2	87
Marion, co., Il., U.S.	E4	90
Marion, co., In., U.S.	E5	91
Marion, co., Ia., U.S.	C4	92
Marion, co., Ks., U.S.	D6	93
Marion, co., Ky., U.S.	C4	94
Marion, co., Ms., U.S.	D4	101
Marion, co., Mo., U.S.	B6	102
Marion, co., Oh., U.S.	B2	112
Marion, co., Or., U.S.	C4	114
Marion, co., S.C., U.S.	C9	117
Marion, co., Tn., U.S.	D8	119
Marion, co., Tx., U.S.	C5	120
Marion, co., W.V., U.S.	B4	125
Marion, Lake, res., S.C., U.S.	E7	117
Marion Center, Pa., U.S.	E3	115
Marion Heights, Pa., U.S.	F3	91
Marion Junction, Al., U.S.	C2	78
Marion Station, Md., U.S.	D7	97
Mariposa, Ca., U.S.	D4	82
Mariposa, co., Ca., U.S.	D3	82
Marissa, Il., U.S.	E4	90
Mariscal Estigarribia, Para.	D3	55
Maristova, Den.	B3	15
Markakol', Sov. Un.	E4	90
Marka, Som.	B2	47
Marka Kul, l., Sov. Un.	B2	31
Markala, Mali	D3	45
Markam, China	F4	31
Markaryd, Swe.	I5	14
Mark Center, Oh., U.S.	A1	112
Markdale, Ont.	C4	73
Marked Tree, Ar., U.S.	B5	81
Markerwaard, reg., Neth.	B5	17
Markesan, Wi., U.S.	E5	126
Market Drayton, Eng., U.K.	B5	12
Market Harborough, Eng., U.K.	B7	12
Markethill, N. Ire., U.K.	C5	11
Market Rasen, Eng., U.K.	C7	12
Market Weighton, Eng., U.K.	G8	13
Markham, Ont.	D5	73
Markham, Il., U.S.	k9	90
Markham, Tx., U.S.	E4	120
Markham, Mount, mtn., Ant.	A29	7
Marki, Pol.	k14	26
Markinch, Sask.	G3	75
Markkleeberg, E. Ger.	B7	19
Markland, In., U.S.	G8	91
Markland Lock and Dam, U.S.	B5	94
Markle, In., U.S.	C7	91
Markleeville, Ca., U.S.	C4	82
Markleville, In., U.S.	E6	91
Markleysburg, Pa., U.S.	G3	115
Markneukirchen, E. Ger.	C7	19
Markópoulon, Grc.	h11	25
Markovka, Sov. Un.	G12	27
Markovo, Sov. Un.	C11	29
Markovo, Sov. Un.	C20	29
Markranstädt, E. Ger.	B7	19
Marks, Ms., U.S.	A3	101
Marksboro, N.J., U.S.	B3	107
Marksville, La., U.S.	C3	95
Marktheidenfeld, W. Ger.	D4	19
Marktredwitz, W. Ger.	C6	19
Markville, Mn., U.S.	D6	100
Marl, W. Ger.	*C3	19
Marland, Ont.	A4	113
Marlboro, Alta.	C2	68
Marlboro, N.J., U.S.	C4	107
Marlboro, N.Y., U.S.	D6	109
Marlboro, Vt., U.S.	F3	122
Marlboro, co., S.C., U.S.	B8	117
Marlborough, Guy.	A3	59
Marlborough, Eng., U.K.	C6	12
Marlborough, Ct., U.S.	C6	84
Marlborough, Ma., U.S.	B4	98
Marlborough, N.H., U.S.	E2	106
Marle, Fr.	E3	17
Marlette, Mi., U.S.	E7	99
Marley, Md., U.S.	*B4	97
Marlin, Tx., U.S.	D4	120
Marlinton, W.V., U.S.	C4	125
Marlow, E. Ger.	D6	15
Marlow, Al., U.S.	D5	78
Marlow, N.H., U.S.	D2	106
Marlow, W.V., U.S.	C4	113
Marlow Heights, Md., U.S.	*C4	97
Marlton, N.J., U.S.	D3	107
Marly-le-Roi, Fr.	g9	16
Marmaduke, Ar., U.S.	A5	81
Marmande, Fr.	E4	16
Marmara, Sea of	B7	40
Marmara Island, i., Tur.	B6	25
Marmaris, Tur.	D7	40
Marmarth, N.D., U.S.	C2	111
Marmelos, Rio dos, stm., Braz.	D2	59
Marmet, W.V., U.S.	C3	125
Marmolada, mtn., Italy	C7	20
Marmora, Ont.	C7	73
Marmora, N.J., U.S.	E3	107
Marmore, stm., Italy	E4	21
Marnay, Fr.	B1	20
Marnaz, Fr.	D2	21
Marne, W. Ger.	E3	15
Marne, Ia., U.S.	C2	92
Marne, Mi., U.S.	E5	99
Marne, dept., Fr.	F4	17
Marne, stm., Fr.	C5	16
Marne au Rhin, Canal de la, Fr.	F4	17
Maroa, Il., U.S.	C5	90
Maroa, Ven.	C4	60
Maroantsetra, Madag.	g9	49
Maromokotro, mtn., Madag.	f9	49
Marondera, Zimb.	A5	49
Marone, Italy	E9	21
Maroni, stm., S.A.	B4	59
Maroochydore-Mooloolaba, Austl.	E9	50
Maro Reef, rf., Hi., U.S.	k13	88
Maroua, Cam.	C2	46
Marovoay, Madag.	g9	49
Marowijne, dept., Sur.	B4	59
Marquam, Or., U.S.	B4	114
Marquand, Mo., U.S.	D7	102
Marquesas Islands, is., Fr. Poly.	G13	6
Marquesas Keys, is., Fl., U.S.	H4	86
Marquette, Man.	D7	70
Marquette, Ia., U.S.	A6	92
Marquette, Ks., U.S.	D6	93
Marquette, Mi., U.S.	B3	99
Marquette, Ne., U.S.	D8	104
Marquette, co., Mi., U.S.	B3	99
Marquette, co., Wi., U.S.	E4	126
Marquette Heights, Il., U.S.	C4	90
Marquez, Tx., U.S.	D4	120
Marquis, Sask.	G3	75
Marquise, Fr.	D9	12
Marrah, Jabal, mts., Sud.	C1	47
Marrakech, Mor.	C3	44
Marree, Austl.	E6	50
Marrero, La., U.S.	k11	95
Marrickville, Austl.	*f9	50
Marriott, Ut., U.S.	*B3	121
Marromeu, Moz.	A6	49
Marrowbone, Ky., U.S.	D4	94
Marrtown, W.V., U.S.	B3	125
Mars, Pa., U.S.	E1	115
Mars, Rivière à, stm., Que.	A7	74
Marsabit, Kenya	A6	48
Marsā Burayqah, Libya	C3	43
Marsala, Italy	F4	23
Marsā Maţrūḩ, Eg.	B2	38
Marsā Sūsah, Libya	C4	43
Marsden, Sask.	E1	75
Marseillan, Fr.	F5	16
Marseille, Fr.	F6	16
Marseilles, Il., U.S.	B5	90
Marshall, Sask.	D1	75
Marshall, Lib.	E2	45
Marshall, Ar., U.S.	B3	81
Marshall, Il., U.S.	D6	90
Marshall, In., U.S.	E3	91
Marshall, Mi., U.S.	F6	99
Marshall, Mn., U.S.	F3	100
Marshall, Mo., U.S.	B4	102
Marshall, N.C., U.S.	f10	110
Marshall, N.D., U.S.	B3	111
Marshall, Ok., U.S.	A4	113
Marshall, Tx., U.S.	C5	120
Marshall, Wa., U.S.	g13	124
Marshall, Wi., U.S.	E4	126
Marshall, co., Al., U.S.	A3	78
Marshall, co., Il., U.S.	B4	90
Marshall, co., In., U.S.	B5	91
Marshall, co., Ia., U.S.	C4	92
Marshall, co., Ks., U.S.	C7	93
Marshall, co., Ky., U.S.	f9	94
Marshall, co., Mn., U.S.	B2	100
Marshall, co., Ms., U.S.	A4	101
Marshall, co., Ok., U.S.	C5	113
Marshall, co., S.D., U.S.	B8	118
Marshall, co., Tn., U.S.	B5	119
Marshall, co., W.V., U.S.	B4	125
Marshallberg, N.C., U.S.	C6	110
Marshall Corner, N.H., U.S.	E4	106
Marshall Islands, ter., T.T.P.I.	F10	6
Marshalls Creek, Pa., U.S.	D11	115
Marshallton, De., U.S.	B3	85
Marshalltown, Ia., U.S.	B5	92
Marshallville, Ga., U.S.	D3	87
Marshallville, Oh., U.S.	B4	112
Marshes Siding, Ky., U.S.	D5	94
Marshfield, Ma., U.S.	B6	98
Marshfield, Mo., U.S.	D5	102
Marshfield, Vt., U.S.	C4	122
Marshfield, Wi., U.S.	D3	126
Marshfield Hills, Ma., U.S.	B6	98
Marsh Fork, stm., W.V., U.S.	n13	125
Marsh Harbour, Bah.	A5	64
Marsh Hill, Pa., U.S.	D8	115
Marsh Hill, N.C., U.S.	f10	110
Mars Hill, mtn., Me., U.S.	B5	96
Marsh Island, i., La., U.S.	E4	95
Marsh Lake, res., Mn., U.S.	E2	100
Marsh Peak, mtn., Ut., U.S.	C6	121
Marshville, N.C., U.S.	C2	110
Marshyhope Creek, stm., Md., U.S.	C6	97
Marsing, Id., U.S.	F2	89
Marsteller, Pa., U.S.	E4	115
Marston, Mo., U.S.	E8	102
Marston, N.C., U.S.	C3	110
Marstons Mills, Ma., U.S.	C7	98
Mart, Tx., U.S.	D4	120
Martaban, Burma	E10	36
Martaban, Gulf of, b., Burma	E10	36
Martap, Cam.	D2	46
Martapura, Indon.	F4	34
Martel, Fl., U.S.	C4	86
Martell, Ne., U.S.	D9	104
Martelle, Ia., U.S.	B6	92
Martensdale, Ia., U.S.	C4	92
Martha, Ok., U.S.	C2	113
Marthasville, Mo., U.S.	C6	102
Martha's Vineyard, i., Ma., U.S.	D6	98
Marthaville, La., U.S.	C2	95
Martí, Cuba	D9	64
Martignano, Lake, l., Italy	g8	23
Martigny[-Ville], Switz.	E3	18
Martigues, Fr.	F6	16
Martin, Czech.	D5	26
Martin, Ga., U.S.	B3	87
Martin, Ky., U.S.	C7	94
Martin, La., U.S.	B2	95
Martin, Mi., U.S.	F5	99
Martin, N.D., U.S.	B5	111
Martin, Oh., U.S.	e7	112
Martin, S.C., U.S.	E5	117
Martin, S.D., U.S.	D4	118
Martin, Tn., U.S.	A3	119
Martin, Ut., U.S.	D5	121
Martin, co., Fl., U.S.	E6	86
Martin, co., In., U.S.	G4	91
Martin, co., Ky., U.S.	C7	94
Martin, co., Mn., U.S.	G4	100
Martin, co., N.C., U.S.	B5	110
Martin, co., Tx., U.S.	C2	120
Martin, co., Ky., U.S.	C4	90
Martina [Franca], Italy	D6	23
Martin City, Mt., U.S.	B3	103
Martindale, Que.	D2	74
Martindale, Tx., U.S.	h8	120
Martinez, Ca., U.S.	C2	82
Martinez, Ga., U.S.	C4	87
Martinique, dep., N.A.	I14	64
Martin Lake, res., Al., U.S.	C4	78
Martin Peninsula, pen., Ant.	B1	7
Martin Point, c., Ak., U.S.	A11	79
Martinsburg, In., U.S.	H5	91
Martinsburg, Mo., U.S.	B6	102
Martinsburg, Ne., U.S.	B9	104
Martinsburg, N.Y., U.S.	B5	109
Martinsburg, Oh., U.S.	B3	112
Martinsburg, Pa., U.S.	F5	115
Martinsburg, W.V., U.S.	B7	125
Martinsdale, Mt., U.S.	D6	103
Martins Ferry, Oh., U.S.	B5	112
Martins Pond, l., Ma., U.S.	f11	98
Martinsville, Il., U.S.	D6	90
Martinsville, In., U.S.	F5	91
Martinsville, Ms., U.S.	D3	101
Martinsville, Mo., U.S.	A3	102
Martinsville, Oh., U.S.	C2	112
Martinsville, Va., U.S.	D3	123
Martinton, Il., U.S.	C5	90
Martinville, Que.	D6	74
Martos, Spain	D4	22
Martre, Lac la, l., N.W. Ter.	D9	66
Martwick, Ky., U.S.	C2	94
Marty, S.D., U.S.	E7	118
Marudi, Malay.	E4	34
Ma'rūf, Afg.	B4	36
Marugame, Japan	I6	33
Marum, Neth.	A5	17
Marumsco Creek, stm., Md., U.S.	D6	97
Mārūn, stm., Iran	F4	39
Marv Dasht, Iran	G6	39
Marvejols, Fr.	E5	16
Marvel, Al., U.S.	B2	78
Marvel, Co., U.S.	D2	83
Marvell, Ar., U.S.	C5	81
Marvin, S.D., U.S.	B9	118
Marvine, Mount, mtn., Ut., U.S.	E4	121
Marvyn, Al., U.S.	C4	78
Marwayne, Alta.	C5	68
Mary, Sov. Un.	F9	29
Mary, Lake, l., Mn., U.S.	E3	100
Mary, Lake, l., Ms., U.S.	D2	101
Maryborough, Austl.	E9	50
Maryborough, Austl.	G7	50
Marydel, De., U.S.	D3	85
Marydel, Md., U.S.	B6	97
Maryfield, Sask.	H5	75
Maryland, state, U.S.	B4	97
Maryland City, Md., U.S.	B4	97
Maryland Heights, Mo., U.S.	f13	102
Maryland Line, Md., U.S.	A4	97
Maryland Point, c., Md., U.S.	D3	97
Maryport, Eng., U.K.	C5	10
Marys, stm., Nv., U.S.	B6	105
Mary's Harbour, Newf.	B4	72
Mary's Igloo, Ak., U.S.	B6	79
Marys Peak, mtn., Or., U.S.	C3	114
Marystown, Newf.	E4	72
Marysvale, Ut., U.S.	E3	121
Marysville, N.B.	D3	71
Marysville, Ca., U.S.	C3	82
Marysville, Id., U.S.	E7	89
Marysville, Ks., U.S.	C7	93
Marysville, Mi., U.S.	F8	99
Marysville, Mt., U.S.	D4	103
Marysville, Oh., U.S.	B2	112
Marysville, Pa., U.S.	F8	115
Marysville, Wa., U.S.	A3	124
Marytown, Wi., U.S.	k9	126
Maryūt, Buḩayrat, l., Eg.	C1	41
Maryville, Mo., U.S.	A3	102
Maryville, Tn., U.S.	D10	119
Marzagão, Braz.	D3	56
Marzūq, Libya	D2	43
Marzūq, Idehan, dunes, Libya	E2	43
Mas'adah, Isr. Occ.	A7	41
Matão, Braz.	C4	56
Masai Steppe, pl., Tan.	B6	48
Masaka, Ug.	B5	48
Masalembu Besar, i., Indon.	G4	34
Masalok, Puntan, c., N. Mar. Is.	D7	52
Masan, S. Kor.	D10	31
Masardis, Me., U.S.	B4	96
Masaryktown, Fl., U.S.	D4	86
Masatiele, S. Afr.	H5	49
Masasi, Tan.	D6	48
Masatepe, Nic.	E7	63
Masaya, Nic.	E7	63
Masbate, Phil.	C6	34
Masbate, i., Phil.	C6	34
Mascoma, stm., N.H., U.S.	C2	106
Mascot, Tn., U.S.	C10	119
Mascota, Mex.	m11	62
Mascotte, Fl., U.S.	D5	86
Mascoutah, Il., U.S.	E4	90
Mascuspana, Mex.	B1	62
Masefield, Sask.	H2	75
Mashḥabbe Sade, Isr.	D4	41
Mashapaug Pond, l., Ct., U.S.	A7	84
Mashiko, Japan	F12	33
Mashīz, Iran	G8	39
Mashkel, Hāmūn-i-, reg., Pak.	G11	39
Māshkīd, stm., Asia	H11	39
Mashpee, Ma., U.S.	C7	98
Mashra'ar Raqq, Sud.	D2	47
Masindi, Ug.	A5	48
Masira, i., Oman	C5	38
Masisea, Peru	E3	58
Masisi, Zaire	B4	48
Mathis, Tx., U.S.	E4	120
Masjed-e Soleymān, Iran	B4	38
Maskanah, Syria	D12	40
Maskell, Ne., U.S.	B9	104
Maskinongé, Que.	C4	74
Maskinongé, co., Que.	C4	74
Masnières, Fr.	D3	17
Masoala, Cap, c., Madag.	g10	49
Mason, Mi., U.S.	F6	99
Mason, Nv., U.S.	E2	105
Mason, N.H., U.S.	E3	106
Mason, Oh., U.S.	C1	112
Mason, Ok., U.S.	B5	113
Mason, Tn., U.S.	B2	119
Mason, Tx., U.S.	D3	120
Mason, W.V., U.S.	B2	125
Mason, Wi., U.S.	B2	126
Mason, co., Il., U.S.	C4	90
Mason, co., Ky., U.S.	B6	94
Mason, co., Mi., U.S.	D4	99
Mason, co., Tx., U.S.	D3	120
Mason, co., Wa., U.S.	B2	124
Mason, co., W.V., U.S.	C3	125
Mason City, Il., U.S.	C4	90
Mason City, Ia., U.S.	A4	92
Mason City, Ne., U.S.	C6	104
Masonhall, Tn., U.S.	A2	119
Masontown, Pa., U.S.	G2	115
Masontown, W.V., U.S.	B5	125
Masonville, Ar., U.S.	D4	81
Masonville, Co., U.S.	B5	83
Masonville, N.Y., U.S.	C5	109
Masqaţ, Oman	C5	38
Massa, Italy	D5	23
Massabesic Lake, l., N.H., U.S.	E4	106
Massac, co., Il., U.S.	F5	90
Massachusetts, state, U.S.	B4	98
Massachusetts Bay, b., Ma., U.S.	B6	98
Massacre Lake, l., Nv., U.S.	B2	105
Massaemett Mountain, mtn., Ma., U.S.	A2	98
Massafra, Italy	D6	23
Massakory, Chad	C3	46
Massa Marittima, Italy	C3	23
Massangena, Moz.	B5	49
Massanutten Mountain, mts., Va., U.S.	B4	123
Massapê, Braz.	B2	57
Massapequa, N.Y., U.S.	*E7	109
Massapequa Park, N.Y., U.S.	*E7	109
Massapoag Lake, l., Ma., U.S.	h11	98
Massasecum, Lake, l., N.H., U.S.	D6	97
Massawa (Mitsiwa), Eth.	B4	47
Massena, Ia., U.S.	C3	92
Massena, N.Y., U.S.	f10	109
Massenya, Chad	C3	46
Masset, B.C.	C1	69
Masset Inlet, b., B.C.	C1	69
Massey, Ont.	A2	73
Massey, Md., U.S.	B6	97
Massies Mill, Va., U.S.	C3	123
Massillon, Oh., U.S.	B4	112
Massinga, Moz.	B6	49
Massive, Mount, mtn., Co., U.S.	B4	83
Masson Island, i., Ant.	C22	7
Masten's Corner, De., U.S.	E3	85
Mastergeehy, Ire.	F1	11
Masterton, N.Z.	N15	51
Mastic, N.Y., U.S.	*n16	109
Mastic Beach, N.Y., U.S.	n16	109
Mastigouche, Réserve, Que.	C4	74
Mastung, Pak.	C4	36
Masturah, Sau. Ar.	C3	38
Masuda, Japan	I5	33
Masuria, reg., Pol.	B6	26
Masury, Oh., U.S.	A5	112
Masvingo (Nyanda), Zimb.	B5	49
Mata, Zaire	C3	48
Mata Amarilla, Arg.	D2	54
Matachewan, Ont.	p19	73
Mata de São João, Braz.	D3	57
Matadi, Zaire	C1	48
Matador, Sask.	G2	75
Matador, Tx., U.S.	B2	120
Matagalpa, Nic.	D7	63
Matagorda, Tx., U.S.	E5	120
Matagorda, co., Tx., U.S.	E5	120
Matagorda Bay, b., Tx., U.S.	E5	120
Matagorda Island, i., Tx., U.S.	E4	120
Matagorda Peninsula, pen., Tx., U.S.	E5	120
Matak, i., Indon.	K7	35
Matam, Sen.	C2	45
Matamoros, Mex.	D12	115
Matamoros, Mex.	B5	63
Matamoros [de la Laguna], Mex.	B4	63
Matane, Que.	k13	74
Matanuska, stm., Ak., U.S.	g18	79
Matanzas, Cuba	C3	64
Matanzas, prov., Cuba	C3	64
Matanzas Inlet, b., Fl., U.S.	C5	86
Matara, Sri L.	G7	36
Mataram, Indon.	G5	34
Matarani, Peru	E3	58
Mataró, Spain	B7	41
Matataula, Cape, c., Am. Sam.	G13	52
Matāʻutu, W. Sam.	F12	52
Mataura, N.Z.	C4	107
Matawan, N.J., U.S.	C4	107
Matehuala, Mex.	C4	63
Matera, Italy	D6	23
Mateszalka, Hung.	B6	24
Mateur, Tun.	F2	23
Matewan, W.V., U.S.	D2	125
Matfield Green, Ks., U.S.	D7	93
Mather, Man.	E2	70
Mather, Pa., U.S.	G1	115
Mather, Wi., U.S.	D3	126
Mather Air Force Base, mil., Ca., U.S.	C3	82
Mather Peaks, mts., Wy., U.S.	B5	127
Matherville, Il., U.S.	B3	90
Mathews, Al., U.S.	D3	101
Mathews, La., U.S.	E5	95
Mathews, Va., U.S.	C6	123
Mathews, co., Va., U.S.	C6	123
Mathews, Lake, l., Ca., U.S.	n14	82
Mathias, W.V., U.S.	B6	125
Mathiston, Ms., U.S.	B4	101
Mathura (Muttra), India	C6	36
Mati, Alb.	B2	25
Matiakoali, Burkina	D5	45
Matinenda Lake, l., Ont.	A2	73
Matinicus, Me., U.S.	E4	96
Matinicus Island, i., Me., U.S.	E3	96
Matlock, Eng., U.K.	A6	12
Matlock, La., U.S.	E5	90
Matlock, In., U.S.	A2	92
Matoaca, Va., U.S.	n18	123
Matoaka, W.V., U.S.	D3	125
Mato Grosso, state, Braz.	B4	55
Mato Grosso, Planalto do, plat., Braz.	E5	53
Mato Grosso do Sul, state, Braz.	B2	56
Matosinhos, Port.	B1	22
Mato Verde, Braz.	B4	56
Matrah, Oman	C5	38
Matrosovo, Sov. Un.	B11	33
Matsqui, B.C.	f13	69
Matsudo, Japan	*I9	33
Matsue, Japan	D11	31
Matsuida, Japan	m17	33
Matsumae, Japan	F10	33
Matsumoto, Japan	H9	33
Matsuyama, Japan	E11	31
Matsuzaka, Japan	I8	33
Matsuzaki, Japan	o17	33
Mattamiscontis Lake, l., Me., U.S.	C4	96
Mattamuskeet, Lake, l., N.C., U.S.	B6	110
Mattapoisett, Ma., U.S.	C6	98
Mattaponi, stm., Va., U.S.	C5	123
Mattawa, Ont.	A6	73
Mattawamkeag, Me., U.S.	C4	96
Mattawamkeag, stm., Me., U.S.	C4	96
Mattawamkeag, East Branch, stm., Me., U.S.	C4	96
Mattawamkeag, West Branch, stm., Me., U.S.	C4	96
Mattawamkeag Lake, l., Me., U.S.	C4	96
Mattawana, Pa., U.S.	F6	115
Mattawoman Creek, stm., Md., U.S.	C3	97
Matterhorn, mtn., Eur.	B1	23
Matterhorn, mtn., Nv., U.S.	B6	105
Matterson Inlet, b., Ant.	g40	7
Matter Vispa, stm., Switz.	D4	21
Matteson, Il., U.S.	k9	90
Matthews, In., U.S.	C7	91
Matthews, Mo., U.S.	E8	102
Matthews, N.C., U.S.	B2	110
Matthews Mountain, mtn., Mo., U.S.	D6	102
Matthews Ridge, Guy.	A2	59
Matthew Town, Bah.	D7	64
Mattituck, N.Y., U.S.	n16	109
Mattoon, Il., U.S.	D5	90
Mattoon, Wi., U.S.	C4	126
Mattoon, Lake, res., Il., U.S.	D5	90
Mattson, Ms., U.S.	A3	101
Mattydale, N.Y., U.S.	B4	109
Matucana, Peru	D2	58
Matuku Island, i., Fiji	I15	52
Matundu, Zaire	A3	48
Matunuck, R.I., U.S.	G3	116
Matura Bay, b., Trin.	N23	65
Maturín, Ven.	B5	60
Maúa, Moz.	D6	48
Mauban, Phil.	o13	34
Maubeuge, Fr.	B5	16
Ma-Ubin, Burma	D1	35
Mauchline, Scot., U.K.	E4	13
Mauckport, In., U.S.	H5	91
Maud, Scot., U.K.	C6	13
Maud, Oh., U.S.	n13	112
Maud, Ok., U.S.	B5	113
Maudlow, Mt., U.S.	D5	103
Maués, Braz.	C3	59
Maués-Açu, stm., Braz.	C3	59
Mauganj, India	E8	36
Maugansville, Md., U.S.	A2	97
Maugerville, N.B.	D3	71
Maughold Head, c., I. of Man	F4	13
Maui, co., Hi., U.S.	B5	88
Maui, i., Hi., U.S.	C6	88
Mauk, Ga., U.S.	D2	87
Mauldin, S.C., U.S.	B3	117
Maule, prov., Chile	B2	54
Mauléon [-Licharre], Fr.	F3	16
Maumakeogh, hill, Ire.	C2	11
Maumee, Oh., U.S.	A2	112
Maumee, stm., U.S.	A5	112
Maumee Bay, b., U.S.	G7	99
Maumelle, Lake, res., Ar., U.S.	C3	81
Maun, Bots.	A3	49
Mauna Kea, vol., Hi., U.S.	D6	88
Maunaloa, Hi., U.S.	B4	88
Mauna Loa, vol., Hi., U.S.	D6	88
Maunalua Bay, b., Hi., U.S.	g10	88
Maunath Bhanjan, India	E9	37
Maunawili, Hi., U.S.	g10	88
Maungdaw, Burma	E5	90
Maunie, Il., U.S.	E5	90
Maunoir, Lac, l., N.W. Ter.	C8	66
Maupin, Or., U.S.	B5	114
Maurepas, La., U.S.	h10	95
Maurepas, Lake, l., La., U.S.	D5	95
Maurertown, Va., U.S.	B4	123
Maurice, La., U.S.	D3	95
Maurice, La., U.S.	B1	92
Maurice, stm., N.J., U.S.	E2	107
Maurice, Lake, l., Austl.	E5	50
Mauricetown, N.J., U.S.	E3	107
Mauritania, ctry., Afr.	B3	45
Mauritius, ctry., Afr.	H24	2
Maury, N.C., U.S.	B5	110
Maury, co., Tn., U.S.	B4	119
Maury City, Tn., U.S.	B2	119
Maury Island, pen., Wa., U.S.	f11	124
Mauston, Wi., U.S.	E3	126
Mauterndorf, Aus.	E6	18
Mauwee Peak, mtn., Ct., U.S.	B2	84
Maverick, co., Tx., U.S.	E2	120
Mavinga, Ang.	B3	49
Mawdesley Lake, l., Man.	B1	70
Mawer, Sask.	G2	75
Mawjib, Wādī al, val., Jord.	C7	41
Mawlamyine, Burma	E10	36
Mawson, Ant.	C19	7
Mawson, Ant.	C19	7
Mawson Coast, Ant.	C19	7
Mawson Escarpment, clf., Ant.	e40	7
Mawson Glacier, ice, Ant.	A7	7
Mawson Peninsula, pen., Ant.	C28	7
Max, Ne., U.S.	D4	104
Max, N.D., U.S.	B4	111
Maxbass, N.D., U.S.	A4	111
Maxcanú, Mex.	C6	63
Maxeys, Ga., U.S.	C3	87

Name	Map Ref.	Page
Maxie, La., U.S.	D3	95
Maxinkuckee, Lake, l., In., U.S.	B5	91
Maxixe, Moz.	B6	49
Max Meadows, Va., U.S.	D2	123
Maxstone, Sask.	H2	75
Maxton, N.C., U.S.	C3	110
Maxville, Ont.	B10	73
Maxville, Mt., U.S.	D3	103
Maxwell, Ca., U.S.	C2	82
Maxwell, In., U.S.	E6	91
Maxwell, Ia., U.S.	C4	92
Maxwell, Ne., U.S.	C5	104
Maxwell, N.M., U.S.	A5	108
Maxwell, Tn., U.S.	B5	119
Maxwell Acres, W.V., U.S.	g8	125
Maxwell Air Force Base, mil., Al., U.S.	C3	78
Maxwell Colony, S.D., U.S.	D8	118
May, Id., U.S.	E5	89
May, Ok., U.S.	A2	113
May, Tx., U.S.	C3	120
May, Isle of, i., Scot., U.K.	D6	13
May, Mount, mtn., Alta.	B1	68
Maya, Mesa de, mtn., Co., U.S.	D7	83
Mayaguana, i., Bah.	C7	64
Mayaguana Passage, strt., Bah.	C7	64
Mayagüez, P.R.	G11	64
Mayagüez, Bahía de, b., P.R.	B1	65
Mayama, Congo	B1	48
Maya Mountains, mts., N.A.	D6	64
Mayari, Cuba	O24	65
Mayaro Bay, b., Trin.	D4	101
Maybank, Ms., U.S.	C6	113
Maybee, Mi., U.S.	F7	99
Maybell, Co., U.S.	A2	83
Mayberry, Md., U.S.	A3	97
Maybeury, W.V., U.S.	*D3	125
Maybole, Scot., U.K.	C4	10
Maydh, Som.	C6	47
Maydī, Yemen	D4	38
Maydūn Pyramid, hist., Egypt	E3	41
Mayen, W. Ger.	C3	18
Mayence see Mainz, W. Ger.	D4	18
Mayenne, Fr.	C3	16
Mayenne, stm., Fr.	D3	16
Mayer, Az., U.S.	C3	80
Mayersville, Ms., U.S.	C2	101
Mayerthorpe, Alta.	C3	68
Mayes, co., Ok., U.S.	A6	113
Mayesville, S.C., U.S.	D7	117
Mayetta, Ks., U.S.	C8	93
Mayetta, N.J., U.S.	D4	107
Mayfair, Sask.	E2	75
Mayfield, Ks., U.S.	E6	93
Mayfield, Mi., U.S.	f9	94
Mayfield, N.Y., U.S.	B4	109
Mayfield, Oh., U.S.	B12	113
Mayfield, Pa., U.S.	C10	115
Mayfield, Ut., U.S.	D4	121
Mayfield Heights, Oh., U.S.	A4	112
Mayfield, Lake, res., Wa., U.S.	C3	124
Mayflower, Ar., U.S.	C3	81
Mayflower Village, Ca., U.S.	*E4	82
Mayger, Or., U.S.	A3	114
Mayhew, Ms., U.S.	B5	101
Mayhill, N.M., U.S.	E4	108
Maykain, Sov. Un.	C9	28
Mayking, Ky., U.S.	C7	94
Maykop, Sov. Un.	G17	8
Mayland, Tn., U.S.	C8	119
Maymont, Sask.	E2	75
Maymyo, Burma	D10	36
Maynard, Ar., U.S.	A5	81
Maynard, Ia., U.S.	B6	92
Maynard, Ky., U.S.	D3	94
Maynard, Ma., U.S.	B5	98
Maynard, Mn., U.S.	F3	100
Maynardville, Tn., U.S.	C10	119
Mayne, B.C.	g12	69
Mayne Island, i., B.C.	g12	69
Maynooth, Ont.	B7	73
Maynooth, Ire.	D5	11
Mayo, Yukon	D5	66
Mayo, Fl., U.S.	B3	86
Mayo, Md., U.S.	C4	97
Mayo, S.C., U.S.	A4	117
Mayo, co., Ire.	D2	11
Mayo, stm., Arg.	D2	54
Mayodan, N.C., U.S.	A3	110
Mayo Lake, l., Yukon	D6	66
Mayon Volcano, vol., Phil.	C6	34
Mayor Pablo Lagerenza, Para.	C3	55
Mayotte, dep., Afr.	f9	49
May Park, Or., U.S.	B8	114
May Pen, Jam.	F5	64
Mayport Naval Station, mil., Fl., U.S.	B5	86
Mayreau, i., St. Vin.	V26	65
Mayrhofen, Aus.	B7	20
Mays Landing, N.J., U.S.	E3	107
Mays Lick, Ky., U.S.	B6	94
Maysville, Al., U.S.	A3	78
Maysville, Ar., U.S.	A1	81
Maysville, Ga., U.S.	B3	87
Maysville, Ia., U.S.	G3	91
Maysville, Ks., U.S.	g10	92
Maysville, Ky., U.S.	B6	94
Maysville, Mo., U.S.	B3	102
Maysville, N.C., U.S.	C5	110
Maysville, Ok., U.S.	C4	113
Maysville, W.V., U.S.	B5	125
Mayumba, Gabon	F2	46
Māyūram, India	F6	36
Mayview, Mo., U.S.	B4	102
Mayville, Mi., U.S.	E7	99
Mayville, N.Y., U.S.	C1	109
Mayville, N.D., U.S.	B8	111
Mayville, Or., U.S.	B6	114
Mayville, Wi., U.S.	E5	126
Maywood, Ca., U.S.	*n12	82
Maywood, Il., U.S.	k9	90
Maywood, Mo., U.S.	B6	102
Maywood, Ne., U.S.	D5	104
Maywood, N.J., U.S.	h8	107
Maywood Park, Or., U.S.	B4	114
Maza, Sask.	B4	54
Maza, N.D., U.S.	A6	111
Mazabuka, Zam.	E4	48
Mazamet, Fr.	F5	16
Mazapil, Mex.	C4	63
Mazara del Vallo, Italy	F4	23
Mazār-e Sharīf, Afg.	A4	36
Mazār'ī an Nūbānī, Isr. Occ.	g11	41
Mazarn Creek, stm., Ar., U.S.	g7	81
Mazarredo, Arg.	D3	54
Mazarrón, Spain	D3	22
Mazaruni, stm., Guy.	A2	59
Mazaruni-Potaro, dept., Guy.	A3	59
Mazatenango, Guat.	E6	63
Mazatlán, Mex.	C3	63
Mazatzal Mountains, mts., Az., U.S.	C4	80
Mazatzal Peak, mtn., Az., U.S.	C4	80
Mažeikiai, Sov. Un.	C4	27
Mazenod, Sask.	H2	75
Mazeppa, Mn., U.S.	F6	100
Mazie, Ok., U.S.	A6	113
Mazomanie, Wi., U.S.	E4	126
Mazon, Il., U.S.	B5	90
Mbabane, Swaz.	C5	49
Mbaïki, Cen. Afr. Rep.	E3	46
Mbala (Abercorn), Zam.	C5	48
Mbale, Ug.	A5	48
Mbalmayo, Cam.	E2	46
Mbamba Bay, Tan.	D5	48
Mbandaka, Zaire	A2	48
M'banza Congo, Ang.	C1	48
Mbanza-Ngungu, Zaire	C1	48
Mbarara, Tan.	B5	48
Mbari, stm., Cen. Afr. Rep.	D4	46
Mbeya, Tan.	C5	48
Mbeya, prov., Tan.	B1	48
Mbinda, Congo	D1	45
Mbout, Maur.	C2	45
Mbuji-Mayi, Zaire	C3	48
Mburucuyá, Arg.	D2	71
McAdam, N.B.	D2	71
McAdams, Ms., U.S.	B4	101
McAdoo, Pa., U.S.	E9	115
McAdoo, Tx., U.S.	C2	120
McAfee, Ms., U.S.	C4	101
McAfee Peak, mtn., Nv., U.S.	B6	105
McAlester, Ok., U.S.	C6	113
McAlester, Lake, res., Ok., U.S.	B6	113
McAlister, N.M., U.S.	C6	108
McAlisterville, Pa., U.S.	E7	115
McAllen, Tx., U.S.	F3	120
McAllister, Mt., U.S.	E5	103
McAlmont, Ar., U.S.	h10	81
McAlpin, Fl., U.S.	B4	86
McAlpine, Md., U.S.	B4	97
McAlpine Lock and Dam, U.S.	H6	91
McAndrews, Ky., U.S.	C7	94
McArthur, Oh., U.S.	C3	112
McAuley, Man.	D1	70
McBain, Mi., U.S.	D5	99
McBaine, Mo., U.S.	C5	102
McBee, S.C., U.S.	C7	117
McBride, B.C.	C7	69
Mcbride, Mo., U.S.	D8	102
McCabe, Mt., U.S.	B12	103
McCall, Id., U.S.	E2	89
McCalla, Al., U.S.	g6	78
McCall Creek, Ms., U.S.	D3	101
McCallsburg, Ia., U.S.	B4	92
McCamey, Tx., U.S.	D1	120
McCammon, Id., U.S.	G6	89
McCandless, Pa., U.S.	h13	115
McCanna, N.D., U.S.	A8	111
McCarley, Ms., U.S.	B4	101
McCarthy, Ak., U.S.	C11	79
McCartney Mountain, mtn., Mt., U.S.	E4	103
McCartys, N.M., U.S.	B2	108
McCaskill, Ar., U.S.	D2	81
McCauley Island, i., B.C.	C2	69
McCaulley, Tx., U.S.	C2	120
McCaysville, Ga., U.S.	B2	87
McChord Air Force Base, mil., Wa., U.S.	f11	124
McClain, co., Ok., U.S.	C4	113
McClave, Co., U.S.	C8	83
McCleary, Wa., U.S.	B2	124
McClellan Air Force Base, mil., Ca., U.S.	C3	82
McClelland, Ar., U.S.	B4	81
McClelland, Ia., U.S.	C2	92
McClellandville, De., U.S.	B2	85
McClellanville, S.C., U.S.	E9	117
McCleod, Mt., U.S.	E6	103
McClintock, Mount, mtn., Ant.	A28	7
McCloud, Ca., U.S.	B2	82
McClure, Oh., U.S.	A2	112
McClure, Pa., U.S.	E7	115
McClure, Va., U.S.	e9	123
McClusky, N.D., U.S.	B5	111
McColl, S.C., U.S.	B8	117
McComas, W.V., U.S.	D3	125
McComb, Ms., U.S.	D3	101
McComb, Oh., U.S.	A2	112
McCondy, Ms., U.S.	B5	101
McCone, co., Mt., U.S.	C11	103
McConnell, Il., U.S.	A4	90
McConnell, Tn., U.S.	A3	119
McConnell Air Force Base, mil., Ks., U.S.	g12	93
McConnells, S.C., U.S.	B5	117
McConnellsburg, Pa., U.S.	G6	115
McConnelstown, Pa., U.S.	F5	115
McConnelsville, Oh., U.S.	C4	112
McCook, Ne., U.S.	D5	104
McCook, co., S.D., U.S.	D8	118
McCook Lake, S.D., U.S.	E9	118
McCool, Ms., U.S.	B4	101
McCool Junction, Ne., U.S.	D8	104
McCord, Sask.	H2	75
McCordsville, In., U.S.	E6	91
McCormick, S.C., U.S.	D3	117
McCormick, co., S.C., U.S.	D3	117
McCoy, Co., U.S.	B4	83
McCracken, Ks., U.S.	D4	93
McCracken, co., Ky., U.S.	e9	94
McCreary, Man.	D2	70
McCreary, co., Ky., U.S.	D5	94
McCrory, Ar., U.S.	B4	81
McCulloch, co., Tx., U.S.	D3	120
McCullough, Al., U.S.	D2	78
McCullough Mountain, mtn., Nv., U.S.	H6	105
McCullum, Al., U.S.	B2	78
McCune, Ks., U.S.	E8	93
McCurtain, Ok., U.S.	B7	113
McCurtain, co., Ok., U.S.	C7	113
McCutchenville, Oh., U.S.	B2	112
McDade, Tx., U.S.	D4	120
McDaniel, Md., U.S.	C5	97
McDavid, Fl., U.S.	u14	86
McDermitt, Nv., U.S.	B4	105
McDermott, Oh., U.S.	D2	112
McDonald, Ks., U.S.	C2	93
McDonald, Ms., U.S.	C4	101
McDonald Peak, mtn., Mt., U.S.	C3	103
McDonald, Tn., U.S.	h12	119
McDonald, co., Mo., U.S.	E3	102
McDonald Creek, stm., Mt., U.S.	C8	103
McDonald Islands, is., Austl.	J1	2
McDonough, Ga., U.S.	C2	87
McDonough, N.Y., U.S.	C5	109
McDonough, co., Il., U.S.	C3	90
McDougal, Ar., U.S.	A5	81
McDougall, Mount, mtn., Wy., U.S.	D2	127
McDowell, Ky., U.S.	C7	94
McDowell, Va., U.S.	B3	123
McDowell, co., N.C., U.S.	f10	110
McDowell, co., W.V., U.S.	D3	125
McDowell Mountains, mts., Az., U.S.	k9	80
McDowell Peak, mtn., Az., U.S.	k9	80
McElhattan, Pa., U.S.	D7	115
McElroy Creek, stm., W.V., U.S.	k9	125
McEwen, Tn., U.S.	A4	119
McFadden, Wy., U.S.	E6	127
McFaddin, Tx., U.S.	E4	120
McFall, Mo., U.S.	A3	102
McFarlan, N.C., U.S.	C3	110
McFarland, Ca., U.S.	E4	82
McFarland, Ks., U.S.	C7	93
McFarland, Mi., U.S.	B3	99
McFarland, Wi., U.S.	E4	126
McGaheysville, Va., U.S.	B4	123
McGee, Sask.	F1	75
McGehee, Ar., U.S.	D4	81
McGill, Nv., U.S.	D7	105
McGillivray, B.C.	D6	69
McGillivray, Lac, l., Que.	A7	73
McGivney, N.B.	C4	71
McGrady, N.C., U.S.	A1	110
McGrath, Ak., U.S.	C8	79
McGrath, Mn., U.S.	D5	100
McGraw, N.Y., U.S.	C4	109
McGraws, W.V., U.S.	D3	125
McGregor, Ia., U.S.	A6	92
McGregor, Mn., U.S.	D5	100
McGregor, N.D., U.S.	A3	111
McGregor, Tx., U.S.	D4	120
McGregor, stm., B.C.	B7	69
McGregor Lake, l., Alta.	D4	68
McGrew, Ne., U.S.	C2	104
McGuffey, Oh., U.S.	B2	112
McGuire, Mount, mtn., Id., U.S.	D4	89
McGuire Air Force Base, mil., N.J., U.S.	C3	107
McHenry, Il., U.S.	A5	90
McHenry, Ky., U.S.	C3	94
McHenry, Md., U.S.	k12	97
McHenry, N.D., U.S.	B7	111
McHenry, co., Il., U.S.	A5	90
McHenry, co., N.D., U.S.	A5	111
Mchinga, Tan.	C6	48
Mchinji, Mwi.	D5	48
McHue, Ar., U.S.	B4	81
McIndoe Falls, Vt., U.S.	C4	122
McIntire, Ia., U.S.	A5	92
McIntosh, Al., U.S.	D1	78
McIntosh, Mn., U.S.	C3	100
McIntosh, N.M., U.S.	C3	108
McIntosh, S.D., U.S.	B4	118
McIntosh, co., Ga., U.S.	E5	87
McIntosh, co., N.D., U.S.	C6	111
McIntosh, co., Ok., U.S.	B6	113
McIntosh Lake, l., Sask.	B3	75
McIntosh Run, stm., Md., U.S.	D4	97
McIntyre, Ga., U.S.	D3	87
McIntyre, Pa., U.S.	D7	115
McKague, Sask.	E4	75
McKean, co., Pa., U.S.	C4	115
McKee, Ky., U.S.	C6	94
McKee City, N.J., U.S.	E3	107
McKeesport, Pa., U.S.	F2	115
McKees Rocks, Pa., U.S.	F1	115
McKenney, Va., U.S.	D5	123
McKenzie, Al., U.S.	D3	78
McKenzie, N.D., U.S.	C5	111
McKenzie, Tn., U.S.	A3	119
McKenzie, co., N.D., U.S.	B2	111
McKenzie, stm., Or., U.S.	C4	114
McKenzie Bridge, Or., U.S.	C4	114
McKerrow, Ont.	A3	73
McKinley, Al., U.S.	C2	78
McKinley, Mn., U.S.	C6	100
McKinley, co., N.M., U.S.	B1	108
McKinley, Mount, mtn., Ak., U.S.	C9	79
McKinley Park, Ak., U.S.	C10	79
McKinney, Ky., U.S.	C5	94
McKinney, Tx., U.S.	C4	120
McKinney, Lake, l., Ks., U.S.	E2	93
McKinnon, Wy., U.S.	E3	127
McKittrick, Ca., U.S.	E4	82
McKittrick, Mo., U.S.	C6	102
McKittrick Summit, mtn., Ca., U.S.	E4	82
McKnight Lake, l., Man.	A1	70
McLain, Ms., U.S.	D5	101
McLaughlin, Alta.	C5	68
McLaughlin, S.D., U.S.	B5	118
McLaughlin, stm., Man.	C3	70
McLaurin, Ms., U.S.	D4	101
McLean, Sask.	G3	75
McLean, Il., U.S.	C4	90
McLean, Ne., U.S.	B8	104
McLean, Tx., U.S.	B2	120
McLean, Va., U.S.	g12	123
McLean, co., Il., U.S.	C4	90
McLean, co., Ky., U.S.	C2	94
McLean, co., N.D., U.S.	B4	111
McLean Lake, l., Sask.	A6	68
McLean Mountain, mtn., Me., U.S.	A4	96
McLeansboro, Il., U.S.	E5	90
McLemoresville, Tn., U.S.	B3	119
McLennan, Alta.	B1	68
McLennan, co., Tx., U.S.	D4	120
McLennan Lake, l., Sask.	B3	75
McLeod, N.D., U.S.	C8	111
McLeod, co., Mn., U.S.	F4	100
McLeod, stm., Alta.	C2	68
McLeod Lake, B.C.	B6	69
McLeod Lake, l., B.C.	B6	69
M'Clintock Channel, strt., N.W. Ter.	B12	66
McLoud, Ok., U.S.	B4	113
McLoughlin, Mount, mtn., Or., U.S.	E4	114
McLouth, Ks., U.S.	C8	93
McMechen, W.V., U.S.	B4	125
McMillan, Mi., U.S.	B5	99
McMillan, Lake, res., N.M., U.S.	E5	108
McMinn, co., Tn., U.S.	D9	119
McMinnville, Or., U.S.	B3	114
McMinnville, Tn., U.S.	D8	119
McMorran, Sask.	F1	75
McMullen, co., Tx., U.S.	E3	120
McMurdo, sci., Ant.	B29	7
McMurdo Sound, strt., Ant.	B29	7
McNab, Ar., U.S.	D2	81
McNabb, Il., U.S.	B4	90
McNair, Ms., U.S.	D2	101
McNairy, co., Tn., U.S.	B3	119
McNary, Az., U.S.	C6	80
McNary, La., U.S.	D3	95
McNary Dam, U.S.	B7	114
McNaughton Lake, res., B.C.	C8	69
McNeal, Az., U.S.	F6	80
McNeil, Ar., U.S.	D2	81
McNeil, Tx., U.S.	D4	120
McNeil, Mount, mtn., B.C.	B2	69
McNeil Island, i., Wa., U.S.	f10	124
McNeill, Ms., U.S.	E4	101
McNulty, Or., U.S.	*B4	114
McNutts Island, i., N.S.	F4	71
McPhail, stm., Man.	C3	70
McPherson, Ks., U.S.	D6	93
McPherson, co., Ks., U.S.	D6	93
McPherson, co., Ne., U.S.	C4	104
McPherson, co., S.D., U.S.	B6	118
McQuady, Ky., U.S.	C3	94
McQueeney, Tx., U.S.	h7	120
McRae, Ar., U.S.	B4	81
McRae, Ga., U.S.	D4	87
McRoberts, Ky., U.S.	C7	94
McSherrystown, Pa., U.S.	G7	115
McTaggart, Sask.	H3	75
McTavish, Man.	E3	70
McVeigh, Ky., U.S.	C7	94
McVeytown, Pa., U.S.	F6	115
McVille, N.D., U.S.	B7	111
McWilliams, Al., U.S.	D2	78
Mdandu, Tan.	C5	48
Mdantsane, Ciskei	*D4	49
Me, i., Viet.		
Meacham, Sask.	E3	75
Meacham, Or., U.S.	B8	114
Mead, Co., U.S.	A6	83
Mead, Ne., U.S.	C9	104
Mead, Ok., U.S.	D5	113
Mead, Wa., U.S.	B8	124
Mead, Lake, res., U.S.	A1	80
Meade, Ks., U.S.	E3	93
Meade, co., Ks., U.S.	E3	93
Meade, co., Ky., U.S.	C3	94
Meade, co., S.D., U.S.	C3	118
Meade, stm., Ak., U.S.	A8	79
Meaden Peak, mtn., Co., U.S.	A3	83
Meade Peak, mtn., Id., U.S.	G7	89
Meador, Ky., U.S.	D3	94
Meadow, S.D., U.S.	B3	118
Meadow, Tx., U.S.	C1	120
Meadow, Ut., U.S.	E3	121
Meadow, stm., W.V., U.S.	C4	125
Meadow Bridge, W.V., U.S.	D4	125
Meadowbrook, Fl., U.S.	*D5	86
Meadowbrook, W.V., U.S.	k10	125
Meadow Creek, stm., W.V., U.S.	D4	125
Meadow Creek, stm., W.V., U.S.	n14	125
Meadow Grove, Ne., U.S.	B8	104
Meadow Lake, Sask.	n7	75
Meadowlands, Mn., U.S.	C6	100
Meadow Lands, Pa., U.S.	F1	115
Meadow Mountain, mtn., Md., U.S.	k12	97
Meadowood, De., U.S.	*B3	85
Meadows, Id., U.S.	E2	89
Meadows, N.H., U.S.	B4	106
Meadow Valley Wash, val., Nv., U.S.	F6	105
Meadowview, Va., U.S.	f10	123
Meadville, Ms., U.S.	D3	101
Meadville, Mo., U.S.	B4	102
Meadville, Pa., U.S.	C1	115
Meaford, Ont.	C4	73
Meagher, co., Mt., U.S.	D6	103
Meaghers Grant, N.S.	E6	71
Mealhada, Port.	E3	22
Mealy Mountains, mts., Newf.	h9	72
Meandarra, Austl.	C7	51
Meander Creek Reservoir, res., Oh., U.S.	A5	112
Means, Ky., U.S.	C6	94
Mearim, stm., Braz.	C1	57
Meath, co., Ire.	C5	11
Meath Park, Sask.	E3	75
Meaux, Fr.	C5	16
Mebane, N.C., U.S.	A3	110
Mecca (Makkah), Sau. Ar.	C3	38
Mecca, Ca., U.S.	F5	82
Mecca, In., U.S.	E3	91
Mechanic Falls, Me., U.S.	D2	96
Mechanicsburg, In., U.S.	D5	91
Mechanicsburg, Oh., U.S.	B2	112
Mechanicsburg, Pa., U.S.	F7	115
Mechanicsville, Ia., U.S.	C6	92
Mechanicsville, Md., U.S.	D4	97
Mechanicsville, Vt., U.S.	C2	122
Mechanicville, N.Y., U.S.	C7	109
Mechant, Lake, l., La., U.S.	E4	95
Mechelen (Malines), Bel.	B6	16
Mechrriya, Alg.	C4	44
Mecklenburg, co., N.C., U.S.	B2	110
Mecklenburg, co., Va., U.S.	D4	123
Mecklenburg, hist. reg., E. Ger.	B5	18
Mecklenburg Bay, b., Eur.	A11	18
Meckling, S.D., U.S.	E8	118
Meconta, Moz.	D7	48
Mecosta, Mi., U.S.	E5	99
Mecosta, co., Mi., U.S.	E5	99
Mecúfi, Moz.	D8	48
Medak, India	C5	37
Medan, Indon.	E2	34
Médanos, Arg.	D4	54
Médanos, Arg.		
Médanos, Punta, c., Arg.	D5	54
Medart, Fl., U.S.	B2	86
Medaryville, In., U.S.	B4	91
Meddybemps, Me., U.S.	C5	96
Meddybumps Lake, l., Me., U.S.	C5	96
Medeglia, Switz.	D6	21
Medellín, Col.	B5	60
Medemblik, Neth.	C5	17
Mederdra, Maur.	C1	45
Medfield, Ma., U.S.	h10	98
Medford, Ma., U.S.	B5	98
Medford, Mn., U.S.	F5	100
Medford, N.J., U.S.	D3	107
Medford, N.Y., U.S.	*n15	109
Medford, Ok., U.S.	A4	113
Medford, Or., U.S.	E4	114
Medford, Wi., U.S.	C3	126
Medford Lakes, N.J., U.S.	D3	107
Medfra, Ak., U.S.	C9	79
Medgidia, Rom.	C9	24
Media, Il., U.S.	C3	90
Media, Pa., U.S.	G11	115
Mediapolis, Ia., U.S.	C6	92
Medias, Rom.	B7	24
Medical Lake, Wa., U.S.	B8	124
Medicina, Italy	E7	20
Medicine Bow, Wy., U.S.	E6	127
Medicine Bow, stm., Wy., U.S.	E6	127
Medicine Bow Mountains, mts., U.S.	E6	127
Medicine Bow Peak, mtn., Wy., U.S.	E6	127
Medicine Creek, stm., Mo., U.S.	B4	102
Medicine Creek, stm., Ne., U.S.	D5	104
Medicine Hat, Alta.	D5	68
Medicine Lodge, Ks., U.S.	E5	93
Medicine Lodge, stm., U.S.	E5	93
Medicine Park, Ok., U.S.	C3	113
Medill, Mo., U.S.	A6	102
Medina (Al Madīnah), Sau. Ar.	C2	38
Medina, N.Y., U.S.	B2	109
Medina, N.D., U.S.	C6	111
Medina, Oh., U.S.	A4	112
Medina, Tn., U.S.	B3	119
Medina, Tx., U.S.	E3	120
Medina, Wa., U.S.	e11	124
Medina, co., Oh., U.S.	A4	112
Medina, co., Tx., U.S.	E3	120
Medina, stm., Tx., U.S.	k7	120
Medina del Campo, Spain	C3	22
Medina de Ríoseco, Spain	B3	22
Medina-Sidonia, Spain	D3	22
Medinīpur, India	D8	36
Mediterranean Sea	H12	8
Medjerda, stm., Tun.	F2	23
Medjerda, Monts de la, mts., Afr.	F2	23
Medjez el Bab, Tun.	C5	28
Mednogorsk, Sov. Un.	D3	96
Medomak, Me., U.S.	D3	96
Medomak, stm., Me., U.S.	D3	96
Medora, Il., U.S.	D3	90
Medora, In., U.S.	G5	91
Medora, Ks., U.S.	D6	93
Medora, N.D., U.S.	C2	111
Médouneu, Gabon	E2	46
Medstead, Sask.	D1	75
Meductic, N.B.	D2	71
Meduxnekeag, North Branch, stm., Me., U.S.	B5	96
Medvedica, stm., Sov. Un.	F15	27
Medvedovskaya, Sov. Un.	I12	27
Medvezhi Islands, is., Sov. Un.	B19	29
Medvezh'yegorsk, Sov. Un.	C6	29
Medway, Me., U.S.	C4	96
Medway, Ma., U.S.	B5	98
Medway, stm., N.S.	E5	71
Medzhibozh, Sov. Un.	G6	27
Meekatharra, Austl.	E2	50
Meeker, Co., U.S.	A3	83
Meeker, Ok., U.S.	B5	113
Meeker, co., Mn., U.S.	E4	100
Meelpaeg Lake, res., Newf.	D3	72
Meerane, E. Ger.	E12	18
Meerbusch, W. Ger.	*C3	18
Meersburg, W. Ger.	A7	21
Meerut, India	*C6	36
Meeteetse, Wy., U.S.	B4	127
Meeting Creek, Alta.	C4	68
Meeting Lake, l., Sask.	D2	75
Mega, Eth.	E4	47
Megali Canal, Grc.	g10	25
Megalópolis, Grc.	D4	25
Mégantic, co., Que.	C6	74
Mégantic, Lac, l., Que.	D7	74
Mégantic, Mont, mtn., Que.	D6	74
Mégara, Grc.	D4	25
Megargel, Al., U.S.	D2	78
Megargel, Tx., U.S.	C3	120
Megève, Fr.	F7	16
Meggett, S.C., U.S.	F7	117
Meghalaya, state, India	C9	36
Megunticook, Mount, mtn., Me., U.S.	D3	96
Mehanga, Mn., U.S.	f13	100
Mehekar, India	B5	37
Meherrin, Va., U.S.	C4	123
Meherrin, stm., U.S.	A4	110
Mehlville, Mo., U.S.	f13	102
Mehoopany, Pa., U.S.	C9	115
Mehrān, Iran	B4	38
Mehsāna, India	I5	36
Mehun-sur-Yèvre, Fr.	D5	16
Meia Ponte, stm., Braz.	B5	56
Meiganga, Cam.	D2	46
Meighen Island, i., N.W. Ter.	K32	66
Meigs, Ga., U.S.	E2	87
Meigs, co., Oh., U.S.	C3	112
Meigs, co., Tn., U.S.	D9	119
Meiktila, Burma	D10	36
Meiners Oaks, Ca., U.S.	*E4	82
Meiningen, E. Ger.	C5	18
Meiringen, Switz.	E4	21
Meissen, E. Ger.	E8	18
Meitan, China	G8	31
Meizhou, China	D1	55
Mejillones, Chile	A1	56
Mejillones, Chile	A2	56
Mekele, Eth.	E2	47
Mékhé, Sen.	B1	45
Mekhtar, Pak.	B3	37
Mékinac, Lac, l., Que.	C4	74
Mekinock, N.D., U.S.	A8	111
Mekong, stm., Asia	C6	34
Mekoryuk, Ak., U.S.	C6	79
Meknès, Mor.	H13	30
Mékrou, stm., Afr.	E6	45
Melaka (Malacca), Malay.	M6	35
Melaka, state, Malay.	K5	35
Melbeta, Ne., U.S.	C2	104
Melber, Ky., U.S.	f9	94
Melbourne Beach, Fl., U.S.	D6	86
Melcher, Ia., U.S.	C4	92
Melder, La., U.S.	C3	95
Meldorf, W. Ger.	D3	15
Meldrim, Ga., U.S.	D5	87
Meldrum Bay, Ont.	B1	73
Meleb, Man.	D3	70
Melekeok, Palau	R17	52
Melekess, Sov. Un.	E18	8
Melenki, Sov. Un.	D13	27
Mélèzes, Rivière aux, stm., Que.	g12	67
Melfi, Chad	C3	46
Melfi, Italy	D5	23
Melfort, Sask.	E3	75
Melghir, Chott, l., Alg.	C6	44
Melilla, Sp. N. Afr.	B4	44
Melipilla, Chile	A2	54
Mélisey, Fr.	A2	21
Melita, Man.	E1	70
Melito di Porto Salvo, Italy	F5	23
Melitopol, Sov. Un.	H10	27
Mella, stm., Italy	D6	20
Melle, Fr.	D3	16
Melle, W. Ger.	A3	19
Mellen, Wi., U.S.	B3	126
Mellette, S.D., U.S.	B7	118
Mellette, co., S.D., U.S.	D5	118
Mellit, Sud.	C2	47
Mellor Glacier, ice, Ant.	B19	7
Mellott, In., U.S.	D3	91
Mellow Valley, Al., U.S.	B4	78
Mellwood, Ar., U.S.	C5	81
Mellrichstadt, W. Ger.	C5	19
Mellum, i., W. Ger.	E2	15
Melmore, Oh., U.S.	A2	112
Mělník, Czech.	n18	26
Melo, Ur.	C6	56
Melocheville, Que.	q19	74
Melrose, N.B.	C6	71
Melrose, N.S.	D7	71
Melrose, Ct., U.S.	B5	84
Melrose, Fl., U.S.	C4	86
Melrose, Ia., U.S.	C4	92
Melrose, La., U.S.	C3	95
Melrose, Ma., U.S.	B5	98
Melrose, Mn., U.S.	E4	100
Melrose, N.M., U.S.	C6	108
Melrose, Oh., U.S.	A1	112
Melrose, Wi., U.S.	D3	126
Melrose Park, Fl., U.S.	r13	86
Melrose Park, Il., U.S.	*k9	90
Mels, Switz.	B7	21
Melstone, Mt., U.S.	D9	103
Melstrand, Mi., U.S.	B4	99
Melsungen, W. Ger.	B4	19
Melton Hill Lake, res., Tn., U.S.	D9	119
Melton Mowbray, Eng., U.K.	B7	12
Melun, Fr.	C5	16
Melvaig, Scot., U.K.	C3	13
Melvern, Ks., U.S.	D8	93
Melville, Austl.	*F2	50
Melville, Sask.	G4	75
Melville, La., U.S.	D4	95
Melville, Mt., U.S.	D7	103
Melville, N.Y., U.S.	*n15	109
Melville, i., Austl.	B5	50
Melville, Cape, c., Austl.	B7	50
Melville Bugt, b., Grnld.	B14	61
Melville Hills, hills, N.W. Ter.	C8	66
Melville Island, i., N.W. Ter.	m30	66
Melville Peninsula, pen., N.W. Ter.	C16	66
Melvin, Al., U.S.	D1	78
Melvin, Il., U.S.	C5	90
Melvin, Ia., U.S.	A2	92
Melvin, Ky., U.S.	C7	94
Melvin, Tx., U.S.	D3	120
Melvin, Lough, l., Eur.	C3	11
Melvindale, Mi., U.S.	*p7	99
Melvin Village, N.H., U.S.	C4	106
Melyana, Alg.	B5	44
Mélykút, Hung.	D7	48
Memba, Moz.	D8	48
Memmingen, W. Ger.	E5	18
Mempawah, Indon.	E3	34
Memphis, Fl., U.S.	p10	86
Memphis, In., U.S.	H6	91
Memphis, Mi., U.S.	F8	99
Memphis, Mo., U.S.	A5	102
Memphis, Ne., U.S.	g12	104
Memphis, Tn., U.S.	B1	119
Memphis, Tx., U.S.	B2	120
Memphis, hist., Eg.	C3	38
Memphis Naval Air Station, mil., Tn., U.S.	B2	119
Memphremagog, Lake, l., N.A.	D5	74
Memramcook, N.B.	C5	71
Mena, Ar., U.S.	C1	81
Menahga, Mn., U.S.	D3	100
Ménaka, Mali	C5	45
Menan, Id., U.S.	F7	89
Menands, N.Y., U.S.	C7	109
Menard, Tx., U.S.	D3	120
Menard, co., Il., U.S.	C4	90
Menard, co., Tx., U.S.	D3	120
Menasha, Wi., U.S.	D5	126
Mendawai, stm., Indon.	F4	34
Mende, Fr.	E5	16
Menden, W. Ger.	B2	19
Mendenhall, Ms., U.S.	D4	101
Mendes, Ga., U.S.	D4	87
Mendham, Sask.	G1	75
Mendham, N.J., U.S.	B3	107
Mendi, Eth.	G8	47
Mendip Hills, hills, Eng., U.K.	C5	12
Mendocino, co., Ca., U.S.	C2	82
Mendocino, Cape, c., Ca., U.S.	C1	82
Mendon, Il., U.S.	C2	90
Mendon, Ma., U.S.	h9	98
Mendon, Mi., U.S.	F5	99
Mendon, Mo., U.S.	B4	102
Mendon, N.Y., U.S.	B1	112
Mendon, Oh., U.S.	B1	112
Mendon, Ut., U.S.	B4	121
Mendon, Vt., U.S.	D3	122
Mendota, Ca., U.S.	D3	82
Mendota, Il., U.S.	B4	90
Mendota, Lake, l., Wi., U.S.	E5	126
Mendota Heights, Mn., U.S.	*m13	100
Mendoza, Arg.	A3	54
Mendoza, Pan.	k11	62
Mendoza, prov., Arg.	A3	54
Mendrisio, Switz.	E6	21
Mene de Mauroa, Ven.	A3	60
Mene Grande, Ven.	B3	60
Menemen, Tur.	C6	25
Menen, Bel.	D3	17
Menfi, Italy	F4	23
Mengcheng, China	E8	31
Menggala, Indon.	F3	34

Name	Map Ref.	Page
Menghai, China	B4	35
Menglian, China	G4	31
Mengzi, China	G5	31
Menifee, Ca.	B3	81
Menifee, co., Ky., U.S.	C6	94
Menihek Lakes, l., Newf.	g8	72
Menindee, Austl.	F7	50
Menindee Lake, l., Austl.	F4	51
Menlo, Ga., U.S.	B1	87
Menlo, Ia., U.S.	C3	92
Menlo, Ks., U.S.	C3	93
Menlo, Wa., U.S.	C2	124
Menlo Park, Ca., U.S.	k8	82
Menno, S.D., U.S.	D8	118
Menoken, N.D., U.S.	C5	111
Meno, Ok., U.S.	A3	113
Menominee, Mi., U.S.	C3	99
Menominee, co., Mi., U.S.	C3	99
Menominee, co., Wi., U.S.	C5	126
Menominee, stm., U.S.	C5	126
Menominee Indian Reservation, Wi., U.S.	C5	126
Menomonee, stm., Wi., U.S.	m11	126
Menomonee Falls, Wi., U.S.	E5	126
Menomonie, Wi., U.S.	D2	126
Menongue, Ang.	D2	48
Menor, Mar, b., Spain	D5	22
Menorca, i., Spain	C8	22
Mentakab, Malay.	K5	35
Mentana, Italy	g9	23
Mentawai Islands, is., Indon.	F1	34
Mentmore, N.M., U.S.	B1	108
Menton, Fr.	F7	16
Mentone, Al., U.S.	A4	78
Mentone, In., U.S.	B5	91
Mentone, Tx., U.S.	D1	120
Mentor, Ky., U.S.	k14	94
Mentor, Mn., U.S.	C2	100
Mentor, Oh., U.S.	A4	112
Mentor, Tn., U.S.	n13	119
Mentor-on-the-Lake, Oh., U.S.	A4	112
Menzel Bourguiba, Tun.	B6	44
Menzies, Austl.	F4	50
Menzies, Mount, mtn., Ant.	B19	7
Menziken, Switz.	B5	21
Meoqui, Mex.	B3	63
Meota, Sask.	D1	75
Meppel, Neth.	A7	16
Meppen, W. Ger.	B3	18
Megerghane, Sebkha, pl., Alg.	D5	44
Mequon, Wi., U.S.	E6	126
Merabolo, Gulf of, b., Grc.	E5	25
Meramec, i., Spain	A3	23
Meramec, stm., Mo., U.S.	C7	102
Merano, Italy	A3	23
Merasheen, Newf.	E4	72
Merasheen Island, i., Newf.	E4	72
Merate, Italy	E7	21
Merauke, Indon.	G10	34
Meraux, La., U.S.	k12	95
Mercâra, India	F6	36
Merced, Ca., U.S.	D3	82
Merced, co., Ca., U.S.	D3	82
Merced, stm., Ca., U.S.	D3	82
Mercedes, Arg.	A3	54
Mercedes, Arg.	A5	54
Mercedes, Arg.	E4	55
Mercedes, Tx., U.S.	F4	120
Mercedes, Ur.	E1	56
Mercer, Me., U.S.	D3	96
Mercer, Mo., U.S.	A4	102
Mercer, N.D., U.S.	B5	111
Mercer, Oh., U.S.	B1	112
Mercer, Pa., U.S.	D1	115
Mercer, Tn., U.S.	B2	119
Mercer, Wi., U.S.	B3	126
Mercer, co., Il., U.S.	B3	90
Mercer, co., Ky., U.S.	C5	94
Mercer, co., Mo., U.S.	A4	102
Mercer, co., N.J., U.S.	C3	107
Mercer, co., N.D., U.S.	B4	111
Mercer, co., Oh., U.S.	B1	112
Mercer, co., Pa., U.S.	D1	115
Mercer, co., W.V., U.S.	D3	125
Mercer Island, Wa., U.S.	B3	124
Mercer Island, i., Wa., U.S.	e11	124
Mercersburg, Pa., U.S.	G6	115
Mercerville, N.J., U.S.	C3	107
Mercês, Braz.	g6	56
Merchantville, N.J., U.S.	*D2	107
Mercier, Que.	D4	74
Mercier, Ks., U.S.	C8	93
Mercoal, Alta.	C2	68
Mercury Bay, b., N.Z.	L15	51
Mercury Islands, is., N.Z.	L15	51
Mercy, Cape, c., N.W. Ter.	D20	66
Meredith, Co., U.S.	B4	83
Meredith, N.H., U.S.	C3	106
Meredith, Lake, l., Co., U.S.	C7	83
Meredith, Lake, res., Tx., U.S.	B2	120
Meredith Center, N.H., U.S.	C3	106
Meredosia, Il., U.S.	D3	90
Meredosia Lake, l., Il., U.S.	D3	90
Mereeg, Som.	E6	47
Merefa, Sov. Un.	G11	27
Merepoint, Me., U.S.	g7	96
Mergui, Burma	F10	36
Mergui Archipelago, is., Burma	F10	36
Meriç (Maritsa) (Évros), stm., Eur.	B6	25
Merid, Sask.	F1	75
Mérida, Mex.	C7	63
Mérida, Spain	C2	22
Mérida, Ven.	B3	60
Mérida, state, Ven.	B3	60
Meriden, Ct., U.S.	C4	84
Meriden, Ia., U.S.	B2	92
Meriden, Ks., U.S.	C8	93
Meriden, N.H., U.S.	C2	106
Meriden, Wy., U.S.	E8	127
Meridian, Ga., U.S.	E5	87
Meridian, Id., U.S.	F2	89
Meridian, Ms., U.S.	C5	101
Meridian, N.Y., U.S.	B4	109
Meridian, Ok., U.S.	B4	113
Meridian, Pa., U.S.	E2	115
Meridian, Tx., U.S.	D4	120
Meridian Hills, In., U.S.	k10	91
Meridian Naval Air Station, mil., Ms., U.S.	C5	101
Meridianville, Al., U.S.	A3	78
Mérignac, Fr.	E3	16
Merigold, Ms., U.S.	B3	101
Merigomish, N.S.	D7	71
Merikarvia, Fin.	G9	14
Meringur, Austl.	G3	51
Merino, Co., U.S.	A7	83
Meriwether, co., Ga., U.S.	C2	87
Merizo, Guam	M9	52
Merkel, Tx., U.S.	C2	120
Merkinė, Sov. Un.	A8	26
Merksem (part of Antwerp), Bel.	B6	16
Merksplas, Bel.	C4	17
Merkys, stm., Sov. Un.	D5	27
Merlin, Ont.	E2	73
Merlin, Or., U.S.	E3	114
Merlo, Arg.	g7	54
Mermentau, La., U.S.	D3	95
Mermentau, stm., La., U.S.	E3	95
Mern, Den.	C6	15
Merna, Ne., U.S.	C6	104
Merom, In., U.S.	F2	91
Meron, Mount, mtn., Isr.	A7	41
Merredin, Austl.	F2	50
Merriam, Ks., U.S.	k16	93
Merrick, N.Y., U.S.	*n15	109
Merrick, co., Ne., U.S.	C7	104
Merrick, mtn., Scot., U.K.	E4	13
Merrick Brook, stm., Ct., U.S.	C7	84
Merrickville, Ont.	C9	73
Merricourt, N.D., U.S.	C7	111
Merrifield, Mn., U.S.	D4	100
Merrifield, Va., U.S.	*B5	123
Merrill, Ia., U.S.	B1	92
Merrill, Mi., U.S.	E6	99
Merrill, Ms., U.S.	E5	101
Merrill, Or., U.S.	E5	114
Merrill, Wi., U.S.	C4	126
Merrillan, Wi., U.S.	D3	126
Merrillville, In., U.S.	B3	91
Merrimac, Ky., U.S.	C4	94
Merrimac, Ma., U.S.	A5	98
Merrimac, Wi., U.S.	E4	126
Merrimack, N.H., U.S.	E4	106
Merrimack, co., N.H., U.S.	D3	106
Merrimack, stm., U.S.	A5	98
Merrimacport, Ma., U.S.	A5	98
Merriman, Ne., U.S.	B4	104
Merrimon, N.C., U.S.	C6	110
Merritt, B.C.	D7	69
Merritt, N.C., U.S.	B6	110
Merritt Island, Fl., U.S.	D6	86
Merritt Reservoir, res., Ne., U.S.	B5	104
Merriwa, Austl.	F8	51
Merriweather, Mi., U.S.	m12	99
Merrow, Ct., U.S.	B6	84
Merry Hill, N.C., U.S.	A6	110
Merrymeeting Lake, l., N.H., U.S.	D4	106
Merry Oaks, N.C., U.S.	B3	110
Merryville, La., U.S.	D2	95
Mersa Fatma, Eth.	D3	47
Merseburg, E. Ger.	C5	18
Mersey, stm., Eng., U.K.	D5	10
Merseyside, co., Eng., U.K.	A4	12
Mershon, Ga., U.S.	E4	87
Mersing, Malay.	E2	34
Merthyr Tydfil, Wales, U.K.	E5	10
Merti, Kenya	A6	48
Mértola, Port.	D2	22
Merton, Ct., U.S.	B4	84
Meru, Kenya	A6	48
Meru, Mount, mtn., Tan.	B6	48
Mervelier, Switz.	B4	21
Merville, Fr.	D2	17
Merwin, Sask.	D1	75
Merwin, Mo., U.S.	C3	102
Merwin Lake, res., Wa., U.S.	C3	124
Méry [-sur-Seine], Fr.	F3	17
Meydān-e Gel, pl., Iran	G7	39
Meydanī, Ra's-e, c., Iran	C5	38
Merzifon, Tur.	B10	40
Merzig, W. Ger.	E6	17
Mesa, Az., U.S.	D4	80
Mesa, Co., U.S.	B2	83
Mesa, Id., U.S.	E2	89
Mesa, co., Co., U.S.	B2	83
Mesabi Range, hills, Mn., U.S.	C6	100
Mesa Mountain, mtn., Co., U.S.	D4	83
Mesa Verde National Park, Co., U.S.	D2	83
Mescalero, N.M., U.S.	D4	108
Mescalero Indian Reservation, N.M., U.S.	D4	108
Meschede, W. Ger.	B3	19
Mesegon, i., Micron.	Q18	52
Mesena, Ga., U.S.	C4	87
Meservey, Ia., U.S.	B4	92
Meshcherskoye, Sov. Un.	n17	27
Meshchovsk, Sov. Un.	D10	27
Meshkovskaya, Sov. Un.	G13	27
Meshomasic Mountain, mtn., Ct., U.S.	C5	84
Meshoppen, Pa., U.S.	C9	115
Mesic, N.C., U.S.	B6	110
Mesick, Mi., U.S.	D5	99
Mesilinka, stm., B.C.	A5	69
Mesilla, N.M., U.S.	E3	108
Mesita, Co., U.S.	D5	83
Mesita, N.M., U.S.	C2	108
Mesocco, Switz.	C5	20
Mesolóngion, Grc.	C3	40
Mesquita, Braz.	B4	56
Mesquite, Nv., U.S.	G7	105
Mesquite, N.M., U.S.	E3	108
Mesquite, Tx., U.S.	n10	120
Messalonskee Lake, l., Me., U.S.	D3	96
Messápion Óros, mtn., Grc.	g10	25
Messen, Switz.	B3	21
Messina, Italy	E5	23
Messina, S. Afr.	B5	49
Messina, Strait of, strt., Italy	E5	23
Messíni, Grc.	D3	25
Messíni, Gulf of, b., Grc.	D4	25
Messkirch, W. Ger.	B5	20
Mesta (Néstos), stm., Eur.	A5	25
Mestghanem (Mostaganem), Alg.	B5	44
Mestre, Italy	A4	23
Mesudiye, Tur.	B11	40
Meta, Mo., U.S.	C5	102
Meta, dept., Col.	C3	60
Meta, stm., S.A.	B4	60
Métabetchouan, Que.	A6	74
Métabetchouane, stm., Que.	A5	74
Meta Incognita Peninsula, pen., N.W. Ter.	D19	66
Metairie, La., U.S.	k11	95
Metaline, Wa., U.S.	A8	124
Metaline Falls, Wa., U.S.	A8	124
Metamora, In., U.S.	F7	91
Metamora, Mi., U.S.	F7	99
Metamora, Oh., U.S.	A2	112
Metán, Arg.	B3	54
Metangula, Moz.	D5	48
Metapán, El Sal.	D4	63
Meta Pond, l., Newf.	D4	72
Metaponto, Italy	D6	23
Metarica, Moz.	D6	48
Métascouac, Lac, l., Que.	A5	74
Metasville, Ga., U.S.	C4	87
Metcalf, Ga., U.S.	F3	87
Metcalf, Il., U.S.	D6	90
Metcalfe, Ont.	B9	73
Metcalfe, Ms., U.S.	B2	101
Metcalfe, co., Ky., U.S.	C4	94
Metchosin, B.C.	h12	69
Metedeconk, North Branch, stm., N.J., U.S.	C4	107
Metedeconk, South Branch, stm., N.J., U.S.	C3	107
Meteghan, N.S.	E3	71
Meteghan River, N.S.	E3	71
Meteghan Station, N.S.	E3	71
Metema, Eth.	C4	47
Meteor Crater, crat., Az., U.S.	C4	80
Methow, Wa., U.S.	A5	124
Methow, stm., Wa., U.S.	A5	124
Methóni, Grc.	D3	25
Methuen, Ma., U.S.	A5	98
Metiskow, Alta.	C5	68
Metković, Yugo.	D3	24
Metlakatla, Ak., U.S.	D13	79
Meto, Bayou, stm., Ar., U.S.	C4	81
Metolius, Or., U.S.	C5	114
Metonga, Lake, l., Wi., U.S.	C5	126
Metropolis, Il., U.S.	F5	90
Metropolitana, prov., Chile	A2	54
Métsovon, Grc.	C3	25
Mettawee, stm., U.S.	E2	122
Metten, W. Ger.	E7	19
Metter, Ga., U.S.	D4	87
Mettingen, W. Ger.	A2	19
Mettlach, W. Ger.	B1	19
Mettmann, W. Ger.	B1	19
Metuchen, N.J., U.S.	B4	107
Metula, Isr.	A7	41
Metz, Fr.	C7	16
Metz, In., U.S.	A8	91
Metz, Mi., U.S.	C7	99
Metz, Mo., U.S.	D3	102
Metzeral, Fr.	B3	20
Metzger, Or., U.S.	h12	114
Metzingen, W. Ger.	g9	16
Meulaboh, Indon.	m11	34
Meulan, Fr.	D4	16
Meung, Fr.	D4	16
Meureudu, Indon.	J2	35
Meurthe, stm., Fr.	F6	17
Meurthe-et-Moselle, dept., Fr.	F6	17
Meuse, dept., Fr.	E5	17
Meuse (Maas), stm., Eur.	C6	16
Meuse, Côtes de, mtn., Fr.	C6	16
Meuselwitz, E. Ger.	B7	19
Mexia, Tx., U.S.	D4	120
Mexia, Lake, res., Tx., U.S.	D4	120
Mexicali, Mex.	A1	63
Mexican Hat, Ut., U.S.	F6	121
Mexican Springs, N.M., U.S.	B1	108
Mexico, Me., U.S.	D2	96
Mexico, Mo., U.S.	B6	102
Mexico, N.Y., U.S.	B4	109
Mexico, Pa., U.S.	E7	115
México, state, Mex.	D5	63
Mexico, ctry., N.A.	D5	63
Mexico, Gulf of, b., N.A.	G11	61
Mexico City, Mex.	D5	63
Meycauayan, Phil.	o13	34
Meyers Chuck, Ak., U.S.	n23	79
Meyersdale, Pa., U.S.	G3	115
Meyísti, i., Grc.	D7	25
Meymaneh, Afg.	A4	36
Meyrin, Switz.	D1	21
Meyronne, Sask.	H2	75
Mèze, Fr.	F5	16
Mezen, Sov. Un.	C7	29
Mezen, stm., Sov. Un.	C7	29
Mezen Bay, b., Sov. Un.	B17	8
Mézenc, Mont, mtn., Fr.	E6	16
Mezhdurechenskiy, Sov. Un.	B7	28
Meziadin Lake, l., B.C.	A3	69
Mézières, Switz.	C2	21
Mézières, Fr.	B5	24
Mezőkövesd, Hung.	B5	24
Mezőtúr, Hung.	B5	24
Mezzana, Italy	C6	20
Mezzolombardo, Italy	C7	20
Mga, stm., Sov. Un.	s32	14
Mga, Sov. Un.	s32	14
Mglin, Sov. Un.	E9	27
Mhór, Beinn, mtn., Scot., U.K.	C11	13
Mhór, Loch, l., Scot., U.K.	C4	13
Mhow, India	F5	37
Miahuatlán de Porfirio Díaz, Mex.	D5	63
Miajadas, Spain	C3	22
Miami, Az., U.S.	D5	80
Miami, Fl., U.S.	G6	86
Miami, In., U.S.	C5	91
Miami, Mo., U.S.	B4	102
Miami, N.M., U.S.	A5	108
Miami, Ok., U.S.	A7	113
Miami, Tx., U.S.	B2	120
Miami, W.V., U.S.	m13	125
Miami, co., In., U.S.	C5	91
Miami, co., Ks., U.S.	D9	93
Miami, co., Oh., U.S.	B1	112
Miami Beach, Fl., U.S.	G6	86
Miami Canal, Fl., U.S.	F6	86
Miami International Airport, Fl., U.S.	*G6	86
Miami Lakes, Fl., U.S.	*G6	86
Miamisburg, Oh., U.S.	C1	112
Miami Shores, Fl., U.S.	G6	86
Miami Springs, Fl., U.S.	G6	86
Miamitown, Oh., U.S.	o12	112
Miāndoāb, Iran	C3	39
Miandrivazo, Madag.	g9	49
Miāneh, Iran	C3	39
Miangas Island, i., Indon.	D7	34
Mianning, China	F5	31
Mianus Reservoir, res., U.S.	E1	84
Miānwāli, Pak.	B5	36
Mianyang, China	I5	32
Mianyang, China	E2	32
Miarinarivo, Madag.	g9	49
Miass, Sov. Un.	C6	28
Miass, stm., Sov. Un.	B6	28
Miasteczko Śląskie, Pol.	f9	26
Miastko, Pol.	A4	26
Mica, Wa., U.S.	B8	124
Mica Creek, B.C.	D8	69
Mica Mountain, mtn., Az., U.S.	E5	80
Micanopy, Fl., U.S.	C4	86
Micco, Fl., U.S.	E6	86
Miccosukee, Fl., U.S.	B2	86
Miccosukee, Lake, res., Fl., U.S.	B2	86
Michael, Il., U.S.	D3	90
Michael, Lake, l., Newf.	A3	72
Michalovce, Czech.	B6	24
Michałów-Reginów, Pol.	k13	26
Michaud, Point, c., N.S.	D9	71
Michelson, Mount, mtn., Ak., U.S.	B11	79
Michendorf, E. Ger.	A8	19
Michichi, Alta.	D4	68
Michie, Tn., U.S.	B3	119
Michigamme, Mi., U.S.	B2	99
Michigamme, Lake, l., Mi., U.S.	B2	99
Michigamme Reservoir, res., Mi., U.S.	B2	99
Michigan, N.D., U.S.	A7	111
Michigan, state, U.S.	E6	99
Michigan, Lake, l., U.S.	A4	99
Michigan, Lake, l., U.S.	B10	76
Michigan Center, Mi., U.S.	F6	99
Michigan City, In., U.S.	A4	91
Michigan City, Ms., U.S.	A4	101
Michigan Island, i., Wi., U.S.	B3	126
Michigan Prairie, reg., Wa., U.S.	C7	124
Michigantown, In., U.S.	D5	91
Michoacán, state, Mex.	D4	63
Michurin (Tsarevo), Bul.	D8	24
Michurinsk, Sov. Un.	E13	27
Micoud, St. Luc.	J14	64
Micro, N.C., U.S.	B4	110
Micronesia, Federated States of, ctry., ter., T.T.P.I.	F9	6
Midai, i., Indon.	K7	35
Midale, Sask.	H4	75
Midas, Id., U.S.	A2	89
Middelburg, Neth.	B5	16
Middelburg, S. Afr.	D4	49
Middelfart, Den.	C3	15
Middelharnis, Neth.	C4	17
Middelkerke, Bel.	C2	17
Middle, stm., B.C.	B5	69
Middle, stm., Ia., U.S.	C3	92
Middle, stm., Mn., U.S.	B2	100
Middle Andaman, i., India	F9	36
Middleboro, Ma., U.S.	C6	98
Middlebourne, W.V., U.S.	B4	125
Middlebranch, Oh., U.S.	B4	112
Middlebro, Man.	E4	70
Middle Brook, Newf.	D4	72
Middlebrook, Va., U.S.	B3	123
Middleburg, Fl., U.S.	B5	86
Middleburg, Ky., U.S.	C5	94
Middleburg, Md., U.S.	A3	97
Middleburg, N.C., U.S.	A4	110
Middleburg, Oh., U.S.	B2	112
Middleburg, Pa., U.S.	E7	115
Middleburg, Tn., U.S.	B2	119
Middleburg, Va., U.S.	B5	123
Middleburg Heights, Oh., U.S.	h9	112
Middlebury, Ct., U.S.	C3	84
Middlebury, In., U.S.	A6	91
Middlebury, Vt., U.S.	C2	122
Middlefield, Ct., U.S.	C5	84
Middlefield, Ma., U.S.	B1	98
Middlefield, Oh., U.S.	A4	112
Middle Granville, N.Y., U.S.	B7	109
Middle Ground, rf., Mid. Is.	J3	52
Middle Haddam, Ct., U.S.	C5	84
Middle Island, N.Y., U.S.	*n16	109
Middle Island Creek, stm., W.V., U.S.	B3	125
Middle Lake, Sask.	E3	75
Middle Loup, stm., Ne., U.S.	C5	104
Middle Musquodoboit, N.S.	D6	71
Middle Nodaway, stm., Ia., U.S.	C3	92
Middle Park, val., Co., U.S.	A4	83
Middle Patuxent, stm., Md., U.S.	B4	97
Middle Point, Oh., U.S.	B1	112
Middleport, N.Y., U.S.	B2	109
Middleport, Oh., U.S.	C3	112
Middle Raccoon, stm., Ia., U.S.	C3	92
Middle River, Md., U.S.	B5	97
Middle River, Mn., U.S.	B2	100
Middlesboro, Ky., U.S.	D6	94
Middlesbrough (Teesside), Eng., U.K.	C6	10
Middlesex, Belize	D7	63
Middlesex, N.J., U.S.	B4	107
Middlesex, N.Y., U.S.	C3	109
Middlesex, N.C., U.S.	B4	110
Middlesex, Vt., U.S.	C3	122
Middlesex, co., Ont.	D3	73
Middlesex, co., Ct., U.S.	D5	84
Middlesex, co., Ma., U.S.	A5	98
Middlesex, co., N.J., U.S.	C4	107
Middlesex, co., Va., U.S.	C6	123
Middlesex Fells Reservation, Ma., U.S.	g11	98
Middle Stewiacke, N.S.	D6	71
Middleton, N.S.	E4	71
Middleton, Id., U.S.	F2	89
Middleton, Ma., U.S.	A5	98
Middleton, Tn., U.S.	B3	119
Middleton, Wi., U.S.	E4	126
Middletown, Ca., U.S.	C2	82
Middletown, Ct., U.S.	C5	84
Middletown, De., U.S.	C3	85
Middletown, Il., U.S.	C4	90
Middletown, Ia., U.S.	D6	92
Middletown, Ky., U.S.	g11	94
Middletown, Md., U.S.	B2	97
Middletown, Mo., U.S.	B6	102
Middletown, N.J., U.S.	C4	107
Middletown, N.Y., U.S.	D6	109
Middletown, Oh., U.S.	C1	112
Middletown, Pa., U.S.	F8	115
Middletown, R.I., U.S.	E5	116
Middletown, Va., U.S.	A4	123
Middletown Springs, Vt., U.S.	E2	122
Middletown Township, Pa., U.S.	*G11	115
Middleville, Ont.	B8	73
Middleville, Mi., U.S.	F5	99
Middleville, N.Y., U.S.	B6	109
Midfield, Al., U.S.	g7	78
Midfield, Tx., U.S.	E4	120
Mid Glamorgan, co., Wales, U.K.	C4	12
Midhurst, Ont.	C5	73
Midi d'Ossau, Pic du, mtn., Fr.	F3	16
Midkiff, Tx., U.S.	D2	120
Midkiff, W.V., U.S.	C2	125
Midland, Ont.	C5	73
Midland, Ar., U.S.	B1	81
Midland, In., U.S.	F3	91
Midland, La., U.S.	D3	95
Midland, Md., U.S.	k13	97
Midland, Mi., U.S.	E6	99
Midland, N.C., U.S.	B2	110
Midland, Oh., U.S.	C2	112
Midland, Pa., U.S.	E1	115
Midland, S.D., U.S.	C4	118
Midland, Tx., U.S.	D1	120
Midland, Va., U.S.	B5	123
Midland, co., Mi., U.S.	E6	99
Midland, co., Tx., U.S.	D1	120
Midland Basin, Co., U.S.	A2	83
Midland City, Al., U.S.	D4	78
Midland Park, Ks., U.S.	g12	93
Midland Park, N.J., U.S.	B4	107
Midland Park, S.C., U.S.	k11	117
Midleton, Ire.	E2	10
Midlothian, Ia., U.S.	k9	90
Midlothian, Md., U.S.	k13	97
Midlothian, Tx., U.S.	C4	120
Midlothian, Va., U.S.	m17	123
Midnapore, Alta.	D3	68
Midnight, Ms., U.S.	B3	101
Midongy Sud, Madag.	h9	49
Midpines, Ca., U.S.	D4	82
Midreshet Ben Gurion, Isr.	D6	41
Midsayap, Phil.	D7	34
Midvale, Id., U.S.	E2	89
Midvale, Oh., U.S.	B4	112
Midvale, Ut., U.S.	C4	121
Midville, Ga., U.S.	D4	87
Midway, B.C.	E8	69
Midway, Al., U.S.	D4	78
Midway, De., U.S.	F5	85
Midway, Fl., U.S.	B2	86
Midway, Ky., U.S.	B5	94
Midway, stm., N.A.	B8	103
Midway, Or., U.S.	*B4	114
Midway, Pa., U.S.	G7	115
Midway, Tn., U.S.	C11	119
Midway, Ut., U.S.	C4	121
Midway Islands, dep., Oc.	E11	6
Midway Naval Station, mil., Mid. Is.	K3	52
Midway Range, mts., B.C.	E8	69
Midwest, Wy., U.S.	C6	127
Midwest City, Ok., U.S.	B4	113
Midyat, Tur.	D13	40
Miechów, Pol.	C6	26
Międzychód, Pol.	B3	26
Międzyrzec [Podlaski], Pol.	C7	26
Międzyrzecz, Pol.	B3	26
Międzyzdroje, Pol.	B2	26
Mielec, Pol.	D7	26
Mien, i., Swe.	B8	15
Mienia, stm., Pol.	m14	26
Mier, Tx., U.S.	C6	91
Miercurea Ciuc, Rom.	B7	24
Mieres, Spain	A3	22
Miesbach, W. Ger.	B7	20
Mieso, Eth.	D5	47
Mifflin, Pa., U.S.	F6	115
Mifflin, Tn., U.S.	B3	119
Mifflin, co., Pa., U.S.	E6	115
Mifflinburg, Pa., U.S.	E7	115
Mifflintown, Pa., U.S.	E7	115
Mifflinville, Pa., U.S.	D9	115
Migdal, Isr.	B7	41
Migennes, Fr.	D5	16
Mignano, Italy	E7	20
Miguel Alemán, Presa, res., Mex.	n15	63
Miguel Alves, Braz.	B2	57
Miguel Auza, Mex.	C4	63
Mihai Viteazu, Rom.	C9	24
Mihama, Japan	o15	33
Mikado, Sask.	F4	75
Mikado, Mi., U.S.	D7	99
Mikawa, Wi., U.S.	C2	126
Mikha Tskhakaya, Sov. Un.	A14	40
Mikhaylov, Sov. Un.	D12	27
Mikhaylov, Cape, c., Ant.	C24	7
Mikhaylovgrad, Bul.	D6	24
Mikhaylovka, Sov. Un.	F14	27
Mikhaylovka, Sov. Un.	H10	27
Mikhaylovskiy, Sov. Un.	C9	28
Mikindani, Tan.	D7	48
Mikkalo, Or., U.S.	B6	114
Mikkeli, Fin.	G12	14
Mikołów, Pol.	g9	26
Mikonos, Grc.	D5	25
Mikonos, i., Grc.	D5	25
Mikope, Zaire	C3	48
Mikulov, Czech.	D4	26
Mikumi Island, i., Japan	J9	33
Mikuni, Japan	G9	33
Milaca, Mn., U.S.	E5	100
Milagro, Ec.	B2	58
Milam, co., Tx., U.S.	D4	120
Milan, Que.	D6	74
Milan (Milano), Italy	D3	20
Milan, Ga., U.S.	D3	87
Milan, Il., U.S.	B3	90
Milan, In., U.S.	F7	91
Milan, Ks., U.S.	E6	93
Milan, Mi., U.S.	F7	99
Milan, Mn., U.S.	E3	100
Milan, Mo., U.S.	A4	102
Milan, N.M., U.S.	B2	108
Milan, N.Y., U.S.	C7	109
Milan, Oh., U.S.	A3	112
Milan, Pa., U.S.	C8	115
Milan, Tn., U.S.	B3	119
Milan, Tx., U.S.	D4	120
Milano, Tx., U.S.	D4	120
Milâs, Tur.	D6	25
Milazzo, Italy	E5	23
Milbank, S.D., U.S.	B9	118
Milbridge, Me., U.S.	D5	96
Milburn, Ky., U.S.	f9	94
Milden, Sask.	F2	75
Mildenhall, Eng., U.K.	B8	12
Mildmay, Ont.	C3	73
Mildred, Sask.	D2	75
Mildred, Mt., U.S.	D12	103
Mildred, Pa., U.S.	D9	115
Mildura, Austl.	F7	50
Miles, Austl.	E9	51
Miles, Ia., U.S.	B7	92
Miles, Tx., U.S.	D2	120
Miles City, Mt., U.S.	D11	103
Miles Mountain, mtn., Vt., U.S.	C5	122
Milestone, Sask.	G3	75
Milesville, S.D., U.S.	C4	118
Miletus, hist., Tur.	D6	25
Milford, N.B.	D3	71
Milford, Ont.	D7	73
Milford, Ct., U.S.	E3	84
Milford, De., U.S.	E4	85
Milford, Il., U.S.	B6	91
Milford, Ia., U.S.	A2	92
Milford, Ks., U.S.	C7	93
Milford, Ky., U.S.	B5	94
Milford, Me., U.S.	D4	96
Milford, Ma., U.S.	B4	98
Milford, Mi., U.S.	F7	99
Milford, Mo., U.S.	D3	102
Milford, Ne., U.S.	D8	104
Milford, N.H., U.S.	E3	106
Milford, N.J., U.S.	B2	107
Milford, N.Y., U.S.	C6	109
Milford, Oh., U.S.	C1	112
Milford, Pa., U.S.	D12	115
Milford, Ut., U.S.	E2	121
Milford, Va., U.S.	B5	123
Milford Center, Oh., U.S.	B2	112
Milford Haven, Wales, U.K.	E4	10
Milford Lake, res., Ks., U.S.	C6	93
Milford Sound, strt., N.Z.	P11	51
Milford Station, N.S.	D6	71
Milh, Ra's al, c., Libya	F5	40
Milicz, Pol.	C4	26
Mililani Town, Hi., U.S.	g9	88
Miling, Austl.	F2	50
Milk, stm., N.A.	B8	103
Milk River, Alta.	E4	68
Milk River Ridge Reservoir, res., Alta.	E4	68
Mill, stm., Ma., U.S.	h9	98
Millard, Mo., U.S.	A5	102
Millard, co., Ut., U.S.	D2	121
Millars Sound, strt., Bah.	n17	64
Millarton, N.D., U.S.	C7	111
Millau, Fr.	E5	16
Millbank, Ont.	D4	73
Millboro, S.D., U.S.	D6	118
Millbrae, Ca., U.S.	h8	82
Millbridge, Ont.	C7	73
Millbrook, Ont.	D7	73
Millbrook, Al., U.S.	C3	78
Millbrook, Mi., U.S.	E5	99
Millbrook, N.Y., U.S.	D7	109
Mill Brook, stm., Vt., U.S.	B5	122
Millburn, N.J., U.S.	B4	107
Millbury, Ma., U.S.	B4	98
Millbury, Oh., U.S.	e7	112
Mill City, Nv., U.S.	C3	105
Mill City, Or., U.S.	C4	114
Mill City, Pa., U.S.	m17	115
Millcreek, Il., U.S.	F4	90
Millcreek, In., U.S.	A4	91
Millcreek, Ok., U.S.	C5	113
Millcreek, Ut., U.S.	C4	121
Mill Creek, W.V., U.S.	C5	125
Mill Creek, stm., In., U.S.	F4	91
Mill Creek, stm., Ks., U.S.	C7	93
Mill Creek, stm., Oh., U.S.	B2	112
Mill Creek, stm., Tn., U.S.	G10	119
Mill Creek, stm., W.V., U.S.	C3	125
Mill Creek, stm., W.V., U.S.	m13	125
Millcreek Township, Pa., U.S.	B1	115
Milldale, Ct., U.S.	C4	84
Milledgeville, Ga., U.S.	C3	87
Milledgeville, Il., U.S.	B4	90
Milledgeville, Tn., U.S.	B3	119
Mille Îles, Rivière des, stm., Que.	p19	74
Mille Lacs, co., Mn., U.S.	E5	100
Mille Lacs Indian Reservation, Mn., U.S.	D5	100
Mille Lacs Lake, l., Mn., U.S.	D5	100
Millen, Ga., U.S.	D5	87
Miller, Ne., U.S.	D6	104
Miller, Oh., U.S.	D3	112
Miller, S.D., U.S.	C7	118
Miller, co., Ar., U.S.	D2	81
Miller, co., Ga., U.S.	E2	87
Miller, co., Mo., U.S.	C5	102
Miller, Mount, mtn., Ak., U.S.	C11	79
Mill Creek, stm., De., U.S.	A3	85
Miller Dale Colony, S.D., U.S.	C6	118
Millerovo, Sov. Un.	G13	27
Miller Peak, mtn., Az., U.S.	F5	80
Miller Place, N.Y., U.S.	*n16	109
Miller Run, stm., Vt., U.S.	B4	122
Millers, Md., U.S.	A4	97
Millers, stm., Ma., U.S.	A3	98
Millersburg, In., U.S.	A6	91
Millersburg, Ky., U.S.	B5	94
Millersburg, Mi., U.S.	C6	99
Millersburg, Oh., U.S.	B4	112
Millersburg, Pa., U.S.	E8	115
Millers Falls, Ma., U.S.	A3	98
Millers Ferry, Al., U.S.	C2	78
Millers Ferry Dam, Al., U.S.	C2	78
Millersport, Oh., U.S.	C3	112
Millersview, Tx., U.S.	D2	120
Millersville, Oh., U.S.	*n12	112
Millerton, N.B.	C4	71
Millerton, Ia., U.S.	D4	92
Millerton, N.Y., U.S.	D7	109
Millerton, Ok., U.S.	C6	113
Milliken, Co., U.S.	A6	83
Millington, Md., U.S.	B6	97
Millington, Mi., U.S.	E7	99
Millington, N.J., U.S.	B3	107
Millington, Tn., U.S.	B2	119
Millinocket, Me., U.S.	C4	96
Millinocket Lake, l., Me., U.S.	C4	96
Millinocket Lake, l., Me., U.S.	C4	96

Name	Map Ref.	Page
Mill Iron, Mt., U.S.	E12	103
Millis, Ma., U.S.	B5	98
Mill Island, i., Ant.	C23	7
Millmerran, Austl.	C8	51
Millom, Eng., U.K.	F5	13
Mill Point, W.V., U.S.	C4	125
Millport, Scot., U.K.	E4	13
Millport, Al., U.S.	B1	78
Millport, Pa., U.S.	C5	115
Millrift, Pa., U.S.	D12	115
Mill River, Ma., U.S.	B1	98
Mill Run, Pa., U.S.	G3	115
Millry, Al., U.S.	D1	78
Mills, Ne., U.S.	B6	104
Mills, N.M., U.S.	A5	108
Mills, Pa., U.S.	C6	115
Mills, Wy., U.S.	D6	127
Mills, co., Ia., U.S.	C2	92
Mills, co., Tx., U.S.	D3	120
Millsboro, De., U.S.	F4	85
Millsboro, Pa., U.S.	G1	115
Mill Shoals, Il., U.S.	E5	90
Mills Lake, l., N.W. Ter.	D9	66
Mill Spring, Mo., U.S.	D7	102
Millstadt, Il., U.S.	E3	90
Millston, Wi., U.S.	D3	126
Mill Stone, N.J., U.S.	B3	107
Millstone, stm., N.J., U.S.	C4	107
Millstreet, Ire.	E2	11
Milltown, Al., U.S.	H5	91
Milltown, In., U.S.	C4	94
Milltown, Ky., U.S.	D3	103
Milltown, Me., U.S.	C4	107
Milltown, N.J., U.S.	C4	107
Milltown, S.D., U.S.	D8	118
Milltown, Wi., U.S.	C1	126
Milltown [-Head of Bay d'Espoir], Newf.	E4	72
Milltown Malbay, Ire.	E2	11
Millvale, Pa., U.S.	k14	115
Mill Valley, Ca., U.S.	D2	82
Mill Village, N.S.	E5	71
Mill Village, Pa., U.S.	C2	115
Millville, N.B.	C2	71
Millville, De., U.S.	F5	85
Millville, Ky., U.S.	B5	94
Millville, Ma., U.S.	B4	98
Millville, N.J., U.S.	E2	107
Millville, Oh., U.S.	n12	112
Millville, Pa., U.S.	D9	115
Millville, Ut., U.S.	B4	121
Millville, W.V., U.S.	B7	125
Millville Lake, N.H., U.S.	E4	106
Millwood, Ga., U.S.	E4	87
Millwood, Oh., U.S.	B3	112
Millwood, Va., U.S.	A4	123
Millwood, Wa., U.S.	g14	124
Millwood Lake, res., Ar., U.S.	D1	81
Milmay, N.J., U.S.	E3	107
Milner, B.C.	f13	69
Milner, Ga., U.S.	A3	83
Milner, Ga., U.S.	C2	87
Milner Dam, Id., U.S.	G5	89
Milner Ridge, Man.	D3	70
Milnesand, N.M., U.S.	D6	108
Milnor, N.D., U.S.	C8	111
Milo, Alta.	D4	68
Milo, Ia., U.S.	C4	92
Milo, Me., U.S.	C4	96
Milo, Or., U.S.	E3	114
Miloli'i, Hi., U.S.	D6	88
Milos, i., Grc.	D5	40
Milparinka, Austl.	D3	51
Milpitas, Ca., U.S.	*k9	82
Milroy, In., U.S.	F7	91
Milroy, Mn., U.S.	F3	100
Milroy, Pa., U.S.	E6	115
Milstead, Al., U.S.	C4	78
Milstead, Ga., U.S.	C3	87
Miltenberg, W. Ger.	D4	19
Milton, N.S.	E5	71
Milton, Ont.	D5	73
Milton, N.Z.	Q12	51
Milton, Ct., U.S.	B2	84
Milton, De., U.S.	E4	85
Milton, Fl., U.S.	u14	86
Milton, Il., U.S.	D3	90
Milton, In., U.S.	E7	91
Milton, Ia., U.S.	D5	92
Milton, Ks., U.S.	E6	93
Milton, Ky., U.S.	B4	94
Milton, Ma., U.S.	B5	98
Milton, N.H., U.S.	D5	106
Milton, N.Y., U.S.	D7	109
Milton, N.C., U.S.	A3	110
Milton, N.D., U.S.	A7	111
Milton, Pa., U.S.	D8	115
Milton, Vt., U.S.	B2	122
Milton, W.V., U.S.	C2	125
Milton, Wi., U.S.	F5	126
Milton, Lake, l., Oh., U.S.	A4	112
Miltona, Mn., U.S.	D3	100
Miltona, Lake, l., Mn., U.S.	D3	100
Milton-Freewater, Or., U.S.	B8	114
Milton Keynes, Eng., U.K.	B7	12
Milton Mills, N.H., U.S.	C5	106
Milton Reservoir, res., Co., U.S.	A6	83
Miltonvale, Ks., U.S.	C6	93
Milverton, Ont.	D4	73
Milwaukee, N.C., U.S.	A5	110
Milwaukee, Wi., U.S.	E6	126
Milwaukee, co., Wi., U.S.	E6	126
Milwaukee, stm., Wi., U.S.	m12	126
Milwaukie, Or., U.S.	B4	114
Mimbres, N.M., U.S.	E2	108
Mimbres Mountains, mts., N.M., U.S.	E2	108
Mimico (part of Etobicoke), Ont.	m15	73
Mimizan, Fr.	E3	16
Mimoň, Czech.	C9	19
Mimongo, Gabon	F2	46
Mimosa Park, La., U.S.	*E5	95
Mims, Fl., U.S.	D6	86
Mina, Nv., U.S.	E3	105
Mina, S.D., U.S.	B7	118
Minā' al Aḥmadi, Kuw.	C4	38
Mīnāb, Iran	H8	39
Minago, stm., Man.	B2	70
Minaki, Ont.	o16	73
Minamata, Japan	J5	33
Minami-iwo, i., Japan	E8	6
Minami-Tori Island, i., Japan	E9	6
Minas, Cuba	D5	64
Minas, Ur.	E1	56
Minas Basin, b., N.S.	D5	71
Minas Channel, strt., N.S.	D5	71
Minas de Corrales, Ur.	E1	56
Minas de Oro, Hond.	G4	64
Minas de Ríotinto, Spain	D2	22
Minas Gerais, state, Braz.	B4	56
Minas Novas, Braz.	B4	56
Minatare, Ne., U.S.	C2	104
Minatitlán, Mex.	D6	63
Minbu, Burma	D9	36
Minburn, Alta.	C5	68
Minburn, Ia., U.S.	C3	92
Minco, Ok., U.S.	B4	113
Mindanao, i., Phil.	D6	34
Mindel, stm., W. Ger.	A6	20
Mindelheim, W. Ger.	A6	20
Mindemoya, Ont.	B2	73
Minden, Ont.	C6	73
Minden, W. Ger.	B4	18
Minden, Ia., U.S.	C2	92
Minden, La., U.S.	B2	95
Minden, Ne., U.S.	D7	104
Minden, Nv., U.S.	E2	105
Minden City, Mi., U.S.	E8	99
Mindoro, i., Phil.	C6	34
Mindoro Strait, strt., Phil.	C6	34
Mine Centre, Ont.	o16	73
Minechoag Mountain, hill, Ma., U.S.	B3	98
Minehead, Eng., U.K.	E5	10
Mine Head, c., Ire.	F4	11
Mine Hill, N.J., U.S.	B3	107
Mine La Motte, Mo., U.S.	D7	102
Mineola, Ia., U.S.	C2	92
Mineola, N.Y., U.S.	E7	109
Mineola, Tx., U.S.	C5	120
Miner, Mo., U.S.	E8	102
Miner, co., S.D., U.S.	D8	118
Mineral, Ca., U.S.	B3	82
Mineral, Il., U.S.	B4	90
Mineral, Va., U.S.	B5	123
Mineral, Wa., U.S.	C3	124
Mineral, co., Co., U.S.	D4	83
Mineral, co., Mt., U.S.	C1	103
Mineral, co., Nv., U.S.	E3	105
Mineral, co., W.V., U.S.	B6	125
Mineral City, Oh., U.S.	B4	112
Mineral del Monte, Mex.	m14	63
Mineral del Oro, Mex.	n13	63
Mineral Hills, Mi., U.S.	B2	99
Mineral Mountains, mts., Ut., U.S.	E3	121
Mineral Park, Tn., U.S.	h11	119
Mineral Point, Mo., U.S.	D7	102
Mineral Point, Wi., U.S.	F3	126
Mineral Springs, Ar., U.S.	D2	81
Mineral Wells, Ms., U.S.	A4	101
Mineral Wells, Tx., U.S.	C3	120
Minersville, Oh., U.S.	C4	112
Minersville, Pa., U.S.	E9	115
Minersville, Ut., U.S.	E3	121
Minerva, N.Y., U.S.	B7	109
Minerva, Oh., U.S.	B4	112
Minervino Murge, Italy	D6	23
Minetto, N.Y., U.S.	B4	109
Mineville, N.Y., U.S.	A7	109
Mingan, Que.	h8	72
Mingechaur, Sov. Un.	G18	8
Mingechaur Reservoir, res., Sov. Un.	E3	28
Mingenew, Austl.	E2	50
Mingo, co., W.V., U.S.	D2	125
Mingo Junction, Oh., U.S.	B5	112
Mingoyo, Tan.	D6	48
Mingshui, China	C4	31
Miniota, Man.	D1	70
Minidoka, co., Id., U.S.	G5	89
Minidoka Dam, Id., U.S.	G5	89
Minier, Il., U.S.	C4	90
Minipi Lake, l., Newf.	h9	72
Minisink Island, i., N.J., U.S.	A3	107
Minitonas, Man.	C1	70
Minna, Nig.	E6	45
Minna Bluff, pen., Ant.	B29	7
Minneapolis, Ks., U.S.	C6	93
Minneapolis, Mn., U.S.	F5	100
Minneapolis, N.C., U.S.	e11	110
Minnedosa, Man.	D2	70
Minnedosa, stm., Man.	D1	70
Minnehaha, co., S.D., U.S.	D9	118
Minneiska, Mn., U.S.	F7	100
Minneola, Ks., U.S.	E3	93
Minneola, Mn., U.S.	F3	100
Minnesota, state, U.S.	F4	100
Minnesota, stm., Mn., U.S.	F2	100
Minnesota Lake, Mn., U.S.	G5	100
Minnetonka, Mn., U.S.	n12	100
Minnetonka, Lake, l., Mn., U.S.	n11	100
Minnewaska, Lake, l., Alta.	D3	68
Minnewaska, Lake, l., Mn., U.S.	E3	100
Minnewaukan, N.D., U.S.	A6	111
Mino, Japan	n15	33
Miño (Minho), stm., Eur.	A1	22
Minocqua, Wi., U.S.	C4	126
Minokamo, Japan	n15	33
Minong, Wi., U.S.	C2	126
Minonk, Il., U.S.	C4	90
Minooka, Il., U.S.	B5	90
Minor Hill, Tn., U.S.	B4	119
Minot, Ma., U.S.	h12	98
Minot, N.D., U.S.	A4	111
Minot Air Force Base, mil., N.D., U.S.	A4	111
Minqin, China	D5	31
Minquadale, De., U.S.	i7	85
Minsen, W. Ger.	A7	17
Minsk, Sov. Un.	D5	29
Mińsk Mazowiecki, Pol.	B6	26
Minster, Oh., U.S.	B1	112
Minter, Al., U.S.	C3	78
Minter City, Ms., U.S.	B3	101
Mint Hill, N.C., U.S.	B2	110
Minto, Man.	E1	70
Minto, Ak., U.S.	C10	79
Minto, Lac, l., Que.	g11	72
Minton, Sask.	H3	75
Minturn, Ar., U.S.	B4	81
Minturn, Co., U.S.	B4	83
Minturn, Me., U.S.	D4	96
Minturno, Italy	D4	23
Minūf, Eg.	D3	41
Minusinsk, Sov. Un.	D12	29
Minute Man National Historical Park, hist., Ma., U.S.	g10	98
Minvoul, Gabon	E2	46
Minyā al Qamḥ, Eg.	D3	41
Minya Konka see Gongga Mountain, mtn., China	F5	31
Mio, Mi., U.S.	D6	99
Miquelon, i., St. P./M.	E3	72
Mira, Port.	B1	22
Mira, La., U.S.	B2	95
Mira, stm., Port.	D1	22
Mira, stm., S.A.	A2	58
Mirabel, Que.	D3	74
Miracema do Norte, Braz.	D5	59
Miracle Hot Springs, Ca., U.S.	E4	82
Mirador, Braz.	C6	57
Miraflores, Col.	C2	57
Miraflores, Peru	*D2	58
Miraflores Locks, Pan.	m17	64
Miragoâne, Haiti	E7	64
Miraj, India	D3	37
Miraí, Braz.	E5	56
Miramar, Arg.	D5	56
Miramar, Fl., U.S.	s13	86
Miramar Naval Air Station, mil., Ca., U.S.	F5	82
Miramichi Bay, b., N.B.	B5	71
Miranda, Braz.	C1	56
Miranda, Col.	C2	60
Miranda, S.D., U.S.	C7	118
Miranda, state, Ven.	A4	60
Miranda, stm., Braz.	C1	56
Miranda de Ebro, Spain	A4	22
Miranda do Douro, Port.	B2	22
Mirande, Fr.	F4	16
Mirandela, Port.	B2	22
Mirando City, Tx., U.S.	F3	120
Mirandola, Italy	E7	20
Mirassol, Braz.	C3	56
Miravalles, Volcán, vol., C.R.	E5	62
Mirbāṭ, Oman	D5	38
Mirebalais, Haiti	E7	64
Mirecourt, Fr.	C7	16
Mirepoix, Fr.	F4	16
Mirgorod, Sov. Un.	G9	27
Miri, Malay.	E4	34
Miriam Vale, Austl.	B8	51
Mirim, Lagoa, b., S.A.	E2	56
Mirnyy, sci., Ant.	C22	7
Mirond Lake, l., Sask.	B4	75
Mirow, E. Ger.	E6	15
Mīrpur, Bngl.	*D9	36
Mīrpur Khās, Pak.	C4	36
Mirror, Alta.	C4	68
Mirror Lake, N.H., U.S.	C4	106
Mirror Lake, l., N.H., U.S.	C4	106
Mirtoan Sea, Grc.	C7	36
Misākhah, Bi'r, well, Eg.	E5	43
Misakubo, Japan	n16	33
Misantla, Mex.	C5	63
Misburg, W. Ger.	A4	19
Miscoe Hill, hill, Ma., U.S.	B4	98
Miscou Centre, N.B.	B5	71
Miscouche, P.E.I.	C6	71
Miscou Island, i., N.B.	B5	71
Miscou Point, c., N.B.	A5	71
Misenheimer, N.C., U.S.	B2	110
Mishan, China	D6	33
Mishawaka, In., U.S.	A5	91
Misheguk Mountain, mtn., Ak., U.S.	B7	79
Mishicot, Wi., U.S.	D6	126
Mishima, Japan	I9	33
Misiones, prov., Arg.	E5	55
Misiones, dept., Para.	E4	55
Miskitos, Cayos, is., Nic.	E8	63
Miskolc, Hung.	A5	24
Mismār, Sud.	B4	47
Misool, i., Indon.	F7	34
Mispillion, stm., De., U.S.	E4	85
Misquamicut, R.I., U.S.	G1	116
Miṣr al Jadīdah (Heliopolis) (part of Cairo), Eg.	D3	41
Misrātah, Libya	C3	43
Missaukee, co., Mi., U.S.	D5	99
Missaukee, Lake, l., Mi., U.S.	D5	99
Missinaibi, stm., Ont.	G16	66
Mission, Ks., U.S.	m16	93
Mission, S.D., U.S.	D5	118
Mission, Tx., U.S.	F3	120
Mission City, B.C.	E6	69
Mission Hill, S.D., U.S.	E8	118
Mission Hills, Ks., U.S.	*k16	93
Mission Mountain, mtn., Ok.	A7	115
Mission Range, mts., Mt., U.S.	C3	103
Mission Ridge, S.D., U.S.	C5	118
Mission Viejo, Ca., U.S.	n13	82
Missisquoi, co., Que.	D4	74
Missisquoi, stm., Vt., U.S.	B3	122
Missisquoi Bay, b., Vt., U.S.	A2	122
Mississauga, Ont.	D5	73
Mississinewa, stm., U.S.	D7	91
Mississinewa Lake, res., In., U.S.	C6	91
Mississippi, co., Ar., U.S.	B5	81
Mississippi, co., Mo., U.S.	E8	102
Mississippi, state, U.S.	C4	101
Mississippi, stm., U.S.	D9	76
Mississippi Delta, La., U.S.	E6	95
Mississippi Lake, l., Ont.	B8	73
Mississippi Sound, strt., U.S.	E5	101
Mississippi State, Ms., U.S.	B5	101
Missoula, Mt., U.S.	D2	103
Missoula, co., Mt., U.S.	D2	103
Missour, Mor.	C4	44
Missouri, state, U.S.	C5	102
Missouri, stm., U.S.	B8	76
Missouri Buttes, mtn., Wy., U.S.	B8	127
Missouri City, Mo., U.S.	h11	102
Missouri City, Tx., U.S.	r14	120
Missouri Valley, Ia., U.S.	C2	92
Mistake Point, c., Newf.	F5	72
Mistassini, Que.	h12	74
Mistassini, Lac, l., Que.	h12	74
Mistastin Lake, l., Newf.	g9	72
Mistatim, Sask.	E4	75
Mistelbach [an der Zaya], Aus.	D8	18
Misti, Volcán, vol., Peru	E3	58
Miston, Tn., U.S.	C10	119
Mistretta, Italy	F5	23
Mita, Punta, c., Mex.	*D2	63
Mitaka, Japan	*I9	33
Mitaka, Japan	I8	33
Mitcham, Austl.	*F6	51
Mitchell, Austl.	E9	51
Mitchell, Ont.	D3	73
Mitchell, Il., U.S.	E3	90
Mitchell, In., U.S.	G5	91
Mitchell, La., U.S.	C2	95
Mitchell, Ne., U.S.	C2	104
Mitchell, Or., U.S.	C6	114
Mitchell, S.D., U.S.	D7	118
Mitchell, co., Ga., U.S.	E2	87
Mitchell, co., Ia., U.S.	A5	92
Mitchell, co., Ks., U.S.	C5	93
Mitchell, co., N.C., U.S.	e10	110
Mitchell, co., Tx., U.S.	C2	120
Mitchell, stm., Austl.	C7	50
Mitchell, Lake, l., Mi., U.S.	D5	99
Mitchell, Lake, res., Al., U.S.	C3	78
Mitchell, Mount, mtn., N.C., U.S.	f10	110
Mitchell Island, i., La., U.S.	E6	95
Mitchellsburg, Ky., U.S.	C5	94
Mitchellville, Ia., U.S.	C4	92
Mitchellville, Tn., U.S.	A5	119
Mitchelstown, Ire.	D2	11
Mit Fāris, Eg.	C3	41
Mit Ghamr, Eg.	D3	41
Mithapur, India	D4	36
Mitilini, Grc.	C6	40
Mitishto, stm., Man.	B2	70
Mitkof Island, i., Ak., U.S.	m23	79
Mitla Pass, Eg.	E4	41
Mito, Japan	H10	33
Mitra do Bispo, mtn., Braz.	h5	56
Mitre, mtn., N.Z.	N15	51
Mitry-Mory, Fr.	E2	17
Mitsinjo, Madag.	g9	49
Mitsiwa, Eth.	A7	47
Mittelland Canal, Eur.	B5	18
Mittenwald, W. Ger.	B7	20
Mittersill, Aus.	B8	20
Mitterteich, W. Ger.	D6	18
Mittie, La., U.S.	D3	95
Mittlerer Isar Kanal, W. Ger.	A7	20
Mittweida, E. Ger.	C6	18
Mitú, Col.	C4	60
Mitumba, Monts, mts., Zaire	C4	48
Mitwaba, Zaire	C4	48
Mitzic, Gabon	E2	46
Miura, Japan	n18	33
Mixquiahuala, Mex.	m14	63
Mixteco, stm., Mex.	o14	63
Miyagi Island, i., Japan	O5	52
Miyake-jima, i., Japan	I9	33
Miyako, Japan	G10	33
Miyakonojō, Japan	K5	33
Miyazaki, Japan	K5	33
Miyazu, Japan	n14	33
Mizdah, Libya	C2	43
Mize, Ms., U.S.	D4	101
Mizen Head, c., Ire.	F2	11
Mizil, Rom.	E8	24
Mizoram, state, India	C4	100
Mizpah, Mn., U.S.	C4	100
Mizpah, N.J., U.S.	E3	107
Mizpah Creek, stm., Mt., U.S.	E11	103
Mizpé Ramon, Isr.	G10	40
Mizque, Bol.	C2	55
Mjölby, Swe.	G4	14
Mjøsa, l., Nor.	A4	19
Mkalama, Tan.	C5	48
Mladá Boleslav, Czech.	C3	26
Mława, Pol.	B6	26
Mljet, i., Yugo.	D3	24
Mnichovo Hradiště, Czech.	C6	19
Mnyusi, Tan.	C6	48
Mo, Nor.	D6	14
Moa, i., Austl.	B7	50
Moab, Ut., U.S.	E6	121
Moala Island, i., Fiji	I15	52
Moamba, Moz.	C5	49
Moanda, Gabon	F2	46
Moapa, Nv., U.S.	G7	105
Moapa River Indian Reservation, Nv., U.S.	G7	105
Moark, Ar., U.S.	A5	81
Moatize, Moz.	D4	70
Moate, Ire.	C4	11
Moba, Zaire	C4	48
Mobara, Japan	n19	33
Mobaye, Cen. Afr. Rep.	A4	48
Mobayi-Mbongo, Zaire	A4	48
Mobeetie, Tx., U.S.	B2	120
Moberly, Mo., U.S.	B5	102
Moberly, stm., B.C.	B7	69
Moberly Lake, l., B.C.	B7	69
Mobile, Al., U.S.	E1	78
Mobile, co., Al., U.S.	E1	78
Mobile, stm., Al., U.S.	E1	78
Mobile Bay, b., Al., U.S.	E1	78
Mobridge, S.D., U.S.	B5	118
Mobula, Zaire	A4	48
Moca, Dom. Rep.	E8	64
Mocajuba, Braz.	D9	57
Moçambique, Moz.	D7	49
Moçâmedes see Namibe, Ang.	E1	48
Mocanaqua, Pa., U.S.	D9	115
Moccasin, Az., U.S.	A3	80
Moccasin, Mt., U.S.	C7	103
Moce, i., Fiji	l16	52
Mocha, Isla, i., Chile	B2	54
Moc Hoa, Viet.	C6	35
Mocho Mountains, mts., Jam.	E14	65
Mochudi, Bots.	C5	49
Mocimboa da Praia, Moz.	D7	48
Möckeln, l., Swe.	B8	15
Mocksville, N.C., U.S.	B2	110
Moclips, Wa., U.S.	B1	124
Môco, Serra, mtn., Ang.	D2	48
Mocoa, Col.	C2	60
Mococa, Braz.	C3	56
Mocomoco, Bol.	C2	55
Mocorito, Mex.	B3	63
Moctezuma, Mex.	B3	63
Moctezuma, stm., Mex.	m14	63
Mocuba, Moz.	A6	49
Mocúburi, Moz.	D7	48
Modale, Ia., U.S.	C2	92
Modane, Fr.	D2	20
Modena, Italy	B3	23
Modena, Ut., U.S.	F2	121
Modena, Wi., U.S.	D2	126
Modeste, La., U.S.	h9	95
Modesto, Il., U.S.	D4	90
Modesto, Ca., U.S.	D3	82
Modica, Italy	F5	23
Modlin, Pol.	k13	26
Mödling, Aus.	D4	87
Modoc, Ga., U.S.	D7	91
Modoc, In., U.S.	D7	91
Modoc, S.C., U.S.	D3	117
Modoc, co., Ca., U.S.	B3	82
Modoc Point, Or., U.S.	E5	114
Moe, Austl.	G8	50
Moehau, mtn., N.Z.	L15	51
Moen, i., Micron.	Q18	52
Moenave, Az., U.S.	A4	80
Moengo, Sur.	A4	59
Moenkopi, Az., U.S.	A4	80
Moenkopi Plateau, plat., Az., U.S.	B4	80
Moenkopi Wash, val., Az., U.S.	A5	80
Moerbeke, Bel.	C3	17
Moers, W. Ger.	B1	19
Moesa, stm., Switz.	D7	21
Moeskroen see Mouscron, Bel.	B5	16
Moffat, Scot., U.K.	E5	13
Moffat, Co., U.S.	C5	83
Moffat, co., Co., U.S.	A2	83
Moffat Tunnel, Co., U.S.	B5	83
Moffett, Ok., U.S.	B7	113
Moffett Field Naval Air Station, mil., Ca., U.S.	k8	82
Moffit, N.D., U.S.	C5	111
Moga, Zaire	A7	49
Mogadishu (Muqdisho), Som.	E6	47
Mogadore, Oh., U.S.	A4	112
Mogaung, Burma	C10	36
Mogi das Cruzes, Braz.	C3	56
Mogielnica, Pol.	C6	26
Mogilev, Sov. Un.	E7	24
Mogilev-Podolskiy, Sov. Un.	G6	27
Mogilno, Pol.	B4	26
Mogi-Mirim, Braz.	C3	56
Mogincual, Moz.	A7	49
Mogocha, Sov. Un.	D14	29
Mogochin, Sov. Un.	B10	28
Mogok, Burma	D10	36
Mogollon, N.M., U.S.	D1	108
Mogollon Mesa, mtn., Az., U.S.	C4	80
Mogollon Mountains, mts., N.M., U.S.	C1	108
Mogollon Rim, clf., Az., U.S.	C5	80
Mogotes, Punta, c., Arg.	B5	54
Moguer, Spain	D2	22
Mohács, Hung.	C4	24
Mohale's Hoek, Leso.	A4	111
Mohall, N.D., U.S.	C3	44
Mohammedia, Mor.	B1	80
Mohave, co., Az., U.S.	H7	105
Mohave, Lake, res., U.S.	C1	80
Mohave Mountains, mts., Az., U.S.	C1	80
Mohave Valley, Az., U.S.	C1	80
Mohawk, Mi., U.S.	A2	99
Mohawk, N.Y., U.S.	C5	109
Mohawk, stm., N.H., U.S.	g7	106
Mohawk, stm., N.Y., U.S.	C6	109
Mohawk Lake, l., N.J., U.S.	A3	107
Mohawk Mountain, mtn., Ct., U.S.	B2	84
Mohawk Mountains, mts., Az., U.S.	E2	80
Mohawk River see Mohawk, stm., N.Y., U.S.	C6	109
Mohe, China	A9	31
Mohegan, Ct., U.S.	D7	84
Mohican, Black Fork, stm., Oh., U.S.	B3	112
Mohican, Clear Fork, stm., Oh., U.S.	B3	112
Mohill, Ire.	D4	11
Mohnton, Wa., U.S.	B7	124
Mohon, Tan.	C6	48
Mohoro, Tan.	C6	48
Moieses, W.S.	C2	103
Moinești, Rom.	B8	24
Moinkum Desert, des., Sov. Un.	E8	28
Moira, N.Y., U.S.	f10	109
Moirans, Fr.	h8	72
Moisie, Que.	h8	72
Moisie, stm., Que.	E4	16
Moissac, Fr.	D3	46
Moïssala, Chad	E4	16
Moita, Port.	B2	120
Mojave, Ca., U.S.	E4	82
Mojave, stm., Ca., U.S.	E5	82
Mojave Desert, des., Ca., U.S.	E5	82
Moji-Guaçu, stm., Braz.	k8	56
Mojo, Eth.	D7	50
Mojokerto, Indon.	*G4	34
Mokāma, India	E10	37
Mokane, Mo., U.S.	C6	102
Mokapu Peninsula, pen., Hi., U.S.	g10	88
Mokapu Point, c., Hi., U.S.	g11	88
Mokelumne, stm., Ca., U.S.	C3	82
Mokelumne Hill, Ca., U.S.	C3	82
Mokena, Il., U.S.	k9	90
Mokhotlong, Leso.	C4	49
Mokolo, Cam.	A2	48
Mokolo, Zaire	A2	48
Mokp'o, S. Kor.	E10	33
Moksha, Sov. Un.	D14	27
Moku Manu, i., Hi., U.S.	g11	88
Mol, Bel.	C5	17
Mola [di Bari], Italy	D6	23
Molalla, Or., U.S.	B4	114
Molanosa, Sask.	C3	75
Mólaoi, Grc.	D4	96
Molasses Pond, l., Me., U.S.	C2	55
Molat, i., Yugo.	B3	24
Moldau see Vltava, stm., Czech.	A6	49
Moldavia, state, Sov. Un.	E5	29
Moldavia, hist. reg., Rom.	B8	24
Molde, Nor.	F2	14
Moldova, stm., Rom.	B8	24
Moldoveanu, mtn., Rom.	C7	24
Molega Lake, l., N.S.	E5	71
Molenbeek-Saint Jean, Bel.	*D4	17
Molepolole, Bots.	D6	109
Môle-Saint-Nicolas, Haiti	E7	64
Molfetta, Italy	D6	23
Molina, Chile	B2	54
Molina de Aragón, Spain	B5	22
Molina de Segura, Spain	C5	22
Moline, Il., U.S.	B3	90
Moline, Ks., U.S.	E7	93
Moline, Mi., U.S.	F5	99
Molinella, Italy	e6	112
Molino, co., Co., U.S.	D2	93
Molino de Rosas (part of Mexico City), Mex.	h9	63
Molinos, Arg.	E2	55
Moliro, Zaire	C5	48
Molise, prov., Italy	D5	23
Moliterno, Italy	D5	23
Möll, stm., Aus.	C9	20
Mölle, Swe.	I5	15
Mollendo, Peru	E3	58
Mollusk, Va., U.S.	C6	123
Mölndal, Swe.	I4	14
Molochansk, Sov. Un.	H10	27
Molodechno, Sov. Un.	D6	27
Molokai, i., Hi., U.S.	B5	88
Molokini, i., Hi., U.S.	C5	88
Molopo, stm., Afr.	C3	49
Moloundou, Cam.	E3	46
Molsheim, Fr.	F7	17
Molson, Man.	D3	70
Molson, Wa., U.S.	A6	124
Molson, stm., Man.	B3	70
Molson Lake, l., Man.	B3	70
Molt, Mt., U.S.	E8	103
Molteno, S. Afr.	D4	49
Moluccas (Maluku), is., Indon.	F7	34
Molucca Sea, Indon.	E7	34
Molus, Ky., U.S.	D6	94
Moma, Moz.	A6	49
Mombasa, Kenya	B6	48
Mombetsu, Japan	D11	33
Mombongo, Zaire	A3	48
Momboyo, stm., Zaire	B2	48
Momence, Il., U.S.	B6	90
Momchilgrad, Bul.	E7	24
Momi, Fiji	H14	52
Momostenango, Guat.	A7	49
Mompog Pass, strt., Phil.	p14	34
Mompono, Zaire	A3	48
Mompós, Col.	B3	60
Møn, i., Den.	C6	15
Mona, Ut., U.S.	D4	121
Mona, Isla de, i., P.R.	G11	64
Mona, Punta, c., C.R.	F6	62
Monaca, Pa., U.S.	E1	115
Monaco, ctry., Eur.	F7	16
Monadhliath Mountains, mts., Scot., U.K.	C4	13
Monadnock, Mount, mtn., N.H., U.S.	E2	106
Monadnock Mountain, mtn., Vt., U.S.	B5	122
Monagas, state, Ven.	B5	60
Monaghan, Ire.	C5	11
Monaghan, co., Ire.	C4	11
Monahans, Tx., U.S.	D1	120
Monamolin, Ire.	E5	11
Mona Passage, strt., N.A.	E10	64
Monarch, Alta.	E4	68
Monarch, Mt., U.S.	C6	103
Monarch Mills, S.C., U.S.	B4	117
Monarch Mountain, mtn., B.C.	D5	69
Monarch Pass, Co., U.S.	C5	83
Monashee Mountains, mts., B.C.	D8	69
Monastir, Tun.	B7	44
Monastyrshchina, Sov. Un.	D7	27
Monavatu, mtn., Fiji	H14	52
Moncalieri, Italy	B1	23
Moncão, Braz.	B1	57
Moncey, Fr.	B1	21
Monchegorsk, Sov. Un.	D15	14
Mönchengladbach, W. Ger.	C3	18
Monchique, Port.	D1	22
Monchique, Serra de, mts., Port.	D1	22
Moncks Corner, S.C., U.S.	E7	117
Monclo, W.V., U.S.	D3	125
Monclova, Mex.	B4	63
Monclova, Oh., U.S.	e6	112
Moncton, N.B.	C5	71
Moncure, N.C., U.S.	B3	110
Mondamin, Ia., U.S.	C1	92
Mondego, Cabo, c., Port.	B1	22
Mondego, stm., Port.	B2	22
Mond Lake, l., B.C.	B9	20
Mondoñedo, Spain	A2	22
Mondorf-les-Bains, Lux.	E6	17
Mondovì, Italy	B1	23
Mondovi, Wi., U.S.	D2	126
Monee, Il., U.S.	B6	90
Monegaw Springs, Mo., U.S.	C4	102
Monemvasía, Grc.	D4	25
Moneron Island, i., Sov. Un.	C10	33
Monessen, Pa., U.S.	F2	115
Moneta, Va., U.S.	C3	123
Monett, Mo., U.S.	E4	102
Monetta, S.C., U.S.	D4	117
Monette, Ar., U.S.	B5	81
Moneygall, Ire.	D?	
Moneymore, N. Ire., U.K.	C5	11
Monfalcone, Italy	B4	23
Monforte de Lemos, Spain	A2	22
Monfort Heights, Oh., U.S.	o12	112
Monga, Zaire	A3	48
Mongala, stm., Zaire	A3	48
Mongalla, Sud.	D4	47
Möng Hsat, Burma	B3	35
Möng Mit, Burma	D10	36
Mongo, Chad	C3	46
Mongo, stm., Afr.	C2	46
Mongolia (part of Markham), Ont.	k15	73
Mongolia, ctry., Asia	B5	31
Mongolia, Plateau of, plat., Mong.	B6	31
Möng Pan, Burma	B3	35
Mongu, Zam.	A3	48
Möng Yai, Burma	A2	35
Monhegan Island, i., Me., U.S.	E3	96
Mönh Hayrhan Mountain, mtn., Mong.	B3	31
Moniac, Ga., U.S.	F4	87
Moniaive, Scot., U.K.	E5	13
Monico, Wi., U.S.	C4	126
Monida Pass, U.S.	E6	89
Monie, Md., U.S.	D6	97
Moninabad see Ambājogāi, India	H6	37
Moniquirá, Col.	B3	60
Moniteau, co., Mo., U.S.	C5	102
Monitor, Alta.	D5	68
Monitor, Or., U.S.	h12	114
Monitor Range, mts., Nv., U.S.	E5	105
Monitor Valley, val., Nv., U.S.	D5	105
Monivea, Ire.	D3	11
Monkey Point, c., Nic.	E8	63
Monkey River, Belize	B3	62
Monkira, Austl.	D3	51
Monkoto, Zaire	B3	48
Monkton, Vt., U.S.	C2	122
Monmouth, Wales, U.K.	C5	12
Monmouth, Il., U.S.	C3	90
Monmouth, Ia., U.S.	B7	92
Monmouth, Me., U.S.	D2	96

Name	Map Ref.	Page

Monmouth, Or., U.S. C3 114
Monmouth, co., N.J., U.S. .. C4 107
Monmouth Beach, N.J., U.S. . C5 107
Monmouth Junction, N.J., U.S. C3 107
Monmouth Mountain, mtn.,
 B.C. D6 69
Monnickendam, Neth. B5 17
Monnow, stm., U.K. C5 12
Mono, co., Ca., U.S. D4 82
Monocacy, stm., Md., U.S. .. B3 97
Mono Lake, l., Ca., U.S. D4 82
Monomonac, Lake, l., U.S. .. E3 106
Monomoy Island, i., Ma., U.S. C7 98
Monomoy Point, c., Ma., U.S. C7 98
Monon, In., U.S. C4 91
Monona, Ia., U.S. A6 92
Monona, Wi., U.S. E4 126
Monona, co., Ia., U.S. B1 92
Monona, Lake, l., Wi., U.S. .. E4 126
Monongah, W.V., U.S. B4 125
Monongahela, Pa., U.S. F2 115
Monongahela, stm., U.S. G2 115
Monongalia, co., W.V., U.S. .. B4 125
Monopoli, Italy D6 23
Monor, Hung. B4 24
Monos Island, i., Trin. N22 65
Monóvar, Spain C5 22
Monoville, Tn., U.S. C8 119
Monowi, Ne., U.S. B7 104
Monowice, Pol. g10 26
Monponsett, Ma., U.S. B6 98
Monreale, Italy E4 23
Monroe, Ar., U.S. C4 81
Monroe, Ct., U.S. D3 84
Monroe, Ga., U.S. C3 87
Monroe, In., U.S. C8 91
Monroe, Ia., U.S. C4 92
Monroe, La., U.S. B3 95
Monroe, Me., U.S. D3 96
Monroe, Mi., U.S. G7 99
Monroe, Ne., U.S. C8 104
Monroe, N.H., U.S. B2 106
Monroe, N.J., U.S. C4 107
Monroe, N.Y., U.S. D6 109
Monroe, N.C., U.S. C2 110
Monroe, Oh., U.S. C11 112
Monroe, Ok., U.S. C7 113
Monroe, Or., U.S. C3 114
Monroe, S.D., U.S. D8 118
Monroe, Tn., U.S. C8 119
Monroe, Ut., U.S. E3 121
Monroe, Va., U.S. C3 123
Monroe, Wi., U.S. F4 126
Monroe, co., Al., U.S. D2 78
Monroe, co., Ar., U.S. C4 81
Monroe, co., Fl., U.S. G5 86
Monroe, co., Ga., U.S. D3 87
Monroe, co., Il., U.S. E3 90
Monroe, co., In., U.S. F4 91
Monroe, co., Ia., U.S. D5 92
Monroe, co., Ky., U.S. D4 94
Monroe, co., Mi., U.S. G7 99
Monroe, co., Ms., U.S. B5 101
Monroe, co., Mo., U.S. B5 102
Monroe, co., N.Y., U.S. B3 109
Monroe, co., Oh., U.S. C4 112
Monroe, co., Pa., U.S. D11 115
Monroe, co., Tn., U.S. D9 119
Monroe, co., W.V., U.S. D4 125
Monroe, co., Wi., U.S. E3 126
Monroe Bridge, Ma., U.S. ... A2 98
Monroe Center, Ct., U.S. ... D3 84
Monroe Center, Il., U.S. A5 90
Monroe City, In., U.S. G3 91
Monroe City, Mo., U.S. B6 102
Monroe Lake, res., In., U.S. . F5 91
Monroe Park, De., U.S. h7 85
Monroeton, Pa., U.S. C9 115
Monroeville, Al., U.S. D2 78
Monroeville, In., U.S. C8 91
Monroeville, N.J., U.S. D2 107
Monroeville, Oh., U.S. A3 112
Monroeville, Pa., U.S. k14 115
Monrovia, Lib. E2 45
Monrovia, Ca., U.S. m13 82
Monrovia, In., U.S. E5 91
Mons (Bergen), Bel. B5 16
Monsarás, Ponta do, c., Braz. E3 57
Monschau, W. Ger. D6 17
Monselice, Italy D7 20
Monsey, N.Y., U.S. *m14 109
Møns Klint, clf., Den. D6 15
Monson, Me., U.S. C3 96
Monson, Ma., U.S. B3 98
Montabaur, W. Ger. C2 19
Montagnais Point, c., Newf. . B1 72
Montagnana, Italy D7 20
Montague, P.E.I. C7 71
Montague, Ca., U.S. B2 82
Montague, Mi., U.S. A2 98
Montague, Mi., U.S. E4 99
Montague, Tx., U.S. C4 120
Montague, co., Tx., U.S. C4 120
Montague Island, i., Ak., U.S. D10 79
Montague Lake, l., Sask. H3 75
Montague Peak, mtn., Ak.,
 U.S. g18 79
Montague Strait, strt., Ak.,
 U.S. h18 79
Montalbán, Spain B5 22
Montalegre, Port. B2 22
Mont Alto, Pa., U.S. G8 115
Montalto, mtn., Italy E5 23
Montana, Ak., U.S. g17 79
Montana, state, U.S. D7 103
Montana-Vermala, Switz. D3 21
Montánchez, Spain C2 22
Montandon, Pa., U.S. E8 115
Montargis, Fr. D5 16
Montataire, Fr. E2 17
Montauban, Fr. E4 16
Montauban-les-Mines, Que. .. C1 74
Montauk, N.Y., U.S. m17 109
Montbard, Fr. D6 16
Montbéliard, Fr. D7 16
Mont Belvieu, Tx., U.S. r14 120
Montblanch, Spain B6 22
Mont Blanc Tunnel, Eur. E5 16
Montbozon, Fr. B1 21
Montbrison, Fr. E3 17
Montcalm, co., Que. C3 74
Montcalm, co., Mi., U.S. E5 99
Montcalm, Pic de, mtn., Fr. .. F4 16
Mont-Carmel, Que. B8 74
Montceau-les-Mines, Fr. D6 16
Mont Cenis Pass, Eur. E7 16
Montcerf, Que. C1 74
Montchanin, Fr. D6 16
Montchanin, De., U.S. h7 85
Montclair, Ca., U.S. m13 82
Montclair, N.J., U.S. B4 107
Mont Clare, Pa., U.S. o19 115
Montcoal, W.V., U.S. D3 125
Montcornet, Fr. E3 17

Mont-de-Marsan, Fr. F3 16
Montdidier, Fr. C5 16
Monteagle, Tn., U.S. D8 119
Monte Alegre, Braz. D3 56
Monte Alegre de Goiás, Braz. C4 59
Monte Azul, Braz. B4 56
Montebello, Que. D3 74
Montebello, Ca., U.S. m12 82
Montebello, Va., U.S. C3 123
Montebelluna, Italy D8 20
Monte Carmelo, Braz. B3 56
Monte Caseros, Arg. A5 54
Montecelio, Italy g9 23
Montecino, Ca., U.S. *E4 82
Monte Comán, Arg. A3 54
Montecristi, Ec. B1 58
Monte Cristo, Bol. B3 55
Monte Cristi, Dom. Rep. E8 64
Montecristo, i., Italy C3 23
Montefrío, Spain D3 22
Montego Bay, Jam. E5 64
Montego Bay, b., Jam. E13 65
Montegut, La., U.S. E5 95
Monteiro, Braz. C3 57
Monteith, Mount, mtn., B.C. . B6 69
Montelavar, Port. f9 22
Montélimar, Fr. E6 16
Montelindo, stm., Para. D4 55
Montellano, Spain D3 22
Montello, Nv., U.S. B7 105
Montello, Wi., U.S. E4 126
Montemayor, Meseta de, plat.,
 Arg. C3 54
Montemorelos, Mex. B5 63
Montemor-o-Novo, Port. C1 22
Montenegro, Braz. D2 56
Montenegro, hist. reg., Yugo. D4 24
Monte Patria, Chile A2 54
Monte Plata, Dom. Rep. E9 64
Monte Porzio Catone, Italy .. h9 23
Montepuez, Moz. D6 48
Montepulciano, Italy C3 23
Monte Quemado, Arg. E3 55
Montereau [-faut-Yonne], Fr. . C5 16
Monterey, Al., U.S. D3 78
Monterey, Ca., U.S. D3 82
Monterey, In., U.S. C7 91
Monterey, Ky., U.S. B5 94
Monterey, La., U.S. C4 95
Monterey, Ma., U.S. B1 98
Monterey, Va., U.S. C8 119
Monterey, co., Ca., U.S. D3 82
Monterey Bay, b., Ca., U.S. . D2 82
Monterey Park, Ca., U.S. ... m12 82
Monteros, Arg. E2 55
Monterotondo, Italy g9 23
Monterrey, Mex. B4 63
Monte Sano Mountain, mtn.,
 Al., U.S. A3 78
Monte Sant'Angelo, Italy D5 23
Monte Santo, Braz. D3 57
Monte Santu, Capo di, c., Italy D2 23
Montes Claros, Braz. B4 56
Montevallo, Al., U.S. B3 78
Montevarchi, Italy C3 23
Montevideo, Mn., U.S. F3 100
Montevideo, Ur. E1 56
Monteview, Id., U.S. F6 89
Monte Vista, Co., U.S. D4 83
Montezuma, Ga., U.S. D2 87
Montezuma, Ia., U.S. C5 92
Montezuma, Ks., U.S. E3 93
Montezuma, N.M., U.S. B4 108
Montezuma, Oh., U.S. B1 112
Montezuma, Tn., U.S. B3 119
Montezuma, co., Co., U.S. .. D2 83
Montezuma Canyon, val., Ut.,
 U.S. F6 121
Montezuma Castle National
 Monument, Az., U.S. C4 80
Montezuma Creek, Ut., U.S. . F6 121
Montezuma Peak, mtn., Az.,
 U.S. D3 80
Montfaucon, Switz. B3 21
Montfort, Que. D3 74
Montfort, Wi., U.S. F3 126
Montfort-sur-Meu, Fr. C3 16
Montgomery, Wales, U.K. ... B4 12
Montgomery, Al., U.S. C3 78
Montgomery, Ga., U.S. E5 87
Montgomery, Il., U.S. B5 90
Montgomery, In., U.S. G3 91
Montgomery, La., U.S. C3 95
Montgomery, Ma., U.S. B2 98
Montgomery, Mi., U.S. G6 99
Montgomery, Mn., U.S. F5 100
Montgomery, N.Y., U.S. D6 109
Montgomery, Oh., U.S. o13 112
Montgomery, Pa., U.S. D8 115
Montgomery, Vt., U.S. B3 122
Montgomery, W.V., U.S. C3 125
Montgomery, co., Al., U.S. .. C3 78
Montgomery, co., Ar., U.S. .. C2 81
Montgomery, co., Ga., U.S. . D4 87
Montgomery, co., Il., U.S. ... D4 90
Montgomery, co., In., U.S. .. D4 91
Montgomery, co., Ia., U.S. .. C2 92
Montgomery, co., Ks., U.S. .. E8 93
Montgomery, co., Ky., U.S. .. B6 94
Montgomery, co., Md., U.S. . B3 97
Montgomery, co., Ms., U.S. . B4 101
Montgomery, co., Mo., U.S. . C6 102
Montgomery, co., N.Y., U.S. . B5 109
Montgomery, co., N.C., U.S. . B3 110
Montgomery, co., Oh., U.S. . C1 112
Montgomery, co., Pa., U.S. .. F11 115
Montgomery, co., Tn., U.S. .. A4 119
Montgomery, co., Tx., U.S. .. D5 120
Montgomery, co., Va., U.S. .. C2 123
Montgomery Center, Vt., U.S. B3 122
Montgomery City, Mo., U.S. . C6 102
Montgomery Village, Md., U.S. *B3 97
Montgomery see Sāhiwāl,
 Pak.
Monthermé, Fr. E4 17
Monthey, Switz. C2 20
Monticello, P.E.I. C7 71
Monticello, Fl., U.S. B3 86
Monticello, Ga., U.S. C3 87
Monticello, Il., U.S. C5 90
Monticello, In., U.S. C4 91
Monticello, Ia., U.S. B6 92
Monticello, Ky., U.S. D5 94
Monticello, Me., U.S. B5 96
Monticello, Ms., U.S. D3 101

Monticello, Mo., U.S. A6 102
Monticello, N.M., U.S. D2 108
Monticello, N.Y., U.S. D6 109
Monticello, Ut., U.S. F6 121
Monticello, Wi., U.S. F4 126
Mont Ida, Ks., U.S. D8 93
Montier, Mo., U.S. D6 102
Montier-en-Der, Fr. F4 17
Montiers-sur-Saulx, Fr. F5 17
Montignac, Fr. E4 16
Montigny [-lès-Metz], Fr. C7 16
Montigny, Port. C1 22
Montijo, Spain C2 22
Montilla, Spain D3 22
Monti Verdi, Ut., U.S. *B4 121
Montivilliers, Fr. C4 16
Mont-Joli, Que. A9 74
Mont-Laurier, Que. C2 74
Montluçon, Fr. D5 16
Montmagny, Que. C7 74
Montmagny, co., Que. C7 74
Montmartre, Sask. G4 75
Montmédy, Fr. E5 17
Montmélian, Fr. D7 20
Montmirail, Fr. F3 17
Montmorenci, In., U.S. D3 91
Montmorenci, S.C., U.S. D4 117
Montmorency, Fr. g10 16
Montmorency, co., Mi., U.S. . C6 99
Montmorency, stm., Que. ... B6 74
Montmorency Number One,
 co., Que. B6 74
Montmorency Number Two,
 co., Que. C7 74
Montmorillon, Fr. D4 16
Montney, B.C. A7 69
Monto, Austl. B8 51
Montone, stm., Italy B3 23
Montoro, Spain C3 22
Montour, Ia., U.S. C5 92
Montour, co., Pa., U.S. D8 115
Montour Falls, N.Y., U.S. C4 109
Montoursville, Pa., U.S. D8 115
Montoya, N.M., U.S. B5 108
Montpelier, Id., U.S. G7 89
Montpelier, In., U.S. C7 91
Montpelier, Ia., U.S. C7 92
Montpelier, La., U.S. D5 95
Montpelier, Ms., U.S. B5 101
Montpelier, N.D., U.S. C7 111
Montpelier, Oh., U.S. A1 112
Montpelier, Vt., U.S. C3 122
Montpelier Station, Va., U.S. . B4 123
Montpelier, Que. D2 74
Montpellier, Fr. F5 16
Montpellier, Fr. F5 16
Montréal, Que. D4 74
Montreal, Wi., U.S. B3 126
Montreal, stm., Sask. C3 75
Montréal, Île de, i., Que. q19 74
Montreal Lake, Sask. C3 75
Montreal Lake, l., Sask. C3 75
Montréal-Nord, Que. p19 74
Montreat, N.C., U.S. f10 110
Montreuil [-sous-Bois], Fr. ... C5 16
Montreuil-sur-Mer, Fr. B4 16
Montreux, Switz. E3 18
Montricher, Switz. C1 21
Mont-Rolland, Que. D3 74
Montrose, B.C. E9 69
Montrose, Scot., U.K. B5 10
Montrose, Al., U.S. E2 78
Montrose, Ar., U.S. D4 81
Montrose, Co., U.S. C3 83
Montrose, Ga., U.S. D3 87
Montrose, Il., U.S. D5 90
Montrose, Ia., U.S. D6 92
Montrose, Ks., U.S. C5 93
Montrose, Mi., U.S. E7 99
Montrose, Ms., U.S. C4 101
Montrose, Mo., U.S. C4 102
Montrose, Pa., U.S. C10 115
Montrose, S.D., U.S. D8 118
Montrose, Va., U.S. m18 123
Montrose, co., Co., U.S. C2 83
Montross, Va., U.S. B6 123
Montrouge, Fr. g10 16
Mont-Royal, Que. p19 74
Mont-Saint-Martin, Fr. C6 16
Mont-Saint-Michel, Fr. C5 16
Montserrat, Mo., U.S. C4 102
Montserrat, dep., N.A. H13 64
Montserrat, mtn., Spain B6 22
Mont-Tremblant, Que. C3 74
Mont-Tremblant, Parc
 Provincial du, Que. C3 74
Montvale, N.J., U.S. A4 107
Montvale, Va., U.S. C3 123
Mont Vernon, N.H., U.S. E3 106
Montville, Ct., U.S. D7 84
Montville, Ma., U.S. B1 98
Montville, N.J., U.S. B4 107
Montz, La., U.S. h11 95
Montzen, Bel. D5 17
Monument, Co., U.S. B6 83
Monument, Ks., U.S. C2 93
Monument, N.M., U.S. E6 108
Monument, Or., U.S. C7 114
Monument Beach, Ma., U.S. . C6 98
Monument Heights, Va., U.S. *C5 123
Monument Peak, mtn., Co.,
 U.S. B3 83
Monument Peak, mtn., Id.,
 U.S. G4 89
Monument Valley, Ut., U.S. . *F5 121
Monument Valley, val., Az.,
 U.S. A5 80
Monywa, Burma D10 36
Monza, Italy B2 23
Monze, Zam. E4 48
Monzón, Peru C2 58
Monzón, Spain B6 22
Moodus, Ct., U.S. C6 84
Moodus Reservoir, res., Ct.,
 U.S. C6 84
Moody, Me., U.S. E2 96
Moody, Mo., U.S. E6 102
Moody, Tx., U.S. D4 120
Moody, co., S.D., U.S. C9 118
Moody Air Force Base, mil.,
 Ga., U.S. F3 87
Moody Beach, Me., U.S. E2 96
Moodys, Ok., U.S. A7 113
Moodys Forks, N.Y., U.S. ... f11 109
Moon, Ok., U.S. D7 113
Moonachie, N.J., U.S. *B4 107
Moonie, stm., Austl. E9 51
Moon Lake, l., Ms., U.S. A3 101
Moon Run, Pa., U.S. k13 115
Moora, Austl. F2 50
Moorabbin, Austl. *G8 51
Moorcroft, Wy., U.S. B8 127
Moore, Id., U.S. F5 89

Moore, Mt., U.S. D7 103
Moore, Ok., U.S. B4 113
Moore, S.C., U.S. B4 117
Moore, Tx., U.S. E3 120
Moore, W.V., U.S. B5 125
Moore, co., N.C., U.S. B3 110
Moore, co., Tn., U.S. B5 119
Moore, co., Tx., U.S. B2 120
Moore, Lake, l., Austl. E2 50
Moore Dam, U.S. B3 106
Moorefield, Ky., U.S. B6 94
Moorefield, W.V., U.S. B6 125
Moore Haven, Fl., U.S. F5 86
Mooreland, In., U.S. E7 91
Mooreland, Ok., U.S. A2 113
Moore Mill, N.B. D2 71
Moore Park, N.B. D5 16
Moore Reservoir, res., U.S. . B3 106
Mooresburg, Tn., U.S. C10 119
Moores Corner, Ma., U.S. .. A3 98
Moores Creek National Military
 Park, N.C., U.S. C4 110
Moores Hill, In., U.S. F7 91
Moorestown, Mi., U.S. D5 99
Moorestown, N.J., U.S. D3 107
Mooresville, In., U.S. E5 91
Mooresville, Mo., U.S. B4 102
Mooresville, N.C., U.S. B2 110
Mooresville, Tn., U.S. B5 119
Mooreton, N.D., U.S. C9 111
Mooreville, Ms., U.S. A5 101
Moorhead, Ia., U.S. B2 92
Moorhead, Mn., U.S. D2 100
Moorhead, Ms., U.S. B3 101
Mooring, Tn., U.S. A2 119
Mooringsport, La., U.S. B2 95
Moor Lake, Ont. A7 73
Moorland, Ia., U.S. B3 92
Moorman, Ky., U.S. C2 94
Moorpark, Ca., U.S. *E4 82
Moosburg, W. Ger. E6 19
Moose, Wy., U.S. C2 127
Moose, stm., N.H., U.S. B4 106
Moose, stm., N.Y., U.S. B5 109
Moose, stm., Vt., U.S. B5 122
Moose Creek, Ont. B10 73
Moose Factory, Ont. F16 66
Moosehead Lake, l., Me., U.S. C3 96
Mooseheart, Il., U.S. B5 90
Moose Heights, B.C. C6 69
Moose Hill, hill, Ma., U.S. ... h11 98
Moosehorn, Man. D3 70
Moose Island, i., Man. D3 70
Moose Jaw, Sask. G3 75
Moose Jaw, stm., Sask. G3 75
Moose Lake, Man. C1 70
Moose Lake, Mn., U.S. D6 100
Moose Lake, l., Man. C1 68
Moose Lake, l., Wi., U.S. ... B2 126
Mooseleuk Stream, stm., Me.,
 U.S. B4 96
Mooselookmeguntic Lake, l.,
 Me., U.S. D2 96
Moose Mountain, mtn., N.H.,
 U.S. C2 106
Moose Mountain Creek, stm.,
 Sask. H4 75
Moose Mountain Provincial
 Park, Sask. H4 75
Moose Pass, Ak., U.S. C10 79
Moose River, Me., U.S. C2 96
Moosic, Pa., U.S. m18 115
Moosilauke, Mount, mtn.,
 N.H., U.S. B3 106
Moosomin, Sask. G5 75
Moosonee, Ont. o19 73
Moosup, Ct., U.S. C8 84
Moosup, stm., U.S. C1 116
Moosup Valley, R.I., U.S. ... D1 116
Mopang Lake, l., Me., U.S. .. D5 96
Mopeia Velha, Moz. A6 49
Mopti, Mali D4 45
Moquegua, Peru E3 58
Moquegua, dept., Peru E3 58
Mór, Hung. B4 24
Mor, i., Den. Q18 52
Mor, Glen, val., Scot., U.K. .. D4 13
Mòr, Sgùrr, mtn., Scot., U.K. . C3 13
Mora, Cam. C2 46
Mora, Spain C4 22
Mora, Swe. G6 14
Mora, Ga., U.S. E4 87
Mora, Mn., U.S. E5 100
Mora, N.M., U.S. B4 108
Mora, co., N.M., U.S. A5 108
Mora, stm., N.M., U.S. B5 108
Morača, stm., Yugo. C3 24
Morādābād, India C6 36
Morada Nova, Braz. D6 57
Mora de Ebro, Spain B6 22
Morafenobe, Madag. g8 49
Morag, Pol. B5 26
Moraga, Ca., U.S. *D2 82
Moraine, Oh., U.S. *C1 112
Morales, Guat. k13 63
Morales, Mex. B6 63
Moramanga, Madag. g9 49
Moran, Ks., U.S. E8 93
Moran, Mi., U.S. B6 99
Moran, Tx., U.S. C3 120
Moran, Wy., U.S. C2 127
Morann, Pa., U.S. E5 115
Morant Bay, Jam. F5 64
Morant Point, c., Jam. F5 64
Morar, Loch, l., Scot., U.K. .. D3 13
Morat, Loch, l., Scot., U.K. .. D3 13
Morata de Tajuña, Spain ... p18 22
Moratalla, Spain C5 22
Morattico, Va., U.S. C6 123
Moratuwa, Sri L. G6 36
Morava, stm., Eur. D4 26
Moravia, N.Y., U.S. C4 109
Moravia, hist. reg., Czech. .. A3 26
Moraya, Bol. H8 58
Moray Firth, est., Scot., U.K. . B5 10
Morbach, W. Ger. F7 19
Morbegno, Italy D4 20
Morbi, India E3 37
Morden, Man. D5 70
More, Ben, mtn., Scot., U.K. . B4 10
More, Ben, mtn., Scot., U.K. . D3 13
More Assynt, Ben, mtn.,
 Scot., U.K. A4 10
Moreau, stm., S.D., U.S. B3 118
Moreau, North Fork, stm.,
 S.D., U.S. B3 118
Moreau, South Fork, stm.,
 S.D., U.S. B2 118

Moreau Peak, mtn., S.D., U.S. B2 118
Moreauville, La., U.S. C4 95
Morecambe, Eng., U.K. F6 13
Morecambe Bay, b., Eng.,
 U.K. D5 10
Moree, Austl. E8 50
Morehead, Ky., U.S. B6 94
Morehead City, N.C., U.S. .. C6 110
Morehouse, Mo., U.S. E8 102
Morehouse, co., La., U.S. ... B4 95
Moreira, Ont. D4 73
Moreland, Ar., U.S. B3 81
Moreland, Ga., U.S. C2 87
Moreland, Id., U.S. F6 89
Moreland, Ky., U.S. C5 94
Morelia, Mex. D4 63
Morella, Spain B5 22
Morelos, state, Mex. D5 63
Morena, Sierra, mts., Spain . C3 22
Morenci, Az., U.S. D6 80
Morenci, Mi., U.S. G6 99
Moreno Valley, Ca., U.S. ... *F5 82
Moresby Island, i., B.C. C2 69
Moreton Bay, b., Austl. C9 51
Moreton-in-Marsh, Eng., U.K. C6 12
Moreton Island, i., Austl. C9 51
Moretown, Vt., U.S. C3 122
Moreuil, Fr. E2 17
Morewood, Ont. B9 73
Morey, Lake, l., Vt., U.S. D4 122
Morey Peak, mtn., Nv., U.S. . E5 105
Morez, Fr. D7 16
Morganza, La., U.S. D4 95
Morgan, Austl. G2 51
Morgan, Ga., U.S. E2 87
Morgan, Ky., U.S. B5 94
Morgan, Mn., U.S. F4 100
Morgan, Tx., U.S. C4 120
Morgan, Ut., U.S. B4 121
Morgan, Vt., U.S. B4 122
Morgan, co., Al., U.S. A3 78
Morgan, co., Co., U.S. A7 83
Morgan, co., Ga., U.S. C3 87
Morgan, co., Il., U.S. D3 90
Morgan, co., In., U.S. F5 91
Morgan, co., Ky., U.S. C6 94
Morgan, co., Mo., U.S. C5 102
Morgan, co., Oh., U.S. C4 112
Morgan, co., Tn., U.S. C9 119
Morgan, co., Ut., U.S. B4 121
Morgan, co., W.V., U.S. B6 125
Morgan City, La., U.S. E4 95
Morgan City, Ms., U.S. B3 101
Morganfield, Ky., U.S. C2 94
Morgan Hill, Ca., U.S. D3 82
Morgan Island, i., S.C., U.S. . G6 117
Morgan Point, c., Ct., U.S. .. E4 84
Morganton, Ar., U.S. B3 81
Morganton, Ga., U.S. B2 87
Morganton, N.C., U.S. B1 110
Morgantown, In., U.S. F5 91
Morgantown, Ky., U.S. C3 94
Morgantown, Ms., U.S. D4 101
Morgantown, Pa., U.S. F10 115
Morgantown, Tn., U.S. D8 119
Morgantown, W.V., U.S. B5 125
Morganville, Ks., U.S. C6 93
Morganville, N.J., U.S. C4 107
Morganza, La., U.S. D4 95
Morges, Switz. C2 20
Morgex, Italy A3 20
Morghāb, stm., Asia A3 36
Morhange, Fr. F6 17
Mori, Japan E10 33
Moriah, Trin. M24 65
Moriah, N.Y., U.S. A7 109
Moriah, Mount, mtn., Nv., U.S. D7 105
Moriah, Mount, mtn., N.H.,
 U.S. B4 106
Moriarty, N.M., U.S. C3 108
Morice, stm., B.C. B4 69
Morice Lake, l., B.C. B4 69
Moriguchi, Japan *I7 33
Morin-Heights, Que. D3 74
Morinville, Alta. C4 68
Morioka, Japan D13 31
Morisset-Station, Que. C7 74
Morjärv, Swe. D10 14
Morkill, stm., B.C. C7 69
Morlaix, Fr. C2 16
Morland, Ks., U.S. C3 93
Morley, Alta. D3 68
Morley, Mi., U.S. E5 99
Morley, Mo., U.S. D8 102
Mormon Lake, Az., U.S. C4 80
Mormon Peak, mtn., Nv., U.S. G7 105
Morne-à-l'Eau, Guad. Q9 65
Morningdale, Ma., U.S. B4 98
Morningside, S.D., U.S. C7 118
Morning Sun, Ia., U.S. C6 92
Mornington, Isla, i., Chile ... D1 54
Morning View, Ky., U.S. k14 94
Moro, Ar., U.S. C5 81
Moro, Or., U.S. B6 114
Morobay, Ar., U.S. D3 81
Morobe, Pap. N. Gui. k12 50
Morocco, In., U.S. C3 91
Morococha, Peru C3 58
Moro Creek, stm., Ar., U.S. . D3 81
Morogoro, Tan. C6 48
Morogoro, prov., Tan. C6 48
Moro Gulf, b., Phil. D6 34
Moroleón, Mex. m13 63
Morombe, Madag. h8 49
Morón, Arg. g7 54
Morón, Cuba C5 64
Morón, Mong. B5 31
Morona, stm., Peru D3 58
Morona-Santiago, prov., Ec. . B2 58
Morón de la Frontera, Spain . D4 22
Moroni, Com. g9 49
Morotai, i., Indon. E7 34
Moroto, Ug. A6 48
Morozovsk, Sov. Un. G13 27
Morpeth, Ont. E3 73
Morpeth, Eng., U.K. E7 13
Morphou Bay, b., Cyp. B3 30
Morral, Oh., U.S. B2 112
Morrill, Ks., U.S. C8 93
Morrill, Ne., U.S. C2 104
Morrilton, Ar., U.S. B3 81
Morrin, Alta. D4 68
Morrinhos, Braz. D4 59
Morrinsville, N.Z. L15 51
Morris, Man. E3 70
Morris, Oh., U.S. A5 112

Morris, Mn., U.S. E3 100
Morris, N.Y., U.S. C5 109
Morris, Ok., U.S. B6 113
Morris, co., Ks., U.S. D7 93
Morris, co., N.J., U.S. B3 107
Morris, co., Tx., U.S. C5 120
Morris, Mount, mtn., N.Y.,
 U.S. A6 109
Morrisburg, Ont. C9 73
Morris Chapel, Tn., U.S. B3 119
Morrisdale, Pa., U.S. E5 115
Morris Island, i., S.C., U.S. .. F8 117
Morris Jesup, Kap, c., Grnld. A17 61
Morrison, Co., U.S. B5 83
Morrison, Il., U.S. B4 90
Morrison, Mo., U.S. C6 102
Morrison, Ok., U.S. A4 113
Morrison, Tn., U.S. D8 119
Morrison, Wi., U.S. h10 126
Morrison, co., Mn., U.S. ... D4 100
Morrison City, Tn., U.S. C11 119
Morrisonville, Il., U.S. D4 90
Morrisonville, N.Y., U.S. ... f11 109
Morris Plains, N.J., U.S. B4 107
Morris Run, Pa., U.S. C7 115
Morriston, Fl., U.S. C4 86
Morristown, Az., U.S. D3 80
Morristown, In., U.S. E6 91
Morristown, Mn., U.S. F5 100
Morristown, N.J., U.S. B4 107
Morristown, N.Y., U.S. f9 109
Morristown, S.D., U.S. B4 118
Morristown, Tn., U.S. C10 119
Morristown, Vt., U.S. B3 122
Morristown National Historical
 Park, N.J., U.S. B3 107
Morrisville, Mo., U.S. D4 102
Morrisville, N.Y., U.S. C5 109
Morrisville, Pa., U.S. F12 115
Morrisville, Vt., U.S. B3 122
Morrito, Nic. I5 63
Morro, Ec. B1 58
Morro, Punta, c., Chile E1 55
Morro, Punta, c., Mex. D6 63
Morro Bay, Ca., U.S. E3 82
Morro do Chapéu, Braz. B3 56
Morropón, Peru C2 58
Morrosquillo, Golfo de, b., Col. B2 60
Morrow, Ga., U.S. C2 87
Morrow, La., U.S. D3 95
Morrow, Oh., U.S. C1 112
Morrow, co., Oh., U.S. B3 112
Morrow, co., Or., U.S. B7 114
Morse, Sask. G2 75
Morse, La., U.S. D3 95
Morse, Tx., U.S. A2 120
Morse, Wi., U.S. B3 126
Morse Bluff, Ne., U.S. C9 104
Morse Mill, Mo., U.S. g12 102
Morse Reservoir, res., In.,
 U.S. D5 91
Morses Creek, stm., N.J., U.S. k8 107
Morshansk, Sov. Un. E13 27
Mortagne, Fr. C4 16
Mortara, Italy B2 23
Morteau, Fr. D7 16
Mortes, Rio das, stm., Braz. . E4 59
Mortlach, Sask. G2 75
Morton, Il., U.S. C4 90
Morton, Mn., U.S. F4 100
Morton, Ms., U.S. C4 101
Morton, Tx., U.S. C1 120
Morton, Wa., U.S. C3 124
Morton, co., Ks., U.S. E2 93
Morton, co., N.D., U.S. C4 111
Morton Grove, Il., U.S. h9 90
Mortons Gap, Ky., U.S. C2 94
Morven, Austl. E4 51
Morven, N.C., U.S. C2 110
Morven, mtn., Scot., U.K. ... B5 13
Moruya, Austl. G8 51
Morvan Mountains, mts., Fr. . D6 16
Morven, Ga., U.S. F3 87
Morven, N.C., U.S. C2 110
Morven, mtn., Scot., U.K. ... B5 13
Moruya, Austl. G8 51
Morwell, Austl. H7 51
Morjärv, Swe. B10 28
Moryakovskiy Zaton, Sov. Un. B10 28
Morye, Sov. Un. r32 14
Mosalsk, Sov. Un. D10 27
Mosbach, W. Ger. D4 19
Mosby, Mo., U.S. h11 102
Mosby, Mt., U.S. D9 103
Mosca, Co., U.S. D5 83
Moscarello, Italy k9 23
Moscos Islands, is., Burma .. F10 36
Moscow, Id., U.S. C2 89
Moscow, Ks., U.S. E3 93
Moscow, Ky., U.S. f8 94
Moscow, Oh., U.S. D1 112
Moscow, Pa., U.S. m18 115
Moscow, R.I., U.S. E2 116
Moscow, Tn., U.S. B2 119
Moscow Mills, Mo., U.S. C7 102
Mosel (Moselle), stm., Eur. .. D3 18
Moseley, Va., U.S. C5 123
Moselle, Ms., U.S. D4 101
Moselle, dept., Fr. C6 16
Moselle (Mosel), stm., Eur. .. D3 18
Mosers River, N.S. E7 71
Moses Coulee, val., Wa., U.S. B6 124
Moses Lake, Wa., U.S. B6 124
Moses Lake, l., Wa., U.S. ... B6 124
Mosgiel, N.Z. P13 51
Mosheim, Tn., U.S. C11 119
Mosher, S.D., U.S. D5 118
Mosherville, N.S. E7 71
Moshi, Tan. B6 48
Moshupa, Bots. g8 49
Mosier, Or., U.S. B5 114
Mosinee, Wi., U.S. D4 126
Mosjöen, Nor. E5 14
Moskva, stm., Sov. Un. n18 27
Mosley Creek, stm., B.C. ... D5 69
Mosomane (Artesia), Bots. .. g8 49
Mosonmagyaróvár, Hung. ... B3 24
Mosquera, Col. C2 60
Mosquero, N.M., U.S. B6 108
Mosquito, Newf. E2 72
Mosquito Coast, N.A. D6 63
Mosquito Creek Lake, res.,
 U.S. C2 92
Mosquito Lagoon, b., Fl., U.S. D6 86
Mosquitos, Golfo de los, b.,
 Pan. F7 62
Moss, Nor. H4 14

185

Name	Map Ref.	Page
Moss, Ms., U.S.	D4	101
Moss, Tn., U.S.	C8	119
Mossaka, Congo	B2	48
Mossbank, Sask.	H3	75
Moss Bluff, La., U.S.	D2	95
Mosselbaai (Mossel Bay), S. Afr.	D3	49
Mossendjo, Congo	B1	48
Mossleigh, Alta.	D4	68
Mossman, Austl.	C8	50
Moss Mountain, mtn., Ar., U.S.	C3	81
Mossoró, Braz.	C3	57
Moss Point, Ms., U.S.	E5	101
Moss Vale, Austl.	G8	51
Mossville, Ar., U.S.	B2	81
Mossy, stm., Man.	C2	70
Mossy, stm., Sask.	C4	75
Mossy Head, Fl., U.S.	u15	86
Mossyrock, Wa., U.S.	C3	124
Most, Czech.	C2	26
Mostar, Yugo.	D3	24
Mostefa, Cap, c., Tun.	F3	42
Móstoles, Spain	p17	22
Mostrim (Edgeworthstown), Ire.	D4	11
Mosul (Al Mawsil), Iraq	B4	38
Moswansicut Pond, l., R.I., U.S.	C3	116
Motagua, stm., N.A.	E6	63
Motala, Swe.	H6	14
Motatán, Ven.	B3	60
Motherwell, Scot., U.K.	C5	10
Motihári, India	D10	37
Motilla del Palancar, Spain	C5	22
Motley, Mn., U.S.	D4	100
Motley, co., Tx., U.S.	B2	120
Motobu, Japan	N5	52
Motomachi, Japan	o18	33
Moto Mountain, hill, Japan	P17	52
Motril, Spain	D4	22
Motru, stm., Rom.	C6	24
Mott, N.D., U.S.	D8	111
Motta di Livenza, Italy	D8	20
Motueka, N.Z.	N14	52
Motul [de Felipe Carrillo Puerto], Mex.	C7	63
Motupe, Peru	C2	58
Moturiki, i., Fiji	H15	52
Mou, Den.	B4	15
Mouaskar, Alg.	C5	25
Moúdhros (Mudros), Grc.	C2	45
Moujéria, Maur.	C2	45
Moudon, Switz.	C2	20
Mouila, Gabon	F2	46
Moulamein Billabong Creek, stm., Austl.	G5	51
Mould Bay, N.W. Ter.	m28	66
Moule, Guad.	H14	64
Moulins, Fr.	D5	16
Moulouya, Oued, stm., Mor.	C4	44
Moulton, Al., U.S.	A2	78
Moulton, Ia., U.S.	D5	92
Moultonboro, N.H., U.S.	C4	106
Moultrie, Ga., U.S.	E3	87
Moultrie, co., Il., U.S.	D5	90
Moultrie, Lake, res., S.C., U.S.	E7	117
Mound, La., U.S.	B4	95
Mound, Mn., U.S.	n11	100
Mound Bayou, Ms., U.S.	B3	101
Mound City, Il., U.S.	F4	90
Mound City, Ks., U.S.	D9	93
Mound City, Mo., U.S.	A2	102
Mound City, S.D., U.S.	B5	118
Mound City Group National Monument, Oh., U.S.	C2	112
Moundou, Chad	D3	46
Moundridge, Ks., U.S.	D6	93
Mounds, Il., U.S.	F4	90
Mounds, Ok., U.S.	B5	113
Mounds View, Mn., U.S.	m12	100
Moundsville, W.V., U.S.	B4	125
Mound Valley, Ks., U.S.	E8	93
Moundville, Al., U.S.	C2	78
Moundville, Mo., U.S.	D3	102
Mounier, Mont, mtn., Fr.	E7	16
Mountain, N.D., U.S.	A8	111
Mountain, W.V., U.S.	B4	125
Mountain, Wi., U.S.	C5	126
Mountainair, N.M., U.S.	C3	108
Mountainaire, Az., U.S.	B4	80
Mountain Ash, Ky., U.S.	D5	94
Mountainboro, Al., U.S.	A3	78
Mountain Brook, Al., U.S.	g7	78
Mountainburg, Ar., U.S.	B1	81
Mountain City, Ga., U.S.	B3	87
Mountain City, Nv., U.S.	B6	105
Mountain City, Tn., U.S.	C12	119
Mountain Dale, N.Y., U.S.	D6	109
Mountain Fork, stm., U.S.	C7	113
Mountain Grove, Ont.	C8	73
Mountain Grove, Mo., U.S.	D5	102
Mountain Home, Ar., U.S.	A3	81
Mountain Home, Id., U.S.	F3	89
Mountainhome, Pa., U.S.	D11	115
Mountain Home, Tx., U.S.	D3	120
Mountain Home, Ut., U.S.	C5	121
Mountain Home Air Force Base, mil., Id., U.S.	F3	89
Mountain Iron, Mn., U.S.	C6	100
Mountain Lake, Mn., U.S.	G4	100
Mountain Lake, l., Sask.	B3	75
Mountain Lake Park, Md., U.S.	m12	97
Mountain Lakes, N.J., U.S.	*B4	107
Mountain Nile (Al Baḥr al Jabal), Sud.	D3	47
Mountain Park, Alta.	C2	68
Mountain Park, Fl., U.S.	*C2	86
Mountain Park, U.S.	C3	113
Mountain Pine, Ar., U.S.	c21	81
Mountain Point, Ak., U.S.	n24	79
Mountainside, N.J., U.S.	B4	107
Mountain Springs, Nv., U.S.	*G6	105
Mountain Valley, Ar., U.S.	C2	81
Mountain View, Alta.	E4	68
Mountain View, Ar., U.S.	B3	81
Mountain View, Ca., U.S.	k8	82
Mountain View, Co., U.S.	*B5	83
Mountain View, Co., U.S.	*A5	83
Mountainview, Hi., U.S.	D6	88
Mountain View, Mo., U.S.	D6	102
Mountain View, N.M., U.S.	B3	113
Mountain View, Wy., U.S.	*E2	127
Mountain Village, Ak., U.S.	C7	79
Mount Airy, Ga., U.S.	B3	87
Mount Airy, Md., U.S.	B3	97
Mount Airy, N.J., U.S.	C3	107
Mount Airy, N.C., U.S.	A2	110
Mount Albert, Ont.	C5	73
Mount Angel, Or., U.S.	B4	114
Mount Arlington, N.J., U.S.	B3	107
Mount Assiniboine Provincial Park, B.C.	D10	69
Mount Athos, ter., Grc.	B5	25
Mount Auburn, Il., U.S.	D4	90
Mount Auburn, Ia., U.S.	B5	92
Mount Ayr, In., U.S.	C3	91
Mount Ayr, Ia., U.S.	D3	92
Mount Barker, Austl.	G2	51
Mount Bellew Bridge, Ire.	D3	11
Mount Berry, Ga., U.S.	B1	87
Mount Blanchard, Oh., U.S.	B2	112
Mount Brydges, Ont.	E3	73
Mount Calvary, Wi., U.S.	E5	126
Mount Carleton Provincial Park, N.B.	B3	71
Mount Carmel, Al., U.S.	C3	78
Mount Carmel, Il., U.S.	E6	90
Mount Carmel, In., U.S.	F8	91
Mount Carmel, N.D., U.S.	A7	111
Mount Carmel, Oh., U.S.	o13	112
Mount Carmel, Pa., U.S.	E9	115
Mount Carmel, S.C., U.S.	C2	117
Mount Carmel, Ut., U.S.	F3	121
Mount Carmel Junction, Ut., U.S.	F3	121
Mount Carmel [-Mitchell's Brook-Saint Catherine's], Newf.	E5	72
Mount Carroll, Il., U.S.	A4	90
Mount Clare, W.V., U.S.	B4	125
Mount Clemens, Mi., U.S.	F8	99
Mount Clinton, Va., U.S.	B4	123
Mount Cory, Oh., U.S.	B2	112
Mount Crawford, Va., U.S.	B4	123
Mount Croghan, S.C., U.S.	B7	117
Mount Darwin, Zimb.	A5	49
Mount Desert, Me., U.S.	*D4	96
Mount Desert Island, i., Me., U.S.	D4	96
Mount Dora, Fl., U.S.	D5	86
Mount Dora, N.M., U.S.	A6	108
Mount Eaton, Oh., U.S.	B4	112
Mount Eden, Ky., U.S.	B4	94
Mount Elgin, Ont.	E4	73
Mount Emmons, Ut., U.S.	*C5	121
Mount Enterprise, Tx., U.S.	D5	120
Mount Ephraim, N.J., U.S.	*D2	107
Mount Erie, Il., U.S.	E5	90
Mount Etna, In., U.S.	C6	91
Mount Etna, Ia., U.S.	C3	92
Mount Forest, Ont.	D4	73
Mount Forest, Mi., U.S.	E6	99
Mount Freedom, N.J., U.S.	B3	107
Mount Gambier, Austl.	G7	50
Mount Gay, W.V., U.S.	D2	125
Mount Gilead, N.C., U.S.	B3	110
Mount Gilead, Oh., U.S.	B3	112
Mount Hagen, Pap. N. Gui.	k11	50
Mount Healthy, Oh., U.S.	o12	112
Mount Hebron, Ca., U.S.	B2	82
Mount Hermon, La., U.S.	D5	95
Mount Hermon, Ma., U.S.	A3	98
Mount Heron, Ar., U.S.	e9	123
Mount Holly, Ar., U.S.	D3	81
Mount Holly, N.J., U.S.	D3	107
Mount Holly, N.C., U.S.	B1	110
Mount Holly, S.C., U.S.	E7	117
Mount Holly, Vt., U.S.	E3	122
Mount Holly Springs, Pa., U.S.	F7	115
Mount Hood, Or., U.S.	B5	114
Mount Hope, Ont.	D5	73
Mount Hope, Al., U.S.	A2	78
Mount Hope, Ks., U.S.	E6	93
Mount Hope, W.V., U.S.	D3	125
Mount Hope, Wi., U.S.	F3	126
Mount Hope, stm., Ct., U.S.	B7	84
Mount Hope Bay, b., U.S.	D6	116
Mount Horeb, Wi., U.S.	E4	126
Mount Ida, Ar., U.S.	C2	81
Mount Idaho, Id., U.S.	D2	89
Mount Isa, Austl.	D6	50
Mount Jackson, Va., U.S.	B4	123
Mount Jewett, Pa., U.S.	C4	115
Mount Joy, Ia., U.S.	h10	92
Mount Joy, Pa., U.S.	F9	115
Mount Judea, Ar., U.S.	B2	81
Mount Juliet, Tn., U.S.	A5	119
Mount Kisco, N.Y., U.S.	D7	109
Mountlake Terrace, Wa., U.S.	*B3	124
Mount Lebanon, Pa., U.S.	F1	115
Mount Lemmon, Az., U.S.	E5	80
Mount Lookout, W.V., U.S.	C4	125
Mount Magnet, Austl.	E2	50
Mount Meigs, Al., U.S.	C3	78
Mountmellick, Ire.	D4	11
Mount Montgomery, Nv., U.S.	F3	105
Mount Morgan, Austl.	D9	50
Mount Moriah, Mo., U.S.	A4	102
Mount Morris, Il., U.S.	A4	90
Mount Morris, Mi., U.S.	E7	99
Mount Morris, N.Y., U.S.	C3	109
Mount Morris, Pa., U.S.	G1	115
Mount of Olives, hill, Isr. Occ.	m14	41
Mount Olive, Al., U.S.	B3	78
Mount Olive, Il., U.S.	D4	90
Mount Olive, Ms., U.S.	D4	101
Mount Olive, N.C., U.S.	B4	110
Mount Olive, Tn., U.S.	n14	119
Mount Olivet, Ky., U.S.	B5	94
Mount Olympus, Ut., U.S.	*C4	121
Mount Orab, Oh., U.S.	C2	112
Mount Pearl, Newf.	E5	72
Mount Penn, Pa., U.S.	F10	115
Mount Pleasant, Ar., U.S.	B4	81
Mount Pleasant, Fl., U.S.	B2	86
Mount Pleasant, Ga., U.S.	E5	87
Mount Pleasant, Ia., U.S.	D6	92
Mount Pleasant, Mi., U.S.	E6	99
Mount Pleasant, Ms., U.S.	A4	101
Mount Pleasant, N.J., U.S.	B2	107
Mount Pleasant, N.C., U.S.	B2	110
Mount Pleasant, Pa., U.S.	F2	115
Mount Pleasant, S.C., U.S.	F8	117
Mount Pleasant, Tn., U.S.	B4	119
Mount Pleasant, Tx., U.S.	C5	120
Mount Pleasant, Ut., U.S.	D4	121
Mount Pocono, Pa., U.S.	D11	115
Mount Prospect, Il., U.S.	A6	90
Mount Pulaski, Il., U.S.	C4	90
Mountrail, co., N.D., U.S.	A3	111
Mount Rainier, Md., U.S.	f9	97
Mount Rainier National Park, Wa., U.S.	C4	124
Mount Revelstoke National Park, B.C.	D8	69
Mount Robson Provincial Park, B.C.	C8	69
Mount Rogers National Recreation Area, Va., U.S.	D1	123
Mount Rushmore National Memorial, hist., S.D., U.S.	D2	118
Mount Savage, Md., U.S.	k13	97
Mount Shasta, Ca., U.S.	B2	82
Mount Sidney, Va., U.S.	B4	123
Mount Sinai, N.Y., U.S.	*n15	109
Mount Solon, Va., U.S.	B3	123
Mount Sterling, Al., U.S.	C1	78
Mount Sterling, Il., U.S.	D3	90
Mount Sterling, Ky., U.S.	B6	94
Mount Sterling, Oh., U.S.	C2	112
Mount Stewart, P.E.I.	C7	71
Mount Storm, W.V., U.S.	B5	125
Mount Summit, In., U.S.	D7	91
Mount Sunapee, N.H., U.S.	D2	106
Mount Tabor, Vt., U.S.	E3	122
Mount Uniacke, N.S.	E6	71
Mount Union, Ia., U.S.	C6	92
Mount Union, Pa., U.S.	F6	115
Mount Upton, N.Y., U.S.	C5	109
Mount Vernon, Al., U.S.	D1	78
Mount Vernon, Ar., U.S.	B3	81
Mount Vernon, Ga., U.S.	D4	87
Mount Vernon, Il., U.S.	E5	90
Mount Vernon, In., U.S.	I2	91
Mount Vernon, Ia., U.S.	C6	92
Mount Vernon, Ky., U.S.	C5	94
Mount Vernon, Me., U.S.	D3	96
Mount Vernon, Md., U.S.	D6	97
Mount Vernon, Mo., U.S.	D4	102
Mount Vernon, N.Y., U.S.	h13	109
Mount Vernon, Oh., U.S.	B3	112
Mount Vernon, Or., U.S.	C7	114
Mount Vernon, S.D., U.S.	D7	118
Mount Vernon, Tn., U.S.	D9	119
Mount Vernon, Tx., U.S.	C5	120
Mount Vernon, Wa., U.S.	A3	124
Mount Victory, Oh., U.S.	B2	112
Mount View, R.I., U.S.	C4	116
Mountville, Ga., U.S.	C2	87
Mountville, S.C., U.S.	C4	117
Mount Washington, Ky., U.S.	B4	94
Mount Washington, Ma., U.S.	B1	98
Mount Wolf, Pa., U.S.	F8	115
Mount Zion, Ga., U.S.	C1	87
Mount Zion, Il., U.S.	D5	90
Moura, Austl.	D8	50
Moura, Braz.	D6	54
Moura, Port.	C2	22
Mourdi, Dépression du, depr., Chad	B4	46
Mourmelon-le-Grand, Fr.	E4	17
Mourne Mountains, mts., N. Ire., U.K.	C6	11
Mouscron (Moeskroen), Bel.	B5	16
Mousie, Ky., U.S.	C7	94
Moussoro, Chad	C3	46
Mouthe, Fr.	C1	21
Moutier, Switz.	B3	21
Moûtiers[-Tarentaise], Fr.	E7	16
Mouy, Fr.	E2	17
Moville, Ire.	B4	11
Moville, Ia., U.S.	B1	92
Moweaqua, Il., U.S.	D4	90
Mower, co., Mn., U.S.	G6	100
Mowrystown, Oh., U.S.	C2	112
Moxahala, Oh., U.S.	C3	112
Moxee City, Wa., U.S.	C5	124
Moxico, dept., Ang.	D3	48
Moxie Pond, l., Me., U.S.	C3	96
Moxley, Ga., U.S.	D4	87
Moy, stm., Ire.	C2	11
Moy, Cnoc, hill, Scot., U.K.	E3	13
Moyale, Eth.	A6	47
Moyale, Kenya	A6	47
Moyamba, S.L.	E2	45
Moycullen, Ire.	D2	11
Moyers, Ok., U.S.	C6	113
Moyeuvre-[Grande], Fr.	C7	16
Moyie, B.C.	E10	69
Moyie Springs, Id., U.S.	A2	89
Moynalty, Ire.	D5	11
Moyo, Ug.	A5	48
Moyobamba, Peru	C2	58
Moyock, N.C., U.S.	A6	110
Moyuta, Guat.	C2	62
Moza, Isr.	h11	41
Mozambique, ctry., Afr.	H9	42
Mozambique Channel, strt., Afr.	H10	42
Mozart, Sask.	F3	75
Mozdok, Sov. Un.	E2	28
Mozelle, Ky., U.S.	D6	94
Mozhaysk, Sov. Un.	D11	27
Mozhga, Sov. Un.	D19	8
Mozyr, Sov. Un.	E7	27
Mpanda, Tan.	C5	48
Mpika, Zam.	D5	48
Mporokoso, Zam.	C5	48
Mpouya, Congo	B2	48
Mpraeso, Ghana	E4	45
Mpulungu, Zam.	C5	48
Mpwapwa, Tan.	C6	48
Mrągowo, Pol.	B6	26
M'Sila, Alg.	A6	44
Msta, stm., Sov. Un.	B9	27
Mstislavl, Sov. Un.	D8	27
Mšeného, Czech.	n16	26
Mšené, Czech.	n17	26
Mtakuja, Tan.	C5	48
Mtsensk, Sov. Un.	E11	27
Mtubatuba, S. Afr.	D7	49
Mtwara, Tan.	D7	48
Mtwara, prov., Tan.	D6	48
Mu, stm., Burma	A1	35
Muaná, Braz.	D9	54
Muang Khammouan, Laos	D6	35
Muang Khong, Laos	C3	34
Muang Khongxedon, Laos	E6	34
Muang Lan, Laos	C5	34
Muang Ou Nua, Laos	A4	34
Muang Ou Tai, Laos	A4	34
Muang Pakxan, Laos	C5	34
Muang Sing, Laos	B4	34
Muang Souy, Laos	C5	34
Muang Xaignabouri, Laos	C4	34
Muang Xepon, Laos	D7	35
Muar (Bandar Maharani), Malay.	*E2	34
Muar, stm., Malay.	K5	34
Muaratewe, Indon.	F5	34
Muări, Cape, c., Pak.	I13	39
Mubārak, Jabal, mtn., Asia	E7	41
Mubende, Ug.	A5	48
Mubi, Nig.	D7	45
Much Wenlock (Wenlock), Eng., U.K.	B5	12
Muck, i., Scot., U.K.	B3	10
Muckalee Creek, stm., Ga., U.S.	D2	87
Muckleshoot Indian Reservation, Wa., U.S.	f11	124
Muconda, Ang.	D3	48
Mucuri, Braz.	E3	57
Mucuri, stm., Braz.	E2	57
Mucusso, Ang.	E3	48
Mud, stm., Ky., U.S.	C3	94
Mud, stm., Mn., U.S.	B3	100
Mud, stm., W.V., U.S.	C2	125
Muda, stm., Malay.	I4	35
Mudanjiang, China	C10	31
Mudan Jiang, stm., China	D4	33
Mudanya, Tur.	B7	25
Mud Butte, S.D., U.S.	C3	118
Mud Creek, stm., Al., U.S.	g6	78
Mud Creek, stm., Co., U.S.	D8	83
Mud Creek, stm., Ia., U.S.	e9	92
Mud Creek, stm., Ne., U.S.	C6	104
Mud Creek, stm., Ok., U.S.	C4	113
Muddy, Il., U.S.	F5	90
Muddy Boggy Creek, stm., Ok., U.S.	C6	113
Muddy Creek, stm., Ks., U.S.	k14	93
Muddy Creek, stm., Ut., U.S.	E4	121
Muddy Creek, stm., Wy., U.S.	C4	127
Muddy Creek, stm., Wy., U.S.	D6	127
Muddy Creek, stm., Wy., U.S.	E2	127
Muddy Creek Mountain, mtn., Ar., U.S.	C2	81
Muddy Lake, l., Sask.	E1	75
Muddy Mountain, mtn., Wy., U.S.	D7	127
Muddy Mountains, mts., Nv., U.S.	G7	105
Muddy Peak, mtn., Nv., U.S.	G7	105
Müden, W. Ger.	F4	15
Mudgee, Austl.	F7	51
Mudjatik, stm., Sask.	A2	75
Mud Lake, Id., U.S.	F6	89
Mud Lake, l., Me., U.S.	A4	96
Mud Lake, l., Nv., U.S.	F4	105
Mud Lick Creek, stm., Ky., U.S.	k13	94
Mudon, Burma	E10	36
Mudros see Moúdhros, Grc.	C5	25
Mudug, prov., Som.	D6	47
Mueda, Moz.	D7	48
Muenster, Tx., U.S.	C4	120
Muff, Ire.	B4	11
Mufulira, Zam.	D5	48
Mugarripug, China	A11	37
Mugia, Spain	A1	22
Mugla, Tur.	D7	40
Mugodzhary Mountains, hills, Sov. Un.	D5	28
Muhammad Qawl, Sud.	A4	47
Mühlacker, W. Ger.	E3	19
Mühldorf, W. Ger.	B2	19
Muhlenberg, co., Ky., U.S.	C2	94
Mühlhausen [in Thüringen], E. Ger.	C5	18
Mühlig-Hofmann Mountains, mts., Ant.	B13	7
Muhulu, Zaire	B4	48
Muhutwe, Tan.	B5	48
Mui, i., Marsh Is.	S18	52
Muine Bheag, Ire.	E5	11
Muir, Mi., U.S.	E6	99
Muirkirk, Scot., U.K.	E4	13
Muirkirk, Md., U.S.	A4	97
Muir Woods National Monument, Ca., U.S.	h7	82
Mukachevo, Sov. Un.	G4	27
Mukah, Malay.	D4	34
Mukdahan, Thai.	D6	35
Mukden see Shenyang, China	C9	31
Mukilteo, Wa., U.S.	B3	124
Mukutawa, stm., Man.	C3	70
Mukwonago, Wi., U.S.	F5	126
Mula, Spain	C5	22
Mulanje, Mwi.	E6	48
Mulberry, Ar., U.S.	B1	81
Mulberry, Fl., U.S.	E4	86
Mulberry, In., U.S.	D4	91
Mulberry, Ks., U.S.	E9	93
Mulberry, N.C., U.S.	A1	110
Mulberry, Oh., U.S.	C1	112
Mulberry, Tn., U.S.	B5	119
Mulberry, stm., Ar., U.S.	B1	81
Mulberry Fork, stm., Al., U.S.	B3	78
Mulberry Grove, Il., U.S.	E4	90
Mulberry Mountain, mtn., Ar., U.S.	B3	81
Mulchén, Chile	D2	56
Mulde, stm., E. Ger.	C6	18
Muldoon, Tx., U.S.	E4	120
Muldraugh, Ky., U.S.	C4	94
Muldrow, Ok., U.S.	B7	113
Mule Creek, N.M., U.S.	D1	108
Mulegé, Mex.	B2	63
Muleshoe, Tx., U.S.	B1	120
Mulga, Al., U.S.	B3	78
Mulgrave, N.S.	D8	71
Mulhacén, mtn., Spain	D4	22
Mulhall, Ok., U.S.	A4	113
Mülheim [an der Ruhr], W. Ger.	D7	16
Mulhouse, Fr.	D7	16
Muling, China	D5	33
Muling He, stm., China	D6	33
Mulino, Or., U.S.	B4	114
Mulinu'u, Cape, c., W. Sam.	F11	52
Mulitapu'ili, Cape, c., W. Sam.	F12	52
Mull, Island of, i., Scot., U.K.	B4	10
Mull, Sound of, strt., Scot., U.K.	D3	13
Mullaghcleevaun, mtn., Ire.	D5	11
Mullan, Id., U.S.	B3	89
Mullan Pass, Mt., U.S.	D4	103
Mullen, Ne., U.S.	B4	104
Mullens, W.V., U.S.	D3	125
Muller Mountains, mts., Indon.	E4	34
Mullet Key, i., Fl., U.S.	p10	86
Mullet Lake, Mi., U.S.	C6	99
Mullet Peninsula, pen., Ire.	C1	10
Mullewa, Austl.	E2	50
Mull Head, c., Scot., U.K.	B6	13
Müllheim, W. Ger.	D6	19
Mullica, stm., N.J., U.S.	D3	107
Mullica Hill, N.J., U.S.	D2	107
Mulliken, Mi., U.S.	F6	99
Mullin, Tx., U.S.	D3	120
Mullinavat, Ire.	E4	11
Mullingar, Ire.	D4	11
Mullins, S.C., U.S.	C9	117
Mullinville, Ks., U.S.	E4	93
Mullröse, E. Ger.	A9	19
Mullumbimby, Austl.	E10	51
Multān, Pak.	B5	36
Multnomah, co., Or., U.S.	B4	114
Mulukuru, Lake, l., Austl.	D6	50
Mulvane, Ks., U.S.	E6	93
Mulvihill, Man.	D2	70
Mumbwa, Zam.	D4	48
Mummy Range, mts., Co., U.S.	A5	83
Mun, stm., Thai.	B2	34
Muna, Mex.	C7	63
Münchberg, W. Ger.	C6	19
Münchenstein, Switz.	A4	21
Münchon, N. Kor.	G3	33
Muncie, In., U.S.	D7	91
Muncy, Pa., U.S.	D8	115
Mundare, Alta.	C4	68
Munday, Tx., U.S.	C3	120
Mundelein, Il., U.S.	A5	90
Münden, W. Ger.	C4	18
Munden, Ks., U.S.	C6	93
Munford, Al., U.S.	B4	78
Munford, Tn., U.S.	B2	119
Munfordville, Ky., U.S.	C4	94
Mungallala Creek, stm., Austl.	D6	51
Mungári, Moz.	A6	49
Mungbere, Zaire	A5	48
Munger, India	C8	36
Mungindi, Austl.	E8	50
Munhall, Pa., U.S.	k14	115
Munich (München), W. Ger.	D5	18
Munich, N.D., U.S.	A7	111
Munising, Mi., U.S.	B4	99
Munith, Mi., U.S.	F6	99
Munjor, Ks., U.S.	D4	93
Munnsville, N.Y., U.S.	C5	109
Muñoz, Phil.	o13	34
Muñoz Gamero, Peninsula, pen., Chile	h11	54
Munro Lake, l., Man.	C3	70
Munsan-ni, S. Kor.	H3	33
Münsingen, W. Ger.	C4	19
Münsingen, Switz.	C4	21
Munson, Alta.	D4	68
Munson, Fl., U.S.	u15	86
Munson, Zaire	B2	48
Munsonville, N.H., U.S.	D2	106
Munster, Fr.	C7	16
Munster, W. Ger.	B5	18
Munster, In., U.S.	A2	91
Munster, hist. reg., Ire.	E3	11
Münster [in Westfalen], W. Ger.	C3	18
Munsungan Lake, l., Me., U.S.	B3	96
Muntenia, hist. reg., Rom.	C7	24
Muntok, Indon.	F3	34
Munuscong Lake, l., Mi., U.S.	B6	99
Muonio, Fin.	D10	14
Muonio, stm., Eur.	D10	14
Muotathal, Switz.	B2	24
Mur (Mura), stm., Eur.	B2	24
Murakami, Japan	G9	33
Murākh, Bi'r, well, Eg.	E6	41
Murano, Italy	D8	20
Murashi, Sov. Un.	B3	28
Murat, Fr.	E5	16
Murat, mtn., Tur.	C7	25
Murat, stm., Tur.	C13	40
Murau, Aus.	E2	19
Muravera, Italy	C11	33
Murchison, stm., Austl.	E2	50
Murchison Falls see Kabalega Falls, wtfl., Ug.	A5	48
Murcia, Spain	C5	22
Murcia, hist. reg., Spain	C5	22
Murcki, Pol.	g10	26
Murderkill, stm., De., U.S.	D4	85
Murdo, S.D., U.S.	D5	118
Murdock, Fl., U.S.	E4	86
Murdock, Il., U.S.	D5	90
Murdock, Ks., U.S.	E6	93
Murdock, Mn., U.S.	E3	100
Murdock, Ne., U.S.	h12	104
Mureş, stm., Eur.	C6	24
Muret, Fr.	A5	16
Murewa, Zimb.	A5	49
Murfreesboro, Ar., U.S.	C2	81
Murfreesboro, N.C., U.S.	A5	110
Murfreesboro, Tn., U.S.	B5	119
Murgha Kibzai, Pak.	B4	36
Murgon, Austl.	E9	51
Muri, Nig.	E7	45
Muriaé, Braz.	C4	56
Muri [-bei Bern], Switz.	C4	21
Murici, Braz.	k6	57
Muriel Lake, l., Alta.	B5	68
Müritz Lake, l., E. Ger.	B6	18
Murmansk, Sov. Un.	C6	29
Murnau, W. Ger.	B7	20
Murom, Sov. Un.	D13	27
Muroran, Japan	C13	31
Muros, Spain	A1	22
Muroto, Japan	J7	33
Muroto, Cape, c., Japan	J7	33
Murphy, Ga., U.S.	E3	87
Murphy, Id., U.S.	F2	89
Murphy, Mo., U.S.	g13	102
Murphy, N.C., U.S.	f8	110
Murphy, Or., U.S.	E3	114
Murphy Island, i., S.C., U.S.	E9	117
Murphy Lake, l., B.C.	C2	69
Murphys, Ca., U.S.	C3	82
Murphysboro, Il., U.S.	F4	90
Murphytown, W.V., U.S.	B3	125
Murr, Bi'r, well, Eg.	E6	43
Murray, Ia., U.S.	C3	92
Murray, Ky., U.S.	f9	94
Murray, Ne., U.S.	D10	104
Murray, Ut., U.S.	C4	121
Murray, co., Ga., U.S.	B2	87
Murray, co., Mn., U.S.	F3	100
Murray, co., Ok., U.S.	C4	113
Murray, stm., Austl.	F7	51
Murray, Cape, c., Pap. N. Gui.	f40	7
Murray, Lake, res., Ok., U.S.	C4	113
Murray, Lake, res., S.C., U.S.	C5	117
Murray Bridge, Austl.	G6	50
Murray City, Oh., U.S.	C3	112
Murray Harbour, P.E.I.	C7	71
Murray Head, c., P.E.I.	C7	71
Murray Lake, l., Alta.	E5	68
Murray River, P.E.I.	C7	71
Murrayville, S. Afr.	D7	49
Murrayville, W.V., U.S.	B3	125
Murrayville, B.C.	f13	69
Murrayville, Il., U.S.	D3	90
Murrells Inlet, S.C., U.S.	D9	117
Murrells Inlet, S.C., U.S.	D10	117
Murrhardt, W. Ger.	E4	19
Murrieta, Ca., U.S.	F5	82
Murrumbidgee, stm., Austl.	F8	50
Murrupula, Moz.	A6	49
Murrysville, Pa., U.S.	*k15	115
Mursala, i., Indon.	K3	35
Murska Sobota, Yugo.	B3	24
Murtaugh, Id., U.S.	G4	89
Murten, Switz.	C3	21
Murtle Lake, l., B.C.	C7	69
Murud, India	E5	36
Murwāra, India	D7	36
Murwillumbah, Austl.	E9	50
Mürz, stm., Aus.	E7	18
Mürzzuschlag, Aus.	E7	18
Muş, Tur.	C13	40
Musaid, Libya	C4	43
Musala, mtn., Bul.	D6	24
Musan, N. Kor.	C10	31
Musangai, Zaire	C3	48
Mūsā Qal'eh, Afg.	E12	39
Musashino, Japan	*I9	33
Muscatatuck, stm., In., U.S.	G5	91
Muscatatuck, Vernon Fork, stm., In., U.S.	G6	91
Muscat see Masqaṭ, Oman	A2	38
Muscatine, Ia., U.S.	C6	92
Muscatine, co., Ia., U.S.	C5	38
Muscle Shoals, Al., U.S.	A2	78
Muscoda, Wi., U.S.	E3	126
Muscogee, co., Ga., U.S.	D2	87
Musconetcong, stm., N.J., U.S.	B4	107
Musconetcong Mountain, mtn., N.J., U.S.	B2	107
Muscooten Bay, l., Il., U.S.	C3	90
Muscotah, Ks., U.S.	C8	93
Muscoy, Ca., U.S.	*E5	82
Muse, Ok., U.S.	C7	113
Mushie, Zaire	B2	48
Mushin, Nig.	E5	45
Mushketovo, Sov. Un.	r20	27
Musi, stm., Indon.	F2	34
Muskeget Channel, strt., Ma., U.S.	D7	98
Muskeget Island, i., Ma., U.S.	D7	98
Muskego, Wi., U.S.	F5	126
Muskego Lake, l., Wi., U.S.	n11	126
Muskegon, Mi., U.S.	E4	99
Muskegon, co., Mi., U.S.	E4	99
Muskegon, stm., Mi., U.S.	E4	99
Muskegon Heights, Mi., U.S.	E4	99
Muskegon Lake, l., Mi., U.S.	E4	99
Muskingum, co., Oh., U.S.	B4	112
Muskingum, stm., Oh., U.S.	C4	112
Muskö, Swe.	u36	14
Muskogee, Ok., U.S.	B6	113
Muskogee, co., Ok., U.S.	B6	113
Muskoka, co., Ont.	C5	73
Muskoka, Lake, l., Ont.	C5	73
Muskrat Dam Lake, res., Ont.	C7	66
Muskwa, stm., Alta.	A3	68
Muskwa, Lake, l., Alta.	A3	68
Muslimbāgh, Pak.	B4	36
Musquacook Lakes, l., Me., U.S.	B3	96
Musquaro, Lac, l., Que.	h14	74
Musquash, N.B.	D3	71
Musquash Mountain, mtn., Me., U.S.	C5	96
Musquodoboit Harbour, N.S.	E6	71
Musselburgh, Scot., U.K.	C5	10
Musselshell, co., Mt., U.S.	D9	103
Musselshell, stm., Mt., U.S.	D9	103
Mussende, Ang.	D2	48
Mussolinia see Arborea, Italy	E2	23
Mussuma, Ang.	D3	48
Mustafakemalpaşa, Tur.	B7	40
Musters, Lago, l., Arg.	D3	54
Mustinka, stm., Mn., U.S.	E2	100
Mustique, i., St. Vin.	V26	65
Mut, Eg.	D5	43
Mut, Tur.	D9	40
Mutá, Ponta do, c., Braz.	D3	57
Mutare, Zimb.	A5	49
Mutayyin, Yemen	B5	47
Mutena, Zaire	C3	48
Mutombo-Mukulu, Zaire	B7	20
Mutoko, Zimb.	A5	49
Mutorashanga, Zimb.	A5	49
Mutsu, Japan	F10	33
Mutsu Bay, b., Japan	F10	33
Mutton Bay, Que.	C2	72
Mutton Mountains, mts., Or., U.S.	C5	114
Mutual, Ok., U.S.	A2	113
Muṭubis, Eg.	C2	41
Mutunópolis, Braz.	A3	56
Mutzig, Fr.	F7	17
Mu Us Shamo (Ordos Desert), des., China	D6	31
Muxima, Ang.	C1	48
Muyinga, Bdi.	B5	48
Muyula, i., Pap. N. Gui.	k13	50
Muzaffargarh, Pak.	B3	37
Muzaffarnagar, India	C6	36
Muzaffarpur, India	C8	36
Muzambinho, Braz.	k8	56
Muzhi, Sov. Un.	B21	8
Muzon, Cape, c., Ak., U.S.	n23	79
Muztag, mtn., China	A8	36
Muztagata, mtn., China	A7	36
Mvuma, Zimb.	A5	49
Mwanza, Zaire	C4	48
Mwami, Zimb.	A5	49
Mwanza, prov., Tan.	B5	48
Mwanza, Tan.	B5	48
Mweelrea, mtn., Ire.	D2	11
Mwene-Ditu, Zaire	C4	48
Mwenezi, stm., Zimb.	B5	49
Mwenga, Zaire	B5	48
Mwimba, Zaire	C3	48
Mwinilunga, Zam.	D4	48
Myakka, stm., Fl., U.S.	E4	86
Myakka City, Fl., U.S.	E4	86
Myanaung, Burma	D2	35
Myaungmya, Burma	D1	35
Mycenae, hist., Grc.	D4	25
Myers Corner, N.Y., U.S.	*D7	109
Myerstown, Pa., U.S.	F9	115
Myersville, Md., U.S.	A2	97

Name	Map Ref.	Page
Myingyan, Burma	D10	36
Myitkyinā, Burma	C10	36
Myitnge, stm., Burma	B2	35
Myjava, Czech.	D4	26
Mylo, N.D., U.S.	A6	111
Mymensingh, Bngl.	D9	36
Mynaral, Sov. Un.	D8	28
Mynard, Ne., U.S.	h13	104
Myrick, Ms., U.S.	D5	101
Myrnam, Alta.	C5	68
Myrtle, Man.	E3	70
Myrtle, Ms., U.S.	A4	101
Myrtle, Mo., U.S.	E6	102
Myrtle Beach, S.C., U.S.	D10	117
Myrtle Beach Air Force Base, mil., S.C., U.S.	D10	117
Myrtle Creek, Or., U.S.	D3	114
Myrtle Grove, Fl., U.S.	u14	86
Myrtle Grove, La., U.S.	k12	95
Myrtle Point, Or., U.S.	D2	114
Myrtlewood, Al., U.S.	C2	78
Mysen, Nor.	p29	14
Myślenice, Pol.	D5	26
Myślibórz, Pol.	B3	26
Mysłowice, Pol.	g10	26
Mysore, India	F6	36
Mysore see Karnataka, state, India	F6	36
Mystic, Ct., U.S.	D8	84
Mystic, Ga., U.S.	E3	87
Mystic, Ia., U.S.	D5	92
Mystic Lakes, l., Ma., U.S.	g11	98
Myszków, Pol.	f10	26
My Tho, Viet.	C3	34
Mytilene see Mitilíni, Grc.	C6	40
Mytishchi, Sov. Un.	n17	27
Myton, Ut., U.S.	C5	121
Mže, stm., Czech.	D8	19
Mzimba, Mwi.	D5	48
Mzuzu, Mwi.	D5	48

N

Name	Map Ref.	Page
Naab, stm., W. Ger.	D7	19
Naalehu, Hi., U.S.	D6	88
Naamans Garden, De., U.S.	*A3	85
Na'an, Isr.	h10	41
Naantali, Fin.	G10	14
Naas, Ire.	D3	10
Nabā, Jabal (Mount Nebo), mtn., Jord.	C7	41
Nabadwīp, India	*D8	36
Nabb, In., U.S.	G6	91
Nabberu, Lake, l., Austl.	E3	50
Nabburg, W. Ger.	D7	19
Nabeina, Kir.	R18	52
Nabekavu, Fiji	H15	52
Naberezhnyye Chelny (Brezhnev), Sov. Un.	D8	29
Nabeul, Tun.	B7	44
Nabi Shuayb, Mount, mtn., Yemen	*D4	38
Nabnasset, Ma., U.S.	A5	98
Naboomspruit, S. Afr.	B4	49
Nabouwalu, Fiji	H15	52
Nabq, Eg.	H10	40
Nābulus, Isr. Occ.	B3	38
Nacala, Moz.	D7	48
Nacaome, Hond.	D4	62
Naches, Wa., U.S.	C5	124
Naches, stm., Wa., U.S.	C5	124
Nachingwea, Tan.	D6	48
Náchod, Czech.	C4	26
Nacilau Point, c., Fiji	H14	52
Nacimiento, Chile	B2	54
Nacimiento Reservoir, res., Ca., U.S.	E3	82
Nacka, Swe.	*H8	14
Nacmine, Alta.	D4	68
Naco, Az., U.S.	F6	80
Nacogdoches, Tx., U.S.	D5	120
Nacogdoches, co., Tx., U.S.	D5	120
Nacozari [de García], Mex.	A3	63
Nacula, i., Fiji	H14	52
Nadarzyn, Pol.	m13	26
Nadeau, Mi., U.S.	C3	99
Naden Harbour, b., B.C.	B1	69
Nadi, Fiji	H14	52
Nadiād, India	F4	37
Nădlac, Rom.	B5	24
Nador, Mor.	B4	44
Naduri, Fiji	H15	52
Nadvornaya, Sov. Un.	G5	27
Nadym, stm., Sov. Un.	B23	8
Næstved, Den.	J4	14
Nafada, Nig.	D7	45
Nafīshah, Eg.	D4	41
Naga, Phil.	C6	34
Naga Hills, mts., Asia	C10	36
Nāgāland, state, India	*C9	36
Nagano, Japan	D12	31
Nagaoka, Japan	D12	31
Nāgappattinam, India	F6	36
Nagarote, Nic.	D4	62
Nagar Pārkar, Pak.	D5	36
Nagasaki, Japan	E10	31
Nāgaur, India	D4	37
Nageezi, N.M., U.S.	A2	108
Nāgercoil, India	G6	36
Nagiba, Phil.	p13	34
Nagles Mountains, mts., Ire.	E3	11
Nago, Japan	N5	52
Nago Bay, b., Japan	N5	52
Nagog Pond, l., Ma., U.S.	f10	98
Nagold, W. Ger.	E3	19
Nagoya, Japan	D12	31
Nāgpur, India	D6	36
Nagqu, China	E3	31
Nags Head, N.C., U.S.	B7	110
Nagua, Dom. Rep.	E9	64
Naguabo, P.R.	B4	65
Nagykanizsa, Hung.	B3	24
Nagykőrös, Hung.	B4	24
Naha, Japan	F10	31
Nahalat Yehuda, Isr.	h10	41
Nahanni National Park, N.W. Ter.	D7	66
Nahant, Ma., U.S.	g12	98
Nahariyya, Isr.	B7	41
Nahāvand, Iran	D4	39
Nahe, stm., W. Ger.	D3	18
Nahma, Mi., U.S.	C4	99
Nahmakanta Lake, l., Me., U.S.	C3	96
Nahuel Huapí, Arg.	C2	54
Nahuel Huapí, Lago, l., Arg.	C2	54
Nahuel Niyeu, Arg.	C3	54
Nahunta, Ga., U.S.	E5	87
Naic, Phil.	o13	34
Naicam, Sask.	E3	75
Naiguatá, Pico, mtn., Ven.	A4	60
Naihāti, India	*D8	36
Naila, W. Ger.	C6	19
Nailaga, Fiji	H14	52
Nain, Newf.	g9	72
Nā'īn, Iran	E6	39
Naini Tāl, India	C7	37
Nairai, i., Fiji	H15	52
Nairn, Scot., U.K.	B5	10
Nairn, stm., Scot., U.K.	C4	13
Nairobi, Kenya	B6	48
Naitonitoni, Fiji	I15	52
Naivasha, Kenya	B6	48
Najafābād, Iran	E5	39
Naj' Ḩammādī, Eg.	D6	43
Najībābād, India	C7	37
Najin, N. Kor.	C11	31
Najran, well, Sau. Ar.	D4	38
Naju, S. Kor.	I3	33
Nakadōri Island, i., Japan	J4	33
Nakagusuku Bay, b., Japan	O5	52
Nakaminato, Japan	m19	33
Nakamura, Japan	J6	33
Nakaosu, Japan	N6	52
Nakatsu, Japan	J5	33
Nakfa, Eth.	B4	47
Nakhichevan, Sov. Un.	F3	28
Nakhodka, Sov. Un.	E6	33
Nakhon Chai Si, stm., Thai.	E4	35
Nakhon Pathom, Thai.	F3	35
Nakhon Phanom, Thai.	B2	34
Nakhon Ratchasima, Thai.	C2	34
Nakhon Sawan, Thai.	B1	34
Nakhon Si Thammarat, Thai.	D2	34
Nakina, Ont.	o18	73
Nakina, N.C., U.S.	C4	110
Nakło [nad Notecią], Pol.	B4	26
Naknek, Ak., U.S.	D8	79
Naknek Lake, l., Ak., U.S.	D8	79
Nakono Island, i., Japan	L4	33
Nakskov, Den.	J4	14
Nakuru, Kenya	B6	48
Nakusp, B.C.	D9	69
Nāl, stm., Pak.	C4	36
Nalchik, Sov. Un.	E2	28
Nallen, W.V., U.S.	m14	125
Nalón, stm., Spain	A2	22
Nālūt, Libya	C2	43
Nam, stm., Asia	B3	35
Nam, stm., S. Kor.	I4	33
Namacurra, Moz.	A6	49
Namak, Daryācheh-ye, l., Iran	D5	39
Namak, Kavīr-e, des., Iran	D8	39
Namaka, Alta.	D4	68
Namakan Lake, l., N.A.	B6	100
Namangan, Sov. Un.	E10	29
Namanock Island, i., N.J., U.S.	A3	107
Namanyere, Tan.	C5	48
Namapa, Moz.	D6	48
Namasagali, Ug.	A5	48
Namatanai, Pap. N. Gui.	h13	50
Nambe Pueblo, N.M., U.S.	B4	108
Nambour, Austl.	E9	50
Nam Co, l., China	E3	31
Nam Dinh, Viet.	A3	34
Nämdö, i., Swe.	t36	14
Nam Du Islands, is., Viet.	H6	35
Namekagon, stm., Wi., U.S.	B2	126
Namekagon Lake, l., Wi., U.S.	B2	126
Namen see Namur, Bel.	B6	16
Nametil, Moz.	A6	49
Namew Lake, l., Can.	C5	75
Namib Desert, des., Afr.	B1	49
Namibe (Moçâmedes), Ang.	E1	48
Namibe, dept., Ang.	E1	48
Namibia (South West Africa), ctry., Afr.	B2	49
Namiquipa, Mex.	B3	63
Namjagbarwa Feng, mtn., China	F4	31
Namlea, Indon.	F7	34
Nam Ngum Reservoir, res., Laos	C5	35
Namoi, stm., Austl.	F8	50
Namoruputh, Kenya	A6	48
Nampa, Alta.	A2	68
Nampa, Id., U.S.	F2	89
Nampala, Mali	C3	45
Nampo (Chinnampo), N. Kor.	D10	31
Nampula, Moz.	A6	49
Nampula, dept., Moz.	D6	48
Namsen, stm., Nor.	E4	14
Namsos, Nor.	E4	14
Namu, B.C.	D4	69
Namu Island, i., Marsh Is.	P18	52
Namur (Namen), Bel.	B6	16
Namur, Que.	D3	74
Namur, prov., Bel.	D4	17
Namur Island, i., Marsh Is.	S17	52
Namutoni, Nmb.	A2	49
Namwala, Zam.	E4	48
Namwŏn, S. Kor.	I3	33
Namysłów, Pol.	C4	26
Nan, Thai.	C4	35
Nan, stm., Thai.	B2	34
Nana, stm., Cen. Afr. Rep.	D3	46
Nanafalia, Al., U.S.	C2	78
Nanaimo, B.C.	E5	69
Nanakuli, Hi., U.S.	B3	88
Nanao, Japan	H8	33
Nanatsu Island, i., Japan	H8	33
Nance, co., Ne., U.S.	C7	104
Nanchang, China	F8	31
Nancheng, China	F8	31
Nanchong, China	E6	31
Nanchuan, China	J2	32
Nancy, Fr.	C7	16
Nancy, Ky., U.S.	C5	94
Nancy Creek, stm., Ga., U.S.	h8	87
Nanda Devi, mtn., India	B7	36
Nānded, India	H6	37
Nandurbār, India	G5	37
Nanfeng, China	K7	32
Nanga Eboko, Cam.	E2	46
Nānga Parbat, mtn., Pak.	A5	36
Nangis, Fr.	F2	17
Nangong, China	F6	32
Nang Rong, Thai.	E5	35
Nanhua, China	F5	31
Nanjemoy, Md., U.S.	D3	97
Nanjing (Nanking), China	E8	31
Nankin, Oh., U.S.	B3	112
Nanking see Nanjing, China	E8	31
Nanning, China	G6	31
Nanoose Bay, B.C.	f11	69
Nanowin, stm., Man.	C3	70
Nanping, China	F8	31
Nansemond, stm., Va., U.S.	k14	123
Nansen Sound, strt., N.W. Ter.	k33	66
Nan Shan see Qilian Shan, mts., China	D4	31
Nansio, Tan.	B5	48
Nanson, N.D., U.S.	A6	111
Nantel, Que.	C3	74
Nanterre, Fr.	g9	16
Nantes, Fr.	D3	16
Nanteuil-le-Haudouin, Fr.	E2	17
Nantian, China	J9	32
Nanticoke, Ont.	E4	73
Nanticoke, Md., U.S.	D6	97
Nanticoke, Pa., U.S.	D10	115
Nanticoke, stm., U.S.	D6	97
Nanton, Alta.	D4	68
Nantong, China	E9	31
Nantua, Fr.	D6	16
Nantucket, Ma., U.S.	D7	98
Nantucket, co., Ma., U.S.	D7	98
Nantucket Island, i., Ma., U.S.	D7	98
Nantucket Sound, strt., Ma., U.S.	C7	98
Nantuxent Point, c., N.J., U.S.	E2	107
Nantwich, Eng., U.K.	A5	12
Nanty Glo, Pa., U.S.	F4	115
Nanuet, N.Y., U.S.	g12	109
Nanukuloa, Fiji	H15	52
Nanuku Passage, strt., Fiji	H16	52
Nanuku Reef, rf., Fiji	H16	52
Nanuque, Braz.	B4	56
Nanyang, China	E7	31
Nanyuki, Kenya	A6	48
Nanzhang, China	I4	32
Nao, Cape, c., Spain	C6	22
Naoli He, stm., China	C6	33
Naoma, W.V., U.S.	n13	125
Naomi Peak, mtn., Ut., U.S.	B4	121
Náousa, Grc.	B4	25
Napa, Ca., U.S.	C2	82
Napa, co., Ca., U.S.	C2	82
Napadogan, N.B.	C3	71
Napakiak, Ak., U.S.	C7	79
Napaktok Bay, b., Newf.	f9	72
Napanee, Ont.	C8	73
Napanoch, N.Y., U.S.	D6	109
Napatree Point, c., R.I., U.S.	G1	116
Napavine, Wa., U.S.	C3	124
Nape, Laos	C6	35
Naper, Ne., U.S.	B6	104
Naperville, Il., U.S.	B5	90
Napetipi, stm., Can.	C2	72
Napf, mtn., Switz.	C4	21
Napier, N.Z.	M16	51
Napier Mountains, mts., Ant.	C18	7
Napierville, Que.	D4	74
Napierville, co., Que.	D4	74
Napinka, Man.	E1	70
Naplate, Il., U.S.	B5	90
Naples (Napoli), Italy	D5	23
Naples, Fl., U.S.	F5	86
Naples, Id., U.S.	A2	89
Naples, Il., U.S.	D3	90
Naples, Me., U.S.	E2	96
Naples, N.Y., U.S.	C3	109
Naples, S.D., U.S.	C8	118
Naples, Tx., U.S.	C5	120
Naples, Ut., U.S.	C6	121
Naples, Gulf of, b., Italy	D5	23
Naples Park, Fl., U.S.	*F5	86
Napo, prov., Ec.	B2	58
Napo, stm., S.A.	B3	58
Napoleon, In., U.S.	F7	91
Napoleon, Mo., U.S.	B3	102
Napoleon, N.D., U.S.	C6	111
Napoleon, Oh., U.S.	A1	112
Napoleonville, La., U.S.	E4	95
Naponee, Ne., U.S.	D6	104
Nappanee, In., U.S.	B5	91
Napton, Mo., U.S.	B4	102
Naqadeh, Iran	C2	39
Nara, Japan	o14	33
Nara, Mali	C3	45
Nāra Canal, Pak.	D2	37
Naracoorte, Austl.	G7	50
Naramata, B.C.	E8	69
Na'rān, Isr. Occ.	A7	41
Naranja, Fl., U.S.	G6	86
Narathiwat, Thai.	D2	34
Nara Visa, N.M., U.S.	B6	108
Nārāyanganj, Bngl.	D9	36
Nārāyanpet, India	I6	37
Narberth, Wales, U.K.	C3	12
Narberth, Pa., U.S.	p20	115
Narbonne, Fr.	F5	16
Narcissa, Ok., U.S.	A7	113
Narcisse, Man.	D3	70
Narcoossee, Fl., U.S.	D5	86
Nardin, Ok., U.S.	A4	113
Nardò, Italy	D7	23
Nares Strait, strt., N.A.	m37	66
Narew, stm., Eur.	B6	26
Nārī, Jabal an, hills, Libya	E4	43
Nariño, dept., Col.	C2	60
Narita, Japan	n19	33
Narka, Ks., U.S.	C6	93
Narmada, stm., India	D6	36
Narodnaya, Mount, mtn., Sov. Un.	C9	29
Naro-Fominsk, Sov. Un.	D11	27
Narok, Kenya	B6	48
Narol, Man.	D3	70
Narrabri, Austl.	F8	50
Narragansett, R.I., U.S.	F4	116
Narragansett Bay, b., R.I., U.S.	E5	116
Narraguagus, stm., Me., U.S.	D5	96
Narran, stm., Austl.	D6	51
Narrandera, Austl.	F8	50
Narran Lake, l., Austl.	D6	51
Narraway, stm., Can.	B7	69
Narrogin, Austl.	F2	50
Narromine, Austl.	F7	51
Narrows, Va., U.S.	C2	123
Narrowsburg, N.Y., U.S.	D5	109
Narsimhapur, India	F7	37
Narsīpatnam, India	I9	37
Naruna, Va., U.S.	C3	123
Narva, Sov. Un.	B7	27
Narvik, Nor.	C7	14
Naryan-Mar, Sov. Un.	C8	29
Naryilco, Austl.	D3	51
Narym, Sov. Un.	D25	8
Naryn, Sov. Un.	E9	28
Naryn, stm., Sov. Un.	E9	28
Narynkol, Sov. Un.	E10	28
Na Sam, Viet.	A7	35
Na San, Thai.	D1	34
Nasarawa, Nig.	E6	45
Nase, Japan	F10	31
Naseby, N.Z.	P13	51
Naselle, Wa., U.S.	C2	124
Nash, N.D., U.S.	A8	111
Nash, Ok., U.S.	A3	113
Nash, Tx., U.S.	C5	120
Nash, co., N.C., U.S.	A4	110
Nashawena Island, i., Ma., U.S.	D6	98
Nash Creek, N.B.	B3	71
Nāshik, India	E5	36
Nashoba, Ok., U.S.	C6	113
Nashoba Hill, hill, Ma., U.S.	f10	98
Nash Stream, stm., N.H., U.S.	A4	106
Nashua, Ia., U.S.	B5	92
Nashua, Mn., U.S.	D2	100
Nashua, Mt., U.S.	B10	103
Nashua, N.H., U.S.	E4	106
Nashua, stm., U.S.	E3	106
Nashville, Ar., U.S.	D2	81
Nashville, Ga., U.S.	E3	87
Nashville, Il., U.S.	E4	90
Nashville, In., U.S.	F5	91
Nashville, Ks., U.S.	E5	93
Nashville, Mi., U.S.	F5	99
Nashville, Mo., U.S.	D3	102
Nashville, N.C., U.S.	B5	110
Nashville, Oh., U.S.	B3	112
Nashville, Tn., U.S.	A5	119
Nashwaak, stm., N.B.	C3	71
Nashwaaksis, N.B.	D3	71
Nashwauk, Mn., U.S.	C5	100
Našice, Yugo.	C4	24
Nasielsk, Pol.	B6	26
Naşīf, Bi'r, well, Eg.	D2	41
Näsijärvi, l., Fin.	G10	14
Nāşir, Sud.	D3	47
Nāsiri see Ahvāz, Iran	B4	38
Naskaupi, stm., Newf.	g9	72
Nason, Il., U.S.	E5	90
Nasonville, R.I., U.S.	B3	116
Nass, stm., B.C.	E7	66
Nassau, Bah.	B5	64
Nassau, De., U.S.	E5	85
Nassau, Mn., U.S.	E2	100
Nassau, N.Y., U.S.	C7	109
Nassau, co., Fl., U.S.	B5	86
Nassau, co., N.Y., U.S.	E7	109
Nassau, stm., Fl., U.S.	k8	86
Nassau, Bahía, b., Chile	k12	54
Nassau International Airport, Bah.	m17	64
Nassau Shores, N.Y., U.S.	*n15	109
Nassau Sound, b., Fl., U.S.	B5	86
Nassauville, Fl., U.S.	B5	86
Nassawadox, Va., U.S.	C7	123
Nassawango Creek, stm., Md., U.S.	D7	97
Nasser, Lake, res., Afr.	E6	43
Nässjö, Swe.	I6	14
Nasugbu, Phil.	o13	34
Nasukoin Mountain, mtn., Mt., U.S.	B2	103
Nata, Bots.	B4	49
Natá, Pan.	F7	62
Natagaima, Col.	C2	60
Natal, Braz.	C3	57
Natal, prov., S. Afr.	C5	49
Natalbany, La., U.S.	D5	95
Natalia, Tx., U.S.	E3	120
Natanes Plateau, plat., Az., U.S.	D5	80
Natashquan, Que.	h9	72
Natashquan, stm., Can.	h9	72
Natawahunan Lake, l., Man.	B3	70
Natchaug, stm., Ct., U.S.	B7	84
Natchez, Ms., U.S.	D2	101
Natchitoches, La., U.S.	C2	95
Natchitoches, co., La., U.S.	C2	95
Natewa Bay, b., Fiji	H15	52
Nathalie, Va., U.S.	D4	123
Nathrop, Co., U.S.	C4	83
Natick, Ma., U.S.	B5	98
Natimuk, Austl.	H3	51
Nation, stm., B.C.	B6	69
National, Wa., U.S.	C3	124
National, W.V., U.S.	B4	125
National City, Ca., U.S.	F5	82
National City, Mi., U.S.	D7	99
National Gardens, Fl., U.S.	C5	86
National Park, N.J., U.S.	*D2	107
Natitingou, Benin	D5	45
Natividade, Braz.	D1	57
Natoma, Ks., U.S.	C4	93
Natron, Lake, l., Afr.	B6	48
Natrona, Wy., U.S.	C6	127
Natrona, co., Wy., U.S.	D5	127
Natrona Heights, Pa., U.S.	E2	115
Nåttarö, i., Swe.	u36	14
Nattaung, mtn., Burma	C2	35
Natuna, is., Indon.	E3	34
Natuna Besar, i., Indon.	E3	34
Natural Bridge, Al., U.S.	A2	78
Natural Bridge, N.Y., U.S.	A5	109
Natural Bridge, Va., U.S.	C3	123
Natural Bridge, Ut., U.S.	F3	121
Natural Bridge, Va., U.S.	C3	123
Natural Bridges National Monument, Ut., U.S.	F6	121
Naturaliste, Cape, c., Austl.	F1	50
Natural Steps, Ar., U.S.	h10	81
Naturita, Co., U.S.	C2	83
Naubinway, Mi., U.S.	B5	99
Nauders, Aus.	E5	18
Nauen, E. Ger.	B6	18
Naugatuck, Ct., U.S.	D3	84
Naugatuck, stm., Ct., U.S.	D3	84
Naumburg, W. Ger.	B4	19
Naumburg [an der Saale], E. Ger.	C5	18
Naunhof, E. Ger.	B7	19
Naupactus see Návpaktos, Grc.	C3	25
Ñaupe, Peru	C2	58
Nauru, ctry., Oc.	G10	6
Naushon Island, i., Ma., U.S.	D6	98
Nauta, Peru	B3	58
Nautilus Park, Ct., U.S.	D7	84
Nautla, Mex.	C5	63
Nauvoo, Al., U.S.	B2	78
Nauvoo, Il., U.S.	C2	90
Nauwigewauk, N.B.	D4	71
Nava, Lake, l., Spain	A3	22
Nava del Rey, Spain	B3	22
Navahermosa, Spain	C3	22
Navajo, Az., U.S.	B6	80
Navajo, co., Az., U.S.	B5	80
Navajo Dam, N.M., U.S.	A2	108
Navajo Indian Reservation, U.S.	A4	80
Navajo Mountain, mtn., Ut., U.S.	F5	121
Navajo National Monument, Az., U.S.	A5	80
Navajo Reservoir, res., U.S.	A2	108
Navalcarnero, Spain	B3	22
Navalmoral de la Mata, Spain	C3	22
Navan, Ont.	B9	73
Navan see An Uaimh, Ire.	D3	10
Navarin, Cape, c., Sov. Un.	C20	29
Navarino, Wi., U.S.	D5	126
Navarino, Isla, i., Chile	k12	54
Navarre, Oh., U.S.	B4	112
Navarre, hist. reg., Spain	A5	22
Navarro, Arg.	B5	54
Navarro, co., Tx., U.S.	D4	120
Navas de Tolosa, Spain	C4	22
Navasota, Tx., U.S.	D4	120
Navassa, N.C., U.S.	C4	110
Navassa Island, i., N.A.	E6	64
Navatu, rf., Fiji	I16	52
Nävekvarn, Swe.	u34	14
Naver, stm., Scot., U.K.	B4	13
Naver, Loch, l., Scot., U.K.	B4	13
Navesink, N.J., U.S.	C4	107
Navet Reservoir, res., Trin.	O23	65
Navia, Arg.	A3	54
Navia, stm., Spain	A2	22
Navidad, Chile	A2	54
Naviti, i., Fiji	H14	52
Navojoa, Mex.	B3	63
Navolato, Mex.	C3	63
Návpaktos (Naupactus), Grc.	C3	25
Návplion, Grc.	D4	25
Navrongo, Ghana	D4	45
Navsāri, India	G4	37
Nawá, Syria	B8	41
Nawābshāh, Pak.	C4	36
Nawāda, India	E10	37
Nāwah, Afg.	E13	39
Nawiliwili Bay, b., Hi., U.S.	B2	88
Náxos, Grc.	D5	40
Náxos, i., Grc.	D5	40
Nay, Fr.	F3	16
Nayarit, state, Mex.	C3	63
Nayau Island, i., Fiji	H16	52
Nāy Band, Iran	C5	38
Nāy Band, Iran	E8	39
Nāy Band, Kūh-e, mtn., Iran	E8	39
Nāy Band, Ra's-e, c., Iran	H6	39
Naylor, Ga., U.S.	F3	87
Naylor, Mo., U.S.	E7	102
Nayoro, Japan	D11	33
Naytahwaush, Mn., U.S.	C3	100
Nazaré, Braz.	D3	57
Nazaré, Port.	C1	22
Nazaré da Mata, Braz.	h6	57
Nazareth (Nazerat), Isr.	B3	38
Nazareth, Ky., U.S.	C4	94
Nazareth, Pa., U.S.	E11	115
Nazareth, Tx., U.S.	B1	120
Nazário, Braz.	B3	56
Nazas, Mex.	B4	63
Nazas, stm., Mex.	B4	63
Nazca, Peru	D3	58
Nazilli, Tur.	D7	40
Nazimovo, Sov. Un.	D27	8
Naziya, Sov. Un.	s32	14
Nazko, stm., B.C.	C6	69
Nazlini, Az., U.S.	B6	80
Nazret, Eth.	D4	47
Nazyvayevsk, Sov. Un.	B8	28
Ncheu, Mwi.	D5	48
Ndala, Tan.	B5	48
N'dalatando, Ang.	C1	48
Ndélé, Cen. Afr. Rep.	D4	46
Ndendé, Gabon	F2	46
N'Djamena (Fort-Lamy), Chad	C3	46
Ndjolé, Gabon	F2	46
Ndola, Zam.	D4	48
Neagh, Lough, l., N. Ire., U.K.	C3	10
Neah Bay, Wa., U.S.	A1	124
Néa Ionía, Grc.	*C4	25
Neal, Ks., U.S.	E7	93
Neales, stm., Austl.	E6	50
Néa Liósia, Grc.	*C4	25
Néa Páfos, Cyp.	E9	40
Néa Palátia, Grc.	g11	25
Neápolis, Grc.	D4	25
Neápolis, Grc.	E5	25
Néa Psará see Erétria, Grc.	g11	25
Near Islands, is., Ak., U.S.	E2	79
Néa Smírni, Grc.	*D4	25
Neath, Wales, U.K.	E5	10
Neavitt, Md., U.S.	C5	97
Neba, Japan	n16	33
Nebel, stm., E. Ger.	E6	15
Nebine Creek, stm., Austl.	D6	51
Nebit-Dag, Sov. Un.	B7	39
Neblina, Pico da, mtn., S.A.	C4	60
Nebo, Il., U.S.	D3	90
Nebo, Ky., U.S.	C2	94
Nebo, La., U.S.	C3	95
Nebo, Mo., U.S.	D5	102
Nebo, Mount, mtn., Ut., U.S.	D4	121
Nebo, Mount see Nabā, Jabal, mtn., Jord.	C7	41
Nebraska, In., U.S.	F7	91
Nebraska, state, U.S.	C6	104
Nebraska City, Ne., U.S.	D10	104
Nebuželу, Czech.	n18	26
Necedah, Wi., U.S.	D3	126
Nechako, stm., B.C.	C5	69
Nechako Range, mts., B.C.	C5	69
Neche, N.D., U.S.	A8	111
Neches, stm., Tx., U.S.	D5	120
Nechí, Col.	B3	60
Nechí, stm., Col.	B3	60
Nechranice Reservoir, res., Czech.	C8	19
Neckar, stm., W. Ger.	D4	18
Neckarsulm, W. Ger.	D4	19
Neck City, Mo., U.S.	D3	102
Necker Island, i., Hi., U.S.	m15	88
Necochea, Arg.	B5	54
Nederland, Co., U.S.	B5	83
Nederland, Tx., U.S.	E6	120
Neder Rijn, mth., Neth.	C5	17
Nedrow, N.Y., U.S.	C4	109
Needham, In., U.S.	E5	91
Needham, Ma., U.S.	g11	98
Needle Mountain, mtn., Wy., U.S.	B3	127
Needles, Ca., U.S.	E6	82
Needmore, In., U.S.	G4	91
Needmore, Pa., U.S.	G5	115
Needville, Tx., U.S.	r14	120
Neelin, Man.	E2	70
Neels Gap, Ga., U.S.	B3	87
Neely, Ms., U.S.	D5	101
Neelyville, Mo., U.S.	E7	102
Ñeembucú, dept., Para.	E4	55
Neenah, Wi., U.S.	D5	126
Neepawa, Man.	D2	70
Neerpelt, Bel.	C5	17
Neeses, S.C., U.S.	D5	117
Neffs, Oh., U.S.	B5	112
Neffsville, Pa., U.S.	F9	115
Nefta, Tun.	C6	44
Neftegorsk, Sov. Un.	G16	8
Nefyn, Wales, U.K.	B3	12
Negage, Ang.	C2	48
Negaunee, Mi., U.S.	B3	99
Negele, Eth.	D4	47
Negeri Sembilan, state, Malay.	K5	35
Negev Desert, des., Isr.	D6	41
Negley, Oh., U.S.	B5	112
Negomano, Moz.	D6	48
Negombo, Sri L.	G6	36
Negotin, Yugo.	C6	24
Negra, Cordillera, mts., Peru	C2	58
Negra, Punta, c., Peru	C1	58
Negreet, La., U.S.	C2	95
Negreira, Spain	A1	22
Negro, stm., Arg.	C4	54
Negro, stm., Bol.	B3	55
Negro, stm., Braz.	D2	56
Negro, stm., Braz.	B1	56
Negro, stm., S.A.	D4	53
Negro, stm., S.A.	E1	56
Negro Mountain, mtn., Md., U.S.	k12	97
Negros, i., Phil.	D6	34
Negru-Vodă, Rom.	D9	24
Neguac, N.B.	B4	71
Nehalem, Or., U.S.	B3	114
Nehalem, stm., Or., U.S.	A3	114
Nehawka, Ne., U.S.	D10	104
Nehbandān, Iran	F10	39
Nehe, China	B2	33
Neheim-Hüsten, W. Ger.	B3	19
Neiba, Dom. Rep.	E8	64
Neiden, Nor.	C13	14
Neidpath, Sask.	G2	75
Neihart, Mt., U.S.	D6	103
Neihuang, China	G6	32
Neijiang, China	F6	31
Neilburg, Sask.	E1	75
Neill Point, c., Wa., U.S.	f11	124
Neillsville, Wi., U.S.	D3	126
Nei Monggol see Inner Mongolia, prov., China	C7	31
Neisse, stm., Eur.	C7	18
Neiva, Col.	C2	60
Neixiang, China	E7	31
Nejd, reg., Sau. Ar.	C4	38
Nejdek, Czech.	C7	19
Nekemte, Eth.	D4	47
Nekoma, Ks., U.S.	D4	93
Nekoma, N.D., U.S.	A7	111
Nekoosa, Wi., U.S.	D4	126
Neksø, Den.	C8	15
Nelagony, Ok., U.S.	A5	113
Nelidovo, Sov. Un.	C9	27
Neligh, Ne., U.S.	B7	104
Nellis Air Force Base, mil., Nv., U.S.	G6	105
Nell Island, i., Marsh Is.	S17	52
Nellore, India	F7	36
Nellysford, Va., U.S.	C4	123
Nelma, Sov. Un.	C9	33
Nelson, B.C.	E9	69
Nelson, N.Z.	N14	51
Nelson, Az., U.S.	B2	80
Nelson, Ga., U.S.	B2	87
Nelson, Il., U.S.	B4	90
Nelson, Ky., U.S.	C2	94
Nelson, Mn., U.S.	E3	100
Nelson, Mo., U.S.	B4	102
Nelson, Ne., U.S.	D7	104
Nelson, Nv., U.S.	H7	105
Nelson, N.H., U.S.	E2	106
Nelson, Pa., U.S.	C7	115
Nelson, Wi., U.S.	D1	126
Nelson, co., Ky., U.S.	C4	94
Nelson, co., N.D., U.S.	B7	111
Nelson, co., Va., U.S.	C4	123
Nelson, stm., Man.	A4	70
Nelson, Cape, c., Austl.	I3	51
Nelson Forks, B.C.	m18	69
Nelson House, Man.	B2	70
Nelson Lake, l., Man.	B2	70
Nelsonville, Oh., U.S.	C3	112
Nelspruit, S. Afr.	C5	49
Néma, Maur.	C3	45
Nemacolin, Pa., U.S.	G2	115
Nemadji, stm., U.S.	B1	126
Nemaha, Ia., U.S.	B2	92
Nemaha, Ne., U.S.	D10	104
Nemaha, co., Ks., U.S.	C7	93
Nemaha, co., Ne., U.S.	D10	104
Nemakščiai, Sov. Un.	A7	26
Neman, Sov. Un.	A7	26
Neman (Nemunas), stm., Sov. Un.	E5	27
Nembe, Nig.	F6	45
Nemeiben Lake, l., Sask.	B3	75
Nemi, Lake, l., Italy	h9	23
Nemiscau, Que.	h11	74
Nemo, S.D., U.S.	C2	118
Nemours, Fr.	C5	16
Nemunas (Neman), stm., Sov. Un.	D4	27
Nemuro, Japan	C14	31
Nemuro Strait, strt., Asia	D12	33
Nenagh, Ire.	D2	10
Nenana, Ak., U.S.	C10	79
Nendeln, Liech.	B8	21
Nene, stm., Eng., U.K.	B8	12
Nenjiang, China	B10	31
Nen Jiang, stm., China	B9	31
Nenzel, Ne., U.S.	B4	104
Nenzing, Aus.	B8	21
Neodesha, Ks., U.S.	E8	93
Neoga, Il., U.S.	D5	90
Neola, Ia., U.S.	C2	92
Neola, Ut., U.S.	C5	121
Néon Karlovásion, Grc.	D6	25
Neopit, Wi., U.S.	D5	126
Neosho, Mo., U.S.	E3	102
Neosho, Wi., U.S.	E5	126
Neosho, co., Ks., U.S.	E8	93
Neosho, stm., Ok., U.S.	A6	113
Neosho Falls, Ks., U.S.	D8	93
Neosho Rapids, Ks., U.S.	D8	93
Neotsu, Or., U.S.	B3	114
Nepal, ctry., Asia	C7	36
Nepālganj, Nepal	C8	36
Nepaug, Ct., U.S.	*B4	84
Nepaug Reservoir, res., Ct., U.S.	B3	84
Nepean, Ont.	B9	73
Nepewassi Lake, l., Ont.	A4	73
Nephi, Ut., U.S.	D4	121
Nephton, Ont.	C7	73
Nepisiguit, stm., N.B.	B3	71
Nepisiguit Bay, b., N.B.	B4	71
Nepomuk, Czech.	D8	19
Neponset, Il., U.S.	B4	90
Neponset, stm., Ma., U.S.	h11	98
Nepton, Ky., U.S.	B6	94
Neptune, Sask.	H3	75
Neptune, N.J., U.S.	C4	107
Neptune Beach, Fl., U.S.	B5	86
Neptune City, N.J., U.S.	C4	107
Nera, stm., Italy	C4	23
Nérac, Fr.	E4	16
Nerchinsk, Sov. Un.	D14	29
Nerchinskiy Zavod, Sov. Un.	A8	31
Nerekhta, Sov. Un.	C13	27
Neretva, stm., Yugo.	D3	24
Neriquinha, Ang.	E3	48
Neris, stm., Sov. Un.	D6	27
Nerja, Spain	D4	22
Nerpichye, Sov. Un.	B12	33
Nerstrand, Mn., U.S.	F5	100
Nerva, Spain	D2	22
Nes, Neth.	A5	17
Nesbit, Ms., U.S.	A3	101
Nesbitt, Man.	E2	70
Nesco, N.J., U.S.	D3	107
Nesconset, N.Y., U.S.	*n15	109

Name	Map Ref.	Page
Nescopeck, Pa., U.S.	D9	115
Nesebŭr, Bul.	D8	24
Neshanic, stm., N.J., U.S.	C3	107
Neshanic Station, N.J., U.S.	B3	107
Nesher, Isr.	B7	41
Neshkoro, Wi., U.S.	E4	126
Neshoba, Ms., U.S.	C4	101
Neshoba, co., Ms., U.S.	C4	101
Nesika Beach, Or., U.S.	E2	114
Neskaupstadur, Ice.	n26	14
Neskowin, Or., U.S.	B3	114
Nesle, Fr.	E2	17
Nesmith, S.C., U.S.	D8	117
Nesodden, Nor.	p28	14
Nesowadnehunk, l., Me., U.S.	B3	96
Nespelem, Wa., U.S.	A7	124
Nesquehoning, Pa., U.S.	E10	115
Ness, co., Ks., U.S.	D4	93
Ness, Loch, l., Scot., U.K.	C4	13
Ness City, Ks., U.S.	D4	93
Nesselrode, Mount, mtn., N.A.	E6	66
Nesselwang, W. Ger.	B6	20
Nesslau, Switz.	B5	20
Nessmersiel, W. Ger.	A7	17
Nesterov, Sov. Un.	C7	26
Nesterov, Sov. Un.	A7	26
Nestórion, Grc.	B3	25
Nestorville, W.V., U.S.	B5	125
Néstos (Mesta), stm., Eur.	B5	25
Nesvizh, Sov. Un.	E6	27
Nes Ziyyona, Isr.	C6	41
Netanya, Isr.	B6	41
Netarts, Or., U.S.	B3	114
Netawaka, Ks., U.S.	C8	93
Netcong, N.J., U.S.	B3	107
Netherhill, Sask.	F1	75
Netherlands, ctry., Eur.	A6	16
Netherlands Antilles, ctry., N.A.	A4	60
Nether Providence Township, Pa., U.S.	*G11	115
Nethy Bridge, Scot., U.K.	C5	13
Netolice, Czech.	D9	19
Netrakona, Bngl.	E13	37
Nettie, W.V., U.S.	C4	125
Nettilling Lake, l., N.W. Ter.	C18	66
Nett Lake, Mn., U.S.	B5	100
Nett Lake, l., Mn., U.S.	B5	100
Nett Lake Indian Reservation, Mn., U.S.	B6	100
Nettleton, Ms., U.S.	A5	101
Nettleton, Mo., U.S.	B4	102
Nettuno, Italy	k9	23
Netvořice, Czech.	o18	26
Netzahualcóyotl, Mex.	h9	63
Neubeckum, W. Ger.	B3	19
Neubrandenburg, E. Ger.	B6	18
Neuburg [an der Donau], W. Ger.	D5	18
Neuchâtel, Switz.	E3	18
Neuchâtel, state, Switz.	C2	20
Neuchâtel, Lake, l., Switz.	E3	18
Neudorf, Sask.	G4	75
Neuenegg, Switz.	C3	21
Neuenkirchen, W. Ger.	E3	19
Neuenrade, W. Ger.	B2	19
Neuerburg, W. Ger.	E6	17
Neufchâteau, Bel.	E5	17
Neufchâteau, Fr.	C6	16
Neufchâtel-en-Bray, Fr.	C4	16
Neufchâtel-sur-Aisne, Fr.	C4	17
Neufelden, Aus.	D6	18
Neugersdorf, E. Ger.	C9	19
Neuharlingersiel, W. Ger.	A7	17
Neuhaus, E. Ger.	E4	15
Neuhaus, E. Ger.	C6	19
Neuilly [-sur-Seine], Fr.	g11	16
Neu-Isenburg, W. Ger.	C3	19
Neukirchen am Grossvenediger, Aus.	B8	20
Neumarkt, W. Ger.	D5	18
Neumarkt-Sankt Veit, W. Ger.	A8	20
Neumünster, W. Ger.	A4	18
Neunburg vorm Wald, W. Ger.	D7	19
Neunkirch, Switz.	A6	21
Neunkirchen, Aus.	E8	18
Neunkirchen, W. Ger.	D2	19
Neuquén, Arg.	B3	54
Neuquén, prov., Arg.	B3	54
Neuquén, stm., Arg.	B3	54
Neurara, Chile	D2	55
Neuruppin, E. Ger.	B6	18
Neuse, stm., N.C., U.S.	B6	110
Neusiedler Lake, l., Eur.	E8	18
Neuss, W. Ger.	B1	19
Neustadt, Ont.	C4	73
Neustadt, E. Ger.	B9	19
Neustadt, E. Ger.	C6	19
Neustadt, W. Ger.	E4	18
Neustadt, W. Ger.	C4	19
Neustadt am Rübenberge, W. Ger.	F3	15
Neustadt [an der Aisch], W. Ger.	D5	18
Neustadt [an der Dosse], E. Ger.	B6	19
Neustadt an der Waldnaab, W. Ger.	D7	19
Neustadt [an der Weinstrasse], W. Ger.	D4	18
Neustadt [bei Coburg], W. Ger.	C5	18
Neustadt-Glewe, E. Ger.	E5	15
Neustadt [in Holstein], W. Ger.	A5	18
Neustrelitz, E. Ger.	B6	18
Neu-Ulm, W. Ger.	D5	18
Neuville, Que.	C6	74
Neuville-lès-Dieppe, Fr.	E9	12
Neuwerk, i., W. Ger.	E2	15
Neuwied, W. Ger.	C2	19
Neva, Tn., U.S.	C12	119
Neva, stm., Sov. Un.	s31	14
Nevada, Ia., U.S.	B4	92
Nevada, Mo., U.S.	D3	102
Nevada, Oh., U.S.	B2	112
Nevada, co., Ar., U.S.	D2	81
Nevada, co., Ca., U.S.	C3	82
Nevada, state, U.S.	D5	105
Nevada, Sierra, mts., Spain	D4	22
Nevada, Sierra, mts., Ca., U.S.	D4	105
Nevada City, Ca., U.S.	C3	82
Nevada Mills, In., U.S.	A7	91
Nevado, Cerro, mtn., Col.	C3	60
Nevel, Sov. Un.	C6	11
Nevelsk, Sov. Un.	B13	31
Nevelski, Mount, mtn., Sov. Un.	A11	33
Nevers, Fr.	D5	16
Neversink, stm., N.Y., U.S.	D6	109
Neversink Reservoir, res., N.Y., U.S.	D6	109
Nevesinje, Yugo.	D4	24
Neville, Sask.	H2	75
Neville, Fr.	E8	12
Nevils, Ga., U.S.	D5	87
Nevinnomyssk, Sov. Un.	G17	8
Nevis, i., St. C.-N.	H13	64
Nevis, Ben, mtn., Scot., U.K.	B4	10
Nevis, Loch, b., Scot., U.K.	C3	13
Nevşehir, Tur.	C10	40
New, stm., U.S.	C3	125
New, stm., Az., U.S.	k8	80
New, stm., N.C., U.S.	C5	110
Newala, Tan.	D6	48
New Albany, In., U.S.	H6	91
New Albany, Ks., U.S.	E8	93
New Albany, Ms., U.S.	A4	101
New Albany, Oh., U.S.	k11	112
New Albany, Pa., U.S.	C9	115
New Albin, Ia., U.S.	A6	92
Newald, Wi., U.S.	C5	126
New Almelo, Ks., U.S.	C3	93
New Alsace, In., U.S.	F8	91
New Amsterdam, Guy.	A3	59
Newark, Ar., U.S.	B4	81
Newark, Ca., U.S.	h8	82
Newark, De., U.S.	B3	85
Newark, Il., U.S.	B5	90
Newark, Md., U.S.	D7	97
Newark, Mo., U.S.	B6	102
Newark, N.J., U.S.	B4	107
Newark, N.Y., U.S.	B3	109
Newark, Oh., U.S.	B3	112
Newark, Tx., U.S.	m9	120
Newark Bay, b., N.J., U.S.	k8	107
Newark Lake, l., Nv., U.S.	D6	105
Newark Valley, N.Y., U.S.	C4	109
New Athens, Il., U.S.	E4	90
New Athens, Oh., U.S.	B4	112
New Auburn, Mn., U.S.	F4	100
New Auburn, Wi., U.S.	C2	126
New Augusta, Ms., U.S.	D4	101
Newaygo, Mi., U.S.	E5	99
Newaygo, co., Mi., U.S.	E5	99
New Baden, Il., U.S.	E4	90
New Baltimore, Mi., U.S.	F8	99
New Baltimore, N.Y., U.S.	C7	109
New Baltimore, Oh., U.S.	n12	112
New Baltimore, Pa., U.S.	G4	115
New Bedford, Il., U.S.	B4	90
New Bedford, Ma., U.S.	C6	98
New Bedford, Pa., U.S.	D1	115
Newberg, Or., U.S.	B4	114
New Berlin, Il., U.S.	D4	90
New Berlin, N.Y., U.S.	C5	109
New Berlin, Pa., U.S.	E7	115
New Berlin, Tx., U.S.	k7	120
New Berlin, Wi., U.S.	n11	126
Newbern, Al., U.S.	C2	78
Newbern, Il., U.S.	D3	90
New Bern, N.C., U.S.	B5	110
Newbern, Tn., U.S.	A2	119
Newberry, Fl., U.S.	C4	86
Newberry, In., U.S.	G3	91
Newberry, Mi., U.S.	B5	99
Newberry, S.C., U.S.	C4	117
Newberry, co., S.C., U.S.	C4	117
Newberry Springs, Ca., U.S.	E5	82
New Bethlehem, Pa., U.S.	D3	115
New Blaine, Ar., U.S.	B2	81
New Bloomfield, Mo., U.S.	C5	102
New Bloomfield, Pa., U.S.	F7	115
New Bloomington, Oh., U.S.	B2	112
Newborn, Ga., U.S.	C3	87
Newboro, Ont.	C8	73
New Boston, Il., U.S.	B3	90
New Boston, Ia., U.S.	D6	92
New Boston, Ma., U.S.	B1	98
New Boston, Mi., U.S.	p15	99
New Boston, N.H., U.S.	E3	106
New Boston, Oh., U.S.	D3	112
New Boston, Tx., U.S.	C5	120
New Braintree, Ma., U.S.	B3	98
New Braunfels, Tx., U.S.	E3	120
New Bremen, N.Y., U.S.	B5	109
New Bremen, Oh., U.S.	B1	112
New Bridge, Or., U.S.	C9	114
New Brigden, Alta.	D5	68
New Brighton, Mn., U.S.	m12	100
New Brighton, Pa., U.S.	E1	115
New Britain, Ct., U.S.	C4	84
New Britain, i., Pap. N. Gui.	k13	50
New Brockton, Al., U.S.	D4	78
Newbrook, Alta.	B4	68
New Brunswick, N.J., U.S.	C4	107
New Brunswick, prov., Can.	C4	71
New Buffalo, Mi., U.S.	G4	99
Newburg, Ia., U.S.	C5	92
Newburg, Mo., U.S.	D6	102
Newburg, N.D., U.S.	A5	111
Newburg, Pa., U.S.	F6	115
Newburg, W.V., U.S.	B5	125
Newburg, Wi., U.S.	E5	126
Newburgh, Ont.	C8	73
Newburgh, Scot., U.K.	C7	13
Newburgh, In., U.S.	I3	91
Newburgh, Me., U.S.	D4	96
Newburgh, N.Y., U.S.	D6	109
Newburgh Heights, Oh., U.S.	h9	112
New Burnside, Il., U.S.	F5	90
Newbury, Ont.	E3	73
Newbury, Eng., U.K.	E6	10
Newbury, Ma., U.S.	A6	98
Newbury, N.H., U.S.	D2	106
Newbury, Vt., U.S.	C4	122
Newburyport, Ma., U.S.	A6	98
New Caledonia, dep., Oc.	H10	6
New Cambria, Ks., U.S.	D6	93
New Cambria, Mo., U.S.	B5	102
New Canaan, Ct., U.S.	E2	84
New Canton, Il., U.S.	D2	90
New Canton, Va., U.S.	C4	123
New Carlisle, Que.	A4	71
New Carlisle, In., U.S.	A4	91
New Carlisle, Oh., U.S.	C1	112
New Carrollton, Md., U.S.	*C4	97
New Cassel, N.Y., U.S.	*n15	109
New Castle, Austl.	F8	51
Newcastle, N.B.	C4	71
Newcastle, Ont.	D6	73
Newcastle, Ire.	E4	11
Newcastle, S. Afr.	C4	49
Newcastle, Ire., U.K.	C6	11
Newcastle, Al., U.S.	B3	78
New Castle, Co., U.S.	B3	83
New Castle, De., U.S.	B3	85
New Castle, In., U.S.	E7	91
New Castle, Ky., U.S.	B4	94
Newcastle, Ne., U.S.	B9	104
New Castle, Pa., U.S.	D1	115
New Castle, Tx., U.S.	C3	120
Newcastle, Tx., U.S.	C3	120
Newcastle, Ut., U.S.	F2	121
New Castle, Va., U.S.	C2	123
New Castle, Wy., U.S.	C8	127
New Castle, co., De., U.S.	B3	85
Newcastle Creek, N.B.	C3	71
Newcastle Emlyn, Wales, U.K.	B3	12
Newcastle Mine, Alta.	D4	68
Newcastle-under-Lyme, Eng., U.K.	A5	12
Newcastle upon Tyne, Eng., U.K.	C6	10
Newcastle West, Ire.	E2	11
Newcestown, Ire.	F3	11
New City, N.Y., U.S.	D6	109
New Columbia, Pa., U.S.	D8	115
Newcomb, N.M., U.S.	A1	108
Newcomb, N.Y., U.S.	B6	109
Newcomb, Tn., U.S.	A7	119
Newcomerstown, Oh., U.S.	B4	112
New Concord, Ky., U.S.	f9	94
New Concord, Oh., U.S.	C4	112
New Cumberland, Pa., U.S.	F8	115
New Cumberland, W.V., U.S.	A4	125
New Cumnock, Scot., U.K.	C4	10
Newdale, Man.	D1	70
Newdale, Id., U.S.	F7	89
New Dayton, Alta.	E4	68
New Delhi, India	C6	36
Newdegate, Austl.	F2	50
New Denmark, N.B.	C2	71
New Denver, B.C.	D9	69
New Diggings, Wi., U.S.	F3	126
New Durham, N.H., U.S.	D4	106
New Edinburg, Ar., U.S.	D3	81
New Effington, S.D., U.S.	B9	118
New Egypt, N.J., U.S.	C3	107
Newell, Al., U.S.	B4	78
Newell, Ar., U.S.	B2	81
Newell, Ia., U.S.	B2	92
Newell, S.D., U.S.	C2	118
Newell, W.V., U.S.	A4	125
Newell, Lake, l., Alta.	D5	68
New Ellenton, S.C., U.S.	E4	117
Newellton, La., U.S.	B4	95
New England, N.D., U.S.	C3	111
Newenham, Cape, c., Ak., U.S.	D7	79
New Enterprise, Pa., U.S.	F5	115
New Era, Mi., U.S.	E4	99
Newe Sha'anan, Isr.	m14	41
New Fairfield, Ct., U.S.	D2	84
Newfane, N.Y., U.S.	B2	109
Newfane, Vt., U.S.	F3	122
Newfield, Me., U.S.	E2	96
Newfield, N.J., U.S.	D2	107
Newfields, N.H., U.S.	D5	106
New Florence, Mo., U.S.	C6	102
New Florence, Pa., U.S.	F3	115
Newfolden, Mn., U.S.	B2	100
New Forest, for., Eng., U.K.	E6	12
Newfound Gap, U.S.	f9	110
Newfound Lake, l., N.H., U.S.	C3	106
Newfoundland, N.J., U.S.	A4	107
Newfoundland, Pa., U.S.	D11	115
Newfoundland, prov., Can.	D4	72
Newfoundland, i., Newf.	D3	72
Newfoundland Mountains, mts., Ut., U.S.	B2	121
New Franken, Wi., U.S.	D6	126
New Franklin, Mo., U.S.	B5	102
New Freedom, Pa., U.S.	G8	115
New Galilee, Pa., U.S.	E1	115
New Galloway, Scot., U.K.	C4	10
Newgate, B.C.	E10	69
New Germany, N.S.	E5	71
New Glarus, Wi., U.S.	F4	126
New Glasgow, N.S.	D7	71
New Gloucester, Me., U.S.	E2	96
New Goshen, In., U.S.	E3	91
New Gretna, N.J., U.S.	D4	107
New Guinea, i.	G8	6
New Hamburg, Ont.	D4	73
New Hampshire, state, U.S.	C3	106
New Hampton, Ia., U.S.	A5	92
New Hampton, Mo., U.S.	A3	102
New Hampton, N.H., U.S.	C3	106
New Hanover, co., U.S.	C5	110
New Hanover, i., Pap. N. Gui.	h12	50
New Harbor, Me., U.S.	E3	96
New Harbour, Newf.	E5	72
New Harmony, In., U.S.	H2	91
New Harmony, Ut., U.S.	F2	121
New Hartford, Ct., U.S.	B4	84
New Hartford, Ia., U.S.	B5	92
New Haven, Ct., U.S.	D4	84
New Haven, Il., U.S.	F5	90
New Haven, In., U.S.	B7	91
New Haven, Ky., U.S.	C4	94
New Haven, Mi., U.S.	F8	99
New Haven, Mo., U.S.	C6	102
New Haven, N.Y., U.S.	B4	109
New Haven, Oh., U.S.	A3	112
New Haven, W.V., U.S.	C3	125
New Haven, co., Ct., U.S.	D4	84
New Haven, stm., Vt., U.S.	C2	122
New Haven Harbor, b., Ct., U.S.	E4	84
New Hebrides see Vanuatu, ctry., Oc.	H10	6
Newhebron, Ms., U.S.	D4	101
New Hill, N.C., U.S.	B4	110
New Holland, Ga., U.S.	B3	87
New Holland, Il., U.S.	C4	90
New Holland, Oh., U.S.	C2	112
New Holland, Pa., U.S.	F9	115
New Holland, S.D., U.S.	D7	118
New Holstein, Wi., U.S.	E5	126
New Hope, Al., U.S.	A3	78
Newhope, Ar., U.S.	C2	81
New Hope, Ky., U.S.	C4	94
New Hope, Mn., U.S.	m12	100
New Hope, N.C., U.S.	*B4	110
New Hope, Pa., U.S.	F12	115
New Hope Mountain, mtn., Al., U.S.	g7	78
New Hradec, N.D., U.S.	B3	111
New Hudson, Mi., U.S.	o14	99
New Hyde Park, N.Y., U.S.	*E7	109
New Iberia, La., U.S.	D4	95
Newington, Ct., U.S.	C5	84
Newington, Ga., U.S.	D5	87
Newington, Va., U.S.	*B5	123
New Inlet, b., N.C., U.S.	D5	110
New Inn, Ire.	E4	11
New Ipswich, N.H., U.S.	E3	106
New Ireland, i., Pap. N. Gui.	h13	50
New Jersey, state, U.S.	C4	107
New Johnsonville, Tn., U.S.	A4	119
New Kensington, Pa., U.S.	E2	115
New Kent, Va., U.S.	C5	123
New Kent, co., Va., U.S.	C5	123
Newkirk, N.M., U.S.	B5	108
Newkirk, Ok., U.S.	A4	113
New Knoxville, Oh., U.S.	B1	112
New Kowloon, H.K.	*G7	31
New Laguna, N.M., U.S.	B2	108
New Lake, l., N.C., U.S.	B6	110
Newland, N.C., U.S.	A1	110
New Lebanon, In., U.S.	F3	91
New Lebanon, N.Y., U.S.	C7	109
New Leipzig, N.D., U.S.	C4	111
New Lenox, Il., U.S.	B6	90
New Lexington, Oh., U.S.	C3	112
New Liberty, Ky., U.S.	B5	94
New Lima, Ok., U.S.	B5	113
New Limerick, Me., U.S.	B5	96
New Lisbon, In., U.S.	E7	91
New Lisbon, N.J., U.S.	D3	107
New Lisbon, Wi., U.S.	E3	126
New Liskeard, Ont.	p20	73
Newllano, La., U.S.	C2	95
New London, Ct., U.S.	D7	84
New London, Ia., U.S.	D6	92
New London, Mn., U.S.	E4	100
New London, Mo., U.S.	B6	102
New London, N.H., U.S.	D3	106
New London, N.C., U.S.	B2	110
New London, Oh., U.S.	A3	112
New London, Wi., U.S.	D5	126
New London, co., Ct., U.S.	C7	84
New London Submarine Base, mil., Ct., U.S.	D7	84
New Lothrop, Mi., U.S.	E7	99
New Lowell, Ont.	C5	73
New Madison, Oh., U.S.	C1	112
New Madrid, Mo., U.S.	E8	102
New Madrid, co., Mo., U.S.	E8	102
Newman, Austl.	D2	50
Newman, Ca., U.S.	D3	82
Newman, Il., U.S.	D6	90
Newman, Ks., U.S.	k15	93
New Manchester, W.V., U.S.	e8	125
Newman Grove, Ne., U.S.	C8	104
Newsoms, Va., U.S.	D5	123
New Market, Al., U.S.	A3	78
New Market, In., U.S.	E4	91
New Market, Ia., U.S.	D3	92
New Market, Md., U.S.	B3	97
New Market, N.H., U.S.	D5	106
New Market, Tn., U.S.	C10	119
New Market, Va., U.S.	B4	123
Newmarket, Eng., U.K.	B8	12
Newmarket, Ont.	C5	73
Newmarket, Ire.	E2	11
New Marlboro, Ma., U.S.	B1	98
New Marshfield, Oh., U.S.	C3	112
New Martinsville, W.V., U.S.	B4	125
New Matamoras, Oh., U.S.	C4	112
New Meadows, Id., U.S.	D2	89
New Melle, Mo., U.S.	C7	102
New Mexico, state, U.S.	C3	108
New Miami, Oh., U.S.	C1	112
New Middletown, In., U.S.	H5	91
New Milford, Ct., U.S.	C2	84
New Milford, N.J., U.S.	h8	107
New Milford, Pa., U.S.	C10	115
New Mills, N.B.	B3	71
New Milton, W.V., U.S.	B4	125
New Minden, Il., U.S.	E4	90
New Munich, Mn., U.S.	E4	100
New Munster, Wi., U.S.	n11	126
Newnan, Ga., U.S.	C2	87
Newnans Lake, l., Fl., U.S.	C4	86
Newnata, Ar., U.S.	B3	81
New Norfolk, Austl.	o15	50
New Norway, Alta.	C4	68
New Offenburg, Mo., U.S.	D7	102
New Orleans, La., U.S.	E5	95
New Orleans Naval Air Station, mil., La., U.S.	k11	95
New Osgoode, Sask.	E4	75
New Oxford, Pa., U.S.	G7	115
New Palestine, In., U.S.	E6	91
New Paltz, N.Y., U.S.	D6	109
New Paris, In., U.S.	B6	91
New Paris, Oh., U.S.	C1	112
New Paris, Pa., U.S.	F4	115
New Perlican, Newf.	E5	72
New Philadelphia, Oh., U.S.	B4	112
New Philadelphia, Pa., U.S.	E9	115
New Pine Creek, Ca., U.S.	B3	82
New Pine Creek, Or., U.S.	E6	114
New Plymouth, N.Z.	M15	51
New Plymouth, Id., U.S.	F2	89
New Plymouth, Oh., U.S.	C3	112
New Point, In., U.S.	F7	91
New Point, Mo., U.S.	A2	102
New Point Comfort, c., Va., U.S.	C6	123
Newport, Ire.	E3	11
Newport, Ire.	D2	11
New Port, Neth. Ant.	H19	65
Newport, Eng., U.K.	E6	10
Newport, Eng., U.K.	B5	12
Newport, Wales, U.K.	E5	10
Newport, Ar., U.S.	B4	81
Newport, De., U.S.	B3	85
Newport, Fl., U.S.	B2	86
Newport, In., U.S.	E3	91
Newport, Ky., U.S.	A5	94
Newport, Me., U.S.	D3	96
Newport, Mi., U.S.	G7	99
Newport, Ne., U.S.	B6	104
Newport, N.H., U.S.	D2	106
Newport, N.J., U.S.	E2	107
Newport, N.C., U.S.	C6	110
Newport, Oh., U.S.	C4	112
Newport, Or., U.S.	C2	114
Newport, Pa., U.S.	F7	115
Newport, R.I., U.S.	F5	116
Newport, S.C., U.S.	B5	117
Newport, Tn., U.S.	D10	119
Newport, Tx., U.S.	C3	120
Newport, Vt., U.S.	B4	122
Newport, Va., U.S.	C2	123
Newport, Wa., U.S.	A8	124
Newport, co., R.I., U.S.	E5	116
Newport Beach, Ca., U.S.	n13	82
Newport Center, Vt., U.S.	B4	122
Newport Hills, Wa., U.S.	*e11	124
New Portland, Me., U.S.	D2	96
Newport News, Va., U.S.	D6	123
New Port Richey, Fl., U.S.	D4	86
New Prague, Mn., U.S.	F5	100
New Preston, Ct., U.S.	C2	84
New Providence, Ia., U.S.	B4	92
New Providence, N.J., U.S.	B4	107
New Providence, i., Bah.	B5	64
New Quay, Wales, U.K.	B3	12
New Raymer, Co., U.S.	A7	83
New Richland, Mn., U.S.	G5	100
New Richmond, Que.	A4	71
New Richmond, In., U.S.	D4	91
New Richmond, Oh., U.S.	D1	112
New Richmond, Wi., U.S.	C1	126
New Riegel, Oh., U.S.	A2	112
New River, Az., U.S.	D3	80
New River, Tn., U.S.	C9	119
New River Gorge, val., W.V., U.S.	m13	125
New River Inlet, b., N.C., U.S.	C5	110
New River Station, N.C., U.S.	*C5	110
New Roads, La., U.S.	D4	95
New Rochelle, N.Y., U.S.	E7	109
New Rockford, N.D., U.S.	B6	111
New Ross, N.S.	E5	71
New Ross, Ire.	D3	10
New Ross, In., U.S.	E4	91
New Salem, Il., U.S.	D3	90
New Salem, In., U.S.	E7	91
New Salem, Ks., U.S.	E7	93
New Salem, Ma., U.S.	A3	98
New Salem, N.D., U.S.	C4	111
New Sarepta, Alta.	C4	68
New Sharon, Ia., U.S.	C5	92
New Sharon, Me., U.S.	D2	96
New Sharon, N.J., U.S.	C3	107
New Siberian Islands, is., Sov. Un.	B18	29
New Site, Al., U.S.	B4	78
New Site, Ms., U.S.	A5	101
New Smyrna Beach, Fl., U.S.	C6	86
New South Wales, state, Austl.	F8	50
New Straitsville, Oh., U.S.	C3	112
New Sweden, Me., U.S.	B4	96
New Tazewell, Tn., U.S.	C10	119
Newtok, Ak., U.S.	C7	79
Newton, Al., U.S.	D4	78
Newton, Ga., U.S.	E2	87
Newton, Il., U.S.	E5	90
Newton, Ia., U.S.	C4	92
Newton, Ks., U.S.	D6	93
Newton, Ma., U.S.	B5	98
Newton, Ms., U.S.	C4	101
Newton, N.H., U.S.	E4	106
Newton, N.J., U.S.	A3	107
Newton, N.C., U.S.	B1	110
Newton, Tx., U.S.	D6	120
Newton, Ut., U.S.	B4	121
Newton, W.V., U.S.	C3	125
Newton, Wi., U.S.	k10	126
Newton, co., Ar., U.S.	B2	81
Newton, co., Ga., U.S.	C3	87
Newton, co., In., U.S.	B3	91
Newton, co., Ms., U.S.	C4	101
Newton, co., Mo., U.S.	E3	102
Newton, co., Tx., U.S.	D6	120
Newton Abbot, Eng., U.K.	D4	12
Newton Aycliffe, Eng., U.K.	F7	13
Newton Falls, N.Y., U.S.	A6	109
Newton Falls, Oh., U.S.	A5	112
Newton Grove, N.C., U.S.	B4	110
Newton Hamilton, Pa., U.S.	F6	115
Newton Junction, N.H., U.S.	E4	106
Newton Stewart, Scot., U.K.	F4	13
Newtonville, Ont.	D6	73
Newtonville, In., U.S.	H4	91
Newtonville, N.J., U.S.	D3	107
New Toronto (part of Etobicoke), Ont.	m14	73
Newtown, Newf.	D5	72
Newtown, Wales, U.K.	D5	10
Newtown, Ct., U.S.	D2	84
Newtown, In., U.S.	D3	91
Newtown, Mo., U.S.	A4	102
Newtown, N.D., U.S.	B3	111
Newtown, Oh., U.S.	o13	112
Newtown, Pa., U.S.	F12	115
Newtown, Va., U.S.	C6	123
New Town, N.D., U.S.	B3	111
Newtownabbey, N. Ire., U.K.	C6	11
Newtownards, N. Ire., U.K.	C6	11
Newtown Cromelin, N. Ire., U.K.	C5	11
Newtownhamilton, N. Ire., U.K.	C5	11
Newtown Mount Kennedy, Ire.	D5	11
Newtown Square, Pa., U.S.	p20	115
Newtownstewart, N. Ire., U.K.	C4	11
New Trenton, In., U.S.	F8	91
New Ulm, Mn., U.S.	F4	100
New Ulm, Tx., U.S.	E4	120
New Underwood, S.D., U.S.	C3	118
New Vienna, Ia., U.S.	B6	92
New Vienna, Oh., U.S.	C2	112
New Village, N.J., U.S.	B2	107
Newville, Al., U.S.	D4	78
Newville, Pa., U.S.	F7	115
New Vineyard, Me., U.S.	D2	96
New Virginia, Ia., U.S.	C4	92
New Washington, In., U.S.	G6	91
New Washington, Oh., U.S.	B3	112
New Washoe City, Nv., U.S.	*D2	105
New Waterford, Ont.	E2	73
New Waterford, Oh., U.S.	B5	112
New Waverly, In., U.S.	C5	91
New Waverly, Tx., U.S.	D5	120
New Westminster, B.C.	E6	69
New Whiteland, In., U.S.	E5	91
New Wilmington, Pa., U.S.	D1	115
New Windsor, Il., U.S.	B3	90
New Windsor, Md., U.S.	A3	97
New Windsor, N.Y., U.S.	D6	109
New Woodstock, N.Y., U.S.	C5	109
New York, N.Y., U.S.	k13	109
New York, co., N.Y., U.S.	C6	109
New York, state, U.S.	C5	109
New York Mills, Mn., U.S.	D3	100
New Zealand, ctry., Oc.	N14	51
New Zion, S.C., U.S.	D7	117
Ney, Oh., U.S.	A1	112
Neya, Sov. Un.	B2	28
Ney Island, i., Guam	M9	52
Ney Lake, l., Can.	B5	70
Neyrīz, Iran	C5	38
Newport Station, N.S.	E5	71
Neyshābūr, Iran	B5	38
Nezhin, Sov. Un.	F8	27
Nezperce, Id., U.S.	*C2	89
Nez Perce, co., Id., U.S.	C2	89
Nez Perce Indian Reservation, Id., U.S.	C2	89
Nezpique, Bayou, stm., La., U.S.	D3	95
Ngabang, Indon.	E3	34
Ngabé, Congo	B2	48
Ngala, Nig.	F8	45
Ngami, Lake, l., Bots.	B3	49
Ngangla Ringco, l., China	B7	36
Ngangzê Lake, l., China	B11	31
Ngaoundéré, Cam.	D2	46
Ngara, Tan.	C3	48
Ngaramasch, Palau	R17	52
Ngaruangl Reef, rf., Palau	R17	52
Ngaruawahia, N.Z.	L15	51
Ngatapa, N.Z.	M16	51
Ngemelis Islands, is., Palau	R17	52
Ngerekebesang, i., Palau	R17	52
Ngerkeel, Palau	R17	52
Ngermechau, Palau	R17	52
Ngeruktabel, i., Palau	R17	52
Ngetbong, Palau	R17	52
Ngidinga, Zaire	C2	48
Ngong, Kenya	B6	48
Ngoring Hu, l., China	D4	31
Ngounié, stm., Gabon	F2	46
Ngounié, stm., Gabon	B2	48
Ngouri, Chad	C3	46
Nguigmi, Niger	D7	45
Nguru, Nig.	D7	45
Nha Trang, Viet.	C3	34
Nhamundá, Braz.	C3	59
Nhamundá, stm., Braz.	C3	59
Nhill, Austl.	H3	51
Nhulunbuy, Austl.	B6	50
Niafounké, Mali	C4	45
Niagara, N.D., U.S.	B8	111
Niagara, Wi., U.S.	C6	126
Niagara, co., N.Y., U.S.	B2	109
Niagara, stm., N.A.	B1	109
Niagara Falls, Ont.	D5	73
Niagara Falls, N.Y., U.S.	B1	109
Niagara-on-the-Lake, Ont.	D5	73
Niamey, Niger	D5	45
Niamtougou, Togo	E5	45
Niangara, Zaire	A4	48
Niangua, stm., Mo., U.S.	D5	102
Niangua, stm., Mo., U.S.	D5	102
Niantic, Ct., U.S.	D7	84
Niarada, Mt., U.S.	C2	103
Nias, i., Indon.	E1	34
Niassa, dept., Moz.	D6	48
Nibe, Den.	B3	15
Nibley, Ut., U.S.	B4	121
Nicaragua, ctry., N.A.	E7	63
Nicaragua, Lago de, l., Nic.	E7	63
Nicastro (Lamezia Terme), Italy	E6	23
Nicatous Lake, l., Me., U.S.	C4	96
Nice, Fr.	F7	16
Niceville, Fl., U.S.	u15	86
Nichicun, Lac, l., Que.	h12	74
Nichinan, Japan	K5	33
Nicholas, co., Ky., U.S.	B6	94
Nicholas, co., W.V., U.S.	C4	125
Nicholas Channel, strt., N.A.	C3	64
Nicholasville, Ky., U.S.	C5	94
Nicholls, Ga., U.S.	E4	87
Nichols, Ia., U.S.	C6	92
Nichols, Mo., U.S.	D4	102
Nichols, N.Y., U.S.	C4	109
Nichols, S.C., U.S.	C9	117
Nichols Hills, Ok., U.S.	B4	113
Nicholson, Ms., U.S.	E4	101
Nicholson, stm., Austl.	C6	50
Nicholson, Pa., U.S.	C10	115
Nicholville, N.Y., U.S.	f10	109
Nickajack Lake, res., Tn., U.S.	D8	119
Nickel Centre, Ont.	p19	73
Nickelsville, Va., U.S.	f9	123
Nickerie, dept., Sur.	B3	59
Nickerie, stm., Sur.	A3	59
Nickerson, Ks., U.S.	D5	93
Nickerson, Ne., U.S.	C9	104
Nickerson Hill, hill, Ct., U.S.	D6	84
Nicobar Islands, is., India	G9	36
Nicodemus, Ks., U.S.	C4	93
Nicola, B.C.	D7	69
Nicola, stm., B.C.	D7	69
Nicolet, Que.	C5	74
Nicolet, stm., Que.	C5	74
Nicolet, co., Que.	C5	74
Nicolet, Lake, l., Mi., U.S.	B6	99
Nicollet, Mn., U.S.	F4	100
Nicollet, co., Mn., U.S.	F4	100
Nicolls Town, Bah.	B4	64
Nicoma Park, Ok., U.S.	B4	113
Nicosia (Levkosia / Lefkoşa), Cyp.	E9	40
Nicosia [Sicilia], Italy	F5	23
Nicotera, Italy	E5	23
Nicoya, C.R.	E7	63
Nicoya, Golfo de, b., C.R.	F5	62
Nicoya, Península de, pen., C.R.	F7	63
Nictaux Falls, N.S.	E4	71
Nid à l'Aigle, Cap du, c., St. P./M.	D4	72
Nidan Rock, hill, Japan	P17	52
Nidda, W. Ger.	C3	19
Nidda, stm., W. Ger.	C4	19
Nidwalden, state, Switz.	C4	20
Nidzica, Pol.	B6	26
Niebüll, W. Ger.	D2	15
Niederbronn-les-Bains, Fr.	F7	17
Niedermarsberg, W. Ger.	B3	19
Niedersachsen, state, W. Ger.	F3	15
Nielsville, Mn., U.S.	C2	100
Niemodlin, Pol.	C4	26
Nienburg, W. Ger.	B4	18
Nienburg, W. Ger.	B4	18
Nierstein, W. Ger.	D3	19
Niesky, E. Ger.	B9	19
Nieszawa, Pol.	B5	26
Nietleben, E. Ger.	B6	19
Nieuw Amsterdam, Sur.	A3	59
Nieuw Nickerie, Sur.	A3	59
Nieuwpoort, Bel.	*B5	17
Nigadoo, N.B.	B4	71
Niger, ctry., Afr.	C6	45
Niger, stm., Afr.	E6	45
Niger Delta, Nig.	F6	45
Nigeria, ctry., Afr.	E6	45
Nigg, Scot., U.K.	C5	13

Name	Map Ref.	Page
Nighthawk, Wa., U.S.	A6	124
Nigríta, Grc.	B4	25
Nihing, stm., Asia	H11	39
Nihoa, i., Hi., U.S.	m15	88
Niigata, Japan	D12	31
Niihama, Japan	J6	33
Niihau, i., Hi., U.S.	B1	88
Nii Island, i., Japan	I9	33
Niimi, Japan	I6	33
Nijar, Spain	D4	22
Nijkerk, Neth.	B5	17
Nijmegen, Neth.	B6	17
Níkaia, Grc.	*D4	25
Nikep, Md., U.S.	k13	97
Nikishka, Ak., U.S.	g16	79
Nikitinka, Sov. Un.	D9	27
Nikitovka, Sov. Un.	q21	27
Nikkí, Benin	E5	45
Nikkō, Japan	D12	31
Nikolayev, Sov. Un.	E6	29
Nikolayevsk, Sov. Un.	F15	29
Nikolayevsk [-na-Amure], Sov. Un.	D17	29
Nikolsk, Sov. Un.	D3	28
Nikolski, Ak., U.S.	E6	79
Nikonovskoye, Sov. Un.	n18	27
Nikopol, Bul.	D7	24
Nikopol, Sov. Un.	H10	27
Niksar, Tur.	B11	40
Nīkshahr, Iran	H10	39
Nikšić, Yugo.	D4	24
Niland, Ca., U.S.	F6	82
Nile, N.Y., U.S.	C2	109
Nile, stm., Afr.	D9	42
Niles, Il., U.S.	h9	90
Niles, Ks., U.S.	D6	93
Niles, Mi., U.S.	G4	99
Niles, Oh., U.S.	A5	112
Nilvange, Fr.	E6	17
Nilwood, Il., U.S.	D4	90
Nimach, India	E5	37
Nimba, Mount, mtn., Afr.	E3	45
Nimba Mountains, mts., Afr.	E3	45
Nîmes, Fr.	F6	16
Nimmons, Ar., U.S.	A5	81
Nimpkish, stm., B.C.	D4	69
Nimrín, Wādī, val., Jord.	h13	41
Nimrod Glacier, ice, Ant.	A29	7
Nimrod Lake, res., Ar., U.S.	C2	81
Nimule, Sud.	E3	47
Ninemile Creek, stm., Ks., U.S.	k15	93
Nine Mile Creek, stm., Ut., U.S.	D5	121
Nine Mile Falls, Wa., U.S.	g13	124
Ninemile Point, c., Mi., U.S.	C6	99
Ninette, Man.	E2	70
Ninety Mile Beach, Austl.	G8	50
Ninety Six, S.C., U.S.	C3	117
Nineveh, Pa., U.S.	G1	115
Nineveh, hist., Iraq	B4	38
Ninga, Man.	E2	70
Ning'an, China	C10	31
Ningbo, China	F9	31
Ningde, China	F8	31
Ningdu, China	K6	32
Ninghai, China	J9	32
Ninghua, China	K7	32
Ningjin, China	F6	32
Ningming, China	A7	35
Ningqiang, China	H2	32
Ningsia Hui see Ningxia Huizu, prov., China		
Ningwu, China	D7	31
Ningxia Huizu, prov., China	D6	31
Ningxian, China	D6	31
Ninh Binh, Viet.	D9	34
Ninigret Pond, l., R.I., U.S.	G2	116
Ninilchik, Ak., U.S.	C9	79
Ninnekah, Ok., U.S.	C4	113
Ninnescah, stm., Ks., U.S.	E6	93
Ninnescah, North Fork, stm., Ks., U.S.	E5	93
Ninnescah, South Fork, stm., Ks., U.S.	E5	93
Ninnis Glacier, ice, Ant.	C27	7
Ninole, Hi., U.S.	D6	88
Ninove, Bel.	D4	17
Nioaque, Braz.	C1	56
Niobe, N.D., U.S.	A3	111
Niobrara, Ne., U.S.	B7	104
Niobrara, co., Wy., U.S.	C8	127
Niobrara, stm., U.S.	B7	104
Nioki, Zaire	B2	48
Niono, Mali	D3	45
Nioro du Rip, Sen.	D1	45
Nioro du Sahel, Mali	C3	45
Niort, Fr.	F3	16
Niota, Tn., U.S.	C2	90
Niota, Tn., U.S.	D9	119
Niotaze, Ks., U.S.	E7	93
Nipawin, Sask.	D4	75
Nipawin Provincial Park, Sask.	C5	75
Nipekamew Lake, l., Sask.	C3	75
Nipew Lake, l., Sask.	B3	75
Nipigon, Ont.	o17	73
Nipigon, Lake, l., Ont.	o17	73
Nipishish Lake, l., Newf.	g9	72
Nipissing, dept., Ont.	A6	73
Nipissing, Lake, l., Ont.	A5	73
Nipomo, Ca., U.S.	E3	82
Nippers Harbour, Newf.	D4	72
Nipple Mountain, mtn., Co., U.S.	D2	83
Nipton, Ca., U.S.	E6	82
Niquelândia, Braz.	A3	56
Niquero, Cuba	D5	64
Nirasaki, Japan	n17	33
Nirmal, India	H7	37
Nirmāli, India	D11	37
Niš, Yugo.	D5	24
Nisa, Port.	C2	22
Nišava, stm., Eur.	D6	24
Nishinomiya, Japan	*I7	33
Nishio, Japan	o16	33
Nísiros, i., Grc.	D6	25
Niskayuna, N.Y., U.S.	C7	109
Nisland, S.D., U.S.	C2	118
Nisqually, stm., Wa., U.S.	C3	124
Nissan, stm., Swe.	B7	15
Nissum Bredning, b., Den.	B2	15
Nissum Fjord, Den.	B2	15
Nisswa, Mn., U.S.	D4	100
Nistowiak Lake, l., Sask.	B3	75
Nisula, Mi., U.S.	B2	99
Niterói, Braz.	C4	56
Nith, stm., Scot., U.K.	E5	13
Nitra, Czech.	D5	26
Nitra, stm., Czech.	D5	26
Nitro, W.V., U.S.	C3	125
Nitta Yuma, Ms., U.S.	B3	101
Nittenau, W. Ger.	F9	18
Niue, ctry., Oc.	H11	6
Nivelles, Bel.	B6	16
Nivernais, hist. reg., Fr.	D5	16

Name	Map Ref.	Page
Nivernais, Côtes du, hills, Fr.	D5	16
Niverville, Man.	E3	70
Nivskiy, Sov. Un.	D15	14
Niwot, Co., U.S.	A5	83
Nixa, Mo., U.S.	D4	102
Nixburg, Al., U.S.	C3	78
Nixon, Nv., U.S.	D2	105
Nixon, Tn., U.S.	B3	119
Nixon, Tx., U.S.	E4	120
Nizāmābād, India	H7	37
Nizām Sāgar, res., India	H7	37
Nizgān, stm., Afg.	E11	39
Nizhnekamsk, Sov. Un.	*D8	29
Nizhnekolymsk, Sov. Un.	C19	29
Nizhne-Leninskoye, Sov. Un.	C6	33
Nizhne Tunguska, stm., Sov. Un.	D12	29
Nizhneudinsk, Sov. Un.	D12	29
Nizhneye, Sov. Un.	q21	27
Nizhniy Chir, Sov. Un.	G14	29
Nizhniy Lomov, Sov. Un.	E14	29
Nizhniy Pyandzh, Sov. Un.	H22	8
Nizhniy Tagil, Sov. Un.	D9	29
Nizhnyaya Tunguska, stm., Sov. Un.	C12	29
Nizhnyaya Tura, Sov. Un.	D21	8
Nizip, Tur.	*D11	40
Nizmennyy, Cape, c., Sov. Un.	E7	33
Nizza Monferrato, Italy	E4	20
Nizzana, Isr.	D6	41
Nizzana, Nahal, val., Isr.	D6	41
Njombe, Tan.	C5	48
Njurunda, Swe.	F7	14
Nkambe, Cam.	D2	46
Nkayi, Zimb.	A4	49
Nkhata Bay, Mwi.	D5	48
Nkhota Kota, Mwi.	D5	48
Nkongsamba, Cam.	E4	46
Nnewi, Nig.	E4	46
Noākhāli, Bngl.	F13	37
Nobel, Ont.	B7	73
Nobeoka, Japan	J5	33
Noble, Il., U.S.	E5	90
Noble, La., U.S.	C2	95
Noble, co., In., U.S.	B7	91
Noble, co., Oh., U.S.	C4	112
Noble, co., Ok., U.S.	A4	113
Nobleboro, Me., U.S.	D3	96
Nobleford, Alta.	E4	68
Nobles, co., Mn., U.S.	G3	100
Noblesville, In., U.S.	D6	91
Nobleton, Fl., U.S.	D4	86
Nobleton, Ont.	C5	73
Noboribetsu, Japan	E10	33
Nobscot Hill, hill, Ma., U.S.	B5	98
Nocatee, Fl., U.S.	E5	86
Nocona, Tx., U.S.	C4	120
Nodaway, Ia., U.S.	D3	92
Nodaway, Mo., U.S.	A3	102
Nodaway, stm., U.S.	A2	102
Node, Wy., U.S.	D8	127
Noel, Mo., U.S.	E3	102
Noel Paul's Brook, stm., Newf.	D3	72
Noelville, Ont.	A4	73
Nogal, N.M., U.S.	D4	108
Nogales, Mex.	n15	63
Nogales, Az., U.S.	F5	80
Nogara, Italy	D7	20
Nogata, Japan	J3	33
Nogent-en-Bassigny, Fr.	C6	16
Nogent-le-Rotrou, Fr.	C4	16
Nogent (-sur-Marne), Fr.	g10	16
Nogent-sur-Seine, Fr.	C5	16
Noginsk, Sov. Un.	D12	27
Nogoa, stm., Austl.	B6	51
Nogoyá, Arg.	A5	54
Nohar, India	C5	36
Noheji, Japan	F10	33
Noirmoutier, Île de, i., Fr.	D2	16
Noisy-le-Sec, Fr.	g10	16
Nojima, Cape, c., Japan	I9	33
Nokesville, Va., U.S.	B5	123
Nok Kundi, Pak.	G11	39
Nokomis, Sask.	F3	75
Nokomis, Fl., U.S.	E4	86
Nokomis, Il., U.S.	D4	90
Nokomis, Lake, res., Wi., U.S.	C4	126
Nokou, Chad	C2	46
Nola, Cen. Afr. Rep.	E3	46
Nola, Italy	D5	23
Nola, Ms., U.S.	D3	101
Nolan, Tx., U.S.	C2	120
Nolan, W.V., U.S.	D2	125
Nolan, co., Tx., U.S.	C2	120
Nolensville, Tn., U.S.	B5	119
Nolichucky, stm., Tn., U.S.	C10	119
Nolin, stm., Ky., U.S.	C3	94
Nolin Lake, res., Ky., U.S.	C3	94
Nolinsk, Sov. Un.	B3	28
Noma, Fl., U.S.	u16	86
Noma, Cape, c., Japan	K5	33
Nomans Land, i., Ma., U.S.	D6	98
Nombre de Dios, Pan.	h12	62
Nome, Ak., U.S.	C6	79
Nome, N.D., U.S.	C8	111
Nomeny, Fr.	F6	17
Nomgon, Mong.	C1	32
Nominingue, Que.	C2	74
Nomonoeas, is., Micron.	Q18	52
Nonacho Lake, l., N.W. Ter.	D11	66
Nondalton, Ak., U.S.	C8	79
Nonesuch, stm., Me., U.S.	g7	96
Nong'an, China	C10	31
Nong Khai, Thai.	B2	34
Nongoma, S. Afr.	B3	49
Nonoava, Mex.	B3	63
Nonquit Pond, l., R.I., U.S.	E6	116
Nonthaburi, Thai.	h5	34
Noonan, N.D., U.S.	A2	111
Noone, N.H., U.S.	E3	106
Noordpunt, c., Neth. Ant.	H18	65
Noordwijk-Binnen, Neth.	B4	17
Noorvik, Ak., U.S.	B7	79
Nootka Island, i., B.C.	E4	69
Nootka Sound, strt., B.C.	E4	69
Nopiming Provincial Park, Man.	D4	70
No Point, Point, c., Md., U.S.	D5	97
Noquebay, Lake, l., Wi., U.S.	C6	126
Nóqui, Ang.	C1	48
Nora, Sask.	D4	75
Nora, Swe.	H6	14
Nora, Il., U.S.	A4	90
Nora Springs, Ia., U.S.	A5	92
Norbertville, Que.	C6	74

Name	Map Ref.	Page
Norborne, Mo., U.S.	B4	102
Norcatur, Ks., U.S.	C3	93
Norco, Ca., U.S.	*n13	82
Norco, La., U.S.	D5	95
Norcross, Ga., U.S.	C2	87
Norcross, Mn., U.S.	E2	100
Nord, dept., Fr.	D2	17
Nord, Canal du, Fr.	D3	17
Nordborg, Den.	C3	15
Nordby, Den.	C2	15
Nordegg, Alta.	C2	68
Nordegg, stm., Alta.	C2	68
Norden, W. Ger.	B3	18
Nordenham, W. Ger.	B4	18
Nordenskjöld Archipelago, is., Sov. Un.	B4	128
Nordenskjöld Ice Tongue, ice, Ant.	e39	7
Norderney, W. Ger.	A7	17
Norderney, i., W. Ger.	B3	18
Norderstedt, W. Ger.	*B5	18
Nordfjord, Nor.	G1	14
Nordhausen, E. Ger.	C5	18
Nordhorn, W. Ger.	B3	18
Nordjylland, co., Den.	B3	15
Nordland, Wa., U.S.	A3	124
Nördlingen, W. Ger.	D5	18
Nordmaling, Swe.	F8	14
Nordman, Id., U.S.	A2	89
Nordostrundingen, c., Grnld.	A19	61
Nordreisa, Nor.	C9	14
Nordrhein-Westfalen, state, W. Ger.	B2	19
Nordstrand, i., W. Ger.	A4	18
Nore, stm., Ire.	D3	10
Norene, Tn., U.S.	A5	119
Norfolk, Ct., U.S.	B3	84
Norfolk, Ma., U.S.	h10	98
Norfolk, Ne., U.S.	B8	104
Norfolk, N.Y., U.S.	f9	109
Norfolk, Va., U.S.	D6	123
Norfolk, co., Ont.	E4	73
Norfolk, co., Eng., U.K.	B8	12
Norfolk Island, dep., Oc.	H10	6
Norfolk Naval Base, mil., Va., U.S.	k15	123
Norfolk Naval Shipyard, mil., Va., U.S.	k15	123
Norfork, Ar., U.S.	A3	81
Norfork Dam, Ar., U.S.	A3	81
Norfork Lake, res., Ar., U.S.	A3	81
Norge, Ok., U.S.	C4	113
Norias, Tx., U.S.	F4	120
Norilsk, Sov. Un.	C11	29
Norland, Ont.	C6	73
Norland, Fl., U.S.	s13	86
Norlina, N.C., U.S.	A4	110
Norma, N.J., U.S.	E2	107
Norma, Tn., U.S.	C9	119
Norma, N.D., U.S.	A4	111
Normal, Al., U.S.	A3	78
Normal, Il., U.S.	C5	90
Norman, In., U.S.	G5	91
Norman, Ne., U.S.	D7	104
Norman, N.C., U.S.	B3	110
Norman, Ok., U.S.	B4	113
Norman, co., Mn., U.S.	C2	100
Normanby, stm., Austl.	B7	50
Normandy, Mo., U.S.	f13	102
Normandy, Tn., U.S.	B5	119
Normandy, hist. reg., Fr.	C3	16
Normandy, Hills of, hills, Fr.	C3	16
Normandy Beach, N.J., U.S.	C4	107
Normangee, Tx., U.S.	D4	120
Norman Island, i., V.I., Br.	B6	65
Normanton, Austl.	C7	50
Normanton, Eng., U.K.	D7	12
Norman Park, Ga., U.S.	E3	87
Normantown, Ga., U.S.	D4	87
Norman Wells, N.W. Ter.	C7	66
Norphlet, Ar., U.S.	D3	81
Norquay, Sask.	F4	75
Norquincó, Arg.	C2	54
Norrahammar, Swe.	A8	15
Nørre Aaby, Den.	C3	15
Nørre Alslev, Den.	D5	15
Nørresundby (part of Ålborg), Den.	A3	15
Norridge, Il., U.S.	k9	90
Norridgewock, Me., U.S.	D3	96
Norris, Il., U.S.	C4	90
Norris, Mt., U.S.	E5	103
Norris, S.C., U.S.	B2	117
Norris, S.D., U.S.	D4	118
Norris, Tn., U.S.	C9	119
Norris Arm, Newf.	D4	72
Norris City, Il., U.S.	F5	90
Norris Dam, Tn., U.S.	C9	119
Norris Lake, res., Tn., U.S.	C10	119
Norris Point, Newf.	D3	72
Norristown, Pa., U.S.	F11	115
Norrisville, Md., U.S.	A4	97
Norrköping, Swe.	H7	14
Norrtälje, Swe.	H8	14
Norseman, Austl.	F3	50
Norte, Cabo, c., Braz.	B5	59
Norte, Canal do, strt., Braz.	B4	59
Norte, Punta, c., Arg.	C4	54
Norte, Serra do, plat., Braz.	E3	59
Norte de Santander, dept., Col.	B3	60
Nortelândia, Braz.	A1	56
North, S.C., U.S.	D5	117
North, Va., U.S.	C6	123
North, stm., Newf.	B3	72
North, stm., Al., U.S.	B2	78
North, stm., Ia., U.S.	f8	92
North, stm., Ma., U.S.	h12	98
North, stm., W.V., U.S.	B6	125
North, Cape, c., N.S.	B9	71
North Abington, Ma., U.S.	B6	98
North Acton, Ma., U.S.	f10	98
North Adams, Ma., U.S.	A1	98
North Adams, Mi., U.S.	G6	99
North Albany, Or., U.S.	k11	114
Northallerton, Eng., U.K.	D7	12
Northam, Austl.	F2	50
North America, cont.	E11	61
North Amherst, Ma., U.S.	B2	98
North Amity, Me., U.S.	C5	96
North Amityville, N.Y., U.S.	*n15	109
Northampton, Austl.	E1	50
Northampton, Eng., U.K.	D6	12
Northampton, Ma., U.S.	B2	98
Northampton, Pa., U.S.	E11	115
Northampton, co., N.C., U.S.	A5	110
Northampton, co., Pa., U.S.	E11	115
Northamptonshire, co., Eng., U.K.	D6	12
North Andaman, i., India	F9	36

Name	Map Ref.	Page
North and Bent Pyramids, hist., Egypt	E3	41
North Andover, Ma., U.S.	A5	98
North Andrews Gardens, Fl., U.S.	r13	86
North Anna, stm., Va., U.S.	B5	123
North Anson, Me., U.S.	D3	96
North Apollo, Pa., U.S.	E2	115
North Arapaho Peak, mtn., Co., U.S.	A5	83
North Arlington, N.J., U.S.	h8	107
North Atlanta, Ga., U.S.	h8	87
North Attleboro, Ma., U.S.	C5	98
North Auburn, Ma., U.S.	*C3	82
North Augusta, Ont.	C9	73
North Augusta, S.C., U.S.	D4	117
North Aulatsivik Island, i., Newf.	f9	72
North Aurora, Il., U.S.	k8	90
North Avondale, Co., U.S.	C6	83
North Babylon, N.Y., U.S.	*n15	109
North Baltimore, Oh., U.S.	A2	112
North Bangor, N.Y., U.S.	f10	109
North Battleford, Sask.	E1	75
North Bay, Ont.	A5	73
North Bay Shore, N.Y., U.S.	*n15	109
North Beach, Md., U.S.	C4	97
North Belgrade, Me., U.S.	D3	96
North Bellmore, N.Y., U.S.	*n15	109
North Bellport, N.Y., U.S.	*n16	109
North Belmont, N.C., U.S.	B1	110
North Bend, B.C.	E7	69
North Bend, Ne., U.S.	C9	104
North Bend, Oh., U.S.	o12	112
North Bend, Or., U.S.	D2	114
North Bend, Pa., U.S.	D6	115
North Bend, Wi., U.S.	D2	126
North Bennington, Vt., U.S.	F2	122
North Bergen, N.J., U.S.	h8	107
North Berwick, Scot., U.K.	D6	13
North Berwick, Me., U.S.	E2	96
North Billerica, Ma., U.S.	A5	98
North Bloomfield, Oh., U.S.	A5	112
North Bonneville, Wa., U.S.	D4	124
Northboro, Ia., U.S.	D2	92
Northborough, Ma., U.S.	B4	98
North Braddock, Pa., U.S.	*k14	115
North Bradley, Mi., U.S.	E6	99
North Branch, Mi., U.S.	E7	99
North Branch, Mn., U.S.	E6	100
North Branch, N.H., U.S.	D3	106
North Branford, Ct., U.S.	D4	84
North Breakers, rf., Mid. Is.	J3	52
North Bridgton, Me., U.S.	D2	96
Northbridge, Ma., U.S.	B4	98
North Brookfield, Ma., U.S.	B3	98
North Brother, mtn., Me., U.S.	C4	96
North Brunswick, N.J., U.S.	C4	107
North Buena Vista, Ia., U.S.	B7	92
North Caldwell, N.J., U.S.	B4	107
North Calais, Vt., U.S.	C4	122
North Canadian, stm., Ok., U.S.	A5	113
North Canton, Ct., U.S.	B4	84
North Canton, Ga., U.S.	B2	87
North Canton, Oh., U.S.	B4	112
North Cape, Wi., U.S.	n11	126
North Cape, c., P.E.I.	B5	71
North Cape, c., Nor.	B11	14
North Cape May, N.J., U.S.	F3	107
North Carolina, state, U.S.	B3	110
North Carrollton, Ms., U.S.	B4	101
North Carver, Ma., U.S.	C6	98
North Cascades National Park, Wa., U.S.	A4	124
North Cay, i., Bah.	m17	64
North Channel, strt., Ont.	A2	73
North Channel, strt., U.K.	C9	10
North Charleston, S.C., U.S.	F8	117
North Charlestown, N.H., U.S.	D2	106
North Chatham, N.H., U.S.	B4	106
North Chicago, Il., U.S.	A6	90
North Chichester, N.H., U.S.	D4	106
North City, Wa., U.S.	*B3	124
North Clarendon, Vt., U.S.	D3	122
Northcliffe, Austl.	F2	50
North Cohasset, Ma., U.S.	g12	98
North Cohocton, N.Y., U.S.	C3	109
North College Hill, Oh., U.S.	o12	112
North Collins, N.Y., U.S.	C2	109
North Concord, Vt., U.S.	C5	122
North Conway, N.H., U.S.	B4	106
North Corbin, Ky., U.S.	D5	94
Northcote, Austl.	*G8	50
North Creek, N.Y., U.S.	B7	109
North Crossett, Ar., U.S.	D4	81
North Crows Nest, In., U.S.	k10	91
North Dakota, state, U.S.	B5	111
North Danville, Vt., U.S.	C4	122
North Dartmouth, Ma., U.S.	C5	98
North Decatur, Ga., U.S.	*h8	87
North Derby, Vt., U.S.	A4	122
North Dighton, Ma., U.S.	C5	98
North Dixmont, Me., U.S.	D3	96
North Downs, plat., Eng., U.K.	E7	10
North Druid Hills, Ga., U.S.	h8	87
North Eagle Butte, S.D., U.S.	B4	118
North East, Md., U.S.	A6	97
North East, Pa., U.S.	B2	115
North East, stm., Md., U.S.	A6	97
Northeast Cape, c., Ak., U.S.	C6	79
Northeast Cape Fear, stm., N.C., U.S.	C5	110
North Eastern, prov., Kenya	A6	48
Northeast Harbor, Me., U.S.	D4	96
Northeast Henrietta, N.Y., U.S.	B3	109
Northeast Pond, l., N.H., U.S.	D5	106
Northeast Providence Channel, strt., Bah.	B5	64
North Edisto, stm., S.C., U.S.	k11	117
North Egremont, Ma., U.S.	B1	98
Northeim, W. Ger.	C4	18
North English, Ia., U.S.	C5	92
North English, stm., Ia., U.S.	C5	92
North Enid, Ok., U.S.	A4	113
Northern, prov., Ghana	E4	45
Northern, prov., Mwi.	C6	48
Northern, prov., Zam.	D5	48
Northern Arm, Newf.	D4	72

Name	Map Ref.	Page
Northern Cheyenne Indian Reservation, Mt., U.S.	E10	103
Northern Donets, stm., Sov. Un.	G13	27
Northern Dvina, stm., Sov. Un.	C7	29
Northern Head, c., N.B.	D4	71
Northern Indian Lake, l., Man.	A3	70
Northern Ireland, ter., U.K.	C3	10
Northern Mariana Islands, ter., T.T.P.I.	E8	6
Northern Range, mts., Trin.	N23	65
Northern Sporades, is., Grc.	C5	25
Northern Territory, ter., Austl.	C5	50
North Esk, stm., Scot., U.K.	D6	13
North Fair Oaks, Ca., U.S.	*k8	82
North Fairfield, Oh., U.S.	A3	112
North Falmouth, Ma., U.S.	C6	98
North Ferrisburg, Vt., U.S.	C2	122
North Fond du Lac, Wi., U.S.	E5	126
North Foreland, c., Eng., U.K.	E7	10
North Fork, Ca., U.S.	D4	82
North Fork, Id., U.S.	D5	89
North Fork Reservoir, res., Or., U.S.	C4	114
North Fort Myers, Fl., U.S.	F5	86
North Fox Island, i., Mi., U.S.	C5	99
North Franklin, Ct., U.S.	C7	84
North Freedom, Wi., U.S.	E4	126
North Frisian Islands, is., Eur.	A4	18
North Fryeburg, Me., U.S.	D2	96
North Galiano, B.C.	f12	69
Northgate, Sask.	H4	75
Northgate, N.D., U.S.	A3	111
Northglenn, Co., U.S.	B6	83
North Gorham, Me., U.S.	g7	96
North Gower, Ont.	B9	73
North Grafton, Ma., U.S.	B4	98
North Granby, Ct., U.S.	B5	84
North Great River, N.Y., U.S.	*n18	109
North Grosvenordale, Ct., U.S.	B8	84
North Gulf of Évvoia, b., Grc.	C4	25
North Gulfport, Ms., U.S.	E4	101
North Halawa Stream, stm., Hi., U.S.	g10	88
North Haledon, N.J., U.S.	B4	107
North Hampton, N.H., U.S.	E5	106
North Hanover, Ma., U.S.	h12	98
North Harpswell, Me., U.S.	g8	96
North Hartland, Vt., U.S.	D4	122
North Hartland Reservoir, res., Vt., U.S.	D4	122
North Hatfield, Ma., U.S.	B2	98
North Hatley, Que.	D6	74
North Haven, Ct., U.S.	D4	84
North Haven, Me., U.S.	D4	96
North Haverhill, N.H., U.S.	B2	106
North Head, N.B.	E3	71
North Henderson, Il., U.S.	B3	90
North Hero, Vt., U.S.	B2	122
North Hero Island, i., Vt., U.S.	B2	122
North Highlands, Ca., U.S.	*C3	82
North Hill, Wa., U.S.	*B3	124
North Holland (Noord-Holland), prov., Neth.	B4	17
North Holston, stm., Va., U.S.	f10	123
North Horn Lake, l., Tn., U.S.	e8	119
North Horr, Kenya	A6	48
North Houston, Tx., U.S.	*E5	120
North Hudson, N.Y., U.S.	B7	109
North Hudson, Wi., U.S.	*C1	126
North Hyde Park, Vt., U.S.	B3	122
North Industry, Oh., U.S.	B4	112
North Inlet, b., S.C., U.S.	E9	117
North Island, i., N.Z.	M15	51
North Island, i., S.C., U.S.	E9	117
North Island Naval Air Station, mil., Ca., U.S.	o15	82
North Islands, is., La., U.S.	E7	95
North Java, N.Y., U.S.	C2	109
North Jay, Me., U.S.	D2	96
North Judson, In., U.S.	B4	91
North Kansas City, Mo., U.S.	h10	102
North Kingstown, R.I., U.S.	E4	116
North Komelik, Az., U.S.	E4	80
North La Junta, Co., U.S.	C7	83
North Lake, Wi., U.S.	*m11	126
North Laramie, stm., Wy., U.S.	D7	127
North Las Vegas, Nv., U.S.	G6	105
North Lauderdale, Fl., U.S.	*r13	86
North La Veta Pass, Co., U.S.	D5	83
North Lawrence, N.Y., U.S.	f10	109
North Lewisburg, Oh., U.S.	B2	112
North Liberty, In., U.S.	A5	91
North Liberty, Ia., U.S.	C6	92
North Lima, Oh., U.S.	B5	112
North Lindenhurst, N.Y., U.S.	*n15	109
North Little Rock, Ar., U.S.	C3	81
North Logan, Ut., U.S.	B4	121
North Long Beach, Ms., U.S.	*E4	101
North Loon Mountain, mtn., Id., U.S.	D3	89
North Loup, Ne., U.S.	C7	104
North Loup, stm., Ne., U.S.	C5	104
North Lubec, Me., U.S.	D5	96
North Madison, Oh., U.S.	A4	112
North Magnetic Pole, N.W. Ter.	m31	66
North Mamm Peak, mtn., Co., U.S.	B3	83
North Manchester, In., U.S.	C6	91
North Manitou Island, i., Mi., U.S.	C4	99
North Mankato, Mn., U.S.	F4	100
North Marshfield, Ma., U.S.	h12	98
North Massapequa, N.Y., U.S.	*E7	109
North Merrick, N.Y., U.S.	*n15	109
North Miami, Fl., U.S.	s13	86
North Miami Beach, Fl., U.S.	s13	86
North Middleboro, Ma., U.S.	C6	98
North Middletown, Ky., U.S.	B5	94
North Monmouth, Me., U.S.	D2	96

Name	Map Ref.	Page
North Montpelier, Vt., U.S.	C4	122
Northmoor, Mo., U.S.	h10	102
North Moose Lake, l., Man.	B1	70
North Mountain, mtn., Pa., U.S.	D9	115
North Muskegon, Mi., U.S.	E4	99
North Myrtle Beach, S.C., U.S.	D10	117
North Naples, Fl., U.S.	F5	86
North Negril Point, c., Jam.	E12	65
North Newcastle, Me., U.S.	D3	96
North New Hyde Park, N.Y., U.S.	*E7	109
North Newport, N.H., U.S.	D2	106
North New Portland, Me., U.S.	D2	96
North New River Canal, Fl., U.S.	F6	86
North Norwich, N.Y., U.S.	C5	109
North Ogden, Ut., U.S.	B4	121
North Olmsted, Oh., U.S.	h9	112
North Omaha, Ne., U.S.	g13	104
North Orange, Ma., U.S.	A3	98
North Oxford, Ma., U.S.	B4	98
North Palisade, mtn., Ca., U.S.	D4	82
North Palm Beach, Fl., U.S.	*F6	86
North Park, Il., U.S.	A4	90
North Park, val., Co., U.S.	A4	83
North Parsonfield, Me., U.S.	D2	96
North Pass, strt., La., U.S.	E7	95
North Patchogue, N.Y., U.S.	*n15	109
North Pembroke, Ma., U.S.	B6	98
North Pitcher, N.Y., U.S.	C5	109
North Plainfield, N.J., U.S.	B4	107
North Plains, Or., U.S.	B4	114
North Plains, pl., N.M., U.S.	C1	108
North Platte, Ne., U.S.	C5	104
North Platte, stm., U.S.	C5	104
North Point, c., Barb.	K20	65
North Point, c., Md., U.S.	B5	97
North Point, c., Md., U.S.	C5	97
North Point, c., Mi., U.S.	C7	99
North Pole,	A1	128
North Pomfret, Vt., U.S.	D4	122
North Pond, l., Me., U.S.	D3	96
North Port, Fl., U.S.	*D4	86
Northport, Al., U.S.	B2	78
Northport, Mi., U.S.	C5	99
Northport, Ne., U.S.	*C2	104
Northport, N.Y., U.S.	*n15	109
Northport, Wa., U.S.	A8	124
North Portal, Sask.	H4	75
North Powder, Or., U.S.	B9	114
North Pownal, Me., U.S.	g7	96
North Pownal, Vt., U.S.	F2	122
North Prairie, Wi., U.S.	F5	126
North Providence, R.I., U.S.	C4	116
North Raccoon, stm., Ia., U.S.	C3	92
North Range Corner, N.S.	E4	71
North Reading, Ma., U.S.	f11	98
North Richland Hills, Tx., U.S.	n9	120
Northridge, Oh., U.S.	C2	112
Northridge, Oh., U.S.	*C1	112
North Ridgeville, Oh., U.S.	A3	112
North Rim, Az., U.S.	A3	80
North River Bridge, N.S.	C9	71
North Riverside, Il., U.S.	*k9	90
North Robinson, Oh., U.S.	B3	112
North Ronaldsay, i., Scot., U.K.	A5	10
Northrop, Mn., U.S.	G4	100
North Rose, N.Y., U.S.	B4	109
North Royalton, Oh., U.S.	h9	112
North Rustico, P.E.I.	C6	71
North Salem, In., U.S.	E4	91
North Salem, N.H., U.S.	E4	106
North Salt Lake, Ut., U.S.	C4	121
North Sanbornton, N.H., U.S.	C3	106
North Sandwich, N.H., U.S.	C4	106
North Santee, stm., S.C., U.S.	E9	117
North Saskatchewan, stm., Can.	F10	66
North Schell Peak, mtn., Nv., U.S.	D7	105
North Scituate, Ma., U.S.	h12	98
North Scituate, R.I., U.S.	C3	116
North Sea, Eur.	D9	8
Norths Highland, plat., Ant.	C25	7
North Shores, De., U.S.	F5	85
North Shoshone Peak, mtn., Nv., U.S.	D4	105
North Shrewsbury, Vt., U.S.	D3	122
North Sioux City, S.D., U.S.	E9	118
Northside, N.C., U.S.	A4	110
North Skunk, stm., Ia., U.S.	C5	92
North Sound, strt., Ire.	D2	11
North Sound, strt., Scot., U.K.	A6	13
North Spicer Island, i., N.W. Ter.	C17	66
North Springfield, Or., U.S.	*C3	114
North Springfield, Pa., U.S.	B1	115
North Springfield, Vt., U.S.	E3	122
North Springfield Reservoir, res., Vt., U.S.	E4	122
North Star, De., U.S.	A3	85
North Star, Oh., U.S.	B1	112
North Stonington, Ct., U.S.	D8	84
North St. Paul, Mn., U.S.	m13	100
North Stradbroke, i., Austl.	E9	50
North Stratford, N.H., U.S.	A3	106
North Sudbury, Ma., U.S.	g10	98
North Sutton, N.H., U.S.	D3	106
North Swansea, Ma., U.S.	C5	98
North Swanzey, N.H., U.S.	E2	106
North Sydney, Austl.	*F9	50
North Sydney, N.S.	C9	71
North Syracuse, N.Y., U.S.	B4	109
North Taranaki Bight, N.Z.	M15	51
North Tea Lake, l., Ont.	B5	73
North Terre Haute, In., U.S.	E3	91
North Tewksbury, Ma., U.S.	A5	98
North Thetford, Vt., U.S.	D4	122
North Thompson, stm., B.C.	D8	69
North Tolsta, Scot., U.K.	A2	13
North Tonawanda, N.Y., U.S.	B2	109
North Troy, Vt., U.S.	A4	122
North Truro, Ma., U.S.	B7	98
North Tunbridge, Vt., U.S.	D4	122
North Tunica, Ms., U.S.	A3	101
North Turner Mountain, mtn., Me., U.S.	C4	96
North Twin Lake, l., Newf.	D4	72
North Twin Lake, l., Wi., U.S.	B4	126
North Tyne, stm., Eng., U.K.	E6	13
North Uist, i., Scot., U.K.	A6	13
Northumberland, N.H., U.S.	A3	106
Northumberland, Pa., U.S.	E8	115
Northumberland, co., Ont.	C6	73
Northumberland, co., Eng., U.K.	E6	13

Name	Map Ref.	Page
Northumberland, co., Pa., U.S.	D8	115
Northumberland, co., Va., U.S.	C6	123
Northumberland Isles, is., Austl.	D9	50
Northumberland Strait, strt., Can.	C6	71
North Umpqua, stm., Or., U.S.	D3	114
North Uxbridge, Ma., U.S.	B4	98
Northvale, N.J., U.S.	g9	107
North Valley Stream, N.Y., U.S.	*n15	109
North Vancouver, B.C.	E6	69
North Vassalboro, Me., U.S.	D3	96
North Vernon, In., U.S.	F6	91
North Versailles, Pa., U.S.	*k14	115
Northview, Mi., U.S.	*E5	99
Northview, Mo., U.S.	*C1	112
Northview, Oh., U.S.	*C1	112
North Village, N.H., U.S.	E3	106
Northville, Ct., U.S.	C2	84
Northville, Mi., U.S.	p15	99
Northville, N.Y., U.S.	B6	109
Northville, S.D., U.S.	B7	118
North Wabasca Lake, l., Alta.	A4	68
North Waldoboro, Me., U.S.	D3	96
North Wales, Pa., U.S.	F11	115
North Walpole, N.H., U.S.	D2	106
North Walsham, Eng., U.K.	D7	10
North Wantagh, N.Y., U.S.	*n15	109
North Warren, Pa., U.S.	C3	115
North Waterford, Me., U.S.	D2	96
Northway, Ak., U.S.	C11	79
North Webster, In., U.S.	B6	91
North West, dept., Guy.	A3	59
North West Cape, c., Austl.	D1	50
North Westchester, Ct., U.S.	C6	84
North-Western, prov., Zam.	D4	48
North West Highlands, plat., Scot., U.K.	B4	10
North Westminster, Vt., U.S.	E4	122
Northwest Miramichi, stm., N.B.	B3	71
Northwest Polder, reg., Neth.	B5	17
Northwest Providence Channel, strt., Bah.	A4	64
North West River, Newf.	B1	72
Northwest Territories, prov., Can.	C13	66
Northwest Upsalquitch, stm., N.B.	B2	71
Northwich, Eng., U.K.	A5	12
North Wildwood, N.J., U.S.	E3	107
North Wilkesboro, N.C., U.S.	A1	110
North Wilmington, Ma., U.S.	f11	98
North Windham, Ct., U.S.	C7	84
North Windham, Me., U.S.	E2	96
Northwood, Ia., U.S.	A4	92
Northwood, N.H., U.S.	D4	106
Northwood, N.D., U.S.	B8	111
Northwood, Oh., U.S.	*e7	112
Northwood Center, N.H., U.S.	D4	106
Northwood Ridge, N.H., U.S.	D4	106
Northwoods, Mo., U.S.	*f13	102
North Woodstock, N.H., U.S.	B3	106
North Yarmouth, Me., U.S.	g7	96
North York, Ont.	D5	73
North York, Pa., U.S.	G8	115
North York Moors, hills, Eng., U.K.	C6	10
North Yorkshire, co., Eng., U.K.	F7	13
North Zulch, Tx., U.S.	D4	120
Norton, N.B.	D4	71
Norton, Eng., U.K.	F8	13
Norton, Ks., U.S.	C4	93
Norton, Ma., U.S.	C5	98
Norton, Oh., U.S.	A4	112
Norton, Tx., U.S.	D2	120
Norton, Va., U.S.	f9	123
Norton, W.V., U.S.	C5	125
Norton, co., Ks., U.S.	C4	93
Norton Air Force Base, mil., Ca., U.S.	E5	82
Norton Bay, b., Ak., U.S.	C7	79
Norton Creek, stm., Al., U.S.	B1	78
Norton Pond, l., Vt., U.S.	B5	122
Norton Reservoir, res., Ks., U.S.	C3	93
Nortons Corner, Az., U.S.	D4	80
Norton Shores, Mi., U.S.	E4	99
Norton Sound, strt., Ak., U.S.	C8	79
Nortonville, Ks., U.S.	C8	93
Nortonville, Ky., U.S.	C2	94
Nortonville, N.D., U.S.	C7	111
Nortorf, W. Ger.	D3	18
Norvegia, Cape, c., Ant.	B11	7
Norwalk, Ca., U.S.	n12	82
Norwalk, Ct., U.S.	E2	84
Norwalk, Ia., U.S.	C4	92
Norwalk, Oh., U.S.	A3	112
Norwalk, stm., Ct., U.S.	E2	84
Norwalk Islands, is., Ct., U.S.	E2	84
Norway, Ia., U.S.	C5	92
Norway, Ks., U.S.	C6	93
Norway, Me., U.S.	D2	96
Norway, Mi., U.S.	C3	99
Norway, Or., U.S.	D2	114
Norway, S.C., U.S.	E5	117
Norway, ctry., Eur.	F4	14
Norway House, Man.	C3	70
Norway Lake, l., Mn., U.S.	E3	100
Norwegian Bay, b., N.W. Ter.	m33	66
Norwegian Sea, Eur.	C14	128
Norwell, Ma., U.S.	h12	98
Norwich, Ont.	E4	73
Norwich, Eng., U.K.	D7	10
Norwich, Ct., U.S.	C7	84
Norwich, Ks., U.S.	E6	93
Norwich, N.Y., U.S.	C5	109
Norwich, Vt., U.S.	D4	122
Norwood, Ont.	C7	73
Norwood, Co., U.S.	C2	83
Norwood, Ga., U.S.	C4	87
Norwood, La., U.S.	D4	95
Norwood, Ma., U.S.	B5	98
Norwood, Mn., U.S.	F5	100
Norwood, Mo., U.S.	D5	102
Norwood, N.J., U.S.	h9	107
Norwood, N.Y., U.S.	f10	109
Norwood, N.C., U.S.	B2	110
Norwood, Oh., U.S.	o13	112
Norwood, Pa., U.S.	p20	115
Norwoodville, Ia., U.S.	e8	92
Norwottock, Mount, mtn., Ma., U.S.	B2	98
Nosbonsing, Lake, l., Ont.	A5	73
Noshiro, Japan	F9	33
Nösjön, l., Swe.	A6	15
Nossa Senhora das Dores, Braz.	D3	57
Nossen, E. Ger.	B8	19
Noss Head, c., Scot., U.K.	B5	13
Nossob, stm., Afr.	C3	49
Nosy Varika, Madag.	h9	49
Notasulga, Al., U.S.	C4	78
Notch Hill, B.C.	D8	69
Notch Mountain, mtn., Ma., U.S.	A3	98
Notch Peak, mtn., Ut., U.S.	D2	121
Noteć, stm., Pol.	B3	26
Notikewin, Alta.	A2	68
Notikewin, stm., Alta.	A1	68
Noto, Italy	F5	23
Noto, Gulf of, b., Italy	F5	23
Notodden, Nor.	H3	14
Noto Island, i., Japan	H8	33
Noto Peninsula, pen., Japan	D12	31
Notoue, Kir.	R18	52
Notre-Dame, N.B.	C5	71
Notre Dame, Monts, mts., Que.	k13	74
Notre Dame Bay, b., Newf.	D4	72
Notre Dame de Lourdes, Man.	E2	70
Notre-Dame-de-Montauban, Que.	C4	74
Notre-Dame-des-Bois, Que.	D6	74
Notre-Dame-du-Lac, Que.	B9	74
Notre-Dame-du-Laus, Que.	C2	74
Nottawa, Ont.	C4	73
Nottawasaga Bay, b., Ont.	C4	73
Nottaway, stm., Que.	h11	74
Nottely Lake, res., Ga., U.S.	B2	87
Nottingham, Eng., U.K.	D6	10
Nottingham, N.H., U.S.	D4	106
Nottingham Island, i., N.W. Ter.	D17	66
Nottinghamshire, co., Eng., U.K.	A7	12
Nottoway, Va., U.S.	C4	123
Nottoway, co., Va., U.S.	C4	123
Nottoway, stm., Va., U.S.	D5	123
Notukeu Creek, stm., Sask.	H2	75
Notus, Id., U.S.	F2	89
Nouadhibou, Maur.	B1	45
Nouakchott, Maur.	C1	45
Nouamrhar, Maur.	C1	45
Nouméa, N. Cal.	H10	6
Nouna, Burkina	D4	45
Noupoort, S. Afr.	D3	49
Noutonice, Czech.	n17	26
Nouvelle-France, Cap de, c., Que.	D18	66
Nouzonville, Fr.	C6	16
Nova, Oh., U.S.	A3	112
Nova Caipemba, Ang.	C1	48
Nova Cruz, Braz.	C3	57
Nova Friburgo, Braz.	C4	56
Nova Iguaçu, Braz.	h6	56
Nova Lima, Braz.	C2	56
Nova Londrina, Braz.	A5	56
Nova Lusitânia, Moz.	B6	49
Nova Mambone, Moz.	F7	49
Nova Olinda do Norte, Braz.	B3	59
Nova Ponte, Braz.	B3	56
Nova Prata, Braz.	B6	56
Novar, Ont.	B5	73
Novara, Italy	B2	23
Nova Roma, Braz.	A3	56
Nova Russas, Braz.	B2	57
Nova Scotia, prov., Can.	D6	71
Nova Sofala, Moz.	B5	49
Nova Soure, Braz.	D3	57
Novate Mezzola, Italy	D7	21
Novato, Ca., U.S.	C2	82
Nova Varoš, Yugo.	D4	24
Nova Venécia, Braz.	B4	56
Nova Vida, Braz.	B3	55
Novaya Astrakhan, Sov. Un.		
Novaya Kazanka, Sov. Un.	F18	8
Novaya Ladoga, Sov. Un.	A9	27
Novaya Lyalya, Sov. Un.	D9	29
Novaya Odessa, Sov. Un.	H8	27
Novaya Sibir Island, i., Sov. Un.	B17	29
Novaya Zemlya, is., Sov. Un.	B8	29
Nova Zagora, Bul.	D8	24
Novelda, Spain	C5	22
Novelty, Mo., U.S.	A5	102
Nové Město [nad Váhom], Czech.	D4	26
Nové Strašecí, Czech.	C8	19
Nové Zámky, Czech.	E5	26
Novgorod, Sov. Un.	D6	29
Novgorod-Severskiy, Sov. Un.	E8	27
Novi, Mi., U.S.	p15	99
Novice, Tx., U.S.	C3	120
Novigrad, Yugo.	C2	23
Novi Ligure, Italy	B2	23
Novinger, Mo., U.S.	A5	102
Novi Pazar, Bul.	D8	24
Novi Pazar, Yugo.	D5	24
Novi Sad, Yugo.	C4	24
Novo, stm., Braz.	g6	56
Novo Airão, Braz.	C2	59
Novoaltaysk, Sov. Un.	E25	8
Novoanninskiy, Sov. Un.	C2	28
Novo Aripuanã, Braz.	B2	59
Novoaydar, Sov. Un.	G12	27
Novocherkassk, Sov. Un.	H13	27
Nôvo Cruzeiro, Braz.	B4	56
Novoekonomicheskoye, Sov. Un.	q20	27
Novograd-Volynskiy, Sov. Un.	F6	27
Novogrudok, Sov. Un.	E5	27
Novokazalinsk, Sov. Un.	E9	28
Novokurovka, Sov. Un.	B7	33
Novokuybyshevsk, Sov. Un.	*D7	29
Novokuznetsk, Sov. Un.	D11	29
Novo Mesto, Yugo.	C2	24
Novomirgorod, Sov. Un.	G8	27
Novomoskovsk, Sov. Un.	G10	27
Novomoskovsk, Sov. Un.	D6	29
Novopokrovskaya, Sov. Un.	I13	27
Novorossiysk, Sov. Un.	E6	29
Novo-Selo, Bul.	C6	24
Novoshakhtinsk, Sov. Un.	H12	27
Novosibirsk, Sov. Un.	D11	29
Novosibirsk Reservoir, res., Sov. Un.	C10	28
Novosil, Sov. Un.	E11	27
Novotroitsk, Sov. Un.	C5	28
Novoukrainka, Sov. Un.	G7	27
Novouzensk, Sov. Un.	G8	27
Novoyeniseyskaya, Sov. Un.	E9	28
Novozybkov, Sov. Un.	E8	27
Nový Bydžov, Czech.	C3	19
Nový Jičín, Czech.	D5	26
Novyye Senzhary, Sov. Un.	G10	27
Novyy Oskol, Sov. Un.	F11	27
Novyy Port, Sov. Un.	C10	29
Novyy Urengoy, Sov. Un.	C10	29
Novyy Uzen, Sov. Un.	G19	8
Novyy Vasyugan, Sov. Un.	B9	29
Nowagród, Pol.	B10	19
Nowa Ruda, Pol.	C3	26
Nowa Sól, Pol.	C3	26
Nowata, Ok., U.S.	A6	113
Nowata, co., Ok., U.S.	A6	113
Nowe Warpno, Pol.	B3	26
Nowogard, Pol.	B3	26
Nowood, stm., Wy., U.S.	B5	127
Nowra-Bomaderry, Austl.	G8	51
Nowshāk, mtn., Asia	k17	39
Nowy Dwór [Mazowiecki], Pol.	k13	26
Nowy Sącz, Pol.	D6	26
Nowy Targ, Pol.	D6	26
Nowy Tomyśl, Pol.	B4	26
Noxapater, Ms., U.S.	C4	101
Noxen, Pa., U.S.	D9	115
Noxon, Mt., U.S.	C1	103
Noxon Reservoir, res., Mt., U.S.	C1	103
Noxontown Lake, res., De., U.S.	C3	85
Noxubee, co., Ms., U.S.	B5	101
Noxubee, stm., U.S.	B5	101
Noya, Spain	A1	22
Noyes, Mn., U.S.	B1	100
Noyes Island, i., Ak., U.S.	n22	79
Noyon, Fr.	C5	16
Nozeroy, Fr.	C1	21
Nsanje, Mwi.	E6	48
Nsawam, Ghana	E4	45
Nsukka, Nig.	E6	45
Ntem, stm., Afr.	E2	46
Nuatabu, Kir.	R18	52
Nubanusit Lake, l., N.H., U.S.	E2	106
Nūbārīyah, Tur'at an, Eg.	D2	41
Nuberg, Ga., U.S.	B4	87
Nubian Desert, des., Sud.	A3	47
Nuckolls, co., Ne., U.S.	D7	104
Nucla, Co., U.S.	C2	83
Nueces, co., Tx., U.S.	F4	120
Nueces, stm., Tx., U.S.	E3	120
Nueltin Lake, l., Can.	D13	66
Nueva, Isla, i., Chile	k12	54
Nueva Antioquia, Col.	B4	60
Nueva Asunción, dept., Para.	D3	55
Nueva Casas Grandes, Mex.	A3	63
Nueva Esparta, state, Ven.	A5	60
Nueva Gerona, Cuba	D2	64
Nueva Imperial, Chile	B2	54
Nueva Lubecka, Arg.	C2	54
Nueva Ocotepeque, Hond.	C3	62
Nueva Palmira, Ur.	E1	56
Nueva Providencia, Pan.	k11	62
Nueva Rosita, Mex.	B4	63
Nueva San Salvador, El Sal.	D3	62
Nueve de Julio, Arg.	B4	54
Nuevitas, Cuba	D5	64
Nuevo, Golfo b., Arg.	C3	54
Nuevo Emperador, Pan.	m11	62
Nuevo Laredo, Mex.	B5	63
Nuevo León, state, Mex.	B5	63
Nuevo San Juan, Pan.	k11	62
Nugaal, prov., Som.	D6	47
Nūh, Rās, c., Pak.	I11	39
Nuits, Fr.	D6	16
Nukhayb, Iraq	G14	40
Nukhaylah, well, Sud.	B2	47
Nuku'alofa, Tonga	H11	6
Nukus, Sov. Un.	E5	29
Nulato, Ak., U.S.	C8	79
Nules, Spain	C6	22
Nulhegan, stm., Vt., U.S.	B5	122
Nullagine, Austl.	D3	50
Nullarbor Plain, pl., Austl.	F4	50
Numa, Ia., U.S.	D5	92
Numan, Nig.	E7	45
Numazu, Japan	I9	33
Numfoor, i., Indon.	F8	34
Numila, Hi., U.S.	B2	88
Nu Mine, Pa., U.S.	E3	115
Nunawading, Austl.	*G8	50
Nunda, N.Y., U.S.	C3	109
Nunda, S.D., U.S.	C8	118
Nuneaton, Eng., U.K.	B6	12
Nunez, Ga., U.S.	D4	87
Nunica, Mi., U.S.	E4	99
Nunivak Island, i., Ak., U.S.	D6	79
Nunn, Co., U.S.	A6	83
Nunnelly, Tn., U.S.	B4	119
Nuoro, Italy	D2	23
Nuquí, Col.	B2	60
Nura, stm., Sov. Un.	E23	8
Nuremberg, Pa., U.S.	E9	115
Nuremberg see Nürnberg, W. Ger.	D5	18
Nuri, Mex.	B3	63
Nurmes, Fin.	F13	14
Nürnberg (Nuremberg), W. Ger.	D5	18
Nürtingen, W. Ger.	D5	18
Nus, Italy	E3	21
Nusaybin, Tur.	D13	40
Nusle (part of Prague), Czech.	n17	26
Nushki, Pak.	C4	36
Nusf, Bi'r an, well, Eg.	C5	43
Nutley, N.J., U.S.	B4	107
Nut Mountain, Sask.	F4	75
Nutrioso, Az., U.S.	D6	80
Nutter Fort, W.V., U.S.	k10	125
Nutting Lake, Ma., U.S.	f10	98
Nutwood, Il., U.S.	D3	90
Nuuanu Pali, Hi., U.S.	g10	88
Nu'utele Island, i., W. Sam.	G12	52
Nuutoi, Cape, c., W. Sam.	G12	52
Nuwara-Eliya, Sri L.	G7	36
Nuwaybi' al Muzayyinah, Eg.	H10	40
Nuyaka, Ok., U.S.	B5	113
Nūzvīd, India	I8	37
Nyac, Ak., U.S.	C8	79
Nyack, N.Y., U.S.	D7	109
Nyala, Sud.	C1	47
Nyamandhlovu, Zimb.	A4	49
Nyamtumbo, Tan.	D7	48
Nyandoma, Sov. Un.	C7	29
Nyanza, prov., Kenya	B5	48
Nyasa, Lake, l., Afr.	D5	48
Nyborg, Den.	C4	15
Nybro, Swe.	I6	14
Nyda, Sov. Un.	B8	29
Nye, Mt., U.S.	E7	103
Nye, co., Nv., U.S.	E5	105
Nyeri, Kenya	B5	48
Nyilumba, Tan.	D7	48
Nyimba, Zam.	D5	48
Nyíregyháza, Hung.		
Nykøbing, Den.	I3	14
Nykøbing Falster, Den.	D5	15
Nykøbing Sjælland, Den.	C5	15
Nyköping, Swe.	H7	14
Nylstroom, S. Afr.	B4	49
Nymagee, Austl.	F6	51
Nymburk, Czech.	C3	26
Nymindegab, Den.	C2	15
Nynäshamn, Swe.	H8	14
Nyngan, Austl.	F8	50
Nyon, Switz.	E3	18
Nyong, stm., Cam.	E2	46
Nyňany, Czech.	D2	26
Nýrsko, Czech.	D8	19
Nysa, Pol.	C4	26
Nyssa, Or., U.S.	D9	114
Nysted, Den.	C4	48
Nyunzu, Zaire	C4	48
Nzega, Tan.	B5	48
Nzérékoré, Gui.	E3	45
N'zeto, Ang.	C1	48
Nzwani, i., Com.	f8	49

O

Oacoma, S.D., U.S.	D6	118
Oahe, Lake, res., U.S.	A7	76
Oahe Dam, S.D., U.S.	C5	118
Oahu, i., Hi., U.S.	B4	88
Oak, Ne., U.S.	D8	104
Oakalla, Tx., U.S.	C4	120
Oak Bay, B.C.	h12	69
Oak Bay, N.B.	D2	71
Oak Bluffs, Ma., U.S.	D6	98
Oak Brook, Il., U.S.	*k9	90
Oakburn, Man.	D1	70
Oak City, N.C., U.S.	B5	110
Oak City, Ut., U.S.	D3	121
Oak Creek, Co., U.S.	A4	83
Oak Creek, Wi., U.S.	n12	126
Oakdale, Ca., U.S.	D3	82
Oakdale, Ct., U.S.	D7	84
Oakdale, Ga., U.S.	h8	87
Oakdale, Il., U.S.	E4	90
Oakdale, La., U.S.	D3	95
Oakdale, Mn., U.S.	*n13	100
Oakdale, Ne., U.S.	B8	104
Oakdale, N.Y., U.S.	*n15	109
Oakdale, Pa., U.S.	k13	115
Oakdale, Tn., U.S.	D9	119
Oakdale Manor, Ct., U.S.	*D2	84
Oakengates, Eng., U.K.	B5	12
Oakes, N.D., U.S.	C7	111
Oakesdale, Wa., U.S.	B8	124
Oakey, Austl.	E3	51
Oakfield, Ga., U.S.	E3	87
Oakfield, Me., U.S.	B4	96
Oakfield, N.Y., U.S.	B2	109
Oakfield, Tn., U.S.	B3	119
Oakfield, Wi., U.S.	E5	126
Oakford, Il., U.S.	C4	90
Oakford, Pa., U.S.	D5	91
Oak Forest, Il., U.S.	k9	90
Oak Grove, Ar., U.S.	A2	81
Oak Grove, Ky., U.S.	D2	94
Oak Grove, La., U.S.	B4	95
Oak Grove, Mi., U.S.	F7	99
Oak Grove, Or., U.S.	B4	114
Oak Grove, S.C., U.S.	C8	117
Oak Grove, S.C., U.S.	*D5	117
Oak Grove, Va., U.S.	B6	123
Oak Harbor, Oh., U.S.	A2	112
Oak Harbor, Wa., U.S.	A3	124
Oak Hill, Fl., U.S.	D6	86
Oak Hill, Fl., U.S.	*B3	86
Oak Hill, Ks., U.S.	*C6	93
Oak Hill, Mi., U.S.	C4	99
Oak Hill, Oh., U.S.	D3	112
Oak Hill, W.V., U.S.	D3	125
Oak Hill, mtn., Ma., U.S.	f9	98
Oakhurst, N.J., U.S.	C4	107
Oakhurst, Ok., U.S.	A5	113
Oak Island, i., Wi., U.S.	B3	126
Oak Lake, Man.	E1	70
Oak Lake, l., Man.	E1	70
Oakland, Ca., U.S.	D2	82
Oakland, Ia., U.S.	C2	92
Oakland, Il., U.S.	D5	90
Oakland, Ky., U.S.	C3	94
Oakland, Md., U.S.	m12	97
Oakland, Me., U.S.	D3	96
Oakland, Ms., U.S.	A4	101
Oakland, Ne., U.S.	C9	104
Oakland, N.J., U.S.	A4	107
Oakland, Or., U.S.	D3	114
Oakland, R.I., U.S.	B3	116
Oakland, Tn., U.S.	B2	119
Oakland, co., Mi., U.S.	F7	99
Oakland City, In., U.S.	H3	91
Oakland Gardens, Ct., U.S.	*C7	84
Oakland Park, Fl., U.S.	r13	86
Oak Lane Manor, De., U.S.	*A3	85
Oak Lawn, Il., U.S.	B6	90
Oaklawn, Ks., U.S.	g12	93
Oakley, Id., U.S.	G5	89
Oakley, Ks., U.S.	C3	93
Oakley, Mi., U.S.	E6	99
Oakley, S.C., U.S.	E7	117
Oakley, Ut., U.S.	C4	121
Oaklyn, N.J., U.S.	*D2	107
Oakman, Al., U.S.	B2	78
Oak Orchard, De., U.S.	*E5	85
Oak Park, Ca., U.S.	*m12	82
Oak Park, Ga., U.S.	D4	87
Oak Park, Il., U.S.	B6	90
Oak Park, Mi., U.S.	p15	99
Oak Point, Man.	D3	70
Oak Ridge, Fl., U.S.	*D5	86
Oak Ridge, La., U.S.	B4	95
Oak Ridge, Mo., U.S.	D8	102
Oak Ridge, N.C., U.S.	A3	110
Oak Ridge, Or., U.S.	D4	114
Oak Ridge, Tn., U.S.	C9	119
Oak Ridge Reservoir, res., N.J., U.S.	A3	107
Oak Ridges (part of Richmond Hill), Ont.	k15	73
Oak River, Man.	D1	70
Oaks, Ok., U.S.	A7	113
Oaks, Pa., U.S.	o20	115
Oakton, Ky., U.S.	f8	94
Oakton, Va., U.S.	g12	123
Oak Vale, Ms., U.S.	D4	101
Oakvale, W.V., U.S.	*D4	125
Oak Valley, N.J., U.S.	D2	107
Oakville, Man.	E2	70
Oakville, Ont.	D5	73
Oakville, Ct., U.S.	C3	84
Oakville, In., U.S.	D7	91
Oakville, Ia., U.S.	C6	92
Oakville, Mo., U.S.	g13	102
Oakville, Wa., U.S.	C2	124
Oakway, S.C., U.S.	B1	117
Oakwood, Ga., U.S.	B3	87
Oakwood, Il., U.S.	C6	90
Oakwood, N.D., U.S.	A8	111
Oakwood, Oh., U.S.	A1	112
Oakwood, Oh., U.S.	C1	112
Oakwood, Ok., U.S.	B3	113
Oakwood, Tx., U.S.	D5	120
Oakwood, Va., U.S.	e9	123
Oakwood Beach, N.J., U.S.	D1	107
Oamaru, N.Z.	P13	51
Ōamishirasato, Japan	n19	33
Oark, Ar., U.S.	B2	81
Oasis, Ut., U.S.	D3	121
Oatman, Az., U.S.	C1	80
Oats, Ut., U.S.	C7	121
Oaxaca, state, Mex.	D5	63
Oaxaca [de Juárez], Mex.	D5	63
Ob, stm., Sov. Un.	C9	29
Oba, Ont.	G16	66
Oba, Japan	n14	33
Obama, Japan	H8	33
Oban, Ont.	D1	70
Oban, Sask.	E1	75
Oban, Scot., U.K.	B4	10
O'Bannon, Ky., U.S.	g11	94
Ob Bay, Sov. Un.	C10	29
Obed, stm., Tn., U.S.	C9	119
Obed, Alta.	C2	68
Oberammergau, W. Ger.	B7	20
Oberdrauburg, Aus.	C8	20
Oberhausen, W. Ger.	C3	18
Oberkirch, W. Ger.	E3	19
Oberlin, Ks., U.S.	C3	93
Oberlin, La., U.S.	D3	95
Oberlin, Oh., U.S.	A3	112
Obernai, Fr.	D7	16
Obernburg [am Main], W. Ger.	D4	19
Oberösterreich, state, Aus.	E9	19
Oberstaufen, W. Ger.	B6	20
Oberstdorf, W. Ger.	E5	18
Obert, Ne., U.S.	B8	104
Oberursel, W. Ger.	C3	19
Oberwald, Switz.	C4	20
Obetz, Oh., U.S.	C3	112
Óbidos, Braz.	D5	91
Obihiro, Japan	C13	31
Obi Islands, is., Indon.	F7	34
Obion, Tn., U.S.	A2	119
Obion, co., Tn., U.S.	A2	119
Obion, stm., Tn., U.S.	A2	119
Obion, Middle Fork, stm., Tn., U.S.	A3	119
Obion, Rutherford Fork, stm., Tn., U.S.	A3	119
Obion, South Fork, stm., Tn., U.S.	A3	119
Obion Creek, stm., Ky., U.S.	f9	94
Oblachnaya, Mount, mtn., Sov. Un.	E7	33
Oblong, Il., U.S.	D6	90
Obluchye, Sov. Un.	E16	29
Obo, Cen. Afr. Rep.	D5	46
Obock, Dji.	C5	47
Oborniki, Pol.	B4	26
Oboyan, Sov. Un.	F11	27
O'Brien, Fl., U.S.	B4	86
O'Brien, co., Ia., U.S.	A2	92
Observation Peak, mtn., Ca., U.S.	B3	82
Obuasi, Ghana	E4	45
Obwalden, state, Switz.	C4	20
Ocala, Fl., U.S.	C4	86
Ocampo, Mex.	B3	63
Ocaña, Col.	B3	60
Ocaña, Spain	C4	22
Ocate, N.M., U.S.	A5	108
Occidental, Cordillera, mts., Col.	C2	60
Occidental, Cordillera, mts., Peru	D3	58
Occidental, Cordillera, mts., S.A.	C2	55
Ocean, co., N.J., U.S.	D4	107
Oceana, W.V., U.S.	D3	125
Oceana, co., Mi., U.S.	E4	99
Oceana Naval Air Station, mil., Va., U.S.	k15	123
Ocean Bluff, Ma., U.S.	B6	98
Ocean City, Fl., U.S.	u15	86
Ocean City, Md., U.S.	D7	97
Ocean City, N.J., U.S.	E3	107
Ocean City, Wa., U.S.	B1	124
Ocean Falls, B.C.	C4	69
Ocean Gate, N.J., U.S.	D4	107
Ocean Grove, Ma., U.S.	C5	98
Ocean Grove, N.J., U.S.	C4	107
Ocean Heights, N.J., U.S.	E3	107
Ocean Park, Wa., U.S.	C1	124
Ocean Port, N.J., U.S.	C4	107
Oceanside, Ca., U.S.	F5	82
Oceanside, N.Y., U.S.	*E7	109
Ocean Springs, Ms., U.S.	E5	101
Ocean [Township], N.J., U.S.	C4	107
Ocean View, De., U.S.	F5	85
Ocean View, N.J., U.S.	E3	107
Oceanville, N.J., U.S.	E4	107
Ochakov, Sov. Un.	H8	27
Ocheda Lake, l., Mn., U.S.	G3	100
Ochelata, Ok., U.S.	A6	113
Ocheyedan, Ia., U.S.	A2	92
Ocheyedan, stm., Ia., U.S.	A2	92
Ochil Hills, hills, Scot., U.K.	B5	10
Ochiltree, co., Tx., U.S.	A2	120
Ochlockonee, stm., Fl., U.S.	B2	86
Ochoco Lake, res., Or., U.S.	C6	114
Ochopee, Fl., U.S.	G5	86
Ochre River, Man.	D2	70
Ochtrup, W. Ger.	A2	19
Ockelbo, Swe.	G7	14
Öckerö, i., Swe.	A5	15
Ocilla, Ga., U.S.	E3	87
Ocmulgee, stm., Ga., U.S.	D3	87
Ocmulgee National Monument, Ga., U.S.	D3	87
Ocna Mureș, Rom.	C7	24
Ocna-Sibiului, Rom.	C7	24
Ocnele Mari, Rom.	C7	24
Ocoee, Fl., U.S.	D5	86
Ocoee, Tn., U.S.	D9	119
Ocoee, Lake, res., Tn., U.S.	D9	119
Ocoltán, Mex.	C4	63
Ocoña, Peru	E3	58
Oconee, Ga., U.S.	D4	87
Oconee, Il., U.S.	D4	90
Oconee, co., Ga., U.S.	C3	87
Oconee, co., S.C., U.S.	B1	117
Oconee, stm., Ga., U.S.	C3	87
Oconee, Lake, res., Ga., U.S.	C3	87
Oconomowoc, Wi., U.S.	E5	126
Oconto, Ne., U.S.	C6	104
Oconto, Wi., U.S.	D6	126
Oconto, co., Wi., U.S.	D5	126
Oconto, stm., Wi., U.S.	C5	126
Oconto Falls, Wi., U.S.	D5	126
Ocós, Guat.	C1	62
Ocotal, Nic.	E7	63
Ocotillo, Az., U.S.	m9	80
Ocracoke, N.C., U.S.	B7	110
Ocracoke Inlet, b., N.C., U.S.	B6	110
Ocracoke Island, i., N.C., U.S.	B7	110
Ocros, Peru	D2	58
Octavia, Ne., U.S.	C8	104
Octavia, Ok., U.S.	C7	113
Octeville, Fr.	C3	16
October Revolution Island, i., Sov. Un.	B4	128
Octoraro Creek, stm., U.S.	A5	97
Ocumare del Tuy, Ven.	A4	60
Oda, Ghana	E4	45
Odanah, Wi., U.S.	B3	126
Ōdate, Japan	F10	33
Odawara, Japan	n18	33
Odd, W.V., U.S.	*D3	125
Odda, Nor.	G2	14
Odder, Den.	C4	15
Odebolt, Ia., U.S.	B2	92
Odei, stm., Man.	A3	70
Odell, Il., U.S.	B5	90
Odell, Ne., U.S.	D9	104
Odell, Or., U.S.	B5	114
Odell, Tx., U.S.	B3	120
Odell Lake, l., Or., U.S.	D5	114
Odem, Tx., U.S.	F4	120
Odemira, Port.	D1	22
Odemiş, Tur.	C7	40
Oden, Ar., U.S.	C2	81
Odendaalsrus, S. Afr.	C4	49
Odensbacken (part of Örebro), Swe.	t35	14
Odense, Den.	J4	14
Odense [å, stm., Den.	C4	15
Odenton, Md., U.S.	B4	97
Odenville, Al., U.S.	B3	78
Odenwald, mts., W. Ger.	D3	19
Oder (Odra), stm., Eur.	B3	26
Oder Spree Canal, E. Ger.	A9	19
Odessa, Ont.	C8	73
Odessa, Sask.	G4	75
Odessa, Sov. Un.	E6	29
Odessa, De., U.S.	C3	85
Odessa, Fl., U.S.	*D4	86
Odessa, Mo., U.S.	C4	102
Odessa, N.Y., U.S.	C4	109
Odessa, Tx., U.S.	D1	120
Odessa, Wa., U.S.	B7	124
Odiel, stm., Spain	D2	22
Odienné, I.C.	E3	45
Odin, Il., U.S.	E4	90
Odin, Mn., U.S.	G4	100
Odin, Mount, mtn., B.C.	D8	69
Odivelas, Port.	f9	22
Odon, In., U.S.	G4	91
O'Donnell, Tx., U.S.	C2	120
Odorheiu Secuiesc, Rom.	B7	24
Odra (Oder), stm., Eur.	B3	26
Odum, Ga., U.S.	E4	87
Odzi, Zimb.	A5	49
Oebisfelde, E. Ger.	A5	19
Oeiras, Braz.	B3	57
Oeiras, Port.	f9	22
Oelde, W. Ger.	B3	19
Oelrichs, S.D., U.S.	D2	118
Oelsnitz [im Erzgebirge], E. Ger.	C6	18
Oelsnitz [im Vogtland], E. Ger.	C7	19
Oelwein, Ia., U.S.	B6	92
Oensingen, Switz.	B4	21
Oesede, W. Ger.	A5	19
Oettingen [in Bayern], W. Ger.	E5	19
Oeyön Island, i., S. Kor.	H2	33
Ofahoma, Ms., U.S.	C4	101
O'Fallon, Il., U.S.	f12	102
O'Fallon, Mo., U.S.	f12	102
O'Fallon Creek, stm., Mt., U.S.	D5	103
Ofanto, stm., Italy	D5	23
Ofaqim, Isr.	D4	43
Offa, Nig.	*E5	45
Offaly, co., Ire.	B4	10
Offenbach [am Main], W. Ger.	C4	18
Offenburg, W. Ger.	D3	18
Offence, Mount of, hist., Isr. Occ.	m14	41
Offerle, Ks., U.S.	E4	93
Offerman, Ga., U.S.	E4	87
Offutt Air Force Base, mil., Ne., U.S.	g3	104
Oficina Pedro de Valdivia, Chile	A2	54
Ofringen, Switz.	B4	21
Ōfunato, Japan	G10	33
Oga, Japan	G9	33
Ōgaki, Japan	I8	33
Ogallah, Ks., U.S.	C4	93
Ogallala, Ne., U.S.	C4	104
Oga Peninsula, pen., Japan	G10	33
Ogbomosho, Nig.	E6	45
Ogden, Ar., U.S.	D1	81
Ogden, Ia., U.S.	B3	92
Ogden, Il., U.S.	C5	90
Ogden, Ks., U.S.	C7	93
Ogden, Ut., U.S.	B4	121
Ogden, Mount, mtn., Ak., U.S.	k23	79
Ogdensburg, N.J., U.S.	A3	107
Ogdensburg, N.Y., U.S.	f9	109
Ogdensburg, Wi., U.S.	D5	126
Ogeechee, stm., Ga., U.S.	D5	87
Ogema, Sask.	C3	75
Ogema, Mn., U.S.	D3	100
Ogema, Wi., U.S.	C3	126
Ogemaw, co., Mi., U.S.	D6	99
Ogilvie, Mn., U.S.	E5	100
Ogilvie Mountains, mts., Yukon	D5	66
Oglala, S.D., U.S.	D3	118
Ogle, co., Il., U.S.	A4	90
Oglesby, Il., U.S.	B5	90
Oglesby, Ok., U.S.	A6	113

Index

Name	Map Ref.	Page
Oglethorpe, Ga., U.S.	D2	87
Oglethorpe, co., Ga., U.S.	C3	87
Oglethorpe, Mount, mtn., Ga., U.S.	B2	87
Oglio, stm., Italy	B3	23
Ognon, stm., Fr.	B1	20
Ogoamas, mtn., Indon.	E6	34
Ogoja, Nig.	E6	45
Ogoki, stm., Ont.	o15	73
Ogooué, stm., Afr.	F2	46
Ogosta, stm., Bul.	D6	24
Ogrodzieniec, Pol.	g11	26
Ogulin, Yugo.	C2	24
Ogunquit, Me., U.S.	E2	96
Ogurchinskiy Island, i., Sov. Un.	B6	39
Ohakune, N.Z.	M15	51
Ohanet, Alg.	D6	44
O'Hanly, stm., Man.	D4	70
Ōhara, Japan	n19	33
Ohatchee, Al., U.S.	B3	78
Ohaton, Alta.	C4	68
O'Higgins, Lago (Lago San Martín), l., S.A.	D2	54
Ohio, Co., U.S.	C4	83
Ohio, Il., U.S.	B4	90
Ohio, N.Y., U.S.	B6	109
Ohio, co., In., U.S.	G7	91
Ohio, co., Ky., U.S.	C3	94
Ohio, co., W.V., U.S.	A4	125
Ohio, state, U.S.	B3	112
Ohio, stm., U.S.	C11	76
Ohio Brush Creek, stm., Oh., U.S.	D2	112
Ohio City, Oh., U.S.	B1	112
Ohio Peak, mtn., Co., U.S.	C3	83
Ohiopyle, Pa., U.S.	G3	115
Ohioville, Pa., U.S.	E1	115
Ohiowa, Ne., U.S.	D8	104
Ohlman, Il., U.S.	D4	90
Ohoopee, Ga., U.S.	D4	87
Ohoopee, stm., Ga., U.S.	D4	87
Ohopoho, Nmb.	A1	49
Ohrdruf, E. Ger.	C5	19
Ohře, stm., Eur.	C2	26
Ohrid, Yugo.	E5	24
Ohrid, Lake, l., Eur.	E5	24
Ohrigstad, S. Afr.	B5	49
Öhringen, W. Ger.	D4	19
Oiapoque, Braz.	B4	59
Oiapoque (Oyapock), stm., S.A.	B4	59
Oies, Île aux, i., Que.	B7	74
Oikull, Palau	R17	52
Oil Center, N.M., U.S.	E6	108
Oil City, La., U.S.	B2	95
Oil City, Ms., U.S.	C3	101
Oil City, Pa., U.S.	D2	115
Oil Creek, stm., Pa., U.S.	C2	115
Oildale, Ca., U.S.	E4	82
Oilmont, Mt., U.S.	B5	103
Oil Springs, Ont.	E2	73
Oilton, Ok., U.S.	A5	113
Oilton, Tx., U.S.	F3	120
Oil Trough, Ar., U.S.	B4	81
Oir, Beinn an, mtn., Scot., U.K.		
Oise, dept., Fr.	E2	17
Oise, stm., Eur.	E2	17
Oiseau, stm., Can.	D4	70
Oisemont, Fr.	E9	12
Ō Island, i., Japan	F9	33
Ō Island, i., Japan	I9	33
Oita, Japan	J5	33
Oiticica, Braz.	C2	57
Ojai, Ca., U.S.	E4	82
Ojinaga, Mex.	B4	63
Ojocaliente, Mex.	C4	63
Ojo Caliente, N.M., U.S.	A3	108
Ojo Feliz, N.M., U.S.	A4	108
Ojo Feliz, N.M., U.S.	A4	108
Ojos del Salado, Nevado, mtn., S.A.	E2	55
Oka, Que.	D3	74
Oka, Nig.	E6	45
Oka, stm., Sov. Un.	C14	27
Okaba, Indon.	G9	34
Okabena, Mn., U.S.	G3	100
Okahandja, Nmb.	B2	49
Okak Islands, is., Newf.	g9	72
Okaloosa, co., Fl., U.S.	u15	86
Okamanpeedan Lake, l., U.S.	A3	92
Okanagan Centre, B.C.	D8	69
Okanagan Falls, B.C.	E8	69
Okanagan Lake, l., B.C.	D8	69
Okanagan Landing, B.C.	D8	69
Okanagan Range, mts., N.A.	E7	69
Okanogan, Wa., U.S.	A6	124
Okanogan, co., Wa., U.S.	A5	124
Okanogan, stm., N.A.	A6	124
Okapilco Creek, stm., Ga., U.S.	E3	87
Okāra, Pak.	B4	37
Okarche, Ok., U.S.	B4	113
Okatibee Reservoir, res., Ms., U.S.	C5	101
Okatoma Creek, stm., Ms., U.S.	D4	101
Okaton, S.D., U.S.	D5	118
Okauchee, Wi., U.S.	*E5	126
Okauchee Lake, l., Wi., U.S.	E5	126
Okaukuejo, Nmb.	A2	49
Okavango, stm., Afr.	H7	42
Okavango Swamps, sw., Bots.	A3	49
Okawville, Il., U.S.	E4	90
Okay, Ok., U.S.	B6	113
Okaya, Japan	H8	33
Okayama, Japan	E11	31
Okazaki, Japan	o16	33
O'Kean, Ar., U.S.	A5	81
Okeana, Oh., U.S.	n12	112
Okęcie (part of Warsaw), Pol.	m13	26
Okeechobee, Fl., U.S.	E6	86
Okeechobee, co., Fl., U.S.	E6	86
Okeechobee, Lake, l., Fl., U.S.	F6	86
Okeene, Ok., U.S.	A3	113
Okefenokee Swamp, sw., U.S.	F4	87
Okehampton, Eng., U.K.	K8	10
Okemah, Ok., U.S.	B5	113
Okemos, Mi., U.S.	*F6	99
Oker, stm., W. Ger.	F4	15
Okesa, Ok., U.S.	A5	113
Oketo, Ks., U.S.	C7	93
Okfuskee, co., Ok., U.S.	B5	113
Okha, Sov. Un.	D17	29
Okhotsk, Sov. Un.	D17	29
Okhotsk, Sea of, Asia	D17	29
Okiep, S. Afr.	D2	49
Oki Islands, is., Japan	D11	31
Okinawa Island, i., Japan	F10	31
Oklahoma, co., Ok., U.S.	B4	113
Oklahoma, state, U.S.	B4	113
Oklahoma City, Ok., U.S.	B4	113
Oklawaha, Fl., U.S.	C5	86
Oklawaha, stm., Fl., U.S.	C5	86
Oklawaha, Lake, res., Fl., U.S.	C5	86
Oklee, Mn., U.S.	C3	100
Okmulgee, Ok., U.S.	B6	113
Okmulgee, co., Ok., U.S.	B5	113
Okoboji, Ia., U.S.	A2	92
Okobojo Creek, stm., S.D., U.S.	C5	118
Okolona, Ar., U.S.	D2	81
Okolona, Ky., U.S.	g11	94
Okolona, Ms., U.S.	B5	101
Okondja, Gabon	F2	46
Okotoks, Alta.	D4	68
Okreek, S.D., U.S.	D5	118
Okrika, Nig.	B6	113
Oktibbeha, co., Ms., U.S.	B5	101
Oktyabrsk, Sov. Un.	D5	28
Oktyabrskiy, Sov. Un.	C4	28
Okulovka, Sov. Un.	C4	28
Okuma Bay, b., Ant.	B32	7
Okushiri, Japan	E9	33
Okushiri Island, i., Japan	E9	33
Ola, Ar., U.S.	B2	81
Ola, Id., U.S.	E2	89
Ólafsfjörður, Ice.	m23	14
Ólafsvík, Ice.	n21	14
Olalla, Wa., U.S.	f10	124
Olamon, Me., U.S.	C4	96
Olancha, Ca., U.S.	D5	82
Olancha Peak, mtn., Ca., U.S.	D4	82
Olanchito, Hond.	C4	62
Öland, i., Swe.	I7	14
Olanta, Pa., U.S.	E4	115
Olanta, S.C., U.S.	D8	117
Olar, S.C., U.S.	E5	117
Olascoaga, Arg.	B4	56
Olathe, Co., U.S.	C3	83
Olathe, Ks., U.S.	D9	93
Olavarría, Arg.	B4	56
Olazagutía, Spain	A4	22
Olberg, Az., U.S.	D4	80
Olbernhau, E. Ger.	C8	19
Olbia, Italy	D2	23
Olcott, N.Y., U.S.	B2	109
Olcott, W.V., U.S.	C3	125
Old Bahama Channel, strt., N.A.	C4	64
Old Bennington, Vt., U.S.	F2	122
Old Bethpage, N.Y., U.S.	*n15	109
Old Bight, Bah.	B6	64
Old Bridge, N.J., U.S.	C4	107
Old Castile, hist. reg., Spain	B4	22
Oldcastle, Ire.	D4	11
Old Crow, Yukon	C5	66
Oldeani, Tan.	B6	48
Olden, Tx., U.S.	C3	120
Oldenburg, W. Ger.	B4	18
Oldenburg [in Holstein], W. Ger.	A5	18
Oldenzaal, Neth.	B6	17
Old Faithful Geyser, Wy., U.S.	B2	127
Old Forge, N.Y., U.S.	B6	109
Old Forge, Pa., U.S.	D10	115
Old Fort, N.C., U.S.	f10	110
Old Fort, Oh., U.S.	A2	112
Old Fort Bay, Que.	C3	72
Oldham, Eng., U.K.	D5	10
Oldham, S.D., U.S.	C8	118
Oldham, co., Ky., U.S.	B4	94
Oldham, co., Tx., U.S.	B1	120
Old Harbor, Ak., U.S.	D9	79
Old Harbour Bay, Jam.	F14	65
Old Head of Kinsale, c., Ire.	E2	10
Old Hickory Lake, res., Tn., U.S.	A5	119
Old Lyme, Ct., U.S.	D6	84
Oldman, stm., Alta.	E4	68
Old Man Mountain, mtn., Newf.	D3	72
Old Man of the Mountain, N.H., U.S.	B3	106
Oldmans Creek, stm., N.J., U.S.	D2	107
Oldmeldrum, Scot., U.K.	C6	13
Old Mkushi, Zam.	D4	48
Old Monroe, Mo., U.S.	C7	102
Old Mystic, Ct., U.S.	D8	84
Old Northwood, N.H., U.S.	D4	106
Old Orchard Beach, Me., U.S.	E2	96
Old Perlican, Newf.	D5	72
Old Point Comfort, c., Va., U.S.	h15	123
Old Rhodes Key, i., Fl., U.S.	G6	86
Old Ripley, Il., U.S.	E4	90
Old River Lake, l., Ar., U.S.	k10	81
Olds, Alta.	D3	68
Olds, Ia., U.S.	C6	92
Old Saybrook, Ct., U.S.	D6	84
Oldsmar, Fl., U.S.	o10	86
Old Speck Mountain, mtn., Me., U.S.	D2	96
Old Tampa Bay, b., Fl., U.S.	p10	86
Old Tappan, N.J., U.S.	g9	107
Old Tate, Bots.	B4	49
Old Topsail Inlet, b., N.C., U.S.	C5	110
Old Town, Fl., U.S.	C4	86
Old Town, Id., U.S.	A1	89
Old Town, Me., U.S.	D4	96
Oldtown, Md., U.S.	k13	97
Old Village, N.Y., U.S.	*E7	109
Old Washington, Oh., U.S.	B4	112
Oldwick, N.J., U.S.	B3	107
Old Wives, Sask.	G2	75
Old Wives Lake, l., Sask.	G2	75
Olean, Mo., U.S.	C5	102
Olean, N.Y., U.S.	C2	109
O'Leary, P.E.I.	C5	71
Olecko, Pol.	A7	26
Oleiros, Spain	A1	22
Olekma, stm., Sov. Un.	D15	29
Olekminsk, Sov. Un.	C15	29
Olenek, stm., Sov. Un.	C14	29
Olentangy, stm., Oh., U.S.	B3	112
Oléron, Île d', i., Fr.	E3	16
Oleśnica (Oels), Pol.	C4	26
Olesno, Pol.	C5	26
Olëtang, Braz.	C3	56
Olin, Ia., U.S.	B6	92
Olinda, Braz.	C4	57
Olionono, Cape, c., W. Sam.	F12	52
Olite, Spain	A5	22
Oliva, Spain	C5	22
Oliva de la Frontera, Spain	C2	22
Olivais, Port.	i9	22
Olive, Mt., U.S.	E11	103
Olive, Ok., U.S.	A5	113
Olive Branch, Il., U.S.	F4	90
Olive Branch, Ms., U.S.	A4	101
Olive Hill, Ky., U.S.	B6	94
Olivehill, Tn., U.S.	B3	119
Olivehurst, Ca., U.S.	C3	82
Oliveira, Braz.	C4	56
Olivenza, Spain	C2	22
Oliver, B.C.	E8	69
Oliver, Al., U.S.	A2	78
Oliver, Ga., U.S.	D5	87
Oliver, Il., U.S.	D6	90
Oliver, Pa., U.S.	G2	115
Oliver, Wi., U.S.	B1	126
Oliver, co., N.D., U.S.	B4	111
Oliver Dam, U.S.	C5	78
Oliver Springs, Tn., U.S.	C9	119
Olivet, Il., U.S.	D6	90
Olivet, Ks., U.S.	D8	93
Olivet, Md., U.S.	D5	97
Olivet, Mi., U.S.	F6	99
Olivet, S.D., U.S.	D8	118
Olivette, Mo., U.S.	*f13	102
Olivia, Mn., U.S.	F4	100
Olivia, N.C., U.S.	B3	110
Öljaren, l., Swe.	t34	14
Ölkusz, Pol.	g11	26
Olla, La., U.S.	C3	95
Ollagüe, Chile	D2	55
Ollei, Palau	R17	52
Ollie, Ia., U.S.	C5	92
Olmito, Tx., U.S.	F4	120
Olmitz, Ks., U.S.	D5	93
Olmos, Peru	C2	58
Olmos Park, Tx., U.S.	k7	120
Olmsted, Ky., U.S.	D2	94
Olmstead, Ut., U.S.	*C4	121
Olmsted, co., Mn., U.S.	G6	100
Olmsted Falls, Oh., U.S.	h9	112
Olmstedville, N.Y., U.S.	B7	109
Olney, Il., U.S.	E5	90
Olney, Md., U.S.	B3	97
Olney, Mo., U.S.	B6	102
Olney, Mt., U.S.	B2	103
Olney, Tx., U.S.	C3	120
Olney Springs, Co., U.S.	C7	83
Oloh, Ms., U.S.	D4	101
Olomouc, Czech.	C4	26
Olongapo, Phil.	o13	34
Oloron, Gave d', stm., Fr.	F3	16
Oloron-Sainte-Marie, Fr.	F3	16
Olot, Spain	A7	22
Olowalu, Hi., U.S.	C5	88
Olpe, W. Ger.	B2	19
Olpe, Ks., U.S.	D7	93
Olsburg, Ks., U.S.	C7	93
Olše, stm., Eur.	h9	26
Olshany, Sov. Un.	F10	27
Olst, Neth.	B6	17
Olsztyn (Allenstein), Pol.	B6	26
Olt, stm., Rom.	C7	24
Olten, Switz.	E3	18
Oltenița, Rom.	C9	24
Oltenia, hist. reg., Rom.	C6	24
Oltet, stm., Rom.	C6	24
Oltu, Tur.	B13	40
Olupona, Nig.	*E5	45
Olustee, Fl., U.S.	*E5	86
Olustee, Ok., U.S.	C2	113
Olvera, Spain	D3	22
Olvey, Ar., U.S.	A3	81
Olympia, Ky., U.S.	B6	94
Olympia, Wa., U.S.	B3	124
Olympia, hist., Grc.	D3	25
Olympia Heights, Fl., U.S.	*s13	86
Olympic Mountains, mts., Wa., U.S.	B2	124
Olympic National Park, Wa., U.S.	B2	124
Olympus, Mount, mtn., Grc.	B4	40
Olympus, Mount, mtn., Ky., U.S.	B6	94
Olympus, Mount, mtn., Wa., U.S.	B2	124
Olyphant, Ar., U.S.	B4	81
Olyphant, Pa., U.S.	D10	115
Olyutorski, Cape, c., Sov. Un.	D20	29
Om, stm., Sov. Un.	B9	28
Oma, Ar., U.S.	g7	81
Oma, Ms., U.S.	D3	101
Oma, stm., Japan	o17	33
Omae, Cape, c., Japan	o17	33
Omagh, N. Ire., U.K.	C3	10
Omaguas, Peru	B3	58
Omaha, Ar., U.S.	A2	81
Omaha, Ga., U.S.	D1	87
Omaha, Il., U.S.	F5	90
Omaha, Ne., U.S.	C10	104
Omaha Indian Reservation, Ne., U.S.	B9	104
Omak, Wa., U.S.	A6	124
Omak Lake, l., Wa., U.S.	A6	124
Oman, ctry., Asia	C5	38
Oman, Gulf of, b., Asia	C6	38
Omao, W.V., U.S.	D3	125
Omarama, N.Z.	P12	51
Omaruru, Nmb.	B2	49
Omas, Peru	D2	58
Omboué, Gabon	F1	46
Ombrone, stm., Italy	C3	23
Omdurman (Umm Durmān), Sud.	B3	47
Omega, Ga., U.S.	E3	87
Omega, N.M., U.S.	C1	108
Omega, Oh., U.S.	C3	112
Omegna, Italy	C2	23
Omemee, Ont.	C6	73
Omeo, Austl.	H6	51
Omer, Mi., U.S.	D7	99
Omerville, Que.	D5	74
Ometepe, Isla de, i., Nic.	C5	62
Ometepec, Mex.	D5	63
Om Hajer, Eth.	C4	47
Omigawa, Japan	n19	33
Omineca, stm., B.C.	B5	69
Omineca Mountains, mts., B.C.	A4	69
Ōmiya, Japan	I9	33
Ōmiya, Japan	o15	33
Ommaney, Cape, c., Ak., U.S.	D12	79
Ommen, Neth.	B6	17
Omø, i., Den.	C5	15
Omo, stm., Eth.	G7	42
Omoa, Braz.	C4	57
Omolon, stm., Sov. Un.	C18	29
Ompompanoosuc, stm., Vt., U.S.	D4	122
Ompompanoosuc, West Branch, stm., Vt., U.S.	D4	122
Omro, Wi., U.S.	D5	126
Ōmuta, Japan	J5	33
Omutninsk, Sov. Un.	D19	8
Ona, Fl., U.S.	E5	86
Onaga, Ks., U.S.	C7	93
Onaka, S.D., U.S.	B6	118
Onalaska, Wa., U.S.	C3	124
Onalaska, Wi., U.S.	E2	126
Onamia, Mn., U.S.	D5	100
Onancock, Va., U.S.	C7	123
Onanole, Man.	D2	70
Onao, Il., Micron.	Q18	52
Onarga, Il., U.S.	C6	90
Onawa, Ia., U.S.	B1	92
Onawa, Me., U.S.	C3	96
Onawa, Lake, l., Me., U.S.	C3	96
Onaway, Id., U.S.	*C2	89
Onaway, Mi., U.S.	C6	99
Onchiota, N.Y., U.S.	f10	109
Onda, Spain	C5	22
Ondangua, Nmb.	A2	49
Ondava, stm., Czech.	D6	26
Ondjiva (Ngiva), Ang.	E2	48
Ondo, Nig.	E5	45
Ondörhaan, Mong.	B7	31
Oneata, i., Fiji	I16	52
Oneco, Ct., U.S.	C8	84
Oneco, Fl., U.S.	E4	86
Onega, Sov. Un.	C6	29
Onega, stm., Sov. Un.	C16	8
Onega, Lake, l., Sov. Un.	C6	29
One Hundred Fifty Mile House, B.C.	C7	69
One Hundred Mile House, B.C.	D7	69
Oneida, Il., U.S.	B3	90
Oneida, Ky., U.S.	C6	94
Oneida, N.Y., U.S.	B5	109
Oneida, Oh., U.S.	C1	112
Oneida, Tn., U.S.	C9	119
Oneida, co., Id., U.S.	G6	89
Oneida, co., N.Y., U.S.	B5	109
Oneida, co., Wi., U.S.	C4	126
Oneida Lake, l., N.Y., U.S.	B5	109
O'Neill, Ne., U.S.	B7	104
Onekama, Mi., U.S.	D4	99
Onekotan, Island, i., Marsh Is.	S17	52
Oneonta, Al., U.S.	B3	78
Oneonta, N.Y., U.S.	C5	109
Ong, Ne., U.S.	D8	104
Ongea Levu, i., Fiji	I16	52
Ongiin Hiid, Mong.	B5	31
Ongjin, stm., Mong.	B5	31
Ongjin, N. Kor.	H2	33
Onida, S.D., U.S.	C5	118
Onilahy, stm., Madag.	h8	49
Oniotto Island, i., Marsh Is.	S17	52
Onitsha, Nig.	E6	45
Onley, Va., U.S.	C7	123
Only, Tn., U.S.	B4	119
Onna, Japan	O5	52
Ōno, Japan	n15	33
Ono, i., Fiji	I15	52
Ono Channel, strt., Fiji	I15	52
Onomichi, Japan	I6	33
Onondaga, Mi., U.S.	F6	99
Onondaga, co., N.Y., U.S.	C4	109
Onondaga Indian Reservation, N.Y., U.S.	C4	109
Onota Lake, l., Ma., U.S.	B1	98
Onoway, Alta.	C3	68
Onset, Ma., U.S.	C6	98
Onslow, Austl.	D2	50
Onslow, co., N.C., U.S.	C5	110
Onslow Bay, b., N.C., U.S.	C5	110
Onsong, N. Kor.	F6	99
Onsted, Mi., U.S.	F6	99
Ontake, Mount, mtn., Japan	n16	33
Ontario, Ca., U.S.	E5	82
Ontario, N.Y., U.S.	B3	109
Ontario, Oh., U.S.	B3	112
Ontario, Or., U.S.	C10	114
Ontario, Wi., U.S.	E3	126
Ontario, co., N.Y., U.S.	C3	109
Ontario, prov., Can.	C6	73
Ontario, Lake, l., N.A.	B12	76
Onteniente, Spain	C5	22
Ontonagon, Mi., U.S.	m12	99
Ontonagon, co., Mi., U.S.	m12	99
Ontonagon Indian Reservation, Mi., U.S.	B1	99
Onward, In., U.S.	C5	91
Oodnadatta, Austl.	E6	50
Ood Weyne, Som.	D6	47
Ooka, Hi., U.S.	G4	91
Oolitic, In., U.S.	G4	91
Oologah, Ok., U.S.	A6	113
Oologah Lake, res., Ok., U.S.	A6	113
Ooltewah, Tn., U.S.	D8	119
Ooltgensplaat, Neth.	C4	17
Oostburg, Wi., U.S.	E6	126
Oostende (Ostende), Bel.	B5	16
Oosterend, Neth.	A5	17
Oosterhout, Neth.	C4	17
Oosterschelde, b., Bel.	C4	17
Oostmahorn, Neth.	A5	17
Oostpunt, c., Neth. Ant.	H19	65
Oost-Vlieland, Neth.	A5	17
Oostvoorne, Neth.	C4	17
Ootsa Lake, B.C.	C4	69
Ootsa Lake, l., B.C.	C4	69
Opal, Alta.	C4	68
Opal, S.D., U.S.	C3	118
Opal, Wy., U.S.	E2	127
Opal Cliffs, Ca., U.S.	*D3	82
Opala, Zaire	B3	48
Opa-Locka, Fl., U.S.	s13	86
Opatów, Pol.	C6	26
Opava, Czech.	C4	26
Opelika, Al., U.S.	C4	78
Opelousas, La., U.S.	D3	95
Opeongo, stm., Ont.	B7	73
Opeongo Lake, l., Ont.	B7	73
Opequon Creek, stm., W.V., U.S.	B6	125
Opfikon, Switz.		
Opheim, Mt., U.S.	B10	103
Ophir, Or., U.S.	E2	114
Ophir, Ut., U.S.	C3	121
Ophir, Mount, mtn., Indon.	E1	34
Opihikao, Hi., U.S.	D7	88
Opiscotéo, Lac, l., Que.	F19	66
Opobo, Nig.	F6	45
Opochka, Sov. Un.	C7	27
Opoczno, Pol.	C6	26
Opole, Pol.	C4	8
Opole Lubelskie, Pol.	C7	26
Oporto see Porto, Port.	B1	22
Opotiki, N.Z.	M16	51
Opp, Al., U.S.	D3	78
Oppdal, Nor.	C4	8
Oppelo, Ar., U.S.	B3	81
Opportunity, Wa., U.S.	B8	124
Optic Lake, Man.	B1	70
Optima, Ok., U.S.	e9	113
Optima Reservoir, res., Ok., U.S.	e9	113
Oppyan, Puntan, c., N. Mar. Is.	D7	52
Oquawka, Il., U.S.	C3	90
Oquossoc, Me., U.S.	D2	96
Ora, Italy	C7	20
Ora, In., U.S.	B4	91
Ora, Ms., U.S.	D4	101
Ora, S.C., U.S.	B4	117
Oracle, Az., U.S.	E5	80
Oradea, Rom.	B5	24
Oradell, N.J., U.S.	h8	107
Oradell Reservoir, res., N.J., U.S.	h9	107
Orai, India	E7	37
Oraibi, Az., U.S.	B5	80
Oraibi Wash, val., Az., U.S.	A5	80
Oral, S.D., U.S.	D2	118
Oran (Wahran), Alg.	A4	44
Oran, Ia., U.S.	B5	92
Oran, Mo., U.S.	D8	102
Orange, Austl.	F8	50
Orange, Fr.	E6	16
Orange, Ca., U.S.	n13	82
Orange, Ct., U.S.	D3	84
Orange, In., U.S.	E7	91
Orange, Ma., U.S.	A3	98
Orange, N.H., U.S.	C3	106
Orange, N.J., U.S.	B4	107
Orange, Tx., U.S.	D6	120
Orange, Vt., U.S.	C4	122
Orange, Va., U.S.	B4	123
Orange, co., Ca., U.S.	F5	82
Orange, co., Fl., U.S.	D5	86
Orange, co., In., U.S.	G4	91
Orange, co., N.Y., U.S.	D6	109
Orange, co., N.C., U.S.	A3	110
Orange, co., Tx., U.S.	D6	120
Orange, co., Vt., U.S.	D3	122
Orange, co., Va., U.S.	B4	123
Orange, Cabo, c., Braz.	B4	59
Orange Beach, Al., U.S.	E2	78
Orangeburg, S.C., U.S.	E6	117
Orangeburg, co., S.C., U.S.	E6	117
Orange City, Fl., U.S.	D5	86
Orange City, Ia., U.S.	B1	92
Orangedale, N.S.	D8	71
Orange Free State, prov., S. Afr.	C4	49
Orange Grove, Ms., U.S.	E5	101
Orange Grove, Tx., U.S.	F4	120
Orange Lake, Fl., U.S.	C4	86
Orange Lake, l., Fl., U.S.	C4	86
Orange Park, Fl., U.S.	B5	86
Orangevale, Ca., U.S.	*C3	82
Orangeville, Ont.	D4	73
Orangeville, Il., U.S.	A4	90
Orangeville, Ut., U.S.	D4	121
Orange Walk, Belize	D7	63
Orléans, Braz.	D3	56
Orani, Phil.	o13	34
Oranienbaum, E. Ger.	B7	19
Oranienburg, E. Ger.	B6	18
Oranje Gebergte, mts., Sur.	B4	59
Oranjemund, Nmb.	C2	49
Oranjestad, Aruba	G17	65
Oranmore, Ire.	D3	11
Or 'Aqiva, Isr.	B4	41
Orăştie, Rom.	C6	24
Oravita, Rom.	C5	24
Orba, stm., Italy	E4	20
Orbe, Switz.	C2	21
Orbetello, Italy	C3	23
Orbey, Fr.	A3	20
Orbigo, stm., Spain	B4	22
Orbisonia, Pa., U.S.	F6	115
Orbost, Austl.	H7	51
Orby, Swe.	A6	15
Orcas Island, i., Wa., U.S.	A3	124
Orchard, Co., U.S.	A6	83
Orchard, Id., U.S.	F2	89
Orchard, Ne., U.S.	B7	104
Orchard City, Co., U.S.	C3	83
Orchard Farm, Mo., U.S.	f13	102
Orchard Homes, Mt., U.S.	D2	103
Orchard Mesa, Co., U.S.	*B2	83
Orchard Park, N.Y., U.S.	C2	109
Orchards, Wa., U.S.	D3	124
Orchard Valley, Wy., U.S.	E8	127
Orchies, Fr.	B10	16
Orchila, Isla, i., Ven.	A4	60
Orcutt, Ca., U.S.	E3	82
Orcutts, Ct., U.S.	B6	84
Ord, Ne., U.S.	C7	104
Ord, stm., Austl.	C4	50
Ord, Mount, mtn., Austl.	C4	50
Ordale, Sask.	D2	75
Ordenes, Spain	A1	22
Orderville, Ut., U.S.	F3	121
Ording, W. Ger.	D2	15
Ordos Desert see Mu Us Shamo, des., China	D6	31
Ordot, Guam	L10	52
Ordu, Tur.	B11	40
Orduña, Spain	A4	22
Ordway, Co., U.S.	C7	83
Ordzhonikidze (Dzaudzhikau), Sov. Un.	E7	29
Oreana, Il., U.S.	D5	90
Oreana, Nv., U.S.	C3	105
Örebro, Swe.	H6	14
Ore City, Tx., U.S.	C5	120
Oregon, Il., U.S.	A4	90
Oregon, Mo., U.S.	B2	102
Oregon, Oh., U.S.	A2	112
Oregon, Wi., U.S.	F4	126
Oregon, co., Mo., U.S.	E6	102
Oregon, state, U.S.	C6	114
Oregon Caves National Monument, Or., U.S.	E2	114
Oregon City, Or., U.S.	B4	114
Orekhovo, Bul.	D6	24
Orekhovo-Zuyevo, Sov. Un.	D12	27
Orel, Sov. Un.	D6	29
Orem, Ut., U.S.	C4	121
Ore Mountains, mts., Eur.	C6	18
Orenburg, Sov. Un.	D8	29
Orense, Spain	A2	22
Orestes, In., U.S.	D6	91
Orestiás, Grc.	B6	40
Øresund (The Sound), strt., Eur.	J5	14
Oretti, stm., N.Z.	P12	51
Oretta, La., U.S.	D2	95
Orford, Mont., mtn., Que.	D5	74
Orford Ness, c., Eng., U.K.	B9	12
Orfordville, N.H., U.S.	C2	106
Orfordville, Wi., U.S.	F4	126
Organ, N.M., U.S.	E3	108
Organ Cave, W.V., U.S.	D4	125
Organ Mountains, mts., N.M., U.S.	E3	108
Organ Pipe Cactus National Monument, Az., U.S.	E3	80
Orgaz, Spain	C4	22
Orgelet, Fr.	C1	20
Orgeyev, Sov. Un.	H7	27
Orgün, Afg.	B4	36
Orhon, stm., Mong.	B6	31
Orick, Ca., U.S.	B1	82
Orient, Il., U.S.	F5	90
Orient, Ia., U.S.	C3	92
Orient, Me., U.S.	C5	96
Orient, N.Y., U.S.	m16	109
Orient, Oh., U.S.	C2	112
Orient, S.D., U.S.	C6	118
Orient, Wa., U.S.	A7	124
Orienta, Ok., U.S.	A3	113
Oriental, N.C., U.S.	B6	110
Oriental, Cordillera, mts., Col.	C3	60
Orihuela, Spain	C5	22
Orillia, Ont.	C5	73
Orinda, Ca., U.S.	*h8	82
Orinoco, stm., S.A.	B6	60
Oriole, Md., U.S.	D6	97
Orion, Alta.	E5	68
Orion, Phil.	o13	34
Orion, Il., U.S.	B3	90
Oriska, N.D., U.S.	C8	111
Oriskany, N.Y., U.S.	B5	109
Oriskany, Va., U.S.	C3	123
Oriskany Falls, N.Y., U.S.	C5	109
Orissa, state, India	E7	36
Oristano, Italy	E2	23
Oristano, Gulf of, b., Italy	E2	23
Orivesi, l., Fin.	F13	14
Oriximiná, Braz.	C3	59
Orizaba, Mex.	D5	63
Orizaba, Pico de (Citlaltépetl), vol., Mex.	n15	63
Orizona, Braz.	B3	56
Orkanger, Nor.	F3	14
Örkelljunga, Swe.	B7	15
Orkla, stm., Nor.	F4	14
Orkney, Sask.	H2	75
Orkney, prov., Scot., U.K.	A5	13
Orkney Islands, is., Scot., U.K.	A5	13
Orla, Tx., U.S.	o13	120
Orland, Ca., U.S.	C2	82
Orland, In., U.S.	A7	91
Orland, Me., U.S.	D4	96
Orlando, Fl., U.S.	D5	86
Orlando, Ok., U.S.	A4	113
Orland Park, Il., U.S.	k9	90
Orléans, Braz.	D3	56
Orléans, hist. reg., Fr.	D4	16
Orléans, Ont.	h12	73
Orléans, Fr.	D4	16
Orleans, Ca., U.S.	B2	82
Orleans, In., U.S.	G5	91
Orleans, Ma., U.S.	C7	98
Orleans, Ne., U.S.	D6	104
Orleans, Vt., U.S.	B4	122
Orleans, co., La., U.S.	E6	95
Orleans, co., N.Y., U.S.	B2	109
Orleans, co., Vt., U.S.	B4	122
Orléans, Île d', i., Que.	C7	74
Orlik Reservoir, res., Czech.	D9	19
Orlinda, Tn., U.S.	A5	119
Orlová, Czech.	*D5	26
Orlovista, Fl., U.S.	*D5	86
Orlovo, Sov. Un.	E17	29
Orly, Fr.	h10	16
Orlyak, Bul.	D8	24
Orman Dam, S.D., U.S.	C2	118
Ormāra, Pak.	C3	36
Ormāra, Rās, c., Pak.	I12	39
Ormiston, Sask.	H3	75
Ormond Beach, Fl., U.S.	C5	86
Ormond By The Sea, Fl., U.S.	*C5	86
Ormsby, Ont.	C7	73
Ormsby, Mn., U.S.	G4	100
Ormskirk, Eng., U.K.	A5	12
Ormstown, Que.	D3	74
Ornans, Fr.	B2	20
Orne, dept., Fr.	A6	16
Orneta, Pol.	t36	14
Örnö, i., Swe.	t36	14
Örnsköldsvik, Swe.	F8	14
Oro, i., Den.	C5	15
Orocué, Col.	C3	60
Orodara, Burkina	D4	45
Oro Grande, Ca., U.S.	E5	82
Orogrande, N.M., U.S.	E3	108
Orohena, mtn., Fr. Poly.	*H13	6
Oromocto, N.B.	D3	71
Oromocto Lake, l., N.B.	D2	71
Oron, Nig.	F6	45
Oron-la-Ville, Switz.	C2	21
Orono, Ont.	D6	73
Orono, Me., U.S.	D4	96
Orono, Mn., U.S.	*n11	100
Oronoco, Mn., U.S.	F6	100
Oronoco, Mo., U.S.	D3	102
Oronsay, i., Scot., U.K.	C3	13
Oropuche, Phil.	O23	52
Orós, Braz.	C3	57
Orosei, Gulf of, b., Italy	D2	23
Orosháza, Hung.	B5	24
Orote Peninsula, pen., Guam	L9	52
Orovada, Nv., U.S.	B4	105
Oroville, Ca., U.S.	C3	82
Oroville, Wa., U.S.	A6	124
Oroville, Lake, res., Ca., U.S.	C3	82
Orpington (part of London), Eng., U.K.	m13	10
Orr, Mn., U.S.	B6	100
Orrick, Mo., U.S.	B3	102
Orrin, N.D., U.S.	A5	111

Name	Map Ref.	Page
Orrington, Me., U.S.	D4	96
Orr Lake, l., Man.	A3	70
Orrs Island, Me., U.S.	E3	96
Orrstown, Pa., U.S.	F6	115
Orrum, N.C., U.S.	C4	110
Orrville, Ont.	B5	73
Orrville, Al., U.S.	C2	78
Orrville, Oh., U.S.	B4	112
Orsa, Swe.	G6	14
Orsay, Fr.	F2	17
Orsha, Sov. Un.	D8	27
Orsières, Switz.	C3	20
Orsk, Sov. Un.	D8	29
Orson, Pa., U.S.	C11	115
Orșova, Rom.	C6	24
Ørsted, Den.	B4	15
Örsundsbro, Swe.	I35	14
Orta, Lake, l., Italy	D4	20
Ortaca, Tur.	D7	25
Orta [San Giulio], Italy	E5	21
Ortegal, Cape, c., Spain	A2	22
Orthez, Fr.	F3	16
Ortigueira, Spain	A2	22
Orting, Wa., U.S.	B3	124
Ortisei, Italy	C7	20
Ortiz, Mex.	B2	63
Ortiz, Co., U.S.	D4	83
Ortiz Mountain, mtn., N.M., U.S.	k8	108
Ortley, S.D., U.S.	B8	118
Ortoire, stm., Trin.	O23	65
Ortona, Italy	C5	23
Ortonville, Mi., U.S.	F7	99
Ortonville, Mn., U.S.	E2	100
Orūmīyeh (Urmia), Iran	B4	38
Oruro, Bol.	C2	55
Oruro, dept., Bol.	C2	55
Orvieto, Italy	C4	23
Orviston, Pa., U.S.	D6	115
Orwell, N.Y., U.S.	B4	109
Orwell, Oh., U.S.	A5	112
Orwell, Vt., U.S.	D2	122
Orwigsburg, Pa., U.S.	E9	115
Or Yehuda, Isr.	g10	41
Orysa, Tn., U.S.	B2	119
Orzesze, Pol.	g9	26
Osa, Península de, pen., C.R.	F6	62
Osage, Sask.	H4	75
Osage, Ia., U.S.	A5	92
Osage, Mn., U.S.	D3	100
Osage, Ok., U.S.	A5	113
Osage, Wy., U.S.	C8	127
Osage, co., Ks., U.S.	D8	93
Osage, co., Mo., U.S.	C6	102
Osage, co., Ok., U.S.	A5	113
Osage, stm., Mo., U.S.	C5	102
Osage Beach, Mo., U.S.	C5	102
Osage City, Ks., U.S.	D8	93
Osage Creek, stm., Ar., U.S.	A2	81
Ōsaka, Japan	E12	31
Ōsaka, Japan	n16	33
Ōsaka Bay, b., Japan	o14	33
Osaka Mountain, hill, Japan	P17	52
Osakis, Mn., U.S.	E3	100
Osakis, Lake, l., Mn., U.S.	E3	100
Osawatomie, Ks., U.S.	D9	93
Osborn, Mo., U.S.	B3	102
Osborne, Ks., U.S.	C5	93
Osborne, co., Ks., U.S.	C5	93
Osbornsville, N.J., U.S.	C4	107
Osburn, Id., U.S.	B3	89
Osby, Swe.	B8	15
Oscar, La., U.S.	D4	95
Oscar, Ok., U.S.	D4	113
Osceola, Ar., U.S.	B6	81
Osceola, In., U.S.	A5	91
Osceola, Ia., U.S.	C4	92
Osceola, Mo., U.S.	C4	102
Osceola, Ne., U.S.	C8	104
Osceola, Pa., U.S.	C7	115
Osceola, S.D., U.S.	C8	118
Osceola, Tx., U.S.	C4	120
Osceola, Wi., U.S.	C1	126
Osceola, co., Fl., U.S.	E5	86
Osceola, co., Ia., U.S.	A2	92
Osceola, co., Mi., U.S.	E5	99
Osceola Mills, Pa., U.S.	E5	115
Oschatz, E. Ger.	C6	18
Oschersleben, E. Ger.	B5	18
Oscoda, Mi., U.S.	D7	99
Oscoda, co., Mi., U.S.	D6	99
Oscura Mountains, mts., N.M., U.S.	D3	108
Osek, Czech.	C8	19
Oselki, Sov. Un.	r31	14
Osgood, Ind., U.S.	F7	91
Osgood, Mo., U.S.	A4	102
Osgood, Oh., U.S.	B1	112
Osgoode, Ont.	B9	73
Osh, Sov. Un.	E10	29
Oshamambe, Japan	E10	33
Oshawa, Ont.	D6	73
Ō-shima, i., Japan	J7	33
Oshkosh, Ne., U.S.	C3	104
Oshkosh, Wi., U.S.	D5	126
Oshnovīyeh, Iran	C2	39
Oshogbo, Nig.	E5	45
Oshoto, Wy., U.S.	B8	127
Oshtorān Kūh, mtn., Iran	E4	39
Oshwe, Zaire	B2	48
Osijek, Yugo.	C4	24
Osilinka, stm., B.C.	A5	69
Osinniki, Sov. Un.	E26	8
Osipovichi, Sov. Un.	E7	27
Oskaloosa, Ia., U.S.	C5	92
Oskaloosa, Ks., U.S.	C8	93
Oskaloosa, Mo., U.S.	D3	102
Oskarshamn, Swe.	I7	14
Oskol, stm., Sov. Un.	G11	27
Oskū, Iran	C2	39
Osler, Sask.	E2	75
Oslo, Nor.	H4	14
Oslo, Mn., U.S.	B1	100
Oslofjorden, Nor.	H4	14
Osma, Spain	B4	22
Osmānābād, India	H6	37
Osmancık, Tur.	B10	40
Osmaneli, Tur.	B7	25
Osmaniye, Tur.	D11	40
Osnabrock, N.D., U.S.	A7	111
Osnabrück, W. Ger.	B4	18
Osório, Braz.	D2	56
Osorno, Chile	B2	56
Osov, Czech.	o17	26
Osoyoos, B.C.	E8	69
Osoyoos Lake, l., Wa., U.S.	A6	124
Ospika, stm., B.C.	A6	69
Osprey, Fl., U.S.	E4	86
Oss, Neth.	B6	16
Ossa, Mount, mtn., Austl.	o15	50
Ossabaw Island, i., Ga., U.S.	E5	87
Ossabaw Sound, strt., Ga., U.S.	E6	87
Osseo, Mn., U.S.	m12	100

Name	Map Ref.	Page
Osseo, Wi., U.S.	D2	126
Ossian, Ind., U.S.	C7	91
Ossian, Ia., U.S.	A6	92
Ossineke, Mi., U.S.	D7	99
Ossining, N.Y., U.S.	D7	109
Ossipee, N.H., U.S.	C4	106
Ossipee, stm., U.S.	C5	106
Ossipee Lake, l., N.H., U.S.	C4	106
Ossipee Mountains, mts., N.H., U.S.	C4	106
Ossokmanuan Lake, l., Newf.	h8	72
Ossora, Sov. Un.	D34	128
Ostașnă, Swe.	t36	14
Ostashkov, Sov. Un.	C9	27
Osteen, Fl., U.S.	D5	86
Ostende see Oostende, Bel.		
Osterburg, E. Ger.	F5	15
Osterburg, Pa., U.S.	F4	115
Osterode, W. Ger.	B5	19
Östersund, Swe.	F6	14
Osterville, Ma., U.S.	C7	98
Osterwieck, E. Ger.	B5	19
Ostia Antica, Italy	h8	23
Ostiglia, Italy	D7	20
Ostrach, W. Ger.	B5	19
Ostrander, Mn., U.S.	G6	100
Ostrander, Oh., U.S.	B2	112
Ostrava, Czech.	D5	26
Ostróda, Pol.	B5	26
Ostrog, Sov. Un.	F6	27
Ostrogozhsk, Sov. Un.	F12	27
Ostrołęka, Pol.	B6	26
Ostrov, Czech.	C2	26
Ostrov, Sov. Un.	C8	24
Ostrov, Rom.	C7	27
Ostrowiec 95Świętokrzyski], Pol.	C6	26
Ostrów Lubelski, Pol.	C7	26
Ostrów Mazowiecka, Pol.	B6	26
Ostrów Wielkopolski, Pol.	C4	26
Ostrzeszów, Pol.	C4	26
Ostseebad Graal-Müritz, E. Ger.	D6	15
Ostseebad Rerik, E. Ger.	D5	15
Ōsuka, Japan	o16	33
Osūm, stm., Bul.	D7	24
Osumi, stm., Alb.	B3	25
Ōsumi Islands, is., Japan	E11	31
Ōsumi Strait, strt., Japan	K5	33
Osuna, Spain	D3	22
Osvaldo Cruz, Braz.	C2	56
Oswayo, Pa., U.S.	C5	115
Oswegatchie, Ct., U.S.	*D7	84
Oswegatchie, N.Y., U.S.	A5	109
Oswegatchie, stm., N.Y., U.S.	f9	109
Oswego, Il., U.S.	B5	90
Oswego, Ks., U.S.	E8	93
Oswego, Mt., U.S.	B11	103
Oswego, N.Y., U.S.	B4	109
Oswego, S.C., U.S.	C7	117
Oswego, co., N.Y., U.S.	B4	109
Oswego, stm., N.J., U.S.	D4	107
Oswego, stm., N.Y., U.S.	B4	109
Oswestry, Eng., U.K.	D5	10
Ōświęcim (Auschwitz), Pol.	C5	26
Osyka, Ms., U.S.	D3	101
Ōta, Japan	*H9	33
Otago Peninsula, pen., N.Z.	P13	51
Ōtaki, Japan	n19	33
Otar, Sov. Un.	E9	28
Otaru, Japan	C13	31
Otava, stm., Czech.	D8	19
Otavalo, Ec.	A2	58
Otavi, Nmb.	A2	49
Otay, Ca., U.S.	*o15	82
Otchinjau, Ang.	E1	48
Oteen, N.C., U.S.	f10	110
Otego, N.Y., U.S.	C5	109
Otero, co., Co., U.S.	D7	83
Otero, co., N.M., U.S.	E3	108
Othello, Wa., U.S.	C6	124
Otho, Ia., U.S.	B3	92
Othonoí, i., Grc.	C4	25
Óthris Mountains, mts., Grc.	C4	25
Oti, stm., Afr.	F5	45
Otis, Co., U.S.	A8	83
Otis, Ind., U.S.	A4	91
Otis, Ks., U.S.	D4	93
Otis, Ma., U.S.	B1	98
Otisco, In., U.S.	G6	91
Otisco, Mn., U.S.	G5	100
Otisco, N.Y., U.S.	C4	109
Otis Orchards, Wa., U.S.	g14	124
Otis Reservoir, res., Ma., U.S.	B1	98
Otisville, Mi., U.S.	E7	99
Otjiwarongo, Nmb.	B2	49
Otley, Ia., U.S.	C4	92
Oto, Ia., U.S.	B2	92
Otočac, Yugo.	C2	24
Otoe, Ne., U.S.	D9	104
Otoe, co., Ne., U.S.	D9	104
Otra, stm., Nor.	H2	14
Otradnoye, Sov. Un.	s31	14
Otranto, Italy	D7	23
Otranto, Strait of, strt., Eur.	B2	40
Otsego, Mi., U.S.	F5	99
Otsego, co., Mi., U.S.	C6	99
Otsego, co., N.Y., U.S.	C5	109
Otsego Lake, l., Mi., U.S.	D6	99
Otsego Lake, l., N.Y., U.S.	C6	109
Ōtsu, Japan	o14	33
Ōtsuki, Japan	n17	33
Ottauquechee, stm., Vt., U.S.	D4	122
Ottawa, Ont.	B9	73
Ottawa, Il., U.S.	B5	90
Ottawa, Ks., U.S.	D8	93
Ottawa, Oh., U.S.	A1	112
Ottawa, W.V., U.S.	n12	125
Ottawa, co., Ks., U.S.	C6	93
Ottawa, co., Mi., U.S.	F4	99
Ottawa, co., Oh., U.S.	A2	112
Ottawa, co., Ok., U.S.	A7	113
Ottawa, stm., Can.	G17	66
Ottawa, stm., Oh., U.S.	e6	112
Ottawa-Carleton, co., Ont.	B9	73
Ottawa Hills, Oh., U.S.	e6	112
Ottawa Islands, is., N.W. Ter.	E16	66
Ottawa Lake, Mi., U.S.	G7	99
Otter, stm., Eng., U.K.	E10	103
Otter, stm., Alta.	A2	68
Otter, stm., Eng., U.K.	D1	13
Otterbein, In., U.S.	D3	91
Otterberg, W. Ger.	F3	19
Otter Brook, stm., N.H., U.S.	E2	106
Otter Brook Lake, res., N.H., U.S.	E2	106
Otterburn, Man.	E3	70
Otterburn Park, Que.	D4	74
Otter Creek, Fl., U.S.	C4	86
Otter Creek, Ut., U.S.	E4	121
Otter Creek, stm., Ut., U.S.	E4	121
Otter Creek, stm., Vt., U.S.	C2	122
Otter Creek Reservoir, res., Ut., U.S.	E4	121

Name	Map Ref.	Page
Otter Islands, is., S.C., U.S.	m11	117
Otter Lake, Ont.	F7	99
Otter Lake, N.Y., U.S.	B5	109
Otter Lake, l., Sask.	B3	75
Otterndorf, W. Ger.	E2	15
Otter River, Ma., U.S.	A3	98
Ottersberg, W. Ger.	E3	15
Ottersleben, E. Ger.	A6	19
Ottertail, Mn., U.S.	D3	100
Otter Tail, co., Mn., U.S.	D3	100
Otter Tail, stm., Mn., U.S.	D2	100
Otter Tail Lake, l., Mn., U.S.	D3	100
Otterup, Den.	C4	15
Otterville, Ont.	E4	73
Otterville, Il., U.S.	D3	90
Otterville, Ia., U.S.	B6	92
Otterville, Mo., U.S.	C4	102
Otthon, Sask.	F4	75
Ottignies, Bel.	E7	99
Otto, Wy., U.S.	B4	127
Ottokee, Oh., U.S.	A1	112
Ottone, Italy	E5	20
Ottosen, Ia., U.S.	B3	92
Ottoville, Oh., U.S.	B1	112
Ottsville, Pa., U.S.	F11	115
Ottumwa, Ia., U.S.	C5	92
Ottumwa, S.D., U.S.	C4	118
Otuzco, Peru	C2	58
Otway, N.C., U.S.	C6	110
Otway, Cape, c., Austl.	G7	50
Otway, Seno, b., Chile	h11	54
Otwell, Ar., U.S.	B5	81
Otwell, In., U.S.	H3	91
Otwock, Pol.	m14	26
Ötztal Alps, mts., Eur.	C6	20
Otztaler Ach, stm., Aus.	B6	20
Ou, stm., Laos	B4	34
Ouachita, Ar., U.S.	D3	81
Ouachita, co., Ar., U.S.	D3	81
Ouachita, co., La., U.S.	B3	95
Ouachita, stm., U.S.	D9	76
Ouachita, Lake, res., Ar., U.S.	C2	81
Ouachita Mountains, mts., U.S.	D9	76
Ouadane, Maur.	B2	45
Ouaddai, hist. reg., Chad	C4	46
Ouagadougou, Burkina	D4	45
Ouahigouya, Burkina	D4	45
Ouaka, stm., Cen. Afr. Rep.	C4	46
Oualâta, Maur.	C3	45
Ouallam, Niger	D5	45
Ouallene, Alg.	E5	44
Ouanary, Fr. Gu.	B4	59
Ouanda Djallé, Cen. Afr. Rep.	D4	46
Ouarzazate, Mor.	B3	45
Oubangui (Ubangi), stm., Afr.	A2	48
Ouddorp, Neth.	D3	17
Oudenaarde, Bel.	C3	17
Oude-Pekela, Neth.	A7	17
Oudtshoorn, S. Afr.	H4	49
Oued Zem, Mor.	*C3	44
Ouellé, I.C.	E4	45
Ouelle, stm., Que.	B8	74
Ouémé, stm., Benin	E5	45
Ouesso, Congo	B3	48
Ouest, Pointe de l', c., Que.	k8	72
Ouest, Pointe du, c., St. P./M.	E3	72
Ouezzane, Mor.	C3	44
Oughter, Lough, l., Ire.	D3	10
Oughterard, Ire.	D2	11
Ouham, stm., Afr.	D3	46
Ouidah, Benin	E5	45
Oujda, Mor.	C4	44
Oullins, Fr.	E6	16
Oulu, Fin.	E11	14
Oulujärvi, l., Fin.	E12	14
Oum Chalouba, Chad	B4	46
Oum Hadjer, Chad	C3	46
Ounâne, Bîr, well, Mali	B4	45
Ounasjoki, stm., Fin.	D11	14
Ounianga Kébir, Chad	B4	46
Ouray, Co., U.S.	C3	83
Ouray, Ut., U.S.	C6	121
Ouray, co., Co., U.S.	C3	83
Ouray, Mount, mtn., Co., U.S.	C4	83
Ouri, Chad	A3	46
Ouricuri, Braz.	C2	57
Ourinhos, Braz.	D3	56
Ourique, Port.	D1	22
Ouro Fino, Braz.	C3	56
Ouro Prêto, Braz.	C4	56
Ourthe, stm., Bel.	D5	17
Ourukaen Island, i., Marsh Is.	P18	52
Ouse, stm., Eng., U.K.	D6	10
Outagamie, co., Wi., U.S.	D5	126
Outardes Quatre, Réservoir, res., Que.	h13	74
Outer Hebrides, is., Scot., U.K.	B3	10
Outer Island, i., Wi., U.S.	A3	126
Outer Santa Barbara Passage, strt., Ca., U.S.	F4	82
Outes, Spain	A1	22
Outing, Mn., U.S.	D5	100
Outlook, Sask.	F2	75
Outlook, Mt., U.S.	B12	103
Outlook, Wa., U.S.	C5	124
Outpost Mountain, mtn., Ak., U.S.	B9	79
Outreau, Fr.	B4	16
Outremont, Que.	p19	74
Ouville-la-Rivière, Fr.	E8	12
Ouzinkie, Ak., U.S.	D9	79
Ovada, Italy	B2	23
Oval, Ca., U.S.	D7	115
Ovalau, i., Fiji	H15	52
Ovalle, Chile	A2	54
Ovana, Cerro, mtn., Ven.	C4	60
Ovando, Mt., U.S.	C3	103
Ovar, Port.	B1	22
Overbach, W. Ger.	D2	81
Overbrook, Ks., U.S.	D8	93
Overbrook, Ok., U.S.	C4	113
Overflowing, stm., Can.	C5	75
Overgaard, Az., U.S.	C5	80
Overijse, Bel.	D4	17
Overijssel, prov., Neth.	B6	17
Overisel, Mi., U.S.	F4	99
Overland, Mo., U.S.	f13	102
Overland Park, Ks., U.S.	m16	93
Overlea, Md., U.S.	B5	97
Overlook, Oh., U.S.	*C1	112
Overly, N.D., U.S.	A5	111
Overstreet, Fl., U.S.	B1	86
Overton, Ne., U.S.	D6	104
Overton, Nv., U.S.	G7	105
Overton, Tx., U.S.	C5	120
Overton, co., Tn., U.S.	C8	119
Övertorneå, Swe.	D10	14
Ovett, Ms., U.S.	D4	101
Ovid, Co., U.S.	A8	83
Ovid, Id., U.S.	G7	89
Ovid, Mi., U.S.	E6	99

Name	Map Ref.	Page
Ovid, N.Y., U.S.	C4	109
Oviedo, Spain	A3	22
Ovruch, Sov. Un.	F7	27
Owando, Congo	B2	48
Owaneco, Il., U.S.	D4	90
Owasco Lake, l., N.Y., U.S.	C4	118
Owasco, Ok., U.S.	A6	113
Owatonna, Mn., U.S.	F5	100
Owbeh, Afg.	D11	39
Owego, N.Y., U.S.	C4	109
Owen, Wi., U.S.	C4	73
Owen, co., In., U.S.	F4	91
Owen, co., Ky., U.S.	B5	94
Owen, Lake, l., Wi., U.S.	B2	126
Owen, Mount, mtn., Co., U.S.	N14	51
Owendale, Mi., U.S.	C3	83
Owens, stm., Ca., U.S.	E7	99
Owensboro, Ky., U.S.	D4	82
Owensburg, In., U.S.	C2	94
Owens Creek, stm., Md., U.S.	G4	91
Owens Cross Roads, Al., U.S.	A3	97
Owens Lake, l., Ca., U.S.	A3	78
Owen Sound, Ont.	D5	82
Owen Sound, b., Ont.	C4	73
Owen Stanley Range, mts., Pap. N. Gui.	C4	73
Owensville, Ar., U.S.	k12	51
Owensville, In., U.S.	C3	81
Owensville, Mo., U.S.	H2	91
Owensville, Oh., U.S.	C6	102
Owenton, Ky., U.S.	C1	112
Owerri, Nig.	B5	94
Owey Island, i., Ire.	E7	45
Owikeno Lake, l., B.C.	B3	11
Owings, Md., U.S.	D4	69
Owings Mills, Md., U.S.	C4	97
Owingsville, Ky., U.S.	B4	97
Owl Creek, stm., Wy., U.S.	B6	94
Owl Creek Mountains, mts., Wy., U.S.	C4	127
Owls Head, Me., U.S.	C4	127
Owo, Nig.	D3	96
Owosso, Mi., U.S.	E6	45
Owsley, co., Ky., U.S.	E6	99
Owyhee, Nv., U.S.	C6	94
Owyhee, co., Id., U.S.	B5	105
Owyhee, stm., U.S.	G2	89
Owyhee, Lake, res., Or., U.S.	E9	114
Owyhee, North Fork, stm., U.S.	D9	114
Owyhee, South Fork, stm., U.S.	E9	114
Owyhee Dam, Or., U.S.	G2	89
Owyhee Mountains, mts., U.S.	D9	114
Öxabäck, Swe.	G2	89
Oxbow, Sask.	A6	15
Oxbow, Me., U.S.	H4	75
Oxbow, Or., U.S.	B4	96
Oxbow Dam, U.S.	B10	114
Oxelösund, Swe.	E9	114
Oxford, N.S.	u35	14
Oxford, Eng., U.K.	D6	71
Oxford, Al., U.S.	E6	10
Oxford, Ar., U.S.	B4	78
Oxford, Ct., U.S.	A4	81
Oxford, Fl., U.S.	D3	84
Oxford, Ga., U.S.	D4	86
Oxford, In., U.S.	C3	87
Oxford, Ia., U.S.	C3	91
Oxford, Ks., U.S.	C6	92
Oxford, Me., U.S.	E6	93
Oxford, Md., U.S.	D2	96
Oxford, Ma., U.S.	C6	97
Oxford, Mi., U.S.	B4	98
Oxford, Ms., U.S.	F7	99
Oxford, Ne., U.S.	A4	101
Oxford, N.J., U.S.	D6	104
Oxford, N.Y., U.S.	B3	107
Oxford, N.C., U.S.	C5	109
Oxford, Oh., U.S.	A4	110
Oxford, Pa., U.S.	C1	112
Oxford, Wi., U.S.	G10	115
Oxford, co., Me.	E4	126
Oxford House, Man.	D2	96
Oxford Junction, Ia., U.S.	B4	70
Oxford Junction, N.S.	C7	92
Oxford Lake, l., Man.	B4	72
Oxfordshire, co., Eng., U.K.	C6	70
Oxly, Mo., U.S.	E7	12
Oxnard, Ca., U.S.	E4	102
Oxon Hill, Md., U.S.	f9	82
Oyace, Italy	E3	97
Oyama, B.C.	D8	21
Oyama, Japan	m18	69
Oyapock (Oiapoque), stm., S.A.	B4	59
Oyat, stm., Sov. Un.	A10	27
Oyem, Gabon	E2	46
Oyen, Alta.	D5	68
Oyens, Ia., U.S.	B1	92
Öyeren, l., Nor.	p29	14
Oykel, stm., Scot., U.K.	C4	13
Oykel Bridge, Scot., U.K.	C4	13
Oymyakon, Sov. Un.	C17	29
Oyo, Nig.	E5	45
Oyonnax, Fr.	D6	16
Oyster Bay, N.Y., U.S.	E7	109
Oyster Keys, is., Fl., U.S.	G6	86
Oyster Ridge, mtn., Wy., U.S.	E2	127
Ozamiz, Phil.	D6	34
Ozan, Ar., U.S.	D2	81
Ozark, Al., U.S.	D4	78
Ozark, Ar., U.S.	B2	81
Ozark, Mo., U.S.	D4	102
Ozark, co., Mo., U.S.	E5	102
Ozark Escarpment, clf., U.S.	C5	81
Ozark Plateau, plat., U.S.	C9	76
Ozark Reservoir, res., Ar., U.S.	B1	81
Ozarks, Lake of the, res., Mo., U.S.	C5	102
Ożarowice, Pol.	g10	26
Ozawkie, Ks., U.S.	k15	93
Ozd, Hung.	A5	24
Ozernoye, Sov. Un.	C6	28
Ozette Lake, l., Wa., U.S.	A1	124
Ozieri, Italy	D2	23
Ozona, Fl., U.S.	o10	86
Ozona, Tx., U.S.	D2	120
Ozone, Ar., U.S.	B2	81
Ozorków, Pol.	J6	26
Özu, Japan	J6	33

Name	Map Ref.	Page
Ozuluama, Mex.	C5	63
P		
Paar, stm., W. Ger.	E6	19
Paarl, S. Afr.	D2	49
Paauhau, Hi., U.S.	C6	88
Pauuilo, Hi., U.S.	C6	88
Pabbay, i., Scot., U.K.	C1	13
Pabianice, Pol.	C5	26
Pablo, Mt., U.S.	C2	103
Pābna, Bngl.	D8	36
Pacaás Novos, Serra dos, mts., Braz.	E2	59
Pacajá, stm., Braz.	C4	59
Pacasmayo, Peru	C2	58
Pace, Fl., U.S.	u14	86
Pachaug Pond, l., Ct., U.S.	C8	84
Pachmarhi, India	F7	37
Pachuca [de Soto], Mex.	C5	63
Pachuta, Ms., U.S.	C5	101
Pacific, B.C.	B3	69
Pacific, Mo., U.S.	C7	102
Pacific, Wa., U.S.	f11	124
Pacific, co., Wa., U.S.	C2	124
Pacifica, Ca., U.S.	h8	82
Pacific Beach, Wa., U.S.	B1	124
Pacific City, Or., U.S.	B3	114
Pacific Creek, stm., Wy., U.S.	D3	127
Pacific Grove, Ca., U.S.	D3	82
Pacific Islands, Trust Territory of the, dep., Oc.	F9	6
Pacific Junction, Ia., U.S.	C2	92
Pacific Ocean	E11	6
Pacific Palisades, Hi., U.S.	g10	88
Pacific Ranges, mts., B.C.	D4	69
Pacific Rim National Park, B.C.	E5	69
Packard Mountain, hill, Ma., U.S.	B3	98
Pack Monadnock Mountain, mtn., N.H., U.S.	E3	106
Packwaukee, Wi., U.S.	E4	126
Packwood, Ia., U.S.	C5	92
Packwood, Wa., U.S.	C4	124
Pacolet, S.C., U.S.	B4	117
Pacolet, stm., S.C., U.S.	A4	117
Pacolet Mills, S.C., U.S.	B4	117
Pacora, Pan.	k12	62
Pacora, stm., Pan.	k12	62
Pacov, Czech.	D9	19
Pacquet, Newf.	D4	72
Pactola Reservoir, res., S.D., U.S.	C2	118
Padang, Indon.	F2	34
Padang, i., Indon.	L5	35
Padang Endau, Malay.	K5	35
Padangpanjang, Indon.	F2	34
Padangsidempuan, Indon.	E1	34
Padauiri, stm., Braz.	D6	71
Paddle Prairie, Alta.	f7	68
Paddling Lake, l., Sask.	D2	75
Paddock Lake, Wi., U.S.	n11	126
Paddockwood, Sask.	D3	75
Paddy Knob, mtn., U.S.	C5	125
Paden, Ms., U.S.	A5	101
Paden City, W.V., U.S.	B4	125
Paderborn, W. Ger.	C4	18
Padilla, Bol.	C3	55
Padova (Padua), Italy	B3	23
Padre Island, i., Tx., U.S.	F4	120
Padre Island National Seashore, Tx., U.S.	F4	120
Padroni, Co., U.S.	A7	83
Padstow, Eng., U.K.	D3	12
Paducah, Ky., U.S.	e9	94
Paducah, Tx., U.S.	B2	120
Paektu, Mount, mtn., Asia	F4	33
Paepaeolei'a, Cape, c., W. Sam.	F11	52
Paeroa, N.Z.	L15	51
Paestum, hist., Italy	D5	23
Pafúri, Moz.	B5	49
Pag, i., Yugo.	C2	24
Pagai Selatan, i., Indon.	F2	34
Pagai Utara, i., Indon.	F2	34
Pagastikós Kólpos (Gulf of Vólos), b., Grc.	C4	40
Pagatan, Indon.	F4	34
Pagosa, stm., Sask.	A4	75
Pagat Point, c., Guam	L10	52
Page, Az., U.S.	A4	80
Page, Ne., U.S.	B7	104
Page, N.D., U.S.	B8	111
Page, Ok., U.S.	C7	113
Page, W.V., U.S.	C3	125
Page, co., Ia., U.S.	D2	92
Page, co., Va., U.S.	B4	123
Pageland, S.C., U.S.	B7	117
Page Manor, Oh., U.S.	*C1	112
Paglia, mtn., Switz.	D6	20
Pagny [-sur-Moselle], Fr.	F5	17
Pago Bay, b., Guam	M10	52
Pagoda Peak, mtn., Co., U.S.	A3	83
Pagoda Point, c., Burma	E9	36
Pago Pago, Am. Sam.	G13	52
Pago Pago Harbor, b., Am. Sam.	F13	52
Pago Point, c., Guam	M10	52
Pagosa Springs, Co., U.S.	D3	83
Paguate, N.M., U.S.	B2	108
Pahala, Hi., U.S.	D6	88
Pahang, state, Malay.	K5	35
Pahang, stm., Malay.	M8	35
Pahaska, Wy., U.S.	B3	127
Pahoa, Hi., U.S.	D7	88
Pahokee, Fl., U.S.	F6	86
Pahra, stm., Yugo.	C3	24
Pahrump, Nv., U.S.	G6	105
Pahute Mesa, mtn., Nv., U.S.	F5	105
Paia, Hi., U.S.	C5	88
Paignton, Eng., U.K.	D1	10
Päijänne, l., Fin.	G11	14
Pailolo Channel, strt., Hi., U.S.	B5	88
Paincourtville, La., U.S.	k9	95
Painesdale, Mi., U.S.	m12	99
Painesville, Oh., U.S.	A4	112
Paint Bank, Va., U.S.	C2	123
Paint Creek, stm., W.V., U.S.	m13	125
Paint Creek, North Fork, stm., Oh., U.S.	C2	112
Paint Creek Lake, res., Oh., U.S.	C2	112
Painted Desert, des., Az., U.S.	B4	80
Painted Post, N.Y., U.S.	C3	109

Name	Map Ref.	Page
Painted Rock Reservoir, res., Az., U.S.	D3	80
Painter, Va., U.S.	C7	123
Paint Lake, l., Man.	B3	70
Paint Lick, Ky., U.S.	C5	94
Paint Mountain, mtn., W.V., U.S.	n13	125
Paint Rock, Al., U.S.	A3	78
Paint Rock, Tx., U.S.	D3	120
Paintsville, Ky., U.S.	C7	94
Paisley, Ont.	C3	73
Paisley, Scot., U.K.	C4	10
Paisley, Fl., U.S.	D5	86
Paisley, Or., U.S.	E6	114
Paita, Peru	C1	58
Pajala, Swe.	D10	14
Pajarito, N.M., U.S.	*B3	108
Pajaros Point, c., V.I., Br.	A7	65
Pajon Point, c., Guam	L10	52
Pakenham, Ont.	B8	73
Pakhra, stm., Sov. Un.	n17	27
Pakistan, ctry., Asia	C4	36
Pakokku, Burma	D9	36
Pakowki Lake, l., Alta.	E5	68
Pakra, stm., Yugo.	C3	24
Paks, Hung.	B4	24
Pakwa Lake, l., Man.	B2	70
Pakxe, Laos	B3	34
Pala, Chad	D2	46
Palacios, Tx., U.S.	E4	120
Palafrugell, Spain	B7	22
Palagruža, is., Yugo.	D3	24
Palaiokhóra, Grc.	E4	25
Palaión Fáliron, Grc.	h11	25
Palamás, Grc.	C4	25
Palamós, Spain	B7	22
Palana, Sov. Un.	D18	29
Palanga, Sov. Un.	D3	27
Palangkaraya, Indon.	F4	34
Pālanpur, India	D5	36
Palaoa Point, c., Hi., U.S.	C4	88
Palapag, Phil.	C7	34
Palapye, Bots.	A2	49
Palas del Rey, Spain	A2	22
Palatine, Il., U.S.	A5	90
Palatka, Fl., U.S.	C5	86
Palau (Belau), ter., T.T.P.I.	F8	6
Palauig, Phil.	o12	34
Palauig Point, c., Phil.	o12	34
Palauli (Vaioa), W. Sam.	F11	52
Palauli Bay, b., W. Sam.	F11	52
Palawan, i., Phil.	C5	34
Palazzolo Acreide, Italy	F5	23
Palco, Ks., U.S.	C4	93
Palembang, Indon.	F2	34
Palena, stm., S.A.	C2	54
Palencia, Spain	A3	22
Palenque, hist., Mex.	B2	62
Palenville, N.Y., U.S.	C6	109
Palermo, Italy	E4	23
Palermo, Me., U.S.	D3	96
Palermo, N.J., U.S.	E3	107
Palermo, N.D., U.S.	A3	111
Palestine, Ar., U.S.	C5	81
Palestine, Ct., U.S.	*D2	84
Palestine, Il., U.S.	D6	90
Palestine, Oh., U.S.	B1	112
Palestine, Tx., U.S.	D5	120
Palestine, W.V., U.S.	B3	125
Palestine, hist. reg., Asia	G10	40
Palestine, Lake, res., Tx., U.S.	C5	120
Palestrina, Italy	h9	23
Paletwa, Burma	D9	36
Pālghāt, India	F6	37
Palhoça, Braz.	D3	56
Pāli, India	E4	37
Palidoro (Baebiana), Italy	h8	23
Palikea, mtn., Hi., U.S.	g9	88
Paliker Point, c., Micron.	Q17	52
Palimé, Togo	E5	45
Palisade, Co., U.S.	B2	83
Palisade, Mn., U.S.	D5	100
Palisade, Ne., U.S.	D4	104
Palisades, Wa., U.S.	B6	124
Palisades Park, N.J., U.S.	h8	107
Palisades Reservoir, res., U.S.	F7	89
Palisadoes, spit, Jam.	F15	65
Paliseul, Bel.	E5	17
Pālitāna, India	G3	37
Palling, B.C.	B5	69
Palliser, Cape, c., N.Z.	N15	51
Pall Mall, Tn., U.S.	C9	119
Palma, Moz.	D7	48
Palma, stm., Braz.	D1	57
Palma del Rio, Spain	D3	22
Palma [de Mallorca], Spain	C7	22
Palmares, Braz.	C3	57
Palmar Sur, C.R.	F6	62
Palmas, Braz.	D2	56
Palmas, Cape, c., Lib.	F3	45
Palmas de Monte Alto, Braz.	A4	56
Palma Sola, Fl., U.S.	*E4	86
Palma Soriano, Cuba	D5	64
Palm Bay, Fl., U.S.	D6	86
Palm Beach, Fl., U.S.	F6	86
Palm Beach, co., Fl., U.S.	F6	86
Palm Beach Gardens, Fl., U.S.	F6	86
Palmdale, Ca., U.S.	E4	82
Palmdale, Fl., U.S.	F5	86
Palm Desert, Ca., U.S.	*F5	82
Palmeira, Braz.	D2	56
Palmeira d'Oeste, Braz.	C2	56
Palmeira dos Índios, Braz.	C3	57
Palmeirinhas, Ponta das, c., Ang.	C1	48
Palmer, Sask.	H2	75
Palmer, Ak., U.S.	C10	79
Palmer, Il., U.S.	D4	90
Palmer, Ia., U.S.	B3	92
Palmer, Ks., U.S.	C6	93
Palmer, Ma., U.S.	B3	98
Palmer, Mi., U.S.	B3	99
Palmer, Ne., U.S.	C7	104
Palmer, Tn., U.S.	D8	119
Palmer, Tx., U.S.	n10	120
Palmer, Wa., U.S.	f12	124
Palmer, stm., Braz.	E2	56
Palmeras do Sul, Braz.	B6	83
Palmer Land, mtn., Ant.	B7	6
Palmer Park, Md., U.S.	*C4	97
Palmerston, Ont.	D4	73
Palmerston, N.Z.	P13	51
Palmerston North, N.Z.	N15	51
Palmerton, Pa., U.S.	E10	115
Palmersville, Tn., U.S.	A3	119
Palmetto, Fl., U.S.	E4	86
Palmetto, Ga., U.S.	C2	87
Palmetto, La., U.S.	D4	95
Palmetto Estates, Fl., U.S.	*G6	86
Palm Harbor, Fl., U.S.	o10	86

Name	Map Ref.	Page
Palmi, Italy	E5	23
Palmira, Col.	C2	60
Palmira, Cuba	C3	64
Palmira, Ec.	B2	58
Palmitas, Ur.	f8	54
Palmitos, Braz.	D2	56
Palms, Mi., U.S.	E8	99
Palms, Isle of, i., S.C., U.S.	F8	117
Palm Springs, Ca., U.S.	F5	82
Palm Springs, Fl., U.S.	F6	86
Palm Valley, Fl., U.S.	m9	86
Palmyra, Il., U.S.	D4	90
Palmyra, In., U.S.	H5	91
Palmyra, Ia., U.S.	f9	92
Palmyra, Me., U.S.	D3	96
Palmyra, Mo., U.S.	B6	102
Palmyra, Ne., U.S.	D9	104
Palmyra, N.J., U.S.	C2	107
Palmyra, N.Y., U.S.	B3	109
Palmyra, N.C., U.S.	A5	110
Palmyra, Pa., U.S.	F8	115
Palmyra, Tn., U.S.	A4	119
Palmyra, Va., U.S.	C4	123
Palmyra, Wi., U.S.	F5	126
Palmyra, atoll, Oc.	F12	5
Palmyras Point, c., India	G11	37
Palo (Alsium), Italy	h8	23
Palo, Ia., U.S.	B6	92
Palo, Mi., U.S.	E6	99
Palo Alto, Ca., U.S.	D2	82
Palo Alto, co., Ia., U.S.	A3	92
Palo Duro Canyon, val., Tx., U.S.	B2	120
Paloich, Sud.	C3	47
Palomar Mountain, mtn., Ca., U.S.	F5	82
Palomas Mountains, mts., Az., U.S.	D2	80
Palombara Sabina, Italy	g9	23
Palo Negro, Col.	C3	60
Palo Pinto, Tx., U.S.	C3	120
Palo Pinto, co., Tx., U.S.	C3	120
Palopo, Indon.	F6	34
Palos, Cape, c., Spain	D5	22
Palos Heights, Il., U.S.	*k9	90
Palos Hills, Il., U.S.	*k9	90
Palos Pk, Il., U.S.	k9	90
Palos Verdes Estates, Ca., U.S.	n12	82
Palourde, Lake, l., La., U.S.	k9	95
Palouse, Wa., U.S.	C8	124
Palouse, stm., Wa., U.S.	C7	124
Palo Verde, Az., U.S.	D3	80
Palo Verde, Ca., U.S.	F6	82
Palpa, Peru	D3	58
Pålsboda, Swe.	t33	14
Palu, Indon.	*F5	34
Palvār, Kūh-e, mtn., Iran	F8	39
Pama, Burkina	D5	45
Pamamaroo Lake, l., Austl.	F4	51
Pambrun, Sask.	H2	75
Pamekasan, Indon.	G4	34
Pamiers, Fr.	F4	16
Pamir, mts., Asia	F10	29
Pamlico, co., N.C., U.S.	B6	110
Pamlico, stm., N.C., U.S.	B6	110
Pamlico Sound, strt., N.C., U.S.	B6	110
Pampa, Tx., U.S.	B2	120
Pampa, reg., Arg.	G4	53
Pampa Grande, Bol.	C3	58
Pampanga, stm., Phil.	o13	34
Pampas, Peru	D3	58
Pampilhosa do Botão, Port.	B1	22
Pamplico, S.C., U.S.	D8	117
Pamplin, Va., U.S.	C4	123
Pamplona, Col.	B3	60
Pamplona, Spain	A5	22
Pamunkey, stm., Va., U.S.	C5	123
Pana, Il., U.S.	D4	90
Panaca, Nv., U.S.	F7	105
Panacea, Fl., U.S.	B2	86
Panache, Lake, l., Ont.	A3	73
Panagyurishte, Bul.	D7	24
Panaitan, i., Indon.	G3	34
Panaji, India	E3	37
Panamá, Braz.	B3	56
Panama, Il., U.S.	D4	90
Panama, Ia., U.S.	C2	92
Panama, Ne., U.S.	D9	104
Panama, N.Y., U.S.	C1	109
Panama, Ok., U.S.	B7	113
Panama, ctry., N.A.	F8	62
Panamá, Bahía de, b., Pan.	F8	62
Panamá, Golfo de, b., Pan.	F8	62
Panama Canal, Pan.	k11	62
Panama City, Fl., U.S.	u16	86
Panama City Beach, Fl., U.S.	u16	86
Panambi, Braz.	D2	56
Panamint Range, mts., Ca., U.S.	D5	82
Panao, Peru	C2	58
Panarea, i., Italy	E5	23
Panaro, stm., Italy	B3	23
Panay, i., Phil.	C6	34
Pancake Range, mts., Nv., U.S.	E6	105
Pančevo, Yugo.	C5	24
Panch'iao (T'aipeihsien), Tai.	*F9	31
Pancoastburg, Oh., U.S.	C2	112
Panda, Moz.	B5	49
Pandharpur, India	E6	36
Pāndhurna, India	G7	37
Pando, Ur.	E1	56
Pando, dept., Bol.	B2	55
Pandora, Oh., U.S.	B2	112
Pandora, Tx., U.S.	E4	120
Pandu, Zaire	A2	48
Panelas, Braz.	k5	57
Panet, Que.	C7	74
Panevėžys, Sov. Un.	D5	27
Panfilov, Sov. Un.	E10	29
Pangala, Congo	B1	48
Pangani, Tan.	C6	48
Pangburn, Ar., U.S.	B4	81
Pangi, Zaire	B4	48
Pangkalanbuun, Indon.	F4	34
Pangkalpinang, Indon.	F3	34
Pangman, Sask.	H3	75
Pangnirtung, N.W. Ter.	C19	66
Pangsau Pass, Asia	C10	36
Panguipulli, Chile	B2	54
Panguitch, Ut., U.S.	F3	121
Panhandle, Tx., U.S.	B2	120
Paniau, mtn., Hi., U.S.	B1	88
Panié, Mont, mtn., N. Cal.	*H10	6
Pānihāti, India	*D8	36
Panipat, India	C6	37
Paniqui, Phil.	o13	34
Panj, stm., Asia	k17	39
Panjāb, Afg.	D13	39
Panjgūr, Pak.	C3	36
Panjim see Panaji, India	E5	36
Panjpāi, Pak.	G13	39
Pankey, Ar., U.S.	h10	81
Pankeyville, Il., U.S.	F5	90
Pankshin, Nig.	E6	45
Panmunjŏm, N. Kor.	H3	33
Panna, India	D7	36
Panola, Al., U.S.	C1	78
Panola, co., Ms., U.S.	A3	101
Panola, co., Tx., U.S.	C5	120
Panora, Ia., U.S.	C3	92
Panorama, Braz.	C2	56
Panshan, China	C12	32
Panshi, China	C11	32
Pantanal, i., Indon.	G6	34
Pantar, i., Indon.	G6	34
Pantego, N.C., U.S.	B6	110
Pantelleria, Italy	F3	23
Pantelleria, i., Italy	F4	23
Panthersville, Ga., U.S.	*h8	87
Pantin, Fr.	g10	16
Panton, Vt., U.S.	C2	122
Pánuco, Mex.	C5	63
Pánuco, stm., Mex.	k14	63
Panulcillo, Chile	F1	55
Panzi, Zaire	C2	48
Panzós, Guat.	D7	63
Pão de Açúcar, Braz.	E2	57
Paola, Italy	E6	23
Paola, Ks., U.S.	D9	93
Paoli, Co., U.S.	A8	83
Paoli, In., U.S.	G5	91
Paoli, Ok., U.S.	C4	113
Paoli, Pa., U.S.	o20	115
Paonia, Co., U.S.	C3	83
Paoua, Cen. Afr. Rep.	D3	46
Paoy Pet, Camb.	F5	35
Pápa, Hung.	B3	24
Papaaloa, Hi., U.S.	D6	88
Papagayo, Golfo de, b., C.R.	E7	63
Papago Indian Reservation, Az., U.S.	E3	80
Papaikou, Hi., U.S.	D6	88
Papantla [de Olarte], Mex.	C5	63
Papawai Point, c., Hi., U.S.	C5	88
Papeete, Fr. Poly.	H13	6
Papenburg, W. Ger.	B3	18
Paper Mill Village, Vt., U.S.	F2	122
Papillion, Ne., U.S.	C9	104
Papineau, Il., U.S.	C6	90
Papineau, co., Que.	D2	74
Papineau Lake, l., Ont.	B7	73
Papineauville, Que.	D2	74
Paposo, Chile	E1	55
Papua, Gulf of, b., Pap. N. Gui.	k11	50
Papua New Guinea, ctry., Oc.	G8	6
Papudo, Chile	A2	54
Papun, Burma	E10	36
Paquette, Que.	D6	74
Paquetville, N.B.	B4	71
Pará, state, Braz.	B4	59
Pará, dept., Sur.	A3	59
Pará, stm., Braz.	C5	59
Parabel, Sov. Un.	B10	28
Pará see Belém, Braz.	B1	57
Paraburdoo, Austl.	D2	50
Paracale, Phil.	o14	34
Paracatu, Braz.	B3	56
Paracatu, stm., Braz.	B3	56
Paracel Islands, is., Asia	B4	34
Parachute, Co., U.S.	B2	83
Paracín, Yugo.	D5	24
Paracuru, Braz.	B3	57
Paradis, La., U.S.	k11	95
Paradise, Ca., U.S.	C3	82
Paradise, Ks., U.S.	C5	93
Paradise, Mi., U.S.	B5	99
Paradise, Mt., U.S.	C2	103
Paradise, Nv., U.S.	G6	105
Paradise, Ut., U.S.	B4	121
Paradise, stm., Newf.	B3	72
Paradise Hill, Sask.	D1	75
Paradise Island, N.M., U.S.	B3	108
Paradise Island, i., Bah.	m18	64
Paradise River, Newf.	B3	72
Paradise Valley, Alta.	C5	68
Paradise Valley, Az., U.S.	k9	80
Paradise Valley, Nv., U.S.	B4	105
Paradise Valley, Wy., U.S.	D6	127
Paradox, Co., U.S.	C2	83
Paragon, In., U.S.	F4	91
Paragonah, Ut., U.S.	F3	121
Paragould, Ar., U.S.	A5	81
Paragua, stm., Ven.	B5	60
Paraguaçu, stm., Braz.	D3	57
Paraguaçu Paulista, Braz.	C2	56
Paraguaná, Península de, pen., Ven.	A4	60
Paraguari, Para.	E4	53
Paraguari, dept., Para.	E4	53
Paraguay, ctry., S.A.	D4	53
Paraguay (Paraguai), stm., S.A.	D4	55
Paraiba, state, Braz.	C3	57
Paraiba, stm., Braz.	h6	57
Paraiba do Sul, Braz.	h6	56
Paraiba do Sul, stm., Braz.	g6	56
Paraiso, Mex.	D6	63
Paraiso, Pan.	k11	62
Paraisópolis, Braz.	C3	56
Parakou, Benin	E5	45
Paralomar, Ar., U.S.	D1	81
Paramaribo, Sur.	A3	59
Paramirim, Braz.	A4	56
Paramithiá, Grc.	C3	25
Paramonga, Peru	C2	58
Paramount, Ca., U.S.	*n12	82
Paramount, Md., U.S.	A2	97
Paramus, N.J., U.S.	h8	107
Paran, Nahal, val.	D6	41
Paraná, Arg.	C4	54
Paraná, Braz.	D1	57
Paraná, state, Braz.	B3	56
Paraná, i., Braz.	D1	57
Paraná, stm., S.A.	G5	53
Paranaguá, Braz.	D3	56
Paranaíba, Braz.	B3	56
Paranaíba, stm., Braz.	B2	56
Paranam, Sur.	A3	59
Paranapanema, stm., Braz.	C2	56
Paranapiacaba, Serra do, mts., Braz.	m8	56
Paranavaí, Braz.	E2	56
Paraopeba, Braz.	E7	57
Parapetí, stm., Bol.	C3	55
Paratinga, Braz.	D2	57
Parauapebas, Serra, hill, Braz.	B4	59
Paraúna, Braz.	B2	56
Paray-le-Monial, Fr.	D6	16
Pārbati, stm., India	E6	37
Parbhani, India	H6	37
Parchim, E. Ger.	B5	18
Parchment, Mi., U.S.	F5	99
Parczew, Pol.	C7	26
Pardee, Va., U.S.	e9	123
Pardeeville, Wi., U.S.	E4	126
Pardes Hanna-Karkur, Isr.	B6	41
Pardo, stm., Braz.	B2	57
Pardo, stm., Braz.	C3	56
Pardo, stm., Braz.	E2	57
Pardo, stm., Braz.	D1	57
Pardo, Pa., U.S.	D1	115
Pardubice, Czech.	C3	26
Parecis, Chapada dos, mts., Braz.	B4	55
Paredes de Nava, Spain	A3	22
Parem, i., Micron.	Q18	52
Parem, i., Micron.	Q17	52
Parempei, i., Micron.	Q17	52
Parent, Que.	k12	74
Parepare, Indon.	F5	34
Párga, Grc.	C3	40
Pargo, Ponta do, c., Port.	h11	22
Pargolovo, Sov. Un.	r31	14
Paria, stm., U.S.	A4	80
Paria, Gulf of, b.	A5	60
Paria, Península de pen., Ven.	A5	60
Pariaguán, Ven.	B5	60
Paria Plateau, plat., Az., U.S.	A4	80
Paricutín, vol., Mex.	n12	63
Parigi, Indon.	F6	34
Parika, Guy.	A3	59
Parima, Serra, mts., S.A.	B2	59
Parima, Sierra (Serra Parima), mts., S.A.	C5	60
Pariñas, Punta, c., Peru	B1	58
Parintins, Braz.	C3	59
Paris, Ont.	D4	73
Paris, Fr.	C5	16
Paris, Ar., U.S.	B2	81
Paris, Id., U.S.	G7	89
Paris, Il., U.S.	D6	90
Paris, Ky., U.S.	B5	94
Paris, Me., U.S.	D2	96
Paris, Mi., U.S.	E5	99
Paris, Ms., U.S.	A4	101
Paris, Mo., U.S.	B5	102
Paris, Tn., U.S.	A3	119
Paris, Tx., U.S.	C5	120
Paris, Va., U.S.	A5	123
Paris Crossing, In., U.S.	G6	91
Parish, N.Y., U.S.	B4	109
Parishville, N.Y., U.S.	f10	109
Paris Peak, mtn., Id., U.S.	G7	89
Parisville, Que.	C5	74
Park, Ks., U.S.	C3	93
Park, co., Co., U.S.	B5	83
Park, co., Mt., U.S.	E6	103
Park, co., Wy., U.S.	B3	127
Park, stm., N.D., U.S.	A8	111
Parkbeg, Sask.	G2	75
Park City, Ks., U.S.	g12	93
Park City, Ky., U.S.	C3	94
Park City, Mt., U.S.	E8	103
Park City, Ut., U.S.	C4	121
Parkdale, P.E.I.	C6	71
Parkdale, Ar., U.S.	D4	81
Parkdale, Mi., U.S.	D4	99
Parkdale, Or., U.S.	B5	114
Parke, co., In., U.S.	E3	91
Parker, Az., U.S.	C1	80
Parker, Co., U.S.	B6	83
Parker, Fl., U.S.	u16	86
Parker, Id., U.S.	F7	89
Parker, Ks., U.S.	D9	93
Parker, Pa., U.S.	D2	115
Parker, S.D., U.S.	D8	118
Parker, Wa., U.S.	C5	124
Parker, co., Tx., U.S.	C4	120
Parker City, In., U.S.	D7	91
Parker Dam, Ca., U.S.	E6	82
Parker Peak, mtn., S.D., U.S.	D2	118
Parkers Prairie, Mn., U.S.	D3	100
Parkersburg, Ia., U.S.	B5	92
Parkersburg, N.C., U.S.	C4	110
Parkersburg, W.V., U.S.	B3	125
Parkertown, N.J., U.S.	D4	107
Parkerview, Sask.	F4	75
Parkerville, Ks., U.S.	D7	93
Parkes, Austl.	F8	50
Parkesburg, Pa., U.S.	G10	115
Park Falls, Wi., U.S.	C3	126
Park Forest, Il., U.S.	k9	90
Park Forest South, Il., U.S.	*k9	90
Park Hall, Md., U.S.	D5	97
Park Head, Ont.	C3	73
Parkhill, Ont.	D3	73
Park Hill, Ok., U.S.	B7	113
Park Hills, Ky., U.S.	h13	94
Parkin, Ar., U.S.	B5	81
Parkland, Alta.	E4	68
Parkland, Wa., U.S.	f11	124
Park Layne, Oh., U.S.	C1	112
Parkman, Sask.	H5	75
Parkman, Me., U.S.	C3	96
Parkman, Oh., U.S.	A4	112
Parkman, Wy., U.S.	B5	127
Park Place, Or., U.S.	h12	114
Park Plateau, plat., Co., U.S.	D6	83
Park Range, mts., Co., U.S.	A4	83
Park Rapids, Mn., U.S.	D3	100
Park Ridge, Il., U.S.	B6	90
Park Ridge, N.J., U.S.	g8	107
Park River, N.D., U.S.	A8	111
Parkrose, Or., U.S.	B4	114
Parks, Ar., U.S.	C1	81
Parks, La., U.S.	D4	95
Parks, Ne., U.S.	D4	104
Parksdale, Sask.	D2	75
Parksley, Va., U.S.	C7	123
Parkston, S.D., U.S.	D8	118
Parksville, B.C.	E5	69
Parksville, N.Y., U.S.	D6	109
Parksville, S.C., U.S.	D3	117
Park Valley, Ut., U.S.	B2	121
Parkville, Md., U.S.	B4	97
Parkville, Mo., U.S.	B3	102
Parkwater, Wa., U.S.	g14	124
Parkway, Ca., U.S.	*C3	82
Parkwood, N.C., U.S.	A3	110
Parla, Spain	p17	22
Parlākimidi, India	H10	37
Parle, Lac qui, l., Mn., U.S.	E3	100
Parlier, Ca., U.S.	D4	82
Parlin, Co., U.S.	C4	83
Parma, Italy	B3	23
Parma, Id., U.S.	F2	89
Parma, Mi., U.S.	F6	99
Parma, Mo., U.S.	E8	102
Parma, Oh., U.S.	A4	112
Parma, stm., Italy	E6	20
Parma Heights, Oh., U.S.	h9	112
Parmele, N.C., U.S.	B5	110
Parmelee, S.D., U.S.	D4	118
Parmer, co., Tx., U.S.	B1	120
Parnaguá, Braz.	D2	57
Parnaíba, Braz.	B2	57
Parnaíba, stm., Braz.	B2	57
Parnassós, mtn., Grc.	C4	25
Parnell, Ia., U.S.	C6	92
Parnell, Mo., U.S.	A3	102
Paro, Bhu.	C8	36
Parnis Óros, mts., Grc.	g11	25
Páros, Grc.	D5	25
Páros, i., Grc.	D5	25
Parowan, Ut., U.S.	F3	121
Par Pond, res., S.C., U.S.	D5	117
Parr, In., U.S.	B3	91
Parral, Chile	D2	54
Parramatta, Austl.	*F9	50
Parramore Island, i., Va., U.S.	C7	123
Parras de la Fuente, Mex.	B4	63
Parrett, stm., Eng., U.K.	C5	12
Parrish, Al., U.S.	B2	78
Parrish, Fl., U.S.	E4	86
Parrish, Wi., U.S.	C4	126
Parris Island, S.C., U.S.	*G6	117
Parrott, Ga., U.S.	E2	87
Parrott, Va., U.S.	C2	123
Parrottsville, Tn., U.S.	C10	119
Parrsboro, N.S.	D5	71
Parrs Ridge, mtn., Md., U.S.	B3	97
Parry, Cape, c., N.W. Ter.	B8	66
Parry, Mount, mtn., B.C.	C3	69
Parry Island, i., Ont.	B4	73
Parry Islands, is., N.W. Ter.	m29	66
Parry Sound, Ont.	B4	73
Parry Sound, dept., Ont.	B5	73
Parsęta, stm., Pol.	A3	26
Parshall, Co., U.S.	A4	83
Parshall, N.D., U.S.	B3	111
Parsippany, N.J., U.S.	B4	107
Parsnip, stm., B.C.	B6	69
Parsons, Ks., U.S.	E8	93
Parsons, Tn., U.S.	B3	119
Parsons, W.V., U.S.	B5	125
Parsonsburg, Md., U.S.	D7	97
Parson's Pond, Newf.	C3	72
Partanna, Italy	E4	23
Parthenay, Fr.	D3	16
Parthenon, Ar., U.S.	B2	81
Partinico, Italy	E4	23
Partlow, Va., U.S.	B5	123
Partridge, Ks., U.S.	E5	93
Partridge Point, c., Newf.	C3	72
Partry, Ire.	D2	11
Paru, stm., Braz.	C4	59
Paru de Oeste, stm., Braz.	C3	59
Parys, S. Afr.	C4	49
Pasadena, Newf.	D3	72
Pasadena, Ca., U.S.	E4	82
Pasadena, Md., U.S.	B4	97
Pasadena, Tx., U.S.	r14	120
Pasado, Cabo, c., Ec.	B1	58
Pasaje, Ec.	B2	58
Pa Sak, stm., Thai.	D4	35
Pascagoula, Ms., U.S.	E5	101
Pascagoula, stm., Ms., U.S.	E5	101
Pascagoula Bay, b., Ms., U.S.	f8	101
Pascani, Rom.	B8	24
Pasco, Wa., U.S.	C6	124
Pasco, dept., Peru	D2	58
Pasco, co., Fl., U.S.	D4	86
Pascoag, R.I., U.S.	B2	116
Pascoag Reservoir, res., R.I., U.S.	B2	116
Pascola, Mo., U.S.	E8	102
Pascua, Isla de (Easter Island), i., Chile	H15	6
Pas-de-Calais, dept., Fr.	B7	18
Pasewalk, E. Ger.	B7	18
Pashkovo, Sov. Un.	B11	31
Pasig, Phil.	o13	34
Pasieka, Pa., U.S.	G10	115
Pasni, Pak.	C3	36
Paso de Indios, Arg.	C3	54
Paso de los Libres, Arg.	E1	56
Paso de los Toros, Ur.	C4	54
Paso Limay, Arg.	C2	54
Paso Robles, Ca., U.S.	E3	82
Pasqua, Sask.	G3	75
Pasque Island, i., Ma., U.S.	D6	98
Pasquia Hills, hills, Sask.	D4	75
Pasquotank, co., N.C., U.S.	A6	110
Pasrur, Pak.	B5	36
Passaconaway, Mount, mtn., N.H., U.S.	C4	106
Passadumkeag, Me., U.S.	C4	96
Passadumkeag Mountain, mtn., Me., U.S.	C4	96
Passage East, Ire.	E5	11
Passage West, Ire.	F3	11
Passaic, N.J., U.S.	B4	107
Passaic, co., N.J., U.S.	A4	107
Passaic, stm., N.J., U.S.	h8	107
Passamaquoddy Bay, b., Me., U.S.	C6	96
Passau, W. Ger.	D6	18
Pass Christian, Ms., U.S.	E4	101
Passekeag, N.B.	D4	71
Passero, Cape, c., Italy	F5	23
Passo Fundo, Braz.	D2	56
Passos, Braz.	C3	56
Passumpsic, Vt., U.S.	C4	122
Passumpsic, stm., Vt., U.S.	C4	122
Passy, Fr.	E2	21
Pastaza, prov., Ec.	B2	58
Pastaza, stm., S.A.	B2	58
Pasto, Col.	C2	60
Pastora Peak, mtn., Az., U.S.	A6	80
Pastura, N.M., U.S.	C5	108
Pasuruan, Indon.	G4	34
Pasvalys, Sov. Un.	D5	27
Pat Cleburne, Lake, res., Tx., U.S.	C4	120
Patea, N.Z.	M15	51
Pateley Bridge, Eng., U.K.	F7	13
Patéras Óros, mtn., Grc.	g10	25
Paternò, Italy	F5	23
Pateros, Wa., U.S.	A6	124
Paterson, N.J., U.S.	B4	107
Paterson, Wa., U.S.	D6	124
Patesville, Ky., U.S.	C3	94
Pathankot, India	B6	36
Pathein, Burma	E9	36
Pathein, mth., Burma	D1	35
Pathfinder Reservoir, res., Wy., U.S.	D6	127
Pathfork, Ky., U.S.	D6	94
Pathlow, Sask.	E3	75
Patía, stm., Col.	C2	60
Patiāla, India	B6	36
Patience Island, i., R.I., U.S.	D5	116
Patman, Lake, res., Tx., U.S.	C5	120
Patmos, Al., U.S.	D2	81
Pátmos, i., Grc.	D6	40
Patna, India	C8	36
Patnanongan Island, i., Phil.	o14	34
Patoka, Il., U.S.	E4	90
Patoka, In., U.S.	H2	91
Patoka, stm., In., U.S.	H2	91
Patoka Lake, res., In., U.S.	H4	91
Paton, Ia., U.S.	B3	92
Patos, Braz.	D5	57
Patos, Lagoa dos, b., Braz.	E2	56
Patos de Minas, Braz.	E5	57
Patosi, Alb.	B2	25
Patquía, Arg.	F2	55
Pátrai (Patras), Grc.	C3	40
Pátrai, Gulf of see Patraïkós Kólpos, b., Grc.	C3	40
Patraïkós Kólpos (Gulf of Pátrai), b., Grc.	C3	40
Patras see Pátrai, Grc.	C3	40
Patricia, Alta.	D5	68
Patricia, Tx., U.S.	C1	120
Patrick, S.C., U.S.	B7	117
Patrick, co., Va., U.S.	D2	123
Patrick Air Force Base, mil., Fl., U.S.	D6	86
Patricksburg, In., U.S.	F4	91
Patrick Springs, Va., U.S.	D2	123
Patriot, In., U.S.	G8	91
Patroon, Tx., U.S.	D6	120
Patsaliga Creek, stm., Al., U.S.	D3	78
Patsville, Nv., U.S.	B6	105
Pattani, Thai.	D2	34
Pattani, stm., Thai.	I4	35
Pattaquattic Hill, hill, Ma., U.S.	B3	98
Patten, Me., U.S.	C4	96
Pattensburg, Mo., U.S.	B3	102
Patterson, Ar., U.S.	B4	81
Patterson, Ca., U.S.	D3	82
Patterson, Ga., U.S.	E4	87
Patterson, Id., U.S.	E5	89
Patterson, Il., U.S.	D3	90
Patterson, Ia., U.S.	C4	92
Patterson, La., U.S.	E4	95
Patterson, Mo., U.S.	D7	102
Patterson, N.Y., U.S.	D7	109
Patterson, Oh., U.S.	B2	112
Patterson, Va., U.S.	C4	123
Patterson, stm., Nv., U.S.	e10	105
Patterson Creek, stm., W.V., U.S.	B5	125
Pattison, Ms., U.S.	D3	101
Patton, Mo., U.S.	D7	102
Patton, Pa., U.S.	E4	115
Pattonsburg, Mo., U.S.	A3	102
Pattullo, Mount, mtn., B.C.	A3	69
Patu, Braz.	C3	57
Patuākhāli, Bngl.	F13	37
Patuca, stm., Hond.	D8	63
Patuca, Punta, c., Hond.	D8	63
Patuxent River Naval Air Test Center, mil., Md., U.S.	D5	97
Patutu, Wi., U.S.	B1	126
Pátzcuaro, Mex.	D4	63
Pátzcuaro, Lago de l., Mex.	n13	63
Patzicía, Guat.	C2	62
Patzún, Guat.	C2	62
Pau, Fr.	F3	16
Pau, Gave de, stm., Fr.	F3	16
Paucarbamba, Peru	D3	58
Paudalho, Braz.	C3	57
Pau dos Ferros, Braz.	C3	57
Paugh Lake, Ont.	B7	73
Pauillac, Fr.	E3	16
Pauini, Braz.	C4	58
Pauk, Burma	D9	36
Paulaya, stm., Hond.	C5	62
Paulden, Az., U.S.	C3	80
Paulding, Mi., U.S.	n12	99
Paulding, Ms., U.S.	C4	101
Paulding, Oh., U.S.	A1	112
Paulding, co., Ga., U.S.	C2	87
Paulding, co., Oh., U.S.	A1	112
Paulette, stm., La., U.S.	B5	101
Paulina, La., U.S.	h10	95
Paulina, Or., U.S.	C6	114
Paulina Mountains, mts., Or., U.S.	D5	114
Paulina Peak, mtn., Or., U.S.	E5	114
Pauline, S.C., U.S.	B4	117
Paulins Kill, stm., N.J., U.S.	A3	107
Paulistana, Braz.	E10	57
Paullina, Ia., U.S.	B2	92
Paulo Afonso, Cachoeira de, wtfl., Braz.	C3	57
Paulsboro, N.J., U.S.	D2	107
Paul Smiths, N.Y., U.S.	f10	109
Paul Stream, stm., Vt., U.S.	B5	122
Pauls Valley, Ok., U.S.	C4	113
Pauto, stm., Col.	B3	60
Pauwela, Hi., U.S.	C5	88
Pavant Range, mts., Ut., U.S.	E3	121
Pavia, Italy	B3	23
Pavilion Key, i., Fl., U.S.	G5	86
Pavillion, Wy., U.S.	C4	127
Pavlodar, Sov. Un.	D10	29
Pavlof Volcano, vol., Ak., U.S.	D7	79
Pavlograd, Sov. Un.	G10	27
Pavlovo, Sov. Un.	D14	27
Pavlovsk, Sov. Un.	s31	14
Pavlovsk, Sov. Un.	F13	27
Pavlovskaya, Sov. Un.	H13	27
Pavlovskiy Posad, Sov. Un.	n18	27
Pavo, Ga., U.S.	F3	87
Pavón, Col.	C3	60
Pawcatuck, Ct., U.S.	D8	84
Pawcatuck, stm., R.I., U.S.	G1	116
Paw Creek, N.C., U.S.	B2	110
Pawhuska, Ok., U.S.	A5	113
Pawlet, Vt., U.S.	E2	122
Pawleys Island, S.C., U.S.	E9	117
Pawling, N.Y., U.S.	D7	109
Pawłowice, Pol.	h9	26
Pawn, stm., Burma	C2	35
Pawnee, Il., U.S.	D4	90
Pawnee, Ok., U.S.	A5	113
Pawnee, co., Ks., U.S.	D4	93
Pawnee, co., Ne., U.S.	D9	104
Pawnee, co., Ok., U.S.	A5	113
Pawnee, stm., Ks., U.S.	D3	93
Pawnee City, Ne., U.S.	D9	104
Pawnee Creek, stm., Co., U.S.	A7	83
Pawnee Rock, Ks., U.S.	D5	93
Paw Paw, Il., U.S.	B5	90
Paw Paw, Mi., U.S.	F5	99
Paw Paw, W.V., U.S.	B6	125
Paw Paw, stm., Mi., U.S.	F4	99
Pawpaw Creek, stm., W.V., U.S.	h10	125
Pawtuckaway Pond, l., N.H., U.S.	D4	106
Pawtucket, R.I., U.S.	C4	116
Pawtuxet, stm., R.I., U.S.	C4	116
Pawtuxet, North Branch, stm., R.I., U.S.	D3	116
Pawtuxet, South Branch, stm., R.I., U.S.	D3	116
Pax, W.V., U.S.	n13	125
Paxico, Ks., U.S.	C7	93
Paxoí, i., Grc.	C3	25
Paxton, Fl., U.S.	u15	86
Paxton, Il., U.S.	C5	90
Paxton, In., U.S.	F3	91
Paxton, Ma., U.S.	B4	98
Paxton, Ne., U.S.	C4	104
Paxtonville, Pa., U.S.	E7	115
Paxville, S.C., U.S.	D7	117
Payakumbuh, Indon.	*F2	34
Payerne, Switz.	C2	21
Payette, Id., U.S.	E2	89
Payette, co., Id., U.S.	E2	89
Payette, North Fork, stm., Id., U.S.	E2	89
Payette, South Fork, stm., Id., U.S.	E3	89
Payette Lake, res., Id., U.S.	D3	87
Payne, Ga., U.S.	A1	112
Payne, Oh., U.S.	A1	112
Payne, co., Ok., U.S.	A4	113
Payne, Lac, l., Que.	g12	74
Paynes Creek, Ca., U.S.	B3	82
Paynesville, Mn., U.S.	E4	100
Paynesville, Mo., U.S.	B7	102
Payneville, Ky., U.S.	C3	94
Paynton, Sask.	D1	75
Paysandú, Ur.	E1	56
Payson, Az., U.S.	C4	80
Payson, Il., U.S.	D2	90
Payson, Ok., U.S.	B5	113
Payson, Ut., U.S.	C4	121
Pazarbaşı, Cape, c., Tur.	B8	40
Pazardzhik, Bul.	D7	24
Pazin, Yugo.	C1	24
Pea, stm., Al., U.S.	D3	78
Peabody, Ks., U.S.	D6	93
Peabody, Ma., U.S.	A6	98
Peabody, stm., N.H., U.S.	B4	106
Peace, stm., Can.	A3	69
Peace, stm., Fl., U.S.	E5	86
Peace Dale, R.I., U.S.	F3	116
Peace River, Alta.	A2	68
Peach, co., Ga., U.S.	D3	87
Peacham, Vt., U.S.	C4	122
Peacham Pond, l., Vt., U.S.	C4	122
Peach Creek, W.V., U.S.	n13	125
Peachland, B.C.	E8	69
Peachland, N.C., U.S.	C2	110
Peach Orchard, Ar., U.S.	A5	81
Peach Orchard, Ga., U.S.	*C4	87
Peach Orchard Knob, mtn., Ky., U.S.	C3	94
Peach Point, c., Ma., U.S.	f12	98
Peach Springs, Az., U.S.	B2	80
Peachtree City, Ga., U.S.	*C2	87
Peacock, Mi., U.S.	D5	99
Peacock Hills, hills, N.W. Ter.	C10	66
Peacock Point, c., Wake I.	B2	52
Peacock Sound, strt., Ant.	B2	7
Peaima Fall, wtfl., Guy.	A2	59
Peak, Ok., U.S.	C5	117
Peaked Mountain, mtn., Me., U.S.	B4	96
Peaks Island, i., Me., U.S.	g7	96
Peale, Mount, mtn., Ut., U.S.	E6	121
Peale, Island, i., Wake I.	A2	52
Pea Patch Island, i., De., U.S.	B3	85
Pearce, Alta.	E4	68
Pearcy, Ar., U.S.	C2	81
Pea Ridge, Ar., U.S.	A1	81
Pea Ridge National Military Park, Ar., U.S.	A1	81
Pearisburg, Va., U.S.	C2	123
Pearl, Il., U.S.	D3	90
Pearl, Ms., U.S.	C3	101
Pearl, stm., U.S.	D3	101
Pearl and Hermes Reef, rf., Hi., U.S.	k12	88
Pearl City, Hi., U.S.	B4	88
Pearl City, Il., U.S.	A4	90
Pearl Harbor, b., Hi., U.S.	B3	88
Pearl Harbor Naval Station, mil., Hi., U.S.	g10	88
Pearlington, Ms., U.S.	E4	101
Pearl River, La., U.S.	D6	95
Pearl River, N.Y., U.S.	g12	109
Pearl River, co., Ms., U.S.	E4	101
Pearl Stream, stm., Vt., U.S.	B5	122
Pearsall, Tx., U.S.	E3	120
Pearsoll Peak, mtn., Or., U.S.	E3	114
Pearson, Ar., U.S.	B3	81
Pearson, Ga., U.S.	E4	87
Pearson Lake, l., Man.	A3	70
Peary Channel, strt., N.W. Ter.	m30	66
Peary Land, reg., Grnld.	A18	128
Pease, Mn., U.S.	E5	100
Pease, stm., Tx., U.S.	B3	120
Pebane, Moz.	A6	49
Pebas, Peru	B3	58
Pebworth, Ky., U.S.	C6	94
Peć, Yugo.	D4	24
Peçanha, Braz.	B5	56
Pecatonica, Il., U.S.	A4	90

Name	Map Ref.	Page

Pecatonica, stm., U.S. — A4 90
Pecatonica, East Branch, stm., Wi., U.S. — F4 126
Pechenga, Sov. Un. — C6 29
Pechora, Sov. Un. — B20 8
Pechora, stm., Sov. Un. — C8 29
Pechora Bay, b., Sov. Un. — B19 8
Peck, Id., U.S. — C2 89
Peck, Ks., U.S. — E6 93
Peck, Mi., U.S. — E8 99
Peckerwood Lake, res., Ar., U.S. — C4 81
Peckham, Ok., U.S. — A4 113
Pecos, N.M., U.S. — B4 108
Pecos, Tx., U.S. — D1 120
Pecos, co., Tx., U.S. — D1 120
Pecos, stm., U.S. — D7 76
Pecos National Monument, N.M., U.S. — B4 108
Pécs, Hung. — B4 24
Peculiar, Mo., U.S. — C3 102
Pedasí, Pan. — G7 62
Peddocks Island, i., Ma., U.S. — g12 98
Pedernales, Ven. — B5 60
Pedra Azul, Braz. — B4 56
Pedregal (part of Panamá), Pan. — k12 62
Pedregal, Pan. — F6 62
Pedregal, Ven. — A3 60
Pedreiras, Braz. — B2 57
Pedricktown, N.J., U.S. — D2 107
Pedro Afonso, Braz. — C1 57
Pedro Antonio Santos, Mex. — A3 62
Pedro Avelino, Braz. — B2 57
Pedro Juan Caballero, Para. — D4 55
Pedro Luro, Arg. — B4 54
Pedro Miguel, Pan. — k11 62
Pedro R. Fernández (Manuel F. Mantilla), Arg. — E4 55
Pedro Velho, Braz. — h6 57
Peebinga, Austl. — G3 51
Peebles, Sask. — G4 75
Peebles, Scot., U.K. — C5 10
Peebles, Oh., U.S. — D2 112
Peebles, Wi., U.S. — k9 126
Peekaboo Mountain, hill, Me., U.S. — C5 96
Peekskill, N.Y., U.S. — D7 109
Peel, N.B. — C2 71
Peel, I. of Man — F4 13
Peel, co., Ont. — D5 73
Peel, stm., Can. — C5 66
Pe Ell, Wa., U.S. — C2 124
Peel Sound, strt., N.W. Ter. — B13 66
Peene, stm., E. Ger. — B6 18
Peer, Bel. — C5 17
Peerless, Mt., U.S. — B11 103
Peerless Lake, l., Alta. — A3 68
Peers, Alta. — C3 68
Peesane, Sask. — E4 75
Peetz, Co., U.S. — A7 83
Peever, S.D., U.S. — B9 118
Pefferlaw, Ont. — C5 73
Pegan Hill, hill, Ma., U.S. — g10 98
Pegasus Bay, b., N.Z. — O14 51
Pegau, E. Ger. — B7 19
Peggs, Ok., U.S. — A6 113
Peggy, Tx., U.S. — E3 120
Pegnitz, W. Ger. — D5 19
Pegnitz, stm., W. Ger. — C5 22
Pego, Spain — B2 22
Pegram, Tn., U.S. — A4 119
Pegu Yoma, mts., Burma — C1 35
Pehčevo, Yugo. —
Pehuajó, Arg. — B4 54
Peine, W. Ger. — B5 18
Peiping see Beijing, China — D8 31
Peipus, Lake, l., Sov. Un. — C6 29
Peixe, Braz. — D1 57
Peixian, China — G7 32
Peixian, China — G7 32
Pejepscot, Me., U.S. — E2 96
Pekalongan, Indon. — G3 34
Pekan, Malay. — E2 34
Pekanbaru, Indon. — E2 34
Pekin, Il., U.S. — C4 90
Pekin, In., U.S. — G5 91
Pekin, N.D., U.S. — B7 111
Peking see Beijing, China — D8 31
Pelabuhan Kelang, Malay. — K4 35
Pélagos, i., Grc. — C5 25
Pelahatchie, Ms., U.S. — C4 101
Pelaihari, Indon. — F4 34
Pelat, Mont, mtn., Fr. — E7 16
Pelée, Montagne, mtn., Mart. — I14 64
Pelee Island, i., Ont. — F2 73
Peleliu, i., Palau — R17 52
Pelham, Ont. — D5 73
Pelham, Al., U.S. — B3 78
Pelham, Ga., U.S. — E2 87
Pelham, Ma., U.S. — B3 98
Pelham, N.H., U.S. — E4 106
Pelham, N.Y., U.S. — *h13 109
Pelham, N.C., U.S. — A3 110
Pelham, S.C., U.S. — B3 117
Pelham, Tn., U.S. — D8 119
Pelham Manor, N.Y., U.S. — h13 109
Pelhřimov, Czech. — D3 26
Pelican, Ak., U.S. — m21 79
Pelican, La., U.S. — C2 95
Pelican Bay, b., Man. — C1 70
Pelican Lake, Wi., U.S. — C4 126
Pelican Lake, l., Alta. — B4 68
Pelican Lake, l., Mn., U.S. — C1 70
Pelican Lake, l., Mn., U.S. — D4 100
Pelican Lake, l., Mn., U.S. — E5 100
Pelican Lake, l., Mn., U.S. — B6 100
Pelican Lake, l., Wi., U.S. — C4 126
Pelican Mountain, mtn., Alta. — B4 68
Pelican Narrows, Sask. — B4 75
Pelican Rapids, Man. — C1 70
Pelican Rapids, Mn., U.S. — D2 100
Péligre, Lac de, res., Haiti — E11 64
Pelion, S.C., U.S. — D5 117
Pella, Ia., U.S. — C5 92
Pell City, Al., U.S. — B3 78
Pellice, stm., Italy — E3 20
Pell Lake, Wi., U.S. — n11 126
Pellston, Mi., U.S. — C6 99
Pellville, Ky., U.S. — C3 94
Pelly, stm., Yukon — D6 66
Pelly, Sask. — F5 75
Pelly Crossing, Yukon — D5 66
Pelly Lake, l., N.W. Ter. — C12 66
Pelly Mountains, mts., Yukon — D6 66
Peloncillo Mountains, mts., U.S. — E1 108
Peloponnesos, hist. reg., Grc. — C5 25
Pelotas, Braz. — E2 56
Pelotas, Braz. — D2 56
Pel'ovo, Bul. — D7 24

Pelton, Lake, l., La., U.S. — E5 95
Pelusium, hist., Eg. — C4 41
Pelusium Bay, b., Eg. — C4 41
Pelzer, S.C., U.S. — B3 117
Pemadumcook Lake, l., Me., U.S. — C3 96
Pemalang, Indon. — *G3 34
Pemanggil, i., Malay. — K6 35
Pemaquid, Me., U.S. — E3 96
Pematangsiantar, Indon. — m11 34
Pemba, Moz. — D7 48
Pemba, prov., Tan. — C6 48
Pemba, i., Tan. — C6 48
Pemberton, B.C. — D6 69
Pemberton, N.J., U.S. — D3 107
Pemberton, Oh., U.S. — B1 112
Pemberville, Oh., U.S. — A2 112
Pembina, N.D., U.S. — A8 111
Pembina, co., N.D., U.S. — A8 111
Pembina, stm., Alta. — C3 68
Pembina, stm., N.A. — E2 70
Pembina Mountains, mts., N.A. — A7 111
Pembine, Wi., U.S. — C6 126
Pembroke, Ont. — B7 73
Pembroke, Wales, U.K. — E4 10
Pembroke, Ga., U.S. — D5 87
Pembroke, Ky., U.S. — D2 94
Pembroke, Me., U.S. — D5 96
Pembroke, Ma., U.S. — B6 98
Pembroke, N.Y., U.S. — B2 109
Pembroke, N.C., U.S. — C3 110
Pembroke, Va., U.S. — C2 123
Pembroke Park, Fl., U.S. — *G6 86
Pembroke Pines, Fl., U.S. — r13 86
Pembuang, stm., Indon. — F4 34
Pemigewasset, stm., N.H., U.S. — C3 106
Pemigewasset, East Branch, stm., N.H., U.S. — B3 106
Pemiscot, co., Mo., U.S. — E8 102
Pemmican Portage, Sask. — D4 75
Pemucco, Chile — B2 54
Pena Blanca, N.M., U.S. — B3 108
Peñafiel, Port. — B1 22
Peñafiel, Spain — B3 22
Peñalara, mtn., Spain — B4 22
Penalosa, Ks., U.S. — E5 93
Penamacor, Port. — B2 22
Penápolis, Braz. — C2 56
Peñaranda de Bracamonte, Spain — B3 22
Pen Argyl, Pa., U.S. — E11 115
Peñarroya-Pueblonuevo, Spain — C3 22
Peñas, Cabo de, c., Spain — A3 22
Penas, Golfo de, b., Chile — D2 54
Penasco, N.M., U.S. — A4 108
Peñasco, Rio, stm., N.M., U.S. — E4 108
Penbrook, Pa., U.S. — F8 115
Pence, In., U.S. — D2 91
Pencer, Mn., U.S. — B3 100
Penck Trough, val., Ant. — B12 7
Pendéli (Pentelicus), mtn., Grc. — g11 25
Pendembu, S.L. — E2 45
Pender, Ne., U.S. — B9 104
Pender, co., N.C., U.S. — C4 110
Pendergrass, Ga., U.S. — B3 87
Pender Island, B.C. — g12 69
Pendleton, In., U.S. — E6 91
Pendleton, Or., U.S. — B8 114
Pendleton, S.C., U.S. — B2 117
Pendleton, co., Ky., U.S. — B5 94
Pendleton, co., W.V., U.S. — C5 125
Pendley Hills, Ga., U.S. — h8 87
Pendra bumulih, Indon. — F2 34
Pendroy, Mt., U.S. — B4 103
Penedo, Braz. — D3 57
Penetanguishene, Ont. — C5 73
Peneus see Piniós, stm., Grc. — C4 40
Penfield, Ga., U.S. — C3 87
Penfield, Il., U.S. — C6 90
Penfield, N.Y., U.S. — *B3 109
Penfield, Pa., U.S. — D4 115
Peng'an, China — I2 32
Penganga, stm., India — H6 37
Penge, Zaire — C3 48
Pengibu, i., Indon. — L7 35
Penglai, China — F9 32
Pengshui, China — J3 32
Penguin Islands, is., Newf. — D3 72
Penha, Braz. — D3 56
Penhold, Alta. — C4 68
Penhook, Va., U.S. — D3 123
Peniche, Port. — C1 22
Penicuik, Scot., U.K. — E5 13
Peninsular Malaysia, hist. reg., Malay. — E2 34
Penitas, Tx., U.S. — F3 120
Penitente, Serra do, hills, Braz. — C1 57
Penitentiary Mountain, hill, Al., U.S. — A2 78
Pénjamo, Mex. — m13 63
Penn, Sask. — D2 75
Penn, N.D., U.S. — A6 111
Penn Acres, De., U.S. — *B3 85
Pennant Point, c., N.S. — E6 71
Pennant Station, Sask. — G1 75
Pennask Mountain, mtn., B.C. — E7 69
Penne, Italy — C4 23
Pennell, Mount, mtn., Ut., U.S. — F5 121
Pennellville, N.Y., U.S. — B4 109
Penner, stm., India — F6 36
Penneshaw, Austl. — G1 51
Penney Farms, Fl., U.S. — C5 86
Pennfield, N.B. — D3 71
Penn Hills, Pa., U.S. — k14 115
Penniac, N.B. — C3 71
Pennine Alps, mts., Eur. — E3 18
Pennines, mts., Eng., U.K. — C5 10
Pennington, Al., U.S. — C1 78
Pennington, N.J., U.S. — C3 107
Pennington, co., Mn., U.S. — B2 100
Pennington, co., S.D., U.S. — D2 118
Pennington Gap, Va., U.S. — f8 123
Pennock, Mn., U.S. — E3 100
Pennsauken, N.J., U.S. — D2 107
Pennsboro, W.V., U.S. — B4 125
Pennsburg, Pa., U.S. — F11 115
Penns Grove, N.J., U.S. — D2 107
Pennsuco, Fl., U.S. — s13 86
Pennsville, N.J., U.S. — D1 107
Pennsville, Oh., U.S. — C4 112
Pennsylvania, state, U.S. — E7 115
Penn Valley, Pa., U.S. — o20 115
Pennville, In., U.S. — D7 91
Penny, B.C. — C7 69
Penn Yan, N.Y., U.S. — C3 109
Pennycutaway, stm., Man. — A5 70

Penobscot, Me., U.S. — D4 96
Penobscot, co., Me., U.S. — C4 96
Penobscot, stm., Me., U.S. — C4 96
Penobscot, East Branch, stm., Me., U.S. — C4 96
Penobscot, North Branch, stm., Me., U.S. — B2 96
Penobscot, West Branch, stm., Me., U.S. — C3 96
Penobscot Bay, b., Me., U.S. — D3 96
Penobscot Lake, l., Me., U.S. — C2 96
Penobsquis, N.B. — D4 71
Penokee, Ks., U.S. — C4 93
Penong, Austl. — F5 50
Penonomé, Pan. — F7 62
Penrhyn, Cape, c., N.W. Ter. — C16 66
Penrith, Austl. — *F9 50
Penrith, Eng., U.K. — F6 13
Pensacola, Fl., U.S. — u14 86
Pensacola, Ok., U.S. — A6 113
Pensacola Bay, b., Fl., U.S. — u14 86
Pensacola Dam, Ok., U.S. — A6 113
Pensacola Mountains, mts., Ant. — A6 7
Pensacola Naval Air Station, mil., Fl., U.S. — u14 86
Pensaukee, Wi., U.S. — D6 126
Pense, Sask. — G3 75
Pentagon Mountain, mtn., Mt., U.S. — C3 103
Pentecostes, Braz. — B3 57
Pentelicus see Pendéli, mtn., Grc. — g11 25
Penticton, B.C. — E8 69
Pentland Firth, strt., Scot., U.K. — A5 10
Pentland Hills, hills, Scot., U.K. — E5 13
Penton, Al., U.S. — D2 107
Pentwater, Mi., U.S. — E4 99
Penwell, Tx., U.S. — D1 120
Penza, Sov. Un. — D7 29
Penzance, Sask. — F3 75
Penzance, Eng., U.K. — F3 13
Penzberg, W. Ger. — E11 18
Penzhina, stm., Sov. Un. — C19 29
Penzlin, E. Ger. — E7 15
Peoa, Ut., U.S. — C4 121
Peonan Point, c., Man. — D2 70
Peoples, Ky., U.S. — C5 94
Peoria, Az., U.S. — D3 80
Peoria, Il., U.S. — C4 90
Peoria, Ok., U.S. — A7 113
Peoria, co., Il., U.S. — C4 90
Peoria Heights, Il., U.S. — C4 90
Pepacton Reservoir, res., N.Y., U.S. — C6 109
Pepeekeo, Hi., U.S. — D6 88
Pepin, Wi., U.S. — D1 126
Pepin, co., Wi., U.S. — D2 126
Pepin, Lake, l., U.S. — D1 126
Pepper Creek, stm., De., U.S. — F5 85
Pepperell, Ma., U.S. — A4 98
Pepper Pike, Oh., U.S. — *h10 112
Peqin, Alb. — B2 25
Pequabuck, Ct., U.S. — C4 84
Pequannock, N.J., U.S. — B4 107
Pequea, stm., Pa., U.S. — k12 62
Pequest, stm., N.J., U.S. — B2 107
Pequop Mountains, mts., Nv., U.S. — C7 105
Pequot Lakes, Mn., U.S. — D4 100
Perabumulih, Indon. — F2 34
Perak, state, Malay. — J4 35
Perak, stm., Malay. — J4 35
Perakhóra, Grc. — g9 25
Perales de Tajuña, Spain — p18 22
Peralta, N.M., U.S. — B3 108
Pérama, Grc. — h11 25
Percival, Ia., U.S. — D2 92
Percy, Il., U.S. — E4 90
Percy, N.H., U.S. — A4 106
Perdido, mtn., Spain — A6 22
Perdido, stm., U.S. — E2 78
Perdido, stm., U.S. — E2 86
Perdido Bay, b., Al., U.S. — E2 78
Perdizes, Braz. — B3 56
Perdões, Braz. — B3 56
Perea, N.M., U.S. — B1 108
Pereira, Col. — C2 60
Pereira Barreto, Braz. — C2 56
Perené, stm., Peru — C3 58
Pereslavl-Zalesskiy, Sov. Un. — C12 27
Pereyaslav-Khmelnitskiy, Sov. Un. — F8 27
Pergamino, Arg. — A4 54
Pergine Valsugana, Italy — A3 23
Perham, Me., U.S. — B4 96
Perham, Mn., U.S. — D3 100
Péribonca, Que. — A5 74
Péribonca, stm., Que. — g20 74
Péridot, Az., U.S. — D5 80
Périgueux, Fr. — E4 16
Perim, i., Yemen — D4 38
Perkasie, Pa., U.S. — F11 115
Perkins, Que. — D2 74
Perkins, Ga., U.S. — D5 87
Perkins, Mi., U.S. — B3 99
Perkins, Ok., U.S. — B4 113
Perkins, co., Ne., U.S. — D4 104
Perkins, co., S.D., U.S. — B3 118
Perkinston, Ms., U.S. — E4 101
Perkinstown, Wi., U.S. — C3 126
Perkinsville, Vt., U.S. — E3 122
Perl-Mack, Co., U.S. — *B6 83
Perlas, Archipiélago de las, is., Pan. — F8 62
Perlas, Laguna de, b., Nic. — E8 63
Perleberg, E. Ger. — B5 18
Perley, Mn., U.S. — C2 100
Perm, Sov. Un. — C5 29
Perma, Mt., U.S. — C2 103
Pérmet, Alb. — B3 25
Pernambuco, state, Braz. — C3 57
Pernambuco see Recife, Braz. — C4 57
Pernik, Bul. — D6 24
Péronne, Fr. — C5 16
Perote, Mex. — D5 63
Perote, Al., U.S. — C4 78
Perow, B.C. — B4 69
Perquimans, co., N.C., U.S. — A6 110
Perrine, Fl., U.S. — G6 86
Perrineville, N.J., U.S. — C4 107

Perris, Ca., U.S. — F5 82
Perro, Laguna del, l., N.M., U.S. — C4 108
Perronville, Mi., U.S. — C3 99
Perros-Guirec, Fr. — C2 16
Perrot, Île, i., Que. — q19 74
Perry, Ar., U.S. — B3 81
Perry, Fl., U.S. — B3 86
Perry, Ga., U.S. — D3 87
Perry, Il., U.S. — D3 90
Perry, Ia., U.S. — C3 92
Perry, Ks., U.S. — C8 93
Perry, La., U.S. — E3 95
Perry, Me., U.S. — D5 96
Perry, Mi., U.S. — F6 99
Perry, Mo., U.S. — B6 102
Perry, N.Y., U.S. — C2 109
Perry, Oh., U.S. — A4 112
Perry, Ok., U.S. — A4 113
Perry, co., Al., U.S. — C2 78
Perry, co., Ar., U.S. — C3 81
Perry, co., Il., U.S. — E4 90
Perry, co., In., U.S. — H4 91
Perry, co., Ky., U.S. — C6 94
Perry, co., Ms., U.S. — D4 101
Perry, co., Mo., U.S. — D8 102
Perry, co., Oh., U.S. — C3 112
Perry, co., Pa., U.S. — F7 115
Perry, co., Tn., U.S. — B4 119
Perrydale, Or., U.S. — B3 114
Perry Hall, Md., U.S. — B5 97
Perry Heights, Oh., U.S. — *B4 112
Perry Lake, res., Ks., U.S. — C8 93
Perryman, Md., U.S. — B5 97
Perry Peak, mtn., Ma., U.S. — B1 98
Perrysburg, N.Y., U.S. — C1 109
Perrysburg, Oh., U.S. — A2 112
Perrysburg Heights, Oh., U.S. — e6 112
Perrysville, Oh., U.S. — B3 112
Perrysville, Pa., U.S. — h13 115
Perryton, Tx., U.S. — A2 120
Perryvale, Alta. — B4 68
Perryville, Ak., U.S. — D8 79
Perryville, Ky., U.S. — C5 94
Perryville, La., U.S. — B4 95
Perryville, Md., U.S. — A5 97
Perryville, Mo., U.S. — D8 102
Perryville, R.I., U.S. — F3 116
Perryville, Tn., U.S. — B3 119
Persan, Fr. — E2 17
Persepolis, hist., Iran — G6 39
Perseverancia, Bol. — E7 91
Pershing, In., U.S. — E5 91
Pershing, Ia., U.S. — C5 92
Pershing, co., Nv., U.S. — C3 105
Persia see Iran, ctry., Asia —
Persian Gulf, b., Asia — C5 38
Persimmon Grove, Ky., U.S. — k14 94
Person, co., N.C., U.S. — A3 110
Perstorp, Swe. — B7 15
Pertek, Tur. — C12 40
Perth, Austl. — F2 50
Perth, Ont. — C8 73
Perth, Scot., U.K. — B5 10
Perth, Ks., U.S. — E6 93
Perth, N.D., U.S. — A6 111
Perth, co., Ont. — D3 73
Perth Amboy, N.J., U.S. — B4 107
Perth-Andover, N.B. — B10 71
Perthshire, Ms., U.S. — B3 101
Pertuis, Fr. — F6 16
Peru, In., U.S. — C5 91
Peru, Ia., U.S. — C4 92
Peru, Ks., U.S. — E7 93
Peru, Me., U.S. — *D2 96
Peru, Ma., U.S. — B1 98
Peru, Ne., U.S. — D10 104
Peru, N.Y., U.S. — f11 109
Peru, Vt., U.S. — E3 122
Peru, ctry., S.A. — C2 58
Perugia, Italy — C4 23
Peruíbe, Braz. — C3 56
Perušić, Yugo. — f12 102
Péruwelz, Bel. — D3 17
Pervomaysk, Sov. Un. — q21 27
Pervomaysk, Sov. Un. — G8 29
Pervouralsk, Sov. Un. — C4 23
Pesaro, Italy — C4 23
Pescadero, Ca., U.S. — D2 82
Pescara, Italy — C5 23
Pescara, stm., Italy — C4 23
Peschanyy, Cape, c., Sov. Un. — G19 8
Peschanyy, Cape, c., Sov. Un. — B10 33
Pesé, Pan. — G7 62
Peshastin, Wa., U.S. — B5 124
Peshāwar, Pak. — B5 36
Peshkopija, Alb. — B3 25
Peshtera, Bul. — D7 24
Peshtigo, Wi., U.S. — C6 126
Peshtigo, stm., Wi., U.S. — C5 126
Peski, Sov. Un. — F14 27
Peski, Sov. Un. — n18 27
Peso da Régua, Port. — C3 22
Pesotum, Il., U.S. — D5 90
Pesqueira, Braz. — C3 57
Pessac, Fr. — E3 16
Petacas, Cerro, mtn., Col. — C2 60
Petal, Ms., U.S. — D4 101
Petaling Jaya, Malay. — K4 35
Petaluma, Ca., U.S. — C2 82
Petatlán, Mex. — D4 63
Petauke, Zam. — D5 48
Petawawa, Ont. — B7 73
Petawawa, stm., Ont. — A6 73
Petén Itzá, Lago, l., Guat. — B3 62
Petenwell Lake, res., Wi., U.S. — D4 126
Peterborough, Austl. — F6 50
Peterborough, Eng., U.K. — D6 10
Peterborough, Ont. — C6 73
Peterborough, N.H., U.S. — E3 106
Peterborough, co., Ont. — C6 73
Peter Dana Point, Me., U.S. — D5 96
Peterhead, Scot., U.K. — B6 10
Peter I Island, i., Ant. — C1 7
Peter Island, i., V.I. Br. — F5 65
Peterlee, Eng., U.K. — F7 13
Peter Lougheed Provincial Park, Ont. — D3 68
Peterman, Al., U.S. — D2 78

Petermann Ranges, mts., Austl. — E4 50
Peter Pond Lake, l., Sask. — m7 75
Petersburg, Ak., U.S. — D13 79
Petersburg, De., U.S. — D3 85
Petersburg, Il., U.S. — C4 90
Petersburg, In., U.S. — H3 91
Petersburg, Ky., U.S. — h13 94
Petersburg, Mi., U.S. — G7 99
Petersburg, Ne., U.S. — C7 104
Petersburg, N.J., U.S. — E3 107
Petersburg, N.Y., U.S. — E7 109
Petersburg, N.D., U.S. — A8 111
Petersburg, Oh., U.S. — B5 112
Petersburg, Pa., U.S. — E5 115
Petersburg, Tn., U.S. — B5 119
Petersburg, Tx., U.S. — C2 120
Petersburg, Va., U.S. — C5 123
Petersburg, W.V., U.S. — B5 125
Peters Creek, stm., W.V., U.S. — m14 125
Petersdorf, W. Ger. — D3 15
Petersfield, Man. — D3 70
Petersfield, Eng., U.K. — C7 12
Petersham, Ma., U.S. — B3 98
Peters Landing, Tn., U.S. — B4 119
Peters Mountain, mtn., U.S. — D4 125
Peterson, Al., U.S. — B2 78
Peterson, Ia., U.S. — B2 92
Peterson, Mn., U.S. — G7 100
Peterson, Ut., U.S. — B4 121
Peterson Field, mil., Co., U.S. — C6 83
Petersville, Al., U.S. — A2 78
Peterstown, W.V., U.S. — D4 125
Peter the Great Bay, b., Sov. Un. — C11 31
Petilia Policastro, Italy — E6 23
Pétionville, Haiti — E7 64
Petitcodiac, N.B. — D4 71
Petitcodiac, stm., N.B. — C5 71
Petit-de-Grat, N.S. — D9 71
Petite Amite, stm., La., U.S. — h10 95
Petite Rivière, N.B. — E5 71
Petite-Rivière-de-l'Artibonite, Haiti — E7 64
Petite-Rivière-de-l'Île, N.B. — B5 71
Petite-Étang, N.S. — C9 71
Petit-Goâve, Haiti — E7 64
Petit Jean, stm., Ar., U.S. — B2 81
Petit Jean Mountain, mtn., Ar., U.S. — C2 81
Petit Lac Des Allemands, l., La., U.S. — k11 95
Petit Lake, l., La., U.S. — k12 95
Petit-Mécatina, Île du, i., Que. — C7 72
Petit-Rocher, N.B. — B4 71
Petitsikapau Lake, l., Newf. — g8 72
Peto, Mex. — C7 63
Petorca, Chile — A2 54
Petoskey, Mi., U.S. — C6 99
Petra, hist., Jord. — D4 41
Petras, Mount, mtn., Ant. — B36 7
Petrey, Al., U.S. — D3 78
Petrich, Bul. — E6 24
Petrified Forest National Park, Az., U.S. — B6 80
Petrikov, Sov. Un. — E7 27
Petrila, Rom. — C6 24
Petrinja, Yugo. — C3 24
Petrodvorets, Sov. Un. — s30 14
Petrohué, Chile — C2 54
Petrokrepost, Sov. Un. — B8 27
Petrolândia, Braz. — C3 57
Petroleum, In., U.S. — C7 91
Petroleum, co., Mt., U.S. — C8 103
Petrolia, Ont. — E2 73
Petrolia, Il., U.S. — E6 90
Petrolia, Ks., U.S. — E8 93
Petrolia, Pa., U.S. — D2 115
Petrolia, Tx., U.S. — C3 120
Petrolina, Braz. — C2 57
Petropavlovsk, Sov. Un. — D9 29
Petropavlovsk [-Kamchatskiy], Sov. Un. — D18 29
Petrópolis, Braz. — C4 56
Petros, Tn., U.S. — C9 119
Petroșani, Rom. — C6 24
Petrovgrad see Zrenjanin, Yugo. — C5 24
Petrovsk, Sov. Un. — E15 27
Petrovsk-Zabaykalskiy, Sov. Un. — D13 29
Petrozavodsk, Sov. Un. — D6 29
Pettaquamscutt Lake Shores, R.I., U.S. — F4 116
Pettibone, N.D., U.S. — B6 111
Pettigo, Ire. — C4 11
Pettigrew, Ar., U.S. — B2 81
Pettingell Peak, mtn., Co., U.S. — B5 83
Pettis, co., Mo., U.S. — C4 102
Pettisville, Oh., U.S. — A1 112
Pettus, Tx., U.S. — E4 120
Petukhovo, Sov. Un. — B7 28
Pevek, Sov. Un. — C33 128
Pevely, Mo., U.S. — g13 102
Pewamo, Mi., U.S. — E6 99
Pewaukee, Wi., U.S. — *E5 126
Pewaukee Lake, l., Wi., U.S. — m11 126
Pewee Valley, Ky., U.S. — B4 94
Peyton, Co., U.S. — B6 83
Pézenas, Fr. — F5 16
Pfaffenhofen [an der Ilm], W. Ger. — E6 19
Pfäffikon, Switz. — B6 21
Pfarrkirchen, W. Ger. — D6 18
Pfeifer, Ks., U.S. — D4 93
Pforzheim, W. Ger. — C6 20
Pfunds, Aus. — C6 20
Pfungstadt, W. Ger. — D3 19
Phalodi, India — C5 36
Phaltan, India — I5 37
Phangan, i., Thai. — H4 35
Phangnga, Thai. — H3 35
Phanom Dongrak Range, mts., Asia — C3 34
Phan Rang, Viet. — C3 34
Phan Thiet, Viet. — C3 34
Pharaoh, Ok., U.S. — B5 113
Pharr, Tx., U.S. — F3 120
Pharsalus see Fársala, Grc. — C4 25
Phatthalung, Thai. —
Phayao, Thai. —
Phelps, Ky., U.S. — C7 94
Phelps, N.Y., U.S. — C3 109
Phelps, Wi., U.S. — C5 126
Phelps, co., Mo., U.S. — D6 102
Phelps, co., Ne., U.S. — D6 104
Phelps City, Mo., U.S. — A2 102
Phelps Lake, l., N.C., U.S. — B6 110
Phenix, Va., U.S. — C4 123
Phenix City, Al., U.S. — C4 78

Petermann Ranges, mts., Austl. — E4 50
Phetchabun, Thai. — B2 34
Phetchabun Range, mts., Thai. — B2 35
Phetchaburi, Thai. — C1 34
Phichit, Thai. — D4 35
Philadelphia, Ms., U.S. — C4 101
Philadelphia, Mo., U.S. — B6 102
Philadelphia, N.Y., U.S. — A5 109
Philadelphia, Pa., U.S. — G11 115
Philadelphia, Tn., U.S. — D9 119
Philadelphia, co., Pa., U.S. — G12 115
Philadelphia Naval Shipyard, mil., Pa., U.S. — P21 115
Phil Campbell, Al., U.S. — A2 78
Philip, S.D., U.S. — C4 118
Philipp, Ms., U.S. — B3 101
Philippeville see Skikda, Alg. — B6 44
Philippeville, Bel. — D4 17
Philippi, W.V., U.S. — B4 125
Philippi Glacier, ice, Ant. — C21 7
Philippine Islands, ctry., Asia — C6 34
Philippine Sea — E7 6
Philipsburg, Que. — D4 74
Philipsburg, Mt., U.S. — D3 103
Philipsburg, Pa., U.S. — E5 115
Philipsville, Ont. — C8 73
Philleo Lake, l., Wa., U.S. — h14 124
Phillip Island, i., Austl. — I5 51
Phillippy, Tn., U.S. — A2 119
Phillips, Me., U.S. — D2 96
Phillips, Ne., U.S. — D7 104
Phillips, Ok., U.S. — C5 113
Phillips, Tx., U.S. — B2 120
Phillips, Wi., U.S. — C3 126
Phillips, co., Ar., U.S. — C5 81
Phillips, co., Co., U.S. — A8 83
Phillips, co., Ks., U.S. — C4 93
Phillips, co., Mt., U.S. — B8 103
Phillips Brook, stm., N.H., U.S. — A4 106
Phillipsburg, Ks., U.S. — C4 93
Phillipsburg, Mo., U.S. — D5 102
Phillipsburg, N.J., U.S. — B2 107
Phillipston, Ma., U.S. — A3 98
Philmont, N.Y., U.S. — C7 109
Philo, Il., U.S. — C5 90
Philo, Oh., U.S. — C4 112
Philomath, Ga., U.S. — C4 87
Philomath, Or., U.S. — C3 114
Philpott Reservoir, res., Va., U.S. — D2 123
Phippen, Sask. — E1 75
Phippsburg, Co., U.S. — A4 83
Phippsburg, Me., U.S. — g8 96
Phitsanulok, Thai. — B2 34
Phlorina see Flórina, Grc. — B3 25
Phnom Penh (Phnom Penh), Camb. — C2 34
Phoenicia, N.Y., U.S. — C6 109
Phoenix, Az., U.S. — D3 80
Phoenix, Il., U.S. — k9 90
Phoenix, Md., U.S. — A4 97
Phoenix, Mi., U.S. — A2 99
Phoenix, N.Y., U.S. — B4 109
Phoenix, Or., U.S. — E4 114
Phoenix Islands, is., Kir. — G11 6
Phoenixville, Pa., U.S. — F10 115
Phong, stm., Thai. — D5 35
Phongsali, Laos — B5 35
Phrae, Thai. — B2 34
Phra Nakhon Si Ayutthaya, Thai. — E4 35
Phuket, Thai. — D1 34
Phuket, i., Thai. — I3 35
Phumi Samraong, Camb. — E5 35
Phu Quoc, Viet. — G5 35
Phu Quoc, i., Viet. — G6 35
Phu Tho, Viet. — B6 35
Phutthaisong, Thai. — B4 35
Piaanu Pass, strt., Micron. — Q18 52
Piacenza, Italy — B2 23
Pialba, Austl. — B9 51
Pianguan, China — E4 32
Pianosa, i., Italy — C3 23
Pianosa Island, i., Italy — C5 23
Piapot, Sask. — H1 75
Piaseczno, Pol. — m14 27
Piastów, Pol. — m13 27
Piatra-Neamţ, Rom. — B8 24
Piatt, co., Il., U.S. — D5 90
Piauí, state, Braz. — C2 57
Piauí, stm., Braz. — C2 57
Piave, stm., Italy — A4 23
Piazza Armerina, Italy — F5 23
Pibor, stm., Afr. — D3 47
Pibor Post, Sud. — D3 47
Picabo, Id., U.S. — F4 89
Picacho, Az., U.S. — E4 80
Picacho, N.M., U.S. — D4 108
Picard, Que. — B8 74
Picardie, hist. reg., Fr. — C5 16
Picayune, Ms., U.S. — E4 101
Piccadilly, Newf. — D2 72
Piceance Creek, stm., Co., U.S. — B2 83
Pichanal, Arg. — D3 55
Picher, Ok., U.S. — A7 113
Pichilemu, Chile — A2 54
Pichincha, prov., Ec. — A2 58
Pickardville, Alta. — B4 68
Pickaway, co., Oh., U.S. — C2 112
Pick City, N.D., U.S. — B4 111
Pickens, Ar., U.S. — C4 81
Pickens, Ms., U.S. — C4 101
Pickens, Ok., U.S. — C5 113
Pickens, S.C., U.S. — B2 117
Pickens, W.V., U.S. — C4 125
Pickens, co., Al., U.S. — B1 78
Pickens, co., Ga., U.S. — B2 87
Pickens, co., S.C., U.S. — B2 117
Pickensville, Al., U.S. — B1 78
Pickerel, Ont. — B4 73
Pickerel, Wi., U.S. — C5 126
Pickerel, stm., Ont. — B4 73
Pickerel Lake, l., Wi., U.S. — C5 126
Pickering, Ont. — D5 73
Pickering, Eng., U.K. — F8 13
Pickering, Mo., U.S. — A3 102
Pickerington, Oh., U.S. — C3 112
Pickett, co., Tn., U.S. — C8 119
Pickford, Mi., U.S. — B6 99
Pickrell, Ne., U.S. — D9 104
Pickstown, S.D., U.S. — D7 118
Pickwick, Mn., U.S. — G7 100
Pickwick Dam, Tn., U.S. — B3 119
Pickwick Lake, res., U.S. — A6 101
Pickworth Point, c., Ma., U.S. — f12 98
Pico, i., Port. — *g8 44
Pico, Ponta do, mtn., Port. — *g8 44
Pico Rivera, Ca., U.S. — n12 82
Picos, Braz. — C2 57
Picton, Ont. — D7 73
Picton, N.Z. — N14 51
Pictou, N.S. — D7 71

Name	Map Ref.	Page

Pictou, co., N.S. — D7 71
Pictou Island, i., N.S. — D7 71
Pictou Landing, N.S. — D7 71
Picture Butte, Alta. — E4 68
Pictured Rocks National Lakeshore, Mi., U.S. — B4 99
Picture Rocks, Pa., U.S. — D8 115
Picuí, Braz. — h5 57
Picún Leufú, Arg. — B3 54
Pidálion, Akrotírion, c., Cyp. — E10 40
Pidurutalagala, mtn., Sri L. — G7 36
Piedade, Braz. — m8 56
Piedal, stm., Mex. — h9 63
Piedmont, Que. — D3 74
Piedmont, Al., U.S. — B4 78
Piedmont, Ca., U.S. — h8 82
Piedmont, Ks., U.S. — E7 93
Piedmont, Mo., U.S. — D7 102
Piedmont, Ok., U.S. — B4 113
Piedmont, S.C., U.S. — B3 117
Piedmont, S.D., U.S. — C2 118
Piedmont, W.V., U.S. — B5 125
Piedmont (Piemonte), prov., Italy — B1 23
Piedmont Lake, res., Oh., U.S. — B4 112
Piedra, Ca., U.S. — D4 82
Piedra, stm., Co., U.S. — D3 83
Piedrabuena, Spain — C3 22
Piedras, stm., Pan. — k12 62
Piedras, stm., Pan. — k11 62
Piedras, Punta, c., Arg. — B5 54
Piedras, Punta, c., Ven. — A5 60
Piedras Blancas, Point, c., Ca., U.S. — B3 82
Piedras Negras, Guat. — D6 63
Piedras Negras, Mex. — B4 63
Piedra Sola, Ur. — E1 56
Piekary Śląskie, Pol. — g9 26
Pieksämäki, Fin. — F12 14
Pielinen, l., Fin. — F13 14
Piemonte, prov., Italy — D3 20
Piendamó, Col. — C2 60
Pierce, Co., U.S. — A6 83
Pierce, Id., U.S. — E5 86
Pierce, Ne., U.S. — C3 89
Pierce, Tn., U.S. — A3 119
Pierce, co., Ga., U.S. — E4 87
Pierce, co., Ne., U.S. — B8 104
Pierce, co., N.D., U.S. — A5 111
Pierce, co., Wa., U.S. — C3 124
Pierce, co., Wi., U.S. — D1 126
Pierce Lake, l., Fl., U.S. — E5 86
Pierce City, Mo., U.S. — E3 102
Piercefield, N.Y., U.S. — A6 109
Pierce Lake, l., Can. — B5 70
Pierce Pond, l., Me., U.S. — C2 96
Pierces Point, N.J., U.S. — E3 107
Pierceton, In., U.S. — B6 91
Pierceville, In., U.S. — F7 91
Pierceville, Ks., U.S. — E3 93
Piercy, Ca., U.S. — C2 82
Piermont, N.H., U.S. — C2 106
Pierowall, Scot., U.K. — A6 13
Pierpont, Oh., U.S. — A5 112
Pierpont, S.D., U.S. — B8 118
Pierre, S.D., U.S. — C5 118
Pierre, Bayou, stm., Ms., U.S. — D3 101
Pierrefitte, Fr. — g10 16
Pierrefitte-sur-Aire, Fr. — F5 17
Pierrefonds, Que. — q19 74
Pierre Part, La., U.S. — k9 95
Pierreville, Que. — C5 74
Pierron, Il., U.S. — E4 90
Pierson, Man. — E1 70
Pierson, Fl., U.S. — C5 86
Pierson, Ia., U.S. — B2 92
Pierz, Mn., U.S. — E4 100
Piešťany, Czech. — D4 26
Pietermaritzburg, S. Afr. — C5 49
Pietersburg, S. Afr. — B4 49
Pie Town, N.M., U.S. — C1 108
Pietrasanta, Italy — C3 23
Piet Retief, S. Afr. — C5 49
Pietrosu, mtn., Rom. — B7 24
Pietrosul, mtn., Rom. — B7 24
Pieve di Cadore, Italy — A4 23
Pigeon, Mi., U.S. — E7 99
Pigeon, stm., Man. — C3 70
Pigeon, stm., U.S. — g9 110
Pigeon, stm., In., U.S. — A6 91
Pigeon, stm., Mn., U.S. — h10 100
Pigeon, stm., Wi., U.S. — k10 126
Pigeon Bay, b., Man. — C3 70
Pigeon Cove, Ma., U.S. — A6 98
Pigeon Creek, stm., In., U.S. — H3 91
Pigeon Falls, Wi., U.S. — D2 126
Pigeon Forge, Tn., U.S. — D10 119
Pigeon Lake, l., Alta. — C4 68
Pigeon Mountain, mtn., U.S. — B1 87
Pigeon Point, c., Mn., U.S. — h10 100
Pigg, stm., Va., U.S. — D3 123
Piggott, Ar., U.S. — A5 81
Pigüé, Arg. — B4 54
Piirai, i., Marsh Is. — S18 52
Pijijiapan, Mex. — D6 63
Pike, N.H., U.S. — B2 106
Pike, N.Y., U.S. — C2 109
Pike, co., Al., U.S. — D4 78
Pike, co., Ar., U.S. — C2 81
Pike, co., Ga., U.S. — C2 87
Pike, co., Il., U.S. — D2 90
Pike, co., In., U.S. — H3 91
Pike, co., Ky., U.S. — C7 94
Pike, co., Ms., U.S. — D3 101
Pike, co., Mo., U.S. — B6 102
Pike, co., Oh., U.S. — C2 112
Pike, co., Pa., U.S. — D11 115
Pike, stm., Wi., U.S. — C6 126
Pike City, Ar., U.S. — C2 81
Pike Island Dam, U.S. — f8 125
Pike Lake, Mn., U.S. — D6 100
Pike Road, Al., U.S. — C3 78
Pikes Peak, mtn., Co., U.S. — C5 83
Pikes Rocks, mtn., Pa., U.S. — C3 115
Piketberg, S. Afr. — B4 49
Piketon, Oh., U.S. — C2 112
Pikeville, Ky., U.S. — C7 94
Pikeville, N.C., U.S. — B5 110
Pikeville, Tn., U.S. — D8 119
Pikou, China — E10 32
Pikwitonei, Man. — B3 70
Piła, Pol. — B4 26
Pilar, Braz. — C3 57
Pilar, Para. — E4 55
Pilar, N.M., U.S. — A4 108
Pilar de Goiás, Braz. — A3 56
Pilar do Sul, Braz. — m8 56
Pilatus, mtn., Switz. — D4 20
Pilcomayo, stm., S.A. — D4 55
Pilger, Sask. — E3 75
Pilger, Ne., U.S. — B8 104
Pilgrims Knob, Va., U.S. — e10 123
Pilgrim, Ky., U.S. — C7 94
Pilibhit, India — C7 37
Pilica, stm., Pol. — C5 26
Pillager, Mn., U.S. — D4 100
Pillaro, Ec. — B2 58
Pillar Point, c., Ca., U.S. — k7 82
Pilley's Island, Newf. — D4 72
Pillow, Pa., U.S. — E6 115
Pillsbury, Pa., U.S. — B8 111
Pilos, Grc. — D3 25
Pilot Butte, Sask. — G3 75
Pilot Grove, Mo., U.S. — C5 102
Pilot Knob, Mo., U.S. — D7 102
Pilot Knob, mtn., Ar., U.S. — B2 81
Pilot Knob, mtn., Id., U.S. — C1 81
Pilot Mound, Man. — E2 70
Pilot Mound, Ia., U.S. — B3 92
Pilot Mountain, N.C., U.S. — A2 110
Pilot Peak, mtn., Nv., U.S. — B7 105
Pilot Peak, mtn., Nv., U.S. — E4 105
Pilot Peak, mtn., Wy., U.S. — B3 127
Pilot Point, Ak., U.S. — D8 79
Pilot Point, Tx., U.S. — C4 120
Pilot Range, mts., Nv., U.S. — B7 105
Pilot Range, mts., N.H., U.S. — A4 106
Pilot Rock, Or., U.S. — B8 114
Pilot Station, Ak., U.S. — C7 79
Pilottown, La., U.S. — E6 95
Pilsen, Wi., U.S. — h10 126
Pilsen see Plzeň, Czech. — D2 103
Pilvo, Sov. Un. — A11 33
Pima, Az., U.S. — E6 80
Pima, co., Az., U.S. — E3 80
Pimmit Hills, Va., U.S. — g12 123
Pimpri-Chinchwad, India — *E5 36
Piña, Pan. — k10 62
Pinal, co., Az., U.S. — E4 80
Pinaleno Mountains, mts., Az., U.S. — E5 80
Pinal Mountains, mts., Az., U.S. — D5 80
Pinang see George Town, Malay. — D2 34
Pinang, state, Malay. — J4 35
Pinang, i., Malay. — D2 34
Pınarbaşı, Tur. — C11 40
Pinar del Río, Cuba — C2 64
Pinar del Río, prov., Cuba — C2 64
Pinardville, N.H., U.S. — E3 106
Pinás, Arg. — A3 54
Pinatubo, Mount, mtn., Phil. — o13 34
Pinawa, Man. — D4 70
Pincher Creek, Alta. — E4 68
Pincher Station, Alta. — E4 68
Pinckard, Al., U.S. — D4 78
Pinckney, Mi., U.S. — F7 99
Pinckney Island, i., S.C., U.S. — G6 117
Pinckneyville, Il., U.S. — E4 90
Pinconning, Mi., U.S. — E7 99
Pińczów, Pol. — C5 26
Pindamonhangaba, Braz. — C3 56
Pindaré, stm., Braz. — B1 57
Pindiga, Nig. — *E7 45
Pindus Mountains, mts., Grc. — C3 40
Pine, Az., U.S. — C4 80
Pine, Co., U.S. — B5 83
Pine, co., Mn., U.S. — D6 100
Pine, stm., B.C. — B6 69
Pine, stm., Man. — D1 70
Pine, stm., Mi., U.S. — D7 99
Pine, stm., Mi., U.S. — D5 99
Pine, stm., N.H., U.S. — C4 106
Pine, stm., Wi., U.S. — C5 126
Pine, stm., Wi., U.S. — C4 126
Pine Apple, Al., U.S. — D3 78
Pine Bank, Pa., U.S. — G1 115
Pine Barrens, reg., N.J., U.S. — D3 107
Pine Bluff, Ar., U.S. — C3 81
Pinebluff, N.C., U.S. — B3 110
Pine Bluffs, Wy., U.S. — E8 127
Pine Bridge, Ct., U.S. — D3 84
Pinebur, Ms., U.S. — D4 101
Pine Bush, N.Y., U.S. — D6 109
Pine Castle, Fl., U.S. — D5 86
Pine City, Ar., U.S. — C4 81
Pine City, Mn., U.S. — E6 100
Pine City, Wa., U.S. — B8 124
Pine Creek, Austl. — B5 50
Pine Creek, stm., Alta. — B4 68
Pine Creek, stm., Nv., U.S. — C5 105
Pine Creek, stm., Pa., U.S. — C6 115
Pine Creek, stm., Wa., U.S. — B8 124
Pine Creek Lake, res., Ok., U.S. — C6 113
Pinecrest, Ca., U.S. — C4 82
Pinedale, Al., U.S. — C3 78
Pinedale, Wy., U.S. — D3 127
Pinnebog, Mi., U.S. — E7 99
Pine Falls, Man. — D3 70
Pine Forest Range, mts., Nv., U.S. — B3 105
Pine Grove, Ga., U.S. — E4 87
Pine Grove, La., U.S. — D5 95
Pine Grove, N.J., U.S. — D3 107
Pine Grove, Pa., U.S. — E9 115
Pine Grove Mills, Pa., U.S. — E6 115
Pine Grove West, W.V., U.S. — B4 125
Pine Hall, N.C., U.S. — A2 110
Pine Hill, Austl. — A6 51
Pine Hill, Al., U.S. — D2 78
Pine Hill, Ky., U.S. — C5 94
Pine Hill, N.J., U.S. — D3 107
Pine Hills, Fl., U.S. — D5 86
Pinehouse Lake, Sask. — B2 75
Pinehouse Lake, l., Sask. — B2 75
Pinehurst, Ga., U.S. — D3 87
Pinehurst, Id., U.S. — B2 89
Pinehurst, Ma., U.S. — f11 98
Pinehurst, N.C., U.S. — B3 110
Pinehurst Lake, l., Alta. — B5 68
Pine Island, Mn., U.S. — F6 100
Pine Island, N.Y., U.S. — D6 109
Pine Island Bay, b., Ant. — B2 7
Pine Island Sound, strt., Fl., U.S. — F4 86
Pine Key, i., Fl., U.S. — p10 86
Pine Knot, Ky., U.S. — D5 94
Pine Lake, Ga., U.S. — h8 87
Pine Lake, Ma., U.S. — g10 98
Pine Lake, l., In., U.S. — A4 91
Pine Lake, l., Wi., U.S. — C5 126
Pineland, S.C., U.S. — F5 117
Pine Lawn, Mo., U.S. — f13 102
Pine Level, Al., U.S. — C3 78
Pine Level, N.C., U.S. — B4 110
Pinellas, co., Fl., U.S. — D4 86
Pinellas Point, c., Fl., U.S. — p10 86
Pinellas Park, Fl., U.S. — E4 86
Pine Meadow, Ct., U.S. — B4 84
Pine Mountain, Ga., U.S. — D2 87
Pine Mountain, mtn., U.S. — D6 94
Pine Mountain, mtn., Ct., U.S. — B4 84
Pine Mountain, mtn., Ga., U.S. — D2 87
Pine Mountain, mtn., Or., U.S. — D6 114
Pine Mountain, mtn., Tn., U.S. — C9 119
Pine Mountain, hills, Ok., U.S. — C6 113
Pineora, Ga., U.S. — D5 87
Pine Orchard, Ct., U.S. — D4 84
Pine Park, Ga., U.S. — F2 87
Pine Plains, N.Y., U.S. — D7 109
Pine Point, N.W. Ter. — D10 66
Pine Point, Me., U.S. — E2 96
Pine Prairie, La., U.S. — D3 95
Pine Rest, Ar., U.S. — g10 98
Pine Ridge, Ar., U.S. — C2 81
Pine Ridge, Ky., U.S. — C6 94
Pine Ridge, Ms., U.S. — D2 101
Pine Ridge, S.D., U.S. — D3 118
Pine Ridge, mtn., Ne., U.S. — B2 104
Pine Ridge Indian Reservation, U.S. — D3 118
Pine River, Man. — D1 70
Pine River, Mn., U.S. — D4 100
Pinerolo, Italy — B1 23
Pines, Isle of see Juventud, Isla de la, i., Cuba — D2 64
Pines, Lake o' the, res., Tx., U.S. — C5 120
Pinesdale, Mt., U.S. — D2 103
Pine Stump Junction, Mi., U.S. — B5 99
Pine Swamp Knob, mtn., W.V., U.S. — B5 125
Pinetops, N.C., U.S. — B5 110
Pinetown, N.C., U.S. — B6 110
Pine Tree Corners, De., U.S. — C5 85
Pinetta, Fl., U.S. — B3 86
Pine Valley, Ca., U.S. — F5 82
Pine Valley, N.H., U.S. — E3 106
Pine Valley, val., Ut., U.S. — F2 121
Pine Valley Mountains, mts., Ut., U.S. — F2 121
Pineview, Ga., U.S. — D3 87
Pine Village, In., U.S. — D3 91
Pineville, Ky., U.S. — D6 94
Pineville, La., U.S. — C3 95
Pineville, Mo., U.S. — E3 102
Pineville, N.C., U.S. — B2 110
Pineville, S.C., U.S. — E7 117
Pineville, W.V., U.S. — D3 125
Pinewald, N.J., U.S. — D4 107
Pinewood, Fl., U.S. — s13 86
Pinewood, Mn., U.S. — C3 100
Pinewood, S.C., U.S. — D7 117
Pinewood Park, Fl., U.S. — *G6 86
Piney, Man. — E4 70
Piney Creek, stm., W.V., U.S. — n13 125
Piney Flats, Tn., U.S. — C11 119
Piney Fork, stm., W.V., U.S. — h9 125
Piney Point, Md., U.S. — D4 97
Piney View, W.V., U.S. — n13 125
Piney Woods, Ms., U.S. — C3 101
Ping, stm., Thai. — E5 34
Pingding, China — F5 32
Pingdingshan, China — H5 32
Pingdu, China — D8 31
Pingjiang, China — J5 32
Pingle, China — G7 31
Pingliang, China — D6 31
Pingluo, China — E2 32
Pingnan, China — G7 31
Pingquan, China — D8 32
Pingree, Id., U.S. — F6 89
Pingree, N.D., U.S. — B7 111
Pingwu, China — E5 31
Pingxiang, China — F7 31
Pingxiang, China — G6 31
Pinhal, Braz. — C3 56
Pinhal Novo, Port. — f10 22
Pinheiro, Braz. — B1 57
Pinheiro, Port. — B2 22
Pinhel, Port. — E4 22
Pini, i., Indon. — E1 34
Piniós (Peneus), stm., Grc. — C4 40
Pink Cliffs, clf., Ut., U.S. — F3 121
Pinkham, Sask. — F1 75
Pinkham Notch, N.H., U.S. — B4 106
Pink Hill, N.C., U.S. — B5 110
Pinkstaff, Il., U.S. — E6 90
Pinnacle, Ar., U.S. — C3 81
Pinnacle, N.C., U.S. — A2 110
Pinnacle, mtn., N.Y., U.S. — B6 109
Pinnacle Buttes, mtn., Wy., U.S. — C3 127
Pinnacles National Monument, Ca., U.S. — D3 82
Pinnaroo, Austl. — G3 51
Pinneberg, W. Ger. — B5 15
Pinnebog, Mi., U.S. — E7 99
Pinola, Ms., U.S. — D4 101
Pinole, Ca., U.S. — h8 82
Pinon, Fr. — E3 17
Pinon, Az., U.S. — A5 80
Pinon, N.M., U.S. — E4 108
Pinopolis Dam, S.C., U.S. — E8 117
Pinos, Mex. — C4 63
Pinos, Mount, mtn., Ca., U.S. — E4 82
Pinos, Point, c., Ca., U.S. — D2 82
Pinos Altos, N.M., U.S. — E1 108
Pinos-Puente, Spain — D4 22
Piñ, Pointe aux, c., Ont. — E3 73
Pinsk, Sov. Un. — E6 27
Pinsk Marshes, sw., Sov. Un. — E6 27
Pinson, Al., U.S. — f7 78
Pinson, Tn., U.S. — B3 119
Pinta, Isla, i., Ec. — f5 58
Pinta, Sierra, mts., Az., U.S. — E2 80
Pintados, Chile — D2 55
Pinto, Spain — p17 22
Pinto, Md., U.S. — k13 97
Pinto Butte, mtn., Sask. — H2 75
Pinto Creek, stm., Sask. — H2 75
Pintura, Braz. — F4 86
Pintwater Range, mts., Nv., U.S. — G6 105
Pinware, stm., Newf. — C3 72
Pinzolo, Italy — p10 86
Pinzón, Isla, i., Ec. — g5 58
Piombino, Italy — C3 23
Pioneer, La., U.S. — B4 95
Pioneer, Oh., U.S. — A1 112
Pioneer Mine, B.C. — D6 69
Pioneer Mountains, mts., Id., U.S. — F5 89
Pioner, i., Sov. Un. — B12 28
Piombino, Italy — C3 23
Piopolis, Que. — D7 74
Piotrków [Trybunalski], Pol. — C5 26
Piove di Sacco, Italy — D8 20
Pipe, Wi., U.S. — k9 126
Pipe Creek, stm., In., U.S. — D6 91
Piper, Ks., U.S. — k16 93
Piper City, Il., U.S. — C5 90
Piperville, Ont. — h12 73
Pipe Spring National Monument, Az., U.S. — A3 80
Pipestem, W.V., U.S. — D4 125
Pipestem Creek, stm., N.D., U.S. — B6 111
Pipestone, Man. — E1 70
Pipestone, Mn., U.S. — G2 100
Pipestone, co., Mn., U.S. — F2 100
Pipestone Creek, stm., Can. — E1 70
Pipestone National Monument, Mn., U.S. — G2 100
Pipestone Pass, Mt., U.S. — E4 103
Pipinas, Arg. — B5 54
Pipmuacan, Réservoir, res., Que. — k12 74
Piqua, Ks., U.S. — E8 93
Piqua, Oh., U.S. — B1 112
Piquiri, stm., Braz. — C2 56
Piracajuba, Braz. — B3 56
Piracicaba, Braz. — C3 56
Piracicaba, stm., Braz. — m8 56
Piracuruca, Braz. — B2 57
Piraeus see Piraiévs, Grc. — D4 40
Piraiévs (Piraeus), Grc. — D4 40
Piraju, Braz. — C3 56
Pirajuba, Braz. — B3 56
Pirajuí, Braz. — C3 56
Piramida, Mount, mtn., Sov. Un. — D12 29
Piran, Yugo. — C1 24
Pirané, Arg. — C4 55
Piranga, Braz. — C4 56
Piranhas, Braz. — C3 57
Pirapora, Braz. — C4 56
Pirassununga, Braz. — C3 56
Piratini, Braz. — D2 87
Pirenópolis, Braz. — B3 56
Pires do Rio, Braz. — B3 56
Pírgos, Grc. — D3 40
Piriápolis, Ur. — C1 56
Piripiri, Braz. — B2 57
Pirmasens, W. Ger. — D3 18
Pirna, E. Ger. — C6 18
Pirot, Yugo. — D6 24
Pirovskoye, Sov. Un. — D27 8
Pirtleville, Az., U.S. — F6 80
Piru, Indon. — F7 34
Piryatin, Sov. Un. — F9 27
Pisa, Italy — C3 23
Pisac, hist., Peru — D3 58
Pisagua, Chile — C1 55
Piscataqua, stm., N.H., U.S. — D5 106
Piscataquis, co., Me., U.S. — C3 96
Piscataquis, stm., Me., U.S. — C3 96
Piscataway, N.J., U.S. — B4 107
Piscataway Creek, stm., Md., U.S. — C4 97
Pisciotta, Italy — D5 23
Pisco, Peru — D2 58
Pisco Lake, l., N.Y., U.S. — B6 109
Písek, Czech. — D3 26
Pisek, N.D., U.S. — A8 111
Pisgah, Al., U.S. — A4 78
Pisgah, Ia., U.S. — C2 92
Pisgah, Oh., U.S. — n13 112
Pisgah, Mount, mtn., Ct., U.S. — B5 84
Pisgah, Mount, mtn., Vt., U.S. — F3 122
Pisgah, Mount, mtn., Wy., U.S. — B8 127
Pisgah Forest, N.C., U.S. — f10 110
Pishīn, Pak. — B4 36
Pishīn Lora, stm., Asia — C4 36
Pisinemo, Az., U.S. — E3 80
Pismo Beach, Ca., U.S. — E3 82
Pisogne, Italy — D6 20
Pissis, Monte, mtn., Arg. — D2 55
Pisticci, Italy — D6 23
Pistoia, Italy — C3 23
Pistol River, Or., U.S. — E2 114
Pisuerga, stm., Spain — A3 22
Pisz, Pol. — B6 26
Pit, stm., Ca., U.S. — B3 82
Pita, Gui. — F2 45
Pital, Cerro el, mtn., N.A. — *C3 62
Pitalito, Col. — C2 60
Pitanga, Braz. — C2 56
Pitangui, Braz. — E5 56
Piteå, Swe. — E9 14
Piteälven, stm., Swe. — E9 14
Pitești, Rom. — C7 24
Pithiviers, Fr. — C5 16
Piti, Guam — L9 52
Pitkin, Co., U.S. — C4 83
Pitkin, co., Co., U.S. — B4 83
Pitlochry, Scot., U.K. — B5 10
Pitman, N.J., U.S. — D2 107
Pitman, Oh., U.S. — C1 112
Pitrufquén, Chile — B2 54
Pitt, Mn., U.S. — B4 100
Pitt, co., N.C., U.S. — B5 110
Pitt Island, i., B.C. — C3 69
Pittman Center, Tn., U.S. — D10 119
Pitts, Ga., U.S. — E3 87
Pittsboro, In., U.S. — E5 91
Pittsboro, Ms., U.S. — B4 101
Pittsboro, N.C., U.S. — B3 110
Pittsburg, Ca., U.S. — g9 82
Pittsburg, Il., U.S. — F5 90
Pittsburg, Ks., U.S. — E9 93
Pittsburg, Ky., U.S. — C5 94
Pittsburg, Ok., U.S. — C5 113
Pittsburg, Tx., U.S. — C5 120
Pittsburg, co., Ok., U.S. — C6 113
Pittsburgh, Pa., U.S. — F1 115
Pittsfield, Me., U.S. — D3 96
Pittsfield, Ma., U.S. — B1 98
Pittsfield, N.H., U.S. — D4 106
Pittsfield, Il., U.S. — D3 90
Pittsfield, Vt., U.S. — D3 122
Pittsford, Mi., U.S. — G6 99
Pittsford, Vt., U.S. — D2 122
Pittston, Pa., U.S. — D10 115
Pittstown, N.J., U.S. — B3 107
Pittsview, Al., U.S. — C4 78
Pittsville, Md., U.S. — D6 97
Pittsville, Wi., U.S. — D3 126
Pittsylvania, co., Va., U.S. — D3 123
Piuí, Braz. — C3 56
Piura, Peru — C1 58
Piura, dept., Peru — C1 58
Piute, co., Ut., U.S. — E3 121
Piute Peak, mtn., Ca., U.S. — E4 82
Piute Reservoir, res., Ut., U.S. — E3 121
Piuthān, Nepal — C9 37
Piva, stm., Yugo. — D4 24
Pixley, Ca., U.S. — E4 82
Pizzo, Italy — E6 23
P. K. le Roux Dam, res., S. Afr. — *D3 49
Placentia, Newf. — E5 72
Placentia, Ca., U.S. — *n13 82
Placentia Bay, b., Newf. — E4 72
Placer, co., Ca., U.S. — C3 82
Placerville, Ca., U.S. — C3 82
Placerville, Id., U.S. — F3 89
Placetas, Cuba — C4 64
Placid, Lake, l., Fl., U.S. — E5 86
Placid, Lake, l., N.Y., U.S. — f11 109
Placida, Fl., U.S. — F4 86
Plácido de Castro, Braz. — D4 58
Placitas, N.M., U.S. — B3 108
Plaffeien, Switz. — C3 21
Plain, Wi., U.S. — E3 126
Plain City, Oh., U.S. — B2 112
Plain City, Ut., U.S. — B3 121
Plain Dealing, La., U.S. — B2 95
Plainedge, N.Y., U.S. — *E7 109
Plainfield, Ct., U.S. — C8 84
Plainfield, In., U.S. — E5 91
Plainfield, Ia., U.S. — B5 92
Plainfield, Ma., U.S. — A2 98
Plainfield, N.J., U.S. — B4 107
Plainfield, Oh., U.S. — B4 112
Plainfield, Vt., U.S. — C4 122
Plainfield, Wi., U.S. — D4 126
Plainfield Heights, Mi., U.S. — E5 99
Plains, Ga., U.S. — D2 87
Plains, Ks., U.S. — E3 93
Plains, Mt., U.S. — C1 103
Plains, Pa., U.S. — n17 115
Plains, Tx., U.S. — C1 120
Plainsboro, N.J., U.S. — C3 107
Plainview, Ar., U.S. — C2 81
Plainview, Mn., U.S. — F6 100
Plainview, Ne., U.S. — B8 104
Plainview, N.Y., U.S. — *E7 109
Plainview, S.D., U.S. — C3 118
Plainview, Tx., U.S. — B2 120
Plainville, Ct., U.S. — C4 84
Plainville, Ga., U.S. — B1 87
Plainville, Il., U.S. — D2 90
Plainville, In., U.S. — G3 91
Plainville, Ks., U.S. — C4 93
Plainville, Ma., U.S. — B5 98
Plainwell, Mi., U.S. — F5 99
Plaisance, Que. — D2 74
Plaisance, Haiti — E7 64
Plaisance, Baie de, b., Que. — B8 71
Plaisance-du-Gers, Fr. — F4 16
Plaisted, Me., U.S. — A4 96
Plaistow, N.H., U.S. — E4 106
Plamondon, Alta. — B4 68
Planá, Czech. — D1 26
Planaltina, Braz. — B3 56
Plane, stm., E. Ger. — A7 19
Plankinton, S.D., U.S. — D7 118
Plano, Il., U.S. — B5 90
Plano, Ia., U.S. — D4 92
Plano, Tx., U.S. — C4 120
Plantagenet, Ont. — B9 73
Plantation, Fl., U.S. — r13 86
Plantersville, Al., U.S. — C3 78
Plantersville, Ms., U.S. — A5 101
Plantersville, S.C., U.S. — D9 117
Plantsite, Az., U.S. — D6 80
Plantsville, Ct., U.S. — C4 84
Plaquemine, La., U.S. — D4 95
Plaquemines, co., La., U.S. — E6 95
Plasencia, Spain — B2 22
Plast, Sov. Un. — E2 8
Plaster Rock, N.B. — C2 71
Plastun, Sov. Un. — D8 33
Plasy, Czech. — C1 16
Plata, mtn., Switz. — D8 21
Plata, Río de la, est., S.A. — C1 56
Plateau, Pa., U.S. — C5 115
Plateau City, Co., U.S. — B3 83
Plate Cove West, Newf. — D5 72
Platina, Ca., U.S. — B2 82
Platinum, Ak., U.S. — D7 79
Platner, Co., U.S. — A7 83
Plato, Sask. — F1 75
Plato, Col. — B3 60
Plato, Mo., U.S. — D5 102
Plato Sánchez, Mex. — m14 63
Platte, S.D., U.S. — D7 118
Platte, co., Mo., U.S. — B3 102
Platte, co., Ne., U.S. — C8 104
Platte, co., Wy., U.S. — D7 127
Platte, stm., Mn., U.S. — E4 100
Platte, stm., Ne., U.S. — C8 104
Platte Center, Ne., U.S. — C8 104
Platte City, Mo., U.S. — B3 102
Platteville, Co., U.S. — A6 83
Platteville, Wi., U.S. — F3 126
Platter, Ok., U.S. — D5 113
Plattling, W. Ger. — E7 19
Plattsburg, Mo., U.S. — B3 102
Plattsburgh, N.Y., U.S. — f11 109
Plattsburgh Air Force Base, mil., N.Y., U.S. — f11 109
Plattsmouth, Ne., U.S. — D10 104
Plattville, Il., U.S. — B5 90
Plaucheville, La., U.S. — k9 95
Plauen, E. Ger. — C6 18
Plaza, N.D., U.S. — A4 111
Pleasant, stm., Me., U.S. — C3 96
Pleasant, Lake, res., Az., U.S. — D3 80
Pleasant, Mount, mtn., Va., U.S. — C3 123
Pleasant Grove, Ms., U.S. — A3 101
Pleasant Grove, Ut., U.S. — C4 121
Pleasant Hill, Ca., U.S. — C3 78
Pleasant Hill, Ca., U.S. — h8 82
Pleasant Hill, Il., U.S. — D3 90
Pleasant Hill, Ia., U.S. — e8 92
Pleasant Hill, La., U.S. — C2 95
Pleasant Hill, Mo., U.S. — C3 102
Pleasant Hill, Oh., U.S. — B1 112
Pleasant Hill, Ok., U.S. — D7 113
Pleasant Hill, S.C., U.S. — C6 117
Pleasant Hills, Pa., U.S. — *k14 115
Pleasant Hope, Mo., U.S. — D4 102
Pleasant Lake, In., U.S. — A7 91
Pleasant Lake, Ma., U.S. — C7 98
Pleasant Lake, N.D., U.S. — A6 111
Pleasant Lake, l., N.H., U.S. — D4 106
Pleasant Mills, In., U.S. — C8 91
Pleasant Mount, Pa., U.S. — C11 115
Pleasanton, Ca., U.S. — h9 82
Pleasanton, Ia., U.S. — D4 92
Pleasanton, Ks., U.S. — D9 93
Pleasanton, Ne., U.S. — D6 104
Pleasanton, Tx., U.S. — E3 120
Pleasant Plain, Ia., U.S. — C6 92
Pleasant Plains, Ar., U.S. — B4 81
Pleasant Plains, Il., U.S. — D4 90
Pleasant Pond, Me., U.S. — C3 96
Pleasant Pond, l., Me., U.S. — C3 96
Pleasant Prairie, Wi., U.S. — n12 126
Pleasants, co., W.V., U.S. — B3 125
Pleasant Shade, Tn., U.S. — C8 119
Pleasant Valley, Ct., U.S. — B4 84
Pleasant Valley, Ia., U.S. — g11 92
Pleasant Valley, Md., U.S. — A3 97
Pleasant Valley, Mo., U.S. — h11 102
Pleasant Valley, Nv., U.S. — *D2 105
Pleasant Valley, Oh., U.S. — C2 112
Pleasant View, Co., U.S. — *B5 83
Pleasant View, Il., U.S. — C3 90
Pleasant View, Ky., U.S. — m11 94
Pleasant View, Tn., U.S. — A4 119
Pleasant View, Ut., U.S. — B3 121
Pleasant View, Wi., U.S. — D3 126
Pleasant Beach, Ct., U.S. — D7 84
Pleasure Ridge Park, Ky., U.S. — g11 94
Pledger, Tx., U.S. — r14 120
Pleebo, Lib. — F3 45
Plenița, Rom. — C6 24
Plenty, Sask. — F1 75
Plenty, Bay of, b., N.Z. — L16 51
Plentywood, Mt., U.S. — B12 103
Plesetsk, Sov. Un. — C7 29
Plessis, N.Y., U.S. — A5 109
Plessisville, Que. — C6 74
Pleszew, Pol. — C4 26
Plétipi, Lac, l., Que. — h12 74
Plettenberg, W. Ger. — B2 19
Pleven, Bul. — D7 24
Plevlja, Yugo. — D4 24
Plevna, Ks., U.S. — E5 93
Plevna, Mo., U.S. — B5 102
Plevna, Mt., U.S. — D12 103
Pliny Range, mts., N.H., U.S. — B4 106
Plochingen, W. Ger. — D5 18
Płock, Pol. — B5 26
Ploemeur, Fr. — D2 16
Ploiești, Rom. — C8 24
Plomárion, Grc. — C6 25
Plomb du Cantal, mtn., Fr. — E5 16
Plombières-les-Bains, Fr. — B2 19
Plomosa Mountains, mts., Az., U.S. — D1 80
Plön, W. Ger. — A5 15
Plonge, Lac la, l., Sask. — B2 75
Płońsk, Pol. — B6 26
Plougastel, Fr. — C1 16
Plovdiv, Bul. — D7 24
Plover, Ia., U.S. — B3 92
Plover, Wi., U.S. — D4 126
Plover, stm., Wi., U.S. — D4 126
Plum, Pa., U.S. — k14 115
Plum, S.D., U.S. — C2 118
Plumas, Man. — D2 70
Plumas, co., Ca., U.S. — B3 82
Plum Bayou, stm., Ar., U.S. — k10 81
Plum Branch, S.C., U.S. — D3 117
Plum City, Wi., U.S. — D1 126
Plum Coulee, Man. — E3 70
Plum Creek, stm., Ne., U.S. — D6 104
Plumerville, Ar., U.S. — B3 81
Plum Island, i., Ma., U.S. — A6 98
Plummer, Id., U.S. — B2 89
Plummer, Mn., U.S. — C2 100
Plum Point, R.I., U.S. — E4 116
Plumsteadville, Pa., U.S. — F11 115
Plumtree, Zimb. — B4 49
Plumwood, Oh., U.S. — B2 112
Plunkett, Sask. — F3 75
Plunketts, Ok., U.S. — C7 113
Plush, Or., U.S. — E7 114
Plymouth, Monts. — H13 64
Plymouth, Eng., U.K. — E4 10
Plymouth, Ct., U.S. — C3 84
Plymouth, Fl., U.S. — D5 86
Plymouth, Il., U.S. — C3 90
Plymouth, In., U.S. — B5 91
Plymouth, Ia., U.S. — A4 92
Plymouth, Ks., U.S. — D7 93
Plymouth, Me., U.S. — D3 96
Plymouth, Ma., U.S. — C6 98
Plymouth, Mi., U.S. — p15 99
Plymouth, Mn., U.S. — m12 100
Plymouth, N.H., U.S. — C3 106
Plymouth, N.C., U.S. — B6 110
Plymouth, Oh., U.S. — B3 112
Plymouth, Pa., U.S. — D10 115
Plymouth, Ut., U.S. — B3 121
Plymouth, W.V., U.S. — E6 125
Plymouth, Wi., U.S. — E6 126
Plymouth, co., Ia., U.S. — B1 92
Plymouth, co., Ma., U.S. — C6 98
Plymouth Bay, b., Ma., U.S. — C6 98
Plymouth Township, Pa., U.S. — *F11 115
Plympton, N.S. — E4 71
Plympton, Ma., U.S. — C6 98
Plzeň, Czech. — D4 45
Pô, Burkina — g7 78

Po, stm., Italy B3 23
Po, stm., Va., U.S. B5 123
Po, Mouths of the, mth., Italy . B4 23
Poamoho Stream, stm., Hi.,
  U.S. f9 88
Pobé, Benin E5 45
Pobeda, Mount, mtn., Sov.
  Un. C36 128
Pobedino, Sov. Un. B11 33
Pobedy, Peak, mtn., Asia . . . E11 29
Poca, W.V., U.S. *C3 125
Pocahontas, Ar., U.S. A5 81
Pocahontas, Il., U.S. E4 90
Pocahontas, Ia., U.S. B3 92
Pocahontas, Tn., U.S. B3 119
Pocahontas, Va., U.S. e10 123
Pocahontas, co., Ia., U.S. . . . B3 92
Pocahontas, co., W.V., U.S. . C4 125
Pocasset, Ma., U.S. C6 98
Pocasset, Ok., U.S. B4 113
Pocatalico, W.V., U.S. C3 125
Pocatalico, stm., W.V., U.S. . C3 125
Pocatello, Id., U.S. G6 89
Pochep, Sov. Un. E9 27
Pochutla, Mex. D5 63
Pocola, Ok., U.S. B7 113
Pocomoke, stm., U.S. D7 97
Pocomoke City, Md., U.S. . . . D6 97
Pocomoke Sound, strt., Md.,
  U.S. E6 97
Poconé, Braz. B1 56
Pocono Mountains, hills, Pa.,
  U.S. E11 115
Pocono Pines, Pa., U.S. D11 115
Poços de Caldas, Braz. C3 56
Pocotopaug Lake, res., Ct.,
  U.S. C6 84
Pocrí, Pan. G7 62
Pocumtuck Mountain, mtn.,
  Ma., U.S. A2 98
Podbořany, Czech. C8 19
Podgornoye, Sov. Un. D25 8
Podhořany, Czech. n17 26
Podkamennaya Tunguska,
  Sov. Un. C27 8
Podkamennaya Tunguska,
  stm., Sov. Un. C12 29
Podolsk, Sov. Un. D11 27
Podor, Sen. C2 45
Podporozhye, Sov. Un. G16 14
Poe, In., U.S. C7 91
Poel, i., E. Ger. E5 15
Pofadder, S. Afr. C2 49
Poge, Cape, c., Ma., U.S. . . . D7 98
Poggibonsi, Italy C3 23
Pöggstall, Aus. D7 18
Pogradeci, Alb. B3 25
Pogranichnoye, Sov. Un. . . . A11 33
Pogranichnyy, Sov. Un. D5 33
Pohang, S. Kor. D10 31
Pohénégamook, Que. B8 74
Pohnpei, i., Micron. F9 6
Pohue Bay, b., Hi., U.S. E6 88
Poinsett, co., Ar., U.S. B5 81
Poinsett, Cape, c., Ant. C24 7
Poinsett, Lake, l., S.D., U.S. . D6 86
Poinsett, Lake, l., S.D., U.S. . C8 118
Point Arena, Ca., U.S. C2 82
Point Baker, Ak., U.S. D13 79
Point Blue, La., U.S. D3 95
Point Cedar, Ar., U.S. C2 81
Point Clear, Al., U.S. E2 78
Pointe a la Hache, La., U.S. . E6 95
Pointe-à-Pierre, Trin. O23 65
Pointe-à-Pitre, Guad. H14 64
Pointe au Baril Station, Ont. . B4 73
Pointe-au-Pic, Que. B7 74
Pointe-aux-Trembles (part of
  Montréal), Que. p20 74
Pointe-Bleue, Que. A5 74
Pointe-Calumet, Que. p19 74
Pointe-Claire, Que. D4 74
Pointe Coupee, co., La., U.S. D4 95
Pointe-des-Cascades, Que. . q19 74
Pointe du Bois, Man. D4 70
Pointe-du-Chêne, N.B. C5 71
Pointe-du-Lac, Que. C5 74
Point Edward, Ont. D2 73
Pointe-Noire, Congo B1 48
Pointe-Noire, Guad. Q8 65
Pointers, N.J., U.S. D2 107
Pointe-Verte, N.B. B4 71
Point Fortin, Trin. O22 65
Point Hope, Ak., U.S. B6 79
Point Imperial, mtn., Az., U.S. A4 80
Point Independence, Ma., U.S. *C6 98
Point Judith, R.I., U.S. G4 116
Point Judith Pond, l., R.I., U.S. F4 116
Point Lake, l., N.W. Ter. C10 66
Point Leamington, Newf. D4 72
Point Lookout, Md., U.S. D5 97
Point Lookout, Mo., U.S. E4 102
Point Marion, Pa., U.S. G2 115
Point Mugu Naval Air Station,
  mil., Ca., U.S. E4 82
Point of Rocks, Md., U.S. . . . B2 97
Point of Rocks, Wy., U.S. . . . E4 127
Point Pelee National Park,
  Ont. F2 73
Point Pleasant, N.J., U.S. . . . C4 107
Point Pleasant, W.V., U.S. . . C2 125
Point Pleasant Beach, N.J.,
  U.S. C4 107
Point Reyes National
  Seashore, Ca., U.S. C2 82
Point Roberts, Wa., U.S. . . . A2 124
Point Sapin, N.B. C5 71
Point Washington, Fl., U.S. . . u15 86
Poipu, Hi., U.S. B2 88
Poirino, Italy E3 20
Poison Creek, stm., Wy., U.S. C5 127
Poison Blanc, Lac du, res.,
  Que. C2 74
Poissy, Fr. C5 16
Poitiers, Fr. D4 16
Poitou, hist. reg., Fr. D3 16
Poix, Fr. E1 17
Pojo, Bol. C3 55
Pojoaque Valley, N.M., U.S. . B3 108
Pokaran, India C5 36
Pokataroo, Austl. D7 51
Pokegama Lake, l., Mn., U.S. C2 100
Pokegama Lake, l., Wi., U.S. . C2 126
Pokhará, Nepal C9 36
Pokkye-ri, N. Kor. G3 33
Poko, Zaire A4 48
Poko Mountain, mtn., Ak.,
  U.S. B7 79
Pokrov, Sov. Un. n19 27
Pokrovskoye, Sov. Un. H12 27
Polacca, Az., U.S. B5 80
Polān, Iran C6 38
Poland, In., U.S. F4 91
Poland, Me., U.S. *D2 96
Poland, N.Y., U.S. B5 109

Poland, ctry., Eur. C5 26
Poland Spring, Me., U.S. . . . D2 96
Polar, Wi., U.S. C5 126
Polar Bear Provincial Park,
  Ont. n18 73
Polaris, Mt., U.S. E3 103
Polar Record Glacier, ice, Ant. C20 7
Polar Times Glacier, ice, Ant. C20 7
Polatlı, Tur. *C9 40
Polbain, Scot., U.K. B3 13
Polch, W. Ger. C2 19
Polcura, Chile B2 54
Pole Mountain, mtn., Wy.,
  U.S. E7 127
Polesella, Italy E7 20
Polessk, Sov. Un. A6 26
Polevskoy, Sov. Un. D21 8
Polgár, Hung. B5 24
Poli, Cam. D2 46
Policastro, Gulf of, b., Italy . . E5 23
Police, Pol. B3 26
Poligny, Fr. D6 16
Polikhnitos, Grc. C6 25
Polillo, Phil. o13 34
Polillo Islands, is., Phil. B6 34
Polillo Strait, strt., Phil. o13 34
Pólis, Cyp. E9 40
Poliyiros, Grc. B4 25
Polk, Ne., U.S. C8 104
Polk, Oh., U.S. B3 112
Polk, Pa., U.S. D2 115
Polk, Tn., U.S. A2 119
Polk, co., Ar., U.S. C1 81
Polk, co., Fl., U.S. E5 86
Polk, co., Ga., U.S. C1 87
Polk, co., Ia., U.S. C4 92
Polk, co., Mn., U.S. C2 100
Polk, co., Mo., U.S. D4 102
Polk, co., Ne., U.S. C8 104
Polk, co., N.C., U.S. f10 110
Polk, co., Or., U.S. C3 114
Polk, co., Tn., U.S. D9 119
Polk, co., Tx., U.S. D5 120
Polk, co., Wi., U.S. C1 126
Polk City, Fl., U.S. D5 86
Polk City, Ia., U.S. C4 92
Polkton, N.C., U.S. B2 110
Polkville, Ms., U.S. C4 101
Pollard, Al., U.S. D2 78
Pollard, Ar., U.S. A5 81
Pollards Point, Newf. D3 72
Pollensa, Spain C7 22
Pollock, Id., U.S. D2 89
Pollock, La., U.S. C3 95
Pollock, Mo., U.S. A4 102
Pollock, S.D., U.S. B5 118
Pollockville, Alta. D5 68
Pollocksville, N.C., U.S. B5 110
Pollockville, Alta. D5 68
Polo, Il., U.S. B4 90
Polo, Mo., U.S. B3 102
Polochic, stm., Guat. C3 62
Pologi, Sov. Un. H11 27
Polonnoye, Sov. Un. F6 27
Polotsk, Sov. Un. D7 27
Polson, Mt., U.S. C2 103
Poltava, Sov. Un. E6 29
Poltimore, Que. D2 74
Polunochnoye, Sov. Un. A6 28
Polvadera, N.M., U.S. C3 108
Polwarth, Sask. D2 75
Polyarnyy, Sov. Un. C15 14
Pomabamba, Peru C2 58
Pombal, Braz. E11 56
Pombal, Port. D2 22
Pomba, stm., Braz. g6 56
Pombal, Braz. C3 57
Pombal, Port. C1 22
Pomerania, hist. reg., Pol. . . . B4 26
Pomeranian Bay, b., Eur. . . . D8 15
Pomerene, Az., U.S. E5 80
Pomeroy, N. Ire., U.K. C5 11
Pomeroy, Ia., U.S. B3 92
Pomeroy, Oh., U.S. C3 112
Pomeroy, Wa., U.S. C8 124
Pomezia, Italy h9 23
Pomfret, Ct., U.S. B8 84
Pomfret, Md., U.S. C3 97
Pomfret, Vt., U.S. D3 122
Pomfret Center, Ct., U.S. . . . B8 84
Pomme de Terre, stm., Mn.,
  U.S. E3 100
Pomme de Terre, stm., Mo.,
  U.S. D4 102
Pomme de Terre Lake, res.,
  Mo., U.S. D4 102
Pomoho, Hi., U.S. f9 88
Pomona, Ca., U.S. E5 82
Pomona, Ks., U.S. D8 93
Pomona, Mo., U.S. E6 102
Pomona, N.J., U.S. E3 107
Pomona Lake, res., Ks., U.S. D7 93
Pompano Beach, Fl., U.S. . . . C5 86
Pompano Beach Highlands,
  Fl., U.S. *F6 86
Pompeii, hist., Italy D5 23
Pompeys Pillar, Mt., U.S. . . . E9 103
Pompton Lakes, N.J., U.S. . . A4 107
Pomquet, N.S. D8 71
Ponaganset, stm., R.I., U.S. . C2 116
Ponaganset Reservoir, res.,
  R.I., U.S. B2 116
Ponape International Airport,
  Micron. Q17 52
Ponask, stm., Ont. B5 70
Ponask Lake, l., Ont. B5 70
Ponass Lakes, l., Sask. E3 75
Ponca, Ar., U.S. A2 81
Ponca, Ne., U.S. B9 104
Ponca City, Ok., U.S. A4 113
Ponca Indian Reservation, Ne.,
  U.S. B7 104
Ponce, P.R. H11 64
Ponce de Leon, Fl., U.S. u16 86
Ponce de Leon Bay, b., Fl.,
  U.S. G5 86
Ponce de Leon Inlet, b., Fl.,
  U.S. C6 86
Poncha Pass, Co., U.S. C4 83
Ponchatoula, La., U.S. D5 95
Pond, stm., Ky., U.S. C2 94
Pond, West Fork, stm., Ky.,
  U.S. C2 94
Ponderay, Id., U.S. A2 89
Ponderosa, N.M., U.S. B3 108
Pond Fork, stm., W.V., U.S. . D3 125
Pond Fork, West Fork, stm.,
  W.V., U.S. n12 125
Pondicherry, India F6 36
Pondicherry, ter., India *F6 36
Pond Inlet, N.W. Ter. B17 66
Ponds, Island of, i., Newf. . . B4 72
Pone Island, i., Md., U.S. . . . D5 97
Poneloya, Nic. D4 62
Ponemah, Mn., U.S. B4 100
Ponferrada, Spain A2 22
Pongoma, Sov. Un. E16 14
Ponhook Lake, l., N.S. E5 71
Ponkapog Pond, l., Ma., U.S. h11 98
Ponoka, Alta. C4 68
Ponoy, Sov. Un. D19 14
Ponoy, stm., Sov. Un. B16 8
Pons, Fr. E3 16
Ponsford, Mn., U.S. D3 100
Ponta Delgada, Port. h9 44
Ponta de Pedras, Braz. C5 59
Ponta Grossa, Braz. D2 56
Pontal, Braz. k7 56
Pontalina, Braz. B3 56
Pont-à-Mousson, Fr. C7 16
Ponta Porã, Braz. C1 56
Pontarlier, Fr. D7 16
Pontchartrain, Lake, l., La.,
  U.S. D5 95
Pont-de-Roide, Fr. B2 20
Pontebba, Italy C3 23
Pontedera, Italy C1 22
Ponte de Sor, Port. C1 22
Ponte di Legno, Italy C6 20
Ponte Nova, Braz. C4 56
Pontevedra, Spain A1 22
Ponte Vedra Beach, Fl., U.S. B5 86
Pontfaverger-Moronvilliers, Fr. E4 17
Pontiac, Il., U.S. C5 90
Pontiac, Mi., U.S. F7 99
Pontiac, S.C., U.S. C6 117
Pontianak, Indon. F3 34
Pontic Mountains, mts., Tur. . B11 40
Pontivy, Fr. C2 16
Pont-l'Abbé, Fr. D1 16
Pontoise, Fr. C5 16
Pontoosuc Lake, l., Ma., U.S. B1 98
Pontotoc, Ms., U.S. A4 101
Pontotoc, Tx., U.S. D3 120
Pontotoc, co., Ms., U.S. A4 101
Pontotoc, co., Ok., U.S. C5 113
Pontremoli, Italy B2 23
Pontresina, Switz. C5 20
Pontrilas, Sask. D3 75
Pont-Rouge, Que. C6 74
Pont-Sainte-Maxence, Fr. . . . E2 17
Pontypool, Ont. C6 73
Pontypool, Wales, U.K. C4 12
Pontypridd (Taff-Ely), Wales,
  U.K. C4 12
Pony, Mt., U.S. E5 103
Ponza, i., Italy D4 23
Ponziane Islands, is., Italy . . D4 23
Poole, Eng., U.K. E5 10
Poole, Ky., U.S. C2 94
Poole, Ne., U.S. D7 104
Pooler, Ga., U.S. D5 87
Pooles Island, i., Md., U.S. . . B5 97
Poolesville, Md., U.S. B3 97
Pooleville, Ok., U.S. C4 113
Poolewe, Scot., U.K. C3 13
Pooley Island, i., B.C. C3 69
Poolville, Tx., U.S. C4 120
Poona see Pune, India E5 36
Poopó, Bol. C2 55
Poopó, Lago, l., Bol. C2 55
Poor Knights Islands, is., N.Z. K15 51
Pootatuck Park, Ct., U.S. . . . *D2 84
Popasnaya, Sov. Un. q21 27
Popayán, Col. C2 60
Pope, Ms., U.S. A4 101
Pope, co., Ar., U.S. B2 81
Pope, co., Il., U.S. F5 90
Pope, co., Mn., U.S. E3 100
Pope Air Force Base, mil.,
  N.C., U.S. B3 110
Popejoy, Ia., U.S. B4 92
Poperinge, Bel. D1 17
Popham Beach, Me., U.S. . . . E3 96
Popham Point, c., Ont. B3 73
Poplar, Mt., U.S. B11 103
Poplar, N.C., U.S. e10 110
Poplar, Wi., U.S. B2 126
Poplar, stm., Can. C3 70
Poplar, stm., N.A. B11 103
Poplar, stm., Mn., U.S. C2 100
Poplar, West Fork, stm., Mn.,
  U.S. B11 103
Poplar Bluff, Mo., U.S. E7 102
Poplar Branch, N.C., U.S. . . . A7 110
Poplar Creek, Man. D3 70
Poplarfield, Man. D3 70
Poplar Grove, Ar., U.S. C5 81
Poplar Grove, Il., U.S. A5 90
Poplar Island, i., Md., U.S. . . C5 97
Poplar Mountain, mtn., Ky.,
  U.S. D5 94
Poplar Plains, Ky., U.S. B6 94
Poplar Point, Man. D3 70
Poplarville, Ms., U.S. E4 101
Popocatépetl, Volcán, vol.,
  Mex. n14 63
Popokabaka, Zaire C2 48
Popondetta, Pap. N. Gui. . . . k12 50
Popovo, Bul. D8 24
Poppel, Bel. B5 17
Popple, stm., Wi., U.S. C5 126
Poprad, Czech. *D6 26
Poquetanuck, Ct., U.S. C7 84
Poquonock, Ct., U.S. B5 84
Poquonock Bridge, Ct., U.S. . D7 84
Poquoson, Va., U.S. C6 123
Porali, stm., Pak. H13 39
Porangatu, Braz. B4 56
Porbandar, India D4 36
Porcher Island, i., B.C. B3 69
Porcuna, Spain D3 22
Porcupine, stm., N.A. B11 79
Porcupine, Cape, c., Newf. . . B3 72
Porcupine Hills, hills, Can. . . E5 75
Porcupine Mountains, mts.,
  Mi., U.S. m12 99
Porcupine Plain, Sask. E4 75
Pordenone, Italy B4 23
Poreč, Yugo. C1 24
Pori, Fin. G9 14
Porirua, N.Z. N15 51
Porjus, Swe. D8 14

Porkhov, Sov. Un. C7 27
Porkkala, Fin. G11 14
Porlamar, Ven. A5 60
Porlezza, Italy D7 21
Pornic, Fr. D2 16
Poroma, Bol. C2 55
Poronaysk, Sov. Un. E17 29
Poroshiri, Mount, mtn., Japan E11 33
Porpoise Bay, b., Ant. C25 7
Porrentruy, Switz. E3 18
Porsangen, Nor. B12 14
Porsgrunn, Nor. p27 14
Portachuelo, Bol. C3 55
Portadown, N. Ire., U.K. C3 10
Portaferry, N. Ire., U.K. C6 11
Portage, P.E.I. C5 71
Portage, In., U.S. A3 91
Portage, Me., U.S. B4 96
Portage, Mi., U.S. F5 99
Portage, Pa., U.S. F4 115
Portage, Ut., U.S. B3 121
Portage, Wi., U.S. E4 126
Portage, co., Oh., U.S. A4 112
Portage, co., Wi., U.S. D4 126
Portage, stm., Oh., U.S. B2 112
Portage, North Branch, stm.,
  Oh., U.S. f7 112
Portage Bay, b., Man. D2 70
Portage Des Sioux, Mo., U.S. f13 102
Portage Head, c., Wa., U.S. . A1 124
Portage Island, i., N.B. B4 71
Portage Lake, l., Me., U.S. . . B4 96
Portage Lakes, Oh., U.S. . . . B4 112
Portage la Prairie, Man. E2 70
Portageville, Mo., U.S. E8 102
Portageville, N.Y., U.S. C2 109
Portal, Ga., U.S. D5 87
Portal, N.D., U.S. A3 111
Port Alberni, B.C. E5 69
Portalegre, Port. C2 22
Portales, N.M., U.S. C6 108
Port Alexander, Ak., U.S. . . . D13 79
Port Alfred, Que. A7 74
Port Alfred (Kowie), S. Afr. . . D4 49
Port Alice, B.C. D4 69
Port Allegany, Pa., U.S. C5 115
Port Allen, La., U.S. D4 95
Port Amherst, W.V., U.S. m12 125
Port Angeles, Wa., U.S. A2 124
Port Anson, Newf. D4 72
Port Antonio, Jam. E5 64
Port Aransas, Tx., U.S. F4 120
Port Arlington, Ire. D3 10
Port Arthur see Lüshun, China D9 31
Port Arthur, Tx., U.S. E6 120
Port Askaig, Scot., U.K. C2 11
Port Augusta, Austl. F6 50
Port au Port Bay, b., Newf. . . D2 72
Port au Port [West-
  Aguathuna-Felix Cove],
  Newf. D2 72
Port-au-Prince, Haiti E7 64
Port au Prince Peninsula, pen.,
  Newf. D2 72
Port Austin, Mi., U.S. D7 99
Port Barre, La., U.S. D4 95
Port-Bergé, Madag. g9 49
Port Birmingham, Al., U.S. . . B2 78
Port Blair, India F9 36
Port Blakely, Wa., U.S. e10 124
Port Blandford, Newf. D4 72
Port Bolivar, Tx., U.S. E5 120
Port Borden, P.E.I. C6 71
Port Burwell, Ont. E4 73
Port Byron, Il., U.S. B3 90
Port Byron, N.Y., U.S. C4 109
Port Canning, India F12 37
Port Carbon, Pa., U.S. E9 115
Port Carling, Ont. B5 73
Port-Cartier-Ouest, Que. k13 74
Port Chalmers, N.Z. P13 51
Port Charlotte, Fl., U.S. F4 86
Port Chester, N.Y., U.S. E7 109
Port Clements, B.C. C1 69
Port Clinton, Oh., U.S. A3 112
Port Clyde, N.S. F4 71
Port Clyde, Me., U.S. E3 96
Port Colborne, Ont. E5 73
Port Colden, N.J., U.S. B3 107
Port Coquitlam, B.C. E6 69
Port Credit, Ont. D5 73
Port-Daniel, Que. A5 71
Port-de-Bouc, Fr. E6 16
Port-de-Paix, Haiti E7 64
Port Deposit, Md., U.S. A5 97
Port Dickinson, N.Y., U.S. . . . C5 109
Port Dickson, Malay. E2 34
Port Dover, Ont. E4 73
Port Eads, La., U.S. E6 95
Port Edward, B.C. B2 69
Port Edwards, Wi., U.S. D4 126
Port Elgin, N.B. C5 71
Port Elgin, Ont. C3 73
Port Elizabeth, S. Afr. D4 49
Port Elizabeth, N.J., U.S. . . . E3 107
Port Ellen, Scot., U.K. C2 11
Porteña, Arg. A4 54
Port Ewen, N.Y., U.S. D7 109
Port Fairy, Austl. I4 51
Port Gamble, Wa., U.S. B3 124
Port Gamble Indian
  Reservation, Wa., U.S. . . . B3 124
Port-Gentil, Gabon F1 46
Port George, N.S. D4 71
Port Gibson, Ms., U.S. D3 101
Port Glasgow, Scot., U.K. . . . F8 13
Portglenone, N. Ire., U.K. . . . C5 11
Port Graham, Ak., U.S. D9 79
Port Greville, N.S. D5 71
Port Harcourt, Nig. F6 45
Port Hardy, B.C. D4 69

Port Hastings, N.S. D8 71
Port Hawkesbury, N.S. D8 71
Porthcawl, Wales, U.K. C4 12
Port Hedland, Austl. D2 50
Port Heiden, Ak., U.S. D7 79
Port Henry, N.Y., U.S. A7 109
Port Hill, P.E.I. C6 71
Porthill, Id., U.S. A2 89
Porthmadog, Wales, U.K. . . . B3 12
Port Hood, N.S. C8 71
Port Hope, Ont. D6 73
Port Hope, Mi., U.S. E8 99
Port Hope Simpson, Newf. . . B3 72
Port Hueneme, Ca., U.S. . . . E4 82
Port Huron, Mi., U.S. F8 99
Portia, Ar., U.S. A4 81
Portimão, Port. D1 22
Portis, Ks., U.S. C5 93
Port Isabel, Tx., U.S. F4 120
Port Jefferson, N.Y., U.S. . . . n15 109
Port Jefferson, Oh., U.S. B1 112
Port Jefferson Station, N.Y.,
  U.S. *n15 109
Port Jervis, N.Y., U.S. D6 109
Port Keats, Austl. B5 50
Port Kent, N.Y., U.S. f11 109
Port Kembla, Austl. G7 50
Port Lairge, Ire. D3 10
Port Lavaca, Tx., U.S. E4 120
Portlaw, Ire. E4 11
Port Leyden, N.Y., U.S. B5 109
Port Lincoln, Austl. F6 50
Port Lions, Ak., U.S. D9 79
Port Loko, S.L. E2 45
Port Loring, Ont. B4 73
Port-Louis, Fr. D2 16
Port-Louis, Guad. Q8 65
Port Louis, Mrts. H24 2
Port Ludlow, Wa., U.S. B3 124
Port Macquarie, Austl. F9 50
Port Madison Indian
  Reservation, Wa., U.S. . . . B3 124
Portmagee, Ire. F1 11
Portmahomack, Scot., U.K. . . C5 13
Port Maitland, N.S. F3 71
Port Maitland (part of
  Dunnville), Ont. E5 73
Port Maria, Jam. E5 64
Port Matilda, Pa., U.S. E5 115
Port Mayaca, Fl., U.S. F6 86
Port McNeill, B.C. D4 69
Port McNicoll, Ont. C5 73
Port Medway, N.S. E5 71
Port Mellon, B.C. E6 69
Port-Menier, Que. k8 72
Port Moller, Ak., U.S. D7 79
Port Monmouth, N.J., U.S. . . . C4 107
Port Morant, Jam. F16 65
Portmore, Jam. *F15 65
Port Moresby, Pap. N. Gui. . . k12 50
Port Morien, N.S. C10 71
Port Morris, N.J., U.S. B3 107
Port Murray, N.J., U.S. B3 107
Port Neches, Tx., U.S. E6 120
Portneuf, Que. C6 74
Portneuf, co., Que. C5 74
Portneuf-sur-Mer, Que. A8 74
Port Nolloth, S. Afr. C2 49
Port Norris, N.J., U.S. E2 107
Portnumber, Ire. E7 11
Porto (Oporto), Port. B1 22
Porto Acre, Braz. C4 58
Porto Alegre, Braz. C2 56
Porto Alexandre see Tombua,
  Ang. D1 48
Porto Amboim, Ang. D2 48
Porto Belo, Braz. D3 56
Portobelo, Pan. F8 62
Porto Calvo, Braz. C5 57
Port O'Connor, Tx., U.S. E4 120
Pôrto de Móis, Port. C1 22
Porto de Moz, Braz. C4 59
Portoferraio, Italy C3 23
Portofino, Italy B2 23
Port of Ness, Scot., U.K. B2 13
Port of Spain, Trin. K14 64
Portogruaro, Italy B4 23
Portola, Ca., U.S. C3 82
Porto Lucena, Braz. D1 56
Portomaggiore, Italy B3 23
Porto Mendes, Braz. C2 56
Porto Murtinho, Braz. D1 57
Porto Nacional, Braz. D1 57
Porto-Novo, Benin E5 45
Porto Santo, i., Port. g12 22
Portoscuso, Italy E2 23
Porto Seguro, Braz. E3 57
Porto Torres, Italy D2 23
Porto União, Braz. D2 56
Porto-Vecchio, Fr. B3 23
Porto Velho, Braz. D2 59
Portoviejo, Ec. B1 58
Portpatrick, Scot., U.K. G7 13
Port Penn, De., U.S. B3 85
Port Perry, Ont. C6 73
Port Phillip Bay, b., Austl. . . . G7 50
Port Pirie, Austl. F6 50
Port Radium, N.W. Ter. C9 66
Portree, Scot., U.K. C2 13
Portreeve, Sask. G1 75

Port Renfrew, B.C. E5 69
Port Republic, N.J., U.S. D4 107
Port Rexton, Newf. D5 72
Port Richey, Fl., U.S. D4 86
Port Rowan, Ont. E4 73
Port Royal, Ky., U.S. B4 94
Port Royal, Pa., U.S. E7 115
Port Royal, S.C., U.S. G6 117
Port Royal, Va., U.S. A4 119
Port Royal, Va., U.S. B5 123
Port Royal Island, i., S.C.,
  U.S. G6 117
Port Royal Sound, strt., S.C.,
  U.S. G6 117
Portrush, N. Ire., U.K. B5 11
Port Said (Būr Sa'īd), Eg. . . . B3 38
Port Saint Joe, Fl., U.S. C1 86
Port Saint Johns, Transkei . . D5 49
Port-Saint-Louis [-du-Rhône],
  Fr. F6 16
Port Saint Lucie, Fl., U.S. . . . E6 86
Port Salerno, Fl., U.S. E6 86
Portsalon, Ire. B4 11
Port Sanilac, Mi., U.S. E8 99
Port Saunders, Newf. C3 72
Port Sewall, Fl., U.S. E6 86
Port Shepstone, S. Afr. D5 49
Portsmouth, Dom. I14 64
Portsmouth, Eng., U.K. E6 10
Portsmouth, Ia., U.S. C2 92
Portsmouth, N.H., U.S. D5 106
Portsmouth, Oh., U.S. D3 112
Portsmouth, R.I., U.S. E6 116
Portsmouth, Va., U.S. D6 123
Portsmouth Naval Shipyard,
  mil., Me., U.S. D5 106
Portsoy, Scot., U.K. C6 13
Port Stanley, Ont. E3 73
Port Sudan (Būr Sūdān), Sud. B4 47
Port Sulphur, La., U.S. E6 95
Port-sur-Saône, Fr. A5 119
Port Talbot (Afan), Wales, U.K. C4 12
Porttipahdan Reservoir, res.,
  Fin. C12 14
Port Tobacco Village, Md.,
  U.S. C3 97
Port Townsend, Wa., U.S. . . . A3 124
Portugal, ctry., Eur. C1 22
Portugalete, Spain A4 22
Portuguesa, state, Ven. B4 60
Portuguesa, stm., Ven. B4 60
Portumna, Ire. D3 11
Port Union, Newf. D5 72
Port-Vendres, Fr. F5 16
Port-Vila, Vanuatu H10 6
Portville, N.Y., U.S. C2 109
Port Vue, Pa., U.S. *k14 115
Port Wakefield, Austl. G2 51
Port Washington, N.Y., U.S. . . h13 109
Port Washington, Oh., U.S. . . B4 112
Port Washington, Wi., U.S. . . E6 126
Port Wentworth, Ga., U.S. . . . D5 87
Port William, Scot., U.K. F4 13
Port William, Oh., U.S. C2 112
Port Wing, Wi., U.S. B2 126
Poruba, Czech. B6 113
Porvenir, Chile h11 54
Porz, W. Ger. C2 19
Posadas, Arg. B5 56
Posadas, Spain D3 22
Poschiavo, Switz. D9 21
Posen, Il., U.S. k9 90
Posen, Mi., U.S. C7 99
Posey, co., In., U.S. H2 91
Posey, co., In., U.S. H2 91
Poshekhonye-Volodarsk, Sov.
  Un. B12 27
Poso, Indon. F6 34
Poso, Lake, l., Indon. F6 34
Posong, S. Kor. I3 33
Pössneck, E. Ger. C6 19
Post, Or., U.S. C6 114
Post, Tx., U.S. C2 120
Poste-de-la-Baleine, Que. . . . g11 74
Post Falls, Id., U.S. B2 89
Postmasburg, S. Afr. C3 49
Post Mills, Vt., U.S. D4 122
Postojna, Yugo. C2 24
Poston, S.C., U.S. D9 117
Postville, Newf. g10 72
Postville, Ia., U.S. A6 92
Potaro Landing, Guy. A3 59
Potato Creek, S.D., U.S. D4 118
Potawatomi
  Reservation, Ks., U.S. . . . C8 93
Potchefstroom, S. Afr. C4 49
Poteau, Ok., U.S. B7 113
Poteau, stm., U.S. B7 113
Poteau Mountain, mtn., U.S. . C1 81
Potenza, Italy D5 23
Potes, Spain A3 22
Potgietersrus, S. Afr. B4 49
Poth, Tx., U.S. E3 120
Potholes Reservoir, res., Wa.,
  U.S. B6 124
Poti, Sov. Un. G17 8
Poti, stm., Braz. C2 57
Potiskum, Nig. D7 45
Potlatch, Id., U.S. C2 89
Potomac, Md., U.S. B3 97
Potomac, Mt., U.S. D3 103
Potomac, stm., U.S. D4 97
Potomac, North Branch, stm.,
  U.S. m12 97
Potomac, South Branch, stm.,
  U.S. B6 125
Potomac, South Branch, North
  Fork, stm., W.V., U.S. C5 125
Potomac, South Branch,
  South Fork, stm., W.V., U.S. B6 125
Potomac Heights, Md., U.S. . C3 97
Potomac Park, Md., U.S. k13 97
Potosí, Bol. D7 55
Potosi, Mo., U.S. D7 102
Potosi, Wi., U.S. F3 126
Potosí, dept., Bol. D2 55
Potosi, Cerro, mtn., S.A. E2 55
Potrerillos, Chile C2 54
Potrerillos, Hond. C4 62
Potro, Cierro el, mtn., S.A. . . E2 55
Potsdam, E. Ger. B6 18
Potsdam, N.Y., U.S. f10 109
Potsdam, Oh., U.S. C1 112
Pottawatomie, co., Ks., U.S. . C7 93
Pottawatomie, co., Ok., U.S. . B4 113
Pottawatomie Creek, stm.,
  Ks., U.S. D8 93
Pottawattamie, co., Ia., U.S. . C2 92
Potter, Ar., U.S. C1 81

Name	Map Ref.	Page

Potter, Ks., U.S. — C8 93
Potter, Ne., U.S. — C2 104
Potter, Wi., U.S. — h9 126
Potter, co., Pa., U.S. — C6 115
Potter, co., S.D., U.S. — B6 118
Potter, co., Tx., U.S. — B2 120
Potter Hill, R.I., U.S. — F1 116
Potter Place, N.H., U.S. — D3 106
Pottersville, Mo., U.S. — E5 102
Pottersville, N.J., U.S. — B3 107
Pottersville, N.Y., U.S. — B7 109
Potter Valley, Ca., U.S. — C2 82
Potterville, Ga., U.S. — D2 87
Potts Camp, Ms., U.S. — A4 101
Potts Creek, stm., U.S. — C2 123
Pottstown, Pa., U.S. — F10 115
Pottsville, Ar., U.S. — B2 81
Pottsville, Pa., U.S. — E9 115
Pottsville, Tx., U.S. — D3 120
Potwin, Ks., U.S. — E6 93
Pouce Coupe, B.C. — B7 69
Pouch Cove, Newf. — E5 72
Poughkeepsie, Ar., U.S. — A4 81
Poughkeepsie, N.Y., U.S. — D7 109
Poulan, Ga., U.S. — E3 87
Poulsbo, Wa., U.S. — B3 124
Poultney, Vt., U.S. — D2 122
Poultney, stm., Vt., U.S. — D2 122
Pound, Va., U.S. — e9 123
Pound, Wi., U.S. — C5 126
Pound Gap, U.S. — C7 94
Pouso Alegre, Braz. — C3 56
Poutasi, W. Sam. — G12 52
Pouthisat, Camb. — C2 34
Pouxeux, Fr. — A2 20
Považská Bystrica, Czech. — *D5 26
Povenets, Sov. Un. — C16 8
Poverty Bay, N.Z. — M16 51
Póvoa de Varzim, Port. — B1 22
Povorino, Sov. Un. — C2 28
Povorotnyy, Cape, c., Sov. Un. — E6 33
Povungnituk, Que. — f11 74
Powassan, Ont. — A5 73
Poway, Ca., U.S. — F5 82
Powder, stm., U.S. — A6 76
Powder, stm., Or., U.S. — C9 114
Powder, Middle Fork, stm., Wy., U.S. — C6 127
Powder, North Fork, stm., Wy., U.S. — C6 127
Powder, South Fork, stm., Wy., U.S. — C6 127
Powderhorn, Co., U.S. — C3 83
Powder River, Wy., U.S. — C6 127
Powder River, co., Mt., U.S. — E11 103
Powder River Pass, Wy., U.S. — B5 127
Powder Springs, Ga., U.S. — h8 87
Powderville, Mt., U.S. — E11 103
Powder Wash, U.S. — A2 83
Powe, Mo., U.S. — E7 102
Powell, Mo., U.S. — E3 102
Powell, Oh., U.S. — B2 112
Powell, Pa., U.S. — C9 115
Powell, Tn., U.S. — m13 119
Powell, Tx., U.S. — C4 120
Powell, Wy., U.S. — B4 127
Powell, co., Ky., U.S. — C6 94
Powell, co., Mt., U.S. — D4 103
Powell, stm., U.S. — C10 119
Powell, Lake, res., U.S. — F5 121
Powell, Mount, mtn., Co., U.S. — B4 83
Powell Butte, Or., U.S. — C5 114
Powellhurst, Or., U.S. — *B4 114
Powell Mountain, mtn., U.S. — C10 119
Powell Mountain, mtn., N.M., U.S. — B1 108
Powell Park, reg., Co., U.S. — A2 83
Powell River, B.C. — E5 69
Powellsville, N.C., U.S. — A6 110
Powellton, W.V., U.S. — C3 125
Powellton, Ga., U.S. — D7 97
Powelton, Ga., U.S. — C4 87
Power, Mt., U.S. — C5 103
Power, co., Id., U.S. — G5 89
Power Head, c., Ire. — F3 11
Powers, Mi., U.S. — C3 99
Powers, Or., U.S. — E2 114
Powers Lake, N.D., U.S. — A3 111
Powersville, Mo., U.S. — A4 102
Powerview, Man. — D3 70
Poweshiek, co., Ia., U.S. — C5 92
Powhatan, Al., U.S. — B2 78
Powhatan, Ar., U.S. — A4 81
Powhatan, La., U.S. — C2 95
Powhatan, Va., U.S. — C5 123
Powhatan, co., Va., U.S. — C5 123
Powhatan Point, Oh., U.S. — C5 112
Powhattan, Ks., U.S. — C8 93
Pownal, Me., U.S. — g7 96
Pownal, Vt., U.S. — F2 122
Pownal Center, Me., U.S. — g7 96
Pownal Center, Vt., U.S. — F2 122
Powys, co., Wales, U.K. — B4 12
Poxoréo, Braz. — C2 57
Poyang Hu, l., China — F8 31
Poyarkovo, Sov. Un. — B4 33
Poydras, La., U.S. — *E6 95
Poyen, Ar., U.S. — C3 81
Poygan, Lake, l., Wi., U.S. — D5 126
Poynette, Wi., U.S. — E4 126
Poynor, Mo., U.S. — E7 102
Poyntzpass, N. Ire., U.K. — C5 11
Poy Sippi, Wi., U.S. — D4 126
Požarevac, Yugo. — C5 24
Poza Rica de Hidalgo, Mex. — m15 63
Poznań, Pol. — B6 26
Pozo Almonte, Chile — D2 55
Pozoblanco, Spain — C3 22
Pozo Colorado, Para. — D4 55
Pozo Redondo Mountains, mts., Az., U.S. — E3 80
Pozos, Mex. — m13 63
Pozuelo de Alarcón, Spain — p17 22
Pozuelos, Ven. — A5 60
Pozuzo, Peru — D2 58
Pozzallo, Italy — F5 23
Pozzuoli, Italy — D5 23
Prachatice, Czech. — E9 19
Prachin Buri, Thai. — C2 34
Prachuap Khiri Khan, Thai. — G3 35
Praco, Al., U.S. — f6 78
Prácticas, Punta de, c., Cuba — D5 64
Prades, Fr. — F5 16
Prado Flood Control Basin, Ca., U.S. — n13 82
Præstø, Den. — C6 15
Praga (part of Warsaw), Pol. — k14 26
Prague (Praha), Czech. — C3 26
Prague, Ne., U.S. — C9 104
Prague, Ok., U.S. — B5 113
Prainha, Braz. — C4 59
Prairie, Al., U.S. — C2 78
Prairie, Ms., U.S. — B5 101

Prairie, co., Ar., U.S. — C4 81
Prairie, co., Mt., U.S. — D11 103
Prairie, stm., Mn., U.S. — C5 100
Prairie, stm., Wi., U.S. — C4 126
Prairie Bayou, stm., Ar., U.S. — g7 81
Prairie City, Il., U.S. — C3 90
Prairie City, Ia., U.S. — C4 92
Prairie City, Or., U.S. — C8 114
Prairie City, S.D., U.S. — B3 118
Prairie Creek, In., U.S. — F3 91
Prairie Creek Reservoir, res., In., U.S. — D7 91
Prairie Dog Creek, stm., U.S. — C3 93
Prairie du Chien, Wi., U.S. — E2 126
Prairie Du Rocher, Il., U.S. — E3 90
Prairie du Sac, Wi., U.S. — E4 126
Prairie Farm, Wi., U.S. — C2 126
Prairie Grove, Ar., U.S. — B1 81
Prairie Hill, Mo., U.S. — B5 102
Prairie Home, Mo., U.S. — C5 102
Prairie Home, Ne., U.S. — h11 104
Prairie Point, Ms., U.S. — B5 101
Prairie River, Sask. — E4 75
Prairies, Lake of the, res., Can. — F5 75
Prairies, Rivière des, stm., Que. — p19 74
Prairieton, In., U.S. — F3 91
Prairie View, Ar., U.S. — B2 81
Prairie View, Ks., U.S. — C4 93
Prairie View, Tx., U.S. — D5 120
Prairie Village, Ks., U.S. — m16 93
Prairieville, La., U.S. — h10 95
Pralognan-la-Vanoise, Fr. — D2 20
Pran Buri, Thai. — C2 34
Praszka, Pol. — C5 26
Prata, Braz. — B3 56
Pratāpgarh, India — E5 37
Prater Mountain, mtn., Wy., U.S. — C2 127
Prato, Italy — C3 23
Prats-de-Mollo, Fr. — F5 16
Pratt, Ks., U.S. — E5 93
Pratt, W.V., U.S. — *C3 125
Pratt, co., Ks., U.S. — E5 93
Pratteln, Switz. — A4 21
Prattsburg, N.Y., U.S. — C3 109
Prattsville, Ar., U.S. — C3 81
Prattsville, N.Y., U.S. — C6 109
Prattville, Al., U.S. — C3 78
Prattville, Mi., U.S. — G6 99
Pravdinsk, Sov. Un. — A6 26
Pravia, Spain — A2 22
Pray, Mt., U.S. — E6 103
Preble, In., U.S. — C7 91
Preble, co., Oh., U.S. — C1 112
Predazzo, Italy — C7 20
Preeceville, Sask. — F4 75
Preetz, W. Ger. — D4 15
Pregel, stm., Sov. Un. — D3 27
Pregolya, stm., Sov. Un. — A6 26
Prelate, Sask. — G1 75
Premana, Italy — D7 21
Premont, Tx., U.S. — F3 120
Prémontré, Fr. — E3 17
Premosello, Italy — D5 21
Prenjasi, Alb. — B3 25
Prenter, W.V., U.S. — C3 125
Prentice, Wi., U.S. — C3 126
Prentiss, Me., U.S. — C4 96
Prentiss, Ms., U.S. — D4 101
Prentiss, co., Ms., U.S. — A5 101
Prenzlau, E. Ger. — B6 18
Přerov, Czech. — D4 26
Prescott, Ont. — C9 73
Prescott, Az., U.S. — C3 80
Prescott, Ar., U.S. — D2 81
Prescott, Ia., U.S. — C3 92
Prescott, Ks., U.S. — D9 93
Prescott, Mi., U.S. — D7 99
Prescott, Wa., U.S. — A4 114
Prescott, Wi., U.S. — D1 126
Prescott, co., Ont. — B10 73
Presho, S.D., U.S. — D5 118
Presidencia Roque Sáenz Peña, Arg. — E3 55
Presidente Epitácio, Braz. — C2 56
Presidente Hayes, dept., Para. — D4 55
Presidente Olegário, Braz. — B3 56
Presidente Prudente, Braz. — C2 56
Presidential Range, mts., N.H., U.S. — B4 106
Presidio, Tx., U.S. — p12 120
Presidio, co., Tx., U.S. — o12 120
Presidio of San Francisco, mil., Ca., U.S. — h8 82
Preslav, Bul. — D8 24
Prešov, Czech. — D6 26
Prespa, Lake, l., Eur. — E5 24
Presque Isle, Me., U.S. — B5 96
Presque Isle, Mi., U.S. — C7 99
Presque Isle, Wi., U.S. — C3 126
Presque Isle, co., Mi., U.S. — C6 99
Pressath, W. Ger. — D6 19
Prestatyn, Wales, U.K. — A4 12
Presteigne, Wales, U.K. — B4 12
Přeštice, Czech. — D1 19
Preston, Austl. — *G8 50
Preston, Eng., U.K. — D5 10
Preston, Ct., U.S. — C8 84
Preston, Ga., U.S. — D2 87
Preston, Id., U.S. — G7 89
Preston, Ia., U.S. — B7 92
Preston, Ks., U.S. — E5 93
Preston, Ky., U.S. — B6 94
Preston, Md., U.S. — C6 97
Preston, Mn., U.S. — G6 100
Preston, Mo., U.S. — D4 102
Preston, Ok., U.S. — B6 113
Preston, Wa., U.S. — e12 124
Preston, W.V., U.S. — B5 125
Preston, co., W.V., U.S. — B5 125
Preston Peak, mtn., Ca., U.S. — B2 82
Prestonburg, Ky., U.S. — C7 94
Prestonville, Ky., U.S. — B4 94
Prestrud Inlet, b., Ant. — B33 7
Prestwick, Scot., U.K. — D2 78
Preti, mtn., Italy — C8 20
Preto, stm., Braz. — h6 56
Preto, stm., Braz. — D2 57
Prêto do Igapó-Açu, stm., Braz. — D2 59
Pretoria, S. Afr. — C4 49
Prettyboy Reservoir, res., Md., U.S. — A4 97
Pretty Prairie, Ks., U.S. — E5 93
Préveza, Grc. — C3 40
Prewitt, N.M., U.S. — B1 108
Prewitt Reservoir, res., Co., U.S. — A7 83

Prey Veng, Camb. — G6 35
Pribilof Islands, is., Ak., U.S. — D5 79
Priboj, Yugo. — D4 24
Příbram, Czech. — D3 26
Price, Md., U.S. — B6 97
Price, Tx., U.S. — C5 120
Price, Ut., U.S. — D5 121
Price, co., Wi., U.S. — C3 126
Price, stm., Ut., U.S. — D5 121
Pricedale, Ms., U.S. — D3 101
Price Inlet, b., S.C., U.S. — k12 117
Price Island, i., B.C. — C3 69
Priceville, Ont. — C4 73
Prichard, Al., U.S. — E1 78
Prichard, W.V., U.S. — C2 125
Priddy, Tx., U.S. — D3 120
Priego [de Córdoba], Spain — D3 22
Prien, La., U.S. — *D2 95
Prienai, Sov. Un. — A7 26
Prieska, S. Afr. — C3 49
Priest Lake, l., Id., U.S. — A2 89
Priestley, Mount, mtn., B.C. — B3 69
Priest Rapids Dam, Wa., U.S. — C6 124
Priest Rapids Lake, res., Wa., U.S. — C6 124
Priest River, Id., U.S. — A2 89
Prievidza, Czech. — *D5 26
Prijedor, Yugo. — C3 24
Prijepolje, Yugo. — D4 24
Prikumsk, Sov. Un. — E2 28
Prilep, Yugo. — E5 24
Prilly, Switz. — F9 27?
Priluki, Sov. Un. — F9 27
Prim, Point, c., P.E.I. — C6 71
Primate, Sask. — E1 75
Primero, stm., Arg. — A4 54
Primghar, Ia., U.S. — A2 92
Primolano, Italy — D7 20
Primorsk, Sov. Un. — A6 26
Primorsk, Sov. Un. — A7 27
Primorsko-Akhtarsk, Sov. Un. — H12 27
Primrose, Ne., U.S. — C7 104
Primrose, R.I., U.S. — B3 116
Primrose Lake, l., Can. — E1 75
Prince, Sask. — E1 75
Prince, co., P.E.I. — C5 71
Prince, Lake, res., Va., U.S. — k14 123
Prince Albert, Sask. — D3 75
Prince Albert Mountains, mts., Ant. — B29 7
Prince Albert National Park, Sask. — C2 75
Prince Albert Sound, strt., N.W. Ter. — B9 66
Prince Alfred, Cape, c., N.W. Ter. — B8 66
Prince Charles Foreland, i., Nor. — B14 128
Prince Charles Island, i., N.W. Ter. — C17 66
Prince Charles Mountains, mts., Ant. — B19 7
Prince Edward, co., Ont. — C7 73
Prince Edward, co., Va., U.S. — C4 123
Prince Edward Island, prov., Can. — C6 71
Prince Edward Island National Park, P.E.I. — C6 71
Prince Edward Islands, is., S. Afr. — J23 2
Prince Frederick, Md., U.S. — C4 97
Prince George, B.C. — C6 69
Prince George, Va., U.S. — C5 123
Prince George, co., Va., U.S. — C5 123
Prince Georges, co., Md., U.S. — C4 97
Prince of Wales, i., Austl. — B7 50
Prince of Wales, Cape, c., Ak., U.S. — B6 79
Prince of Wales Island, i., N.W. Ter. — B13 66
Prince of Wales Island, i., Ak., U.S. — n23 79
Prince of Wales Strait, strt., N.W. Ter. — B9 66
Prince Olav Coast, Ant. — C17 7
Prince Patrick Island, i., N.W. Ter. — m27 66
Prince Regent Inlet, b., N.W. Ter. — B14 66
Prince Rupert, B.C. — B2 69
Princes Lakes, In., U.S. — F5 91
Princes Risborough, Eng., U.K. — C7 12
Princess Anne, Md., U.S. — D6 97
Princess Astrid Coast, Ant. — B14 7
Princess Charlotte Bay, b., Austl. — B7 50
Princess Martha Coast, Ant. — B11 7
Princess Ragnhild Coast, Ant. — B15 7
Princess Royal Channel, strt., B.C. — C3 69
Princess Royal Island, i., B.C. — C3 69
Princes Town, Trin. — O23 65
Princeton, B.C. — E7 69
Princeton, Newf. — D5 72
Princeton, Ont. — D4 73
Princeton, Al., U.S. — A3 78
Princeton, Ca., U.S. — C2 82
Princeton, Fl., U.S. — G6 86
Princeton, Il., U.S. — B4 90
Princeton, In., U.S. — H2 91
Princeton, Ia., U.S. — C7 92
Princeton, Ks., U.S. — D8 93
Princeton, Ky., U.S. — C2 94
Princeton, Me., U.S. — C5 96
Princeton, Mn., U.S. — E5 100
Princeton, Mo., U.S. — A4 102
Princeton, N.J., U.S. — C3 107
Princeton, N.C., U.S. — B4 110
Princeton, Wi., U.S. — E4 126
Princeton, W.V., U.S. — D3 125
Princeton, Mount, mtn., Co., U.S. — C4 83
Princeton Junction, N.J., U.S. — C3 107
Princeville, Que. — C6 74
Princeville, Il., U.S. — C4 90
Princeville, N.C., U.S. — B5 110
Prineville, Or., U.S. — C6 114
Prineville Reservoir, res., Or., U.S. — C6 114
Pringle, S.D., U.S. — D2 118

Prinsburg, Mn., U.S. — F3 100
Prinzapolka, Nic. — E8 63
Prinzapolka, stm., Nic. — D6 62
Prior Lake, Mn., U.S. — F5 100
Priozersk, Sov. Un. — A8 27
Pripyat, Sov. Un. — F7 27
Pripyat (Pripet), stm., Sov. Un. — B4 30
Prishib, Sov. Un. — D8 83
Priština, Yugo. — D5 24
Pritchards Island, i., S.C., U.S. — G6 117
Pritchett, Tx., U.S. — C5 120
Pritzerbe, E. Ger. — F6 18
Pritzwalk, E. Ger. — B6 18
Privas, Fr. — E6 16
Privert, Lac, l., Que. — g8 72
Privolnoye, Sov. Un. — H9 27
Prizren, Yugo. — D5 24
Prizzi, Italy — F4 23
Probolinggo, Indon. — G4 34
Procious, W.V., U.S. — m13 125
Procter, B.C. — E9 69
Proctor, Mn., U.S. — D6 100
Proctor, Mt., U.S. — C2 103
Proctor, Ok., U.S. — B7 113
Proctor, Tx., U.S. — D3 120
Proctor, Vt., U.S. — D2 122
Proctor, W.V., U.S. — g8 125
Proctor Lake, res., Tx., U.S. — C3 120
Proctorsville, Vt., U.S. — E3 122
Proctorville, N.C., U.S. — C3 110
Proctorville, Oh., U.S. — D3 112
Proença-a-Nova, Port. — C2 22
Progreso, Mex. — C7 63
Prokhladnyy, Sov. Un. — E2 28
Prokopyevsk, Sov. Un. — D11 29
Prokuplje, Yugo. — D5 24
Prole, Ia., U.S. — f8 92
Proletarsk, Sov. Un. — H13 27
Proletarsk, Sov. Un. — q21 27
Prome (Pye), Burma — E10 36
Promise City, Ia., U.S. — D4 92
Promissão, Braz. — C3 56
Promontory Mountains, mts., Ut., U.S. — B3 121
Pronsfeld, W. Ger. — C6 17
Prophetstown, Il., U.S. — B4 90
Proprià, Braz. — D7 57
Prorer Wiek, b., E. Ger. — D7 15
Prorva, Sov. Un. — D5 28
Proserpine, Austl. — D8 50
Prosna, stm., Pol. — C5 26
Prosotsáni, Grc. — B4 25
Prospect, N.S. — E6 71
Prospect, Ct., U.S. — C4 84
Prospect, In., U.S. — g11 94
Prospect, Oh., U.S. — B2 112
Prospect, Or., U.S. — E4 114
Prospect, Pa., U.S. — E1 115
Prospect, Tn., U.S. — B4 119
Prospect, Va., U.S. — C4 123
Prospect Harbor, Me., U.S. — D4 96
Prospect Heights, Co., U.S. — *C5 83
Prospect Heights, Il., U.S. — *h9 90
Prospect Hill, N.C., U.S. — A3 110
Prospect Hill, mtn., Or., U.S. — k11 114
Prospect Hill, hill, Ma., U.S. — D6 98
Prospect Hill, hill, Ma., U.S. — g10 98
Prospect Park, N.J., U.S. — B4 107
Prospect Park, Pa., U.S. — p20 115
Prospect Plains, N.J., U.S. — C4 107
Prosperity, S.C., U.S. — C4 117
Prosperity, W.V., U.S. — n13 125
Prosser, Ne., U.S. — D7 104
Prosser, Wa., U.S. — C6 124
Prostějov, Czech. — D4 26
Prostki, Pol. — B7 26
Protection, Ks., U.S. — E4 93
Proton Station, Ont. — C4 73
Prouts Neck, Me., U.S. — g7 96
Provadiya, Bul. — D8 24
Provadiyska, stm., Bul. — D8 24
Provencal, La., U.S. — C2 95
Provence, hist. reg., Fr. — F7 16
Providence, Fl., U.S. — G4 86
Providence, Ky., U.S. — C2 94
Providence, R.I., U.S. — C4 116
Providence, Ut., U.S. — B4 121
Providence, co., R.I., U.S. — C2 116
Providence, stm., R.I., U.S. — C5 116
Providence Bay, Ont. — B2 73
Providence Forge, Va., U.S. — C5 123
Providence Point, c., R.I., U.S. — D5 116
Providencia, Isla de, i., Col. — H7 63
Province Lake, l., N.H., U.S. — C5 106
Provincetown, Ma., U.S. — B7 98
Provins, Fr. — C5 16
Provo, Ar., U.S. — C1 81
Provo, S.D., U.S. — D2 118
Provo, Ut., U.S. — C4 121
Provo, stm., Ut., U.S. — C4 121
Provost, Alta. — C5 68
Prowers, co., Co., U.S. — D8 83
Prozor, Yugo. — D3 24
Pruden, Tn., U.S. — C10 119
Prudence Island, R.I., U.S. — E5 116
Prudence Island, i., R.I., U.S. — D5 116
Prudentópolis, Braz. — B2 56
Prudenville, Mi., U.S. — D6 99
Prudhoe Bay, Ak., U.S. — A10 79
Prudhoe Bay, b., Ak., U.S. — A10 79
Prud'homme, Sask. — E3 75
Prudnik, Pol. — C4 26
Prue, Ok., U.S. — A5 113
Prüm, W. Ger. — C6 18
Pruszków, Pol. — B6 26
Prut, stm., Eur. — B9 24
Pruzhany, Sov. Un. — E5 27
Prydz Bay, b., Ant. — C20 7
Pryor, Mt., U.S. — E8 103
Pryor, Ok., U.S. — A6 113
Pryor, stm., Mt., U.S. — E8 103
Pryor Mountains, mts., Mt., U.S. — E8 103
Przasnysz, Pol. — B6 26
Przedbórz, Pol. — C5 26
Przemsza, stm., Pol. — g10 26
Przemyśl, Pol. — D7 26
Przeworsk, Pol. — C7 26
Przewóz, Pol. — B9 19
Przheválsk, Sov. Un. — E9 28
Psakhná, Grc. — C5 25
Psará, i., Grc. — C5 40
Psary, Pol. — g10 29
Psel, stm., Sov. Un. — G9 27
Pskov, Sov. Un. — C5 27
Pskov, Lake, l., Sov. Un. — B7 27
Pszczyna, Pol. — D5 26
Pszczynka, stm., Pol. — h10 29
Ptich, stm., Sov. Un. — E7 27
Ptolemaís, Grc. — B3 25
Ptuj, Yugo. — B2 24

Puako, Hi., U.S. — D6 88
Puán, Arg. — B4 54
Pu'apu'a, W. Sam. — F11 52
Pucallpa, Peru — C3 58
Pucheng, China — K8 32
Pucheng, China — G6 32
Puchŏn, S. Kor. — *H3 33
Puck, Pol. — A5 26
Puckaway Lake, l., Wi., U.S. — E4 126
Puckett, Ms., U.S. — C4 101
Pudasjärvi, Fin. — E12 14
Pudozh, Sov. Un. — A11 27
Puebla, state, Mex. — D5 63
Puebla de Don Fadrique, Spain — D4 22
Puebla del Caramiñal, Spain — A1 22
Puebla [de Zaragoza], Mex. — D5 63
Pueblo, Co., U.S. — C6 83
Pueblo, co., Co., U.S. — C6 83
Pueblo Colorado Wash, val., Az., U.S. — B6 80
Pueblo Hundido, Chile — E1 55
Pueblo Libre, Peru — *D2 58
Pueblo Mountain, mtn., Or., U.S. — E8 114
Pueblo Mountains, mts., Or., U.S. — E8 114
Pueblo Nuevo (part of Panamá), Pan. — k11 63
Pueblo Nuevo, Ven. — A4 60
Pueblo Reservoir, res., Co., U.S. — C6 83
Pueblo Viejo, Ec. — B2 58
Pueblonuevo, Ec. — B2 58
Puenteareas, Spain — A1 22
Puente-Ceso, Spain — A1 22
Puentedeume, Spain — A1 22
Puente-Genil, Spain — D3 22
Puerco, stm., U.S. — C6 83
Puerco, Rio, stm., N.M., U.S. — B2 108
Pueo Point, c., Hi., U.S. — B1 88
Pu'er, China — G5 31
Puerca, Punta, c., P.R. — B4 65
Puercos, co., U.S. — C6 83
Punia, Zaire — B4 48
Punjab, state, India — B5 36
Puerto Acosta, Bol. — C5 55
Puerto Aisén, Chile — D2 54
Puerto Alegre, Bol. — B5 55
Puerto Armuelles, Pan. — F6 62
Puerto Asís, Col. — C2 60
Puerto Ayacucho, Ven. — B4 60
Puerto Alta, Arg. — B4 54
Puerto Baquerizo Moreno, Ec. — g6 58
Puerto Barrios, Guat. — D7 63
Puerto Belgrano, Arg. — B4 54
Puerto Bermúdez, Peru — D3 58
Puerto Berrío, Col. — B3 60
Puerto Bolívar, Ec. — B1 58
Puerto Cabello, Ven. — A4 60
Puerto Cabezas, Nic. — E8 63
Puerto Carreño, Col. — B4 60
Puerto Casado, Para. — D4 55
Puerto Chicama, Peru — C2 55
Puerto Colombia, Col. — A3 60
Puerto Constanza, Arg. — f7 54
Puerto Cortés, Hond. — D7 63
Puerto Cumarebo, Ven. — A4 60
Puerto de la Cruz, Spain — m13 22
Puerto del Rosario, Spain — m15 22
Puerto del Son, Spain — A1 22
Puerto de Luna, N.M., U.S. — C5 108
Puerto Deseado, Arg. — D3 54
Puerto Eten, Peru — C2 58
Puerto Francisco de Orellana, Ec. — B2 58
Puerto Guaraní, Para. — D4 55
Puerto Heath, Bol. — B5 55
Puerto Inírida, Col. — B4 60
Puerto Jiménez, C.R. — F6 62
Puerto la Cruz, Ven. — A5 60
Puerto Leguízamo, Col. — D3 60
Puerto Lobos, Arg. — C3 54
Puerto López, Col. — C3 60
Puerto Madryn, Arg. — C3 54
Puerto Maldonado, Peru — D4 58
Puerto México see Coatzacoalcos, Mex. — D6 63
Puerto Mineral, Arg. — E4 55
Puerto Montt, Chile — D2 54
Puerto Morazán, Nic. — D4 62
Puerto Nariño, Col. — C4 60
Puerto Natales, Chile — E2 54
Puerto Padre, Cuba — D9 64
Puerto Páez, Col. — B4 60
Puerto Peñasco, Mex. — A2 63
Puerto Pilón, Pan. — k11 63
Puerto Pinasco, Para. — D4 55
Puerto Pirámides, Arg. — C4 54
Puerto Plata, Dom. Rep. — E8 64
Puerto Portillo, Peru — C3 58
Puerto Presidente Stroessner, Para. — E5 55
Puerto Princesa, Phil. — D5 34
Puerto Real, Spain — D2 22
Puerto Rico, ctry., N.A. — G11 64
Puerto Saavedra, Chile — D2 54
Puerto Sastre, Para. — D4 55
Puerto Siles, Bol. — B5 55
Puerto Suárez, Bol. — C6 55
Puerto Supe, Peru — D2 58
Puerto Tejada, Col. — C2 60
Puerto Toledo, Col. — D3 60
Puerto Vallarta, Mex. — C3 63
Puerto Varas, Chile — D2 54
Puerto Victoria, Peru — C3 58
Puerto Viejo, C.R. — F6 62
Puerto Villamizar, Col. — B3 60
Puerto Visser, Arg. — D3 54
Puerto Wilches, Col. — B3 60
Pugachev, Sov. Un. — D6 28
Puget Sound, strt., Wa., U.S. — B3 124
Puget Sound Naval Shipyard, mil., Wa., U.S. — e10 124
Puget-Théniers, Fr. — F7 16
Pugwash, N.S. — D6 71
Puhi, Hi., U.S. — B2 88
Puhsi, China — B7 33
Puigcerdá, Spain — A2 22
Pujehun, S.L. — E2 45
Pujili, Ec. — B2 58
Puka, Alb. — g10 29
Pukalani, Hi., U.S. — C5 88
Pukaskwa National Park, Ont. — o18 73
Pukch'ŏng, N. Kor. — F4 33
Pukeashun Mountain, mtn., B.C. — F3 90
Pukekohe, N.Z. — L15 51
Pukhan, stm., Asia — H3 33
Pukou, China — H8 32
Puksubaek, Mount, mtn., N. Kor. — F3 33
Pukwana, S.D., U.S. — D6 118
Pula, Italy — B2 23
Pula, Yugo. — C1 24
Pulacayo, Bol. — C5 55
Pulaski, Ga., U.S. — D5 87
Pulaski, Il., U.S. — F4 90

Pulaski, In., U.S. — C4 91
Pulaski, Ia., U.S. — D5 92
Pulaski, Ms., U.S. — C4 101
Pulaski, N.Y., U.S. — B4 109
Pulaski, Tn., U.S. — B4 119
Pulaski, Va., U.S. — C2 123
Pulaski, Wi., U.S. — D5 126
Pulaski, co., Ar., U.S. — C3 81
Pulaski, co., Ga., U.S. — D3 87
Pulaski, co., Il., U.S. — F4 90
Pulaski, co., In., U.S. — B4 91
Pulaski, co., Ky., U.S. — C5 94
Pulaski, co., Mo., U.S. — D5 102
Pulaski, co., Va., U.S. — C2 123
Puławy, Pol. — D2 26
Pulheim, W. Ger. — *C3 18
Pulicat Lake, l., India — F4 99
Pulkovo, Sov. Un. — C8 124
Pullman, Wa., U.S. — B4 125
Pulog, Mount, mtn., Phil. — B6 34
Pulozero, Sov. Un. — C15 14
Pułtusk, Pol. — B6 26
Pumphrey, Md., U.S. — h11 97
Pumpkin Buttes, mtn., Wy., U.S. — C7 127
Pumpkin Creek, stm., Mt., U.S. — E11 103
Pumpkin Creek, stm., Ne., U.S. — C2 104
Pumpville, Tx., U.S. — E2 120
Puna, Bol. — C5 55
Puna, Isla, i., Ec. — B1 58
Punakha, Bhu. — C8 36
Punat, Yugo. — C2 24
Punata, Bol. — C5 55
Punchaw, B.C. — C6 69
Pune, India — E5 36
Pungo Lake, l., N.C., U.S. — B6 110
Pungsan, N. Kor. — F4 33
Punia, Zaire — B4 48
Punjab, state, India — B5 36
Punjab, prov., Pak. — B5 36
Punnichy, Sask. — F3 75
Puno, Peru — E3 58
Puno, dept., Peru — E3 58
Punta Alta, Arg. — B4 54
Punta Arenas, Chile — h11 54
Punta de Díaz, Chile — E1 55
Punta del Este, Ur. — E2 56
Punta de Piedras, Ven. — A5 60
Punta de Vacas, Arg. — A3 54
Punta Gorda, Belize — D7 63
Punta Gorda, Fl., U.S. — F4 86
Punta Gorda, Bahía de, b., Nic. — E8 63
Punta Moreno, Peru — C2 58
Puntarenas, C.R. — E5 62
Punto Fijo, Ven. — A3 60
Puntzi Lake, l., B.C. — C5 69
Punxsutawney, Pa., U.S. — E4 115
Puposky, Mn., U.S. — C4 100
Puquio, Peru — D3 58
Pur, stm., Sov. Un. — C10 29
Pūranpur, India — C6 37
Purari, stm., Pap. N. Gui. — k11 50
Purcell, Mo., U.S. — D3 102
Purcell, Ok., U.S. — B4 113
Purcell Mountains, mts., N.A. — D9 69
Purcellville, Va., U.S. — A5 123
Purdham Hill, mtn., Ar., U.S. — h10 81
Purdin, Mo., U.S. — B4 102
Purdum, Ne., U.S. — B5 104
Purdy, Mo., U.S. — E4 102
Purépero, Mex. — n12 63
Purgatoire, stm., Co., U.S. — D7 83
Purgatoire Peak, mtn., Co., U.S. — D5 83
Puri, India — E8 36
Purmerend, Neth. — B4 17
Pūrna, stm., India — H6 37
Pūrnia, India — C8 36
Purple Springs, Alta. — E5 68
Purpus, W.V., U.S. — B4 125
Puruándiro, Mex. — m13 63
Puruliya, India — B4 36
Purús, stm., S.A. — D4 53
Purvis, Ms., U.S. — D4 101
Purwakarta, Indon. — *G3 34
Purwokerto, Indon. — *G3 34
Puryear, Tn., U.S. — A3 119
Puryŏng-dong, N. Kor. — D10 31
Pusan, S. Kor. — D10 31
Pushaw Lake, l., Me., U.S. — D4 96
Pushkin, Sov. Un. — D6 29
Pushkino, Sov. Un. — C11 27
Pushmataha, Al., U.S. — C1 78
Pushmataha, co., Ok., U.S. — C6 113
Pushthrough, Newf. — E3 72
Pusiano, Lago di, l., Italy — E7 21
Püspökladány, Hung. — B5 24
Pustelnik, Pol. — k14 26
Pustynnaya, Sov. Un. — B8 33
Putao, Burma — C10 36
Puteaux, Fr. — g9 16
Putian, China — F8 31
Putilovo, Sov. Un. — s32 14
Puting, Cape, c., Indon. — F4 34
Putivl, Sov. Un. — F9 27
Putlitz, E. Ger. — E2 15
Putnam, Ct., U.S. — B8 84
Putnam, Ok., U.S. — B3 113
Putnam, Tx., U.S. — C3 120
Putnam, co., Fl., U.S. — C5 86
Putnam, co., Ga., U.S. — C3 87
Putnam, co., Il., U.S. — B4 90
Putnam, co., In., U.S. — E4 91
Putnam, co., Mo., U.S. — A4 102
Putnam, co., N.Y., U.S. — D7 109
Putnam, co., Oh., U.S. — B1 112
Putnam, co., Tn., U.S. — C8 119
Putnam, co., W.V., U.S. — C3 125
Putnam Station, N.Y., U.S. — B7 109
Putnamville, In., U.S. — E4 91
Putnamville, Vt., U.S. — C3 122
Putney, Ga., U.S. — E2 87
Putney, S.D., U.S. — B7 118
Putney, Vt., U.S. — F3 122
Putre, Chile — C5 55
Puttalam, Sri L. — G6 36
Putte, Neth. — C4 17
Püttlingen, W. Ger. — D1 19
Putumayo, dept., Col. — C2 60
Putumayo (Içá), stm., S.A. — C12 40
Pütürge, Tur. — C12 40
Puukohola Heiau National Historic Site, hist., Hi., U.S. — D6 88
Puunene, Hi., U.S. — C5 88
Puurs, Bel. — C5 88
Puxico, Mo., U.S. — E7 102
Puyallup, Wa., U.S. — B3 124

Name	Map Ref.	Page

Puyallup, stm., Wa., U.S. — C3 124
Puyang, China — G6 32
Puyehue, Chile — C2 54
Puyo, Ec. — B2 58
Pūzak, Hāmūn-e, l., Afg. — F10 39
Pwani, prov., Tan. — C6 48
Pweto, Zaire — C4 48
Pwllheli, Wales, U.K. — D4 10
Pyaozero, l., Sov. Un. — D14 14
Pyapon, Burma — E10 36
Pyasina, stm., Sov. Un. — B12 29
Pyatigorsk, Sov. Un. — E2 28
Pyatt, Ar., U.S. — A3 81
Pyhäjärvi, l., Fin. — G10 14
Pyinmana, Burma — E10 36
Pyland, Ms., U.S. — B4 101
Pyles Fork, stm., W.V., U.S. — h10 125
Pymatuning Reservoir, res., U.S. — C1 115
Pyŏngchang, S. Kor. — H4 33
Pyŏngtaek, S. Kor. — H3 33
Pyŏngyang, N. Kor. — D10 31
Pyote, Tx., U.S. — D1 120
Pyramid Lake, l., Nv., U.S. — C2 105
Pyramid Lake Indian Reservation, Nv., U.S. — D2 105
Pyramid Mountains, mts., N.M., U.S. — E1 108
Pyramid Peak, mtn., N.M., U.S. — E1 108
Pyramid Peak, mtn., Wy., U.S. — C2 127
Pyramids, hist., Eg. — C3 38
Pyrenees, mts., Eur. — A6 22
Pyrites, N.Y., U.S. — f9 109
Pyrmont, In., U.S. — D4 91
Pyrzyce, Pol. — B3 26
Pyskowice, Pol. — g9 26
Pytalovo, Sov. Un. — C6 27
Pyu, Burma — E10 36

Q

Qabātiyah, Isr. Occ. — B7 41
Qā'emshahr, Iran — C6 39
Qā'en, Iran — E9 39
Qahar Youyi Zhongqi, China — D5 32
Qaidam Pendi (Tsaidam Basin), China — D3 31
Qalamshāh, Eg. — H8 40
Qalāt, Afg. — B4 36
Qal'at Bīshah, Sau. Ar. — C4 38
Qal'at Ṣāliḥ, Iraq — F3 39
Qal'at Sukkar, Iraq — F3 39
Qal'eh-ye Now, Afg. — D11 39
Qallābāt, Sud. — C4 47
Qalyūb, Eg. — D3 41
Qamdo, China — E4 31
Qamea, i., Fiji — H16 52
Qamīnīs, Libya — C4 43
Qānā, Leb. — A7 41
Qandahār see Kandahar, Afg. — B4 36
Qandala, Som. — C6 47
Qārah, Egypt — H6 40
Qardho, Som. — D6 47
Qareh, stm., Iran — D5 39
Qārūn, Birkat, l., Eg. — D6 43
Qaryat Abu Nujaym, Libya — C3 43
Qaṣr al Farāfirah, Eg. — C2 38
Qasr el Boukhari, Alg. — B5 44
Qaṣr-e Shīrīn, Iran — D2 39
Qa'ṭabah, Yemen — D4 38
Qatar, ctry., Asia — C5 38
Qattara Depression, depr., Eg. — C2 38
Qawz Rajab, Sud. — B4 47
Qazvīn, Iran — B4 38
Qeshm, Iran — H8 39
Qeshm, i., Iran — C5 38
Qezel Owzan, stm., Iran — C4 39
Qian'an, China — D8 32
Qianjiang, China — J3 32
Qianshan, China — I7 32
Qiantang Jiang, stm., China — J8 32
Qianxian, China — G3 32
Qianyang, China — F7 31
Qiaojia, China — F5 31
Qichun, China — I6 32
Qiemo, China — A8 36
Qijiang, China — J2 32
Qila Lādgasht, Pak. — C3 36
Qila Saifullāh, Pak. — B2 37
Qilian Shan, mts., China — D4 31
Qimen, China — J7 32
Qina, China — C3 38
Qing'an, China — C3 33
Qingdao (Tsingtao), China — D9 31
Qinghai Hu, l., China — D4 31
Qingjian, China — D7 31
Qingjiang, China — J6 32
Qingliu, China — F8 31
Qingpu, China — E9 31
Qingyang, China — D6 31
Qingyuan, China — C11 31
Qingyun, China — F7 32
Qing Zang Gaoyuan (Plateau of Tibet), plat., China — G11 30
Qin He, stm., China — G5 32
Qinhuangdao, China — D8 31
Qin Ling (Tsinling Shan), mts., China — E6 31
Qinxian, China — F5 32
Qinyang, China — G5 32
Qinzhou, China — B8 35
Qiongshan, China — B4 34
Qiongzhou Haixia, strt., China — B8 35
Qiqian, China — A9 31
Qiqihar (Tsitsihar), China — B9 31
Qiryat Ata, Isr. — B7 41
Qiryat Gat, Isr. — C6 41
Qiryat Mal'akhi, Isr. — C6 41
Qiryat Ono, Isr. — g10 41
Qiryat Shemona, Isr. — A7 41
Qiryat Yam, Isr. — B7 41
Qishn, Yemen — B7 47
Qishon, stm., Isr. — B7 41
Qitai, China — C4 31
Qitaihe, China — *B11 31
Qiyang, China — F7 31
Qīzān, Sau. Ar. — D4 38
Qnadsa, Alg. — C4 44
Qom, Iran — B5 38
Qom, stm., Iran — C5 39
Qomemiyyut (Talbiya) (part of Jerusalem), Isr. — m14 41
Qomsheh, Iran — E5 39
Quabbin Reservoir, res., Ma., U.S. — B3 98
Quaco Head, c., N.B. — D4 71
Quaddick Reservoir, res., Ct., U.S. — B8 84
Quail Oaks, Va., U.S. — n18 123
Quakenbrück, W. Ger. — B3 18

Quaker City, Oh., U.S. — C4 112
Quaker Hill, Ct., U.S. — D7 84
Quakertown, N.J., U.S. — B3 107
Quakertown, Pa., U.S. — F11 115
Qualicum Beach, B.C. — E5 69
Quality, Ky., U.S. — C3 94
Quamba, Mn., U.S. — E5 100
Quanah, Tx., U.S. — B3 120
Quang Ngai, Viet. — B3 34
Quang Trach, Viet. — D7 35
Quang Tri, Viet. — B3 34
Quannapowitt, Lake, l., Ma., U.S. — f11 98
Quantico, Md., U.S. — D6 97
Quantico, Va., U.S. — B5 123
Quantico Marine Corps Air Station, mil., Va., U.S. — B5 123
Quantico Station, Va., U.S. — *B5 123
Quanzhou, China — F7 31
Quanzhou, China — G8 31
Quapaw, Ok., U.S. — A7 113
Qu'Appelle, Sask. — G4 75
Qu'Appelle, stm., Can. — G4 75
Quaraí, Braz. — E1 56
Quaraí, stm., S.A. — E1 56
Quarles Mountains, mts., Indon. — F5 34
Quarryville, N.B. — C4 71
Quarryville, Ct., U.S. — B6 84
Quarryville, Pa., U.S. — G9 115
Quartu Sant' Elena, Italy — E2 23
Quartz Hill, Ca., U.S. — *E4 82
Quartz Mountain, mtn., Or., U.S. — D4 114
Quartzsite, Az., U.S. — D1 80
Quasqueton, Ia., U.S. — B6 92
Quassapaug, Lake, l., Ct., U.S. — C3 84
Quatre, Isle, i., St. Vin. — V26 65
Quatsino Sound, strt., B.C. — D3 69
Quay, N.M., U.S. — C6 108
Quay, Ok., U.S. — A5 113
Quay, co., N.M., U.S. — C6 108
Québec, Que. — B5 74
Québec, prov., Can. — C5 74
Quebeck, Tn., U.S. — D8 119
Quechee, Vt., U.S. — D4 122
Quechee Gorge, val., Vt., U.S. — D4 122
Quecreek, Pa., U.S. — F3 115
Quedlinburg, E. Ger. — C5 18
Queen, stm., R.I., U.S. — E3 116
Queen, Cape, c., N.W. Ter. — D17 66
Queen Alexandra Range, mts., Ant. — A29 7
Queen Anne, Md., U.S. — C5 97
Queen Annes, co., Md., U.S. — B5 97
Queen Bess, Mount, mtn., B.C. — D5 69
Queenborough [-in-Sheppey], Eng., U.K. — E7 10
Queen Charlotte, B.C. — C1 69
Queen Charlotte Islands, is., B.C. — C1 69
Queen Charlotte Mountains, mts., B.C. — C1 69
Queen Charlotte Sound, strt., B.C. — n17 69
Queen Charlotte Strait, strt., B.C. — D4 69
Queen City, Mo., U.S. — A5 102
Queen City, Tx., U.S. — C5 120
Queen Creek, Az., U.S. — m9 80
Queen Elizabeth Islands, is., N.W. Ter. — k30 66
Queen Fabiola Mountains, mts., Ant. — B16 7
Queen Mary Coast, Ant. — C22 7
Queen Maud Gulf, b., N.W. Ter. — C12 66
Queen Maud Land, reg., Ant. — B15 7
Queen Maud Mountains, mts., Ant. — A31 7
Queens, co., N.B. — D4 71
Queens, co., N.S. — E4 71
Queens, co., P.E.I. — C6 71
Queens, co., N.Y., U.S. — E7 109
Queensborough, Ont. — C7 73
Queensborough, Wa., U.S. — *B3 124
Queensferry, Scot., U.K. — E5 13
Queensferry see South Queensferry, Scot., U.K. — E5 13
Queen Shoals, W.V., U.S. — C3 125
Queensland, Ga., U.S. — E3 87
Queensland, state, Austl. — D7 51
Queensport, N.S. — D8 71
Queens Sound, strt., B.C. — D3 69
Queenstown, Austl. — o15 50
Queenstown, Alta. — D4 68
Queenstown, N.B. — D3 71
Queenstown, N.Z. — P12 51
Queenstown, S. Afr. — D4 49
Queenstown, Md., U.S. — C5 97
Queen Victoria Sea, Eur. — A5 29
Queets, Wa., U.S. — B1 124
Queguay Grande, stm., Ur. — E1 56
Queimadas, Braz. — D3 57
Queimadinhas, Braz. — A4 56
Queixada, Braz. — B4 56
Quela, Ang. — C2 48
Quelelevu, i., Fiji — H16 52
Quelimane, Moz. — A6 49
Quemado, N.M., U.S. — C1 108
Quemado, Tx., U.S. — E2 120
Quemado de Güines, Cuba — C3 64
Quemú Quemú, Arg. — D4 54
Quenemo, Ks., U.S. — D8 93
Quentin, Ms., U.S. — D3 101
Quepos, C.R. — F5 62
Quequén, Arg. — D5 54
Querétaro, Mex. — C4 63
Querétaro, state, Mex. — C5 63
Querfurt, E. Ger. — B6 19
Quers, Fr. — A1 21
Quesada, Spain — D4 22
Queshan, China — H6 32
Qūesnel, B.C. — C6 69
Quesnel, stm., B.C. — C7 69
Quesnel Lake, l., B.C. — C7 69
Questa, N.M., U.S. — A4 108
Quetena, Bol. — D2 55
Quetico Provincial Park, Ont. — o17 73
Quetta, Pak. — B4 36
Quevedo, Ec. — B2 58
Quezaltenango, Guat. — E6 63
Quezaltepeque, El Sal. — D3 63
Quezon City, Phil. — C6 34
Quibala, Ang. — D1 48
Quibdó, Col. — B2 60
Quibell, Ont. — E5 70
Quiberon, Fr. — D2 16
Quiberon Peninsula, pen., Fr. — D2 16
Quicksand Pond, l., R.I., U.S. — E6 116

Quicksburg, Va., U.S. — B4 123
Quidnessett, R.I., U.S. — E4 116
Quidnick, R.I., U.S. — D3 116
Quidnick Reservoir, res., R.I., U.S. — D2 116
Quiindy, Para. — E4 55
Quilá, Mex. — C3 63
Quilcene, Wa., U.S. — B3 124
Quilengues, Ang. — D1 48
Quileute Indian Reservation, Wa., U.S. — B1 124
Quilino, Arg. — F3 55
Quillagua, Chile — D2 55
Quillan, Fr. — F5 16
Quill Lake, Sask. — E3 75
Quillota, Chile — A2 54
Quilmes, Arg. — g7 54
Quilon, India — G6 36
Quilpie, Austl. — E7 50
Quilpué, Chile — A2 54
Quilty, Ire. — E2 11
Quimbele, Ang. — C2 48
Quimby, Ia., U.S. — B2 92
Quimby, Me., U.S. — B4 96
Quimili, Arg. — E3 55
Quimper, Fr. — C1 16
Quimperlé, Fr. — D2 16
Quinaby, Or., U.S. — B4 114
Quinault, stm., Wa., U.S. — B1 124
Quinault, Lake, l., Wa., U.S. — B2 124
Quinault Indian Reservation, Wa., U.S. — B1 124
Quince Orchard, Md., U.S. — *B3 97
Quincy, Ca., U.S. — C3 82
Quincy, Fl., U.S. — B2 86
Quincy, Il., U.S. — D2 90
Quincy, In., U.S. — F4 91
Quincy, Ks., U.S. — E8 93
Quincy, Ky., U.S. — B6 94
Quincy, Ma., U.S. — B5 98
Quincy, Mi., U.S. — G6 99
Quincy, Ms., U.S. — B5 101
Quincy, Mo., U.S. — C4 102
Quincy, Oh., U.S. — B2 112
Quincy, Pa., U.S. — G6 115
Quincy, Wa., U.S. — B6 124
Quincy Bay, b., Ma., U.S. — g12 98
Quindío, dept., Col. — C2 60
Quinebaug, Ct., U.S. — A8 84
Quinebaug, stm., Ct., U.S. — C8 84
Quines, Arg. — A3 54
Quinga, Moz. — A7 49
Quinhagak, Ak., U.S. — D7 79
Qui Nhon, Viet. — C4 34
Quinlan, Ok., U.S. — A2 113
Quinlan, Tx., U.S. — C4 120
Quinn, S.D., U.S. — D3 118
Quinn, stm., Nv., U.S. — B3 105
Quinn Canyon Range, mts., Nv., U.S. — F6 105
Quinnesec, Mi., U.S. — C3 99
Quinnipiac, stm., Ct., U.S. — D4 84
Quinnville, R.I., U.S. — B4 116
Quintana de la Serena, Spain — C3 22
Quintanar [de la Orden], Spain — C4 22
Quintana Roo, state, Mex. — D7 63
Quinter, Ks., U.S. — C3 93
Quintero, Chile — A2 54
Quinton, Sask. — F3 75
Quinton, Ky., U.S. — D5 94
Quinton, N.J., U.S. — D2 107
Quinton, Ok., U.S. — B6 113
Quinwood, W.V., U.S. — C4 125
Quipapá, Braz. — C3 57
Quipungo, Ang. — D1 48
Quiraba, Braz. — C3 57
Quirauk Mountain, mtn., Md., U.S. — A2 97
Quirindi, Austl. — E8 51
Quirinópolis, Braz. — B2 56
Quiriquire, Ven. — B5 60
Quiroga, Spain — A2 22
Quirpon Island, i., Newf. — C4 72
Quissanga, Moz. — D7 48
Quitaque, Tx., U.S. — B2 120
Quita Sueño Bank, Col. — C7 62
Quitman, Ar., U.S. — B3 81
Quitman, Ga., U.S. — F3 87
Quitman, La., U.S. — B3 95
Quitman, Ms., U.S. — C5 101
Quitman, Mo., U.S. — A2 102
Quitman, Tx., U.S. — C5 120
Quitman, co., Ga., U.S. — E1 87
Quitman, co., Ms., U.S. — A3 101
Quitman Mountains, mts., Tx., U.S. — o12 120
Quito, Ec. — B2 58
Quixadá, Braz. — B3 57
Quixeramobim, Braz. — C3 57
Qulin, Mo., U.S. — E7 102
Quoi, i., Micron. — Q18 52
Quonnipaug Lake, l., Ct., U.S. — D5 84
Quonochontaug, R.I., U.S. — G2 116
Quonochontaug Pond, l., R.I., U.S. — G2 116
Quonset Point, c., R.I., U.S. — E4 116
Quorn, Austl. — F2 51
Qurayyah, Wādī, val., Eg. — C3 38
Qūs, Eg. — C3 38
Quṣrah, Isr. Occ. — g12 41
Quthing, Leso. — D4 49
Quxian, China — E6 31
Quxian, China — F8 31
Quzhou, China — *F8 31

R

Raab (Rába), stm., Eur. — B2 24
Raabs [an der Thaya], Aus. — D7 18
Raahe, Fin. — E11 14
Raalte, Neth. — B6 17
Ra'ananna, Isr. — g10 41
Raasay, i., Scot., U.K. — C3 13
Rab, i., Yugo. — E5 24
Raba, Indon. — G5 34
Rába (Raab), stm., Eur. — B2 24
Rabastens, Fr. — F4 16
Rabat, Mor. — B4 44
Rabaul, Pap. N. Gui. — h13 50
Rabbit Creek, stm., S.D., U.S. — B3 118
Rabbit Ears Pass, Co., U.S. — A4 83
Rabbit Hash, Ky., U.S. — k13 94
Rabbit Lake, Sask. — D2 75
Rabi, i., Fiji — H16 52
Rābigh, Sau. Ar. — C3 38
Rabun, Al., U.S. — D2 78
Rabun, co., Ga., U.S. — B3 87
Rabun, Bald, mtn., Ga., U.S. — B3 87
Rača, Yugo. — C5 24
Raccoon Creek, stm., Oh., U.S. — D3 112
Raccourci Island, i., La., U.S. — D4 95
Race, Cape, c., Newf. — E5 72

Raceland, Ky., U.S. — B7 94
Raceland, La., U.S. — E5 95
Race Point, c., Ma., U.S. — B7 98
Race Pond, Ga., U.S. — F4 87
Rach Gia, Viet. — C4 34
Raciborz, Pol. — C5 26
Racine, Mn., U.S. — G6 100
Racine, Mo., U.S. — E3 102
Racine, Oh., U.S. — D4 112
Racine, W.V., U.S. — C3 125
Racine, Wi., U.S. — F6 126
Racine, co., Wi., U.S. — F5 126
Racine Dam, U.S. — C3 125
Račinĕves, Czech. — n17 26
Racket, Mo., U.S. — C4 102
Raco, Mi., U.S. — B6 99
Rădăuţi, Rom. — B7 24
Rāmādi Barrage, Iraq — F14 40
Radbuza, stm., Czech. — D8 19
Radcliff, Ky., U.S. — C4 94
Radcliff, Oh., U.S. — C3 112
Radcliffe, Ia., U.S. — B4 92
Råde, Nor. — p28 14
Radeberg, E. Ger. — C6 18
Radebeul, E. Ger. — B8 19
Radersburg, Mt., U.S. — D5 103
Radford, Va., U.S. — C2 123
Rādhanpur, India — F3 37
Radisson, Sask. — E2 75
Radisson, Wi., U.S. — C2 126
Radium, Ks., U.S. — D5 93
Radium, Mn., U.S. — B2 100
Radium Hot Springs, B.C. — D9 69
Radium Springs, N.M., U.S. — E3 108
Radix, Point, c., Trin. — O24 65
Radley, Ks., U.S. — *E9 93
Radnice, Czech. — D8 19
Radnor, In., U.S. — C4 91
Radnor, Oh., U.S. — B2 112
Radnor Township, Pa., U.S. — *F11 115
Radom, Pol. — C6 26
Radomsko, Pol. — C5 26
Radomyshl, Sov. Un. — F7 27
Radoviš, Yugo. — E6 18
Radstadt, Aus. — H3 75
Radville, Sask. — H3 75
Radway, Alta. — B4 68
Radzików, Pol. — g9 26
Radzymin, Pol. — k14 26
Radzyń [Podlaski], Pol. — C7 26
Rāe Bareli, India — C7 36
Rae, N.W. Ter. — D9 66
Raeford, N.C., U.S. — B3 110
Raeside, Lake, l., Austl. — E3 50
Rae Strait, strt., N.W. Ter. — C14 66
Rafaela, Arg. — A4 54
Rafah, Isr. Occ. — G10 40
Rafaï, Cen. Afr. Rep. — D4 46
Rafḥā', Sau. Ar. — C3 38
Rafsanjān, Iran — F8 39
Raft, stm., Id., U.S. — G5 89
Raft River Mountains, mts., Ut., U.S. — B2 121
Raga, Sud. — D2 47
Ragan, Ne., U.S. — D6 104
Ragay, Phil. — p14 34
Ragay Gulf, b., Phil. — p14 34
Ragged Island, i., Me., U.S. — E4 96
Ragged Island Range, is., Bah. — C6 64
Ragged Lake, l., Me., U.S. — C3 96
Ragged Top Mountain, mtn., Wy., U.S. — E7 127
Raghza, Pak. — B4 36
Raglan, N.Z. — B5 51
Raglesville, In., U.S. — G4 91
Ragley, La., U.S. — D2 95
Rago, Ks., U.S. — E5 93
Ragunda, Swe. — F7 14
Ragusa, Italy — F5 23
Rahad al Bardī, Sud. — C1 47
Rahden, W. Ger. — F2 15
Rahīmyār Khān, Pak. — C5 36
Rahway, N.J., U.S. — k7 107
Rahway, stm., N.J., U.S. — k7 107
Rāichūr, India — E6 36
Raiford, Fl., U.S. — B4 86
Raigarh, India — D7 36
Railroad Valley, val., Nv., U.S. — E6 105
Raimbault, stm., Que. — A5 74
Rainbow Bridge National Monument, Ut., U.S. — F5 121
Rainbow City, Pan. — k11 62
Rainbow City, Al., U.S. — *A3 78
Rainbow Falls, wtfl., Tn., U.S. — D10 119
Rainbow Flowage, res., Wi., U.S. — C4 126
Rainbow Lake, l., Me., U.S. — C3 96
Rainelle, W.V., U.S. — D4 125
Raines, Ut., U.S. — A2 121
Rainier, Or., U.S. — A4 114
Rainier, Wa., U.S. — C3 124
Rainier, Mount, mtn., Wa., U.S. — C4 124
Rainsboro, Oh., U.S. — C2 112
Rainsville, Al., U.S. — A4 78
Rainy, stm., N.A. — B5 100
Rainy Lake, l., N.A. — B5 100
Rainy Lake, l., Mn., U.S. — B5 100
Rainy River, dept., Ont. — o16 73
Raipur, India — D7 36
Ra'īs, Sau. Ar. — C3 38
Raismes, Fr. — A5 21
Raja, Cape, c., Indon. — K2 35
Rājahmundry, India — E7 36
Rajang, stm., Malay. — D5 34
Rājapālaiyam, India — *G6 36
Rājasthān, state, India — C5 36
Rājkot, India — D5 36
Rājpīpla, India — J7 37
Rājshāhi, Bngl. — D8 36
Rakaia, stm., N.Z. — O13 51
Raka Zangbo, stm., China — C11 37
Rakhov, Sov. Un. — A7 24
Rakovník, Czech. — C2 26
Rakvere, Sov. Un. — B6 27
Raleigh, Newf. — C4 72
Raleigh, Fl., U.S. — C4 86
Raleigh, Il., U.S. — F5 90
Raleigh, Ms., U.S. — C4 101
Raleigh, N.C., U.S. — B4 110
Raleigh, N.D., U.S. — C4 111
Raleigh, co., W.V., U.S. — D3 125
Raleigh Bay, b., N.C., U.S. — B6 110
Raleigh Hills, Or., U.S. — *B4 114

Ralls, Tx., U.S. — C2 120
Ralls, co., Mo., U.S. — B6 102
Ralph, Al., U.S. — B2 78
Ralph, Mi., U.S. — B3 99
Ralph, S.D., U.S. — B2 118
Ralston, Ia., U.S. — B3 92
Ralston, Ne., U.S. — g12 104
Ralston, Ok., U.S. — A5 113
Ralston, Pa., U.S. — D8 115
Ralston, Tn., U.S. — A3 119
Ralston, Wy., U.S. — B4 127
Ralston Valley, val., Nv., U.S. — E4 105
Rānīganj, India — D8 36
Rankin, Il., U.S. — C6 90
Rankin, Pa., U.S. — k14 115
Rankin, Tx., U.S. — D2 120
Rankin, co., Ms., U.S. — C4 101
Rannoch, Loch, res., Scot., U.K. — D4 13
Ranong, Thai. — H3 35
Ransom, Il., U.S. — B5 90
Ransom, Ks., U.S. — D4 93
Ransom, Pa., U.S. — m17 115
Ransom, co., N.D., U.S. — C8 111
Ransomville, N.Y., U.S. — B2 109
Ranson, W.V., U.S. — B7 125
Rantauprapat, Indon. — K3 35
Rantekombola, mtn., Indon. — F6 34
Rantoul, Il., U.S. — C5 90
Rantoul, Ks., U.S. — D8 93
Rantowles, S.C., U.S. — k11 117
Ranum, Den. — B3 15
Raohe, China — B11 31
Raon-[l'Étape], Fr. — A2 20
Raoui, Erg er, des., Alg. — D4 44
Raoul, Ga., U.S. — B3 87
Rapallo, Italy — B2 23
Rāpch, stm., Iran — I9 39
Raphine, Va., U.S. — C3 123
Raphoe, Ire. — C4 11
Rapid, stm., Mn., U.S. — B4 100
Rapid, North Branch, stm., Mn., U.S. — B4 100
Rapidan, Va., U.S. — B4 123
Rapid City, Man. — D1 70
Rapid City, Mi., U.S. — D5 99
Rapid City, S.D., U.S. — C2 118
Rapides, co., La., U.S. — C3 95
Rapid River, Mi., U.S. — C4 99
Rapids City, Il., U.S. — B3 90
Rappahannock, co., Va., U.S. — B4 123
Rappahannock, stm., Va., U.S. — B5 123
Rappahannock Academy, Va., U.S. — B5 123
Rapperswil, Switz. — B6 21
Rāpti, stm., Asia — D9 37
Raquette, stm., N.Y., U.S. — f10 109
Raquette Lake, N.Y., U.S. — h12 109
Raquette Lake, l., N.Y., U.S. — B6 109
Rarden, Oh., U.S. — D2 112
Rardin, Il., U.S. — D5 90
Raritan, Il., U.S. — C3 90
Raritan, N.J., U.S. — B3 107
Raritan, stm., N.J., U.S. — C4 107
Raritan, South Branch, stm., N.J., U.S. — B3 107
Raritan Bay, b., N.J., U.S. — C4 107
Ra's al 'Ayn, Syria — D13 40
Ra's al Khaymah, U.A.E. — C5 38
Ra's al Unūf, Libya — C3 43
Ra's an Naqb, Jord. — C3 38
Ra's Gharib, Eg. — D6 43
Raseiniai, Sov. Un. — A7 26
Ra's Dashen Terara, mtn., Eth. — B4 78
Rashāyyā, Leb. — F10 40
Rashīd (Rosetta), Eg. — B9 24
Rāshidah, Ma'tan, well, Libya — H3 40
Rashkov, Sov. Un. — B9 24
Rasht, Iran — B4 38
Raška, stm., Yugo. — D5 24
Raso, Cabo, c., Arg. — C3 54
Raspberry Peak, mtn., Ar., U.S. — C1 81
Rasskazovo, Sov. Un. — E13 27
Rastatt, W. Ger. — C4 18
Rastede, W. Ger. — A8 17
Rastibonne Monastery, Isr. — m14 41
Raszyn, Pol. — m13 26
Rat, stm., Man. — A2 70
Rat, stm., Man. — E3 70
Ratcliff, Ar., U.S. — B2 81
Ratekau, W. Ger. — B2 15
Rathbun, Ia., U.S. — D5 92
Rathbun Lake, res., Ia., U.S. — D5 92
Rathdrum, Ire. — E5 11
Rathdrum, Id., U.S. — B2 89
Rathenow, E. Ger. — B6 18
Rathfriland, N. Ire., U.K. — B6 11
Rathkeale, Ire. — E3 11
Rathlin Island, i., N. Ire., U.K. — A6 11
Rathlin Sound, strt., N. Ire. — A6 11
Ráth Luirc, Ire. — B5 11
Rathmelton, Ire. — E2 11
Rathmore, Ire. — E2 11
Rathmullen, Ire. — D5 11
Rathnew, Ire. — E5 36
Rathowen, Ire. — E2 70
Rathwell, Man. — B1 19
Ratingen, W. Ger. — C5 81
Ratio, Braz. — B8 104
Rat Lake, l., Man. — A2 70
Rat Lake, l., Man. — A2 70
Ratlām, India — E5 36
Ratnagiri, India — E5 36
Ratne, Sask. — F3 75
Raton, N.M., U.S. — A5 108
Raton Pass, N.M., U.S. — A5 108
Rattan, Ok., U.S. — C6 113
Rattenburg, Aus. — E5 18
Rattlesnake Creek, stm., Ks., U.S. — E4 93
Rattlesnake Creek, stm., Oh., U.S. — C2 112
Rattlesnake Creek, stm., Wa., U.S. — C6 124
Rattlesnake Flat, pl., Wa., U.S. — C7 124
Rattlesnake Hills, hills, Wa., U.S. — C6 124
Rattlesnake Hills, hills, Wy., U.S. — D5 127
Rattlesnake Mountain, mtn., Ct., U.S. — C4 84
Rattling Brook, Newf. — D3 72
Rattray Head, c., Scot., U.K. — C7 13
Rättvik, Swe. — G6 14
Ratzeburg, W. Ger. — E4 15

Name	Map Ref.	Page

Ratzeburger, I., Eur. — E4 15
Raub, Malay. — K4 35
Raub, In., U.S. — C3 91
Raub, N.D., U.S. — B3 111
Rauch, Arg. — B5 54
Raufarhöfn, Ice. — m25 14
Rauer, i., Nor. — p28 14
Raukumara, mtn., N.Z. — L17 51
Rauland, Nor. — H2 14
Rauma, Fin. — G9 14
Raurkela, India — F10 37
Rausu, Mount, mtn., Japan — D12 33
Rautalampi, Fin. — F12 14
Ravalli, Mt., U.S. — C2 103
Ravalli, co., Mt., U.S. — D2 103
Ravanna, Ar., U.S. — D1 81
Ravanna, Mo., U.S. — A4 102
Rāvar, Iran — B5 38
Rava-Russkaya, Sov. Un. — F4 27
Raven, Va., U.S. — e10 123
Ravena, N.Y., U.S. — C7 109
Ravendale, Ca., U.S. — B3 82
Ravenden, Ar., U.S. — A4 81
Ravenden Springs, Ar., U.S. — A4 81
Ravenel, S.C., U.S. — k11 117
Ravenglass, Eng., U.K. — F5 13
Ravenna, Italy — B4 23
Ravenna, Ky., U.S. — C6 94
Ravenna, Mi., U.S. — E5 99
Ravenna, Ne., U.S. — C7 104
Ravenna, Oh., U.S. — A4 112
Raven Park, reg., Co., U.S. — A2 83
Raven Rock, N.J., U.S. — C2 107
Ravensburg, W. Ger. — E4 18
Ravenscrag, Sask. — H1 75
Ravenscroft, Tn., U.S. — D8 119
Ravensdale, Wa., U.S. — f12 124
Ravensthorpe, Austl. — F3 50
Ravenswood, In., U.S. — k10 91
Ravenswood, W.V., U.S. — C3 125
Ravensworth, Ont. — B5 73
Ravenwood, Mo., U.S. — A3 102
Rāvi, stm., Asia — B4 37
Ravia, Ok., U.S. — C5 113
Ravinia, S.D., U.S. — D7 118
Rāwalpindi, Pak. — B5 36
Rāwalpindi Cantonment, Pak. — *B5 36
Rawa Mazowiecka, Pol. — C6 26
Rawāndūz, Iraq — D15 40
Rawdon, Que. — C4 74
Rawḍ Sālim, Bi'r, well, Eg. — D5 41
Rawhide Creek, stm., Wy., U.S. — D8 127
Rawicz, Pol. — C4 26
Rawlings, Md., U.S. — k13 97
Rawlings, Va., U.S. — D5 123
Rawlinna, Austl. — F4 50
Rawlins, Wy., U.S. — E5 127
Rawlins, co., Ks., U.S. — C2 93
Rawson, Arg. — C3 54
Rawson, Arg. — g6 54
Rawson, N.D., U.S. — B2 111
Rawson, Oh., U.S. — B2 112
Rawsonville, Vt., U.S. — E3 122
Ray, In., U.S. — A8 91
Ray, Mn., U.S. — B5 100
Ray, N.D., U.S. — A2 111
Ray, co., Mo., U.S. — B3 102
Ray, Cape, c., Newf. — E2 72
Raya, mtn., Indon. — F4 34
Raya, i., Indon. — J1 35
Rāyagarha, India — H9 37
Raychikhinsk, Sov. Un. — H20 29
Ray City, Ga., U.S. — E3 87
Raygorodka, Sov. Un. — q22 27
Rayle, Ga., U.S. — C4 87
Raymond, Alta. — E4 68
Raymond, Ca., U.S. — D4 82
Raymond, Ga., U.S. — C2 87
Raymond, Il., U.S. — D4 90
Raymond, In., U.S. — F7 91
Raymond, Ks., U.S. — D5 93
Raymond, Me., U.S. — E2 96
Raymond, Mn., U.S. — E3 100
Raymond, Ms., U.S. — C3 101
Raymond, Mt., U.S. — B12 103
Raymond, Ne., U.S. — D9 104
Raymond, N.H., U.S. — D4 106
Raymond, S.D., U.S. — C7 118
Raymond, Wa., U.S. — C2 124
Raymond Terrace, Austl. — F8 51
Raymondville, Mo., U.S. — D6 102
Raymondville, N.Y., U.S. — f10 109
Raymondville, Tx., U.S. — F4 120
Raymore, Sask. — F3 75
Raymore, Mo., U.S. — C3 102
Rayne, La., U.S. — D3 95
Rayner Glacier, ice, Ant. — C17 7
Raynesford, Mt., U.S. — C6 103
Raynham, Ma., U.S. — C5 98
Raynham Center, Ma., U.S. — C5 98
Rayón, Mex. — B2 63
Rayong, Thai. — F4 35
Rayside-Balfour, Ont. — *p19 73
Raytown, Mo., U.S. — h11 102
Rayville, La., U.S. — B4 95
Rayville, Mo., U.S. — B3 102
Razan, Iran — D4 39
Razgrad, Bul. — D8 24
Razlog, Bul. — E6 24
Razorback Mountain, mtn., B.C. — D5 69
Re, i., Viet. — E8 35
Ré, Île de, i., Fr. — D3 16
Rea, Mo., U.S. — A3 102
Rea, Lough, l., Ire. — D3 11
Reader, Ar., U.S. — D2 81
Reader, W.V., U.S. — B4 125
Reader Lake, l., Man. — C1 70
Readfield, Me., U.S. — D3 96
Reading, Eng., U.K. — E6 10
Reading, Ks., U.S. — D8 93
Reading, Ma., U.S. — A5 98
Reading, Mi., U.S. — G6 99
Reading, Mn., U.S. — G3 100
Reading, Oh., U.S. — C1 112
Reading, Pa., U.S. — F10 115
Reading Center, N.Y., U.S. — C4 109
Readland, Ar., U.S. — D4 81
Readlyn, Sask. — H3 75
Readlyn, Ia., U.S. — B5 92
Readsboro, Vt., U.S. — F3 122
Readstown, Wi., U.S. — E3 126
Readyville, Tn., U.S. — B5 119
Reagan, Tn., U.S. — B3 119
Reagan, co., Tx., U.S. — D2 120
Real, co., Tx., U.S. — E3 120
Real, Cordillera, mts., S.A. — C2 55
Realicó, Arg. — F3 54
Realitos, Tx., U.S. — F3 120
Reamstown, Pa., U.S. — F9 115
Reardan, Wa., U.S. — B8 124
Reasnor, Ia., U.S. — C4 92
Reata, Mex. — B4 63

Reaville, N.J., U.S. — C3 107
Reay, Scot., U.K. — B5 13
Rebecca, Ga., U.S. — E3 87
Rebersburg, Pa., U.S. — E7 115
Rebiana, well, Libya — E4 43
Rebiana Sand Sea, des., Libya — E3 43
Reboly, Sov. Un. — F14 14
Rebun Island, i., Japan — D10 33
Recanati, Italy — C4 23
Recalde, Arg. — B4 54
Recherche, Archipelago of the, is., Austl. — F3 50
Rechitsa, Sov. Un. — E8 27
Recife, Braz. — C4 57
Recinto, Chile — B2 54
Recklinghausen, W. Ger. — C3 18
Recluse, Wy., U.S. — B7 127
Recogne, Bel. — E5 17
Reconquista, Arg. — E4 55
Recovery, Ga., U.S. — F2 87
Recreo, Arg. — E2 55
Rector, Ar., U.S. — A5 81
Red, stm., N.A. — A8 76
Red, stm., U.S. — D9 76
Red, stm., Ky., U.S. — C6 94
Red, stm., Tn., U.S. — A4 119
Red, Elm Fork, stm., U.S. — B2 113
Red, North Fork, stm., U.S. — B1 113
Red, Salt Fork, stm., U.S. — C2 113
Red, South Fork, stm., U.S. — A5 113
Red, West Fork, stm., U.S. — A4 113
Redang, i., Malay. — J5 35
Redange, Lux. — E5 17
Red Bank, N.J., U.S. — C4 107
Red Bank, S.C., U.S. — D5 117
Red Bank, Tn., U.S. — D8 119
Red Banks, Ms., U.S. — A4 101
Red Bay, Newf. — C3 72
Red Bay, Al., U.S. — A1 78
Redbay, Fl., U.S. — u16 86
Red Bay, b., N. Ire., U.K. — B6 11
Redberry Lake, l., Sask. — E2 75
Redbird, Ok., U.S. — A4 112
Redbird, Ok., U.S. — B6 113
Red Bird, stm., Ky., U.S. — C6 94
Red Bluff, Ca., U.S. — B2 82
Red Bluff Lake, res., U.S. — o12 120
Red Boiling Springs, Tn., U.S. — C8 119
Red Bud, Il., U.S. — E4 90
Red Butte, mtn., Ut., U.S. — B2 121
Red Buttes Village, Wy., U.S. — D6 127
Redby, Mn., U.S. — C4 100
Redcar, Eng., U.K. — F7 13
Red Cedar, stm., Wi., U.S. — C2 126
Red Cedar Lake, l., Wi., U.S. — C2 126
Redcliff, Alta. — D5 68
Redcliff, Co., U.S. — B4 83
Red Cliff, Wi., U.S. — B3 126
Redcliffe, Austl. — E9 50
Red Cliff Indian Reservation, Wi., U.S. — B2 126
Red Cloud, Ne., U.S. — D7 104
Redcloud Peak, mtn., Co., U.S. — D3 83
Red Creek, N.Y., U.S. — B4 109
Red Creek, stm., Ms., U.S. — E4 101
Red Cross Lake, l., Man. — B5 70
Red Deer, Alta. — C4 68
Red Deer, stm., Can. — D4 68
Red Deer, stm., Can. — E4 75
Red Deer Lake, l., Man. — C1 70
Reddell, La., U.S. — D3 95
Red Desert, Wy., U.S. — E4 127
Reddick, Fl., U.S. — C4 86
Redding, Ca., U.S. — B2 82
Redding, Ct., U.S. — D2 84
Redding Ridge, Ct., U.S. — D2 84
Reddish, Eng., U.K. — h10 13
Redditt, Ont. — E4 70
Rede, stm., Eng., U.K. — F6 13
Redenção, Braz. — D3 57
Redeye, stm., Mn., U.S. — D3 100
Red Feather Lakes, Co., U.S. — A5 83
Redfield, Ar., U.S. — C3 81
Redfield, Ia., U.S. — C3 92
Redfield, Ks., U.S. — E9 93
Redfield, N.Y., U.S. — B5 109
Redfield, S.D., U.S. — C7 118
Redford, Mi., U.S. — F7 99
Redford, N.Y., U.S. — f11 109
Redford, Tx., U.S. — p12 120
Red Hook, N.Y., U.S. — C7 109
Redhouse, Ky., U.S. — C5 94
Red House, Va., U.S. — C4 123
Red House, W.V., U.S. — C3 125
Redig, S.D., U.S. — B2 118
Red Indian Lake, l., Newf. — D3 72
Red Island, i., Newf. — E4 72
Red Jacket, W.V., U.S. — D2 125
Redkey, In., U.S. — D7 91
Red Lake, Ont. — o16 73
Red Lake, co., Mn., U.S. — C2 100
Red Lake, l., Az., U.S. — B1 80
Red Lake, stm., Mn., U.S. — C2 100
Red Lake Falls, Mn., U.S. — C2 100
Red Lake Indian Reservation, Mn., U.S. — B3 100
Redlands, Ca., U.S. — E5 82
Red Level, Al., U.S. — D3 78
Red Lick, Ms., U.S. — D3 101
Red Lion, Pa., U.S. — G8 115
Red Lodge, Mt., U.S. — E7 103
Redmon, Il., U.S. — D6 90
Red Mill Pond, l., De., U.S. — E5 85
Redmond, Or., U.S. — C5 114
Redmond, Ut., U.S. — E4 121
Redmond, Wa., U.S. — e11 124
Red Mountain, Ca., U.S. — E5 82
Red Mountain, mtn., Al., U.S. — B3 78
Red Mountain, mtn., Mt., U.S. — C4 103
Red Mountain Pass, Co., U.S. — D3 83
Rednitz, stm., W. Ger. — D5 18
Red Oak, Ia., U.S. — h7 87
Red Oak, Ia., U.S. — D2 92
Red Oak, N.C., U.S. — A5 110
Red Oak, Ok., U.S. — C6 113
Red Oak, Tx., U.S. — n10 120
Red Oak, Va., U.S. — D4 123
Red Oak Mill, N.Y., U.S. — *D7 109
Red Lake, res., Sask. — G1 75
Redon, Fr. — E4 16
Redonda Islands, is., B.C. — D5 69
Redondela, Spain — A1 22
Redondo, Port. — C2 22
Redondo, Wa., U.S. — f11 124
Redondo Beach, Ca., U.S. — n12 82

Redoubt Volcano, vol., Ak., U.S. — g15 79
Redowl, S.D., U.S. — C3 118
Red Pass, B.C. — C8 69
Red Peak, mtn., Co., U.S. — B4 83
Red Pheasant, Sask. — E1 75
Red Rapids, N.B. — C2 71
Red River, N.M., U.S. — A4 108
Red River, co., La., U.S. — B2 95
Red River, co., Tx., U.S. — C5 120
Red Rock, B.C. — C6 69
Red Rock, Ont. — o18 73
Red Rock, Az., U.S. — E4 80
Redrock, N.M., U.S. — E1 108
Red Rock, Ok., U.S. — A4 113
Red Rock, stm., Mt., U.S. — F4 103
Red Rock, Lake, res., Ia., U.S. — C4 92
Red Scaffold, S.D., U.S. — C4 118
Red Sea — C3 38
Red Shirt, S.D., U.S. — D3 118
Red Springs, N.C., U.S. — C3 110
Redstone, B.C. — C6 69
Redstone, Co., U.S. — B3 83
Redstone, Mt., U.S. — B12 103
Red Sucker, stm., Man. — B5 70
Red Sucker Lake, l., Man. — B5 70
Red Table Mountain, mts., Co., U.S. — B4 83
Redvale, Co., U.S. — C2 83
Redvers, Sask. — H5 75
Redwater, Alta. — C4 68
Redwater, stm., Mt., U.S. — C11 103
Red Willow, Alta. — C4 68
Red Willow, co., Ne., U.S. — D5 104
Redwillow, stm., Can. — B7 69
Red Willow Creek, stm., Ne., U.S. — D5 104
Redwine, Ky., U.S. — B6 94
Red Wing, Co., U.S. — D5 83
Red Wing, Mn., U.S. — F6 100
Redwood, Ms., U.S. — C3 101
Redwood, Ut., U.S. — *C4 121
Redwood, co., Mn., U.S. — F3 100
Redwood City, Ca., U.S. — D2 82
Redwood Falls, Mn., U.S. — F3 100
Redwood National Park, Ca., U.S. — B2 82
Redwood Valley, Ca., U.S. — C2 82
Red see Yuan Jiang, stm., Asia — G5 36
Ree, Lough, l., Ire. — D2 10
Reece City, Al., U.S. — A3 78
Reece, Ks., U.S. — E7 93
Reed City, Mi., U.S. — E5 99
Reed Lake, l., Man. — B1 70
Reed Lake, l., Sask. — G2 75
Reedley, Ca., U.S. — D4 82
Reedpoint, Mt., U.S. — E7 103
Reeds Beach, N.J., U.S. — E3 107
Reeds Peak, mtn., N.M., U.S. — D2 108
Reedsport, Or., U.S. — D2 114
Reeds Spring, Mo., U.S. — E4 102
Reedsville, Oh., U.S. — C4 112
Reedsville, Pa., U.S. — E6 115
Reedsville, W.V., U.S. — B5 125
Reedurban, Oh., U.S. — *B4 112
Reedville, Va., U.S. — C6 123
Reedy, W.V., U.S. — C3 125
Reedy, stm., S.C., U.S. — C3 117
Reedy Lake, l., Fl., U.S. — E5 86
Reefton, N.Z. — O13 51
Ree Heights, S.D., U.S. — C6 118
Reelfoot Lake, l., Tn., U.S. — A2 119
Reelsville, In., U.S. — E4 91
Reere Island, i., Marsh Is. — P18 52
Reese, Mi., U.S. — E7 99
Reese, stm., Nv., U.S. — C4 105
Reese Air Force Base, mil., Tx., U.S. — C1 120
Reese Station, Oh., U.S. — m11 112
Reeseville, Wi., U.S. — E5 126
Reesville, Oh., U.S. — C2 112
Reeth, Eng., U.K. — F7 13
Reeves, La., U.S. — D2 95
Reeves, co., Tx., U.S. — o13 120
Reeves, Mn., U.S. — F3 100
Reevesville, Il., U.S. — F5 90
Reevesville, S.C., U.S. — E6 117
Reform, Al., U.S. — B1 78
Refosco, Chile — E2 55
Reftele, Swe. — A7 15
Refuge Cove, B.C. — D5 69
Refugio, Tx., U.S. — E4 120
Refugio, co., Tx., U.S. — E4 120
Regan, N.D., U.S. — B5 111
Regen, W. Ger. — E8 19
Regen, stm., W. Ger. — D6 18
Regensburg, W. Ger. — D6 18
Reggâne, Alg. — D5 44
Reggio di Calabria, Italy — E5 23
Reggio nell'Emilia, Italy — B3 23
Reghin, Rom. — B7 24
Regina, Sask. — G3 75
Régina, Fr. Gu. — B4 59
Regina, Ms., U.S. — C9 103
Regina, N.M., U.S. — A2 108
Regina Beach, Sask. — G3 75
Register, Ga., U.S. — D5 87
Regna, Swe. — u33 14
Reguengos de Monsaraz, Port. — C2 22
Rehau, W. Ger. — C7 19
Rehavya (part of Jerusalem), Isr. — m14 41
Rehoboth, Nmb. — B2 49
Rehoboth, Ma., U.S. — C5 98
Rehoboth, N.M., U.S. — B1 108
Rehoboth Bay, b., De., U.S. — F5 85
Rehoboth Beach, De., U.S. — F5 85
Reichenbach, E. Ger. — C6 18
Reichenbach, W. Ger. — B2 20
Reid, Mount, mtn., Ak., U.S. — n24 79
Reid Lake, res., Sask. — G1 75
Reidland, Ky., U.S. — e9 94
Reids Grove, Md., U.S. — C6 97
Reidsville, Ga., U.S. — D5 87
Reidsville, N.C., U.S. — A3 110
Reidville, S.C., U.S. — B3 117
Reigate, Eng., U.K. — E6 10
Retie, Bel. — C5 17
Retlaw, Alta. — D4 68

Reina Adelaida, Archipiélago, is., Chile — E2 54
Reinach, Switz. — B5 21
Reinbeck, Ia., U.S. — B5 92
Reindeer, stm., Sask. — B4 75
Reindeer Island, i., Man. — C3 70
Reindeer Lake, l., Can. — m8 75
Reinersville, Oh., U.S. — C4 112
Reinfeld, W. Ger. — E4 15
Reinosa, Spain — A3 22
Reinosa see Reynosa, Mex. — B5 63
Reinstown, Md., U.S. — B4 97
Reit im Winkl, W. Ger. — B8 20
Reitz, S. Afr. — C4 49
Reliance, De., U.S. — F3 85
Reliance, S.D., U.S. — D6 118
Reliance, Tn., U.S. — D9 119
Reliance, Wy., U.S. — E3 127
Remada, Tun. — C7 44
Remagen, W. Ger. — C2 19
Remanso, Braz. — C2 57
Rembert, S.C., U.S. — C6 117
Rembertów (part of Warsaw), Pol. — k14 26
Rembrandt, Ia., U.S. — B2 92
Remecó, Arg. — B4 54
Remedios, Cuba — C4 64
Remedios, Pan. — F7 62
Remer, Mn., U.S. — C5 100
Remerton, Ga., U.S. — F3 87
Remeshk, Iran — H9 39
Remington, In., U.S. — C3 91
Remington, Va., U.S. — B5 123
Rémire, Fr. Gu. — B4 59
Remiremont, Fr. — C7 16
Remmel Dam, Ar., U.S. — g8 81
Rems, stm., W. Ger. — E4 19
Remscheid, W. Ger. — C3 18
Remsen, Ia., U.S. — B2 92
Remsen, N.Y., U.S. — B5 109
Remus, Mi., U.S. — E5 99
Rena Lara, Ms., U.S. — A3 101
Renault, Il., U.S. — E3 90
Renco, Ks., U.S. — k15 93
Rencontre East, Newf. — E4 72
Rend Lake, res., Il., U.S. — E5 90
Rendsburg, W. Ger. — A4 18
Renedo, Spain — A4 22
Renews [-Cappahayden], Newf. — E5 72
Renforth, N.B. — D4 71
Renfrew, Ont. — B8 73
Renfrew, S.C., U.S. — B3 117
Renfrew, co., Ont. — B7 73
Renfrow, Ok., U.S. — A4 113
Rengo, Chile — A2 54
Reni, Sov. Un. — C9 24
Renick, Mo., U.S. — B5 102
Renick, W.V., U.S. — D4 125
Renish Point, c., Scot., U.K. — C2 13
Renmark, Austl. — F7 50
Renner, S.D., U.S. — D9 118
Rennerod, W. Ger. — C3 19
Rennert, N.C., U.S. — C3 110
Rennes, Fr. — C3 16
Rennick Bay, b., Ant. — C29 7
Rennick Glacier, ice, Ant. — B29 7
Rennie, Man. — E4 70
Rheinfelden, Switz. — A4 21
Reno, Mn., U.S. — G7 100
Reno, Nv., U.S. — D2 105
Reno, Oh., U.S. — C4 112
Reno, co., Ks., U.S. — E5 93
Reno, stm., Italy — B3 23
Reno Hill, mtn., Wy., U.S. — D6 127
Renous, N.B. — C4 71
Renovo, Pa., U.S. — D6 115
Renshou, China — E5 31
Renssdorf, In., U.S. — C3 91
Rensselaer, N.Y., U.S. — C7 109
Rensselaer, co., N.Y., U.S. — C7 109
Rensselaer Falls, N.Y., U.S. — f9 109
Rensselaerville, N.Y., U.S. — C6 109
Rentiesville, Ok., U.S. — B6 113
Renton, Wa., U.S. — B3 124
Rentz, Ga., U.S. — D4 87
Renville, Mn., U.S. — F3 100
Renville, co., Mn., U.S. — F4 100
Renville, co., N.D., U.S. — A4 111
Renwick, Ia., U.S. — B4 92
Repentigny, Que. — D4 74
Repton, Al., U.S. — D2 78
Republic, Ks., U.S. — C6 93
Republic, Mi., U.S. — B3 99
Republic, Mo., U.S. — D4 102
Republic, Oh., U.S. — A2 112
Republic, Pa., U.S. — G2 115
Republic, Wa., U.S. — A7 124
Republic, co., Ks., U.S. — C6 93
Republican, stm., U.S. — C6 93
Republican, North Fork, stm., U.S. — A8 93
Republican, South Fork, stm., U.S. — E4 104
Republican City, Ne., U.S. — D6 104
Repulse Bay, N.W. Ter. — C15 66
Repulse Bay, b., Austl. — D8 50
Requena, Spain — C5 22
Riacho de Santana, Braz. — A4 56
Requena, Peru — E2 58
Rescue, Va., U.S. — k14 123
Reserve, Sask. — E4 75
Reserve, La., U.S. — h10 95
Reserve, N.M., U.S. — D1 108
Reservoir Pond, l., Ma., U.S. — h11 98
Reshef, Isr. — g10 41
Resistencia, Arg. — E4 55
Reşiţa, Rom. — C5 24
Resko, Pol. — B3 26
Resolution Island, i., N.W. Ter. — D20 66
Resplendor, Braz. — D4 56
Resthaven Mountain, mtn., Alta. — C1 68
Restigouche, co., N.B. — B2 71
Restigouche, stm., N.B. — B2 71
Restinga Sêca, Braz. — D4 56
Restingué, Punta, c., Pan. — G7 62
Restoule, Ont. — B4 73
Retalhuleu, Guat. — E3 63
Rethel, Fr. — C6 16
Rethimnon, Grc. — E5 40
Retie, Bel. — C5 17
Retlaw, Alta. — D4 68

Retsof, N.Y., U.S. — C3 109
Reubens, Id., U.S. — *C2 89
Reuland, Bel. — D6 17
Reunion, dep., Afr. — H24 2
Reus, Spain — B6 22
Reuss, stm., Switz. — B5 21
Reusel, Neth. — C5 17
Reutlingen, W. Ger. — D4 18
Reutte, Aus. — E5 18
Reva, S.D., U.S. — B5 118
Revda, Sov. Un. — B5 28
Revel, Fr. — F5 16
Revelo, Ky., U.S. — D5 94
Revelstoke, B.C. — D8 69
Revelstoke, Lake, res., B.C. — D8 69
Reventazón, Peru — C1 58
Revenue, Sask. — E1 75
Revere, Ma., U.S. — g11 98
Revere, Mo., U.S. — A6 102
Reverie, Tn., U.S. — B2 119
Revigny [-sur-Ornain], Fr. — C6 16
Revillagigedo, Islas, is., Mex. — D2 63
Revillagigedo Island, i., Ak., U.S. — n24 79
Revillo, S.D., U.S. — B9 118
Revin, Fr. — C6 16
Revloc, Pa., U.S. — F4 115
Ŗevnice, Czech. — o17 26
Rew, Pa., U.S. — C4 115
Rewa, India — D7 36
Reward, Sask. — E1 75
Rewāri, India — C6 36
Rex, Mount, mtn., Ant. — B5 7
Rexburg, Id., U.S. — F7 89
Rexford, Ks., U.S. — C3 93
Rexford, Mt., U.S. — B1 103
Rexham, Ma., U.S. — h13 98
Rexton, N.B. — C5 71
Rexton, Mi., U.S. — B5 99
Rey Bouba, Cam. — D2 46
Reydell, Ar., U.S. — C3 81
Reydon, Ok., U.S. — B2 113
Reyes, Point, c., Ca., U.S. — C2 82
Reyes, Ga., U.S. — h8 87
Reykjavík, Ice. — m22 14
Reynaud, Sask. — E3 75
Reyno, Ar., U.S. — A5 81
Reynolds, Ga., U.S. — D2 87
Reynolds, Il., U.S. — B3 90
Reynolds, Mo., U.S. — D6 102
Reynolds, Ne., U.S. — D8 104
Reynolds, N.D., U.S. — B8 111
Reynolds, co., Mo., U.S. — D6 102
Reynoldsburg, Oh., U.S. — C3 112
Reynoldsville, Pa., U.S. — D4 115
Reynosa (Reinosa), Mex. — B5 63
Rezā'īyeh see Orūmīyeh, Iran — B4 38
Rezé, Fr. — D3 16
Rēzekne, Sov. Un. — C6 27
Rezeny, Sov. Un. — B9 24
Rhaetian Alps, mts., Eur. — A3 23
Rhea, co., Tn., U.S. — D9 119
Rheda-Wiedenbrück, W. Ger. — B3 18
Rheden, Neth. — A7 16
Rhein, Sask. — F4 75
Rheine, W. Ger. — B3 18
Rheinfelden, Switz. — A4 21
Rheinhausen, W. Ger. — B1 19
Rheinland, hist. reg., W. Ger. — C3 18
Rheinland-Pfalz, state, W. Ger. — C2 19
Rheinsberg, E. Ger. — B3 18
Rheinwaldhorn, mtn., Switz. — C5 20
Rhenen, Neth. — A6 16
Rheydt, W. Ger. — C6 17
Rhinau, Fr. — A3 20
Rhin Canal, E. Ger. — F6 15
Rhine, Ga., U.S. — E3 87
Rhine, stm., Eur. — C3 18
Rhinebeck, N.Y., U.S. — D7 109
Rhineland, N.C., U.S. — C6 120
Rhinelander, Wi., U.S. — C4 126
Rhinow, E. Ger. — F6 15
Rhir, Cap, c., Mor. — C3 44
Rhode Island, state, U.S. — D3 116
Rhode Island, i., R.I., U.S. — E5 116
Rhode Island Sound, strt., U.S. — F5 116
Rhodell, W.V., U.S. — D3 125
Rhodes, Al., U.S. — C4 92
Rhodes, Mi., U.S. — E6 99
Rhodes see Ródhos, i., Grc. — D7 40
Rhodes Peak, mtn., Id., U.S. — C5 89
Rhodes Point, Md., U.S. — D5 97
Rhodhiss, N.C., U.S. — B1 110
Rhodope Mountains, mts., Eur. — E7 24
Rhome, Tx., U.S. — m9 120
Rhondda, Wales, U.K. — E5 10
Rhône, stm., Eur. — E6 16
Rhône au Rhin, Canal du, Fr. — C7 16
Rhum, i., Scot., U.K. — B3 10
Rhum, Sound of, strt., Scot., U.K. — D2 13
Rhyl, Wales, U.K. — D5 10
Rhymney, Wales, U.K. — C4 12
Rialma, Braz. — A4 56
Rialto, Ca., U.S. — m14 82
Rianjo, Spain — A1 22
Riau Islands, is., Indon. — E2 34
Riaza, Spain — B4 22
Ribadavia, Spain — A1 22
Ribadeo, Spain — A2 22
Ribadesella, Spain — A3 22
Ribas do Rio Pardo, Braz. — D6 48
Ribauè, Moz. — D6 48
Ribble, stm., Eng., U.K. — G6 13
Ribe, Den. — C2 15
Ribeauvillé, Fr. — C7 16
Ribeira, stm., Braz. — C3 56
Ribeirão Bonito, Braz. — m7 56
Ribeirão Branco, Braz. — C1 68
Ribeirão Preto, Braz. — C3 56
Ribera, Italy — E4 23
Ribera, N.M., U.S. — B4 108
Riberalta, Bol. — *B2 55
Ribinsk see Rybinsk, Sov. Un. — B5 28
Ribnitz-Damgarten, E. Ger. — D6 15
Ribstone, Alta. — C5 68
Ribstone Creek, stm., Alta. — C5 68
Ŗíčany, Czech. — o18 26
Riccione, Italy — B4 23
Rice, Mn., U.S. — E4 100

Rice, Va., U.S. — C4 123
Rice, co., Ks., U.S. — D5 93
Rice, co., Mn., U.S. — F5 100
Riceboro, Ga., U.S. — E5 87
Rice Creek, stm., Mn., U.S. — m12 100
Rice Lake, Wi., U.S. — C2 126
Rice Lake, l., Ont. — C6 73
Rice Lake, l., Mn., U.S. — D5 100
Rices Landing, Pa., U.S. — G1 115
Riceton, Sask. — G3 75
Riceville, Ia., U.S. — A5 92
Riceville, Tn., U.S. — D9 119
Rich, Ms., U.S. — A3 101
Rich, co., Ut., U.S. — B4 121
Rich, Cape, c., Ont. — C4 73
Richard, Sask. — E2 75
Richard City, Tn., U.S. — D8 119
Richards, Mo., U.S. — D3 102
Richards, Tx., U.S. — D5 120
Richards-Gebaur Air Force Base, mil., Mo., U.S. — C3 102
Richard's Harbour, Newf. — E3 72
Richardson, Sask. — G3 75
Richardson, Ky., U.S. — C7 94
Richardson, Tx., U.S. — n10 120
Richardson, co., Ne., U.S. — D10 104
Richardson Lakes, l., Me., U.S. — D2 96
Richardson Mountains, mts., Can. — C5 66
Richardson Park, De., U.S. — *B3 85
Richards Spur, Ok., U.S. — C3 113
Richardton, N.D., U.S. — C3 111
Richboro, Pa., U.S. — *F11 115
Richburg, N.Y., U.S. — C2 109
Richburg, S.C., U.S. — B5 117
Rich Creek, Va., U.S. — C2 123
Richdale, Alta. — D5 68
Riche, Pointe c., Newf. — C3 72
Richelieu, co., Que. — D4 74
Richer, Man. — E3 70
Richey, Mt., U.S. — C11 103
Richfield, Id., U.S. — F4 89
Richfield, Ks., U.S. — E2 93
Richfield, Mn., U.S. — F5 100
Richfield, Ne., U.S. — g12 104
Richfield, N.C., U.S. — B2 110
Richfield, Pa., U.S. — E7 115
Richfield, Ut., U.S. — E3 121
Richfield, Wi., U.S. — m11 126
Richfield Springs, N.Y., U.S. — C5 109
Richford, N.Y., U.S. — C4 109
Richford, Vt., U.S. — B3 122
Rich Fountain, Mo., U.S. — C6 102
Rich Hill, Mo., U.S. — C3 102
Richibucto, N.B. — C5 71
Rich Lake, Alta. — B5 68
Richland, Ga., U.S. — D2 87
Richland, Ia., U.S. — C6 92
Richland, Mi., U.S. — F5 99
Richland, Mo., U.S. — D5 102
Richland, Mt., U.S. — B10 103
Richland, Ne., U.S. — C8 104
Richland, N.J., U.S. — E3 107
Richland, N.Y., U.S. — B4 109
Richland, Or., U.S. — C9 114
Richland, S.D., U.S. — E9 118
Richland, Wa., U.S. — C6 124
Richland, co., Il., U.S. — E5 90
Richland, co., La., U.S. — B4 95
Richland, co., Mt., U.S. — C12 103
Richland, co., N.D., U.S. — C8 111
Richland, co., Oh., U.S. — B3 112
Richland, co., S.C., U.S. — D6 117
Richland, co., Wi., U.S. — E3 126
Richland Balsam, mtn., N.C., U.S. — f10 110
Richland Center, Wi., U.S. — E3 126
Richland Creek, stm., Tn., U.S. — B5 119
Richland Hills, Tx., U.S. — *C4 120
Richlands, N.C., U.S. — C5 110
Richlands, Va., U.S. — e10 123
Richland Springs, Tx., U.S. — D3 120
Richlandtown, Pa., U.S. — F11 115
Richlea, Sask. — F1 75
Richmond, Austl. — D7 50
Richmond, B.C. — E6 69
Richmond, Ont. — B9 73
Richmond, P.E.I. — C6 71
Richmond, Que. — D5 74
Richmond, N.Z. — N14 51
Richmond, S. Afr. — C5 49
Richmond (part of London), Eng., U.K. — C7 12
Richmond, Eng., U.K. — F7 13
Richmond, Ca., U.S. — C3 82
Richmond, Il., U.S. — A5 90
Richmond, In., U.S. — E8 91
Richmond, Ia., U.S. — C6 92
Richmond, Ks., U.S. — D8 93
Richmond, Ky., U.S. — C5 94
Richmond, Me., U.S. — D3 96
Richmond, Mi., U.S. — F8 99
Richmond, Mo., U.S. — B4 102
Richmond, N.H., U.S. — E2 106
Richmond, R.I., U.S. — E5 120
Richmond, Ut., U.S. — B4 121
Richmond, Vt., U.S. — C3 122
Richmond, Va., U.S. — C5 123
Richmond, co., Ga., U.S. — C4 87
Richmond, co., N.C. — C3 110
Richmond, co., N.Y., U.S. — k12 109
Richmond, co., Va., U.S. — C6 123
Richmond Beach, Wa., U.S. — B3 124
Richmond Dale, Oh., U.S. — C3 112
Richmond Heights, Fl., U.S. — s13 86
Richmond Heights, Mo., U.S. — f13 102
Richmond Heights, Oh., U.S. — *g9 112
Richmond Highlands, Wa., U.S. — B3 124
Richmond Hill, Ont. — D5 73
Richmond Hill, Ga., U.S. — E5 87
Richmond National Battlefield Park, Va., U.S. — n18 123
Richmond Park, Eng., U.K. — m12 10
Richmondville, N.Y., U.S. — C6 109
Richmound, Sask. — G1 75
Rich Mountain, mtn., U.S. — C5 125
Rich Mountain, mtn., Va., U.S. — C1 123
Rich Mountain, mtn., W.V., U.S. — C5 125
Rich Square, N.C., U.S. — A5 110
Richthofen, Mount, mtn., Co., U.S. — A5 83
Richton, Ms., U.S. — D5 101
Richton Park, Il., U.S. — *m9 90
Richvalley, In., U.S. — C6 91

Name	Map Ref.	Page
Richview, Il., U.S.	E4	90
Richville, Mi., U.S.	E7	99
Richville, Mn., U.S.	D7	100
Richville, N.Y., U.S.	f9	109
Richwood, Ky., U.S.	k13	94
Richwood, Oh., U.S.	B2	112
Richwood, W.V., U.S.	C4	125
Richwoods, Mo., U.S.	C7	102
Rickenbacker Air Force Base, mil., Oh., U.S.	m11	112
Ricketts, Ia., U.S.	B2	92
Rickman, Tn., U.S.	C8	119
Rickmansworth, Eng., U.K.	k12	10
Rickreall, Or., U.S.	C3	114
Rico, Co., U.S.	D2	83
Riddle, Id., U.S.	G2	89
Riddle, N.C., U.S.	A6	110
Riddle, Or., U.S.	E3	114
Riddle Mountain, mtn., Or., U.S.	D8	114
Riddlesburg, Pa., U.S.	F5	115
Rideau, stm., Ont.	B9	73
Riderwood, Al., U.S.	C1	78
Ridge, N.Y., U.S.	*n16	109
Ridgebury, Ct., U.S.	D1	84
Ridgecrest, Ca., U.S.	E5	82
Ridgecrest, N.C., U.S.	f10	110
Ridgecrest, Wa., U.S.	*B3	124
Ridgedale, Sask.	D3	75
Ridgedale, Mo., U.S.	E4	102
Ridge Farm, Il., U.S.	D6	90
Ridgefield, Ct., U.S.	D2	84
Ridgefield, N.J., U.S.	h8	107
Ridgefield, Wa., U.S.	D3	124
Ridgefield Park, N.J., U.S.	B4	107
Ridgeland, Ms., U.S.	C3	101
Ridgeland, S.C., U.S.	G6	117
Ridgeland, Wi., U.S.	C2	126
Ridgeley, W.V., U.S.	B6	125
Ridgely, Md., U.S.	C6	97
Ridgely, Tn., U.S.	A2	119
Ridgeside, Tn., U.S.	h11	119
Ridge Spring, S.C., U.S.	D4	117
Ridgetop, Tn., U.S.	A5	119
Ridgetown, Ont.	E3	73
Ridgeview, S.D., U.S.	B5	118
Ridgeview, W.V., U.S.	C3	125
Ridgeville, Man.	E3	70
Ridgeville, In., U.S.	E5	87
Ridgeville, In., U.S.	D7	91
Ridgeville, S.C., U.S.	E7	117
Ridgeville Corners, Oh., U.S.	A1	112
Ridgeway, Ia., U.S.	A6	92
Ridgeway, Mi., U.S.	F7	99
Ridgeway, Mo., U.S.	A4	102
Ridgeway, N.J., U.S.	C4	107
Ridgeway, Oh., U.S.	B2	112
Ridgeway, S.C., U.S.	C6	117
Ridgeway, Va., U.S.	D3	123
Ridgeway, Wi., U.S.	E4	126
Ridgewood, N.J., U.S.	B4	107
Ridgewood Park, Ct., U.S.	D7	84
Ridgway, Co., U.S.	C3	83
Ridgway, Il., U.S.	F5	90
Ridgway, Pa., U.S.	D4	115
Riding Mountain, hills, Man.	D1	70
Riding Mountain National Park, Man.	D1	70
Ridley Park, Pa., U.S.	p20	115
Ridley Township, Pa., U.S.	*G11	115
Ridott, Il., U.S.	A4	90
Ried [im Innkreis], Aus.	D6	18
Riehen, Switz.	A4	21
Rienza, st., Italy	C7	20
Rienzi, Ms., U.S.	A5	101
Riesa, E. Ger.	C6	18
Riesco, Isla, i., Chile	h11	54
Riesel, Tx., U.S.	D4	120
Rieth, Or., U.S.	B8	114
Rieti, Italy	C4	23
Riffe Lake, res., Wa., U.S.	C3	124
Rifle, Co., U.S.	B3	83
Rifle, stm., Mi., U.S.	D6	99
Rift Valley, prov., Kenya	A6	48
Rift Valley, val., Afr.	*F9	42
Rīga, Sov. Un.	D5	29
Rīga, Gulf of, b., Sov. Un.	C4	27
Rīgān, Iran	C5	38
Rīgān, Iran	G9	39
Rigaud, Que.	D3	74
Rigby, Id., U.S.	F7	89
Rīgestān, reg., Afg.	B4	36
Riggins, Id., U.S.	D2	89
Riggisberg, Switz.	C3	21
Rigi, mtn., Switz.	B4	20
Rigili, i., Marsh Is.	S18	52
Rigney, Fr.	B1	21
Rigo, Pap. N. Gui.	k12	50
Rigolet, Newf.	A2	72
Riihimäki, Fin.	G11	14
Riiser-Larsen Peninsula, pen., Ant.	C16	7
Rijeka (Fiume), Yugo.	C2	24
Rijssen, Neth.	B6	17
Riley, In., U.S.	F3	91
Riley, Ks., U.S.	C7	93
Riley, Ks., U.S.	C4	94
Riley, Or., U.S.	D7	114
Riley, co., Ks., U.S.	C7	93
Riley, Mount, mtn., N.M., U.S.	F2	108
Rillito, Az., U.S.	E4	80
Rilly-la-Montagne, Fr.	E4	17
Rímac, Peru	*D2	58
Rimava, Sobota, Czech.	D6	26
Rimbey, Alta.	C3	68
Rimbo, Swe.	t36	14
Rimella, Italy	E5	21
Rimersburg, Pa., U.S.	D3	115
Rimini, Italy	B4	23
Rîmnicu-Sărat, Rom.	C8	24
Rîmnicu-Vîlcea, Rom.	C7	24
Rimouski, Que.	A9	74
Rimouski, stm., Que.	A9	74
Rimouski-Est, Que.	A9	74
Rimrock, Az., U.S.	C4	80
Rimrock Lake, res., Wa., U.S.	C4	124
Rinard, Ia., U.S.	B3	92
Rincon, Ga., U.S.	D5	87
Rincon, N.M., U.S.	E2	108
Rincón, Bahía de, b., P.R.	C5	65
Rinconada, Arg.	D2	55
Rincon del Bonete, Lago Artificial de, res., Ur.	E1	56
Rincón de Romos, Mex.	k12	63
Rincon Mountains, mts., Az., U.S.	E5	80
Rindge, N.H., U.S.	E2	106
Riner, Va., U.S.	C2	123
Rineyville, Ky., U.S.	C4	94
Rīngas, India	D5	37
Ringe, Den.	C4	15
Ringelheim, W. Ger.	A5	19
Ringel Spitze, mtn., Switz.	C7	21
Ringerike, Nor.	*G4	14
Ringgold, Ga., U.S.	B1	87
Ringgold, Md., U.S.	A2	97
Ringgold, Tx., U.S.	C4	120
Ringgold, Va., U.S.	D3	123
Ringgold, co., La., U.S.	B2	95
Ringgold Isles, is., Fiji	H16	52
Ringim, Nig.	D6	45
Ringkøbing, Den.	I3	14
Ringkøbing, co., Den.	B2	15
Ringkøbing Fjord, Den.	B2	15
Ringling, Mt., U.S.	D6	103
Ringling, Ok., U.S.	C4	113
Ringoes, N.J., U.S.	C3	107
Ringold, Ok., U.S.	C6	113
Ringsaker, Nor.	B4	14
Ringsted, I., Swe.	C7	15
Ringsjön, i., Swe.	u35	14
Ringsted, Den.	C5	15
Ringsted, Ia., U.S.	A3	92
Ringvassøya, i., Nor.	C8	14
Ringville, Ire.	E4	11
Ringwood, N.J., U.S.	A4	107
Ringwood, Ok., U.S.	A3	113
Riñihue, Chile	B2	54
Rinjani, mtn., Indon.	G5	34
Rinnes, Ben, mtn., Scot., U.K.	C5	13
Rinns Point, c., Scot., U.K.	E2	13
Rinteln, W. Ger.	A4	19
Rio, Fl., U.S.	E6	86
Rio, Il., U.S.	B3	90
Rio, W.V., U.S.	B6	125
Rio, Wi., U.S.	E4	126
Rio Arriba, co., N.M., U.S.	A2	108
Riobamba, Ec.	B2	58
Rio Benito, Eq. Gui.	E1	46
Rio Blanco, co., Co., U.S.	B2	83
Rio Branco, Braz.	A5	55
Rio Branco, Ur.	E2	56
Rio Brilhante, Braz.	C2	56
Rio Bueno, Chile	C2	54
Río Caribe, Ven.	A5	60
Río Chico, Ven.	A4	60
Río Claro, Braz.	C3	56
Rio Claro, Trin.	O23	65
Río Cuarto, Arg.	A4	54
Rio de Janeiro, Braz.	C4	56
Rio de Janeiro, state, Braz.	C4	56
Rio de Jesús, Pan.	G7	62
Rio Dell, Ca., U.S.	B1	82
Rio Del Mar, Ca., U.S.	*D3	82
Rio de Oro, Col.	B3	60
Rio do Prado, Braz.	B4	56
Rio do Sul, Braz.	D3	56
Río Gallegos, Arg.	h12	54
Río Grande, Arg.	G2	56
Rio Grande, Braz.	E2	56
Rio Grande, Mex.	C4	63
Rio Grande, Oh., U.S.	D3	112
Río Grande, co., Co., U.S.	D4	83
Rio Grande City, Tx., U.S.	F3	120
Rio Grande do Norte, state, Braz.	C3	57
Rio Grande do Sul, state, Braz.	D2	56
Rio Grande Reservoir, res., Co., U.S.	D3	83
Ríohacha, Col.	A3	60
Río Hato, Pan.	F7	62
Río Hondo, Mex.	h9	63
Rio Hondo, Tx., U.S.	F4	120
Rioja, Peru	C2	58
Riolândia, Braz.	B3	56
Rio Linda, Ca., U.S.	*C3	82
Riom, Fr.	E5	16
Rio Maior, Port.	C1	22
Río Mayo, Arg.	D2	54
Río Mulatos, Bol.	C2	55
Rio Muni, prov., Eq. Gui.	E2	46
Rio Negro, Braz.	D3	56
Río Negro, prov., Arg.	C3	54
Rionero in Vulture, Italy	D5	23
Río Pardo, Braz.	D2	56
Rio Pardo de Minas, Braz.	B4	56
Rio Pomba, Braz.	g6	56
Rio Preto da Eva, Braz.	C2	59
Rio Primero, Arg.	A4	54
Rio Rancho, N.M., U.S.	B3	108
Ríosucio, Col.	B2	60
Ríosucio, Col.	B2	60
Rio Tercero, Arg.	A4	54
Rio Tinto, Sierra, mtn., Hond.	C5	62
Rio Verde, Braz.	B3	56
Ríoverde, Mex.	m13	63
Rio Verde de Mato Grosso, Braz.	B2	56
Rio Vermelho, Braz.	B35	56
Rio Vista, Ca., U.S.	C3	82
Rioz, Fr.	B1	21
Ripley, Ont.	C3	73
Ripley, Eng., U.K.	A6	12
Ripley, Ca., U.S.	F6	82
Ripley, Il., U.S.	C3	90
Ripley, Me., U.S.	D3	96
Ripley, Ms., U.S.	A5	101
Ripley, N.Y., U.S.	C1	109
Ripley, Oh., U.S.	D2	112
Ripley, Ok., U.S.	A5	113
Ripley, Tn., U.S.	B2	119
Ripley, W.V., U.S.	C3	125
Ripley, co., In., U.S.	F7	91
Ripley, co., Mo., U.S.	E7	102
Riplinger, Wi., U.S.	D3	126
Ripogenus Pond, l., Me., U.S.	C3	96
Ripoll, Spain	A7	22
Ripon, Que.	D2	74
Ripon, Eng., U.K.	C6	10
Ripon, Ca., U.S.	D3	82
Ripon, Wi., U.S.	E5	126
Rippey, Ia., U.S.	C3	92
Ripples, N.B.	C3	71
Rippowam, stm., Ct., U.S.	E1	84
Ripton, Vt., U.S.	C2	122
Ririe, Id., U.S.	F7	89
Ririe Lake, res., Id., U.S.	F7	89
Risaralda, dept., Col.	B2	60
Rishiri Island, i., Japan	D10	33
Rishon LeZiyyon, Isr.	C6	40
Rising City, Ne., U.S.	C8	104
Rising Star, Tx., U.S.	C3	120
Rising Sun, De., U.S.	D3	85
Rising Sun, In., U.S.	G8	91
Risingsun, Oh., U.S.	e9	92
Rising Sun, Md., U.S.	A5	97
Risingsun, Oh., U.S.	A2	112
Risle, stm., Fr.	C4	16
Rison, Ar., U.S.	D3	81
Rison, Md., U.S.	C3	97
Risør, Nor.	H3	14
Ritchey, Mo., U.S.	E3	102
Ritchie, co., W.V., U.S.	B3	125
Ritidian Point, c., Guam	L10	52
Ritscher Upland, plat., Ant.	B12	7
Ritter, Or., U.S.	C7	114
Ritter, Mount, mtn., Ca., U.S.	D4	82
Rittman, Oh., U.S.	B4	112
Ritzville, Wa., U.S.	B7	124
Rivadavia, Arg.	A3	54
Rivadavia, Arg.	B4	54
Rivadavia, Arg.	D3	55
Rivadavia, Chile	E1	55
Riva [del Garda], Italy	B3	23
Rivanna, stm., Va., U.S.	C4	123
Rivare, In., U.S.	C8	91
Rivas, Nic.	E7	62
Rivas, Nic.	E6	61
Rive-de-Gier, Fr.	B4	54
Rivera, Arg.	B5	54
Rivera, Ur.	E1	56
Riverbank, Ca., U.S.	D3	82
River Bourgeois, N.S.	D9	71
River Cess, Lib.	E3	45
Riverdale, Ga., U.S.	*C2	87
Riverdale, Il., U.S.	k9	90
Riverdale, Ia., U.S.	g11	92
Riverdale, Ks., U.S.	E6	93
Riverdale, Md., U.S.	C4	97
Riverdale, Ne., U.S.	D6	104
Riverdale, N.J., U.S.	B4	107
Riverdale, N.D., U.S.	B4	111
Riverdale, Ut., U.S.	*B3	121
Riverdale, Va., U.S.	D4	123
River Edge, N.J., U.S.	h8	107
River Falls, Al., U.S.	D3	78
River Falls, Wi., U.S.	D1	126
River Forest, Il., U.S.	k9	90
Rivergaro, Italy	E5	20
River Grove, Il., U.S.	k9	90
Riverhaven, In., U.S.	B7	91
Riverhead, N.Y., U.S.	n16	109
River Hebert, N.S.	D5	71
River Heights, Ut., U.S.	B4	121
River Hills, Wi., U.S.	m12	126
Riverhurst, Sask.	G2	75
River John, N.S.	D6	71
River Jordan, B.C.	h11	69
River Oaks, Tx., U.S.	*n9	120
River of Ponds, Newf.	C3	72
River Pines, Ma., U.S.	f10	98
Riverport, N.S.	E5	71
River Ridge, La., U.S.	k11	95
River Road, Or., U.S.	C3	114
River Rouge, Mi., U.S.	p15	99
Rivers, Man.	D1	70
Rivers, Lake of the, l., Sask.	H3	75
Riverside, Al., U.S.	B3	78
Riverside, Ca., U.S.	F5	82
Riverside, Ct., U.S.	E1	84
Riverside, Il., U.S.	k9	90
Riverside, Ia., U.S.	C6	92
Riverside, Ma., U.S.	*A2	98
Riverside, N.J., U.S.	C3	107
Riverside, Or., U.S.	D8	114
Riverside, Pa., U.S.	E8	115
Riverside, Ut., U.S.	B3	121
Riverside, Wa., U.S.	A6	124
Riverside, Wy., U.S.	E6	127
Riverside, co., Ca., U.S.	F5	82
Riverside Reservoir, res., Co., U.S.	A6	83
Riverside-Albert, N.B.	D5	71
Rivers Inlet, b., B.C.	D4	69
River Sioux, Ia., U.S.	C1	92
Riverton, Man.	D3	70
Riverton, N.Z.	Q12	51
Riverton, Ct., U.S.	B3	84
Riverton, Il., U.S.	D4	90
Riverton, Ia., U.S.	D2	92
Riverton, Ks., U.S.	E9	93
Riverton, La., U.S.	B3	95
Riverton, Mn., U.S.	D4	100
Riverton, Ne., U.S.	D7	104
Riverton, N.J., U.S.	C3	107
Riverton, Or., U.S.	D2	114
Riverton, Ut., U.S.	C4	121
Riverton, Vt., U.S.	C3	122
Riverton, Va., U.S.	B4	123
Riverton, Wy., U.S.	C5	127
Riverton Heights, Wa., U.S.	f11	124
River Vale, N.J., U.S.	h8	107
River View, Al., U.S.	C4	78
Riverview, Fl., U.S.	p11	86
Riverview, Mi., U.S.	p15	99
Rives, Mo., U.S.	E7	102
Rives, Tn., U.S.	A2	119
Rivesaltes, Fr.	F5	16
Rives Junction, Mi., U.S.	F6	99
Riviera, Az., U.S.	B1	80
Riviera, Tx., U.S.	F4	120
Riviera Beach, Fl., U.S.	F6	86
Riviera Beach, Md., U.S.	B4	97
Riviera Beach, N.J., U.S.	C4	107
Rivière-à-Pierre, Que.	B5	74
Rivière-Bleue, Que.	B8	74
Rivière-du-Loup, Que.	B8	74
Rivière-du-Loup, co., Que.	B8	74
Rivière-Ouelle, Que.	B8	74
Rivière-Trois-Pistoles, Que.	A8	74
Rivière-Verte, N.B.	B1	71
Rivière-Verte, Que.	B8	74
Rivulet, Mt., U.S.	D2	103
Rixford, Pa., U.S.	C4	115
Rixie's, Nv., U.S.	*C5	105
Riyadh (Ar Riyāḍ), Sau. Ar.	C4	38
Rize, Tur.	B13	40
Rizhao, China	D8	31
Rizzuto, Cape, c., Italy	E6	23
Rjukan, Nor.	H3	14
Roachdale, In., U.S.	E4	91
Roads, Oh., U.S.	C3	112
Roadstown, N.J., U.S.	E2	107
Road Town, V.I., Br.	Q2	65
Roan Cliffs, clf., U.S.	B1	83
Roan Creek, stm., Co., U.S.	B2	83
Roane, co., Tn., U.S.	D9	119
Roane, co., W.V., U.S.	C3	125
Roan High Knob, mtn., U.S.	C11	119
Roan Mountain, Tn., U.S.	C11	119
Roann, In., U.S.	C6	91
Roanne, Fr.	B6	16
Roanoke, Al., U.S.	B4	78
Roanoke, Il., U.S.	C4	90
Roanoke, In., U.S.	C7	91
Roanoke, La., U.S.	D3	95
Roanoke, Tx., U.S.	m9	120
Roanoke, Va., U.S.	C3	123
Roanoke, W.V., U.S.	C4	125
Roanoke, co., Va., U.S.	C2	123
Roanoke, stm., U.S.	A5	110
Roanoke Island, i., N.C., U.S.	B7	110
Roanoke Rapids, N.C., U.S.	A5	110
Roanoke Rapids Lake, res., U.S.	A5	110
Roan Plateau, plat., U.S.	B2	83
Roaring Branch, Pa., U.S.	C8	115
Roaring Fork, stm., Co., U.S.	C4	83
Roaring Spring, Pa., U.S.	F5	115
Roaring Springs, Tx., U.S.	C2	120
Roaringwater Bay, b., Ire.	F2	11
Roark, Ky., U.S.	C6	94
Roatán, Hond.	D7	63
Roba, Al., U.S.	C4	78
Robards, Ky., U.S.	C2	94
Robbin, Mn., U.S.	B1	100
Robbins, Il., U.S.	k9	90
Robbins, N.C., U.S.	B3	110
Robbinsdale, Mn., U.S.	m12	100
Robbinston, Me., U.S.	C5	96
Robbinsville, N.J., U.S.	C3	107
Robbinsville, N.C., U.S.	f9	110
Robbins, Il., U.S.	F5	90
Robe, stm., Ire.	D2	11
Robeline, La., U.S.	C2	95
Robersonville, N.C., U.S.	B5	110
Robert, La., U.S.	D5	95
Robert Lee, Tx., U.S.	D2	120
Roberts, Id., U.S.	F6	89
Roberts, Il., U.S.	C5	90
Roberts, Mt., U.S.	E7	103
Roberts, Wi., U.S.	C1	126
Roberts, co., S.D., U.S.	B8	118
Roberts, co., Tx., U.S.	B2	120
Roberts, Cape, c., Ont.	A2	73
Roberts, Point, c., Wa., U.S.	A2	124
Roberts Creek Mountain, mtn., Nv., U.S.	D5	105
Robertsdale, Al., U.S.	E2	78
Robertsdale, Pa., U.S.	F5	115
Robert S. Kerr Reservoir, res., Ok., U.S.	B6	113
Roberts Mountain, mtn., Ak., U.S.	C6	79
Roberts Mountain, mtn., Wy., U.S.	D3	127
Robertson, S. Afr.	D3	49
Robertson, Wy., U.S.	E2	127
Robertson, co., Ky., U.S.	B5	94
Robertson, co., Tn., U.S.	A5	119
Robertson, co., Tx., U.S.	D4	120
Robertson, Lac, l., Que.	C2	72
Robertson Bay, b., Ant.	B29	7
Robertsonville, Que.	C6	74
Roberta, Ga., U.S.	D2	87
Roberta Mills, N.C., U.S.	B2	110
Robert Lee, Tx., U.S.	D2	120
Roberts Peak, mtn., B.C.	F8	66
Robertsport, Lib.	E2	45
Robertstown, Ga., U.S.	B3	87
Robertson, S.D., U.S.	C7	118
Robertsville, Ct., U.S.	B3	84
Robertsville, N.J., U.S.	*C4	107
Roberval, Que.	A5	74
Roca, co., N.C., U.S.	C3	110
Rockhill Furnace, Pa., U.S.	F6	115
Rockholds, Ky., U.S.	D5	94
Rockingham, N.C., U.S.	C3	110
Rockingham, Vt., U.S.	E4	122
Rockingham, co., N.H., U.S.	D4	106
Rockingham, co., N.C., U.S.	A3	110
Rockingham, co., Va., U.S.	B4	123
Rock Island, Que.	D5	74
Rock Island, Il., U.S.	B3	90
Rock Island, Ok., U.S.	B7	113
Rock Island, Wa., U.S.	B5	124
Rock Island, i., Fl., U.S.	C3	86
Rock Island, i., Wi., U.S.	C7	126
Rocklake, N.D., U.S.	A6	111
Rock Lake, i., Man.	E2	70
Rock Lake, i., Wa., U.S.	B8	124
Rockland, Ont.	B9	73
Rockland, Id., U.S.	G6	89
Rockland, Me., U.S.	D3	96
Rockland, Ma., U.S.	B6	98
Rockland, Man.	D1	70
Rockland, N.Y., U.S.	A5	70
Rockland, N.Y., U.S.	D6	109
Rockland, co., N.Y., U.S.	D6	109
Rocklands Reservoir, res., Austl.	H3	51
Rockledge, Fl., U.S.	D6	86
Rockledge, Ga., U.S.	D4	87
Rockledge, Pa., U.S.	o20	115
Rockleigh, N.J., U.S.	g9	107
Rockmart, Ga., U.S.	B1	87
Rock Mountain, mtn., Al., U.S.	B2	78
Rock Mountain, mtn., Co., U.S.		
Rock Point, Az., U.S.	A6	80
Rock Point, Md., U.S.	D4	97
Rockport, Ar., U.S.	g8	81
Rockport, Il., U.S.	D2	90
Rockport, In., U.S.	I3	91
Rockport, Ky., U.S.	C3	94
Rockport, Me., U.S.	D3	96
Rockport, Ma., U.S.	A6	98
Rock Port, Mo., U.S.	A2	102
Rockport, N.J., U.S.	B3	107
Rockport, Wa., U.S.	A4	124
Rock Rapids, Ia., U.S.	A1	92
Rock River, Wy., U.S.	E7	127
Rock Run, Al., U.S.	A4	78
Rock Springs, Tx., U.S.	D2	120
Rock Springs, Wi., U.S.	E3	126
Rock Springs, Wy., U.S.	E4	127
Rockstone, Guy.	A5	60
Rockton, Il., U.S.	A4	90
Rockton, Pa., U.S.	D5	115
Rockvale, Co., U.S.	C5	83
Rock Valley, Ia., U.S.	A1	92
Rockville, In., U.S.	E3	91
Rockville, Md., U.S.	B3	97
Rockville, Mn., U.S.	E4	100
Rockville, N.H., U.S.	E4	106
Rockville, R.I., U.S.	E1	116
Rockville Centre, N.Y., U.S.	n15	109
Rockwall, Tx., U.S.	C4	120
Rockwall, co., Tx., U.S.	C4	120
Rockwell, Ia., U.S.	B4	92
Rockwell, N.C., U.S.	B2	110
Rockwell City, Ia., U.S.	B3	92
Rockwell Park, N.C., U.S.	B2	110
Rockwood, Ont.	D4	73
Rociada, N.M., U.S.	B4	108
Rock, Ks., U.S.	E7	93
Rock, Ma., U.S.	*C6	98
Rock, Mi., U.S.	B3	99
Rock, co., Mn., U.S.	G2	100
Rock, co., Ne., U.S.	B6	104
Rock, co., Wi., U.S.	F4	126
Rock, stm., U.S.	B3	90
Rock, stm., U.S.	A1	92
Rockaway, N.J., U.S.	B3	107
Rockaway, Or., U.S.	B3	114
Rockaway Beach, Mo., U.S.	E4	102
Rock Bay, B.C.	D5	69
Rock Bluff, Fl., U.S.	B2	86
Rockbridge, Il., U.S.	D3	90
Rockbridge, Oh., U.S.	C3	112
Rockbridge, co., Va., U.S.	C3	123
Rockcastle, co., Ky., U.S.	C5	94
Rockcastle, stm., Ky., U.S.	C5	94
Rockcliffe Park, Ont.	h12	73
Rock Creek, B.C.	E8	69
Rock Creek, Ks., U.S.	k14	93
Rock Creek, Mn., U.S.	E6	100
Rock Creek, Oh., U.S.	A5	112
Rock Creek, stm., N.A.	H2	75
Rock Creek, stm., Il., U.S.	B3	97
Rock Creek, stm., Il., U.S.	h14	124
Rock Creek, stm., Il., U.S.	B4	90
Rock Creek, stm., Ks., U.S.	g10	93
Rock Creek, stm., Ne., U.S.	g11	104
Rock Creek, stm., Nv., U.S.	C5	105
Rock Creek, stm., Or., U.S.	B6	114
Rock Creek, stm., Wa., U.S.	B8	124
Rock Creek, stm., Wa., U.S.	D5	124
Rock Creek Butte, mtn., Or., U.S.	C8	114
Rockdale, Austl.	*F9	50
Rockdale, Il., U.S.	B5	90
Rockdale, In., U.S.	B7	92
Rockdale, Md., U.S.	B4	97
Rockdale, Tn., U.S.	B4	119
Rockdale, Tx., U.S.	D4	120
Rockdale, co., Ga., U.S.	C3	87
Rockefeller Plateau, plat., Ant.	A35	7
Rockford, Al., U.S.	C3	78
Rockford, Il., U.S.	A5	90
Rockford, Ia., U.S.	A5	92
Rockford, Mi., U.S.	E5	99
Rockford, Mn., U.S.	E5	100
Rockford, Oh., U.S.	B1	112
Rockford, Tn., U.S.	D10	119
Rockford, Wa., U.S.	B8	124
Rockglen, Sask.	H3	75
Rock Hall, Md., U.S.	B5	97
Rockham, S.D., U.S.	C7	118
Rockhampton, Austl.	D9	50
Rockaway, Or., U.S.	B3	114
Rockwood, Al., U.S.	A2	78
Rockwood, Il., U.S.	F4	90
Rockwood, Me., U.S.	C3	96
Rockwood, Mi., U.S.	F7	99
Rockwood, Or., U.S.	*B4	114
Rockwood, Pa., U.S.	G3	115
Rockwood, Tn., U.S.	D9	119
Rockwood, Tx., U.S.	D3	120
Rocky, Ok., U.S.	B2	113
Rocky, stm., Alta.	C2	68
Rocky, stm., N.C., U.S.	B2	110
Rocky, stm., S.C., U.S.	C2	117
Rocky, East Branch, stm., Oh., U.S.	h9	112
Rocky, West Branch, stm., Oh., U.S.	h9	112
Rocky Bay, b., Newf.	B4	72
Rocky Boy, Mt., U.S.	B7	103
Rocky Boys Indian Reservation, U.S.	B7	103
Rocky Comfort, Mo., U.S.	E3	102
Rocky Coulee, val., Wa., U.S.	B6	124
Rocky Creek, Fl., U.S.	*o10	86
Rockyford, Alta.	D4	68
Rocky Ford, Co., U.S.	C7	83
Rocky Ford, Ga., U.S.	D5	87
Rocky Fork Lake, l., Oh., U.S.	C2	112
Rocky Gap, Va., U.S.	C1	123
Rocky Harbour, Newf.	D3	72
Rocky Hill, Ct., U.S.	C5	84
Rocky Hill, Ky., U.S.	C3	94
Rocky Hill, N.J., U.S.	C3	107
Rocky Lake, l., Man.	B1	70
Rocky Lake, l., Me., U.S.	D5	96
Rocky Mount, N.C., U.S.	B5	110
Rocky Mount, Va., U.S.	D3	123
Rocky Mountain, mtn., Mt., U.S.	C4	103
Rocky Mountain House, Alta.	C3	68
Rocky Mountain National Park, Co., U.S.	A5	83
Rocky Mountains, mts., N.A.	E9	61
Rocky Point, N.Y., U.S.	*n16	109
Rocky Point, N.C., U.S.	C5	110
Rocky Ripple, In., U.S.	k10	91
Rocky River, Oh., U.S.	A4	112
Rocky Top, mtn., Or., U.S.	C4	114
Rocroi, Fr.	E4	17
Roda, Va., U.S.	f9	123
Rodach, W. Ger.	C5	19
Rodanthe, N.C., U.S.	B7	110
Rodarte, N.M., U.S.	*A4	108
Rødby, Den.	D5	15
Rødbyhavn, Den.	D5	15
Roddickton, Newf.	C3	72
Rødding, Den.	C2	15
Roddy, Tn., U.S.	D9	119
Rødekro, Den.	C3	15
Rødovre, Den.	C5	15
Rodeo, Ca., U.S.	*g8	82
Rodeo, N.M., U.S.	F1	108
Roderfield, W.V., U.S.	D3	125
Roderick Island, i., B.C.	C3	69
Rodessa, La., U.S.	B2	95
Rodewisch, E. Ger.	C7	19
Rodey, N.M., U.S.	E2	108
Rodez, Fr.	E5	16
Ródhos, Grc.	D7	40
Ródhos (Rhodes), i., Grc.	D7	40
Roding, W. Ger.	D7	19
Rodman, Ia., U.S.	A3	92
Rodney, Ont.	E3	73
Rodney, Ms., U.S.	D2	101
Rodney, Cape, c., Ak., U.S.	C6	79
Rodney Pond, l., Newf.	D4	72
Rodney Village, De., U.S.	D3	85
Roduco, N.C., U.S.	A6	110
Roe, Ar., U.S.	C4	81
Roebling, N.J., U.S.	C3	107
Roebourne, Austl.	D2	50
Roebuck, S.C., U.S.	B4	117
Roebuck Bay, b., Austl.	C3	50
Roeland Park, Ks., U.S.	k16	93
Roermond, Neth.	B6	16
Roeselare (Roulers), Bel.	B5	16
Roessleville, N.Y., U.S.	*C7	109
Roes Welcome Sound, strt., N.W. Ter.	D15	66
Roetgen, W. Ger.	D6	17
Roff, Ok., U.S.	C5	113
Rogaguado, Laguna, l., Bol.	B2	55
Rogagua, Laguna, l., Bol.	B2	55
Roganville, Tx., U.S.	D6	120
Rogatica, Yugo.	D4	24
Roger Mills, co., Ok., U.S.	B1	113
Rogers, Ar., U.S.	A1	81
Rogers, Ct., U.S.	B8	84
Rogers, Mn., U.S.	E5	100
Rogers, N.D., U.S.	C8	111
Rogers, N.M., U.S.	D6	108
Rogers, Oh., U.S.	B5	112
Rogers, Tx., U.S.	D4	120
Rogers, co., Ok., U.S.	A6	113
Rogers, Mount, mtn., Va., U.S.	f10	123
Rogers City, Mi., U.S.	C7	99
Rogers Lake, res., Ct., U.S.	D6	84
Rogerson, Id., U.S.	G4	89
Rogers Pass, Mt., U.S.	C4	103
Rogersville, Al., U.S.	A2	78
Rogersville, Mo., U.S.	D4	102
Rogersville, Pa., U.S.	G1	115
Rogersville, Tn., U.S.	C10	119
Roggen, Co., U.S.	A6	83
Rogozhina, Alb.	B2	25
Rogoźno, Pol.	B4	26
Rogue, stm., Or., U.S.	E2	114
Rogue River, Or., U.S.	E3	114
Rohnert Park, Ca., U.S.	*C2	82
Rohrersville, Md., U.S.	B2	97
Rohri Canal, Pak.	D3	37
Rohtak, India	D6	37
Roi Et, Thai.	B2	34
Roi Island, i., Marsh Is.	S17	52
Roissy-en-France, Fr.	g11	16
Rojas, Arg.	A4	54
Rojo, Cabo, c., Mex.	m15	63
Rojo, Cabo, c., P.R.	H11	64
Rokan, stm., Indon.	L4	35
Rokeby, Sask.	F4	75
Rokel, stm., S.L.	E2	45
Rokitno, Sov. Un.	F6	27
Rokycany, Czech.	D2	26
Roland, Man.	E3	70
Roland, Ar., U.S.	C3	81
Roland, Ia., U.S.	B4	92
Roland, Ok., U.S.	B7	113
Roland, Lake, res., Md., U.S.	g11	97
Rolesville, N.C., U.S.	B4	110
Rolette, N.D., U.S.	A6	111
Rolette, co., N.D., U.S.	B3	111
Rolfe, Ia., U.S.	B3	92

Name	Map Ref.	Page
Roll, Az., U.S.	E2	80
Roll, In., U.S.	C7	91
Roll, Ok., U.S.	B2	113
Rolla, B.C.	B7	69
Rolla, Ar., U.S.	C3	81
Rolla, Ks., U.S.	E2	93
Rolla, Mo., U.S.	D6	102
Rolla, N.D., U.S.	A6	111
Rolle, Switz.	E3	18
Rolleston, Bah.	C6	64
Rollingbay, Wa., U.S.	e10	124
Rolling Fork, Ms., U.S.	C3	101
Rolling Fork, stm., Ar., U.S.	C1	81
Rolling Fork, stm., Ky., U.S.	C4	94
Rolling Hills Estates, Ca., U.S.	*n12	82
Rolling Meadows, Il., U.S.	h8	90
Rollingstone, Mn., U.S.	F7	100
Rollins, Mt., U.S.	C2	103
Rollinsford, N.H., U.S.	D5	106
Rolvsøya, i., Nor.	B10	14
Roma, Austl.	E8	50
Roma, Alta.	A2	68
Roma, Tx., U.S.	F3	120
Romain, Cape, c., S.C., U.S.	F9	117
Romaine, stm., Can.	h9	72
Romania, ctry., Eur.	C7	24
Roman Nose Mountain, mtn., Md., U.S.	m12	97
Roman Nose Mountain, mtn., Or., U.S.	D3	114
Romano, Cape, c., Fl., U.S.	G5	86
Romano, Cayo, i., Cuba	C5	64
Romanshorn, Switz.	A7	21
Romans [-sur-Isère], Fr.	E6	16
Romanzof, Cape, c., Ak., U.S.	C6	79
Romanzof Mountains, mts., Ak., U.S.	B11	79
Romayor, Tx., U.S.	D5	120
Rombauer, Mo., U.S.	E7	102
Rome (Roma), Italy	D4	23
Rome, Ga., U.S.	B1	87
Rome, Il., U.S.	C4	90
Rome, In., U.S.	I4	91
Rome, Ia., U.S.	D6	92
Rome, Ms., U.S.	B3	101
Rome, N.Y., U.S.	B5	109
Rome, Oh., U.S.	D3	112
Rome, Pa., U.S.	C9	115
Rome City, In., U.S.	B7	91
Romema (part of Jerusalem), Isr.	m14	41
Romeo, Co., U.S.	D4	83
Romeo, Mi., U.S.	F7	99
Romeoville, Il., U.S.	k8	90
Romeville, La., U.S.	h10	95
Romford (part of London), Eng., U.K.	k13	10
Romilly, Fr.	C5	16
Romita, Mex.	m13	63
Romney, In., U.S.	D4	91
Romney, W.V., U.S.	B6	125
Romny, Sov. Un.	F9	27
Rømø, i., Den.	C2	15
Romona, In., U.S.	F4	91
Romont, Switz.	C2	21
Romorantin, Fr.	D4	16
Rompin, stm., Malay.	K5	35
Romsey, Eng., U.K.	D6	12
Romulus, Mi., U.S.	p15	99
Romulus, N.Y., U.S.	C4	109
Romunum, i., Micron.	C18	52
Romurikku Island, i., Marsh Is.	P18	52
Ron, Viet.	D7	35
Ron, Cape, c., Viet.	C7	35
Rona, i., Scot., U.K.	C3	13
Rona, i., Scot., U.K.	A3	13
Ronald, Wa., U.S.	B4	124
Ronan, Mt., U.S.	C2	103
Roncador, Serra do, plat., Braz.	E4	59
Roncador Bank, Col.	D7	62
Ronceverte, W.V., U.S.	D4	125
Ronciglione, Italy	C4	23
Ronda, Spain	D2	22
Ronda, N.C., U.S.	A2	110
Rønde, Den.	B4	15
Rønde Island, i., Gren.	W25	65
Rondo, Ar., U.S.	C5	81
Rondônia, state, Braz.	E2	59
Rondonópolis, Braz.	B2	56
Roneys Point, W.V., U.S.	f8	125
Ronge, Lac la, l., Sask.	B3	75
Rongjiang, China	L3	32
Rongxian, China	G7	31
Ronkiti Harbor, b., Micron.	Q17	52
Ronkonkoma, N.Y., U.S.	*n15	109
Rønne, Den.	J6	14
Rönne, stm., Swe.	B6	15
Ronneburg, E. Ger.	C7	19
Ronne Entrance, b., Ant.	B5	7
Ronne Ice Shelf, ice, Ant.	B6	7
Ronse, Bel.	B5	16
Ronuro, stm., Braz.	E4	59
Roodepoort-Maraisburg, S. Afr.	*C4	49
Roodeschool, Neth.	A6	17
Roodhouse, Il., U.S.	D3	90
Roof Butte, mtn., Az., U.S.	A6	80
Rooks, co., Ks., U.S.	C4	93
Roopville, Ga., U.S.	C1	87
Roosendaal, Neth.	B6	16
Roosevelt, Az., U.S.	D4	80
Roosevelt, Mn., U.S.	B3	100
Roosevelt, N.J., U.S.	C4	107
Roosevelt, N.Y., U.S.	*n15	109
Roosevelt, Ut., U.S.	C5	121
Roosevelt, co., Mt., U.S.	B11	103
Roosevelt, co., N.M., U.S.	C6	108
Roosevelt, stm., Braz.	D2	59
Roosevelt Campobello International Park, N.A.	E3	71
Roosevelt Island, i., Ant.	B32	7
Roosevelt Park, Mi., U.S.	E4	99
Root, stm., Mn., U.S.	G7	100
Root, stm., Wi., U.S.	n12	126
Rootstown, Oh., U.S.	A4	112
Ropczyce, Pol.	C6	26
Roper, N.C., U.S.	B6	110
Roper, stm., Austl.	B5	50
Ropesville, Tx., U.S.	C1	120
Roque Bluffs, Me., U.S.	D5	96
Roquefort, Fr.	E3	16
Roquetas, Spain	E4	22
Rora Head, c., Scot., U.K.	B5	13
Roraima, ter., Braz.	A2	59
Roraima, Mount, mtn., S.A.	A2	59
Rorke Lake, l., Can.	B5	70
Rorketon, Man.	D2	70
Røros, Nor.	F4	14
Rorschach, Switz.	E4	18
Rosa, La., U.S.	D3	95
Rosa, Monte, mtn., Eur.	B1	23
Rosa, Punta, c., Mex.	B3	63
Rosales, Phil.	o13	34
Rosalia, Ks., U.S.	E7	93
Rosalia, Wa., U.S.	B8	124
Rosalie, Ne., U.S.	B9	104
Rosalind, Alta.	C4	68
Rosamond, Ca., U.S.	E4	82
Rosamond, Il., U.S.	D4	90
Rosamorada, Mex.	k11	63
Rosário, Arg.	A4	54
Rosário, Braz.	B2	57
Rosario, Mex.	C3	63
Rosário, Para.	D4	55
Rosario, Ur.	E1	56
Rosario, [Villa del], Ven.	A3	60
Rosario de la Frontera, Arg.	E3	55
Rosario del Tala, Arg.	A5	54
Rosário Oeste, Braz.	A1	56
Rosário do Sul, Braz.	E2	56
Rosati, Mo., U.S.	C6	102
Rosburg, Wa., U.S.	C2	124
Roscoe, Il., U.S.	A5	90
Roscoe, Mn., U.S.	E4	100
Roscoe, Mo., U.S.	D4	102
Roscoe, Ne., U.S.	C4	104
Roscoe, N.Y., U.S.	D6	109
Roscoe, Pa., U.S.	F2	115
Roscoe, S.D., U.S.	B6	118
Roscoe, Tx., U.S.	C2	120
Roscoe Glacier, ice, Ant.	C22	7
Roscommon, Ire.	D2	10
Roscommon, Mi., U.S.	D6	99
Roscommon, co., Ire.	D3	11
Roscommon, co., Mi., U.S.	D6	99
Roscrea, Ire.	D3	10
Rose, Ne., U.S.	B6	104
Rose, Ok., U.S.	A6	113
Rose, Mount, mtn., Nv., U.S.	D2	105
Roseau, Dom.	f14	64
Roseau, Mn., U.S.	B3	100
Roseau, co., Mn., U.S.	B3	100
Roseau, stm., N.A.	E3	70
Roseau, South Fork, stm., Mn., U.S.	B3	100
Rosebery, B.C.	D9	69
Rose-Blanche [-Harbour le Cou], Newf.	E2	72
Roseboro, N.C., U.S.	C4	110
Rosebud, Alta.	D4	68
Rosebud, Mo., U.S.	C6	102
Rosebud, S.D., U.S.	D5	118
Rosebud, Tx., U.S.	D4	120
Rosebud, co., Mt., U.S.	D10	103
Rosebud, stm., Alta.	D4	68
Rosebud Creek, stm., Mt., U.S.	E10	103
Rosebud Indian Reservation, S.D., U.S.	D5	118
Roseburg, Or., U.S.	D3	114
Rosebush, Mi., U.S.	E6	99
Rose City, Mi., U.S.	D6	99
Rose Creek, Mn., U.S.	G6	100
Rosedale, Alta.	D4	68
Rosedale, B.C.	f14	69
Rosedale, In., U.S.	E3	91
Rosedale, Md., U.S.	g11	97
Rosedale, Ms., U.S.	B2	101
Rosedale, Ok., U.S.	C4	113
Rosedale, Tn., U.S.	C9	119
Rosedale, Wa., U.S.	f10	124
Rosedale, W.V., U.S.	C4	125
Rosedale Colony, S.D., U.S.	*D8	118
Rose Farm, Oh., U.S.	C3	112
Rosehearty, Scot., U.K.	C6	13
Rose Hill, Ia., U.S.	C5	92
Rose Hill, Ks., U.S.	E6	93
Rose Hill, Ms., U.S.	C4	101
Rose Hill, N.C., U.S.	C4	110
Rose Hill, Va., U.S.	*B5	123
Rose Hill, Va., U.S.	f8	123
Roseisle, Man.	E2	70
Roseland, Ca., U.S.	*C2	82
Roseland, Fl., U.S.	E6	86
Roseland, La., U.S.	D5	95
Roseland, Ne., U.S.	D7	104
Roseland, N.J., U.S.	*B4	107
Roseland, Oh., U.S.	B3	112
Roselawn, In., U.S.	B3	91
Roselle, Il., U.S.	k8	90
Roselle, N.J., U.S.	k7	107
Roselle Park, N.J., U.S.	k7	107
Rose Lynn, Alta.	D5	68
Rosemark, Tn., U.S.	B2	119
Rosemary, Alta.	D5	68
Rosemead, Ca., U.S.	*m15	82
Rosemère, Que.	p19	74
Rosemont, Ca., U.S.	*C3	82
Rosemont, N.J., U.S.	C3	107
Rosemont, W.V., U.S.	k10	125
Rosemount, Mn., U.S.	F5	100
Rosenberg, Tx., U.S.	E5	120
Rosendale, Mo., U.S.	A3	102
Rosendale, Wi., U.S.	E5	126
Roseneath, Ont.	C6	73
Rosenfeld, Man.	E3	70
Rosenhayn, N.J., U.S.	E2	107
Rosenheim, W. Ger.	E6	18
Rose Peak, mtn., Az., U.S.	D6	80
Rosepine, La., U.S.	D2	95
Rose Point, c., B.C.	B2	69
Rose Prairie, B.C.	A7	69
Roseray, Sask.	G1	75
Rosetown, Sask.	F1	75
Rosetta, Ms., U.S.	D2	101
Rosetta Branch, stm., Eg.	D2	41
Rosetta Mouth, mth., Eg.	C2	41
Rosetta see Rashīd, Eg.	B3	38
Rose Valley, Sask.	E4	75
Rosevear, Alta.	C2	68
Roseville, Ca., U.S.	C3	82
Roseville, Il., U.S.	C3	90
Roseville, Mi., U.S.	o16	99
Roseville, Mn., U.S.	m12	100
Roseville, Oh., U.S.	C3	112
Rosewood, Mn., U.S.	B2	100
Rosewood, Oh., U.S.	B1	112
Rosewood Heights, Il., U.S.	E3	90
Rosharon, Tx., U.S.	r14	120
Rosheim, Fr.	F7	17
Rosh Ha`Ayin, Isr.	B6	41
Rosholt, S.D., U.S.	B9	118
Rosholt, Wi., U.S.	D4	126
Rosh Pinna, Isr.	B7	41
Rosiclare, Il., U.S.	F5	90
Rosie, Ar., U.S.	B4	81
Rosier, Ga., U.S.	D4	87
Rosières-en-Santerre, Fr.	E2	17
Rosignano Marittimo, Italy	C3	23
Rosignol, Guy.	A3	59
Roşiorii de Vede, Rom.	C7	24
Roskilde, Den.	C6	15
Roskilde, co., Den.	C6	15
Roslavl, Sov. Un.	E9	27
Roslyn, Pa., U.S.	o21	115
Roslyn, S.D., U.S.	B8	118
Roslyn, Wa., U.S.	B4	124
Roslyn Heights, N.Y., U.S.	h13	109
Rosman, N.C., U.S.	f10	110
Ross, N.Z.	O13	51
Ross, Mn., U.S.	B3	100
Ross, N.D., U.S.	A3	111
Ross, Oh., U.S.	C1	112
Ross, co., Oh., U.S.	C2	112
Ross, Mount, mtn., N.Z.	N15	51
Rossa, Switz.	D7	21
Rossano, Italy	E6	23
Ross Barnett Reservoir, res., Ms., U.S.	C3	101
Rossburg, Oh., U.S.	B1	112
Rossburn, Man.	D1	70
Ross Carbery, Ire.	F2	11
Ross Dam, Wa., U.S.	A4	124
Rosseau, Ont.	B5	73
Rossendale, Man.	E2	70
Rosser, Tx., U.S.	n10	120
Rosses Bay, b., Ire.	B3	11
Rosses Point, Ire.	C3	11
Rossford, Oh., U.S.	A2	112
Ross Ice Shelf, ice, Ant.	A31	7
Rossie, N.Y., U.S.	f9	109
Rossignol, Lake, l., N.S.	E4	71
Rossinière, Switz.	D21	21
Rossiter, Pa., U.S.	E4	115
Ross Island, i., Ant.	B29	7
Ross Island, i., Man.	B3	70
Rossiter, Pa., U.S.	E4	115
Ross Lake, res., N.A.	A4	124
Ross Lake National Recreation Area, Wa., U.S.	A5	124
Rossland, B.C.	E9	69
Rosslare, Ire.	E5	11
Rosslau, E. Ger.	B7	19
Rosslea, N. Ire., U.K.	C4	11
Rossmoor, Ca., U.S.	*n12	82
Rosso, Maur.	C1	45
Ross-on-Wye, Eng., U.K.	C5	12
Rossosh, Sov. Un.	F12	27
Ross River, Yukon	D6	66
Rosston, Ar., U.S.	D2	81
Rosston, Ok., U.S.	A2	113
Ross Township, Pa., U.S.	*E1	115
Rossville, Ga., U.S.	B1	87
Rossville, Il., U.S.	C6	90
Rossville, In., U.S.	D4	91
Rossville, Ia., U.S.	A6	92
Rossville, Ks., U.S.	C8	93
Rossville, Ok., U.S.	B5	113
Rossville, Tn., U.S.	B2	119
Rossway, N.S.	E4	71
Rosthern, Sask.	E2	75
Rostock, E. Ger.	A6	18
Rostov, Sov. Un.	C12	27
Rostov-na-Donu, Sov. Un.	E6	29
Roşul Pass, Rom.	C7	24
Roswell, Ga., U.S.	B2	87
Roswell, Id., U.S.	F2	89
Roswell, N.M., U.S.	D5	108
Roswell, S.D., U.S.	C8	118
Rota, Spain	D2	22
Rotan, Tx., U.S.	C2	120
Rotenburg [an der Fulda], W. Ger.	C4	18
Roth, La., U.S.	k11	95
Roth, N.D., U.S.	A5	111
Rothaar Mountains, mts., W. Ger.	C4	18
Rothbury, Eng., U.K.	E7	13
Rothbury, Mi., U.S.	E4	99
Röthenbach [bei Sankt Wolfgang], W. Ger.	D6	19
Röthenbach im Emmental, Switz.	C4	21
Rothenburg, E. Ger.	B9	19
Rothenburg [ob der Tauber], W. Ger.	D5	18
Rothenthurm, Switz.	B6	21
Rother, stm., Eng., U.K.	D8	12
Rothera, sci., Ant.	C6	7
Rotherham, Eng., U.K.	A6	12
Rothes, Scot., U.K.	C5	13
Rothesay, N.B.	D4	71
Rothesay, Scot., U.K.	C4	10
Rothsay, Mn., U.S.	D2	100
Rothschild, Wi., U.S.	D4	126
Rothville, Pa., U.S.	F9	115
Rothville, Mo., U.S.	B4	102
Rothwell, N.B.	C3	71
Roto, Austl.	F5	51
Rotondella, Italy	D6	23
Rotonde, Monte, mtn., Fr.	C2	23
Rotorua, N.Z.	M16	51
Rott, stm., W. Ger.	E8	19
Rottenburg, W. Ger.	E3	19
Rottenmann, Aus.	E7	18
Rotterdam, Neth.	B6	16
Rotterdam, N.Y., U.S.	C6	109
Rottumeroog, i., Neth.	A6	17
Rottweil, W. Ger.	D4	18
Roubaix, Fr.	B5	16
Roubideau Creek, stm., Co., U.S.	C2	83
Roudnice [nad Labem], Czech.	n17	26
Rouen, Fr.	C4	16
Rouge, stm., Que.	D3	74
Rougemont, Fr.	B2	20
Rougemont, N.C., U.S.	A4	110
Rougon, La., U.S.	D4	95
Rough River Lake, res., Ky., U.S.	C3	94
Rouleau, Sask.	G3	75
Roulers see Roeselare, Bel.	B5	16
Roulette, Pa., U.S.	C5	115
Round Harbour, Newf.	D4	72
Roundhead, Oh., U.S.	B2	112
Round Hill, Alta.	C4	68
Round Hill, N.S.	E4	71
Round Hill, Va., U.S.	A5	123
Round Island, i., Ms., U.S.	g8	101
Round Island Passage, strt., Fiji	H14	52
Round Lake, Il., U.S.	h8	90
Round Lake, Mn., U.S.	G3	100
Round Lake, N.Y., U.S.	C7	109
Round Lake, l., Ont.	B7	73
Round Lake, l., Sask.	G4	75
Round Lake Beach, Il., U.S.	h8	90
Round Mound, hill, Ks., U.S.	D4	93
Round Mountain, Nv., U.S.	E4	105
Round Mountain, Tx., U.S.	D3	120
Round Mountain, mtn., Austl.	F9	50
Round Oak, Ga., U.S.	C3	87
Round Pond, Ar., U.S.	B5	81
Round Pond, Me., U.S.	E3	96
Round Pond, l., Newf.	D4	72
Round Rock, Az., U.S.	A6	80
Round Rock, Tx., U.S.	D4	120
Round Spring, Mo., U.S.	D6	102
Roundstone, Ire.	D2	11
Round Top Hill, mtn., Ma., U.S.	B2	98
Roundup, Mt., U.S.	D8	103
Round Valley Indian Reservation, Ca., U.S.	C2	82
Round Valley Reservoir, res., N.J., U.S.	B3	107
Roura, Fr. Gu.	B4	59
Rousay, i., Scot., U.K.	A5	10
Rouses Point, N.Y., U.S.	f11	109
Rouseville, Pa., U.S.	D2	115
Routon, Tn., U.S.	A3	119
Routt, co., Co., U.S.	A3	83
Rouville, co., Que.	D4	74
Rouyn, Que.	k11	74
Rouzerville, Pa., U.S.	G6	115
Rovaniemi, Fin.	D11	14
Rovato, Italy	B2	23
Rovenki, Sov. Un.	G12	27
Rovenki, Sov. Un.	G12	27
Rover, Ar., U.S.	C2	81
Rover, Tn., U.S.	B5	119
Roveredo, Switz.	D7	21
Rovereto, Italy	B3	23
Rovigo, Italy	B3	23
Rovinj, Yugo.	C1	24
Rovno, Sov. Un.	D5	29
Rovnoye, Sov. Un.	F16	27
Row, Ok., U.S.	A7	113
Rowan, co., Ky., U.S.	B6	94
Rowan, co., N.C., U.S.	B2	110
Rowan Lake, l., Ont.	E5	70
Rowan's Ravine Provincial Park, Sask.	G3	75
Rowe, Ma., U.S.	A2	98
Rowe, N.M., U.S.	B4	108
Rowena, S.D., U.S.	D9	118
Rowena, Tx., U.S.	D2	120
Rowesville, S.C., U.S.	E6	117
Rowland, N.C., U.S.	C5	94
Rowland, Pa., U.S.	D11	115
Rowland Heights, Ca., U.S.	*n13	82
Rowlesburg, W.V., U.S.	B5	125
Rowlett, Tx., U.S.	*n9	120
Rowletts, Ky., U.S.	C4	94
Rowley, Alta.	D4	68
Rowley, Ma., U.S.	B6	98
Rowley Shoals, rf., Austl.	C2	50
Roxana, De., U.S.	G5	85
Roxas (Capiz), Phil.	C6	34
Roxboro, N.C., U.S.	A4	110
Roxbury, Ct., U.S.	C2	84
Roxbury, Ks., U.S.	D6	93
Roxbury, Me., U.S.	D2	96
Roxbury, N.Y., U.S.	C6	109
Roxbury, Vt., U.S.	C3	122
Roxie, Ms., U.S.	D2	101
Roxobel, N.C., U.S.	A5	110
Roxton, Tx., U.S.	C5	120
Roxton Falls, Que.	D5	74
Roxton Pond, Que.	D5	74
Roy, La., U.S.	B2	95
Roy, Mt., U.S.	C8	103
Roy, N.M., U.S.	B5	108
Roy, Ut., U.S.	B3	121
Roy, Wa., U.S.	B3	124
Roy, Peña, mtn., Spain	B5	22
Royal, Ar., U.S.	C2	81
Royal, Ne., U.S.	B7	104
Royal, N.C., U.S.	B6	110
Royal, stm., Me., U.S.	g7	96
Royal Canal, Ire.	D4	11
Royal Center, In., U.S.	C4	91
Royale, Isle, i., Mi., U.S.	h9	99
Royal Gorge, val., Co., U.S.	C5	83
Royal Leamington Spa, Eng., U.K.	D6	10
Royal Oak, B.C.	h12	69
Royal Oak, Md., U.S.	C5	97
Royal Oak, Mi., U.S.	F7	99
Royal Oak, Mi., U.S.	*F7	99
Royal Pines, N.C., U.S.	f10	110
Royalston, Ma., U.S.	A3	98
Royalties, Alta.	D3	68
Royalton, Il., U.S.	F4	90
Royalton, Ky., U.S.	C6	94
Royalton, Mn., U.S.	E4	100
Royalton, Vt., U.S.	D3	122
Royalton, Wi., U.S.	D5	126
Royalty, Tx., U.S.	D1	120
Royan, Fr.	E3	16
Roye, Fr.	C5	16
Royersford, Pa., U.S.	F10	115
Royerton, In., U.S.	D7	91
Royse City, Tx., U.S.	C4	120
Royston, B.C.	E5	69
Royston, Ga., U.S.	B3	87
Royston, Eng., U.K.	C6	12
Rozel, Ks., U.S.	D4	93
Rozet, Wy., U.S.	B7	127
Rožňava, Czech.	D6	26
Rtishchevo, Sov. Un.	E14	27
Ruapehu, Mount, mtn., N.Z.	M15	51
Rub' al Khali, des., Sau. Ar.	D5	38
Rubiataba, Braz.	B3	56
Rubidoux, Ca., U.S.	n14	82
Rubim, Braz.	B4	56
Rubonia, Fl., U.S.	p10	86
Rubottom, Ok., U.S.	D4	113
Ruby, Ak., U.S.	C8	79
Ruby, La., U.S.	C3	95
Ruby, S.C., U.S.	B7	117
Ruby Dome, mtn., Nv., U.S.	C6	105
Ruby Lake, l., Nv., U.S.	C6	105
Ruby Mountains, mts., Nv., U.S.	C6	105
Ruby Range, mts., Co., U.S.	C3	83
Ruby Range, mts., Mt., U.S.	E4	103
Ruby Valley, Nv., U.S.	C6	105
Rucker, Tn., U.S.	B5	119
Ruda, stm., Pol.	g9	26
Ruda Śląska, Pol.	g9	26
Rūdbār, Afg.	B3	36
Ruddell, Sask.	E2	75
Ruddels Mills, Ky., U.S.	B5	94
Rüdesheim, W. Ger.	C3	18
Rudkøbing, Den.	D4	15
Rudnichnyy, Sov. Un.	B4	28
Rudnyy, Sov. Un.	*D9	29
Rudolf, Lake, l., Afr.	A6	48
Rudolph, Oh., U.S.	A2	112
Rudolph, i., Sov. Un.	A8	28
Rudolstadt, E. Ger.	C5	18
Rüdsar, Iran	B5	38
Rudy, Ar., U.S.	*B1	81
Rudyard, Mi., U.S.	B6	99
Rudyard, Mt., U.S.	B6	103
Rue, Fr.	D9	12
Rueil-Malmaison, Fr.	g9	16
Ruelle, Fr.	E4	16
Rueun, Switz.	C7	21
Rufā'ah, Sud.	C3	47
Rufe, Ok., U.S.	C6	113
Ruffec, Fr.	D4	16
Ruffin, N.C., U.S.	A3	110
Ruffin, S.C., U.S.	E6	117
Rufiji, stm., Tan.	C6	48
Rufino, Arg.	A4	54
Rufisque, Sen.	D1	45
Rufus, Or., U.S.	B6	114
Rufus Woods Lake, res., Wa., U.S.	A6	124
Rugao, China	H9	32
Rugby, Eng., U.K.	B6	12
Rugby, N.D., U.S.	A6	111
Rugeley, Eng., U.K.	B6	12
Rugged Mountain, mtn., B.C.	E4	69
Rügen, i., E. Ger.	A6	18
Rugozero, Sov. Un.	E15	14
Ruhengeri, Rw.	B5	48
Ruhla, E. Ger.	C5	19
Ruhland, E. Ger.	B8	19
Ruhr, stm., W. Ger.	C4	18
Rui'an, China	F9	31
Ruidosa, Tx., U.S.	p12	120
Ruidoso, N.M., U.S.	D4	108
Ruidoso Downs, N.M., U.S.	D4	108
Rujiyou, i., Marsh Is.	S18	52
Rukoji Island, i., Marsh Is.	P18	52
Rukoji Pass, strt., Marsh Is.	P18	52
Rukuruku Bay, b., Fiji	H15	52
Rukwa, prov., Tan.	C5	48
Rukwa, Lake, l., Tan.	C5	48
Rule, Tx., U.S.	C3	120
Rule Creek, stm., Co., U.S.	D7	83
Ruleville, Ms., U.S.	B3	101
Rulo, Ne., U.S.	D10	104
Rum, stm., Mn., U.S.	D5	100
Ruma, Il., U.S.	E3	90
Ruma, Yugo.	C4	24
Rumbek, Sud.	D2	47
Rumbley, Md., U.S.	D6	97
Rumburk, Czech.	C9	19
Rumely, Mi., U.S.	B3	99
Rumford, Me., U.S.	D2	96
Rumilly, Fr.	D1	20
Rummah, Wādī ar, val., Sau. Ar.	C4	38
Rummānah, Eg.	C4	41
Rumney, N.H., U.S.	C3	106
Rumney Depot, N.H., U.S.	C3	106
Rumoi, Japan	E10	33
Rumphi, Mwi.	D5	48
Rump Mountain, mtn., Me., U.S.	C1	96
Rumsey, Alta.	D4	68
Rumsey, Ky., U.S.	C2	94
Rumson, N.J., U.S.	C4	107
Rumstick Point, c., R.I., U.S.	D5	116
Runan, China	H6	32
Runcorn, Eng., U.K.	A5	12
Rung, i., Camb.	G5	35
Runge, Tx., U.S.	E4	120
Rungwa, Tan.	C5	48
Runit Island, i., Marsh Is.	S18	52
Runnells, Ia., U.S.	C4	92
Runnels, co., Tx., U.S.	D2	120
Runnemede, N.J., U.S.	D2	107
Runnymede, Sask.	F5	75
Runtu, Nmb.	A2	49
Ruo Shui, stm., China	C5	31
Rupanco, Chile	C2	54
Rupat, i., Indon.	L4	35
Rupert, Id., U.S.	G5	89
Rupert, Vt., U.S.	E2	122
Rupert, W.V., U.S.	D4	125
Rupert, Rivière de, stm., Que.	h11	74
Rupununi, dept., Guy.	B3	59
Rupununi, stm., Guy.	B3	59
Rur, stm., Eur.	D6	17
Rural Hall, N.C., U.S.	A2	110
Rural Retreat, Va., U.S.	D1	123
Rurrenabaque, Bol.	B2	55
Rusagonis, N.B.	D3	71
Rusape, Zimb.	A5	49
Ruşaynş, Khazzān ar, res., Afr.	C3	47
Ruse, Bul.	D7	24
Rush, Ky., U.S.	B7	94
Rush, co., In., U.S.	E7	91
Rush, co., Ks., U.S.	D4	93
Rush, stm., Wi., U.S.	D1	126
Rush City, Mn., U.S.	E6	100
Rush Creek, stm., Co., U.S.	C7	83
Rush Creek, stm., Oh., U.S.	C3	112
Rush Creek, stm., Ok., U.S.	C4	113
Rushden, Eng., U.K.	C6	12
Rushford, Mn., U.S.	G7	100
Rushford, N.Y., U.S.	C2	109
Rush Hill, Mo., U.S.	B6	102
Rush Lake, Sask.	G1	75
Rush Lake, l., Mn., U.S.	D3	100
Rush Lake, l., Wi., U.S.	E5	126
Rushmere, Va., U.S.	h14	123
Rushmore, Mn., U.S.	G3	100
Rushsylvania, Oh., U.S.	B2	112
Rush Valley, Ut., U.S.	C3	121
Rushville, Il., U.S.	C3	90
Rushville, In., U.S.	E7	91
Rushville, Mo., U.S.	B2	102
Rushville, N.Y., U.S.	C3	109
Rushville, Ne., U.S.	B3	104
Rushville, Oh., U.S.	C3	112
Rusk, Tx., U.S.	D5	120
Rusk, co., Tx., U.S.	C5	120
Rusk, co., Wi., U.S.	C2	126
Ruskin, Fl., U.S.	E4	86
Ruskin, Ne., U.S.	D8	104
Russa, N.D., U.S.	B5	111
Russas, Braz.	B3	57
Russell, Man.	D1	70
Russell, Ont.	B9	73
Russell, Fl., U.S.	m8	86
Russell, Ia., U.S.	D4	92
Russell, Ks., U.S.	D5	93
Russell, Ky., U.S.	B7	94
Russell, Ma., U.S.	B2	98
Russell, Mn., U.S.	F3	100
Russell, N.Y., U.S.	f9	109
Russell, N.D., U.S.	A5	111
Russell, Pa., U.S.	C3	115
Russell, co., Ont.	B9	73
Russell, co., Al., U.S.	C4	78
Russell, co., Ks., U.S.	D5	93
Russell, co., Ky., U.S.	D4	94
Russell, co., Va., U.S.	f9	123
Russell, Mount, mtn., Ak., U.S.	f16	79
Russell Cave National Monument, Al., U.S.	A4	78
Russell Fork, stm., U.S.	e9	94
Russell Lake, l., Alta.	A3	68
Russell Lake, l., Man.	A1	70
Russell Springs, Ks., U.S.	D2	93
Russell Springs, Ky., U.S.	C4	94
Russellville, Al., U.S.	A2	78
Russellville, Ar., U.S.	B2	81
Russellville, Il., U.S.	E6	90
Russellville, In., U.S.	E4	91
Russellville, Ky., U.S.	D3	94
Russellville, Mo., U.S.	C5	102
Russellville, Oh., U.S.	D2	112
Russellville, Or., U.S.	*B4	114
Russellville, S.C., U.S.	E8	117
Russellville, Tn., U.S.	C10	119
Rüsselsheim, W. Ger.	D3	19
Russia, Oh., U.S.	B1	112
Russian Soviet Federative Socialist Republic, state, Sov. Un.	C12	29
Russiaville, In., U.S.	D5	91
Russum, Ms., U.S.	D2	101
Rustad, Mn., U.S.	D2	100
Rustavi, Sov. Un.	B15	40
Rustburg, Va., U.S.	C3	123
Rustenburg, S. Afr.	C4	49
Ruston, La., U.S.	B3	95
Ruston, Wa., U.S.	B3	124
Ruswil, Switz.	B5	21
Ruszów, Pol.	B10	19
Rutana, Bdi.	B4	48
Rute, Spain	D3	22
Ruteng, Indon.	G6	34
Ruth, Mi., U.S.	E8	99
Ruth, Ms., U.S.	D3	101
Ruth, Nv., U.S.	D6	105
Ruth, N.C., U.S.	f11	110
Ruth, W.V., U.S.	n12	125
Rutherford, N.J., U.S.	B4	107
Rutherford, co., N.C., U.S.	B1	110
Rutherford, co., Tn., U.S.	B5	119
Rutherfordton, N.C., U.S.	B1	110
Rutherglen, Ont.	A5	73
Rutherglen, Scot., U.K.	C4	13
Ruthilda, Sask.	F1	75
Ruthin, Wales, U.K.	A4	12
Ruthton, Mn., U.S.	F2	100
Ruthven, Ia., U.S.	A2	92
Rüti, Switz.	B4	20
Rutland, B.C.	E8	69
Rutland, Il., U.S.	C4	90
Rutland, Ma., U.S.	B3	98
Rutland, N.D., U.S.	C8	111
Rutland, Oh., U.S.	C3	112
Rutland, S.D., U.S.	C9	118
Rutland, Vt., U.S.	D3	122
Rutland, co., Vt., U.S.	D2	122
Rutledge, Al., U.S.	D3	78
Rutledge, Ga., U.S.	C3	87
Rutledge, Mn., U.S.	D6	100
Rutledge, Mo., U.S.	A5	102
Rutledge, Tn., U.S.	C10	119
Rutog, China	B6	36
Rutshuru, Zaire	B4	48
Rutter, Ont.	A4	73
Ruvo [di Puglia], Italy	D6	23
Ruvu, Tan.	C6	48
Ruvuma, prov., Tan.	D6	48
Ruvuma, stm., Afr.	D6	48
Ruwenzori, mts., Afr.	A4	48
Ruza, Sov. Un.	D11	27
Ruzayevka, Sov. Un.	D15	27
Ružomberok, Czech.	B5	26
Rwanda, ctry., Afr.	B5	48
Ry, Den.	B3	15
Ryå, stm., Den.	A3	15
Ryan, Ia., U.S.	B6	92
Ryan, Ok., U.S.	C4	113
Ryan Creek, stm., Al., U.S.	A3	78
Ryan Park, Wy., U.S.	E6	127
Ryan Peak, mtn., Id., U.S.	F4	89
Ryazan, Sov. Un.	E13	27
Ryazhsk, Sov. Un.	E9	27
Rybachye, Sov. Un.	E9	27
Rybatskoye (part of Leningrad), Sov. Un.	s31	27
Rybinsk see Andropov, Sov. Un.	D6	29
Rybinsk Reservoir, res., Sov. Un.	D6	29
Rybnik, Pol.	g10	26
Rybnitsa, Sov. Un.	B9	24
Rychnov [nad Kněžnou], Czech.	C4	26
Rycroft, Alta.	B1	68
Ryde, Austl.	*F9	50
Ryde, Eng., U.K.	D8	12
Ryder, N.D., U.S.	B4	111
Ryderwood, Wa., U.S.	C2	124
Rye, Eng., U.K.	D8	12
Rye, Co., U.S.	C6	83
Rye, N.H., U.S.	D5	106
Rye, N.Y., U.S.	h13	109
Rye Beach, N.H., U.S.	E5	106
Rye Brook, N.Y., U.S.	*D7	109
Ryegate, Mt., U.S.	D7	103
Ryegate, Vt., U.S.	C4	122
Rye Patch Dam, Nv., U.S.	C3	105
Rye Patch Reservoir, res., Nv., U.S.	C3	105
Ryerson, Sask.	H5	75
Rygge, Nor.	p28	14

Name	Map Ref.	Page
Ryley, Alta.	C4	68
Rylsk, Sov. Un.	F10	27
Rynda, Sov. Un.	C17	14
Ryomgård, Den.	B4	15
Ryōtsu, Japan	G9	33
Rypin, Pol.	B5	26
Rysy, mtn., Eur.	*D6	26
Ryukyu Islands, is., Japan	F10	31
Rzadza, stm., Pol.	k14	26
Rzepin, Pol.	B3	26
Rzeszów, Pol.	C6	26
Rzhev, Sov. Un.	C10	27

S

Name	Map Ref.	Page
Saale, stm., Eur.	C5	18
Saaler Bodden, b., E. Ger.	D6	15
Saalfeld, E. Ger.	C5	18
Saalfelden, Aus.	B8	20
Saanen, Switz.	D3	21
Saar, hist. reg., W. Ger.	D3	18
Saar, stm., Eur.	E6	17
Saarbrücken, W. Ger.	D3	18
Saaremaa, i., Sov. Un.	B4	27
Saarland, state, W. Ger.	E6	17
Saarlouis, W. Ger.	D3	18
Saas-Almagell, Switz.	D4	21
Saas-Fee, Switz.	D4	21
Saavedra, Arg.	B4	54
Saba, i., Neth. Ant.	H13	64
Šabac, Yugo.	C4	24
Sabadell, Spain	B7	22
Sabae, Japan	n15	33
Sabael, N.Y., U.S.	B6	109
Sabah (North Borneo), state, Malay.	D5	34
Sa'bah, Qārat as, mtn., Libya	D3	43
Sabana, Archipiélago de, is., Cuba	C8	64
Sabana de la Mar, Dom. Rep.	E9	64
Sabanagrande, Hond.	D4	62
Sabanalarga, Col.	A3	60
Sabaneta, Puntan, c., N. Mar. Is.	C8	52
Sabang, Indon.	k11	34
Sabará, Braz.	B4	56
Sābarmati, stm., India	D5	36
Sabastīyah, Isr. Occ.	f11	41
Sabattus, Me., U.S.	D2	96
Sabattus Pond, l., Me., U.S.	D2	96
Sabaudia, Italy	D4	23
Sabbathday Pond, l., Me., U.S.	g7	96
Sabetha, Ks., U.S.	C8	93
Sabhah, Libya	D2	43
Sabillasville, Md., U.S.	A3	97
Sabin, Mn., U.S.	D2	100
Sabina, Oh., U.S.	C2	112
Sabinal, Tx., U.S.	E3	120
Sabinas, Mex.	B4	63
Sabinas Hidalgo, Mex.	B4	63
Sabine, Tx., U.S.	E6	120
Sabine, co., La., U.S.	C2	95
Sabine, co., Tx., U.S.	D6	120
Sabine, stm., U.S.	D6	120
Sabine, Mount, mtn., Ant.	B29	7
Sabine Lake, l., U.S.	E2	95
Sabine Pass, Tx., U.S.	E6	120
Sabine Pass, strt., U.S.	E2	95
Sabinópolis, Braz.	B4	56
Sabinsville, Pa., U.S.	C7	115
Sablé, Fr.	D3	16
Sable, Cape, c., N.S.	H19	64
Sable, Cape, c., Fl., U.S.	G5	86
Sable Island, i., N.S.	F10	71
Sable River, N.S.	F4	71
Sabon Birni, Nig.	D6	45
Sabor, stm., Port.	B2	22
Şabrātah, Libya	*C2	43
Sabrina Coast, Ant.	C25	7
Sabula, Ia., U.S.	B7	92
Sabula, Mo., U.S.	D7	102
Sabzevār, Iran	B5	38
Sac, co., Ia., U.S.	B2	92
Sac, stm., Mo., U.S.	D4	102
Sacaba, Bol.	C2	55
Sacajawea, Lake, res., Wa., U.S.	C7	124
Sacajawea Peak, mtn., Or., U.S.	B9	114
Sacandaga Lake, l., N.Y., U.S.	B6	109
Sac and Fox Indian Reservation, Ia., U.S.	C5	92
Sacaton, Az., U.S.	D4	80
Sacavém, Port.	f9	22
Sac City, Ia., U.S.	B2	92
Sācele, Rom.	C7	24
Sachem Head, Ct., U.S.	E5	84
Sachigo Lake, l., Ont.	C5	70
Sachse, Tx., U.S.	n10	120
Sachs Harbour, N.W. Ter.	B8	66
Sachuest Point, c., R.I., U.S.	F6	116
Sacile, Italy	D8	20
Sackets Harbor, N.Y., U.S.	A4	109
Säckingen, W. Ger.	A4	21
Sackville, N.B.	D5	71
Saclay, Fr.	h9	16
Saco, Al., U.S.	D4	78
Saco, Me., U.S.	E2	96
Saco, Mt., U.S.	B9	103
Saco, stm., U.S.	E2	96
Saco, East Branch, stm., N.H., U.S.	B4	106
Sacramento, Ca., U.S.	C3	82
Sacramento, Ky., U.S.	C2	94
Sacramento, N.M., U.S.	E4	108
Sacramento, co., Ca., U.S.	C3	82
Sacramento, stm., Ca., U.S.	C3	82
Sacramento, stm., N.M., U.S.	E4	108
Sacramento Mountains, mts., N.M., U.S.	D4	108
Sacramento Valley, val., Az., U.S.	B1	80
Sacramento Valley, val., Ca., U.S.	C2	82
Sacré-Coeur-Saguenay, Que.	A8	74
Sacred Heart, Mn., U.S.	F3	100
Sacrofano, Italy	g8	23
Sacul, Tx., U.S.	D5	120
Sa'dah, Yemen	D4	38
Sadani, Tan.	C6	48
Saddle (Burnt), stm., Alta.	B1	68
Saddle, mtn., Az., U.S.	h8	107
Saddleback Mountain, mtn., Az., U.S.	k8	80
Saddleback Mountain, mtn., Me., U.S.	D2	96
Saddleback Mountain, mtn., Me., U.S.	B4	96
Saddle Ball Mountain, mtn., Ma., U.S.	A1	98
Saddle Brook, N.J., U.S.	h8	107

Name	Map Ref.	Page
Saddlebunch Keys, is., Fl., U.S.	H5	86
Saddle Mountain, mtn., Or., U.S.	B3	114
Saddle Mountains, mts., Wa., U.S.	C5	124
Saddle River, N.J., U.S.	A4	107
Saddlestring, Wy., U.S.	B6	127
Sadieville, Ky., U.S.	B5	94
Sadiya, India	C10	36
Sado, stm., Port.	C1	22
Sado Island, i., Japan	D12	31
Sadorus, Il., U.S.	D5	90
Sadská, Czech.	n18	26
Sæby, Den.	A4	15
Saegertown, Pa., U.S.	C1	115
Safājah, Bür, well, Egypt	H9	40
Safety Harbor, Fl., U.S.	E4	86
Saffell, Ar., U.S.	B4	81
Safford, Al., U.S.	C2	78
Safford, Az., U.S.	E6	80
Saffron Walden, Eng., U.K.	B12	12
Safi, Mor.	C3	44
Safīd Kūh, Selseleh-ye, mts., Afg.	D12	39
Safonovo, Sov. Un.	D9	27
Safranbolu, Tur.	B9	40
Safune, W. Sam.	F11	52
Safune Bay, b., W. Sam.	F11	52
Saga, China	C8	36
Saga, Japan	J5	33
Sagaing, Burma	D10	36
Sagamihara, Japan	*l9	33
Sagami Sea, b., Japan	n18	33
Sagamore, Ma., U.S.	C6	98
Sagamore, Pa., U.S.	E2	115
Sagamore Beach, Ma., U.S.	*C6	98
Sagamore Hills, Oh., U.S.	h9	112
Sagan, stm., Swe.	t34	14
Saganaga Lake, l., Mn., U.S.	B7	100
Sāgar, India	D6	36
Sagara, Japan	o17	33
Saggart, Ire.	D5	11
Sag Harbor, N.Y., U.S.	m16	109
Saginaw, Al., U.S.	B3	78
Saginaw, Mi., U.S.	E7	99
Saginaw, Or., U.S.	D3	114
Saginaw, Tx., U.S.	n9	120
Saginaw, co., Mi., U.S.	E6	99
Saginaw Bay, b., Mi., U.S.	E7	99
Sagiz, Sov. Un.	D4	28
Sagiz, stm., Sov. Un.	D5	28
Saglek Bay, b., Newf.	f9	72
Sagle, Id., U.S.	A2	89
Sagola, Mi., U.S.	B2	99
Sagua de Tánamo, Cuba	D6	64
Sagua la Grande, Cuba	C3	64
Saguache, Co., U.S.	C4	83
Saguache, co., Co., U.S.	C4	83
Saguache Creek, stm., Co., U.S.	C4	83
Saguaro National Monument, Az., U.S.	E5	80
Saguaro National Monument (Tucson Mountain Section), Az., U.S.	E4	80
Saguenay, co., Que.	A8	74
Saguenay, stm., Que.	A7	74
Sagunto, Spain	C5	22
Şahbā, Jord.	C8	41
Sahagún, Col.	B2	60
Sahand, Kūh-e, mtn., Iran	C3	39
Sahara, des., Afr.	D6	42
Sāharanpur, India	C6	36
Sāhīwal (Montgomery), Pak.	B5	36
Sahrajat al Kubrā, Eg.	D3	41
Sahuaripa, Mex.	B3	63
Sahuayo [de Díaz], Mex.	m12	59
Saïda, Sov. Un.	E6	28
Saïda, Alg.	C5	44
Saïdpur, Bngl.	C8	36
Saigō, Japan	H6	33
Saigon see Ho Chi Minh City, Viet.	C3	34
Saiki, Japan	J5	33
Sailor Springs, Il., U.S.	E5	90
Saimaa, l., Fin.	G13	14
Saint Abb's Head, c., Scot., U.K.	E6	13
Saint Adelphe, Que.	C5	74
Saint Adolphe, Man.	E3	70
Saint-Affrique, Fr.	F5	16
Saint-Agapit, Que.	C6	74
Saint Agatha, Me., U.S.	A4	96
Sainte-Agathe, Man.	E3	70
Sainte-Agathe, Que.	C5	74
Sainte-Agathe-des-Monts, Que.	C3	74
Saint-Agnès-de-Dundee, Que.	D3	74
Saint-Aimé (Massueville), Que.	D5	74
Saint-Alban, Que.	C5	74
Saint Alban's, Newf.	E4	72
Saint Albans, Eng., U.K.	B6	12
Saint Albans, Me., U.S.	D3	96
Saint Albans, Vt., U.S.	B2	122
Saint Albans, W.V., U.S.	C3	125
Saint Albans Bay, Vt., U.S.	B2	122
Saint Albans Bay, b., Vt., U.S.	B2	122
Saint Albert, Alta.	C4	68
Saint Aldhelm's Head, c., Eng., U.K.	E6	10
Sainte-Alexandre, Que.	D4	74
Saint-Alexandre [de-Kamouraska], Que.	B8	74
Saint-Alexis-des-Monts, Que.	C4	74
Saint-Alphonse [de-Granby], Que.	D5	74
Saint-Amand-les-Eaux, Fr.	D3	17
Saint-Amand-Mont-Rond, Fr.	D5	17
Saint Amant, La., U.S.	h10	95
Saint-Amarin, Fr.	B1	20
Saint-Ambroise, Que.	A6	74
Saint-Anaclet, Que.	A9	74
Saint-André, Cap, c., Madag.	g8	49
Saint-André-Avellin, Que.	D2	74
Saint-André-Est, Que.	D3	74
Saint Andrew, Fl., b., U.S.	u16	86
Saint-André [d'Apcher], Fr.	E5	16
Saint Andrews, N.B.	D2	71
Saint Andrew's, Newf.	E2	72
Saint Andrews, Scot., U.K.	B5	10
Saint Andrews, S.C., U.S.	F7	117
Saint Andrews, S.C., U.S.	C5	117
Saint Andrews, S.C., U.S.	D8	119
Saint Andrews Bay, b., Scot., U.K.	D6	13
Saint Andrew Sound, strt., Ga., U.S.	F5	87
Sainte-Angèle [de-Monnoir], Que.	D4	74
Sainte-Anicet, Que.	D3	74

Name	Map Ref.	Page
Saint Ann, Mo., U.S.	*f13	102
Saint Anna, Mi., U.S.	k9	126
Sainte-Anne, Guad.	H14	64
Saint Anne, Il., U.S.	B6	90
Sainte-Anne, stm., Que.	B6	74
Sainte-Anne-de-Beaupré, Que.	B7	74
Sainte-Anne [-de-Bellevue], Que.	q19	74
Sainte-Anne-de-la-Pérade, Que.	C5	74
Sainte-Anne-de-Madawaska, N.B.	B1	71
Sainte-Anne-des-Chênes, Man.	E3	70
Sainte-Anne [-des-Plaines], Que.	D4	74
Sainte-Anne-du-Lac, Que.	k11	74
Sainte-Anne du Nord, stm., Que.	B7	74
Saint Anns, N.S.	C9	71
Saint Ann's Bay, Jam.	E5	64
Saint Anns Peak, mtn., Trin.	N23	65
Saint-Anselme, Que.	C7	74
Saint Ansgar, Ia., U.S.	A5	92
Saint Anthony, Newf.	C4	72
Saint Anthony, Id., U.S.	F7	89
Saint Anthony, In., U.S.	H4	91
Saint Anthony, Mn., U.S.	*E5	100
Saint Anthony, N.D., U.S.	C5	111
Saint Antoine [-de-Tilly], Que.	C6	74
Saint-Antoine [-sur-Richelieu], Que.	D4	74
Saint-Antonin, Que.	B8	74
Saint-Apollinaire, Que.	C6	74
Saint-Apolline, Que.	C7	74
Saint Arnaud, Austl.	H4	51
Saint Arsène, Que.	B8	74
Saint Arthur, N.B.	B3	71
Saint-Athanase, Que.	B8	74
Saint-Aubert, Que.	B7	74
Saint-Augustin, Que.	o17	74
Saint-Augustin, stm., Can.	C2	72
Saint-Augustin-Deux-Montagnes, Que.	p19	74
Saint Augustin, Fl., U.S.	C5	86
Saint-Augustin-Nord-Quest, stm., Que.	C2	72
Saint-Augustin-Saguenay, Que.	C2	72
Saint Austell, Eng., U.K.	D3	12
Saint-Avold, Fr.	C7	16
Sainte-Barbe, Que.	D3	74
Saint-Barnabé-Nord, Que.	C5	74
Saint-Barnabé-Sud, Que.	D5	74
Saint-Barthélemy, Que.	C4	74
Saint-Barthélemy, i., Guad.	H13	64
Saint Basile, N.B.	B1	71
Saint Basile [-Sud], Que.	C6	74
Saint-Béatrix, Que.	C4	74
Saint Bees Head, c., Eng., U.K.	C5	10
Saint Benedict, Sask.	E3	75
Saint Benedict, Ia., U.S.	A3	92
Saint Benedict, Ks., U.S.	C7	93
Saint Benedict, Or., U.S.	h12	114
Saint-Benoît-Labre, Que.	C7	74
Saint Bernard, Que.	C6	74
Saint Bernard, Al., U.S.	A3	78
Saint Bernard, La., U.S.	E6	95
Saint Bernard, Ne., U.S.	C8	104
Saint Bernard, Oh., U.S.	o13	112
Saint Bernard, co., La., U.S.	E6	95
Saint Bernice, In., U.S.	E2	91
Saint Bethlehem, Tn., U.S.	A4	119
Sainte-Blandine, Que.	A9	74
Sainte-Bonaventure, Que.	D5	74
Saint Boswells, Sask.	G2	75
Saint Brendan's, Newf.	D4	72
Saint Bride, Mount, mtn., Alta.	D3	68
Saint Bride's, Newf.	E4	72
Saint Brides Bay, b., Wales, U.K.	E4	10
Saint-Brieuc, Fr.	C2	16
Saint Brieux, Sask.	E3	75
Sainte-Brigide [d'Iberville], Que.	D4	74
Sainte-Brigitte [-des-Saults], Que.	C5	74
Saint-Bruno, Que.	A6	74
Saint-Calais, Fr.	D4	16
Saint-Calixte, Que.	D4	74
Saint-Camille, Que.	D6	74
Saint-Camille [-de-Bellechasse], Que.	C7	74
Saint Casimir, Que.	C5	74
Saint Catharine, Ky., U.S.	C4	94
Saint Catharines, Ont.	D5	73
Sainte-Catherine, Que.	C6	74
Saint Catherine, Lake, l., Vt., U.S.	E2	122
Saint Catherine, Mount, mtn., Gren.	W25	65
Saint Catherines Island, i., Ga., U.S.	E5	87
Saint Catherine's Point, c., Eng., U.K.	D6	12
Saint Catherines Sound, strt., Ga., U.S.	E5	87
Sainte-Cécile [-de-Frontenac], Que.	D7	74
Sainte-Célestin (Annaville), Que.	D5	74
Saint-Césaire, Que.	D4	74
Saint-Chamond, Fr.	E6	16
Saint Charles, Que.	C7	74
Saint Charles, Ar., U.S.	C4	81
Saint Charles, Id., U.S.	G7	89
Saint Charles, Il., U.S.	B5	90
Saint Charles, Ia., U.S.	C4	92
Saint Charles, Md., U.S.	*C4	97
Saint Charles, Mi., U.S.	E6	99
Saint Charles, Mn., U.S.	G6	100
Saint Charles, Mo., U.S.	C7	102
Saint Charles, S.D., U.S.	D6	118
Saint Charles, Va., U.S.	f8	123
Saint Charles, co., La., U.S.	E5	95
Saint Charles, co., Mo., U.S.	C7	102
Saint Charles, Cape, c., Newf.	*D6	83
Saint Charles Mesa, Co., U.S.	C6	83
Saint-Chély-d'Apcher, Fr.	E5	16
Saint Christopher (Saint Kitts), Nevis, ctry., N.A.	H13	64
Saint-Chrysostome, Que.	D4	74
Saint Clair, Mi., U.S.	F8	99
Saint Clair, Mn., U.S.	F5	100
Saint Clair, Mo., U.S.	C6	102
Saint Clair, Pa., U.S.	E9	115
Saint Clair, co., Al., U.S.	B3	78
Saint Clair, co., Il., U.S.	E3	90
Saint Clair, co., Mi., U.S.	F8	99
Saint Clair, co., Mo., U.S.	C4	102
Saint Clair, stm., N.A.	E2	73
Saint Clair, Lake, l., N.A.	E2	73

Name	Map Ref.	Page
Sainte-Claire, Que.	C7	74
Saint Clair Shores, Mi., U.S.	p16	99
Saint Clairsville, Oh., U.S.	B5	112
Saint Claude, Man.	E2	70
Saint-Claude, Que.	D6	74
Saint Claude, Fr.	D6	16
Saint-Clément, Que.	B8	74
Saint Clements Creek, stm., Md., U.S.	D4	97
Sainte-Clothilde, Que.	D5	74
Saint-Cloud, Fr.	g9	16
Saint Cloud, Fl., U.S.	D5	86
Saint Cloud, Mn., U.S.	E4	100
Saint-Côme, Que.	C4	74
Sainte Croix, N.B.	D2	71
Sainte-Croix, Que.	C6	74
Sainte-Croix, Switz.	C2	20
Saint Croix, In., U.S.	H4	91
Saint Croix, i., V.I.U.S.	H12	64
Saint Croix, co., Wi., U.S.	C1	126
Saint Croix, stm., N.A.	C1	126
Saint Croix, Lake, l., U.S.	D1	126
Saint Croix Falls, Wi., U.S.	C1	126
Saint Croix Stream, stm., Me., U.S.	B4	96
Saint-Cuthbert, Que.	C4	74
Saint-Cyrille [-de-L'Islet], Que.	B7	74
Saint-Cyrille [-de-Wendover], Que.	D5	74
Saint-Cyr [-sur-Loire], Fr.	D4	16
Saint-Damase, Que.	D4	74
Saint-Damase-des-Aulnaies, Que.	B7	74
Saint-Damien-de-Brandon, Que.	C4	74
Sainte-Damien [-de-Buckland], Que.	C7	74
Saint-Damien, Que.	D5	74
Saint David, Az., U.S.	F5	80
Saint David, Il., U.S.	C3	90
Saint David, Me., U.S.	A4	96
Saint-David-de-l'Auberivière, Que.	n17	74
Saint-David [-d'Yamaska], Que.	D5	74
Saint David's, Newf.	D2	72
Saint David's, Wales, U.K.	E2	12
Saint David's Head, c., Wales, U.K.	E4	10
Saint David's Island, i., Ber.	o21	64
Saint-Denis, Fr.	D4	16
Saint-Denis, Que.	C5	16
Saint-Denis, Reu.	H24	2
Saint-Denis [-de-la-Bouteillerie], Que.	B8	74
Saint-Didace, Que.	C4	74
Saint-Dié, Fr.	C7	16
Saint-Dizier, Fr.	D6	16
Saint-Dominique, Que.	D5	74
Saint-Dominique, Que.	q18	74
Saint-Donat-de-Montcalm, Que.	C3	74
Saint Donatus, Ia., U.S.	B7	92
Saint-Édouard [-de-Napierville], Que.	D4	74
Sainte-Edwidge, Que.	D6	74
Saint Eleanor's, P.E.I.	C6	71
Saint Elias, Cape, c., Ak., U.S.	D11	79
Saint Elias Mountains, mts., N.A.	C11	79
Saint-Élie, Fr. Gu.	B4	59
Sainte-Élie-d'Orford, Que.	D5	74
Saint Elizabeth, Mo., U.S.	C5	102
Saint Elmo, Al., U.S.	E1	78
Saint Elmo, Il., U.S.	D5	90
Saint-Éloi, Que.	A8	74
Sainte-Émélie-de-l'Énergie, Que.	C4	74
Saint-Émile [-de-Suffolk], Que.	D3	74
Saint-Éphrem [-de-Tring], Que.	C7	74
Saint-Esprit, Que.	D4	74
Saint-Étienne, Fr.	E6	16
Saint-Étienne [-de-Beauharnois], Que.	q19	74
Sainte-Eulalie, Que.	C5	74
Sainte-Eusèbe, Que.	B9	74
Saint-Eustache, Que.	D4	74
Saint-Fabien, Que.	A9	74
Sainte-Famille, Que.	C7	74
Saint-Famille-de-l'Aumond, Que.	C2	74
Saint-Faustin, Que.	C3	74
Saint-Félicien, Que.	A5	74
Saint-Félix-de-Valois, Que.	C4	74
Saint-Ferdinand (Bernierville), Que.	C6	74
Saint-Ferréol [-les-Neiges], Que.	B7	74
Saint-Fidèle, Que.	B7	74
Saint Fintan's, Newf.	D2	72
Saint-Flavien, Que.	C6	74
Saint-Florent, Fr.	D5	16
Saint Florian, Al., U.S.	A2	78
Saint-Flour, Fr.	F5	16
Saint-Fortunat, Que.	D6	74
Sainte-Foy, Que.	n17	74
Sainte-Foy-la-Grande, Fr.	E4	16
Saint Francis, Ar., U.S.	A5	81
Saint Francis, Ks., U.S.	C2	93
Saint Francis, Me., U.S.	A4	96
Saint Francis, Mn., U.S.	E5	100
Saint Francis, S.D., U.S.	D5	118
Saint Francis, Wi., U.S.	n12	126
Saint Francis, co., Ar., U.S.	B5	81
Saint Francis, stm., N.A.	B8	74
Saint Francis, Cape, c., Newf.	E5	72
Saint Francisville, Il., U.S.	D6	90
Saint Francisville, La., U.S.	D4	95
Saint-François, Guad.	Q9	65
Saint-François, co., Mo., U.S.	D7	102
Saint-François, Que.	B7	74
Saint-François, Lac, l., Que.	D6	74
Saint François Mountains, hills, Mo., U.S.	D7	102
Saint-François-Xavier [de-Brompton], Que.	D5	74
Saint-Frédéric, Que.	C7	74
Saint Froid Lake, l., Me., U.S.	B4	96
Saint-Fulgence, Que.	A7	74
Saint-Gabriel, Que.	C4	74
Saint Gabriel, La., U.S.	D4	95
Saint-Gaudens, Fr.	F4	16
Saint-Gédéon, Que.	D7	74
Sainte Genevieve, Mo., U.S.	D7	102
Sainte Genevieve, co., Mo., U.S.	D7	102
Sainte-Geneviève-de-Batiscan, Que.	C5	74

Name	Map Ref.	Page
Saint George, Austl.	E8	50
Saint George, Ber.	o20	64
Saint George, N.B.	D3	71
Saint George, Ont.	D4	73
Saint George, Ga., U.S.	F4	87
Saint George, Ks., U.S.	C7	93
Saint George, Me., U.S.	D3	96
Saint George, S.C., U.S.	E6	117
Saint George, Ut., U.S.	F2	121
Saint George, Cape, c., Newf.	D2	72
Saint George, Cape, c., Fl., U.S.	C1	86
Saint George Island, Md., U.S.	D4	97
Saint George Island, i., Ak., U.S.	D6	79
Saint George Island, i., Fl., U.S.	C2	86
Saint Georges, Bel.	D5	17
Saint-Georges, Newf.	D2	72
Saint-Georges, Que.	C5	74
Saint-Georges, Fr. Gu.	B4	59
Saint George's, Gren.	J14	64
Saint Georges, De., U.S.	B3	85
Saint George's Bay, b., Newf.	D2	72
Saint George's Bay, b., N.S.	D8	71
Saint George's Cathedral, Isr. Occ.	m14	41
Saint George's Channel, strt., Eur.	E3	10
Saint George's Island, i., Ber.	o20	64
Saint-Gérard, Que.	D6	74
Saint Germain, Wi., U.S.	C4	126
Saint-Germain, Forêt de, Fr.	g9	16
Saint-Germain-de-Kamouraska, Que.	B8	74
Saint-Germain-en-Laye, Fr.	g9	16
Sainte-Germaine-Station, Que.	C7	74
Saint-Gervais, Que.	C7	74
Saint-Gervais-les-Bains, Fr.	D2	20
Saint-Gilles (Sint-Gillis), Bel.	*D4	17
Saint-Gilles, Que.	C6	74
Saint-Gilles-Croix-de-Vie, Fr.	D3	16
Saint-Gilles-du-Gard, Fr.	F6	16
Saint-Gingolph, Switz.	D2	21
Saint-Girons, Fr.	F4	16
Saint-Gobain, Fr.	C5	16
Saint Gotthard Tunnel, Switz.	E4	18
Saint Govan's Head, c., Wales, U.K.	C3	12
Saint-Grégoire (Larochelle), Que.	C5	74
Saint Gregor, Sask.	E3	75
Saint Gregory, Mount, mtn., Newf.	D2	72
Saint-Guillaume-d'Upton, Que.	D5	74
Saint Helen, Lake, l., Mi., U.S.	D6	99
Saint Helena, Ca., U.S.	C2	82
Saint Helena, Ne., U.S.	B8	104
Saint Helena, co., La., U.S.	D5	95
Saint Helena, dep., Afr.	H5	42
Saint Helena Island, i., S.C., U.S.	G6	117
Saint Helena Sound, strt., S.C., U.S.	G7	117
Sainte-Hélène [de-Kamouraska], Que.	B8	74
Saint Helens, Eng., U.K.	A5	12
Saint Helens, Or., U.S.	B4	114
Saint Helens, Mount, vol., Wa., U.S.	C3	124
Saint Helier, Jersey	F5	10
Saint-Hénédine, Que.	C7	74
Saint-Henri [-de-Lévis], Que.	C6	74
Saint Henry, Oh., U.S.	B1	112
Saint-Herménégilde, Que.	D6	74
Saint Hilaire, Mn., U.S.	B2	100
Saint-Hilaire-de-Dorset, Que.	C7	74
Saint-Hilarion, Que.	B7	74
Saint-Hippolyte, Que.	D3	74
Saint-Honoré, Que.	D7	74
Saint-Honoré-de-Témiscouata, Que.	B8	74
Saint-Hubert, Bel.	D5	17
Saint-Hubert, Que.	q20	74
Saint-Hubert-de-Témiscouata, Que.	B8	74
Saint-Hugues, Que.	D5	74
Saint-Hyacinthe, Que.	D5	74
Saint-Hyacinthe, co., Que.	D4	74
Saint Ignace, Mi., U.S.	C6	99
Saint Ignace, Mi., U.S.	C6	99
Saint Ignatius, Guy.		
Saint Ignatius, Mt., U.S.	C2	103
Saint Inigoes, Md., U.S.	D5	97
Saint-Irénée, Que.	B7	74
Saint-Isidore, N.B.	B4	71
Saint-Isidore, Que.	q19	74
Saint-Isidore-d'Auckland, Que.	D6	74
Saint Isidore de Prescott, Ont.	B10	73
Saint Ives, Eng., U.K.	D2	12
Saint Ives, Eng., U.K.	B6	12
Saint Jacob, Il., U.S.	E4	90
Saint Jacobs, Ont.	D4	73
Saint Jacques, N.B.	B1	71
Saint-Jacques, Que.	D4	74
Saint-Jacques-le-Mineur, Que.	q20	74
Saint James, Ar., U.S.	m14	81
Saint James, La., U.S.	k10	95
Saint James, Mi., U.S.	C5	99
Saint James, Mn., U.S.	G4	100
Saint James, Mo., U.S.	C6	102
Saint James, N.Y., U.S.	*n15	109
Saint James, co., La., U.S.	D5	95
Saint James, Cape, c., B.C.	D2	69
Saint James City, Fl., U.S.	F4	86
Saint-Jean, stm., Que.	F4	72
Saint-Jean, Lac, l., Que.	A5	74
Saint Jean Baptiste, Man.	E3	70
Saint-Jean-Chrysostome, Que.	o17	74
Saint-Jean-d'Angély, Fr.	E4	16
Saint-Jean-de-Dieu, Que.	A8	74
Saint-Jean-de-Luz, Fr.	F3	16
Saint-Jean-de-Matha, Que.	C4	74
Saint-Jean-Port-Joli, Que.	B7	74
Saint-Jérôme, Que.	D3	74
Saint Jo, Tx., U.S.	C4	120
Saint-Joachim, Que.	B7	74
Saint-Joachim [-de-Courval], Que.	D5	74
Saint Joe, Ar., U.S.	A3	81
Saint Joe, In., U.S.	B7	91
Saint Joe, stm., Id., U.S.	B3	89
Saint John, N.B.	D3	71
Saint John, Ks., U.S.	E5	93
Saint John, Me., U.S.	A4	96
Saint John, N.D., U.S.	A6	111

Name	Map Ref.	Page
Saint John, Wa., U.S.	B8	124
Saint John, i., co., N.B.	D3	71
Saint John, i., V.I.U.S.	G12	64
Saint John, Cape, c., Newf.	D4	72
Saint John, Southeast Branch, stm., N.A.	B2	96
Saint John Bay, b., Newf.	C3	72
Saint John Island, i., Newf.	C3	72
Saint Johns, Antig.	H14	64
Saint John's, Newf.	E5	72
Saint Johns, Az., U.S.	C6	80
Saint Johns, Mi., U.S.	E6	99
Saint Johns, Mo., U.S.	*f13	102
Saint Johns, co., Fl., U.S.	C2	86
Saint Johns, co., Fl., U.S.	B1	112
Saint Johnsbury, Vt., U.S.	C4	122
Saint Johnsbury Center, Vt., U.S.	C4	122
Saint John's Point, c., Ire.	C3	11
Saint John's Point, c., N. Ire., U.K.	C6	11
Saint Johnsville, N.Y., U.S.	B6	109
Saint John the Baptist, co., La., U.S.	D5	95
Saint Johns, stm., De., U.S.	D5	85
Saint Joseph, N.B.	D5	71
Saint Joseph, Dom.	I14	64
Saint Joseph, Il., U.S.	C5	90
Saint Joseph, Mi., U.S.	F4	99
Saint Joseph, Mn., U.S.	E4	100
Saint Joseph, Mo., U.S.	B3	102
Saint Joseph, Tn., U.S.	B4	119
Saint Joseph, co., In., U.S.	A5	91
Saint Joseph, co., Mi., U.S.	G5	99
Saint-Joseph, Lac, l., Que.	n16	74
Saint-Joseph, Lake, l., Ont.	o17	73
Saint-Joseph-Bay, b., Fl., U.S.	C1	86
Saint-Joseph-de-Beauce, Que.	C7	74
Saint-Joseph-de-la-Rive, Que.	B7	74
Saint-Joseph-du-Lac, Que.	p18	74
Saint Joseph Point, c., Fl., U.S.	v16	86
Saint Joseph Sound, strt., Fl., U.S.	o10	86
Saint-Jovite, Que.	C3	74
Saint-Jude, Que.	D5	74
Saint-Julien [-en-Genevois], Fr.	D1	21
Sainte-Julienne, Que.	C4	74
Sainte-Julie-Station, Que.	E4	16
Saint-Junien, Fr.	E4	16
Saint Just, Eng., U.K.	D2	12
Saint-Just-en-Chaussée, Fr.	E2	17
Sainte-Justine, Que.	C7	74
Sainte-Justine [-de-Newton], Que.	D3	74
Saint-Lambert, Que.	p19	74
Saint-Lambert [-de-Lévis], Que.	C6	74
Saint Landry, La., U.S.	D3	95
Saint Landry, co., La., U.S.	D3	95
Saint Laurent, Man.	D3	70
Saint-Laurent, Que.	p19	74
Saint-Laurent-Blangy, Fr.	D2	17
Saint-Laurent-de-la-Salanque, Fr.	F5	16
Saint-Laurent [-du-Maroni], Fr. Gu.	A4	59
Saint Laurent [du Maroni], ter., Fr. Gu.	B4	59
Saint-Laurent-en-Grandvaux, Fr.	C1	20
Saint Lawrence, Austl.	D8	50
Saint Lawrence, Newf.	E4	72
Saint Lawrence, S.D., U.S.	C7	118
Saint Lawrence, co., N.Y., U.S.	A5	109
Saint Lawrence, stm., N.A.	G19	66
Saint Lawrence, Cape, c., N.S.	B9	71
Saint Lawrence, Gulf of, b., Can.	G20	66
Saint Lawrence Island, i., Ak., U.S.	C5	79
Saint Lawrence Islands National Park, Ont.	C9	73
Saint Lazare, Man.	D1	70
Saint-Lazare, Que.	q18	74
Saint Leo, Fl., U.S.	D4	86
Saint Leon, In., U.S.	F8	91
Saint Léonard, N.B.	B2	71
Saint-Léonard, Que.	p19	74
Saint-Léonard [-d'Aston], Que.	C5	74
Saint-Léonard-de-Portneuf, Que.	C6	74
Saint Lewis Sound, strt., Newf.	B4	72
Saint-Liboire, Que.	D5	74
Saint Libory, Ne., U.S.	C7	104
Saint-Lô, Fr.	C3	16
Saint Louis, P.E.I.	C6	71
Saint-Louis, Sask.	E3	75
Saint Louis, Guad.	C1	65
Saint-Louis, Sen.	C1	45
Saint Louis, Mi., U.S.	E6	99
Saint Louis, Mo., U.S.	C7	102
Saint Louis, Ok., U.S.	B5	113
Saint Louis, co., Mn., U.S.	C6	100
Saint Louis, co., Mo., U.S.	C7	102
Saint Louis, stm., U.S.	D6	100
Saint Louis Bay, b., Ms., U.S.	f7	101
Saint Louis Crossing, In., U.S.	F6	91
Saint-Louis [-de-Bonsecours], Que.		
Saint-Louis-de-Gonzague, Que.	D3	74
Saint Louis-de-Kent, N.B.	C5	71
Saint-Louis-du-Ha! Ha!, Que.	B8	74
Sainte-Louise, Que.	B7	74
Saint-Loup-sur-Semouse, Fr.	D7	16
Saint-Luc, Que.	D4	74
Saint-Luc, Switz.	D4	21
Saint Lucas, Ia., U.S.	A5	92
Saint Lucia, ctry., N.A.	J14	64
Saint Lucia, Cape, c., S. Afr.	C5	49
Saint Lucia, Lake, l., S. Afr.	C5	49
Saint Lucia Channel, strt., N.A.	I14	64
Saint Lucie, Fl., U.S.	E6	86
Saint Lucie, co., Fl., U.S.	E6	86
Saint Lucie Canal, Fl., U.S.	F6	86
Sainte-Lucie-de-Beauregard, Que.	C7	74
Saint Lucie Inlet, b., Fl., U.S.	E6	86

Index

Name	Map Ref.	Page
Saint-Ludger, Que.	D7	74
Sainte-Madeleine, Que.	D4	74
Saint-Magloire, Que.	C7	74
Saint Magnus Bay, b., Scot., U.K.	g10	10
Saint-Maixent-l'École, Fr.	D3	16
Saint-Malachie, Que.	C7	74
Saint Malo, Man.	E3	70
Saint Malo, Fr.	C2	16
Saint Malo, Gulf of, b., Fr.	C2	16
Saint-Mandé, Fr.	g10	16
Saint-Marc, Que.	D4	74
Saint-Marc, Haiti	E7	64
Saint-Marc [-des-Carrières], Que.	C5	74
Saint-Marcel-de-L'Islet, Que.	C7	74
Saint-Marcellin, Fr.	E6	16
Saint Margaret Bay, b., Newf.	C3	72
Saint Margaret's Hope, Scot., U.K.	B6	13
Sainte-Marguerite, stm., Que.	h8	72
Sainte-Marguerite, stm., Que.	A7	74
Sainte-Marguerite-de-Dorchester, Que.	C7	74
Sainte-Marguerite Nord-Est, stm., Que.	A7	74
Sainte-Marie, Que.	C5	74
Sainte-Marie, Que.	C6	74
Sainte-Marie, Mart.	S11	65
Sainte Marie, Il., U.S.	E5	90
Sainte-Marie, Cap, c., Madag.	i8	49
Sainte-Marie-aux-Mines, Fr.	A3	20
Saint Maries, Id., U.S.	B2	89
Sainte Marie-sur-Mer, N.B.	B5	71
Saint Mark, Ks., U.S.	g11	93
Saint Marks, Fl., U.S.	B2	86
Sainte-Marthe, Que.	D3	74
Saint-Martin, Fr.	D3	16
Saint Martin, co., La., U.S.	D4	95
Saint Martin, i., N.A.	G13	64
Saint Martin, stm., Md., U.S.	D7	97
Saint Martin, Lake, l., Man.	D2	70
Saint-Martin-Boulogne, Fr.	D9	12
Sainte-Martine, Que.	D4	74
Saint Martin Island, i., Mi., U.S.	C4	99
Saint Martins, N.B.	D4	71
Saint Martin Station, Man.	D2	70
Saint Martinville, La., U.S.	D4	95
Saint-Martory, Fr.	F4	16
Saint Mary, Ky., U.S.	C4	94
Saint Mary, Mo., U.S.	D8	102
Saint Mary, co., La., U.S.	E4	95
Saint Mary, stm., B.C.	E2	68
Saint Mary, stm., N.A.	E4	68
Saint Mary-of-the-Woods, In., U.S.	E3	91
Saint Mary Peak, mtn., Austl.	F6	50
Saint Mary Reservoir, res., Alta.	E4	68
Saint Mary's, Newf.	E5	72
Saint Mary's, Ont.	D3	73
Saint Marys, Ak., U.S.	C7	79
Saint Marys, Ga., U.S.	F5	87
Saint Marys, In., U.S.	A5	91
Saint Marys, Ks., U.S.	C7	93
Saint Marys, Oh., U.S.	B1	112
Saint Marys, Pa., U.S.	D4	115
Saint Marys, W.V., U.S.	B3	125
Saint Marys, co., Md., U.S.	D4	97
Saint Marys, stm., N.S.	D8	71
Saint Marys, stm., U.S.	F5	87
Saint Marys, stm., U.S.	C8	91
Saint Marys, stm., Md., U.S.	D5	97
Saint Mary's, Cape, c., Newf.	E4	72
Saint Mary's Bay, b., N.S.	E3	71
Saint Mary's Bay, b., Newf.	E5	72
Saint Marys City, Md., U.S.	D5	97
Saint Marys Entrance, strt., Ga., U.S.	F5	87
Saint-Mathieu, Que.	q19	74
Saint-Mathieu, Que.	A9	74
Saint Matthew Island, i., Ak., U.S.	C5	79
Saint Matthews, Ky., U.S.	B4	94
Saint Matthews, S.C., U.S.	D6	117
Saint-Maur-des-Fossés, Fr.	g10	16
Saint-Maurice, Que.	C5	74
Saint-Maurice, Switz.	C3	20
Saint-Maurice, Que.	C3	95
Saint-Maurice, co., Que.	C4	74
Saint-Maurice, stm., Que.	C5	74
Saint Meinrad, In., U.S.	H4	91
Sainte-Mélanie, Que.	C4	74
Saint-Memmie, Fr.	F4	17
Sainte-Menehould, Fr.	C6	16
Saint-Méthode [-de-Frontenac], Que.	C6	74
Saint Michael, Alta.	C4	68
Saint Michael, Ak., U.S.	C7	79
Saint Michael, Mn., U.S.	E5	100
Saint Michael, N.D., U.S.	B7	111
Saint Michaels, Az., U.S.	B6	80
Saint Michaels, Md., U.S.	C5	97
Saint Michaels Bay, b., Newf.	B4	72
Saint-Michel, Fr.	E4	17
Saint-Michel, Que.	D2	20
Saint-Michel [-de-Bellechasse], Que.	C7	74
Saint-Michel-de-Napierville, Que.	q19	74
Saint-Michel-des-Saints, Que.	C4	74
Saint-Mihiel, Fr.	C6	16
Saint-Modeste, Que.	B8	74
Sainte-Monique [-de-Nicolet], Que.	C5	74
Saint-Nazaire, Que.	C5	74
Saint-Nazaire, Fr.	D2	16
Saint-Nazaire [-de-Buckland], Que.	C7	74
Saint-Nazaire-de-Chicoutimi, Que.	A6	74
Saint Nazianz, Wi., U.S.	D6	126
Saint Neots, Eng., U.K.	B7	12
Saint-Nérée, Que.	C7	74
Saint-Nicolas, Que.	o17	74
Saint-Nicolas-de-Port, Fr.	F6	17
Saint-Nicolas see Sint-Niklaas, Bel.	B6	16
Saint-Odilon, Que.	C7	74
Saint Olaf, Ia., U.S.	B6	92
Saint-Omer, Fr.	B9	12
Saint Onge, S.D., U.S.	C2	118
Saintonge, hist. reg., Fr.	E4	16
Saint-Ouen, Fr.	g10	16
Saint-Ours, Que.	D4	74
Saint-Pacôme, Que.	B8	74
Saint-Pamphile, Que.	B8	74
Saint Paris, Oh., U.S.	B2	112
Saint-Pascal, Que.	B8	74
Saint Patrice, Lac, l., Que.	A7	73
Saint Paul, Alta.	B5	68
Saint Paul, Ak., U.S.	D5	79
Saint Paul, Ar., U.S.	B2	81
Saint Paul, In., U.S.	F6	91
Saint Paul, Ks., U.S.	E8	93
Saint Paul, Mn., U.S.	F5	100
Saint Paul, Mo., U.S.	f12	102
Saint Paul, Ne., U.S.	C7	104
Saint Paul, Or., U.S.	h12	114
Saint Paul, S.C., U.S.	D7	117
Saint Paul, Va., U.S.	f9	123
Saint Paul, stm., Can.	C3	72
Saint Paul, stm., Lib.	E2	45
Saint-Paul, Île, i., F.S.A.T.	I2	2
Saint-Paul-de-Chester, Que.	D6	74
Saint-Paul-de-la-Croix, Que.	A8	74
Saint-Paul-de-Montminy, Que.	B8	74
Saint-Paul-du-Nord, Que.	A8	74
Saint-Paulin, Que.	C4	74
Saint Paul Island, i., N.S.	B9	71
Saint Paul Island, i., Ak., U.S.	D5	79
Saint Paul Park, Mn., U.S.	n12	100
Saint Pauls, N.C., U.S.	C4	110
Saint-Perpétue-de-L'Islet, Que.	B8	74
Saint Peter, Il., U.S.	E5	90
Saint Peter, Ks., U.S.	C3	93
Saint Peter, Mn., U.S.	F5	100
Saint Peter Port, Guernsey	F5	10
Saint Peters, N.S.	D9	71
Saint Peters, In., U.S.	F7	91
Saint Peters, Mo., U.S.	C7	102
Saint Peters Bay, P.E.I.	C7	71
Saint Petersburg, Fl., U.S.	E4	86
Saint Petersburg, Pa., U.S.	D2	115
Saint Petersburg Beach, Fl., U.S.	p10	86
Saint-Philémon, Que.	C7	74
Saint Philip, In., U.S.	I2	91
Saint-Philippe [-de-Laprairie], Que.	D4	74
Saint-Philippe-de-Néri, Que.	B8	74
Saint Phillips Island, i, S.C., U.S.	G6	117
Saint-Pie, Que.	D5	74
Saint-Pierre, Mart.	I14	64
Saint-Pierre, St. P./M.	E3	72
Saint-Pierre, i., St. P./M.	E3	72
Saint Pierre and Miquelon, dep., N.A.	E3	72
Saint-Pierre-d'Albigny, Fr.	D2	20
Saint-Pierre-en-Port, Fr.	E8	12
Saint-Pierre-Jolys, Man.	E3	70
Saint-Pierre-Montmagny, Que.	C7	74
Saint-Placide, Que.	p18	74
Saint-Pol-de-Léon, Fr.	C2	16
Saint-Pol-sur-Mer, Fr.	C2	17
Saint-Pol [-sur-Ternoise], Fr.	B5	16
Saint-Pourçain, Fr.	D5	16
Saint-Prime, Que.	A5	74
Saint-Prosper, Que.	C5	74
Saint-Prosper-de-Dorchester, Que.	C7	74
Saint Quentin, N.B.	B2	71
Saint-Quentin, Fr.	C5	16
Saint-Raphaël, Que.	C7	74
Saint-Raphaël, Fr.	F7	16
Saint-Raphaël-sur-Mer, N.B.	B5	71
Saint-Raymond, Que.	C6	74
Saint-Rédempteur, Que.	o17	74
Saint Regis, Mt., U.S.	C1	103
Saint Regis, stm., N.A.	f10	109
Saint Regis, West Branch, stm., N.Y., U.S.	f10	109
Saint Regis Falls, N.Y., U.S.	f10	109
Saint-Rémi, Que.	D4	74
Saint-Rémi-d'Amherst, Que.	C3	74
Saint-Rémi [-de-Tingwick], Que.	D6	74
Saint-Roch [-de-Richelieu], Que.	D4	74
Saint-Roch-des-Aulnaies, Que.	B7	74
Saint-Romuald, Que.	C7	74
Sala'ilua, W. Sam.	F11	52
Sala'ilua Bay, b., W. Sam.	F11	52
Sainte-Rose, Guad.	H14	64
Saint Rose, La., U.S.	k11	95
Sainte Rose du Lac, Man.	D2	70
Saintes, Fr.	E3	16
Saintes, Île des, is., Guad.	R8	65
Sainte-Sabine-de-Bellechasse, Que.	C7	74
Saint Samuel, Que.	D7	74
Saint Sanford, Man.	E3	70
Saint-Sauveur, N.B.	B4	71
Saint-Sauveur-des-Monts, Que.	D3	74
Sainte-Savine, Fr.	C6	16
Saint-Sébastien, Que.	D7	74
Saint-Sébastien, Cap, c., Madag.	f9	49
Saint-Sébastien [-sur-Loire], Fr.	D4	16
Saint-Sever, Fr.	F3	16
Saint-Séverin-de-Beauce, Que.	C6	74
Saint Shotts, Newf.	E5	72
Saint-Siméon, Que.	B8	74
Saint-Simon-de-Rimouski, Que.	A8	74
Saint Simons Island, Ga., U.S.	E5	87
Saint Simons Island, i., Ga., U.S.	E5	87
Saint Simons Sound, strt., Ga., U.S.	E5	87
Saint-Sixte, Que.	D2	74
Sainte-Sophie [-de-Lévrard], Que.	C5	74
Sainte-Sophie [-de-Mégantic], Que.	C6	74
Saint Stephen, N.B.	D2	71
Saint Stephens, S.C., U.S.	E8	117
Saint Stephens, Al., U.S.	D1	78
Saint Stephens, N.C., U.S.	*B1	110
Saint Stephen's Church, Isr. Occ.	m14	41
Saint Stephen's Gate, hist., Isr. Occ.	m14	41
Saint-Sylvère, Que.	C5	74
Saint-Sylvestre, Que.	C6	74
Saint Tammany, co., La., U.S.	D5	95
Sainte-Thècle, Que.	C5	74
Saint-Théophile, Que.	D7	74
Sainte-Thérèse, Que.	D4	74
Saint Thomas, Ont.	E3	73
Saint Thomas, Mo., U.S.	C5	102
Saint Thomas, N.D., U.S.	A8	111
Saint Thomas, Pa., U.S.	G6	115
Saint Thomas, i., V.I.U.S.	G12	64
Saint-Thomas [-de-Joliette], Que.	D4	74
Saint Timothée, Que.	q18	74
Saint-Tite, Que.	C5	74
Saint-Tite-des-Caps, Que.	B7	74
Saint-Tropez, Fr.	F7	16
Saint-Ubalde, Que.	C5	74
Saint-Urbain-de-Charlevoix, Que.	B7	74
Saint-Urbain [-de-Châteauguay], Que.	q19	74
Saint-Valère, Que.	C5	74
Saint-Valérien, Que.	D5	74
Saint-Valéry-en-Caux, Fr.	C4	16
Saint-Valéry-sur-Somme, Fr.	B4	16
Saint-Vallier, Que.	C7	74
Saint-Vallier, Fr.	E6	16
Sainte-Véronique, Que.	C3	74
Saint-Victor, Que.	C7	74
Saint Vincent, Mn., U.S.	B1	100
Saint Vincent, i., St. Vin.	U26	65
Saint Vincent, Cap, c., Madag.	h8	49
Saint Vincent, Cape, c., Port.	D1	22
Saint Vincent, Gulf, b., Austl.	G6	50
Saint Vincent and the Grenadines, ctry., N.A.	J14	64
Saint Vincent Island, i., Fl., U.S.	C1	86
Saint Vincent Passage, strt., N.A.	J14	64
Saint Vincent's [-Saint Stephens-Peter's River], Newf.	E5	72
Saint-Vith, Bel.	D6	17
Saint Vrain, N.M., U.S.	C6	108
Saint Walburg, Sask.	D1	75
Saint Wendelins, In., U.S.	H2	91
Saint Williams, Ont.	E4	73
Saint Xavier, Mt., U.S.	E9	103
Saint-Yrieix-la-Perche, Fr.	E4	16
Saint-Zacharie, Que.	C7	74
Saint-Zéphirin, Que.	C5	74
Saipan, i., N. Mar. Is.	E8	6
Saipan Channel, strt., N. Mar. Is.	D7	52
Saipan International Airport, N. Mar. Is.	D7	52
Sairecábur, Cerro, mtn., S.A.	D2	55
Sai Yok, Thai.	F4	35
Sajama, Nevado, mtn., Bol.	C2	55
Saka, Kenya	B6	48
Sa Kaeo, Thai.	F5	35
Sakai, Japan	o14	33
Sakākah, Sau. Ar.	C4	38
Sakakawea, Lake, res., N.D., U.S.	B3	111
Sakami, Lac, l., Que.	F17	66
Sakania, Zaire	D4	48
Sakaraha, Madag.	h8	49
Sakarya, stm., Tur.	B8	40
Sakashita, Japan	n16	33
Sakata, Japan	D12	31
Sakchu, N. Kor.	F2	33
Sakhalin, i., Sov. Un.	D17	29
Sakishima Islands, is., Japan	G9	31
Sakon Nakhon, Thai.	B2	34
Sakonnet, R.I., U.S.	F6	116
Sakonnet, stm., R.I., U.S.	E6	116
Sakonnet Point, c., R.I., U.S.	F6	116
Sakskøbing, Den.	D5	15
Sakti, India	D7	36
Saku, Japan	m10	33
Sal, Point, c., Ca., U.S.	E3	82
Sala, Swe.	H7	14
Salaberry-de-Valleyfield, Que.	D3	74
Sala Consilina, Italy	D5	23
Saladas, Arg.	E4	55
Saladillo, Arg.	B5	54
Salado, stm., Arg.	B5	54
Salado, stm., Arg.	B3	54
Salado, stm., Arg.	F3	55
Salado, stm., Mex.	B4	63
Salado, Rio, stm., N.M., U.S.	C2	108
Salado, Arroyo, stm., Arg.	C3	54
Salaga, Ghana	E4	45
Sala'ilua, W. Sam.	F11	52
Sala'ilua Bay, b., W. Sam.	F11	52
Šalālah, Oman	D5	38
Salamá, Guat.	C2	62
Salamá, Hond.	E7	63
Salamanca, Chile	A2	54
Salamanca, Mex.	m13	63
Salamanca, Spain	B3	22
Salamanca, N.Y., U.S.	C2	109
Salamat, Bahr, stm., Chad	C3	46
Salamaua, Pap. N. Gui.	k12	50
Salamina, Col.	B2	60
Salamís, Grc.	D4	25
Salamís, i., Grc.	h10	25
Salamonia, In., U.S.	D8	91
Salamonie, stm., In., U.S.	C6	91
Salamonie Lake, res., In., U.S.	C6	91
Salani, W. Sam.	G12	52
Salar de Pocitos, Arg.	D2	55
Salas, Spain	A2	22
Salatiga, Indon.	*G4	34
Salavat, Sov. Un.	C5	28
Salaverry, Peru	C2	58
Salaverry, Arg.	E3	55
Salawati, i., Indon.	F8	34
Sala y Gómez, Isla, i., Chile	H15	6
Salbris, Fr.	D5	16
Salcantay, Nevado, mtn., Peru	F4	58
Salcedo, Ec.	B2	58
Saldaña, S. Afr.	D2	49
Saldus, Sov. Un.	C4	27
Sale, Austl.	I6	51
Sale City, Ga., U.S.	E2	87
Sale Creek, Tn., U.S.	D8	119
Salée, Rivière, strt., Guad.	Q8	65
Salekhard, Sov. Un.	C9	29
Salem, India	F6	36
Salem, Al., U.S.	C4	78
Salem, Ar., U.S.	A4	81
Salem, Ct., U.S.	D6	84
Salem, Fl., U.S.	C3	86
Salem, Il., U.S.	E5	90
Salem, In., U.S.	G5	91
Salem, Ky., U.S.	e9	94
Salem, Ma., U.S.	A6	98
Salem, Mi., U.S.	p14	99
Salem, Mo., U.S.	D6	102
Salem, N.H., U.S.	E4	106
Salem, N.J., U.S.	D2	107
Salem, N.Y., U.S.	B7	109
Salem, Oh., U.S.	B5	112
Salem, Or., U.S.	C4	114
Salem, S.C., U.S.	B2	117
Salem, S.D., U.S.	D8	118
Salem, Ut., U.S.	C4	121
Salem, Va., U.S.	C2	123
Salem, W.V., U.S.	B4	125
Salem, Wi., U.S.	n11	126
Salem, co., N.J., U.S.	D2	107
Salem, stm., N.J., U.S.	D2	107
Salem, Lake, l., Vt., U.S.	B4	122
Salemburg, N.C., U.S.	B4	110
Salemi, Italy	F4	23
Salen, Scot., U.K.	D3	13
Salen, Scot., U.K.	D3	13
Salerno, Italy	D5	23
Salerno, Gulf of, b., Italy	D5	23
Salfit, Isr. Occ.	B7	41
Salford, Eng., U.K.	D5	10
Salgótarján, Hung.	A4	24
Salgueiro, Braz.	C3	57
Salida, Co., U.S.	C5	83
Salies-de-Béarn, Fr.	F3	16
Salihli, Tur.	C7	25
Salima, Mwi.	D5	48
Salimah, Wāhat, well, Sud.	A2	47
Salin, Burma	B1	35
Salina, Az., U.S.	A6	80
Salina, Ks., U.S.	D6	93
Salina, Ok., U.S.	A6	113
Salina, Ut., U.S.	E4	121
Salina, i., Italy	E5	23
Salina Cruz, Mex.	D5	63
Salinas, Braz.	B4	56
Salinas, Ec.	B1	58
Salinas, Ca., U.S.	D3	82
Salinas, stm., Ca., U.S.	D3	82
Salinas, Cape, c., Spain	C7	22
Salinas, Pampa de las, pl., Arg.	A3	54
Salinas de Garci Mendoza, Bol.	C2	55
Salinas National Monument, N.M., U.S.	C3	108
Salinas Peak, mtn., N.M., U.S.	D3	108
Saline, La., U.S.	B3	95
Saline, Mi., U.S.	F7	99
Saline, co., Ar., U.S.	C3	81
Saline, co., Il., U.S.	F5	90
Saline, co., Ks., U.S.	D6	93
Saline, co., Mo., U.S.	B4	102
Saline, co., Ne., U.S.	D8	104
Saline, stm., Ar., U.S.	C1	81
Saline, stm., Ar., U.S.	D4	81
Saline, stm., Ks., U.S.	C3	93
Saline, North Fork, stm., Il., U.S.	F5	90
Saline, South Fork, stm., Ar., U.S.	E4	81
Saline Bayou, stm., La., U.S.	B3	95
Saline Lake, res., La., U.S.	C3	95
Salineno, Tx., U.S.	F3	120
Salines, Point, c., Gren.	W25	65
Salines, Pointe des, c., Mart.	T11	65
Salineville, Oh., U.S.	B5	112
Salinópolis, Braz.	B1	57
Salins-les-Bains, Fr.	D6	16
Salisbury, Austl.	*F6	50
Salisbury, N.B.	C4	71
Salisbury, Mo., Sov. Un.	C5	28
Salisbury, Eng., U.K.	E6	10
Salisbury, Ct., U.S.	B2	84
Salisbury, Md., U.S.	D6	97
Salisbury, Ma., U.S.	A6	98
Salisbury, Mo., U.S.	B5	102
Salisbury, N.H., U.S.	D3	106
Salisbury, N.C., U.S.	B2	110
Salisbury, Pa., U.S.	G3	115
Salisbury, Vt., U.S.	D2	122
Salisbury Center, N.Y., U.S.	B6	109
Salisbury see Harare, Zimb.	A5	49
Salisbury Heights, N.S.	D6	106
Salisbury Island, i., N.W. Ter.	D17	66
Salisbury Plain, pl., Eng., U.K.	C6	12
Salish Mountains, mts., Mt., U.S.	B2	103
Salitpa, Al., U.S.	D1	78
Salix, Ia., U.S.	B1	92
Salkehatchie, stm., S.C., U.S.	E5	117
Salkum, Wa., U.S.	C3	124
Salladasburg, Pa., U.S.	D7	115
Sallanches, Fr.	D2	20
Salley, S.C., U.S.	D5	117
Salliqueló, Arg.	B4	54
Sallis, Ms., U.S.	B4	101
Sallisaw, Ok., U.S.	B7	113
Salluit, Que.	f11	74
Sallūm, Khalīj as, b., Afr.	G5	40
Salm, i., Sov. Un.	B9	128
Salmās, Iran	B2	38
Salmo, B.C.	E9	69
Salmon, Id., U.S.	D5	89
Salmon, stm., B.C.	C4	69
Salmon, stm., N.B.	B7	71
Salmon, stm., N.A.	f10	109
Salmon, stm., N.B.	C3	71
Salmon, Middle Fork, stm., Id., U.S.	E4	89
Salmon, South Fork, stm., Id., U.S.	E4	89
Salmon Arm, B.C.	D8	69
Salmon-Bay, Que.	C3	72
Salmon Creek, Wa., U.S.	D3	124
Salmon Creek Reservoir, res., Id., U.S.	G4	89
Salmon Falls, stm., U.S.	G5	89
Salmon Falls Creek, stm., U.S.	G4	89
Salmon Mountain, mtn., N.H., U.S.	f7	106
Salmon Mountains, mts., Ca., U.S.	B2	82
Salmon Peak, mtn., Tx., U.S.	E2	120
Salmon Point, c., Ont.	D7	73
Salmon River Mountains, mts., Id., U.S.	E3	89
Salmon River Reservoir, res., N.Y., U.S.	B5	109
Salmon Valley, B.C.	B6	69
Salo, Fin.	G10	14
Salò, Italy	D6	20
Salol, Mn., U.S.	B3	100
Salome, Az., U.S.	D2	80
Salome-de-Provence, Fr.	F6	16
Samokov, Bul.	D6	40
Sámos, Grc.	D6	40
Salonika see Thessaloníki, Grc.	B4	40
Salonika, Gulf of see Thermaïkós Kólpos, b., Grc.	B4	40
Salonta, Rom.	B5	24
Salsacate, Arg.	A3	54
Salsk, Sov. Un.	H13	27
Salsomaggiore Terme, Italy	B2	23
Salt, stm., Az., U.S.	C4	80
Salt, stm., Ky., U.S.	C4	94
Salt, stm., Mo., U.S.	B6	102
Salt, Middle Fork, stm., Mo., U.S.	B5	102
Salt, North Fork, stm., Mo., U.S.	B5	102
Salt, South Fork, stm., Mo., U.S.	B5	102
Salta, Arg.	D5	120
Salta, prov., Arg.	A3	55
Saltash, Eng., U.K.	D3	12
Saltburn-by-the-Sea, Eng., U.K.	F8	13
Salt Cay, i., Bah.	m18	64
Saltcoats, Sask.	F4	75
Saltcoats, Scot., U.K.	E4	13
Salt Creek, stm., Il., U.S.	C4	90
Salt Creek, stm., Ks., U.S.	f10	93
Salt Creek, stm., Ne., U.S.	h11	104
Salt Creek, stm., N.M., U.S.	D5	108
Salt Creek, stm., Oh., U.S.	C3	112
Salt Creek, stm., Wy., U.S.	C6	127
Salt Fork, Ok., U.S.	A4	113
Salt Fork Lake, res., Oh., U.S.	B4	112
Saltholm, i., Den.	C6	15
Saltillo, Mex.	B4	63
Saltillo, In., U.S.	G5	91
Saltillo, Ms., U.S.	A5	101
Saltillo, Pa., U.S.	F6	115
Saltillo, Tn., U.S.	B3	119
Salt Lake, co., Ut., U.S.	C3	121
Salt Lake, l., Hi., U.S.	g10	88
Salt Lake, l., N.M., U.S.	E6	108
Salt Lake City, Ut., U.S.	C4	121
Salt Lick, Ky., U.S.	B6	94
Salto, Braz.	m8	56
Salto, Ur.	E1	56
Salto Grande, Braz.	C3	54
Salton Sea, l., Ca., U.S.	F5	82
Saltonstall, Lake, l., Ct., U.S.	D4	84
Salt Point, c., Ca., U.S.	C2	82
Salt River Indian Reservation, Az., U.S.	k9	80
Salt River Range, mts., Wy., U.S.	D2	127
Salt Rock, W.V., U.S.	C2	125
Saltsburg, Pa., U.S.	F3	115
Saltsjöbaden (part of Nacka), Swe.	t36	14
Saltspring Island, i., B.C.	E6	69
Salt Springs, Fl., U.S.	C5	86
Saltville, Va., U.S.	f10	123
Saltwater, Wa., U.S.	*B3	124
Salt Wells Creek, stm., Wy., U.S.	E4	127
Salud, Pan.	k10	62
Saluda, N.C., U.S.	f10	110
Saluda, S.C., U.S.	C4	117
Saluda, Va., U.S.	C6	123
Saluda, co., S.C., U.S.	C4	117
Saluda, stm., S.C., U.S.	C4	117
Saluda Dam, S.C., U.S.	C5	117
Salūr, India	E7	36
Salus, Ar., U.S.	B2	81
Saluvia, Pa., U.S.	F5	115
Saluzzo, Italy	B1	23
Salvador, Braz.	D3	57
Salvador, Sask.	E1	75
Salvador, Lake, l., La., U.S.	E5	95
Salvage, Newf.	D5	72
Salvatierra, Mex.	m13	63
Salvisa, Ky., U.S.	C5	94
Salwa Bay, b., Asia	I5	39
Salween (Thanlwin), stm., Asia	D10	36
Salyān, Nepal	C9	37
Salyany, Sov. Un.	F3	28
Salyer, Ca., U.S.	B2	82
Salyersville, Ky., U.S.	C6	94
Salym Marsh, sw., Sov. Un.	B8	28
Salzach, stm., Eur.	E6	18
Salzburg, Aus.	E6	18
Salzburg, state, Aus.	B88	20
Salzgitter, W. Ger.	B5	18
Salzwedel, E. Ger.	B5	18
Sama [de Langreo], Spain	A3	22
Samaipata, Bol.	C3	55
Samalá, stm., Guat.	C2	62
Samālūt, Eg.	D6	43
Samana, Dom. Rep.	E9	64
Samaná, Bahía de, b., Dom. Rep.	E9	64
Samana Cay, i., Bah.	C7	64
Samandağı, Tur.	D10	40
Samani, Japan	E11	33
Samaniego, Col.	C2	60
Samannūd, Eg.	D3	41
Samar, Isr.	E6	41
Samar, i., Phil.	C7	34
Samara, stm., B.C.	C4	69
Samaria, Pap. N. Gui.	m13	50
Samarga, Sov. Un.	G6	29
Samaria, Id., U.S.	G6	89
Samariapo, Ven.	D3	89
Samarinda, Indon.	F5	34
Samarkand, Sov. Un.	A2	29
Sāmarrā', Iraq	B4	38
Sāmarrā' Barrage, Iraq	E14	40
Samataua, W. Sam.	F11	52
Samatan, Fr.	F4	16
Sambalpur, India	J11	37
Sambar, Cape, c., Indon.	F4	34
Sambas, Indon.	E3	34
Sambava, Madag.	f10	49
Sambhal, India	C7	37
Sāmbhar, India	G6	37
Sambor, Sov. Un.	G4	27
Sambre, Eur.	D4	17
Samburg, Tn., U.S.	A2	119
Samch'ŏk, S. Kor.	H4	33
Samch'ŏnpo, S. Kor.	H3	33
Same, Tan.	B6	48
Samedan, Switz.	C5	20
Sammamish Lake, l., Wa., U.S.	e11	124
Samnorwood, Tx., U.S.	B2	120
Samnū, Libya	C3	46
Samoa, Ca., U.S.	B1	82
Samoa de-Provence, Fr.	F6	16
Samokov, Bul.	D6	40
Sámos, Grc.	D6	40
Sámos, i., Grc.	E1	34
Samosir, i., Indon.	E1	34
Samoset, Fl., U.S.	q10	86
Samosir, i., Indon.	E1	34
Samoth, Il., U.S.	F5	90
Samothrace see Samothráki, i., Grc.	B5	40
Samothráki (Samothrace), i., Grc.	B5	40
Sampacho, Arg.	B5	54
Sampaloc Point, c., Phil.	o13	34
Sampit, Indon.	F4	34
Sampit, stm., S.C., U.S.	E9	117
Sampson, co., N.C., U.S.	C4	110
Sampwe, Zaire	C4	48
Sam Rayburn Reservoir, res., Tx., U.S.	D5	120
Samsang, China	D7	37
Samsø, i., Den.	C4	15
Samsø Bælt, strt., Den.	C4	15
Samson, Al., U.S.	D3	78
Samsun, Tur.	B11	40
Samtown, La., U.S.	*C3	95
Samtredia, Sov. Un.	A14	40
Samuels, Id., U.S.	A2	89
Samui, i., Thai.	H4	35
Samus, Sov. Un.	D25	8
Samut Sakhon, Thai.	C2	34
San, Mali	D4	45
San, stm., Asia	F7	35
San, stm., Eur.	C7	26
Şan'ā', Yemen	D4	38
Sanaag, prov., Som.	C6	47
San Acacia, N.M., U.S.	C3	108
San Acacio, Co., U.S.	D5	83
Sanaga, stm., Cam.	E2	46
San Agustín, Col.	C2	60
San Agustín, Plains of, pl., N.M., U.S.	*C2	108
San Agustín de Valle Fértil, Arg.	A3	54
Sanak Islands, is., Ak., U.S.	E7	79
San Ambrosio, Isla, i., Chile	F3	53
Sanana, i., Indon.	F7	34
Sanandaj, Iran	B4	38
San Andreas, Ca., U.S.	C3	82
San Andrés, Col.	D7	62
San Andrés, Isla de, i., Col.	D7	62
San Andres, de Giles, Arg.	g7	54
San Andres Mountains, mts., N.M., U.S.	E3	108
San Andres Peak, mtn., N.M., U.S.	E3	108
San Andrés Tetepilco (part of Mexico City), Mex.	h9	63
San Andrés Tuxtla, Mex.	D5	63
San Andrés y Providencia, dept., Col.	*D7	62
San Angelo, Tx., U.S.	D2	120
San Anselmo, Ca., U.S.	h7	82
San Antonio, Chile	A2	54
San Antonio, Chile	E2	55
San Antonio, N. Mar. Is.	D7	52
San Antonio, Phil.	o13	34
San Antonio, Fl., U.S.	D4	86
San Antonio, N.M., U.S.	k8	108
San Antonio, Tx., U.S.	E3	120
San Antonio, Cabo, c., Arg.	B5	54
San Antonio, Cabo, c., Cuba	D1	64
San Antonio Abad, Spain	C6	22
San Antonio Bay, b., Tx., U.S.	E4	120
San Antonio de Areco, Arg.	g7	54
San Antonio de los Baños, Cuba	C2	64
San Antonio de los Cobres, Arg.	D2	55
San Antonio Mountain, mtn., N.M., U.S.	A3	108
San Antonio Oeste, Arg.	C4	54
San Ardo, Ca., U.S.	D3	82
Sanare, Guat.	C2	62
Sanatorium, Ms., U.S.	D4	101
San Augustine, Tx., U.S.	D5	120
San Augustine, co., Tx., U.S.	D5	120
San Bartolomeo [in Galdo], Italy	D5	23
San Benedetto del Tronto, Italy	C4	23
San Benito, Tx., U.S.	F4	120
San Benito, co., Ca., U.S.	D3	82
San Benito Mountain, mtn., Ca., U.S.	D3	82
San Bernardino, Switz.	D7	21
San Bernardino, Ca., U.S.	E5	82
San Bernardino, co., Ca., U.S.	E5	82
San Bernardo, Chile	A2	54
San Blas, Mex.	m11	63
San Blas, Cape, c., Fl., U.S.	v16	86
San Blas, Cordillera de, mts., Pan.	F8	62
San Blas, Punta, c., Pan.	F8	62
San Bonifacio, Italy	D7	20
San Borja, Bol.	B2	55
San Borja, stm., Mex.	h9	63
Sanborn, Ia., U.S.	A2	92
Sanborn, In., U.S.	F3	100
Sanborn, N.D., U.S.	C7	111
Sanborn, Wi., U.S.	B3	126
Sanborn, co., S.D., U.S.	D7	118
Sanborn, co., N.H., U.S.	D3	106
Sanbornton, N.H., U.S.	C4	106
Sanbornville, N.H., U.S.	C4	106
San Bruno, Ca., U.S.	D2	82
San Candido, Italy	C8	20
San Carlos, Arg.	A3	54
San Carlos, Chile	B2	54
San Carlos, Nic.	E8	63
San Carlos, Phil.	o13	34
San Carlos, Az., U.S.	D5	80
San Carlos, Ur.	C5	56
San Carlos, co., Az., U.S.	D5	80
San Carlos de Bariloche, Arg.	C2	54
San Carlos del Zulia, Ven.	B3	60
San Carlos de Río Negro, Ven.	C4	60
San Carlos Indian Reservation, Az., U.S.	D5	80
San Carlos Lake, res., Az., U.S.	D5	80
San Cataldo, Italy	F4	23
Sancerre, Fr.	D5	16
Sánchez, Dom. Rep.	E9	64
San Ciro de Acosta, Mex.	m14	63
San Clemente, Spain	C4	22
San Clemente Island, i., Ca., U.S.	F5	82
San Cristóbal, Arg.	A4	54
San Cristóbal, Dom. Rep.	E8	64
San Cristóbal, Ven.	A4	108
San Cristóbal, i., Sol.Is.	G9	6
San Cristóbal, Isla (Chatham), i., Ec.	g6	58
San Cristóbal, Volcán, vol., Nic.	D4	63
San Cristóbal de las Casas, Mex.	D6	63
Sancti-Spíritus, Cuba	D4	64
Sancti-Spíritus, prov., Cuba	D4	64
Sanctuary, Sask.	G1	75
Sancy, Puy de, mtn., Fr.	E5	16
Sanda, Japan	o14	33
Sanda Island, i., Scot., U.K.	D5	34
Sandakan, Malay.	D5	34
Sandalfoot Cove, Fl., U.S.	*F6	86
San Daniele del Friuli, Italy	C9	20
Sandaré, Mali	C3	45
Sanday, i., Scot., U.K.	A5	10
Sanday Sound, strt., Scot.	A6	10
Sandborn, In., U.S.	G3	91
Sand Brook, N.J., U.S.	C3	107

Name	Map Ref.	Page

Sand Coulee, Mt., U.S. — C5 103
Sand Creek, Wi., U.S. — C2 126
Sand Creek, stm., In., U.S. — F6 91
Sand Creek, stm., Ks., U.S. — g12 93
Sand Creek, stm., Wy., U.S. — C7 127
Sand Draw, Wy., U.S. — *D4 127
Sande, Nor. — p28 14
Sandefjord, Nor. — p28 14
Sanders, Az., U.S. — B6 80
Sanders, Ky., U.S. — B5 94
Sanders, Mt., U.S. — D9 103
Sanders, co., Mt., U.S. — C1 103
Sanderson, Tx., U.S. — D1 120
Sandersville, Ga., U.S. — D4 87
Sandersville, Ms., U.S. — D4 101
Sandfly Lake, l., Sask. — B2 75
Sandford, Il., U.S. — E2 91
Sand Fork, W.V., U.S. — C4 125
Sandhammaren, c., Swe. — C8 15
Sand Hill, Ma., U.S. — h13 98
Sand Hill, Mn., U.S. — D5 101
Sandhill, Ms., U.S. — C4 101
Sand Hill, stm., Newf. — B3 72
Sand Hill, stm., Mn., U.S. — C2 100
Sandi, India — C7 36
Sandia, Peru — D4 58
Sandia, N.M., U.S. — *B3 109
Sandia, Tx., U.S. — E4 120
Sandia Crest, mtn., N.M., U.S. — k8 108
Sandia Indian Reservation, N.M., U.S. — k7 108
Sandia Mountains, mts., N.M., U.S. — k8 108
Sandia Park, N.M., U.S. — k8 108
San Diego, Ca., U.S. — F5 82
San Diego, Tx., U.S. — F3 120
San Diego, co., Ca., U.S. — F5 82
San Diego, stm., Ca., U.S. — o15 82
San Diego, Cabo, c., Arg. — h12 54
San Diego Naval Station, mil., Ca., U.S. — o15 82
San Diego Naval Training Center, mil., Ca., U.S. — o15 82
Sandikli, Tur. — C8 40
Sandilands, Man. — E3 70
San Dimas, Mex. — C3 63
San Dimas, Ca., U.S. — *m13 82
Sand Island, i., Mid. Is. — K3 52
Sand Island, i., Hi., U.S. — g10 88
Sand Island, i., Wi., U.S. — B3 126
Sand Islet, i., Mid. Is. — J3 52
Sand Key, i., Fl., U.S. — E4 86
Sand Lake, Mi., U.S. — E5 99
Sandlick Creek, stm., W.V., U.S. — n13 125
Sand Mountain, mtn., U.S. — A3 78
Sandnes, Nor. — H1 14
Sandoa, Zaire — C3 48
Sandomierz, Pol. — C6 26
Sandon, B.C. — D9 69
Sandoná, Col. — C2 60
San Donà di Piave, Italy — B4 23
Sandoval, Il., U.S. — E4 90
Sandoval, co., N.M., U.S. — B2 108
Sandover, stm., Austl. — D6 50
Sandoway, Burma — E9 36
Sandown, Eng., U.K. — D6 12
Sandown, N.H., U.S. — E4 106
Sand Point, Ont. — B8 73
Sand Point, Ak., U.S. — D7 79
Sandpoint, Id., U.S. — A2 89
Sands, Mi., U.S. — B3 99
Sands Key, i., Fl., U.S. — s3 86
Sandspit, B.C. — C2 69
Sand Springs, Mt., U.S. — C9 103
Sand Springs, Ok., U.S. — A5 113
Sandston, Va., U.S. — m18 123
Sandstone, Austl. — E2 50
Sandstone, Mn., U.S. — D6 100
Sandstone, W.V., U.S. — D4 125
Sandtown, De., U.S. — D3 85
Sandusky, Mi., U.S. — E8 99
Sandusky, N.Y., U.S. — C2 109
Sandusky, co., Oh., U.S. — A3 112
Sandusky, stm., Oh., U.S. — A2 112
Sandusky, Oh., U.S. — B2 112
Sandusky Bay, b., Oh., U.S. — A3 112
Sandvig (part of Allinge-Sandvig), Den. — C8 15
Sandviken, Swe. — G7 14
Sandwich, Il., U.S. — B5 90
Sandwich, Ma., U.S. — C7 98
Sandwich, N.H., U.S. — C4 106
Sandwich Bay, b., Newf. — B3 72
Sandwich Range, mts., N.H., U.S. — C3 106
Sandwick, B.C. — E5 69
Sandwith, Sask. — D1 75
Sandy, Or., U.S. — B4 114
Sandy, Ut., U.S. — C4 121
Sandy, stm., Me., U.S. — D2 96
Sandy Bay Mountain, mtn., Me., U.S. — C2 96
Sandy Brook, stm., Ct., U.S. — A3 84
Sandy Cape, c., Austl. — D9 50
Sandy Creek, N.Y., U.S. — B4 109
Sandy Creek, stm., Oh., U.S. — B4 112
Sandy Creek, stm., Ok., U.S. — C2 113
Sandy Hook, Ct., U.S. — D2 84
Sandy Hook, Ky., U.S. — B6 94
Sandy Hook, Md., U.S. — B2 97
Sandy Hook, Ms., U.S. — D4 101
Sandy Hook, spit, N.J., U.S. — C5 107
Sandy Island, i., S.C., U.S. — D9 117
Sandy Lake, Man. — D1 70
Sandy Lake, l., Newf. — D3 72
Sandy Lake, l., Ont. — n16 73
Sandy Lake, l., Sask. — B2 75
Sandy Neck, pen., Ma., U.S. — C7 98
Sandy Point, Me., U.S. — D4 96
Sandy Point, c., Trin. — M24 65
Sandy Point, c., R.I., U.S. — h7 116
Sandy Point, c., V.I.U.S. — C6 65
Sandy Pond, l., Ma., U.S. — g10 98
Sandy Ridge, Al., U.S. — C3 78
Sandy Ridge, N.C., U.S. — A2 110
Sandy Ridge, Pa., U.S. — E5 115
Sandy Ridge, mtn., Va., U.S. — e9 123
Sandy Springs, S.C., U.S. — B2 117
Sandyville, Mi., U.S. — A4 97
Sandyville, W.V., U.S. — C3 125
San Elizario, Tx., U.S. — o11 120
San Enrique, Arg. — B4 54
San Estanislao, Para. — D4 55
San Esteban, Hond. — D7 63
San Felice sul Panaro, Italy — E7 20
San Felipe, Chile — A2 54
San Felipe, Col. — E7 60
San Felipe, Mex. — m13 63
San Felipe, Ven. — A4 60
San Felipe, Punta, c., Mex. — A2 63
San Felipe Indian Reservation, N.M., U.S. — k8 108

San Felipe Pueblo, N.M., U.S. — B3 108
San Feliu de Guixols, Spain — B7 22
San Félix, Isla, i., Chile — F2 53
San Fernando, Arg. — A5 54
San Fernando, Chile — A2 54
San Fernando, Mex. — C5 63
San Fernando, Phil. — B6 34
San Fernando, Phil. — o13 34
San Fernando, Spain — D2 22
San Fernando, Trin. — K14 64
San Fernando, Ca., U.S. — m12 82
San Fernando de Apure, Ven. — B4 60
San Fernando de Atabapo, Ven. — C4 60
San Fernando de Henares, Spain — p17 22
San Fidel, N.M., U.S. — B2 108
Sånfjället, mtn., Swe. — F5 14
Sånfjället National Park, Swe. — F5 14
Sanford, Co., U.S. — D5 83
Sanford, Fl., U.S. — D5 86
Sanford, Me., U.S. — E2 96
Sanford, Mi., U.S. — E6 99
Sanford, N.C., U.S. — B3 110
Sanford, Tx., U.S. — B2 120
Sanford, Mount, mtn., Ak., U.S. — C11 79
San Francisco, Ec. — A4 54
San Francisco, Col. — C2 60
San Francisco, co., Ca., U.S. — D2 82
San Francisco, stm., N.A. — E8 63
San Francisco, stm., U.S. — C6 76
San Francisco, stm., U.S. — D6 80
San Francisco, Cabezas de, c., P.R. — B4 65
San Francisco Bay, b., Ca., U.S. — h8 82
San Francisco de Borja, Mex. — B3 63
San Francisco del Oro, Mex. — B3 63
San Francisco del Rincón, Mex. — m13 63
San Francisco de Macorís, Dom. Rep. — E8 64
San Francisco Mountains, mts., Ut., U.S. — E2 121
San Francisco Solano, Punta, c., Col. — B2 60
San Gabriel, Ec. — A2 58
San Gabriel, Ca., U.S. — m12 82
San Gabriel, Punta, c., Mex. — B2 63
San Gabriel Chilac, Mex. — D5 63
San Gabriel Mountains, mts., Ca., U.S. — m12 82
San Gallan, Isla, i., Peru — D2 58
Sangamner, India — H5 37
Sangamon, co., Il., U.S. — D4 90
Sangamon, stm., Il., U.S. — C3 90
Sangay, Volcán, vol., Ec. — B2 58
Sange-Māsheh, Afg. — E13 39
Sanger, Ca., U.S. — D4 82
Sanger, Tx., U.S. — C4 120
Sangerhausen, E. Ger. — C5 18
San Germán, P.R. — B1 65
Sangerville, Me., U.S. — C3 96
Sanggau, Indon. — E4 34
Sangha, stm., Afr. — E3 46
San Giacomo Pass, Eur. — D5 21
Sangihe, i., Indon. — E7 34
San Gil, Col. — B3 60
San Gimignano, Italy — C3 23
San Giovanni in Fiore, Italy — E6 23
San Giovanni in Persiceto, Italy — E7 20
Sangju, S. Kor. — H4 33
Sångli, India — *E5 36
Sangmélima, Cam. — E2 46
San Gorgonio Mountain, mtn., Ca., U.S. — E5 82
Sangre de Cristo Mountains, mts., U.S. — C6 76
San Gregorio, Ca., U.S. — k8 82
San Gregorio, Ur. — E1 56
Sangre Grande, Trin. — N23 65
Sangro, stm., Italy — D5 23
Sangrūr, India — B5 37
Sangudo, Alta. — C3 68
Sangue, Rio do, stm., Braz. — B4 55
Sangüesa, Spain — A5 22
Sanguinaro, stm., Italy — h8 23
Sanhedriyya (part of Jerusalem), Isr. — m14 41
Sanibel, Fl., U.S. — F4 86
Sanibel Island, i., Fl., U.S. — F4 86
San Ignacio, Belize — B3 62
San Ignacio, Bol. — B2 55
San Ignacio, Bol. — C3 55
San Ignacio, Mex. — B2 63
San Ignacio, Para. — E4 55
Sanilac, co., Mi., U.S. — E8 99
San Ildefonso, Cape, c., Phil. — B6 34
San Ildefonso [o la Granja], Spain — p17 22
San Ildefonso Peninsula, pen., Phil. — n14 34
Sanish, N.D., U.S. — B3 111
San Isidro, Arg. — g7 54
San Isidro, Peru — *D2 58
San Isidro [del General], C.R. — F6 62
Sanitz, E. Ger. — D6 15
Saniyah, Hawr as, l., Iraq — E3 39
San Jacinto, Ca., U.S. — F5 82
San Jacinto, co., Tx., U.S. — D5 120
San Jacinto, stm., Tx., U.S. — r14 120
San Jacinto Peak, mtn., Ca., U.S. — F5 82
San Javier, Arg. — A4 54
San Javier, Bol. — C3 55
San Javier, Mex. — F3 55
San Javier [de Loncomilla], Chile — B2 54
San Jerónimo, Serranía de, mts., Col. — B2 60
San Jerónimo Lídice (part of Mexico City), Mex. — h9 63
Sanjiang, China — L3 32
Sanjō, Japan — H9 33
San Joaquin, Para. — D4 55
San Joaquin, co., Ca., U.S. — D3 82
San Joaquin, stm., Ca., U.S. — D3 82
San Joaquin Valley, val., Ca., U.S. — D3 82

San José, dept., Ur. — g8 54
San Jose, stm., B.C. — D7 69
San José, stm., Ur. — g8 54
San José, Isla, i., Mex. — B2 63
San José [de Chiquitos, Bol.] — C3 55
San José de Feliciano, Arg. — A5 54
San José de Guanipa (El Tigrito), Ven. — B5 60
San José de Jáchal, Arg. — F2 55
San José del Boquerón, Arg. — E3 55
San José del Cabo, Mex. — m12 82
San José del Guaviare, Col. — C3 60
San José de los Molinos, Peru — E1 56
San José de Mayo, Ur. — E1 56
San José de Ocuné, Col. — C3 60
San Jose Island, i., Tx., U.S. — E4 120
San Juan, Arg. — A3 55
San Juan, Phil. — p13 34
San Juan, Phil. — n13 34
San Juan, P.R. — G11 64
San Juan, Co., U.S. — D6 83
San Juan, Tx., U.S. — F3 120
San Juan, prov., Arg. — A3 54
San Juan, co., Co., U.S. — D3 83
San Juan, co., N.M., U.S. — A1 108
San Juan, co., Ut., U.S. — F5 121
San Juan, co., Wa., U.S. — A2 124
San Juan, stm., Arg. — A3 54
San Juan, stm., B.C. — g11 69
San Juan, stm., Col. — C2 60
San Juan, stm., N.A. — E8 63
San Juan, stm., U.S. — C6 76
San Juan, Cabezas de, c., P.R. — B4 65
San Juan Bautista, Para. — E4 55
San Juan Capistrano, Ca., U.S. — F5 82
San Juan de Aragón (part of Mexico City), Mex. — h9 63
San Juan de Colón, Ven. — B3 60
San Juan [de la Maguana], Dom. Rep. — E8 64
San Juan de Lima, Punta, c., Mex. — D4 63
San Juan del Norte, Nic. — A4 60
San Juan de los Cayos, Ven. — A4 60
San Juan de los Lagos, Mex. — m12 63
San Juan del Río, Mex. — m13 63
San Juan de los Morros, Ven. — B4 60
San Juan del Sur, Nic. — E7 63
San Juan Mountains, mts., Co., U.S. — D3 83
San Juan Nepomuceno, Col. — B2 60
San Juan Pueblo, N.M., U.S. — *A3 108
San Juan y Martínez, Cuba — C2 64
San Julián, Arg. — D3 54
San Justo, Arg. — A4 54
Sankarani, stm., Afr. — D3 45
Sankt Anton [am Arlberg], Aus. — B6 20
Sankt Blasien, W. Ger. — B4 20
Sankt Gallen, Switz. — E4 18
Sankt Gallen, state, Switz. — B5 20
Sankt Gallenkirch, Aus. — B8 21
Sankt Georgen [im Attergau], Aus. — B9 20
Sankt Goarshausen, W. Ger. — C2 19
Sankt Johann [in Tirol], Aus. — B8 20
Sankt Margrethen, Switz. — B6 20
Sankt Michaelisdonn, W. Ger. — E3 15
Sankt Moritz, Switz. — E4 18
Sankt Olof, Swe. — C8 15
Sankt Pölten, Aus. — E7 20
Sankt Veit [an der Glan], Aus. — E7 18
Sankt Wendel, W. Ger. — D2 19
Sankuru, stm., Zaire — B3 48
San Leandro, Ca., U.S. — h8 82
San Lorenzo, Arg. — A4 54
San Lorenzo, Ec. — A2 58
San Lorenzo, Hond. — D4 62
San Lorenzo, P.R. — B4 65
San Lorenzo, Ur. — *h8 82
San Lorenzo, N.M., U.S. — E2 108
San Lorenzo, Cerro, mtn., S.A. — D2 54
San Lorenzo de El Escorial, Spain — B3 22
Sanlúcar [de Barrameda], Spain — D2 22
San Lucas, Mex. — C2 63
San Lucas, Cabo, c., Mex. — F4 62
San Lucas, Serranía de, mts., Col. — B3 60
San Luis, Arg. — A3 54
San Luis, Cuba — D6 64
San Luis, Guat. — D7 63
San Luis, Az., U.S. — E1 80
San Luis, Co., U.S. — D5 83
San Luis, prov., Arg. — A3 54
San Luis, stm., Mex. — h9 63
San Luis Creek, stm., Co., U.S. — C5 83
San Luis de la Paz, Mex. — m13 63
San Luis Jilotepeque, Guat. — C3 62
San Luis Obispo, Ca., U.S. — E3 82
San Luis Obispo, co., Ca., U.S. — E3 82
San Luis Pass, strt., Tx., U.S. — r14 120
San Luis Peak, mtn., Co., U.S. — D4 83
San Luis Potosí, Mex. — C4 63
San Luis Potosí, state, Mex. — C4 63
San Luis Río Colorado, Mex. — A2 63
San Luis Valley, val., Co., U.S. — D4 83
San Manuel, Az., U.S. — E5 80
San Marco [in Lamis], Italy — D5 23
San Marcos, Col. — B2 60
San Marcos, Guat. — C2 62
San Marcos, Tx., U.S. — E4 120
San Marcos, stm., Tx., U.S. — h8 120
San Marcos de Colón, Hond. — D4 62
San Marino, Ca., U.S. — m12 82
San Marino, Eur. — F7 20
San Martín, Arg. — A3 54
San Martín, dept., Peru — C2 58
San Martín, Lago (Lago O'Higgins), l., S.A. — F2 53
San Martín de la Vega, Spain — p17 22
San Martino di Castrozza, Italy — C7 20
San Mateo, Spain — B6 22
San Mateo, Ca., U.S. — D2 82
San Mateo, Fl., U.S. — C5 86
San Mateo, N.M., U.S. — B2 108
San Mateo, co., Ca., U.S. — D2 82
San Mateo, Cabo, c., Ec. — B1 58
San Mateo Mountains, mts., N.M., U.S. — D2 108
San Mateo Mountains, mts., N.M., U.S. — B2 108

San Matías, Bol. — C4 55
San Matías, Golfo, b., Arg. — C4 54
Sanmen Bay, b., China — J9 32
Sanmenxia, China — E7 31
San Miguel, El Sal. — E7 63
San Miguel, Pan. — F8 62
San Miguel, Az., U.S. — F4 80
San Miguel, Ca., U.S. — E3 82
San Miguel, N.M., U.S. — E3 108
San Miguel, co., Co., U.S. — D2 83
San Miguel, co., N.M., U.S. — B5 108
San Miguel, stm., Bol. — C5 55
San Miguel, stm., S.A. — C2 83
San Miguel, stm., Co., U.S. — C2 83
San Miguel de Allende, Mex. — m13 63
San Miguel de Tucumán, Arg. — E2 55
San Miguel Island, i., Ca., U.S. — E3 82
San Miguelito, Pan. — *F8 62
San Miguel Mountains, mts., Co., U.S. — D2 83
Sanming, China — K7 32
Sannär, Sud. — C3 47
San Narciso, Phil. — o13 34
San Narciso, Phil. — p14 34
Sannar Dam, Sud. — C3 47
San Nicolás [de los Arroyos], Arg. — A4 54
San Nicolás de las Garzas, Mex. — *B4 63
San Nicolas Island, i., Ca., U.S. — F4 82
Sanniquellie, Lib. — E3 45
Sannois, Fr. — g10 16
Sano, Japan — m18 33
Sanok, Pol. — D7 26
San Onofre, Col. — B2 60
San Pablo, Phil. — o13 34
San Pablo, Co., U.S. — D5 83
San Pablo, stm., Bol. — C3 55
San Pablo Bay, b., Ca., U.S. — g8 82
San Patricio, N.M., U.S. — D4 108
San Patricio, co., Tx., U.S. — E4 120
San Patricio, Bayou, stm., La., U.S. — C2 95
San Pedrillo, Punta, c., C.R. — F6 62
San Pedro, Arg. — A5 54
San Pedro, Bol. — B3 55
San Pedro, Chile — D4 55
San Pedro, Para. — D4 55
San Pedro, N.M., U.S. — *B3 108
San Pedro, dept., Para. — D4 55
San Pedro, stm., Mex. — k11 63
San Pedro, stm., N.A. — B2 63
San Pedro, stm., Az., U.S. — E5 80
San Pedro, Punta, c., Chile — E1 55
San Pedro de Atacama, Chile — A2 54
San Pedro [de Buena Vista], Bol. — C2 55
San Pedro de las Colonias, Mex. — B4 63
San Pedro de Macorís, Dom. Rep. — E9 64
San Pedro Mártir, Sierra, mts., Mex. — A1 63
San Pedro Peaks, mts., N.M., U.S. — A3 108
San Pedro Sula, Hond. — D7 63
San Pedro Tlaquepaque see Tlaquepaque, Mex. — m12 63
Sanpete, co., Ut., U.S. — D4 121
San Pierre, In., U.S. — B4 91
San Pitch Mountains, mts., Ut., U.S. — D4 121
Sanpoil, stm., Wa., U.S. — A7 124
Sanpoil, West Fork, stm., Wa., U.S. — A7 124
Sanquhar, Scot., U.K. — E5 13
San Quintin, Phil. — o13 34
San Quintín, Cabo, c., Mex. — A1 63
San Rafael, Arg. — A3 54
San Rafael, Ca., U.S. — D2 82
San Rafael, N.M., U.S. — B2 108
San Rafael, Ven. — A3 60
San Rafael, stm., Ut., U.S. — D5 121
San Rafael del Norte, Nic. — E7 63
San Rafael Desert, des., Ut., U.S. — E5 121
San Rafael Knob, mtn., Ut., U.S. — E5 121
San Rafael Mountains, mts., Ca., U.S. — E4 82
San Rafael Swell, plat., Ut., U.S. — E5 121
San Ramón, Peru — C2 58
San Ramon, Ca., U.S. — h9 82
San Ramón de la Nueva Orán, Arg. — A3 54
San Remo, Italy — C1 23
San Remo, N.Y., U.S. — *n15 109
San Román, Spain — D3 22
San Roque, Spain — D3 22
San Roque, N. Mar. Is. — D8 52
San Rosendo, Chile — B2 54
San Saba, Tx., U.S. — D3 120
San Saba, co., Tx., U.S. — D3 120
San Saba, stm., Tx., U.S. — D3 120
San Salvador, Arg. — A5 54
San Salvador (Watling Island), i., Bah. — B6 64
San Salvador, Isla (James), i., Ec. — g5 58
San Salvador de Jujuy, Arg. — A3 54
Sansanné-Mango, Togo — D5 45
Sans Bois Mountains, mts., Ok., U.S. — B6 113
San Sebastián (part of San José), C.R. — F5 62
San Sebastián, Arg. — A4 54
San Sebastián, Cabo, c., Arg. — h12 54
San Sebastián de los Reyes, Spain — o17 22
Sansepolcro, Italy — C4 23
San Severo, Italy — D5 23
San Simeon, Ca., U.S. — E3 82
San Simon, Az., U.S. — E6 80
San Simon, stm., Az., U.S. — E6 80
Sans Souci, S.C., U.S. — *B3 117
Santa, Id., U.S. — B2 89
Santa, stm., Peru — C2 58
Santa Ana, Bol. — C4 55
Santa Ana, El Sal. — D3 62
Santa Ana, Mex. — A2 63
Santa Ana, Peru — D3 58
Santa Ana, Ca., U.S. — F5 82

Santa Ana, Ven. — B5 60
Santa Ana, stm., Ca., U.S. — n13 82
Santa Ana Indian Reservation, N.M., U.S. — h7 108
Santa Ana Mountains, mts., Ca., U.S. — n13 82
Santa Ana Pueblo, N.M., U.S. — B3 108
Santa Anita (part of Mexico City), Mex. — h9 63
Santa Anna, Tx., U.S. — D3 120
Santa Bárbara, Braz. — B4 56
Santa Bárbara, Chile — B2 54
Santa Bárbara, Hond. — C3 62
Santa Bárbara, Mex. — B3 63
Santa Bárbara, Ca., U.S. — E4 82
Santa Barbara, co., Ca., U.S. — E3 82
Santa Barbara Channel, strt., Ca., U.S. — E3 82
Santa Bárbara d'Oeste, Braz. — m8 57
Santa Barbara Island, i., Ca., U.S. — F4 82
Santa Catalina, Arg. — D2 55
Santa Catalina, Gulf of, b., Ca., U.S. — F5 82
Santa Catalina Island, i., Ca., U.S. — F4 82
Santa Catalina Mountains, mts., Az., U.S. — E5 80
Santa Catarina, state, Braz. — D2 56
Santa Catarina, Ilha de, i., Braz. — D3 56
Santa Clara, Cuba — D2 64
Santa Clara, Ca., U.S. — D2 82
Santa Clara, N.Y., U.S. — f10 109
Santa Clara, Or., U.S. — *C3 114
Santa Clara, Ut., U.S. — F2 121
Santa Clara, co., Ca., U.S. — D3 82
Santa Clara, stm., Ca., U.S. — E4 82
Santa Clara Pueblo, N.M., U.S. — *B3 108
Santa Claus, In., U.S. — H4 91
Santa Clotilde, Peru — D2 58
Santa Coloma de Farnés, Spain — B7 22
Santa Coloma [de Gramanet], Spain — B7 22
Santa Croce, Cape, c., Italy — F5 23
Santa Cruz, Arg. — E3 54
Santa Cruz, Bol. — C5 55
Santa Cruz, Braz. — D3 57
Santa Cruz, Chile — A2 54
Santa Cruz, C.R. — E7 63
Santa Cruz, N.M., U.S. — *B3 108
Santa Cruz, Phil. — p13 34
Santa Cruz, Phil. — o13 34
Santa Cruz, Phil. — o12 34
Santa Cruz, Ca., U.S. — D2 82
Santa Cruz, prov., Arg. — D3 54
Santa Cruz, dept., Bol. — C5 55
Santa Cruz, co., Az., U.S. — F5 80
Santa Cruz, co., Ca., U.S. — D2 82
Santa Cruz, stm., Arg. — E2 54
Santa Cruz, stm., Az., U.S. — E4 80
Santa Cruz, Isla (Indefatigable Island), i., Ec. — g5 58
Santa Cruz de la Palma, Spain — m13 22
Santa Cruz de la Zarza, Spain — C4 22
Santa Cruz del Quiché, Guat. — C2 62
Santa Cruz del Sur, Cuba — D5 64
Santa Cruz de Tenerife, Spain — m13 22
Santa Cruz do Rio Pardo, Braz. — C3 56
Santa Cruz [do Sul], Braz. — D2 56
Santa Cruz Island, i., Ca., U.S. — F4 82
Santa Cruz Mountains, mts., Jam. — F13 65
Santa Elena, Ec. — B1 58
Santa Elena, Bahía de, b., Ec. — B1 58
Santa Elena, Cabo, c., C.R. — E7 63
Santa Elena, Punta, c., Ec. — C5 60
Santa Elena de Uairén, Ven. — C5 60
Santa Eugenia, Spain — A1 22
Santa Eulalia del Río, Spain — C6 22
Santa Fe, Arg. — A4 54
Santa Fé, Cuba — D2 64
Santa Fe (part of Mexico City), Mex. — h9 63
Santa Fe, N.M., U.S. — B3 108
Santa Fe, Spain — D4 22
Santa Fe, co., N.M., U.S. — B3 108
Santa Fe, Oh., U.S. — B1 112
Santa Fe, Tn., U.S. — B4 119
Santa Fe, Tx., U.S. — r14 120
Santa Fe, prov., Arg. — A4 54
Santa Fe, co., N.M., U.S. — B3 108
Santa Fe, Isla, i., Ec. — g5 58
Sante Fe Baldy, mtn., N.M., U.S. — B4 108
Santa Fe Springs, Ca., U.S. — *n12 82
Santa Filomena, Braz. — C1 57
Santai, China — E6 31
Santa Inés, Isla, i., Chile — h11 54
Santa Isabel Ahuatempan, Mex. — n14 63
Santa Isabel, P.R. — B3 65
Santa Isabel, Pico de, mtn., Eq. Gui. — *E1 46
Santa Isabel de Sihuas, Peru — E3 58
Santa Isabel do Rio Negro, Braz. — C2 59
Santa Isabel see Malabo, Eq. Gui. — E1 46
Santa Lucía, Cuba — D6 64
Santa Lucía, Ur. — E1 56
Santa Lucía, stm., Ur. — g8 54
Santa Lucia Range, mts., Ca., U.S. — E3 82
Santa Magdalena, Isla, i., Mex. — E3 63
Santa Margarita, Ca., U.S. — E3 82
Santa Margarita, Isla de, i., Mex. — E3 63

Santa Marta, Spain — C2 22
Santa Marta Grande, Cabo de, c., Braz. — D3 56
Santa Monica, Ca., U.S. — m12 82
Santan, Az., U.S. — m9 80
Santana, Braz. — D2 57
Santana, Port. — h12 22
Santana, Coxilha de, hills, S.A. — E2 56
Santana do Cariri, Braz. — C3 57
Santana do Ipanema, Braz. — C3 57
Santana do Livramento, Braz. — E1 56
Santander, Col. — C2 60
Santander, Spain — A4 22
Santander, dept., Col. — B3 60
Santander, co., Col. — C5 63
Sant'Angelo Romano, Italy — g9 23
Santanilla, Islas, is., Hond. — B6 62
Santanoni Peak, mtn., N.Y., U.S. — A6 109
Santañy, Spain — C7 22
Sant'Antioco, i., Italy — E2 23
Santa Paula, Ca., U.S. — E4 82
Santaquin, Ut., U.S. — D4 121
Santa Quitéria, Braz. — B2 57
Santarém, Braz. — C4 59
Santarém, Port. — C1 22
Santaren Channel, strt., Bah. — B4 64
Santa Rita, Braz. — C4 57
Santa Rita, Guam — M9 52
Santa Rita, Mt., U.S. — B4 103
Santa Rita, Ven. — A3 60
Santa Rita do Weil, Braz. — B4 58
Santa Rita Park, Ca., U.S. — D3 82
Santa Rosa, Arg. — A3 54
Santa Rosa, Arg. — A3 54
Santa Rosa, Bol. — B4 54
Santa Rosa, Braz. — D2 56
Santa Rosa, Col. — C4 60
Santa Rosa, Ec. — C2 82
Santa Rosa, Ca., U.S. — C2 82
Santa Rosa, Mo., U.S. — B3 102
Santa Rosa, N.M., U.S. — C5 108
Santa Rosa, co., Fl., U.S. — u14 86
Santa Rosa, Mount, hill, Guam — L10 52
Santa Rosa Beach, Fl., U.S. — u15 86
Santa Rosa de Aguán, Hond. — C5 62
Santa Rosa de Copán, Hond. — C3 62
Santa Rosa de Osos, Col. — B2 60
Santa Rosa [de Río Primero], Arg. — A4 54
Santa Rosa Island, i., Ca., U.S. — F3 82
Santa Rosa Island, i., Fl., U.S. — u14 86
Santa Rosalía, Mex. — B2 63
Santa Rosa Range, mts., Nv., U.S. — B4 105
Santa Teresa Gallura, Italy — D2 23
Santa Úrsula Coapa (part of Mexico City), Mex. — h9 63
Santa Venetia, Ca., U.S. — *D2 82
Santa Vitória do Palmar, Braz. — E2 56
Santa Ynez, Ca., U.S. — E3 82
Santa Ynez, stm., Ca., U.S. — E4 80
Santee, Ne., U.S. — B8 104
Santee, stm., S.C., U.S. — E8 117
Santee Dam, S.C., U.S. — E7 117
Santee Indian Reservation, Ne., U.S. — B8 104
Sant'Eufemia, Gulf of, b., Italy — E6 23
Santiago, Braz. — D2 56
Santiago, Chile — A2 54
Santiago, Mex. — C3 63
Santiago, Pan. — F7 62
Santiago, Para. — E4 55
Santiago, Phil. — n13 34
Santiago, stm., S.A. — B2 58
Santiago, c., Phil. — p13 34
Santiago de Cao, Peru — C2 58
Santiago [de Compostela], Spain — A1 22
Santiago de Cuba, Cuba — E6 64
Santiago de Cuba, prov., Cuba — D6 64
Santiago del Estero, Arg. — E3 55
Santiago del Estero, prov., Arg. — A3 54
Santiago de Machaca, Bol. — C2 55
Santiago Island, i., Phil. — n12 34
Santiago Ixcuintla, Mex. — C3 63
Santiago Papasquiaro, Mex. — B4 63
Santiago Peak, mtn., Ca., U.S. — n13 82
Santiago Reservoir, res., Ca., U.S. — n13 82

Santiam Pass, Or., U.S. — C4 114
Säntis, mtn., Switz. — B7 21
Santisteban del Puerto, Spain — C3 22
Santo, Tx., U.S. — C3 120
Santo Amaro, Braz. — m8 56
Santo Amaro, Ilha de, i., Braz. — m8 56
Santo Anastácio, Braz. — C2 56
Santo Ângelo, Braz. — D2 56
Santo Antônio, Ponta de, c., Braz. — E3 57
Santo Antônio de Jesus, Braz. — C3 57
Santo Antônio do Içá, Braz. — C2 58
Santo Corazón, Bol. — C4 55
Santo Domingo, Dom. Rep. — E9 64
Santo Domingo, Nic. — E8 63
Santo Domingo de la Calzada, Spain — A4 22
Santo Domingo de los Colorados, Ec. — D6 64
Santo Domingo Indian Reservation, N.M., U.S. — h8 108
Santo Domingo Pueblo, N.M., U.S. — B3 108
Santorini see Thíra, i., Grc.
Santos, Braz. — A7 57
Santos Dumont, Braz. — D5 57
Santo Tomás, Nic. — E8 63
Santo Tomás, Peru — D3 58
Santo Tomé, Ven. — B5 60
Santo Tomé, Arg. — *C7 54
Santuit, Ma., U.S. — C7 98
San Valentín, Cerro, mtn., Chile — E2 53
San Vicente, El Sal. — E7 63
San Vicente, N. Mar. Is. — D7 52
San Vicente de Alcántara, Spain — C3 22
San Vicente de Cañete, Peru — D2 58
San Vicente de la Barquera, Spain — A3 22
San Vicente del Caguán, Col. — C3 60
San Vicente Reservoir, res., Ca., U.S. — o16 82
San Vito al Tagliamento, Italy — B4 20
San Xavier Indian Reservation, Az., U.S. — E4 80

Name	Map Ref.	Page
San Ygnacio, Tx., U.S.	F3	120
San Ysidro, N.M., U.S.	B3	108
Sanza Pombo, Ang.	C2	48
Sanzhan, China	B3	33
São Bento do Sul, Braz.	D3	56
São Bento do Una, Braz.	k5	57
São Bernardo do Campo, Braz.	C3	56
São Borja, Braz.	D1	56
São Carlos, Braz.	D3	56
São Cristóvão, Braz.	D3	57
São Domingos, Braz.	A3	56
São Félix do Araguaia, Braz.	E4	59
São Félix do Xingu, Braz.	D4	59
São Fidélis, Braz.	C4	56
São Francisco, Braz.	B4	56
São Francisco, stm, Braz.	C3	57
São Francisco do Sul, Braz.	D3	56
São Gabriel, Braz.	E2	56
São Gabriel da Cachoeira, Braz.	D4	60
São Gotardo, Braz.	B3	56
Sao Hill, Tan.	C6	48
São Jerônimo, Braz.	E2	56
São Jerônimo, Serra de, plat., Braz.	B2	56
São João da Barra, Braz.	C4	56
São João da Boa Vista, Braz.	C3	56
São João da Ponte, Braz.	B4	56
São João das Lampas, Port.	f9	22
São João del Rei, Braz.	C4	56
São João do Cariri, Braz.	h5	57
São João do Piauí, Braz.	C2	57
São João Nepomuceno, Braz.	C4	56
São Joaquim, Braz.	D3	56
São Joaquim National Park, Braz.	D2	56
São Jorge, I., Port.	g8	44
São José de Mipibu, Braz.	h6	57
São José do Barreiro, Braz.	h5	56
São José do Rio Pardo, Braz.	k8	56
São José do Rio Preto, Braz.	C3	56
São José dos Campos, Braz.	C3	56
São José dos Pinhais, Braz.	D3	56
São Leopoldo, Braz.	D2	56
São Lourenço, Braz.	C3	56
São Lourenço, stm., Braz.	B1	56
São Lourenço do Sul, Braz.	E2	56
São Luís, Braz.	B2	57
São Luís do Quitunde, Braz.	k6	57
São Luís Gonzaga, Braz.	D2	56
São Manuel, Braz.	C3	56
São Manuel, stm., Braz.	B3	59
São Mateus, Braz.	E3	57
São Miguel, i., Port.	h9	44
São Miguel Arcanjo, Braz.	m7	56
São Miguel dos Campos, Braz.	k5	57
Saona, Isla, i., Dom. Rep.	E9	64
Saône, stm., Fr.	D6	16
São Paulo, Braz.	C3	56
São Paulo, state, Braz.	C3	56
São Paulo de Olivença, Braz.	D4	60
São Pedro, Braz.	m8	56
São Pedro do Piauí, Braz.	C2	57
São Raimundo Nonato, Braz.	C2	57
São Romão, Braz.	B3	56
São Roque, Braz.	m8	56
São Roque, Cabo de, c., Braz.	C3	57
Saorre, Mount, mtn., N.W. Ter.	D16	66
São Sebastião, Ilha de, i., Braz.	C3	56
São Sebastião, Ponta, c., Moz.	B6	49
São Sebastião do Caí, Braz.	D2	56
São Sebastião do Paraíso, Braz.	C3	56
São Sepé, Braz.	E2	56
São Simão, Braz.	C3	56
São Tomé, S. Tom./P.	E1	46
São Tomé, i., S. Tom./P.	E1	46
São Tomé, Cabo de, c., Braz.	C4	56
São Tomé, Pico de, mtn., S. Tom./P.	*E1	46
Sao Tome and Principe, ctry., Afr.	E1	46
Saoura, Oued, val., Alg.	C4	44
São Vicente, Braz.	C3	56
São Vicente, Port.	h11	22
São Vicente do Sul, Braz.	D2	56
Sápai, Grc.	B5	25
Sapele, Nig.	E6	45
Sapello, N.M., U.S.	B4	108
Sapelo Island, i., Ga., U.S.	E5	87
Sapelo Sound, strt., Ga., U.S.	E5	87
Sapinero, Co., U.S.	C3	83
Sapitwa, mtn., Mwi.	E6	48
Saposoa, Peru	C2	58
Sapozhok, Sov. Un.	E13	27
Sappa Creek, stm., U.S.	E5	104
Sappa Creek, Middle Fork, stm., Ks., U.S.	C2	93
Sappa Creek, South Fork, stm., Ks., U.S.	C3	93
Sappemeer (part of Hoogezand), Neth.	A6	17
Sapphire Mountains, mts., Mt., U.S.	D3	103
Sappington, Mo., U.S.	f13	102
Sapporo, Japan	C13	31
Sapri, Italy	D5	23
Sapulpa, Ok., U.S.	B5	113
Şaqqārah, Eg.	E3	41
Saqqez, Iran	C3	39
Saquarema, Braz.	C4	56
Saquena, Peru	B3	58
Sarāb, Iran	C3	39
Sarābīān, Eg.	D4	41
Saraburi, Thai.	E4	35
Saragosa, Tx., U.S.	D1	120
Saragossa, Al., U.S.	B2	78
Saraguro, Ec.	B2	58
Sarah, Ms., U.S.	A3	101
Sarajevo, Yugo.	D4	24
Sarakhs, Iran	C10	39
Saraktash, Sov. Un.	E20	8
Saraland, Al., U.S.	E1	78
Saramacca, dept., Sur.	B3	59
Saranac, Mi., U.S.	F5	99
Saranac, N.Y., U.S.	f11	109
Saranac, stm., N.Y., U.S.	F11	109
Saranac Inn, N.Y., U.S.	f10	109
Saranac Lake, N.Y., U.S.	f10	109
Saranac Lakes, l., N.Y., U.S.	f10	109
Saranda, Alb.	C3	40
Sarandi, Braz.	D2	56
Sarandi del Yi, Ur.	E1	56
Sarandí Grande, Ur.	E1	56
Sarangani Bay, b., Phil.	D6	34
Sārangpur, India	F6	37
Saranley, Som.	E5	47
Saransk, Sov. Un.	D7	29
Sarapuí, Braz.	m8	56
Sarapul, Sov. Un.	B4	28
Sarasota, Fl., U.S.	E4	86
Sarasota, co., Fl., U.S.	E4	86
Sarasota Bay, b., Fl., U.S.	E4	86
Saratoga, Sov. Un.	B9	24
Saratoga, Ar., U.S.	D2	81
Saratoga, Ca., U.S.	k8	82
Saratoga, In., U.S.	D8	91
Saratoga, Ia., U.S.	A5	92
Saratoga, N.C., U.S.	B5	110
Saratoga, Tx., U.S.	D5	120
Saratoga, Wy., U.S.	E6	127
Saratoga, co., N.Y., U.S.	B7	109
Saratoga National Historical Park, N.Y., U.S.	B7	109
Saratoga Springs, Fl., U.S.	*E4	86
Saratoga Springs, N.Y., U.S.	B7	109
Sarāvān, Iran	H11	39
Saravan, Laos	E7	35
Sarawak, state, Malay.	E4	34
Saray, Tur.	B6	25
Sarayköy, Tur.	D7	40
Sarbāz, Iran	C6	38
Sárbogárd, Hung.	B4	24
Sarca, stm., Italy	C6	20
Sarcelles, Fr.	g10	16
Sarcoxie, Mo., U.S.	D3	102
Sárda, stm., Asia	C8	37
Sardalas, Libya	D2	43
Sardina, Col.	C4	60
Sardinia, In., U.S.	F6	91
Sardinia, Oh., U.S.	C2	112
Sardinia, i., Italy	D2	23
Sardis, B.C.	f14	69
Sardis, Al., U.S.	C2	78
Sardis, Ga., U.S.	D5	87
Sardis, Ky., U.S.	B6	94
Sardis, Ms., U.S.	A4	101
Sardis, Oh., U.S.	C5	112
Sardis, Ok., U.S.	C6	113
Sardis, Tn., U.S.	B3	119
Sardis Lake, res., Ms., U.S.	A4	101
Sarektjåkkå, mtn., Swe.	C7	14
Sar-e Pol, Afg.	C12	39
Sarepta, La., U.S.	B2	95
Sarepta, Ms., U.S.	A4	101
Sargans, Switz.	B5	20
Sargeant, Mn., U.S.	G6	100
Sargent, Ga., U.S.	C2	87
Sargent, Ne., U.S.	C6	104
Sargent, co., N.D., U.S.	C8	111
Sargents, Co., U.S.	C4	83
Sargodha, Pak.	*B5	36
Sarh (Fort-Archambault), Chad	D3	46
Sārī, Iran	C6	39
Saría, i., Grc.	E6	25
Sarıkamış, Tur.	B14	40
Sarina, Austl.	D8	50
Sarine, stm., Switz.	C3	20
Sariñena, Spain	B5	22
Sarita, Tx., U.S.	F4	120
Sariwŏn, N. Kor.	G2	33
Sark, i., Guernsey	F5	10
Sarkand, Sov. Un.	F24	8
Şarkışla, Tur.	C11	40
Şarköy, Tur.	B6	40
Şarlat, Fr.	E4	16
Sarles, N.D., U.S.	A6	111
Sarmiento, Arg.	D3	54
Sarmiento, Cerro, mtn., Chile	h11	54
Särna, Swe.	G5	14
Sarnen, Switz.	C4	20
Sarnen, Lake, l., Switz.	C4	20
Sarnia, Ont.	E2	73
Sarny, Sov. Un.	F6	27
Sárö, Swe.	A5	15
Sarona, Wi., U.S.	C2	126
Saronic Gulf, b., Grc.	D4	25
Saronno, Italy	B2	23
Saronville, Ne., U.S.	D8	104
Saros, Gulf of, b., Tur.	B6	25
Sárospatak, Hung.	A5	24
Sárova, Sov. Un.	D14	27
Šar Planina, mts., Yugo.	E5	24
Sarpsborg, Nor.	p29	14
Sarpy, co., Ne., U.S.	C9	104
Sarrebourg, Fr.	F7	17
Sarreguemines, Fr.	C7	16
Sarre-Union, Fr.	F7	17
Sarria, Spain	B3	22
Sarsfield, Ont.	h13	73
Sarstedt, W. Ger.	A4	19
Sarstún, stm., N.A.	C3	62
Sartell, Mn., U.S.	E4	100
Sartène, Fr.	D2	23
Sarthe, stm., Fr.	D6	16
Sartrouville, Fr.	g9	16
Sarufutsu, Japan	D11	31
Sárvár, Hung.	B3	24
Sarvestān, Iran	G6	39
Sary-Ishikotrau Desert, des., Sov. Un.	G8	27
Sary-Ozek, Sov. Un.	E9	28
Sarysu, stm., Sov. Un.	D7	28
Sarzana, Italy	B2	23
Sasabe, Az., U.S.	F4	80
Sasaginnigak Lake, l., Man.	D4	70
Sasakwa, Ok., U.S.	C5	113
Sāsarām, India	D7	36
Sasebo, Japan	E10	31
Sashemene, Eth.	D4	47
Saskatchewan, prov., Can.	E3	66
Saskatchewan, stm., Can.	F12	66
Saskatoon, Sask.	E2	75
Sasovo, Sov. Un.	D13	27
Sassafras, Tx., U.S.	k7	120
Sassafras, stm., Md., U.S.	B5	97
Sassafras Mountain, mtn., U.S.	A2	117
Sassandra, I.C.	F3	45
Sassandra, stm., I.C.	E3	45
Sassari, Italy	D2	23
Sassenberg, W. Ger.	B3	19
Sasser, Ga., U.S.	E2	87
Sassnitz, E. Ger.	A6	18
Sasso Marconi, Italy	E7	20
Sassuolo, Italy	E6	20
Sastown, Lib.	F3	45
Sastre, Arg.	A4	54
Sasu-ri, N. Kor.	F3	33
Sasykkol, Lake, l., Sov. Un.	D10	28
Satah Mountain, mtn., B.C.	C5	69
Satanta, Ks., U.S.	E3	93
Sātāra, India	I4	37
Satartia, Ms., U.S.	C3	101
Satauaa, W. Sam.	F11	52
Satellite Beach, Fl., U.S.	*D6	86
Säter, Swe.	G6	14
Satilla, stm., Ga., U.S.	E5	87
Satipo, Peru	D3	58
Satīrlar, Tur.	B9	12
Satka, Sov. Un.	D8	29
Sătmāla Range, mts., India	H7	37
Satna, India	E8	37
Sátoraljaújhely, Hung.	A5	24
Sātpura Range, mts., India	D6	36
Sātrabrunn, Swe.	t34	14
Satsop, Wa., U.S.	B2	124
Satsuma, Al., U.S.	E1	78
Satsuma, Fl., U.S.	C5	86
Sattahip, Thai.	F4	35
Sattler, Tx., U.S.	h7	120
Satu Mare, Rom.	B6	24
Satun, Thai.	I4	35
Satupa'itea, W. Sam.	F11	52
Satus Creek, stm., Wa., U.S.	C5	124
Şaydā (Sidon), Leb.	B3	38
Saydel, Ia., U.S.	e8	92
Sayhūt, Yemen	D5	38
Saylesville, R.I., U.S.	B4	116
Saylorsburg, Pa., U.S.	E11	115
Saylorville, Ia., U.S.	e8	92
Saylorville Lake, res., Ia., U.S.	C4	92
Sayner, Wi., U.S.	B4	126
Saynshand, Mong.	C7	31
Sayre, Al., U.S.	B3	78
Sayre, Ok., U.S.	B2	113
Sayre, Pa., U.S.	C8	115
Sayreton, Al., U.S.	B3	78
Sayreville, N.J., U.S.	C4	107
Sayr Usa, Mong.	C6	31
Sayula, Mex.	D4	63
Sayula, Laguna de, l., Mex.	m12	63
Say'ūn, Yemen	D4	38
Sayville, N.Y., U.S.	n15	109
Sayward, B.C.	D5	69
Sazani, i., Alb.	B2	25
Sazava, Czech.	o18	26
Sázava, stm., Czech.	D3	26
Sazliyka, stm., Bul.	G9	24
Scafell Pikes, mtn., Eng., U.K.	F5	13
Scales Mound, Il., U.S.	A3	90
Scalp Level, Pa., U.S.	F4	115
Scaly Mountain, N.C., U.S.	f9	110
Scammon, Ks., U.S.	E9	93
Scammon Bay, Ak., U.S.	C6	79
Scandia, Alta.	D4	68
Scandia, Ks., U.S.	C6	93
Scandicci, Italy	C3	23
Scandinavia, Wi., U.S.	D4	126
Scanlon, Mn., U.S.	D6	100
Scansano, Italy	C3	23
Scanterbury, Man.	D3	70
Scantic, Ct., U.S.	B5	84
Scanzano, Italy	D6	23
Scapa, Alta.	D5	68
Scapa Flow, b., Scot., U.K.	A5	10
Scapegoat Mountain, mtn., Mt., U.S.	C3	103
Scappoose, Or., U.S.	B4	114
Scarba, i., Scot., U.K.	D3	13
Scarboro, Ga., U.S.	D5	87
Scarborough, Ont.	m15	73
Scarborough, Trin.	K14	64
Scarborough, Eng., U.K.	C6	10
Scarborough, Me., U.S.	E2	96
Scarbro, W.V., U.S.	n13	125
Scariff Island, i., Ire.	F1	11
Scariff, Ire.	E3	11
Scarsdale, N.Y., U.S.	h13	109
Scartaglin, Ire.	E2	11
Scarth, Man.	E1	70
Scarville, Ia., U.S.	A4	92
Scauri, Italy	F4	23
Sceaux, Fr.	g10	16
Scenic, S.D., U.S.	D3	118
Sceptre, Sask.	G1	75
Schaal, l., Eur.	E4	15
Schaefferstown, Pa., U.S.	F9	115
Schaerbeek (Schaarbeek), Bel.	*D4	17
Schaffer, Mt., U.S.	C3	99
Schaffhausen, Switz.	E4	15
Schaffhausen, state, Switz.	B4	20
Schagen, Neth.	B4	17
Schaghticoke, N.Y., U.S.	C7	109
Schaller, Ia., U.S.	B2	92
Schangnau, Switz.	C4	21
Schärding, Aus.	E8	19
Scharnhörn, i., W. Ger.	E2	15
Schaumburg, Il., U.S.	h8	90
Schefferville, Que.	h13	74
Schell City, Mo., U.S.	C3	102
Schell Creek Range, mts., Nv., U.S.	D7	105
Schellsburg, Pa., U.S.	F4	115
Schenectady, N.Y., U.S.	C7	109
Schenectady, co., N.Y., U.S.	C6	109
Schenefeld, W. Ger.	D9	15
Schenevus, N.Y., U.S.	C6	109
Scherer, Lake, res., Ga., U.S.	C3	87
Schererville, In., U.S.	B3	91
Scherfede, W. Ger.	B4	19
Schertz, Tx., U.S.	h7	120
Scheveningen (part of The Hague), Neth.	B4	17
Schiedam, Neth.	B6	16
Schiermonnikoog, i., Neth.	A6	17
Schifferstadt, W. Ger.	D3	19
Schilpario, Italy	C6	20
Schiltigheim, Fr.	C7	16
Schio, Italy	B3	23
Schkeuditz, E. Ger.	B7	19
Schladming, Aus.	E6	18
Schlater, Ms., U.S.	B3	101
Schlei, stm., W. Ger.	D3	15
Schleicher, co., Tx., U.S.	D2	120
Schleiz, E. Ger.	C6	19
Schleswig, W. Ger.	A4	18
Schleswig, Ia., U.S.	B2	92
Schleswig-Holstein, state, W. Ger.	D3	15
Schleswig-Holstein, hist. reg., W. Ger.	A4	18
Schley, Va., U.S.	C6	123
Schley, co., Ga., U.S.	D2	87
Schleusingen, W. Ger.	C5	19
Schlitz, W. Ger.	C4	19
Schloss Neuhaus, W. Ger.	B3	19
Schmalkalden, E. Ger.	C5	19
Schmölln, E. Ger.	C7	19
Schmölln, E. Ger.	B5	19
Schnackenburg, W. Ger.	B6	19
Schneeberg, E. Ger.	C7	19
Schneeberg, mtn., W. Ger.	C6	19
Schneider, In., U.S.	B3	91
Schoenchen, Ks., U.S.	D4	93
Schofield, Wi., U.S.	D4	126
Schofield Barracks, mil., Hi., U.S.	g9	88
Schoharie, N.Y., U.S.	C6	109
Schoharie, co., N.Y., U.S.	C6	109
Schoharie Creek, stm., N.Y., U.S.	C6	109
Scholls, Or., U.S.	h12	114
Schönbach, Aus.	G15	18
Schönebeck, E. Ger.	B5	18
Schöneck, E. Ger.	C7	19
Schongau, W. Ger.	E5	18
Schöningen, W. Ger.	A5	19
Schoodic Lake, l., Me., U.S.	C4	96
Schoolcraft, Mi., U.S.	F5	99
Schoolcraft, co., Mi., U.S.	B4	99
Schooleys Mountain, mtn., N.J., U.S.	B3	107
Schoonhoven, Neth.	B3	20
Schopfheim, W. Ger.	B3	20
Schorndorf, W. Ger.	C4	19
Schoten, Bel.	C4	17
Schöttmar, W. Ger.	A3	19
Schouten Islands, is., Indon.	F9	34
Schramberg, W. Ger.	D4	18
Schram City, Il., U.S.	D4	90
Schriever, La., U.S.	E5	95
Schrobenhausen, W. Ger.	D5	18
Schroeder, Mn., U.S.	C8	100
Schroon Lake, N.Y., U.S.	B7	109
Schroon Lake, l., N.Y., U.S.	B7	109
Schuchk, Az., U.S.	E4	80
Schuchuli, Az., U.S.	E3	80
Schulenburg, Tx., U.S.	E4	120
Schuler, Alta.	D5	68
Schulte, Ks., U.S.	g12	93
Schulter, Ok., U.S.	B6	113
Schüpfheim, Switz.	B5	21
Schurz, Nv., U.S.	E3	105
Schussen, stm., W. Ger.	A8	21
Schüttorf, W. Ger.	A2	19
Schuyler, Ne., U.S.	C8	104
Schuyler, Va., U.S.	C4	123
Schuyler, co., Il., U.S.	C3	90
Schuyler, co., Mo., U.S.	A5	102
Schuyler, co., N.Y., U.S.	C4	109
Schuyler Lake, N.Y., U.S.	C5	109
Schuylerville, N.Y., U.S.	B7	109
Schuylkill, co., Pa., U.S.	E9	115
Schuylkill, stm., Pa., U.S.	F10	115
Schuylkill Haven, Pa., U.S.	E9	115
Schwabach, W. Ger.	D5	18
Schwäbische Alb, mts., W. Ger.	E4	19
Schwäbisch Gmünd, W. Ger.	D4	18
Schwäbisch Hall, W. Ger.	D4	18
Schwabmünchen, W. Ger.	A6	20
Schwanden, Switz.	E4	18
Schwandorf, W. Ger.	D6	18
Schwaner Mountains, mts., Indon.	F4	34
Schwarmstedt, W. Ger.	A4	19
Schwarza, stm., W. Ger.	A5	21
Schwarze Elster, stm., E. Ger.	B8	19
Schwarzenbach [an der Saale], W. Ger.	C6	19
Schwarzenbek, W. Ger.	E4	15
Schwarzenberg, E. Ger.	C7	19
Schwarzheide, E. Ger.	B8	19
Schwaz, Aus.	E5	18
Schwedt, E. Ger.	B7	18
Schweinfurt, W. Ger.	C5	19
Schwerin, E. Ger.	B5	18
Schwerin, Lake, l., E. Ger.	B5	18
Schwetzingen, W. Ger.	D3	19
Schwyz, Switz.	E4	18
Schwyz, state, Switz.	B4	20
Sciacca, Italy	C4	21
Science Hill, Ky., U.S.	C5	94
Scilly, Isles of, is., Eng., U.K.	F3	10
Scio, N.Y., U.S.	C3	109
Scio, Oh., U.S.	B4	112
Scio, Or., U.S.	C4	114
Sciota, Il., U.S.	C3	90
Scioto, co., Oh., U.S.	D3	112
Scioto, stm., Oh., U.S.	C3	112
Scioto Furnace, Oh., U.S.	D3	112
Scipio, In., U.S.	F6	91
Scipio, Ok., U.S.	B6	113
Scipio, Ut., U.S.	D3	121
Scircleville, In., U.S.	D5	91
Scituate, Ma., U.S.	B6	98
Scituate Reservoir, res., R.I., U.S.	C3	116
Scobey, Mt., U.S.	B11	103
Scofield, Ut., U.S.	D4	121
Scofield Reservoir, res., Ut., U.S.	D4	121
Scollard, Alta.	D4	68
Scone, Austl.	F8	51
Scooba, Ms., U.S.	C5	101
Scopus, Mount, mtn., Isr.	m14	41
Scoresbysund, Grnld.	B17	128
Scotch Plains, N.J., U.S.	B4	107
Scotia, Ca., U.S.	B1	82
Scotia, Ne., U.S.	C7	104
Scotia, N.Y., U.S.	C7	109
Scotia, S.C., U.S.	F5	117
Scotland, Ont.	D4	73
Scotland, Ct., U.S.	B7	84
Scotland, Ga., U.S.	D4	87
Scotland, Il., U.S.	D6	90
Scotland, In., U.S.	G4	91
Scotland, S.D., U.S.	D8	118
Scotland, co., Mo., U.S.	A5	102
Scotland, co., N.C., U.S.	C3	110
Scotland, ter., U.K.	D6	10
Scotland Neck, N.C., U.S.	A5	110
Scotlandville, La., U.S.	D4	95
Scotrun, Pa., U.S.	D11	115
Scotsburn, N.S.	D7	71
Scotsguard, Sask.	H1	75
Scotstown, Que.	D6	74
Scott, Sask.	E1	75
Scott, Ar., U.S.	C3	81
Scott, Ga., U.S.	D4	87
Scott, La., U.S.	D3	95
Scott, Ms., U.S.	B2	101
Scott, Oh., U.S.	B1	112
Scott, co., Ar., U.S.	C1	81
Scott, co., Il., U.S.	D3	90
Scott, co., In., U.S.	G6	91
Scott, co., Ia., U.S.	C7	92
Scott, co., Ks., U.S.	D3	93
Scott, co., Ky., U.S.	B5	94
Scott, co., Mn., U.S.	F5	100
Scott, co., Mo., U.S.	D8	102
Scott, co., Ms., U.S.	C4	101
Scott, co., Tn., U.S.	C9	119
Scott, co., Va., U.S.	f9	123
Scott, i., Ant.	C31	7
Scott, sci., Ant.	B29	7
Scott, Cape, c., B.C.	D3	69
Scott, Mount, mtn., Ok., U.S.	C3	113
Scott, Mount, mtn., Or., U.S.	E4	114
Scott Air Force Base, mil., Il., U.S.	E4	90
Scott City, Ks., U.S.	D3	93
Scott City, Mo., U.S.	D8	102
Scottdale, Ga., U.S.	h8	87
Scottdale, Pa., U.S.	F2	115
Scott Glacier, ice, Ant.	C23	7
Scott Glacier, ice, Ant.	A33	7
Scott Islands, is., B.C.	D3	69
Scott Lake, Fl., U.S.	*G6	86
Scott Mountain, mtn., Id., U.S.	E3	89
Scott Peak, mtn., Id., U.S.	E6	89
Scott Reef, rf., Austl.	B3	50
Scott Reservoir, res., N.C., U.S.	A1	110
Scotts, Mi., U.S.	F5	99
Scottsbluff, Ne., U.S.	C2	104
Scotts Bluff, co., Ne., U.S.	C2	104
Scotts Bluff National Monument, Ne., U.S.	C2	104
Scottsboro, Al., U.S.	A3	78
Scottsburg, In., U.S.	G6	91
Scottsburg, Or., U.S.	D3	114
Scottsburg, Va., U.S.	D4	123
Scottsdale, Az., U.S.	D4	80
Scotts Hill, N.C., U.S.	C5	110
Scotts Hill, Tn., U.S.	B3	119
Scotts Mills, Or., U.S.	B4	114
Scotts Mountain, mtn., N.J., U.S.	B2	107
Scotts Valley, Ca., U.S.	*D2	82
Scottsville, Ar., U.S.	B2	81
Scottsville, Ks., U.S.	C6	93
Scottsville, Ky., U.S.	D3	94
Scottsville, N.Y., U.S.	B3	109
Scottsville, Va., U.S.	C4	123
Scott Township, Pa., U.S.	*k13	115
Scottville, Il., U.S.	D3	90
Scottville, Mi., U.S.	E4	99
Scourie, Scot., U.K.	B3	13
Scout Lake, Sask.	H3	75
Scow Bay, Ak., U.S.	m23	79
Scraggly Lake, l., Me., U.S.	B4	96
Scranton, Ar., U.S.	B2	81
Scranton, Ia., U.S.	B3	92
Scranton, Ks., U.S.	D8	93
Scranton, Ky., U.S.	C6	94
Scranton, N.C., U.S.	B6	110
Scranton, N.D., U.S.	C2	111
Scranton, Pa., U.S.	D10	115
Scranton, S.C., U.S.	D8	117
Screven, Ga., U.S.	E4	87
Screven, co., Ga., U.S.	D5	87
Scribner, Ne., U.S.	C9	104
Scridain, Loch, b., Scot., U.K.	D2	13
Scrivia, stm., Italy	B2	23
Scugog, Lake, l., Ont.	C6	73
Scullville, N.J., U.S.	E3	107
Scunthorpe, Eng., U.K.	D6	10
Scuol (Schuls), Switz.	E5	18
Scurry, co., Tx., U.S.	C2	120
Scutari, Lake, l., Eur.	D4	24
Scutari see Shkodra, Alb.	A2	40
Scyrene, Al., U.S.	D2	78
Scyros see Skíros, i., Grc.	C5	40
Seaboard, N.C., U.S.	A5	110
Seabreeze, De., U.S.	F5	85
Sea Bright, N.J., U.S.	C5	107
Seabrook, Md., U.S.	*C4	97
Seabrook, N.H., U.S.	E5	106
Seabrook, N.J., U.S.	E2	107
Seabrook, Tx., U.S.	r14	120
Seabrook Beach, N.H., U.S.	E5	106
Seabrook Island, i., S.C., U.S.	F7	117
Sea Cliff, N.Y., U.S.	*E7	109
Seadrift, Tx., U.S.	E4	120
Seaford, De., U.S.	F3	85
Seaford, N.Y., U.S.	*E7	109
Seaford, Va., U.S.	h15	123
Seaforth, Ont.	D3	73
Seaforth, Mn., U.S.	F3	100
Sea Girt, N.J., U.S.	C4	107
Seagoville, Tx., U.S.	n10	120
Seagram Lakes, l., Sask.	E1	75
Seagrave, Ont.	C6	73
Seagraves, Tx., U.S.	C1	120
Seagrove, N.C., U.S.	B3	110
Seaham, Eng., U.K.	F7	13
Seahouses, Eng., U.K.	F7	13
Sea Isle City, N.J., U.S.	E3	107
Seal, stm., Man.	f8	70
Seal Bay, b., Ant.	B11	7
Seal Beach, Ca., U.S.	*n12	82
Seal Cove, N.B.	E3	71
Seal Cove, Newf.	D3	72
Seal Cove, Me., U.S.	D4	96
Sealevel, N.C., U.S.	C6	110
Seal Harbor, Me., U.S.	D4	96
Seal Lake, l., Newf.	g9	72
Sealston, Va., U.S.	B5	123
Sealy, Tx., U.S.	E4	120
Seama, N.M., U.S.	B2	108
Seaman, Oh., U.S.	D2	112
Seaman Range, mts., Nv., U.S.	F6	105
Seanor, Pa., U.S.	F4	115
Searchlight, Nv., U.S.	H7	105
Searcy, Ar., U.S.	B4	81
Searcy, co., Ar., U.S.	B3	81
Searight, Al., U.S.	D3	78
Searles, Al., U.S.	B2	78
Searles, Mn., U.S.	F4	100
Searles Lake, l., Ca., U.S.	E5	82
Searsboro, Ia., U.S.	C5	92
Searsburg, Vt., U.S.	F3	122
Sears Falls, wtfll., Ne., U.S.	B5	104
Searsmont, Me., U.S.	D3	96
Searsport, Me., U.S.	D4	96
Searston, Newf.	E2	72
Seaside, Ca., U.S.	*D3	82
Seaside, Or., U.S.	B3	114
Seaside Heights, N.J., U.S.	D4	107
Seaside Park, N.J., U.S.	D4	107
Seaton, Il., U.S.	B3	90
Seat Pleasant, Md., U.S.	C4	97
Seattle, Wa., U.S.	B3	124
Seattle-Tacoma International Airport, Wa., U.S.	f11	124
Sea View, Ma., U.S.	*H13	98
Seaview, Wa., U.S.	C1	124
Seaville, N.J., U.S.	E3	107
Seaward Roads, strt., Mid. Is.	J3	52
Seba Beach, Alta.	C3	68
Sebaco, Nic.	D4	62
Sebago Lake, Me., U.S.	E2	96
Sebago Lake, l., Me., U.S.	g8	96
Sebasco Estates, Me., U.S.	E3	96
Sebastian, Fl., U.S.	E6	86
Sebastian, co., Ar., U.S.	B1	81
Sebastian, Cape, c., Or., U.S.	E2	114
Sebastian Inlet, b., Fl., U.S.	E6	86
Sebastián Vizcaíno, Bahía, b., Mex.	B2	63

Name	Map Ref.	Page
Sebasticook Lake, l., Me., U.S.	D3	96
Sebastopol, Ca., U.S.	C2	82
Sebastopol, Ms., U.S.	C4	101
Sebatik Island, i., Asia	E5	34
Sebderat, Eth.	B4	47
Sebec, Me., U.S.	C3	96
Sebec Lake, l., Me., U.S.	C3	96
Sebeka, Mn., U.S.	D3	100
Sebeş, Rom.	C6	24
Sebewaing, Mi., U.S.	E7	99
Şebinkarahisar, Tur.	B12	40
Sebnitz, E. Ger.	C7	18
Seboeis, Me., U.S.	C4	96
Seboeis, stm., Me., U.S.	B4	96
Seboeis Lake, l., Me., U.S.	C4	96
Seboomook Lake, l., Me., U.S.	C3	96
Seboyeta, N.M., U.S.	B2	108
Sebree, Ky., U.S.	C2	94
Sebrell, Va., U.S.	D5	123
Sebring, Fl., U.S.	E5	86
Sebring, Oh., U.S.	B4	112
Sebringville, Ont.	D3	73
Secaucus, N.J., U.S.	h8	107
Secchia, stm., Italy	B3	23
Sechelt, B.C.	E6	69
Sechura, Peru	C1	58
Sechura, Bahía de, b., Peru	C1	58
Sechura, Desierto de, des., Peru	C1	58
Seclin, Fr.	D3	17
Seco, Ky., U.S.	C7	94
Second Lake, l., N.H., U.S.	f7	106
Second Mesa, Az., U.S.	B5	80
Secor, Il., U.S.	C4	90
Secretan, Sask.	G2	75
Secretary, Md., U.S.	C6	97
Secretary Island, i., N.Z.	P11	51
Secret Lake, l., R.I., U.S.	E4	116
Section, Al., U.S.	A4	78
Sector Popular (part of Mexico City), Mex.	h9	63
Security, Co., U.S.	C6	83
Sedalia, Alta.	D5	68
Sedalia, Co., U.S.	B6	83
Sedalia, In., U.S.	D4	91
Sedalia, Ky., U.S.	f9	94
Sedalia, Mo., U.S.	C4	102
Sedalia, Oh., U.S.	C2	112
Sedan, Fr.	C6	16
Sedan, Ks., U.S.	E7	93
Sedan, Mn., U.S.	E3	100
Sedan, N.M., U.S.	A6	108
Sedbergh, Eng., U.K.	F6	13
Sederot, Isr.	C6	41
Sedgewick, Alta.	C5	68
Sedgewick, Mount, mtn., N.M., U.S.	B1	108
Sedgewickville, Mo., U.S.	D8	102
Sedgwick, Ar., U.S.	B5	81
Sedgwick, Co., U.S.	A8	83
Sedgwick, Ks., U.S.	E6	93
Sedgwick, Me., U.S.	D4	96
Sedgwick, co., Co., U.S.	A8	83
Sedgwick, co., Ks., U.S.	E6	93
Sédhiou, Sen.	D1	45
Sedillo Hill, N.M., U.S.	k8	108
Sedlčany, Czech.	D9	19
Sedley, Sask.	G3	75
Sedley, Va., U.S.	D6	123
Sedom, Isr.	C7	41
Sedona, Az., U.S.	C4	80
Sedot Yam, Isr.	B6	41
Sedro Woolley, Wa., U.S.	A3	124
Sedrun, Switz.	C6	21
Seebe, Alta.	D3	68
Seeber, stm., Can.	C5	70
Seebert, W.V., U.S.	C4	125
Seehausen, E. Ger.	F5	15
Seeheim, Nmb.	B2	49
Seeis, Nmb.	B2	49
Seekonk, Ma., U.S.	C5	98
Seekonk, stm., R.I., U.S.	E3	116
Seeley, Ca., U.S.	F6	82
Seeley Lake, Mt., U.S.	C3	103
Seeleys Bay, Ont.	C8	73
Seelow, E. Ger.	F8	15
Seelyville, In., U.S.	F3	91
Seelyville, Pa., U.S.	C11	115
Sées, Fr.	C4	16
Seesen, W. Ger.	B5	19
Seez, stm., Switz.	C7	21
Sefadu, S.L.	E2	45
Seferihisar, Tur.	C6	25
Sefíd, stm., Iran	C4	39
Sefíd Ábeh, Iran	F10	39
Segamat, Malay.	K5	35
Sena, N.M., U.S.	B4	108
Segbwema, S.L.	E2	45
Segesta, hist., Italy	F4	23
Segezha, Sov. Un.	F16	14
Segorbe, Spain	C5	22
Ségou, Mali	D3	45
Segovia, Spain	B3	22
Segozero, l., Sov. Un.	F15	14
Segré, Fr.	D3	16
Segre, stm., Eur.	B6	22
Segreganset, Ma., U.S.	C5	98
Seguam Island, i., Ak., U.S.	E5	79
Seguam Pass, strt., Ak., U.S.	E5	79
Séguédine, Niger	B7	45
Séguéla, I.C.	E3	45
Seguin, Tx., U.S.	E4	120
Seguin Falls, Ont.	B5	73
Segundo, Co., U.S.	D6	83
Segura, stm., Spain	C5	22
Sehnkwehn, Lib.	E3	45
Sehore, India	F6	37
Sehwan, Pak.	D1	37
Seibert, Co., U.S.	B8	83
Seiling, Ok., U.S.	A3	113
Seille, stm., Fr.	F6	17
Seinäjoki, Fin.	F10	14
Seine, stm., Fr.	C4	16
Seine, Bay of the, est., Fr.	C3	16
Seine-et-Marne, dept., Fr.	F3	17
Seixal, Port.	f9	22
Sejerby, Den.	C5	15
Sejerø, i., Den.	C5	15
Sejerø Bugt, b., Den.	C5	15
Sekenke, Tan.	C6	48
Seki, Japan	o15	33
Sekiu, Wa., U.S.	A1	124
Sekondi-Takoradi, Ghana	F4	45
Sekota, Eth.	C4	47
Selah, Wa., U.S.	C5	124
Selangor, state, Malay.	K4	35
Selanovtsi, Bul.	D7	24
Selaru, i., Indon.	G8	34
Selatan, Cape, c., Indon.	F4	34
Selatpanjang, Indon.	L5	35
Selawik, Ak., U.S.	B7	79
Selawik Lake, l., Ak., U.S.	B7	79
Selayar, i., Indon.	G6	34
Selb, W. Ger.	C6	18
Selbourne, Cape, c., Ant.	g40	7
Selbu, Nor.	F4	14
Selby, Eng., U.K.	A6	12
Selby, S.D., U.S.	B5	118
Selbyville, De., U.S.	G5	85
Selbyville, W.V., U.S.	C4	125
Selde, Den.	C3	93
Selden, Ks., U.S.	C3	93
Selden, N.Y., U.S.	*n15	109
Seldovia, Ak., U.S.	D10	79
Selebi, stm., Asia	B5	31
Selenga, stm., Asia	A5	31
Selenica, Alb.	B2	25
Selenter, l., W. Ger.	D4	15
Sélestat, Fr.	C7	16
Seletyteniz, Lake, l., Sov. Un.	C8	28
Selfridge, N.D., U.S.	C5	111
Sélibaby, Maur.	C2	45
Selidovo, Sov. Un.	q20	27
Seligenstadt, W. Ger.	C3	19
Seliger, Lake, l., Sov. Un.	C9	27
Seligman, Az., U.S.	B3	80
Seligman, Mo., U.S.	E4	102
Selinsgrove, Pa., U.S.	E8	115
Selinunte, hist., Italy	F4	23
Selizharovo, Sov. Un.	C9	27
Selkirk, Man.	D3	70
Selkirk, Ont.	E5	73
Selkirk, Scot., U.K.	C5	10
Selkirk, Ks., U.S.	D2	93
Selkirk Mountains, mts., N.A.	D9	69
Selle, Pic la, mtn., Haiti	E8	64
Selleck, Wa., U.S.	B4	124
Seller Lake, l., Man.	B4	70
Sellers, Al., U.S.	C3	78
Sellers, S.C., U.S.	C9	117
Sellersburg, In., U.S.	H6	91
Sellersville, Pa., U.S.	F11	115
Sells, Az., U.S.	F4	80
Selm, W. Ger.	B2	19
Selma, N.S.	D6	71
Selma, Al., U.S.	C2	78
Selma, Al., U.S.	D4	81
Selma, Ca., U.S.	D4	82
Selma, In., U.S.	D7	91
Selma, N.C., U.S.	B4	110
Selma, Or., U.S.	E3	114
Selman, Ok., U.S.	A2	113
Selmer, Tn., U.S.	B3	119
Selsey, Eng., U.K.	D7	12
Selsey Bill, c., Eng., U.K.	D7	12
Selva, Arg.	B3	55
Selvagens, Ilhas is., Port.	m14	22
Selvas, for., Braz.	C3	56
Selvin, In., U.S.	H3	91
Selway, stm., Id., U.S.	C3	89
Selwyn, Mount, mtn., B.C.	A6	69
Selwyn Lake, l., Can.	k8	75
Selwyn Mountains, mts., Can.	D6	66
Selz, N.D., U.S.	B6	111
Seman, Alb.	C3	78
Semani, stm., Alb.	B2	25
Semans, Sask.	F3	75
Semara, W. Sah.	D2	44
Semarang, Indon.	G4	34
Semenovka, Sov. Un.	E9	27
Semeru, mtn., Indon.	G4	34
Seminary, Ms., U.S.	D4	101
Seminoe Dam, Wy., U.S.	D6	127
Seminoe Mountains, mts., Wy., U.S.	D6	127
Seminoe Reservoir, res., Wy., U.S.	D6	127
Seminole, Al., U.S.	E2	78
Seminole, Ok., U.S.	B5	113
Seminole, Tx., U.S.	C1	120
Seminole, co., Fl., U.S.	D5	86
Seminole, co., Ga., U.S.	F2	87
Seminole, co., Ok., U.S.	B5	113
Seminole, Lake, res., U.S.	F2	87
Seminole Park, Fl., U.S.	*p10	86
Semipalatinsk, Sov. Un.	D11	29
Semisopochnoi Island, i., Ak., U.S.	E3	79
Semitau, Indon.	E4	34
Semiyarskoye, Sov. Un.	C9	28
Semliki, stm., Afr.	A5	48
Semmens Lake, l., Man.	B4	70
Semmering Pass, Aus.	H15	19
Semmes, Al., U.S.	E1	78
Semnān, Iran	D5	39
Semois, stm., Eur.	E5	17
Semora, N.C., U.S.	A3	110
Semporna, Malay.	E6	34
Sempach Lake, l., Switz.	B4	20
Semur-en-Auxois, Fr.	D6	16
Sen, stm., Camb.	F6	35
Sena, N.M., U.S.	B4	108
Senachwine Lake, l., Il., U.S.	B4	90
Senador Pompeu, Braz.	C3	57
Sena Madureira, Braz.	C4	58
Senanga, Zam.	E3	48
Senate, Sask.	H1	75
Senath, Mo., U.S.	E7	102
Senatobia, Ms., U.S.	A4	101
Sendai, Japan	K5	33
Sendai, Japan	D13	31
Sendai Bay, b., Japan	G10	33
Setúbal, Port.	C1	22
Setúbal, Bay of, b., Port.	C1	22
Seul, Lac, l., Ont.	o16	73
Seul Choix Point, c., Mi., U.S.	C5	99
Sevan, Lake, l., Sov. Un.	E3	28
Sevastopol, Sov. Un.	E6	29
Seven Devils Lake, res., Ar., U.S.	D4	81
Seven Devils Mountains, mts., Id., U.S.	D2	89
Seven Heads, c., Ire.	F3	11
Seven Hills, Oh., U.S.	h9	112
Seven Islands Bay, b., Newf.	f9	72
Seven Mile, Oh., U.S.	C1	112
Seven Mile Beach, N.J., U.S.	E3	107
Sevenoaks, Eng., U.K.	m13	10
Seven Oaks, Pa., U.S.	*C5	117
Seven Persons, Alta.	E5	68
Seven Sisters Peaks, mts., B.C.	B3	69
Seven Springs, N.C., U.S.	B5	110
Seventy Mile House, B.C.	D7	69
Severance, Co., U.S.	A6	83
Severance, Ks., U.S.	C9	93
Severance, N.H., U.S.	D4	106
Severka, stm., Sov. Un.	n18	27
Severn, Md., U.S.	B4	97
Severn, N.C., U.S.	D12	39
Severn, Va., U.S.	C6	123
Severn, stm., Ont.	n17	73
Severn, stm., U.K.	D5	10
Severn, Mouth of the, mth., U.K.	C5	12
Severna Park, Md., U.S.	B4	97
Severnaya Zemlya, is., Sov. Un.	B11	29
Severo, stm., Sov. Un.	B4	97
Severočeský, prov., Czech.	C9	19
Severodonetsk, Sov. Un.	q21	27
Severodvinsk, Sov. Un.	C16	8
Severomorsk, Sov. Un.	C15	14
Severouralsk, Sov. Un.	C21	8
Severy, Ks., U.S.	E7	93
Sevier, co., Ar., U.S.	D1	81
Sevier, co., Tn., U.S.	D10	119
Sevier, co., Ut., U.S.	E4	121
Sevier, stm., Ut., U.S.	D3	121
Sevier, East Fork, stm., Ut., U.S.	F3	121
Sevier Bridge Reservoir, res., Ut., U.S.	D4	121
Sevier Desert, des., Ut., U.S.	D3	121
Sevier Lake, l., Ut., U.S.	E2	121
Sevierville, Tn., U.S.	D10	119
Sevilla, Col.	C2	60
Sevilla, Spain	D3	22
Seville, Fl., U.S.	C5	86
Seville, Ga., U.S.	E3	87
Seville, Oh., U.S.	A4	112
Seville, O., U.S.	D7	24
Sevran, Fr.	g11	16
Sèvre, stm., Fr.	D3	16
Sèvre Niortaise, stm., Fr.	D3	16
Sèvres, Fr.	g9	16
Sewal, La., U.S.	D4	92
Sewanee, Tn., U.S.	D8	119
Seward, Ak., U.S.	C10	79
Seward, Ks., U.S.	D5	93
Seward, Ne., U.S.	D8	104
Seward, N.Y., U.S.	C6	109
Seward, Ok., U.S.	B4	113
Seward, Pa., U.S.	F3	115
Seward, co., Ks., U.S.	E3	93
Seward, co., Ne., U.S.	D8	104
Seward Peninsula, pen., Ak., U.S.	B7	79
Sewaren, N.J., U.S.	k7	107
Sewell, Chile	A2	54
Sewell, N.J., U.S.	D2	107
Sewen, Fr.	A2	21
Sewickley, Pa., U.S.	E1	115
Sexsmith, Alta.	B1	68
Sextonville, Wi., U.S.	E3	126
Seychelles, ctry., Afr.	G24	2
Seydişehir, Tur.	n26	14
Seydisfjördur, Ice.	n26	14
Seyhan (Sarus), stm., Tur.	C10	40
Seylac, Som.	C5	47
Seym, stm., Sov. Un.	F9	27
Seymchan, Sov. Un.	C18	29
Seymour, Austl.	H5	51
Seymour, Ct., U.S.	D3	84
Seymour, Il., U.S.	C5	90
Seymour, In., U.S.	G6	91
Seymour, Ia., U.S.	D4	92
Seymour, Mo., U.S.	D5	102
Seymour, Tn., U.S.	D10	119
Seymour, Tx., U.S.	C3	120
Seymour, Wi., U.S.	D5	126
Seymour Inlet, b., B.C.	D4	69
Seymour Johnson Air Force Base, mil., N.C., U.S.	B5	110
Seymour Lake, l., Vt., U.S.	B4	122
Seymourville, La., U.S.	h9	95
Sézanne, Fr.	C5	16
Sezimbra, Port.	C1	22
Sezze, Italy	D4	23
Sfax, Tun.	C7	44
Shaanxi, prov., China	D6	31
Shabbona, Il., U.S.	B5	90
Shabeellaha Dhexe, prov., Som.	E6	47
Shabeellaha Hoose, prov., Som.	E5	47
Shabeelle (Shebele), stm., Afr.	E5	47
Shabogamo Lake, l., Newf.	h8	72
Shabunda, Zaire	B4	48
Shabwah, Yemen	B6	47
Shache, China	F10	29
Shackelford, co., Tx., U.S.	C3	120
Shackleton, Sask.	G1	75
Shackleton Glacier, ice, Ant.	A31	7
Shackleton Ice Shelf, ice, Ant.	C23	7
Shackleton Range, mts., Ant.	A10	7
Shadehill, S.D., U.S.	B3	118
Shadehill Dam, S.D., U.S.	B3	118
Shadehill Reservoir, res., S.D., U.S.	B3	118
Shades Creek, stm., Al., U.S.	g7	78
Shades Mountain, mtn., Al., U.S.	g7	78
Shadeville, Oh., U.S.	m10	112
Shadow Mountain National Recreation Area, Co., U.S.	A4	83
Shadrinsk, Sov. Un.	B6	28
Shady Cove, Or., U.S.	E4	114
Shady Dale, Ga., U.S.	C3	87
Shady Grove, Al., U.S.	D3	78
Shady Grove, Fl., U.S.	B3	86
Shady Grove, Ky., U.S.	e10	94
Shady Point, Ok., U.S.	B7	113
Shady Rest, Ct., U.S.	*D2	84
Shady Side, Md., U.S.	C4	97
Shadyside, Oh., U.S.	C5	112
Shady Spring, W.V., U.S.	D3	125
Shady Valley, Tn., U.S.	C12	119
Shafer, Lake, l., In., U.S.	C4	91
Shafer Butte, mtn., Id., U.S.	F2	89
Shafter, Ca., U.S.	E4	82
Shafter, Nv., U.S.	C7	105
Shafter, Tx., U.S.	p12	120
Shaftesbury, Eng., U.K.	C5	12
Shaftsbury, Vt., U.S.	E2	122
Shaftsbury Center, Vt., U.S.	*E5	45
Shagamu, Nig.	D9	32
Shageluk, Ak., U.S.	C7	79
Shag Harbour, N.S.	F4	71
Shaguotun, China	D9	32
Shah Alam, Malay.	*K4	35
Shahbanou Farah Dam, Iran	D1	37
Shāhdādkot, Pak.	H2	37
Shahdol, India	F8	37
Shāhgarh, India	C4	36
Shaḩḩāt, Libya	A3	47
Shāhī, i., Iran	C4	36
Shājahānpur, India	C7	36
Shāh Jūy, Afg.	E13	39
Shāhpur, India	I6	37
Shāhpur, Pak.	E3	37
Shāhpura, India	E5	36
Shahrak, Afg.	D12	39
Shahr-e Bābak, Iran	E5	39
Shahr-e Kord, Iran	C5	39
Shāhrūd, stm., Iran	C5	39
Shāhrūd see Emāmshahr, Iran	B5	38
Shakawe, Bots.	A3	49
Shaker Heights, Oh., U.S.	A4	112
Shakhrisyabz, Sov. Un.	B13	39
Shakhty, Sov. Un.	E7	29
Shakhunya, Sov. Un.	B7	28
Shaki, Nig.	E5	45
Shakopee, Mn., U.S.	F5	100
Shakotan, Cape, c., Japan	E10	33
Shaktoolik, Ak., U.S.	C7	79
Shala, Lake, l., Eth.	D4	47
Shalath, B.C.	D6	69
Shaler Mountains, mts., N.W. Ter.	B10	66
Shaler Township, Pa., U.S.	*E2	115
Shalkar, Lake, l., Sov. Un.	C4	28
Shallmar, Md., U.S.	m12	97
Shallotte, N.C., U.S.	D4	110
Shallotte Inlet, b., N.C., U.S.	D4	110
Shallowater, Tx., U.S.	C2	120
Shallow Lake, Ont.	C3	73
Shallow Water, Ks., U.S.	D3	93
Shambat, Sud.	B3	47
Shambaugh, Ia., U.S.	D2	92
Shambe, Sud.	D3	47
Shamīl, Iran	H8	39
Shamokin, Pa., U.S.	E8	115
Shamokin Dam, Pa., U.S.	E8	115
Shamrock, Fl., U.S.	C3	86
Shamrock, Sask.	G2	75
Shamrock, Ok., U.S.	B5	113
Shamrock, Tx., U.S.	B2	120
Shamva, Zimb.	A5	49
Shandaken, N.Y., U.S.	C6	109
Shandī, Sud.	B3	47
Shandon, Ca., U.S.	E3	82
Shandon, Oh., U.S.	n12	112
Shandong, prov., China	D8	31
Shandong Bandao, pen., China	D9	31
Shanghai, China	D5	32
Shanghai, China	E9	31
Shangnan, China	H4	32
Shangqiu, China	E8	31
Shangrao, China	F8	31
Shangshui, China	E7	31
Shangxian, China	H4	32
Shanhaiguan, China	D9	31
Shanhe, China	B6	114
Shannock, R.I., U.S.	F2	116
Shannon, Ga., U.S.	B1	87
Shannon, Il., U.S.	A4	90
Shannon, Ms., U.S.	A5	101
Shannon, co., Mo., U.S.	D6	102
Shannon, co., S.D., U.S.	D3	118
Shannon, i., Grnld.	B16	128
Shannon, stm., Ire.	D2	10
Shannon Lake, l., Wa., U.S.	A4	124
Shannon Airport, Ire.	E3	11
Shannon City, Ia., U.S.	D3	92
Shannontown, S.C., U.S.	D7	117
Shanshan, China	C3	31
Shantou (Swatow), China	G8	31
Shantung see Shandong, prov., China	D8	31
Shantung Peninsula see Shandong Bandao, pen., China	D9	31
Shanwa, Tan.	B5	48
Shanxi, prov., China	D7	31
Shaobo, China	H8	32
Shaoguan, China	G7	31
Shaowu, China	F7	31
Shaoxing, China	F9	31
Shaoyang, China	F7	31
Shap, Eng., U.K.	F6	13
Shapinsay, i., Scot., U.K.	A6	13
Shapki, Sov. Un.	g9	72
Shapio Lake, l., Newf.	s32	14
Shapleigh, Me., U.S.	*E2	96
Shaqqam, Bi'r ash, well, Egypt	G5	40
Sharafkhāneh, Iran	B5	39
Sharangad, Mong.	B2	32
Sharbatāt, Ra's ash-, c., Oman	D5	38
Sharbot Lake, Ont.	C8	73
Sharefford, co., Que.	D5	74
Shari, Japan	E12	33
Sharifah, Ra's, c., Oman	H8	39
Shark Bay, b., Austl.	E1	50
Sharkey, co., Ms., U.S.	C3	101
Shark Point, c., Fl., U.S.	H5	86
Sharktooth Mountain, mtn., B.C.	E7	66
Sharm ash Shaykh, Eg.	D6	43
Sharon, Ct., U.S.	B2	84
Sharon, Ga., U.S.	C4	87
Sharon, Ks., U.S.	E5	93
Sharon, Ma., U.S.	B5	98
Sharon, N.H., U.S.	E3	106
Sharon, N.D., U.S.	B8	111
Sharon, Ok., U.S.	A2	113
Sharon, Pa., U.S.	D1	115
Sharon, S.C., U.S.	B5	117
Sharon, Tn., U.S.	A3	119
Sharon, Vt., U.S.	D4	122
Sharon, W.V., U.S.	m13	125
Sharon, Wi., U.S.	F5	126
Sharon Grove, Ky., U.S.	C2	94
Sharon Hill, Pa., U.S.	p20	115
Sharon Park, Oh., U.S.	n12	112
Sharon Springs, Ks., U.S.	C2	93
Sharon Springs, N.Y., U.S.	C6	109
Sharon Valley, Ct., U.S.	B2	84
Sharonville, Oh., U.S.	n13	112
Sharp, co., Ar., U.S.	A4	81
Sharp, Cape, c., N.S., U.S.	D5	71
Sharpe Lake, l., Man.	B5	70
Sharples, Fl., U.S.	D6	86
Sharples, W.V., U.S.	D3	125
Sharpley, De., U.S.	h7	85
Sharpsburg, Ia., U.S.	D3	92
Sharpsburg, Ky., U.S.	B6	94
Sharpsburg, Md., U.S.	B2	97
Sharpsburg, N.C., U.S.	B5	110
Sharpsburg, Pa., U.S.	k14	115
Sharps Chapel, Tn., U.S.	C10	119
Sharpsville, In., U.S.	D5	91
Sharpsville, Pa., U.S.	D1	115
Sharp Top Mountain, mtn., Ar., U.S.	C2	81
Sharptown, Md., U.S.	C6	97
Sharptown, N.J., U.S.	D2	107
Sharya, Sov. Un.	B7	28
Shashi, China	E8	31
Shashke, Sov. Un.	B4	49
Shasta, co., Ca., U.S.	B2	82
Shasta, Mount, vol., Ca., U.S.	B2	82
Shasta Lake, res., Ca., U.S.	B2	82
Shatney Mountain, mtn., N.H., U.S.	f7	106
Shatsk, Sov. Un.	D13	27
Shatt al 'Arab, stm., Asia	H8	39
Shattuck, Ok., U.S.	A2	113
Shattuckville, Ma., U.S.	A2	98
Shatura, Sov. Un.	E7	29
Shauck, Oh., U.S.	B3	112
Shaunavon, Sask.	H1	75
Shaw, Ms., U.S.	B3	101
Shaw, Or., U.S.	k12	114
Shaw Air Force Base, mil., S.C., U.S.	D7	117
Shawanaga, Ont.	B4	73
Shawangunk Mountains, mts., N.Y., U.S.	D6	109
Shawano, Wi., U.S.	D5	126
Shawano, co., Wi., U.S.	D5	126
Shawano Lake, l., Wi., U.S.	D5	126
Shawboro, N.C., U.S.	A6	110
Shawbridge, Que.	D3	74
Shawhan, Ky., U.S.	B5	94
Shawinigan, Que.	C5	74
Shawinigan Lake, B.C.	g12	69
Shawinigan-Sud, Que.	C5	74
Shawmut, Al., U.S.	C4	78
Shawmut, Mt., U.S.	D7	103
Shawnee, Co., U.S.	B5	83
Shawnee, Ga., U.S.	D5	87
Shawnee, Ks., U.S.	k16	93
Shawnee, Oh., U.S.	C3	112
Shawnee, Ok., U.S.	B5	113
Shawnee, Wy., U.S.	D7	127
Shawnee, co., Ks., U.S.	D8	93
Shawnee Hills, Oh., U.S.	B2	112
Shawnee, Ok., U.S.	B5	113
Shawnee, Tx., U.S.	B2	120
Shawneetown, Il., U.S.	F5	90
Shawsheen, stm., Ma., U.S.	f11	98
Shawsville, Md., U.S.	A4	97
Shawsville, Va., U.S.	C2	123
Shawville, Que.	B8	73
Shaxian, China	F8	31
Shayang, China	I5	32
Shay Gap, Austl.	D3	50
Shaykh Miskīn, Syria	B8	41
Shchekino, Sov. Un.	D11	27
Shchelkovo, Sov. Un.	n18	27
Shchetovo, Sov. Un.	q22	27
Shchigry, Sov. Un.	F11	27
Shchors, Sov. Un.	E9	27
Shchuchinsk, Sov. Un.	C8	28
Shchurovo, Sov. Un.	n18	27
Shebele (Shabeelle), stm., Afr.	D5	47
Sheberghān, Afg.	A4	36
Sheboygan, Wi., U.S.	E6	126
Sheboygan, co., Wi., U.S.	E5	126
Sheboygan, stm., Wi., U.S.	k10	126
Sheboygan Falls, Wi., U.S.	E6	126
Shedd, Or., U.S.	C3	114
Shedden, Ont.	E3	73
Shediac, N.B.	C5	71
Sheekh, Som.	D6	47
Sheelin, Lough, l., Ire.	D3	10
Sheenjek, stm., Ak., U.S.	B11	79
Sheep Creek, stm., Alta.	C1	68
Sheep Haven, b., Ire.	B4	11
Sheep Mountain, mtn., Az., U.S.	E1	80
Sheep Mountain, mtn., Wy., U.S.	C2	127
Sheep Mountain, mtn., Wy., U.S.	B5	127
Sheep Peak, mtn., Nv., U.S.	G6	105
Sheep Range, mts., Nv., U.S.	G6	105
Sheep's Head, c., Ire.	F2	11
Sheeps Heaven Mountain, mtn., Ma., U.S.	A1	98
Sheerness, Alta.	D5	68
Sheerness, Eng., U.K.	C8	12
Sheet Harbour, N.S.	E7	71
Shefar'am, Isr.	B7	41
Shefayim, Isr.	g10	41
Sheffield, N.Z.	O14	51
Sheffield, Eng., U.K.	D6	10
Sheffield, Al., U.S.	A2	78
Sheffield, Il., U.S.	B4	90
Sheffield, Ia., U.S.	B4	92
Sheffield, Ma., U.S.	B1	98
Sheffield, Pa., U.S.	C3	115
Sheffield, Tx., U.S.	D2	120
Sheffield, Vt., U.S.	B4	122
Sheffield Lake, Oh., U.S.	A3	112
Sheffield Lake, l., Newf.	D3	72
Shefford, co., Que.	D5	74
Sheguiandah, Ont.	B3	73
Sheho, Sask.	F3	75
Shehuen, stm., Arg.	D2	54
Sheila, N.B.	B5	71
Shekhūpura, Pak.	B4	37
Shelagski, Cape, c., Sov. Un.	B33	128
Shelbiana, Ky., U.S.	C7	94
Shelbina, Mo., U.S.	B5	102
Shelburn, In., U.S.	F3	91
Shelburne, N.S.	F4	71
Shelburne, Ont.	C4	73
Shelburne, Ma., U.S.	A2	98
Shelburne, Vt., U.S.	C2	122
Shelburne, co., N.S.	F4	71
Shelburne Falls, Ma., U.S.	A2	98
Shelburne Falls, Vt., U.S.	C2	122
Shelburne Pond, l., Vt., U.S.	C2	122
Shelby, Al., U.S.	B3	78
Shelby, In., U.S.	B3	91
Shelby, Ia., U.S.	C2	92
Shelby, Mi., U.S.	E4	99
Shelby, Ms., U.S.	B3	101
Shelby, Mt., U.S.	B5	103
Shelby, Ne., U.S.	C8	104
Shelby, N.C., U.S.	B1	110
Shelby, Oh., U.S.	B3	112
Shelby, co., Al., U.S.	B3	78
Shelby, co., Il., U.S.	D5	90
Shelby, co., In., U.S.	E6	91
Shelby, co., Ia., U.S.	C2	92
Shelby, co., Ky., U.S.	B4	94
Shelby, co., Mo., U.S.	B5	102
Shelby, co., Oh., U.S.	B1	112
Shelby, co., Tn., U.S.	B2	119
Shelby, co., Tx., U.S.	D5	120
Shelbyville, Il., U.S.	D5	90
Shelbyville, In., U.S.	F6	91
Shelbyville, Ky., U.S.	B4	94
Shelbyville, Mo., U.S.	B5	102
Shelbyville, Tn., U.S.	B5	119
Shelbyville, Lake, res., Il., U.S.	D5	90
Sheldahl, Ia., U.S.	e8	92
Sheldon, Il., U.S.	C6	90
Sheldon, Ia., U.S.	A2	92
Sheldon, Mo., U.S.	D3	102
Sheldon, N.D., U.S.	C8	111
Sheldon, S.C., U.S.	F6	117
Sheldon, Tx., U.S.	r14	120
Sheldon, Wi., U.S.	C3	126
Sheldon Springs, Vt., U.S.	B3	122
Sheldonville, Ma., U.S.	B5	98
Shelekhov, Gulf of, b., Sov. Un.	C18	29
Shelikof Strait, strt., Ak., U.S.	D9	79
Shell, Wy., U.S.	B5	127
Shell, stm., Man.	D1	70
Shell, Loch, b., Scot., U.K.	C2	13
Shellbrook, Sask.	D2	75
Shell Creek, Tn., U.S.	C11	119

Name	Map Ref.	Page

Shell Creek, stm., U.S. — A2 83
Shell Creek, stm., Wy., U.S. — B5 127
Shelley, B.C. — C6 69
Shelley, Id., U.S. — F6 89
Shellharbour, Austl. — G8 51
Shell Lake, Sask. — D2 75
Shell Lake, Wi., U.S. — C2 126
Shell Lake, l., Mn., U.S. — D3 100
Shell Lake, l., Wi., U.S. — C2 126
Shellman, Ga., U.S. — E2 87
Shellman Bluff, Ga., U.S. — E5 87
Shellmouth, Man. — D1 70
Shellpot Creek, stm., De., U.S. — h7 85
Shell Rock, Ia., U.S. — B5 92
Shell Rock, stm., Ia., U.S. — B5 92
Shell Rock, West Fork, stm., Ia., U.S. — B5 92
Shellsburg, Ia., U.S. — B6 92
Shelly, Mn., U.S. — C2 100
Shelly Mountain, mtn., Id., U.S. — F5 89
Shelter Harbor, R.I., U.S. — G2 116
Shelter Island, N.Y., U.S. — m16 109
Shelton, Ct., U.S. — D3 84
Shelton, Ne., U.S. — D7 104
Shelton, Wa., U.S. — B2 124
Shemogue, N.B. — C5 71
Shemya Air Force Base, mil., Ak., U.S. — E2 79
Shenandoah, Ia., U.S. — D2 92
Shenandoah, Pa., U.S. — E9 115
Shenandoah, Va., U.S. — B4 123
Shenandoah, co., Va., U.S. — B4 123
Shenandoah, stm., U.S. — A5 123
Shenandoah, North Fork, stm., Va., U.S. — B4 123
Shenandoah, South Fork, stm., Va., U.S. — B4 123
Shenandoah Mountain, mtn., U.S. — B3 123
Shenandoah National Park, Va., U.S. — B4 123
Shenandoah Valley, val., U.S. — B4 123
Shenango River Lake, res., U.S. — D1 115
Shengxian, China — J9 32
Shenipsit Lake, l., Ct., U.S. — B6 84
Shenmu, China — D7 31
Shenqiu, China — H6 32
Shensi see Shaanxi, prov., China — D6 31
Shenyang, China — C9 31
Sheopur, India — E6 37
Shepard, Alta. — D4 68
Shepard Island, i., Ant. — B35 7
Shepardsville, In., U.S. — E3 91
Shepaug, stm., Ct., U.S. — C2 84
Shepaug Dam, Ct., U.S. — D2 84
Shepaug Reservoir, res., Ct., U.S. — C2 84
Shepetovka, Sov. Un. — F6 27
Shepherd, Mi., U.S. — E6 99
Shepherd, Mt., U.S. — E8 103
Shepherd, Tx., U.S. — D5 120
Shepherdstown, W.V., U.S. — B7 125
Shepherdsville, Ky., U.S. — C4 94
Sheppard Air Force Base, mil., Tx., U.S. — C3 120
Shepparton, Austl. — G8 50
Sheppey, Isle of, i., Eng., U.K. — C8 12
Sheppton, Pa., U.S. — E9 115
Shepton Mallet, Eng., U.K. — C5 12
Sheqi, China — H5 32
Sherabad, Sov. Un. — C13 39
Sherard, Ms., U.S. — A3 101
Sherborn, Ma., U.S. — h10 98
Sherborne, Eng., U.K. — D5 12
Sherbrooke, Que. — D6 74
Sherbrooke, co., Que. — D6 74
Sherbrooke Lake, l., N.S. — E5 71
Sherburn, Mn., U.S. — G4 100
Sherburne, N.Y., U.S. — C5 109
Sherburne, co., Mn., U.S. — E5 100
Shercock, Ire. — C5 11
Shereshevo, Sov. Un. — B8 26
Sheridan, Ar., U.S. — C3 81
Sheridan, Co., U.S. — *B6 83
Sheridan, Il., U.S. — B5 90
Sheridan, In., U.S. — D5 91
Sheridan, Ky., U.S. — e9 94
Sheridan, Me., U.S. — B4 96
Sheridan, Mi., U.S. — E5 99
Sheridan, Mo., U.S. — A3 102
Sheridan, Mt., U.S. — E4 103
Sheridan, Or., U.S. — B3 114
Sheridan, Wy., U.S. — B6 127
Sheridan, co., Ks., U.S. — C3 93
Sheridan, co., Mt., U.S. — B12 103
Sheridan, co., Ne., U.S. — B3 104
Sheridan, co., N.D., U.S. — B5 111
Sheridan, co., Wy., U.S. — B5 127
Sheridan, Mount, mtn., Wy., U.S. — B2 127
Sheridan Beach, Wa., U.S. — *B3 124
Sheridan Gardens, Wy., U.S. — *B6 127
Sheridan Lake, Co., U.S. — C8 83
Sheringham, Eng., U.K. — D7 10
Sherman, Ct., U.S. — C2 84
Sherman, Me., U.S. — C4 96
Sherman, Ms., U.S. — A5 101
Sherman, Mo., U.S. — f12 102
Sherman, N.Y., U.S. — C1 109
Sherman, S.D., U.S. — D9 118
Sherman, Tx., U.S. — C4 120
Sherman, co., Ks., U.S. — C2 93
Sherman, co., Ne., U.S. — C6 104
Sherman, co., Or., U.S. — B6 114
Sherman, co., Tx., U.S. — A2 120
Sherman Mills, Me., U.S. — C4 96
Sherman Mountain, mtn., Ar., U.S. — A2 81
Sherman Reservoir, res., Ne., U.S. — C7 104
Sherman Station, Me., U.S. — C4 96
Sherpur, Bngl. — E12 37
Sherrard, Il., U.S. — B3 90
Sherrelwood, Co., U.S. — B6 83
Sherridon, Man. — B1 70
Sherrill, Ar., U.S. — C3 81
Sherrill, N.Y., U.S. — B5 109
Sherrodsville, Oh., U.S. — B4 112
's Hertogenbosch, Neth. — B6 16
Sherwood, P.E.I. — C6 71
Sherwood, Ar., U.S. — C3 81
Sherwood, Ms., U.S. — B5 101
Sherwood, N.D., U.S. — A4 111
Sherwood, Oh., U.S. — A1 112
Sherwood, Or., U.S. — h12 114
Sherwood, Tn., U.S. — D8 119
Sherwood, Wi., U.S. — h9 126
Sherwood Manor, Ct., U.S. — A5 84
Sherwood Park, Alta. — C4 68
Sherwood Park, De., U.S. — i7 85

Shetek, Lake, l., Mn., U.S. — G3 100
Shetland Islands, is., Scot., U.K. — g10 10
Shetucket, stm., Ct., U.S. — C7 84
Shevchenko, Sov. Un. — E8 29
Shevlin, Mn., U.S. — C3 100
Shevut 'Am, Isr. — f10 41
Shewa, prov., Eth. — D4 47
Shewa Gimira, Eth. — D4 47
Shexian, China — J8 32
Sheyenne, N.D., U.S. — B6 111
Sheyenne, stm., N.D., U.S. — C8 111
Sheyenne Lake, res., N.D., U.S. — B5 111
Sheykhābād, Afg. — D14 39
Shiant Islands, is., Scot., U.K. — C2 13
Shiawassee, co., Mi., U.S. — F6 99
Shibām, Yemen — D4 38
Shibecha, Japan — E12 33
Shibata, Japan — H9 33
Shibetsu, Japan — D11 33
Shibetsu, Japan — E12 33
Shibīn al Kawm, Eg. — D3 41
Shibīn al Qanāṭir, Eg. — D3 41
Shicheng, China — K7 32
Shickley, Ne., U.S. — D8 104
Shickshinny, Pa., U.S. — D9 115
Shidao, China — F10 32
Shideler, In., U.S. — D7 91
Shiderty, stm., Sov. Un. — C8 28
Shidler, Ok., U.S. — A5 113
Shiel, Loch, l., Scot., U.K. — D3 13
Shieldaig, Scot., U.K. — C3 13
Shields, Ks., U.S. — D3 93
Shields, N.D., U.S. — C4 111
Shihezi, China — C2 31
Shijiazhuang, China — D7 31
Shikārpur, Pak. — C4 36
Shikohābād, India — D7 37
Shikoku, i., Japan — E11 33
Shiliguri, India — C8 36
Shilka, Sov. Un. — D14 29
Shilka, stm., Sov. Un. — A8 31
Shillington, Pa., U.S. — F10 115
Shillong, India — C9 36
Shiloh, Ga., U.S. — D2 87
Shiloh, N.J., U.S. — E2 107
Shiloh, N.C., U.S. — A6 110
Shiloh, Oh., U.S. — B3 112
Shiloh, Pa., U.S. — *G8 115
Shiloh, Tn., U.S. — B3 119
Shiloh National Military Park, Tn., U.S. — B3 119
Shimabara, Japan — J5 33
Shimanovsk, Sov. Un. — D15 29
Shimber Berris, mtn., Som. — C6 47
Shimen, China — F7 31
Shimizu, Japan — I9 33
Shimoda, Japan — o17 33
Shimodate, Japan — m19 33
Shimoga, India — F6 36
Shimo Island, i., Japan — J4 33
Shimonoseki, Japan — E11 31
Shimotsuma, Japan — m18 33
Shinall Mountain, mtn., Ar., U.S. — h10 81
Shinano, stm., Japan — H9 33
Shīndand, Afg. — B3 36
Shiner, Tx., U.S. — E4 120
Shingbwiyang, Burma — C10 36
Shinglehouse, Pa., U.S. — C5 115
Shingleton, Mi., U.S. — B4 99
Shingū, Japan — J8 33
Shinjō, Japan — G10 33
Shinkolobwe, Zaire — D4 48
Shinnston, W.V., U.S. — B4 125
Shin Pond, Me., U.S. — B4 96
Shinshiro, Japan — o16 33
Shinyanga, Tan. — B5 48
Shinyanga, prov., Tan. — B5 48
Shiocton, Wi., U.S. — D5 126
Shiogama, Japan — G10 33
Shiojiri, Japan — m16 33
Shioya, Cape, c., Japan — H10 33
Ship Bottom, N.J., U.S. — D4 107
Ship Cove, Newf. — E4 72
Ship Harbour, N.S. — E7 71
Ship Island, i., Ms., U.S. — E5 101
Ship Island Pass, strt., Ms., U.S. — g7 101
Shipka Pass, Bul. — D7 24
Shipki Pass, India — B7 37
Shipley, Eng., U.K. — G7 13
Shipman, Sask. — D3 75
Shipman, Il., U.S. — D4 90
Shipman, Va., U.S. — C4 123
Shippagan, N.B. — B5 71
Shippensburg, Pa., U.S. — F6 115
Shippenville, Pa., U.S. — D2 115
Shiprock, N.M., U.S. — A1 108
Ship Rock, mtn., N.M., U.S. — A1 108
Shipshewana, In., U.S. — A6 91
Shipyard, Belize — D7 63
Shiquan, China — E6 31
Shirane, Mount, mtn., Japan — H9 33
Shirase Glacier, ice, Ant. — B16 7
Shīrāz, Iran — C5 38
Shirbīn, Eg. — C3 41
Shire, stm., Afr. — E5 48
Shiretoko, Cape, c., Japan — D12 33
Shiribetsu, Mount, mtn., Japan — E10 33
Shiriya, Cape, c., Japan — F10 33
Shīr Kūh, mtn., Iran — F7 39
Shirley, Ar., U.S. — B3 81
Shirley, Il., U.S. — C4 90
Shirley, In., U.S. — E6 91
Shirley, Ma., U.S. — A4 98
Shirley, N.Y., U.S. — *n16 109
Shirley, W.V., U.S. — B4 125
Shirley Basin, Wy., U.S. — D6 127
Shirley Center, Ma., U.S. — A4 98
Shirley Mills, Me., U.S. — C3 96
Shirley Mountains, mts., Wy., U.S. — D6 127
Shirleysburg, Pa., U.S. — F6 115
Shiroishi, Japan — H10 33
Shirotori, Japan — n15 33
Shirvān, Iran — C8 39
Shishaldin Volcano, vol., Ak., U.S. — E7 79
Shishmaref, Ak., U.S. — B6 79
Shishou, China — J5 32
Shitara, Japan — n16 33
Shively, Ky., U.S. — B4 94
Shivpuri, India — E6 37
Shivwits, l., U.S. — F2 121
Shivwits Plateau, plat., Az., U.S. — A2 80
Shiyan, China — *E7 31
Shizuishan, China — D6 31

Shizuoka, Japan — E12 31
Shkhara, Mount, mtn., Sov. Un. — *E7 29
Shkodra (Scutari), Alb. — A2 40
Shkotovo, Sov. Un. — E6 33
Shoal, stm., Man. — C1 70
Shoal Creek, stm., U.S. — B4 119
Shoal Harbour, Newf. — D4 72
Shoal Lake, Man. — D1 70
Shoal Lake, l., Can. — E4 70
Shoals, In., U.S. — G4 91
Shoals, Isles of, is., Me., U.S. — E2 96
Shoalwater, Cape, c., Wa., U.S. — C1 124
Shobonier, Il., U.S. — E4 90
Shoe Cove, Newf. — D4 72
Shoemakersville, Pa., U.S. — F10 115
Sholes, Ne., U.S. — B8 104
Shomolu, Nig. — *E5 45
Shongaloo, La., U.S. — B2 95
Shongopovi, Az., U.S. — B5 80
Shonkin, Mt., U.S. — C6 103
Shonto, Az., U.S. — A5 80
Shooting Creek, N.C., U.S. — f9 110
Shop Springs, Tn., U.S. — A5 119
Shoreacres, B.C. — E9 69
Shore Acres, Ma., U.S. — h13 98
Shore Acres, N.J., U.S. — C4 107
Shore Acres, R.I., U.S. — E4 116
Shoreham, Mi., U.S. — F4 99
Shoreham, Vt., U.S. — D2 122
Shoreview, Mn., U.S. — m12 100
Shorewood, Il., U.S. — k8 90
Shorewood, Mn., U.S. — n11 100
Shorewood, Wi., U.S. — E6 126
Shorewood Hills, Wi., U.S. — *E4 126
Short Beach, Ct., U.S. — D4 84
Shorter, Al., U.S. — C4 78
Shorterville, Al., U.S. — D4 78
Short Falls, N.H., U.S. — D4 106
Short Mountain, mtn., Tn., U.S. — D8 119
Shortsville, N.Y., U.S. — C3 109
Shoshone, Ca., U.S. — E5 82
Shoshone, Id., U.S. — G4 89
Shoshone, co., Id., U.S. — B2 89
Shoshone, stm., Wy., U.S. — B4 127
Shoshone, North Fork, stm., Wy., U.S. — B3 127
Shoshone, South Fork, stm., Wy., U.S. — B3 127
Shoshone Falls, wtfl., Id., U.S. — G4 89
Shoshone Lake, l., Wy., U.S. — B2 127
Shoshone Mountains, mts., Nv., U.S. — E4 105
Shoshone Peak, mtn., Nv., U.S. — G5 105
Shoshone Range, mts., Nv., U.S. — C5 105
Shoshong, Bots. — B4 49
Shoshoni, Wy., U.S. — C4 127
Shostka, Sov. Un. — F9 27
Shouldice, Alta. — D4 68
Shouns, Tn., U.S. — C12 119
Shoup, Id., U.S. — D4 89
Showell, Md., U.S. — D7 97
Show Low, Az., U.S. — C5 80
Shpola, Sov. Un. — G8 27
Shreve, Oh., U.S. — B3 112
Shreveport, La., U.S. — B2 95
Shrewsbury, Eng., U.K. — D5 10
Shrewsbury, Ma., U.S. — B4 98
Shrewsbury, Mo., U.S. — *f13 102
Shrewsbury, N.J., U.S. — C4 107
Shrewsbury, Pa., U.S. — G8 115
Shrīrangapattana, India — F6 36
Shropshire (Salop), co., Eng., U.K. — B5 12
Shrule, Ire. — D2 11
Shuangcheng, China — B10 31
Shuangjiang, China — G4 31
Shuangliao, China — C9 31
Shuangshan, China — C10 32
Shuangyang, China — C11 32
Shuangyashan, China — B11 31
Shubenacadie, N.S. — D6 71
Shubenacadie Lake, l., N.S. — E6 71
Shubert, Ne., U.S. — D10 104
Shubrā al Khaymah, Eg. — C6 43
Shubrā Khīt, Eg. — C3 41
Shubuta, Ms., U.S. — D5 101
Shucheng, China — I7 32
Shueyville, Ia., U.S. — C6 92
Shū'fāt, Isr. Occ. — h13 41
Shujāābād, Pak. — C3 37
Shuksan, Mount, mtn., Wa., U.S. — A4 124
Shulan, China — D3 33
Shulaps Peak, mtn., B.C. — D6 69
Shule He, stm., China — C4 31
Shulerville, S.C., U.S. — E8 117
Shullsburg, Wi., U.S. — F3 126
Shumagin Islands, is., Ak., U.S. — E7 79
Shumaykh, Libya — C2 43
Shumen, Bul. — D8 24
Shumerlya, Sov. Un. — D16 27
Shumikha, Sov. Un. — B6 28
Shumway, Il., U.S. — D5 90
Shunan Nimrīn, Jord. — h13 41
Shunchang, China — K7 32
Shungnak, Ak., U.S. — B8 79
Shuoxian, China — D7 31
Shuqrah, Yemen — D4 38
Shuqualak, Ms., U.S. — C5 101
Shūr, stm., Iran — D5 39
Shūr, stm., Iran — F7 39
Shuri, Japan — O5 52
Shurugwi, Zimb. — A5 49
Shushan, N.Y., U.S. — B7 109
Shūshtar al Maghārah, mtn., Eg. — D5 41
Shūshtar, Iran — E4 39
Shuswap, stm., B.C. — D8 69
Shuswap Lake, l., B.C. — D8 69
Shutesbury, Ma., U.S. — B3 98
Shuwak, Sud. — C4 47
Shuwaykah, Isr. Occ. — f11 41
Shuya, Japan — N6 52
Shuya, Sov. Un. — C13 27
Shuzenji, Japan — o17 33
Shwebo, Burma — D10 36
Shwegyin, Burma — D2 35
Shyok, stm., India — B7 37
Sialkot, Pak. — B5 36
Siam, Gulf of see Thailand, Gulf of, b., Asia — C2 34
Siam see Thailand, ctry., Asia — B2 34
Sian see Xi'an, China — E6 31
Siantan, i., Indon. — K7 35
Siasconset, Ma., U.S. — D8 98
Siátista, Grc. — B3 25
Siauliai, Sov. Un. — D4 27
Sibay, Sov. Un. — C5 28

Sibbald, Alta. — D5 68
Siberia, In., U.S. — H4 91
Siberia, reg., Sov. Un. — C13 29
Sibert, Ky., U.S. — C6 94
Siberut, i., Indon. — F1 34
Sibi, Pak. — C4 36
Sibiryakov, i., Sov. Un. — B7 128
Sibiti, Congo — B1 48
Sibiu, Rom. — C7 24
Sibley, Ia., U.S. — A2 92
Sibley, La., U.S. — B2 95
Sibley, Ms., U.S. — D2 101
Sibley, Mo., U.S. — h11 102
Sibley, N.D., U.S. — B8 111
Sibley, co., Mn., U.S. — F4 100
Sibolga, Indon. — E1 34
Sibsāgar, India — C9 36
Sibu, Malay. — E4 34
Sibuatan, mtn., Indon. — K3 35
Sibutu Island, i., Phil. — E5 34
Sibutu Passage, strt., Asia — E5 34
Sibuyan Sea, Phil. — C6 34
Sicamous, B.C. — D8 69
Si Chang, i., Thai. — F4 35
Sichomovi, Az., U.S. — B5 80
Sichuan, prov., China — E5 31
Sicily, i., Italy — F4 23
Sicily Island, La., U.S. — C4 95
Sicklerville, N.J., U.S. — D3 107
Sicuani, Peru — D3 58
Sidamo, prov., Eth. — E4 47
Sideling Hill, mtn., U.S. — A1 97
Sideling Hill Creek, stm., Md., U.S. — A1 97
Sidell, Il., U.S. — D6 90
Siderno Marina, Italy — F6 23
Sídheros, Ákra, c., Grc. — E6 40
Sidi bel Abbès, Alg. — C5 43
Sidi Bennour, Mor. — C3 44
Sidi Ifni, Mor. — D2 44
Sidi Kacem, Mor. — *C3 44
Sidikalang, Indon. — m11 34
Sīdī Muḥammad, 'Ayn, well, Libya — H3 40
Sīdī Sālim, Eg. — C2 41
Sidi Slimane, Mor. — *C3 44
Sidlaw Hills, hills, Scot., U.K. — D5 13
Sidley, Mount, mtn., Ant. — B36 7
Sidmouth, Eng., U.K. — D4 12
Sidnaw, Mi., U.S. — B2 99
Sidney, B.C. — E6 69
Sidney, Man. — E2 70
Sidney, Ar., U.S. — A4 81
Sidney, Il., U.S. — C5 90
Sidney, Ia., U.S. — D2 92
Sidney, Me., U.S. — D3 96
Sidney, Mt., U.S. — C12 103
Sidney, Ne., U.S. — C3 104
Sidney, N.J., U.S. — B3 107
Sidney, N.Y., U.S. — C5 109
Sidney, Oh., U.S. — B1 112
Sidney Center, N.Y., U.S. — C5 109
Sidney Lanier, Lake, res., Ga., U.S. — B2 87
Sidon, Ms., U.S. — B3 101
Sidonia, Tn., U.S. — A3 119
Sidon see Ṣaydā, Leb. — B3 38
Sidorovka, Sov. Un. — D25 8
Sidra, Gulf of (Khalīj Surt), b., Libya — C3 43
Sidrolândia, Braz. — C2 56
Siedlce, Pol. — B7 26
Sieg, stm., W. Ger. — C3 18
Siegburg, W. Ger. — C3 18
Siegen, W. Ger. — C4 18
Sieglar, W. Ger. — *C2 19
Siegle, La., U.S. — *B3 95
Siemianowice Śląskie, Pol. — g10 26
Siemiatycze, Pol. — B7 26
Siemreab, Camb. — C2 34
Siena, Italy — C3 23
Sieper, La., U.S. — C3 95
Sieradz, Pol. — C5 26
Sierck, Fr. — A3 21
Siero, Spain — A3 22
Sierpc, Pol. — B5 26
Sierra, co., Ca., U.S. — C3 82
Sierra, co., N.M., U.S. — D2 108
Sierra Blanca, Tx., U.S. — o12 120
Sierra Blanca Peak, mtn., N.M., U.S. — D4 108
Sierra City, Ca., U.S. — C3 82
Sierra Colorada, Arg. — E3 59
Sierra Estrella, mts., Az., U.S. — m8 80
Sierra Gorda, Chile — D2 55
Sierra Leone, ctry., Afr. — E2 45
Sierra Madre, Ca., U.S. — m12 82
Sierra Mojada, Mex. — B4 63
Sierra Nevada, (Simón Bolívar) National Park, Ven. — B3 60
Sierraville, Ca., U.S. — C3 82
Sierra Vista, Az., U.S. — F5 80
Sierre, Switz. — C3 21
Siesta Key, Fl., U.S. — *E4 86
Siesta Key, i., Fl., U.S. — E4 86
Sievierz, Pol. — g10 26
Sífnos, i., Grc. — D5 40
Sifton, Man. — D1 70
Sigatoka, Fiji — I14 52
Sigean, Fr. — F5 16
Sigel, Il., U.S. — D5 90
Sigel, Pa., U.S. — D3 115
Sighetu Marmaţiei, Rom. — B6 24
Sighişoara, Rom. — B7 24
Sighty Crag, mtn., Eng., U.K. — E6 13
Sigli, Indon. — k11 34
Siglufjördur, Ice. — m23 14
Sigmaringen, W. Ger. — A5 20
Signachi, Sov. Un. — B6 29
Signal Hill, U.S. — *n12 82
Signal Mountain, Tn., U.S. — D8 119
Signal Mountain, mtn., Vt., U.S. — C4 122
Signal Mountain, mtn., Va., U.S. — g11 123
Signal Peak, mtn., Az., U.S. — D1 80
Signal Peak, mtn., Ut., U.S. — F2 121
Signy, Switz. — C1 21
Signy-l'Abbaye, Fr. — E4 17
Sigourney, Ia., U.S. — C5 92
Sigsbee, Ga., U.S. — E3 87
Sigsig, Ec. — B2 58
Sigtuna, Swe. — t35 14
Siguatepeque, Hond. — G4 63
Sigüenza, Spain — B4 22
Siguiri, Gui. — D3 45
Sigurd, Ut., U.S. — E4 121
Sími, i., Grc. — D6 40
Similan Islands, is., Thai. — H2 35
Similkameen, stm., N.A. — E7 69
Sihabuhabu, mtn., Indon. — K3 35

Sihanoukville see Kampong Saom, Camb. — C2 34
Sihl Lake, l., Switz. — B6 21
Sihuas, Peru — C2 58
Siˊir, Isr. Occ. — C7 41
Siirt, Tur. — D13 40
Siis, i., Micron. — Q18 52
Sikar, India — C6 36
Sikasso, Mali — D3 45
Sikes, La., U.S. — B3 95
Sikeston, Mo., U.S. — E8 102
Sikhote-Alin Mountains, mts., Sov. Un. — E16 29
Sikiá, Grc. — C5 40
Sikinos, i., Grc. — D5 40
Sikkim, state, India — C8 36
Siklós, Hung. — C4 24
Sil, stm., Spain — A2 22
Silandro, Italy — A3 23
Silang, Phil. — o13 34
Silao, Mex. — m13 63
Silas, Al., U.S. — D1 78
Silat Az Zahr, Isr. Occ. — f11 41
Silchar, India — D9 36
Sile, Tur. — B7 40
Siler City, N.C., U.S. — B3 110
Silerton, Tn., U.S. — B3 119
Silesia, Mt., U.S. — E8 103
Silesia, hist. reg., Pol. — C4 26
Siletz, Or., U.S. — C3 114
Silex, Mo., U.S. — B6 102
Silgarhi-Doti, Nepal — C8 37
Silica, Oh., U.S. — e6 112
Silifke, Tur. — D9 40
Siling Co, l., China — B8 36
Silisili, Mount, mtn., W. Sam. — F11 52
Silistra, Bul. — C8 24
Silivri, Tur. — B7 40
Siljan, Nor. — p27 14
Siljan, l., Swe. — G6 14
Silkeborg, Den. — B3 15
Sillery, Que. — n17 74
Silloth, Eng., U.K. — F5 13
Sil Nakaya, Az., U.S. — E4 80
Siloam, Ga., U.S. — C3 87
Siloam Springs, Ar., U.S. — A1 81
Silsbee, Tx., U.S. — D5 120
Silsby Lake, l., Man. — B4 70
Sils im Domleschg, Switz. — D8 21
Silt, Co., U.S. — B3 83
Silton, Sask. — G3 75
Silva, Mo., U.S. — D7 102
Silva, N.D., U.S. — A6 111
Silva Jardim, Braz. — h6 56
Silvânia, Braz. — B3 56
Silver, S.C., U.S. — D7 117
Silver Bay, Mn., U.S. — C7 100
Silver Bay, N.Y., U.S. — B7 109
Silver Bow, co., Mt., U.S. — E4 103
Silver City, Ia., U.S. — C2 92
Silver City, N.C., U.S. — B3 101
Silver City, Nv., U.S. — D2 105
Silver City, N.M., U.S. — E1 108
Silver Cliff, Co., U.S. — C2 118
Silver Creek, Ga., U.S. — B1 87
Silver Creek, Ms., U.S. — D3 101
Silver Creek, Ne., U.S. — C8 104
Silver Creek, N.Y., U.S. — C1 109
Silver Creek, stm., In., U.S. — H6 91
Silver Creek, stm., Ne., U.S. — g11 104
Silver Creek, stm., Or., U.S. — D7 114
Silverdale, Ks., U.S. — E7 93
Silverdale, Wa., U.S. — B3 124
Silver Fork, Ut., U.S. — *C4 121
Silver Gate, Mt., U.S. — E7 103
Silver Grove, Ky., U.S. — h14 94
Silverhill, Al., U.S. — E2 78
Silver Hill, Md., U.S. — f9 97
Silver Island Mountains, mts., Ut., U.S. — C2 121
Silver Lake, Ks., U.S. — C8 93
Silver Lake, Mn., U.S. — F4 100
Silver Lake, N.H., U.S. — C4 106
Silver Lake, Or., U.S. — D5 114
Silver Lake, Wi., U.S. — F5 126
Silver Lake, l., Ont. — B7 73
Silver Lake, l., De., U.S. — D3 85
Silver Lake, l., Ia., U.S. — A3 92
Silver Lake, l., Me., U.S. — C3 96
Silver Lake, l., N.H., U.S. — C4 106
Silver Lake, l., N.H., U.S. — D7 106
Silver Lake, l., Wa., U.S. — g13 124
Silvermines, Ire. — E3 11
Silverpeak, Nv., U.S. — F4 105
Silver Peak Range, mts., Nv., U.S. — F4 105
Silver Plume, Co., U.S. — *B5 83
Silver Point, Tn., U.S. — C8 119
Silver Run, Md., U.S. — A3 97
Silver Spring, Md., U.S. — C3 97
Silver Springs, Fl., U.S. — C4 86
Silver Springs, Nv., U.S. — D2 105
Silver Springs, N.Y., U.S. — C2 109
Silver Star, Mt., U.S. — E4 103
Silver Star Mountain, mtn., Wa., U.S. — A5 124
Silverstreet, S.C., U.S. — C4 117
Silverthrone Mountain, mtn., B.C. — D4 69
Silvertip Mountain, mtn., Mt., U.S. — C3 103
Silverton, B.C. — E9 69
Silverton, Co., U.S. — D3 83
Silverton, Id., U.S. — B3 89
Silverton, N.J., U.S. — C4 107
Silverton, Oh., U.S. — o13 112
Silverton, Or., U.S. — C4 114
Silverton, Tx., U.S. — B2 120
Silverville, In., U.S. — G4 91
Silvia, Col. — C2 60
Silvies, stm., Or., U.S. — D7 114
Silview, De., U.S. — B3 85
Silwān (part of Jerusalem), Isr. Occ. — h11 41
Simanggang, Malay. — E4 34
Simav, Tur. — C8 40
Simav, stm., Tur. — B7 25
Simcoe, Ont. — E4 73
Simcoe, co., Ont. — C4 73
Simcoe, Lake, l., Ont. — C5 73
Simdega, India — F10 37
Simeulue, i., Indon. — m11 34
Simferopol, Sov. Un. — E6 29
Sími, i., Grc. — D6 40
Simikot, India — C8 37
Similaun, mtn.?

Simití, Col. — B3 60
Simi Valley, Ca., U.S. — E4 82
Simla, Co., U.S. — B6 83
Simleu Silvaniei, Rom. — B6 24
Simmern, W. Ger. — D2 19
Simmesport, La., U.S. — D4 95
Simmie, Sask. — H1 75
Simmons, Mo., U.S. — D5 102
Simms, Mt., U.S. — C5 103
Simms Point, c., Bah. — m16 64
Simms Stream, stm., N.H., U.S. — g7 106
Simonette, stm., Alta. — B1 68
Simonhouse Lake, l., Man. — B1 70
Simonstorp (part of Norrköping), Swe. — u34 14
Simonstown (Simonstad), S. Afr. — D2 49
Simonsville, Vt., U.S. — E3 122
Simoom Sound, B.C. — D4 69
Simpang-kiri, stm., Indon. — K2 35
Simplício Mendes, Braz. — C2 57
Simplon Pass, Switz. — C4 20
Simplon Tunnel, Eur. — A2 23
Simpson, Sask. — F3 75
Simpson, Il., U.S. — F5 90
Simpson, Ks., U.S. — C6 93
Simpson, La., U.S. — C3 95
Simpson, Mn., U.S. — G6 100
Simpson, N.C., U.S. — B5 110
Simpson, Ok., U.S. — C5 113
Simpson, Pa., U.S. — C11 115
Simpson, W.V., U.S. — k10 125
Simpson, co., Ky., U.S. — D3 94
Simpson, co., Ms., U.S. — D4 101
Simpson Creek, stm., W.V., U.S. — k10 125
Simpson Desert, des., Austl. — E6 50
Simpson Peninsula, pen., N.W. Ter. — C15 66
Simpsonville, Ky., U.S. — B4 94
Simpsonville, S.C., U.S. — B3 117
Simrishamn, Swe. — J6 14
Sims, Ar., U.S. — C2 81
Sims, Il., U.S. — E5 90
Sims, In., U.S. — D6 91
Sims, N.C., U.S. — B4 110
Simsboro, La., U.S. — B3 95
Simsbury, Ct., U.S. — B4 84
Sims Chapel, Al., U.S. — D1 78
Sinabang, Indon. — K2 35
Sinai, S.D., U.S. — C8 118
Sinaia, Rom. — C7 24
Sinai Peninsula, pen., Eg. — C3 38
Sinajana, Guam — L10 52
Sinaloa, state, Mex. — B3 63
Sinaloa [de Leyva], Mex. — B3 63
Sinan, China — F6 31
Sinanju, N. Kor. — G2 33
Sinarūl, Eg. — E2 41
Sīnāwan, Libya — C2 43
Sincan, Tur. — *C9 40
Sincé, Col. — B2 60
Sincelejo, Col. — B2 60
Sinclair, Man. — E1 70
Sinclair, Me., U.S. — A4 96
Sinclair, Wy., U.S. — E5 127
Sinclair, Lake, res., Ga., U.S. — C3 87
Sinclair's Bay, b., Scot., U.K. — B5 13
Sinclairville, N.Y., U.S. — C1 109
Sind, co., Pak. — C4 36
Sind, stm., India — D7 37
Sindal, Den. — A4 15
Sindara, Gabon — F2 46
Sindelfingen, W. Ger. — E3 19
Sindirgi, Tur. — C7 40
Sinel'nikovo, Sov. Un. — G10 27
Sines, Port. — D1 22
Sinfra, I.C. — E3 45
Singapore, Sing. — E2 34
Singapore, ctry., Asia — E2 34
Singapore Strait, strt., Asia — L5 35
Singaraja, Indon. — G5 34
Singer, (Hohentwiel), W. Ger. — B4 20
Singer, La., U.S. — D2 95
Singhampton, Ont. — C4 73
Singida, Tan. — B5 48
Singida, prov., Tan. — B5 48
Singitic Gulf, b., Grc. — B4 25
Singkawang, Indon. — E3 34
Singkep, i., Indon. — F2 34
Singkil, Indon. — E1 34
Singleton, Austl. — F8 51
Sinhūng, N. Kor. — F3 33
Siniscola, Italy — D3 23
Sinj, Yugo. — C3 24
Sinjil, Isr. Occ. — g12 41
Sinkāt, Sud. — B4 47
Sinkiang see Xinjiang Uygur, prov., China — C2 31
Sinking Creek, stm., Ky., U.S. — C4 94
Sinking Spring, Oh., U.S. — C2 112
Sinks Grove, W.V., U.S. — D4 125
Sinnamahoning, Pa., U.S. — D5 115
Sinnamary, Fr. Gu. — A4 59
Sinnemahoning Creek, stm., Pa., U.S. — D5 115
Sinnemahoning Creek, First Fork, stm., Pa., U.S. — B5 115
Sînnicolau Mare, Rom. — B5 24
Sinnūris, Eg. — D3 41
Sinop, Tur. — A10 40
Sinpo, N. Kor. — F4 33
Sintaluta, Sask. — G4 75
Sint-Amandsberg (part of Gent), Bel. — C3 17
Sintang, Indon. — E4 34
Sint Christoffelberg, hill, Neth. Ant. — o13 112
Sint Eustatius, i., Neth. Ant. — H13 64
Sint Helenabaai, b., S. Afr. — D2 49
Sint Jacobiparochie, Neth. — A5 17
Sint Kruis, Neth. Ant. — H18 65
Sint-Lenaarts, Bel. — C4 17
Sint Marie, Kaap, c., Neth. Ant. — H18 65
Sint Nicolaas, Aruba — H17 65
Sint-Niklaas (Saint-Nicolas), Bel. — B6 16
Sinton, Tx., U.S. — E4 120
Sintra, Port. — f9 22
Sint-Truiden, Bel. — D5 17
Sinú, stm., Col. — B2 60
Sinŭiju, N. Kor. — D9 31
Sinzig, W. Ger. — s32 14
Sion, Switz. — C3 21
Sioux, co., Ia., U.S. — A1 92
Sioux, co., Ne., U.S. — B2 104
Sioux, co., N.D., U.S. — C4 111
Sioux Center, Ia., U.S. — A1 92
Sioux City, Ia., U.S. — B1 92

Name	Map Ref.	Page
Sioux Falls, S.D., U.S.	D9	118
Sioux Lookout, Ont.	o17	73
Sioux Rapids, Ia., U.S.	B2	92
Sipanok Channel, mth., Sask.	D4	75
Siparia, Trin.	O22	65
Siping, China	C9	31
Sipiwesk Lake, l., Man.	B3	70
Siple, sci., Ant.	B4	7
Siple, Mount, mtn., Ant.	B36	7
Siple Coast, Ant.	A33	7
Sipsey, Al., U.S.	B2	78
Sipsey, stm., Al., U.S.	B2	78
Sipsey Fork, stm., Al., U.S.	A2	78
Sipura, i., Indon.	F1	34
Siquirres, C.R.	E6	62
Siquisique, Ven.	A4	60
Şīr Abū NuʿAyr, i., U.A.E.	I7	39
Siracusa (Syracuse), Italy	F5	23
Sirāiganj, Bngl.	D8	38
Sir Alexander, Mount, mtn., B.C.	C7	69
Sirdar, B.C.	E9	69
Sir Douglas, Mount, mtn., Can.	D3	68
Sir Edward Pellew Group, is., Austl.	C6	50
Siren, Wi., U.S.	C1	126
Siret, Rom.	B8	24
Siret, stm., Eur.	B8	24
Sirhān, Wādī as, val., Asia	C7	43
Sirik, Cape, c., Malay.	E4	34
Sírina, i., Grc.	D6	25
Sir James MacBrien, Mount, mtn., N.W. Ter.	D7	66
Sīrjān, Iran	G7	39
Sirmans, Fl., U.S.	B3	86
Sirmione, Italy	D6	20
Sironj, India	E6	37
Síros, i., Grc.	D5	25
Sirpur, India	H7	37
Sirr, Mushāsh as, well, Eg.	D5	41
Sīrrī, i., Iran	I7	39
Sirsa, India	C6	36
Sir Sandford, Mount, mtn., B.C.	D9	69
Sirvintos, Sov. Un.	A8	26
Sir-Wilfrid, Mont, mtn., Que.	C2	74
Sir Wilfrid Laurier, Mount, mtn., B.C.	C8	69
Sisak, Yugo.	C3	24
Si Sa Ket, Thai.	B2	34
Sishui, China	G7	32
Sisib Lake, l., Man.	C2	70
Sisipuk Lake, l., Can.	B1	70
Siskiyou, co., Ca., U.S.	B2	82
Siskiyou Mountains, mts., U.S.	F3	114
Siskiyou Pass, Or., U.S.	E4	114
Sisquoc, Ca., U.S.	E3	82
Sissach, Switz.	B4	21
Sisseton, S.D., U.S.	B8	118
Sisseton Indian Reservation, U.S.	B8	118
Sissiboo, stm., N.S.	E4	71
Sisson Branch Reservoir, res., N.B.	B2	71
Sissonville, W.V., U.S.	C3	125
Sisteron, Fr.	E12	16
Sisterdale, Tx., U.S.	E3	120
Sisters, Or., U.S.	C5	114
Sistersville, W.V., U.S.	B4	125
Sītāpur, India	C7	36
Sitía, Grc.	E6	40
Sítio da Abadia, Braz.	A3	56
Sitionuevo, Col.	A3	60
Sitka, Ak., U.S.	D12	79
Sitka National Historical Park, Ak., U.S.	m22	79
Sitka Sound, strt., Ak., U.S.	m22	79
Sittard, Neth.	D5	17
Sittoung, stm., Burma.	E10	36
Sittwe (Akyab), Burma	D9	36
Siuna, Nic.	D5	62
Siuri, India	D8	36
Sivas, Tur.	C11	40
Siverek, Tur.	D12	40
Sīwah, Eg.	C4	38
Siwalik Range, mts., India	B6	36
Six-Fours-la-Plage, Fr.	F6	16
Sixian, China	H7	32
Si see Xi Jiang, stm., China	G7	31
Six Mile, S.C., U.S.	B2	117
Sixmile Creek, stm., Fl., U.S.	n8	86
Sixmilecross, N. Ire., U.K.	C4	11
Sixt, Fr.	D2	21
Sizhan, China	B2	33
Sjælland, i., Den.	J4	14
Sjællands Odde, pen., Den.	B5	15
Sjenica, Yugo.	D5	24
Sjöbo, Swe.	C7	15
Skælskør, Den.	C5	15
Skærbæk, Den.	C2	15
Skagen, Den.	A4	15
Skagerrak, strt., Eur.	I3	14
Skagit, co., Wa., U.S.	A4	124
Skagit, stm., N.A.	A3	69
Skagway, Ak., U.S.	D12	79
Skælderviken, b., Swe.	C6	15
Skalka Reservoir, res., Czech.	C7	19
Skamania, Wa., U.S.	D3	124
Skamania, co., Wa., U.S.	D3	124
Skamokawa, Wa., U.S.	C2	124
Skanderborg, Den.	B3	15
Skaneateles, N.Y., U.S.	C4	109
Skaneateles Lake, l., N.Y., U.S.	C4	109
Skanee, Mi., U.S.	B2	99
Skånes-Fagerhult, Swe.	B7	15
Skanör, Swe.	C6	15
Skántzoura, i., Grc.	C5	25
Skara, Swe.	H5	14
Skarven, l., Swe.	t35	14
Skarzysko-Kamienna, Pol.	C6	26
Skawa, stm., Pol.	h11	26
Skawina, Pol.	D5	26
Skedee, Ok., U.S.	A5	113
Skeena, stm., B.C.	F7	66
Skeena Mountains, mts., B.C.	E7	66
Skegness, Eng., U.K.	D7	10
Skeldon, Guy.	A3	59
Skeleton Lake, l., Ont.	B5	73
Skellefteå, Swe.	E9	14
Skellefteå, stm., Swe.	E8	14
Skellytown, Tx., U.S.	B2	120
Skelton, W.V., U.S.	n13	125
Skelton Glacier, ice, Ant.	f40	7
Skene, Ms., U.S.	B3	101
Skerries, Ire.	D5	11
Skerry, Stack, rock, Scot., U.K.	A4	13
Skhimatárion, Grc.	g11	25
Skiáthos, Grc.	C4	25
Skiáthos, i., Grc.	C4	25
Skiatook, Ok., U.S.	A5	113
Skiatook Reservoir, res., Ok., U.S.	A5	113
Skibbereen, Ire.	E2	10
Skibby, Den.	C5	15
Skiddaw, mtn., Eng., U.K.	F5	13
Skidegate, B.C.	C2	69
Skidegate Inlet, b., B.C.	C2	69
Skidmore, Mo., U.S.	A2	102
Skidmore, Tx., U.S.	E4	120
Skien, Nor.	H3	14
Skierniewice, Pol.	C6	26
Skihist Mountain, mtn., B.C.	D7	69
Skikda (Philippeville), Alg.	B6	44
Skillet Fork, stm., Il., U.S.	E5	90
Skillman, N.J., U.S.	C3	107
Skipperville, Al., U.S.	D4	78
Skipton, Eng., U.K.	G7	13
Skíros, Grc.	C5	40
Skíros (Scyros), i., Grc.	C5	40
Skive, Den.	B3	15
Skjern, Den.	C2	15
Skjern Å, stm., Den.	C2	15
Skoczów, Pol.	h9	26
Skofja Loka, Yugo.	B2	24
Škofja Loka, Yugo.	A6	90
Skokie, Il., U.S.	A6	90
Skokomish Indian Reservation, Wa., U.S.	B2	124
Skole, Sov. Un.	D7	26
Skópelos, i., Grc.	C4	40
Skopin, Sov. Un.	E12	27
Skopje, Yugo.	D5	24
Skørping, Den.	B3	15
Skotovataya, Sov. Un.	q20	27
Skotselv, Nor.	p27	14
Skövde, Swe.	H5	14
Skovorodino, Sov. Un.	D15	29
Skowhegan, Me., U.S.	D3	96
Skownan, Man.	D2	70
Skradin, Yugo.	D2	24
Skreen, Ire.	C3	11
Skull, Ire.	F2	11
Skull Valley, Az., U.S.	C3	80
Skull Valley, val., Ut., U.S.	C3	121
Skull Valley Indian Reservation, Ut., U.S.	C3	121
Skuna, stm., Ms., U.S.	B4	101
Skurup, Swe.	D6	92
Skutskär, Swe.	C7	15
Skvira, Sov. Un.	G7	27
Skwentna, Ak., U.S.	g16	79
Skwentna, stm., Ak., U.S.	g15	79
Skwierzyna (Schwerin), Pol.	B3	26
Skye, Island of, i., Scot., U.K.	B3	10
Skykomish, Wa., U.S.	B4	124
Skykomish, stm., Wa., U.S.	B4	124
Sky Lake, Fl., U.S.	*D5	86
Skyland, Nv., U.S.	D2	105
Skyland, N.C., U.S.	f10	110
Skylight, Ky., U.S.	g11	94
Skylight Mountain, mtn., Ar., U.S.	B1	81
Skyline, Al., U.S.	A3	78
Skyline, Co., U.S.	C6	83
Skyway, Co., U.S.	*f11	114
Skyway, Wa., U.S.	*C3	107
Slackwood, N.J., U.S.	C6	94
Slade, Ky., U.S.	C2	95
Slagle, La., U.S.	G3	34
Slamet, mtn., Indon.	D5	11
Slane, Ire.	E5	11
Slaney, stm., Ire.	C6	15
Slangerup, Den.	C7	24
Slánic, Rom.	n17	26
Slaný, Czech.	A1	113
Slapout, Ok., U.S.	o17	26
Slapy Reservoir, res., Czech.	D9	19
Slater, Co., U.S.	A3	83
Slater, Ia., U.S.	C4	92
Slater, Mo., U.S.	B4	102
Slater, S.C., U.S.	A3	117
Slatersville, R.I., U.S.	A3	116
Slatersville Reservoir, res., R.I., U.S.	B3	116
Slate Spring, Ms., U.S.	B4	101
Slatina, Rom.	C7	24
Slatington, Pa., U.S.	E10	115
Slaton, Tx., U.S.	C2	120
Slave, stm., Can.	D10	66
Slaughter, La., U.S.	D4	95
Slaughter Beach, De., U.S.	E4	85
Slaughters, Ky., U.S.	C2	94
Slave, stm., Can.	D10	66
Slave Lake, Alta.	B3	68
Slavgorod, Sov. Un.	D10	29
Slavonia, hist. reg., Yugo.	C3	24
Slavonska Požega, Yugo.	C3	24
Slavonski Brod, Yugo.	C4	24
Slavsk, Sov. Un.	A6	26
Slavyanoserbsk, Sov. Un.	q21	27
Slavyansk, Sov. Un.	G11	27
Slavyansk-na-Kubani, Sov. Un.	I12	27
Stawków, Pol.	g10	26
Stawno, Pol.	A4	26
Slayden, Ms., U.S.	A4	101
Slayton, Mn., U.S.	G3	100
Slaytonville, De., U.S.	E3	85
Sleaford, Eng., U.K.	A7	12
Slea Head, c., Ire.	E1	11
Sleat, Point of, c., Scot., U.K.	C2	13
Sleat, Sound of, strt., Scot., U.K.	C3	13
Sledge, Ms., U.S.	A3	101
Sled Lake, l., Sask.	C2	75
Sleeper, Ms., U.S.	D5	102
Sleeping Bear Dunes National Lakeshore, Mi., U.S.	D4	99
Sleeping Bear Point, c., Mi., U.S.	D4	99
Sleepy Creek, W.V., U.S.	B6	125
Sleepy Eye, Mn., U.S.	F4	100
Sleepy Point, c., Fiji	H15	52
Sleetmute, Ak., U.S.	C8	79
Slemp, Ky., U.S.	C6	94
Slick, Ok., U.S.	B5	113
Slick Rock, Co., U.S.	C2	83
Slickville, Pa., U.S.	F2	115
Slidell, La., U.S.	D6	95
Slide Mountain, mtn., N.Y., U.S.	D6	109
Sliderock Mountain, mtn., Mt., U.S.	D3	103
Slieve Aughty Mountains, mts., Ire.	D3	11
Slievecallan, hill, Ire.	E2	11
Slievekimalta, mtn., Ire.	E3	11
Slieve Mish Mountains, mts., Ire.	E2	11
Slievenamon, mtn., Ire.	E4	11
Sligo, Ire.	C3	10
Sligo, Pa., U.S.	D3	115
Sligo, co., Ire.	C3	11
Sligo Bay, b., Ire.	C2	10
Slim Buttes, hills, S.D., U.S.	B2	118
Slinger, Wi., U.S.	E5	126
Slippery Rock, Pa., U.S.	D1	115
Sliven, Bul.	D8	24
Slivenec, Czech.	n17	26
Sloan, Ia., U.S.	B1	92
Sloan, Nv., U.S.	H6	105
Sloan, N.Y., U.S.	C2	109
Sloans Valley, Ky., U.S.	D5	94
Sloat, Ca., U.S.	*C3	82
Sloatsburg, N.Y., U.S.	*D6	109
Slobodskoy, Sov. Un.	B4	28
Slobozia, Rom.	C8	24
Slocan, B.C.	E9	69
Slocan Lake, l., B.C.	E9	69
Slocomb, Al., U.S.	D4	78
Slocum, R.I., U.S.	E3	116
Slonim, Sov. Un.	E5	27
Slope, co., N.D., U.S.	C2	111
Slough, Eng., U.K.	k11	10
Slovak, Ar., U.S.	C4	81
Slovakia, hist. reg., Czech.	D5	26
Slovan, Pa., U.S.	F1	115
Slovenia, hist. reg., Yugo.	C2	24
Stubice, Pol.	A9	19
Sluch, stm., Sov. Un.	F6	27
Slunj, Yugo.	C2	24
Stupca, Pol.	B4	26
Stupia, stm., Pol.	A4	26
Stupsk, Pol.	A4	26
Slutsk, Sov. Un.	E6	27
Slyne Head, c., Ire.	D1	10
Slyudyanka, Sov. Un.	D13	29
Smackover, Ar., U.S.	D3	81
Smackover Creek, stm., Ar., U.S.	D3	81
Smålandsfarvandet, strt., Den.	C5	15
Small Point, Me., U.S.	g8	96
Small Point, c., Me., U.S.	g8	96
Smallwood Reservoir, res., Newf.	g8	72
Smarr, Ga., U.S.	D3	87
Smarts Mountain, mtn., N.H., U.S.	C2	106
Smeaton, Sask.	D3	75
Smečno, Czech.	n17	26
Smederevo, Yugo.	C5	24
Smela, Sov. Un.	G8	27
Smelterville, Id., U.S.	B2	89
Smethport, Pa., U.S.	C5	115
Smethwick (Warley), Eng., U.K.	D5	10
Smíchov (part of Prague), Czech.	n17	26
Smicksburg, Pa., U.S.	E3	115
Smidovich, Sov. Un.	B6	33
Smiley, Sask.	F1	75
Smiley, Tx., U.S.	E4	120
Smirnov, Sov. Un.	H11	27
Smith, Alta.	B3	68
Smith, Nv., U.S.	E2	105
Smith, co., Ks., U.S.	C5	93
Smith, co., Ms., U.S.	C4	101
Smith, co., Tn., U.S.	A5	119
Smith, co., Tx., U.S.	C5	120
Smith, stm., U.S.	D23	123
Smith, stm., Mt., U.S.	D5	103
Smith, Cape, c., Ont.	B3	73
Smith and Sayles Reservoir, res., R.I., U.S.	B2	116
Smith Bay, b., Ak., U.S.	A9	79
Smithboro, Il., U.S.	E4	90
Smithburg, W.V., U.S.	B4	125
Smith Canyon, val., Co., U.S.	D7	83
Smith Center, Ks., U.S.	C5	93
Smithdale, Ms., U.S.	D3	101
Smithers, B.C.	B4	69
Smithers, W.V., U.S.	C3	125
Smithfield, Il., U.S.	C3	90
Smithfield, Me., U.S.	D3	96
Smithfield, Mo., U.S.	D5	102
Smithfield, Ne., U.S.	D6	104
Smithfield, N.C., U.S.	B4	110
Smithfield, Oh., U.S.	B5	112
Smithfield, Pa., U.S.	G2	115
Smithfield, Ut., U.S.	B4	121
Smithfield, Va., U.S.	D6	123
Smithfield, W.V., U.S.	k9	125
Smith Island, i., B.A.T.	C6	7
Smith Island, i., Md., U.S.	D5	97
Smith Island, i., Va., U.S.	*C2	123
Smithland, Ia., U.S.	B2	92
Smithland, Ky., U.S.	e9	94
Smithmill, Pa., U.S.	E5	115
Smith Mills, Ky., U.S.	C2	94
Smith Mountain Lake, res., Va., U.S.	C3	123
Smith Peak, mtn., Id., U.S.	A2	89
Smith Peninsula, pen., Ant.	B6	7
Smith Point, c., N.S.	D6	71
Smith Point, c., Ma., U.S.	D7	98
Smith Point, c., Va., U.S.	C6	123
Smith River, Ca., U.S.	B1	82
Smiths, Al., U.S.	C4	78
Smithsburg, Md., U.S.	A3	97
Smiths Cove, N.S.	E4	71
Smiths Falls, Ont.	C8	73
Smiths Ferry, Id., U.S.	E2	89
Smiths Grove, Ky., U.S.	C3	94
Smithshire, Il., U.S.	C2	90
Smithsonia, Ga., U.S.	B3	87
Smith Sound, strt., B.C.	C3	69
Smithton, Austl.	o15	50
Smithton, Il., U.S.	E4	90
Smithton, Mo., U.S.	C4	102
Smith Town, Ky., U.S.	D5	102
Smithtown, N.Y., U.S.	n15	109
Smithville, Ar., U.S.	A4	81
Smithville, Ga., U.S.	E2	87
Smithville, In., U.S.	F5	91
Smithville, Mo., U.S.	A5	101
Smithville, Ms., U.S.	B5	101
Smithville, N.H., U.S.	E3	106
Smithville, Oh., U.S.	B4	112
Smithville, Ok., U.S.	C7	113
Smithville, Tn., U.S.	D8	119
Smithville, Tx., U.S.	D4	120
Smithville, W.V., U.S.	B3	125
Smithville Flats, N.Y., U.S.	C5	109
Smithville Lake, res., Mo., U.S.	B3	102
Smoaks, S.C., U.S.	E6	117
Smoke Creek Desert, des., Nv., U.S.	C2	105
Smokerun, Pa., U.S.	E5	115
Smokey, Cape, c., N.S.	C9	71
Smokey Dome, mtn., Id., U.S.	F4	89
Smoky, stm., Alta.	B1	68
Smoky, Cape, c., Austl.	E9	51
Smoky Hill, stm., U.S.	D5	93
Smoky Hill, North Fork, stm., U.S.	C2	93
Smoky Junction, Tn., U.S.	C9	119
Smoky Lake, Alta.	B4	68
Smoky Mountains, mts., Id., U.S.	F4	89
Sodus, N.Y., U.S.	B3	109
Sodus Point, N.Y., U.S.	B4	109
Soest, W. Ger.	C4	18
Sofádhes, Grc.	C4	25
Sofala, dept., Moz.	A5	49
Sofia (Sofiya), Bul.	D6	24
Sofia, stm., Madag.	g9	49
Sofiyevka, Sov. Un.	G9	27
Sogamoso, Col.	B3	60
Sögel, W. Ger.	B7	17
Sogndal, Nor.	G1	14
Söğüt, Tur.	C8	25
Soham, N.M., U.S.	B4	108
Soignies, Bel.	D4	17
Sointula, B.C.	D4	69
Soissons, Fr.	C5	16
Sokal, Sov. Un.	F5	27
Sokcho, S. Kor.	G4	33
Söke, Tur.	D2	40
Sokehs Passage, strt., Micron.	Q17	52
Sokhondo, Mount, mtn., Sov. Un.	E14	29
Sokodé, Togo	E5	45
Sokol, Sov. Un.	B13	27
Sokółka, Pol.	B7	26
Sokolo, Mali	D3	45
Sokolov, Czech.	C7	19
Sokoto, Nig.	D6	45
Sol, Pico do, mtn., Braz.	C4	56
Sofa, stm., Pol.	h10	26
Songjiang, China	E9	31
Sŏngjin see Kimchaek, N. Kor.	C10	31
Solana Beach, Ca., U.S.	*F5	82
Solano, co., Ca., U.S.	C2	82
Solano, N.M., U.S.	B5	108
Solano, Phil.	n13	34
Solano, stm., Co., U.S.	C3	82
Solapūr, India	E6	36
Solbad Hall [in Tirol], Aus.	E5	18
Soldatovo, Sov. Un.	C2	92
Soldier, Ia., U.S.	C8	93
Soldier, Ks., U.S.	B6	94
Soldier, Ky., U.S.	*D5	118
Soldier Creek, stm., S.D., U.S.	C8	93
Soldier Creek, stm., Ks., U.S.	s3	86
Soldier Key, i., Fl., U.S.	A4	96
Soldier Pond, Me., U.S.	D4	121
Soldiers Grove, Wi., U.S.	E3	126
Soldier Summit, Ut., U.S.	g16	79
Soldotna, Ak., U.S.	A3	60
Soledad, Col.	D3	82
Soledad, Ca., U.S.	B5	60
Soledad, Ven.	*C4	63
Soledad Diez Gutiérrez, Mex.	B1	124
Soleduck, stm., Wa., U.S.	C5	111
Solen, N.D., U.S.	D3	17
Solesmes, Fr.	E6	12
Solihull, Eng., U.K.	D8	29
Solikamsk, Sov. Un.	C5	28
Sol-Iletsk, Sov. Un.	F3	11
Soliman, Tun.	D5	38
Solingen, W. Ger.	C13	14
Sollas, Scot., U.K.	*H8	14
Sollefteå, Swe.	C7	22
Soller, Spain	C3	109
Sollihögda, Nor.	H7	14
Solna, Swe.	B2	86
Solomon, Az., U.S.	D5	93
Solomon, Ks., U.S.	C6	93
Solomon, stm., Ks., U.S.	C4	93
Solomon, North Fork, stm., Ks., U.S.	C4	93
Solomon, South Fork, stm., Ks., U.S.	*D3	82
Solomon Islands, ctry., Oc.	G9	6
Solomons, Md., U.S.	D5	97
Solomon Sea, Oc.	B9	31
Solon, China	C6	92
Solon, Ia., U.S.	A4	112
Solon, Oh., U.S.	h8	90
Solon Mills, Il., U.S.	C6	126
Solon Springs, Wi., U.S.	E3	18
Solothurn, Switz.	E3	18
Solothurn, state, Switz.	D15	29
Solovyevsk, Sov. Un.	F4	91
Solsberry, In., U.S.	D3	24
Šolta, i., Yugo.	B4	18
Soltau, W. Ger.	B4	109
Solvay, N.Y., U.S.	C5	100
Solway, Mn., U.S.	C5	13
Solway Firth, est., U.K.	D4	48
Solwezi, Zam.	D6	47
Soma, Tur.	C4	24
Somalia, ctry., Afr.	E2	73
Sombor, Yugo.	C4	63
Sombra, Ont.	G9	36
Sombrerete, Mex.	D3	56
Sombrero Channel, strt., India	D2	107
Sombrio, Braz.	B6	34
Somerdale, N.J., U.S.	A8	27
Somers, Ct., U.S.	B6	84
Somers, Ia., U.S.	B3	92
Somers, Mt., U.S.	B2	103
Somers, Wi., U.S.	F6	126
Somerset, Ber.	p19	64
Somerset, Co., U.S.	C3	83
Somerset, In., U.S.	C6	91
Somerset, Ky., U.S.	C5	94
Somerset, Ma., U.S.	C5	98
Somerset, Oh., U.S.	C3	112
Somerset, Pa., U.S.	F3	115
Somerset, Tx., U.S.	k7	120
Somerset, Wi., U.S.	C1	126
Somerset, co., Eng., U.K.	C5	12
Somerset, co., Md., U.S.	D6	97
Somerset, co., N.J., U.S.	B3	107
Somerset, co., Pa., U.S.	G3	115
Somerset East, S. Afr.	D4	48
Somerset Island, i., Ber.	p19	64
Somerset Island, i., N.W. Ter.	B14	67
Somerset Reservoir, res., Vt., U.S.	E3	122
Somers Point, N.J., U.S.	E3	107
Somersville, Ct., U.S.	B6	84
Somersworth, N.H., U.S.	D5	106
Somerton, Az., U.S.	E1	80
Somervell, co., Tx., U.S.	C4	120
Somerville, In., U.S.	H3	91
Somerville, Ma., U.S.	B5	98
Somerville, N.J., U.S.	B3	107
Somerville, Tn., U.S.	B2	119
Somerville, Tx., U.S.	D4	120
Somerville Lake, res., Tx., U.S.	D4	120
Someş (Szamos), stm., Eur.	B6	24
Sommatino, Italy	L9	23
Somme, dept., Fr.	B2	17
Somme, stm., Fr.	B4	16
Sommepy [-Tahure], Fr.	E4	17
Sömmerda, E. Ger.	B6	19
Semmesous, Fr.	F4	17
Somonauk, Il., U.S.	B5	90
Somosomo, Fiji	H16	52
Somosomo Strait, strt., Fiji	H15	52
Somoto, Nic.	E7	62
Sompeta, India	H10	37
Somuncurá, Meseta de, plat., Arg.	C3	54
Somvix, Switz.	C6	21
Son, stm., India	D7	36
Soná, Pan.	F7	62
Sönchön, N. Kor.	G2	33
Soncino, Italy	D5	20
Sønder, stm., Den.	D3	15
Sønderborg, Den.	D3	15
Sønderho, Den.	C2	15
Sønderjylland, co., Den.	C3	15
Sønder Omme, Den.	C2	15
Sondershausen, E. Ger.	C5	18
Søndervig, Den.	B2	15
Sondheimer, La., U.S.	B4	95
Sondrio, Italy	A2	23
Sonepur, India	D7	36
Sonestown, Pa., U.S.	D8	115
Song, Nig.	E7	45
Song Cau, Viet.	F8	35
Songea, Tan.	D6	48
Songhua Jiang, stm., China	B10	31
Songjiang, China	E9	31
Songkhla, Thai.	G2	33
Songnim (Kyōmipo), N. Kor.	C1	48
Songololo, Zaire	J3	32
Songtao, China	C5	32
Sonid Youqi, China	E6	36
Sonid Zuoqi, China	E5	18
Son La, Viet.	B5	35
Sonmiāni, Pak.	C4	36
Sonmiāni Bay, b., Pak.	I13	39
Sonneberg, E. Ger.	C5	18
Sonnette, Mt., U.S.	E11	103
Sonningdale, Sask.	E2	75
Sono, Rio do, stm., Braz.	C1	57
Sonobe, Japan	n14	33
Sonoita, Az., U.S.	F5	80
Sonoma, Ca., U.S.	C2	82
Sonoma, co., Ca., U.S.	C2	82
Sonoma Peak, mtn., Nv., U.S.	C4	105
Sonoma Range, mts., Nv., U.S.	C4	105
Sonora, Ca., U.S.	D3	82
Sonora, Ky., U.S.	C4	94
Sonora, Oh., U.S.	C4	112
Sonora, Tx., U.S.	D2	120
Sonora, state, Mex.	B2	63
Sonqor, Iran	D3	39
Sonsón, Col.	B2	60
Sonsonate, El Sal.	E7	63
Sontag, Ms., U.S.	D3	101
Sonthofen, W. Ger.	A9	21
Sonyea, N.Y., U.S.	C3	109
Sooke, B.C.	E6	69
Soo Locks, N.A.	B6	99
Sopchoppy, Fl., U.S.	B2	86
Soper, Ok., U.S.	C6	113
Soperton, Ga., U.S.	D4	87
Sophia, N.C., U.S.	B3	110
Sophia, W.V., U.S.	D3	125
Sopot, Pol.	A5	26
Sopron, Hung.	*D3	82
Soquel, Ca., U.S.	*D3	82
Sor, stm., Port.	C1	22
Sora, Italy	D4	23
Sŏrak, Mount, mtn., S. Kor.	G4	33
Sorata, Bol.	C2	55
Sorbas, Spain	D4	22
Sorel, Que.	C4	74
Sorell, Cape, c., Austl.	o15	73
Sorento, Il., U.S.	E4	90
Soreq, stm., Isr.	h10	41
Soresina, Italy	D5	20
Soria, Spain	B4	22
Soriano, Ur.	f7	54
Soriano, dept., Ur.	f8	54
Sorocaba, Braz.	C6	56
Sorochinsk, Sov. Un.	C4	28
Soroki, Sov. Un.	G7	27
Sorong, Indon.	F8	34
Soroti, Ug.	A5	48
Sørøya, i., Nor.	B10	14
Sorrento, Italy	D5	23
Sorrento, Fl., U.S.	D5	86
Sorrento, La., U.S.	D5	95
Sorris Sorris, Nmb.	B1	49
Sør Rondane Mountains, mts., Ant.	B15	7
Sorsogon, Phil.	C6	34
Sortavala, Sov. Un.	A8	27
Sorum, S.D., U.S.	B3	118
Sörumsand, Nor.	p29	14
Sōsan, S. Kor.	H3	33
Soscook, Ms., U.S.	D4	101
Soudan, Mn., U.S.	C6	100
Souderton, Pa., U.S.	F11	115
Souflíon, Grc.	B6	25
Soufrière, St. Luc.	J14	64
Soufrière, mtn., Guad.	Q18	65
Soufrière, mtn., St. Vin.	U26	65
Souhegan, stm., N.H., U.S.	E3	106
Souilac	E3	16
Soulac, Fr.	D7	74
Soulanges, co., Que.	D7	74
Sound Beach, N.Y., U.S.	*n16	103
Sounding Creek, stm., Alta.	D5	68
Sounding Lake, l., Alta.	C5	68
Sound View, Ct., U.S.	D6	84
Sources, Mount aux, mtn., Afr.	C4	49
Soure, Braz.	C5	59
Soure, Port.	B1	22
Souris, Man.	E1	70
Souris, P.E.I.	C7	71
Souris, N.D., U.S.	A5	111
Souris, stm., N.A.	A7	76
Sous, Oued, val., Mor.	C3	44
Sousa, Braz.	C3	57

Name	Map Ref.	Page
Sousse, Tun.	B7	44
Soustons, Fr.	F3	16
South, stm., Ont.	B5	73
South, stm., Ga., U.S.	h8	87
South, stm., Ia., U.S.	C4	92
South, stm., N.C., U.S.	C4	110
South Acton, Ma., U.S.	g10	98
South Acworth, N.H., U.S.	D2	106
South Addison, Me., U.S.	D5	96
South Africa, ctry., Afr.	C4	49
South America, cont.	E5	53
South Amboy, N.J., U.S.	C4	107
South Amherst, Ma., U.S.	B2	98
South Amherst, Oh., U.S.	A3	112
Southampton, N.B.	D2	71
Southampton, N.S.	D5	71
Southampton, Ont.	C3	73
Southampton, Eng., U.K.	E6	10
Southampton, Ma., U.S.	B2	98
Southampton, N.Y., U.S.	n16	109
Southampton, co., Va., U.S.	D5	123
Southampton, Cape, c., N.W. Ter.	D16	66
Southampton Island, i., N.W. Ter.	D16	66
South Andaman, i., India	F9	36
South Anna, stm., Va., U.S.	C5	123
Southard, Ok., U.S.	A3	113
South Ashburnham, Ma., U.S.	A4	98
South Ashfield, Ma., U.S.	A2	98
South Aulatsivik Island, i., Newf.	g9	72
South Australia, state, Austl.	E5	50
Southaven, Ms., U.S.	A3	101
South Bald Mountain, mtn., Co., U.S.	A5	83
South Baldy, mtn., N.M., U.S.	D2	108
Southbank, B.C.	C5	69
South Barnstead, N.H., U.S.	D4	106
South Barre, Ma., U.S.	B3	98
South Barre, Vt., U.S.	C3	122
South Barrule, hill, I. of Man	F4	13
South Bay, Fl., U.S.	F6	86
South Bay, b., Ont.	B3	73
Southbeach, Or., U.S.	C2	114
South Belmar, N.J., U.S.	C4	107
South Beloit, Il., U.S.	A4	90
South Bend, In., U.S.	A5	91
South Bend, Ne., U.S.	h12	104
South Bend, Tx., U.S.	C3	120
South Bend, Wa., U.S.	C2	124
South Bentinck Arm, b., B.C.	C4	69
South Berwick, Me., U.S.	E2	96
South Bethany, De., U.S.	F5	85
South Bethlehem, N.Y., U.S.	C7	109
South Bloomfield, Oh., U.S.	C3	112
South Boardman, Mi., U.S.	D5	99
South Bolton, Que.	D5	74
Southborough, Ma., U.S.	B4	98
South Boston, Va., U.S.	D4	123
Sound Bound Brook, N.J., U.S.	B3	107
South Bradenton, Fl., U.S.	*E4	86
South Branch, Newf.	E2	72
South Branch, Mi., U.S.	D7	99
South Branch Lake, l., Me., U.S.	C4	96
South Branch Mountain, mtn., W.V., U.S.	B6	125
Southbridge, Ma., U.S.	B3	98
South Bristol, Me., U.S.	E3	96
South Britain, Ct., U.S.	D3	84
South Broadway, Wa., U.S.	C5	124
South Brookfield, N.S.	E5	71
South Bruny, i., Austl.	o15	50
South Burlington, Vt., U.S.	C2	122
Southbury, Ct., U.S.	D3	84
South Byfield, Ma., U.S.	A6	98
South Byron, N.Y., U.S.	B2	109
South Canaan, Pa., U.S.	D11	115
South Cape, c., Nor.	B13	128
South Carolina, state, U.S.	D6	117
South Carver, Ma., U.S.	C6	98
South Channel, strt., Marsh Is.	S18	52
South Charleston, Oh., U.S.	C2	112
South Charleston, W.V., U.S.	C3	125
South Charlestown, N.H., U.S.	D2	106
South Chatham, Ma., U.S.	C7	98
South Chatham, N.H., U.S.	B4	106
South Chicago Heights, Il., U.S.	m9	90
South China, Me., U.S.	D3	96
South China Sea, Asia	H14	30
South Cle Elum, Wa., U.S.	B5	124
South Coffeyville, Ok., U.S.	A6	113
South Colby, Wa., U.S.	e10	124
South Colton, N.Y., U.S.	f10	109
South Congaree, S.C., U.S.	D5	117
South Connellsville, Pa., U.S.	G2	115
South Corning, N.Y., U.S.	C3	109
South Cottonwood, Ut., U.S.	*C4	121
South Dakota, state, U.S.	C5	118
South Danville, N.H., U.S.	D4	106
South Dartmouth, Ma., U.S.	C6	98
South Dayton, N.Y., U.S.	C1	109
South Daytona, Fl., U.S.	C5	86
South Decatur, Ga., U.S.	*h8	87
South Deerfield, Ma., U.S.	B2	98
South Deerfield, N.H., U.S.	D4	106
South Deer Isle, Me., U.S.	D4	96
South Dennis, Ma., U.S.	C7	98
South Dennis, N.J., U.S.	E3	107
South Dorset, Vt., U.S.	E2	122
South Dos Palos, Ca., U.S.	D3	82
South Downs, plat., Eng., U.K.	E6	10
South Dum Dum, India	F12	37
South Duxbury, Ma., U.S.	B6	98
Southeast Cape, c., Ak., U.S.	C6	79
South Easton, Ma., U.S.	B5	98
Southeast Pass, strt., La., U.S.	E7	95
Southeast Point, c., R.I., U.S.	h7	116
South Effingham, N.H., U.S.	C5	106
South Egremont, Ma., U.S.	B1	98
South Elgin, Il., U.S.	B5	90
South El Monte, Ca., U.S.	*m12	82
Southend-on-Sea, Eng., U.K.	E7	10
South English, Ia., U.S.	C5	92
Southern, prov., Mwi.	E4	48
Southern, prov., Zam.	E4	48
Southern Alps, mts., N.Z.	O13	51
Southern Bug, stm., Sov. Un.	H8	22
Southern Cross, Austl.	F2	50
Southern Indian Lake, l., Man.	f8	70
Southern Pines, N.C., U.S.	B3	110
Southern Uplands, plat., Scot., U.K.	C5	10
Southern Ute Indian Reservation, Co., U.S.	D2	83
South Esk, stm., Scot., U.K.	C5	10
South Euclid, Oh., U.S.	g9	112
Southey, Sask.	G3	75
South Fabius, stm., Mo., U.S.	A5	102
South Fallsburg, N.Y., U.S.	D6	109
South Farmingdale, N.Y., U.S.	*n15	109
Southfield, Ma., U.S.	B1	98
Southfield, Mi., U.S.	o15	99
South Flevoland, reg., Neth.	B5	17
South Fork, Sask.	H1	75
South Fork, Co., U.S.	D4	83
South Fork, Pa., U.S.	F4	115
South Fort George, B.C.	C6	69
South Foster, R.I., U.S.	C2	116
South Fox Island, i., Mi., U.S.	C5	99
South Freeport, Me., U.S.	g7	96
South Fulton, Tn., U.S.	A3	119
South Gastonia, N.C., U.S.	B1	110
South Gate, Ca., U.S.	n12	82
Southgate, Fl., U.S.	*E4	86
Southgate, Ky., U.S.	h14	94
South Gate, Md., U.S.	*B4	97
Southgate, Mi., U.S.	p15	99
South Gifford, Mo., U.S.	A5	102
South Glamorgan, co., Wales, U.K.	C4	12
South Glastonbury, Ct., U.S.	C5	84
Southglenn, Co., U.S.	*B6	83
South Glens Falls, N.Y., U.S.	B7	109
South Grafton, Ma., U.S.	B4	98
South Grand, stm., Mo., U.S.	C3	102
South Greenfield, Mo., U.S.	D4	102
South Gulf of Évvoia, b., Grc.	g11	25
South Hadley, Ma., U.S.	B2	98
South Hadley Falls, Ma., U.S.	B2	98
South Hamilton, Ma., U.S.	A6	98
South Hampton, N.H., U.S.	E5	106
South Hanover, Ma., U.S.	h12	98
South Harpswell, Me., U.S.	g7	96
South Harwich, Ma., U.S.	C7	98
South Haven, In., U.S.	A3	91
South Haven, Ks., U.S.	E6	93
South Haven, Mi., U.S.	F4	99
South Heart, N.D., U.S.	C3	111
South Heart, stm., Alta.	B2	68
South Hero, Vt., U.S.	B2	122
South Hero Island, i., Vt., U.S.	B2	122
South Hill, N.Y., U.S.	*C4	109
South Hill, Va., U.S.	D4	123
South Hingham, Ma., U.S.	h12	98
South Holland, Il., U.S.	k9	90
South Holland (Zuid-Holland), prov., Neth.	B4	17
South Holston Lake, res., U.S.	A9	119
South Hooksett, N.H., U.S.	D4	106
South Hopkinton, R.I., U.S.	F1	116
South Houston, Tx., U.S.	r14	120
South Huntington, N.Y., U.S.	*n15	109
South Hutchinson, Ks., U.S.	f11	93
South Indian Lake, Man.	A2	70
Southington, Ct., U.S.	C4	84
South International Falls, Mn., U.S.	B5	100
South Jacksonville, Il., U.S.	D3	90
South Jordan, Ut., U.S.	C3	121
South Junction, Man.	E4	70
South Kenosha, Wi., U.S.	F6	126
South Kensington, Md., U.S.	*B3	97
South Kent, Ct., U.S.	C2	84
South Killingly, Ct., U.S.	B8	84
South Komelik, Az., U.S.	F4	80
South Laguna, Ca., U.S.	*F5	82
South Lake Tahoe, Ca., U.S.	C4	82
South Lancaster, Ma., U.S.	B4	98
Southland, Ky., U.S.	C6	94
South Laramie, Wy., U.S.	*E7	127
South Laurel, Md., U.S.	B4	97
South Lebanon, Me., U.S.	E2	96
South Lebanon, Oh., U.S.	C1	112
South Lee, Ma., U.S.	B1	98
South Lincoln, Vt., U.S.	C3	122
South Londonderry, Vt., U.S.	E3	122
South Loup, stm., Ne., U.S.	C6	104
South Lunenburg, Vt., U.S.	C5	122
South Lyme, Ct., U.S.	D6	84
South Lyndeborogh, N.H., U.S.	E3	106
South Lyon, Mi., U.S.	F7	99
South Magnetic Pole, Ant.	C26	7
South Manitou Island, i., Mi., U.S.	C4	99
South Mansfield, La., U.S.	B2	95
South Medford, Or., U.S.	E4	114
South Merrimack, N.H., U.S.	E3	106
South Miami, Fl., U.S.	G6	86
South Miami Heights, Fl., U.S.	s13	86
South Middleboro, Ma., U.S.	C6	98
South Milford, In., U.S.	A7	91
South Mills, N.C., U.S.	A6	110
South Milwaukee, Wi., U.S.	F6	126
Southminster, Eng., U.K.	C8	12
South Modesto, Ca., U.S.	*D3	82
South Molton, Eng., U.K.	C4	12
South Montrose, Pa., U.S.	C10	115
South Moose Lake, l., Man.	C1	70
South Mountain, Pa., U.S.	G7	115
South Mountain, mtn., Id., U.S.	G2	89
South Mountain, mtn., N.M., U.S.	k8	108
South Mountains, mts., Az., U.S.	m8	80
South Mountains, mts., N.C., U.S.	B1	110
South Naknek, Ak., U.S.	D8	79
South Negril Point, c., Jam.	E4	64
South New Berlin, N.Y., U.S.	C5	109
South Newbury, N.H., U.S.	D2	106
South Newbury, Vt., U.S.	C4	122
South Newfane, Vt., U.S.	F3	122
South New River Canal, Fl., U.S.	r3	86
South Northfield, Vt., U.S.	C3	122
South Nyack, N.Y., U.S.	*D7	109
South Ogden, Ut., U.S.	B4	121
South Orange, N.J., U.S.	m16	109
South Orkney Islands, is., B.A.T.	C8	7
South Orrington, Me., U.S.	D4	96
South Otselic, N.Y., U.S.	C5	109
South Paris, Me., U.S.	D2	96
South Park, val., Co., U.S.	B5	83
South Pasadena, Ca., U.S.	*m12	82
South Pass, Wy., U.S.	D4	127
South Pass, strt., Marsh Is.	S17	52
South Pass, strt., La., U.S.	F6	95
South Pass City, Wy., U.S.	D4	127
South Patrick Shores, Fl., U.S.	D6	86
South Peacham, Vt., U.S.	C4	122
South Pekin, Il., U.S.	C4	90
South Pittsburg, Tn., U.S.	D8	119
South Plainfield, N.J., U.S.	B4	107
South Platte, stm., U.S.	B7	76
South Point, c., Austl.	I6	51
South Point, c., Barb.	K20	65
South Point, c., Newf.	C4	72
South Point, c., Mi., U.S.	D7	99
South Pole, Ant.	A7	7
South Pomfret, Vt., U.S.	D3	122
Southport (Gold Coast), Austl.	E9	50
Southport, Eng., U.K.	D5	10
Southport, Fl., U.S.	u16	86
Southport, In., U.S.	E5	91
Southport, N.Y., U.S.	C4	109
Southport, N.C., U.S.	D4	110
South Portland, Me., U.S.	E2	96
South Portsmouth, Ky., U.S.	B6	94
South Poultney, Vt., U.S.	E12	122
South Prairie, Wa., U.S.	B3	124
South Range, Mi., U.S.	A2	99
South Range, Wi., U.S.	B2	126
South Reading, Vt., U.S.	E3	122
South Renovo, Pa., U.S.	D6	115
South Revelstoke, B.C.	D8	69
South River, Ont.	B5	73
South River, N.J., U.S.	C4	107
South River, b., Md., U.S.	C4	97
South Ronaldsay, i., Scot., U.K.	A5	10
South Royalston, Ma., U.S.	A3	98
South Royalton, Vt., U.S.	D3	122
South Rustico, P.E.I.	C6	71
South Ryegate, Vt., U.S.	C4	122
South Salem, Oh., U.S.	C2	112
South Salt Lake, Ut., U.S.	*C4	121
South Sandwich Islands, is., S.A.	D10	7
South San Francisco, Ca., U.S.	h8	82
South San Gabriel, Ca., U.S.	*m12	82
South San Jose Hills, Ca., U.S.	*m13	82
South Saskatchewan, stm., Can.	F11	66
South Seaville, N.J., U.S.	E3	107
South Setauket, N.Y., U.S.	*n15	109
South Shetland Islands, is., B.A.T.	C7	7
South Shields, Eng., U.K.	C6	10
South Shore, Mo., U.S.	f12	102
South Shore, S.D., U.S.	B9	118
Southside, Al., U.S.	B3	78
Southside, N.C., U.S.	B1	110
Southside, Tn., U.S.	A4	119
Southside Place, Tx., U.S.	r14	120
South Sioux City, Ne., U.S.	B9	104
South Skunk, stm., Ia., U.S.	C4	92
South Slocan, B.C.	E9	69
South Solon, Oh., U.S.	C2	112
South Sound, strt., Ire.	D2	11
South Spicer Island, i., N.W. Ter.	C17	66
South Sterling, Pa., U.S.	D11	115
South Stony Brook, N.Y., U.S.	n15	109
South Strafford, Vt., U.S.	D4	122
South Streator, Il., U.S.	B5	90
South Sumter, S.C., U.S.	*D7	117
South Superior, Wy., U.S.	E4	127
South Sutton, N.H., U.S.	D3	106
South Swansea, Ma., U.S.	C5	98
South Tamworth, N.H., U.S.	C4	106
South Taranaki Bight, N.Z.	M15	51
South Toms River, N.J., U.S.	D4	107
South Torrington, Wy., U.S.	D8	127
South Tucson, Az., U.S.	E5	80
South Twin Lake, l., Newf.	D4	72
South Twin Mountain, mtn., N.H., U.S.	B3	106
South Tyne, stm., Eng., U.K.	F6	13
South Uist, i., Scot., U.K.	B3	10
South Valley Stream, N.Y., U.S.	n15	109
South Van Buren, Mo., U.S.	E6	102
South Venice, Fl., U.S.	E4	86
South Ventana Cone, vol., Ca., U.S.	D3	82
South Vienna, Oh., U.S.	C2	112
South Wabasca Lake, l., Alta.	B4	68
South Wadesboro, N.C., U.S.	C2	110
South Wallingford, Vt., U.S.	E3	122
South Walpole, Ma., U.S.	h10	98
South Waterford, Me., U.S.	D2	96
South Waverly, Pa., U.S.	C8	115
South Wayne, Wi., U.S.	F4	126
South Weare, N.H., U.S.	D3	106
South Webster, Oh., U.S.	D3	112
South Wellfleet, Ma., U.S.	C8	98
South Wellington, B.C.	f12	69
Southwest, Pa., U.S.	F3	115
South West Africa see Namibia, dep., Afr.	B2	49
South West Bay, b., Bah.	n16	64
South Westbury, N.Y., U.S.	n15	109
South West Cape, c., Austl.	o15	50
Southwest Cape, c., N.Z.	Q11	51
Southwest Channel, strt., Fl., U.S.	E4	86
South West City, Mo., U.S.	E3	102
Southwest Harbor, Me., U.S.	D4	96
Southwest Head, c., N.B.	E3	71
Southwest Miramichi, stm., N.B.	C3	71
Southwest Mountains, mts., Va., U.S.	B4	123
Southwest Pass, strt., La., U.S.	E3	95
Southwest Pass, strt., La., U.S.	F6	95
Southwest Passage, strt., Marsh Is.	S18	52
Southwest Point, c., R.I., U.S.	h7	116
South Weymouth Naval Air Station, mil., Ma., U.S.	h12	98
South Whitley, In., U.S.	B6	91
South Whittier, Ca., U.S.	*n13	82
Southwick, Ma., U.S.	B2	98
South Williamson, Ky., U.S.	C7	94
South Williamsport, Pa., U.S.	D7	115
South Willington, Ct., U.S.	B6	84
South Wilmington, Il., U.S.	B5	90
South Windham, Ct., U.S.	C7	84
South Windham, Me., U.S.	E2	96
South Windsor, Ct., U.S.	B5	84
Southwold, Eng., U.K.	B9	12
South Wolfeboro, N.H., U.S.	C4	106
South Wolf Island, i., Newf.	C4	72
Southwood Acres, Ct., U.S.	A5	84
South Woodbury, Vt., U.S.	C4	122
South Woodstock, Ct., U.S.	B8	84
South Woodstock, Vt., U.S.	D3	122
South Yarmouth, Ma., U.S.	C7	98
South Yorkshire, co., Eng., U.K.	A6	12
South Yuba River, Ca., U.S.	*C3	82
South Zanesville, Oh., U.S.	*C3	112
Soverato, Italy	E6	23
Sovereign, Sask.	F2	75
Sovetsk (Tilsit), Sov. Un.	D3	27
Sovetskaya Gavan, Sov. Un.	E16	29
Sovetskaya Gavan, Sov. Un.	B10	33
Soviet Union, ctry., Asia	D11	29
Soweto, S. Afr.	C4	49
Soyo, Ang.	C1	48
Sozopol, Bul.	D8	24
Spa, Bel.	B6	16
Spadra, Ar., U.S.	B2	81
Spain, ctry., Eur.	B4	22
Spalding, Austl.	F2	51
Spalding, Sask.	E3	75
Spalding, Eng., U.K.	D6	10
Spalding, Id., U.S.	C2	89
Spalding, Ne., U.S.	C7	104
Spalding, co., Ga., U.S.	C2	87
Spanaway, Wa., U.S.	B3	124
Spangle, Wa., U.S.	B8	124
Spaniard's Bay, Newf.	E5	72
Spanish, stm., Ont.	A2	73
Spanish Fork, Ut., U.S.	C4	121
Spanish Lake, Mo., U.S.	f13	102
Spanish North Africa, dep., Afr.	*B4	44
Spanish Peak, mtn., Or., U.S.	C7	114
Spanish Ranch, Ca., U.S.	C3	82
Spanish Town, Jam.	F5	64
Sparkman, Ar., U.S.	D3	81
Sparks, Ga., U.S.	E3	87
Sparks, Ne., U.S.	B5	104
Sparks, Nv., U.S.	D2	105
Sparks, Ok., U.S.	B5	113
Sparland, Il., U.S.	B4	90
Sparr, Fl., U.S.	C4	86
Sparrevohn, Swe.	t34	14
Sparrows Point, Md., U.S.	B5	97
Sparta see Spárti, Grc.	D4	40
Sparta, Ga., U.S.	C4	87
Sparta, Il., U.S.	E4	90
Sparta, Ky., U.S.	B5	94
Sparta, Mi., U.S.	E5	99
Sparta, Mo., U.S.	D4	102
Sparta, N.J., U.S.	A3	107
Sparta, N.C., U.S.	A1	110
Sparta, Oh., U.S.	B3	112
Sparta, Tn., U.S.	D8	119
Sparta, Wa., U.S.	B8	124
Sparta, Wi., U.S.	E3	126
Sparta Mountains, mts., N.J., U.S.	B3	107
Spartanburg, In., U.S.	D8	91
Spartanburg, S.C., U.S.	B4	117
Spartanburg, co., S.C., U.S.	B3	117
Spartansburg, Pa., U.S.	C2	115
Spárti (Sparta), Grc.	D4	40
Spartivento, Cape, c., Italy	F6	23
Spartivento, Cape, c., Italy	E2	23
Sparwood, B.C.	E10	69
Spas-Demensk, Sov. Un.	F16	29
Spassk-Dalniy, Sov. Un.	E16	29
Spassk-Ryazanskiy, Sov. Un.	D17	27
Spáta, Grc.	h11	25
Spátha, Ákra, c., Grc.	E4	40
Spaulding, Ok., U.S.	B5	113
Spavinaw, Ok., U.S.	A6	113
Spavinaw Creek, stm., Ok., U.S.	A7	113
Spear, Cape, c., Newf.	E5	72
Spearfish, S.D., U.S.	C2	118
Spearhill, Man.	D2	70
Spearman, Tx., U.S.	A2	120
Spearsville, La., U.S.	B3	95
Spearville, Ks., U.S.	E3	93
Spectacle Pond, l., Me., U.S.	D4	96
Speculator, N.Y., U.S.	B6	109
Spednic Lake, l., N.A.	C5	96
Speed, In., U.S.	H6	91
Speed, Ks., U.S.	C4	93
Speed, N.C., U.S.	B5	110
Speed, W.V., U.S.	C3	125
Speedway, In., U.S.	E5	91
Speedwell, Tn., U.S.	C10	119
Speedwell, Va., U.S.	D1	123
Speers, Sask.	E2	75
Speigle, Al., U.S.	C4	78
Speight, Ky., U.S.	C7	94
Speke, W.V., U.S.	k10	125
Spenard (part of Anchorage), Ak., U.S.	g17	79
Spencer, Id., U.S.	E6	89
Spencer, Ia., U.S.	A2	92
Spencer, Ma., U.S.	B4	98
Spencer, Ne., U.S.	B7	104
Spencer, N.Y., U.S.	C4	109
Spencer, N.C., U.S.	B2	110
Spencer, Oh., U.S.	A3	112
Spencer, Tn., U.S.	D8	119
Spencer, Wi., U.S.	D3	126
Spencer, W.V., U.S.	C3	125
Spencer, co., In., U.S.	H4	91
Spencer, co., Ky., U.S.	B4	94
Spencer, Cape, c., Ak., U.S.	k21	79
Spencer Gulf, b., Austl.	F6	50
Spencer Lake, l., Me., U.S.	C2	96
Spencerport, N.Y., U.S.	B3	109
Spencers Island, N.S.	D5	71
Spencerville, In., U.S.	B8	91
Spencerville, Md., U.S.	B4	97
Spencerville, Oh., U.S.	B1	112
Spencerville, Ok., U.S.	C6	113
Spences Bridge, B.C.	D7	69
Spennymoor, Eng., U.K.	F7	13
Sperling, Man.	E3	70
Sperchiós, stm., Grc.	k9	25
Sperrin Mountains, mts., N. Ire., U.K.	C3	10
Sperry, Ok., U.S.	A6	113
Sperryville, Va., U.S.	B4	123
Spesutie Island, i., Md., U.S.	B5	97
Spey, stm., Scot., U.K.	B5	10
Speyer, W. Ger.	F7	19
Sphinx, hist., Eg.	C3	41
Spiceland, In., U.S.	E7	91
Spicer, In., U.S.	E4	100
Spickard, Mo., U.S.	A4	102
Spider Lake, l., Wi., U.S.	B2	126
Spiekeroog, W. Ger.	A7	17
Spiekeroog, i., W. Ger.	B3	18
Spiez, Switz.	C4	21
Spigno Monferrato, Italy	E4	20
Spijkenisse, Neth.	*C4	17
Spillville, Ia., U.S.	A6	92
Spinazzola, Italy	D6	23
Spindale, N.C., U.S.	B1	110
Spink, S.D., U.S.	E9	118
Spink, co., S.D., U.S.	C7	118
Spirit Lake, Id., U.S.	B2	89
Spirit Lake, Ia., U.S.	A2	92
Spirit Lake, l., Man.	A2	70
Spirit Lake, l., Wa., U.S.	C3	124
Spirit River, Alta.	B1	68
Spirit River Flowage, res., Wi., U.S.	C4	126
Spiritwood, Sask.	D2	75
Spiritwood, N.D., U.S.	C7	111
Spiro, Ok., U.S.	B7	113
Spišská Nová Ves, Czech.	D6	26
Spit Island, i., Mid. Is.	K3	52
Spitsbergen, i., Nor.	B13	128
Spittal, Aus.	E12	19
Spivey, Ks., U.S.	E5	93
Split, Yugo.	D3	24
Split, Cape, c., N.S.	D5	71
Split Lake, l., Man.	A4	70
Split Rock Creek, stm., U.S.	G2	100
Splügen, Switz.	C5	20
Splügen Pass, Eur.	C5	20
Spofford, N.H., U.S.	E2	106
Spofford, Tx., U.S.	E2	120
Spofford Lake, l., N.H., U.S.	E2	106
Spokane, La., U.S.	C4	95
Spokane, Wa., U.S.	B8	124
Spokane, co., Wa., U.S.	B8	124
Spokane, stm., U.S.	B8	124
Spokane, Mount, mtn., Wa., U.S.	B8	124
Spokane Indian Reservation, Wa., U.S.	B8	124
Spöl, stm., Eur.	C9	21
Spoleto, Italy	C4	23
Spondin, Alta.	D5	68
Spoon, stm., Il., U.S.	C3	90
Spooner, Wi., U.S.	C2	126
Spooner Lake, l., Wi., U.S.	C2	126
Spotswood, N.J., U.S.	C4	107
Spotsylvania, Va., U.S.	B5	123
Spotsylvania, co., Va., U.S.	B5	123
Spotted Island, i., Newf.	B4	72
Spottsville, Ky., U.S.	C2	94
Spragge, Ont.	A2	73
Sprague, Man.	E4	70
Sprague, Al., U.S.	C3	78
Sprague, Ne., U.S.	D9	104
Sprague, Wa., U.S.	B8	124
Sprague, stm., Or., U.S.	E5	114
Sprague River, Or., U.S.	E5	114
Spragueville, Ia., U.S.	B7	92
Spratly Island, i., Asia	D4	34
Spray, Or., U.S.	C7	114
Spread Eagle, Wi., U.S.	C5	126
Spreckelsville, Hi., U.S.	*C5	88
Spremberg, E. Ger.	B7	18
Spring, Tx., U.S.	q141	120
Sprigg, W.V., U.S.	D2	125
Spring, stm., Ar., U.S.	A4	81
Spring, South Fork, stm., U.S.	E6	102
Spring Arbor, Mi., U.S.	F6	99
Spring Bay, b., Ut., U.S.	B3	121
Springboro, Oh., U.S.	C1	112
Springboro, Pa., U.S.	C1	115
Springbrook, Ont.	C7	73
Springbrook, Wi., U.S.	B2	126
Spring Brook, N.D., U.S.	A2	111
Spring Brook, stm., Pa., U.S.	n18	115
Spring City, Pa., U.S.	F10	115
Spring City, Tn., U.S.	D9	119
Spring City, Ut., U.S.	D4	121
Spring Coulee, Alta.	E4	68
Spring Creek, Pa., U.S.	C2	115
Spring Creek, Tn., U.S.	B3	119
Spring Creek, stm., Co., U.S.	B8	83
Spring Creek, stm., Nv., U.S.	C4	105
Spring Creek Colony, S.D., U.S.	*B7	118
Springdale, Newf.	D3	72
Springdale, Ar., U.S.	A1	81
Springdale, Mt., U.S.	E8	103
Springdale, Oh., U.S.	n13	112
Springdale, Or., U.S.	B4	114
Springdale, Pa., U.S.	E2	115
Springdale, S.C., U.S.	D5	117
Springdale, Ut., U.S.	F3	121
Spring Dale, W.V., U.S.	D4	125
Springdell, Ut., U.S.	*C4	121
Springe, W. Ger.	A4	19
Springer, N.M., U.S.	A5	108
Springer, Ok., U.S.	C4	113
Springerton, Il., U.S.	E5	90
Springerville, Az., U.S.	C6	80
Springfield, N.B.	D4	71
Springfield, N.S.	E5	71
Springfield, Ont.	E4	73
Springfield, Co., U.S.	D8	83
Springfield, Fl., U.S.	u16	86
Springfield, Ga., U.S.	D5	87
Springfield, Id., U.S.	F6	89
Springfield, Il., U.S.	D4	90
Springfield, Ky., U.S.	C4	94
Springfield, La., U.S.	D5	95
Springfield, Me., U.S.	C4	96
Springfield, Ma., U.S.	B2	98
Springfield, Mn., U.S.	F4	100
Springfield, Mo., U.S.	D4	102
Springfield, Ne., U.S.	C9	104
Springfield, N.H., U.S.	D3	106
Springfield, N.J., U.S.	B4	107
Springfield, Oh., U.S.	C2	112
Springfield, Or., U.S.	C4	114
Springfield, Pa., U.S.	p20	115
Springfield, S.C., U.S.	E5	117
Springfield, S.D., U.S.	E8	118
Springfield, Tn., U.S.	A5	119
Springfield, Vt., U.S.	E3	122
Springfield, Va., U.S.	g12	123
Springfield, W.V., U.S.	B6	125
Springfield, Lake, res., Il., U.S.	D4	90
Springfield Township, Pa., U.S.	*F11	115
Springfontein, S. Afr.	D4	49
Spring Garden, Al., U.S.	B4	78
Spring Garden, Pa., U.S.	*G8	115
Spring Glen, Ut., U.S.	D5	121
Spring Green, Wi., U.S.	E3	126
Spring Grove, Il., U.S.	h8	90
Spring Grove, Mn., U.S.	G7	100
Spring Grove, Pa., U.S.	G8	115
Springhill, N.S.	D5	71
Spring Hill, Ct., U.S.	B7	84
Spring Hill, Fl., U.S.	D4	86
Springhill, La., U.S.	A2	95
Spring Hill, In., U.S.	k10	91
Spring Hill, Ks., U.S.	D9	93
Spring Hill, Tn., U.S.	B5	119
Springhill Junction, N.S.	D5	71
Spring Hope, N.C., U.S.	B4	110
Springhouse, B.C.	D6	69
Spring Island, i., S.C., U.S.	G6	117
Spring Lake, Fl., U.S.	D4	86
Spring Lake, Mi., U.S.	E4	99
Spring Lake, N.J., U.S.	C4	107
Spring Lake, N.C., U.S.	B4	110
Spring Lake, l., Me., U.S.	C2	96
Spring Lake, l., Wi., U.S.	D3	126
Spring Lake Heights, N.J., U.S.	C4	107
Spring Lake Park, Mn., U.S.	*E5	100
Spring Lick, Ky., U.S.	C3	94
Spring Mills, Pa., U.S.	E6	115
Spring Mountains, mts., Nv., U.S.	G6	105
Spring Place, Ga., U.S.	B2	87
Springport, In., U.S.	D7	91
Springs, S. Afr.	C5	49
Springside, Sask.	F4	75
Springstein, Man.	E3	70
Springvale, Austl.	A3	51
Springvale, Ga., U.S.	E2	87
Springvale, Me., U.S.	E2	96
Spring Valley, Sask.	H3	75
Spring Valley, Al., U.S.	A2	78
Spring Valley, Ca., U.S.	o16	82
Spring Valley, Il., U.S.	B4	90
Spring Valley, Mn., U.S.	G6	100
Spring Valley, N.Y., U.S.	g12	109
Spring Valley, Oh., U.S.	C1	112
Spring Valley, Wi., U.S.	D1	126
Springview, Ne., U.S.	B6	104
Springville, Al., U.S.	B3	78
Springville, Ia., U.S.	B6	92
Springville, N.Y., U.S.	C2	109
Springville, Tn., U.S.	A3	119
Springville, Ut., U.S.	C4	121
Springwater, Sask.	F1	75
Springwater, N.Y., U.S.	C3	109
Spruce, Mi., U.S.	D7	99
Spruce, stm., Sask.	D5	75
Spruce Creek, Pa., U.S.	E5	115
Sprucedale, Ont.	B5	73
Spruce Fork, stm., W.V., U.S.	m12	125
Spruce Grove, Alta.	C4	68
Spruce Knob, mtn., W.V., U.S.	C6	125
Spruce Knob-Seneca Rocks National Recreation Area, W.V., U.S.	C5	125
Spruce Lake, Sask.	D1	75
Spruce Mountain, mtn., Az., U.S.	C3	80
Spruce Mountain, mtn., Nv., U.S.	C7	105
Spruce Pine, Al., U.S.	A2	78
Spruce Pine, N.C., U.S.	f10	110
Spruce Run Reservoir, res., N.J., U.S.	B3	107
Spruga, Switz.	D6	21
Spur, Tx., U.S.	C2	120
Spurfield, Alta.	B3	68
Spurgeon, In., U.S.	H3	91
Spurn Head, c., Eng., U.K.	A8	12
Spurr, Mount, mtn., Ak., U.S.	g15	79
Spy Hill, Sask.	G5	75
Squamish, B.C.	E6	69
Squam Lake, l., N.H., U.S.	C4	106
Squam Mountains, mts., N.H., U.S.	C3	106
Squantum, N.H., U.S.	B4	96
Squapan Lake, l., Me., U.S.	B4	96
Square Islands, Newf.	B4	72
Square Lake, l., Me., U.S.	A4	96
Squatec, Que.	B9	74
Squaw Cap Mountain, mtn., N.B.	B3	71
Squaw Harbor, Ak., U.S.	D7	79
Squaw Hill, mtn., Wy., U.S.	E7	127
Squaw Lake, Mn., U.S.	C4	100
Squaw Peak, mtn., Mt., U.S.	C2	103
Squaw Rapids, Sask.	D4	75
Squibnocket Point, c., Ma., U.S.	D6	98
Squillace, Gulf of, b., Italy	E6	23
Squire, W.V., U.S.	D3	125
Squires, Mo., U.S.	E5	102
Squirrel, Id., U.S.	E7	89
Srbobran, Yugo.	C4	24
Srednekolymsk, Sov. Un.	C18	29
Sredniy Vasyugan, Sov. Un.	D24	8
Šrem, Pol.	C4	26
Sremska Mitrovica, Yugo.	C4	24
Sremski Karlovci, Yugo.	C4	24
Srepok, stm., Asia	C3	34
Sri Lanka, ctry., Asia	G7	36
Srinagar, India	C6	36
Środa Śląska, Pol.	C4	26
Środa [Wielkopolska], Pol.	B4	26
Staatsburg, N.Y., U.S.	D7	109
Stab, Ky., U.S.	C4	94
Stack Reservoir, res., R.I., U.S.	C3	116
Stack's Mountains, mts., Ire.	E2	11
Stacy, N.C., U.S.	C6	110
Stacy, Mn., U.S.	E6	100
Stacyville, Ia., U.S.	A5	92
Stacyville, Me., U.S.	C4	96
Stade, W. Ger.	B9	18
Stadskanaal, Neth.	A6	17
Stadthagen, W. Ger.	A4	19
Stadtlohn, W. Ger.	B1	19
Stadtroda, E. Ger.	C6	19

Name	Map Ref.	Page
Sturgeon Landing, Sask.	C5	75
Sturgeon-weir, stm., Sask.	C4	75
Sturgis, Sask.	F4	75
Sturgis, Ky., U.S.	e10	94
Sturgis, Mi., U.S.	G5	99
Sturgis, Ms., U.S.	B4	101
Sturgis, S.D., U.S.	C2	118
Sturt Creek, stm., Austl.	C4	50
Sturt Desert, des., Austl.	D3	51
Sturtevant, Wi., U.S.	F6	126
Stutsman, co., N.D., U.S.	B6	111
Stutterheim, S. Afr.	D4	49
Stuttgart, W. Ger.	D4	18
Stuttgart, Ar., U.S.	C4	81
Stuttgart, Ks., U.S.	C4	93
Styr, stm., Sov. Un.	F5	27
Styria, hist. reg., Aus.	E7	18
Subarnarekha, stm., India	F11	37
Subi, i., Indon.	K8	35
Subiaco, Ar., U.S.	B2	81
Subic, Phil.	o13	34
Subic Bay, b., Phil.	o13	34
Sublette, Il., U.S.	B4	90
Sublette, Ks., U.S.	E3	93
Sublette, co., Wy., U.S.	D2	127
Sublett Range, mts., Id., U.S.	G6	89
Sublimity, Or., U.S.	C4	114
Subotica, Yugo.	B4	24
Sucarnoochee, stm., Al., U.S.	C1	78
Succasunna, N.J., U.S.	B3	107
Success, Sask.	G1	75
Success, Ar., U.S.	A5	81
Success, Mo., U.S.	D5	102
Success, Mount, mtn., N.H., U.S.	B4	106
Suceava, Rom.	B8	24
Suceava, stm., Rom.	B8	24
Sucha [Beskidzka], Pol.	D5	26
Suchdol, Czech.	n17	26
Suches, Ga., U.S.	B2	87
Suchitoto, El Sal.	D3	62
Süchow see Xuzhou, China	E8	31
Suck, stm., Ire.	D2	10
Sucre, Bol.	C2	55
Sucre, state, Ven.	A5	60
Sucre, dept., Col.	B2	60
Sucuaro, Col.	C4	60
Sucuriú, stm., Braz.	C2	56
Sucy-en-Brie, Fr.	g11	16
Sudan, Tx., U.S.	B1	120
Sudan, ctry., Afr.	C2	47
Sudan, reg., Afr.	E7	42
Sudbury, Ont.	A4	73
Sudbury, Eng., U.K.	B8	12
Sudbury, Ma., U.S.	B5	98
Sudbury, Vt., U.S.	D2	122
Sudbury, dept., Ont.	p19	73
Sudbury, stm., Ma., U.S.	B5	98
Sudbury Center, Ma., U.S.	g10	98
Sudbury Reservoir, res., Ma., U.S.	g10	98
Suddie, Guy.	A3	59
Süderbrarup, W. Ger.	D3	15
Suderburg, W. Ger.	B5	18
Sudetes, mts., Eur.	C4	26
Sudlersville, Md., U.S.	B6	97
Süd-Nord Canal, W. Ger.	B7	17
Sudogda, Sov. Un.	D13	27
Sudr, 'Ayn, well, Eg.	D5	41
Sudzha, Sov. Un.	F10	27
Sue, stm., Sud.	D2	47
Sueca, Spain	C5	22
Suez (As Suways), Eg.	C3	38
Suez, Gulf of, b., Eg.	C3	38
Suez Canal, Eg.	B3	38
Suffern, N.Y., U.S.	D6	109
Suffield, Alta.	D5	68
Suffield, Ct., U.S.	B5	84
Suffolk, Va., U.S.	D6	123
Suffolk, co., Eng., U.K.	B8	12
Suffolk, co., Ma., U.S.	B5	98
Suffolk, co., N.Y., U.S.	n15	109
Sugar, stm., U.S.	F4	126
Sugar, stm., U.S.	D2	106
Sugar, North Branch, stm., N.H., U.S.	D2	106
Sugar City, Co., U.S.	C7	83
Sugar City, Id., U.S.	F7	89
Sugar Creek, Mo., U.S.	h11	102
Sugarcreek, Pa., U.S.	D2	115
Sugar Creek, stm., In., U.S.	F6	91
Sugar Creek, stm., In., U.S.	E3	91
Sugar Creek, stm., Oh., U.S.	C2	112
Sugar Creek, stm., Pa., U.S.	C8	115
Sugar Grove, N.C., U.S.	A1	110
Sugar Grove, Oh., U.S.	C3	112
Sugar Grove, Pa., U.S.	C3	115
Sugar Grove, Va., U.S.	D1	123
Sugar Grove, W.V., U.S.	C5	125
Sugar Hill, Ga., U.S.	B2	87
Sugar Hill, N.H., U.S.	B3	106
Sugar Island, i., Mi., U.S.	B6	99
Sugar Land, Tx., U.S.	E5	120
Sugar Run, Va., U.S.	A5	123
Sugar Loaf, Va., U.S.	C3	123
Sugar Loaf, mtn., Braz.	h6	56
Sugarloaf, mtn., N.H., U.S.	A4	106
Sugarloaf, hill, Oh., U.S.	A4	112
Sugarloaf Mountain, mtn., Me., U.S.	C2	96
Sugar Loaf Mountain, mtn., Md., U.S.	B3	97
Sugarloaf Mountain, mtn., Mt., U.S.	C4	103
Sugar Loaf Mountain, mtn., Ok., U.S.	B7	113
Sugarloaf Point, c., Austl.	F9	51
Sugar Mountain, mtn., Mi., U.S.	k9	99
Sugar Notch, Pa., U.S.	n17	115
Sugartown, La., U.S.	D2	95
Sugar Valley, Ga., U.S.	B1	87
Sugden, Ok., U.S.	C4	113
Suggi Lake, l., Sask.	C4	75
Suggsville, Al., U.S.	D2	78
Şuḩār, Oman	C5	38
Sühbaatar, Mong.	A6	31
Suhl, E. Ger.	C5	18
Suiattle, stm., Wa., U.S.	A4	124
Suibin, China	C5	33
Suichuan, China	F7	31
Suide, China	D7	31
Suifenhe, China	C11	31
Suihua, China	B10	31
Suijiang, China	F5	31
Suileng, China	B10	31
Suining, China	E6	31
Suipacha, Arg.	g7	54
Suipacha, Bol.	D2	55
Suippes, Fr.	E4	17
Suir, stm., Ire.	D3	10
Suisun City, Ca., U.S.	*C2	82
Suit, N.C., U.S.	f8	110
Suita, Japan	*I7	33
Suitland, Md., U.S.	C4	97
Suixian, China	E7	31
Suixian, China	G6	32
Suizhong, China	D9	32
Sukabumi, Indon.	G3	34
Sukadana, Indon.	F3	34
Sukaraja, Indon.	F4	34
Sukarnapura see Jayapura, Indon.	F10	34
Sukhaya Tunguska, Sov. Un.	B26	8
Sukhobuzimskoye, Sov. Un.	D27	8
Sukhona, stm., Sov. Un.	C7	29
Sukhothai, Thai.	B1	34
Sukhumi, Sov. Un.	G17	8
Sukkur, Pak.	C4	36
Sukumo, Japan	J6	33
Sula, Mt., U.S.	E3	103
Sula, stm., Sov. Un.	F9	27
Sulaco, stm., Hond.	C4	62
Sulaiman Range, mts., Pak.	C4	36
Sula Islands, is., Indon.	F7	34
Sula Sgeir, i., Scot., U.K.	A2	13
Sulecin, Pol.	B3	26
Sulejówek, Pol.	m14	26
Sule Skerry, rock, Scot., U.K.	A4	13
Sulina, Rom.	C9	24
Sulingen, W. Ger.	F2	15
Sulitelma, mtn., Eur.	D7	14
Sullana, Peru	B1	58
Sulligent, Al., U.S.	B1	78
Sullivan, Il., U.S.	D5	90
Sullivan, In., U.S.	F3	91
Sullivan, Ky., U.S.	C2	94
Sullivan, Mo., U.S.	C6	102
Sullivan, N.H., U.S.	D2	106
Sullivan, Oh., U.S.	A3	112
Sullivan, Wi., U.S.	E5	126
Sullivan, co., In., U.S.	F3	91
Sullivan, co., Mo., U.S.	A4	102
Sullivan, co., N.H., U.S.	D2	106
Sullivan, co., N.Y., U.S.	D6	109
Sullivan, co., Pa., U.S.	D9	115
Sullivan, co., Tn., U.S.	C11	119
Sullivan Lake, l., Alta.	D5	68
Sullivans Island, S.C., U.S.	k12	117
Sully, Ia., U.S.	C5	92
Sully, co., S.D., U.S.	C5	118
Sulmona, Italy	C4	23
Sulphide, Ont.	C7	73
Sulphur, Ky., U.S.	B4	94
Sulphur, La., U.S.	D2	95
Sulphur, Ok., U.S.	C5	113
Sulphur, stm., Alta.	C1	68
Sulphur Rock, Ar., U.S.	B4	81
Sulphur Spring Range, mts., Nv., U.S.	C5	105
Sulphur Springs, Ar., U.S.	A1	81
Sulphur Springs, In., U.S.	D7	91
Sulphur Springs, Mo., U.S.	g13	102
Sulphur Springs, Oh., U.S.	B3	112
Sulphur Springs, Tx., U.S.	C5	120
Sulphur Springs Valley, val., Az., U.S.	E6	80
Sultan, Wa., U.S.	B4	124
Sultānpur, India	D9	37
Sulu Archipelago, is., Phil.	D6	34
Sulu Sea, Asia	C4	43
Sulzbach, W. Ger.	D2	19
Sulzbach-Rosenberg, W. Ger.	D6	19
Sulzberger Bay, b., Ant.	B33	7
Sumas, Wash., U.S.	A3	124
Sumatra, Fl., U.S.	B2	86
Sumatra, i., U.S.	D9	103
Sumatra (Sumatera), i., Indon.	F2	34
Sumava Resorts, In., U.S.	B3	91
Sumba, i., Indon.	G6	34
Sumba, i., Indon.	B7	39
Sumbawa, i., Indon.	G5	34
Sumbawa Besar, Indon.	G5	34
Sumbawanga, Tan.	C5	48
Sumbay, Peru	E3	58
Sumbe (Ngunza), Ang.	D1	48
Sumburgh Head, c., Scot., U.K.	h10	10
Sümeg, Hung.	B3	24
Sumenep, Indon.	G4	34
Sumgait, Sov. Un.	A4	39
Sumiswald, Switz.	B4	21
Sumiton, Al., U.S.	B2	78
Summerberry, Sask.	G4	75
Summerdale, Al., U.S.	E2	78
Summerfield, Fl., U.S.	C4	86
Summerfield, Ks., U.S.	C7	93
Summerfield, La., U.S.	B3	95
Summerfield, Mo., U.S.	C6	102
Summerfield, N.C., U.S.	A3	110
Summerfield, Oh., U.S.	C4	112
Summerford, Newf.	D4	72
Summerhill, Ire.	D5	11
Summer Hill, Il., U.S.	D3	90
Summer Island, i., Mi., U.S.	C4	99
Summer Lake, Or., U.S.	E6	114
Summer Lake, l., Or., U.S.	E6	114
Summerland, B.C.	E8	69
Summerland Key, Fl., U.S.	H5	86
Summers, co., W.V., U.S.	D4	125
Summer Shade, Ky., U.S.	D4	94
Summerside, P.E.I.	C6	71
Summersville, Mo., U.S.	D6	102
Summersville, W.V., U.S.	C4	125
Summersville Lake, res., W.V., U.S.	C4	125
Summerton, S.C., U.S.	D7	117
Summertown, Ga., U.S.	D4	87
Summerville, Ga., U.S.	B1	87
Summerville, Or., U.S.	B8	114
Summerville, Pa., U.S.	D3	115
Summerville, S.C., U.S.	E7	117
Summit, Az., U.S.	A3	81
Summit, Il., U.S.	k9	90
Summit, Ms., U.S.	D3	101
Summit, N.J., U.S.	B4	107
Summit, Ok., U.S.	B6	113
Summit, R.I., U.S.	C3	116
Summit, S.D., U.S.	B8	118
Summit, Tn., U.S.	h11	119
Summit, Ut., U.S.	F3	121
Summit, co., Co., U.S.	B4	83
Summit, co., Oh., U.S.	A4	112
Summit, co., Ut., U.S.	C5	121
Summit, stm., N.Z.	N16	51
Summit Grove, In., U.S.	E3	91
Summit Hill, Pa., U.S.	E10	115
Summit Lake, B.C.	B6	69
Summit Lake, l., Ia., U.S.	C3	92
Summit Lake Indian Reservation, Nv., U.S.	*C2	82
Summit Mountain, mtn., Nv., U.S.	B2	105
	D5	105
Summit Peak, mtn., Co., U.S.	D4	83
Summit Point, W.V., U.S.	B7	125
Summit Station, Oh., U.S.	k11	112
Summitville, Co., U.S.	D4	83
Summitville, In., U.S.	D6	91
Summitville, Tn., U.S.	D8	119
Summum, Il., U.S.	C3	90
Sumner, Ga., U.S.	E3	87
Sumner, Il., U.S.	E6	90
Sumner, Ia., U.S.	B5	92
Sumner, Ms., U.S.	B3	101
Sumner, Mo., U.S.	B4	102
Sumner, Ne., U.S.	D6	104
Sumner, Wa., U.S.	A4	113
Sumner, wa., U.S.	B3	124
Sumner, co., Ks., U.S.	E6	93
Sumner, co., Tn., U.S.	A5	119
Sumner, Lake, res., N.M., U.S.	C5	108
Sumner Strait, strt., Ak., U.S.	m23	79
Sumoto, Japan	I7	33
Šumperk, Czech.	D4	26
Sumpter, Or., U.S.	C8	114
Sumrall, Ms., U.S.	D4	101
Sumter, Ga., U.S.	E2	87
Sumter, S.C., U.S.	D7	117
Sumter, co., Al., U.S.	C1	78
Sumter, co., Fl., U.S.	D4	86
Sumter, co., Ga., U.S.	D2	87
Sumter, co., S.C., U.S.	D7	117
Sumterville, Al., U.S.	C1	78
Sumy, Sov. Un.	D6	29
Sun, La., U.S.	D6	95
Sun, stm., Mt., U.S.	C4	103
Sunapee, N.H., U.S.	D2	106
Sunapee Lake, l., N.H., U.S.	D2	106
Sunapee Mountain, mtn., N.H., U.S.	D2	106
Sunart, Loch, i., Scot., U.K.	D5	13
Sunbright, Tn., U.S.	C9	119
Sunburg, Mn., U.S.	E3	100
Sunburst, Mt., U.S.	B5	103
Sunbury, N.C., U.S.	A6	110
Sunbury, Oh., U.S.	B3	112
Sunbury, Pa., U.S.	E8	115
Sunbury, co., N.B.	D3	71
Sunchales, Arg.	A4	54
Suncho Corral, Arg.	E3	55
Sunchŏn, N. Kor.	G2	33
Sunchŏn, S. Kor.	I3	33
Sun City, Az., U.S.	k8	80
Sun City, Ca., U.S.	*F5	82
Sun City, Fl., U.S.	p10	86
Sun City, Ks., U.S.	E5	93
Sun City Center, Fl., U.S.	*E4	86
Suncook, N.H., U.S.	D4	106
Suncook, stm., N.H., U.S.	D4	106
Suncook Lakes, l., N.H., U.S.	D4	106
Sundance, Wy., U.S.	B8	127
Sundance Mountain, mtn., Wy., U.S.	B8	127
Sundarbans, reg., Asia	D8	36
Sunda Strait, strt., Indon.	G3	34
Sunday Strait, strt., Austl.	C3	50
Sundbyberg, Swe.	t35	14
Sunderland, Ont.	C5	73
Sunderland, Eng., U.K.	C6	10
Sunderland, Md., U.S.	C4	97
Sunderland, Ma., U.S.	B2	98
Sunderland, Vt., U.S.	E2	122
Sundown, Man.	E3	70
Sundown, Tx., U.S.	C1	120
Sundre, Alta.	D3	68
Sundridge, Ont.	B5	73
Sunds, Den.	B3	15
Sundsvall, Swe.	F7	14
Sunfield, Mi., U.S.	F5	99
Sunflower, Ms., U.S.	B3	101
Sunflower, co., Ms., U.S.	B3	101
Sunflower, Mount, mtn., Ks., U.S.	C2	93
Sungaigontung, Indon.	E2	34
Sungaipenuh, Indon.	F2	34
Sungai Petani, Malay.	J4	35
Sungari Reservoir, res., China	E3	33
Sungari see Songhua Jiang, stm., China	B10	31
Sungurlu, Tur.	B10	40
Sunland Park, N.M., U.S.	F3	108
Sunlight Creek, stm., Wy., U.S.	B3	127
Sunman, In., U.S.	F7	91
Sunne, Swe.	H5	14
Sunnybrae, N.S.	D7	71
Sunnybrook, Alta.	C3	68
Sunny Isles, Fl., U.S.	*G6	86
Sunnyland, Fl., U.S.	q11	86
Sunnymead, Ca., U.S.	*F5	82
Sunnynook, Alta.	D5	68
Sunnyside, Newf.	E5	72
Sunnyside, Ca., U.S.	*D4	82
Sunnyside, Fl., U.S.	u16	86
Sunnyside, Ut., U.S.	D5	121
Sunnyside, Wa., U.S.	C5	124
Sunny South, Al., U.S.	D2	78
Sunnyvale, Ca., U.S.	k8	82
Sunnyvale, S.D., U.S.	C9	118
Sunol, Ca., U.S.	h9	82
Sun Prairie, Wi., U.S.	E4	126
Sunray, Ok., U.S.	A2	113
Sunray, Tx., U.S.	A2	120
Sunrise, Fl., U.S.	*r13	86
Sunrise, Wy., U.S.	D8	127
Sunrise Manor, Nv., U.S.	G6	105
Sunrise Mountain, mtn., N.J., U.S.	A3	107
Sun River, Mt., U.S.	C5	103
Sunset, Fl., U.S.	*G6	86
Sunset, La., U.S.	D3	95
Sunset, Me., U.S.	D4	96
Sunset, Tx., U.S.	C4	120
Sunset, Ut., U.S.	B4	121
Sunset Beach, Hi., U.S.	f9	88
Sunset Crater National Monument, Az., U.S.	B4	80
Sunset Hill, hill, U.S.	B7	84
Sunset Lake, l., Vt., U.S.	D2	122
Sunset Park, Ks., U.S.	D6	93
Sunshine, Austl.	*G7	50
Sunshine, Ak., U.S.	f16	79
Sunshine, Me., U.S.	D4	96
Sunspot, N.M., U.S.	E4	108
Suntar, Sov. Un.	C14	29
Suntaug Lake, l., Ma., U.S.	f11	98
Suntrana, Ak., U.S.	C10	79
Sun Valley, Id., U.S.	F4	89
Sun Valley, Nv., U.S.	D2	105
Sunyani, Ghana	E4	45
Suoyarvi, Sov. Un.	F15	14
Suozhou, China	E9	31
Superb, Sask.	F1	75
Superior, Az., U.S.	D4	80
Superior, Mt., U.S.	A3	92
	C2	103
Superior, Ne., U.S.	D7	104
Superior, Wi., U.S.	B1	126
Superior, Wy., U.S.	E4	127
Superior, Lake, l., N.A.	A10	76
Superstition Mountains, mts., Az., U.S.	m10	80
Suphan Buri, Thai.	E4	35
Supi Oidak, Az., U.S.	F4	80
Supply, N.C., U.S.	C4	110
Supreme, La., U.S.	k9	95
Supung Reservoir, res., Asia	F3	33
Sūq ash Shuyūkh, Iraq	F3	39
Suquamish, Wa., U.S.	B3	124
Sur, Point, c., Ca., U.S.	D3	82
Sura, stm., Sov. Un.	D16	27
Surabaya, Indon.	G4	34
Surakarta, Indon.	G4	34
Surakhany, Sov. Un.	E4	28
Surat, Austl.	C7	51
Sūrat, India	D5	36
Sūratgarh, India	C4	37
Surat Thani, Thai.	D1	34
Surazh, Sov. Un.	E9	27
Şūr Bāhir, Isr. Occ.	k11	41
Surco, Peru	*D2	58
Surendranagar, India	F3	37
Suresnes, Fr.	g9	16
Suretka, C.R.	F6	62
Surettes Island, N.S.	F4	71
Surf City, N.J., U.S.	D4	107
Surfside, Fl., U.S.	s13	86
Surfside Beach, S.C., U.S.	D10	117
Surgères, Fr.	D3	16
Surgoinsville, Tn., U.S.	C11	119
Surgut, Sov. Un.	C4	28
Surgut, Sov. Un.	C10	29
Suriāpet, India	I7	37
Suribachi, Mount, hill, Japan	P17	52
Surigao, Phil.	D7	34
Suriname, dept., Sur.	A3	59
Suriname, ctry., S.A.	B3	59
Suring, Wi., U.S.	D5	126
Surkhan Darya, stm., Sov. Un.	C13	39
Surprise, Az., U.S.	k8	80
Surprise, Ne., U.S.	C8	104
Surquillo, Peru	*D2	58
Surrency, Ga., U.S.	E4	87
Surrey, N.D., U.S.	A4	111
Surrey, co., Eng., U.K.	C7	12
Surry, Me., U.S.	D4	96
Surry, N.H., U.S.	D2	106
Surry, Va., U.S.	C6	123
Surry, co., N.C., U.S.	A2	110
Surry, co., Va., U.S.	C6	123
Surry Mountain Lake, res., N.H., U.S.	D2	106
Sursee, Switz.	B5	21
Surt, Libya	C3	43
Sürüç, Tur.	D12	40
Suruga Bay, b., Japan	o17	33
Surveyor, W.V., U.S.	n13	125
Suryānī, Dayr as, hist., Eg.	D2	41
Susa, Italy	B1	23
Sušac, i., Yugo.	D3	24
Sušak (part of Rijeka), Yugo.	C2	24
Susak, i., Yugo.	C2	24
Susami, Japan	s31	14
Susanino, Sov. Un.	s31	14
Susank, Ks., U.S.	D5	93
Susanville, Ca., U.S.	B3	82
Suşice, Czech.	D2	26
Susitna, stm., Ak., U.S.	C10	79
Susoh, Indon.	K2	35
Susong, China	I7	32
Susquehanna, Pa., U.S.	C10	115
Susquehanna, co., Pa., U.S.	C10	115
Susquehanna, stm., U.S.	A5	97
Susquehanna, West Branch, stm., Pa., U.S.	D5	115
Susques, Arg.	D2	55
Sussex, N.B.	D4	71
Sussex, N.J., U.S.	A3	107
Sussex, Va., U.S.	D5	123
Sussex, Wi., U.S.	m11	126
Sussex, co., De., U.S.	F4	85
Sussex, co., N.J., U.S.	A3	107
Sussex, co., Va., U.S.	D5	123
Sussex Shores, De., U.S.	F5	85
Sustut, stm., B.C.	A4	69
Susurluk, Tur.	C7	40
Sutcliffe, Nv., U.S.	D2	105
Sutherland, S. Afr.	D3	49
Sutherland, Ia., U.S.	B2	92
Sutherland, Ne., U.S.	C4	104
Sutherland, Ut., U.S.	D3	121
Sutherland, Va., U.S.	C5	123
Sutherland Springs, Tx., U.S.	k7	120
Sutherlin, Or., U.S.	D3	114
Sutlej (Langqên Zangbo), stm., Asia	B6	36
Sutter, Ca., U.S.	C3	82
Sutter Creek, Ca., U.S.	C3	82
Suttle, Al., U.S.	C2	78
Sutton, Que.	D5	74
Sutton, Ak., U.S.	g17	79
Sutton, Ma., U.S.	*B4	98
Sutton, Ne., U.S.	D8	104
Sutton, N.H., U.S.	D3	106
Sutton, N.D., U.S.	B7	111
Sutton, Vt., U.S.	B4	122
Sutton, W.V., U.S.	C4	125
Sutton, co., Tx., U.S.	D2	120
Sutton Coldfield, Eng., U.K.	B6	12
Sutton in Ashfield, Eng., U.K.	D6	10
Sutton Lake, res., W.V., U.S.	C4	125
Sutton Park, N.J., U.S.	C4	107
Suttons Bay, Mi., U.S.	D5	99
Sutton West, Ont.	C5	73
Suttsu, Japan	E10	33
Sutwik Island, i., Ak., U.S.	D8	79
Suva, Fiji	I15	52
Suva Harbour, b., Fiji	I15	52
Suwa, Japan	m17	33
Suwałki, Pol.	A7	26
Suwannee, Fl., U.S.	B2	86
Suwannee, co., Fl., U.S.	B3	86
Suwannee, stm., U.S.	C3	86
Suwannee Lake, l., Man.	A1	70
Suwannee Sound, strt., Fl., U.S.	C3	86
Suwanose Island, i., Japan	L3	33
Suwaylih, Jord.	B7	41
Suwayqimah, Thamilāt, well, Eg.	D6	41
Suwaywah, Jord.	h13	41
Suwŏn, S. Kor.	H3	33
Suxian, China	H7	32
Suyo, Peru	B1	58
Suzhou, China	E9	31
Suzu, Cape, c., Japan	H8	33
Suzuka, Japan	o15	33
Suzzara, Italy	E6	20
Svalbard, ter., Nor.	B13	128
Svaneke, Den.	C8	15
Svärtagård, Swe.	u35	14
Svartån, stm., Swe.	t34	14
Svatovo, Sov. Un.	G12	27
Svay Rieng, Camb.	C3	34
Svedala, Swe.	C7	15
Svedrup, i., Sov. Un.	B7	128
Sveg, Swe.	F6	14
Svendborg, Den.	C4	15
Svenljunga, Swe.	A7	15
Svensen, Or., U.S.	A3	114
Svenstrup, Den.	B3	15
Sverdlovsk, Sov. Un.	q22	27
Sverdlovsk, Sov. Un.	D9	29
Sverdrup Islands, is., N.W. Ter.	m32	66
Svetlaya, Sov. Un.	C9	33
Svetlograd, Sov. Un.	I14	27
Svicha, stm., Sov. Un.	D8	26
Svilajnac, Yugo.	C5	24
Svilengrad, Bul.	E8	24
Svindal, Nor.	p29	14
Svir, stm., Sov. Un.	A10	27
Svirstroy, Sov. Un.	A9	27
Svishtov, Bul.	D7	24
Svisloch, Sov. Un.	D4	26
Svitavy, Czech.	D4	26
Svobodnyy, Sov. Un.	D15	29
Svobodnyy, Cape, c., Sov. Un.	C11	33
Svyatoy Nos, Cape, c., Sov. Un.	B16	29
Swadlincote, Eng., U.K.	B6	12
Swaffham, Eng., U.K.	B8	12
Swain, co., N.C., U.S.	f9	110
Swain Reefs, rf., Austl.	D9	50
Swainsboro, Ga., U.S.	D4	87
Swakopmund, Nmb.	B1	49
Swaledale, Ia., U.S.	B4	92
Swalwell, Alta.	D4	68
Swampscott, Ma., U.S.	B6	98
Swan, stm., Alta.	B3	68
Swan, stm., Can.	C1	70
Swanage, Eng., U.K.	D6	12
Swan Creek, Il., U.S.	C3	90
Swan Creek, stm., Oh., U.S.	e6	112
Swandale, W.V., U.S.	m14	125
Swan Falls, wtfl., Id., U.S.	F2	89
Swan Hill, Austl.	G7	50
Swan Hills, Alta.	B3	68
Swan Hills, hills, Alta.	B3	68
Swan Lake, Man.	E2	70
Swan Lake, l., Man.	C1	70
Swan Lake, l., Ms., U.S.	B3	101
Swan Lake, l., Id., U.S.	G6	89
Swan Lake, l., Ne., U.S.	C5	104
Swan Peak, mtn., Mt., U.S.	C3	103
Swanquarter, N.C., U.S.	B6	110
Swan Range, mts., Mt., U.S.	C3	103
Swan River, Man.	C1	70
Swan River, Mn., U.S.	C5	100
Swansboro, N.C., U.S.	C5	110
Swansea, Wales, U.K.	E4	10
Swansea, Il., U.S.	E3	90
Swansea, Ma., U.S.	C5	98
Swansea, S.C., U.S.	D5	117
Swansea Bay, b., Wales, U.K.	C4	12
Swansea Center, Ma., U.S.	C5	98
Swans Island, Me., U.S.	D4	96
Swanson, Sask.	F2	75
Swanson Lake, res., Ne., U.S.	D4	104
Swanton, Md., U.S.	m12	97
Swanton, Oh., U.S.	A2	112
Swanton, Vt., U.S.	B2	122
Swan Valley, Id., U.S.	F7	89
Swanville, Mn., U.S.	E4	100
Swanwick, Il., U.S.	E4	90
Swanwyck Estates, De., U.S.	*B3	85
Swanzey Center, N.H., U.S.	E2	106
Swarthmore, Pa., U.S.	p20	115
Swartswood, N.J., U.S.	A3	107
Swartswood Lake, l., N.J., U.S.	A3	107
Swartz, La., U.S.	B4	95
Swartz Creek, Mi., U.S.	F7	99
Swatara, Mn., U.S.	D5	100
Swatara Township, Pa., U.S.	*F8	115
Swatow see Shantou, China	G8	31
Swayzee, In., U.S.	C6	91
Swaziland, ctry., Afr.	C5	49
Swea City, Ia., U.S.	A3	92
Sweatman, Ms., U.S.	B4	101
Swedeborg, Mo., U.S.	D5	102
Swedeburg, Ne., U.S.	g11	104
Sweden, ctry., Eur.	C6	14
Swedesboro, N.J., U.S.	D2	107
Sweeny, Tx., U.S.	r14	120
Sweet, Id., U.S.	F2	89
Sweet Briar, Va., U.S.	C3	123
Sweetgrass, Mt., U.S.	B5	103
Sweet Grass, co., Mt., U.S.	E7	103
Sweet Home, Or., U.S.	C4	114
Sweet Home, Tx., U.S.	E4	120
Sweetser, In., U.S.	C6	91
Sweet Springs, Mo., U.S.	C4	102
Sweet Springs, W.V., U.S.	D4	125
Sweet Valley, Pa., U.S.	D9	115
Sweet Water, Al., U.S.	C2	78
Sweetwater, Fl., U.S.	*G6	86
Sweetwater, Ok., U.S.	B2	113
Sweetwater, Tn., U.S.	D9	119
Sweetwater, co., Wy., U.S.	E3	127
Sweetwater Creek, Fl., U.S.	p10	86
Sweetwater Creek, stm., Ok., U.S.	B1	113
Sweetwater Station, Wy., U.S.	D5	127
Swellendam, S. Afr.	D3	49
Swenson, Tx., U.S.	C3	120
Swepsonville, N.C., U.S.	A3	110
Świder, stm., Pol.	m14	26
Świdnica, Pol.	C4	26
Świdwin, Pol.	B3	26
Świebodzice, Pol.	C4	26
Świebodzin, Pol.	B3	26
Świecie, Pol.	B5	26
Świetochłowice, Pol.	g9	26
Świętokrzyskie, Góry, mts., Pol.	C6	26
Swift Creek, stm., N.C., U.S.	B5	110
Swift Creek, stm., Va., U.S.	n17	123
Swift Creek Reservoir, res., Wa., U.S.	C3	124
Swift Current, Sask.	G2	75
Swiftcurrent Creek, stm., Sask.	H1	75
Swift Diamond, stm., N.H., U.S.	g7	106
Swifton, Ar., U.S.	B4	81
Swiftown, Ms., U.S.	B3	101
Swiftwater, N.H., U.S.	B3	106
Swilly, Lough, b., Ire.	B4	11
Swinburne, Cape, c., N.W. Ter.	B13	66
Swindle Island, i., B.C.	C3	69
Swindon, Eng., U.K.	E6	10
Swinford, Ire.	D3	11
Swink, Co., U.S.	C7	83
Swink, Ok., U.S.	C6	113
Swinomish Indian Reservation, Wa., U.S.	A3	124
Świnoujście, Pol.	B3	26
Swisher, Ia., U.S.	C6	92
Swisher, co., Tx., U.S.	B2	120
Swiss, W.V., U.S.	C3	125
Swisshome, Or., U.S.	C3	114
Swissvale, Pa., U.S.	I 14	115
Switz City, In., U.S.	F3	91
Switzer, W.V., U.S.	D3	125
Switzerland, Fl., U.S.	m8	86
Switzerland, S.C., U.S.	G5	117
Switzerland, co., In., U.S.	G7	91
Switzerland, ctry., Eur.	E4	18
Swords, Ire.	D5	11
Swords, Ga., U.S.	C3	87
Swoyerville, Pa., U.S.	D10	115
Sycamore, Al., U.S.	B3	78
Sycamore, Ga., U.S.	E3	87
Sycamore, Il., U.S.	B5	90
Sycamore, Ks., U.S.	E8	93
Sycamore, Mo., U.S.	E5	102
Sycamore, Oh., U.S.	B2	112
Sycamore, S.C., U.S.	E5	117
Sycamore Creek, stm., Tn., U.S.	A4	119
Sycamore Creek, stm., W.V., U.S.	m13	125
Sychevka, Sov. Un.	D10	27
Syców, Pol.	C4	26
Sydenham, Ont.	C8	73
Sydney, Austl.	F9	50
Sydney, N.S.	C9	71
Sydney Mines, N.S.	C9	71
Sykeston, N.D., U.S.	B6	111
Sykesville, Md., U.S.	B4	97
Sykesville, Pa., U.S.	D4	115
Syktyvkar, Sov. Un.	C8	29
Sylacauga, Al., U.S.	B3	78
Sylamore, Ar., U.S.	B3	81
Sylling, Nor.	p28	14
Sylt, i., W. Ger.	A4	18
Sylva, N.C., U.S.	f9	110
Sylvan, Pa., U.S.	G5	115
Sylvan Beach, N.Y., U.S.	B5	109
Sylvan Grove, Ks., U.S.	C5	93
Sylvan Hills, Ar., U.S.	h10	81
Sylvania, Sask.	E3	75
Sylvania, Al., U.S.	A4	78
Sylvania, Ga., U.S.	D5	87
Sylvania, Oh., U.S.	A2	112
Sylvan Lake, Alta.	C3	68
Sylvan Lake, Mi., U.S.	o15	99
Sylvan Pass, Wy., U.S.	B2	127
Sylvarena, Ms., U.S.	C4	101
Sylvester, Ga., U.S.	E3	87
Sylvester, Tx., U.S.	C2	120
Sylvester, Mount, hill, Newf.	D4	72
Sylvia, Ks., U.S.	E5	93
Sylvia, Tn., U.S.	A4	119
Symmes Creek, stm., Oh., U.S.	D3	112
Symsonia, Ky., U.S.	f9	94
Syosset, N.Y., U.S.	*E7	109
Syracuse, In., U.S.	B6	91
Syracuse, Ks., U.S.	E2	93
Syracuse, Mo., U.S.	C5	102
Syracuse, N.Y., U.S.	B4	109
Syracuse, Ne., U.S.	D9	104
Syracuse, Ut., U.S.	B3	121
Syracuse see Siracusa, Italy	F5	23
Syr Darya, stm., Sov. Un.	E9	29
Syria, ctry., Asia	B3	38
Syriam, Burma	D2	35
Syrian Desert, des., Asia	B3	38
Syros see Ermoúpolis, Grc.	D5	40
Sysladobsis Lake, l., Me., U.S.	C4	96
Sysola, stm., Sov. Un.	C19	8
Syurkum, Cape, c., Sov. Un.	A10	33
Syzran, Sov. Un.	D7	29
Szabadszállás, Hung.	B4	24
Szamos (Someş), stm., Eur.	B6	24
Szamotuły, Pol.	B4	26
Szarvas, Hung.	B5	24
Szczakowa (part of Jaworzno), Pol.	g10	26
Szczebrzeszyn, Pol.	C7	26
Szczecin (Stettin), Pol.	B3	26
Szczecinek, Pol.	B4	26
Szczuczyn, Pol.	B7	26
Szczytno, Pol.	B6	26
Szechwan see Sichuan, prov., China	E5	31
Szeged, Hung.	B5	24
Székesfehérvár, Hung.	B4	24
Szekszárd, Hung.	B4	24
Szentendre, Hung.	B4	24
Szentes, Hung.	B5	24
Szigetvár, Hung.	B3	24
Szolnok, Hung.	B5	24
Szombathely, Hung.	B3	24
Szprotawa, Pol.	C3	26
Sztum, Pol.	B5	26
Szydłowiec, Pol.	C6	26
Szymanów, Pol.	m12	26

T

Taal, Phil.	p13	34
Taal, Lake, l., Phil.	p13	34
Tab, In., U.S.	D3	91
Tabar Islands, is., Pap. N. Gui.	h13	52
Tabarka, Tun.	F2	23
Tabas, Iran	D6	38
Tabasco, state, Mex.	D6	63
Tabas Masīnā, Iran	E10	39
Tabatinga, Braz.	k7	56

Name	Map Ref.	Page
Tabayin, Burma	A1	35
Tabbys Peak, mtn., Ut., U.S.	C3	121
Tabelbala, Alg.	D4	44
Taber, Alta.	E4	68
Tabernacle, N.J., U.S.	D3	107
Tabernas, Spain	D4	22
Tabernash, Co., U.S.	B5	83
Taberville, Mo., U.S.	C4	102
Tabik Island, i., Marsh Is.	S17	52
Tabiona, Ut., U.S.	C5	121
Tabiteuea, Kir.	R18	52
Tabla, Cerro de la, mtn., P.R.	B3	65
Tablas, Cabo, c., Chile	A2	54
Tablas Island, i., Phil.	C6	34
Table Bay, b., Newf.	B3	72
Table Bay, b., S. Afr.	D2	49
Table Grove, Il., U.S.	C3	90
Table Head, c., Newf.	B4	72
Table Mountain, mtn., Newf.	E2	72
Table Mountain, mtn., Az., U.S.	E5	80
Table Rock, Ne., U.S.	D9	104
Table Rock Lake, res., U.S.	E4	102
Table Top, mtn., Az., U.S.	E3	80
Taboada, Spain	A2	22
Tábor, Czech.	D3	26
Tabor, Ia., U.S.	D2	92
Tabor, Mn., U.S.	B2	100
Tabor, S.D., U.S.	E8	118
Tabor, Mount, mtn., Isr.	B7	41
Tabora, Tan.	C5	48
Tabora, prov., Tan.	C5	48
Tabor City, N.C., U.S.	C4	110
Tabou, I.C.	F3	45
Tabrīz, Iran	B4	38
Tabuaeran Island (Fanning Island), atoll, Kir.	F12	6
Tabūk, Sau. Ar.	C3	38
Tabusintac, stm., N.B.	B5	71
Täby, Swe.	*H8	14
Tacámbaro de Codallos, Mex.	n13	63
Tacheng, China	B1	31
Tachie, stm., B.C.	B5	69
Tachiiwa Point, c., Japan	P17	33
Tachikawa, Japan	n18	33
Táchira, state, Ven.	B3	60
Tachov, Czech.	D2	26
Tacloban, Phil.	C7	34
Tacna, Peru	E3	58
Tacna, Az., U.S.	E1	80
Tacna, dept., Peru	E3	58
Tacoma, Wa., U.S.	B3	124
Taconic, Ct., U.S.	A2	84
Taconic Range, mts., U.S.	A1	98
Taconite, Mn., U.S.	C5	100
Tacoronte, Spain	m13	22
Tacuarembo, Ur.	E1	56
Tacuati, Para.	C4	55
Tad, W.V., U.S.	m13	125
Tademaït, Plateau du, plat., Alg.	D5	44
Tadjoura, Dji.	C5	47
Tadoule Lake, l., Man.	f8	70
Tadoussac, Que.	A8	74
T'aebaek-Sanmaek, mts., Asia	H4	33
Taegu, S. Kor.	D10	31
Taejon, S. Kor.	D10	31
Taeyu-dong, N. Kor.	F2	33
Tafalla, Spain	A5	22
Tafí Viejo, Arg.	E2	55
Tafo, Ghana	*E4	45
Taft, Ca., U.S.	E4	82
Taft, La., U.S.	k11	95
Taft, Ok., U.S.	B6	113
Taft, Tn., U.S.	B5	119
Taft, Tx., U.S.	F4	120
Taftān, mtn., Iran	G10	39
Taftsville, Vt., U.S.	D4	122
Tafuna International Airport, Am. Sam.	G13	52
Taganrog, Sov. Un.	H12	27
Taganrog, Gulf of, b., Sov. Un.	H12	27
Tagaytay, Phil.	o13	34
Tagbilaran, Phil.	D6	34
Taghmon, Ire.	E5	11
Taghrīfāt, Libya	D3	43
Tagolo Point, c., Phil.	D6	34
Taguan Point, c., Guam	L10	52
Taguatinga, Braz.	D1	57
Tagus, N.D., U.S.	A4	111
Tagus (Tejo) (Tajo), stm., Eur.	C1	22
Tahan, mtn., Malay.	E2	34
Tahat, mtn., Alg.	E6	44
Tahgong, Puntan, c., N. Mar. Is.	D7	52
Tahiti, i., Fr. Poly.	H13	6
Tahlequah, Ok., U.S.	B7	113
Tahmā wa Minshāt 'Abd as Sayyid, Eg.	E3	41
Tahoe, Lake, l., U.S.	E1	105
Tahoe City, Ca., U.S.	C3	82
Tahoka, Tx., U.S.	C2	120
Taholah, Wa., U.S.	B1	124
Tahoma, Ca., U.S.	C3	82
Tahoua, Niger	D6	45
Tahquamenon, stm., Mi., U.S.	B5	99
Tahsis, B.C.	E4	69
Tahtā, Eg.	C3	38
Tahtsa Lake, l., B.C.	C4	69
Tahtsa Peak, mtn., B.C.	C4	69
Tahuya, Wa., U.S.	B2	124
Taï, I.C.	G4	45
Tai'an, China	D10	32
Tai'an, China	F7	32
Taiban, N.M., U.S.	C5	108
Taibus Qi, China	D6	32
T'aichung, Tai.	G9	31
Taigu, China	F5	32
Taihape, N.Z.	M15	51
Taiho, Japan	N6	52
Tai Hu, l., China	E8	31
Tailai, China	A10	32
Tailem Bend, Austl.	G6	50
Tailevu Point, c., Fiji	H15	52
Tain, Scot., U.K.	B4	10
Tainan, Tai.	G9	31
Tainaron, Ákra, c., Grc.	D4	40
Taining, China	K7	32
Taioberas, Braz.	B4	56
Taipei, Tai.	G9	31
Taiping, Malay.	E2	34
Taipu, Braz.	g6	57
Taira see Iwaki, Japan	H10	33
Taishun, China	K8	32
Taitao, Peninsula de, pen., Chile	D2	54
T'aitung, Tai.	G9	31
Taivalkoski, Fin.	E13	14
Taiwan, ctry., Asia	G9	31
Taiwan Strait, strt., Asia	G8	31
Taiyiba, Isr.	B7	41
Taiyuan, China	D7	31
Taizhao, China	E3	31
Taizhou, China	H8	32
Ta'izz, Yemen	D4	38
Tajarhī, Libya	E2	43
Tajik S.S.R., state, Sov. Un.	F9	29
Tajimi, Japan	I8	33
Tajique, N.M., U.S.	C3	108
Tajumulco, Volcán, vol., Guat.	C2	62
Tajuña, stm., Spain	B4	22
Tājūrā', Libya	C2	43
Tak, Thai.	B1	34
Takabanare Island, i., Japan	O6	52
Takahe, Mount, mtn., Ant.	B1	7
Takaka, N.Z.	N14	51
Takamatsu, Japan	E11	31
Takaoka, Japan	H8	33
Takapuna, N.Z.	L15	51
Takara Island, i., Japan	L4	33
Takasaki, Japan	H9	33
Takashippu, Japan	O5	52
Takatō, Japan	n17	33
Takatsuki, Japan	o14	33
Takaw, Burma	B3	35
Takayama, Japan	H8	33
Takefu, Japan	n15	33
Take Islands see Tok Islands, is., Asia	H5	33
Takengon, Indon.	J2	35
Tākestān, Iran	C4	39
Takev, Camb.	G6	35
Takhta-Bazar, Sov. Un.	D11	39
Takhtakupyr, Sov. Un.	E6	28
Takigawa, Japan	E10	33
Takijuq Lake, l., N.W. Ter.	C10	66
Takishiri Island, i., Japan	D10	33
Takla, Lake, l., B.C.	B5	69
Taklamakan Shamo, des., China	F11	29
Takoma Park, Md., U.S.	f8	97
Takotna, Ak., U.S.	C8	79
Takpocha, Okso, mtn., N. Mar. Is.	D7	52
Taku, stm., N.A.	k23	79
Takua Pa, Thai.	H3	35
Taku Glacier, ice, Ak., U.S.	k22	79
Takut, Burma	A3	35
Talā, Eg.	D2	41
Tala, Mex.	m12	63
Tala, Ur.	E1	56
Talagante, Chile	A2	54
Talakan, Sov. Un.	B6	33
Talala, Ok., U.S.	A6	113
Talanga, Hond.	C4	62
Talara, Peru	B1	58
Talas, Sov. Un.	E8	28
Talasea, Pap. N. Gui.	k13	50
Talata Mafara, Nig.	D6	45
Talaud Islands, is., Indon.	E7	34
Talavera de la Reina, Spain	C3	22
Talbert, Ky., U.S.	C6	94
Talbot, In., U.S.	D3	91
Talbot, co., Ga., U.S.	D2	87
Talbot, co., Md., U.S.	C5	97
Talbot Lake, l., Man.	B2	70
Talbotton, Ga., U.S.	D2	87
Talca, Chile	B2	54
Talcahuano, Chile	B2	54
Tālcher, India	D8	36
Talco, Tx., U.S.	C5	120
Talcott, W.V., U.S.	D4	125
Talcottville, N.Y., U.S.	B5	109
Taldy-Kurgan, Sov. Un.	D9	28
Tālesh, Iran	C4	39
Taliabu, i., Indon.	F6	34
Taliaferro, co., Ga., U.S.	C4	87
Talica, Sov. Un.	B6	28
Talihina, Ok., U.S.	C6	113
Talim Island, i., Phil.	o13	34
Tali Post, Sud.	D3	47
Talisay, Phil.	o14	34
Talisheek, La., U.S.	D6	95
Talish Mountains, mts., Asia	B4	38
Talkeetna, Ak., U.S.	C10	79
Talkeetna Mountains, mts., Ak., U.S.	f17	79
Talkha, Eg.	C3	41
Tall, Isr. Occ.	g11	41
Talla Bena, U.S.	B4	95
Talladega, Al., U.S.	B3	78
Talladega, co., Al., U.S.	B3	78
Talladega Mountain, mtn., Al., U.S.	B3	78
Talladega Springs, Al., U.S.	B3	78
Tallahala Creek, stm., Ms., U.S.	D4	101
Tallahassee, Fl., U.S.	B2	86
Tallahatchie, co., Ms., U.S.	B3	101
Tallahatchie, stm., Ms., U.S.	B3	101
Tall al Abyaḍ, Syria	B3	38
Tallangatta, Austl.	H6	51
Tallant, Ok., U.S.	A5	113
Tallapoosa, Ga., U.S.	C1	87
Tallapoosa, Mo., U.S.	E8	102
Tallapoosa, co., Al., U.S.	C4	78
Tallapoosa, stm., Al., U.S.	C4	78
Tallard, Fr.	E2	20
Tallassee, Al., U.S.	C4	78
Talleyville, De., U.S.	A3	85
Tallinn, Sov. Un.	D5	29
Tall Kalakh, Syria	E11	40
Tallmadge, Oh., U.S.	A4	112
Tallow, Ire.	E3	11
Tallulah, La., U.S.	B4	95
Tallulah, stm., U.S.	B3	87
Talluža, Isr. Occ.	f12	41
Talmage, Sask.	H4	75
Talmage, Ks., U.S.	C6	93
Talmage, Ne., U.S.	D9	104
Talmage, Ut., U.S.	C5	121
Talnoye, Sov. Un.	G8	27
Talofofo, Guam	M10	52
Talofofo Bay, b., Guam	M10	52
Taloga, Ok., U.S.	A3	113
Talon, Lake, l., Ont.	A5	73
Talowah, Ms., U.S.	D4	101
Talpa de Allende, Mex.	m11	63
Talquin, Lake, res., Fl., U.S.	B2	86
Talsi, Sov. Un.	C6	27
Taltal, Chile	E1	55
Taltson, stm., N.W. Ter.	D10	66
Tama, i., U.S.	C5	92
Tama, co., Ia., U.S.	B5	92
Tamacuari, Pico, mtn., S.A.	C5	60
Tamaha, Ok., U.S.	B7	113
Tamalameque, Col.	B3	60
Tamale, Ghana	E4	45
Tamalpais, Mount, mtn., Ca., U.S.	h7	82
Tamalpais Valley, Ca., U.S.	*D2	82
Taman, Sov. Un.	I11	27
Tamana, Mount, hill, Trin.	O23	65
Tamanar, Mor.	C3	44
Tamano, Japan	I6	33
Tamaqua, Pa., U.S.	E10	115
Tamar, stm., Eng., U.K.	D3	12
Tamarac, Fl., U.S.	*r13	86
Tamarack, Mn., U.S.	D5	100
Tamarite [de Litera], Spain	B4	22
Tamaroa, Il., U.S.	E4	90
Tamassee, S.C., U.S.	B1	117
Tamaulipas, state, Mex.	C5	63
Tamazula de Gordiano, Mex.	n12	63
Tamazulapan [del Progreso], Mex.	o15	63
Tamazunchale, Mex.	C5	63
Tambacounda, Sen.	D2	45
Tambaú, Braz.	k8	56
També, Braz.	C3	57
Tambelan Besar, i., Indon.	L7	35
Tambelan Islands, is., Indon.	L7	35
Tambo, Austl.	B6	51
Tambo, stm., Peru	E3	58
Tambo, stm., Peru	D3	58
Tambo Grande, Peru	B1	58
Tambohorano, Madag.	g8	49
Tambov, Sov. Un.	D7	29
Tambre, stm., Spain	A1	22
Tambura, Sud.	D2	47
Tamchaket, Maur.	C2	45
Tamdybulak, Sov. Un.	E6	28
Tame, Col.	B3	60
Tāmega, stm., Port.	D2	22
Tamel Aike, Arg.	D2	54
Tamenghest, Alg.	E5	44
Tamenghest, Oued, val., Alg.	E5	44
Tamguê, Massif du, mts., Gui.		
Tamiahua, Mex.	C5	63
Tamiahua, Laguna de, b., Mex.	C5	63
Tamiami, Fl., U.S.	*G6	86
Tamiami Canal, Fl., U.S.	G6	86
Tamil Nadu (Madras), state, India	G6	36
Tamina, Tx., U.S.	D5	120
Tamins, Switz.	C7	21
Tamiš, stm., Eur.	C5	24
Tam Ky, Viet.	E8	35
Tamms, Il., U.S.	F4	90
Tamo, Ar., U.S.	C4	81
Tamora, Ne., U.S.	D8	104
Tampa, Fl., U.S.	E4	86
Tampa, Ks., U.S.	D6	93
Tampa Bay, b., Fl., U.S.	E4	86
Tampere, Fin.	G10	14
Tampico, Mex.	C5	63
Tampico, Il., U.S.	B4	90
Tampico, In., U.S.	G6	91
Tampico, Mt., U.S.	B10	103
Tams, W.V., U.S.	D3	125
Tamsagbulag, Mong.	B8	31
Tamshiyacu, Peru	B3	58
Tamuning, Guam	L10	52
Tamworth, Austl.	F9	50
Tamworth, Ont.	C8	73
Tamworth, Eng., U.K.	B6	12
Tamworth, N.H., U.S.	C4	106
Tana, stm., Eur.	B12	14
Tana, stm., Kenya	B7	48
Tana, Lake, l., Eth.	C4	47
Tanabe, Japan	J7	33
Tanabi, Braz.	C3	56
Tanacross, Ak., U.S.	C11	79
Tanafjorden, Nor.	B13	14
Tanaga Island, i., Ak., U.S.	E4	79
Tanahbala, i., Indon.	F1	34
Tanahgrogot, Indon.	F5	34
Tanahmasa, i., Indon.	F1	34
Tanakpur, India	F8	36
Tanami, Austl.	C4	50
Tan An, Viet.	G7	35
Tanana, Ak., U.S.	B9	79
Tanana, stm., Ak., U.S.	C10	79
Tananarive see Antananarivo, Madag.	g9	49
Tanapag, N. Mar. Is.	D8	52
Tanapag, Lagunan b., N. Mar. Is.	D7	52
Tanaro, stm., Italy	B2	23
Tanavuso Point, c., Fiji	H15	52
Tancheng, China	G8	32
Tanchon, N. Kor.	F4	33
Tancook Island, N.S.	E5	71
Tānda, India	D9	37
Tandalți, Sud.	E4	47
Tāndārei, Rom.	C8	24
Tandil, Arg.	B5	54
Tando Ādam, Pak.	E2	37
Tandou Lake, l., Austl.	F3	51
Tanega Island, i., Japan	E11	31
Tanegashima Strait, strt., Japan	K5	33
Taney, co., Mo., U.S.	E4	102
Taneycomo, Lake, res., Mo., U.S.	E4	102
Taneytown, Md., U.S.	A3	97
Tanezrouft, des., Afr.	E4	44
Tanga, Tan.	C6	48
Tanga, prov., Tan.	B6	48
Tanganyika, Lake, l., Afr.	C4	48
Tangent, Or., U.S.	C3	114
Tangerhütte, E. Ger.	A6	19
Tangermünde, E. Ger.	B5	18
Tangghe, China	E7	31
Tangier (Tanger), Mor.	B3	44
Tangier, In., U.S.	E3	91
Tangier, Va., U.S.	C7	123
Tangier Island, i., Va., U.S.	C6	123
Tangier Sound, strt., Md., U.S.	D6	97
Tangipahoa, co., La., U.S.	D5	95
Tangipahoa, stm., La., U.S.	D5	95
Tanglewood, Fl., U.S.	*F5	86
Tangra Yumco, l., China	B8	36
Tangshan, China	D8	31
Tanguiéta, Benin	E5	45
Tanguisson Point, c., Guam	L10	52
Tanimbar Islands, is., Indon.	G8	34
Taninges, Fr.	C7	20
Tanjore see Thanjāvūr, India	F6	36
Tanjung, Indon.	F5	34
Tanjungbalai, Indon.	E1	34
Tanjungkarang-Telukbetung, Indon.	G3	34
Tanjungpandan, Indon.	F3	34
Tanjungselor, Indon.	E5	34
Tānk, Pak.	B5	36
Tännäs, Swe.	F5	14
Tanner, Al., U.S.	A3	78
Tanner, W.V., U.S.	C4	125
Tannersville, N.Y., U.S.	C6	109
Tannis Bugt, b., Den.	A4	15
Tānout, Niger	C6	45
Tanpok, stm., Fr. Gu.	B4	59
Tanque Verde, Az., U.S.	E5	80
Tanțā, Eg.	B3	38
Tantallon, Sask.	G5	75
Tantani, mtn., Peru	C5	58
Tantoyuca, Mex.	m14	63
Tanum (Tanumshede), Swe.	H4	14
Tanzania, ctry., Afr.	C5	48
Tao, i., Thai.	H4	35
Tao'an, China	B9	31
Tao'er He, stm., China	B9	31
Taopi, Mn., U.S.	G6	100
Taormina, Italy	F5	23
Taos, Mo., U.S.	C5	102
Taos, N.M., U.S.	A4	108
Taos, co., N.M., U.S.	A4	108
Taos Pueblo, N.M., U.S.	A4	108
Taoudenni, Mali	B4	45
Taoyuan, China	J4	32
Tapachula, Mex.	C2	55
Tapaga, Cape, c., W. Sam.	G12	52
Tapajós, stm., Braz.	C3	59
Tapaktuan, Indon.	m11	34
Tapalquén, Arg.	B5	54
Tapanahony, stm., Sur.	B3	59
Tapanui, N.Z.	P12	51
Tapauá, Braz.	D2	59
Tapauá, stm., Braz.	C4	58
Tapejara, Braz.	D2	56
Taperoá, Braz.	h5	57
Tapeta, Lib.	E3	45
Tāpi, stm., India	D5	36
Tapirapé, stm., Braz.	E4	59
Tapoco, N.C., U.S.	f9	110
Tappahannock, Va., U.S.	C6	123
Tappan, N.Y., U.S.	g13	109
Tappan, Lake, res., N.J., U.S.	g9	107
Tappan Lake, res., Oh., U.S.	B4	112
Tappen, N.D., U.S.	C6	111
Tapuaenuku, mtn., N.Z.	N14	51
Taputapu, Cape, c., Am. Sam.	G13	52
Taqātu' Hayyā, Sud.	B4	47
Taquara, Braz.	D2	56
Taquari, stm., Braz.	D2	56
Taquari, stm., Braz.	B1	56
Taquaritinga, Braz.	k7	56
Taquaritinga do Norte, Braz.	h5	57
Tar, stm., N.C., U.S.	B5	110
Tara, Ont.	C3	73
Tara, Sov. Un.	D10	29
Tara, stm., Sov. Un.	B9	28
Tara, stm., Yugo.	D4	24
Tara, Hill of, hist., Ire.	D5	11
Tarabai, Braz.	C2	56
Tara Hills, Ca., U.S.	*h8	82
Tarakan, Indon.	E5	34
Tarakliya, Sov. Un.	C9	24
Tarancón, Spain	C4	22
Taransay, i., Scot., U.K.	C1	13
Taranto, Italy	E6	23
Taranto, Gulf of, b., Italy	E6	23
Tarapacá, Col.	D4	60
Tarapacá, prov., Chile	C2	55
Tarapoto, Peru	C2	58
Tarare, Fr.	E6	16
Tarascon-sur-Ariège, Fr.	F4	16
Tarascon-sur-Rhône, Fr.	F6	16
Tarasp, Switz.	C9	21
Tarata, Bol.	C2	55
Tarata, Peru	E3	58
Tarauacá, Braz.	C3	58
Tarauacá, stm., Braz.	C3	58
Tarawa, atoll, Kir.	F10	6
Tarawera, N.Z.	M16	51
Tarazona, Spain	B5	22
Tarazona [de la Mancha], Spain	C5	22
Tarbagatay Range, mts., Asia	D10	28
Tarbat Ness, c., Scot., U.K.	B5	10
Tarbellville, Vt., U.S.	E3	122
Tarbert, Ire.	E2	11
Tarbert, Scot., U.K.	E3	13
Tarbert, Scot., U.K.	C1	13
Tarbes, Fr.	F4	16
Tarbet, Scot., U.K.	E4	13
Tarboro, Ga., U.S.	E5	87
Tarboro, N.C., U.S.	B5	110
Tarbū, Libya	D3	43
Tarcenay, Fr.	B1	21
Tarcento, Italy	C9	21
Tarcoola, Austl.	F5	50
Tardoki-Yani, Mount, mtn., Sov. Un.	D17	29
Taree, Austl.	F9	50
Tarentum, Pa., U.S.	E2	115
Tarfawi, Bi'r, well, Sud.	A3	47
Tarfaya, Mor.	C2	44
Tarfside, Scot., U.K.	D6	13
Targhee Pass, U.S.	E7	89
Tarhūnah, Libya	C2	43
Tarifa, Spain	D3	22
Tarifa, Point, c., Spain	D3	22
Tariffville, Ct., U.S.	B4	84
Tarija, Bol.	D3	55
Tarija, dept., Bol.	D3	55
Tarim He, stm., China	E11	29
Tarim Pendi, des., China	E11	30
Tarkastad, S. Afr.	D4	49
Tarkiln, R.I., U.S.	B3	116
Tarkiln Hill, mtn., Me., U.S.	g7	96
Tarkio, Mo., U.S.	A2	102
Tarko-Sale, Sov. Un.	C24	8
Tarkwa, Ghana	E4	45
Tarland, Scot., U.K.	C6	13
Tarlton, Oh., U.S.	C3	112
Tarm, Den.	C2	15
Tarma, Peru	C2	58
Tarn, stm., Fr.	F4	16
Tarna, stm., Hung.	B5	24
Tarnobrzeg, Pol.	C6	26
Tarnopol, Sask.	E5	75
Tarnów, Pol.	C6	26
Tarnowskie Góry, Pol.	C5	26
Taro, stm., Italy	B2	23
Taroom, Austl.	B7	51
Taroudant, Mor.	C3	44
Tarp, W. Ger.	A5	18
Tarpey, Ca., U.S.	D4	82
Tarpley, Tx., U.S.	E3	120
Tarpon, Lake, l., Fl., U.S.	o10	86
Tarpon Springs, Fl., U.S.	D4	86
Tarqui, Peru	B2	58
Tarquinia, Italy	C3	23
Tarragona, Spain	B6	22
Tarrant, co., Tx., U.S.	C4	120
Tarrant City, Al., U.S.	B3	78
Tarrasa, Spain	B7	22
Tárrega, Spain	B6	22
Tarrytown, Fl., U.S.	D4	86
Tarrytown, Ga., U.S.	D4	87
Tarrytown, N.Y., U.S.	D7	109
Tårs, Den.	A4	15
Tarsus, Tur.	D10	40
Tartagal, Arg.	D3	55
Tartu, Sov. Un.	D5	29
Tartuguan Point, c., Guam	M10	52
Tartūs, Syria	E10	40
Tārūt, i., Sau. Ar.	H5	39
Tarutung, Indon.	L3	35
Tarver, Ga., U.S.	F4	87
Tasaral, Sov. Un.	D8	28
Tāsāwah, Libya	D2	43
Taseko, stm., B.C.	D6	69
Taseko Lakes, l., B.C.	D6	69
Taseko Mountain, mtn., B.C.	D6	69
Tashauz, Sov. Un.	E5	28
Tashkent, Sov. Un.	E9	29
Tashkumyr, Sov. Un.	E8	28
Tasikmalaya, Indon.	G3	34
Tåsinge, i., Den.	C4	15
Taskan, Sov. Un.	C18	29
Taşköprü, Tur.	B10	40
Tasman Bay, b., N.Z.	N14	51
Tasmania, state, Austl.	o15	50
Tasman Peninsula, pen., Austl.	o15	50
Tasman Sea, Oc.	I9	6
Tasso, Tn., U.S.	D9	119
Taswell, In., U.S.	H4	91
Tata, Hung.	B4	24
Tatabánya, Hung.	B4	24
Tatamagouche, N.S.	D6	71
Tatarbunary, Sov. Un.	C9	24
Tatarsk, Sov. Un.	B9	28
Tatar Strait, strt., Sov. Un.	D17	29
Tate, Sask.	F3	75
Tate, co., Ms., U.S.	A4	101
Tateville, Ky., U.S.	D5	94
Tateyama, Japan	I9	33
Tatitlek, Ak., U.S.	C10	79
Tatla Lake, l., B.C.	C5	69
Tatlayoko Lake, l., B.C.	D5	69
Tatnam, Cape, c., Man.	f9	70
Tattershall, Eng., U.K.	A7	12
Tattnall, co., Ga., U.S.	D4	87
Tatuí, Braz.	C3	56
Tatum, N.M., U.S.	D6	108
Tatum, S.C., U.S.	B8	117
Tatumville, Tn., U.S.	A2	119
Tatvan, Tur.	C14	40
Tauá, Braz.	C2	57
Taubaté, Braz.	C3	56
Tauber, stm., W. Ger.	D4	19
Tauberbischofsheim, W. Ger.	D4	19
Taucha, E. Ger.	B7	19
Tauern Tunnel, Aus.	C9	21
Taughmaconnell, Ire.	D3	11
Taumarunui, N.Z.	L15	51
Taum Sauk Mountain, mtn., Mo., U.S.	D6	102
Taung, Boph.	C3	49
Taungdwingyi, Burma	D10	36
Taunggyi, Burma	D10	36
Taunton, Eng., U.K.	E5	10
Taunton, Ma., U.S.	C5	98
Taunton, Mn., U.S.	F2	100
Taunton, stm., Ma., U.S.	C5	98
Taunton Lakes, N.J., U.S.	D3	107
Taunus, mts., W. Ger.	E4	19
Taupo, Lake, l., N.Z.	M15	51
Tauranga, N.Z.	L16	51
Taurage, Sov. Un.	D4	27
Taureau, Réservoir, res., Que.	C4	74
Tauroa Point, c., N.Z.	K14	51
Taurus Mountains, mts., Tur.	D8	40
Tavares, Fl., U.S.	D5	86
Tavas, Tur.	D7	25
Tavda, Sov. Un.	D9	29
Tavda, stm., Sov. Un.	D9	29
Tavernier, Fl., U.S.	G6	86
Taveuni, i., Fiji	H16	52
Tavira, Port.	D3	22
Tavistock, Ont.	D4	73
Tavistock, Eng., U.K.	D3	12
Tavoy, stm., Burma	F3	35
Tavoy Point, c., Burma	F2	35
Tavşanlı, Tur.	C7	40
Taw, stm., Eng., U.K.	D4	12
Tawakoni, Lake, res., Tx., U.S.	C4	120
Tawas City, Mi., U.S.	D7	99
Tawas Lake, l., Mi., U.S.	D7	99
Tawatinaw, Alta.	B4	68
Tawau, Malay.	E5	34
Tawitawi Group, is., Phil.	D6	34
Tawi-Tawi Island, i., Phil.	D5	34
Tawkar, Sud.	B4	47
Tawny, Ire.	B4	11
Tāwurghā', Libya	C3	43
Taxco de Alarcón, Mex.	n14	63
Tay, stm., Scot., U.K.	B5	10
Tay, Firth of, est., Scot., U.K.	B5	10
Tay, Loch, l., Scot., U.K.	B5	10
Tayabamba, Peru	C2	58
Tayasīr, Isr. Occ.	f12	41
Taycheedah, Wi., U.S.	E5	126
Tayga, Sov. Un.	B11	28
Taylor, B.C.	A7	69
Taylor, Az., U.S.	C5	80
Taylor, Mi., U.S.	p15	99
Taylor, Ne., U.S.	C6	104
Taylor, Pa., U.S.	D10	115
Taylor, Tx., U.S.	D4	120
Taylor, Wi., U.S.	D2	126
Taylor, co., Fl., U.S.	B3	86
Taylor, co., Ga., U.S.	D2	87
Taylor, co., Ia., U.S.	D3	92
Taylor, co., Ky., U.S.	C4	94
Taylor, co., Tx., U.S.	C3	120
Taylor, co., W.V., U.S.	B4	125
Taylor, co., Wi., U.S.	C3	126
Taylor, stm., Man.	B2	70
Taylor, stm., Co., U.S.	C4	83
Taylor, Mount, mtn., N.Z.	O13	51
Taylor, Mount, mtn., N.M., U.S.	B2	108
Taylor Knob, hill, Tn., U.S.	G10	119
Taylor Mill, Ky., U.S.	k14	94
Taylor Mountain, mtn., Id., U.S.	E4	89
Taylor Park Reservoir, res., Co., U.S.	C4	83
Taylor Ridge, mtn., Ga., U.S.	B1	87
Taylors, S.C., U.S.	B3	117
Taylors Bridge, De., U.S.	C3	85
Taylors Falls, Mn., U.S.	E6	100
Taylors Island, Md., U.S.	D5	97
Taylor Springs, Il., U.S.	D4	90
Taylorsville, Ga., U.S.	B2	87
Taylorsville, In., U.S.	F6	91
Taylorsville, Ky., U.S.	B4	94
Taylorsville, Ms., U.S.	D4	101
Taylorsville, N.C., U.S.	B1	110
Taylorsville, Ut., U.S.	*C4	121
Taylorville, Il., U.S.	D4	90
Taymā', Sau. Ar.	D7	43
Taymouth, N.B.	C3	71
Taymyr Lake, l., Sov. Un.	B13	29
Taymyr Peninsula, pen., Sov. Un.	B12	29
Tay Ninh, Viet.	G7	35
Tayport, Scot., U.K.	D6	13
Tayshet, Sov. Un.	D12	29
Tayside, prov., Scot., U.K.	D5	13
Taytay, Phil.	C5	34
Taytsy, Sov. Un.	s31	14
Taz, stm., Sov. Un.	C11	29
Taza, Mor.	C4	44
Taz Bay, b., Sov. Un.	C7	128
Tazerbo, well, Libya	D4	43
Tazewell, Ga., U.S.	D2	87
Tazewell, Tn., U.S.	C10	119
Tazewell, Va., U.S.	e10	123
Tazewell, co., Il., U.S.	C4	90
Tazewell, co., Va., U.S.	e10	123
Tazrouk, Alg.	E6	44
Tbessa, Alg.	B6	44
Tbilisi, Sov. Un.	E7	29
Tchefuncta, stm., La., U.S.	D5	95
Tchibanga, Gabon	F2	46
Tchien, Lib.	E3	45
Tchula, Ms., U.S.	B3	101
Tczew, Pol.	A5	26
Tea, S.D., U.S.	D9	118
Tea, stm., Braz.	D4	60
Teachey, N.C., U.S.	C4	110
Tea Creek, stm., Sask.	C2	75
Teague, Tx., U.S.	D4	120
Teakean Butte, mtn., Id., U.S.	C2	89
Te Anau, Lake, l., N.Z.	P11	51
Teaneck, N.J., U.S.	h8	107
Teangue, Scot., U.K.	C3	13
Tearaght, i., Ire.	E1	11
Tearinibai, Kir.	R18	52
Teasdale, Ut., U.S.	E4	121
Teaticket, Ma., U.S.	C6	98
Tea Tree Gully, Austl.	*F6	50
Te Awamutu, N.Z.	M15	51
Tebbetts, Mo., U.S.	C6	102
Tebicuary, stm., Para.	E4	55
Tebingtinggi, Indon.	E1	34
Tecalitlán, Mex.	n12	63
Tecate, Mex.	F5	63
Teche, Bayou, stm., La., U.S.	D4	95
Techirghiol, Rom.	C9	24
Tecka, Arg.	C2	54
Tecolotito, N.M., U.S.	B4	108
Tecolutla, stm., Mex.	m15	63
Tecopa, Ca., U.S.	E5	82
Tecpan de Galeana, Mex.	C3	63
Tecuala, Mex.	C3	63
Tecuci, Rom.	C8	24
Tecumseh, Ont.	E2	73
Tecumseh, Ks., U.S.	k14	93
Tecumseh, Mi., U.S.	G7	99
Tecumseh, Ne., U.S.	D9	104
Tecumseh, Ok., U.S.	B5	113
Tecumseh, Mount, mtn., N.H., U.S.	C4	106
Ted Ceidaar Dabole, Som.	E5	47
Tedrow, Oh., U.S.	A1	112
Teec Nos Pos, Az., U.S.	A6	80
Teegarden, In., U.S.	B5	91
Tees, Alta.	C4	68
Tees, stm., Eng., U.K.	C6	10
Teesside see Middlesbrough, Eng., U.K.	C6	10
Teeswater, Ont.	C3	73
Tefé, Braz.	C2	59
Tefé, stm., Braz.	B4	58
Tefé, Lago de, l., Braz.	C2	59
Tefenni, Tur.	D7	25
Tefft, In., U.S.	B4	91
Tegal, Indon.	G3	34
Tegelen, Neth.	C6	17
Tegernsee, W. Ger.	H11	19
Teglio, Italy	D9	21
Tegucigalpa, Hond.	C4	62
Teguise, Spain	m15	22
Tehachapi, Ca., U.S.	E4	82
Tehachapi Mountains, mts., Ca., U.S.	E4	82
Tehama, co., Ca., U.S.	B2	82
Tehek Lake, l., N.W. Ter.	C13	66
Tehrān, Iran	B5	38
Tehri, India	B4	11
Tehuacán, Mex.	D5	63
Tehuantepec, Mex.	D5	63
Tehuantepec, Golfo de, b., Mex.	D6	63
Tehuitzingo, Mex.	n14	63
Teide, Pico de, mtn., Spain	m13	22
Teifi, stm., Wales, U.K.	B3	12
Teignmouth, Eng., U.K.	D4	12
Teiuş, Rom.	B7	24
Tejakula, Indon.	G5	34
Tekamah, Ne., U.S.	C9	104
Tekapo, Lake, l., N.Z.	O13	51
Tekax de Álvaro Obregón, Mex.	C7	63
Tekeli, Sov. Un.	E9	28
Tekes, Sov. Un.	C4	31
Tekirdağ, Tur.	B6	40
Tekkali, India	H10	37
Tekoa, Wa., U.S.	B8	124
Tekonsha, Mi., U.S.	F5	99
Tel, stm., India	D7	36
Tela, Hond.	D7	63

Name	Map Ref.	Page
Telavi, Sov. Un.	E3	28
Tel Aviv-Yafo (Tel Aviv-Jaffa), Isr.	B3	38
Telde, Sp.	m14	22
Telegraph Creek, B.C.	m16	69
Telén, Arg.	B3	54
Teleneshty, Sov. Un.	B9	24
Teleorman, stm., Rom.	C7	24
Telephone, Tx., U.S.	C4	120
Télérthéba, Djebel, mtn., Alg.	E6	44
Telescope Peak, mtn., Ca., U.S.	D5	82
Telfair, co., Ga., U.S.	E4	87
Telford, Eng., U.K.	C5	12
Telford, Pa., U.S.	F11	115
Telford, Tn., U.S.	C11	119
Telfs, Aus.	B7	20
Télimélé, Gui.	D2	45
Telkwa, B.C.	B4	69
Tell, Tx., U.S.	B2	120
Tell City, In., U.S.	I4	91
Teller, Ak., U.S.	B6	79
Teller, co., Co., U.S.	C5	83
Telluride, Co., U.S.	D3	83
Tel Mond, Isr.	B6	41
Telogia, Fl., U.S.	B2	86
Telok Anson (Teluk Intan), Malay.	E2	34
Teloloapan, Mex.	D5	63
Telos Lake, l., Me., U.S.	B3	96
Telsen, Arg.	C3	54
Tema, Ghana	E5	45
Temax, Mex.	C7	63
Tembo, Zaire	C2	48
Temecula, Ca., U.S.	F5	82
Temelli, Tur.	C8	40
Temirtau, Sov. Un.	E26	8
Temirtau, Sov. Un.	D10	29
Témiscaming, Que.	G17	66
Témiscouata, co., Que.	B9	74
Témiscouata, Lac, l., Que.	B9	74
Te-Moak Indian Reservation, Nv., U.S.	C6	105
Temora, Austl.	G6	51
Temósachic, Mex.	B3	63
Tempe, Az., U.S.	D4	80
Tempe Downs, Austl.	D5	50
Temperance, Mi., U.S.	G7	99
Temperance, stm., Mn., U.S.	C8	100
Temperanceville, Va., U.S.	C7	123
Tempio Pausania, Italy	D2	23
Temple, Ga., U.S.	C1	87
Temple, Mi., U.S.	D5	99
Temple, N.H., U.S.	E3	106
Temple, Ok., U.S.	C3	113
Temple, Pa., U.S.	F10	115
Temple, Tx., U.S.	D4	120
Temple City, Ca., U.S.	*m12	82
Temple Hill, Ky., U.S.	D4	94
Templemore, Ire.	E4	11
Temple Terrace, Fl., U.S.	o11	86
Templeton, In., U.S.	C3	91
Templeton, Ia., U.S.	C3	92
Templeton, Ma., U.S.	A3	98
Templeton, Pa., U.S.	E3	115
Templeville, Md., U.S.	B6	97
Templin, E. Ger.	B6	18
Tempoal, stm., Mex.	m14	63
Temryuk, Sov. Un.	I11	27
Temuco, Chile	B2	54
Temuka, N.Z.	P13	51
Temwen, i., Micron.	Q17	51
Tena, Ec.	B2	58
Tenafly, N.J., U.S.	B5	107
Tenaha, Tx., U.S.	D5	120
Tenakee Springs, Ak., U.S.	D12	79
Tenāli, India	*E7	36
Tenancingo [de Degollado], Mex.	D5	63
Tenango del Valle, Mex.	n14	63
Tenant Mountain, mtn., N.Y., U.S.	B6	109
Tenants Harbor, Me., U.S.	E3	96
Tenasserim, Burma	F10	36
Tenay, Fr.	E6	16
Tenby, Wales, U.K.	C3	12
Tendaho, Eth.	C5	47
Tende, Fr.	E7	16
Ten Degree Channel, strt., India	G9	36
Tendoy, Id., U.S.	E5	89
Tendre, Mont, mtn., Switz.	C2	20
Ténéré, des., Niger	C7	45
Tenerife, i., Spain	m13	22
Ténès, Alg.	B5	44
Teng, stm., Burma	B2	35
Tengah Islands, is., Indon.	G5	34
Tengchong, China	F4	31
Tengiz, Lake, l., Sov. Un.	D9	29
Tengxian, China	G7	32
Tenino, Wa., U.S.	C3	124
Tenke, Zaire	D4	48
Tenkiller Ferry Lake, res., Ok., U.S.	B6	113
Tenkodogo, Burkina	D4	45
Ten Mile, stm., U.S.	D9	119
Tenmile, stm., U.S.	B5	116
Tenmile Creek, stm., W.V., U.S.	k10	125
Ten Mile Lake, l., Newf.	C3	72
Tenmile Lake, l., Mn., U.S.	D4	100
Tennant, Ia., U.S.	C2	92
Tennant Creek, Austl.	C5	50
Tennent, N.J., U.S.	C4	107
Tennessee, Il., U.S.	C3	90
Tennessee, state, U.S.	B5	119
Tennessee, stm., U.S.	D10	76
Tennessee City, Tn., U.S.	A4	119
Tennessee Pass, Co., U.S.	B4	83
Tennessee Ridge, Tn., U.S.	A4	119
Tennga, Ga., U.S.	B2	87
Tennille, Ga., U.S.	D4	87
Tennyson, In., U.S.	H3	91
Tenosique [de Pino Suárez], Mex.	D6	63
Tenryū, stm., Japan	n16	33
Tensas, co., La., U.S.	B4	95
Tensas, stm., La., U.S.	B4	95
Tensaw, stm., Al., U.S.	E2	78
Tensed, Id., U.S.	B2	89
Ten Sleep, Wy., U.S.	B5	127
Tenstrike, Mn., U.S.	C4	100
Tenterfield, Austl.	E9	50
Ten Thousand Islands, is., Fl., U.S.	G5	86
Teocaltiche, Mex.	m12	63
Teófilo Otoni, Braz.	B4	56
Tepa, Indon.	G7	34
Tepalcatepec, Mex.	n12	63
Tepalcatepec, stm., Mex.	n12	63
Tepatitlán [de Morelos], Mex.	m12	63
Tepeji del Río, Mex.	n14	63
Tepelena, Alb.	B2	25
Tepepan (part of Mexico City), Mex.	h9	63
Tepic, Mex.	C4	63
Teplice, Czech.	C2	26
Tepoca, Cabo, c., Mex.	A2	63
Tequila, Mex.	m12	63
Ter, stm., Spain	A7	22
Téra, Niger	D5	45
Teraina Island (Washington Island), i., Kir.	F12	6
Teramo, Italy	C4	23
Ter Apel, Neth.	B7	17
Tercan, Tur.	C13	40
Tercero, stm., Arg.	A4	54
Terceira, i., Port.	g9	44
Terebovlya, Sov. Un.	G5	27
Terek, stm., Sov. Un.	G18	13
Terek Pass, Sov. Un.	G23	8
Terekty, Sov. Un.	D7	28
Terengganu, state, Malay.	J5	35
Terenos, Braz.	C2	56
Teresina, Braz.	C2	57
Teresinha, Braz.	B4	59
Teresópolis, Braz.	C4	56
Tergnier, Fr.	E3	17
Teriberka, Sov. Un.	C16	14
Terlingua, Tx., U.S.	D1	120
Terlton, Ok., U.S.	A5	113
Termez, Sov. Un.	F9	29
Termini Imerese, Italy	F4	23
Términos, Laguna de, b., Mex.	D6	63
Termoli, Italy	C5	23
Tern, i., Indon.	E7	34
Ternate, Indon.	E7	34
Ternate, i., Indon.	E7	34
Terneuzen, Neth.	B5	16
Terney, Sov. Un.	D8	33
Terni, Italy	C4	23
Ternopol, Sov. Un.	G5	27
Terpeniya Bay, b., Sov. Un.	B11	33
Terpeniya, Cape, c., Sov. Un.	B12	33
Terra Alta, W.V., U.S.	B5	125
Terrace, B.C.	B3	69
Terrace, Mn., U.S.	E3	100
Terrace Bay, Ont.	G15	66
Terracina, Italy	D4	23
Terral, Ok., U.S.	D4	113
Terra Nova, Newf.	D4	72
Terra Nova National Park, Newf.	D4	72
Terra Rica, Braz.	C2	56
Terrasson, Fr.	E4	16
Terrebonne, Bayou, stm., La., U.S.	k10	95
Terrebonne, Que.	D4	74
Terrebonne, Or., U.S.	C5	114
Terrebonne, co., Que.	C3	74
Terrebonne, co., La., U.S.	E5	95
Terrebonne Bay, b., La., U.S.	E5	95
Terre Haute, Il., U.S.	C3	90
Terre Haute, In., U.S.	F3	91
Terre Hill, Pa., U.S.	F9	115
Terrell, N.C., U.S.	B2	110
Terrell, Tx., U.S.	C4	120
Terrell, co., Ga., U.S.	E2	87
Terrell, co., Tx., U.S.	D1	120
Terrell Hills, Tx., U.S.	k7	120
Terrenceville, Newf.	E4	72
Terreton, Id., U.S.	F6	89
Terril, Ia., U.S.	A3	92
Terror, Mount, mtn., Ant.	e38	7
Terry, La., U.S.	B4	95
Terry, Ms., U.S.	C3	101
Terry, Mt., U.S.	D11	103
Terry, co., Tx., U.S.	C1	120
Terry Peak, mtn., S.D., U.S.	C2	118
Terrytown, La., U.S.	*E5	95
Terrytown, Ne., U.S.	C2	104
Terryville, Ct., U.S.	C3	84
Terryville, N.Y., U.S.	*n15	109
Tersakkan, stm., Sov. Un.	C7	28
Terschelling, i., Neth.	A6	16
Terskey-Alatau Range, mts., Sov. Un.	E9	28
Teruel, Col.	C2	60
Teruel, Spain	B5	22
Terutao, i., Thai.	I3	35
Terwagne, Bel.	D5	17
Tešanj, Yugo.	C3	24
Tescott, Ks., U.S.	C6	93
Teshekpuk Lake, l., Ak., U.S.	A9	79
Teshie, Ghana	*E5	45
Teshio, Japan	D10	33
Tesiyn, stm., Asia	B4	31
Teslin, Yukon	D6	66
Teslin Lake, l., Can.	D6	66
Tessalit, Mali	B5	45
Tessaoua, Niger	D6	45
Tessier, Sask.	F2	75
Tessin, E. Ger.	D6	15
Test, stm., Eng., U.K.	E6	10
Tesuque, N.M., U.S.	B4	108
Tesuque Pueblo, N.M., U.S.	B4	108
Tetachuck Lake, l., B.C.	C5	69
Tetagouche, stm., N.B.	B3	71
Tetas, Punta, c., Chile	F3	53
Tetbury, Eng., U.K.	C5	12
Tete, Moz.	A5	49
Tête-à-la-Baleine, Que.	C2	72
Tête Jaune Cache, B.C.	C8	69
Teterow, E. Ger.	B6	18
Teteven, Bul.	D7	24
Tetlin, Ak., U.S.	C11	79
Teton, co., Id., U.S.	F7	89
Teton, co., Mt., U.S.	C4	103
Teton, co., Wy., U.S.	C2	127
Teton, stm., Mt., U.S.	C5	103
Tetonia, Id., U.S.	F7	89
Teton Pass, Wy., U.S.	C2	127
Teton Range, mts., Wy., U.S.	C2	127
Teton Village, Wy., U.S.	C2	127
Tétouan, Mor.	B3	44
Tetovo, Yugo.	E5	24
Tetschen, Sov. Un.	D18	14
Tettnang, W. Ger.	A8	21
Teuchern, E. Ger.	B7	19
Teuco, stm., Arg.	D3	55
Teufen, Switz.	B7	21
Teulada, Italy	E2	23
Teúl de González Ortega, Mex.	m12	63
Teulon, Man.	D3	70
Teuri Island, i., Japan	D10	33
Teutopolis, Il., U.S.	D5	90
Teviot, stm., Scot., U.K.	E6	13
Tevriz, Sov. Un.	C8	28
Te Waewae Bay, b., N.Z.	Q11	51
Tewantin-Noosa, Austl.	E9	50
Tewkesbury, Eng., U.K.	C5	12
Tewksbury, Ma., U.S.	A5	98
Texada Island, i., B.C.	E5	69
Texanna, Ok., U.S.	B6	113
Texarkana, Ar., U.S.	D1	81
Texarkana, Tx., U.S.	C5	120
Texas, co., Mo., U.S.	D5	102
Texas, co., Ok., U.S.	e9	113
Texas, state, U.S.	D3	120
Texas City, Tx., U.S.	E5	120
Texcaltitlán, Mex.	n14	63
Texcoco, Lago de, l., Mex.	g10	63
Texcoco [de Mora], Mex.	n14	63
Texel, i., Neth.	A6	16
Texhoma, Ok., U.S.	e9	113
Texhoma, Tx., U.S.	A2	120
Texico, N.M., U.S.	C6	108
Texline, Tx., U.S.	A1	120
Texola, Ok., U.S.	B2	113
Texoma, Lake, res., U.S.	D5	113
Texon, Tx., U.S.	D2	120
Teywarah, Afg.	E12	39
Teziutlán, Mex.	D5	63
Tezpur, India	C9	36
Tezzeron Lake, l., B.C.	B5	69
Thabana Ntlenyana, mtn., Leso.	C4	49
Thacker, W.V., U.S.	D2	125
Thackeray, Il., U.S.	E5	90
Thackerville, Ok., U.S.	D4	113
Thai Binh, Viet.	B7	35
Thailand, ctry., Asia	B2	34
Thailand, Gulf of, b., Asia	C2	34
Thai Nguyen, Viet.	B6	35
Thal, Pak.	B5	36
Thale, E. Ger.	B6	19
Thale Luang, b., Thai.	I4	35
Thalia, Tx., U.S.	C3	120
Thame, Eng., U.K.	C7	12
Thames, N.Z.	L15	51
Thames, stm., Ont.	E3	73
Thames, stm., Eng., U.K.	E6	10
Thames, stm., Ct., U.S.	D7	84
Thames, Firth of, b., N.Z.	L15	51
Thamesville, Ont.	E3	73
Thāna, India	H4	37
Thanh Hoa, Viet.	C6	35
Thanjāvūr, India	F6	36
Thann, Fr.	D7	16
Thānnhausen, W. Ger.	A6	20
Thāno Bula Khān, Pak.	E1	37
Thar Desert (Great Indian Desert), des., Asia	D2	37
Tharrawaddy, Burma	E10	36
Thásos, Grc.	B5	25
Thásos, i., Grc.	B5	40
Thatcher, Az., U.S.	E6	80
Thatcher, Id., U.S.	G7	89
Thaton, Burma	E10	36
Thawville, Il., U.S.	C5	90
Thaxton, Ms., U.S.	A4	101
Thayer, Il., U.S.	D4	90
Thayer, In., U.S.	B3	91
Thayer, Ia., U.S.	C3	92
Thayer, Ks., U.S.	E8	93
Thayer, Mo., U.S.	E6	102
Thayer, Ne., U.S.	D8	104
Thayer, W.V., U.S.	n13	125
Thayer, co., Ne., U.S.	D8	104
Thayetmyo, Burma	C1	35
Thayne, Wy., U.S.	D1	127
Thazi, Burma	B2	35
Thealka, Ky., U.S.	C7	94
Theba, Az., U.S.	E3	80
The Backway, b., Bah.	A2	72
The Barrens, plat., Tn., U.S.	B5	119
The Basin, Il., U.S.	F4	90
The Bight, Bah.	B6	64
The Cheviot, mtn., Eng., U.K.	E6	13
The Cheviot Hills, hills, U.K.	C5	10
The Colony, Tx., U.S.	C4	120
The Dalles, Or., U.S.	B5	114
The Dells, val., Wi., U.S.	E4	126
Thedford, Ont.	D3	73
Thedford, Ne., U.S.	C5	104
The Dome, mtn., Vt., U.S.	F2	122
The Entrance, Austl.	F8	51
The Everglades, sw., Fl., U.S.	G6	86
The Father, mtn., Pap. N. Gui.	k13	50
The Fens, sw., Eng., U.K.	B8	12
The Fishing Lake, l., Sask.	G3	75
The Flat Tops, mts., Co., U.S.	B3	83
The Flume, wtfl., N.H., U.S.	B3	106
The Graves, is., Ma., U.S.	g12	98
The Hague ('s Gravenhage), Neth.	A6	16
The Heads, c., Or., U.S.	E2	114
The Hummocks, R.I., U.S.	D6	116
The Landes, reg., Fr.	E3	16
The Little Minch, strt., Scot., U.K.	B3	10
Thelma, N.C., U.S.	A5	110
Thelon, stm., N.W. Ter.	D12	66
The Minch, strt., Scot., U.K.	A4	10
The Narrows, strt., Wa., U.S.	f10	124
The Naze, c., Nor.	I2	14
The Naze, c., Eng., U.K.	C9	12
The Oa, pen., Scot., U.K.	C2	13
Theodore, Austl.	D9	50
Theodore, Sask.	F4	75
Theodore, Al., U.S.	E1	78
Theodore Roosevelt Lake, res., Az., U.S.	D4	80
Theodore Roosevelt National Park (South Unit), N.D., U.S.	C2	111
Theodore Roosevelt National Park (North Unit), N.D., U.S.	B2	111
Theodosia, Mo., U.S.	E5	102
Theologos, Grc.	B5	25
The Palisades, clf., N.J., U.S.	h9	107
The Pas, Man.	C1	70
The Peak, mtn., N.C., U.S.	A1	110
The Pinnacle, hill, Ct., U.S.	B4	84
The Pinnacle, hill, Mo., U.S.	B7	102
The Plains, Oh., U.S.	C3	112
The Plains, Va., U.S.	B5	123
Thérain, stm., Fr.	E2	17
The Range, N.B.	C4	71
The Raven Point, c., Ire.	E5	11
Theresa, N.Y., U.S.	A5	109
Theresa, Wi., U.S.	E5	126
Therien, Alta.	B5	68
Thermaikós Kólpos (Gulf of Salonika), b., Grc.	B4	40
Thérmon, Grc.	C3	25
Thermopolis, Wy., U.S.	C4	127
The Rock, Austl.	D3	87
The Rockies, mts., Wa., U.S.	C3	124
Theron Mountains, mts., Ant.	B10	7
The Solent, strt., Eng., U.K.	D6	12
The Sound see Øresund, strt., Eur.	J5	14
Thessalon, Ont.	p19	73
Thessaloníki (Saloníka), Grc.	B4	40
Thessaly, hist. reg., Grc.	C4	25
The Storr, mtn., Scot., U.K.	C2	13
Theta, Tn., U.S.	B4	119
Thetford, Eng., U.K.	D7	10
Thetford, Vt., U.S.	D4	122
Thetford Center, Vt., U.S.	D4	122
Thetford Mines, Que.	C6	74
The Thimbles, is., Ct., U.S.	E5	84
The Village, Ok., U.S.	B4	113
The Village of India, Oh., U.S.	*C1	112
The Wash, b., Eng., U.K.	D7	10
The Wolds, hills, Eng., U.K.	D6	10
The Woodlands, Tx., U.S.	*E5	120
Thibar, Tun.	F2	23
Thibaudeau, Man.	A4	70
Thibodaux, La., U.S.	E5	95
Thicket Portage, Man.	B3	70
Thickwood Hills, hills, Sask.	E2	75
Thida, Ar., U.S.	B4	81
Thief, stm., Mn., U.S.	B2	100
Thief Lake, l., Mn., U.S.	B3	100
Thief River Falls, Mn., U.S.	B2	100
Thiel Mountains, mts., Ant.	A2	7
Thielsen, Mount, mtn., Or., U.S.	D4	114
Thiene, Italy	D7	20
Thiensville, Wi., U.S.	E6	126
Thiers, Fr.	E5	16
Thiès, Sen.	D1	45
Thika, Kenya	B6	48
Thimbu see Thimphu, Bhu.	C8	36
Thimphu (Thimbu), Bhu.	C8	36
Thingangyun, Burma	*E10	36
Thionville, Fr.	C7	16
Thíra, i., Grc.	D5	40
Third Lake, l., N.H., U.S.	f7	106
Thirsk, Eng., U.K.	F7	13
Thisted, Den.	B2	15
Thívai (Thebes), Grc.	C4	25
Thu Chu, is., Viet.	H5	35
Tholen, Neth.	C4	17
Thomas, Ok., U.S.	B3	113
Thomas, Wa., U.S.	f11	124
Thomas, W.V., U.S.	B5	125
Thomas, co., Ga., U.S.	F3	87
Thomas, co., Ks., U.S.	C2	93
Thomas, co., Ne., U.S.	C5	104
Thomasboro, Il., U.S.	C5	90
Thomas Creek, stm., Fl., U.S.	k8	86
Thomas Mountains, mts., Ant.	B5	7
Thomaston, Al., U.S.	C2	78
Thomaston, Ct., U.S.	C3	84
Thomaston, Ga., U.S.	D2	87
Thomaston, Me., U.S.	D3	96
Thomaston, Tx., U.S.	E4	120
Thomaston Reservoir, res., Ct., U.S.	C3	84
Thomastown, Ire.	E4	11
Thomastown, Ms., U.S.	C4	101
Thomasville, Al., U.S.	D2	78
Thomasville, Ga., U.S.	F3	87
Thomasville, Mo., U.S.	E6	102
Thomasville, N.C., U.S.	B2	110
Thomasville, Pa., U.S.	G8	115
Thomlinson, Mount, mtn., B.C.	B4	69
Thompson, Man.	B3	70
Thompson, Ct., U.S.	B8	84
Thompson, Ia., U.S.	A4	92
Thompson, Mi., U.S.	C4	99
Thompson, Mo., U.S.	B6	102
Thompson, N.D., U.S.	B8	111
Thompson, Oh., U.S.	A4	112
Thompson, Pa., U.S.	C10	115
Thompson, Ut., U.S.	E6	121
Thompson, stm., B.C.	D7	69
Thompson, stm., U.S.	A4	102
Thompson Creek, stm., Ms., U.S.	D5	101
Thompson Falls, Mt., U.S.	C1	103
Thompson Island, i., Ma., U.S.	g11	98
Thompson Lake, l., Mi., U.S.	D2	96
Thompson Peak, mtn., Ca., U.S.	B2	82
Thompson Peak, mtn., N.M., U.S.	h9	108
Thompson Reservoir, res., Or., U.S.	E5	114
Thompsons Station, Tn., U.S.	B5	119
Thompsontown, Pa., U.S.	E7	115
Thompsonville, Il., U.S.	F5	90
Thompsonville, Mi., U.S.	D5	99
Thomson, Ga., U.S.	C4	87
Thomson, Il., U.S.	B3	90
Thomson, Mn., U.S.	D6	100
Thomson, stm., Austl.	D7	50
Thomson's Falls, Kenya	A6	48
Thônes, Fr.	E1	21
Thonon-les-Bains, Fr.	C2	20
Thonotosassa, Fl., U.S.	D4	86
Thor, Ia., U.S.	B3	92
Thorburn, N.S.	D7	71
Thoreau, N.M., U.S.	B1	108
Thorhild, Alta.	B4	68
Thornburg, Ar., U.S.	C3	81
Thornbury, Ont.	C4	73
Thorndale, Ont.	D3	73
Thorndale, Tx., U.S.	D4	120
Thorndike, Me., U.S.	D3	96
Thornfield, Mo., U.S.	E5	102
Thornhill, Man.	E2	70
Thornhill, Ont.	k15	73
Thornhill, Scot., U.K.	C5	13
Thornton, Ar., U.S.	D3	81
Thornton, Co., U.S.	*B6	83
Thornton, Ia., U.S.	B4	92
Thornton, Il., U.S.	k9	90
Thornton, N.H., U.S.	C3	106
Thornton, Tx., U.S.	D4	120
Thornton, Wa., U.S.	B8	124
Thornton, W.V., U.S.	k11	125
Thornton Gap, Va., U.S.	B4	123
Thorntown, In., U.S.	D4	91
Thorntonville, Tx., U.S.	D1	120
Thornville, Oh., U.S.	*C3	112
Thornwood, N.Y., U.S.	*m15	109
Thorny Mountain, mtn., Mo., U.S.	D6	102
Thorofare, N.J., U.S.	D2	107
Thorold, Ont.	D5	73
Thorp, Wi., U.S.	D3	126
Thorp, Wa., U.S.	C5	124
Thorsby, Alta.	C3	68
Thorsby, Al., U.S.	C3	78
Thouars, Fr.	D3	16
Thousand Islands, is., N.Y., U.S.	A4	109
Thousand Lake Mountain, mtn., Ut., U.S.	*E4	121
Thousand Oaks, Ca., U.S.	*E4	82
Thousand Springs Creek, stm., U.S.	B7	105
Thrace, hist. reg., Eur.	B6	25
Thrapston, Eng., U.K.	B7	12
Thrashers, Ms., U.S.	A5	101
Three Bridges, N.J., U.S.	B3	107
Three Fingered Jack, mtn., Or., U.S.	C5	114
Three Forks, Mt., U.S.	E5	103
Three Hills, Alta.	D4	68
Three Kings Islands, is., N.Z.	K14	51
Three Lakes, Wi., U.S.	C4	126
Three Mile Bay, N.Y., U.S.	A4	109
Three Mile Plains, N.S.	E5	71
Three Nunataks, mtn., Ant.	g41	7
Three Oaks, Mi., U.S.	G4	99
Threepoint Lake, l., Man.	B2	70
Three Points, Cape, c., Ghana	F4	45
Three Rivers, Mi., U.S.	G5	99
Three Rivers, N.M., U.S.	E3	108
Three Rivers, Tx., U.S.	E3	120
Three Rock Cove, Newf.	D2	72
Three Springs, Pa., U.S.	F6	115
Three Springs, Austl.	F3	51
Throckmorton, Tx., U.S.	C3	120
Throckmorton, co., Tx., U.S.	C3	120
Throop, Pa., U.S.	m18	115
Thu, i., Viet.	G8	35
Thu Dau Mot, Viet.	G7	35
Thule (Qaanaaq), Grnld.	B14	61
Thun, Switz.	E3	18
Thun, Lake, l., Switz.	E3	18
Thunder Bay, Ont.	o17	73
Thunder Bay, dept., Ont.	o17	73
Thunder Bay, b., Mi., U.S.	D7	99
Thunder Bay, stm., Mi., U.S.	D6	99
Thunder Bay, North Branch, stm., Mi., U.S.	C6	99
Thunderbird, Lake, res., Ok., U.S.	B4	113
Thunderbolt, Ga., U.S.	D5	87
Thunder Butte, S.D., U.S.	B4	118
Thunder Butte, mtn., S.D., U.S.	B4	118
Thunder Butte Creek, stm., S.D., U.S.	B3	118
Thunder Hawk, S.D., U.S.	B4	118
Thunder Hills, hills, Sask.	C2	75
Thung Song, Thai.	H3	35
Thur, stm., Switz.	A6	21
Thurgau, state, Switz.	A6	21
Thüringer Wald, mts., E. Ger.	C5	18
Thuringia, hist. reg., E. Ger.	C5	18
Thurles, Ire.	D3	10
Thurlow Dam, Al., U.S.	C4	78
Thurman, Ia., U.S.	D2	92
Thurman, Oh., U.S.	D3	112
Thurmont, Md., U.S.	A3	97
Thurø, i., Den.	C4	15
Thursday Island, Austl.	B7	50
Thurso, Que.	D2	74
Thurso, Scot., U.K.	B5	13
Thurso, stm., Scot., U.K.	B5	13
Thurston, Ne., U.S.	B9	104
Thurston, Oh., U.S.	C3	112
Thurston, co., Ne., U.S.	B9	104
Thurston, co., Wa., U.S.	C2	124
Thurston Island, i., Ant.	B1	7
Thusis, Switz.	E4	18
Thuvu, Fiji	I14	52
Thwaites Iceburg Tongue, ice, Ant.	B2	15
Thyborøn, Den.	B2	15
Thyborøn Kanal, strt., Den.	B2	15
Tiahuanaco, Bol.	C2	55
Tiancang, China	C5	31
Tianjin (Tientsin), China	D8	31
Tianjun, China	D4	31
Tianmen, China	I5	32
Tianshui, China	C7	31
Tianzhen, China	D6	32
Tianzhu, China	D6	31
Tiawah, Ok., U.S.	A6	113
Tibagi, Braz.	C2	56
Tibagi, stm., Braz.	C2	56
Tibati, Cam.	D2	46
Tibbie, Al., U.S.	D1	78
Tibé, Pic de, mtn., Gui.	E3	45
Tiber (Tevere), stm., Italy	C4	23
Tiberias (Teverya), Isr.	F10	40
Tibesti, mts., Chad	A3	46
Tibet (Xizang), prov., China	E5	30
Tibiri, Niger	E7	50
Tibooburra, Austl.	E7	50
Tiburón, Isla, i., Mex.	B2	63
Tice, Fl., U.S.	F5	86
Tichborne, Ont.	C8	73
Tichfield, Sask.	C3	75
Tichît, Maur.	C3	45
Tichnor, Ar., U.S.	C4	81
Ticino, state, Switz.	C4	20
Ticino, stm., Eur.	C3	20
Tickfaw, La., U.S.	D5	95
Tickfaw, stm., U.S.	C5	95
Ticomán (part of Mexico City), Mex.	g9	63
Ticonderoga, N.Y., U.S.	B7	109
Ticul, Mex.	C7	63
Tide Head, N.B.	B3	71
Tidikelt, pl., Alg.	C5	44
Tidioute, Pa., U.S.	C3	115
Tidjikdja, Maur.	C2	45
Tídra, Ïle, i., Maur.	C1	45
Tiel, Neth.	C5	17
Tièl, Sen.	D1	45
Tieli, China	*B10	31
Tieling, China	C11	31
Tielmes de Tajuña, Spain	p18	22
Tielt, Bel.	B3	17
Tienen, Bel.	B6	16
Tien Shan, mts., Asia	E10	30
Tientsin see Tianjin, China		
Tien Yen, Viet.	B7	35
Tierp, Swe.	B4	14
Tierra Amarilla, Chile	E1	55
Tierra Amarilla, N.M., U.S.	A3	108
Tierra Blanca, Mex.	D5	63
Tierra del Fuego, Antártida e Islas del Atlántico Sur, ter., Arg.	h12	54
Tierra del Fuego, Isla Grande de, i., S.A.	*h12	54
Tie Siding, Wy., U.S.	E7	127
Tietê, Braz.	G5	57
Tietê, stm., Braz.	C3	56
Tieton, Wa., U.S.	C5	124
Tieton, stm., Wa., U.S.	C4	124
Tieton Dam, Wa., U.S.	C4	124
Tiffany Mountain, mtn., Wa., U.S.	A6	124
Tiff City, Mo., U.S.	E3	102
Tiffin, Ia., U.S.	C6	92
Tiffin, Oh., U.S.	A2	112
Tiffin, stm., Oh., U.S.	A1	112
Tiflis see Tbilisi, Sov. Un.	E7	29
Tift, co., Ga., U.S.	E3	87
Tifton, Ga., U.S.	E3	87
Tigard, Or., U.S.	h12	114
Tiger, Ga., U.S.	B3	87
Tigerton, Wi., U.S.	D4	126
Tigerville, S.C., U.S.	A3	117
Tighnabruaich, Scot., U.K.	C3	13
Tigil, Sov. Un.	D18	29
Tignall, Ga., U.S.	C4	87
Tignère, Cam.	D2	46
Tignish, P.E.I.	C5	71
Tigray (Tigre), prov., Eth.	C4	47
Tigre, Arg.	g7	54
Tigre, stm., Peru	B2	58
Tigre, stm., Ven.	B5	60
Tigrett, Tn., U.S.	B2	119
Tigris (Dicle), stm., Asia	B4	38
Tiguabos, Cuba	D6	64
Tiguentourine, Alg.	D6	44
Tih, Jabal at, plat., Eg.	E5	41
Tihert, Alg.	B5	44
Tihuatlán, Mex.	m15	63
Tijeras, N.M., U.S.	B3	108
Tíjí, Libya	C2	43
Tijuana, Mex.	A1	63
Tijucas, Braz.	D5	56
Tikal, hist., Guat.	D7	63
Tikamgarh, India	E7	37
Tikhoretsk, Sov. Un.	I13	27
Tikhvin, Sov. Un.	B9	27
Tiko, Cam.	E1	46
Tikrīt, Iraq	E14	40
Tiksi, Sov. Un.	B15	29
Tilamuta, Indon.	E6	34
Tilarán, C.R.	I5	63
Tilburg, Neth.	B6	16
Tilbury, Ont.	E2	73
Tilbury, Eng., U.K.	m13	10
Tilcara, Arg.	D2	55
Tilden, Il., U.S.	E4	90
Tilden, Ne., U.S.	B8	104
Tilden, Tx., U.S.	E3	120
Tilemsès, Niger	C5	45
Tilemsi, Vallée du, val., Mali	C5	45
Tilford, S.D., U.S.	C2	118
Tilghman, Md., U.S.	C5	97
Tilghman Island, i., Md., U.S.	C5	97
Tilimsen (Tlemcen), Alg.	C4	44
Tiline, Ky., U.S.	e9	94
Till, stm., Eng., U.K.	E6	13
Tillabéry, Niger	D5	45
Tillamook, Or., U.S.	B3	114
Tillamook, co., Or., U.S.	B3	114
Tillar, Ar., U.S.	D4	81
Tillatoba, Ms., U.S.	B4	101
Tillberga (part of Västerås), Swe.	t34	14
Tiller, Or., U.S.	E4	114
Tillery, Lake, res., N.C., U.S.	B2	110
Tilley, Alta.	D5	68
Tillman, S.C., U.S.	G5	117
Tillman, co., Ok., U.S.	C2	113
Tillmans Corner, Al., U.S.	E1	78
Tillson, N.Y., U.S.	D6	109
Tillsonburg, Ont.	E4	73
Tilly, Ar., U.S.	B3	81
Tillyfourie, Scot., U.K.	C6	13
Tilos, i., Grc.	D6	40
Tilpa, Austl.	F5	51
Tilrhemt, Alg.	C5	44
Tilston, Man.	E1	70
Tilting, Newf.	D4	72
Tilton, Ga., U.S.	B2	87
Tilton, Il., U.S.	C6	90
Tilton, N.H., U.S.	D3	106
Tiltonsville, Oh., U.S.	B5	112
Tim, Sov. Un.	F11	27
Timaná, Col.	C2	60
Timaru, N.Z.	P13	51
Timashevsk, Sov. Un.	I12	27
Timbalier Bay, b., La., U.S.	E5	95
Timbalier Island, i., La., U.S.	E5	95
Timbaúba, Braz.	h6	57
Timbédra, Maur.	C3	45
Timber, Or., U.S.	B3	114
Timbered Knob, mtn., Mo., U.S.	E5	102
Timberlake, N.C., U.S.	A4	110
Timber Lake, S.D., U.S.	B4	118
Timberville, Va., U.S.	B4	123
Timblin, Pa., U.S.	D3	115
Timbo, Ar., U.S.	B3	81
Timbuktu see Tombouctou, Mali	C4	45
Timerzit, Mor.	C4	44
Timewell, Il., U.S.	C3	90
Timimoun, Alg.	C5	44
Timiris, Cap, c., Maur.	C1	45
Timiskaming, dept., Ont.	o19	73
Timișoara, Rom.	C5	24
Timken, Ks., U.S.	D4	93
Timmendorfer Strand, W. Ger.	E4	15
Timmins, Ont.	o19	73
Timmonsville, S.C., U.S.	C8	117
Timms Hill, hill, Wi., U.S.	C3	126
Timnath, Co., U.S.	A5	83
Timok, stm., Eur.	C5	24
Timor, i., Indon.	G6	34
Timor Sea	B4	50
Timpanogos Cave National Monument, Ut., U.S.	C4	121
Timpas, Co., U.S.	D7	83
Timpas Creek, stm., Co., U.S.	D5	120
Timrå, Swe.	F7	14
Tims Ford Lake, res., Tn., U.S.	B5	119
Tin, Ra's at, c., Libya	B10	43
Tina, Mo., U.S.	B4	102
Tinaca Point, c., Phil.	D7	34
Tinahely, Ire.	E5	11
Tinaquillo, Ven.	B4	60
Tindouf, Alg.	C3	44
Tineo, Spain	A2	22
Tinghert, Ḥammādat, plat.	D2	43
Tinghert, Plateau du (Ḥammādat Tinghert), plat., Afr.	D6	44
Tinglev, Den.	D3	15
Tingley, Ia., U.S.	D3	92
Tingmerkpuk Mountain, mtn., Ak., U.S.	B7	79
Tingo María, Peru	C2	58
Tingréla, I.C.	D3	45
Tingri, China	C11	37

Name	Map Ref.	Page
Tingsryd, Swe.	B8	15
Tinguipaya, Bol.	C2	55
Tingwick, Que.	D6	74
Tinian, i., N. Mar. Is.	F8	6
Tinian Harbor, b., N. Mar. Is.	E7	52
Tinizong, Switz.	C8	21
Tinker Air Force Base, mil., Ok., U.S.	B4	113
Tinkerville, N.H., U.S.	B3	106
Tinkisso, stm., Gui.	D2	45
Tinley Park, Il., U.S.	k9	90
Tinnie, N.M., U.S.	D4	108
Tinniswood, Mount, mtn., B.C.	D6	69
Tinogasta, Arg.	E2	55
Tinos, Grc.	D5	40
Tínos, i., Grc.	D5	40
Tinqueux, Fr.	E3	17
Tinsley, Ms., U.S.	C3	101
Tinsman, Ar., U.S.	D3	81
Tinsukia, India	C10	99
Tintah, Mn., U.S.	D2	100
Tintigny, Bel.	E5	17
Tintina, Arg.	E3	55
Tintinara, Austl.	G3	51
Tinton Falls, N.J., U.S.	C4	107
Ti-n-Zaouatene, Alg.	E5	44
Tio, Eth.	C5	47
Tioga, Il., U.S.	C2	90
Tioga, La., U.S.	C3	95
Tioga, N.D., U.S.	A3	111
Tioga, Pa., U.S.	C7	115
Tioga, W.V., U.S.	C4	125
Tioga, co., N.Y., U.S.	C4	109
Tioga, co., Pa., U.S.	C7	115
Tioga, stm., Pa., U.S.	B7	115
Tiogue Lake, res., R.I., U.S.	D3	116
Tioman, i., Malay.	K6	35
Tiona, Pa., U.S.	C3	115
Tione di Trento, Italy	C6	20
Tionesta, Pa., U.S.	C3	115
Tionesta Creek, stm., Pa., U.S.	C3	115
Tionesta Lake, res., Pa., U.S.	D3	115
Tioughnioga, stm., N.Y., U.S.	C4	109
Tipler, Wi., U.S.	C5	126
Tiplersville, Ms., U.S.	A5	101
Tippah, co., Ms., U.S.	A5	101
Tippah, stm., Ms., U.S.	A4	101
Tipp City, Oh., U.S.	C1	112
Tippecanoe, In., U.S.	B5	91
Tippecanoe, co., In., U.S.	D4	91
Tippecanoe, stm., In., U.S.	C4	91
Tipperary, Ire.	D2	10
Tipperary, co., Ire.	E4	11
Tippo, Ms., U.S.	B3	101
Tipton, Ca., U.S.	D4	82
Tipton, In., U.S.	D5	91
Tipton, Ia., U.S.	C6	92
Tipton, Ks., U.S.	C5	93
Tipton, Mo., U.S.	C5	102
Tipton, Ok., U.S.	C2	113
Tipton, Tn., U.S.	B2	119
Tipton, co., In., U.S.	D5	91
Tipton, co., Tn., U.S.	B2	119
Tipton, Mount, mtn., Az., U.S.	B1	80
Tiptonville, Tn., U.S.	A2	119
Tip Top, Ky., U.S.	C6	94
Tiptop, Va., U.S.	C1	123
Tip Top Mountain, mtn., Ont.	o18	73
Tiquisate, Guat.	C2	62
Tīra, Isr.	B6	41
Tīrān, Jazīrat, i., Sau. Ar.	I10	40
Tirana (Tiranë), Alb.	B2	40
Tiranë see Tirana, Alb.	B2	40
Tirano, Italy	A3	23
Tiraque, Bol.	C2	55
Tiraspol, Sov. Un.	H7	27
Tirat Karmel, Isr.	B6	41
Tirat Zevi, Isr.	B7	41
Tire, Tur.	C6	40
Tirebolu, Tur.	B12	40
Tiree, i., Scot., U.K.	B3	10
Tire Hill, Pa., U.S.	F4	115
Tîrgovişte, Rom.	C7	24
Tîrgu-Frumos, Rom.	B8	24
Tîrgu-Jiu, Rom.	C6	24
Tîrgu-Neamţ, Rom.	B8	24
Tîrgu-Ocna, Rom.	B8	24
Tîrgu-Secuiesc, Rom.	B8	24
Tirich Mīr, mtn., Pak.	A5	36
Tiro, Oh., U.S.	B3	112
Tirlyanskiy, Sov. Un.	E20	8
Tîrnava Mică, stm., Rom.	B7	24
Tîrnăveni, Rom.	B7	24
Tîrnavos, Grc.	C4	25
Tiro, Oh., U.S.	B3	112
Tirol (Tyrol), state, Aus.	B7	20
Tirol, hist. reg., Aus.	E5	18
Tiros, Braz.	B3	56
Tirschenreuth, W. Ger.	D7	19
Tirso, stm., Italy	D2	23
Tirstrup, Den.	B4	15
Tiruchchirāppalli (Trichinopoly), India	F6	36
Tirunelveli (Tinnevelly), India	G6	36
Tiruppur, India	*F6	36
Tisa (Tisza), stm., Eur.	C5	24
Tisaren, l., Swe.	t33	14
Tisch Mills, Wi., U.S.	h10	126
Tisdale, Sask.	E3	75
Tishomingo, Ms., U.S.	A5	101
Tishomingo, Ok., U.S.	C5	113
Tishomingo, co., Ms., U.S.	A5	101
Tiskilwa, Il., U.S.	B4	90
Tisnaren, l., Swe.	u33	14
Tissemsilt, Alg.	B5	44
Tista, stm., Asia	D12	37
Tisza (Tisa), stm., Eur.	B6	15
Tiszaföldvár, Hung.	B5	24
Tiszakécske, Hung.	B5	24
Titicaca, Lago, l., S.A.	E4	58
Titograd, Yug.	D4	24
Titonka, Ia., U.S.	A3	92
Titovo Užice, Yug.	C3	24
Titov Veles, Yug.	E5	24
Titule, Zaire	A4	48
Titus, co., Tx., U.S.	C5	120
Titusville, Fl., U.S.	D6	86
Titusville, N.J., U.S.	C3	107
Titusville, Pa., U.S.	C2	115
Tivaouane, Sen.	C1	45
Tiverton, N.S.	E3	71
Tiverton, Ont.	C3	73
Tiverton, Eng., U.K.	E5	10
Tiverton, R.I., U.S.	D6	116
Tiverton Four Corners, R.I., U.S.	E6	116
Tivoli, Italy	D4	23
Tivoli, N.Y., U.S.	C7	109
Tivoli, Tx., U.S.	E4	120
Tixtla [de Guerrero], Mex.	o14	63
Tizapán (part of Mexico City), Mex.	h9	63
Tizard Bank, atoll, Asia	C4	34
Tizimín, Mex.	C7	63
Tizi-Ouzou, Alg.	B5	44
Tiznit, Mor.	D3	44
Tjeukemeer, l., Neth.	B5	17
Tlacolula [de Matamoros], Mex.	D5	63
Tlacotalpan, Mex.	D5	63
Tlacotepec, Mex.	o13	63
Tláhuac (part of Mexico City), Mex.	h9	63
Tlahualilo de Zaragoza, Mex.	g9	63
Tlalnepantla, stm., Mex.	g9	63
Tlalnepantla [de Comonfort], Mex.	g9	63
Tlalpan (part of Mexico City), Mex.	h9	63
Tlaltenango [de Sánchez Román], Mex.	C4	63
Tlaltenco (part of Mexico City), Mex.	h9	63
Tlapa, Mex.	o14	63
Tlapacoyan, Mex.	n15	63
Tlapaneco, stm., Mex.	o14	63
Tlaquepaque (San Pedro Tlaquepaque), Mex.	m12	63
Tlaxcala, state, Mex.	D5	63
Tlaxcala [de Xicohténcatl], Mex.	D5	63
Tlaxco [de Morelos], Mex.	n14	63
Tlaxiaco, Mex.	D5	63
Tłuszcz, Pol.	k14	26
Tmassah, Libya	D3	43
Toadlena, N.M., U.S.	A1	108
Toamasina, Madag.	g9	49
Toamasina, prov., Madag.	g9	49
Toano, Va., U.S.	C6	123
Toano Range, mts., Nv., U.S.	C7	105
Toast, N.C., U.S.	A2	110
Toay, Arg.	B4	54
Toba, Japan	o15	33
Toba, stm., B.C.	D5	69
Toba, Lake, l., Indon.	E1	34
Tobacco Root Mountains, mts., Mt., U.S.	E5	103
Tobago, i., Trin.	K14	64
Tobago Cays, is., St. Vin.	V26	65
Toba Inlet, b., B.C.	D5	69
Tobarra, Spain	C5	22
Tobaru, Japan	O5	52
Tobercurry, Ire.	C3	11
Tobermory, Ont.	B3	73
Tobermory, Scot., U.K.	D2	13
Tobias, Ne., U.S.	D8	104
Tobiishi Point, c., Japan	P17	52
Tobi Island, i., Japan	G9	33
Tobin, Mount, mtn., Nv., U.S.	C4	105
Tobin Lake, l., Austl.	D4	50
Tobin Lake, l., Sask.	D4	75
Tobin Range, mts., Nv., U.S.	C4	105
Tobins Harbor, Mi., U.S.	h10	99
Tobique, stm., N.B.	B2	71
Tobol, Sov. Un.	C6	26
Tobol, stm., Sov. Un.	C6	26
Tobolsk, Sov. Un.	D9	29
Tobruk see Ţubruq, Libya	C4	43
Toby, Mount, mtn., Ma., U.S.	B2	98
Tobyhanna, Pa., U.S.	D11	115
Tochio, Japan	H9	33
Toccoa, Ga., U.S.	B3	87
Toccoa, stm., Ga., U.S.	B2	87
Toccoa Falls, Ga., U.S.	B3	87
Toccopola, Ms., U.S.	A4	101
Toce, stm., Italy	C4	20
Tochchia Lake, l., B.C.	B5	69
Tochigi, Japan	H9	33
Toco, Chile	D2	55
Toco, Trin.	N24	65
Tocoa, Hond.	C4	62
Tocopilla, Chile	D1	55
Tocsin, In., U.S.	C7	91
Tocumen, Pan.	F8	62
Tocumwal, Austl.	G5	51
Tocuyo, stm., Ven.	A4	60
Todd, N.C., U.S.	A1	110
Todd, co., Ky., U.S.	D2	94
Todd, co., Mn., U.S.	D4	100
Todd, co., S.D., U.S.	D5	118
Todd Estates, De., U.S.	*B3	85
Toddville, Md., U.S.	D4	97
Toddy Pond, l., Me., U.S.	D4	96
Tödi, mtn., Switz.	C4	20
Todos os Santos, Baia de, b., Braz.	D3	57
Todos Santos, Bol.	C2	55
Todos Santos, Mex.	C2	63
Todtnau, W. Ger.	B3	20
Toe Head, c., Ire.	F2	11
Toe Head, c., Scot., U.K.	C1	13
Tofield, Alta.	C4	68
Tofino, B.C.	E5	69
Tofte, Mn., U.S.	C8	100
Toftlund, Den.	C3	15
Togdheer, prov., Som.	D6	47
Togiak, Ak., U.S.	D7	79
Togian Islands, is., Indon.	F6	34
Togo, Sask.	F5	75
Togo, ctry., Afr.	E5	45
Togtoh, China	D4	32
Togwotee Pass, Wy., U.S.	C2	127
Tohakum Peak, mtn., Nv., U.S.	C2	105
Tohatchi, N.M., U.S.	B1	108
Tohopekaliga, Lake, l., Fl., U.S.	D5	86
Toi, Cape, c., Japan	K5	33
To Island, i., Japan	I9	33
Toivola, Mi., U.S.	B2	99
Toivola, Mn., U.S.	C6	100
Toiyabe Range, mts., Nv., U.S.	D4	105
Tok, Ak., U.S.	C11	79
Tokachi, Mount, mtn., Japan	E11	33
Tokaj, Hung.	A5	24
Tokara Islands, is., Japan	F10	31
Tokara Strait, strt., Japan	K5	33
Tokat, Tur.	B11	40
Tôkchön, N. Kor.	G3	33
Tokeland, Wa., U.S.	C2	124
Tokelau, dep., Oc.	G11	6
Tokio, N.D., U.S.	B7	111
Tokio, Tx., U.S.	C1	120
Toki Point, c., Wake I.	A1	52
Tok Islands (Take Islands), is., Asia	H5	33
Tokmak, Sov. Un.	H10	27
Tokmak, Sov. Un.	E9	28
Tokoroa, N.Z.	M15	51
Tokuno Island, i., Japan	F10	31
Tokushima, Japan	E11	31
Tokuyama, Japan	J5	33
Tōkyō, Japan	D12	33
Tōkyō Bay, b., Japan	n18	33
Tokzār, Afg.	B10	32
Tol, i., Micron.	Q18	52
Tolar, N.M., U.S.	C6	108
Tolbukhin (Dobrich), Bul.	D8	24
Toleak Point, c., Wa., U.S.	B1	124
Toledo, Braz.	C8	73
Toledo, Ont.	C8	73
Toledo, Spain	C3	22
Toledo, Il., U.S.	D5	90
Toledo, Ia., U.S.	B5	92
Toledo, Oh., U.S.	A2	112
Toledo, Or., U.S.	C3	114
Toledo, Wa., U.S.	C3	124
Toledo, Montes de, mts., Spain	C3	22
Toledo Bend Reservoir, res., U.S.	C2	95
Toler, Ky., U.S.	C7	94
Tolga, Alg.	C6	44
Toliara, Madag.	h8	49
Toliara, prov., Madag.	h8	49
Tolima, dept., Col.	C2	60
Tolima, Nevado del, mtn., Col.	C2	60
Tolimán, Mex.	m14	63
Tolitoli, Indon.	E6	34
Tolken, l., Swe.	A6	15
Tolland, Ct., U.S.	B6	84
Tolland, co., Ct., U.S.	B6	84
Tollense, l., E. Ger.	E7	15
Tollense, stm., E. Ger.	E7	15
Tollesboro, Ky., U.S.	B6	94
Tolleson, Az., U.S.	m8	80
Tollette, Ar., U.S.	D2	81
Tolley, N.D., U.S.	A4	111
Tollhouse, Ca., U.S.	D4	82
Tolloche, Arg.	E3	55
Tolmezzo, Italy	A4	23
Tolmin, Yugo.	B1	24
Tolna, Hung.	B4	24
Tolna, N.D., U.S.	B7	111
Tolo, Gulf of, b., Indon.	F6	34
Tolono, Il., U.S.	D5	90
Tolosa, Spain	A4	22
Tolovana Park, Or., U.S.	B3	114
Tolsta Head, c., Scot., U.K.	C2	13
Tolstoi, Man.	E3	70
Tolstoy, S.D., U.S.	B6	118
Toltén, Chile	D1	54
Tolt Reservoir, res., Wa., U.S.	B4	124
Tolú, Col.	B2	60
Toluca, Il., U.S.	C4	90
Toluca, Nevado de, vol., Mex.	n14	63
Toluca [de Lerdo], Mex.	D5	63
Tolyatti, Sov. Un.	D7	113
Tom, Ok., U.S.	D7	113
Tom, Mount, hill, Ct., U.S.	C2	84
Tomah, Wi., U.S.	E3	126
Tomahawk, Wi., U.S.	C4	126
Tomahawk Lake, l., Wi., U.S.	C4	126
Tomakomai, Japan	E10	33
Tomakovka, Sov. Un.	H10	27
Tomanivi, mtn., Fiji	H15	52
Tomar, Port.	C1	22
Tomari, Sov. Un.	E17	29
Tomaszów Lubelski, Pol.	C7	26
Tomaszów Mazowiecki, Pol.	C6	26
Tomatlán, Mex.	D3	63
Tomato, Ar., U.S.	B6	81
Tomave, Bol.	C2	55
Tombador, Serra do, plat., Braz.	B4	55
Tomball, Tx., U.S.	D5	120
Tombigbee, stm., U.S.	D1	78
Tomboco, Ang.	C1	48
Tombouctou (Timbuktu), Mali	F5	80
Tombstone, Az., U.S.	F5	80
Tombstone Mountain, mtn., Yukon	D5	66
Tombua (Porto Alexandre), Ang.	E1	48
Tomé, Chile	B2	54
Tome, N.M., U.S.	C3	108
Tomelilla, Swe.	C7	15
Tomelloso, Spain	C4	22
Tom Green, co., Tx., U.S.	D2	120
Tomichi Creek, stm., Co., U.S.	C4	83
Tomini, Gulf of, b., Indon.	E6	34
Tominian, Mali	C4	45
Tomintoul, Scot., U.K.	C5	13
Tomkins Cove, N.Y., U.S.	D6	109
Tommot, Sov. Un.	D15	29
Tom Nevers Head, c., Ma., U.S.	D8	98
Tomnolen, Ms., U.S.	B4	101
Tomo, stm., Col.	B4	60
Tomobe, Japan	m19	33
Tomori, Japan	O5	33
Toms, stm., N.J., U.S.	C4	107
Toms, Ridgeway Branch, stm., N.J., U.S.	C4	107
Toms Creek, Va., U.S.	f9	123
Tomsk, Sov. Un.	D11	29
Toms River, N.J., U.S.	D4	107
Tonalá, Mex.	D6	63
Tonalea, Az., U.S.	A5	80
Tonantins, Braz.	D4	60
Tonasket, Wa., U.S.	A6	124
Tonawanda, N.Y., U.S.	B2	109
Tonawanda Indian Reservation, N.Y., U.S.	C2	109
Tonbridge, Eng., U.K.	C8	12
Tondano, Indon.	E6	34
Tønder, Den.	D2	15
Tone, stm., Japan	n19	33
Tonekābon, Iran	B5	38
Toney, Al., U.S.	A3	78
Tonga, ctry., Oc.	H11	6
Tonganoxie, Ks., U.S.	C8	93
Tongbei, China	B3	33
Tongcheng, China	D5	33
Tongchuan, China	G3	32
Tongeren, Bel.	D5	17
Tongguan, China	E7	31
Tonghe, China	B4	33
Tonghua, China	C10	31
Tongjiang, China	B6	33
Tongjiang, China	C6	33
Tongjiao Bay, b., N. Kor.	C9	33
Tongliao, China	E8	31
Tongling, China	D5	33
Tongoy, Chile	F1	55
Tongren, China	K3	32
Tongue, Scot., U.K.	B4	13
Tongue, stm., Mt., U.S.	E10	103
Tongue, stm., Tx., U.S.	p13	120
Tongue, Kyle of, b., Scot., U.K.	B4	13
Tongyu, China	B10	32
Tongzi, China	J2	32
Tonica, Il., U.S.	B4	90
Tōnichi, Mex.	B3	63
Tonj, Sud.	D2	47
Tönjum, Nor.	G2	14
Tonk, India	C6	36
Tonkawa, Ok., U.S.	A4	113
Tonkin, hist. reg., Viet.	B5	35
Tonkin, Gulf of, b., Asia	B3	34
Tonle Sap, l., Camb.	C3	35
Tonneins, Fr.	E4	16
Tonnerre, Fr.	D5	16
Tönning, W. Ger.	D2	15
Tonoloway Ridge, mtn., Md., U.S.	A1	97
Tonopah, Az., U.S.	D3	80
Tonopah, Nv., U.S.	E4	105
Tonosí, Pan.	G7	62
Tönsberg, Nor.	H4	14
Tontitown, Ar., U.S.	A1	81
Tonto, stm., Mex.	n15	63
Tonto Basin, Az., U.S.	D4	80
Tontogany, Oh., U.S.	f6	112
Tonto National Monument, Az., U.S.	D4	80
Tonto Natural Bridge, Az., U.S.	C4	80
Tony, Wi., U.S.	C3	126
Tooele, Ut., U.S.	C3	121
Tooele, co., Ut., U.S.	C2	121
Toole, co., Mt., U.S.	B5	103
Toombs, co., Ga., U.S.	D4	87
Toomsboro, Ga., U.S.	D3	87
Toomsuba, Ms., U.S.	C5	101
Toomyvara, Ire.	E3	11
Toone, Tn., U.S.	B3	119
Toormakeady, Ire.	D2	11
Toowoomba, Austl.	E9	50
Topawa, Az., U.S.	F4	80
Topaz, Ca., U.S.	C4	82
Topeka, In., U.S.	A6	91
Topeka, Ks., U.S.	C8	93
Topinabee, Mi., U.S.	C6	99
Topki, Sov. Un.	B11	28
Topley, B.C.	B4	69
Toplica, stm., Yugo.	D4	24
Topock, Az., U.S.	C1	80
Topol'čany, Czech.	D5	26
Topolino, stm., Bul.	D7	24
Topolobampo, Mex.	B3	63
Topolovgrad, Bul.	A4	24
Topozero, l., Sov. Un.	E14	14
Toppenish, Wa., U.S.	C5	124
Toppenish Ridge, mtn., Wa., U.S.	C5	124
Top Pond, l., Newf.	E3	72
Topsfield, Me., U.S.	C5	96
Topsfield, Ma., U.S.	A6	98
Topsham, Me., U.S.	E3	96
Topsham, Vt., U.S.	C4	122
Topton, N.C., U.S.	f9	110
Topton, Pa., U.S.	F10	115
Toquerville, Ut., U.S.	F2	121
Toquima Range, mts., Nv., U.S.	E5	105
Torbali, Tur.	C6	25
Torbat-e Heydarīyeh, Iran	D9	39
Torbat-e Jām, Iran	D10	39
Torbay, Newf.	E5	72
Tor Bay, b., Eng., U.K.	D4	12
Torbert, Mount, mtn., Ak., U.S.	g15	79
Torbrook, N.S.	E5	71
Torcello, Italy	D8	20
Torch, stm., Sask.	D4	75
Torch Lake, l., Mi., U.S.	D5	99
Torekov, Swe.	B6	15
Torez, Sov. Un.	q21	27
Torgau, E. Ger.	C6	19
Torhout, Bel.	B5	16
Toride, Japan	n19	33
Tori Island, i., Japan	J4	33
Torit, Sud.	E3	47
Tormes, stm., Spain	B3	22
Tornado Mountain, mtn., Can.	E3	68
Torneälven, stm., Eur.	D10	14
Torneträsk, l., Swe.	C9	14
Torngat Mountains, mts., Can.	f8	72
Tornillo, Tx., U.S.	o11	120
Tornquist, Arg.	B4	54
Toro, Spain	B3	22
Torö, Swe.	u35	14
Törökszentmiklós, Hung.	B5	24
Toronto, Ont.	D5	73
Toronto, Ks., U.S.	E8	93
Toronto, Oh., U.S.	B5	112
Toronto, S.D., U.S.	C9	118
Toronto Lake, res., Ks., U.S.	E7	93
Toro Peak, mtn., Ca., U.S.	F5	82
Toropets, Sov. Un.	C8	27
Tororo, Ug.	A5	48
Toro Rumi, mtn., Peru	D3	58
Torote, stm., Spain	o18	22
Torpsbruk, Swe.	A8	15
Torquay, Sask.	H4	75
Torquay, Eng., U.K.	E5	10
Torrance, Ca., U.S.	n12	82
Torrance, co., N.M., U.S.	C3	108
Torre Annunziata, Italy	D5	23
Torre de Cerredo, mtn., Spain	A3	22
Torre del Greco, Italy	D5	23
Torredonjimeno, Spain	D4	22
Torrejón de Ardoz, Spain	p18	22
Torrelavega, Spain	A3	22
Torremaggiore, Italy	D5	23
Torrens, Lake, l., Austl.	F6	50
Torrente, Spain	C5	22
Torreón, Mex.	B4	63
Torres, Braz.	C3	56
Torres-Pacheco, Spain	D5	22
Torres Novas, Port.	C1	22
Torres Strait, strt., Austl.	A7	50
Torres Vedras, Port.	C1	22
Torrevieja, Spain	D5	22
Torrey, Ut., U.S.	E4	121
Torridge, stm., Eng., U.K.	D3	12
Torridon, Loch, b., Scot., U.K.	C3	13
Torriglia, Italy	E5	23
Tørring, Den.	C3	57
Torrington, Alta.	D4	68
Torrington, Ct., U.S.	B3	84
Torrington, Wy., U.S.	D8	127
Torrinha, Braz.	m7	56
Torrox, Spain	D4	22
Torsby, Swe.	C5	14
Torshälla (part of Eskilstuna), Swe.	t34	14
Tórshavn, Faer. Is.	C7	8
Tongyu, China	B10	32
Tortola, i., V.I., Br.	G12	64
Tortona, Italy	B2	23
Tortosa, Spain	B6	22
Tortosa, Cape, c., Spain	B6	22
Tortue, Île de la, i., Haiti	D7	64
Tortugas, Golfo b., Col.	C2	60
Toruń, Pol.	B5	26
Torup, Swe.	B7	15
Tory Hill, Ont.	C6	73
Tory, Ia., U.S.	B5	92
Tory Island, i., Ire.	C2	10
Torysa, stm., Czech.	D6	26
Tory Sound, strt., Ire.	B3	11
Trafalgar, Cape, c., Spain	D2	22
Torzhok, Sov. Un.	C10	27
Torzym, Pol.	A10	19
Traiguén, Chile	B2	54
Tosa-shimizu, Japan	J6	33
Tosno, Sov. Un.	B8	27
Tostado, Arg.	E3	55
Tosya, Tur.	B10	40
Toszek, Pol.	g9	26
Totagatic, stm., Wi., U.S.	B2	126
Totana, Spain	D5	22
Toteng, Bots.	B3	49
Totma, Sov. Un.	B2	28
Totness, Sur.	A3	59
Toto, Guam	L10	52
Totolapan (part of Mexico City), Mex.	h9	63
Totonicapán, Guat.	E6	63
Totora Palca, Bol.	C2	55
Totowa, N.J., U.S.	B4	107
Totoya Island, i., Fiji	I16	52
Totson Mountain, mtn., Ak., U.S.	C8	79
Tótkomlós, Hung.	B5	24
Totma, Sov. Un.	B2	28
Tottenham, Austl.	F6	51
Tottenham, Ont.	C5	73
Tottenham (part of London), Eng., U.K.	k12	12
Tottori, Japan	D11	31
Totz, Ky., U.S.	D6	94
Touba, I.C.	D3	45
Touba, Sen.	D1	45
Touchet, Wa., U.S.	C7	124
Touchet, stm., Wa., U.S.	C7	124
Touchwood Lake, l., Man.	B4	70
Tougan, Burkina	D4	45
Touggourt, Alg.	C6	44
Tougué, Gui.	D2	45
Touhy, Ne., U.S.	C9	104
Touisset, Ma., U.S.	C5	98
Toul, Fr.	C6	16
Toulépleu, I.C.	E3	45
Toulon, Fr.	F6	16
Toulon, Il., U.S.	B4	90
Toulouse, Fr.	F4	16
Toungoo, Nig.	E7	45
Toungoo, Burma	E10	36
Touraine, hist. reg., Fr.	D4	16
Tourlaville, Fr.	C3	16
Tournai (Doornik), Bel.	D3	17
Tournon, Fr.	E6	16
Tournus, Fr.	D6	16
Touros, Braz.	C3	57
Tourville, Que.	B8	74
Touside, Pic, mtn., Chad	A3	46
Toussaint Creek, stm., Oh., U.S.	f7	112
Toutle, North Fork, stm., Wa., U.S.	C3	124
Tovar, Ven.	C6	60
Tovarkovskiy, Sov. Un.	C11	27
Tovey, Il., U.S.	D4	90
Towac, N.J., U.S.	B4	107
Towada, Il., U.S.	C5	90
Towanda, Ks., U.S.	E7	93
Towanda, Pa., U.S.	C9	115
Towanda Creek, stm., Pa., U.S.	C8	115
Towaoc, Co., U.S.	D2	83
Tower, Mi., U.S.	C6	99
Tower, Mn., U.S.	C6	100
Tower City, N.D., U.S.	C8	111
Tower City, Pa., U.S.	E8	115
Tower Hill, Il., U.S.	D5	90
Town and Country, Wa., U.S.	*B8	124
Town Creek, Al., U.S.	A2	78
Town Creek Manor, Md., U.S.	D5	97
Towner, Co., U.S.	C8	83
Towner, N.D., U.S.	A5	111
Towner, co., N.D., U.S.	A6	111
Town Hill, Ct., U.S.	B3	84
Town Hill, hill, Ber.	p20	64
Townley, Al., U.S.	B2	78
Town 'n Country, Fl., U.S.	*E4	86
Town of Tonawanda, N.Y., U.S.	C2	109
Towns, co., Ga., U.S.	B3	87
Towns, co., Ga., U.S.	B3	87
Townsend, De., U.S.	C3	85
Townsend, Mt., U.S.	D5	103
Townsend, Tn., U.S.	D10	119
Townsend, Va., U.S.	C7	123
Townsend, Vt., U.S.	E3	122
Townshend Reservoir, res., Vt., U.S.	E3	122
Townsville, Austl.	C8	50
Townville, N.C., U.S.	A4	110
Townville, Pa., U.S.	C2	115
Townville, S.C., U.S.	B2	117
Towrzī, Afg.	E4	36
Towson, Md., U.S.	B4	97
Towuti, Lake, l., Indon.	F6	34
Toxey, Al., U.S.	D1	78
Toyah, Tx., U.S.	o13	120
Toyahvale, Tx., U.S.	o13	120
Toyama Bay, b., Japan	H8	33
Toyohashi, Japan	D12	33
Toyokawa, Japan	*I8	33
Toyonaka, Japan	o14	33
Toyota, Japan	n16	33
Trabancos, stm., Spain	B3	22
Trabzon, Tur.	B12	40
Tracadie, N.B.	B5	71
Tracadie, N.S.	D8	71
Tracy, Que.	C4	74
Tracy, Ca., U.S.	D3	82
Tracy, Ia., U.S.	C5	92
Tracy, Mn., U.S.	F3	100
Tracy, Mo., U.S.	B3	102
Tracy City, Tn., U.S.	D8	119
Tracys Creek, stm., Md., U.S.	C4	97
Tracyton, Wa., U.S.	e10	124
Tradewater, stm., Ky., U.S.	C2	94
Trading Post, Ks., U.S.	D9	93
Traer, Ia., U.S.	B5	92
Traer, Ks., U.S.	C3	93
Trafalgar, In., U.S.	F5	91
Trafford, Pa., U.S.	k14	115
Trafford, Lake, l., Fl., U.S.	F5	86
Trail, B.C.	E9	69
Trail, Mn., U.S.	C3	100
Trail, Or., U.S.	E4	114
Trail City, S.D., U.S.	B5	118
Trail Creek, In., U.S.	A4	91
Trail Ridge, mtn., U.S.	F4	87
Trains, Swe.	H6	14
Tramandaí, Braz.	h9	22
Tramelan [-Dessus], Switz.	B3	21
Tramore, Ire.	E4	11
Trampas, N.M., U.S.	A4	108
Tramping Lake, Sask.	E1	75
Tramping Lake, l., Sask.	E1	75
Tranås, Swe.	H6	14
Trancão, stm., Port.	E2	55
Trancas, Arg.	B2	22
Trancoso, Port.	C4	15
Tranebjerg, Den.	A7	15
Tranemo, Swe.	D1	34
Trang, Thai.	G8	34
Trangan, i., Indon.	D6	23
Trani, Italy	C5	35
Tranninh, Plateau du, plat., Laos	C5	35
Tranquility, N.J., U.S.	B3	107
Tranquility, Ca., U.S.	D3	82
Transfer, Pa., U.S.	D1	115
Transkei, ctry., Afr.	D4	49
Transvaal, prov., S. Afr.	B4	49
Transylvania, co., N.C., U.S.	f10	110
Transylvania, hist. reg., Rom.	B6	24
Transylvanian Alps, mts., Rom.	C7	24
Trapani, Italy	E4	23
Trap Mountain, mtn., Ar., U.S.	g7	81
Trappe, Md., U.S.	C5	97
Trappe Creek, stm., Md., U.S.	D7	97
Trapper Peak, mtn., Mt., U.S.	E2	103
Traralgon, Austl.	G8	50
Traryd, Swe.	B7	15
Trasimeno, Lake, l., Italy	C4	23
Trask, Mo., U.S.	E6	102
Traskwood, Ar., U.S.	C3	81
Tras-os-Montes, hist. reg., Port.	B2	22
Trat, Thai.	C2	34
Traun, Aus.	D7	18
Traunik, Mi., U.S.	B4	99
Traun Lake, l., Aus.	E6	18
Traunstein, W. Ger.	E6	18
Trautenau (Trutnov), Czech.	D3	117
Travelers Rest, S.C., U.S.	B3	117
Travers, Alta.	D4	68
Travers, Switz.	C2	21
Traverse, co., Mn., U.S.	E2	100
Traverse, Lake, l., U.S.	B9	118
Traverse City, Mi., U.S.	D5	99
Traverspine, stm., Newf.	B1	72
Travers Reservoir, res., Alta.	D4	68
Tra Vinh, Viet.	H7	35
Travis, co., Tx., U.S.	D4	120
Travis Air Force Base, mil., Ca., U.S.	C2	82
Travnik, Yugo.	C3	24
Tray Mountain, mtn., Ga., U.S.	B3	87
Treadway, Tn., U.S.	C10	119
Treasure, co., Mt., U.S.	D9	103
Treasure Island, Fl., U.S.	*p10	86
Treasure Island Naval Station, Ca., U.S.	h8	82
Trebbia, stm., Italy	E5	20
Trebel, stm., E. Ger.	E6	15
Třebíč, Czech.	D3	26
Trebinje, Yugo.	D4	24
Trebišov, Czech.	D6	26
Treble Mountain, mtn., B.C.	B3	69
Trebloc, Ms., U.S.	B5	101
Třeboň, Czech.	D3	26
Trece Martires, Phil.	o13	34
Treece, Ks., U.S.	E9	93
Trees, La., U.S.	B1	95
Tregaron, Wales, U.K.	D5	10
Tregarva, Sask.	G3	75
Trego, Mt., U.S.	B2	103
Trego, Wi., U.S.	C2	126
Trego, co., Ks., U.S.	D4	93
Treherne, Man.	E2	70
Treig, Loch, res., Scot., U.K.	D4	13
Treinta y Tres, Ur.	E2	56
Treis, W. Ger.	D3	16
Trelew, Arg.	C3	54
Trelleborg, Swe.	J5	14
Tremadog Bay, b., Wales, U.K.	D4	10
Tremblant, Mont, mtn., Que.	C3	74
Tremblay, Fr.	g11	16
Trembleur Lake, l., B.C.	B5	69
Trementina, N.M., U.S.	B5	108
Tremiti Islands, is., Italy	C5	23
Tremont, Il., U.S.	C4	90
Tremont, Ma., U.S.	A5	101
Tremont, Pa., U.S.	E9	115
Tremont City, Oh., U.S.	B2	112
Tremonton, Ut., U.S.	B3	121
Tremp, Spain	A6	22
Tremošná, Czech.	D8	19
Trempealeau, co., Wi., U.S.	D2	126
Trempealeau, stm., Wi., U.S.	D2	126
Trenary, Mi., U.S.	B4	99
Trenče, Tun.	C6	44
Trenčín, Czech.	D5	26
Trent, E. Ger.	D7	15
Trent, S.D., U.S.	D9	118
Trent, Tx., U.S.	C2	120
Trent, stm., Eng., U.K.	D6	10

Trent, stm., N.C., U.S. — B5 — 110
Trente et un Milles, Lac des, l., Que. — C2 — 74
Trentino-Alto Adige, prov., Italy — C7 — 20
Trento (Trent), Italy — A3 — 23
Trenton, N.S. — D7 — 71
Trenton, Ont. — C7 — 73
Trenton, Al., U.S. — A3 — 78
Trenton, Fl., U.S. — C4 — 86
Trenton, Ga., U.S. — B1 — 87
Trenton, Il., U.S. — E4 — 90
Trenton, Ky., U.S. — D2 — 94
Trenton, Mo., U.S. — F7 — 99
Trenton, Ne., U.S. — A4 — 102
Trenton, N.J., U.S. — D4 — 104
Trenton, N.J., U.S. — C3 — 107
Trenton, N.C., U.S. — B5 — 110
Trenton, N.D., U.S. — A2 — 111
Trenton, Oh., U.S. — C1 — 112
Trenton, S.C., U.S. — D4 — 117
Trenton, Tn., U.S. — B3 — 119
Trenton, Tx., U.S. — C4 — 120
Trenton, Ut., U.S. — B4 — 121
Trepassey, Newf. — E5 — 72
Trepassey Bay, b., Newf. — E5 — 72
Tres Algarrobos, Arg. — B4 — 54
Tres Árboles, Ur. — E1 — 56
Tres Arroyos, Arg. — B4 — 54
Tres Cerros, Arg. — D3 — 54
Tres Corações, Braz. — C3 — 56
Três Esquinas, Col. — C2 — 60
Treshnish Point, c., Scot., U.K. — D2 — 13
Tres Irmãos, Serra dos, hills, Braz. — D2 — 59
Treska, stm., Yugo. — E5 — 24
Três Lagoas, Braz. — C2 — 56
Três Marias, Represa, res., Braz. — B3 — 56
Tres Piedras, N.M., U.S. — A4 — 108
Tres Puntas, Cabo, c., Arg. — A4 — 54
Três Rios, Braz. — h6 — 56
Tres Ritos, N.M., U.S. — A4 — 108
Trestle Creek, Id., U.S. — A2 — 89
Treuchtlingen, W. Ger. — E5 — 19
Treuenbrietzen, E. Ger. — A7 — 19
Treutlen, co., Ga., U.S. — D4 — 87
Treviglio, Italy — B2 — 23
Trévillers, Fr. — B2 — 21
Treviño, Spain — A4 — 22
Treviso, Italy — B4 — 23
Trevlac, In., U.S. — F5 — 91
Trevor, Wi., U.S. — n11 — 126
Trevorton, Pa., U.S. — E8 — 115
Trevose, Pa., U.S. — o22 — 115
Trevose Head, c., Eng., U.K. — D2 — 12
Treynor, Ia., U.S. — C2 — 92
Treysa, W. Ger. — C4 — 19
Trezevant, Tn., U.S. — A3 — 119
Trhové Sviny, Czech. — E9 — 19
Triadelphia, W.V., U.S. — A4 — 125
Triadelphia Reservoir, res., Md., U.S. — B3 — 97
Triánda, Grc. — D7 — 25
Triangle, Va., U.S. — B5 — 123
Triaucourt [-en-Argonne], Fr. — F5 — 17
Tribbett, Ms., U.S. — B3 — 101
Tribbey, Ok., U.S. — B4 — 113
Tribune, Sask. — H4 — 75
Tribune, Ks., U.S. — D2 — 93
Trichinopoly see Tiruchchirāppalli, India — F6 — 36
Trichūr, India — F6 — 36
Tri City, Or., U.S. — E3 — 114
Tridell, Ut., U.S. — C6 — 121
Trident, Mt., U.S. — E5 — 103
Trident Peak, mtn., Nv., U.S. — B3 — 105
Trier, W. Ger. — D3 — 18
Trieste, Italy — B4 — 23
Trieste, Gulf of, b., Eur. — B4 — 23
Trigg, co., Ky., U.S. — D2 — 94
Triglav, mtn., Yugo. — B1 — 24
Trigo Mountains, mts., Az., U.S. — D1 — 80
Trigueros, Spain — D2 — 22
Trikala, Grc. — C3 — 40
Trikhonís, Lake, l., Grc. — C3 — 40
Trikora Peak, mtn., Indon. — F9 — 34
Tri Lakes, In., U.S. — B7 — 91
Trilby, Fl., U.S. — D4 — 86
Trilla, Il., U.S. — D5 — 90
Trillick, N. Ire., U.K. — C4 — 11
Trim, Ire. — D5 — 11
Trimble, Mo., U.S. — B3 — 102
Trimble, Tn., U.S. — A2 — 119
Trimble, co., Ky., U.S. — B4 — 94
Trimont, Mn., U.S. — G4 — 100
Trimountain, Mi., U.S. — A2 — 99
Trinchera, Co., U.S. — D6 — 83
Trinchera Creek, stm., Co., U.S. — D5 — 83
Trincomalee, Sri L. — G7 — 36
Trindade, i., Braz. — H8 — 5
Třinec, Czech. — *D5 — 26
Tring Jonction, Que. — C6 — 74
Trinidad, Bol. — B3 — 55
Trinidad, Col. — B3 — 60
Trinidad, Cuba — D4 — 64
Trinidad, Co., U.S. — D6 — 83
Trinidad, Tx., U.S. — C4 — 120
Trinidad, Ur. — E1 — 56
Trinidad, i., Trin. — K14 — 64
Trinidad, Bahía, b., Pan. — k11 — 62
Trinidad, Isla, i., Arg. — B4 — 54
Trinidad and Tobago, ctry., N.A. — K14 — 64
Trinidad Head, c., Ca., U.S. — B1 — 82
Trinity, Newf. — D5 — 72
Trinity, Newf. — D5 — 72
Trinity, Al., U.S. — A2 — 78
Trinity, N.C., U.S. — *B3 — 110
Trinity, Tx., U.S. — D5 — 120
Trinity, co., Ca., U.S. — B2 — 82
Trinity, co., Tx., U.S. — D5 — 120
Trinity, stm., Ca., U.S. — B2 — 82
Trinity, stm., Tx., U.S. — D5 — 120
Trinity, East Fork, stm., Tx., U.S. — n10 — 120
Trinity, Elm Fork, stm., Tx., U.S. — m10 — 120
Trinity, South Fork, stm., Ca., U.S. — B2 — 82
Trinity, West Fork, stm., Tx., U.S. — n9 — 120
Trinity Bay, b., Newf. — D5 — 72
Trinity Center, Ca., U.S. — B2 — 82
Trinity Islands, is., Ak., U.S. — D9 — 79
Trinity Mountain, mtn., Id., U.S. — F3 — 89
Trinity Mountains, mts., Ca., U.S. — B2 — 82
Trinity Peak, mtn., Nv., U.S. — C3 — 105
Trinity Range, mts., Nv., U.S. — C3 — 105
Trinity Springs, In., U.S. — G4 — 91

Trino, Italy — B2 — 23
Trinway, Oh., U.S. — B3 — 112
Trio, S.C., U.S. — E8 — 117
Trion, Ga., U.S. — B1 — 87
Triplett, Mo., U.S. — B4 — 102
Tripoli (Țarābulus), Leb. — B3 — 38
Tripoli (Țarābulus), Libya — C2 — 43
Tripoli, Ia., U.S. — B5 — 92
Tripoli, Wi., U.S. — C4 — 126
Tripolis, Grc. — D4 — 40
Tripolitania (Țarābulus), hist. reg., Libya — C3 — 43
Tripura, state, India — D9 — 36
Trisanna, stm., Aus. — B9 — 21
Trischen, i., W. Ger. — A4 — 18
Triste, Golfo, b., Ven. — A4 — 60
Triumph, La., U.S. — E6 — 95
Triune, Tn., U.S. — B5 — 119
Trivandrum, India — G6 — 36
Triunfo, Braz. — C3 — 57
Trnava, Czech. — D4 — 26
Trobriand Islands, is., Pap. N. Gui. — k13 — 50a
Trochu, Alta. — D4 — 68
Trogir, Yugo. — D3 — 24
Trøgstad, Nor. — p29 — 14
Troisdorf, W. Ger. — C2 — 19
Trois-Pistoles, Que. — A8 — 74
Trois-Rivières, Que. — C5 — 74
Trois-Rivières-Ouest, Que. — C5 — 74
Trois-Saumons, Que. — B7 — 74
Troitsk, Sov. Un. — D9 — 29
Troitskoye, Sov. Un. — B8 — 33
Trollheim, Nor. — p28 — 14
Trollhättan, Swe. — H5 — 14
Trombetas, stm., Braz. — C3 — 59
Trombly, Mi., U.S. — B3 — 99
Tromper Wiek, b., E. Ger. — D7 — 15
Tromsø, Nor. — C8 — 14
Trona, Ca., U.S. — E5 — 82
Tronador, Monte, mtn., S.A. — C2 — 54
Trondheim, Nor. — F4 — 14
Trondheimsfjorden, Nor. — F4 — 14
Troon, Scot., U.K. — E4 — 13
Trooper, Pa., U.S. — *F11 — 115
Tropea, Italy — E5 — 23
Trophy Mountain, mtn., B.C. — D8 — 69
Tropic, Ut., U.S. — F3 — 121
Trosa, Swe. — u35 — 14
Trosky, Mn., U.S. — G2 — 100
Trossachs, Sask. — H3 — 75
Trostan, mtn., N. Ire., U.K. — B5 — 11
Trotters, N.D., U.S. — B2 — 111
Trotwood, Oh., U.S. — C1 — 112
Troup, Tx., U.S. — C5 — 120
Troup, co., Ga., U.S. — C1 — 87
Trousdale, Ks., U.S. — E5 — 93
Trousdale, co., Tn., U.S. — A5 — 119
Troussers Lake, l., N.B. — B3 — 71
Trout, La., U.S. — C3 — 95
Trout, stm., Alta. — A3 — 68
Trout, stm., Fl., U.S. — m8 — 86
Trout, stm., Vt., U.S. — B3 — 122
Trout Creek, Ont. — B5 — 73
Trout Creek, Mi., U.S. — n12 — 99
Trout Creek, Mt., U.S. — C1 — 103
Trout Creek, Ut., U.S. — D2 — 121
Trout Creek Pass, Co., U.S. — C5 — 83
Troutdale, Me., U.S. — E5 — 83
Troutdale, Or., U.S. — *B4 — 114
Trout Lake, Ont. — *D4 — 114
Troutdale, Va., U.S. — D1 — 123
Trout Lake, Mi., U.S. — B6 — 99
Trout Lake, Wa., U.S. — D4 — 124
Trout Lake, l., B.C. — D9 — 69
Trout Lake, l., N.W. Ter. — D8 — 66
Trout Lake, l., Ont. — A5 — 73
Trout Lake, l., Ont. — o16 — 73
Trout Lake, l., Mn., U.S. — B6 — 100
Trout Lake, l., Wi., U.S. — B4 — 126
Troutman, N.C., U.S. — B2 — 110
Trout Peak, mtn., Wy., U.S. — B3 — 127
Trout River, Newf. — D2 — 72
Trout Run, Pa., U.S. — D7 — 115
Troutville, [-sur-Mer], Fr. — C4 — 16
Trowbridge, Eng., U.K. — E5 — 12
Troy, Al., U.S. — D4 — 78
Troy, Id., U.S. — C2 — 89
Troy, Il., U.S. — E4 — 90
Troy, In., U.S. — H4 — 91
Troy, Ia., U.S. — D5 — 92
Troy, Ks., U.S. — C8 — 93
Troy, Mo., U.S. — o15 — 99
Troy, Ms., U.S. — A5 — 101
Troy, Mt., U.S. — C7 — 102
Troy, Mt., U.S. — B1 — 103
Troy, N.H., U.S. — E2 — 106
Troy, N.Y., U.S. — C7 — 109
Troy, N.C., U.S. — B3 — 110
Troy, Oh., U.S. — C6 — 20
Troy, Oh., U.S. — B1 — 112
Troy, Ok., U.S. — C5 — 113
Troy, Or., U.S. — B9 — 114
Troy, S.C., U.S. — D3 — 117
Troy, S.D., U.S. — B9 — 118
Troy, Tn., U.S. — A2 — 119
Troy, Vt., U.S. — B4 — 122
Troy, W.V., U.S. — B4 — 125
Troy (Ilion), hist., Tur. — C6 — 25
Troyes, Fr. — C6 — 16
Troy Grove, Il., U.S. — B5 — 90
Troy Mills, Ia., U.S. — B6 — 92
Troy Peak, mtn., Nv., U.S. — E6 — 105
Trstenik, Yugo. — H3 — 75
Truax, Sask. — H3 — 75
Trubchevsk, Sov. Un. — E9 — 27
Trubschachen, Switz. — C3 — 26
Truchas, N.M., U.S. — A4 — 108
Truchas Peak, mtn., N.M., U.S. — B4 — 108
Truckee, Ca., U.S. — C3 — 82
Truckee, stm., U.S. — D2 — 105
Trujillo, Hond. — D7 — 63
Trujillo, Peru — B2 — 58
Trujillo, Spain — C3 — 22
Trujillo, Ven. — B3 — 60
Trujillo, state, Ven. — B3 — 60
Truk, is., Micron. — F9 — 6
Truk International Airport, Micron. — Q18 — 52
Truk Lagoon, b., Micron. — Q18 — 52
Trumann, Mn., U.S. — G4 — 100
Trumann, Ar., U.S. — B5 — 81
Trumann, Tx., U.S. — B5 — 120
Trumansburg, N.Y., U.S. — C4 — 109
Trumbull, Ct., U.S. — E3 — 84
Trumbull, Ne., U.S. — D7 — 102
Trumbull, co., Oh., U.S. — A5 — 112
Trumbull, Mount, mtn., Az., U.S. — A2 — 80
Trún, Bul. — D6 — 24

Truro, N.S. — D6 — 71
Truro, Eng., U.K. — E4 — 10
Truro, Ia., U.S. — C4 — 92
Truro, Ma., U.S. — C7 — 98
Truscott, Tx., U.S. — C3 — 120
Truskmore, mtn., Ire. — C3 — 11
Trussville, Al., U.S. — B3 — 78
Trustom Pond, l., R.I., U.S. — G3 — 116
Trust Territory of the Pacific Islands see Pacific Islands, Trust Territory of the, dep., Oc. — F9 — 6
Truth or Consequences (Hot Springs), N.M., U.S. — D2 — 108
Trutnov, Czech. — C3 — 26
Truxton, Az., U.S. — B2 — 80
Truxton, Mo., U.S. — B6 — 102
Truxton, N.Y., U.S. — C4 — 109
Tryon, Ne., U.S. — C5 — 104
Tryon, N.C., U.S. — f10 — 110
Tryon, Ok., U.S. — B5 — 113
Trysil, Nor. — G5 — 14
Trzcianka, Pol. — B4 — 26
Trzciatów, Pol. — A3 — 26
Trzebinia, Pol. — C5 — 26
Trzebnica, Pol. — C4 — 26
Tsagaan Tologoy Hiid, Mong. — C2 — 32
Tsaidam Basin see Qaidam Pendi, China — D3 — 31
Tsakir, Sov. Un. — A5 — 31
Tsala Apopka Lake, l., Fl., U.S. — D4 — 86
Tsaratanana, Madag. — g9 — 49
Tsast Bogd Mountain, mtn., Mong. — B3 — 31
Tsau, Bots. — B3 — 49
Tsavo, Kenya — B6 — 48
Tschetter Colony, S.D., U.S. — D8 — 118
Tschida, Lake, res., N.D., U.S. — C4 — 111
Tselinograd, Sov. Un. — D10 — 29
Tsentralnyy, Sov. Un. — D26 — 8
Tsetserleg, Mong. — B5 — 31
Tshabong, Bots. — C3 — 49
Tshane, Bots. — B3 — 49
Tshela, Zaire — B1 — 48
Tshikapa, Zaire — C3 — 48
Tshilongo, Zaire — D4 — 48
Tshimbo, Zaire — C4 — 48
Tshofa, Zaire — C4 — 48
Tshuapa, stm., Zaire — B3 — 48
Tshukudu, Bots. — B3 — 49
Tshwaane, Bots. — B3 — 49
Tsiafajavona, mtn., Madag. — g9 — 49
Tsihombe, Madag. — i9 — 49
Tsimlyansk Reservoir, res., Sov. Un. — E7 — 29
Tsinan see Jinan, China — D8 — 31
Tsing Hai see Qinghai, prov., China — D4 — 31
Tsingtao see Qingdao, China — D9 — 31
Tsinling Shan see Qin Ling, mts., China — E6 — 31
Tsintsabis, Nmb. — A2 — 49
Tsiroanomandidy, Madag. — g9 — 49
Tsitsihar see Qiqihar, China — B9 — 31
Tsitsutl Peak, mtn., B.C. — C5 — 69
Tsivory, Madag. — h9 — 49
Tshinvali, Sov. Un. — E2 — 28
Tsna, stm., Sov. Un. — E13 — 27
Tsodilo Hill, hill, Bots. — A3 — 49
Tsomo, stm., S. Afr. — H5 — 49
Tsu, Japan — I8 — 33
Tsuchiura, Japan — H10 — 33
Tsugaru Strait, strt., Japan — F10 — 33
Tsuken Island, i., Japan — O5 — 52
Tsulukidze, Sov. Un. — A14 — 40
Tsumeb, Nmb. — A2 — 49
Tsumis Park, Nmb. — B2 — 49
Tsun Wan, H.K. — *G7 — 31
Tsuruga, Japan — I8 — 33
Tsurugi, Mount, mtn., Japan — J7 — 33
Tsuruoka, Japan — G9 — 33
Tsushima, is., Japan — n15 — 33
Tsu Shima, is., Japan — E10 — 31
Tsuyama, Japan — I6 — 33
Tua, stm., Port. — B2 — 22
Tual, Indon. — G8 — 34
Tuam, Ire. — C3 — 11
Tuao, Phil. — B7 — 34
Tuamotu Archipelago, is., Fr. Poly. — H13 — 6
Tuangku, i., Indon. — K2 — 35
Tuangku, i., Indon. — G16 — 8
Tuasivi, W. Sam. — F11 — 52
Tuasivi, Cape, c., W. Sam. — F11 — 52
Tuatapere, N.Z. — Q11 — 51
Tuba, Az., U.S. — o15 — 99
Tuba City, Az., U.S. — A4 — 80
Tubarão, Braz. — D3 — 56
Tūbās, Isr. Occ. — B7 — 41
Tuberose, Sask. — G1 — 75
Tubize, Bel. — C6 — 20
Tubruq (Tobruk), Libya — C4 — 43
Tucacas, Ven. — A4 — 60
Tuchola, Pol. — B4 — 26
Tuckahoe, N.J., U.S. — E3 — 107
Tuckahoe, N.Y., U.S. — h13 — 109
Tuckahoe, stm., N.J., U.S. — E3 — 107
Tuckahoe Creek, stm., Md., U.S. — C6 — 97
Tucker, Ar., U.S. — C4 — 81
Tucker, Ga., U.S. — h8 — 87
Tucker, Tx., U.S. — D5 — 120
Tucker, co., W.V., U.S. — B5 — 125
Tucker Island, i., N.J., U.S. — E4 — 107
Tuckerman, Ar., U.S. — B4 — 81
Tuckernuck Island, i., Ma., U.S. — D7 — 98
Tuckers Crossing, Ms., U.S. — D4 — 101
Tuckerton, N.J., U.S. — D4 — 107
Tucson, Az., U.S. — E5 — 80
Tucson, prov., Arg. — B3 — 54
Tucumcari, N.M., U.S. — B6 — 108
Tucumcari Mountain, mtn., N.M., U.S. — B6 — 108
Tucupita, Bol. — D2 — 55
Tucupita, Ven. — B6 — 60
Tucuruí, Braz. — C5 — 59
Tuczno, Pol. — g10 — 29
Tudela, Spain — A5 — 22
Tudor (Palmyra), Syria — E12 — 40
Tufi, Pap. N. Gui. — k12 — 50a
Tugaloo Lake, res., U.S. — B1 — 117
Tugela, stm., S. Afr. — G5 — 49
Tug Fork, stm., U.S. — C2 — 125
Tuguegarao, Phil. — B6 — 34
Tuira, stm., Pan. — G9 — 62

Tükrah, Libya — C4 — 43
Tuktoyaktuk, N.W. Ter. — C6 — 66
Tukums, Sov. Un. — C4 — 27
Tukuyu, Tan. — C5 — 48
Tukwila, Wa., U.S. — f11 — 124
Tula, Mex. — C5 — 63
Tula, Sov. Un. — D6 — 29
Tula, Ms., U.S. — A4 — 101
Tula de Allende, Mex. — m14 — 63
Tulalip Indian Reservation, Wa., U.S. — A3 — 124
Tulancingo, Mex. — C5 — 63
Tulare, Ca., U.S. — D4 — 82
Tulare, S.D., U.S. — C7 — 118
Tulare, co., Ca., U.S. — D4 — 82
Tulare Lake, l., Ca., U.S. — D4 — 82
Tularosa, N.M., U.S. — D3 — 108
Tularosa Mountains, mts., N.M., U.S. — D1 — 108
Tularosa Valley, val., N.M., U.S. — E3 — 108
Tulbagh, S. Afr. — D2 — 49
Tulcán, Ec. — A2 — 58
Tulcea, Rom. — C9 — 24
Tulchin, Sov. Un. — G7 — 27
Tule, stm., Ca., U.S. — B3 — 82
Tule Lake Sump, sw., Ca., U.S. — B3 — 82
Tule River Indian Reservation, Ca., U.S. — E4 — 82
Tuleta, Tx., U.S. — E4 — 120
Tule Valley, val., Ut., U.S. — D2 — 121
Tuli, Zimb. — B4 — 49
Tuli, stm., Zimb. — B4 — 49
Tūlkarm, Isr. Occ. — B7 — 41
Tulla, Ire. — E3 — 11
Tullahassee, Ok., U.S. — B6 — 113
Tullahoma, Tn., U.S. — B5 — 119
Tullamore, Ire. — D3 — 10
Tulle, Fr. — E4 — 16
Tullins, Fr. — E6 — 16
Tulln, Aus. — D8 — 18
Tullos, La., U.S. — C3 — 95
Tully, Austl. — C8 — 50
Tully, N.Y., U.S. — C4 — 109
Tulmaythah, Libya — F3 — 40
Tuloma, stm., Sov. Un. — B15 — 8
Tulot, Ar., U.S. — B5 — 81
Tulsa, Ok., U.S. — A6 — 113
Tulsa, co., Ok., U.S. — B6 — 113
Tulsequah, B.C. — E6 — 66
Tulsk, Ire. — D3 — 11
Tuluá, Col. — C2 — 60
Tulun, Sov. Un. — D13 — 29
Tulungagung, Indon. — G4 — 34
Tulu Welel, mtn., Eth. — D3 — 47
Tuma, stm., Nic. — D5 — 62
Tumacacori, Az., U.S. — F4 — 80
Tumacacori National Monument, Az., U.S. — F4 — 80
Tumaco, Col. — C2 — 60
Tumaco, Ensenada de, b., Col. — C2 — 60
Tumalo, Or., U.S. — C5 — 114
Tumatumari, Guy. — A3 — 59
Tumba, Swe. — t35 — 14
Tumba, Lac, l., Zaire — B2 — 48
Tumbarumba, Austl. — G7 — 51
Tumbaya, Arg. — D2 — 55
Tumbes, Peru — B1 — 58
Tumbes, dept., Peru — B1 — 58
Tumble Mountain, mtn., Mt., U.S. — E7 — 103
Tumbler Ridge, B.C. — B7 — 69
Tumbling Shoals, Ar., U.S. — B3 — 81
Tumen, China — C10 — 31
Tumen Jiang, stm., Asia — E4 — 33
Tumereng, Ven. — B5 — 60
Tumkūr, India — F6 — 36
Tumnin, stm., Sov. Un. — A10 — 33
Tumon Bay, b., Guam — L10 — 52
Tumtum, Wa., U.S. — B8 — 124
Tumu, Ghana — D4 — 45
Tumuc-Humac Mountains, mts., S.A. — B3 — 59
Tumut, Austl. — G7 — 51
Tumwater, Wa., U.S. — B3 — 124
Tumayn, Trin. — N23 — 65
Tumez, Austl. — D2 — 10
Tunas de Zaza, Cuba — D4 — 64
Tunaycha, l., Sov. Un. — C11 — 33
Tunbridge, Vt., U.S. — D4 — 122
Tunbridge Wells see Royal Tunbridge Wells, Eng., U.K. — E7 — 10
Tunduru, Tan. — D6 — 48
Tundzha, stm., Eur. — D8 — 24
Tunga, stm., India — F6 — 36
Tungla, Nic. — D5 — 62
Tungurahua, prov., Ec. — B2 — 58
Tuni, India — I9 — 37
Tunica, La., U.S. — D4 — 95
Tunica, Ms., U.S. — A3 — 101
Tunica, co., Ms., U.S. — A3 — 101
Tunis, Tun. — B7 — 44
Tunis, Gulf of, b., Tun. — F3 — 23
Tunisia, ctry., Afr. — C6 — 44
Tunis Mills, Md., U.S. — C5 — 97
Tunja, Col. — C6 — 60
Tunkhannock, Pa., U.S. — C10 — 115
Tunk Lake, l., Me., U.S. — D4 — 96
Tunnel Hill, Ga., U.S. — B1 — 87
Tunnel Springs, Al., U.S. — D2 — 78
Tunnelton, In., U.S. — G5 — 91
Tunnelton, W.V., U.S. — B5 — 125
Tunø, i., Den. — C4 — 15
Tunø, i., Den. — C4 — 15
Tunstall, Va., U.S. — C5 — 123
Tuntutuliak, Ak., U.S. — C7 — 79
Tununak, Ak., U.S. — C6 — 79
Tunungayualok Island, i., Newf. — g9 — 72
Tunuyán, Arg. — A3 — 54
Tunuyán, stm., Arg. — A3 — 54
Tunxi, China — F8 — 31
Tuolumne, Ca., U.S. — D3 — 82
Tuolumne, co., Ca., U.S. — C4 — 82
Tuolumne, stm., Ca., U.S. — D3 — 82
Tupã, Braz. — C3 — 56
Tupaciretã, Braz. — D2 — 56
Tupelo, Ar., U.S. — B4 — 81
Tupelo, Ms., U.S. — A5 — 101
Tupelo, Ok., U.S. — C5 — 113
Tupiza, Bol. — D2 — 55
Tupman, Ca., U.S. — E4 — 82
Tupper, B.C. — B7 — 69
Tupper Lake, l., N.Y., U.S. — A6 — 109
Tupper Lake, l., N.Y., U.S. — A6 — 109
Tuppers Plains, Oh., U.S. — C4 — 112
Tupperville, Ont. — E2 — 73
Tupungato, Arg. — A3 — 54
Tupungato, Cerro, mtn., S.A. — A3 — 54
Tuquerres, Col. — C2 — 60
Tuquan, China — B9 — 32
Tura, India — E13 — 37
Tura, Sov. Un. — C13 — 29
Tura, stm., Sov. Un. — B6 — 28

Turan Lowland, pl., Sov. Un. — E5 — 28
Turayf, Sau. Ar. — B3 — 38
Turbaco, Col. — A2 — 60
Turbat, Pak. — C3 — 36
Turbenthal, Switz. — B6 — 21
Turbo, Col. — B2 — 60
Turbotville, Pa., U.S. — D8 — 115
Turda, Rom. — B6 — 24
Turek, Pol. — B5 — 26
Turgay, Sov. Un. — E9 — 29
Turgay, stm., Sov. Un. — D6 — 28
Türgen Mountain, mtn., Mong. — B3 — 31
Türgovishte, Bul. — D8 — 24
Turgutlu, Tur. — D3 — 39
Turhal, Tur. — *B11 — 40
Turi, Sov. Un. — B5 — 27
Turia, stm., Spain — C5 — 22
Turiaçu, Braz. — B1 — 57
Turiaçu, stm., Braz. — B1 — 57
Turimiquire, Cerro, mtn., Ven. — A5 — 60
Turin, Alta. — E4 — 68
Turin (Torino), Italy — B1 — 23
Turin, Ga., U.S. — C2 — 87
Turin, Ia., U.S. — B1 — 92
Turin, N.Y., U.S. — B5 — 109
Turinsk, Sov. Un. — B6 — 28
Turiy Rog, Sov. Un. — D5 — 33
Turka, Sov. Un. — G4 — 27
Turkestan, Sov. Un. — E9 — 29
Túrkeve, Hung. — B5 — 24
Turkey, N.C., U.S. — C4 — 110
Turkey, Tx., U.S. — B2 — 120
Turkey, ctry., Asia — C10 — 40
Turkey, stm., Ia., U.S. — B6 — 92
Turkey Creek, La., U.S. — D3 — 95
Turkey Creek, stm., Ne., U.S. — D8 — 104
Turkey Creek, stm., Ok., U.S. — A3 — 113
Turkey Point, c., Md., U.S. — B5 — 97
Turkmen S.S.R., state, Sov. Un. — F8 — 29
Turk Mine, Zimb. — A4 — 49
Turks and Caicos Islands, dep., N.A. — D8 — 64
Turks Island Passage, strt., T./C. Is. — D8 — 64
Turks Islands, is., T./C. Is. — D8 — 64
Turku (Åbo), Fin. — G10 — 14
Turkwel, stm., Kenya — A6 — 48
Turley, Ok., U.S. — A6 — 113
Turlock, Ca., U.S. — D3 — 82
Turmalina, Braz. — B4 — 56
Turmus 'Ayyā, Isr. Occ. — B7 — 41
Turnbull, Mount, mtn., Az., U.S. — D5 — 80
Turneffe Islands, is., Belize — D7 — 63
Turner, Ar., U.S. — C4 — 81
Turner, Me., U.S. — D2 — 96
Turner, Mi., U.S. — D7 — 99
Turner, Or., U.S. — C4 — 114
Turner, co., Ga., U.S. — E3 — 87
Turner, co., S.D., U.S. — D8 — 118
Turner Falls, Ma., U.S. — A2 — 98
Turner Valley, Alta. — D3 — 68
Turney, Mo., U.S. — B3 — 102
Turnhout, Bel. — B6 — 16
Turnor Lake, l., Sask. — m7 — 75
Turnov, Czech. — C3 — 26
Turnu-Măgurele, Rom. — D7 — 24
Turochak, Sov. Un. — E26 — 8
Turon, Ks., U.S. — E5 — 93
Turpan, China — C2 — 31
Turpan Pendi, China — C3 — 31
Turpin, Ok., U.S. — e10 — 113
Turquino, Pico, mtn., Cuba — E5 — 64
Turrell, Ar., U.S. — B5 — 81
Turret Peak, mtn., Az., U.S. — C4 — 80
Turriff, Scot., U.K. — D6 — 13
Turshīz see Kāshmar, Iran — C6 — 38
Turtkul, Sov. Un. — E9 — 29
Turtle, stm., Wi., U.S. — A3 — 126
Turtle, stm., Ont. — D5 — 73
Turtle Creek, N.B. — D5 — 71
Turtle Creek, Pa., U.S. — k14 — 115
Turtle Flambeau Flowage, res., Wi., U.S. — B3 — 126
Turtleford, Sask. — D1 — 75
Turtle Lake, N.D., U.S. — B5 — 111
Turtle Lake, Wi., U.S. — C1 — 126
Turtle Lake, l., Sask. — D1 — 75
Turtle Mountain Indian Reservation, N.D., U.S. — A6 — 111
Turtle Mountains, hills, N.A. — A5 — 111
Turtle River, Mn., U.S. — C3 — 100
Turton, S.D., U.S. — B7 — 118
Turukhansk, Sov. Un. — C11 — 29
Turuya, stm., Sov. Un. — F5 — 27
Tuscaloosa, Al., U.S. — B2 — 78
Tuscaloosa, co., Al., U.S. — B2 — 78
Tuscany (Toscana), prov., Italy — C3 — 23
Tuscarawas, co., Oh., U.S. — B4 — 112
Tuscarawas, stm., Oh., U.S. — B4 — 112
Tuscarora, Nv., U.S. — B5 — 105
Tuscarora Indian Reservation, N.Y., U.S. — B2 — 109
Tuscarora Mountain, mtn., Pa., U.S. — F6 — 115
Tuscarora Mountains, mts., Nv., U.S. — B5 — 105
Tuscola, Il., U.S. — D5 — 90
Tuscola, Tx., U.S. — C3 — 120
Tuscola, co., Mi., U.S. — E7 — 99
Tusculum, hist., Italy — h9 — 23
Tuscumbia, Al., U.S. — A2 — 78
Tuscumbia, Mo., U.S. — C5 — 102
Tushka, Ok., U.S. — C6 — 113
Tuskahoma, Ok., U.S. — C6 — 113
Tuskegee, Al., U.S. — C4 — 78
Tusket, N.S. — F4 — 71
Tusket, stm., N.S. — E4 — 71
Tustin, Ca., U.S. — *n13 — 82
Tustin, Mi., U.S. — D5 — 99
Tustumena Lake, l., Ak., U.S. — g16 — 79
Tutayev, Sov. Un. — C12 — 27
Tuthill, S.D., U.S. — D4 — 118
Tuticorin, India — G6 — 36
Tutrakan, Bul. — E8 — 24
Tutshi, S.D., U.S. — C1 — 118
Tuttle, Ok., U.S. — B4 — 113
Tuttle Creek Dam, Ks., U.S. — C7 — 93
Tuttle Creek Lake, res., Ks., U.S. — C7 — 93
Tuttlingen, W. Ger. — E4 — 18
Tutubu, Tan. — C5 — 48
Tutuila, i., Am. Sam. — G13 — 52
Tutupaca, Volcán, vol., Peru — A3 — 58
Tututalak Mountain, mtn., Ak., U.S. — B7 — 79
Tutwiler, Ms., U.S. — A3 — 101
Tuvalu, ctry., Oc. — G10 — 6
Tuvuca, i., Fiji — H16 — 52
Tuwayq, Jabal, mts., Sau. Ar. — C4 — 38

Tuxedo, N.C., U.S. — f10 — 110
Tuxedo Park, De., U.S. — i7 — 85
Tuxford, Sask. — G3 — 75
Tuxpan, Mex. — n12 — 63
Tuxpan, Mex. — B6 — 63
Tuxpan, Mex. — C3 — 63
Tuxpan, stm., Mex. — m15 — 63
Tuxpan de Rodríguez Cano, Mex. — C5 — 63
Tuxtepec, Mex. — m15 — 63
Tuxtla Gutiérrez, Mex. — D6 — 63
Túy, Spain — A1 — 22
Tuyen Quang, Viet. — B6 — 35
Tuy Hoa, Viet. — F8 — 35
Tuymazy, Sov. Un. — C4 — 35
Tüysarkän, Iran — D4 — 39
Tuz, Lake, l., Tur. — C9 — 40
Tuzigoot National Monument, Az., U.S. — C4 — 80
Tūz Khurmātū, Iraq — E15 — 40
Tuzla, Yugo. — C4 — 24
Tweed, Ont. — C7 — 73
Tweed, stm., U.K. — C5 — 10
Tweedsmuir Provincial Park, B.C. — C4 — 69
Tweedy Mountain, mtn., Mt., U.S. — E4 — 103
Twelve Mile, In., U.S. — C5 — 91
Twelve Mile Lake, l., Sask. — H2 — 75
Twelvepole Creek, stm., W.V., U.S. — C2 — 125
Twelvepole Creek, East Fork, stm., W.V., U.S. — D2 — 125
Twelvepole Creek, West Fork, stm., W.V., U.S. — D2 — 125
Twentymile Creek, stm., W.V., U.S. — C3 — 125
Twentynine Palms, Ca., U.S. — E5 — 82
Twentynine Palms Base, Ca., U.S. — *E5 — 82
Twentynine Palms Marine Corps Base, mil., Ca., U.S. — E5 — 82
Twig, Mn., U.S. — D6 — 100
Twiggs, co., Ga., U.S. — D3 — 87
Twillingate, Newf. — D4 — 72
Twin Bridges, Mt., U.S. — E4 — 103
Twin Brooks, S.D., U.S. — B9 — 118
Twin Buttes, stm., Or., U.S. — C3 — 114
Twin Buttes Reservoir, res., Tx., U.S. — D2 — 120
Twin City, Ga., U.S. — D4 — 87
Twin Creek, stm., Oh., U.S. — C1 — 112
Twin Falls, Id., U.S. — G4 — 89
Twin Falls, co., Id., U.S. — G4 — 89
Twining, Mi., U.S. — D7 — 99
Twin Knolls, Az., U.S. — m9 — 80
Twin Lakes, Co., U.S. — B4 — 83
Twin Lakes, Ga., U.S. — F3 — 87
Twin Lakes, In., U.S. — B5 — 91
Twin Lakes, Wi., U.S. — F5 — 126
Twin Lakes, l., Ct., U.S. — A2 — 84
Twin Lakes, l., Ia., U.S. — B3 — 92
Twin Lakes Mountain, mtn., Ca., U.S. — B6 — 109
Twin Mountain, N.H., U.S. — B3 — 106
Twin Mountains, mts., Wy., U.S. — E7 — 127
Twin Peaks, mts., Id., U.S. — E4 — 89
Twin Rivers, N.J., U.S. — C4 — 107
Twin Rocks, Pa., U.S. — F4 — 115
Twinsburg, Oh., U.S. — A4 — 112
Twinton, Tn., U.S. — C8 — 119
Twin Valley, Mn., U.S. — C2 — 100
Twisp, Wa., U.S. — A5 — 124
Twist, Ar., U.S. — B5 — 81
Two Butte Creek, stm., Co., U.S. — D8 — 83
Two Buttes, Co., U.S. — D8 — 83
Two Creeks, Man. — D1 — 70
Twodot, Mt., U.S. — D6 — 103
Twoforks, stm., Sask. — C2 — 75
Two Harbors, Mn., U.S. — C7 — 100
Two Hills, Alta. — C5 — 68
Two Mile Beach, N.J., U.S. — F3 — 107
Two Prairie, Bayou, stm., Ar., U.S. — h11 — 81
Two Rivers, Wi., U.S. — D6 — 126
Two Rivers, North Branch, stm., Mn., U.S. — B2 — 100
Two Rivers, South Branch, stm., Mn., U.S. — B2 — 100
Tyachev, Sov. Un. — D7 — 26
Tyaskin, Md., U.S. — D6 — 97
Tybee Island, Ga., U.S. — g9 — 26
Tychy, Pol. — C4 — 123
Tye River, Va., U.S. — C4 — 123
Tygart Lake, res., W.V., U.S. — B5 — 125
Tygart River, Falls of the, wtfl., W.V., U.S. — k10 — 125
Tygarts Creek, stm., Ky., U.S. — B7 — 94
Tygart Valley, stm., W.V., U.S. — B4 — 125
Tyger, stm., S.C., U.S. — B3 — 117
Tygh Valley, Or., U.S. — B5 — 114
Tyler, Mn., U.S. — F2 — 100
Tyler, Pa., U.S. — C5 — 115
Tyler, Tx., U.S. — C5 — 120
Tyler, co., Tx., U.S. — D5 — 120
Tyler, co., W.V., U.S. — B4 — 125
Tyler, Lake, res., Tx., U.S. — C5 — 120
Tyler Branch, stm., Vt., U.S. — B3 — 122
Tyler Heights, W.V., U.S. — C3 — 125
Tylersburg, Pa., U.S. — E7 — 115
Tylersville, Pa., U.S. — E7 — 115
Tylerton, Md., U.S. — E5 — 97
Tylertown, Ms., U.S. — D3 — 101
Tym, stm., Sov. Un. — C25 — 8
Tymochtee Creek, stm., Oh., U.S. — B2 — 112
Tynagh, Ire. — D3 — 11
Tyndall, Man. — D3 — 70
Tyndall, S.D., U.S. — D8 — 118
Tyndall Air Force Base, mil., Fl., U.S. — u16 — 86
Tyndinskiy, Sov. Un. — D15 — 29
Tyndrum, Scot., U.K. — D4 — 13
Tyne, stm., Eng., U.K. — C5 — 10
Tyne, stm., Scot., U.K. — E6 — 13
Tyne and Wear, co., Eng., U.K. — E7 — 13
Týnec, Czech. — C6 — 18
Tynemouth, Eng., U.K. — o18 — 13
Tyner, In., U.S. — B5 — 91
Tyner, N.C., U.S. — A6 — 110
Tyne Valley, P.E.I. — C6 — 71
Tyngsboro, Ma., U.S. — A5 — 98
Týn nad Vltavou, Czech. — F14 — 19
Tynset, Nor. — F4 — 14
Tyonek, Ak., U.S. — g16 — 79
Tyre (Şūr), Leb. — B3 — 38
Tyringham, Ma., U.S. — B1 — 98
Tyrma, Sov. Un. — A6 — 33
Tyro, Ks., U.S. — E8 — 93

Tyrone, Ky., U.S. — B5 94
Tyrone, N.M., U.S. — E1 108
Tyrone, Ok., U.S. — e9 113
Tyrone, Pa., U.S. — E5 115
Tyronza, Ar., U.S. — B5 81
Tyrrell, co., N.C., U.S. — B6 110
Tyrrell, Lake, l., Austl. — G4 51
Tyrrhenian Sea, Eur. — D3 23
Tysons Corner, Va., U.S. — *B5 123
Ty Ty, Ga., U.S. — E3 87
Ty Ty Creek, stm., Ga., U.S. — E3 87
Tyub-Karagan Peninsula, pen., Sov. Un. — E4 28
Tyukalinsk, Sov. Un. — B8 28
Tyuleniy Island, i., Sov. Un. — B12 33
Tyumen, Sov. Un. — D9 29
Tyuratam, Sov. Un. — D6 28
Tyvan, Sask. — G4 75
Tywyn, Wales, U.K. — B3 12
Tzaneen, S. Afr. — B5 49

U

Uatumã, stm., Braz. — C3 59
Uaupés (Vaupés), stm., S.A. — C4 60
Ubá, Braz. — C4 56
Ubaíra, Braz. — D3 57
Ubaitaba, Braz. — D3 57
Ubangi (Oubangui), stm., Afr. — A2 48
Ubaye, stm., Fr. — E2 20
Ubayyid, Wādī al, val., Asia — B4 38
Ube, Japan — E11 31
Úbeda, Spain — C4 22
Uberaba, Braz. — B3 56
Uberlândia, Braz. — B3 56
Überlingen, W. Ger. — E4 18
Ubiaja, Nig. — E6 45
Ubly, Mi., U.S. — E8 99
Ubombo, S. Afr. — C5 49
Ubon Ratchathani, Thai. — B2 34
Uborka, Sov. Un. — D7 33
Ubort, stm., Sov. Un. — F6 27
Ubrique, Spain — D3 22
Ubundu (Ponthierville), Zaire — B4 48
Ucayali, dept., Peru — *C3 58
Ucayali, stm., Peru — C3 58
Uccle, Bel. — B6 16
Ucharal, Sov. Un. — D10 28
Uchiura Bay, b., Japan — E10 33
Uchiza, Peru — C2 58
Uchoa, Braz. — C3 56
Uckange, Fr. — E6 17
Ucluelet, B.C. — E5 69
Ucon, Id., U.S. — F7 89
Udagamandalam, India — F6 36
Udaipur, India — D5 36
Udall, Ks., U.S. — E6 93
Udall, Mo., U.S. — E5 102
Udaquiola, Arg. — B5 54
Uddevalla, Swe. — G7 14
Uden, Neth. — C5 17
Udgīr, India — H6 37
Udhampur, India — B6 36
Udine, Italy — A4 23
Udmurt, Aut. — B6 29
Udon Thani, Thai. — B2 34
Udot, i., Micron. — Q18 52
Udu Point, c., Fiji — H16 52
Uecker, stm., E. Ger. — B6 18
Ueckermünde, E. Ger. — B6 18
Ueda, Japan — H9 33
Uehling, Ne., U.S. — C9 104
Uele, stm., Zaire — A3 48
Uelen, Sov. Un. — C21 29
Uelkal, Sov. Un. — C21 29
Uelsen, W. Ger. — B6 17
Uelzen, W. Ger. — B5 18
Ueno, Japan — o15 33
Uere, stm., Zaire — A4 48
Uesslingen, Switz. — A6 21
Uetendorf, Switz. — C4 21
Uetersen, W. Ger. — E3 15
Ufa, Sov. Un. — D8 29
Ufa, stm., Sov. Un. — B5 28
Uffenheim, W. Ger. — D5 19
Ugab, stm., Nmb. — B2 49
Ugalla, stm., Tan. — C5 48
Uganda, ctry., Afr. — A5 48
Ugashik, Ak., U.S. — D8 79
Ugashik Lakes, l., Ak., U.S. — D8 79
Ugep, Nig. — E6 45
Ugine, Fr. — D2 20
Uglegorsk, Sov. Un. — B13 31
Uglich, Sov. Un. — C12 27
Ugra, stm., Sov. Un. — D10 27
Ugurchin, Bul. — D7 26
Uh, stm., Eur. — D7 26
Uherské Hradiště, Czech. — D4 26
Úhlava, stm., Czech. — D8 19
Uhlingen, W. Ger. — A5 21
Uhlman Lake, l., Man. — A2 70
Uhrichsville, Oh., U.S. — B4 112
Uhříněves, Czech. — n18 26
Uig, Scot., U.K. — B2 13
Uig, Scot., U.K. — C2 13
Uíge, Ang. — C2 48
Uíge, dept., Ang. — C2 48
Uijŏngbu, S. Kor. — H3 33
Uiju, N. Kor. — C9 31
Uil, Sov. Un. — D4 28
Uil, stm., Sov. Un. — D4 28
Uinkaret Plateau, plat., Az., U.S. — A2 80
Uinta, co., Wy., U.S. — E2 127
Uinta, stm., Ut., U.S. — C5 121
Uintah, Ut., U.S. — *B4 121
Uintah, co., Ut., U.S. — D6 121
Uintah and Ouray Indian Reservation, Ut., U.S. — C5 121
Uinta Mountains, mts., Ut., U.S. — C5 121
Uitenhage, S. Afr. — D4 49
Uithuizen, Neth. — A6 17
Uivak, Cape, c., Newf. — f9 72
Uji Islands, is., Japan — K4 33
Ujiji, Tan. — B4 48
Uji-yamada see Ise, Japan — I8 33
Ujjain, India — D6 36
Ujungpandang (Makasar), Indon. — G5 34
Uka, Japan — N6 52
Uka, Sov. Un. — D19 29
Ukerewe, i., Tan. — B5 48
Ukhta, Sov. Un. — C8 29
Ukiah, Ca., U.S. — C2 82
Ukiah, Or., U.S. — B8 114
Ukmergė, Sov. Un. — D5 27
Ukraine, state, Sov. Un. — E5 29
Uku, Ang. — D1 48
Ulaangom, Mong. — B3 31
Ulak Island, i., Ak., U.S. — E4 79
Ulan Bator (Ulaanbaatar), Mong. — B6 31
Ulan-Ude, Sov. Un. — D13 29
Ulba, Sov. Un. — E25 8

Ulchin, S. Kor. — H4 33
Ulcinj, Yugo. — E4 24
Uldza, stm., Asia — B7 31
Ulen, In., U.S. — D5 91
Ulen, Mn., U.S. — C2 100
Ulhāsnagar, India — *E5 36
Uliastay, Mong. — B4 31
Ulíndi, stm., Zaire — B4 48
Ulla, Sov. Un. — D7 27
Ulla, stm., Spain — A1 22
Ulladulla, Austl. — G8 51
Ullapool, Scot., U.K. — B4 10
Ullared, Swe. — A6 15
Ullin, Il., U.S. — F4 90
Ullswater, l., Eng., U.K. — F6 13
Ullŭng Island, i., S. Kor. — H5 33
Ulm, W. Ger. — D4 18
Ulm, Ar., U.S. — C4 81
Ulm, Mt., U.S. — C5 103
Ulman, Mo., U.S. — C5 102
Ulongué, Moz. — D5 48
Ulricehamn, Swe. — I5 14
Ulsan, S. Kor. — I4 33
Ulster, Pa., U.S. — C9 115
Ulster, co., N.Y., U.S. — D6 109
Ulster, hist. reg., Eur. — C4 11
Ulúa, stm., Hond. — C3 62
Ulubat Lake, l., Tur. — B7 25
Uluborlu, Tur. — C8 40
Uludağ, mtn., Tur. — B7 40
Ulukışla, Tur. — D10 40
Ulva, i., Scot., U.K. — D2 13
Ulverston, Eng., U.K. — C5 10
Ulverstone, Austl. — o15 50
Ulyanovka, Sov. Un. — s31 14
Ulyanovsk, Sov. Un. — D7 29
Ulysses, Ks., U.S. — E2 93
Ulysses, Ne., U.S. — C8 104
Ulysses, Pa., U.S. — C6 115
Ulzburg, W. Ger. — E3 15
Uman, Sov. Un. — G8 27
Uman, i., Micron. — Q18 52
Umarkot, Pak. — C4 36
Umatac, Guam — M9 52
Umatac Bay, b., Guam — M9 52
Umatilla, Fl., U.S. — D5 86
Umatilla, co., Or., U.S. — B7 114
Umatilla, Or., U.S. — B8 114
Umatilla, stm., Or., U.S. — B7 114
Umatilla Indian Reservation, Or., U.S. — B8 114
Umba, Sov. Un. — D16 14
Umbagog Lake, l., U.S. — A4 106
Umboi, i., Pap. N. Gui. — k12 50
Umbrail Pass, Eur. — C9 21
Umbria, prov., Italy — C4 23
Umbuzeiro, Braz. — C3 57
Umcolcus Lake, l., Me., U.S. — B4 96
Umeå, Swe. — F9 14
Umeälven, stm., Swe. — E8 14
Umhausen, Aus. — B6 20
Umlazi, S. Afr. — *C5 49
Umm el Fahm, Isr. — B7 41
Umm Kaddādah, Sud. — C2 47
Umm Lajj, Sau. Ar. — C3 38
Umm Ruwābah, Sud. — C2 47
Umnak Island, i., Ak., U.S. — E6 79
Umniati, stm., Zimb. — A4 49
Umpire, Ar., U.S. — C1 81
Umpqua, Or., U.S. — D3 114
Umpqua, stm., Or., U.S. — D3 114
'Umrān, Yemen — B5 47
Umsaskis Lake, l., Me., U.S. — B3 96
Umtanum Ridge, mtn., Wa., U.S. — C5 124
Umtata, Transkei — D4 49
Umuahia, Nig. — E6 45
Umzinto, S. Afr. — D5 49
Una, stm., Braz. — k6 57
Una, stm., Yugo. — C2 24
Unadilla, Ga., U.S. — D3 87
Unadilla, Ne., U.S. — h12 104
Unadilla, N.Y., U.S. — C5 109
Unadilla, stm., N.Y., U.S. — C5 109
Unaí, Braz. — B3 56
Unaka, N.C., U.S. — f8 110
Unaka Mountains, mts., U.S. — C11 119
Unalakleet, Ak., U.S. — C7 79
Unalaska Island, i., Ak., U.S. — E6 79
'Unayzah, Sau. Ar. — C4 38
Uncasville, Ct., U.S. — D7 84
Uncia, Bol. — C2 55
Uncompahgre, stm., Co., U.S. — C3 83
Uncompahgre Butte, mtn., Co., U.S. — C2 83
Uncompahgre Mountains, mts., Co., U.S. — C3 83
Uncompahgre Peak, mtn., Co., U.S. — C3 83
Uncompahgre Plateau, plat., Co., U.S. — C2 83
Underhill, Vt., U.S. — B3 122
Underhill Center, Vt., U.S. — B3 122
Underwood, Al., U.S. — B3 78
Underwood, In., U.S. — G6 91
Underwood, Ia., U.S. — C2 92
Underwood, Mn., U.S. — D3 100
Underwood, N.D., U.S. — B4 111
Underwood, Wa., U.S. — D4 124
Unecha, Sov. Un. — E9 27
Uneiuxi, stm., Braz. — D4 60
Unezhma, Sov. Un. — F17 14
Ungarie, Austl. — F4 51
Ungava, Péninsule d', pen., Que. — g12 74
Ungava Bay, b., Can. — E19 66
Unggi, N. Kor. — C11 31
Unhošt', Czech. — n17 26
União, Braz. — B2 57
União da Victória, Braz. — D2 56
União dos Palmares, Braz. — C3 57
Unicoi, Tn., U.S. — C11 119
Unicoi, co., Tn., U.S. — C11 119
Unicoi Mountains, mts., U.S. — D9 119
Unije, i., Yugo. — C2 24
Unimak Island, i., Ak., U.S. — D7 79
Unimak Pass, strt., Ak., U.S. — E6 79
Unini, stm., Braz. — C2 59
Unión, Arg. — B3 54
Union, Ar., U.S. — A4 81
Union, Il., U.S. — A5 90
Union, In., U.S. — H3 91
Union, Ia., U.S. — B4 92
Union, Ky., U.S. — k13 94
Union, La., U.S. — h10 95
Union, Me., U.S. — D3 96
Union, Ms., U.S. — C4 101
Union, Mo., U.S. — C6 102
Union, N.H., U.S. — D4 106
Union, N.J., U.S. — *B4 107

Union, N.C., U.S. — A5 110
Union, N.D., U.S. — A8 111
Union, Oh., U.S. — *C1 112
Union, Or., U.S. — B9 114
Union, S.C., U.S. — B4 117
Union, Ut., U.S. — *C4 121
Union, Wa., U.S. — B2 124
Union, W.V., U.S. — D4 125
Union, co., Ar., U.S. — D3 81
Union, co., Fl., U.S. — B4 86
Union, co., Ga., U.S. — B2 87
Union, co., Il., U.S. — F4 90
Union, co., In., U.S. — E8 91
Union, co., Ia., U.S. — C3 92
Union, co., Ky., U.S. — C2 94
Union, co., La., U.S. — B3 95
Union, co., Ms., U.S. — A4 101
Union, co., N.J., U.S. — B4 107
Union, co., N.M., U.S. — A6 108
Union, co., N.C., U.S. — B2 110
Union, co., Oh., U.S. — B2 112
Union, co., Or., U.S. — B8 114
Union, co., Pa., U.S. — E7 115
Union, co., S.C., U.S. — B4 117
Union, co., S.D., U.S. — E9 118
Union, co., Tn., U.S. — C10 119
Union Bay, B.C. — E5 69
Union Beach, N.J., U.S. — C4 107
Union Bridge, Md., U.S. — A3 97
Union Center, S.D., U.S. — C3 118
Union Center, Wi., U.S. — E3 126
Union Church, Ms., U.S. — D3 101
Union City, Ca., U.S. — h8 82
Union City, Ga., U.S. — C2 87
Union City, In., U.S. — D8 91
Union City, Mi., U.S. — F5 99
Union City, N.J., U.S. — h8 107
Union City, Oh., U.S. — B1 112
Union City, Ok., U.S. — B4 113
Union City, Pa., U.S. — C2 115
Union City, Tn., U.S. — A2 119
Union Creek, Or., U.S. — E4 114
Union Flat Creek, stm., Wa., U.S. — C8 124
Union Furnace, Oh., U.S. — C3 112
Union Gap, Wa., U.S. — C5 124
Union Grove, Wi., U.S. — F5 126
Union Hall, Va., U.S. — C3 123
Union Island, i., St. Vin. — V26 65
Union Lake, l., N.J., U.S. — E2 107
Union Lake, Mi., U.S. — *o15 99
Union Mill, Hi., U.S. — C6 88
Union Mills, In., U.S. — B4 91
Union Mills, Md., U.S. — A3 97
Union of Soviet Socialist Republics see Soviet Union, ctry., Asia — D11 29
Union Park, Fl., U.S. — *D5 86
Union Point, Ga., U.S. — C3 87
Union Springs, Al., U.S. — C4 78
Union Springs, N.Y., U.S. — C4 109
Union Star, Mo., U.S. — B3 102
Uniontown, Al., U.S. — C2 78
Uniontown, Ks., U.S. — E9 93
Uniontown, Ky., U.S. — C2 94
Uniontown, Md., U.S. — A3 97
Uniontown, Oh., U.S. — B4 112
Uniontown, Pa., U.S. — G2 115
Uniontown, Wa., U.S. — C8 124
Union Village, R.I., U.S. — B3 116
Union Village, Vt., U.S. — D4 122
Union Village Reservoir, res., Vt., U.S. — D4 122
Unionville, Ont. — k15 73
Unionville, Ct., U.S. — B4 84
Unionville, Il., U.S. — F5 90
Unionville, In., U.S. — F5 91
Unionville, Ia., U.S. — D5 92
Unionville, Me., U.S. — D5 96
Unionville, Mi., U.S. — E7 99
Unionville, Mo., U.S. — A4 102
Unionville, Nv., U.S. — C3 105
Unionville, N.C., U.S. — B2 110
Unionville, Oh., U.S. — A4 112
Unionville, Tn., U.S. — B5 119
Unionville, Va., U.S. — B5 123
Unionville Center, Oh., U.S. — B2 112
Unisan, Phil. — p13 34
United, Pa., U.S. — F3 115
United Arab Emirates, ctry., Asia — C5 38
United Kingdom, ctry., Eur. — C5 10
United Nations Headquarters, N.Y., U.S. — h12 109
United Pueblos Indian Reservations, N.M., U.S. — A3 108
United States, ctry., N.A. — C8 76
United States Air Force Academy, mil., Co., U.S. — B6 83
United States Military Academy, mil., N.Y., U.S. — C6 109
United States Naval Academy, mil., Md., U.S. — C4 97
Unity, Sask. — E1 75
Unity, Il., U.S. — F4 90
Unity, Me., U.S. — D3 96
Unity, N.H., U.S. — D2 106
Unity, Or., U.S. — C8 114
Unity Pond, l., Me., U.S. — D3 96
Unity Reservoir, res., Or., U.S. — C8 114
Unityville, S.D., U.S. — D8 118
Universal, In., U.S. — E3 91
Universal City, Tx., U.S. — *E3 120
Universales, Montes, mts., Spain — B5 22
University, Fl., U.S. — *D4 86
University City, Mo., U.S. — C7 102
University Gardens, N.Y., U.S. — *n15 109
University Heights, Ia., U.S. — C6 92
University Heights, Oh., U.S. — h9 112
University Park, Ia., U.S. — C5 92
University Park, N.M., U.S. — E3 108
University Park, Tx., U.S. — n10 120
University Place, Wa., U.S. — f10 124
Unlingen, W. Ger. — A5 20
Unna, W. Ger. — B2 19
Unnen, I., Swe. — B7 15
Unst, i., Scot., U.K. — g10 10
Unterwasser, Switz. — B7 21
Unuk, stm., N.A. — E4 69
Unuwhao, hill, N.Z. — K14 51
Unwin, Sask. — E1 75
Ünye, Tur. — B11 40
Unzha, stm., Sov. Un. — C4 29
Uozu, Japan — H8 33

Upata, Ven. — B5 60
Upatoi Creek, stm., Ga., U.S. — D2 87
Upemba, Lac, l., Zaire — C4 48
Upernavik, Grnld. — B15 61
Upia, stm., Col. — C3 60
Upington, S. Afr. — C3 49
Upland, Ca., U.S. — E5 82
Upland, In., U.S. — D7 91
Upland, Ne., U.S. — D7 104
Upolu, W. Sam. — G11 52
Upolu Point, c., Hi., U.S. — C6 88
Upper Ammonoosuc, stm., N.H., U.S. — A4 106
Upper Arlington, Oh., U.S. — B2 112
Upper Arrow Lake, res., B.C. — D9 69
Upper Black Eddy, Pa., U.S. — E11 115
Upper Blackville, N.B. — C4 71
Upper Chichester Township, Pa., U.S. — *G11 115
Upperco, Md., U.S. — A4 97
Upper Darby, Pa., U.S. — p20 115
Upper Dublin Township, Pa., U.S. — *F11 115
Upper Fairmount, Md., U.S. — D6 97
Upper Fraser, B.C. — B7 69
Upper Frenchville, Me., U.S. — A4 96
Upper Gagetown, N.B. — D3 71
Upper Ganges Canal, India — C6 37
Upper Gloucester, Me., U.S. — E2 96
Upper Granteville, Vt., U.S. — C4 122
Upper Greenwood Lake, N.J., U.S. — A4 107
Upper Humber, stm., Newf. — D3 72
Upper Indian Pond, l., Newf. — D3 72
Upper Iowa, stm., Ia., U.S. — A5 92
Upper Island Cove, Newf. — E5 72
Upper Jay, N.Y., U.S. — f11 109
Upper Kapuas Mountains, mts., Asia — E4 34
Upper Kent, N.B. — C2 71
Upper Klamath Lake, l., Or., U.S. — E4 114
Upper Manitou Lake, l., Ont. — E5 70
Upper Marlboro, Md., U.S. — C4 97
Upper Merion Township, Pa., U.S. — *F11 115
Upper Moreland Township, Pa., U.S. — *F11 115
Upper Musquodoboit, N.S. — D7 71
Upper New York Bay, b., U.S. — k8 107
Upper Providence Township, Pa., U.S. — *G11 115
Upper Red Lake, l., Mn., U.S. — B4 100
Upper Saddle River, N.J., U.S. — A4 107
Upper Saint Clair, Pa., U.S. — *F1 115
Upper Sandusky, Oh., U.S. — B2 112
Upper Sheila, N.B. — B5 71
Upper Silesia, hist. reg., Pol. — g9 26
Upper Southampton Township, Pa., U.S. — *F11 115
Upper Strasburg, Pa., U.S. — F6 115
Upper Tract, W.V., U.S. — C5 125
Upperville, Va., U.S. — B5 123
Upper Volta see Burkina Faso, ctry., Afr. — D4 45
Upper Wilson Pond, l., Me., U.S. — C3 96
Upper Woods Harbour, N.S. — F4 71
Uppsala, Swe. — H7 14
Upright, Cape, c., Ak., U.S. — C5 79
Upsala, Mn., U.S. — E4 100
Upsalquitch, N.B. — B3 71
Upsalquitch, stm., N.B. — B3 71
Upshur, co., Tx., U.S. — C5 120
Upshur, co., W.V., U.S. — C4 125
Upson, Wi., U.S. — B3 126
Upson, co., Ga., U.S. — D2 87
Upton, Que. — D5 74
Upton, Ky., U.S. — C4 94
Upton, Me., U.S. — D1 96
Upton, Ma., U.S. — B4 98
Upton, co., Tx., U.S. — D2 120
Upton, Wy., U.S. — B8 127
Uraba, Golfo de, b., Col. — B2 60
Uracoa, Ven. — B5 60
Urad Qianqi, China — D9 32
Ural, stm., Sov. Un. — E8 29
Ural Mountains, mts., Sov. Un. — D8 29
Uralsk, Sov. Un. — D5 29
Urandi, Braz. — A4 56
Urania, La., U.S. — C3 95
Uranium City, Sask. — m7 75
Uraricoera, Braz. — B2 59
Uraricoera, stm., Braz. — B2 59
Urasoe, Japan — O5 52
Ura-Tyube, Sov. Un. — H22 8
Uravan, Co., U.S. — C2 83
Urawa, Japan — I9 33
Urbana, Ar., U.S. — D3 81
Urbana, Il., U.S. — C5 90
Urbana, In., U.S. — C6 91
Urbana, Md., U.S. — B3 97
Urbana, Mo., U.S. — D4 102
Urbana, Oh., U.S. — B2 112
Urbancrest, Oh., U.S. — m10 112
Urbandale, Ia., U.S. — C4 92
Urbank, Mn., U.S. — D3 100
Urbanna, Va., U.S. — C6 123
Urbino, Italy — C4 23
Urcos, Peru — C3 58
Urdaneta, Phil. — o13 34
Urdzhar, Sov. Un. — D10 28
Ure, stm., Eng., U.K. — F7 13
Ures, Mex. — B3 63
Urfa, Tur. — D12 40
Urga, Sov. Un. — E8 29
Urgench, Sov. Un. — E6 29
Uri, state, Switz. — C4 21
Uriah, Al., U.S. — D2 78
Uribia, Col. — A3 60
Urich, Mo., U.S. — C4 102
Urique, Mex. — B3 63
Uritsk (part of Leningrad), Sov. Un. — s31 14
Urk, Neth. — B5 17
Urla, Tur. — C6 25
Uroyán, Montañas de, mts., P.R. — B2 65
Urr, stm., Scot., U.K. — F5 13
Urrao, Col. — B2 60
Ursa, Il., U.S. — C2 90
Ursina, Pa., U.S. — G3 115
Ursus (part of Warsaw), Pol. — m13 26
Uruaçu, Braz. — A3 56
Uruana, Braz. — B3 56
Uruapan [del Progreso], Mex. — D4 63
Urubamba, Peru — C3 58

Urubamba, stm., Peru — D3 58
Urubu, stm., Braz. — C3 59
Urucará, Braz. — C3 59
Uruçuí, Braz. — C2 57
Urucuia, stm., Braz. — B3 56
Urucurituba, Braz. — C3 59
Uruguaiana, Braz. — D1 56
Uruguay, ctry., S.A. — E1 56
Uruguay (Uruguai), stm., S.A. — E1 56
Urumchi see Ürümqi, China — C2 31
Ürümqi (Urumchi), China — C2 31
Uruno Point, c., Guam — L10 52
Urusha, Sov. Un. — D15 29
Urutaí, Braz. — B3 56
Uryu, stm., Japan — D11 33
Uryupinsk, Sov. Un. — F14 27
Urziceni, Rom. — C8 24
Uşak, Tur. — C7 40
Usakos, Nmb. — B2 49
Usedom, E. Ger. — B7 15
Usedom, i., Eur. — B4 18
Ushaki, Sov. Un. — s32 14
Ushibuka, Japan — J4 33
Ushtobe, Sov. Un. — D9 28
Ushuaia, Arg. — h12 54
Usingen, W. Ger. — B3 19
Uslar, W. Ger. — B4 19
Usman, Sov. Un. — E12 27
Usolye-Sibirskoye, Sov. Un. — D13 29
Uspenskiy, Sov. Un. — D8 28
Usquepaug, R.I., U.S. — F3 116
Ussel, Fr. — E5 16
Ussuri (Wusuli), stm., Asia — B11 31
Ussuriysk, Sov. Un. — E16 29
Ust-Bolsheretsk, Sov. Un. — D18 29
Uster, Switz. — B4 20
Ustica, i., Italy — E4 23
Ústí nad Labem, Czech. — C3 26
Ustinov see Izhevsk, Sov. Un. — D8 29
Ust-Ishim, Sov. Un. — B8 28
Ust-Kamchatsk, Sov. Un. — D19 29
Ust-Kamenogorsk, Sov. Un. — E11 29
Ust-Kut, Sov. Un. — D13 29
Ust-Maya, Sov. Un. — C16 29
Ust-Olenek, Sov. Un. — B14 29
Ust-Shchugor, Sov. Un. — C9 28
Ust-Srednekan, Sov. Un. — C18 29
Ust-Tsilma, Sov. Un. — C8 29
Ust-Tym, Sov. Un. — B9 28
Ust-Urt Plateau, plat., Sov. Un. — E8 29
Ust-Usa, Sov. Un. — C8 29
Ustyuzhna, Sov. Un. — B11 27
Usu, China — C1 31
Usu, China — D9 114
Usulután, El Sal. — E7 63
Usumacinta, stm., N.A. — D6 63
Utah, co., Ut., U.S. — C4 121
Utah, state, U.S. — D4 121
Utah Lake, l., Ut., U.S. — C4 121
Utajärvi, Fin. — E12 14
Ute, Ia., U.S. — B2 92
Ute Creek, stm., N.M., U.S. — A6 108
Ute Mountain Indian Reservation, U.S. — D2 83
Ute Park, N.M., U.S. — A4 108
Ute Reservoir, res., N.M., U.S. — B6 108
Utete, Tan. — C6 48
Uthai Thani, Thai. — B1 34
Utiariti, Braz. — B1 56
Utica, Il., U.S. — B5 90
Utica, In., U.S. — H6 91
Utica, Ky., U.S. — C2 94
Utica, Mi., U.S. — F7 99
Utica, Ms., U.S. — C3 101
Utica, Mo., U.S. — B4 102
Utica, N.Y., U.S. — B5 109
Utica, Oh., U.S. — B3 112
Utica, Pa., U.S. — D2 115
Utica, S.D., U.S. — E8 118
Utiel, Spain — C5 22
Utikuma Lake, l., Alta. — B3 68
Utö, i., Swe. — u36 14
Utopia, Tx., U.S. — E3 120
Utrata, stm., Pol. — m13 26
Utrecht, Neth. — C5 17
Utrecht, prov., Neth. — B5 17
Utrera, Spain — D3 22
Utsjoki, Fin. — B13 14
Utsunomiya, Japan — D12 31
Uttaradit, Thai. — B2 34
Uttar Pradesh, state, India — C8 37
Uttoxeter, Eng., U.K. — B6 12
Utuado, P.R. — B2 65
Utulei, Am. Sam. — F13 52
Uusikaupunki, Fin. — G9 14
Uva, stm., Col. — C3 60
Uvalda, Ga., U.S. — D4 87
Uvalde, Tx., U.S. — E3 120
Uvalde, co., Tx., U.S. — E3 120
Uvarovo, Sov. Un. — E14 27
Uverite Point, c., Fiji — H14 52
Uvinza, Tan. — C5 48
Uvira, Zaire — B4 48
Uvs Lake, l., Asia — A3 31
Uwajima, Japan — J6 33
'Uwaynāt, Jabal al, mtn., Afr. — E4 43
Uwharrie, stm., N.C., U.S. — B3 110
Uxbridge, Ont. — C5 73
Uxbridge (part of London), Eng., U.K. — k12 12
Uxbridge, Ma., U.S. — B4 98
Uxmal, hist., Mex. — C7 63
Uyar, Sov. Un. — D11 29
Uyo, Nig. — *E6 45
Uyuni, Bol. — C2 55
Uyuni, Salar de, pl., Bol. — D2 55
Uzbek S.S.R., state, Sov. Un. — E6 29
Uzès, Fr. — E6 16
Uzhgorod, Sov. Un. — G4 27
Uzlovaya, Sov. Un. — E11 27
Uzunköprü, Tur. — B6 40
Uzwil, Switz. — B7 21

V

Vaal, stm., S. Afr. — C4 49
Vaals, Neth. — D6 17
Vaasa, Fin. — F9 14
Vác, Hung. — B4 24
Vaca Key, i., Fl., U.S. — H5 86

Vacaria, Braz. — D2 56
Vacaville, Ca., U.S. — C3 82
Vacha, E. Ger. — C5 19
Vacherie, La., U.S. — h10 95
Vader, Wa., U.S. — C3 124
Vadito, N.M., U.S. — A4 108
Vadnais Heights, Mn., U.S. — *m12 100
Vado, N.M., U.S. — E3 108
Vadodara, India — D5 36
Vadsö, Nor. — B13 14
Vaduz, Liech. — B4 18
Vaggeryd, Swe. — A8 15
Vaggyay, Sov. Un. — B7 28
Vagnhärad, Swe. — u35 14
Vagos, Port. — B1 22
Váh, stm., Czech. — D4 26
Vahsel Bay, b., Ant. — B9 7
Vaiden, Ms., U.S. — B4 101
Vail, stm., Sov. Un. — B20 8
Vaigai, stm., India — G6 36
Vaihingen, W. Ger. — E3 19
Vail, Az., U.S. — E5 80
Vail, Co., U.S. — B4 83
Vail, Ia., U.S. — B2 92
Vail Homes, N.J., U.S. — *C4 107
Vailoa see Palauli, W. Sam. — F11 52
Vails, N.J., U.S. — h12 107
Vaitele Bay, b., W. Sam. — F12 52
Vakh, stm., Sov. Un. — C25 8
Vakhan, reg., Afg. — k17 39
Vakhrushev, Sov. Un. — B11 33
Valais, state, Switz. — C3 20
Valatie, N.Y., U.S. — C7 109
Val-Barrette, Que. — C2 74
Val-Bélair, Que. — n17 74
Valcartier-Village, Que. — C6 74
Valcheta, Arg. — C3 54
Valcourt, Que. — D5 74
Valdagno, Italy — D7 20
Valdai Hills, hills, Sov. Un. — C9 27
Val-David, Que. — C3 74
Valday, Sov. Un. — C9 27
Valdemarsvik, Swe. — H7 14
Valdemorillo, Spain — o16 22
Valdepeñas, Spain — C4 22
Valderaduey, stm., Spain — A3 22
Valders, Wi., U.S. — D6 126
Valdés, Península, pen., Arg. — C4 54
Valdese, N.C., U.S. — B1 110
Valdez, Ak., U.S. — C10 79
Valdez, N.M., U.S. — A4 108
Valdilecha, Spain — p18 22
Valdivia, Chile — B2 54
Valdivia, Col. — B2 60
Valdobbiadene, Italy — D7 20
Val-d'Or, Que. — k11 74
Valdosta, Ga., U.S. — F3 87
Vale, Nor. — p28 14
Vale, Or., U.S. — D9 114
Vale, S.D., U.S. — C2 118
Vale, Tn., U.S. — A3 119
Valeene, In., U.S. — H5 91
Valemount, B.C. — C8 69
Valença, Braz. — C4 56
Valença, Port. — A1 22
Valença do Piauí, Braz. — E6 56
Valence, Fr. — E6 16
Valencia, Spain — C5 22
Valencia, Az., U.S. — m7 80
Valencia, Ca., U.S. — *E4 82
Valencia, co., N.M., U.S. — C3 108
Valencia, Pa., U.S. — E2 115
Valencia, Ven. — A4 60
Valencia, hist. reg., Spain — C5 22
Valencia [de Alcántara], Spain — C3 22
Valencia Heights, S.C., U.S. — D6 117
Valencia, i., Ire. — E1 10
Valenciennes, Fr. — B5 16
Valendas, Switz. — C7 21
Valentigney, Fr. — D7 16
Valentine, Az., U.S. — B2 80
Valentine, Ne., U.S. — B5 104
Valentine, Tx., U.S. — o12 120
Valera, Ven. — B3 60
Valhermoso Springs, Al., U.S. — A3 78
Valiente, Punta, c., Pan. — F7 62
Valier, Il., U.S. — E4 90
Valier, Mt., U.S. — B4 103
Valier, Pa., U.S. — E3 115
Valinda, Ca., U.S. — *m13 82
Val-Jalbert, Que. — A5 74
Valjevo, Yugo. — C4 24
Valka, Sov. Un. — C6 27
Valkeakoski, Fin. — G11 14
Valkenswaard, Neth. — C5 17
Valladolid, Ec. — B2 58
Valladolid, Mex. — C7 63
Valladolid, Spain — B3 22
Vallákra, Swe. — C6 15
Vallauris, Fr. — F7 16
Vall de Uxó, Spain — C5 22
Vallecas, Spain — B4 22
Vallecito, Co., U.S. — D3 83
Vallecito Reservoir, res., Co., U.S. — D3 83
Vallecitos, N.M., U.S. — A3 108
Valle d'Aosta, prov., Italy — D3 20
Valle de la Pascua, Ven. — B4 60
Valle del Cauca, dept., Col. — C2 60
Valle de Santiago, Mex. — m13 63
Valledupar, Col. — A3 60
Vallée-Jonction, Que. — C7 74
Vallegrande, Bol. — C3 55
Vallejo, Ca., U.S. — C2 82
Vallenar, Chile — E1 55
Valletta, Malta — H11 8
Valle Vista, Ca., U.S. — *F5 82
Valley, co., Id., U.S. — E3 89
Valley, co., Mt., U.S. — B10 103
Valley, co., Ne., U.S. — C6 104
Valley, stm., Man. — D1 70
Valley, Wa., U.S. — A8 124
Valley Bend, W.V., U.S. — C5 125
Valley Center, Ca., U.S. — F5 82
Valley Center, Ks., U.S. — E6 93
Valley Centre, Sask. — F2 75
Valley City, Il., U.S. — D3 90
Valley City, N.D., U.S. — C8 111
Valley City, Oh., U.S. — A4 112
Valley Cottage, N.Y., U.S. — g13 109
Valley Creek, stm., Al., U.S. — g6 78
Valley East, Ont. — p19 73
Valley Falls, Ks., U.S. — C8 93
Valley Falls, Or., U.S. — E6 114
Valley Falls, R.I., U.S. — B4 116
Valley Farms, Az., U.S. — E4 80
Valleyfield (part of Badger's Quay-Valleyfield-Pool's Island), Newf. — D5 72

Name	Map Ref.	Page
Valleyford, Wa., U.S.	B8	124
Valley Forge, Pa., U.S.	o20	115
Valley Grove, W.V., U.S.	A4	125
Valley Head, Al., U.S.	A4	78
Valley Head, W.V., U.S.	C4	125
Valley Lee, Md., U.S.	D4	97
Valley Mills, Tx., U.S.	D4	120
Valley Park, Ms., U.S.	C3	101
Valley Park, Mo., U.S.	f12	102
Valley Ridge, W.V., U.S.	*B3	124
Valley Spring, Tx., U.S.	D3	120
Valley Springs, Ar., U.S.	A3	81
Valley Springs, S.D., U.S.	D9	118
Valley Station, Ky., U.S.	g11	94
Valley Stream, N.Y., U.S.	n15	109
Valleyview, Alta.	B2	68
Valley View, Ky., U.S.	C5	94
Valley View, Pa., U.S.	E8	115
Valley View, Tx., U.S.	C4	120
Valliant, Ok., U.S.	D6	113
Vallo della Lucania, Italy	D5	23
Vallonia, In., U.S.	G5	91
Vallorbe, Switz.	E3	18
Valls, Spain	B6	22
Vallscreek, W.V., U.S.	D3	125
Val Marie, Sask.	H2	75
Valmeyer, Il., U.S.	E3	90
Valmiera, Sov. Un.	C5	27
Valmont, Que.	C5	74
Valmontone, Italy	h9	23
Valmora, N.M., U.S.	B5	108
Val-Morin, Que.	C3	74
Valognes, Fr.	C3	16
Valois, N.Y., U.S.	C4	109
Valona see Vlora, Alb.	B2	40
Valparaíso, Sask.	E3	75
Valparaíso, Chile	A2	54
Valparaíso, Mex.	C4	63
Valparaiso, Fl., U.S.	u15	86
Valparaiso, In., U.S.	B3	91
Valparaiso, Ne., U.S.	C9	104
Valparaíso, prov., Chile	A2	54
Val-Racine, Que.	D6	74
Valréas, Fr.	E6	16
Vals, Cape, c., Indon.	G9	34
Val-Saint-Michel, Que.	n17	74
Valsetz, Or., U.S.	C3	114
Vals Platz, Switz.	C7	21
Valtournanche, Italy	E4	21
Valuyki, Sov. Un.	F12	27
Val Verda, Ut., U.S.	C4	121
Val Verde, co., Tx., U.S.	E2	120
Valverde del Camino, Spain	D2	22
Vamdrup, Den.	C3	15
Vamori, Az., U.S.	F4	80
Van, Tur.	C14	40
Van, Tx., U.S.	C5	120
Van, W.V., U.S.	n12	125
Van, Lake, l., Tur.	C14	40
Vanadium, N.M., U.S.	E1	108
Van Alstyne, Tx., U.S.	C4	120
Vananda, B.C.	E5	69
Van-Bruyssel, Que.	B5	74
Van Buren, Ar., U.S.	B1	81
Van Buren, In., U.S.	C6	91
Van Buren, Me., U.S.	A5	96
Van Buren, Mo., U.S.	E6	102
Van Buren, co., Ar., U.S.	A2	112
Van Buren, co., Ar., U.S.	B3	81
Van Buren, co., Ia., U.S.	D6	92
Van Buren, co., Mi., U.S.	F4	99
Van Buren, co., Tn., U.S.	D8	119
Vance, Ms., U.S.	A3	101
Vance, S.C., U.S.	E7	117
Vance, co., N.C., U.S.	A4	110
Vance Air Force Base, mil., Ok., U.S.	A3	113
Vanceboro, Me., U.S.	C5	96
Vanceboro, N.C., U.S.	B5	110
Vanceburg, Ky., U.S.	B6	94
Vancleave, Ms., U.S.	E5	101
Vanclieve, Ky., U.S.	C6	94
Vancorum, Co., U.S.	C2	83
Vancouver, B.C.	E6	69
Vancouver, Wa., U.S.	D3	124
Vancouver Island, i., B.C.	E4	69
Vancouver Island Ranges, mts., B.C.	D4	69
Vandalia, Il., U.S.	E4	90
Vandalia, Mo., U.S.	B6	102
Vandalia, Mt., U.S.	B10	103
Vandalia, Oh., U.S.	*C1	112
Vandemere, N.C., U.S.	B6	110
Vandenberg Air Force Base, mil., Ca., U.S.	E3	82
Vandenberg Village, Ca., U.S.	*E3	82
Vander, N.C., U.S.	B4	110
Vanderbilt, Mi., U.S.	C6	99
Vanderbilt, Pa., U.S.	F2	115
Vanderbilt, Tx., U.S.	E4	120
Vanderbilt Peak, mtn., N.M., U.S.	E1	108
Vanderburgh, co., In., U.S.	H2	91
Vandercook Lake, Mi., U.S.	*F6	99
Vandergrift, Pa., U.S.	E2	115
Vanderhoof, B.C.	C5	69
Vanderpool, Tx., U.S.	E3	120
Vandervoort, Ar., U.S.	C1	81
Vanderwagen, N.M., U.S.	B1	108
Van Diemen, Cape, c., Austl.	B5	50
Van Diemen Gulf, b., Austl.	B5	50
Vandiver, Al., U.S.	B3	78
Vandling, Pa., U.S.	C11	115
Vanduser, Mo., U.S.	E8	102
Vandyne, Wi., U.S.	k9	126
Vanegas, Mex.	C4	63
Vänern, l., Swe.	H5	14
Vänersborg, Swe.	H5	14
Van Etten, N.Y., U.S.	C4	109
Vang, Mount, mtn., Ant.	B6	7
Vanga, Kenya	B6	48
Vangaindrano, Madag.	h9	49
Vanguard, Sask.	H2	75
Van Horn, Tx., U.S.	o12	120
Van Horne, Ia., U.S.	B5	92
Vanier, Ont.	h12	73
Vanimo, Pap. N. Gui.	h11	50
Vankleek Hill, Ont.	B10	73
Van Kull, Kill, stm., N.J., U.S.	k8	107
Van Lear, Ky., U.S.	C7	94
Vanleer, Tn., U.S.	A4	119
Vanlue, Oh., U.S.	B2	112
Van Meter, Ia., U.S.	C4	92
Vanna, Ga., U.S.	B3	81
Vanndale, Ar., U.S.	B5	81
Vannes, Fr.	D2	16
Vanoss, Ok., U.S.	C5	113
Van Phong Bay, b., Viet.	F8	34
Van Rees Mountains, mts., Indon.	F9	34
Vanrhynsdorp, S. Afr.	D2	49
Vansant, Va., U.S.	e9	123
Vanscoy, Sask.	E2	75
Vantaa (Vanda), Fin.	*G11	14
Vantage, Sask.	H2	75
Van Tassell, Wy., U.S.	D8	127
Vanua Balavu, i., Fiji	H16	52
Vanua Levu, i., Fiji	H15	52
Vanuatu, ctry., Oc.	H10	6
Vanua Vatu, i., Fiji	I16	52
Vanves, Fr.	g10	16
Van Vleck, Tx., U.S.	r14	120
Van Vleet, Ms., U.S.	B5	101
Van Wert, Ga., U.S.	C1	87
Van Wert, Ia., U.S.	D4	92
Van Wert, Oh., U.S.	B1	112
Van Wert, co., Oh., U.S.	B1	112
Van Wyck, S.C., U.S.	B6	117
Vanwyksvlei, S. Afr.	D3	49
Van Zandt, co., Tx., U.S.	C5	120
Vanzant, Mo., U.S.	E5	102
Varallo, Italy	D4	20
Varāmīn, Iran	D5	39
Vārānasi (Benares), India	C7	36
Varangerfjorden, Nor.	B14	14
Varano, Lake, b., Italy	D5	23
Varaždin, Yugo.	B3	24
Varazze, Italy	B2	23
Varberg, Swe.	I5	14
Vardaman, Ms., U.S.	B4	101
Vardar (Axiós), stm., Eur.	B4	40
Varde, Den.	C2	15
Varde Å, stm., Den.	C2	15
Vardenis, Sov. Un.	B15	40
Vardö, Nor.	B14	14
Varel, W. Ger.	B4	18
Varena, Sov. Un.	A8	26
Varennes, Que.	D4	74
Varennes, Fr.	D5	16
Vareš, Yugo.	C4	24
Varese, Italy	B2	23
Varese, Lake, l., Italy	E6	21
Varginha, Braz.	C3	56
Vári, Grc.	h11	25
Varina, Ia., U.S.	B3	92
Varina, Va., U.S.	C5	123
Varjão, Braz.	B3	56
Varkaus, Fin.	F12	14
Varkhān, stm., Afg.	E12	39
Varna (Stalin), Bul.	D8	24
Varna, Ont.	D3	73
Varna, Il., U.S.	B4	90
Varnado, La., U.S.	D6	95
Varnamo, Swe.	I6	14
Varney, Ont.	C4	73
Varnsdorf, Czech.	C3	26
Varnville, S.C., U.S.	F5	117
Varö, Swe.	A6	15
Varös, Ont.	h13	73
Varysburg, N.Y., U.S.	C2	109
Várzea, stm., Braz.	D2	56
Várzea da Palma, Braz.	B4	56
Várzea Grande, Braz.	B1	56
Varzi, Italy	E5	20
Varzuga, stm., Sov. Un.	D17	14
Vashon, Wa., U.S.	B3	124
Vashon, Point, c., Wa., U.S.	E11	124
Vashon Island, i., Wa., U.S.	f11	124
Vasilkov, Sov. Un.	F8	27
Vaslui, Rom.	B8	24
Vass, N.C., U.S.	B3	110
Vassalboro, Me., U.S.	*D3	96
Vassar, Man.	E4	70
Vassar, Ks., U.S.	D8	93
Vassar, Mi., U.S.	E7	99
Vassouras, Braz.	h6	56
Västerås, Swe.	H7	14
Västerhaninge, Swe.	t36	14
Västervik, Swe.	I7	14
Vasto, Italy	C5	23
Vaternish Point, c., Scot., U.K.	C2	13
Vatican City, ctry., Eur.	D4	23
Vatnajökull, ice, Ice.	n24	14
Vatomandry, Madag.	g9	49
Vatra Dornei, Rom.	B7	24
Vättern, l., Swe.	H6	14
Vatulele, i., Fiji	I14	52
Vatu Vara, i., Fiji	H16	52
Vaucluse, S.C., U.S.	D4	117
Vaucouleurs, Fr.	F5	17
Vaud, state, Switz.	C2	20
Vaudreuil, Que.	D3	74
Vaudreuil, co., Que.	D3	74
Vaughan, Ont.	D5	73
Vaughan, Ms., U.S.	C3	101
Vaughan, N.C., U.S.	A4	110
Vaughan, W.V., U.S.	m13	125
Vaughn, Mt., U.S.	C5	103
Vaughn, N.M., U.S.	C4	108
Vaughn, Or., U.S.	C3	114
Vaughnsville, Oh., U.S.	B1	112
Vaupés, dept., Col.	C3	60
Vaupés (Uaupés), stm., S.A.	C3	60
Vauvillers, Fr.	B2	20
Vauxhall, Alta.	D4	68
Vavoua, I.C.	E3	45
Vavuniya, Sri L.	I6	36
Vaxholm, Swe.	t36	14
Växjö, Swe.	I6	14
Vaxtorp, Swe.	B7	15
Vayia, Grc.	g10	25
Vazante, Braz.	B3	56
Vealmoor, Tx., U.S.	C2	120
Veazie, Me., U.S.	D4	96
Veberöd, Swe.	C7	15
Veblen, S.D., U.S.	B8	118
Vechta, W. Ger.	F2	15
Vechte, stm., Eur.	A7	16
Veckholm, Swe.	t35	14
Veddige, Swe.	A6	15
Vedia, Arg.	A4	54
Veedersburg, In., U.S.	D4	91
Veendam, Neth.	A6	17
Vega, Tx., U.S.	B1	120
Vega, i., Nor.	E4	14
Vega Alta, P.R.	B3	65
Vega Baja, P.R.	B3	65
Vegreville, Alta.	C4	68
Veguita, N.M., U.S.	C3	108
Veinticinco de Mayo, Arg.	B3	54
Veinticinco de Mayo, Arg.	A3	54
Veinticinco de Mayo, Arg.	B4	54
Vejen, Den.	C3	15
Vejer [de la Frontera], Spain	D2	22
Vejle, co., Den.	C3	15
Vejprty, Czech.	C2	26
Vela, Cabo de la, c., Col.	A3	60
Velarde, N.M., U.S.	A4	108
Velas, Cabo, c., C.R.	E5	62
Velbert, W. Ger.	B2	19
Velda Rose Estates, Az., U.S.	D4	80
Velden, W. Ger.	A8	20
Velebit Mountains, mts., Yugo.	C2	24
Velestínon, Grc.	C4	25
Vélez, Col.	B3	60
Vélez Blanco, Spain	D4	22
Vélez-Málaga, Spain	D3	22
Vélez Rubio, Spain	D4	22
Velgast, E. Ger.	D6	15
Velhas, Rio das, stm., Braz.	B4	56
Velika Morava, stm., Yugo.	C5	24
Velikaya, stm., Sov. Un.	C7	27
Velikaya Lepetikha, Sov. Un.	H10	27
Velikiye Luki, Sov. Un.	C8	27
Velikiy Ustyug, Sov. Un.	C7	29
Velikiy Tŭrnovo, Bul.	D7	24
Vélingara, Sen.	D2	45
Vélingara, Sen.	D2	45
Velizh, Sov. Un.	D8	27
Velké Meziříčí, Czech.	D4	26
Velletri, Italy	h9	23
Vellinge, Swe.	C7	15
Vellore, India	F6	36
Velma, Ok., U.S.	C4	113
Velpen, In., U.S.	H3	91
Velsen (part of IJmuiden), Neth.	B4	17
Velsk, Sov. Un.	C7	29
Veltrusy, Czech.	n17	26
Velva, N.D., U.S.	A5	111
Velvary, Czech.	n17	26
Vemb, Den.	B2	15
Ven, i., Swe.	C6	15
Venaco, Fr.	C2	23
Venado Tuerto, Arg.	A4	54
Venango, Ne., U.S.	D3	104
Venango, Pa., U.S.	C1	115
Venango, co., Pa., U.S.	D2	115
Venceslau Brás, Braz.	C4	56
Venda, ctry., Afr.	B5	49
Vendôme, Fr.	D4	16
Vendrell, Spain	B6	22
Venedocia, Oh., U.S.	B1	112
Venedy, Il., U.S.	E4	90
Veneta, Or., U.S.	C3	114
Veneta, Laguna, b., Italy	D8	20
Venetia (Veneto), prov., Italy	A3	23
Venetie, Ak., U.S.	B10	79
Veneto, prov., Italy	D7	20
Venev, Sov. Un.	D12	27
Venezuela, ctry., S.A.	B4	60
Venezuela, Golfo de, b., S.A.	A3	60
Veniaminof, Mount, mtn., Ak., U.S.	D8	79
Venice, Alta.	B4	68
Venice (Venezia), Italy	B4	23
Venice, Fl., U.S.	E4	86
Venice, Il., U.S.	E3	90
Venice, La., U.S.	E6	95
Venice, Ne., U.S.	g12	104
Venice, Ut., U.S.	E4	121
Venice, Gulf of, b., Eur.	A4	23
Venice Gardens, Fl., U.S.	*E4	86
Vénissieux, Fr.	B5	73
Venlo, Neth.	B7	16
Venn, Sask.	F3	75
Vennachar, Ont.	B7	73
Venø, i., Den.	B2	15
Vent, Aus.	C6	20
Venta, stm., Sov. Un.	C3	27
Ventana, Az., U.S.	E3	80
Ventimiglia, Italy	C1	23
Ventnor, Ont.	C9	73
Ventnor, Eng., U.K.	D6	12
Ventnor City, N.J., U.S.	E4	107
Venton, Md., U.S.	D6	97
Ventoux, Mont, mtn., Fr.	E6	16
Ventry, Ire.	E1	11
Ventspils, Sov. Un.	C3	27
Venturi, stm., Ven.	C4	60
Ventura (San Buenaventura), Ca., U.S.	E4	82
Ventura, Ia., U.S.	A4	92
Ventura, co., Ca., U.S.	E4	82
Venturia, N.D., U.S.	D6	111
Venus, Fl., U.S.	E5	86
Venus, Pa., U.S.	D2	115
Venus, Tx., U.S.	n9	120
Venustiano Carranza, Mex.	D6	63
Vera, Arg.	E3	55
Vera, Spain	D5	22
Vera, Ok., U.S.	A6	113
Vera, Tx., U.S.	C3	120
Veracruz, state, Mex.	C5	63
Veracruz [Llave], Mex.	D5	63
Veradale, Wa., U.S.	*B8	124
Veranópolis, Braz.	B6	56
Verāval, India	J5	36
Verbania, Italy	D4	20
Verbena, Al., U.S.	C3	78
Vercel, Fr.	B1	21
Vercelli, Italy	B2	23
Verchères, Que.	D4	74
Verchères, co., Que.	D4	74
Verda, Ky., U.S.	D6	94
Verde, stm., Braz.	B4	56
Verde, stm., Braz.	C2	56
Verde, stm., Braz.	D4	55
Verde, stm., Mex.	C2	63
Verde, stm., Mex.	m14	63
Verde, stm., Para.	D4	55
Verde, Point, c., Newf.	E4	72
Verde Island, i., Phil.	p13	34
Verde Island Passage, strt., Phil.	p13	34
Verdel, Ne., U.S.	B7	104
Verden, W. Ger.	B4	18
Verden, Ok., U.S.	B3	113
Verdi, Mn., U.S.	F2	100
Verdi, Nv., U.S.	D2	105
Verdigre, Ne., U.S.	B7	104
Verdigris, Ok., U.S.	A6	113
Verdigris, stm., U.S.	E8	93
Verdon, Ne., U.S.	D10	104
Verdun, Que.	q19	74
Verdun, Fr.	C6	16
Verdun, S.D., U.S.	D7	118
Verdunville, W.V., U.S.	*D2	125
Vereeniging, S. Afr.	C4	49
Vereshchagino, Sov. Un.	D19	8
Vergara, Spain	A4	22
Vergara, Ur.	C2	56
Vergennes, Il., U.S.	F4	90
Vergennes, Vt., U.S.	C2	122
Verigin, Sask.	F4	75
Verín, Spain	B2	22
Verismo Sarmento see Camissombo, Ang.	C3	48
Veríssimo, Braz.	B3	56
Verkhnedvinsk, Sov. Un.	D7	27
Verkhneimbatsk, Sov. Un.	C26	8
Verkhnekolymsk, Sov. Un.	C18	29
Verkhneuralsk, Sov. Un.	E20	8
Verkhneusinskoye, Sov. Un.	E27	8
Verkhniy Baskunchak, Sov. Un.	D3	28
Verkhniy Ufaley, Sov. Un.	B6	28
Verkhnyaya Tura, Sov. Un.	D21	8
Verkhoyansk, Sov. Un.	C16	29
Verkhoyansk Mountains, mts., Sov. Un.	C15	29
Verlo, Sask.	G1	75
Vermilion, Alta.	C5	68
Vermilion, Il., U.S.	D6	90
Vermilion, Oh., U.S.	A3	112
Vermilion, co., Il., U.S.	C6	90
Vermilion, co., La., U.S.	E3	95
Vermilion, stm., Alta.	C5	68
Vermilion, stm., Il., U.S.	B5	90
Vermilion, stm., La., U.S.	E3	95
Vermilion, stm., Mn., U.S.	B6	100
Vermilion, stm., Oh., U.S.	A3	112
Vermilion Bay, Ont.	o17	73
Vermilion Bay, b., La., U.S.	E3	95
Vermilion Lake, l., Mn., U.S.	C6	100
Vermilion Pass, Can.	D2	68
Vermilion Range, hills, Mn., U.S.	C7	100
Vermillion, Ks., U.S.	C7	93
Vermillion, S.D., U.S.	E9	118
Vermillion, co., In., U.S.	E2	91
Vermillion, East Fork, stm., S.D., U.S.	D8	118
Vermillion Bluffs, clf., Co., U.S.	A2	83
Vermillion Creek, stm., Co., U.S.	A2	83
Vermillon, stm., Que.	B4	74
Vermont, Il., U.S.	C3	90
Vermont, state, U.S.	D3	122
Vermontville, Mi., U.S.	F6	99
Vernal, Ut., U.S.	C6	121
Vernalis, Ca., U.S.	h10	82
Verndale, Mn., U.S.	D3	100
Verner, Ont.	A4	73
Verneuil, Fr.	C4	16
Verneukpan, pl., S. Afr.	D3	49
Vernon, B.C.	D8	69
Vernon, Fr.	C4	16
Vernon, Al., U.S.	B1	78
Vernon, Az., U.S.	*C6	80
Vernon, Co., U.S.	B8	83
Vernon, Ct., U.S.	C6	84
Vernon, Fl., U.S.	u16	86
Vernon, Il., U.S.	E4	90
Vernon, In., U.S.	G6	91
Vernon, Ok., U.S.	B6	113
Vernon, Tn., U.S.	B4	119
Vernon, Tx., U.S.	B3	120
Vernon, Vt., U.S.	F3	122
Vernon, N.Y., U.S.	B5	109
Vernon, co., La., U.S.	C2	95
Vernon, co., Mo., U.S.	D3	102
Vernon, co., Wi., U.S.	E3	126
Vernon, stm., Ga., U.S.	E5	87
Vernon Bridge, P.E.I.	C7	71
Vernon Center, Mn., U.S.	G4	100
Vernon Hill, Va., U.S.	D3	123
Vernon Hills, Il., U.S.	h9	90
Vernonia, Or., U.S.	B3	114
Vernon River, P.E.I.	C7	71
Vero Beach, Fl., U.S.	E6	86
Véroia, Grc.	B4	40
Verona, Ont.	C8	73
Verona, Italy	B3	23
Verona, Il., U.S.	B5	90
Verona, Ky., U.S.	k13	94
Verona, Ms., U.S.	A5	101
Verona, Mo., U.S.	E4	102
Verona, N.J., U.S.	B4	107
Verona, N.C., U.S.	C5	110
Verona, N.D., U.S.	C7	111
Verona, Oh., U.S.	C1	112
Verona, Pa., U.S.	k14	115
Verona, Va., U.S.	A3	123
Verona, Wi., U.S.	F4	126
Verónica, Arg.	g8	54
Verret, N.B.	B1	71
Verret, Lake, l., La., U.S.	E4	95
Verrières-le-Buisson, Fr.	h10	16
Versailles, Fr.	C5	16
Versailles, Ct., U.S.	C7	84
Versailles, Il., U.S.	D3	90
Versailles, In., U.S.	F7	91
Versailles, Ky., U.S.	B5	94
Versailles, Mo., U.S.	C5	102
Versailles, Oh., U.S.	B1	112
Vershire, Vt., U.S.	D4	122
Versmold, W. Ger.	B3	19
Versoix, Switz.	C2	20
Vert, Cap, c., Sen.	E4	42
Verte, stm., Que.	B8	74
Verte, Île, i., Que.	B8	74
Verton, Fr.	D9	12
Vertou, Fr.	B1	21
Vertus, Fr.	F4	17
Verviers, Bel.	C5	16
Vervins, Fr.	C5	16
Verwall Group, mts., Aus.	B6	20
Verwood, Sask.	H3	75
Verzasca, stm., Switz.	C6	21
Verzenay, Fr.	C6	16
Veseleyville, N.D., U.S.	A8	111
Veselí nad Lužnicí, Czech.	D9	13
Veseloye, Sov. Un.	H10	27
Vesoul, Fr.	D7	16
Vesper, Ks., U.S.	C5	93
Vesper, Wi., U.S.	D4	126
Vesta, C.R.	F6	62
Vesta, Mn., U.S.	F3	100
Vestaburg, Mi., U.S.	E6	99
Vestal, N.Y., U.S.	C4	109
Vestal Center, N.Y., U.S.	C4	109
Vestavia Hills, Al., U.S.	g7	78
Vestby, Nor.	p28	14
Vesterålen, is., Nor.	A4	15
Vesterø Havn, Den.	A4	15
Vestervig, Den.	B2	15
Vestfjorden, Nor.	D5	14
Vestmannaeyjar, Ice.	o22	14
Vestsjælland, co., Den.	C5	15
Vesuvius, Va., U.S.	C3	123
Vesuvius, mtn., Italy	D5	23
Vesyegonsk, Sov. Un.	B11	27
Veszprém, Hung.	B3	24
Vészto, Hung.	B5	24
Vetal, S.D., U.S.	D4	118
Veteran, Alta.	C5	68
Veteran, Wy., U.S.	E8	127
Vetlanda, Swe.	I6	14
Vetluga, stm., Sov. Un.	H10	29
Vetlužskiy, Sov. Un.	G10	29
Vetovo, Bul.	D8	24
Vetren, Bul.	D7	24
Veurne, Bel.	C2	17
Vevay, In., U.S.	G7	91
Vevey, Switz.	E3	18
Veynes, Fr.	E6	16
Veyo, Ut., U.S.	F2	121
Veyrier-du-Lac, Fr.	E1	21
Viesca, Mex.	B4	63
Vézère, stm., Fr.	D6	23
Vezirköprü, Tur.	B10	40
Viacha, Bol.	C2	55
Viadana, Italy	B3	23
Vian, Ok., U.S.	B7	113
Viana, Braz.	B2	57
Viana del Bollo, Spain	A2	22
Viana do Alentejo, Port.	C1	22
Viana do Castelo, Port.	B1	22
Vianópolis, Braz.	B3	56
Viar, stm., Spain	D3	22
Viareggio, Italy	C3	23
Vibank, Sask.	G4	75
Viborg, Den.	B3	15
Viborg, S.D., U.S.	D8	118
Vibo Valentia, Italy	E6	23
Viburnum, Mo., U.S.	D6	102
Vic, Fr.	F4	16
Vicálvaro, Spain	p17	22
Vicco, Ky., U.S.	C6	94
Vicente, Point, c., Ca., U.S.	n12	82
Vicenza, Italy	B3	23
Viceroy, Sask.	H3	75
Vichada, dept., Col.	C4	60
Vichada, stm., Col.	C4	60
Vichuga, Sov. Un.	C13	27
Vichuquén, Chile	A2	54
Vichy, Fr.	D5	16
Vichy, Mo., U.S.	C6	102
Vici, Ok., U.S.	A2	113
Vick, Ar., U.S.	D3	81
Vick, La., U.S.	C3	95
Vickery, Oh., U.S.	A3	112
Vicksburg, In., U.S.	F3	91
Vicksburg, Mi., U.S.	F5	99
Vicksburg, Ms., U.S.	C3	101
Vicksburg National Military Park, Ms., U.S.	C3	101
Viçosa, Braz.	C4	56
Viçosa, Braz.	D3	57
Viçosa do Ceará, Braz.	B2	57
Vicosoprano, Switz.	D8	21
Vicovaro, Italy	g9	23
Vic [-sur-Seille], Fr.	F6	17
Victor, Co., U.S.	C5	83
Victor, Id., U.S.	F7	89
Victor, Ia., U.S.	C5	92
Victor, Mt., U.S.	D2	103
Victor, N.Y., U.S.	C3	109
Victor, S.D., U.S.	B9	118
Victor Harbor, Austl.	A4	54
Victoria, Arg.	A4	54
Victoria, B.C.	E6	69
Victoria, Newf.	E5	72
Victoria, P.E.I.	C6	71
Victoria, Chile	B2	54
Victoria, Gren.	W25	65
Victoria (Hong Kong), H.K.	G7	31
Victoria, Malay.	D5	33
Victoria, Phil.	o13	34
Victoria, Il., U.S.	B3	90
Victoria, Ks., U.S.	D4	93
Victoria, Ms., U.S.	A4	101
Victoria, Mo., U.S.	C7	102
Victoria, Tn., U.S.	D8	119
Victoria, Tx., U.S.	E4	120
Victoria, Va., U.S.	D4	123
Victoria, state, Austl.	G7	50
Victoria, co., N.B.	B2	71
Victoria, co., N.S.	C9	71
Victoria, co., Ont.	C6	73
Victoria, co., Tx., U.S.	E4	120
Victoria, stm., Austl.	C5	50
Victoria, stm., Newf.	D3	72
Victoria, Lake, l., Afr.	B5	48
Victoria, Lake, l., Austl.	F3	51
Victoria, Mount, mtn., Burma	D9	36
Victoria, Mount, mtn., Pap. N. Gui.	k12	50
Victoria Beach, Man.	D3	70
Victoria de Durango see Durango, Mex.	C4	63
Victoria de las Tunas, Cuba	D5	64
Victoria Falls, Zimb.	A4	49
Victoria Falls, wtfl., Afr.	A4	49
Victoria Harbour, Ont.	C5	73
Victoria Island, i., N.W. Ter.	B10	66
Victoria Lake, l., Newf.	D3	72
Victoria Land, reg., Ant.	B28	7
Victoria Peak, mtn., Belize	B3	62
Victoria Road, Ont.	C6	73
Victoria Strait, strt., N.W. Ter.	C12	66
Victoriaville, Que.	C6	74
Victoria West, S. Afr.	D3	49
Victorica, Arg.	B3	54
Victorino, Ven.	C4	60
Victorino de la Plaza, Arg.	B4	54
Victorville, Ca., U.S.	E5	82
Victory, Ok., U.S.	C3	113
Victory, Wi., U.S.	E2	126
Vicuña, Chile	F1	55
Vicuña Mackenna, Arg.	A4	54
Vida, Mt., U.S.	C11	103
Vidal, Ca., U.S.	E6	82
Vidalia, Ga., U.S.	D4	87
Vidalia, La., U.S.	C4	95
Vidette, Ga., U.S.	D4	87
Vidin, Bul.	C6	24
Vidisha, India	F6	37
Vidor, Tx., U.S.	D5	120
Vidora, Sask.	H1	75
Viechtach, W. Ger.	D7	19
Viedma, Arg.	E3	53
Viedma, Lago, l., Arg.	D2	54
Vieja, Sierra, mts., U.S.	o12	120
Viejo, Cerro el, mtn., Col.	B3	60
Vielsalm, Bel.	B5	19
Vienenburg, W. Ger.	B5	19
Vienna (Wien), Aus.	E4	73
Vienna, Il., U.S.	F5	90
Vienna, Ga., U.S.	B3	95
Vienna, Md., U.S.	C6	102
Vienna, Mo., U.S.	C6	102
Vienna, S.D., U.S.	C8	118
Vienna, Va., U.S.	B5	123
Vienna, W.V., U.S.	B3	125
Vienne, Fr.	D6	16
Vienne, stm., Fr.	D4	16
Vientiane see Viangchan, Laos	B2	34
Vieques, P.R.	B5	65
Vieques, Isla de, i., P.R.	G12	64
Vieques, Pasaje de, strt., P.R.	B4	65
Vieques, Sonda de, strt., P.R.	B5	65
Viernheim, W. Ger.	F3	19
Viersen, W. Ger.	C6	17
Vierzon, Fr.	D5	16
Viesca, Mex.	B4	63
Vieste, Italy	D6	23
Vietnam, ctry., Asia	B3	34
Viet Tri, Viet.	B3	34
Vieux Desert, Lac, l., Wi., U.S.	B4	126
Vieux-Fort, St. Luc.	J14	64
Vieux-Fort, Pointe du, c., Guad.	R8	65
View Park, Ca., U.S.	*m12	82
Vigan, Phil.	B6	34
Vigevano, Italy	B2	23
Vignola, Italy	E6	20
Vigo, Spain	A1	22
Vigo, co., In., U.S.	F3	91
Vigsø Bugt, b., Den.	A2	15
Vihowa, Pak.	B5	36
Vijayawāda (Bezwada), India	E7	36
Vikersund, Nor.	p27	14
Viking, Alta.	C5	68
Viking, Mn., U.S.	B2	100
Vila Alferes Chamusca, Moz.	B5	49
Vila Bela de Santíssima Trinidade, Braz.	B4	55
Vila da Maganja, Moz.	A6	49
Vila de Manica, Moz.	A5	49
Vila de Rei, Port.	C1	22
Vila de Sena, Moz.	A6	49
Vila do Conde, Port.	B1	22
Vila Fontes, Moz.	A6	49
Vilafranca del Penedés, Spain	B6	22
Vila Franca de Xira, Port.	C1	22
Vilaine, stm., Fr.	D2	16
Vilanculos, Moz.	B6	49
Vila Nova de Foz Côa, Port.	B2	22
Vila Nova de Gaia, Port.	B1	22
Vila Nova de Milfontes, Port.	D1	22
Vila Real, Port.	B2	22
Vila Real de Santo António, Port.	D2	22
Vilas, Co., U.S.	D8	83
Vilas, S.D., U.S.	C8	118
Vilas, co., Wi., U.S.	B4	126
Vila São Luís, Braz.	B3	59
Vila Vasco da Gama, Moz.	A5	49
Vila Velha, Moz.	C4	56
Vila Viçosa, Port.	C2	22
Vildbjerg, Den.	B2	15
Vildo, Italy	g9	23
Vileyka, Sov. Un.	D6	27
Vilhelmina, Swe.	E7	14
Vilhena, Braz.	B3	55
Vília, Grc.	g10	25
Viliya, stm., Sov. Un.	A8	26
Viljandi, Sov. Un.	B5	27
Vilkaviškis, Sov. Un.	A7	26
Vilkitsky, i., Sov. Un.	B7	128
Vilkovo, Sov. Un.	I7	27
Villa Abecia, Bol.	D2	55
Villa Adriana, hist., Italy	h9	23
Villa Ahumada, Mex.	A3	63
Villa Ángela, Arg.	E3	55
Villa Aroma, Bol.	C2	55
Villa Bella, Bol.	B2	55
Villablino, Spain	A2	22
Villacañas, Spain	C4	22
Villacarrillo, Spain	C4	22
Villa Clara, prov., Cuba	C3	64
Villa Constitución, Arg.	A4	54
Villa Cuauhtémoc, Mex.	k15	63
Villa de Arriaga, Mex.	m13	63
Villa de Cura, Ven.	A3	60
Villa Delgado, El Sal.	*D3	62
Villa del Rosario, Arg.	A4	54
Villa de Méndez, Mex.	B5	63
Villa Dolores, Arg.	B3	54
Villadossola, Italy	D4	21
Villa Eufronio Viscarra, Bol.	C2	55
Villafamés, Spain	B5	22
Villafranca del Bierzo, Spain	A2	22
Villafranca de los Barros, Spain	C2	22
Villafranca [di Verona], Italy	B3	23
Villa Frontera, Mex.	B4	63
Villa García, Mex.	k13	63
Villagarcía, Spain	A1	22
Villa García, Arg.	D2	81
Village, Va., U.S.	C6	123
Village Creek, stm., Al., U.S.	f7	78
Village Springs, Al., U.S.	B3	78
Villa González, Mex.	C5	63
Villa Grove, Co., U.S.	C5	83
Villa Grove, Il., U.S.	D5	90
Villaguay, Arg.	E4	55
Villa Hayes, Para.	E4	55
Villahermosa, Mex.	D6	63
Villa Hills, Ky., U.S.	*A5	94
Villa Huidobro, Arg.	B4	55
Villa Iris, Arg.	B4	55
Villajoyosa, Spain	C5	22
Villalba, Spain	A2	22
Villalonga, Arg.	B4	55
Villalpando, Spain	B3	22
Villa María, Arg.	A4	54
Villa María Grande, Arg.	A5	54
Villamartín, Spain	D3	22
Villa Mazán, Arg.	E2	55
Villamil, Ec.	g5	58
Villa Montes, Bol.	D3	55
Villanueva, Col.	A3	60
Villanueva, N.M., U.S.	B4	108
Villanueva de Córdoba, Spain	C3	22
Villanueva del Arzobispo, Spain	C4	22
Villanueva de la Serana, Spain	C3	22
Villanueva de los Infantes, Spain	C4	22
Villanueva [del Río y Minas], Spain	C4	22
Villanueva y Geltrú, Spain	B6	22
Villa Obregón (part of Mexico City), Mex.	h9	63
Villa Ocampo, Arg.	E4	55
Villa Oliva, Arg.	E4	55
Villa Park, Ca., U.S.	*n13	82
Villa Park, Il., U.S.	k8	90
Villaputzu, Italy	J4	23
Villard, Mn., U.S.	E3	100
Villard-Bonnot, Fr.	E6	16
Villa Rica, Ga., U.S.	C2	87
Villa Ridge, Il., U.S.	F4	90
Villa Ridge, Mo., U.S.	C7	102
Villarreal, Spain	C5	22
Villarrica, Chile	C2	54
Villarrica, Para.	E4	55
Villarrobledo, Spain	C4	22
Villarrubia [de los Ojos], Spain	C4	22
Villas, N.J., U.S.	E3	107
Villa San Martín (Loreto), Arg.	E3	55
Villa Unión, Arg.	E2	55

Name	Map Ref.	Page
Villa Unión, Mex.	B4	63
Villa Unión, Mex.	C3	63
Villa Valeria, Arg.	A4	54
Villaverde, Spain	p17	22
Villavicencio, Col.	C3	60
Villaviciosa, Spain	A3	22
Villefranche, Fr.	D6	16
Villefranche [-sur-Saône], Fr.	D6	16
Villegreen, Co., U.S.	D7	83
Villejuif, Fr.	g10	16
Ville Marie, Que.	G17	66
Villemomble, Fr.	g11	16
Villena, Spain	C5	22
Villenauxe-la-Grande, Fr.	F3	17
Villeneuve-d'Ascq, Fr.	*B5	16
Villeneuve-le-Roi, Fr.	h10	16
Villeneuve [-lès-Avignon], Fr.	F6	16
Villeneuve-Saint-Georges, Fr.	h10	16
Villeneuve-sur-Lot, Fr.	E4	16
Villeneuve-sur-Yonne, Fr.	C5	16
Villepinte, Fr.	g11	16
Ville Platte, La., U.S.	D3	95
Villeroy, Que.	C6	74
Villers-Bretonneux, Fr.	E2	17
Villers-Cotterêts, Fr.	C5	16
Villersexel, Fr.	A1	21
Villers-Outréaux, Fr.	D3	17
Villers-Semeuse, Fr.	E4	17
Villerupt, Fr.	C6	16
Ville Saint-Georges, Que.	C7	74
Villeta, Para.	E4	55
Villeurbanne, Fr.	E6	16
Villingen-Schwenningen, W. Ger.	D4	18
Villisca, Ia., U.S.	D3	92
Vilna, Alta.	B5	68
Vilnius, Sov. Un.	D5	29
Vilonia, Ar., U.S.	B3	81
Vilppula, Fin.	F11	14
Vils, stm., W. Ger.	E7	19
Vils, stm., W. Ger.	D6	19
Vilsbiburg, W. Ger.	E7	19
Vilseck, W. Ger.	D6	19
Vilshofen, W. Ger.	E8	19
Vilvoorde, Bel.	B6	16
Vilyuy, stm., Sov. Un.	C15	29
Vilyuysk, Sov. Un.	C15	29
Vimianzo, Spain	A1	22
Vimmerby, Swe.	I6	14
Vimperk, Czech.	D2	26
Vimy Ridge, Ar., U.S.	k10	81
Vina, Al., U.S.	A1	78
Vina, Ca., U.S.	C2	82
Viña del Mar, Chile	A2	54
Vinalhaven, Me., U.S.	D4	96
Vinalhaven Island, i., Me., U.S.	D4	96
Vinaroz, Spain	B6	22
Vincennes, Fr.	g10	16
Vincennes, In., U.S.	G2	91
Vincennes Bay, b., Ant.	C23	7
Vincent, Al., U.S.	B3	78
Vincent, Ia., U.S.	B3	92
Vincent, Oh., U.S.	C4	112
Vincent, Tx., U.S.	C2	120
Vincentown, N.J., U.S.	D3	107
Vinces, Ec.	B2	58
Vinchina, Arg.	E2	55
Vinchina, stm., Arg.	E2	55
Vinco, Ok., U.S.	B4	113
Vindelälven, stm., Swe.	E8	14
Vindeln, Swe.	E8	14
Vinderup, Den.	B2	15
Vindhya Range, mts., India	D6	36
Vine Brook, stm., Ma., U.S.	g11	98
Vinegar Hill, mtn., Or., U.S.	C8	114
Vine Grove, Ky., U.S.	C4	94
Vineland, N.J., U.S.	E2	107
Vinemont, Al., U.S.	A3	78
Vineyard Haven, Ma., U.S.	D6	98
Vineyard Sound, strt., Ma., U.S.	D6	98
Vingåker, Swe.	t33	14
Vinh, Viet.	B3	34
Vinhais, Port.	B2	22
Vinh Long, Viet.	C3	34
Vining, Ks., U.S.	C6	93
Vining, Mn., U.S.	D3	100
Vinita, Ok., U.S.	A6	113
Vinkovci, Yugo.	C4	24
Vinland, Ks., U.S.	m15	93
Vinnitsa, Sov. Un.	E5	29
Vinson, Ok., U.S.	C2	113
Vinson Massif, mtn., Ant.	B4	7
Vinton, Ia., U.S.	B5	92
Vinton, La., U.S.	D2	95
Vinton, Oh., U.S.	C3	112
Vinton, Va., U.S.	C3	123
Vinton, co., Oh., U.S.	C3	112
Vintondale, Pa., U.S.	F4	115
Viola, Ar., U.S.	A4	81
Viola, De., U.S.	D3	85
Viola, Id., U.S.	C1	89
Viola, Il., U.S.	B3	90
Viola, Ks., U.S.	E6	93
Viola, N.Y., U.S.	*D6	109
Viola, Tn., U.S.	D8	119
Viola, Wi., U.S.	E3	126
Violet, La., U.S.	k12	95
Vipiteno, Italy	C7	20
Virden, Man.	E1	70
Virden, Il., U.S.	D4	90
Virden, N.M., U.S.	E1	108
Vire, Fr.	C3	16
Vire, stm., Fr.	C3	16
Viren, i., Swe.	t34	14
Virgem da Lapa, Braz.	B4	56
Vírgenes, Cabo, c., S.A.	E3	54
Virgil, Ks., U.S.	E7	93
Virgil, N.Y., U.S.	C4	109
Virgil, S.D., U.S.	C7	118
Virgilina, Va., U.S.	D4	123
Virgin, Ut., U.S.	F2	121
Virgin, stm., U.S.	G8	105
Virgin Gorda, i., V.I. Br.	G12	64
Virginia, Ire.	D4	11
Virginia, S. Afr.	C4	49
Virginia, Al., U.S.	g6	78
Virginia, Il., U.S.	D3	90
Virginia, Mn., U.S.	C6	100
Virginia, Ne., U.S.	D9	104
Virginia, state, U.S.	C4	123
Virginia Beach, Va., U.S.	D7	123
Virginia City, Mt., U.S.	E5	103
Virginia City, Nv., U.S.	D2	105
Virginia Peak, mtn., Nv., U.S.	D2	105
Virgin Islands, dep., N.A.	G12	64
Virgin Islands, is., N.A.	B6	65
Virgin Mountains, mts., U.S.	A1	80
Virginópolis, Braz.	B4	56
Virgin Passage, strt., N.A.	B5	65
Virgolândia, Braz.	B4	56
Virochey, Camb.	C3	34
Viroflay, Fr.	g10	16
Viron, Grc.	*D4	25
Viroqua, Wi., U.S.	E3	126
Virovitica, Yugo.	C3	24
Virpazar, Yugo.	D4	24
Virrat, Swe.	F10	14
Virserum, Swe.	I6	14
Virton, Bel.	E5	17
Virú, Peru	C2	58
Vis, Yugo.	D3	24
Vis, i., Yugo.	D3	24
Visalia, Ca., U.S.	D4	82
Visalia, Ky., U.S.	k14	94
Visayan Sea, Phil.	C6	34
Visby, Swe.	I8	14
Visconde do Rio Branco, Braz.	C4	56
Viscount, Sask.	F3	75
Viscount Melville Sound, strt., N.W. Ter.	B11	66
Visé, Bel.	D5	17
Višegrad, Yugo.	D4	24
Vislanda, Swe.	H5	14
Viso, Mount, mtn., Italy	B1	23
Visoko, Yugo.	D4	24
Visp, Switz.	E3	18
Vista, Man.	D1	70
Vista, Ca., U.S.	F5	82
Vista, Mo., U.S.	D5	102
Vista, Nv., U.S.	*D2	105
Vista Alegre, Braz.	C4	60
Vistonís, Lake, l., Grc.	B5	25
Vistula, In., U.S.	A6	91
Vistula Lagoon, b., Eur.	A5	26
Vistula see Wisła, stm., Pol.	B5	26
Vit, stm., Bul.	D7	24
Vita, Man.	E3	70
Vitanovac, Yugo.	D5	24
Vitarte, Peru	D2	58
Vitebsk, Sov. Un.	D6	29
Viterbo, Italy	C4	23
Vitichi, Bol.	D2	55
Viti Levu, i., Fiji	H14	52
Viti Levu Bay, b., Fiji	H15	52
Vitim, Sov. Un.	D14	29
Vitim, stm., Sov. Un.	D14	29
Vitor, Peru	E3	58
Vitória, Braz.	C4	56
Vitória, Braz.	C4	59
Vitoria, Spain	A4	22
Vitória da Conquista, Braz.	A4	56
Vitória [de Santo Antão], Braz.	C3	57
Vitória do Mearim, Braz.	B2	57
Vitória Quebrangulo, Braz.	k5	57
Vitré, Fr.	C3	16
Vitry-le-François, Fr.	C6	16
Vitry [-sur-Seine], Fr.	g10	16
Vittel, Fr.	C6	16
Vittoria, Ont.	E4	73
Vittoria, Italy	F5	23
Vittorio Veneto, Italy	B4	23
Vivero, Spain	A2	22
Vivian, La., U.S.	B2	95
Vivian, S.D., U.S.	D5	118
Vivian Park, Ut., U.S.	C4	121
Vivoratá, Arg.	B5	54
Viwa, i., Fiji	H14	52
Vize, Tur.	B6	40
Vizianagaram, India	E7	36
Vizille, Fr.	E6	16
Viziru, Rom.	C8	24
Vizzini, Italy	F5	23
Vjosa, stm., Eur.	B3	25
Vlaardingen, Neth.	B6	16
Vladimir, Sov. Un.	D7	29
Vladimir-Aleksandrovskoye, Sov. Un.	C11	31
Vladimirovo, Sov. Un.	B12	33
Vladimir-Volynskyi, Sov. Un.	F5	27
Vladivostok, Sov. Un.	E16	29
Vlasenica, Yugo.	C4	24
Vlašim, Czech.	D9	19
Vlasotince, Yugo.	D6	24
Vlčany, Czech.	H18	19
Vlieland, i., Neth.	A6	16
Vlissingen, Neth.	B5	16
Vlkava, Czech.	n18	26
Vltava, stm., Czech.	n18	26
Vlora (Valona), Alb.	B2	40
Vlotho, W. Ger.	A3	19
Vltava, stm., Czech.	D3	26
Voca, Tx., U.S.	D3	120
Vodlozero, l., Sov. Un.	F17	14
Vodňany, Czech.	D9	19
Voghera, Italy	B2	23
Vohibinany, Madag.	g9	49
Vohimarina, Madag.	f9	49
Vohipeno, Madag.	h9	49
Voi, Kenya	B6	48
Void, Fr.	F5	17
Voil, Loch, l., Scot., U.K.	D4	13
Voinjama, Lib.	E3	45
Voiron, Fr.	E6	16
Voisin, Lac, l., Sask.	C2	75
Voitsberg, Aus.	E7	18
Vojens, Den.	C3	15
Vokhma, Sov. Un.	B3	28
Vokhma, stm., Sov. Un.	B3	28
Volary, Czech.	E9	19
Volborg, Mt., U.S.	E11	103
Volcano, Hi., U.S.	D6	88
Volcano Island, i., Phil.	o13	34
Volcano Islands, is., Japan	E8	6
Volchansk, Sov. Un.	F11	27
Volga, Ia., U.S.	B6	92
Volga, S.D., U.S.	C9	118
Volga, W.V., U.S.	B4	125
Volga, stm., Sov. Un.	E7	29
Volga Plateau, plat., Sov. Un.	C3	28
Volgodonsk, Sov. Un.	H13	27
Volgograd (Stalingrad), Sov. Un.	E7	29
Volgograd Reservoir, res., Sov. Un.	D7	29
Volkach, W. Ger.	D5	19
Volkhov, Sov. Un.	B9	27
Volkovysk, Sov. Un.	E5	27
Vollenhove, Neth.	B5	17
Volney, Va., U.S.	D1	123
Volnovakha, Sov. Un.	H11	27
Volochayevka Vtoraya, Sov. Un.	B7	33
Volochisk, Sov. Un.	G6	27
Volodarskiy (part of Leningrad), Sov. Un.		
Volodarskoye, Sov. Un.	C7	28
Vologda, Sov. Un.	D7	29
Vólos, Grc.	C4	40
Vólos, Gulf of see Pagasitikós Kólpos, b., Grc.	C4	40
Volsk, Sov. Un.	C3	28
Volta, prov., Ghana	E5	45
Volta, Lake, res., Ghana	E5	45
Voltaire, N.D., U.S.	A5	111
Volta Noire (Black Volta), stm., Afr.	D4	45
Volta Redonda, Braz.	C4	56
Volterra, Italy	C3	23
Voltri, Italy	B2	23
Volturno, stm., Italy	D5	23
Voluntown, Ct., U.S.	C8	84
Volusia, co., Fl., U.S.	C5	86
Vólvi, Lake, l., Grc.	B4	25
Volzhskiy, Sov. Un.	G15	27
Vombsjön, l., Swe.	C7	15
Vona, Co., U.S.	B8	83
Vonda, Sask.	E2	75
Von Frank Mountain, mtn., Ak., U.S.	C9	79
Vónitsa, Grc.	C3	25
Vonore, Tn., U.S.	D9	119
Von Ormy, Tx., U.S.	k7	120
Vopnafjördur, Ice.	n25	14
Vorarlberg, state, Aus.	B5	20
Vorderrhein, stm., Switz.	C7	21
Vorderthal, Switz.	B6	21
Vordingborg, Den.	C5	15
Vorkuta, Sov. Un.	C9	29
Vorona, stm., Sov. Un.	E14	27
Voronezh, Sov. Un.	D6	29
Voronezh, stm., Sov. Un.	E12	27
Voronya, stm., Sov. Un.	C16	14
Voroshilovgrad, Sov. Un.	E6	29
Vorskla, stm., Sov. Un.	G10	27
Vørterkaka Nunatak, mtn., Ant.	B15	7
Vosburg, S. Afr.	D3	49
Vosges, dept., Fr.	A2	20
Vosges, mts., Fr.	C7	16
Voskresensk, Sov. Un.	n18	27
Voss, Nor.	G2	14
Voss, N.D., U.S.	A8	111
Vossburg, Ms., U.S.	D5	101
Vostochnyy, Sov. Un.	B11	33
Vostok, sci., Ant.	B23	7
Vostok Island, i., Kir.	G12	6
Votaw, Tx., U.S.	D5	120
Votice, Czech.	D9	19
Votkinsk, Sov. Un.	B4	28
Votuporanga, Braz.	A4	59
Vouga, stm., Port.	B1	22
Vouliagméni, Grc.	h11	25
Vouvray, Fr.	D4	16
Vouziers, Fr.	C6	16
Voyageurs National Park, Mn., U.S.	B5	100
Voyeykov Ice Shelf, ice, Ant.	C25	7
Vozhega, Sov. Un.	A13	27
Voznesensk, Sov. Un.	H8	27
Voznesenskoye, Sov. Un.	A8	33
Voznesenye, Sov. Un.	A10	27
Vrå, Den.	A3	15
Vranje, Yugo.	D5	24
Vratsa, Bul.	D6	24
Vrbas, Yugo.	C4	24
Vrbas, stm., Yugo.	C3	26
Vrchlabí, Czech.	C3	26
Vrede, S. Afr.	C4	49
Vreden, W. Ger.	A1	19
Vredenburg, S. Afr.	D2	78
Vreed en Hoop, Guy.	A3	59
Vrena, Swe.	u34	14
Vriezenveen, Neth.	B6	17
Vrigstad, Swe.	A8	15
Vrin, Switz.	C7	21
Vršac, Yugo.	C5	24
Vršovice (part of Prague), Czech.	n17	26
Vrútky, Czech.	D5	26
Vryburg, S. Afr.	C3	49
Vryheid, S. Afr.	C5	49
Vsetaty, Czech.	n18	26
Vsetín, Czech.	D5	26
Vsevidof, Mount, mtn., Ak., U.S.	E6	79
Vsevolozhsk, Sov. Un.	r31	14
Vuaqava, i., Fiji	I16	52
Vúcha, stm., Bul.	E7	24
Vuda Point, c., Fiji	H14	52
Vukovar, Yugo.	C4	24
Vulcan, Alta.	D4	68
Vulcan, Mi., U.S.	C3	99
Vulcan, Mo., U.S.	D7	102
Vulcano, i., Italy	E5	23
Vúlchedrúma, Bul.	D6	24
Vung Tau, Viet.	G7	35
Vung Tau, Cape, c., Viet.	H15	52
Vuya Point, c., Fiji	H15	52
Vyartsilya, Sov. Un.	F14	14
Vyatka, stm., Sov. Un.	D7	29
Vyazemskiy, Sov. Un.	C7	33
Vyazma, Sov. Un.	D10	27
Vyazniki, Sov. Un.	C14	27
Vyborg, Sov. Un.	C5	29
Vychegda, stm., Sov. Un.	C18	8
Vygozero, l., Sov. Un.	F16	14
Vyksa, Sov. Un.	D14	29
Vyritsa, Sov. Un.	s31	14
Výrovka, stm., Czech.	n19	26
Vyshniy Volochek, Sov. Un.	C10	27
Vyškov, Czech.	D4	26
Vysočany (part of Prague), Czech.	n17	26
Vysoká, Czech.	n18	26
Vysoké Mýto, Czech.	D4	26
Vyšší Brod, Czech.	E9	19
Vytegra, Sov. Un.	C6	29

W

Name	Map Ref.	Page
Wa, Ghana	D4	45
Waal, stm., Neth.	B6	16
Waalwijk, Neth.	C5	17
Waawaa, Puu, mtn., Hi., U.S.	D6	88
Wabamun, Alta.	C3	68
Wabamun Lake, l., Alta.	C3	68
Wabana (Bell Island), Newf.	E5	72
Wabasca, stm., Alta.	f1	68
Wabash, Ar., U.S.	C6	91
Wabash, In., U.S.	C6	91
Wabash, Ne., U.S.	h12	104
Wabash, co., Il., U.S.	E6	90
Wabash, co., In., U.S.	C6	91
Wabash, stm., U.S.	H2	91
Wabasha, Mn., U.S.	F6	100
Wabasha, co., Mn., U.S.	F6	100
Wabasso, Fl., U.S.	E6	86
Wabasso, Mn., U.S.	F3	100
Wabaunsee, Ks., U.S.	C7	93
Wabaunsee, co., Ks., U.S.	D7	93
Wabasca, Ar., U.S.	C4	81
Wabeno, Wi., U.S.	C5	126
Wabigoon, Ont.	E5	70
Wabigoon Lake, l., Ont.	E5	70
Wabowden, Man.	B2	70
Wabrzeźno, Pol.	B5	26
Wabuska, Nv., U.S.	D2	105
Waccamaw, stm., U.S.	D9	117
Waccamaw, Lake, l., N.C., U.S.	C4	110
Waccasassa Bay, b., Fl., U.S.	C4	86
Wachapreague, Va., U.S.	C7	123
Wachusett Mountain, mtn., Ma., U.S.	B4	98
Wachusett Reservoir, res., Ma., U.S.	B4	98
Wacissa, Fl., U.S.	B3	86
Wacker, Il., U.S.	A3	90
Waco, Ga., U.S.	C1	87
Waco, Ks., U.S.	g12	93
Waco, Ne., U.S.	D8	104
Waco, N.C., U.S.	B1	110
Waco, Tx., U.S.	D4	120
Waco Lake, res., Tx., U.S.	C5	93
Waconda Lake, res., Ks., U.S.	C5	93
Waconia, Mn., U.S.	F5	100
Waddān, Libya	D3	43
Waddān, Jabal, mtn., Libya	D3	43
Waddell, Az., U.S.	D3	80
Wadden Zee, Neth.	A6	16
Waddington, N.Y., U.S.	f9	109
Waddington, Mount, mtn., B.C.	D5	69
Waddy, Ky., U.S.	B4	94
Wade, N.C., U.S.	B4	110
Wade, Ok., U.S.	D5	113
Wade, Mount, mtn., Ant.	A32	7
Wade Hampton, S.C., U.S.	*B3	117
Wadena, Sask.	F4	75
Wadena, In., U.S.	C3	91
Wadena, Ia., U.S.	B6	92
Wadena, Mn., U.S.	D3	100
Wadena, co., Mn., U.S.	D4	100
Wadesboro, N.C., U.S.	C2	110
Wadesville, In., U.S.	H2	91
Wadham Islands, is., Newf.	D5	72
Wadhwān see Surendranagar, India	F3	37
Wādī al Jayb (Ha Arava), val., Asia	G10	40
Wādī al Jōz (part of Jerusalem), Isr. Occ.	m14	41
Wading, stm., N.J., U.S.	D3	107
Wading, West Branch, stm., N.J., U.S.	D3	107
Wading River, N.J., U.S.	D4	107
Wading River, N.Y., U.S.	n16	109
Wadley, Al., U.S.	B4	78
Wadley, Ga., U.S.	D4	87
Wad Madanī, Sud.	C3	47
Wadmalaw Island, i., S.C., U.S.	F7	117
Wadowice, Pol.	D5	26
Wadsworth, Al., U.S.	C3	78
Wadsworth, Il., U.S.	h9	90
Wadsworth, Nv., U.S.	D2	105
Wadsworth, Oh., U.S.	A4	112
Waelder, Tx., U.S.	E4	120
Wagarville, Al., U.S.	D1	78
Wagener, S.C., U.S.	D5	117
Wageningen, Sur.	A3	59
Wager Bay, b., N.W. Ter.	C15	66
Wagga, Sud.	B4	47
Wagga Wagga, Austl.	G8	50
Waggoner, Il., U.S.	D4	90
Waging [am See], W. Ger.	E6	18
Waginger Lake, l., W. Ger.	E6	18
Wagner, Mt., U.S.	B8	103
Wagner, S.D., U.S.	D7	118
Wagners Lake, Ne., U.S.	*C8	104
Wagoner, Ok., U.S.	B6	113
Wagoner, co., Ok., U.S.	B6	113
Wagon Mound, N.M., U.S.	A5	108
Wagontire Mountain, mtn., Or., U.S.	D7	114
Wagram, N.C., U.S.	C3	110
Wagrowiec, Pol.	B4	26
Waha, Libya	D3	43
Wahai, Indon.	F7	34
Wah Cantonment, Pak.	*B5	36
Wahiawa, Hi., U.S.	B3	88
Wahiawa Reservoir, res., Hi., U.S.	g9	88
Wahkiakum, co., Wa., U.S.	C2	124
Wahkon, Mn., U.S.	D5	100
Wahlen, Lake, l., Switz.	B5	21
Wahoo, Ne., U.S.	C9	104
Wahoo Creek, stm., Ne., U.S.	g11	104
Wahpeton, N.D., U.S.	C9	111
Wah Wah Mountains, mts., Ut., U.S.	E2	121
Wahweap Creek, stm., Ut., U.S.	F4	121
Waialae-Kahala, Hi., U.S.	g10	88
Waialua, Hi., U.S.	B3	88
Waialua Bay, b., Hi., U.S.	B3	88
Waianae, Hi., U.S.	B3	88
Waianae Range, mts., Hi., U.S.	B3	88
Waiau, stm., N.Z.	f9	88
Waiblingen, W. Ger.	E4	19
Waidhofen [an der Thaya], Aus.	D7	18
Waidhofen [an der Ybbs], Aus.	D7	18
Waigeo, i., Indon.	F8	34
Waihee, Hi., U.S.	*C5	88
Wai Islands, is., Camb.	H5	35
Waikabubak, Indon.	G5	34
Waikapu, Hi., U.S.	C5	88
Waikari, N.Z.	O14	51
Waikato, stm., N.Z.	L15	51
Waikawa, N.Z.	Q12	51
Waikelo, Indon.	G5	34
Waikiki Beach, Hi., U.S.	g10	88
Wailagi Lala, i., Fiji	H16	52
Wailea, Hi., U.S.	D6	88
Wailua, Hi., U.S.	A2	88
Wailuku, Hi., U.S.	C5	88
Wailuku, stm., Hi., U.S.	D6	88
Waimanalo, Hi., U.S.	B4	88
Waimate, N.Z.	P13	51
Waimea, Hi., U.S.	B2	88
Waimea, Hi., U.S.	C5	88
Waingapu, Indon.	G6	34
Waini Point, c., Guy.	A3	59
Wainunu Bay, b., Fiji	H15	52
Wainwright, Alta.	C5	68
Wainwright, Ak., U.S.	A8	79
Wainwright, Ok., U.S.	B6	113
Waiohinu, Hi., U.S.	D6	88
Waipahu, Hi., U.S.	B3	88
Waipara, N.Z.	O14	51
Waipio Acres, Hi., U.S.	g9	88
Waipio Peninsula, pen., Hi., U.S.	g10	88
Waipukurau, N.Z.	N16	51
Wairau, N.Z.	N14	51
Wairoa, N.Z.	M16	51
Waitaki, stm., N.Z.	P13	51
Waitara, N.Z.	M15	51
Waite, Me., U.S.	C5	96
Waite Park, Mn., U.S.	E4	100
Waitsburg, Wa., U.S.	C7	124
Waitsfield, Vt., U.S.	C3	122
Waits River, Vt., U.S.	C4	122
Waitville, Sask.	E3	75
Waiwo, Indon.	H8	34
Wajima, Japan	B13	31
Wajir, Kenya	A7	48
Waka, Eth.	A4	47
Waka, Zaire	A3	48
Waka, Tx., U.S.	A2	120
Wakarusa, In., U.S.	A5	91
Wakarusa, Ks., U.S.	D8	93
Wakarusa, stm., Ks., U.S.	D8	93
Wakasa Bay, b., Japan	I7	33
Wakatipu, Lake, l., N.Z.	P12	51
Wakatomika Creek, stm., Oh., U.S.	B3	112
Wakaw, Sask.	E3	75
Wakaya, i., Fiji	H15	52
Wakayama, Japan	E12	31
Wake, co., N.C., U.S.	B4	110
Wa Keeney, Ks., U.S.	C4	93
Wakefield, Que.	D2	74
Wakefield, Eng., U.K.	A6	12
Wakefield, Ks., U.S.	C6	93
Wakefield, La., U.S.	D4	95
Wakefield, Ma., U.S.	B5	98
Wakefield, Mi., U.S.	n12	99
Wakefield, Ne., U.S.	B9	104
Wakefield, N.H., U.S.	C4	106
Wakefield, Oh., U.S.	D2	112
Wakefield, R.I., U.S.	F3	116
Wakefield, Va., U.S.	D6	123
Wake Forest, N.C., U.S.	B4	110
Wake Island, dep., Oc.	E10	6
Wake Island Air Force Base, mil., Wake I.	B2	52
Wakema, Burma	D1	35
Wakeman, Oh., U.S.	A3	112
Wakenda, Mo., U.S.	B4	102
Wakita, Ok., U.S.	A4	113
Wakonda, S.D., U.S.	D8	118
Wakopa, Pol.	D5	26
Wakpala, S.D., U.S.	B5	118
Wakuach, Lac, l., Que.	g9	72
Wakunga, Ang.	D2	48
Wakulla, Fl., U.S.	B2	86
Wakulla, co., Fl., U.S.	B2	86
Walachia, hist. reg., Rom.	C7	24
Walbourg, Fr.	F7	17
Walbridge, Oh., U.S.	e6	112
Wałbrzych (Waldenburg), Pol.	C4	26
Walchen Lake, l., W. Ger.	B7	20
Walcott, Ar., U.S.	A5	81
Walcott, Ia., U.S.	C7	92
Walcott, N.D., U.S.	C9	111
Walcott, Wy., U.S.	E6	127
Walcott, Lake, res., Id., U.S.	G5	89
Wałcz, Pol.	B3	26
Wald, Switz.	B6	21
Waldbröl, W. Ger.	C2	19
Waldeck, Sask.	G2	75
Walden, Ont.	A3	73
Walden, Co., U.S.	A4	83
Walden, N.Y., U.S.	D6	109
Walden Pond, l., Ma., U.S.	g10	98
Walden Ridge, mtn., Tn., U.S.	D8	119
Waldheim, Sask.	E2	75
Waldheim, E. Ger.	B8	19
Waldkappel, W. Ger.	B4	19
Waldkirchen, W. Ger.	E8	19
Waldmünchen, W. Ger.	D7	19
Waldo, B.C.	E10	69
Waldo, Ar., U.S.	D2	81
Waldo, Fl., U.S.	C4	86
Waldo, Ks., U.S.	C5	93
Waldo, Oh., U.S.	B3	112
Waldo, co., Me., U.S.	D3	96
Waldoboro, Me., U.S.	D3	96
Waldo Lake, l., Or., U.S.	D4	114
Waldorf, Md., U.S.	C4	97
Waldorf, Mn., U.S.	G5	100
Waldport, Or., U.S.	C2	114
Waldron, Sask.	G4	75
Waldron, Ar., U.S.	C1	81
Waldron, In., U.S.	F6	91
Waldron, Mo., U.S.	h10	102
Waldsassen, W. Ger.	C7	19
Waldshut, W. Ger.	E4	19
Waldwick, N.J., U.S.	A4	107
Walen, Lake, l., Switz.	B5	21
Wales, Ak., U.S.	B6	79
Wales, N.D., U.S.	A7	111
Wales, Ut., U.S.	D4	121
Wales, ter., U.K.	D5	10
Waleska, Ga., U.S.	B2	87
Walford Station, Ont.	A2	73
Walgett, Austl.	B8	50
Walgreen Coast, Ant.	B2	7
Walhalla, N.D., U.S.	A8	111
Walhalla, S.C., U.S.	B1	117
Walhonding, stm., Oh., U.S.	B3	112
Walikale, Zaire	B5	48
Walker, Ia., U.S.	B6	92
Walker, La., U.S.	g10	95
Walker, Mn., U.S.	C4	100
Walker, Mo., U.S.	D3	102
Walker, S.D., U.S.	B4	118
Walker, co., Al., U.S.	B2	78
Walker, co., Ga., U.S.	B1	87
Walker, co., Tx., U.S.	D5	120
Walker, stm., Nv., U.S.	D3	105
Walker Lake, l., Man.	B3	70
Walker Lake, l., Nv., U.S.	E3	105
Walker Mill, Md., U.S.	*C4	97
Walker Mountain, mtn., Ga., U.S.	B3	87
Walker Mountain, mtn., Va., U.S.	C1	123
Walker River Indian Reservation, Nv., U.S.	D3	105
Walker Springs, Al., U.S.	D2	78
Walkersville, Md., U.S.	B3	97
Walkersville, W.V., U.S.	C4	125
Walkerton, Ont.	C3	73
Walkerton, In., U.S.	B5	91
Walkerville, Mi., U.S.	E4	99
Walkerville, Mt., U.S.	D4	103
Wall, S.D., U.S.	D3	118
Walla, N.S.	D6	71
Wallace, Ont.	B6	73
Wallace, Id., U.S.	B3	89
Wallace, In., U.S.	E3	91
Wallace, Ks., U.S.	D2	93
Wallace, Mi., U.S.	C3	99
Wallace, N.C., U.S.	C5	110
Wallace, Ne., U.S.	D4	104
Wallace, N.Y., U.S.	C3	109
Wallace, S.D., U.S.	B8	118
Wallace, Va., U.S.	f9	123
Wallace, W.V., U.S.	B4	125
Wallace, co., Ks., U.S.	D2	93
Wallaceburg, Ont.	E2	73
Wallace Lake, res., La., U.S.	B2	95
Wallacetown, Ont.	E3	73
Wallagrass, Me., U.S.	A4	96
Walland, Tn., U.S.	D10	119
Wallaroo, Austl.	F6	50
Wallasey, Eng., U.K.	D5	10
Walla Walla, Wa., U.S.	C7	124
Walla Walla, co., Wa., U.S.	C7	124
Walla Walla, stm., U.S.	C7	124
Walled Lake, Mi., U.S.	o15	99
Wallen Ridge, mtn., Tn., U.S.	C10	119
Waller, Tx., U.S.	q14	120
Waller, co., Tx., U.S.	E4	120
Wallingford, Eng., U.K.	C6	12
Wallingford, Ct., U.S.	D4	84
Wallingford, Ia., U.S.	A3	92
Wallingford, Vt., U.S.	E3	122
Wallis, Tx., U.S.	E4	120
Wallis and Futuna, dep., Oc.	G11	6
Wallis Sands, N.H., U.S.	D5	106
Wallkill, N.Y., U.S.	D6	109
Wallkill, stm., N.Y., U.S.	D6	109
Wall Lake, Ia., U.S.	B2	92
Wall Lake, l., Ia., U.S.	B4	92
Walloomsac, stm., Vt., U.S.	F2	122
Walloon Lake, l., Mi., U.S.	C6	99
Wallowa, Or., U.S.	B9	114
Wallowa, co., Or., U.S.	B9	114
Wallowa Mountains, mts., Or., U.S.	B9	114
Wallpack Center, N.J., U.S.	A3	107
Walls, Ms., U.S.	A3	101
Wallsburg, Ut., U.S.	C4	121
Wallsend, Eng., U.K.	C6	10
Wallula, Wa., U.S.	C7	124
Wallula, Lake, res., U.S.	C7	124
Wallum Lake, l., U.S.	A1	116
Walney, Isle of, i., Eng., U.K.	C5	10
Walnut, Ca., U.S.	*m13	82
Walnut, Il., U.S.	B4	90
Walnut, Ia., U.S.	C2	92
Walnut, Ks., U.S.	E8	93
Walnut, Ms., U.S.	A5	101
Walnut, N.C., U.S.	f10	110
Walnut, stm., Ks., U.S.	E6	93
Walnut Bottom, Pa., U.S.	F7	115
Walnut Canyon National Monument, Az., U.S.	B4	80
Walnut Cove, N.C., U.S.	A2	110
Walnut Creek, Ca., U.S.	h8	82
Walnut Creek, stm., Ks., U.S.	D4	93
Walnut Creek West, Ca., U.S.	*D2	82
Walnut Grove, Al., U.S.	A3	78
Walnut Grove, Mn., U.S.	F3	100
Walnut Grove, Ms., U.S.	C4	101
Walnut Grove, Mo., U.S.	D4	102
Walnut Hill, Fl., U.S.	u14	86
Walnut Hill, Il., U.S.	E5	90
Walnut Hill, Ma., U.S.	g7	98
Walnut Mountain, hill, Ct., U.S.	B3	84
Walnut Park, Ca., U.S.	*n12	82
Walnutport, Pa., U.S.	E10	115
Walnut Ridge, Ar., U.S.	A5	81
Walpole, Sask.	H5	75
Walpole, Ma., U.S.	B5	98
Walpole, N.H., U.S.	D2	106
Walsall, Eng., U.K.	D6	10
Walsenburg, Co., U.S.	D6	83
Walsh, Alta.	E5	68
Walsh, Co., U.S.	D8	83
Walsh, co., N.D., U.S.	A8	111
Walsingham, Cape, c., N.W. Ter.	C20	66
Walsrode, W. Ger.	F3	15
Walston, Pa., U.S.	E4	115
Walter Bathurst, Cape, c., N.W. Ter.	B17	66
Walterboro, S.C., U.S.	F6	117
Walter F. George Dam, U.S.	D4	78
Walter F. George Lake, res., U.S.	D4	78
Walterhill, Tn., U.S.	B5	119
Walters, La., U.S.	C4	95
Walters, Mn., U.S.	G5	100
Walters, Ok., U.S.	C3	113
Walters, Va., U.S.	D6	123
Walters Falls, Ont.	C4	73
Walthausen, E. Ger.	C5	19
Walthall, Ms., U.S.	B4	101
Walthall, co., Ms., U.S.	D3	101
Waltham, Que.	D1	74
Waltham, Ma., U.S.	B5	98
Waltham, Mn., U.S.	G6	100
Walthourville, Ga., U.S.	E5	87
Walton, N.S.	D6	71
Walton, Ont.	C4	73
Walton, In., U.S.	C5	91
Walton, Ky., U.S.	B5	94
Walton, N.Y., U.S.	C5	109
Walton, W.V., U.S.	C3	125

Name	Map Ref.	Page

Walton, Ks., U.S. — D6 93
Walton, Ky., U.S. — B5 94
Walton, Ne., U.S. — h11 104
Walton, N.Y., U.S. — C5 109
Walton, W.V., U.S. — C3 125
Walton, co., Fl., U.S. — u15 86
Walton, co., Ga., U.S. — C3 87
Waltonville, Il., U.S. — E4 90
Walvisbaai (Walvis Bay), S. Afr. — B1 49
Walvis Bay see Walvisbaai, S. Afr. — B1 49
Walworth, N.Y., U.S. — B3 109
Walworth, Wi., U.S. — F5 126
Walworth, co., S.D., U.S. — B5 118
Walworth, co., Wi., U.S. — F5 126
Wamac, Il., U.S. — E4 90
Wamba, Nig. — E6 45
Wamba, Zaire — A4 48
Wamba, stm., Afr. — C2 48
Wamego, Ks., U.S. — C7 93
Wamesit, Ma., U.S. — A5 98
Wami, stm., Tan. — C6 48
Wamic, Or., U.S. — B5 114
Wampsville, N.Y., U.S. — B5 109
Wampum, Pa., U.S. — E1 115
Wamsutter, Wy., U.S. — E5 127
Wāna, Pak. — A3 36
Wanaka, N.Z. — P12 51
Wanaka, Lake, l., N.Z. — P12 51
Wanakena, N.Y., U.S. — A6 109
Wanamie, Pa., U.S. — D9 115
Wanamingo, Mn., U.S. — F6 100
Wan'an, China — K6 32
Wanapitei, stm., Ont. — A4 73
Wanapum Dam, Wa., U.S. — C6 124
Wanapum Lake, res., Wa., U.S. — B6 124
Wanaque, N.J., U.S. — A4 107
Wanaque Reservoir, res., N.J., U.S. — A4 107
Wanatah, In., U.S. — B4 91
Wanblee, S.D., U.S. — D4 118
Wanchese, N.C., U.S. — B7 110
Wanda, Mn., U.S. — F3 100
Wandering River, Alta. — B4 68
Wando, S. Kor. — I3 33
Wando, S.C., U.S. — F8 117
Wando, stm., S.C., U.S. — F8 117
Wandoan, Austl. — C7 51
Wando Woods, S.C., U.S. — k11 117
Wandsworth (part of London), Eng., U.K. — m12 10
Wanette, Ok., U.S. — C4 113
Wang, stm., Thai. — D3 35
Wanganui, N.Z. — M15 51
Wangaratta, Austl. — G8 50
Wangen [im Allgäu], W. Ger. — B5 20
Wangerooge, i., W. Ger. — B3 18
Wangkui, China — A12 32
Wangqing, China — C10 31
Wanham, Alta. — B1 68
Wanilla, Ms., U.S. — D3 101
Wanipigow, stm., Can. — D4 70
Wankie National Park, Zimb. — A4 49
Wann, Ne., U.S. — g12 104
Wann, Ok., U.S. — A6 113
Wannaska, Mn., U.S. — B3 100
Wanship, Ut., U.S. — C4 121
Wantage, Eng., U.K. — C6 12
Wantagh, N.Y., U.S. — *E7 109
Wanup, Ont. — A4 73
Wanxian, China — E6 31
Wanzai, China — J6 32
Wapakoneta, Oh., U.S. — B1 112
Wapanucka, Ok., U.S. — C5 113
Wapato, Wa., U.S. — C5 124
Wapawekka Hills, hills, Sask. — C3 75
Wapawekka Lake, l., Sask. — C3 75
Wapella, Sask. — G5 75
Wapella, Il., U.S. — C5 90
Wapello, Ia., U.S. — C6 92
Wapello, co., Ia., U.S. — C5 92
Wapisu Lake, l., Man. — B2 70
Wapiti, Wy., U.S. — B3 127
Wapiti, stm., Can. — B1 68
Wapiti Ridge, mtn., Wy., U.S. — B3 127
Wappapello, Mo., U.S. — E7 102
Wappapello, Lake, res., Mo., U.S. — D7 102
Wappingers Falls, N.Y., U.S. — D7 109
Wapsipinicon, stm., Ia., U.S. — B6 92
Wapske, N.B. — C2 71
Wapus Lake, l., Sask. — A4 75
Wapwallopen, Pa., U.S. — D9 115
Wāqid, Eg. — D2 41
Waqqās, Jord. — B7 41
Waquoit, Ma., U.S. — C6 98
War, W.V., U.S. — D3 125
Waramaug, Lake, l., Ct., U.S. — C2 84
Warangal, India — E6 36
Warba, Mn., U.S. — C5 100
Warburg, Alta. — C3 68
Warburg, W. Ger. — B4 19
Warburton, Austl. — H5 51
Warburton Creek, stm., Austl. — E6 50
Ward, Al., U.S. — C1 78
Ward, Ar., U.S. — B4 81
Ward, Co., U.S. — *A5 83
Ward, S.C., U.S. — D4 117
Ward, S.D., U.S. — C9 118
Ward, co., N.D., U.S. — A4 111
Ward, co., Tx., U.S. — D1 120
Ward, Mount, mtn., Ant. — B6 7
Wardell, Mo., U.S. — E8 102
Warden, Que. — C4 68
Warden, Wa., U.S. — B6 124
Warden, La., U.S. — B4 95
Wardensville, W.V., U.S. — B6 125
Warder, l., W. Ger. — E4 15
Wardha, India — D6 36
Wardha, stm., India — D6 36
Ward Hill, hill, Scot., U.K. — B5 13
Wardlow, Alta. — D5 68
Ward Mountain, mtn., Mt., U.S. — D2 103
Wardner, B.C. — E10 69
Wardsboro, Vt., U.S. — E3 122
Wardsville, Ont. — E3 73
Wardville, Ok., U.S. — C5 113
Ware, Ma., U.S. — B3 98
Ware, Ga., U.S. — E4 87
Ware, stm., Ma., U.S. — B3 98
War Eagle, W.V., U.S. — D3 125
War Eagle Creek, stm., Ar., U.S. — A2 81
War Eagle Mountain, mtn., Id., U.S. — G2 89
Wareham, Eng., U.K. — D5 12
Wareham, Ma., U.S. — C6 98
Warehouse Point, Ct., U.S. — B5 84
Waren, E. Ger. — B6 18
Waren, Indon. — F9 34

Warendorf, W. Ger. — B2 19
Waresboro, Ga., U.S. — E4 87
Ware Shoals, S.C., U.S. — C3 117
Waretown, N.J., U.S. — D4 107
Warfield, B.C. — E9 69
Warfield, Ky., U.S. — C7 94
Warfield, Va., U.S. — D5 123
Warfordsburg, Pa., U.S. — G5 115
Wargla, Alg. — C6 44
Warin, E. Ger. — E5 15
Waring, Tx., U.S. — E3 120
Wark, Eng., U.K. — E6 13
Warkworth, Ont. — C7 73
Warkworth, N.Z. — L15 51
Warley see Smethwick, Eng., U.K. — D5 10
Warman, Sask. — E2 75
Warman, Mn., U.S. — D5 100
Warmbad, Nmb. — C2 49
Warmbad, S. Afr. — B4 49
Warm Beach, Wa., U.S. — A3 124
Warminster, Eng., U.K. — C5 12
Warminster, Pa., U.S. — F11 115
Warm Lake, Id., U.S. — E3 89
Warm River, Id., U.S. — E7 89
Warm Springs, Ar., U.S. — A4 81
Warm Springs, Ga., U.S. — D2 87
Warm Springs, Nv., U.S. — E5 105
Warm Springs, Or., U.S. — C5 114
Warm Springs, Va., U.S. — B3 123
Warm Springs Indian Reservation, Or., U.S. — C5 114
Warm Springs Reservoir, res., Or., U.S. — D8 114
Warnemünde (part of Rostock), E. Ger. — A6 18
Warner, Alta. — E4 68
Warner, N.H., U.S. — D3 106
Warner, Oh., U.S. — C4 112
Warner, Ok., U.S. — B6 113
Warner, S.D., U.S. — B7 118
Warner, stm., N.H., U.S. — D3 106
Warner Mountain, mtn., Ma., U.S. — B1 98
Warner Mountains, mts., Ca., U.S. — B3 82
Warner Peak, mtn., Or., U.S. — E7 114
Warner Robins, Ga., U.S. — D3 87
Warner Springs, Ca., U.S. — F5 82
Warnes, Bol. — C3 55
Warnow, stm., E. Ger. — B5 18
Warpath, stm., Man. — C2 70
Warracknabeal, Austl. — H4 51
Warr Acres, Ok., U.S. — B4 113
Warragul, Austl. — I5 51
Warrego, stm., Austl. — E8 50
Warren, Austl. — E6 51
Warren, Ont. — A4 73
Warren, Ar., U.S. — D3 81
Warren, Ct., U.S. — C2 84
Warren, Id., U.S. — D3 89
Warren, Il., U.S. — A4 90
Warren, In., U.S. — C7 91
Warren, Me., U.S. — D3 96
Warren, Ma., U.S. — B3 98
Warren, Mi., U.S. — F7 99
Warren, Mn., U.S. — B2 100
Warren, N.H., U.S. — C3 106
Warren, N.Y., U.S. — C6 109
Warren, Oh., U.S. — A5 112
Warren, Ok., U.S. — C2 113
Warren, Or., U.S. — B4 114
Warren, Pa., U.S. — C3 115
Warren, R.I., U.S. — D5 116
Warren, Tx., U.S. — D5 120
Warren, Vt., U.S. — C3 122
Warren, co., Ga., U.S. — C4 87
Warren, co., Il., U.S. — C3 90
Warren, co., In., U.S. — D3 91
Warren, co., Ia., U.S. — C4 92
Warren, co., Ky., U.S. — C3 94
Warren, co., Ms., U.S. — C3 101
Warren, co., Mo., U.S. — C6 102
Warren, co., N.J., U.S. — B3 107
Warren, co., N.Y., U.S. — B7 109
Warren, co., N.C., U.S. — A4 110
Warren, co., Oh., U.S. — C1 112
Warren, co., Pa., U.S. — C3 115
Warren, co., Tn., U.S. — D8 119
Warren, co., Va., U.S. — B4 123
Warren, stm., U.S. — D5 116
Warren Center, Pa., U.S. — C9 115
Warrendale, Pa., U.S. — h13 115
Warren Park, In., U.S. — k10 91
Warren Peaks, mts., Wy., U.S. — B8 127
Warrenpoint, N. Ire., U.K. — C5 11
Warren Point, R.I., U.S. — F6 116
Warrens, Wi., U.S. — D3 126
Warrensburg, Il., U.S. — D4 90
Warrensburg, Mo., U.S. — C4 102
Warrensburg, N.Y., U.S. — B7 109
Warrensville, Pa., U.S. — D8 115
Warrensville Heights, Oh., U.S. — h9 112
Warrenton, S. Afr. — C3 49
Warrenton, Ga., U.S. — C4 87
Warrenton, Mo., U.S. — C6 102
Warrenton, N.C., U.S. — A4 110
Warrenton, Or., U.S. — A3 114
Warrenton, Va., U.S. — B5 123
Warrenville, Ct., U.S. — B7 84
Warrenville, Il., U.S. — k8 90
Warrenville, S.C., U.S. — D4 117
Warri, Nig. — E6 45
Warrick, co., In., U.S. — H3 91
Warrington, Eng., U.K. — D5 10
Warrington, Fl., U.S. — u14 86
Warrior, Al., U.S. — B3 78
Warrior, stm., Pa., U.S. — *F11 115
Washington Park, Fl., U.S. — *F6 86
Washington Park, Il., U.S. — E3 90
Washington Terrace, Ut., U.S. — B4 121
Warrior Reservoir, res., Al., U.S. — C2 78
Warriors Mark, Pa., U.S. — E5 115
Warrnambool, Austl. — G7 50
Warroad, Mn., U.S. — B3 100
Warsaw (Warszawa), Pol. — B6 26
Warsaw, Il., U.S. — C2 90
Warsaw, In., U.S. — B6 91
Warsaw, Ky., U.S. — B5 94
Warsaw, Mo., U.S. — C4 102
Warsaw, N.Y., U.S. — C2 109
Warsaw, N.C., U.S. — B4 110
Warsaw, Oh., U.S. — B3 112
Warsaw, Va., U.S. — C6 123
Warspite, Alta. — B4 68
Warstein, W. Ger. — B3 19
Warta, Pol. — C5 26
Warta, stm., Pol. — B3 26
Wartburg, Tn., U.S. — C9 119
Warth, Aus. — B6 20
Warthen, Ga., U.S. — C4 87
Wartime, Sask. — F1 75

Wartrace, Tn., U.S. — B5 119
Warwick, Austl. — D8 51
Warwick, Ont. — D3 73
Warwick, Que. — D6 74
Warwick, Eng., U.K. — D6 10
Warwick, Ga., U.S. — E3 87
Warwick, Md., U.S. — B6 97
Warwick, Ma., U.S. — A3 98
Warwick, N.Y., U.S. — D6 109
Warwick, N.D., U.S. — B7 111
Warwick, Ok., U.S. — B4 113
Warwick, Pa., U.S. — F10 115
Warwick, R.I., U.S. — D4 116
Warwick Dam, R.I., U.S. — E3 87
Warwickshire, co., Eng., U.K. — B6 12
Wasaga Beach, Ont. — C4 73
Wasatch, co., Ut., U.S. — C4 121
Wasatch Plateau, plat., Ut., U.S. — D4 121
Wasatch Range, mts., U.S. — B5 76
Wascana Creek, stm., Sask. — G3 75
Wasco, Ca., U.S. — E4 82
Wasco, Or., U.S. — B6 114
Wasco, co., Or., U.S. — B5 114
Waseca, Sask. — D1 75
Waseca, Mn., U.S. — F5 100
Waseca, co., Mn., U.S. — F5 100
Washademoak Lake, l., N.B. — D4 71
Washago, Ont. — C5 73
Washakie, co., Wy., U.S. — C4 127
Washakie Needles, mts., Wy., U.S. — C3 127
Washburn, Il., U.S. — C4 90
Washburn, Ia., U.S. — B5 92
Washburn, Me., U.S. — B4 96
Washburn, Mo., U.S. — E4 102
Washburn, N.D., U.S. — B5 111
Washburn, Tn., U.S. — C10 119
Washburn, Wi., U.S. — B3 126
Washburn, co., Wi., U.S. — C2 126
Washburn, Mount, mtn., Wy., U.S. — B2 127
Washington, Ar., U.S. — D2 81
Washington, Ct., U.S. — C2 84
Washington, D.C., U.S. — C3 97
Washington, Ga., U.S. — C4 87
Washington, Il., U.S. — C4 90
Washington, In., U.S. — G3 91
Washington, Ia., U.S. — C6 92
Washington, Ks., U.S. — C6 93
Washington, Ky., U.S. — B6 94
Washington, La., U.S. — D3 95
Washington, Ma., U.S. — B1 98
Washington, Ms., U.S. — D2 101
Washington, Mo., U.S. — C6 102
Washington, Ne., U.S. — g12 104
Washington, N.H., U.S. — D2 106
Washington, N.J., U.S. — B3 107
Washington, N.C., U.S. — B5 110
Washington, Ok., U.S. — B4 113
Washington, Pa., U.S. — F1 115
Washington, Tn., U.S. — D9 119
Washington, Ut., U.S. — F2 121
Washington, Va., U.S. — B4 123
Washington, W.V., U.S. — B3 125
Washington, co., Al., U.S. — D1 78
Washington, co., Ar., U.S. — A1 81
Washington, co., Co., U.S. — B7 83
Washington, co., Fl., U.S. — u16 86
Washington, co., Ga., U.S. — C4 87
Washington, co., Id., U.S. — E2 89
Washington, co., Il., U.S. — E4 90
Washington, co., In., U.S. — G5 91
Washington, co., Ia., U.S. — C6 92
Washington, co., Ks., U.S. — C6 93
Washington, co., Ky., U.S. — C4 94
Washington, co., Me., U.S. — D5 96
Washington, co., Md., U.S. — A2 97
Washington, co., Mn., U.S. — E6 100
Washington, co., Ms., U.S. — B3 101
Washington, co., Mo., U.S. — D7 102
Washington, co., Ne., U.S. — C9 104
Washington, co., N.Y., U.S. — B7 109
Washington, co., N.C., U.S. — B6 110
Washington, co., Oh., U.S. — C4 112
Washington, co., Ok., U.S. — A6 113
Washington, co., Or., U.S. — B3 114
Washington, co., Pa., U.S. — F1 115
Washington, co., R.I., U.S. — E2 116
Washington, co., Tn., U.S. — C11 119
Washington, co., Tx., U.S. — D4 120
Washington, co., Ut., U.S. — F2 121
Washington, co., Va., U.S. — f9 123
Washington, co., Vt., U.S. — C3 122
Washington, co., Wi., U.S. — E5 126
Washington, state, U.S. — B5 124
Washington, Cape, c., Fiji — I14 52
Washington, Lake, l., Fl., U.S. — D6 86
Washington, Lake, l., Mn., U.S. — E4 100
Washington, Lake, l., Ms., U.S. — B3 101
Washington, Lake, l., Wa., U.S. — e11 124
Washington, Mount, mtn., N.H., U.S. — B4 106
Washington Court House, Oh., U.S. — C2 112
Washington Crossing, N.J., U.S. — C3 107
Washington Depot, Ct., U.S. — C2 84
Washington Island, i., Wi., U.S. — C7 126
Washington Island see Teraina Island, i., Kir. — F12 6
Washington Park, Fl., U.S. — *F6 86
Washington Park, Il., U.S. — E3 90
Washington Terrace, Ut., U.S. — B4 121
Washington Township, N.J., U.S. — *B4 107
Washingtonville, Pa., U.S. — D8 115
Washita, Ok., U.S. — B3 113
Washita, co., Ok., U.S. — B2 113
Washita, stm., Ok., U.S. — C4 113
Washoe, co., Nv., U.S. — C2 105
Washoe City, Nv., U.S. — D2 105
Washougal, Wa., U.S. — D3 124
Washow Bay, b., Man. — D3 70
Washta, Ia., U.S. — B2 92
Washtenaw, co., Mi., U.S. — F7 99
Washtucna, Wa., U.S. — C7 124
Wasilków, Pol. — A8 111
Wasilla, Ak., U.S. — C10 79
Wasioja, Mn., U.S. — F6 100
Waskada, Man. — E1 70
Waskaganish, Que. — h11 74
Waskaiowaka Lake, l., Man. — A3 70
Waskatenau, Alta. — B4 68
Waskesiu Lake, l., Sask. — D2 75
Waskish, Mn., U.S. — B4 100
Waskom, Tx., U.S. — C5 120
Waspam, Nic. — C5 62

Wasque Point, c., Ma., U.S. — D7 98
Wassaw Sound, strt., Ga., U.S. — E6 87
Wassenaar, Neth. — B4 17
Wasseralfingen, W. Ger. — E5 19
Wasserburg [am Inn], W. Ger. — D6 18
Wasserkuppe, mtn., W. Ger. — C4 19
Wass Lake, l., Man. — C4 70
Wassookeag, Lake, l., Me., U.S. — C3 96
Wassuk Range, mts., Nv., U.S. — E3 105
Wassy-sur-Blaise, Fr. — F4 17
Wasta, S.D., U.S. — C3 118
Waswanipi, Que. — o20 74
Watampone, Indon. — F6 34
Watapi Lake, l., Sask. — B6 68
Watatic, Mount, mtn., Ma., U.S. — A4 98
Watauga, S.D., U.S. — B4 118
Watauga, Tn., U.S. — C11 119
Watauga, Tx., U.S. — *n9 120
Watauga, co., N.C., U.S. — A1 110
Watauga, stm., Tn., U.S. — C12 119
Watauga Lake, res., Tn., U.S. — C12 119
Watchaug Pond, l., R.I., U.S. — F2 116
Watchet, Eng., U.K. — C4 12
Watch Hill, R.I., U.S. — G1 116
Watch Hill Point, c., R.I., U.S. — G1 116
Watchung, N.J., U.S. — B4 107
Waterboro, Me., U.S. — E2 96
Waterbury, Ct., U.S. — C3 84
Waterbury, Ne., U.S. — B9 104
Waterbury, Vt., U.S. — C3 122
Waterbury Center, Vt., U.S. — C3 122
Waterbury Reservoir, res., Vt., U.S. — C3 122
Waterdown, Ont. — D5 73
Wateree, stm., S.C., U.S. — D6 117
Wateree Lake, res., S.C., U.S. — C6 117
Waterfall, Ak., U.S. — n23 79
Waterflow, N.M., U.S. — A1 108
Waterford, Ont. — E4 73
Waterford, P.E.I. — C5 71
Waterford, Ire. — D10 10
Waterford, Ct., U.S. — D7 84
Waterford, In., U.S. — A4 91
Waterford, Mi., U.S. — *F7 99
Waterford, N.Y., U.S. — C7 109
Waterford, Oh., U.S. — C4 112
Waterford, Wi., U.S. — F5 126
Waterford, co., Ire. — E4 11
Waterford Harbour, b., Ire. — E5 11
Waterford Mills, In., U.S. — A6 91
Waterford Works, N.J., U.S. — D3 107
Watergrasshill, Ire. — E3 11
Waterhen Lake, l., Man. — C2 70
Waterloo, Bel. — D4 17
Waterloo, Ont. — D4 73
Waterloo, Que. — D5 74
Waterloo, S.L. — E2 45
Waterloo, Al., U.S. — A1 78
Waterloo, Ar., U.S. — D2 81
Waterloo, Il., U.S. — E3 90
Waterloo, Ia., U.S. — B5 92
Waterloo, Ks., U.S. — E4 103
Waterloo, Ne., U.S. — g12 104
Waterloo, N.Y., U.S. — C4 109
Waterloo, Or., U.S. — C4 114
Waterloo, S.C., U.S. — C3 117
Waterloo, Wi., U.S. — E5 126
Waterloo, co., Ont. — D4 73
Waterman, Il., U.S. — B5 90
Waterman Four Corners, R.I., U.S. — C3 116
Waterman Reservoir, res., R.I., U.S. — B3 116
Waterport, N.Y., U.S. — B2 109
Waterproof, La., U.S. — C4 95
Waters, Mi., U.S. — D6 99
Watersmeet, Mi., U.S. — n12 99
Waterton, Mn., U.S.A. — E4 68
Waterton-Glacier International Peace Park, N.A. — B3 103
Waterton Lakes National Park, Alta. — E4 68
Waterton Park, Alta. — E4 68
Watertown, Ct., U.S. — C3 84
Watertown, Fl., U.S. — B4 86
Watertown, Ma., U.S. — g11 98
Watertown, N.Y., U.S. — B5 109
Watertown, S.D., U.S. — C8 118
Watertown, Tn., U.S. — A5 119
Watertown, Wi., U.S. — E5 126
Water Valley, Ky., U.S. — f9 94
Water Valley, Ms., U.S. — A4 101
Water View, Va., U.S. — C6 123
Water Village, N.H., U.S. — C4 106
Waterville, N.S. — D5 71
Waterville, Ire. — F1 11
Waterville, Ia., U.S. — A6 92
Waterville, Ks., U.S. — C7 93
Waterville, Me., U.S. — D3 96
Waterville, Ma., U.S. — A3 98
Waterville, Mn., U.S. — F5 100
Waterville, N.Y., U.S. — C5 109
Waterville, Oh., U.S. — A2 112
Waterville, Pa., U.S. — D7 115
Waterville, Vt., U.S. — B3 122
Waterville, Wa., U.S. — B5 124
Waterville Valley, N.H., U.S. — C3 106
Watervliet, Bel. — C3 17
Watervliet, Mi., U.S. — F4 99
Watervliet, N.Y., U.S. — C7 109
Watford, Ont. — E3 73
Watford, Eng., U.K. — k12 10
Watford City, N.D., U.S. — B2 111
Watha, N.C., U.S. — C5 110
Wathena, Ks., U.S. — C9 93
Watino, Alta. — B2 68
Watkins, Co., U.S. — *B6 83
Watkins, Ia., U.S. — B5 92
Watkins, Mn., U.S. — E4 100
Watkins Glen, N.Y., U.S. — C4 109
Watkinsville, Ga., U.S. — C3 87
Watonga, Ok., U.S. — B3 113
Watonwan, co., Mn., U.S. — F4 100
Watonwan, stm., Mn., U.S. — G4 100
Watou, Bel. — D1 17
Watova, Ok., U.S. — A6 113
Watrous, Sask. — F3 75
Watrous, N.M., U.S. — B5 108
Watsa, Zaire — A5 48
Watseka, Il., U.S. — C6 90
Watson, Sask. — E3 75

Watson, Ar., U.S. — D4 81
Watson, Il., U.S. — D5 90
Watson, In., U.S. — H6 91
Watson, Mn., U.S. — E3 100
Watson, Mo., U.S. — A2 102
Watson, Ok., U.S. — C7 113
Watson Chapel, Ar., U.S. — C3 81
Watson Lake, Yukon — D7 66
Watsontown, Pa., U.S. — D8 115
Watsonville, Ca., U.S. — D3 82
Watten, Fr. — D10 12
Watten, Fr. — D2 17
Watten, Loch, l., Scot., U.K. — B5 13
Wattenberg, Co., U.S. — A6 83
Wattensaw Bayou, stm., Ar., U.S. — C4 81
Watton, Mi., U.S. — B2 99
Wattrelos, Fr. — B5 16
Watts (part of Los Angeles), U.S. — n12 82
Watts, Ok., U.S. — A7 113
Watts Bar Dam, Tn., U.S. — D9 119
Watts Bar Dam, Tn., U.S. — D9 119
Watts Bar Lake, res., Tn., U.S. — D9 119
Wattsburg, Pa., U.S. — B2 115
Wattsville, Al., U.S. — B3 78
Wattsville, S.C., U.S. — B4 117
Wattwil, Switz. — B5 20
Watu, Zaire — B3 48
Watubela Islands, is., Indon. — F8 34
Watuppa Pond, l., Ma., U.S. — C5 98
Waubamik, Ont. — B4 73
Waubaushene, Ont. — C5 73
Waubay, S.D., U.S. — B8 118
Waubay Lake, l., S.D., U.S. — B8 118
Waubun, Mn., U.S. — C3 100
Wauchope, Austl. — F9 51
Wauchope, Sask. — H5 75
Wauchula, Fl., U.S. — E5 86
Wauconda, Il., U.S. — h8 90
Wauconda, Wa., U.S. — A6 124
Waukau, Wi., U.S. — E5 126
Waukeenah, Fl., U.S. — B3 86
Waukegan, Il., U.S. — A6 90
Waukesha, Wi., U.S. — F5 126
Waukesha, co., Wi., U.S. — E5 126
Waukewan, Lake, l., N.H., U.S. — C3 106
Waukomis, Ok., U.S. — A4 113
Waukon, Ia., U.S. — A6 92
Wauna, Wa., U.S. — f10 124
Waunakee, Wi., U.S. — E4 126
Wauneta, Ne., U.S. — D4 104
Waungumbaug Lake, l., Ct., U.S. — B6 84
Waupaca, Wi., U.S. — D5 126
Waupaca, co., Wi., U.S. — D5 126
Waupun, Wi., U.S. — E5 126
Wauregan, Ct., U.S. — C8 84
Waurika, Ok., U.S. — C4 113
Waurika Lake, res., Ok., U.S. — C3 113
Wausa, Ne., U.S. — B8 104
Wausau, Fl., U.S. — u16 86
Wausau, Wi., U.S. — D4 126
Wausau, Lake, res., Wi., U.S. — D4 126
Wausaukee, Wi., U.S. — C6 126
Wauseon, Oh., U.S. — A1 112
Waushara, co., Wi., U.S. — E4 126
Wautoma, Wi., U.S. — E4 126
Wauwatosa, Wi., U.S. — m12 126
Wauzeka, Wi., U.S. — E3 126
Waveland, In., U.S. — E3 91
Waveland, Ms., U.S. — E4 101
Waveney, stm., Eng., U.K. — D7 10
Waverley, Austl. — *F9 50
Waverley, Austl. — *G8 50
Waverly, N.S. — E6 71
Waverly, Al., U.S. — C4 78
Waverly, Ga., U.S. — E5 87
Waverly, Il., U.S. — D4 90
Waverly, Ia., U.S. — B5 92
Waverly, Ks., U.S. — D8 93
Waverly, Ky., U.S. — C2 94
Waverly, Mn., U.S. — E5 100
Waverly, Mo., U.S. — B4 102
Waverly, Ne., U.S. — D9 104
Waverly, N.Y., U.S. — C4 109
Waverly, Oh., U.S. — C3 112
Waverly, Tn., U.S. — A4 119
Waverly, Va., U.S. — C5 123
Waverly, W.V., U.S. — B3 125
Waverly Hall, Ga., U.S. — D2 87
Wavre, Bel. — D4 17
Wāw, Sud. — D2 47
Wawa, Ont. — o18 73
Wawa, Nig. — E5 45
Wawa, stm., Nic. — C6 62
Wawaka, In., U.S. — B7 91
Wāw al Kabīr, Libya — D3 43
Wawanesa, Man. — E2 70
Wawasee, Lake, l., In., U.S. — B6 91
Wawayanda Lake, l., N.J., U.S. — A4 107
Wawayanda Mountain, mtn., N.J., U.S. — A4 107
Waweig, Que. — D7 74
Wawota, Sask. — H4 75
Waxahachie, Tx., U.S. — C4 120
Waxhaw, N.C., U.S. — C2 110
Waxweiler, W. Ger. — D6 17
Waya, i., Fiji — H14 52
Wayagamac, Lac, l., Que. — B5 74
Wayan, Id., U.S. — G7 89
Waycross, Ga., U.S. — E4 87
Wayland, Ia., U.S. — C6 92
Wayland, Ky., U.S. — C7 94
Wayland, Ma., U.S. — g10 98
Wayland, Mi., U.S. — F5 99
Wayland, Mo., U.S. — A6 102
Wayland, N.Y., U.S. — C3 109
Wayland Springs, Tn., U.S. — B4 119
Waylyn, S.C., U.S. — k12 117
Waymart, Pa., U.S. — C11 115
Wayne, Alta. — D4 68
Wayne, Mi., U.S. — p15 99
Wayne, N.J., U.S. — B4 107
Wayne, N.Y., U.S. — C3 109
Wayne, Oh., U.S. — A2 112
Wayne, Ok., U.S. — C4 113
Wayne, Pa., U.S. — F11 115
Wayne, W.V., U.S. — C2 125
Wayne, co., Ga., U.S. — E5 87
Wayne, co., Il., U.S. — E5 90
Wayne, co., Ia., U.S. — D4 92
Wayne, co., Ky., U.S. — D5 94

Wayne, co., Mi., U.S. — F7 99
Wayne, co., Ms., U.S. — D5 101
Wayne, co., Mo., U.S. — D7 102
Wayne, co., Ne., U.S. — B8 104
Wayne, co., N.Y., U.S. — B3 109
Wayne, co., N.C., U.S. — B4 110
Wayne, co., Oh., U.S. — B4 112
Wayne, co., Pa., U.S. — C11 115
Wayne, co., Tn., U.S. — B4 119
Wayne, co., Ut., U.S. — E4 121
Wayne, co., W.V., U.S. — C2 125
Wayne City, Il., U.S. — E5 90
Waynesboro, Ms., U.S. — D5 101
Waynesboro, Ga., U.S. — C4 87
Waynesboro, Ms., U.S. — D5 101
Waynesboro, Pa., U.S. — G6 115
Waynesboro, Tn., U.S. — B4 119
Waynesboro, Va., U.S. — B3 123
Waynesburg, Ky., U.S. — C5 94
Waynesburg, Pa., U.S. — G1 115
Waynesville, Ga., U.S. — E5 87
Waynesville, Il., U.S. — C4 90
Waynesville, Mo., U.S. — D5 102
Waynesville, N.C., U.S. — f10 110
Waynetown, In., U.S. — C1 112
Waynoka, Ok., U.S. — A3 113
Wayside, Ks., U.S. — E8 93
Wayside, Ms., U.S. — B2 101
Wayside, Tx., U.S. — B2 120
Wayside, Wi., U.S. — h10 126
Wayzata, Mn., U.S. — n11 100
We, i., Indon. — J1 35
Weakley, co., Tn., U.S. — A3 119
Weare, N.H., U.S. — D3 106
Weatherby, Mo., U.S. — B3 102
Weatherford, Ok., U.S. — B3 113
Weatherford, Tx., U.S. — C4 120
Weatherly, Pa., U.S. — E10 115
Weatogue, Ct., U.S. — B4 84
Weaubleau, Mo., U.S. — D4 102
Weaver, Al., U.S. — B4 78
Weaver Lake, l., Man. — C3 70
Weaver Mountains, mts., Az., U.S. — C3 80
Weaverville, Ca., U.S. — B2 82
Weaverville, N.C., U.S. — f10 110
Webb, Sask. — G1 75
Webb, Al., U.S. — D4 78
Webb, Ia., U.S. — B2 92
Webb, Ms., U.S. — B3 101
Webb, co., Tx., U.S. — F3 120
Webb Air Force Base, mil., Tx., U.S. — C2 120
Webb City, Ar., U.S. — B2 81
Webb City, Mo., U.S. — D3 102
Webb City, Ok., U.S. — A5 113
Webber, Ks., U.S. — C5 93
Webber Lake, l., Man. — B5 70
Webbers Falls, Ok., U.S. — B6 113
Webberville, Mi., U.S. — F6 99
Webb Hill, hill, Ma., U.S. — B3 98
Webb Lake, l., Me., U.S. — D2 96
Webbville, Ky., U.S. — B7 94
Webbwood, Ont. — A3 73
Weber, co., Ut., U.S. — B4 121
Weber, Mount, mtn., B.C. — B3 69
Weber City, Va., U.S. — f9 123
Webster, Alta. — B1 68
Webster, Fl., U.S. — D4 86
Webster, In., U.S. — E8 91
Webster, Ma., U.S. — B4 98
Webster, Mn., U.S. — F5 100
Webster, N.H., U.S. — D3 106
Webster, N.Y., U.S. — B3 109
Webster, N.D., U.S. — A7 111
Webster, Oh., U.S. — B1 112
Webster, Pa., U.S. — F2 115
Webster, S.D., U.S. — B8 118
Webster, Tx., U.S. — r14 120
Webster, Wi., U.S. — C1 126
Webster, co., Ga., U.S. — D2 87
Webster, co., Ia., U.S. — B3 92
Webster, co., Ky., U.S. — C2 94
Webster, co., Ms., U.S. — B4 101
Webster, co., Mo., U.S. — D5 102
Webster, co., Ne., U.S. — D7 104
Webster, co., W.V., U.S. — C4 125
Webster City, Ia., U.S. — B4 92
Webster Groves, Mo., U.S. — f13 102
Webster Mills, Pa., U.S. — G5 115
Webster Reservoir, res., Ks., U.S. — C4 93
Webster Springs, W.V., U.S. — C4 125
Websterville, Vt., U.S. — C4 122
Wecota, S.D., U.S. — B6 118
Weda, Indon. — E7 34
Weddell Sea, Ant. — C9 7
Wedderburn, Or., U.S. — E2 114
Wedgefield, S.C., U.S. — D6 117
Wedgeport, N.S. — F4 71
Wedgewood, Mo., U.S. — f13 102
Wedowee, Al., U.S. — B4 78
Wedron, Il., U.S. — B5 90
Weed, Ca., U.S. — B2 82
Weed, N.M., U.S. — E4 108
Weed Heights, Nv., U.S. — E2 105
Weedon, Que. — D6 74
Weed Patch Hill, hill, In., U.S. — F5 91
Weedsport, N.Y., U.S. — B4 109
Weedville, Pa., U.S. — D5 115
Weehawken, N.J., U.S. — h8 107
Weekapaug, R.I., U.S. — G1 116
Weekes, Sask. — E4 75
Weeksbury, Ky., U.S. — C7 94
Weekstown, N.J., U.S. — D3 107
Weeksville, N.C., U.S. — A6 110
Weems, Va., U.S. — C6 123
Weener, W. Ger. — A7 19
Weeping Water, Ne., U.S. — D9 104
Weeping Water Creek, stm., Ne., U.S. — h12 104
Weert, Neth. — B6 16
Weesen, Switz. — B7 21
Weesp, Neth. — B5 16
Weferlingen, E. Ger. — A6 19
Wegdahl, Mn., U.S. — F2 100
Wegorzewo, Pol. — A7 26
Węgrów, Pol. — B7 26
Weggis, Switz. — B5 21
Wehr, W. Ger. — E4 21
Weiang, China — C7 31
Weida, E. Ger. — C7 19
Weiden, W. Ger. — D6 18
Weidman, Mi., U.S. — E6 99
Weifang, China — F11 31
Weigelstown, Pa., U.S. — *G8 115
Weihai, China — D9 31
Wei He, stm., China — E6 31
Weilburg, W. Ger. — C3 19
Weiler, W. Ger. — A8 21
Weilheim, W. Ger. — E5 18

Name	Map Ref.	Page
Weimar, E. Ger.	C5	18
Weimar, Tx., U.S.	E4	120
Weinan, China	E6	31
Weinböhla, E. Ger.	B8	19
Weiner, Ar., U.S.	B5	81
Weinert, Tx., U.S.	C3	120
Weinfelden, Switz.	A7	21
Weingarten, W. Ger.	D3	19
Weingarten, W. Ger.	A8	21
Weinheim, W. Ger.	D4	18
Weining, China	F5	31
Weinsberg, W. Ger.	D4	19
Weipa, Austl.	B7	50
Weippe, Id., U.S.	C3	89
Weir, Que.	D3	74
Weir, Ks., U.S.	E9	93
Weir, Ky., U.S.	C2	94
Weir, Ms., U.S.	B4	101
Weir, stm., U.S.	A4	70
Weir, Lake, l., Fl., U.S.	C5	86
Weirdale, Sask.	D3	75
Weir River, Man.	A4	70
Weirsdale, Fl., U.S.	D5	86
Weirton, W.V., U.S.	A4	125
Weisburg, In., U.S.	F7	91
Weiser, Id., U.S.	E2	89
Weiser, stm., Id., U.S.	E2	89
Weishan Lake, l., China	G7	32
Weishi, China	G6	32
Weisner Mountain, hill, Al., U.S.	A4	78
Weisse Elster, stm., E. Ger.	B7	19
Weissenburg, W. Ger.	D5	18
Weissenburg, Switz.	C3	21
Weissenfels, E. Ger.	B6	19
Weissenhorn, W. Ger.	A6	20
Weissert, Ne., U.S.	C6	104
Weisshorn, mtn., Switz.	C3	20
Weiss Lake, res., U.S.	A4	78
Weisswasser, E. Ger.	B9	19
Weitra, Aus.	E9	19
Weixi, China	F4	31
Weizhou Dao, i., China	B8	35
Wejherowo, Pol.	A5	26
Wekiva Springs, Fl., U.S.	*D5	86
Wekusko Lake, l., Man.	B2	70
Welaka, Fl., U.S.	C5	86
Welch, Ok., U.S.	A6	113
Welch, Tx., U.S.	C1	120
Welch, W.V., U.S.	D3	125
Welches, Or., U.S.	h10	95
Welcome, La., U.S.	h10	95
Welcome, Mn., U.S.	G4	100
Welcome, S.C., U.S.	B3	117
Weld, Me., U.S.	D2	96
Weld, co., Co., U.S.	A6	83
Welda, Ks., U.S.	D8	93
Welden, W. Ger.	B3	20
Weldon, Sask.	D3	75
Weldon, Ar., U.S.	B4	81
Weldon, Il., U.S.	C5	90
Weldon, Ia., U.S.	D4	92
Weldon, N.C., U.S.	A5	110
Weldon, Tx., U.S.	D5	120
Weldona, Co., U.S.	A7	83
Weldon Spring, Mo., U.S.	f12	102
Weleetka, Ok., U.S.	B5	113
Welega, prov., Eth.	D4	47
Welkom, S. Afr.	C4	49
Welland, Ont.	E5	73
Welland, stm., Eng., U.K.	D6	10
Wellandport, Ont.	D5	73
Wellborn, Fl., U.S.	B4	86
Wellborn, Tx., U.S.	D4	120
Wellersburg, Pa., U.S.	G4	115
Welles Harbor, b., Mid. Is.	K3	52
Wellesley, Ont.	D4	73
Wellesley, Ma., U.S.	B5	98
Wellesley Islands, is., Austl.	C6	50
Wellfleet, Ma., U.S.	C7	98
Wellfleet, Ne., U.S.	D5	104
Wellford, S.C., U.S.	B3	117
Wellin, Bel.	C5	17
Welling, Ok., U.S.	B7	113
Wellingborough, Eng., U.K.	F7	12
Wellington, Austl.	F7	51
Wellington, B.C.	f11	69
Wellington, Ont.	D7	73
Wellington, N.Z.	N15	51
Wellington, S. Afr.	D2	49
Wellington, Eng., U.K.	B5	12
Wellington, Co., U.S.	A6	83
Wellington, Il., U.S.	C6	90
Wellington, Ks., U.S.	E6	93
Wellington, Me., U.S.	C3	96
Wellington, Mo., U.S.	B4	102
Wellington, Nv., U.S.	E2	105
Wellington, Oh., U.S.	A3	112
Wellington, Tx., U.S.	B2	120
Wellington, Ut., U.S.	D5	121
Wellington, co., U.S.	D4	73
Wellington, Isla, i., Chile	D2	54
Wellington Channel, strt., N.W. Ter.	m33	66
Wellington Station, N.S.	E6	71
Wellington Station, P.E.I.	C5	71
Wellman, Ia., U.S.	C6	92
Wellman, Tx., U.S.	C1	120
Wellpinit, Wa., U.S.	B8	124
Wells, B.C.	C7	69
Wells, Eng., U.K.	C5	12
Wells, Ks., U.S.	C6	93
Wells, Me., U.S.	E2	96
Wells, Mi., U.S.	C3	99
Wells, Mn., U.S.	G5	100
Wells, Nv., U.S.	B7	105
Wells, N.Y., U.S.	B6	109
Wells, Tx., U.S.	D5	120
Wells, Vt., U.S.	E2	122
Wells, co., In., U.S.	C7	91
Wells, co., N.D., U.S.	B6	111
Wells, stm., Vt., U.S.	C4	122
Wells, Lake, l., Austl.	E3	50
Wells Beach, Me., U.S.	E2	96
Wellsboro, In., U.S.	B4	91
Wellsboro, Pa., U.S.	C7	115
Wellsburg, Ia., U.S.	B5	92
Wellsburg, N.Y., U.S.	C4	109
Wellsburg, W.V., U.S.	A4	125
Wellsford, B.C.	E4	93
Wells Gray Provincial Park, B.C.	C8	69
Wells Lake, l., Man.	A1	70
Wells-next-the-Sea, Eng., U.K.	D7	10
Wells River, Vt., U.S.	C4	122
Wells Tannery, Pa., U.S.	F5	115
Wellston, Mi., U.S.	D5	99
Wellston, Oh., U.S.	C3	112
Wellston, Ok., U.S.	B4	113
Wellsville, Mi., U.S.	D8	93
Wellsville, Mo., U.S.	B6	102
Wellsville, N.Y., U.S.	C3	109
Wellsville, Oh., U.S.	B5	112
Wellsville, Pa., U.S.	F8	115
Wellsville, Ut., U.S.	B4	121
Wells see Wells-next-the-Sea, Eng., U.K.	D7	10
West Berkshire, Vt., U.S.	B3	122
West Berlin, N.J., U.S.	D3	107
West Berlin see Berlin (West), W. Ger.	B6	18
West Bethel, Me., U.S.	D2	96
West Billerica, Ma., U.S.	f10	98
West Blocton, Al., U.S.	B2	78
West Bloomfield, N.Y., U.S.	C3	109
West Bloomfield Township, Mi., U.S.	*F7	99
Westboro, Mo., U.S.	A2	102
Westboro, Wi., U.S.	C3	126
Westborough, Ma., U.S.	B4	98
West Bountiful, Ut., U.S.	C4	121
Westbourne, Man.	D2	70
West Bowdoin, Me., U.S.	f7	96
West Boylston, Ma., U.S.	B4	98
West Bradenton, Fl., U.S.	*E4	86
West Branch, Ia., U.S.	C6	92
West Branch, Mi., U.S.	D6	99
West Branch Reservoir, res., Ct., U.S.	B3	84
West Brentwood, N.H., U.S.	E4	106
West Bridgewater, Ma., U.S.	B5	98
West Bridgewater, Vt., U.S.	D3	122
West Bromwich, Eng., U.K.	D6	10
Westbrook, Ct., U.S.	D6	84
Westbrook, Me., U.S.	E2	96
Westbrook, Mn., U.S.	F3	100
Westbrook, Tx., U.S.	C2	120
West Brookfield, Ma., U.S.	B3	98
West Brooklyn, Il., U.S.	B4	90
Westbrookville, N.Y., U.S.	D6	109
West Burke, Vt., U.S.	B5	122
West Burlington, Ia., U.S.	D6	92
Westbury, N.Y., U.S.	*n15	109
West Butte, mtn., Mt., U.S.	B5	103
Westby, Mt., U.S.	B12	103
Westby, Wi., U.S.	E3	126
West Cache Creek, stm., Ok., U.S.	C3	113
West Caldwell, N.J., U.S.	B4	107
West Campton, N.H., U.S.	C3	106
West Canaan, N.H., U.S.	C2	106
West Canada Creek, stm., N.Y., U.S.	B6	109
West Cape Howe, c., Austl.	G2	50
West Cape May, N.J., U.S.	F3	107
West Carroll, co., La., U.S.	B4	95
West Carrollton, Oh., U.S.	C1	112
West Carry Pond, l., Me., U.S.	C2	96
West Carson, Ca., U.S.	*n12	82
West Carthage, N.Y., U.S.	B5	109
West Castleton, Vt., U.S.	D2	122
West Charleston, Vt., U.S.	B4	122
West Chatham, Ma., U.S.	C8	98
West Chazy, N.Y., U.S.	f11	109
Westchester, Fl., U.S.	*s13	86
Westchester, Il., U.S.	k9	90
West Chester, Ia., U.S.	C6	92
West Chester, Oh., U.S.	n13	112
West Chester, Pa., U.S.	G10	115
Westchester, co., N.Y., U.S.	D7	109
Westchester Station, N.S.	D6	71
West Chicago, Il., U.S.	k8	90
West Chop, c., Ma., U.S.	D6	98
West City, Il., U.S.	F5	90
Westcliffe, Co., U.S.	C5	83
West Coffeyville, Ks., U.S.	A6	113
West College Corner, In., U.S.	E8	91
West Columbia, S.C., U.S.	D5	117
West Columbia, Tx., U.S.	E5	120
West Compton, Ca., U.S.	*F4	82
West Concord, Ma., U.S.	B5	98
West Concord, Mn., U.S.	F6	100
West Concord, N.C., U.S.	B2	110
Westconnaug Reservoir, res., R.I., U.S.	C2	116
West Cornwall, Ct., U.S.	B2	84
West Cote Blanche Bay, b., La., U.S.	E4	95
West Covina, Ca., U.S.	m13	82
West Creek, N.J., U.S.	D4	107
West Crossett, Ar., U.S.	D4	81
West Cumberland, Me., U.S.	g7	96
West Cummington, Ma., U.S.	B2	98
West Danby, N.Y., U.S.	C4	109
West Danville, Vt., U.S.	C4	122
West Decatur, Pa., U.S.	D5	115
West Demerara-Essequibo Coast, dept., Guy.	A3	59
West Dennis, Ma., U.S.	C7	98
West Des Moines, Ia., U.S.	C4	92
West Dover, Vt., U.S.	F3	122
West Dudley, Ma., U.S.	B4	98
West Dummerston, Vt., U.S.	F3	122
West Elk Mountains, mts., Co., U.S.	C3	83
West Elk Peak, mtn., Co., U.S.	C3	83
West Elkton, Oh., U.S.	C1	112
West Elmira, N.Y., U.S.	*C4	109
West Elwood, In., U.S.	D6	91
West Eminence, Mo., U.S.	D6	102
West Emma Creek, stm., Ks., U.S.	D6	93
West End, Bah.	A4	64
Westend, Ca., U.S.	E5	82
West End, N.C., U.S.	B3	110
West Enfield, Me., U.S.	C4	96
West Enosburg, Vt., U.S.	B3	122
West Epping, N.H., U.S.	D4	106
Westerkappeln, W. Ger.	A2	19
Westerland, W. Ger.	A4	18
Westerly, R.I., U.S.	F1	116
Western, Ne., U.S.	D8	104
Western, prov., Ghana	E4	45
Western, prov., Kenya	A5	48
Western, prov., Zam.	E3	48
Western Australia, state, Austl.	D3	50
Western Desert, des., Eg.	C2	38
Western Dvina (Daugava), stm., Sov. Un.		
Western Ghâts, mts., India	E5	36
Western Grove, Ar., U.S.	A3	81
Western Head, c., Newf.	D2	72
Western Head, c., N.S.	F5	71
Western Hills, Co., U.S.	*B6	83
Western Island, i., Newf.	C4	72
Western Isles, prov., Scot., U.K.	B2	13
Westernport, Md., U.S.	m12	97
Westernport Reservoir, res., Md., U.S.	k12	97
Western Sahara, dep., Afr.	C2	44
Western Samoa, ctry., Oc.	G11	6
Western Shore, N.S.	E5	71
Western Springs, Il., U.S.	k9	90
West Melbourne, Fl., U.S.	*D6	86
West Memphis, Ar., U.S.	B5	81
Westerstede, W. Ger.	A7	19
Westervelt, Il., U.S.	D5	90
Westerville, Ne., U.S.	C6	104
Westerville, Oh., U.S.	B3	112
West Middleton, In., U.S.	C4	91
Westerwald, mts., W. Ger.	C4	18
West Fairlee, Vt., U.S.	D4	122
West Fairview, Pa., U.S.	*F8	115
Westfall, Or., U.S.	D9	95
West Falmouth, Ma., U.S.	C6	98
West Fargo, N.D., U.S.	C9	111
West Farmington, Me., U.S.	D2	96
West Farmington, Oh., U.S.	A5	112
West Feliciana, co., La., U.S.	D4	95
Westfield, N.B.	D3	71
Westfield, Il., U.S.	D6	90
Westfield, In., U.S.	D5	91
Westfield, Ia., U.S.	B1	92
Westfield, Me., U.S.	B5	96
Westfield, Ma., U.S.	B2	98
Westfield, N.J., U.S.	B4	107
Westfield, N.Y., U.S.	C1	109
Westfield, N.C., U.S.	A2	110
Westfield, N.D., U.S.	C5	111
Westfield, Pa., U.S.	C6	115
Westfield, Vt., U.S.	B4	122
Westfield, Wi., U.S.	E4	126
Westfield, stm., Ma., U.S.	B2	98
Westfield Center, Oh., U.S.	A4	112
Westfir, Or., U.S.	D4	114
West Flanders, prov., Bel.	C3	17
Westford, Ct., U.S.	B7	84
Westford, Ma., U.S.	f10	98
Westford, Vt., U.S.	B2	122
West Fork, Ar., U.S.	B1	81
West Fork, stm., W.V., U.S.	B4	125
West Frankfort, Il., U.S.	F5	90
West Freehold, N.J., U.S.	C4	107
West Friendship, Md., U.S.	B4	97
West Frisian Islands, is., Neth.	A6	16
Westgate, Fl., U.S.	F6	86
Westgate, Ia., U.S.	B6	92
Westby, Wi., U.S.	*B5	123
West Gate of Lomond, Va., U.S.	*B5	123
West Germany see Germany, Federal Republic of, ctry., Eur.	C4	18
West Glacier, Mt., U.S.	B3	103
West Glamorgan, co., Wales, U.K.	C4	12
West Glens Falls, N.Y., U.S.	*B7	109
West Glocester, R.I., U.S.	B1	116
West Glover, Vt., U.S.	B4	122
West Gorham, Me., U.S.	g7	96
West Goshen, Ct., U.S.	B2	84
West Gouldsboro, Me., U.S.	D4	96
West Granby, Ct., U.S.	B4	84
West Grand, l., Me., U.S.	C5	96
West Granville, Ma., U.S.	B2	98
West Green, Ga., U.S.	E4	87
West Greene, Al., U.S.	C1	78
West Greenville, R.I., U.S.	B3	116
West Groton, Ma., U.S.	A4	98
West Grove, Ia., U.S.	D5	92
West Grove, Pa., U.S.	G10	115
West Halifax, Vt., U.S.	F3	122
West Hamlin, W.V., U.S.	C2	125
West Hampstead, N.H., U.S.	E4	106
Westhampton, Ma., U.S.	B2	98
West Hanover, Ma., U.S.	h12	98
West Harrison, Ct., U.S.	F8	91
West Hartford, Ct., U.S.	B4	84
West Hartford, Vt., U.S.	D4	122
West Hartland, Ct., U.S.	A4	84
West Hatfield, Ma., U.S.	B2	98
West Haven, Ct., U.S.	D4	84
West Haven, Or., U.S.	*B4	114
West Haverstraw, N.Y., U.S.	*D7	109
West Hazleton, Pa., U.S.	E9	115
West Helena, Ar., U.S.	C5	81
West Hempstead, N.Y., U.S.	*k13	109
West Hickory, Pa., U.S.	C3	115
West Hill Reservoir, res., Ma., U.S.	B4	98
Westhoff, Tx., U.S.	E4	120
West Hollywood, Ca., U.S.	*m12	82
Westhope, N.D., U.S.	A4	111
West Hopkinton, N.H., U.S.	D3	106
West Huntington, N.Y., U.S.	*n15	109
West Hyannisport, Ma., U.S.	C7	98
West Ice Shelf, ice, Ant.	C21	7
West Indies, is.	A3	53
West Island, i., Ma., U.S.	C6	98
West Islip, N.Y., U.S.	*E7	109
West Jefferson, N.C., U.S.	A1	110
West Jefferson, Oh., U.S.	C2	112
West Jersey, Il., U.S.	B4	90
West Jordan, Ut., U.S.	C4	121
Westkapelle (part of Knokke-Heist), Bel.	C3	17
Westkapelle, Neth.	C3	17
West Kennebunk, Me., U.S.	E2	96
West Kingston, R.I., U.S.	F3	116
West Lafayette, In., U.S.	D4	91
West Lafayette, Oh., U.S.	B4	112
Westlake, La., U.S.	D2	95
Westlake, Oh., U.S.	h9	112
Westlake, Or., U.S.	D2	114
West Lake, l., Me., U.S.	C4	96
Westlake Village, Ca., U.S.	*E4	82
Westland, Mi., U.S.	F7	99
West Laramie, Wy., U.S.	E7	127
West Lawn, Pa., U.S.	F10	115
West Lebanon, In., U.S.	D3	91
West Lebanon, Me., U.S.	E2	96
West Leisenring, Pa., U.S.	G2	115
West Leyden, N.Y., U.S.	B5	109
West Liberty, Il., U.S.	E5	90
West Liberty, Ia., U.S.	C6	92
West Liberty, Ky., U.S.	C6	94
West Liberty, Oh., U.S.	B2	112
West Liberty, W.V., U.S.	f8	125
West Lima, Wi., U.S.	E3	126
West Lincoln, Wi., U.S.	C2	122
Westline, Pa., U.S.	C4	115
West Linn, Or., U.S.	B4	114
West Loch Roag, b., Scot., U.K.	B2	13
West Long Branch, N.J., U.S.	C4	107
West Lorne, Ont.	E3	73
West Louisville, Ky., U.S.	C2	94
West Manchester, Oh., U.S.	C1	112
West Mansfield, Oh., U.S.	B2	112
West Marion, N.C., U.S.	f10	110
Westmeath, Ont.	B8	73
Westmeath, co., Ire.	D4	11
Westmoreland, Ks., U.S.	C7	93
Westmoreland, N.H., U.S.	E2	106
Westmoreland, Tn., U.S.	A5	119
Westmoreland, co., Pa., U.S.	F2	115
Westmoreland, co., Va., U.S.	B6	123
Westmorland, Ca., U.S.	F6	82
Westmorland, co., N.B.	C4	71
Westmount, co., N.B.		
West Mountain, mtn., Ar., U.S.	f7	81
West Mountain, mtn., N.Y., U.S.		
Westmont, Il., U.S.	k9	90
Westmont, N.J., U.S.	D2	107
Westmont, Pa., U.S.	F4	115
West Monterey, Pa., U.S.	D2	115
Westmoreland, Ks., U.S.	C7	93
West Muncie, In., U.S.	D7	91
West Musquash Lake, l., Me., U.S.	C5	96
West Mystic, Ct., U.S.	D8	84
West Newbury, Ma., U.S.	A6	98
West Newbury, Vt., U.S.	C5	122
West Newfield, Me., U.S.	E2	96
West New York, N.J., U.S.	h8	107
West Nicholson, Zimb.	B4	49
West Nishnabotna, stm., Ia., U.S.	C2	92
West Norriton, Pa., U.S.	o20	115
West Nottingham, N.H., U.S.	D4	106
West Nyack, N.Y., U.S.	*D7	109
West Olive, In., U.S.	F7	99
West Orange, N.J., U.S.	B4	107
West Ossipee, N.H., U.S.	C4	106
Westover, Al., U.S.	B3	78
Westover, Md., U.S.	D6	97
Westover, Pa., U.S.	E4	115
Westover, Tn., U.S.	B3	119
Westover, W.V., U.S.	B5	125
Westover Air Force Base, mil., Ma., U.S.	B2	98
West Palm Beach, Fl., U.S.	F6	86
West Paris, Me., U.S.	D2	96
West Park, N.Y., U.S.	D7	109
West Pasco, Wa., U.S.	*C6	124
West Paterson, N.J., U.S.	*B4	107
West Pawlet, Vt., U.S.	D2	122
West Pearl, stm., La., U.S.	D6	95
West Pelham, Ma., U.S.	*B2	98
West Pelzer, S.C., U.S.	B3	117
West Pembroke, Me., U.S.	D5	96
West Pensacola, Fl., U.S.	u14	86
West Peoria, Il., U.S.	C4	90
West Peru, Me., U.S.	D2	96
West Peterborough, N.H., U.S.	E3	106
Westphalia, In., U.S.	G3	91
Westphalia, Ks., U.S.	D8	93
Westphalia, Mi., U.S.	F6	99
Westphalia, Mi., U.S.	C5	102
Westphalia, hist. reg., W. Ger.	C3	18
West Pittsburg, Ca., U.S.	*g9	82
West Pittston, Pa., U.S.	m17	115
West Plains, Mo., U.S.	E6	102
West Plymouth, N.H., U.S.	C3	106
West Point, Al., U.S.	A3	78
West Point, Ar., U.S.	B4	81
West Point, Ca., U.S.	C3	82
West Point, Ga., U.S.	D1	87
West Point, Il., U.S.	C2	90
West Point, Ia., U.S.	D6	92
West Point, Ky., U.S.	C4	94
West Point, Ms., U.S.	B5	101
West Point, Ne., U.S.	C9	104
West Point, N.Y., U.S.	D7	109
West Point, Va., U.S.	C6	123
West Point, mtn., Ak., U.S.	C11	79
West Point Lake, res., U.S.	C1	87
Westport, Newf.	D3	72
Westport, N.S.	E3	71
Westport, Ont.	C8	73
Westport, Ire.	D2	10
Westport, N.Z.	N13	51
Westport, Ct., U.S.	E2	84
Westport, In., U.S.	F6	91
Westport, Ky., U.S.	B4	94
Westport, Mn., U.S.	E3	100
Westport, N.Y., U.S.	A7	109
Westport, S.D., U.S.	B7	118
Westport, Tn., U.S.	B3	119
Westport, Wa., U.S.	C1	124
Westport Point, Ma., U.S.	f10	98
West Portsmouth, Oh., U.S.	D2	112
West Prairie, stm., Alta.	B2	68
West Pubnico, N.S.	F4	71
West Puente Valley, Ca., U.S.	*m13	82
West Quoddy Head, c., Me., U.S.	D6	96
Westray, i., Scot., U.K.	A5	10
Westray Firth, strt., Scot., U.K.	A5	13
West Reading, Pa., U.S.	F10	115
West Redding, Ct., U.S.	D2	84
Westrhauderfehn, W. Ger.	A7	17
West Ridge, Ar., U.S.	B5	81
West Rindge, N.H., U.S.	E2	106
West River, Md., U.S.	C4	97
West River, stm., B.C.	C5	69
West Rumney, N.H., U.S.	C3	106
West Rupert, Vt., U.S.	E2	122
West Rutland, Vt., U.S.	D2	122
West Rye, N.H., U.S.	D5	106
West Sacramento, Ca., U.S.	*C3	82
West Saint Modeste, Newf.	C3	72
West Saint Paul, Mn., U.S.	n12	100
West Salem, Il., U.S.	E5	90
West Salem, Oh., U.S.	B3	112
West Salem, Wi., U.S.	E2	126
West Salt Creek, stm., Co., U.S.	B2	83
West Sayville, N.Y., U.S.	*n15	109
West Scarborough, Me., U.S.	E2	96
West Seneca, N.Y., U.S.	C2	109
West Siberian Lowland, pl., Sov. Un.	C10	29
Westside, Ia., U.S.	B2	92
West Simsbury, Ct., U.S.	B4	84
West Slope, Or., U.S.	g12	114
West Spanish Peak, mtn., Co., U.S.	D6	83
West Springfield, Ma., U.S.	B2	98
West Springfield, N.H., U.S.	D2	106
West Springfield, Va., U.S.	g12	123
West Stafford, Ct., U.S.	B6	84
West Stockbridge, Ma., U.S.	B1	98
West Suffield, Ct., U.S.	B5	84
West Sullivan, Me., U.S.	D4	96
West Sumner, Me., U.S.	D2	96
West Sunbury, Pa., U.S.	D2	115
West Sussex, co., Eng., U.K.	D7	12
West Swanzey, N.H., U.S.	E2	106
West Terre Haute, In., U.S.	F3	91
West-Terschelling, Neth.	A5	17
West Thompson Lake, res., Ct., U.S.	B8	84
West Thornton, N.H., U.S.	C3	106
West Tisbury, Ma., U.S.	D6	98
West Topsham, Vt., U.S.	C4	122
West Townsend, Ma., U.S.	A4	98
West Townshend, Vt., U.S.	E3	122
West Union, Il., U.S.	D6	90
West Union, Ia., U.S.	B6	92
West Union, Oh., U.S.	D2	112
West Union, S.C., U.S.	B1	117
West Union, W.V., U.S.	B4	125
West Unity, Oh., U.S.	A1	112
West University Place, Tx., U.S.	r14	120
West Upton, Ma., U.S.	B4	98
Westvale, N.Y., U.S.	*B4	109
West Valley, N.Y., U.S.	C2	109
West Valley City, Ut., U.S.	C4	121
West Vancouver, B.C.	f12	69
West Van Lear, Ky., U.S.	*C7	94
Westville, N.S.	D7	71
Westville, Fl., U.S.	u16	86
Westville, Il., U.S.	C6	90
Westville, In., U.S.	A4	91
Westville, N.H., U.S.	E4	106
Westville, Oh., U.S.	D2	112
Westville, Ok., U.S.	A7	113
Westville, Pa., U.S.	D4	115
Westville, S.C., U.S.	C6	117
Westville Lake, res., Ma., U.S.	B3	98
West Virginia, state, U.S.	C4	125
West Walker, stm., U.S.	E2	105
West Wardsboro, Vt., U.S.	E3	122
West Wareham, Ma., U.S.	C6	98
West Warren, Ma., U.S.	B3	98
West Warwick, R.I., U.S.	D3	116
West Webster, N.Y., U.S.	*B3	109
Westwego, La., U.S.	k11	95
West Whittier, Ca., U.S.	*n12	82
West Willington, Ct., U.S.	B6	84
West Willow, Mi., U.S.	*F7	99
West Wilton, N.H., U.S.	E3	106
West Winfield, N.Y., U.S.	C5	109
West Winfield, Pa., U.S.	E2	115
Westwold, B.C.	D8	69
Westwood, Ca., U.S.	B3	82
Westwood, Ks., U.S.	k16	93
Westwood, Ky., U.S.	B7	94
Westwood, Ma., U.S.	B5	98
Westwood, Mi., U.S.	*F5	99
Westwood, N.J., U.S.	B4	107
Westwood Lakes, Fl., U.S.	s13	86
West Woodstock, Vt., U.S.	D3	122
West Wyalong, Austl.	F8	50
West Wyoming, Pa., U.S.	n17	115
West Yarmouth, Ma., U.S.	C7	98
West Yellowstone, Mt., U.S.	F5	103
West York, Il., U.S.	D6	90
West York, Pa., U.S.	G8	115
West Yorkshire, co., Eng., U.K.	*G7	13
Wetar, i., Indon.	G7	34
Wetaskiwin, Alta.	C4	68
Wete, Tan.	C6	48
Wethersfield, Ct., U.S.	C5	84
Wetmore, Co., U.S.	C5	83
Wetmore, Ks., U.S.	C8	93
Wetmore, Or., U.S.	C7	114
Wet Mountains, mts., Co., U.S.	C5	83
Wetonka, S.D., U.S.	B7	118
Wettingen, Switz.	A4	20
Wetumka, Ok., U.S.	B5	113
Wetumpka, Al., U.S.	C3	78
Wetwang, Eng., U.K.	D7	10
Wetzikon, Switz.	B6	21
Wetzlar, W. Ger.	C4	18
Wevelgem, Bel.	D3	17
Wever, Ia., U.S.	D6	92
Wewahitchka, Fl., U.S.	B1	86
Wewak, Pap. N. Gui.	h11	50
Wewela, S.D., U.S.	D6	118
Wewoka, Ok., U.S.	B5	113
Wexford, Ire.	D3	10
Wexford, co., Ire.	E5	11
Wexford, S.D., U.S.	D5	99
Wexford Harbour, b., Ire.	E5	11
Weyakwin Lake, l., Sask.	C3	75
Weyanoke, La., U.S.	D4	95
Weyauwega, Wi., U.S.	D5	126

Name	Map Ref.	Page

Weybridge, Eng., U.K. — m12 10
Weyburn, Sask. — H4 75
Weyerhaeuser, Wi., U.S. — C2 126
Weyers Cave, Va., U.S. — B4 123
Weymouth, N.S. — E4 71
Weymouth, Ma., U.S. — B6 98
Weymouth, Ma., U.S. — D3 107
Weymouth [and Melcombe Regis], Eng., U.K. — E5 10
Weymouth Bay, b., Eng., U.K. — D5 12
Whakatane, N.Z. — L16 51
Whalan, Mn., U.S. — G7 100
Whales, Bay of, b., Ant. — B32 7
Whaleysville, Md., U.S. — D7 97
Whalom, Ma., U.S. — A4 98
Whangarei, N.Z. — K15 51
Wharfe, stm., Eng., U.K. — D6 10
Wharton, N.J., U.S. — B3 107
Wharton, Oh., U.S. — B2 112
Wharton, Tx., U.S. — E4 120
Wharton, W.V., U.S. — n12 125
Wharton, co., Tx., U.S. — E4 120
Whataroa, N.Z. — O13 51
What Cheer, Ia., U.S. — C5 92
Whatcom, co., Wa., U.S. — A4 124
Whatcom, Lake, l., Wa., U.S. — A3 124
Whately, Ma., U.S. — B2 98
Whatley, Al., U.S. — D2 78
Wheatcroft, Ky., U.S. — C2 94
Wheatfield, In., U.S. — B3 91
Wheatfield, Ca., U.S. — C3 82
Wheatland, In., U.S. — G3 91
Wheatland, Ia., U.S. — C7 92
Wheatland, Mo., U.S. — D4 102
Wheatland, N.D., U.S. — C8 111
Wheatland, Pa., U.S. — D1 115
Wheatland, Wy., U.S. — D8 127
Wheatland, co., Mt., U.S. — D7 103
Wheatland Reservoir, res., Wy., U.S. — E7 127
Wheatley, Ont. — E2 73
Wheatley, Ar., U.S. — C4 81
Wheaton, Il., U.S. — B5 90
Wheaton, Ks., U.S. — C7 93
Wheaton, Md., U.S. — B3 97
Wheaton, Mn., U.S. — E2 100
Wheaton, Mo., U.S. — E3 102
Wheat Ridge, Co., U.S. — B5 83
Wheelbarrow Peak, mtn., Nv., U.S. — F5 105
Wheeler, Al., U.S. — A2 78
Wheeler, Ar., U.S. — A1 81
Wheeler, Il., U.S. — D5 90
Wheeler, In., U.S. — B3 91
Wheeler, Ks., U.S. — C2 93
Wheeler, Ms., U.S. — A5 101
Wheeler, Or., U.S. — B3 114
Wheeler, Tx., U.S. — B2 120
Wheeler, Wi., U.S. — C2 126
Wheeler, co., Ga., U.S. — D4 87
Wheeler, co., Ne., U.S. — C7 104
Wheeler, co., Or., U.S. — C6 114
Wheeler, co., Tx., U.S. — B2 120
Wheeler Air Force Base, mil., Hi., U.S. — g9 88
Wheeler Dam, Al., U.S. — A2 78
Wheeler Lake, res., Al., U.S. — A2 78
Wheeler Peak, mtn., Ca., U.S. — C7 82
Wheeler Peak, mtn., Nv., U.S. — E7 105
Wheeler Peak, mtn., N.M., U.S. — A4 108
Wheelersburg, Oh., U.S. — D3 112
Wheeling, Il., U.S. — h9 90
Wheeling, Mo., U.S. — B4 102
Wheeling, W.V., U.S. — A4 125
Wheeling Creek, stm., W.V., U.S. — f8 125
Wheelock, N.D., U.S. — A2 111
Wheelock, Vt., U.S. — B4 122
Wheelock Mountain, mtn., Vt., U.S. — B4 122
Wheelockville, Ma., U.S. — *B4 98
Wheelon, Ut., U.S. — *B3 121
Wheelwright, Ky., U.S. — C7 94
Wheelwright, Ma., U.S. — B3 98
Whelen Springs, Ar., U.S. — D2 81
Whernside, mtn., Eng., U.K. — F6 13
Whetstone, stm., U.S. — E2 100
Whickham, Eng., U.K. — F7 13
Whidbey Island, i., Wa., U.S. — A3 124
Whidbey Island Naval Air Station, mil., Wa., U.S. — A3 124
Whigham, Ga., U.S. — F2 87
Whigville, Ct., U.S. — C4 84
Whipholt, Mn., U.S. — C4 100
Whipple, W.V., U.S. — n13 125
Whiskey Gap, Alta. — E4 68
Whiskey Peak, mtn., Wy., U.S. — D5 127
Whiskeytown-Shasta-Trinity National Recreation Area, Ca., U.S. — B2 82
Whisky Chitto Creek, stm., La., U.S. — C2 95
Whistler, B.C. — D6 69
Whitacres, Ct., U.S. — A5 84
Whitakers, N.C., U.S. — A5 110
Whitbourne, Newf. — E5 72
Whitby, Ont. — D6 73
Whitby, Eng., U.K. — G6 10
Whitchurch, Eng., U.K. — B5 12
Whitchurch-Stouffville, Ont. — D5 73
Whitcombe, Mount, mtn., N.Z. — O13 51
Whitcomb Mountain, mtn., N.H., U.S. — A4 106
White, Ga., U.S. — B2 87
White, S.D., U.S. — C9 118
White, co., Ar., U.S. — B4 81
White, co., Ga., U.S. — B3 87
White, co., Il., U.S. — E5 90
White, co., In., U.S. — C4 91
White, co., Tn., U.S. — D8 119
White, stm., B.C. — D3 68
White, stm., U.S. — C4 81
White, stm., U.S. — D5 118
White, stm., U.S. — C7 121
White, stm., Az., U.S. — D5 80
White, stm., In., U.S. — H2 91
White, stm., Mi., U.S. — E4 99
White, stm., Tx., U.S. — C2 120
White, stm., Vt., U.S. — D4 122
White, stm., Wa., U.S. — B5 124
White, stm., Wa., U.S. — B4 124
White, East Fork, stm., In., U.S. — G5 91
White, Lake, l., Austl. — D4 50
White Bay, b., Newf. — D3 72
White Bear, Sask. — G1 75
White Bear, stm., Newf. — E3 72
White Bear, stm., Newf. — E3 72
White Bear Lake, Mn., U.S. — E5 100
White Bear Lake, l., Newf. — A2 72
White Bear Lake, l., Sask. — H4 75
White Bird, Id., U.S. — D2 89

White Bluff, Tn., U.S. — A4 119
White Breast Creek, stm., Ia., U.S. — C4 92
White Butte, mtn., N.D., U.S. — C2 111
White Cap Mountain, mtn., Me., U.S. — C3 96
White Carpathians, mts., Czech. — D4 26
White Castle, La., U.S. — D4 95
White Center, Wa., U.S. — e11 124
White City, Fl., U.S. — C1 86
White City, Ks., U.S. — D7 93
White City, Or., U.S. — E4 114
White City, Ut., U.S. — *C4 121
Whiteclay, Ne., U.S. — B3 104
White Clay Creek, stm., U.S. — A3 104
White Clay Creek, stm., De., U.S. — B3 85
White Cliffs, Austl. — E4 51
White Cloud, Ks., U.S. — C8 93
White Cloud, Mi., U.S. — E5 99
White Coomb, mtn., Scot., U.K. — C5 10
Whitecourt, Alta. — B3 68
White Creek, stm., U.S. — E2 122
White Deer, Pa., U.S. — D8 115
White Deer, Tx., U.S. — B2 120
White Earth, Mn., U.S. — C3 100
White Earth, N.D., U.S. — A3 111
White Earth Indian Reservation, Mn., U.S. — C3 100
White Earth Lake, l., Mn., U.S. — C3 100
Whiteface, stm., Mn., U.S. — C6 100
Whiteface Mountain, mtn., N.Y., U.S. — f10 109
White Face Mountain, mtn., Vt., U.S. — B3 122
White Fathers, N.Y., U.S. — *f10 109
Whitefield, Me., U.S. — *D3 96
Whitefield, N.H., U.S. — B3 106
Whitefield, Ok., U.S. — B6 113
Whitefish Bay, Wi., U.S. — m12 126
Whitefish Bay, b., Mi., U.S. — B6 99
Whitefish Falls, Ont. — A3 73
Whitefish Lake, l., Alta. — B4 68
Whitefish Lake, l., Mn., U.S. — D4 100
Whitefish Point, Mi., U.S. — B6 99
Whitefish Range, mts., Mt., U.S. — B2 103
Whiteford, Md., U.S. — A5 97
White Fox, Sask. — D3 75
White Fox, stm., Sask. — D3 75
White Gull Creek, stm., Sask. — D3 75
Whitehall, Ire. — E4 11
White Hall, Al., U.S. — C3 78
White Hall, Ar., U.S. — C3 81
White Hall, Ga., U.S. — C3 87
White Hall, Il., U.S. — D3 90
Whitehall, La., U.S. — D5 95
White Hall, Md., U.S. — A4 97
Whitehall, Mi., U.S. — E4 99
Whitehall, Mt., U.S. — E4 103
Whitehall, N.Y., U.S. — B7 109
Whitehall, Oh., U.S. — m11 112
Whitehall, Pa., U.S. — *E11 115
Whitehall, Pa., U.S. — *k14 115
White Hall, S.C., U.S. — F6 117
Whitehall, Wi., U.S. — D2 126
Whitehall Reservoir, res., Ma., U.S. — h9 98
Whitehaven, Eng., U.K. — C5 10
Whitehaven, Md., U.S. — D6 97
White Haven, Pa., U.S. — D10 115
Whitehead, N. Ire., U.K. — C6 11
White Horse, N.J., U.S. — C3 107
Whitehorse, S.D., U.S. — B5 118
White Horse Beach, Ma., U.S. — C6 98
Whitehouse, Scot., U.K. — C6 13
Whitehouse, Oh., U.S. — A2 112
White House, Tn., U.S. — A5 119
White House Station, N.J., U.S. — B3 107
Whiteman Air Force Base, mil., Mo., U.S. — C4 102
Whitemarsh Township, Pa., U.S. — *F11 115
White Meadow Lake, N.J., U.S. — B3 107
White Mesa Natural Bridge, Az., U.S. — A4 80
White Mills, Pa., U.S. — C11 115
White Mountain, Ak., U.S. — C7 79
White Mountain Peak, mtn., Ca., U.S. — D4 82
White Mountains, mts., U.S. — D4 82
White Mountains, mts., N.H., U.S. — B3 106
Whitemouth, Man. — E4 70
Whitemouth, stm., Man. — E4 70
Whitemouth Lake, l., Man. — E4 70
Whitemud, stm., Alta. — A2 68
White Nile (Al Bahr al Abyad), stm., Sud. — C3 47
White Nile Dam, Sud. — E5 87
White Oak, Ga., U.S. — E5 87
White Oak, Oh., U.S. — o12 112
White Oak, Pa., U.S. — *k14 115
White Oak, S.C., U.S. — C5 117
White Oak Creek, stm., Oh., U.S. — D2 112
Whiteoak Creek, stm., Tn., U.S. — A4 119
White Oak Lake, res., Ar., U.S. — D2 81
White Oak Mountain, mtn., U.S. — C2 81
White Owl, S.D., U.S. — C3 118
White Pass, N.A. — D12 79
White Pigeon, Mi., U.S. — G5 99
White Pine, Mi., U.S. — m12 99
White Pine, Tn., U.S. — C10 119
White Pine, co., Nv., U.S. — D6 105
White Plains, Al., U.S. — B4 78
White Plains, Ga., U.S. — C3 87
White Plains, Ky., U.S. — C2 94

White Plains, Md., U.S. — C4 97
White Plains, N.Y., U.S. — D7 109
White Plains, N.C., U.S. — A2 110
White Pond, S.C., U.S. — E5 117
Whiteriver, Az., U.S. — D6 80
White River, S.D., U.S. — D5 118
White River Junction, Vt., U.S. — D4 122
White River Plateau, plat., Co., U.S. — B3 83
White Rock, B.C. — E6 69
White Rock, N.M., U.S. — *B3 108
White Rock, R.I., U.S. — F1 116
White Rock, S.C., U.S. — C5 117
White Rock, S.D., U.S. — B9 118
White Rock Creek, stm., Ks., U.S. — C5 93
Whiterocks, Ut., U.S. — C6 121
White Rocks, mtn., Ky., U.S. — D6 94
White Russia, see Byelorussia, state, Sov. Un. — D5 29
Whites, Ms., U.S. — B5 101
Whites, Wa., U.S. — B2 124
Whitesail Lake, l., B.C. — C4 69
White Salmon, Wa., U.S. — D4 124
White Salmon, stm., Wa., U.S. — D4 124
Whitesand, stm., Sask. — F4 75
Whitesand Bay, b., Eng., U.K. — D3 12
White Sands Missile Range, mil., N.M., U.S. — E3 108
White Sands National Monument, N.M., U.S. — E3 108
Whitesbog, N.J., U.S. — D3 107
Whitesboro, N.J., U.S. — E3 107
Whitesboro, N.Y., U.S. — B5 109
Whitesboro, Ok., U.S. — C7 113
Whitesboro, Tx., U.S. — C4 120
White Sea, Sov. Un. — C6 29
Whites Brook, N.B. — C2 71
Whitesburg, Ga., U.S. — C2 87
Whitesburg, Ky., U.S. — C7 94
Whites City, N.M., U.S. — E5 108
Whites Creek, stm., Tn., U.S. — g10 119
Whiteshell Provincial Park, Man. — D4 70
Whiteshore Lake, l., Sask. — E1 75
Whiteside, Mo., U.S. — B6 102
Whiteside, Tn., U.S. — D8 119
Whiteside, co., Il., U.S. — B3 90
Whiteson, Or., U.S. — B3 114
White Springs, Fl., U.S. — B4 86
Whitestone, Ga., U.S. — B2 87
White Stone, Va., U.S. — C6 123
White Stone, l., Man. — A3 70
Whitestown, In., U.S. — C5 91
White Sulphur Springs, Mt., U.S. — D6 103
White Sulphur Springs, W.V., U.S. — D4 125
Whitesville, De., U.S. — G4 85
Whitesville, Ky., U.S. — C3 94
Whitesville, N.Y., U.S. — C3 109
Whitesville, W.V., U.S. — D3 125
Whiteswan Lakes, l., Sask. — C3 75
Whitetail, Mt., U.S. — B11 103
White Tank Mountains, mts., Az., U.S. — k7 80
Whiteville, N.C., U.S. — C4 110
Whiteville, Tn., U.S. — B2 119
White Volta, stm., Afr. — D4 45
Whitewater, Man. — E1 70
Whitewater, Co., U.S. — C2 83
Whitewater, Ks., U.S. — E6 93
Whitewater, Mo., U.S. — D8 102
Whitewater, Mt., U.S. — B9 103
Whitewater, Wi., U.S. — F5 126
Whitewater, stm., U.S. — F7 91
Whitewater, stm., Ks., U.S. — E6 93
Whitewater, East Fork, stm., U.S. — E8 91
Whitewater, West Branch, stm., Ks., U.S. — g12 93
Whitewater Baldy, mtn., N.M., U.S. — D1 108
Whitewater Bay, b., Fl., U.S. — G6 86
White Woman Creek, stm., Ks., U.S. — D2 93
Whitewood, Sask. — G4 75
Whitewood, S.D., U.S. — C2 118
Whitewright, Tx., U.S. — C4 120
Whitfield, Al., U.S. — C1 78
Whitfield, co., Ga., U.S. — B2 87
Whitfield Estates, Fl., U.S. — q10 86
Whithorn, Scot., U.K. — C4 10
Whiting, In., U.S. — A3 91
Whiting, Ia., U.S. — B1 92
Whiting, Ks., U.S. — C8 93
Whiting, Me., U.S. — D5 96
Whiting, N.J., U.S. — D4 107
Whiting, Vt., U.S. — D2 122
Whiting, Wi., U.S. — D4 126
Whiting Bay, Scot., U.K. — E3 13
Whiting Field Naval Air Station, mil., Fl., U.S. — u14 86
Whitingham, Vt., U.S. — F3 122
Whitinsville, Ma., U.S. — B4 98
Whitkow, Sask. — E2 75
Whitla, Alta. — E5 68
Whitlash, Mt., U.S. — B5 103
Whitley, co., In., U.S. — B6 91
Whitley, co., Ky., U.S. — D5 94
Whitley City, Ky., U.S. — D5 94
Whitlock, Tn., U.S. — B3 119
Whitman, Ma., U.S. — B6 98
Whitman, Ne., U.S. — B4 104
Whitman, N.D., U.S. — A7 111
Whitman, W.V., U.S. — D2 125
Whitman, co., Wa., U.S. — B8 124
Whitmans Pond, l., Ma., U.S. — h12 98
Whitman Square, N.J., U.S. — D2 107
Whitmell, Va., U.S. — D3 123
Whitmire, S.C., U.S. — B5 117
Whitmire, W.V., U.S. — C5 125
Whitmire Lake, l., Sask. — C4 75
Whitmore Mountains, mts., Ant. — A2 7
Whitney, Ont. — B6 73
Whitney Village, Hi., U.S. — f9 88
Whitney, Id., U.S. — G7 89
Whitney, Pa., U.S. — F3 115
Whitney, S.C., U.S. — B4 117
Whitney, Tx., U.S. — C4 120
Whitney, Lake, res., Tx., U.S. — C4 120
Whitney, Mount, mtn., Ca., U.S. — D4 82
Whitney Point, N.Y., U.S. — C5 109
Whitney Point Lake, res., N.Y., U.S. — C5 109
Whitsett, N.C., U.S. — A3 110
Whitstable, Eng., U.K. — C9 12
Whittaker, Mount, mtn., Pap. N. Gui. — k12 50
Whittemore, Ia., U.S. — A3 92
Whittemore, Mi., U.S. — D7 99

Whitten, Ia., U.S. — B4 92
Whittier, Ak., U.S. — C10 79
Whittier, Ca., U.S. — F4 82
Whittier, N.H., U.S. — C4 106
Whittier, N.C., U.S. — f9 110
Whittlesey, Eng., U.K. — B7 12
Whittlesey, Mount, hill, Wi., U.S. — B3 126
Whitwell, Tn., U.S. — D8 119
Wholdaia Lake, l., N.W. Ter. — D12 66
Whyalla, Austl. — F6 50
Whycocomagh, N.S. — D8 71
Wiarton, Ont. — C3 73
Wiau Lake, l., Alta. — B5 68
Wiawso, Ghana — E4 45
Wibaux, Mt., U.S. — D12 103
Wibaux, co., Mt., U.S. — D12 103
Wiborg, Ky., U.S. — D5 94
Wichita, Ks., U.S. — E6 93
Wichita, co., Ks., U.S. — D2 93
Wichita, co., Tx., U.S. — B3 120
Wichita Falls, Tx., U.S. — C3 120
Wichita Mountains, mts., Ok., U.S. — C3 113
Wick, Scot., U.K. — A5 10
Wickatunk, N.J., U.S. — C4 107
Wickenburg, Az., U.S. — D3 80
Wickes, Ar., U.S. — C1 81
Wickes, Mt., U.S. — D4 103
Wickett, Tx., U.S. — D1 120
Wickham, Que. — D5 74
Wickiup Reservoir, res., Or., U.S. — E5 114
Wickliffe, Ky., U.S. — f8 94
Wickliffe, Oh., U.S. — *A5 112
Wickliffe, Oh., U.S. — A4 112
Wicklow, Ire. — D3 10
Wicklow, co., Ire. — E5 11
Wicklow Head, c., Ire. — E5 11
Wicklow Mountains, mts., Ire. — D3 10
Wicomico, co., Md., U.S. — D6 97
Wicomico, stm., Md., U.S. — D6 97
Wiconisco, Pa., U.S. — E8 115
Widefield, Co., U.S. — C6 83
Widen, W.V., U.S. — C4 125
Widener, Ar., U.S. — B5 81
Widerøe, Mount, mtn., Ant. — B15 7
Wide Ruins, Az., U.S. — B6 80
Widnes, Eng., U.K. — A5 12
Widuchowa, Pol. — B8 15
Wiebelskirchen, W. Ger. — D2 19
Wiehl, N.Y., U.S. — C5 109
Wieliczka, Pol. — C6 26
Wieluń, Pol. — C5 26
Wiener Neustadt, Aus. — E8 18
Wieprz, stm., Pol. — C7 26
Wieprza, stm., Pol. — h10 26
Wiesau, W. Ger. — D7 19
Wiesbaden, W. Ger. — C4 18
Wiese, stm., W. Ger. — A4 21
Wiesenburg, E. Ger. — A7 19
Wiesental, W. Ger. — D3 19
Wiesloch, W. Ger. — D3 19
Wigan, Eng., U.K. — A5 12
Wiggins, Co., U.S. — A6 83
Wiggins, Ms., U.S. — E4 101
Wiggins Peak, mtn., Wy., U.S. — C3 127
Wight, Isle of, i., Eng., U.K. — E6 10
Wigston, Eng., U.K. — F5 13
Wigtown, Scot., U.K. — C4 10
Wigtown Bay, b., Scot., U.K. — C4 10
Wijhe, Neth. — B6 17
Wikieup, Az., U.S. — C2 80
Wikwemikong, Ont. — B3 73
Wilayah Persekutuan (Federal Territory), ter., Malay. — *K4 35
Wilbar, N.C., U.S. — A1 110
Wilbarger, co., Tx., U.S. — B3 120
Wilber, Ne., U.S. — D9 104
Wilberforce, Ont. — B6 73
Wilberforce, Oh., U.S. — C2 112
Wilbraham, Ma., U.S. — B3 98
Wilbur, Or., U.S. — D3 114
Wilbur, Wa., U.S. — B7 124
Wilburn, Ar., U.S. — B4 81
Wilburton, Ok., U.S. — C6 113
Wilcannia, Austl. — F7 50
Wilcox, Sask. — G3 75
Wilcox, Ne., U.S. — D6 104
Wilcox, co., Al., U.S. — D2 78
Wilcox, co., Ga., U.S. — E3 87
Wilcox, Mount, mtn., Ma., U.S. — B1 98
Wilczek, i., Sov. Un. — A8 128
Wild Ammonoosuc, stm., N.H., U.S. — B3 106
Wildbad [im Schwarzwald], W. Ger. — D4 21
Wild Branch, stm., Vt., U.S. — B4 122
Wildcat Creek, South Fork, stm., In., U.S. — D4 91
Wildcat Hill, hill, Sask. — D4 75
Wildcat Top, mtn., Tn., U.S. — D10 119
Wilder, Id., U.S. — F2 89
Wilder, Vt., U.S. — D4 122
Wilder Dam, U.S. — D4 122
Wildersville, Tn., U.S. — B3 119
Wildervank (part of Veendam), Neth. — A7 16
Wilderville, Or., U.S. — E3 114
Wildeshausen, W. Ger. — B4 21
Wildhaus, Switz. — B7 21
Wildhay, stm., Alta. — C2 68
Wildhorn, mtn., Switz. — D3 21
Wild Horse, Co., U.S. — C7 83
Wildhorse Creek, stm., Ok., U.S. — C4 113
Wild Horse Reservoir, res., U.S. — B6 105
Wild Rice, stm., Mn., U.S. — C2 100
Wild Rice, stm., N.D., U.S. — C8 111
Wild Rice, South Branch, stm., Mn., U.S. — C2 100
Wildrose, N.D., U.S. — A2 111
Wild Rose, Wi., U.S. — D4 126
Wildspitze, mtn., Aus. — C6 20
Wildsville, La., U.S. — C4 95
Wildwood, Alta. — C3 68
Wildwood, Fl., U.S. — D4 86
Wildwood, Il., U.S. — h9 90
Wildwood, N.J., U.S. — F3 107
Wildwood, Ut., U.S. — *C4 121
Wildwood Crest, N.J., U.S. — F3 107
Wiley, Co., U.S. — C8 83
Wiley, Wa., U.S. — C5 124
Wilhelm, Mount, mtn., Pap. N. Gui. — k12 50
Wilhelmina Gebergte, mts., Sur. — B3 59

Wilhelm-Pieck-Stadt Guben, E. Ger. — C7 18
Wilhelmshaven, W. Ger. — B4 18
Wilhoit, Az., U.S. — C3 80
Wilkau [-Hasslau], E. Ger. — C7 19
Wilkes, co., Ga., U.S. — C4 87
Wilkes, co., N.C., U.S. — A1 110
Wilkes-Barre, Pa., U.S. — D10 115
Wilkesboro, N.C., U.S. — A1 110
Wilkes Island, i., Wake I. — A1 52
Wilkes Land, reg., Ant. — B25 7
Wilkeson, Wa., U.S. — B3 124
Wilkesville, Oh., U.S. — C3 112
Wilkie, Sask. — E1 75
Wilkin, co., Mn., U.S. — D2 100
Wilkinsburg, Pa., U.S. — F2 115
Wilkinson, In., U.S. — E6 91
Wilkinson, co., Ga., U.S. — D3 87
Wilkinson, co., Ms., U.S. — D2 101
Wilkinson Hills, Oh., U.S. — A4 112
Willacoochee, Ga., U.S. — E3 87
Willacy, co., Tx., U.S. — F4 120
Willamette, stm., Or., U.S. — C3 114
Willamette, Middle Fork, stm., Or., U.S. — D4 114
Willamette Pass, Or., U.S. — D4 114
Willamina, Or., U.S. — B3 114
Willangee, Austl. — E3 51
Willapa, Wa., U.S. — C2 124
Willapa Bay, b., Wa., U.S. — C1 124
Willard, Co., U.S. — C8 83
Willard, Ky., U.S. — B7 94
Willard, Mo., U.S. — D4 102
Willard, N.M., U.S. — C3 108
Willard, N.Y., U.S. — C4 109
Willard, N.C., U.S. — C5 110
Willard, Oh., U.S. — A3 112
Willard, Ut., U.S. — B3 121
Willard, Wi., U.S. — D3 126
Willard Bay, b., Ut., U.S. — B3 121
Willards, Md., U.S. — D7 97
Willard Stream, stm., Vt., U.S. — B4 122
Willcox, Az., U.S. — E6 80
Willcox Playa, l., Az., U.S. — E5 80
Willemstad, Neth. — C4 17
Willemstad, Neth. Ant. — H19 65
Willet, N.Y., U.S. — C5 109
Willette, Tn., U.S. — C8 119
William "Bill" Dannelly Reservoir, res., Al., U.S. — C2 78
William Lake, l., Man. — C2 70
William P. Lane, Jr. Memorial Bridge, Md., U.S. — B5 97
Williams, Az., U.S. — B3 80
Williams, Ca., U.S. — C2 82
Williams, In., U.S. — G4 91
Williams, Ia., U.S. — B4 92
Williams, Mn., U.S. — B4 100
Williams, co., N.D., U.S. — A2 111
Williams, co., Oh., U.S. — A1 112
Williams, stm., Vt., U.S. — E3 122
Williams, stm., W.V., U.S. — C4 125
Williams, Cape, c., Ant. — B29 7
Williams Air Force Base, mil., Az., U.S. — D4 80
Williams Bay, Wi., U.S. — F5 126
Williamsburg, Ont. — C9 73
Williamsburg, Co., U.S. — *C5 83
Williamsburg, In., U.S. — E8 91
Williamsburg, Ia., U.S. — C5 92
Williamsburg, Ks., U.S. — D8 93
Williamsburg, Ky., U.S. — D5 94
Williamsburg, Md., U.S. — C6 97
Williamsburg, Mi., U.S. — D5 99
Williamsburg, N.M., U.S. — D2 108
Williamsburg, Oh., U.S. — C1 112
Williamsburg, Pa., U.S. — F5 115
Williamsburg, Va., U.S. — C6 123
Williamsburg, W.V., U.S. — D4 125
Williamsburg, co., S.C., U.S. — D8 117
Williamsfield, Il., U.S. — C3 90
Williams Fork, stm., Co., U.S. — A3 83
Williams Harbour, Newf. — B4 72
Williams Lake, B.C. — C6 69
Williams Mountain, mtn., Ok., U.S. — C7 113
Williamson, Ga., U.S. — C2 87
Williamson, Ia., U.S. — C4 92
Williamson, N.Y., U.S. — B3 109
Williamson, W.V., U.S. — D2 125
Williamson, co., Il., U.S. — F4 90
Williamson, co., Tn., U.S. — B5 119
Williamson, co., Tx., U.S. — D4 120
Williamson, Mount, mtn., Ca., U.S. — *D4 82
Williamson Head, c., Ant. — C28 7
Williamsport, Newf. — C3 72
Williamsport, In., U.S. — D3 91
Williamsport, Md., U.S. — A2 97
Williamsport, Oh., U.S. — C2 112
Williamsport, Pa., U.S. — D7 115
Williamsport, Tn., U.S. — B4 119
Williamston, Mi., U.S. — F6 99
Williamston, N.C., U.S. — B5 110
Williamston, S.C., U.S. — B3 117
Williamstown, Ont. — B10 73
Williamstown, Ky., U.S. — B5 94
Williamstown, Ma., U.S. — A1 98
Williamstown, N.J., U.S. — D3 107
Williamstown, Pa., U.S. — E8 115
Williamstown, Vt., U.S. — C3 122
Williamstown, W.V., U.S. — B3 125
Williamsville, Il., U.S. — D4 90
Williamsville, Mo., U.S. — E7 102
Williamsville, N.Y., U.S. — C2 109
Williamsville, Vt., U.S. — F3 122
Willimantic, Ct., U.S. — C7 84
Willimantic, stm., Ct., U.S. — B6 84
Willimantic Reservoir, res., Ct., U.S. — C7 84
Willingboro, N.J., U.S. — C3 107
Willis, Ks., U.S. — C8 93
Willis, Tx., U.S. — D5 120
Willis, Va., U.S. — C2 123
Willisburg, Ky., U.S. — C4 94
Willis Island, i., Newf. — D5 72
Williston, S. Afr. — D3 49
Williston, Fl., U.S. — C4 86
Williston, N.C., U.S. — C6 110

Williston, N.D., U.S. — A2 111
Williston, S.C., U.S. — E5 117
Williston, Tn., U.S. — B2 119
Williston, Vt., U.S. — C2 122
Williston Basin, U.S. — B2 111
Williston Lake, res., B.C. — B6 69
Williston Park, N.Y., U.S. — *E7 109
Willisville, Ar., U.S. — D2 81
Willisville, Il., U.S. — F4 90
Willits, Ca., U.S. — C2 82
Willis Wharf, Va., U.S. — C7 123
Willmar, Sask. — H4 75
Willmar, Mn., U.S. — E3 100
Willmore Wilderness Park, Alta. — C1 68
Willoughby, Austl. — *F9 50
Willoughby, Oh., U.S. — A4 112
Willoughby, Lake, l., Vt., U.S. — B4 122
Willoughby Hills, Oh., U.S. — A4 112
Willow, Ak., U.S. — g17 79
Willow, Ar., U.S. — C3 81
Willow, Ok., U.S. — B2 113
Willow Branch, In., U.S. — E6 91
Willowbrook, Sask. — F4 75
Willow Brook, Ca., U.S. — *n12 82
Willowbrook, Il., U.S. — *B6 89
Willow Bunch, Sask. — H3 75
Willow Bunch Lake, l., Sask. — H3 75
Willow City, N.D., U.S. — A5 111
Willow City, Tx., U.S. — D3 120
Willow Creek, Mt., U.S. — E5 103
Willow Creek, stm., Alta. — D4 68
Willow Creek, stm., Nv., U.S. — E5 105
Willow Creek, stm., Ut., U.S. — D6 121
Willow Creek, stm., Wy., U.S. — C6 127
Willow Glen, La., U.S. — C3 95
Willow Grove, De., U.S. — D3 85
Willow Grove, Pa., U.S. — F11 115
Willow Grove Naval Air Station, mil., Pa., U.S. — F11 115
Willow Hill, Il., U.S. — E5 90
Willow Hill, Pa., U.S. — F6 115
Willowick, Oh., U.S. — A4 112
Willow Island, Ne., U.S. — D5 104
Willow Lake, S.D., U.S. — C8 118
Willowmore, S. Afr. — D3 49
Willow Reservoir, res., Wi., U.S. — C3 126
Willow River, B.C. — B6 69
Willow River, Mn., U.S. — D6 100
Willow Run, De., U.S. — i7 85
Willow Run, Mi., U.S. — p14 99
Willows, Sask. — H3 75
Willows, Ca., U.S. — C2 82
Willow Springs, Il., U.S. — k9 90
Willow Springs, Mo., U.S. — E6 102
Willsboro, N.Y., U.S. — f11 109
Wills Hill, hill, Ma., U.S. — f11 98
Willshire, Oh., U.S. — B1 112
Wills Mountain, mtn., U.S. — k13 97
Willston, Va., U.S. — B5 123
Wilmar, Ar., U.S. — D4 81
Wilmer, Al., U.S. — E1 78
Wilmer, Tx., U.S. — n10 120
Wilmerding, Pa., U.S. — k14 115
Wilmersdorf, E. Ger. — E7 15
Wilmette, Il., U.S. — A6 90
Wilmington, Austl. — F2 51
Wilmington, De., U.S. — B3 85
Wilmington, Il., U.S. — B5 90
Wilmington, Ma., U.S. — A5 98
Wilmington, N.Y., U.S. — f11 109
Wilmington, N.C., U.S. — C5 110
Wilmington, Oh., U.S. — C2 112
Wilmington, Vt., U.S. — F3 122
Wilmington Island, Ga., U.S. — *E5 87
Wilmington Manor, De., U.S. — i7 85
Wilmington Manor Gardens, De., U.S. — *B3 85
Wilmont, Mn., U.S. — G3 100
Wilmore, Ks., U.S. — E4 93
Wilmore, Ky., U.S. — C5 94
Wilmot, Ar., U.S. — D4 81
Wilmot, In., U.S. — B6 91
Wilmot, N.H., U.S. — D3 106
Wilmot, Oh., U.S. — B4 112
Wilmot, S.D., U.S. — B9 118
Wilmot Flat, N.H., U.S. — D3 106
Wilmslow, Eng., U.K. — A5 12
Wilno, Ont. — B7 73
Wilsall, Mt., U.S. — E6 103
Wilsey, Ks., U.S. — D7 93
Wilseyville, Ca., U.S. — C3 82
Wilson, Ar., U.S. — B5 81
Wilson, Ks., U.S. — D5 93
Wilson, La., U.S. — D4 95
Wilson, Mi., U.S. — C3 99
Wilson, N.Y., U.S. — B2 109
Wilson, N.C., U.S. — B5 110
Wilson, Ok., U.S. — C4 113
Wilson, Pa., U.S. — E11 115
Wilson, Tx., U.S. — C2 120
Wilson, Wy., U.S. — C2 127
Wilson, co., Ks., U.S. — E8 93
Wilson, co., N.C., U.S. — B5 110
Wilson, co., Tn., U.S. — A5 119
Wilson, co., Tx., U.S. — E3 120
Wilson, Austl. — A4 51
Wilson, Mount, mtn., Az., U.S. — B1 80
Wilson, Mount, mtn., Ca., U.S. — m12 82
Wilson, Mount, mtn., Co., U.S. — D2 83
Wilson, Mount, mtn., Nv., U.S. — F6 105
Wilson, Mount, mtn., Or., U.S. — B5 114
Wilson Creek, stm., Wa., U.S. — B6 124
Wilson Creek, stm., Wa., U.S. — B6 124
Wilson Lake, res., Al., U.S. — A2 78
Wilson Lake, res., Ks., U.S. — D4 93
Wilson Piedmont Glacier, ice, Ant. — e39 7
Wilsons, Va., U.S. — C5 123
Wilsons Beach, N.B. — E3 71
Wilsons Mills, Me., U.S. — D1 96
Wilsons Mills, N.C., U.S. — B4 110
Wilsons Promontory, c., Austl. — G8 50
Wilsonville, Al., U.S. — B3 78
Wilsonville, Il., U.S. — D4 90
Wilsonville, Ne., U.S. — D5 104
Wilsonville, Or., U.S. — h12 114
Wilstedt, W. Ger. — E3 15
Wilster, W. Ger. — B5 15
Wilton, Al., U.S. — B3 78
Wilton, Ct., U.S. — E2 84
Wilton, Me., U.S. — D2 96
Wilton, N.H., U.S. — E3 106
Wilton, N.Y., U.S. — B7 109
Wilton, N.D., U.S. — B5 111

Name	Map Ref.	Page
Wilton, Wi., U.S.	E3	126
Wilton Center, N.H., U.S.	E3	106
Wilton Manors, Fl., U.S.	*r13	86
Wiltshire, co., Eng., U.K.	C6	12
Wiltz, Lux.	C6	16
Wiluna, Austl.	E3	50
Wimapedi, stm., Man.	B2	70
Wimauma, Fl., U.S.	E4	86
Wimbledon (part of London), Eng., U.K.	m12	10
Wimbledon, N.D., U.S.	B7	111
Wimborne, Alta.	D4	68
Wimborne Minster, Eng., U.K.	D6	12
Wimico, Lake, l., Fl., U.S.	C1	86
Winagami Lake, l., Alta.	B2	68
Winamac, In., U.S.	B4	91
Winburg, S. Afr.	C4	49
Winburne, Pa., U.S.	E5	115
Wincheck Pond, l., R.I., U.S.	E1	116
Winchell Mountain, mtn., Ma., U.S.	B2	98
Winchendon, Ma., U.S.	A3	98
Winchendon Springs, Ma., U.S.	A3	98
Winchester, Ont.	B9	73
Winchester, Eng., U.K.	E6	10
Winchester, Ar., U.S.	D4	81
Winchester, Id., U.S.	C2	89
Winchester, Il., U.S.	D3	90
Winchester, In., U.S.	D8	91
Winchester, Ks., U.S.	k15	93
Winchester, Ky., U.S.	C5	94
Winchester, Ma., U.S.	g11	98
Winchester, Ms., U.S.	D5	101
Winchester, Mo., U.S.	A6	102
Winchester, Nv., U.S.	G6	105
Winchester, N.H., U.S.	E2	106
Winchester, Oh., U.S.	D2	112
Winchester, Tn., U.S.	B5	119
Winchester, Va., U.S.	A4	123
Winchester Bay, Or., U.S.	D2	114
Winchester Center, Ct., U.S.	B3	84
Wind, stm., Wa., U.S.	D4	124
Wind, stm., Wy., U.S.	C4	127
Windber, Pa., U.S.	F4	115
Wind Cave National Park, S.D., U.S.	D2	118
Wind Creek, stm., Wy., U.S.	C7	127
Windcrest, Tx., U.S.	*E3	120
Winder, Ga., U.S.	C3	87
Windermere, B.C.	D10	69
Windermere, Ont.	B5	73
Windermere, Eng., U.K.	C5	10
Windermere, l., Eng., U.K.	F6	13
Windfall, Alta.	B2	68
Windfall, In., U.S.	D6	91
Windgap, Pa., U.S.	E11	115
Windham, Ct., U.S.	C7	84
Windham, Mt., U.S.	C6	103
Windham, N.Y., U.S.	C6	109
Windham, Oh., U.S.	A4	112
Windham, co., Ct., U.S.	B7	84
Windham, co., Vt., U.S.	F3	122
Windham Center, Me., U.S.	*E2	96
Windhoek, Nmb.	B2	49
Windigo, stm., Que.	B4	74
Winding Stair Mountain, mts., Ok., U.S.	C6	113
Wind Lake, Wi., U.S.	F5	126
Wind Lake, l., Wi., U.S.	n11	126
Windmill Point, c., Va., U.S.	C6	123
Windom, Ks., U.S.	D6	93
Windom, Mn., U.S.	G3	100
Windom Peak, mtn., Co., U.S.	D3	83
Window Rock, Az., U.S.	B6	80
Wind Point, Wi., U.S.	n12	126
Wind Ridge, Pa., U.S.	G1	115
Wind River Indian Reservation, Wy., U.S.	C4	127
Wind River Peak, mtn., Wy., U.S.	D3	127
Wind River Range, mts., Wy., U.S.	C3	127
Windsbach, W. Ger.	D5	19
Windsor, Newf.	D4	72
Windsor, N.S.	E5	71
Windsor, Ont.	E1	73
Windsor, Que.	D5	74
Windsor (New Windsor), Eng., U.K.	E6	10
Windsor, Co., U.S.	A6	83
Windsor, Ct., U.S.	B5	84
Windsor, Il., U.S.	D5	90
Windsor, Ma., U.S.	A1	98
Windsor, Mo., U.S.	C4	102
Windsor, N.J., U.S.	C3	107
Windsor, N.C., U.S.	B6	110
Windsor, N.D., U.S.	C6	111
Windsor, Pa., U.S.	G8	115
Windsor, S.C., U.S.	E4	117
Windsor, Vt., U.S.	E4	122
Windsor, Va., U.S.	D6	123
Windsor, co., Vt., U.S.	D3	122
Windsor Heights, Ia., U.S.	e8	92
Windsor Hills, Ca., U.S.	*n12	82
Windsor Locks, Ct., U.S.	B5	84
Windsorville, Ct., U.S.	B5	84
Windthorst, Sask.	G4	75
Windthorst, Tx., U.S.	C3	120
Windward Islands, is., N.A.	I14	64
Windward Passage, strt., N.A.	E7	64
Windygates, Man.	E2	70
Windy Hill, S.C., U.S.	C8	117
Windy Hills, De., U.S.	*B3	85
Windy Lake, l., Sask.	C4	75
Windy Peak, mtn., Wa., U.S.	A6	124
Windy Point, c., Newf.	C4	72
Winefred, Alta.	B5	68
Winefred Lake, l., Alta.	B5	68
Winfall, N.C., U.S.	A6	110
Winfield, Alta.	C3	68
Winfield, Al., U.S.	B2	78
Winfield, Ia., U.S.	C6	92
Winfield, Ks., U.S.	E7	93
Winfield, Md., U.S.	B3	97
Winfield, Mo., U.S.	C7	102
Winfield, N.J., U.S.	k7	107
Winfield, Pa., U.S.	E8	115
Winfield, Tn., U.S.	C9	119
Winfield, W.V., U.S.	C3	125
Winfred, S.D., U.S.	D8	118
Wing, N.D., U.S.	D3	78
Wing, Ar., U.S.	C2	81
Wing, N.D., U.S.	B5	111
Wing, stm., Mn., U.S.	D3	100
Wingate, In., U.S.	D3	91
Wingate, Md., U.S.	D5	97
Wingate, N.C., U.S.	C2	110
Winger, Mn., U.S.	C3	100
Wingham, Ont.	D3	73
Wingo, Ky., U.S.	f9	94
Winifred, Mt., U.S.	C7	103
Winifreda, Arg.	B4	54
Winifrede, W.V., U.S.	m12	125
Winigan, Mo., U.S.	A5	102
Winisk, Ont.	n18	73
Winisk, stm., Ont.	n18	73
Winisk Lake, l., Ont.	n18	73
Winkelman, Az., U.S.	E5	80
Winkler, Man.	E3	70
Winkler, co., Tx., U.S.	D1	120
Winlaw, B.C.	E9	69
Winlock, Wa., U.S.	C3	124
Winn, Me., U.S.	C4	96
Winn, Mi., U.S.	E6	99
Winn, co., La., U.S.	C3	95
Winnabow, N.C., U.S.	C4	110
Winneba, Ghana	E4	45
Winnebago, Mn., U.S.	G4	100
Winnebago, Ne., U.S.	B9	104
Winnebago, Wi., U.S.	h8	126
Winnebago, co., Il., U.S.	A4	90
Winnebago, co., Ia., U.S.	A4	92
Winnebago, stm., Ia., U.S.	A4	92
Winnebago, Lake, l., Wi., U.S.	E5	126
Winnebago Indian Reservation, Ne., U.S.	B9	104
Winneconne, Wi., U.S.	D5	126
Winnemucca, Nv., U.S.	C4	105
Winnemucca Lake, l., Nv., U.S.	C2	105
Winner, S.D., U.S.	D6	118
Winneshiek, co., Ia., U.S.	A6	92
Winnetka, Il., U.S.	A6	90
Winnetoon, Ne., U.S.	B8	104
Winnett, Mt., U.S.	C8	103
Winnfield, La., U.S.	C3	95
Winnibigoshish, Lake, l., Mn., U.S.	C4	100
Winnifred, Alta.	E5	68
Winnipeg, Man.	E3	70
Winnipeg, stm., Can.	D4	70
Winnipeg, Lake, l., Man.	C3	70
Winnipeg Beach, Man.	D2	70
Winnipegosis, Man.	D2	70
Winnipegosis, Lake, l., Man.	C2	70
Winnipesaukee, Lake, l., N.H., U.S.	C4	106
Winnisquam, N.H., U.S.	C3	106
Winnisquam Lake, l., N.H., U.S.	C3	106
Winnsboro, La., U.S.	B4	95
Winnsboro, S.C., U.S.	C5	117
Winnsboro, Tx., U.S.	C5	120
Winnsboro Mills, S.C., U.S.	C5	117
Winona, Ks., U.S.	C2	93
Winona, Mn., U.S.	F7	100
Winona, Ms., U.S.	B4	101
Winona, Mo., U.S.	D6	102
Winona, N.H., U.S.	C3	106
Winona, Wa., U.S.	C8	124
Winona, W.V., U.S.	C4	125
Winona, co., Mn., U.S.	F7	100
Winona Lake, In., U.S.	B6	91
Winona Lake, l., Vt., U.S.	C2	122
Winooski, Vt., U.S.	C2	122
Winooski, stm., Vt., U.S.	C3	122
Winooski, North Branch, stm., Vt., U.S.	C3	122
Winschoten, Neth.	A7	16
Winsen, W. Ger.	E4	15
Winsford, Eng., U.K.	A5	12
Winside, Ne., U.S.	B8	104
Winslow, Az., U.S.	C5	80
Winslow, Ar., U.S.	B1	81
Winslow, Il., U.S.	A4	90
Winslow, In., U.S.	H3	91
Winslow, Me., U.S.	D3	96
Winslow, Ne., U.S.	C9	104
Winslow, N.J., U.S.	D3	107
Winsted, Ct., U.S.	B3	84
Winsted, Mn., U.S.	F4	100
Winston, Fl., U.S.	D4	86
Winston, Mo., U.S.	B3	102
Winston, Mt., U.S.	D5	103
Winston, N.M., U.S.	D2	108
Winston, Or., U.S.	D3	114
Winston, co., Al., U.S.	A2	78
Winston, co., Ms., U.S.	B4	101
Winston-Salem, N.C., U.S.	A2	110
Winstonville, Ms., U.S.	B3	101
Winsum, Neth.	A6	17
Winter, Sask.	E1	75
Winter, Wi., U.S.	C2	126
Winter Beach, Fl., U.S.	E6	86
Winterberg, W. Ger.	B3	19
Winter Garden, Fl., U.S.	D5	86
Winter Harbor, Me., U.S.	D4	96
Winter Harbour, B.C.	D3	69
Winter Haven, Fl., U.S.	D5	86
Wintering Lake, l., Man.	B3	70
Winter Park, Co., U.S.	B5	83
Winter Park, Fl., U.S.	D5	86
Winter Park, N.C., U.S.	C5	110
Winterpock, Va., U.S.	C5	123
Winterport, Me., U.S.	D4	96
Winter Ridge, mtn., Or., U.S.	E6	114
Winters, Ca., U.S.	C2	82
Winters, Tx., U.S.	D3	120
Winterset, Ia., U.S.	C4	92
Winter Springs, Fl., U.S.	*D5	86
Wintersville, Oh., U.S.	B5	112
Winterswijk, Neth.	C6	17
Winterthur, Switz.	E4	21
Winterthur, De., U.S.	h7	85
Winterton, Newf.	E5	72
Winterville, Ga., U.S.	C3	87
Winterville, Me., U.S.	B4	96
Winterville, Ms., U.S.	B2	101
Winterville, N.C., U.S.	B5	110
Winthrop, Ar., U.S.	D1	81
Winthrop, Ct., U.S.	C5	84
Winthrop, Ia., U.S.	B6	92
Winthrop, Me., U.S.	D3	96
Winthrop, Ma., U.S.	B6	98
Winthrop, Mn., U.S.	F4	100
Winthrop, N.Y., U.S.	f10	109
Winthrop, Wa., U.S.	A5	124
Winthrop Harbor, Il., U.S.	A6	90
Winton, Austl.	D7	50
Winton, Bah.	m18	64
Winton, N.C., U.S.	A6	110
Winton, co., Res., Oh., U.S.	o12	113
Wintzenheim, Fr.	A3	20
Winyah Bay, b., S.C., U.S.	E9	117
Wiota, Ia., U.S.	C3	92
Wiratnagar, Nepal	C8	36
Wirral, N.B.	D3	71
Wirt, co., W.V., U.S.	B3	125
Wirtz, Va., U.S.	C3	123
Wisbech, Eng., U.K.	D7	10
Wiscasset, Me., U.S.	D3	96
Wisconsin, state, U.S.	D4	126
Wisconsin, stm., Wi., U.S.	E3	126
Wisconsin, Lake, res., Wi., U.S.	E4	126
Wisconsin Dells, Wi., U.S.	E4	126
Wisconsin Rapids, Wi., U.S.	D4	126
Wisdom, Mt., U.S.	E3	103
Wise, N.C., U.S.	A4	110
Wise, Va., U.S.	f9	123
Wise, co., Tx., U.S.	C4	120
Wise, co., Va., U.S.	e9	123
Wiseman, Ak., U.S.	B9	79
Wise River, Mt., U.S.	E4	103
Wiseton, Sask.	F2	75
Wishart, Sask.	F3	75
Wishart, Mo., U.S.	D4	102
Wishaw, Scot., U.K.	E5	13
Wishek, N.D., U.S.	C6	111
Wishram, Wa., U.S.	D4	124
Wisła (Vistula), stm., Pol.	B5	26
Wisłok, stm., Pol.	C7	26
Wismar, E. Ger.	B5	18
Wismar Bucht, b., E. Ger.	D5	15
Wisner, La., U.S.	C4	95
Wisner, Ne., U.S.	C9	104
Wissant, Fr.	D9	12
Wissembourg, Fr.	C7	16
Wissota, Lake, res., Wi., U.S.	D2	126
Wister, Ok., U.S.	C7	113
Wister Lake, res., Ok., U.S.	C7	113
Witbank, S. Afr.	C4	49
Witchekan Lake, l., Sask.	D2	75
Witch Lake, Mi., U.S.	B3	99
Witham, Eng., U.K.	C8	12
Witham, stm., Eng., U.K.	A7	12
Withamsville, Oh., U.S.	C1	112
Withee, Wi., U.S.	D3	126
Witherbee, N.Y., U.S.	A7	109
Witherspoon, Mount, mtn., Ak., U.S.	g18	79
Withlacoochee, stm., U.S.	B3	86
Withlacoochee, stm., Fl., U.S.	C4	86
Witless Bay, Newf.	E5	72
Witney, Eng., U.K.	C6	12
Witry-lès-Reims, Fr.	D17	12
Witt, Il., U.S.	D4	90
Witten, W. Ger.	B2	19
Witten, S.D., U.S.	D5	118
Witten, l., W. Ger.	D3	15
Wittenberg, E. Ger.	B6	18
Wittenberg, Wi., U.S.	D4	126
Wittenberge, E. Ger.	B5	18
Wittenheim, Fr.	B3	20
Wittingen, W. Ger.	B5	18
Wittlich, W. Ger.	D3	18
Wittman, Md., U.S.	C5	97
Wittmann, Az., U.S.	D3	80
Wittmund, W. Ger.	A7	17
Wittstock, E. Ger.	B6	18
Witu Islands, is., Pap. N. Gui.	h12	50
Witvlei, Nmb.	B2	49
Witzenhausen, W. Ger.	B4	19
Wiveliscombe, Eng., U.K.	C4	12
Wiwŏn, N. Kor.	F3	33
Wixom, Mi., U.S.	o14	99
Wixom Lake, res., Mi., U.S.	E6	99
Wkra, stm., Pol.	B6	26
Władysławowo, Pol.	A5	26
Włocławek, Pol.	B5	26
Włodawa, Pol.	C7	26
Włoszczowa, Pol.	C5	26
Woburn, Que.	D7	74
Woburn, Ma., U.S.	B5	98
Woden, Ia., U.S.	A4	92
Wodzisław Śląski, Pol.	*C5	26
Woerden, Neth.	B4	17
Wohlen, Switz.	B5	21
Wohlthat Mountains, mts., Ant.	B14	7
Woito, Ont.	B7	73
Wokam, i., Indon.	G8	34
Woking, Alta.	B1	68
Woking, Eng., U.K.	m11	10
Wokingham, Eng., U.K.	C7	12
Wolbach, Ne., U.S.	C7	104
Wolcott, Co., U.S.	B4	83
Wolcott, Ct., U.S.	C4	84
Wolcott, In., U.S.	C3	91
Wolcott, N.Y., U.S.	B4	109
Wolcott, Vt., U.S.	B4	122
Wolcottville, In., U.S.	A7	91
Woldegk, E. Ger.	E7	15
Wolf, Ok., U.S.	B5	113
Wolf, Wy., U.S.	B5	127
Wolf, stm., Ms., U.S.	E4	101
Wolf, stm., Tn., U.S.	e9	119
Wolf, Isla, i., Ec.	f5	58
Wolf, North Fork, stm., Tn., U.S.	B2	119
Wolf, Volcán, vol., Ec.	f5	58
Wolf Creek, Mt., U.S.	C4	103
Wolf Creek, Or., U.S.	E3	114
Wolf Creek, stm., U.S.	A2	113
Wolf Creek, stm., Ia., U.S.	B5	92
Wolf Creek, stm., Mi., U.S.	D7	99
Wolf Creek, stm., W.V., U.S.	m13	125
Wolf Creek Pass, Co., U.S.	D3	83
Wolfe, co., Que.	D6	74
Wolfe, co., Ky., U.S.	C6	94
Wolfeboro, N.H., U.S.	C4	106
Wolfeboro Falls, N.H., U.S.	C4	106
Wolfe City, Tx., U.S.	C4	120
Wolfegg, W. Ger.	A8	21
Wolfen, E. Ger.	B7	19
Wolfenbüttel, W. Ger.	B5	18
Wolfenschiessen, Switz.	C5	21
Wolfhagen, W. Ger.	B4	19
Wolf Island, Mo., U.S.	E8	102
Wolflake, In., U.S.	B7	91
Wolf Lake, Mi., U.S.	E4	99
Wolf Lake, Mn., U.S.	D3	100
Wolf Lake, l., Alta.	B5	68
Wolf Lake, l., Il., U.S.	k9	90
Wolf Mountain, mtn., Ak., U.S.	B9	79
Wolford, N.D., U.S.	A6	111
Wolf Point, Mt., U.S.	B11	103
Wolfratshausen, W. Ger.	D6	19
Wolfsberg, Aus.	E7	18
Wolfsburg, W. Ger.	B5	18
Wolfsville, Md., U.S.	A2	97
Wolf Swamp, sw., N.C., U.S.	E9	117
Wolf Trap, Va., U.S.	*B5	123
Wolfville, N.S.	D5	71
Wolgast, E. Ger.	A6	18
Wolhusen, Switz.	C4	20
Wolin, Pol.	B4	26
Wolin, i., Pol.	E8	15
Wollaston, Cape, c., N.W. Ter.	B9	66
Wollaston, Islas, is., Chile	k12	54
Wollaston Lake, l., Sask.	m8	75
Wollongong, Austl.	F9	50
Wolmaransstad, S. Afr.	C4	49
Wolmirstedt, E. Ger.	A6	19
Wołomin, Pol.	k14	26
Wołów, Pol.	C4	26
Wolseley, Sask.	G4	75
Wolsey, S.D., U.S.	C7	118
Wolsztyn, Pol.	B4	26
Wolverhampton, Eng., U.K.	D5	10
Wolverine, Mi., U.S.	C6	99
Wolverton, Eng., U.K.	D6	10
Wolverton, Mn., U.S.	D2	100
Womack Hill, Al., U.S.	D1	78
Woman Lake, l., Mn., U.S.	D4	100
Wŏnam, N. Kor.	D10	31
Wonowon, B.C.	A7	69
Wŏnsan, N. Kor.	D10	31
Wonthaggi, Austl.	G8	50
Wood, N.C., U.S.	A4	110
Wood, Pa., U.S.	F5	115
Wood, S.D., U.S.	D5	118
Wood, co., Oh., U.S.	A2	112
Wood, co., Tx., U.S.	C5	120
Wood, co., W.V., U.S.	B3	125
Wood, co., Wi., U.S.	D3	126
Wood, stm., B.C.	C8	69
Wood, stm., Sask.	H2	75
Wood, stm., R.I., U.S.	F2	116
Wood, Mount, mtn., Mt., U.S.	E7	103
Woodall Mountain, mtn., Ms., U.S.	A5	101
Woodberry, Ar., U.S.	D3	81
Woodbine, Ga., U.S.	F5	87
Woodbine, Ia., U.S.	C2	92
Woodbine, Ks., U.S.	D7	93
Woodbine, Ky., U.S.	D5	94
Woodbine, N.J., U.S.	E3	107
Woodbourne, N.Y., U.S.	D6	109
Woodbourne, Oh., U.S.	*C1	112
Woodbridge, Eng., U.K.	B9	12
Woodbridge, Ct., U.S.	D3	84
Woodbridge [Township], N.J., U.S.	B4	107
Woodburn, In., U.S.	B8	91
Woodburn, Ky., U.S.	D3	94
Woodburn, Or., U.S.	B4	114
Woodbury, Ct., U.S.	C3	84
Woodbury, Ga., U.S.	D2	87
Woodbury, Mn., U.S.	F6	100
Woodbury, N.J., U.S.	D2	107
Woodbury, N.Y., U.S.	*E7	109
Woodbury, Pa., U.S.	F5	115
Woodbury, Tn., U.S.	B5	119
Woodbury, Vt., U.S.	C4	122
Woodbury, co., Ia., U.S.	B1	92
Woodbury Mountain, mtn., Vt., U.S.	C4	122
Woodcliff, Ga., U.S.	D5	87
Woodcliff Lake, N.J., U.S.	g8	107
Woodcliff Lake, l., N.J., U.S.	g8	107
Wood Dale, Il., U.S.	k9	90
Wood End, spit, Ma., U.S.	B7	98
Woodfibre, B.C.	E6	69
Woodfield, S.C., U.S.	C6	117
Woodford, Ire.	D3	11
Woodford, S.C., U.S.	D5	117
Woodford, co., Il., U.S.	B4	90
Woodford, co., Ky., U.S.	B5	94
Woodfords, Ca., U.S.	C3	82
Woodhaven, Mi., U.S.	*F7	99
Woodhull, Il., U.S.	B3	90
Woodhull, N.Y., U.S.	C3	109
Woodlake, Ca., U.S.	D4	82
Wood Lake, Mn., U.S.	F3	100
Wood Lake, Ne., U.S.	B5	104
Woodlake, Tx., U.S.	D5	120
Wood Lake, l., Sask.	B4	75
Woodland, Al., U.S.	B4	78
Woodland, Ca., U.S.	C3	82
Woodland, Ga., U.S.	D2	87
Woodland, Il., U.S.	C6	90
Woodland, Me., U.S.	C5	96
Woodland, Mi., U.S.	F5	99
Woodland, N.C., U.S.	A5	110
Woodland, Pa., U.S.	E5	115
Woodland, Wa., U.S.	D3	124
Woodland Acres, Co., U.S.	C6	83
Woodland Beach, De., U.S.	C4	85
Woodland Mills, Tn., U.S.	A2	119
Woodland Park, Co., U.S.	C5	83
Woodlawn, Ont.	h11	73
Woodlawn, Il., U.S.	E4	90
Woodlawn, Ky., U.S.	e9	94
Woodlawn, Md., U.S.	g10	97
Woodlawn, Oh., U.S.	n13	112
Woodlawn, Va., U.S.	A4	119
Woodleaf, N.C., U.S.	B2	110
Woodlynne, N.J., U.S.	*D2	107
Woodman, N.H., U.S.	C5	106
Woodmere, N.Y., U.S.	*k13	109
Woodmont, Ct., U.S.	E2	115
Woodmont, Md., U.S.	B1	92
Wood Mountain, Sask.	H2	75
Wood Mountain, mtn., Sask.	H2	75
Woodport, N.J., U.S.	B3	107
Woodridge, Man.	E3	70
Woodridge, Il., U.S.	k8	90
Wood-Ridge, N.J., U.S.	h8	107
Wood River, Il., U.S.	E3	90
Wood River, Ne., U.S.	D7	104
Wood River Junction, R.I., U.S.	F2	116
Woodroffe, Mount, mtn., Austl.	E6	50
Woodrow, Sask.	H2	75
Woodruff, Az., U.S.	C5	80
Woodruff, S.C., U.S.	B3	117
Woodruff, Ut., U.S.	B4	121
Woodruff, Wi., U.S.	C4	126
Woodruff, co., Ar., U.S.	B4	81
Woods, co., Ok., U.S.	A3	113
Woods, Lake, l., Austl.	C5	50
Woods, Lake, res., Tn., U.S.	B5	119
Woods, Lake of the, l., N.A.	E4	70
Woodsboro, Md., U.S.	A3	97
Woodsboro, Tx., U.S.	E4	120
Woods Cross, Ut., U.S.	C4	121
Woodsdale, N.C., U.S.	A4	110
Woodsfield, Oh., U.S.	C4	112
Woods Hole, Ma., U.S.	C6	98
Woodstock, Austl.	I6	51
Woodside, Ca., U.S.	*k8	82
Woodson, Ar., U.S.	C3	81
Woodson, Il., U.S.	D3	90
Woodson, co., Ks., U.S.	E8	93
Woodstock, N.B.	C2	71
Woodstock, Ont.	D4	73
Woodstock, Al., U.S.	B2	78
Woodstock, Ct., U.S.	B8	84
Woodstock, Ga., U.S.	B2	87
Woodstock, Il., U.S.	A5	90
Woodstock, Md., U.S.	B4	97
Woodstock, N.H., U.S.	C3	106
Woodstock, N.Y., U.S.	C6	109
Woodstock, Oh., U.S.	B2	112
Woodstock, Vt., U.S.	D3	122
Woodstock Valley, Ct., U.S.	B7	84
Woodston, Ks., U.S.	C4	93
Woodstown, N.J., U.S.	D2	107
Woodsville, N.H., U.S.	B3	106
Woodville, Austl.	*F6	50
Woodville, Ont.	C6	73
Woodville, N.Z.	N15	51
Woodville, Ga., U.S.	C3	87
Woodville, Fl., U.S.	B2	86
Woodville, Ga., U.S.	C3	87
Woodville, Id., U.S.	F6	89
Woodville, Ky., U.S.	e9	94
Woodville, Ma., U.S.	h9	98
Woodville, Mi., U.S.	E5	99
Woodville, Ms., U.S.	D2	101
Woodville, Oh., U.S.	A2	112
Woodville, Tx., U.S.	D5	120
Woodville, Wi., U.S.	D1	126
Woodward, Al., U.S.	B3	78
Woodward, Ok., U.S.	A2	113
Woodward, co., Ok., U.S.	A2	113
Woodway, Tx., U.S.	*D4	120
Woodway, Va., U.S.	f9	123
Woodworth, La., U.S.	C3	95
Woodworth, N.D., U.S.	B6	111
Woody, stm., Can.	C1	70
Woodridge, Mo., U.S.	C5	102
Wooler, Eng., U.K.	E6	13
Woolford, Md., U.S.	C5	97
Woollahra, Austl.	*F9	50
Woolmarket, Ms., U.S.	E5	101
Woolper Creek, stm., Ky., U.S.	h13	94
Woolsey Peak, mtn., Az., U.S.	D3	80
Woolstock, Ia., U.S.	B4	92
Woolwich, Me., U.S.	g8	96
Woomera, Austl.	F6	50
Woonsocket, R.I., U.S.	A3	116
Woonsocket, S.D., U.S.	C7	118
Woonsocket Reservoir Number Three, res., R.I., U.S.	B3	116
Wooster, Ar., U.S.	B3	81
Wooster, Oh., U.S.	B4	112
Woosung, Il., U.S.	B4	90
Woqooyi Galbeed, prov., Som.	C5	47
Worb, Switz.	C4	21
Worbis, E. Ger.	B5	19
Worcester, S. Afr.	D2	49
Worcester, Eng., U.K.	D5	10
Worcester, Ma., U.S.	B4	98
Worcester, N.Y., U.S.	C6	109
Worcester, co., Md., U.S.	D7	97
Worcester, co., Ma., U.S.	A3	98
Worcester Mountains, mts., Vt., U.S.	C3	122
Worden, Il., U.S.	E4	90
Worden, Mt., U.S.	E8	103
Worden, Or., U.S.	E5	114
Worden Pond, l., R.I., U.S.	F3	116
Wordsworth, Sask.	H4	75
Workington, Eng., U.K.	C5	10
Worksop, Eng., U.K.	A6	12
Workum, Neth.	B5	17
Worland, Mo., U.S.	A6	102
Worland, Wy., U.S.	C5	127
Wormerveer, Neth.	B4	17
Worms, W. Ger.	D4	18
Worms Head, c., Wales, U.K.	C3	12
Woronoco, Ma., U.S.	B2	98
Worth, Il., U.S.	k9	90
Worth, Mo., U.S.	A3	102
Worth, co., Ga., U.S.	E3	87
Worth, co., Ia., U.S.	A4	92
Worth, co., Mo., U.S.	A3	102
Wortham, Tx., U.S.	D4	120
Worthing, Eng., U.K.	E6	10
Worthing, S.D., U.S.	D9	118
Worthington, In., U.S.	F4	91
Worthington, Ia., U.S.	B6	92
Worthington, Ky., U.S.	B7	94
Worthington, Ma., U.S.	B2	98
Worthington, Mn., U.S.	G3	100
Worthington, Oh., U.S.	B2	112
Worthington, Pa., U.S.	E2	115
Worthington, W.V., U.S.	h10	125
Worthington Knob, mtn., Tn., U.S.	D10	119
Worthington Peak, mtn., Nv., U.S.	F6	105
Worthington Springs, Fl., U.S.	C4	86
Worthville, Ky., U.S.	B4	94
Worthville, N.C., U.S.	B3	110
Worton, Md., U.S.	B5	97
Wostok, Alta.	B4	68
Wotton, Que.	D6	74
Wounded Knee, S.D., U.S.	D3	118
Wounta, Nic.	E8	63
Wowoni, i., Indon.	F6	34
Woy Woy, Austl.	F9	50
Woźniki, Pol.	f10	26
Wrangel Island, i., Sov. Un.	B21	29
Wrangell, Ak., U.S.	D13	79
Wrangell, Mount, mtn., Ak., U.S.	f19	79
Wrangell Island, i., Ak., U.S.	m24	79
Wrangell Mountains, mts., N.A.	D4	66
Wrangell Mountains, mts., Ak., U.S.	C11	79
Wrangell-Saint Elias National Park, Ak., U.S.	C11	79
Wrath, Cape, c., Scot., U.K.	A4	10
Wray, Co., U.S.	A8	83
Wray, Ga., U.S.	E3	87
Wren, Oh., U.S.	B1	112
Wrens, Ga., U.S.	C4	87
Wrenshall, Mn., U.S.	D6	100
Wrentham, Alta.	E4	68
Wrentham, Ma., U.S.	B5	98
Wrexham, Wales, U.K.	D5	10
Wriezen, E. Ger.	B7	18
Wright, Al., U.S.	A2	78
Wright, Ar., U.S.	C3	81
Wright, Fl., U.S.	*u15	86
Wright, Ia., U.S.	C5	92
Wright, Ks., U.S.	E4	93
Wright, Mn., U.S.	D5	100
Wright, co., Ia., U.S.	B4	92
Wright, co., Mn., U.S.	E4	100
Wright, co., Mo., U.S.	D5	102
Wright, Mount, mtn., Mt., U.S.	C4	103
Wright Brothers National Memorial, hist., N.C., U.S.	A7	110
Wright City, Mo., U.S.	C8	102
Wright City, Ok., U.S.	C6	113
Wright-Patterson Air Force Base, mil., Oh., U.S.	C1	112
Wrightson, Mount, mtn., Az., U.S.	F5	80
Wrightstown, N.J., U.S.	C3	107
Wrightstown, Wi., U.S.	D5	126
Wrightsville, Ar., U.S.	C3	81
Wrightsville, Ga., U.S.	D4	87
Wrightsville, Pa., U.S.	F8	115
Wrightsville Beach, N.C., U.S.	C5	110
Wrightsville Reservoir, res., Vt., U.S.	C3	122
Wrightwood, Ca., U.S.	E5	82
Wrigley, N.W. Ter.	D8	66
Wrigley, Tn., U.S.	B4	119
Wrigley Gulf, b., Ant.	B36	7
Wrocław (Breslau), Pol.	C4	26
Wrong Lake, l., Man.	C3	70
Wroxeter, Ont.	D3	73
Wroxham, Eng., U.K.	B9	12
Wroxton, Sask.	F5	75
Września, Pol.	B4	26
Wschowa, Pol.	C4	26
Wuchang, China	D3	33
Wuchou see Wuzhou, China	G7	31
Wuchuan, China	J3	32
Wuchuan, China	D4	32
Wuchuan, China	B9	35
Wuda, China	D6	31
Wudaoliang, China	D3	31
Wuding, China	E6	31
Wufeng, China	I4	32
Wugang, China	F7	31
Wuhai, China	E2	32
Wuhan, China	E7	31
Wuhu, China	H7	32
Wuhu, China	E8	31
Wukari, Nig.	G7	45
Wum, Cam.	D2	46
Wümme, stm., W. Ger.	E3	15
Wünnewil, Switz.	C6	19
Wunsiedel, W. Ger.	C6	19
Wunstorf, W. Ger.	A4	19
Wupatki National Monument, Az., U.S.	B4	80
Wuppertal, W. Ger.	C3	18
Wurtsboro, N.Y., U.S.	D6	109
Wurtsmith Air Force Base, mil., Mi., U.S.	D7	99
Württemberg, hist. reg., W. Ger.	D4	18
Würzburg, W. Ger.	D4	18
Wurzen, E. Ger.	C6	18
Wushan, China	E6	31
Wuskwatim Lake, l., Man.	B2	70
Wusong, China	I9	32
Wusuli (Ussuri), stm., Asia	B11	31
Wutongqiao, China	F5	31
Wuwei, China	D7	31
Wuwei, China	I7	32
Wuxi, China	I9	31
Wuxing, China	E9	31
Wuyi, China	F6	32
Wuyiling, China	B10	31
Wuyuan, China	C6	31
Wuyuan, China	E5	31
Wuzhai, China	A2	33
Wuzhi Peak, mtn., China	B3	34
Wuzhong, China	F2	32
Wuzhou (Wuchou), China	G7	31
Wyaconda, stm., Mo., U.S.	A6	102
Wyalusing, Pa., U.S.	C9	115
Wyandanch, N.Y., U.S.	*n15	109
Wyandot, co., Oh., U.S.	B2	112
Wyandotte, Mi., U.S.	F7	99
Wyandotte, Ok., U.S.	A7	113
Wyandotte, co., Ks., U.S.	C9	93
Wyandra, Austl.	E9	51
Wyanet, Il., U.S.	B4	90
Wyarno, Wy., U.S.	B6	127
Wyatt, Mo., U.S.	E8	102
Wyckoff, N.J., U.S.	*A4	107
Wyco, W.V., U.S.	D3	125
Wye, stm., U.S.	C5	12
Wyebridge, Ont.	C5	73
Wye Mills, Md., U.S.	C5	97
Wyevale, Ont.	C5	73
Wykoff, Mn., U.S.	G6	100
Wylie, Lake, res., U.S.	A5	117
Wylliesburg, Va., U.S.	D4	123
Wymark, Sask.	G2	75
Wyman Lake, res., Me., U.S.	C2	96
Wymondham, Eng., U.K.	B9	12
Wymore, Ne., U.S.	D9	104
Wyndham, Austl.	C4	50
Wyndmere, N.D., U.S.	C8	111
Wynnburg, Tn., U.S.	A2	119
Wynndel, B.C.	E9	69
Wynne, Ar., U.S.	B5	81
Wynnewood, Ok., U.S.	C4	113
Wynona, Ok., U.S.	A5	113
Wynoochee, stm., Wa., U.S.	B2	124
Wynyard, Austl.	o15	50
Wynyard, Sask.	F3	75
Wyocena, Wi., U.S.	E4	126
Wyodak, Wy., U.S.	B7	127
Wyola, Mt., U.S.	E9	103
Wyoming, Ont.	E2	73
Wyoming, De., U.S.	D3	85
Wyoming, Il., U.S.	B4	90
Wyoming, Mi., U.S.	F5	99
Wyoming, Mn., U.S.	E6	100

Name	Map Ref.	Page
Wyoming, N.Y., U.S.	C2	109
Wyoming, Oh., U.S.	o13	112
Wyoming, Pa., U.S.	n17	115
Wyoming, R.I., U.S.	E2	116
Wyoming, co., N.Y., U.S.	C2	109
Wyoming, co., Pa., U.S.	D9	115
Wyoming, co., W.V., U.S.	D3	125
Wyoming, state, U.S.	C5	127
Wyoming Peak, mtn., Wy., U.S.	D2	127
Wyoming Range, mts., Wy., U.S.	D2	127
Wyomissing, Pa., U.S.	F10	115
Wyrzysk, Pol.	B4	26
Wysocking Bay, b., N.C., U.S.	B7	110
Wysokie Mazowieckie, Pol.	B7	26
Wyszków, Pol.	B6	26
Wythe, co., Va., U.S.	D1	123
Wytheville, Va., U.S.	D1	123
Wytopitlock, Me., U.S.	C4	96
Wyvis, Ben, mtn., Scot., U.K.	C4	13

X

Name	Map Ref.	Page
Xaafuun, Som.	C7	47
Xainza, China	B8	36
Xai-Xai (João Belo), Moz.	C5	49
Xalin, Som.	D6	47
Xambioá, Braz.	D5	59
Xam Nua, Laos	A2	34
Xangongo, Ang.	E1	48
Xánthi, Grc.	B5	40
Xapecó, stm., Braz.	D2	56
Xapuri, Braz.	B2	55
Xarardheere, Som.	E6	47
Xau, l., Bots.	B3	49
Xbonil, Mex.	D6	63
Xcalak, Mex.	D7	63
Xenia, Il., U.S.	E5	90
Xenia, Oh., U.S.	C2	112
Xiaguan, China	F5	31
Xiajiang, China	F8	31
Xiajin, China	F6	32
Xiamen (Amoy), China	G8	31
Xi'an (Sian), China	E6	31
Xiangfan, China	E7	31
Xiang Jiang, stm., China	J5	32
Xiangkhoang, Laos	B2	34
Xiangtan, China	F3	32
Xiangxiang, China	K5	32
Xianning, China	J6	32
Xianyang, China	E6	31
Xianyou, China	F8	31
Xiao Hinggan Ling (Lesser Khingan Range), mts., China	B10	31
Xiapu, China	F9	31
Xichang, China	F5	31
Xifeng, China	C11	32
Xigazê, China	C8	36
Xi Jiang, stm., China	G7	31
Xilitla, Mex.	m14	63
Xin Barag Zuoqi, China	B8	31
Xinbin, China	D11	32
Xincai, China	H6	32
Xingcheng, China	D9	32
Xinghua, China	H8	32
Xingkai Hu (Lake Khanka), l., Asia	B11	31
Xingtai, China	D7	31
Xingu, stm., Braz.	C4	59
Xinhua, China	K4	32
Xining, China	D5	31
Xinjiang, China	G4	32
Xinjiang Uygur, prov., China	C2	31
Xinjin, China	D9	32
Xinmin, China	C9	31
Xinning, China	K4	32
Xintai, China	*D8	31
Xinwen, China	G7	32
Xinxian, China	D7	31
Xinxiang, China	D7	31
Xinyang, China	.E7	31
Xinye, China	H5	32
Xinyi He, stm., China	G8	32
Xinzhou, China	C8	35
Xique-Xique, Braz.	D2	57
Xishui, China	I6	32
Xi Ujimqin Qi, China	B7	32
Xiushui, China	J6	32
Xixabangma Mountain, mtn., Asia	C8	36
Xixian, China	F4	32
Xizang see Tibet, prov., China	E3	31
Xochimilco (part of Mexico City), Mex.	h9	63
Xuancheng, China	I8	32
Xuanhua, China	C8	31
Xuchang, China	E7	31
Xuddun, Som.	D6	47
Xuddur, Som.	E5	47
Xuguit Qi (Yakeshi), China	*B9	31
Xunhe, China	B4	33
Xunke, China	B4	33
Xupu, China	K4	32
Xuwen, China	B9	35
Xuyi, China	H8	32
Xuy Nong, is., Viet.	B7	35
Xuyong, China	F6	31
Xuzhou (Süchow), China	E8	31

Y

Name	Map Ref.	Page
Ya'an, China	F5	31
Ya'bad, Isr. Occ.	B7	41
Yabassi, Cam.	E2	46
Yabbenohr Island, i., Marsh Is.	S17	52
Yablis, Nic.	C6	62
Yablonovy Mountains, mts., Sov. Un.	D14	29
Yabu, Japan	N5	52
Yabucoa, P.R.	B4	65
Yacata, i., Fiji	H16	52
Yachats, Or., U.S.	C2	114
Yacheng, China	B3	34
Yaco (Iaco), stm., S.A.	D3	58
Yacolt, Wa., U.S.	D3	124
Yacuiba, Bol.	D3	55
Yad Eli'ezer, Isr.	h10	41
Yadkin, co., N.C., U.S.	A2	110
Yadkin, stm., N.C., U.S.	A2	110
Yadkinville, N.C., U.S.	A2	110
Yad Mordekhay, Isr.	C6	41
Yadong, China	D12	37
Yadua, i., Fiji	H15	52
Yagasa Cluster, is., Fiji	I16	52
Yagoua, Cam.	C3	46
Yaguajay, Cuba	C4	64
Yaguas, stm., Peru	B3	58
Yahk, B.C.	E9	69
Yahuma, Zaire	A3	48
Yainax Butte, mtn., Or., U.S.	E5	114
Yaizu, Japan	o17	33
Yakima, Wa., U.S.	C5	124
Yakima, co., Wa., U.S.	C4	124
Yakima, stm., Wa., U.S.	C6	124
Yakima Indian Reservation, Wa., U.S.	C5	124
Yakima Ridge, mtn., Wa., U.S.	C5	124
Yakima Valley, val., Wa., U.S.	C5	124
Yako, Burkina	D4	45
Yakobi Island, i., Ak., U.S.	m21	79
Yakoma, Zaire	A3	48
Yaku Island, i., Japan	E11	31
Yakutat, Ak., U.S.	D12	79
Yakutat Bay, b., Ak., U.S.	D11	79
Yakutsk, Sov. Un.	C15	29
Yala, Thai.	D2	34
Yalinga, Cen. Afr. Rep.	D2	48
Yalobusha, co., Ms., U.S.	A4	101
Yalobusha, stm., Ms., U.S.	B3	101
Yalova, Tur.	B7	40
Yalta, Sov. Un.	I10	27
Yalu, China	B9	31
Yalu Jiang, stm., Asia	C9	31
Yalutorovsk, Sov. Un.	B7	28
Yalvaç, Tur.	C8	40
Yama, Sov. Un.	q21	27
Yamachiche, Que.	C5	74
Yamagata, Japan	D13	31
Yamaguchi, Japan	I5	33
Yamal Peninsula, pen., Sov. Un.	B9	29
Yamantau, Mount, mtn., Sov. Un.	D8	29
Yamaska (Saint-Michel), Que.	C5	74
Yamaska, co., Que.	C5	74
Yambio, Sud.	E2	47
Yambol, Bul.	D8	24
Yamdena, i., Indon.	G8	34
Yamethin, Burma	D10	36
Yamhill, Or., U.S.	h11	114
Yamhill, co., Or., U.S.	B3	114
Yamkino, Sov. Un.	n18	27
Yamma Yamma, Lake, l., Austl.	E7	50
Yamoussoukro, I.C.	E3	45
Yampa, Co., U.S.	A4	83
Yampa, stm., Co., U.S.	A2	83
Yampa Plateau, plat., U.S.	A1	83
Yamparáez, Bol.	C2	55
Yamsay Mountain, mtn., Or., U.S.	E5	114
Yamsk, Sov. Un.	D18	29
Yamuna, stm., India	C7	36
Yamzho Yumco, l., China	C16	36
Yana, stm., Sov. Un.	C16	29
Yanac, Austl.	H3	51
Yanam, India	E7	36
Yan'an, China	D6	31
Yanaoca, Peru	D3	58
Yanaul, Sov. Un.	D20	8
Yanbu' al Bahr, Sau. Ar.	C3	38
Yancey, co., N.C., U.S.	f10	110
Yanceyville, N.C., U.S.	A3	110
Yancheng, China	*E9	31
Yancheng, China	H9	32
Yancheng, China	H5	32
Yanfolila, Mali	D3	45
Yangambi, Zaire	A3	48
Yangbajain, China	B13	37
Yangchou see Yangzhou, China	E8	31
Yangchun, China	G7	31
Yangdŏk, N. Kor.	G3	33
Yangiyul, Sov. Un.	G22	8
Yangjiang, China	G7	31
Yangquan, China	D7	31
Yangtze (Chang Jiang), stm., China	E8	31
Yangxian, China	H2	32
Yangyang, S. Kor.	G4	33
Yangzhou (Yangchou), China	E8	31
Yanji, China	C10	31
Yankeetown, Fl., U.S.	C4	86
Yankeetown, In., U.S.	I3	91
Yankton, S.D., U.S.	D8	118
Yankton, co., S.D., U.S.	D8	118
Yanonge, Zaire	A3	48
Yanqi, China	C2	31
Yanshan, China	E7	32
Yanshi, China	G5	32
Yanshou, China	D4	33
Yantai, China	D9	31
Yantic, stm., Ct., U.S.	C7	84
Yantley, Al., U.S.	C1	78
Yantra, stm., Bul.	D7	24
Yanzhou, China	D8	31
Yao, Chad	C3	46
Yao, Japan	*I7	33
Yaosca, Nic.	D5	62
Yaoundé, Cam.	E2	46
Yap, i., Micron.	F8	6
Yapen, i., Indon.	F9	34
Yaphank, N.Y., U.S.	*n16	109
Yaqeta, i., Fiji	H14	52
Yaqui, stm., Mex.	B3	63
Yaracuy, state, Ven.	A4	60
Yaraka, Austl.	D7	50
Yardley, Pa., U.S.	F12	115
Yardville, N.J., U.S.	C3	107
Yarensk, Sov. Un.	C18	8
Yarí, stm., Col.	C3	60
Yarīm, Yemen	C5	47
Yaritagua, Ven.	A4	60
Yarkovo, Sov. Un.	B7	28
Yarmouth, N.S.	F3	71
Yarmouth, I., U.S.	C6	92
Yarmouth, Me., U.S.	E2	96
Yarmouth, Ma., U.S.	C7	98
Yarmouth, co., N.S.	E4	71
Yarmouth Port, Ma., U.S.	*C7	98
Yarmūk, Nahr al, stm., Asia	B7	41
Yarnell, Az., U.S.	C3	80
Yaroslavl, Sov. Un.	F18	14
Yarqah, Mayyat, well, Eg.	E5	41
Yarqon, stm., Isr.	B6	41
Yarram, Austl.	I6	51
Yarrow, B.C.	f13	69
Yarrowsburg, Md., U.S.	B2	97
Yartsevo, Sov. Un.	C27	8
Yartsevo, Sov. Un.	D9	27
Yarumal, Col.	B2	60
Yasawa, i., Fiji	H14	52
Yasawa Group, is., Fiji	H14	52
Yashi, Nig.	D6	45
Yasinovataya, Sov. Un.	q20	27
Yasinya, Sov. Un.	A7	24
Yasothon, Thai.	E6	35
Yass, Austl.	F8	50
Yata, Bol.	B2	55
Yatesboro, Pa., U.S.	E3	115
Yates Center, Ks., U.S.	E8	93
Yates City, Il., U.S.	C3	90
Yatesville, Ga., U.S.	D2	87
Yathkyed Lake, l., N.W. Ter.	D13	66
Yatsuga, Mount, mtn., Japan	*G7	33
Yatsushiro, Japan	J5	33
Yatsushiro Sea, Japan	J4	33
Yattah, Isr. Occ.	C7	41
Yauca, Peru	E3	58
Yauco, P.R.	B2	65
Yauco, Embalse de, res., P.R.	B2	65
Yauli, Peru	D2	58
Yaupi, Ec.	B2	58
Yauri, Peru	D3	58
Yautepec, Mex.	n14	63
Yauyos, Peru	D2	58
Yavapai, co., Az., U.S.	C3	80
Yavarí (Javari), stm., S.A.	B3	58
Yavatmāl, India	G7	37
Yaví, Cerro, mtn., Ven.	B4	60
Yaviza, Pan.	F9	62
Yavne, Isr.	C4	41
Yavorov, Sov. Un.	G4	27
Yawatahama, Japan	J6	33
Yawgoog Pond, l., R.I., U.S.	E1	116
Yaxian, China	B3	34
Yazd (Yezd), Iran	B5	38
Yazoo, co., Ms., U.S.	C3	101
Yazoo, stm., Ms., U.S.	C3	101
Yazoo City, Ms., U.S.	C3	101
Yding Skovhøj, hill, Den.	B3	15
Ye, Burma	E10	36
Yeadon, Pa., U.S.	p21	115
Yeager, Ok., U.S.	B5	113
Yeagertown, Pa., U.S.	E6	115
Yebbi Bou, Chad	A3	46
Yecla, Spain	C5	22
Yeddo, In., U.S.	D3	91
Yefremov, Sov. Un.	E12	27
Yegindybulak, Sov. Un.	D9	28
Yegoryevsk, Sov. Un.	D12	27
Yeguas, Punta, c., P.R.	B4	65
Yehud, Isr.	g10	41
Yei, Sud.	E3	47
Yekaterinoslavka, Sov. Un.	A4	33
Yelabuga, Sov. Un.	D19	8
Yelabuga, Sov. Un.	B7	33
Yelan, Sov. Un.	F14	27
Yelan-Kolenovskiy, Sov. Un.	F13	27
Yelanskoye, Sov. Un.	C15	29
Yélimané, Mali	C2	45
Yell, co., Ar., U.S.	B2	81
Yell, i., Scot., U.K.	A12	13
Yellandu, India	I8	37
Yellow, stm., U.S.	u15	86
Yellow, stm., Ga., U.S.	h8	87
Yellow, stm., In., U.S.	B4	91
Yellow, stm., Wi., U.S.	D3	126
Yellow Creek, Sask.	E3	75
Yellow Creek, stm., Tn., U.S.	A4	119
Yellow Grass, Sask.	H3	75
Yellowhead Pass, Can.	C1	68
Yellow see Huang He, stm., China	D8	31
Yellow Jacket, Co., U.S.	D2	83
Yellowjacket Mountains, mts., Id., U.S.	D4	89
Yellowknife, N.W. Ter.	D10	66
Yellow Lake, l., Wi., U.S.	C1	126
Yellow Medicine, co., Mn., U.S.	F2	100
Yellow Pine, Al., U.S.	D1	78
Yellow Pine, Id., U.S.	E3	89
Yellow Sea, Asia	D9	31
Yellow Springs, Md., U.S.	B3	97
Yellow Springs, Oh., U.S.	C2	112
Yellowstone, co., Mt., U.S.	D8	103
Yellowstone, stm., U.S.	D10	103
Yellowstone, Clarks Fork, stm., U.S.	F7	103
Yellowstone Lake, l., Wy., U.S.	B2	127
Yellowstone National Park, Wy., U.S.	B2	127
Yellowstone National Park, co., Mt., U.S.	E6	103
Yellowstone National Park, U.S.	B2	127
Yellville, Ar., U.S.	A3	81
Yelm, Wa., U.S.	C3	124
Yelnya, Sov. Un.	D9	27
Yeltes, stm., Spain	B2	22
Yelverton Bay, b., N.W. Ter.	k35	66
Yelvington, Ky., U.S.	C5	94
Yelwa, Nig.	D5	45
Yemanzhelinsk, Sov. Un.	C6	28
Yemassee, S.C., U.S.	F6	117
Yemen, ctry., Asia	D4	38
Yen Bai, Viet.	B6	35
Yendéré, Burkina	D4	45
Yendi, Ghana	E4	45
Yenice, stm., Tur.	B9	40
Yenisei, stm., Sov. Un.	C11	29
Yenisei Ridge, mts., Sov. Un.	D27	8
Yeniseysk, Sov. Un.	D12	29
Yeo Lake, l., Austl.	E4	50
Yeoman, In., U.S.	C4	91
Yeotmal see Yavatmāl, India	G7	37
Yeovil, Eng., U.K.	E5	13
Yeppoon, Austl.	D9	50
Yeránia Óri, mts., Grc.	g10	25
Yerba Buena, Chile	E1	55
Yerevan, Sov. Un.	E7	29
Yermentau, Sov. Un.	C8	28
Yermo, Ca., U.S.	E5	82
Yermolayevo, Sov. Un.	C5	28
Yerres, Fr.	h10	16
Yerres, stm., Fr.	F2	17
Yerseke, Neth.	C4	17
Yershov, Sov. Un.	D9	27
Yerupaja, Nevado, mtn., Peru	D2	58
Yeso, N.M., U.S.	C5	108
Yessentuki, Sov. Un.	G17	13
Yessey, Sov. Un.	C13	29
Yeste, Spain	C4	22
Yetter, Ia., U.S.	B3	92
Yeu, Île d', i., Fr.	D2	16
Yevlach, Sov. Un.	E3	28
Yevpatoriya, Sov. Un.	I9	27
Yexian, China	F8	32
Yeya, stm., Sov. Un.	H12	27
Yeysk, Sov. Un.	H12	27
Yezd see Yazd, Iran	B5	38
Yi, stm., Ur.	E1	56
Yi'an, China	B10	31
Yiannitsá, Grc.	B4	25
Yiáros, i., Grc.	D5	25
Yibin, China	F5	31
Yichang, China	E7	31
Yicheng, China	I5	32
Yichuan, China	D7	31
Yichun, China	B10	31
Yichun, China	K6	32
Yidu, China	I4	32
Yidu, China	F8	32
Yigo, Guam	L10	52
Yilan, China	B10	31
Yiliang, China	G5	31
Yimianpo, China	D4	33
Yinchuan, China	D6	31
Yingde, China	E8	31
Ying He, stm., China	E8	31
Yingkou, China	D9	31
Yingshang, China	H7	32
Yingxian, China	E5	32
Yining, China	E11	29
Yin Mountains, mts., China	D4	32
Yioúra, i., Grc.	C5	25
Yirga Alem, Eth.	D4	47
Yirol, Sud.	D4	47
Yishan, China	G6	31
Yíthion, Grc.	D4	40
Yitong, China	C11	32
Yixian, China	D9	32
Yixing, China	I8	32
Yiyang, China	F7	31
Yiyang, China	C7	31
Ylig Bay, b., Guam	M10	52
Ylikitka, l., Fin.	D13	14
Ymers, i., Grnld.	B16	128
Ymir, B.C.	E9	69
Yoakum, Tx., U.S.	E4	120
Yoakum, co., Tx., U.S.	C1	120
Yockanookany, stm., Ms., U.S.	C4	101
Yocona, stm., Ms., U.S.	A4	101
Yoder, In., U.S.	C7	91
Yoder, Ks., U.S.	g11	93
Yoder, Wy., U.S.	E8	127
Yogyakarta, Indon.	G4	34
Yoho National Park, B.C.	D9	69
Yoichi, Japan	E10	33
Yojoa, Lago de, l., Hond.	C3	62
Yokadouma, Cam.	E2	46
Yokkaichi, Japan	E12	31
Yoko, Cam.	D2	46
Yokoate Island, i., Japan	L4	33
Yokohama, Japan	D12	31
Yokoshiba, Japan	n19	33
Yokosuka, Japan	D12	31
Yokote, Japan	G10	33
Yokum Seat, mtn., Ma., U.S.	B1	98
Yola, Nig.	E7	45
Yolo, co., Ca., U.S.	C2	82
Yolyn, W.V., U.S.	n12	125
Yom, stm., Thai.	B1	34
Yona, Guam	M10	52
Yonabaru, Japan	O5	52
Yonago, Japan	I6	33
Yonaha Mountain, hill, Japan	N6	52
Yoncalla, Or., U.S.	D3	114
Yonezawa, Japan	H10	33
Yong'an, China	F8	31
Yŏngan, N. Kor.	F4	33
Yonges Island, S.C., U.S.	F7	117
Yŏnghŭng, N. Kor.	G3	33
Yŏngil Bay, b., S. Kor.	H4	33
Yongji, China	G4	32
Yongnian, China	F6	32
Yongshou, China	G2	32
Yongshun, China	F6	31
Yongxiu, China	J6	32
Yonkers, N.Y., U.S.	E7	109
Yonne, stm., Fr.	D5	16
Yopal, Col.	B3	60
Yorba Linda, Ca., U.S.	*n13	82
York, Austl.	F2	50
York, Ont.	D5	73
York, Eng., U.K.	D6	10
York, Al., U.S.	C1	78
York, In., U.S.	D6	90
York, Me., U.S.	A8	91
York, Ne., U.S.	E2	96
York, N.D., U.S.	A6	104
York, Pa., U.S.	G8	115
York, S.C., U.S.	B5	117
York, co., N.B.	C3	71
York, co., Ont.	D5	73
York, co., Ne., U.S.	D8	104
York, co., Pa., U.S.	G8	115
York, co., S.C., U.S.	A5	117
York, co., Va., U.S.	C6	123
York, Cape, c., Austl.	B8	50
York, Kap, c., Grnld.	B14	61
York Beach, Me., U.S.	E5	96
York Factory, Man.	A5	70
York Harbor, Me., U.S.	E5	96
York Haven, Pa., U.S.	F8	115
Yorklyn, De., U.S.	A3	85
York Point, c., Newf.	C4	72
Yorkshire, N.Y., U.S.	C2	109
York Springs, Pa., U.S.	F7	115
Yorkton, Sask.	F4	75
Yorktown, Ar., U.S.	C4	81
Yorktown, Ia., U.S.	D2	92
Yorktown, N.Y., U.S.	*D7	109
Yorktown, Tx., U.S.	E4	120
Yorktown, Va., U.S.	C6	123
Yorktown Heights, N.Y., U.S.	*D7	109
Yorktown Manor, R.I., U.S.	*C3	116
Yorkville, Il., U.S.	B5	90
Yorkville, N.Y., U.S.	B5	109
Yorkville, Tn., U.S.	A2	119
Yoro, Hond.	C4	62
Yorosso, Mali	D4	45
Yoshkar-Ola, Sov. Un.	B3	28
Yos Sudarsa Islands, i., Indon.	G9	34
Yosemite, Ky., U.S.	C5	94
Yosemite National Park, Ca., U.S.	D4	82
Yosemite National Park, Ca., U.S.	D4	82
Yŏsu, S. Kor.	I3	33
Yotala, Bol.	C2	55
Yotvata, Isr.	E7	41
Youbou, B.C.	g11	69
Youghal, Ire.	D2	10
Youghal Bay, b., Ire.	E3	10
Youghioheny, stm., U.S.	F2	115
Youghiogheny River Lake, res., U.S.	G13	115
You Jiang, stm., China	G6	31
Youkounkoun, Gui.	E2	45
Young, Austl.	G7	51
Young, Sask.	F3	75
Young, Az., U.S.	C5	80
Young, co., Tx., U.S.	C3	120
Young America, In., U.S.	C5	91
Young Harris, Ga., U.S.	B3	87
Youngs, Lake, l., Wa., U.S.	f11	124
Youngs Creek, In., U.S.	H4	91
Youngs Point, Ont.	C6	73
Youngstown, Alta.	D5	68
Youngstown, Fl., U.S.	B1	86
Youngstown, In., U.S.	F3	91
Youngstown, N.Y., U.S.	B1	109
Youngstown, Oh., U.S.	A5	112
Youngsville, La., U.S.	D3	95
Youngsville, N.M., U.S.	A3	108
Youngsville, N.C., U.S.	A4	110
Youngsville, Pa., U.S.	C3	115
Youngtown, Az., U.S.	k8	80
Youngwood, Pa., U.S.	F2	115
Youssoufia, Mor.	C3	44
Youxi, China	K8	32
Youyang, China	C7	31
Youyu, China	C7	31
Yozgat, Tur.	C10	40
Ypacaraí, Para.	E4	55
Ypané, stm., Para.	D4	55
Ypres see Ieper, Bel.	B5	16
Ypsilanti, Mi., U.S.	F7	99
Ypsilanti, N.D., U.S.	C7	111
Yreka, Ca., U.S.	B2	82
Yssingeaux, Fr.	F8	16
Ystad, Swe.	J5	14
Ythan, stm., Scot., U.K.	C6	13
Yu'alliq, Jabal, mtn., Eg.	D5	41
Yuan'an, China	I4	32
Yuanjiang, China	G5	31
Yuan Jiang (Red), stm., Asia	G5	31
Yuan Jiang (Red), stm., Asia	G5	36
Yuan Jiang, stm., China	F7	31
Yuanling, China	F7	31
Yuanping, China	F7	32
Yuanshi, China	F6	32
Yuba, co., Ca., U.S.	C3	82
Yuba, stm., Ca., U.S.	C3	82
Yuba City, Ca., U.S.	C3	82
Yūbari, Japan	E10	33
Yucaipa, Ca., U.S.	*E5	82
Yucatán, state, Mex.	C7	63
Yucatan Channel, strt., N.A.	C7	63
Yucca, Az., U.S.	C1	80
Yucca Lake, l., Nv., U.S.	F5	105
Yucca Mountain, mtn., Nv., U.S.	D4	105
Yucca Valley, Ca., U.S.	*E5	82
Yucheng, China	F7	32
Yuci, China	F5	32
Yudu, China	F8	31
Yueqing, China	F9	31
Yueyang, China	F7	31
Yug, stm., Sov. Un.	A3	28
Yugoslavia, ctry., Eur.	C4	24
Yuhuan, China	J9	32
Yukhnov, Sov. Un.	D10	27
Yukon, Ok., U.S.	B4	113
Yukon, W.V., U.S.	D3	125
Yukon, prov., Can.	D5	66
Yukon, stm., N.A.	C9	79
Yule Bay, b., Ant.	B29	7
Yulee, Fl., U.S.	B5	86
Yulin, China	D6	31
Yulin, China	F3	31
Yulin, China	B3	34
Yuma, Az., U.S.	E1	80
Yuma, Co., U.S.	A8	83
Yuma, Mi., U.S.	D5	99
Yuma, co., Az., U.S.	E1	80
Yuma, co., Co., U.S.	A8	83
Yuma Desert, des., N.A.	E1	80
Yuma Marine Corps Air Station, mil., Az., U.S.	E1	80
Yumbi, Zaire	B4	48
Yumen, China	D4	31
Yumenzhen, China	C4	31
Yuna, Japan	N6	52
Yuna, stm., Dom. Rep.	E8	64
Yuncheng, China	D7	31
Yungas, reg., Bol.	C2	55
Yungay, Chile	B2	54
Yungay, Peru	B2	58
Yunhe, China	J8	32
Yunnan, prov., China	G5	31
Yunnan Plateau see Yun Gui Plateau, plat., China	F5	31
Yunta, Austl.	F2	51
Yunxian, China	E7	31
Yurécuaro, Mex.	m12	63
Yurga, Sov. Un.	D25	8
Yurimaguas, Peru	C2	58
Yurino, Sov. Un.	C16	27
Yuriria, Mex.	m13	63
Yurochi Island, i., Marsh Is.	P18	52
Yuryevets, Sov. Un.	C14	27
Yuryev-Polskiy, Sov. Un.	C12	27
Yuscarán, Hond.	D4	62
Yushan, China	J8	32
Yü Shan, mtn., Tai.	G9	31
Yushkozero, Sov. Un.	E15	14
Yushu, China	B3	31
Yutan, Ne., U.S.	C9	104
Yutian, China	C9	31
Yuty, Para.	E4	55
Yuwang, China	E3	32
Yuxian, China	E6	32
Yuyao, China	I9	32
Yuza, Sov. Un.	C13	27
Yuzhno-Sakhalinsk, Sov. Un.	E17	29
Yuzhnoye, Sov. Un.	C11	33
Yverdon, Switz.	E3	18
Yvetot, Fr.	C4	16
Yvonand, Switz.	C2	21
Yzeure, Fr.	D5	16

Z

Name	Map Ref.	Page
Zaanstad, Neth.	A6	16
Zabīd, Yemen	D4	38
Ząbki, Pol.	k14	26
Zabkowice, Pol.	g10	26
Zabkowice 95Śląskie], Pol.	C4	26
Zābol, Iran	B6	38
Zāboli, Iran	H10	39
Zabré, Burkina	D4	45
Zabrze, Pol.	C5	26
Zacapa, Guat.	E7	63
Zacapu, Mex.	n13	63
Zacatecas, Mex.	C4	63
Zacatecas, state, Mex.	C4	63
Zacatecoluca, El Sal.	D3	62
Zachary, La., U.S.	D4	95
Zacoalco [de Torres], Mex.	C4	63
Zacualpan, Mex.	m14	63
Zacualtipán, Mex.	m14	63
Zadar, Yugo.	C2	24
Zadetkale, i., Burma	G3	35
Zadetkyi, i., Burma	H3	35
Zadonsk, Sov. Un.	E12	27
Zafer, Cape, c., N. Cyp.	E10	40
Zafra, Spain	C2	22
Zag, B.C., U.S.	C7	113
Zagań, Pol.	C3	26
Zaghouan, Tun.	B7	44
Zagora, Grc.	C4	25
Zagora, Mor.	C12	44
Zagreb, Yugo.	C2	24
Zagros Mountains, mts., Iran	E3	39
Zagyva, stm., Hung.	B5	24
Zāhedān, Iran	C6	38
Zahl, N.D., U.S.	A2	111
Zahna, E. Ger.	B7	19
Zailiyskiy Alatau Mountains, mts., Sov. Un.	E9	28
Zaire, dept., Ang.	C1	48
Zaire, ctry., Afr.	B3	48
Zaire Basin (Congo Basin), Afr.	B3	48
Zaječar, Yugo.	D6	24
Zaka, Zimb.	B5	49
Zakataly, Sov. Un.	B16	40
Zákinthos, Grc.	D3	40
Zákinthos (Zante), i., Grc.	D3	40
Zakopane, Pol.	D5	26
Zakroczym, Pol.	B6	26
Zala, dept., Hung.	B3	24
Zalaegerszeg, Hung.	B3	24
Zalamea de la Serana, Spain	C2	22
Zalamea la Real, Spain	D2	22
Zalău, Rom.	B6	24
Zaleski, Oh., U.S.	C3	112
Zalewo, Pol.	B5	26
Zalingei, Sud.	C1	47
Zalma, Mo., U.S.	D7	102
Zaltbommel, Neth.	C5	17
Zama, Ms., U.S.	C4	101
Zambales Mountains, mts., Phil.	o13	34
Zambezi (Balovale), Zam.	D3	48
Zambezi, stm., Afr.	H8	42
Zambézia, dept., Moz.	A6	49
Zamboanga, Phil.	D6	34
Zambrano, Col.	B3	60
Zambrów, Pol.	B7	26
Zamora, Ec.	B2	58
Zamora, Spain	B2	22
Zamora, stm., Ec.	B2	58
Zamora-Chinchipe, prov., Ec.	B2	58
Zamora de Hidalgo, Mex.	D4	63
Zamość, Pol.	C7	26
Zanaga, Congo	B1	48
Zandvoort, Neth.	B4	17
Zanesville, Oh., U.S.	C4	112
Zanjān, Iran	B4	38
Zanpa Cape, c., Japan	O5	52
Zante see Zákinthos, i., Grc.	D3	40
Zanzibar, Tan.	C6	48
Zanzibar, i., Tan.	C6	48
Zaozhuang, China	G7	32
Zapadna Morava, stm., Yugo.	D5	24
Západočeský, prov., Czech.	D8	19
Zapala, Arg.	B2	54
Zapata, Tx., U.S.	F3	120
Zapata, co., Tx., U.S.	F3	120
Zapata, Peninsula de, pen., Cuba	C3	64
Zapatoca, Col.	B3	60
Zapopan, Mex.	m12	63
Zaporozhye, Sov. Un.	E6	29
Zapotillo, Ec.	B1	58
Zara, Tur.	C11	40
Zaragoza, Mex.	B3	60
Zaragoza, Mex.	B4	63
Zaragoza, Mex.	k13	63
Zaragoza, Spain	B5	22
Zarand, Iran	F8	39
Zárate, Arg.	A5	54
Zaraysk, Sov. Un.	D12	27
Zaraza, Ven.	B4	60
Zard Kūh, mtn., Iran	E5	39
Zarembo Island, i., Ak., U.S.	m23	79
Zarephath, N.J., U.S.	B3	107
Zaria, Nig.	D6	45
Zarnekow, E. Ger.	E7	15
Zarqā', Nahr az, stm., Jord.	B7	41
Zarrentin, E. Ger.	E4	15
Zarrīn Shahr, Iran	E5	39
Zarumilla, Peru	B1	58
Żary, Pol.	C3	26
Zarzal, Col.	B2	60
Zarzis, Tun.	C7	44
Zasenbeck, W. Ger.	F4	15
Zasieki, Pol.	C3	26
Zásmuky, Czech.	o19	26
Zastavna, Sov. Un.	A7	24
Zastron, S. Afr.	D4	49
Zatec, Czech.	C6	19
Zator, Pol.	h10	26
Zavala, co., Tx., U.S.	E3	120
Zavalla, Tx., U.S.	D5	120
Zavitinsk, Sov. Un.	D15	29
Zavodo-Petrovsky, Sov. Un.	B7	28
Zawiercie, Pol.	C5	26
Zawīlah, Libya	D3	43

Index

Name	Map Ref.	Page
Zāwiyat Masūs, Libya	C4	43
Zawr, Ra's az, c., Sau. Ar.	H4	39
Zaysan, Sov. Un.	E11	29
Zaysan, Lake, l., Sov. Un.	E11	29
Zaza, stm., Cuba	C4	64
Zbraslav, Czech.	o17	26
Žd'ár [nad Sazavou], Czech.	D3	26
Zdice, Czech.	o16	26
Zdolbunov, Sov. Un.	F6	27
Zduńska Wola, Pol.	C5	26
Zealandia, Sask.	F2	75
Zearing, Ia., U.S.	B4	92
Zeballos, B.C.	D4	69
Zebla, mtn., Tun.	F2	23
Zebrzydowice, Pol.	h9	26
Zebulon, Ga., U.S.	C2	87
Zebulon, Ky., U.S.	C7	94
Zebulon, N.C., U.S.	B4	110
Zeebrugge (part of Brugge), Bel.	B5	16
Zeeland, Mi., U.S.	F5	99
Zeeland, N.D., U.S.	D6	111
Zeeland, prov., Neth.	C3	17
Zeerust, S. Afr.	C4	49
Zefat (Safad), Isr.	F10	40
Zegrze, Pol.	k14	26
Zehdenick, E. Ger.	B6	18
Zeigler, Il., U.S.	F4	90
Zeil, Mount, mtn., Austl.	D5	50
Zeist, Neth.	A6	16
Zeitz, E. Ger.	C6	18
Zekiah Swamp Run, stm., Md., U.S.	D4	97
Żelechów, Pol.	C6	26
Zelenodolsk, Sov. Un.	B3	28
Zelenogorsk, Sov. Un.	A7	27
Zelenograd, Sov. Un.	C11	27
Železná Ruda, Czech.	D8	19
Zelienople, Pa., U.S.	E1	115
Zell, S.D., U.S.	C7	118
Zell am Ziller, Aus.	B7	20
Zeller Lake, l., Aus.	B8	20
Zelma, Sask.	F3	75
Zelzate, Bel.	C3	17
Zembra, i., Tun.	F3	23
Zemetchino, Sov. Un.	E14	27
Zemio, Cen. Afr. Rep.	D5	46
Zenda, Ks., U.S.	E5	93
Zendeh Jān, Afg.	D10	39
Zenica, Yugo.	C3	24
Zenith, Ks., U.S.	E5	93
Zenith, Wa., U.S.	f11	124
Zenobia Peak, mtn., Co., U.S.	A2	83
Zenon Park, Sask.	D4	75
Zeona, S.D., U.S.	B3	118
Zephyr, Tx., U.S.	D3	120
Zephyr Cove, Nv., U.S.	E2	105
Zephyrhills, Fl., U.S.	D4	86
Zerbst, E. Ger.	C6	18
Zereh, Gowd-e, depr., Afg.	C3	36
Zermatt, Switz.	C3	20
Zernez, Switz.	C6	20
Zeulenroda, E. Ger.	C6	19
Zeven, W. Ger.	E3	15
Zevenaar, Neth.	C6	17
Zevgolation, Grc.	D3	25
Zeya, Sov. Un.	D15	29
Zeya, stm., Sov. Un.	D15	29
Zeya Reservoir, res., Sov. Un.	D15	29
Zêzere, stm., Port.	B2	22
Zgierz, Pol.	C5	26
Zgorzelec, Pol.	C3	26
Zhanatas, Sov. Un.	E7	28
Zhangbei, China	D6	32
Zhangiztobe, Sov. Un.	D10	28
Zhangjiakou, China	C7	31
Zhangwu, China	C10	32
Zhangye, China	D5	31
Zhangzhou (Changchou), China	G8	31
Zhanjiang, China	G7	31
Zhanyu, China	B10	32
Zhao'an, China	G8	31
Zhaodong, China	A11	32
Zhaoqing, China	G7	31
Zhaotong, China	F5	31
Zhaoxing, China	C5	33
Zhaoyuan, China	B11	32
Zhaozhou, China	D2	33
Zhari Namco, l., China	B8	36
Zharkamys, Sov. Un.	D5	28
Zhashui, China	H3	32
Zhaxigang, China	A7	37
Zhdanov see Mariupol, Sov. Un.	E6	29
Zhecheng, China	G6	32
Zhejiang, prov., China	F9	31
Zhelaniya, Cape, c., Sov. Un.	B9	29
Zhen'an, China	H3	32
Zhenba, China	H2	32
Zheng'an, China	J2	32
Zhenglan Qi, China	C6	32
Zhengyangguan, China	H7	32
Zhengzhou (Chengchou), China	E7	31
Zhenjiang, China	E8	31
Zhenlai, China	B10	32
Zhenping, China	I3	32
Zhenyuan, China	K3	32
Zhidachov, Sov. Un.	D8	26
Zhidan, China	D6	31
Zhigansk, Sov. Un.	C15	29
Zhijiang, China	K3	32
Zhilaya Kosa, Sov. Un.	D4	28
Zhilevo, Sov. Un.	o18	27
Zhitomir, Sov. Un.	D5	29
Zhizdra, Sov. Un.	E10	27
Zhmerinka, Sov. Un.	G7	27
Zhob, Pak.	B4	36
Zhob, stm., Pak.	B2	37
Zhongba, China	C7	36
Zhongdian, China	F5	31
Zhongwei, China	D6	31
Zhongxian, China	E6	31
Zhongxiang, China	I5	32
Zhoukou, China	*E7	31
Zhoushan Qundao, is., China	E9	31
Zhuanghe, China	E10	32
Zhucheng, China	F8	32
Zhuji, China	J9	31
Zhukovskiy, Sov. Un.	n18	27
Zhumadian, China	H6	32
Zhuoxian, China	E6	32
Zhushan, China	E7	31
Zhuzhou, China	F7	31
Zia Indian Reservation, N.M., U.S.	h7	108
Zia Pueblo, N.M., U.S.	*B3	108
Zibo, China	D8	31
Ziebach, co., S.D., U.S.	C4	118
Zielona Góra, Pol.	C3	26
Zierikzee, Neth.	C3	17
Ziesar, E. Ger.	A7	19
Ziftã, Eg.	D3	41
Zigazinskiy, Sov. Un.	C5	28
Zigey, Chad	C3	46
Zigong, China	F5	31
Zigui, China	E7	31
Ziguinchor, Sen.	D1	45
Zikhron Ya'aqov, Isr.	B6	41
Zile, Tur.	B10	40
Zillah, Libya	D3	43
Zillah, Wa., U.S.	C5	124
Ziller, stm., Aus.	B7	20
Zilwaukee, Mi., U.S.	E7	99
Zima, Sov. Un.	D13	29
Zimapán, Mex.	C5	63
Zimba, Zam.	E4	48
Zimbabwe, ctry., Afr.	A5	49
Zimmerman, Mn., U.S.	E5	100
Zimnicea, Rom.	D7	24
Zin, Naḥal, val., Isr.	D7	41
Zinal, Switz.	D4	21
Zinc, Ar., U.S.	A3	81
Zincville, Ok., U.S.	A7	113
Zinder, Niger	D6	45
Zingst, E. Ger.	D6	15
Zion, Il., U.S.	A6	90
Zion, N.J., U.S.	C3	107
Zion, S.C., U.S.	C9	117
Zion Gate, hist., Isr. Occ.	m14	41
Zion National Park, Ut., U.S.	F3	121
Zion Reservoir, res., Az., U.S.	C6	80
Zionsville, In., U.S.	E5	91
Zionville, N.C., U.S.	A1	110
Zipaquirá, Col.	B3	60
Zirándaro, Mex.	n13	63
Zirkel, Mount, mtn., Co., U.S.	A4	83
Zirndorf, W. Ger.	D5	19
Zistersdorf, Aus.	D8	18
Zitácuaro, Mex.	n13	63
Zittau, E. Ger.	C7	18
Ziwa Magharibi, prov., Tan.	B5	48
Ziway, Lake, l., Eth.	D4	47
Ziyang, China	E6	31
Ziyuan, China	K4	32
Žižkov (part of Prague), Czech.	n17	26
Zlatograd, Bul.	E7	24
Zlatoust, Sov. Un.	D9	29
Złoczew, Pol.	C5	26
Zlonice, Czech.	n17	26
Zlotoryja, Pol.	C3	26
Złotów, Pol.	B4	26
Zlynka, Sov. Un.	E8	27
Zmeinogorsk, Sov. Un.	C10	28
Znamenka, Sov. Un.	G9	27
Żnin, Pol.	B4	26
Znojmo, Czech.	D4	26
Žilina, Czech.	D5	26
Zofingen, Switz.	B4	21
Zogno, Italy	E8	21
Zohreh, stm., Iran	F5	39
Zolfo Springs, Fl., U.S.	E5	86
Zollikofen, Switz.	B3	21
Zollikon, Switz.	B6	21
Zolochev, Sov. Un.	G5	27
Zolotonosha, Sov. Un.	G9	27
Zolotoy, Cape, c., Sov. Un.	B12	31
Zomba, Mwi.	E6	48
Zomergem, Bel.	C3	17
Zongo, Zaire	A2	48
Zonguldak, Tur.	B8	40
Zörbig, E. Ger.	B7	19
Zorita, Spain	C3	22
Zorritos, Peru	B1	58
Zortman, Mt., U.S.	C8	103
Zossen, E. Ger.	B6	18
Zouar, Chad	A3	46
Zoutkamp, Neth.	A6	17
Zreigat, Bir, well, Maur.	B3	45
Zrenjanin (Petrovgrad), Yugo.	C5	24
Zrmanja, stm., Yugo.	C2	24
Zschopau, E. Ger.	C8	19
Zuata, stm., Ven.	B4	60
Zubtsov, Sov. Un.	C10	27
Zuénoula, I.C.	E3	45
Zuera, Spain	B5	22
Zug, Switz.	E4	18
Zug, W. Sah.	E2	44
Zug, state, Switz.	E4	18
Zug, Lake, l., Switz.	E4	18
Zugdidi, Sov. Un.	A13	40
Zugspitze, mtn., Eur.	B6	20
Zuider Zee see IJsselmeer, l., Neth.	A6	16
Zulia, state, Ven.	B3	60
Zülpich, W. Ger.	C1	19
Zumbi, Ponta do, c., Braz.	B2	57
Zumbo, Moz.	A5	49
Zumbro, stm., Mn., U.S.	F6	100
Zumbro Falls, Mn., U.S.	F6	100
Zumbrota, Mn., U.S.	F6	100
Zumpango, Mex.	n14	63
Zungeru, Nig.	E6	45
Zunhua, China	C8	31
Zuni, N.M., U.S.	B1	108
Zuni, Va., U.S.	k14	123
Zuni, stm., U.S.	C6	80
Zuni Indian Reservation, N.M., U.S.	B1	108
Zuni Mountains, mts., N.M., U.S.	B1	108
Zunyi, China	F6	31
Zuoquan, China	F5	32
Zuqar, i., Yemen	C5	47
Zurich, Ont.	D3	73
Zurich, Switz.	E4	18
Zurich, Ks., U.S.	C4	93
Zurich, Mt., U.S.	B7	103
Zürich, state, Switz.	E4	18
Zürich, Lake, l., Switz.	E4	18
Zusam, stm., W. Ger.	E5	19
Zussdorf, W. Ger.	A7	21
Zutphen, Neth.	A7	16
Zuwārah, Libya	C2	43
Zuwayzā, Jord.	C7	41
Zuyevka, Sov. Un.	B4	28
Zvishavane, Zimb.	B5	49
Zvolen, Czech.	D5	26
Zvornik, Yugo.	C4	24
Zweibrücken, W. Ger.	D3	18
Zweisimmen, Switz.	C3	20
Zwenkau, E. Ger.	B7	19
Zwettl, Aus.	D7	18
Zwickau, E. Ger.	C6	18
Zwickauer Mulde, stm., E. Ger.	C7	19
Zwiesel, W. Ger.	D8	19
Zwingle, Ia., U.S.	B7	92
Zwischenahn, W. Ger.	A7	17
Zwolle, Neth.	A7	16
Zwolle, La., U.S.	C2	95
Zylks, La., U.S.	A1	95
Żyrardów, Pol.	B6	26
Zyryanovsk, Sov. Un.	D10	28
Żywiec, Pol.	D5	26

WORLD POLITICAL INFORMATION

This table lists the area, population, population density, form of government, political status, capital and predominant languages for every country in the world.

The populations are estimates for January 1, 1990 made by Rand McNally on the basis of official data, United Nations estimates, and other available information. Area figures include inland water.

The political units listed in the table are categorized by political status, as follows: A–independent countries; B–internally independent political entities which are under the protection of other countries in matters of defense and foreign affairs; C–colonies and other dependent political units; D–the major administrative subdivisions of Australia, Canada, China, the Soviet Union, the United Kingdom, and the United States. For comparison, the table also includes the continents and the world.

All footnotes to this table appear on page 228.

Country, Division or Region English (Conventional)	Area in sq. mi.	Estimated Population 1/1/90	Pop. per sq. mi.	Form of Government and Political Status	Capital	Predominant Languages
Afars and Issas *see* Djibouti	—	—	—			
† Afghanistan	251,826	15,210,000	60	Socialist republic A	Kabul (Kābol)	Dari, Pashto, Uzbek, Turkmen
Africa	11,700,000	648,300,000	55			
† Alabama	51,704	4,203,000	81	State (U.S.) D	Montgomery	English
Alaska	591,004	543,000	0.9	State (U.S.) D	Juneau	English, indigenous languages
† Albania	11,100	3,233,000	291	Socialist republic A	Tirana	Albanian, Greek
Alberta	255,287	2,475,000	9.7	Province (Canada) D	Edmonton	English
† Algeria	919,595	24,880,000	27	Socialist republic A	Algiers (El Djazaïr)	Arabic, Berber dialects, French
American Samoa	77	44,000	571	Unincorporated territory (U.S.) C	Pago Pago	Samoan, English
Andorra	175	51,000	291	Coprincipality (Spanish and French protection) B	Andorra	Spanish, French
† Angola	481,354	8,668,000	18	Socialist republic A	Luanda	Portuguese, indigenous languages
Anguilla	35	7,000	200	Dependent territory (U.K. protection) B	The Valley	English
Anhui	53,668	53,800,000	1,003	Province (China) D	Hefei	Chinese (Mandarin)
Antarctica	5,400,000	(1)	—			
† Antigua and Barbuda	171	79,000	462	Parliamentary state A	St. Johns	English, local dialects
† Argentina	1,073,400	32,680,000	30	Republic A	Buenos Aires	Spanish, English, Italian, German, French
Arizona	114,002	3,577,000	31	State (U.S.) D	Phoenix	English
Arkansas	53,191	2,451,000	46	State (U.S.) D	Little Rock	English
Armenia	11,506	3,324,000	289	Soviet socialist republic (Soviet Union) D	Yerevan	Armenian, Azerbaijani, Russian
Aruba	75	63,000	840	Self-governing territory (Netherlands protection) B	Oranjestad	Dutch, Papiamento, English, Spanish
Ascension	34	1,300	38	Dependency (St. Helena) C	Georgetown	English
Asia	17,300,000	3,156,100,000	182			
† Australia	2,966,155	16,950,000	5.7	Federal parliamentary state A	Canberra	English, indigenous languages
Australian Capital Territory	927	280,000	302	Territory (Australia) D	Canberra	English
† Austria	32,377	7,644,000	236	Federal republic A	Vienna (Wien)	German
Azerbaijan	33,436	7,081,000	212	Soviet socialist republic (Soviet Union) D	Baku	Azerbaijani, Russian, Armenian
† Bahamas	5,380	251,000	47	Parliamentary state A	Nassau	English, Creole
† Bahrain	267	478,000	1,790	Monarchy A	Manama	Arabic, English, Farsi, Urdu
† Bangladesh	55,598	107,510,000	1,934	Islamic republic A	Dhaka	Bangla, English
† Barbados	166	255,000	1,536	Parliamentary state A	Bridgetown	English
Beijing	6,487	10,045,000	1,548	Autonomous city (China) D	Beijing (Peking)	Chinese (Mandarin)
† Belgium	11,783	9,877,000	838	Constitutional monarchy A	Brussels (Bruxelles)	Dutch (Flemish), French, German
† Belize	8,866	189,000	21	Parliamentary state A	Belmopan	English, Spanish, Garifuna, Mayan
† Benin	43,475	4,667,000	107	Socialist republic A	Porto-Novo and Cotonou	French, Fon, Adja, indigenous languages
Bermuda	21	57,000	2,714	Dependent territory (U.K.) C	Hamilton	English
† Bhutan	17,954	1,550,000	86	Monarchy (Indian protection) B	Thimphu	Dzongkha, Tibetan and Nepalese dialects
† Bolivia	424,165	7,298,000	17	Republic A	La Paz and Sucre	Spanish, Quechua, Aymara
Bophuthatswana(2)	15,641	2,251,000	144	National state (South African protection) B	Mmabatho	Tswana
† Botswana	224,711	1,280,000	5.7	Republic A	Gaborone	English, Tswana
† Brazil	3,286,488	148,980,000	45	Federal republic A	Brasília	Portuguese, Spanish, English, French
British Columbia	365,948	3,011,000	8.2	Province (Canada) D	Victoria	English
British Indian Ocean Territory	23	(1)	—	Dependent territory (U.K.) C		English
† Brunei	2,226	253,000	114	Monarchy A	Bandar Seri Begawan	Malay, English, Chinese
† Bulgaria	42,823	9,015,000	211	Socialist republic A	Sofia (Sofiya)	Bulgarian
† Burkina Faso	105,869	9,019,000	85	Provisional military government A	Ouagadougou	French, indigenous languages
† Burma (Myanmar)	261,228	40,865,000	156	Provisional military government A	Rangoon (Yangon)	Burmese, indigenous languages
† Burundi	10,745	5,380,000	501	Provisional military government A	Bujumbura	French, Kirundi, Swahili
† Byelorussia	80,155	10,290,000	128	Soviet socialist republic (Soviet Union) D	Minsk	Byelorussian, Russian
California	158,704	28,815,000	182	State (U.S.) D	Sacramento	English
† Cambodia	69,898	8,153,000	117	Socialist republic A	Phnum Penh (Phnom Penh)	Khmer, French
† Cameroon	183,569	11,580,000	63	Republic A	Yaoundé	English, French, indigenous languages
† Canada	3,849,674	26,415,000	6.9	Federal parliamentary state A	Ottawa	English, French, indigenous languages
† Cape Verde	1,557	370,000	238	Republic A	Praia	Portuguese, Crioulo
Cayman Islands	100	25,000	250	Dependent territory (U.K.) C	Georgetown	English
† Central African Republic	240,535	2,843,000	12	Republic A	Bangui	French, Sango, Arabic, indigenous languages
Ceylon *see* Sri Lanka	—	—	—			
† Chad	495,755	4,984,000	10	Republic A	N'Djamena	Arabic, French, indigenous languages
Channel Islands	75	138,000	1,840	Dependent territory (U.K.) C		English, French
† Chile	292,135	13,140,000	45	Republic A	Santiago	Spanish
† China (excl. Taiwan)	3,689,631	1,092,100,000	296	Socialist republic A	Beijing (Peking)	Chinese dialects
Christmas Island	52	2,000	38	External territory (Australia) C	The Settlement	English, Chinese, Malay
Ciskei(2)	2,996	1,268,000	423	National state (South African protection) B	Bisho	English, Xhosa, Afrikaans
Cocos (Keeling) Islands	5.4	600	111	Part of Australia		English, Cocos-Malay, Malay
† Colombia	440,831	30,860,000	70	Republic A	Bogotá	Spanish
Colorado	104,094	3,402,000	33	State (U.S.) D	Denver	English
† Comoros (excl. Mayotte)	863	452,000	524	Federal Islamic republic A	Moroni	Arabic, French, Swahili, Malagasy
† Congo	132,047	2,267,000	17	Socialist republic A	Brazzaville	French, indigenous languages
Connecticut	5,019	3,302,000	658	State (U.S.) D	Hartford	English
Cook Islands	91	18,000	198	Self-governing territory (New Zealand protection) B	Avarua	English, Malay-Polynesian languages
† Costa Rica	19,730	2,958,000	150	Republic A	San José	Spanish
† Cuba	42,804	10,640,000	249	Socialist republic A	Havana (La Habana)	Spanish
† Cyprus	2,276	524,000	230	Republic A	Nicosia (Levkosía)	Greek, English
† Cyprus, North(3)	1,295	173,000	134	Republic A	Nicosia (Lefkoşa)	Turkish
† Czechoslovakia	49,382	15,670,000	317	Federal republic A	Prague (Praha)	Czech, Slovak, Hungarian
Delaware	2,045	650,000	318	State (U.S.) D	Dover	English
† Denmark	16,638	5,135,000	309	Constitutional monarchy A	Copenhagen (København)	Danish
District of Columbia	69	625,000	9,058	Federal district (U.S.) D	Washington	English
† Djibouti	8,958	333,000	37	Republic A	Djibouti	French, Somali, Afar, Arabic
† Dominica	305	86,000	282	Republic A	Roseau	English, French
† Dominican Republic	18,704	7,094,000	379	Republic A	Santo Domingo	Spanish
† Ecuador	109,484	10,650,000	97	Republic A	Quito	Spanish, Quechua, indigenous languages
† Egypt	386,662	52,830,000	137	Socialist republic A	Cairo (Al Qāhirah)	Arabic
Ellis Islands *see* Tuvalu	—	—	—			
† El Salvador	8,124	5,260,000	647	Republic A	San Salvador	Spanish, Nahua
England	50,363	47,730,000	948	Administrative division (U.K.) D	London	English
† Equatorial Guinea	10,831	357,000	33	Republic A	Malabo	Spanish, indigenous languages, English
Estonia	17,413	1,590,000	91	Soviet socialist republic (Soviet Union) D	Tallinn	Estonian, Russian
† Ethiopia	483,123	49,628,000	103	Socialist republic A	Addis Ababa	Amharic, Tigrinya, Orominga, Arabic
Europe	3,800,000	688,000,000	181			
† Faeroe Islands	540	47,000	87	Self-governing territory (Danish protection) B	Tórshavn	Danish, Faroese
Falkland Islands(4)	4,700	2,000	0.4	Dependent territory (U.K.) C	Stanley	English
† Fiji	7,078	720,000	102	Republic A	Suva	English, Fijian, Hindustani
† Finland	130,559	4,985,000	38	Republic A	Helsinki (Helsingfors)	Finnish, Swedish, Lapp
Florida	58,668	12,610,000	215	State (U.S.) D	Tallahassee	English
† France (excl. Overseas Departments)	211,208	56,210,000	266	Republic A	Paris	French
French Guiana	35,135	96,000	2.7	Overseas department (France) C	Cayenne	French
French Polynesia	1,544	194,000	126	Overseas territory (France) C	Papeete	French, Tahitian, Chinese
Fujian	46,332	28,395,000	613	Province (China) D	Fuzhou	Chinese dialects
† Gabon	103,347	1,065,000	10	Republic A	Libreville	French, Fang, indigenous languages

World Political Information

Country, Division or Region English (Conventional)	Area in sq. mi.	Estimated Population 1/1/90	Pop. per sq. mi.	Form of Government and Political Status		Capital	Predominant Languages
† Gambia	4,361	805,000	185	Republic	A	Banjul	English, Malinke, Wolof, Fula, indigenous languages
Gansu	173,746	21,405,000	123	Province (China)	D	Lanzhou	Chinese (Mandarin), Mongolian, Tibetan dialects
Georgia	58,914	6,504,000	110	State (U.S.)	D	Atlanta	English
Georgia	26,911	5,491,000	204	Soviet socialist republic (Soviet Union)	D	Tbilisi	Georgian, Russian, Armenian
† German Democratic Republic (East Germany)	41,828	16,740,000	400	Socialist republic	A	Berlin (East)	German
† Germany, Federal Republic of (West Germany)	96,028	61,460,000	640	Federal republic	A	Bonn	German
† Ghana	92,098	14,160,000	154	Provisional military government	A	Accra	English, Akan, indigenous languages
Gibraltar	2.3	31,000	13,478	Dependent territory (U.K.)	C	Gibraltar	English, Spanish
Gilbert Islands see Kiribati	—	—	—				
† Great Britain see United Kingdom	—	—	—				
† Greece	50,962	10,010,000	196	Republic	A	Athens (Athínai)	Greek
Greenland	840,004	57,000	0.1	Self-governing territory (Danish protection)	B	Godthåb	Danish, Greenlandic, Inuit dialects
† Grenada	133	97,000	729	Parliamentary state	A	St. George's	English, French
Guadeloupe (incl. Dependencies)	687	346,000	504	Overseas department (France)	C	Basse-Terre	French, Creole
Guam	209	154,000	737	Unincorporated territory (U.S.)	C	Agana	English, Chamorro, Filipino dialects
Guangdong	68,726	58,970,000	858	Province (China)	D	Guangzhou (Canton)	Chinese dialects, Miao-Yao
Guangxi Zhuangzu	91,236	40,735,000	446	Autonomous region (China)	N	Nanning	Chinese dialects, Thai, Miao-Yao
† Guatemala	42,042	9,059,000	215	Republic	A	Guatemala	Spanish, indigenous languages
Guernsey (incl. Dependencies)	30	57,000	1,900	Bailiwick (Channel Islands)	C	St. Peter Port	English, French
† Guinea	94,926	7,178,000	76	Provisional military government	A	Conakry	French, indigenous languages
† Guinea-Bissau	13,948	986,000	71	Republic	A	Bissau	Portuguese, Crioulo, indigenous languages
Guizhou	65,637	31,125,000	474	Province (China)	D	Guiyang	Chinese (Mandarin), Thai, Miao-Yao
† Guyana	83,000	765,000	9.2	Republic	A	Georgetown	English, indigenous languages
Hainan	13,127	6,553,000	499	Province (China)	D	Haikou	Chinese, Min, Tai
† Haiti	10,714	6,456,000	603	Provisional military government	A	Port-au-Prince	Creole, French
Hawaii	6,473	1,126,000	174	State (U.S.)	D	Honolulu	English, Hawaiian, Japanese
Hebei	73,359	57,990,000	790	Province (China)	D	Shijiazhuang	Chinese (Mandarin)
Heilongjiang	181,082	34,400,000	190	Province (China)	D	Harbin	Chinese dialects, Mongolian, Tungus
Henan	64,479	80,800,000	1,253	Province (China)	D	Zhengzhou	Chinese (Mandarin)
Holland see Netherlands							
† Honduras	43,277	5,039,000	116	Republic	A	Tegucigalpa	Spanish, indigenous
Hong Kong	414	5,888,000	14,222	Dependent territory (U.K.)	C	Victoria (Hong Kong)	Chinese (Cantonese), English
Hubei	72,356	51,550,000	712	Province (China)	D	Wuhan	Chinese dialects
Hunan	81,081	58,860,000	726	Province (China)	D	Changsha	Chinese dialects, Miao-Yao
† Hungary	35,920	10,565,000	294	Republic	A	Budapest	Hungarian
† Iceland	39,769	254,000	6.4	Republic	A	Reykjavík	Icelandic
Idaho	83,566	1,026,000	12	State (U.S.)	D	Boise	English
Illinois	57,872	11,780,000	204	State (U.S.)	D	Springfield	English
† India (incl. part of Jammu and Kashmir)	1,237,062	841,750,000	680	Federal republic	A	New Delhi	English, Hindi, Hindustani, indigenous languages
Indiana	36,417	5,653,000	155	State (U.S.)	D	Indianapolis	English
† Indonesia	741,101	189,460,000	256	Republic	A	Jakarta	Indonesian, Javanese, Sundanese, other indigenous languages
Inner Mongolia (Nei Monggol)	456,759	20,970,000	46	Autonomous region (China)	D	Hohhot	Mongolian
Iowa	56,275	2,877,000	51	State (U.S.)	D	Des Moines	English
† Iran	636,296	55,280,000	87	Islamic republic	A	Tehrān	Farsi, Turkish, Kurdish, Arabic, English, French
† Iraq	169,235	17,745,000	105	Republic	A	Baghdād	Arabic, Kurdish, Assyrian, Armenian
† Ireland	27,137	3,536,000	130	Republic	A	Dublin (Baile Átha Cliath)	English, Irish Gaelic
Isle of Man	221	67,000	303	Self-governing territory (U.K. protection)	B	Douglas	English, Manx Gaelic
† Israel (excl. Occupied Areas)	8,019	4,460,000	556	Republic	A	Jerusalem (Yerushalayim)	Hebrew, Arabic, English, Yiddish
Israeli Occupied Areas[5]	2,947	1,876,000	637	None			Arabic, Hebrew, English
† Italy	116,324	57,625,000	495	Republic	A	Rome (Roma)	Italian
† Ivory Coast	124,518	11,845,000	95	Republic	A	Abidjan and Yamoussoukro[6]	French, indigenous languages
† Jamaica	4,244	2,386,000	562	Parliamentary state	A	Kingston	English, Creole
† Japan	145,870	123,350,000	846	Constitutional monarchy	A	Tōkyō	Japanese
Jersey	45	81,000	1,800	Bailiwick (Channel Islands)	C	St. Helier	English, French
Jiangsu	39,614	64,760,000	1,635	Province (China)	D	Nanjing (Nanking)	Chinese dialects
Jiangxi	64,325	36,260,000	564	Province (China)	D	Nanchang	Chinese dialects
Jilin	72,201	23,915,000	331	Province (China)	D	Changchun	Chinese (Mandarin), Mongolian, Korean
† Jordan (excl. West Bank)	35,135	3,011,000	86	Constitutional monarchy	A	'Ammān	Arabic
Kansas	82,282	2,527,000	31	State (U.S.)	D	Topeka	English
Kazakh S.S.R.	1,049,156	16,675,000	16	Soviet socialist republic (Soviet Union)	D	Alma-Ata	Kazakh, Russian, German, Ukrainian
Kentucky	40,414	3,802,000	94	State (U.S.)	D	Frankfort	English
† Kenya	224,961	25,350,000	113	Republic	A	Nairobi	English, Swahili, indigenous languages
Kirghiz S.S.R.	76,641	4,335,000	57	Soviet socialist republic (Soviet Union)	D	Frunze	Kirghiz, Russian, Uzbek
Kiribati	280	70,000	250	Republic	A	Bairiki	English, Gilbertese
Korea, North	46,540	22,790,000	490	Socialist republic	A	Pyŏngyang	Korean
Korea, South	38,230	42,590,000	1,114	Republic	A	Seoul (Sŏul)	Korean
† Kuwait	6,880	1,971,000	286	Constitutional monarchy	A	Kuwait	Arabic, English
† Laos	91,429	3,980,000	44	Socialist republic	A	Viangchan (Vientiane)	Lao, French, Thai, indigenous languages
Latvia	24,595	2,717,000	110	Soviet socialist republic (Soviet Union)	D	Rīga	Latvian, Russian
† Lebanon	4,015	3,377,000	841	Republic	A	Beirut (Bayrūt)	Arabic, French, Armenian, English
† Lesotho	11,720	1,772,000	151	Constitutional monarchy	A	Maseru	English, Sesotho, Zulu, Xhosa
Liaoning	56,255	38,440,000	683	Province (China)	D	Shenyang (Mukden)	Chinese (Mandarin), Mongolian
† Liberia	38,250	2,670,000	70	Republic	A	Monrovia	English, indigenous languages
† Libya	679,362	4,143,000	6.1	Socialist republic	A	Tripoli (Ṭarābulus)	Arabic
Liechtenstein	62	28,000	452	Constitutional monarchy	A	Vaduz	German
Lithuania[7]	25,174	3,728,000	148	Soviet socialist republic (Soviet Union)	D	Vilnius	Lithuanian, Russian, Polish
Louisiana	47,750	4,503,000	94	State (U.S.)	D	Baton Rouge	English
† Luxembourg	998	381,000	382	Constitutional monarchy	A	Luxembourg	French, Luxembourgish, German, English
Macao	6.6	454,000	68,788	Chinese territory under Portuguese administration	C	Macao	Portuguese, Chinese (Cantonese)
† Madagascar	226,658	11,615,000	51	Republic	A	Antananarivo	Malagasy, French
Maine	33,265	1,226,000	37	State (U.S.)	D	Augusta	English
† Malawi	45,747	8,335,000	182	Republic	A	Lilongwe	Chichewa, English, Tombuka
† Malaysia	129,251	17,480,000	135	Federal constitutional monarchy	A	Kuala Lumpur	Malay, Chinese dialects, English, Tamil
† Maldives	115	211,000	1,835	Republic	A	Male	Divehi
† Mali	478,767	9,293,000	19	Republic	A	Bamako	French, Bambara, indigenous languages
† Malta	122	347,000	2,844	Republic	A	Valletta	English, Maltese
Manitoba	250,947	1,115,000	4.4	Province (Canada)	D	Winnipeg	English
Marshall Islands	70	43,000	614	Republic (U.S. protection)	B	Majuro (island)	English, Malay-Polynesian languages, Japanese
Martinique	425	347,000	816	Overseas department (France)	C	Fort-de-France	French, Creole
Maryland	10,461	4,703,000	450	State (U.S.)	D	Annapolis	English
Massachusetts	8,286	5,954,000	719	State (U.S.)	D	Boston	English
† Mauritania	395,956	2,008,000	5.1	Provisional military government	A	Nouakchott	Arabic, French, indigenous languages
† Mauritius (incl. Dependencies)	788	1,105,000	1,402	Parliamentary state	A	Port Louis	English, Creole, French, Bhojpuri
Mayotte[8]	144	82,000	569	Territorial collectivity (France)	C	Dzaoudzi and Mamoudzou[6]	French, Swahili (Mahorian)
† Mexico	756,066	85,090,000	113	Federal republic	A	Mexico City (Ciudad de México)	Spanish, indigenous languages
Michigan	97,107	9,431,000	97	State (U.S.)	D	Lansing	English
Micronesia, Federated States of	271	90,000	332	Republic (U.S. protection)	B	Kolonia	English, Malay-Polynesian languages
Midway Islands	2.0	500	250	Unincorporated territory (U.S.)	C		English
Minnesota	86,614	4,378,000	51	State (U.S.)	D	St. Paul	English
Mississippi	47,691	2,702,000	57	State (U.S.)	D	Jackson	English

Country, Division or Region English (Conventional)	Area in sq. mi.	Estimated Population 1/1/90	Pop. per sq. mi.	Form of Government and Political Status	Capital	Predominant Languages
Missouri	69,697	5,253,000	75	State (U.S.) ... D	Jefferson City	English
Moldavia	13,012	4,365,000	335	Soviet socialist republic (Soviet Union) ... D	Kishinev	Moldavian, Russian, Ukrainian
Monaco	0.7	29,000	41,429	Constitutional monarchy ... A	Monaco	French, English, Italian, Monegasque
†Mongolia	604,250	2,155,000	3.6	Socialist republic ... A	Ulan Bator (Ulaanbaatar)	Khalkha Mongol, Kazakh, Russian, Chinese
Montana	147,045	825,000	5.6	State (U.S.) ... D	Helena	English
Montserrat	39	12,000	308	Dependent territory (U.K.) ... C	Plymouth	English
†Morocco (excl. Western Sahara)	172,414	25,930,000	150	Constitutional monarchy ... A	Rabat	Arabic, Berber dialects, French
†Mozambique	308,642	15,535,000	50	Socialist republic ... A	Maputo	Portuguese, indigenous languages
Namibia (excl. Walvis Bay)	317,818	1,386,000	4.4	Republic ... A	Windhoek	Afrikaans, English, German, indigenous languages
Nauru	8.1	9,000	1,111	Republic ... A	Yaren District	Nauruan, English
Nebraska	77,350	1,626,000	21	State (U.S.) ... D	Lincoln	English
†Nepal	56,827	18,930,000	333	Constitutional monarchy ... A	Kathmandu (Kāṭmāṇḍau)	Nepali, Maithili, Bhojpuri, other indigenous languages
†Netherlands	16,133	14,825,000	919	Constitutional monarchy ... A	Amsterdam and The Hague ('s-Gravenhage)	Dutch
Netherlands Antilles	309	207,000	670	Self-governing territory (Netherlands protection) ... B	Willemstad	Dutch, Papiamento, English, Spanish
Nevada	110,562	1,076,000	9.7	State (U.S.) ... D	Carson City	English
New Brunswick	28,355	740,000	26	Province (Canada) ... D	Fredericton	English, French
New Caledonia	7,358	153,000	21	Overseas territory (France) ... C	Nouméa	French, Malay-Polynesian languages
Newfoundland	156,649	592,000	3.8	Province (Canada) ... D	St. John's	English
New Hampshire	9,278	1,101,000	119	State (U.S.) ... D	Concord	English
New Hebrides *see* Vanuatu	—	—	—	...	...	...
†New Jersey	7,787	7,830,000	1,006	State (U.S.) ... D	Trenton	English
New Mexico	121,594	1,551,000	13	State (U.S.) ... D	Santa Fe	English, Spanish
New South Wales	309,500	5,823,000	19	State (Australia) ... D	Sydney	English
New York	52,737	18,185,000	345	State (U.S.) ... D	Albany	English
†New Zealand	103,519	3,408,000	33	Parliamentary state ... A	Wellington	English, Maori
†Nicaragua	50,193	3,555,000	71	Republic ... A	Managua	Spanish, English, indigenous languages
†Niger	489,191	7,609,000	16	Provisional military government ... A	Niamey	French, Hausa, Djerma, indigenous languages
†Nigeria	356,669	111,010,000	311	Provisional military government ... A	Lagos and Abuja(6)	English, Hausa, Fulani, Yorbua, Ibo, indigenous languages
Ningxia Huizu	25,637	4,368,000	170	Autonomous region (China) ... D	Yinchuan	Chinese (Mandarin)
Niue	102	1,600	16	Self-governing territory (New Zealand protection) ... B	Alofi	English, Malay-Polynesian languages
Norfolk Island	14	1,900	136	External territory (Australia) ... C	Kingston	English, Norfolk
North America	9,400,000	423,600,000	45	...	...	...
†North Carolina	52,669	6,604,000	125	State (U.S.) ... D	Raleigh	English
North Dakota	70,702	699,000	9.9	State (U.S.) ... D	Bismarck	English
Northern Ireland	5,452	1,588,000	291	Administrative division (U.K.) ... D	Belfast	English
Northern Mariana Islands	184	24,000	130	Commonwealth (U.S. protection) ... B	Saipan (island)	English, Malay-Polynesian languages
Northern Territory	519,771	158,000	0.3	Territory (Australia) ... D	Darwin	English, indigenous languages
Northwest Territories	1,322,910	55,000	—	Territory (Canada) ... D	Yellowknife	English, indigenous languages
†Norway (incl. Svalbard and Jan Mayen)	149,412	4,202,000	28	Constitutional monarchy ... A	Oslo	Norwegian, Lapp
Nova Scotia	21,425	909,000	42	Province (Canada) ... D	Halifax	English
Oceania (incl. Australia)	3,300,000	26,300,000	8.0	...	...	...
†Ohio	44,786	11,005,000	246	State (U.S.) ... D	Columbus	English
Oklahoma	69,957	3,352,000	48	State (U.S.) ... D	Oklahoma City	English
†Oman	82,030	1,325,000	16	Monarchy ... A	Mascāt (Muscat)	Arabic, English, Baluchi, Urdu, Indian dialects
Ontario	412,581	9,495,000	23	Province (Canada) ... D	Toronto	English
Oregon	97,076	2,777,000	29	State (U.S.) ... D	Salem	English
Pacific Islands, Trust Territory of the	196	15,000	77	United Nations trusteeship (U.S. administration) ... B	Saipan (island)	English, Palauan
†Pakistan (incl. part of Jammu and Kashmir)	339,732	112,360,000	331	Federal Islamic republic ... A	Islāmābād	English, Urdu, Punjabi, Pashto, Sindhi, Saraiki
Palau (Belau)	196	15,000	77	Part of Trust Territory of the Pacific Islands ... B	Koror	English, Palauan
†Panama	29,762	2,396,000	81	Republic ... A	Panamá	Spanish, English, indigenous languages
†Papua New Guinea	178,704	3,653,000	20	Parliamentary state ... A	Port Moresby	English, Motu, Pidgin, indigenous languages
†Paraguay	157,048	4,221,000	27	Republic ... A	Asunción	Spanish, Guarani
Pennsylvania	46,047	12,155,000	264	State (U.S.) ... D	Harrisburg	English
†Peru	496,225	22,085,000	45	Republic ... A	Lima	Quechua, Spanish, Aymara
†Philippines	115,831	60,835,000	525	Republic ... A	Manila	English, Pilipino, Tagalog, Cebuano
Pitcairn (incl. Dependencies)	19	60	3.2	Dependent territory (U.K.) ... C	Adamstown	English, Tahitian
†Poland	120,728	37,840,000	313	Republic ... A	Warsaw (Warszawa)	Polish
†Portugal	35,516	10,495,000	296	Republic ... A	Lisbon (Lisboa)	Portuguese
Prince Edward Island	2,185	132,000	60	Province (Canada) ... D	Charlottetown	English
Puerto Rico	3,515	3,368,000	958	Commonwealth (U.S. protection) ... B	San Juan	Spanish, English
†Qatar	4,416	417,000	94	Monarchy ... A	Doha (Ad Dawḩah)	Arabic, English
Qinghai	277,994	4,259,000	15	Province (China) ... D	Xining	Tibetan dialects, Mongolian, Turkish dialects, Chinese (Mandarin)
Quebec	594,860	6,815,000	11	Province (Canada) ... D	Québec	French, English
Queensland	666,876	2,843,000	4.3	State (Australia) ... D	Brisbane	English
Reunion	969	590,000	609	Overseas department (France) ... C	Saint-Denis	French, Creole
Rhode Island	1,212	1,001,000	826	State (U.S.) ... D	Providence	English
Rhodesia *see* Zimbabwe	—	—	—	...	...	...
†Romania	91,699	23,210,000	253	Socialist republic ... A	Bucharest (Bucureşti)	Romanian, Hungarian, German
Russian Soviet Federative Socialist Republic	6,592,849	148,550,000	23	Soviet socialist republic (Soviet Union) ... D	Moscow (Moskva)	Russian, Tatar, Ukrainian
†Rwanda	10,169	7,463,000	734	Republic ... A	Kigali	French, Kinyarwanda
†St. Christopher-Nevis	104	46,000	442	Parliamentary state ... A	Basseterre	English
St. Helena (incl. Dependencies)	162	7,600	47	Dependent territory (U.K.) ... C	Jamestown	English
†St. Lucia	238	151,000	634	Parliamentary state ... A	Castries	English, French
St. Pierre and Miquelon	93	6,800	73	Territorial collectivity (France) ... C	Saint-Pierre	French
†St. Vincent and the Grenadines	150	114,000	760	Parliamentary state ... A	Kingstown	English, French
San Marino	24	24,000	1,000	Republic ... A	San Marino	Italian
†Sao Tome and Principe	372	123,000	331	Republic ... A	São Tomé	Portuguese, indigenous languages
Saskatchewan	251,866	1,051,000	4.2	Province (Canada) ... D	Regina	English
†Saudi Arabia	830,000	14,645,000	18	Monarchy ... A	Riyadh (Ar Riyāḑ)	Arabic
Scotland	30,414	5,150,000	169	Administrative division (U.K.) ... D	Edinburgh	English, Scots Gaelic
†Senegal	75,955	7,367,000	97	Republic ... A	Dakar	French, Wolof, indigenous languages
†Seychelles	175	69,000	394	Republic ... A	Victoria	English, French, Creole
Shaanxi	79,151	31,450,000	397	Province (China) ... D	Xi'an (Sian)	Chinese (Mandarin)
Shandong	59,074	80,380,000	1,361	Province (China) ... D	Jinan	Chinese (Mandarin)
Shanghai	2,394	12,780,000	5,338	Autonomous city (China) ... D	Shanghai	Chinese (Wu)
Shanxi	60,232	27,410,000	455	Province (China) ... D	Taiyuan	Chinese (Mandarin)
Sichuan	220,078	106,590,000	484	Province (China) ... D	Chengdu	Chinese (Mandarin), Tibetan dialects, Miao-Yao
†Sierra Leone	27,925	4,116,000	147	Republic ... A	Freetown	English, Krio, indigenous languages
†Singapore	246	2,710,000	11,016	Republic ... A	Singapore	Chinese (Mandarin), English, Malay, Tamil
†Solomon Islands	10,954	312,000	28	Parliamentary state ... A	Honiara	English, Malay-Polynesian languages
†Somalia	246,201	8,332,000	34	Socialist republic ... A	Mogadishu (Muqdisho)	Arabic, Somali, English, Italian
†South Africa (incl. Walvis Bay)	433,680	36,790,000	85	Republic ... A	Pretoria, Cape Town, and Bloemfontein	Afrikaans, English, Zulu, Xhosa, other indigenous languages
South America	6,900,000	293,700,000	43	...	...	...
†South Australia	379,925	1,437,000	3.8	State (Australia) ... D	Adelaide	English
South Carolina	31,116	3,552,000	114	State (U.S.) ... D	Columbia	English

World Political Information

Country, Division or Region English (Conventional)	Area in sq. mi.	Estimated Population 1/1/90	Pop. per sq. mi.	Form of Government and Political Status		Capital	Predominant Languages
South Dakota	77,120	725,000	9.4	State (U.S.)	D	Pierre	English
South Georgia and the South Sandwich Islands	1,450	(1)	—	Dependent territory (U.K.)	C		English
† Soviet Union	8,600,387	289,010,000	34	Federal socialist republic	A	Moscow (Moskva)	Russian and other Slavic languages, various ethnic languages
† Spain	194,885	39,520,000	203	Constitutional monarchy	A	Madrid	Spanish (Castilian), Catalan, Galician, Basque
Spanish North Africa(9)	12	100,000	8,333	Five possessions (Spain)	C		Spanish, Arabic, Berber dialects
Spanish Sahara see Western Sahara	—						
† Sri Lanka	24,962	16,935,000	678	Socialist republic	A	Colombo and Sri Jayawardenapura	English, Sinhala, Tamil
† Sudan	967,500	24,775,000	26	Provisional military government	A	Khartoum (Al Kharṭūm)	Arabic, indigenous, English
† Suriname	63,251	405,000	6.4	Republic	A	Paramaribo	Dutch, Sranan Tongo, English, Hindustani, Javanese
† Swaziland	6,704	787,000	117	Monarchy	A	Mbabane and Lobamba(6)	English, siSwati
† Sweden	173,732	8,503,000	49	Constitutional monarchy	A	Stockholm	Swedish
Switzerland	15,943	6,623,000	415	Federal republic	A	Bern (Berne)	German, French, Italian, Romansch
† Syria	71,498	11,915,000	167	Socialist republic	A	Damascus (Dimashq)	Arabic, Kurdish, Armenian, Aramaic, Circassian
Taiwan	13,900	20,345,000	1,464	Republic	A	T'aipei	Chinese dialects
Tajik S.S.R.	55,251	5,144,000	93	Soviet socialist republic (Soviet Union)	D	Dushanbe	Tajik, Uzbek, Russian
† Tanzania	364,900	25,220,000	69	Republic	A	Dar es Salaam and Dodoma(6)	English, Swahili, indigenous languages
Tasmania	26,178	456,000	17	State (Australia)	D	Hobart	English
Tennessee	42,143	5,003,000	119	State (U.S.)	D	Nashville	English
Texas	266,805	17,060,000	64	State (U.S.)	D	Austin	English, Spanish
† Thailand	198,115	55,925,000	282	Constitutional monarchy	A	Bangkok (Krung Thep)	Thai, indigenous languages
Tianjin (Tientsin)	4,363	8,409,000	1,927	Autonomous city (China)	D	Tianjin (Tientsin)	Chinese (Mandarin)
Tibet (Xizang)	471,045	2,075,000	4.4	Autonomous region (China)	D	Lhasa	Tibetan dialects
† Togo	21,925	3,508,000	160	Republic	A	Lomé	French, indigenous languages
Tokelau	4.6	1,700	370	Island territory (New Zealand)	C		English, Tokelauan
Tonga	290	97,000	334	Constitutional monarchy	A	Nuku'alofa	Tongan, English
Transkei(2)	16,816	3,636,000	216	National state (South African protection)	B	Umtata	Xhosa, Afrikaans
† Trinidad and Tobago	1,980	1,248,000	630	Republic	A	Port of Spain	English, Hindi, French, Spanish
Tristan da Cunha	40	300	7.5	Dependency (St. Helena)	C	Edinburgh	English
† Tunisia	63,170	8,079,000	128	Republic	A	Tunis	Arabic, French
† Turkey	300,948	54,075,000	180	Republic	A	Ankara	Turkish, Kurdish, Arabic
Turkmen S.S.R.	188,456	3,555,000	19	Soviet socialist republic (Soviet Union)	D	Ashkhabad	Turkmen, Russian, Uzbek, Kazakh
Turks and Caicos Islands	166	11,000	66	Dependent territory (U.K.)	C	Grand Turk	English
Tuvalu	10	8,800	880	Parliamentary state	A	Funafuti	Tuvaluan, English
† Uganda	93,104	17,300,000	186	Provisional military government	A	Kampala	English, Luganda, Swahili, indigenous languages
† Ukraine	233,090	52,110,000	224	Soviet socialist republic (Soviet Union)	D	Kiev	Ukrainian, Russian
† United Arab Emirates	32,278	2,183,000	68	Federation of monarchs	A	Abu Dhabi (Abū Ẓaby)	Arabic, English, Farsi, Hindi, Urdu
† United Kingdom	94,248	57,335,000	608	Constitutional monarchy	A	London	English, Welsh, Gaelic
† United States	3,679,245	250,150,000	68	Federal republic	A	Washington	English, Spanish
Upper Volta see Burkina Faso	—	—	—				
† Uruguay	68,500	3,120,000	46	Republic	A	Montevideo	Spanish
Utah	84,902	1,726,000	20	State (U.S.)	D	Salt Lake City	English
Uzbek S.S.R.	172,742	20,055,000	116	Soviet socialist republic (Soviet Union)	D	Tashkent	Uzbek, Russian, Kazakh, Tajik, Tatar
† Vanuatu	4,706	158,000	34	Republic	A	Port-Vila	Bislama, English, French
Vatican City	0.2	800	4,000	Ecclesiastical city-state	A	Vatican City	Italian, Latin
Venda(2)	2,393	588,000	246	National state (South African protection)	B	Thohoyandou	Afrikaans, English, Venda
† Venezuela	352,145	19,485,000	55	Federal republic	A	Caracas	Spanish, indigenous
Vermont	9,614	563,000	59	State (U.S.)	D	Montpelier	English
Victoria	87,877	4,355,000	50	State (Australia)	D	Melbourne	English
† Vietnam	127,242	65,475,000	515	Socialist republic	A	Hanoi (Ha Noi)	Vietnamese, French, Chinese, English, indigenous languages
Virginia	40,763	6,104,000	150	State (U.S.)	D	Richmond	English
Virgin Islands (U.S.)	133	114,000	857	Unincorporated territory (U.S.)	C	Charlotte Amalie	English, Spanish, Creole
Virgin Islands, British	59	13,000	220	Dependent territory (U.K.)	C	Road Town	English
Wake Island	3.0	300	100	Unincorporated territory (U.S.)	C		English
Wales	8,019	2,867,000	358	Administrative division (U.K.)	D	Cardiff	English, Welsh Gaelic
Wallis and Futuna	98	16,000	163	Overseas territory (France)	C	Mata-Utu	French, Uvean, Futunan
Washington	68,139	4,678,000	69	State (U.S.)	D	Olympia	English
Western Australia	975,101	1,598,000	1.6	State (Australia)	D	Perth	English
Western Sahara	102,703	196,000	1.9	Occupied by Morocco	C	El Aaiún	Arabic
† Western Samoa	1,093	184,000	168	Constitutional monarchy	A	Apia	English, Samoan
West Virginia	24,236	1,926,000	79	State (U.S.)	D	Charleston	English
Wisconsin	66,213	4,903,000	74	State (U.S.)	D	Madison	English
Wyoming	97,808	500,000	5.1	State (U.S.)	D	Cheyenne	English
Xinjiang Uygur	617,764	14,305,000	23	Autonomous region (China)	D	Ürümqi	Turkish dialects, Mongolian, Tungus, English
† Yemen	205,356	13,019,000	63	Islamic republic	A	Ṣanʿāʾ	Arabic
† Yugoslavia	98,766	23,765,000	241	Federal socialist republic	A	Belgrade (Beograd)	Macedonian, Serbo-Croatian, Slovene, Albanian, Hungarian
Yukon Territory	186,661	25,000	0.1	Territory (Canada)	D	Whitehorse	English, Inuktitut, indigenous languages
Yunnan	152,124	35,710,000	235	Province (China)	D	Kunming	Chinese (Mandarin), Tibetan dialects, Khmer, Miao-Yao
† Zaire	905,568	35,165,000	39	Republic	A	Kinshasa	French, Kikongo, Lingala, Swahili, Tshiluba
† Zambia	290,586	7,995,000	28	Republic	A	Lusaka	English, Bemba, Nyanja, Tonga, indigenous languages
Zhejiang	39,305	42,045,000	1,070	Province (China)	D	Hangzhou	Chinese dialects
† Zimbabwe	150,873	9,252,000	61	Republic	A	Harare (Salisbury)	English, ChiShona, SiNdebele
WORLD	57,800,000	5,236,000,000	91				

† Member of the United Nations (1989).
(1) No permanent population.
(2) Bophuthatswana, Ciskei, Transkei, and Venda are not recognized by the United Nations.
(3) North Cyprus unilaterally declared its independence from Cyprus in 1983.
(4) Claimed by Argentina.
(5) Includes West Bank, Golan Heights, and Gaza Strip.
(6) Future capital.
(7) Lithuania unilaterally declared its independence from the Soviet Union in 1990.
(8) Claimed by Comoros.
(9) Comprises Ceuta, Melilla, and several small islands.

WORLD GEOGRAPHICAL INFORMATION

GENERAL

MOVEMENTS OF THE EARTH

The earth makes one complete revolution around the sun every 365 days, 5 hours, 48 minutes, and 46 seconds.

The earth makes one complete rotation on its axis in 23 hours, 56 minutes and 4 seconds.

The earth revolves in its orbit around the sun at a speed of 66,700 miles per hour.

The earth rotates on its axis at an equatorial speed of more than 1,000 miles per hour.

MEASUREMENTS OF THE EARTH

Estimated age of the earth, at least 4.6 billion years.

Equatorial diameter of the earth, 7,926.38 miles.

Polar diameter of the earth, 7,899.80 miles.

Mean diameter of the earth, 7,917.52 miles.

Equatorial circumference of the earth, 24,901.46 miles.

Polar circumference of the earth, 24,855.34 miles.

Difference between equatorial and polar circumferences of the earth, 46.12 miles.

Weight of the earth, 6,600,000,000,000,000,000,000 tons, or 6,600 billion billion tons.

THE EARTH'S SURFACE

Total area of the earth, 197,000,000 square miles.

Total land area of the earth (including inland water and Antarctica), 57,800,000 square miles.

Highest point on the earth's surface, Mt. Everest, Asia, 29,028 feet.

Lowest point on the earth's land surface, shores of the Dead Sea, Asia, –1,322 feet below sea level.

Greatest known depth of the ocean, the Mariana Trench, southwest of Guam, Pacific Ocean, 35,810 feet.

THE EARTH'S INHABITANTS

Population of the earth is estimated to be 5,236,000,000 (January 1, 1990).

Estimated population density of the earth, 91 per square mile.

EXTREMES OF TEMPERATURE AND RAINFALL OF THE EARTH

Highest temperature ever recorded, 136° F. at Al' 'Azīzīyah, Libya, Africa, on September 13, 1922.

Lowest temperature ever recorded, –129° F. at Vostok, Antarctica on July 21, 1983.

Highest mean annual temperature, 94° F. at Dallol, Ethiopia.

Lowest mean annual temperature, –70° F. at Plateau Station, Antarctica.

The greatest local average annual rainfall is at Mt. Waialeale, Kauai, Hawaii, 460 inches.

The greatest 24-hour rainfall, 74 inches, is at Cilaos, Reunion Island, March 15-16, 1952.

The lowest local average annual rainfall is at Arica, Chile, .03 inches.

The longest dry period, over 14 years, is at Arica, Chile, October 1903 to January 1918.

THE CONTINENTS

CONTINENT	Area (sq. mi.)	Estimated Population Jan. 1, 1990	Population per sq. mi.	Mean Elevation (feet)	Highest Elevation (Feet)	Lowest Elevation (Feet)	Highest Recorded Temperature	Lowest Recorded Temperature
North America	9,400,000	423,600,000	45	2,000	Mt. McKinley, Alaska, United States, 20,320	Death Valley, California, United States 282 below sea level	Death Valley, California 134° F	Northice, Greenland –87° F
South America	6,900,000	293,700,000	43	1,800	Cerro Aconcagua, Argentina 22,831	Salinas Chicas, Argentina 138 below sea level	Rivadavia, Argentina 120° F	Sarmiento, Argentina –27° F
Europe	3,800,000	688,000,000	181	980	Mt. Elbrus, Soviet Union 18,510	Caspian Sea, Soviet Union-Iran 92 below sea level	Sevilla, Spain 122° F	Ust-Shchugor, Soviet Union –67° F
Asia............	17,300,000	3,156,100,000	182	3,000	Mt. Everest, China-Nepal 29,028	Dead Sea, Israel-Jordan 1,322 below sea leve	Tirat Zevi, Israel 129° F	Oymyakon and Verkhoyansk, Soviet Union –90° F
Africa	11,700,000	648,300,000	55	1,900	Kilimanjaro, Tanzania 19,340	Lac Assal, Djibouti 509 below sea level	Al 'Azīzīyah, Libya 136° F	Ifrane, Morocco –11° F
Oceania, incl. Australia	3,300,000	26,300,000	8.0	....	Mt. Wilhelm, Papua New Guinea 14,793	Lake Eyre, South Australia 52 below sea level	Cloncurry, Queensland, Australia 128° F	Charlotte Pass, New South Wales, Australia –8° F
Australia	2,966,155	16,950,000	5.7	1,000	Mt. Kosciusko, New South Wales 7,310	Lake Eyre, South Australia 52 below sea level	Cloncurry, Queensland 128° F	Charlotte Pass, New South Wales –8° F
Antarctica........	5,400,000	Uninhabited	....	6,000	Vinson Massif 16,864	sea level	Vanda Station 59° F	Vostok –129° F
World	57,800,000	5,236,000,000	91	....	Mt. Everest, China-Nepal 29,028	Dead Sea, Israel-Jordan 1,322 below sea leve	Al 'Azīzīyah, Libya 136° F	Vostok, Antarctica –129°

HISTORICAL POPULATIONS *

AREA	1650	1750	1800	1850	1900	1914	1920	1939	1950	1990
North America	5,000,000	5,000,000	13,000,000	39,000,000	106,000,000	141,000,000	147,000,000	186,000,000	219,000,000	423,600,000
South America	8,000,000	7,000,000	12,000,000	20,000,000	38,000,000	55,000,000	61,000,000	90,000,000	111,000,000	293,700,000
Europe	100,000,000	140,000,000	190,000,000	265,000,000	400,000,000	470,000,000	453,000,000	526,000,000	530,000,000	688,000,000
Asia..................	335,000,000	476,000,000	593,000,000	754,000,000	932,000,000	1,006,000,000	1,000,000,000	1,247,000,000	1,418,000,000	3,156,100,000
Africa.................	100,000,000	95,000,000	90,000,000	95,000,000	118,000,000	130,000,000	140,000,000	170,000,000	199,000,000	648,300,000
Oceania, incl. Australia ..	2,000,000	2,000,000	2,000,000	2,000,000	6,000,000	8,000,000	9,000,000	11,000,000	13,000,000	26,300,000
Australia					4,000,000	5,000,000	6,000,000	7,000,000	8,000,000	16,950,000
World	550,000,000	725,000,000	900,000,000	1,175,000,000	1,600,000,000	1,810,000,000	1,810,000,000	2,230,000,000	2,490,000,000	5,236,000,000

* Figures prior to 1990 are rounded to the nearest million.   *Figures in italics represent very rough estimates.*

LARGEST COUNTRIES : POPULATION

		Population 1/1/90
1	China (excl. Taiwan) .	1,092,100,000
2	India (incl. part of Jammu and Kashmir)	841,750,000
3	Soviet Union........	289,010,000
4	United States	250,150,000
5	Indonesia	189,460,000
6	Brazil	148,980,000
7	Japan	123,350,000
8	Pakistan (incl. part of Jammu and Kashmir)	112,360,000
9	Nigeria.............	111,010,000
10	Bangladesh.........	107,510,000
11	Mexico	85,090,000
12	Vietnam............	65,475,000
13	Germany, Federal Republic of (West Germany)	61,460,000
14	Philippines..........	60,835,000
15	Italy	57,625,000
16	United Kingdom	57,335,000
17	France.............	56,210,000
18	Thailand	55,925,000
19	Iran	55,280,000
20	Turkey	54,075,000
21	Egypt..............	52,830,000
22	Ethiopia	49,628,000
23	Korea, South	42,590,000
24	Burma	40,865,000
25	Spain	39,520,000

LARGEST COUNTRIES : AREA

		Area (sq. mi.)
1	Soviet Union...........	8,600,387
2	Canada	3,849,674
3	China (excl. Taiwan)	3,689,631
4	United States	3,679,245
5	Brazil.................	3,286,488
6	Australia	2,966,155
7	India (incl. part of Jammu and Kashmir)	1,237,062
8	Argentina	1,073,400
9	Sudan	967,500
10	Algeria	919,595
11	Zaire	905,568
12	Greenland	840,004
13	Saudi Arabia...........	830,000
14	Mexico	756,066
15	Indonesia	741,101
16	Libya	679,362
17	Iran	636,296
18	Mongolia	604,250
19	Peru	496,225
20	Chad	495,755
21	Niger	489,191
22	Ethiopia	483,123
23	Angola	481,354
24	Mali	478,767
25	Colombia.............	440,831
26	South Africa	433,680
27	Bolivia	424,165
28	Mauritania	395,956
29	Egypt...............	386,662
30	Tanzania	364,900
31	Nigeria..............	356,669

World Geographical Information

PRINCIPAL MOUNTAINS

NORTH AMERICA

Height (feet)

McKinley, Mt., Δ Alaska (Δ United States;
  Δ North America) 20,320
Logan, Mt., Δ Canada (Δ Yukon; Δ St. Elias
  Mts.) 19,524
Orizaba, Pico de, Δ Mexico 18,406
St. Elias, Mt., Alaska—Canada 18,008
Popocatépetl, Volcán, Mexico 17,930
Foraker, Mt., Alaska 17,400
Iztaccíhuatl, Mexico 17,159
Lucania, Mt., Canada 17,147
Fairweather, Mt., Alaska—Canada (Δ British
  Columbia) 15,300
Whitney, Mt., Δ California 14,491
Elbert, Mt., Δ Colorado (Δ Rocky Mts.) 14,433
Massive, Mt., Colorado 14,421
Harvard, Mt., Colorado 14,420
Rainier, Mt., Δ Washington (Δ Cascade
  Range) 14,410
Williamson, Mt., California 14,375
Blanca Pk., Colorado (Δ Sangre de Cristo
  Mts.) 14,345
La Plata Pk., Colorado 14,336
Uncompahgre Pk., Colorado (Δ San Juan
  Mts.) 14,309
Grays Pk., Colorado (Δ Front Range) 14,270
Evans, Mt., Colorado 14,264
Longs Pk., Colorado 14,255
Wrangell, Mt., Alaska 14,163
Shasta, Mt., California 14,162
Pikes Pk., Colorado 14,110
Colima, Nevado de, Mexico 13,911
Tajumulco, Volcán, Δ Guatemala (Δ Central
  America) 13,846
Gannett Pk., Δ Wyoming 13,804
Mauna Kea, Δ Hawaii 13,796
Grand Teton Mtn., Wyoming 13,770
Mauna Loa, Hawaii 13,679
Kings Pk,, Δ Utah 13,528
Cloud Pk., Wyoming (Δ Bighorn Mts.) 13,167
Wheeler Pk., Δ New Mexico 13,161
Boundary Pk., Δ Nevada 13,143
Waddington, Mt., Canada (Δ Coast Mts.) 13,104
Robson, Mt., Canada (Δ Canadian Rockies) 12,972
Granite Pk., Δ Montana 12,799
Borah Pk., Δ Idaho 12,662
Humphreys Pk., Δ Arizona 12,633
Chirripó, Cerro, Δ Costa Rica 12,533
Columbia, Mt., Canada (Δ Alberta) 12,294
Adams, Mt., Washington 12,276
Gunnbjørn Mtn., Δ Greenland 12,139
San Gorgonio Mtn., California 11,499
Barú, Volcán, Δ Panama 11,411
Hood, Mt., Δ Oregon 11,235
Lassen Pk., California 10,457
Duarte, Pico, Δ Dominican Rep. (Δ West
  Indies) 10,417
Haleakala Crater, Hawaii (Δ Maui) 10,023
Paricutín, Mexico 9,213
El Pital, Cerro, Δ El Salvador—Honduras 8,957
La Selle, Pic, Δ Haiti 8,773
Guadalupe Pk., Δ Texas 8,749
Olympus, Mt., Washington (Δ Olympic Mts.) 7,965
Blue Mountain Pk., Δ Jamaica 7,402
Harney Pk., Δ South Dakota (Δ Black Hills) 7,242
Mitchell, Mt., Δ North Carolina (Δ Appalachian
  Mts.) 6,684
Clingmans Dome, North
  Carolina—Δ Tennessee (Δ Great Smoky
  Mts.) 6,643
Turquino, Pico, Δ Cuba 6,542
Washington, Mt., Δ New Hampshire (Δ White
  Mts.) 6,288
Rogers, Mt., Δ Virginia 5,729
Marcy, Mt., Δ New York (Δ Adirondack Mts.) 5,344
Katahdin, Mt., Δ Maine 5,268
Kawaikini, Mt., Δ Kauai) 5,243
Spruce Knob, Δ West Virginia 4,862
Pelée, Montagne, Δ Martinique 4,583
Mansfield, Mt., Δ Vermont (Δ Green Mts.) 4,393
Punta, Cerro de, Δ Puerto Rico 4,389
Black Mtn., Δ Kentucky—Virginia 4,145
Kaala, Hawaii (Δ Oahu) 4,040

SOUTH AMERICA

Aconcagua, Cerro, Δ Argentina (Δ Andes
  Mts.; Δ South America) 22,831
Ojos del Salado, Nevado,
  Argentina—Δ Chile 22,615
Illimani, Nevado, Δ Bolivia 22,579
Bonete, Cerro, Argentina 22,546
Pissis, Monte, Argentina 22,241
Huascarán, Nevado, Δ Peru 22,123
Llullaillaco, Volcán, Argentina—Chile 22,110

Yerupaja, Nevado, Peru 21,765
Tupungato, Cerro, Argentina—Chile 21,490
Sajama, Nevado, Bolivia 21,463
Illampu, Nevado, Bolivia 20,873
Chimborazo, Δ Ecuador 20,702
Antofalla, Volcán, Argentina 20,013
Cotopaxi, Ecuador 19,347
Misti, Volcán, Peru 19,101
Cristóbal Colón, Pico, Δ Colombia 19,028
Huila, Nevado del, Colombia (Δ Cordillera
  Central) 18,865
Bolívar, Pico, Δ Venezuela 16,427
Fitzroy, Monte (Cerro Chaltel),
  Argentina—Chile 11,073
Neblina, Pico da, Δ Brazil—Venezuela 9,888

EUROPE

Elbrus, Mt., Soviet Union (Δ Caucasus Mts.;
  Δ Europe) 18,510
Dykh—Tau, Mt., Soviet Union 17,073
Shkhara, Mt., Soviet Union 16,512
Blanc, Mont (Monte Bianco),
  Δ France—Δ Italy (Δ Alps) 15,771
Rosa, Monte (Dufourspitze),
  Italy—Δ Switzerland 15,203
Weisshorn, Switzerland 14,780
Matterhorn, Italy—Switzerland 14,692
Finsteraarhorn, Switzerland 14,022
Jungfrau, Switzerland 13,642
Écrins, Barre des, France 13,458
Viso, Mt., Italy (Δ Cottian Alps) 12,602
Grossglockner, Δ Austria 12,457
Teide, Pico de, Δ Spain (Δ Canary Is.) 12,198
Mulhacén, Δ Spain (continental) 11,411
Aneto, Pico de, Spain (Δ Pyrenees) 11,168
Perdido (Perdu), Spain 11,007
Etna, Mt., Italy (Δ Sicily) 10,902
Zugspitze, Austria—Δ Germany,
  Fed. Rep. of 9,718
Musala, Δ Bulgaria 9,596
Olympus, Mt., Δ Greece 9,570
Corno Grande, Italy (Δ Apennines) 9,554
Triglav, Δ Yugoslavia 9,393
Korab, Δ Albania—Yugoslavia 9,026
Cinto, Monte, France (Δ Corsica) 8,878
Gerlachovka, Δ Czechoslovakia (Δ Carpathian
  Mts.) 8,711
Moldoveanu, Δ Romania 8,343
Rysy, Czechoslovakia—Δ Poland 8,199
Glittertinden, Δ Norway (Δ Scandinavia) 8,110
Parnassós, Greece 8,061
Ida, Mount, Greece (Δ Crete) 8,058
Pico, Ponta do, Δ Portugal (Δ Azores Is.) 7,713
Hvannadalshnúkur, Δ Iceland 6,952
Kebnekaise, Δ Sweden 6,926
Estrêla, Serra da, Δ Portugal (continental) 6,539
Narodnaya, Mt., Soviet Union (Δ Ural Mts.) 6,217
Sancy, Puy de, France (Δ Massif Central) 6,184
La Marmora, Punta, Italy (Δ Sardinia) 6,017
Hekla, Mt., Iceland 4,892
Nevis, Ben, Δ United Kingdom (Δ Scotland) 4,406
Haltia, Δ Finland—Norway 4,357
Vesuvius, Italy 4,190
Snowdon, United Kingdom (Δ Wales) 3,560
Carrauntoohil, Δ Ireland 3,406
Kékes, Δ Hungary 3,327
Scafell Pikes, United Kingdom (Δ England) 3,210

ASIA

Everest, Mt., Δ China—Δ Nepal (Δ Tibet;
  Δ Himalayas; Δ Asia; Δ World) 29,028
K2 (Godwin Austen/Qogir Feng),
  China—Δ Pakistan (Δ Kashmir;
  Δ Karakoram Range) 28,250
Kānchenjunga, Δ India—Nepal 28,208
Makālu, China—Nepal 27,825
Dhawalāgiri, Nepal 26,810
Nānga Parbat, Pakistan 26,660
Annapurna, Nepal 26,504
Gasherbrum, China—Pakistan 26,470
Xixabangma Mtn. (Gosainthan), China 26,286
Nanda Devi, India 25,645
Kāmet, China—India 25,446
Namjagbarwa Feng, China 25,446
Muztag, China (Δ Kunlun Shan) 25,338
Tirich Mīr, Pakistan (Δ Hindu Kush) 25,230
Gongga Shan, China 24,790
Kula Kangri, Δ Bhutan 24,784
Muztagata, China 24,757
Communism Pk., Δ Soviet Union (Δ Pamir
  Mts.) 24,590
Nowshāk, Δ Afghanistan—Pakistan 24,557
Pobedy, Pk., China—Soviet Union 24,406
Chomo Lhāri, Bhutan—China 23,996
Lenin Pk., Soviet Union 23,406

Api, Nepal 23,399
Kangrinboqê Mtn., China 22,028
Hkakabo Razi, Δ Burma 19,296
Demavend, Mt., Δ Iran 18,386
Fūlādī, Kūh-e, Afghanistan 16,847
Ararat, Mt., Δ Turkey 16,804
Jaya Pk., Δ Indonesia (Δ New Guinea) 16,503
Klyuchevskaya Sopka, Soviet Union
  (Δ Kamchatka Peninsula) 15,584
Trikora Pk., Indonesia 15,584
Belukha, Mt., Soviet Union 14,783
Kinabalu, Mt., Δ Malaysia (Δ Borneo) 13,455
Türgen Mtn., Mongolia 13,051
Yu Shan, Δ Taiwan 12,959
Erciyes Mtn., Turkey 12,848
Kerinci, Indonesia (Δ Sumatra) 12,467
Fuji, Mt., Δ Japan (Δ Honshu) 12,388
Rinjani, Indonesia (Δ Lombok) 12,224
Semeru, Indonesia (Δ Java) 12,060
Nabi Shuayb, Mt., Δ Yemen (Δ Arabian
  Peninsula) 12,008
Rantekombola, Indonesia (Δ Celebes) 11,335
Slamet, Indonesia 11,247
Fan Si Pan, Δ Vietnam 10,312
Sham, Mt., Δ Oman 9,957
Apo, Mt., Δ Philippines (Δ Mindanao) 9,692
Pulog, Mt., Philippines (Δ Luzon) 9,626
Bia, Mt., Δ Laos 9,249
Hermon, Mt., Lebanon—Δ Syria 9,232
Paektu, Mt., Δ North Korea—China 9,003
Inthanon, Mt., Δ Thailand 8,530
Pidurutalagala, Δ Sri Lanka 8,281
Mayon Volcano, Philippines 8,077
Asahi, Mt., Japan (Δ Hokkaido) 7,513
Tahan, Malaysia (Δ Malaya) 7,174
Ólimbos, Δ Cyprus 6,401
Halla, Mt., Δ South Korea 6,398
Aoral, Mt., Δ Cambodia 5,948
Kujū, Mt., Japan (Δ Kyushu) 5,866
Ramm, Jabal, Δ Jordan 5,755
Meron, Mt., Δ Israel 3,963
Carmel, Mt., Israel 1,791

AFRICA

Kilimanjaro, Δ Tanzania (Δ Africa) 19,340
Kirinyaga (Mt. Kenya), Δ Kenya 17,058
Margherita Pk., Δ Uganda—Δ Zaire 16,763
Ras Dashen Terara, Δ Ethiopia 15,158
Meru, Mt., Tanzania 14,978
Karisimbi, Volcan, Δ Rwanda—Zaire 14,787
Elgon, Mt., Kenya—Uganda 14,178
Toubkal, Jbel, Δ Morocco (Δ Atlas Mts.) 13,665
Cameroun, Mont, Δ Cameroon 13,353
Ntlenyana, Thabana, Δ Lesotho 11,425
eNjesuthi, Δ South Africa 11,306
Koussi, Emi, Δ Chad (Δ Tibesti Mts.) 11,204
Kinyeti, Δ Sudan 10,456
Santa Isabel, Pico de, Δ Equatorial Guinea
  (Δ Bioko) 9,869
Tahat, Δ Algeria (Δ Ahaggar Mts.) 9,541
Maromokotro, Δ Madagascar 9,436
Kātrīnā, Jabal, Δ Egypt 8,668
São Tomé, Pico de, Δ Sao Tome 6,640

OCEANIA

Wilhelm, Mt., Δ Papua New Guinea 14,793
Giluwe, Mt., Papua New Guinea 14,331
Bangeta, Mt., Papua New Guinea 13,520
Victoria, Mt., Papua New Guinea (Δ Owen
  Stanley Range) 13,240
Cook, Mt., Δ New Zealand (Δ South Island) 12,349
Ruapehu, Mt., New Zealand (Δ North Island) 9,177
Balbi, Papua New Guinea (Δ Solomon Is.) 9,000
Egmont, Mt., New Zealand 8,260
Orohena, Mont, Δ French Polynesia (Δ Tahiti) 7,352
Kosciusko, Mt., Δ Australia (Δ New South
  Wales) 7,310
Silisili, Mt., Δ Western Samoa 6,096
Panié, Mont, Δ New Caledonia 5,341
Ossa, Mt., Australia (Δ Tasmania) 5,305
Bartle Frere, Mt., Australia (Δ Queensland) 5,285
Woodroffe, Mt., Australia (Δ South Australia) 4,721
Sinewit, Mt., Papua New Guinea (Δ Bismarck
  Archipelago) 4,462
Tomanivi (Victoria), Δ Fiji (Δ Viti Levu) 4,341
Meharry, Mt., Australia (Δ Western Australia) 4,104
Ayers Rock, Australia 2,844

ANTARCTICA

Vinson Massif, Δ Antarctica 16,864
Kirkpatrick, Mt. 14,856
Markham,Mt. 14,275
Jackson, Mt. 13,750
Sidley, Mt. 13,717
Wade, Mt. 13,399

Δ Highest mountain in state, country, range, or region named.

OCEANS, SEAS AND GULFS

	Area (sq. mi.)	Greatest Depth (ft.)
Pacific Ocean	63,800,000	35,810
Atlantic Ocean	31,800,000	28,232
Indian Ocean	28,900,000	23,376
Arctic Ocean	5,400,000	17,881
Arabian Sea	1,492,000	19,029
South China Sea	1,331,000	18,241
Caribbean Sea	1,063,000	25,197
Mediterranean Sea	967,000	16,470
Bering Sea	876,000	13,438
Bengal, Bay of	839,000	17,251
Okhotsk, Sea of	619,000	11,063
Norwegian Sea	597,000	13,189
Mexico, Gulf of	596,000	14,370
Hudson Bay	475,000	850
Greenland Sea	465,000	15,899

PRINCIPAL LAKES

	Area (sq. mi.)
Caspian Sea, Iran—Soviet Union (salt)	143,240
Superior, L., Canada—United States	31,700
Victoria, L., Kenya—Tanzania—Uganda	26,820
Aral Sea, Soviet Union (salt)	24,700
Huron, L., Canada—United States	23,000
Michigan, L., United States	22,300
Tanganyika. L., Burundi—Tanzania—Zaire—Zambia	12,350
Baikal, L., Soviet Union	12,200
Great Bear Lake, Canada	12,095
Nyasa, L., Malawi—Mozambique—Tanzania	11,150
Great Slave Lake, Canada	11,030
Erie, L., Canada—United States	9,910
Winnipeg, L., Canada	9,416
Ontario, L., Canada—United States	7,540
Balkhash, L., Soviet Union	Δ 7,100
Ladoga, L., Soviet Union	6,833
Chad, L., Cameroon—Chad—Nigeria	6,300
Onega, L., Soviet Union	3,753
Eyre, L., Australia (salt)	Δ 3,700
Titicaca, Lago, Bolivia—Peru	3,200
Nicaragua, Lago, de Nicaragua	3,150
Mai-Ndombe, Lac, Zaire	Δ 3,100
Athabasca, L., Canada	3,064
Reindeer Lake, Canada	2,568
Tonle Sap, Cambodia	Δ 2,500
Rudolf, L., Ethiopia—Kenya (salt)	2,473
Issyk-Kul, L., Soviet Union (salt)	2,425
Torrens, L., Australia (salt)	2,300
Albert, L., Uganda—Zaire	2,160
Vänern, Sweden	2,156
Nettilling Lake, Canada	2,140
Winnipegosis, L., Canada	2,075
Bangweulu, L., Zambia	1,930
Nipigon, L. Canada	1,872
Urmia, L., Iran (salt)	Δ 1,815
Manitoba, L., Canada	1,785
Woods, Lake of the, Canada—United States	1,727
Kyoga, L., Uganda	1,710
Great Salt Lake, United States (salt)	1,680
Mweru, L., Zaire—Zambia	1,680
Gairdner, L., Australia (salt)	Δ 1,700
Peipus, L., Soviet Union	1,660
Qinghai Hu, China (salt)	1,650
Khanka, L., (Xingkai Hu) China—Soviet Union	1,618
Van, Lake, Turkey (salt)	1,420

Δ Due to seasonal fluctuations in water level, areas of these lakes vary considerably.

PRINCIPAL RIVERS

	Length (miles)
Nile, Africa	4,145
Amazon—Ucayali, South America	4,000
Yangtze (Chang Jiang), Asia	3,900
Mississippi—Missouri, North America	3,740
Huang He (Yellow), Asia	3,395
Ob—Irtysh, Asia	3,362
Río de la Plata—Paraná, South America	3,030
Congo (Zaïre), Africa	2,900
Paraná, South America	2,800
Amur—Argun, Asia	2,761
Amur (Heilong Jiang), Asia	2,744
Lena, Asia	2,700
Mackenzie, North America	2,635
Mekong, Asia	2,600
Niger, Africa	2,600
Yenisey, Asia	2,543
Missouri—Red Rock, North America	2,533
Mississippi, North America	2,348
Murray—Darling, Australia	2,330
Missouri, North America	2,315
Volga, Europe	2,194
Madeira, South America	2,013
São Francisco, South America	1,988
Grande, Rio, North America	1,885
Purús, South America	1,860
Indus, Asia	1,800
Danube, Europe	1,776
Yukon, North America	1,770
Brahmaputra, Asia	1,770
Salween (Nu Jiang) (Thanlwin), Asia	1,750
Zambezi, Africa	1,700
Vilyuy, Asia	1,647
Tocantins, South America	1,640
Paraguay (Paraguai), South America	1,610
Orinoco, South America	1,600
Amu Darya, Asia	1,578
Murray, Australia	1,566
Ganges, Asia	1,560
Pilcomayo, South America	1,550
Euphrates, Asia	1,510
Ural, Asia	1,509
Arkansas, North America	1,459
Colorado, North America (U.S.—Mexico)	1,450
Aldan, Asia	1,412
Araguaia, South America	1,400
Dnepr, Europe	1,400
Syr Darya, Asia	1,370
Kasai, Africa	1,338
Tarim He, Asia	1,328
Kolyma, Asia	1,323
Ayeyarwady (Irrawaddy), Asia	1,300
Negro, South America	1,300
Orange, Africa	1,300
Red, North America	1,270
Juruá, South America	1,250
Xingu, South America	1,230
Ucayali, South America	1,220
Saskatchewan—Bow, North America	1,205
Columbia, North America	1,200
Peace, North America	1,195
Tigris, Asia	1,180
Don, Europe	1,162
Songhua Jiang, Asia	1,140
Pechora, Europe	1,124
Kama, Europe	1,122
Angara, Asia	1,105
Limpopo, Africa	1,100
Snake, North America	1,038
Uruguay (Uruguai), South America	1,025
Churchill, North America	1,000
Marañón, South America	1,000
Tobol, Asia	989
Ohio, North America	981
Magdalena, South America	950
Roosevelt, South America	950
Xiang Jiang, Asia	930
Godāvari, Asia	930
Canadian, North America	906
Brazos, North America	900
Salado, South America	900
Oka, Europe	900
Darling, Australia	864
Fraser, North America	851
Parnaíba, South America	850
Colorado, North America (Texas)	840
Dnestr, Europe	840
Rhine, Europe	820
Saint Lawrence, North America	800
Narmada, Asia	800
Ottawa, North America	790
Athabasca, North America	765
Northern Donets, Europe	735
Pecos, North America	735
Green, North America	730
Elbe (Labe), Europe	720
White, North America (Ar.—Mo.)	720
Cumberland, North America	720
James, North America (N./S. Dakota)	710
Gambia, Africa	680
Yellowstone, North America	671
Tennessee, North America	652
Gila, North America	630
Wisła (Vistula), Europe	630
Loire, Europe	625
Tagus (Tejo) (Tajo), Europe	625
North Platte, North America	618
Albany, North America	610
Tisza (Tisa), Europe	607
Ouachita, North America	605
Back, North America	605
Cimarron, North America	600
Sava, Europe	585
Nemunas (Neman), Europe	582
Branco, South America	580
Meuse, Europe	575
Oder (Odra), Europe	565
Rhône, Europe	500

PRINCIPAL ISLANDS

	Area (sq. mi.)
Greenland, North America	840,000
New Guinea, Asia—Oceania	309,000
Borneo (Kalimantan), Asia	287,300
Madagascar, Africa	226,500
Baffin I., Canada	195,928
Sumatra (Sumatera), Indonesia	182,860
Honshū, Japan	89,176
Great Britain, United Kingdom	88,795
Victoria I., Canada	83,897
Ellesmere I., Canada	75,767
Celebes (Sulawesi), Indonesia	73,057
South I., New Zealand	57,870
Java (Jawa) Indonesia	51,038
Ceram, Indonesia	45,801
North I., New Zealand	44,274
Cuba, North America	42,800
Newfoundland, Canada	42,031
Luzon, Philippines	40,420
Iceland, Europe	39,800
Mindanao, Philippines	36,537
Ireland, Europe	32,600
Hokkaidō, Japan	32,245
Novaya Zemlya, Soviet Union	31,900
Sakhalin, Soviet Union	29,500
Hispaniola, North America	29,400
Banks I., Canada	27,038
Tasmania, Austl.	26,200
Sri Lanka, Asia	24,900
Devon I., Canada	21,331
Tierra del Fuego, Isla Grande de, South America	18,600
Kyūshū, Japan	17,129
Melville I., Canada	16,274
Southampton I., Canada	15,913
Spitsbergen, Norway	15,260
New Britain, Papua New Guinea	14,093
Taiwan, Asia	13,900
Hainan I., China	13,100
Prince of Wales I., Canada	12,872
Vancouver I., Canada	12,079
Sicily, Italy	9,926
Somerset I., Canada	9,570
Sardinia, Italy	9,301
Shikoku, Japan	7,258
North East Land, Norway	6,350
New Caledonia, Oceania	6,252
Timor, Indonesia	5,743
Flores, Indonesia	5,502
Samar, Philippines	5,100
Negros, Philippines	4,907
Palawan, Philippines	4,550
Panay, Philippines	4,446
Jamaica, North America	4,200
Hawaii, United States	4,034
Cape Breton I., Canada	3,981
Mindoro, Philippines	3,759
Kodiak I., United States	3,670
Bougainville, Papua New Guinea	3,600
Cyprus, Asia	3,572
New Ireland, Papua New Guinea	3,500
Puerto Rico, North America	3,500
Corsica, France	3,367
Crete, Greece	3,189
Wrangel I., Soviet Union	2,800
Leyte, Philippines	2,785
Guadalcanal, Solomon Is.	2,060
Long I., United States	1,377

WORLD METROPOLITAN AREAS

This table lists the major metropolitan areas of the world according to their estimated population on January 1, 1989. For convenience in reference, the areas are grouped by major region, and the number of areas in each region and size group is given.

The metropolitan areas are listed alphabetically within population classifications. Altogether these 282 metropolitan areas have an estimated 1989 population of about 811,000,000, or 15.6 percent of the world total. The 33 metropolitan areas of 5 million or more account for about 338,000,000 population.

For ease of comparison, each metropolitan area has been defined by Rand McNally according to consistent rules. A metropolitan area includes a central city, neighboring communities linked to it by continuous built-up areas, and more distant communities if the bulk of their population is supported by commuters to the central city. Some metropolitan areas have more than one central city, for example Tōkyō-Yokohama or San Francisco-Oakland-San Jose.

POPULATION CLASSIFICATION	UNITED STATES and CANADA	LATIN AMERICA	EUROPE (excl. Soviet Union)	SOVIET UNION	WEST ASIA	EAST ASIA	AFRICA and OCEANIA
Over 15,000,000 (6)	New York, U.S.	Mexico City, Mex. São Paulo, Brazil				Ōsaka-Kōbe-Kyōto, Japan Seoul, Kor. S. Tōkyō-Yokohama, Japan	
10,000,000-15,000,000 (9)	Los Angeles, U.S.	Buenos Aires, Arg. Rio de Janeiro, Brazil	London, Eng. Paris, France	Moscow	Bombay, India Calcutta, India		Cairo, Egypt
5,000,000-10,000,000 (18)	Chicago, U.S. Philadelphia-Trenton-Wilmington, U.S. San Francisco-Oakland-San Jose, U.S.	Lima, Peru		Leningrad	Delhi-New Delhi, India İstanbul, Tur. Karāchi, Pak. Madras, India Tehrān, Iran	Bangkok (Krung Thep), Thai. Beijing (Peking), China Jakarta, Indon. Manila, Phil. Shanghai, China T'aipei, Taiwan Tianjin (Tientsin), China Victoria (Hong Kong), Hong Kong	
3,000,000-5,000,000 (38)	Boston, U.S. Dallas-Fort Worth, U.S. Detroit, U.S.-Windsor, Can. Houston, U.S. Miami-Fort Lauderdale, U.S. Toronto, Can. Washington, U.S.	Belo Horizonte, Brazil Bogotá, Col. Caracas, Ven. Guadalajara, Mex. Santiago, Chile	Athens, Greece Barcelona, Spain Berlin, Ger. Essen-Dortmund-Duisburg (The Ruhr), F.R. Ger. Madrid, Spain Milan, Italy Rome, Italy		Baghdād, Iraq Bangalore, India Dhaka (Dacca), Bngl. Hyderābād, India Lahore, Pak.	Guangzhou (Canton), China Ho Chi Minh City (Saigon), Viet. Nagoya, Japan Pusan, Kor. S. Rangoon (Yangoon), Burma Shenyang, China Singapore, Sing. Wuhan, China	Alexandria, Egypt Johannesburg, S. Afr. Kinshasa, Zaire Lagos, Nigeria Melbourne, Austl. Sydney, Austl.
2,000,000-3,000,000 (49)	Atlanta, U.S. Baltimore, U.S. Cleveland, U.S. Minneapolis-St. Paul, U.S. Montréal, Can. Phoenix, U.S. Pittsburgh, U.S. St. Louis, U.S. San Diego, U.S.-Tijuana, Mex. Seattle-Tacoma, U.S.	Fortaleza, Brazil Havana, Cuba Medellín, Col. Monterrey, Mex. Porto Alegre, Brazil Recife, Brazil Salvador, Brazil	Birmingham, Eng. Brussels, Bel. Bucharest, Rom. Budapest, Hung. Hamburg, F.R. Ger. Katowice-Bytom-Gliwice, Pol. Lisbon, Port. Manchester, Eng. Naples, Italy Warsaw, Pol.	Baku Donetsk-Makeyevka Gorkiy Kiev Tashkent	Ahmadābād, India Ankara, Tur. Colombo, Sri Lan. Kānpur, India Pune (Poona), India	Bandung, Indon. Chongqing (Chungking), China Harbin, China Kuala Lumpur, Malay. Nanjing (Nanking), China Sapporo-Otaru, Japan Surabaya, Indon. Taegu, Kor. S. Xi'an (Sian), China	Algiers, Alg. Cape Town, S. Afr. Casablanca, Mor.
1,500,000-2,000,000 (57)	Cincinnati, U.S. Denver, U.S.	Brasília, Brazil Cali, Col. Curitiba, Brazil Guayaquil, Ec. Montevideo, Ur. San Juan, P.R. Santo Domingo, Dom. Rep.	Amsterdam, Neth. Belgrade, Yugo. Cologne, F.R. Ger. Copenhagen, Den. Frankfurt am Main, F.R. Ger. Glasgow, Scot. Leeds-Bradford, Eng. Liverpool, Eng. Munich, F.R. Ger. Stuttgart, F.R. Ger. Turin, Italy Vienna, Aus.	Dnepropetrovsk Kharkov Kuybyshev Minsk Novosibirsk Sverdlovsk	'Ammān, Jordan Beirut, Leb. Chittagong, Bngl. Damascus, Syria İzmir, Tur. Jiddah, Sau. Ar. Kuwait (Al Kuwayt), Kuwait Mashhad, Iran Nāgpur, India Riyadh, Sau. Ar. Tel Aviv-Yafo, Isr.	Changchun, China Chengdu (Chengtu), China Dalian (Dairen), China Fukuoka, Japan Hanoi, Viet. Hiroshima-Kure, Japan Jinan (Tsinan), China Kaohsiung, Taiwan Kitakyūshū-Shimonoseki, Japan Medan, Indon. Pyŏngyang, Kor. N. Semarang, Indon. Taiyuan, China	Abidjan, I.C. Addis Ababa, Eth. Dakar, Sen. Dar es Salaam, Tan. Durban, S. Afr. Khartoum-Omdurman, Sudan
1,000,000-1,500,000 (105)	Buffalo-Niagara Falls, U.S.-St. Catharines-Niagara Falls, Can. Columbus, U.S. El Paso, U.S.-Ciudad Juárez, Mex. Hartford-New Britain, U.S. Indianapolis, U.S. Kansas City, U.S. Milwaukee, U.S. New Orleans, U.S. Portland, U.S. Riverside-San Bernardino, U.S. Sacramento, U.S. St. Petersburg-Clearwater, U.S. San Antonio, U.S. Vancouver, Can.	Barranquilla, Col. Belém, Brazil Campinas, Brazil Córdoba, Arg. Goiânia, Brazil Guatemala, Guat. La Paz, Bol. Maracaibo, Ven. Puebla, Mex. Quito, Ec. Rosario, Arg. Santos, Brazil	Antwerp, Bel. Dublin, Ire. Düsseldorf, F.R. Ger. Hannover, F.R. Ger. Lille-Roubaix, France Łódź, Pol. Lyon, France Mannheim, F.R. Ger. Marseille, France Newcastle-Sunderland, Eng. Nürnberg, F.R. Ger. Porto, Port. Prague, Czech. Rotterdam, Neth. Sofia, Bul. Stockholm, Swe. Valencia, Spain	Alma-Ata Chelyabinsk Kazan Odessa Omsk Perm Rīga Rostov-na-Donu Saratov Tbilisi Ufa Volgograd Yerevan	Aleppo, Syria Āsānsol, India Coimbatore, India Eşfahān, Iran Faisalabad, Pak. Indore, India Jaipur, India Kabul (Kābol), Afg. Lucknow, India Madurai, India Patna, India Rāwalpindi-Islāmābād, Pak. Sūrat, India Tabrīz, Iran Vārānasi (Benares), India	Anshan, China Baotou, China Changsha, China Fushun, China Guiyang, China Hangzhou (Hangchou), China Jilin (Kirin), China Kunming, China Kwangju, Kor. S. Lanzhou (Lanchou), China Nanchang, China Palembang, Indon. Qingdao (Tsingtao), China Qiqihar (Tsitsihar), China Sendai, Japan Shijiazhuang, China Tangshan, China Ujungpandang (Makasar), Indon. Ürümqi, China Zhengzhou (Chengchou), China	Accra, Ghana Adelaide, Austl. Brisbane, Austl. Douala, Cam. Harare, Zimb. Ibadan, Nigeria Luanda, Ang. Maputo, Moz. Nairobi, Kenya Perth, Austl. Pretoria, S. Afr. Rabat-Salé, Mor. Tripoli, Libya Tunis, Tun.
Total by Region (282)	38	36	48	26	43	61	30

WORLD POPULATIONS

This table includes every urban center of 50,000 or more population in the world (excluding the United States), as well as many other important or well-known cities and towns. The table also lists major political subdivisions (states, provinces, etc.) of many countries.

The population figures are all from recent censuses (designated C) or official estimates (designated E), except for a few cities for which only unofficial estimates are available (designated UE). The date of the census or estimate is specified for each country. Individual exceptions are dated in parentheses.

For many cities, a second population figure is given accompanied by a star (★). The starred population refers to the city's entire metropolitan area, including suburbs. These metropolitan areas have been defined by Rand McNally, following consistent rules to facilitate comparisons among the urban centers of various countries. Where a place is part of the metropolitan area of another city, that city's name is specified in parentheses preceded by (★). Some important places that are considered to be secondary central cities of their areas are designated by (★★) preceding the name of the metropolitan area's main city. A population preceded by a triangle (▲) refers to an entire municipality, commune, or other district, which includes rural areas in addition to the urban center itself. The names of capital cities appear in CAPITALS; the largest city in each country is designated by the symbol (•).

For more recent population totals for countries, see the Rand McNally population estimates in the World Political Information table. For lists of the largest metropolitan areas, see the World Metropolitan Areas and United States Metropolitan Areas tables.

AFGHANISTAN / Afghānestān

1984 E	17,672,000

Cities and Towns

Andkhvoy (1981 E)	13,469
Baghlān (1982 E)	41,000
Chārīkār (1981 E)	22,994
Ghaznī (1981 E)	31,196
Herāt	160,000
Jalālābād (1982 E)	58,000
• KABUL (KĀBOL)	1,179,000
Kandahar (Qandahār)	203,000
Khānābād (1981 E)	27,482
Kholm (1981 E)	28,788
Kondūz (1982 E)	57,000
Lashkar Gāh (1981 E)	22,147
Mazār-e Sharīf	118,000
Meymaneh (1981 E)	39,218
Pol-e Khomrī (1981 E)	31,888
Sheberghān (1981 E)	19,475
Tāloqān (1981 E)	20,429

ALBANIA / Shqipëri

1983 E	2,841,300

Cities and Towns

Berati (Berat)	36,600
Durrësi (Durrës)	72,400
Elbasani (Elbasan)	69,900
Fieri (Fier)	37,000
Gjirokastra (Gjirokastër)	21,400
Kavaja (Kavajë)	22,500
Korça (Korçë)	57,100
Lushnja (Lushnje)	24,200
Shkodra (Scutari)	71,200
Stalin (Kuçovë)	18,900
• TIRANA (TIRANË) (1984 E)	210,800
Vlora (Valona)	61,100

ALGERIA / Djazaïr

1987 C	23,038,942

Cities and Towns

Adrar	28,580
Aflou	29,890
Aïn Benian (★ Algiers)	34,084
Aïn Defla	25,251
Aïn el Beïda	61,997
Aïn Fekroun	25,432
Aïn M'lila	33,345
Aïn Oussera	44,270
Aïn Sefra	23,799
Aïn Témouchent	47,479
Aïn Touta	28,915
• ALGIERS (EL DJAZAÏR) (★ 2,547,983)	1,507,241
Annaba (Bône)	305,526
Arzew	35,784
Bab Ezzouar (★ Algiers)	55,211
Barika	56,488
Batna	181,601
Béchar (Colomb-Béchar)	107,311
Bejaïa (Bougie)	114,534
Beni Saf	29,921
Beskra (Biskra)	128,281
Bir el Ater	33,364
Birkhadem (★ Algiers)	28,217
Bordj Bou Arreridj	84,264
Bordj el Kiffan (★ Algiers)	61,035
Bordj Menaïel	28,520
Boufarik	41,305
Bougara	29,650
Bouïra	36,550
Bou Saâda	66,688
Chelghoum-el Aïd	29,896
Cherchell	18,727
Cheria	32,953
Constantine (Qacentina)	440,842
Douéra	11,873
Ech Cheliff (Orléansville)	129,976
El Affroun	23,247
El Beyyadh	41,119
El Boulaïda (Blida)	170,935
El Djelfa	84,207
El Eulma	67,933
El Ghazawet	24,936
El Grara	33,912
El Kroub	36,924
El Menia	30,413
El Qoll	21,113
El Wad	70,073
Frenda	30,640
Ghardaïa	89,415
Ghilizane	80,091
Guelma	77,821
Hadjout	24,251
Hamma Bouziane	29,203
Hassi Bahbah	34,176
Jijel	62,793
Khemis Miliana	55,335
Khenchla	69,743
Koléa	33,115
Ksar Chellala	27,058
Laghouat	67,214
Lakhdaria	28,023
Larbaa	35,896
Lemdiyya (Médéa)	85,195
Maghnia	52,275
Mechriyya	39,145
Melyana	27,183
Messaad	47,460
Mestghanem (Mostaganem)	114,037
Mila	33,456
Mohammadia	42,123
Mouaskar (Mascara)	64,691
M'Sila	65,805
Oran (Wahran)	628,558
Oued Rhiou	27,056
Oued Zenati	17,772
Ouenza	36,096
Ouled Djellal	28,438
Oum el Bouaghi	34,257
Qasr el Boukhari	39,003
Reghaïa	26,542
Rouiba	16,435
Saïda	80,825
Sedrata	31,464
Sidi Aïssa	31,455
Sidi bel Abbès	152,778
Sidi Moussa	25,074
Sig	42,197
Skikda (Philippeville)	128,747
Sougueur	38,407
Souk Ahras	83,015
Sour el Ghozlane	24,527
Stif (Sétif)	170,182
Tbessa	107,559
Tihert	95,821
Tilimsen	126,882
Tissemsilt	26,250
Tizi-Ouzou	61,163
Touggourt	70,645
Wargla (Ouargla)	81,721

AMERICAN SAMOA / Amerika Samoa

1980 C	32,279

Cities and Towns

• PAGO PAGO	3,075

ANDORRA

1982 C	38,051

Cities and Towns

• ANDORRA	14,928

ANGOLA

1986 E	8,981,000

Cities and Towns

Benguela (1983 E)	155,000
Cabinda (1970 C)	21,124
Huambo (Nova Lisboa) (1983 E)	203,000
Lobito (1983 E)	150,000
• LUANDA	1,082,000
Lubango (1984 E)	105,000
Malanje (1970 C)	31,599
Namibe (Moçâmedes) (1981 E)	100,000

ANGUILLA

1984 C	6,680

Cities and Towns

South Hill	961
• THE VALLEY	1,042

ANTIGUA AND BARBUDA

1977 E	72,000

Cities and Towns

• SAINT JOHN'S	24,359

ARGENTINA

1980 C	27,947,446

Cities and Towns

Alm (★ Buenos Aires)	331,919
Alta Gracia	30,668
Avellaneda (★ Buenos Aires)	334,145
Azul	44,062
Bahía Blanca	223,818
Balcarce	29,406
Bell Ville	26,494
Berazategui (★ Buenos Aires)	201,862
Berisso (★ Buenos Aires)	66,152
Bragado	27,406
• BUENOS AIRES (★ 10,750,000)	2,922,829
Campana (★ Buenos Aires)	54,832
Cañada de Gómez	24,569
Caseros (Tres de Febrero) (★ Buenos Aires)	345,424
Casilda	23,074
Chacabuco	26,860
Chivilcoy	44,579
Cipolletti	40,268
Comodoro Rivadavia	96,817
Concepción	29,355
Concepción del Uruguay	46,247
Concordia	94,222
Córdoba (★ 1,070,000)	993,055
Coronel Rosales	56,620
Corrientes	180,612
Cruz del Eje	23,255
Curuzú Cuatiá	24,962
Cutral-Có	25,911
Ensenada (★ Buenos Aires)	41,323
Esquel	17,277
Esteban Echeverría (★ Buenos Aires)	188,923
Florencio Varela (★ Buenos Aires)	173,452
Formosa	93,603
General Pico	30,173
General Roca	38,419
General San Martín (★ Buenos Aires)	385,625
General Sarmiento (San Miguel) (★ Buenos Aires)	502,926
Godoy Cruz (★ Mendoza)	142,408
Goya	47,395
Gualeguay	25,075
Gualeguaychú	51,400
Guaymallén (★ Mendoza)	164,670
Junín	62,458
La Banda (★★ Santiago del Estero)	46,837
Lanús (★ Buenos Aires)	466,980
La Plata (★★ Buenos Aires)	477,175
La Rioja	67,043
Las Heras (★ Mendoza)	101,579
Lomas de Zamora (★ Buenos Aires)	510,130
Luján (★ Buenos Aires)	48,377
Maipú	7,247
Mar del Plata	414,696
Mendoza (★ 650,000)	119,088
Mercedes (★ Buenos Aires)	41,484
Mercedes	50,992
Merlo (★ Buenos Aires)	292,587
Moreno (★ Buenos Aires)	194,440
Morón (★ Buenos Aires)	598,420
Necochea	51,069
Neuquén	90,089
Olavarría	64,097
Paraná	161,638
Pergamino	68,612
Pilar (★ Buenos Aires)	84,429
Posadas	143,889
Presidencia Roque Sáenz Peña	49,341
Quilmes (★ Buenos Aires)	446,587
Rafaela	53,273
Reconquista	33,106
Resistencia	220,104
Río Cuarto	110,254
Río Tercero	34,745
Rosario (★ 1,045,000)	938,120
Salta	260,744
San Carlos de Bariloche	48,980
San Carlos de Bolívar	16,426
San Fernando (★ Buenos Aires)	133,624
San Fernando del Valle de Catamarca (★ 90,000)	78,799
San Francisco (★ 58,536)	51,932
San Isidro (★ Buenos Aires)	289,170
San Juan (★ 300,000)	118,046
San Justo (La Matanza) (★ Buenos Aires)	949,566
San Lorenzo (★ Rosario)	96,891
San Luis	70,999
San Miguel de Tucumán (★ 525,000)	392,888
San Nicolás [de los Arroyos]	98,495
San Pedro	27,386
San Pedro [de Jujuy]	37,101
San Rafael	70,959
San Ramón de la Nueva Orán	32,910
San Salvador de Jujuy	124,950
Santa Fe	292,165
Santiago del Estero (★ 200,000)	148,758
Santo Tomé	35,840
San Vicente (★ Buenos Aires)	55,803
Tafí Viejo	26,660
Tandil	79,429
Tartagal	31,556
Tigre (★ Buenos Aires)	206,349
Trelew	52,372
Tres Arroyos	41,265
Ushuaia	11,029
Venado Tuerto	47,501
Vicente López (★ Buenos Aires)	291,072
Victoria	18,894
Viedma	24,346
Villa Ángela	25,744
Villa Carlos Paz	29,655
Villa Constitución	36,425
Villa Krause (★ San Juan)	66,693
Villa María	67,560
Zárate	67,143

Provinces

Buenos Aires	10,865,408
Catamarca	207,717
Chaco	701,392
Chubut	263,116
Córdoba	2,407,754
Corrientes	661,454
Distrito Federal	2,922,829
Entre Ríos	908,313
Formosa	295,887
Jujuy	410,008
La Pampa	208,260
La Rioja	164,217
Mendoza	1,196,228
Misiones	588,977
Neuquén	243,850
Río Negro	383,354
Salta	662,870
San Juan	465,976
San Luis	214,416
Santa Cruz	114,941
Santa Fe	2,465,546
Santiago del Estero	594,920
Tierra del Fuego, Antártida e Islas del Atlántico Sur (Ter.)	27,358
Tucumán	972,655

ARUBA

1987 E	64,763

Cities and Towns

• ORANJESTAD	19,800

AUSTRALIA

1986 C	15,602,156

Cities and Towns

Adelaide (★ 977,721)	14,157
Albany	13,258
Albury (★ 62,697)	38,704
Alice Springs	22,759
Altona (★ Melbourne)	32,838
Armadale (★ Perth)	41,248
Armidale	19,525
Ashfield (★ Sydney)	40,401
Auburn (★ Sydney)	47,147
Ballarat (★ 75,210)	34,806
Bankstown (★ Sydney)	151,570
Bathurst	24,460
Bendigo (★ 62,380)	30,704
Berwick (★ Melbourne)	48,677
Blacktown (★ Sydney)	192,442
Blue Mountains (★ Sydney)	63,866
Botany (★ Sydney)	34,271
Box Hill (★ Melbourne)	45,785
Brighton (★ Melbourne)	33,195
Brisbane (★ 1,149,401)	705,755
Broadmeadows (★ Melbourne)	101,144
Broken Hill	24,460
Brunswick (★ Melbourne)	41,362
Bunbury	23,031
Bundaberg (★ 42,036)	31,421
Burnside (★ Adelaide)	37,198
Burwood (★ Sydney)	28,556
Cairns (★ 74,358)	42,227
Camberwell (★ Melbourne)	83,792
Campbelltown (★ Adelaide)	43,352
Campbelltown (★ Sydney)	121,297
CANBERRA (★ 271,362)	247,194
Canning (★ Perth)	60,736
Canterbury (★ Sydney)	128,502
Caulfield (★ Melbourne)	67,718
Cessnock (★★ Newcastle)	41,733
Chelsea (★ Melbourne)	25,803
Coburg (★ Melbourne)	52,885
Cockburn (★ Perth)	40,711
Croydon (★ Melbourne)	40,096
Dandenong (★ Melbourne)	56,461
Darwin (★ 72,937)	66,131
Devonport	24,417
Doncaster and Templestowe (★ Melbourne)	99,269
Drummoyne (★ Sydney)	30,605
Dubbo	30,918
Elizabeth (★ Adelaide)	30,687
Enfield (★ Adelaide)	63,528
Essendon (★ Melbourne)	53,977
Fairfield (★ Sydney)	153,522
Footscray (★ Melbourne)	47,330
Frankston (★ Melbourne)	83,819
Fremantle (★ Perth)	22,709
Gawler	11,354
Geelong (★ 139,792)	13,441
Geraldton	18,801
Glenorchy (★ Hobart)	40,883
Gosford	109,278
Gosnells (★ Perth)	60,610
Goulburn	21,552
Grafton	16,647
Hawthorn (★ Melbourne)	29,623
Heidelberg (★ Melbourne)	61,917
Hobart (★ 175,082)	47,356
Holroyd (★ Sydney)	78,237
Horsham	12,174
Hurstville (★ Sydney)	63,219
Ipswich (★ Brisbane)	71,861
Kalgoorlie (★ 22,232)	10,087
Keilor (★ Melbourne)	93,327
Knox (★ Melbourne)	104,207
Kogarah (★ Sydney)	45,949
Lake Macquarie (★ Newcastle)	153,540
Launceston (★ 88,486)	61,492
Leichhardt (★ Sydney)	56,303
Lismore	37,053
Liverpool (★ Sydney)	93,215
Logan (★ Brisbane)	117,191
Mackay (★ 48,725)	22,199
Maitland (★ Newcastle)	44,315
Malvern (★ Melbourne)	41,777
Manly (★ Sydney)	35,730
Marion (★ Adelaide)	69,695
Marrickville (★ Sydney)	81,647
Maryborough	7,705
Melbourne (★ 2,832,893)	60,828
Melville (★ Perth)	67,131
Mitcham (★ Adelaide)	61,213
Moe	16,999
Moorabbin (★ Melbourne)	95,291
Mordialloc (★ Melbourne)	26,817
Morwell	16,387
Mosman (★ Sydney)	25,781
Mount Gambier (★ 25,858)	18,729
Mount Isa	23,927
Murray Bridge	11,893
Newcastle (★ 405,089)	129,490
Noarlunga (★ Adelaide)	69,809
Northcote (★ Melbourne)	48,552
North Sydney (★ Sydney)	49,927
Nunawading (★ Melbourne)	93,482
Oakleigh (★ Melbourne)	55,764
Orange	31,710
Parramatta (★ Sydney)	130,783
Penrith (★ Sydney)	135,342
Perth (★ 994,472)	79,409
Port Adelaide (★ Adelaide)	37,296
Port Augusta	15,621
Port Lincoln	11,943
Port Pirie	14,597
Prahran (★ Melbourne)	43,051
Preston (★ Melbourne)	80,551
Queanbeyan (★ Canberra)	22,698
Randwick (★ Sydney)	115,620
Redcliffe (★ Brisbane)	44,933
Richmond (★ Melbourne)	23,275
Ringwood (★ Melbourne)	40,289
Rockdale (★ Sydney)	83,350
Rockhampton (★ 59,056)	56,742

C Census. E Official estimate. UE Unofficial estimate.
• Largest city in country.

★ Population or designation of metropolitan area, including suburbs (see headnote).
▲ Population of an entire municipality, commune, or district, including rural area.

Rockingham 30,635
Ryde (★ Sydney) 89,252
Saint Kilda (★ Melbourne) 45,889
Sale 13,559
Salisbury (★ Adelaide) 96,618
Sandringham (★ Melbourne) 30,416
Shellharbour (★ Wollongong) 43,872
Shepparton (★ 37,086) 24,744
Shoalhaven 55,980
South Barwon (★ Geelong) 38,019
South Perth (★ Perth) 32,626
Southport (★ 215,663) 130,304
Springvale (★ Melbourne) 83,385
Stirling (★ Perth) 164,687
Sunshine (★ Melbourne) 94,413
• Sydney (★ 3,364,858) 86,311
Tamworth 33,321
Taree (Greater Taree) 35,921
Tea Tree Gully (★ Adelaide) 73,838
Thuringowa 30,104
Toowoomba 73,390
Townsville (★ 106,416) 82,809
Unley (★ Adelaide) 36,195
Wagga Wagga 49,401
Wangaratta 16,598
Wanneroo (★ Perth) 126,053
Warrnambool 22,706
Waverley (★ Melbourne) 122,935
Waverley (★ Sydney) 59,847
West Torrens (★ Adelaide) 43,639
Whyalla 27,102
Willoughby (★ Sydney) 51,893
Wollongong (★ 225,178) 167,863
Woodville (★ Adelaide) 79,886
Woollahra (★ Sydney) 51,057

States

Australian Capital Territory (Ter.) 249,407
New South Wales 5,401,881
Northern Territory (Ter.) 154,848
Queensland 2,587,315
South Australia 1,345,945
Tasmania 436,353
Victoria 4,019,478
Western Australia 1,406,929

AUSTRIA / Österreich

1981 C 7,555,338

Cities and Towns

Amstetten (★ 30,000) 21,989
Baden [bei Wien] (★ Vienna) 23,140
Bad Ischl 12,970
Braunau [am Inn] 16,318
Bregenz (★ 73,000) 24,561
Bruck [an der Mur] (★ 52,000) 15,068
Dornbirn 38,641
Feldkirch (★ 52,000) 23,745
Gmunden (★ 27,000) 12,653
Graz (★ 325,000) 243,166
Hallein (★ Salzburg) 15,377
Hohenems (★ 31,000) 12,666
Innsbruck (★ 185,000) 117,287
Kapfenberg (★★ Bruck an der Mur) 25,716
Kitzbühel 7,840
Klagenfurt (★ 115,000) 87,321
Klosterneuburg (★ Vienna) 22,975
Knittelfeld (★ 59,000) 14,136
Krems [an der Donau] (★ 37,000) 23,056
Kufstein (★ 20,000) 13,118
Leoben (★ 52,000) 31,989
Leonding (★ Linz) 19,389
Lienz (★ 17,000) 11,661
Linz (★ 335,000) 199,910
Lustenau 17,401
Mödling (★ Vienna) 19,276
Mürzzuschlag (★ 16,000) 10,751
Neunkirchen (★ 45,000) 10,764
Salzburg (★ 220,000) 139,426
Sankt Pölten (★ 67,000) 50,419
Sankt Veit [an der Glan] 12,007
Solbad Hall [in Tirol] (★ Innsbruck) 12,614
Spittal (★ 24,000) 14,736
Steyr (★ 65,000) 38,942
Stockerau (★ Vienna) 12,679
Ternitz (★★ Neunkirchen) 16,120
Traun (★ Linz) 21,464
• VIENNA (WIEN) (★ 1,875,000) (1988 E) 1,480,688
Villach (★ 65,000) 52,692
Vöcklabruck (★ 48,000) 11,019
Voitsberg (★ 37,000) 10,945
Wels (★ 76,000) 51,060
Wiener Neustadt (★ 62,000) 35,006
Wolfsberg (★ 39,000) 28,097

States

1988 ESTIMATE

Burgenland 267,120
Kärnten (Carinthia) 541,900
Niederösterreich (Lower Austria) 1,427,636
Oberösterreich (Upper Austria) 1,297,171
Salzburg 463,422
Steiermark (Styria) 1,180,625
Tirol (Tyrol) 613,205
Vorarlberg 314,649
Wien (Vienna) 1,480,688

BAHAMAS

1982 E 218,000

Cities and Towns

Freeport 25,000
Matthew Town (1980 C) 939
• NASSAU 135,000
West End (1980 C) 1,834

BAHRAIN / Al Baḩrayn

1981 C 350,798

Cities and Towns

Al Muḩarraq (★ Manama) 57,688
• MANĀMA (★ 224,643) 115,054

BANGLADESH

1981 C 87,119,965

Cities and Towns

Barisāl 172,905
Begumganj 69,623
Bhairab Bāzār 63,563
Bogra 68,749
Brāhmanbāria 87,570
Chāndpur 85,656
Chittagong (★ 1,391,877) 980,000
Chuādānga 76,000
Comilla 184,132
• DHAKA (DACCA) (★ 3,430,312) 2,365,695
Dinājpur 96,718
Farīdpur 66,579
Gopālpur 31,725
Gulshan (★ Dhaka) 215,444
Jamālpur 91,815
Jessore 148,927
Jhenida 47,953
Khulna 648,359
Kishorganj 52,302
Kurīgrām 47,641
Kushtia 74,892
Mādārīpur 63,917
Mīrpur (★ Dhaka) 349,031
Mymensingh (Nasirābād) 190,991
Naogaon 52,975
Nārāyanganj (★★ Dhaka) 405,562
Narsingdi 76,841
Nawābganj 87,724
Netrakona 37,455
Noākhāli 59,065
Pābna 109,065
Pārbatipur 18,979
Patuākhāli 48,121
Rājshāhi (Rampur Boalia) 253,740
Rangpur 153,174
Saidpur 126,608
Sātkhira 52,156
Sherpur 48,214
Sirājganj 106,774
Sītākunda (★ Chittagong) 237,520
Sylhet 168,371
Tangail 77,518
Tongi (★ Dhaka) 94,580

BARBADOS

1980 C 244,228

Cities and Towns

• BRIDGETOWN (★ 115,000) 7,466

BELGIUM / Belgique / België

1987 E 9,864,751

Cities and Towns

Aalst (Alost) (★ Brussels) 77,113
Anderlecht (★ Brussels) 88,849
Antwerp (Antwerpen) (Anvers) (★ 1,100,000) 479,748
Arlon (▲ 22,208) 16,600
Ath (Aat) (▲ 23,535) 14,200
Auderghem (★ Brussels) 29,063
Bastogne (▲ 11,699) 6,900
Berchem-Sainte-Agathe (Sint-Agatha-Berchem) (★ Brussels) 18,942
Binche 32,647
Braine-l'Alleud (★ Brussels) 31,070
Brasschaat (★ Antwerp) 33,372
Brugge (Bruges) (★ 223,000) 117,755
• BRUSSELS (BRUXELLES) (BRUSSEL) (★ 2,385,000) 136,920
Charleroi (★ 480,000) 209,395
Châtelet (★ Charleroi) 37,351
Dendermonde 42,389
Edegem (★ Antwerp) 23,595
Eeklo 19,211
Etterbeek (★ Brussels) 44,240
Eupen 16,967
Evere (★ Brussels) 30,303
Forest (Vorst) (★ Brussels) 48,266
Ganshoren (★ Brussels) 20,629
Geel (▲ 31,981) 17,600
Genk (★★ Hasselt) 61,391
Gent (Ghent) (Gand) (★ 465,000) 233,856
Geraardsbergen (Grammont) (▲ 30,079) 14,800
Halle (Hal) (★ Brussels) 32,332
Hamme 22,694
Harelbeke (★ Kortrijk) 25,491
Hasselt (★ 290,000) 65,563
Herentals 24,162
Herstal (★ Liège) 36,849
Huy (▲ 17,230) 12,500
Ieper (Ypres) (▲ 34,757) 21,200
Ixelles (Elseue) (★ Brussels) 76,241
Izegem 26,377
Jette (★ Brussels) 38,623
Knokke [-Heist] 30,618
Kortrijk (Courtrai) (★ 202,000) 76,216
La Louvière (★ 147,000) 76,340
Leuven (Louvain) (★ 173,000) 84,583
Liège (Luik) (★ 750,000) 200,891
Lier (Lierre) (★ Antwerp) 30,867
Lokeren 34,256
Maasmechelen (Mechelen) 33,432
Mechelen (Malines) (★ 121,000) 75,808
Menen 32,804
Mol (▲ 30,179) 17,000
Molenbeek Saint-Jean (Sint-Jans-Molenbeek) (★ Brussels) 69,764
Mons (Bergen) (★ 242,000) 89,697
Mortsel (★ Antwerp) 26,085
Mouscron (Moeskroen) (★ Lille, France) 53,713
Namur (Namen) (★ 147,000) 102,670
Nivelles (Nijvel) 22,130
Oostende (Ostende) (★ 122,000) 68,318
Oudenaarde (Audenarde) (▲ 27,233) 26,926
Roeselare (Roulers) 51,963
Ronse (Renaix-Gleiche) 23,981
Saint-Gilles (Sint-Gillis) (★ Brussels) 42,482
Schaerbeek (Schaarbeek) (★ Brussels) 104,919
Schoten (★ Antwerp) 30,785
Seraing (★ Liège) 61,731
Sint-Niklaas (Saint-Nicolas) 68,082
Sint-Truiden (Saint-Trond) (▲ 36,612) 17,300
Soignies (Zinnik) (▲ 23,407) 11,600
Spa 9,645
Tienen (Tirlemont) 31,900
Tongeren (Tongres) (▲ 29,643) 18,600
Tournai (Doornik) (▲ 66,998) 44,900
Turnhout 37,462
Uccle (Ukkel) (★ Brussels) 75,876
Verviers (★ 101,000) 53,498
Veurne (Furnes) (▲ 11,284) 7,500
Vilvoorde (★ Brussels) 32,895
Waregem 33,945
Waterloo (★ Brussels) 25,232
Woluwe-Saint-Lambert (Sint-Lambrechts-Woluwe) (★ Brussels) 47,887
Woluwe-Saint-Pierre (Sint-Pieters-Woluwe) (★ Brussels) 39,492
Zottegem (▲ 24,596) 12,700

Provinces

Antwerp (Antwerpen) (Anvers) 1,585,163
Brabant 2,219,272
East Flanders (Oost-Vlaanderen) (Flandre Orientale) 1,328,931
Hainaut (Henegouwen) 1,274,034
Liège (Luik) 991,089
Limburg (Limbourg) 734,382
Luxembourg (Luxemburg) 225,563
Namur (Namen) 413,621
West Flanders (West-Vlaanderen) (Flandre Occidentale) 1,092,696

BELIZE

1985 E 166,400

Cities and Towns

• Belize City 47,000
BELMOPAN 4,500
Corozal 10,000
Orange Walk 9,600
Punta Gorda (1980 C) 2,219
San Ignacio (1980 C) 5,553
Stann Creek 7,700

BENIN / Bénin

1984 E 3,825,000

Cities and Towns

Abomey 53,000
• Cotonou 478,000
Natitingou (1975 E) 51,000
Ouidah (1979 E) 53,000
Parakou 92,000
PORTO-NOVO 164,000

BERMUDA

1985 E 56,000

Cities and Towns

• HAMILTON (★ 15,000) 1,676
Saint George 1,707

BHUTAN / Druk-Yul

1982 E 1,333,000

Cities and Towns

• THIMPHU 12,000

BOLIVIA

1985 E 6,429,226

Cities and Towns

Cobija 4,989
Cochabamba 317,251
• LA PAZ 992,592
Oruro 178,393
Potosí 113,380
Santa Cruz 441,717
SUCRE 86,609
Tarija 60,621
Trinidad 40,288

Departments

Beni 239,810
Chuquisaca 462,904
Cochabamba 979,171
La Paz 2,091,429
Oruro 412,756
Pando 46,933
Potosí 878,232
Santa Cruz 1,047,964
Tarija 270,027

BOPHUTHATSWANA

1982 E 1,347,000

Cities and Towns

• Ga-Rankuwa (1980 C) 48,300
Mabopane (1970 C) 22,559
Mafikeng (★ 16,000) (1980 C) 6,500
MMABATHO (★ Mafikeng) (1977 E) 9,062

BOTSWANA

1986 E 1,127,900

Cities and Towns

Francistown 43,837
• GABORONE (GABERONES) 95,163
Kanye (1982 E) 22,000
Lobatse 23,832
Mahalatswe (1982 E) 19,000
Mochudi (1982 E) 20,000
Molepolole (1982 E) 19,000
Seiebi Phikwe 41,382

BRAZIL / Brasil

1985 E 135,564,395

Cities and Towns

Alagoinhas (▲ 116,959) 87,500
Alegrete (▲ 71,898) 56,700
Alvorada 105,730
Americana 156,030
Anápolis 225,840
Andradina 45,888
Apucarana (▲ 92,812) 73,700
Aracaju 360,013
Araçatuba 129,304
Araguari (▲ 96,035) 84,300
Arapiraca (▲ 147,879) 91,400
Araraquara (▲ 145,042) 87,500
Araras (▲ 71,652) 59,900
Araxá 61,418
Assis (▲ 74,238) 63,100
Bagé (▲ 106,155) 70,800
Barbacena (▲ 99,337) 80,200
Barra do Piraí (▲ 71,931) 55,700
Barra Mansa (★ Volta Redonda) 149,200
Barretos 80,202
Bauru 220,105
Bayeux (★ João Pessoa) 67,182
Belém (★ 1,200,000) 1,116,578
Belford Roxo (★ Rio de Janeiro) 340,700
Belo Horizonte (★ 2,950,000) 2,114,429
Betim (★ Belo Horizonte) 96,810
Blumenau 192,074
Boa Vista 66,028
Botucatu (▲ 71,139) 62,600
Bragança Paulista (▲ 105,099) 76,300
BRASÍLIA 1,567,709
Caçapava (▲ 64,213) 56,600
Cachoeira do Sul (▲ 91,492) 58,900
Cachoeirinha (★ Porto Alegre) 73,117
Cachoeiro de Itapemirim (▲ 138,156) 95,000
Campina Grande 279,929
Campinas (★ 1,125,000) 841,016
Campo Grande 384,398
Campos (▲ 366,716) 187,900
Campos Elyseos (★ Rio de Janeiro) 188,200
Canoas (★ Porto Alegre) 261,222
Carapicuíba (★ São Paulo) 265,856
Carazinho (▲ 62,108) 48,500
Cariacica (★ Vitória) 74,300
Caruaru (▲ 190,794) 152,100
Cascavel (▲ 200,485) 123,100
Castanhal (▲ 89,703) 71,200
Catanduva (▲ 80,309) 71,400
Caucaia (★ Fortaleza) 78,500
Cavaleiro (★ Recife) 106,600
Caxias (▲ 148,230) 66,300
Caxias do Sul 266,809
Chapecó (▲ 100,997) 64,200
Coelho da Rocha (★ Rio de Janeiro) 164,400
Colatina (▲ 106,260) 58,600
Colombo (★ Curitiba) 65,900
Conselheiro Lafaiete 77,958
Contagem (★ Belo Horizonte) 152,700
Corumbá (▲ 80,666) 65,800
Crato (▲ 86,371) 52,700
Criciúma (▲ 128,410) 85,900
Cruz Alta (▲ 71,817) 58,300
Cruzeiro 63,918
Cubatão (★ Santos) 98,322
Cuiabá (▲ 279,651) 220,400
Curitiba (★ 1,700,000) 1,279,205
Diadema (★ São Paulo) 320,187
Divinópolis 139,940
Dourados (▲ 123,757) 89,200
Duque de Caxias (★ Rio de Janeiro) 353,200
Embu (★ São Paulo) 119,791
Erexim (▲ 70,709) 54,300
Esteio (★ Porto Alegre) 58,964
Feira de Santana (▲ 355,201) 278,600
Ferraz de Vasconcelos (★ São Paulo) 68,831
Florianópolis (★ 365,000) 178,400
Fortaleza (★ 1,825,000) 1,582,414
Foz do Iguaçu (▲ 182,101) 124,900
Franca 182,820
Garanhuns 73,100
Goiânia (★ 990,000) 923,333
Governador Valadares (▲ 216,957) 192,300
Guaratinguetá (▲ 93,534) 80,400
Guarujá (★ Santos) 83,500
Guarulhos (★ São Paulo) 571,700
Ijuí (▲ 82,064) 64,400
Ilhéus (▲ 145,810) 79,400
Imperatriz (▲ 235,453) 119,500
Ipatinga (★ 270,000) 149,100
Ipiíba (★ Rio de Janeiro) 116,200
Itabira (▲ 81,771) 66,300
Itabuna (▲ 167,543) 142,200
Itajaí 104,232
Itajubá (▲ 69,675) 61,500
Itapecerica da Serra (★ São Paulo) 65,500
Itapetininga (▲ 105,512) 76,700
Itapevi (★ São Paulo) 66,825
Itaquaquecetuba (★ São Paulo) 91,366
Itaquari (★ Vitória) 163,900
Itaúna 61,446
Itu (▲ 92,786) 77,900
Ituiutaba (▲ 85,365) 74,900
Itumbiara (▲ 78,844) 57,200
Jaboatão (★ Recife) 82,900
Jacareí 149,061
Jandira 45,069
Jaú (▲ 92,547) 74,500
Jequié (▲ 127,070) 92,100
João Pessoa (Paraíba) (★ 550,000) 348,500
Joinville 302,877
Juazeiro (★ Petrolina) 78,600
Juazeiro do Norte 159,806
Juiz de Fora 349,720

C Census. E Official estimate. UE Unofficial estimate.
• Largest city in country.

★ Population or designation of metropolitan area, including suburbs (see headnote).
▲ Population of an entire municipality, commune, or district, including rural area.

Jundiaí (▲ 313,652)	268,900
Lajes (▲ 143,246)	103,600
Lavras	52,100
Limeira	186,986
Linhares (▲ 122,453)	53,400
Londrina (▲ 346,676)	296,400
Lorena	63,230
Luziânia (▲ 98,408)	71,400
Macapá (▲ 168,839)	109,400
Maceió	482,195
Manaus	809,914
Marabá (▲ 133,559)	92,700
Marília (▲ 136,187)	116,100
Maringá	196,871
Mauá (★ São Paulo)	269,321
Mesquita (★ Rio de Janeiro)	161,300
Mogi das Cruzes (★ São Paulo)	144,800
Mogi-Guaçu (▲ 91,994)	81,800
Mogi-Mirim (▲ 63,313)	52,300
Monjolo (★ Rio de Janeiro)	113,900
Montes Claros (▲ 214,472)	183,500
Mossoró (▲ 158,723)	128,300
Muriaé (▲ 80,466)	57,600
Muribeca dos Guararapes (★ Recife)	171,200
Natal	510,106
Neves (★ Rio de Janeiro)	163,600
Nilópolis (★ Rio de Janeiro)	112,800
Niterói (★ Rio de Janeiro)	441,684
Nova Friburgo (▲ 143,529)	103,500
Nova Iguaçu (★ Rio de Janeiro)	592,800
Novo Hamburgo (★ Porto Alegre)	167,744
Olinda (★ Recife)	316,600
Osasco (★ São Paulo)	591,568
Ourinhos (▲ 65,841)	58,100
Paranaguá (▲ 94,809)	82,300
Paranavaí (▲ 75,511)	60,900
Parnaíba (▲ 116,206)	90,200
Parque Industrial (★ Belo Horizonte)	228,400
Passo Fundo (▲ 137,843)	117,500
Passos (▲ 79,393)	65,500
Patos	74,298
Patos de Minas (▲ 99,027)	69,000
Paulo Afonso (▲ 86,182)	75,300
Pelotas (▲ 277,730)	210,300
Petrolina (★ 225,000)	92,100
Petrópolis (★ Rio de Janeiro)	170,300
Pindamonhangaba (▲ 86,990)	64,100
Pinheirinho (★ Curitiba)	51,600
Piracicaba (▲ 252,079)	211,000
Poá (★ São Paulo)	66,006
Poços de Caldas	100,004
Ponta Grossa	223,154
Porto Alegre (★ 2,600,000)	1,272,121
Porto Velho (▲ 202,011)	152,700
Pouso Alegre (▲ 65,958)	58,300
Praia Grande (★ Santos)	67,800
Presidente Prudente	155,883
Queimados (★ Rio de Janeiro)	113,700
Recife (★ 2,625,000)	1,287,623
Ribeirão Preto	383,125
Rio Branco (▲ 145,486)	109,800
Rio Claro	129,859
Rio de Janeiro (★ 10,150,000)	5,603,388
Rio Grande	164,221
Rio Verde (▲ 92,954)	59,400
Rondonópolis (▲ 101,642)	65,500
Salvador (★ 2,050,000)	1,804,438
Santa Bárbara d'Oeste	95,818
Santa Cruz [do Sul] (▲ 115,288)	60,300
Santa Maria (▲ 196,827)	163,900
Santana do Livramento	60,100
Santarém (▲ 226,618)	120,800
Santa Rita (★ João Pessoa)	60,100
Santo André (★ São Paulo)	635,129
Santo Ângelo (▲ 107,559)	57,700
Santos (★ 1,065,000)	460,100
São Bernardo [do Campo] (★ São Paulo)	562,485
São Caetano do Sul (★ São Paulo)	171,005
São Carlos	140,383
São Gonçalo (★ Rio de Janeiro)	262,400
São João da Boa Vista (▲ 61,653)	50,400
São João del Rei (▲ 74,385)	61,400
São João de Meriti (★ Rio de Janeiro)	241,700
São José do Rio Preto	229,221
São José dos Campos	372,578
São José dos Pinhais (★ Curitiba)	64,100
São Leopoldo (★ Porto Alegre)	114,065
São Lourenco da Mata (★ Recife)	65,936
São Luís (★ 600,000)	227,900
• São Paulo (★ 15,175,000)	10,063,110
São Vicente (★ Santos)	239,778
Sapucaia do Sul (★ Porto Alegre)	91,820
Sete Lagoas	121,418
Sete Pontes (★ Rio de Janeiro)	72,300
Sobral (▲ 112,275)	69,400
Sorocaba	327,468
Suzano (★ São Paulo)	128,924
Taboão da Serra (★ São Paulo)	122,112
Tatuí (▲ 69,358)	56,000
Taubaté	205,120
Teófilo Otoni (▲ 126,265)	82,700
Teresina (★ 525,000)	425,300
Teresópolis (▲ 115,859)	92,600
Timon (★ Teresina)	68,300
Tubarão (▲ 82,082)	70,400
Uberaba	244,875
Uberlândia	312,024
Uruguaiana (▲ 105,862)	91,500
Varginha	74,630
Vicente de Carvalho (★ Santos)	102,700
Vila Velha (Espírito Santo) (★ Vitória)	91,900
Vitória (★ 735,000)	201,500
Vitória da Conquista (▲ 198,150)	145,800
Vitória de Santo Antão (▲ 100,450)	67,800
Volta Redonda (★ 375,000)	219,267

States

Acre	366,103
Alagoas	2,224,238
Amapá (Ter.)	217,027
Amazonas	1,739,540
Bahia	10,654,453
Ceará	5,890,414
Distrito Federal	1,567,709
Espírito Santo	2,287,888
Fernando de Noronha (Ter.)	1,294
Goiás	4,437,483
Maranhão	4,655,123
Mato Grosso	1,486,111
Mato Grosso do Sul	1,592,489
Minas Gerais	14,609,062
Pará	4,318,420
Paraíba	3,008,534
Paraná	8,130,905
Pernambuco	6,742,169
Piauí	2,419,502
Rio de Janeiro	12,695,417
Rio Grande do Norte	2,111,947
Rio Grande do Sul	8,471,943
Rondônia	908,938
Roraima (Ter.)	102,491
Santa Catarina	4,085,847
São Paulo	29,541,863
Sergipe	1,297,485

BRUNEI

1981 C	192,832

Cities and Towns

• BANDAR SERI BEGAWAN (BRUNEI) (★ 64,000)	22,777
Seria	23,415

BULGARIA / Bâlgarija

1986 E	9,913,000

Cities and Towns

Asenovgrad (1985 E)	47,143
Blagoevgrad (Gorna Dzhumaya)	67,766
Burgas	186,369
Dimitrovgrad	54,898
Gabrovo	81,688
Gorna Oryakhovitsa (1985 E)	40,704
Kazanlŭk	61,780
Khaskovo	89,273
Kŭrdzhali	56,906
Kyustendil	54,773
Lom (1985 E)	32,121
Lovech (1985 E)	48,862
Mikhaylovgrad	53,529
Pazardzhik	79,198
Pernik (Dimitrovo)	96,277
Pleven	132,206
Plovdiv	349,148
Razgrad	51,277
Ruse	186,428
Shumen (Kolarovgrad)	102,886
Silistra	54,627
Sliven	104,345
Smolyan (1985 E)	31,539
• SOFIA (SOFIYA) (★ 1,205,000)	1,119,152
Stanke Dimitrov (1985 E)	42,153
Stara Zagora	153,538
Svishtov (1985 E)	30,550
Tolbukhin (Dobrich)	110,471
Tŭrgovishte (1985 E)	46,522
Varna	303,071
Veliko Tŭrnovo (Tŭrnovo)	70,610
Vidin	63,813
Vratsa	77,934
Yambol	92,321

Provinces

1985 ESTIMATE

Blagoevgrad	346,266
Burgas	449,314
Gabrovo	175,120
Khaskovo	301,249
Kŭrdzhali	302,578
Kyustendil	190,410
Lovech	202,708
Mikhaylovgrad	223,292
Pazardzhik	326,315
Pernik	174,419
Pleven	362,130
Plovdiv	754,393
Razgrad	198,007
Ruse	304,443
Shumen	254,789
Silistra	174,052
Sliven	239,479
Smolyan	164,223
Sofiya	305,251
Sofiya (Sofia) (city)	1,199,405
Stara Zagora	411,506
Tolbukhin	257,298
Tŭrgovishte	171,167
Varna	464,701
Veliko Tŭrnovo	339,120
Vidin	166,388
Vratsa	287,841
Yambol	203,754

BURKINA FASO

1985 C	7,964,705

Cities and Towns

Bobo Dioulasso	228,668
Koudougou	51,926
• OUAGADOUGOU	441,514
Ouahigouya	38,902

BURMA / Myanmar

1983 C	35,306,189

Cities and Towns

Bago	150,447
Chauk (1953 C)	24,466
Dawei (1970 E)	53,000
Henzada (1970 E)	85,000
Mandalay	532,895
Mawlamyine	219,991
Meiktila (1953 C)	25,180
Mergui (1953 C)	33,697
Monywa	106,873
Myaungmya (1953 C)	24,532
Myingyan (1970 E)	65,000
Myitkyinā (1953 C)	12,833
Pakokku (1953 C)	30,943
Pathein	144,092
Prome (Pyè) (1970 E)	65,000
• RANGOON (YANGON) (★ 2,800,000)	2,458,712
Sagaing (1953 C)	15,439
Sittwe (Akyab)	107,607
Taunggyi	107,907
Thaton (1953 C)	38,047
Toungoo (1953 C)	31,589
Yenangyaung (1953 C)	24,416

BURUNDI

1986 E	4,782,000

Cities and Towns

• BUJUMBURA	273,000
Bururi (1979 E)	7,800
Gitega	95,000
Muyinga (1982 E)	5,400

CAMEROON / Cameroun

1986 E	10,446,000

Cities and Towns

Bafoussam (1985 E)	89,000
Bamenda (1985 E)	72,000
• Douala	1,029,731
Foumban (1985 E)	50,000
Garoua (1985 E)	96,000
Kumba (1985 E)	67,000
Limbe (Victoria) (1976 C)	27,016
Maroua	103,653
Ngaoundéré (1985 E)	61,000
Nkongsamba	123,149
YAOUNDÉ	653,670

CAMBODIA / Kâmpŭchéa

1986 E	7,492,000

Cities and Towns

Batdambang (1962 C)	38,780
Kampong Cham (1971 E)	35,000
Kampong Saom (1981 E)	53,000
• PHNUM PENH	700,000

CANADA

1986 C	25,354,064

CANADA: ALBERTA

1986 C	2,375,278

Cities and Towns

Banff (1981 C)	4,208
Calgary (★ 671,326)	636,104
Camrose	12,968
Edmonton (★ 785,465)	573,982
Fort McMurray (★ 48,497)	34,949
Fort Saskatchewan (★ Edmonton)	11,983
Grande Prairie	26,471
Jasper (1981 C)	3,269
Leduc	13,126
Lethbridge	58,841
Lloydminster, Alta. and Sask. prov.	17,356
Medicine Hat (★ 50,734)	41,804
Red Deer	54,425
Saint Albert (★ Edmonton)	36,710
Sherwood Park (★ Edmonton) (1981 C)	29,285
Spruce Grove	11,918

CANADA: BRITISH COLUMBIA

1986 C	2,889,207

Cities and Towns

Burnaby (★ Vancouver)	145,161
Campbell River (1981 C)	15,370
Chilliwack (★ 50,288)	41,337
Courtenay (★ 37,553)	9,631
Cranbrook	15,893
Dawson Creek	10,544
Esquimalt (★ Victoria)	15,972
Fort Saint John	13,355
Kamloops	61,773
Kelowna (★ 89,730)	61,213
Kitimat (★ Terrace)	11,196
Langley (★ Vancouver)	16,557
Matsqui (★ 88,420)	51,449
Nanaimo (★ 60,420)	49,029
New Westminster (★ Vancouver)	39,972
North Vancouver (★ Vancouver)	35,698
Oak Bay (★ Victoria)	17,065
Penticton (★ 38,966)	23,588
Port Alberni (★ 26,134)	18,241
Port Coquitlam (★ Vancouver)	29,115
Port Moody (★ Vancouver)	15,754
Powell River (★ 18,374)	12,440
Prince George	67,621
Prince Rupert (★ 17,581)	15,755
Richmond (★ Vancouver)	108,492
Terrace (★ 17,390)	10,532
Trail (★ 20,257)	7,948
Vancouver (★ 1,380,729)	431,147
Vernon (★ 42,802)	20,241
Victoria (★ 255,547)	66,303
West Vancouver (★ Vancouver)	36,266
White Rock (★ Vancouver)	14,387

CANADA: MANITOBA

1986 C	1,071,232

Cities and Towns

Brandon	38,708
Churchill (1981 C)	1,186
Flin Flon, Man. and Sask. prov. (★ 9,211)	7,591
Portage la Prairie	13,198
Selkirk	10,013
Thompson (★ 14,729)	14,701
Winnipeg (★ 625,304)	594,551

CANADA: NEW BRUNSWICK

1986 C	710,422

Cities and Towns

Bathurst (★ 34,895)	14,683
Campbellton (★ 17,418)	9,077
Edmundston (★ 22,614)	11,497
Fredericton (★ 65,768)	44,352
Moncton (★ 102,084)	55,468
Oromocto	9,656
Riverview (★ Moncton)	15,638
Saint John (★ 121,265)	76,381

CANADA: NEWFOUNDLAND

1986 C	568,349

Cities and Towns

Carbonear (★ 13,082)	5,337
Channel-Port-aux-Basques	5,901
Conception Bay South (★ Saint John's)	15,531
Corner Brook (★ 33,730)	22,719
Gander (★ 10,899)	10,207
Grand Falls (★ 25,612)	9,121
Happy Valley-Goose Bay	7,248
Kilbride (★ Saint John's) (1981 C)	5,014
Labrador City (★ 11,301)	8,664
Marystown	6,660
Mount Pearl (★ Saint John's)	20,293
Saint John's (★ 161,901)	96,216
Saint John's Metropolitan Area (★ Saint John's)	6,254
Stephenville	7,994
Windsor (★ Grand Falls)	5,545

CANADA: NORTHWEST TERRITORIES

1986 C	52,238

Cities and Towns

Eskimo Point	1,189
Fort Smith	2,460
Hay River	2,964
Inuvik	3,389
Iqaluit (1981 C)	2,333
Pine Point	1,558
Rae	1,378
Rankin Inlet	1,374
Yellowknife	11,753

CANADA: NOVA SCOTIA

1986 C	873,199

Cities and Towns

Dartmouth (★ Halifax)	65,243
Glace Bay (★★ Sydney)	20,467
Halifax (★ 295,990)	113,577
Kentville	5,208
Louisbourg	1,355
New Glasgow (★ 38,737)	10,022
Sydney (★ 119,470)	27,754
Sydney Mines	8,063
Truro (★ 41,516)	12,124

CANADA: ONTARIO

1986 C	9,113,515

Cities and Towns

Ajax (★ Toronto)	36,550
Ancaster (★ Hamilton)	17,264
Aurora (★ Toronto)	20,905
Barrie (★ 67,703)	48,287
Belleville (★ 87,530)	36,041
Brampton (★ Toronto)	188,498
Brantford (★ 90,521)	76,146
Brockville (★ 37,115)	20,880
Burlington (★ Hamilton)	116,675
Caledon (★ Toronto)	29,666
Cambridge (Galt) (★★ Kitchener)	79,920
Chatham	42,211
Cobourg	13,197
Collingwood	12,172
Cornwall (★ 51,719)	46,425
Dundas (★ Hamilton)	20,118
Dunnville	11,589
East Gwillimbury	14,644
East York (★ Toronto)	101,085
Elliot Lake (★ 19,071)	17,984
Etobicoke (★ Toronto)	302,973
Fergus	6,372
Fort Erie	23,253
Gloucester (★ Ottawa)	89,810
Grimsby (★ Hamilton)	16,956
Guelph (★ 85,962)	78,235
Haileybury (★ 14,781)	4,820
Haldimand	17,701
Halton Hills	35,570
Hamilton (★ 557,029)	306,728
Hawkesbury (★ 11,064)	9,710
Huntsville	12,131
Kanata (★ Ottawa)	27,519
Kapuskasing	11,378
Kenora (★ 15,456)	9,621
Kingston (★ 122,350)	55,050
Kirkland Lake	11,604
Kitchener (★ 311,195)	150,604
Leamington	12,828
Lincoln	14,391
Lindsay (★ 17,913)	14,455
London (★ 342,302)	269,140
Markham (★ Toronto)	114,597
Midland (★ 35,003)	12,092
Milton	32,037
Mississauga (★ Toronto)	374,005
Nanticoke	20,202
Nepean (★ Ottawa)	95,490
Newcastle	34,073
Newmarket (★ Toronto)	34,923

C Census. E Official estimate. UE Unofficial estimate.
• Largest city in country.

★ Population or designation of metropolitan area, including suburbs (see headnote).
▲ Population of an entire municipality, commune, or district, including rural area.

Niagara Falls (★★ Saint Catharines) 72,107
Niagara-on-the-Lake (★ Saint Catharines) 12,494
Nickel Centre (★ Sudbury) 11,469
North Bay (★ 57,422) 50,623
North York (★ Toronto) 556,297
Oakville (★ Toronto) 87,107
Orangeville 14,440
Orillia (★ 31,252) 24,077
Oshawa (★ 203,543) 123,651
OTTAWA (★ 819,263) 300,763
Owen Sound (★ 27,364) 19,804
Pelham (★ Saint Catharines) 12,137
Pembroke (★ 22,560) 14,131
Petawawa 5,580
Peterborough (★ 87,083) 61,049
Pickering (★ Toronto) 48,959
Port Colborne (★ Saint Catharines) 18,281
Rayside-Balfour (★ Sudbury) 14,231
Richmond Hill (★ Toronto) 46,766
Saint Catharines (★ 343,258) 123,455
Saint Thomas 28,851
Sarnia (★ 85,700) 49,033
Sault Sainte Marie (★ 84,617) 80,905
Scarborough (★ Toronto) 484,676
Simcoe 14,290
Smiths Falls 9,163
Stoney Creek (★ Hamilton) 43,554
Stratford 26,451
Sudbury (★ 148,877) 88,717
Thorold (★ Saint Catharines) 16,131
Thunder Bay (★ 122,217) 112,272
Tillsonburg 10,745
Timmins 46,657
• Toronto (★ 3,427,168) 612,289
Trenton 15,311
Valley East (★ Sudbury) 19,233
Vanier (Eastview) (★ Ottawa) 18,426
Vaughan (Woodbridge) (★ Toronto) 65,058
Walden (★ Sudbury) 9,442
Wallaceburg 11,367
Waterloo (★ Kitchener) 58,718
Welland (★★ Saint Catharines) 45,054
Whitby (★ Oshawa) 45,819
Whitchurch-Stouffville (★ Toronto) 15,135
Windsor (★ 253,988) 193,111
Woodstock 26,386
York (★ Toronto) 135,401

CANADA: PRINCE EDWARD ISLAND

1986 C 126,646

Cities and Towns

Charlottetown (★ 53,868) 15,776
Summerside (★ 15,614) 8,020

CANADA: QUEBEC / Québec

1986 C 6,540,276

Cities and Towns

Alma (★ 29,977) 25,923
Ancienne-Lorette (Notre-Dame-de-Lorette) (★ Québec) 13,747
Anjou (★ Montréal) 36,916
Asbestos 6,961
Aylmer East (★ Ottawa) 28,976
Baie-Comeau (★ 33,047) 26,244
Beaconsfield (★ Montréal) 19,301
Beauport (★ Québec) 62,869
Bécancour 10,472
Beloeil (★ Montréal) 17,958
Blainville (★ Montréal) 16,175
Boisbriand (★ Montréal) 14,360
Boucherville (★ Montréal) 31,116
Brossard (★ Montréal) 57,441
Cap-de-la-Madeleine (★ Trois-Rivières) 32,800
Chambly (★ Montréal) 12,869
Charlesbourg (★ Québec) 68,996
Châteauguay (★ Montréal) 37,865
Chibougamau 9,922
Chicoutimi (★ 158,468) 61,083
Côte-Saint-Luc (★ Montréal) 28,582
Cowansville (★ 12,114) 11,643
Dolbeau (★ 15,288) 8,554
Dollard-des-Ormeaux (★ Montréal) 43,089
Dorval (★ Montréal) 17,354
Drummondville (★ 56,283) 36,020
Gaspé 17,350
Gatineau (★ Ottawa) 81,244
Granby (★ 51,176) 38,508
Grand-Mère (★ Shawinigan) 14,582
Greenfield Park (★ Montréal) 18,290
Hauterive (★ Baie-Comeau) (1981 C) 13,995
Hull (★ Ottawa) 58,722
Joliette (★ 34,897) 16,845
Jonquière (★★ Chicoutimi) 58,467
Kirkland (★ Montréal) 13,376
La Baie 20,753
Lachine (★ Montréal) 34,906
Lachute 11,586
La Prairie (★ Montréal) 11,072
LaSalle (★ Montréal) 75,621
La Tuque (★ 13,468) 10,723
Lauzon (★ Québec) 13,620
Laval (★ Montréal) 284,164
Lévis (★ Québec) 18,310
Longueuil (★ Montréal) 125,441
Loretteville (★ Québec) 14,335
Magog (★ 18,738) 13,530
Mascouche (★ Montréal) 21,285
Matane (★ 15,361) 13,243
Mirabel 13,875
Montmagny 11,958
Montréal (★ 2,921,357) 1,015,420
Montréal-Nord (★ Montréal) 90,303
Mont-Royal (★ Montréal) 18,350
Mont-Saint-Hilaire (★ Montréal) 10,588
Outremont (★ Montréal) 23,080
Pierrefonds (★ Montréal) 39,605
Pointe-Claire (★ Montréal) 26,026
Québec (★ 603,267) 164,580
Repentigny (★ Montréal) 40,778
Rimouski (★ 46,210) 29,672
Rivière-du-Loup (★ 22,471) 13,321
Roberval 11,448
Rouyn (★ 36,495) 17,319
Saint-Bruno-de-Montarville (★ Montréal) 23,103
Saint-Eustache (★ Montréal) 32,226
Sainte-Foy (★ Québec) 69,615
Saint-Hubert (★ Montréal) 66,218
Saint-Hyacinthe (★ 48,303) 38,603
Saint-Jean-sur-Richelieu (★ 59,958) 34,745
Saint-Jérôme (★ 44,048) 23,316
Sainte-Julie (★ Montréal) 15,502
Saint-Lambert (★ Montréal) 20,030
Saint-Laurent (★ Montréal) 67,002
Saint-Léonard (★ Montréal) 75,947
Sainte-Thérèse-de-Blainville (★ Montréal) 19,336
Salaberry-de-Valleyfield (★ 38,797) 27,942
Sept-Îles (Seven Islands) (★ 28,050) 25,637
Shawinigan (★ 61,965) 21,470
Shawinigan-Sud (★ Shawinigan) 11,412
Sherbrooke (★ 129,960) 74,438
Sillery (★ Québec) 12,784
Sorel (★ 46,096) 19,522
Terrebonne (★ Montréal) 31,310
Thetford Mines (★ 31,940) 18,561
Tracy (★ Sorel) 12,546
Trois-Rivières (★ 128,888) 50,122
Trois-Rivières-Ouest (★ Trois-Rivières) 15,538
Val-Bélair (★ Québec) 13,105
Val-d'Or (★ 27,178) 22,252
Vanier (Québec-Ouest) (★ Québec) 10,208
Verdun (★ Montréal) 60,246
Victoriaville (★ 38,003) 21,587
Ville-Saint-Georges (★ 21,022) 11,723
Westmount (★ Montréal) 20,011

CANADA: SASKATCHEWAN

1986 C 1,010,198

Cities and Towns

Lloydminster, Sask. and Alta. prov. 17,356
Moose Jaw (★ 37,219) 35,073
North Battleford (★ 18,709) 14,876
Prince Albert (★ 40,841) 33,686
Regina (★ 186,521) 175,064
Saskatoon (★ 200,665) 177,641
Swift Current 15,666
Yorkton (★ 18,525) 15,574

CANADA: YUKON

1986 C 23,504

Cities and Towns

Dawson 896
Faro 400
Whitehorse 15,199

CAPE VERDE / Cabo Verde

1980 C 296,093

Cities and Towns

Mindelo 36,265
• PRAIA 37,480

CAYMAN ISLANDS

1987 E 23,000

Cities and Towns

• GEORGETOWN 11,500

CENTRAL AFRICAN REPUBLIC / République centrafricaine

1984 E 2,517,000

Cities and Towns

Bambari (1982 E) 35,000
• BANGUI 473,817
Berbérati (1982 E) 40,000
Bossangoa (1982 E) 36,000
Bouar (1982 E) 48,000

CHAD / Tchad

1979 E 4,405,000

Cities and Towns

Abéché 54,000
Kélo 27,000
Koumra 27,000
Moundou 66,000
• N'DJAMENA (FORT-LAMY) 303,000
Sarh (Fort-Archambault) 65,000

CHILE

1982 C 11,329,736

Cities and Towns

Angol 31,005
Antofagasta 185,486
Arica 139,320
Calama 81,684
Cauquenes 23,908
Cerrillos (★ Santiago) 67,013
Cerro Navia (★ Santiago) 137,777
Chillán 118,163
Chuquicamata 16,891
Concepción (★ 675,000) 267,891
Conchalí (★ Santiago) 157,884
Copiapó 69,045
Coquimbo 62,186
Coronel (★ Concepción) 65,918
Curicó 60,550
El Bosque (★ Santiago) 143,717
Estación Central (★ Santiago) 147,918
Huechuraba (★ Santiago) 56,313
Independencia (★ Santiago) 86,724
Iquique 110,153
La Calera 38,322
La Cisterna (★ Santiago) 95,863
La Florida (★ Santiago) 191,883
La Granja (★ Santiago) 109,168
La Pintana (★ Santiago) 73,932
La Reina (★ Santiago) 80,452
Las Condes (★ Santiago) 175,735
La Serena 83,283
La Unión 16,925
Lebu 16,952
Limache 22,711
Linares 46,433
Lo Barnechea (★ Santiago) 24,258
Lo Espejo (★ Santiago) 124,462
Lo Prado (★ Santiago) 103,575
Los Andes 34,613
Los Ángeles 70,529
Lota (★ Concepción) 47,133
Macul (★ Santiago) 113,100
Maipú (★ Santiago) 114,117
Melipilla 33,654
Ñuñoa (★ Santiago) 168,919
Osorno 95,286
Ovalle 43,023
Parral 21,221
Pedro Aguirre Cerda (★ Santiago) 145,207
Peñalolén (★ Santiago) 137,298
Penco (★ Concepción) 30,939
Providencia (★ Santiago) 115,449
Pudahuel (★ Santiago) 97,578
Puente Alto (★ Santiago) 109,239
Puerto Aisén 9,176
Puerto Montt 84,410
Puerto Natales 14,250
Punta Arenas 95,332
Quillota 44,824
Quilpué (★ Valparaíso) 84,136
Quinta Normal (★ Santiago) 128,989
Rancagua 139,925
Recoleta (★ Santiago) 164,292
Renca (★ Santiago) 93,928
San Antonio 61,486
San Bernardo (★ Santiago) 117,132
San Carlos 21,919
San Felipe 31,656
San Fernando 32,432
San Joaquín (★ Santiago) 123,904
San Miguel (★ Santiago) 88,764
San Ramón (★ Santiago) 99,410
• SANTIAGO (★ 4,100,000) 232,667
Talca 128,544
Talcahuano (★★ Concepción) 202,368
Temuco 157,297
Tocopilla 21,883
Tomé (★ Concepción) 34,107
Valdivia 100,046
Vallenar 38,375
Valparaíso (★ 675,000) 265,355
Victoria 19,743
Villa Alemana (★ Valparaíso) 55,766
Viña del Mar (★ Valparaíso) 244,899
Vitacura (★ Santiago) 72,038

Regions

1984 ESTIMATE

Aisén del General Carlos Ibáñez del Campo 71,369
Antofagasta 338,219
Atacama 214,718
Biobío 1,569,431
Coquimbo 439,938
La Araucanía 677,951
Libertador General Bernardo O'Higgins 589,347
Los Lagos 904,557
Magallanes y Antártica Chilena 117,401
Maule 739,329
Metropolitana 4,722,528
Tarapacá 266,428
Valparaíso 1,326,834

CHINA / Zhongguo

1987 E 1,057,210,000

Cities and Towns

Abagnar Qi (Xilin Hot) (▲ 100,700) (1986 E) 71,700
Acheng (1985 E) 100,304
Aksu (▲ 345,900) (1986 E) 143,100
Altay (▲ 141,700) (1986 E) 62,800
Anci (Langfang) (▲ 522,800) (1986 E) 122,100
Anda (▲ 425,500) (1986 E) 130,200
Ankang (1985 E) 89,188
Anlu (1985 E) 35,199
Anqing (▲ 433,900) (1986 E) 213,200
Anqiu (1985 E) 18,969
Anshan 1,300,000
Anshun (▲ 214,700) (1986 E) 128,800
Anyang (▲ 541,900) (1986 E) 361,200
Arxan (1985 E) 36,343
Baicheng (▲ 282,000) (1986 E) 198,600
Baiquan (1985 E) 50,996
Baiyin (▲ 301,900) (1986 E) 157,100
Baoding (▲ 535,100) (1986 E) 423,200
Baoji (▲ 359,500) (1986 E) 286,200
Baoqing (1985 E) 38,364
Baoshan (▲ 688,400) (1986 E) 52,300
Baotou 1,120,000
Baoying (1985 E) 50,479
Bayan (1985 E) 42,299
Bei'an (▲ 440,500) (1986 E) 199,500
Beihai (▲ 175,900) (1986 E) 119,000
BEIJING (PEKING) (★ 6,450,000) 5,970,000
Beipiao (▲ 603,700) (1986 E) 180,900
Bengbu (▲ 612,600) (1986 E) 403,900
Benxi (Xiaoshi) (1985 E) 29,442
Benxi 840,000
Bijie (1985 E) 54,871
Binhai (Dongkan) (1985 E) 37,565
Binxian (Binzhou) (▲ 177,900) (1986 E) 86,700
Binxian (Beizhen) (1982 C) 127,326
Bo'ai (Qinghua) (1985 E) 25,471
Bole (Bortala) (▲ 137,300) (1986 E) 41,400
Boli (1985 E) 61,990
Bose (▲ 271,400) (1986 E) 82,000
Boshan (1975 UE) 100,000
Boxian (Bozhou) (1985 E) 63,222
Boxing (1982 C) 57,554
Boyang (1985 E) 60,688
Butha Qi (▲ 389,500) (1986 E) 111,300
Cangshan (Bianzhuang) (1982 C) 79,334
Cangzhou (▲ 293,600) (1986 E) 196,700
Chaihe (1985 E) 40,328
Changchun (▲ 1,910,000) 1,740,000
Changde (▲ 220,800) (1986 E) 178,200
Changge (1982 C) 67,002
Changji (▲ 233,400) (1986 E) 110,500
Changle (1982 C) 43,092
Changli (1985 E) 29,966
Changqing (1982 C) 65,094
Changsha 1,190,000
Changshou (1985 E) 51,923
Changshu (Yushan) (▲ 998,000) (1986 E) 281,300
Changtu (1985 E) 49,937
Changyi (1982 C) 64,513
Changzhi (▲ 463,400) (1986 E) 273,000
Changzhou (1986 E) 522,700
Chao'an (▲ 1,214,500) (1986 E) 265,400
Chaoxian (▲ 739,500) (1986 E) 116,800
Chaoyang (Miancheng, Guangdong prov. (1985 E) 85,968
Chaoyang, Liaoning prov. (▲ 318,900) (1986 E) 180,300
Chengde (▲ 330,400) (1986 E) 226,600
Chengdu (Chengtu) (▲ 2,640,000) 1,810,000
Chenghai (1985 E) 50,631
Chengwu (1982 C) 43,244
Chenxian (Chenzhou) (▲ 191,900) (1986 E) 143,500
Chifeng (Ulanhad) (▲ 882,900) (1986 E) 299,000
Chiping (1982 C) 44,036
Chongqing (Chungking) (▲ 2,830,000) 2,450,000
Chuxian (▲ 365,000) (1986 E) 113,300
Chuxiong (Lucheng) (▲ 379,400) (1986 E) 67,700
Da'an (Dalai) (1985 E) 70,552
Dachangzhen (1975 UE) 50,000
Dalian (Lüda) (Dairen) 1,680,000
Dandong (Antung) (1986 E) 579,800
Danyang (1985 E) 48,449
Daqing (Anda) (▲ 850,000) 620,000
Dashiqiao (1985 E) 68,898
Dashitou (1985 E) 45,550
Datong (▲ 1,020,000) 790,000
Datong (Qiaotou) (1985 E) 55,529
Dawa (1985 E) 142,581
Daxian (▲ 209,400) (1986 E) 142,000
Daxing (Huangcun) (1985 E) 39,271
Dehui (1985 E) 60,247
Dengfeng (1982 C) 49,746
Dengxian (1985 E) 32,130
Deqing (1982 C) 48,726
Deyang (▲ 753,400) (1986 E) 184,800
Dezhou (▲ 276,200) (1986 E) 161,300
Didao (1975 UE) 50,000
Dinghai (1985 E) 50,161
Dingshuzhen (1985 E) 46,373
Dingtao (1982 C) 44,955
Dingxian (1985 E) 40,037
Dongchuan (Xincun) (▲ 275,100) (1986 E) 67,400
Dongfeng (1985 E) 44,747
Dongguan (Guancheng) (▲ 1,208,500) (1986 E) 254,900
Dongjingcheng (1985 E) 40,531
Dongming (1982 C) 44,660
Dongning (1985 E) 29,937
Dongshan (1985 E) 37,023
Dongsheng (▲ 121,300) (1986 E) 57,500
Dongtai (1985 E) 65,788
Dongying (▲ 514,400) (1986 E) 178,100
Dorbod (Taikang) (1985 E) 34,100
Dukou (▲ 551,200) (1986 E) 380,200
Dunhua (▲ 448,000) (1986 E) 217,100
Duyun (▲ 386,600) (1986 E) 123,800
Echeng (▲ 938,000) (1986 E) 217,400
Enshi (▲ 679,000) (1986 E) 84,300
Erenhot (1986 E) 7,200
Ergun Zuoqi (Genhe) (1985 E) 55,970
Fanjiatun (1985 E) 33,035
Feixian (1982 C) 73,246
Fengcheng, Liaoning prov. (1985 E) 66,745
Fengzhen (1985 E) 38,267
Fenyang (1985 E) 30,222
Foshan (▲ 312,700) (1986 E) 243,500
Fu'an (1985 E) 31,077
Fujin (1985 E) 60,948
Fuling (▲ 973,500) (1986 E) 166,300
Fushan (1982 C) 43,685
Fushun 1,270,000
Fuxian (Wafangdian) (▲ 960,700) (1986 E) 246,200
Fuxin 690,000

C Census. E Official estimate. UE Unofficial estimate.
• Largest city in country.
★ Population or designation of metropolitan area, including suburbs (see headnote).
▲ Population of an entire municipality, commune, or district, including rural area.

Fuxin (1985 E) ... 36,438
Fuyang (▲ 195,200) (1986 E) ... 143,400
Fuyu, Heilongjiang prov. (1985 E) ... 48,670
Fuyu, Jilin prov. (1985 E) ... 98,373
Fuzhou (Fuchou) (▲ 1,210,000) ... 890,000
Fuzhou (▲ 171,800) (1986 E) ... 106,700
Gaixian (Gaizhou) (1985 E) ... 67,587
Ganhe (1985 E) ... 48,128
Gannan (1985 E) ... 38,623
Ganzhou (Kanchow) (▲ 346,000) (1986 E) ... 191,600
Gaomi (1985 E) ... 34,542
Gaoqing (Tianzhen) (1982 C) ... 70,411
Gaoyou (1985 E) ... 57,844
Gaozhou (1985 E) ... 41,919
Gejiu (▲ 341,700) (1986 E) ... 193,600
Golmud (1986 E) ... 60,300
Gongchangling (1982 C) ... 49,281
Gongxi (1985 E) ... 24,612
Gongxian (Xiaoyi) (1985 E) ... 22,669
Guanghan (Luocheng) (1985 E) ... 47,577
Guangyuan (Jialing) (▲ 805,500) (1986 E) ... 162,200
Guangzhou (Canton) (▲ 3,360,000) ... 3,050,000
Guanxian (1982 C) ... 49,782
Guanxian (Guankou) (1985 E) ... 65,039
Gucheng (1985 E) ... 27,643
Guichi (Chizhou) (1985 E) ... 36,623
Guilin (Kweilin) (▲ 457,500) (1986 E) ... 324,200
Guixian (Guicheng) (1985 E) ... 61,970
Guiyang (▲ 1,400,000) ... 1,010,000
Gushi (1985 E) ... 38,152
Haicheng (▲ 984,800) (1986 E) ... 210,700
Haifeng (Haicheng) (1985 E) ... 50,401
Haikang (Leizhou) (1985 E) ... 24,422
Haikou (▲ 289,600) (1986 E) ... 209,200
Hailar (1986 E) ... 180,000
Hailin (1985 E) ... 58,909
Hailong (Meihekou) (▲ 534,200) (1986 E) ... 117,500
Hailun (1985 E) ... 83,448
Haimen (1985 E) ... 46,341
Haining (Xiashi) (1985 E) ... 43,426
Haiyang (Dongcun) (1982 C) ... 77,098
Hami (▲ 270,300) (1986 E) ... 146,400
Hancheng (▲ 304,200) (1986 E) ... 66,600
Handan (▲ 1,010,000) ... 850,000
Hangu (1975 UE) ... 100,000
Hangzhou (Hangchou) ... 1,270,000
Hanzhong (▲ 415,000) (1986 E) ... 151,700
Harbin (Haerhpin) ... 2,670,000
Hebi (▲ 321,600) (1986 E) ... 158,500
Hechi (Jinchengjiang) (▲ 266,800) (1986 E) ... 74,400
Hechuan (1985 E) ... 65,237
Hefei (▲ 900,000) ... 720,000
Hegang (1986 E) ... 588,300
Heihe (Aihui) (▲ 135,000) (1986 E) ... 76,700
Heishan (1985 E) ... 39,271
Helong (1985 E) ... 62,665
Hengshui (▲ 286,500) (1986 E) ... 83,100
Hengyang (▲ 601,300) (1986 E) ... 419,200
Hepu (Lianzhou) (1985 E) ... 42,524
Heshan (▲ 109,600) (1986 E) ... 42,000
Hexian (Babu) (1985 E) ... 34,298
Heyuan (Yuancheng) (1985 E) ... 43,124
Heze (Caozhou) (▲ 1,001,500) (1986 E) ... 115,400
Hohhot (Kweisui) (▲ 810,000) ... 650,000
Honghu (Xindi) (1985 E) ... 44,057
Hongjiang (▲ 67,000) (1986 E) ... 54,300
Horinger (1986 E) ... 29,900
Horqin Youyi Qianqi (Ulan Hot) (▲ 192,100) (1986 E) ... 129,100
Hotan (▲ 122,800) (1986 E) ... 71,700
Houma (▲ 158,500) (1986 E) ... 67,000
Huadian (1985 E) ... 75,183
Huai'an (Huaicheng) (1985 E) ... 65,673
Huaibei (▲ 447,200) (1986 E) ... 252,100
Huaide (Gongzhuling) (▲ 899,400) (1986 E) ... 187,600
Huaihua (▲ 427,100) (1986 E) ... 102,000
Huainan (Hwainan) (▲ 1,090,000) ... 690,000
Huaiyang (Huizu) (1985 E) ... 35,679
Huaiyin (Wangying) (▲ 382,500) (1986 E) ... 201,700
Huanan (1985 E) ... 66,596
Huangchuan (1985 E) ... 45,574
Huanggang (Huangzhou) (1982 C) ... 65,961
Huangnihe (1985 E) ... 33,072
Huangshi (1986 E) ... 451,900
Huangyan (1985 E) ... 39,284
Huanren (1985 E) ... 33,345
Huantai (Suozhen) (1982 C) ... 44,903
Huayun (Huarong) (▲ 313,500) (1986 E) ... 81,000
Huilai (Huicheng) (1985 E) ... 30,671
Huinan (Chaoyang) (1985 E) ... 52,429
Huixian (1985 E) ... 25,031
Huizhou (▲ 182,100) (1986 E) ... 117,000
Hulan (1985 E) ... 74,989
Hunjiang (▲ 687,700) (1986 E) ... 442,600
Huzhou (▲ 964,400) (1986 E) ... 208,500
Jiading (1985 E) ... 60,718
Jiamusi (▲ 557,700) (1986 E) ... 429,800
Ji'an (▲ 184,300) (1986 E) ... 132,200
Jiangdu (1985 E) ... 32,638
Jiangjin (1985 E) ... 44,378
Jiangling (Jingzhou) (1985 E) ... 77,887
Jiangmen (▲ 231,700) (1986 E) ... 168,800
Jiangyin (Chengjiang) (1985 E) ... 66,476
Jiangyou (Zhongba) (1985 E) ... 72,663
Jian'ou (1985 E) ... 55,180
Jianping (Yebaishou) (1985 E) ... 39,690
Jianyang (Jiancheng) (1985 E) ... 45,977
Jiaohe (1985 E) ... 51,504
Jiaojiang (▲ 385,200) (1986 E) ... 82,300
Jiaoxian (1985 E) ... 51,869
Jiaozuo (▲ 509,900) (1986 E) ... 335,400
Jiawang (1975 UE) ... 50,000
Jiaxing (▲ 686,500) (1986 E) ... 210,200
Jiayuguan (▲ 102,100) (1986 E) ... 73,800
Jiazi (1985 E) ... 46,073
Jidong (1985 E) ... 38,948
Jieshi (1985 E) ... 37,502
Jiexiu (1985 E) ... 51,300
Jieyang (Rongcheng) (1985 E) ... 98,531
Jilin (Kirin) ... 1,170,000
Jimo (1985 E) ... 22,845
Jinan (Tsinan) ... 1,460,000
Jinchang (Baijiazui) (▲ 136,000) (1986 E) ... 90,500
Jincheng (▲ 612,700) (1986 E) ... 99,900
Jingdezhen (▲ 569,700) (1986 E) ... 304,000
Jinghong (Yunjinghong) (1985 E) ... 28,029
Jingmen (▲ 946,500) (1986 E) ... 227,000
Jinhua (▲ 799,900) (1986 E) ... 147,800
Jining, Inner Mongolia prov. (1986 E) ... 163,300
Jining, Shandong prov. (▲ 765,700) (1986 E) ... 222,600
Jinshi (▲ 219,700) (1986 E) ... 73,700
Jinxi (▲ 634,300) (1986 E) ... 223,100
Jinxian (Jinzhou) (1985 E) ... 95,761
Jinzhou (▲ 790,000) ... 690,000
Jishou (▲ 194,500) (1986 E) ... 59,500
Jishu (1985 E) ... 75,587
Jiujiang (▲ 382,300) (1986 E) ... 248,500
Jiuquan (Suzhou) (▲ 269,900) (1986 E) ... 56,300
Jiutai (1985 E) ... 63,021
Jixi (Chihsi) (▲ 820,000) ... 700,000
Jixian (1985 E) ... 59,725
Jixian (Fulitun) (1985 E) ... 35,705
Juancheng (1982 C) ... 54,110
Junan (Shizilu) (1982 C) ... 90,222
Junxian (Danjiang) (▲ 423,400) (1986 E) ... 97,000
Juxian (1982 C) ... 51,666
Kaifeng (▲ 629,100) (1986 E) ... 458,800
Kaili (▲ 342,100) (1986 E) ... 96,600
Kaiping (Sanbu) (1985 E) ... 54,145
Kaiyuan (▲ 342,100) (1986 E) ... 96,600
Kaiyuan (1985 E) ... 85,762
Karamay (1986 E) ... 185,300
Kashi (Kaxgar) (▲ 194,500) (1986 E) ... 146,300
Keshan (1985 E) ... 65,088
Korla (▲ 219,000) (1986 E) ... 129,400
Kunming (Yünnanfu) (▲ 1,520,000) ... 1,280,000
Kunshan (Yushan) (1985 E) ... 44,645
Kuqa (1985 E) ... 63,847
Kuytun (1986 E) ... 60,200
Laiwu (▲ 1,041,800) (1986 E) ... 143,500
Laixi (Shuiji) (1982 C) ... 41,117
Laiyang (1985 E) ... 42,813
Langxiang (1985 E) ... 64,658
Lanxi (▲ 606,800) (1986 E) ... 70,500
Lanxi (1985 E) ... 53,236
Lanzhou (Lanchou) (▲ 1,390,000) ... 1,270,000
Laohekou (Guanghua) (▲ 420,000) (1986 E) ... 104,400
Lechang (1986 E) ... 56,913
Leiyang (1985 E) ... 27,572
Lengshuijiang (▲ 277,600) (1986 E) ... 101,700
Lengshuitan (▲ 362,000) (1986 E) ... 60,900
Leping (1985 E) ... 45,620
Leshan (▲ 972,300) (1986 E) ... 307,300
Lhasa (▲ 107,700) (1986 E) ... 84,400
Lianxian (Lianzhou) (1985 E) ... 34,720
Lianyungang (▲ 459,400) (1986 E) ... 288,000
Liaocheng (▲ 724,300) (1986 E) ... 119,000
Liaoyang (▲ 576,900) (1986 E) ... 442,600
Liaoyuan (1986 E) ... 370,400
Lihu (1985 E) ... 30,204
Lijiang Naxi (Dayan) (1985 E) ... 36,939
Liling (▲ 856,300) (1986 E) ... 107,100
Linfen (▲ 530,100) (1986 E) ... 157,600
Lingling (Yongzhou) (▲ 515,300) (1986 E) ... 72,700
Lingxian (1982 C) ... 40,617
Lingyuan (1985 E) ... 66,825
Linhai (1985 E) ... 52,653
Linhe (▲ 365,900) (1986 E) ... 99,800
Linkou (1985 E) ... 52,936
Linqing (▲ 603,000) (1986 E) ... 87,000
Linqu (1982 C) ... 84,196
Linru (1985 E) ... 21,403
Linxia (▲ 150,200) (1986 E) ... 72,900
Linyi (▲ 1,365,000) (1986 E) ... 190,000
Linying (1982 C) ... 44,516
Lishi (1985 E) ... 32,083
Lishu (1985 E) ... 40,838
Lishui (1985 E) ... 42,004
Liuhe (1985 E) ... 42,695
Liujiachang (1985 E) ... 25,296
Liupanshui (Shuicheng) (▲ 2,216,500) (1986 E) ... 363,500
Liuzhou ... 660,000
Liyang (Licheng) (1985 E) ... 43,974
Longhai (Shima) (1985 E) ... 40,817
Longjiang (1985 E) ... 51,156
Longyan (▲ 378,500) (1986 E) ... 114,500
Loudi (▲ 254,300) (1986 E) ... 84,200
Lu'an (▲ 163,400) (1986 E) ... 122,600
Luanchuan (1982 C) ... 40,297
Lufeng (Donghai) (1985 E) ... 53,015
Luhe (Lucheng) (1985 E) ... 45,183
Lujiang (1985 E) ... 32,021
Luohe (▲ 159,100) (1986 E) ... 102,300
Luoyang (▲ 1,060,000) ... 740,000
Lushan (1985 E) ... 22,205
Luzhou (Luchou) (▲ 360,300) (1986 E) ... 237,800
Ma'anshan (▲ 367,000) (1986 E) ... 258,900
Manzhouli (1986 E) ... 116,600
Maoming (▲ 434,900) (1986 E) ... 118,600
Meizhou (▲ 740,600) (1986 E) ... 169,100
Mengjin (1982 C) ... 41,706
Mengxian (1982 C) ... 45,599
Mengyin (1982 C) ... 70,602
Mianduhe (1982 C) ... 46,629
Mianyang (Xiantao), Hubei prov. (1985 E) ... 41,008
Mianyang, Sichuan prov. (▲ 848,500) (1986 E) ... 233,900
Mingshui (1985 E) ... 42,956
Minhang (1975 UE) ... 60,000
Mishan (1985 E) ... 54,919
Mixian (1982 C) ... 64,776
Mudanjiang ... 630,000
Muling (Bamiantong) (1985 E) ... 38,638
Muling (1985 E) ... 30,416
Naizishan (1985 E) ... 51,982
Nancha (1975 UE) ... 50,000
Nanchang (▲ 1,190,000) ... 1,030,000
Nanchang (Liantang) (1985 E) ... 37,661
Nanchong (▲ 238,100) (1986 E) ... 158,000
Nanjing (Nanking) ... 2,290,000
Nanning (▲ 960,000) ... 690,000
Nanpiao (1982 C) ... 67,274
Nanping (▲ 420,800) (1986 E) ... 157,100
Nantong (▲ 411,000) (1986 E) ... 308,800
Nanxiong (1985 E) ... 33,424
Nanyang (▲ 294,800) (1986 E) ... 199,400
Nanzhang (1985 E) ... 22,398
Nehe (1985 E) ... 49,725
Neihuang (1982 C) ... 56,039
Neijiang (▲ 298,500) (1986 E) ... 191,100
Nenjiang (1985 E) ... 59,276
Ning'an (1985 E) ... 49,334
Ningbo (▲ 1,030,000) ... 560,000
Ningde (1985 E) ... 36,529
Ningyang (1982 C) ... 55,424
Nong'an (1985 E) ... 55,966
Orogen Zizhiqi (Alihe) (1985 E) ... 48,042
Orqohan (1982 C) ... 44,875
Panshan (▲ 343,100) (1986 E) ... 248,100
Panshi (1985 E) ... 59,270
Panyu (Shiqiao) (1985 E) ... 46,705
Penglai (1985 E) ... 21,502
Pengxian (Tianpeng) (1985 E) ... 41,190
Pingdingshan (▲ 819,900) (1986 E) ... 363,200
Pingdu (1985 E) ... 23,362
Pingliang (▲ 362,500) (1986 E) ... 85,400
Pingnan (1985 E) ... 22,601
Pingxiang, Guangxi Zhuangzu prov. (▲ 81,100) (1986 E) ... 14,600
Pingxiang, Jiangxi prov. (▲ 1,286,700) (1986 E) ... 368,700
Pingyao (1985 E) ... 34,007
Pingyi (1982 C) ... 89,373
Pingyin (1982 C) ... 62,827
Potou (▲ 456,100) (1986 E) ... 59,000
Puqi (1985 E) ... 65,239
Putian (▲ 265,400) (1986 E) ... 64,600
Putuo (Shenjiamen) (1985 E) ... 50,962
Puyang (▲ 1,086,100) (1986 E) ... 131,000
Qian Gorlos (Qianguozhen) (1985 E) ... 79,494
Qianyang (Anjiang) (1985 E) ... 38,836
Qihe (Yancheng) (1982 C) ... 43,556
Qilimiao (1985 E) ... 48,692
Qing'an (1985 E) ... 41,990
Qingdao (Tsingtao) ... 1,270,000
Qinggang (1985 E) ... 43,075
Qingjiang (Zhangshu), Jiangxi prov. (1985 E) ... 42,698
Qingjiang, Jiangsu prov. (▲ 246,617) (1982 C) ... 150,000
Qingyuan (Qingcheng) (1985 E) ... 51,756
Qinhuangdao (★ 436,000) (1986 E) ... 307,500
Qinzhou (▲ 923,400) (1986 E) ... 97,100
Qiqihar (Tsitsihar) (▲ 1,300,000) ... 1,150,000
Qitaihe (▲ 309,900) (1986 E) ... 166,400
Qixia (1982 C) ... 54,158
Qixian (1982 C) ... 53,041
Qizhou (1982 C) ... 48,010
Quanyang (1985 E) ... 36,623
Quanzhou (▲ 436,000) (1986 E) ... 157,000
Qujing (▲ 758,000) (1986 E) ... 135,000
Quzhou (▲ 704,800) (1986 E) ... 124,000
Raoping (Huanggang) (1985 E) ... 54,831
Rizhao (▲ 970,300) (1986 E) ... 93,300
Roncheng (Yatou) (1982 C) ... 52,878
Rugao (Rucheng) (1985 E) ... 50,643
Rui'an (1985 E) ... 57,993
Sandu (1985 E) ... 37,804
Sanmenxia (▲ 150,000) (1986 E) ... 79,000
Sanming (▲ 214,300) (1986 E) ... 144,900
Shache (Yarkant) (1985 E) ... 45,331
Shahe (Dalian) (1985 E) ... 29,943
• Shanghai (★ 9,300,000) ... 7,100,000
Shangqiu (Zhuji) (▲ 199,400) (1986 E) ... 135,400
Shangrao (▲ 142,500) (1986 E) ... 113,000
Shangshui (1982 C) ... 50,191
Shangzhi (1985 E) ... 41,326
Shanhetun (1985 E) ... 42,148
Shantou (Swatow) (▲ 770,000) ... 550,000
Shanwei (1985 E) ... 61,234
Shanxian (1985 E) ... 31,197
Shaoguan (1986 E) ... 363,100
Shaowu (▲ 266,700) (1986 E) ... 81,400
Shaoxing (▲ 250,900) (1986 E) ... 167,100
Shaoyang (▲ 465,900) (1986 E) ... 218,600
Shashi (1986 E) ... 253,700
Shengfang (1982 C) ... 45,999
Shenqiu (Huaidian) (1985 E) ... 29,311
Shenxian (1982 C) ... 50,208
Shenyang (Mukden) (▲ 4,290,000) ... 3,840,000
Shenzhen (▲ 231,900) (1986 E) ... 189,600
Shiguaigou (1975 UE) ... 50,000
Shihezi (▲ 549,300) ... 304,700
Shijiazhuang ... 1,190,000
Shijiusuo (1985 E) ... 22,660
Shilong (1985 E) ... 39,189
Shiyan (▲ 332,600) (1986 E) ... 227,300
Shizuishan (▲ 317,400) (1986 E) ... 225,500
Shouguang (1982 C) ... 83,400
Shuangcheng (1985 E) ... 91,163
Shuangfeng (1985 E) ... 34,456
Shuangliao (1985 E) ... 67,326
Shuangyashan (1986 E) ... 427,300
Shulan (1986 E) ... 50,582
Shunde (Daliang) (1985 E) ... 50,262
Shuyang (Shucheng) (1985 E) ... 42,053
Simao (1985 E) ... 36,891
Siping (▲ 357,800) (1986 E) ... 280,100
Sishui (1982 C) ... 82,990
Siyang (Zhongxing) (1985 E) ... 31,090
Songjiang (1985 E) ... 71,864
Songjianghe (1985 E) ... 53,023
Suifenhe (▲ 21,700) (1986 E) ... 13,900
Suihua (▲ 732,100) (1986 E) ... 200,400
Suileng (1985 E) ... 68,399
Suining (▲ 1,174,900) (1986 E) ... 118,500
Suixian (Suizhou) (▲ 1,281,600) (1986 E) ... 187,700
Suqian (Sucheng) (1985 E) ... 50,742
Suxian (Suzhou) (▲ 218,600) (1986 E) ... 123,300
Suzhou (Soochow) ... 720,000
Tacheng (Qoqek) (▲ 119,000) (1986 E) ... 40,000
Tai'an (▲ 1,325,400) (1986 E) ... 215,900
Tailai (1985 E) ... 44,866
Taishan (Taicheng) (1985 E) ... 48,759
Taixian (Jiangyan) (1985 E) ... 45,156
Taixing (1985 E) ... 40,580
Taiyuan (▲ 1,930,000) ... 1,660,000
Taizhou (▲ 210,800) ... 143,200
Tancheng (1982 C) ... 61,857
Tangshan (▲ 1,410,000) ... 1,060,000
Tao'an (Taonan) (1985 E) ... 76,269
Tengxian (1985 E) ... 53,254
Tianjin (Tientsin) (▲ 5,460,000) ... 4,880,000
Tianmen (1985 E) ... 42,706
Tianshui (Beidaobu) (▲ 186,460) (1985 E) ... 38,595
Tianshui (▲ 953,200) (1986 E) ... 209,500
Tiefa (▲ 146,367) (1982 C) ... 60,000
Tieli (1985 E) ... 102,527
Tieling (▲ 454,100) (1986 E) ... 326,100
Tongchuan (▲ 393,200) (1986 E) ... 268,900
Tonghua (▲ 367,400) (1986 E) ... 290,200
Tongliao (▲ 253,100) (1986 E) ... 190,100
Tongling (▲ 216,400) (1986 E) ... 182,900
Tongren (1985 E) ... 50,307
Tongxian (Tongzhou) (1985 E) ... 97,168
Tongyu (Kaitong) (1985 E) ... 47,781
Tumen (▲ 99,700) (1986 E) ... 77,600
Tunxi (▲ 104,500) (1986 E) ... 61,800
Turpan (▲ 196,800) (1986 E) ... 52,300
Ürümqi (Urumchi) ... 1,040,000
Wangkui (1985 E) ... 52,021
Wangqing (1985 E) ... 61,237
Wanxian (▲ 280,800) (1986 E) ... 138,700
Weifang (▲ 1,042,200) (1986 E) ... 312,500
Weihai (▲ 220,800) (1986 E) ... 83,000
Weihe (1985 E) ... 30,226
Weinan (▲ 699,400) (1986 E) ... 111,300
Weishan (Xiazhen) (1982 C) ... 57,932
Weixian (Hanting) (1982 C) ... 50,180
Wenling (1985 E) ... 20,273
Wenxian (1982 C) ... 44,781
Wenzhou (▲ 530,600) (1986 E) ... 372,200
Wuchang (1985 E) ... 64,403
Wuchuan (Meilü) (1985 E) ... 44,146
Wuhai (1986 E) ... 266,000
Wuhan (Hankow) ... 3,490,000
Wuhu (▲ 502,200) (1986 E) ... 396,000
Wulian (Hongning) (1982 C) ... 51,718
Wuqing (Yangcun) (1985 E) ... 24,225
Wusong (1982 C) ... 64,017
Wuwei (Liangzhou) (▲ 804,000) (1986 E) ... 115,500
Wuxi ... 860,000
Wuzhong (▲ 402,400) (1986 E) ... 48,600
Wuzhou (Wuchou) (▲ 261,500) (1986 E) ... 194,800
Xiaguan (▲ 395,800) (1986 E) ... 112,100
Xiamen (Amoy) (▲ 546,400) (1986 E) ... 343,700
Xi'an (Sian) (▲ 2,390,000) ... 2,050,000

C Census. E Official estimate. UE Unofficial estimate.
• Largest city in country.
★ Population or designation of metropolitan area, including suburbs (see headnote).
▲ Population of an entire municipality, commune, or district, including rural area.

Xiangfan (▲ 421,200) (1986 E) 314,900
Xiangtan (Siangtan) (▲ 511,100) (1986 E) 389,500
Xiangxiang (1985 E) 38,509
Xiangyin (1985 E) 37,830
Xianning (▲ 402,200) (1986 E) 122,200
Xianyang (Sienyang) (▲ 641,800) (1986 E) 285,900
Xiaogan (▲ 1,204,400) (1986 E) 125,500
Xiaoshan (1985 E) 63,074
Xichang (▲ 161,000) (1986 E) 105,000
Xifeng (▲ 229,500) (1986 E) 37,200
Xihua (1985 C) 40,022
Xin'an (1982 C) 46,823
Xinghua (Xinxing) (1985 E) 75,573
Xinglongzhen (1982 C) 52,961
Xingning (Xingcheng) (1985 E) 42,983
Xingtai (▲ 350,800) (1986 E) 265,600
Xingyi (1985 E) 36,416
Xinhua (1985 E) 33,260
Xinhui (Huicheng) (1985 E) 77,381
Xining 610,000
Xinjin (Pulandian) (1985 E) 43,196
Xinmin (1985 E) 47,900
Xintai (▲ 1,157,300) (1986 E) 171,400
Xinwen (Suncun) (1975 UE) 50,000
Xinxian (▲ 398,600) (1986 E) 74,200
Xinxiang (▲ 540,500) (1986 E) 411,000
Xinyang (▲ 234,200) (1986 E) 169,100
Xinyu (▲ 610,600) (1986 E) 140,200
Xiuyan (1985 E) 46,087
Xuancheng (1985 E) 52,387
Xuanhua (1975 UE) 140,000
Xuanwei (1982 C) 70,081
Xuchang (▲ 247,200) (1986 E) 167,800
Xuguit Qi (Yakeshi) (1986 E) 390,000
Xuzhou 840,000
Ya'an (▲ 277,600) (1986 E) 89,200
Yan'an (▲ 259,800) (1986 E) 86,700
Yancheng (▲ 1,251,400) (1986 E) 258,400
Yangcheng (1982 C) 57,255
Yanggu (1982 C) 45,839
Yangjiang (Jiangcheng) (1986 E) 91,433
Yangjiazhangzi (1985 E) 44,916
Yangquan (▲ 478,900) (1986 E) 295,100
Yangzhou (▲ 417,300) (1986 E) 321,500
Yanji (Longjing) (1985 E) 55,035
Yanji (▲ 216,900) (1986 E) 175,000
Yanling (1982 C) 52,679
Yanshou (1985 E) 34,294
Yantai (▲ 717,300) (1986 E) 327,000
Yanzhou (1985 E) 48,972
Yaxian (Sanya) (▲ 321,700) (1986 E) 70,500
Yexian (1985 E) 26,543
Yi'an (1986 E) 54,253
Yibin (▲ 636,500) (1986 E) 218,800
Yichang (Ichang) (1986 E) 410,500
Yichuan (1982 C) 58,914
Yichun, Heilongjiang prov. 830,000
Yichun, Jiangxi prov. (▲ 770,200) (1986 E) 132,600
Yidu (1985 E) 54,838
Yilan (1985 E) 50,436
Yima (▲ 84,800) (1986 E) 53,700
Yimianpo (1985 E) 23,518
Yinan (Jiehu) (1982 C) 67,803
Yinchuan (▲ 396,900) (1986 E) 268,200
Yingcheng (1985 E) 59,072
Yingkou (▲ 480,000) (1986 E) 366,900
Yingtan (▲ 116,200) (1986 E) 64,500
Yining (Gulja) (▲ 232,000) (1986 E) 153,200
Yishan (Qingyuan) (1985 E) 39,447
Yiyang (▲ 365,000) (1986 E) 155,300
Yiyuan (Nanma) (1982 C) 53,800
Yong'an (▲ 269,000) (1986 E) 105,100
Yongchuan (1985 E) 70,444
Yuci (▲ 420,700) (1986 E) 171,000
Yueyang (▲ 411,300) (1986 E) 239,500
Yulin, Guangxi Zhuangzu prov. (▲ 1,228,800) (1986 E) 115,600
Yulin, Shaanxi prov. (1985 E) 51,610
Yumen (Laojunmiao) (▲ 160,100) (1986 E) 84,300
Yuncheng, Shandong prov. (1982 C) 54,262
Yuncheng, Shansi prov. (▲ 434,900) (1986 E) 87,000
Yunxiao (1985 E) 32,701
Yunyang (1982 C) 54,903
Yushu (1985 E) 57,222
Yutai (Guting) (1982 C) 41,990
Yuxi (▲ 291,500) (1986 E) 47,400
Yuxian (1985 E) 40,271
Yuyao (▲ 772,700) (1986 E) 169,700
Zaoyang (1985 E) 30,446
Zaozhuang (▲ 1,592,000) (1986 E) 292,200
Zhangjiakou (▲ 626,500) (1986 E) 492,800
Zhangye (▲ 394,200) (1986 E) 73,000
Zhangzhou (Changchou) (▲ 310,400) (1986 E) 159,400
Zhanhua (Fuguo) (1982 C) 48,193
Zhanjiang (▲ 920,900) (1986 E) 335,500
Zhao'an (1985 E) 42,047
Zhaodong (1985 E) 99,836
Zhaoqing (▲ 187,600) (1986 E) 145,700
Zhaotong (▲ 546,600) (1986 E) 77,500
Zhaoyuan (1985 E) 42,426
Zhaoyuan (1982 C) 56,389
Zhaozhou (1985 E) 38,500
Zhengzhou (Chengchou) (▲ 1,610,000) 1,170,000
Zhenjiang (Chinkiang) (1986 E) 412,400
Zhenlai (1985 E) 40,928
Zhongshan (Shiqizhen) (▲ 1,059,700) (1986 E) 238,700
Zhoucun (1975 UE) 50,000
Zhoukou (▲ 220,400) (1986 E) 110,500
Zhuanghe (1985 E) 42,502
Zhucheng (1985 E) 32,852
Zhuhai (▲ 155,000) (1986 E) 88,800
Zhumadian (▲ 149,500) (1986 E) 99,400
Zhuoxian (Zhouzhou) (1985 E) 54,523
Zhuzhou (▲ 499,600) (1986 E) 344,800
Zibo (Zhangdian) (▲ 2,330,000) 830,000
Zigong (▲ 909,300) (1986 E) 361,700
Zixing (▲ 334,300) (1986 E) 97,100
Ziyang (1985 E) 57,349
Zouping (1982 C) 49,274
Zouxian (1985 E) 61,578
Zunyi (▲ 347,600) (1986 E) 236,600

Political Divisions

Anhui 52,170,000
Beijing (Peking) (Auton. City) 9,750,000
Fujian 27,490,000
Gansu 20,710,000
Guangdong 63,460,000
Guangxi Zhuangzu (Auton. Region) 39,460,000
Guizhou (Kweichow) 30,080,000
Hainan
Hebei 56,170,000
Heilongjiang 33,320,000
Henan (Honan) 78,080,000
Hubei (Hupeh) 49,890,000
Hunan 56,960,000
Inner Mongolia (Nei Mongol) 20,290,000
Jiangsu (Kiangsu) 62,700,000
Jiangxi 35,090,000
Jilin 23,150,000
Liaoning 37,260,000
Ningxia Huizu 4,240,000
Qinghai 4,120,000
Shaanxi (Shensi) 30,430,000
Shandong 77,760,000
Shanghai (Municipality) 12,320,000
Shanxi 26,550,000
Sichuan 103,200,000
Tianjin (Tientsin) (Municipality) 8,190,000
Xinjiang Uygur 13,840,000
Xizang (Tibet) (Auton. Region) 2,030,000
Yunnan 34,560,000
Zhejiang (Chekiang) 40,700,000

CISKEI

1986 E 882,200

Cities and Towns

BISHO 2,850
• Mdantsane (★ East London, S. Afr.) 242,823
Zwelitsha (★ King William's Town, S. Afr.) 30,760

COLOMBIA

1985 C 27,867,326

Cities and Towns

Apartadó 29,151
Armenia 187,130
Armero 20,962
Barrancabermeja 137,406
Barranquilla (★ 1,140,000) 899,781
Bello (★ Medellín) 212,861
• BOGOTÁ (★ 4,260,000) 3,982,941
Bucaramanga (★ 550,000) 352,326
Buenaventura 160,342
Buga 82,992
Caldas (★ Medellín) 36,203
Cali (★ 1,400,000) 1,350,565
Cartagena 531,426
Cartago 97,791
Ciénaga 56,860
Cúcuta (★ 445,000) 379,478
Dos Quebradas (★ Pereira) 101,480
Duitama 56,390
Envigado (★ Medellín) 91,391
Espinal 37,563
Facatativá 44,331
Florencia 66,430
Florida 30,040
Floridablanca (★ Bucaramanga) 143,824
Girardot 70,078
Ibagué 292,965
Ipiales 45,419
Itagüí (★ Medellín) 137,623
La Dorada 48,572
Líbano 23,703
Lorica 24,264
Magangué 49,160
Maicao 46,033
Malambo (★ Barranquilla) 52,584
Manizales (★ 330,000) 299,352
Medellín (★ 2,095,000) 1,468,089
Montería 157,466
Neiva 194,556
Ocaña 51,443
Palmira 175,186
Pamplona 34,213
Pasto 197,407
Pereira (★ 390,000) 233,271
Piedecuesta 34,646
Planeta Rica 24,238
Popayán 141,964
Puerto Berrío 21,414
Quibdó 47,950
Ríohacha 46,667
Ríonegro 28,706
Sabanalarga 35,786
Santa Marta 177,922
Santa Rosa de Cabal 37,112
Sevilla 31,309
Sincelejo 120,537
Soacha (★ Bogotá) 109,051
Sogamoso 64,437
Soledad (★ Barranquilla) 165,791
Sonsón 15,535
Tuluá 99,721
Tumaco 45,456
Tunja 93,792
Valledupar 142,771
Villa Rosario (★ Cúcuta) 63,615
Villavicencio 178,685
Yumbo (★ Cali) 43,508
Zipaquirá 45,676

Departments

Amazonas (Comisaría) 30,327
Antioquia 3,888,067
Arauca (intendencia) 70,085
Atlántico 1,428,601
Bolívar 1,197,623
Boyacá 1,097,618
Caldas 838,094
Caquetá 214,473
Casanare (intendencia) 110,253
Cauca 795,838
Cesar 584,631
Chocó 242,768
Córdoba 913,636
Cundinamarca 1,382,360
Distrito Especial (Bogotá) 3,982,941
Guainía (comisaría) 9,214
Guajira 255,310
Guaviare (comisaría) 35,305
Huila 647,756
Magdalena 769,141
Meta 412,312
Nariño 1,019,098
Norte de Santander 883,884
Putumayo (intendencia) 119,815
Quindío 377,860
Risaralda 625,451
San Andrés y Providencia (intendencia) 35,936
Santander 1,438,226
Sucre 529,059
Tolima 1,051,852
Valle del Cauca 2,847,087
Vaupés (Comisaría) 18,935
Vichada (comisaría) 13,770

COMOROS / Comores / Al Qumur

1980 C 346,992

Cities and Towns

• MORONI 20,112
Mutsamudu 14,000

CONGO (PEOPLE'S REPUBLIC OF THE CONGO)

1984 C 1,912,429

Cities and Towns

• BRAZZAVILLE 585,812
Jacob 36,540
Loubomo 49,134
Pointe-Noire 294,203

COOK ISLANDS

1981 C 17,753

Cities and Towns

• AVARUA 9,525

COSTA RICA

1984 C 2,416,809

Cities and Towns

Alajuela (▲ 34,556) 29,273
Cartago 23,928
Cinco Esquinas 27,140
Desamparados (★ San José) 43,352
Guadalupe (★ San José) 25,506
Heredia 21,440
Ipís (★ San José) 25,586
Limón (▲ 52,602) 33,925
Puntarenas 29,224
• SAN JOSÉ (★ 670,000) 241,464
San Juan (★ San José) 22,415
San Pedro (★ San José) 24,519
San Vicente (★ San José) 24,661

CUBA

1981 C 9,723,605

Cities and Towns

Amancio Rodríguez 21,097
Artemisa 33,907
Banes 31,237
Baracoa 35,754
Bayamo (1985 E) 105,302
Cabaiguán 26,460
Caibarién 31,872
Camagüey (1985 E) 260,782
Cárdenas 59,352
Ciego de Avila (1985 E) 80,500
Cienfuegos (1985 E) 109,304
Colón 34,744
Contramaestre 22,168
Florida 39,482
Guanajay 20,548
Guantánamo (1985 E) 174,383
Güines 41,591
Güira de Melena 21,088
• HAVANA (LA HABANA) (★ 2,125,000) (1987 E) 2,036,800
Holguín (1985 E) 194,728
Jobabo 14,895
Jovellanos 20,635
Manzanillo 87,830
Matanzas (1985 E) 105,382
Mayarí 21,076
Moa 26,893
Morón 39,779
Nueva Gerona (1985 E) 34,400
Nuevitas 34,869
Palma Soriano 55,851
Pinar del Río (1985 E) 100,906
Placetas 37,310
Puerto Padre 23,310
Ranchuelo (▲ 60,829) 14,700
Remedios (▲ 47,347) 16,200
Sagua de Tánamo 15,435
Sagua la Grande 42,291
San Antonio de los Baños (★ Havana) 27,488
Sancti-Spíritus (1985 E) 75,600
San José de las Lajas 26,917
San Luis 24,347
Santa Clara (1985 E) 178,278
Santiago de Cuba (1985 E) 358,764
Trinidad 32,935
Vertientes 22,432
Victoria de las Tunas (1985 E) 91,400

CYPRUS / Kípros / Kıbrıs

1982 C 512,097

Cities and Towns

Lárnax (Larnaca) (★ 48,330) 35,823
Lemesós (Limassol) (★ 107,161) 74,782
• NICOSIA (LEVKOSÍA) (★ 185,000) 48,221
Páfos (★ 20,824) 13,122

CYPRUS, NORTH / Kuzey Kıbrıs

1985 E 160,287

Cities and Towns

Gazimağusa (Famagusta) 19,428
• NICOSIA (LEFKOŞA) 37,400

CZECHOSLOVAKIA / Československo

1989 E 15,624,021

Cities and Towns

Banská Bystrica 85,327
Bardejov 30,157
Beroun 24,018
Bratislava 435,499
Břeclav 26,141
Brno (★ 450,000) 389,892
Česká Lípa 39,047
České Budějovice (Budweis) (★ 114,000) 97,340
Český Těšín (★★ Třinec) 28,647
Cheb 31,600
Chomutov (★ 80,000) 56,715
Děčín (★ 72,000) 56,200
Frýdek-Místek (★ Ostrava) 65,481
Gottwaldov (Zlín) (★ 124,000) 86,742
Havířov (★ Ostrava) 92,279
Havlíčkův Brod 25,157
Hlohovec 23,499
Hodonín 33,449
Hradec Králové (★ 113,000) 100,454
Humenné 34,636
Jablonec [nad Nisou] (★★ Liberec) 46,200
Jihlava 53,987
Karlovy Vary (Carlsbad) 55,907
Karviná (★★ Ostrava) 71,742
Kladno (★ 88,500) 73,180
Kolín 32,036
Komárno 37,569
Košice 232,253
Krnov 25,976
Kroměříž (★ 38,500) 29,396
Levice 32,951
Liberec (★ 175,000) 103,752
Liptovský Mikuláš 30,449
Litoměřice 26,322
Litvínov (★★ Most) 30,344
Louny 25,994
Lučenec 29,783
Mariánské Lázně (Marienbad) 18,513
Martin 65,218
Michalovce 38,242
Mladá Boleslav 48,600
Most (★ 135,000) 69,557
Náchod 21,751
Nitra 89,306
Nové Zámky 41,718
Nový Jičín 32,917
Olomouc (★ 126,000) 106,662
Opava (★ 77,500) 63,084
Orlová (★ Ostrava) 36,233
Ostrava (★ 760,000) 330,614
Ostrov 19,566
Pardubice 95,668
Partizánske 26,255
Piešťany 33,667
Písek 29,395
Plzeň (Pilsen) (★ 210,000) 174,635
Poprad 50,300
Považská Bystrica 39,569
• PRAGUE (PRAHA) (★ 1,325,000) 1,211,106
Přerov 51,800
Prešov 87,396
Příbram 40,110
Prievidza 51,200
Prostějov 51,900
Ružomberok 29,509
Sokolov (★ 36,000) 28,382
Spišská Nová Ves 44,600
Šumperk 36,940
Tábor (★ 55,500) 35,703
Teplice (★ 94,000) 55,756
Topoľčany 37,259
Třebíč 38,847
Trenčín 56,843
Třinec (★ 87,500) 45,600
Trnava 72,200
Trutnov 31,640
Uherské Hradiště 38,871
Ústí nad Labem (★ 115,000) 105,854
Valašské Meziříčí 26,786
Vsetín 31,944
Žďár nad Sazavou 26,759
Žilina 96,418
Znojmo 37,364
Zvolen 41,800

Republics

Česká Socialistická Republika 10,360,480
Slovenská Socialistická Republika 5,263,541

Regions

Bratislava (city) 435,499
Jihočeský 697,785
Jihomoravský 2,058,530
Praha (Prague) (city) 1,211,106

C Census. E Official estimate. UE Unofficial estimate.
• Largest city in country.

★ Population or designation of metropolitan area, including suburbs (see headnote).
▲ Population of an entire municipality, commune, or district, including rural area.

Severočeský 1,190,606
Severomoravský 1,969,991
Středočeský 1,122,023
Stredoslovenský 1,608,192
Východočeský 1,240,847
Východoslovenský 1,494,084
Západočeský 869,592
Západoslovenský 1,725,766

Historic Provinces

Bohemia (Čechy) 6,331,959
Moravia (Morava) 4,028,521
Sloviakia (Slovensko) 5,263,541

DENMARK / Danmark

1988 E 5,129,254

Cities and Towns

Åbenrå (▲ 21,363) 15,500
Albertslund (★ Copenhagen) 29,001
Ålborg (▲ 154,739) 113,800
Århus (▲ 258,028) 199,700
Ballerup (★ Copenhagen) 45,791
Brøndby (★ Copenhagen) 34,704
• COPENHAGEN (KØBENHAVN) (★ 1,685,000) 468,704
Esbjerg (▲ 81,385) 71,800
Fredericia (▲ 45,970) 28,300
Frederiksberg (★ Copenhagen) 85,814
Frederikshavn (▲ 35,531) 25,336
Gentofte (★ Copenhagen) 65,467
Gladsakse (★ Copenhagen) 61,424
Glostrup (★ Copenhagen) 19,896
Greve (★ Copenhagen) 45,121
Haderslev (▲ 30,208) 19,500
Helsingør (Elsinore) (★ Copenhagen) 56,607
Herlev (★ Copenhagen) 27,068
Herning (▲ 56,191) 28,900
Hillerød (★ Copenhagen) 25,300
Hjørring (▲ 34,426) 23,658
Høje Tåstrup (★ Copenhagen) 44,266
Holbæk (▲ 30,860) 21,300
Holstebro (▲ 38,256) 29,300
Horsens (▲ 54,776) 46,900
Hvidovre (★ Copenhagen) 49,332
Køge (★ Copenhagen) 30,400
Kolding (▲ 57,043) 42,000
Lyngby (Kongens Lyngby) [-Tårbæk] (★ Copenhagen) 49,601
Middelfart (▲ 18,468) 12,100
Næstved (▲ 45,132) 38,000
Nakskov 16,229
Nykøbing Falster (▲ 25,121) 18,800
Odense (▲ 174,016) 138,400
Randers 61,155
Ringsted (▲ 28,445) 17,000
Rødovre (★ Copenhagen) 35,787
Rønne 15,397
Roskilde (★ Copenhagen) 39,700
Silkeborg (▲ 47,917) 33,775
Skagen (▲ 13,890) 11,653
Skive (▲ 26,854) 19,500
Slagelse (▲ 34,022) 29,000
Søllerød (★ Copenhagen) 31,253
Sønderborg 27,793
Svendborg (▲ 40,623) 25,800
Tårnby (★ Copenhagen) 39,829
Thisted (▲ 29,781) 12,363
Vejle (▲ 50,817) 44,800
Viborg (▲ 39,631) 29,400
Vordingborg (▲ 19,947) 8,800

Counties

Århus 591,993
Bornholm 46,642
Fredericksberg (City) 85,814
Frederiksborg 339,914
Fyn 457,070
København (City) 468,704
København 605,127
Nordjylland 483,675
Ribe 217,973
Ringkøbing 266,554
Roskilde 215,164
Sønderjylland 250,132
Storstrøm 257,161
Vejle 329,590
Vestsjælland 282,775
Viborg 230,966

DJIBOUTI

1976 E 226,000

Cities and Towns

• DJIBOUTI 120,000

DOMINICA

1984 E 77,000

Cities and Towns

• ROSEAU 9,348

DOMINICAN REPUBLIC / República Dominicana

1981 C 5,647,977

Cities and Towns

Azua 31,481
Bajos de Haina 33,135
Baní 36,705
Barahona 49,334
Bonao 44,486
La Romana 91,571
La Vega 52,432
Mao (Valverde) 33,527
Moca 31,176
Puerto Plata 45,348
Salvaleón de Higüey 33,501
San Cristóbal 58,520
San Francisco de Macorís 64,906
San Juan [de La Maguana] 49,764
San Pedro de Macorís 78,562
Santiago [de los Caballeros] 278,638
• SANTO DOMINGO 1,313,172

ECUADOR

1982 C 8,050,630

Cities and Towns

Alfaro (★ Guayaquil) 51,023
Ambato 100,454
Azogues 14,548
Babahoyo 42,266
Chone 33,839
Cuenca 157,213
Esmeraldas 91,382
Guaranda 13,685
• Guayaquil (★ 1,255,000) 1,204,532
Ibarra 53,428
Jipijapa 27,146
Latacunga 28,764
Loja 71,652
Machala 108,156
Manta 103,609
Milagro 77,010
Pasaje 26,224
Portoviejo 102,628
Quevedo 67,023
QUITO (★ 1,050,000) 890,355
Riobamba 75,455
Santo Domingo de los Colorados 69,235
Tulcán 30,985

Provinces

Azuay 443,044
Bolívar 141,566
Cañar 174,674
Carchi 125,452
Chimborazo 320,268
Cotopaxi 279,765
El Oro 337,818
Esmeraldas 247,311
Galápagos (Ter.) 6,119
Guayas 2,047,001
Imbabura 245,745
Loja 358,952
Los Ríos 457,065
Manabí 858,780
Morona-Santiago 70,217
Napo 115,110
Pastaza 31,779
Pichincha 1,376,831
Tungurahua 324,286
Zamora-Chinchipe 46,691
Zones in dispute with Peru 42,156

EGYPT / Miṣr

1986 C 48,205,049

Cities and Towns

Abnūb 48,519
Abū Kabīr 69,509
Abū Tīj 48,711
Akhmīm 70,602
Al 'Arīsh 67,638
Al Badārī 34,858
Al Badrashayn 40,159
Alexandria (Al Iskandarīyah) (★ 3,350,000) 2,917,327
Al Fashn 43,347
Al Fayyūm 212,523
Al Ghurdaqah 22,801
Al Ḥawāmidīyah (★ Cairo) 73,060
Al Karnak 20,842
Al Khārijah 38,544
Al Madīnah al Fikrīyah 45,629
Al Maḥallah al Kubrā 358,844
Al Manshāh 37,788
Al Manṣūrah (El Mansura) (★ 375,000) 316,870
Al Manzilah 55,090
Al Maṭarīyah 74,554
Al Minyā 179,136
Al Qanāṭir al Khayrīyah 48,909
Al Qaṣr 5,263
Al Quṣayr 19,997
Al Qūṣīyah 42,175
Armant 54,650
Ashmūn 54,450
Ash Shuhadā' 34,695
As Sallūm 3,601
As Sinbillāwayn 60,285
Aswān 191,461
Asyūṭ 273,191
Az Zaqāzīq 245,496
Bahtīm (★ Cairo) 275,807
Banhā 115,571
Banī Mazār 47,964
Banī Suwayf 151,813
Bibā 40,668
Bilbays 96,540
Bilqās Qism Awwal 73,162
Biyalā 47,781
Būlāq ad Dakrūr (★ Cairo) 148,787
Būsh 54,482
• CAIRO (AL QĀHIRAH) (★ 9,300,000) 6,052,836
Damanhūr 190,840
Dayr Mawās 25,518
Dayrūṭ 44,498
Dishnā 37,978
Disūq 78,119
Dumyāṭ (Damietta) 89,498
Fāqūs 48,625
Fuwah 46,014
Giheina al Gharbiya 34,395
Giza (Al Jīzah) (★ Cairo) 1,870,508
Ḥawsh'Īsā (1980 C) 53,619
Hihyā 29,334
Idfū 45,737
Idkū 70,729
Ismailia (Al Ismā'īlīyah) (★ 235,000) 212,567
Isnā 43,055
Jirjā 70,899
Kafr ad Dawwār (★ Alexandria) 195,102
Kafr ash Shaykh 102,910
Kafr az Zayyāt 58,061
Kafr Salīm (★ Alexandria) 2,956
Kawm Umbū 52,131
Luxor (Al Uqṣur) 125,404
Maghāghah 50,807
Mallawī 99,062
Manfalūṭ 52,644
Marsā Maṭrūḥ 43,192
Minūf 69,883
Minyā al Qamḥ 45,871
Mīt Ghamr (★ 100,000) 92,253
Nafīshah (★ Al Ismā'īlīyah) 46,188
Naj'Ḥammādī 28,493
Port Said (Būr Sa'īd) 399,793
Qalyūb 86,684
Qinā 119,794
Qūṣ 42,467
Ra's Gharib 20,617
Rashīd (Rosetta) 52,014
Rummānah 50,014
Samālūt 62,404
Samannūd 41,670
Sāqiyat Makkī 51,062
Sawhāj 132,965
Shibīn al Kawm 132,751
Shibīn al Qanāṭir 35,519
Shirbīn 40,441
Shubrā al Khaymah (★ Cairo) 710,794
Sīdī Barrānī 19,359
Sīdī Sālim 31,674
Sinnūris 55,323
Sīwah 7,329
Suez (As Suways) 326,820
Ṭahṭā 58,516
Talā 38,584
Ṭalkhā (★ Al Manṣūrah) 55,757
Ṭanṭā 334,505
Ṭimā 47,223
Warrāq al 'Arab (★ Cairo) 127,108
Ziftā (★★ Mīt Ghamr) 69,050

EL SALVADOR

1985 E 5,337,896

Cities and Towns

Ahuachapán 20,376
Chalchuapa (▲ 62,340) 26,158
Cojutepeque 32,043
Cuscatancingo (★ San Salvador) 27,638
Ilopango (★ San Salvador) 31,294
La Unión (▲ 56,063) 27,917
Mejicanos (★ San Salvador) 91,465
Nueva San Salvador (★ San Salvador) 53,688
Quezaltepeque (▲ 44,496) 18,887
San Marcos (★ San Salvador) 37,202
San Miguel 88,520
• SAN SALVADOR (★ 920,000) 462,652
Santa Ana 137,879
San Vicente 27,205
Sonsonate 48,436
Soyapango (★ San Salvador) 60,000
Usulután 32,172
Villa Delgado (★ San Salvador) 67,684
Zacatecoluca 26,646

EQUATORIAL GUINEA / Guinea Ecuatorial

1983 C 300,000

Cities and Towns

Bata 24,100
• MALABO 30,710

ETHIOPIA / Ityopiya

1984 C 42,019,418

Cities and Towns

• ADDIS ABABA (★ 1,500,000) 1,412,575
Adwa 13,823
Akaki Beseka (★ Addis Ababa) 54,146
Akordat 5,948
Aseb 30,385
Asela 36,720
Asmara 275,385
Awasa 36,169
Bahir Dar 54,800
Debre Birhan 25,753
Debre Markos 39,808
Debre Zeyit 51,143
Dese 68,848
Dire Dawa 98,104
Gonder 68,958
Harer 62,160
Jima 60,992
Keren 26,149
Massawa (Mitsiwa) 15,441
Mekele 61,583
Nazret 76,284
Nekemte 28,824
Sashemene 31,531
Wenji Gefersa 35,420

FAEROE ISLANDS / Føroyar

1988 E 47,653

Cities and Towns

• TÓRSHAVN 14,547

FALKLAND ISLANDS

1986 C 1,916

Cities and Towns

• STANLEY 1,200

FIJI

1986 C 715,375

Cities and Towns

Lautoka (★ 39,057) 28,728
• SUVA (★ 141,273) 69,665

FINLAND / Suomi

1988 E 4,938,602

Cities and Towns

Borgå (Porvoo) 19,858
Espoo (Esbo) (★ Helsinki) 164,569
Hämeenlinna 42,486
• HELSINKI (HELSINGFORS) (★ 900,000) 490,034
Hyvinkää 39,185
Iisalmi (▲ 23,695) 17,000
Imatra 34,566
Jakobstad (Pietarsaari) 20,118
Järvenpää (★ Helsinki) 29,001
Joensuu 47,099
Jyväskylä (★ 89,000) 65,719
Kajaani 36,056
Kemi 25,984
Kerava (★ Helsinki) 26,829
Kokkola (Gamlakarleby) 34,599
Kotka 57,745
Kouvola (★ 55,000) 31,933
Kuopio 78,916
Kuusankoski (★★ Kouvola) 21,888
Lahti (★ 109,000) 74,300
Lappeenranta (▲ 53,780) 47,400
Mariehamn (Maarianhamina) 9,966
Mikkeli 31,728
Nokia (★ Tampere) 21,900
Oulu (★ 112,000) 98,582
Pori 77,395
Rauma 30,757
Riihimäki 24,674
Rovaniemi 32,911
Salo 20,838
Savonlinna (▲ 28,510) 24,500
Seinäjoki 26,837
Tampere (★ 241,000) 170,533
Turku (Åbo) (★ 221,000) 160,456
Vaasa (Vasa) 53,737
Vantaa (Vanda) (★ Helsinki) 149,063
Varkaus (▲ 24,791) 19,200

Provinces

Ahvenanmaa (Åland) 23,761
Häme 681,550
Keski-Suomi 248,441
Kuopio 255,705
Kymi 337,254
Lappi 200,174
Mikkeli 207,927
Oulu (Uleåborg) 433,715
Pohjois-Karjala 176,699
Turku-Pori 714,196
Uusimaa (Nyland) 1,214,775
Vaasa (Vasa) 444,405

FRANCE

1982 C 54,334,871

Cities and Towns

Abbeville 24,915
Agen (★ 58,288) 31,593
Aigues-Mortes 4,472
Aix-en-Provence (★ 126,552) 121,327
Aix-les-Bains (★ 31,680) 23,451
Ajaccio 54,089
Albi (★ 60,181) 45,947
Alençon (★ 43,101) 31,608
Alès (★ 70,180) 43,268
Alfortville (★ Paris) 36,231
Amiens (★ 154,498) 131,332
Angers (★ 195,859) 136,038
Angoulême (★ 103,552) 46,197
Annecy (★ 112,632) 49,965
Antibes (★★ Cannes) 62,859
Antony (★ Paris) 54,610
Arcachon (★ 39,931) 13,293
Argenteuil (★ Paris) 95,347
Arles (★ 52,547) 37,571
Armentières (★ 59,000) 24,834
Arras (★ 80,477) 41,736
Asnières [-sur-Seine] (★ Paris) 71,077
Athis-Mons (★ Paris) 28,496
Aubervilliers (★ Paris) 67,719
Auch (▲ 23,258) 20,273
Aulnay-sous-Bois (★ Paris) 75,996
Aurillac (★ 35,829) 30,963
Autun 20,587
Auxerre (★ 42,126) 38,741
Avignon (★ 174,264) 89,132
Avranches (★ 14,889) 9,468
Bagneux (★ Paris) 40,385
Bagnolet (★ Paris) 32,557
Barentin (★ 19,499) 12,364
Bar-le-Duc 18,471
Bastia (★ 50,596) 44,020
Bayeux 14,721
Bayonne (★ 127,477) 41,381
Beauvais (★ 55,817) 52,365
Belfort (★ 76,221) 51,206
Besançon (★ 120,772) 113,283
Béthune (★ 258,383) 25,508
Béziers (★ 81,347) 76,647
Biarritz (★★ Bayonne) 26,598
Blois (★ 61,049) 47,243
Bobigny (★ Paris) 42,723
Bois-Colombes (★ Paris) 23,780
Bondy (★ Paris) 44,301
Bordeaux (★ 640,012) 208,159
Boulogne-Billancourt (★ Paris) 102,582
Boulogne-sur-Mer (★ 98,566) 47,653
Bourg [-en-Bresse] (★ 53,463) 41,098
Bourges (★ 92,202) 76,432
Brest (★ 201,145) 156,060
Briançon (★ 13,123) 9,710
Brive [-la-Gaillarde] (★ 64,301) 51,511
Bron (★ Lyon) 40,638
Bruay [-en-Artois] (★★ Béthune) 22,893
Caen (★ 183,526) 114,068
Cagnes-sur-Mer (★ Nice) 35,214
Cahors 19,707
Calais (★ 100,823) 76,527
Caluire [-et-Cuire] (★ Lyon) 41,931
Cambrai (★ 49,581) 35,272
Cannes (★ 295,525) 72,259
Carcassonne 41,153
Carmaux (★ 19,422) 12,113
Castres (★ 46,891) 45,578
Châlons-sur-Marne (★ 63,061) 51,137
Chalon-sur-Saône (★ 78,064) 56,194
Chambéry (★ 96,163) 53,427
Chamonix [-Mont-Blanc] (★ 10,512) 7,406
Champigny-sur-Marne (★ Paris) 76,176
Chantilly (★ 28,128) 10,065
Charleville-Mézières (★ 67,694) 58,667
Chartres (★ 77,795) 37,119
Châteauroux (★ 66,851) 51,942
Château-Thierry (★ 22,696) 14,557
Châtellerault 35,838
Châtenay-Malabry (★ Paris) 28,580

C Census. E Official estimate. UE Unofficial estimate.
• Largest city in country.
★ Population or designation of metropolitan area, including suburbs (see headnote).
▲ Population of an entire municipality, commune, or district, including rural area.

Châtillon (★ Paris) 24,834
Chatou (★ Paris) 28,437
Chaumont 27,554
Chauny (★ 20,078) 13,435
Chelles (★ Paris) 41,838
Cherbourg (★ 85,485) 28,442
Chinon (▲ 8,622) 6,032
Choisy-le-Roi (★ Paris) 35,476
Cholet 55,524
Clamart (★ Paris) 48,353
Clermont-Ferrand (★ 256,189) 147,361
Clichy (★ Paris) 46,895
Cognac (★ 31,189) 20,660
Colmar (★ 82,468) 62,483
Colombes (★ Paris) 78,777
Compiègne (★ 62,778) 40,384
Concarneau (★ 23,893) 15,747
Corbeil [-Essonnes] (★ Paris) 37,846
Courbevoie (★ Paris) 59,830
Coutances 9,930
Creil (★ 82,505) 34,709
Créteil (★ Paris) 71,693
Dax (★ 33,475) 18,648
Deauville 4,682
Decazeville (★ 21,925) 8,804
Denain (★★ Valenciennes) 21,825
Dieppe (★ 41,812) 35,957
Dijon (★ 215,865) 140,942
Dinard (★ 15,838) 9,590
Dives-sur-Mer (★ 11,204) 5,508
Dôle (★ 31,546) 26,889
Douai (★ 202,366) 42,576
Douarnenez 17,653
Drancy (★ Paris) 60,183
Dreux (★ 44,706) 33,379
Dunkerque (★ 195,705) 73,120
Elbeuf (★ 51,083) 17,224
Épernay (★ 34,355) 27,668
Épinal (★ 51,495) 37,818
Espinay [-sur-Seine] (★ Paris) 50,314
Étaples (★ 22,701) 11,292
Eu (★ 20,506) 8,588
Évreux (★ 54,654) 46,045
Évry (★ Paris) 29,471
Falaise 8,597
Fécamp 21,436
Foix 9,282
Fontaine (★ Grenoble) 22,827
Fontainebleau (★ 35,629) 15,679
Fontenay [-sous-Bois] (★ Paris) 52,627
Forbach (★ 99,606) 27,187
Fougères 24,362
Fréjus (★ 60,289) 31,662
Gagny (★ Paris) 34,861
Gap (▲ 30,676) 21,874
Garges-lès-Gonesse (★ Paris) 40,182
Gennevilliers (★ Paris) 45,396
Givors (★ Lyon) 20,544
Granville (★ 17,890) 13,546
Grasse (★★ Cannes) 24,553
Grenoble (★ 392,021) 156,637
Guebwiller (★ 25,427) 10,689
Guéret 15,720
Hagondange (★ 119,669) 9,091
Haguenau (★ 32,403) 26,629
Hayange (★★ Thionville) 17,848
Hendaye 10,572
Hénin-Beaumont (Hénin-Liétard) (★★ Lens) 26,037
Houilles (★ Paris) 29,537
Hyères (★★ Toulon) 32,191
Issy [-les-Moulineaux] (★ Paris) 45,772
Ivry-sur-Seine (★ Paris) 55,699
Jœuf (★ Hagondange) 9,016
La Baule-Escoublac (★ Saint-Nazaire) 14,553
La Ciotat (★ 39,956) 31,727
La Courneuve (★ Paris) 33,537
La Garenne-Colombes (★ Paris) 20,990
La Grand'Combe (★ 13,743) 8,329
Lambersart (★ Lille) 28,520
Laon 26,682
La Rochelle (★ 102,143) 75,840
La Roche-sur-Yon 45,098
La Seyne [-sur-Mer] (★ Toulon) 57,659
Laval (★ 55,984) 50,360
Le Blanc-Mesnil (★ Paris) 47,037
Le Creusot (★ 44,389) 32,149
Le Grand-Quevilly (★ Rouen) 31,650
Le Havre (★ 254,595) 199,388
Le Mans (★ 191,080) 147,697
Lens (★ 327,383) 38,244
Le Perreux-sur-Marne (★ Paris) 27,647
Le Puy [-en-Velay] (★ 42,382) 24,064
Les Sables-d'Olonne (★ 32,436) 16,100
Levallois-Perret (★ Paris) 53,500
Le Vésinet (★ Paris) 17,272
L'Haÿ-les-Roses (★ Paris) 29,568
Libourne (★ 26,992) 22,119
Liévin (★ Lens) 33,096
Lille (★ 1,020,000) 168,424
Limoges (★ 171,689) 140,400
Lisieux (★ 29,063) 24,940
Livry-Gargan (★ Paris) 32,778
Loches (▲ 6,772) 5,847
Lomme (★ Lille) 28,281
Longwy (★ 77,000) 17,338
Lons-le-Saunier (★ 26,410) 20,105
Lorient (★ 104,025) 62,554
Lourdes 17,425
Lunéville 21,468
Lyon (★ 1,275,000) 413,095
Mâcon (★ 47,274) 38,404
Maisons-Alfort (★ Paris) 51,065
Maisons-Laffitte (★ Paris) 22,595
Malakoff (★ Paris) 32,553
Mantes [-la-Jolie] (★ 170,265) 43,564
Marcq-en-Baroeul (★ Lille) 35,278
Marignane (★ Marseille) 31,109
Marseille (★ 1,225,000) 874,436
Martigues (★ Marseille) 31,157
Massy (★ Paris) 40,135
Maubeuge (★ 105,714) 36,061
Mazamet (★ 26,676) 12,840
Meaux (★ 55,797) 45,005
Melun (★ 82,479) 35,005
Mende 10,929
Menton (★★ Monaco, Monaco) 25,072
Mérignac (★ Bordeaux) 51,306
Metz (★ 186,437) 114,232
Meudon (★ Paris) 48,450
Millau 21,695
Montargis (★ 51,954) 16,110
Montauban (▲ 50,682) 36,758
Montbéliard (★ 128,194) 31,836
Montceau-les-Mines (★ 51,290) 26,925
Mont-de-Marsan (★ 33,616) 27,326
Montélimar (★ 38,292) 29,161
Montereau [-faut-Yonne] (★ 26,663) 19,413
Montigny [-lès-Metz] (★ Metz) 22,114
Montluçon (★ 67,963) 49,912
Montmorency (★ Paris) 20,798
Montpellier (★ 221,307) 197,231
Montreuil [-sous-Bois] (★ Paris) 93,368
Montrouge (★ Paris) 38,517
Morlaix (★ 27,829) 15,558
Moulins (★ 43,082) 25,159
Moyeuvre [-Grande] (★ Hagondange) 10,287
Mulhouse (★ 220,613) 112,157
Nancy (★ 306,982) 96,317
Nanterre (★ Paris) 88,578
Nantes (★ 464,857) 240,539
Narbonne 41,565
Neuilly [-sur-Seine] (★ Paris) 64,170
Nevers (★ 59,274) 43,013
Nice (★ 449,496) 337,085
Nîmes (★ 132,343) 124,220
Niort (★ 61,959) 58,203
Nogent [-sur-Marne] (★ Paris) 24,630
Noisy-le-Grand (★ Paris) 40,585
Noisy-le-Sec (★ Paris) 36,880
Noyon 14,041
Orange (▲ 26,499) 18,727
Orléans (★ 220,478) 102,710
Orly (★ Paris) 23,766
Oullins (★ Lyon) 27,168
Oyonnax (★ 28,107) 22,739
Palaiseau (★ Paris) 28,369
Pantin (★ Paris) 43,553
Paray-le-Monial 10,639
• PARIS (★ 9,775,000) (1987 E) 2,078,900
Pau (★ 131,265) 83,790
Périgueux (★ 59,716) 32,916
Perpignan (★ 137,915) 111,669
Pessac (★ Bordeaux) 50,267
Poissy (★ Paris) 36,389
Poitiers (★ 103,204) 79,350
Pont-à-Mousson (★ 22,661) 14,942
Pontoise (★ Paris) 28,434
Port-de-Bouc 20,106
Privas (★ 14,108) 10,345
Puteaux (★ Paris) 36,117
Quimper 56,907
Reims (★ 199,388) 194,656
Rennes (★ 234,418) 117,234
Rezé (★ Nantes) 33,562
Riom (★ 23,316) 18,346
Rive-de-Gier (★★ Saint-Chamond) 15,806
Roanne (★ 81,786) 48,705
Rochefort (★ 35,122) 26,167
Rodez (★ 37,953) 24,368
Romans [-sur-Isère] (★ 47,083) 33,152
Rosny-sous-Bois (★ Paris) 36,970
Roubaix (★★ Lille) 101,602
Rouen (★ 379,879) 101,945
Royan (★ 28,327) 17,540
Rueil-Malmaison (★ Paris) 63,412
Saint-Avold (★ 26,543) 12,389
Saint-Brieuc (★ 83,900) 48,563
Saint-Chamond (★ 82,059) 40,267
Saint-Cyr-l'École (★ Paris) 14,996
Saint-Denis (★ Paris) 90,829
Saint-Dié (★ 27,708) 23,759
Saint-Dizier 35,189
Saint-Étienne (★ 317,228) 204,955
Saint-Étienne-du-Rouvray (★ Rouen) 32,444
Saint-Germain-en-Laye (★ Paris) 38,499
Saint-Jean-de-Luz (★ 23,868) 12,769
Saint-Lô (★ 27,656) 23,212
Saint-Malo 46,347
Saint-Martin-d'Hères (★ Grenoble) 35,188
Saint-Maur-des-Fossés (★ Paris) 80,811
Saint-Nazaire (★ 130,271) 68,348
Saint-Omer (★ 53,748) 15,415
Saint-Ouen (★ Paris) 43,606
Saint-Quentin (★ 71,887) 63,567
Saintes 25,471
Saint-Tropez (▲ 6,213) 4,961
Salon-de-Provence (★ 41,091) 34,846
Sarcelles (★ Paris) 53,630
Sarreguemines 24,763
Sartrouville (★ Paris) 46,197
Saumur 32,149
Savigny-sur-Orge (★ Paris) 32,502
Schiltigheim (★ Strasbourg) 29,574
Sedan (★ 30,871) 23,477
Senlis 14,514
Sens (★ 35,178) 26,602
Sète (★ 58,865) 39,545
Sèvres (★ Paris) 20,208
Soissons (★ 47,305) 30,213
Sotteville-lès-Rouen (★ Rouen) 30,558
Stains (★ Paris) 36,079
Strasbourg (★ 400,000) 248,712
Suresnes (★ Paris) 35,187
Tarbes (★ 78,056) 51,422
Thann (★ 28,406) 7,788
Thionville (★ 138,034) 40,573
Thonon-les-Bains (★ 45,372) 27,161
Toul (★ 22,878) 17,406
Toulon (★ 410,393) 179,423
Toulouse (★ 541,271) 347,995
Tourcoing (★★ Lille) 96,908
Tours (★ 262,786) 132,209
Trouville [-sur-Mer] (★ 18,533) 6,008
Troyes (★ 125,240) 63,581
Tulle 18,880
Valence (★ 106,041) 66,356
Valenciennes (★ 349,505) 40,275
Vannes 42,178
Vanves (★ Paris) 22,868
Vénissieux (★ Lyon) 64,804
Verdun (★ 26,944) 21,516
Versailles (★ Paris) 91,494
Vesoul (★ 26,592) 18,412
Vichy (★ 63,501) 30,527
Vienne (★ 41,019) 28,294
Vierzon 34,209
Villefranche-sur-Mer (★ Nice) 7,363
Villefranche [-sur-Saône] (★ 50,143) 28,881
Villejuif (★ Paris) 52,448
Villemomble (★ Paris) 27,571
Villeneuve-d'Ascq (★ Lille) 59,527
Villeneuve-Saint-Georges (★ Paris) 28,119
Villeurbanne (★ Lyon) 115,960
Vincennes (★ Paris) 42,870
Viry-Châtillon (★ Paris) 30,224
Vitry-le-François (★ 21,192) 18,261
Vitry-sur-Seine (★ Paris) 85,263
Voiron (★ 33,492) 18,911
Wattrelos (★ Lille) 44,626

Departments

1987 ESTIMATE

Ain 453,200
Aisne 532,600
Allier 364,500
Alpes-de-Haute-Provence (Basses-Alpes) 125,900
Alpes-Maritimes 907,200
Ardèche 274,500
Ardennes 297,900
Ariège 136,100
Aube 294,600
Aude 288,800
Aveyron 276,100
Bas-Rhin 941,600
Belfort, Territoire de 130,000
Bouches-du-Rhône 1,754,500
Calvados 608,000
Cantal 159,600
Charente 342,500
Charente-Maritime 522,500
Cher 322,700
Corrèze 238,900
Corse-du-Sud 111,400
Côte-d'Or 485,300
Côtes-du-Nord 541,700
Creuse 135,700
Deux-Sèvres 346,000
Dordogne 379,200
Doubs 478,800
Drôme 412,200
Essonne 1,042,600
Eure 490,200
Eure-et-Loir 378,800
Finistère 834,200
Gard 566,000
Gers 175,200
Gironde 1,161,700
Haute-Corse 134,600
Haute-Garonne 858,800
Haute-Loire 209,100
Haute-Marne 207,600
Hautes-Alpes 108,700
Haute-Saône 234,100
Haute-Savoie 535,200
Hautes-Pyrénées 232,300
Haute-Vienne 360,100
Haut-Rhin 663,800
Hauts-de-Seine 1,371,300
Hérault 769,200
Ille-et-Vilaine 777,900
Indre 238,300
Indre-et-Loire 524,600
Isère 982,700
Jura 245,100
Landes 308,600
Loire 739,200
Loire-Atlantique 1,032,600
Loiret 568,900
Loir-et-Cher 300,600
Lot 154,700
Lot-et-Garonne 304,300
Lozère 72,400
Maine-et-Loire 707,600
Manche 476,600
Marne 557,700
Mayenne 280,400
Meurthe-et-Moselle 709,000
Meuse 197,600
Morbihan 609,400
Moselle 1,030,500
Nièvre 235,400
Nord 2,507,200
Oise 695,600
Orne 294,800
Paris 2,078,900
Pas-de-Calais 1,424,300
Puy-de-Dôme 596,000
Pyrénées-Atlantiques (Basses Pyrénées) 569,800
Pyrénées-Orientales 357,200
Rhône 1,443,600
Saône-et-Loire 571,000
Sarthe 515,400
Savoie 334,200
Seine-et-Marne 975,400
Seine-Maritime 1,209,400
Seine-Saint-Denis 1,343,700
Somme 548,200
Tarn 341,500
Tarn-et-Garonne 194,900
Val-de-Marne 1,198,600
Val-d'Oise 985,900
Var 754,800
Vaucluse 461,400
Vendée 506,600
Vienne 380,500
Vosges 389,900
Yonne 318,900
Yvelines 1,262,900

Historic Regions

1987 ESTIMATE

Alsace 1,605,300
Aquitaine 2,723,600
Auvergne 1,329,200
Basse-Normandie 1,379,400
Bourgogne 1,610,600
Bretagne 2,763,100
Centre 2,333,800
Champagne-Ardenne 1,357,900
Corse (Corsica) 246,000
Franche-Comté 1,088,000
Haute-Normandie 1,699,600
Île-de-France 10,259,400
Languedoc-Roussillon 2,053,600
Limousin 734,700
Lorraine 2,326,900
Midi-Pyrénées 2,369,500
Nord-Pas-de-Calais 3,931,500
Pays de la Loire 3,042,500
Picardie 1,776,400
Poitou-Charentes 1,591,500
Provence-Alpes-Côte D'Azur 4,112,500
Rhône-Alpes 5,174,800

FRENCH GUIANA / Guyane française

1982 C 73,022

Cities and Towns

• CAYENNE 38,091
Kourou 7,061
Saint-Laurent [-du-Maroni] (▲ 6,971) 4,500

FRENCH POLYNESIA / Polynésie française

1983 C 166,753

Cities and Towns

• PAPEETE (★ 80,000) 23,496

GABON

1985 E 1,312,000

Cities and Towns

Franceville 58,800
Lambaréné 49,500
• LIBREVILLE 235,700
Port-Gentil 124,400

GAMBIA

1983 C 696,000

Cities and Towns

• BANJUL (BATHURST) (★ 95,000) 44,536
Brikama 20,208

GERMAN DEMOCRATIC REPUBLIC (EAST GERMANY) / Deutsche Demokratische Republik

1987 E 16,639,877

Cities and Towns

Altenburg 53,602
Annaberg-Buchholz 26,002
Apolda 28,230
Arnstadt 30,207
Aschersleben 34,166
Aue 27,935
Bautzen 52,354
• BERLIN (EAST) (★★ Berlin) 1,236,248
Bernburg 40,834
Bitterfeld (★ 105,000) 20,869
Blankenburg 19,279
Borna 24,397
Brandenburg 94,755
Burg bei Magdeburg 28,359
Coswig (★ Dresden) 27,590
Cottbus 126,592
Crimmitschau 24,440
Delitzsch 27,636
Dessau (★ 140,000) 103,538
Döbeln 27,706
Dresden (★ 670,000) 519,810
Eberswalde [-Finow] 54,566
Eilenburg 21,931
Eisenach 49,534
Eisenhüttenstadt 51,729
Eisleben 26,484
Erfurt 217,134
Falkensee (★ Berlin) 23,024
Finsterwalde 23,857
Forst [Lausitz] 26,501
Frankfurt [an der Oder] 86,441
Freiberg 50,415
Freital (★ Dresden) 43,092
Fürstenwalde [Spree] 35,282
Gera 132,319
Glauchau 28,309
Görlitz 78,856
Gotha 57,423
Greifswald 67,298
Greiz 34,858
Güstrow 38,971
Halberstadt 47,017
Halle (★ 475,000) 236,148
Halle-Neustadt (★ Halle) 93,477
Heidenau (★ Dresden) 19,133
Henningsdorf bei Berlin (★ Berlin) 26,574
Hettstedt 21,861
Hoyerswerda 69,113
Ilmenau 29,338
Jena 107,610
Karl-Marx-Stadt (Chemnitz) (★ 450,000) 313,799
Köthen 34,617
Lauchhammer 24,391
Leipzig (★ 700,000) 550,641
Limbach-Oberfrohna (★ Karl-Marx-Stadt) 22,059
Lübbenau 20,815
Luckenwalde 26,761
Ludwigsfelde 22,290
Magdeburg (★ 400,000) 288,975
Markkleeberg (★ Leipzig) 19,240
Meerane 21,879
Meiningen 25,823
Meissen 37,757
Merseburg (★★ Halle) 46,188
Mühlhausen (Thomas-Müntzer-Stadt) 43,046
Naumburg [an der Saale] 32,100
Neubrandenburg 87,235
Neuruppin 26,934
Neustrelitz 27,300
Nordhausen 47,681
Oranienburg (★ Berlin) 28,667
Parchim 23,454
Pirna 46,991
Plauen 77,514
Potsdam (★ Berlin) 141,231
Prenzlau 23,642
Quedlinburg 29,168
Radebeul (★ Dresden) 33,757
Rathenow 31,302
Reichenbach 24,749
Riesa 49,108
Rostock 249,349
Rudolstadt 32,264
Saalfeld 33,453
Salzwedel 23,163
Sangerhausen 33,064
Sassnitz 14,077
Schmalkalden 17,409
Schneeberg 22,105
Schönebeck 45,155
Schwedt 51,753
Schwerin 128,328
Senftenberg 32,428
Sömmerda 23,398
Sondershausen 24,178
Sonneberg 28,152
Spremberg 24,815
Stassfurt 27,372
Stendal 47,880
Stralsund 75,857
Strausberg (★ Berlin) 27,527
Suhl 55,295
Tangermünde 11,720
Torgau 22,749
Waren 24,318
Weimar 63,910
Weissenfels 38,763

C Census. E Official estimate. UE Unofficial estimate.
• Largest city in country.

★ Population or designation of metropolitan area, including suburbs (see headnote).
▲ Population of an entire municipality, commune, or district, including rural area.

Weisswasser 36,472
Werdau 19,451
Wernigerode 36,499
Wilhelm-Pieck-Stadt Guben 34,665
Wismar 58,066
Wittenberge 30,389
Wittenberg [Lutherstadt] 53,670
Wolfen (★★ Bitterfeld) 43,606
Wurzen 19,330
Zeitz 42,985
Zerbst 18,717
Zittau 39,305
Zwickau (★ 165,000) 120,923

Districts

Berlin, [East] (city) 1,236,248
Cottbus 883,591
Dresden 1,768,990
Erfurt 1,235,785
Frankfurt 710,634
Gera 739,856
Halle 1,783,987
Karl-Marx-Stadt 1,866,321
Leipzig 1,371,427
Magdeburg 1,249,636
Neubrandenburg 620,057
Potsdam 1,121,640
Rostock 909,550
Schwerin 592,519
Suhl 549,636

GERMANY, FEDERAL REPUBLIC OF (WEST GERMANY) / Bundesrepublik Deutschland

1987 E 61,140,461

Cities and Towns

Aachen (★ 535,000) 239,170
Aalen (★ 80,000) 63,337
Achern 20,667
Achim (★ Bremen) 28,122
Ahaus 29,604
Ahlen 51,895
Ahrensburg (★ Hamburg) 27,203
Albstadt 45,973
Alfeld (Leine) 22,453
Alsdorf (★ Aachen) 45,925
Altena 22,103
Amberg 43,348
Andernach (★★ Neuwied) 26,520
Ansbach 37,451
Arnsberg 74,641
Aschaffenburg (★ 145,000) 59,646
Augsburg (★ 405,000) 245,962
Aurich 35,063
Backnang 29,695
Baden-Baden 49,257
Bad Harzburg (★ Goslar) 23,701
Bad Hersfeld 27,239
Bad Homburg vor der Höhe (★ Frankfurt am Main) 51,081
Bad Honnef am Rhein (★ Bonn) 20,495
Bad Kissingen 21,092
Bad Kreuznach 39,713
Bad Nauheim (★ Frankfurt am Main) 26,521
Bad Neuenahr-Ahrweiler 24,749
Bad Oeynhausen 43,237
Bad Oldesloe 20,775
Bad Reichenhall 17,506
Bad Salzuflen (★★ Herford) 51,187
Bad Vilbel (★ Frankfurt am Main) 24,984
Balingen 29,917
Bamberg (★ 120,000) 69,591
Barsinghausen (★ Hannover) 32,521
Bayreuth (★ 90,000) 72,326
Beckum 36,542
Bensheim 33,537
Berchtesgaden 8,051
Bergheim (Erft) (★ Cologne) 54,413
Bergisch Gladbach (★ Cologne) 101,776
Bergkamen (★ Essen) 47,912
Berlin (West) (★ 3,825,000) 1,879,225
Biberach [an der Riss] 28,015
Bielefeld (★ 515,000) 299,360
Bietigheim-Bissingen (★ Stuttgart) 35,618
Bingen am Rhein 22,138
Böblingen (★ Stuttgart) 41,485
Bocholt 66,443
Bochum (★★ Essen) 381,216
BONN (★ 570,000) 291,439
Borken 33,696
Bornheim (★ Bonn) 36,168
Bottrop (★ Essen) 112,256
Brake 16,862
Bramsche 23,648
Braunschweig (Brunswick) (★ 330,000) 247,836
Bremen (★ 800,000) 521,976
Bremerhaven (★ 190,000) 132,194
Bretten 23,668
Brilon 24,565
Bruchsal 36,549
Brühl (★ Cologne) 40,680
Buchholz in der Nordheide (★ Hamburg) 30,870
Bückeburg 20,409
Bünde 38,360
Burgdorf (★ Hannover) 28,674
Butzbach 21,252
Buxtehude (★ Hamburg) 32,474
Calw 22,401
Castrop-Rauxel (★ Essen) 76,110
Celle 70,245
Cloppenburg 22,008
Coburg 44,412
Coesfeld 31,584
Cologne (Köln) (★ 1,760,000) 914,336
Crailsheim 25,097
Cuxhaven 56,076
Dachau (★ Munich) 32,871
Darmstadt (★ 305,000) 133,572
Datteln (★ Essen) 36,276
Deggendorf 30,243
Delmenhorst (★★ Bremen) 70,512
Detmold 66,660
Dietzenbach (★ Frankfurt am Main) 27,127
Dillingen / Saar (★ Saarlouis) 20,061
Dinkelsbühl 10,520
Dinslaken (★ Essen) 61,330
Ditzingen (★ Stuttgart) 22,196
Dormagen (★ Cologne) 57,513
Dorsten (★ Essen) 74,115
Dortmund (★★ Essen) 568,164
Dreieich (★ Frankfurt am Main) 38,082
Duderstadt 22,815
Duisburg (★★ Essen) 514,628
Dülmen 40,136
Düren (★ 110,000) 84,100
Düsseldorf (★ 1,190,000) 560,572
Eckernförde 24,470
Einbeck 27,440
Elmshorn 41,467
Emden 49,557
Emmendingen 25,111
Emmerich 29,075
Emsdetten 31,121
Ennepetal (★ Essen) 33,744
Erftstadt (★ Cologne) 45,010
Erkelenz 36,865
Erkrath (★ Düsseldorf) 45,204
Erlangen (★★ Nürnberg) 100,200
Eschwege 22,893
Eschweiler (★★ Aachen) 53,082
Espelkamp 21,725
• Essen (★ 4,950,000) 615,421
Esslingen am Neckar (★ Stuttgart) 86,886
Ettlingen (★ Karlsruhe) 37,081
Euskirchen 45,676
Fellbach (★ Stuttgart) 39,819
Filderstadt (★ Stuttgart) 37,355
Flensburg (★ 103,000) 85,714
Forchheim 28,808
Frankenthal (★ Mannheim) 44,269
Frankfurt [am Main] (★ 1,855,000) 592,411
Frechen (★ Cologne) 42,327
Freiburg [im Breisgau] (★ 225,000) 186,156
Freising 36,209
Friedberg (★ Augsburg) 25,562
Friedrichshafen 52,064
Fulda (★ 79,000) 54,131
Fürstenfeldbruck (★ Munich) 31,458
Fürth (★★ Nürnberg) 98,203
Gaggenau 27,915
Ganderkesee (★ Bremen) 26,233
Garbsen (★ Hannover) 57,541
Garmisch-Partenkirchen 27,701
Geesthacht (★ Hamburg) 25,495
Geislingen an der Steige (★ Göppingen) 26,164
Geldern 27,239
Gelsenkirchen (★★ Essen) 283,560
Georgsmarienhütte (★ Osnabrück) 30,636
Germering (★ Munich) 35,565
Gevelsberg (★ Essen) 30,444
Giessen (★ 160,000) 71,095
Gifhorn 34,501
Gladbeck (★ Essen) 76,625
Goch 28,477
Göppingen (★ 155,000) 51,416
Goslar (★ 84,000) 49,034
Göttingen 133,796
Greven 28,753
Grevenbroich (★ Düsseldorf) 57,463
Gronau (★ Enschede, Netherlands) 39,858
Gummersbach 48,359
Gütersloh (★★ Bielefeld) 79,432
Haan (★ Wuppertal) 27,838
Hagen (★★ Essen) 206,070
Haltern (★ Essen) 32,158
Hamburg (★ 2,225,000) 1,571,267
Hameln (★ 72,000) 55,390
Hamm 165,957
Hanau [am Main] (★★ Frankfurt am Main) 85,217
Hannover (★ 1,000,000) 505,718
Hattingen (★ Essen) 54,964
Heide 20,652
Heidelberg (★★ Mannheim) 136,227
Heidenheim an der Brenz (★ 89,000) 47,611
Heilbronn (★ 230,000) 111,713
Heiligenhaus (★ Essen) 28,514
Heinsberg 36,638
Helmstedt 25,471
Hemer 31,486
Hennef (★ Siegburg) 30,236
Heppenheim (★ Mannheim) 24,028
Herdecke (★ Essen) 24,703
Herford (★ 120,000) 59,495
Herne (★ Essen) 171,274
Herrenberg (★ Stuttgart) 26,072
Herten (★ Essen) 67,829
Herzogenrath (★ Aachen) 43,326
Hilden (★ Düsseldorf) 53,820
Hildesheim (★ 140,000) 100,558
Hof 50,623
Hofheim am Taunus (★ Frankfurt am Main) 33,985
Holzminden 20,978
Homburg (★★ Zweibrücken) 40,836
Höxter 31,506
Hückelhoven 35,629
Hürth (★ Cologne) 51,286
Husum 23,795
Ibbenbüren 42,664
Idar-Oberstein 33,980
Ingolstadt (★ 138,000) 92,593
Iserlohn 89,466
Itzehoe 31,727
Jüchen (★ Mönchengladbach) 20,479
Jülich 30,156
Kaarst (★ Düsseldorf) 39,321
Kaiserslautern (★ 138,000) 96,766
Kamen (★ Essen) 44,509
Kamp-Lintfort (★ Essen) 36,596
Karlsruhe (★ 485,000) 268,309
Kassel (★ 360,000) 185,370
Kaufbeuren 41,475
Kehl (★ Strasbourg, France) 28,768
Kelkheim (★ Frankfurt am Main) 26,961
Kempen (★ Essen) 31,882
Kempten [in Allgäu] 56,950
Kerpen (★ Cologne) 55,158
Kiel (★ 335,000) 243,626
Kirchheim unter Teck (★ Stuttgart) 34,000
Kleve (Cleves) 44,725
Koblenz (★ 180,000) 110,277
Königswinter (★ Bonn) 33,685
Konstanz 70,539
Korbach 22,213
Kornwestheim (★ Stuttgart) 26,956
Korschenbroich (★ Düsseldorf) 27,427
Krefeld (★★ Essen) 216,598
Kreuztal (★ Siegen) 28,989
Kulmbach 27,364
Laatzen (★ Hannover) 36,884
Lage 32,207
Lahnstein (★ Koblenz) 18,086
Lahr / Schwarzwald 34,566
Lampertheim (★ Mannheim) 30,660
Landau in der Pfalz 35,284
Landshut 57,067
Langen (★ Frankfurt am Main) 29,302
Langenfeld (Rheinland) (★ Düsseldorf) 45,463
Langenhagen (★ Hannover) 46,630
Leer 30,075
Lehrte (★ Hannover) 39,238
Leinfelden-Echterdingen (★ Stuttgart) 35,349
Lemgo 39,108
Lengerich 20,182
Lennestadt 25,985
Leonberg (★ Stuttgart) 40,235
Leverkusen (★ Cologne) 154,703
Limburg [an der Lahn] 28,905
Lindau (Bodensee) 23,053
Lingen 45,722
Lippstadt 60,141
Lohmar (★ Siegburg) 25,334
Löhne 36,209
Lörrach (★ Basel, Switzerland) 41,198
Lübeck (★ 260,000) 209,159
Lüdenscheid 73,442
Ludwigsburg (★ Stuttgart) 76,898
Ludwigshafen am Rhein (★★ Mannheim) 152,162
Lüneburg 59,497
Lünen (★ Essen) 84,352
Maintal (★ Frankfurt am Main) 36,589
Mainz (★★ Wiesbaden) 189,005
Mannheim (★ 1,400,000) 294,648
Marburg [an der Lahn] 77,114
Marl (★ Essen) 87,766
Meerbusch (★ Düsseldorf) 49,158
Melle 39,862
Memmingen 37,284
Menden 52,175
Meppen 29,087
Merzig 29,228
Meschede 29,313
Mettmann (★ Düsseldorf) 36,297
Minden (★ 125,000) 75,384
Moers (★ Essen) 95,407
Mönchengladbach (★ 410,000) 255,087
Monheim (★ Düsseldorf) 40,838
Mörfelden-Walldorf (★ Frankfurt am Main) 29,406
Mülheim [am der Ruhr] (★ Essen) 170,392
Münden 24,215
Munich (München) (★ 1,955,000) 1,274,716
Münster 267,628
Neckarsulm (★ Heilbronn) 21,891
Nettetal 37,123
Neuburg [an der Donau] 24,267
Neu-Isenburg (★ Frankfurt am Main) 35,170
Neukirchen-Vluyn (★ Essen) 25,391
Neumarkt [in der Oberpfalz] 32,059
Neumünster 77,877
Neunkirchen [Saar] (★ 135,000) 49,536
Neuss (★ Düsseldorf) 143,832
Neustadt am Rübenberge (★ Hannover) 37,893
Neustadt [an der Weinstrasse] 48,391
Neu-Ulm (★ Ulm) 46,409
Neuwied (★ 150,000) 58,263
Niederkassel (★ Bonn) 27,734
Nienburg 29,827
Norden 23,553
Nordenham (★★ Bremerhaven) 28,817
Norderstedt (★ Hamburg) 68,724
Nordhorn 48,015
Nördlingen 18,084
Northeim 30,638
Nürnberg (Nuremberg) (★ 1,030,000) 467,392
Nürtingen (★ Stuttgart) 35,858
Oberammergau 4,664
Oberhausen (★★ Essen) 221,542
Oberursel (★ Frankfurt am Main) 38,781
Oelde 26,991
Oer-Erkenschwick (★ Essen) 27,306
Offenbach am Main (★ Frankfurt am Main) 107,078
Offenburg 50,468
Oldenburg 139,256
Olpe 22,371
Osnabrück (★ 270,000) 153,776
Osterode am Harz 26,990
Ostfildern (★ Stuttgart) 28,384
Overath (★ Cologne) 23,169
Paderborn 110,296
Papenburg 28,652
Passau 52,733
Peine 45,576
Pforzheim (★ 220,000) 104,452
Pinneberg (★ Hamburg) 35,615
Pirmasens 46,077
Plettenberg 27,568
Porta Westfalica (★ Minden) 33,200
Pulheim (★ Cologne) 47,673
Rastatt 37,595
Ratingen (★ Düsseldorf) 89,161
Ravensburg (★ 75,000) 43,245
Recklinghausen (★ Essen) 117,585
Regensburg (★ 205,000) 123,821
Reinbek (★ Hamburg) 25,315
Remagen (★ Bonn) 14,270
Remscheid (★★ Wuppertal) 121,005
Rendsburg 30,647
Reutlingen (★ 160,000) 97,920
Rheda-Wiedenbrück (★ Bielefeld) 37,684
Rheinberg (★ Essen) 26,192
Rheine 70,412
Rheinfelden 27,145
Rietberg 23,479
Rinteln 25,377
Rodgau (★ Frankfurt am Main) 37,319
Rosenheim 53,168
Rösrath (★ Cologne) 21,450
Rothenburg [ob der Tauber] 11,171
Rottenburg am Neckar 33,601
Rottweil 23,297
Rüsselsheim (★★ Wiesbaden) 57,303
Saarbrücken (★ 385,000) 184,353
Saarlouis (★ 115,000) 37,411
Salzgitter 105,392
Sankt Augustin (★ Bonn) 51,105
Sankt Ingbert 40,455
Sankt Wendel 26,278
Schleswig 28,291
Schmallenberg 24,429
Schorndorf (★ Stuttgart) 34,722
Schwabach (★ Nürnberg) 35,627
Schwäbisch Gmünd 56,137
Schwäbisch Hall 30,942
Schwandorf 26,368
Schweinfurt (★ 110,000) 50,568
Schwelm (★ Wuppertal) 29,831
Schwerte (★ Essen) 48,456
Seelze (★ Hannover) 29,469
Seesen 21,648
Seevetal (★ Hamburg) 37,258
Selb 20,044
Selm (★ Essen) 25,641
Siegburg (★ 170,000) 34,085
Siegen (★ 200,000) 107,319
Sindelfingen (★ Stuttgart) 55,715
Singen (Hohentwiel) 41,454
Sinsheim 27,716
Soest 42,028
Solingen (★★ Wuppertal) 158,401
Speyer 42,865
Springe 29,042
Stade 42,979
Stadthagen 22,251
Steinfurt 31,432
Stolberg (★★ Aachen) 56,421
Straubing 41,622
Stuhr (★ Bremen) 26,966
Stuttgart (★ 1,925,000) 565,486
Sulzbach-Rosenberg 17,638
Sulzbach [Saar] (★ Saarbrücken) 19,591
Sundern [Sauerland] 25,223
Taunusstein (★ Wiesbaden) 26,178
Trier (★ 125,000) 93,076
Troisdorf (★★ Siegburg) 61,832
Tübingen 76,122
Tuttlingen 30,780
Uelzen 35,093
Ulm (★ 210,000) 100,745
Unna (★ Essen) 59,587
Vaihingen an der Enz (★ Stuttgart) 22,920
Varel 23,859
Vechta 24,220
Velbert (★ Essen) 88,573
Verden 24,172
Viernheim (★ Mannheim) 29,076
Viersen (★★ Mönchengladbach) 78,124
Villingen-Schwenningen 76,155
Voerde (★ Essen) 33,534
Völklingen (★★ Saarbrücken) 43,146
Waiblingen (★ Stuttgart) 45,062
Walsrode 22,669
Waltrop (★ Essen) 27,427
Warburg 21,790
Warendorf 33,545
Warstein 27,616
Wedel (★ Hamburg) 30,534
Wegberg (★ Mönchengladbach) 24,626
Weiden [in der Oberpfalz] 41,807
Weil am Rhein (★ Basel, Switzerland) 26,038
Weingarten (★ Ravensburg) 22,187
Weinheim (★ Mannheim) 40,616
Werdohl 20,336
Werl 26,025
Wermelskirchen (★ Wuppertal) 33,871
Werne an der Lippe (★ Essen) 28,303
Wesel 54,604
Wesseling (★ Cologne) 30,356
Wetter (★ Essen) 28,737
Wetzlar (★ 105,000) 50,284
Wiesbaden (★ 795,000) 266,542
Wilhelmshaven (★ 135,000) 94,896
Willich (★ Essen) 39,990
Winsen (Luhe) (★ Hamburg) 27,406
Witten (★ Essen) 102,232
Wolfenbüttel (★★ Braunschweig) 48,623
Wolfsburg 121,951
Worms (★★ Mannheim) 72,045
Wunstorf (★ Hannover) 37,344
Wuppertal (★ 830,000) 374,217
Würselen (★ Aachen) 33,592
Würzburg (★ 210,000) 127,050
Zweibrücken (★ 105,000) 32,722

States

Baden-Württemberg 9,326,780
Bayern (Bavaria) 11,026,490
Berlin, [West] (city) 1,879,225
Bremen 654,170
Hamburg 1,571,267
Hessen (Hesse) 5,543,657
Niedersachsen (Lower Saxony) 7,196,127
Nordrhein-Westfalen (North Rhinewestphalia) 16,676,501
Rheinland-Pfalz (Rhineland-Palatinate) 3,611,437
Saarland 1,042,135
Schleswig-Holstein 2,612,672

Districts

Arnsberg 3,564,601
Berlin, [West] (city) 1,879,225
Braunschweig 1,593,212
Bremen 654,170
Darmstadt 3,405,524
Detmold 1,787,042
Düsseldorf 5,034,721
Freiburg 1,891,169
Giessen 966,909
Hamburg 1,571,267
Hannover 2,008,858
Karlsruhe 2,410,098
Kassel 1,171,224
Koblenz 1,346,018
Köln 3,887,576
Lüneburg 1,469,236
Mittelfranken 1,521,262
Münster 2,402,561
Niederbayern 1,017,984
Oberbayern 3,736,358
Oberfranken 1,037,245
Oberpfalz 963,034
Rheinhessen-Pfalz 1,797,847
Saarland 1,042,135
Schleswig-Holstein 2,612,672
Schwaben 1,548,811
Stuttgart 3,490,434
Trier 467,572
Tübingen 1,535,079
Unterfranken 1,201,796
Weser-Ems 2,124,821

C Census. E Official estimate. UE Unofficial estimate.
• Largest city in country.

★ Population or designation of metropolitan area, including suburbs (see headnote).
▲ Population of an entire municipality, commune, or district, including rural area.

GHANA

1984 C 12,205,574

Cities and Towns

• ACCRA (★ 1,250,000) 859,640
Ashiaman (★ Accra) 49,427
Bawku 33,900
Bolgatanga 31,547
Cape Coast 86,620
Ho 37,231
Keta 12,666
Koforidua 54,400
Kumasi (★ 600,000) 348,880
Nkawkaw 34,068
Nsawam 31,900
Obuasi 60,146
Oda 24,384
Sekondi (★ 175,352) 32,355
Tafo (★ Kumasi) 50,432
Takoradi (★★ Sekondi) 61,527
Tamale (★ 168,091) 136,828
Tarkwa 21,971
Tema (★★ Accra) 99,608
Teshie (★ Accra) 62,954
Wa 35,993
Winneba 26,218
Yendi 30,733

GIBRALTAR

1987 E 30,000

Cities and Towns

• GIBRALTAR 30,000

GREECE / Ellás

1981 C 9,740,417

Cities and Towns

Agrínion (★ 45,087) 35,774
Aiyáleo (★ Athens) 81,906
Aíyion (Aegion) (★ 25,723) 20,955
Akharnaí (Acharnae) 40,185
Alexandroúpolis 34,535
Amaliás 14,698
Amaroúsion (★ Athens) 48,151
Ampelókipoi (★ Thessaloníki) 40,033
Árgos 20,702
Árta 18,283
• ATHENS (ATHÍNAI) (★ 3,027,331) 885,737
Ayía Paraskeví (★ Athens) 32,904
Ayía Varvára (★ Athens) 29,259
Áyioi Anáryiroi (★ Athens) 30,320
Áyios Dhimítrios (★ Athens) 51,421
Dháfni (★ Athens) 26,887
Dráma 36,109
Édhessa (Edessa) 16,054
Elevsís (Eleusis) 20,320
Ermoúpolis (Syros) (★ 16,595) 13,876
Flórina (Phlorina) 12,562
Galátsion (★ Athens) 50,096
Glifádha (★ Athens) 44,018
Ilioúpolis (★ Athens) 69,560
Ioánnina 44,829
Iráklion (★ Athens) 37,833
Iráklion (Canadia) (★ 110,958) 102,398
Kaisarianí (★ Athens) 28,972
Kalámai (★ 43,235) 42,075
Kalamariá (★ Thessaloníki) 51,676
Kallithéa (★ Athens) 117,319
Kardhítsa 27,291
Kastoría 17,133
Kateríni (★ 39,895) 38,404
Kavála 56,375
Keratsínion (★ Athens) 74,179
Kérkira (Corfu) 33,561
Khaïdhárion (★ Athens) 47,396
Khalándrion (★ Athens) 54,320
Khalkís (Chalcis) 44,867
Khaniá (Canea) (★ 61,976) 47,451
Khíos (Chios) (★ 29,742) 24,070
Kholargós (★ Athens) 31,703
Kifisiá (★ Athens) 31,876
Komotiní 34,051
Koridhallós (★ Athens) 61,313
Kórinthos (Corinth) 22,658
Kozáni 30,994
Lamía 41,667
Lárisa 102,048
Levádhia (Lebadea) 16,864
Mégara 17,719
Mitilíni (Mytilene) 24,115
Návplion (Nauplia) 10,609
Néa Ionía (★ Athens) 59,202
Néa Liósia (★ Athens) 72,427
Neápolis (★ Thessaloníki) 31,464
Néa Smírni (★ Athens) 67,408
Níkaia (★ Athens) 90,368
Palaión Fáliron (★ Athens) 53,273
Pátrai (Patras) (★ 154,596) 142,163
Peristérion (★ Athens) 140,858
Piraiévs (Piraeus) (★★ Athens) 196,389
Pírgos (Pyrgos) 21,958
Ródhos (Rhodes) 40,392
Salamís 20,437
Sérrai 45,213
Spárti (Sparta) (★ 14,388) 12,975
Thessaloníki (Salonika) (★ 706,180) 406,413
Thívai (Thebes) 18,712
Tríkala 40,857
Trípolis (Tripolitza) 21,311
Véroia 37,087
Víron (★ Athens) 57,880
Vólos (★ 107,407) 71,378
Xánthi 31,541
Zográfos (★ Athens) 84,548

GREENLAND / Kalaallit Nunaat / Gronland

1989 E 55,171

Cities and Towns

Angmagssalik 2,861
Egedesminde 3,601
Godhavn 1,143
• GODTHÅB (NUUK) 12,426
Holsteinsborg 5,024
Julianehåb 3,514
Sukkertoppen 4,024
Thule 849

GRENADA

1981 C 89,088

Cities and Towns

• SAINT GEORGE'S (★ 25,000) 4,788

GUADELOUPE

1982 C 328,400

Cities and Towns

BASSE-TERRE (★ 26,600) 13,656
Capesterre (▲ 17,472) 7,572
Les Abymes (★ Pointe-à-Pitre) 56,165
• Pointe-à-Pitre (★ 83,000) 25,310

GUAM

1980 C 105,979

Cities and Towns

• AGANA (★ 44,000) 896
Tamuning (★ Agana) 8,862

GUATEMALA

1981 C 6,054,227

Cities and Towns

Amatitlán 20,407
Antigua Guatemala 15,801
Chimaltenango 14,967
Chiquimula 18,965
Coatepeque 19,307
Cobán 14,152
Escuintla 36,931
• GUATEMALA (★ 1,100,000) 754,243
Huehuetenango 12,422
Mazatenango 20,918
Puerto Barrios 24,235
Quezaltenango 62,719
Retalhuleu 22,001
Tiquisate 12,096
Zacapa 12,482

GUERNSEY

1986 C 55,482

Cities and Towns

• SAINT PETER PORT (★ 36,000) 16,085

GUINEA / Guinée

1986 E 6,225,000

Cities and Towns

• CONAKRY 800,000
Kankan 100,000
Kindia 80,000
Labé 110,000
Mamou (1983 C) 35,748
Nzérékoré (1983 C) 55,356
Siguiri (1983 C) 37,361

GUINEA-BISSAU / Guiné-Bissau

1979 C 777,214

Cities and Towns

• BISSAU 109,486

GUYANA

1983 E 918,000

Cities and Towns

• GEORGETOWN (★ 188,000) 78,500
Linden (1980 C) 30,043
New Amsterdam (1982 E) 20,000

HAITI / Haïti

1982 C 5,053,791

Cities and Towns

Cap-Haïtien (1986 E) 70,500
Gonaïves (1986 E) 36,500
Jacmel 13,730
Jérémie 18,493
Les Cayes (1986 E) 36,500
Pétionville (★ Port-au-Prince) 35,333
• PORT-AU-PRINCE (★ 760,000) 684,284
Port-de-Paix 15,540
Saint-Marc 24,165

HONDURAS

1986 E 4,514,000

Cities and Towns

Choluteca 60,700
Comayagua 30,100
Danlí 18,800
El Progreso 58,300
Juticalpa 13,900
La Ceiba 63,800
La Lima (1974 C) 14,631
Puerto Cortés 40,900
San Pedro Sula 399,700
• TEGUCIGALPA 604,600
Tela 27,200

HONG KONG

1986 C 5,395,997

Cities and Towns

Kowloon (★★ Victoria) 774,781
Kwai Chung (★ Victoria) 131,362
New Kowloon (Xinjiulong) (★★ Victoria) 1,526,910
Sha Tin (★ Victoria) 355,810
Sheung Shui 87,206
Tai Po 119,679
Tsun Wan (★ Victoria) 514,241
Tuen Mun (★ Victoria) 262,458
• VICTORIA (HONG KONG) (XIANGGANG) (★ 4,770,000) 1,175,860
Yuen Long 75,740

HUNGARY / Magyarország

1989 E 10,589,000

Cities and Towns

Ajka 34,390
Baja 40,426
Békés (▲ 22,140) 18,200
Békéscsaba (▲ 70,978) 61,700
• BUDAPEST (★ 2,565,000) 2,113,645
Cegléd (▲ 39,574) 32,400
Csongrád (▲ 20,449) 17,900
Debrecen 219,251
Dunakeszi (★ Budapest) 29,148
Dunaújváros 62,386
Eger 67,252
Érd (★ Budapest) 48,037
Esztergom 32,303
Gödöllő (★ Budapest) 30,261
Gyöngyös 36,420
Győr 131,503
Gyula (▲ 36,025) 30,900
Hajdúböszörmény (▲ 30,799) 27,500
Hajdúszoboszló 24,494
Hatvan 24,816
Hódmezővásárhely (▲ 53,311) 44,600
Jászberény (▲ 30,001) 24,200
Kaposvár 76,834
Karcag 24,473
Kazincbarcika 39,233
Kecskemét (▲ 106,869) 85,400
Kiskunfélegyháza (▲ 34,889) 26,500
Kiskunhalas (▲ 31,991) 23,100
Komló 32,845
Makó 28,178
Miskolc 207,826
Mohács (▲ 21,081) 17,800
Mosonmagyaróvár 29,779
Nagykanizsa 55,023
Nagykőrös (▲ 26,193) 20,500
Nyíregyháza (▲ 119,333) 92,500
Orosháza (▲ 36,475) 31,900
Ózd 44,617
Paks 26,240
Pápa 34,412
Pécs 183,082
Salgótarján 48,785
Sopron 57,107
Szeged 189,484
Székesfehérvár 113,935
Szekszárd 39,005
Szentes (▲ 34,950) 30,700
Szolnok 81,907
Szombathely 87,997
Tata 25,931
Tatabánya 76,455
Törökszentmiklós (▲ 23,973) 20,900
Vác 36,070
Várpalota 28,095
Veszprém 66,280
Zalaegerszeg 63,785

Counties

Bács-Kiskun 552,000
Baranya 251,000
Békés 413,000
Borsod-Abaúj-Zemplén 564,000
Budapest (Independent city) 2,114,000
Csongrád 267,000
Debrecen (city) 219,000
Fejér 426,000
Győr (city) 132,000
Győr-Sopron 294,000
Hajdú-Bihar 330,000
Heves 336,000
Komárom 320,000
Miskolc (city) 208,000
Nógrád 227,000
Pécs (city) 183,000
Pest 990,000
Somogy 348,000
Szabolcs-Szatmár 564,000
Szeged (city) 189,000
Szolnok 426,000
Tolna 262,000
Vas 276,000
Veszprém 386,000
Zala 310,000

ICELAND / Ísland

1987 E 247,357

Cities and Towns

Akureyri 13,856
Hafnarfjördur (★ Reykjavík) 13,780
Keflavík 7,133
Kópavogur (★ Reykjavík) 15,037
• REYKJAVÍK (★ 137,941) 93,425

INDIA / Bhārat

1981 C 685,184,692

Cities and Towns

Abohar 86,334
Achalpur (Ellichpur) 81,186
Ādilābād 53,482
Adītyapur (★ Jamshedpur) 53,421
Ādoni 108,939
Agartala 132,186
Āgra (★ 747,318) 694,191
Ahmadābād (★ 2,400,000) 2,059,725
Ahmadnagar (★ 181,210) 143,937
Aijal 74,493
Ajmer 375,593
Akola 225,412
Akot 51,936
Alandur (★ Madras) 97,449
Alīgarh 320,861
Ālīpur Duār (★ 71,573) 45,324
Allahābād (★ 650,070) 616,051
Alleppey 169,940
Almora (★ 22,705) 20,758
Alwar 145,795
Amalner 67,516
Ambāla (★ 233,110) 104,565
Ambāla Sadar (★ Ambāla) 80,741
Ambarnāth (★ Bombay) 96,347
Ambāsamudram (★ 52,591) 29,761
Ambattur (★ Madras) 115,901
Āmbūr 66,042
Amrāvati (Amraoti) 261,404
Amreli (★ 58,241) 56,598
Amritsar 594,844
Amroha 112,682
Anakāpalle 73,179
Ānand 83,936
Anantapur 119,531
Ara 125,111
Arakkonam 59,405
Arcot (★ 94,363) 38,836
Arni 49,365
Aruppukkottai 72,245
Āsānsol (★ 1,050,000) 183,375
Ashoknagar-Kalyangarh (★ Hābra) 55,176
Āttūr 50,517
Aurangābād (★ 316,421) 284,607
Avadi (★ Madras) 124,701
Āzamgarh 66,523
Badagara 64,174
Bāgalkot 67,858
Baharampur (★ 102,311) 92,889
Bahraich 99,889
Baidyabāti (★ Calcutta) 70,573
Bālāghāt (★ 53,183) 49,564
Balāngīr 54,943
Bāleshwar 65,779
Ballarpur 61,398
Ballia 61,704
Bālly (★ Calcutta) 147,735
Bālly (★ Calcutta) 54,859
Balrāmpur 46,058
Bālurghāt (★ 112,621) 104,646
Bānda 72,379
Bangalore (★ 2,950,000) 2,476,355
Bangaon 69,885
Bānkura 94,954
Bānsbāria (★ Calcutta) 77,020
Bānswāra (★ 48,070) 46,749
Bāpatla 55,347
Bārākpur (★ Calcutta) 115,253
Baranagar (★ Calcutta) 170,343
Bārāsat (★ Calcutta) 66,504
Barauni 56,366
Baraut 46,292
Barddhamān 167,364
Bareilly (★ 449,425) 386,734
Bāripada (★ 52,989) 40,314
Bārmer 55,554
Bārsi 72,537
Basīrhāt 81,040
Basti 69,357
Batala (★ 101,966) 87,135
Bathinda (★ 127,363) 124,453
Beāwar 89,998
Begusarai (★ 68,305) 56,633
Behāla (South Suburban) (★ Calcutta) 378,765
Bela (Pratapgarh) 49,932
Belgaum (★ 300,372) 274,430
Bellary 201,579
Bettiah 72,167
Betūl 46,293
Bhadrak 60,600
Bhadrāvati (★ 130,606) 53,551
Bhadrāvati New Town (★★ Bhadrāvati) 77,055
Bhadreswar (★ Calcutta) 58,858
Bhāgalpur 225,062
Bhandāra 56,025
Bharatpur 105,274
Bharūch (★ 120,524) 110,070
Bhātpāra (★ Calcutta) 260,761
Bhavāni (★ 80,472) 28,898
Bhāvnagar (★ 308,642) 307,121
Bhilai (Bhilainagar) (★ 490,214) 290,090
Bhīlwāra 122,625
Bhīmavaram 101,894
Bhind 74,515
Bhiwandi (★ Bombay) 115,298
Bhiwāni 101,277
Bhopāl 671,018
Bhubaneshwar 219,211
Bhuj (★ 70,211) 69,693
Bhusāwal (★ 132,142) 123,133
Bīdar 78,856
Bihār 151,343
Bijāpur 147,313
Bijnor 56,713
Bīkāner (★ 287,712) 253,174
Bilāspur (★ 187,104) 147,218
Bīr (Bhir) 80,287
Birlapur (★ 50,831) 20,470
Birnagar (★ 67,066) 14,581
Bishnupur 47,529
Bodhan 50,807
Bodināyakkanūr 59,168
Bokāro Steel City (★ 264,480) 224,099
Bombay (★ 9,950,000) 8,243,405
Botād 50,274
Brahmapur 162,550
Brajrajnagar 54,033
Budaun 93,004
Budge Budge (★ Calcutta) 66,424
Bulandshahr 103,436
Būndi (★ 48,027) 47,736
Burhānpur 140,896
• Calcutta (★ 11,100,000) 3,305,006
Calicut (Kozhikode) (★ 546,058) 394,447
Cannanore (★ 157,797) 60,904
Chākdaha 59,308
Chakradharpur (★ 44,532) 29,272
Chālisgaon 59,342
Champdāni (★ Calcutta) 76,138
Chandannagar (Chandernagore) (★ Calcutta) 101,925
Chandausi 66,970
Chandīgarh (★ 422,841) 373,789
Chandrapur 115,777
Changanācheri 51,955
Channapatna 50,725
Chhapra 111,564
Chhatarpur 51,959
Chhindwāra 75,178

C Census. E Official estimate. UE Unofficial estimate.
• Largest city in country.

★ Population or designation of metropolitan area, including suburbs (see headnote).
▲ Population of an entire municipality, commune, or district, including rural area.

Chidambaram (★ 62,543) 55,920
Chikmagalūr 60,582
Chilakalūrupet 61,645
Chīrāla 72,040
Chitradurga 74,580
Chittaranjan (★ 61,045) 50,748
Chittoor 86,230
Chūru (★ 62,070) 61,811
Cochin (★ 685,836) 513,249
Coimbatore (★ 965,000) 704,514
Coonoor (★ 92,242) 44,750
Cuddalore 127,625
Cuddapah 103,125
Cuttack (★ 327,412) 269,950
Dabgram 76,402
Dabhoi 44,357
Dabra 33,421
Dāhod (★ 82,256) 55,256
Dalhousie (★ 4,189) 2,936
Dāltenganj 51,952
Damān 21,003
Damoh (★ 76,758) 75,573
Dānāpur (★ Patna) 58,684
Darbhanga 176,301
Darjeeling 57,603
Datia 49,386
Dāvangere 196,621
Dehra Dūn (★ 293,010) 211,416
Dehra Dūn Cantonment (★ Dehra Dūn) 43,566
Dehri 90,409
Delhi (★ 7,200,000) 4,884,234
Delhi Cantonment (★ Delhi) 85,166
Deoband 51,270
Deoghar (★ 59,120) 52,904
Deolāli (★★ Nāsik) 77,666
Deolāli Cantonment (★ Nāsik) 57,745
Deoria 55,720
Dewās 83,465
Dhamtari 55,797
Dhanbād (★ 825,000) 120,221
Dhār 48,870
Dharmapuri 51,223
Dharmavaram 50,969
Dhorāji (★ 77,716) 76,556
Dhrāngadhra 51,280
Dhuburi (★ 45,580) (1971 C) 36,503
Dhule 210,759
Dibrugarh (1971 C) 80,348
Digboi (★ 32,388) (1971 C) 16,538
Dindigul 164,103
Dombivli (★ Bombay) 103,222
Dum-Dum (★ Calcutta) 33,604
Durg (★★ Bhilai) 114,637
Durgāpur 311,798
Dwārka 21,375
Elūru (Ellore) 168,154
Erode (★ 275,999) 142,252
Etah 53,784
Etāwah 112,174
Faizābād (Fyzabad) (★ 143,167) 101,873
Farīdābād New Township (★ Delhi) 330,864
Farrukhābād (★ 160,796) 145,793
Fatehpur, Rājasthān state 51,084
Fatehpur, Uttar Pradesh state 84,831
Fatehpur Sīkri 17,908
Fīrozābād 202,338
Fīrozpur (Ferozepore) (★ 105,840) 61,162
Gadag 117,368
Gandhidham (★ 61,489) 61,415
Gāndhinagar 62,443
Gangāvathi 58,735
Garden Reach (★ Calcutta) 191,107
Gārulia (★ Calcutta) 57,061
Gaya 247,075
Ghāziābād (★ 287,170) 271,730
Ghāzīpur 60,725
Girīdīh 65,444
Godhra (★ 86,228) 85,784
Gonda 70,847
Gondal (★ 66,818) 66,096
Gondia 100,423
Gorakhpur (★ 307,501) 290,814
Gudivāda 80,198
Gudiyāttam (★ 80,674) 75,044
Gulbarga 221,325
Guna (★ 64,659) 60,255
Guntakal 84,599
Guntūr 367,699
Gurgaon (★ 100,877) 89,115
Guruvayur (★ 59,467) 17,858
Guwāhāti (★ 200,377) (1971 C) 123,783
Gwalior (★ 555,862) 539,015
Hābra (★ 129,610) 74,434
Hājīpur 62,520
Haldwāni 77,300
Hālisahar (★ Calcutta) 95,579
Hānsi 50,365
Hanumangarh 60,071
Hāora (★ Calcutta) 744,429
Hāpur 102,837
Hardoi 67,259
Haridwār (★ 145,946) 114,180
Hassan 71,534
Hāthras 92,962
Hazārībāg 80,155
Hindupur 55,901
Hinganghāt 59,075
Hisār (★ 137,369) 131,309
Hooghly-Chinsura (★ Calcutta) 125,193
Hoshiārpur 85,648
Hospet (★ 115,351) 90,572
Hubli-Dhārwār 527,108
Hyderābād (★ 2,750,000) 2,187,262
Ichalkaranji 133,751
Imphāl 156,622
Indore (★ 850,000) 829,327
Ingrāj Bāzār (English Bāzār) 79,010
Itārsi (★ 69,619) 62,499
Jabalpur (★ 757,303) 614,162
Jabalpur Cantonment (★ Jabalpur) 61,026
Jadabpur (★ Calcutta) 251,968
Jagādhri (★★ Yamunānagar) 43,102
Jagdalpur (★ 63,632) 51,286
Jagtiāl 53,213
Jaipur (★ 1,025,000) 977,165
Jalandhar (★ 441,552) 408,186
Jālgaon 145,335
Jālna 122,276
Jalpāiguri 61,743
Jamālpur 78,356
Jammu (★ 223,361) 206,135
Jamnagar (Navanagar) (★ 317,362) 277,615
Jamshedpur (★ 669,580) 438,385
Jangaon 70,727
Jaora (★ 47,548) 47,129
Jaridih Bazar (★ 101,946) 46,477
Jaunpur 105,140
Jaypur 53,981
Jetpur (★ 63,074) 62,806
Jhānsi (★ 284,141) 246,172
Jharia (★★ Dhanbād) 57,496
Jhārsuguda 54,859
Jīnd 56,748
Jodhpur 506,345
Jorhāt (★ 70,674) (1971 C) 30,247
Jūnāgadh (★ 120,416) 118,646
Kadaiyanallūr 60,306
Kadiri 52,774
Kaithal 58,385
Kākināda (Cocanada) 226,409
Kālol (★ Ahmadābād) 69,946
Kalyān (★ Bombay) 136,052
Kāmārhāti (★ Calcutta) 234,951
Kambam 50,340
Kamptee (★ Nāgpur) 67,364
Kānchipuram (Conjeeveram) (★ 145,254) 130,926
Kānchrāpāra (★ Calcutta) 88,798
Kānpur (★ 1,875,000) 1,481,789
Kānpur Cantonment (★ Kānpur) 90,311
Kapūrthala 50,300
Karād 54,364
Kāraikkudi (★ 100,141) 66,993
Karīmnagar 86,125
Karnāl 132,107
Karūr (★ 93,810) 72,692
Kāsganj 61,402
Kashīpur 51,773
Katihār (★ 122,005) 104,781
Kātwa (★ 44,430) 32,890
Kāvali 48,119
Kayankulam (Kayamkulam) 61,327
Kerkend (★ Dhānbād) 75,186
Khambhāt 68,791
Khāmgaon 61,992
Khammam 98,757
Khandwa 114,725
Khanna 53,761
Kharagpur (★ 232,575) 150,475
Kharagpur Railway Settlement (★ Kharagpur) 82,100
Khargone 52,749
Khurja 67,119
Kirkee Cantonment (★ Pune) 80,835
Kishanganj 51,790
Kishangarh 62,032
Koch Bihār (★ 80,101) 62,127
Kohīma 34,340
Kolār 65,834
Kolār Gold Fields (★ 144,385) 77,679
Kolhāpur (★ 351,392) 340,625
Konnagar (★ Calcutta) 51,211
Korba 83,387
Kota 358,241
Kot Kapūra 47,550
Kottagūdem 94,894
Kottayam 64,431
Kovilpatti 63,964
Krishnagiri 48,335
Krishnanagar 98,141
Kulti (★★ Āsansol) 41,323
Kumba-konam (★ 141,794) 132,832
Kundla (★ 51,431) 49,740
Kurasia (★ 53,015) 12,963
Kurichi (★ Coimbatore) 48,936
Kurnool 206,362
Lakhīmpur 61,003
Lātūr 111,986
Leh 8,718
Lucknow (★ 1,060,000) 895,721
Lucknow Cantonment (★ Lucknow) 59,614
Ludhiāna 607,052
Machilīpatnam 138,530
Madanapalle 54,938
Madgaon (Margao) (★ 64,858) 53,076
Madras (★ 4,475,000) 3,276,622
Madurai (★ 960,000) 820,891
Mahbūbnagar 87,503
Mahesāna (★ 73,024) 72,872
Mahuva (★ 56,072) 53,625
Mainpuri 58,928
Mālegaon 245,883
Māler Kotla 65,756
Malkajgiri (★ Hyderābād) 65,776
Mandsaur 77,603
Mandya 100,285
Mangalore (★ 306,078) 172,252
Mango (★ Jamshedpur) 67,284
Manjeri 53,959
Manmād 51,439
Mannārgudi 51,738
Mathura (Muttra) (★ 160,995) 147,493
Maunath Bhanjan 86,326
Māyūram 67,675
Medinīpur 86,118
Meerut (★ 536,615) 417,395
Meerut Cantonment (★ Meerut) 94,210
Melappālaiyam (★ Tirunelveli) 57,683
Mettuppālaiyam 59,537
Mhow Cantonment (★ 76,037) 70,130
Miraj (★★ Sāngli) 105,455
Mirzāpur 127,787
Modinagar (★ 87,665) 78,243
Moga 80,272
Mokāma 51,047
Morādābād (★ 345,350) 330,051
Morbi 73,327
Morena 69,864
Mormugão 69,684
Motihāri (★ 63,212) 57,971
Muktsar 50,941
Munger 129,260
Murwāra (Katni) (★ 123,017) 77,862
Muzaffarnagar 171,816
Muzaffarpur 190,416
Mysore (★ 479,081) 441,754
Nabadwīp (★ 129,800) 109,108
Nadiād 142,689
Nāgappattinam (★ 90,650) 82,828
Nāgaur 48,005
Nāgda 56,602
Nāgercoil 171,648
Nagīna 50,405
Nāgpur (★ 1,302,066) 1,219,461
Naihāti (★ Calcutta) 114,607
Naini Tāl (★ 26,093) 24,835
Najībābād 55,109
Nalgonda 62,458
Nānded 191,269
Nandurbār 65,394
Nandyāl 88,185
Nangi (★ Calcutta) 54,035
Narasapur 46,033
Narasaraopet 67,032
Nāshik (★ 429,034) 262,428
Navsāri (★ 129,266) 106,793
Nawābganj (★ 62,216) 51,518
Neemuch (★ 68,853) 65,860
Nellore 237,065
NEW DELHI (★★ Delhi) 273,036
Neyveli (★ 98,866) 88,000
Nizāmābād 183,061
North Barrackpore (★ Calcutta) 81,758
North Dum Dum (★ Calcutta) 96,418
Nowgong (1971 C) 56,537
Ongole 85,302
Orai 66,397
Outer Burnpur (★ Asansol) 86,803
Pālakollu 46,146
Pālanpur 61,262
Pālayankottai (★★ Tirunelveli) 87,302
Pālghāt (★ 117,986) 111,245
Pāli 91,568
Pallavaram (★ Madras) 83,901
Palni (★ 68,389) 64,444
Palwal 47,328
Panaji (★ 77,226) 43,165
Pānchur (★ Calcutta) 51,223
Pandharpur 64,380
Pānihāti (★ Calcutta) 205,718
Pānīpat 137,927
Panruti 43,042
Paramagudi 61,149
Parbhani 109,364
Parli 48,946
Pātan 79,196
Pathānkot 110,039
Patiāla (★ 206,254) 205,141
Patna (★ 1,025,000) 776,371
Pattukkottai 49,484
Periyakulam 44,310
Petlād 47,020
Phagwāra (★ 75,961) 72,499
Pīlibhīt 88,548
Pimpri-Chinchwad (★ Pune) 220,966
Pollāchi (★ 114,971) 82,354
Pondicherry (★ 251,420) 162,636
Ponmalai (★ Tiruchchirāppalli) 55,995
Ponnāni 43,226
Ponnur 50,206
Porbandar (★ 133,307) 115,182
Port Blair 49,634
Proddatūr 107,070
Pudukkottai 87,952
Pune (★ 1,775,000) 1,203,351
Pune Cantonment (★ Pune) 85,986
Puri 100,942
Pūrnia (★ 109,875) 91,144
Puruliya 73,904
Quilon (★ 167,598) 137,943
Rabkavi Banhatti 51,693
Rāe Bareli 89,697
Rāichūr 124,762
Raiganj (★ 66,705) 60,343
Raigarh (★ 69,791) 68,060
Raipur 338,245
Rājahmundry (★ 268,370) 203,358
Rājapālaiyam 101,640
Rajhara-Jharandalli 55,307
Rājkot 445,076
Rāj Nāndgaon 86,367
Rājpur (★ 60,734) 43,985
Rājpura 58,645
Rāmanāthapuram 45,719
Ramgarh [Cantonment] (★ 65,268) 41,257
Rāmpur 204,610
Rānāghāt (★ 83,744) 58,356
Rānchi (★ 502,771) 489,626
Rānībennur 58,118
Rānīganj (★ 119,101) 48,702
Ratlām (★ 155,578) 142,319
Ratnāgiri 47,036
Raurkela (★ 322,610) 206,821
Raurkela Civil Township (★ Raurkela) 96,000
Rewa 100,641
Rewāri 51,562
Rishra (★ Calcutta) 81,001
Robertson Pet (★ Kolār Gold Fields) 61,099
Rohtak 166,767
Roorkee (★ 79,076) 61,851
Sāgar (★ 207,479) 160,392
Sahāranpur 295,355
Saharsa 57,580
Sahijpur Bogha (★ Ahmadābād) 65,327
Salem (★ 518,615) 361,394
Sambalpur (★ 162,214) 110,282
Sambhal 108,232
Sāngli (★ 268,988) 152,339
Sardarnagar (★ Ahmadābād) 50,128
Sardārshahr (★ 56,388) 55,473
Sāsarām 73,457
Sātāra 83,336
Satna (★ 96,667) 90,476
Saunda (★ 99,990) 70,780
Sawai Mādhopur (★ 59,083) 28,139
Secunderābād Cantonment (★ Hyderābād) 135,994
Sehore 52,190
Seoni 54,017
Serampore (★ Calcutta) 127,304
Shahdol (★ 49,631) 44,342
Shāhjahānpur (★ 205,095) 185,396
Shāmli 51,850
Shāntipur 82,980
Shikohābād 47,083
Shiliguri 154,378
Shillong (★ 174,703) 109,244
Shimla 70,604
Shimoga 151,783
Shivpuri 75,738
Shrirampur 55,491
Sidhpur (★ 52,706) 51,953
Sīkar 102,970
Silchar (1971 C) 52,596
Sindri (★★ Dhānbād) 70,645
Sirsa 89,068
Sītāpur 101,210
Sivakāsi (★ 83,072) 59,827
Siwān 51,284
Solāpur (★ 514,860) 511,103
Sonīpat 109,369
South Dum Dum (★ Calcutta) 230,266
Sri Gangānagar (Gangānagar) 123,692
Srīkākulam 68,145
Srikalahasti 51,306
Srīnagar (★ 606,002) 594,775
Srīrangam (★ Tiruchchirāppalli) 64,241
Srīvilliputtūr 61,458
Sūjāngarh 55,546
Sultānpur 48,782
Sūrat (★ 913,806) 776,583
Surendranagar (★ 130,602) 89,619
Tādepallegūdem 62,574
Tādpatri 53,920
Tāmbaram (★ Madras) 86,923
Tānda 54,474
Tanuku 53,618
Tellicherry (★ 98,704) 75,561
Tenāli 119,257
Tenkāsi 49,214
Thāna (★ Bombay) 309,897
Thānesar 49,052
Thanjāvūr 184,015
Theni-Allinagaram 53,018
Tindivanam 56,520
Tinsukia (1971 C) 54,911
Tiruchchirāppalli (Trichinopoly) (★ 609,548) 362,045
Tiruchendūr (★ 68,884) 24,233
Tiruchengodu 53,941
Tirunelveli (Tinnevelly) (★ 323,344) 128,850
Tirupati 115,292
Tiruppattūr 52,422
Tiruppur (★ 215,859) 165,223
Tiruvannāmalai 89,462
Tiruvottiyūr (★ Madras) 134,014
Titāgarh (★ Calcutta) 104,534
Tonk 77,653
Trichūr (★ 170,122) 77,923
Trivandrum (★ 520,125) 483,086
Tumkūr 108,670
Tuticorin (★ 250,677) 192,949
Udagamandalam 78,277
Udaipur 232,588
Udamalpet 54,852
Udgīr 50,564
Ujjain (★ 282,203) 278,454
Ulhāsnagar (★ Bombay) 273,668
Unnāo 75,983
Upleta 54,907
Uttarpara-Kotrung (★ Calcutta) 79,598
Vadodara (★ 744,881) 734,473
Valparai 115,452
Valsad (Bulsar) (★ Bombay) 54,017
Vāniyambādi (★ 75,042) 59,107
Vārānasi (Benares) (★ 925,000) 708,647
Vasai (Bassein) (★ 52,398) 34,940
Vellore (★ 274,041) 174,247
Verāval (★ 105,307) 85,048
Vidisha 65,521
Vijayawāda (Bezwada) (★ 543,008) 454,577
Vikramasingapuram 49,319
Villupuram 77,091
Viramgām 48,275
Virudunagar 68,047
Vishākhapatnam (Vizagapatam) (★ 603,630) 565,321
Visnagar 46,631
Vizianagaram 114,806
Warangal 335,150
Wardha 88,495
Yamunānagar (★ 160,424) 109,304
Yavatmāl 89,071
Yemmiganur 50,701

States

Andaman and Nicobar Islands (Ter.) 188,741
Andhra Pradesh 53,549,673
Arunachal Pradesh 631,839
Assam 19,896,843
Bihār 69,914,734
Chandīgarh (Ter.) 451,610
Dādra and Nagar Haveli (Ter.) 103,676
Damān and Diu (Ter.) 79,981
Delhi (Ter.) 6,220,406
Goa 1,007,749
Gujarat 34,085,799
Haryana 12,922,618
Himachal Pradesh 4,280,818
Jammu and Kashmir 5,987,389
Karnataka (Mysore) 37,135,714
Kerala 25,453,680
Lakshadweep (Ter.) 40,249
Madhya Pradesh 52,178,844
Mahārāshtra 62,784,171
Manipur 1,420,953
Meghalaya 1,335,819
Mizoram 493,757
Nāgāland 774,930
Orissa 26,370,271
Pondicherry (Ter.) 604,471
Punjab 16,788,915
Rājasthān 34,261,862
Sikkim 316,385
Tamil Nadu (Madras) 48,408,077
Tripura 2,053,058
Uttar Pradesh 110,862,013
West Bengal 54,580,647

INDONESIA

1980 C 147,490,298

Cities and Towns

Amahai (1961 C) 18,256
Ambon (▲ 207,702) 111,914
Balikpapan (▲ 279,852) 208,040
Banda Aceh (Kuturaja) 71,868
Bandung (★ 1,800,000) 1,461,407
Bangil 42,241
Bangkalan 34,947
Banjarmasin 380,884
Bantul 12,268
Banyuwangi 90,378
Batang 49,328
Baubau 17,771
Bekasi (★ Jakarta) 144,290
Bengkulu (▲ 64,733) 32,478
Binjai 71,444
Blitar (★ 100,000) 78,503
Blora 31,978
Bogor (★ 560,000) 246,946
Bojonegoro 57,483
Bondowoso 35,496
Brebes 40,971
Bukittinggi (▲ 70,691) 55,577
Ciamis 18,897
Cianjur 105,655
Cibinong 87,580
Cikampek 46,124
Cilacap 127,017
Ciledug 43,959
Cimahi (★ Bandung) (1971 C) 72,367
Ciparay 66,854
Cirebon (★ 275,000) 223,504
Denpasar 159,233
Depok (★ Jakarta) 126,693
Dili (▲ 67,039) 6,890
Dumai 44,644
Ende 27,074
Garut 145,624
Genteng 59,481
Gorontalo (▲ 97,610) 63,554

C Census. E Official estimate. UE Unofficial estimate.
• Largest city in country.

★ Population or designation of metropolitan area, including suburbs (see headnote).
▲ Population of an entire municipality, commune, or district, including rural area.

Gresik 86,418
Indramayu 32,273
• JAKARTA (★ 8,600,000) (1985 E) 7,885,000
Jambi (▲ 230,046) 155,761
Jayapura 60,641
Jember 171,284
Jepara 30,315
Jombang 58,800
Kandangan 13,498
Kebumen 44,139
Kediri (▲ 221,830) 176,261
Kendari 42,999
Kisaran 58,129
Klangenang 64,013
Klaten 117,560
Kotabumi 40,090
Krawang 72,195
Kualakapuas 15,685
Kudus 154,478
Kuningan 32,702
Kupang 84,587
Lahat 25,972
Langsa 16,426
Lawang 28,647
Lhokseumawe 22,611
Lumajang 58,495
Madiun (★ 180,000) 150,562
Magelang (★ 160,000) 123,358
Magetan 23,517
Majalaya 87,474
Majalengka 19,294
Majene 31,016
Malang 511,780
Manado 217,091
Martapura 26,405
Mataram 210,485
Medan 1,373,747
Metro 42,387
Mojokerto 68,849
Muncar 47,009
Muntilan 43,090
Nganjuk 33,916
Ngawi 20,887
Padang (▲ 480,607) 296,675
Padangpanjang (▲ 34,443) 13,661
Padangsidempuan 56,984
Palangkaraya (▲ 60,447) 51,686
Palembang 786,607
Palopo 44,611
Palu 41,779
Pamekasan 39,026
Pangkalpinang 90,078
Pare 47,262
Parepare (▲ 86,360) 62,865
Pasuruan (★ 125,000) 95,864
Pati 50,159
Payakumbuh (▲ 78,789) 24,567
Pekalongan (▲ 260,000) 132,413
Pekanbaru 186,199
Pemalang 72,663
Pematangsiantar (★ 175,000) 150,296
Perabumulih 43,846
Pinrang 21,263
Ponorogo 55,523
Pontianak 304,490
Praya 22,087
Pringsewu 56,115
Probolinggo 100,296
Purbolinggo 41,997
Purwakarta 61,995
Purwokerto 143,787
Purworejo 38,276
Raba 39,921
Rangkasbitung 18,674
Rantauprapat 25,043
Rembang 27,850
Salatiga 85,740
Samarinda (▲ 264,012) 182,473
Sampit 16,377
Semarang 1,024,940
Serang 78,209
Sibolga 59,466
Sidoarjo 56,090
Singaraja 53,368
Singkawang 58,693
Situbondo 58,299
Solok (▲ 31,700) 6,976
Sorong 52,041
Sragen 39,349
Subang 52,041
Sukabumi (★ 225,000) 109,898
Sumedang 42,549
Sumenep 48,705
Surabaya 2,027,913
Surakarta (★ 575,000) 469,532
Taman 64,358
Tangerang 97,091
Tanjungbalai 41,776
Tanjungkarang-Telukbetung (★ 375,000) 284,167
Tanjungpandan 33,433
Tanjungpinang 36,999
Tarakan 46,657
Tasikmalaya 192,267
Tebingtinggi (▲ 92,068) 69,569
Tegal (★ 340,000) 131,440
Tembilahan 52,140
Tuban 48,558
Tulungagung 91,585
Ujungpandang (Makasar) 708,465
Watampone 37,869
Yogyakarta (★ 510,000) 394,965

Provinces

Aceh 2,611,271
Bali 2,469,930
Bengkulu 768,064
Irian Jaya 1,173,875
Jakarta Raya (Greater Jakarta) 6,503,449
Jambi 1,445,994
Jawa Barat (West Java) 27,453,525
Jawa Tengah (Central Java) 25,372,889
Jawa Timur (East Java) 29,188,852
Kalimantan Barat (West Borneo) 2,486,068
Kalimantan Selatan (South Borneo) 2,064,649
Kalimantan Tengah (Central Borneo) 954,353
Kalimantan Timur (East Borneo) 1,218,016
Lampung 4,624,785
Maluku (Moluccas) 1,411,006
Nusa Tenggara Barat (West Nusa Tenggara) 2,724,664
Nusa Tenggara Timur (East Nusa Tenggara) 2,737,166
Riau 2,168,535
Sulawesi Selatan (South Celebes) 6,062,212
Sulawesi Tengah (Central Celebes) 1,289,635
Sulawesi Tenggara (Tenggara Celebes) 942,302
Sulawesi Utara (North Celebes) 2,115,384
Sumatera Barat (West Sumatra) 3,406,816
Sumatera Selatan (South Sumatra) 4,629,801
Sumatera Utara (North Sumatra) 8,360,894
Timor Timur 555,350
Yogyakarta 2,750,813

IRAN / Īrān

1986 C 49,445,010

Cities and Towns

Ābādān (1976 C) 296,081
Ābādeh (1982 E) 45,000
Abhar (1982 E) 31,000
Āghā Jārī (1982 E) 64,000
Ahar (1982 E) 52,000
Ahvāz 579,826
Āmol 118,242
Andīmeshk (1982 E) 53,000
Arāk 265,349
Ardabīl 281,973
Bābol 115,320
Bākhtarān (Kermānshāh) 560,514
Bam (1982 E) 46,000
Bandar-e ʿAbbās 201,642
Bandar-e Anzalī (Bandar-e Pahlavī) (1982 E) 83,000
Bandar-e Būshehr 120,787
Bandar-e Khomeynī (Bandar-e Shāhpūr) (1982 E) 47,000
Bandar-e Māhshahr (1982 E) 88,000
Behbahān (1982 E) 84,000
Behshahr (1982 E) 45,000
Bīrjand (1982 E) 68,000
Bojnūrd (1982 E) 82,000
Borāzjān (1982 E) 53,000
Borūjerd 183,879
Dezfūl 151,420
Do Gonbadān (1982 E) 47,000
Do Rūd (1982 E) 52,000
Emāmshahr (Shāhrūd) (1982 E) 68,000
Eṣfahān (Isfahan) 986,753
Eslāmābād (1982 E) 71,000
Eslāmshahr (★ Tehrān) 215,129
Fasā (1982 E) 67,000
Gonbad-e Qābūs (1982 E) 75,000
Gorgān 139,430
Hamadān 272,499
Īlām (1982 E) 75,000
Jahrom (1982 E) 68,000
Karaj (★ Tehrān) 275,100
Kāshān 138,599
Kāshmar (1982 E) 40,000
Kāzerūn (1982 E) 63,000
Kermān 257,284
Khomeynīshahr (Homāyūnshahr) 104,647
Khorramābād 208,592
Khorramshahr (1976 C) 146,709
Khvoy 115,343
Lāhījān (1982 E) 35,000
Mahābād (1982 E) 63,000
Malāyer 103,640
Marāgheh 100,679
Marand (1982 E) 59,000
Marv Dasht (1982 E) 72,000
Mashhad (Meshed) 1,463,508
Masjed-e Soleymān 104,787
Miāndoāb (1982 E) 52,000
Mīāneh (1982 E) 57,000
Nahāvand (1982 E) 45,000
Najafābād 129,058
Neyshābūr 109,258
Orūmīyeh (Rezāʾīyeh) 300,746
Qāʾemshahr (Shāhī) 109,288
Qazvīn 248,591
Qom 543,139
Qomsheh (1982 E) 67,000
Qūchān (1982 E) 61,000
Rafsanjān (1982 E) 61,000
Rāmhormoz (1982 E) 53,000
Rasht 290,897
Robāṭ Karīm (1982 E) 40,000
Sabzevār 129,103
Salmās (1982 E) 44,000
Sanandaj 204,537
Saqqez (1982 E) 76,000
Sārī 141,020
Sāveh (1982 E) 46,000
Semnān (1982 E) 54,000
Shahr-e Kord (1982 E) 63,000
Shīrāz 848,289
Sīrjān (1982 E) 67,000
Tabrīz 971,482
• TEHRĀN (★ 6,400,000) 6,042,584
Torbat-e Ḩeydarīyeh (1982 E) 62,000
Varāmīn (1982 E) 51,000
Yazd 230,483
Zābol (1982 E) 58,000
Zāhedān 281,923
Zanjān 215,261
Zarrīn Shahr (1982 E) 69,000

IRAQ / Al ʿIrāq

1985 E 15,584,987

Cities and Towns

Ad Dīwānīyah (1970 E) 62,300
Al ʿAmārah 131,758
Al Fallūjah (1965 C) 38,072
Al Ḩillah (Hilla) 215,249
Al Kūfah (1965 C) 30,862
Al Kūt (Kūt al Imāra) (1965 C) 42,116
An Najaf 242,603
An Nāṣirīyah 138,842
Ar Ramādī 137,388
As Samāwah (1965 C) 33,473
As Sulaymānīyah 279,424
Az Zubayr (1965 C) 41,408
• BAGHDĀD (1987 C) 3,841,268
Baʿqūbah 114,516
Basra (Al Baṣrah) 616,700
Irbīl 333,903
Karbalāʾ 184,574
Kirkūk (1970 E) 207,900
Mosul (Al Mawṣil) 570,926
Sāmarrāʾ (1965 C) 24,746
Tall ʿAfar (1965 C) 36,837

IRELAND / Éire

1986 C 3,540,643

Cities and Towns

An Uaimh (Navan) (★ 11,929) 3,660
Arklow (Inbhear Mór) 8,388
Athlone (Áth Luain) (★ 15,571) 8,815
Balbriggan (★ 7,555) 5,680
Bray (Brí Chualann) (★ Dublin) 24,686
Carlow (Ceatharlach) (★ 13,816) 11,509
Castlebar (Caisleán an Bharraigh) (★ 7,645) 6,349
Clonmel (Cluain Meala) (★ 15,517) 11,759
Cobh (★ 8,282) 6,369
Cork (Corcaigh) (★ 173,694) 133,271
Drogheda (Droichead Átha) (★ 24,681) 24,086
Droichead Nua (★ 11,503) 5,983
• DUBLIN (BAILE ÁTHA CLIATH) (★ 1,140,000) 502,749
Dundalk (Dún Dealgan) (★ 30,608) 26,669
Dún Laoghaire (★ Dublin) 54,715
Ennis (Inis) (★ 15,547) 5,917
Enniscorthy (Inis Coirthe) (★ 7,753) 4,483
Galway (Gaillimh) 47,104
Kilkenny (Cill Choinnigh) (★ 17,537) 8,969
Killarney (Cill Áirne) (★ 10,189) 7,837
Leixlip (★ Dublin) 11,938
Letterkenny (★ 9,809) 6,691
Limerick (Luimneach) (★ 76,557) 56,279
Lucan (★ Dublin) 12,259
Mallow (Mala) (★ 7,685) 6,488
Monaghan (Muineachán) (★ 6,284) 6,075
Mullingar (Muileann Cearr) (★ 12,127) 8,077
Naas (Nás na Ríogh) (★ Dublin) 10,017
Nenagh (Aonach Urmhumhan) (★ 5,777) 5,483
Port Laoise (Portlaoighise) (★ 8,384) 3,773
Shannon 8,005
Sligo (Sligeach) (★ 18,018) 17,259
Swords (★ Dublin) 15,312
Thurles (Durlas éile) (★ 7,338) 7,049
Tipperary (Tiobrad Árann) (★ 5,209) 5,033
Tralee (Tráighlí) (★ 17,620) 17,109
Tuam (Tuaim) (★ 6,039) 4,109
Tullamore (Tulach Mhór) (★ 9,442) 8,484
Waterford (Port Láirge) (★ 41,054) 39,529
Wexford (Loch Garman) (★ 15,365) 10,336

Counties

Carlow 40,988
Cavan 53,965
Clare 91,344
Cork 412,735
Donegal 129,664
Dublin 1,021,449
Galway 178,552
Kerry 124,159
Kildare 116,247
Kilkenny 73,186
Laois 53,284
Leitrim 27,035
Limerick 164,569
Longford 31,496
Louth 91,810
Mayo 115,184
Meath 103,881
Monaghan 52,379
Offaly 59,835
Roscommon 54,592
Sligo 56,046
Tipperary 136,619
Waterford 91,151
Westmeath 63,379
Wexford 102,552
Wicklow 94,542

Historic Provinces

Connaught 431,409
Leinster 1,852,649
Munster 1,020,577
Ulster 236,008

ISLE OF MAN

1986 C 64,282

Cities and Towns

Castletown 3,019
• DOUGLAS (★ 28,500) 20,368
Peel 3,660
Ramsey 5,778

ISRAEL / Yisra'el / Isrāʾīl

1989 E 4,386,000

Cities and Towns

ʿAfula 24,500
ʿAkko (★ Haifa) 37,200
Ashdod 74,700
Ashqelon 56,300
Bat Yam (★ Tel Aviv-Yafo) 133,100
Be'er Shevaʿ 113,200
Bene Beraq (★ Tel Aviv-Yafo) 109,400
Dimona 25,000
Elat (Elath) 24,700
Giv'atayim (★ Tel Aviv-Yafo) 45,600
Ḩadera 41,600
Haifa (Ḩefa) (★ 435,000) 222,600
Herzliyya (★ Tel Aviv-Yafo) 71,600
Hod HaSharon (★ Tel Aviv-Yafo) 24,500
Ḩolon (★ Tel Aviv-Yafo) 146,100
JERUSALEM (YERUSHALAYIM) (AL-QUDS) (★ 490,000) 493,500
Karmi'el (Carmiel) 20,100
Kefar Sava (★ Tel Aviv-Yafo) 54,800
Lod (Lydda) (★ Tel Aviv-Yafo) 41,300
Nahariyya 28,800
Nazareth (Naẕerat) (★ 74,000) 50,600
Naẕerat ʿIllit (★ Nazareth) 24,900
Nes Ẕiyyona (★ Tel Aviv-Yafo) 18,600
Netanya (★ Tel Aviv-Yafo) 117,800
Or Yehuda (★ Tel Aviv-Yafo) 20,000
Petaḩ Tiqwa (★ Tel Aviv-Yafo) 133,600
Qiryat Atta (★ Haifa) 35,500
Qiryat Bialik (★ Haifa) 32,600
Qiryat Gat 27,400
Qiryat Motzkin (★ Haifa) 30,000
Qiryat Ono (★ Tel Aviv-Yafo) 22,200
Qiryat Shemona 15,400
Qiryat Yam (★ Haifa) 31,800
Ra'anana (★ Tel Aviv-Yafo) 49,400
Ramat Gan (★ Tel Aviv-Yafo) 115,700
Ramat HaSharon (★ Tel Aviv-Yafo) 36,100
Ramla (★ Tel Aviv-Yafo) 44,500
Reḩovot (★ Tel Aviv-Yafo) 72,500
Rishon leẔiyyon (★ Tel Aviv-Yafo) 123,800
Ṭaiyibe 20,000
• Tel Aviv-Yafo (Tel Aviv-Jaffa) (★ 1,670,000) 317,800
Tiberias (Teverya) 31,200
Tirat Karmel (★ Haifa) 14,600
Umm el Faḩm 23,800
Yavne (★ Tel Aviv-Yafo) 20,800
Ẕefat 16,400

Districts

Central 949,400
Haifa 605,000
Jerusalem 544,200
Northern 722,200
Southern 533,000
Tel Aviv 1,032,200

ISRAELI OCCUPIED TERRITORIES

1989 E 1,574,700

Cities and Towns

Bethlehem (Bayt Laḩm) (1971 E) 25,000
• Gaza (Ghazzah) (1967 C) 118,272
Hebron (Al Khalīl) (1971 E) 43,000
Jabālyah (1967 C) 43,604
Janīn (1971 E) 20,000
Jericho (Arīḩā) (1967 C) 6,829
Jerusalem (Al-Quds) (★ Jerusalem, Israel) (1976 E) 90,000
Khān Yūnus (1967 C) 52,997
Nābulus (1971 E) 64,000
Rafaḩ (1967 C) 49,812

Territories

Gaza Strip 591,700
Golan Heights 24,300
West Bank 958,700

ITALY / Italia

1987 E 57,290,519

Cities and Towns

Abano Terme (▲ 17,044) 14,000
Acerra (★ Naples) 39,067
Acireale 46,997
Adrano 35,066
Afragola (★ Naples) 59,397
Agrigento (▲ 54,600) 41,200
Alassio 12,204
Alba (▲ 30,932) 25,500
Albano Laziale (★ Rome) 29,967
Alberobello (▲ 10,309) 8,700
Alcamo 43,072
Alessandria (▲ 96,014) 76,100
Alghero 39,795
Altamura 54,784
Amalfi (▲ 6,026) 4,400
Ancona 104,409
Andria 88,348
Anzio 30,806
Aosta 36,856
Arezzo (▲ 91,681) 74,200
Ascoli Piceno (▲ 53,281) 43,600
Assisi (▲ 24,492) 4,700
Asti (▲ 75,459) 63,600
Augusta 39,735
Avellino 56,407
Aversa (★ Naples) 57,827
Avezzano 35,966
Avola 31,809
Bagheria 43,725
Barcellona [Pozzo di Gotto] (▲ 39,295) 34,400
Bari (★ 475,000) 362,524
Barletta 86,954
Bassano del Grappa (▲ 38,666) 33,900
Battipaglia (▲ 43,845
Belluno (▲ 36,157) 28,200
Benevento (▲ 65,661) 54,400
Bergamo (★ 345,000) 118,959
Biella 51,788
Bisceglie 47,771
Bitonto 51,962
Bollate (★ Milan) 42,921
Bologna (★ 525,000) 432,406
Bolzano (Bozen) 101,515
Bordighera (▲ 11,511) 10,100
Brescia 199,286
Bressanone (▲ 16,466) 12,800
Bresso (★ Milan) 31,570
Brindisi 92,280
Busto Arsizio (★ Milan) 78,056
Cagliari (★ 305,000) 220,574
Caltagirone 38,331
Caltanissetta 62,352
Camaiore (▲ 30,836) 24,500
Campobasso (▲ 50,801) 44,000
Canicattì 34,009
Canosa [di Puglia] 31,003
Cantù 36,349
Capannori 44,084
Capua (▲ 18,966) 15,500
Carbonia (▲ 33,495) 26,167
Carpi (▲ 60,614) 49,500
Carrara (★★ Massa) 69,229
Casale Monferrato (▲ 40,408) 35,800
Cascina 35,781
Caserta 65,974
Casoria (★ Naples) 54,100
Cassino (▲ 33,927) 24,200
Castel Gandolfo (★ Rome) 6,918

C Census. E Official estimate. UE Unofficial estimate.
• Largest city in country.
★ Population or designation of metropolitan area, including suburbs (see headnote).
▲ Population of an entire municipality, commune, or district, including rural area.

Castellammare di Stabia (★ Naples) ... 68,491
Castelvetrano ... 31,809
Catania (★ 550,000) ... 372,486
Catanzaro ... 102,558
Cattolica ... 15,735
Cava de'Tirreni (★ Salerno) ... 52,028
Cefalù ... 14,322
Cerignola ... 53,463
Cesano Maderno (★ Milan) ... 31,338
Cesena (▲ 90,012) ... 72,600
Cesenatico (▲ 20,123) ... 15,700
Chiavari ... 29,103
Chieri ... 30,981
Chieti ... 55,827
Chioggia (▲ 53,744) ... 47,000
Chivasso (▲ 25,884) ... 21,600
Ciampino (★ Rome) ... 32,524
Cinisello Balsamo (★ Milan) ... 78,917
Cittadella (▲ 17,783) ... 12,400
Città di Castello (▲ 38,159) ... 21,800
Civitanova Marche (▲ 36,648) ... 28,500
Civitavecchia ... 50,806
Collegno (★ Turin) ... 49,334
Cologno Monzese (★ Milan) ... 52,554
Como (★ 165,000) ... 91,738
Conegliano ... 36,074
Corato ... 42,704
Corsico (★ Milan) ... 40,908
Cortina d'Ampezzo (▲ 7,738) ... 6,800
Cortona (▲ 22,679) ... 3,200
Cosenza (★ 150,000) ... 106,026
Crema ... 33,784
Cremona ... 76,979
Crotone (▲ 61,005) ... 53,600
Cuneo (▲ 55,878) ... 47,900
Desio (★ Milan) ... 33,357
Domodossola ... 19,902
Eboli (▲ 33,413) ... 26,000
Empoli (▲ 43,940) ... 33,200
Enna ... 29,124
Ercolano (Resina) (★ Naples) ... 62,783
Erice (▲ 28,878) ... 24,300
Este (▲ 17,931) ... 14,900
Faenza (▲ 54,622) ... 40,300
Fano (▲ 54,442) ... 42,700
Fasano (▲ 37,705) ... 24,400
Favara ... 32,357
Fermo (▲ 35,168) ... 17,600
Ferrara (▲ 143,950) ... 113,300
Fiesole (★ Florence) ... 3,900
Florence (Firenze) (★ 640,000) ... 425,835
Foggia ... 155,051
Foligno (▲ 53,568) ... 42,500
Forlì (▲ 110,482) ... 91,200
Francavilla Fontana ... 34,439
Frascati (★ Rome) ... 19,593
Frattamaggiore (★ Naples) ... 37,740
Frosinone ... 46,814
Gaeta ... 24,154
Gallarate (★ Milan) ... 46,857
Gela ... 79,378
Genoa (Genova) (★ 805,000) ... 727,427
Giugliano in Campania (★ Naples) ... 51,187
Gorizia ... 40,187
Gravina [in Puglia] ... 38,088
Grosseto (▲ 70,592) ... 56,400
Grottaglie ... 30,169
Grugliasco (★ Turin) ... 27,500
Gubbio (▲ 32,354) ... 14,100
Guidonia [Montecelio] (★ Rome) ... 11,700
Iesi (Jesi) ... 40,855
Iglesias (▲ 30,390) ... 26,500
Imola (▲ 61,587) ... 48,200
Imperia ... 41,481
Isernia (▲ 21,083) ... 17,700
Ivrea ... 26,624
L'Aquila (▲ 66,438) ... 42,200
La Spezia (★ 185,000) ... 108,937
Latina (▲ 98,479) ... 67,800
Lecce ... 100,981
Lecco ... 48,844
Legnago (▲ 26,890) ... 23,100
Legnano (★ Milan) ... 48,711
Lentini ... 30,855
Licata ... 42,484
Limbiate (★ Milan) ... 32,308
Lissone (★ Milan) ... 30,676
Livorno (Leghorn) ... 174,065
Lodi ... 42,460
Loreto (▲ 10,528) ... 6,400
Lucca ... 88,024
Lucera ... 34,479
Lugo (▲ 33,282) ... 20,900
Macerata (▲ 43,719) ... 34,400
Maddaloni (▲ 36,223) ... 32,400
Magenta ... 23,625
Manduria ... 32,443
Manfredonia ... 57,707
Mantova (▲ 56,817) ... 49,000
Marino (★ Rome) ... 33,105
Marsala ... 80,468
Martina [Franca] (▲ 44,663) ... 36,300
Massa (★ 145,000) ... 66,872
Matera ... 52,819
Mazara del Vallo ... 47,628
Merano ... 33,323
Messina ... 268,896
Mestre (★ Venice) ... 189,700
• Milan (Milano) (★ 3,750,000) ... 1,495,260
Milazzo ... 32,016
Modena ... 176,880
Modica (▲ 49,550) ... 36,100
Molfetta ... 64,519
Moncalieri (★ Turin) ... 62,306
Monfalcone ... 28,629
Monopoli (▲ 46,257) ... 35,600
Monreale (▲ 26,636) ... 20,700
Montecatini Terme (▲ 21,063) ... 18,700
Montepulciano (▲ 14,094) ... 3,400
Monte Sant'Angelo ... 16,379
Monza (★ Milan) ... 122,064
Naples (Napoli) (★ 2,875,000) ... 1,204,211
Nardò ... 30,135
Nettuno ... 33,145
Nicastro (Lamezia Terme) (▲ 67,562) ... 52,100
Nichelino (★ Turin) ... 46,260
Nocera Inferiore ... 48,151
Nola (▲ 32,675) ... 25,300
Novara ... 102,742
Novi Ligure ... 30,848
Nuoro ... 37,542
Oristano (▲ 31,890) ... 25,900
Orvieto (▲ 22,386) ... 7,300
Otranto ... 5,077
Paderno Dugnano (★ Milan) ... 42,099
Padova (★ 270,000) ... 225,769
Pagani ... 32,961
Palermo ... 723,732
Parma ... 175,842
Partinico ... 28,966
Paternò ... 45,513
Pavia ... 82,065
Perugia (▲ 146,713) ... 106,700
Pesaro (▲ 90,336) ... 78,700
Pescara ... 131,027
Piacenza ... 105,626
Piazza Armerina ... 22,300
Pietrasanta (▲ 25,404) ... 20,400
Pinerolo ... 36,288
Piombino ... 38,266
Pisa ... 104,384
Pistoia (▲ 90,689) ... 76,800
Poggibonsi (▲ 26,553) ... 22,800
Pompei (★ Naples) ... 16,200
Pontedera (▲ 27,325) ... 20,700
Pordenone ... 50,825
Portici (★ Naples) ... 76,302
Portoferraio (▲ 11,587) ... 8,700
Portofino (▲ 664) ... 560
Potenza (▲ 67,114) ... 57,600
Pozzuoli (★ Naples) ... 65,000
Prato (★ 215,000) ... 164,595
Quartu Sant' Elena ... 52,838
Ragusa ... 67,748
Rapallo ... 29,451
Ravello (▲ 2,373) ... 1,300
Ravenna (▲ 136,016) ... 86,500
Reggio di Calabria ... 178,821
Reggio nell'Emilia (▲ 130,086) ... 107,300
Rho (★ Milan) ... 50,876
Riccione ... 32,193
Rieti (▲ 43,921) ... 34,300
Rimini (▲ 130,698) ... 114,600
Riva [del Garda] ... 13,171
Rivoli (★ Turin) ... 50,786
ROME (ROMA) (★ 3,175,000) ... 2,815,457
Rosignano Marittimo (▲ 29,827) ... 2,200
Rovereto ... 33,017
Rovigo (▲ 52,594) ... 41,400
Salerno (★ 250,000) ... 154,848
Salsomaggiore Terme (▲ 17,713) ... 14,800
San Benedetto del Tronto ... 45,397
San Donà di Piave (▲ 32,775) ... 24,300
San Gimignano (▲ 7,175) ... 3,900
San Giorgio a Cremano (★ Naples) ... 63,656
San Remo ... 60,797
San Severo ... 55,239
Santa Maria [Capua Vetere] ... 32,610
Sarno ... 31,160
Saronno ... 37,963
Sassari ... 120,152
Sassuolo ... 39,234
Savona (★ 112,000) ... 62,300
Scandicci (★ Florence) ... 54,367
Schio (▲ 36,187) ... 30,900
Sciacca ... 39,539
Senigallia (▲ 40,814) ... 28,000
Seregno (★ Milan) ... 37,988
Sesto [Fiorentino] (★ Florence) ... 46,355
Sesto San Giovanni (★ Milan) ... 91,624
Sestri Levante ... 21,218
Settimo Torinese (★ Turin) ... 45,430
Siena ... 59,712
Siracusa ... 122,857
Sondrio (▲ 22,914) ... 20,100
Sora (▲ 26,876) ... 21,300
Sorrento (★ 45,000) ... 17,722
Spoleto (▲ 37,932) ... 22,000
Sulmona ... 24,540
Taormina (▲ 10,606) ... 7,300
Taranto ... 244,997
Taurianova (▲ 16,911) ... 13,000
Teramo (▲ 52,378) ... 36,000
Termini Imerese ... 26,440
Terni (▲ 111,157) ... 94,500
Terracina (▲ 38,528) ... 28,600
Tivoli (★ Rome) ... 31,100
Todi (▲ 16,976) ... 6,200
Torre Annunziata (★ Naples) ... 57,508
Torre del Greco (★ Naples) ... 105,066
Torremaggiore ... 17,489
Tortona (▲ 28,541) ... 25,000
Trani ... 47,872
Trapani (▲ 73,083) ... 63,000
Trento (▲ 100,202) ... 81,500
Treviglio ... 25,413
Treviso ... 85,083
Trieste ... 239,031
Turin (Torino) (★ 1,550,000) ... 1,035,565
Udine (★ 126,000) ... 100,211
Urbino (▲ 15,639) ... 8,000
Varese ... 88,353
Velletri ... 43,899
Venice (Venezia) (★ 420,000) ... 88,700
Verbania ... 31,299
Vercelli ... 51,008
Verona ... 259,151
Viareggio (▲ 59,146) ... 50,300
Vibo Valentia (▲ 33,216) ... 19,900
Vicenza ... 110,449
Vigevano ... 62,671
Villa San Giovanni ... 12,780
Viterbo (▲ 59,267) ... 47,900
Vittoria ... 54,795
Vittorio Veneto (▲ 29,584) ... 25,500
Voghera ... 41,524

Regions

Abruzzi ... 1,254,129
Basilicata (Lucania) ... 620,260
Calabria ... 2,139,301
Campania ... 5,690,431
Emilia-Romagna ... 3,931,014
Friuli-Venezia-Giulia ... 1,214,557
Lazio (Latium) ... 5,116,125
Liguria ... 1,758,961
Lombardia (Lombardy) ... 8,876,787
Marche (Marches) ... 1,426,965
Molise ... 334,195
Piemonte (Piedmont) ... 4,389,430
Puglia (Apulia) ... 4,026,151
Sardegna (Sardinia) ... 1,643,789
Sicilia (Sicily) ... 5,112,073
Toscana (Tuscany) ... 3,571,538
Trentino-Alto Adige ... 880,237
Umbria ... 817,852
Valle d'Aosta ... 113,855
Veneto (Venetia) ... 4,372,869

Provinces

Agrigento ... 488,768
Alessandria ... 452,493
Ancona ... 438,045
Aosta ... 113,855
Arezzo ... 313,396
Ascoli Piceno ... 358,827
Asti ... 211,041
Avellino ... 447,822
Bari ... 1,515,742
Belluno ... 216,763
Benevento ... 298,159
Bergamo ... 912,688
Bologna ... 917,016
Bolzano ... 435,377
Brescia ... 1,030,360
Brindisi ... 406,162
Cagliari ... 759,076
Caltanissetta ... 294,247
Campobasso ... 240,753
Caserta ... 803,438
Catania ... 1,060,527
Catanzaro ... 771,585
Chieti ... 382,765
Como ... 783,881
Cosenza ... 777,000
Cremona ... 328,613
Cuneo ... 547,116
Enna ... 197,701
Ferrara ... 372,240
Firenze (Florence) ... 1,197,310
Foggia ... 699,624
Forlì ... 608,159
Frosinone ... 478,931
Genova (Genoa) ... 1,006,711
Gorizia ... 141,215
Grosseto ... 220,170
Imperia ... 222,067
Isernia ... 93,442
L'Aquila ... 298,299
La Spezia ... 236,625
Latina ... 463,141
Lecce ... 808,294
Livorno ... 345,175
Lucca ... 382,882
Macerata ... 294,759
Mantova ... 372,802
Massa-Carrara ... 205,001
Matera ... 207,899
Messina ... 687,776
Milano (Milan) ... 3,978,658
Modena ... 595,610
Napoli (Naples) ... 3,087,246
Novara ... 501,706
Nuoro ... 277,107
Oristano ... 159,551
Padova ... 816,226
Palermo ... 1,249,005
Parma ... 396,491
Pavia ... 501,470
Perugia ... 591,166
Pesaro e Urbino ... 335,334
Pescara ... 293,669
Piacenza ... 273,606
Pisa ... 388,620
Pistoia ... 265,509
Pordenone ... 276,102
Potenza ... 412,361
Ragusa ... 287,927
Ravenna ... 353,375
Reggio di Calabria ... 590,716
Reggio nell'Emilia ... 414,517
Rieti ... 145,475
Roma (Rome) ... 3,752,360
Rovigo ... 250,734
Salerno ... 1,053,766
Sassari ... 448,055
Savona ... 293,558
Siena ... 253,475
Siracusa ... 409,509
Sondrio ... 176,120
Taranto ... 596,329
Teramo ... 279,396
Terni ... 226,686
Torino (Turin) ... 2,292,068
Trapani ... 436,613
Trento ... 444,860
Treviso ... 731,893
Trieste ... 269,878
Udine ... 527,362
Varese ... 792,195
Venezia (Venice) ... 837,170
Vercelli ... 385,006
Verona ... 782,754
Vicenza ... 737,329
Viterbo ... 276,218

IVORY COAST / Côte d'Ivoire

1983 E ... 9,300,000

Cities and Towns

Abengourou (1975 C) ... 31,239
• ABIDJAN ... 1,950,000
Agboville (1975 C) ... 27,192
Bouaké ... 275,000
Daloa ... 70,000
Danané (1975 C) ... 19,872
Dimbokro (1975 C) ... 30,986
Divo (1975 C) ... 37,896
Gagnoa (1975 C) ... 42,362
Grand-Bassam (1975 C) ... 25,808
Korhogo ... 125,000
Man ... 55,000
YAMOUSSOUKRO ... 80,000

JAMAICA

1982 C ... 2,190,357

Cities and Towns

• KINGSTON (★ 770,000) ... 586,930
Mandeville ... 34,502
May Pen ... 40,962
Montego Bay ... 70,265
Ocho Rios ... 7,777
Port Antonio ... 12,285
Portmore (★ Kingston) ... 73,426
Savanna-la-Mar ... 14,912
Spanish Town (★ Kingston) ... 89,097

JAPAN / Nihon

1985 C ... 121,048,923

Cities and Towns

Abashiri ... 44,283
Abiko (★ Tōkyō) ... 111,659
Ageo (★ Tōkyō) ... 178,587
Aioi ... 39,868
Aizu-wakamatsu ... 118,140
Akashi (★ Ōsaka) ... 263,363
Akigawa (★ Tōkyō) ... 45,735
Akishima (★ Tōkyō) ... 97,543
Akita ... 296,400
Akō ... 52,374
Amagasaki (★ Ōsaka) ... 509,115
Amagi (▲ 43,575) ... 33,600
Anan (▲ 60,749) ... 48,100
Anjō ... 133,059
Annaka (▲ 44,601) ... 34,500
Aomori ... 294,045
Arao (★ Ōmuta) ... 62,570
Arida (▲ 35,401) ... 29,600
Asahikawa ... 363,631
Asaka (★ Tōkyō) ... 94,431
Ashibetsu (▲ 30,017) ... 25,500
Ashikaga ... 167,656
Ashiya (★ Ōsaka) ... 87,127
Atami ... 49,374
Atsugi (★ Tōkyō) ... 175,600
Ayabe (▲ 41,903) ... 31,800
Ayase (★ Tōkyō) ... 71,152
Beppu ... 134,775
Bibai (▲ 37,414) ... 29,400
Bisai (★ Nagoya) ... 56,234
Bizen ... 32,243
Chiba (★ Tōkyō) ... 788,930
Chichibu ... 61,013
Chigasaki (★ Tōkyō) ... 185,030
Chikugo (▲ 43,359) ... 35,600
Chikushino (★ Fukuoka) ... 63,242
Chino (▲ 47,273) ... 38,300
Chiryū (★ Nagoya) ... 50,506
Chita (★ Nagoya) ... 70,013
Chitose ... 73,610
Chōfu (★ Tōkyō) ... 191,071
Chōshi ... 87,883
Daitō (★ Ōsaka) ... 122,441
Dazaifu (★ Fukuoka) ... 57,737
Ebetsu (★ Sapporo) ... 90,328
Ebina (★ Tōkyō) ... 93,159
Ena (▲ 35,356) ... 30,700
Eniwa ... 48,305
Fuchū ... 47,798
Fuchū (★ Tōkyō) ... 201,972
Fuchū ... 48,833
Fuji (★ 370,000) ... 214,448
Fujieda (★ Shizuoka) ... 111,985
Fujiidera (★ Ōsaka) ... 65,252
Fujimi (★ Tōkyō) ... 85,697
Fujinomiya (★★ Fuji) ... 112,642
Fujioka (▲ 57,082) ... 46,900
Fujisawa (★ Tōkyō) ... 328,387
Fuji-yoshida ... 54,796
Fukaya (▲ 89,121) ... 71,600
Fukuchiyama (▲ 65,995) ... 56,200
Fukui ... 250,261
Fukuoka (★ 1,750,000) ... 1,160,440
Fukuroi (▲ 49,480) ... 40,700
Fukushima ... 270,762
Fukuyama ... 360,261
Funabashi (★ Tōkyō) ... 506,966
Furukawa (▲ 60,718) ... 48,400
Fussa (★ Tōkyō) ... 51,478
Futtsu (▲ 56,777) ... 48,200
Gamagōri ... 85,580
Gifu ... 411,743
Ginowan ... 69,206
Gobō (▲ 30,450) ... 24,800
Gose (★ Ōsaka) ... 36,693
Gosen (▲ 40,261) ... 33,000
Goshogawara (▲ 49,543) ... 34,500
Gotemba ... 74,882
Gushikawa ... 51,351
Gyōda ... 79,359
Habikino (★ Ōsaka) ... 111,394
Hachinohe ... 241,430
Hachiōji (★ Tōkyō) ... 426,654
Hadano (★ Tōkyō) ... 141,803
Hagi ... 52,740
Hakodate ... 319,194
Hamada ... 51,071
Hamakita ... 77,228
Hamamatsu ... 514,118
Hanamaki (▲ 69,886) ... 54,500
Handa (★ Nagoya) ... 92,883
Hannō (★ Tōkyō) ... 66,550
Hanyū (▲ 51,504) ... 44,700
Haramachi (▲ 48,411) ... 40,200
Hashima ... 59,760
Hasuda (★ Tōkyō) ... 53,991
Hatogaya (★ Tōkyō) ... 55,424
Hatsukaichi (★ Hiroshima) ... 52,020
Hekinan ... 63,778
Higashihiroshima (★ Hiroshima) ... 84,717
Higashikurume (★ Tōkyō) ... 110,079
Higashimatsuyama ... 70,426
Higashimurayama (★ Tōkyō) ... 123,798
Higashine (▲ 41,874) ... 30,400
Higashiōsaka (★ Ōsaka) ... 522,805
Higashiyamato (★ Tōkyō) ... 69,881
Hikari (★ Tokuyama) ... 49,246
Hikone ... 94,204
Himeji (★ 660,000) ... 452,917
Himi (▲ 62,112) ... 52,300
Hino (★ Tōkyō) ... 156,031
Hirakata (★ Ōsaka) ... 382,257
Hiratsuka (★ Tōkyō) ... 229,990
Hirosaki (▲ 176,082) ... 134,800
Hiroshima (★ 1,575,000) ... 1,044,118
Hisai ... 39,134
Hita (▲ 65,730) ... 57,900
Hitachi ... 206,074
Hitoyoshi (▲ 42,292) ... 35,600
Hōfu ... 118,067
Hondo (▲ 42,641) ... 35,800
Honjō, Saitama pref. ... 56,495
Hōya (★ Tōkyō) ... 9,156
Hyūga ... 59,163
Ibara ... 37,212
Ibaraki (★ Ōsaka) ... 250,463
Ichihara (★ Tōkyō) ... 237,617
Ichikawa (★ Tōkyō) ... 397,822
Ichinomiya (★★ Nagoya) ... 257,388
Ichinoseki (▲ 60,941) ... 49,200
Iida (▲ 92,401) ... 65,000
Iizuka (★ 110,000) ... 81,868
Ikeda (★ Ōsaka) ... 101,683
Ikoma (★ Ōsaka) ... 86,293
Imabari ... 125,115
Imaichi (▲ 53,113) ... 44,000
Imari (▲ 62,044) ... 50,700
Ina (▲ 59,010) ... 48,600
Inagi (★ Tōkyō) ... 50,766
Inazawa (★ Nagoya) ... 94,479
Innoshima (▲ 37,239) ... 32,100
Inuyama (★ Nagoya) ... 68,723
Iruma (★ Tōkyō) ... 118,603
Isahaya ... 88,376
Ise (Uji-yamada) ... 105,455
Isehara (★ Tōkyō) ... 7,776
Isesaki ... 112,459
Ishigaki (▲ 41,177) ... 34,600
Ishinomaki ... 122,674
Ishioka (▲ 49,059) ... 41,400
Itami (★ Ōsaka) ... 182,731
Itō ... 70,197
Itoigawa (▲ 35,797) ... 27,700
Itoman (▲ 45,921) ... 37,000
Iwai (▲ 42,177) ... 29,100
Iwaki (Taira) ... 350,569
Iwakuni ... 111,833
Iwakura (★ Nagoya) ... 42,508
Iwamizawa ... 81,664
Iwanuma (▲ 36,519) ... 31,800
Iwata ... 80,810
Iwatsuki (★ Tōkyō) ... 100,903
Iyo-mishima ... 38,603
Izumi (★ Sendai) ... 124,216
Izumi (▲ 40,084) ... 30,500

C Census. E Official estimate. UE Unofficial estimate.
• Largest city in country.

★ Population or designation of metropolitan area, including suburbs (see headnote).
▲ Population of an entire municipality, commune, or district, including rural area.

Izumi (★ Ōsaka) 137,641
Izumi-ōtsu (★ Ōsaka) 67,755
Izumi-sano (★ Ōsaka) 91,563
Izumo (▲ 80,749) 68,000
Joetsu 130,659
Jōyō (★ Ōsaka) 81,850
Kadoma (★ Ōsaka) 140,590
Kaga 68,630
Kagoshima 530,502
Kainan (★ Wakayama) 50,779
Kaizuka (★ Ōsaka) 79,591
Kakamigahara 124,464
Kakegawa (▲ 68,724) 55,600
Kakogawa (★ Ōsaka) 227,311
Kamagaya (★ Tōkyō) 85,705
Kamaishi 60,007
Kamakura (★ Tōkyō) 175,495
Kameoka 76,207
Kameyama 35,510
Kamifukuoka (★ Tōkyō) 57,638
Kamo 35,959
Kanazawa 430,481
Kani (★ Nagoya) 69,630
Kanonji (▲ 45,569) 38,300
Kanoya (▲ 76,029) 60,200
Kanuma (▲ 88,078) 73,200
Karatsu (▲ 78,744) 70,100
Kariya (★ Nagoya) 112,403
Karuizawa 15,050
Kasai 52,107
Kasaoka (▲ 60,598) 53,500
Kashihara (★ Ōsaka) 112,888
Kashiwa (★ Tōkyō) 273,128
Kashiwara (★ Ōsaka) 73,252
Kashiwazaki (▲ 86,020) 73,350
Kasuga (★ Fukuoka) 75,555
Kasugai (★ Nagoya) 256,990
Kasukabe (★ Tōkyō) 171,890
Katano (★ Ōsaka) 64,205
Katsuta 102,763
Kawachi-nagano
(★ Ōsaka) 91,313
Kawagoe (★ Tōkyō) 285,437
Kawaguchi (★ Tōkyō) 403,015
Kawanishi (★ Ōsaka) 136,376
Kawanoe 38,538
Kawasaki (★ Tōkyō) 1,088,624
Kazo (▲ 50,537) 41,200
Kazuno (▲ 44,499) 32,600
Kesennuma 68,137
Kimitsu (▲ 84,310) 71,900
Kiryū 131,267
Kisarazu 120,201
Kishiwada (★ Ōsaka) 185,731
Kita-ibaraki 51,035
Kitakami (▲ 56,741) 46,200
Kitakyūshū (★ 1,525,000) 1,056,402
Kitami 107,281
Kitamoto (★ Tōkyō) 58,114
Kiyose (★ Tōkyō) 65,066
Kobayashi (▲ 40,976) 27,300
Kōbe (★★ Ōsaka) 1,410,834
Kōchi 312,241
Kodaira (★ Tōkyō) 158,673
Kōfu 202,405
Koga (★ Tōkyō) 57,541
Koganei (★ Tōkyō) 104,642
Kokubu (▲ 40,931) 33,000
Kokubunji (★ Tōkyō) 95,467
Komae (★ Tōkyō) 73,784
Komaki (★ Nagoya) 113,284
Komatsu 106,041
Komatsushima
(▲ 43,998) 38,300
Komoro (▲ 43,705) 33,900
Kōnan (★ Nagoya) 92,049
Kōnosu (★ Tōkyō) 60,565
Kōriyama 301,673
Kosai 41,371
Koshigaya (★ Tōkyō) 253,479
Kōshoku (▲ 36,849) 30,500
Kudamatsu
(★★ Tokuyama) 54,445
Kuki (★ Tōkyō) 58,636
Kumagaya 143,496
Kumamoto 555,719
Kunitachi (★ Tōkyō) 64,881
Kurashiki 413,632
Kurayoshi (▲ 52,351) 43,000
Kure (★★ Hiroshima) 226,488
Kurobe (▲ 36,135) 31,400
Kuroishi (▲ 40,501) 28,500
Kuroiso (▲ 49,742) 39,800
Kurume 222,847
Kusatsu (★ Ōsaka) 87,542
Kushiro 214,541
Kuwana (★ Nagoya) 94,731
Kyōto (★★ Ōsaka) 1,479,218
Machida (★ Tōkyō) 321,188
Maebashi 277,319
Maizuru 98,775
Marugame 74,272
Masuda (▲ 54,049) 46,200
Matsubara (★ Ōsaka) 136,455
Matsudo (★ Tōkyō) 427,473
Matsue 140,005
Matsumoto 197,340
Matsuyama 426,658
Matsuzaka 116,886
Mihara 85,975
Miki (★ Ōsaka) 74,527
Minamata (▲ 36,520) 31,700
Minamiashigara 41,706
Minō (★ Ōsaka) 114,770
Minokamo 41,700
Misato (★ Tōkyō) 107,964
Misawa (▲ 41,425) 34,500
Mishima (★★ Numazu) 99,600
Mitaka (★ Tōkyō) 166,252
Mito 228,985
Mitsuke (▲ 42,546) 37,400
Miura (★ Tōkyō) 50,471
Miyako 61,654
Miyakonojō (▲ 132,098) 107,600
Miyazaki 279,114
Miyoshi (▲ 38,968) 31,500
Mizunami 40,078
Mizusawa (▲ 57,257) 47,900
Mobara 76,929
Mōka (▲ 57,261) 43,500
Mombetsu 32,163
Moriguchi (★ Ōsaka) 159,400
Morioka 235,469
Moriyama 53,052
Mukō (★ Ōsaka) 52,216
Munakata 60,971
Murakami 33,325
Muroran (★ 195,000) 136,208
Musashi-murayama
(★ Tōkyō) 60,930
Musashino (★ Tōkyō) 138,783
Mutsu 49,292
Nabari 56,474
Nagahama 55,531
Nagano 336,973
Nagaoka 183,756
Nagaokakyō (★ Ōsaka) 75,242
Nagareyama (★ Tōkyō) 124,682
Nagasaki 449,382
Nago (▲ 49,038) 40,800
Nagoya (★ 4,800,000) 2,116,381
Naha 303,674
Nakama (★ Kitakyūshū) 50,294
Nakatsu 66,260
Nakatsugawa 53,277
Nanao 50,582
Nankoku (▲ 47,554) 36,700
Nara (★ Ōsaka) 327,702
Narashino (★ Tōkyō) 136,365
Narita 77,181
Naruto 64,329
Natori (★ Sendai) 43,200
Naze 49,765
Nemuro 40,675
Neyagawa (★ Ōsaka) 258,228
Nichinan (▲ 51,966) 44,900
Niigata 475,630
Niihama 132,184
Niitsu (▲ 63,846) 55,600
Niiza (★ Tōkyō) 129,287
Nikkō 21,705
Nishinomiya (★ Ōsaka) 421,267
Nishio 91,930
Nishiwaki 38,770
Nobeoka 136,598
Noboribetsu (★ Muroran) 58,370
Noda (★ Tōkyō) 105,937
Nōgata 64,479
Noshiro (▲ 59,170) 50,400
Numata (▲ 47,179) 38,400
Numazu (★ 495,000) 210,490
Obihiro 162,932
Ōbu (★ Nagoya) 66,696
Ōda (▲ 38,242) 29,400
Ōdate (▲ 71,794) 60,900
Odawara 185,941
Ōfunato 39,300
Oga (▲ 36,949) 30,900
Ōgaki 145,910
Ogōri 43,811
Ōita 390,096
Ojiya (▲ 44,204) 35,200
Ōkawa 47,837
Okaya 61,747
Okayama 572,479
Okazaki 284,996
Okegawa (★ Tōkyō) 61,499
Okinawa 101,210
Ōmagari (▲ 41,545) 32,500
Ōme (★ Tōkyō) 110,828
Ōmi-hachiman (★ Ōsaka) 63,791
Ōmiya (★ Tōkyō) 373,022
Ōmura 69,472
Ōmuta (★ 225,000) 159,424
Ono 45,686
Ōno (▲ 41,926) 33,500
Onoda (★ Ube) 46,364
Ōnojō (★ Fukuoka) 69,435
Onomichi 100,640
Ōsaka (★ 16,450,000) 2,636,249
Ōta 133,670
Ōtake 34,760
Otaru (★★ Sapporo) 172,486
Ōtawara (▲ 49,542) 37,000
Ōtsu (★ Ōsaka) 234,551
Ōtsuki 34,914
Owari-asahi (★ Nagoya) 57,415
Oyabe (▲ 36,711) 31,000
Oyama (▲ 134,242) 113,100
Rumoi 35,542
Ryōtsu (▲ 20,412) 14,700
Ryūgasaki (★ 48,857) 40,400
Sabae 61,452
Saga 168,252
Sagamihara (★ Tōkyō) 482,778
Saijō 56,516
Saiki 54,708
Sakado (★ Tōkyō) 87,586
Sakai (★ Ōsaka) 818,271
Sakaide 66,087
Sakaiminato 37,351
Sakata 101,392
Saku (▲ 59,974) 48,400
Sakura (★ Tōkyō) 121,213
Sakurai 58,894
Sanda (▲ 40,716) Ōsaka) 34,300
Sanjō 86,325
Sano 80,753
Sapporo (★ 1,900,000) 1,542,979
Sasebo 250,633
Satte 51,462
Sawara (▲ 49,784) 36,800
Sayama (★ Ōsaka) 50,246
Sayama (★ Tōkyō) 144,366
Seki 64,149
Sendai, Kagoshima pref.
(▲ 71,444) 57,800
Sendai, Miyagi pref.
(★ 1,175,000) 700,254
Sennan (★ Ōsaka) 60,059
Seto 124,623
Settsu (★ Ōsaka) 86,332
Shibata (▲ 77,219) 62,800
Shibukawa 47,814
Shijōnawate (★ Ōsaka) 50,352
Shiki (★ Tōkyō) 58,935
Shimabara (▲ 46,061) 39,500
Shimada (▲ 72,388) 63,200
Shimizu (★★ Shizuoka) 242,166
Shimminato (★ Takaoka) 41,707
Shimodate (▲ 63,958) 52,400
Shimonoseki
(★★ Kitakyūshū) 269,169
Shingū 38,231
Shinjō (▲ 43,033) 33,500
Shinnayō 33,895
Shiogama (★ Sendai) 61,825
Shiojiri (▲ 55,960) 44,500
Shiraoka (▲ 44,678) 39,100
Shiroishi (▲ 42,262) 34,300
Shizuoka (★ 975,000) 468,362
Sōja (▲ 51,240) 43,500
Sōka (★ Tōkyō) 194,205
Suita (★ Ōsaka) 348,948
Sukagawa (▲ 58,786) 44,100
Sukumo (▲ 26,255) 21,500
Sumoto (▲ 44,563) 38,500
Susono (★ Numazu) 45,149
Suwa 52,329
Suzaka (▲ 53,611) 44,500
Suzuka 164,936
Tachikawa (★ Tōkyō) 146,523
Tagajō (★ Sendai) 54,436
Tagawa 59,727
Tajimi (★ Nagoya) 84,829
Takahama 31,270
Takaishi (★ Ōsaka) 66,974
Takamatsu 326,999
Takaoka (★ 220,000) 175,780
Takarazuka (★ Ōsaka) 194,273
Takasago (★ Ōsaka) 91,434
Takasaki 231,766
Takatsuki (★ Ōsaka) 348,784
Takayama 65,033
Takefu 69,148
Takehara (▲ 36,286) 32,000
Takikawa 52,004
Tama (★ Tōkyō) 122,135
Tamana (▲ 46,115) 35,900
Tamano 76,954
Tanabe (▲ 70,835) 59,800
Tanashi (★ Tōkyō) 71,331
Tatebayashi 75,141
Tateyama (▲ 56,035) 47,100
Tatsuno (★ Himeji) 41,157
Tendō (▲ 55,123) 42,800
Tenri 69,129
Tenryū (▲ 25,008) 21,900
Toba 28,363
Tochigi 86,290
Toda (★ Tōkyō) 76,960
Tōkai (★ Nagoya) 95,278
Tōkamachi (▲ 48,005) 39,700
Toki 65,308
Tokoname (★ Nagoya) 53,077
Tokorozawa (★ Tōkyō) 275,168
Tokushima 257,884
Tokuyama (★ 250,000) 112,638
• TŌKYŌ (★ 27,700,000) 8,354,615
Tomakomai 158,061
Tomioka (▲ 48,551) 37,400
Tondabayashi (★ Ōsaka) 102,619
Toride (★ Tōkyō) 78,608
Tosa-shimizu (▲ 23,014) 20,600
Tosu 55,791
Tottori 137,060
Towada (▲ 61,295) 46,000
Toyama 314,111
Toyoake (★ Nagoya) 57,969
Toyohashi 322,142
Toyokawa 107,430
Toyonaka (★ Ōsaka) 413,213
Toyooka 47,712
Toyosaka (▲ 44,534) 35,100
Toyota 308,111
Tsu 150,690
Tsubame 44,651
Tsuchiura 120,175
Tsuru 33,158
Tsuruga 65,670
Tsuruoka 100,200
Tsushima (★ Nagoya) 58,735
Tsuyama 86,837
Ube (★ 230,000) 174,855
Ueda 116,178
Ueno (▲ 60,812) 51,800
Uji (★ Ōsaka) 165,411
Uozu 49,825
Urasoe 81,611
Urawa (★ Tōkyō) 377,235
Urayasu (★ Tōkyō) 93,756
Usa (▲ 52,217) 39,500
Ushiku 51,926
Usuki (▲ 39,719) 34,200
Utsunomiya 405,375
Uwajima 71,381
Wakayama (★ 495,000) 401,352
Wakkanai 51,854
Wakō (★ Tōkyō) 55,212
Warabi (★ Tōkyō) 70,408
Yachiyo (★ Tōkyō) 142,184
Yaizu (★ Shizuoka) 108,558
Yamagata 245,158
Yamaguchi 124,213
Yamato (★ Tōkyō) 177,669
Yamato-kōriyama
(★ Ōsaka) 89,624
Yamato-takada
(★ Ōsaka) 65,223
Yame (▲ 40,286) 33,000
Yanagawa (▲ 44,942) 38,000
Yanai (▲ 37,414) 30,800
Yao (★ Ōsaka) 276,394
Yashio (★ Tōkyō) 67,635
Yatsushiro (▲ 108,790) 88,700
Yawata (★ Ōsaka) 72,356
Yawatahama (▲ 41,600) 33,000
Yōkaichi 39,744
Yokkaichi 263,001
Yokohama (★★ Tōkyō) 2,992,926
Yokosuka (★ Tōkyō) 427,116
Yokote (▲ 43,266) 34,800
Yonago 131,792
Yonezawa 93,721
Yono (★ Tōkyō) 71,597
Yotsukaidō (★ Tōkyō) 67,008
Yūbari 31,665
Yūki (▲ 52,283) 40,200
Yukuhashi 65,527
Yuzawa (▲ 37,079) 28,000
Zama (★ Tōkyō) 100,000
Zentsūji 33,900
Zushi (★ Tōkyō) 57,656

Prefectures

Aichi 6,455,172
Akita 1,254,032
Aomori 1,524,448
Chiba 5,148,163
Ehime 1,529,983
Fukui 817,633
Fukuoka 4,719,259
Fukushima 2,080,304
Gifu 2,028,536
Gumma 1,921,259
Hiroshima 2,819,200
Hokkaidō 5,679,439
Hyōgo 5,278,050
Ibaraki 2,725,005
Ishikawa 1,152,325
Iwate 1,433,611
Kagawa 1,022,569
Kagoshima 1,819,270
Kanagawa 7,431,974
Kōchi 839,784
Kumamoto 1,837,747
Kyōto 2,586,574
Mie 1,747,311
Miyagi 2,176,295
Miyazaki 1,175,543
Nagano 2,136,927
Nagasaki 1,593,968
Nara 1,304,866
Niigata 2,478,470
Ōita 1,250,214
Okayama 1,916,906
Okinawa 1,179,097
Ōsaka 8,668,095
Saga 880,013
Saitama 5,863,678
Shiga 1,155,844
Shimane 794,629
Shizuoka 3,574,692
Tochigi 1,866,066
Tokushima 834,889
Tōkyō 11,829,363
Tottori 616,024
Toyama 1,118,369
Wakayama 1,087,206
Yamagata 1,261,662
Yamaguchi 1,601,627
Yamanashi 832,832

JERSEY

1986 C 80,212

Cities and Towns

• SAINT HELIER
(★ 46,500) 27,083

JORDAN / Al Urdunn

1986 E 2,796,100

Cities and Towns

Al Buq'ah 57,860
Al Karak 15,700
Al Mafraq 27,980
• 'AMMĀN (★ 1,250,000) 833,500
Aqaba (Al 'Aqabah) 37,360
Ar Ramthā 35,470
Ar Ruṣayfah (★ 'Ammān) 65,560
As Salṭ 42,690
Az Zarqā' 285,000
Irbid 150,000
Ma'ān 14,720
Ma'dabā 36,150
Ṣuwayliḥ 31,340

KENYA

1989 E 24,506,000

Cities and Towns

Eldoret (1979 C) 50,503
Kakamega (1979 C) 32,025
Kisumu (1984 E) 167,100
Machakos (1983 E) 92,300
Meru (1979 C) 72,049
Mombasa (1985 E) 442,369
• NAIROBI 1,286,200
Nakuru (1984 E) 101,700
Nyeri (1979 C) 35,753
Thika (1979 C) 41,324

KIRIBATI

1985 C 63,883

Cities and Towns

BAIRIKI 2,086
• Bikenibeu 4,293

KOREA, NORTH / Chosŏn-minjujuŭi-inmin-konghwaguk

1981 E 18,317,000

Cities and Towns

Aoji-ri (1944 C) 39,616
Chŏngjin 490,000
Haeju (1983 E) 213,000
Hamhŭng (1970 E) 150,000
Hŭngnam (1976 E) 260,000
Kaesŏng 259,000
Kanggye (1967 E) 130,000
Kilchu (1944 C) 30,026
Kimchaek (Sŏngjin)
(1967 E) 265,000
Najin (1944 C) 34,338
Nampo (Chinnampo) 241,000
Ongjin (1949 C) 32,965
Pukchŏng (1944 C) 30,709
• PYŎNGYANG
(★ 1,600,000) 1,283,000
Sariwŏn (1944 C) 42,957
Sinŭiju 305,000
Songnim (1944 C) 53,035
Tanchŏn (1944 C) 32,761
Wŏnsan 398,000

Provinces

1982 ESTIMATE

Chagang-do (Jagang) 1,020,000
Chŏngjin 720,000
Hamgyŏng-namdo (South
Hamgyeong) 2,400,000
Hamgyŏng-pukto (North
Hamgyeong) 1,110,000
Hwanghae-namdo (South
Hwanghae) 1,770,000
Hwanghae-pukto (North
Hwanghae) 1,350,000
Kaesŏng (Gaeseong)
(City) 330,000
Kangwŏn-do (Gangweon) 1,350,000
Nampo 660,000
P'yŏngan-namdo (South
Pyeongan) 2,490,000
P'yŏngan-pukto (North
Pyeongan) 2,160,000
P'yŏngyang (Pyeongyang) 2,520,000
Yanggang-do 570,000

KOREA, SOUTH / Taehan-min'guk

1985 C 40,448,486

Cities and Towns

Andong 114,216
Anyang (★ Seoul) 361,577
Changwŏn (★ Masan) 173,508
Chechŏn 102,274
Cheju 202,911
Chinhae 121,341
Chinju 227,309
Chŏnan 170,196
Chŏngju 79,323
Chŏngju, Ch'ungch'ŏng
Pukto prov. 350,256
Chŏnju 426,473
Chunchŏn 162,988
Chungju 113,331
Chungmu 87,459
Inchŏn (★★ Seoul)
(1989 E) 1,604,000
Iri 192,269
Kangnŭng 132,897
Kimchŏn 77,254
Kimhae 77,903
Kumi 142,094
Kŭmsŏng 58,897
Kunsan 185,649
Kwangju (1989 E) 1,165,000
Kwangmyŏng (★ Seoul) 219,611
Kyŏngju 127,544
Masan (★ 625,000) 448,746
Mokpo 236,085
Namwŏn 61,447
Pohang 260,691
Puchŏn (★ Seoul) 456,292
Pusan (★ 3,800,000)
(1989 E) 3,754,000
Pyŏngtaek (▲ 180,513) 63,400
Samchŏnpo 62,466
Sangju (▲ 180,575) 28,300
Seongnam (★ Seoul) 447,692
• SEOUL (SŎUL)
(★ 15,850,000)
(1989 E) 10,513,000
Sŏgwipo 82,311
Sŏkcho 69,501
Songjŏng (▲ 136,612) 35,300
Songtan 66,357
Sunchŏn (▲ 116,323) 121,958

C Census. E Official estimate. UE Unofficial estimate.
• Largest city in country.

★ Population or designation of metropolitan area, including suburbs (see headnote).
▲ Population of an entire municipality, commune, or district, including rural area.

Suwŏn (★ Seoul) ... 430,752
Taebaek ... 113,997
Taegu (1989 C) ... 2,206,000
Taejŏn ... 866,148
Tongduchŏn ... 68,633
Tonghae ... 91,691
Ŭijŏngbu (★ Seoul) ... 162,700
Ulsan ... 551,014
Wŏnju ... 151,165
Yŏngchŏn ... 52,811
Yŏngju ... 84,742
Yŏsu ... 171,933

Provinces

1989 ESTIMATE

Cheju Do (Jeju) ... 505,000
Chŏlla Namdo (South Jeonia) ... 2,540,000
Chŏlla Pukto (North Jeonia) ... 2,118,000
Ch'ungch'ŏng Namdo (South Chungcheong) ... 3,008,000
Ch'ungch'ŏng Pukto (North Chungcheong) ... 1,356,000
Inchŏn (City) ... 1,604,000
Kangwŏn Do (Gangweon) ... 1,663,000
Kwangju ... 1,165,000
Kyŏnggi Do (Gyeonggi) ... 5,466,000
Kyŏngsang Namdo (South Gyeongsang) ... 3,636,000
Kyŏngsang Pukto (North Gyeongsang) ... 2,846,000
Pusan (Busan) (City) ... 3,754,000
Sŏul (Seoul) (City) ... 10,513,000
Taegu (City) ... 2,206,000

KUWAIT / Al Kuwayt

1985 C ... 1,697,301

Cities and Towns

Abraq Khīṭān (★ Kuwait) ... 45,120
Aḥmadī (★ 285,000) ... 26,899
Al Farwānīyah (★ Kuwait) ... 68,701
Al Fuḥayḥīl (★ Aḥmadī) ... 50,081
Al Jahrah (★ Kuwait) ... 111,222
Ar Rumaythīyah (★ Kuwait) ... 39,058
As Sālimīyah (★ Kuwait) ... 153,359
Aṣ Ṣulaybīyah (★ Kuwait) ... 51,314
Ḥawallī (★ Kuwait) ... 145,126
Jaleeb al Shuyūkh (★ Kuwait) ... 114,771
• KUWAIT (AL KUWAYT) (★ 1,375,000) ... 44,335
Salwa and Messellah (★ Kuwait) ... 24,948
South Khīṭān (★ Kuwait) ... 69,256
Subahiya (★ Aḥmadī) ... 60,787
Umm al Himan (★ Aḥmadī) ... 31,588

LAOS / Lao

1985 C ... 3,584,803

Cities and Towns

Louangphrabang (1975 E) ... 46,000
Pakxe (1975 E) ... 47,000
Savannakhet (1975 E) ... 53,000
• VIENTIANE (VIANGCHAN) ... 377,409

LEBANON / Al Lubnān

1982 E ... 2,637,000

Cities and Towns

Ba'labakk ... 24,000
• BEIRUT (BAYRŪT) (★ 1,675,000) ... 509,000
Jūniyah ... 29,000
Ṣaydā (Sidon) ... 105,000
Tripoli (Ṭarābulus) ... 198,000
Tyre (Ṣūr) (1970 E) ... 12,500
Zaḥlah ... 45,000

LESOTHO

1986 C ... 1,577,536

Cities and Towns

• MASERU ... 109,382

LIBERIA

1986 E ... 2,221,000

Cities and Towns

Buchanan (1981 E) ... 30,000
• MONROVIA ... 465,000

LIBYA / Lībiya

1984 C ... 3,637,488

Cities and Towns

Benghazi (Banghāzī) ... 435,886
Darnah ... 62,179
Misrātah ... 131,031
• TRIPOLI (ṬARĀBULUS) ... 990,697
Ṭubruq (Tobruk) ... 75,282
Zāwiyat al Bayḍā' (Beida) ... 67,120

LIECHTENSTEIN

1989 E ... 28,181

Cities and Towns

• VADUZ ... 4,919

LUXEMBOURG

1985 E ... 366,000

Cities and Towns

Differdange (1981 C) ... 8,588
Dudelange (1981 C) ... 14,074
Esch-sur-Alzette (★ 83,000) (1981 C) ... 25,142
• LUXEMBOURG (★ 133,000) ... 76,130

MACAO / Macau

1987 E ... 429,000

Cities and Towns

• MACAO ... 429,000

MADAGASCAR / Madagasikara

1984 E ... 9,731,000

Cities and Towns

• ANTANANARIVO (1985 E) ... 663,000
Antsirabe (▲ 95,000) ... 50,100
Antsiranana ... 100,000
Fianarantsoa ... 130,000
Mahajanga ... 85,000
Manakara (1975 C) ... 20,037
Marovoay (1975 C) ... 16,303
Toamasina ... 100,000
Toliara ... 55,000

MALAWI / Malaŵi

1987 C ... 7,982,607

Cities and Towns

• Blantyre ... 331,588
LILONGWE ... 233,973
Mzuzu ... 44,238
Zomba ... 42,878

MALAYSIA

1980 C ... 13,136,109

Cities and Towns

Alor Setar ... 69,435
Ayer Itam (★ George Town) ... 35,550
Batu Pahat ... 64,727
Bukit Mertajam ... 28,675
Butterworth (★★ George Town) ... 77,982
George Town (Pinang) (★ 495,000) ... 248,241
Ipoh ... 293,849
Johor Baharu (★ Singapore) ... 246,395
Kajang ... 29,301
Kampar ... 24,626
Kelang ... 192,080
Keluang ... 50,315
Kota Baharu ... 167,872
Kota Kinabalu (Jesselton) ... 55,997
• KUALA LUMPUR (★ 1,475,000) ... 919,610
Kuala Terengganu ... 180,296
Kuantan ... 131,547
Kuching ... 72,555
Kulim ... 26,817
Melaka (Malacca) ... 87,494
Miri ... 52,125
Muar (Bandar Maharani) ... 65,151
Petaling Jaya (★ Kuala Lumpur) ... 207,805
Port Dickson ... 24,389
Sandakan ... 70,420
Segamat ... 34,008
Seremban ... 132,911
Sibu ... 85,231
Sungai Petani ... 45,343
Taiping ... 146,000
Tawau ... 43,200
Telok Anson (Teluk Intan) ... 49,148

States

Johor ... 1,580,423
Kedah ... 1,077,815
Kelantan ... 859,270
Melaka ... 446,769
Negeri Sembilan ... 551,442
Pahang ... 768,801
Perak ... 1,743,655
Perlis ... 144,782
Pinang ... 900,772
Sabah (North Borneo) ... 955,712
Sarawak ... 1,235,553
Selangor ... 1,426,250
Terengganu ... 525,255
Wilayah Persekutuan (Federal Territory) ... 919,610

MALDIVES

1985 C ... 181,453

Cities and Towns

• MALE ... 46,334

MALI

1987 C ... 7,620,225

Cities and Towns

• BAMAKO ... 646,163
Djénné (1976 C) ... 10,275
Gao ... 54,874
Goundam (1976 C) ... 10,468
Kati ... 34,092
Kayes ... 48,216
Kita ... 22,629
Koulikoro ... 20,354
Koutiala ... 48,010
Mopti ... 73,979
Nioro du Sahel ... 17,197
San ... 30,688
Ségou ... 88,877
Sikasso ... 73,050
Tombouctou (Timbuktu) ... 31,925

MALTA

1987 E ... 343,334

Cities and Towns

Birkirkara (★ Valletta) ... 20,300
Ħamrun (★ Valletta) ... 13,651
Qormi (★ Valletta) ... 18,413
Rabat (Victoria), Gozo I. ... 5,922
Sliema (★ Valletta) ... 13,650
• VALLETTA (★ 215,000) ... 9,263

MARTINIQUE

1982 C ... 328,566

Cities and Towns

• FORT-DE-FRANCE (★ 116,017) ... 99,844
Le Lamentin (▲ 26,367) ... 7,207
Saint-Pierre ... 5,438
Schœlcher (★ Fort-de-France) ... 18,094

MAURITANIA / Mauritanie / Mūrītāniyā

1987 E ... 2,007,000

Cities and Towns

Aleg (1962 C) ... 1,360
Atar (1986 E) ... 19,000
'Ayoûn el'Atroûs (1962 C) ... 4,877
Fdérik (1976 C) ... 18,000
Kaédi (1986 E) ... 20,000
Kiffa (1976 C) ... 10,700
Néma (1962 C) ... 3,893
Nouadhibou (1986 E) ... 24,400
• NOUAKCHOTT ... 285,000
Rosso (1986 E) ... 18,500
Zouîrât (1986 E) ... 22,000

MAURITIUS

1987 E ... 1,008,864

Cities and Towns

Beau Bassin-Rose Hill (★ Port Louis) ... 93,125
Curepipe (★ Port Louis) ... 64,243
• PORT LOUIS (★ 420,000) ... 139,730
Quatre Bornes (★ Port Louis) ... 65,480
Vacoas-Phoenix (★ Port Louis) ... 55,667

MAYOTTE

1985 E ... 67,205

Cities and Towns

• DZAOUDZI (★ 6,979) ... 5,865

MEXICO / México

1980 C ... 67,395,826

Cities and Towns

Acámbaro ... 38,224
Acaponeta ... 15,272
Acapulco [de Juárez] ... 301,902
Acayucan ... 32,398
Actopan ... 16,215
Agua Dulce ... 27,242
Agua Prieta ... 28,862
Aguascalientes ... 293,152
Alvarado ... 22,633
Ameca ... 25,946
Amecameca [de Juárez] ... 23,508
Apatzingán ... 55,522
Apizaco ... 30,498
Arandas ... 19,835
Arriaga ... 17,848
Atlixco ... 53,207
Atotonilco el Alto ... 21,276
Autlán de Navarro ... 27,926
Caborca ... 33,696
Cadereyta Jiménez ... 26,539
Campeche ... 128,434
Cananea ... 19,551
Cancún ... 33,273
Cárdenas, Michoacán state ... 26,217
Cárdenas, Tabasco state ... 34,078
Celaya ... 141,675
Cerro Azul ... 29,082
Chetumal ... 56,709
Chihuahua ... 385,603
Chilpancingo [de los Bravos] ... 67,498
Cholula [de Rivadabia] (★ Puebla de Zaragoza) ... 26,748
Ciudad Acuña ... 38,898
Ciudad Camargo ... 29,433
Ciudad del Carmen ... 72,489
Ciudad de Naucalpan de Juárez (★ Mexico City) ... 723,723
Ciudad de Valles ... 65,609
Ciudad Guzmán ... 60,938
Ciudad Hidalgo ... 32,311
Ciudad Ixtepec ... 13,302
Ciudad Jiménez ... 23,786
Ciudad Juárez (★★ El Paso, Tex., U.S.A.) ... 544,496
Ciudad Lerdo (★ Torreón) ... 33,470
Ciudad Madero (★ Tampico) ... 132,444
Ciudad Mante ... 70,647
Ciudad Melchor Múzquiz ... 22,115
Ciudad Mendoza (★ Orizaba) ... 25,330
Ciudad Obregón ... 165,572
Ciudad Serdán ... 12,824
Ciudad Victoria ... 140,161
Coatepec ... 28,499
Coatzacoalcos ... 127,170
Colima ... 86,044
Comalcalco ... 25,021
Comitán [de Domínguez] ... 27,374
Córdoba ... 99,972
Cortazar ... 35,330
Cosamaloapan [de Carpio] ... 29,457
Cuauhtémoc ... 43,546
Cuautla ... 24,153
Cuernavaca ... 192,770
Culiacán ... 304,826
Delicias ... 65,504
Dolores Hidalgo ... 23,143
Durango ... 257,915
Ecatepec de Morelos (★ Mexico City) ... 741,821
El Grullo ... 16,595
Empalme ... 31,555
Encarnación de Díaz ... 14,795
Ensenada ... 120,483
Escuinapa [de Hidalgo] ... 20,247
Etzatlán ... 10,309
Fortín de las Flores ... 14,046
Fresnillo [de González Echeverría] ... 56,066
Garza García (★ Monterrey) ... 81,974
Gómez Palacio (★★ Torreón) ... 116,967
Guadalajara (★ 2,325,000) ... 1,626,152
Guadalupe (★ Monterrey) ... 370,524
Guadalupe ... 25,395
Guamúchil ... 36,308
Guanajuato ... 48,981
Guasave (1970 C) ... 26,080
Guaymas ... 54,826
Hermosillo ... 297,175
Heroica Nogales ... 65,603
Hidalgo del Parral ... 75,590
Huajuapan de León ... 16,743
Huamantla ... 21,944
Huatabampo ... 22,635
Huauchinango ... 25,776
Huixtla ... 21,578
Iguala ... 66,005
Irapuato ... 170,138
Izúcar de Matamoros ... 27,714
Jacona de Plancarte ... 29,955
Jalapa Enríquez ... 204,594
Jalostotitlán ... 13,031
Jerez de García Salinas ... 28,629
Jiquilpan de Juárez ... 22,149
Jojutla ... 21,243
Juchitán [de Zaragoza] ... 38,801
La Barca ... 20,889
Lagos de Moreno ... 44,223
La Paz ... 91,453
La Piedad [Cavadas] ... 47,441
Las Choapas ... 35,807
León [de los Aldamas] ... 593,002
Linares ... 33,012
Loma Bonita ... 24,344
Los Mochis ... 122,531
Los Reyes [de Salgado] ... 23,633
Magdalena ... 13,618
Manzanillo ... 39,088
Martínez de la Torre ... 25,837
Matamoros (★★ Brownsville, Tex., U.S.A.) ... 188,745
Matamoros [de la Laguna] (★ Torreón) ... 28,175
Matehuala ... 41,550
Matías Romero ... 15,092
Mazatlán ... 199,830
Meoqui ... 14,859
Mérida ... 400,142
Mexicali (★ 365,000) ... 341,559
• MEXICO CITY (CIUDAD DE MÉXICO) (★ 14,100,000) ... 8,831,079
Minatitlán ... 106,765
Mineral del Monte ... 8,605
Monclova ... 115,786
Montemorelos ... 28,342
Monterrey (★ 2,015,000) ... 1,090,009
Morelia ... 297,544
Moroleón ... 37,500
Motul [de Felipe Carrillo Puerto] ... 15,919
Múgica ... 21,239
Navojoa ... 62,901
Netzahualcóyotl (★ Mexico City) ... 1,341,230
Nogales (★ Orizaba) ... 22,499
Nueva Casas Grandes ... 28,514
Nueva Rosita ... 33,121
Nuevo Laredo (★★ Laredo, Tex., U.S.A.) ... 201,731
Oaxaca [de Juárez] ... 154,223
Ocotlán ... 48,931
Ojinaga ... 18,162
Orizaba (★ 215,000) ... 114,848
Pachuca [de Soto] ... 110,351
Pánuco ... 26,652
Papantla [de Olarte] ... 43,935
Parras de la Fuente ... 23,453
Pátzcuaro ... 32,902
Pénjamo ... 17,307
Piedras Negras ... 67,455
Poza Rica de Hidalgo ... 166,799
Progreso ... 24,257
Puebla [de Zaragoza] (★ 1,055,000) ... 835,759
Puerto Vallarta ... 38,645
Puruándiro ... 17,535
Querétaro ... 215,976
Reynosa ... 194,693
Río Bravo ... 55,236
Ríoverde ... 30,267
Romita ... 14,492
Rosario ... 12,171
Sabinas ... 27,413
Sabinas Hidalgo ... 23,187
Sahuayo [de Díaz] ... 43,258
Salamanca ... 96,703
Salina Cruz ... 40,010
Saltillo ... 284,937
Salvatierra ... 28,878
San Andrés Tuxtla ... 40,412
San Cristóbal de las Casas ... 42,026
San Francisco del Oro ... 10,813
San Francisco del Rincón ... 40,943
San Juan de los Lagos ... 26,204
San Juan del Río ... 27,204
San Juan Teotihuacán (★ Mexico City) ... 6,815
San Luis de la Paz ... 19,306
San Luis Potosí (★ 470,000) ... 362,371
San Luis Río Colorado ... 76,684
San Martín Texmelucan ... 36,712
San Miguel de Allende ... 30,003
San Miguel el Alto ... 13,949
San Nicolás de los Garzas (★ Monterrey) ... 280,696
San Pedro de las Colonias ... 35,879
Santa Ana Chiautempan ... 13,204
Santa Bárbara ... 14,894
Santa Catarina (★ Monterrey) ... 87,673
Santa Cruz de Juventino Rosas ... 20,436
Santa Inés Zacatelco (★ Puebla de Zaragoza) ... 19,421
Santa Rosalía ... 8,221
Santiago Ixcuintla ... 17,516
Sayula ... 17,809

C Census. E Official estimate. UE Unofficial estimate.
• Largest city in country.

★ Population or designation of metropolitan area, including suburbs (see headnote).
▲ Population of an entire municipality, commune, or district, including rural area.

Silao 32,248
Soledad Díez Gutiérrez (★ San Luis Potosí) 49,173
Sombrerete 13,562
Tala 19,680
Tamazula de Gordiano 14,080
Tamazunchale 12,863
Tampico (★ 435,000) 267,957
Tangancícuaro [de Arista] 14,433
Tantoyuca 19,552
Tapachula 85,766
Taxco de Alarcón 36,315
Tecate 23,909
Tecomán 46,371
Tecuala 14,755
Tehuacán 79,547
Tehuantepec 22,019
Teocaltiche 16,559
Tepatitlán [de Morelos] 41,813
Tepic 145,741
Tequila 15,514
Texcoco [de Mora] (★ Mexico City) 30,593
Teziutlán 25,119
Ticul 18,255
Tierra Blanca 31,653
Tijuana (★★ San Diego, Calif., U.S.A.) 429,500
Tizimín 26,305
Tlalnepantla [de Comonfort] (★ Mexico City) 778,173
Tlapacoyan 14,000
Tlaquepaque (★ Guadalajara) 133,500
Tlaxcala [de Xicohténcatl] 14,437
Toluca [de Lerdo] 199,778
Tonalá 19,013
Torreón (★ 575,000) 328,086
Tula de Allende 18,744
Tulancingo 53,400
Tuxpan 24,476
Tuxpan de Rodríguez Cano 56,037
Tuxtepec 29,060
Tuxtla Gutiérrez 131,096
Umán 10,273
Unión de Tula 7,670
Uriangato 19,845
Uruapan [del Progreso] 122,828
Valladolid 28,201
Valle de Santiago 37,645
Valle Hermoso 27,966
Venustiano Carranza 8,546
Veracruz [Llave] (★ 385,000) 284,822
Vicente Guerrero (★ Orizaba) (1970 C) 11,688
Vicente Guerrero (★ Puebla de Zaragoza) 27,589
Villa Flores 20,313
Villa Frontera 32,568
Villahermosa 158,216
Xicotepec de Juárez 18,473
Yautepec 17,899
Yurécuaro 16,123
Yuriria 14,960
Zaachila 8,474
Zacapu 39,570
Zacatecas 80,088
Zacatepec 18,042
Zacoalco [de Torres] 13,105
Zamora de Hidalgo 86,998
Zapopan (★ Guadalajara) 345,390
Zapotiltic 14,552
Zihuatanejo (1970 C) 4,879
Zitácuaro 47,520
Zumpango 19,389

States

Aguascalientes 519,439
Baja California Norte 1,177,886
Baja California Sur 215,139
Campeche 420,553
Chiapas 2,084,717
Chihuahua 2,005,477
Coahuila 1,557,265
Colima 346,293
Distrito Federal (Federal District) 8,831,079
Durango 1,182,320
Guanajuato 3,006,110
Guerrero 2,109,513
Hidalgo 1,547,493
Jalisco 4,371,998
México 7,564,335
Michoacán 2,868,824
Morelos 947,089
Nayarit 726,120
Nuevo León 2,513,044
Oaxaca 2,369,076
Puebla 3,347,685
Querétaro 739,605
Quintana Roo 225,985
San Luis Potosí 1,673,893
Sinaloa 1,849,879
Sonora 1,513,731
Tabasco 1,062,961
Tamaulipas 1,924,484
Tlaxcala 556,597
Veracruz 5,387,680
Yucatán 1,063,733
Zacatecas 1,136,830

MONACO

1982 C 27,063

Cities and Towns

• MONACO (★ 87,000) 27,063

MONGOLIA / Mongol Ard Uls

1987 E 1,966,000

Cities and Towns

Choybalsan (1979 C) 29,800
Darhan (1985 E) 69,800
Erdene (1985 E) 42,900
• ULAN BATOR (ULAANBAATAR) 511,100

MONTSERRAT

1980 C 11,606

Cities and Towns

• PLYMOUTH 1,568

MOROCCO / Al Maghrib

1982 C 20,419,555

Cities and Towns

Agadir 110,479
Al Hoceima 41,662
Beni Mellal 95,003
Berkane 60,490
Berrechid (★ Casablanca) 29,738
• Casablanca (Dar el Beida) (★ 2,475,000) 2,139,204
Dcheïra 39,760
El Jadida (Mazagan) 81,455
El Kelaa des Srarhna 33,353
Essaouira (Mogador) 42,035
Fès (Fez) (★ 535,000) 448,823
Fkih Ben Salah 47,540
Jerada 43,016
Kenitra 188,194
Khemisset 58,925
Khenifra 38,840
Khouribga 127,181
Ksar el Kebir 73,541
Ksar es Souk 27,040
Larache 63,893
Marrakech (★ 535,000) 439,728
Meknès (★ 375,000) 319,783
Mohammedia (Fedala) (★ Casablanca) 105,120
Nador 62,040
Ouarzazate 17,227
Oued Zem 58,744
Ouezzane 40,485
Oujda 260,082
RABAT (★ 980,000) 518,616
Safi 197,309
Salé (★★ Rabat) 289,391
Sefrou 38,833
Settat 65,203
Sidi Ifni 16,188
Sidi Kacem 55,833
Sidi Slimane 50,457
Tangier (Tanger) (★ 370,000) 266,346
Tan-Tan 41,451
Taourirt 32,667
Taroudant 35,848
Taza 77,216
Temera (★ Rabat) 48,644
Tétouan 199,615
Youssoufia 42,195

MOZAMBIQUE / Moçambique

1980 C 12,130,000

Cities and Towns

Beira 230,744
Chimoio (Vila Pery) 74,372
Inhambane 54,990
Lichinga 39,487
• MAPUTO (LOURENÇO MARQUES) (1987 E) 1,006,765
Nacala 80,426
Nampula (1986 E) 183,000
Pemba 42,962
Quelimane 62,174
Tete 48,064
Xai-Xai (João Belo) 44,164

NAMIBIA

1981 C 1,033,196

Cities and Towns

Gobabis 5,528
Keetmanshoop 11,502
Lüderitz 4,748
Mariental 5,367
Otjiwarongo 9,087
Rehoboth 12,378
Swakopmund 12,219
Tsumeb 11,269
• WINDHOEK (1984 E) 120,000

NAURU / Naoero

1987 E 8,000

NEPAL / Nepāl

1981 C 15,022,839

Cities and Towns

Bhaktapur 48,472
Bīrganj 43,642
Dharān Bāzār 42,146
• KATHMANDU (KĀTHMĀNḌAU) (★ 320,000) 235,160
Mahendranagar 43,834
Nepālganj 34,015
Pokharā 46,642
Wirātnagar 93,544

NETHERLANDS / Nederland

1986 E 14,529,430

Cities and Towns

Aalsmeer 21,293
Alkmaar (★ 121,000) 86,509
Almelo 62,421
Alphen aan den Rijn 55,812
Amersfoort (★ 130,158) 89,596
Amstelveen (★ Amsterdam) 68,090
• AMSTERDAM (★ 1,860,000) 679,140
Apeldoorn 145,773
Arnhem (★ 294,085) 127,968
Assen 47,462
Bergen op Zoom 46,103
Beverwijk (★ Amsterdam) 34,889
Breda (★ 154,565) 119,174
Brunssum (★ Heerlen) 29,726
Bussum (★ Amsterdam) 32,706
Capelle aan den IJssel (▲ 54,862) 41,100
Castricum (★ Amsterdam) 22,815
De Bilt (★ Utrecht) 31,470
Delft (★★ The Hague) 87,440
Delfzijl 24,320
Den Helder 63,231
Deventer 64,806
Doetinchem (▲ 40,406) 30,400
Dordrecht (★ 200,396) 106,968
Drachten (Smallingerland) (▲ 50,635) 40,400
Edam [-Volendam] (★ Amsterdam) 24,158
Ede (▲ 88,866) 46,700
Eindhoven (★ 376,185) 190,839
Emmen (▲ 91,775) 36,400
Enschede (★ 288,000) 144,048
Etten-Leur (▲ 31,465) 26,900
Geldrop (★ Eindhoven) 26,051
Geleen (★ 177,243) 34,292
Goes 31,422
Gorinchem 28,003
Gouda 60,927
Groningen (★ 207,060) 168,006
Haarlem (★ Amsterdam) 149,776
Haarlemmermeer (★ Amsterdam) (1984 E) 11,400
Harderwijk 33,195
Harlingen 16,320
Heemstede (★ Amsterdam) 26,106
Heerenveen (▲ 37,304) 20,700
Heerlen (★ 266,617) 93,871
Helmond 63,043
Hengelo (★★ Enschede) 76,694
Hilversum (★ Amsterdam) 86,125
Hoogeveen (▲ 45,233) 34,200
Hoorn 52,720
IJmuiden (Velsen) (★ Amsterdam) 57,157
Kampen 32,230
Katwijk aan Zee 38,882
Kerkrade (★ Heerlen) 52,885
Leeuwarden 84,966
Leiden (★ 178,731) 105,262
Lelystad (▲ 57,952) 15,100
Maassluis (★ Rotterdam) 32,770
Maastricht (★ 158,915) 114,579
Meppel 22,923
Middelburg 39,105
Nieuwegein (★ Utrecht) 55,644
Nijmegen (★ 238,187) 147,182
Oldenzaal 29,128
Oss 50,343
Papendrecht (★ Dordrecht) 26,492
Purmerend (★ Amsterdam) 50,664
Renkum (★ Arnhem) 12,500
Ridderkerk (★ Rotterdam) 46,419
Rijswijk (★ The Hague) 48,886
Roermond 38,307
Roosendaal 57,385
Rotterdam (★ 1,110,000) 571,372
Schiedam (★ Rotterdam) 69,078
's-Hertogenbosch (★ 189,067) 89,039
Sittard (★★ Geleen) 44,037
Sliedrecht 22,696
Sneek 29,504
Soest (★ Amersfoort) 40,562
Spijkenisse (★ Rotterdam) 60,221
Tegelen (★ Venlo) 18,565
Terneuzen (▲ 35,250) 22,200
THE HAGUE ('s-GRAVENHAGE) (★ 770,000) 443,961
Tiel 30,251
Tilburg (★ 223,043) 153,703
Utrecht (★ 511,195) 229,933
Veendam 28,323
Veenendaal 44,866
Veldhoven (★ Eindhoven) 36,492
Venlo (★ 87,000) 63,475
Vlaardingen (★ Rotterdam) 75,536
Vlissingen (Flushing) (▲ 45,339) 26,000
Voorburg (★ The Hague) 41,433
Vught (★ 's-Hertogenbosch) 23,347
Waalwijk 28,581
Wageningen 32,358
Wassenaar (★ The Hague) 26,513
Weert (▲ 39,542) 28,700
Winschoten 20,286
Woerden 26,955
Zaandam (Zaanstad) (★ Amsterdam) 128,248
Zeist (★ Utrecht) 59,743
Zoetermeer (★ The Hague) 82,334
Zutphen 31,298
Zwijndrecht (★★ Dordrecht) 40,182
Zwolle 88,438

Provinces

Drenthe 431,997
Flevoland 177,334
Friesland 598,068
Gelderland 1,761,492
Groningen 560,029
Limburg 1,088,331
North Brabant (Noord-Brabant) 2,124,656
North Holland (Noord-Holland) 2,322,708
Overijssel 998,751
South Holland (Zuid-Holland) 3,164,652
Utrecht 944,372
Zeeland 355,781

NETHERLANDS ANTILLES / Nederlandse Antillen

1984 E 178,744

Cities and Towns

Kralendijk (1981 C) 1,270
• WILLEMSTAD (★ 130,000) (1981 C) 31,883

Political Divisions

Bonaire 10,001
Curacao 147,481
Saba 977
Sint Eustatius 1,638
Sint Maarten 18,647

NEW CALEDONIA / Nouvelle-Calédonie

1983 C 145,368

Cities and Towns

• NOUMÉA (★ 83,000) 60,112

NEW ZEALAND

1986 C 3,307,084

Cities and Towns

• Auckland (★ 850,000) 149,046
Birkenhead (★ Auckland) 22,582
Blenheim (★ 22,681) 18,308
Christchurch (★ 320,000) 168,200
Dunedin (★ 109,000) 76,964
East Coast Bays (★ Auckland) 31,325
Gisborne (★ 32,238) 30,020
Hamilton (★ 101,814) 94,511
Hastings (★★ Napier) 37,658
Invercargill (★ 52,807) 48,197
Kapiti (★ Wellington) 17,357
Levin (★ 18,962) 15,368
Lower Hutt (★ Wellington) 63,862
Manukau (★ Auckland) 177,248
Masterton (★ 20,145) 18,511
Mount Albert (★ Auckland) 27,579
Mount Eden (★ Auckland) 18,877
Mount Roskill (★ Auckland) 35,158
Mount Wellington (★ Auckland) 20,397
Napier (★ 107,060) 49,428
Nelson (★ 44,593) 34,274
New Plymouth (★ 47,384) 36,865
Palmerston North (★ 67,405) 60,503
Papakura (★ Auckland) 23,357
Papatoetoe (★ Auckland) 21,883
Porirua (★ Wellington) 43,213
Rotorua (★ 52,001) 40,597
Takapuna (★ Auckland) 69,419
Tauranga (★ 59,435) 41,611
Timaru (★ 28,621) 27,757
Tokoroa (★ 18,193) 17,628
Upper Hutt (★ Wellington) 31,130
Wainuiomata (★ Wellington) 18,810
Waitemata (★ Auckland) 96,365
Wanganui (★ 40,758) 38,084
WELLINGTON (★ 350,000) 137,495
Whangarei (★ 44,043) 40,179

NICARAGUA

1985 E 3,272,100

Cities and Towns

Bluefields (1981 E) 20,608
Chinandega 75,000
Granada (1981 E) 64,642
León 101,000
• MANAGUA 682,000
Masaya 75,000
Matagalpa 68,000
Rivas (1981 E) 18,360

NIGER

1988 C 7,250,383

Cities and Towns

Agadez 50,164
Arlit 31,993
Birni Nkonni 29,948
Dosso 27,092
Maradi 112,965
• NIAMEY 398,265
Tahoua 51,607
Zinder 120,892

NIGERIA

1987 E 101,907,000

Cities and Towns

Aba 239,800
Abakaliki 56,800
Abeokuta 341,300
Ado-Ekiti 287,000
Afikpo 65,790
Agege 83,810
Akure 129,600
Amaigbo 53,690
Apomu 49,570
Aramoko 48,280
Asaba 47,410
Awka 88,800
Azare 50,020
Bauchi 68,840
Benin City 183,200
Bida 100,200
Birnin Kebbi 48,250
Calabar 139,800
Deba 110,600
Dukku 52,880
Ede 245,200
Effon-Alaiye 122,300
Ejigbo 84,570
Emure-Ekiti 58,750
Enugu 252,500
Epe 80,560
Erin-Oshogbo 59,940
Eruwa 49,140
Fiditi 49,440
Garko 46,400
Gboko 49,390
Gbongan 53,990
Gombe 86,120
Gusau 126,200
Ibadan 1,144,000
Idah 50,550
Idanre 56,080
Ife 237,000
Ifon-Oshogbo 65,980
Igbasa-Odo 48,040
Igboho 85,230
Igbo-Ora 68,060
Igede-Ekiti 56,570
Ihiala 73,240
Ijebu Igbo 78,680
Ijebu Ode 124,900
Ijero-Ekiti 76,420
Ikare 112,500
Ikerre 195,400
Ikire 94,450
Ikirun 144,900
Ikole 71,860
Ikorodu 147,700
Ikot Ekpene 69,440
Ila 210,800
Ilawe-Ekiti 147,300
Ilesha 302,100
Ilobu 159,000
Ilorin 380,000
Inisa 95,630
Ipetu-Ekiti 53,220
Ise-Ekiti 82,580
Iseyin 173,500
Iwo 289,100

C Census. E Official estimate. UE Unofficial estimate.
• Largest city in country.

★ Population or designation of metropolitan area, including suburbs (see headnote).
▲ Population of an entire municipality, commune, or district, including rural area.

Jega (1985 E) 47,000
Jimeta 66,130
Jos 164,700
Kaduna 273,200
Kano 538,300
Katsina 165,000
Kaura Namoda 52,910
Keffi 57,790
Kishi 77,210
Kumo 118,200
Lafia 97,810
Lafiagi 57,580
• LAGOS (★ 3,800,000) 1,213,000
Lalupon 56,130
Lere 49,670
Lokoja 45,550
Maiduguri 255,100
Makurdi 98,350
Minna 109,300
Mubi 51,190
Mushin (★ Lagos) 266,100
Nembe 45,600
Nguru 78,770
Nsukka 47,760
Ode-Ekiti 48,910
Offa 157,500
Ogbomosho 582,900
Oka 114,400
Oke-Mesi 55,040
Okwe 52,550
Olupona 65,720
Ondo 135,300
Onitsha 298,200
Opobo 64,620
Oron 62,260
Oshogbo 380,800
Owerri (1982 E) 52,670
Owo 146,600
Oyan 50,930
Oyo 204,700
Pindiga 64,130
Port Harcourt 327,300
Potiskum 56,490
Sapele 111,200
Shagamu 93,610
Shaki 139,000
Shomolu (★ Lagos) 120,700
Sokoto 163,700
Ugep 81,910
Umuahia 52,550
Uyo 60,500
Warri 100,700
Zaria 302,800

NIUE

1986 C 2,531

Cities and Towns

• ALOFI 811

NORWAY / Norge

1985 E 4,153,000

Cities and Towns

Ålesund 35,000
Arendal (★ 22,500) (1983 E) 11,743
Asker (★ Oslo) 37,800
Bærum (★ Oslo) 83,000
Bergen (★ 239,000) 207,374
Bodø 34,000
Drammen (★ 73,000) 50,700
Fredrikstad (★ 52,000) (1983 E) 27,618
Gjøvik (1983 E) 26,077
Halden (1983 E) 26,223
Hamar (★ 28,000) (1983 E) 15,837
Hammerfest (1983 E) 7,208
Harstad (1983 E) 21,765
Haugesund (★ 31,000) (1983 E) 27,043
Kongsberg (1983 E) 20,629
Kristiansand 62,200
Kristiansund (1983 E) 17,895
Larvik (★ 19,000) (1983 E) 8,226
Lillehammer (1983 E) 21,954
Molde (1983 E) 21,057
Moss (★ 30,000) (1983 E) 24,967
Narvik (1983 E) 19,080
• OSLO (★ 720,000) 447,304
Porsgrunn (★★ Skien) 31,400
Ringerike (1983 E) 26,839
Sandefjord 35,000
Sandnes (★ Stavanger) 39,700
Sarpsborg (★ 41,500) (1983 E) 12,143
Skien (★ 77,981) 46,700
Stavanger (★ 132,000) 94,200
Steinkjer (1983 E) 20,694
Tønsberg (★ 37,500) (1983 E) 8,921
Tromsø 47,800
Trondheim 134,019
Vadsø (1983 E) 5,995

Counties

1984 ESTIMATE

Akershus 386,400
Aust-Agder 94,200
Buskerud 219,300
Finnmark 76,700
Hedmark 187,000
Hordaland 397,500
Møre og Romsdal 237,400
Nordland 243,600
Nord-Trøndelag 126,900
Oppland 182,100
Oslo 447,304
Østfold 235,000
Rogaland 320,200
Sogn og Fjordane 106,200
Sør-Trøndelag 246,400
Telemark 162,300
Troms 147,100
Vest-Agder 139,800
Vestfold 190,500

OMAN / ʿUmān

1981 E 919,000

Cities and Towns

• MASQAṬ (MUSCAT) 50,000
Maṭraḥ (1971 E) 14,000
Nazwá (1980 E) 25,000
Ṣuḥār (1980 E) 20,000
Ṣūr (1980 E) 30,000

PACIFIC ISLANDS, TRUST TERRITORY OF THE

1980 C 132,929

Cities and Towns

Garapan 2,063
• Jarej-Uliga-Delap 8,583
Kolonia 5,549
Koror 6,222

Political Divisions

Federated States of Micronesia 73,160
Marshall Islands 30,873
Northern Mariana Islands 16,780
Palau (Belau) 12,116

PAKISTAN / Pākistān

1981 C 84,253,644

Cities and Towns

Abbottābād (★ 65,996) 32,188
Ahmadpur East 56,979
Attock (★ 39,986) 26,233
Bahāwalnagar 74,533
Bahāwalpur (★ 180,263) 152,009
Bannu (★ 43,210) 35,170
Bhakkar 41,934
Chārsadda 62,530
Chīchāwatni 50,241
Chiniot 105,559
Chishtiān Mandi 61,959
Dādu 39,298
Daska 55,555
Dera Ghāzi Khān 102,007
Dera Ismāīl Khān (★ 68,145) 64,358
Drigh Road Cantonment (★ Karāchi) 56,742
Faisalabad (Lyallpur) 1,104,209
Gojra 68,000
Gujrānwāla (★ 658,753) 600,993
Gujrānwāla Cantonment (★ Gujrānwāla) 57,760
Gujrāt 155,058
Gwādar 17,000
Hāfizābād 83,464
Hyderābād (★ 800,000) 702,539
Hyderābād Cantonment (★ Hyderābād) 48,990
ISLĀMĀBĀD (★★ Rāwalpindi) 204,364
Jacobābād 79,365
Jarānwāla 69,459
Jhang Sadar 195,558
Jhelum (★ 106,462) 92,646
Kamālia 61,107
Kāmoke 71,097
• Karāchi (★ 5,300,000) 4,901,627
Karāchi Cantonment (★ Karāchi) 181,981
Kasūr 155,523
Khairpur 61,447
Khānewāl 89,090
Khānpur 70,589
Khāriān (★ 51,506) 16,042
Khushāb 56,274
Kohāt (★ 77,604) 55,832
Lahore (★ 3,025,000) 2,707,215
Lahore Cantonment (★ Lahore) 245,474
Lārkāna 123,890
Leiah 51,482
Malir Cantonment (★ Karāchi) 47,588
Mandi Būrewāla 86,311
Mardān (★ 147,977) 141,842
Miānwāli 59,159
Mingāora 88,078
Mīrpur Khās 124,371
Multān (★ 732,070) 696,316
Muzaffargarh 53,000
Nawābshāh 102,139
Nowshera (★ 74,913) 38,875
Okāra (★ 153,483) 127,455
Pākpattan 69,820
Peshāwar (★ 566,248) 506,896
Peshāwar Cantonment (★ Peshāwar) 59,352
Quetta (★ 285,719) 244,842
Rahīmyār Khān (★ 132,635) 119,036
Rāwalpindi (★ 1,040,000) 457,091
Rāwalpindi Cantonment (★ Rāwalpindi) 337,752
Sādiqābad 63,935
Sāhīwal (Montgomery) 150,954
Sargodha (★ 291,362) 231,895
Sargodha Cantonment (★ Sargodha) 59,467
Shekhūpura 141,168
Shikārpur 88,138
Shorkot (★ 50,568) 18,533
Siālkot (★ 302,009) 258,147
Sibi 23,043
Sukkur 190,551
Tando Ādam 62,744
Turbat 52,337
Vihāri 53,799
Wāh Cantonment 122,335
Wazīrābād 62,725

PANAMA / Panamá

1980 C 1,795,012

Cities and Towns

Balboa (★ Panamá) 1,904
Colón (★ 88,000) (1982 E) 64,763
David 49,472
La Chorrera 37,566
La Concepción 10,823
• PANAMÁ (★ 625,000) (1984 E) 424,204
Puerto Armuelles 12,562
San Miguelito (★ Panamá) (1984 E) 200,584
Santiago 24,205

PAPUA NEW GUINEA

1984 E 3,239,000

Cities and Towns

Lae 73,400
Madang 23,700
• PORT MORESBY 144,300
Rabaul (1980 C) 14,954
Wewak 22,100

PARAGUAY

1985 E 3,279,000

Cities and Towns

• ASUNCIÓN (★ 700,000) 477,100
Caacupé (1972 C) 7,278
Concepción (1984 E) 25,000
Coronel Oviedo (1982 C) 21,782
Encarnación (1984 E) 31,000
Fernando de la Mora (★ Asunción) 80,000
Lambaré (★ Asunción) 84,000
Luque (★ Asunción) (1972 C) 13,921
Paraguarí (1972 C) 5,036
Pedro Juan Caballero (1982 C) 37,331
Pilar (1982 C) 13,135
Puerto Presidente Stroessner 64,000
San Lorenzo (★ Asunción) (1982 C) 74,632
Villa Hayes (1972 C) 4,749
Villarrica (1982 C) 21,203

Departments

Alto Paraguay 10,100
Alto Paraná 255,000
Amambay 69,400
Asunción (Distrito Federal) 477,100
Boquerón 12,000
Caaguazú 333,000
Caazapá 111,400
Canendiyu 77,100
Central 572,500
Chaco 300
Concepción 143,000
Cordillera 194,000
Guairá 149,600
Itapúa 284,500
Misiones 80,100
Ñeembucú 69,500
Nueva Asunción 200
Paraguarí 201,900
Presidente Hayes 27,800
San Pedro 210,500

PERU / Perú

1981 C 17,031,221

Cities and Towns

Abancay 19,863
Arequipa (★ 446,942) 108,023
Ayacucho (★ 69,533) 57,432
Barranco (★ Lima) 46,478
Barrio Obrero Industrial (★ Lima) 404,856
Breña (★ Lima) 112,398
Cajamarca 62,259
Callao (★★ Lima) 264,133
Cerro de Pasco (★ 66,373) 55,597
Chachapoyas 11,853
Chiclayo (★ 279,527) 213,095
Chimbote 223,341
Chincha Alta 41,369
Chorrillos (★ Lima) 141,881
Chosica 65,139
Chulucanas (▲ 63,163) 35,000
Cuzco (★ 184,550) 89,563
Huacho 43,398
Huancavelica 21,137
Huancayo (★ 164,954) 84,845
Huánuco 61,812
Huaraz 44,814
Ica 114,786
Iquitos 178,738
Jesús María (★ Lima) 83,179
Juliaca 87,651
Lambayeque (▲ 30,784) 24,000
La Oroya 34,940
La Victoria (★ Lima) 270,778
• LIMA (★ 4,608,010) 371,122
Lince (★ Lima) 80,456
Magdalena del Mar (★ Lima) 55,535
Miraflores (★ Lima) 103,453
Moyobamba 14,376
Pisco 55,604
Piura (★ 207,934) 144,609
Pucallpa 112,263
Pueblo Libre (★ Lima) 83,985
Puerto Maldonado 12,693
Puno 67,397
Rímac (★ Lima) 184,484
San Isidro (★ Lima) 71,203
Sullana 89,037
Surco (★ Lima) 146,636
Surquillo (★ Lima) 134,158
Tacna 97,173
Talara 57,351
Trujillo (★ 354,301) 202,469
Tumbes 47,936
Vitarte (★ Lima) 145,504

Departments

Amazonas 254,560
Ancash 818,289
Apurímac 323,346
Arequipa 706,580
Ayacucho 503,392
Cajamarca 1,045,569
Callao (Province) 443,413
Cuzco (Cusco) 832,504
Huancavelica 346,797
Huánuco 484,780
Ica 433,897
Junín 852,238
La Libertad 962,949
Lambayeque 674,442
Lima 4,745,877
Loreto 445,368
Madre de Dios 33,007
Moquegua 101,610
Pasco 213,125
Piura 1,125,865
Puno 890,258
San Martín 319,751
Tacna 143,085
Tumbes 103,839
Ucayali 200,669

PHILIPPINES / Pilipinas

1980 C 48,098,460

Cities and Towns

Angeles (1984 E) 213,305
Angono 26,571
Antipolo (▲ 68,912) 54,117
Bacolod (1984 E) 287,830
Bacoor (★ Manila) 90,364
Baguio (1984 E) 133,726
Bais (▲ 49,301) 8,225
Balagtas 28,654
Baliuag 70,555
Basista 17,191
Batangas (▲ 143,570) 24,678
Binalbagan (▲ 49,428) 21,589
Biñan (★ Manila) 83,684
Binangonan 80,980
Bislig (▲ 81,615) 49,498
Bocaue 49,693
Bulan (▲ 60,911) 14,234
Butuan (▲ 172,489) (1984 E) 74,900
Cabanatuan (▲ 153,899) (1984 E) 67,300
Cadiz (▲ 129,632) 25,215
Cagayan de Oro (▲ 275,938) (1984 E) 207,000
Cainta (★ Manila) 59,025
Calamba (▲ 121,175) 72,359
Calapan (▲ 67,370) 16,435
Calbayog (▲ 113,954) (1984 E) 15,000
Caloocan (★ Manila) (1984 E) 524,624
Calumpit 45,454
Carmona (★ Manila) 65,014
Catarman (▲ 59,021) 17,714
Catbalogan (▲ 58,737) 23,739
Cavite (★ 175,000) 87,666
Cebu (★ 600,000) (1984 E) 552,155
Cordoba 16,455
Cotabato 83,871
Daet (▲ 54,789) 27,812
Dagupan (1984 E) 103,401
Davao (▲ 610,375) 408,775
Digos (▲ 70,065) 26,919
Dinagat 36,726
Dipolog (▲ 61,919) 26,211
Dumaguete 63,411
Escalante (▲ 71,293) 19,639
General Santos (Dadiangas) (▲ 183,255) (1984 E) 115,600
Gingoog (▲ 79,937) 20,128
Guagua 72,609
Guiguinto 27,751
Ilagan (▲ 79,336) 12,168
Iligan (▲ 181,865) (1984 E) 23,300
Iloilo (1984 E) 263,422
Iriga (▲ 66,113) 18,252
Isabela (Basilan) (▲ 49,891) 11,491
Jolo 52,429
Kawit (★ Cavite) 39,368
Koronadal (▲ 80,566) 33,526
La Carlota (▲ 45,812) 20,943
Laoag (▲ 69,648) 32,357
Lapu-Lapu 98,723
Las Piñas (★ Manila) (1984 E) 190,364
Legaspi (▲ 108,864) (1984 E) 56,600
Lingayen (▲ 65,187) 19,367
Lipa (▲ 133,540) (1984 E) 25,200
Lucena (1984 E) 124,355
Maasin (▲ 59,731) 11,151
Mabalacat (▲ 80,966) 54,988
Macabebe 45,830
Makati (★ Manila) (1984 E) 408,991
Malabon (★ Manila) (1984 E) 212,930
Malaybalay (▲ 60,779) 14,018
Malolos 95,699
Manaoag 36,742
Mandaluyong (★ Manila) (1984 E) 226,670
Mandaue (★ Cebu) (1984 E) 137,300
Mangaldan 50,434
• MANILA (★ 6,800,000) (1984 E) 1,728,441
Marawi 53,812
Marikina (★ Manila) (1984 E) 248,183
Mati (▲ 78,178) 19,400
Meycauayan (★ Manila) 83,579
Muntinglupa (★ Manila) (1984 E) 172,421
Naga 90,712
Navotas (★ Manila) (1984 E) 146,899
Noveleta (★ Cavite) 14,460
Olongapo (1984 E) 173,701
Ormoc (▲ 116,474) (1984 E) 15,600
Ozamiz (▲ 77,832) 25,827
Pagadian (▲ 80,861) 39,561
Parañaque (★ Manila) (1984 E) 252,791
Pasay (★ Manila) (1984 E) 320,889
Pasig (★ Manila) (1984 E) 318,853
Puerto Princesa (▲ 60,234) 34,003
Pulilan 38,110
Quezon City (★ Manila) (1984 E) 1,326,035
Rosario (★ Cavite) 33,312
Roxas (Capiz) (▲ 81,183) 19,399
Sagay (▲ 99,118) 43,662
San Carlos (▲ 107,080) (1984 E) 26,300
San Fernando 110,891
San Juan del Monte (★ Manila) (1984 E) 139,126
San Pablo (▲ 143,023) (1984 E) 74,500
San Pedro 74,556
Santa Cruz 60,620
Santa Rosa (★ Manila) 64,325
Santo Tomas, Pampanga prov. 24,951
Santo Tomas, Pangasinan prov. 8,946
Silay (▲ 111,131) 37,173
Surigao (▲ 79,745) 28,482
Tacloban (1984 E) 117,243
Tagaytay (▲ 16,322) 3,678
Tagbilaran 42,683
Tagig (★ Manila) (1984 E) 130,719
Tagum (▲ 86,201) 35,785
Talisay (▲ 53,624) 26,463
Tarlac (▲ 175,691) 38,205
Taytay (★ Manila) 75,328
Toledo (▲ 102,565) (1984 E) 8,900
Trece Martires (▲ 8,579) 1,455
Tuguegarao (▲ 73,507) 30,107
Valenzuela (★ Manila) (1984 E) 275,725
Victorias (▲ 55,959) 27,407
Vigan 33,483
Zamboanga (▲ 379,194) (1984 E) 91,300

C Census. E Official estimate. UE Unofficial estimate.
• Largest city in country.

★ Population or designation of metropolitan area, including suburbs (see headnote).
▲ Population of an entire municipality, commune, or district, including rural area.

PITCAIRN

1988 C 59

Cities and Towns

• ADAMSTOWN 59

POLAND / Polska

1988 E 37,663,800

Cities and Towns

Augustów 27,900
Będzin (★ Katowice) 77,300
Bełchatów 54,900
Biała Podlaska 49,700
Białogard 23,700
Białystok 259,600
Bielawa (★★ Dzierżoniów) 34,100
Bielsko-Biała 177,700
Bochnia 28,200
Bolesławiec (Bunzlau) 43,300
Brzeg (Brieg) 37,700
Bydgoszcz 372,600
Bytom (★★ Katowice) 239,800
Chełm 62,700
Chojnice 36,500
Chorzów (★★ Katowice) 138,200
Chrzanów 40,400
Ciechanów 41,000
Cieszyn 36,900
Czechowice-Dziedzice 35,100
Czeladź (★ Katowice) 38,000
Częstochowa 252,900
Dąbrowa Górnicza (★ Katowice) 140,000
Dębica 42,700
Dzierżoniów (Reichenbach) (★ 89,000) 37,800
Elbląg (Elbing) 121,800
Ełk (Lyck) 45,300
Gdańsk (Danzig) (★ 909,000) 469,100
Gdynia (★★ Gdańsk) 249,500
Giżycko 29,000
Gliwice (Gleiwitz) (★★ Katowice) 211,300
Głogów 70,100
Gniezno 70,000
Gorzów [Wielkopolski] 119,500
Grodzisk Mazowiecki (★ Warsaw) 25,200
Grudziądz 98,300
Inowrocław 74,600
Jarosław 41,700
Jasło 35,900
Jastrzębie-Zdrój 102,200
Jaworzno (★ Katowice) 97,500
Jelenia Góra (Hirschberg) 92,500
Kalisz 105,300
Kamienna Góra (Landeshut) 23,300
• Katowice (★ 2,778,000) 368,600
Kędzierzyn-Koźle 72,900
Kętrzyn 29,600
Kielce 208,100
Kłodzko (Glatz) 29,500
Knurów (★ Katowice) 45,600
Kołobrzeg (Kolberg) 43,100
Konin 78,100
Kościan 23,100
Koszalin (Köslin) 104,700
Kraków (★ 828,000) 744,900
Kraśnik 35,800
Krosno 47,300
Krotoszyn 27,000
Kutno 47,400
Kwidzyn (Marienwerder) 36,200
Lębork 32,900
Legionowo (★ Warsaw) 47,600
Legnica (Liegnitz) 100,700
Leszno 56,300
Łódź (★ 1,061,000) 844,900
Łomża 54,800
Łowicz 29,500
Lubań 23,300
Lubin 77,600
Lublin (★ 389,000) 333,000
Lubliniec 24,700
Łuków 29,600
Malbork (Marienburg) 38,200
Mielec 56,900
Mikołów (★ Katowice) 36,800
Mińsk Mazowiecki 34,000
Mława 26,800
Mysłowice (★ Katowice) 91,900
Myszków 32,300
Nowa Ruda 26,600
Nowa Sól 42,700
Nowy Sącz 73,200
Nowy Targ 31,300
Nysa (Neisse) 45,800
Oława 31,400
Oleśnica 36,400
Olkusz 37,700
Olsztyn (Allenstein) 154,900
Opole (Oppeln) 128,200
Ostróda (Osterode) 32,500
Ostrołęka 46,900
Ostrowiec [Świętokrzyski] 75,500
Ostrów Wielkopolski 70,400
Oświęcim 45,500
Otwock (★ Warsaw) 44,700
Pabianice (★ Łódź) 73,600
Piaseczno (★ Warsaw) 24,500
Piekary Śląskie (★ Katowice) 69,400
Piła (Schneidemühl) 69,700
Piotrków [Trybunalski] 80,200
Płock 117,600
Poznań (★ 672,000) 585,900
Prudnik 24,600
Pruszków (★ Warsaw) 53,700
Przemyśl 67,200
Pszczyna 39,100
Puławy 51,200
Racibórz (Ratibor) 62,500
Radom 221,800
Radomsko 49,600
Ruda Śląska (★ Katowice) 167,900
Rumia (★ Gdańsk) 36,100
Rybnik 141,000
Rzeszów 147,300
Sanok 37,500
Siedlce 68,400
Siemianowice Śląskie (★ Katowice) 82,200
Sieradz 39,500
Skarżysko-Kamienna 49,500
Skierniewice 42,600
Słupsk (Stolp) 96,200
Sochaczew 37,400
Sopot (Zoppot) (★ Gdańsk) 49,700
Sosnowiec (★★ Katowice) 259,600
Stalowa Wola 68,800
Starachowice 56,000
Stargard [Szczeciński] 68,500
Starogard [Gdański] 46,900
Suwałki 55,900
Świdnica (Schweidnitz) 61,900
Świdnik (★ Lublin) 38,800
Świecie 26,000
Świętochłowice (★ Katowice) 60,900
Świnoujście (Swinemünde) 44,100
Szczecin (Stettin) (★ 449,000) 396,600
Szczecinek 39,200
Szczytno (Ortelsburg) 26,200
Tarnobrzeg 44,700
Tarnów 118,400
Tarnowskie Góry (★ Katowice) 74,300
Tczew 59,000
Tomaszów Mazowiecki 67,400
Toruń 197,000
Trzebinia 20,900
Turek 28,000
Tychy (★ Katowice) 187,800
Wałbrzych (Waldenburg) (★ 207,000) 141,100
Wałcz 26,200
WARSAW (WARSZAWA) (★ 2,323,000) 1,671,400
Wejherowo 46,500
Włocławek 119,200
Wodzisław Śląski 111,500
Wołomin (★ Warsaw) 35,300
Wrocław (Breslau) 640,200
Września 26,300
Zabrze (Hindenburg) (★★ Katowice) 199,400
Żagań (Sagan) 27,000
Zakopane 30,100
Zamość 58,400
Żary (Sorau) 39,700
Zawiercie 56,100
Zduńska Wola 43,800
Zgierz (★ Łódź) 56,200
Zgorzelec 35,900
Zielona Góra (Grünberg) 113,300
Żory 65,300
Żyrardów (★ Warsaw) 40,900
Żywiec 30,100

Voivodships

Biała Podlaska 300,300
Białystok 678,100
Bielsko-Biała 881,400
Bydgoszcz 1,093,500
Chełm 242,900
Ciechanów 421,200
Częstochowa 770,300
Elbląg 470,800
Gdańsk 1,416,000
Gorzów Wielkopolski 488,600
Jelenia Góra 513,200
Kalisz 701,900
Katowice 3,957,600
Kielce 1,113,900
Konin 462,400
Koszalin 496,500
Kraków 1,215,300
Krosno 481,600
Legnica 499,700
Leszno 379,400
Łódź 1,149,300
Łomża 341,200
Lublin 994,100
Nowy Sącz 676,300
Olsztyn 735,800
Opole 1,022,000
Ostrołęka 388,300
Piła 470,900
Piotrków Trybunalski 637,600
Płock 512,000
Poznań 1,311,900
Przemyśl 399,100
Radom 734,800
Rzeszów 700,400
Siedlce 640,500
Sieradz 403,000
Skierniewice 412,300
Słupsk 402,000
Suwałki 456,400
Szczecin 955,000
Tarnobrzeg 585,500
Tarnów 649,100
Toruń 647,600
Wałbrzych 738,900
Warszawa 2,425,900
Włocławek 427,500
Wrocław 1,119,600
Zamość 489,400
Zielona Góra 652,800

PORTUGAL

1981 C 9,833,014

Cities and Towns

Agualva-Cacém (★ Lisbon) 34,341
Águas Santas (★ Porto) 26,523
Algés (★ Lisbon) 20,377
Algueirão-Mem Martins (★ Lisbon) 28,154
Almada (★ Lisbon) 42,607
Amadora (★ Lisbon) 95,518
Angra do Heroísmo, Azores Is. 12,292
Aveiro 28,625
Baixa da Banheira (★ Lisbon) 21,358
Barreiro (★ Lisbon) 50,863
Beja 19,643
Braga 63,033
Bragança 14,181
Castelo Branco 21,256
Coimbra 74,616
Cova da Piedade (★ Lisbon) 28,251
Covilhã 21,807
Damaia (★ Lisbon) 23,261
Évora 34,851
Faro 27,974
Funchal, Madeira Is. 44,111
Guimarães 21,947
Horta, Azores Is. 5,749
Laranjeiro (★ Lisbon) 20,374
• LISBON (LISBOA) (★ 2,250,000) 807,167
Matosinhos (★ Porto) 26,404
Montijo (★ Lisbon) 23,017
Moscavide (★ Lisbon) 17,797
Odivelas (★ Lisbon) 38,322
Oeiras (★ Lisbon) 32,529
Olhão 20,080
Ponta Delgada, Azores Is. 21,187
Portimão 19,605
Porto (Oporto) (★ 1,225,000) 327,368
Póvoa de Varzim 23,729
Queluz (★ Lisbon) 42,241
Sacavém (★ Lisbon) 24,116
Santarém 19,761
Setúbal 77,885
Sintra (★ Lisbon) 9,322
Vila do Conde 20,613
Vila Nova de Gaia (★ Porto) 62,469
Viseu 20,070

Districts

Açores (Azores) (Auton. Region) 243,410
Aveiro 622,988
Beja 188,420
Braga 708,924
Bragança 184,252
Castelo Branco 234,230
Coimbra 436,324
Évora 180,277
Faro 323,534
Guarda 205,631
Leiria 420,229
Lisboa (Lisbon) 2,069,467
Madeira (Auton. Region) 252,844
Portalegre 142,905
Porto 1,562,287
Santarém 454,123
Setúbal 658,326
Viana do Castelo 256,814
Vila Real 264,381
Viseu 423,648

PUERTO RICO

1980 C 3,196,520

Cities and Towns

Adjuntas (▲ 18,786) 5,239
Aguadilla (★ 152,793) 22,039
Aibonito (▲ 22,167) 9,331
Arecibo (★ 160,336) 48,779
Bayamón (★ San Juan) 185,087
Caguas (★ San Juan) 87,214
Carolina (★ San Juan) 147,835
Cataño (★ San Juan) 26,243
Cayey (▲ 41,099) San Juan) 23,305
Coamo (▲ 30,822) 12,851
Corozal (★ San Juan) 5,889
Fajardo (▲ 32,087) San Juan) 26,928
Guánica (▲ 18,799) 9,628
Guayama (▲ 40,183) 21,097
Guayanilla (▲ 21,050) 6,163
Guaynabo (★ San Juan) 65,075
Humacao (★ San Juan) 19,147
Isabela (★ Aguadilla) 12,087
Manatí (★ San Juan) 17,347
Mayagüez (★ 200,464) 82,968
Ponce (★ 232,551) 161,739
San Germán (★ Mayagüez) 13,054
• SAN JUAN (★ 1,775,260) 424,600
San Sebastián (▲ 35,690) 10,619
Trujillo Alto (★ San Juan) 41,141
Utuado (▲ 34,505) 11,113
Vega Alta (★ San Juan) 10,582
Vega Baja (★ San Juan) 18,233
Yabucoa (▲ 31,425) 6,797
Yauco (▲ 37,742) 14,594

QATAR / Qaṭar

1986 C 369,079

Cities and Towns

Ar Rayyān (★ Doha) 91,996
• DOHA (AD DAWḤAH) (★ 310,000) 217,294

REUNION / Réunion

1982 C 515,814

Cities and Towns

Le Port (▲ 30,131) 26,000
• SAINT-DENIS (▲ 109,072) 84,400
Saint-Pierre (▲ 58,412) 28,000

ROMANIA / România

1986 E 22,823,479

Cities and Towns

Aiud 29,250
Alba Iulia 66,100
Alexandria 52,802
Arad 187,744
Bacău 179,877
Baia-Mare 139,704
Bîrlad 70,365
Bistrița 77,267
Blaj 23,438
Borșa 29,494
Botoșani 108,775
Brăila 235,620
Brașov 351,493
• BUCHAREST (BUCUREȘTI) (★ 2,250,000) 1,989,823
Buzău 136,080
Călărași 69,350
Caracal 36,963
Caransebeș 32,787
Carei 27,727
Cîmpia Turzii 28,342
Cîmpina 39,032
Cîmpulung 41,895
Cluj-Napoca 310,017
Codlea 24,039
Constanța 327,676
Craiova 281,044
Cugir 33,325
Curtea-de-Argeș 30,019
Dej 39,229
Deva 77,976
Dorohoi 29,721
Drobeta-Turnu-Severin 99,366
Făgăraș 41,851
Fetești 32,504
Focșani 86,411
Galați 295,372
Gheorghe Gheorghiu-Dej 52,329
Giurgiu 68,002
Hunedoara 88,514
Huși 28,963
Iași 313,060
Lugoj 53,665
Lupeni 30,949
Mangalia 38,803
Medgidia 48,409
Mediaș 72,816
Miercurea Ciuc 46,494
Moinești 23,004
Odorheiu Secuiesc 41,071
Oltenița 29,367
Oradea 213,846
Pașcani 36,420
Petrila (★ Petroșani) 26,468
Petroșani (★ 74,000) 49,131
Piatra-Neamț 109,393
Pitești 157,190
Ploiești (★ 300,000) 234,886
Rădăuți 28,740
Reghin 36,423
Reșița 105,914
Rîmnicu-Sărat 36,501
Rîmnicu-Vîlcea 96,051
Roman 72,415
Roșiorii de Vede 35,622
Săcele 33,502
Satu Mare 130,082
Sebeș 30,793
Sfîntu Gheorghe 67,587
Sibiu 177,511
Sighetu Marmației 43,274
Sighișoara 36,775
Slatina 76,714
Slobozia 46,324
Suceava 96,317
Tecuci 44,075
Timișoara 325,272
Tîrgoviște 91,990
Tîrgu-Jiu 87,693
Tîrgu Mureș 158,998
Tîrnăveni 29,341
Tulcea 86,336
Turda 61,594
Turnu-Măgurele 35,094
Vaslui 65,070
Vulcan 34,117
Zalău 57,283
Zărnești 26,773

RWANDA

1983 E 5,762,000

Cities and Towns

Butare 30,000
• KIGALI 181,600

SAINT CHRISTOPHER-NEVIS

1980 C 44,404

Cities and Towns

• BASSETERRE 14,725
Charlestown 1,771

SAINT HELENA

1987 C 5,644

Cities and Towns

• JAMESTOWN 1,413

SAINT LUCIA

1987 E 142,342

Cities and Towns

• CASTRIES 53,933

SAINT PIERRE AND MIQUELON / Saint-Pierre-et-Miquelon

1982 C 6,041

Cities and Towns

• SAINT-PIERRE 5,371

SAINT VINCENT AND THE GRENADINES

1987 E 112,589

Cities and Towns

• KINGSTOWN (★ 28,936) 19,028

SAN MARINO

1988 E 22,304

Cities and Towns

• SAN MARINO 4,137

SAO TOME AND PRINCIPE / São Tomé e Príncipe

1970 C 73,631

Cities and Towns

• SÃO TOMÉ 17,380

SAUDI ARABIA / Al 'Arabīyah as Su'ūdīyah

1980 E 9,229,000

Cities and Towns

Abhā (1974 C) 30,150
Ad Dammām 200,000
Al Hufūf (Hofuf) (1974 C) 101,271
Al Khubar (1974 C) 48,817
Al Mubarraz (1974 C) 54,325
Aṭ Ṭā'if 300,000
Aẓ Ẓahrān (Dhahran) (1974 UE) 25,000
Buraydah (1974 C) 69,940
Hā'il (1974 C) 40,502
• Jiddah 1,300,000
Khamīs Mushayṭ (1974 C) 49,581

C Census. E Official estimate. UE Unofficial estimate.
• Largest city in country.

★ Population or designation of metropolitan area, including suburbs (see headnote).
▲ Population of an entire municipality, commune, or district, including rural area.

Mecca (Makkah) 550,000
Medina (Al Madīnah) 290,000
Najran (1974 C) 47,501
Qīzān (1974 C) 32,812
RIYADH (AR RIYĀḌ) 1,250,000
Tabūk (1974 C) 74,825

SENEGAL / Sénégal

1985 E 6,566,988

Cities and Towns

• DAKAR 1,428,084
Diourbel 76,409
Kaolack 132,386
Kolda 42,180
Louga 49,436
Saint-Louis 91,485
Tambacounda 44,510
Thiès 156,200
Ziguinchor 106,460

SEYCHELLES

1984 E 64,718

Cities and Towns

• VICTORIA 23,000

SIERRA LEONE

1985 C 3,515,812

Cities and Towns

Bo 59,768
• FREETOWN (★ 525,000) 469,776
Kenema 52,473
Koidu 82,474
Lunsar 16,073
Makeni 49,038
Port Loko 15,248

SINGAPORE

1988 E 2,631,000

Cities and Towns

• SINGAPORE (★ 3,000,000) 2,631,000

SOLOMON ISLANDS

1986 C 285,176

Cities and Towns

• HONIARA 30,413

SOMALIA / Soomaaliya

1984 E 5,423,000

Cities and Towns

Berbera 65,000
Hargeysa 70,000
Kismaayo 70,000
Marka 60,000
• MOGADISHU (MUQDISHO) 600,000

SOUTH AFRICA / Suid-Afrika

1985 C 23,385,645

Cities and Towns

Alberton (★ Johannesburg) 66,155
Alexandra (★ Johannesburg) 67,276
Aliwal North 5,399
Atlantis (★ Cape Town) 29,524
Atteridgeville (★ Pretoria) 73,439
Beaufort West (★ 24,487) 18,979
Bellville (★ Cape Town) 68,915
Benoni (★ Johannesburg) 94,926
Bethal (★ 23,510) 8,721
Bethlehem (★ 35,301) 12,871
Bloemfontein (★ 235,000) 104,381
Boksburg (★ Johannesburg) 110,832
Botshabelo (★ Bloemfontein) 95,625
Brakpan (★ Johannesburg) 46,416
CAPE TOWN (KAAPSTAD) (★ 1,790,000) 776,617
Carletonville (★ 120,499) 97,874
Clermont (★ Durban) 27,136
Constantia (★ Cape Town) 25,749
Cradock (★ 22,930) 10,911
Daveyton (★ Johannesburg) 99,056
De Aar (★ 22,484) 17,540
Diepmeadow (★ Johannesburg) 192,682
Dobsonville (★ Johannesburg) 38,166
Duduza (★ Johannesburg) 27,649
Dundee 9,737
Durban (★ 1,550,000) 634,301
East London (Oos-Londen) (★ 320,000) 85,699
Edendale (★ Pietermaritzburg) 47,001
Edenvale (★ Johannesburg) 30,699
Elsies River (★ Cape Town) 70,067
Empumalanga (★ Durban) 47,938
Ermelo (★ 32,047) 12,746
Evaton (★ Vereeniging) 52,559
Ezakheni 27,277
Galeshewe (★ Kimberley) 63,238
George (★ 55,935) 41,920
Germiston (★★ Johannesburg) 116,718
Goodwood (★ Cape Town) 33,451
Graaff-Reinet (★ 23,758) 18,106
Grahamstown (★ 48,452) 19,188
Grassy Park (★ Cape Town) 50,193
Guguletu (★ Cape Town) 63,893
Harrismith 4,518
Ikageng (★ Potchefstroom) 35,099
Imbali (★ Pietermaritzburg) 27,866
• Johannesburg (★ 3,650,000) 632,369
Jouberton (★ Klerksdorp) 33,180
Kagiso (★ Johannesburg) 50,647
Katlehong (★ Johannesburg) 137,745
Kayamnandi (★ Port Elizabeth) 220,548
Kempton Park (★ Johannesburg) 87,721
Kimberley (★ 145,000) 74,061
King William's Town (★ 48,300) 16,123
Klerksdorp (★ 205,000) 48,947
Kraaifontein (★ Cape Town) 29,431
Kroonstad (★ 65,165) 22,886
Krugersdorp (★ Johannesburg) 73,767
Kwaguqa (★ Witbank) 35,387
Kwa Makuta (★ Durban) 71,378
Kwa Mashu (★ Durban) 111,593
Kwanobuhle (★ Port Elizabeth) 52,376
Kwathema (★ Johannesburg) 78,640
Ladysmith (★ 31,670) 25,102
Langa (★ Cape Town) 22,998
Lekoa (Shapeville) (★ Vereeniging) 218,392
Madadeni (★ Newcastle) 65,832
Mamelodi (★ Pretoria) 127,033
Mangaung (★ Bloemfontein) 79,851
Middelburg (★ 44,762) 25,627
Mohlakeng (★ Johannesburg) 27,706
Mosselbaai (★ 22,180) 20,404
Nelspruit (★ 40,300) 15,519
Newcastle (★ 155,000) 34,931
Nigel (★ Johannesburg) 27,138
Ntuzuma (★ Durban) 61,834
Nyanga (★ Cape Town) 148,882
Odendaalsrus (★★ Welkom) 8,819
Orkney (★★ Klerksdorp) 19,431
Oudtshoorn (★ 37,112) 34,124
Ozisweni (★ Newcastle) 51,934
Paarl (★★ Cape Town) 63,671
Parow (★ Cape Town) 60,294
Parys (★ 22,320) 7,345
Phalaborwa (★ 29,740) 9,284
Pietermaritzburg (★ 230,000) 133,809
Pietersburg (★ 62,804) 29,909
Pinetown (★ Durban) 55,770
Port Elizabeth (★ 690,000) 272,844
Potchefstroom (★ 78,865) 43,766
Potgietersrus (★ 22,140) 8,195
PRETORIA (★ 960,000) 443,059
Queenstown (★ 32,699) 17,996
Randburg (★ Johannesburg) 74,347
Randfontein (★ Johannesburg) 43,763
Rhini (★ Grahamstown) 29,264
Roodepoort-Maraisburg (★ Johannesburg) 141,764
Rustenburg 37,712
Sandton (★ Johannesburg) 86,089
Sasolburg (★★ Vereeniging) 29,310
Seeisoville (★ Kroonstad) 42,279
Seshego (★ Pietersburg) 32,895
Soshanguve (★ Pretoria) 68,598
Soweto (★ Johannesburg) 521,948
Springs (★ Johannesburg) 68,235
Standerton (★ 31,728) 15,301
Stellenbosch (★★ Cape Town) 38,602
Stilfontein (★★ Klerksdorp) 13,782
Strand (★ Cape Town) 28,474
Tembisa (★ Johannesburg) 149,282
Thabong (★ Welkom) 43,470
Tokoza (★ Johannesburg) 44,589
Tsakane (★ Johannesburg) 42,280
Uitenhage (★★ Port Elizabeth) 54,987
Umlazi (★ Durban) 194,933
Upington (★ 40,463) 32,182
Vanderbijlpark (★★ Vereeniging) 59,865
Vereeniging (★ 525,000) 60,584
Verwoerdburg (★ Pretoria) 49,891
Virginia (★ 65,000) 17,624
Vosloosrus (★ Johannesburg) 52,061
Vredenburg-Saldanha 26,091
Vryburg (★ 20,993) 10,071
Vryheid (★ 18,680) 12,313
Walvisbaai (Walvis Bay) (★ 16,607) 9,687
Welkom (★ 215,000) 54,488
Westonaria (★ Johannesburg) 46,523
Westville (★ Durban) 24,933
Witbank (★ 77,171) 41,784
Worcester (★ 54,007) 46,043

Provinces

Cape 5,041,137
Natal 5,892,033
Orange Free State 1,958,462
Transvaal 10,494,013

SOVIET UNION / Sovetskiy Soyuz

1989 C 286,717,000

Cities and Towns

Abakan 154,000
Abay (1974 E) 41,000
Abdulino (1974 E) 25,000
Abovyan (1987 E) 53,000
Achinsk 122,000
Agryz (1974 E) 19,000
Akhtubinsk (1987 E) 53,000
Akhtyrka (1974 E) 43,000
Aktyubinsk 253,000
Alapajevsk (1987 E) 51,000
Alatyr (1974 E) 46,000
Aleksandriya 103,000
Aleksandrov (1987 E) 66,000
Aleksin (1987 E) 72,000
Aleysk (1974 E) 37,000
Ali-Bayramly (1987 E) 51,000
Alma-Ata (★ 1,190,000) 1,128,000
Almalyk 114,000
Almetyevsk 129,000
Alytus (1987 E) 71,000
Amursk (1987 E) 54,000
Anapa (1974 E) 30,000
Andizhan 293,000
Angarsk 266,000
Angren 131,000
Antratsit (★★ Krasnyy Luch) (1987 E) 70,000
Anzhero-Sudzhensk 108,000
Apatity (1987 E) 80,000
Apsheronsk (1974 E) 33,000
Aralsk (1974 E) 39,000
Arkalyk (1987 E) 71,000
Arkhangelsk 416,000
Armavir 161,000
Arsenyev (1987 E) 67,000
Artem (1987 E) 73,000
Artemovsk (1987 E) 91,000
Artemovskiy (1974 E) 38,000
Arzamas 109,000
Asbest (1987 E) 83,000
Asha (1974 E) 38,000
Ashkhabad 398,000
Asino (1974 E) 31,000
Astrakhan 509,000
Atbasar (1974 E) 39,000
Atkarsk (1974 E) 30,000
Avdeyevka (★ Donetsk) (1974 E) 33,000
Ayaguz (1974 E) 40,000
Azov (1987 E) 81,000
Baku (★ 2,020,000) 1,150,000
Balakhna (★ Gorkiy) (1974 E) 37,000
Balakleya (1974 E) 31,000
Balakovo 198,000
Balashikha (★ Moscow) 136,000
Balashov (1987 E) 99,000
Balkhash (1987 E) 84,000
Barabinsk (1974 E) 37,000
Baranovichi 159,000
Barnaul (★ 665,000) 602,000
Bataysk (★ Rostov-na-Donu) (1987 E) 98,000
Batumi 136,000
Bayram-Ali (1974 E) 36,000
Bekabad (Begovat) (1987 E) 80,000
Belaya Kalitva (1974 E) 35,000
Belaya Tserkov 197,000
Belebey (1987 E) 51,000
Belgorod 300,000
Belgorod-Dnestrovskiy (1987 E) 54,000
Belogorsk (1987 E) 71,000
Belorechensk (1974 E) 38,000
Beloretsk (1987 E) 75,000
Belovo (1987 E) 118,000
Beltsy 159,000
Bendery 130,000
Berdichev (1987 E) 89,000
Berdsk (★ Novosibirsk) (1987 E) 77,000
Berdyansk 132,000
Berezniki 201,000
Berezovskiy (1987 E) 51,000
Bezhetsk (1974 E) 30,000
Birobidzan (1987 E) 82,000
Biysk 233,000
Blagoveshchensk 206,000
Bobruysk 223,000
Bogoroditsk (1974 E) 32,000
Bogorodsk (★ Gorkiy) (1974 E) 37,000
Bologoye (1974 E) 34,000
Bor (★ Gorkiy) (1987 E) 65,000
Borislav (1974 E) 36,000
Borisoglebsk (1987 E) 69,000
Borisov 144,000
Borispol (1974 E) 36,000
Borovichi (1987 E) 64,000
Boyarka (★ Kiev) (1974 E) 31,000
Bratsk 255,000
Brest 258,000
Brovary (★ Kiev) (1987 E) 73,000
Bryanka (★ Stakhanov) (1987 E) 65,000
Bryansk 452,000
Budennovsk (1987 E) 54,000
Bugulma (1987 E) 88,000
Buguruslan (1987 E) 53,000
Bukhara 224,000
Buy (1974 E) 28,000
Buynaksk (1987 E) 53,000
Buzuluk (1987 E) 82,000
Chapayevsk (1987 E) 87,000
Chardzhou 161,000
Chaykovskij (1987 E) 83,000
Chebarkul (1974 E) 42,000
Cheboksary 420,000
Chekhov (1987 E) 57,000
Chelyabinsk (★ 1,325,000) 1,143,000
Cheremkhovo (1987 E) 73,000
Cherepovets 310,000
Cherkassy 290,000
Cherkessk 113,000
Chernigov 296,000
Chernogorsk (1987 E) 80,000
Chernovtsy 257,000
Chernyakhovsk (Insterburg) (1974 E) 34,000
Chervonograd (1987 E) 71,000
Chimkent 393,000
Chirchik (★ Tashkent) 156,000
Chistopol (1987 E) 65,000
Chita 366,000
Chu (1974 E) 35,000
Chusovoy (1987 E) 59,000
Chust (1974 E) 31,000
Daugavpils 127,000
Debaltsevo (1983 E) 37,000
Denau (1987 E) 53,000
Derbent (1987 E) 83,000
Dimitrov (★★ Krasnoarmeysk) (1987 E) 62,000
Dimitrovgrad (Melekess) 124,000
Dmitrov (1987 E) 64,000
Dneprodzerzhinsk (★★ Dnepropetrovsk) 282,000
Dnepropetrovsk (★ 1,600,000) 1,179,000
Dobropolye (1974 E) 31,000
Dolgoprudnyy (★ Moscow) (1987 E) 71,000
Domodedovo (★ Moscow) (1987 E) 51,000
Donetsk, Donetsk oblast (★ 2,200,000) 1,110,000
Donetsk, Rostov oblast (1974 E) 42,000
Donskoy (★ Novomoskovsk) (1974 E) 34,000
Drogobych (1987 E) 76,000
Druzhkovka (★ Kramatorsk) (1987 E) 70,000
Dubna (1987 E) 64,000
Dushanbe 595,000
Dzerzhinsk (★ Gorlovka) (1974 E) 46,000
Dzerzhinsk (★ Gorkiy) 285,000
Dzhalal-Abad (1987 E) 74,000
Dzhambul 307,000
Dzhankoy (1987 E) 51,000
Dzhetygara (1974 E) 39,000
Dzhezkazgan 109,000
Dzhizak 102,000
Echmiadzin (★ Yerevan) (1987 E) 53,000
Ekibastuz 135,000
Elektrostal 153,000
Elista (1987 E) 85,000
Engels (★★ Saratov) 182,000
Fastov (1987 E) 55,000
Feodosiya (1987 E) 83,000
Fergana 200,000
Frolovo (1974 E) 38,000
Frunze 616,000
Fryazino (★ Moscow) (1987 E) 52,000
Furmanov (1974 E) 41,000
Gatchina (★ Leningrad) (1987 E) 81,000
Gelendzhik (1974 E) 31,000
Geokchay (1974 E) 30,000
Georgiu-Dez (Liski) (1987 E) 54,000
Georgiyevsk (1987 E) 62,000
Glazov 104,000
Glukhov (1974 E) 30,000
Gomel 500,000
Gori (1987 E) 62,000
Gorkiy (Gorki) (★ 2,025,000) 1,438,000
Gorlovka (★ 710,000) 337,000
Gorno-Altaysk (1974 E) 39,000
Gorodets (1974 E) 35,000
Grodno 270,000
Groznyy 401,000
Gryazi (1974 E) 42,000
Gubakha (1974 E) 32,000
Gubkin (1987 E) 75,000
Gudermes (1974 E) 34,000
Gukovo (1987 E) 72,000
Gulistan (1987 E) 51,000
Guryev 149,000
Gus-Khrustalnyy (1987 E) 75,000
Ilichevsk (★ Odessa) (1987 E) 52,000
Ingulets (1974 E) 35,000
Inta (1987 E) 58,000
Irbit (1987 E) 53,000
Irkutsk 626,000
Ishim (1987 E) 65,000
Ishimbay (1987 E) 67,000
Iskitim (1987 E) 69,000
Ivano-Frankovsk 214,000
Ivanovo 481,000
Ivanteyevka (★ Moscow) (1987 E) 53,000
Izhevsk (Ustinov) 635,000
Izmail (1987 E) 90,000
Izyum (1987 E) 63,000
Jelgava (1987 E) 72,000
Jurmala (★ Rīga) (1987 E) 65,000
Kachkanar (1974 E) 38,000
Kafan (1974 E) 31,000
Kagan (1974 E) 38,000
Kagul (1974 E) 31,000
Kakhovka (1974 E) 35,000
Kalinin 451,000
Kaliningrad (★ Moscow) 160,000
Kaliningrad (Königsberg) 401,000
Kaluga 312,000
Kalush (1987 E) 67,000
Kamenets-Podolskiy 102,000
Kamenka (1974 E) 32,000
Kamen-na-Obi (1974 E) 40,000
Kamensk-Shakhtinskiy (1987 E) 75,000
Kamensk-Uralskiy 209,000
Kamyshin 122,000
Kamyshlov (1974 E) 31,000
Kanash (1987 E) 53,000
Kandalaksha (1974 E) 43,000
Kansk 110,000
Kapsukas (1974 E) 33,000
Kara-Balty (1987 E) 55,000
Karaganda 614,000
Karpinsk (1974 E) 37,000
Karshi 156,000
Kartaly (1974 E) 44,000
Kashira (1974 E) 42,000
Kasimov (1974 E) 34,000
Kaspiysk (1987 E) 61,000
Kattakurgan (1987 E) 63,000
Kaunas 423,000
Kazan (★ 1,140,000) 1,094,000
Kemerovo 520,000
Kentau (1987 E) 60,000
Kerch 174,000
Khabarovsk 601,000
Khanty-Mansiysk (1974 E) 26,000
Kharkov (★ 1,940,000) 1,611,000
Khartsyzsk (★ Donetsk) (1987 E) 69,000
Khasavyurt (1987 E) 74,000
Kherson 355,000
Khimki (★ Moscow) 133,000
Khmelnitskiy 237,000
Khodzheyli (1987 E) 55,000
Kholmsk (1987 E) 50,000
Kiev (Kiyev) (★ 2,900,000) 2,587,000
Kimovsk (1974 E) 44,000
Kimry (1987 E) 61,000
Kinel (1974 E) 40,000
Kineshma 105,000
Kirishi (1987 E) 51,000
Kirov 441,000
Kirovabad 278,000
Kirovakan (1987 E) 169,000
Kirovo-Chepetsk (1987 E) 89,000
Kirovograd 269,000
Kirovsk (★ Stakhanov) (1974 E) 40,000
Kirovsk (1974 E) 40,000
Kiselevsk (★★ Prokopyevsk) 128,000
Kishinev 665,000
Kislovodsk 114,000
Kizel (1974 E) 42,000
Klaipėda (Memel) 204,000
Klimovsk (★ Moscow) (1987 E) 57,000
Klin (1987 E) 95,000
Klintsy (1987 E) 72,000
Kohtla-Järve (1987 E) 78,000
Kokand 182,000
Kokchetav 137,000
Kolchugino (1974 E) 43,000
Kolomna 162,000
Kolomyya (1987 E) 63,000
Kolpino (★ Leningrad) 142,000
Kommunarsk (★ Stakhanov) 126,000
Komsomolsk-na-Amure 315,000
Konakovo (1974 E) 33,000
Kondopoga (1974 E) 32,000
Konotop (1987 E) 93,000

C Census. E Official estimate. UE Unofficial estimate.
• Largest city in country.

★ Population or designation of metropolitan area, including suburbs (see headnote).
▲ Population of an entire municipality, commune, or district, including rural area.

Konstantinovka 108,000
Kopeysk (★ Chelyabinsk) (1987 E) 99,000
Korkino (1981 E) 63,000
Korosten (1987 E) 72,000
Korsakov (1974 E) 40,000
Kostroma 278,000
Kotelnich (1974 E) 31,000
Kotlas (1987 E) 69,000
Kotovsk (1974 E) 39,000
Kovel (1987 E) 66,000
Kovrov 160,000
Kramatorsk (★ 465,000) 198,000
Krasnoarmeysk (★ 175,000) (1987 E) 70,000
Krasnodar 620,000
Krasnodon (1987 E) 52,000
Krasnogorsk (★ Moscow) (1987 E) 89,000
Krasnokamensk (1987 E) 70,000
Krasnokamsk (1987 E) 58,000
Krasnoturinsk (1987 E) 66,000
Krasnoufimsk (1974 E) 40,000
Krasnouralsk (1974 E) 40,000
Krasnovodsk (1987 E) 59,000
Krasnoyarsk 912,000
Krasnyy Luch (★ 250,000) 113,000
Krasnyy Sulin (1974 E) 43,000
Kremenchug 236,000
Krivoy Rog 713,000
Kronshtadt (★ Leningrad) (1970 C) 39,477
Kropotkin (1987 E) 73,000
Krymsk (Krymskaya) (1983 E) 50,000
Kstovo (★ Gorkiy) (1987 E) 64,000
Kuba (1974 E) 19,000
Kulebaki (1974 E) 46,000
Kulyab (1987 E) 71,000
Kumertau (1987 E) 62,000
Kungur (1987 E) 83,000
Kupyansk (1974 E) 34,000
Kurgan 356,000
Kurganinsk (1974 E) 38,000
Kurgan-Tyube (1987 E) 55,000
Kursk 424,000
Kushva (1974 E) 43,000
Kustanay 224,000
Kutaisi 235,000
Kuybyshev (★ 1,505,000) 1,257,000
Kuybyshev (1987 E) 51,000
Kuznetsk (1987 E) 98,000
Kyshtym (1974 E) 39,000
Kyzyl (1987 E) 80,000
Kyzyl-Kiya (1974 E) 33,000
Kzyl-Orda 153,000
Labinsk (1987 E) 58,000
Leninabad 160,000
Leninakan 120,000
Leningrad (★ 5,825,000) 4,456,000
Leninogorsk, Tatarskaya Auton. S. S. R. (1987 E) 69,000
Leninogorsk, Vostochno-Kazakhstanskaya oblast' (1987 E) 61,000
Leninsk (1974 E) 31,000
Leninsk-Kuznetskiy 165,000
Lenkoran (1974 E) 38,000
Lesozavodsk (1974 E) 38,000
Lida (1987 E) 81,000
Liepāja 114,000
Lipetsk 450,000
Lisichansk (★ 410,000) 127,000
Livny (1987 E) 51,000
Lobnya (★ Moscow) (1987 E) 59,000
Lomonosov (★ Leningrad) (1980 E) 46,000
Lozovaya (1987 E) 68,000
Lubny (1987 E) 58,000
Luga (1974 E) 35,000
Lutsk 198,000
Lvov 790,000
Lysva (1987 E) 77,000
Lytkarino (★ Moscow) (1987 E) 51,000
Lyubertsy (★ Moscow) 165,000
Lyubotin (1974 E) 33,000
Lyudinovo (1974 E) 36,000
Magadan 152,000
Magnitogorsk 440,000
Makeyevka (★★ Donetsk) 430,000
Makhachkala 315,000
Marganets (1987 E) 55,000
Margilan 125,000
Mariinsk (1974 E) 40,000
Mariupol 517,000
Mary (1987 E) 89,000
Maykop 149,000
Mednogorsk (1974 E) 36,000
Melitopol 174,000
Mezhdurechensk 107,000
Miass 168,000
Michurinsk 109,000
Mikhaylovka (1987 E) 58,000
Millerovo (1974 E) 37,000
Mineralnyye Vody (1987 E) 75,000
Mingechaur (1987 E) 78,000
Minsk (★ 1,650,000) 1,589,000
Minusinsk (1987 E) 72,000
Mogilev 356,000
Molodechno (1987 E) 87,000
Monchegorsk (1987 E) 65,000
Morshansk (1987 E) 51,000
• MOSCOW (MOSKVA) (★ 13,100,000) 8,769,000
Mozdok (1974 E) 33,000
Mozhga (1974 E) 41,000
Mozyr 101,000
Mtsensk (1974 E) 34,000
Mukachevo (1987 E) 88,000
Murmansk 468,000
Murom 124,000
Myski (1974 E) 38,000
Mytishchi (★ Moscow) 154,000
Naberezhnyye Chelny 501,000
Nakhichevan (1987 E) 51,000
Nakhodka 165,000
Nalchik 235,000
Namangan 308,000
Naro-Fominsk (1987 E) 60,000
Narva (1987 E) 81,000
Navoy 107,000
Nazarovo (1987 E) 63,000
Nebit-Dag (1987 E) 85,000
Neftekamsk 107,000
Nefteyugansk (1987 E) 86,000
Neryungri (1987 E) 68,000
Nevinnomyssk 121,000
Nevyansk (1974 E) 31,000
Nezhin (1987 E) 81,000
Nikolayev 503,000
Nikolayevsk [-na-Amure] (1974 E) 33,000
Nikolskiy (1987 E) 64,000
Nikopol 158,000
Nizhnekamsk 191,000
Nizhneudinsk (1974 E) 42,000
Nizhnevartovsk 242,000
Nizhniy Tagil 440,000
Noginsk 123,000
Norilsk 174,000
Novaya Kakhovka (1987 E) 53,000
Novgorod 229,000
Novoaltaysk (★ Barnaul) (1987 E) 51,000
Novocheboksarsk 115,000
Novocherkassk 187,000
Novodvinsk (1987 E) 50,000
Novoekonomicheskoye (★★ Krasnoarmeysk) (1970 C) 31,214
Novograd-Volynskiy (1987 E) 52,000
Novokazalinsk (1970 C) 34,815
Novokuybyshevsk (★ Kuybyshev) 113,000
Novokuznetsk 600,000
Novomoskovsk, Dnepropetrovsk oblast (1987 E) 76,000
Novomoskovsk, Tula oblast (★ 365,000) 146,000
Novopolotsk (1987 E) 90,000
Novorossiysk 186,000
Novoshakhtinsk 106,000
Novosibirsk (★ 1,600,000) 1,436,000
Novotroitsk 106,000
Novovolynsk (1987 E) 54,000
Novozybkov (1974 E) 39,000
Novyy Urengoy (1987 E) 79,000
Noyabrsk (1987 E) 77,000
Nukus 169,000
Obninsk 100,000
Odessa (★ 1,185,000) 1,115,000
Odintsovo (★ Moscow) 125,000
Okha (1974 E) 31,000
Oktyabr'sk (1974 E) 33,000
Oktyabrskiy 105,000
Omsk (★ 1,175,000) 1,148,000
Ordzhonikidze 300,000
Orekhovo-Zuyevo (★ 205,000) 137,000
Orel 337,000
Orenburg 547,000
Orsha 123,000
Orsk 271,000
Osh 213,000
Osinniki (1987 E) 63,000
Otradnyy (1974 E) 46,000
Panevėžys 126,000
Pärnu (1987 E) 53,000
Partizansk (Suchan) (1974 E) 49,000
Pavlodar 331,000
Pavlograd 131,000
Pavlovo (1987 E) 72,000
Pavlovskiy Posad (1987 E) 71,000
Pechora (1987 E) 64,000
Penza 543,000
Pereslavl-Zalesskiy (1974 E) 33,000
Perevalsk (★ Stakhanov) (1974 E) 32,000
Perm (★ 1,160,000) 1,091,000
Pervomaysk (1987 E) 79,000
Pervomaysk (★ Stakhanov) (1974 E) 46,000
Pervouralsk 142,000
Petrodvorets (★ Leningrad) (1987 E) 77,000
Petropavlovsk 241,000
Petropavlovsk [-Kamchatskiy] 269,000
Petrovsk (1974 E) 34,000
Petrozavodsk 270,000
Pinsk 119,000
Podolsk (★ Moscow) 210,000
Polevskoy (1987 E) 71,000
Polotsk (1987 E) 80,000
Poltava 315,000
Poti (1977 E) 54,000
Priluki (1987 E) 73,000
Prokhladnyy (1987 E) 53,000
Prokopyevsk (★ 410,000) 274,000
Przhevalsk (1987 E) 64,000
Pskov 204,000
Pugachev (1974 E) 35,000
Pushkin (★ Leningrad) (1987 E) 97,000
Pushkino (1987 E) 74,000
Pyatigorsk 129,000
Ramenskoye (1987 E) 86,000
Rasskazovo (1974 E) 40,000
Razdan (1987 E) 56,000
Rechitsa (1987 E) 71,000
Reutov (★ Moscow) (1987 E) 68,000
Revda (1987 E) 66,000
Rēzekne (1974 E) 34,000
Rezh (1974 E) 34,000
Rīga (★ 1,005,000) 915,000
Rodniki (1974 E) 30,000
Romny (1987 E) 53,000
Roslavl (1987 E) 61,000
Rossosh (1987 E) 55,000
Rostov (1974 E) 31,000
Rostov-na-Donu (★ 1,165,000) 1,020,000
Rovenki (1987 E) 68,000
Rovno 228,000
Rtishchevo (1974 E) 41,000
Rubezhnoye (★★ Lisichansk) (1987 E) 72,000
Rubtsovsk 172,000
Rudnyy 124,000
Rustavi (★ Tbilisi) 159,000
Ruzayevka (1987 E) 53,000
Ryazan 515,000
Rybachye (1974 E) 33,000
Rybinsk 252,000
Rybnitsa (1987 E) 58,000
Rzhev (1987 E) 70,000
Safonovo (1987 E) 56,000
Salavat 150,000
Salsk (1987 E) 62,000
Samarkand 366,000
Saran (1987 E) 64,000
Saransk 312,000
Sarapul 111,000
Saratov (★ 1,155,000) 905,000
Satka (1974 E) 44,000
Segezha (1974 E) 33,000
Semipalatinsk 334,000
Serdobsk (1974 E) 37,000
Serov 104,000
Serpukhov 144,000
Sevastopol 356,000
Severodonetsk (★★ Lisichansk) 131,000
Severodvinsk (Molotovsk) 249,000
Severomorsk (1987 E) 55,000
Shadrinsk (1987 E) 87,000
Shakhtersk (★★ Torez) (1987 E) 73,000
Shakhtinsk (1987 E) 62,000
Shakhty 224,000
Shchekino (1987 E) 70,000
Shchelkovo (★ Moscow) 109,000
Shchuchinsk (1987 E) 53,000
Shebekino (1974 E) 36,000
Sheki (Nukha) (1987 E) 54,000
Shepetovka (1974 E) 42,000
Shevchenko 159,000
Shostka (1987 E) 87,000
Shumerlya (1974 E) 35,000
Shuya (1987 E) 72,000
Šiauliai 145,000
Sibay (1974 E) 40,000
Simferopol 344,000
Slantsy (1974 E) 42,000
Slavyansk (★★ Kramatorsk) 135,000
Slavyansk-na-Kubani (1987 E) 57,000
Slobodskoy (1974 E) 36,000
Slutsk (1987 E) 55,000
Smela (1987 E) 76,000
Smolensk 341,000
Snezhnoye (★ Torez) (1987 E) 68,000
Sochi 337,000
Sokol (1974 E) 48,000
Soligorsk (1987 E) 92,000
Solikamsk 110,000
Solnechnogorsk (★ Moscow) (1987 E) 53,000
Solntsevo (★ Moscow) (1984 E) 62,000
Sosnovyy Bor (1987 E) 56,000
Sovetsk (Tilsit) (1974 E) 40,000
Spassk-Dalniy (1987 E) 60,000
Stakhanov (Kadiyevka) (★ 610,000) 112,000
Staraya Russa (1974 E) 37,000
Staryy Oskol 174,000
Stavropol 318,000
Sterlitamak 248,000
Stryy (1987 E) 63,000
Stupino (1987 E) 73,000
Sukhumi 121,000
Sumgait (★ Baku) 231,000
Sumy 291,000
Surgut 248,000
Suzdal (1959 C) 9,000
Sverdlovsk (★ 1,620,000) 1,367,000
Sverdlovsk (1987 E) 84,000
Svetlogorsk (1987 E) 68,000
Svetlovodsk (Kremges) (1987 E) 55,000
Svobodnyy (1987 E) 78,000
Syktyvkar 233,000
Syzran 174,000
Taganrog 291,000
Taldy-Kurgan 119,000
Talgar (1974 E) 35,000
Tallinn 482,000
Talnakh (1987 E) 54,000
Tambov 305,000
Tartu 114,000
Tashauz 112,000
Tashkent (★ 2,325,000) 2,073,000
Tatarsk (1974 E) 31,000
Tavda (1974 E) 47,000
Tayshet (1974 E) 35,000
Tbilisi (★ 1,460,000) 1,260,000
Temirtau 212,000
Termez (1987 E) 72,000
Ternopol 205,000
Teykovo (1974 E) 42,000
Tikhoretsk (1987 E) 67,000
Tikhvin (1987 E) 70,000
Tiraspol 182,000
Tobolsk (1987 E) 82,000
Tokmak (1987 E) 71,000
Tokmak (1974 E) 39,000
Tolyatti (Stavropol) 630,000
Tomsk 502,000
Topki (1974 E) 30,000
Torez (Chistyakovo) (★ 290,000) (1987 E) 88,000
Torzhok (1987 E) 51,000
Troitsk (1987 E) 91,000
Tselinograd (Akmolinsk) 277,000
Tskhinvali (1975 E) 34,000
Tuapse (1987 E) 64,000
Tula (★ 640,000) 540,000
Tulun (1987 E) 56,000
Turkestan (1987 E) 77,000
Tuymazy (1987 E) 54,000
Tynda (1987 E) 61,000
Tyumen 477,000
Ufa (★ 1,100,000) 1,083,000
Uglich (1974 E) 37,000
Ukhta 111,000
Ulan-Ude 353,000
Ulyanovsk 625,000
Uman (1987 E) 89,000
Uralsk 200,000
Ura-Tyube (1974 E) 36,000
Urgench 128,000
Uryupinsk (1974 E) 39,000
Usolye-Sibirskoye 107,000
Ussuriysk 162,000
Ust-Ilimsk 109,000
Ust-Kamenogorsk 324,000
Ust-Kut (1987 E) 58,000
Ust'-Labinsk (1974 E) 38,000
Uzhgorod 117,000
Uzlovaya (1987 E) 63,000
Valuyki (1974 E) 30,000
Velikiye Luki 114,000
Velikiy Ustyug (1974 E) 38,000
Ventspils (1987 E) 52,000
Verkhniy Ufaley (1974 E) 38,000
Verkhnyaya Pyshma (★ Sverdlovsk) (1974 E) 40,000
Verkhnyaya Salda (1987 E) 56,000
Vichuga (1987 E) 51,000
Vidnoye (1974 E) 40,000
Vilnius 582,000
Vinnitsa 374,000
Vitebsk 350,000
Vladimir 350,000
Vladivostok 648,000
Volgodonsk 176,000
Volgograd (Stalingrad) (★ 1,360,000) 999,000
Volkhov (1987 E) 51,000
Vologda 283,000
Volsk (1987 E) 66,000
Volzhsk (1987 E) 60,000
Volzhskiy (★ Volgograd) 269,000
Vorkuta 116,000
Voronezh 887,000
Voroshilovgrad (Lugansk) 497,000
Voskresensk (1987 E) 80,000
Votkinsk 103,000
Voznesensk (1974 E) 39,000
Vyatskiye Polyany (1974 E) 35,000
Vyazma (1987 E) 57,000
Vyazniki (1974 E) 44,000
Vyborg (1987 E) 81,000
Vyksa (1987 E) 60,000
Vyshniy Volochek (1987 E) 70,000
Yakutsk 187,000
Yalta (1987 E) 89,000
Yangiyul (1987 E) 71,000
Yaroslavl 633,000
Yartsevo (1974 E) 39,000
Yasinovataya (1974 E) 39,000
Yefremov (1987 E) 58,000
Yegoryevsk (1987 E) 73,000
Yelabuga (1974 E) 35,000
Yelets 120,000
Yemanzhelinsk (1974 E) 34,000
Yenakiyevo (★★ Gorlovka) 121,000
Yerevan (★ 1,315,000) 1,199,000
Yermak (1974 E) 40,000
Yessentuki (1987 E) 84,000
Yevpatoriya 108,000
Yeysk (1987 E) 77,000
Yoshkar-Ola 242,000
Yurga (1987 E) 92,000
Yuzhno-Sakhalinsk 157,000
Yuzhno-Uralsk (1974 E) 37,000
Zagorsk 115,000
Zaporozhye 884,000
Zavolzhye (1974 E) 38,000
Zelenograd (★ Moscow) 158,000
Zel'onodol'sk (1987 E) 93,000
Zhanatas (1987 E) 53,000
Zheleznodorozhnyy (★ Moscow) (1987 E) 90,000
Zheleznogorsk (1987 E) 81,000
Zheltyye Vody (1987 E) 61,000
Zhigulevsk (1977 E) 50,000
Zhitomir 292,000
Zhlobin (1987 E) 52,000
Zhmerinka (1974 E) 38,000
Zhodino (1987 E) 51,000
Zhukovskiy 101,000
Zima (1987 E) 51,000
Zlatoust 208,000
Zugdidi (1974 E) 41,000
Zyryanovsk (1987 E) 55,000

Republics

Armenia 3,283,000
Azerbaijan S.S.R. 7,029,000
Byelorussia (White Russia) 10,200,000
Estonia 1,573,000
Georgia 5,449,000
Kazakh S.S.R. 16,538,000
Kirghiz S.S.R. 4,291,000
Latvia 2,681,000
Lithuania 3,690,000
Moldavia 4,341,000
Russian Soviet Federative Socialist Republic 147,386,000
Tajik S.S.R. 5,112,000
Turkmen S.S.R. 3,534,000
Ukraine 51,704,000
Uzbek S.S.R. 19,906,000

SPAIN / España

1987 E 38,606,576

Cities and Towns

Águilas 23,162
Albacete 125,764
Alcalá [de Guadaira] 50,567
Alcalá de Henares (★ Madrid) 145,320
Alcalá la Real (▲ 20,410) 12,184
Alcantarilla 27,454
Alcázar de San Juan 26,302
Alcira 40,234
Alcobendas (★ Madrid) 71,542
Alcorcón (★ Madrid) 138,448
Alcoy 66,312
Algeciras 97,601
Algemesí 25,195
Algorta (Guecho) (▲ 78,672) 37,800
Alicante 258,004
Almadén (1981 C) 9,521
Almendralejo 25,137
Almería 154,911
Andújar (▲ 36,027) 31,400
Antequera (▲ 40,844) 31,900
Aranjuez 37,079
Arcos de la Frontera (▲ 26,915) 19,300
Arizgoiti (Basauri) (★ Bilbao) 45,600
Arrecife, Canary Is. 33,272
Ávila 44,221
Avilés (★ 131,000) 86,858
Badajoz (▲ 120,240) 104,500
Badalona (★ Barcelona) 224,233
Baracaldo (★ Bilbao) 114,090
Barcelona (★ 4,040,000) 1,703,744
Baza 20,682
Benidorm 34,831
Bilbao (★ 985,000) 382,413
Burgos 158,857
Burjasot (★ Valencia) 35,024
Burriana 25,369
Cabra (▲ 20,181) 17,900
Cáceres 69,770
Cádiz (★ 240,000) 156,113
Camas (★ Sevilla) 25,427
Carmona 24,029
Cartagena (▲ 169,036) 68,500
Castellón de la Plana 128,664
Cerdanyola de Vallès (★ Barcelona) 42,700
Chiclana [de la Frontera] 42,226
Cieza 30,419
Ciudad Real 55,072
Colmenar Viejo 30,328
Córdoba 298,372
Cornellá (★ Barcelona) 86,971
Coslada (★ Madrid) 65,598
Cuenca 41,407
Daimiel (1981 C) 16,260
Don Benito (▲ 28,829) 24,100
Dos Hermanas (▲ 67,330) 59,600
Écija (▲ 35,434) 30,600
Éibar 34,545
Elche (▲ 177,629) 156,000
Elda 56,189
El Ferrol [del Caudillo] (★ 129,000) 86,329
El Puerto de Santa María (▲ 61,032) 48,900
Esplugas Llobregat (★ Barcelona) 47,598
Figueras 32,035
Fuenlabrada (★ Madrid) 122,752
Gandía (▲ 51,092) 44,700
Gavá (★ Barcelona) 33,076
Gerona (▲ 67,447) 30,200
Getafe (★ Madrid) 132,786
Gijón 258,759
Granada 256,800
Granollers (★ Barcelona) 48,380
Guadalajara 59,492
Guadix (▲ 20,286) 16,500
Guernica y Luno (▲ 17,836) (1981 C) 12,214
Hellín (▲ 24,487) 19,000
Hospitalet (★ Barcelona) 277,688
Huelva 135,938
Huesca 40,949
Ibiza 27,685
Igualada 31,107
Irún 54,301

C Census. E Official estimate. UE Unofficial estimate.
• Largest city in country.

★ Population or designation of metropolitan area, including suburbs (see headnote).
▲ Population of an entire municipality, commune, or district, including rural area.

Jaén	103,698
Játiva	24,237
Jerez de la Frontera (▲ 179,349)	153,100
La Coruña	242,437
La Línea	59,260
La Orotava, Canary Is. (▲ 35,528)	11,500
Las Palmas de Gran Canaria, Canary Is. (▲ 358,272)	312,000
Leganés (★ Madrid)	167,748
León (★ 159,000)	135,521
Lérida (▲ 108,207)	90,200
Linares (▲ 57,401)	57,526
Logroño	116,273
Loja (▲ 21,883)	14,000
Lorca (▲ 65,458)	26,300
Lucena (▲ 31,243)	25,800
Lugo (▲ 77,043)	67,200
• MADRID (★ 4,650,000)	3,100,507
Mahón	22,028
Málaga	566,330
Manacor	24,397
Manresa	65,285
Marbella (▲ 75,351)	44,900
Martos (▲ 22,036)	16,800
Mataró	100,189
Mérida	52,225
Mieres (▲ 57,532)	26,500
Miranda de Ebro	35,892
Mislata (★ Valencia)	35,815
Mollet	38,568
Morón de la Frontera	28,653
Móstoles (★ Madrid)	176,993
Motril (▲ 44,882)	37,700
Murcia (▲ 305,278)	145,600
Olot (▲ 24,892)	18,573
Onteniente	29,162
Orense	103,397
Orihuela (▲ 45,938)	20,300
Oviedo (▲ 186,363)	165,600
Palencia	75,951
Palma [de Mallorca] (▲ 306,840)	242,900
Pamplona	178,666
Parla (★ Madrid)	64,546
Peñarroya-Pueblonuevo (1981 C)	13,219
Plasencia	32,902
Ponferrada (▲ 59,399)	33,600
Pontevedra (▲ 67,314)	40,000
Portugalete (★ Bilbao)	58,117
Prat de Llobregat (★ Barcelona)	63,411
Priego [de Córdoba] (▲ 20,788)	14,200
Puente-Genil (▲ 26,961)	24,000
Puerto de la Cruz, Canary Is.	25,418
Puertollano	51,755
Rentería (★ San Sebastián)	43,653
Reus	81,816
Ronda (▲ 32,556)	25,600
Rota (▲ 21,583)	18,900
Rubí (★ Barcelona)	47,069
Sabadell (★ Barcelona)	187,506
Sagunto (▲ 55,957)	19,400
Salamanca	155,612
Sama [de Langreo] (▲ 53,889)	9,800
San Adrián de Besós (★ Barcelona)	34,673
San Baudilio de Llobregat (★ Barcelona)	76,008
San Cristóbal de la Laguna, Canary Is. (▲ 107,593)	25,000
San Felíu de Llobregat	37,626
San Fernando (★★ Cádiz)	80,791
Sanlúcar [de Barrameda] (▲ 53,566)	37,300
San Sebastián (★ 285,000)	176,586
San Sebastián de los Reyes (★ Madrid)	50,531
Santa Coloma [de Gramanet] (★ Barcelona)	135,310
Santa Cruz de Tenerife, Canary Is.	211,209
Santander (▲ 187,222)	163,700
Santiago [de Compostela] (▲ 86,818)	67,800
Santurce-Antiguo (★ Bilbao)	52,480
Segovia	53,849
Sestao (★ Bilbao)	38,217
Sevilla (Seville) (★ 945,000)	655,435
Soria	31,507
Sueca	24,400
Talavera de la Reina	67,680
Tarragona (▲ 107,356)	62,200
Tarrasa (★ Barcelona)	160,245
Telde, Canary Is. (▲ 75,106)	18,300
Teruel	27,475
Toledo	58,297
Tolosa (▲ 18,894) (1981 C)	13,015
Tomelloso	28,344
Torrejón de Ardoz (★ Madrid)	81,658
Torrelavega (▲ 58,885)	28,600
Torrente (★ Valencia)	54,739
Tortosa (▲ 28,862)	19,300
Totana (▲ 18,394) (1981 C)	15,420
Úbeda	30,720
Utrera (▲ 41,021)	35,500
Valdepeñas	25,337
Valencia (★ 1,270,000)	732,491
Valladolid	329,206
Vall de Uxó	27,565
Vélez-Málaga (▲ 51,132)	31,600
Vich	28,609
Vigo (▲ 262,560)	173,800
Viladecáns	45,423
Villanueva y Geltrú	45,258
Villarreal [de los Infantes] (▲ 37,035)	33,100
Villarrobledo	20,829
Villena	30,428
Vitoria	200,742
Zamora	60,708
Zaragoza (Saragossa)	575,317

Regions

Andalusia	6,842,464
Aragón	1,185,840
Asturias	1,115,016
Baleares	700,307
Canarias (Canary Is.)	1,479,549
Cantabria	524,844
Castilla-La Mancha	1,680,780
Castilla-León	2,592,287
Cataluña	6,000,522
Extremadura	1,092,398
Galicia	2,858,130
La Rioja	260,964
Madrid	4,846,100
Murcia	1,013,647
Navarra	516,872
País Vasco	2,142,631
Palencia	189,898
Valencia	3,754,225

Provinces

Alava	268,863
Albacete	346,793
Alicante	1,226,657
Almería	446,200
Asturias	1,115,016
Ávila	182,634
Badajoz	670,051
Baleares	700,307
Barcelona	4,629,176
Burgos	359,711
Cáceres	422,347
Cádiz	1,052,419
Cantabria (Santander)	524,844
Castellón	439,266
Ciudad Real	485,639
Córdoba	753,102
Cuenca	213,812
Gerona	492,028
Granada	788,187
Guadalajara	146,669
Guipúzcoa	691,410
Huelva	436,813
Huesca	210,257
Jaén	650,844
La Coruña	1,116,398
La Rioja	260,964
Las Palmas	761,793
León	532,890
Lérida	352,350
Lugo	406,123
Madrid	4,846,100
Málaga	1,160,739
Murcia	1,013,647
Navarra	516,872
Orense	432,714
Pontevedra	902,895
Salamanca	362,477
Santa Cruz de Tenerife	717,756
Segovia	151,036
Sevilla	1,554,160
Soria	97,915
Tarragona	526,968
Teruel	149,423
Toledo	487,867
Valencia	2,088,302
Valladolid	493,486
Vizcaya	1,182,358
Zamora	222,240
Zaragoza	826,160

SPANISH NORTH AFRICA / Plazas de Soberanía en el Norte de África

1987 E 118,380

Cities and Towns

• Ceuta	65,141
Melilla	53,239

SRI LANKA

1985 E 15,837,000

Cities and Towns

Anuradhapura	46,000
Badulla	44,000
Battaramulla (★ Colombo) (1981 C)	56,535
Batticaloa	47,000
• COLOMBO (★ 2,050,000)	664,000
Dalugama (★ Colombo) (1981 C)	47,723
Dehiwala-Mount Lavinia (★ Colombo)	188,000
Galle	102,000
Jaffna	138,000
Kalutara	47,000
Kandy	125,000
Kegalla (1981 C)	15,000
Kelaniya (★ Colombo) (1981 C)	36,738
Kolonnawa (★ Colombo) (1981 C)	41,005
Kotikawatta (★ Colombo) (1981 C)	48,262
Kotte (★ Colombo)	102,000
Kurunegala	44,000
Maharagama (★ Colombo) (1981 C)	49,765
Matale	57,000
Matara (1981 C)	39,000
Moratuwa (★ Colombo)	138,000
Negombo	76,000
Puttalam (1981 C)	21,000
Ratnapura	51,000
Trincomalee	51,000

SUDAN / As Sūdān

1983 C 20,564,364

Cities and Towns

Al Junaynah (1973 C)	35,424
Al Qaḍārif (1973 C)	66,465
An Nuhūd (1973 C)	26,002
'Aṭbarah	73,000
Barbar (1973 C)	11,303
El Fasher (1973 C)	51,932
El Obeid (Al Ubayyiḍ)	140,000
Jūbā (1973 C)	56,737
Kassalā	143,000
• KHARTOUM (AL KHARṬŪM) (★ 1,450,000)	476,218
Khartoum North (Al Kharṭūm Baḥrī) (★ Khartoum)	341,146
Kūstī (1973 C)	65,257
Malakāl (1973 C)	34,898
Nyala (1973 C)	59,852
Omdurman (Umm Durmān) (★★ Khartoum)	526,287
Port Sudan (Būr Sūdān)	206,727
Sannār (1973 C)	28,546
Sinjah (1973 C)	19,452
Ṭawkar (1973 C)	13,394
Umm Ruwābah (1973 C)	19,713
Wad Madanī	141,000
Wāw (1973 C)	52,752

SURINAME

1988 E 392,000

Cities and Towns

• PARAMARIBO	241,000
Wanica	55,000

SWAZILAND

1986 C 712,131

Cities and Towns

LOBAMBA	
Manzini (★ 30,000)	18,084
• MBABANE	38,290

SWEDEN / Sverige

1988 E 8,414,083

Cities and Towns

Alingsås (▲ 32,051)	20,900
Ängelholm (▲ 32,443)	18,600
Arvika (▲ 26,532)	13,600
Avesta (▲ 24,731)	17,300
Boden (▲ 29,117)	18,800
Bollnäs (▲ 27,659)	13,000
Borås	100,395
Borlänge	45,990
Enköping (▲ 33,290)	18,900
Eskilstuna	88,508
Eslöv (▲ 26,566)	13,300
Falkenberg (▲ 36,095)	16,100
Falun (▲ 52,202)	33,500
Gällivare (▲ 22,908)	7,600
Gävle (▲ 87,474)	67,000
Göteborg (Gothenburg) (★ 710,894)	431,521
Halmstad (▲ 77,942)	50,000
Härnösand (▲ 27,252)	19,200
Hässleholm (▲ 48,493)	16,000
Helsingborg	106,982
Huddinge (★ Stockholm)	71,910
Hudiksvall (▲ 37,568)	14,800
Järfälla (★ Stockholm)	56,563
Jönköping	108,962
Kalmar (▲ 54,915)	31,000
Karlshamn (▲ 31,429)	17,700
Karlskoga	34,395
Karlskrona (▲ 58,650)	31,700
Karlstad	74,892
Katrineholm (▲ 31,884)	21,600
Kiruna	26,551
Köping (▲ 26,280)	19,100
Kristianstad (▲ 70,180)	31,200
Kristinehamn (▲ 26,061)	13,500
Kungsbacka (▲ 50,804)	14,500
Landskrona	35,371
Lidingö (★ Stockholm)	38,818
Lidköping (▲ 35,082)	21,400
Lindesberg (▲ 24,446)	8,300
Linköping	118,602
Ljungby (▲ 27,199)	13,500
Ludvika (▲ 29,414)	16,400
Luleå	66,719
Lund (★★ Malm320)	84,342
Malmö (★ 445,000)	230,838
Mariestad (▲ 24,465)	15,700
Mjölby (▲ 25,828)	12,300
Mölndal (★ Göteborg)	50,549
Motala (▲ 41,444)	29,400
Nacka (★ Stockholm)	61,084
Nässjö (▲ 30,739)	17,000
Norrköping	119,001
Norrtälje (▲ 43,140)	13,700
Nyköping (▲ 64,428)	28,300
Örebro	119,066
Örnsköldsvik (▲ 59,248)	29,400
Oskarshamn (▲ 27,351)	18,600
Östersund (▲ 56,914)	41,200
Partille (★ Göteborg)	29,604
Piteå (▲ 38,828)	16,300
Ronneby (▲ 28,988)	11,600
Sandviken	39,876
Skellefteå (▲ 74,091)	30,000
Skövde (▲ 46,438)	30,000
Söderhamn (▲ 29,709)	13,400
Södertälje (★ Stockholm)	80,263
Sollefteå (▲ 25,184)	9,200
Sollentuna (★ Stockholm)	49,757
Solna (★ Stockholm)	50,450
• STOCKHOLM (★ 1,449,972)	666,810
Sundbyberg (★ Stockholm)	30,569
Sundsvall (▲ 92,721)	50,200
Täby (★ Stockholm)	55,661
Trelleborg (▲ 34,362)	22,200
Trollhättan	49,914
Tumba (Botkyrka) (★ Stockholm)	67,536
Uddevalla (▲ 46,257)	30,500
Umeå (▲ 86,816)	56,600
Upplands Väsby (★ Stockholm)	35,023
Uppsala	159,962
Vänersborg (▲ 35,948)	20,700
Varberg (▲ 47,040)	21,100
Värnamo (▲ 30,894)	23,800
Västerås	117,563
Västervik (▲ 39,558)	20,800
Växjö (▲ 67,350)	44,500
Vetlanda (▲ 27,727)	12,100
Visby (Gotland) (▲ 56,269)	20,100

Counties

Älvsborg	430,129
Blekinge	149,600
Gävleborg	286,907
Göteborg och Bohus	726,325
Gotland	56,269
Halland	244,377
Jämtland	133,389
Jönköping	302,475
Kalmar	237,356
Kopparberg	283,330
Kristianstad	281,907
Kronoberg	174,116
Malmöhus	757,643
Norrbotten	260,833
Örebro	269,341
Östergötland	395,580
Skaraborg	270,847
Södermanland	250,073
Stockholm	1,606,157
Uppsala	257,739
Värmland	279,402
Västerbotten	245,703
Västernorrland	260,332
Västmanland	254,253

Historic Provinces

Ångermanland	155,632
Blekinge	149,600
Bohuslän	237,749
Dalarna	283,845
Dalsland	55,769
Gästrikland	145,476
Gotland	56,269
Halland	248,567
Hälsingland	142,344
Härjedalen	11,430
Jämtland	115,779
Lappland	114,348
Medelpad	123,855
Närke	173,174
Norrbotten	192,638
Öland	23,924
Östergötland	392,674
Skåne	1,037,834
Småland	699,690
Södermanland	982,985
Uppland	1,152,482
Värmland	324,131
Västerbotten	185,147
Västergötland	1,125,461
Västmanland	283,280

SWITZERLAND / Schweiz / Suisse / Svizzera

1987 E 6,523,413

Cities and Towns

Aarau (★ 57,900)	15,750
Adliswil (★ Zürich)	15,848
Allschwil (★ Basel)	18,339
Altdorf	8,163
Appenzell	4,914
Arbon (★ 41,100)	12,292
Arosa	2,399
Baar (★ Zug)	15,481
Baden (★ 70,700)	14,058
Basel (Bâle) (★ 575,000)	173,160
Bellinzona (★ 36,500)	16,886
BERN (BERNE) (★ 298,800)	137,134
Biel (Bienne) (★ 81,900)	51,341
Bülach	13,292
Burgdorf	15,072
Château d'Oex	2,797
Chiasso (★ 38,600)	8,687
Chur (Coire) (★ 42,500)	30,740
Davos	10,377
Delémont	11,298
Einsiedeln	9,973
Emmen (★ Luzern)	23,451
Frauenfeld	18,944
Fribourg (Freiburg) (★ 56,800)	33,935
Geneva (Genève) (★ 460,000)	160,645
Glarus	5,593
Grenchen (★ 23,800)	15,705
Grindelwald	3,560
Herisau (★★ Sankt Gallen)	14,947
Illnau [-Effretikon] (★ Zürich)	14,624
Interlaken	4,899
Köniz (★ Bern)	35,664
Kreuzlingen (★ 22,200)	16,149
Kriens (★ Luzern)	21,327
La Chaux-de-Fonds	35,726
Langenthal	13,868
Lausanne (★ 259,900)	124,206
Lauterbrunnen	2,829
Le Locle	10,953
Liestal (★ Basel)	12,161
Locarno (★ 42,350)	14,473
Lugano (★ 94,800)	27,462
Luzern (Lucerne) (★ 159,500)	59,904
Martigny	12,359
Meiringen	4,000
Monthey	11,809
Montreux (★★ Vevey)	18,970
Morges (★ Lausanne)	13,565
Neuchâtel (Neuenburg) (★ 65,900)	32,650
Nyon	13,587
Olten (★ 43,450)	17,800
Riehen (★ Basel)	20,054
Rorschach (★★ Arbon)	9,325
Sankt Gallen (Saint-Gall) (★ 125,000)	72,910
Sankt Moritz	5,335
Sarnen	7,980
Schaffhausen (★ 53,000)	33,826
Schwyz	12,350
Sierre	13,063
Sion	23,504
Solothurn (Soleure) (★ 56,800)	15,499
Stans	5,969
Thun (Thoune) (★ 77,200)	37,074
Uster	25,227
Vernier (★ Genève)	27,426
Vevey (★ 63,100)	15,021
Wädenswil	19,084
Wettingen (★ Baden)	17,799
Wil (★ 23,200)	16,124
Winterthur (★ 107,400)	84,548
Wohlen	11,553
Yverdon (Iferten) (★ 21,500)	21,004
Zermatt	3,929
Zug (Zoug) (★ 67,100)	21,569
• Zürich (★ 860,000)	349,549

Cantons

Aargau	472,685
Appenzell Ausser-Rhoden	49,342
Appenzell Inner-Rhoden	13,137
Basel-Land	225,836
Basel-Stadt	194,340
Bern (Berne)	925,463
Fribourg (Freiburg)	194,645
Genève	363,550
Glarus	36,580
Graubünden (Grisons)	166,494
Jura	64,711
Luzern (Lucerne)	306,132
Neuchâtel	156,216
Nidwalden	31,041
Obwalden	27,594
Sankt Gallen	403,931
Schaffhausen	69,781
Schwyz	103,358
Solothurn	219,458
Thurgau	192,439
Ticino (Tessin)	277,220
Uri	33,456
Valais (Wallis)	232,550
Vaud (Waadt)	550,336
Zug (Zoug)	81,634
Zürich	1,131,484

SYRIA / As Sūrīyah

1987 E 10,969,000

Cities and Towns

Aleppo (Ḥalab)	1,216,000
Al Ḥasakah (1981 C)	73,426

C Census. E Official estimate. UE Unofficial estimate.
• Largest city in country.

★ Population or designation of metropolitan area, including suburbs (see headnote).
▲ Population of an entire municipality, commune, or district, including rural area.

Al Qāmishlī (1988 E) 126,236
Ar Raqqah 126,700
As Suwaydā' (1981 C) 43,414
• DAMASCUS (DIMASHQ) (★ 1,850,000) (1988 E) 1,326,000
Dar'ā (1981 C) 49,534
Dārayyā (1988 E) 53,204
Dayr az Zawr (1986 E) 106,500
Dūmā (★ Damascus) (1988 E) 66,130
Hajar Aswad (1988 E) 36,820
Ḥamāh 214,000
Ḥimṣ (Homs) 431,000
Idlib (1981 C) 51,682
Jaramānah (★ Damascus) (1988 E) 96,681
Kābir aş Şaghīr (1988 E) 47,728
Latakia (Al Lādhiqīyah) 241,000
Madīnat ath Thawrah (1988 E) 58,151
Manbij (1988 E) 36,085
Salamīyah (1988 E) 46,844
Ṭarṭūs (1981 C) 52,589

TAIWAN / T'aiwan

1988 E 19,672,612

Cities and Towns

Changhua (▲ 206,603) 158,400
Chiai 254,875
Chilung (Keelung) 348,541
Chungho (★ T'aipei) 343,389
Chungli (Chunli) 247,639
Chutung 104,797
Fengshan (Kaohsiunghsien) (★ Kaohsiung) 276,259
Fengyüan (T'aichunghsien) (▲ 144,434) 115,300
Hsichih (★ T'aipei) (1980 C) 70,031
Hsinchu 309,899
Hsinchuang (★ T'aipei) 259,001
Hsintien (★ T'aipei) 205,094
Hualien 106,658
Ilan (▲ 81,751) (1980 C) 70,900
Kangshan (1980 C) 78,049
Kaohsiung (★ 1,845,000) 1,342,797
Lotung (1980 C) 57,925
Lukang (Luchiang) (1980 C) 72,019
Makung (▲ 55,678) (1980 C) 23,000
Miaoli (1980 C) 81,500
Nant'ou (1980 C) 84,038
Panch'iao (T'aipeihsien) (★ T'aipei) 506,220
P'ingchen (★ T'aipei) 134,925
P'ingtung (▲ 204,990) 167,600
Quemoy (Chinmen) (▲ 51,958) (1980 C) 14,000
Sanch'ung (★ T'aipei) 362,171
Shulin (★ T'aipei) (1980 C) 75,700
Tach'i (1980 C) 67,209
T'aichung 715,107
T'ainan 656,927
• T'AIPEI (★ 6,130,000) 2,637,100
T'aitung (▲ 109,358) 79,800
Tanshui (★ T'aipei) (1980 C) 28,000
T'aoyüan 220,255
T'oufen (1980 C) 66,536
T'uch'eng (★ T'aipei) 70,500
Yangmei (1980 C) 84,353
Yüanlin (▲ 116,936) 51,300
Yungho (★ T'aipei) 242,252
Yungkang (▲ 114,904) 59,600

TANZANIA

1984 E 21,062,000

Cities and Towns

Arusha 69,000
• DAR ES SALAAM 1,300,000
Dodoma 54,000
Iringa 67,000
Kigoma (1978 C) 50,044
Mbeya 93,000
Morogoro 72,000
Moshi 62,000
Mtwara (1978 C) 48,510
Musoma (1978 C) 32,658
Mwanza (1978 C) 110,611
Singida (1987 C) 29,252
Tabora 87,000
Tanga 121,000
Ujiji (1967 C) 21,369
Zanzibar (1980 E) 119,000

THAILAND / Prathet Thai

1986 E 52,969,204

Cities and Towns

• BANGKOK (KRUNG THEP) (★ 6,450,000) 5,468,915
Ban Phai 36,393
Ban Pong 24,749
Buri Ram 29,402
Chachoengsao 43,117
Chanthaburi 37,885
Chiang Mai 157,843
Chiang Rai 37,847
Chon Buri 48,203
Hat Yai (Ban Hat Yai) 131,302
Hua Hin 31,889
Kalasin 32,436
Kanchanaburi 33,616
Khon Kaen 130,773
Lampang 47,493
Lop Buri 39,447
Maha Sarakham 37,547
Nakhon Pathom 45,284
Nakhon Phanom 32,700
Nakhon Ratchasima 206,758
Nakhon Sawan 101,498
Nakhon Si Thammarat 72,558
Narathiwat 38,066
Nong Khai 24,024
Nonthaburi (★ Bangkok) 40,502
Pattani 38,775
Pattaya 49,548
Phatthalung 33,075
Phayao 24,457
Phetchabun 27,955
Phetchaburi 34,268
Phitsanulok 75,804
Phra Nakhon Si Ayutthaya 60,511
Phuket 47,430
Ratchaburi 43,239
Rayong 42,594
Roi Et 33,994
Sakon Nakhon 23,454
Samut Prakan (★ Bangkok) 69,218
Samut Sakhon 53,274
Samut Songkhram 35,477
Saraburi 57,364
Songkhla 84,738
Suphan Buri 25,581
Surat Thani (Ban Don) 41,473
Surin 40,044
Trang 47,065
Ubon Ratchathani 100,145
Udon Thani 82,706
Uttaradit 32,884
Warin Chamrap 30,721
Yala 64,695

TOGO

1981 C 2,702,945

Cities and Towns

Atakpamé 24,377
Lama-Kara 28,480
• LOMÉ (1984 E) 400,000
Palimé 27,669
Sokodé 48,098
Tsévié 20,247

TOKELAU

1986 C 1,690

TONGA

1986 C 94,535

Cities and Towns

• NUKU'ALOFA 21,265

TRANSKEI

1982 E 2,400,000

Cities and Towns

• UMTATA (1978 E) 30,000

TRINIDAD AND TOBAGO

1980 C 1,055,763

Cities and Towns

Arima 24,112
Barataria 14,983
Chaguanas 6,122
Morvant 25,416
Point Fortin 6,538
• PORT OF SPAIN (★ 370,000) (1982 E) 59,649
Princes Town 8,288
San Fernando (★ 75,000) 33,395
Sangre Grande 8,948
Scarborough 6,057
Tunapuna (★ Port of Spain) 10,251

TUNISIA / Tunisie / Tunis

1984 C 6,975,450

Cities and Towns

Ariana (★ Tunis) 98,655
Bardo (★ Tunis) 65,669
Béja 46,708
Ben Arous (★ Tunis) 52,105
Bizerte 94,509
El Kairouan 72,254
El Kasserine 47,606
El Kef 34,519
El Mahdia 36,828
Gabès 92,258
Gafsa 60,970
Hammamet 30,441
Hammam Lif (★ Tunis) 47,009
Houmt Essouk (Djerba) 92,269
Jendouba (Souk el Arba) 23,249
Kalaa Kebira (★★ Sousse) 31,406
La Goulette (★ Tunis) 61,609
La Marsa (★ Tunis) 38,319
Manouba (★ Tunis) 31,758
Médenine 26,602
Menzel Bourguiba 51,399
Monastir 35,546
Msaken 41,217
Nabeul (★ 75,000) 39,531
Rades (★ Tunis) 30,218
Sfax (★ 310,000) 231,911
Sousse (★ 160,000) 83,509
Tataouine 30,371
• TUNIS (★ 1,225,000) 596,654
Zarzis 49,063

TURKEY / Türkiye

1985 C 50,664,458

Cities and Towns

Adana 777,554
Adapazarı 152,291
Adıyaman 71,644
Afyonkarahisar 87,033
Ağrı (Karaköse) 54,492
Akhisar 68,553
Aksaray 81,056
Akşehir 45,320
Alaşehir 29,484
Amasya 53,431
ANKARA (★ 2,400,000) 2,235,035
Antakya (Antioch) 107,821
Antalya 261,114
Artvin 18,720
Aydın 90,449
Bafra 53,482
Balıkesir 149,989
Bandırma 70,137
Batman 110,036
Bayburt 28,068
Bergama 38,849
Bilecik 18,506
Bingöl 34,024
Bitlis 36,073
Bolu 50,288
Bolvadin 35,509
Burdur 53,995
Bursa 612,510
Çanakkale 48,059
Çankırı 41,420
Çarşamba 34,189
Ceyhan 72,624
Çorlu 59,107
Çorum 96,725
Denizli 169,130
Diyarbakır 305,940
Doğubeyazıt 31,134
Dörtyol 30,722
Düzce 45,077
Düziçi 35,750
Edirne 86,909
Edremit 30,159
Elazığ 182,296
Elbistan 48,756
Erciş 36,582
Ereğli, Konya prov. 68,749
Ereğli, Zonguldak prov. 54,837
Ergani 33,209
Erzincan 82,616
Erzurum 246,053
Eskişehir 366,765
Gaziantep 478,635
Gebze (★ İstanbul) 92,592
Gelibolu (Gallipoli) 16,715
Gemlik 36,693
Giresun 55,887
Gölcük 56,087
Gümüşhane 22,067
Hakkâri 20,754
İçel (Mersin) 314,350
İnegöl 54,659
İskenderun (Alexandretta) 152,096
Isparta 101,215
• İstanbul (★ 5,750,000) 5,475,982
İzmir (Smyrna) (★ 1,550,000) 1,489,772
İzmit (Kocaeli) 233,338
Kadirli 47,609
Kahramanmaraş (Maraş) 210,371
Karabük 94,818
Karaman 64,735
Karş 69,293
Kastamonu 46,986
Kayseri 373,937
Keşan 34,518
Kilimli (★ Zonguldak) 34,748
Kilis 59,876
Kırıkhan 52,780
Kırıkkale 208,018
Kırklareli 40,881
Kırşehir 64,754
Kızıltepe 40,852
Konya 439,181
Kozan 50,324
Kozlu (★ Zonguldak) 35,691
Kütahya 118,773
Lüleburgaz 43,420
Malatya 243,138
Manisa 127,012
Mardin 44,085
Merzifon 37,027
Muğla 31,279
Muş 42,159
Mustafakemalpaşa 33,904
Nazilli 77,627
Nevşehir 50,204
Niğde 49,068
Nizip 50,067
Nusaybin 45,178
Ödemiş 47,475
Ordu 80,828
Osmaniye 103,824
Polatlı 52,737
Reyhanlı 37,471
Rize 50,221
Salihli 63,759
Samsun 240,674
Seydişehir 37,226
Siirt 53,884
Silvan (Miyafarkin) 45,825
Sincan (★ Ankara) 50,869
Sinop 23,148
Sivas 198,553
Siverek 48,333
Söke 44,556
Soma 39,088
Suluova (Suluca) 32,717
Tarsus 146,502
Tatvan 51,906
Tavşanlı 30,506
Tekirdağ 63,215
Tire 35,044
Tokat 73,008
Trabzon 142,008
Tunceli 18,471
Turgutlu 65,740
Turhal 60,097
Ünye 35,508
Urfa 194,969
Uşak 88,267
Uzunköprü 33,878
Van 110,653
Viranşehir 45,329
Yalova 53,857
Yarımca 48,420
Yozgat 43,686
Zile 37,097
Zonguldak (★ 210,000) 117,879

TURKS AND CAICOS ISLANDS

1980 C 7,436

Cities and Towns

• GRAND TURK 3,146

TUVALU

1979 C 7,349

Cities and Towns

• FUNAFUTI 2,191

UGANDA

1980 C 12,636,179

Cities and Towns

Entebbe 21,289
Fort Portal (Kabarole) 26,806
Gulu 14,958
Jinja (1982 E) 55,000
• KAMPALA (1982 E) 460,000
Masaka 29,123
Mbale 28,039
Mbarara 23,255
Tororo 16,707

UNITED ARAB EMIRATES / Al Imārāt al 'Arabīyah al Muttaḥidah

1980 C 980,000

Cities and Towns

ABU DHABI (ABŪ ẒABY) 242,975
'Ajmān (1968 C) 3,725
Al 'Ayn 101,663
Al Fujayrah (1968 C) 2,001
Ash Shāriqah 125,149
• Dubai (Dubayy) 265,702
Ra's al Khaymah 42,000
Umm al Qaywayn (1968 C) 2,928

UNITED KINGDOM

1981 C 55,678,079

Political Divisions

England 46,220,955
Northern Ireland 1,578,500
Scotland 5,117,146
Wales 2,790,462

UNITED KINGDOM: ENGLAND

1981 C 46,220,955

Cities and Towns

Abingdon (★ Oxford) 29,130
Accrington (★★ Blackburn) 36,459
Aldershot (Rushmoor) (★ London) 53,665
Altrincham (★ Manchester) 39,528
Andover 30,632
Arnold (★ Nottingham) 37,721
Ashford 45,198
Ashington 27,786
Ashton-in-Makerfield (★ Manchester) 28,517
Ashton-under-Lyne (★ Manchester) 43,605
Aylesbury 51,999
Banbury 37,463
Banstead and Tadworth (★ London) 35,360
Barnsley 76,783
Barnstaple 24,490
Barrow-in-Furness 50,174
Basildon (★ London) 94,800
Basingstoke 73,027
Bath 84,283
Batley (★ Leeds) 45,582
Battle 4,662
Bebington (★ Liverpool) 62,618
Bedford (North Bedfordshire) 75,632
Bedlington 15,074
Beeston and Stapleford (Broxtowe) (★ Nottingham) 64,785
Benfleet (★ London) 50,783
Bentley 34,273
Berkhamsted (★ London) 16,874
Berwick-upon-Tweed 12,772
Bexhill-on-Sea 34,625
Billericay (★ London) 30,397
Billingham (★ Middlesbrough) 36,855
Birkenhead (★ Liverpool) 99,075
Birmingham (★ 2,675,000) 1,013,995
Bishop Auckland 23,560
Bishop's Stortford (★ London) 22,535
Blackburn (★ 221,900) 109,564
Blackpool (★ 280,000) 146,297
Bletchley 37,903
Blyth 35,101
Bodmin 11,992
Bognor Regis 50,323
Bolton (★★ Manchester) 143,960
Bootle 70,860
Borehamwood (★ London) 28,426
Boston 33,908
Bournemouth (★ 315,000) 142,829
Bracknell (★ London) 52,257
Bradford (★★ Leeds) 293,336
Bradford-on-Avon 8,921
Braintree 30,975
Bredbury and Romiley (★ Manchester) 28,600
Brentwood (★ London) 51,212
Bridgwater 30,782
Bridlington 28,426
Brighouse (★ Leeds) 32,597
Brighton (★ 420,000) 134,581
Bristol (★ 630,000) 413,861
Bromsgrove (★ Birmingham) 24,576
Broxtowe see Beeston and Stapleford
Burgess Hill 23,577
Burnham-on-Sea / Highbridge 17,022
Burnley (★ 160,000) 76,365
Burntwood (★ Birmingham) 28,938
Burton upon Trent 59,040
Bury (★ Manchester) 61,785
Bury Saint Edmunds 30,563
Buxton 19,502
Camberley see Frimley and Camberley
Camborne [-Redruth] (Kerrier) 34,262
Cambridge 87,111
Cannock (★ Birmingham) 54,503
Canterbury 34,546
Canvey (★ London) 35,243
Carlisle 72,206
Carlton (★ Nottingham) 46,053
Castleford (★ Leeds) 39,308
Caterham and Warlingham (Tandridge) (★ London) 30,331
Chadderton (★ Manchester) 33,512
Chalfont Saint Giles 5,216
Chatham (★ London) 65,835
Cheadle and Gatley (★ Manchester) 59,478
Chelmsford (★ London) 91,109
Cheltenham 87,188

C Census. E Official estimate. UE Unofficial estimate.
• Largest city in country.

★ Population or designation of metropolitan area, including suburbs (see headnote).
▲ Population of an entire municipality, commune, or district, including rural area.

Chertsey (★ London) 10,198
Chesham (★ London) 20,883
Cheshunt (★ London) 49,616
Chester 80,154
Chesterfield (★ 127,000) 73,352
Chester-le-Street (★ Newcastle upon Tyne) 34,776
Chichester 26,050
Chippenham 21,325
Chipping Sodbury (★ Bristol) 26,882
Chorley (★★ Preston) 33,465
Christchurch (★ Bournemouth) 32,854
Cirencester 13,491
Clacton-on-Sea 39,618
Cleckheaton and Liversedge (★ Leeds) 26,340
Cleethorpes (★ Grimsby) 33,238
Clevedon 17,875
Coalville 28,831
Colchester 87,476
Consett (★ Newcastle upon Tyne) 22,409
Corby 48,704
Coventry (★ 645,000) 318,718
Cowes 16,134
Cramlington (★ Newcastle upon Tyne) 25,324
Crawley (★ London) 80,113
Crewe 59,097
Crosby (★ Liverpool) 54,103
Darlington 85,519
Dartford (★ London) 62,032
Dartmouth 5,282
Darwen (★ Blackburn) 30,883
Deal 26,311
Denton (★ Manchester) 37,784
Derby (★ 275,000) 218,026
Dewsbury (★★ Leeds) 49,612
Doncaster 74,727
Dorchester 13,734
Dorking (★ London) 14,602
Dover 33,461
Dronfield (★ Sheffield) 22,641
Dudley (★★ Birmingham) 186,513
Dunstable (★ Luton) 48,436
Durham 38,105
Eastbourne 86,715
East Grinstead (★ London) 23,867
Eastleigh (★ Southampton) 58,585
East Retford 19,308
Eccles (★ Manchester) 37,497
Ellesmere Port (★ Liverpool) 65,829
Ely 9,006
Epsom [and Ewell] (★ London) 65,830
Esher / Molesey (★ London) 46,688
Eston and South Bank (★ Middlesbrough) 37,694
Eton see Windsor / Eton
Evesham 15,069
Exeter 88,235
Exmouth 28,037
Falmouth 17,810
Fareham / Portchester (★ Portsmouth) 55,563
Farnborough (★ London) 48,063
Farnham (★ London) 34,541
Farnworth (★ Manchester) 25,591
Faversham 15,914
Felixstowe 24,207
Felling (★ Newcastle upon Tyne) 36,377
Fleet (★ London) 27,406
Fleetwood (★★ Blackpool) 27,899
Folkestone 42,949
Formby (Shepway) (★ Liverpool) 26,852
Frimley and Camberley (Surrey Heath) (★ London) 45,108
Frome 19,678
Gainsborough 20,326
Gateshead (★ Newcastle upon Tyne) 91,429
Gillingham (★ London) 92,531
Glastonbury 6,751
Glossop / Hollingworth (★ Manchester) 29,923
Gloucester (★ 115,000) 106,526
Golborne (★ Manchester) 20,633
Goole 19,394
Gosforth (★ Newcastle upon Tyne) 25,128
Gosport (★ Portsmouth) 69,664
Grantham 30,700
Gravesend (Gravesham) (★ London) 53,450
Grays (★ London) 45,881
Greasby / Moreton (★ Liverpool) 56,410
Great Malvern 30,153
Great Sankey 26,222
Great Yarmouth 54,777
Grimsby (Great Grimsby) (★ 145,000) 91,532
Guildford (★ London) 61,509
Guiseley / Yeadon (★ Leeds) 30,811
Halesowen (★ Birmingham) 57,533
Halifax 76,675
Harlow (★ London) 79,150
Harpenden (★ London) 28,589
Harrogate 63,637
Hartlepool (★★ Middlesbrough) 91,749
Harwich 17,245
Haslemere (★ London) 10,544
Hastings 74,979
Hatfield 33,174
Havant (★ Portsmouth) 50,098
Haverhill 16,970
Haywards Heath 27,958
Hazel Grove and Bramhall (★ Manchester) 40,819
Heanor 21,863
Hemel Hempstead (Dacorum) (★ London) 80,110
Hemsworth 9,608
Henley-on-Thames 10,910
Hereford 48,277
Herne Bay 26,523
Hertford (★ London) 21,350
Heswall (★ Liverpool) 31,037
Hexham 8,914
Heywood (★ Manchester) 29,639
High Wycombe (Wycombe) (▲ 156,800) 69,575
Hinckley (★★ Coventry) 35,510
Hitchin 33,480
Hoddesdon (★ London) 37,960
Horsham (★ London) 38,356
Houghton-le-Spring (★ Newcastle upon Tyne) 35,337
Hove (★ Brighton) 65,587
Hucknall (★ Nottingham) 27,463
Huddersfield (Kirklees) (▲ 377,400) 147,825
Huntingdon 14,395
Huyton-with-Roby (★ Liverpool) 62,011
Hyde (★ Manchester) 30,461
Hythe 13,118
Ilkeston (★ Nottingham) 34,683
Ipswich 129,661
Jarrow (★ Newcastle upon Tyne) 31,345
Keighley (★ Leeds) 49,188
Kendal 23,710
Kenilworth (★ Coventry) 18,782
Keswick 4,777
Kettering 44,758
Kidderminster 50,385
Kidsgrove (★ Stoke-on-Trent) 27,999
King's Lynn 37,323
Kingston upon Hull (★ 350,000) 322,144
Kingswood (★ Bristol) 54,736
Kirkby (★ Liverpool) 52,825
Kirkby in Ashfield (★ Mansfield) 26,098
Lancaster 43,902
Leatherhead (Mole Valley) (★ London) 42,399
Leeds (★ 1,540,000) 445,242
Leek 18,495
Leicester (★ 495,000) 324,394
Leigh (★ Manchester) 42,627
Leighton Buzzard 29,554
Letchworth 31,146
Lewes 14,499
Leyland (★ Preston) 36,694
Lichfield 25,408
Lincoln 79,980
Littlehampton 46,028
Liverpool (★ 1,525,000) 538,809
• LONDON (★ 11,100,000) 6,574,009
Longbenton / Backworth (★ Newcastle upon Tyne) 36,780
Long Eaton (★ Nottingham) 42,285
Loughborough (Charnwood) 44,895
Loughton (★ London) 39,162
Lowestoft (Waveney) 59,430
Ludlow 7,496
Luton (★ 220,000) 163,209
Lymington 11,614
Lytham Saint Anne's (Fylde) (★ Blackpool) 39,559
Macclesfield 47,525
Maidenhead (★ London) 59,809
Maidstone 86,067
Manchester (★ 2,775,000) 437,612
Mangotsfield (★ Bristol) 28,664
Mansfield (★ 198,000) 71,325
Margate 53,137
Market Harborough 15,852
Marlborough 5,330
Matlock 13,706
Melton Mowbray 23,379
Middlesbrough (Teesside) (★ 580,000) 158,516
Middleton (★ Manchester) 51,373
Milton Keynes 36,886
Morecambe (★★ Lancaster) 41,432
Morley (★ Leeds) 44,652
Nelson (★★ Burnley) 30,449
Newark-on-Trent 33,143
Newburn (★ Newcastle upon Tyne) 43,713
Newbury 31,488
Newcastle-under-Lyme (★★ Stoke-on-Trent) 73,208
Newcastle upon Tyne (★ 1,300,000) 199,064
Newmarket 15,861
Newport 19,758
Newton Abbot 20,567
Newton Aycliffe 24,375
Newtown 8,906
Northampton 154,172
North Shields (★ Newcastle upon Tyne) 41,519
Northwich 32,664
Norwich (★ 230,000) 169,814
Nottingham (★ 655,000) 273,300
Nuneaton (★★ Coventry) 60,337
Oadby (★ Leicester) 18,331
Oakengates / Donnington 26,890
Oakham 7,914
Oldbury / Smethwick (★ Birmingham) 153,268
Oldham (★★ Manchester) 107,095
Ormskirk (★ Liverpool) 22,308
Oxford (★ 230,000) 113,847
Paignton (★ Torquay) 39,565
Penrith 12,086
Penzance 18,501
Peterborough 113,404
Peterlee 31,405
Plymouth (★ 290,000) 238,583
Pontefract (★ Leeds) 28,621
Poole (★★ Bournemouth) 122,815
Portsmouth (★ 485,000) 174,218
Prescot (★ Liverpool) 40,191
Preston (★ 250,000) 166,675
Prestwich (★ Manchester) 31,854
Pudsey (★ Leeds) 31,943
Radcliffe (★ Manchester) 27,664
Ramsgate 36,678
Rawtenstall 21,247
Rayleigh (★ London) 28,574
Reading (★ 200,000) 194,727
Redcar (★ Middlesbrough) 35,373
Redditch (★ Birmingham) 61,639
Reigate / Redhill (★ London) 48,241
Rickmansworth (★ London) 15,960
Ripon 13,036
Rochdale (★★ Manchester) 97,292
Rotherham (★★ Sheffield) 122,374
Royal Leamington Spa (★★ Coventry) 56,552
Royal Tunbridge Wells 57,699
Rugby 59,039
Runcorn (★ Liverpool) 63,995
Rushden 22,394
Ryde 19,384
Rye 4,127
Saint Albans (★ London) 76,709
Saint Austell 20,267
Saint Helens 114,397
Sale (★ Manchester) 57,872
Salford (★ Manchester) 96,525
Salisbury 36,890
Sandwich 4,184
Scarborough 36,665
Scunthorpe 79,043
Seaford 16,367
Seaham (★ Newcastle upon Tyne) 21,807
Selby 12,224
Sevenoaks (★ London) 24,493
Sheffield (★ 710,000) 470,685
Shipley (★ Leeds) 28,815
Shoreham-by-Sea (★ Brighton) 20,562
Shrewsbury 57,731
Sittingbourne 35,893
Skelmersdale (★ Manchester) 42,611
Slough (★ London) 106,341
Solihull (★ Birmingham) 93,940
Sompting / Lancing (★ Brighton) 25,585
Southampton (★ 415,000) 211,321
Southend-on-Sea (★ London) 155,720
Southport (Sefton) (★★ Liverpool) 88,596
South Shields (★★ Newcastle) 86,488
Spalding 18,182
Spennymoor 18,563
Stafford 60,915
Staines (Spelthorne) (★ London) 51,949
Stamford 16,127
Stanford le Hope / Corringham (★ London) 32,150
Stanley (★ Newcastle) 20,058
Stapleford see Beeston and Stapleford
Stevenage 74,757
Stockport (★ Manchester) 135,489
Stockton-on-Tees (★★ Middlesbrough) 86,699
Stoke-on-Trent (★ 440,000) 272,446
Stourbridge (★ Birmingham) 55,136
Stratford-upon-Avon 20,941
Stretford (★ Manchester) 47,522
Strood (★ London) 32,822
Stroud 37,791
Sudbury 17,723
Sunbury (★ London) 28,240
Sunderland (★★ Newcastle) 195,064
Surrey Heath see Frimley and Camberley
Sutton Coldfield (★ Birmingham) 102,572
Sutton in Ashfield (Ashfield) (★★ Mansfield) 39,536
Swadlincote 33,667
Swindon 127,348
Swinton and Pendlebury (★ Manchester) 44,416
Tamworth 63,260
Taunton 47,793
Telford 28,645
Tewkesbury 9,454
Thetford 19,529
Thornaby-on-Tees (★ Middlesbrough) 26,319
Thornton / Cleveleys (★ Blackpool) 26,697
Tiverton 14,745
Todmorden 11,936
Tonbridge (★ London) 34,407
Torquay (Torbay) (★ 112,400) 54,430
Trowbridge 27,299
Truro 17,852
Tyldesley (★ Manchester) 27,773
Tynemouth (★ Newcastle upon Tyne) 17,877
Ulverston 11,976
Urmston (★ Manchester) 43,706
Wakefield (★★ Leeds) 74,764
Walkden (★ Manchester) 39,413
Wallasey (★ Liverpool) 62,465
Wallsend (★ Newcastle upon Tyne) 44,542
Walsall (★★ Birmingham) 177,923
Walton and Weybridge (★ London) 50,031
Warlingham see Caterham and Warlingham
Warrington 81,366
Warwick (★★ Coventry) 21,701
Washington (★ Newcastle upon Tyne) 48,856
Waterlooville (★ Portsmouth) 57,296
Watford (★ London) 109,503
Wellingborough 38,598
Wells 9,252
Welwyn Garden City (★ London) 40,665
West Bridgford (★ Nottingham) 27,463
West Bromwich (★ Birmingham) 153,725
Weston-super-Mare 60,821
Weybridge see Walton and Weybridge
Weymouth 38,384
Whitby 12,982
Whitefield (★ Manchester) 27,715
Whitehaven 27,512
Whitley Bay (★ Newcastle upon Tyne) 36,040
Whitstable 26,227
Widnes 55,973
Wigan (★★ Manchester) 88,725
Wigston (★ Leicester) 32,373
Wilmslow (★ Manchester) 28,827
Winchester 34,127
Windermere 6,835
Windsor / [Eton] (★ London) 30,832
Winsford 26,548
Woking / [Byfleet] (★ London) 92,667
Wokingham 30,344
Wolverhampton (★★ Birmingham) 263,501
Worcester 75,466
Workington 25,978
Worksop 34,551
Worthing (★★ Brighton) 90,687
Yeovil 36,114
York (★ 145,000) 123,126

Counties

Avon 909,408
Bedfordshire 504,986
Berkshire 675,153
Buckinghamshire 565,992
Cambridgeshire 575,177
Cheshire 926,293
Cleveland 565,775
Cornwall and Isles of Scilly 430,506
Cumbria 483,427
Derby 906,929
Devon 952,000
Dorset 591,990
Durham 604,728
East Sussex 652,568
Essex 1,469,065
Gloucestershire 499,351
Greater London 6,696,008
Greater Manchester 2,594,778
Hampshire 1,456,367
Hereford and Worcester 630,218
Hertfordshire 954,535
Humberside 847,666
Isle of Wight 118,192
Kent 1,463,055
Lancashire 1,372,118
Leicestershire 842,577
Lincolnshire 547,560
Merseyside 1,513,070
Norfolk 693,490
Northamptonshire 527,532
Northumberland 299,905
North Yorkshire 666,610
Nottinghamshire 982,631
Oxfordshire 515,079
Shropshire 375,610
Somerset 424,988
South Yorkshire 1,301,813
Staffordshire 1,012,320
Suffolk 596,354
Surrey 999,393
Tyne and Wear 1,143,245
Warwickshire 473,620
West Midlands 2,644,634
West Sussex 658,562
West Yorkshire 2,037,510
Wiltshire 518,167

UNITED KINGDOM: NORTHERN IRELAND

1987 E 1,575,200

Cities and Towns

Antrim (1981 C) 22,342
Armagh (1981 C) 12,700
Ballymena (1981 C) 28,166
Bangor (North Down) (★ Belfast) 70,700
Belfast (★ 685,000) 303,800
Castlereagh (★ Belfast) 57,900
Enniskillen (1981 C) 10,429
Larne (1981 C) 18,224
Lisburn (★ Belfast) (1981 C) 40,391
Londonderry (Derry) (★ 97,200) 97,500
Lurgan (★ 63,000) (1981 C) 20,991
Newry (1981 C) 19,426
Newtownabbey (★ Belfast) 72,300
Newtownards (1981 C) 20,531
Omagh (1981 C) 14,627
Portadown (★★ Lurgan) (1981 C) 21,333

UNITED KINGDOM: SCOTLAND

1981 C 5,035,315

Cities and Towns

Aberdeen 186,757
Airdrie (★ Glasgow) 45,320
Alexandria (★ Glasgow) 25,947
Alloa 26,378
Arbroath 23,934
Ardrossan (★★ Irvine) 11,386
Ayr (★ 100,000) 48,493
Bearsden (★ Glasgow) 27,146
Bellshill (★ Glasgow) 39,713
Clydebank (★ Glasgow) 51,832
Coatbridge 50,831
Cumbernauld (★ Glasgow) 47,517
Dumbarton (★ Glasgow) 23,345
Dumfries 31,307
Dundee 172,294
Dunfermline (★ 125,817) 52,105
East Kilbride (★ Glasgow) 70,454
Edinburgh (★ 630,000) 408,822
Elgin 18,702
Falkirk (★ 148,171) 36,372
Forfar 12,652
Giffnock (★ Glasgow) 33,585
Glasgow (★ 1,800,000) 754,586
Glenrothes (★★ Kirkcaldy) 33,639
Grangemouth (★★ Falkirk) 21,744
Greenock (★ 101,000) 58,436
Hamilton (★ Glasgow) 51,666
Hawick 16,213
Helensburgh (★ Glasgow) 16,432
Inverness 38,204
Irvine (★ 94,000) 32,507
Johnstone (★ Glasgow) 42,731
Kilmarnock (★ 84,000) 51,799
Kirkcaldy (★ 148,171) 46,356
Kirkintilloch (★ Glasgow) 33,024
Kirkwall 5,867
Lerwick 7,149
Livingston 38,671
Montrose 12,127
Motherwell (★ Glasgow) 30,616
Oban 7,476
Paisley (★ Glasgow) 84,330
Perth 41,916
Peterhead 16,804
Port Glasgow 22,636
Prestwick (★ Ayr) 13,355
Saint Andrews 10,525
Stirling (★ 61,000) 36,640
Stonehouse 5,092
Stranraer 10,766
Thurso 8,828
Wick 7,770
Wishaw (★ Glasgow) 37,717

Regions

Borders 99,248
Central 273,078
Dumfries and Galloway 145,078
Fife 326,480
Grampian 470,596
Highland 200,030
Lothian 735,892
Orkney (island area) 18,906
Shetland (island area) 26,716
Strathclyde 2,397,827
Tayside 391,529
Western Isles (island area) 31,766

UNITED KINGDOM: WALES

1981 C 2,790,462

C Census. E Official estimate. UE Unofficial estimate.
• Largest city in country.
★ Population or designation of metropolitan area, including suburbs (see headnote).
▲ Population of an entire municipality, commune, or district, including rural area.

Cities and Towns

Aberdare (Cynon Valley)	31,617
Aberdare / Brynmawr	28,239
Aberystwyth	10,290
Bangor	12,244
Bargoed (★ Newport)	15,321
Barry (Vale of Glamorgan) (★ Cardiff)	44,443
Brecon	7,166
Bridgend	31,008
Caernarfon	9,271
Caerphilly (★ Cardiff)	28,681
Cardiff (★ 625,000)	262,313
Carmarthen	13,860
Colwyn Bay	27,002
Cwmbran (★ Newport)	44,592
Ebbw Vale (Blaenau Gwent)	21,048
Flint	11,411
Llandudno	13,202
Llanelli	45,336
Merthyr Tydfil	38,893
Milford Haven	13,883
Monmouth	7,379
Neath (★★ Swansea)	48,687
Newport (★ 310,000)	115,896
Pembroke	7,049
Pontypool (★★ Newport)	36,064
Pontypridd (Taff-Ely) (★ Cardiff)	29,465
Port Talbot (Afan) (★ 130,000)	40,078
Prestatyn	16,246
Rhondda (★★ Cardiff)	70,980
Rhyl (Rhuddlan)	23,130
Swansea (★ 275,000)	172,433
Wrexham	39,929

Counties

Clwyd	390,173
Dyfed	329,977
Gwent	439,684
Gwynedd	230,468
Mid Glamorgan	537,866
Powys	110,467
South Glamorgan	384,633
West Glamorgan	367,194

URUGUAY

1985 C 2,940,200

Cities and Towns

Artigas	31,200
Canelones	15,800
Durazno	26,500
Florida	26,200
Fray Bentos	18,800
La Paz (★ Montevideo)	17,200
Las Piedras (★ Montevideo)	61,300
Maldonado	32,300
Melo	39,600
Mercedes	33,300
Minas	33,700
• MONTEVIDEO (★ 1,550,000)	1,246,500
Pando (★ Montevideo)	21,000
Paysandú	75,200
Punta del Este	6,500
Rivera	55,400
Rocha	25,200
Salto	77,400
San Carlos	20,000
San José de Mayo	32,100
Santa Lucía	15,600
Tacuarembó	38,600
Treinta y Tres	27,500
Trinidad	16,500

Departments

Artigas	68,994
Canelones	359,913
Cerro Largo	77,985
Colonia	112,348
Durazno	53,864
Flores	24,381
Florida	65,873
Lavalleja	61,241
Maldonado	92,618
Montevideo	1,303,942
Paysandú	103,487
Río Negro	48,590
Rivera	83,801
Rocha	66,440
Salto	105,617
San José	88,020
Soriano	79,042
Tacuarembó	82,809
Treinta y Tres	46,599

VANUATU

1986 C 140,154

Cities and Towns

• PORT-VILA (★ 18,000)	14,184

VATICAN CITY / Città del Vaticano

1987 E 752

VENDA

1985 C 459,819

Cities and Towns

Makwarela	3,712
• Shayandima	4,853
THOHOYANDOU	3,641

VENEZUELA

1981 C 14,516,735

Cities and Towns

Acarigua	91,662
Altagracia de Orituco	31,582
Anaco	43,607
Araure	41,747
Bachaquero (1971 C)	17,896
Barcelona	156,461
Barinas	110,462
Barquisimeto	497,635
Baruta (★ Caracas)	200,063
Boconó	18,906
Cabimas	140,435
Cagua	53,704
Calabozo	61,995
• CARACAS (★ 3,600,000)	1,816,901
Caripito	18,172
Carora	58,694
Carúpano	64,579
Catia La Mar (★ Caracas)	87,916
Chacao (★ Caracas)	72,703
Charallave	29,410
Chivacoa	27,500
Ciudad Bolívar	182,941
Ciudad Guayana (Santo Tomé de Guayana)	314,497
Ciudad Ojeda	83,565
Coro	96,339
Cumaná	179,814
El Hatillo	27,999
El Limón	65,122
El Tigre	73,595
El Tocuyo	22,854
El Vigía	40,753
Guacara	72,727
Guanare	64,025
Guarenas (★ Caracas)	101,742
Guatire	37,827
Güigüe	27,662
La Guaira (★ Caracas)	21,815
La Victoria	70,828
Los Dos Caminos (★ Caracas)	63,346
Los Teques (★ Caracas)	112,857
Machiques	27,242
Maiquetía (★ Caracas)	66,056
Maracaibo	890,643
Maracay	322,560
Mariara	47,242
Maturín	154,976
Mérida	143,209
Morón	33,973
Ocumare del Tuy	40,666
Palo Negro	27,789
Petare (★ Caracas)	395,715
Porlamar	51,079
Pozuelos	80,342
Puerto Cabello	71,759
Puerto la Cruz	53,881
Punto Fijo	71,114
San Antonio del Táchira	26,939
San Carlos	37,892
San Carlos del Zulia	31,437
San Cristóbal	198,793
San Felipe	57,526
San Fernando de Apure	57,308
San José de Guanipa (El Tigrito)	35,689
San Juan de los Morros	57,219
San Mateo	22,841
Santa Teresa	34,460
Trujillo	31,774
Tucupita	27,299
Turmero	111,186
Upata	33,238
Valencia	616,224
Valera	102,068
Valle de la Pascua	55,761
Villa de Cura	39,228
Yaritagua	31,936

States

Amazonas (Ter.)	45,667
Anzoátegui	683,717
Apure	188,187
Aragua	891,623
Barinas	326,166
Bolívar	668,340
Carabobo	1,062,268
Cojedes	133,991
Delta Amacuro (Ter.)	56,720
Dependencias Federales (Ter.)	850
Distrito Federal (Federal District)	2,070,742
Falcón	503,896
Guárico	393,467
Lara	945,064
Mérida	459,361
Miranda	1,421,442
Monagas	388,536
Nueva Esparta	197,198
Portuguesa	424,984
Sucre	585,698
Táchira	660,234
Trujillo	433,735
Yaracuy	300,597
Zulia	1,674,252

VIETNAM / Viet Nam

1979 C 52,741,766

Cities and Towns

Bac Giang	54,506
Bac Lieu (1967 E)	41,700
Bac Ninh	38,097
Ben Tre	28,672
Bien Hoa	187,254
Bien Son	29,482
Buon Me Thuot	71,815
Ca Mau	67,484
Cam Pha	76,697
Cam Ranh (1973 E)	118,111
Can Tho	182,856
Cao Bang	26,741
Chau Doc	45,245
Da Lat	87,136
Da Nang	318,653
Dong Ha	28,796
Dong Hoi	39,521
Ha Dong	37,378
Hai Duong	54,579
Hai Phong (▲ 1,279,067)	385,210
HANOI (HA NOI) (★ 1,500,000)	897,500
Hoa Binh	51,187
• Ho Chi Minh City (Thanh Pho Ho Chi Minh) (★ 3,100,000)	2,700,849
Hoi An	23,490
Hon Gai	114,573
Hue	165,710
Kon Tum	28,378
Lang Son	20,204
Lao Cai	18,618
Long Xuyen	112,485
Minh Hai	72,517
My Tho	101,493
Nam Dinh	160,179
Nha Trang	172,663
Phan Rang (1967 E)	21,900
Phan Thiet	75,241
Phu Tho	22,273
Play Cu	58,088
Qui Nhon	127,211
Rach Gia	81,075
Sa Dec	73,104
Soc Trang	74,967
Soc Trang (1967 E)	40,300
Son La	14,810
Tam Ky (1971 E)	18,100
Tan An	43,364
Tay Ninh	32,151
Thai Binh	79,566
Thai Nguyen	138,023
Thanh Hoa	72,646
Thu Dau Mot	40,759
Tra Vinh	44,020
Tuyen Quang	22,279
Tuy Hoa	46,617
Uong Bi	34,400
Viet Tri	72,108
Vinh	159,753
Vinh Long	71,505
Vinh Yen	9,590
Vung Tau	81,694
Yen Bai	40,017

VIRGIN ISLANDS, BRITISH

1980 C 12,034

Cities and Towns

• ROAD TOWN	2,479

VIRGIN ISLANDS OF THE UNITED STATES

1980 C 96,569

Cities and Towns

• CHARLOTTE AMALIE (★ 32,000)	11,842

WALLIS AND FUTUNA / Wallis et Futuna

1983 E 12,408

Cities and Towns

• MATA-UTU	815
Ono (1976 C)	624

WESTERN SAHARA

1982 E 142,000

Cities and Towns

• EL AAIÚN (LA'YOUN)	93,875

WESTERN SAMOA / Samoa i Sisifo

1981 C 156,349

Cities and Towns

• APIA	33,170

YEMEN / Al Yaman

1990 E 15,267,000

Cities and Towns

Aden ('Adan) (★ 318,000) (1984 E)	176,100
Al Mukallā (1984 E)	58,000
Dhamār (1981 C)	30,367
Hodeida (Al Ḥudaydah) (1986 C)	155,110
• ṢAN'Ā' (1986 C)	427,150
Say'ūn (1984 E)	25,400
Ta'izz (1986 C)	178,043

YUGOSLAVIA / Jugoslavija

1987 E 23,417,188

Cities and Towns

Banja Luka (▲ 193,890)	130,900
Bečej (1971 C)	26,470
• BELGRADE (BEOGRAD) (★ 1,400,000)	1,130,000
Bihać (1971 C)	24,026
Bijeljina (1971 C)	24,722
Bitola (▲ 143,090)	76,200
Bor (1971 C)	29,039
Brčko (1971 C)	25,422
Čačak (1971 C)	38,170
Celje (1971 C)	31,788
Cetinje (1971 C)	11,892
Đakovica (1971 C)	29,638
Dubrovnik (1971 C)	31,106
Karlovac (1971 C)	47,532
Kikinda (1971 C)	37,487
Kosovska Mitrovica (1971 C)	42,241
Kragujevac (▲ 171,609)	94,800
Kraljevo (1971 C)	27,817
Kranj (1971 C)	27,209
Kruševac (1971 C)	29,469
Kumanovo (1971 C)	46,406
Leskovac (1971 C)	44,255
Ljubljana (▲ 316,607)	233,200
Maribor (▲ 187,651)	107,400
Mostar (1971 C)	47,606
Nikšić (1971 C)	28,547
Niš (▲ 240,219)	168,400
Novi Pazar (1971 C)	29,072
Novi Sad (▲ 266,772)	176,000
Ohrid (1971 C)	26,370
Osijek (▲ 162,490)	106,800
Pančevo (★ Belgrade)	62,700
Peć (1971 C)	42,113
Pirot (1971 C)	29,228
Požarevac (1971 C)	33,121
Prilep (1971 C)	48,242
Priština (▲ 244,830)	125,400
Prizren (1971 C)	41,661
Pula (1971 C)	47,414
Rijeka (▲ 199,282)	166,400
Šabac (1971 C)	42,307
Sarajevo (▲ 479,688)	341,200
Šibenik (1971 C)	30,090
Sisak (1971 C)	38,421
Skopje (▲ 547,214)	444,900
Slavonski Brod (1971 C)	38,762
Smederevo (1971 C)	40,289
Sombor (1971 C)	43,971
Split	191,074
Sremska Mitrovica (1971 C)	31,921
Štip (1971 C)	27,289
Subotica (▲ 153,306)	100,500
Svetozarevo (1971 C)	27,542
Tetovo (1971 C)	35,792
Titograd (▲ 145,163)	82,500
Titovo Užice (1971 C)	34,312
Titov Veles (1971 C)	36,026
Tuzla (▲ 129,967)	67,300
Valjevo (1971 C)	26,367
Varaždin (1971 C)	34,270
Vinkovci (1971 C)	29,072
Vranje (1971 C)	25,685
Vršac (1971 C)	34,231
Vukovar (1971 C)	30,149
Zadar (1971 C)	43,187
Zagreb	697,925
Zenica (▲ 144,869)	67,500
Zrenjanin (▲ 140,009)	65,400

Republics

Bosnia-Hercegovina (Bosna i Hercegovina)	4,400,464
Croatia (Hrvatska)	4,673,517
Macedonia (Makedonija)	2,064,581
Montenegro (Crna Gora)	625,882
Serbia (Srbija)	9,716,138
Slovenia (Slovenija)	1,936,606

ZAIRE / Zaïre

1984 C 29,671,407

Cities and Towns

Bandundu	63,189
Beni	73,319
Boma	88,556
Bukavu	171,064
Bumba	46,823
Bunia	46,224
Butembo	78,633
Gandajika	60,263
Gemena	62,641
Goma	76,745
Ilebo	48,831
Isiro	78,871
Kabalo	38,787
Kabinda	81,752
Kalemie (Albertville)	70,694
Kalima	22,716
Kamina	5,970
Kananga (Luluabourg)	290,898
Kikwit	146,784
Kindu	68,044
• KINSHASA (LÉOPOLDVILLE) (1986 E)	3,000,000
Kisangani (Stanleyville)	282,650
Kolwezi	201,382
Likasi (Jadotville)	194,465
Lisala	40,471
Lubumbashi (Élisabethville)	543,268
Matadi	144,742
Mbandaka (Coquilhatville)	125,263
Mbanza-Ngungu	43,900
Mbuji-Mayi (Bakwanga)	423,363
Mwene-Ditu	72,567
Tshikapa	105,484
Yangambi	53,726

ZAMBIA

1980 C 5,661,801

Cities and Towns

Chililabombwe (Bancroft) (★ 56,582)	25,900
Chingola	130,872
Kabwe (Broken Hill)	127,420
Kalulushi	53,383
Kitwe (★ 283,962)	207,500
Livingstone	61,296
Luanshya (★ 113,422)	61,600
• LUSAKA	535,830
Mufulira (★ 138,824)	77,100
Ndola	250,490

ZIMBABWE

1982 C 7,539,000

Cities and Towns

Bulawayo	413,814
Chinhoyi	24,322
Chitungwiza (★ Harare)	172,556
Gweru	78,918
• HARARE (SALISBURY) (★ 890,000)	656,011
Hwange	39,202
Kadoma	44,613
Kwekwe	47,607
Masvingo (Nyanda)	30,642
Mutare	69,621
Zvishavane	26,758

C Census. E Official estimate. UE Unofficial estimate.
• Largest city in country.

★ Population or designation of metropolitan area, including suburbs (see headnote).
▲ Population of an entire municipality, commune, or district, including rural area.